D0138883

Smith and Roberson's
BUSINESS LAW
Sixth Edition

Smith and Roberson's
BUSINESS LAW
Sixth Edition

Len Young Smith
Chairman of the Department of Business Law
Northwestern University (Retired)
Member of the Illinois Bar

G. Gale Roberson
Professorial Lecturer in Business Law
Northwestern University (Retired)
Member of the Illinois Bar

Richard A. Mann
Professor of Business Law
The University of North Carolina at Chapel Hill
Member of the North Carolina Bar

Barry S. Roberts
Professor of Business Law
The University of North Carolina at Chapel Hill
Member of the North Carolina and Pennsylvania Bars

WEST PUBLISHING COMPANY
St. Paul   New York   Los Angeles   San Francisco

A study guide has been developed to assist you in mastering concepts presented in this text. Prepared by Dennis R. Hower and Peter T. Kahn of the University of Minnesota, this practical student study guide includes chapter overviews, key terms, and exercises that match key terms to definitions. Your comprehension can be tested with multiple choice, true/false, and short essay problems. Answers are provided for all exercises and are keyed to the text material. The study guide is available from your local bookstore under the title *Study Guide to Accompany Smith and Roberson's Business Law, Sixth Edition*. If you cannot locate it in the bookstore, ask your bookstore manager to order it for you.

COPYRIGHT © 1962, 1966, 1971, 1977, 1982 by WEST PUBLISHING CO.

COPYRIGHT © 1985   By WEST PUBLISHING CO.
50 West Kellogg Boulevard
P.O. Box 43526
St. Paul, Minnesota   55164–0526

All rights reserved.

Printed in the United States of America.

Library of Congress Cataloging in Publication Data

Main entry under title:

Business law.

    Rev. ed. of: Smith and Roberson's Business Law / Len Young Smith . . . [et al.]. 5th ed. c1982.
    Includes index.
    1. Commercial law—United States.   I. Smith, Len Young, 1901– . II. Smith, Len Young, 1901– . Business law.
KF888.S554   1985   346.73′07′02632   84–19633
ISBN 0–314–85302–2   347.306702632

PREFACE

The format of the Sixth Edition is the same as that of the five prior editions, in that each chapter contains narrative text, cases consisting of selected court decisions, and problems. Six new chapters have been added: Chapter 3, Constitutional and Administrative Law; Chapter 4, Criminal Law; Chapter 32, Limited Partnerships; Chapter 38, Suretyship; Chapter 43, Employment Law; and Chapter 45, Accountants' Legal Liability.

This text is designed for use in Business Law and Legal Environment courses generally offered in universities, colleges, and schools of business and commerce. By reason of the broad coverage and variety of the material, this volume may be readily adapted to specially designed courses in Business Law by assigning and emphasizing different combinations of the subject matter. With the addition of the chapters on Employment Law, Suretyship, and Accountants' Legal Liability, all topics included in the CPA exam are covered by the text.

The Sixth Edition has been made more readable and understandable by reorganization within sections, chapters, and parts. Unnecessary "legalese" has been eliminated while necessary legal terms are printed in boldface and clearly defined, explained and illustrated. The text has been enriched by the addition of numerous new, illustrative hypothetical and case examples which help students relate material to real life experiences. The end of chapter cases are cross-referenced in the text as are related topics covered in other chapters.

Greater emphasis has been placed upon the regulatory environment of Business Law:

The first six chapters are devoted to introductory coverage of the legal environment of business; Part IX (Chapters 40 to 45) thoroughly addresses the area of government regulation of business; and parts open with an introductory discussion of the public policy, social issues and business ethics pertaining to that part.

From long classroom experience we are of the opinion that fundamental legal principles can be more effectively learned from text and case materials having at least a degree of human interest. To accomplish this objective a large number of recent cases have been included. Landmark cases, on the other hand, have not been neglected. The Sixth Edition contains a total of 241 cases, 87 of which are new to this edition. Cases have been placed at the end of the chapter and cross-referenced to the text. They have been carefully edited to show the essential facts of the case, the issue or issues involved, the decision of the court, and the reason for its decision.

Strong classroom tested problems appear at the end of chapters to test the student's understanding of major concepts. We have used the problems and consider them excellent stimulants to classroom discussion. Students have found the problems helpful in enabling them to apply the basic rules of law to factual situations, many of which are taken from reported court decisions. The problems serve as a springboard for discussion and readily suggest other and related problems to the inquiring, analytical mind.

We have used over 70 classroom tested figures, charts, and diagrams. The diagrams help the student conceptualize the many ab-

v

stract concepts in the law; the charts not only summarize prior discussions but also aid in pointing out relationships among legal rules. In addition, each chapter begins with an outline which summarizes the topics to be covered.

The text contains comprehensive appendixes, including the United States Constitution (Appendix A); selected provisions of the Restatements of Torts, Contracts and Agency (Appendix B); the Uniform Commercial Code (Appendix C); the Uniform Partnership Act (Appendix D); the Uniform Limited Partnership Act (Appendix E); the Uniform Revised Limited Partnership Act (Appendix F); the Model Business Corporation Act (Appendix G); and selected provisions of the Revised Model Business Corporation Act (Appendix H).

Classroom use and study of this book should provide for the student the following benefits and skills:

(1) Perception and appreciation of the scope, extent, and importance of the law.

(2) Basic knowledge of the fundamental concepts, principles, and rules of law that apply to business transactions.

(3) Acquisition of knowledge of the function and operation of courts and governmental administrative agencies.

(4) Ability to recognize the possibility of potential legal problems which may arise in a doubtful or complicated situation, and the necessity of consulting a lawyer and obtaining competent professional legal advice.

(5) Development of analytical skills and reasoning power.

We express our gratitude to the following Professors for their helpful comments: Michael Garrison, North Dakota State University; Herbert McLaughlin, Bryant College; Leonard Tripodi, St. Joseph's College; Al Stauber, Florida State University; Donald Boren, Bowling Green University; William Day, Cleveland State University; Alex DeVience, Jr., DePaul University; Donald Nelson, University of Denver; Richard Paxton, San Diego Community College; Richard Luke, Ricks College; Tim Rueth, Marquette University.

We express our thanks and deep appreciation to Jean Riggsbee and Denise Smith for typing the manuscript. For their support we extend our thanks to Helen T. Smith, Jo Roberson, Karlene Fogelin Knebel, and Joanne Erwick Roberts. And we are grateful to Richard Fenton, Tad Bornhoft and Tim Danielson of West Publishing Company for their invaluable assistance and cooperation in connection with the preparation of this text.

Len Young Smith
G. Gale Roberson
Richard A. Mann
Barry S. Roberts

SUMMARY OF CONTENTS

TABLE OF CONTENTS

**PART ONE
The Legal
Environment
of Business
1**

PART FOUR
Sales
393

—PUBLIC POLICY,
SOCIAL ISSUES AND
BUSINESS ETHICS
394

Appendices

TABLE OF STATUTES

TABLE OF CASES

Cases in roman are those cited in text.
References are to pages.

Smith and Roberson's
BUSINESS LAW
Sixth Edition

Chapter 1

INTRODUCTION TO LAW

THE laws of the United States affect and influence the lives of every American citizen, and the laws of each State affect and influence the life of each of its citizens as well as a large number of noncitizens. The rights possessed and the duties owing by every individual to others as well as the safety and security of every individual and his property depend upon the law.

The law is pervasive. It interacts with and influences the political, economic, and social systems of every civilized society. It permits, forbids, and/or regulates practically every known human activity and affects all persons either directly or indirectly.

It will be helpful in studying the several branches of law known collectively as business law first to consider law as a whole. Law is an instrument of social control. Its function is the regulation, within certain limitations, of human conduct and human relations. Accordingly, each branch of law is related to a greater or lesser extent to every other branch. Hence, even a brief survey of law as a whole will enable the student not only better to comprehend any given branch of law, but also to understand its relation to other branches of law which he may study as well as to law as a whole.

NATURE OF LAW

The law did not spring full blown from the mind of any person nor the minds of any combination of persons at any one time. It evolved slowly, and it contains the seed of future change and development as new conditions and new needs arise in an era of technology and expanding population. The law has improved by change and will continue to change.

The law is not a pure science based upon unchanging and universal truths. "The life of the law has not been logic;" writes Oliver Wendell Holmes in *The Common Law*, "it has been experience. The felt necessities of the time, the prevalent moral and political theories, avowed or unconscious, even the prejudices which judges share with their fellow-men, have had a good deal more to do than the syllogism in determining the rules by which men should be governed. The law embodies the story of a nation's development through many centuries, and it cannot be dealt with as if it contained only the axioms and corrollaries of a book of mathematics." Rather, it is a continuous striving to attain a workable set of rules that adjust the individual and group rights of a society within the fixed framework of its political ideology and the constant progression of its sociology and technology. Nonetheless, the fundamental question remains: What should the law be? Numerous philosophers and jurists (legal scholars) have attempted to answer this question.

Definition of Law

The American jurists and Supreme Court Justices, Holmes and Cardozo, defined law in a functional sense as predictions of the way that a court will probably decide specific legal questions. Blackstone, an English jurist, on the other hand, defined law as "a rule of civil conduct prescribed by the supreme power in a state, commanding what is right, and prohibiting what is wrong." Similarly, Austin, a nineteenth-century English jurist, defined law as a general command of a state or sovereign to those who are subject to its authority by laying down a course of action which is enforced by judicial or administrative tribunals.

Judge Jerome Frank, in his classic work, "Law and the Modern Mind," observes that the fluidity of the law is what makes it most meaningful, yet elusive of definition:

The law always has been, is now, and will ever continue to be, largely vague and variable. And how could this well be otherwise? The law deals with human relations in their most complicated aspects. The whole confused, shifting helter-skelter of life parades before it—more confused than ever, in our kaleidoscopic age.

Even in a relatively static society, men have never been able to construct a comprehensive, eternized, set of rules anticipating all possible legal disputes and formulating in advance the rules which would apply to them. Even in such a social order no one can foresee all the future permutations and combinations of events; situations are bound to occur which were never contemplated when the original rules were made. How much less is such a frozen legal system possible in modern times. New instruments of production, new modes of travel and of dwelling, new credit and ownership devices, new concentrations of capital, new social customs, habits, aims and ideals—all these factors of innovation make vain the hope that definitive legal rules can be drafted that will forever after solve all legal problems. When human relationships are transforming daily, legal relationships cannot be expressed in enduring form. The constant development of unprecedented problems requires a legal system capable of fluidity and pliancy. Our society would be strait-jacketed were not the courts, with the able assistance of the lawyers, constantly overhauling the law and adapting it to the realities of ever-changing social, industrial, and political conditions; although changes cannot be made lightly, yet rules of law must be more or less impermanent, experimental and therefore not nicely calculable. *Much of the uncertainty of law is not an unfortunate accident: it is of immense social value.*

Roscoe Pound, a distinguished American jurist and former dean of the Harvard Law School, stated that law may mean any of three things:

First, we may mean the legal order, that is, the régime of ordering human activities and relations through systematic application of the force of politically organized society, or through social pressure in such a society backed by such force. We use the term "law" in this sense when we speak of "respect for law" or for the "end of law."

Second, we may mean the aggregate of laws or legal precepts; the body of authoritative grounds of judicial and administrative action established in such a society. We may mean the body of received and established materials on which judicial and administrative determinations proceed. We use the term in this sense when we speak of "systems of law" or of "justice according to law."

Third, we may mean what Mr. Justice Cardozo has happily styled "the judicial process." We may mean the process of determining controversies, whether as it actually takes place, or as the public, the jurists, and the practitioners in the courts hold it ought to take place.

Legal Sanctions

A primary function of the legal system is to insure that legal rules are enforced. Sanctions are the means by which the law enforces the judgments and decrees of the courts. Laws without sanctions would be ineffectual and unenforceable.

Examples of sanctions in a <u>civil</u> (non-criminal) case to enforce a court's judgment include the seizure and sale of the debtor's property. Moreover, under certain circumstances the court may enforce its orders and decrees by finding the offender in contempt of court and sentencing him to jail until he obeys the court's order. The principal sanctions for convictions of a crime are the imposition of a fine, imprisonment, and capital punishment.

The mere existence of sanctions is not enough. It is essential that there be a widespread willingness on the part of individuals in the community to submit to law. Important attitudes which make the law respected and obeyed without the necessity of the State's invoking legal sanctions include: public sentiment and opinion, habits of obedience to law, and a desire to conform to societal standards.

Law and Morals

The law is greatly affected and determined by moral and ethical concepts. Morals and law are, however, not synonymous but may be considered as two circles, one partially superimposed upon the other, as shown in Figure 1-1. The area covered by both the mo-

---

FIGURE 1-1 Law and Morals

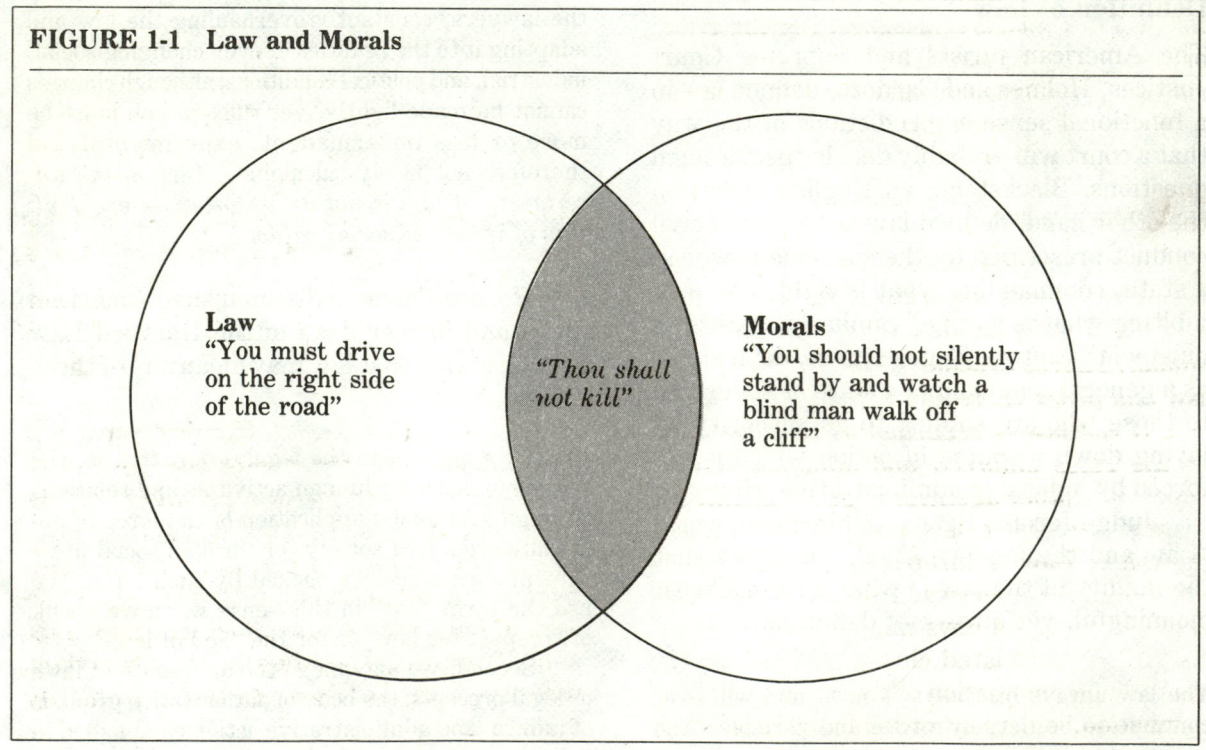

Law
"You must drive on the right side of the road"

"Thou shall not kill"

Morals
"You should not silently stand by and watch a blind man walk off a cliff"

rality circle and the legal circle includes the vast body of ideas which are both moral and legal. For instance, "thou shall not kill" and "thou shall not steal" are both moral precepts and legal constraints.

On the other hand, the part of the legal circle not covering the morality circle includes many rules of law that are completely unrelated to morals, such as, you must drive on the right side of the road or you must register before you can vote. Likewise, the part of the morality circle not also covered by the legal circle includes moral precepts which are not enforced by law, such as, you should not silently stand by and watch a blind man walk off a cliff, or you should not foreclose a poor widow's mortgage.

While law and ethics are essentially similar in that they are bodies of rules for the regulation of human conduct, they differ in one all-important respect. Rules of law, as such, have sanctions; rules of ethics, as such, do not. Rules of law are enforceable by a political government; rules of ethics or morals are not so enforceable. In the realm of morals and ethics as contrasted with law, sanction for the individual is conscience. For the group or community it takes the form of contempt, ridicule, or ostracism, and sometimes illegal force or even "lynch law."

Law and Justice

The law is no guarantee of justice, and these terms represent separate and distinct concepts. Justice is an ideal which good law continually strives to achieve. However, without law and order there can be no justice.

If the law is regarded as the sum total of the rules enforced and administered by courts and other agencies of government, the disparity between law and justice becomes apparent. Law is inseparable from a politically organized society. In a government by a dictatorship its laws might be oppressive, harsh, and calculated chiefly to maintain the control and domination of the dictator. A rule, regulation, edict, or order is no less a law

because it is harsh, unwise, or unjust. Alexander Hamilton regarded justice as the "great cement of society." Law is ever changing and its change should be in the direction of fair, reasonable, and impartial treatment of competing interests and desires of individuals with due regard for the common good. To the extent that it fails to do so, it fails to achieve justice.

CLASSIFICATION OF LAW

Because of the enormous scope and extent of law, it is helpful to classify the law into categories. There are a number of ways in which this can be done, but the most useful is (1) substantive and procedural, (2) public and private, and (3) civil and criminal. See Figure 1-2.

Substantive and Procedural Law

A common classification divides substantive law from procedural law. The former includes laws which create, define, and regulate legal rights and obligations. Thus, the rules of contract law that determine when a binding contract is formed are rules of substantive law. Procedural law establishes the rules for enforcing rights which exist by reason of the substantive law. One turns to procedural law to ascertain the method by which to obtain a remedy in court.

Public and Private Law

Public law is that branch of substantive law which deals with the rights and powers of government in its political or sovereign capacity, and its relation to individuals or groups. Public law consists of constitutional, administrative, and criminal law. Private law is the part of substantive law which governs individuals and legal entities in their relations with one another. Business law is primarily private law.

Civil and Criminal Law

The civil law defines duties the violation of which constitutes a wrong against the injured party. In contrast, the criminal law establishes duties the violation of which is a wrong against the whole community. Civil law is a part of private law, while criminal law is a part of public law. In a civil action the injured party **sues** to recover **compensation** for the damage and injury that he has sustained as a result of the defendant's wrongful conduct. The party bringing a civil action (the plaintiff) has the burden of proof which he must sustain by a **preponderance** (greater weight) of the evidence. The purpose of the civil law is to compensate the aggrieved party, not to punish the wrongdoer as in the case of criminal law. The principal forms of relief afforded by the civil law are a judgment for money damages and a decree ordering the defendant to specifically perform a certain act or to desist from specified conduct.

A crime is any act or omission prohibited by public law in the interest of protection of the public and made punishable by the government in a judicial proceeding brought (**prosecuted**) by it. The government must prove criminal guilt **beyond a reasonable doubt** which is a significantly higher burden of proof than that required in a civil action. Crimes are prohibited and **punished** upon the ground of public policy, which may include the protection and safeguarding of government, human life, or private property. Additional purposes of the criminal law include deterrence and rehabilitation. A comparison of civil and criminal law is shown in Figure 1-3.

Within recent times the scope of the criminal law has increased substantially. Traditional crimes have been augmented by a multitude of regulations and laws to which are attached criminal penalties. These pertain to nearly every phase of modern living. Typical examples in the business law field are those respecting the licensing and conduct of a business, the laws governing the sale of securities, and antitrust law. Criminal law is more fully discussed in Chapter 4.

SOURCES OF LAW

The sources of law in the American legal system are the Federal and State constitutions,

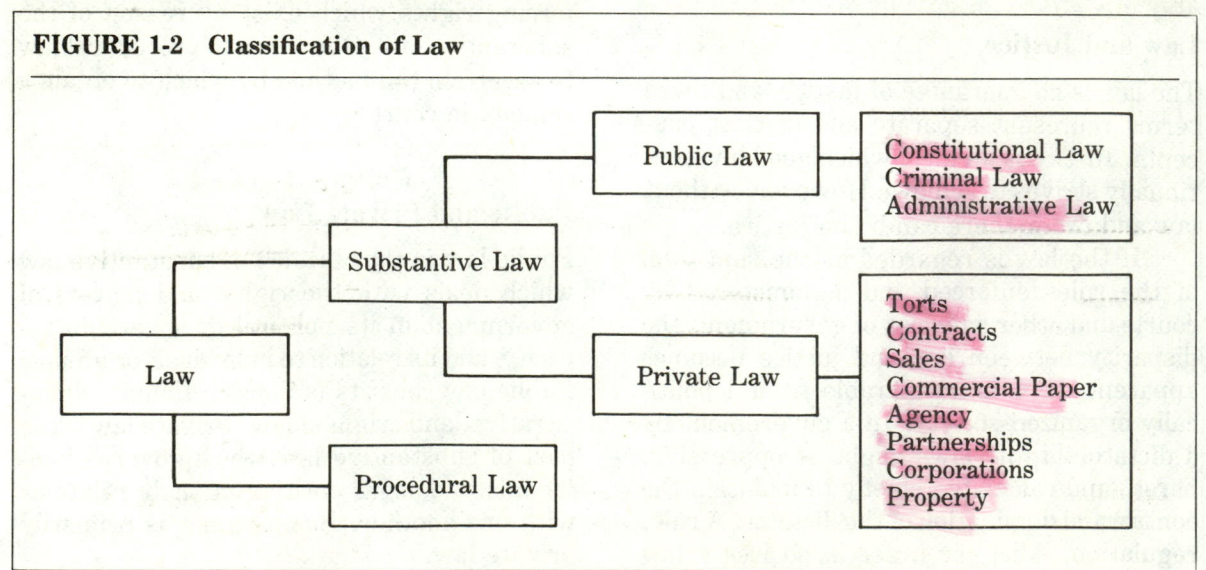

FIGURE 1-2   Classification of Law

Federal treaties, interstate compacts, Federal and State statutes, the ordinances of countless local municipal governments, Federal and State executive orders, the rules and regulations of Federal and State administrative agencies, and an ever increasing volume of reported Federal and State court decisions.

The **supreme law** of the land is the United States Constitution. The Constitution also provides that treaties made under the authority of the United States shall be the supreme law of the land. Federal treaties are, therefore, paramount to State constitutions and statutes. Federal legislation is of next significance as a source of law. The importance and complexity of new bills enacted at each congressional session results from the interplay of tremendous economic and social forces within this nation. Federal activity having the force of law is also manifest in the promulgation of executive orders by the President and in the rules and regulations of Federal administrative officials, agencies, and commissions. The Federal courts also contribute considerably to the body of law in the United States.

The same pattern exists in every State. The paramount law of each State is contained in its written constitution. Subordinate to this are the statutes enacted by its legislature and the case law developed by its judiciary. Likewise, State administrative agencies issue rules and regulations having the force of law as do executive orders promulgated by the Governor. In addition, cities, towns, and villages have limited legislative powers within their respective municipal areas to pass ordinances and resolutions.

These sources of law will be considered under the headings of constitutional, judicial, legislative, and administrative law.

Constitutional Law

Constitutions are the fundamental law of a particular level of government and serve a number of critical functions. They establish the governmental structure and allocate power among the levels of government, thereby defining political relationships. They also impose restrictions upon the powers of government and enumerate the rights and liberties of the people. For example, the framers of the Constitution of the United States deemed it necessary to state precisely what rights and authority were vested in the people's creation—the national government—but considered it unnecessary to list those liberties the people reserved to themselves, which the government could not restrict nor officials ignore. Alexander Hamilton, a co-author of *The*

FIGURE 1-3   Comparison of Civil and Criminal Law

	Civil Law	Criminal Law
Commencement of action	Aggrieved individual (plaintiff) sues	State or Federal government prosecutes
Purpose	Compensation Deterrence	Punishment Deterrence Rehabilitation Preservation of peace
Burden of proof	Preponderance of the evidence	Beyond a reasonable doubt
Principal sanctions	Monetary damages Equitable remedies	Capital punishment Imprisonment Fines

Federalist, put it this way: "Here in strictness the people surrender nothing; and as they retain everything, they have no need of particular reservations."

All law in the United States, whether case law, statutory law, or administrative law, is subject to the Federal Constitution. No law, Federal or State, is valid if it violates the Federal Constitution. The final arbiter as to constitutionality is the Supreme Court of the United States. This principle of **judicial review** is one of the basic ideas incorporated in the Federal Constitution, which William Gladstone (a British statesman) once characterized as "the greatest [document] ever struck off at one time by the brain and the purpose of man." Alexander Hamilton forcefully expressed this idea when he stated: "The interpretation of the laws is the proper and peculiar province of the courts. A constitution is, in fact, and must be regarded by the judges, a fundamental law. It therefore belongs to them to ascertain its meaning as well as the meaning of any particular act or proceeding from the legislative body. If there should happen to be an irreconcilable variance between the two, that which has the superior obligation and validity ought of course to be preferred; or in other words, the Constitution ought to be preferred to the statute, the intention of the people to the intention of their agents." (*The Federalist*, No. 78, Lodge Ed., pp. 485–6.)

One of the fundamental principles upon which our government is founded is that of separation of powers. As incorporated into our Constitution it means that there are three distinct and independent branches of government—the Federal judiciary, the Congress, and the Executive branch.

Because of the continuing importance of constitutional law, this source of law is more fully discussed in Chapter 3.

Judicial Law

The American legal system is a **common law system** that relies heavily upon the judiciary

as a source of law and upon the **adversary** method for adjudication of disputes. In an adversary system it is generally incumbent upon the parties, not the court, to initiate and to conduct litigation. This approach is based upon the belief that the truth is more likely to emerge from the investigation and presentation of evidence by two opposing parties, both motivated by self-interest, than from judicial investigation motivated only by official duty. The common law system is utilized by other English-speaking countries, among them England, Canada, and Australia.

In distinct contrast to the common law system are the **civil law systems** (as opposed to civil or non-criminal law) which are based upon Roman law. These systems depend upon comprehensive legislative enactments (called Codes) and the **inquisitorial** method of adjudication. The inquisitorial approach relies upon the judiciary to initiate litigation, to investigate pertinent facts, and to conduct the presentation of evidence. The civil law system prevails in most of Europe, Scotland, the State of Louisiana, the province of Quebec, Mexico, and South America.

Common Law The courts in common law systems have developed a body of law which serves as precedent for determination of later controversies. This law is called "case law," "judge-made law," or "common law." In this sense, common law is distinguished from other sources of law, such as legislation and administrative rulings.

The principle of **stare decisis** (to stand by the decisions), whereby rules of law announced and applied by courts in prior decisions are later adhered to and relied upon in deciding cases of a similar nature, upholds the stability of the common law. Judicial decisions have two uses: first, to determine with finality the case decided; and, second, to indicate to the public how similar cases will be decided if and when they arise. Thus, as defined by the jurist Jerome Frank, the law "as to any given situation is either (a) actual law, i.e., a specific past decision, as to that situation, or (b) probable law, i.e., a guess as to a specific future decision."

Stare decisis does not preclude correction of erroneous decisions or judicial choice among conflicting precedents. Thus, the doctrine allows sufficient flexibility for the common law to change. Justice Musmanno of the Supreme Court of Pennsylvania paid tribute to the doctrine of *stare decisis* when he stated:

Without *stare decisis*, there would be no stability in our system of jurisprudence.

Stare decisis channels the law. It erects lighthouses and flys the signals of safety. The ships of jurisprudence must follow that well-defined channel which, over the years, has been proved to be secure and trustworthy. But it would not comport with wisdom to insist that, should shoals rise in a heretofore safe course and rocks emerge to encumber the passage, the ship should nonetheless pursue the original course, merely because it presented no hazard in the past. The principle of *stare decisis* does not demand that we follow precedents which shipwreck justice.

Stare decisis is not an iron mold into which every utterance by a Court—regardless of circumstances, parties, economic barometer and sociological climate—must be poured, and, where, like wet concrete, it must acquire an unyielding rigidity which nothing later can change.

The history of law through the ages records numerous inequities pronounced by courts because the society of the day sanctioned them. Reason revolts, humanity shudders, and justice recoils before much of what was done in the past under the name of law. Yet, we are urged to retain a forbidding incongruity in the law simply because it is old.

While age adds venerableness to moral principles and physical objects, it sometimes becomes necessary, and it is not sacrilegious to do so, to scrape away the moss of the years to study closely the thing which is being accepted as authoritative, inviolable, and untouchable. When a rule offends against reason, when it is at odds with every precept of natural justice, and when it cannot be defended on its own merits, but has to depend alone on a discredited genealogy, courts not only possess the inherent power to repudiate, but, indeed, it is required, by the very nature of judicial function,

to abolish such a rule. *Flagiello v. Pennsylvania Hospital*, 417 Pa. 486, 208 A.2d 193 (1965).

The genius of the common law is its ability to adapt to change without losing its sense of direction. As Cardozo said: "The inn that shelters for the night is not the journey's end. The law, like the traveler, must be ready for the morrow. It must have a principle of growth."

Equity As the common law developed in England, it had a tendency to become overly rigid and beset with technicalities. As a consequence, for many wrongs no remedies were provided because the judges insisted that a claim be within the scope of one of the recognized forms of action. Moreover, courts of common law were extremely limited in the remedies they could provide; the principal type of relief obtainable was a money judgment. Consequently, individuals who could not obtain adequate relief from monetary awards began to petition the king directly for justice. He, in turn, came to delegate these petitions to his chancellor.

Gradually, there evolved what was in effect a new and supplementary system of needed judicial relief to those who had no adequate remedy at common law. It was called Equity and was administered by a Court of Chancery presided over by the chancellor. The latter, deciding cases on "equity and good conscience," afforded relief in many instances in which the common law judges refused to act or where the remedy at law was inadequate. Thus, there grew up, side by side, two systems of law administered by different tribunals, the common law courts and courts of equity. Alexander Hamilton stated "that great advantages result from the separation of the equity from the law jurisdiction, and that the causes which belong to the former would be improperly committed to juries. The great and primary use of a court of equity is to give relief in extraordinary cases, which are exceptions to general rules."

An important difference between law and equity is that the chancellor had the power to order a defendant personally to do or refrain from doing a specific act. If the defendant did not comply with the order or **decree**, he could be held in contempt of court and punished by fine or imprisonment. This power of compulsion available in a court of equity opened the door to many needed remedies not available in a court of common law.

Equity jurisdiction, in some cases, recognized rights which were enforceable at common law but provided more effective remedies. For example, for breach of a land contract the buyer could obtain **specific performance** in a court of equity. The defendant seller would be commanded to perform his part of the contract by transferring title to the land. Another powerful and effective remedy available only in the courts of equity was the **injunction**, a court order requiring a party to do or refrain from doing a specified act. No comparable remedies were available in the common law courts. There were other remedies in equity, which were not available elsewhere, among them the remedy of **reformation** where, upon the ground of mutual mistake, an action could be brought to reform or change the language of a written agreement to conform to the actual intention of the contracting parties. Another was an action for **rescission** of a contract which allowed a party to invalidate a contract under certain circumstances.

While courts of equity provided remedies not available in courts of law, they granted them only at their discretion, not as a matter of right. This discretion was exercised according to the general legal principles formulated by equity courts over the years called **maxims.** A few of these familiar maxims of equity are: Equity will not suffer a wrong to be without a remedy. Equity regards the substance rather than the form. Equity abhors a forfeiture. Equity delights to do justice and not by halves. He who comes into equity must come with clean hands. He who seeks equity must do equity. For a comparison of law and equity, see Figure 1-4.

In nearly every jurisdiction in the United States there has been a union of courts of common law and equity into a single court which administers both systems of law. However, vestiges of the old division continue. For example, the right to a trial by jury applies only to actions at law and not to suits filed in equity.

Restatements of Law The common law of the United States results from the independent decisions of the State and Federal courts. The rapid increase in the number of decisions by these courts led to the establishment of the American Law Institute in 1923, composed of a distinguished group of lawyers, judges, and law teachers who assumed the immediate task of preparing "an orderly restatement of the general common law of the United States,

---

FIGURE 1-4   Comparison of Law and Equity

	Law	Equity
Remedy	Judgment	Decree *injunction, for relief*
Availability	Primarily	Secondarily if remedy at law is inadequate
Jury	If either party demands	None
Formality	Technical	Relaxed
Precedents	*Stare decisis*	Equitable maxims

including in that term not only the law developed solely by judicial decision, but also the law that has grown from the application by the courts of statutes that were generally enacted and were in force for many years." Wolkin, "Restatements of the Law: Origin, Preparation, Availability," 21 *Ohio B.A.Rept.* 663 (1940).

The Restatements cover many of the important areas of the common law including torts, contracts, agency, property, and trusts. Although not law by themselves, they are highly persuasive and have frequently been utilized by courts in support of their opinions. The Restatements are regarded as the authoritative statement of the common law of the United States. Because they provide a concise and clear statement of much of the common law, relevant portions of the Restatements are frequently relied upon in this book.

Legislative Law

Since the end of the nineteenth century, legislation has become the primary source of new law and ordered social change in the United States. The total annual volume of legislative law is enormous. Justice Felix Frankfurter's remarks to the New York City Bar in 1947 are even more appropriate today:

. . . Inevitably the work of the Supreme Court reflects the great shift in the center of gravity of law-making. Broadly speaking, the number of cases disposed of by opinions has not changed from term to term. But even as late as 1875 more than 40 percent of the controversies before the Court were common-law litigation, fifty years later only 5 percent, while today cases not resting on statutes are reduced almost to zero. It is therefore accurate to say that courts have ceased to be the primary makers of law in the sense in which they "legislated" the common law. It is certainly true of the Supreme Court that almost every case has a statute at its heart or close to it.

This modern emphasis upon statutory law has occurred because case law develops evolutionarily and haphazardly; thus it is not well suited for making drastic or comprehensive changes. Moreover, courts tend to be hesitant about overruling prior decisions, while it is a common practice for legislatures to repeal prior enactments. In addition, legislatures are independent and able to choose the issues they wish to address, while courts may deal only with those issues presented by actual cases. As a result, legislatures are better equipped to make the dramatic, sweeping, and relatively rapid changes in the law that are needed to respond to the numerous and vast technological, social, and economic innovations that arise.

Some business law topics remain governed principally by the common law, such as contracts, agency, property, and trusts. Most areas of commercial law, however, have become largely statutory, including partnerships, corporations, sales, commercial paper, secured transactions, insurance, securities regulation, antitrust, and bankruptcy. Since most States enacted statutes dealing with these branches of commercial law, a great diversity developed among the States and hampered the conduct of commerce on a national scale. The increased need for greater uniformity brought about the codification of large parts of commercial law.

The most successful example is the **Uniform Commercial Code**, which was prepared under the joint sponsorship and direction of the National Conference of Commissioners on Uniform State Laws and the American Law Institute. The entire Official Text of the Code is set forth in Appendix C of this book. All fifty States (although Louisiana has adopted only Articles 1, 3, 4, and 5), the District of Columbia, and the Virgin Islands have adopted the Uniform Commercial Code. The underlying purposes and policies of the Code are to:

1. simplify, clarify, and modernize the law governing commercial transactions;
2. permit the continued expansion of commercial practices through custom, usage and agreement of the parties;

3. make uniform the law among the various jurisdictions.

Other uniform laws include the Uniform Partnership Act, the Uniform Limited Partnership Act, the Model Business Corporation Act, and the Uniform Probate Code.

Administrative Law

This branch of public law deals with the various regulatory functions and activities of the government in its executive capacity as performed, supervised, and regulated by public officials, departments, boards, and commissions. It also involves controversies arising between individuals and such public officials and agencies. Administrative functions and activities concern such important matters of national safety, welfare, and convenience as the establishment and maintenance of military forces, police, citizenship and naturalization, taxation, coinage of money, elections, environmental protection, the regulation of transportation, interstate highways, waterways, television, radio, trade and commerce, and, in general, public health, safety, and welfare.

Because of the increasing complexity of the social, economic, and industrial life of the nation, the scope of administrative law has expanded enormously. Justice Jackson stated that "the rise of administrative bodies has been the most significant legal trend of the last century, and perhaps more values today are affected by their decisions than by those of all the courts, review of administrative decisions apart." *Federal Trade Commission v. Ruberoid Co.*, 343 U.S. 470. This is evidenced by the great increase in the number and activities of Federal government boards, commissions, and other agencies. Certainly, agencies create more legal rules and adjudicate more controversies than all the legislatures and all the courts combined. Administrative law is more fully discussed in Chapter 3.

LEGAL ANALYSIS

Trial court decisions are not generally reported or published. The weight of the precedent set by a trial court is not sufficient to warrant permanent reporting. Except for the Federal courts, New York, and a few other States where selected opinions of trial courts are published, decisions in trial courts are simply filed in the office of the clerk of the court where they are available for public inspection.

The reported appellate decisions are published in volumes called "reports" which are numbered consecutively. Most State court decisions are found in the State reports of that particular State. In addition, the State reports are published in a regional reporter published by West Publishing Company and called the National Reporter System, comprised of the following: Atlantic (A. or A.2d); South Eastern (S.E. or S.E.2d); South Western (S.W. or S.W.2d); New York Supplement (N.Y.S. or N.Y.S.2d); North Western (N.W. or N.W.2d); North Eastern (N.E. or N.E.2d); Southern (So. or So.2d); and Pacific (P. or P.2d). After they are published, these opinions or "cases" are referred to ("cited") by giving the name of the case, the volume, name, and page of the official State report, if any, in which it is published; the volume, name, and page of the particular set and series of the National Reporter System; and the volume, name, and page of any other selected case series. For instance, the case of *Lefkowitz v. Great Minneapolis Surplus Store, Inc.*, 251 Minn. 188, 86 N.W.2d 689 (1957), indicates that the opinion in this case may be found in Volume 251 of the official Minnesota Reports at page 188; and in Volume 86 of the Northwestern Reporter, Second Series, at page 689. The Federal Court decisions are found in the Federal Reporter (Fed. or F.2d); Federal Supplement (F.Supp.); Federal Rules Decisions (F.R.D.); and United States Supreme Court Reports (U.S.), Supreme Court Reporter (S.Ct.), and Lawyers Edition (L.Ed.).

In reading the title of a case, such as "*Jones v. Brown*," the "*v*" or "*vs*" means versus or against. In the trial court, Jones is the **plaintiff**, the person who filed the suit, and Brown is the **defendant**, the person against whom the suit was brought. When the case is appealed, some, but not all, appellate courts place the name of the party who appeals, or the **appellant**, first, so that "*Jones v. Brown*" in the trial court becomes, if Brown loses and is the appellant, "*Brown v. Jones*" in the appellate court. Since some appellate courts retain the trial court order of names, it is not always possible to determine from the title itself who was the plaintiff and who the defendant. The student must carefully read the facts of each case and clearly identify each party in his mind in order to understand the discussion by the appellate court.

Study of the reported cases requires an understanding and application of legal analysis. Normally, the reported opinion in a case sets forth (a) essential facts, nature of the action, the parties, what happened to precipitate the controversy, what happened in the lower court, and what pleadings are material to the issues; (b) the issues of law or fact; (c) the legal principles involved; (d) the application of these principles; and (e) the decision.

A serviceable method of analyzing and briefing cases after a careful reading and comprehension of the opinion is for the student to write in his own language a brief containing the:

1. Facts of the case;
2. Issue or question involved;
3. Decision of the court;
4. Reasons for the decision.

The following excerpt from Professor Karl Llewellyn's *The Bramble Bush* contains a number of useful suggestions for reading cases:

The first thing to do with an opinion, then, is read it. The next thing is to get clear the actual decision, the judgment rendered. Who won, the plaintiff or defendant? And watch your step here. You are after in first instance the plaintiff and defendant *below*, in the trial court. In order to follow through what happened you must therefore first know the outcome *below*; else you do not see what was appealed from, nor by whom. You now follow through in order to see exactly what *further* judgment has been rendered on appeal. The stage is then cleared of form—although of course you do not yet know all that these forms mean, that they imply. You can turn now to what you want peculiarly to know. Given the actual judgments below and above as your indispensable framework—what has the case decided, and what can you derive from it as to what will be decided later?

You will be looking, in the opinion, or in the preliminary matter plus the opinion, for the following: a statement of the facts the court assumes; a statement of the precise way the question has come before the court—which includes what the plaintiff wanted below, and what the defendant did about it, the judgment below, and what the trial court did that is complained of; then the outcome on appeal, the judgment; and, finally the reasons this court gives for doing what it did. This does not look so bad. But it is much worse than it looks.

For all our cases are decided, all our opinions are written, all our predictions, all our arguments are made, on certain four assumptions. They are the first presuppositions of our study. They must be rutted into you till you can juggle with them standing on your head and in your sleep.

1) *The court must decide the dispute that is before it.* It cannot refuse because the job is hard, or dubious, or dangerous. *very imp Bacon*

2) *The court can decide only the particular dispute which is before it.* When it speaks to that question it speaks ex cathedra, with authority, with finality, with an almost magic power. When it speaks to the question before it, it announces *law*, and if what it announces is new, it legislates, it *makes* the law. But when it speaks to any other question at all, it says mere words, which no man needs to follow. Are such words worthless? They are not. We know them as judicial *dicta*; when they are wholly off the point at issue we call them *obiter dicta*—words dropped along the road, wayside remarks. Yet even wayside remarks shed light on the remarker. They may be very useful in the future to him, or to us. But he will not feel bound to them, as to his ex cathedra utterance. They

came not hallowed by a Delphic frenzy. He may be slow to change them; but not so slow as in the other case.

3) *The court can decide the particular dispute only according to a* general *rule which covers a whole class of like disputes.* Our legal theory does not admit of single decisions standing on their own. If judges are free, are indeed forced, to decide new cases for which there is no rule, they must at least make a new rule as they decide. So far, good. But how wide, or how narrow, is the general rule in this particular case? That is a troublesome matter. The practice of our case-law, however, is I think fairly stated thus: it pays to be suspicious of general rules which look too wide; it pays to go slow in feeling *certain* that a wide

rule has been laid down at all, or that, if seemingly laid down, it will be followed. For there is a fourth accepted canon:

4) *Everything, everything, everything, big or small, a judge may say in an opinion, is to be read with primary reference to the particular dispute, the particular question before him.* You are not to think that the words mean what they might if they stood alone. You are to have your eye on the case in hand, and to learn how to interpret all that has been said *merely* as a reason for deciding *that* case *that* way.

By way of example, the following edited case of *Caldwell v. Bechtel, Inc.* is presented and then briefed using the suggested format.

CASE

CALDWELL v. BECHTEL, INC.

United States Court of Appeals, District of Columbia Circuit, 1980.
631 F.2d 989.

MacKinnon, J.

We are here concerned with a claim for damages by a worker who allegedly contracted silicosis while he was mucking in a tunnel under construction as part of the metropolitan subway system [WMATA]. The basic issue is whether a consultant engineering firm owed the worker a duty to protect him against unreasonable risk of harm.

* * *

In attempting to convince the court that it owes no duty of reasonable care to protect appellant's safety, Bechtel argues that by its contract with WMATA it assumed duties only to WMATA. Appellant has not brought action, however, for breach of contract but rather seeks damages for an asserted breach of the duty of reasonable care. Unlike contractual duties, which are imposed by agreement of the parties to a contract, a duty of due care under tort law is based primarily upon social policy. The law imposes upon individuals certain expectations of conduct, such as the ex-

pectancy that their actions will not cause foreseeable injury to another. These societal expectations, as formed through the common law, comprise the concept of duty.

Society's expectations, and the concomitant duties imposed, vary in response to the activity engaged in by the defendant. If defendant is driving a car, he will be held to exercise the degree of care normally exercised by a reasonable person in like circumstances. Or if defendant is engaged in the practice of his profession, he will be held to exercise a degree of care consistent with his superior knowledge and skill. Hence, when defendant Bechtel engaged in consulting engineering services, the company was required to observe a standard of care ordinarily adhered to by one providing such services, possessing such skill and expertise.

A secondary but equally important principle involved in a determination of duty is to whom the duty is owed. The answer to this question is usually framed in terms of the foreseeable plaintiff, in other words, one who might foreseeably be injured by defendant's conduct. This secondary principle also serves to distinguish tort law from contract law. While in contract law, only one to whom the contract specifies that a duty be rendered will have a cause of action for its breach, in tort law, society, not the contract, specifies to whom the duty is owed, and this has traditionally been the foreseeable plaintiff.

It is important to keep these differences between contract and tort duties in mind when examining whether Bechtel's undertaking of contractual duties to WMATA created a duty of reasonable care toward Caldwell. Dean Prosser expressed the relationship in this terse fashion:

[B]y entering into a contract with A, the defendant may place himself in such a relation toward B that the law will impose upon him an obligation, sounding in tort and not in contract, to act in such a way that B will not be injured. The incidental fact of the existence of the contract with A does not negative the responsibility of the actor when he enters upon a course of affirmative conduct which may be expected to affect the interests of another person.

*   *   *

Analyzing the common law, Prosser noted that courts have found a duty to act for the protection of another when certain relationships exist, such as carrier—passenger, innkeeper—guest, shipper—seaman, employer—employee, shopkeeper—visitor, host—social guest, jailor—prisoner, and school—pupil. These holdings suggest that courts have been eroding the general rule that there is no duty to act to help another in distress, by creating exceptions based upon a relationship between the actors.

*   *   *

We find that case law provides many such analogous situations from which the principles deserving of application to this case may be culled. The foregoing concepts of duty converge in this case, as the facts include both the WMATA-Bechtel contractual relationship from which it was foreseeable that a negligent undertaking by Bechtel might injure the appellant, and a special relationship established between Bechtel and the appellant because of Bechtel's superior skills, knowledge of the dangerous condition, and ability to protect appellant.

*   *   *

We reverse the summary judgment of the district court, and hold that as a matter of law, on the record as we are required to view it at this time, Bechtel owed Caldwell a duty of due care to take reasonable steps to protect him from the foreseeable risk of harm to his health posed by the excessive concentration of silica dust in the Metro tunnels. We remand so that Caldwell will have an opportunity to prove, if he can, the other elements of his negligence action.

BRIEF OF CALDWELL V. BECHTEL, INC.

I. FACTS: Caldwell was a laborer who now suffers from silicosis. He claims that he contracted the disease while he was working in a tunnel under construction as part of the Washington Metropolitan Area Transportation Authority (WMATA). He brought this action for damages against Bechtel, Inc., a consultant engineering firm under contract with WMATA for the project.

II. ISSUE: Did Bechtel owe a duty of due care to Caldwell to take reasonable steps to protect him from the foreseeable risk of harm to his health posed by the excessive concentration of silica dust in the subway tunnels?

III. DECISION: In favor of Caldwell. Summary judgment reversed and case remanded to the district court.

IV. REASONS: Caldwell has not brought an action for breach of contract. Rather, he seeks damages for an alleged breach of the duty of reasonable care. Unlike contractual duties, which are imposed by agreement of the parties to a contract, a duty of due care under tort law is based primarily on social policy. That is, the law imposes upon individuals the expectation that their actions will not cause foreseeable injury to another. These societal expectations comprise the concept of duty— a concept that varies in response to the activity engaged in by the individual. Moreover, the duty is owed by anyone who might foreseeably be injured by the conduct of the actor in question. In contrast, under contract law, a duty is owed only to those parties specified in the contract.

Here, by entering into a contract with WMATA, Bechtel placed itself in such a relation toward Caldwell that the law will impose upon it an obligation in tort, and not in contract, to act in such a way that Caldwell would not be injured.

Chapter 2

LEGAL PROCESS

A S discussed in Chapter 1, substantive law establishes the rights and duties of individuals and other legal entities while procedural law governs the means by which these rights are asserted. Pursuant to this role, procedural law attempts to accomplish two competing objectives that may at times conflict with each other. First, the judicial process should be perceived by all parties to the dispute as being fair and impartial. Second, the process should operate with administrative efficiency. The judicial process in the United States represents a balance between these two objectives as well as an expression of this country's commitment to the adversary system.

The first part of this chapter describes the structure and function of the Federal and State court systems. The second part deals with jurisdiction while the final section covers the procedure in civil lawsuits.

THE COURT SYSTEM

Courts are impartial tribunals (seats of judgment) established by governmental bodies to settle disputes. A court may render a binding decision only when it has jurisdiction over the dispute and the parties to that dispute. The United States has a dual court system: each of the fifty States plus the District of Columbia has its own system as does the Federal government.

The Federal Courts

Article III of the United States Constitution states that the judicial power of the United States shall be vested in one Supreme Court and such lower courts as Congress may establish. Congress has established a Federal court system consisting of a number of special courts, district courts, and courts of appeals.

The Federal court system is staffed by judges who receive lifetime appointments from the president, subject to confirmation by the Senate. The structure of the Federal court system is illustrated in Figure 2-1.

District Courts *TRIAL Courts* The district courts are the trial courts of general jurisdiction in the Federal system. Most cases begin in the district court, and it is here that issues of fact are decided. The district court is generally presided over by *one* judge, although in certain cases three judges preside. In a few cases, an appeal from a judgment or decree of a district court is taken directly to the Supreme Court. In most cases, however, appeals are taken to the Circuit Court of Appeals of the appropriate circuit, the decision of which is, in most cases, final.

Congress has established judicial districts, each of which is located entirely in a particular State. All States have at least one district, while certain States contain more than one district. For instance, New York has four districts, Illinois has three, Wisconsin has two, while a number of less populated States comprise a single district.

Courts of Appeals Congress has established twelve judicial circuits, each having a court known as the Court of Appeals, which primarily hears appeals from the district courts

located within its circuit. See map of Federal circuits, Figure 2-2. In addition, they review orders of certain administrative agencies. The United States Courts of Appeals generally hear cases in panels of *three* judges.

The Courts of Appeals exercise no original jurisdiction, being solely courts of review. Accordingly, they do *not* hear witnesses. The function of appellate courts is to examine the record of a case on appeal and to determine whether the trial court committed prejudicial error. If so, the appellate court will reverse or modify the judgment of the lower court and whenever necessary remand or send it back to the lower court for further proceeding. If there is no prejudicial error, the appellate court will affirm the decision of the lower court.

The Supreme Court The nation's highest tribunal is the United States Supreme Court, consisting of nine justices (a Chief Justice and eight Associate Justices), who sit as a group in Washington, D.C. The United States Supreme Court has original jurisdiction (the right to hear a case first) in certain types of cases described in the second paragraph of Section 2 of Article III of the United States Constitution:

In all Cases affecting Ambassadors, other public Ministers and Consuls, and those in which a State

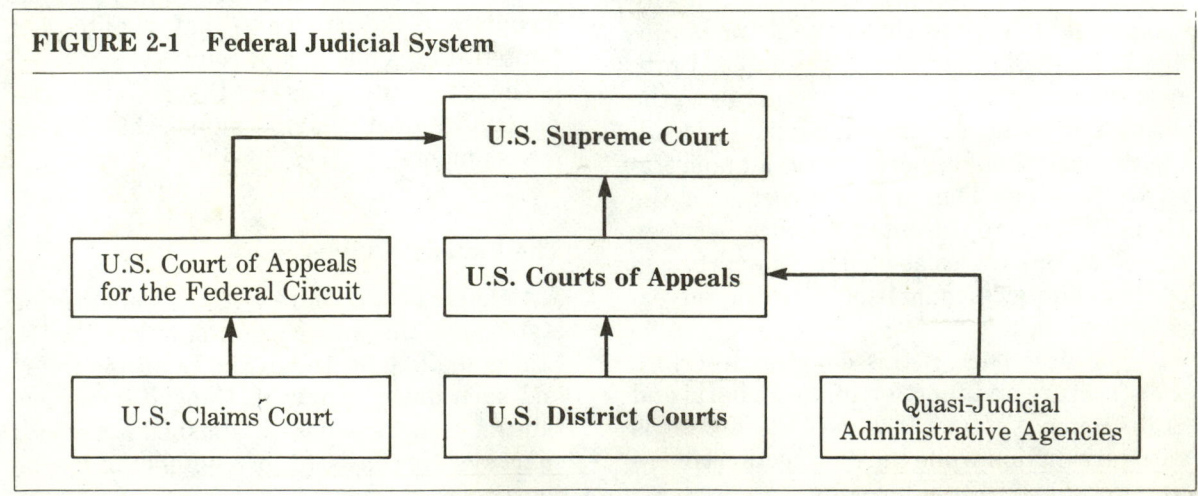

FIGURE 2-1   Federal Judicial System

FIGURE 2-2   The Twelve Federal Judicial Circuits

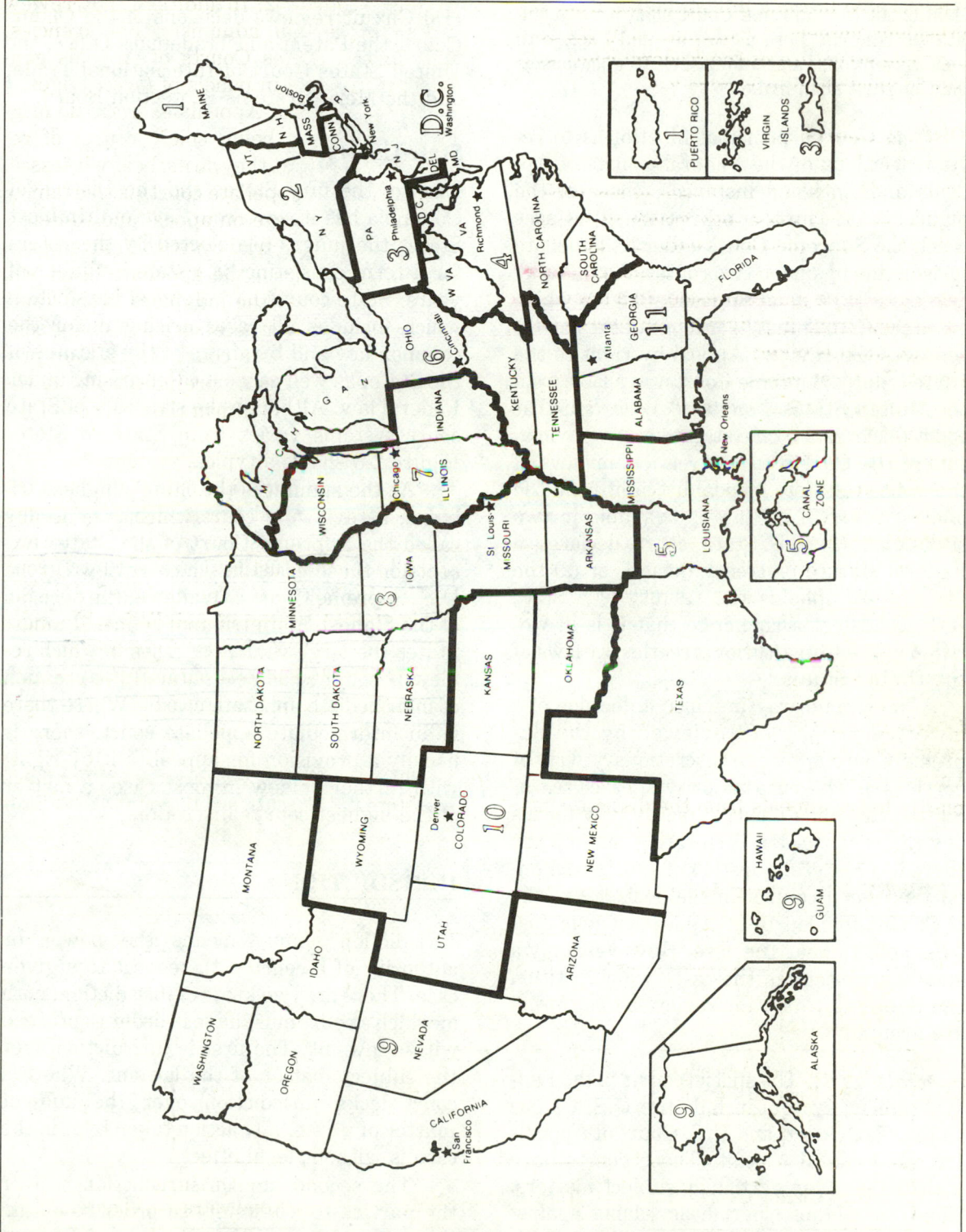

shall be Party, the supreme Court shall have original Jurisdiction. In all the other Cases before mentioned, the supreme Court shall have appellate Jurisdiction, both as to Law and Fact, with such Exceptions, and under such Regulations as the Congress shall make.

The Court's principal function is to review decisions of the Federal Courts of Appeals and, in some instances, those of the highest State courts or other tribunals. Cases reach the Supreme Court under its appellate jurisdiction by one of two routes. A relatively few come by way of **appeal by right**, which cases the Court must hear if one of the parties requests the review. Appeal by right to the United States Supreme Court is available from the United States *Courts of Appeals* if that court declares a State statute to be in violation of the Constitution, treaties, or laws of the United States. Appeal by right from the highest court of a *State* is available in two situations: (1) the State court declares a Federal statute or treaty invalid, or (2) the State court upholds the validity of a State statute against a challenge that it is in violation of the Constitution, treaties, or laws of the United States.

The second way in which a decision of a lower court may be reviewed by the Supreme Court is by the discretionary **writ of certiorari**. The vast majority of cases reaching the Supreme Court come to it by means of writs of *certiorari*. Writs are granted when there is a Federal question of substantial importance or a conflict in the decisions of the U.S. Circuit Courts of Appeals if four Justices vote to hear the case. However, only a small percentage of the cases which petition the Supreme Court for review by *certiorari* are granted.

Special Courts The special courts in the Federal judicial system include the U.S. Claims Court, Tax Court, and U.S. Court of Appeals for the Federal Circuit. These courts have jurisdiction over particular subject matters. The U.S. Claims Court hears claims against the United States. The Tax Court has juris-

diction over certain cases involving Federal taxes. The U.S. Court of Appeals for the Federal Circuit reviews decisions of the Claims Court, the Patent and Trademark Office, the United States Court of International Trade, and the Merit Systems Protection Board.

State Courts

Each of the fifty States and the District of Columbia has its own court system. In most States the judges are elected by the voters for a term consisting of a stated number of years. State courts have general jurisdiction which includes all cases arising under the common law and by virtue of the statutes of the State, as well as most cases arising under Federal law. Although the structure of State court systems varies from State to State, Figure 2-3 shows a typical system.

At the summit is the State's highest tribunal, a reviewing court which is generally called the Supreme Court of the State. Except for those cases in which review by the U.S. Supreme Court is available, the decision of the highest State tribunal is final. In most States the large volume of cases in which review is sought has necessitated the creation of intermediate appellate courts. Where there is an intermediate appellate court, there is usually a provision for appeal to it by right, with further review in most cases a matter of the highest court's discretion.

JURISDICTION

Jurisdiction simply means the power or authority of a court with respect to a given case. There are two kinds of jurisdiction, both of which a court must have in order to proceed with a lawsuit. The first is jurisdiction over the subject matter of the lawsuit. Where a court lacks jurisdiction over the **subject matter** of a case, any action taken by it in the case is without legal effect.

The second kind of jurisdiction is over the **parties** to a lawsuit. In order to obtain this type of jurisdiction over the defendant

FIGURE 2–3   State Court System

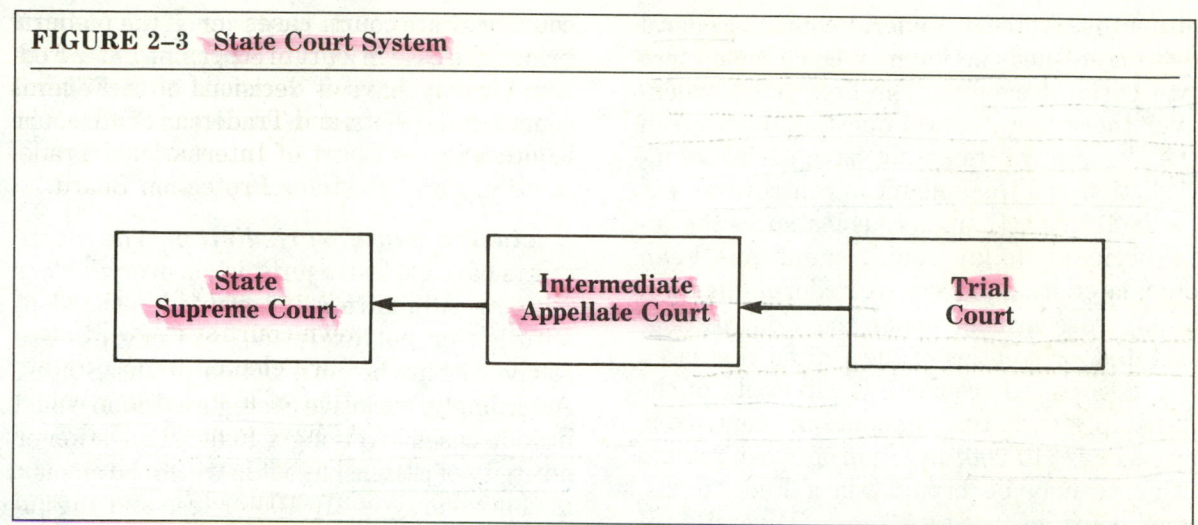

named in a lawsuit, in most instances the defendant must either be present or domiciled in the court's territory or the transaction out of which the case has arisen must have a substantial connection to the court's territory. The court obtains jurisdiction over the plaintiff by the plaintiff's voluntary submission to the court's power through filing his complaint with the court.

In addition to having jurisdiction over the subject matter and the parties, a valid exercise of jurisdiction requires that the parties to the dispute are accorded fair notice and a reasonable opportunity to be heard. This overriding limitation is imposed upon the Federal and State courts by the U.S. Constitution.

Subject Matter Jurisdiction

Subject matter jurisdiction refers to the authority of a particular court to adjudicate a controversy of a particular kind. Federal courts have *limited* subject matter jurisdiction. Article III, Section 2, of the Federal Constitution sets forth the subject matter jurisdiction of the Federal courts as follows:

The judicial Power shall extend to all Cases, in Law and Equity, arising under this Constitution,

the Laws of the United States, and Treaties made, or which shall be made, under their Authority;—to all Cases affecting Ambassadors, other public Ministers and Consuls;—to all Cases of admiralty and maritime Jurisdiction;—to Controversies to which the United States shall be a Party—to Controversies between two or more States;—between a State and Citizens of another State;—between Citizens of different States;—between Citizens of the same State claiming Lands under Grants of different States, and between a State, or the Citizens thereof, and foreign States, Citizens or Subjects.

State courts have jurisdiction over *all* matters that have not been exclusively given to the Federal courts or expressly taken away by the Constitution or Congress.

Exclusive Federal Jurisdiction The Federal courts have exclusive jurisdiction over Federal criminal prosecutions, admiralty, bankruptcy, antitrust, patent, trademark and copyright cases, suits against the United States, and cases arising under certain Federal statutes that expressly provide for exclusive Federal jurisdiction.

Concurrent Federal Jurisdiction All instances of Federal jurisdiction other than exclusive are concurrent and thus may be heard either by State or Federal courts. Federal concurrent jurisdiction may be classified into two basic categories. The first arises whenever there is a Federal question over which the Federal courts do not have exclusive jurisdiction and the amount in controversy exceeds $10,000. In numerous instances the jurisdictional dollar requirement has been eliminated by Congress. A **Federal question** is any case arising under the Constitution, statutes, or treaties of the United States.

Second, where there is "diversity of citizenship" and the amount in controversy exceeds $10,000, an action between private litigants may be brought in a Federal district court or a State court. **Diversity of citizenship** exists (1) when the plaintiff or plaintiffs are all citizens of a State or States different from the State or States of which the defendants are citizens; (2) when a foreign country is bringing an action against citizens of the United States; *or* (3) when the controversy is between citizens of the United States and citizens of a foreign country. The citizenship of an individual litigant is the State of her residence or domicile, while that of a corporate litigant is both the State of incorporation and the State in which its principal place of business is located. For example, if the amount in controversy exceeds $10,000, then diversity of citizenship jurisdiction would be satisfied if A, a citizen of California, sues B, a citizen of Idaho. However, if A, a citizen of Virginia, and B, a citizen of North Carolina, sue C, a citizen of Georgia, and D, a citizen of North Carolina, there would *not* be diversity of citizenship because there are citizens of North Carolina as both plaintiff and defendant.

When a Federal district court hears a case solely under diversity of citizenship jurisdiction, there is no Federal question involved, and accordingly the Federal courts must apply State law. *See Erie Railroad Co. v. Tompkins.*

In any case involving concurrent jurisdiction, the plaintiff has the choice of bringing the action in either an appropriate Federal court or State court. However, if the plaintiff brings the case in a State court, the defendant usually may have it removed to a Federal court for the district in which the State court is located.

Exclusive State Jurisdiction The State courts have exclusive jurisdiction over *all other matters*. All matters not granted in the Constitution or not exercised by Congress are solely within the jurisdiction of the States. Accordingly, exclusive State jurisdiction would include cases involving a Federal question or diversity of citizenship but in which the amount in controversy is $10,000 or less and the jurisdictional amount has not been statutorily waived by Congress. In addition, all cases to which the Federal judicial power does not reach would be exclusively within the jurisdiction of the State courts. These matters include, but are by no means limited to, property, torts, contract, agency, commercial transactions, and most crimes.

The jurisdiction of the Federal and State courts is illustrated by Figure 2-4.

Stare Decisis in the Dual Court System The doctrine of *stare decisis* presents certain problems when there are two parallel court systems. As a consequence, in the United States *stare decisis* functions approximately as follows (also illustrated in Figure 2–5):

1. The United States Supreme Court has never held itself to be rigidly bound by its own decisions, and lower Federal courts and State courts have followed that course in respect to their own decisions.
2. A decision of the U.S. Supreme Court on Federal questions is binding on all other courts, Federal or State.
3. While a decision of a Federal court other than the Supreme Court may be persuasive in a State court on a Federal question, it is nevertheless not binding.
4. A decision of a State court may be persuasive in the Federal courts, but it is not

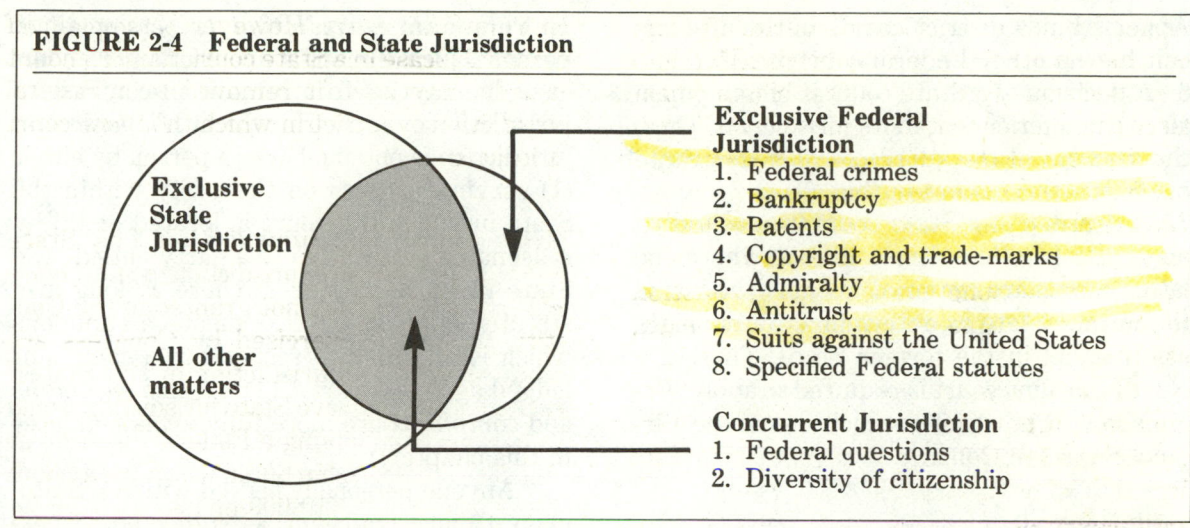

FIGURE 2-4　Federal and State Jurisdiction

Exclusive State Jurisdiction

All other matters

Exclusive Federal Jurisdiction
1. Federal crimes
2. Bankruptcy
3. Patents
4. Copyright and trade-marks
5. Admiralty
6. Antitrust
7. Suits against the United States
8. Specified Federal statutes

Concurrent Jurisdiction
1. Federal questions
2. Diversity of citizenship

binding except where Federal jurisdiction is based on diversity of citizenship, in which case the Federal courts are required to apply local State law as determined by the highest State tribunal and not by a trial or intermediate appellate court.

5. Decisions of the Federal courts (other than the U.S. Supreme Court) are not binding upon other Federal courts of coordinate rank, or of inferior rank, unless the latter owe obedience to the court rendering the decision. Thus, a decision of the Fifth Circuit Court of

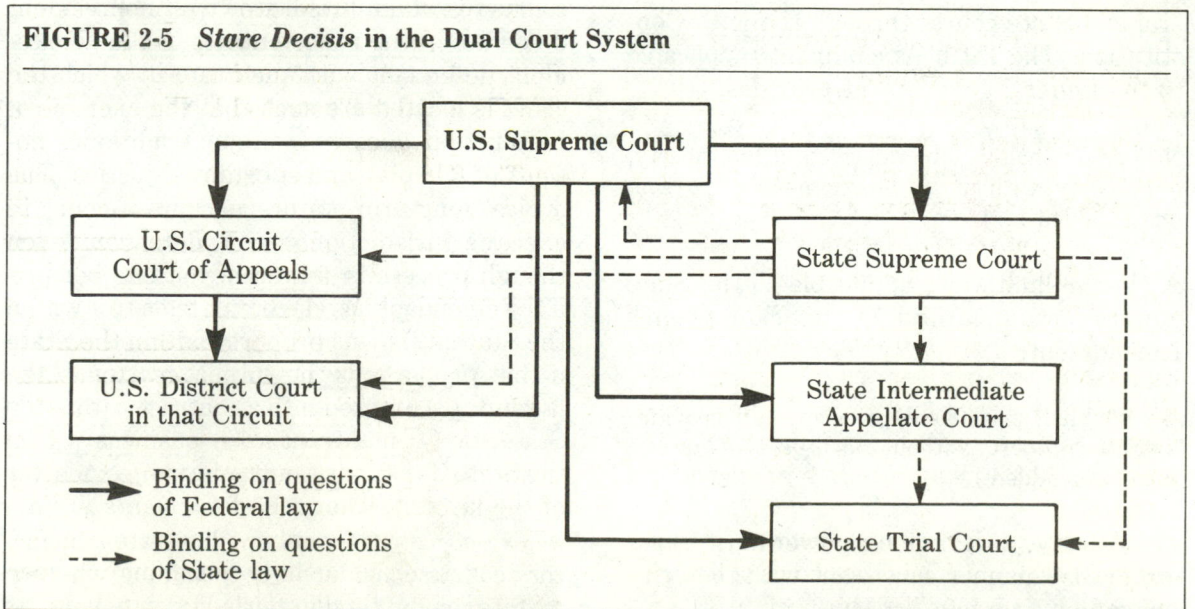

FIGURE 2-5　*Stare Decisis* in the Dual Court System

U.S. Supreme Court

U.S. Circuit Court of Appeals

U.S. District Court in that Circuit

State Supreme Court

State Intermediate Appellate Court

State Trial Court

Binding on questions of Federal law

Binding on questions of State law

Appeals binds district courts in the fifth circuit but no other Federal court.

6. A decision of a State court is binding upon all courts inferior to it in its jurisdiction. Thus, the decision of the supreme court in a State binds all other courts in that State.

7. A decision of a State court is not binding on courts in other States except where the latter courts are required to apply the law of the former State as determined by the highest tribunal in the former State. Thus, if a North Carolina court is required to apply Virginia law, it must follow decisions of the Virginia Supreme Court.

Jurisdiction Over the Parties

The second essential type of jurisdiction is the power of a court to bind the parties involved in the dispute. This type of jurisdiction is called jurisdiction over the parties and its requirements may be met in any of three ways: (1) *in personam* jurisdiction, (2) *in rem* jurisdiction, or (3) attachment jurisdiction. In addition, the constitutionally imposed requirements of reasonable notification and a reasonable opportunity to be heard must also be satisfied. This overriding limitation on jurisdictional power is imposed upon the Federal and State courts through the U.S. Constitution. The Fifth Amendment, applicable to the Federal government provides:

No person shall . . . be deprived of life, liberty, or property, without *due process of law*. . . . (Emphasis added.)

A similar limitation, applicable to the State courts, is contained in the Fourteenth Amendment:

. . . Nor shall any State deprive any person of life, liberty or property without *due process of law* . . . (Emphasis added.)

Accordingly, jurisdictional power must be asserted in a manner consistent with the principle of "due process" of law.

In Personam *Jurisdiction* *In personam,* or personal jurisdiction, is jurisdiction of a court over the parties to a lawsuit in contrast to jurisdiction over their property. *In personam* jurisdiction is obtained over a person by either (1) serving process on the party within the State in which the court is located or (2) by reasonable notification to a party outside the State in those instances where a "long arm statute" applies. *Process* means a summons which is an order to respond to a complaint lodged against a party. (The terms *summons* and *complaint* are more fully explained later in this chapter.)

Anyone personally served within a State, even a mere transient, is subjected to personal jurisdiction of courts within that State. For instance, A, a resident of Ohio, while driving his automobile through Texas, is served with a summons from a Texas court. The Texas court has obtained personal jurisdiction over A because A was personally served within Texas. The same is true of B, a resident of New Jersey, who is served in Dallas when the airplane in which he is flying touches down for a brief stop.

In addition, most States have adopted **long-arm statutes** in order to expand their jurisdictional reach. These statutes allow courts to obtain jurisdiction over nonresident defendants when the contacts of the nonresident defendant with the State in which the court is located are such that the exercise of jurisdiction does not offend traditional notions of fair play and substantial justice. The typical long-arm statute permits a court to exercise jurisdiction over a defendant even though process is served beyond its borders if the defendant has (1) committed a tort within the State, (2) owns property within the State if that property is the subject matter of the lawsuit, (3) entered into a contract within the State, or (4) has transacted business within the State if that business is the subject matter of the lawsuit. The case of *Clements v. Barney's Sporting Goods Store* illustrates the factors courts consider in determining whether a State may extend its jurisdiction beyond its territorial borders through the use of a long-arm statute.

In Rem *Jurisdiction* Courts in a State have the jurisdiction to adjudicate claims to property situated within the State if provision is made for giving reasonable notice and opportunity to be heard to those persons who have an interest in the property. Such jurisdiction over property is called *in rem* jurisdiction from the Latin word *"res"* which means thing. For example, if A and B are involved in a lawsuit over property located in Kansas, then an appropriate court in Kansas would have *in rem* jurisdiction to adjudicate claims with respect to this property so long as both parties are given notice of the lawsuit and a reasonable opportunity to contest the claim.

Attachment Jurisdiction Attachment jurisdiction or **quasi** *in rem* jurisdiction is jurisdiction over property rather than over a person. Attachment jurisdiction is invoked by seizing the defendant's property located within the State in order to obtain payment of a claim against the defendant that is *unrelated* to the property seized. The basis of jurisdiction, therefore, is the State's connection with the property and does not depend upon any connection between the State and the defendant. Attachment jurisdiction differs from *in rem* jurisdiction. The purpose of *in rem* jurisdiction is to resolve conflicting claims to the property while in attachment jurisdiction both parties accept that the property is owned by the defendant but the plaintiff seeks to seize it to obtain payment for his claim against the defendant. For example, A, a resident of Ohio, has obtained a valid judgment in the amount of $20,000 against B, a citizen of Kentucky. A can attach B's automobile which is located in Ohio to satisfy her court judgment against B.

However, in attachment jurisdiction, as with all forms of jurisdiction, the State must have sufficient, minimum contacts with the controversy so as to comport with due process. Accordingly, in the example above, the fact that A was a resident of Ohio satisfies this requirement. On the other hand, if the automobile had been located in West Virginia it is doubtful that a court in West Virginia could assert attachment jurisdiction over B's automobile.

Venue Venue, which is often confused with jurisdiction, deals with the location where a lawsuit *should* be brought. State rules of venue typically provide that suit must be initiated in the county in which one of the defendants resides. In matters involving real estate most venue rules require suit to be initiated in the county in which the property is situated. However, a court may remove a case from one proper court to another where it suits the convenience of witnesses and the ends of justice.

A defendant may object to the venue for various reasons. For instance, a defendant may object to venue based on the principle of *forum non-conveniens*. This basically means that the presentation of the case in that court will create a hardship on the defendant or on relevant witnesses because of the great distance the individuals must travel. The court does not dismiss the case in such a situation. Rather, it shifts the case to a more convenient forum.

CIVIL PROCEDURE

Civil disputes that enter the judicial system are subject to the rules of civil procedure which are designed to effect a just, prompt, and inexpensive resolution of the dispute.

To acquaint the student with civil procedure, it will be helpful to carry a hypothetical action through the trial court to the highest court of review in the State. Although there are technical differences in trial and appellate procedure among the States, the following illustration will serve to provide a general understanding of the trial and appeal of cases. Assume that A, a pedestrian, while crossing a street in Chicago, is struck by an automobile driven by B. A suffers serious personal injuries, incurs heavy medical and hospital expenses, and is unable to work for several months. A desires that B pay her for the loss and damages that she sustained. Attempts at settlement failing, A brings an action at law against B. A is the plaintiff, and B the defendant. Each is represented by a lawyer. Let us follow the progress of the case.

The Pleadings

The purpose of pleadings is to establish the issues of fact and law presented and disputed. A lawsuit is commenced by A, the plaintiff, filing with the clerk of the trial court a complaint against B which alleges: (1) the relevant facts, (2) the existence of a duty owing by the defendant to the plaintiff by reason of the facts, (3) a breach of that duty by the defendant, (4) loss and damage sustained by the plaintiff proximately resulting from that breach, and (5) prayer for relief requesting a judgment for money damages or other appropriate remedy.

The sheriff of the county, or one of his deputies, serves a summons and a copy of the complaint upon B, the defendant, commanding him to file his appearance and answer with the clerk of the court within a specific time, usually thirty days from the date of service of the summons. The **summons** serves the important function of notifying the defendant that a suit has been commenced against him. Proper service of the summons establishes the court's jurisdiction over the person of the defendant.

In this example A's complaint alleges that while in the exercise of due and reasonable care for her own safety, she was struck by B's automobile, which was negligently being driven by B, causing personal injuries and damages of $50,000 for which A requests judgment.

At this point B, the defendant, has several options. He may make **pre-trial motions** contesting the court's jurisdiction over him or asserting that the action is barred by the Statute of Limitations, which requires suits to be brought within a specified time. B may also move that the complaint be made more definite and certain, or B may instead move that the complaint be dismissed for failure to state a claim upon which relief may be granted. Such a motion is sometimes called a **demurrer** and essentially asserts that even if all of A's allegations are true, A would, nevertheless, not be entitled to the relief she seeks, and, therefore, there is no need for a trial of the facts. The court rules on this motion as a matter of law. If it rules in favor of the defendant, the plaintiff may appeal the ruling.

Most likely, B will respond to the complaint by filing an **answer** which may contain admissions, denials, affirmative defenses, and counterclaims. Thus, B might answer the complaint by denying its allegations of negligence and stating, on the other hand, that he, B, was driving his car at a low speed and with reasonable care (a denial) when his car struck A (an admission) who had dashed across the street in front of B's car without looking in any direction to see whether cars or other vehicles were approaching; that, accordingly, A's injuries were caused by her own negligence (an **affirmative defense**) and therefore she should not be permitted to recover any damages. B might further state that A caused damages to his car and request a judgment for $2,000 (a **counterclaim**). An issue of fact is thus made by the pleadings as to whether A or B, or both, had failed to exercise due and reasonable care under the circumstances and were thus negligent and liable for their carelessness.

If the defendant counterclaims, the plaintiff must respond by a **reply** which may contain admissions, denials or affirmative defenses.

After the pleadings, either party may move for **judgment on the pleadings** which requests the judge to rule as a matter of law whether the facts as alleged in the pleadings, which for the purpose of the motion are taken to be as alleged by the nonmoving party, form a sufficient basis to grant the requested relief.

Pretrial Procedure

In preparation for trial and even before completion of the pleadings stage, each party has the right to obtain evidence, or facts which may lead to evidence, from the other party. This procedure is known as **discovery**. It includes (1) pretrial **depositions** consisting of sworn testimony of the opposing party, or other witnesses, taken out of court; (2) sworn answers by the opposing party to **written interrogatories**; (3) **production** of documents and physical objects in the possession of the opposing party; (4) **examination** by a physician of the physical condition of the opposing party, to the extent relevant; and (5) admissions of facts set forth in a **request for admissions** submitted to the opposing party. By proper use of discovery each party may become fully informed of the evidence and avoid surprise at the trial. Another purpose of this procedure is to encourage and facilitate settlements by providing both parties with as much relevant information as possible.

The evidence disclosed by discovery may be so clear that a trial to determine the facts becomes unnecessary. Thus, after discovery, either party may move for a **summary judgment** which requests the judge to rule that, since there are no issues of fact to be determined by trial, as a matter of law that party should prevail. *See Parker v. Twentieth Century-Fox Film Corp.*

3. Trial

Either by statute or court rule, either party desiring trial by jury, in cases in which one is available, must file a written jury demand not later than the date when his first written pleading is due. Assuming a timely demand for a jury has been made, the trial begins by selection of a jury. The jury selection process involves an examination of the jurors called *voir dire.* Each party has an unlimited number of **challenges for cause** which allow a party to prevent a prospective juror from serving on the jury if the prospective juror is biased or cannot be fair and impartial. In addition, each party has a limited number of **peremptory challenges** for which no cause is required to disqualify a prospective juror.

After the jury has been selected, each attorney makes an **opening statement** concerning the facts that he expects to prove in the trial. The plaintiff and her witnesses then testify upon **direct examination**. Each is subject to **cross-examination** by the defendant's attorney. Thus, in our hypothetical case, the plaintiff has her witnesses testify that the traffic light at the street intersection where A was struck was green for traffic in the direction in which A was crossing but changed to orange when A was about one-third of the way across.

In the course of the trial the judge rules upon the admission and exclusion of evidence. If the judge refuses to allow certain evidence to be introduced or certain testimony to be given, the only way the attorney can preserve for review on appeal the question of its admissibility is by making an **offer of proof**. This is not regarded as evidence, and the offer, which is made outside of the presence of the jury, consists of oral statements of counsel or witnesses for the purpose of the record to show the substance of the evidence which the judge has ruled inadmissible.

After cross-examination, followed by redirect examination of each of her witnesses, the plaintiff rests her case. At this point the defendant may move for a **directed verdict** in his favor. If the judge concludes that the evidence introduced by the plaintiff, which is assumed to be true, would not be sufficient for the jury to find in favor of the plaintiff, then the judge will grant the directed verdict in favor of the defendant.

If the judge denies the motion for a directed verdict, then the defendant has the opportunity to present evidence. The defendant and his witnesses testify that B was driving his car at a low speed when it struck A and that B at the time had the green light at the intersection. After the defendant has presented his evidence and both parties have rested, then each party may move for a directed verdict. By this motion the party is contending that the evidence is so clear that reasonable persons could not differ as to the outcome of the case. If the judge grants the motion for a directed verdict, the judge takes the case away from the jury and enters a judgment for the party making the motion.

If these motions are denied, then the plaintiff's attorney makes an argument to the jury, reviewing the evidence and urging a verdict in favor of his client, A, followed by defendant's attorney, who summarizes the evidence in the light most favorable to her client, B. A's attorney is permitted to make a short argument in rebuttal.

The attorneys have previously tendered written **jury instructions** on the applicable law to the trial judge, who gives those which he approves and denies those which he considers incorrect. The judge may also give the jury instructions of his own. These instructions (called "charges" in some States) are for the purpose of advising the jury of the particular rules of law which it is to apply to the facts as determined by it from the evidence. The jury then retires to the jury room to deliberate and to reach its verdict in favor of one party or the other. If it finds the issues in favor of defendant, its verdict is that the defendant is not liable. If, however, it finds the issues for the plaintiff and against defendant, its verdict is that the defendant is liable and specifies the amount of plaintiff's damages, in this case, $35,000. Upon returning to the jury box, the foreman either announces the verdict or hands it in written form to the clerk, who then gives it to the judge, who reads the verdict in open court. The unsuccessful party may then file a written motion for a new trial or for **judgment notwithstanding the verdict** (also referred to as a judgment n.o.v.). The latter motion is similar to a motion for a directed verdict, only it is made after the jury's verdict. Upon denial of these motions, the judge enters judgment on the verdict for $35,000 in favor of the plaintiff.

In the event that B does not appeal, or of affirmance by the reviewing court if he does appeal, and B does not pay the judgment, the task of enforcement remains. A requests the clerk to issue a **writ of execution** which is served by the sheriff upon the defendant demanding payment of the judgment. Upon return of the writ "unsatisfied," A may post bond or other security and order a levy on and sale of specific nonexempt property belonging to the defendant which is then seized by the sheriff, advertised for sale, and sold at public sale under the writ of execution. If the proceeds of the sale do not produce sufficient funds to pay the judgment, plaintiff A's attorney may institute a supplementary proceeding in an attempt to locate money or other property belonging to defendant. He may also proceed by **garnishment** against B's employer to collect from B's wages or a bank in which B has an account in an attempt to collect the judgment.

Appeal

Assume that B directs his attorney to appeal. A notice of appeal is filed with the clerk of the trial court within the prescribed time. Later B, the party appealing or appellant, files in the reviewing court the record on appeal which contains the pleadings, transcript of the testimony, rulings by the judge on motions made by the parties, arguments of counsel, jury instructions, verdict, post-trial motions, and the judgment order from which the appeal is taken. In States where there is an intermediate court of appeals, it will usually be the reviewing court. In States where there are no intermediate courts of appeal, a party may appeal directly from the trial court to the State supreme court.

B, as appellant, is required to prepare a condensation of the record, known as an abstract, or pertinent excerpts from the record which he files together with a **brief** and argument with the reviewing court. His brief contains a statement of the facts, the issues, the rulings by the trial court which B contends are erroneous and prejudicial, grounds for reversal of the judgment, statement of the applicable law, and arguments on his behalf. A, the appellee, files an answering brief and argument. B may, but is not required to, file a reply brief. The case is now ready for consideration by the reviewing court.

The appellate court does not hear any evidence. It takes the case upon the record, abstracts, and briefs. After **oral argument** by the attorneys, if the court elects to hear one, the case is taken under advisement. The appellate court then makes a decision based upon majority rule. The court prepares a written opinion containing the reasons for its decision, the rules of law which apply, and its judgment. The judgment may affirm the judgment of the trial court, or if it finds that reversible error was committed, the judgment may be reversed, or the case may be reversed and remanded for a new trial. The losing party may file a petition for rehearing, which is usually denied.

If the reviewing court is an intermediate appellate court, the party losing in that court may decide to seek a reversal of its judgment by filing within a prescribed time a notice of appeal, if the appeal is by right, or a petition for leave to appeal to the State supreme court, if the appeal is by discretion. This petition corresponds to a petition for a writ of *certiorari* in the United States Supreme Court. The party winning in the appellate court may file an answer to the petition for leave to appeal. If the petition is granted, or if the appeal is by right, the record is certified to the higher court, and each party files a new brief and argument in the supreme court. Oral argument may be held, and the case is taken under advisement. If the supreme court concludes that the judgment of the appellate court is correct, it affirms. If it decides otherwise, it reverses the judgment of the appellate court and enters a reversal or an order of remand. The unsuccessful party may again file a petition for a rehearing which is likely to be denied. Barring the remote possibility of an application for still further review by the United States Supreme Court, the case has either reached its termination or, upon remand, is about to start its second journey through the courts, beginning as originally in the trial court.

The various stages in civil procedure are illustrated in Figure 2-6.

ARBITRATION

Arbitration is a nonjudicial means whereby matters in dispute may be decided by a neutral person or persons (arbitrators) selected by the parties. The presentation of the case is informal, and the arbitrator is not bound to adhere to established rules of evidence.

The decision of the arbitrator, called an award, is binding upon the parties. Nevertheless, it is subject to limited judicial review for such matters as lack of due process, excess of the arbitrator's jurisdiction, or violation of law.

In commercial cases, resolution by arbitration normally comes about by reason of (1) the inclusion of a provision in a contract which requires that any controversy pertaining to a matter or matters covered by the agreement shall be determined by arbitration; or (2) a written agreement called a "submission agreement" by which the parties to a dispute agree to submit the controversy to arbitration rather than to a court. The increasing popularity of arbitration stems from congestion and delay in the courts and the cost of a court trial. However, arbitration is not a panacea for these problems. Depending upon the type of case, arbitration is not always faster or less expensive.

Both Federal and State statutes have been widely used to enforce arbitration agreements in labor disputes and in commercial disputes. In addition, many States have enacted compulsory uninsured motorists statutes which require automobile public liability insurance policies to include uninsured motorist coverage, which provides that if the

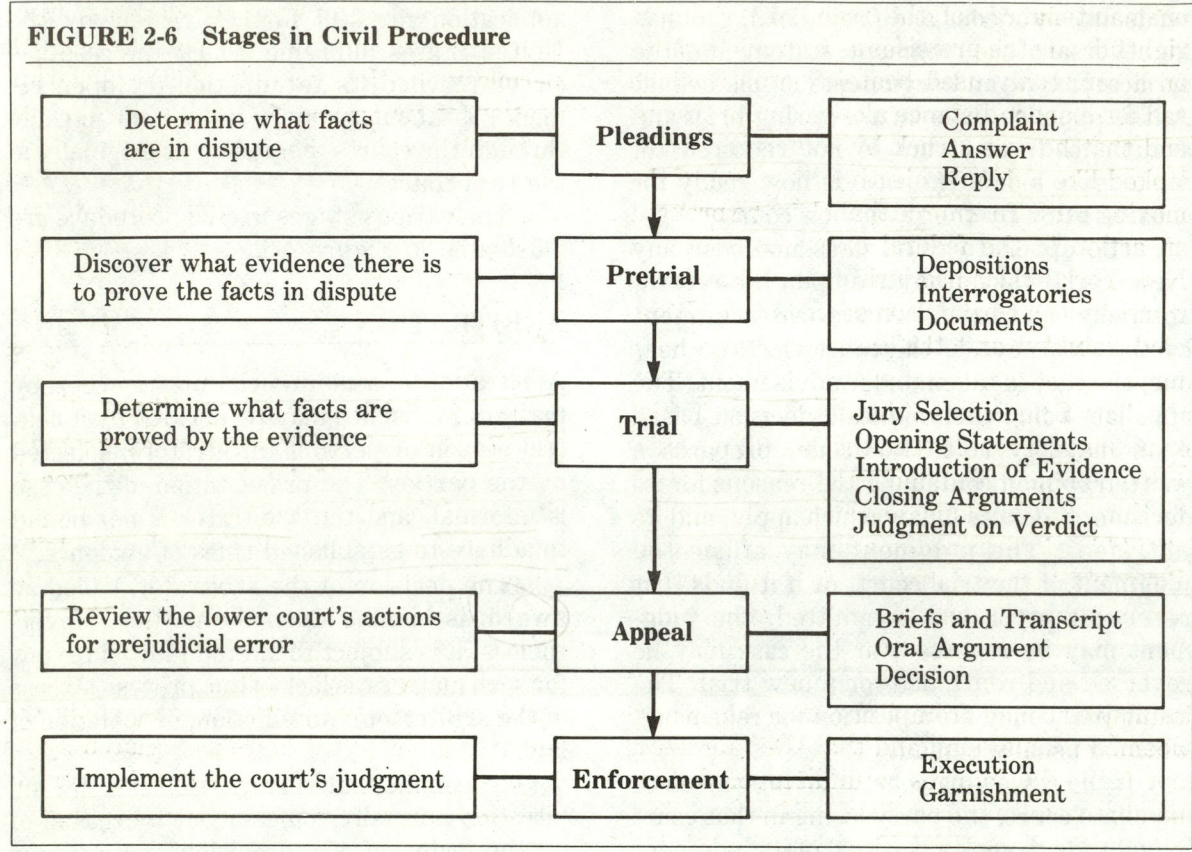

FIGURE 2-6   Stages in Civil Procedure

Determine what facts are in dispute	**Pleadings**	Complaint Answer Reply
Discover what evidence there is to prove the facts in dispute	**Pretrial**	Depositions Interrogatories Documents
Determine what facts are proved by the evidence	**Trial**	Jury Selection Opening Statements Introduction of Evidence Closing Arguments Judgment on Verdict
Review the lower court's actions for prejudicial error	**Appeal**	Briefs and Transcript Oral Argument Decision
Implement the court's judgment	**Enforcement**	Execution Garnishment

insured motorists are involved in an automobile accident with an uninsured owner or operator of an automobile, they may recover from their own insurance carrier up to a specified amount for bodily injuries for which the uninsured motorist is liable. An arbitration clause is customarily incorporated into this type of coverage. Moreover, a number of States have enacted compulsory arbitration statutes requiring arbitration of unresolved labor disputes involving police officers and firefighters.

CASES

Concurrent Federal Jurisdiction

ERIE RAILROAD CO. v. TOMPKINS

Supreme Court of the United States, 1938.
304 U.S. 64, 58 S.Ct. 817, 82 L.Ed. 1188.

MR. JUSTICE BRANDEIS delivered the opinion of the Court.

The question for decision is whether the oft-challenged doctrine of Swift v. Tyson shall now be disapproved.

Tompkins, a citizen of Pennsylvania, was injured on a dark night by a passing freight train of the Erie Railroad Company while walking along its right of way at Hughestown in that state. He claimed that the accident occurred through negligence in the operation, or maintenance, of the train; that he was rightfully on the premises as licensee because on a commonly used beaten footpath which ran for a short distance alongside the tracks; and that he was struck by something which looked like a door projecting from one of the moving cars. To enforce that claim he brought an action in the federal court for Southern New York, which had jurisdiction because the company is a corporation of that state. It denied liability; and the case was tried by a jury.

The Erie insisted that its duty to Tompkins was no greater than that owed to a trespasser. It contended, among other things, that its duty to Tompkins, and hence its liability, should be determined in accordance with the Pennsylvania law; that under the law of Pennsylvania, as declared by its highest court, persons who use pathways along the railroad right of way—that is, a longitudinal pathway as distinguished from a crossing—are to be deemed trespassers; and that the railroad is not liable for injuries to undiscovered trespassers resulting from its negligence, unless it be wanton or willful. Tompkins denied that any such rule had been established by the decisions of the Pennsylvania courts; and contended that, since there was no statute of the state on the subject, the railroad's duty and liability is to be determined in federal courts as a matter of general law.

The trial judge refused to rule that the applicable law precluded recovery. The jury brought in a verdict of $30,000; and the judgment entered thereon was affirmed by the Circuit Court of Appeals, which held [citation], that it was unnecessary to consider whether the law of Pennsylvania was as contended, because the question was one not of local, but of general, law, and that "upon questions of general law the federal courts are free, in absence of a local statute, to exercise their independent judgment as to what the law is; and it is well settled that the question of the responsibility of a railroad for injuries caused by its servants is one of general law. * * * Where the public has made open and notorious use of a railroad right of way

for a long period of time and without objection, the company owes to persons on such permissive pathway a duty of care in the operation of its trains. * * * It is likewise generally recognized law that a jury may find that negligence exists toward a pedestrian using a permissive path on the railroad right of way if he is hit by some object projecting from the side of the train."

The Erie had contended that application of the Pennsylvania rule was required, among other things, by section 34 of the Federal Judiciary Act of September 24, 1789 * * *.

Because of the importance of the question whether the federal court was free to disregard the alleged rule of the Pennsylvania common law, we granted certiorari, [citation].

Swift v. Tyson, [citation], held that federal courts exercising jurisdiction on the ground of diversity of citizenship need not, in matters of general jurisprudence, apply the unwritten law of the state as declared by its highest court; that they are free to exercise an independent judgment as to what the common law of the state is—or should be * * *.

* * *

Experience in applying the doctrine of Swift v. Tyson, had revealed its defects, political and social; and the benefits expected to flow from the rule did not accrue. Persistence of state courts in their own opinions on questions of common law prevented uniformity; and the impossibility of discovering a satisfactory line of demarcation between the province of general law and that of local law developed a new well of uncertainties.

* * * [T]he mischievous results of the doctrine had become apparent. Diversity of citizenship jurisdiction was conferred in order to prevent apprehended discrimination in state courts against those not citizens of the State. Swift v. Tyson introduced grave discrimination by noncitizens against citizens. It made rights enjoyed under the unwritten "general law" vary according to whether enforcement was sought in the state or in the federal court; and the privilege of selecting the court in which the right should be determined was conferred

upon the noncitizen. Thus, the doctrine rendered impossible equal protection of the law. In attempting to promote uniformity of law throughout the United States, the doctrine had prevented uniformity in the administration of the law of the state.

* * *

The injustice and confusion incident to the doctrine of Swift v. Tyson have been repeatedly urged as reasons for abolishing or limiting diversity of citizenship jurisdiction. Other legislative relief has been proposed. If only a question of statutory construction were involved, we should not be prepared to abandon a doctrine so widely applied throughout nearly a century. But the unconstitutionality of the course pursued has now been made clear, and compels us to do so.

* * *

The fallacy underlying the rule declared in Swift v. Tyson is * * * clear * * *. The doctrine rests upon the assumption that there is a "transcendental body of law outside of any particular State but obligatory within it unless and until changed by statute," that federal courts have the power to use their judgment as to what the rules of common law are; and that in the federal courts "the parties are entitled to an independent judgment on matters of general law":

"But law in the sense in which courts speak of it today does not exist without some definite authority behind it. The common law so far as it is enforced in a State, whether called common law or not, is not the common law generally but the law of that State existing by the authority of that State without regard to what it may have been in England or anywhere else. * * *

"The authority and only authority is the State, and if that be so, the voice adopted by the State as its own (whether it be of its Legislature or of its Supreme Court) should utter the last word."

Thus the doctrine of Swift v. Tyson is * * * "an unconstitutional assumption of powers by Courts of the United States which no lapse of time or respectable array of opinion should make us hesitate to correct." * * * We merely declare that in applying the doctrine this Court and the lower courts have invaded rights which in our opinion are reserved by the Constitution to the several states.

* * *

Reversed.

Jurisdiction: Long-Arm Statute

CLEMENTS v. BARNEY'S SPORTING GOODS STORE

Appellate Court of Illinois, First District, Fifth Division, 1980.
84 Ill.App.3d 600, 40 Ill.Dec. 342, 406 N.E.2d 43.

LORENZ, J.

This appeal raises the frequently litigated question of when has a foreign corporation submitted itself to the jurisdiction of our courts by the transaction of business within this State. [Citation.] Plaintiff, Thomas Clements, brought this action to recover damages for breach of warranty against defendant, Signa Corporation. According to plaintiff's complaint, he purchased a motor boat from Barney's Sporting Goods, an Illinois corporation, in 1974. The boat was manufactured by defendant, and defendant has allegedly breached its warranty of fitness for a particular purpose. Plaintiff further alleges that defendant, an Indiana Corporation, is subject to the jurisdiction of Illinois courts under the "transaction of business" section of the Illinois Long-Arm Statute [citation], because of its sale of this boat to Barney's Sporting Goods in Illinois. Although defendant was served with summons, it failed to enter an appearance in this case. A default order was entered against defendant and, subsequently an ex-parte judgment of $6,220 was entered against defendant. Approximately one month later, defendant filed a special and limited appearance and affidavit contesting the jurisdiction of the trial court to enter a default judgment against defendant. A counter-affidavit was filed by the plaintiff.

The affidavit of defendant's authorized agent, M. M. Loman, states that defendant is an Indiana corporation with its principal place of business in Decatur, Indiana. Defendant has no office in Illinois and no agent authorized to do business on its behalf within Illinois. All shipments of merchandise sold by defendant are F.O.B. Decatur, Indiana.

Plaintiff's affidavit states that in 1974 he saw defendant's boats on display at the Chicago Boat Show. In addition, literature on defendant's boats was distributed at the Chicago Boat Show. Several boating magazines, delivered to plaintiff in Illinois, contained advertisements for defendant's boats. Plaintiff has also seen defendant's boats on display at Barney's Sporting Goods Store in Palatine, Illinois, where he eventually purchased the boat. A written warranty issued by defendant was delivered to plaintiff in Illinois.

After a hearing on defendant's motion, the trial court ruled for defendant. Plaintiff moved for a rehearing, and at the rehearing, the trial court reversed its earlier ruling. Defendant's subsequent motion for rehearing was denied by the trial court. Defendant now appeals.

Plaintiff seeks to sustain jurisdiction over defendant under the Illinois Long-Arm Statute. [Citation.] Section 17 provides in pertinent part:

(1) Any person, whether or not a citizen or resident of this State, who in person or through an agent does any of the acts hereinafter enumerated, thereby submits such person, and, if an individual, his personal representative, to the jurisdiction of the courts of this State as to any cause of action arising from the doing of any such acts:

    (a) The transaction of any business within this State;

* * *

The purpose of section 17 is to exert in personam jurisdiction over non-resident defendants to the extent permitted by the due process clause of the fourteenth amendment to the United States Constitution. [Citation.] Due process requires the existence of sufficient "minimum contacts" between the forum state and the non-resident defendant so that the exercise of personal jurisdiction is consistent with traditional notions of fair play and substantial justice. [Citations.] This determination is to be made on the facts of each case and turns on an assessment of the quality and nature of defendant's activities. [Citations.] Thus, we must decide whether defendant has by some voluntary act or conduct purposely availed itself of the privilege of conducting business within Illinois and thereby invoked the benefits and protection of Illinois law. [Citations.]

After examining the affidavits submitted by both parties, we believe the defendant has intentionally and consistently engaged in practices designed to promote sale of its boats in Illinois. By displaying its boats and distributing literature at the Chicago Boat Show, advertising in magazines which have Illinois subscribers, and selling its boats to Illinois retailers, defendant has entered the Illinois marketplace and invoked the benefits and protection of Illinois law. Defendant's conduct constitutes direct solicitation of Illinois customers. Solicitation of business inside the State of Illinois has been found sufficient to sustain personal jurisdiction over a non-resident defendant. [Citations.] Additionally, defendant has indirectly entered the Illinois marketplace through the sale of its boat to the Illinois corporation, Barney's Sporting Goods Store. Although defendant was not a participant in the sale of this boat to the plaintiff, we believe defendant cannot insulate itself from the jurisdiction of our courts by using an intermediary or by professing ignorance of the ultimate destination of his goods. [Citation.] In *Gray v. American Radiator &*

Standard Sanitary Corp. (1961), [citation], our supreme court said:

As a general proposition, if a corporation elects to sell its products for ultimate use in another State, it is not unjust to hold it answerable there for any damage caused by defects in those products. Advanced means of distribution and other commercial activity have made possible these modern methods of doing business, and have largely effaced the economic significance of State lines. By the same token, today's facilities for transportation and communication have removed much of the difficulty and inconvenience formerly encountered in defending lawsuits brought in other States.

Unless they are applied in recognition of the changes brought about by technological and economic progress, jurisdictional concepts which may have been reasonable enough in a simpler economy lose their relation to reality, and injustice rather than justice is promoted. Our unchanging principles of justice, whether procedural or substantive in nature, should be scrupulously observed by the courts. But the rules of law which grow and develop within those principles must do so in the light of the facts of economic life as it is lived today. Otherwise the need for adaptation may become so great that basic rights are sacrificed in the name of reform, and the principles themselves become impaired. [Citation.]

Although the *Gray* court was applying the "commission of a tortious act" section of the Long-Arm Statute [citation], we believe its analysis is equally applicable to the "transaction of business" section of that statute. [Citations.] Accordingly, we believe that defendant has transacted business as provided in section 17(1)(a) of the Civil Practice Act.

* * * In this case, plaintiff's purchase of the defective boat was, at least in part, a result of defendant's solicitation in Illinois. Therefore, we hold that defendant has submitted itself to the jurisdiction of our courts under section 17(1)(a) of the Illinois Long-Arm Statute. The order of the circuit court denying defendant's motion to reconsider is hereby affirmed.

Affirmed.

Pretrial Procedure: Summary Judgment

PARKER v. TWENTIETH CENTURY-FOX FILM CORP.

Supreme Court of California, 1970.
3 Cal.3d 176, 89 Cal.Rptr. 737, 474 P.2d 689.

BURKE, J.

Defendant Twentieth Century-Fox Film Corporation appeals from a summary judgment granting to plaintiff [Shirley MacLaine Parker] the recovery of agreed compensation under a written contract for her services as an actress in a motion picture. As will appear, we have concluded that the trial court correctly ruled in plaintiff's favor and that the judgment should be affirmed.

Plaintiff is well known as an actress, and in the contract between plaintiff and defendant is sometimes referred to as the "Artist." Under the contract, dated August 6, 1965, plaintiff was to play the female lead in defendant's contemplated production of a motion picture entitled "Bloomer Girl." The contract provided that defendant would pay plaintiff a minimum "guaranteed compensation" of $53,571.42 per week for 14 weeks commencing May 23, 1966, for a total of $750,000. Prior to May 1966 defendant decided not to produce the picture and by a letter dated April 4, 1966, it notified plaintiff of that decision and that it would not "comply with our obligations to you under" the written contract.

By the same letter and with the professed purpose "to avoid any damage to you," defendant instead offered to employ plaintiff as the leading actress in another film tentatively entitled "Big Country, Big Man" (hereinafter, "Big Country"). The compensation offered was identical, as were 31 of the 34 numbered provisions or articles of the original contract. Unlike "Bloomer Girl," however, which was to have been a musical production, "Big Country" was a dramatic "western type" movie. "Bloomer Girl" was to have been filmed in California; "Big Country" was to be produced in Australia. Also, certain terms in the proffered contract varied from those of the original. Plaintiff was given one week within which to accept; she did not and the offer lapsed. Plaintiff then commenced this action seeking recovery of the agreed guaranteed compensation.

The complaint sets forth two causes of action. The first is for money due under the contract; the second, based upon the same allegations as the first, is for damages resulting from defendant's breach of contract. Defendant in its answer admits the existence and validity of the contract, that plaintiff complied with all the conditions, covenants and promises and stood ready to complete the performance, and that defendant breached and "anticipatorily repudiated" the contract. It denies, however, that any money is due to plaintiff either under the contract or as a result of its breach, and pleads as an affirmative defense to both causes of action plaintiff's allegedly deliberate failure to mitigate damages, asserting that she unreasonably refused to accept its offer of the leading role in "Big Country."

Plaintiff moved for summary judgment under Code of Civil Procedure section 437c, the motion was granted, and summary judgment for $750,000 plus interest was entered in plaintiff's favor. This appeal by defendant followed.

The familiar rules are that the matter to be determined by the trial court on a motion for summary judgment is whether facts have been presented which give rise to a triable factual issue. The court may not pass upon the issue itself. Summary judgment is proper only if the affidavits or declarations in support of the moving party would be sufficient to sustain a judgment in his favor and his opponent does not by affidavit show facts sufficient to present a triable issue of fact. The affidavits of the moving party are strictly construed, and doubts as to the propriety of summary judgment should be resolved against granting the motion. Such summary procedure is drastic and should be used with cau-

tion so that it does not become a substitute for the open trial method of determining facts. The moving party cannot depend upon allegations in his own pleadings to cure deficient affidavits, nor can his adversary rely upon his own pleadings in lieu or in support of affidavits in opposition to a motion; however, a party can rely on his adversary's pleadings to establish facts not contained in his own affidavits. [Citations.] Also, the court may consider facts stipulated to by the parties and facts which are properly the subject of judicial notice. [Citations.]

As stated, defendant's sole defense to this action which resulted from its deliberate breach of contract is that in rejecting defendant's substitute offer of employment plaintiff unreasonably refused to mitigate damages.

The general rule is that the measure of recovery by a wrongfully discharged employee is the amount of salary agreed upon for the period of service, less the amount which the employer affirmatively proves the employee has earned or with reasonable effort might have earned from other employment. [Citations.] However, before projected earnings from other employment opportunities not sought or accepted by the discharged employee can be applied in mitigation, the employer must show that the other employment was comparable, or substantially similar, to that of which the employee has been deprived; the employee's rejection of or failure to seek other available employment of a different or inferior kind may not be resorted to in order to mitigate damages. [Citations.]

In the present case defendant has raised no issue of *reasonableness of efforts* by plaintiff to obtain other employment; the sole issue is whether plaintiff's refusal of defendant's substitute offer of "Big Country" may be used in mitigation. Nor, if the "Big Country" offer was of employment different or inferior when compared with the original "Bloomer Girl" employment, is there an issue as to whether or not plaintiff acted reasonably in refusing the substitute offer. Despite defendant's arguments to the contrary, no case cited or which our research has discovered holds or suggests that reasonableness is an element of a wrongfully discharged employee's option to reject, or fail to seek, different or inferior employment lest the possible earnings therefrom be charged against him in mitigation of damages.

Applying the foregoing rules to the record in the present case, with all intendments in favor of the party opposing the summary judgment motion—here, defendant—it is clear that the trial court correctly ruled that plaintiff's failure to accept defendant's tendered substitute employment could not be applied in mitigation of damages because the offer of the "Big Country" lead was of employment both different and inferior, and that no factual dispute was presented on that issue. The mere circumstance that "Bloomer Girl" was to be a musical review calling upon plaintiff's talents as a dancer as well as an actress, and was to be produced in the City of Los Angeles, whereas "Big Country" was a straight dramatic role in a "Western Type" story taking place in an opal mine in Australia, demonstrates the difference in kind between the two employments; the female lead as a dramatic actress in a western style motion picture can by no stretch of imagination be considered the equivalent of or substantially similar to the lead in a song-and-dance production.

Additionally, the substitute "Big Country" offer proposed to eliminate or impair the director and screenplay approvals accorded to plaintiff under the original "Bloomer Girl" contract * * * and thus constituted an offer of inferior employment. No expertise or judicial notice is required in order to hold that the deprivation or infringement of an employee's rights held under an original employment contract converts the available "other employment" relied upon by the employer to mitigate damages, into inferior employment which the employee need not seek or accept. [Citation.]

Statements found in affidavits submitted by defendant in opposition to plaintiff's summary judgment motion, to the effect that the "Big Country" offer was not of employment different from or inferior to that under the "Bloomer Girl" contract, merely repeat the allegations of defendant's answer to the complaint in this action, constitute only conclusionary assertions with respect to undisputed facts, and do not give rise to a triable factual issue so as to defeat the motion for summary judgment. [Citations.]

In view of the determination that defendant failed to present any facts showing the existence of a factual issue with respect to its sole defense—plaintiff's rejection of its substitute employment offer in mitigation of damages—we need not consider plaintiff's further contention that for various reasons, including the provisions of the original contract, plaintiff was excused from attempting to mitigate damages.

The judgment is affirmed.

Chapter 3

CONSTITUTIONAL AND ADMINISTRATIVE LAW

A S mentioned in Chapter 1, public law is that branch of substantive law which deals with the rights and powers of government in its political or sovereign capacity and its relation to individuals or groups. Public law consists of (1) constitutional law, (2) administrative law, and (3) criminal law. The first two are discussed in this chapter; criminal law is covered in the next chapter.

The importance of public law to the study of business is continually increasing. Large and significant areas of the regulation of business arise from public law. For example, bankruptcy (Chapter 39), antitrust (Chapter 41), employment law (Chapter 43), and securities regulation (Chapter 44) are principally public law. In addition, other areas of the law such as products liability and warranties (Chapter 21), unfair competition (Chapter 40), and consumer protection (Chapter 42) are also greatly affected by public law.

CONSTITUTIONAL LAW

Constitutions are the organic law of a particular jurisdiction and serve a number of critical functions. They establish the governmental structure and allocate power among the levels of government, thereby defining political relationships. They also impose restrictions upon the powers of government and enumerate the rights and liberties of the people.

The Constitution of the United States (reprinted in Appendix A) was adopted on September 17, 1787, at Philadelphia by representatives of the thirteen newly created States. Its purpose is stated in the preamble:

We the People of the United States, In Order to form a more perfect Union, establish Justice, insure domestic Tranquility, provide for the common defence, promote the general Welfare, and secure the Blessings of Liberty to ourselves and our Posterity, do ordain and establish this Constitution for the United States of America.

The framers of the Constitution of the United States deemed it imperative to state precisely what rights and authority were vested in the people's creation—the national government—which was to be a government of enumerated powers. On the other hand, they considered it unnecessary to list those liberties the people reserved to themselves, which the government could not restrict nor officials ignore. Alexander Hamilton, a co-author of *The Federalist*, put it this way: "Here in strictness the people surrender nothing; and as they retain everything, they have no need of particular reservations." Nonetheless, at the time of its adoption, all the representatives at the convention understood and were agreed that the Constitution would contain a Bill of Rights which should guarantee protection of individuals from oppression by the newly formed Federal government which it created. The Bill of Rights, which consists of the first ten amendments to the Constitution, was adopted on December 15, 1791. Its provisions were insisted upon by the States as curbs and restrictions upon the power and authority of the Federal government.

This part of the chapter will discuss constitutional law as it applies to business and commerce. It will begin by surveying some of the basic principles of constitutional law. Then it will examine the allocation of power between the Federal and State governments with respect to the regulation of business. Finally, it will discuss the constitutional restrictions imposed upon the power of government to regulate business.

BASIC PRINCIPLES

There are a number of concepts that are basic to constitutional law in the United States. These principles apply to analysis of both the powers of government and the limitations upon governmental action. These principles are (1) Federal supremacy and preemption, (2) ju-

dicial review, (3) separation of powers, and (4) state action.

Federal Supremacy and Preemption

All law in the United States, whether case law, statutory law, or administrative law, is subject to the Federal Constitution which is the **"supreme law of the land."** Article VI of the United States Constitution states:

This Constitution, and the Laws of the United States which shall be made in Pursuance thereof; and all Treaties made, or which shall be made, under the Authority of the United States, shall be the supreme Law of the Land; and the Judges in every State shall be bound thereby, any Thing in the Constitution or Laws of any State to the Contrary notwithstanding.

Accordingly, no statute, Federal or State, is valid if it violates the Federal Constitution. In the landmark case of *McCulloch v. Maryland*, 17 U.S. (4 Wheat.) 316 (1819), Chief Justice Marshall stated, "This great principle is, that the Constitution and the laws made in pursuance thereof are supreme; that they control the Constitution and laws of the respective states, and cannot be controlled by them."

Whenever Congress exercises a power granted it by the Constitution any conflicting State legislation is **preempted** (overridden) by the Federal action. Even where the State regulation is not obviously in conflict it must nevertheless give way if Congress has clearly manifested the intent that its enactment should preempt the field. Such intent may be expressly stated in the legislation or inferred from the pervasiveness of the Federal regulation, the need for uniformity, or the danger of conflict between concurrent Federal and State regulation. For example, Congress enacted legislation making it unlawful for any railroad to operate locomotives which were not safe and inspected. The statute did not, however, impose any requirement concerning the type of firebox door to be employed. In striking down statutes of Wisconsin and

Georgia which mandated that the engine contain an automatic firebox door the United States Supreme Court stated:

The Federal and the State statutes are directed to the same subject—the equipment of locomotives. They operate upon the same object. It is suggested that the power delegated to the Commission has been exerted only in respect to minor changes or additions. But this, if true, is not of legal significance. It is also urged that, even if the Commission has power to prescribe an automatic firebox door and a cab curtain, it has not done so; and that it has made no other requirement inconsistent with the state legislation. This, also, if true, is without legal significance. The fact that the Commission has not seen fit to exercise its authority to the full extent conferred, has no bearing upon the construction of the Act delegating the power. We hold that state legislation is precluded, because the Boiler Inspection Act, as we construe it, was intended to occupy the field. *Napier v. Atlantic Coast Line Railroad Co.*, 272 U.S. 605 (1926).

Where Congress has not acted, the fact that Congress has the power to act does not preclude the States from acting. Until Congress exercises its power to preempt, State regulation is *not* forbidden or displaced.

Judicial Review

A corollary to the basic principle of Federal supremacy is that the Supreme Court of the United States acts as the final arbiter as to the constitutionality of any law. The Constitution in Article III states "The judicial Power shall extend to all Cases, in Law and Equity, arising under this Constitution, the Laws of the United States, and Treaties made, or which shall be made, under their Authority. . . ." This provision, together with the one in regard to the judicial power of the United States being vested in the courts, gives the courts the power to test the validity of legislative enactments. Alexander Hamilton forcefully expressed the idea when he stated, "The interpretation of the laws is the proper and peculiar province of the courts. A con-

stitution is, in fact, and must be regarded by the judges, a fundamental law. It therefore belongs to them to ascertain its meaning as well as the meaning of any particular act or proceeding from the legislative body. If there should happen to be an irreconcilable variance between the two, that which has the superior obligation and validity ought of course to be preferred; or, in other words, the Constitution ought to be preferred to the statute, the intention of the people to the intention of their agents." *The Federalist*, No. 78, Lodge Ed., pp. 485–86.

The principle stated by Hamilton was adopted by the Supreme Court in *Marbury v. Madison*, 5 U.S. (1 Cranch) 137 (1803). Chief Justice Marshall wrote the landmark opinion which stated:

It is a proposition too plain to be contested, that the Constitution controls any legislative Act repugnant to it; or, that the legislature may not alter the Constitution by an ordinary Act.

* * *

It is emphatically the province and duty of the judicial department to say what the law is. Those who apply the rule to particular cases, must of necessity expound and interpret that rule. If two laws conflict with each other, the courts must decide on the operation of each.

So if a law be in opposition to the Constitution; if both the law and the Constitution apply to a particular case, so that the court must either decide that case conformably to the law, disregarding the Constitution; or conformably to the Constitution, disregarding the law; the court must determine which of these conflicting rules governs the case. This is the very essence of judicial duty.

If, then, the courts are to regard the Constitution and the Constitution is superior to any ordinary Act of the Legislature, the Constitution, and not such ordinary Act, must govern the case to which they both apply.

Separation of Powers

One of the fundamental principles upon which our government is founded is that of separation of powers, a doctrine which can be traced back to the philosophers Baron Montesquieu and John Locke. As incorporated into our Constitution it means that there are three distinct and independent branches of government, consisting of the executive, legislative, and judicial branches. The basic rationale behind this doctrine is to avoid the concentration of excessive power in any group or branch of government. Basically, the legislative branch is granted the power to make the law, the executive branch to enforce the law, and the judicial branch to interpret the law. The principle of separation of powers arose in the case of *United States v. Nixon*, 418 U.S. 683 (1974). In March, 1974, a grand jury indicted seven individuals charging them with various offenses, including conspiracy to defraud the United States and obstruction of justice. On motion of the Special Prosecutor, a *subpoena duces tecum* was issued to Richard M. Nixon, President of the United States, requiring the production of certain tapes, memoranda, papers, transcripts, and other writings. The President filed his appearance and a motion to quash the *subpoena* on the grounds of executive privilege, contending that the separation of powers doctrine precludes judicial review of a President's claim of privilege. The Supreme Court rejected this claim and upheld the *subpoena*. Chief Justice Burger wrote the opinion which stated in part:

In the performance of assigned constitutional duties each branch of the Government must initially interpret the Constitution, and the interpretation of its powers by any branch is due great respect from the others. * * * Many decisions of this Court, however, have unequivocally reaffirmed the holding of *Marbury v. Madison*, 5 U.S. (1 Cranch.) 137, 2 L.Ed. 60 (1803), that "it is emphatically the province and duty of the judicial department to say what the law is."

* * *

Our system of government "requires that federal courts on occasion interpret the Constitution in a manner at variance with the construction given the document by another branch." [Citations.] Notwithstanding the deference each branch must accord the others, the "judicial power of the United States" vested in the federal courts

by Art. III, § 1 of the Constitution can no more be shared with the Executive Branch than the Chief Executive, for example, can share with the Judiciary the veto power, or the Congress share with the Judiciary the power to override a presidential veto. Any other conclusion would be contrary to the basic concept of the separation of powers and the checks and balances that flow from the scheme of a tripartite government.

State Action

In order for most of the protections provided by the U.S. Constitution and its amendments to apply there must be governmental action, Federal or State, collectively referred to as "state" action. Only the Thirteenth Amendment, which abolishes slavery or involuntary servitude, applies to the actions of private individuals. "State action" includes any actions of the Federal and State governments, as well as their subdivisions such as city or county governments and agencies.

In addition, if "private" individuals or entities engage in public functions, their actions may be considered state action subject to constitutional limitations. For example, in *Marsh v. Alabama*, 326 U.S. 501 (1946), it was held that a company town was subject to the First Amendment because the State had allowed the company to exercise all of the public functions and activities that usually were conducted by a town government. Since that case the Supreme Court has been less willing to find state action based upon private entities performing public functions. For instance, in *Jackson v. Metropolitan Edison Co.* (see below) the Court held that a privately owned electric utility was *not* subject to the due process clause because operating a utility is not state action even though the utility had been granted a monopoly by the State. In reaching this conclusion the Court held that the fact that the State could have operated its own utilities did not make the activity of providing electric services state action.

POWERS OF GOVERNMENT

The United States Constitution created a Federal government of enumerated powers.

Moreover, as the Tenth Amendment declares, "the powers not delegated to the United States by the Constitution, nor prohibited by it to the States, are reserved to the States respectively, or to the people." Therefore, "the sovereign powers vested in the State governments, by their respective constitutions, remained unaltered and unimpaired, except so far as they were granted to the government of the United States." *Martin v. Hunter's Lessee*, 14 U.S. (1 Wheat.) 304 (1816).

This part of the chapter examines the sources and extent of the powers of the Federal government—as well as the residual power of the States—to regulate business and commerce.

Federal Commerce Power

Article I, Section 8 of the U.S. Constitution provides in part that "The Congress shall have Power * * * To regulate Commerce with foreign Nations, and among the several States * * *." This clause has two important effects: (1) it is a broad source of power for the Federal government to regulate the economy, and (2) it operates as a restriction upon State regulations that obstruct or unduly burden interstate commerce. As the U.S. Supreme Court has stated: "The Clause is both a prolific sourc[e] of national power and an equally prolific source of conflict with legislation of the state[s]." This section will discuss the first of these effects; the next section will discuss the second effect.

The U.S. Supreme Court interprets the commerce clause as granting virtually complete power to Congress to regulate the economy and business. A court may invalidate legislation enacted under the commerce clause only if it is clear either that there is no rational basis for a congressional finding that the regulated activity affects interstate commerce, or that there is no reasonable connection between the regulatory means selected and the asserted ends. For example, activities that are carried on solely in one State, such as the practice of law or real estate brokerage agreements, are subject to the Federal antitrust laws under the power granted by the commerce clause provided: (1) the local activity substantially affects interstate commerce or (2) the local activity is in the flow of commerce. *See McLain v. Real Estate Board of New Orleans, Inc.*

As a consequence of the broad and permissive interpretation of the commerce power, Congress currently regulates a vast range of activities. Justice Douglas in *Perez v. United States*, 402 U.S. 146 (1971) summarized these activities as follows:

The Commerce Clause reaches in the main three categories of problems. First, the use of channels of interstate or foreign commerce which Congress deems are being misused, as for example, the shipment of stolen goods or of persons who have been kidnapped. Second, protection of the instrumentalities of interstate commerce, as for example, the destruction of an aircraft, or persons or things in commerce, as for example, thefts from interstate shipments. Third, those activities affecting commerce.

By way of further illustration, many of the activities discussed in this text are regulated by the Federal government based upon the commerce power including:

1. crimes under Federal law (Chapter 4);
2. consumer warranties under the Magnuson-Moss Warranty Act (Chapters 21 and 42);
3. consumer credit transactions under the Federal Trade Commission rule (Chapter 26);
4. electronic fund transfers under the Federal Electronic Fund Transfer Act (Chapter 28);
5. trademarks under the Lanham Act (Chapter 40);
6. unfair trade practices under the Sherman Antitrust Act, Clayton Act, Robinson-Patman Act, and Federal Trade Commission Act (Chapter 41);
7. consumer transactions under the Federal Trade Commission Act, Consumer Credit Protection Act, Fair Credit Billing Act, Fair Debt Collection Practices Act, Real Estate Settlement Procedures Act, and Consumer Product Safety Act (Chapter 42);

8. employee safety under the Occupational Safety and Health Act and Fair Labor Standards Act (Chapter 43);

9. labor relations under the Norris-La Guardia Act, National Labor Relations Act, Taft-Hartley Act, and Landrum-Griffin Act (Chapter 43);

10. civil rights in employment under the Civil Rights Act, Equal Pay Act, Age Discrimination in Employment Act, and Rehabilitation Act (Chapter 43); and

11. transaction in securities under the Securities Act of 1933 and the Securities Exchange Act of 1934 (Chapter 44).

State Regulation of Commerce

The commerce clause, as previously discussed, specifically grants to Congress the power to regulate commerce among the States. In addition to acting as a broad source of Federal power, the clause also operates as a restriction upon the States' power to regulate activities if the result obstructs or unduly burdens interstate commerce. In *Kassel v. Consolidated Freightways Corp.*, 450 U.S. 662 (1981), the Supreme Court explained this limitation as follows:

The Commerce Clause does not, of course, invalidate all state restrictions on commerce. It has long been recognized that, "in the absence of conflicting legislation by Congress, there is a residuum of power in the State to make laws governing matters of local concern which nevertheless in some measure affect interstate commerce or even, to some extent, regulate it." The extent of permissible state regulation is not always easy to measure. It may be said with confidence, however, that a State's power to regulate commerce is never greater than in matters traditionally of local concern.

Regulations The Supreme Court ultimately decides the extent of permissible State regulation affecting interstate commerce. In doing so, the Court weighs and balances several factors: (1) the necessity and importance of the State regulation, (2) the burden it imposes upon interstate commerce, and (3) the extent to which it discriminates against interstate commerce in favor of local concerns. The application of these factors involves case by case analysis that often defies prediction but may be summarized as follows:

Although the criteria for determining the validity of state statutes affecting interstate commerce have been variously stated, the general rule that emerges can be phrased as follows: Where the statute regulates even-handedly to effectuate a legitimate local public interest, and its effects on interstate commerce are only incidental, it will be upheld unless the burden imposed on such commerce is clearly excessive in relation to the putative local benefits. If a legitimate local purpose is found, then the question becomes one of degree. And the extent of the burden that will be tolerated will of course depend on the nature of the local interest involved, and on whether it could be promoted as well with a lesser impact on interstate activities. Occasionally the Court has candidly undertaken a balancing approach in resolving these issues, but more frequently it has spoken in terms of "direct" and "indirect" benefits and burdens. *Pike v. Bruce Church, Inc.*, 397 U.S. 137 (1970).

Taxation The commerce clause in conjunction with the import-export clause serves as a limitation upon the power of the States to tax. The import-export clause provides: "No State shall, without the Consent of the Congress, lay any Imposts or Duties on Imports or Exports." Article I, Section 10. Together, the commerce clause and the import-export clause immunize from State taxation goods that have entered the stream of commerce, whether they are interstate or foreign and whether as imports or exports. The purpose of this immunity is to protect goods in commerce from both discriminatory and cumulative State taxes. Once the goods enter the stream of interstate or foreign commerce, the power of the State to tax ceases and does not resume until the goods are delivered to the purchaser or the owner terminates the movement of the goods through interstate or foreign commerce. This principle has been explained by the Supreme Court:

* * * a State "cannot impose taxes upon persons passing through the State, or coming into it merely for a temporary purpose" such as itinerant drummers. * * * Moreover, it is beyond dispute that a State may not lay a tax on the "privilege" of engaging in interstate commerce. * * * Nor may a State impose a tax which discriminates against interstate commerce either by providing a direct commercial aadvantage to local business * * * or by subjecting interstate commerce to the burden of "multiple taxation." * * * Such impositions have been stricken because the States, under the Commerce Clause, are not allowed "one single tax-dollar worth of direct interference with the free flow of commerce." *Northwestern States Portland Cement Co. v. Minnesota*, 358 U.S. 450 (1959).

Federal Fiscal Powers

The Federal government exerts a dominating influence over the national economy. A good deal of this impact results from the exercise of its regulatory powers under the commerce clause, as previously discussed. In addition, a substantial portion of its influence derives from powers arising independent of the commerce clause. These include (1) the power to tax and spend, (2) the power to borrow and coin money, and (3) the power of eminent domain.

Taxation and Spending Express provisions of the Constitution grant Congress broad powers to tax. Article I, Section 8, states, "The Congress shall have Power To lay and collect Taxes, Duties, Imposts, and Excises, to pay the Debts and provide for the common Defence and general Welfare of the United States; but all Duties, Imposts, and Excises shall be uniform throughout the United States." In addition, the Sixteenth Amendment states: "The Congress shall have power to lay and collect taxes on incomes, from whatever source derived, without apportionment among the several States, and without regard to any census or enumeration."

The Federal government's power to tax, although extremely broad, is subject to three major limitations: (1) direct taxes other than income taxes must be apportioned among the States, (2) all custom duties and excise taxes must be uniform throughout the United States, and (3) no duties may by levied upon exports from any State (Article I, Section 9).

Beyond raising revenues, taxes inevitably have regulatory and socio-economic effects. For example, import taxes and custom duties can protect domestic industry from foreign competition. Graduated or progressive tax rates and exemptions may further social policies of redistributing wealth. Tax credits encourage investment in favored enterprises to the disadvantage of unfavored businesses. Nevertheless, a tax will be upheld:

So long as the motive of Congress and the effect of its legislative action are to secure revenue for the benefit of the general government, the existence of other motives in the selection of the subjects of taxes cannot invalidate Congressional action. *J. W. Hampton Co. v. United States*, 276 U.S. 394 (1928).

As mentioned above, Article I, Section 8, authorizes the Federal government to pay debts and spend for the common defense and general welfare of the United States. The spending power of congress is extremely broad and will be upheld so long as it does not violate a specific constitutional limitation upon Federal power. In *United States v. Butler*, 297 U.S. 1 (1936), the Supreme Court defined the limits of the spending power as follows:

Funds in the Treasury as a result of taxation may be expended only through appropriation. (Article I, § 9, cl. 7.) They can never accomplish the objects for which they were collected unless the power to appropriate is as broad as the power to tax. The necessary implication from the terms of the grant is that the public funds may be appropriated "to provide for the general welfare of the United States." * * * The conclusion must be that they were intended to limit and define the granted power to raise and to expend money.

Moreover, the power to spend is an important way in which the Federal government regulates the economy. In some cases this is accomplished directly as the level and type of government expenditure has a significant impact upon economic cycles and activity. More indirectly, governmental appropriations may be conditioned upon recipients of Federal grants engaging in, or refraining from, specified conduct. For instance, under an executive order issued in 1965, many contractors who enter into contracts with the Federal government must comply with affirmative action requirements in their employment practices. (This is discussed more fully in Chapter 43.) Whether directly or indirectly, the power of the Federal government to spend money represents an important regulatory force in the economy and significantly affects the general welfare of the United States.

Borrowing and Coining Money Article I, Section 8, states: "The Congress shall have Power * * * To borrow money on the credit of the United States * * *." The broad extent of this grant of power is evidenced by the current size of the Federal deficit. Article I, Section 8, also states: "The Congress shall have Power * * * to coin Money, regulate the Value thereof, and of foreign Coin * * *." The power to borrow and the power to coin money together have enabled the Federal government to establish a national banking system, the Federal Reserve System, and specialized Federal lending programs such as the Federal Land Bank. Through these and other institutions and agencies the Federal government wields extensive control over national fiscal and monetary policies and exerts considerable influence over interest rates, money supply, and foreign exchange rates.

Eminent Domain Supplementing the government's power to tax is its power to take private property for public use, known as the power of eminent domain, which is recognized as one of the inherent powers of government in the Federal constitution and in the constitutions of the States. At the same time, how-

ever, the power is carefully circumscribed and controlled. The Fifth Amendment to the Federal Constitution provides: "nor shall private property be taken for public use, without just compensation." This amendment is applicable to the States through the Fourteenth Amendment, which is discussed later. Moreover, similar or identical provisions are to be found in the constitutions of the States. There is, therefore, a direct constitutional prohibition against taking private property without just compensation and an implicit prohibition against taking private property for other than public use. Under both Federal and State constitutions, the individual is entitled to due process of law in connection with the taking. Eminent domain is discussed further in Chapter 49.

LIMITATIONS UPON GOVERNMENT

The Constitution of the United States enumerates certain powers which are granted to the Federal government. Other powers, without enumeration, have been reserved to the States. However, all of these powers have been circumscribed by limitations imposed by the Constitution and its amendments. This part of the chapter will discuss those limitations most applicable to business: (1) the contract clause, (2) the First Amendment, (3) due process, and (4) equal protection.

Contract Clause

Article I, Section 10, of the Constitution provides: "No State shall * * * pass any * * * Law impairing the Obligation of Contracts * * *." The Supreme Court has used this clause to restrict States from retroactively modifying public charters and private contracts. For example, the charter of a corporation formed under a State incorporation statute is protected against impairment by the contract clause. In *Dartmouth College v. Woodward*, 17 U.S. (4 Wheat.) 518 (1819), the incorporation of Dartmouth College by charter granted by King George III in 1769 provided for its creation, corporate structure, and administration and control by a self-perpetuating board of trustees. In 1816 New Hampshire enacted a statute creating a board of twenty-five overseers of the College to be appointed by the State and empowered to have access to the books and records of Dartmouth College; to appoint and remove its president, faculty members, and administration personnel; to establish departments and professorships; to provide for the erection of new buildings; and in other ways to exercise control over the affairs of the College given by its charter to the board of trustees. The Supreme Court held the statute unconstitutional as impairing the obligation of contract.

To avoid the impact of this decision, incorporation and other enabling statutes commonly reserve to the State the power to prescribe such regulations, provisions, and limitations as it shall deem advisable, and to amend, repeal, or modify the statute at its pleasure. As such reservation is a material part of the contract between the State and the other party, any amendment or modification does not impair the obligation of contract because it was expressly permitted by the contract or charter.

Moreover, the Supreme Court has held that the contract clause does **not** preclude the States from exercising eminent domain or their police powers. As the Supreme Court stated: "No legislature can bargain away the public health or the public morals." *Stone v. Mississippi*, 101 U.S. 814 (1880).

First Amendment

The First Amendment states:

Congress shall make no law respecting an establishment of religion, or prohibiting the free exercise thereof; or abridging the freedom of speech, or of the press; or the right of the people peaceably to assemble, and to petition the Government for a redress of grievances.

This amendment is the constitutional source of much of the civil and political rights enjoyed in the United States. Accordingly, it gives rise to an extrememly wide range of issues, far too broad for this text to address fully. This section will examine the application of the First Amendment's guarantee of free speech to (1) commercial speech and (2) defamation.

Commercial Speech Commercial speech is expression related to the economic interests of the speaker and its audience, such as advertisements of a product or service. Within the past decade, United States Supreme Court decisions have eliminated the doctrine that commercial speech is wholly outside the protection of the First Amendment and in its place have established the principle that speech that does no more than propose a commercial transaction is entitled to a "lesser degree" of constitutional protection. This limited grant of shelter is warranted due to interest in the communication by the advertiser, consumer, and general public. Such messages provide important information for the proper and efficient allocation of resources in our free market system. At the same time, commercial speech is less valuable and less vulnerable than other varieties of speech and therefore does not merit complete First Amendment protection.

These Supreme Court cases establish an *ad hoc* balancing test to determine the constitutional validity of governmental regulations that suppress commercial expression. The analysis weighs—with *close* scrutiny—the implicated First Amendment interests against the State's justification for its regulation, and focuses specifically upon whether the regulation substantially furthers a legitimate state interest and whether a less drastic alternative is available. Although this standard is less rigorous than the traditional First Amendment test—*exacting* scrutiny to determine whether a compelling state interest exists—the commercial speech is far from undemanding. For example, in *Virginia State Board of Pharmacy v. Virginia Citizens Consumer Council*, 425 U.S. 748 (1976), the Supreme Court decided a case arising out of a challenge by prescription drug consumers to a Virginia statute which in essence prohibited pharmacists from advertising prescription drug prices. The Court invalidated the statute as being violative of the First Amendment to the United States Constitution and stated:

In concluding that commercial speech enjoys First Amendment protection, we have *not* held that it is wholly undifferentiable from other forms. There are commonsense differences between speech that does "no more than propose a commercial transaction," * * * and other varieties. Even if the differences do not justify the conclusion that commercial speech is valueless, and thus subject to complete suppression by the State, they nonetheless suggest that a different degree of protection is necessary to insure that the flow of truthful and legitimate commercial information is unimpaired.

Because the constitutional protection extended to commercial speech is based upon the informational function of advertising, governments may regulate or suppress commercial messages that do not accurately inform the public about lawful activity. "The government may ban forms of communication more likely to deceive the public than to inform it, or commercial speech related to illegal activity." *Central Hudson Gas and Electric Corp. v. Public Service Commission*, 447 U.S. 557 (1980). Therefore, governmental regulation of false and misleading advertising is permissible under the First Amendment. *See Warner-Lambert Co. v. FTC* in Chapter 42.

Defamation Defamation is tortious conduct that consists of a communication which injures a person's reputation by disgracing him and diminishing the respect in which he is held. An example would be the publication of a statement that a person had committed a crime or had a loathsome disease. For a discussion of defamation refer to Chapter 5.

Because defamation involves a communication, the protection extended to speech by the First Amendment applies. The case of *New York Times Co. v. Sullivan*, 376 U.S. 254 (1964), held that a public official who was defamed in regard to his conduct, fitness, or role as public official may *not* recover in an action of defamation unless the statement was made with actual malice which requires proof that the defendant had knowledge of the falsity of the communication or acted in reckless disregard of its truth or falsity. This restriction upon the right to recover for defamation is based upon "a profound national commitment to the principle that debate on public issues should be uninhibited, robust and wide-open, and that it may well include vehement, caustic and sometimes unpleasantly sharp attacks on government and public officials." The communication may deal with the official's qualifications for office and his performance in it, which would likely include most aspects of his character and his public conduct.

In addition, subsequent Supreme Court cases have extended the same rule to candidates for public office and public figures. *See Hutchinson v. Proxmire* in Chapter 5. The court, however, has not precisely defined the term "public figure." Examples of persons held to be public figures include a well-known football coach of a State university and a retired army general who had taken a prominent and controversial position regarding racial segregation. More recently, in *Gertz v. Robert Welch, Inc.*, 418 U.S. 323 (1974), the Court has explained:

For the most part [public figures are] those who attain this status [by assuming] roles of especial prominence in the affairs of society. Some occupy positions of such persuasive power and influence that they are deemed public figures for all purposes. More commonly, those classed as public figure have thrust themselves to the forefront of particular public controversies in order to influence the resolution of the issues involved.

Due Process

The Fifth and Fourteenth Amendments respectively prohibit the Federal and State governments from depriving any person of life, liberty, or property without due process of law. The Fifth Amendment provides:

No person shall be held to answer for a capital, or otherwise infamous crime, unless on a presentment or indictment of a Grand Jury, except in cases arising in the land or naval forces, or in the Militia, when in actual service in time of War or public danger; nor shall any person be subject for the same offence to be twice put in jeopardy of life or limb; nor shall be compelled in any criminal case to be a witness against himself, *nor be deprived of life, liberty, or property, without due process of law*; nor shall private property be taken for public use, without just compensation [emphasis added.]

The Fourteenth Amendment similarly states in Section 1:

All persons born or naturalized in the United States, and subject to the jurisdiction thereof, are citizens of the United States and of the State wherein they reside. No State shall make or enforce any law which shall abridge the privileges or immunities of citizens of the United States; *nor shall any State deprive any person of life, liberty, or property, without due process of law*; nor deny any person within its jurisdiction the equal protection of the laws [emphasis added.]

Due process has two different aspects: *substantive* due process and *procedural* due process. As discussed in Chapter 1, substantive law creates, defines, or regulates legal rights whereas procedural law establishes the rules for enforcing rights created by the substantive law. Accordingly, **substantive due process** concerns the compatibility of a law or governmental action with fundamental constitutional rights such as free speech. In contrast, **procedural due process** involves the review of the decision-making process that enforces substantive laws and results in depriving a person of life, liberty, or property.

Substantive Due Process Substantive due process involves a court's determination of whether a particular governmental action is compatible with individual liberties. During the period from 1885 until 1937 the Supreme Court viewed substantive due process as authorizing it to act as a "super legislature" and enabling it to invalidate any law it considered unwise. Since 1937 the Court has abandoned this approach and no longer overturns legislation affecting economic and social interests so long as the legislation is rationally related to legitimate governmental objectives. This drastic shift has been explained as follows:

The doctrine that prevailed in *Lochner, Coppage, Adkins, Burns*, [early 1900 Supreme Court decisions] and like cases—that due process authorizes courts to hold laws unconstitutional when they believe the legislature has acted unwisely—has long since been discarded. We have returned to the original constitutional proposition that courts do not substitute their social and economic beliefs for the judgment of legislative bodies, who are elected to pass laws * * *. Legislative bodies have broad scope to experiment with economic problems, and this Court does not sit to "subject the State to an intolerable supervision hostile to the basic principles of our Government and wholly beyond the protection which the general clause of the Fourteenth Amendment was intended to secure." *Ferguson v. Skrupa*, 372 U.S. 726 (1963).

Where fundamental rights of individuals under the Constitution are affected, however, the Court will carefully scrutinize the legislation to determine that it is necessary to promote a compelling or overriding state interest. Included among the fundamental rights that trigger the strict scrutiny standard of substantive due process are (1) the First Amendment rights of freedom of speech, religion, press, peaceful assembly, and petition; (2) the right to engage in interstate travel; (3) the right to vote; (4) the right to privacy; and (5) the right to marry.

Procedural Due Process Procedural due process pertains to the governmental decision making process that results in depriving a person of life, liberty, or property. As the Supreme Court has interpreted procedural due process the government is required to provide persons with a fair procedure if, but only if, the person is faced with deprivation of life, liberty, or property. When governmental action adversely affects an individual but does not deny life, liberty, or property, the government is not required to give the person any hearing at all.

Liberty for the purposes of procedural due process generally includes the ability of individuals to engage in freedom of action and choice regarding their personal lives. Any significant physical restraint constitutes a deprivation of liberty which requires procedural safeguards. The most important and common example is criminal proceedings. In addition, civil proceedings which result in depriving a person of freedom of action are also subject to the requirements of procedural due process. For example, in *Jackson v. Indiana*, 406 U.S. 715 (1972), a mentally defective deaf-mute, age twenty-seven, with the mental level of a pre-school child, who could not read, write, or otherwise communicate except through limited sign language, was indicted by the State on two charges of robbery, one of a purse containing four dollars, the other of five dollars. Following an examination by two court appointed psychiatrists, at a competency hearing the court held that the defendant lacked sufficient comprehension to make a defense to the charges and ordered him committed to the State Department of Mental Health until such time as the department should certify to the court that the defendant is competent to stand trial. Although the defendant had pleaded insanity as a defense, his guilt or innocence of the crimes charged was not determined but only his competency to stand trial. The Supreme Court held that, under this commitment, the defendant would probably never be entitled to a release at any time because of the extreme unlikelihood of improvement in his condition, and that such a commitment therefore was a denial of due process of law. The Court reversed the order and remanded the case with directions that the State either institute civil proceedings applicable to indefinite commitment of those not charged with crime or release the defendant.

Governmental action impairing a person's right to exercise fundamental constitutional rights is also considered a deprivation of liberty subject to due process. As mentioned above, these fundamental rights include the First Amendment rights of freedom of speech, religion, press, peaceful assembly, and petition; the right to engage in interstate travel; and the rights to vote, to privacy, and to marry. Moreover, other rights may also be protected by procedural due process. In *Meyer v. Nebraska*, 262 U.S. 390 (1923), the Supreme Court stated:

While this Court has not attempted to define with exactness the liberty * * * guaranteed (by the Fourteenth Amendment), the term has received much consideration and some of the included things have been definitely stated. Without doubt, it denotes not merely freedom from bodily restraint, but also the right of the individual to contract; to engage in any of the common occupations of life; to acquire useful knowledge; to marry, establish a home, and bring up children; to worship God according to the dictates of his own conscience; and generally to enjoy those privileges long recognized * * * as essential to the orderly pursuit of happiness by free men.

Property for the purposes of procedural due process not only includes all forms of real and personal property but also certain entitlements conferred by government, such as social security payments and food stamps. In *Logan v. Zimmerman Brush Co.*, 455 U.S. 422 (1982), the Supreme Court stated:

The hallmark of property, the Court has emphasized, is an individual entitlement grounded in state law, which cannot be removed except "for cause." Once that characteristic is found, the types of interests protected as "property" are varied and, as often as not, intangible, relating "to the whole domain of social and economic fact."

"While the legislature may elect not to confer a property interest * * * it may not constitutionally authorize the deprivation of such an interest, once conferred, without appropriate procedural safeguards. * * * "

To put it as plainly as possible, the State may not finally destroy a property interest without first giving the putative owner an opportunity to present his claim of entitlement. * * *

If a person is hired by the government and is given assurances of continued employment or dismissal only for specified reasons, then there must be a fair procedure to discharge the employee. On the other hand, if the employment is terminable at any time by the government there is no property interest in the employee and, therefore, no requirement of procedural due process applies to a dismissal of the employee. *Board of Regents v. Roth*, 408 U.S. 564 (1972).

See *Board of Curators of the University of Missouri v. Horowitz.*

When applicable, procedural due process requires that the procedure be fundamentally fair and impartial in the resolution of the factual and legal basis for the governmental actions which result in the deprivation of life, liberty, or property. The essential elements of such a process, as summarized from *Constitutional Law* (2d ed.) by Nowak, Rotunda, and Young, pp. 555–56, are:

1. adequate notice of the charges or basis for government action;
2. a neutral decision maker;
3. an opportunity to make an oral presentation to the decision maker;
4. an opportunity to present evidence or witnesses to the decision maker;
5. a chance to confront and cross-examine witnesses or evidence to be used against the individual;
6. the right to have an attorney present the individual's case to the decision maker; and
7. a decision based on the record with a statement of reasons for the decision.

In addition, there are six other procedural safeguards which tend to appear only in connection with criminal trials or formal judicial process of some type. These are:

1. the right to compulsory process of witnesses;
2. a right to pre-trial discovery of evidence;

3. a public hearing;
4. a transcript of the proceedings;
5. a jury trial; and
6. a burden of proof on the government greater than the preponderance of the evidence standard.

Equal Protection

The Fourteenth Amendment states that "nor shall any State * * * deny to any person within its jurisdiction the equal protection of the laws." Although this amendment applies only to the actions of State governments, the Supreme Court has interpreted the due process clause of the Fifth Amendment to subject Federal actions to the same standards of review. Basically, the guarantee of equal protection requires that similarly situated persons be treated similarly by governmental actions. Since 1937, when the Supreme Court abandoned substantive due process as a critical check on legislation, the equal protection guarantee has become the most important constitutional concept protecting individual rights.

When governmental action involves classification of people, the equal protection guarantee comes into play. In some instances legislation will appear neutral on its face but its application is discriminatory. For example, in *Yick Wo v. Hopkin*, 118 U.S. 356 (1886), the ordinances of the city of San Francisco gave the board of supervisors authority, at their discretion, to refuse permission to carry on laundries, except where located in buildings of brick or stone. Some 200 Chinese persons were denied permission to operate laundries in wooden buildings while 80 non-Chinese persons were granted permission to operate laundries in wooden buildings. The Court held this to be a denial of equal protection: "Though the law itself be fair on its face, and impartial in appliance, yet, if it is applied and administered by public authority with an evil eye and an unequal hand, so as practically to make unjust and illegal discriminations between persons in similar circumstances, material to their rights, the denial of equal justice is still within the prohibition of the constitution."

In determining whether or not legislation satisfies the equal protection guarantee, the Supreme Court utilizes either of two standards of review: (1) the rational relationship test and (2) the strict scrutiny test.

Rational Relationship Test This standard applies to economic legislation and simply requires that it is *conceivable* that the classification bears some rational relationship to a legitimate governmental interest furthered by the legislation. Basic tenets of this standard of review are that there is a strong presumption of constitutionality which requires clear and convincing evidence to be rebutted; every reasonable basis—including any conceivable state of justifying facts—must be negated; and the legislature is permitted to attack part of the evil to which the statute is addressed.

For example, in *Minnesota v. Clover Leaf Creamery Co.*, 449 U.S. 456 (1981), a Minnesota statute banning the retail sale of milk in plastic nonreturnable, nonrefillable containers, but permitting such sale in other nonreturnable, nonrefillable containers, such as paperboard milk cartons, was attacked as violating the equal protection clause. It was stipulated by the parties that the purposes of the statute cited by the legislature—promoting resource conservation, easing solid waste disposal problems, and conserving energy—were legitimate State purposes. The Court upheld the statute because those challenging it failed to "convince the court that the legislative facts on which the classification is apparently based could not reasonably be conceived to be true by the governmental decision maker."

Strict Scrutiny Test This test is far more exacting than the rational relationship test. Under the strict scrutiny test the courts do not defer to the legislature; rather they independently determine whether the classification is constitutionally permissible. This determination requires that the legislature's classification is necessary to promote a compelling or overriding governmental interest.

The strict scrutiny test is applied when the legislation impinges upon fundamental rights or involves suspect classifications. Fundamental rights include most of the provisions of the Bill of Rights. Suspect classifications include those made on the basis of race or national origin. A classic and important example of strict scrutiny of classifications based upon race is the 1954 school desegregation case in which the Supreme Court ruled that segregated public school systems violated the equal protection guarantee. *See Brown v. Board of Education of Topeka.* Subsequently, the Court invalidated segregated public beaches, municipal golf courses, buses, parks, public golf courses, and courtroom seating.

Another important example of strict scrutiny is the "one person, one vote" rule based upon the fundamental right to vote. Chief Justice Warren formulated the rule as follows:

Legislators represent people, not trees or acres. * * * And, if a State should provide that the votes of citizens in one part of the State should be given two times, or five times, or ten times the weight of votes of citizens in another part of the State, it could hardly be contended that the right to vote of those residing in the disfavored areas had not been effectively diluted * * * the Equal Protection Clause requires that the seats in both houses of a bicameral state legislature must be apportioned on a population basis. *Reynolds v. Sims*, 377 U.S. 533 (1964).

Classifications based upon gender have been subject to an intermediate standard of review. This standard has been expressed by the Supreme Court:

The Equal Protection Clause of that amendment does, however, deny to States the power to legislate that different treatment be accorded to persons placed by statute into different classes on the basis of criteria wholly unrelated to the objective of that statute. A classification must be reasonable, not arbitrary, and must rest upon some ground of difference having a fair and substantial relation to the object of the legislation, so that all persons similarly circumstanced shall be treated alike. *Reed v. Reed*, 404 U.S. 71 (1971).

Under this test there must be a substantial relationship to an important governmental objective. The intermediate standard eliminates the strong presumption of constitutionality adhered to by the rational relationship test. For example, in *Orr v. Orr*, 440 U.S. 268 (1979), the Court invalidated an Alabama law which allowed courts to grant alimony awards only from husbands to wives and not from wives to husbands. Similarly, in *Reed v. Reed*, an Idaho statute gave preference to males over females in qualifying for selection as administrators of estates. The Court invalidated the statute because the preference did not bear a fair and substantial relationship to any legitimate objective of the legislation. On the other hand, not all legislation based upon gender is invalid. For example, the Court has upheld a California statutory rape law which imposed penalties only upon males as well as the Federal military selective service act which exempted women from registering for the draft.

In cases involving classifications based upon legitimacy the Court has adopted a standard more rigorous than the rational relationship test but not as demanding as the strict scrutiny test. For instance, legislation denying wrongful death recoveries, worker's compensation benefits, and welfare benefits to illegitimate children have been invalidated as violative of equal protection.

Finally, classifications based upon alienage (citizenship) have been subjected to different standards of review for different types of alienage cases:

* * * When a state or local government distributes economic benefits on the basis of United States citizenship, the classification will be deemed "suspect" and subject to heightened judicial scrutiny and some form of the compelling interest test. When the State seeks to allocate political power, including the opportunity to hold important government positions, it will be able to do so whenever a majority of the justices believe that the law is reasonably tailored to further a legitimate po-

litical end. When the federal government employs an alienage classification, the Court will invoke only the rational basis test and defer to Congressional judgment over the dispensation of either economic benefits or political rights on the basis of citizenship. *Constitutional Law* (2d ed.), Nowak, Rotunda, and Young, p. 698.

ADMINISTRATIVE LAW

This branch of public law deals with various regulatory functions and activities of the government in its executive capacity as performed, supervised, and regulated by public officials, departments, boards, and commissions, as well as with controversies arising between individuals and such public officials and agencies. Administrative functions and activities concern such important matters of national safety, welfare, and convenience as the establishment and maintenance of military forces, police, citizenship and naturalization, taxation, coinage of money, elections, environmental protection, consumer protection, the regulation of transportation, interstate highways, labor relations, television, radio, trade and commerce, and, in general, public health, safety, and welfare.

Because of the increasing complexity of the social, economic, and industrial life of the nation, the scope of administrative law has expanded enormously. Justice Jackson stated that "the rise of administrative bodies has been the most significant legal trend of the last century, and perhaps more values today are affected by their decisions than by those of all the courts, review of administrative decisions apart." *Federal Trade Commission v. Ruberoid Co.*, 343 U.S. 470 (1952). This is evidenced by the great increase in the number and activities of Federal government boards, commission, and other agencies. Certainly, agencies create more legal rules and adjudicate more controversies than all the legislatures and all the courts combined.

Among the more important boards and commissions in the States are those supervising and regulating banking, insurance, communications, transportation, public utilities, pollution control, and Worker's Compensation Boards for the administration of employers' liability laws.

Much of Federal, State, and local law in this country, therefore, is established by the countless administrative agencies. These agencies, which many label the "fourth branch of government," possess tremendous power and have long been criticized as being "in reality miniature independent governments * * * [which are] a haphazard deposit of irresponsible agencies * * * ." 1937 Presidential Task Force Report. In 1979 an article in *Fortune* magazine stated:

In recent years, economists have joined the chorus of criticism, and have blamed excessive regulation for the nation's baffling troubles with innovation, productivity, shortages, unemployment, and inflation. The total cost of complying with government regulation, variously estimated at $50 billion to $150 billion a year, is now in the same league as industry's outlays on new plant and equipment.

Despite this criticism against administrative regulations, it is clear that these agencies play a significant and necessary role in our society. Administrative agencies serve the important function of relieving legislatures from the impossible burden of fashioning legislation which deals with every detail of the specific problem addressed. As a result, Congress can enact legislation, such as the Federal Trade Commission Act, which prohibits unfair and deceptive trade practices without having to define this phrase or anticipate all the particular problems that may arise. Instead, Congress created an agency—in this example, the Federal Trade Commission—to which it could delegate the power to issue rules, regulations, and guidelines to carry out the statutory mandate. In addition, the establishment of separate, specialized bodies enables administrative agencies to be staffed by individuals with expertise in the field being regulated. Moreover, a number of administrative agencies have responsibility to protect the public from powerful entities, such as large business corporations. For example,

the Federal government has established the Consumer Product Safety Commission and the Environmental Protection Agency to safeguard the public against unreasonably dangerous consumer products and damage to the environment.

FEDERAL ADMINISTRATIVE AGENCIES

Federal administrative agencies can be classified as either independent or executive branch. Executive agencies are those agencies which are housed within the executive branch of government, while independent agencies are not. *All* agencies, whether executive or independent, receive their authority from the legislative branch. The following listing provides an overview of the more significant, business related Federal agencies, their classification as either independent or executive, when they were created, and their purpose as stated in the United States Government Manual.

Independent Agencies

1. Civil Aeronautics Board (CAB) (1938): to promote and regulate the air transport industry.

2. Consumer Products Safety Commission (CPSC) (1972): to reduce the risk of injury to consumers from consumer products.

3. Environmental Protection Agency (EPA) (1970): to assure protection of the environment by the systematic abatement and control of pollution.

4. Equal Employment Opportunity Commission (EEOC) (1955): to end discrimination based on race, color, religion, sex, or national origin in hiring, promotion, and firing.

5. Federal Communication Commission (FCC) (1934): to regulate interstate and foreign communications by wire and radio in the public interest.

6. Federal Deposit Insurance Corporation (FDIC) (1935): to promote and preserve confidence in banks and to protect the money

supply through provision of insurance coverage for bank deposits.

7. Federal Reserve Board (Fed) (1913): to furnish an elastic currency, afford means of rediscounting commercial paper, and establish a more effective supervision of banking in the United States.

8. Federal Trade Commission (FTC) (1911): to prevent the free enterprise system from being stifled or fettered by monopoly or corrupted by unfair or deceptive trade practices.

9. Interstate Commerce Commission (ICC) (1887): to regulate, in the public interest, carriers subject to the Interstate Commerce Act which are engaged in transportation, in interstate commerce, and in foreign commerce to the extent it takes place within the United States.

10. National Labor Relations Board (NLRB) (1935): to promote the right of employees to self-organization and to bargain collectively through representatives of their own choosing or to refrain from such activities.

11. Securities and Exchange Commission (SEC) (1934): to provide the fullest possible disclosure to the investing public and protect the interests of the public and investors against malpractices in the securities and financial markets.

12. Small Business Administration (SBA) (1953): to aid, counsel, assist, and protect the interests of small business; insure that small business concerns receive a fair proportion of government purchases, contracts, and subcontracts, as well as of the sales of government property; make loans to small business concerns, State and local development companies, and the victims of floods or other catastrophies; license, regulate, and make loans to small business investment companies; improve the management skills of small business owners, potential owners, and managers; and conduct studies of the economic environment.

Executive Agencies and Departments

1. Council of Economic Advisors (CEA) (1946): to analyze the national economy and its var-

ious segments, advise the President on economic developments, appraise the economic programs and policies of the Federal government, recommend to the President policies for economic growth and stability, and assist in the preparation of the economic reports of the President to Congress.

2. Department of Agriculture (1862): to acquire and diffuse useful information on agricultural subjects; perform functions relating to research, education, conservation, marketing, regulatory work, agricultural adjustment, surplus disposal, and rural development.

3. Department of Commerce (1913): to foster, serve, and promote the nation's economic development and technological advancement.

4. Department of Defense (1949): to provide for the security of the United States through establishment of integrated policies and procedures for the departments, agencies, and functions of the government concerned with national security.

5. Department of Health and Human Services (1953; originally Department of Health, Education and Welfare): to promote the general welfare of the public and its health and social services. Included in the departments operating division are the Food and Drug Administration (FDA) and Social Services Administration (SSA).

6. Department of Justice (1870): to enforce the law of the United States.

7. Department of Labor (1913): to administer and enforce statutes designed to advance the public interest by promoting the welfare of the wage earners of the United States, improving their working conditions, and advancing their opportunities for profitable employment. The Occupational Safety and Health Administration (OSHA) is a division of the Department of Labor.

8. Department of Transportation (DOT) (1966): to develop national transportation policies and programs conducive to the provision of fast, safe, efficient, and convenient transportation at the lowest cost consistent therewith. Among the department's divisions are the Federal Aviation Administration, Fed-

eral Highway Administration, Federal Railroad Administration, National Highway Traffic Safety Administration, and National Transportation Safety Board.

9. Office of Management and Budget (1970): to assist the President in bringing about more efficient and economical conduct of government service; assist in developing efficient coordinating mechanisms to implement government activities and expand interagency cooperation; assist the President in the preparation of the budget and the formulation of the fiscal program of the government; assist the President by clearing and coordinating departmental advice on proposed legislation and by making recommendations as to presidential action on legislative enactments; and assist in the consideration and clearance and, where necessary, in the preparation of proposed executive orders and proclamations.

Many of these agencies are discussed in other parts of the text. More specifically, the FTC and Department of Justice are discussed in Chapter 41; the FTC and the Consumer Product Safety Commission in Chapter 42; the Department of Labor, NLRB, and EEOC in Chapter 43; and the SEC in Chapters 44 and 45.

OPERATION

Most administrative agencies perform three basic functions: (1) make rules and regulations, (2) enforce the law, and (3) adjudicate controversies. Thus, administrative agencies exercise powers that have been allocated by the Constitution to the three separate branches of government. More specifically, agencies exercise legislative power when they make rules, executive power when they enforce the statute and their rules, and judicial power when they adjudicate disputes. This concentration of power has raised questions regarding the propriety of having the same persons who establish the rules also act as prosecutor and as judge in determining whether the rules have been violated.

Rulemaking

Rulemaking is the process by which an administrative agency promulgates rules of law. Under the Administrative Procedure Act (APA) a rule is "the whole or a part of an agency statement of general or particular applicability and future effect designed to implement, interpret, or process law or policy." Section 551(4). Once promulgated, rules are applicable to all parties. In many situations this is preferable to individual, case-by-case adjudication because it treats all parties equally. Moreover, the process of rulemaking puts all parties on notice that the impending rule is being considered and provides concerned individuals with an opportunity to be heard.

Legislative rules must be promulgated in accordance with the APA. In addition, they may not involve an unconstitutional delegation of legislative power from the legislature to the agency. To be constitutionally permissible, the statute granting power to an agency must establish reasonable standards guiding the agency in implementing the statute. This requirement has been met by statutory language such as "unfair methods of competition," "fair and equitable," "public interest, convenience, and necessity," and other equally broad expressions. In any event, agencies may not exceed the actual authority granted by the enabling statute. See *American Textile Mfrs. Institute Inc. v. Donovan.*

To be distinguished from this type of rulemaking—which has the force of law —are interpretative and procedural rules. **Interpretative rules** are statements issued by the agency which provide guidance to the agency's construction of its governing statute. However, these rules, which are exempt from APA requirements, are *not* law in that they are not binding on the agency or the courts, although they are given substantial weight. **Procedural rules**, which are also exempt from the APA, establish rules of conduct for practice before the agency.

Enforcement

Agencies are also charged with investigating conduct to determine whether the statute or the agency's legislative rules have been violated. In carrying out this function the agencies have traditionally been accorded great discretion to compel the disclosure of information.

Adjudication

So extensive and numerous have become the activities of these administrative agencies that, in their entirety, such activities are referred to as the **administrative process**. This term is used in contradistinction to the term "judicial process." The former term implies the administration of law by non-judicial agencies; the latter, the administration of law by judicial bodies or courts. The courts have held that the agencies may adjudicate (by admin-

istrative process) subject to review by the courts.

The scope of judicial review of administrative agencies is limited to determining whether the agency has (1) exceeded its authority, (2) properly interpreted the applicable law, (3) violated any constitutional provision, (4) acted contrary to the procedural requirements of the law, (5) acted arbitrarily or capriciously, or (6) reached conclusions that are not supported by substantial evidence.

The procedures employed by the various administrative agencies to adjudicate cases are nearly as varied as the agencies themselves. Nevertheless, the APA does establish certain standards which must be followed by those Federal agencies which are covered by the act. The hearing is presided over by an administrative law judge and is prosecuted by the agency. Thus, the agency serves as both the prosecutor and decision maker. In order to mitigate this conflict of interest, the APA provides for the separation of functions between those engaged in investigation and prosecution from those involved in decision making. Section 554(d).

CASES

State Action

JACKSON v. METROPOLITAN EDISON CO.

Supreme Court of the United States, 1974.
419 U.S. 345, 95 S.Ct. 449, 42 L.Ed.2d 477.

REHNQUIST, J.

Respondent Metropolitan Edison Co. is a privately owned and operated Pennsylvania corporation which holds a certificate of public convenience issued by the Pennsylvania Public Utility Commission empowering it to deliver electricity to a service area which includes the city of York, Pa. As a condition of holding its certificate, it is subject to extensive regulation by the Commission. Under a provision of its general tariff filed with the

Commission, it has the right to discontinue service to any customer on reasonable notice of nonpayment of bills.

Petitioner Catherine Jackson is a resident of York, who has received electricity in the past from respondent. [Her account with respondent was terminated in 1970 because of alleged delinquency in payments, but a new account was opened for her residence in the name of James Dodson, another occupant of the residence. In August 1971 Dodson moved away and no payments were subsequently made to the account. Finally, in October 1971 Catherine Jackson's service was disconnected without any prior notice. She brought suit in Federal court, claiming that her electric service could not be terminated without notice and hearing.]

* * *

She urged that under state law she had an entitlement to reasonably continuous electrical service to her home and that Metropolitan's termination of her service for alleged nonpayment, action allowed by a provision of its general tariff filed with the Commission, constituted "state action" depriving her of property in violation of the Fourteenth Amendment's guarantee of due process of law.

* * *

* * * In 1883, this Court in the Civil Rights Cases [citation] affirmed the essential dichotomy set forth in [the Fourteenth] Amendment between deprivation by the State, subject to scrutiny under its provisions, and private conduct, "however discriminatory or wrongful," against which the Fourteenth Amendment offers no shield. [Citation.]

* * * While the principle that private action is immune from the restrictions of the Fourteenth Amendment is well established and easily stated, the question whether particular conduct is "private," on the one hand, or "state action," on the other, frequently admits of no easy answer. [Citations.]

Here the action complained of was taken by a utility company which is privately owned and operated, but which in many particulars of its business is subject to extensive state regulation. The mere fact that a business is subject to state regulation does not by itself convert its action into that of the State for purposes of the Fourteenth Amendment. [Citation.] Nor does the fact that the regulation is extensive and detailed, as in the case of most public utilities do so. [Citation.] It may well be that acts of a heavily regulated utility with at least something of a governmentally protected monopoly will more readily be found to be "state" acts than will the acts of an entity lacking these characteristics. But the inquiry must be whether there is a sufficiently close nexus between the State and the challenged action of the regulated entity so that the action of the latter may be fairly treated as that of the State itself. [Citation.]

* * *

* * *

All of petitioner's arguments taken together show no more than that Metropolitan was a heavily regulated privately owned utility enjoying at least a partial monopoly in the providing of electrical service within its territory, and that it elected to terminate service to petitioner in a manner which the Pennsylvania Public Utility Commission found permissible under state law. Under our decision this is not sufficient to connect the State of Pennsylvania with respondent's action so as to make the latter's conduct attributable to the State for purposes of the Fourteenth Amendment.

We conclude that the State of Pennsylvania is not sufficiently connected with respondent's action in terminating petitioner's service so as to make respondent's conduct in so doing attributable to the State for purposes of the Fourteenth Amendment. We therefore have no occasion to decide whether petitioner's claim to continued service was "property" for purposes of that Amendment, or whether "due process of law" would require a State taking similar action to accord petitioner the procedural rights for which she contends.

* * *

[Judgment for defendant Metropolitan Edison Company affirmed.]

Federal Commerce Power

McLAIN v. REAL ESTATE BOARD OF NEW ORLEANS, INC.

Supreme Court of the United States, 1980.
444 U.S. 232, 100 S.Ct. 502, 62 L.Ed.2d 441.

BURGER, C. J.

The question in this case is whether the Sherman Act extends to an agreement among real estate brokers in a market area to conform to a fixed rate of brokerage commissions on sales of residential property.

I

The complaint in this private antitrust action, filed in the Eastern District of Louisiana in 1975, alleges that real estate brokers in the Greater New Orleans area have engaged in a price-fixing conspiracy in violation of § 1 of the Sherman [Antitrust] Act, [citation]. No trial has as yet been had on the merits of the claims since the complaint was dismissed for failure to establish the interstate commerce component of Sherman Act jurisdiction.

The complaint asserts a claim individually and on behalf of that class of persons who employed the services of a respondent real estate broker in the purchase or sale of residential property in the Louisiana parishes of Jefferson or Orleans (the Greater New Orleans area) during the four years preceding the filing of the complaint. The respondents are two real estate trade associations, six named real estate firms, and that class of real estate brokers who at some time during the period covered by the complaint transacted realty brokerage business in the Greater New Orleans area and charged a brokerage fee for their services. The unlawful conduct alleged is a continuing combination and conspiracy among the respondents to fix, control, raise, and stabilize prices for the purchase and sale of residential real estate by the systematic use of fixed commission rates, widespread fee splitting, suppression of market information useful to buyers and sellers, and other allegedly anticompetitive practices. The complaint asserts that respondents' conduct has injured petitioners in their business or property because the fees and commissions charged for brokerage services have been maintained at an artificially high and noncompetitive level, with the effect that the prices of residential properties have been artificially raised. The complaint seeks treble damages and injunctive relief as authorized by §§ 4 and 16 of the Clayton [Antitrust] Act, [citation].

The allegations of the complaint pertinent to establishing federal jurisdiction are:

(1) that the activities of the respondents are "within the flow of interstate commerce and have an effect upon that commerce";

(2) that the services of respondents were employed in connection with the purchase and sale of real estate by "persons moving into and out of the Greater New Orleans area";

(3) that respondents "assist their clients in securing financing and insurance involved with the purchase of real estate in the Greater New Orleans area," which "financing and insurance are obtained from sources outside the State of Louisiana and move in interstate commerce into the State of Louisiana through the activities of the [respondents]"; and

(4) that respondents have engaged in an unlawful restraint of "interstate trade and commerce in the offering for sale and sale of real estate brokering services."

Respondents moved in the District Court to dismiss the complaint for failure to state a claim within the ambit of the Sherman Act [which the District Court granted.]

* * *

The United States Court of Appeals for the Fifth Circuit affirmed the dismissal of the complaint. * * *

II

The broad authority of Congress under the Commerce Clause has, of course, long been interpreted to extend beyond activities actually *in* interstate commerce to reach other activities that, while wholly local in nature, nevertheless substantially *affect* interstate commerce. [Citations.] This Court has often noted the correspondingly broad reach of the Sherman Act. [Citations.] During the near century of Sherman Act experience, forms and modes of business and commerce have changed along with changes in communication and travel, and innovations in methods of conducting particular businesses have altered relationships in commerce. Application of the Act reflects an adaptation to these changing circumstances. [Citations.]

The conceptual distinction between activities "in" interstate commerce and those which "affect" interstate commerce has been preserved in the cases, for Congress has seen fit to preserve that distinction in the antitrust and related laws by limiting the applicability of certain provisions to activities demonstrably "in commerce." [Citations.] It can no longer be doubted, however, that the jurisdictional requirement of the Sherman Act may be satisfied under either the "in commerce" or the "effect on commerce" theory. [Citations.]

Although the cases demonstrate the breadth of Sherman Act prohibitions, jurisdiction may not be invoked under that statute unless the relevant aspect of interstate commerce is identified; it is not sufficient merely to rely on identification of a relevant local activity and to presume an interrelationship with some unspecified aspect of interstate commerce. To establish jurisdiction a plaintiff must allege the critical relationship in the pleadings and if these allegations are controverted must proceed to demonstrate by submission of evidence beyond the pleadings either that the defendants' activity is itself in interstate commerce or, if it is local in nature, that it has an effect on some other appreciable activity demonstrably in interstate commerce. [Citation.]

To establish the jurisdictional element of a Sherman Act violation it would be sufficient for petitioners to demonstrate a substantial effect on interstate commerce generated by respondents' brokerage activity. Petitioners need not make the more particularized showing of an effect on interstate commerce caused by the alleged conspiracy to fix commission rates, or by those other aspects of respondents' activity that are alleged to be unlawful. The validity of this approach is confirmed by an examination of the case law. If establishing jurisdiction required a showing that the unlawful conduct itself had an effect on interstate commerce, jurisdiction would be defeated by a demonstration that the alleged restraint failed to have its intended anticompetitive effect. This is not the rule of our cases. [Citations.] A violation may still be found in such circumstances because in a civil action under the Sherman Act, liability may be established by proof of *either* an unlawful purpose or an anticompetitive effect. [Citations.]

*   *   *

On the record thus far made, it cannot be said that there is an insufficient basis for petitioners to proceed at trial to establish Sherman Act jurisdiction. It is clear that an appreciable amount of commerce is involved in the financing of residential property in the Greater New Orleans area and in the insuring of titles to such property. The presidents of two of the many lending institutions in the area stated in their deposition testimony that those institutions committed hundreds of millions of dollars to residential financing during the period covered by the complaint. The testimony further demonstrates that this appreciable commercial activity has occurred in interstate commerce. Funds were raised from out-of-state investors and from interbank loans obtained from interstate financial institutions. Multistate lending institutions took mortgages insured under federal programs which entailed interstate transfers of premiums and settlements. Mortgage obligations physically and constructively were traded as financial instruments in the interstate secondary mortgage market. Before making a mortgage loan in the Greater New Orleans area, lending institutions usually, if not always required title insurance, which was furnished by interstate corporations. Reading the pleadings, as supplemented, most favorably to petitioners, for present purposes we take these facts as established.

At trial, respondents will have the opportunity, if they so choose, to make their own case contradicting this factual showing. On the other hand, it may be possible for petitioners to establish that, apart from the commerce in title insurance and real estate financing, an appreciable amount of interstate commerce is involved with the local residential real estate market arising out of the interstate movement of people, or otherwise.

To establish federal jurisdiction in this case, there remains only the requirement that respondents' activities which allegedly have been infected by a price-fixing conspiracy be shown "as a matter of practical economics" to have a not insubstantial effect on the interstate commerce involved. [Citations.] It is clear, as the record shows, that the function of respondent real estate brokers is to bring the buyer and seller together on agreeable terms. For this service the broker charges a fee generally calculated as a percentage of the sale price. Brokerage activities necessarily affect both the frequency and the terms of residential sales transactions. Ultimately, whatever stimulates or retards the volume of residential sales, or has an impact on the purchase price, affects the demand for financing and title insurance, those two commercial activities that on this record are shown to have occurred in interstate commerce. Where, as here, the services of respondent real estate brokers are often employed in transactions in the relevant market, petitioners at trial may be able to show that respondents' activities have a not insubstantial effect on interstate commerce.

* * * Here, what was submitted to the District Court shows a sufficient basis for satisfying the Act's jurisdictional requirements under the effect-on-commerce theory so as to entitle the petitioners to go forward. We therefore conclude that it was error to dismiss the complaint at this stage of the proceedings. The judgment of the Court of Appeals is vacated, and the case is remanded for further proceedings consistent with this opinion.

Vacated and remanded.

Due Process

BOARD OF CURATORS OF THE UNIVERSITY OF MISSOURI v. HOROWITZ

Supreme Court of the United States, 1978.
435 U.S. 78, 98 S.Ct. 948, 55 L.Ed.2d 124.

REHNQUIST, J.

Respondent, a student at the University of Missouri-Kansas City Medical School, was dismissed by petitioner officials of the school during her final year of study for failure to meet academic standards. Respondent sued petitioners * * * alleging, among other constitutional violations, that petitioners had not accorded her procedural due process prior

to her dismissal. The District Court, after conducting a full trial, concluded that respondent had been afforded all of the rights guaranteed her by the Fourteenth Amendment to the United States Constitution and dismissed her complaint. The Court of Appeals for the Eighth Circuit reversed. * * *

I

Respondent was admitted with advanced standing to the Medical School in the fall of 1971. During the final years of a student's education at the school, the student is required to pursue in "rotational units" academic and clinical studies pertaining to various medical disciplines such as obstetrics-gynecology, pediatrics, and surgery. Each student's academic performance at the School is evaluated on a periodic basis by the Council on Evaluation, a body composed of both faculty and students, which can recommend various actions including probation and dismissal. The recommendations of the Council are reviewed by the Coordinating Committee, a body composed solely of faculty members, and must ultimately be approved by the Dean. Students are not typically allowed to appear before either the Council or the Coordinating Committee on the occasion of their review of the student's academic performance.

In the spring of respondent's first year of study, several faculty members expressed dissatisfaction with her clinical performance during a pediatrics rotation. The faculty members noted that respondent's "performance was below that of her peers in all clinical patient-oriented settings," that she was erratic in her attendance at clinical sessions, and that she lacked a critical concern for personal hygiene. Upon the recommendation of the Council on Evaluation, respondent was advanced to her second and final year on a probationary basis.

Faculty dissatisfaction with respondent's clinical performance continued during the following year. For example, respondent's docent, or faculty adviser, rated her clinical skills as "unsatisfactory." In the middle of the year, the Council again reviewed respondent's academic progress and concluded that respondent should not be considered for graduation in June of that year; furthermore, the Council recommended that, absent "radical improvement," respondent be dropped from the school.

Respondent was permitted to take a set of oral and practical examinations as an "appeal" of the decision not to permit her to graduate. Pursuant to this "appeal," respondent spent a substantial portion of time with seven practicing physicians in the area who enjoyed a good reputation among their peers. The physicians were asked to recommend whether respondent should be allowed to graduate on schedule and, if not, whether she should be dropped immediately or allowed to remain on probation. Only two of the doctors recommended that respondent be graduated on schedule. Of the other five, two recommended that she be immediately dropped from the school. The remaining three recommended that she not be allowed to graduate in June and be continued on probation pending further reports on her clinical progress. Upon receipt of these recommendations, the Council on Evaluation reaffirmed its prior position.

The Council met again in mid-May to consider whether respondent should be allowed to remain in school beyond June of that year. Noting that the report on respondent's recent surgery rotation rated her performance as "low-satisfactory," the Council unanimously recommended that "barring receipt of any reports that Miss Horowitz has improved radically, [she] not be allowed to re-enroll in the . . . School of Medicine." The Council delayed making its recommendation official until receiving reports on other rotations; when a report on respondent's emergency rotation also turned out to be negative, the Council unanimously reaffirmed its recommendation that respondent be dropped from the school. The Coordinating Committee and the Dean approved the recommendation and notified respondent, who appealed the decision in writing to the University's Provost for Health Sciences. The Provost sustained the school's actions after reviewing the record compiled during the earlier proceedings.

II
A

To be entitled to the procedural protections of the Fourteenth Amendment, respondent must in a case such as this demonstrate that her dismissal from the school deprived her of either a "liberty" or a "property" interest. Respondent has never alleged that she was deprived of a property interest. Because property interests are creatures of state law, [Citation], respondent would have been required to show at trial that her seat at the Medical School was a "property" interest recognized by Missouri state law. Instead, respondent argued that her dismissal deprived her of "liberty" by substantially impairing her opportunities to continue her medical education or to return to employment in a medically related field.

The Court of Appeals agreed, citing this Court's opinion in [Citation]. In that case, we held that the State had not deprived a teacher of any liberty or property interest in dismissing the teacher from a nontenured position, but noted:

[T]here is no suggestion that the State, in declining to re-employ the respondent, imposed on him a stigma or other disability that foreclosed his freedom to take advantage of other employment opportunities. The State, for example, did not invoke any regulations to bar the respondent from all other public employment in state universities. [Citation].

We have recently had an opportunity to elaborate upon the circumstances under which an employment termination might infringe a protected liberty interest. In [Citation], we upheld the dismissal of a policeman without a hearing; we rejected the theory that the mere fact of dismissal, absent some publicizing of the reasons for the action, could amount to a stigma infringing one's liberty * * *.

The opinion of the Court of Appeals, * * *, does not discuss whether a state university infringes a liberty interest when it dismisses a student without publicizing allegations harmful to the student's reputation. * * *

B

We need not decide, however, whether respondent's dismissal deprived her of a liberty interest in pursuing a medical career. Nor need we decide whether respondent's dismissal infringed any other interest constitutionally protected against deprivation without procedural due process. Assuming the existence of a liberty or property interest, respondent has been awarded at least as much due process as the Fourteenth Amendment requires. The school fully informed respondent of the faculty's dissatisfaction with her clinical progress and the danger that this posed to timely graduation and continued enrollment. The ultimate decision to dismiss respondent was careful and deliberate. These procedures were sufficient under the Due Process Clause of the Fourteenth Amendment. We agree with the District Court that respondent

was afforded full procedural due process by the (school). In fact, the Court is of the opinion, and so finds, that the school went beyond (constitutionally required) procedural due process by affording (respondent) the opportunity to be examined by seven independent physicians in order to be absolutely certain that their grading of the (respondent) in her medical skills was correct [Citation].

In *Goss v. Lopez*, [Citation], we held that due process requires, in connection with the suspension of a student from public school for disciplinary reasons, "that the student be given oral or written notice of the charges against him and, if he denies them, an explanation of the evidence the authorities have and an opportunity to present his side of the story." [Citation.] The Court of Appeals apparently read *Goss* as requiring some type of formal

hearing at which respondent could defend her academic ability and performance. All that *Goss* required was an "informal give-and-take" between the student and the administrative body dismissing him that would, at least, give the student "the opportunity to characterize his conduct and put it in what he deems the proper context." [Citation.] But we have frequently emphasized that "[t]he very nature of due process negates any concept of inflexible procedures universally applicable to every imaginable situation." [Citation.] The need for flexibility is well illustrated by the significant difference between the failure of a student to meet academic standards and the violation by a student of valid rules of conduct. This difference calls for far less stringent procedural requirements in the case of an academic dismissal.

* * *

* * * A school is an academic institution, not a courtroom or administrative hearing room. In *Goss*, this Court felt that suspensions of students for disciplinary reasons have a sufficient resemblance to traditional judicial and administrative factfinding to call for a "hearing" before the relevant school authority. While recognizing that school authorities must be afforded the necessary tools to maintain discipline, the Court concluded:

[I]t would be a strange disciplinary system in an educational institution if no communication was sought by the disciplinarian with the student in an effort to inform him of his dereliction and to let him tell his side of the story in order to make sure that an injustice is not done.

* * *

[R]equiring effective notice and informal hearing permitting the student to give his version of the events will provide a meaningful hedge against erroneous action. At least the disciplinarian will be alerted to the existence of disputes about facts and arguments about cause and effect. [Citation.]

Even in the context of a school disciplinary proceeding, however, the Court stopped short of requiring a *formal* hearing since "further formalizing the suspension process and escalating its formality and adversary nature may not only make it too costly as a regular disciplinary tool but also destroy its effectiveness as a part of the teaching process." [Citation.]

Academic evaluations of a student, in contrast to disciplinary determinations, bear little resemblance to the judicial and administrative factfinding proceedings to which we have traditionally attached a full-hearing requirement. In *Goss*, the school's decision to suspend the students rested on factual conclusions that the individual students had participated in demonstrations that had disrupted classes, attacked a police officer, or caused physical damage to school property. The requirement of a hearing, where the student could present his side of the factual issue, could under such circumstances "provide a meaningful hedge against erroneous action." [Citation.] The decision to dismiss respondent, by comparison, rested on the academic judgment of school officials that she did not have the necessary clinical ability to perform adequately as a medical doctor and was making insufficient progress toward that goal. Such a judgment is by its nature more subjective and evaluative than the typical factual questions presented in the average disciplinary decision. Like the decision of an individual professor as to the proper grade for a student in his course, the determination whether to dismiss a student for academic reasons requires an expert evaluation of cumulative information and is not readily adapted to the procedural tools of judicial or administrative decisionmaking.

Under such circumstances, we decline to ignore the historic judgment of educators and thereby formalize the academic dismissal process by requiring a hearing. The educational process is not by nature adversary; instead it centers around a continuing relationship between faculty and students, "one in which the teacher must occupy many roles—educator, adviser, friend, and, at times, parent-substitute." [Citation]. This is especially true as one advances through the varying regimes of the educational system, and the instruction becomes both more individualized and more specialized.

* * *

The judgment of the Court of Appeals is therefore reversed.

Equal Protection

BROWN v. BOARD OF EDUCATION OF TOPEKA

Supreme Court of the United States, 1954.
347 U.S. 483, 74 S.Ct. 686, 98 L.Ed. 873.

WARREN, C. J.

These cases come to us from the States of Kansas, South Carolina, Virginia, and Delaware. They are premised on different facts and different local conditions, but a common legal question justifies their consideration together in this consolidated opinion.

In each of the cases, minors of the Negro race, through their legal representatives, seek the aid of the courts in obtaining admission to the public schools of their community on a nonsegregated basis. In each instance, they have been denied admission to schools attended by white children under laws requiring or permitting segregation according to race. This segregation was alleged to deprive the plaintiffs of the equal protection of the laws under the Fourteenth Amendment. In each of the cases other than the Delaware case, a three-judge federal district court denied relief to the plaintiffs on the so-called "separate but equal" doctrine announced by this Court in *Plessy v. Ferguson*, [citation]. Under that doctrine, equality of treatment is accorded when the races are provided substantially equal facilities, even though these facilities be separate. In the Delaware case, the Supreme Court of Delaware adhered to that doctrine, but ordered that the plaintiffs be admitted to the white schools because of their superiority to the Negro schools.

The plaintiffs contend that segregated public schools are not "equal" and cannot be made "equal" and that hence they are deprived of the equal protection of the laws. Because of the obvious importance of the question presented, the Court took jurisdiction. * * *

Reargument was largely devoted to the circumstances surrounding the adoption of the Fourteenth Amendment in 1868. It covered exhaustively consideration of the Amendment in Congress, ratification by the states, then existing practices in racial segregation, and the views of proponents and opponents of the Amendment. This discussion and our own investigation convince us that, although these sources cast some light, it is not enough to resolve the problem with which we are faced. At best, they are inconclusive. The most avid proponents of the post-War Amendments undoubtedly intended them to remove all legal distinctions among "all persons born or naturalized in the United States." Their opponents, just as certainly, were antagonistic to both the letter and the spirit of the Amendments and wished them to have the most limited effect. What others in Congress and the state legislatures had in mind cannot be determined with any degree of certainty.

An additional reason for the inconclusive nature of the Amendment's history, with respect to segregated schools, is the status of public education at that time. In the South, the movement toward free common schools, supported by general taxation, had not yet taken hold. Education of white children was largely in the hands of private groups. Education of Negroes was almost nonexistent, and practically all of the race were illiterate. In fact, any education of Negroes was forbidden by law in some states. Today, in contrast, many Negroes have achieved outstanding success in the arts and sciences as well as in the business and professional world. It is true that public school education at the time of the Amendment had advanced further in the North, but the effect of the Amendment on Northern States was generally ignored in the congressional debates. Even in the North, the conditions of public education did not approx-

imate those existing today. The curriculum was usually rudimentary; ungraded schools were common in rural areas; the school term was but three months a year in many states; and compulsory school attendance was virtually unknown. As a consequence, it is not surprising that there should be so little in the history of the Fourteenth Amendment relating to its intended effect on public education.

In the first cases in this Court construing the Fourteenth Amendment, decided shortly after its adoption, the Court interpreted it as proscribing all state-imposed discriminations against the Negro race. The doctrine of "separate but equal" did not make its appearance in this Court until 1896 in the case of *Plessy v. Ferguson*, involving not education but transportation. American courts have since labored with the doctrine for over half a century. In this Court, there have been six cases involving the "separate but equal" doctrine in the field of public education. * * * In none of these cases was it necessary to reexamine the doctrine to grant relief to the Negro plaintiff. And in *Sweatt v. Painter*, [citation], the Court expressly reserved decision on the question whether *Plessy v. Ferguson* should be held inapplicable to public education.

In the instant cases, that question is directly presented. Here, unlike *Sweatt v. Painter*, there are findings below that the Negro and white schools involved have been equalized, or are being equalized, with respect to buildings, curricula, qualifications and salaries of teachers, and other "tangible" factors. Our decision, therefore, cannot turn on merely a comparison of these tangible factors in the Negro and white schools involved in each of the cases. We must look instead to the effect of segregation itself on public education.

* * *

Today, education is perhaps the most important function of state and local governments. Compulsory school attendance laws and the great expenditures for education both demonstrate our recognition of the importance of education to our democratic society. It is required in the performance of our most basic public responsibilities, even service in the armed forces. It is the very foundation of good citizenship. Today it is a principal instrument in awakening the child to cultural values, in preparing him for later professional training, and in helping him to adjust normally to his environment. In these days, it is doubtful that any child may reasonably be expected to succeed in life if he is denied the opportunity of an education. Such an opportunity, where the state has undertaken to provide it, is a right which must be made available to all on equal terms.

We come then to the question presented: Does segregation of children in public schools solely on the basis of race, even though the physical facilities and other "tangible" factors may be equal, deprive the children of the minority group of equal educational opportunities? We believe that it does.

In *Sweatt v. Painter*, [citation], in finding that a segregated law school for Negroes could not provide them equal educational opportunities, this Court relied in large part on "those qualities which are incapable of objective measurement but which make for greatness in a law school." In *McLaurin v. Oklahoma State Regents*, [citation], the Court in requiring that a Negro admitted to a white graduate school be treated like all other students, again resorted to intangible considerations: " * * * his ability to study, to engage in discussions and exchange views with other students, and, in general, to learn his profession." Such considerations apply with added force to children in grade and high schools. To separate them from others of similar age and qualifications solely because of their race generates a feeling of inferiority as to their status in the community that may affect their hearts and minds in a way unlikely ever to be undone. The effect of this separation on their educational opportunities was well stated by a finding in the Kansas case by a court which nevertheless felt compelled to rule against the Negro plaintiffs:

"Segregation of white and colored children in public schools has a detrimental effect upon the colored children. The impact is greater when it has the sanction of the law, for the policy of separating the races usually interpreted as denoting the inferiority of the Negro group. A sense of inferiority affects the motivation of a child to learn. Segregation with the sanction of law, therefore, has a tendency to (retard) the educational and mental development of Negro children and to deprive them of some of the benefits they would receive in a racial(ly) integrated school system."

Whatever may have been the extent of psychological knowledge at the time of *Plessy v. Ferguson*, this finding is amply supported by modern authority. Any language in *Plessy v. Ferguson* contrary to this finding is rejected.

We conclude that in the field of public education the doctrine of "separate but equal" has no place. Separate educational facilities are inherently unequal. Therefore, we hold that the plaintiffs and others similarly situated for whom the actions have been brought are, by reason of the segregation complained of, deprived of the equal protection of the laws guaranteed by the Fourteenth Amendment. This disposition makes unnecessary any discussion whether such segregation also violates the Due Process Clause of the Fourteenth Amendment.

Administrative Law

AMERICAN TEXTILE MANUFACTURERS INSTITUTE INC. v. DONOVAN

Supreme Court of the United States, 1981.
452 U.S. 490, 101 S.Ct. 2478, 69 L.Ed.2d 185.

BRENNAN, J.

Congress enacted the Occupational Safety and Health Act of 1970 (the Act) "to assure so far as possible every working man and woman in the Nation safe and healthful working conditions . . . " [Citation.] The Act authorizes the Secretary of Labor to establish, after notice and opportunity to comment, mandatory nationwide standards governing health and safety in the workplace. [Citation.] In 1978, the Secretary, acting through the Occupational Safety and Health Administration (OSHA), promulgated a standard limiting occupational exposure to cotton dust, an airborne particle byproduct of the preparation and manufacture of cotton products, exposure to which induces a "constellation of respiratory effects" known as "byssinosis." [Citation.] * * *

Petitioners in these consolidated cases, representing the interests of the cotton industry, challenged the validity of the "Cotton Dust Standard" * * *. They contend in this Court, as they did below, that the Act requires OSHA to demonstrate that its Standard reflects a reasonable relationship between the costs and benefits associated with the Standard. Respondents, the Secretary of Labor and two labor organizations, counter that Congress balanced the costs and benefits in the Act itself, and that the Act should therefore be construed not to require OSHA to do so. They interpret the Act as mandating that OSHA enact the most protective standard possible to eliminate a significant risk of material health impairment, subject to the constraints of economic and technological feasibility.

* * *

I

Byssinosis, known in its more severe manifestations as "brown lung" disease, is a serious and potentially disabling respiratory disease primarily caused by the inhalation of cotton dust. [Citations.]

* * *

Estimates indicate that at least 35,000 employed and retired cotton mill workers, or 1 in 12 such workers, suffers from the most disabling form of byssinosis. [Citation.] The Senate Report accompanying the Act cited estimates that 100,000 active and retired workers suffer from some grade of the disease. [Citation.] One study found that over 25% of a sample of active cotton preparation and yarn manufacturing workers suffer at least some form of the disease at a dust exposure level common prior to adoption of the current standard. [Citation.] * * *

Not until the early 1960's was byssinosis recognized in the United States as a distinct occupational hazard associated with cotton mills. [Citation.] In 1966, the American Conference of Governmental Industrial Hygienists (ACGIH), a private organization, recommended that exposure to total cotton dust be limited to a "threshold limit value" of 1,000 micrograms per cubic meter of air (1000 µg/m³) averaged over an 8-hour workday. [Citation.] The United States Government first regulated exposure to cotton dust in 1968, when the Secretary of Labor, [citation,] promulgated airborne contaminant threshold limit values, applicable to public contractors, that included the 1000 µg/m³ limit for total cotton dust. [Citation.] Following passage of the Act in 1970, the 1000 µg/m³ standard was adopted as an "established Federal standard" * * *.

In 1974, ACGIH, adopting a new measurement unit of respirable rather than total dust, lowered its previous exposure limit recommendation to 200 µg/m³ * * *.

On December 28, 1976, OSHA published a proposal to replace the existing Federal standard on cotton dust with a new permanent standard, [citation.] The proposed standard contained a PEL of 200 µg/m³ of vertical elutriated lint-free respirable cotton dust for all segments of the cotton industry. [Citation.] It also suggested an implementation strategy for achieving the PEL that relied on respirators for the short-term and engineering controls for the long-term. [Citation.] OSHA invited interested parties to submit written comments within a 90-day period.

Following the comment period, OSHA conducted three hearings in Washington, D.C., Greenville, Miss., and Lubbock, Tex. that lasted over 14 days. Public participation was widespread, involving representatives from industry and the workforce, scientists, economists, industrial hygienists, and many others. By the time the informal rule-making procedure had terminated, OSHA had received 263 comments and 109 notices of intent to appear at the hearings. [Citation.] The voluminous record, composed of a transcript of written and oral testimony, exhibits, and post-hearing comments and briefs, totaled some 105,000 pages. OSHA issued its final Cotton Dust Standard—the one challenged in the instant case—on June 23, 1978. Along with an accompanying statement of findings and reasons, the Standard occupied 69 pages of the Federal Register. [Citation.]

The Cotton Dust Standard promulgated by OSHA establishes mandatory PELs over an 8-hour period of 200 μg/m³ for yarn manufacturing, 750 μg/m³ for slashing and weaving operations, and 500 μg/m³ for all other processes in the cotton industry [Citation.] * * *

OSHA chose an implementation strategy for the Standard that depended primarily on a mix of engineering controls, such as installation of ventilation systems, and work practice controls, such as special floor sweeping procedures. Full compliance with the PELs is required within 4 years, except to the extent that employers can establish that the engineering and work practice controls are infeasible. [Citation.] During this compliance period, and at certain other times, the Standard requires employers to provide respirators to employees.

* * *

On the basis of the evidence in the record as a whole, the Secretary determined that exposure to cotton dust represents a "significant health hazard to employees", [citation] and that "the prevalence of byssinosis should be significantly reduced" by the adoption of the Standard's PELs, [citation]. * * *

In enacting the Cotton Dust Standard, OSHA interpreted the Act to require adoption of the most stringent standard to protect against material health impairment, bounded only by technological and economic feasibility. OSHA therefore rejected the industry's alternative proposal for a PEL of 500 μg/m³

in yarn manufacturing, a proposal which would produce a 25% prevalence of at least Grade ½. byssinosis. The agency expressly found the Standard to be both technologically and economically feasible based on the evidence in the record as a whole. Although recognizing that permitted levels of exposure to cotton dust would still cause some byssinosis, OSHA nevertheless rejected the union proposal for a 100 μg/m³ PEL because it was not within the "technological capabilities of the industry." [Citation.]

* * *

II

The principal question presented in this case is whether the Occupational Safety and Health Act requires the Secretary, in promulgating a standard [citation] to determine that the costs of the standard bear a reasonable relationship to its benefits.

* * *

The starting point of our analysis is the language of the statute itself. [Citations.] Section 6(b)(5) of the Act provides:

The secretary, in promulgating standards dealing with toxic materials or harmful physical agents under this subsection, shall set the standard which most adequately assures, *to the extent feasible*, on the basis of the best available evidence, that no employee will suffer material impairment of health or functional capacity even if such employee has regular exposure to the hazard dealt with by such standard for the period of his working life.

Although their interpretations differ, all parties agree that the phrase "to the extent feasible" contains the critical language in § 6(b)(5) for purposes of this case.

* * *

Thus, § 6(b)(5) directs the Secretary to issue the standard that "most adequately assures . . . that no employee will suffer material impairment of health," limited only by the extent to which this is "capable of being done." In effect then, as the Court of Appeals held, Congress itself defined the basic relationship between costs and benefits, by placing the "benefit" of worker health above all other considerations save those making attainment of this "benefit" unachievable. Any standard based on a balancing of costs and benefits by the Secretary that strikes a different balance than that struck by Congress would be inconsistent with the command set forth in § 6(b)(5). Thus, cost-benefit analysis by OSHA is not required by the statute because feasibility analysis is. [Citation.]

* * *

III

Section 6(f) of the Act provides that "[t]he determinations of the Secretary shall be conclusive if supported by substantial evidence in the record considered as a whole." [Citation.] Petitioners contend that the Secretary's determination that the Cotton Dust Standard is "economically feasible" is not supported by substantial evidence in the record considered as a whole. In particular, they claim (1) that OSHA underestimated the financial costs necessary to meet the Standard's requirements; and (2) that OSHA incorrectly found that the Standard would not threaten the economic viability of the cotton industry.

In statutes with provisions virtually identical to § 6(f) of the Act, we have defined substantial evidence as "such relevant evidence as a reasonable mind might accept as adequate to support a conclusion." [Citation.] The reviewing court must take into account contradictory evidence in the record, [Cita-

tion], but "the possibility of drawing two inconsistent conclusions from the evidence does not prevent an administrative agency's finding from being supported by substantial evidence," [Citation.]

* * *

The Court of Appeals found that the agency "explained the economic impact it projected for the textile industry," and that OSHA has "substantial support in the record for its . . . findings of economic feasibility for the textile industry." [Citation.] On the basis of the whole record, we cannot conclude that the Court of Appeals "misapprehended or grossly misapplied" the substantial evidence test.

* * *

V

When Congress passed the Occupational Safety and Health Act in 1970, it chose to place pre-eminent value on assuring employees a safe and healthful working environment, limited only by the feasibility of achieving such an environment. We must measure the validity of the Secretary's actions against the requirements of that Act. For "[t]he judicial function does not extend to substantive revision of regulatory policy. That function lies elsewhere—in Congressional and Executive oversight or amendatory legislation." [Citations.]

* * *

[Judgment for OSHA affirmed.]

PROBLEMS

1. In May, Patricia Allen left her automobile on the shoulder of a road in the city of Erewhon after the car stopped running. A member of the Erewhon city police department came upon the car later that day and placed on the car a sticker which stated that unless the car were moved it would be towed. After a week the car had not been removed and the police department authorized Baldwin Auto

Wrecking Co. to tow it away and store it on its property. Allen was told by a friend that her car was at Baldwin's. Allen asked Baldwin to allow her to take possession of her car but Baldwin refused to relinquish the car until the $70 towing fee was paid. Allen could not afford to pay the fee and the car remained at Baldwin's for six weeks. At that time Baldwin requested the police department for a permit to dispose of the automobile. After the police department tried unsuccessfully to telephone Allen, the department issued the permit. In late July, Baldwin destroyed the automobile. Allen brings an action against the city and Baldwin for damages for loss of the vehicle, arguing that she was denied due process. Decision?

2. In 1967, large oil reserves were discovered in the Prudhoe Bay area of Alaska. As a result the State revenues increased from $124 million in 1969 to $3.7 billion in 1981. In 1980 the State legislature enacted a dividend program that would distribute annually a portion of these earnings to the State's adult residents. Under the plan, each citizen eighteen years of age or older receives one unit for each year of residency subsequent to 1959, the year Alaska became a State. Crawford, a resident since 1978, brings suit challenging the dividend distribution plan as violative of the equal protection guarantee. Decision?

3. Maryland enacted a statute prohibiting any producer or refiner of petroleum products from operating retail service stations within the State. The statute also required that any producer or refiner discontinue operating their company-owned retail service stations. Approximately 3,800 retail service stations in Maryland sell over twenty different brands of gasoline. However, no petroleum products are produced or refined in Maryland and only five percent of the total number of retailers are operated by a producer or refiner. Maryland enacted the statute because a survey conducted by the State Comptroller indicated that gasoline stations operated by producers or refiners had received preferential treatment during periods of gasoline shortage. Seven major producers and refiners bring an action challenging the statute on the ground that it discriminates against interstate commerce in violation of the commerce clause of the United States Constitution. Decision?

4. The Federal Aviation Act of 1958 provides that "The United States of America is declared to possess and exercise complete and exclusive national sovereignty in the airspace of the United States." The city of Orion adopted an ordinance which makes it unlawful for jet aircraft to take off from its airport between 11:00 P.M. of one day and 7:00 A.M. of the next day. The Jordan Airlines, Inc. is adversely affected by this ordinance and brings suit challenging it under the supremacy clause of the United States Constitution. Decision?

5. The Public Service Commission of State X issued a regulation completely banning all advertising that "promotes the use of electricity" by any electric utility company in State X. The Commission issued the order in order to conserve energy. Central Electric Corporation of State X challenges the order in the State courts arguing that the commission had restrained commercial speech in violation of the First Amendment. Decision?

6. E-Z-Rest Motel is a motel with 216 rooms located in the center of a large city in State Y. It is readily accessible from two interstate highways and three major state highways. The motel solicits patronage from outside of State Y through various national advertising media including magazines of national circulation. It accepts convention trade from outside State Y and approximately 75 percent of its registered guests are from out of State Y. An action under the Federal Civil Rights Act of 1964 has been brought against E-Z-Rest Motel alleging that the motel discriminates on the basis of race and color. The motel contends that the statute cannot be applied to it because it is not engaged in interstate commerce. Decision?

7. State Z enacted a Private Pension Benefits Protection Act requiring private employers with 100 or more employees to pay a pension funding charge upon terminating a pension plan or closing an office in State Z. Acme Steel Company closed its offices in State Z, whereupon the State assessed the company $185,000 under the vesting provisions of the Act. Acme challenged the constitutionality of the Act under the Contract clause (Article I, Section 10) of the U.S. Constitution. Decision?

8. In 1942 Congress passed the Emergency Price Control Act in the interest of national defense and security. The stated purpose of the Act was "to stabilize prices and to prevent speculative, unwarranted and abnormal increases in prices and rents. . . ." The Act established the office of Price Administration which was authorized to establish maximum prices and rents which were to be "generally fair and equitable and [were to] effectuate the purposes of this Act." Stark was convicted for selling beef at prices in excess of those set by the agency. Stark appeals on the ground that the Act was an unconstitutional delegation to the agency of the legislative power of Congress to control prices. Decision?

Chapter 4

CRIMINAL LAW

THE civil law, as discussed in Chapter 1, defines duties the violation of which constitutes a wrong against the injured party. In contrast, the criminal law establishes duties the violation of which is a wrong against the whole community. Civil law is a part of private law, while criminal law is a part of public law. In a civil action the injured party sues to recover compensation for the damage and injury that he has sustained as a result of the defendant's wrongful conduct. The party bringing a civil action (the plaintiff) has the burden of proof which he must sustain by a preponderance (greater weight) of the evidence. The purpose of the civil law is to compensate the aggrieved party. Criminal law, on the other hand, is designed to prevent harm to society by declaring what conduct is criminal and prescribing punishment for such conduct. Punishment for criminal conduct includes (1) fines, (2) imprisonment, and (3) death. In a criminal case the defendant is prosecuted by the government. The government must prove the defendant's guilt beyond a reasonable doubt, which is a significantly higher burden of proof than that required in a civil action. Moreover, under Anglo-American law, guilt is never presumed. Indeed, the law presumes the innocence of the accused, and this presumption is not diminished by his failure to testify in his own defense. The government still has the burden of affirmatively proving the guilt of the accused beyond a reasonable doubt.

Of course, the same conduct may, and often does, constitute both a crime and a tort, which is a civil wrong discussed in Chapters 5 and 6. But an act may be criminal without being tortious, and by the same token an act may be a tort but not a crime.

This chapter will cover the general principles of criminal law as well as the definitions of particular crimes under the following headings (1) nature of crimes, (2) offenses against the person, (3) offenses against property, (4) criminal defenses, and (5) criminal procedure.

NATURE OF CRIMES

A crime is any act or omission prohibited by public law in the interest of protecting society and made punishable by the government in a judicial proceeding brought by it. Crimes are prohibited and punished upon grounds of public policy, which may include the protection and safeguarding of government (as in treason), human life (as in murder), or private property (as in larceny). Additional purposes of the criminal law include deterrence, rehabilitation, and retribution.

Within recent times the scope of the criminal law has increased substantially. Traditional crimes have been augmented by a multitude of regulations and laws to which are attached criminal penalties. These pertain to nearly every phase of modern living. Typical examples in the business law field are those respecting the licensing and conduct of a business, antitrust laws discussed in Chapter 41, and the laws governing the sales of securities discussed in Chapter 44.

Essential Elements

In general, a crime consists of two elements: (1) the wrongful or overt act (*actus reus*) and (2) the criminal intent (*mens rea*). For example, it is not enough in order to sustain a larceny conviction to show that the defendant took another's goods; it must also be established that he *intended* to steal the goods. Conversely, criminal intent without an overt act is not a crime. For instance, A says to herself that she ought to rob the neighborhood grocery store and then really "live it up." Without more, A has commited no crime. Although most crimes do require intent, some statutory crimes do not. Most of these are regulatory statutes which deal with health and safety and impose only fines.

Intent under criminal law has traditionally included both those consequences a person desires to cause as well as those consequences he knows, or should know, are substantially certain to result from his conduct. Thus, if A shoots his rifle at D, who is seemingly out of gunshot range, with the desire to kill D and in fact does kill D, A had the requisite criminal intent to kill D. Likewise, if B, desiring to poison P, places a toxic chemical in the water cooler in P's office and unwittingly poisons U and V, B will be found to have intended to kill U and V, regardless of B's feelings toward U and V.

One of the essential elements of most crimes is a guilty mind or criminal intent, and it has been argued that since a corporation is artificial, intangible, and incorporeal, it, therefore, is incapable of committing a crime. The modern trend is to make corporations criminally responsible for the criminal conduct of their agents, if the conduct is attributable to the corporation. The American Law Institute's proposed Model Penal Code provides that a corporation may be convicted of a criminal offense for the conduct of its employees if:

1. the legislative purpose of the statute defining the offense is to impose liability on corporations and the conduct is within the scope of the agent's office or employment;
2. the offense consists of an omission to discharge a specific, affirmative duty imposed upon corporations by law; or
3. the offense was authorized, requested, commanded, performed, or recklessly tolerated by the board of directors or by a high managerial agent of the corporation.

The punishment necessarily is by fine and not imprisonment.

Classification

Historically, crimes were classified *mala in se* (wrongs in themselves or morally wrong, such as murder) or *mala prohibita* (not morally wrong but declared wrongful by law, such as the prohibition against making a U-turn).

From the standpoint of the seriousness of the offense, crimes are also classified as a (1) *felony* (any crime punishable by death or imprisonment in the penitentiary), or (2) *misdemeanor* (any crime punishable by a fine or imprisonment in a local jail). Under Federal law, there is another category known as a (3) petty crime (any misdemeanor punishable by fine or imprisonment of six months or less).

Another classification of crime has been labeled **white collar crime** and has been variously defined. The Justice Department defines it as nonviolent crime involving deceit, corruption, or breach of trust. It has also been defined as "crimes in the [corporate] suites" which includes crimes committed by individuals such as embezzlement and forgery as well as crimes committed on behalf of a corporation such as commercial bribery, product safety and health crimes, and antitrust violations. A less precise definition is crime "committed by a person of respectability and high social status in the course of his occupation," while a more narrow definition is fraud or deceit practiced through misrepresentation, to gain an unfair advantage. Regardless of the definition of white collar crime, it is clear that such crime is costing society billions of dollars; estimates range from $40 billion to over $200 billlion per year.

One special type of white collar crime is computer crime. **Computer crime** involves the use of a computer to steal money or services, to remove personal or business information, or to tamper with information. Detection of crimes involving the computer not only is extremely difficult but also is frequently not disclosed by business in order to avoid the impression of being lax in its security. Losses due to computer crime are estimated to be in the tens of billions of dollars.

OFFENSES AGAINST THE PERSON

The more serious crimes against an individual include homicide, rape, mayhem, assault and battery. Although these crimes infrequently occur in a business setting, an understanding of them is basic to understanding our criminal law system.

Homicide

Homicide is the unlawful taking of another's life. It can be classified into two categories—murder and manslaughter—each of which may be further classified. Murder is the more serious of the two.

Murder Murder has traditionally been defined as the unlawful killing of another with malice aforethought. Historically, "malice aforethought" meant that the perpetrator had an evil intent to kill and had planned the killing in advance; in short, it was a premeditated, intentional killing. Gradually this definition was expanded by the courts and legislatures to cover several additional types of murder: (1) murder with intent to cause serious bodily harm (2) gross recklessness murder, and (3) felony murder. The sentence for these different types of murder vary from State to State and, within a State, among the types of murder.

The first of these, murder with intent to cause serious bodily harm, involves a situation in which a person intends to cause serious bodily injury to another, without the intent to kill, but nonetheless does cause the death of the other. Thus, if A intends to shoot B in the arm but misses and hits B in the heart causing B's death, A is guilty of the murder of B.

The second type of murder arises out of a situation in which the defendant's conduct is grossly negligent or grossly reckless: although there is no actual intent to kill, the conduct creates an unreasonably high degree of risk of death or serious bodily injury to others and it does cause the death of another. Thus, if A drives his automobile 90 m.p.h. down Fifth Avenue in New York City on Friday at 12:00 noon and "unintentionally" kills six people, A is guilty of gross recklessness murder. Similarly, in one case a defendant was found guilty of this type of murder when he fired two shots into the caboose of a passing train, one of which killed the brakeman. *Banks v. State*, 85 Tex.Crim.R. 165, 211 S.W. 217 (1919).

Finally, the unintentional killing of another during the course of a felony is considered murder. Thus, if A, while burning a building which he believes is unoccupied, causes B, a child asleep in the building, to die by burning, A is guilty of a felony murder. Likewise, if during a robbery the robber ties up the victim and accidentally suffocates her, the robber is guilty of felony murder. Most jurisdictions now limit the scope of felony murder to prescribed felonies (e.g., those dangerous to life, common law felonies, or *mala in se* felonies) and/or to situations in which the death of the victim is foreseeable.

Manslaughter Manslaughter has traditionally been defined as the "unlawful killing of another without malice aforethought." Manslaughter has been divided into two types: voluntary and involuntary.

Voluntary manslaughter is generally defined as an intentional killing of another which, although not justified, is committed under extenuating circumstances, typically the defendant's heated passion provoked by the victim. To be manslaughter rather than murder, the provocation must be sufficient to cause a reasonable man to become enraged and there must be insufficient time between the provocation and the attack for a reasonable person to have calmed himself. For example, if a woman discovers her husband in the act of committing adultery and kills either her husband or his lover, she is guilty of voluntary manslaughter and not murder. However, if the woman takes a week to track down her husband after discovering the adultery, she would be guilty of murder and not voluntary manslaughter.

Involuntary manslaughter, on the other hand, involves a death caused during the course of a misdemeanor or by the defendant's criminal negligence. Criminal negligence is more than mere carelessness creating an unreasonable risk of harm but less than

recklessness constituting murder. For example, an individual, who is aware that he is subject to relatively frequent epileptic seizures, suffers one while driving his car causing the car to run onto the sidewalk killing four small children, is guilty of involuntary manslaughter. *See also Thiede v. State.*

Rape

At common law rape was defined as unlawful sexual intercourse with a woman against her will by force or threat of immediate force. The victim of a rape was limited to females and a husband could not be convicted of raping his wife. Today the crime of rape is statutorily defined and varies greatly from State to State. In addition, nonforcible sexual intercourse with a minor—*statutory rape*—is considered criminal rape.

Mayhem

At common law the crime of mayhem consisted of the intentional disfigurement which interfered with the victim's capacity to serve the sovereign as a fighting man. Thus, the intentional cutting off of a man's finger would constitute the crime of mayhem, while the cutting off of a man's ear would not. Modern criminal statutes eliminate this distinction and make any intentional disfigurement of another the criminal act of mayhem.

Assault and Battery

Assault and battery are two distinct crimes, although frequently the word assault is used to cover both. Battery is the unlawful touching of another. The touching may be direct, such as the striking of another with one's fist or the shooting of another, or indirect, such as by placing poison in another's drink. Assault is an unlawful attempt, coupled with a present ability, to commit a battery. In addition, most States have also classified as a criminal assault intentional conduct by the defendant which is of a threatening nature and which does in fact place the victim in reasonable apprehension of immediate bodily harm.

OFFENSES AGAINST PROPERTY

Offenses against property greatly affect businesses and amount to losses in the hundreds of billions of dollars each year. This section will cover the following crimes against property: (1) larceny, (2) embezzlement, (3) false pretenses, (4) robbery, (5) extortion and bribery, (6) burglary, (7) forgery, and (8) bad checks.

Larceny

The crime of larceny is the (1) trespassory (2) taking and (3) carrying away of (4) personal property (5) of another (6) with intent to deprive the victim permanently of the goods. All six elements must be present for the crime to exist. Thus, B pays A $5,000 for an automobile which A agrees to deliver the following week and A does not. A is *not* guilty of larceny because she has not trespassed on B's property. A has not taken anything from B; she has simply refused to turn over the automobile to B. Larceny only applies when a person takes possession of personal property from another without the other's consent. Here B voluntarily paid the money to A who has not committed larceny but has obtained the $5,000 by false pretenses as discussed below. Likewise, if C takes D's 1968 automobile without D's permission intending to use it for a "joyride" and then to return it to D, C has not committed larceny since C did not intend to deprive D permanently of the automobile. On the other hand, if C left D's 1968 car in a junk yard after the "joyride", C would most likely be held to have committed a larceny because of the high risk that D would be permanently deprived of the car.

Embezzlement

Embezzlement is the fraudulent taking of a principal's property by an agent who through her employment was entrusted with receiving the money or property. This statutory crime was first enacted in response to a 1799 English case in which a bank employee was found not guilty of larceny for taking money given to him for deposit in the bank because the money had been voluntarily handed to him. Thus, embezzlement is a crime intended to prevent individuals who are lawfully in possession of property of another from taking the property for their own use. The key distinction between larceny and embezzlement, therefore, is whether the thief is in lawful possession of the property. In both there is a misappropriation of the property of another but in larceny the thief unlawfully possesses the property while in embezzlement the thief lawfully possesses the property. *See United States v. Waronek.*

False Pretenses

False pretenses, like embezzlement, is a statutory crime enacted to close a loophole in the requirements of larceny. False pretenses is the crime of obtaining title to property of another by means of materially false representations of fact, with knowledge of their falsity, and made with the intent to defraud. Larceny does not cover this situation because possession of the property is voluntarily transferred to the thief. The crime of false pretense would thus cover the situation in which a con artist goes door to door stating that he is selling stereo equipment, which indeed he is not selling, and thus gaining possession of the victim's money. The test of deception is *subjective*, so if the victim was actually deceived it is satisfied even though a reasonable man would not have been deceived by the defendant's misrepresentation. Therefore, gullibility or lack of due care on the part of the victim is no defense: "Any pretense which deceives the person designed to be deceived thereby is sufficient, although it would not deceive a person of ordinary prudence." *Clarke v. People*, 64 Colo. 164, 171 P. 69 (1918).

Robbery

Under the common law as well as most statutes, robbery is a larceny with the additional elements that (1) it is from the person or in the immediate presence of the victim and (2) it is accomplished through either force or threat of force. The defendant's force or threat of force need not be against the person from whom the property is taken. To illustrate: a robber threatens A that unless A relinquishes his wallet the robber will shoot B. Moreover, the victim's presence may be actual or constructive. By constructive presence it is meant that the victim is prevented from being present by either the defendant's actual or threatened force. For example, if the defendant knocks the victim unconscious or ties him up, the victim is considered constructively present.

Many statutes further differentiate between simple robbery and aggravated robbery. **Aggravated robbery** is generally defined as (1) robbery with a deadly weapon, (2) robbery where the robber had the intent to kill or would kill if faced with resistance, (3) robbery which involved serious bodily injury, *or* (4) robbery by two or more perpetrators.

Extortion and Bribery

Extortion and bribery are frequently confused; nevertheless, they are two distinct crimes. Extortion, or "blackmail" as it is sometimes called, is generally held to be the making of threats for the purpose of obtaining money or property. In a minority of jurisdictions, however, the crime of extortion only occurs if the defendant actually causes the victim to relinquish his property.

Bribery, on the other hand, is the offer of money or property to a public official in order to influence the official's decision. The crime of bribery is committed when the illegal offer is made, whether accepted or not. Thus, if A offered M, the mayor of Town Y, a 20% interest in A's planned real estate development if M would use her influence to have the development proposal approved, A would be guilty of criminal bribery. In contrast, if M had threatened A that unless she received a 20% interest in A's development she would use her influence to prevent the approval of the development, M would be guilty of criminal extortion. Bribery of foreign officials is addressed by the Foreign Corrupt Practices Act discussed in Chapter 44.

Some jurisdictions have gone beyond the general bribery law and have adopted statutes that make commercial bribery illegal. Commercial bribery is the use of bribery to acquire new business, obtain secret information or processes, or obtain kickbacks. One State court described its commercial bribery statute as follows:

First, it provides that "[a]ny person who gives, offers, or promises to an agent, employee or servant any gift or gratuity whatever with intent to influence his action in relation to his principal's, employer's or master's business" shall be guilty of a [crime]. The intent specified is an essential element of the offense. The acts prohibited are stated in words sufficiently explicit, clear and definite to inform any man of ordinary intelligence what conduct on his part will render him liable to its penalties. If a person does the prohibited act or acts specified in this part of the statute with the intent explicitly stated therein, he is guilty of what is commonly called "comercial bribery." In [citation] the Court said: "The vice of conduct labeled 'commercial bribery,' as related to unfair trade practices, is the advantage which one competitor secures over his fellow competitors by his secret and corrupt dealing with employees or agents of prospective purchasers."

* * *

The second part of the statute provides that "any agent, employee or servant who requests or accepts a gift or gratuity or a promise to make a gift or to do an act beneficial to himself, under an agreement or with an understanding that he shall act in any particular manner in relation to his principal's, employer's or master's business" shall be guilty of a [crime]. * * * The plain intent and purpose of this part of [the statute] is to prohibit any agent, employee or servant from being disloyal and unfaithful to his principal, employer or master. *North Carolina v. Brewer*, 258 N.C. 533, 129 S.E.2d 262 (1963).

Burglary

At common law, burglary was defined as a breaking and entering of a dwelling house of another in the nighttime with the intent to commit a felony in the house. Of these elements the three which caused the greatest degree of confusion was (1) breaking, (2) entering, and (3) dwelling house. A breaking required that the defendant had to create the breach or opening; the opening could not have been created by the resident. Therefore, a person would not be guilty of common law burglary if he entered another's home in the nighttime through an *open* window in order to steal jewelry. Moreover, the crime of burglary would not be committed even if the defendant had to open the window further in order to climb into the house. On the other hand, the common law was extremely lenient with respect to entry and required only that any part of the defendant's person enter the house, regardless of the duration of the entry. To illustrate, A punches in a window of a dwelling house at nighttime in order to gain entry and steal a television. Upon reaching his hand in the broken window A triggers the burglar alarm and he flees. A has committed a burglary. Finally, the dwelling house of another means that it is someone's residence, regardless of whether she is present at the time of the burglary.

Modern statutes vary significantly from the common law definition. Many of them simply require that there be (1) an entry (2) into a building (3) with the intent to commit a felony in the building. Thus, these statutory definitions omit three elements of the common law crime as the building need not be a dwelling house, the entry need not be at nighttime, and the entry need not be a technical breaking. The modern statutes vary so greatly it is impossible to generalize, except that each of the statutes include some, but not all, of the common law elements.

Forgery

Forgery is the intentional falsification or false making of a legally significant instrument with the intent to defraud. Accordingly, if A prepares a false certification of title to a stolen automobile, he is guilty of the crime of forgery. Likewise, if an individual alters some receipts in order to increase his income tax deductions he has committed the crime of forgery.

Bad Checks

A statutory crime that has some relation to both forgery and false pretenses is the passing of "bad" checks, that is issuing a check when there are insufficient funds on deposit to cover the check. All jurisdictions have now enacted legislation making it a crime to issue bad checks; however, these statutes vary greatly from jurisdiction to jurisdiction. Most jurisdictions simply require that the check be issued and do not require that the issuer receive anything in return for the check. A majority of the jurisdictions require that the defendant issue a check with knowledge that she has insufficient funds on deposit to pay the check upon presentation, while a minority only require that there be insufficient funds.

CRIMINAL DEFENSES

Even though a defendant is found to have committed a criminal act he will not be convicted if he has a valid defense. Most criminal law defenses are valid against both crimes against the person and crimes against property. The one exception to this rule is that the defense of person or property only serves as a defense to crimes against the person.

Defense of Person or Property

Individuals may use reasonable force to protect themselves, other individuals, and their property. These defenses entitle a person to commit without any criminal liability what would otherwise be considered the crime of assault, battery, manslaughter, or murder. The law confers this privilege in order to further important societal interests.

Self-Defense An individual need not submit to the application of force or violence against his person but may use force to protect himself. More specifically, an individual may use *reasonable* force to protect himself against an attack provided he reasonably believes that he is in immediate danger of unlawful bodily harm and that the use of force is necessary to protect himself from such harm. Accordingly, even though an individual acts on the mistaken belief that he is defending himself against an unlawful attack, so long as the belief is based upon reasonable grounds he is entitled to the same defense as if the attack had been as it appeared. An individual who acts in self-defense has a complete defense against any crime based upon his infliction of physical harm upon the aggressor.

What constitutes "reasonable force" has given rise to a great deal of litigation and considerable commentary. As a general rule, a person may use *non-deadly* force to protect herself against unlawful bodily harm and *deadly* force to protect herself against an attack threatening death or serious bodily harm. Thus, A may not shoot B in order to protect himself against B's punching A in the mouth. On the other hand, if B attacked A with a knife, A could properly defend himself by shooting B, even if B's knife was in fact plastic so long as A reasonably believed it to be real. A minority of States and the Model Penal Code require a person to retreat before using deadly force provided that he can safely do so. The objective of this rule is to protect human life even though it requires the avoidance of confrontation. The majority of States, on the other hand, do not require retreat on the view that a person should not be forced to take "cowardly" action against a criminal aggressor. Moreover, even in the jurisdictions following the minority rule retreat is not required before a person may reasonably use deadly force in his own home.

Defense of Another Under the general rule, an individual has a complete defense against criminal prosecution if he uses reasonable force in defense of another provided he reasonably believes the other to be in immediate danger of unlawful bodily harm and that use of such force is necessary to prevent this harm. Most States permit this defense to be used by an individual in defense of *any* other person, even a stranger, although some States limit its use to the defense of individuals who have some defined relationship to the intervenor. Moreover, some States limit the rule's application by permitting the defense only in those situations in which the original victim had the right of self-defense. In other words, these States place the intervenor in the shoes of the party whom he is assisting. Under this rule, therefore, if one goes to the aid of the original aggressor in a fight the intervenor would not enjoy the privilege of defense of others.

Defense of Property An individual also has the right to use reasonable force to protect her property. Under the majority rule deadly force is *never* reasonable to protect property because life is deemed more important than the protection of property. For this reason, an individual cannot use a deadly mechanical device, such as a spring gun, to protect her property.

Incapacity

Under some circumstances an individual will not be deemed to have the capacity to form criminal intent. Accordingly, even though that person commits the overt act constituting the crime, he will not be criminally liable because of the lack of criminal intent. In these situations the person has a complete criminal defense based upon his incapacity. The criminal capacity of persons will be discussed in the following order (1) insanity, (2) infancy, and (3) intoxication.

Insanity The extent to which insanity should be a defense to criminal conduct has long troubled the legal system. While it is difficult to conceive how any "sane" person could commit a brutal murder or a rape, it is not in that sense that the term criminally insane is used. The criminal law defense of insanity is directed at those for whom criminal sanctions are not appropriate. Those who are found "not guilty by reason of insanity" are generally not allowed to go free but are typically committed to a mental institution for treatment.

The traditional and majority test for insanity is the *McNaughton* test. Under this test a defendant is *not* criminally responsible for her conduct if, at the time of committing the act, she did not understand the nature and quality of her act or she could not distinguish between right or wrong. For example, if A axed B believing that B's body was a tree trunk that he was splitting for firewood, A would be found to be not guilty by reason of insanity.

Some States have aded to the *McNaughton* test the irresistible impulse test. Under this additional provision a defendant is relieved of criminal responsibility if he had a mental disease which prevented him from controlling his conduct, even though he understood the nature of his act and that it was wrong. To illustrate: A kills B knowing it to be illegal and wrong because he believed God's messenger had ordered him to do so. Under the irresistible impulse test A would be not guilty by reason of insanity.

A third test of insanity has been accepted by some States and incorporated into the American Law Institute's Model Penal Code. This test provides:

1. A person is not responsible for criminal conduct if at the time of such conduct as a result of mental disease or defect he lacks substantial capacity either to appreciate the criminality (wrongfulness) of his conduct or to conform his conduct to the requirements of law.

2. As used in this Article, the terms "mental disease or defect" do not include an abnormality manifested only by repeated criminal or otherwise antisocial conduct. Section 4.01.

Infancy Under the common law and most modern statutes a child under the age of seven is conclusively presumed to be incapable of committing a crime. From the ages of seven to fourteen there is a rebuttable presumption that the child is incapable of committing a crime. Above the age of fourteen there is a rebuttable presumption that the child is capable of committing a crime. The common law defense of infancy has been rendered moot, however, by the enactment of juvenile court acts, which require that all individuals below a certain age—varying among States between fourteen and eighteen—be brought before a juvenile, and not a criminal, court. Juvenile courts are not criminal in nature but rather attempt to deal with the welfare of the youth and decide if the youth is a delinquent.

Intoxication The great majority of the States follow what is commonly known as the voluntary/involuntary test, which makes voluntary intoxication *not* a defense. Thus, if A commits a burglary while so intoxicated as not to know what he is doing, A would not be guilty of criminal burglary if he involuntarily drank the alcohol as a result of B's forcing A to drink the liquor against his free will. On the hand, if A had drunk the liquor voluntarily, he would not have the defense of intoxication. *See Coots v. Commonwealth.*

Other Defenses

Duress A person who is threatened with immediate, serious bodily harm to himself or another unless he engages in criminal activity has a valid defense to criminal conduct other than murder. For example, A threatens to kill B if B does not assist A in committing larceny. B complies. B would not be guilty of the larceny because of duress. However, if A threatens B with death unless B kills C, B would *not* be relieved of the crime of homicide although the crime may be reduced from murder to manslaughter. The Model Penal Code has rejected the "murder limitation" and relieves a person of all criminal responsibility if "a person of reasonable firmness would have been unable to resist." Section 2.09.

Mistake of Fact If a person reasonably believes the facts to be such that his conduct would not constitute a crime, then the law will treat the facts as he reasonably believed. Accordingly, an honest and reasonable mistake of fact will justify the defendant's conduct. For example, if A gets into a car which he reasonably believes to be his—the car is the same color, model, and year as his, is parked in the same parking lot and is started by his key—he will be relieved of criminal responsibility for taking B's automobile.

Entrapment The defense of entrapment arises when a law enforcement official induces a person, who is not otherwise predisposed to do so, to commit a crime. The rationale behind the rule is to prevent law enforcement officials from instigating crime and from engaging in reprehensible conduct. The doctrine is only aimed at government officials and agents and does not apply to private individuals. For example, if A, a police officer, entices B to commit a robbery, B would possess the valid defense of entrapment; whereas if A were a private citizen, B would be guilty of criminal robbery.

CRIMINAL PROCEDURE

Each of the States and the Federal government have procedures for initiating and coordinating criminal prosecutions. In addition, many defenses and rights of an accused are guaranteed by the Constitution: the Fourth Amendment to the Federal Constitution prohibits unreasonable searches and seizures to obtain incriminating evidence. The Fifth Amendment requires indictment for capital crimes by a grand jury, prevents double jeopardy and self-incrimination, and prohibits deprivation of life or liberty without due process of law. The Sixth Amendment requires a speedy and public trial by jury, that the accused be informed of the nature of the accusation, confronted with the witnesses who testify against him, be given the power to obtain witnesses in his favor, and have the right to competent counsel for his defense. The Eighth Amendment prohibits excessive bail, excessive fines, and cruel or unusual punishment. Prejudicial pretrial publicity is also the basis for a change of venue before trial or for a new trial after conviction.

Most State constitutions have similar provisions protecting the rights of accused persons.

This section will first discuss the steps in a criminal prosecution and then will focus on the major constitutional protections afforded the accused in our system of criminal justice.

Steps in Criminal Prosecution

Although the particulars of criminal procedure vary from State to State, the following provides a basic overview. After arrest, the accused is booked and makes his initial appearance before a magistrate, commissioner, or justice of the peace when formal notice of the charges are given, he is given advice of his rights, and bail is set. Next, a preliminary hearing is held to ascertain whether there is probable cause to believe the defendant is the one who committed the crime. The defendant is entitled to be represented by counsel.

Prosecution is initiated for less serious crimes by the issuance of a warrant which is served upon the accused together with an "information" of the charge at the time of his arrest. Serious crimes are prosecuted by an indictment or "true bill" after presentment to a grand jury, which determines only whether or not a criminal action should be brought. A grand jury consists of not less than sixteen nor more than twenty-three people. If there is sufficient evidence the grand jury "indicts" the defendant. Information, which is used in most misdemeanor cases and some felony cases, is a formal accusation of a crime brought by a prosecuting officer and not a grand jury.

At the arraignment the accused is informed of the charge against him and he enters his plea. The arraignment must be held promptly after the indictment or information has been filed. If his plea is "not guilty," he must stand trial. He is entitled to a jury trial, but if he chooses, he may have his guilt or innocence determined by the court sitting without a jury, which is called a "bench trial."

The trial begins with the selection of the jury and the opening statements by the prosecutor and the attorney for the defense. The prosecution presents evidence first; then the defendant presents his. At the conclusion of the testimony, closing statements are made and the jury is instructed as to the applicable law and retires to arrive at a verdict. In most States the verdict must be unanimous. If the verdict is "not guilty," the matter ends there. The State has no right to appeal from an acquittal, and the accused having been placed in "jeopardy," cannot be tried a second time for the same offense. If the verdict is "guilty" and judgment is entered, the defendant has further recourse. He may make a motion for a new trial, asserting that prejudicial error occurred at the trial, necessitating a retrial of the case. Or he may assert that the evidence was insufficient upon which to predicate guilt beyond any reasonable doubt and ask for his discharge. He may perfect an appeal to a reviewing court, alleging error by the trial court and asking for either his discharge or a remandment of the case for a new trial. In addition, there may be other proceedings in a criminal case, including, for example, a request for probation.

Fourth Amendment

The Fourth Amendment protects all individuals against unreasonable searches and seizures:

The right of the people to be secure in their persons, houses, papers, and effects, against unreasonable searches and seizures, shall not be violated, and no Warrants shall issue, but upon probable cause, supported by Oath or affirmation, and particularly describing the place to be searched, and the persons or things to be seized.

This Amendment is designed to protect the privacy and security of individuals against arbitrary invasions by government officials. Although the Fourth Amendment directly applies only to the Federal government it has been made applicable to the States through the Fourteenth Amendment.

When there is a violation of the Fourth Amendment the general rule prohibits the introduction of the illegally seized evidence. The purpose of this **exclusionary rule** is to deter illegal police conduct and to protect individual liberty, not to hinder the search for the truth. In *Weeks v. United States*, 232 U.S. 383 (1914), the United States Supreme Court stated:

If letters and private documents can thus be seized and held and used in evidence against a citizen accused of an offense, the protection of the Fourth Amendment declaring his right to be secure against such searches and seizures is of no value, and, so far as those thus placed and concerned, might as well be stricken from the Constitution. The efforts of the courts and their officials to bring the guilty to punishment, praiseworthy as they are, are not to be aided by the sacrifice of those great principles established by years of endeavor and suffering which have resulted in their embodiment in the fundamental law of the land.

Nonetheless, in recent years the Supreme Court has limited the exclusionary rule. *See United States v. Leon.*

In order to obtain a search warrant of a particular person, place, or thing, the law enforcement official must demonstrate to a magistrate that he has probable cause to believe that the search will reveal evidence of criminal activity. Probable cause means that "the apparent facts set out in the affidavit [of the requesting authority] are such that a reasonably discreet and prudent man would be led to believe that there was a commission of the offense charged . . . ." *Dumbra v. United States*, 268 U.S. 435 (1925).

Even though the Fourth Amendment requires that a search and seizure generally be made pursuant to a valid search warrant, there are instances in which a search warrant is not necessary. For example, it has been held that a warrant is not necessary where (1) there is hot pursuit of a fugitive, (2) voluntary consent is given, (3) an emergency requires such action, (4) there has been a lawful arrest, (5) evidence of a crime is in plain view of the law enforcement officer, or (6) delay would present a significant obstacle to the investigation.

Fifth Amendment

The Fifth Amendment protects persons against self-incrimination, double jeopardy, and charging a person with a capital or infamous crime except by grand jury indictment.

No person shall be held to answer for a capital, or otherwise infamous crime, unless on a presentment or indictment of a Grand Jury, except in cases arising in the land or naval forces, or in the Militia, when in actual service in time of War or public danger; nor shall any person be subject for the same offense to be twice put in jeopardy of life or limb; nor shall be compelled in any criminal case to be a witness against himself, nor be deprived of life, liberty, or property, without due process of law; . . . .

The prohibitions against self-incrimination and double jeopardy, but not the grand jury clause, have been made applicable to the States through the Due Process Clause of the Fourteenth Amendment.

The privilege against self-incrimination only extends to testimonial evidence and not physical evidence. The Fifth Amendment "privilege protects an accused only from being compelled to testify against himself, or otherwise provide the State with evidence of a testimonial or communicative nature." *Schmerber v. California*, 384 U.S. 757 (1966). Therefore, a person can be forced to stand in a "lineup" for identification purposes, provide

a handwriting sample, or take a blood test. Most significantly, the Fifth Amendment does not protect business records as it only applies to papers of individuals and does not extend to records of business organizations. *Bellis v. United States*, 417 U.S. 85 (1974).

The Fifth Amendment and the Fourteenth Amendment also guarantee due process of law which is basically the requirement of a fair trial. Every person is entitled to have charges or complaints against him, whether in civil or criminal proceedings, made publicly and in writing, and be given the opportunity to defend against them. In criminal prosecutions, it includes the right to counsel, confront and cross-examine adverse witnesses, testify in his own behalf if desired, produce witnesses and offer other evidence, and be free from any and all prejudicial conduct and statements.

See generally Miranda v. Arizona.

Sixth Amendment

The Sixth Amendment provides that the Federal government shall provide the accused with a speedy and public trial by an impartial jury, to be informed of the nature and cause of the accusation, to be confronted with the witnesses against him, to have compulsory process for obtaining witnesses in his favor, and to have the assistance of counsel for his defense. The guarantees of the Sixth Amendment have been made applicable to the States by the Fourteenth Amendment.

The Supreme Court has explained the purpose of guaranteeing the right to a trial by jury as follows: "[T]he purpose of trial by jury is to prevent oppression by the Government by providing a safeguard against the corrupt or overzealous prosecutor and against the compliant, biased, or eccentric judge . . . [T]he essential factors of a jury trial obviously lies in the interposition between the accused and his accuser of the common sense judgment of a group of laymen." *Apodaca v. Oregon*, 406 U.S. 404 (1972). Nevertheless, a defendant may waive his right to a jury trial.

Historically, juries consisted of twelve jurors, but in the Federal courts and in the courts of certain States the number has been reduced to six. In *Williams v. Florida*, 399 U.S. 78 (1970), the Supreme Court held that the use of a six-member jury in a criminal case does not violate a defendant's right to a jury trial under the Sixth Amendment. The Supreme Court recognized that there was no discernible difference between the results reached by a jury of twelve or by a jury of six, nor was there any evidence to suggest that a jury of twelve is more advantageous to a defendant. The jury needs only be large enough "to promote group deliberation, free from outside attempts at intimidation, and to provide a fair possibility for obtaining a representative cross section of the community." Moreover, State court jury verdicts need not be unanimous provided the vote is sufficient to assure adequate deliberations. Thus, the Supreme Court has upheld jury votes of 11–1, 10–2, and 9–3 but rejected as insufficient a 5–1 vote.

CASES

Involuntary Manslaughter

THIEDE v. STATE

Supreme Court of Nebraska, 1921.
106 Neb. 48, 182 N.W. 570.

FLANSBURG, J.

Criminal prosecution for manslaughter, charged to have been committed by defendant through the unlawful act of giving deceased intoxicating liquor, which the deceased drank and which caused his death. Defendant was found guilty and brings the case here for review.

It is his contention that the evidence introduced by the prosecution is insufficient upon which to base the charge.

The evidence in behalf of the state shows that the defendant, Thiede, and others, some weeks previously had attempted to make intoxicating liquor on the Nelson farm; that they had a coil and a kettle and had distilled some liquor. Just what the nature of the liquor was and what quantity they made is not shown. On the day in question, defendant, with one Stromer and Forney, who were also originally charged with the commission of the offense in this case, went to the Nelson farm. Defendant dug up three jugs of white whisky which had been buried on the place, and he and Forney then went to the town of Prosser. In the course of an hour they returned with two girls. Stromer was found lying on the ground in a drunken stupor, with the jugs near him. At this time the farmer, Nelson, was present and defendant gave him a drink from the jug. He testified that it tasted like hot acids and temporarily paralyzed him, and that, at the time of trial, he still felt the effects. The defendant, Stromer and Forney drank of the liquor, and the girls each drank once from a coffee cup, containing a mixture of the liquor and grape juice. One of the girls testified that she had used whisky before, but that this was the first time she had taken too much.

That evening, at about 7:30, a party was made up with four young men from the town of Prosser, and these seven boys and the two girls went into the country.

* * *

The state's testimony shows that neither deceased nor any of the other Prosser boys took more than two drinks. They then drove to Prosser, a mile and a quarter distant. When they arrived, Lambrecht, Hendriks and the deceased were very drunk. Lambrecht went into a picture show, and he testifies that the next he remembered was when he awoke at home the next morning. Hendriks, stupefied, remained in the seat of his car all night and went home at 6 o'clock the next morning. The deceased was unable to talk when he reached

Prosser, and was utterly helpless. He began vomiting and was taken home by his brother and placed upon the floor, where he remained unconscious. A doctor arrived at midnight and administered strychnine and atropin, and at 3 a. m. Kroll was dead. The doctor testified that death was the result of alcoholic poisoning.

Defendant the next morning, before he had heard of the death of Kroll, made a test of the liquor by touching a match to some that had been poured on the ground, and it was found to burn. A chemist testified that he made a gravity test and also an analysis by distilling the liquor, and found that it contained 57 per cent "pure alcohol," but that he made no analysis for the discovery of other ingredients.

The testimony in defendant's behalf conflicts in many material aspects with that just related, but, to determine the question presented, it is unnecessary to consider his version of the case.

Under our statutes, it is manslaughter to "unlawfully kill another without malice, * * * or unintentionally, while the slayer is in the commission of some unlawful act." [Citation.]

It is not questioned that the giving of liquor to the deceased, under the circumstances shown in this case, was in violation of the prohibitory law of this state, and that for the act the defendant was subject to fine and imprisonment. It is the defendant's contention, however, that the act of giving liquor is an act merely malum prohibitum and is not in its nature such an unlawful act as carries with it that intentional wrong toward another which will supply the place of the criminal intent otherwise necessary to any criminal homicide.

In the commission of those unlawful acts which are criminal in their nature and which the law characterizes as malum in se, there is always found an intent on the part of the perpetrator of the offense to commit a wrong as against the person or property of another, and, though the wrong or injury committed may not be calculated nor intended to do great injury, nor to produce death, the person committing the act is not allowed to stop with the effect he intended to produce, but is held, in law, responsible for the full consequences of his act, and, where the result in such a case is death, a wrongful intent being present, the act is held to be involuntary manslaughter.

It is obvious, however, that there are acts prohibited by law which are not in their nature criminal, and in the commission of which the perpetrator of the act has no intent to do harm nor to injure another in his person or property. Where such a wrongful intent is not present and the act is wrong only because prohibited, it is an act malum prohibitum, and, where in the perpetration of such an act death results, the law will not convert the act, innocently done and done with no intent to injure and with no disregard for the safety of another, into a criminal act and pronounce the act manslaughter.

* * *

[I]t is our opinion that the giving or furnishing of intoxicating liquors, unaccompanied by any negligent conduct, though unlawful, is but an act merely malum prohibitum. The person who treats his friend, even though the act be unlawful, has no intent to harm, nor is such an act calculated or intended to endanger the recipient of the liquor. We cannot go so far as to say that such an act, prompted perhaps by the spirit of good-fellowship, though prohibited by law, could ever, by any resulting consequence, be converted into the crime of manslaughter; but, where the liquor, by reason of its extreme potency or poisonous ingredients, is dangerous to use as an intoxicating beverage, where the drinking of it is capable of producing direct physical injury, other than as an ordinary intoxicant, and of perhaps endangering life itself, the case is different, and the question of negligence enters; for, if the party furnishing the liquor knows, or was apprised of such facts that he should have known, of the danger, there then appears from his act a recklessness which is indifferent to results.

Such recklessness in the furnishing of intoxicating liquors, in violation of law, may constitute such an unlawful act as, if it results in causing death, will constitute manslaughter.

The evidence here was sufficient, as we view it, to warrant a submission of the charge of manslaughter to the jury.

The defendant, it seems, distilled this liquor himself. It was at least home-made whisky. The danger of drinking such liquor, by reason of its extreme potency and its frequently containing poisonous ingredients, is commonly known. The defendant may have been dealing with an unknown quantity, but, * * * he was handling a dangerous weapon. There is evidence to show that he knew this particular liquor was extremely powerful. He saw its effect on Chris Nelson and on Stromer in the morning; yet that evening he offered it to the Prosser boys and invited them to drink all they wanted. There is substantial proof that the liquor was dangerous. That two drinks of it should paralyze three men within a few minutes after drinking, and that one of these men, as a result, should die in a few hours, as happened in this case, sufficiently raised the issue of its dangerous character for the jury.

Defendant contends that the drinking of liquor by deceased was his voluntary act and served as an intervening cause, breaking the causal connection between the giving of the liquor by defendant and the resulting death. The drinking of the liquor, in consequence of defendant's act, was, however, what the defendant contemplated. Deceased, it is true, may have been negligent in drinking, but, where the defendant was negligent, then the contributory negligence of the deceased will be no defense in a criminal action. The act of the deceased, as we view it, was no more than a concurring cause.

Defendant complains of the court's instructions, which directed the jury that, if defendant furnished intoxicating liquor to deceased, and the liquor caused death, defendant was guilty, but failed to instruct upon the question of recklessness on the part of the defendant. We believe the instructions are erroneous in that regard and that the defendant is entitled to a new trial.

Reversed and remanded.

Larceny/Embezzlement

UNITED STATES v. WARONEK

United States Court of Appeals, Seventh Circuit, 1978.
582 F.2d 1158.

CAMPBELL, J.

The sole issue raised in this appeal is whether the district court erred in refusing to instruct the jury that an essential element of the crime of theft from an interstate shipment is the accused's intent to permanently deprive the owner of his property. We hold that the district court did not so err, and affirm the defendant's conviction.

The relevant facts are undisputed. Defendant-Appellant Waronek owned and operated a tractor. Pursuant to a written agreement, Waronek undertook to haul loads for L. T. L. Perishables, Inc., of South St. Paul, Minnesota. On June 7, 1977, defendant accepted an offer to haul a trailer load of beef from Illini Beef Packers, Inc. in Joslin, Illinois to Midtown Packing Company, in New York City. After his truck was loaded by the shipper's personnel, Waronek signed a bill of lading for 95 forequarters and 95 hindquarters of beef.

Upon leaving Joslin, Illinois, Waronek proceeded northward to his home in Watertown, Wisconsin, instead of heading eastward to New York. Waronek testified that his reason for making this detour was to drop off some of his advance money with his wife and to make a minor repair in his refrigeration unit. While in Watertown defendant contacted employees of the Royal Meat Company, and requested the butchering and preparation of four hindquarters of the beef. He instructed the employees that two quarters be prepared for himself, and two quarters to be prepared and stored for friends. Lowell

Pritchard of Royal Meat Company testified that Waronek asked him if he would be interested in purchasing ten hindquarters at sixty cents per pound—a price substantially lower than the prevailing wholesale rate. Pritchard became suspicious and contacted an officer of the Watertown Police Department, who instructed Pritchard to proceed with the transaction and to obtain information regarding Waronek.

Upon arrival in New York, defendant's truck was unloaded and found to be short nineteen hindquarters of beef. Waronek then telephoned his dispatcher in St. Paul and told him that he was short nineteen hindquarters, that he knew where the beef went, and that he would make good on it out of future settlements. Although instructed to contact the New York police, Waronek failed to do so. Thereafter, defendant was arrested by agents of the Federal Bureau of Investigation.

A grand jury in the Western District of Wisconsin, where part of Watertown is located, charged in an indictment that Waronek willfully, knowingly, and with intent to convert to his own use, did embezzle and unlawfully take from a motor truck fourteen hindquarters of beef valued at approximately $2149.00. The indictment further alleged that the hindquarters were moving as, were a part of, and constituted an interstate shipment of freight from Joslin, Illinois, to New York, New York. The indictment specified that the alleged acts constituted a violation of 18 U.S.C. § 659[2] [theft from interstate shipment].

At the close of the evidence, during the conference on jury instructions, counsel for defendant requested the court to instruct the jury as follows:

---

2. In relevant part, 18 U.S.C. § 659 provides:

"Whoever embezzles, steals, or unlawfully takes, carries away, or conceals . . . from any . . . motortruck . . . with intent to convert to his own use any goods or chattels moving as or which are a part of or which constitute an interstate or foreign shipment of freight, express, or other property . . . [s]hall in each case be fined not more than $5,000 or imprisoned not more than ten years, or both; . . . ."

Three essential elements are required to be proved in order to establish the offense charged in the indictment:

FIRST: The act of unlawfully taking away, from a motor truck, property moving as, or which constitutes a part of, an interstate shipment of freight or express, as charged in the indictment; and

SECOND: Doing such act unlawfully, and with the intent to convert the property to the use of the accused.

THIRD: Doing such act with the intent to permanently deprive the owner of the property.

The district court refused to instruct the jury on the elements of the offense as tendered by the defendant, but rather instructed the jury in language substantially tracking the pattern instruction in Devitt and Blackmar, *Federal Jury Practice and Instructions*, § 46.06:

Two essential elements are required to be proved in order to establish the offense charged in the indictment:

FIRST: The act of embezzling, or unlawfully taking from a motor truck, goods moving as, or which constitute a part of, an interstate shipment of freight as charged in the indictment; and

SECOND: Doing such act willfully, knowingly, and unlawfully, and with the intent to convert the goods or property to the use of the accused.

On the basis of a line of Third Circuit cases, defendant argues here, as he did below that an essential element of a violation of 18 U.S.C. § 659 is the accused's intent to permanently deprive the owner of the property. If the proposed instruction correctly propounded the law, and had the trial judge agreed to give the proposed instruction, the defendant would have been able to argue to the jury the evidence of his intent to pay back L.T.L. Perishables, Inc. out of future settlements for the hindquarters he converted. Waronek asserts that this evidence, if believed by the jury, would be sufficient to enable the jury to find that he did not intend to permanently deprive the owner of the value of the hindquarters.

In contending that an element of the crimes embraced by 18 U.S.C. § 659 is the intent permanently to deprive the owner of his property, defendant proceeds on the assumption that the crime charged in the indictment and the facts proven at trial amount to larceny, as that crime existed at common law, and the 18 U.S.C. § 659 is limited in application to the common law crime of larceny. There is no basis for either assumption.

The indictment in this case charged the defendant with embezzling and unlawfully taking fourteen beef hindquarters with intent to convert them to his own use. Larceny, as defined in the common law, generally consists of the taking and carrying away of the personal property of another with the intent to deprive the owner of his property permanently, and to convert the property to the use of someone other than the owner. [Citation.] Larceny involves an unlawful trespass to the possessory interest of the owner in the property. Hence, if the owner is not in possession of the property taken, there can be no larceny. [Citations.] Where the taker has been entrusted with possession of the property, the taking is more aptly described as embezzlement. [Citation.] In this case it is clear that Waronek was entrusted with possession of the hindquarters under a contract of carriage, and that he took and converted to his own use these hindquarters while they were in his possession. Thus, the indictment correctly charged embezzlement, and the facts adduced at trial proved that charge. Consequently, even if defendant's proposed instruction correctly stated an element of the crime of larceny, there were simply no allegations in the indictment or factual basis developed at trial to warrant the giving of such an instruction.[4]

* * *

The judgment of conviction is affirmed.

---

4. The intent to permanently deprive the owner of his property is not an element of the crime of embezzlement. Rather, cases indicate that the "felonious" intent with

Intoxication

COOTS v. COMMONWEALTH

Court of Appeals of Kentucky, 1967.
418 S.W.2d 752.

WADDILL, J.

Appellant, Felix Coots, Jr., was convicted of the crime of rape and his punishment fixed at confinement in prison for ten years. His grounds for reversal of the conviction are that the verdict is flagrantly against the evidence, the instructions did not cover the whole law of the case and the trial court erred in failing to grant a new trial.

The prosecuting witness testified unequivocally that appellant forced her to submit to sexual intercourse with him by threats of physical injury. Appellant denied he had sexual intercourse with her and stated that he was so drunk that he was unable to do so. His testimony did not entitle him to a directed verdict of acquittal or render the verdict flagrantly against the evidence. It merely placed in issue the credibility of the prosecutrix's testimony since we are unwilling to hold that her testimony is without probative value. Her version of the affair is not so incredible and improbable as to be patently untrue but is a lucid account of an unfortunate experience for her.

Moreover, there is other testimony that strongly tends to support her claim that she was raped by appellant. We find no merit in appellant's first contention. Appellant next contends that he was entitled to an instruction to the effect that if the jury believed from the evidence that appellant was so drunk at the time of the alleged offense he did not realize the consequences of his act it should find him not guilty. Ordinarily, voluntary intoxication constitutes no excuse or justification for the commission of crime. Whenever an act

---

which embezzlement is committed consists of the intent to appropriate or convert the property of the owner; the simultaneous intent to return the property or to make restitution does not make the offense any less embezzlement. [Citation.]

constitutes the offense, drunkenness is no defense to its commission * * *.

* * *

The judgment is affirmed.
All concur.

*Fourth Amendment
Exclusionary Rule*

UNITED STATES v. LEON

Supreme Court of the United States, 1984.
— US. —, 104 S.Ct. 3405, — L.Ed.2d —.

WHITE, J.

This case presents the question whether the Fourth Amendment exclusionary rule should be modified so as not to bar the use in the prosecution's case-in-chief of evidence obtained by officers acting in reasonable reliance on a search warrant issued by a detached and neutral magistrate but ultimately found to be unsupported by probable cause. To resolve this question, we must consider once again the tension between the sometimes competing goals of, on the one hand, deterring official misconduct and removing inducements to unreasonable invasions of privacy and, on the other, establishing procedures under which criminal defendants are "acquitted or convicted on the basis of all the evidence which exposes the truth." [Citation.]

I

In August 1981, a confidential informant of unproven reliability informed an officer of the Burbank Police Department that two persons known to him as "Armando" and "Patsy" were selling large quantities of cocaine and methaqualone from their residence at 620 Price Drive in Burbank, Cal. The informant also indicated that he had witnessed a sale of methaqualone by "Patsy" at the residence approximately five months earlier and had observed at that time a shoebox containing a large amount of cash that belonged to "Patsy." He further declared that "Armando" and

"Patsy" generally kept only small quantities of drugs at their residence and stored the remainder at another location in Burbank.

On the basis of this information, the Burbank police initiated an extensive investigation focusing first on the Price Drive residence and later on two other residences as well. Cars parked at the Price Drive residence were determined to belong to respondents Armando Sanchez, who had previously been arrested for possession of marihuana, and Patsy Stewart, who had no criminal record. During the course of the investigation, officers observed an automobile belonging to respondent Ricardo Del Castillo, who had previously been arrested for possession of 50 pounds of marihuana, arrive at the Price Drive residence. The driver of that car entered the house, exited shortly thereafter carrying a small paper sack, and drove away. A check of Del Castillo's probation records led the officers to respondent Alberto Leon, whose telephone number Del Castillo had listed as his employer's. Leon had been arrested in 1980 on drug charges, and a companion had informed the police at that time that Leon was heavily involved in the importation of drugs into this country. Before the current investigation began, the Burbank officers had learned that an informant had told a Glendale police officer that Leon stored a large quantity of methaqualone at his residence in Glendale. During the course of this investigation, the Burbank officers learned that Leon was living at 716 South Sunset Canyon in Burbank.

Subsequently, the officers observed several persons, at least one of whom had prior drug involvement, arriving at the Price Drive residence and leaving with small packages; observed a variety of other material activity at the two residences as well as at a condominium at 7902 Via Magdalena; and witnessed a variety of relevant activity involving respondents' automobiles. The officers also observed respondents Sanchez and Stewart board separate flights for Miami. The pair later returned to Los Angeles together, consented to a search of their luggage that revealed only a small amount of marihuana, and left the airport. Based on these and other observations summarized in the affidavit, Officer Cyril Rombach of the Burbank Police Department, an experienced and well-trained narcotics investigator, prepared an application for a warrant to search 620 Price Drive, 716 South Sunset Canyon, 7902 Via Magdalena, and automobiles registered to each of the respondents for an extensive list of items believed to be related to respondents' drug-trafficking activities. Officer Rombach's extensive application was reviewed by several Deputy District Attorneys.

A facially valid search warrant was issued in September 1981 by a state superior court judge. The ensuing searches produced large quantities of drugs at the Via Magdalena and Sunset Canyon addresses and a small quantity at the Price Drive residence. Other evidence was discovered at each of the residences and in Stewart's and Del Castillo's automobiles. Respondents were indicted by a grand jury in the District Court for the Central District of California and charged with conspiracy to possess and distribute cocaine and a variety of substantive counts.

The respondents then filed motions to suppress the evidence seized pursuant to the warrant. The District Court held an evidentiary hearing and, while recognizing that the case was a close one, granted the motions to suppress in part. It concluded that the affidavit was insufficient to establish probable cause, but did not suppress all of the evidence as to all of the respondents because none of the respondents had standing to challenge all of the searches. In response to a request from the Government, the court made clear that Officer Rombach had acted in good faith, but it rejected the Government's suggestion that the Fourth Amendment exclusionary rule should not apply where evidence is seized in reasonable, good-faith reliance on a search warrant.

The District Court denied the Government's motion for reconsideration and a divided panel of the Court of Appeals for the Ninth Circuit affirmed. The Court of Appeals * * * concluded that Officer Rombach's affidavit could not establish probable cause to search the Price Drive residence. To the extent that the affidavit set forth facts demonstrating the basis of the informant's knowledge of criminal activity, the information included was fatally stale. The affidavit, moreover, failed to establish the informant's credibility.

* * *

II
A

The Fourth Amendment contains no provision expressly precluding the use of evidence obtained in violation of its commands, and an examination of its origin and purposes makes clear that the use of fruits of a past unlawful search or seizure "work[s] no new Fourth Amendment wrong." [Citation.] The wrong condemned by the Amendment is "fully accomplished" by the unlawful search or seizure itself, and the exclusionary rule is neither intended nor able to "cure the invasion of the defendant's rights which he has already suffered." [Citation] The rule thus operates as "a judicially created remedy designed to safeguard Fourth Amendment rights generally through its deterrent effect, rather than a personal constitutional right of the person aggrieved." [Citation.]

Whether the exclusionary sanction is appropriately imposed in a particular case, our decisions make clear, is "an issue separate from the question whether the Fourth Amendment rights of the party seeking to invoke the rule were violated by police conduct." [Citation.] Only the former question is currently before us, and it must be resolved by weighing the costs and benefits of preventing the use in the prosecution's case-in-chief of inherently trustworthy tangible evidence obtained in reliance on a search warrant issued by a detached and neutral magistrate that ultimately is found to be defective.

The substantial social costs exacted by the exclusionary rule for the vindication of Fourth Amendment rights have long been a source of concern. "Our cases have consistently recognized that unbending application of the exclusionary sanction to enforce ideals of governmental rectitude would impede unacceptably the truth-finding functions of judge and jury." [Citation]. An objectionable collateral consequence of this interference with the criminal justice system's truth-finding function is that some guilty defendants may go free or receive reduced sentences as a result of favorable plea bargains. Particularly when law enforcement officers have acted in objective good faith or their transgressions have been minor, the magnitude of the benefit conferred on such guilty defendants offends basic concepts of the criminal justice system. [Citation.] Indiscriminate application of the exclusionary rule, therefore, may well "generat[e] disrespect for the law and the administration of justice." [Citation.] Accordingly, "[a]s with any remedial device, the application of the rule has been restricted to those areas where its remedial objectives are thought most efficaciously served." [Citation.]

B

Close attention to those remedial objectives has characterized our recent decisions concerning the scope of the Fourth Amendment exclusionary rule. The Court has, to be sure, not seriously questioned, "in the absence of a more efficacious sanction, the continued application of the rule to suppress evidence from the [prosecution's] case where a Fourth Amendment violation has been substantial and deliberate . . . ." [Citation.] Nevertheless, the balancing approach that has evolved in various contexts including criminal trials—"forcefully suggest[s] that the exclusionary rule be more generally modified to

permit the introduction of evidence obtained in the reasonable good-faith belief that a search or seizure was in accord with the Fourth Amendment." [Citation.]

* * *

As yet, we have not recognized any form of good-faith exception to the Fourth Amendment exclusionary rule. But the balancing approach that has evolved during the years of experience with the rule provides strong support for the modification currently urged upon us. As we discuss below, our evaluation of the costs and benefits of suppressing reliable physical evidence seized by officers reasonably relying on a warrant issued by a detached and neutral magistrate leads to the conclusion that such evidence should be admissible in the prosecution's case-in-chief.

III
A

Because a search warrant "provides the detached scrutiny of a neutral magistrate, which is a more reliable safeguard against improper searches than the hurried judgment of a law enforcement officer 'engaged in the often competitive enterprise of ferreting out crime,' " [Citations], we have expressed a strong preference for warrants and declared that "in a doubtful or marginal case a search under a warrant may be sustainable where without one it would fail." [Citations.] Reasonable minds frequently may differ on the question whether a particular affidavit establishes probable cause, and we have thus concluded that the preference for warrants is most appropriately effectuated by according "great deference" to a magistrate's determination. [Citations.]

Deference to the magistrate, however, is not boundless. It is clear, first, that the deference accorded to a magistrate's finding of probable cause does not preclude inquiry into the knowing or reckless falsity of the affidavit on which that determination was based. [Citation.] Second, the courts must also insist that the magistrate purport to "perform his 'neutral and detached' function and not serve merely as a rubber stamp for the police." [Citations.] A magistrate failing to "manifest that neutrality and detachment demanded of a judicial officer when presented with a warrant application" and who acts instead as "an adjunct law enforcement officer" cannot provide valid authorization for an otherwise unconstitutional search. [Citation.]

Third, reviewing courts will not defer to a warrant based on an affidavit that does not "provide the magistrate with a substantial basis for determining the existence of probable cause." [Citation.] "Sufficient information must be presented to the magistrate to allow that official to determine probable cause; his action cannot be a mere ratification of the bare conclusions of others." [Citation]. * * *

Only in the first of these three situations, however, has the Court set forth a rationale for suppressing evidence obtained pursuant to a search warrant; in the other areas, it has simply excluded such evidence without considering whether Fourth Amendment interests will be advanced. To the extent that proponents of exclusion rely on its behavioral effects on judges and magistrates in these areas, their reliance is misplaced. First, the exclusionary rule is designed to deter police misconduct rather than to punish the errors of judges and magistrates. Second, there exists no evidence suggesting that judges and magistrates are inclined to ignore or subvert the Fourth Amendment or that lawlessness among these actors requires application of the extreme sanction of exclusion.

Third, and most important, we discern no basis, and are offered none, for believing that exclusion of evidence seized pursuant to a warrant will have a significant deterrent effect on the issuing judge or magistrate. Many of the factors that indicate that the exclusionary rule cannot provide an effective "special" or "general" deterrent for individual offending law enforcement officers apply as well to judges or magistrates. And, to the extent that the rule is thought to operate as a "systematic" deterrent on a wider audience, it

clearly can have no such effect on individuals empowered to issue search warrants. Judges and magistrates are not adjuncts to the law enforcement team; as neutral judicial officers, they have no stake in the outcome of particular criminal prosecutions. The threat of exclusion thus cannot be expected significantly to deter them. Imposition of the exclusionary sanction is not necessary meaningfully to inform judicial officers of their errors, and we cannot conclude that admitting evidence obtained pursuant to a warrant while at the same time declaring that the warrant was somehow defective will in any way reduce judicial officers' professional incentives to comply with the Fourth Amendment, encourage them to repeat their mistakes, or lead to the granting of all colorable warrant requests.

B

If exclusion of evidence obtained pursuant to a subsequently invalidated warrant is to have any deterrent effect, therefore, it must alter the behavior of individual law enforcement officers or the policies of their departments. One could argue that applying the exclusionary rule in cases where the police failed to demonstrate probable cause in the warrant application deters future inadequate presentations or "magistrate shopping" and thus promotes the ends of the Fourth Amendment. Suppressing evidence obtained pursuant to a technically defective warrant supported by probable cause also might encourage officers to scrutinize more closely the form of the warrant and to point out suspected judicial errors. We find such arguments speculative and conclude that suppression of evidence obtained pursuant to a warrant should be ordered only on a case-by-case basis and only in those unusual cases in which exclusion will further the purposes of the exclusionary rule.

We have frequently questioned whether the exclusionary rule can have any deterrent effect when the offending officers acted in the objectively reasonable belief that their conduct did not violate the Fourth Amendment.

"No empirical researcher, proponent, or opponent of the rule, has yet been able to establish with any assurance whether the rule has a deterrent effect . . . ." [Citation.] But even assuming that the rule effectively deters some police misconduct and provides incentives for the law enforcement profession as a whole to conduct itself in accord with the Fourth Amendment, it cannot be expected, and should not be applied, to deter objectively reasonable law enforcement activity.

In short, where the officer's conduct is objectively reasonable,

excluding the evidence will not further the ends of the exclusionary rule in any appreciable way; for it is painfully apparent that . . . the officer is acting as a reasonable officer would and should act under the circumstances. Excluding the evidence can in no way affect his future conduct unless it is to make him less willing to do his duty. [Citation.]

This is particularly true, we believe, when an officer acting with objective good faith has obtained a search warrant from a judge or magistrate and acted within its scope. In most such cases, there is no police illegality and thus nothing to deter. It is the magistrate's responsibility to determine whether the officer's allegations establish probable cause and, if so, to issue a warrant comporting in form with the requirements of the Fourth Amendment. In the ordinary case, an officer cannot be expected to question the magistrate's probable-cause determination or his judgment that the form of the warrant is technically sufficient. "[O]nce the warrant issues, there is literally nothing more the policeman can do in seeking to comply with the law." [Citation.] Penalizing the officer for the magistrate's error, rather than his own, cannot logically contribute to the deterrence of Fourth Amendment violations.

C

We conclude that the marginal or nonexistent benefits produced by suppressing evidence obtained in objectively reasonable reliance on a subsequently invalidated search warrant cannot justify the substantial costs of exclusion. * * * Nevertheless, the officer's reliance on the magistrate's probable-cause determination and on the technical sufficiency of the warrant he issues must be objectively reasonable, [citation.] and it is clear that in some circumstances the officer will have no reasonable grounds for believing that the warrant was properly issued.

* * *

Accordingly, the judgment of the Court of Appeals is *Reversed*.

Fifth Amendment

MIRANDA v. ARIZONA

Supreme Court of the United States, 1964.
384 U.S. 436, 86 S.Ct. 1602, 16 L.Ed.2d 694.

WARREN, C. J.

Our holding will be spelled out with some specificity in the pages which follow but briefly stated it is this: the prosecution may not use statements, whether exculpatory or inculpatory, stemming from custodial interrogation of the defendant unless it demonstrates the use of procedural safeguards effective to secure the privilege against self-incrimination. By custodial interrogation, we mean questioning initiated by law enforcement officers after a person has been taken into custody or otherwise deprived of his freedom of action in any significant way. * * *

* * *

I

The constitutional issue we decide in each of these cases is the admissibility of statements obtained from a defendant questioned while in custody or otherwise deprived of his freedom of action in any significant way. In each, the defendant was questioned by police officers, detectives, or a prosecuting attorney in a room in which he was cut off from the outside world. In none of these cases was the defendant given a full and effective warning of his rights at the outset of the interrogation process. In all the cases, the questioning elicited oral admissions, and in three of them, signed statements as well which were admitted at their trials. They all thus share salient features—incommunicado interrogation of individuals in a police-dominated atmosphere, resulting in self-incriminating statements without full warnings of constitutional rights.

An understanding of the nature and setting of this in-custody interrogation is essential to our decisions today. The difficulty in depicting what transpires at such interrogations stems from the fact that in this country they have largely taken place incommunicado.

* * *

A valuable source of information about present police practices, however, may be found in various police manuals and texts which document procedures employed with success in the past, and which recommend various other effective tactics. These texts are used by law enforcement agencies themselves as guides. It should be noted that these texts professedly present the most enlightened and effective means presently used to obtain statements through custodial interrogation. By considering these texts and other data, it is possible to describe procedures observed and noted around the country.

The officers are told by the manuals that the "principal psychological factor contributing to a successful interrogation is privacy—being alone with the person under interrogation."

* * *

To highlight the isolation and unfamiliar surroundings, the manuals instruct the police to display an air of confidence in the suspect's guilt and from outward appearance to maintain only an interest in confirming certain details. The guilt of the subject is to be posited as a fact. The interrogator should direct his comments toward the reasons why the subject committed the act, rather than court failure by asking the subject whether he did it. Like other men, perhaps the subject has had a bad family life, had an unhappy childhood, had too much to drink, had an unrequited desire for women. The officers are instructed to minimize the moral seriousness of the offense, to cast blame on the victim or on society. These tactics are designed to put the subject in a psychological state where his story is but an elaboration of what the police purport to know already—that he is guilty. Explanations to the contrary are dismissed and discouraged.

* * *

The manuals suggest that the suspect be offered legal excuses for his actions in order to obtain an initial admission of guilt. * * *

When the techniques described above prove unavailing, the texts recommend they be alternated with a show of some hostility. One ploy often used has been termed the "friendly-unfriendly" or the "Mutt and Jeff" act:

* * * In this technique, two agents are employed. Mutt, the relentless investigator, who knows the subject is guilty and is not going to waste any time. He's sent a dozen men away for this crime and he's going to send the subject away for the full term. Jeff, on the other hand, is obviously a kindhearted man. He has a family himself. He has a brother who was involved in a little scrape like this. He disapproves of Mutt and his tactics and will arrange to get him off the case if the subject will cooperate. He can't hold Mutt off for very long. The subject would be wise to make a quick decision. The technique is applied by having both investigators present while Mutt acts out his role. Jeff may stand by quietly and demur at some of Mutt's tactics. When Jeff makes his plea for cooperation, Mutt is not present in the room.

The interrogators sometimes are instructed to induce a confession out of trickery. The technique here is quite effective in crimes which require identification or which run in series. In the identification situation, the interrogator may take a break in his questioning to place the subject among a group of men in a line-up. "The witness or complainant (previously coached, if necessary) studies the line-up and confidently points out the subject as the guilty party." Then the questioning resumes "as though there were now no doubt about the guilt of the subject." * * *

The manuals also contain instructions for police on how to handle the individual who refuses to discuss the matter entirely, or who asks for an attorney or relatives. The examiner is to concede him the right to remain silent. "This usually has a very undermining effect. First of all, he is disappointed in his expectation of an unfavorable reaction on the part of the interrogator. Secondly, a concession of this right to remain silent impresses the subject with the apparent fairness of his interrogator." After this psychological conditioning, however, the officer is told to point out the incriminating significance of the suspect's refusal to talk. * * *

In the event that the subject wishes to speak to a relative or an attorney, the following advise is tendered:

[T]he interrogator should respond by suggesting that the subject first tell the truth to the interrogator himself rather than get anyone else involved in the matter. If the request is for an attorney, the interrogator may suggest that the subject save himself or his family the expense of any such professional service, particularly if he is innocent of the offense under investigation. The interrogator may also add, "Joe, I'm only looking for the truth, and if you're telling the truth, that's it. You can handle this by yourself."

* * *

Even without employing brutality, the "third degree" or the specific stratagems described above, the very fact of custodial interrogation exacts a heavy toll on individual liberty and trades on the weakness of individuals.

* * *

II

The question in these cases is whether the privilege [against self-incrimination] is fully applicable during a period of custodial interrogation.

* * *

This question, in fact, could have been taken as settled in federal courts almost 70 years ago, when, in *Bram v. United States*, [citation], this Court held:

In criminal trials, in the courts of the United States, wherever a question arises whether a confession is incompetent because not voluntary, the issue is controlled by that portion of the fifth amendment * * * commanding that no person "shall be compelled in any criminal case to be a witness against himself."

Our decision in *Malloy v. Hogan*, [citation] * * * squarely held the privilege applicable to the States, and held that the substantive standards underlying the privilege applied with full force to state court proceedings.

* * *

Aside from the holding itself, the reasoning in *Malloy* made clear what had already become apparent—that the substantive and procedural safeguards surrounding admissibility of confessions in state cases had become exceedingly exacting, reflecting all the policies embedded in the privilege. The voluntariness doctrine in the state cases, as *Malloy* indicates, encompasses all interrogation practices which are likely to exert such pressure upon an individual as to disable him from making a free and rational choice. The implications of this proposition were elaborated in our decision in *Escobedo v. Illinois*, decided one week after *Malloy* applied the privilege to the States.

* * *

* * * In *Escobedo* * * * the police did not relieve the defendant of the anxieties which they had created in the interrogation rooms. Rather, they denied his request for the assistance of counsel, [citation]. This heightened his dilemma, and made his later statements the product of this compulsion.

* * *

It was in this manner that *Escobedo* explicated another facet of the pre-trial privilege, noted in many of the Court's prior decisions: the protection of rights at trial. That counsel is present when statements are taken from an individual during interrogation obviously enhances the integrity of the fact-finding processes in court. The presence of an attorney, and the warnings delivered to the individual, enable the defendant under otherwise compelling circumstances to tell his story without fear, effectively, and in a way that eliminates the evils in the interrogation process.

* * *

III

Today, then, there can be no doubt that the Fifth Amendment privilege is available outside of criminal court proceedings and serves to protect persons in all settings in which their freedom of action is curtailed in any significant way from being compelled to incriminate themselves. We have concluded that without proper safeguards the process of in-custody interrogation of persons suspected or accused of crime contains inherently compelling pressures which work to undermine the individual's will to resist and to compel him to speak where he would not otherwise do so freely. In order to combat these pressures and to permit a full opportunity to exercise the privilege against self-incrimination, the accused must be adequately and effectively apprised of his rights and the exercise of those rights must be fully honored.

It is impossible for us to foresee the potential alternatives for protecting the privilege which might be devised by Congress or the States in the exercise of their creative rule-making capacities. Therefore we cannot say that the Constitution necessarily requires adherence to any particular solution for the inherent compulsions of the interrogation process as it is presently conducted. Our decision in no way creates a constitutional straitjacket which will handicap sound efforts at reform, nor is it intended to have this effect. We encourage Congress and the States to continue their laudable search for increasingly effective ways of protecting the rights of the individual while promoting efficient enforcement of our criminal laws. However, unless we are shown other procedures which are at least as effective in apprising accused persons of their right of silence and in assuring a continuous opportunity to exercise it, the following safeguards must be observed.

At the outset, if a person in custody is to be subjected to interrogation, he must first be informed in clear and unequivocal terms that he has the right to remain silent. For those unaware of the privilege, the warning is needed simply to make them aware of it— the threshold requirement for an intelligent decision as to its exercise. More important, such a warning is an absolute prerequisite in overcoming the inherent pressures of the interrogation atmosphere. It is not just the subnormal or woefully ignorant who succumb to an interrogator's imprecations, whether implied or expressly stated, that the interrogation will continue until a confession is obtained or that silence in the face of accusation is itself damning and will bode ill when presented to a jury. Further, the warning will show the individual that his interrogators are prepared to recognize his privilege should he choose to exercise it.

The Fifth Amendment privilege is so fundamental to our system of constitutional rule and the expedient of giving an adequate warning as to the availability of the privilege so simple, we will not pause to inquire in individual cases whether the defendant was aware of his rights without a warning being given. Assessments of the knowledge the defendant possessed, based on information as to his age, education, intelligence, or prior contact with authorities, can never be more than speculation; a warning is a clearcut fact. More important, whatever the background of the person interrogated, a warning at the time of the interrogation is indispensable to overcome its pressures and to insure that the individual knows he is free to exercise the privilege at that point in time.

The warning of the right to remain silent must be accompanied by the explanation that anything said can and will be used against the individual in court. This warning is needed in order to make him aware not only of the privilege, but also of the consequences of foregoing it. It is only through an awareness of these consequences that there can be any assurance of real understanding and intelligent exercise of the privilege. Moreover, this warning may serve to make the individual more acutely aware that he is faced with a phase of the adversary system—that he is not in the presence of persons acting solely in his interest.

The circumstances surrounding in-custody interrogation can operate very quickly to overbear the will of one merely made aware of his privilege by his interrogators. Therefore the right to have counsel present at the interrogation is indispensable to the protection of the Fifth Amendment privilege under the system we delineate today.

* * *

The presence of counsel at the interrogation may serve several significant subsidiary functions as well. If the accused decides to talk to his interrogators, the assistance of counsel can mitigate the dangers of untrustworthiness. With a lawyer present the likelihood that the police will practice coercion is reduced, and if coercion is nevertheless exercised the lawyer can testify to it in court. The presence of a lawyer can also help to guarantee that the accused gives a fully accurate statement to the police and that the statement is rightly reported by the prosecution at trial.

An individual need not make a pre-interrogation request for a lawyer. While such request affirmatively secures his right to have one, his failure to ask for a lawyer does not constitute a waiver. No effective waiver of the right to counsel during interrogation can be recognized unless specifically made after the warnings we here delineate have been given. The accused who does not know his rights and therefore does not make a request may be the person who most needs counsel.

* * *

Accordingly we hold that an individual held for interrogation must be clearly informed that he has the right to consult with a lawyer and to have the lawyer with him during interrogation under the system for protecting the privilege we delineate today. As with the warnings of the right to remain silent and that anything stated can be used in evidence against him, this warning is an absolute prerequisite to interrogation. No amount of circumstantial evidence that the person may have been aware of this right will suffice to stand in its stead. Only through such a warning is there ascertainable assurance that the accused was aware of this right.

If an individual indicates that he wishes the assistance of counsel before any interrogation occurs, the authorities cannot rationally ignore or deny his request on the basis that the individual does not have or cannot afford a retained attorney.

* * *

Denial of counsel to the indigent at the time of interrogation while allowing an attorney to those who can afford one would be no more supportable by reason or logic than the similar situation at trial and on appeal struck down in *Gideon v. Wainwright*.

In order fully to apprise a person interrogated of the extent of his rights under this system then, it is necessary to warn him not only that he has the right to consult with an attorney, but also that if he is indigent a lawyer will be appointed to represent him. Without this additional warning, the admonition of the right to consult with counsel would often be understood as meaning only that he can consult with a lawyer if he has one or has the funds to obtain one. The warning of a right to counsel would be hollow if not couched in terms that would convey to the indigent— the person most often subjected to interrogation—the knowledge that he too has a right to have counsel present. As with the warnings of the right to remain silent and of the general right to counsel, only by effective and express explanation to the indigent of this right can there be assurance that he was truly in a position to exercise it.

Once warnings have been given, the subsequent procedure is clear. If the individual indicates in any manner, at any time prior to or during questioning, that he wishes to remain silent, the interrogation must cease. At this point he has shown that he intends to exercise his Fifth Amendment privilege; any statement taken after the person invokes his privilege cannot be other than the product of compulsion, subtle or otherwise. Without the right to cut off questioning, the setting of in-custody interrogation operates on the individual to overcome free choice in producing a statement after the privilege has been once invoked. If the individual states that he wants an attorney, the interrogation must cease until an attorney is present. At that time, the individual must have an opportunity to confer with the attorney and to have him present during any subsequent questioning. If the individual cannot obtain an attorney and he indicates that he wants one before speaking to police, they must respect his decision to remain silent.

This does not mean, as some have suggested, that each police station must have a "station house lawyer" present at all times to advise prisoners. It does mean, however, that if police propose to interrogate a person they must make known to him that he is entitled to a lawyer and that if he cannot afford one, a lawyer will be provided for him prior to any interrogation. If authorities conclude that they will not provide counsel during a reasonable period of time in which investigation in the field is carried out, they may refrain from doing so without violating the person's Fifth Amendment privilege so long as they do not question him during that time.

If the interrogation continues without the presence of an attorney and a statement is taken, a heavy burden rests on the government to demonstrate that the defendant knowingly and intelligently waived his privilege against self-incrimination and his right to retained or appointed counsel. * * *

Whatever the testimony of the authorities as to waiver of rights by an accused, the fact of lengthy interrogation or incommunicado incarceration before a statement is made is strong evidence that the accused did not validly waive his rights. In these circumstances the fact that the individual eventually made a statement is consistent with the conclusion that the compelling influence of the interrogation finally forced him to do so. It is inconsistent with any notion of a voluntary relinquishment of the privilege. Moreover, any evidence that the accused was threatened, tricked, or cajoled into a waiver will, of course, show that the defendant did not voluntarily waive his privilege. The requirement of warnings and waiver of rights is a fundamental with respect to the Fifth Amendment privilege and not simply a preliminary ritual to existing methods of interrogation.

The warnings required and the waiver necessary in accordance with our opinion today are, in the absence of a fully effective equivalent, prerequisites to the admissibility of any statement made by a defendant. No distinction can be drawn between statements which are direct confessions and statements which amount to "admissions" of part or all of any offense. The privilege against self-incrimination protects the individual from being compelled to incriminate himself in any manner; it does not distinguish degrees of incrimination. Similarly, for precisely the same reason, no distinction may be drawn between inculpatory statements and statements alleged to be merely "exculpatory." If a statement made were in fact truly exculpatory it would, of course, never be used by the prosecution. In fact, statements merely intended to be exculpatory by the defendant are often used to impeach his testimony at trial or to demonstrate untruths in the statement given under interrogation and thus to prove guilt by implication. These statements are incriminating in any meaningful sense of the word and may not be used without the full warnings and effective waiver required for any other statement. * * *

Our decision is not intended to hamper the traditional function of police officers in investigating crime. [Citation.] When an individual is in custody on probable cause, the police may, of course, seek out evidence in the field to be used at trial against him. Such investigation may include inquiry of persons not under restraint. General on-the-scene questioning as to facts surrounding a crime or other general questioning of citizens in the fact-finding process is not affected by our holding. It is an act of responsible citizenship for individuals to give whatever information they may have to aid in law enforcement. In such situations the compelling atmosphere inherent in the process of in-custody interrogation is not necessarily present.

In dealing with statements obtained through interrogation, we do not purport to find all confessions inadmissible. Confessions remain a proper element in law enforcement. Any statement given freely and voluntarily without any compelling influences is, of course, admissible in evidence. The fundamental import of the privilege while an individual is in custody is not whether he is allowed to talk to the police without the benefit of warnings and counsel, but whether he can be interrogated. There is no requirement that police stop a person who enters a police station and states that he wishes to confess to a crime, or a person who calls the police to offer a confession or any other statement he desires to make. Volunteered statements of any kind are not barred by the Fifth Amendment and their admissibility is not affected by our holding today.

* * *

PROBLEMS

1. X said to Y, "B is going to sell me a good used car next Monday and then I'll deliver it to you in exchange for your microcomputer, but I'd like to have the computer now." Relying on this statement, Y delivered the computer to X. X knew B had no car, would have none in the future, and had no such arrangement with B. The appointed time of exchange passed and X failed to deliver the car to Y. Has a crime been committed? Discuss.

2. X, a lawyer, drew a deed for Y by which Y was to convey land to B. The deed was correct in every detail. Y examined and verbally approved it but did not sign it. X erased B's name and substituted his own. Y signed the deed with all required legal formalities without noticing the change. Was X guilty of forgery? Discuss.

3. A took B's watch before B was aware of the theft. B discovered his loss immediately and pursued A. A pointed a loaded pistol at B, who, in fear of being shot, allowed A to escape. Was A guilty of robbery? Any other crime?

4. X and Y were on trial, separately, for larceny of a $1,000 bearer bond (payable to the holder of the bond not a named individual) issued by A, Inc. The Commonwealth's evidence showed that the owner of the bond had dropped it accidentally in the street enclosed in an envelope bearing his name and address; that X found the envelope with the bond in it; that X could neither read nor write; that X presented the envelope and bond to Y, an educated man, and asked Y what he should do with it; that Y told X that the finder of lost property becomes the owner of it; that Y told X that the bond was worth $100 but that the money could only be collected at the issuer's home office; that X than handed the bond to Y, who redeemed it at the corporation's home office and received $1,000; that Y gave X $100 of the proceeds. What rulings?

5. Truck drivers for a hauling company, while loading a desk, found a $100 bill that fell out of the desk. They agreed to get it exchanged for small bills and divide the proceeds. En route to a bank, one of them changed his mind and refused to proceed with the scheme, whereupon the other

pulled a knife and demanded the bill. A police officer intervened. It turned out that the bill was confederate money. What crimes have been committed?

6. W was adjudged legally insane and committed as an inmate of a State hospital. Six months after his commitment he escaped and met his friend R. After R and W had drunk several drinks of hard liquor, they rode to a liquor store in a car driven by W. In accordance with a previous plan W waited in the car while R held up the proprietor of the liquor store. W and R were later apprehended and are now being prosecuted for robbery. W pleaded not guilty by reason of insanity and intoxication and on the further ground that he did not enter the building or receive any part of the stolen property. Discuss and decide.

7. P, an undercover police agent, was trying to locate a laboratory where it was believed that methamphetamine or "speed"—a controlled substance—was being manufactured illegally. P went to D's home and said that he represented a large organization that was interested in obtaining methamphetamine. P offered to supply a necessary ingredient for the manufacture of the drug, which was very difficult to obtain, in return for one-half of the drug produced. D agreed and processed the chemical given to him by P in P's presence. Later P returned with a search warrant and arrested D. D was charged with various narcotics law violations. D asserted the defense of entrapment. Decision?

8. The police obtained a search warrant based upon an affidavit which contained the following allegations: (a) D was seen crossing a State line on four occasions during a five-day period and going to a particular apartment; (b) telephone records disclosed that the apartment had two telephones; (c) D had a reputation as a bookmaker and as an associate of gamblers; and (d) the FBI was informed by a "confidential reliable informant" that D was conducting gambling operations. When a search was made based upon the warrant, evidence was obtained which resulted in D's conviction of violating certain gambling laws. D challenged the constitutionality of the search warrant. Decision?

9. A national bank was robbed by a man with a small strip of tape on each side of his face. He drove away with an accomplice who was waiting in a stolen car outside. An indictment was returned against D, and another for robbing the bank. D was then arrested, and counsel appointed to represent him. Two weeks later, without notice to D's lawyer, an FBI agent arranged to have the two bank employees observe a lineup, including D and five or six other prisoners. Each person in the lineup wore strips of tape, as had the robber, and each was directed to repeat the words "Put the money in the bag," as had the robber. Both of the bank employees identified D as the robber. At D's trial he was again identified by the two, in the courtroom, and the prior lineup identification was elicited upon cross examination by D's counsel. D's counsel moved the court either to grant a judgment of acquittal, or, alternatively to strike the courtroom identifications, on the ground that the lineup had violated D's Fifth Amendment privilege against self-incrimination, and his Sixth Amendment right to counsel. Decision?

Chapter 5

INTENTIONAL TORTS

ALL types and forms of liability are either (1) voluntarily assumed, as by contract, or (2) involuntarily imposed by law independent of contract. Tort liability is of the second type. Tort law protects a person from civil wrongs or injuries to his person, property, and economic interests. A tort is committed when

1. a duty owing by one person to another,
2. is breached, and
3. proximately causes,
4. injury or damage to the owner of a legally protected interest.

Each person is legally responsible for the damages that are proximately caused by his tortious conduct. Moreover, as discussed in Chapter 18, businesses that employ agents to conduct their business activities are also lia-

ble for the torts committed by their agents in the course of the agent's employment. The tort liability of employers makes the study of tort law essential to business managers.

In a tort action the injured party *sues* to recover *compensation* for the damage and injury that she has sustained as a result of the defendant's wrongful conduct. The primary purpose of tort law is to compensate the injured party, not to punish the wrongdoer as in the case of criminal law.

Of course, the same conduct may, and often does, constitute both a crime and a tort. An example is an assault and battery committed by A against B. For the commission of this crime, the state may take appropriate action against A. In addition, however, A has violated B's right to be secure in his person, and so has committed a tort against B. B, regardless of the criminal action by the state against A, may bring a civil action against A for damages. On the other hand, an act may be criminal without being tortious and, by the same token, an act may be a tort but not a crime. The closest that tort law comes to an implementation of the objectives of the criminal law is in certain cases where courts may award *"punitive"* or "exemplary" damages. Where the defendant's tortious conduct has been intentional and deliberate, exhibiting "malice" or a fraudulent or evil motive, many courts permit a jury to award damages over and above the amount necessary to compensate the plaintiff. The allowance of punitive damages is designed to punish and make an example of the defendant and thus deter others from similar conduct.

Harms or injuries may be inflicted (1) intentionally or (2) negligently or (3) without fault (strict liability). This chapter will discuss intentional torts. The following chapter will cover negligence and strict liability.

Tort law is primarily common law. The Restatement of Torts provides an orderly presentation of this law. The first Restatement was adopted and promulgated by the American Law Institute during the years from 1934 to 1939. Since then, it has served as a vital force in shaping the law of torts. Between 1965 and 1978 the institute adopted and promulgated a revised edition of the Restatement of Torts which supersedes the First Restatement. The revised Restatement will be referred to simply as the Restatement. Selected provisions of the Restatement are included in Appendix B of this book.

INTENT

Intent, as used in tort law, does not require a hostile or evil motive but rather denotes that the actor desires to cause the consequences of his act, or that he believes that the consequences are substantially certain to result from it. Restatement, Section 8A. The following examples should help to clarify the definition of intent: (1) If A fires a gun in the middle of the Mojave Desert, he intends to fire the gun, but when the bullet hits B who is in the desert without A's knowledge, A does not intend that result. (2) A throws a bomb into B's office in order to kill B. A knows that C is in B's office and that the bomb is substantially certain to injure C, although A has no desire to do so. A is, nonetheless, liable to C for any injury caused C. A's intent to injure B is *transferred* to C.

INJURY OR DAMAGE TO THE PERSON

The most common intentional torts involve interference with personal rights and include the following: (1) battery, (2) assault, (3) false imprisonment, (4) malicious prosecution, (5) infliction of emotional distress, (6) defamation, and (7) invasion of privacy. These torts will be separately discussed in that order.

Battery

Battery is an intentional infliction of **harmful or offensive bodily contact.** It may cause serious injury, as a gunshot wound or a blow on the head with a club, or it may cause little or no physical injury, such as knocking a hat off of a person's head or flicking a glove in another's face. Bodily contact is offensive if it would offend a reasonable person's sense of dignity. Restatement, Section 19. Bodily contact may be accomplished by the use of objects, such as A's throwing a rock at B with the intention of hitting her. If the rock hits B or any other person, A has committed a battery.

In *Capune v. Robbins*, 273 N.C. 581, 160 S.E.2d 881 (1968), Captune was attempting a trip from New York to Florida on an eighteen-foot-long paddleboard. The trip was being covered by various media to gain publicity for Capune and certain products he endorsed. On August 15, 1965, Capune approached a pier by water. The pier was owned by Robbins who had posted signs prohibiting surfing and swimming around the pier. Capune was unaware of these notices and attempted to continue his journey by passing under the pier. Robbins ran up yelling and threw two bottles at Capune. Capune was frightened and tried to maneuver his paddle to go around the pier. Robbins then threw a third bottle that hit Capune on the head. Capune had to be helped out of the water and taken to the hospital. He suffered a physical wound which required twenty-four sutures and as a result had to discontinue his trip. Judgment for Capune for compensatory and punitive damages. Robbins's throwing the bottles with the intent to frighten Capune constituted sufficient intent to make Robbins liable in battery for any injuries that resulted. The harmful physical contact resulted from Capune being hit by the bottle thrown by Robbins.

Assault

Assault is intentional conduct by one person directed at another which places him in **apprehension** of immediate bodily harm or offensive contact. It is usually committed immediately preceding a battery, but if the intended battery fails, the assault remains. *See Continental Casualty Co. v. Mirabile.* An essential element of this tort is that the person in danger of immediate bodily harm have *knowledge* of the danger and be apprehensive of its imminent threat to his safety. For example, A aims a loaded gun at B's back but is subdued by C before B becomes aware of the danger. A has not committed an assault upon B.

False Imprisonment

The tort of false imprisonment is the intentional **confining** of a person within fixed boundaries if such person is conscious of the confinement or harmed by it. Merely obstructing a person's freedom of movement is not false imprisonment so long as there is a reasonable alternative exit available.

Merchants occasionally have a problem when they seek to question a suspected shoplifter. If the merchant detains an innocent person, she may be facing a lawsuit for false imprisonment. Most States have statutes which protect the merchant, provided she detains the suspect in a reasonable manner, for not more than a reasonable time, and upon probable cause.

See National Bond & Investment Co. v. Whithorn.

Malicious Prosecution

The tort of malicious prosecution or wrongful use of civil proceedings consists in bringing about a criminal proceeding or filing and maintaining a civil suit against another person if the proceeding or civil suit is initiated (1) without probable cause, (2) for an improper purpose, and (3) results in the case of a criminal proceeding in a finding of not guilty, and in the case of a civil suit in a judgment for the defendant. Restatement, Sections 653, 674. A public prosecutor acting in his official capacity in bringing about and maintaining a criminal proceeding is cloaked with absolute immunity from liability for malicious prosecution. Restatement, Section 656.

Infliction of Emotional Distress

The law is not static, and the most recent type of wrongdoing recognized as tortious and imposing liability upon the wrongdoer for money damages is that of intentional infliction of emotional distress. William L. Prosser, principal author of the Restatement of Torts, states in his book, *Law of Torts* (4th ed.), pp. 49–50:

Notwithstanding its early recognition in the assault cases, the law has been slow to accept the interest in peace of mind as entitled to independent legal protection, even as against intentional invasions. It is not until comparatively recent years that there has been any general admission that the infliction of mental distress, standing alone, may serve as the basis of an action, apart from any other tort. In this respect, the law is clearly in a process of growth, the ultimate limits of which cannot as yet be determined.

Various reasons have been advanced for this reluctance to redress mental injuries. One is the difficulty of proof, or of measurement of the damages. "Mental pain or anxiety," said Lord Wensleydale in a famous English case, "the law cannot value, and does not pretend to redress, when the unlawful act causes that alone." It was regarded as something "metaphysical," "too subtle and speculative to be capable of admeasurement by any standard known to the law." But mental suffering is scarcely more difficult of proof, and certainly no harder to estimate in terms of money, than the physical pain of a broken leg, which never has been denied compensation; and the courts have been quite willing to allow large sums as damages for such "mental anguish" itself, where it accompanies a slight physical injury.

The Restatement, Section 46 states the rule as follows:

One who by extreme and outrageous conduct intentionally or recklessly causes severe emotional distress to another is subject to liability for such emotional distress, and if bodily harm to the other results from it, for such bodily harm.

This cause of action does not protect a person from abusive language or rudeness, but rather from atrocious, intolerable conduct beyond all bounds of decency. Examples of this tort include leading to a person's home, when he is present, a noisy demonstrating mob yelling threats to lynch him unless he leaves town, or placing a rattlesnake in another's bed as a practical joke. *See LaBrier v. Anheuser Ford. Co.*

A defendant is liable to a plaintiff for infliction of emotional distress where the defendant's outrageous conduct is directed at a member of the plaintiff's immediate family, provided the plaintiff is present at the time and is known by the defendant to be present. For example, C notices A and his pregnant wife, B, walking down the street and intentionally drives his car into A. As a consequence of viewing this, B suffers severe mental distress resulting in a miscarriage. C is liable to B for intentional infliction of mental distress. If B, however, was not walking with A but instead observed, without C's knowledge, the accident through a window in her home, C would not be liable to B for the tort of emotional distress.

Defamation

The tort of defamation is a communication which injures a person's reputation by disgracing him and diminishing the respect in which he is held. An example would be the publication of a statement that a person had committed a crime or had a loathsome disease. In *Beckman v. Dunn*, 276 Pa.Super. 527, 419 A.2d. 583 (1979), the court stated:

A communication is defamatory if it tends to harm the reputation of another so as to lower him in the estimation of the community or deter third persons from associating or dealing with him, and necessarily involves the idea of disgrace.

Libel and Slander If the defamatory communication is handwritten, typewritten, printed, pictorial, or by other means with like communicative power, such as television or radio, it is designated **libel.** If it is spoken or oral, it is designated **slander.** Restatement, Sections 568 and 568A. In either case it must be communicated to another person or persons. This is referred to as its *publication*. If A writes a defamatory letter about B's character which he hands or mails to B, this is not a publication as it is intended only for B.

Defenses *Truth* and *privilege* are complete defenses to defamation. There are three types of privileges: (1) absolute, (2) conditional, and (3) constitutional.

In most States, truth is a complete defense without regard to the purpose or intent in publishing the defamation. The law presumes that all defamation is false and places the burden upon the defendant of proving its truth.

As with the defense of truth, **absolute privilege** protects the defendant regardless of his motive or intent. Absolute privilege has been confined to those few situations where public policy clearly favors complete freedom of speech and includes: (1) statements made regarding a judicial proceeding; (2) statements made by members of Congress on the floor of Congress; (3) statements made by certain executive officers in the discharge of their governmental duty; and (4) statements made between spouses when they are alone.

Conditional or qualified **privilege** is conditioned upon proper use of the privilege. A person has conditional privilege to publish defamatory matter to protect his own legitimate interests, or in some cases the interests of another. Conditional privilege also extends to many cases where the publisher and the recipient have a common interest as with letters of reference. Conditional privilege, however, is forfeited by the publisher if she acts in an excessive manner, without probable cause or for an improper purpose.

The First Amendment to the United States Constitution guarantees freedom of speech and freedom of press. The courts have applied these rights to the law of defamation by extending a form of **constitutional privilege** to comment regarding public officials or public figures so long as it is done without *malice*. Restatement, Section 580A. For these purposes "malice" is not ill will but proof of the publisher's knowledge of falsity or reckless disregard of the truth.

See Hutchinson v. Proxmire.

Invasion of Privacy

The invasion of a person's right to privacy actually consists of four distinct torts: (a) appropriation of a person's name or likeness; (b) unreasonable intrusion upon the seclusion of another; (c) unreasonable public disclosure of private facts; or (d) unreasonable publicity which places another in a false light in the public eye. Restatement, Section 652A.

It is entirely possible and not uncommon for a person's right of privacy to be invaded in such a way that two or more of these related torts are committed. For example, A forces his way into B's hospital room, takes a photograph of B, and publishes it to promote A's cure for B's illness along with false statements about B that would be highly objectionable to a reasonable person. B would be entitled to recover on any or all of the four torts comprising invasion of privacy.

Appropriation Appropriation is the use of plaintiff's name or likeness for the benefit of the defendant, as for example in promoting or advertising a product or service. Restatement, Section 652C. The tort of appropriation seeks to protect the individual's right to the exclusive use of his identity. In the example above, A's use of B's photograph to promote A's business constitutes the tort of appropriation.

Intrusion This type of invasion of privacy is the unreasonable and highly offensive interference with the solitude or seclusion of another. Restatement, Section 652B. Such unreasonable interference would include improper entry into another's dwelling, unauthorized eavesdropping upon another's private conversations, and unauthorized examination of another's private papers and records. The intrusion must be offensive or objectionable to a reasonable person and must involve matters which are private. Thus, there is no liability if the defendant examines public records or observes the plaintiff in a public place. This form of invasion of privacy is committed once the intrusion occurs as publicity is not required.

The case of *Nader v. General Motors Corp.*, 25 N.Y.2d 560, 307 N.Y.S. 2d 647, 255 N.E.2d 765, (1970), involved the following facts: Ralph Nader had been a critic of General Motors for several years. When General Motors learned that Nader was about to publish a book entitled *Unsafe at Any Speed,* criticizing one of its automobiles, it decided to conduct a campaign of intimidation against him. Specifically, Nader claimed that GM (1) conducted a series of interviews with Nader's acquaintances, questioning them about his political, social, racial, and religious views; (2) kept him under surveillance in public places for an unreasonable length of time; (3) caused him to be accosted by women for the purpose of entrapping him into illicit relationships; (4) made threatening, harassing, and obnoxious telephone calls to him; (5) tapped his telephone and eavesdropped by means of mechanical and electronic equipment on his private conversations with others; and (6) conducted a "continuing" and harassing investigation of him. Nader brought an action against GM for invasion of privacy and GM moved to have the action dismissed. The lower court ruled against GM and GM appealed. The appellate court held that Nader's complaint in part was legally sufficient. The tort of invasion of privacy includes instances of intrusion by physical trespass or otherwise into areas from which an ordinary man would reasonably expect that others should be excluded. In the present case, only two of the activities complained of could constitute an invasion of Nader's privacy: (1) the unauthorized wiretapping and eavesdropping by electronic means, and (2) certain potentially overzealous surveillance of Nader in a public place.

Public Disclosure of Private Facts The law of privacy imposes liability for offensive *publicity* given to private information about another. As with intrusion, this tort only applies to private, not public, information regarding an individual, but unlike intrusion it requires publicity. The publicity required differs in degree from "publication" as used in the law of defamation. Under this tort the private facts must be communicated to the public at large or become public knowledge, whereas publication of a defamatory statement need only be made to a single third party. Thus A, a creditor of B, will not invade B's privacy by writing a letter to B's employer informing the employer of B's failure to pay the debt, but A would be liable if she posted in the window of her store a statement that B will not pay a debt owed to A. Also unlike defamation, this tort applies to truthful private information if the matter published would be offensive and objectionable to a reasonable person of ordinary sensibilities.

False Light This invasion of privacy imposes liability for *publicity* which places another in a false light that is highly offensive if the defendant *knew* or acted in *reckless disregard* that the matter publicized was false. Restatement, Section 652E. For example, A includes B's name and photograph in a public "rogues' gallery" of convicted criminals. B has never been convicted of any crime. A is liable to B for placing him in a false light.

As with defamation, the matter must be untrue, but unlike defamation it must be "publicized," not merely "published." Although the matter must be objectionable to a reasonable person, it need not be defamatory. In many instances, the same facts will give rise to both an action for defamation and false light.

Defenses *Absolute, conditional*, and *constitutional* privilege apply to the same extent to the torts of disclosure of private facts and false light as they do to defamation.

See Kinsey v. Macur.

INTERFERENCE WITH PROPERTY RIGHTS

In addition to protecting against intentional interference with the person, the law also provides protection against invasions of a person's interests in property. Intentional interference with property rights includes the torts of (1) trespass to real property, (2) nuisance, (3) trespass to personal property and (4) conversion.

Real Property

Real property is land and anything attached to it, such as buildings, trees, and minerals. The law protects the rights of the possessor of land to its exclusive use and quiet enjoyment.

Trespass Section 158 of the Restatement provides:

One is subject to liability to another for trespass, irrespective of whether he thereby causes harm to any legally protected interest of the other, if he intentionally

    (a) enters land in the possession of the other, or causes a thing or a third person to do so, or

    (b) remains on the land, or

    (c) fails to remove from the land a thing which he is under a duty to remove.

It is no defense that the intruder acted upon the mistaken belief of law or fact that he was not trespassing. If the intruder intended to be upon the particular property, it is irrelevant that he reasonably believed that he owned the land or had permission to enter upon the land. Restatement, Section 164. An intruder is not liable if his presence on the land of another is not caused by his own actions. For example, if A is thrown onto B's land by C, A is not liable to B for trespass, but C is.

A trespass may be committed on, beneath, or above the surface of the land, although the law regards the upper air, above the prescribed minimum altitude of flight, as a public highway. Therefore, there is no trespass unless the aircraft enters into the lower reaches of the air space and substantially interferes with the landowner's use and enjoyment. Restatement, Section 159.

Nuisance A nuisance is a non-trespassory invasion of another's interest in the private use and enjoyment of land. Restatement, Section 821D. In contrast to trespass, nuisance does not require interference with another's right to exclusive possession of land, but rather imposes liability for significant harm to another's use or enjoyment of land. Examples of nuisances include the emission of unpleasant odors, smoke, dust, or gas as well as the pollution of a stream, pond, or underground water supply.

Personal Property

Personal property or **chattel** is any type of property other than an interest in land. The law protects a number of interests in the possession of personal property including an interest in their physical condition and usability, an interest in the retention of possession, and an interest in their availability for future use.

Trespass Trespass to personal property consists of the intentional dispossession or unauthorized use of the personal property of another. The interference with the right to exclusive use and possession may be direct or indirect, but liability is limited to instances in which the trespasser (a) dispossesses the other of the property; (b) substantially impairs the condition, quality, or value of the property; or (c) deprives the possessor of the use of the property for a substantial time. Restatement, Section 218. For example, A parks his car in front of his house. B pushes A's car around the corner. A subsequently looks for his car but cannot find it for several hours. B is liable to A for trespass.

Conversion Conversion is the intentional exercise of dominion or control over another's personal property which so seriously interferes with the other's right of control as to justly require the payment of full value for the property. Restatement, Section 222A. The Restatement considers the following factors in determining whether justice requires the wrongdoing actor to pay full value:

1. the extent and duration of the actor's exercise of dominion or control;

2. the actor's intent to assert a right in fact inconsistent with the other's right of control;
3. the actor's good faith;
4. the extent and duration of the resulting interference with the other's right of control;
5. the harm done to the chattel; and
6. the inconvenience and expense caused to the other. Section 222A.

Conversion may consist of the intentional destruction of the personal property or the use of the property in an unauthorized manner. For example, A entrusts an automobile to B, a dealer, for sale. B drives the car 8,000 miles on his own business. B is liable to A for conversion. On the other hand, in the example above in which B pushed A's car around the corner, B would *not* be liable to A for conversion.

A major distinction between trespass to personal property and conversion is the measure of damages. In trespass, the possessor recovers damages for actual harm to the property or for the loss of possession. In conversion, the possessor recovers the full value of the property, and the convertor takes possession of it upon payment of the judgment.

INTERFERENCE WITH ECONOMIC INTERESTS

A third set of interests protected by the law against intentional interference is economic interests. The following are covered under this heading: (1) interference with contractual relations, (2) disparagement, and (3) fraudulent misrepresentation.

Interference with Contractual Relations

Section 766 of the Restatement provides:

One who intentionally and improperly interferes with the performance of a contract (except a contract to marry) between another and a third person by inducing or otherwise causing the third person not to perform the contract, is subject to liability to the other for the pecuniary loss resulting to the other from the failure of the third person to perform the contract.

Similar liability is imposed for intentional and improper interference with another's prospective contractual relation. Restatement, Section 766B.

In either case, the rule applies whenever a person acts with the purpose or motive of interfering with another's contract or with the knowledge that such interference is substantially certain to occur as a natural consequence of her actions. The interference may be by prevention through the use of physical force or by threats. Frequently, it is accomplished by inducement such as the offer of a better contract. For instance, A may offer B, an employee of C, a yearly salary of $5,000 per year more than the contractual arrangement between B and C. If A is aware of the contract between B and C and that his offer to B interferes with that contract, then A is liable to C for intentional interference with contractual relations.

Disparagement

The tort of disparagement or injurious falsehood imposes liability for the publication of a false statement which results in harm to another's interests which have pecuniary value if the publisher knows that the statement is false or acts in reckless disregard of its truth or falsity. This tort most commonly involves false statements intended by the party making them to cast doubt upon the title or quality of another's property or products. Thus, A, while contemplating the purchase of a stock of merchandise which belongs to B, reads an advertisement in a newspaper in which C falsely asserts she owns the merchandise. C has disparaged B's property in the goods. Absolute, conditional, and constitutional privilege apply to the same extent to the tort of disparagement as they do to defamation.

FIGURE 5-1   Intentional Torts

Interest Protected	Tort
Person	
Freedom from contact	Battery
Freedom from apprehension	Assault
Freedom of movement	False imprisonment
Freedom from wrongful criminal actions	Malicious prosecution
Freedom from distress	Infliction of emotional distress
Reputation	Defamation
Privacy	Appropriation
	Intrusion
	Public disclosure of private facts
	False light
Property	
Real	Trespass
	Nuisance
Personal	Trespass
	Conversion
Economic	
Contracts	Interference with contractual rights
Good will	Disparagement
Freedom from deception	Fraudulent misrepresentation

Fraudulent Misrepresentation

Section 525 of the Restatement provides:

One who fraudulently makes a misrepresentation of fact, opinion, intention, or law for the purpose of inducing another to act or to refrain from action in reliance upon it, is subject to liability to the other in deceit for pecuniary loss caused to him by his justifiable reliance upon the misrepresentation.

For example, A misrepresents to B that a tract of land in Texas is located in an area where drilling for oil had recently commenced. A made this statement knowing it was not true. In reliance upon the statement, B purchased the land from A. A is liable to B for fraudulent misrepresentation. Although intentional, or fraudulent, misrepresentation is a tort action, it is closely connected with contractual negotiations and is discussed in Chapter 9.

Figure 5–1 lists the intentional torts and the interests they protect.

DEFENSES TO INTENTIONAL TORTS

Even though the defendant has intentionally invaded the interests of the plaintiff, the defendant will not be liable if such conduct was privileged. A defendant's conduct is privileged if it furthers an interest of such social importance that the law confers immunity from tort liability for damage to others. Examples of privilege include self-defense, defense of property, and defense of others. In addition, the plaintiff's consent to the defendant's conduct is a defense to intentional torts.

Infants (i.e., persons who have not reached the age of majority) are held liable for their intentional torts. The infant's age and knowledge, however, are critical in determining whether the infant had sufficient intelligence to form the requisite intent. **Incompetents**, like infants, are generally held liable for their intentional torts.

CONSENT

If one consents to conduct resulting in damage or harm done to his own person, property, or economic interests, no liability will generally attach to the intentional infliction of injury. Consent to an act is the willingness that it shall occur. It may be manifested expressly or impliedly, by words or by conduct. For example, A states that he wishes to kiss B. Although B does not wish A to do so, she does not object or resist by word or act. A kisses B. A is not liable to B for battery since B has impliedly consented to A's conduct.

Consent must be given by an individual with capacity to do so. Consent given by a minor, mental incompetent, or intoxicated individual is invalid if he is not capable of appreciating the nature, extent, or probable consequences of the conduct to which he has consented.

The defendant's privilege is limited to the conduct to which the plaintiff consents. For example, A consents to an exploratory operation by B, a surgeon, but refuses to have any further operation performed. While A is under ether, B discovers a condition which indicates that an operation is needed and proceeds to operate. B is liable to A, even though the operation is properly and successfully performed, because B exceeded the consent given. On the other hand, assume that A consents to a particular operation to be performed by B. A submits to anesthesia. Upon opening A's body, B discovers conditions which make it necessary to extend the operation in order to save A's life. A reasonable man would consent to the operation if he knew of the conditions discovered by B. B performs the operation. B is not liable to A.

Consent to Participate in a Game

By agreeing to participate in a game, a person consents to encounter such bodily contact and limitations upon freedom of movement as is permitted by or general to the game. However, such consent does not extend to intentional acts of violence or restrictions beyond the rules and usages of the game. Thus, if A participates in a game of ice hockey, he does not consent to be intentionally attacked by B, another player, wielding his hockey stick as a weapon.

Consent to a Criminal Act

The jurisdictions are divided as to whether consent to conduct that constitutes a crime is a valid defense to an intentional tort. However, if conduct is made criminal in order to protect a certain class of persons, the consent of members of that class will *not* be effective as a defense to a tort action. For example, a statute makes it a crime to sell alcoholic beverages to a person who is intoxicated. A sells liquor to B in violation of the statute. B consumes the liquor and suffers physical injury from it. B's consent in purchasing the liquor does not bar his suit against A.

PRIVILEGE

This section deals with that form of privilege which entitles an individual to injure another's person without that person's consent. These privileges are created by law to enable an individual to protect himself, others, or his property against tortious interference. By virtue of these privileges an individual may inflict or impose what would otherwise constitute battery, assault, or false imprisonment. This section covers the following privileges: (1) self-defense, (2) defense of others, and (3) defense of property.

Self-Defense

The law permits a person to take appropriate action to prevent harm to himself where time does not allow resort to the law. Section 63 of the Restatement provides:

(1) An actor is privileged to use reasonable force, not intended or likely to cause death or serious bodily harm, to defend himself against unprivileged harmful or offensive contact or other bodily harm which he reasonably believes that another is about to inflict intentionally upon him.

The privilege of self-defense exists whether or not the danger actually exists, provided that the defendant reasonably believed that self-defense was necessary. The reasonableness of the defendant's actions is based upon what a person of average courage would have thought under the circumstances.

Self-defense is warranted even if the defendant reasonably believed that she could avoid the threatened contact or confinement by retreating. However, the defendant is not privileged to retaliate, as revenge is not self-defense. The defendant, to protect herself from offensive or nonserious bodily contact, is limited to reasonable force, which is proportionate in extent to the harm from which the defendant is seeking to protect herself.

The defendant is privileged to defend by the use of force intended or likely to cause death or serious bodily harm if she reasonably believes that the plaintiff is about to inflict death, serious bodily harm, or ravishment upon the defendant. Most States limit the right to use deadly force in self-defense to those situations in which the defendant does not have a completely safe means of escape. If the defendant, however, has the slightest doubt, if reasonable, as to the safety of her escape, she may stand her ground. One may also stand her ground and use deadly force if the attack occurs in her own residence, even though a reasonable means of escape exists. Restatement, Section 65.

Defense of Others

An individual is privileged to defend third persons from harmful or offensive contact to the same extent that he is privileged to protect himself, provided that the defendant correctly or reasonably believes that the third person possesses the privilege of self-defense and that the defendant's intervention is necessary for the safety of the third person. Restatement, Section 76. Thus, A sees B about to strike A's friend C. B is, in fact, privileged to do so to repel C's attack. A has no reason to suspect that C is the aggressor and intercedes to assist C. A is privileged to use reasonable force to assist C against B.

Defense of Property

A possessor of property is permitted to use reasonable force, not intended or likely to cause death or serious bodily harm, to protect his real and personal property. Such force can only be employed if the possessor reasonably believes that the intrusion can only be terminated or prevented by use of force and the intruder has disregarded requests to cease. Restatement, Section 77. For example, A sees B walking across his vacant lot. A is not privileged to use even the mildest of force to eject B until A has requested B to leave and B has disregarded the warning. Once reasonable force has been used, the defendant may use such greater force as is necessary to protect himself and his property. The intruder is not entitled to invoke the privilege of self-defense. Nonetheless, there is no privilege to use any force calculated to cause death or serious bodily injury in order to protect property unless there is also a threat to the defendant's personal safety justifying the use of such force.

A person may not through indirect means, such as mechanical devices, employ deadly force to protect his property unless he would, if present, have been privileged to employ such force. Restatement, Section 85. This applies to spring guns, electrified fences, and other traps that are intended or likely to cause death or serious bodily harm. *See Katko v. Briney*.

CASES

Assault and Battery

CONTINENTAL CASUALTY CO. v. MIRABILE

Court of Special Appeals of Maryland, 1982.
52 Md.App. 387, 449 A.2d 1176.

MORTON, J.

* * *

The testimony at trial disclosed that Russell Mirabile, appellee and cross-appellant, had worked nearly five years as a trainee and then a claims representative at the Towson branch of Continental Casualty Company (hereinafter Continental) investigating claims, preparing reports and maintaining files. Phillip E. Klingler was the Towson office manager who directly supervised Mr. Mirabile's work. Klinger, in turn, reported to William F. Sheehan, the claims manager of the Silver Spring regional office, and ultimately to Ronald Lewis, the general branch manager of that office.

* * *

[As a result of a "needs improvement" evaluation and consequent denial of raise, Mirabile sued his three supervisors for defamation in March of 1978.]

Although Mirabile's performance became more acceptable as reflected in the "competent" ratings for the periods from July 1 to October 1, 1977; July 7 to October 7, 1977; and July 8, 1977, to April 28, 1978, he contends that a pattern of workplace harassment was at this point initiated.

Mirabile testified that his desk was first moved against a blank wall; then he was assigned by Sheehan to various uncomfortable, inconvenient desks—a desk near a noisy copying machine, a stick desk that was used as a lunch table, the "wrong side" of another adjuster's desk. With each move his supervisors would "smirk" and "laugh." Mirabile also noticed that he was being sent on distant assignments, files were not being delivered to him from the file room, completed work was disappearing from his case files, and his mail was not always delivered. He further testified that Klingler would often "direct his hum at me . . . hum, hum, hum, hum," put his face rather close, raise his eyebrows, chuckle and walk away. Sheehan called him a "hyena" and on another occasion a "jackass" in the presence of coworkers.

There was also evidence that all employees had to share desks due to cramped conditions; that Mirabile himself would occasionally make bird calls, sing out loud, and make loud sarcastic remarks about the company; and an expert witness testified that Mirabile showed signs of "paranoid thinking."

The culminating incident which prompted Mirabile to stop working and formed the basis of his assault and battery claim occurred on June 27, 1979, after more than a year of such "harassment." The most violent version of the facts follows. On that day Sheehan, having repeatedly asked Mirabile to sit at a desk by himself rather than with Ed Hrica, whose desk he had previously been told to share, became annoyed when he saw Mirabile sitting at Hrica's desk in the morning. He called Mirabile into his office, told him to stay away from Hrica, and at one point "swung his hand into" Mirabile. That afternoon when Sheehan saw Mirabile standing at Hrica's desk making a phone call, Sheehan grabbed the receiver and slammed it down; stood chin to chin with Mirabile, waving a finger in his face and screaming that he had 15 . . . 10 seconds to get out of the area; rushed at Mirabile and started tapping his nose with his finger; repeatedly pushed Mirabile; grabbed Mirabile's arm and pulled him back, saying he was going to fire him. Mirabile, crying "worse than a baby," was so upset and "shocked" that it took him one-half hour to find his car in the parking lot.

He sought comfort of his priest that night and that of a psychiatrist the next day, whom he has continued to see twice a week. Having suffered what three experts agreed was a disabling psychological injury, Mirabile did not return to work and a year later he was terminated.

[Mirabile brought a tort action against Sheehan and Continental for *inter alia* assault and battery. The jury returned a verdict of $80,000 compensatory damages against Sheehan and Continental, with $25,000 punitive damages against Continental and $10,000 punitive damages against Sheehan.]

Defendants' motions for a new trial and for a judgment notwithstanding the verdict were denied and final judgment was entered on the jury's verdicts.

* * *

An assault is any unlawful attempt to cause a harmful or offensive contact with the person of another or to cause an apprehension of such a contact. A battery is its consummation. *See* Restatement (Second) of Torts §§ 13, 21 (1965); Prosser, *Law of Torts*, §§ 9, 10 (4th ed. 1971).

Sheehan first asserts that the essential element of threat of a harmful or offensive contact was not present, citing as support [citation], wherein it was held that plaintiff's work place supervisor did not commit an actionable assault and battery when he called plaintiff "sweetheart" and gave him "pats on the rear."

While it may be true that "the law disregards trifles," [citation], we think there was sufficient evidence from which this jury could have concluded that such a threat existed. Appellants' counsel conceded at trial that the assault and battery claim, which it characterized as a "pushing and shoving incident," was an issue of credibility to be determined by the jury. It cannot now be reviewed on appeal.

* * *

The rationale is sound and the arguments are strong against allowing a common law tort action against an employer for the intentional torts of a supervisory employee who cannot

be said to be the employer's alter ego. To do so would mean that in all tort incidents arising between co-employees, of which there are no doubt a multitude, the plaintiff need only "show that the assailant was one notch higher on the totem-pole than the victim" in order to recover against the employer. * * * Were it otherwise, there would be a subversion of the very purpose of the workmen's compensation scheme of spreading the risk of loss for injuries arising out of and in the course of covered employment, in that an employer would be required not only to provide workmen's compensation but also to defend tort actions of employees.

* * *

Judgment as to assault and battery award, reversed as to Continental Casualty Co., and affirmed as to William F. Sheehan.

False Imprisonment

NATIONAL BOND & INVESTMENT CO. v. WHITHORN
Court of Appeals of Kentucky, 1939.
276 Ky. 204, 123 S.W.2d 263.

FULTON, J.

Appellee, William Whithorn, brought this action for false imprisonment against the appellant, National Bond and Investment Company, in the Jefferson circuit court and on a trial before a jury verdict was rendered in his favor for $700 comensatory damages and $900 punitive damages. Judgment was entered on this verdict and from that judgment this appeal is prosecuted.

* * *

The evidence discloses that the appellant had, or at least claimed to have, a conditional sales contract on a car in possession of appellee, and that payments due under this contract had not been made. Appellant desired to repossess the car and assigned its employees, O'Brien and Baer, to this task. Baer appears to have been a high-powered repossessor in the employ of appellant in Chicago and was imported to Louisville for some special work along this line. These employees, after making inquiry from a relative of appellee, and after a little "fast work" connected with this inquiry, learned where appellee lived and by so doing managed to find him driving the car on a street in Louisville. In their car they followed appellee in his car for some distance and hailed him down for the purpose of making a repossession.

There is considerable conflict in the testimony as to what occurred between appellee and these two employees of appellant on the occasion of this repossession, but the jury evidently accepted appellee's version of the melee * * *.

* * * When O'Brien and Baer hailed appellee he thought they were officers and stopped his car, whereupon O'Brien got out of his car, walked up to appellee's car, and invited him to get out and come back and talk to Baer. This appellee refused to do, so finally Baer also came to appellee's car and from that time things began to move rapidly. Appellee was informed that these employees desired to repossess the car and was notified to get out and take his personal belongings. Appellee demanded evidence of their authority, which they assured him they had, but their assurance did not satisfy appellee and the argument as to authority continued for some time. The repossessors became impatient at being balked of their quarry and finally one of them said, "Don't you move this machine, I will have an officer here in about two minutes." * * * After O'Brien came back he made the statement that "the officers will be here any minute." Shortly after O'Brien returned, a wrecker, which had been called by O'Brien, pulled up and one of the appellant's employees motioned for the wrecker to pull in front of appellee's car to hook on, whereupon appellee started the motor in his car for the purpose of driving off, but O'Brien raised the hood of the car and jerked loose the distributor wire. Appellee, not desiring to see his car put hors du combat, opened the door of his car and started out after him. When

appellee opened the door of his car and started out, Baer attempted to reach through the window of the car on the other side and get the car key, but appellee sensing what was in the wind, beat Baer to the key, and this seemed to "peeve" the repossessors very much. O'Brien then said, "He has acted so smart I will have him put in jail," and got in his machine and left. He came back in a short while and it does not clearly appear whether or not he called the police officers, but at any rate a police officer pursuant to a telephone call from someone, showed up a while afterwards.

When O'Brien returned from this second departure Baer directed the driver operating the wrecker to hook to appellee's car and pull out with it, but in view of appellee's vehement protests the driver of the wrecker hesitated to act, but after repeated demands by O'Brien finally coupled up with appellee's car and hoisted the front wheels off the ground. Baer then climbed in appellee's car and the wrecker started pulling the car down the street, whereupon appellee put on the emergency brake and threw the car into reverse, thereby managing to stall the wrecker and bring the car to a stop after it had been pulled down the street something like 75 to 100 feet. During the progress down the street, appellee, who says he tried to prevent Baer from getting in the car with him, attempted to eject Baer from the car by kicks on the shins, which Baer says in his testimony were rather forcefully administered, but his attempts to dislodge this Chicago repossessor were wholly unavailing.

While all this was occurring numerous cars were passing up and down the street; some of them stopping and looking and then driving on. In other words, the passing public seemed to realize that a good act was being put on and did not miss the opportunity to enjoy at least a portion of it. After appellee had managed to bring the procession to a halt by stalling the wrecker, a policeman came up and inquired as to the meaning of the controversy, and the contestants on the respective sides stated their case. The policeman says that he refused to pass on the merits of the controversy, but he did demand appellee's driver's license, which it appears appellee had but had left at home. Appellee seemed to think the policeman was taking sides with the repossessors and became rather angry, demanding the policeman's badge number and name, whereupon the policeman placed him under arrest. The drama of repossession ended with the policeman departing with appellee in tow and O'Brien and Baer departing with appellee's car in tow, the result being a complete and satisfying repossession, at least satisfying in its results to appellant's employees, O'Brien and Baer, but highly unsatisfactory to appellee.

*   *   *

If appellant had a valid conditional sales contract on appellee's car, and he was behind in the payments, appellant had the right to repossess the car if it could do so peaceably, but, of course, had no right to create a breach of the peace in doing so, or to put appellee under any kind of restraint, or to use any force directed against him in making the repossession. [Citation.]

Appellant contends the transaction above recited did not amount to false imprisonment, its theory being that Whithorn was in no wise restrained or impeded, and that he was perfectly at liberty at any time to go his way. *   *   *.

We are unable to agree with appellant's contention *   *   *. A reading of the evidence we have quoted above makes it immediately apparent that appellee, in the present case, was placed under restraint by O'Brien and Baer. They had him in his car under forcible control, being pulled down the street some 75 to 100 feet, against his vehement protest, and we are firmly of the opinion that such conduct on their part was a false imprisonment.

It is true, as [National Bond] argues, that [Whithorn] was at liberty to depart and these employees were not preventing him from doing so, but the result of his departure would have been an automatic parting with his automo-

bile, which he did not desire to part with, and which he did not have to part with, and which O'Brien and Baer had no right to take over his protests. While he was in the car he was in a place he had a legal right to be, and in which neither O'Brien or Baer had a legal right to be, by force, and when these men hooked the wrecker on and hoisted the front wheels in the air, forcibly dragging [Whithorn] down the street in his car, this was unquestionably a restraint imposed upon him and a detention of his person, such as constitutes a false imprisonment.

*   *   *

Wherefore, the judgment is affirmed.

Infliction of Emotional Distress

LABRIER v. ANHEUSER FORD CO.

Missouri Court of Appeals, Eastern District, Division Two, 1981.
612 S.W.2d 790.

WEIER, J.

This is a suit for damages for injury caused by outrageous conduct. From a directed verdict in favor of defendants at the close of plaintiff's evidence, plaintiff appeals.

The question presented is whether plaintiff's evidence made a case of outrageous conduct. If the elements of such a case have been established by some of the evidence, then plaintiff is entitled to a reversal and remand of the case for retrial so that the issues of liability and damages can be presented to the jury. If not, then the lower court must be affirmed.

Plaintiff Mary Jane LaBrier is the wife of James LaBrier, a former employee of Anheuser Ford, Inc. Prior to April 17, 1975, Mr. LaBrier had been employed as a used car salesman by the company for about seven years. On that date he discussed his need for time away from his duties with his superiors. A doctor had advised him to take four to six weeks away from his employment. He first spoke to the general manager Mr. Zeiser who told him that if he needed rest he had some three weeks' vacation due. He then came back the next day and talked to Mr. Gilmour who was his immediate superior. The discussion centered around whether he should take sick leave or vacation time. He had some three weeks coming to him on vacation but company rules required thirty days' notice prior to taking a vacation and it was also policy that he receive his check for the time off before he left. To avoid any complications he requested that it be considered sick leave.

It had apparently been the custom to allow employees to take their demonstrator car with them on vacation but not on sick leave. On this matter after some discussion, Mr. Zeiser the manager talked to a Mr. Fritz at the company office. Zeiser then returned and told LaBrier that the company did not want him to take the car on vacation or on sick leave. But after discussing the matter with a union representative, Mr. LaBrier decided to take the automobile.

LaBrier left home the next morning about 5:30 in the demonstrator. That afternoon Mr. Zeiser and Mr. Gilmour came to the home where Mr. and Mrs. LaBrier resided. Plaintiff Mary Jane LaBrier came to the front porch and the men asked her repeatedly where her husband had gone and where the car was located. They told her that he had stolen the car and if it was not returned there would be an all-points bulletin sent to the State Highway Patrol. He would be detained and the car brought back. They kept repeating these questions and statements for approximately twenty to twenty-five minutes in a loud and angry tone of voice. Mrs. LaBrier, who had been under the care of a doctor and had been hospitalized for emotional problems for approximately two weeks in October of the preceding year, became very upset and she began to cry. Her eyes became swollen and itching and she developed a rash over her body. She had not been taking any medication prior to this event for several months. After this occurrence, however, she had to return

to taking the medicine and was prevented from taking care of her household duties for several months. LaBrier returned within a day or two after he found out about the occurrence at the home and returned the automobile to the defendants.

Two other witnesses testified with regard to the confrontation on the porch between the two employees of Anheuser Ford and Mrs. LaBrier. A next door neighbor Annie McKay testified that she and her little son were sitting on the steps of her house when the two men drove up, got out of the car and walked up on the LaBrier porch. When they got real loud she could hear the conversation. One of the men kept asking where Mr. LaBrier had gone and then she heard him say: "Well, he stole the car and we are going to put an all-points bulletin out to get it back." She characterized these statements as being loud and angry. She noticed as they kept repeating the questions and asking them in a loud and angry fashion, Mrs. LaBrier became very nervous and her voice was trembling. Another neighbor Sandra Lee Rishan was in the LaBrier residence in the kitchen visiting with Mrs. LaBrier when the men came to the door. She also overheard the conversation and related that the questions and remarks of the two men became loud and she heard them say: "We need our car, we want it back, we are going to put out an all-points bulletin." She also heard them tell Mrs. LaBrier that her husband stole the car and that they wanted it. In reply Mrs. LaBrier informed them she didn't know exactly where he was and then one of them told her: "Oh, yes you do, and we want to know where he is, and we want our car."

Since . . . 1965, Missouri has recognized the tort of outrageous conduct as defined by § 46 of the Restatement (Second) of Torts wherein it is said: "One who by extreme and outrageous conduct intentionally or recklessly causes severe emotional distress to another is subject to liability for such emotional distress, and if bodily harm to the other results from it, for such bodily harm." The elements of this tort are * * * (1) Defendant's conduct must be extreme and outrageous; (2) the defendant acts in an intentional or reckless manner; and (3) by reason of said acts, plaintiff is caused to suffer severe emotional distress from which bodily harm results.

We first consider whether the two employees of Anheuser Ford acted in a manner that could be characterized as extreme or outrageous. If in the favorable view of plaintiff's evidence, giving plaintiff all the benefit of favorable inferences to be drawn therefrom, the question is reasonably debatable, then the issue should go to the jury. "Mere insults, indignities, inconsiderations or petty oppressions do not rise to the level of the outrageous conduct essential to plaintiff's right of recovery." [Citation] * * * [G]enerally a case of outrageous conduct "is one in which the recitation of the facts to an average member of the community would arouse his resentment against the actor, and lead him to exclaim, 'Outrageous!' " [Citation.] * * *

We believe that the action of the employees of Anheuser Ford in appearing at plaintiff's residence in the presence of two neighbors and in a loud and threatening voice attempting to harass and humiliate plaintiff by repeatedly questioning her as to the whereabouts of her husband and the demonstrator automobile and threatening to have her husband arrested by the issuance of an "all-points bulletin" to the police could be characterized as "extreme and outrageous." Defendants suggest they had a legitimate interest in determining the whereabouts of the demonstrator. We have no doubt that this is a legitimate interest, but in light of the prior condition of plaintiff as a highly emotional and easily distraught individual who had suffered severe emotional problems before this episode that had caused her to be hospitalized, a condition known to defendants, it would appear that Mr. Gilmour and Mr. Zeiser may have exceeded the bounds of normal human conduct to such a point that the jury could find them and through them defendant Anheuser Ford guilty of outrageous conduct. As

is stated in Restatement (Second) of Torts, *supra*, Comment (f) to § 46, [t]he extreme and outrageous character of the conduct may arise from the actor's knowledge that the other is peculiarly susceptible to emotional distress, by reason of some physical or mental condition or peculiarity. The conduct may become heartless, flagrant, and outrageous when the actor proceeds in the face of such knowledge, where it would not be so if he did not know. It must be emphasized again, however, that major outrage is essential to the tort; and the mere fact that the actor knows that the other will regard the conduct as insulting, or will have his feelings hurt, is not enough." Mrs. LaBrier had previously lost her father and her daughter. Because of this and several other crises in the family, she had been hospitalized for two weeks because of emotional problems. Defendants Zeiser and Gilmour were both aware that she had been in the hospital. She had received a house plant from defendant Anheuser Ford when she was in the hospital. The knowledge of her prior condition was clear.

We next test the evidence to determine whether * * * the acts of Zeiser and Gilmour could be determined by the jury to be intentional or reckless as required in the second standard hereinabove set out. * * * Knowing that Mrs. LaBrier had previously had emotional problems as was shown here, it can easily be seen that defendants could be charged with intentional commission of an outrageous act or such a reckless disregard of a previously known condition so as to supply the necessary element of intentional infliction of an emotional crisis resulting in physical harm.

The last element, that of causation, would seem to be supplied by the evidence that was given by Mrs. LaBrier and by the neighbors to the effect that following the ordeal plaintiff was nervous, upset, confused and crying. During this time, the plaintiff continually dug at her face as a result of an itch that occurred under her skin. Thereafter, Mrs. Rishar a neighbor visited plaintiff almost daily to aid her in caring for her children. During that time plaintiff would break down and cry and begin scratching her face. Mr. LaBrier also related that when he arrived home he found plaintiff in bed. She had blotches over her entire body and her eyes were swollen.

After examining the evidence and considering the case law, we have concluded that plaintiff by her evidence made a jury case. * * * We are therefore constrained to reverse the judgment of the court sustaining the motion for directed verdict at the close of plaintiff's case and remand the case for new trial.

The case is reversed and remanded.

Defamation

HUTCHINSON v. PROXMIRE

Supreme Court of the United States, 1979.
443 U.S. 111, 99 S.Ct. 2675, 61 L.Ed.2d 411.

BURGER, C. J.

[In March 1975, William Proxmire, a United States Senator from Wisconsin, initiated the "Golden Fleece of the Month Award" to publicize what he believed to be wasteful government spending. The second of these awards was given to the Federal agencies that had for seven years funded Dr. Hutchinson's research on stress levels in animals. The award was made in a speech Proxmire gave in the Senate; the text was also incorporated into an advance press release that was sent to 275 members of the national news media. Proxmire also referred to the research again in two subsequent newsletters sent to 100,000 constituents and during a television interview. Hutchinson then brought this action alleging defamation resulting in personal and economic injury. The District Court granted summary judgment for Proxmire and the Court of Appeals affirmed based on (1) absolute privilege under the Speech or Debate Clause of the U.S. Constitution and (2) constitutional privilege. Hutchinson (plaintiff) then brought this appeal.]

* * *

The purpose of the Speech or Debate Clause is to protect Members of Congress "not only from the consequences of ligitation's results but also from the burden of defending themselves." [Citations.] If the respondents [Proxmire] have immunity under the Clause, no other questions need be considered for they may "not be questioned in any other place."

* * *

Whatever imprecision there may be in the term "legislative activities," it is clear that nothing in history or in the explicit language of the Clause suggests any intention to create an absolute privilege from liability or suit for defamatory statements made outside the Chamber . . .

The immunities of the Speech or Debate Clause were not written into the Constitution simply for the personal or private benefit of Members of Congress, but to protect the integrity of the legislative process by insuring the independence of individual legislators.

* * *

A speech by Proxmire in the Senate would be wholly immune and would be available to other Members of Congress and the public in the Congressional Record. But neither the newsletters nor the press release was "essential to the deliberations of the Senate" and neither was part of the deliberative process.

* * *

Newsletters and press releases * * * are primarily means of informing those outside the legislative forum; they represent the views and will of a single Member. It does not disparge either their value or their importance to hold that they are not entitled to the protection of the Speech or Debate Clause.

Since *New York Times v. Sullivan*, [citation], this Court has sought to define the accommodation required to assure the vigorous debate on public issues that the First Amendment was designed to protect while at the same time affording protection to the reputations of individuals. [Citations.] In *Gertz v. Robert Welch, Inc.*, the court offered a general definition of "public figures":

For the most part those who attain this status [of public figure] have assumed roles of especial prominence in the affairs of society. Some occupy positions of such persuasive power and influence that they are deemed public figures for all purposes. More commonly, those classed as public figures have thrust themselves to the forefront of particular public controversies in order to influence the resolution of the issues involved. In either event, they invite attention and comment. [Citation.]

It is not contended that Hutchinson attained such prominence that he is a public figure for all purposes. Instead, respondents have argued that the District Court and the Court of Appeals were correct in holding that Hutchinson is a public figure for the limited purpose of comment on his receipt of federal funds for research projects. That conclusion was based upon two factors: first, Hutchinson's successful application for federal funds and the reports in local newspapers of the federal grants; second, Hutchinson's access to the media, as demonstrated by the fact that some newspapers and wire services reported his response to the announcement of the Golden Fleece Award. Neither of those factors demonstrates that Hutchinson was a public figure prior to the controversy engendered by the Golden Fleece Award; his access such as it was, came after the alleged libel.

On this record Hutchinson's activities and public profile are much like those of countless members of his profession. His published writings reach a relatively small category of professionals concerned with research in human behavior. To the extent the subject of his published writings became a matter of controversy it was a consequence of the Golden Fleece Award. Clearly those charged with defamation cannot, by their own conduct, create their own defense by making the claimant a public figure. [Citation.]

Hutchinson did not thrust himself or his views into public controversy to influence others. * * *

Moreover, Hutchinson at no time assumed any role of public prominence in the broad question of concern about expenditures. Neither his applications for federal grants nor his publications in professional journals can be said to have invited that degree of public attention and comment on his receipt of federal grants essential to meet the public figure level.

* * *

Finally, we cannot agree that Hutchinson had such access to the media that he should be classified as a public figure. Hutchinson's access was limited to responding to the announcement of the Golden Fleece Award. He did not have the regular and continuing access to the media that is one of the accouterments of having become a public figure.

* * *

Reversed and remanded.

Invasion of Privacy

KINSEY v. MACUR

Court of Appeals of California, First District, 1980.
107 Cal.App.3d 265, 165 Cal.Rptr. 608.

MILLER, J.

In this action for invasion of privacy, appellant Mary Macur Appeals from a judgment entered upon a non-jury verdict in the amount of $5,000 in favor of respondent Bill Kinsey.

The record discloses that, while respondent Bill Kinsey was in the Peace Corps in Tanzania in 1966, his wife died when they were on a picnic. Kinsey was charged with her murder and spent six months awaiting trial. He was subsequently acquitted. The case attracted some notoriety as evidenced by articles published in TIME magazine. Kinsey later returned to Africa on many occasions in different capacities.

In December 1971, Kinsey met appellant Mary Macur at a cocktail party given by the World Affairs Council in San Francisco. At that time he was a graduate student at Stanford University while Macur worked as a researcher at a medical institute. * * * Kinsey then left for a four to five week trip to England. Upon his return, he received a postcard from appellant and they renewed their relationship. * * *

On April 5, 1972, after Kinsey and Macur had attended the symphony together, they returned to appellant's apartment * * *. Kinsey then told Macur that he would no longer be seeing her since a woman was coming from England to live with him. Kinsey testified that she did not ask him to leave, and that he left the next morning with Macur maintaining a "stony silence."

On the other hand, Macur testified that Kinsey went into a "rage" that evening and that he terrorized her. She also claimed that he had lunged at her, and that he had tried to have sexual intercourse with her.

After the evening of April 5, appellant wrote Kinsey a "mildly recriminatory" letter which was "somewhat questioning in tone" but the two did not otherwise maintain any contact with each other. In the fall of 1972, Kinsey accepted a business and study assignment to work in Central Africa. Sally Allen, who was living with Kinsey at this time, accompanied him to Africa. Kinsey subsequently married Sally in February of 1973.

Shortly before they left the United States, Kinsey received a letter from appellant addressed to "the most deceitful, . . . selfish bastard I know." Sally Kinsey also received a letter from Macur which was ostensibly designed to expose Kinsey and his mistreatment of appellant.

During the time the Kinseys were in Africa, they received more letters which had been written by Macur. Some were directed to Bill, while others were addressed to acquaintances who had in turn forwarded them to the Kinseys. In several of these letters, appellant enclosed copies of various magazine articles and documents which she believed supported her claims concerning Kinsey's character. However, other letters contained statements which accused Kinsey of murdering his first wife, spending six months in jail for the crime, being a rapist, and other questionable behavior.

Several letters also contained references to matters which respondent had never disclosed to Macur, and he concluded that she must have broken into his apartment. For example, in one letter, she referred to the presence of marijuana in his apartment. Other letters contained copies of Sally Kinsey's divorce certificate from a previous marriage which was missing from Bill Kinsey's apartment. Macur testified that she had written to London and Cambridge in order to obtain copies of the divorce decree. The trial court concluded that Macur had not broken into respondent's apartment.

Appellant also visited a psychologist whom Kinsey had known while at Stanford. In some letters she suggested that the psychologist tended to agree with her evaluation of respondent.

On July 9, 1973, both Sally and Bill Kinsey filed a complaint for permanent injunction. The complaint prayed for $10,000 in general damages based on mental anguish, suffering and expenses incurred in trying to protect the Kinseys from appellant Macur's reach. A preliminary injunction was stipulated to by the parties on July 30, 1973.

On August 15, 1973, Macur filed a cross-complaint for assault, intentional infliction of emotional distress and conspiracy to cause intentional infliction of emotional distress. An amended cross-complaint further alleged false imprisonment and sought $25,000 general damages as well as $100,000 punitive damages for each cause of action. On June 28, 1977, after a trial without jury, judgment was entered for Bill Kinsey in the amount of $5,000.

The trial court found that Kinsey did not assault, batter or attempt to rape appellant. The court also denied Macur's cross-complaint for false imprisonment and intentional infliction of emotional and physical distress.

Since the main issues before the court relate to invasion of privacy, a brief review of this tort follows.

Courts now recognize four separate torts within the broad designation of "invasion of privacy": (1) the commercial appropriation of the plaintiff's name or likeness * * *; (2) intrusion upon the plaintiff's physical solitude or seclusion; (3) public disclosure of true, embarrassing private facts concerning the plaintiff; and (4) publicity which places the plaintiff in a false light in the public eye. (Prosser, Law of Torts (4th ed., 1971) § 117, pp. 804–814.) In the present case, only the latter two forms of invasion of privacy are alleged.

As discussed in [citation], the concept of a legal right to privacy was first suggested in a now famous Harvard Law Review article by Warren and Brandeis, *The Right to Privacy* (1890) 4 Harv.L.Rev. 193. While they had difficulty tracing a common law basis for the right, Warren and Brandeis expressed the belief that it was mass exposure to the public gaze and not just backyard gossip which provided the raison d'etre for the tort.

Subsequently, in discussing the right of privacy in the area of public disclosure of embarrassing private facts, Prosser stated: "The disclosure of the private facts must be a public disclosure, and not a private one; there must be, in other words, publicity." [Citation.]

Thus, except in cases involving physical intrusion, the tort must be accompanied by publicity in the sense of communication to the public in general or to a large number of persons as distinguished from one individual or a few. [Citation.] "The gravamen of the tort is unwarranted publication of intimate details of plaintiff's private life. [Citations.] The interest to be protected is individual freedom from the wrongful publicizing of private affairs and activities which are outside the realm of legitimate public concern. [Citations.]

Appellant first contends that her mailing of letters to "perhaps twenty [people] at most" was insufficient publicity to justify a finding that respondent's privacy had been invaded. Since these mailings were ostensibly to only a small select group of people, appellant ar-

gues that the requirement of mass exposure to the public as opposed to a few people has not been satisfied. Appellant's contention misstates the applicable law.

* * *

While it may be true that no California case has defined the number of people necessary to justify a finding of publicity, an examination of some of the cases in this area provides sufficient guidance for the matter before us. In *Porten v. University of San Francisco*, [citation], the court held that the disclosure by the University of plaintiff's transcript to the State Scholarship and Loan Commission was not a "communication to the public in general." [Citation.] In *Timperley v. Chase Collection Service* [citation], the defendant wrote a letter to plaintiff's employer informing it of an attorney's bill allegedly owed by plaintiff and threatening legal action against the employee plaintiff. There, a judgment for defendant on demurrer was affirmed by the court which declared that it would have been an invasion of plaintiff's privacy to inform the public generally. [Citation.] In both cases, communication was to a single recipient for a specific, nonmalicious purpose.

In the instant case, appellant, in her professed attempts to "tell the whole world what a bastard he is," sought to reach a large group of people whom she knew had nothing in common except the possible acquaintance of Bill Kinsey. Unlike the State Commission in *Porten* or the employer in *Timperley*, recipients of appellant Macur's letters comprised a diverse group of people living in several states and totally unconnected either socially or professionally. Recipients of her letters included the Kinseys, their former spouses, their parents, their neighbors, their parents' neighbors, members of Bill Kinsey's dissertation committee, other faculty and the President of Stanford University. Since this court believes these recipients adequately reflect "mass exposure" we decline to yield to appellant's claim of insufficient publicity. To do so, we conclude, would only emasculate the legal remedy available to individuals for the invasion of their privacy by another individual.

As the Supreme Court noted: "Men fear exposure not only to those closest to them; much of the outrage underlying the asserted right to privacy is a reaction to exposure to persons known only through business or other secondary relationships. The claim is not so much one of total secrecy as it is the right to *define* one's circle of intimacy . . ." [Citation.]

Under this standard, appellant clearly has violated Bill Kinsey's right of privacy. While it may be true that there is little to admire in Kinsey's treatment of appellant, this does not justify the harassment of Kinsey and his wife which followed.

* * *

Appellant next contends that, even if respondent's privacy had been invaded, the invasion was privileged since Kinsey was a public figure. This status, she contends, was achieved "by virtue of his entry into the Peace Corps and through his trial for the murder of his first wife." Given this "public figure" status, she asserts that she may exercise her constitutional privilege to disseminate critical material if done without malice. [Citation.] We disagree.

Contrary to appellant's assertion that "the definition of 'public figure' for the purposes of the qualified privilege to publish is not clearly defined," the United States Supreme Court opinion in the leading case of *Gertz v. Robert Welch, Inc.* [citation] is particularly instructive: "Hypothetically, it may be possible for someone to become a public figure through no purposeful action of his own, but the instances of truly involuntary public figures must be exceedingly rare. For the most part those who attain this status have assumed roles of especial prominence in the affairs of society. Some occupy positions of such persuasive power and influence that they are deemed

public figures for all purposes. More commonly, those classified as public figures have thrust themselves to the forefront of particular public controversies in order to influence the resolution of the issues involved. In either event, they invite attention and comment." [Citation.]

Additionally, *Gertz* cautioned against lightly assuming ". . . that a citizen's participation in community and professional affairs rendered him a public figure for all purposes . . . It is preferable to reduce the public-figure question to a more meaningful context by looking to the nature and extent of an individual's participation in the particular controversy . . . ." [Citation.]

Under this standard, it is difficult to see how respondent could become a public figure simply because of his participation in the Peace Corps or his employment with the United Nations.

With respect to Kinsey's notoriety by virtue of his trial, respondent was involuntarily thrust into the public limelight through the unfortunate death of his first wife. Offered the opportunity to be released on bail, he declined in favor of waiting some six months in jail for his trial at which time he was acquitted.

In the leading case of *Melvin v. Reid* [citation], plaintiff, a prostitute, was charged with murder and acquitted after a very long and very public trial. She abandoned her life of shame, married and assumed a place in respectable society, making many friends who were not aware of the incidents of her earlier life. The court held that she had stated a cause of action for privacy against defendants who had made a movie based entirely on Mrs. Melvin's life some seven years after the trial.

* * * Since Kinsey, like Mrs. Melvin, had been acquitted of the murder charge, there is a strong societal interest in allowing him "to melt into the shadows of obscurity" once again.

* * *

The judgment is affirmed.

Defense of Property

KATKO v. BRINEY

Supreme Court of Iowa, 1971.
183 N.W.2d 657.

MOORE, C. J.

The primary issue presented here is whether an owner may protect personal property in an unoccupied boarded-up farm house against trespassers and thieves by a spring gun capable of inflicting death or serious injury.

We are not here concerned with a man's right to protect his home and members of his family. Defendants' home was several miles from the scene of the incident to which we refer * * *.

Plaintiff's action is for damages resulting from serious injury caused by a shot from a 20-gauge spring shotgun set by defendants in a bedroom of an old farm house which had been uninhabited for several years. Plaintiff and his companion, Marvin McDonough, had broken and entered the house to find and steal old bottles and dated fruit jars which they considered antiques.

* * * The jury returned a verdict for plaintiff and against defendants for $20,000 actual and $10,000 punitive damages. [The defendants appealed.]

Most of the facts are not disputed. In 1957 defendant Bertha L. Briney inherited her parents' farm land in Mahaska and Monroe Counties. Included was an 80-acre tract in southwest Mahaska County where her grandparents and parents had lived. No one occupied the house thereafter. Her husband, Edward, attempted to care for the land. He kept no farm machinery thereon. The outbuildings became dilapidated.

For about 10 years, 1957 to 1967, there occurred a series of trespassing and housebreaking events with loss of some household items, the breaking of windows and "messing up of the property in general." The latest occurred June 8, 1967, prior to the event on July 16, 1967, herein involved.

Defendants through the years boarded up the windows and doors in an attempt to stop the intrusions. They had posted "no trespass" signs on the land several years before 1967. The nearest one was 35 feet from the house. On June 11, 1967, defendants set "a shotgun trap" in the north bedroom. After Mr. Briney cleaned and oiled his 20-gauge shotgun, the power of which he was well aware, defendants took it to the old house where they secured it to an iron bed with the barrel pointed at the bedroom door. It was rigged with wire from the doorknob to the gun's trigger so it would fire when the door was opened. Briney first pointed the gun so an intruder would be hit in the stomach but at Mrs. Briney's suggestion it was lowered to hit the legs. He admitted he did so "because I was mad and tired of being tormented" but "he did not intend to injure anyone." He gave no explanation of why he used a loaded shell and set it to hit a person already in the house. Tin was nailed over the bedroom window. The spring gun could not be seen from the outside. No warning of its presence was posted.

Plaintiff lived with his wife and worked regularly as a gasoline station attendant in Eddyville, seven miles from the old house. He had observed it for several years while hunting in the area and considered it as being abandoned. He knew it had long been uninhabited. In 1967 the area around the house was covered with high weeds. Prior to July 16, 1967, plaintiff and McDonough had been to the premises and found several old bottles and fruit jars which they took and added to their collection of antiques. On the latter date about 9:30 p.m. they made a second trip to the Briney property. They entered the old house by removing a board from a porch window which was without glass. While McDonough was looking around the kitchen area plaintiff went to another part of the house. As he started to open the north bedroom door the shotgun went off striking him in the right leg above the ankle bone. Much of his leg, including part of the tibia, was blown away. Only by McDonough's assistance was plaintiff able to get out of the house and after crawling some distance was put in his vehicle and rushed to a doctor and then to a hospital. He remained in the hospital 40 days.

Plaintiff's doctor testified he seriously considered amputation but eventually the healing process was successful. Some weeks after his release from the hospital plaintiff returned to work on crutches. He was required to keep the injured leg in a cast for approximately a year and wear a special brace for another year. He continued to suffer pain during this period.

There was undenied medical testimony plaintiff had a permanent deformity, a loss of tissue, and a shortening of the leg.

The record discloses plaintiff to trial time had incurred $710 medical expense, $2,056.85 for hospital service, $61.80 for orthopedic service and $750 as loss of earnings. In addition thereto the trial court submitted to the jury the question of damages for pain and suffering and for future disability.

* * *

The main thrust of defendants' defense in the trial court and on this appeal is that "the law permits use of a spring gun in a dwelling or warehouse for the purpose of preventing the unlawful entry of a burglar or thief." * * *

* * *

The overwhelming weight of authority, both textbook and case law, supports the trial court's statement of the applicable principles of law.

Prosser on Torts, Third Edition, pages 116–118, states:

* * * the law has always placed a higher value upon human safety than upon mere rights in property, it is the accepted rule that there is no privilege to use any force calculated to cause death or serious bodily injury to repel the threat to land or chattels, unless there is also such a threat to the defendant's personal safety as to justify a self-defense. * * * spring guns and other man-killing devices are not justifiable against a mere trespasser, or even a petty thief. They are privileged only against those upon whom the landowner, if he were present in person, would be free to inflict injury of the same kind.

Restatement of Torts, section 85 * * * states: "The value of human life and limb, not only to the individual concerned but also to society, so outweighs the interest of a possessor of land in excluding it from those whom he is not willing to admit thereto that a possessor of land has, as is stated in § 79, no privilege to use force intended or likely to cause death or serious harm against another whom the possessor sees about to enter his premises or meddle with his chattel, unless the intrusion threatens death or serious bodily harm to the occupiers or users of the premises. * * *"

Judgment affirmed.

PROBLEMS

1. The Penguin intentionally hits Batman with his umbrella. Batman, stunned by the blow, falls backwards, knocking Robin down. Robin's leg is broken in the fall, and he cries out, "Holy broken bat bones! My leg is broken." Who, if anyone, is liable to Robin? Why?

2. For the purpose of frightening N. C. Kure, Bob comes up behind Kure in the desert and sounds a buzzer which is an excellent imitation of a rattlesnake. Kure, believing that he is about to be bitten, is frightened but suffers no bodily harm. May Kure recover from Bob for:

(a) the tort of assault?

(b) the tort of intentional infliction of mental distress?

3. A kisses B while she is asleep but does not waken or harm her. B sues A for battery. Decision?

4. Cole Lect, a creditor, seeking to collect a debt, calls on Over Due and demands payment in a rude and insolent manner. When Due says that he cannot pay, Cole calls Due a deadbeat and says that he will never trust Due again. Is Cole liable to Due? If so, for what tort?

5. A, a 10-year-old child, is run over by a car negligently driven by B. A, at the time of the accident, was acting reasonably and without negligence. C, a newspaper reporter, photographs A while she is lying in the street in great pain. Two years later, D, the publisher of a newspaper, prints C's picture of A in his newspaper as a lead to an article concerning the negligence of children. The caption under the picture reads: "They ask to be killed." A, who has recovered from the accident, brings suit against C and D. What result?

6. In 1963 the Saturday Evening Post featured an article entitled "The Story of a College Football Fix," characterized in the subtitle as "A Shocking Report of How Wally Butts and Bear Bryant Rigged a Game Last Fall." Butts was athletic director of the University of Georgia, and Bryant was head coach of the University of Alabama. The article was based on a claim by one George Burnett that he had accidentally overheard a long distance telephone conversation between Butts and Bryant in the course of which Butts divulged information on plays Georgia would use in the upcoming game against Alabama. The writer assigned to the story by the Post was not a football expert and did not interview either Butts or Bryant, nor did he personally see the notes Burnett had made of the telephone conversation. Butts admitted that he had a long distance telephone conversation with Bryant but denied that any advance information on prospective football plays was given. Butts brought a libel suit against the Post. Decision?

7. A is a patient confined in a hospital with a rare disease that is of great interest to the public. B, a television reporter, requests A to consent to an interview. A refuses, but B, nonetheless, enters A's room over her objection and photographs her. A brings a suit against B. Decision?

8. Proper T. Owner has a place on his land where he piles trash. The pile has been there for a period of three months. John, a neighbor of Owner and without Owner's consent or knowledge, throws trash onto the trashpile. Owner learns that John has done this and sues him. What tort, if any, has John committed?

9. Chris leaves her car parked in front of a store. There are no signs that say Chris cannot park there. The store owner, however, needs the car moved to enable a delivery truck to unload. He releases the brake and pushes Chris's car three or four feet, doing no harm to the car. Chris returns and sees that her car has been moved and is very angry. She threatens to sue the store owner for trespass to her personal property. Can she recover?

10. N. O. Carr borrowed John's brand new Ford Escort for the purpose of going to the store. He told John he would be right back. N. O. then decided, however, to go to the beach while he had the car. Can John recover from N. O. the value of the automobile? If so, for what tort?

Chapter 6

NEGLIGENCE AND STRICT LIABILITY

N EGLIGENCE involves conduct that creates an **unreasonable** risk of harm, whereas intentional torts deal with conduct that has a substantial certainty of causing harm. The failure to exercise reasonable care under the circumstances for the safety of another person or his property, which proximately causes injury to such person or damage to his property, or both, is the basis of liability for negligence. Thus, if the driver of an automobile runs down a person, intending to do so, she has committed the intentional tort of battery. However, if the driver hits and injures a person while driving unreasonably for the safety of others, she is negligent.

Strict liability is not based upon the negligence or intent of the defendant but rather upon the nature of the activity in which he is engaging. Both negligence and strict liability are the subject matter of this chapter.

NEGLIGENCE

The Restatement defines negligence as "conduct which falls below the standard established by law for the protection of others against unreasonable risk of harm." Restatement, Section 282. The standard established by law is the conduct of a **reasonable man** acting prudently and with due care under the circumstances.

A person is not liable for injury caused to another by an unavoidable accident—an occurrence which was not intended and could not have been prevented by the exercise of reasonable care. Thus, no liability results from the sudden loss of control of an automobile because the driver is suddenly and unforeseeably stricken with a heart attack, stroke, or fainting spell. If the driver, however, had warning of the imminent heart attack or other infirmity, it would be negligent for him to drive at all.

An action for negligence consists of four elements, each of which must be proved by the plaintiff:

1. that a legal duty required the defendant to conform to the standard of conduct established by law for the protection of others,
2. that the defendant failed to conform to the required standard of conduct,
3. that the injury and harm sustained by the plaintiff was proximately caused by defendant's failure to conform to the required standard of conduct, and
4. that the injury and harm is protected against negligent interference.

The first two elements will be discussed under the heading duty of care, the third under proximate cause, and the last under injury.

DUTY OF CARE

Negligence consists of conduct which creates an unreasonable risk of harm. In determining whether a given risk of harm is unreasonable the following factors are considered: (1) the probability that the harm will occur, (2) the gravity or seriousness of the resulting harm, (3) the utility of the conduct creating the risk, and (4) the cost of taking precautions that will reduce the risk. As Prosser stated:

It is fundamental that the standard of conduct which is the basis of the law of negligence is usually determined upon a risk-benefit form of analysis: by balancing the risk, in the light of the social value of the interest threatened, and the probability and extent of the harm, against the value of the interest which the actor is seeking to protect, and the expedience of the course pursued. For this reason, it is usually very difficult, and often simply not possible, to reduce negligence to any definite rules; it is "relative to the need and the occasion," and conduct which would be proper under some circumstances becomes negligence under others.

Reasonable Man Standard

The duty of care imposed by law is measured by the degree of carefulness which a reasonable man would exercise in a given situation. The reasonable man is a fictitious individual who is always careful, prudent, and never negligent. What the judge or jury determines that a reasonable man would have done in the light of the facts brought out by the evidence in a particular case sets the standard of conduct for that case. The reasonable man standard is thus external and *objective*, as described by Justice Holmes:

If, for instance, a man is born hasty and awkward, is always hurting himself or his neighbors, no doubt his congenital defects will be allowed for in the courts of Heaven, but his slips are no less troublesome to his neighbors than if they sprang from guilty neglect. His neighbors accordingly require him, at his peril, to come up to their standard, and the courts which they establish decline to take his personal equation into account. Holmes, *The Common Law.*

Children The standard of conduct to which a child must conform to avoid being negligent is that of a reasonable person of like age, intelligence, and experience under like circumstances. Restatement, Section 283A. The law applies an individualized test because children are incapable of exercising the judgment, intelligence, knowledge, and experience of an adult. Moreover, children as a general rule do not engage in activities entailing high risk to others, and their conduct does not involve the same magnitude of harm. However, a child who engages in an adult activity, such as flying an airplane or driving a boat or car, is held to the standard of care applicable to adults.

Physical Disability If a person is ill or otherwise physically disabled, the standard of conduct to which he must conform to avoid being negligent is that of a reasonable man under like disability. Thus, a blind man must act as a reasonable man who is blind.

Mental Deficiency The law makes no allowance for the insanity or other mental deficiency of the defendant in a negligence case, and the defendant is held to the standard of conduct of a reasonable man who is *not* mentally deficient even though it is, in fact, beyond his capacity to conform to the standard. The Restatement, Section 283B, Comment b, justifies this rule as follows:

1. The difficulty of drawing any satisfactory line between mental deficiency and those variations of temperament, intellect, and emotional balance which cannot, as a practical matter, be taken into account in imposing liability for damage done.

2. The unsatisfactory character of the evidence of mental deficiency in many cases, together with the ease with which it can be feigned, the difficulties which the triers of fact must encounter in determining its existence, nature, degree, and effect, * * *

3. The feeling that if mental defectives are to live in the world, they should pay for the damage they do, and that it is better that their wealth, if any, should be used to compensate innocent victims than that it should remain in their hands.

4. The belief that their liability will mean that those who have charge of them or their estates will be stimulated to look after them, keep them in order, and see that they do not do harm.

Superior Skill or Knowledge Persons who are qualified and who practice a profession or trade which calls for special skill and expertise are required to exercise that care and skill which are normally possessed by members in good standing of their profession or trade. This standard applies to such professionals as physicians, surgeons, dentists, attorneys, pharmacists, architects, accountants, and engineers and to such skilled trades as airline pilots, electricians, carpenters, and plumbers. If a member of a profession or skilled trade possesses greater skill than that common to the profession or trade, she is required to exercise that skill.

To illustrate: In *Waynick v. Reardon*, 236 N.C. 116, 72 S.E.2d 4 (1956), Waynick entered Duke University Hospital suffering from fallen arches and pain in his feet. Although a definite diagnosis of his condition was never reached and the symptoms soon subsided, doctors of the hospital persuaded Waynick to undergo what they described as minor neural surgery to relieve the problem. Waynick reluctantly agreed. The operation was performed by Dr. Reardon, Assistant Resident in Surgery, with the aid of two interns. Although the procedure began smoothly, severe complications soon developed, and the Chief of Surgical Service at the hospital, Dr. Hart, had to be summoned from his home to save Waynick's life. The physicians were successful in that respect, but the patient lost both legs and suffered a heart attack as a direct result of the operation. Waynick finally left the hospital four months after the operation, weighing half of what he did when he entered. When asked to describe what happened during the operation, Dr. Reardon could only reply, "I played hell; that is what happened." Waynick brought an action to recover damages for Dr. Reardon's negligence. The trial court dismissed the case and Waynick appealed. The appellate court reversed. Hospitals and members of the medical profession are not guarantors of effective cures or of perfect operative results. Nevertheless, the law of negligence holds a physician or surgeon liable for an injury to a patient proximately resulting from an absence of that degree of knowledge and skill ordinarily possessed by other members of his profession or for his failure to exercise his best judgment in the treatment of his patient. Moreover, the question of whether Dr. Reardon or any physician proceeded with that degree of ordinary care required of him under the circumstances is a question of fact for the jury to decide.

Emergencies In determining whether a defendant's conduct is reasonable, the fact that he was at the time confronted with a sudden emergency is taken into consideration. Restatement, Section 296. An emergency is a sudden, unexpected event which calls for immediate action and does not permit time for deliberation. The standard is still that of a reasonable man under the circumstances— the emergency is simply part of the circumstances. However, an emergency is not helpful to a defendant if his own negligent or tortious conduct created the emergency.

In *Cordas v. Peerless Transportation Co.*, 27 N.Y.S.2d 198 (1941), an unidentified man was held up by two thugs in an alley in Manhattan. When the thieves departed with his possessions, the man quickly gave chase. He had almost caught one when the thief managed to force his way into an unengaged taxicab stopped at a traffic light. The cab was owned by the Peerless Transport Company. The thief pointed his gun at the driver's head and ordered him to drive on. The driver started to follow the directions while closely pursued by a "posse of good citizens" but then suddenly jammed on the brakes and jumped out of the car to safety. The thief also jumped out, but the car traveled on and injured Mrs. Cordas and her two children. The Cordases then brought an action for damages against the cab company, claiming that the cab driver was negligent in jumping to safety and leaving the moving vehicle uncontrolled. Judgment for Peerless Transport Company. The court stated that the test of actionable negligence is what a reasonably prudent person would have done under like conditions or circumstances. Therefore, to determine if the cab driver was negligent in abandoning his cab, his actions must be compared with what a reasonable person would have done in a similar circumstance. In general, one faced with an emergency is not required to exercise the same mature judgment that is expected of him under circumstances where he has an opportunity for deliberate action. Here, the cab driver was faced with a most frightening experience and made a split-second decision in an attempt to extricate himself from the danger. The court concluded that it could not be said that he had acted unreasonably under the emergency circumstances, and, therefore, the Cordases are not entitled to recover.

Violation of Statute The reasonable man standard of conduct may be established by legislation. Restatement, Section 285. Some statutes expressly impose civil liability upon violators. Absent such a provision, courts may adopt the requirements of the statute as the standard of conduct if the statute is intended to protect a class of persons, which includes the plaintiff, against the particular hazard and kind of harm which resulted. The Restatement, Section 286, provides:

The court may adopt as the standard of conduct of a reasonable man the requirements of a legislative enactment or an administrative regulation whose purpose is found to be exclusively or in part:

(a) to protect a class of persons which includes the one whose interest is invaded, and

(b) to protect the particular interest which is invaded, and

(c) to protect that interest against the kind of harm which has resulted, and

(d) to protect that interest against the particular hazard from which the harm results.

If the statute is found to be applicable, the majority of the courts hold that an unexcused violation is **negligence *per se*;** that is, it is conclusive on the issue of negligent conduct. In a minority of States the violation is considered merely evidence of negligence. In either event, the plaintiff must also prove legal causation and injury.

For example, a statute enacted to protect employees from injuries requires that all factory elevators be equipped with specified safety devices. A, an employee in B's factory, and C, a business visitor to the factory, are injured when the elevator falls because of the failure to install the safety devices. The court may adopt the statute as a standard of conduct as to A, and hold B negligent *per se* to A, but not as to C, because A, and not C, is within the class of persons intended to be protected by the statute. C would have to establish that a reasonable person in the position of B under the circumstances would have installed the safety device.

See *Vance v. United States.*

Duty of Affirmative Action

Absent special circumstances, no one is under an affirmative duty to aid another in peril. As Prosser has explained, "[b]ecause of [the] reluctance to countenance 'nonfeasance' as a basis of liability, the law has persistently refused to recognize the moral obligation of common decency and common humanity, to come to the aid of another human being who is in danger, even though the outcome is to cost him his life." For example, A, an adult standing along the edge of a steep cliff, observes a baby carriage with a crying infant in it slowly heading toward the edge and certain doom. A could easily prevent the baby's fall at no risk to her own safety. Nonetheless, A does nothing, and the baby falls to his death. A is under no legal duty to act and, therefore, incurs no liability for failing to do so.

Section 314 of the Restatement reflects this position: "The fact that the actor realizes or should realize that action on his part is necessary for another's aid or protection does not of itself impose upon him a duty to take such action." However, special relations between the parties may exist that impose a duty upon the defendant to aid or protect the other. Thus, if in the example above, A were the baby's mother or babysitter, A would be under a duty to act and would therefore be liable for not taking action. The special relations giving rise to the duty to aid or protect another include: common carrier—passenger, innkeeper—guest, employer—employee, and parent—child. Restatement, Sections 314A and 314B. *See Caldwell v. Bechtel, Inc.* in Chapter 1.

A duty of affirmative action is also imposed upon those whose conduct, whether tortious or innocent, has injured another and left him helpless and in danger of further harm.

For example, A drives her car into B who is rendered unconscious. A leaves B lying in the middle of the road where he is run over by a second car driven by C. A is liable to B for the additional injuries inflicted by C. Moreover, a person incurs a duty to exercise care by voluntarily coming to the assistance of another in need of aid. In such instance, the actor is liable if his failure to exercise reasonable care increases the risk of harm, causes harm to be suffered by reliance upon the undertaking, or leaves the other in a worse position. For example, A finds B drunk and stumbling along a dark sidewalk. A leads B halfway up a steep and unguarded stairway where he abandons B. B attempts to climb the stairs but trips and falls, suffering serious injury. A is liable to B for having left him in a worse position.

A parent is not liable for the torts of his minor child simply because of the parental relationship. Where, however, the parent authorizes, encourages, or participates in, the tort of his child, or ratifies it by knowingly participating in the benefits, he is liable. So, also, tort liability may be attributed to the parents on the grounds of their negligence, as where the parent places a dangerous instrumentality, such as a gun or knife, in the hands of the child, and the child thereby causes injury to another. The Restatement, Section 316, provides:

A parent is under a duty to exercise reasonable care so to control his minor child as to prevent it from intentionally harming others or from so conducting itself as to create an unreasonable risk of bodily harm to them, if the parent

(a) knows or has reason to know that he has the ability to control his child, and

(b) knows or should know of the necessity and opportunity for exercising such control.

For example, "A is informed that his six-year-old child is shooting at a target in the street with a .22 rifle, in a manner which endangers the safety of those using the street. A fails to take the rifle away from the child, or to take any other action. The child unintentionally shoots B, a pedestrian, in the leg. A is subject to liability to B." Restatement, Section 316, Illustration 1.

Special Duties of Possessors of Land

The duty of a possessor of land to persons who come upon the land depends upon whether that person is a trespasser, a licensee, or an invitee.

Duty to Trespassers A trespasser is a person who enters or remains on the land of another without permission or privilege to do so. The lawful possessor of the land is *not* liable to trespassers for her failure to maintain the land in a reasonably safe condition. Nonetheless, trespassers are not criminals, and the lawful possessor is not free to inflict intentional injury on them. Some courts have held that the lawful possessor is required to exercise reasonable care for the safety of trespassers, upon discovery of their presence on the land.

The law, however, extends greater protection to a child who trespasses by imposing upon a possessor of land liability for physical harm caused by artificial conditions upon the land if:

(a) the place where the condition exists is one upon which the possessor knows or has reason to know that children are likely to trespass, and

(b) the condition is one of which the possessor knows or has reason to know and which he realizes or should realize will involve an unreasonable risk of death or serious bodily harm to such children, and

(c) the children because of their youth do not discover the condition or realize the risk involved in intermeddling with it or in coming within the area made dangerous by it, and

(d) the utility to the possessor of maintaining the condition and the burden of eliminating the danger are slight as compared with the risk to children involved; and

(e) the possessor fails to exercise reasonable care to eliminate the danger or otherwise to protect the children. Restatement, Section 339.

The Restatement provides the following illustration: "A has on his land a small artificial pond full of goldfish. A's land adjoins a nursery in which children from two to five years of age are left by their parents for the day, and such children are, as A knows, in the habit of trespassing on A's land and going near the pond. A could easily prevent this by closing and locking his gate. A does not do so. B, a child three years of age, trespasses, enters the pond to catch goldfish, and is drowned. A is subject to liability for the death of B." Section 339, Illustration 7.

Duty to Licensees A licensee is a person who is privileged to enter or remain upon land only by virtue of the consent of the lawful possessor. Restatement, Section 330. Licensees include members of the possessor's household and **social guests.** A licensee, however, will become a trespasser if he enters a portion of the land to which he is not invited or remains upon the land after his invitation has expired.

The possessor owes a higher duty of care to licensees than to trespassers. The licensee is entitled to be warned of dangerous activities and conditions of which the possessor has knowledge and which the licensee does not and is not likely to discover. If he is not warned, the licensee may recover if the activity or dangerous condition resulted from the possessor's failure to exercise reasonable care to protect him from the danger. Restatement, Section 342. To illustrate: A invites a friend, B, to his place in the country at eight o'clock on a winter evening. A knows that a bridge in his driveway is in a dangerous condition which is not noticeable in the dark. A does not inform B of this fact. The bridge gives way under B's car, causing serious harm to B. A is liable to B.

Duty to Invitees An invitee is either a public invitee or a business visitor. A person is a **public invitee** if she enters upon land which is open to the public, such as a public park, beach, swimming pool, or a governmental facility where business with the public is transacted openly such as a post office or office of the Recorder of Deeds. A **business visitor** is a person who enters upon the premises to engage in private business, such as one who enters a store or a workman who enters a residence to make repairs.

The duty of the possessor of land to invitees with respect to the condition of the premises is to exercise reasonable care to protect them against dangerous conditions they are unlikely to discover. Restatement, Section 343. For example, supermarket A has in its store a large, glass front door which is well lighted and plainly visible. B, a customer, mistakes the glass for an open doorway and walks into the glass, injuring himself. A is not liable to B. If, on the other hand, the glass was difficult to see and it was foreseeable that a person might mistake the glass for an open doorway, then A would be liable to B if B crashed into the glass while exercising reasonable care. *See H. E. Butt Grocery Co. v. Hawkins.*

These three categories of duties are illustrated in Figure 6-1.

Res Ipsa Loquitur

A rule has developed which permits the jury to infer *both* negligent conduct and causation from the mere occurrence of certain types of events. This rule is called *res ipsa loquitur*, which means "the thing speaks for itself," and applies when the event is of a kind which ordinarily does not occur in the absence of negligence and other possible causes are sufficiently eliminated by the evidence. Section 328D of the Restatement provides as follows:

(1) It may be inferred that harm suffered by the plaintiff is caused by negligence of the defendant when

(a) the event is of a kind which ordinarily does not occur in the absence of negligence;

(b) other responsible causes, including the conduct of the plaintiff and third persons, are sufficiently eliminated by the evidence; and

(c) the indicated negligence is within the scope of the defendant's duty to the plaintiff.

For example, A rents a room in B's motel and is injured during the night by a large piece of plaster which falls upon her from the

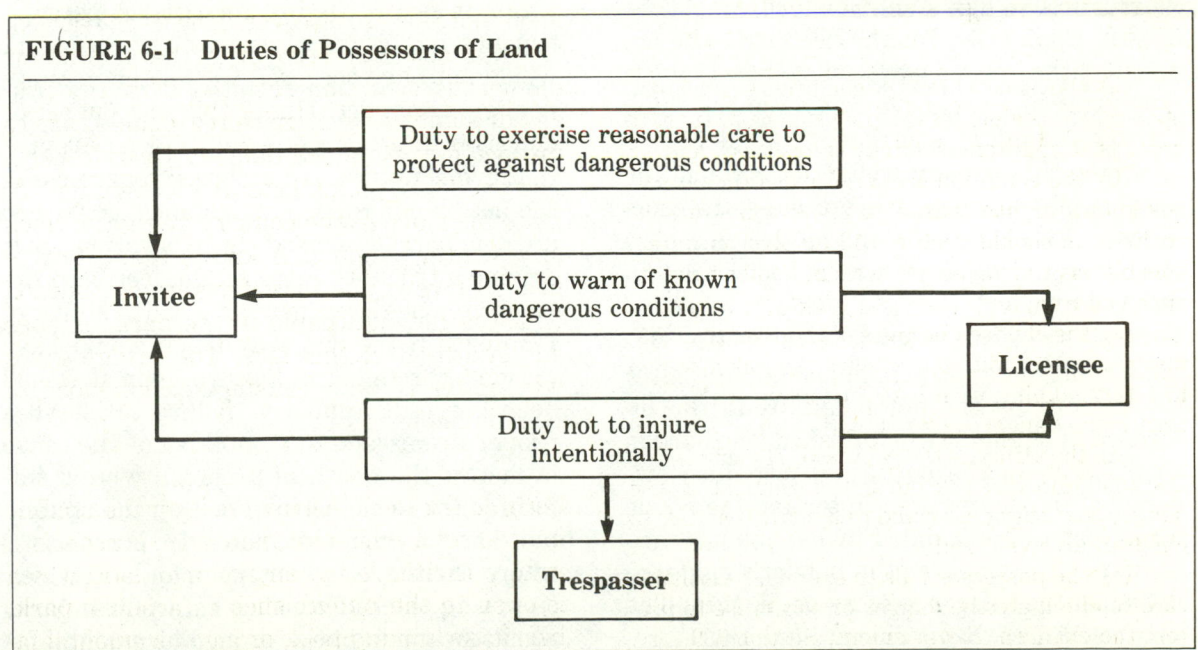

FIGURE 6-1 Duties of Possessors of Land

ceiling. In the absence of other evidence the jury may infer that the harm resulted from B's negligence in permitting the plaster to become defective. B is permitted, however, to introduce evidence to contradict the inference of negligence. *See Uzdavines v. Metropolitan Baseball Club, Inc.*

In *Escola v. Coca Cola Bottling Co. of Fresno*, 24 Cal.2d 453, 150 P.2d 436 (1944), Escola, a waitress, was injured when a bottle of Coca Cola exploded in her hand while she was putting it into the restaurant's cooler. The bottle came from a shipment that had remained under the counter for thirty-six hours after being delivered by the bottling company. The bottler had subjected the bottle to the method of testing for defects commonly used in the industry, and there was no evidence that Escola or anyone else did anything to damage the bottle between its delivery and the explosion. Escola brought an action against the bottler for damages. Since she was unable to show any specific acts of negligence on its part, she sought to rely on the doctrine of *res ipsa loquitur.* Judgment for Escola. The doctrine of *res ipsa loquitur* permits a jury to infer both negligent conduct and causation from the mere occurrence of certain types of events where actual negligent conduct cannot be shown. Ordinarily, for the doctrine to be applicable, the injured party must show that the defendant had exclusive control of the thing causing the injury and that the accident was of a type that usually would not occur in the absence of negligence. Nevertheless, the court allowed Escola to rely on the doctrine here even though the bottle was not in the defendant's exclusive possession when it exploded because she had shown that the bottle was not damaged by any extraneous force after its delivery by the defendant. With the inference of negligence established, the burden then fell upon the bottler to introduce evidence of due care taken in testing the bottle for defects. This it did. Finally, the jury had to determine whether the bottler's evidence dispelled the inference of its negligence. The jury concluded that it did not, and, therefore, Escola is entitled to recover.

PROXIMATE CAUSE

One of the requirements of imposing liability for the negligent conduct of a defendant is that it not only caused injury to the plaintiff, but that it was the proximate cause of the injury. Referring to proximate cause, Dean Prosser has stated, "[t]here is perhaps nothing in the entire field of law which has called forth more disagreement, or upon which the opinions are in such a welter of confusion." Most simply expressed, proximate cause consists of the judicially imposed limitations upon a person's liability for the consequences of his or her negligence. As a matter of social policy, legal responsibility has not been permitted to follow all the consequences of a negligent act. Responsibility has been limited to those persons and results which are closely connected with the negligent conduct.

Causation in Fact

In order to support a finding that the defendant's negligence was the proximate cause of the plaintiff's injury, it is first necessary that the defendant's conduct was the *actual cause* of the injury. A widely applied test for causation in fact is the **but for rule:** A person's conduct is a cause of an event if the event would not have occurred *but for* the person's negligent conduct. Under this test, an act or omission to act is *not* a cause of an event if that event would have occurred regardless of the act or omission. For instance, A fails to erect a barrier around an excavation. B is driving a truck when its accelerator becomes stuck. A's negligence is not a cause in fact of B's death if the runaway truck would have crashed through the barrier even if it had been erected. Similarly, failure to install a proper fire escape to a hotel is not the cause in fact of the death of a person who is suffocated while sleeping in bed by the smoke.

The "but for" test, however, is not useful where there are two or more forces actively operating, each of which is sufficient to bring about the harm in question. For example, A accidentally stabs C with a knife while B negligently fractures C's skull with a rock. Either wound would be fatal, and C dies from both. Under the "but for" test, either A or B, or both, could argue that C would have died from the wound inflicted by the other and therefore he is not liable. The **substantial factor test** addresses this problem by stating that negligent conduct is a legal cause of harm to another if the conduct is a substantial factor in bringing about the harm. Restatement, Section 431. Under this test the conduct of both A and B would be found to be a cause in fact of C's death.

Limitations upon Causation in Fact

As a matter of policy, the law imposes limitations upon the causal connection between the defendant's negligence and the plaintiff's injury. Two of the factors that are taken into consideration in determining such limitations are (a) unforeseeable consequences and (b) superseding causes.

Unforeseeable Consequences The liability of a negligent defendant for unforeseeable consequences has proved to be troublesome and controversial. The Restatement and a majority of the courts have adopted the following position:

(1) If the actor's conduct is a substantial factor in bringing about harm to another, the fact that the actor neither foresaw nor should have foreseen the extent of the harm or the manner in which it occurred does not prevent him from being liable.

(2) The actor's conduct may be held not to be a legal cause of harm to another where after the event and looking back from the harm to the actor's negligent conduct, it appears to the court highly extraordinary that it should have brought about the harm. Section 435.

Even if the defendant's negligent conduct is a cause in fact of harm to the plaintiff, the defendant is *not* liable to the plaintiff *unless* the defendant could have reasonably anticipated injuring the plaintiff or a class of persons of which the plaintiff is a member.

Restatement, Section 281, Comment c. Proximate cause involves a recognition of the risk of harm to the plaintiff individually or to a class of persons of which the plaintiff is a member. *See Palsgraf v. Long Island Railroad Co., and Petition of Kinsman Transit Co.*

For example, A, while negligently driving an automobile, collides with a car which is carrying dynamite. A is unaware of the contents of the other car and has no reason to know about it. The collision causes the dynamite to explode, shattering glass in a building a block away. The shattered glass injures B, who was inside the building. The explosion also injures C, who was walking on the sidewalk near the collision. A would be liable to C because A should have realized that his negligent driving might result in a collision that would endanger pedestrians nearby, and the fact that the actual harm resulted in an unforeseeable manner does not affect his liability. B, however, was beyond the zone of danger, and A, accordingly, is not liable to B. A's negligent driving is not deemed to be the "proximate cause" of B's injury because, looking back from the harm to A's negligence, it appears highly extraordinary that A's conduct should have brought about the harm to B.

Superseding Cause A superseding cause is an *intervening* event or act which occurs subsequently to the defendant's negligent conduct and relieves him of liability for harm to the plaintiff caused in fact by both the defendant's negligence and the intervening event or act. Section 442 of the Restatement provides the following list of considerations that are of importance in determining whether an intervening force is a superseding cause that relieves the defendant of liability:

(a) the fact that its intervention brings about harm different in kind from that which would otherwise have resulted from the actor's negligence;

(b) the fact that its operation or the consequences thereof appear after the event to be extraordinary rather than normal in view of the circumstances existing at the time of its operation;

(c) the fact that the intervening force is operating independently of any situation created by the actor's negligence, or, on the other hand, is or is not a normal result of such a situation;

(d) the fact that the operation of the intervening force is due to a third person's act or to his failure to act;

(e) the fact that the intervening force is due to an act of a third person which is wrongful toward the other and as such subjects the third person to liability to him;

(f) the degree of culpability of a wrongful act of a third person which sets the intervening force in motion.

For example, A negligently runs down a cow which is left lying stunned in the road. Several minutes later the cow regains consciousness, takes fright, and charges into B, a bystander. The cow's conduct is an intervening, but not a superseding, cause of harm to B because it is a normal consequence of the situation caused by A's negligence. Therefore, A is liable to B. In contrast, A negligently leaves an excavation in a public sidewalk into which B intentionally hurls C. A is not liable to C because B's conduct is a superseding cause that relieves A of liability.

INJURY

The plaintiff must prove that the defendant's negligent conduct caused harm to a legally protected interest. Certain interests receive little or no protection from negligent interference, while others receive full protection. The extent of protection for a particular interest is determined by the courts as a matter of law on the basis of social policy and expediency. For example, negligent conduct that is the proximate cause of harmful contact with the person of another is actionable. Thus, if A negligently runs into B, a pedestrian, who is carefully crossing the street, A is liable for physical injuries sustained by B as a result of the collision. On the other hand, if A's careless conduct causes only offensive contact with

B's person, A is not liable. "In general, however, it may be said that the law gives protection against negligent acts to the interest in security of the person, and to the various interests in tangible property. In other words, negligence may result in liability for personal injury or property damage." *Prosser and Keeton on the Law of Torts*, p. 359.

The courts have traditionally been reluctant to allow recovery for negligently inflicted emotional distress. This view has gradually changed during this century, and the majority of courts now hold a person liable for negligently causing emotional distress if bodily harm results from the distress. Restatement, Section 436. However, if the defendant's conduct merely results in emotional disturbance without resultant bodily harm, the defendant is not liable. Restatement, Section 436A.

DEFENSES

Although a plaintiff has established by the preponderance of the evidence all the required elements of a negligence action, he may, nevertheless, be denied recovery if the defendant proves a valid defense. As a general rule, any defense to an intentional tort is also available in an action in negligence. In addition, there are defenses available in negligence cases that are not defenses to intentional torts.

Contributory Negligence

Contributory negligence is defined as "conduct on the part of the plaintiff which falls below the standard to which he should conform for his own protection, and which is a legally contributing cause co-operating with the negligence of the defendant in bringing about the plaintiff's harm." Restatement, Section 463.

If negligence of the plaintiff in conjunction with negligence of the defendant proximately caused the injury and damage sustained by the plaintiff, he cannot recover *any* damages from the defendant. It does not matter whether the plaintiff's contributory negligence was slight or extensive.

Notwithstanding the contributory negligence of the plaintiff, if the defendant had a **last clear chance** to avoid injury to the plaintiff but did not avail himself of such chance, the contributory negligence of the plaintiff does not bar his recovery of damages. Restatement, Section 479. For example, A negligently stops his car on the highway. B, who is driving along, sees A's car in sufficient time to stop. However, B negligently puts her foot on the accelerator instead of the brake and runs into A's car. Because B had the last clear chance to stop her car before striking A's car, A's contributory negligence does not bar his recovery from B.

Comparative Negligence

The harshness of the contributory negligence doctrine has caused the great majority of the States to reject the all-or-nothing rule of contributory negligence and to substitute the doctrine of comparative negligence. Under comparative negligence, damages are apportioned between the parties in proportion to the degree of fault or negligence found against the parties. For instance, B negligently drives his automobile into A, who is crossing against the light. A sustains damages in the amount of $10,000 and sues B. If the trier of fact determines that B's negligence contributed 70 percent to A's injury and that A's contributory negligence contributed 30 percent to her injury, then A would recover $7,000.

Most States that have adopted the doctrine of comparative negligence have enacted statutes that do not permit the plaintiff any recovery if his contributory negligence was "as great as" or "greater than" that of the defendant. Thus, in the example above, if the trier of fact determined that B's negligence contributed 40 percent to A's injury and A's contributory negligence contributed 60 percent to her injury, then A would not recover anything from B.

Assumption of Risk

A plaintiff who has *voluntarily* and *knowingly* assumed the risk of harm arising from the negligent or reckless conduct of the defendant cannot recover from such harm. Basically, assumption of risk is the plaintiff's express or implied consent to encounter a known danger. Thus, a spectator entering a baseball park may be regarded as consenting that the players may proceed with the game without taking precautions to protect him from being hit by the ball. *See Falgout v. Wardlaw.*

Considerable confusion has arisen by reason of the use of the term "assumption of risk" in several different senses. Comment c to Section 496A of the Restatement explains four of these meanings:

1. In its simplest form, assumption of risk means that the plaintiff has given his express consent to relieve the defendant of an obligation to exercise care for his protection, and agrees to take his chances as to injury from a known or possible risk. The result is that the defendant, who would otherwise be under a duty to exercise such care, is relieved of that responsibility, and is no longer under any duty to protect the plaintiff. * * *

2. A second, and closely related, meaning is that the plaintiff has entered voluntarily into some relation with the defendant which he knows to involve the risk, and so is regarded as tacitly or impliedly agreeing to relieve the defendant of responsibility, and to take his own chances. * * *

3. In a third type of situation, the plaintiff, aware of a risk created by the negligence of the defendant, proceeds or continues voluntarily to encounter it. * * * The same policy of the common law which denies recovery to one who expressly consents to accept a risk will, however, prevent his recovery in such a case. * * *

4. To be distinguished from these three situations is the fourth, in which the plaintiff's conduct in voluntarily encountering a known risk is itself unreasonable, and amounts to contributory negligence. There is thus negligence on the part of both plaintiff and defendant; and the plaintiff is barred from recovery, not only by his implied consent to accept the risk, but also by the policy of the law which refuses to allow him to impose upon

FIGURE 6-2 Defenses to a Negligence Action

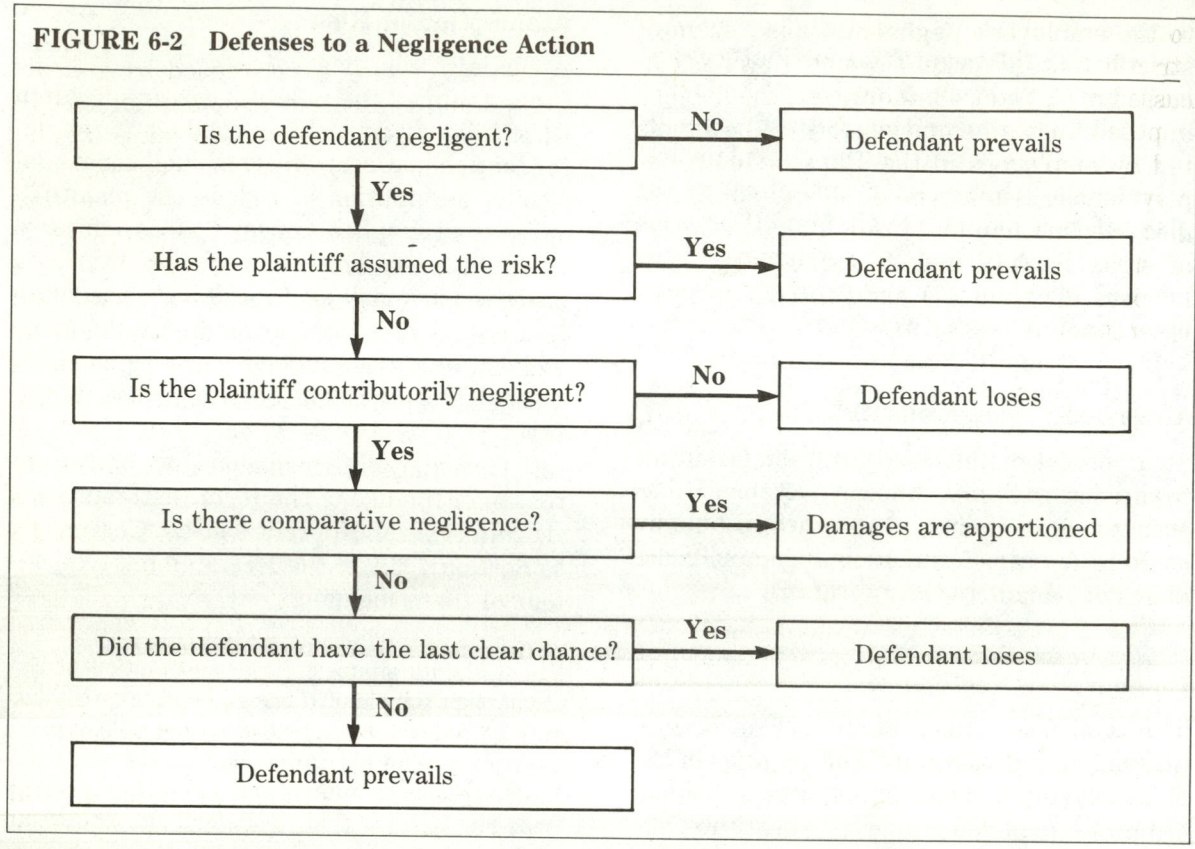

the defendant a loss for which his own negligence was in part responsible.

Figure 6-2 illustrates the defenses to a negligence action.

STRICT LIABILITY

In some instances, people may be held liable for injuries they have caused even though they have not acted intentionally or negligently. Such liability is called strict liability, absolute liability, or liability without fault. The law has determined that certain types of otherwise socially desirable activities pose sufficiently high risks of harm regardless of how carefully they are conducted, and, therefore, those who carry on these activities should bear the cost of all harm they cause. The doctrine of strict liability is *not* predicated upon any particular fault of the defendant, but rather upon the nature of the activity in which he is engaging. In effect, strict liability makes those who conduct these activities insurers of all who may be harmed by the activity.

ACTIVITIES GIVING RISE TO STRICT LIABILITY

The following activities giving rise to strict liability will be discussed in this section: (1) abnormally dangerous activities, (2) keeping of animals, and (3) products liability. In addition, strict liability is also imposed upon other activities. All States have enacted Worker's Compensation statutes which make employers liable to employees for injuries arising out of the course of employment. Because this liability is imposed without regard to the employer's negligence it is a form of strict liability. Worker's compensation is discussed in Chapter 43. Moreover, the liability imposed upon an employer for torts committed by employees in the scope of their employment is also a type of strict liability, as discussed in Chapter 18. Additional instances of strict liability include carriers and innkeepers (Chapter 47) and innocent misrepresentation (Chapter 9).

Abnormally Dangerous Activities

Strict liability is imposed for harm resulting from extraordinary, unusual, abnormal, or exceptional activities, as determined in light of the place, time, and manner in which the activity is conducted. Activities to which the rule has been applied include collecting water in such quantity and location as to make it dangerous; storing explosives or flammable liquids in large quantities; blasting or pile driving; crop dusting; drilling for or refining oil in populated areas; and emitting noxious gases or fumes into a settled community. On the other hand, courts have refused to apply the rule where the activity is a "natural" use of the land, such as drilling for oil in the oil fields of Texas, collecting water in a stock watering tank, and transmitting gas through a gas pipe or electricity in electric wiring.

Sections 519 and 520 of the Restatement impose strict liability for abnormally dangerous activities which are to be determined by considering the following six factors:

1. whether the activity involves a high degree of risk of some harm to the person, land, or chattels of others;
2. whether the gravity of the harm which may result from it is likely to be great;
3. whether the risk cannot be eliminated by the exercise of reasonable care;
4. whether the activity is not a matter of common usage;
5. whether the activity is inappropriate to the place where it is carried on; and
6. the value of the activity to the community.

Keeping of Animals

Strict liability for harm caused by animals existed at common law and continues today with some modification. As a general rule, those who possess animals for their own purposes do so at their peril and must protect against harm to people and property.

Trespassing Animals Keepers of animals are generally held liable for any damage done by their animals trespassing on the property of another. There are three exceptions to this rule: (1) keepers of cats and dogs are liable only for negligence; (2) keepers of animals are not strictly liable for animals straying from a highway on which they are being lawfully driven, although the owner may be liable for negligence if he fails to properly control them; and (3) keepers of farm animals, typically cattle, in some Western states are not strictly liable for harm caused by their trespassing animals which are allowed to graze freely.

Nontrespassing Animals Keepers of **wild animals** are strictly liable for harm caused by such animals, whether or not they are trespassing. Wild animals are defined as those which in the particular region are known to be likely to inflict serious damage and cannot be considered safe no matter how domesticated. Animals included in this category are bears, lions, elephants, monkeys, tigers, wolves, zebras, deer, and raccoons.

Domestic animals are those which are traditionally devoted to the service of mankind and as a class are considered safe. Examples of domestic animals are dogs, cats, horses, cattle, and sheep. Keepers of domestic animals are liable if they knew, or should have known, of the animal's dangerous propensity. Restatement, Section 509. The dangerous propensity of the animal must be the cause of the harm. For example, a keeper is not liable for a dog which bites a human merely because he knows that the dog has a propensity to engage in combat with other dogs. On the other hand, if a person's 150-pound sheep dog has a propensity to jump enthusiastically on visitors, the animal's keeper would be liable for any damage done by the dog's playfulness. *See Allen v. Whitehead.*

Products Liability

A recent and important trend in the law is the imposition of strict liability upon manufacturers and merchants who sell goods in a defective condition unreasonably dangerous to the user or consumer. Restatement, Section 402A. Liability is imposed regardless of the seller's due care and applies to all merchant sellers. This topic is covered in Chapter 21.

DEFENSES

This section will discuss the availability in a strict liability action of the following defenses: (1) contributory negligence, (2) comparative negligence, and (3) assumption of risk.

Contributory Negligence

Since the strict liability of one who carries on an abnormally dangerous activity, keeps animals, or sells products is not based on his negligence, the ordinary contributory negli-

gence of the plaintiff is *not* a defense to such liability. The law in imposing strict liability places the full responsibility for preventing harm upon the defendant. For example, A negligently fails to observe a sign on a highway warning of blasting operation conducted by B. As a result A is injured by these operations. A may nonetheless recover from B.

Comparative Negligence

Despite the rationale that disallows contributory negligence as a defense to strict liability, some States apply the doctrine of comparative negligence to some types of strict liability, in particular, products liability.

Assumption of Risk

Voluntary assumption of risk *is* a defense to an action based upon strict liability. If the owner of an automobile knowingly and voluntarily parks the vehicle in a blasting zone, he may not recover for harm to his automobile. The assumption of risk, however, must be voluntary. If blasting operations are established, the possessor of nearby land is not required to move away and may recover for harm suffered.

CASES

Violation of Statute

VANCE v. UNITED STATES

United States District Court, D. Alaska, 1973.
355 F.Supp. 756.

PLUMMER, C. J.

    This case comes before the court on defendant's second motion for summary judgment. Plaintiff is seeking recovery in this action for injuries to John C. Vance and his dependents resulting from injuries sustained by Mr. Vance while he was intoxicated. Plaintiff's action is brought against the United States under the Federal Tort Claims Act,

[citation], on the theory that Mr. Vance was negligently served intoxicating liquors at the Non-Commissioned Officers' Club at Clear Air Force Station, Alaska.

           *   *   *

    It is necessary to begin with an examination of the effect on this case of A. S. [Alaska Statute] 04.15.020(a), which makes it a crime to give or sell liquor to minors or intoxicated persons. Plaintiff does not contend that this statute creates a new civil cause of action. [Citations.] Rather, plaintiff contends that this statute sets a minimum standard of care for purposes of the common law cause of action based upon ordinary negligence. That is, plaintiff is contending that a violation of this statute is negligence *per se.*

* * *

Under the Restatement rule [Sections 286 and 288], an unexcused violation of a statute or regulation is negligence in itself if the court adopts the statute as defining the conduct of a reasonable man. (If the statute is not so adopted, a violation may be considered as evidence of negligence.) The court may and usually must adopt the statute as the minimum standard of care if the purpose of the statute is at least in part: (a) to protect a class of persons which includes the one whose interest is invaded, and (b) to protect the particular interest which is invaded, and (c) to protect that interest against the kind of harm which has resulted, and (d) to protect that interest against the particular hazard from which the harm results.

Applying this test to the statute in question, it is clear that requirements (b), (c) and (d) are satisfied; the statute unquestionably is designed at least in part to protect against personal injuries caused by intoxication. The principal issue is whether requirement (a) is met; that is, whether the consumer himself is within the protected class.

* * *

Turning to the nub of the issue, it is apparent that, although the principal purpose of the statute may have been to protect innocent third parties from the negligence of an intoxicated consumer, the purpose at least in part was also to protect the consumer himself. If the consumer involved in this case were a minor rather than an alleged intoxicated person, it would be logical to conclude that the statute was enacted by the Legislature to protect minors. The statute does not purport to discriminate between minors and intoxicated persons and therefore it should logically follow that both are protected. Accordingly, the court adopts [the statute] as the minimum standard of conduct for defendant's agent in the present case.

* * *

In summary, the court holds as follows. Defendant had a duty to Mr. Vance to exercise reasonable care in dispensing intoxicants, and a breach of this duty may be found to have been the proximate cause of plaintiff's injuries. Such a breach occurred if defendant violated [the statute], but a breach may also be found if defendant failed to take additional reasonable precautions.

* * *

It is hereby ordered that defendant's second motion for summary judgment is denied.

Duty to Invitees

H. E. BUTT GROCERY CO. v. HAWKINS

Court of Civil Appeals of Texas, Corpus Christi, 1980.
594 S.W.2d 187.

NYE, C. J.

This is a slip-and-fall * * * case. Lucille Hawkins brought suit against defendant, H. E. Butt Grocery Company, for personal injuries she allegedly sustained when she slipped and fell in the defendant's grocery store in Bay City, Matagorda County, Texas. After hearing evidence, the trial judge overruled defendant's [motion for verdict] * * *, and this appeal resulted.

* * *

In a slip-and-fall suit, such as the one that is before us, the plaintiff must establish that: 1) the defendant placed the substance on the floor; or 2) the defendant knew that the substance was on the floor and willfully or negligently failed to remove it; or 3) the substance had been on the floor for such a period of time that it would have been discovered and removed by defendant in the exercise of ordinary care. [Citations.]

Plaintiff testified by deposition that she entered the H. E. B. store at approximately 3:30 or 3:35 p. m. on the occasion in question. She described the door which opened automatically and stated in essence that she had taken approximately one or two steps off of the mat which was located on the inside of the store next to the door when she slipped and fell in some rain water that had accumulated there. The water on the floor was approximately one-half inch deep and covered approximately two feet of floor space. Plaintiff testified that she did not see anything on the floor until she fell. It was undisputed that she was injured as a result of her fall.

Kaiser, the manager on duty at the time plaintiff fell, testified in substance that he was aware that the combination of a heavy rainfall and a North wind, on prior occasions, had caused water to be tracked into the store by customers and had caused water to be blown through the door as it opened and to accumulate in dangerous quantities on the floor near the door mat inside. He further testified to the effect that: 1) such weather conditions existed on the day in question; 2) water accumulated so rapidly that he and another employee had to mop the floor in that area at least four or five times during the hour or so immediately preceding the time plaintiff fell; 3) at the time of each mopping, several minutes were required to remove such accumulation and 4) he spent about the same amount of time to remove the water which had accumulated when he mopped the floor immediately after plaintiff fell. Kaiser testified specifically:

Q. Did it surprise you that someone fell at that time?
A. No.
Q. I am sorry?
A. No, sir.
Q. It didn't surprise?
A. No, sir.

Kaiser also testified concerning his knowledge of the short length of time required for the water to accumulate under the particular weather conditions then existing. Kaiser admitted that no signs were erected to warn store patrons of the wet condition of the floor, nor was anybody posted at the door to tell people there was a water hazard. He stated that "we usually kept it (the water) mopped up."

Appellant, as an occupier of premises, had the duty to use ordinary care to keep its premises in a reasonable safe condition for its invitees or to warn them of the hazard. [Citations.] What constitutes a hazard or danger depends upon the facts or circumstances of each case. As stated by our Supreme Court in [citation]:

Whether a condition constitutes a danger is a function of reasonableness. That is, if the ordinarily prudent man could foresee that harm was a likely result of a condition, then it is a danger.

[Citation.]

We are of the opinion that the direct and circumstantial evidence adduced at the * * * hearing was sufficient for the able trial judge (sitting as a fact finder) to conclude that, at the time of plaintiff's fall, defendant's employees knew or should have known that water was present and continuing to accumulate on the floor, and they negligently failed to remove the water.

The trial court's order * * * is affirmed.

Res Ipsa Loquitur

UZDAVINES v. METROPOLITAN BASEBALL CLUB, INC.

Civil Court of the City of New York, Queens County, 1982.
115 Misc.2d 343, 454 N.Y.S.2d 238.

HENTEL, J.

[The plaintiff, Marie Uzdavines, was struck on the head by a foul ball while she was watching defendant, the Metropolitan Baseball Club, play against the Philadelphia Phillies. The ball came through a hole in the screen which protects spectators who are behind the home plate. The screen in front of the plaintiff contained several holes which had been repaired with baling wire, a lighter weight wire than that used in the original screen. Although the manager of the stadium makes no formal inspections of the screen, his employees do try to repair the holes as they find them. These holes are generally caused by weather conditions, rust deterioration, and baseballs hitting the screen. The owner of the stadium, the City of New York, leases the stadium to the defendant and replaces the entire screen every two years. Plaintiff sued defendant for negligence under the *res ipsa loquitur* doctrine.]

Defendant's motion to set aside the verdict fixing defendant's liability under the doctrine of *res ipsa loquitur* presents an issue of apparent first impression under this particular set of facts. The court must undertake an analysis of the duty owned to plaintiff by defendant, and once having established that, seek to determine whether this duty supports a finding of "*exclusive control*" under the *res ipsa loquitur* doctrine. Only an affirmative answer to this query will support the jury's finding of liability. Fortunately, guidance is furnished as to the duty of care owed to baseball game spectators by our state's highest court.

In *Akins v. Glens Falls City School Dist.*, [citation], * * * the Court of Appeals chose to adopt the majority rule and set it forth as follows:

We hold that, in the exercise of reasonable care, the proprietor of a ball park need only provide screening for the area of the field behind home plate where the danger of being struck by a ball is the greatest * * * In * * * providing adequate protection in the most dangerous area of the field for those spectators who wish to avail themselves of it, a proprietor fulfills its duty of reasonable care under such circumstances. [Citation.]

* * *

The Court adopts the position that professional sports teams charging admission to assigned seats cannot shirk responsibility for personal injury, nor deny a duty to keep structures free from defects. They must be held to a standard of reasonable care at a minimum. [Citation.]

The Court believes that a duty has clearly been imposed on "The Mets" via the *Akins* decision. It is equally well-settled that even where one has no duty to plaintiff, but assumes a duty and chooses to perform, he is then under an affirmative duty to use reasonable care to see that the instrumentality provided, or acts done, are safe for the purpose for which they were to be used. [Citation.]

The testimony reveals that "The Mets," through its responsible employees, did notice and repair holes which developed in the safety screen in the ordinary course of events. The law requires that such repairs be done in a non-negligent manner. Thus, the Court finds that "The Mets" had a duty to provide protected seating, consonant to its duty to use reasonable care; and to keep the people seated in the area behind home plate free from foreseeable danger, because of the duty imposed upon it as *primary user* of the ball field, the benefits obtained by it from its use, and the reliance of the public on the safety of seats behind home plate, generally.

* * *

The more complex question before the Court involves whether there is a legal basis for a verdict of negligence under the theory of *res ipsa loquitur*. * * *

The elements of *res ipsa loquitur*, having been set forth many times by our courts, are well known:

(1) the event must be of a kind which ordinarily does not occur in the absence of someone's negligence;
(2) it must be caused by an agency or instrumentality within the *exclusive control* of the defendant; (*emphasis added*)
(3) it must not be due to any voluntary action or contribution on the part of the plaintiff; and
(4) evidence as to the true explanation of the event must be more readily accessible to the defendant than to plaintiff. [Citation.]

There is no question that requirements (1), (3), and (4) have been met by plaintiff.

The words *"exclusive control,"* however, have been the subject of much interpretation. The trend evident to this Court is that *"The requirement of exclusive possession and control is not an absolutely rigid concept."* [Citation.]

* * *

"Reliance on *res ipsa* would not require plaintiff to establish exclusive control over the (instrumentality) but merely a degree of domination sufficient to identify defendant with probability as the party responsible for plaintiff's injuries * * *" [Citation.]

* * *

The court finds that defendant, by its own testimony, has admitted either exclusive or at least joint control of the safety screen in fact as interpreted under the law. Both "The Mets" and the City of New York owed an independent duty to a spectator, and indeed a heightened duty arising out of the dangers reasonably to be anticipated from extending an invitation to the public to sit in the most dangerous area of the stadium. This duty mandates that "The Mets" exercise strict control of the screen, assuring the public that they may rely on the implied safety of sitting in that area.

Considering all the circumstances, the indicia of sole, joint, or concurrent dominion or control over the safety nets to qualify for the application of the *res ipsa* doctrine are compelling: * * *

Accordingly, on this record, the jury was free to conclude logically that defendant was at all times under a duty to maintain and control the protective screening for the safety of plaintiff who has purchased a ticket seating her behind the safety screen, thereby causing her to rely on its protection; and the injury from a foul ball was an accident that would not have occurred in the absence of defendant's negligence.

Thus, the Court denies defendant's motion to set aside the jury's verdict under the doctrine of *res ipsa loquitur.*

Proximate Cause

PALSGRAF v. LONG ISLAND RAILROAD CO.

Court of Appeals of New York, 1928.
248 N.Y. 339, 162 N.E. 99.

CARDOZO, C. J.

Plaintiff was standing on a platform of defendant's railroad after buying a ticket to go to Rockaway Beach. A train stopped at the station, bound for another place. Two men ran forward to catch it. One of the men reached the platform of the car without mishap, though the train was already moving. The other man, carrying a package, jumped aboard the car, but seemed unsteady as if about to fall. A guard on the car, who had held the door open, reached forward to help him in, and another guard on the platform pushed him from behind. In this act, the package was dislodged, and fell upon the rails. It was a package of small size, about fifteen inches long, and was covered by a newspaper. In fact it contained fireworks, but there was nothing in its appearance to give notice of its contents. The fireworks when they fell exploded. The shock of the explosion threw down some scales at the other end of the platform many feet away. The scales struck the plaintiff, causing injuries for which she sues.

The conduct of the defendant's guard, if a wrong in its relation to the holder of the package, was not a wrong in its relation to the plaintiff, standing far away. Relatively to her it was not negligence at all. Nothing in the situation gave notice that the falling package had in it the potency of peril to persons thus removed. Negligence is not actionable unless it involves the invasion of a legally protected interest, the violation of a right. "Proof of negligence in the air, so to speak, will not do." [Citations.] "Negligence is the absence of care, according to the circumstances." [Citations.]

* * *

If no hazard was apparent to the eye of ordinary vigilance, an act innocent and harmless, at least to outward seeming, with reference to her, did not take to itself the quality of a tort because it happened to be a wrong, though apparently not one involving the risk of bodily insecurity, with reference to someone else. "In every instance, before negligence can be predicated of a given act, back of the act must be sought and found a duty to the individual complaining, the observance of which would have averted or avoided the injury." [Citations.]

* * *

A different conclusion will involve us, and swiftly too, in a maze of contradictions. A guard stumbles over a package which has been left upon a platform. It seems to be a bundle of newspapers. It turns out to be a can of dynamite. To the eye of ordinary vigilance, the bundle is abandoned waste, which may be kicked or trod on with impunity. Is a passenger at the other end of the platform protected by the law against the unsuspected hazard concealed beneath the waste? If not, is the result to be any different, so far as the distant passenger is concerned, when the guard stumbles over a valise which a truckman or a porter has left upon the walk? The passenger far away, if the victim of a wrong at all, has a cause of action, not derivative, but original and primary. His claim to be protected against invasion of his bodily security is neither greater nor less because the act resulting in the invasion is a wrong to another far removed. In this case, the rights that are said to have been violated, the interests said to have been invaded, are not even of the same order. The man was not injured in his person nor even put in danger. The purpose of the act, as well as its effect, was to make his person safe. If there was a wrong to him at all, which may very well be doubted, it was a wrong to a property interest only, the safety of his package. Out of this wrong to property, which threatened injury to nothing else, there has passed, we are told, to the plaintiff by derivation or succession a right of action for the invasion of an interest of another order,

the right to bodily security. The diversity of interests emphasizes the futility of the effort to build the plaintiff's right upon the basis of a wrong to someone else. * * * One who jostles one's neighbor in a crowd does not invade the rights of others standing at the outer fringe when the unintended contact casts a bomb upon the ground. The wrongdoer as to them is the man who carries the bomb, not the one who explodes it without suspicion of the danger. Life will have to be made over, and human nature transformed, before prevision so extravagant can be accepted as the norm of conduct, the customary standard to which behavior must conform.

* * *

The judgment of the Appellate Division and that of the Trial Term should be reversed, and the complaint dismissed, with costs in all courts.

Proximate Cause

PETITION OF KINSMAN TRANSIT CO.

United States Court of Appeals, Second Circuit, 1964.
338 F.2d 708.

FRIENDLY, J.

[The MacGilvray Shiras was a ship owned by the Kinsman Transit Company. During the winter months when Lake Erie was frozen, the ship and others moored at docks on the Buffalo River. As oftentimes happened, one night an ice jam disintegrated upstream, sending large chunks of ice downward. Chunks of ice began to pile up against the Shiras which at that time was without power and manned only by a shipman. The ship broke loose when a negligently constructed "deadman" to which one mooring cable was attached pulled out of the ground. The "deadman" was operated by Continental Grain Company. The ship began moving down the S-shaped river stern first and struck another ship, the Tewksbury. The Tewksbury also broke loose from its mooring, and the two ships floated down the river together. Although the crew manning the Michigan Avenue Bridge downstream had been notified of the runaway ships, they failed to raise the bridge in time to avoid the collision because of a mixup in the shift changeover. As a result, both ships crashed into the bridge and were wedged against the bank of the river. The two vessels substantially dammed the flow of the river, causing ice and water to back up and flood installations as far as three miles upstream. The injured parties brought this action for damages against Kinsman, Continental, and the City of Buffalo.]

The very statement of the case suggests the need for considering *Palsgraf v. Long Island RR.*, [citation], and the closely related problem of liability for unforeseeable consequences.

* * *

We see little similarity between the Palsgraf case and the situation before us. The point of Palsgraf was that the appearance of the newspaper-wrapped package gave no notice that its dislodgement could do any harm save to itself and those nearby, and this by impact, perhaps with consequent breakage, and not by explosion. In contrast, a ship insecurely moored in a fast flowing river is a known danger not only to herself but to the owners of all other ships and structures downriver, and to persons upon them. No one would dream of saying that a shipowner who "knowingly and willfully" failed to secure his ship at a pier on such a river "would not have threatened" persons and owners of property downstream in some manner. The shipowner and the wharfinger in this case having thus owed a duty of care to all within the reach of the ship's known destructive power, the impossibility of advance identification of the particular person who would be hurt is without legal consequences. [Citations.] Similarly the foreseeable consequences of the City's failure to raise the bridge were not limited to the Shiras and the Tewksbury. Collision plainly created a danger that the bridge towers might fall onto adjoining property, and the crash of

two uncontrolled lake vessels, one 425 feet and the other 525 feet long, into a bridge over a swift ice-ridden stream, with a channel only 177 feet wide, could well result in a partial damming that would flood property upstream.

* * *

All the claimants here met the Palsgraf requirement of being persons to whom the actors owed a "duty of care," * * *. But this does not dispose of the alternative argument that the manner in which several of the claimants were harmed, particularly by flood damage, was unforeseeable and that recovery for this may not be had—whether the argument is put in the forth-right form that unforeseeable damages are not recoverable or is concealed under a formula of lack of "proximate cause."

So far as concerns the City, the argument lacks factual support. Although the obvious risks from not raising the bridge were damage to itself and to the vessels the danger of a fall of the bridge and of flooding would not have been unforeseeable under the circumstances to anyone who gave them thought. And the same can be said as to the failure of Kinsman's shipkeeper to ready the anchors after the danger had become apparent. * * *

Continental's position on the facts is stronger. It was indeed foreseeable that the improper construction and lack of inspection of the "deadman" might cause a ship to break loose and damage persons and property on or near the river—that was what made Continental's conduct negligent. With the aid of hindsight one can also say that a prudent man, carefully pondering the problem, would have realized that the danger of this would be greatest under such water conditions as developed during the night of January 21, 1959, and that if a vessel should break loose under those circumstances, events might transpire as they did. But such *post hoc* step by step analysis would render "foreseeable" almost anything that has in fact occurred; if the argument relied upon has legal validity, it ought not be circumvented by characterizing as foreseeable what almost no one would in fact have foreseen at the time.

* * *

Foreseeability of danger is necessary to render conduct negligent; where as here the damage was caused by just those forces whose existence required the exercise of greater care than was taken—the current, the ice, and the physical mass of the Shiras, the incurring of consequences other and greater than foreseen does not make the conduct less culpable or provide a reasoned basis for insulation. [Citation.] The oft encountered argument that failure to limit liability to foreseeable consequences may subject the defendant to a loss wholly out of proportion to his fault seems scarcely consistent with the universally accepted rule that the defendant takes the plaintiff as he finds him and will be responsible for the full extent of the injury even though a latent susceptibility of the plaintiff renders this far more serious than could reasonably have been anticipated. [Citation.]

The weight of authority in this country rejects the limitation of damages to consequences foreseeable at the time of the negligent conduct when the consequences are "direct," and the damage, although other and greater than expectable, is of the same general sort that was risked.

* * *

Here it is surely more equitable that the losses from the operators' negligent failure to raise the Michigan Avenue Bridge should be ratably borne by Buffalo's taxpayers than left with the innocent victims of the flooding; yet the mind is also repelled by a solution that would impose liability solely on the City and exonerate the persons whose negligent acts of commission and omission were the precipitating force of the collision with the bridge and its sequelae. We go only so far as to hold that where, as here, the damages resulted from the same physical forces whose existence required the exercise of greater care than was displayed and were of the same general sort that was expectable, unforeseeability of the exact developments and of the ex-

tent of the loss will not limit liability. Other fact situations can be dealt with when they arise.

* * *

[Judgment for plaintiffs.]

Assumption of Risk

FALGOUT v. WARDLAW

Court of Appeal of Louisiana, Second Circuit, 1982.
423 So.2d 707.

MARVIN, J.

Ms. Falgout appeals a judgment rejecting her demands for personal injury damages arising out of her fall on a partially decked pier on Lake Bistineau.

The factual and legal issues relate to the trial court's finding that Ms. Falgout's recovery was barred by her fault. We affirm.

The pier is supported by posts or pilings * * *. Each pair of posts is about six feet from the next pair. Ms. Falgout was the social guest of defendant William Wardlaw, who partially decked the pier and frequented the camp with the tacit permission of his brother, Glenn, who owned the once community camp and began construction of the pier. Glenn Wardlaw and his wife, divorced co-owner, were also made defendants in this action.

Ms. Falgout accompanied William to the camp on a Saturday afternoon, arriving there from Shreveport about 3:30 p. m. After the two had consumed an eight-pack of "little" beers purchased on the way to the camp, Ms. Falgout also drank some vodka she found in the kitchen of the camp, according to William. While it was still daylight about 7:00 p. m., Ms. Falgout, with a drink in hand, went with William outside the camp while he checked on the camp utilities. William says that he told her not to go on the pier and that she told him, "don't tell me what to do, ... [I have] walked on every pier on Lake Bistineau . . . . ."

William said that Ms. Falgout went all the way to the end of the pier and sat there. Ms. Falgout was returning toward the camp when she fell near post four. William said that after she got on the pier he told her not to go past where the boards were close together ($^{25}/_{32}$ inch spacing between posts one and three almost to post four). In any event Ms. Falgout says that her shoe "got caught between two boards under a board . . ." and she fell, suspended by her foot with her head and arms in the water. She suffered serious injuries to her knee and leg.

William, who at one time went on the pier . . . by this time was back on the ground and heard, but did not see, Ms. Falgout hit the water. He went to her aid and later helped her obtain medical attention.

Notwithstanding that the trial court found the pier, because of its partially constructed state, to be defective and to pose an unreasonable risk of harm to anyone who might walk on it, Ms. Falgout's demands were rejected because the circumstances constituted [plaintiff fault.]

* * *

As a defense to * * * liability, [plaintiff] fault in some circumstances may encompass either or both assumption of the risk and contributory negligence * * *.

Knowledge is the mainstay of assumption of risk and is imputed to a plaintiff, not because he was in a position to make observations, but only when he actually made the observations and it is found that plaintiff should reasonably have known that a particular risk existed. [Citation.] Assumption of risk is a subjective inquiry. [Citation.]

Contributory negligence is conduct which falls below the reasonable man standard and is determined by objective inquiry on a case to case basis. As a defense to liability, it is applied only where the policy considerations imposing the liability on the defendant in the first place are not present, such as where the defendant's conduct is not ultra hazardous, not abnormally dangerous, is not that of a manufacturer whose product causes injury, and is not commercial in the sense that it is designed to render a profit. Where these policy considerations are not present, [plaintiff] fault includes contributory negligence. [Ci-

tation.] Some circumstances which may not constitute assumption of risk, may constitute contributory negligence. [Citation.]

Here Ms. Falgout was told by her host not to go on the pier and, after she was on it, she was effectively told not to walk on the area where the decking boards were widely spaced. She had knowledge and, having traversed the pier to its end, she admittedly observed the variance in spacing of the decking. She was returning to the safer area where the decking was more closely and uniformly spaced when her foot or shoe got caught. The trial court's conclusions that she *saw* and *understood* the risk are supported by competent evidence which the trial court could believe. We find no error in the ultimate conclusion that Ms. Falgout assumed the risk because she *observed* and she was effectively told of the risk. Under these circumstances she should reasonably have known of the existence of the particular risk of getting her foot or her shoe caught in the wider spacing. [Citation.]

These circumstances also constitute contributory negligence. [Citation.] The defendants here were not engaged in an ultra hazardous or abnormally dangerous activity and were not engaged in a commercial enterprise. While the Wardlaw brothers manufactured or constructed the partially completed pier, they cannot be deemed to have been manufacturers of a product to gain a profit. The policy considerations or factors which impose strict liability to which contributory negligence is not a defense are sorely lacking and, in such circumstances, contributory negligence is encompassed in the defense of [plaintiff] fault. [Citation.]

[Judgment for defendant affirmed.]

Keeping of Animals

ALLEN v. WHITEHEAD

Supreme Court of Alabama, 1982.
423 So.2d 835.

PER CURIAM.

On November 22, 1978, David Allen, then two years old, was playing on a porch at the

Allen residence when a dog attacked him. The dog that bit David was later identified as the dog which had taken up at the home of Whitehead, the defendant and appellee herein, approximately one and a half years prior to the incident in question. As a result of the attack, David suffered facial cuts, a severed muscle in his left eye, a hole in his left ear, and scarring over his forehead.

After the attack, the dog was picked up by the Humane Society and placed in quarantine. Whitehead subsequently had the dog placed in a private veterinary clinic, from which the dog allegedly escaped. Following the dog's escape, David underwent rabies treatment. Whitehead later found the dog and placed it in another veterinary hospital for the duration of the quarantine period.

On July 10, 1981, David, through his father, appellant herein, filed a complaint against Whitehead, the alleged owner of the dog. The complaint alleged that "as a proximate result of defendant's negligence and violation of various state and municipal ordinances plaintiff's child was injured . . . ." On November 5, 1981, Whitehead filed an affidavit and a motion for summary judgment based on the ground that there was no genuine issue as to whether Whitehead had any reason to believe his dog had vicious propensities at the time of the attack.

A hearing on the motion for summary judgment was scheduled for December 10, 1981.* * *

On December 22, 1981, the trial court granted Whitehead's motion for summary judgment and, further, dismissed plaintiff's amended complaint. We affirm the trial court's order granting summary judgment directed to the claim in appellant's original complaint and reverse the trial court's order dismissing the claims of Appellant's amended complaint.

This court in *Kershaw v. McKown*, [citation], reiterated the common law rule that the owner of a dog is not liable for acts of the dog unless the owner had knowledge of the vicious propensities of the dog that resulted in the injury complained of. In *McCullar v. Williams*, [citation], the court stated,

"[p]revious knowledge of the animal's vicious habits must be alleged and proved," although positive proof is not always necessary. [Citation.] This court held in *Owen v. Hampson*, [citation], that the common law rule was still applicable in Alabama: * * * that previous knowledge of the animal's dangerous propensity, whether it be shown by positive proof or inferred from the circumstances, must be alleged and proved.

* * *

Appellant Allen asserts that there is a genuine issue of material fact relating to the alleged vicious propensities of the dog and the knowledge of appellee as to such propensities. Our examination of the record in its factual context reveals the following. In answers to interrogatories propounded by appellee, appellant stated in substance that (1) the dog was large and mean looking and frequently barked at neighbors; (2) the dog was allowed to run wild; and (3) the dog frequently chased cars and barked at them. On the other hand, appellee, by way of affidavit and also in answers to interrogatories propounded by appellant to him, in effect, stated: (1) the dog was friendly and "enjoyed" playing with his children and other children in the neighborhood; (2) appellee had never received any complaints from anyone nor had any reason to believe that the dog represented any kind of threat to anyone; (3) there was nothing aggressive or threatening about the dog's manner or behavior, but on the contrary, his disposition was quiet and gentle, and the dog was affectionate and enjoyed being petted; and (4) that to the best of the knowledge and belief of appellee, the dog had never bitten anyone prior to the instance in question. Appellee admitted that the dog was not confined.

Considering the evidence submitted to the trial court on appellee's motion for summary judgment most favorably to appellant, the nonmoving party, we cannot find that there existed a genuine issue of material fact. Accordingly, we hold as a matter of law that evidence that a dog was large and mean looking, chased and barked at cars, and frequently barked at neighbors is not sufficient to present an issue of fact as to the dangerous propensities of such an animal.

In support of his contention that Whitehead had notice of the dog's dangerous propensities, appellant also points out that Whitehead had admitted in an affidavit that the dog had a playful nature. * * *

* * * In his treatise, Professor Prosser has also stated that notice of the character of the animal "must extend to the trait or propensity which caused the damage." [Citation.] Accordingly, notice of an animal's playful character is not notice that it will viciously attack and bite a person. Liability is limited to the particular risk known to the defendant.

In *Owen v. Hampson*, [citation], the defendant's dog ran out and overturned plaintiff's motorcycle while plaintiff was riding on a public street. This court stated that the law makes no distinction between an animal dangerous from playfulness and one dangerous from viciousness, but places on the owner a burden of restraint when he knows of the animal's dangerous propensities. [Citation.] The crucial issue remains whether the owner knows or has reason to know of the animal's dangerous propensities. This is not a case where the plaintiff was knocked down or injured in a manner traditionally associated with an overly friendly dog. The claim and the evidence is that David was attacked and bitten. Knowledge of an animal's playfulness would not provide sufficient notice that the dog would be likely to act in the harmful manner alleged in this incident.

* * *

* * * The Court concludes that the order dismissing the amended complaint is due to be reversed and the cause remanded for consideration of the claims stated in the amended complaint.

The judgment appealed from, therefore, is affirmed in part, and reversed in part, and the cause remanded.

PROBLEMS

1. A statute, which requires railroads to fence their tracks, is construed as intended solely to prevent injuries to animals straying onto the right of way who may be hit by trains. B. & A. Railroad Company fails to fence its tracks. Two of C's cows wander onto the track. Nellie is hit by a train. Elsie is poisoned by weeds growing beside the track. For which cows, if any, is B. & A. Railroad liable to C? Why?

2. Martha invites John to come to lunch. Martha knows that her private road is dangerous to travel, having been guttered by recent rains. She doesn't warn John of the condition, reasonably believing that he will notice the gutters and exercise sufficient care. John's attention, while driving over, is diverted from the road by the screaming of his child, who has been stung by a bee. He fails to notice the condition of the road, hits a gutter, and skids into a tree. If John is not contributorily negligent, is Martha liable to John?

3. N is run over by a car and left lying in the street. Samaritan Sam, seeing N's helpless state, places him in his car for the purpose of taking him to the hospital. Sam drives negligently into a ditch, causing additional injury to N. Is Sam liable to N?

4. Led Foot drives his car carelessly into another car. The second car contains dynamite which Led had no way of knowing. The collision causes an explosion which shatters a window of a building half a block away on another street. The flying glass inflicts serious cuts on Sally, who is working at a desk near the window. The explosion also harms Vic Jones, who is walking on the sidewalk near the point of the collision. Toward whom is Led Foot negligent?

5. A statute requires all vessels traveling on the Great Lakes to provide lifeboats. One of W Steamship Company's boats is sent out of port without a lifeboat. P, a sailor, falls overboard in a storm so heavy that had there been a lifeboat it could

not have been launched. P drowns. Is W liable to P's estate?

6. L is negligently driving an automobile at excessive speed. R's negligently driven car crosses the center line of the highway and scrapes the side of L's car, damaging its fenders. As a result L loses control of his car, which goes into the ditch, where L's car is wrecked and L suffers personal injuries. What, if anything, can L recover?

7. (a) E, the owner of a baseball park, is under a duty to the entering public to provide a reasonably sufficient number of screened seats to protect those who desire it against the risk if being hit by batted balls. E fails to do so. F, a customer entering the park, is unable to find a screened seat and, although fully aware of the risk, sits in an unscreened seat. F is struck and injured by a batted ball. Is E liable?

(b) G, F's wife, has just arrived from Germany and is viewing baseball for the first time. Without asking any questions, she follows F to a seat. After the batted ball hits F, it caroms into G, injuring her. Is E liable to G?

8. CC Railroad is negligent in failing to give warning of the approach of its train to a crossing, and thereby endangers L, a blind man who is about to cross. M, a bystander, in a reasonable effort to save L, rushes onto the track to push L out of danger. Although M acts as carefully as possible, she is struck and injured by the train.

(a) Can M recover from L?

(b) Can M recover from CC Railroad?

9. S, constructing a building, operates pile-driving machinery that causes excessive vibrations abnormally dangerous to buildings in the vicinity. Cy, in an adjoining building, is conducting scientific experiments with extremely delicate instruments. Although the vibration causes no other harm to Cy or to the building, it ruins the instruments and prevents the experiments. Is S liable for the harm caused Cy?

10. T keeps a pet chimpanzee, which is thoroughly tamed and accustomed to playing with its owner's children. The chimpanzee escapes, despite every precaution to keep it upon its owner's premises. It approaches a group of children. W, the mother of one of the children, erroneously thinking the chimpanzee is about to attack the children rushes to her child's assistance; and in her hurry and excitement, she stumbles and falls, breaking her leg. Can W recover for her personal injuries?

Part Two—Contracts

PUBLIC POLICY AND SOCIAL ISSUES

IN examining Part Two, Contracts, it should be recognized that contract law has undergone—and is still undergoing—enormous changes. In the nineteenth century virtually absolute autonomy in forming contracts was the rule. As the noted legal scholar Samuel Williston wrote: "Economic writers adopted the same line of thought. Adam Smith, Ricardo, Bentham and John Stuart Mill successfully insisted on freedom of bargaining as the fundamental and indispensable requisite of progress; and imposed their theories on the educational thought of their times with a thoroughness not common in economic speculation." Williston, Freedom of Contract, 6 *Cornell L.Q.* 365, 366 (1921). Accordingly, contract liability was imposed only where the parties strictly complied with the required formalities. The same principle also dictated that once a contract was formed it should be enforced according to its terms and neither party should be lightly excused from performance.

This view was consistent with the then dominant philosophy of governmental *laissez-faire*. As Professor Friedmann has explained it, "[t]he idea that the state on behalf of the community should intervene to dictate or alter terms of contracts in the public interest, is, on the whole, alien to the classical theory of common-law contract." W. Friedmann, *Law in a Changing Society*, 123 (2d ed. 1972). Consequently, the watchword of the day was *caveat emptor*—let the buyer beware. The following excerpt further describes the nineteenth century doctrines as well as outlining the social forces and policies that have brought about the decline of these earlier doctrines:

The general principle that the buyer should and could look after himself had its roots in the idea that a system of robust trading was a good system in which the final outcome with respect to resource allocation and income distribution was desirable. This attitude was itself supported by three ideas. The value judgment was widespread that if a fool and his money were soon parted then that was no more than was to be expected and was 'right': just as a tone-deaf person could not expect a career as a professional musician, so a fool could not expect to engage in other than foolhardy actions. The second idea which consolidated the *caveat emptor* approach was the Adam Smith argument that a free market led to the best resource use. The third idea, running parallel to the second, was that if a buyer and seller made a 'contract' then, save for such cases as overt fraud, that contract was sacred.

If contracts, voluntarily entered into, were not going to be supported by the courts, then it was believed that fewer people would trade and so there would be less benefit from specialization and division of labour. This whole system of ideas seemed to be interlocking whole—and what is more a sensible way of running society, for it was also consistent with the notion of individual freedom and individual responsibility.

This system of values thus gave a low priority to consumer protection. The rising role of consumer protection law is an example of the point that—whatever lawyers claim—the law is not an immutable system but manmade. Changes in the law are largely the result of men perceiving the world differently from hitherto.

A least four reasons may be found for the rise of consumer protection law and the associated consumer lobbies. First, *caveat emptor* makes much sense in a primitive society where there is little trade but much self-reliance within the family and the village and what trade there is concerns goods such as farm produce where both buyer and seller might be equally knowledgeable. The buyer at the occasional fair or market would indeed be expected to take care, since he might never see the itinerant seller again. In many cases, the value of the sale would in any event be less than the likely transaction costs of going to court.

The twentieth-century consumer lives in a very different world. A far greater proportion of the family consumption of goods and services is bought and the average consumer is at some disadvantage compared to the retailer and manufacturer of electrical goods, consumer durables, and so forth—*that is, information is asymmetrically distributed*. This means that the concept of a bargain struck between equals is quite inappropriate and so, as in the case of monopoly legislation, attempts are made to defend the weaker party against any unfortunate outcomes of the bargains into which he freely enters—because he may have entered them innocently. It should be said that in many trivial transactions the costs of going to court far outweigh the losses and so many breaches of the letter or the spirit of the law go unpunished. The disgruntled shopper simply takes his business elsewhere in future.

If one reason for the attack on *caveat emptor* is because the world is more complex, and the distribution of information and bargaining power unequal, a second reason is that free market systems have come to be seen, at least technically, as not necessarily leading to the optimal use of resources. A third reason is that the value judgement implicit in the 'devil take the hindmost' attitude to the parting of a fool from his money is now much less widely held. People are commonly seen as the products of their own history and environment rather than as responsible in any direct sense for their own foolhardiness. J. M. Oliver, *Law and Economics*, 82–83 (1979).

As a result of these forces contract law has experienced tremendous changes during this century. As will be discussed in the next ten chapters, many of the formalities of contract formation have been relaxed and today contractual obligations are usually recognized whenever the parties manifest an intent to be bound. In addition, an increasing number of promises are now enforced in the absence of consideration on the basis of reliance under the doctrine of promissory estoppel. While in the past contract liability was absolute and there were few, if any, escapes from liability once assumed, presently the law allows a party to be excused from contractual duties where fraud, duress, undue influence, mistake, un-

Today, the duty of good faith is imposed upon parties to a contract and the doctrine of unconscionability protects against grossly unfair dealings.

In brief, the twentieth century has left its mark on contract law by limiting the absolute freedom of contract and, at the same time, by relaxing the requirements of contract formation. The external, objective and formal contract model of the nineteenth century has been replaced by one that is more individualized, subjective and informal. Accordingly, it is accurate to say that now it is considerably easier to get into a contract and correspondingly less difficult to get out of one. Last century's narrow view of contract damages has been expanded to embrace equitable remedies and restitution as remedies for breach of contract. The older doctrines of privity of contract sharply restricting which parties could enforce contracts rights has given way to the current view that permits intended third party beneficiaries to sue in their own right. Earlier contract theory did not require good faith and fair dealing among contracting parties who dealt at arm's length. As Grant Gilmore noted:

It seems apparent to the twentieth century mind, as perhaps it did not to the nineteenth century mind, that a system in which everybody is invited to do his own thing, at whatever cost to his neighbor, must work ultimately to the benefit of the rich and powerful, who are in a position to look after themselves and to act, so to say, as their own self-insurers. As we look back on the nineteenth century theories, we are struck most of all, I think, by the narrow scope of social duty which they implicitly assumed. No man is his brother's keeper; the race is to the swift; let the devil take the hindmost. For good or ill, we have changed all that. We are now all cogs in a machine, each dependent on the other. The decline and fall of the general theory of contract and, in most quarters, of laissez-faire economics may be taken as remote reflections of the transition from nineteenth century individualism to the welfare state and beyond. Gilmore, *The Death of Contract*, 95–96 (1974).

Chapter 7

INTRODUCTION TO CONTRACTS

IT is impossible to over-estimate the importance of the contract in the field of business. Every business enterprise, whether large or small, must necessarily enter into contracts with its employees, its suppliers, and its customers in order to conduct its business operations. The study of contract law is, therefore, a most important subject for the business manager. Contract law is also significant in that it is basic to other fields of law which are treated in other parts of this book, such as agency, sales of personal property, commercial paper, and secured transactions.

Even the most common transaction may involve a multitude of contracts. In a typical contract for the sale of land, the seller promises to transfer title to the land, and the buyer promises to pay an agreed-upon purchase price. In addition, the seller may promise to pay certain taxes or assessments; the buyer may promise to assume a mortgage on the property or may promise to pay the purchase price to a creditor of the seller. A portion of the purchase price may consist of the buyer's check, which is a contract containing the buyer's written order to his bank to pay a sum certain in money. If the parties are represented by counsel, they very likely have contracts with their attorneys. If the seller deposits the proceeds of the sale in a bank, he enters into a contract with the bank. If the buyer leases the property, he enters into a contract with the tenant. When one of the parties leaves his car in a parking lot to attend to any of these matters, he assumes a contractual relationship with the proprietor of the lot. In short, nearly every business transaction is based upon contract and the expectations created by the agreed-upon promises.

It is a truism that law arises from social necessity. This is obviously true of the law of contracts. The vast and complicated institution known as business can be conducted efficiently and successfully only upon the certainty of fulfillment of promises. Business must have complete assurance with regard to supplies of raw materials or manufactured goods, as well as with respect to labor, management, capital, insurance, and so forth. Common experience has shown that promises based solely on personal honesty or integrity will not suffice. Such promises do not have the assurance and reliability which are essential to business. Hence the development of the law of contracts, which, briefly, is the law of enforceable promises. This branch of law, like all branches of business law, is the response of society to the needs of business. It is, therefore, essential to know what the law requires in order that a promise or set of promises be binding on the promisor.

DEVELOPMENT OF THE LAW OF CONTRACTS

Common Law

Contracts are primarily governed by State common law. An orderly presentation of this law is found in the Restatements of the Law of Contracts. The first Restatement was adopted and promulgated on May 6, 1932, by the American Law Institute. On May 17, 1979, the Institute adopted and promulgated a revised edition of the Restatement—the Restatement, Second, Contracts—which will be referred to as the Restatement. Selected provisions of the Restatement cited in the text are included in Appendix B of this book. For more than fifty years the Restatements have been regarded as a valuable authoritative reference work and extensively relied upon and quoted in reported judicial opinions.

The Uniform Commercial Code

The sale of personal property forms a substantial portion of commercial activity. Article 2 of the Uniform Commercial Code (the

Code or U.C.C.) governs sales in all States except Louisiana. (The U.C.C. is set forth in Appendix C of this text.) A sale is a contract involving the transfer of title to goods from a seller to a buyer for a price. Section 2–106. The Code essentially defines goods as tangible personal property. Section 2–105(1). **Personal property** is any type of property other than an interest in land. For example, the purchase of a television set, automobile, or textbook is considered a sale of goods. All such transactions are governed by Article 2 of the Code, but, where general contract law has not been specifically modified by the Code, the common law of contracts continues to apply. "Unless displaced by the particular provisions of this Act, the principles of law [including contract law] and equity shall supplement its provisions." Section 1–103. See Figure 7–1.

Types of Contracts Outside the Code

General contract law governs all contracts outside the scope of the Code. Such contracts play a significant role in commercial activities. For example, the Code does *not* apply to employment contracts, service contracts, insurance contracts, contracts involving **real property** (land and anything attached to it, including buildings), and contracts for the sale of intangibles such as patents and copyrights. These transactions continue to be governed by general contract law. See Figure 7–1.

DEFINITION OF A CONTRACT

Section 1 of the Restatement defines a contract as "a promise or a set of promises for the breach of which the law gives a remedy, or the performance of which the law in some way recognizes as a duty." "A promise is a manifestation of the intention to act or refrain from acting in a specified manner." Restatement, Section 2. Only those promises that meet *all* of the essential requirements of a binding contract will be enforced. All other

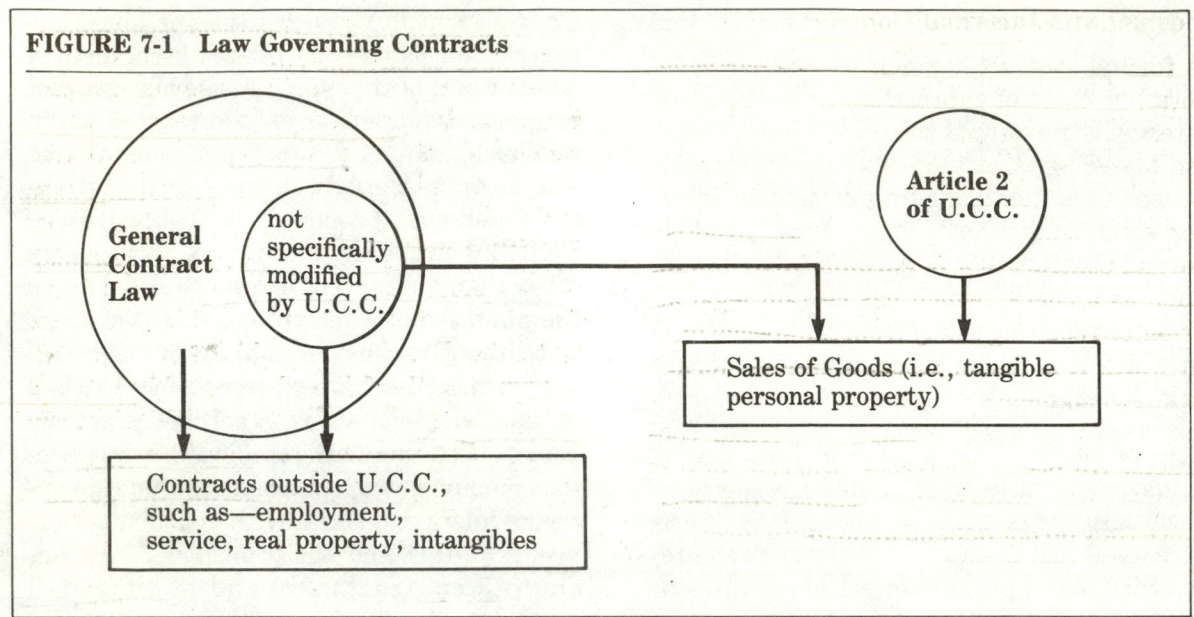

FIGURE 7-1 Law Governing Contracts

promises are *not* contractual and no legal remedy is available for a **breach** (a failure to properly perform) of these promises. Thus, a promise may be binding (contractual) or not binding (noncontractual). In other words, all contracts are promises, but not all promises are contracts.

For example, if A pays B $5,000 in return for B's promise to burn down C's factory, B's promise is noncontractual and not binding because it is for an illegal purpose. As a result, the law will not provide a remedy to B for A's failure to fulfill his promise. A is not under any contractual or legal obligation to perform his promise.

See Steinberg v. Chicago Medical School.

NATURE OF A CONTRACT

The true nature of a contract lies in the fact that it is not a physical thing, but a relationship existing between the parties to the contract. The elements of this relationship are the mutual rights and duties of the parties. It is true, of course, that where the terms of the contract are reduced to writing, the written instrument itself will be frequently re-ferred to as the contract. This, however, is done simply as a matter of convenience, and does not alter the fact that a contract is basically a certain type of legal relationship. The written instrument signed by the parties, the oral agreement spoken by the parties, or the conduct of the parties, as the case may be, constitute, not the contract itself, but simply the evidence of the contract. A contract is essentially a certain type of agreement or promise or set of promises. And contractual agreements and promises, while not physical realities, are nevertheless very important legal realities.

CLASSIFICATION OF CONTRACTS

Contracts have been classified from various standpoints such as their method of formation, their content, and their legal effect. The standard classifications are: (1) Formal and Informal Contracts; (2) Express and Implied Contracts; (3) Unilateral and Bilateral Contracts; (4) Void, Voidable, and Unenforceable Contracts; and (5) Executed and Executory Contracts.

Formal and Informal Contracts

A **formal** contract depends upon a particular form, or mode of expression, for its legal existence. For example, at common law a promise under **seal**, a particular symbol which serves to authenticate an instrument, is enforceable without anything more. Another formal contract is a **negotiable instrument**, such as a check, which has certain legal attributes resulting solely from the special form in which it is made. **Recognizances**, formal acknowledgments of indebtedness made in court, are another example of formal contracts. All other contracts, whether oral or written, are **informal** or simple contracts, since they do not depend upon mere formality for their legal validity.

Express and Implied Contracts

Parties to a contract may indicate their assent either by express language or by conduct which implies such willingness. Thus, a contract may be (1) entirely oral; (2) partly oral and partly written; (3) entirely written; (4) partly oral or written and partly implied from the conduct of the parties; and (5) wholly implied from the conduct of the parties. The first three are known as express contracts, and the last two as implied contracts. An **express** contract is therefore one in which all the terms have been definitely and specifically stated and agreed upon by the parties in oral or written language, or both. Nothing is left to implication.

An **implied** contract is one which is inferred, wholly or in part, from the parties' conduct and not from the expression of words. In an implied contract, the intention or promise of one or both parties is not definitely expressed in oral or written words, but is reasonably inferred from the conduct of the parties in relation to each other. Thus, if A orders and receives a meal in B's restaurant, a promise is implied on A's part to pay B the price stated in the menu, or B's customary price, as the case may be. Again, when one boards a bus as a passenger, a wholly implied contract is formed, by which the passenger undertakes to pay the customary fare, and the bus company undertakes to provide the passenger transportation to the extent of its facilities. In still another example, A telephones an order to B's store for certain goods, and B delivers the goods to A. Nothing is said by either party about the price or payment of the price. Clearly, however, B delivered the goods to A upon the implied intention and understanding that A would pay her the market price or the fair and reasonable value of the goods, as the case may be. It is equally obvious that the only reasonable interpretation of A's conduct in ordering the goods is an implied promise on his part to pay for them. These contracts are said to be **implied in fact**. This is simply another way of saying that it is implied from the facts and circumstances of the situation, that is, from the conduct and actions of the parties. It should be noted that both express and implied contracts are genuine contracts, equally enforceable. The difference between them is merely the manner in which assent is manifested. *See Richardson v. J. C. Flood Co.*

Unilateral and Bilateral Contracts

In the typical contractual transaction, each party makes at least one promise. For example, A says to B, "If you promise to mow my lawn, I will give you ten dollars," and B agrees to mow A's lawn. A and B have made mutual promises, each undertaking to do something in exchange for the promise of the other. When a contract comes into existence by the exchange of promises, each is under a duty to the other. This kind of contract is called **bilateral**, because each party is both a *promisor* (a person making a promise) and a *promisee* (the person to whom a promise is made).

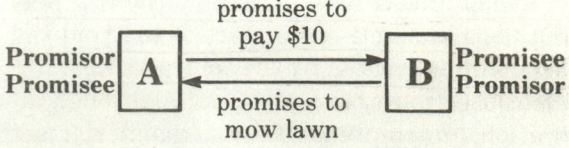

But suppose that only one of the parties makes a promise. A says to B, "If you will mow my lawn, I will give you ten dollars." A contract will be formed when B has finished mowing the lawn and not before. At that time A becomes contractually obligated to pay ten dollars to B. A's offer was in exchange for B's act of mowing the lawn, and not for a promise of B to mow it. B was under no duty to mow the lawn. This is a **unilateral** contract because only *one* of the parties made a promise.

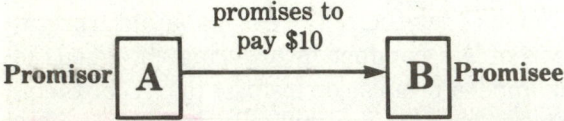

Thus, a bilateral contract results from the exchange of a promise for a return promise. A unilateral contract results from the exchange of a promise for an act or for a forbearance to act. Where it is not clear whether a unilateral or bilateral contract has been formed, the courts presume that the parties intended a bilateral contract. Thus, in the above example, if A says to B, "if you will mow my lawn, I will pay you ten dollars," and B replies, "O.K., I will mow your lawn," a bilateral contract is formed.

Void, Voidable, and Unenforceable Contracts

By definition a contract is an enforceable promise or agreement. Thus, a **void** contract is no contract at all. It is merely a promise or agreement which has no legal effect. An example of a void agreement is an agreement entered into by an *adjudicated* (judicially declared) incompetent.

A **voidable** contract, on the other hand, is not wholly lacking in legal effect. It is a contract, but because of the manner or method in which it was brought about, the law permits one or more of the parties to avoid the legal duties created by the contract. Restatement, Section 7. For instance, A through intentional misrepresentation of a material fact

(*fraud*) induces B to enter into a contract. B may, upon discovery of the fraud, notify A that by reason of the misrepresentation she will not perform her promise, and the law will support B. The contract induced by fraud is not void, but is voidable at the election of B, the defrauded party. A, the fraudulent party, has no such election.

A contract may be neither void nor voidable, yet may be unenforceable. An **unenforceable** contract is one for the breach of which the law does not provide a remedy. Restatement, Section 8. For example, a contract may be unenforceable because of a failure to satisfy the requirements of the Statute of Frauds, which requires certain kinds of contracts to be in writing in order to be enforceable. Also, the right to bring a lawsuit for breach of contract may be barred by running of the time within which such a suit may be filed, as provided in the Statute of Limitations. After the time period has run, the contract is referred to as unenforceable, rather than void or voidable.

Executed and Executory Contracts

These terms pertain to the state of performance of a contract. If a contract has been fully performed by all of the parties, it is an **executed** contract. Strictly, an executed contract is no contract in the present tense, as all duties under it have been performed, but it is useful to have a term for the completed contract. The word "executed" is also used to mean signed, as in to execute or sign a certain document. The term **executory** contract means unperformed and applies to situations where there are one or more unperformed promises by any party to the contract, or the contract is wholly unperformed by one or more of the parties. Thus, A and B make a contract under which A is to sell and deliver certain goods to B in ten days and B is to pay the agreed price in thirty days. Prior to the delivery of the goods by A on the tenth day, the contract is wholly executory. Upon A's delivery of the goods to B, the contract is executed as to A and executory as to B. When B duly pays for the goods the contract is wholly executed, and thereby completely fulfilled.

QUASI CONTRACTS

In addition to implied-in-fact contracts, there are **implied-in-law** contracts or **quasi contracts** which were not mentioned in the foregoing classification of contracts for the reason that a quasi (meaning "as if") contract is not a contract at all.

This is because it is not based either upon an express or an implied promise. For example, A by mistake delivers to B a plain, unaddressed envelope containing $100 intended for C. B is under no contractual obligation to return it. However, A is permitted to recover the $100 from B. The law imposes an obligation upon B in order to prevent his unjust enrichment at the expense of A.

One court has summarized the doctrine of quasi-contract in the following manner:

Quasi contracts are not contracts at all, although they give rise to obligations more akin to those stemming from contract than from tort. The contract is a mere fiction, a form imposed in order to adapt the case to a given remedy. . . . Briefly stated, a quasi-contractual obligation is one imposed by law where there has been no agreement or expression of assent, by word or act, on the part of either party involved. The law creates it, regardless of the intention of the parties, to assure a just and equitable result. *Bradkin v. Leverton*, 26 N.Y.2d 192, 309 N.Y.S.2d 192, 257 N.E.2d 643 (1970).

See also *Puttkammer v. Minth*.

ESSENTIALS OF A CONTRACT

The four essential ingredients of a binding promise are:

1. manifestation of mutual assent,
2. consideration,
3. legality of object, and
4. capacity of the parties.

In addition, in a limited number of instances, a contract must be in writing to be enforceable, although in most cases an oral contract is binding and enforceable. If all of these essentials are present, the promise is contractual and legally binding. If any of them is lacking, the promise is non-contractual. These essentials will be separately considered in succeeding chapters.

CASES

Definition and Essentials of a Contract

STEINBERG v. CHICAGO MEDICAL SCHOOL

Illinois Court of Appeals, 1976.
41 Ill.App.3d 804, 354 N.E.2d 586.

DEMPSEY, J.

In December 1973 the plaintiff, Robert Steinberg, applied for admission to the defendant, the Chicago Medical School, as a first-year student for the academic year 1974-75 and paid an application fee of $15. The Chicago Medical School is a private, not-for-profit educational institution, incorporated in the State of Illinois. His application for admission was rejected and Steinberg filed a[n] * * * action against the school, claiming that it had failed to evaluate his application * * * according to the academic entrance criteria printed in the school's bulletin. Specifically, his complaint alleged that the school's decision to accept or reject a particular applicant for the first-year class was primarily based on such nonacademic considerations as the prospective student's familial relationship to members of the school's faculty and to members of its board of trustees, and the ability of the applicant or his family to pledge or make payment of large sums of money to the school. The complaint further alleged that, by using such unpublished criteria to evaluate applicants, the school had breached the contract which Steinberg contended was created when the school accepted his application fee.

* * *

The defendant filed a motion to dismiss, arguing that the complaint failed to state a cause of action because no contract came into existence during its transaction with Steinberg inasmuch as the school's informational publication did not constitute a valid offer. The trial court sustained [ruled in favor of] the motion to dismiss and Steinberg appeals from this order.

* * *

A contract is an agreement between competent parties, based upon a consideration sufficient in law, to do or not do a particular thing. It is a promise or a set of promises for the breach of which the law gives a remedy, or the performance of which the law in some way recognizes as a duty. [Citation.] A contract's essential requirements are: competent parties, valid subject matter, legal consideration, mutuality of obligation and mutuality of agreement. Generally, parties may contract in any situation where there is no legal prohibition, since the law acts by restraint and not by conferring rights. [Citation.] However, it is basic contract law that in order for a contract to be binding the terms of the contract must be reasonably certain and definite. [Citation.]

A contract, in order to be legally binding, must be based on consideration. [Citation.] Consideration has been defined to consist of some right, interest, profit or benefit accruing to one party or some forbearance, disadvantage, detriment, loss or responsibility given, suffered, or undertaken by the other. [Citation.] Money is a valuable consideration and its transfer or payment or promises to pay it or the benefit from the right to its use, will support a contract.

In forming a contract, it is required that both parties assent to the same thing in the same sense [citation] and that their minds meet on the essential terms and conditions. [Citation.] Furthermore, the mutual consent essential to the formation of a contract, must be gathered from the language employed by the parties or manifested by their words or acts. The intention of the parties gives character to the transaction, and if either party contracts in good faith he is entitled to the benefit of his contract no matter what may have been the secret purpose or intention of the other party. [Citation.]

Steinberg contends that the Chicago Medical School's informational brochure constituted an invitation to make an offer; that his subsequent application and the submission of his $15 fee to the school amounted to an offer; that the school's voluntary reception of his fee constituted an acceptance and because of these events a contract was created between the school and himself. He contends that the school was duty bound under the terms of the contract to evaluate his application according to its stated standards and that the deviation from these standards not only breached the contract, but amounted to an arbitrary selection which constituted a violation of due process and equal protection. He concludes that such a breach did in fact take place each and every time during the past ten years that the school evaluated applicants according to their relationship to the school's faculty members or members of its board of trustees, or in accordance with their ability to make or pledge large sums of money to the school. Finally, he asserts that he is a member and a proper representative of the class that has been damaged by the school's practice.

The school counters that no contract came into being because informational brochures, such as its bulletin, do not constitute offers, but are construed by the courts to be general proposals to consider, examine and negotiate. The school points out that this doctrine has been specifically applied in Illinois to university informational publications.

* * *

We agree with Steinberg's position. We believe that he and the school entered into an enforceable contract; that the school's obligation under the contract was stated in the school's bulletin in a definitive manner and that by accepting his application fee—a valuable consideration—the school bound itself to fulfill its promises. Steinberg accepted the school's promises in good faith and he was entitled to have his application judged according to the school's stated criteria.

* * *

[Reversed and remanded.]

Implied Contracts

RICHARDSON v. J. C. FLOOD CO.

District Court of Appeals, 1963.
190 A.2d 259.

MYERS, J.

This is an appeal by a property owner from a judgment against her for costs of labor and material furnished by appellee plumbing company.

Appellant contends there was error in the findings of the trial court that all work done by appellee was authorized by her and that there was sufficient competent evidence to substantiate the amount of recovery.

Appellant requested appellee to correct a stoppage in the sewer line of her house. In the course of the work a "snake" used to clear the line leading to the main sewer became caught and to secure its release a portion of the sewer line in the backyard was excavated. It was then discovered that the instrument was embedded in pieces of wood which had become lodged in a sewer trap from surface debris. At this time numerous leaks were found in a rusty, defective water pipe which ran parallel with the sewer line. In order to meet District regulations, the water pipe, of a type no longer approved for such service, had to

be replaced then or at a later date when the yard would have to be redug for that purpose. Appellee's agent testified he so informed appellant's agent. Appellant testified she had requested appellee to clear the sewer line but denied she was told about the need for replacement of the water line and contested the total amount of the charges for all the work done by appellee.

In the absence of a written contract, but with appellant admitting she had requested correction of a sewer obstruction but denying she had agreed to replace the water pipe, the existence of an implied agreement between the parties to replace the water pipe at the same time became an issue for the trial court.

It seems clear from the record that there was evidence to support a finding that appellant and her agent through daily inspections of the repairs knew of the magnitude of the work required and made no objection to the performance of the extra work in replacing the water pipe until after the entire job was finished when appellant refused to pay any part of the total bill submitted.

Contracts for work to be done are either express or implied—*express* when their terms are stated by the parties, *implied* when arising from a mutual agreement and promise not set forth in words. Direct evidence is not essential to prove a contract which may be presumed from the acts and conduct of the parties as a reasonable man would view them under all the circumstances. The testimony was conflicting but we cannot say that the trial court was wrong in holding that the burden of proving its right to recover had been carried by appellee.

With respect to the costs of both jobs the record reveals that no testimony was offered by appellant to show that itemized amounts for labor and materials furnished by appellee were wrong or excessive and unreasonable or that the work performed was either unnecessary or unsatisfactory. Appellee produced testimony that the charges were fair and reasonable and that the work on both the sewer and the water lines was fully completed. We find no merit in appellant's claim of error that the evidence on the costs of labor and material was insufficient to support the finding on this point.

[Affirmed.]

Quasi Contracts

PUTTKAMMER v. MINTH

Supreme Court of Wisconsin, 1978.
83 Wis.2d 686, 266 N.W.2d 361.

HANSEN, J.

On November 20, 1974, Victor Puttkammer, d/b/a Asphalt Spraying Co., plaintiff-appellant, commenced this action against the defendant-respondent, Arthur Minth, seeking compensation for improvements made to certain real property owned by Minth. * * *

The defendant, Minth, is the owner of the Hiawatha Supper Club in Eagle River, Wisconsin, which he leased during 1972 and 1973 to James Piekarski. During the period of the lease, the plaintiff, at the request of Piekarski, resurfaced the access and service areas of the supper club, providing labor and materials with a reasonable value of $2,540, and increasing the value of the property by the same amount.

The defendant was aware that this work was being done and "stood by and acquiesced" in its completion. Piekarski did not pay for the work and was subsequently adjudged bankrupt, with no assets in his estate for the payment of plaintiff. The defendant now has the benefit of the improvements but refuses to pay for them, and the plaintiff has not been paid for any portion of the work.

The complaint further alleges that the plaintiff has exhausted his remedy against Piekarski and that if the defendant is not required to pay for the improvements, he will be unjustly enriched at the plaintiff's expense. The * * * complaint therefore prays for damages in the amount of $2,540, plus costs and disbursements.

The defendant demurred to this * * * complaint on the ground that it failed to state a cause of action. The trial court [ruled in favor of the defendant].

The issues on this appeal are whether the complaint alleges facts sufficient to state a cause of action * * *.

* * *

The plaintiff maintains that the complaint states a cause of action in equity for unjust enrichment. The elements of such a cause of action are: (1) a benefit conferred upon the defendant by the plaintiff; (2) an appreciation or knowledge by the defendant of the benefit; and (3) acceptance or retention by the defendant of the benefit under circumstances making it inequitable for the defendant to retain the benefit without payment of its value. [Citations.]

The amended complaint in the present case alleges facts sufficient to satisfy the first and second of these requirements. The complaint alleges that a benefit has been conferred on the defendant in that the value of his property has been enhanced by $2,540. The complaint also alleges appreciation by the defendant of the fact of the benefit, since it is alleged the defendant was aware the work was being performed and stood by and acquiesced in its completion.

The question is whether the complaint alleges facts sufficient to establish, either expressly or by inference, the third requirement: that the benefit was accepted or retained under such circumstances as to make retention of the benefit of the resurfacing, without payment therefor, inequitable.

In an action for unjust enrichment, " '. . . [r]ecovery is based upon the universally recognized moral principle that one who has received a benefit has the duty to make restitution when to retain such benefit would be unjust.' . . ." [Citations.] It is not enough to establish that a benefit was conferred and retained; the retention must be inequitable.

The law in this state thus recognizes the principle set forth in the Restatement, *Restitution*, sec. 1, Comment c., p. 13, that:

. . . Even where a person has received a benefit from another, he is liable to pay therefor only if the circumstances of its receipt or retention are such that, as between the two persons, it is unjust for him to retain it. The mere fact that a person benefits another is not of itself sufficient to require the other to make restitution therefor . . .

* * *

In the instant case the complaint does not allege or reasonably imply that the work was ordered or ratified by the defendant; that the plaintiff performed the work expecting to be paid by the defendant; that the plaintiff was prejudiced by any misconduct or fault on the part of the defendant; or that the interests of Piekarski and the defendant were so related or intermingled that it can be said that the contract was executed for the defendant's benefit. The most that can be said from the complaint is that the defendant knowingly acquiesced in the performance of the work. This is insufficient basis to impose liability on one who did not request the work and may not have desired it. The trial court was correct in ruling that the complaint fails to state a cause of action.

* * *

Chapter 8

MUTUAL ASSENT

WHILE each requirement for the formation of a contract is essential to its existence, mutual assent is so basic that frequently a contract is referred to as the agreement between the parties. The Restatement, Section 3, has this definition: "An agreement is a manifestation of mutual assent on the part of two or more parties." When the contract is enforced, it is the agreement that is enforced. The agreement between the parties is the very core of the contract.

A contractual agreement always involves either a promise exchanged for a promise (*bilateral contract*), or a promise exchanged for an act or forbearance to act (*unilateral contract*) as manifested by what the parties communicated to one another. The manner in which parties usually manifest mutual assent is by offer and acceptance.

To form a contract the agreement must be objectively manifested. The important thing is what the parties manifest to one another by spoken or written words or by conduct. The law applies an **objective** standard and is, therefore, concerned only with the assent, agreement, or intention of a party as it reasonably appears from his words or actions. The law of contracts is not concerned with what a party may have actually thought or the meaning that he intended to convey, insofar as his subjective understanding or intention differed from the meaning objectively manifested. For example, if A offers to sell to B her Chevrolet automobile but intends to offer and believes that she is offering her Ford automobile, and B accepts the offer reasonably believing it was for the Chevrolet, a contract has been formed for the sale of the Chevrolet. Subjectively, there is no agreement as to the subject matter, but objectively there is a manifestation of agreement, and this is binding.

OFFER

An offer is a definite proposal or undertaking made by one person to another which manifests a willingness to enter into a bargain. The person making the proposal is the **offeror**. The person to whom it is made is the **offeree**. Upon receipt the offer confers upon the offeree the power of acceptance, which is an expression of willingness to comply with the terms of the offer. If unequivocal, the offeree's expression of willingness is an acceptance.

An offer may take several forms. (1) It may consist of a promise for a promise. An example is an offer to sell and deliver goods in thirty days to be paid in sixty days. If this offer is accepted, the resulting contract consists of the mutual promises of the parties, each made in exchange for the other. (2) An offer may be a promise for an act. A common example is an offer of a reward, as for certain information or the return of lost property. Such an offer can be accepted only by the performance of the act called for. (3) An offer may be in the form of an act for a promise. Thus, A tenders the necessary price to a clerk in a theater ticket office and asks for a ticket for a certain performance. This offer of an act can be accepted only by the delivery of the requested ticket, which amounts, in effect, to the theater owner's promise to admit A to the designated performance.

ESSENTIALS OF AN OFFER

An offer need not take any particular form to have legal effect. However, (1) it must be communicated to the offeree; (2) it must manifest an intent to enter into a contract; and (3) it must be sufficiently definite and certain. If these essentials are present, an offer which has not terminated grants the offeree the power to form a contract by accepting the offer. The communication of an offer to an offeree does not of itself confer any rights or impose any duties on either of the parties.

The offeror, by making his offer, simply confers upon the offeree a power to create a contract between the parties by duly accepting the offer. Until the offeree exercises this power, the outstanding offer creates neither rights nor liabilities.

Communication

In order to have the mutual assent required to form a contract the offeree must have knowledge of the offer, and the offer must have been communicated by the offeror. An offeree cannot agree to something of which he has no knowledge.

Assume that A signs a letter containing an offer to B and leaves it on top of the desk in his office. Later that day, B, without prearrangement, goes to A's office, discovers that A is away, notices the letter on A's desk, reads it, and then writes on it an acceptance which she dates and signs. No contract is formed because the offer never became effective for the reason that it was never communicated by A to B. If A had mailed the letter, and it had gone astray in the mail, the offer would likewise never have become effective. The offer must be communicated to the offeree and the communication must be made or authorized by the offeror. For instance, if J tells K that she is going to offer $600 to L for his piano, and K promptly informs L of this expressed intention of J, no offer has been made. There was no authorized communication of any offer by J to L. By the same token, if X should offer to sell his diamond ring to Y, an acceptance of this offer by Z would not be effective, as X made the offer to Y and not to Z.

An offer need not be stated or communicated by words. Conduct from which a reasonable person may infer a promise in return for either an act or a promise will amount to an offer.

An offer may be made generally or to the public. However, no person can accept such an offer until and unless he has knowledge that the offer exists. For example, if a person, without knowledge of the existence of an advertised reward for information leading to the arrest of a particular criminal, gives information which leads to such arrest, he is not entitled to the reward. His act was not an acceptance of the offer because he could not accept something of which he had no knowledge.

Intent

To have legal effect an offer must further manifest an intent to enter into a contract. Some proposals lack such intent and are therefore not deemed offers. As a result, a purported acceptance does not bring about a contract but operates only as an offer.

Invitations Seeking Offers It is important to distinguish language which constitutes an offer from that which merely solicits or invites offers. Communications between the parties in many cases take the form of preliminary negotiations. The parties are either requesting or supplying the terms of an offer which may or may not be given. A statement which may indicate a willingness to offer is not itself an offer. If A writes to B, "Will you buy my automobile for $3000?" and B replies "Yes," there is no contract. A has not made an offer to sell her automobile to B for $3000.

A businessperson desirous of selling merchandise is interested in informing potential customers about the goods, the terms of sale, and the price. But if he makes widespread promises to sell to each person on his mailing list, it is conceivable that the number of acceptances and resulting contracts might exceed his ability to perform. Consequently, he might refrain from making offers by merely announcing that he has goods for sale, describing the goods, and quoting prices. He is inviting his customers and, in the case of published advertisements, the public, to make offers to him to buy the goods. His advertisements, circulars, quotation sheets, and display of merchandise are *not* offers because (1) they do not contain a promise, and (2) they leave unexpressed many terms which would

be necessary to the making of a contract. Accordingly, the responses are not acceptances because no offer to sell has been made.

However, a seller is not free to advertise goods at one price and then raise the price once demand has been stimulated. Although as far as contract law is concerned no offer has been made, such conduct is prohibited by the Federal Trade Commission as well as legislation in many States.

Moreover, in some circumstances a public announcement or advertisement may constitute an offer. This is so if the advertisement or announcement contains a definite promise of something in exchange for something else and confers a power of acceptance upon a specified person or class of persons. The typical offer of a reward is an example as is the landmark case of *Lefkowitz v. Great Minneapolis Surplus Store, Inc.* In this case, the court held that a newspaper advertisement was an offer because it contained a promise of performance in definite terms in return for a requested act.

Objective Standard for Intent Occasionally, a person exercises her sense of humor by speaking or writing words which—taken literally and without regard to context or surrounding circumstances—could be construed as an offer. However, the promise is intended as a joke, and the promisee as a reasonable person understands it to be such. Therefore it is not an offer. It does not create a sense of reasonable expectancy in the mind of the person to whom it is made because of his realization that it is not being made in earnest. There is no contractual intent on the part of the promisor, and the promisee is or reasonably ought to be aware of that fact. However, if the intended jest is so successful that the promisee as a reasonable man under all the circumstances reasonably believes that it has been made as an offer, and so believing accepts, the objective standard applies and the parties have thus entered into a contract.

A promise made under circumstances of obvious excitement or emotional strain is likewise not an offer. For example, A, after having her month-old Cadillac break down for the third time in two days, screams in disgust, "I will sell this car to anyone for $10.00!" B hears A and hands her a ten-dollar bill. Under the circumstances, A's statement was not an offer, if a reasonable person in B's position would have not so considered it.

See *City of Everett v. Estate of Sumstad.*

Definiteness

The terms of a contract must be reasonably certain so as to provide a court with a basis for determining the existence of a breach and for giving an appropriate remedy. It is a fundamental policy that contracts should be made by the parties and not by the courts; accordingly, remedies for breach must have a basis in the parties' contract.

However, where the parties have intended to form a contract, the courts will attempt to find a basis for granting a remedy. Missing terms may be supplied by course of dealing, usage of trade, or by inference. Thus, uncertainty as to incidental matters will seldom be fatal so long as the parties intend to form a contract.

Open Terms Under the Code With respect to agreements for the sale of goods, the Code provides standards by which omitted terms may be ascertained, provided the parties intended to enter into a binding contract. The Restatement, Section 34, has adopted an approach similar to the Code's in supplying terms omitted in the parties' contract. Under the Code, an offer for the purchase or sale of goods may leave open particulars of performance to be specified by one of the parties. Any such specification must be made in good faith and within limits set by commercial reasonableness. Section 2–311(1). "Good faith" is defined as honesty in fact in the conduct or transaction concerned. Section 1–201(19). "Commercial reasonableness" is a standard measured by the business judgment of reasonable persons familiar with the customary practices in the type of transaction involved and with regard to the facts and circumstances of the case.

Moreover, a contract formed by acceptance of an offer which in certain respects is indefinite is reinforced by the obligation of good faith which the Code makes generally applicable. "Every contract or duty within this Act imposes an obligation of good faith in its performance or enforcement." Section 1–203. Commercial standards and reasonable practices of business supply those terms omitted by parties who have reached an agreement intended by them to be mutually binding.

For instance, the parties may enter into a contract for the sale of goods even though they have reached no agreement on the price. Thus, a contract for the sale of goods may contain an open price term. In such a case the price is a reasonable one at the time for delivery where the agreement (1) says nothing as to price; (2) provides that the parties shall agree later on the price and they fail to so agree; or (3) fixes the price in terms of some agreed market or other standard or as set by a third person or agency, and the price is not so set. Section 2–305. Whenever an agreement provides that the price is to be fixed by the seller or buyer, it must be fixed in good faith.

If the price is to be fixed otherwise than by agreement and is not so fixed through the fault of one of the parties, the other party has an option to treat the contract as cancelled or to fix a reasonable price in good faith for the goods. However, where the parties intend not to be bound unless the price is fixed or agreed upon as provided in the agreement, and it is not so fixed or agreed upon, the Code provides in accordance with the parties' intent that there is no contractual liability. In such case the seller must refund to the buyer any portion of the price received, and the buyer must return the goods to the seller or, if unable to do so, pay the reasonable value of the goods. Section 2–305(4).

The Code also provides missing terms in a number of other instances, such as where the contract fails to specify the time or place of delivery or payment. Sections 2–204(3), 2–308, and 2–310.

Output, Requirements, and Exclusive Dealings An agreement of a buyer to purchase the entire output of a seller's factory for a stated period, or an agreement of a seller to supply a buyer with all his requirements of certain goods used in his business operations, may appear to lack definiteness and mutuality of obligation. The exact quantity of goods is not specified; moreover, the seller may have some degree of control over her output and the buyer over his requirements. However, under the Code and the Restatement such agreements are enforceable by the application of an objective standard based upon good faith of both parties. Thus, the seller cannot operate her factory twenty-four hours a day and insist upon the buyer's taking all of the output where she only operated it eight hours a day before the agreement was made. Nor can the buyer expand his business abnormally and insist that the seller supply all of his requirements.

A valid agreement between buyer and seller for exclusive dealing in goods, unless otherwise agreed, imposes an obligation upon the seller to use her best efforts to supply the goods and upon the buyer to use his best efforts to promote the sale of the goods. Section 2–306(2).

DURATION OF OFFERS

An offer confers upon the offeree a power of acceptance, which power continues until the offer terminates. The ways in which an offer may be terminated, other than by acceptance, are: (1) lapse of time; (2) revocation; (3) rejection; (4) counter-offer; (5) death or incompetency of the offeror or offeree; (6) destruction of the specific subject matter to which the offer relates; and (7) subsequent illegality of the type of contract contemplated by the offer.

Lapse of Time

The offeror may specify the time within which the offer is to be accepted, just as he may specify any other term or condition in the offer. Unless otherwise terminated, the offer remains open for the **specified** time period. After the expiration of that time, the offer no longer exists and cannot be accepted. As to time, it may be provided that the offer is to be accepted immediately, or by return mail, or within a specified period, as a week or ten days. "Return mail" does not necessarily mean the next mail. The acceptance is valid if sent by the last mail of the same day. If there is no further mail on that day, an acceptance sent by the next mail is sufficient.

If no time is stated in the offer within which the offeree may accept, the offer will terminate upon the expiration of a **reasonable** period of time. What is a reasonable period of time is a question of fact, depending on the nature of the contract proposed, the usages of business, and other circumstances of the case. Restatement, Section 41. For instance, an offer to sell a perishable good would be open for a shorter period of time than an offer to sell undeveloped real estate.

An offer, as previously discussed, becomes effective at the time it becomes known by the offeree. This is apparent when the offer is made orally or by telephone. In either of these cases, the offer goes into effect when it is heard by the offeree. The importance of the time when an offer goes into effect lies in the determination of the time within which the offer must be accepted, whether immediately, within a stated time, or within a reasonable time, as the case may be. If A makes an offer to B orally and tells B that he can have five days in which to accept, no difficulty arises. The five-day period begins on the day on which B was told of the offer by A. Nor is there any difficulty, ordinarily, when the offer is sent by mail. In such case, the time within which the offer must be accepted commences on the day on which the offer is received by the offeree, and not on the day it was written or mailed.

Revocation

Inasmuch as an offer is made gratuitously, the offeror may generally withdraw it at any time before it has been accepted, even though he has definitely promised to keep it open for a stated time. To be effective, notice of revocation of the offer must actually reach the offeree before he has accepted it. *See Cushing v. Thomson.* If the offeror originally promises that the offer would be open for thirty days, but after five days wishes to terminate it, he may do so merely by giving the offeree notice that he is withdrawing the offer. This notice may be given by any means of communication and effectively terminates the offer when **received** by the offeree. However, an offer made to the general public is only revoked by giving publicity to the revocation equivalent to that given the offer.

Notice of revocation may be indirectly communicated to the offeree, as where he receives reliable information from a third person that the offeror has disposed of the goods which he has offered for sale or has otherwise placed himself in a position which indicates an unwillingness or inability to perform the promise contained in the offer. Restatement, Section 43. For example, A offers to sell her portable television set to B and tells B that he has ten days in which to accept. One week later B observes the television set in C's house and is informed that C had purchased it from A. The next day B sends to A an acceptance of the offer. There is no contract, as A's offer was effectively revoked when B learned of A's inability to sell the television set to B by reason of her having sold it to C.

Certain limitations, however, have been imposed upon the offeror's power to revoke the offer at any time prior to its acceptance. These limitations pertain to the following four situations.

Option Contracts An option is a contract by which the offeror is bound to hold open an offer for a specified period of time. It must comply with all of the requirements of a contract, including **consideration** being given to the offeror by the offeree. For example, if in consideration of $500 paid to A by B, A gives B an option to buy Blackacre at a price of $80,000 exercisable at any time within thirty days, A's offer is irrevocable. A is legally bound to keep the offer open for thirty days, and any communication by A to B of notice of withdrawal of the offer is ineffective. B is not bound to accept the offer, but the option contract entitles her to thirty days in which to consider acceptance. B now has the right, not merely the power, to accept the offer if she so chooses. If B does not exercise her option within the agreed time, the offer is terminated by lapse of time as in other cases. If, within the option period, A should revoke his offer or sell the property to another person, B could still accept the offer, and then maintain a suit against A for damages for breach of contract. An option agreement is itself a contract. It is a contract to keep an offer open for an agreed time.

Firm Offers Under the Code The Code provides that a *merchant* is bound to keep an offer to buy or sell **goods** open for a stated period not in excess of three months, if the merchant gives assurance in a **signed writing** that it will be held open. Section 2–205. The Code, therefore, makes a merchant's written promise not to revoke an offer for a stated period of time enforceable even though no consideration is given the offeror for that promise. A **merchant** is defined as a person (1) who is a dealer in the goods, (2) who by his occupation holds himself out as having knowledge or skill peculiar to the goods or practices involved, or (3) who employs an agent or broker whom he holds out as having such knowledge or skill. Section 2–104.

Statutory Irrevocability Certain offers are made irrevocable by statute, such as bids for the construction of a building or some public work made to the State, municipality, or other governmental body. Another example is preincorporation stock subscription agreements, which are irrevocable for a period of six months under many State corporation statutes. See Section 17 of the Model Business Corporation Act (Appendix G).

Irrevocable Offers of Unilateral Contracts Where the offer contemplates a unilateral contract, that is, a promise for an act, injustice to the offeree may result if revocation is permitted after the offeree has started to perform the act requested in the offer and has substantially but not completely accomplished it. Traditionally, such an offer is not accepted and no contract is formed until the offeree has completed the requested act. By commencing performance the offeree does not bind himself to complete performance and historically did not bind the offeror to keep the offer open. Thus, the offeror could revoke the offer at any time prior to the offeree's completion of performance. For example, A offers B $300 if B will climb to the top of the flagpole in the center of campus. B commences his ascent, and when he is five feet from the top, A yells to him, "I revoke."

Some courts have attempted to solve this difficulty by treating the offer as if it were an offer for a bilateral contract or a promise for a promise, which is accepted by the offeree's commencing performance. Such construction does violence to the terms of the offer, and causes the offeree as well as the offeror to become bound, which may not have been within the contemplation of the parties. The Restatement deals with this problem by providing that where the performance of the requested act necessarily requires time and effort to be expanded by the offeree, the offeror is obligated not to revoke the offer for a reasonable period of time:

(1) Where an offer invites an offeree to accept by rendering a performance and does not invite a promissory acceptance, an option contract is created when the offeree tenders or begins the invited performance or tenders a beginning of it.

(2) The offeror's duty of performance under any option contract so created is conditional on completion or tender of the invited performance in accordance with the terms of the offer. Restatement, Section 45.

It is reasoned that the offeree's commencement of performance is equivalent to consideration being given to keep the offer open.

This rule, however, presents another difficulty for it does not require the offeree to give notice to the offeror that performance has been commenced or is being given by the offeree. Where the offeror is not informed or notified that performance has been undertaken by the offeree, the situation is one in which the offeree knows that a contract has been formed, but the offeror does not know. To alleviate this hardship upon the offeror, the Code provides in Section 2–206(2):

Where the beginning of a requested performance is a reasonable mode of acceptance an offeror who is not notified of acceptance within a reasonable time may treat the offer as having lapsed before acceptance.

Rejection

An offeree is at liberty to accept or reject the offer as he sees fit. If he decides not to accept it, he is not required to reject it. If he does reject the offer, it is thereby terminated. Just as the acceptance of an offer is a manifestation of the willingness of the offeree to accept, a rejection of an offer is a manifestation by the offeree of his unwillingness to accept. The power of acceptance is terminated by a communicated rejection. From the effective moment of rejection, which is the **receipt** of the rejection by the offeror, the offeree may no longer accept the offer. Rejection by the offeree may consist of express language, or may be implied from language or from conduct.

Counter-offer

A counter-offer is a counter-proposal from the offeree to the offeror and indicates a willingness to contract with reference to the subject matter of the offer but upon terms or conditions different from those contained in the offer. It is not an unequivocal acceptance and, by indicating an unwillingness to agree to the terms of the offer, it operates as a rejection. For instance, assume that A writes B a letter stating that he will sell to B a secondhand color television set for $300. B replies that she will pay A $250 for the set. This is a counter-offer which, upon **receipt** by A, terminates the original offer. However, if B in her reply states that she wishes to consider the $300 offer but is willing to pay $250 at once for the set, that is a counter-offer which does *not* terminate A's original offer. In the first instance, after making the $250 counter-offer, B may not accept the $300 offer. In the second instance she may do so, as the counter-offer was stated in such a manner as not to indicate an unwillingness to accept the original offer, and B therefore did not terminate it. *See Zeller v. First National Bank & Trust.*

Another common type of counter-offer is the **conditional acceptance**. A conditional acceptance purports to accept the offer but expressly makes the acceptance conditional upon the offeror's assent to additional or different terms. Nonetheless, it is a counter-offer and terminates the original offer. However, a mere inquiry about the possibility of obtaining different or new terms is not a counter-offer and does not terminate the offer. The Code's treatment of acceptances containing terms that vary from the offer are discussed later in this chapter.

Death or Incompetency

The death or incompetency of either the offeror or the offeree ordinarily terminates an offer. Upon his death or incompetency the offeror no longer has legal capacity to enter into a contract, and thus all outstanding offers are terminated. Death or incompetency of the offeree likewise terminates the offer, because an ordinary offer is not assignable and can be accepted only by the person to whom it was made. When the offeree dies or ceases to have legal capability to enter into a contract, there is, in effect, no one who can accept the offer. Therefore, the offer necessarily terminates.

The death or incompetency of the offeror or offeree, however, does *not* terminate an offer contained in an option. An option is a contract and upon the death or insanity of the offeror becomes the property of his estate. If during the option period the offeree possessing the option, should die or become incompetent, his personal representative would

possess the right to exercise the option within the option time period.

Destruction of Subject Matter

Destruction of the specific subject matter of an offer terminates the offer. The impossibility of performance prevents a contract from being consummated and thus terminates all outstanding offers with respect to the destroyed property. Suppose that A, owning a Buick car, offers to sell this particular car to B, and allows B five days in which to accept. Three days later the car is destroyed by fire. On the following day B, in ignorance of the destruction of the car, notifies A that he accepts A's offer. There is no contract. A's offer was terminated by the destruction of the car. Clearly, there can be no agreement made concerning a specific car which is no longer in existence.

Subsequent Illegality

One of the four essential ingredients of a contract, as previously mentioned, is legality of purpose or subject matter. If performance of a valid contract is subsequently made illegal, the obligations of both parties under the contract are discharged. Illegality taking effect after the making of an offer but prior to acceptance has the same effect. The offer is legally terminated.

ACCEPTANCE

The acceptance of an offer is essential to the formation of a contract. An acceptance can only be made by an offeree. Acceptance of an offer for a bilateral contract is some overt act by the offeree which manifests his assent to the terms of the offer, such as speaking or sending a letter, a telegram, or other communication to the offeror. If the offer is for a unilateral contract, acceptance is the performance of the requested act with the intention of accepting. For example, if A publishes an offer of a reward to anyone who returns the diamond ring which she has lost (a unilateral contract offer), and B with knowledge of the offer finds and returns the ring to A, B has accepted the offer. However, if B returns the ring to A but in doing so disclaims the reward and says that he does not accept the offer, there is no contract. Merely doing the act requested by the offeror is not sufficient to form a contract where it is not done with the intention of accepting the offer.

Since acceptance is the manifestation of the offeree's assent to the offer, it must necessarily be communicated to the offeror. This is the rule as to all bilateral offers and also as to some unilateral offers. In some cases of unilateral offers, however, notice of acceptance to the offeror is not required. This occurs, for example, when the offeree furnishes the requested information or restores the lost property to the offeror of a reward for the information or the return of the lost property. In such cases, no other notice of acceptance is necessary. Generally, where the offeror has knowledge of the performance of the act by the offeree, he is not entitled to any other notice of acceptance from the offeree. Where, however, the offeror has no adequate means of learning of the acceptance of his offer, he is not bound unless the offeree gives him notice of the acceptance of his offer within a reasonable time after such acceptance.

Once an acceptance has been given, the contract is formed.

DEFINITENESS

An acceptance must be *positive* and *unequivocal*. It may not change any of the terms of the offer, nor add to, subtract from, or qualify in any way the provisions of the offer. It must be the **mirror image** of the offer. Except as modified by the Code, any communication by the offeree which attempts to modify the offer is not an acceptance but is a mere counteroffer.

The common law "mirror image" rule, by which the acceptance cannot vary or deviate from the terms of the offer, is modified by the Code. This modification is necessitated by the realities of modern business practices. A vast number of business transactions utilize standardized business forms. For example, a buyer sends to the seller on the buyer's order form a purchase order for 1,000 dozen cotton shirts at $60.00 per dozen with delivery by October 1 at the buyer's place of business. On the reverse side of this standard form are twenty-five numbered paragraphs containing provisions generally favorable to the buyer. When the seller receives the buyer's order, he sends to the buyer on his acceptance form an unequivocal acceptance of the offer. However, despite the fact that the seller agrees to the buyer's quantity, price, and delivery terms on the back of his acceptance form, the seller has thirty-two numbered paragraphs generally favorable to himself and in significant conflict with the buyer's form. Under the common law's *mirror image* rule no contract would exist, for there has not been an unequivocal acceptance of all of the material terms of the buyer's offer.

The Code alleviates this **Battle of the Forms** problem by focusing upon the intent of the parties. Section 2–207 of the Code provides as follows:

(1) A definite and seasonable expression of acceptance or a written confirmation which is sent within a reasonable time operates as an acceptance even though it states terms additional to or different from those offered or agreed upon, unless acceptance is expressly made conditional on assent to the additional or different terms.

(2) The additional terms are to be construed as proposals for addition to the contract. Between merchants such terms become part of the contract unless:

    (a) the offer expressly limits acceptance to the terms of the offer;

    (b) they materially alter it; or

    (c) notification of objection to them has already been given or is given within a reasonable time after notice of them is received.

(3) Conduct by both parties which recognizes the existence of a contract is sufficient to establish a contract for sale although the writings of the parties do not otherwise establish a contract. In such case the terms of the particular contract consist of those terms on which the writings of the parties agree, together with any supplementary terms incorporated under any other provisions of this Act.

If the seller definitely and seasonably expresses her acceptance of the offer and does not expressly make her acceptance conditional upon the buyer's assent to the additional or different terms, a contract is formed. The issue then becomes whether the seller's different or additional terms become part of the contract. If both buyer and seller are merchants, additional terms will be part of the contract provided they do not materially alter the agreement and are not objected to either in the offer itself or within a reasonable period of time. If both parties are not merchants, then the additional terms are merely construed as proposals for addition to the contract. Different terms proposed by the offeree will not become part of the contract unless accepted by the offeror.

　　See *Leonard Pevar & Co. v. Evans Product Co.*

EFFECTIVE MOMENT

A contract is formed when and where the last act necessary to its formation is done. Accordingly, when the offer is accepted in full compliance with its terms, unconditionally and unequivocally, and at the proper time and place, a contract is created. Where the parties live in different States (such as A, the offeror, living in Chicago and B, the offeree, living in New York), the contract is made in the State in which the acceptance became effective. With some exceptions, it is a rule of law that the validity of a contract is governed by the law of the State where it was made.

　　As previously discussed, an offer, a revocation, a rejection, and a counter-offer are effective when they are *received*. An acceptance, on the other hand, is generally effective upon **dispatch**. This is true unless the offer specifically provides otherwise or the offeree uses an unauthorized means of communication. *See Morrison v. Thoelke.*

Authorized Means

Historically, an authorized means of communication was the means expressly authorized by the offeror in the offer, or, if none was authorized, it was the means utilized by the offeror. For example, if in reply to an offer by mail, the offeree places in the mail a letter of acceptance properly stamped and addressed to the offeror, a contract is formed at the time and place that the offeree mails the letter. This assumes, of course, that the offer at that time was open and had not been terminated by any of the methods previously discussed. The reason for this rule is that the offeror, by using the mail, impliedly authorized the offeree to use the same channel of communication, and his mailing of an acceptance is an overt act of manifestation of assent. It is immaterial if the letter of acceptance goes astray in the mails and is never received.

　　The Restatement, Section 30, and the Code Section 2–206(1)(a) both now provide that where the language in the offer or the circumstances do not otherwise indicate, an offer to make a contract shall be construed as authorizing acceptance in any **reasonable manner**. These provisions are intended to allow flexibility of response and the ability to keep pace with new modes of communication.

Unauthorized Means

When the medium of communication used by the offeree is unauthorized, the traditional rule is that acceptance is effective when and if received by the offeror, provided that it is received within the time the authorized means would have arrived. The Restatement, Section 67, provides that if these conditions are met the acceptance is effective upon dispatch.

Stipulated Provisions in the Offer

If the offer specifically stipulates the means of communication to be utilized by the offeree, the acceptance to be effective must conform to that specification. Thus, if an offer states that acceptance must be made by registered mail, any purported acceptance not made by registered mail would be ineffective. Moreover, the rule that an acceptance is effective when dispatched or sent does not apply where the offer provides that the acceptance must be received by the offeror. If the offeror states that a reply must be received by a certain date or that he must hear from the offeree, or uses other language indicating that the acceptance must be received by him, the effective moment of the acceptance is when it is received by the offeror and not when it is sent or dispatched by the offeree.

Acceptance Following a Prior Rejection

After dispatching a rejection, an acceptance is not effective when sent by the offeree, but is only effective when and if received by the offeror prior to his receipt of the rejection. Thus, when an acceptance follows a prior rejection, the first communication to be received by the offeror is the effective one. For example, A in New York sends by air mail to B in San Francisco an offer which is expressly stated to be open for one week. On the fourth day B sends to A by air mail a letter of rejection which is delivered on the morning of the sixth day. At noon on the fifth day B dispatches a telegram of acceptance which is received by A before the close of business on that day. A contract was formed when B's telegram of acceptance was received by A as it was received before the letter of rejection.

Defective Acceptances

A late acceptance or defective acceptance does not create a contract. After the offer has expired, there can be no acceptance of it. However, a late or defective acceptance does manifest a willingness on the part of the offeree to enter into a contract and therefore constitutes a new offer. In order to create a contract based upon this offer, the original offeror must accept the new offer by manifesting his assent.

MODE OF ACCEPTANCE

Silence as Acceptance

An offeree is generally under no legal duty to reply to an offer. Silence or inaction is therefore *not* an acceptance of the offer. However, by custom, usage, or course of dealing, silence or inaction by the offeree may operate as an acceptance.

Salespeople employed by a manufacturing company or by a distributor to solicit orders for its merchandise from its customers usually have no authority to bind their employer by contract. The order forms usually recite that no contract is formed until the order of the buyer is accepted at the home office of the seller. Upon receipt of purchase orders, however, the manufacturer or distributor is under a duty to notify the customer within a reasonable time of its non-acceptance in the event of its inability or unwillingness to ship the merchandise ordered. Silence or inaction by the soliciting company is treated as an acceptance of the order.

Silence or inaction of an offeree who fails to reply to an offer also operates as an acceptance and causes a contract to be formed where by previous dealings or otherwise the offeree has given the offeror reason to understand that silence or inaction by the offeree is intended by the offeree as a manifestation of assent, and the offeror does so understand.

Furthermore, if an offeror sends unordered or unsolicited merchandise to a person with an offer stating that the goods are sent for examination, that the addressee may purchase the goods at a specified price, and that unless the goods are returned within a stated period of time the offer will be deemed to have been accepted, the offer is one for an inverted unilateral contract (i.e., an act for a promise). However, this practice led to abuse, which has prompted the Federal government as well as most States to enact statutes which provide that in such cases the offeree-recipient of the goods may keep them as a gift and is under no obligation either to return them or to pay for them.

Contract Formed by Conduct

A contract may be formed by conduct. Thus, there may be no definite offer and acceptance, or definite acceptance of an offer, yet a contract exists if both of the parties have acted in a manner which manifests a recognition by each of them of the existence of a contract. Recognition may result from the cumulative effect of a number of occurrences or events which indicate reliance of both parties upon the existence of a contract. Thus, it may be impossible to determine the exact moment when such a contract formed by conduct was made.

Auction Sales

The auctioneer at an auction sale does not make offers to sell the property which is being auctioned but invites offers to buy. The classic statement by the auctioneer is, "How much am I offered?" The persons attending the auction may make progressively higher bids for the property, and each bid or statement of a price or a figure is an offer to buy at that figure. If the bid is accepted, which is customarily by the fall of the hammer in the hands of the auctioneer, a contract results. A bidder is free to withdraw his bid at any time prior to its acceptance. The auctioneer is likewise free to withdraw the goods from sale *unless* the sale is advertised or announced to be *without reserve.*

If the auction sale is advertised or announced in explicit terms to be *without reserve*, the auctioneer may not withdraw an article or lot put up for sale unless no bid is made within a reasonable time. Unless so advertised or announced the sale is with reserve. Whether with or without reserve, a bidder may retract his bid at any time prior to acceptance by the auctioneer. Such retraction does not revive any previous bid.

Under the Code, if the auctioneer knowingly receives a bid by or on behalf of the seller, and notice has not been given that the seller reserves the right to bid at the auction sale, any such bid by or on behalf of the seller gives the bidder to whom the goods are sold an election either (1) to avoid the sale, or (2) to take the goods at the price of the last good faith bid. Section 2–328.

FIGURE 8-1   Offer and Acceptance

	Time Effective	Effect
Communications by Offeror		
Offer	Received by offeree	Creates power to form a contract
Revocation	Received by offeree	Terminates power
Communications by Offeree		
Rejection	Received by offeror	Terminates offer
Counter-offer	Received by offeror	Terminates offer
Acceptance	Sent by offeree	Forms a contract
Acceptance after prior rejection	Received by offeror	If received before rejection, forms a contract

CASES

Invitations Seeking Offers

LEFKOWITZ v. GREAT MINNEAPOLIS SURPLUS STORE, INC.

Supreme Court of Minnesota, 1957.
251 Minn. 188, 86 N.W.2d 689.

MURPHY, J.

This is an appeal from an order of * * * judgment award[ing] the plaintiff the sum of $138.50 as damages for breach of contract.

This case grows out of the alleged refusal of the defendant to sell to the plaintiff a certain fur piece which it had offered for sale in a newspaper advertisement. It appears from the record that on April 6, 1956, the defendant published the following advertisement in a Minneapolis newspaper:

> Saturday 9 A.M. Sharp
> 3 Brand New
> Fur
> Coats
> Worth to $100.00
> First Come
> First Served
> $1
> Each

On April 13, the defendant again published an advertisement in the same newspaper as follows:

> Saturday 9 A.M.
> 2 Brand New Pastel
> Mink 3-Skin Scarfs
> Selling for $89.50
> Out they go
> Saturday. Each .   . $1.00
> 1 Black Lapin Stole
> Beautiful,
> worth $139.50 .   . $1.00
> First Come
> First Served

The record supports the findings of the court that on each of the Saturdays following the publication of the above-described ads the plaintiff was the first to present himself at the appropriate counter in the defendant's store and on each occasion demanded the coat and the stole so advertised and indicated his readiness to pay the sale price of $1. On both occasions, the defendant refused to sell the merchandise to the plaintiff, stating on the first occasion that by a "house rule" the offer was intended for women only and sales would not be made to men, and on the second visit that plaintiff knew defendant's house rules.
* * *

The defendant contends that a newspaper advertisement offering items of merchandise for sale at a named price is a "unilateral offer" which may be withdrawn without notice. He relies upon authorities which hold that, where an advertiser publishes in a newspaper that he has a certain quantity or quality of goods which he wants to dispose of at certain prices and on certain terms, such advertisements are not offers which become contracts as soon as any person to whose notice they may come signifies his acceptance by notifying the other that he will take a certain quantity of them. Such advertisements have been construed as an invitation for an offer of sale on the terms stated, which offer, when received, may be accepted or rejected and which therefore does not become a contract of sale until accepted by the seller; and until a contract has been so made, the seller may modify or revoke such prices or terms. [Citations.] * * *

On the facts before us we are concerned with whether the advertisement constituted an offer, and, if so, whether the plaintiff's conduct constituted an acceptance.
* * *

The test of whether a binding obligation may originate in advertisements addressed to the general public is "whether the facts show that some performance was promised in positive terms in return for something requested."

* * *

Whether in any individual instance a newspaper advertisement is an offer rather than an invitation to make an offer depends on the legal intention of the parties and the surrounding circumstances. [Citations.] We are of the view on the facts before us that the offer by the defendent of the sale * * * was clear, definite, and explicit, and left nothing open for negotiation. The plaintiff, having successfully managed to be the first one to appear at the seller's place of business to be served, as requested by the advertisement, and having offered the stated purchase price of the article, was entitled to performance on the part of the defendant. We think the trial court was correct in holding that there was in the conduct of the parties a sufficient mutuality of obligation to constitute a contract of sale.

* * *

Affirmed.

Objective Standard

CITY OF EVERETT v. ESTATE OF SUMSTAD

Supreme Court of Washington, 1981.
95 Wn.2d 853, 631 P.2d 366.

DOLLIVER, J.

The City of Everett commenced an * * * action against the seller (the Sumstad Estate) and the buyer (Al and Rosemary Mitchell) of a safe to determine who is entitled to a sum of money found in the safe. Both the Estate and the Mitchells moved for summary judgment. The trial court entered summary judgment in favor of the Estate. The Court of Appeals affirmed. [Citation.]

Petitioners, Mr. and Mrs. Mitchell, are the proprietors of a small secondhand store. On August 12, 1978, the Mitchells attended Alexander's Auction, where they frequently had shopped to obtain merchandise for their own use and for use as inventory in their business. At the auction the Mitchells purchased a used safe with an inside compartment for $50. As they were told by the auctioneer when they purchased the safe, the Mitchells found that the inside compartment of the safe was locked. The safe was part of the Sumstad Estate.

Several days after the auction, the Mitchells took the safe to a locksmith to have the locked compartment opened. The locksmith found $32,207 inside. The Everett Police Department, notified by the locksmith, impounded the money.

* * * The issue is whether there was in fact a sale of the safe and its unknown contents at the auction. In contrast to the Court of Appeals, we find that there was.

A sale is a consensual transaction. The subject matter which passes is to be determined by the intent of the parties as revealed by the terms of their agreement in light of the surrounding circumstances. [Citation.] The objective manifestation theory of contracts, which is followed in this state [citation] lays stress on the outward manifestation of assent made by each party to the other. The subjective intention of the parties is irrelevant.

A contract has, strictly speaking, nothing to do with the personal, or individual, intent of the parties. A contract is an obligation attached by the mere force of law to certain acts of the parties, usually words, which ordinarily accompany and represent a known intent. If, however, it were proved by twenty bishops that either party, when he used the words, intended something else than the usual meaning which the law imposes upon them, he would still be held, unless there were some mutual mistake, or something else of the sort. [Citation.]

As stated in *Washington Shoe Mfg. Co. v. Duke* [citation.]

The apparent mutual assent of the parties, essential to the formation of a contract, must be gathered from their outward expressions and acts, and not from an unexpressed intention.

The inquiry, then, is into the outward manifestations of intent by a party to enter into a contract. We impute an intention corresponding to the reasonable meaning of a

Ape 3 offer   Apr 3 contract
" 4
" 5 postmarked
6 Received

person's words and acts. [Citation.] If the offeror, judged by a reasonable standard manifests an intention to agree in regard to the matter in question, that agreement is established. [Citation.]

* * *

In the case before us, * * * the Mitchells were aware of the rule of the auction that all sales were final. Furthermore, the auctioneer made no statement reserving rights to any contents of the safe to the estate. Under these circumstances, we hold reasonable persons would conclude that the auctioneer manifested an objective intent to sell the safe and its contents and that the parties mutually assented to enter into that sale of the safe and the contents of the locked compartment.

* * *

This matter is remanded to the trial court for entry of the summary judgment in favor of the Mitchells.

Revocation of Offers

CUSHING v. THOMSON

Supreme Court of New Hampshire, 1978.
118 N.H. 292, 386 A.2d 805.

PER CURIAM.

This is a bill in equity brought by five members of an antinuclear protest group called the Portsmouth Area Clamshell Alliance against Governor Meldrim Thomson, Jr., and John Blatsos, adjutant general of the State of New Hampshire. The bill seeks specific performance of a contract allegedly entered into by the parties for the use of the New Hampshire National Guard armory in Portsmouth.

* * *

The [trial] court ruled that a binding contract existed, granted the plaintiffs specific performance, and enjoined the defendants from any and all acts that would impede performance.

* * *

On or about March 30, 1978, the adjutant general's office received an application from plaintiff Cushing for the use of the Portsmouth armory to hold a dance on the evening of April 29, 1978. On March 31 the adjutant general mailed a signed contract offer agreeing to rent the armory to the Portsmouth Clamshell Alliance for the evening of April 29. The agreement required acceptance by the renter affixing his signature to the accompanying copy of the agreement and returning the same to the adjutant general within five days after its receipt. On Monday, April 3, plaintiff Cushing received the contract offer and signed it on behalf of the Portsmouth Clamshell Alliance. At 6:30 on the evening of Tuesday, April 4, Mr. Cushing received a telephone call from the adjutant general advising him that the governor had ordered withdrawal of the rental offer, and accordingly the offer was being withdrawn. During that conversation Mr. Cushing stated that he had already signed the contract. A written confirmation of the withdrawal was sent by the adjutant general to the plaintiffs on April 5. On April 6 defendants received by mail the signed contract dated April 3, postmarked April 5.

The first issue presented is whether the trial court erred in determining that a binding contract existed. Neither party challenges the applicable law. "To establish a contract of this character . . . there must be . . . an offer and an acceptance thereof in accordance with its terms . . . . [W]hen the parties to such a contract are at a distance from one another and the offer is sent by mail . . . the reply accepting the offer may be sent through the same medium, and the contract will be complete when the acceptance is mailed . . . properly addressed to the party making the offer and beyond the acceptor's control." [Citation.] Withdrawal of the offer is ineffectual once the offer has been accepted by posting in the mail. [Citation.]

* * *

Plaintiffs introduced the sworn affidavit of Mr. Cushing in which he stated that on April 3, he executed the contract and placed it in the outbox for mailing. Moreover plaintiffs' counsel represented to the court that it was customary office practice for outgoing letters to be picked up from the outbox daily and put in the U.S. mail. * * * Thus the representation that it was customary office procedure for the letters to be sent out the same day that they are placed in the office outbox, together with the affidavit, supported the implied finding that the completed contract was mailed before the attempted revocation. [Citation.]

[Judgment for plaintiff.]

Counter-offer

ZELLER v. FIRST NATIONAL BANK & TRUST

Appellate Court of Illinois, First District, 1979.
79 Ill.App.3d 170, 34 Ill.Dec. 473, 398 N.E.2d 148.

McNamara, J.

Plaintiff filed a complaint * * * alleging a contract to sell real estate to him. * * * The trial court entered summary judgment against plaintiff * * * and he appeals.

The property in question is held in trust. Defendant First National Bank and Trust Company of Evanston was trustee. William Jennings, who is not party to these proceedings, was beneficiary of the trust and executor of the estate containing the trust property. Austin L. Wyman, Jr., an attorney, and the law firm of Tenney & Bentley represented the estate.

In November, 1977, plaintiff and Jennings began negotiations with respect to the sale of the property. On December 23, 1977, Wyman wrote plaintiff, stating that he had been instructed by his principals to offer plaintiff the building for $240,000. The letter also recited interest rates and loan fees. Following receipt of this letter, plaintiff met with his attorney, Roger Jamma, and instructed him to communicate a counter-offer to Wyman. Accordingly, on January 10, 1978, Jamma sent Wyman a written counter-offer offering $230,000 and suggesting varying interest and loan arrangements.

On the same day, Jamma telephoned Wyman, and the two men discussed the offer and counter-offer. In his discovery deposition, Jamma stated that he might have mentioned the contents of the counter-offer to Wyman. Wyman testified at his deposition that Jamma informed him that a counter-offer of $230,000 had been sent and detailed the substance of the counter-offer.

* * *

On review, we deem it necessary to consider only the finding that the contract under which relief is sought was never properly formed.

It is elementary that for a contract to exist, there must be an offer and acceptance. [Citations.] Moreover, to create a binding contract, an acceptance must comply strictly with the terms of the offer. An acceptance requesting modification or containing terms which vary from those offered constitutes a rejection of the original offer, and becomes a counterproposal which must be accepted by the original offeror before a valid contract is formed. [Citations.]

On December 23, 1977, Wyman offered to sell plaintiff the property for $240,000. In a telephone conversation with Wyman on January 10, 1978, plaintiff's attorney discussed the counter-offer of $230,000. This counter-offer, containing terms varying from the original offer, operated as a rejection and terminated plaintiff's power to accept Wyman's offer. There was no suggestion that Wyman, the offeror, assented to the price modification in plaintiff's counter-offer so as to create a contract. Once having rejected Wyman's offer, plaintiff could not revive the offer by later telegraphing acceptance. [Citation.]

* * *

Plaintiff urges, however, that the counter-offer which was disclosed in the telephone conversation had no legal significance because it was oral rather than written. We do not agree. It is clear that the language of an offer may govern the mode of acceptance required. [Citation.] Where an offer requires a written acceptance, no other mode of acceptance may be used. [Citation.] Since the offer in the present case did not require acceptance or other communications regarding the sale to be in writing, verbal communication of the counter-offer was an effective rejection. Thus, contrary to plaintiff's contention, it is not determinative that the subsequent written acceptance arrived prior to the written counter-offer. In view of plaintiff's rejection prior to acceptance, no binding contract was created.

*   *   *

Judgment affirmed.

Definiteness

LEONARD PEVAR CO. v. EVANS PRODUCTS CO.

United States District Court, District of Delaware, 1981.
524 F.Supp. 546.

LATCHUM, C. J.

This is a diversity action by the Leonard Pevar Company ("Pevar") against the Evans Products Company ("Evans") for an alleged breach of express and implied warranties in Evans' sale to Pevar of medium density overlay plywood. Defendant denies liability, claiming that it expressly disclaimed warranties and limited its liability in its contract with Pevar. The parties agree that their respective rights and liabilities in this action are governed by the Uniform Commercial Code. The parties have both filed *   *   * motions for summary judgment *   *   *.

In the fall of 1977, Pevar [plaintiff] began obtaining price quotations for the purchase of medium density overlay plywood to be used in the construction of certain buildings for the State of Pennsylvania. Evans [defendant] was one of the manufacturers contacted and was the supplier that quoted the lowest price for this material.

On October 12, 1977, Marc Pevar had a telephone conversation with Kenneth Kruger of Evans to obtain this price quotation. It is at this juncture that a material fact appears in dispute that precludes this court from granting summary judgment. Pevar claims

that on October 14 it again called Evans, ordered plywood, and entered into an oral contract of sale. Evans admits that Pevar called Evans, but denies that Evans accepted that order.

After the October 14th telephone conversation, Pevar sent a written purchase order to Evans for the plywood. In the purchase order, Pevar simply ordered the lumber specifying the price, quantity, and shipping instructions. On October 19, 1977, Evans sent an acknowledgment to Pevar stating, on the reverse side of the acknowledgment *   *   * that the contract of sale would be expressly contingent upon Pevar's acceptance of all terms contained in the document. One of these terms disclaim most warranties and another limited the "buyer's remedy" by restricting liability if the plywood proved to be defective.

*   *   *

Turning now to § 2–207 it provides:

(1) A definite and seasonal expression of acceptance or a written confirmation which is sent within a reasonable time operates as an acceptance even though it states terms additional to or different from those offered or agreed upon, unless acceptance is expressly made conditional on assent to the additional or different terms.

(2) The additional terms are to be construed as proposals for addition to the contract. Between merchants such terms become part of the contract unless:

> (a) the offer expressly limits acceptance to the terms of the offer;

> (b) they materially alter it; or

> (c) notification of objection to them has already been given or is given within a reasonable time after notice of them is received.

(3) Conduct by both parties which recognizes the existence of a contract is sufficient to establish a contract for sale although the writings of the parties do not otherwise establish a contract. In such case the terms of the particular contract consist of those terms on which the writings of the parties agree, together with any supplementary terms incorporated under any other provisions of this Act.

Section 2–207 was intended to eliminate the "ribbon matching" or "mirror" rule of common law, under which the terms of an acceptance or confirmation were required to be identical to the terms of the offer or oral agreement, respectively. [Citation.] The drafters of the Code intended to preserve an agreement, as it was originally conceived by the parties, in the face of additional material terms included in standard forms exchanged by merchants in the normal course of dealings. [Citation.] Section 2–207 recognizes that a buyer and seller can enter into a contract by one of three methods. First, the parties may agree orally and thereafter send confirmatory memoranda. Section 2–207(1). Second, the parties, without oral agreement, may exchange writings which do not contain identical terms, but nevertheless constitute a seasonable acceptance. Section 2–207(1). Third, the conduct of the parties may recognize the existence of a contract, despite the previous failure to agree orally or in writing. Section 2–207(3).

A. Oral agreement followed by confirmation.

Section 2–207(1) applies to those situations where an "oral agreement has been reached . . . followed by one or both of the parties sending formal memoranda embodying the terms so far as agreed upon and adding terms not discussed." [Citation.] These additional terms are treated as proposals under Section 2–207(2) and will become part of the agreement unless they materially alter it. [Citation.]

* * * If the trier of fact determines that the acknowledgment includes additional terms which do not materially alter the oral agreement, then the terms will be incorporated into the agreement. If they materially alter it, however, the terms will not be included in the agreement, and the standardized "gap filler" provisions of Article Two will provide the terms of the contract.

* * *

B. Written documents not containing identical terms.

The second situation in which Section 2–207(1) may apply is where the parties have not entered into an oral agreement but have exchanged writings which do not contain identical terms. If the court determines that Pevar and Evans did not orally agree prior to the exchange of documents, then this second situation may apply. In such a case, both Pevar and Evans agree that Pevar's purchase order constituted an offer to purchase. The parties, however, disagree with the characterization of Evans' acknowledgment and Pevar's acceptance of and payment for the shipped goods. Evans contends that the terms disclaiming warranties and limiting liability in the acknowledgment should control because the acknowledgment consituted a counteroffer which Pevar accepted by receiving and paying for the goods. Evans argues that by inserting the "unless" proviso in the terms and conditions of acceptance of the acknowledgment, it effectively rejected and terminated Pevar's offer, and initiated a counteroffer; and when Pevar received and paid for the goods, it accepted the terms of the counteroffer.

* * * The drafters of the Code intended to change the common law in an attempt to conform contract law to modern day business transactions. They believed that businessmen rarely read the terms on the back of standardized forms and that the common law, therefore, unduly rewarded the party who sent the last form prior to the shipping of the goods. The Code disfavors any attempt by one party to unilaterally impose conditions that would create hardship on another party. Thus, before a counteroffer is accepted, the counterofferee must expressly assent to the new terms.

This court joins those courts that have rejected the [mirror image rule and] . . . "finds that [t]he consequence of a clause conditioning acceptance on assent to the additional or different terms is that *as of the exchanged writings there is no contract.* Either party may at this point in their dealing walk away from the transaction" or reach an express assent. [Citation.] Without the express assent by the parties no contract is created pursuant to Section 2–207(1). Nevertheless, the parties' conduct may create a contract pursuant to Section 2–207(3).

C. Conduct establishing the existence of a contract.

Section 2–207(3) is the third method by which parties may enter into a contract. This section applies when the parties have not entered into an oral or written contract. Section 2–207(3) provides that "[c]onduct by both parties which recognizes the existence of a contract is sufficient to establish a contract for sale although the writing of the parties do not otherwise establish a contract."

* * *

Section 2–207(3) also provides that where a contract has been consummated by the conduct of the parties, "the terms of the particular contract consist of those terms in which the writings of the parties agree, together with any supplementary terms incorporated under any other provisions of this Act."

In this case, the parties' conduct indicates that they recognized the existence of a contract. If this court finds after trial that Pevar and Evans did not enter into an oral agreement, Section 2–207(3) will apply. The terms of the contract will include those terms in which Pevar's purchase order and Evans' acknowledgment agree. For those terms where the writings do not agree, the standardized "gap filler" provisions of Article Two will provide the terms of the contract. [Citation.]

* * *

[Both motions for summary judgment denied.]

*Effective Moment of
Acceptance*

MORRISON v. THOELKE

Florida Court of Appeals, 1963.
155 So.2d 889.

ALLEN, C. J.

* * *

A number of undisputed facts were established by the pleadings, including the facts that appellees are the owners of the subject [real] property, located in Orange County; that on November 26, 1957, appellants, as purchasers, executed a contract for the sale and purchase of the subject property and mailed the contract to appellees who were in Texas; and that on November 27, 1957, appellees executed the contract and placed it in the mails addressed to appellants' attorney in Florida. It is also undisputed that after mailing said contract, but prior to its receipt in Florida, appellees called appellants' attorney and cancelled and repudiated the execution and contract. Nonetheless, appellants, upon receipt of the contract caused the same to be recorded.

* * *

On the basis of the foregoing facts, the lower court entered summary decree for the appellees, quieting [awarding] title in them. The basis of this decision was, in the words of the able trial judge:

"The contract executed by the parties hereto * * * constituted a cloud on the title of Paintiffs. * * * The Court finds said contract to have been cancelled and repudiated by Plaintiffs prior to its receipt by Defendants * * * and that on this basis there was no legal contract binding on the parties * * *."

* * * The question is whether a contract is complete and binding when a letter of acceptance is mailed, thus barring repudiation prior to delivery to the offeror, or when the letter of acceptance is received, thus permitting repudiation prior to receipt. Appellants, of course, argue that posting the acceptance creates the contract; appellees contend that only receipt of the acceptance bars repudiation.

* * *

A * * * statement of the general rule is found in 1 Williston, Contracts § 81 (3rd ed. 1957):

Contracts are frequently made between parties at some distance and therefore it is of vital importance to determine at what moment the contract is complete. If the mailing of an acceptance completes the contract, what happens thereafter, whether the death of either party, the receipt of a revocation or rejection, or a telegraphic recalling of the acceptance, though occurring before the receipt of the acceptance, will be of no avail; whereas, if a contract is not completed until the acceptance has been received, in all the sitations supposed no contract will arise.

It was early decided that the contract was completed upon the mailing of the acceptance. The reason influencing the court was evidently that when the acceptance was mailed, there had been an overt manifestation of assent to the proposal. The court failed to consider that since the proposed contract was bilateral, as is almost invariably any contract made by mail, the so-called acceptance must also have become effective as a promise to the offeror in order to create a contract. The result thus early reached, however, has definitely established the law not only in England but also in the United States, Canada, and other common law jurisdictions. It is, therefore, immaterial that the acceptance never reaches its destination.

The same work, in Section 86, negatives the possible effect of a power to recall an acceptance after mailing. In the author's words:

"By the United States Postal Regulations, the sender of a letter may regain it by complying with certain specified formalities, and yet a contract is completed by mailing an acceptance in the authorized channel. Since the acceptance is binding when it is mailed, the fact that the sender of a letter may regain possession of it should have no effect on the validity of the acceptance. * * * "

* * *

The rule that a contract is complete upon deposit of the acceptance in the mails, hereinbefore referred to as the "deposited acceptance rule" and also known as the "rule in *Adams v. Lindsell*" had its origin, insofar as the common law is concerned, in *Adams v. Lindsell*, [citation]. In that case, the defendants had sent an offer to plaintiffs on September 2nd, indicating that they expected an answer "in course of post." The offer was misdirected and was not received and accepted until the 5th, the acceptance being mailed that day and received by defendant-offerors on the 9th. However, the defendants, who had expected to receive the acceptance on or before the 7th, sold the goods offered on the 8th of September. It was conceded that the delay had been occasioned by the fault of the defendants in initially misdirecting the offer.

* * * As [Professor] Corbin indicated, there must be a choice made, and such choice may, by the nature of things, seem unjust in some cases. Weighing the arguments with reference not to specific cases but toward a rule of general application and recognizing the general and traditional acceptance of the rule as well as the modern changes in effective long-distance communication, it would seem that the balance tips, whether heavily or near imperceptibly, to continued adherence to the "Rule in *Adams v. Lindsell*." This rule, although not entirely compatible with ordered, consistent, and sometimes artificial principles of contract advanced by some theorists, is, in our view, in accord with the practical considerations and essential concepts of contract law. [Citation.]

* * *

In choosing to align this jurisdiction with those adhering to the deposited acceptance rule, we adopt a view contrary to that of the very able judge below, * * *.

In the instant case, an unqualified offer was accepted and the acceptance made manifest. Later, the offerees sought to repudiate their initial assent. Had there been a delay in their determination to repudiate permitting the letter to be delivered to appellant, no question as to the invalidity of the repudiation would have been entertained. As it were, the repudiation antedated receipt of the letter. However, adopting the view that the acceptance was effective when the letter of acceptance was deposited in the mails, the repudiation was equally invalid and cannot alone, support the summary decree for appellees.

The summary decree is reversed and the cause remanded for further proceedings.

PROBLEMS

1. Ames, seeking business for his lawn maintenance firm, posted the following notice in the meeting room of the Antlers, a local lodge: "To the members of the Antlers—Special this month. I will resod your lawn for two dollars per square foot using Fairway brand sod. This offer expires July 15."

The notice also included Ames's name, address, and signature and specified that the acceptance was to be in writing.

Bates, a member of the Antlers, and Cramer, the janitor, read the notice and became interested. Bates wrote a letter to Ames saying he would accept the offer if Ames would use Putting Green brand sod. Ames received this letter July 14 and wrote to Bates saying he would not use Putting Green sod. Bates received Ames's letter on July 16 and promptly wrote Ames that he would accept Fairway sod. Cramer wrote to Ames on July 10, saying he accepted Ames's offer.

By July 15, Ames had found more profitable ventures and refused to resod either lawn at the specified price. Bates and Cramer brought an appropriate action against Ames for breach of contract. Decision as to the respective claims of Bates and Cramer?

2. A owned four speedboats named Porpoise, Priscilla, Providence, and Prudence. On April 2, A made written offers to sell the four boats in the order named for $4,200 each to C, D, E, and F, respectively, allowing ten days for acceptance. In which, if any, of the following four situations described was a contract formed?

(a) Five days later, C received notice from A that he had contracted to sell Porpoise to M. The next day, April 8, C notified A that he accepted A's offer.

(b) On the third day, April 5, D mailed a rejection to A which reached A on the morning of the fifth day. But at 10:00 A.M., on the fourth day, D sent an acceptance by telegram to A who received it at noon on the same day.

(c) E, on April 3, replied that she was interested in buying Providence but declared the price asked appeared slightly excessive and wondered if, perhaps, A would be willing to sell the boat for $3,900. Five days later, having received no reply

from A, E, by letter, accepted A's offer and enclosed a certified check for $4,200.

(d) F was accidently killed in an automobile accident on April 9. The following day, the executor of F's estate mailed an acceptance of A's offer to A.

3. Alpha Rolling Mill Corporation, by letter dated June 8, offered to sell Brooklyn Railroad Company 2,000 to 5,000 tons of fifty-pound iron rails upon certain specified terms adding that, if the offer was accepted, Alpha Corporation would expect to be notified prior to June 20. Brooklyn Company, on June 16, by telegram, referring to Alpha Corporation's offer of June 8, directed Alpha Corporation to enter an order for 1,200 tons of fifty-pound iron rails on the terms specified. The same day, June 16, Brooklyn Company, by letter to Alpha Corporation, confirmed the telegram. On June 18, Alpha Corporation by telegram, declined to fulfill the order. Brooklyn Company, on June 19, telegraphed Alpha Corporation: "Please enter an order for 2,000 tons rails as per your letter of the eighth. Please forward written contract. Reply." To Brooklyn Company's repeated inquiries whether the order for 2,000 tons of rails had been entered, Alpha denied the existence of any contract between Brooklyn Company and itself. Thereafter, Brooklyn Company sues Alpha Corporation for breach of contract. Decision?

4. On April 8, X received a telephone call from A, a truck dealer, who told X that a new model truck in which X was interested would arrive in one week. Although A initially wanted $10,500, the conversation ended after A agreed to sell and X to purchase the truck for $10,000, with $1,000 down payment and the balance upon delivery. The next day, X sent A a check for $1,000 which A promptly cashed.

One week later, when X called A and inquired about the truck, A informed X he had several prospects looking at the truck and would not sell for less than $10,500. The following day A sent X a properly executed check for $1,000 with the following notation thereon: "Return of down payment on sale of truck."

After notifying A that she will not cash the check, X sues A for damages. Decision?

5. On November 15, I. Sellit, a manufacturer of crystalware, mailed to Benny Buyer a letter stating that Sellit would sell to Buyer 100 crystal "A" goblets at $100 per goblet and that "the offer would remain open for fifteen (15) days." On November 18, Sellit, noticing the sudden rise in the price of crystal "A" goblets, decided to withdraw her offer to Buyer and so notified Buyer. Buyer chose to ignore Sellit's letter of revocation and gleefully watched as the price of crystal "A" goblets continued to skyrocket. On November 30, Buyer mailed to Sellit a letter accepting Sellit's offer to sell the goblets. The letter was received by Sellit on December 4. Buyer demands delivery of the goblets; what result?

6. On May 1, Melforth Realty Company offered to sell Greenacre to Dallas, Inc., for $1,000,000. The offer was made by telegraph and stated that the offer would expire on May 15. Dallas decided to purchase the property and sent a registered letter to Melforth on May 10, accepting the offer. Due to unexplained delays in the postal service, the letter was not received by Melforth until May 22. Melforth wishes to sell Greenacre to another buyer, who is offering $1,200,000 for the tract of land. Has a contract resulted between Melforth and Dallas?

7. Rowe advertised in newspapers of wide circulation and otherwise made known that she would pay $5,000 for a complete set consisting of ten volumes of certain rare books. Ford, not knowing of the offer, gave Rowe all but one of the set of rare books as a Christmas present. Ford later learned of the offer, obtained the one remaining book, tendered it to Rowe, and demanded the $5,000. Rowe refused to pay. Is Ford entitled to the $5,000?

8. Scott, manufacturer of a carbonated beverage, entered into a contract with Otis, owner of a baseball park, whereby Otis rented to Scott a large signboard on top of the center field wall. The contract provided that Otis should letter the sign as desired by Scott and would change the lettering from time to time within forty-eight hours after receipt of written request from Scott. As directed by Scott, the signboard originally stated in large letters that Scott would pay $100 to any ball player hitting a home run over the sign.

In the first game of the season, Hume, the best hitter in the League, hit one home run over the sign. Scott immediately served written notice on Otis instructing Otis to replace the offer on the signboard with an offer to pay fifty dollars to every pitcher who pitched a no hit game in the park. A week after receipt of Scott's letter, Otis had not changed the wording on the sign, and on that day Perry, a pitcher for a scheduled game, pitched a no hit game while Todd, one of his teammates, hit a home run over Scott's sign.

Scott refuses to make any payment to any of the three players. What are the rights of Scott, Hume, Perry, and Todd?

9. B accepted C's offer to sell to him a portion of C's coin collection. C forgot that his prized $20 gold piece at the time of the offer and acceptance was included in the portion which he offered to sell to B. C did not intend to include the gold piece in the sale. B, at the time of inspecting the offered portion of the collection, and prior to accepting the offer, saw the gold piece. Is B entitled to the $20 gold piece?

10. Small, admiring Jasper's watch, asked Jasper where and at what price he had purchased it. Jasper replied: "I bought it at West Watch Shop about two years ago for around $85, but I am not certain as to that." Small then said: "Those fellows at West are good people and always sell good watches. I'll buy that watch from you." Jasper replied: "It's a deal." The next morning Small telephoned Jasper and said he had changed his mind and did not wish to buy the watch.

Jasper sued Small for breach of contract. In defense, Small has pleaded that he made no enforceable contract with Jasper (a) because the parties did not agree on the price to be paid for the watch, and (b) because the parties did not agree on the place and time of delivery of the watch to Small. Are either, or both, of these defenses good?

Chapter 9

CONDUCT INVALIDATING ASSENT

THE preceding chapter considered one of the essential requirements of a contract, namely, the objective manifestation of mutual assent by each party to the other. It is possible, in the case of a given contract, that as far as appears on the surface all the appropriate rules of offer and acceptance leading up to an agreement have been satisfied. Further inquiry, however, may disclose that the agreement is defective in some way or that there was no real assent or agreement. Since a knowing and voluntary agreement is essential to the validity of a contract, it follows that if there is no actual agreement, or if the agreement is defective, the contract is either voidable or void. This chapter deals with situations in which the manifested consent by one of the parties to the contract is not effective because it was not knowingly and voluntarily given. These situations are considered under the headings of duress, undue influence, fraud, misrepresentation, and mistake.

DURESS

A person should not be held to an agreement which he has not entered into voluntarily. Accordingly, the law will not enforce any contract induced by duress, which consists of improper physical or mental coercion. There are two basic types of duress. The first occurs when a party is compelled to manifest assent to contract through actual physical force, such as pointing a gun at a person or taking a person's hand and compelling him to sign a written contract. This type of duress is extremely rare, but it renders the agreement void. Restatement, Section 174(1).

The second type of duress involves the use of improper threats or acts, including economic and social coercion, to compel a person to enter into a contract. The threat may be explicit or inferred from words or conduct. This type of duress makes the contract **voidable** at the option of the coerced party. Restatement, Section 175(2). For example, if A, a landlord, induces B, an infirm bedridden tenant, to enter into a new lease on the same premises at a greatly increased rent by wrongfully threatening to terminate B's lease and evict her, B can avoid the new lease by reason of the duress exerted upon her. *See International Underwater Contractors, Inc. v. New England Telephone and Telegraph Co.*

With respect to the second and more common type of duress, the fact that the act or threat would not affect a person of average strength and intelligence is not determinative if it places the particular person in fear and induces an action against his will. The test is **subjective,** and the question is, did the threat actually induce assent on the part of the person claiming to be the victim of duress? Threats that would suffice to induce assent by one person may not suffice to induce assent by another. All circumstances must be considered, including the age, background, and relationship of the parties. Restatement, Section 175.

Ordinarily, the acts or threats constituting duress are themselves crimes or torts. But this is not true in all cases. The acts need not be criminal or tortious in order to be *wrongful*; they merely need be contrary to public policy or morally reprehensible. For example, if the threat involves a breach of a contractual duty of good faith and fair dealing or the use of the civil process in bad faith, it is improper.

Moreover, it has generally been held that contracts induced by threats of criminal prosecution are voidable, regardless of whether the coerced party had committed an unlawful act. Likewise, a threat of criminal prosecution of a near relative, as a son or husband, is duress, regardless of the guilt or innocence of the relative. As Justice Cardozo observed, "The principle thus vindicated is simple and commanding. *There is to be no traffic in the privilege of invoking the public justice of the state. One may press a charge or withhold it as one will. One may not make action or inaction dependent on a price."* Union Exchange Nat. Bank of New York v. Joseph, 231 N.Y. 250, 131 N.E. 905 (1921). *See also Great American Indemnity Co. v. Berryessa.*

To be distinguished are threats to resort to ordinary civil remedies in order to recover a debt due from another. It is not wrongful to threaten to bring a civil suit against an individual to recover a debt. It is the inducement of the payment by the threat to use criminal prosecution that is prohibited.

UNDUE INFLUENCE

Undue influence is taking unfair advantage of a person by reason of a dominant position based upon a **confidential relationship.** The law has traditionally scrutinized very carefully contracts between those in a relationship of trust and confidence which is likely to permit unfair persuasion being exerted by one party upon the other. Examples are the relationships of guardian and ward, trustee and beneficiary, principal and agent, husband and wife, parent and child, attorney and client, physician and patient, and clergyman and parishioner.

Where one party is under the domination of another, or by virtue of the relation between them is justified in assuming that the other party will not act in a manner inconsistent with his welfare, a transaction induced by unfair persuasion on the part of the latter is induced by undue influence and is **voidable.** The ultimate question in undue influence cases is whether the transaction was induced by influencing a freely exercised and competent judgment, or by dominating the mind or emotions of a submissive party. The weakness or dependence of the person persuaded is a strong circumstance tending to show that persuasion may have been unfair. For example, A, a person without business experience, has for years been accustomed to rely in business matters on the advice of B, who is experienced in business. B, without making any false representations of fact, induces A to enter into a contract with B's confederate, C, that is disadvantageous to A, as both B and C know. The transaction is voidable on the grounds of undue influence.

Undue influence, as previously mentioned, generally arises in the context of the relationships in which one person is in a position of dominance over another, or is likely to be. Where such a relationship exists at the time of the transaction and it appears that the dominant party has gained at the expense of the other party, the transaction is presumed to be voidable. For example, in a legally challenged contract between a guardian and his ward, the law presumes that advantage was taken by the guardian. It is, therefore, incumbent upon the guardian to rebut this presumption. Important factors in determining whether the contract is fair are (1) whether the guardian made full disclosure of all relevant information known to him, (2) whether the consideration was adequate, and (3) whether the ward had competent and independent advice before completing the transaction. Without limitation, in every situation in which a confidential relationship exists the dominant party is held to utmost good faith in his dealings with the other. *See Schaneman v. Schaneman.*

FRAUD

Another factor bearing upon the validity of consent manifested by a contracting party is fraud. Fraud prevents the assent from being knowingly given. There are two distinct types of fraud, namely, fraud in the execution and fraud in the inducement.

Fraud in the Execution

This type of fraud, which is extremely rare, consists of a misrepresentation which deceives the defrauded person as to the very nature of the contract. In cases of this type of fraud, the innocent party, without fault on her part, is wholly unaware that she is entering into a contract, and has no intention to do so. For example, A delivers a package to B, requests B to sign a receipt for it, holds out a simple printed form headed "Receipt," and indicates the line on which B is to sign. This line appears to B to be the bottom line of the form, but instead it is the bottom line of a promissory note cleverly concealed underneath the receipt. B signs where directed without knowing that she is signing a note. This is fraud in the execution. The note is void and of no legal effect. The reason is simply that, although the signature is genuine and appears to be a manifestation of assent to the terms of the note, there is no actual assent. The nature of A's fraud precluded consent to the signing of the note because it prevented B from knowing what she was signing.

Fraud in the Inducement

Fraud in the inducement, generally referred to as fraud or deceit, is an intentional misrepresentation of material fact by one party to the other who consents to enter into a contract in reliance upon the misrepresentation. For example, A, in offering to sell her dog to B, tells B that the dog won first prize in its class in the recent National Dog Show. In fact, the dog had not even been entered in the show. This statement induces B to accept the offer and pay a high price for the dog. There is a contract, but it is **voidable** by B because of A's fraud which induced his assent.

The requisite elements of fraud in the inducement are:

1. a false representation
2. of a fact
3. that is material
4. and made with knowledge of its falsity and the intention to deceive
5. which is justifiably relied upon.

False Representation A basic element of fraud is a false representation. There must be some positive statement or conduct that misleads. As a general rule, **silence** alone does *not* amount to fraud. There is generally no obligation on the part of a seller to tell a purchaser everything he knows about the subject of the sale, although if there is a latent (hidden) defect of a substantial character, one that would not be discovered by an ordinary examination, the seller is obliged to reveal it. Suppose, for example, that A owns a valuable horse, which, known to A, is suffering from a certain disease which is discoverable only by a competent veterinary surgeon. A offers to sell this horse to B, but does not inform B as to the condition of her horse. B makes a reasonable examination of the horse, and finding it in apparently normal condition, purchases it from A. B, on later discovering the disease in question, can have the sale set aside. A's silence, under the circumstances, was fraud. On the facts assumed, A was under a legal duty to disclose to B the condition of the horse as she knew it.

There are other situations in which the law imposes a duty of disclosure. For example, one may have a duty of disclosure because of prior representations innocently made but which are later discovered to be untrue before making a contract. The Restatement, Section 161 gives this illustration: "A makes to B, a credit rating company, a true statement of his financial condition, intending that its substance be published to B's subscribers. B summarizes the information and transmits the summary to C, a subscriber. Shortly thereafter, A's financial condition becomes seriously impaired, but he does not disclose this to B. C makes a contract to lend money to A. A's nondisclosure is equivalent to an assertion that his financial condition is not seriously impaired, and this assertion is a misrepresentation."

Another instance in which silence may constitute fraud is a transaction involving a fiduciary. A **fiduciary** is a person who owes a duty of trust, loyalty, and confidence to another. For example, an agent owes a fiduciary duty to his principal as does a trustee to the beneficiary of the trust and a partner to her copartners. A fiduciary may not deal at *arm's length* but rather owes a duty to make full disclosure of all relevant facts when he enters into a transaction with the other party to the relationship. In contrast, in most every-day business or market transactions, the parties are said to deal at "arm's length." By this expression it is meant that, in legal theory, the parties deal with each other on equal terms. It implies the absence of a fiduciary or confidential relation between the parties. Neither is required to make disclosures to the other.

Active **concealment** can likewise form the basis for fraud, as where the seller put heavy oil or grease in an engine to conceal a knock. Truth may be suppressed by concealment quite as much as by active misrepresentation. An express denial of knowledge of a fact which a party knows to exist, or the statement of misleading half-truth, can be fraudulent. Such conduct is clearly more than mere silence and is considered the equivalent of a false representation.

On the other hand, silence or nondisclosure is not fraud where a buyer possesses advantageous information about the seller's property, of which he knows the seller to be ignorant, and does not disclose such information to the seller. A buyer is under no duty to inform the seller of the greater value or other advantages of his property. Assume that A owns a farm which, as a farm, is worth $10,000. B knows that there is oil under A's farm, and knows that A is ignorant of this fact. B, without disclosing this information to A, makes an offer to A to buy the farm for $10,000. A accepts the offer and a contract is duly made. A, on later learning the facts, can do nothing about the matter, either at law or in equity. As one case puts it, "a purchaser is not bound by our laws to make the man he buys from as wise as himself."

It was assumed, in the above example, that B merely remained silent as to his knowledge of the oil under A's farm. If, however, when B made his offer to A, A had asked questions of B, the true answers to which would have disclosed the presence of oil, and B had lied or evaded the questions, he would have been guilty of fraud. Again, if A had hesitated about accepting B's offer, and B then made statements tending to mislead A and to discourage investigation by A, with the result that a contract was then made, B again would have been guilty of fraud, and the contract would have been voidable at A's option.

Fact The basic element of fraud is the misrepresentation of a material fact; actionable fraud can rarely be predicated upon what is merely a statement of **opinion.** A representation is one of opinion if it expresses only the belief of the representor as to the existence of a fact or one's judgment as to quality, value, authenticity, or other matters of judgment. The line between fact and opinion is not an easy one to draw and in close cases presents an issue for the jury. Suppose that A induces B to purchase shares in a company unknown to B at a price of $100 per share by representing that she had the preceding year paid $150 per share for them, when in fact she had paid only $50. This is a representation of a past event, definitely ascertainable, verifiable, and fraudulent. If, on the other hand, A said to B that the shares were "a good investment," she is merely stating her opinion, and in the usual case B ought to regard it as no more than that. Suppose, however, that A said the company "had a good year last year," when in fact it failed to show a profit. Is this opinion or fact? It is difficult, if not impossible, to decide without additional evidence. The solution will often turn upon the superior knowledge of the person making the statement and the information available to the other party. If the representor is a professional broker advising a client, the courts are more likely to regard an untrue statement of opinion as actionable. When the expression of opinion is of one holding himself out as having **expert** knowledge, the tendency is to grant relief to those who have sustained loss by reasonable reliance upon the expert evaluation. *See Vokes & Arthur Murray, Inc.*

The distinction between statements of fact and opinion is also considered in connection with sales of goods. Statements of **value,** such as "This is the best car for your money in town" or "This deluxe model will give you twice the wear of a cheaper model," are not grounds for the avoidance of a contract. Such exaggerations and commendations of articles offered for sale are to be expected from dealers who are merely **puffing** their wares with "sales talk."

Also to be distinguished from a representation of fact is a **prediction** of the future. Predictions are closely akin to opinions, as one cannot know with certainty what will happen in the future, and normally they are not regarded as factual statements. Likewise, promissory statements ordinarily do not constitute a basis of fraud, as a breach of promise does not necessarily indicate that the promise was fraudulently made. However, a promise which the promisor at the time of making had no intention of keeping is fraudulent as a misrepresentation of fact. Most courts take the position that the state of a person's mind, which is being misrepresented, "is as much a fact as the state of a person's digestion." *Edgigton v. Fitzmaurice,* 29 Ch.D. 459 (1885). If a dealer promises, "I will service this machine free for the next year," but at the time has no intention of doing so, his conduct is actionable if the other elements of fraud are present.

Misrepresentations of law are also generally distinguished from those of fact. Suppose that the seller of land induces a sale by misrepresenting that a certain zoning classification will permit the type of commercial activity contemplated by the purchaser or that the zoning ordinance is unconstitutional as applied to the property. Has she made a misrepresentation of fact? Practically all courts will agree that she has not. Rather, she has misrepresented the state of the law, and since everyone is presumed to know the law, the purchaser is not justified in relying upon the seller's representation of this type, and the sale is not fraudulent. There are, however, a few exceptions to this rule. If the seller occupies a fiduciary or confidential relationship with the purchaser, the latter will be able to avoid the transaction. A misrepresentation by one who is learned in the law, as a practicing attorney, may be fraudulent. It is not unreasonable to rely upon a legal expert's statement of the law.

Materiality In addition to the requirement that the misrepresentation be one of fact, it is necessary that it be material. It must relate to something of sufficient substance to induce reliance. In the sale of a race horse it may not be material whether the horse was ridden in its most recent race by a certain jockey, but its running time for the race probably would be. In determining the materiality of a representation, courts look to the impression made upon the mind of the party to whom it was made. It is usually material if, but for the representation, he would not have entered into the transaction. Most courts deem the misrepresentation to be material if, to a substantial degree, it influenced the making of a decision, even though it was not the decisive factor.

Knowledge of Falsity and Intention to Deceive To establish fraud the misrepresentation must have been known by the one making it to be false and must be made with an intention to deceive. This element of fraud is known as *scienter.* Knowledge of falsity can consist of (a) actual knowledge, (b) lack of belief in the statement's truthfulness, or (c) reckless indifference as to its truthfulness.

Moreover, many courts have implied knowledge to the representor and have held him strictly responsible where the situation or his means of knowledge were such as to make it his duty to know the truth or falsity of his representation. This frequently happens in business dealings or cases relating to sales of land or stock where the superior knowledge of the seller is made apparent.

Justifiable Reliance A person is not entitled to relief unless he has justifiably relied upon the misrepresentation to his detriment or injury. If the complaining party's decision was in no way influenced by the misrepresentation, he must abide by the terms of the contract. He is not deceived if he does not rely. Moreover, if the complaining party knew or should have known that the representation of the defendant was untrue, but still entered into the contract, he has not justifiably relied. For example, A, seeking to purchase a six-passenger car, was told by the salesman that a two-seat sports car was appropriate and took A for a test drive in the car. If A, nevertheless, relied on the salesman's statement, such reliance would not be justified, and A would not have been legally defrauded.

See *Gibson v. Home Folks Mobile Home Plaza, Inc.*

NON-FRAUDULENT MISREPRESENTATION

At common law it is necessary for the injured party in a fraud action, whether seeking rescission or damages, to prove an intention by the defendant to deceive. Hence, the necessity for showing knowledge of the falsity, or at least culpable ignorance. Today, a majority of courts permit a rescission for negligent or innocent (non-negligent) misrepresentation, provided, of course, that all of the remaining elements of fraud are present. Thus, a contract induced by negligent or innocent misrepresentation is **voidable.** See *Whipp v. Iverson.* Moreover, some courts also permit the recovery of damages for non-fraudulent misrepresentation.

MISTAKE

Mistake is an understanding or belief that is not in accord with existing fact. An elusive branch of the law is that which is concerned with the effect of "mistake" upon the formation of a contract. Certain problems have been settled, but many have not. There is, however, one concept that runs through the cases and which will at least help to place the issues in a meaningful context as well as assist in predicting results. In the chapter on "Manifestation of Mutual Assent," attention was given to the standard by which the assent of the parties is to be tested. The courts favor an objective approach. A person is bound by the reasonable impression which he has created in the mind of the other party, even if this differs from his own subjective intention.

An illustration is an offer in language manifesting an intention different from that actually intended by the offeror, a mistake resulting from carelessness, inattention, or failure to double check. This occurs in the case of A offering to sell her Chevrolet when she intended to offer her Ford automobile. If the offer is accepted before it is corrected, A is bound by the intention that she manifested. In the absence of duress, fraud, or breach of fiduciary duty by the buyer, she has no legal remedy.

The problem is how far can the objective theory be extended in mistake cases? At what point is there a lack of "real consent"? The law grants relief in a situation involving mistake only where there has been a **mutual mistake of material fact** by both parties to the contract. *See Ferris v. Ferris.*

Existence or Identity of Subject Matter

Suppose A offers to sell B a certain boat but unknown to both parties the boat has been destroyed. If B accepts, is he entitled to damages upon A's failure to deliver the boat as promised? He is not. The Code provides that, where the contract requires for its performance goods identified when the contract is made, and the goods suffer casualty without fault of either party before the risk of loss passes to the buyer, then, if the loss is total, the contract is avoided. Section 2-613.

The rationale of this rule is based upon the presumed intention of the parties in or-dinary transactions; that is, *no subject matter, no contract.* To be distinguished is the case in which the parties are mutually mistaken, but the contract contemplates an assumption of the risk. For instance, a ship at sea may be sold "lost or not lost." In such case the buyer is liable whether the ship was lost or not lost at the time of the making of the contract. There is no mistake; instead, there is a conscious allocation of risk.

Possibly the most famous decision involving mutual mistake is *Raffles v. Wichelhaus,* 2 Hurlstone & Coltman 906 (1864), popularly known as the "Peerless Case." A contract of purchase was made for 125 bales of cotton to arrive on the Peerless from Bombay. It happened, however, that there were two ships by the name of "Peerless," each sailing from Bombay, one in October and the other in December. The buyer had in mind the ship that sailed in October, while the seller reasonably believed the agreement referred to the Peerless sailing in December. Neither party was at fault, but both believed in good faith that a different ship was intended. The English court held that no contract existed. The Restatement, Section 20 is in accord:

(1) There is no manifestation of mutual assent to an exchange if the parties attach materially different meanings to their manifestations and (a) neither party knows or has reason to know the meaning attached by the other or (b) each party knows or each party has reason to know the meaning attached by the other.

(2) The manifestations of the parties are operative in accordance with the meaning attached to them by one of the parties if (a) that party does not know of any different meaning attached by the other, and the other knows the meaning attached by the first party; or (b) that party has no reason to know of any different meaning attached by the other, and the other has reason to know the meaning attached by the first party.

There is no manifestation of mutual assent where the parties attach materially different meanings to their manifestations *and* neither party knows or has reason to know the meaning attached by the other. However, if **blame** can be ascribed to either party, that party will be held responsible. Thus, if the seller knew of the sailing from Bombay of two ships by the name of Peerless, then he would be at fault, and the contract would be for the ship sailing in October as the buyer expected. If neither is to blame or both are to blame, there is **no** contract at all.

Nature of Subject Matter

If B contracts to purchase A's automobile under the belief that she can sell it at a profit to C, she obviously is not excused from liability if she is mistaken in this belief. Nor can she rescind the agreement simply because she was mistaken as to her estimate of what the automobile was worth. These are the ordinary risks of business, and courts do not undertake to relieve against them. But suppose that the parties contract upon the assumption that the automobile is a 1984 Cadillac, with 15,000-miles use, when, in fact, the engine is that of a cheaper model and has been run in excess of 50,000 miles? Here, a court would likely allow a rescission because of mutual mistake of a material fact. Another example of mutual mistake of fact was presented in a California case where a noted violinist purchased two violins from a collector for $8,000, the bill of sale reading: " *   *   * I have on this date sold to Mr. Efrem Zimbalist one Joseph Guarnerius violin and one Stradivarius violin dated 1717." Actually, unknown to either party, neither violin was genuine. Taken together they were worth no more than $300. The sale was **voidable** by the purchaser for mutual mistake. In a New Zealand case, the plaintiff purchased a "stud bull" at an auction. There were no express warranties as to "sex, condition, or otherwise." Actually, the bull was sterile. Rescission was allowed, the court observing that it was a "bull in name only."

The foregoing cases are to be contrasted with situations in which the parties are aware that they do not know the character or value of the item sold. For example, the Supreme Court of Wisconsin refused to set aside the sale of a stone for which the purchaser paid one dollar, but which was subsequently discovered to be an uncut diamond valued at $700. The parties did not know at the time of sale what the stone was and knew they did not know. Each consciously assumed the risk that the value might be more or less than the selling price.

A mistake unknown to the party making it becomes voidable if the other party recognizes it as a mistake. For example, suppose a building contractor submits a bid for a job that is one-half of what it should be, because he made a serious error in his computations. If the other party knows that he made such an error, or reasonably should have known of it, he cannot, as a general rule, take advantage of the other's mistake and accept the offer. In one such case the plaintiff, in computing his bid on a city sewer project, by mistake omitted the cost of one item—the steel. Accordingly, his bid was substantially lower than the others. He bid $429,444.20; the next higher bid was $671,600. All other bids were even higher. An estimate made by the city engineers, undisclosed to the bidders prior to the submission of the bids, was $632,000. The plaintiff received a sympathetic ear from the Oregon Supreme Court which stated in the course of its opinion: "It is our belief that although the plaintiff alone made the mistake, the City was aware of it. When it accepted the plaintiff's bid, with knowledge of the mistake, it sought to take an unconscionable advantage of an inadvertent error." *Rushlight Automatic Sprinkler Co. v. City of Portland*, 189 Or. 194, 219 P.2d 732 (1950). Some courts refer to a case of this type as one of **palpable unilateral mistake**, to distinguish it from the situation where the other had no suspicion nor any good reason to suspect that an error had been committed. In the latter type of case no judicial relief from the unilateral mistake is available.

Failure to Read Document

As a general proposition, a party is held to what she signs. Her signature authenticates the writing, and she cannot repudiate that which she has voluntarily approved. As a Louisiana court expressed it: "Signatures to obligations are not mere ornaments." Generally, one who assents to a writing is presumed to know its contents and cannot escape being bound by its terms merely by contending that she did not read them; her assent is deemed to cover unknown as well as known terms. Restatement, Section 157, Comment b. However, there are instances where one is relieved of obligations to which she has apparently assented; namely, where the character of the writing was misrepresented by the other party or where the writing was such that a reasonable person would not think it contained contractual provisions. An example of the latter would be a coatcheck stub containing in fine print a limitation of the proprietor's liability in case of loss or damage to the item checked. Ordinarily, stubs of this type are used for identification purposes only; hence, in the usual case one is not held to have assented to the limitation of proprietor liability merely by accepting the stub.

Mistake of Law

In the absence of fraud, one cannot obtain a release from contractual liability upon the ground that he did not understand the legal effect of the contract. Courts will not grant relief from a mistake of law. By the majority view in this country, one paying money to another under a mistake of law cannot recover that money even though it was not legally due, provided the payee's claim was asserted in good faith. There are, however, some exceptions. Payments made by governmental agencies or payments made to a court or court official under mistake of law are recoverable. The general reluctance to grant relief for mistake of law has been subjected to serious criticism and has been changed by statute in some States. In these States relief for mistake of law is placed upon the same basis as mutual mistake of a material fact.

CASES

Duress

INTERNATIONAL UNDERWATER CONTRACTORS, INC. v. NEW ENGLAND TELEPHONE AND TELEGRAPH CO.

Massachusetts Court of Appeals, 1979.
8 Mass.App.Ct. 340, 393 N.E.2d 968.

BROWN, J.

The plaintiff, International Underwater Contractors, Inc. (IUC), appeals from the entry of summary judgment for the defendant, New England Telephone and Telegraph Company (NET).

The plaintiff, which had entered into a written contract with the defendant to assemble and install certain conduits under the Mystic River for a lump sum price of $149,680, to be paid semimonthly in installments in proportion to the progress of the work, seeks additional compensation in a total amount of $811,816.73 for a major change in the system from that specified in the contract. The plaintiff asserts that the change, which was necessitated by delays caused by the defendant, forced the work to be performed in the winter months instead of during the summer, as originally bid, making the equipment originally specified unusable. This major change was made, the plaintiff alleges, at the direction of the defendant, and upon the defendant's assurances that it would pay the resulting additional costs.

The defendant moved for summary judgment with a supporting affidavit, wherein it argued in defense a release signed by the plaintiff settling the additional claim for a total sum of $575,000. The plaintiff, which submitted countervailing affidavits in opposition to the motion, argues that the release is not binding because it was signed under economic duress.

A special master appointed to hear summary judgment motions found that "as a matter of law, the economic duress required to vitiate the subject release was not present." Summary judgment was entered for the defendant, and the plaintiff's motions for reconsideration and to vacate judgment were denied. The instant appeal ensued.

* * *

A release signed under duress is not binding. [Citation.] "Coercion sufficient to avoid a contract need not, of course, consist of physical force or threats of it. Social or economic pressure illegally or immorally applied may be sufficient." [Citations.]

To show economic duress (1) a party "must show that he has been the victim of a wrongful or unlawful act or threat, and (2) such act or threat must be one which deprives the victim of his unfettered will." [Citation.] "As a direct result of these elements, the party threatened must be compelled to make a disproportionate exchange of values." [Citation.]

The elements of economic duress have also been described as follows: "(1) that one side involuntarily accepted the terms of another; (2) that circumstances permitted no other alternative; and (3) that said circumstances were the result of coercive acts of the opposite party." [Citations.] "Merely taking advantage of another's financial difficulty is not duress. Rather, the person alleging financial difficulty must allege that it was contributed to or caused by the one accused of coercion." [Citation.] Thus "[i]n order to substantiate the allegation of economic duress or business compulsion . . . [t]here must be a showing of acts on the part of the defendant which produced [the financial embarrassment]. The assertion of duress resulted from defendant's wrongful and oppressive conduct and not by plaintiff's necessities." [Citation.]

* * * Here, if the plaintiff's allegations are true, the defendant's acts in (1) insisting on a deviation from the contract and repeatedly assuring the plaintiff that it would pay the additional cost, which was substantially greater than the original, if the plaintiff would complete the work and (2) then refusing to make payments for almost a year caused the plaintiff's financial difficulties. Such acts could be considered "wrongful" acts and indications of bad faith.

* * *

The unequal bargaining power of the two parties (both in terms of their comparative size and resources as well as the financial difficulties into which the plaintiff had fallen, allegedly because of the defendant's acts) is a factor to be considered in determining whether the transaction involved duress. [Citations.] In addition, the disparity between not only the plaintiff's alleged costs ($811,816) but also the amount NET's engineers had recommended in November, 1974, to the board for settlement ($775,000) and the amount offered on a "take-it-or-leave-it" basis in December and accepted in settlement ($575,000) raises the possibility there may have been a disproportionate exchange of values and should be considered in determining whether the release was signed under duress. [Citation.]

The defendant argues that it did not have to settle the case but could have "exercised its lawful right to litigate the rights of the parties under the agreement" and that "[d]oing or threatening to do what a party has a legal right to do cannot form the basis of a claim of economic duress." [Citation.] However, if the assertions of the plaintiff are true, the defendant did more than assert a legal right, as its acts created the financial difficulties of the plaintiff, of which it then took advantage.

* * *

In summary, we are therefore unable to say as matter of law that the signing of the release was voluntary. Accordingly, it was error to enter summary judgment.

Judgment reversed.

Duress

GREAT AMERICAN INDEMNITY CO. v. BERRYESSA

Supreme Court of Utah, 1952.
122 Utah 243, 248 P.2d 367.

WADE, J.

The Great American Indemnity Company, appellant herein, brought this suit against Frank Berryessa and W. S. Berryessa, the obligors [debtors] on a joint promissory note [debt]. * * * W. S. Berryessa pleaded as defenses duress and lack of consideration and also counterclaimed for the return of $1,500 paid by him and the cancellation of a personal check given by him and not cashed at time of suit. This appeal is from a jury verdict and judgment thereon in favor of respondent W. S. Berryessa.

Viewing the evidence in the light most favorable to respondent, * * * it discloses that Frank Berryessa, a son of W. S. Berryessa, misappropriated some funds of his employer the Eccles Hotel Company, which operates the Ben Lomond Hotel in Ogden, Utah. When the father first learned of this, it was thought that the sum involved was approximately $2,000 and he agreed to repay this amount if the bonding company would not be notified and no publicity given to the matter and gave the hotel his promissory note for $2,186 to cover the shortage. Before this note became due, it was discovered that the shortage would probably be over $6,000 and therefore the manager of the hotel called W. S. Berryessa in for a conference. W. S. Berryessa knew he couldn't pay this larger sum and it was decided that the bonding company, the appellant herein, should be advised of the shortages. The hotel didn't try to collect the note for $2,186 after the bonding company was notified, apparently expecting that company to reimburse the hotel for the entire shortage discovered. After the bonding company was notified, its agent had several conferences with the Berryessas and the hotel management in which there was ascertained that the total shortage amounted to $6,865.28,

and Frank Berryessa signed a statement that he had misappropriated that amount. Frank Berryessa had stated that he had given a brother-in-law some of the money he had embezzled and it was suggested that he sign a note along with the Berryessas. The brother-in-law did not sign the note and at a further meeting of the Berryessas with the agent, W. S. Berryessa indicated that he did not think his son Frank would be able to make the payments of $250 quarterly suggested and that he was sure that he personally would not be able to do so and therefore did not want to sign the note. Mr. Berryessa then testified, although this was denied by the agent, that the agent thereupon swore, pounded his fists on his desk, and told him, "You can't come here and tell me what you will do," and then told them that if W. S. Berryessa would pay $2,000 in cash and sign a note with Frank Berryessa for $4,865.20, payable at the rate of $50 a month, that Frank would not be prosecuted but that if he did not sign Frank would have to be prosecuted. Thereupon, W. S. Berryessa agreed to do this and a couple of days later signed the note sued upon herein and about a month later, having secured a loan by mortgaging his home, gave the agent a cashier's check in the amount of $1,500 and a personal check in the amount of $500 as payment for the $2,000 cash agreed upon. Mr. Berryessa asked the agent not to cash the $500 check for about a month until he could get some more funds to pay it. This is the check which was never presented for payment by the appellant.

* * *

It is well settled that a note given to suppress a criminal prosecution is against public policy and is not enforceable between the parties. * * *

In this case respondent relied on two separate defenses, duress and illegal consideration, either one of which is sufficient to nullify this note. So if the jury found that the note was the result of duress or that respondent signed the note because appellant promised to refrain from criminal prosecution of his son, either one would be sufficient to invalidate the note and would constitute a defense thereto.

The uncashed check and the payment of $1,500 cash, present a different problem. Respondent had given the hotel a note for slightly over $2,000 to pay for the son's defalcations. At the time this note was given, there can be no question that no coercion was exercised against respondent and that his act was voluntary and at his own suggestion. There is nothing in the record to indicate that this note was given under duress or a promise to suppress prosecution.

* * *

The judgment against appellant on its complaint [to collect on the $4,865.20 promissory note] is affirmed. The judgment in favor of the respondent on his counterclaim [to recover the $2,000 paid the appellant] is reversed.

Undue Influence

SCHANEMAN v. SCHANEMAN

Supreme Court of Nebraska, 1980.
206 Neb. 113, 291 N.W.2d 412.

CLARK, J.

This is an action in equity to set aside and cancel a deed executed by Conrad Schaneman, Sr., hereinafter called Conrad, in favor of his eldest son, the defendant, Laurence Schaneman.

* * *

By his answer, the defendant admitted the execution of the deed but alleged that the conveyance was pursuant to an oral understanding and agreement between Conrad and the defendant.

The District Court of Scotts Bluff County, Nebraska, found that the execution of the deed was a result of fraud and undue influence, set aside the deed, and quieted title in Conrad. Defendant appeals.

* * *

We affirm the judgment of the District Court.

The property in question was purchased in January 1945 for a price of $23,500. Defendant helped arrange the purchase and loaned his father $10,500 toward the purchase price. The grantees were Conrad and the defendant as joint tenants. There is some testimony that another son, Conrad, Jr., loaned his father $2,500 toward the purchase price also. In any event, it is agreed that Conrad was the real purchaser. By October 1946, Conrad had repaid the loans to his sons * * *.

Conrad, who was born in Russia, could not read or write the English language. He was the father of eight sons and five daughters, * * *.

Over the years, the family had been closeknit, especially the father and the sons. It had been customary for Conrad and his sons to help one another financially in the purchase of farms. Conrad helped his sons; the sons helped Conrad; and the brothers helped one another in this fashion.

After Conrad's retirement from farming, all the children had frequent contact with Conrad and helped him with his personal needs, although defendant, as the oldest son, perhaps had more contact and a closer relationship with Conrad.

* * *

[T]he defendant was the primary person who advised Conrad and handled Conrad's business matters, although the other sons did continue to help Conrad to some extent.

On March 18, 1975, Conrad deeded the farm in question to the defendant for a stated consideration of $23,500, which was the original purchase price of the property in 1945. The value of the farm in March 1975 was between $145,000 and $160,000.

In March of 1975, Conrad was a man 82 years of age whose health had been deteriorating since at least 1971. He had numerous periods of hospitalization and suffered from heart problems, diabetes with extremely high and uncontrollable blood sugar levels at times, and obesity. He weighed between 325 and 350 pounds, had difficulty breathing, could not walk more than 15 feet, and was no longer able to drive an automobile. He was unable to shave himself and a special jackhoist had to be utilized to get him in and out of the bathtub. He was, for all intents and purposes, an invalid, completely dependent on others for most of his personal needs and for transportation, banking, and other business matters.

Conrad's children, other than the defendant, testified that during early 1975 Conrad had some days when he was sharper and more alert mentally than on other days, that at times he was confused, had difficulty communicating, and, on occasion, seemed to lapse into times long past. * * *

In about the spring of 1977, one of Conrad's sons discovered by accident that defendant's name was on Conrad's bank account as a joint tenant with right of survivorship. At about the same time, it was discovered that defendant had bought, with Conrad's money, a $20,000 certificate of deposit and that this also listed defendant as joint owner with right of survivorship. It was also later discovered that Conrad had executed a power of attorney in favor of defendant on August 20, 1975.

* * *

At trial, defendant testified that in March 1975 his father trusted and relied on the defendant; that defendant held a "special place" with his father, and that Conrad had complete trust and confidence in defendant. He did not recall any period that he and Conrad were not speaking and said that he and his father had never had a falling out. He further stated that, in March 1975, he was handling Conrad's business affairs generally.

* * *

An examination of the evidence reflects, in our opinion, that from the fall of 1974 until the conservatorship proceedings were commenced, there existed between the defendant and Conrad a confidential relationship and that, during that period, Conrad relied on the defendant for advice in his business affairs.

"[A confidential] relationship exists between two persons if one has gained the confidence of the other and purports to act or advise with the other's interest in mind." [Citation.]

"In a confidential or fiduciary relationship in which confidence is rightfully reposed on one side and a resulting superiority and opportunity for influence is thereby created on the other, equity will scrutinize the transaction critically, especially where age, infirmity, and instability are involved, to see that no injustice has occurred." [Citation.]

Here the evidence reflects that, due to age and physical infirmities, Conrad was, for all intents and purposes, an invalid at the time of the conveyance. It further supports a finding that Conrad's mental acuity was impaired at times and that he sometimes suffered from disorientation and lapse of memory. Considering all the evidence, we find that, in March 1975, Conrad was subject to the influence of the defendant, who was acting in a confidential relationship; that the opportunity to exercise undue influence existed; that there was a disposition on the part of the defendant to exercise such undue influence; and that the conveyance appears to be the effect of such influence. These findings establish a *prima facie* case of undue influence and cast upon the defendant the burden of going forward with the evidence.

A *prima facie* case of undue influence is made out in case of a deed where it is shown by clear and satisfactory evidence (1) that the grantor was subject to such influence; (2) that the opportunity to exercise it existed; (3) that there was a disposition to exercise it; and (4) that the result appears to be the effect of such influence. . . . In an action based on undue influence, when a confidential relationship exists between the parties, and a *prima facie* case is established, the burden of proof remains on the plaintiff, but the burden of going forward with the evidence shifts to the defendant.

* * *

We find that the defendant has not rebutted the presumption of undue influence which was raised by the plaintiff's *prima facie* case.

The judgment of the trial court was correct and is affirmed.

AFFIRMED.

Fraud:
False Representation of Fact

VOKES v. ARTHUR MURRAY, INC.

Florida Court of Appeals, 1968.
212 So.2d 906.

PIERCE, J.

[Audrey E. Vokes, plaintiff, appeals from a final order dismissing her complaint, for failure to state a cause of action.]

Defendant Arthur Murray, Inc., a corporation, authorizes the operation throughout the nation of dancing schools under the name of "Arthur Murray School of Dancing" through local franchised operators, one of whom was defendant J. P. Davenport whose dancing establishment was in Clearwater.

Plaintiff Mrs. Audrey E. Vokes, a widow of 51 years and without family, had a yen to be "an accomplished dancer" with the hopes of finding "new interest in life." So, on February 10, 1961, a dubious fate, with the assist of a motivated acquaintance, procured her to attend a "dance party" at Davenport's "School of Dancing" where she whiled away the pleasant hours, sometimes in a private room, absorbing his accomplished sales technique, during which her grace and poise were elaborated upon and her rosy future as "an excellent dancer" was painted for her in vivid and glowing colors. As an incident to this interlude, he sold her eight ½-hour dance lessons to be utilized within one calendar month therefrom, for the sum of $14.50 cash in hand paid, obviously a baited "come-on."

Thus she embarked upon an almost endless pursuit of the terpsichorean art during which, over a period of less than sixteen months, she was sold fourteen "dance courses" totalling in the aggregate 2,302 hours of dancing lessons for a total cash outlay of $31,090.45, all at Davenport's dance emporium.

*   *   *

These dance lesson contracts and the monetary consideration therefor of over $31,000 were procured from her by means and methods of Davenport and his associates which went beyond the unsavory, yet legally permissible, perimeter of "sales puffing" and intruded well into the forbidden area of undue influence, the suggestion of falsehood, the suppression of truth, and the free exercise of rational judgment, if what plaintiff alleged in her complaint was true. From the time of her first contact with the dancing school in February, 1961, she was influenced unwittingly by a constant and continuous barrage of flattery, false praise, excessive compliments, and panegyric encomiums, to such extent that it would be not only inequitable, but unconscionable, for a court exercising inherent chancery power to allow such contracts to stand.

She was incessantly subjected to overreaching blandishment and cajolery. She was assured she had "grace and poise"; that she was "rapidly improving and developing in her dancing skill"; that the additional lessons would "make her a beautiful dancer, capable of dancing with the most accomplished dancers"; that she was "rapidly progressing in the development of her dancing skill and gracefulness"; etc. She was given "dance aptitude tests" for the ostensible purpose of "determining" the number of remaining hours of instruction needed by her from time to time.

At one point she was sold 545 additional hours of dancing lessons to be entitled to the award of the "Bronze Medal" signifying that she had reached "the Bronze Standard," a supposed designation of dance achievement by students of Arthur Murray, Inc.

Later she was sold an additional 926 hours in order to gain the "Silver Medal," indicating she had reached "the Silver Standard," at a cost of $12,501.35.

At one point, while she still had to her credit about 900 unused hours of instructions, she was induced to purchase an additional 24 hours of lessons to participate in a trip to Miami at her own expense, where she would be "given the opportunity to dance with members of the Miami Studio."

She was induced at another point to purchase an additional 126 hours of lessons in order to be not only eligible for the Miami trip but also to become "a life member of the Arthur Murray Studio," carrying with it certain dubious emoluments, at a further cost of $1,752.30.

At another point, while she still had over 1,000 unused hours of instruction she was induced to buy 151 additional hours at a cost of $2,049.00 to be eligible for a "Student Trip to Trinidad," at her own expense as she later learned.

Also, when she still had more than 1,000 unused hours to her credit, she was prevailed upon to purchase an additional 347 hours at a cost of $4,235.74 to qualify her to receive a "Gold Medal" for achievement, indicating she had advanced to "the Gold Standard."

On another occasion, while she still had over 1,200 unused hours, she was induced to buy an additional 175 hours of instruction at a cost of $2,472.75, to be eligible "to take a trip to Mexico."

Finally, sandwiched in between other lesser sales promotions, she was influenced to buy an additional 481 hours of instruction at a cost of $6,523.81 in order to "be classified as a Gold Bar Member, the ultimate achievement of the dancing studio."

All the foregoing sales promotions, illustrative of the entire fourteen separate contracts, were procured by defendant Davenport and Arthur Murray, Inc., by false representations to her that she was improving in her dancing ability, that she had excellent potential, that she was responding to instructions in dancing grace, and that they were developing her into a beautiful dancer, whereas in truth and in fact she did not develop in her dancing ability, she had no "dance aptitude," and in fact had difficulty in "hearing the musical beat." The complaint alleged that such representations to her "were in fact false and known by the defendant to be false and contrary to the plaintiff's true ability, the

truth of plaintiff's ability being fully known to the defendants, but withheld from the plaintiff for the sole and specific intent to deceive and defraud the plaintiff and to induce her in the purchasing of additional hours of dance lessons." It was averred that the lessons were sold to her "in total disregard to the true physical, rhythm, and mental ability of the plaintiff." In other words, while she first exulted that she was entering the "spring of her life," she finally was awakened to the fact there was "spring" neither in her life nor in her feet.

* * *

It is true that "generally a misrepresentation, to be actionable, must be one of fact rather than of opinion." [Citation.] But this rule has significant qualifications, applicable here. * * * As stated by Judge Allen of this court [citation]: "A statement of a party having * * * superior knowledge may be regarded as a statement of fact although it would be considered as opinion if the parties were dealing on equal terms."

It could be reasonably supposed here that defendants had "superior knowledge" as to whether plaintiff had "dance potential" and as to whether she was noticeably improving in the art of terpsichore. And it would be a reasonable inference from the undenied averments of the complaint that the flowery eulogiums heaped upon her by defendants as a prelude to her contracting for 1,944 additional hours of instruction in order to attain the rank of the Bronze Standard, thence to the bracket of the Silver Standard, thence to the class of the Gold Bar Standard, and finally to the crowning plateau of a Life Member of the Studio, proceeded as much or more from the urge to "ring the cash register" as from any honest or realistic appraisal of her dancing prowess or a factual representation of her progress.

Even in contractual situations where a party to a transaction owes no duty to disclose facts within his knowledge or to answer inquiries respecting such facts, the law is if he undertakes to do so he must disclose the *whole truth*. [Citations.] From the face of the complaint, it should have been reasonably apparent to defendants that her vast outlay of cash for the many hundreds of additional hours of instruction was not justified by her slow and awkward progress, which she would have been made well aware of if they had spoken the "whole truth."

* * *

Reversed.

Fraud: Justifiable Reliance

GIBSON v. HOME FOLKS MOBILE HOME PLAZA, INC.

United States District Court, S.D. Georgia, 1982.
533 F.Supp. 1211.

BOWEN, J.

Prior to September 17, 1976, defendant Home Folks Mobile Home Plaza, Inc. [Home Folks] owned fifteen and one-half acres of land in Richmond County, Georgia, upon which it operated a mobile home park. The business was essentially twofold: (1) leasing to tenants some seventeen mobile homes owned by defendant and located in the park, and (2) leasing spaces in the park on which tenants could place their own mobile homes. The total 116 park spaces for mobile homes were equipped with connections for water, electric, natural gas, and sewer services. Sewage disposal was provided by a septic system in the park and water service was provided by park wells; natural gas was sold by Home Folks to the tenants in the park.

Sometime in 1975, Home Folks listed the land and business, constituting the mobile home park, for sale with a real estate broker. Plaintiff, a New Jersey resident interested in an investment property, saw an advertisement for the park in December, 1975, and subsequently in the spring and summer of 1976, entered into discussions with Mr. W. S. May, Sr., president of Home Folks, concerning the possible purchase of the park.

Pursuant to these discussions, plaintiff first visited the park in May, 1976, at which time plaintiff counted ninety-two spaces occupied, and thus a concomitant vacancy of twenty-four spaces. During this visit also, various statements were made by Mr. May concerning the mobile home park, its facilities, and the conditions of its business. While the exact content of these statements is in dispute, plaintiff, by writing in his own hand dated May 18 and 19, 1976, purports to show a series of questions about the property and answers thereto by Mr. May. Of relevance to this case, the question and answers purport to show that the following representations were made by Mr. May: (1) the water and sewage systems were in good condition and no major expenditures could be expected in the short term; (2) the profit on natural gas sold to tenants was 40%; (3) the normal vacancy was 5% with fluctuations. Separate from these questions and answers transcribed by plaintiff, Mr. May gave plaintiff an income statement for the park prepared by an accountant showing a gross rental income of $55,776.42 and a net rental income of $38,220.80 for an eight-month period, January 1, 1975 through August 31, 1975. The income statement did not provide a separate accounting for income derived from the sale of natural gas as opposed to rental income.

Following receipt of this income statement, plaintiff, by letter to Mr. May dated June 2, 1976, projected a twelve-month gross income of $83,664.63 and a net profit before debt service in the amount of $57,331.20. In his letter, plaintiff asked Mr. May if this twelve-month figure, derived from the income statement, was accurate for the last three years of Home Folks' business. By letter dated June 16, 1976, Mr. May responded in part as follows: "The figures you gave on your letter are very accurate. Our business is steadily improving. We have at this time five vacant spaces and have two different customers that want to park four mobile homes each."

Plaintiff again visited the park in July, 1976, and determined that ninety-five of the park spaces were occupied. During this visit, as well as his prior inspection, plaintiff visually ascertained no problems with the sewage and water systems. Furthermore, during his visits, plaintiff never asked to inspect the books and records of Home Folks, and there is no indication that the records were in any way concealed; nor is there any indication that plaintiff was prevented from inspecting any part of the premises.

After these negotiations and visits to the park, plaintiff decided to make the purchase. The sale was consummated on September 17, 1976, at which time the parties executed a sales contract, promissory note and security deed and a sales closing statement. Additionally, a schedule was prepared by the secretary-treasurer of Home Folks, Louise M. May, listing the park's present tenants and prorating the amounts due from those tenants for the month of September between the parties. Both parties at closing were represented by counsel.

The sales contract provided for a total purchase price of $275,000 paid as follows: a down payment of $60,000 and a promissory note for the balance, secured by certain personal property in the park.

* * *

After plaintiff purchased the park, he made certain expenditures on the water and septic systems. In the first six months of his ownership, plaintiff spent $3,899.00 on repairing the wells and $1,485.00 on the septic system. According to plaintiff's resident manager, who had previously been employed by Mr. May, the water and septic systems in the park had presented recurring problems prior to September 17, 1976. Ultimately, when plaintiff sold the park some three years after the purchase, he expended $7,531.00 on the water wells and $8,125.00 on the septic system.

In the first year of plaintiff's operation of the park, the number of spaces occupied never exceeded ninety-eight. Plaintiff raised the rent, as well as the charges for natural gas, and made a gross income for the year in the amount of $69,764.00. Since plaintiff's op-

erating expenses exceeded $45,572.00, his net income before debt service was approximately $24,192.00. After payment of his debt to Mr. May, in the sum of $27,244.00, plaintiff was operating at a deficit. Plaintiff first notified Mr. May of his financial problems with the park in April, 1977, and again in May, 1977.

Plaintiff filed the present case on January 5, 1981, some four years and four months after the date of the sale closing on September 17, 1976. The complaint alleges that Mr. May, on behalf of defendant Home Folks, made certain false, untrue, and fraudulent statements to plaintiff for the purpose of inducing plaintiff to purchase the mobile home park. Specifically, the alleged fraudulent representations include the following: (1) the eight-month income statement and Mr. May's assurance that the twelve-month income projection by plaintiff was accurate; (2) statements that the property had three water wells in good operating condition; (3) statement that an approximate forty percent profit was realized on the sale of natural gas to the park's tenants; (4) statement that the sewage disposal system was in good condition and functioned satisfactorily; and (5) statement that the number of vacancies in the park was as low as five in June, 1976. Plaintiff seeks $100,000.00 actual damages and $100,000.00 punitive damages.

The case is presently before the court on defendant's motion for summary judgment. The bases for the motion appear to be [that the] * * * plaintiff, in the exercise of due diligence, should have discovered the verity of any alleged representations made by defendant.

* * *

As gleaned from the complaint, plaintiff is seeking actual damage through an action at law in tort for fraud and deceit in the procurement of the sales contract, which fraud consisted of certain prior representations, both oral and written, allegedly made by defendant. [Citations.]

The elements of this cause of action, which plaintiff has alleged with the requisite specificity, [citation] are: "(1) false representation made by the defendant; (2) scienter; (3) an intention to induce the plaintiff to act or refrain from acting in reliance by the plaintiff; (4) justifiable reliance by the plaintiff; (5) damage to the plaintiff." [Citation.] Central to defendant's motion for summary judgment is the applicability * * * to the facts in this case of the fourth of these elements—"justifiable reliance by the plaintiff."

As a general rule, a defrauded party cannot state a claim of justifiable reliance upon the false representations of another, when such person, in the exercise of ordinary diligence, could have discovered the falsity of the representations before acting thereon. [Citation.] The scope of the defrauded party's duty to discover, as defined by the "ordinary", "reasonable", or "due" diligence standard, does not go so far as to require the exhaustion of all available means to ascertain the truth of the representations. [Citation.] Furthermore, as recognized by Georgia appellate courts, questions of whether the defrauded party "could have protected himself by the exercise of proper diligence are, except in plain and indisputable cases, questions for the jury." [Citation.]

* * * [P]ositive misrepresentations by words or act are clearly actionable unless it appears as a matter of law that plaintiff was not justified in relying on them in the exercise of common prudence and diligence. [Citation.] A lack of diligence may appear as a matter of law where plaintiff blindly relies upon the representations of another without rhyme or reason. [Citation.] "Blind reliance exists where 'it cannot be said that the purchase originated in fraud so much as in the carelessness of the purchaser to exercise ordinary care for his own interest.'" [Citations.] In a similar manner, a failure of due diligence by plaintiff may exist as a matter of law, where the alleged fraud consisted of defendant's silence on a particular matter and plaintiff could have discovered the existence of the unspoken fact by simple inspection.

Allegations of fraud also may not be actionable if it appears as a matter of law that the person relying on the fraud had an equal and ample opportunity to prevent the happening of the occurrence causing injury. * * * Finally, plaintiff's lack of diligence may exist as a matter of law where he clearly had notice of the allegedly misrepresented fact and yet proceeded with the sale. * * *

On review of the foregoing Georgia appellate decisions, it is apparent that the facts in the present case do not show, as a matter of law, that plaintiff failed to exercise common prudence and ordinary diligence before acting on the alleged misrepresentations. Certainly, this is not a case of "blind reliance." Plaintiff visited the park on several occasions and corresponded with and questioned Mr. May extensively about the operation of the park. [Citation.] ("[W]e are not aware of any rule of law, or decision of any court, that goes to the extent of saying that one who has been imposed upon by a deceitful and false statement can have no relief unless, before acting upon such a statement, he had exhausted all means at his command to ascertain its truth." [Citation.]) During the course of these discussions, plaintiff sought verification from Mr. May of several items, most notably the eight-month income statement and the yearly projection therefrom. Such conduct cannot be termed blind reliance as a matter of law. [Citation.] The Georgia Court of Appeals has commented:

[W]here the basis upon which the contract was entered upon lies in the existence or nonexistence of certain material facts, the verity of which needs must be ascertained from the statement of one acquainted with such facts, each of the contracting parties has a right to rely upon the truth of the other's statements with reference thereto, when such statements relate to matters apparently within the knowledge of the party asserting them; and to do this without checking up the statement with the declarations of other and different persons, in order, by such and investigation, to test their probable truth. [Citations.]

Furthermore, the fraud at issue is not mere silence as to a material fact which could have been discovered by simple inspection [citations], but rather pertains to certain affirmative or positive misrepresentations. Even if defendant's silence had formed the basis of plaintiff's action, it is by no means shown, as a matter of law, that plaintiff could have discovered the septic and water system problems [citations]. Once again, Georgia law does not require a defrauded party to exhaust all means at his disposal to ascertain the truth of representations before acting theron. [Citation.]

* * *

Accordingly, on the basis of the foregoing discussion, defendant's motion for summary judgment is denied.

Misrepresentation

WHIPP v. IVERSON

Supreme Court of Wisconsin, 1969.
43 Wis.2d 166, 168 N.W.2d 201.

HALLOWS, C. J.

The complaint alleges the defendants were the owners of a business known as the Iverson Motor Company at Amery, Wisconsin. The company was engaged in general automobile and farm implement repair work and the sale of Oldsmobile, Rambler, and International Harvester Scout automobiles. The Oldsmobile agency consisted of 40 percent of the volume of sales and net earnings. On October 18, 1966, the plaintiffs and the defendant Robert Iverson discussed the sale of the business. The complaint alleges Iverson falsely represented the sale included the Oldsmobile agency and franchise and he was selling the business to the plaintiffs as he was operating it. It is alleged this representation and others Iverson knew or ought to have known were false and the plaintiffs, relying on them, were

induced to enter into an agreement to purchase the business and to lease the real estate occupied by the business.

In December, 1966, the Oldsmobile division of General Motors refused to transfer the franchise to the plaintiff Blaine Whipp, who returned possession of the business and property to the defendants and demanded the return of the down payment and the amount of capital invested in the business. The defendants demurred to the complaint and argue it states no cause of action because it fails to allege the defendants made the false representation intentionally for the purpose of inducing the plaintiffs to sign the agreements. We think the trial court was correct in overruling the demurrer.

Rescission of a contract in equity may be grounded on misrepresentations not intentionally made for the purpose of defrauding or inducing a person to act to his detriment for the speaker's economic benefit.

At law in the action for deceit the basis of responsibility for misrepresentation was intention, generally called *scienter* or the intent to deceive. [Citations.] This elusive state of mind may be proved by proof the speaker believes his statement to be false or the representation is made without any belief as to its truth. [Citations.] As [Professor] Prosser puts it, "A defendant who asserts a fact as of his own knowledge, or so positively as to imply that he has knowledge, under circumstances where he is aware that he will be so understood when he knows that he does not in fact know whether what he says is true is found to have the intent to deceive. * * *"

* * *

It is not necessary for rescission of a contract "that the party making a misrepresentation should have known that it was false." Recovery is allowed even though misrepresentation is innocently made because "It would be unjust to allow one who has made false representations, even innocently, to retain the fruits of a bargain induced by such representations." [Citation.] This statement of law is adopted by the Restatement of Contracts, s.

476, which states "Where a party is induced to enter into a transaction with another party that he was under no duty to enter into by means of the latter's fraud or material misrepresentation, the transaction is voidable as against the latter and all who stand in no better position, subject to" certain qualifications. A misrepresentation may be innocent, negligent, or known to be false. Restatement, 2 Contracts, p. 890, s. 470, Comment a, and if innocently made is voidable, s. 476(2). See also Restatement, Restitution, p. 123, s. 28(b).

*   *   *

We think an express allegation of *scienter* is not required for rescission which is asked for in this complaint. The defendants are alleged to have known or ought to have known the Oldsmobile franchise could not be sold as part of the business. Iverson was the owner of the franchise he was purporting to sell and should know whether he could or could not sell the franchise. There is no question of Iverson's economic interest in the sale and his lack of intent to deceive is not material to the cause of action. We think therefore a cause of action is stated for rescission *   *   *.

Order affirmed.

Mistake

FERRIS v. FERRIS

Supreme Court of Vermont, 1981.
140 Vt. 12, 433 A.2d 304.

HILL, J.

The parties to this action were divorced in 1972. A stipulation regarding alimony was incorporated into the decree whereby plaintiff, Barbara Ferris, was to receive $8,500.00 per year. Payments were to terminate upon occurrence of any one of certain events, including the inheritance by plaintiff of her mother's estate. Also, alimony payments were to be reduced by such amounts as plaintiff received from any sources resulting from lifetime gifts from, or trusts created by, her mother, or from any outright bequests arising from her mother's death.

Plaintiff's mother, Violet Healy, was alive at the time of the 1972 divorce. She had made a will in 1964 establishing a trust of all her assets with plaintiff as sole beneficiary. In 1969, Violet Healy executed a codicil calling for cash bequests to plaintiff and her three children in the amount of $15,000 each. The remainder of the will was unaltered. Shortly thereafter, Violet Healy suffered a second, crippling stroke. Both parties admit they assumed she was thereafter incompetent to rewrite her will or to make a valid lifetime transfer of property.

During the interim between the 1964 execution of the will and her second stroke, Violet Healy's first husband died and she married Francis X. Healy. Unbeknownst to the parties, Violet Healy before her death in 1975 transferred to the joint ownership of Francis and Violet Healy her certificates of deposit, which had amounted to $180,000 at the time of the 1972 stipulation between the parties. Also, Violet Healy had drawn a new will leaving all her remaining estate to her husband.

Amidst a will contest and accusations that Francis X. Healy had used undue influence in causing his wife to rewrite her will, negotiations ensued between Francis X. Healy and plaintiff. An irrevocable trust was established providing for substantially the same result as Violet Healy's original will envisioned except that Francis X. Healy was named the first life beneficiary. Francis X. Healy died in late 1977 or early 1978. Plaintiff is currently life beneficiary of the trust and received income therefrom of $8,925.20 in 1978.

Defendant terminated alimony payments when plaintiff commenced receipt of monies from the trust. Plaintiff moved to find defendant in contempt for refusing to pay $3,541.65 in payments she claimed were owed. She prayed that defendant be ordered to pay that amount and, due to changed circumstances caused by inflation, requested that alimony payments be increased. Defendant countersued, requesting that the court adjudge that he was not liable for past alimony payments and terminated his future obligation.

The lower court concluded that the conditions specified in the divorce stipulation to bring about an end to alimony payments substantially occurred when plaintiff received money from the trust. * * *

Plaintiff claims that she has not received any income from lifetime gifts from, or trusts created by, her mother as specified in the divorce stipulation. The income, she contends, was from a trust created by an intervenor, Francis X. Healy. Citing *Braine v. Braine*, [citation] plaintiff urges this Court to preclude a rewriting of the contract terms involved in the divorce settlement.

In *Braine*, this Court noted a reluctance to alter an arrangement stipulated to by the parties to a divorce. Noting the similarity with a commercial contract agreement, we stated: "For the parties have contracted, and, if modification is freely indulged or granted without warrant, a party may have forfeited rights or positions of advantage for consideration that suddenly becomes insecure or inadequate." [Citation.]

The case at bar, however, presents a tangent to the *Braine* situation. Both parties when they agreed to the divorce arrangements felt that Violet Healy had become incapacitated from illness and thus could not revise her will. Based upon that circumstance, the parties came to a mutually satisfactory settlement. That aspect of the parties' consideration, however, was not accurate, and where a contract has been entered into under a mutual mistake regarding a material fact, the contract may be avoided in a court of law. [Citation.] "The mistake must be one vitally affecting a fact or facts on the basis of which the parties have contracted; and where they have mutually assumed a certain state of facts to exist and contracted on the faith of that assumption, relief from the bargain should be given if the assumption is erroneous." [Citation.]

The evidence clearly reveals circumstances intervening beyond the expectation of the parties. When such a situation is presented, a court may exercise discretion in amending an alimony agreement. [Citation.] Consequently, the modification reached by the lower court is affirmed.

* * *

Affirmed.

PROBLEMS

1. A and B were negotiating, and A's attorney prepared a long and carefully drawn contract which was given to B for examination. Five days later and prior to its execution, B's eyes became so infected that it was impossible for him to read. Ten days thereafter and during the continuance of the illness A called upon B and urged him to sign the contract, telling him that time was running out. B signed the contract despite the fact he was unable to read it. In a subsequent action by A, B claimed that the contract was not binding upon him because it was impossible for him to read and he did not know what it contained prior to his signing it. Decision?

2. (a) A tells B that he paid $150,000 for his farm in 1981, and that he believes it is worth twice that at the present time. Relying upon these statements, B buys the farm from A for $225,000. A did pay $150,000 for the farm in 1981, but its value has increased only slightly, and it is presently not worth $300,000. On discovering this, B offers to reconvey the farm to A and sues for the return of his $225,000. Result?

(b) Modify the facts in (a) by assuming that A had paid $100,000 for the property in 1981, what result?

3. On September 1, A in Portland, Oregon, wrote a letter to B in New York City offering to sell to B 1,000 tons of chromite at $48.00 per ton, to be shipped by *S. S. Malabar* sailing from Portland, Oregon, to New York City via the Panama Canal. Upon receiving the letter on September 5, B im-

mediately mailed to A a letter stating that she accepted the offer. There were two ships by the name of *S. S. Malabar* sailing from Portland to New York City via the Panama Canal, one sailing in October and the other sailing in December. At the time of mailing her letter of acceptance B knew of both sailings and further knew that A knew only of the December sailing. Is there a contract? If so, to which *S. S. Malabar* does it relate?

4. A owes B, a police captain, $500. A threatens B that unless B gives him a discharge from the debt, A will disclose the fact that B has on several occasions become highly intoxicated and has been seen in the company of certain disreputable persons. B, induced by fear that such a disclosure would cost him his position or in any event lead to social disgrace, gives A a release, but subsequently sues to set it aside and recover on his claim. Decision?

5. A owned a farm which was worth about $600 an acre. By false representations of fact, A induced B to buy the farm at $1,500 an acre. Shortly after taking possession of the farm, B discovered oil under the land. A, on learning this, sues to have the sale set aside on the ground that it was voidable because of fraud. Decision?

6. On February 2, A induced B to purchase from her fifty (50) shares of stock in the XYZ Corporation for $10,000, representing that the actual book value of each share was $200. A certificate for fifty (50) shares was delivered to B. On February 16, B discovered that the book value was only $50 per share on February 2. Thereafter, B sues A. Decision?

7. D mistakenly accused P's son, S, of negligently burning down D's barn. P believed that his son, S, was guilty of the wrong, and that he, P, was personally liable for the damage, since S was only fifteen years old. Upon demand made by D, P paid D $2,500 for the damage to D's barn. After making this payment, P learned that his son, S, had not caused the burning of D's barn and was in no way responsible for its burning. P then sued D to recover $2,500 which he had paid D. Decision?

8. Jones, a farmer, found an odd-looking stone in his fields. He went to Smith, the town jeweler, and asked him what he thought it was. Smith said he did not know but thought it might be a ruby. Jones asked Smith what he would pay for it, and Smith said two hundred dollars; whereupon Jones sold it to Smith for $200. The stone turned out to be an uncut diamond worth $3,000. Jones brought an action against Smith to recover the stone. On trial, it was proved that Smith actually did not know the stone was a diamond when he bought it, but thought it might be a ruby. Decision?

9. Decedent, a bedridden, lonely woman of eighty-six years, owned outright Greenacre, her ancestral estate. F, her physician and friend, visited her weekly and was held in the highest regard by Decedent. Decedent was extremely fearful of pain and suffering and depended upon F to ease her anxiety and pain. Several months before her death Decedent deeded Greenacre to F for $5,000. The fair market value of Greenacre at this time was $125,000. Decedent was survived by two children and six grandchildren. Decedent's children challenge the validity of the deed. Decision?

Chapter 10

CONSIDERATION

IN order for a promise or agreement to be binding, the requirement of legally sufficient consideration must be satisfied. If consideration is absent, neither party can enforce the promise or agreement. The doctrine of consideration has been used to ensure that promises are enforced only where the parties have exchanged something of value in the eye of the law. *Gratuitous* (gift) promises, accordingly, are not legally enforceable.

Consideration is whatever is given in exchange for something else and is present only when the parties intend an exchange, whether it be a promise exchanged for a promise, a promise for an act, or a promise exchanged for a forbearance to act. Thus, there are two basic elements to consideration: (1) legal sufficiency (something of value), and (2) bargained for exchange. Both must be present for the requirement of consideration to be satisfied.

Section 71 of the Restatement, defines consideration for a promise as (a) an act other than a promise; (b) a forbearance; (c) the creation, modification, or destruction of a legal relation; or (d) a return promise bargained for and given in exchange for the promise. The consideration may be given to the promisor or to some other person. It may be given by the promisee or by some other person.

LEGAL SUFFICIENCY

The doctrine of consideration requires that the promises or performance of *both* parties be legally sufficient. If the requisite mutuality of consideration does not exist, the contract is void. To be legally sufficient, the promise must be something of "value in the eye of the law," either a benefit to the promisor *or* a detriment to the promisee.

Definition

The definition of legal sufficiency is technical, and in certain cases its application produces a result which is artificial. To be legally sufficient, the consideration exchanged for the promise must be either a legal detriment to the promisee *or* a legal benefit to the promisor.

Legal detriment means (1) the doing (or undertaking to do) that which the promisee was under no prior legal obligation to do *or* (2) the refraining from doing (or undertaking to refrain from doing) that which he was previously under no legal obligation to refrain from doing. On the other hand, **legal benefit** means the obtaining by the promisor of that which he had no prior legal right to obtain.

Unilateral Contracts

In the unilateral contract a promise is exchanged for an act or a forbearance to act. Accordingly only one party is the promisor, while the other party is the promisee. For example, A promises to pay B $500 if B paints A's house. B paints A's house.

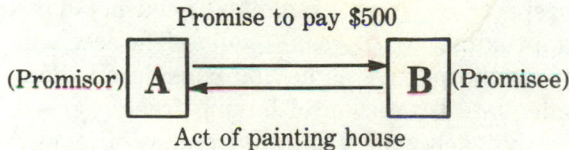

Promise to pay $500

(Promisor) A   B (Promisee)

Act of painting house

In order for A's promise to be binding, it must be supported by consideration consisting of either a legal detriment to B, the promisee, or a legal benefit to A, the promisor. B's having painted the house is a legal detriment to B, the promisee, because she was under no prior legal duty to paint A's house. Also, B's painting A's house is a legal benefit to A, the promisor, because A had no prior legal right to have his house painted by B.

A unilateral contract may also consist of a promise exchanged for a forbearance. To illustrate, A negligently injures B, for which B may recover damages in a tort action. A

promises B $5,000 if B forbears from bringing suit. B accepts by not filing suit.

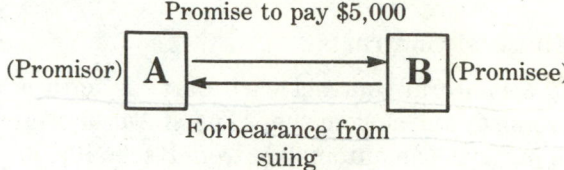

Promise to pay $5,000

(Promisor) A   B (Promisee)

Forbearance from suing

A's promise to pay B $5,000 is binding because it is supported by consideration; B, the promisee, has incurred a legal detriment by refraining from bringing suit which he was under no prior legal obligation to refrain from doing. A, the promisor, has received a legal benefit because she had no prior legal right to B's forbearance from bringing suit.

To illustrate further, suppose that A promises B, a high school graduate, that if B will attend and graduate from the XYZ College, A will pay to B upon graduation the entire cost of her college education. B enters XYZ College and duly graduates. The college education which she received is an actual benefit to B, but legally she suffered a detriment in graduating from XYZ College in that she gave up her freedom to attend any other college, or to not attend college at all, in consideration for A's promise. Consequently, the consideration which B, the promisee, gave for A's promise, although not actually detrimental, was legally detrimental to the promisee B. It is therefore legally sufficient, and A's promise is enforceable by B. Furthermore, A, the promisor, may have received no actual benefit from B's having obtained a college education at XYZ College, yet A received a legal benefit in that he obtained from B something that he had no previous right to have, namely, B's attendance at XYZ College and her graduation. This legal benefit may be of no value or usefulness to A, but nevertheless A's promise resulted in A's obtaining a performance from B which A was not otherwise entitled to have. Thus, in this illustration the promisor (A) received a legal benefit and the promisee (B) suffered a legal detriment, although **either** one of these would satisfy the test of legal sufficiency.

Bilateral Contracts

In a bilateral contract each party is **both** a promisor and a promisee. Thus, if A promises to purchase an automobile from B for $10,000 and B promises to sell the automobile to A for $10,000, the following relationship exists:

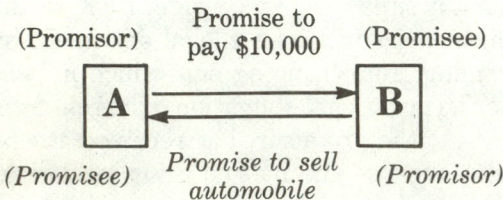

(Promisor)   Promise to pay $10,000   *(Promisee)*

(Promisee)   Promise to sell automobile   *(Promisor)*

A's promise to pay B $10,000 is binding if that promise is supported by legal consideration which may consist of either a legal detriment to B, the *promisee*, or a legal benefit to A, the *promisor*. B's promise to sell A the automobile is a legal detriment to B because he was under no prior legal duty to sell the automobile to A. Moreover, B's promise is also a legal benefit to A because A had no prior legal right to that automobile. Consequently, A's promise to pay $10,000 to B *is* supported by consideration and is binding.

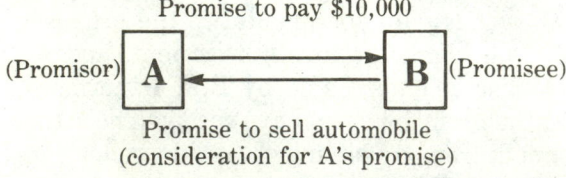

Promise to pay $10,000

(Promisor) A   B (Promisee)

Promise to sell automobile
(consideration for A's promise)

For **B's promise** to sell the automobile to A to be binding, it likewise must be supported by consideration, which may be either a legal detriment to A, the *promisee*, or a legal benefit to B, the *promisor*. A's promise to pay B $10,000 is a legal detriment to A because he was under no prior legal duty to pay $10,000 to B. At the same time, A's promise is also a legal benefit to B because B had no prior legal right to the $10,000. Thus, B's promise

to sell the automobile is supported by consideration and *is* binding.

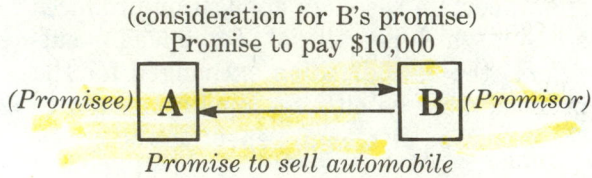

(consideration for B's promise)
Promise to pay $10,000

(Promisee) A   B *(Promisor)*

Promise to sell automobile

To summarize, in order for *A's promise* to B to be binding, it must be supported by legally sufficient consideration, which requires that the promise or forbearance received from B in exchange provide either a legal benefit to A *(the promisor)* or a legal detriment to B *(the promisee)*. In most cases where there is legal detriment to the promisee, a legal benefit to the promisor will also be found. However, the presence of **either** one is sufficient. In a bilateral contract where B makes a return promise to A, that *promise* must also be supported by consideration.

See Collins v. Parsons College.

Adequacy

Legal sufficiency has nothing to do with adequacy of consideration. Restatement, Section 79. The subject matter which the parties respectively have exchanged need not have approximately the same value. The law will treat the parties as having considered them adequate by reason of having freely agreed to the exchange. The requirement of legally sufficient consideration is, therefore, *not* at all concerned with whether the bargain was good or bad, or whether one party received disproportionately more or less than what he gave or promised in exchange for it. Such an inquiry might be relevant if a question of fraud, duress, or undue influence were involved. However, the requirement of legally sufficient consideration is simply (1) that the parties have agreed to an exchange; and (2) that with respect to each party the subject matter exchanged, or promised in exchange, either imposed a legal detriment upon the promisee or conferred a legal benefit upon the promisor.

Mutuality of Obligation

Both parties to a contract must give consideration in order for the contract to be enforceable. Each promise is the consideration for the other, and the parties are mutually obligated to perform their respective promises. However, it must appear that each promise is definite enough to be capable of being broken. This is in accord with the rule that the terms of a contract must be certain and definite. By mutuality of obligation it is meant that each party or promisor must be bound or neither is bound. This presents some problems in instances involving illusory promises, output and requirement contracts, and exclusive dealing contracts. The former destroys the mutuality of consideration while the latter two do not.

Illusory Promises It is fundamental to the formation of a bilateral contract that if one party is not bound, neither party is bound. A promise by its literal terms may impose no obligation upon the promisor. Thus, a promise to purchase such quantity of goods as the promisor may "desire" or "want" or "wish to buy" imposes no obligation to buy any goods, as its performance is entirely optional. Thus, if A offers to sell to B as many barrels of oil as B shall choose at forty dollars per barrel, there is no contract for lack of consideration. B may wish or desire to buy none of the oil, for in buying none he would fulfill his promise. An offer containing such a promise, although accepted by the offeree, does not create a contract because the promise is illusory—performance is entirely optional with B, and no constraint is placed upon his freedom. He is not bound to do anything nor can A reasonably expect to receive any performance. Thus, B, by his promise, suffers no legal detriment and confers no legal benefit. Consequently B's promise does not provide legally sufficient consideration for A's promise and thus A's promise is not binding upon A. The rule is that both parties must be bound or neither is bound.

Output and Requirement Contracts An agreement to sell the entire production of a particular plant, factory, or mine is called an output contract. It affords the seller an assured market for her product. An agreement to purchase all materials of a particular kind is called a requirements contract. It assures the buyer of a ready source of inventory or supplies. These contracts when made may or may not be accompanied by an estimate of the quantity to be sold or to be purchased. Nevertheless, these promises are *not* illusory. The buyer under a requirements contract does not promise to buy as much as she desires to buy, but rather to buy as much as is needed. Similarly, under an output contract the seller promises to sell to the buyer the seller's entire production, not merely as much as the seller desires.

Furthermore, the Code, Section 2-306(1), as well as the Restatement, Section 77, impose a good faith limitation upon the quantity to be sold or purchased under an output or requirements contract. Thus, an output or requirements contract means such actual output or requirements as may occur in good faith, except that no quantity unreasonably disproportionate to any stated estimate or, in the absence of a stated estimate, to any normal prior output or requirements may be demanded. B, therefore, after contracting with A to sell to A its entire output cannot increase its production from one eight-hour shift per day to three eight-hour shifts per day.

Exclusive Dealing Contracts Where a manufacturer of goods grants an exclusive franchise or license to a distributor to sell its products in a designated territory, unless otherwise agreed, an implied obligation is imposed on the manufacturer to use its best efforts to supply the goods and on the distributor to use his best efforts to promote their sale. U.C.C. Section 2-306(2). The obligations which arise upon acceptance of the exclusive franchise are sufficient consideration to bind both parties to the contract. *See Otis F. Wood v. Lucy, Lady Duff-Gordon.*

Conditional Contracts The fact that the obligation to perform a contract may not arise until the happening of a specified event does not invalidate the contract. This is so even though the specified event may never occur. The requisite mutuality of obligation nonetheless exists, since neither party need perform if the event does not occur. The same result obtains where the obligation to perform terminates upon the occurrence of a specified event.

Thus, if A offers to pay B $8,000 for B's automobile, provided that A receives such amount as an inheritance from the estate of her deceased uncle, and B accepts the offer, the duty of A to pay $8,000 to B is *conditioned* upon her receiving $8,000 from her deceased uncle's estate. The consideration moving from B to A is the transfer of title to the automobile. The consideration moving from A to B is the promise of $8,000 subject to the condition. Although the contract is conditional, it is complete, definite, and certain. If the express condition was an event the occurrence of which was impossible, then no contract would exist because the agreement would be illusory. Restatement, Section 76.

Pre-existing Public Obligation

The law does not regard the performance of or promise to perform a pre-existing public duty as either a legal detriment to the party under the prior legal obligation or as a benefit to the other party. A public duty is one which does not arise out of a contract but is imposed upon members of society by force of the common law or by statute. Illustrations are found in the law of torts, such as the duty not to commit an assault, battery, false imprisonment, or defamation. The criminal law also imposes upon everyone numerous duties of a public nature. Thus, if A promises to pay B, the village ruffian, $100 not to abuse him physically, A's promise is unenforceable since B is under a pre-existing public obligation imposed by both tort and criminal law to refrain from so acting.

Public officials, such as the mayor of a city, members of a city council, policemen, and firemen, are under a pre-existing obligation to perform their duties by virtue of their public office. If A's house catches fire and A telephones the chief of the city fire department and promises him $500 if he will immediately send a fire truck and firemen to A's house to put out the fire, and he does so, the promise is not enforceable. A public official will not be allowed to gain privately by performing his duty.

See Denney v. Reppert.

Pre-existing Contractual Obligation

The performance of a pre-existing contractual duty, which is neither doubtful nor the subject of honest dispute, is also legally insufficient consideration because the doing of what one is legally bound to do is neither detriment to the promisee nor benefit to the promisor. For example, if A employs B for one year at a salary of $1,000 per month, and at the end of six months promises B that in addition to the salary she will pay B $3,000 if B remains on the job for the remainder of the period originally agreed upon, A's promise is not binding for lack of legally sufficient consideration. However, if B's duties were by agreement changed even to a small extent in nature or amount, A's promise would be binding.

In a case involving a building contract, the parties entered into an oral contract in June, 1969, under which plaintiff agreed to construct a building for defendant on a time and materials basis, at a maximum cost of $56,146, plus sales tax and extras ordered by defendant. When the building was 90 percent completed defendant told plaintiff he was unhappy with the whole job as "the thing wasn't just being run right." The parties then on October 17 signed a written agreement lowering the maximum cost to $52,000 plus sales tax. Plaintiff thereafter completed the building at a cost of $64,155. The maximum under the June oral agreement, plus extras and sales tax, totalled $61,040. Defendant contended that he was obligated to pay only the lower maximum fixed by the October 17 agreement. The Supreme Court of Washington held that the October 17 modification agreement was not binding for lack of consideration and plaintiff was entitled to recover under the original agreement, stating:

Applying our holding to the facts in this case, we must conclude that no consideration existed to support the October 17th agreement. Under the oral contract plaintiff had an antecedent duty to complete the building; defendant had an antecedent duty to pay a maximum of $56,146 plus extras, plus sales tax. Under the October 17th agreement plaintiff had the same duty while defendant had a lesser duty, unsupported by consideration. This is not a case of the mutual surrender of rights constituting consideration. *Rosellini v. Banchero*, 83 Wash.2d 268, 272, 517 P.2d 955, 958 (1974). *See also Denney v. Reppert.*

Modification of a Pre-existing Contract To be enforceable, a modification of an existing contract, under the common law, must be supported by mutual consideration. The key is that the modification be supported by some new consideration beyond that which is already owing. For example, A and B agree that A shall put in a gravel driveway for B at a cost of $2,000. Subsequently, B agrees to pay an additional $1,000 if A will blacktop the driveway. Since A was not bound by the original contract to provide blacktopping, he would incur a legal detriment in doing so and is therefore entitled to the additional $1,000. *See Brenner v. Little Red School House, Limited.*

The Code has modified the common law rule by providing that a contract for the sale of goods can be effectively modified by the parties without new consideration, provided they so intend and act in good faith. Section 2-209(1). Moreover, the Restatement has moved toward this position by providing that a modification of an executory contract is binding if it is fair and equitable in light of the surrounding facts which were not antic-ipated by the parties when the contract was made. Restatement, Section 89.

Settlement of an Undisputed Debt An "undisputed" debt is an uncontested obligation to pay a sum certain in money or to pay an amount which by computation can be reduced to a sum certain in money. If the debtor has made an express promise to pay a specific sum of money, e.g., $100, the debt is *undisputed*. If she has agreed to pay three dollars per bushel for apples delivered and fifty bushels of apples have been delivered, the debt is liquidated in the amount of $150.

Under the common law, the payment of a sum of money in consideration of a promise to discharge a fully matured undisputed debt in an amount larger than the sum paid is legally insufficient to support the promise of discharge. To illustrate, assume that B owes A $100, and in consideration of B's paying A fifty dollars, A agrees to accept the lesser sum in full satisfaction of the debt. In a subsequent suit by A against B to recover the remaining fifty dollars, at common law A is entitled to judgment for fifty dollars on the ground that A's promise of discharge is not binding for the reason that B's payment of fifty dollars was no legal detriment to the promisee, B, as he was under a *pre-existing legal obligation* to pay that much and more. By the same token, the receipt of fifty dollars was no legal benefit to the promisor A. Consequently, the consideration for A's promise of discharge was legally insufficient, and A is not bound on his promise. However, if A had accepted from B any new or different consideration, such as the sum of forty dollars and a fountain pen worth ten dollars or less or even the fountain pen with no payment of money, in full satisfaction of the $100 debt, the consideration moving from B would be legally sufficient inasmuch as B was under no legal obligation to give a fountain pen to A. In this example, consideration would also exist if A had agreed to accept fifty dollars *before* the debt became due, in full satisfaction of the debt. B was under no legal obligation to pay any of the debt before its due date. Consequently, B's early payment is a legal detriment to B as well as a legal benefit to A. The law is not concerned with the amount of the discount, as that is simply a question of adequacy. Likewise, B's payment of a lesser amount on the due date at an agreed-upon different place of payment would be legally sufficient consideration.

Settlement of a Disputed Debt A disputed debt is an obligation which is either contested as to its existence or as to its amount. Implied contracts frequently create obligations to pay uncertain amounts. For example, where a person has requested professional services from a doctor or a dentist and no agreement was made with respect to the amount of the fee to be charged, the doctor or dentist is entitled to receive from her patient a reasonable fee for the services which have been rendered. As no definite amount has been agreed upon, the obligation of the patient is uncertain or unliquidated. The legal obligation of the patient is to pay the reasonable worth of the services that were performed. When the doctor or dentist sends the patient a bill for her services, the amount stated in the bill is her estimate of the reasonable value of the services, but the debt does not in this manner become liquidated until and unless the patient agrees to pay the amount of the bill. If the patient honestly disputes the amount that is owing and tenders in full settlement an amount less than the bill, acceptance of the lesser amount by the creditor discharges the debt. Thus, if A sends to B, an accountant, a check for $120 in payment of his debt to B for services rendered, which services A considered worthless but for which B billed A $600, B's acceptance of the check releases A from any further liability. A has given up his right to further dispute the billing, while B has forfeited his right to further collection. Thus, there is mutuality of consideration.

In order for the giving up of a disputed claim to constitute legally sufficient consideration, the dispute must be *honest* and not

frivolous. Where the dispute is based upon contentions which are non-meritorious or not made in good faith, giving up such contentions by the debtor is no legal detriment.

Substituted Contracts Distinguished A substituted contract occurs when the parties to a contract mutually agree to rescind their original contract and enter into a new one. Substituted contracts are perfectly valid and effective to discharge the original contract and to impose obligations under the new contract. The rescission is binding in that each party by giving up his rights under the original contract has provided consideration to the other, as long as each party still has rights under the original contract.

BARGAINED FOR EXCHANGE

The central idea behind consideration is that the parties have intentionally entered into a bargained exchange with one another and have each given to the other something in exchange for his promise or performance. Bargain as used in this context does not mean making an advantageous deal or buying something at a price less than its fair market value. "Bargain" as used in the phrase "bargained for exchange" means simply that the parties have negotiated and mutually agreed upon the terms of what each party is giving to the other party in exchange for what he is receiving. Thus, a promise to give someone a birthday present is without consideration, as the promisor received nothing in exchange for his promise of a present.

Past Consideration

The element of exchange is absent where a promise is given for a past transaction. Hence, past consideration is no consideration. A promise made on account of something which the promisee has already done is not enforceable. For example, A gives emergency care to B's adult son while the son is ill. B subsequently promises to reimburse A for her expenses. B's promise is not binding because there is no bargained for exchange. Consideration is the inducement for a promise or performance. Therefore, unbargained for past events are not consideration, despite their designation as "past consideration."

Moral Obligation

A promise made in order to satisfy a pre-existing moral obligation is unenforceable for lack of consideration. Instances involving such moral obligation include promises to pay for board and lodging previously furnished to a needy relative of the promisor, promises to pay debts owed by a relative of the promisor, and promises of an employer to pay a completely disabled former employee a sum of money in addition to the amount of an award made under a worker's compensation statute. Although in many cases the moral obligation may be strong by reason of the particular facts and circumstances, no liability attaches to the promise. *See Harrington v. Taylor.*

Third Parties

Consideration to support a promise may be given to a person other than the promisor if the promisor bargains for that exchange. For example, A promises to pay B fifteen dollars if B delivers a specified book to C.

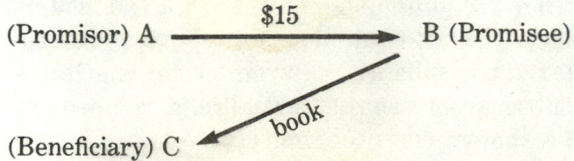

A's promise is binding because B incurred a legal detriment by delivering the book to C, as B was under no prior legal obligation to do so. A's promise to pay $15 is also consideration for B's promise to give C the book.

Conversely, consideration may be given by some person other than the promisee. For example, A promises to pay B twenty-five dollars in return for D's promise to give A a radio.

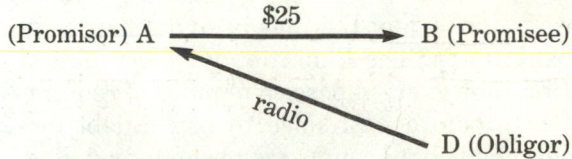

A's promise to pay twenty-five dollars is consideration for D's promise to give A a radio and vice versa.

CONTRACTS WITHOUT CONSIDERATION

Certain transactions, even though they are not supported by consideration, are nevertheless enforceable. These transactions include the following:

Promise to Pay Debt Barred by the Statute of Limitations

Every State has in effect statutes which provide that actions to enforce debts must be commenced within a prescribed period of time after the debts become due. Actions not commenced within the specified time period will be dismissed. The time periods vary among the States and also vary with the nature of the claim sought to be enforced. These statutes are known as Statutes of Limitations.

A new promise by the debtor to pay the debt renews the running of the Statute of Limitations for a second statutory period. This new promise requires no consideration. The following facts operate as a sufficient promise unless circumstances indicate otherwise: (1) a voluntary, unqualified admission that the debt is owing; (2) a partial payment of the debt; or (3) a statement that the Statute of Limitations will not be pleaded as a defense. Restatement, Section 82.

Promise to Pay Debt Discharged in Bankruptcy

Another exception to the requirement that consideration be given in exchange for a promise in order to make it binding is a promise to pay a debt that has been discharged in bankruptcy. The Bankruptcy Reform Act of 1978, however, imposes a number of requirements before a promise to pay a debt discharged in bankruptcy may be enforced. Section 524(c) of this Act provides the following requirements:

1. The debtor's promise must be made before the discharge of the debt is granted;
2. The debtor does not revoke the promise within thirty days after the promise becomes enforceable;
3. The debtor, if an individual, must be informed by the bankruptcy court of his legal rights and the effects of his new promise; and
4. The debtor's promise, if the debtor is an individual and the debt is a consumer obligation, must be approved by the bankruptcy court as being in the best interest of the debtor.

Although these new limitations do not prohibit promises to pay a debt discharged in bankruptcy, they should reduce the frequency of such promises, especially in cases involving consumer debts.

Promissory Estoppel

When a promise is made under circumstances which should lead the promisor reasonably to expect that the promisee will be induced by the promise to take definite and substantial action or forbearance in reliance on the promise, and the promisee does take such action or forbearance, the promisor is estopped, or prohibited, from denying the promise. The basis of the promisor's liability is the doctrine of promissory estoppel, and consideration for the promise is not required. Section 90 of the Restatement, provides: "(1) A promise which the promisor should reasonably expect to induce action or forbearance on the part of the promisee or a third person and which does induce such action or forbearance is binding if injustice can be avoided only by enforcement of the promise. The remedy granted for breach may be limited as justice requires."

Promissory estoppel does not mean that every gratuitous promise is binding simply because it is followed by a change of position on the part of the promisee. Liability is created by the change of position in justifiable reliance on the promise. For example, A promises B not to foreclose on a mortgage A owns on B's land for a period of six months. B then expends $100,000 on a building constructed on the land. A's promise not to foreclose is binding on A under the doctrine of promissory estoppel.

The most frequently occurring application of the doctrine of promissory estoppel is to charitable subscriptions. Numerous churches, memorials, college buildings, stadia, hospitals, and other structures used for religious, educational, and charitable purposes have been built with the assistance of contributions made through fulfillment of pledges or promises to contribute to particular worthwhile causes. Although the pledgor regards herself as making a gift for a charitable purpose and gift promises are generally not enforceable, the courts have generally enforced charitable subscription promises. Despite the fact that various reasons and theories have been advanced in support of liability, the one most accepted is that the subscription has induced a change of position by the promisee (the church, school, or charitable organization) in reliance on the promise. *See Mount Sinai Hospital of Greater Miami, Inc. v. Jordan.* The Restatement, moreover, has relaxed the reliance requirement for charitable subscriptions so that actual reliance need not be shown; the probability or reliance is sufficient.

Contracts under Seal

A contract executed under seal is a formal contract, in contrast with a simple or informal contract. A sealed contract, as a formal contract, derives its validity and binding force from the formality with which it is executed, namely, its execution under seal. A **seal,** at common law, is an impression on wax or other adhesive substance attached to the parchment or paper, or on the parchment or paper itself. The word "seal," whether handwritten, typewritten or printed is now sufficient as a seal. The law which made sealed promises or contracts binding was developed before the law of simple or informal contracts. Consequently, the presence of a seal on a written contract or promise does not import consideration, nor can it be said that it renders consideration unnecessary. The matter of consideration is simply not in point. A contract under seal is binding solely because of the fact of its execution under seal.

In some States a promise under seal is still binding without consideration. Nevertheless, most states have abolished by statute the distinction between contracts under seal and written unsealed contracts. In these states the seal is no longer recognized as a substitute for consideration. The U.C.C. specifically makes seals inoperative with respect to contracts for the sale of goods.

Other Promises which Require No Consideration

Renunciation Under both the Code, Section 1-107, and the Restatement, Section 74, any claim or right arising out of an alleged breach of contract can be discharged in whole or in part without consideration by a written waiver or renunciation signed and delivered by the aggrieved party.

Firm Offer Under the Code a written offer signed by a merchant offeror to buy or sell goods is not revocable for lack of consideration during the time stated that it is open, not to exceed three months, or if no time is stated, for a reasonable time. Section 2-205.

CASES

Legal Sufficiency

COLLINS v. PARSONS COLLEGE

Supreme Court of Iowa, 1973.
203 N.W.2d 594.

UHLENHOPP, J.

This appeal involves the enforceability of an employment agreement between a teacher and Parsons College.

Ben L. Collins holds bachelor and master of arts degrees and a doctor of philosophy degree. He studied at Harvard University in addition and taught for a number of years. In the spring of 1966 he was a full professor with tenure at Wisconsin State University at Whitewater.

In March of 1966, Collins was invited to confer with Dr. W. B. Munson, vice president for academic affairs of Parsons College. Collins testified that the following transpired at that conference:

Dr. Munson asked me to his office and told me he was prepared to offer me a contract for $25,000.00, that he would give me the rank of full professor and that I would be on full tenure.

Further regarding the conference, Collins testified concerning salary increments:

Yes, he told me there would be annual increments of $1,000.00 per year until I reached $30,000.00 in 1971.

The college introduced no evidence contradicting Collins' testimony about the conference.

Munson tendered Collins a written contract for the first year incorporating the terms stated at the conference. Collins was to t two trimesters in the academic year ning October 1, 1966, at a salary of with the academic rank of "Profe glish and Humanities with tenu tract covered the 1966-1967 school year and incorporated Parsons' faculty bylaws by reference. The last two paragraphs of the contract stated:

4. You are hereby placed on tenure.
5. You will receive annual increments of $1,000.00 to the level of $30,000.00 by 1971.

The faculty bylaws provided in part:

The service of a Faculty member on permanent tenure shall be terminated before retirement or his rank reduced only for just cause. Charges which may lead to the dismissal or reduction in rank of Faculty members with permanent tenure shall be made in writing through the Professional Problems Committee whose recommendation will be presented to a meeting of the tenured Faculty.

* * *

After considering the offer of the college, Collins accepted it and gave up his teaching position in Wisconsin. He signed the contract covering the first year and Munson signed it on behalf of the college.

* * *

In February 1968, however, Collins was tendered a different contract, to cover the following year. He was still to have the rank of "Professor of English with tenure," but at a salary of $15,000 with no provision for increment. The tendered contract also stated:

By accepting this contract, the Faculty member agrees that it shall constitute the only contract of employment with the College for the period set forth above and that he waives any rights or claims arising from any other contract of employment with the College, save and except any rights he may have to any unpaid salary or fringe benefits for service performed by him under any previous contract with the College.

* * *

Collins did not sign this contract and in ʼie course the college notified him that he ʼuld not be employed the following year. desired to teach at the college under the ʼnal agreement, but in view of the action of the college he sought employment elsewhere. He secured a position at the University of North Dakota and taught there at a salary of $15,000 for the academic year commencing in the fall of 1968, $15,800 commencing in 1969, $16,400 commencing in 1970, and $16,700 commencing in 1971.

No one suggests that Collins did not perform his work properly at Parsons College or that the college had grounds to discharge him or to depart from the original agreement. No written charge was made against him before the tenured faculty, or before anyone else for that matter.

In Collins' present action against the college, he asks as damages the difference between the amount he was promised by the college to 1971 and the amount he was able to earn elsewhere. The trial court tried the case by ordinary proceedings without a jury and held for the college. The controlling facts on liability are really uncontroverted. The dispute is over the legal conclusions to be drawn from the facts.

* * *

Consideration. We have considerable doubt that an agreement for tenure such as this one requires mutuality in any event, *as to duration of the employment.* Tenured teachers in institutions of higher learning have permanent positions as spelled out in the bylaws of their institutions, just as civil servants have permanent positions as spelled out in statutes. Yet such teachers and servants are free to resign if they wish. But a different situation exists *as to compensation to be paid.* This case presents both the duration and compensation aspects.

We do not place the decision, however, on the issue of whether mutuality is required in the case of tenured positions such as the present one. The contention of the college that mutuality of obligation is essential is not strictly an accurate statement of the law. Promises must be mutually obligatory if they constitute the only consideration for each other. But if a promise is supported by other consideration, it is enforceable although the promisee has the right to terminate his undertaking or indeed makes no promise at all, as in the case of unilateral contracts. Speaking for the court, Judge Evans stated the principle thus:

If the lack of mutuality amounts to a lack of consideration, then the contract is invalid. But mere lack of mutuality in and of itself does not render a contract invalid. If mutual promises be the mutual consideration of a contract, then each promise must be enforceable in order to render the other enforceable. Though consideration is essential to the validity of a contract, it is not essential that such consideration consist of a mutual promise. A promissory note for a consideration is valid, though no mutuality appear thereon. This is true of all unilateral contracts which are supported by a consideration.

[Citations.]

The question before us, then, becomes one of consideration. Collins did not promise to serve permanently or even until 1971, and so we have no promise from him in exchange for the promise of the college to employ him permanently at a specified salary with increments to 1971. Did he provide other consideration?

Collins points to his surrender of his tenured position at Wisconsin State University to accept this position, to the knowledge of Parsons College. The evidence shows that he had good academic credentials as well as experience in teaching, and evidently the college believed he would be a valuable addition and would lend stature to its staff. The college appeared eager to get him and was aware that he was surrendering a secure position to accept its offer. Once Collins left Wisconsin, he lost his tenure there. Did his surrender of that position constitute consideration for the agreement of Parsons College?

Courts are divided on such a question, some holding yes and some no. [Citations.] This court has adverted to the question but does not appear to have decided it squarely. [Citations.] Some courts hold the surrender of employment to take a new job constitutes

consideration if the new employer is aware that the employee is giving up the other position. [Citations.] Generally consideration may, of course, consist of a detriment to the promisee. [Citations.] Consideration need not move to the promisor. Restatement, Contracts § 75, Comment *e*: "It matters not from whom the consideration moves or to whom it goes."

After considering the question, we think the better rule to be that an employee who gives up other employment to accept an offer of a permanent job provides independent consideration—at least, when as here the employment surrendered was itself permanent and the new employer is aware of the facts. [Citations.]

The result is that the college agreed to employ Collins permanently and at the salary and increments promised to 1971, and that Collins provided consideration for the agreement of the college.

* * *

Reversed and remanded with directions.

Exclusive Dealing Contracts

OTIS F. WOOD v. LUCY, LADY DUFF-GORDON

Court of Appeals of New York, 1917.
222 N.Y.88, 118 N.E. 214.

CARDOZO, J.

The defendant styles herself "a creator of fashions." Her favor helps a sale. Manufacturers of dresses, millinery, and like articles are glad to pay for a certificate of her approval. The things which she designs, fabrics, parasols and what not have a new value in the public mind when issued in her name. She employed the plaintiff to help her turn this vogue into money. He was to have the exclusive right, subject always to her approval, to place her indorsements on the designs of others. He was also to have the exclusive right to place her own designs on sale, or to license others to market them. In return, she was to have one-half of "all profits and revenues" derived from any contracts he might make. The exclusive right was to last at least one year from April 1, 1915, and thereafter from year to year unless terminated by notice of ninety days. The plaintiff says that he kept the contract on his part, and that the defendant broke it. She placed her indorsement on fabrics, dresses, and millinery without his knowledge, and withheld the profits. He sues her for the damages, and the case comes here on demurrer.

The agreement of employment is signed by both parties. It has a wealth of recitals. The defendant insists, however, that [the agreement] lacks the elements of a contract. She says that the plaintiff does not bind himself to anything. It is true that he does not promise in so many words that he will use reasonable efforts to place the defendant's indorsements and market her designs. We think, however, that such a promise is fairly to be implied. The law has outgrown its primitive stage of formalism when the precise word was the sovereign talisman, and every slip was fatal. It takes a broader view today. A promise may be lacking, and yet the whole writing may be "instinct with an obligation," imperfectly expressed [citation]. If that is so, there is a contract.

The implication of a promise here finds support in many circumstances. The defendant gave an *exclusive* privilege. She was to have no right for at least a year to place her own indorsements or market her own designs except through the agency of the plaintiff. The acceptance of the exclusive agency was an assumption of its duties. [Citations.] We are not to suppose that one party was to be placed at the mercy of the other. [Citations.] Many other terms of the agreement point the same way. We are told at the outset by way of recital that "the said Otis F. Wood possesses a business organization adapted to the placing of such indorsements as the said Lucy, Lady Duff-Gordon has approved." The implication is that the plaintiff's business organization will be used for the purpose for which it is adapted. But the terms of the defendant's compensation are even more significant. Her

sole compensation for the grant of an exclusive agency is to be one-half of all the profits resulting from the plaintiff's efforts. Unless he gave his efforts, she could never get anything. Without an implied promise, the transaction cannot have such business "efficacy as both parties must have intended that at all events it should have." [Citation.]

But the contract does not stop there. The plaintiff goes on to promise that he will account monthly for all moneys received by him, and that he will take out all such patents and copyrights and trademarks as may in his judgment be necessary to protect the rights and articles affected by the agreement. It is true, of course, as the appellate division has said, that if he was under no duty to try to market designs or to place certificates of indorsement, his promise to account for profits or take out copyrights would be valueless. But in determining the intention of the parties, the promise *has* a value. It helps to enforce the conclusion that the plaintiff *had* some duties. His promise to pay the defendant one-half of the profits and revenues resulting from the exclusive agency and to render accounts monthly, was a promise to use reasonable efforts to bring profits and revenues into existence. For this conclusion, the authorities are ample. * * *

Judgment reversed.

Pre-existing Obligation

DENNEY v. REPPERT

Court of Appeals of Kentucky, 1968.
432 S.W.2d 647.

MYRE, SPECIAL COMMISSIONER.

The sole question presented in this case is which of several claimants is entitled to an award for information leading to the apprehension and conviction of certain bank robbers.

* * *

On June 12th or 13th, 1963, three armed men entered the First State Bank, Eubank, Kentucky, and with a display of arms and threats robbed the bank of over $30,000. Later in the day they were apprehended by State Policemen Garret Godby, Johnny Simms, and Tilford Reppert, placed under arrest, and the entire loot was recovered. Later all of the prisoners were convicted and Garret Godby, Johnny Simms, and Tilford Reppert appeared as witnesses at the trial.

The First State Bank of Eubank was a member of the Kentucky Bankers Association which provided and advertised a reward of $500.00 for the arrest and conviction of each bank robber. Hence the outstanding reward for the three bank robbers was $1,500.00. Many became claimants for the reward and the Kentucky State Bankers Association, being unable to determine the merits of the claims for the reward, asked the circuit court to determine the merits of the various claims and to adjudge who was entitled to receive the reward or share in it. All of the claimants were made defendants in the action.

At the time of the robbery the claimants Murrell Denney, Joyce Buis, Rebecca McCollum, and Jewell Snyder were employees of the First State Bank of Eubank and came out of the grueling situation with great credit and glory. Each one of them deserves approbation and an accolade. They were vigilant in disclosing to the public and the peace officers the details of the crime, and in describing the culprits, and giving all the information that they possessed that would be useful in capturing the robbers. Undoubtedly, they performed a great service. It is in the evidence that the claimant Murrell Denney was conspicuous and energetic in his efforts to make known the robbery, to acquaint the officers as to the personal appearance of the criminals, and to give other pertinent facts.

The first question for determination is whether the employees of the robbed bank are eligible to receive or share in the reward? The great weight of authority answers in the negative. In Re Waggoner [citation] states the rule thusly:

To the general rule that, when a reward is offered to the general public for the performance of some

specified act, such reward may be claimed by any person who performs such act, is the exception of agents, employees, and public officials who are acting within the scope of their employment or official duties. * * *

Or, as the rule was set forth in *Forsythe v. Murnane et al.*, [citation]:

" * * * The defendent Delaney is and during all the times herein mentioned has been, employed by defendant Great Northern Railway Company * * * and by virtue of such employment it was his duty to do and perform all the things that were done and performed by him in the matter of the arrest, identification, and prosecution * * *.

"It is clear that defendant Delaney is not, in view of * * * his contractual relations and the duties in the premises * * * entitled to any part of the reward. * * *."

In *Stacy v. President, etc., of State Bank of Ill.* [citation] it was held that a director of a bank was not entitled to share in the reward offered by the bank for the arrest of a robber because it was his duty as a director to further the best interests of the bank, and apprehending one who had robbed the bank was in the best interest of the bank. [Citations.]

At the time of the robbery the claimants Murrell Denney, Joyce Buis, Rebecca McCollum, and Jewell Snyder were employees of the First State Bank of Eubank. They were under duty to protect and conserve the resources and moneys of the bank, and safeguard every interest of the institution furnishing them employment. Each of these employees exhibited great courage and cool bravery, in a time of stress and danger. The community and the county have recompensed them in commendation, admiration, and high praise, and the world looks on them as heroes. But in making known the robbery and assisting in acquainting the public and the officers with details of the crime and with identification of the robbers, they performed a duty to the bank and the public, for which they cannot claim a reward.

The claims of Corbin Reynolds, Julia Reynolds, Alvie Reynolds, and Gene Reynolds also must fail. According to their statements they gave valuable information to the arresting officers. However, they did not follow the procedure as set forth in the offer of reward in that they never filed a claim with the Kentucky Bankers Association. It is well established that a claimant of a reward must comply with the terms and conditions of the offer of reward. [Citation.]

State Policemen Garret Godby, Johnny Simms, and Tilford Reppert made the arrest of the bank robbers and captured the stolen money. All participated in the prosecution. At the time of the arrest, it was the duty of the state policemen to apprehend the criminals. Under the law they cannot claim or share in the reward and they are interposing no claim to it.

This leaves the defendant, Tilford Reppert the sole eligible claimant. The record shows that at the time of the arrest he was a deputy sheriff in Rockcastle County, but the arrest and recovery of the stolen money took place in Pulaski County. He was out of his jurisdiction, and was thus under no legal duty to make the arrest, and is thus eligible to claim and receive the reward. In *Kentucky Bankers Ass'n et al. v. Cassady* [citation], it was said:

It is * * * well established that a public officer with the authority of the law to make an arrest may accept an offer of reward or compensation for acts or services performed outside of his bailiwick or not within the scope of his official duties. * * *.

The claimant Tilford Reppert was present with Garret Godby and Johnny Simms at the time of the arrest and all cooperated in its consummation. The claimant Tilford Reppert personally recovered the stolen money. He recovered $2,000.00 more than the bank records show was stolen. This record does not reveal what became of the $2,000.00 excess.

It is manifest from the record that Tilford Reppert is the only claimant qualified and eligible to receive the reward. Therefore, it is the judgment of the circuit court that he is entitled to receive payment of the $1,500.00

reward now deposited with the clerk of this court.

The judgment is affirmed.

Modification of a Pre-existing Contract

BRENNER v. LITTLE RED SCHOOL HOUSE, LIMITED

Court of Appeals of North Carolina, 1982.
59 N.C.App. 68, 295 S.E.2d 607.

ARNOLD, J.

[Plaintiff Brenner, entered into a contract with the defendant, Little Red School House, Ltd., which stated that in return for nonrefundable tuition of $1,080, Brenner's son could attend defendant's school for a year. When Brenner's ex-wife refused to enroll their son, plaintiff sought and received a verbal promise of a refund. Defendant now refuses to refund plaintiff's money for lack of consideration.]

* * *

Before a contract modification is effective there must be consideration to support it. [Citation.] Consideration can be found in benefit to the promisor or detriment to the promisee.

[T]here is a consideration if the promisee, in return for the promise, does anything legal which he is not bound to do, or refrains from doing anything which he has a right to do, whether there is any actual loss or detriment to him or actual benefit or not. [Citation.]

The defendant argues that there was no consideration given by the plaintiff because the plaintiff as promisee suffered no detriment. But as the Supreme Court observed [in a prior case]:

[I]n return for the defendant's promise to refund the tuition paid, plaintiff would relinquish his right to have his child educated in defendant school . . . . . It is well established that any benefit, right, or interest bestowed upon the promisor, or any forbearance, detriment, or loss undertaken by the promisee, is sufficient consideration to support a contract. [Citation.]

The record shows that plaintiff was relinquishing the opportunity to have his child educated by the defendant when he testified "From the time . . . . [the defendant] first told me that she would refund the tuition to me and from that point on, I did not expect the school to do anything else in regard to providing services or anything else on behalf of Russ Brenner." [Citation.] * * * [Thus,] the record as quoted above shows sufficient consideration to support the modification in this case.

* * *

[Judgment for plaintiff.]

Moral Obligation

HARRINGTON v. TAYLOR

Supreme Court of North Carolina, 1945.
225 N.C. 690, 36 S.E.2d 227.

PER CURIAM.

The plaintiff in this case sought to recover of the defendant upon a promise made by him under the following peculiar circumstances:

The defendant had assaulted his wife, who took refuge in plaintiff's house. The next day the defendant gained access to the house and began another assault upon his wife. The defendant's wife knocked him down with an axe, and was on the point of cutting his head open or decapitating him while he was laying on the floor, and the plaintiff intervened, caught the axe as it was descending, and the blow intended for defendant fell upon her hand, mutilating it badly, but saving defendant's life.

Subsequently, defendant orally promised to pay the plaintiff her damages; but, after paying a small sum, failed to pay anything more. So, substantially, states the complaint.

The defendant demurred to the complaint as not stating a cause of action, and the demurrer was sustained. Plaintiff appealed.

The question presented is whether there was a consideration recognized by our law as sufficient to support the promise. The court is of the opinion that however much the defendant should be impelled by common gratitude to alleviate the plaintiff's misfortune, a humanitarian act of this kind, voluntarily performed, is not such consideration as would entitle her to recover at law.

The judgment sustaining the demurrer is affirmed.

Charitable Subscription Promises

MOUNT SINAI HOSPITAL OF GREATER MIAMI, INC. v. JORDAN

Supreme Court of Florida, 1974.
290 So.2d 484.

McCAIN, J.

* * *

The salient facts establish that Harry M. Burt executed two pledges of $50,000.00 each in 1968. These pledges were delivered to the petitioner and provided in pertinent part:

In consideration of and to induce the subscriptions of others, I (We) promise to pay to Mount Sinai Hospital of Greater Miami, Inc. or order the sum of *Fifty Thousand and no/100 dollars* $50,000.00 payable herewith: Balance in *nine* equal annual installments commencing on *Janaury [sic] 1* of * * *.

Mr. Burt made payments totalling $20,000.00, which were applied equally to the two pledges and upon his death on November 18, 1969, there remained an unpaid balance of $80,000.00. Upon Mr. Burt's death, the petitioner filed a claim for the unpaid balance of the pledges against his estate. The respondents, executors, objected to this claim. On the basis of these facts, the trial court held in favor of the charities and the respondents appealed.

There being no claim that the petitioner had suffered any material detriment or that any substantial liability had been incurred in reliance upon the subscriptions, the District Court proceeded to reverse and answered negatively the question certified to this Court. That question is:

[W]hether the recitation in a charitable pledge that it is given in consideration of and to induce the subscription of others constitutes consideration rendering it enforceable by the promisee against the promisor, in the absence of any reliant action thereon by the promisee such as would create promissory estoppel.

* * *

A mere gratuitous promise of a future gift, lacking consideration, is simply unenforceable as a *nudum pactum*. When the gratuitous promise is coupled with an inducement for others to subscribe, the promise is no longer void on its face. This is the situation in this case. The pledge specifically recites that the subscription is made "[in] consideration * * * to induce the subscriptions of other, * * *."

The District Court was eminently correct when it recited the law that:

For the doctrine of promissory estoppel to be applicable, the promisor must make a promise which he should reasonably expect to induce action or forbearance of a substantial character on the part of the promisee, * * *.

Therefore, in order for a pledge to survive the death of the donor and be considered a valid claim against the estate, two elements must coincidentally exist. First, the document stating the conditions of the pledge must recite with particularity the specific purpose for which the funds are to be used. It would, for example, be insufficient if the pledge designated the general operating fund. The rationale for such a decision is obvious. While the donor is alive, he has the opportunity to monitor the use of the pledged funds and, to some extent, manifest his intent as to their proper disposition. However, upon his death, and in the absence of an express written intention, the donee would have unfettered discretion as to the expenditures of these pledged monies and could spend it in a manner which might have offended the donor had he still been alive. Therefore, the donative intent as to the specific material plan, for example, for the establishment of an engineering school as in *Rouff v. Washington & Lee University* [citation], must be made an integral part of the pledge instrument, limiting the exercise of discretion by the donee within the boundaries set forth by the instrument.

* * *

Secondly, the donee must affirmatively show actual reliance of a substantial character in furtherance of the specified purpose set forth in the pledge instrument before the claim may be honored by the estate. Text writers have expressed a similar view:

* * * The view most commonly held is that such a subscription is an offer to contract which becomes binding as soon as the work towards which the subscription was promised has been done or begun, or liability incurred in regard to such work on the faith of the subscription.

Since the subscription in its inception is regarded as an offer, until the work has been done or liability incurred, the subscription is revocable by the death, insanity, or otherwise. 1 Williston on Contracts, Sec. 116, pp. 250–51 (1st ed. 1920).

In the light of this pronouncement we must view the facts in this case to see if the doctrine of promissory estoppel should be applied to enforce the pledge against the estate of the donor.

A review of the record reveals that the pledge in question was not made for any specified purpose, clearly was not used to induce others to subscribe and the Hospital undertook no work in reliance upon Burt's subscription.

The District Court correctly interpreted the facts when it stated:

Neither can the appellee find solace in the doctrine of promissory estoppel. The record is devoid of any evidence that the promisee was induced in reliance upon decedent's promise to take any substantial action, or to forego any material right, so that an injustice could only be avoided by applying this equitable doctrine. [Citations.]

Courts should act with restraint in respect to the public policy arguments endeavoring to sustain a mere charitable subscription. To ascribe consideration where there is none, or to adopt any other theory which affords charities a different legal rationale than other entities, is to approve fiction.

[Judgment for defendant affirmed.]

PROBLEMS

1. In consideration of $800 paid to him by Joyce, Hill gave Joyce a written option to purchase his house for $80,000 on or before April 1. Prior to April 1, Hill verbally agreed to extend the option until July 1. On May 18, Hill, known to Joyce, sold the house to Gray, who was ignorant of the unrecorded option. Joyce brought suit against Hill. Decision?

2. A owed $500 to B for services B rendered to A. The debt was due June 30, 1983. In March 1984, the debt was still unpaid. B was in urgent need of ready cash and told A that if he would pay $150 on the debt at once, B would release him from the balance. A paid $150 and B stated to A that all claims had been paid in full. In August 1984, B demanded the unpaid balance and subsequently sued A for $350. Decision?

3. (a) Modify the facts in (2) by assuming that B gave A a written receipt which stated that all claims had been paid in full. Result?

(b) Modify the facts in (2) by assuming that A owed B the $500 on A's purchase of a motorcycle from B. Result?

4. A owed B $800 on a personal loan. Neither the amount of the debt nor A's liability to pay the $800 was disputed. B had also rendered services as a carpenter to A without any agreement as to the price to be paid. When the work was completed, an honest and reasonable difference of opinion developed between A and B with respect to the value of B's services. Upon receiving B's bill for the carpentry services for $800, A mailed in a properly stamped and addressed envelope his check for $800 to B. In an accompanying letter, A stated that the enclosed check was in full settlement of both claims. B indorsed and cashed the check. Thereafter, B unsuccessfully sought to collect from A an alleged unpaid balance of $800. B then sued A for $800. Decision?

5. The Snyder Mfg. Co., being a large user of coal, entered into separate contracts with several coal companies, in each of which it was agreed that the coal company would supply coal during the year 1985 in such amounts as the manufacturing company might desire to order, at a price of forty-nine dollars per ton. In February 1985, the Snyder Company ordered 1,000 tons of coal from Union Coal Company, one of the contracting parties. Union Coal Company delivered 500 tons of the order and then notified Snyder Company that no more deliveries would be made and that it denied any obligation under the contract. In an action by Union Coal to collect forty-nine dollars per ton for the 500 tons of coal delivered, Snyder files a counterclaim, claiming damages of $1,500 for failure to deliver the additional 500 tons of the order and damages of $4,000 for breach of the agreement to deliver coal during the balance of the year. Decision?

6. On February 5, D entered into a written agreement with P whereby P agreed to drill a well on D's property for the sum of $5,000 and to complete the well on or before April 15. Before entering into the contract, P made test borings and had satisfied himself as to the character of the subsurface. After two days of drilling P struck hard rock. On February 17, P removed his equipment and advised D that the project had proved unprofitable and that he would not continue. On March 17, D went to P and told P that he would assume the risk of the enterprise and would pay P $100 for each day required to drill the well, as compensation for labor, the use of P's equipment, and P's services in supervising the work, provided P would furnish certain special equipment designed to cut through hard rock. P said that the proposal was satisfactory. The work was continued by P and completed in an additional fifty-eight days. Upon completion of the work D failed to pay, and P brought an action to recover $5,800. D answered that he had never become obligated to pay $100 a day and filed a counterclaim for damages in the amount of $500 for the month's delay based on an alleged breach of contract by P. Decision?

7. Discuss and explain whether there is valid consideration for each of the following promises:

(a) A and B entered into a contract for the purchase and sale of goods. A subsequently promised to pay a higher price for the goods upon B's refusal to deliver at the contract price.

(b) A promised in writing to pay a debt, which was due from B to C, upon C's agreement to extend the time of payment for one year.

(c) A executed a promissory note to her son, B, solely in consideration of past services rendered to A by B, for which there had been no agreement or request to pay. *NO 3 — past consideration*

8. A purchased shoes from B on an open account. B sent A a bill for $10,000. A wrote back stating that 200 pairs of the shoes were defective and offered to pay $6,000 and give B his promissory note for $1,000. B accepted the offer, and A sent his check for $6,000 and his note conformably to the agreement. B cashed the check, collected on the note, and, one month later, sued A for $3,000. Decision?

9. B owed A $1,500, but A did not initiate a law suit to collect the debt within the time period prescribed by the Statute of Limitations. Nevertheless, B promises A that she will pay the barred debt. Thereafter, B refuses to pay. A brings suit to collect on this new promise. Decision?

Chapter 11

ILLEGAL BARGAINS

MANIFESTLY, an unlawful act, whether criminal or civil, is not made lawful because it was committed under the terms of an agreement. It cannot be imagined that the law, which, for example, makes arson a crime, would regard as valid and enforceable an agreement between A and B by which B, in consideration of money to be paid to him by A, undertakes to destroy C's house by fire. Such an agreement itself would be a crime—an unlawful conspiracy. An agreement to commit a tort or civil wrong would likewise be illegal. The same is true of a contract which is opposed to public policy, as technically distinguished from a crime or tort.

An essential requirement of a binding promise or agreement is therefore legality of objective. When the formation or performance of an agreement is criminal, tortious, or otherwise contrary to public policy, the agreement is illegal and **unenforceable**. An unenforceable agreement is one for the breach of which the law does *not* provide a remedy and thus "leaves the parties where it finds them." In this connection, it is preferable to use the term "illegal bargain" or "illegal agreement" rather than "illegal contract," for the reason that the word "contract," by definition, denotes a legal and enforceable agreement. The illegal bargain is rendered unenforceable in order (1) to discourage such undesirable conduct and (2) to avoid the inappropriate use of the judicial process in carrying out the socially undesirable bargain.

Discussion of this subject will be in terms of agreements (a) in violation of a statute and (b) contrary to public policy.

VIOLATIONS OF STATUTES

An agreement declared illegal by statute will not be enforced by the courts. For example, "wagering contracts" are typically expressly declared unenforceable. In addition, an agreement to violate a statute prohibiting crimes, such as murder, robbery, embezzlement, forgery, and price fixing is unenforceable. Likewise, an agreement which is induced by criminal conduct will not be enforced. For example, in a New York case the plaintiff sued for the purchase price, $1,555, of certain hosiery and wrappers delivered to defendant's store. The defense was that the order for the goods was obtained through the bribing of defendant's purchasing agent, to whom the plaintiff paid five per cent of the purchase price. This type of commercial bribery constituted a criminal offense. There was no showing that the price of the goods was excessive, nor did the defendant return them or offer to do so. Under these circumstances, the court denied recovery, stating that in view of the purpose of the statute to eradicate commercial bribery, a refusal to aid the plaintiff who obtained the sale by a secret bribe of defendant's employee would contribute to that end.

Licensing Statutes

In every jurisdiction there are laws requiring a license for those who engage in certain trades, professions, or businesses. Common examples are licensing statutes which apply to lawyers, doctors, dentists, accountants, brokers, plumbers, and contractors. Whether a person may recover for services rendered if he has failed to comply with a licensing requirement depends upon the terms or type of licensing statute.

The statute itself may expressly provide that an unlicensed person engaged in a business or profession for which a license is required shall not recover for services rendered. Where there is no such statutory provision, the courts commonly distinguish between those statutes or ordinances which are regulatory in character and those which are enacted merely to raise revenue. If the statute is regulatory, there can be no recov-

ery for professional services rendered by a person not having the required license, provided the interest in enforcement of the promise is clearly outweighed by the public policy behind the regulatory purpose. Restatement, Section 181. However, if the law is for revenue purposes only, agreements for such services are enforceable.

A regulatory measure is one designed for the protection of the public against unqualified persons, such as statutes prescribing standards for those who seek to practice law or medicine. *See Tovar v. Paxton Community Memorial Hospital.* A revenue measure, on the other hand, does not seek to protect against the incompetent or unqualified, but simply to furnish revenue. An example is a statute requiring a license of plumbers but not establishing standards of competence for those who seek to follow the trade. It is regarded as a taxing measure and lacking in any expression of legislative intent to preclude unlicensed plumbers from enforcing their business contracts.

Gambling Statutes

All States have legislation pertaining to gambling, and American courts generally refuse to recognize the enforceability of a gambling agreement. Thus, if A makes a bet with B on the outcome of a ball game, the agreement is unenforceable by either party. Some States, however, now permit certain kinds of regulated gambling; these include State operated lotteries.

In a wager the parties stipulate that one shall win and the other lose depending upon the outcome of an event in which they have no "interest" other than that arising from the possibility of such gain or loss. To be distinguished are ordinary insurance contracts in which the insured, having an "insurable interest," pays a certain sum of money or premium in exchange for a promise of the company to pay a larger amount upon the occurrence of some event such as a fire which causes loss to the insured. Here, the agreement is one which compensates for loss under an existing risk, rather than one which creates an entirely new risk. In a wager the parties contemplate gain through mere chance, whereas in an insurance contract they seek to distribute possible loss.

In the past, lotteries, which are a form of wager, were generally prohibited by statute. Now many States operate lotteries for revenue producing purposes. A common statutory definition of lottery is as follows: "a scheme for the distribution of property by chance among persons who have paid or agreed to pay a valuable consideration for the chance, whether called a lottery, a raffle, a gift enterprise, or by some other name." Most fast food games and grocery store drawings have been held not to be lotteries because the participants need not make a purchase to be eligible for the prize.

Sunday Statutes

At common law a valid contract may be entered into on Sunday as on any other day. Some States have legislation referred to as **Blue Laws** modifying this common law rule and prohibiting certain types of commercial activity on Sunday. The modern tendency is to permit week-day "ratification" or "adoption" of a contract executed on Sunday. Even in a State which prohibits contracts on Sunday, a court will enforce a subsequent week-day ratification of a loan made on Sunday or a promise to pay for goods sold and delivered on Sunday. Activities of "necessity" and "charity" are usually exempted from the application of Blue Laws.

Usury Statutes

Historically, every State had a "usury law," a statute establishing a maximum rate of permissible interest which may be contracted for between a lender and borrower of money. Recently, however, there has been a trend to limit or relax usury statutes. Maximum rates permitted vary greatly from State to

State and among types of transactions. These statutes typically are general in their application, although certain specified types of transactions are exempted. For example, numerous States impose no limit on the rate of interest which may be charged on loans to corporations. Furthermore, some States permit the parties to contract for any rate of interest on loans made to individual proprietorships or partnerships for the purpose of carrying on a business.

In addition to the exceptions accorded certain designated types of borrowers, a number of States have exempted specific lenders. For example, the majority of the States have enacted installment loan laws, which permit eligible lenders a higher return on installment loans than would otherwise be permitted under the applicable general interest statute. These *specific* lender usury statutes, which have all but abrogated the general usury statute, vary greatly but have generally encompassed small consumer loans, corporate loans, loans by small lenders, real estate mortgages, and numerous other transactions.

General usury statutes, moreover, have traditionally exempted credit terms granted by vendors. Nevertheless, vendor credit has been covered by the judicially created time-price doctrine. The **time-price** doctrine provides that sellers may have two prices for their merchandise—a cash price and a credit or "time price," and that the credit price may exceed the cash price by more than the statutorily allowed interest on the cash price. Today, most States have rendered the time-price doctrine moot by adopting state retail installment sales acts, which apply specific usury statutes to specific consumer transactions and are beyond the scope of the general usury statutes.

In order for a transaction to be usurious, courts usually require evidence of the following factors: (a) a loan or forbearance, (b) of money, (c) which is repayable absolutely and in all events, (d) for which an interest charge is exacted in excess of the interest rate allowed by law. Transactions which, in fact, are loans may not be clothed with the trappings of a sale for the purpose of avoiding the usury laws.

Assuming that it is established that the arrangement is for a loan, certain expenses or charges are permitted in addition to the maximum legal interest. Payments made by a borrower to the lender for expenses incurred or for services rendered in good faith in making a loan or in obtaining security for its repayment are generally not included in determining whether the loan is usurious. Ordinary expenses by the lender which are permissible include costs of examining title, investigating the credit rating of the borrower, drawing necessary documents, and inspecting the property. If not excessive, they are not considered in determining the rate of interest with respect to usury statutes. However, payments made to the lender or from which he derives an advantage if they exceed the reasonable value of services actually rendered are included.

The legal effect to be given a usurious loan varies from State to State. In a few States both principal and interest are forfeited. In some jurisdictions the lender can recover the principal but forfeits all interest. In other States only that portion of interest exceeding the maximum permitted is forfeited. In several States the amount forfeited is a multiple (double or treble) of the interest charged. Disposition of usurious interest already paid also varies. Some States do not allow any recovery of usurious interest paid; others allow a recovery of the usurious interest paid or a multiple of it.

See *Abramowitz v. Barnett Bank of West Orlando.*

VIOLATIONS OF PUBLIC POLICY

The reach of a statute may extend beyond its language as courts, by analogy, use the statute and the policy sought to be served by it as a guide in determining the private contract rights of one harmed by a violation of the statute. In addition, the courts are frequently called upon to articulate the "public policy" of the State without significant help from statutory sources. See *Marvin v. Marvin.* This judicially declared public policy is very broad in scope, it often being said that agreements which have "a tendency to be injurious to the public or the public good" are contrary to public policy. The public policy of a State concerns the general welfare of the people of the State. While the public policy of all the States is substantially the same, differences will be found in its relation to some few matters. Again, the public policy of a given State may change with time in respect to some particular matter. Furthermore, certain acts which were formerly regarded as being opposed to public policy are now definitely prohibited by statute. On the other hand, some acts which were formerly considered as being contrary to public policy are no longer so regarded. Thus, the term "public policy" is broad and general, and not subject to precise definition. Examples to be considered are agreements that involve (1) tortious conduct, (2) restrain trade, (3) tend to obstruct the administration of justice, (4) tend to corrupt public officials or impair the legislative process, (5) exempt a party from liability for his own tortious conduct, or (6) are unconscionable.

Tortious Conduct

"A promise to commit a tort or to induce the commission of a tort is unenforceable on grounds of public policy." Restatement, Section 192. The courts will not permit contract law to violate the law of torts. Any agreement attempting to do so is considered contrary to public policy. For example, A and B enter into an agreement under which A promises B that in return for $5,000 he will disparage the product of B's competitor C in order to provide B with a competitive advantage. A's promise is to commit the tort of disparagement and is unenforceable as contrary to public policy.

Common Law Restraint of Trade

At early common law any restraint upon an individual's right to engage in his trade or calling was illegal. Such restraints were viewed with disfavor because of the belief that they would diminish the individual's means of earning a living, deprive the public of useful services, adversely affect competition, and otherwise be harmful to the welfare of the community. But this strict view has been modified so that reasonable restraints of trade are enforceable.

Today an agreement to refrain from a particular trade, profession, or business is enforceable if (1) the purpose of the restraint is to protect a property interest of the promisee and (2) the restraint is no more extensive than is reasonably necessary to protect that interest. Restraints typically arise in two situations: the sale of a business and employment contracts.

It is necessary at this point to distinguish between a contract which has for its primary purpose the imposition of a restraint of trade upon one of the parties and a contract in which the agreement in restraint of trade is merely ancillary to some other and major purpose of the contract. A common example of the latter is a contract for the sale of a business in which the seller agrees to refrain from engaging in the same business in a specified territory. A contract in which the agreement in restraint of trade is primary and not ancillary is illegal, regardless of the possible reasonableness of the restraint. Suppose, for example, that A and B each owns a drug store in the city of Wye. They make a contract under which, in consideration of $50,000 paid by A to B, B closes his store and also agrees to refrain from engaging in the drug store business in Wye. This contract is opposed to public policy and unenforceable. B is not bound by it and may re-enter the drug store business in Wye as and when he sees fit. Assume instead that A and B learn that C is planning to open a drug store in Wye. A and B then make a contract with C under which they pay C $5,000 in consideration for her agreement not to engage

in the drug store business in the city of Wye at any time. This contract is likewise opposed to public policy and unenforceable, and C may establish a drug store in Wye whenever she chooses. In both of these examples, the contracts were primarily for the purpose of restraining trade and hence opposed to public policy and void. Assume now that A sells his drug store and business to C, and that, as part of the transaction, A agrees not to engage in the drug store business in the city of Wye at any time. In this case, the agreement in restraint of trade is ancillary to the primary purpose of the contract, namely, the sale and purchase of A's store. The only question raised by this contract is whether the restraint is reasonable or not. If the restraint is reasonable, A is bound by his agreement. If it is not, and A should break his agreement, the courts will give C no relief.

Sale of a Business In the purchase of a business, the buyer naturally seeks to acquire not only the business itself but also the goodwill of the business. In other words, he seeks assurance and protection against competition on the part of the seller. It is for this purpose that a provision restraining the seller from engaging in the same business is included in the contract. The seller's promise in restraint of trade must of course be supported by consideration. Where, as is ordinarily the case, the stipulation in restraint of trade is a part of the contract for the sale of the business, the purchase price paid by the purchaser furnishes the consideration both for the sale of the business and the seller's promise not to compete. The restraint may cover territory or time or both. While in some cases the extent of time is the major issue, most cases involve the area or territory covered by the restraint. In any event the restraint must be reasonable. *See Haynes v. Monson.* The rule is that the restraint is reasonable if it is coextensive only with the interest to be protected. As one case puts it, the test is "whether the restraint is such only as to afford a fair protection to the interests of the party in whose

good will factor

favor it is given, and not so large as to interfere with the interests of the public."

A few examples will illustrate this point. Suppose that A owns a store in Chicago and that his trade extends throughout the city but not beyond the city limits. He sells his store to B, and as part of the transaction agrees not to engage in the same business anywhere within the state of Illinois. This restraint is unreasonable and the agreement unenforceable. The restraint imposed on A is greater than is co-extensive with the interest (that of B) to be protected. It also imposes an unnecessary hardship on A. Finally, it unduly interferes with the interests of the public. Assume instead that A agreed not to engage in the same business in the city of Chicago. This restraint is reasonable and binding. It gives B only the protection he is fairly and reasonably entitled to and no more, since A's trade extended throughout the city. In some cases, a restraint covering a single city would be held unreasonable. Suppose that G owns a strictly local or neighborhood business, such as a barber shop or delicatessen, in New York City. She sells the business to L, and agrees with L not to again conduct the same business in the city of New York. This restraint is too extensive and is unreasonable. Suppose now that the A Corporation sells its products in every State in the country. It decides to drop the manufacture of one of its products, and then sells this department of its business to the B Corporation. The contract under which this sale is made provides that the A Corporation shall not again engage in the manufacture or sale of this product anywhere within the United States. This restraint is reasonable and is binding on the A Corporation. In view of the fact that it sold the product in question throughout the United States, the restraint covering that entire territory amounted only to fair protection to the B Corporation and no more.

The same type of inquiry must be made with respect to time limitations. In the sale of a service station twenty-five years would be unreasonable, but one year probably would

not. Each case must be considered on its own facts, with the court determining what is reasonable under the particular circumstances.

Employment Contracts Salespeople, management personnel, and other employees are frequently required to sign employment contracts prohibiting them from competing with their employers during the time of employment and for some additional stated period after termination. The courts readily enforce a covenant not to compete during the period of employment. The promise not to compete after termination of employment, however, is subjected to an even stricter test of reasonableness than that applied to non-competition promises included in a contract for the sale of a business. As stated by one court, "restrictive stipulations in agreements between employer and employee are not viewed with the same indulgence as such stipulations between a vendor and vendee of a business and its good will." One reason for this is that the employer is in a stronger bargaining position than the employee.

A court order enjoining the former employee from competing in a described territory for a stated period of time is the usual method by which the employer seeks enforcement of the promise not to compete made by the employee. Before granting such injunctions, the courts insist that the employer demonstrate that the restriction is necessary to protect his legitimate interests, such as trade secrets or customer lists. Because issuance of the injunction may have the practical effect of placing the employee out of work, the courts must carefully balance the public policy favoring the employer's right to protect his business interests against the public policy favoring full opportunity for individuals to gain employment.

Thus, one court has held that a covenant in a contract that a travel agency employee after termination of her employment would not engage in a like business in any capacity in either of two named towns or within a radius of sixty miles of the towns for a period of two years was unreasonable. There was no indication that the employee had such dominion over customers as would cause them to move their business to her new agency, and it was not shown that any trade secrets were involved.

Some courts, instead of refusing to enforce an unreasonable covenant, will if considered justifiable under the circumstances of the particular case, reform the agreement to make it reasonable and enforceable. This is an extension of the familiar "blue pencil" rule by which courts have upheld reasonable restrictions in a contract while deleting the unreasonable ones. In one case in which a former employer sought to enforce the noncompetitive agreement of a former employee, the Supreme Court of New Jersey refused to declare the covenant invalid. It said that, "we are entirely satisfied that the time is well due for the abandonment of New Jersey's void per se rule in favor of the rule which permits the total or partial enforcement of noncompetitive agreements to the extent reasonable under the circumstances." *See also Bob Pagan Ford, Inc. v. Smith.*

Obstructing the Administration of Justice

Agreements which are harmful to the administration of justice are illegal and unenforceable. For example, a promise by an employer not to press criminal charges against an embezzling employee who restores the stolen funds is not enforceable. Similarly, a promise to conceal evidence or to give false testimony tends to obstruct the administration of justice and for that reason is illegal and unenforceable. Contacts tending to obstruct the administration of public justice include the following: agreements to pay a witness a sum of money contingent upon the outcome of the litigation; agreements under which a witness is to testify falsely or is to absent himself from the State during the progress of the trial; agreements to induce a juror to vote to bring in a certain verdict for one of the parties;

agreements to stifle a criminal prosecution; and agreements to encourage litigation by one having no actual interest.

Corrupting Public Officials

Agreements which have a tendency to affect adversely the public interest through the corruption of public officials or the impairment of the legislative process are unenforceable. Examples are improper means to influence legislation, to secure some official action, or to procure a government contract.

To illustrate, a bargain by a candidate for public office to make a certain appointment following his election is illegal. In addition, an agreement to pay a public officer something extra for performing his official duty, as a promise to a policeman for strictly enforcing the traffic laws on his beat, is illegal. The same is true of an agreement in which a citizen promises to perform, or to refrain from performing, duties imposed upon her by citizenship. Thus, a promise by X to pay fifty dollars to Y if she will register and vote is opposed to public policy and unenforceable.

Exculpatory Clauses

Some contracts for services contain an exculpatory clause which excuses one party from liability for her own tortious conduct. This type of clause is generally looked upon with disfavor since there is a policy to discourage overreaching and to assure that wrongdoers will pay the damages caused by their tortious conduct. Restatement, Section 195. Accordingly, an exculpatory clause on the reverse side of a parking lot claim check which attempts to relieve the parking lot operator of liability for negligently damaging the customer's automobile is unenforceable as against public policy. On the other hand, the policy of freedom of contract is also a factor in determining the validity of contractual clauses exempting a party from liability for his tortious conduct, and thus not all such clauses are held to be against public policy.

Where a public service or a specific legal duty is involved, an exculpatory clause is generally held to be violative of public policy and, therefore, unenforceable. Thus, a public service company cannot by contract insulate itself from liability for negligence in performing its duties of public service, nor may a common carrier exempt itself from liability for negligence in the performance of its duties as a carrier.

Further, where one party has a superior bargaining position which has enabled him to impose upon the other party such a provision, the courts are inclined to nullify the provision. Such a situation may arise in residential leases exempting a landlord from liability for his negligence. *See Henrioulle v. Marin Ventures, Inc.*

Unconscionable Contracts

Every contract of sale may be scrutinized by the court to determine whether in its commercial setting, purpose, and effect, it is unconscionable. The court may refuse to enforce an unconscionable contract or any part of the contract found to be unconscionable. Section 2-302 provides:

If the court as a matter of law finds the contract or any clause of the contract to have been unconscionable at the time it was made the court may refuse to enforce the contract, or it may enforce the remainder of the contract without the unconscionable clause, or it may so limit the application of any unconscionable clause as to avoid any unconscionable result.

Similarly, Section 208 of the Restatement provides:

If a contract or term thereof is unconscionable at the time the contract is made, a court may refuse to enforce the contract, or may enforce the remainder of the contract without the unconscionable term, or may so limit the application of any unconscionable term as to avoid any unconscionable result.

Neither the Code nor the Restatement define the word "unconscionable." However, the Oxford Universal Dictionary (3rd ed.) definition is: "Monstrously extortionate, harsh, showing no regard for conscience."

The U.C.C. and Restatement deny or limit enforcement of an unconscionable contract or provision in the interest of fairness and decency, and to correct harshness in contracts resulting from unequal bargaining positions of the parties. The determination that a contract or term is or is not unconscionable is made taking into account its setting, purpose and effect. Inadequacy of consideration does not of itself invalidate a bargain, but gross disparity in the values exchanged may be a significant factor in a determination that a contract is unconscionable and may be sufficient ground, without more, for denying specific performance.

In many cases a contract between a necessitous buyer in an unequal bargaining position with the seller has been held unconscionable by reason of the exorbitant price. For instance, a price of $749 ($920 on time) for a vacuum cleaner which cost the seller $140 was held unconscionable. In another case the buyers, welfare recipients, purchased by time payment contract a home freezer unit for $900 which, added to time credit charges, credit life insurance, credit property insurance, and sales tax, amounted to $1,235. The purchase resulted from a visit to the buyer's home by a salesman representing Your Shop At Home Service, Inc., and the maximum retail value of the freezer unit at time of purchase was $300. The court held the contract unconscionable and reformed it by reducing the price to the total payment ($620) made by the buyers. *See also Williams v. Walker-Thomas Furniture Co.*

EFFECT OF ILLEGALITY

Illegal contracts are unenforceable unless they fall into one of several exceptions. The unenforceability of these contracts will be discussed in this section of the chapter.

Unenforceability

When an agreement is illegal with but few exceptions, **neither** party can successfully sue the other for breach nor recover for any performance rendered. Whichever party is plaintiff is immaterial to the courts. As is frequently said in these cases, the court will leave the parties where it finds them. Even though the defendant does not plead illegality as a defense, the courts in most cases, on finding the contract to be illegal, will of their own motion declare it to be illegal and deny relief to the plaintiff. It may thus happen that a defendant, who has received the benefit of an illegal contract, gains an unfair advantage. This, however, is not the concern of the courts. They will refuse to enforce illegal contracts, regardless of a possible benefit or advantage to the plaintiff or defendant.

Exceptions

To the general rule as to the effect of illegality on a contract there are several exceptions. The circumstances surrounding the particular contract may be such that the courts will grant relief to one of the parties although not to the other. These exceptions will now be considered.

Party Withdrawing Before Performance

Under some circumstances a party to an illegal agreement may, prior to performance, withdraw from the transaction and recover whatever she has contributed. Restatement, Section 199. A common example is recovery of money left with a stake holder pursuant to a wager before it is paid over to the winner, but the rule has also been applied to more serious misconduct.

Party Protected by Statute

Sometimes an agreement is illegal because it violates a statute designed to protect persons in the position of one of the parties. For example, State "Blue-Sky Laws" prohibiting the sale of unregistered securities are designed primarily for the protection of investors. In such case, even though there is an unlawful agreement, the statute usually expressly gives the purchaser a right to rescind the sale and recover the money paid.

Party Not Equally at Fault

Where one of the parties is less at fault than the other, he will be allowed to recover payments made or property transferred. Restatement, Section 198. For example, this exception would apply where one party is induced to enter into an illegal bargain through the fraud, duress, or undue influence of the other party.

Party Ignorant of Facts Making Bargain Illegal

An agreement which appears to be entirely permissible on its face may, nevertheless, be illegal by reason of facts and circumstances of which one of the parties is completely unaware. For example, a man and woman make mutual promises to marry, but unknown to the woman, the man is already married. This is an agreement to commit the crime of bigamy. It is illegal, and the marriage, if entered into, is void. In such case the courts permit the party who is ignorant of the illegality to maintain a lawsuit against the other party for damages.

Partial Illegality

A contract may be partly unlawful and partly lawful. In such case there are two possibilities. (1) The partial illegality may be held to taint the entire contract with illegality, so that it is wholly unenforceable. (2) It may be possible to separate the illegal from the legal part, in which case, the illegal part only will be held unenforceable, but the legal part valid and enforceable. Ordinarily, the entire agreement is unenforceable if any part of the agreement is illegal. For example, a promise to pay $1,000 for the delivery of two different kinds of goods, one type legal and the other illegal, is unenforceable. The seller may not recover payment for any of the goods delivered. But, if within the same agreement there is a separate price allocation for the different goods, as $250 for the legal and $750 for the illegal, a successful action may be maintained for the legal goods costing $250. Even though the agreement is tainted with illegality, there is a tendency to disregard this if the legal and illegal portions can be "severed" and to permit recovery for the legal portion.

CASES

Licensing Statutes

MANUEL TOVAR v. PAXTON COMMUNITY MEMORIAL HOSPITAL

Appellate Court of Illinois, 1975.
29 Ill.App.3d 218, 330 N.E.2d 247.

CRAVEN, J.

Plaintiff appeals the dismissal of his complaint which contained a count for breach of an employment contract and a count alleging the tort of misrepresentation. The trial court granted a motion to dismiss the complaint * * *.

Plaintiff's complaint alleges he was informed of the defendant hospital's desire to hire a full-time resident physician. He responded in a letter in which he inquired about the position and informed the defendant hospital he was presently employed by the department of mental health for the State of Kansas. He claims this letter fully described the nature and extent of his education, training, and licensing as a physician. Plaintiff then personally appeared at the office of the defendant and informed its agents that he was employed in a full-time position and would only be interested in a position of resident physician if it would provide for permanent employment. Plaintiff alleges defendant's agents represented to him that the position would last for plaintiff's natural life or for so long as the defendant hospital required the services of a resident physician, and plaintiff was willing and able to do such work competently. Plaintiff alleges he thoroughly described the nature and extent of his academic background, professional experience, and licensing to defendant's agents during this interview, and that these agents then and there told and assured plaintiff that his professional credentials were satisfactory for the employment.

Plaintiff further claims that as a result of defendant's promise of permanent employment he resigned his position in Kansas and entered into defendant's service as a resident physician on August 1, 1972. However, on or about August 15, 1972, defendant discharged plaintiff. Plaintiff's complaint alleges that the defendant hospital wrongfully breached the employment contract and also misrepresented to plaintiff that his professional credentials were fully satisfactory to the defendant hospital for employment as a resident physician. Plaintiff seeks damages for the period following the termination of his employment.

In response to the defendant hospital's request to admit facts, plaintiff denies that he has never held a license to practice medicine as required under section 2 of the Medical Practice Act (Ill.Rev.Stat. 1973, ch. 91, ¶ 2), but admits he has never been licensed to practice medicine in Illinois. Plaintiff denied that he had not passed an examination of his qualifications as is required by section 3 of the Medical Practice Act because "plaintiff feels he has passed an examination of his qualifications that Illinois would accept from another state." He admitted he had taken the examination called for in section 3 of the Medical Practice Act and had never passed it in Illinois.

The trial court found plaintiff's complaint to be substantially insufficient at law because he had not complied with sections 2 and 3 of the Act, had not obtained a license pursuant to licensing requirements of that Act, and that it would be against public policy to enforce an employment contract where the plaintiff had not obtained the requisite license. The court found the employment contract to be in violation of public policy, illegal and void.

*   *   *

It has long been the law of Illinois that one who has failed to comply with the licensing provisions of the Medical Practice Act cannot maintain an action for fees or services as a physician or surgeon. [Citations.] The purpose of the statutes establishing a licensing requirement is not to generate revenue, but rather to protect the public by assuring them of adequately trained practitioners. [Citation.] Any agreement the purpose of which is to induce a breach of one of these licensing statutes is illegal. [Citation.] A person who practices medicine without obtaining the required license cannot maintain an action for his promised compensation or *in quantum meruit*. [Citations.] While the action on the employment contract involved here is not to recover for services rendered but rather for claimed wrongful termination of the employment contract, the same doctrine applies. The agreement sued upon is unenforceable as contrary to public policy.

In Count II of his complaint, plaintiff asked for damages from the date of termination of his employment as a result of the defendant hospital's alleged misrepresentation that his credentials were satisfactory to them. However, as plaintiff could not be a resident physician for the defendant hospital under the law of this State, public policy will not allow him to sue on the tort of misrepresentation when the alleged misrepresentations concerned the unauthorized practice of medicine. Our courts will not lend their aid to a man who founds his cause of action upon an illegal act. [Citation.] A plaintiff is not permitted to profit by his own wrong by recovering damages. [Citation.] This rule applies to a complaint that alleges the same acts amounted to a breach of contract and a tort. [Citation.] The trial court was correct in dismissing Count II of plaintiff's complaint.

The judgment of the circuit court dismissing both counts of plaintiff's complaint is affirmed.

Judgment affirmed.

Usury Statutes

ABRAMOWITZ v. BARNETT BANK OF WEST ORLANDO

Florida Court of Appeals, 1981.
394 So.2d 1033.

SHARP, J.

Abramowitz appeals from a judgment denying him any relief in his suit against the Barnett Bank of West Orlando, appellee, in which he sought damages for an allegedly "usurious" loan.

*   *   *

The record established that Abramowitz filed three or more loan applications with the bank from February 1973 through October 1973. Originally he sought a construction loan to build a building to be leased to Ford Motor Company on land he owned near the John Young Parkway. C. Lee Maynard, president of the bank, wanted the loan for his bank, although the $300,000 to $400,000 loan requests considerably exceeded the bank's lending limits. In anticipation of making the loan, Maynard made "inspections" of the site and building being constructed, although Ford was financing the construction itself and the bank had made no loan commitment.

When the building was completed in November of 1973, the parties rushed into a mortgage loan closing without the benefit of a written loan commitment and without a carefully prepared loan closing statement. Maynard had verbally promised Abramowitz a $400,000 loan for one year, at 9% interest, with a 1% "point" or "service fee." The $4,000 "service fee" was shown on the closing statement as a "discount," but everyone agreed no "discount" was involved because the bank was not purchasing a mortgage loan from another party at less than face value.

The $4,000 service fee was deducted in full from the loan proceeds, and it was immediately received by the bank as income. During the one year term of this loan, Abramowitz was charged and he paid $36,347.78 in "interest." If the $4,000 charge was also "interest," Abramowitz paid more than $40,000 or 10% of his $400,000 loan in total interest charges. If viewed as a "discount" loan where interest is paid in advance, the rate should be properly gauged on the amount of principal actually disbursed to the borrower plus legitimate expenses—($396,000 or a somewhat larger figure if any part of the $4,000 were attributable to a legitimate expense of the lender).

Maynard testified that the $4,000 charge was meant to be a "service charge" or "points." He was the only mortgage loan officer at his bank, so he made "in-house" inspections of the construction of the building and a final inspection. He reported verbally to the bank's loan committee. He admitted that part of the $4,000 went to pay the bank's normal overhead expenses, such as salaries and utilities. Another expense attributed to this loan was Maynard's contacting other Barnett banks to obtain the participation of other lenders, and the preparation of loan participation agreements.

The other banker witnesses at trial testified that their banks normally imposed "service fees" or "points" on real estate loans in addition to interest, but they were careful not to exceed the usury limits when the two amounts were combined. Sometimes inspection fees were paid to architects or engineers for which the customer was charged; sometimes the inspections were done "in-house," and the borrower was charged a small amount, or was not charged at all.

* * *

A lender will not be allowed to impose any miscellaneous fees or service charges on the front end of a loan when that sum, added to the interest charged, exceeds the maximum legal rate of interest allowable. [Citations.] Application of such fees to pay the general overhead of a lender or the cost of participating out the loan are not sufficient to alter the characterization of these charges as interest. [Citation.]

It is also well established that a borrower can be charged the actual reasonable expenses of making a particular loan. [Cita-

tions.] However "bogus" charges for services not actually rendered will not be allowed to cloak the extraction of illegal interest. [Citation.]

The only basis to characterize the "service fee" in this case as something other than interest, is to allocate part of it as an "inspection" fee performed "in-house" by the bank's president. Such fees are usually paid to third-parties, and are documented on the mortgage loan closing statement. We are not prepared to say, however, that in all cases the inspection must be done by a third-person or that it must be documented on the closing statement, although that obviously is the better practice. The fact that Maynard himself performed the inspection does not flaw the charges although any charge for this "service" is inconsistent with his testimony that he did the inspection "in-house" to save the borrower money.

It is fundamental that the charges must be "reasonable." [Citations.] This loan was not a "construction" loan which requires more inspections to insure the lender's construction funds are being properly used as the building progresses. Rather, it was a loan on a completed building, and similar to a "take-out" loan for a permanent lender, only a final inspection fee is required. The only testimony in the record on this point established that $300 was the maximum a third party expert would have charged.

The conclusion thus follows inescapably that Abramowitz was charged in excess of 10% interest on this one year loan.

"Service Fee"	$ 4,000.00
Less "Reasonable Expenses"	−300.00
"Hidden Interest"	$ 3,700.00
Principle of Loan	$400,000.00
Less Prepaid Interest	−3,700.00
Actual Principal	$396,300.00
Maximum legal amount of interest collectible on this loan (10%) of actual principal	$ 39,630.00

Actual interest charged and billed	36,347.78
Plus "hidden interest"	+3,700.00
	$ 40,047.78
Amount of over-charge	$ 40,047.78
	−39,630.00
	$ 417.78

The lower court found there was no "corrupt" intent on the part of the bank to charge a usurious rate of interest because the bank did not deliberately charge more than 10%. It charged 9% on the loan plus 1% in points only. The difficulty here was that the 1% was taken up-front, resulting in a reduction in principal received, and an increase in the rate paid. [Citation.] The "intent" to exceed the legal rate of interest need not be to consciously decide to charge a borrower greater than the legal rate, when the lender consciously intends and does in fact make the charges which add up to usury. [Citations.]

In this case, the closing statement showing a 1% point or service fee was prepared by the bank; and it calculated and billed the borrower interest throughout the year. No errors were shown to have occurred in the billing. In fact during two quarters, the lender billed on a 360-day year basis, which for a 10% or maximum rate loan, was usurious in and of itself. [Citation.] We conclude the bank had the requisite intent to make the usurious charges. [Citation.]

Accordingly, the judgment is reversed and this case is remanded for imposition of damages against the bank * * *.

Reversed and remanded.

Public Policy

MARVIN v. MARVIN

Supreme Court of California, 1976.
18 Cal.3d 660, 134 Cal.Rpt. 815, 557 P.2d 106.

TOBRINER, J.

During the past 15 years, there has been a substantial increase in the number of couples living together without marrying. Such nonmarital relationships lead to legal controversy when one partner dies or the couple separates. Courts of Appeal, faced with the task of determining property rights in such cases, have arrived at conflicting positions * * *.

In the instant case plaintiff and defendant lived together for seven years without marrying; all property acquired during this period was taken in defendant's name. When plaintiff sued to enforce a contract under which she was entitled to half the property and to support payments, the trial court granted judgment on the pleadings for defendant, thus leaving him with all property accumulated by the couple during their relationship. * * *

Plaintiff avers that in October of 1964 she and defendant "entered into an oral agreement" that while "the parties lived together they would combine their efforts and earnings and would share equally any and all property accumulated as a result of their efforts whether individual or combined." Furthermore, they agreed to "hold themselves out to the general public as husband and wife" and that "plaintiff would further render her services as a companion, homemaker, housekeeper and cook to . . . defendant."

Shortly thereafter plaintiff agreed to "give up her lucrative career as an entertainer (and) singer" in order to "devote her full time to defendant . . . as a companion, homemaker, housekeeper and cook"; in return defendant agreed to "provide for all of plaintiff's financial support and needs for the rest of her life."

Plaintiff alleges that she lived with defendant from October of 1964 through May of 1970 and fulfilled her obligations under the agreement. During this period the parties as a result of their efforts and earnings acquired in defendant's name substantial real and personal property, including motion picture rights worth over $1 million. In May of 1970, however, defendant compelled plaintiff to leave his household. He continued to support plaintiff until November of 1971, but thereafter refused to provide further support.

*   *   *

In *Trutalli v. Meraviglia* (1932) [Citation] we established the principle that nonmarital partners may lawfully contract concerning the ownership of property acquired during the relationship. We reaffirmed this principle in *Vallera v. Vallera* (1943) [Citation], stating that "If a man and woman (who are not married) live together as husband and wife under an agreement to pool their earnings and share equally in their joint accumulations, equity will protect the interests of each in such property."

*   *   *

Defendant first and principally relies on the contention that the alleged contract is so closely related to the supposed "immoral" character of the relationship between plaintiff and himself that the enforcement of the contract would violate public policy. He points to cases asserting that a contract between nonmarital partners is unenforceable if it is "involved in" an illicit relationship [Citations] or made in "contemplation" of such a relationship. [Citations.]

A review of the numerous California decisions concerning contracts between nonmarital partners, however, reveals that the courts have not employed such broad and uncertain standards to strike down contracts. The decisions instead disclose a narrower and more precise standard: a contract between nonmarital partners is unenforceable only *to the extent* that it *explicitly* rests upon the immoral and illicit consideration of meretricious sexual services.

*   *   *

In summary, we base our opinion on the principle that adults who voluntarily live together and engage in sexual relations are nonetheless as competent as any other persons to contract respecting their earnings and property rights. Of course, they cannot lawfully contract to pay for the performance of sexual services, for such a contract is, in essence, an agreement for prostitution and unlawful for that reason. But they may agree to pool their earnings and to hold all property acquired during the relationship in accord with the law governing community property; conversely they may agree that each partner's earnings and the property acquired from those earnings remains the separate property of the earning partner. So long as the agreement does not rest upon illicit meretricious consideration, the parties may order their economic affairs as they choose, and no policy precludes the courts from enforcing such agreements.

In the present instance, plaintiff alleges that the parties agreed to pool their earnings, that they contracted to share equally in all property acquired, and that defendant agreed to support plaintiff. The terms of the contract as alleged do not rest upon any unlawful consideration. We therefore conclude that the complaint furnishes a suitable basis upon which the trial court can render *   *   * relief. [Citation.] The trial court consequently erred in granting defendant's motion for judgment on the pleadings.

Common Law Restraint of Trade: Sale of Business

HAYNES v. MONSON

Supreme Court of Minnesota, 1974.
301 Minn. 327, 224 N.W.2d 482.

Scott, J.

In this action for breach of contract, plaintiffs appeal from a summary judgment dismissing their action, but preserving for trial defendants' counterclaim for breach of a covenant not to compete. We affirm.

Plaintiffs entered into a contract for the sale of Haynes Bookkeeping and Tax Service in Austin, Minnesota, on March 18, 1970. The total purchase price agreed upon was to be $20,000, with $3,500 down, $2,500 to be paid at a later date, and the balance payable in 36 equal monthly installments of $425.91. On February 1, 1972, defendant purchasers discontinued payment of the monthly installments, leaving a balance of approximately

$7,000. This action for breach of contract was commenced in March 1972, and defendants counterclaimed for breach of a covenant not to compete set out in the contract. Summary judgment was entered for defendants and plaintiffs appeal.

Paragraph 3 of the contract for sale provided as follows:

The Sellers agree that they will not within five (5) years from date hereof, either solely or jointly, with or as manager or agent of any person or corporation, directly or indirectly, carry on or be engaged or interested in the business of bookkeeping, accounting, or tax practice, or permit his name to be used in connection with any such business within fifty (50) miles of Austin, Minnesota.

Following the sale of the business, plaintiff Paul E. Haynes [seller] worked for the defendants for approximately 1½ years. In July 1971, he moved to Red Wing, Minnesota, 199 miles from Austin, and opened his new office. However, he neither sold his Austin residence nor disconnected the telephone service and returned to his home every week or two.

Evidence from Haynes' deposition indicates that he continued to furnish bookkeeping and tax services for residents of the city of Austin and that he further filed tax returns for residents of Austin from his Red Wing office. Although he testified that he did work for 45–50 Austin clients through his Red Wing office, he admitted that only two actually came to his office.

The deposition also illuminates the various methods utilized by Haynes to continue his contact with former clients. The information necessary for him to provide his services was either mailed to Red Wing, delivered to Haynes' Austin residence, or left with Haynes' relatives for delivery to him. In an affidavit, Duane Grafe indicated that he had telephoned Haynes' Austin residence, at the suggestion of defendant [purchaser] Gerhard A. Monson, to arrange to have some tax work done. Someone identifying himself as Haynes

returned Grafe's call and agreed to do the necessary work. The caller further agreed either to pick up the information or to have Grafe deliver it to the Austin home.

* * *

The basic issue for our determination is whether the lower court erred in granting summary judgment in favor of defendants. This court has construed covenants not to compete so as to effectuate the purpose for their inception, i.e., to protect purchasers of a going concern from an infringement upon their investment and the continuation of the business for a profit. To allow one to sell his business, with its accompanying customer lists and files, and then allow him to compete for the patronage of these former customers would be contrary to the covenant, and would frustrate the intent of the parties.

This court has long held that where the restraint is for a "just and honest purpose, for the protection of a legitimate interest of the party in whose favor it is imposed, reasonable as between the parties, and not injurious to the public," that restraint is valid. [Citations.] Under these standards, covenants, such as the one before us, should be strictly construed. [Citation.]

Furthermore, covenants with rather specific geographic and economic limitations have been enforced. [Citation.]

Plaintiffs contend that the absence of the element of solicitation should be controlling. [Citation.] We, however, are of the opinion that when one has conducted a business in the same area for many years and has built a sizable clientele, active solicitation on his part is unnecessary to compete so as to defeat the covenant. Solicitation by mere reputation and past business practices is more than sufficient.

Therefore, we conclude that on the basis of the record before us, there existed no genuine issue of material fact, and that the defendants were entitled to judgment as a matter of law.

Affirmed.

Common Law Restraint of
Trade: Employment Contract

BOB PAGEN FORD, INC. v. SMITH

Court of Appeals of Texas, Houston (1st Dist.),
1982.
638 S.W.2d 176.

EVANS, C. J.

[The defendant, Charles Smith, was employed by plaintiff Bob Pagan Ford, Inc. under a written contract which prohibited defendant from selling automobiles or automobile parts in Galveston County, Texas, for a period of three years after terminating his employment. Several months after signing the contract, Smith voluntarily left the company to accept a position as auto salesman with a competing dealer. Plaintiff sued defendant to enforce the noncompetition clause of the contract. The trial court held in favor of the plaintiff, but limited the restrictive covenant to six months. Plaintiff appeals.]

* * *

Covenants against competition are not favored by our courts because of the public policy against restraints of trade and the hardships resulting from interference with a person's means of livelihood. [Citation.] Because such a covenant is in restraint of trade, its terms will not be enforced by the courts unless they are reasonable. [Citation.]

Whether a restrictive covenant is reasonable as to time and area is a question of law to be determined by the court, [Citation], usually on the basis of whether the restriction imposes greater restraint on the employee than is reasonably necessary to protect the employer's business and goodwill. Thus, the trial court must examine the circumstances of each case to determine whether the restrictions sought to be imposed are greater than those required to protect the employer's interests, and whether they impose undue hardship upon the employee. [Citation.]

In determining whether a restrictive covenant is reasonable as to duration, the trial court is accorded considerable discretion, and it is appropriate for the court to consider

whether the interests which the covenant was designed to protect are still outstanding and to balance those interests against the hardships which would be imposed upon the employee by enforcement of the restrictions. [Citation.] The proceeding is in equity, and the court may reduce the duration of the restrictive covenant to that which it considers reasonable under the circumstances. [Citation.] The record tends to support the trial court's determination that a full and liberal application of the contractual restrictions would impose a much more onerous burden on Smith than would, on balance, be required to protect the business and goodwill of Bob Pagan Ford. Thus, we hold that the trial court did not abuse its discretion in reducing the duration of the restrictive covenant.

Exculpatory Clauses

HENRIOULLE v. MARIN VENTURES, INC.

Supreme Court of California, 1978.
20 Cal.3d 512, 573 P.2d 465, 143 Cal.Rptr. 247.

BIRD, C. J.

Appellant, John Henrioulle, seeks to set aside orders of the superior court granting his landlord, respondent Marin Ventures, Inc., a judgment notwithstanding the jury's verdict and a new trial. Appellant contends that the exculpatory clause in his lease could not relieve the landlord of liability for the personal injuries appellant sustained in a fall on a common stairway in the apartment building. This court agrees.

* * *

From the record, it appears that on April 3, 1974, appellant entered into a lease agreement with respondent for an apartment in San Rafael, California. At that time, appellant was an unemployed widower with two children who received public assistance in the form of a rent subsidy from the Marin County Department of Social Services. There was also evidence of a shortage of housing accommodations for person of low income in Marin County.

The printed form lease agreement which appellant signed contained the following exculpatory clause: "INDEMNIFICATION: Owner shall not be liable for any damage or injury to Tenant, or any other person, or to any property, occurring on the premises, or any part thereof, or in the common areas thereof, and Tenant agrees to hold Owner harmless from any claims for damages no matter how caused."

On May 22, 1974, appellant fractured his wrist when he tripped over a rock on a common stairway in the apartment building. At the time of the accident the landlord had been having difficulty keeping the common areas of the apartment building clean. An on-site manager, whose duties included keeping these areas clean, had proven unsatisfactory and had been terminated in the month prior to the accident. The landlord had also employed an additional person to do maintenance work, but he had worked only a few hours at the apartment building in the month preceding the accident.

* * *

In *Tunkl v. Regents of the University of California* [Citation], this court held invalid a clause in a hospital admission form which released the hospital from liability for future negligence. This court noted that although courts have made "diverse" interpretations of [California] Civil Code section 1668, which invalidates contracts which exempt one from responsibility for certain wilful or negligent acts, all the decisions were in accord that exculpatory clauses affecting the public interest are invalid. [Citation.]

In *Tunkl*, six criteria are used to identify the kind of agreement in which an exculpatory clause is invalid as contrary to public policy. "(1) It concerns a business of a type generally thought suitable for public regulation. (2) The party seeking exculpation is engaged in performing a service of great importance to the public, which is often a matter of practical necessity for some members of the public. (3) The party holds himself out as willing to perform this service for any member of the public who seeks it, or at least any member coming within certain established standards. (4) As a result of the essential nature of the service, in the economic setting of the transaction, the party invoking exculpation possesses a decisive advantage of bargaining strength against any member of the public who seeks his services. (5) In exercising a superior bargaining power, the party confronts the public with a standardized adhesion contract of exculpation, and makes no provision whereby a purchaser may pay additional fees and obtain protection against negligence. (6) Finally, as a result of the transaction, the person or property of the purchaser is placed under the control of the seller, subject to the risk of carelessness by the seller or his agents." [Citation.]

The transaction before this court, a residential rental agreement, meets the *Tunkl* criteria.

* * *

In holding that exculpatory clauses in residential leases violate public policy, this court joins an increasing number of jurisdictions. [Citations.]

* * *

The orders of the superior court granting respondent's motions for judgment notwithstanding the jury's verdict and a new trial are reversed, and the cause is remanded with direction to enter judgment for appellant on the verdict.

Unconscionable Contracts

WILLIAMS v. WALKER-THOMAS FURNITURE CO.

Court of Appeals, District of Columbia, 1965.
350 F.2d 445.

WRIGHT, C. J. *one against whom an appeal is taken*

Appellee, Walker-Thomas Furniture Company, operates a retail furniture store in the District of Columbia. During the period from 1957 to 1962 each appellant in these cases purchased a number of household items from

Walker-Thomas, for which payment was to be made in installments. The terms of each purchase were contained in a printed form contract which set forth the value of the purchased item and purported to lease the item to appellant for a stipulated monthly rent payment. The contract then provided, in substance, that title would remain in Walker-Thomas until the total of all the monthly payments made equaled the stated value of the item, at which time appellants could take title. In the event of a default in the payment of any monthly installment, Walker-Thomas could repossess the item.

The contract further provided that "the amount of each periodical installment payment to be made by [purchaser] to the Company under this present lease shall be inclusive of and not in addition to the amount of each installment payment to be made by [purchaser] under such prior leases, bills, or accounts; *and all payments now and hereafter made by [purchaser] shall be credited pro rata on all outstanding leases, bills, and accounts* due the Company by [purchaser] at the time each such payment is made." (Emphasis added.) The effect of this rather obscure provision was to keep a balance due on every item purchased until the balance due on all items, whenever purchased, was liquidated. As a result, the debt incurred at the time of purchase of each item was secured by the right to repossess all the items previously purchased by the same purchaser, and each new item purchased automatically became subject to a security interest arising out of the previous dealings.

On May 12, 1962, appellant Thorne purchased an item described as a Daveno, three tables, and two lamps, having total stated value of $391.10. Shortly thereafter, he defaulted on his monthly payments and appellee sought to replevy all the items purchased since the first transaction in 1958. Similarly, on April 7, 1962, appellant Williams bought a stereo set of stated value of $514.95. She too defaulted shortly thereafter, and appellee sought to replevy all the items purchased since De-

cember 1957. The Court of General Sessions granted judgment for appellee. The District of Columbia Court of Appeals affirmed, and we granted appellants' motion for leave to appeal to this court.

Appellants' principal contention, rejected by both the trial and the appellate courts * * *, is that these contracts, or at least some of them, are unconscionable and, hence, not enforceable. * * *

Unconscionability has generally been recognized to include an absence of meaningful choice on the part of one of the parties together with contract terms which are unreasonably favorable to the other party. Whether a meaningful choice is present in a particular case can only be determined by consideration of all the circumstances surrounding the transaction. In many cases the meaningfulness of the choice is negated by a gross inequality of bargaining power. The manner in which the contract was entered is also relevant to this consideration. Did each party to the contract, considering his obvious education or lack of it, have a reasonable opportunity to understand the terms of the contract, or were the important terms hidden in a maze of fine print and minimized by deceptive sales practices? Ordinarily, one who signs an agreement without full knowledge of its terms might be held to assume the risk that he has entered a one-sided bargain. But when a party of little bargaining power, and hence little real choice, signs a commercially unreasonable contract with little or no knowledge of its terms, it is hardly likely that his consent, or even an objective manifestation of his consent, was ever given to all the terms. In such a case the usual rule that the terms of the agreement are not to be questioned should be abandoned and the court should consider whether the terms of the contract are so unfair that enforcement should be withheld.

In determining reasonableness or fairness, the primary concern must be with the terms of the contract considered in light of the circumstances existing when the contract was made. The test is not simple, nor can it be mechanically applied. The terms are to be considered "in the light of the general commercial background and the commercial needs of the particular trade or case." Corbin suggests the test as being whether the terms are "so extreme as to appear unconscionable according to the mores and business practices of the time and place." [Citation.] We think this formulation correctly states the test to be applied in those cases where no meaningful choice was exercised upon entering the contract.

Because the trial court and the appellate court did not feel that enforcement could be refused, no findings were made on the possible unconscionability of the contracts in these cases. Since the record is not sufficient for our deciding the issue as a matter of law, the cases must be remanded to the trial court for further proceedings.

Reversed and remanded.

PROBLEMS

Business By-out Agreement

1. A and B were the principal shareholders in XYZ Corporation located in the city of Jonesville, Wisconsin. This corporation was engaged in the business of manufacturing paper novelties which were sold over a wide area in the Middle West. The corporation was also in the business of binding books. A purchased B's shares of the XYZ Corporation and, in consideration thereof, B agreed that for a period of two years he would not: (a) manufacture or sell in Wisconsin any paper novelties of any kind which would compete with those sold by the XYZ Corporation, (b) engage in the book binding business in the city of Jonesville. Discuss the validity and effect, if any, of this agreement.

2. Wilkins, a resident of and licensed by the State of Texas as a certified public accountant, rendered service in his professional capacity in Louisiana to Coverton Cosmetics Company. He was not registered as a certified public accountant in Louisiana. His service under his contract with the cosmetics company was not the only occasion on which he had practiced his profession in that State. The company denied liability and refused to pay him relying upon a Louisiana statute declaring it unlawful for any person to perform or offer to perform services as a CPA for compensation until he has been registered by the designated agency of the State and holds an unrevoked registration card. Provision is made for issuance of a certificate as a CPA without examination to any applicant who holds a valid unrevoked certificate as a CPA under the laws of any other State. The statute provides further that rendition of services of the character performed by Wilkins, without registration, is a misdemeanor punishable by a fine or imprisonment in the county jail, or by both fine and imprisonment. Wilkins brought an action against Coverton seeking to recover a fee in the amount of $1,500 as the reasonable value of his services. Decision?

3. A is interested in promoting the passage of a bill in the State legislature. He agrees with B, an attorney, to pay B for her services in drawing the required bill, procuring its introduction in the legislature and making an argument for its passage before the legislative committee to which it will be referred. B renders these services. Subsequently, upon A's refusal to pay B, B sues A for damage for breach of contract. Decision?

4. Anthony promises to pay McCarthy $10,000 if McCarthy reveals to the public that Washington is a Communist. Washington is not a Communist and never has been. McCarthy successfully persuades the media to report that Washington is a Communist and now seeks to recover the $10,000 from Anthony, who refuses to pay. McCarthy initiates a lawsuit against Anthony. What result?

5. The XYZ Corporation was engaged in the business of making and selling harvesting machines. It sold everything pertaining to the business to the ABC Company agreeing not again to go into the manufacture of harvesting machines anywhere in the United States." The seller had a national and international goodwill in its business. It now begins the manufacture of such machines contrary to its agreement. Should the court enjoin it?

6. Charles Leigh, engaged in the industrial laundry business in Central City, employed Tim Close, previously employed in the home laundry business, as a route salesman on July 1, 1984. Leigh rents linens and industrial uniforms to commercial customers; the soiled linens and uniforms are picked up at regular intervals by the routemen and replaced with clean ones. Every employee is assigned a list of customers whom he services. The contract of employment stated that in consideration of being employed, upon termination of the employment, Close would not "directly or indirectly engage in the linen supply business or any competitive business within Central City, Illinois, for a period of one year from the date when his employment under this contract ceases." On May 10 of the following year, Close's employment was terminated by Leigh for valid reasons. Thereafter, Close accepted employment with Ajax Linen Service, a direct competitor of Leigh in Central City. He commenced soliciting former customers whom he had called on for Leigh, and obtained some of them as customers for Ajax.

Leigh brings an action to enforce the provisions of the contract. Decision?

7. On July 5, 1980, Billy and Nancy entered into a bet on the outcome of the 1980 presidential election. On January 28, 1982, Nancy, who bet on Ronald Reagan, approached Billy seeking to collect the $3,000 which Billy had wagered on Jimmy Carter. Billy paid Nancy the wager and now seeks to recover the funds from Nancy. Result?

8. C, a salesman for S, comes to B's home and sells him a complete set of "gourmet cooking utensils," which are worth approximately $300. B, a man of eighty years, lives alone in a one-room efficiency apartment. B signs a contract to buy the utensils for $1,450 plus a credit charge of $145 and to make payment in ten equal monthly installments. After C leaves with the signed contract, B decides he cannot afford and has no use for cooking utensils. What can B do?

9. A rents a bicycle from B. The bicycle rental contract which A signed provides that B is not liable for any injury to the renter caused by any defect in the bicycle or the negligence of B. A is injured when she is involved in an accident due to B's improper maintenance of the bicycle. A sues B for her damage. Decision?

Chapter 12

CONTRACTUAL CAPACITY

A binding promise or agreement requires that the parties to the agreement have contractual capacity. Everyone is regarded as having such capacity unless the law for reason of public policy holds that the individual lacks such capacity. This essential ingredient of a contract will be discussed by considering those classes and conditions of persons who are legally limited in their capacity to contract. The contracting capacity of persons will be discussed in the following order: (1) minors; (2) incompetent persons; and (3) intoxicated persons.

MINORS

A minor, also called an infant, is a person who has not attained the age of legal majority. At common law, a minor was a person who was under twenty-one years of age. To-day the age limit has been changed in nearly all jurisdictions by statute, usually reduced to age eighteen. Almost without exception a minor's contract is **voidable** at his option. Restatement, Section 14; *See also Robertson v. King*. Even an "emancipated" minor, one who by reason of marriage or otherwise is no longer subject to strict parental control, may avoid contractual liability in most jurisdictions. Consequently, businesspeople deal with minors at their peril.

Liability for Necessaries

Contractual immunity does not excuse a minor from an obligation to pay for necessaries, those things which suitably and reasonably supply her personal needs, such as food, shelter, and clothing. Even here the minor is not contractually liable for the agreed price but, instead, the *reasonable value* of the items furnished. Recovery is based upon quasi contract. Suppose that A, a minor, actually needs an overcoat and purchases one from B on credit at the agreed price of $100. Suppose further that the fair and reasonable value of the coat is only $75. If A were an adult, and there was no fraud on B's part, A would be liable to B for the contract price of $100. As a minor, however, A is not liable on his express contract but on a quasi contract. He is liable to B, therefore, for only $75. In no case, however, even though the reasonable value of the coat exceeded the contract price, would A be liable for more than the contract price.

Determining what are necessaries is a difficult problem. In general, those things are regarded as necessary which the minor needs to maintain himself in his particular station in life. Items necessary for subsistence and health are obviously included, such as food, lodging, clothing, medicine, and medical services. But others less essential may be included as well, such as text books, school instruction, and legal advice. Further, there may be a tendency to enlarge the concept of necessaries to include such articles of property and services as are reasonably necessary to enable a minor to earn the money required to provide the necessities of life for himself and his dependents. *See Gastonia Personnel Corp. v. Rogers.*

A minor is not liable for anything on the ground that it is a necessary unless it has been actually furnished to him and used or consumed by him. In other words, a minor may repudiate his executory contracts for necessaries, and refuse to accept the clothing, lodging, or other thing contracted for by him. Again, a minor is generally not liable for anything that would come within the general classification of necessaries if he is already supplied or is being supplied by his parents or guardian. If, for example, a minor who is being supplied by his parents with all usual essentials should purchase, without the authority of his parents, a suit of clothes, he could not be held liable by the seller. Nor of course would the parents be liable in such

case. Parents are liable only where they authorize the minor to procure the necessaries, or authorize the other party to furnish them to the minor, or where they fail or refuse to supply the minor with necessaries and he procures them himself. The burden of ascertaining whether the infant is supplied or being supplied rests upon the other party.

Ordinarily, luxury items, such as cameras, tape recorders, phonographs, television sets, and motor boats, seldom qualify as necessaries. Whether automobiles and trucks are necessaries has caused considerable controversy, but some courts have recognized that under certain circumstances an automobile may be a necessary where it is used by the minor for his business activities. *See Rose v. Sheehan Buick, Inc.*

Liability on Contracts

A minor's contract is not entirely void and of no legal effect, but rather it is *voidable* at the minor's option. He has a power of avoidance. This exercise of power is called a **disaffirmance,** and the minor is released from any liability on the contract. On the other hand, after the minor becomes of age, she may choose to adopt or **ratify** the contract, in which case she becomes bound.

Ratification Suppose that a minor makes a contract to buy property from an adult. The contract is voidable by the minor, and she can escape liability. But, suppose that after reaching her majority, she promises to go through with the purchase. Her promise is binding, and the adult can sue for breach upon her failure to perform. She has *expressly* ratified the contract entered into when she was a minor. Ratification makes the contract binding *ab initio.* That is, the result is the same as if the contract had been valid and binding from the beginning. Ratification, once effected, is final and cannot be withdrawn.

Ratification must be in total; it must validate the entire contract. The minor can ratify the contract only as a whole, both as to burdens and benefits. He cannot, for example, ratify so as to retain the consideration he received and escape payment or other performance on his part. For example, Langstraat, age seventeen, owned a motorcycle which he insured against liability with Midwest Mutual Insurance Company. He signed a notice of rejection attached to the policy indicating that he did not desire to purchase uninsured motorists coverage from the insurance company. Later he was involved in an accident with another motorcycle owned and operated by a party who was uninsured. Langstraat sought to recover from the insurance company asserting that his rejection was not a valid rejection because he was a minor. Langstraat cannot ratify the benefits from the insurance policy while disaffirming the uninsured motorist provision which has become burdensome. A minor is not permitted this selective choice. Ratification and disaffirmance, if asserted, go to the whole contract. *Langstraat v. Midwest Mutual Ins. Co.*, 217 N.W.2d 570 (Iowa 1974).

A ratification need not be express; it may be *implied* from the minor's conduct. If, for example, the minor should, after attaining her majority, use the property, or undertake to sell it to someone else, or perform some other act showing an intention to affirm the contract, she may not thereafter disaffirm but is liable on the contract. Perhaps the most common form of implied ratification occurs when the minor, after attaining her majority, continues to use the property which she purchased as a minor. This use is obviously inconsistent with the nonexistence of the contract, and whether the contract is performed or still partly executory, it will amount to a ratification and prevent a disaffirmance by the minor. Mere retention of the goods for an unreasonable time after attaining majority has also been construed as a ratification. Although there is a division of authority, payments by the minor either upon principal or interest or upon the purchase price of goods have been held to amount to a ratification. Some courts require some additional evidence

of an intention to abide by the contract, such as an express promise to that effect or the use of the subject matter of the contract.

It should be noted that a minor has *no* power to ratify a contract while he remains a minor. A ratification *cannot* be based on words or conduct occurring while he is still under age, for his ratification at that time would be no more effective than his original contractual promise. The ratification must take place after the individual has acquired contractual capacity by attaining his majority.

Disaffirmance   As stated, a minor's contract is voidable at his option, conferring upon him a power to avoid liability. He may exercise his power to disaffirm through words or conduct manifesting an intention not to abide by it. A contract once disaffirmed cannot thereafter be ratified. Aspects of this power will be considered in the following order: (1) When can the minor disaffirm? (2) How can he disaffirm? (3) What, if anything, must he do upon a disaffirmance?

In general, a minor's disaffirmance must come either during his minority or within a reasonable time after reaching majority, the precise time period varying with the circumstances and local law.

As is true of ratification, a disaffirmance may be either *express* or *implied*. No particular form of words is essential, so long as they show an intention not to be bound. This intention may be manifested by acts or by conduct, e.g., where a minor agrees to sell property to A and then sells that property to B. The sale to B would constitute a disaffirmance of the contract with A.

A troublesome and, at the same time, very important problem in this area pertains to the minor's duty upon a disaffirmance. There is no unanimity of opinion on this question. By the majority view, it is only necessary that the minor return any property he has received from the other party, provided he has it in his possession at the time of disaffirmance. Nothing more. If the minor is disaffirming the purchase of an automobile and the vehicle has been wrecked, he need only return the wrecked vehicle. A few States, however, either by statute or common law, recognize a duty upon the part of the minor to make *restitution*, i.e., return an equivalent of what has been received in order to place the seller in approximately the same position she would have occupied had the sale not occurred. Others require at least the payment of a reasonable amount for the use of the property or the amount of its depreciation while in the hands of the minor. *See Halbman v. Lemke*.

Finally, can a minor disaffirm and recover property which has been transferred by his buyer to a good faith purchaser for value? Traditionally, he could avoid the contract and recover the property, despite the fact that the third person gave value for it and had no notice of the minority. This, however, has been changed regarding sales of goods by Section 2-403 of the U.C.C., which provides that a person with voidable title (e.g., the person buying goods from a minor) has power to transfer valid title to a good faith purchaser for value. For example, a minor sells his car to an individual who resells it to a used car dealership, a good faith purchaser for value. The used car dealer would acquire legal title even though he bought the car from a seller who had only voidable title. However, in the case of the sale of real estate the traditional rule applies, and a minor's deed of conveyance may be rescinded even against a good faith purchaser of the land who did not know of the minority.

Further mention should be made of a minor's transactions concerning real property. Until his contract for the sale or purchase of land has been consummated by the conveyance of the land by or to the minor, he can disaffirm it in accordance with the rules already considered. If, however, the contract has been consummated, and the title to the land conveyed by or to the minor, he can not disaffirm such conveyance until he has reached his majority. The reason for this rule is that lands and improvements on it, in contrast with personal property, are of a permanent nature, and will be available and intact after the minor reaches majority, should he then wish to regain them. Where a minor has sold his land he may, while still a minor, re-enter the premises and enjoy the use of the land, but he cannot finally disaffirm his conveyance until he has attained his majority. If he still has the consideration he received from the other party, he must upon disaffirmance restore it. If he has disposed of it and so cannot return it, he can, under the general rule, still disaffirm his conveyance without placing the other party in his original position. Where he purchased land during minority, he can likewise disaffirm upon reaching majority, and recover in full what he paid or delivered to the other party.

Liability for Misrepresentation of Age

The law is not uniform on the effect to be given a fraudulent misrepresentation by a minor with respect to her age at the time of entering into a contract. Suppose a minor says that she is eighteen years of age (or twenty-one if that is the year of attaining majority) and actually looks that old or even older? By the prevailing view in this country the minor may nevertheless disaffirm the contract. However, some States prohibit disaffirmance if a minor misrepresents her age and the adult, in good faith, reasonably relied upon the misrepresentation. Other States not following the majority rule either (a) require the minor to restore the other party to the position she occupied before the making of the contract or (b) allow the defrauded party to recover damages against the minor in tort.

Liability for Tort Connected with Contract

It is well settled that minors are, as a general proposition, liable for their torts. There is, however, a doctrine in the law that if a tort and a contract are so connected or "interwoven" that to enforce the tort action the court must enforce the contract, the minor is not liable in tort. Thus, if a minor rents an automobile from an adult, he enters into a contractual relationship obliging him to exercise reasonable care and diligence to protect the property from injury. By negligently damaging the automobile, he breaches that contractual undertaking. But his contractual immunity protects him from an action by the adult based on the contract. However, can the adult sue for damages on a tort theory? By the majority view he cannot. For, it is reasoned, a tort recovery would, in effect, be an enforcement of the contract and would defeat the protection which contract law affords the minor. This rationale has been stated by the Supreme Court of Michigan as follows:

But it is also a general rule that if the tort with which an infant is charged is so connected with the contract that commission of the tort constitutes a breach of the contract, or if the tort is predicated on a transaction with the infant based upon contract, so, that holding the infant liable in tort would in effect enforce a liability arising out of his contract, then, since the infant cannot be held *ex contractu*, he cannot be held liable for his tort. The injured party is not permitted to enforce against the infant indirectly by an action in tort a liability which he could not enforce directly against the infant by an action upon contract. *Brown v. Wood*, 293 Mich. 148, 291 N.W. 255, 127 A.L.R. 1436 (1940).

INCOMPETENT PERSONS

Mental Illness or Defect

Since a contract is a consensual transaction, it is necessary to a valid contract that the parties have requisite mental capacity. If one is lacking in such capacity, or mentally incompetent, he may avoid liability under the agreement (i.e., the contract is **voidable**).

A person who is lacking in sufficient mental capacity to enter into a contract is one

unable to comprehend the subject of the contract, its nature, and probable consequences. To avoid the contract it is not necessary that he be proved permanently incompetent; but his mental defect must be something more than a weakness of intellect or a lack of average intelligence. In short, a person is competent unless he is unable to understand the nature and effect of his act.

Section 15 of the Restatement provides:

(1) A person incurs only voidable contractual duties by entering into a transaction if by reason of mental illness or defect

    (a) he is unable to understand in a reasonable manner the nature and consequences of the transaction or

    (b) he is unable to act in a reasonable manner in relation to the transaction and the other party has reason to know of his condition.

See G.A.S. v. S.I.S.

As in the case of a minor, an incompetent person is liable for *necessaries* furnished on the principle of quasi contract, the measure of recovery being the reasonable value of the goods or services. Moreover, an incompetent person's voidable contracts may be *ratified* or *disaffirmed* by him when he becomes competent, or during a lucid period.

The predominant view in this country respecting an incompetent person's responsibility upon disaffirmance varies somewhat from that of a minor. If the contract is fair and the competent party had no reason to suspect the incompetency of the other, the incompetent must restore the competent party to the *status quo* by a return of the consideration received by the incompetent or its equivalent in money.

Person under Guardianship

If the property of a person is under guardianship by **court order**, her contracts are **void** and of no legal effect. Restatement, Section 13. A *guardian* is appointed by a court, generally under the terms of a statute, to control and preserve the property of a person (the

FIGURE 12-1   Contractual Incapacity

Incapacity	Effect
Minority	Voidable
Mental illness or defect	Voidable
Guardianship for incompetency	Void
Intoxication	Voidable

ward) with impaired capacity to manage her own property. As with the case of incompetents not under guardianship, a party dealing with an individual under guardianship may be able to recover the fair value of any necessaries provided to the incompetent. Moreover, the contracts of the ward may be ratified by her guardian or by herself upon termination of the guardianship.

INTOXICATED PERSONS

A person may *avoid* any contract that he enters into if the other party has reason to know that, because of intoxication, he is unable to understand the nature and consequences of his actions or that he is unable to act in a reasonable manner. Restatement, Section 16. Such contracts are voidable. Slight intoxication will not destroy one's contractual ca-

pacity, but neither is it essential that one be so drunk as to be totally without reason or understanding. *See Williamson v. Matthews.*

The effect of intoxication on contractual capacity is generally the same as that given to contracts that are voidable because of incompetency. The options of *ratification* or *disaffirmance* remain, although the courts are even more strict with respect to the requirement of restitution upon disaffirmance than they are in the area of an incompetent person's agreements. The rule is only relaxed where the person dealing with the intoxicated person fraudulently took advantage of the intoxicated individual. As with incompetent persons, intoxicated persons are liable in quasi contract for necessaries furnished during their incapacity.

Figure 12-1 illustrates the various types of contractual incapacities and the resulting effects.

CASES

Minors: Contractual Incapacity

ROBERTSON v. KING

Supreme Court of Arkansas, 1955.
225 Ark. 276, 280 S.W.2d 402.

ROBINSON, J.

The principal issue here is whether appellant, [Robertson], a minor, may rescind a contract to purchase a pick-up truck. On the

20th day of March, 1954, L. D. Robertson, a minor, entered into a conditional sales agreement whereby he purchased from Turner King and J. W. Julian, doing business as the Julian Pontiac Company, a pick-up truck for the agreed price of $1,743.85. On the day of the purchase, Robertson was 17 years of age, and did not have his 18th birthday until April 8th. Robertson traded in a passenger car for which he was given a credit of $723.85 on the purchase price, leaving a balance of $1,020 payable in 23 monthly installments of $52.66 plus one payment of $52.83. He paid the April installment of $52.66.

It appears that Robertson had considerable trouble with the wiring on the truck. He returned it to the automobile dealers for repairs, but the defective condition was not remedied. On May 2nd, the truck caught fire and was practically destroyed. He notified the automobile concern and they stated that they would send the insurance man to see him. It appears that the insurance representative, upon finding out that Robertson was only 17 years of age, refused to deal with him.

On June 7th, appellees [King and Julian] filed suit to replevy [recover] the damaged truck from Robertson. * * * Robertson filed a cross-complaint in which he alleged that he is a minor and asked that the contract of purchase be rescinded and sought to recover that part of the purchase price he had paid, which he alleges is the amount of $723.85, allowed by the dealers on the car traded in, plus the one monthly payment of $52.66 totalling $776.51. A jury [returned] * * * judgment for King and Julian on the complaint and the cross-complaint. On Appeal, Robertson contends that he was 17 years of age at the time of the alleged purchase and that he has a right under the law to rescind the contract and to recover the portion of the purchase price he has paid.

Appellees contend * * * that the judgment should be sustained because Robertson did not return the damaged truck to the automobile dealers. However, the judgment of the court states: "The court further finds the proof to be that the plaintiff has possession of the said GMC pick-up truck." Hence, there is no merit to this contention. * * *

Appellees further contend that the minor is bound by the contract because the automobile was a necessary. The record does not contain any substantial evidence to support this contention. The only evidence on this issue is that the boy quit school in 1951 and has been earning his own living since that time,

and that he has been working for a construction company and traveling around the country to different jobs with his father in his father's truck. The boy lives at home with his parents and there is no showing whatever that he needed the truck in connection with any work he was doing. One of the witnesses for the appellees testified that the boy stated he wanted to use the truck in a farming operation. The record contains no evidence that he was engaged in farming at any time. * * * He was allowed a sum on the car which he traded in, amounting to more than one-third of the purchase price of the new truck, and he was to make substantial monthly payments for the balance. It is a matter of common knowledge that the plan under which the boy bought the truck is the usual method of making purchases of automobiles. In a suit by a minor to rescind a contract the burden is on the defendant to show that the article was a necessary. [Citation.]

It is our conclusion that the evidence does not sustain a finding that the truck was a necessary to Robertson. * * * The law is settled in this State that a minor may rescind a contract to purchase where the property involved is not a necessary. [Citations.]

The automobile dealers have disposed of the car they received in the trade, and cannot restore it to the minor. In a situation of this kind, the weight of authority is that the actual value of the property given as part of the purchase price by the minor is the correct measure of damages. Neither side is bound by the agreement reached as to the value of the car at the time the trade was made. This is true because the contract has been rescinded and there is no contract fixing the value. "While it is generally held that, where property traded in by the infant as part of the price is beyond reach of the seller, the infant is entitled to the reasonable value of the property at the time of the purchase, rather than the value fixed in the purchase agreement, it has also been held that he is entitled to receive the value fixed in the agreement." [Citation.]

In support of the rule that a reasonable value of the property at the time of purchase governs, [one] court said: "Where the infant parts with personal property, he may, upon disaffirmance, recover the value of such property, as of the date of the contract, but he is neither bound by, nor entitled to be awarded, the price fixed by the contract, for its real value may be more or less than the amount so stipulated." * * *

In the case at bar, although the minor was allowed over $700 on his car in the trade, there is evidence to the effect that it was actually worth about $350. Although there is conflict among the authorities as pointed out above, we believe the better rule holds that the value of an article given in trade by a minor as a part of the purchase price is the reasonable market value of the article at the time of the purchase, and that neither party is bound by the value fixed in the purchase agreement.

Young Robertson is a minor; the truck was not a necessary. * * * Hence, the court erred in finding for the automobile dealers, and the cause is therefore reversed and remanded for a new trial

Minors: Liability for
Necessaries

GASTONIA PERSONNEL CORP. v. ROGERS

Supreme Court of North Carolina, 1970.
276 N.C. 279, 172 S.E.2d 19.

BOBBITT, C. J.

[Rogers (defendant) was a nineteen-year-old (the age of majority being twenty-one) high school graduate pursuing a civil engineering degree when he learned that his wife was expecting a child. As a result he quit school and sought assistance from Gastonia Personnel Corporation (plaintiff) in finding a job. Rogers signed a contract with the employment agency providing that he would pay the agency a service charge if it obtained suitable employment for him. The employment

agency found him such a job, but Rogers refused to pay the service charge asserting that he was a minor when he signed the contract. Plaintiff sued to recover the agreed upon service charge from Rogers.]

Under the common law, persons, whether male or female, are classifed and referred to as *infants* until they attain the age of twenty-one years. [Citations.]

"By the fifteenth century it seems to have been well settled that an infant's bargain was in general void at his election (that is voidable), and also that he was liable for necessaries." [Citation.]

An early commentary on the common law, after the general statement that contracts made by persons (infants) before attaining the age of twenty-one "may be avoided," sets forth "some exceptions out of this generality," to wit: *An infant may bind himself to pay for his necessary meat, drinke, apparell, necessary physicke, and such other necessaries, and likewise for his good teaching or instruction, whereby he may profit himself afterwards.*" (Our italics.) [Citations.] * * * If the infant married, "necessaries" included necessary food and clothing for his wife and child. [Citation.]

In accordance with this ancient rule of the common law, this Court has held an infant's contract, unless for "necessaries" or unless authorized by statute, is voidable by the infant, at his election, and may be disaffirmed during infancy or upon attaining the age of twenty-one. [Citations.]

* * *

In general, our prior decisions are to the effect that the "necessaries" of an infant, his wife and child, include only such necessities of life as food, clothing, shelter, medical attention, etc. In our view, the concept of "necessities" should be enlarged to include such articles of property and such services as are reasonably necessary to enable the infant to earn the money required to provide the necessities of life for himself and those who are legally dependent upon him.

The evidence before us tends to show that defendant, when he contracted with plaintiff, was nineteen years of age, emancipated, married, a high school graduate, within "a quarter or 22 hours" of obtaining his degree in applied science, and capable of holding a job at a starting annual salary of $4,784.00. To hold, as a matter of law, that such a person cannot obligate himself to pay for services rendered him in obtaining employment suitable to his ability, education, and specialized training, enabling him to provide the necessities of life for himself, his wife and his expected child, would place him and others similarly situated under a serious economic handicap.

In the effort to protect "older minors" from improvident or unfair contracts, the law should not deny to them the opportunity and right to obligate themselves for articles of property or services which are reasonably necesssary to enable them to provide for the proper support of themselves and their dependents. The minor should be held liable for the reasonable value of articles of property or services received pursuant to such contract.

Applying the foregoing legal principles, which modify *pro tanto* the ancient rule of the common law, we hold that the evidence offered by plaintiff was sufficient for submission to the jury for its determination of issues substantially as indicated below.

To establish liability, plaintiff must satisfy the jury by the greater weight of the evidence that defendant's contract with plaintiff was an appropriate and reasonable means for defendant to obtain suitable employment. If this issue is answered in plaintiff's favor, plaintiff must then establish by the greater weight of the evidence the reasonable value of the services received by defendant pursuant to the contract. Thus, plaintiff's recovery, if any, cannot exceed the reasonable value of its services to defendant.

[Judgment for plaintiff awarding a new trial in accordance with legal principles stated in this opinion.]

Minors: Liability for Necessaries

ROSE v. SHEEHAN BUICK, INC.

Florida Court of Appeals, 1967.
204 So.2d 903.

BARKDULL, J.

* * *

The record reveals that on or about August 11, 1965, the appellee [Sheehan] sold a 1965 Buick Riviera to the appellant [Rose] for a cash sales price of $5,176.87. At the time of the sale, the appellant was a minor. On March 1, 1966, while still a minor under the age of 21 years [the age of majority], the appellant elected to disaffirm the purchase and notified the appellee of his intention, offering to return the vehicle upon a refund of the purchase price in full. The appellee refused to accept the return of the vehicle or to refund the purchase price thereof, so the appellant [who reached the age of 21 years on April 11, 1966] brought the instant action seeking invalidation of the contract and refund of the purchase price in full. The appellee answered admitting the sale and value of the vehicle, but denying the appellant had ever disaffirmed the contract while still a minor. The answer further alleged the vehicle was purchased as a necessity for the minor appellant; * * * and that the appellee was entitled to deterioration in the event of disaffirmance by the appellant. The court's decree in favor of defendant made findings that: * * * The Plaintiff, at age twenty, gave all the appearance of being of legal age. He acted and negotiated for the purchase of the car as an experienced adult. He traded, as part of the purchase price of the new car, his personal car titled in his father's name. His mother advanced part of the cash purchase price. Both his mother and father ratified and confirmed the sale. The car has been used by the Plaintiff since August 11, 1965, to carry on his school, business and social activities. The car is a necessity for this plaintiff. The attempted disaffirmance of the sale by the plaintiff was made for trivial claimed defects in the car. If the disaffirmance were to be allowed, the Defendant would be entitled to an allowance or set-off for the use and depreciation of the car while in the possession of the Plaintiff. However, equity and good conscience will not allow a rescission or disaffirmance of this contract by the Plaintiff. * * *

* * *

The appellant has preserved five points for review on this appeal. * * *

The second point contends that the [lower court] erred in finding that the vehicle was a necessity for the plaintiff. This was a finding of fact, amply supported by the record [citations] and, therefore, this court will not disturb the decree on this basis.

* * *

The appellant also urges that the [lower court] erred in holding that even if the plaintiff were entitled to rescission or disaffirmance, the defendant would be entitled to depreciation or depletion in value as of the date of the disaffirmance. This is an equity court and one who seeks equity must do equity. [Citations.] We concur with the [lower court's] decision and, in the event the plaintiff were permitted to disaffirm the agreement, we hold that the defendant would be entitled to take into account depreciation on the returned chattel as of the date of the election to disaffirm.

* * *

Affirmed.

Disaffirmance

HALBMAN v. LEMKE

Supreme Court of Wisconsin, 1980.
99 Wis.2d 241, 298 N.W.2d 562.

CALLOW, J.

* * *

This matter was before the trial court upon stipulated facts. On or about July 13, 1973, James Halbman, Jr. (Halbman), a minor, entered into an agreement with Michael Lemke (Lemke) whereby Lemke agreed to sell Halbman a 1968 Oldsmobile for the sum of $1,250. Lemke was the manager of L & M Standard Station in Greenfield, Wisconsin, and Halbman was an employe at L & M. At the time the agreement was made Halbman paid Lemke $1,000 cash and took possession of the car. Arrangements were made for Halbman to pay $25 per week until the balance was paid, at which time title would be transferred. About five weeks after the purchase agreement, and after Halbman had paid a total of $1,100 of the purchase price, a connecting rod on the vehicle's engine broke. Lemke, while denying any obligation, offered to assist Halbman in installing a used engine in the vehicle if Halbman, at his expense, could secure one. Halbman declined the offer and in September took the vehicle to a garage where it was repaired at a cost of $637.40. Halbman did not pay the repair bill.

In October of 1973 Lemke endorsed the vehicle's title over to Halbman, although the full purchase price had not been paid by Halbman, in an effort to avoid any liability for the operation, maintenance, or use of the vehicle. On October 15, 1973, Halbman returned the title to Lemke by letter which disaffirmed the purchase contract and demanded the return of all money theretofore paid by Halbman. Lemke did not return the money paid by Halbman.

The repair bill remained unpaid, and the vehicle remained in the garage where the repairs had been made. In the spring of 1974, in satisfaction of a garageman's lien for the outstanding amount, the garage elected to remove the vehicle's engine and transmission and then towed the vehicle to the residence of James Halbman, Sr., the father of the plaintiff minor. Lemke was asked several times to remove the vehicle from the senior Halbman's home, but he declined to do so, claiming he was under no legal obligation to remove it. During the period when the vehicle was at the garage and then subsequently at the home of the plaintiff's father, it was subjected to vandalism, making it unsalvageable.

Halbman initiated this action seeking the return of the $1,100 he had paid toward the purchase of the vehicle, and Lemke counterclaimed for $150, the amount still owing on the contract. Based upon the uncontroverted facts, the trial court granted judgment in favor of Halbman, concluding that when a minor disaffirms a contract for the purchase of an item, he need only offer to return the property remaining in his hands without making restitution for any use or depreciation.

*   *   *

The sole issue before us is whether the minor, having disaffirmed a contract for the purchase of an item which is not a necessity and having tendered the property back to the vendor, must make restitution to the vendor for damage to the property prior to the disaffirmance. Lemke argues that he should be entitled to recover for the damage to the vehicle up to the time of disaffirmance, which he claims equals the amount of the repair bill.

Neither party challenges the absolute right of a minor to disaffirm a contract for the purchase of items which are not necessities. That right, variously known as the doctrine of incapacity or the "infancy doctrine," is one of the oldest and most venerable of our common law traditions. [Citations.] Although the origins of the doctrine are somewhat obscure, it is generally recognized that its purpose is the protection of minors from foolishly squandering their wealth through improvident contracts with crafty adults who would take advantage of them in the marketplace. [Citation.] Thus it is settled law in this state that a contract of a minor for items which are not necessities is *   *   * voidable at the minor's option. [Citations.]

Once there has been a disaffirmance, however, as in this case between a minor vendee and an adult vendor, unresolved problems arise regarding the rights and responsibilities of the parties relative to the disposition of the consideration exchanged on the contract. As a general rule a minor who disaffirms a contract is entitled to recover all consideration he has conferred incident to the transaction. [Citation.] In return the minor is expected to restore as much of the consideration as, at the time of disaffirmance, remains in the minor's possession. [Citations.] The minor's right to disaffirm is not contingent upon the return of the property, however, as disaffirmance is permitted even where such return cannot be made.

*   *   *

A minor, as we have stated, is under an enforceable duty to return to the vendor, upon disaffirmance, as much of the consideration as remains in his possession. When the contract is disaffirmed, title to that part of the purchased property which is retained by the minor revests in the vendor; it no longer belongs to the minor. [Citation.] The rationale for the rule is plain: a minor who disaffirms a purchase and recovers his purchase price should not also be permitted to profit by retaining the property purchased. The infancy doctrine is designed to protect the minor, sometimes at the expense of an innocent vendor, but it is not to be used to bilk merchants out of property as well as proceeds of the sale. Consequently, it is clear that, when the minor no longer possesses the property which was the subject matter of the contract, the rule requiring the return of property does not apply. The minor will not be required to give up what he does not have.

*   *   *

Here Lemke seeks restitution of the value of the depreciation by virtue of the damage to the vehicle prior to disaffirmance. Such a recovery would require Halbman to return more than that remaining in his possession. It seeks compensatory value for that which he cannot return. Where there is misrepresentation by a minor or willful destruction of property, the vendor may be able to recover damages in tort. [Citations.] But absent these factors, as in the present case, we believe that to require a disaffirming minor to make restitution for diminished value is, in effect, to bind the minor to a part of the obligation which by law he is privileged to avoid.

*   *   *

Incompetent Persons

G. A. S. v. S. I. S.

Family Court of Delaware, 1978.
407 A.2d 253.

JAMES, J.

Action by petitioner to rescind the separation agreement he and his former wife, respondent S.I.S., executed on February 20, 1975.

Petitioner and respondent were married on January 19, 1957, and four children were born of this marriage. Petitioner's mental health problems began in 1970 when he was hospitalized at the Delaware State Hospital for eight weeks. Similar illnesses occurred in 1972 and the early part of 1974, with petitioner suffering such symptoms as acceleration of the mind followed by paranoia and loss of a sense of reality. During the two to three-day onset of the illness, petitioner generally becomes violent toward himself, but not other people. After commitment, and drug therapy, petitioner slowly comes down from this state of aggressiveness, begins to communicate with others and, according to psychiatric testimony, becomes extremely dependent. After release from the hospital, petitioner usually continues to take medication for thirty to ninety days. Petitioner has been diagnosed as suffering from schizophrenia, paranoid type, and manic-depression.

On December 23, 1974, petitioner suffered a reoccurrence of this illness and was committed again to the Delaware State Hospital by police after being called by respondent. At this time, petitioner was employed by Hercules as a design engineer at a yearly salary of approximately $21,000. Although petitioner claims there had been no marital discord prior to the December 23, 1974 mental breakdown, respondent testified that she consulted an attorney in March of 1974, during petitioner's previous reoccurrence of this illness, for the purpose of securing a legal separation. However, petitioner pleaded with her to stay with him and she agreed if he promised to take his medication. In any event, respondent filed for a divorce in Superior Court alleging the mental illness of petitioner as the sole ground for the action, and petitioner was personally served with the divorce summons on January 10, 1975, while still committed to the Delaware State Hospital.

Petitioner told respondent that he did not want the divorce and he was referred, by the hospital's patient advocate, to an attorney with whom he had a very brief consultation of January 16, 1975, the details of which are the subject of some dispute. However, all parties agree that petitioner was primarily concerned with returning to the marital home and reconciling with respondent. While there may have been some discussion as to what property petitioner owned, he did not discuss with the attorney any type of proposed written separation agreement between petitioner and respondent. Although the attorney indicated he was willing to take the case, petitioner never followed up on the initial visit.

The separation agreement which is the subject of the current dispute was prepared by respondent's attorney and signed by petitioner on February 20, 1975 at her attorney's office, at her request. Petitioner never spoke with respondent's attorney about the contents of the agreement, nor did petitioner read it in the office prior to signing the document. It is clear that petitioner was not independently represented by counsel when he executed this agreement, although at the time he was still committed to the Delaware State Hospital in the night hospital program, under which he left during working hours to attend his job and returned to the hospital at night for continuing treatment.

* * *

The Court must answer the following questions in order to resolve the issue of the validity of the February 20, 1975 separation agreement: first, whether petitioner had the legal capacity to contract on that date; * * *

Only competent persons can make a contract, and where there is no capacity to understand or agree, there can be no contact. [Citations.]

Although petitioner was still under commitment to Delaware State Hospital at the time of execution of the separation agreement, he had not been judicially adjudicated mentally incompetent, and therefore the agreement is not void but may be voidable. [Citations.]

The mental incapacity sufficient to permit the cancellation of an agreement must render the afflicted individual incapable of understanding the nature and effect of the transaction. [Citation.] The court must determine whether his mental faculties have been impaired to such an extent that he is unable to properly, intelligently, and fairly protect and preserve his property rights. [Citation.]

At the time of the execution of the separation agreement not only was petitioner a diagnosed paranoid schizophrenic still receiving in-patient treatment, but he was also receiving significant amounts of "antipsychotic" medication. The only psychiatrist to testify, Dr. S., treated petitioner in February of 1978, and based his testimony upon direct knowledge of petitioner and a review of the existing medical records. Dr. S's opinion, based upon reasonable medical certainty, was that when petitioner executed the separation agreement on February 20, 1975, he would not have been fully able to understand or comprehend what he was signing nor the implications thereof.

* * *

Delaware courts have held that mental incapacity, resulting from the use of drugs, may furnish a ground for voiding a contract, [citation] however,

[I]f no circumstances of unfairness, fraud, duress, or undue influence appear, the reasoning powers must be so impaired as to render the person actually incapable of comprehending and acting rationally in the particular transaction.

The facts of this case do not require this Court to make the extremely difficult decision as to whether petitioner was, in fact, incapable of comprehending and acting rationally in executing the separation agreement. For even if the mental weakness of the petitioner in this case did not rise to the level of contractual incapacity, such weakness is a circumstance that operates to make the separation agreement voidable when coupled with the evidence of lack of independent counsel, undue influence, and unfairness in the transaction that is present in this case.

Intoxicated Persons/
Incompetent Persons

WILLIAMSON v. MATTHEWS

Supreme Court of Alabama, 1980.
379 So.2d 1245.

PER CURIAM

This is an appeal from an order denying appellant Williamson * * * relief seeking to cancel a deed and to set aside a sale of property from Williamson to the Matthews. We reverse and remand.

The Matthews learned from members of their family that Williamson wanted to sell her home. Her mortgage was in default, and the mortgagee was threatening foreclosure. There was some evidence to the effect that Williamson wanted to get enough equity to help her finance a mobile home. When they went to Williamson's house to inquire about it, Williamson showed the Matthews through the house. Bobby Matthews asked Williamson how much she wanted for it. Williamson told the Matthews to come back the next day. It is at this point that the parties are in disagreement. The Matthews contend that Williamson offered to sell her equity for $1,700, and Williamson contends that she offered to sell her equity for $17,000, and that the Matthews agreed to pay off the mortgage. It is undisputed that on September 27, 1978, the parties went to attorney Arthur J. Cook's office to execute a contract for the sale of the property. The contract of sale stated the purchase price to be $1,800 ($100 increase reflecting an agreement between the parties concerning some of the furniture in the home) plus the unpaid balance of the mortgage. Attorney Cook testified that he read the terms of the sale to both parties.

The parties then met on October 10, 1978, at attorney Larry Keener's office to sign the deed and to close a loan from appellee Family Savings Federal Credit Union to the Matthews so that the Matthews could buy the property from Williamson. Appellee The Brooklyn Savings Bank was about to foreclose the mortgage on Williamson's property. Keener disbursed part of the loan proceeds to Williamson. Williamson signed the deed to the property.

* * *

Immediately after the sale, Williamson became concerned that she had not received her full consideration and consulted an attorney.

Two days later, on October 12, 1978, Williamson filed a petition for injunctive relief alleging inadequate consideration and mental weakness. * * *

* * *

Williamson contends that the "something else" in the case at bar is mental weakness, either due to some form of permanent mental incapacity or due to intoxication. * * * Williamson, however, is not contending that she was insane at the time of the contract, but rather is contending that she had a mental incapacity, which coupled with inadequacy of consideration requires the setting aside of the transaction.

Our rule in such a case is that a party cannot avoid, free from fraud or undue influence, a contract on the ground of mental incapacity, unless it be shown that the incapacity was of such a character that, at the time of execution, the person had no reasonable perception or understanding of the nature and terms of the contract. [Citation.]

Our rule regarding incapacity due to intoxication is much the same. The drunkenness of a party at the time of making a contract may render the contract voidable, but it does not render it void; and to render the contract voidable, it must be made to appear that the party was intoxicated to such a degree that he was, at the time of the contracting, incapable of exercising judgment, understanding the proposed engagement, and of knowing what he was about when he entered into the contract sought to be avoided. [Citation.] Proof merely that the party was drunk on the day the sale was executed does not per se show that he was without contractual capacity; there must be some evidence of a resultant condition indicative of that extreme impairment of the faculties which amounts to contractual incapacity. [Citation.]

The burden was therefore cast on Williamson to show, by clear and convincing evidence, that she was incapable, at the time of execution, of executing the contract for sale and of executing the deed. [Citation.]

We hold that Williamson met this burden.

* * *

Indulging the usual presumption due the trial court, we nevertheless hold that, under the facts of this case, it appears to us that Williamson was not, at the time of execution, capable of fully and completely understanding the nature and terms of the contract and of the deed. [Citation.] Williamson's contention that she was intoxicated supports this holding. Testimony was admitted from various witnesses to the effect that Williamson had a history of drinking, that she still had the problem at the time she executed the contract, and that she had in fact taken a couple of drinks before leaving for the meeting in attorney Arthur Cook's office. We do not hold that Williamson was so intoxicated as to render her incapable of contracting. However, numerous factors combine to warrant the conclusion that she was operating under diminished capacity. Testimony showed that Williamson's capacity to transact business was impaired, that she had a history of drinking, that she had been drinking the day she conducted negotiations, and that she had an apparent weakened will because she was pressured by the possibility of an impending foreclosure. Moreover, Williamson made complaint to an attorney only hours after the transaction. These factors are combined with a gross inadequacy of consideration. [The property was appraised twice, once at $16,500 and once at $19,500.]

Reversed and remanded.

PROBLEMS

1. M, a minor, operates a one-man automobile repair shop. A, having heard of M's good work on other cars, takes her car to M's shop for a thorough engine overhaul. M, while overhauling A's engine, carelessly fits an unsuitable piston ring on one of the pistons, with the result that A's engine is seriously damaged. M offers to return the sum which A paid him for his work, but refuses to make good the damage. A sues M in tort for the damage to her engine. Decision?

2. (a) On March 20, Andy Small became seventeen years old, but he appeared to be at least twenty-one. On April 1, he moved into a rooming house in Chicago where he orally agreed to pay the landlady $300 a month for room and board, payable at the end of each month for services and room during that month.

(b) On April 4, he went to Honest Hal's Carfeteria and signed a contract to buy a used car on time with a small down payment. He made no representation as to his age, but Honest Hal represented the car to be in A-1 condition, which it subsequently turned out not to be.

(c) On April 7, Andy sold and conveyed to Adam Smith a parcel of real estate which he owned.

On April 30, he refused to pay his landlady for his room and board for the month of April; he returned the car to Honest Hal and demanded a refund of his down payment; and he demanded that Adam Smith reconvey the land although the purchase price, which Andy received in cash, had been spent in riotous living. Decisions as to each claim?

3. Jones, a minor, owned a 1982 automobile. She traded it to Stone for a 1983 car. Jones went on a three-week trip and found that the 1983 car was not as good as the 1982 car. She asked Stone to return the 1982 car but was told that it had been sold to Tate. Jones thereupon sued Tate for the return of the 1982 car. Decision?

4. On May 7, Roy, a minor, a resident of Smithton, purchased an automobile from Royal Motors, Inc., for $12,750 in cash. On the same day he bought a motor scooter from Marks, also a minor, for $750 and paid him in full. On June 5, two days before attaining his majority, Roy disaffirmed the contracts and offered to return the car and the motor scooter to the respective sellers. Royal Motors, Inc., and Marks each refused the offers. On June 16, Roy brought separate appropriate actions against Royal Motors, Inc., and Marks to recover the purchase price of the car and the motor scooter. By agreement on July 30, Royal Motors, Inc., accepted the automobile. Royal filed a counterclaim against Roy for the reasonable rental value of the car between June 5 and July 30. The car was not damaged during this period. Royal knew that Roy lived twenty-five miles from his place of employment in Smithton and that he would probably drive the car, as he did, to provide himself transportation. Decision as to (a) Roy's action against Royal Motors, Inc., and its counterclaim against Roy; (b) Roy's action against Marks?

5. George Jones on October 1, being then a minor, entered into a contract with Johnson Motor Company, a dealer in automobiles, to buy a car for $10,850. He paid $1,100 down and, under the agreement, was to make monthly payments thereafter of $325 each. After making the first payment on November 1, he failed to make any more payments. Jones was seventeen years old at the time he made the contract. He represented to the company that he was twenty-one years old, and the reason he made the representation was because he was afraid that if the company knew his real age, it would not sell the car to him. His appearance was that of a man of twenty-one years of age. On December 15, the company repossessed the car under the terms provided in the contract. At that time, the car had been damaged and was in need of repairs. On December 20, George Jones became of age and at once disaffirmed the contract and demanded the return of the $1,425 paid on the contract. On refusal of the company to do so, George Jones brought an action to recover the $1,425, and

the company set up a counterclaim for $1,500 for expenses to which it was put in repairing the car. Decision?

6. A entered into a written contract to sell certain real estate to M, a minor, for $80,000, payable $4,000 upon the execution of the contract and $400 on the first day of each month thereafter until paid. M paid the $4,000 down payment and eight monthly installments before attaining her majority. Thereafter, M made two additional monthly payments and caused the contract to be recorded in the county in which the real estate was located. M was then advised by her attorney that her contract was voidable. Immediately upon being so advised, M tendered the contract to A, together with a deed reconveying all of M's interest in the property to A. Also, M demanded that A return to her the money which she had paid under the contract. A refused the tender and declined to repay any portion of the money paid to her by M. M then brought an action to cancel the contract and recover the amount paid to A. Decision?

7. A sold and delivered an automobile to B, a minor. B, during his minority, returned the automobile to A, saying that he disaffirmed the sale. A accepted the automobile and said she would return the purchase price to B the next day. Later in the day, without A's having paid B, he (B) changed his mind, took the automobile without A's knowledge, and sold it to C. Upon what theory, if any, can A recover from B?

8. N, who in 1982 had been found innocent of a criminal offense based upon his insanity, had been released from the hospital for the criminally insane during the summer of 1983 and has since that time been a reputable and well-respected citizen and businessman. On February 1, 1985, N and S enter into a contract in which N would sell his farm to S for $100,000. N seeks to void the contract. S insists that N is fully competent and has no right to avoid the contract. Who will prevail? Why?

9. I, while under the influence of alcohol, agreed to sell to B his 1980 automobile for $8,000. The next morning when B went to I's house with the $8,000 in cash, I stated that he did not remember the transaction but "a deal is a deal." One week after completing the sale I decides that he wishes to avoid the contract. What result?

Chapter 13

CONTRACTS IN WRITING

AN **oral** contract, that is, one not evidenced by any writing, is in every way as enforceable as a written contract unless otherwise provided by statute. Although most contracts are not required by statute to be in writing to be enforceable, it is highly desirable that significant contracts be written. Written contracts avoid the numerous problems inevitably involved in proving the terms of oral contracts. The process of setting down the contractual terms in a written document also tends to clarify the terms and bring to light a number of problems the parties might not otherwise foresee. Moreover, the terms of a written contract do not change over time, while the parties' recollections of the terms might.

When the parties do reduce their agreement to a complete and final written expression, the law (the parol evidence rule) honors this document by not allowing the parties to introduce any evidence in a lawsuit that would alter, modify, or vary the terms of the written contract. Nevertheless, the parties may differ as to the proper or intended meaning of language contained in the written agreement where such language is ambiguous or susceptible to different interpretations. To ascertain the proper meaning requires a construction of the contract. The rules of interpretation or construction permit the introduction of evidence in order to resolve ambiguity and to show the meaning of the language employed and the sense in which both parties used it.

This chapter will examine (1) the types of contracts which must be in writing to be enforceable, (2) the parol evidence rule, and (3) the rules of contractual interpretation.

STATUTE OF FRAUDS

The Statute of Frauds requires that certain designated types of contracts be evidenced in a particular manner in order to be enforceable. The original statute became law in 1677 when the English Parliament adopted "An Act for Prevention of Frauds and Perjuries," commonly referred to as the Statute of Frauds. From the early days of American history practically every State has and continues to have a Statute of Frauds patterned upon the original English statute.

The reason for enactment of the original Statute of Frauds three centuries ago has long ceased to exist. At that time the law of England did not permit a person to testify as a witness in a lawsuit in which he had an interest in its outcome. The law regarded both the plaintiff and the defendant as incompetent to testify.

In *Azevedo v. Minister*, 86 Nev. 576, 471 P.2d 661 (1970), the Court comments on the rationale and development of the statute as follows:

The development of the action of *assumpsit* [breach of contract] in the fourteenth century gave rise to the enforceability of the oral promise. Although parties to an action could not be witnesses, the alleged promise could be enforced on the strength of oral testimony of others not concerned with the litigation. Because of this practice, a party could readily suborn perjured testimony, resulting in marked injustice to innocent parties who were held legally obligated to promises they had never made. The statute of frauds was enacted to preclude the practice. The passage of the statute did not eliminate the problem, but rather, has precipitated a controversy as to the relative merits of the statute. Those favoring the statute of frauds insist that it prevents fraud by prohibiting the introduction of perjured testimony. They also suggest that it deters hasty action, in that the formality of a writing will prevent a person from obligating himself without a full appreciation of the nature of his acts. Moreover, it is said, since business customs almost entirely conform to the mandates of the statute, an abolition of the statute would seriously disrupt such affairs.

On the other hand, in England the statute of frauds has been repealed. The English base their position upon the reasoning that the assertion of the technical defense of the statute aids a person

in breaking a contract and effects immeasurable harm upon those who have meritorious claims.

It is further maintained by the advocates of the English position that the rationale for the necessity of the statute has been vitiated because parties engaged in litigation today may testify as witnesses and readily defend against perjured testimony.

The Statute of Frauds has no relation whatever to any kind of fraud practiced in the making of contracts. The rules relating to such fraud are rules of common law and are discussed in Chapter 9. For example, A claims that B fraudulently misrepresented a material fact and thereby induced A to make a certain contract. A cannot rely upon the Statute of Frauds in support of his claim. It has been frequently stated that the word "frauds" in the title of this statute is misleading. The purpose of the statute is to prevent fraud in the proof of certain oral contracts by perjured testimony in court. This purpose is accomplished by the requirement that certain contracts be proved by a signed writing. On the other hand, the statute does not prevent the performance of oral contracts if the parties are willing to perform. In brief, the statute relates only to the proof or evidence of a contract. It has nothing to do with the circumstances surrounding the making of a contract or with the validity of a contract.

CONTRACTS WITHIN THE STATUTE OF FRAUDS

There are many more types of contracts that are not subject to the Statute of Frauds than those that are subject to it. Most oral contracts, as previously indicated, are as enforceable and valid as a written contract. However, if a given contract is subject to the Statute of Frauds, the contract is said to be **"within"** the statute, and it must, therefore, comply with the requirements of the statute in order to be enforceable. All other types of contracts are said to be "not within" or "outside" the statute and need not comply with its requirements to be enforceable.

The following five types of contracts are within the original English statute and remain within most State statutes. Restatement, Section 110. Compliance requires a writing signed by the party to be charged.

1. Promises to answer for the duty of another;

2. Promises of an executor or administrator to answer personally for a duty of the decedent whose funds he is administering;

3. Agreements upon consideration of marriage;

4. Agreements for the sale of an interest in land; and

5. Agreements not to be performed within one year.

A sixth type of contract within the statute applied to contracts for the sale of goods. The enforceability of contracts of this type is now governed by Section 2-201 of the U.C.C.

In addition to those contracts specified in the original statute, some modern statutes require that others be written; for example, a contract to make a will, to authorize an agent to sell real estate, or to pay a commission to a real estate broker. Moreover, the U.C.C. requires that a contract for the sale of securities and contracts creating certain types of security interests be in writing.

Suretyship Provision

This provision applies to a contractual promise by a *promisor* (called a **surety**) to a **creditor** *(promisee)* to perform the duties or obligations of a third person (**principal debtor**). Thus, if a mother tells a merchant to extend $1,000 worth of credit to her son and says, "If he doesn't pay, I will," the promise must be in writing to be enforceable. The factual situation can be reduced to the simple "If X doesn't pay, I will." The promise is said to be **collateral,** in that the promisor is not the one who is primarily liable. She does not promise to pay in any event; her promise is to pay only upon the default of the one primarily obligated.

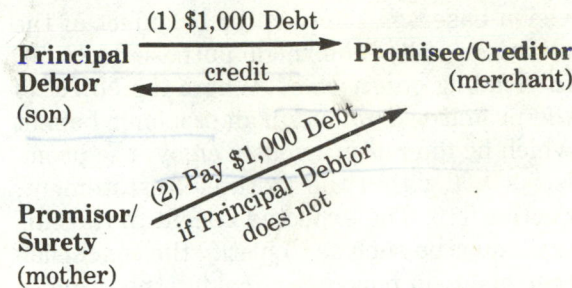

The rule applies only to cases where three parties and two contracts are involved. The primary contract is between the principal debtor and the creditor and creates the indebtedness. The collateral contract is made by the third person (surety) directly with the creditor, whereby she promises to pay the debt to the creditor in case the principal debtor (son) fails to do so. For a complete discussion of suretyship see Chapter 38.

Promise Must Be Collateral It is sometimes difficult to ascertain whether a promise is "collateral" ("I'll pay if X doesn't") or whether the promisor undertakes to become primarily liable, or, as the courts say, makes an **"original"** promise ("I'll pay"). For example, a father tells a merchant to deliver certain items to his daughter and says, "I will pay $400 for them." The Statute of Frauds does not apply, and the promise may be oral. Here, the father is not promising to answer for the debt of another, but rather he is making the debt his own. It is to the father, and to the father alone, that the merchant extends credit and may look for payment.

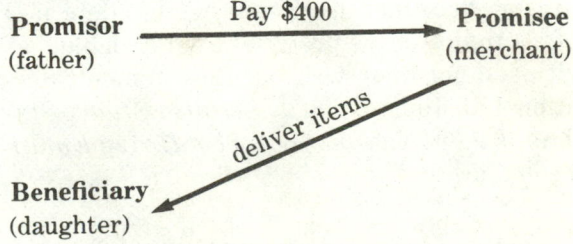

See Shane Quadri v. Goodyear Service Stores.

Main Purpose Doctrine The courts have developed an exception to the suretyship provision based on the purpose or object of the promisor, called the "main purpose doctrine" or "leading object rule." Where the object of the promisor is to obtain an economic benefit which he did not previously enjoy, the promise is *not* within the statute. Restatement, Section 116. The expected benefit to the surety "must be such as to justify the conclusion that his main purpose in making the promise is to advance his own interest." Restatement, Section 116, Comment b. The fact that the surety received consideration for his promise or that he might receive a slight and indirect advantage is insufficient to bring the promise within the main purpose doctrine.

Suppose that a supply company has refused to furnish materials upon the credit of a building contractor. Faced with a possible slow down in construction of his building, the owner of the land promises the supplier that if he will extend credit to the contractor, the owner will pay if the contractor does not. Here, the purpose of the promisor was to serve an economic interest of his own, even though the performance of the promise would discharge the duty of another. The intent to benefit the contractor was at most incidental, and courts will uphold oral promises of this type. Another application of the rule is shown as follows: "D owes C $1,000. C is about to levy an attachment [take possession by court order] on D's factory. S, who is also a creditor of D, fearing that the attachment will ruin D's business and thereby destroy his own chance of collecting his claim, orally promises C that if C will forbear to take legal proceedings against D for three months, S will pay D's debt if D fails to do so. S's promise is enforceable," as it need not be in writing. Restatement, Section 116, Illustration 2. *See also Stuart Studio, Inc. v. National School of Heavy Equipment, Inc.*

Promise Made to Debtor Courts do not regard promises made to a *debtor* as being within the statute. For example, D owes a debt to C. S promises D to pay her debt. Since the promise of S was made to the debtor, not the creditor, the promise may be oral.

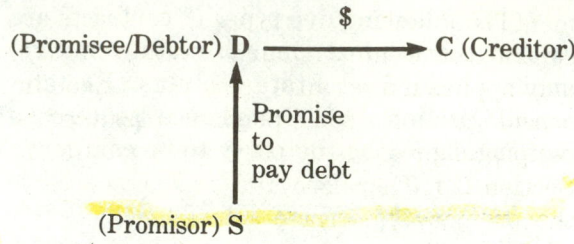

For this reason contracts of "indemnity," as where S says to D, "Buy goods from C and I will insure you against loss," are also not required to be in writing.

Executor-Administrator Provision

This provision applies to promises of an executor of a decedent's will, or the administrator of his estate if he dies without a will, to answer personally for a duty of the decedent. An executor or administrator is a person appointed by a court to carry on, subject to order of court, the administration of the estate of a deceased person. If the will of a decedent nominates a certain person as executor, the court customarily appoints such person. If an executor or administrator agrees to pay a debt of his decedent or, as the English statute puts it, "answer damages" out of his own estate, the promise must be in writing, signed by him or his agent, in order to be binding. For example, B, who is A's son and executor of A's will, recognizes that A's estate will not have sufficient funds to pay all of the decedent's debts and orally promises C, one of A's creditors, that he (B) will personally pay all of his father's creditors in full. B's oral promise is not enforceable. The statute does not, however, apply to an original undertaking by the executor or administrator and, accordingly, a promise by an executor to pay an heir-at-law money if he will refrain from contesting the will does not fall within the statute.

Marriage Provision

The notable feature of this section is that it does not apply to mutual promises to marry. If, for example, A and B each orally promise and agree to marry each other, the agreement is *not* within the statute and is a binding contract between the parties. The provision only applies if a promise to marry is made in consideration for some promise other than a reciprocal promise to marry. Restatement, Section 124. Therefore, this provision covers the ordinary "marriage settlement," as for example, where a man orally promises a woman to convey title to a certain farm to her if she accepts his proposal of marriage.

The following are additional examples of the promises which are within this section of the Statute of Frauds: "In consideration of a woman's promise to marry him, a man promises to make a settlement of money or other property in trust for her. In consideration of Mary's promising to marry or actually marrying John, John promises to pay her an allowance or to execute a will leaving Mary some or all of John's property at death. In consideration of Mary's marrying John, Peter [Mary's father] promises to convey property or to pay her an annuity. John and Mary mutually agree that their marriage shall not affect the existing property rights of each. Mary marries John in return for John's promise to give Sarah [Mary's daughter] a share in his estate, or to adopt and care for Sarah. Mary promises to release a money judgment against John in consideration of his marrying her." Corbin on Contracts, Section 462.

Land Contract Provision

This provision covers promises to transfer "any interest in land," which includes any right, privilege, power, or immunity in real property. Restatement, Section 125. Thus, all promises to transfer, buy, or pay for an interest in land, including ownership interests, leases, mortgages, options, and easements, are within the provision.

The land contract provision does not include contracts to transfer an interest in personal property. It also does not cover short-term leases which by statute in most States are those for one year or less.

Moreover, an oral contract for the transfer of an interest in land may be enforced if the party seeking enforcement has so changed his position in reasonable reliance upon the contract, that injustice can only be prevented by enforcing the contract. Restatement, Section 129. For example, A orally agrees to sell land to B for $30,000. With A's consent, B takes possession of the land, pays A $10,000, builds a house on the land, and occupies it. Several years later A repudiates the contract. The courts will enforce the contract against A.

One Year Provision

The statute requires all contracts that cannot be fully performed within one year of the making of the contract to be in writing. Restatement, Section 130.

The Possibility Test The test here is not whether the agreement is one which is likely to be performed within one year from the date of the making of the contract or whether the parties contemplate that performance will be within the year, but whether it is *possible* for the contract to be performed within a year. The enforceability of the contract does not depend upon probabilities or on the actuality of subsequent events. For example, an oral contract between A and B for A to build a bridge, which should reasonably take three years, is enforceable if it is possible, although extremely unlikely and difficult, for A to perform the contract in one year. Similarly, if A agrees to employ B for life, the contract is not within the Statute of Frauds. It is possible that B may die within the year, in which case the contract would be completely performed. The contract is therefore one which is *fully performable* within a year. However, an oral contract to employ another person for thirteen months is not possible of performance within a year and is unenforceable.

Computation of Time The year runs from the time the *agreement is made*, not from the time when the performance is to begin. For example, on January 1, 1984, A hires B to work for eleven months starting on April 1, 1984 under the terms of an oral contract. That contract will be fully performed on March 31, 1985 which is more than one year after January 1, 1984, the date the contract was made. Consequently, it is *within* the Statute of Frauds and unenforceable since it is oral.

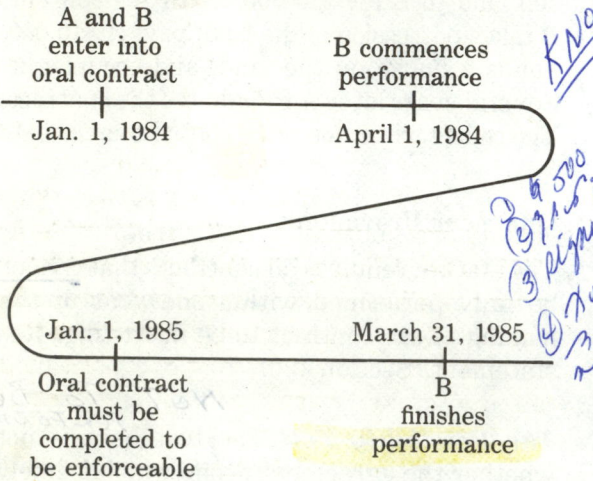

A and B enter into oral contract	B commences performance
Jan. 1, 1984	April 1, 1984

Jan. 1, 1985	March 31, 1985
Oral contract must be completed to be enforceable	B finishes performance

Similarly, a contract for a year's performance which is to begin three days from the date of the making of the contract is within the statute and if oral, is unenforceable. If, however, the performance is to begin the following day or under the terms of the agreement could have begun the following day, it is not within the statute and need not be in writing, as the one year's performance would be completed on the anniversary date of the making of the contract.

See *Co-op Dairy, Inc. v. Dean.*

Full Performance by One Party Where a contract has been fully performed on one side, most courts hold that the promise of the other party is enforceable even though by its terms its performance was not possible within the period of a year. The Restatement, Section 130, provides the following: "When one party to a contract has completed his performance, the one-year provision of the statute does not prevent enforcement of the promises of other parties." For example, A borrows $4,800 from B. A orally promises C to pay B $4,800 in three annual installments of $1,600. A's promise is enforceable, notwithstanding the one-

year provision, because B has fully performed by making the loan.

Sales of Goods

The original Statute of Frauds applied to contracts for the sale of goods and has been used as a prototype for the U.C.C. Article 2 Statute of Frauds provision. Section 2-201 of the U.C.C. provides that a contract for the sale of goods for the price of $500 or more is not enforceable unless there is some writing sufficient to indicate that a contract for sale has been made between the parties. "*Goods,*" as previously indicated, are defined as tangible personal property. Section 2-105(1). The definition expressly includes growing crops and unborn animals.

Other U.C.C. Statute of Frauds Provisions

The U.C.C. also contains Statute of Frauds provisions for sale of securities, security interests in personal property, and a catchall provision for all other kinds of personal property.

Sale of Securities The Code, in Section 8–319, contains a separate Statute of Frauds applicable to contracts for the sale of securities (stocks and bonds). Every contract for the sale of securities is within the statute, as no minimum amount in terms of price is excluded, and therefore must be in writing to be enforceable.

Security Interest in Personal Property Section 9-203 of the U.C.C., as discussed in Chapter 37, requires that agreements which create or provide a non-possessory security interest in personal property be contained in a signed writing to be effective.

Sale of Other Kinds of Personal Property The U.C.C. also contains a catchall Statute of Frauds provision applicable to contracts for the sale of personal property, other than goods, securities, or security agreements, in amount or value beyond $5,000. This section makes such contracts unenforceable unless there is some writing which indicates that a contract for sale has been made between the parties. This provision of the Code covers contractual rights, royalty rights, patent rights, and "general intangibles."

Figure 13-1 illustrates contracts that are within the Statute of Frauds.

Modification or Rescission of Contracts Within the Statute of Frauds

Oral contracts modifying previously existing contracts are unenforceable if the resulting contract is within the Statute of Frauds. The reverse is also true: an oral modification of a prior contract is enforceable if the new contract is not within the Statute of Frauds.

Thus, an oral promise to guarantee additional duties of another and an oral agreement to substitute different land for that described in the original contract are both examples of unenforceable oral contracts. On the other hand, an oral agreement to modify an employee's contract from two years to six months at a higher salary is not within the Statute of Frauds and is enforceable.

By extension, an oral rescission is effective and discharges all unperformed duties under the original contract. For example, A and B enter into a written contract of employment for a two-year term. Later they orally agree to rescind the contract. The oral agreement is effective and the written contract is rescinded. However, where land has been transferred, an agreement to rescind the transaction is a contract to retransfer the land and is within the Statute of Frauds.

Under the U.C.C., if the parties enter into an oral contract to sell a motorcycle for $450 to be delivered to the buyer and later, prior to delivery, orally agree that the seller shall paint the motorcycle and install new tires and the buyer pay a price of $550, the modified contract is unenforceable. Conversely, if the parties have a written contract for the sale of 200 bushels of wheat at a price of $4.00 per bushel and later, upon oral agreement, decrease the quantity to 100 bushels at the same price per bushel, the agreement, as modified, is enforceable. Section 2-209(3).

METHODS OF COMPLIANCE

The most common way to satisfy the Statute of Frauds is for the parties to enter into a

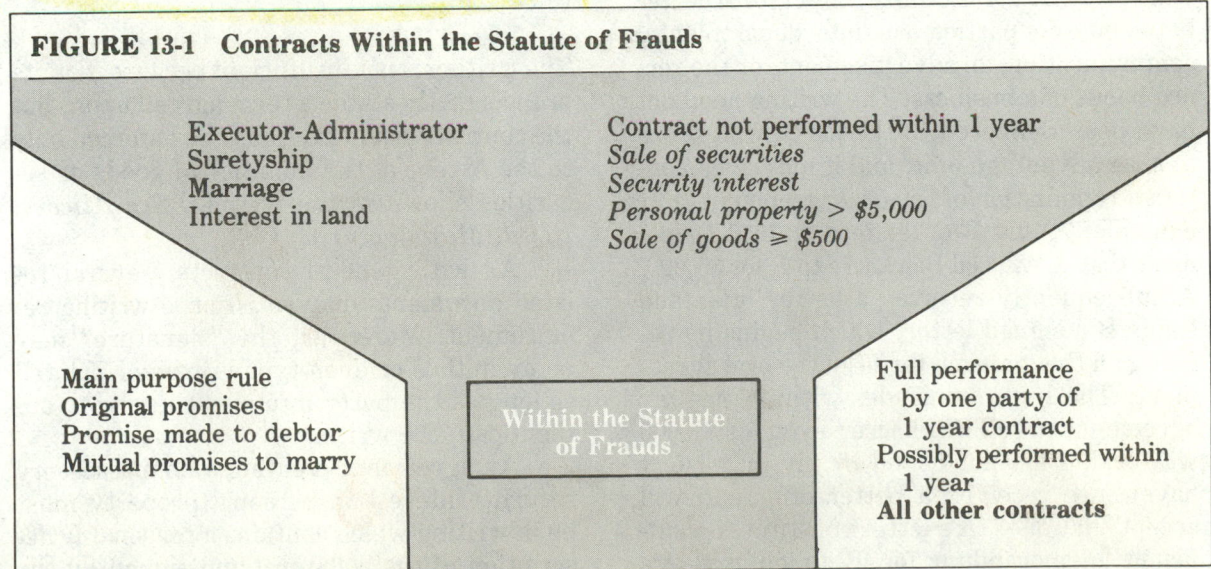

FIGURE 13-1   Contracts Within the Statute of Frauds

Executor-Administrator
Suretyship
Marriage
Interest in land

Contract not performed within 1 year
Sale of securities
Security interest
Personal property > $5,000
Sale of goods ≥ $500

Main purpose rule
Original promises
Promise made to debtor
Mutual promises to marry

Within the Statute of Frauds

Full performance
by one party of
1 year contract
Possibly performed within
1 year
All other contracts

written agreement; nevertheless there are several other methods by which the parties may comply with the statutory mandates.

Writing or Memorandum

General Contract Provisions The original Statute of Frauds and most modern Statutes of Frauds require that the agreement be in writing to be enforceable. Such writing or memorandum must:

1. be signed by the party to be charged or by his agent;
2. specify the parties to the contract; and
3. specify with reasonable certainty the subject matter and the essential terms of the unperformed promises.

The note or memorandum may be formal or informal; all that is necessary is that it contain the required information and be signed by the party to be charged. The "signature" may be by initials or even typewritten or printed so long as the party intended it to authenticate the writing. Furthermore, the "signature" need not be at the bottom of the page or at the customary place for a signature.

The memorandum may be such that the parties view it as having no legal significance whatever, as for example, a personal letter between the parties, an interdepartmental communication, an advertisement, or the record books of a business. The writing need not have been delivered to the party who seeks to take advantage of it, and it may even contain a repudiation of the oral agreement. For example, A and B enter into an oral agreement that A will sell Blackacre to B for $5,000. A subsequently receives a better offer and sends B a signed letter, which begins by reciting all the material terms of the oral agreement. The letter concludes with: "Since my agreement to sell Blackacre to you for $5,000 was oral, I am not bound by my promise. I have since received a better offer and will accept that one." A's letter constitutes a sufficient memorandum for B to enforce A's

promise to sell Blackacre. It should be recognized that since B did not sign the memorandum, the writing does not bind B. Thus, a contract may be enforceable against only one of the parties.

The memorandum may consist of *several* papers or documents, none of which would be sufficient by itself. The several memoranda, however, must together satisfy all of the requirements of a writing to comply with the Statute of Frauds and must clearly indicate that they relate to the same transaction. Restatement, Section 132. The latter requirement can be satisfied if (1) the writings are physically attached, (2) the writings refer to each other, or (3) an examination of the writings shows them to be in reference to each other.

U.C.C. Provisions The Statute of Frauds provisions under the U.C.C. are more liberal. Section 2-201. For a sale of goods or securities the Code requires merely some writing:

1. sufficient to indicate that a contract has been made between the parties;
2. signed by the party against whom enforcement is sought or by her authorized agent or broker; and
3. specify the **quantity** of goods or securities to be sold.

The writing is not insufficient because it omits or incorrectly states a term agreed upon, but the contract can in such case be enforced only to the extent of the quantity of goods or securities shown in the writing. *See Alice v. Robett Manufacturing Co.*

As with general contracts, several related documents may satisfy the writing requirement. Moreover, the "signature" may be by initials or even typewritten or printed so long as the party intended thereby to authenticate the writing.

An agreement creating a nonpossessory security interest in personal property must be in writing which contains a reasonable description of the collateral and signed by the debtor. A contract for the sale of personal property other than goods, securities or security agreements requires some writing which contains (1) that a contract for sale has been entered into between the parties, (2) at a defined or stated price, (3) reasonably identifies the subject matter, and (4) is signed by the party against whom enforcement is sought or by his authorized agent. Section 8-319(a).

Other Methods of Compliance Under the U.C.C.

Forget this

An oral contract for the *sale of goods* is enforceable in the following instances: (1) where written confirmation of a contract between merchants is sent and no objection is made within ten days; (2) where the party defending against the contract admits it by pleading, testimony, or otherwise in court; (3) under certain circumstances where the goods are to be specially manufactured; and (4) where there has been payment or delivery and acceptance. Similar alternative methods of compliance applies to sales of securities but *not* to security agreements in personal property or sales of other kinds of personal property.

Written Confirmation The Code provides relief to a merchant who has confirmed an oral agreement for the sale of goods by letter or signed writing to the other party if he too is a merchant. As between merchants, the written confirmation, if sufficient against the sender, is also sufficient against the recipient of the confirmation unless the recipient gives written notice of his objection within ten days after receiving the confirmation. Section 2-201(2).

Admission The Code permits an oral contract for the sale of goods to be enforced against a party who in his pleading, testimony, or otherwise in court admits that a contract was made, but limits enforcement to the quantity of goods so admitted. Section 2-201(3)(b). The language "otherwise in court" may include pretrial deposition of the defendant.

Specially Manufactured Goods The Code permits enforcement of an oral contract for goods specially manufactured for the buyer but only if there is evidence indicating that the goods were made for the buyer and the seller can show that he has made a *substantial beginning* of their manufacture prior to receipt of any notice of repudiation. Section 2-201(3)(a). If the goods, although manufactured on special order, are readily marketable in the ordinary course of the seller's business, this exception does not apply.

If B brings an action against A alleging that pursuant to a contract A ordered from B three million balloons with A's trademark imprinted on them at a price of $30,000, the action is not subject to the defense of the statute, unless A can show (1) that the balloons are suitable for sale to other buyers, which is highly improbable in view of the trademark, or (2) that notice of repudiation was received by B before he had made a substantial start on the production of the balloons or had otherwise substantially committed himself for their procurement. *See Impossible Electronic Techniques, Inc. v. Wackenhut Protective Systems, Inc.*

Delivery or Payment and Acceptance Prior to the Code, delivery and acceptance of part of the goods or payment of part of the price made enforceable the entire oral contract against the buyer who had received part delivery or against the seller who had received part payment. Under the Code, such "partial performance," as a substitute for the required memorandum, validates the contract only for the goods which have been accepted or for which payment has been accepted. Section 2-201(3)(c). To illustrate, A orally agrees to buy 1,000 watches from B for $15,000. B delivers 300 watches to A, who receives and accepts the watches. The oral contract is enforceable to the extent of 300 watches ($4,500)—those received and accepted; but is unenforceable to the extent of 700 watches ($10,500).

But what if the contract is indivisible, such as one for the sale of an automobile, so that if part payment is made there is only a choice between not enforcing the contract or enforcing the contract as a whole? Presently, there is a division of authority on this issue although the better rule appears to be that such part payment and acceptance makes the entire contract enforceable.

Figure 13-2 summarizes the methods of compliance with the Statute of Frauds.

EFFECT OF NONCOMPLIANCE

The original statute provided that "no action shall be brought" upon a contract to which the Statute of Frauds applied *and* which did not comply with its requirements. The Code states that the contract "is not enforceable by way of action or defense." Despite the difference in language the basic legal effect is the same: a contracting party has a defense to an action by the other for enforcement of an oral contract which is within the statute and does not comply with its requirements. In short, the oral contract is **unenforceable**.

If A, a painter, and B, a home owner, make an oral contract under which B is to give A a certain tract of land in return for the painting of B's house, the contract is unenforceable under the Statute of Frauds. It is a contract for the sale of an interest in land. Either party can repudiate and has a defense to an action by the other to enforce the contract.

However, after *all* the promises of an oral contract have been *performed* by all the parties, the Statute of Frauds no longer applies. In any such case, neither party can have the contract set aside on the ground that it should have been in writing. The purpose of the statute is simply to exclude parol evidence of contracts within its provisions, and not to prohibit the performance of oral contracts. Courts, in other words, will not "unscramble" a fully performed contract merely because it was not in writing as required by the statute. In short, the statute applies to executory contracts only.

If the painter has already performed a *part* of the work is she completely without a

Type of Contract	Written memos	Full Performance by both parties	Written Confirmation	Admission	Specially Manufactured	Delivery or payment and acceptance
General Contracts Executor—Administrator	•	•				
Suretyship	•	•				
Marriage	•	•				
Interest in Land	•	•				
One-year	•	•				
UCC Sale of Goods ≥ $500	•	•	•	•	•	•
Sale of Securities	•		•	•	•	•
Security Interest	•					
Personal Property > $5,000	•					

FIGURE 13-2 Methods of Compliance

remedy? Clearly, she cannot enforce the contract, but courts may still permit a recovery in quasi contract to prevent an unjust enrichment. The remedy of restitution allows the painter to recover damages equal to the amount of the benefit that she has conferred upon the home owner. Thus, all may not be lost to a party unable to enforce an oral contract. However, this possibility should prompt a contracting party to use the utmost caution to assure compliance with the statute. Only by complying with the Statute of Frauds can one be reasonably certain of obtaining the benefit of the bargain that has been made.

Figure 13-3 summarizes the operation of the Statute of Frauds.

PAROL EVIDENCE RULE

The execution of a written contract may be, and often is, preceded by preliminary negotiations between the parties. Letters and memoranda are written and exchanged; personal conferences are held; proposals and counter proposals are made; tentative or definite agreements are entered into. In time, the parties may come to a final and definite agreement, reduce the agreement to writing, and sign it. Thereupon, and whether the contract is required by law to be in writing or not, the writing is now the sole evidence of the contract. It may be that some definite agreement concerning the subject matter of the written contract was made by the parties during their negotiations, which was not included in the written contract. Notwithstanding that such was the case, the agreement so made is no part of the written contract. In the event of a law suit on the contract, no evidence of such agreement would be admitted by the court. The evidence would be excluded by the parol or oral evidence rule. This rule presumes that the parties included in the

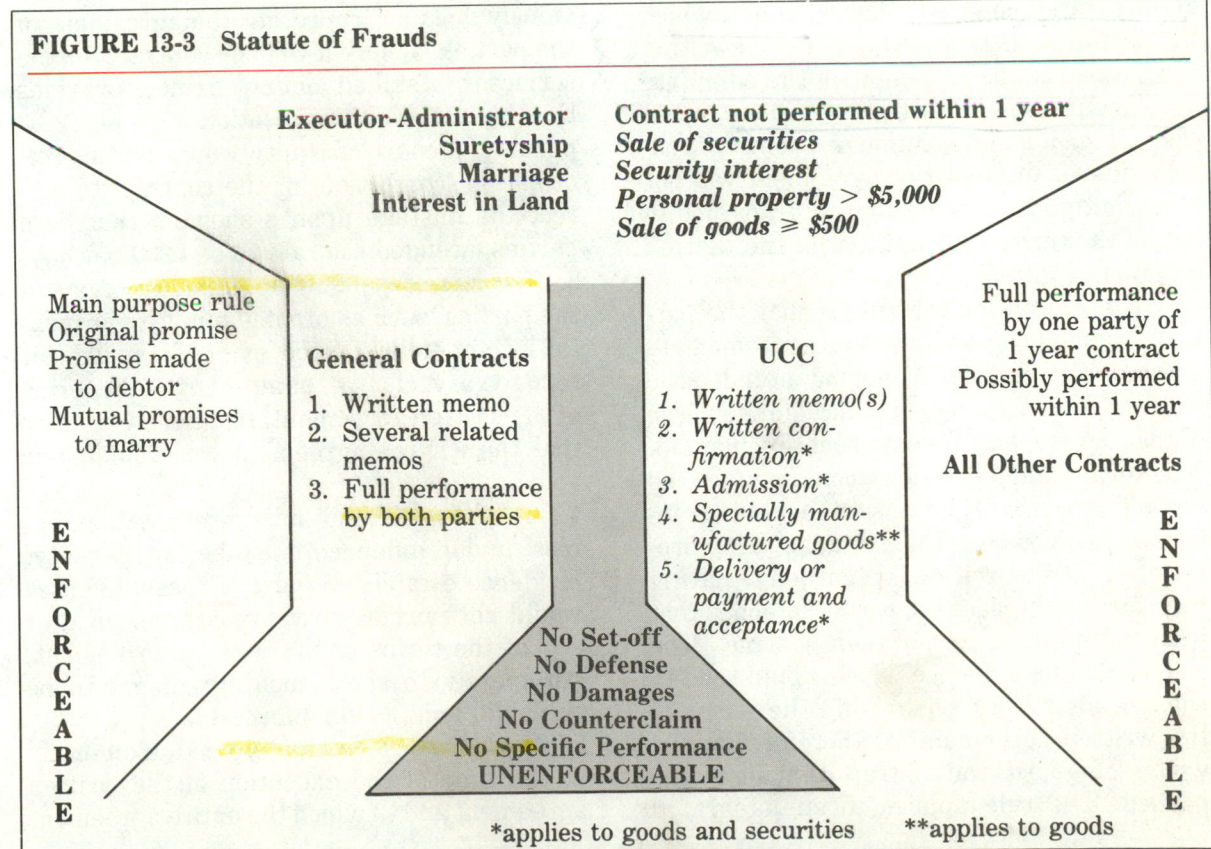

FIGURE 13-3   Statute of Frauds

Executor-Administrator
Suretyship
Marriage
Interest in Land

Contract not performed within 1 year
Sale of securities
Security interest
Personal property > $5,000
Sale of goods ≥ $500

Main purpose rule
Original promise
Promise made
to debtor
Mutual promises
to marry

General Contracts

1. Written memo
2. Several related memos
3. Full performance by both parties

UCC

1. *Written memo(s)*
2. *Written confirmation**
3. *Admission**
4. *Specially manufactured goods***
5. *Delivery or payment and acceptance**

Full performance
by one party of
1 year contract
Possibly performed
within 1 year

All Other Contracts

No Set-off
No Defense
No Damages
No Counterclaim
No Specific Performance
UNENFORCEABLE

E N F O R C E A B L E

E N F O R C E A B L E

*applies to goods and securities   **applies to goods written contract *everything* they intended to include, and omitted everything not intended to be part of their contract. The result is, as it is sometimes put, that the writing is the sole repository of the contract.

THE RULE

When a contract is expressed in a writing which is intended to be the complete and final expression of the rights and duties of the parties, parol evidence of (1) **prior** oral or written negotiations or agreements of the parties or (2) their **contemporaneous** oral agreements which **vary** or **change** the written contract are not admissible. The word "parol" means literally "speech" or "words." The term "parol evidence" refers to any evidence, whether oral or in writing, which is extrinsic to the written contract and not incorporated into the contract either directly or by reference.

The parol evidence rule applies only to an integrated contract, that is, one in which the parties have assented to a certain writing or writings as the statement of the **complete** agreement or contract between them. When there is such an integration of a contract, parol evidence of any prior agreement will not be permitted to vary, change, alter, or modify any of the terms or provisions of the written contract.

The reason for the rule is that the parties, by reducing their entire agreement to writing, are regarded as having intended the writing which they signed to include the whole of their agreement. Restatement, Section 213. The terms and provisions contained in the writing are there because the parties intended them to be in their contract. Any provision not in the writing is regarded as having been omitted because the parties intended that it should not be a part of their contract. The rule excluding evidence which would tend to change, alter, vary, or modify the terms of the written agreement is, therefore, a rule which safeguards the contract as made by the parties. The rule applies to all integrated

written contracts and deals with what terms are part of the contract. The rule differs from the Statute of Frauds which governs what contracts must be in writing to be enforceable.

See Mitchill v. Lath.

SITUATIONS TO WHICH THE RULE DOES NOT APPLY

The parol evidence rule, in spite of its name, is not an exclusionary rule of evidence, nor is it a rule of construction or interpretation. It is a rule of substantive law which defines the limits of a contract. Bearing this in mind, as well as the reason underlying the rule, it will be readily understood that the rule does **not** apply to any of the following:

1. A contract which is *partly written* and partly oral, that is, the parties do not intend the writing to be their entire agreement.

2. A clerical or *typographical error* which obviously does not represent the agreement of the parties. Where a written contract for the services of a skilled mining engineer provides that his rate of compensation is to be $2.00 per day, a court of equity would permit reformation (correction) of the contract to correct the mistake upon a showing that both parties intended the rate to be $200 per day.

3. The lack of *contractual capacity* of one of the parties, such as proof of minority or mental incompetency. Such evidence would not tend to vary, change, or alter any of the terms of the written agreement, but merely to show that the written agreement was voidable or void.

4. A *defense* of fraud, misrepresentation, duress, undue influence, mistake, or illegality. Evidence establishing any of these defenses would not purport to vary, change, or alter any of the terms of the written agreement, but merely to show such agreement to be voidable, void, or unenforceable.

5. A *condition precedent* agreed upon orally at the time of the execution of the written agreement and to which the entire agreement

was made subject. For example, if A signs a subscription agreement to buy stock in a corporation to be formed and delivers it to B with the mutual understanding that the agreement is not to be operative unless the other financially responsible persons shall each agree to buy at least an equivalent amount of such stock, A is permitted to show by parol evidence this condition. Such evidence does not tend to vary, alter, or change any of the terms of the stock subscription, but merely to show that the entire written agreement, unchanged and unaltered, never became effective.

6. A *subsequent mutual rescission* or *modification* of the written contract. Parol evidence of a later agreement does not tend to show that the integrated writing did not represent the contract between the parties at the time it was made. Parties to an existing contract, whether written or oral, may agree to change the terms of their contract as they see fit, or to cancel it completely, if they so desire.

7. Parol evidence of *usage* and *custom* which is not inconsistent with the terms of the written agreement is admissible to define the meaning of the language in the agreement where both parties knew or should have known of the existence of the usage or custom in the particular trade or locality. Such evidence does not alter, change, or vary any of the terms or language of the written contract, but simply shows the meaning which the parties attached to the particular language.

8. Parol evidence is admissible to explain *ambiguous* terms in the contract. To enforce a contract, it is necessary to understand its intended meaning. Such interpretation is not to alter, change, or vary the terms of the contract.

SUPPLEMENTAL EVIDENCE

Under the Restatement, Section 216, and the Code, Section 2-202, although a written agreement may not be contradicted by evidence of a prior agreement or of a contemporaneous oral agreement, a written contract may be explained or supplemented by (1) course of dealing between the parties, (2) usage of trade, (3) course of performance, or (4) evidence of consistent additional terms unless the writing was intended by the parties as a complete and exclusive statement of their agreement.

A **course of dealing** is a sequence of previous conduct between the parties to an agreement which may fairly be regarded as establishing a common basis of understanding for interpreting their expressions and other conduct.

A **usage of trade** is a practice or method of dealing regularly observed and followed in a place, vocation, or trade.

Course of performance refers to the manner and extent to which the respective parties to a contract have accepted successive tenders of performance by the other party without objection.

The Restatement and the Code permit *supplemental consistent evidence* to be introduced into a court proceeding. Such evidence is only admissible if it does not contradict a term or terms of the original agreement and would probably not have been included in the original contract.

Figure 13-4 illustrates the parol evidence rule.

INTERPRETATION OF CONTRACTS

While the written words or language in which the parties embodied their agreement or contract may not be changed by parol evidence, the ascertainment of the meaning to be given to the written language is outside the scope of the parol evidence rule. The written words embody the terms of the contract. However, words are but symbols. If their meaning is not clear, it may be made clear by the application of rules of interpretation or construction and by the use of extrinsic evidence for this purpose where necessary.

FIGURE 13-4   Parol Evidence Rule

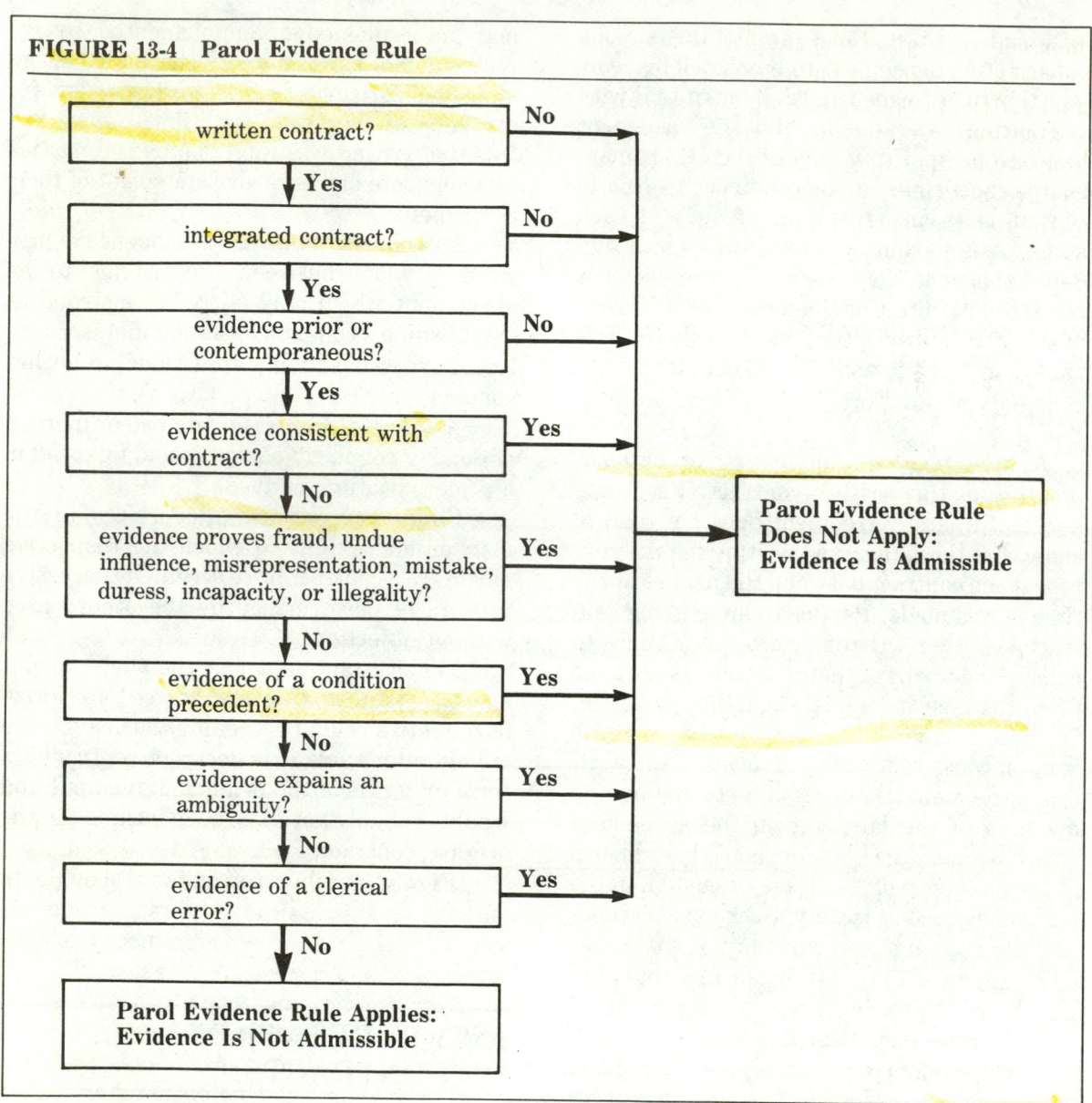

The Restatement, Section 200, defines interpretation as the ascertainment of the meaning of a promise or agreement or a term of the promise or agreement. In most cases involving the necessity of construction, the disputed language is usually, though not necessarily, in writing. Among writings, in addition to contracts, which sometimes require construction by the courts, are wills, deeds, corporate charters, statutes, and constitutions. With regard only to contracts, where the language of the contract is clear and unequivocal, which is usually the case, there is of course no necessity for construction by the court. In such case, the court will simply enforce the contract according to its plain terms. Where the language of the contract is ambiguous, that is, susceptible of different meanings, it becomes necessary for the court to resort to construction of the disputed language in order to ascertain and give effect to the intentions of the parties as expressed in their contract. It is not the function of the court, in such case, to make or remake a contract for the parties. Its function, instead, is to ascertain the intention of the parties, not from what they now claim to be their respective intentions, but from the language used by them in the contract now before the court. As stated in one case:

> The great object of construction is to collect from the terms or language of the instrument, the manner and extent to which the parties intended to be bound. To facilitate this, the law has devised certain rules, which are not merely conventional, but are the canons by which all writings are to be construed, and the meaning and intention of men to be ascertained. These rules are to be applied with consistency and uniformity. They constitute a part of the common law, and the application of them, in the interpretation and construction of dispositive writings, is not discretionary with courts of justice, but an imperative duty. *Johnson County v. Wood*, 84 Mo. 489 (1884)

As indicated in the above passage, a number of rules of construction of contracts have been developed by the courts in many cases over a long period of time. It is these rules to which a court has recourse when the language of the contract before it is ambiguous and contradictory. There is a large number of these rules, but not all of them can be stated or considered here. Those given below, however, are the more important and basic rules.

1. The primary purpose of the construction of contracts by courts is to ascertain the intention of the parties from the language used by them in their agreement.
2. Words and other conduct are interpreted in the light of all the circumstances, and if the principal purpose of the parties is ascertainable, it is given great weight.
3. A writing is interpreted as a whole, and all writings that are part of the same transaction are interpreted together.
4. Unless a different intention is manifested, where language has a generally prevailing meaning, it is interpreted in accordance with that meaning. In a note due one

year after date, the word "year" obviously means a calendar year. On the other hand, where an instructor is employed by a university to teach for a year at a stipulated salary, the word "year" means an academic or school year of approximately nine months.
5. Unless a different intention is manifested, technical terms and words of art are given their technical meaning. Certain technical words are commonly used in building construction contracts, for example. However, if such words are used by persons who are ignorant of their technical meaning, and it appears that the parties intended another meaning, they will be construed to mean what the parties intended.
6. Wherever reasonable, the manifestations of intention of the parties to a promise or agreement are interpreted as consistent with each other and with any relevant course of performance, course of dealing, or usage of trade.
7. An interpretation which gives a reasonable, lawful, and effective meaning to all the terms is preferred to an interpretation which leaves a part unreasonable, unlawful, or of no effect. The reason for this rule lies in the presumption that persons who go through the formality of making a contract intend their contract to be valid or lawful rather than invalid or illegal and reasonable in its meaning rather than unreasonable or absurd.
8. Specific terms and exact terms are given greater weight than general language.
9. Separately negotiated or added terms are given greater weight than standardized terms or other terms not separately negotiated.
10. Express terms, course of performance, course of dealing, and usage of trade are weighted in that order.
11. Where a term or promise is susceptible of multiple meanings it will be interpreted against the party who supplied the contract or the term. One reason for this rule, in any such case, is that the party who prepares the contract will tend to use language most favorable to himself. Another reason is that the party who undertakes to draft the contract should do so in clear and unambiguous lan-

guage. If he fails to do so, he is held responsible for the ambiguities of his own expressions.

Restatement, Sections 201, 202, and 203.

Through the application of the parol evidence rule, where it is properly applicable, and the above rules of interpretation and construction, it may be observed that the law not only enforces a contract but in doing so exercises great care that the contract being enforced is the one which the parties made, and that the sense and meaning of the manifested intentions of the parties is carefully ascertained and given effect. *See Phelps Dodge Corp. v. Brown.*

CASES

Suretyship Provision

SHANE QUADRI v. GOODYEAR SERVICE STORES

Court of Appeals of Indiana, Third District, 1980. 412 N.E.2d 315.

HOFFMAN, J.

[The defendant, Shane Quadri, contacted Don Hoffman, employee of defendant Al J. Hoffman & Co., to procure car insurance. Later, Quadri's car was stolen on October 25 or 26, 1977. Quadri contacted Hoffman who arranged with Budget Rent-a-Car, a plaintiff in this case, for a rental car for Quadri until his car was recovered. Hoffman authorized Budget Rent-a-Car to bill the Hoffman Agency. Later, when the stolen car was recovered, Hoffman telephoned plaintiff, Goodyear, and arranged to have four new tires put on Quadri's car to replace those damaged during the theft. The plaintiff's (Budget and Goodyear) sued the defendants (Quadri and Hoffman) for payment for the car rental and tires, respectively.]

* * *

The Hoffman Agency's liability must be based on Don Hoffman's oral promises. The Hoffman Agency asserts that these promises are promises to pay the debts of Shane Quadri and are therefore made unenforceable by the Statute of Frauds [Citation.]

The Hoffman Agency is correct in the theoretical statement of the law but errs in its application in this case. Although the statute makes unenforceable contracts to pay the debts of a third person, it does not affect the enforceability of oral contracts between two parties for the benefit of a third party. [Citation.] The statute therefore does not apply to original promises to pay for services rendered to a third person. [Citation.] The evidence in the present case is clear that Don Hoffman made original promises to both Budget and Goodyear that the Hoffman Agency would pay for goods and services rendered to Quadri.

* * *

The evidence discloses that Don Hoffman initiated the transactions with both Goodyear and Budget through a telephone call. Hoffman indicated that Quadri was insured and authorized the billing of the Hoffman Agency. Hoffman also gave both Goodyear and Budget a claim number to use in their records. Quadri merely went to Goodyear and Budget to obtain the benefits as negotiated by Hoffman. Although Quadri's signature appears on the Budget rental agreement and the Goodyear invoice, both documents indicate that Don Hoffman authorized the transaction. Based on this evidence it cannot be said that the trial court erred in determing that credit was extended solely to the Hoffman Agency. Don Hoffman's oral promises are not within the Statute of Frauds.

* * *

[Judgment of the trial court in favor of Budget and Goodyear against Hoffman and in favor of Quadri affirmed.]

Main Purpose Doctrine

STUART STUDIO, INC. v. NATIONAL SCHOOL OF HEAVY EQUIPMENT, INC.

Court of Appeals of North Carolina, 1975.
25 N.C.App. 544, 214 S.E.2d 192.

CLARK, J.

In this action plaintiff seeks to recover from the defendant, National School of Heavy Equipment, Inc., (hereafter School), and the individual defendants the sum of $18,010.02 under a contract whereby it produced catalogues for use by the School in promoting its services. The School has been adjudged a bankrupt corporation, and plaintiff has obtained a judgment against the School in the sum claimed, plus interest. By amended complaint plaintiff seeks to recover from individual defendant, Gilbert S. Shaw, the sum of $17,828.02 for purchasing and supervising the printing of the catalogues, claiming that Shaw promised, when the contract was made on 6 March 1972, to stand behind or guarantee payment.

It was stipulated that all work pursuant to the contract was completed and catalogues delivered to and accepted by the School on 7 July 1972.

It appeared from the evidence that Gilbert S. Shaw was Chairman of the Board of Directors of the School and drew a salary of $2,000 per month. He held 100% of the voting stock and 49% of the Class B stock of the School; he employed various members of his family in the operation of the School, including his son, Donald T. Shaw, as President.

Plaintiff is an art studio. Its president, Keith Stuart, had a conversation with Gilbert Shaw and Donald Shaw in August 1971, about the preparation of a new catalogue for the School, and in September 1971, all agreed that plaintiff was to produce the camera-ready art for the catalogue. Plaintiff completed this work and the School accepted the format. There was a discussion between Stuart and the Shaws about the printing. Plaintiff does not do printing but in some cases purchased the printing

for its clients. In a meeting on 6 March 1972, when the camera-ready art work was virtually finished, Gilbert Shaw requested Stuart to purchase and supervise the printing of 25,000 catalogues. They discussed payment of printing costs, and Gilbert Shaw told Stuart that payment would be made within ten days after billing and that if the *National School could not pay the full total that he would stand good for the entire bill.*

Plaintiff then contracted in its name for the printing. The School made an advance payment of $2,000 to plaintiff on 23 March 1972. Plaintiff delivered the catalogues to the School on 7 July 1972 with its invoice. To requests for payment thereafter, Donald T. Shaw, Gilbert S. Shaw being overseas, replied that the School did not have the money but expected to get it.

At the completion of plaintiff's evidence, the individual defendants moved for directed verdicts, and from judgment granting the motions, the plaintiff appeals. It appears from the amended complaint, filed after entry of judgment, that plaintiff has elected to proceed only against the individual defendant, Gilbert S. Shaw.

* * *

The North Carolina Statute of Frauds, a substantial prototype of the historic English statute [citation] contains the provision that "no action shall be brought * * * upon a special promise to answer the debt * * * of another person, unless the agreement upon which such action shall be brought, or some memorandum or note thereof, shall be in writing, and signed by the party charged therewith or some other person thereunto by him lawfully authorized." [Citations.]

The promise of Gilbert S. Shaw to stand good for the debt of National School of Heavy Equipment, Inc., to be incurred for the printing of catalogues was not in writing and was within the Statute of Frauds unless plaintiff has offered evidence to invoke the application of the "main purpose rule," which is a well-known exception to the rule requiring that such promises be evidenced by a written memorandum.

The "main purpose rule" is * * * as follows:

* * * [W]henever the main purpose and object of the promisor is not to answer for another, but to subserve some pecuniary or business purpose of his own, involving either a benefit to himself, or damage to the other contracting party, his promise is not within the statute, although it may be in form a promise to pay the debt of another, and although the performance of it may incidentally have the effect of extinguishing that liability.

* * *

Shaw's personal and pecuniary interest in the transaction was evident; he was the founder of the School, owned 100% of the Class A voting stock and 49% of the Class B stock, was Chairman of the Board of Directors, and as an officer drew a monthly salary of $2,000. At this time, 6 March 1972, it is reasonable to assume that the School was facing financial difficulty; Shaw personally advanced $12,000 to the School during this period of financial distress. The School went into receivership in December 1972, and bankruptcy in March 1973. Apparently, Shaw sought, in a final effort to avoid the School's financial ruin, to attract new students through an advertising campaign, which included the production and circulation of new catalogues.

Burlington Industries v. Foil [Citation] a 1974 decision, culminates a line of cases which have developed the "main purpose rule" and prescribed its limitations. The *Foil* case holds that the benefit accruing to a party merely by virtue of his position as a stockholder, officer, or director is not alone such personal, immediate, and pecuniary benefit as to invoke the main purpose rule, and that Foil's evidence failed to establish the required *direct interest* on the part of Foil.

In *Foil*, the court cited with approval the cases of *May v. Haynes*, [Citation] and *Warren v. White*, [Citation]. In *Warren v. White*, defendant promisor was the principal investor and owned most of the capital stock, and during a period of financial difficulty advanced in excess of $23,000 to the corporation. In *May v. Haynes*, the defendant and his wife owned the entire capital stock of the corporation, and he was its president, managing officer, and controlling stockholder. In both of these cases it was held that the evidence was sufficient to invoke the main purpose rule and in doing so it is obvious that the significant, if not controlling, factor was the extent of the promisor's control over the corporation.

In this case the evidence offered by the plaintiff tends to show that Gilbert S. Shaw had a personal and direct interest in the School; and the evidence is clearly sufficient to raise an issue for jury determination. We find that the trial court improvidently granted defendant's motion for directed verdict and the judgment is modified and the cause remanded for trial on the issue of the liability of Gilbert S. Shaw on the printing contract of 6 March 1972.

Modified and Remanded.

One Year Provision

CO-OP DAIRY, INC. v. DEAN
Supreme Court of Arizona, 1968.
102 Ariz. 573, 435 P.2d 470.

McFARLAND, J.

Plaintiff-appellee Charles W. Dean, hereinafter referred to as Dean, sued defendant-appellant Co-Op Dairy, Inc., hereinafter referred to as Dairy, for damages for breach of an oral contract to employ Dean and to reimburse him for his moving expenses from Ardmore, Oklahoma, to Phoenix, Arizona. From a judgment on a jury verdict in Superior Court, Dairy has appealed.

The facts, stated most favorably to Dean, are as follows:

On February 12, 1962, Dairy's general manager, Gerald J. Patsey, hired Dean as sales manager at a guaranteed salary of $1,000 per month. The employment period was to be "for a minimum period of one year," and the agreement provided for the payment of Dean's moving expenses. The day after Dean was hired, he signed a one-year lease on a Phoenix apartment. He then went to Oklahoma, picked up his family, arranged to have household goods moved to Phoenix, and, on February 26, 1962, he "reported for active work." After he had worked a few days, all the delivery and supervisory personnel of Dairy resigned, and refused to return to work unless and until Patsey and Dean were fired. In order to avoid a massive loss of customers from lack of service, and a large loss of milk from spoilage, Dairy capitulated to the drivers' demands and fired the two men. For the approximately nine days that he worked, Dean was paid $1,000 "for the period ending March 8, 1962." He sued for his salary for the year, less what he was paid, and less what he earned in another job after being fired, plus his moving expenses. It was conceded that what work Dean did for Dairy was eminently satisfactory.

The jury, in addition to bringing in a general verdict for $6,000.38 for wages and $776.53 for moving expense, answered two special interrogatories by finding that there was an agreement between the parties to hire Dean for one year, and that Dairy agreed to pay Dean's moving expenses. The evidence was ample to justify the verdict and special findings.

Dairy contends that a contract of employment to start in the future, and to continue for one year, is within the Statute of Frauds, and that therefore this action cannot be maintained. As a general rule of law this is true. [Arizona statute] provides that no action shall be brought upon any oral agreement "which is not to be performed within one year from the making thereof." [Citations.]

Dean contends that a contract for one year's employment, to commence the day following the making of the contract, is not within the Statute of Frauds, [Citation.] We agree. So does Dairy in its brief. The difficulty in the instant case is that the facts are not entirely clear, and the special interrogatories submitted to the jury contained no requirement that they find when the employment contract was to begin. We know that the contract was made, orally, between Patsey and Dean on February 12, 1962. We know that the contract was to guarantee Dean $1,000 per month, and that it was to run for one year. But, nowhere in the record is there a scintilla of evidence from which one can determine when the contract was to start. It is undisputed that Dean reported for work February 26th, after having gone back to Oklahoma to get his family and to arrange for the transportation of his household goods. On cross-examination, Dean was asked whether there was any specific time that he was to start working, and he answered that there was not. However, he was also asked: "When you left * * * Mr. Patsey on February 12th it was understood that you would not start work until you had moved your family out from Ardmore, Oklahoma?" and the answer was "That is correct, sir."

We need not take this statement literally. That could mean that he did not *have* to come to work until he had moved his family. It could mean that he would not come to work until he had *arranged* to move his family. However, it does not show they agreed he *could not* commence work until he had returned to Oklahoma and personally made all the arrangements. It did not mean that he could not call his wife that night, tell her to arrange for shipping the furniture and to take a plane or bus to Phoenix, so that he could start work the next day.

The conversations between Dean and Patsey, leading up to the contract of hiring, show that Dean was somewhat timid about nailing down the term of the contract. Patsey testified that Dean inquired about a contract, and Patsey told him:

"Any man that comes in on a job like this has always got a year to prove himself. I pointed out that I had no contract with Co-op Dairy. I said that I have never been too much for contracts."

* * * Clearly, Dean's leasing of an apartment is no proof that the contract had begun to operate. At the same time, Dean's failure to report to work until February 26 does not prove that he could not have reported for work on February 13th.

* * * One principle that generally has been upheld is that the words "not to be performed within one year" mean "*impossible to be performed within one year.*"

"In its actual application, however, the courts have been perhaps even less friendly to this provision than to the other provisions of the statute. * * * In general, the cases indicate that there must not be the *slightest possibility* that it can be fully performed within one year. It makes no difference how long the agreed performance may be delayed or over how long a period it may in fact be continued. It makes no difference how long the parties expect performance to take, or how reasonable and accurate those expectations are, if the agreed performance can *possibly* be completed within one year." [Citation.]

* * *

We are inclined to agree with the court in *Farmer v. Arabian American Oil Company*, [Citation] in which it said that the Statute of Frauds, applied to an employment contract, "is an anachronism in modern life and we are not disposed to expand its destructive force." We therefore hold that there was nothing to prevent Dean from turning over the moving details to his wife and going to work the next day. Had he done so, the Statute of Frauds would not be applicable. Though he did not do so, the mere fact that he could have done so takes the contract out of the Statute of Frauds.

Judgment affirmed.

A Writing or Memorandum

ALICE v. ROBETT MANUFACTURING CO.

United States District Court, District of Georgia, 1970.
328 F.Supp. 1377

SMITH, C. J.

* * *

Plaintiff alleges that in response to an invitation to bid from the General Services Administration, he solicited an offer from the defendant to manufacture certain clothing, which plaintiff intended to supply to the Government. It is undisputed that on April 29, 1969, the defendant offered to produce 3,500 shirts at $4.00 each, and 3,500 pairs of pants at $3.00 each for the plaintiff. Plaintiff asserts that he accepted the offer and informed the defendant that its price quotation would be the basis for his bid to GSA.

On or about May 8, 1969, defendant having received the same invitation to bid as had plaintiff, the defendant submitted its own bid to GSA, offering to produce 3,500 "uniforms" at $7.78 each. On June 10, 1969, the defendant was awarded the contract for the production of this clothing. Eleven months later plaintiff filed this action. The thrust of Count I is that having entered a binding sub-contract with plaintiff for the production of this clothing for the Government, the defendant breached that contract by bidding directly with GSA for the same job.

* * *

The thrust of defendant's motion as to Count I of the complaint is that since plaintiff never accepted the defendant's offer, there was never any contract between them.

Apparently, the defendant contends that its offer was in writing. But plaintiff argues, and defendant's letter * * * shows that on the same day the letter was written the parties had a telephone conversation concerning the defendant's production of clothing for the plaintiff. It is the plaintiff's contention, supported by his affidavit, that during that conversation the defendant made an oral offer which was immediately accepted in the same fashion. Under such a theory, the defendant's letter would serve as a memorandum of the telephonic agreement. In order to recover on this theory, that memorandum would have to satisfy the statute of frauds, since the alleged transaction involved a sale of goods for more than $500.

Under Georgia law prior to the adoption of the Uniform Commercial Code, a writing was not sufficient to comply with the requirements of the statute of frauds unless it contained *all* the terms of the agreement. [Citations.] It is clear, however, that Ga. Code [U.C.C., Section] 2–201 (1962) changes that rule of law. First, the Legislature repealed the old statute of frauds relating to the sale of goods * * * in adopting the Uniform Commercial Code. [Citation.] Secondly, according to the Official [U.C.C.] Comments:

The changed phraseology of this section is intended to make it clear that:

1. The required writing need not contain all the material terms of the contract and such material terms as are stated need not be precisely stated. All that is required is that the writing afford a basis for believing that the offered oral evidence rests on a real transaction. It may be written in lead pencil on a scratch pad. It need not indicate which party is the buyer and which the seller. The only term which must appear is the quantity term which need not be accurately stated but recovery is limited to the amount stated. The price, time, and place of payment or delivery, the general quality of the goods, or any particular warranties may all be omitted.

* * *

Only three definite and invariable requirements as to the memorandum are made by this subsection. First, it must evidence a contract for the sale of goods; second, it must be "signed," a word which includes any authentication which identifies the party to be charged; and third, it must specify a quantity. U.C.C. § 2–201, Comment 1.

The courts of other states have given effect to the changes which this Comment states were intended. [Citation.] (§ 2–201(1) doesn't require a writing which embodies all the essential terms of the contract); [citations] (the memorandum need contain only the three elements specified in the Comment.)

But it does not appear that the letter upon which the plaintiff must rely is a sufficient memorandum to satisfy even the minimal requirements of * * * § 2–201. The letter states:

Confirming our telephone conversation, we are pleased to offer the 3,500 shirts at $4.00 each and

the trousers at $3.00 each with delivery approximately ninety days after receipt of order. We will try to cut this to sixty days if at all possible.

This, of course, is quoted f. o. b. Atlanta and the order will not be subject to cancellation, domestic pack only.

Thanking you for the opportunity to offer these garments, we are

Very truly yours,

ROBETT MANUFACTURING CO., INC.

Although it is not signed, the defendant admits its authenticity. Nevertheless, it does not evidence a contract for the sale of goods, but very clearly is only an offer.

* * *

Accordingly, the defendant's motion for summary judgment must be, and hereby is, granted.

It is so ordered.

Specially Manufactured Goods

IMPOSSIBLE ELECTRONIC TECHNIQUES, INC. v. WACKENHUT PROTECTIVE SYSTEMS, INC.

United States Court of Appeals, Fifth Circuit, 1982.
669 F.2d 1026.

ANDERSON, C. J.

In this . . . action, the appellant, Impossible Electronic Techniques, Inc., sued the appellee, Wackenhut Protective Systems, Inc., for breach of an oral contract to buy certain electronic closed-circuit cameras. Wackenhut denied that such a contract had been made and interposed the Statute of Frauds as a defense. The district court granted Wackenhut's motion for summary judgment and dismissed the case. * * *

* * *

Sometime in late 1973, George Wackenhut, chairman of the board and president of the Wackenhut Corporation, the parent company of the appellee, decided that his personal home, known as the "Castle," in Coral Gables, Florida, needed a little extra security. Thereafter, the appellee began looking to purchase a closed-circuit television camera security system, and contacted the six or eight companies in the United States that manufacture such equipment. Two of these companies, one of which was the appellant, were invited in January, 1974, to conduct a demonstration of their equipment at the "Castle." Mr. Wackenhut personally decided that the appellant's camera produced the best picture.

At this point, the appellant's and the appellee's versions of the facts diverge. The appellant contends that after its demonstration the price for its cameras was discussed, Mr. Wackenhut decided to use appellant's cameras, and an oral contract for the sale was made. The appellee, conversely, claims that while Mr. Wackenhut concluded that he wanted the appellant's cameras, no further negotiations were conducted and no agreement was reached.

The parties agree, however, that the appellee stated that it would need a local company to install and to maintain the system. In response, the appellant recommended Jackson & Church Electronics, Inc., a local dealer of the appellant's equipment. Appellee had never heard of Jackson & Church before this time. Although the appellee's brief implies that the appellee next contacted Jackson & Church the record appears to indicate that the appellant first contacted Jackson & Church to inquire whether that company would be willing to handle the installation and maintenance.

The appellant apparently initiated the documentary aspects of the transaction by preparing in late March a shipping instructions form for the first camera and accessories to be sent to Jackson & Church. The president of Jackson & Church next mailed a letter to the appellant explaining how payment for the equipment would be made, thanking the appellant for the referral, and describing the appellee as "yours [i.e., the appellant's] and our [i.e., Jackson & Church's] customer."

Jackson & Church forwarded a purchase order to the appellant listing three cameras, two auto-zoom lenses, one auto-iris, three lens control units, and one rack mount assembly, all totaling $32,119. The appellee sent Jackson & Church a purchase order listing the same items and quantities as in the Jackson & Church purchase order (although for prices totaling $43,420) and assorted additional electronic paraphernalia, amounting to a total price of $47,678. The appellant contends that the price differences between the purchase orders merely represents the additional charges imposed by Jackson & Church for the installation and maintenance services. The appellee claims that Jackson & Church bought the equipment from the appellant at a dealer discount for resale to the appellee at retail prices.

After these documents were issued, the appellant commenced assembling the cameras. Due to some delays in obtaining parts and the special nature of the cameras, the first camera was not completed until early June, 1974, at which time the appellant's president, Jesse Wagner, personally delivered it to the Wackenhut residence. An employee of Jackson & Church installed the camera in the presence of Wagner and representatives of the appellee. George Wackenhut would occasionally visit the installation locations and at one point discussed with Wagner the service life and warranties of the camera. In response to a question, Wagner informed Wackenhut that the picture tube, an essential component of each camera, had an operational life expectancy of about six months and a replacement cost of approximately $5,000. Not surprisingly, George Wackenhut was unhappy upon discovering that the camera system his company had bought for him had a yearly maintenance cost of possibly $30,000, more than half the purchase price of the system. One week later, before the remaining two cameras were shipped, the appellee sent a letter to Jackson & Church cancelling its purchase order. Jackson & Church in response notified the appellant that Jackson & Church was cancelling its purchase order. Appellee thereafter arranged to purchase through Jackson & Church a less expensive camera system manufactured by one of appellant's competitors. Distressed by this turn of events, the appellant filed this suit.

* * *

The major ground for summary judgment advanced by the appellee and the district court is that even if the parties did enter into an oral contract, the Statute of Frauds renders such a contract unenforceable. The Florida Uniform Commercial Code Statute of Frauds provides in relevant part that "a contract for the sale of goods for the price of $500 or more is not enforceable by way of action or defense unless there is some writing sufficient to indicate that a contract for sale has been made between the parties and signed by the party against whom enforcement is sought or by his authorized agent or broker." Section 2–201(1). Such a writing is not required "[i]f the goods are to be specially manufactured for the buyer and are not suitable for sale to others in the ordinary course of the seller's business and the seller, before notice of repudiation is received and under circumstances which reasonably indicate that the goods are for the buyer, has made a substantial beginning of their manufacture or commitments for their procurement.   . . ." Id. 2–201(3)(a). The appellee contends that the undisputed facts show that the alleged contract falls within the general statutory provisions, that no writing exists sufficient to satisfy the statute, and that the goods in question are not "specially manufactured" within the meaning of the statute.

* * *

The Statute of Frauds does not require that *the* contract for the sale of goods be in writing; rather, the statute requires only "*some* writing sufficient to indicate that a contract for sale has been made between the parties." A writing that omits or incorrectly states a term (other than the quantity of the goods to be sold) may nonetheless satisfy the statute. Section 2.2–201(1). An adequate memorandum "may be in almost any possible form."

[Citation.] The Uniform Commercial Code Official Comment No. 1 explains that:

Only three definite and invariable requirements as to the memorandum are made by this subsection. First, it must evidence a contract for the sale of goods; second, it must be 'signed,' a word which includes any authentication which identifies the party to be charged; and third, it must specify a quantity.

Appellant relies upon the Wackenhut purchase order as a sufficient writing to satisfy the statute. Judged by the above standards, the purchase order clearly meets the last two requirements: there is no doubt that it was signed by an authorized employee of the appellee or that it correctly specifies the quantity of goods to be sold. Regarding the first requirement, the purchase order does evidence a contract. The question, however, is a contract between whom—appellant and appellee or appellee and Jackson & Church?

* * *

In the present case, various invoices, Jackson & Church's purchase order, and other documents, viewed in the light of the testimony of the appellant's president, might connect the Wackenhut purchase order to a contract between the appellant and the appellee. This is a question of fact much akin to the issue of whether there was any contract between the appellant and the appellee. The record reveals that there is indeed a genuine issue of fact as to whether the Wackenhut purchase order evidences a contract between the appellant and the appellee. * * * Summary judgment for the defendant based on the Statute of Frauds is therefore inappropriate.

* * *

[T]here is a [another] reason why the appellee could not obtain summary judgment based on the Statute of Frauds. As noted above, the statute does not apply "if the goods are to be specially manufactured for the buyer and are not suitable for sale to others in the ordinary course of the seller's business." In opposing the motion for summary judgment, the appellant argued that the cameras in question are such specially made goods. The district court rejected this argument on the ground that "[s]ince IET's [i.e., appellant's] normal operations consist of designing, manufacturing, and selling low-light level closed-circuit television cameras and related night-viewing devices, it would appear that the cameras, indeed, were *not* specially manufactured within the meaning of the statute" (emphasis in original).

If the district court meant by this assertion that as a factual matter there must be a ready market for these cameras because appellant is regularly in the business of making them (i.e., supplying this market), then the district court's reasoning ignores the substantial possibility that the appellant, as part or all of his business operations, manufactures custom-made cameras suitable for use by and sale to only the immediate buyer. If the district court meant that as a matter of statutory interpretation the cameras were not *specially* manufactured because the appellant as part of his normal business operations *ordinarily* builds custom-made products, then this reasoning ignores the purpose underlying the statutory exception for specially-made goods. The statute exempts contracts involving "specially manufactured" goods from the writing requirement because in these cases the very nature of the goods serves as a reliable indication that a contract was indeed formed. Where the seller has commenced or completed the manufacture of goods that conform to the special needs of a particular buyer, and thereby are not suitable for sale to others, not only is the likelihood of a perjured claim of a contract diminished, but denying enforcement to such a contract would impose substantial hardship on the aggrieved party (i.e., a seller is left with goods that are difficult or impossible to sell to others; a buyer may have difficulty locating an alternative supply of the goods). The unfairness is especially acute where, as in the present case, the seller has incurred substantial, unrecov-

erable expense in reliance on the oral promise of the buyer. The term "specially manufactured," therefore, refers to the nature of the particular goods in question and not to whether the goods were made in an unusual, as opposed to the regular, business operation or manufacturing process of the seller. That the seller may be in the business of manufacturing custom designed and made goods does not necessarily preclude his goods from being deemed "specially manufactured" within the meaning of this exception. The crucial inquiry is whether the manufacturer could sell the goods in the ordinary course of his business to someone other than the original buyer. If with slight alterations the goods could be so sold, then they are not specially manufactured; if, however, essential changes are necessary to render the goods marketable by the seller to others, then the exception does not apply. [Citation.]

Other than testimony that the appellant is in the business of manufacturing and selling cameras of this general kind, the appellee introduced very little evidence to support his contention that these cameras were not "specially manufactured" goods. Appellee argues that the appellant has made little nor no effort to sell the cameras to another buyer. The deposition testimony cited on this point, however, reveals that the appellant could not resell the cameras because they had been specially adapted to adjust automatically to the extreme nighttime darkness at the Wackenhut residence and to the glaring daytime sunlight reflecting off the beach and the sea. Indeed, the deposition testimony of Jesse Wagner contains numerous references to the specialized nature of the cameras themselves, the manufacturing process, and the market for them. The depositions, as well as the briefs submitted on the motion for summary judgment, raise the legal issue of whether the Statute of Frauds exception for specially manufactured goods applies in this case. The appellee has made virtually no attempt to show the absence of a genuine issue of fact with respect to this issue, and thus has failed to carry its initial burden. Moreover, the depositions themselves more than amply raise a genuine question of fact regarding whether the cameras were specially manufactured within the meaning of 2–201(3)(a). On this record, the appellee could not properly obtain summary judgment based on the Statute of Frauds.

Reversed and remanded.

Parol Evidence Rule

MITCHILL v. LATH

New York Court of Appeals, 1928.
247 N.Y. 377, 160 N.E. 646, 68 A.L.R. 239.

ANDREWS, J.

[The plaintiff brought an action seeking to compel specific performance by the defendants of an alleged oral contract to remove an ice house. The trial court entered a decree for the plaintiff. Defendants appeal.]

In the fall of 1923 the Laths owned a farm. This they wished to sell. Across the road, on land belonging to Lieutenant-Governor Lunn, they had an ice house which they might remove. Mrs. Mitchill looked over the land with a view to its purchase. She found the ice house objectionable. Thereupon "the defendants *orally* promised and agreed, for and in consideration of the purchase of their farm by the plaintiff to remove the said ice house in the spring of 1924." Relying upon this promise, she made a written contract to buy the property for $8,400, for cash and a mortgage and containing various provisions usual in such papers. Later receiving a deed, she entered into possession and has spent considerable sums in improving the property for use as a summer residence. The defendants have not fulfilled their promise as to the ice house and do not intend to do so. We are not dealing, however, with their moral delinquencies. The question before us is whether their oral agreement may be enforced in a court of equity.

This requires a discussion of the parol evidence rule—a rule of law which defines the limits of the contract to be construed. * * * It applies, however, to attempts to modify such a contract by parol. It does not affect a parol collateral contract distinct from and independent of the written agreement. It is, at times, troublesome to draw the line. Williston, in his work on Contracts (sec. 637) points out the difficulty. "Two entirely distinct contracts," he says, "each for a separate consideration may be made at the same time and will be distinct legally. Where, however, one agreement is entered into wholly or partly in consideration of the simultaneous agreement to enter into another, the transactions are necessarily bound together. * * * Then if one of the agreements is oral and the other is written, the problem arises whether the bond is sufficiently close to prevent proof of the oral agreement." That is the situation here. It is claimed that the defendants are called upon to do more than is required by their written contract in connection with the sale as to which it deals.

The principle may be clear, but it can be given effect by no mechanical rule. As so often happens, it is a matter of degree, for as Professor Williston also says where a contract contains several promises on each side it is not difficult to put any one of them in the form of a collateral agreement. If this were enough written contracts might always be modified by parol. Not form, but substance is the test.

In applying this test the policy of our courts is to be considered. We have believed that the purpose behind the rule was a wise one not easily to be abandoned. Notwithstanding injustice here and there, on the whole it works for good. Old precedents and principles are not to be lightly cast aside unless it is certain that they are an obstruction under present conditions.

* * *

Under our decisions, before such an oral agreement as the present is received to vary the written contract, at least three conditions must exist: (1) the agreement must in form be a collateral one; (2) it must not contradict express or implied provisions of the written contract; and (3) it must be one that parties would not ordinarily be expected to embody in the writing; or put in another way, an inspection of the written contract, read in the light of surrounding circumstances, must not indicate that the writing appears "to contain the engagement of the parties, and to define the object and measure the extent of such engagement." Or again, it must not be so clearly connected with the principal transaction as to be part and parcel of it.

* * * At least, however, an inspection of this contract shows a full and complete agreement, setting forth in detail the obligations of each party. On reading it one would conclude that the reciprocal obligations of the parties were fully detailed. Nor would his opinion alter if he knew the surrounding circumstances. The presence of the ice house, even the knowledge that Mrs. Mitchill thought it objectionable, would not lead to the belief that a separate agreement existed with regard to it. Were such an agreement made it would seem most natural that the inquirer should find it in the contract. Collateral in form it is found to be, but it is closely related to the subject dealt with in the written agreement—so closely that we hold it may not be proved.

* * *

Judgment reversed.

Interpretation

PHELPS DODGE CORP. v. BROWN

Supreme Court of Arizona, 1975.
112 Ariz. 179, 540 P.2d 651.

STRUCKMEYER, C. J.

This is an appeal from a judgment for the appellee, Louie E. Brown, against the appellant, Phelps Dodge Corporation, for $1,950.00.

The relevant facts reveal that appellant terminated appellee's employment on April 26, 1968. Prior to his termination, appellee had worked for appellant under an oral contract for approximately twenty-three years. In 1967, appellee was suspended from work forty-five days for unauthorized possession of tires belonging to the company, and in 1968, upon discovering that appellee was constructing a trailer on company time and using company property without authorization, appellant fired appellee. Appellee brought suit for damages for wrongful discharge, for a pension, and for benefits under an Unemployment Benefit Plan (hereinafter referred to as the Plan). The only issue remaining for trial was whether or not appellee was entitled to recover under the Plan. The jury found for appellee. Reversed.

* * *

[The Plan provides] in order to be eligible for unemployment benefits, a laid-off employee must: (1) Have completed two or more years of continuous service with the company, and (2) Have been laid off from work because the company had determined that work was not available for him.

* * *

The trial court ruled, in denying appellant's Motion for Directed Verdict, that an ambiguity existed in the Plan as to who was eligible for the benefits since the requirement "Have been laid off from work because the company had determined that work was not available for him" was open to at least two possible interpretations. The trial court noted that the two possible interpretations were (1) that the company had determined it would not hire or continue to employ appellee under any circumstance and, therefore, work was not available for him, individually, and (2) it could be interpreted that the work category was not available for appellee or anyone else in his category. Because of the ambiguity, the trial court construed the contract against the party who chose the wording, in this case appellant.

It then determined that appellee was eligible for the payments since by firing appellee, appellant was saying that there was no work for appellee individually. The only issue thus left for the jury was whether appellant acted arbitrarily, capriciously, and without good faith in denying appellee eligibility to receive benefits under the Plan.

The object of all rules of interpretation is to arrive at the intention of the parties as it is expressed in the contract. [Citation.] There are many rules of interpretation which can be utilized in reaching the intent of the parties. These include giving words their ordinary meaning, giving technical terms their technical meaning, reading the contract as a whole, giving effect to the main purpose of the instrument, and interpreting the contract so as to make it effective and reasonable. [Citation.]

We believe the trial court, in construing the terms most strongly against the party who chose the wording, without first utilizing other rules of construction, acted contrary to standard principles. [Citation.]

Professor Corbin, criticizing the rules of construction used by the trial court, said:

It is frequently said that this rule is to be applied only as a last resort. It should not be applied until other rules of interpretation have been exhausted; nor should it be applied unless there remain two possible and reasonable interpretations. The rule is hardly to be regarded as truly a rule of interpretation; its application does not help to determine the meaning that the two parties gave to the words, or even the meaning that a reasonable person would have given to the language used. 3 Corbin on Contracts § 559 (1960).

From a reading of the entire contract, it becomes obvious that no ambiguity exists. It is clear that the contract was not meant to apply to someone who was dismissed for cause.

The Purpose of the Plan, Article III, specifically states who the Plan covers. This Article reads: "It is the purpose of this Plan to provide unemployment payments for laid-off employees to the extent and in the manner prescribed hereunder."

Article V, Part A, Eligibility for and Payment of Benefits, was quoted by the trial court in its instructions to the jury. Part B of that Article reads:

B. Determination of Eligibility.

When an employee is laid off the Company shall determine whether he is eligible for a Benefit. * * *

From a reading of the Plan as a whole, it is clear that it was to cover employees who were laid-off and not employees who were dismissed for cause.

The words "lay-off" and "discharge" have a normal and understood meaning in both common and industrial usage and the use of one instead of the other is sufficient to escape the charge of ambiguity. [Citation.]

* * *

In support of the finding that appellant had failed to specifically state who was eligible for benefits under the Plan, the trial court also noted that the terms "a quit," "discharge," "lay off," "disciplinary lay-off," and "laid off" were all used in the Plan but that none was defined. By reading the Plan as a whole and noting the context within which each of the terms was used, it becomes obvious that no ambiguity exists merely because the different terms were used but not defined.

The three terms, "a quit," "discharge," and "lay off" were used in defining what is meant by a break in employment. The Plan, in defining "Continuous Service," Article XIII, reads in part: " *   *   * The employment of an Employee shall be deemed to have been broken (a) by a quit, discharge, or failure to return to work upon recall; or (b) except as otherwise provided in this definition, by a lay-off, absence for sickness, or leave of absence of one year or more. *   *   * "

* * *

The term "disciplinary lay-off" is included in the terms that signify why an employee is not actively at work. All the reasons apply to people who are on the payroll of the company and who are expected to return to work. An employee such as appellee, whose employment is terminated for cause, is not one who would still be on the payroll, nor would the company expect him to return to work. The term "disciplinary lay-off" must be understood to mean a situation where a person, while still an employee, is refused work for a temporary period of time because of wrongdoings. It cannot be construed to mean an employee in appellee's position.

The terms "laid-off" and "lay-off" are used in other places in the Plan. The context in which they are used support our construction.

* * *

Since as a matter of law no ambiguity existed and appellee was not entitled to recover under the Plan, it follows that there were no issues left for the jury to decide.

Judgment reversed with directions that judgment be entered for appellant.

PROBLEMS

1. A was the principal shareholder in X Corporation, and, as a result, he received the lion's share of X Corporation's dividends. X Corporation was anxious to close an important deal for iron ore products to use in its business. A written contract was on the desk of Z Corporation for the sale of the iron ore to X Corporation. Z Corporation, however, was cautious about signing the contract, and it was not until A called Z Corporation on the telephone and stated that, if X Corporation did not pay for the ore, he would, that Z Corporation signed the contract. Business reverses struck X Corporation and it failed. Z Corporation sues A. What defense, if any, has A? Decision?

2. Green was the owner of a large department store. On Wednesday, January 26, he talked to Smith and said, "I will hire you to act as sales manager in my store for one year at a salary of $18,000; you are to begin work next Monday." Smith accepted and started work on Monday, January 31. At the end of three months, Smith was discharged by Green. On May 15, Smith brings an action against Green to recover the unpaid portion of the $18,000 salary. Decision?

3. A, while driving, ran into B, injuring B and rendering her unconscious. There was some doubt as to who was at fault. A took B to a hospital, where she remained unconscious for twenty-four hours. On arriving at the hospital, A told the official in charge to treat B for her injuries and stated that he would pay the bill. B was duly treated and cured by the hospital, but A refused to pay the bill. On being sued by the hospital, A pleads the Statute of Frauds as a defense. Decision?

4. Ames, Bell, Cain, and Dole each orally ordered color television sets from Marvel Electronics Company which accepted the orders. Ames's set was to be specially designed and encased in an ebony cabinet. Bell, Cain, and Dole ordered standard sets described as "Alpha Omega Theatre." The price of Ames's set was $1,800 and of the sets ordered by Bell, Cain, and Dole, $700 each. Bell paid the company seventy-five dollars to apply on his purchase; Ames, Cain, and Dole paid nothing. The next day, Marvel sent Ames, Bell, Cain, and Dole written confirmations captioned "Purchase Memorandum," numbered 12345, 12346, 12347, and 12348, respectively, containing the essential terms of the oral agreements. Each memorandum was sent in duplicate with the request that one copy be signed and returned to the company. None of the four purchasers returned a signed copy. Ames promptly sent the company a repudiation of the oral contract, which it received before beginning manufacture of the set for Ames or making commitments to carry out the contract. Cain sent the company a letter reading in part, "Referring to your Contract No. 12347, please be advised I have cancelled this contract. Yours truly, (Signed) Cain." The four television sets were duly tendered by Marvel to Ames, Bell, Cain, and Dole, all of whom refused to accept delivery. Marvel brings four separate actions against Ames, Bell, Cain, and Dole for breach of contract.

Decide each claim.

5. A and B enter into an oral contract by which A promises to sell and B promises to buy Blackacre for $10,000. A repudiates the contract by writing

a letter to B in which she states accurately the terms of the bargain, but adds "our agreement was oral. It, therefore, is not binding upon me, and I shall not carry it out." Thereafter, B sues A for specific performance of the contract. A interposes the defense of the Statute of Frauds, arguing that the contract is within the Statute and, hence, unenforceable. Decision?

6. On March 1, Lucas called Craig on the telephone and offered to pay him $90,000 for a house and lot which Craig owned. Craig accepted the offer immediately on the telephone. Later in the same day, Lucas told Annabelle that if she would marry him, he would convey to her the property then owned by Craig which was the subject of the earlier agreement. On March 2, Lucas called Penelope and offered her $15,000 if she would work for him for the year commencing March 15, and she agreed. Lucas and Annabelle were married on June 25. By this time Craig had refused to convey the house to Lucas. Thereafter, Lucas renounced his promise to convey the property to Annabelle. Penelope, who had been working for Lucas, was discharged without cause on July 5; Annabelle left Lucas and instituted divorce proceedings in July 1984.

What rights, if any, have (a) Lucas against Craig for his failure to convey the property; (b) Annabelle against Lucas for failure to convey the house to her; (c) Penelope against Lucas for discharging her before the end of the agreed term of employment?

7. A orally promises B to sell him five crops of potatoes to be grown on Blackacre, a farm in Minnesota, and B promises to pay a stated price for them on delivery. Is the contract enforceable?

8. A leased an apartment to B for the term May 1, 1982, to April 30, 1983, at $250 a month "payable in advance on the first day of each and every month of said term." At the time the lease was signed, B told A that he received his salary on the 10th of the month, and that he would be unable to pay the rent before that date each month. A replied that would be satisfactory. On June 2, B not having paid the June rent, A sued B for such rent. At the trial, B offered to prove the oral agreement as to the date of payment each month. Decision?

9. A bought a car from the B Used Car Agency under a written contract. She purchased the same in reliance on B's agent's oral representations that the car had never been in a wreck and could be driven at least 2,000 miles without adding oil. Thereafter A discovered that the car had, in fact, been previously wrecked and rebuilt, that it used excessive quantities of oil, and that B's agent was aware of these facts when the car was sold. A brings an action to rescind the contract and recover the purchase price. B objects to the introduction of oral testimony concerning representations of its agent, contending that the written contract alone governed the rights of the parties. Decision on the objection?

10. In a contract drawn up by X Company, it agreed to sell and Y Contracting Company agreed to buy wood shingles at $6.50. After the shingles were delivered and used, X Company billed Y Company at $6.50 per bunch of 900 shingles. Y Company refused to pay because it thought the contract meant $6.50 per thousand shingles. X Company brought action to recover on the basis of $6.50 per bunch. The evidence showed that there was no applicable custom or usage in the trade and that each party held its belief in good faith. Decision?

Chapter 14

RIGHTS OF THIRD PARTIES

PRIOR chapters considered situations in which essentially only two parties were involved. This chapter deals with the rights of third parties, namely, persons who are not parties to the contract but have acquired a right to its performance. These rights arise either by reason of (1) an assignment of the rights of a party to the contract or (2) the express terms of a contract entered into for the benefit of a third person. We shall consider these two situations in that order.

ASSIGNMENT OF RIGHTS AND DELEGATION OF DUTIES

A clear distinction must be made between an **assignment** of rights and a **delegation** of duties. Every contract creates both rights and duties. For instance, A promises to sell to B an automobile for which B promises to pay $10,000 in monthly installments over the next three years. A's right under the contract is to receive payment from B, while A's duty is to deliver the automobile. B's right is to receive the automobile; his duty is to pay for the automobile.

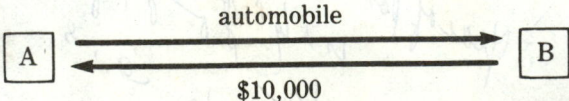

An assignment of rights is the voluntary transfer to a third party of the rights arising from the contract. In the above example, if A were to transfer his right under the contract (the installment payments due from B) to C for $8,500 in cash, this would constitute a valid **assignment of rights.** In this case, A would be the **assignor**, C would be the **assignee**, and B would be the **obligor**.

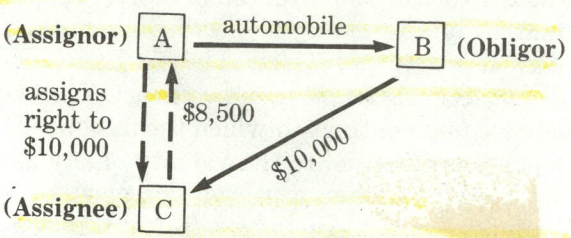

An effective assignment extinguishes the assignor's right to performance by the obligor. After an assignment *only* the assignee has a right to the obligor's performance.

On the other hand, if A agreed with D that D should deliver the automobile to B, this would constitute a **delegation**, not an assignment, **of duties**. In this instance, A would be the **delegator**, D would be the **delegatee**, and B would be the **obligee**.

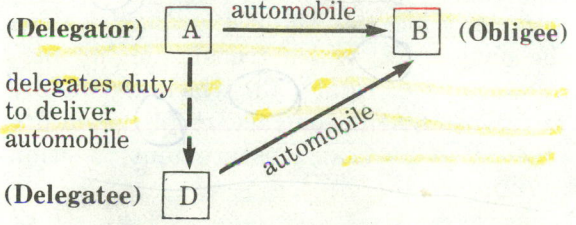

A delegation of duty, however, does *not* extinguish the delegator's obligation to perform, but rather an additional party (the delegatee) is also obligated to perform. A delegation of duties results in **both** the delegator and delegatee being held liable for performance of the contractual duty to the obligee.

ASSIGNMENT OF RIGHTS

At early common law an assignment of a contractual right was wholly ineffective. At that time the law regarded the personal relationship between the parties to the contract as a vital part of the agreement. It could not be changed unilaterally any more than any other term of the contract. As commerce increased,

the need to sell contract rights also increased. In response, courts of equity began to enforce assignments. Relief was allowed in equity so consistently that ultimately courts of law began to enforce assignments, and, as this afforded assignees an adequate remedy, courts of equity no longer were called upon to grant relief for assignments.

Requirements of an Assignment

The Restatement, Section 317(1), defines an assignment of a right as a "manifestation of the assignor's intention to transfer it by virtue of which the assignor's right to performance by the obligor is extinguished in whole or in part and the assignee acquires the right to such performance."

What Amounts to an Assignment No special form or particular words are necessary to create an assignment. Any words which fairly indicate an intention to make the assignee the owner of the right are sufficient, and the assignment, unless otherwise provided by statute, may be oral or written.

Consideration is *not* required for an effective assignment. Consequently, gratuitous assignments are valid and enforceable. However, a gratuitous assignment is revocable by the assignor and is terminated by the assignor's death, incapacity, or subsequent assignment of the right, *unless* an effective delivery of the assignment has been made by the assignor to the assignee. Such delivery can be accomplished by transferring a deed or other document evidencing the right, such as a stock certificate or savings passbook. Delivery may also consist of physically delivering a signed, written assignment of the contract right. A gratuitous assignment is further rendered irrevocable if, prior to the attempted revocation, the donee-assignee has received payment of the claim from the obligor, has obtained a judgment against the obligor, or has obtained a new contract of the obligor. For example, B owes A $50,000. A signs a written statement granting C a gratuitous assignment of his rights from B. A dies prior to delivering to C the signed, written assignment of the contract right. The assignment is terminated and therefore ineffective. On the other hand, had A delivered the signed, written assignment to C before A died, the assignment would have been effective and irrevocable.

Partial Assignments A partial assignment is a transfer of a portion of the contractual rights to one or more assignees. At early common law, partial assignments were not enforceable because it was believed that they could materially increase the burden upon the obligor. For instance, it was argued that the obligor who possessed a valid defense against performance would be compelled to relitigate the issue with each and every assignee. Today, partial assignments are permitted and are enforceable. However, the obligor may require all the parties entitled to the promised performance to litigate the matter in one action. This insures that all parties are present and avoids the undue hardship of multiple suits. For example, B owes A $2,500. A assigns $1,000 to C. If B objects, neither A nor C can maintain an action against B, unless the other is joined in the proceeding against B.

Rights That Are Assignable

As a general rule most contract rights, including rights under an option contract, are assignable. So long as the assignment merely substitutes the assignee for the assignor and does not materially increase the burden or risk upon the obligor, the assignment is effective and valid. *See Munchak Corporation v. Cunningham.*

The most common contractual right which may be assigned is the right to the payment of money, as represented by wages or an account receivable. The right to property other than money, such as goods or lands, is also frequently assignable. In the case of money absolutely owing, such as wages earned but not paid or the purchase price of goods ac-

tually sold and delivered, the right to the payment of such money may be assigned without regard to the employer or debtor. The potential right to money is likewise assignable, such as wages to be earned in the future under an existing employment contract. The existence of a contract to which the assignor is a party is essential to the validity of any assignment. In other words, there must be a contract in existence upon which the assignment can operate. There cannot be an assignment of rights under a contract which is yet to be made. Such a purported assignment "operates only as a promise to assign the right when it arises and as a power to enforce it." Restatement, Section 321.

Rights That Are Not Assignable

In order to protect the obligor, some contract rights are not assignable. These non-assignable contract rights include those (1) which materially increase the risk or burden upon the obligor, (2) which transfer highly personal contract rights, (3) which are validly prohibited by the contract, or (4) which are prohibited by law. Restatement, Section 317(2).

Assignments which Materially Increase the Risk or Burden An assignment is ineffective where performance by the obligor to the asignee would be materially different from performance to the assignor; that is, where the assignment would significantly change the nature or extent of the obligor's duty. Thus, an automobile liability insurance policy issued to A is not assignable by A to B. The risk assumed by the insurance company was liability for A's negligent operation of the automobile. Liability for operation of the same automobile by B would be an entirely different risk and one which the insurance company had not assumed. Similarly, A would not be allowed to assign her contractual right to have B paint her small, two bedroom house to C, the owner of a twenty–five room mansion. Clearly, such an assignment would materially increase B's duty of performance. By comparison, the right to receive monthly payments under a contract may be assigned, for it costs no more to mail the check to the assignee than it does to mail it to the assignor.

Assignments of Personal Rights Where the rights under a contract are of a highly personal nature, they are not assignable. An extreme example of such a contract is an agreement of two persons to marry one another. The prospective groom obviously cannot transfer the prospective bride's promise to marry him to some third party. A more common example of contracts of a personal character is a contract for the personal services of one of the parties. See *Schupack v. McDonald's System, Inc.*

Express Prohibition Against Assignment At common law the courts enforced a contract term prohibiting assignment of rights under the contract. Such prohibitions, however, are now strictly construed; most courts interpret a general prohibition against assignments as a mere promise not to assign. As a consequence, the prohibition, if violated, gives the obligor a right to damages for breach of the terms forbidding assignment but does *not* render the assignment ineffective.

Section 322(1) of the Restatement and Section 2-210(3) of the Code provide that, unless circumstances indicate the contrary, a contract term prohibiting assignment of the *contract* bars only the delegation to the assignee (delegatee) of the assignor's (delegator's) *duty* of performance and not the assignment of *rights*. Thus, A and B contract for the sale of land by B to A for $30,000 and provide in their contract that A may not assign his rights under it. A pays B $30,000 and thereby fully performs his obligations under the contract. A then assigns his rights to C. C is entitled to receive the land from B (the obligor) despite the contractual prohibition of assignment.

A contract term prohibiting assignment of rights under the contract, unless a differ-

ent intention is manifested, does not forbid assignment of a right to damages for breach of the whole contract or a right arising out of the assignor's due performance of his entire obligation. Restatement, Section 322(2). For example, A and B contract for the sale of land by B to A. The contract contains a clause prohibiting the assignment of the contract. A fully performs the contract and becomes entitled to specific performance on B's refusal to convey the land. A then assigns his rights to C. C is entitled to specific performance against B.

Assignments Prohibited by Law Various Federal and State statutes, as well as public policy, prohibit or regulate the assignment of certain types of contract rights. For instance, assignments of future wages are subject to statutes, some of which prohibit them altogether while others require them to be in writing and subject to certain restrictions. An assignment that violates public policy will be unenforceable even in the absence of a prohibiting statute.

Rights of the Assignee

Obtains Rights of Assignor The general rule is that an assignee **stands in the shoes** of the assignor. He acquires the rights of the assignor but *no* new rights by reason of the assignment and takes the assigned right with all of the defenses, defects, and infirmities to which it would be subject in an action against the obligor by the assignor. Thus, in an action brought by the assignee against the obligor, the obligor may plead fraud, duress, undue influence, failure of consideration, breach of contract, or any other defense arising *before* notification of the assignment which he may have against the assignor. The obligor may also assert rights of set-off or counterclaim arising out of entirely separate matters which he may have against the assignor, provided they arose prior to his receiving notice of the assignment. See *Wiscombe v. Lockhart Co.*

Standing in the shoes of the assignor also permits the assignee to have the benefit of any outstanding security for the claim, even though not expressly assigned. If the claim has any right of priority in the hands of the assignor, such as a wage claim in bankruptcy, the assignee is entitled to the same priority as he is enforcing the right of the assignor.

The Code permits the buyer under a contract of sale to agree as part of the contract that he will not assert against an assignee who takes an assignment for value and in good faith any claim or defense which the buyer may have against the seller. U.C.C. Section 9-206. Such provision in an agreement affords greater marketability to the rights of the seller. The Federal Trade Commission, however, has invalidated such waiver of defense provisions in consumer credit transactions. This rule is discussed more fully in Chapter 26.

Notice A valid assignment does not require that notice be given to the obligor. Nonetheless, it is advisable that such notice be given because an assignee will lose his rights against the obligor if the latter pays the assignor without notice of the assignment. It would be unfair to compel an obligor to pay a claim a second time when she has paid it once to the only person whom she knew to be entitled to receive payment. Also, as already indicated, defenses to the contract, as well as set-offs and counterclaims of the obligor that arise out of entirely separate matters, cannot be used against the assignee if they arise *after* the notice has been given.

Implied Warranties of Assignor

In the absence of an express intention to the contrary, an assignor who receives value makes the following implied warranties to the assignee with respect to the assigned right:

1. that he will do nothing to defeat or impair the assignment;
2. that the assigned right actually exists and is subject to no limitations or defenses other than those stated or apparent at the time of the assignment;
3. that any writing evidencing the right delivered to the assignee or exhibited to him as an inducement to accept the assignment is genuine and what it purports to be; and
4. that he has no knowledge of any fact that would impair the value of the assignment.

Thus, A has a right against B and assigns it for value to C. Thereafter A gives B a release. C can recover damages from A for any harm this causes C. The amount of harm may be greater if B is released for value before he receives notification of the assignment than if B remains liable to C. Restatement, Section 333, Illustration 1.

The assignor is further bound by any express warranties he makes to the assignee with respect to the right assigned. However, unless explicitly stated, the assignor does *not* guarantee that the obligor will pay the assigned debt or otherwise perform.

Successive Assignments of the Same Right

The owner of a right could conceivably make successive assignments of the same claim to different persons. Assume that B owes A $1,000. On June 1, A for value assigns the debt to C. Thereafter, on June 15, A assigns it to D, who in good faith gives value and has no knowledge of the prior assignment by A to C. The majority rule in the United States is that the **first assignee in point of time** (C) prevails over subsequent assignees. In England and in a minority of the States, priority of notice of the assignment to the obligor determines which assignee prevails. *See Boulevard National Bank of Miami v. Air Metal Industries.*

The Restatement adopts the majority American rule and provides that a prior assignee is entitled to the assigned right and its proceeds to the exclusion of a subsequent assignee, except where the prior assignment is revocable or voidable by the assignor or the subsequent assignee in good faith and without knowledge of the prior assignment gives value and obtains one of the following: (1) payment or satisfaction of the obligor's duty, (2) a judgment against the obligor, (3) a new contract with the obligor, or (4) possession of a writing of a type customarily accepted as a symbol or as evidence of the right assigned. Restatement, Section 342.

DELEGATION OF DUTIES

As already indicated, contractual **duties** are *not* assignable, but their performance may generally be *delegated* to a third person. For example, A has entered into a contract with B to deliver to B a specified amount of copper for $5,000. A may properly delegate the performance of this contract to C. The courts, however, will scrutinize a delegation more closely than an assignment because, with a delegation, the non-delegating party to the contract (the obligee) is being compelled to receive performance from a party with which she has not dealt.

A delegation will not be permitted if:

1. the nature of the duties are personal;
2. the performance is expressly made nondelegable; or
3. the delegation is prohibited by statute or public policy.

For example, a school teacher may not delegate her performance to another teacher, even if the substitute is equally competent, for this is a contract which is personal in nature. In the frequently quoted words of an English case: "You have a right to the benefit you contemplate from the character, credit and substance of the person with whom you contract." On the other hand, where performance by a party involves no peculiar or special skill, and where no personal trust or confidence is involved, he may delegate the performance of his duty. *See Macke Company v. Pizza of Gaithersburg, Inc.*

Even when permitted, a delegation of a duty to a third person still leaves the delegator bound to perform. If the delegator desires to be discharged of the duty, it may be possible for her to enter into an agreement obtaining the consent of the obligee to substitute a third person (the delgatee) in her place. This is a **novation** whereby the delegator is discharged and the third party becomes directly bound upon his promise to the obligee. Nevertheless, unlike an assignment which extinguishes the assignor's rights under the original contract or a novation which extinguishes the duties of the original obligor, a **delegation** leaves **both** the delegator and delegatee **liable** for proper performance of the original contractual duty. A delegation, therefore, amounts to no more than a third party's being authorized to perform the duty for the delegator.

Since a delegatee becomes liable for performance, the delegatee must assent to the delegation. But if A and C agree to an assignment of A's contract with B, does this include both an assignment of rights and a delegation of duties? The common law rule is unclear as there is a division of authority among the jurisdictions. The Code clearly resolves this conflict by providing that, unless the language or circumstances indicate the contrary, an assignment of "the contract" or of "all my rights under the contract" or an assignment in similar general terms is an assignment of rights *and* a delegation of performance of the duties of the assignor, and its acceptance by the assignee constitutes a promise by her to perform those duties. Section 2-210(4). The Restatement, Section 328, has also adopted this position. For example, A, an oil company, has a contract to sell and deliver oil to B. A delivers to C, another oil company, a writing assigning to C "all A's rights and duties under the contract." C is under a duty to B to deliver the oil called for by the contract, and A is liable to B if C does not perform. It should also be recalled that the Restatement and the Code provide that a clause prohibiting an assignment of "the contract" is to be construed as barring only the delegation to the assignee (delegatee) of the assignor's (delegator's) performance, unless the circumstances indicate the contrary.

THIRD PARTY BENEFICIARY CONTRACTS

A contract in which a party (the **promisor**) promises to render a certain performance not to the other party (the **promisee**) but to a third person (the **beneficiary**) is called a third party beneficiary contract. The third person is not a party to the contract but is merely a beneficiary of the contract. Such contracts may be divided into two types: (1) **intended** beneficiary and (2) **incidental** beneficiary. The first type of beneficiary is intended by the two parties to the contract (the promisor and promisee) to receive a benefit from the performance of their agreement. Accordingly, the courts generally enforce the intended beneficiary type of third party contracts. For example, A promises B to deliver an automobile to C if B promises to pay $10,000. C is the intended beneficiary.

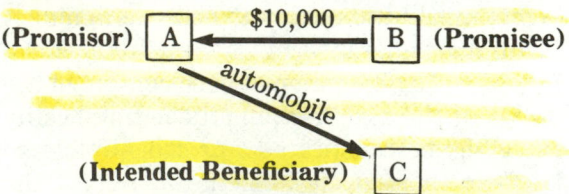

However, where the third party incidentally and not intentionally is to receive a benefit under the contract, no court will enforce the third party's right to the benefits of the contract. For example, A promises to purchase and deliver to B an automobile for $10,000. In all probability A would acquire the automobile from D. D would be an incidental beneficiary.

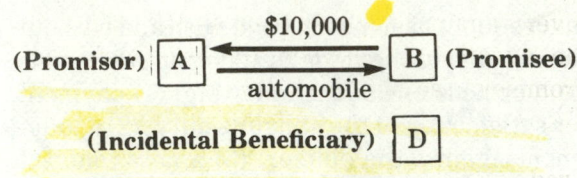

INTENDED BENEFICIARY

Gift Promise

A third party is an **intended donee beneficiary** if the purpose of the promisee in bargaining for and obtaining the promise from the promisor was to make a gift to the beneficiary. The ordinary life insurance policy is an illustration of this type of intended beneficiary third party contract. The insured (the promisee) makes a contract with an insurance company (the promisor) which promises, in consideration of premiums paid to it by the insured, to pay upon the death of the insured a stated sum of money to the named beneficiary, who is an intended donee beneficiary.

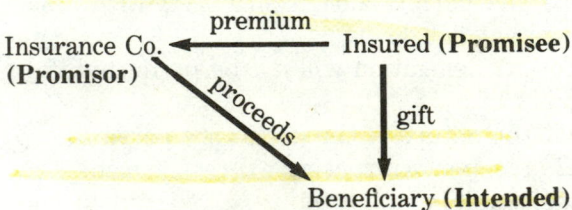

    The desirability of allowing intended donee beneficiaries to recover on contracts made for their benefit is manifest. Upon breach by the promisor and a suit against him by the promisee, the damages which could be established by the promisee would be nominal. Unless the donee beneficiary is given the right to recover against the promisor, even though he furnished no consideration and is not in privity of contract with the promisor, the purpose of the parties to the contract is defeated and the content of the promisor's consideration loses its value. The donee beneficiary has no right of action against the promisee, who is his donor, and a denial of his right of recovery against the promisor would frustrate the agreement between the promisee and promisor. *See Saylor v. Saylor.*

Creditor Beneficiary

A third person is also an intended beneficiary if the promisee intends the performance of the promise to satisfy a legal duty owed to the beneficiary, who is a creditor of the promisee. The contract involves consideration moving from the promisee to the promisor in exchange for the promisor's engaging to pay some debt or discharge some obligation of the promisee to the third person.

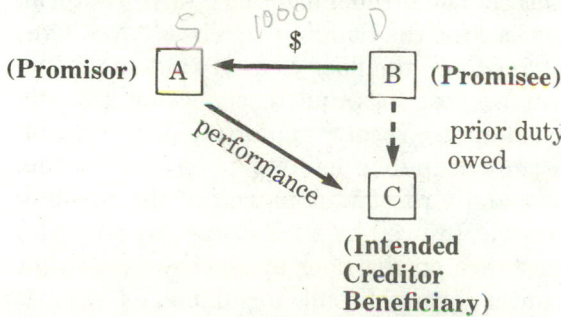

(Promisor) A ← $ → B (Promisee)

performance

prior duty owed

C

(Intended Creditor Beneficiary)

To illustrate, in the contract for the sale by B of his business to A, A promises B that she will pay all of B's outstanding business debts, as listed in the contract. Here, B's creditors are creditor beneficiaries. Similarly, in the classic case of *Lawrence v. Fox*, 20 N.Y. 268 (1859), Holly loaned Fox $300 in consideration for Fox's promise to pay that sum to Lawrence, a creditor of Holly's. Fox failed to pay Lawrence, who sued Fox for the $300. The court held for Lawrence, who was permitted to recover as a third party creditor beneficiary to the contract between Holly and Fox. Where a party to a contract promises to render performance, not to the promisee but to a third party who is a creditor of the promisee, the third party is a creditor beneficiary of the promise and may maintain an action for breach of contract.

The making of the contract, however, does not (as with delegation of duties) in any way change or affect the obligation of the promisee to the beneficiary as it previously existed. The beneficiary in this situation has **both** rights against the promisee based upon the original obligation and rights against the promisor based upon the third party beneficiary contract. If neither performs, the third person can maintain separate suits against both and obtain judgments against both, although he can only collect his debt once.

Rights of Intended Beneficiary

A promise in a contract creates a duty in the promisor to an intended beneficiary to perform the promise, and the intended beneficiary may enforce this duty. Generally, the rights of an intended beneficiary vest at the time of the making of the contract, whether she has knowledge of it or not. However, within a reasonable time after learning of the contract's existence, the intended beneficiary may reject the promised benefit.

If the contract between the promisor and promisee provides that its terms may not be varied without the consent of the beneficiary, such a provision is effective. Otherwise, the parties to the contract may rescind or vary the contract unless the intended beneficiary has brought an action upon the promise or has changed her position in reliance upon it. Restatement, Section 311.

An intended *donee* beneficiary may sue the promisor only. He cannot maintain an action against the promisee, since the promisee was under no legal obligation to him. An intended *creditor* beneficiary, however, may sue either or both parties. If B owes C $500, and A contracts with B to pay this debt to C, B is not thereby relieved of his liability to C. If A breaks the contract, C, as a creditor beneficiary, may sue him. In addition, C may sue B as his debtor. If C should recover judgments against both A and B, he is, of course, entitled to collect only one judgment. If C recovers against B, B has a right of reimbursement from A, the promisor. Restatement, Section 310.

The fact that a beneficiary brings suit against the promisor does not prevent the promisee from likewise suing the promisor. The promisor has not only violated the right of the beneficiary, but he has also broken his contract with the promisee. The promisee may, therefore, also sue the promisor.

In an action by the intended beneficiary of a third party contract to enforce the promise, the promisor may assert any defense which would be available to him if the action had been brought by the promisee. The rights of the third party are based upon the promisor's contract with the promisee. Thus, the absence of mutual assent or consideration, lack of capacity, fraud, mistake, and the like may be asserted by the promisor against the intended beneficiary. But claims and defenses of the promisor against the promisee arising out of *separate* transactions do not affect the rights of the intended beneficiary unless the contract so provides. Likewise, the right of the intended beneficiary against the promisor is not subject to the promisee's claims or defenses against the beneficiary.

INCIDENTAL BENEFICIARY

An incidental third party beneficiary is a person whom the parties to a contract did not intend to benefit, but who nevertheless would derive some benefit by its performance. For instance, a contract to raze an old, unsightly building and replace it with a costly modern house would benefit the owner of the adjoining property by increasing its value. However, he would have no rights under the contract, as the benefit to him is unintended and incidental.

A third person who may be incidentally benefited by the performance of a contract to which he is not a party has no rights under the contract. It was not the intention of either the promisee or the promisor that the third person be benefited. Assume that for a stated consideration B promises A that he will purchase and deliver to A a brand new Sony television of the latest model. A performs. B does not. C, the local exclusive Sony dealer, has no rights under the contract although performance by B would produce a sale from which C would derive a benefit. C is only an incidental beneficiary.

In *Northwest Airlines, Inc. v. Crosetti Bros. Inc.*, 483 P.2d 70 (Or.1971), plaintiff Northwest leased space in the terminal building at the Portland Airport from the Port of Portland. Defendant Crosetti entered into a contract with the Port to furnish janitorial services for the building which required Crosetti to keep the floor clean, to indemnify the Port against loss due to claims or lawsuits based upon Crosetti's failure to perform, and to provide public liability insurance for the Port and Crosetti. A patron of the building who was injured by a fall caused by a foreign substance on the floor at Northwest's ticket counter brought suit for damages against Northwest, the Port, and Crosetti. Upon settlement of this suit, Northwest sued Crosetti to recover the amount of its contribution to the settlement and other expenses on the grounds that Northwest was a third party beneficiary of Crosetti's contract with the Port to keep the floors clean and, therefore, within the protection of Crosetti's indemnification agreement. The court held that only two types of third party beneficiaries are entitled to recover; and that Northwest was not a creditor beneficiary as it was not a creditor of the Port since its lease contained no agreement by the Port to indemnify it; nor was it a donee beneficiary as there was no evidence of any intention of the Port in its contract with Crosetti to make a gift to Northwest or confer upon Northwest a right to indemnity. At most, Northwest was an incidental beneficiary, and as such had no right of recovery.

CASES

Rights That Are Assignable

MUNCHAK CORPORATION v. CUNNINGHAM

United States Court of Appeals, Fourth Circuit, 1972.
457 F.2d 721.

WINTER, J.

Plaintiffs, the owners and operators of the basketball club "The Carolina Cougars" (the "Cougars"), sued to enjoin defendant, William John Cunningham ("Cunningham"), a professional basketball player, from performing services as a basketball player for any basketball club other than the Cougars in violation of a contract between the Cougars and Cunningham. The district court, finding that Cunningham had contracted to play for the Cougars, nevertheless concluded that even if Cunningham had failed and refused to perform his contract, plaintiffs had unclean hands and had breached their contract with Cunningham. It, therefore, denied injunctive relief.

In this appeal, we conclude that plaintiffs did not have unclean hands, that any breach of contract on the part of plaintiffs was too insubstantial to justify the denial of injunctive relief, and that Cunningham's additional argument that his contract was not assignable is lacking in merit. Accordingly, we reverse and remand the case for entry of an injunction restraining Cunningham from playing for any team, other than the Cougars, for the duration of his contract with that club.

* * *

The district judge made detailed findings of fact to support his opinion and conclusions of law that plaintiffs were not entitled to injunctive relief. Munchak Corporation v. Cunningham, 331 F.Supp. 872 (M.D.N.C. 1971), and, consequently, we need not repeat all of the facts. It suffices to say that Cun-

ningham is a basketball player of special, exceptional, and unique knowledge, skills, and ability. For the period October 1, 1969, until October 1, 1970, as well as for four earlier seasons, he had contracted to play professional basketball for the Philadelphia 76ers. For the period October 1, 1969, to October 1, 1970, Cunningham received $40,000.00 compensation under the contract, together with a bonus of $15,000.00, a total of $55,000.00. The contract contained a "reserve clause," which gave that club the right on or before September 1, 1970, to tender a contract to Cunningham to play the next season. If Cunningham failed, neglected, or omitted to sign the tendered contract and to return it by October 1, 1970, the existing contract would be continued for another year, but at the rate of compensation fixed in the tendered contract, provided that that compensation was not less than 75% of the compensation being paid Cunningham under the contract then in force.

During May or early June of 1969, the Cougars, with knowledge that Cunningham was under contract with the Philadelphia 76ers, and that that club had an option to Cunningham's services for the 1970–71 basketball season, through intermediaries, entered into contract negotiations with Cunningham. On August 5, 1969, the negotiations ripened into a three-year contract *commencing on the 2nd day of October, 1971*. For the first year of the contract Cunningham was to receive a salary of $100,000.00, for the second year $110,000.00, and for the third year $120,000.00. Additionally, Cunningham was to receive $125,000.00 as a bonus for signing the contract. The bonus was payable $45,000.00 on August 5, 1969, and the balance of $80,000.00 was evidenced by a promissory note wherein the Cougars promised to pay Cunningham $80,000.00 not later than May 15, 1970. The contract contained a provision which recited that Cunningham had special, exceptional and unique knowledge, skill and ability as a basketball player, the loss of which was not readily translatable into money damages; and, therefore, Cunningham agreed that the Cougars could enjoin him from playing basketball for another team during the term of his contract with the Cougars. The validity and enforceability of this provision in a proper case is not disputed. The litigation revolves about whether Cunningham has meritorious defenses to obviate plaintiffs' equitable remedy.

* * *

Cunningham's contention that his contract was not assignable and that by reason of a purported assignment he is excused from performance arises from these facts. Cunningham's contracts with the Cougars were made at a time when Southern Sports Corporation, owned and operated primarily by James C. Gardner, was the owner of the Cougars' franchise. His contract with Southern Sports Corporation prohibited its assignment to another "*club*" without his consent, but it contained no prohibition against its assignment to another owner of the same club. In 1971, Southern Sports Corporation assigned its franchise and Cunningham's contracts to the plaintiffs, who, as joint venturers, operate the franchise. Cunningham was not asked to consent, nor has he consented, to this assignment. While Cunningham's contracts require him to perform personal services, the services were to the club.

We recognize that under North Carolina law the right to performance of a personal service contract requiring special skills and based upon the personal relationship between the parties cannot be assigned without the consent of the party rendering those services. [Citation.] But, as discussed in [citation], some of such contracts may be assigned when the character of the performance and the obligation will not be changed. To us it is inconceivable that the rendition of services by a professional basketball player to a professional basketball club could be affected by the personalities of successive corporate owners. Cf. Washington Capitols Basketball Club, Inc. v. Barry, [citation]. Indeed, Cunningham had met only Gardner of Southern Sports Club, and had not met, nor did he know, the other stockholders. If Gardner had sold all or part of his stock to another person, Cunningham could not seriously contend that his consent would be required.

The policy against assignability of certain personal service contracts is to prohibit an assignment of a contract in which the obligor undertakes to serve only the original obligee. [Citations.] This contract is not of that type, since Cunningham was not obligated to perform differently for plaintiffs than he was obligated to perform for Southern Sports Club. We, therefore, see no reason to hold that the contract was not assignable under the facts here.

For the reasons stated, we reverse the judgment of the district court and remand the case for entry of appropriate equitable relief.

Reversed and remanded.

Assignment of Personal Rights

SCHUPACK v. McDONALD'S SYSTEM, INC.

Supreme Court of Nebraska, 1978.
200 Neb. 485, 264 N.W.2d 827.

WHITE, C. J.

This is an action by the plaintiffs against the defendants, McDonald's Corporation and McDonald's System, Inc., its wholly owned subsidiary (hereinafter referred to as McDonald's), for a declaratory judgment to determine the respective rights and obligations of the parties to and under a certain Right of First Refusal (or Right) originally granted by McDonald's to Bernard L. Copeland and now allegedly possessed by the plaintiffs, and for specific performance and injunctive relief requiring McDonald's to accord the plaintiffs the Right of First Refusal to acquire a McDonald's unit in Bellevue, Nebraska, and any additional units which might be in the future developed by McDonald's in the Omaha, Nebraska, or Council Bluffs, Iowa, area.

*   *   *

The Right in question was granted to Bernard Copeland by McDonald's in a letter dated July 1, 1959, which reads:

This letter, Mr. Copeland, will confirm our understanding regarding any additional McDonald's units that may be developed in the Omaha, Nebraska, or Council Bluffs, Iowa area.

Providing you or any corporation you are involved with, is not in default on a McDonald's franchise, or a franchise Realty Corporation lease; any locations that we might develop in the Omaha, Nebraska or Council Bluffs, Iowa area will be offered to Bernard L. Copeland first.

This letter was signed by Donald R. Conley, then vice president of McDonald's.

The intial question for us to decide is whether the Right was assignable as transferable without the consent of McDonald's. "Subject to certain exceptions in case of contracts involving relations of personal confidence or trust or being for personal services all contracts are assignable." [Citation.] "A contract, which shows by its nature or terms that it is personal in character, that is, that reliance for its performance is placed on the integrity, credit, or responsibility of a party, or that confidence or trust is reposed in him personally for its performance, is not assignable, even in the sense of its performance being delegated to another, without the consent of the other party to the contract, *   *   * " [Citation.]

*   *   *

Whether the Right granted to Copeland was personal to him, and thus not assignable without the consent of McDonald's, is a question to be resolved by ascertaining the intent of the parties to the transaction. *   *   *

Summarizing, the evidence is overwhelming and almost undisputed to establish the following factual conclusions:

(1) That it was the basic and undeviating policy of McDonald's to retain the rigid and absolute control over *who* received new franchises in the rapidly expanding demand for new franchises.

(2) That the Right of First Refusal was intended to be personal in nature and was separately a grant independent of the terms of the franchise contract itself.

(3) That the grant depended upon the personal confidence and trust that McDonald's placed in the grantee, and that to permit assignability or transfer by the grantee without the permission of McDonald's, would serve to destroy the basic policy of control of the quality and confidence in performance in the event any new franchises were to be granted in the locality.

(4) That by its terms, the letter granting the Right granted it only to Bernard L. Copeland, even though it expressly recognized and extended Copeland's Right to corporate involvement in his operation and management of the franchise.

*   *   *

(6) That the intent and the purpose of the letter granting the Right to Copeland was to look to the personal performance of Mr. Copeland.

*   *   *

We hold that the Right of First Refusal granted to Copeland by McDonald's was personal to Copeland, and could not be transferred or assigned without the consent of McDonald's. *   *   *

The next question for us to determine is whether Copeland's Right was transferred and assigned to the plaintiff [Schupack], and whether McDonald's has ever consented to a transfer or assignment of Copeland's Right to the plaintiffs.

*   *   *

On November 24, 1964, plaintiffs and the sellers executed a purchase and sale agreement. *   *   *

We hold that McDonald's did not consent to a transfer of the Right of First Refusal from Copeland to the plaintiffs, but that they only consented to a sale of the stock in the then existing franchises. We also find Mc-Donald's has consistently maintained the position that the Right of First Refusal was personal only to Copeland and did not pass to the plaintiffs, and has acted in accordance with that position, and has not at any time subsequent to the 1964 purchase of the Omaha-Council Bluffs franchises by the plaintiffs, recognized the existence of the Right of First Refusal in the plaintiffs.

Accordingly, plaintiffs possess no Right of First Refusal to additional McDonald's franchises in the Omaha-Council Bluffs area.
* * *

[Judgment for McDonald's.]

Rights of Assignee

WISCOMBE v. LOCKHART CO.

Supreme Court of Utah, 1980.
608 P.2d 236.

WILKINS, J.

[On January 1, 1976, Beardall purchased by contract certain real property from Wiscombe. The contract called for annual payments of $15,000, due on the first day of January of each year. On November 5, 1976, Beardall assigned his rights under this contract to Lockhart. However, Lockhart did not notify Wiscombe of the assignment. The $15,000 payment due on January 1, 1977 was not received by Wiscombe. Wiscombe notified Beardall of the default on February 2, 1977 and gave him five days in which to remedy his default. Beardall did not do so and left the premises on or before February 7, 1977. Wiscombe first learned of the assignment in late February, and shortly thereafter Lockhart tendered to Wiscombe $15,000 representing the payment due on January 1, 1977. Wiscombe rejected the tender and brought suit to establish his title to the property.]

* * *

Fundamental to the law of assignments is the concept that an assignee takes nothing more by his assignment than his assignor had. In *Tanner v. Lawler*, we stated:

An assignment merely sets over or transfers the interest of one party in certain property to another. Such an assignment does not have the effect of canceling any rights which other persons have in connection with such property.

The . . . [c]ontract between Wiscombe and Beardall was properly foreclosed by Wiscombe in accordance with the terms of the [c]ontract after Beardall's default. Beardall quit the premises in question on or before February 7, 1977, and so certainly after February 7, the . . . [c]ontract had no further viability of its own. Title to the property remained in Wiscombe no longer subject to the [c]ontract.

Lockhart's tender on March 1 and 2, 1977, was therefore wholly ineffectual because it came almost three weeks after the [c]ontract terminated. There was nothing which could be performed by Lockhart by way of its tender.

* * *

[Judgment for Wiscombe affirmed.]

*Successive Assignments of
Same Right*

BOULEVARD NATIONAL BANK OF MIAMI v. AIR METAL INDUSTRIES

Supreme Court of Florida, 1965.
176 So.2d 94.

WILLIS, J.

The suit commenced as an action at law by the plaintiff bank against several defendants, including the respondent Tompkins-Beckwith, Inc., in whose favor the summary final judgment involved here was rendered.

Tompkins-Beckwith was the contractor on a construction project which had entered into a subcontract with a division of Air Metal Industries, Inc. Air Metal procured American Fire and Casualty Company to be surety on certain bonds in connection with contracts it was performing for Tompkins-Beckwith and others. As security for such bonds, Air Metal executed, on January 3, 1962, a "Contractor's General Agreement of Indemnity" which contains an assignment to American Fire of [all accounts receivable under the Tompkins-Beckwith contract.]

On November 26, 1962, the petitioner bank lent money to Air Metal and to secure the loans Air Metal purported to assign to the bank certain accounts receivable it had with Tompkins-Beckwith which arose out of subcontracts being done for that contractor.

In June, 1963 Air Metal defaulted on various contracts bonded by American Fire. On July 1, 1963 American Fire served formal notice on Tompkins-Beckwith of Air Metal's assignment. Tompkins-Beckwith acknowledged the assignment and agreed to pay. On August 12, 1963, the petitioner bank notified Tompkins-Beckwith of its assignment and claim thereunder. The claim was not recognized and on September 26, 1963, this action was filed in the trial court. On October 9, 1963 Tompkins-Beckwith paid all remaining funds which had accrued to Air Metal to American Fire.

* * * The "question" * * * is whether the law of Florida requires recognition of the so-called "English" rule or "American" rule of priority between assignees of successive assignments of an account receivable or other similar chose in action. Stated in its simplest form, the American rule would give priority to the assignee first in point of time of assignment, while the English rule would give preference to the assignment of which the debtor was first given notice. Both rules presuppose the absence of any estoppel or other special equities in favor of or against either assignee. The English rule giving priority to the assignee first giving notice to the debtor is specifically qualified as applying "unless he takes a later assignment with notice of a previous one or without a valuable consideration." [Citations.]

* * *

The American rule for which petitioner contends is based upon the reasoning that an account or other chose in action may be assigned at will by the owner; that notice to the debtor is not essential to complete the assignment; and that when such assignment is made the property rights become vested in the assignee so that the assignor no longer has any interest in the account or chose which he may subsequently assign to another. [Citations.]

* * *

It is undoubted that the creditor of an account receivable or other similar chose in action arising out of contract may assign it to another so that the assignee may sue on it in his own name and make recovery. Formal requisites of such an assignment are not prescribed by statute and it may be accomplished by parol, by instrument in writing, or other mode, such as delivery of evidences of the debt, as may demonstrate an intent to transfer and an acceptance of it. * * *

It seems to be generally agreed that notice to a debtor of an assignment is necessary to impose on the debtor the duty of payment to the assignee, and that if before receiving such notice he pays the debt to the assignor, or to a subsequent assignee, he will be discharged from the debt. [Citation.] To regard the debtor as a total nonparticipant in the assignment by the creditor of his interests to another is to deny the obvious. An account receivable is only the right to receive payment of a debt which ultimately must be done by the act of the debtor. For the assignee to acquire the right to stand in the shoes of the assigning creditor he must acquire some "delivery" or "possession" of the debt constituting a means of clearly establishing his right to collect. The very nature of an account receivable renders "delivery" and "possession" matters very different and more difficult than in the case of tangible personalty and negotiable instruments which are readily capable of physical handling and holding. However, the very principles which render a sale of personal property with possession remaining in the vendor unexplained fraudulent and void as to creditors applies with equal urgency to choses in action which are the subject of assignment. It would seem to follow that the mere private dealing between the creditor and his assignee unaccompanied by any manifestations discernable to others having or considering the acquiring of an interest in the account would not meet the requirement of delivery and acceptance of possession which is essential to the consummation of the assignment. Proper notice to the debtor of the assignment is a manifestation of such delivery. It fixes the accountability of the debtor to the assignee instead of the assignor and enables all involved to deal more safely.

We thus find that the so-called English rule which the trial and appellate court approved and applied is harmonious with our jurisprudence, whereas the so-called American rule is not. * * *

[Judgment for Air Metal.]

Delegation of Duties

MACKE COMPANY v. PIZZA OF GAITHERSBURG, INC.

Court of Appeals of Maryland, 1970.
259 Md. 479, 270 A.2d 645.

SINGLEY, J.

The appellees and defendants below, Pizza of Gaithersburg, Inc.; Pizzeria, Inc.; The Pizza Pie Corp., Inc.; and Pizza Oven, Inc., four corporations under the common ownership of Sidney Ansell, Thomas S. Sherwood, and Eugene Early and the same individuals as partners or proprietors (the Pizza Shops) operated at six locations in Montgomery and Prince George's Counties. The appellees had arranged to have installed in each of their locations cold drink vending machines owned by Virginia Coffee Service, Inc., and on 30 December 1966, this arrangement was formalized at five of the locations, by contracts for terms of one year, automatically renewable for a like term in the absence of 30 days'

written notice. A similar contract for the sixth location, operated by Pizza of Gaithersburg, Inc., was entered into on 25 July 1967.

On 30 December 1967, Virginia's assets were purchased by The Macke Company (Macke) and the six contracts were assigned to Macke by Virginia. In January, 1968, the Pizza Shops attempted to terminate the five contracts having the December anniversary date, and in February, the contract which had the July anniversary date.

Macke brought suit in the Circuit Court for Montgomery County against each of the Pizza Shops for damages for breach of contract. From judgments for the defendants, Macke has appealed.

* * *

In the absence of a contrary provision— and there was none here—rights and duties under an executory bilateral contract may be assigned and delegated, subject to the exception that duties under a contract to provide personal services may never be delegated, nor rights be assigned under a contract where *delectus personae* [choice of person] was an ingredient of the bargain. [Citations.] Crane Ice Cream Co. v. Terminal Freezing & Heating Co. [citation], held that the right of an individual to purchase ice under a contract which by its terms reflected a knowledge of the individual's needs and reliance on his credit and responsibility could not be assigned to the corporation which purchased his business. In [citation], our predecessors held that an advertising agency could not delegate its duties under a contract which had been entered into by an advertiser who had relied on the agency's skill, judgment and taste.

The six machines were placed on the appellees' premises under a printed "Agreement-Contract" which identified the "customer," gave its place of business, described the vending machine, and * * *.

We cannot regard the agreements as contracts for personal services. They were either a license or concession granted Virginia by the appellees, or a lease of a portion of the appellees' premises, with Virginia agreeing to pay a percentage of gross sales as a license or concession fee or as rent, [citations], and were assignable by Virginia unless they imposed on Virginia duties of a personal or unique character which could not be delegated, [citation].

The appellees earnestly argue that they had dealt with Macke before and had chosen Virginia because they preferred the way it conducted its business. Specifically, they say that service was more personalized, since the president of Virginia kept the machines in working order, that commissions were paid in cash, and that Virginia permitted them to keep keys to the machines so that minor adjustments could be made when needed. Even if we assume all this to be true, the agreements with Virginia were silent as to the details of the working arrangements and contained only a provision requiring Virginia to "install * * * the above listed equipment and * * * maintain the equipment in good operating order and stocked with merchandise." We think the Supreme Court of California put the problem of personal service in proper focus a century ago when it upheld the assignment of a contract to grade a San Francisco street:

All painters do not paint portraits like Sir Joshua Reynolds, nor landscapes like Claude Lorraine, nor do all writers write dramas like Shakespeare or fiction like Dickens. Rare genius and extraordinary skill are not transferable, and contracts for their employment are therefore personal, and cannot be assigned. But rare genius and extraordinary skill are not indispensable to the workmanlike digging down of a sand hill or the filling up of a depression to a given level, or the construction of brick sewers with manholes and covers, and contracts for such work are not personal, and may be assigned. [Citation.]

* * * Moreover, the difference between the service the Pizza Shops happened to be getting from Virginia and what they expected to get from Macke did not mount up to such a material change in the performance of obligations under the agreements as would justify the appellees' refusal to recognize the assignment, [citation].

* * *

* * * Modern authorities * * * hold that, absent provision to the contrary, a duty may be delegated, as distinguished from a right which can be assigned, and that the promisee cannot rescind, if the quality of the performance remains materially the same. * * *

As we see it, the delegation of duty by Virginia to Macke was entirely permissible under the terms of the agreements.

* * *

[Judgment reversed.]

Intended Beneficiary

SAYLOR v. SAYLOR

Court of Appeals of Kentucky, 1965.
389 S.W.2d 904.

PALMORE, J.

This is a declaratory judgment action to determine the ownership of a bank savings account. The facts are stipulated. The contest is between the administrator and the widow of Adrian M. Saylor. The trial court found in favor of the widow, and the administrator appeals.

The account was opened by Mr. Saylor on March 19, 1962; with the deposit of $6,540.65 derived from the sale of government bonds owned exclusively by him. The pass book issued by the bank to Mr. Saylor on March 19, 1962, was made out in the names of "Mr. or Mrs. Adrian M. Saylor," and the bank's ledger card for the account was established and thenceforth maintained in the names of "Adrian M. Saylor or Kathleen B. Saylor." Kathleen is the widow.

* * *

On June 15, 1963, Mr. Saylor deposited $2,132.60 of his own money in the account, and the deposit was entered in the pass book. There were no other deposits, and for purposes of this opinion it may be assumed that there were no withdrawals whatever, prior to the death of Mr. Saylor on May 15, 1964.

The question is whether the balance of the account at Mr. Saylor's death is payable wholly to the administrator, wholly to the widow, or half to each. The trial court held it was a survivorship account, passing wholly to the widow.

It is recognized in this state that a person may by depositing his own money in the names of himself and another create the equivalent of a tenancy in common or a tenancy by the entirety, depending upon his intent. [Citations.] As in the case of other intangibles such as bonds or stock certificates, the right gratuitously conferred on the other party is recognized and is enforceable on the theory of third party beneficiary contract. It is not necessary that such a contract be supported by a consideration moving from the beneficiary, and it is not necessary that a "gift" be proved. [Citation.]

"The prevailing modern view is that a donee-beneficiary has a right of action to enforce a promise made for his benefit. In this respect, the courts so holding have rejected any requirement of consideration, privity, or obligation as between the promisee and the third person." [Citation.]

"In this jurisdiction a party beneficiary of a contract may look to the promisor directly and sue him in his own name to enforce a promise made for plaintiff's benefit, even though he is a stranger, it being sufficient that there is a consideration between the parties who made the agreement for the benefit of the third party." [Citation.]

"It is not essential, in order to enable a third person to recover on a contract made and intended for his benefit, that he knew of the contract at the time it was made." [Citation.] A fortiori, that Mrs. Saylor did not sign the signature card or otherwise participate in the establishment of the account is immaterial.

By his deposit of money a contract was created between Mr. Saylor and the bank. By causing the account to be established and maintained in the names of himself and his wife, in the absence of evidence to the contrary there is a rebuttable presumption that Mr. Saylor intended to and did make his wife a third party beneficiary of the contract. * * *

The judgment is affirmed.

PROBLEMS

1. On December 1, A, a famous singer, contracted with B to sing at B's theatre on December 31st for a fee of $25,000 to be paid immediately after the performance.

(a) A, for value received, assigns this fee to C.

(b) A, for value received, assigns this contract to sing to D, an equally famous singer.

(c) B sells his theatre to E, and assigns his contract with A to E.

State the effect of each of these assignments.

2. The Smooth Paving Company entered into a paving contract with the city of Chicago. The contract contained the clause "contractor shall be liable for all damages to buildings resulting from the work performed." In the process of construction one of the bulldozers of the Smooth Paving Company struck a gas main, breaking the main which caused an explosion and a fire which destroyed the house of John Puff. Puff brought an appropriate action against the Smooth Paving Company to recover damages for the loss of this house. Decision?

3. A, who was unemployed, registered with the X Employment Agency. A contract was then made under which A, in consideration of such position as the Agency would obtain for A, agreed to pay

No contract at time of assign)

the Agency one-half of her first month's salary. The contract also contained an assignment by A to the Agency of one-half of such first month's salary. Two weeks later, the Agency obtained a permanent position for A with the B Co. at a monthly salary of $900. The agency also notified the B Co. of the assignment by A. At the end of the first month, the B Co. paid A her salary in full. A then quit and disappeared. The Agency now sues the B Co. for $450 under the assignment. Decision?

4. B purchased an option on Blackacre from S for $1,000. The option contract contained a provision by which B promised not to assign the option contract without S's permission. B, without S's permission, assigns the contract to A. A seeks to exercise the option, and S refuses to sell Blackacre to him. Decision? *if obligor? damages on recover*
assignor

5. B contracts to sell to A, an ice cream manufacturer, the amount of ice A may need in his business for the ensuing three years to the extent of not more than 250 tons a week at a stated price per ton. A makes a corresponding promise to B to buy such an amount of ice. A sells his ice cream plant to C and assigns to C all A's rights under the contract with B. Upon learning of the sale, B refused to furnish ice to C. C sues B for damages. Decision?

6. Brown enters into a written contract with Ideal Insurance Company under which, in consideration of the payment of the premiums, the Insurance Company promises to pay XYZ College the face amount of the policy, $100,000, on Brown's death. Brown pays the premiums until her death. Thereafter, XYZ College makes demand for the $100,000 of Insurance Company, which refuses to pay upon the ground that XYZ College was not a party to the contract. Decision?

7. A and B enter into a contract binding A personally to do some delicate cabinet work. A assigns his rights and delegates performance of his duties to C. On being informed of this, B agrees with C, in consideration of C's promise to do the work, that B will accept C's work, if properly done, instead of the performance promised by A. Later, without cause, B refuses to allow C to proceed with the work, though C is ready to do so, and makes demand on A that A perform. A refuses.

Can C recover damages from B? Can B recover from A? *yes—or su or A*

No—delegation

8. A, a homeowner, enters into a valid, written contract with B, a carpenter, for the construction of various book shelves and cabinets in A's house. Prior to the commencement of the work B assigns his interest in the contract to C, another carpenter. A refuses to permit C to do the work, employs another carpenter, and brings an action against B claiming as damages the difference between the contract price and the cost to employ the other carpenter. Decision?

9. S hired G in the spring, as she had for many years, to set out in beds the flowers S had grown during the winter in her greenhouses. The work was to be done in S's absence for $300. G became ill the day after S departed and requested his friend, B, to set out the flowers, promising to pay him $250 when he was paid; B agreed. Upon completion of the planting, an agent of S's, who had authority to dispense the money, paid G, and G paid B. Within two days it became obvious that the planting was a disaster. Everything set out by B had died of water rot, due to his inability to properly operate S's automatic watering system.

May S recover damages from B? May S recover damages from G, and, if so, does G have an action against B?

10. Caleb, operator of a window washing business, dictated a letter to his secretary addressed to Apartments, Inc. stating: "I will wash the windows of your apartment buildings at $4.10 per window to be paid upon completion of the work." The secretary typed the letter, signed Caleb's name and mailed it to Apartments, Inc. Apartments, Inc. replied: "Accept your offer."

Caleb wrote back: "I will wash them during the week commencing July 10 and direct you to pay the money you will owe me to my son, Bernie. I am giving it to him as a wedding present." Caleb sent a signed copy of the letter to Bernie.

Caleb washed the windows during the time stated and demanded payment to him of $8,200 (2,000 windows at $4.10 each), informing Apartments, Inc. that he had changed his mind about having the money paid to Bernie.

What are the rights of the parties?

Chapter 15

PERFORMANCE, BREACH AND DISCHARGE

THE subject of discharge of contracts pertains to the termination of contractual duties. In earlier chapters we have seen how parties may become bound to their promises by a contract. It may be equally desirable for a person to know how she may become unbound from a contract. When a contract is made, it is not intended by either party that the duties created shall exist forever. Contractual promises are made for a purpose, and the parties reasonably expect this purpose to be fulfilled by performance. However, performance of a contractual duty is only one method of discharge.

Whatever causes a binding promise to cease to be binding is a discharge of the contract. In general, there are four types of discharge: (1) by performance of the parties, (2) by breach of the parties, (3) by agreement of the parties, and (4) by operation of law. In addition, there are various ways in which each type of discharge may occur. Closely allied to discharge is an excuse for non-performance of a contractual duty.

Moreover, many contractual promises are not absolute and unconditional promises to perform but rather are conditional promises. The obligation to perform conditional promises is dependent upon the happening or non-happening of a specific event. This makes necessary a brief discussion of the subject of conditions.

CONDITIONS

A condition is an operative event the happening or non-happening of which affects a duty of performance under a contract. Some conditions must be satisfied before any duty to perform arises; others terminate the duty to perform; still others either limit or modify the duty to perform. A condition is therefore the natural enemy of a promise. It is inserted for the protection and benefit of the promisor. The more conditions to which a promise is subject, the less content the promise has. A promise to pay $8,000 provided that such sum is realized from the sale of an automobile, provided the automobile is sold within sixty days, and provided that the automobile which has been stolen can be found, is clearly different from and worth considerably less than an unconditional promise by the same promisor to pay $8,000.

A fundamental distinction exists between the breach or non-performance of a promise and the failure or non-happening of a condition. A breach of contract subjects the promisor to liability. It may or may not, depending upon its materiality, excuse non-performance by the other party, the promisee, of his duty under the contract. The happening or non-happening of a condition, on the other hand, either prevents the promisee from acquiring a right or deprives him of a right, but subjects neither party to any liability.

Conditions may be either (1) express, (2) implied-in-fact, or (3) implied-in-law. They are also classified as (4) conditions concurrent, (5) conditions precedent, and (6) conditions subsequent.

These conditions do not relate to the formation or existence of the contract, but are either a part of the contract as entered into between the parties or arise by reason of events occurring subsequent to its formation. Consequently, none of the essentials to the existence of a contract, discussed in earlier chapters, are treated as conditions.

Express Conditions

A condition is express when it is set forth in language usually preceded by such words as "provided that," "on condition that," "while," "after," "upon," or "as soon as." While no particular form of words is necessary to create an express condition, the operative event to which the performance of the promise is made subject is in some manner clearly expressed. An illustration is the provision frequently found in building contracts to the effect that before the owner is required to pay, the builder shall furnish a certificate of the architect that the building has been constructed according to the plans and specifications. The price is being paid for the building, not for the certificate, yet before the owner is obliged to pay, he must have both the building and the certificate, as the duty of payment was made expressly conditional upon the presentation of the certificate. This condition is excused if the architect dies, or becomes insane, or capriciously refuses to give a certificate, or if there is collusion between the owner and the architect.

The parties to a contract may also agree that performance by one of them shall be to the satisfaction of the other who shall not be obligated to pay for it unless he is satisfied. This is an express condition to the duty to pay for the performance. It is a valid condition. Assume that tailor A contracts to make a suit of clothes to B's satisfaction, and that B promises to pay A $250 for the suit if she is satisfied with it when completed. A completes the suit using materials ordered by B. The suit fits B beautifully, but B tells A that she is not satisfied with it and refuses to accept or pay for it. A is not entitled to recover $250 or any amount from B by reason of the non-happening of the express condition. This is so even if the dissatisfaction of B, although honest and sincere, is unreasonable. Where satisfaction relates to a matter of personal taste, opinion, or judgment, the law applies the *subjective* standard, and the condition has not occurred if the promisor is actually dissatisfied. The condition relates to the individual satisfaction of B and no one else, including a reasonable person. However, if the contract does not clearly indicate that satisfaction is subjective, or if the performance contracted for relates to mechanical fitness or utility, the condition of satisfaction would be regarded as applying an *objective* standard. For example, the sale of a building or goods would apply the objective standard of satisfaction; it would be assumed that the satisfaction standard applies to the marketability, utility, or mechanical fitness of the item being sold. In such cases, the question would not be whether the promisor was actually satisfied with the performance tendered to him by the other party, but whether as a reasonable man, he ought to be satisfied.

Implied-in-Fact Conditions

Such conditions are similar to express conditions, in that they are understood by the parties to be part of the agreement, although not found in express language. They are necessarily inferred from the promise contained in the contract. Thus, if A for $750 contracts to paint B's house any color desired by B, it is necessarily implied in fact that B will inform A of the desired color before A begins to paint. The notification of choice of color is an implied-in-fact condition, an operative event which must occur before A is subject to the duty of painting the house.

Implied-in-Law Conditions

A condition implied-in-law differs from an express condition and a condition implied-in-fact in that it is not contained in the language of the contract or necessarily implied from the contract, but is imposed by law in order to accomplish a just and fair result. For example, if A contracts to sell a certain tract of land to B for $18,000 and the contract is silent as to the time of delivery of the deed and payment of the price, the law will imply that the respective performances are not independent of one another. The law will treat the promises as mutually dependent, and, therefore, that a delivery or tender of the deed by A to B is a condition to the duty of B to pay the price, and, conversely, payment or tender of $18,000 by B to A is a condition to the duty of A to deliver the deed to B. If the contract specified a sale on credit and A

gave B thirty days after delivery within which to pay the price, these conditions would not be implied as the parties by their contract have made their respective duties of performance independent of each other.

Concurrent Conditions

Where the proposed reciprocal and agreed performances of two mutual promisors are to take place at the same time, such performances are concurrent conditions. As previously indicated, in the absence of agreement to the contrary, the law assumes that the respective performances under a contract are concurrent conditions. Thus, if A has contracted to sell B a watch for $100, with delivery and payment to take place concurrently, neither party may maintain an action against the other without first performing or tendering performance. The party who is suing must have first placed the other party in default. *See Monroe Street Properties, Inc. v. Carpenter.*

Conditions Precedent

A condition precedent is an operative event the happening of which must precede the creation of a duty of performance under a contract. Where the immediate duty of one party to perform is subject to the condition that some event must first occur, such event is a condition precedent. For instance, if A is to deliver shoes to B on June 1, with A's duty to pay for the shoes on July 15, A's delivery of the shoes is a condition precedent to B's performance. Similarly, if A promises to buy B's land for $50,000, provided A can obtain financing in the amount of $40,000 at 13 percent or less for thirty years within sixty days of signing the contract, A's obtaining the specified financing is a condition precedent to A's duty. If the condition is met, A is bound to perform; if it does not occur, A is not bound to perform. A, however, is under an implied-in-law duty to use her best efforts to obtain financing under these terms.

Conditions Subsequent

A condition subsequent is an operative event which terminates an existing duty. Where goods are sold under terms of "sale or return," the buyer has the right to return the goods to the seller within a stated period, but is under an immediate duty to pay the price unless credit has been agreed upon. The duty to pay the price is terminated by a return of the goods which operates as a condition subsequent.

DISCHARGE BY PERFORMANCE

Undoubtedly, this is the most frequent method of discharging a contractual duty. If a promisor exactly performs his duty under the contract he is no longer subject to that duty. Less than exact performance, but substantial performance, does not fully discharge a promisor, although under the common law, substantial performance by one party deprives the other party of an excuse for non-performance of her promise.

Tender is attempted performance. It is an offer by one party, having the present ability to perform, to the other party, to perform his obligation according to the terms of the contract. Where the contract is bilateral, a tendered or offered performance by one party to the other which is refused or rejected may be treated as a repudiation which excuses or discharges the tendering party from further duty of performance under the contract. A valid tender of payment is an unconditional offer by a debtor to pay to his creditor the exact amount of the debt in money which is legal tender, at the proper time and place. However, a tender of payment of a debt past due does not discharge the debt if the creditor refuses to accept the tender. The effect of such refusal is to stop further accrual of interest on the debt and to deprive the creditor of court costs in a subsequent suit by him to recover the amount due. The debtor, to be free from further interest, damages, or costs, must keep his tender good. This simply means

that he must remain ready, able and willing to pay upon reasonable demand by the creditor.

Payment by a debtor to his creditor is performance or part performance, as the case may be, of the debtor's obligation. If a debtor owes money on several accounts and tenders to his creditor less than the total amounts due, the debtor has the right to designate the account or debt to which the payment is to be applied. This direction by the debtor must be accepted by the creditor. If the debtor does not direct the application of the payment, the creditor may apply it to any account owing to him by the debtor or distribute it among several such accounts. Once the debtor has made payment without specifying its application, he may not subsequently direct its application. The payment was unconditionally made by him and may not thereafter become conditional. The application of payment may be a matter of importance, as where one of several debts is secured and others not, or where one is barred by the Statute of Limitations and the others are not barred.

DISCHARGE BY BREACH

Breach of contract is the failure of a party to perform his promise.

Breach by One Party as a Discharge of the Other

Breach of contract always gives rise to a cause of action for damages by the aggrieved (injured) party. It may, however, have a more important effect. Because of the rule that one party need not perform unless the other party performs, an uncured (uncorrected) material breach by one party operates as an excuse for non-performance by the other party and discharges the aggrieved party from any further duty under the contract. If the breach, on the other hand, is nonmaterial, the aggrieved party is not discharged from the contract although she may recover money damages.

goes to heart or ...

Material Breach An unjustified failure to perform *substantially* the obligations promised in a contract constitutes a material breach. The key is whether the aggrieved party obtained substantially what he bargained for. A material breach discharges the aggrieved party from his duty of performance. For instance, A orders a specially made, tailored suit from B to be made of wool, but B instead makes the suit of cotton. B has materially breached the contract. Consequently, A is discharged from his duty to pay for the suit. A may also collect money damages from B due to B's breach.

Although there are no clear-cut rules as to what constitutes a material breach, several basic principles are applicable. First, partial performance materially breaches a contract if it omits some essential part of the contract. Second, a breach will be considered material if it is quantitatively serious. Third, an *intentional* breach of contract is generally held to be material. Fourth, a failure to perform promptly a promise is a material breach if time is of the essence, i.e., if the parties have clearly indicated that a failure to perform by the stated time is material. Otherwise, the aggrieved party may only recover damages for loss caused by the delay. Finally, the parties to a contract may, within limits, specify what breaches are to be considered material.

A contract may expressly provide that one party is to perform to the **satisfaction** of the other. The question presented by this provision in a contract is whether, upon performance, the other party can arbitrarily take the position that he is not satisfied, and so refuse to pay or perform on his part. The rule is substantially this: If performance on the other's satisfaction involves personal taste, fancy, or judgment, as in a contract to make a suit or a dress, to paint a portrait, or to write a book or article, the other party is the sole judge as to whether he is satisfied or not. The first party cannot complain, since he expressly undertook to perform to the other's satisfaction. If, however, performance involves only mechanical operation, fitness, or utility, as in the installation of a heating system, the other party is not the judge as to whether performance is satisfactory, but can require only such performance as would satisfy a reasonable man. In other words, the question is one for the jury.

The Code greatly alters the common law doctrine of material breach by adopting what is known as the **perfect tender rule**. This rule, which is discussed more fully in Chapter 22, essentially provides that *any* deviation from the promised performance in a sales contract under the Code constitutes a material breach of the contract and discharges the aggrieved party of his duty of performance. Thus, if a seller of camera accessories delivers to buyer ninety-nine of the hundred ordered pieces, or ninety-nine correct accessories and one incorrect accessory, the buyer can rightfully reject the improper delivery.

Substantial Performance If a party substantially, but not completely, performs her obligations under a contract, the law will generally allow that party to obtain the other party's performance less any damages caused by the partial performance. Thus, in the specially ordered suit illustration, if B, the tailor, improperly used black buttons instead of blue, B would, nevertheless, be permitted to collect from A the contract price of the suit less the damage caused to A by the substitution of the wrongly colored buttons. The doctrine of substantial performance assumes particular importance in the construction industry where the structure is being built on the aggrieved party's land. Consider the following: A builds a $300,000 house for B but deviates from the specifications, causing B $10,000 worth of damages. If this breach were considered material, then B need not pay for the house which is now on her land. However, this breach would probably not be deemed material, and A's performance would be substantial. As a result, A would be able to collect $290,000 from B.

Prevention of Performance

Material breach

If one party to a contract substantially interferes with or prevents performance by the other, such action generally constitutes a material breach which discharges the other party to the contract. For instance, A prevents an architect from giving a certificate which is a condition to A's liability to pay B a certain sum of money. A may not set up B's failure to produce a certificate as an excuse for A's nonpayment. Likewise, if A has contracted to grow a certain crop for B, and after A has planted the seed, B plows the field and destroys the seedling plants, his interference with A's performance discharges A from his duty under the contract. It does not, however, discharge B from his duty under the contract.

Anticipatory Repudiation

A party to a contract, prior to the time fixed for his performance, may notify the other party that he will not perform his contract. That is, he repudiates the contract in advance. This is a form of breach. The party so notified has two alternatives. He may take the other party at his word, and consider the contract as broken. He may thereupon, and without waiting for the time set for the other's performance, bring suit and recover such damages as he can show he has suffered by reason of the other's anticipatory breach. *See Hochster v. De La Tour.* His other alternative is to ignore the repudiation of the contract and to regard it as still in force. If, then, the other party fails to perform at the stipulated time, he, the injured party, has his right of action for damages. However, if he elects to keep the contract open he does so for the benefit of the other party as well as his own. Thus, if the party giving notice of repudiation is a seller, and the buyer elects to keep the contract open, and on the date of delivery of the goods the market price is lower than the contract price, the buyer must accept delivery

tendered by the seller and pay him the contract price.

Section 2–610 of the Uniform Commercial Code provides that an anticipatory repudiation of a contract for the sale of goods entitles the aggrieved party to suspend performance on her part and either (1) to await performance for a commercially reasonable time, or (2) to resort to any remedy for breach of contract.

Material Alteration of Written Contract

To operate as a discharge, the alteration must have been made by a party to the contract, intentionally, without the consent of the other party, and must be material, that is, of such a nature as to change the legal effect of the contract. An unauthorized alteration or change of *any* of the material terms or provisions of a written contract or document is a discharge of the *entire* contract.

A material alteration is defined in Section 286 of the Restatement, as follows:

By one of the parties

(1) If one to whom a duty is owed under a contract alters a writing that is an integrated agreement or that satisfies the Statute of Frauds with respect to that contract, the duty is discharged if the alteration is fraudulent and material.

(2) An alteration is material if it would, if effective, vary any party's legal relations with the maker of the alteration or adversely affect that party's legal relations with a third person. The unauthorized insertion in a blank space in a writing is an alteration.

An unauthorized change in the terms of a written contract by one who is not a party to the contract does not discharge the contract.

Most cases of alteration arise in connection with negotiable instruments, such as checks and notes. Suppose that M borrows $1000 from P and gives P his negotiable promisory note for that amount. P skillfully changes the amount of the note to $10,000. The change in the amount of the note was a material alteration and M is discharged of *all* liability to P.

DISCHARGE BY AGREEMENT OF THE PARTIES

Mutual Rescission

A rescission is an agreement between the parties to a contract to terminate their respective duties under the contract. It is a contract to end a contract. All of the essentials of a contract must be present.

Discharge by mutual agreement may take several forms. Where the contract is wholly executory, and the parties mutually agree that it shall no longer be binding on them, it is thereby discharged. Each party has surrendered his rights under the contract, and so furnished the necessary consideration for the other's agreement to rescind the contract. See *Watts Construction Co. v. Cullman County.* If one party has partly performed, a mere agreement to terminate the contract is insufficient to discharge it, because of lack of consideration. For example, A and B make a contract for A to repair B's car for $1,000, of which sum B pays A $100. The service is to be performed in a week. On the following day, A tells B that he wishes to take the week off and offers to return the $100 payment to B if B will agree to cancel the contract. B so agrees, and receives the $100 from A. Because of B's part performance of the contract, a mutual agreement, alone, to cancel the contract would be ineffective. It is only because of A's actual return of the $100 to B that their agreement operates to discharge the contract. An oral agreement of mutual rescission is valid and will discharge a written contract unless the contract to rescind involves the retransfer of a subject matter which is within the Statute of Frauds, or unless under the U.C.C. the written contract provides that it cannot be modified or rescinded except by a signed writ-

ing. Section 2-209(2). The Restatement, however, explicitly rejects this rule and provides that a prior written provision that a contract can only be rescinded or modified in writing does not impair the effectiveness of an oral modification or rescission. Section 283, Comment b.

A contract containing a provision which is contrary to or inconsistent with a provision in a prior contract between the same parties is a mutual rescission of the inconsistent provision in the prior contract. Whether the later contract completely supersedes and discharges all of the provisions of the prior contract is a matter of interpretation.

Substituted Contracts

A substituted contract occurs when the parties to a contract mutually agree to rescind their original contract and enter into a new one. Restatement, Section 279. Substituted contracts are perfectly valid and effective to discharge the original contract and to impose obligations under the new contract. For example, the Restatement, Section 279, gives the following illustration:

A and B make a contract under which A promises to build on a designated spot a building, for which B promises to pay $100,000. Later, before this contract is performed, A and B make a new contract under which A is to build on the same spot a different building, for which B is to pay $200,000. The new contract is a substituted contract and the duties of A and B under the original contract are discharged.

Accord and Satisfaction

An *accord* is a contract between a promisee and his promisor by which the former agrees to accept and the latter agrees to render a substituted performance in *satisfaction* of an existing contractual duty. Restatement, Section 281. Thus, if B owes A $500 and the parties agree that B shall paint A's house in satisfaction of the debt, the agreement is an executory accord. The debt, however, is not discharged until B performs the accord by painting A's house; the $500 debt is then discharged by accord and satisfaction.

Novation

A novation is a substituted contract which involves *three* parties and an agreement among to substitute a new promisee in place of an existing promisee, or to replace an existing promisor with a new one. Restatement, Section 280. The effect is to discharge the old obligation by the creation of a new contract in which there is either a new promisee or a new promisor. Thus, if B owes A $500 and A, B, and C agree that C will pay the debt and B will be discharged, the novation is the substitution of the new debtor C for B. Alternatively, if the three parties agree that B will pay $500 to D instead of to A, the novation is the substitution of a new creditor D for A. In each instance the debt owed by B to A is discharged.

Release and Covenant Not to Sue

A release is technically a discharge under seal of an existing obligation. The term is also applied to any formal writing supported by sufficient consideration which recites a present relinquishment and termination of the rights described in the agreement. A covenant or promise not to sue does not effect a discharge of the obligation, as does a release. It may, however, be raised as a bar to any suit brought in violation of the covenant and to this extent has the effect of a release. Covenants not to sue are usually employed where an obligee of joint obligors makes a settlement with one of them and wishes to preserve his rights against the others. A release of one joint obligor releases all of them. A covenant not to sue one or more but less than all obligors does not release the remaining ones.

Renunciation

A duty to pay damages for breach of a bilateral contract which is unperformed on both sides may be discharged by a manifestation by the promisee to treat his excuse for non-performance as a termination of the contract. Thus, if A contracts to employ B to work for one year at an agreed salary commencing July 1, and B on June 25 repudiates the contract by informing A that he will not work for him, A has an excuse for non-performance and may promptly fill the job by employing C. If this is all that happens, B would remain liable to A for breach of contract. However, if when B repudiates, A tells B that he is satisfied and will regard the contract as terminated, both B and A are discharged by this act of mutual renunciation.

DISCHARGE BY OPERATION OF LAW

Subsequent Illegality

Performance of a contract which was legal when formed may become illegal or impractical by reason of a subsequently enacted law. In such case the duty of performance is discharged. Restatement, Section 264. For example, A contracts to sell and deliver to B ten cases of a certain whiskey each month for one year. A subsequent prohibition law makes unlawful the manufacture, transportation, or sale of intoxicating liquor. The contract, to the extent unperformed by A, is discharged.

War is another illustration of supervening illegality. A pre-existing contract between a citizen and an alien may be discharged by the outbreak of war between the countries of the respective parties. This is true, at least, if the performance of the contract will involve communication with the alien enemy in enemy territory, or if performance will aid the enemy or lessen the power of this country to carry on the war. If one of the parties performed before the outbreak of war, it will depend on the nature of the contract whether his rights will be preserved and become enforceable after the close of the war.

Impossibility *Objective*

It may be impossible for a promisor to perform his contract because he is financially unable or because he personally lacks the capability or competence. This is **subjective** impossibility and does not excuse the promisor from liability for breach of contract. On the other hand, performance may be impossible not because the particular promisor is unable to perform, but because no one is able to perform. This is **objective** impossibility which in a great number of situations will be held to excuse the promisor or discharge his duty to perform.

The **death** or **incapacity** of a person who has contracted to render personal services is a discharge of his contractual duty. If a jockey contracts to ride a certain horse in the Kentucky Derby and the horse dies prior to the Derby, the contract is discharged. It is objectively impossible for this or any other jockey to perform this contract. Also, a singer, unable to perform her contractual engagement because of a severe cold, is excused from performance, as is a pianist or violinist who is unable to perform because of an injury to his hand.

Destruction of the **subject matter** or of the agreed upon means of performance of a contract is also excusable impossibility. Subject matter here means specific subject matter. Suppose that A contracts to sell to B five office chairs at an agreed price. A has 100 of these chairs in stock, out of which he expects to deliver five to B. Before he can do so, the entire 100 chairs are destroyed by fire without A's fault. A is not excused from performance. This was not a contract for the sale of specific goods. A can perform this contract by delivering to B any five chairs of the kind and grade specified in the contract. His failure to do so will render him liable to B for breach of contract. Suppose now that A and B make a contract for A to manufacture these five chairs in his factory but prior to their manufacture the factory is destroyed by fire without A's fault. Although, the chairs are available from other manufacturers, A's duty to deliver the chairs is discharged by the destruction of the factory. Suppose further that A and B enter into a contract for the sale by A to B of the particular desk which A uses in his private office. This desk and no other is the specific subject matter of the contract. If, before the sale is completed, this desk is destroyed by fire without A's fault, it is then impossible for A to perform. The contract is therefore discharged.

Where the purpose of a contract has been frustrated by fortuitous circumstances which deprives the performance of the value attached to it by the parties, although performance is not impossible, the courts generally regard the frustration as a discharge. This rule developed from the so-called "coronation cases." When Edward VII became King of England upon the death of his mother Queen Victoria, impressive coronation ceremonies were planned including a procession along a designated route through certain streets in London. Contracts were made by owners and lessees of buildings along the route to permit the use of rooms with a view on the date scheduled for the procession. The King became ill, and the procession did not take place. The purpose for using the rooms having failed, the rooms were not used. Numerous suits were filed, some by landowners seeking to hold the would-be viewers liable on their promises, and some by the would-be viewers seeking to recover back money paid in advance for the rooms. The principle involved was novel, but from these cases evolved the **frustration of purpose** doctrine under which a contract is discharged if supervening circumstances make fulfillment of the purpose which both parties had in mind impossible, unless one of the parties contractually assumed that risk.

The Restatement, Section 261, and the Code, Section 2-615, views of impossibility conform to this position and provide that performance need not be actually or literally impossible, but that **commercial impracticability** will excuse non-performance. This does not mean mere hardship or that the cost of performance would be more than expected. In order for a party to be discharged from performing his duty such performance must be rendered impracticable as a result of a supervening event. Moreover, the nonoccurrence of the subsequent event must have been a "basic assumption" upon which both parties made when entering into the contract. See *Kennedy v. Reece* and *Northern Corp. v. Chugach Electrical Association.*

Bankruptcy

Bankruptcy is a method of discharge of a contractual duty by operation of law available to a debtor who, by compliance with the requirements of the Bankruptcy Act, obtains an order of discharge by the bankruptcy court. It is applicable only to obligations which the Statute provides are dischargeable in bankruptcy. The subject of bankruptcy is treated in Chapter 39.

Statute of Limitations

Every state has in force a statute of limitations. The purpose of these statutes is to fix or limit the time in which actions of various kinds may be brought. Their effect is to bar the remedy if the action is not commenced within the prescribed time. The period of limitation varies as to different actions in each State, and these periods differ in different States. The statute begins to run from the time of the breach of contract, at which time a right of action vests in the creditor or injured party. It should be emphasized that a

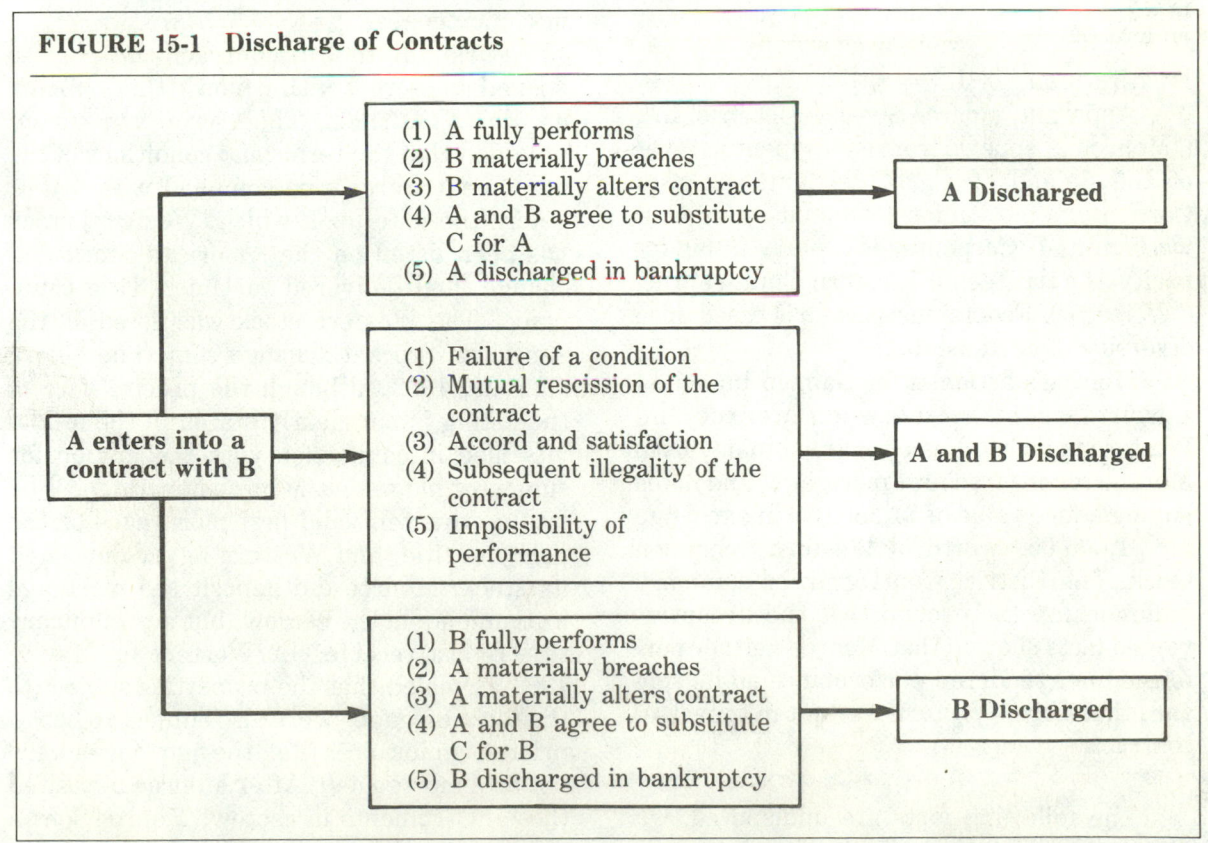

FIGURE 15-1   Discharge of Contracts

A enters into a contract with B

(1) A fully performs
(2) B materially breaches
(3) B materially alters contract
(4) A and B agree to substitute C for A
(5) A discharged in bankruptcy
→ **A Discharged**

(1) Failure of a condition
(2) Mutual rescission of the contract
(3) Accord and satisfaction
(4) Subsequent illegality of the contract
(5) Impossibility of performance
→ **A and B Discharged**

(1) B fully performs
(2) A materially breaches
(3) A materially alters contract
(4) A and B agree to substitute C for B
(5) B discharged in bankruptcy
→ **B Discharged**

statute of limitations does not operate to discharge the debt or other obligation, but only to bar the creditor's action. One result of this is that if, in an action by a creditor, the defendant does not specially plead the statute as a defense, he is held to have waived it.

Merger

A contract is said to be merged, and thereby discharged, when its terms are embodied by the parties in another contract of a higher legal standing or order. Merger is said to take place by the acceptance of a higher security in the place of a lower one. In States where the common-law effect of a seal is still recognized, a merger takes place when the terms of an oral contract or an unsealed written contract are embodied by the parties in a contract under seal. The "lower" contract is thus discharged. Where a creditor accepts a note executed by his debtor as unconditional payment of the debt, the debt is merged into the note and is thereby discharged. The debtor is now liable on the note only. For a summary of discharge of contracts, see Figure 15-1.

CASES

Concurrent Conditions

MONROE STREET PROPERTIES, INC. v. CARPENTER

United States Court of Appeals, Ninth Circuit, 1969.
407 F.2d 379.

HUFSTEDLER, C. J.

Appellant, Monroe Street Properties, Inc. ("Monroe"), appeals from a judgment in favor of the defendant Carpenter entered after Carpenter's motion for a summary judgment was granted. Carpenter is a party in his capacity as a trustee for Western Equities, Inc. ("Western"). Federal jurisdiction is based upon diversity of citizenship.

Monroe's action is for claimed breach of a written contract between Monroe and Western in which Western agreed to buy from Monroe ten insured first mortgages and notes having a face value of $1,250,000 in exchange for $1,000,000 worth of Western's common stock. The District Court granted summary judgment on the ground that the uncontroverted facts showed that Monroe neither performed nor tendered performance on its side and, therefore, Western was not in breach of contract.

*   *   *

The following facts are undisputed. On March 27, 1962, Western submitted its written offer to Monroe to buy the ten first mortgages and notes. Monroe promptly accepted the offer. Western's offer was expressly subject to "verification by Union Title Company that the ten first mortgages * * * are valid first mortgages." * * *

Pursuant to the contract the parties opened an escrow with Union Title Company on March 30, 1962. The escrow agreement provided that the terms and conditions of the agreement were to be complied with "on or before the date upon which [Western] stock has been listed on the American Stock Exchange, and delivered to Union Title Company." The Western stock was listed on the American Stock Exchange sometime before June 29, 1962, although the precise date of the listing is not clearly stated in the affidavits filed in connection with the motion for summary judgment. Monroe never deposited into escrow ten valid first mortgages or the policy of title, and Western never deposited its stock. Monroe did deposit the mortgage instruments in the escrow, but a preliminary title report received by Western on May 7, 1962, revealed that the properties subject to the ten mortgages were also subject to heavy prior encumbrances [i.e., the mortgages were not first mortgages]. After Monroe deposited those instruments in escrow, Monroe sent a demand to Western to deposit the stock.

Western did not comply with the demand. Nothing further was done by either of the parties to perform the agreement and Monroe brought this action in October 1966.

* * *

The District Court correctly decided that Monroe never made an adequate tender of its own performance. Monroe's duty to deposit the insured first mortgages and Western's duty to deposit its stock were concurrent conditions. [Citations.] Neither party could place the other in breach for failure to perform without a tender of its own performance. "Tender" as used in this connection means " 'a readiness and willingness to perform in case of the *concurrent* performance by the other party, with present ability to do so, and notice to the other party of such readiness.' " [Citation.] Monroe's offer to perform its concurrent condition upon condition that Western perform first was not an adequate tender and could not be relied upon by Monroe to place Western in breach of contract.

The judgment is affirmed.

Anticipatory Breach

HOCHSTER v. DE LA TOUR

2 Ellis and Blackburn Reports 678 (Q.B. 1853) (England).

LORD CAMPBELL, C. J.

[On April 12, 1852, Hochster contracted with De La Tour to serve as a guide for De La Tour on his three-month trip to Europe, beginning on June 1 at an agreed upon salary. On May 11, De La Tour notified Hochster that he would not need Hochster's services. He also refused to pay Hochster any compensation. Hochster brings this action to recover damages for breach of contract.]

On this motion * * * the question arises, Whether, if there be an agreement between A. and B., whereby B. engages to employ A. on and from a future day for a given period of time, to travel with him into a foreign country as a [guide], and to start with him in that capacity on that day, A. being

to receive a monthly salary during the continuance of such service, B. may, before the day, refuse to perform the agreement and break and renounce it, so as to entitle A. before the day to commence an action against B. to recover damages for breach of the agreement; A. having been ready and willing to perform it, till it was broken and renounced by B.

* * *

If the plaintiff has no remedy for breach of the contract unless he treats the contract as in force, and acts upon it down to the 1st June, 1852, it follows that, till then, he must enter into no employment which will interfere with his promise "to start with the defendant on such travels on the day and year" and that he must then be properly equipped in all respects as a [guide] for a three months' tour on the continent of Europe. But it is surely much more rational, and more for the benefit of both parties, that, after the renunciation of the agreement by the defendant, the plaintiff should be at liberty to consider himself absolved from any future performance of it, retaining his right to sue for any damage he has suffered from the breach of it. Thus, instead of remaining idle and laying out money in preparations which must be useless, he is at liberty to seek service under another employer, which would go in mitigation of the damages to which he would otherwise be entitled for a breach of the contract. It seems strange that the defendant after renouncing the contract, and absolutely declaring that he will never act under it, should be permitted to object that faith is given to his assertion, and that an opportunity is not left to him of changing his mind. * * *

* * * The man who wrongfully renounces a contract into which he has deliberately entered cannot justly complain if he is immediately sued for a compensation in damage by the man whom he has injured: and it seems reasonable to allow an option to the injured party, either to sue immediately, or to wait till the time when the act was to be done, still holding it as prospectively binding for the exercise of this option, which may be

advantageous to the innocent party, and cannot be prejudicial to the wrongdoer.

Judgment for plaintiff.

Mutual Rescission

WATTS CONSTRUCTION CO. v. CULLMAN COUNTY

Supreme Court of Alabama, 1980.
382 So.2d 520.

SHORES, J.

This is a contract case. Appellant Watts Construction Company submitted the low bid on a County Water Works Improvement Project and was awarded the contract in May of 1976. In July, Robert L. Harbison, chairman of the Cullman County Commission, executed a construction contract for the project, separate copies of which had earlier been executed by Watts. Item V, Section II, of the contract provides that "[t]his contract shall not be effective unless and until approved by the State Director of the Farmers Home Administration, U.S. Department of Agriculture or his delegated representative." FHA approval for the project was not obtained. However, when a portion of the project which was being funded by the city, rather than the county, was deleted during the summer, the change order was signed by a representative of the State Director of the FHA.

Construction on the project was delayed until the fall, allegedly due to the lowering of the county's debt limit. In September, construction still had not been authorized, and Watts requested a 5 percent increase in the contract price due to seasonal and inflational price increases. The county countered with an offer of 3.5 percent. By a letter dated September 21, 1976 * * *, Watts notified the commission that he could not accept less than a 5 percent increase, and concluded: "If this is not agreeable with you, please consider this letter a withdrawal of our bid." This letter was discussed at a meeting of the county commission on September 24, 1976, where it was agreed that the county could not pay a 5 percent increase. Negotiations were begun with the next lowest bidder to take the project on at the low bid price. On October 4, 1976, the commission re-awarded the contract to Tucker Brothers Construction Company at the low bid made by Watts. Watts alleges that the award to Tucker Brothers included project specification changes which reduced the cost of the project and which were not offered to Watts. He was notified by letter dated October 14, 1976, that his withdrawal of the bid had been accepted by the commission. On October 19, 1976, Watts informed the commission that he was willing to perform the contract at bid price with certain modifications in specifications. His offer was not accepted.

Watts then brought this action to recover damages for breach of contract, * * *. The trial court granted the county's motion for summary judgment, and this appeal followed. For the reasons discussed herein, we affirm.

* * *

We find it unnecessary to discuss the issue of whether FHA approval was a condition precedent to creation of a valid contract. Watt's letter of September 21 withdrawing his bid and the commission's letter of October 14 accepting that withdrawal effectively rescinded any contract that might have existed. Parties to a written contract may by mutual consent and without other consideration rescind the contract. [Citation.] Where the acts and conduct of one party inconsistent with the existence of a contract are acquiesced in by the other, such contract will be treated as abandoned or rescinded. [Citation.] Watt's demand for an increase in the contract price demonstrated his intention not to be bound by the original contract. The commission acquiesced in his desire not to be so bound, and the contract was rescinded. Once a party to a contract has repudiated or broken it, he cannot reinstate the contract by an offer to perform. [Citation.] Where the parties have by mutual agreement rescinded a contract, one of the parties thereto cannot recover damages in an action for breach of contract. [Citation.] Where parties agree to rescind the contract, each gives up the provisions for its benefit, and the parties are then competent to contract with others. [Citation.]

* * *

The judgment appealed from is affirmed.

Impossibility

KENNEDY v. REECE

California Court of Appeal, 1964.
225 Cal.App.2d 717, 37 Cal.Rpt. 708.

CONLEY, J.

This is an appeal by the plaintiff from a judgment adverse to him on his complaint and favorable to the defendants on their counterclaim. The plaintiff, Fred Kennedy, made a contract with Reece and Thomas, mining partners, to drill a water well for them; the agreement, on the letterhead of the Fred Kennedy Company, reads as follows:

We propose to furnish all materials and perform all labor necessary to complete the following:

drill 12" hole to estimated depth of 400'

3.50 per ft

case with new 6" well casing with bottom half perforated gravel pack, wash well and bail.

1.50 per ft

All of the above work to be completed in a substantial and workmanlike manner according to standard practices for the sum of two thousand Dollars ($2,000.00)

Payments to be made $1,000.00 on signing this agreement bal when cased $ _____ as the work progresses to the value of _____ per cent (_____%) of all work completed. The entire amount of contract to be paid within _____ days after completion.

Any alteration or deviation from the above specifications involving extra cost of materials or labor will only be executed upon written orders for same, and will become an extra charge over the sum mentioned in this contract. All agreements must be made in writing.

Respectfully submitted,

FRED KENNEDY CO.
Drilling and Sewer Contractors

By: /s/Fred Kennedy _____

An acceptance is endorsed by Louis H. Reece and Steven Thomas.

The complaint alleges with respect to the contract:

That on or about the 31st day of March, 1961, plaintiff and defendants entered into a written contract wherein plaintiff agreed to drill for defendants certain water well at an estimated cost of Two Thousand Dollars; that after commencing drilling operations it was determined that it was not possible to obtain water in the area selected by defendants, hence, by mutual agreements the parties discontinued drilling operations, at which time there was due to plaintiff the sum of Four Hundred Dollars, demand for which has been made and no part of which has been paid.

The answer and counterclaim avers, on the contrary, that the agreement was to drill a 12-inch hole for a water well to an estimated depth of 400 feet, case it with new 6-inch well casing with the bottom half perforated, and further to gravel pack, wash and bail the well for a fixed price of $2,000.00, payable $1,000.00 upon execution of the contract and the balance when the casing was installed; that the sum of $1,000.00 was paid upon the execution of the contract and that plaintiff "failed and refused to perform the contract and breached the same and after abandoning one hole at a depth of 130 feet, commenced a second hole, which he abandoned at 270 feet, and failed and refused and continues to fail and refuse to drill a hole to the depth of 400 feet and case the same." The pleading further alleges that the two holes in question were placed at points selected by the plaintiff as most likely to yield water; that plaintiff breached the contract by failing and refusing to complete the well* * *.

* * *

It is obvious that the finding that the plaintiff failed to comply with the terms of his contract is supported by substantial evidence; the well driller did not dig the well to a depth of 400 feet; he did not case it; he did not gravel pack, or wash, or bail it. Appellant contends, however, that he was relieved from the duty of completing his contract because of "impossibility" resulting when he hit hard rock at the 270 foot level.

The enlargement of the meaning of "impossibility" as a defense, (which at common law originally meant literal or physical impossibility of performance) to include "impracticability" is now generally recognized [Citation]. In the leading California case approving this expanded meaning, [Citation] the court accepted the defense of impracticability in an action which involved a contract to take all gravel necessary to effect the construction of a fill and complete the cement work on a proposed bridge when the evidence showed that the defendant used all gravel that was available except submerged gravel, the cost of the extraction of which would have been ten or twelve times the cost of removing the surface gravel. As is said in 6 Corbin on Contracts, Section 1325, page 338:

A performance may be so difficult and expensive that it is described as 'impracticable,' and enforcement may be denied on the ground of impossibility.

[Citations.] However, this does not mean that any facts, which make performance more difficult or expensive than the parties anticipated, discharge a duty that has been created by the contract (Rest., Contracts, § 467, pp. 882–884). Facts which make performance harder or more costly than the parties contemplated when the agreement was made do not constitute a ground for the successful interposition of the defense of "impracticability" unless such facts are of the gravest importance. If it be noted that this is merely a difference of degree rather than a difference in kind, such notation is accurate.

In Snow Mountain W. & P. Co. v. Kraner, * * * it is said:

Appellant was not absolved from his contract by the natural obstacles intervening, unless they rendered peformance practically impossible. Mere difficulty, or unusual or unexpected expense, would not excuse him.

Principles applicable to the present case are thus stated in [citation]:

The rule is that if performance of a contract is possible, it is none the less a breach although the obligor himself may have become wholly unable to perform. The impossibility must consist in the nature of the thing to be done, and not in the inability of the party to do it. If what is agreed to be done is possible and lawful, it must be done. Difficulty of accomplishing the undertaking will not avail the party who commits a breach of the contract. If a party expressly undertakes to do a thing, lawful in itself, and not necessarily impossible under all the circumstances, and does not do it, he must make compensation in damages, though the performance was rendered impracticable, or even impossible, by some unforeseen cause for which no provision is made and over which he had no control, but against which he might have provided in his contract. The rule has its foundation in common sense and honesty, and compels parties to abide by their contracts. Any other rule would leave all contracts in a sea of uncertainty, without rudder or compass.

That increased difficulties and heightened costs of a reasonable nature, even though originally unforeseen, do not render the performance of a contract "impracticable" is illustrated [in a number of] California cases: [Citations.] For example, if a contractor agrees to build a structure and it is destroyed by fire or other casualty when only partly completed, the contractor is not relieved from his duty to rebuild merely because of the additional expense he must incur or the added difficulties he must overcome. [Citations.]

In the present case, neither the pleadings nor the facts as found by the court warrant the application of the doctrine of impossibility, or impracticability. * * *

More important still, the findings do not establish, but actually negate, the necessary basis for a defense of impracticability. The plaintiff testified that it would be almost impossible and extremely expensive to drill through the rock formation at the 270-foot level, but the defendants' testimony indicated that the rock encountered by the drill was not so hard a formation as plaintiff claimed and inferentially that, with some increased difficulty, it could be pierced. The evidence also showed that two other drillers had expressed to defendants a willingness to complete the well to the 400-foot level and that a charge of $5.00 per foot besides the cost of moving the drilling equipment would be adequate. Every intendment is in favor of the judgment, and the court's findings on controverted issues, if supported as here, by substantial evidence must be accepted. It is clear, therefore, that the necessary factual basis for a successful plea of impracticability was not present.

Impossibility

NORTHERN CORP. v. CHUGACH ELECTRICAL ASSOCIATION

Supreme Court of Alaska, 1974.
518 P.2d 76.

BOOCHEVER, J.

[Northern Corporation entered into a contract with Chugach in August 1966 to repair and upgrade the upstream face of Cooper Lake Dam in Alaska. The contract required Northern to obtain rock from a quarry site at the opposite end of the lake and to transport the rock to the dam during the winter across the ice on the lake. In December 1966, Northern cleared the road on the ice to permit deeper freezing, but thereafter water overflowed on the ice preventing its use. Northern complained of unsafe conditions of the lake ice, but Chugach insisted on performance. In March 1967, one of Northern's loaded trucks broke through the ice and sank. Northern continued to encounter difficulties and ceased operations with the approval of Chugach. On January 8, 1968 Chugach notified Northern that it would be in default unless all rock was hauled by April 1. After two more trucks broke through the ice, causing the deaths of the drivers, Northern ceased operations and notified Chugach that it would make no more attempts to haul across the lake. Northern advised Chugach it considered the contract terminated for impossibility of performance

and commenced suit to recover the cost incurred in attempting to complete the contract.]

* * *

The focal question is whether the * * * contract was impossible of performance. The September 27, 1966 directive specified that the rock was to be transported "across Cooper Lake to the dam site when such lake is frozen to a sufficient depth to permit heavy vehicle traffic thereon," and * * * specified that the hauling to the dam site would be done during the winter of 1966–67. It is therefore clear that the parties contemplated that the rock would be transported across the frozen lake by truck. Northern's repeated efforts to perform the contract by this method during the winter of 1966–67 and subsequently in February 1968, culminating in the tragic loss of life, abundantly support the trial court's findings that the contract was impossible of performance by this method.

Chugach contends, however, that Northern was nevertheless bound to perform, and that it could have used means other than hauling by truck across the ice to transport the rock. The answer to Chugach's contention is that * * * the parties contemplated that the rock would be hauled by truck once the ice froze to a sufficient depth to support the weight of the vehicles. The specification of this particular method of performance presupposed the existence of ice frozen to the requisite depth. Since this expectation of the parties was never fulfilled, and since the provisions relating to the means of performance was clearly material, Northern's duty to perform was discharged by reason of impossibility.

There is an additional reason for our holding that Northern's duty to perform was discharged because of impossibility. It is true that in order for a defendant to prevail under the original common law doctrine of impossibility, he had to show that no one else could have performed the contract. However, this harsh rule has gradually been eroded, and the Restatement of Contracts has departed from the early common law rule by recognizing the principle of "commercial impracticability". Under this doctrine, a party is discharged from his contract obligations, even if it is technically possible to perform them, if the costs of performance would be so disproportionate to that reasonably contemplated by the parties as to make the contract totally impractical in a commercial sense. * * * Removed from the strictures of the common law, "impossibility" in its modern context has become a coat of many colors, including among its hues the point argued here—namely, impossibility predicated upon "commercial impracticability." This concept—which finds expression both in case law * * * and in other authorities * * * is grounded upon the assumption that in legal contemplation something is impracticable when it can only be done at an excessive and unreasonable cost. As stated in *Transatlantic Financing Corp. v. United States* [Citation]

* * * The doctrine ultimately represents the ever-shifting line, drawn by courts hopefully responsive to commercial practices and mores, at which the community's interest in having contracts enforced according to their terms is outweighed by the commercial senselessness of requiring performance * * *

* * *

In the case before us the detailed opinion of the trial court clearly indicates that the appropriate standard was followed. There is ample evidence to support its findings that "[t]he ice haul method of transporting riprap ultimately selected was within the comtemplation of the parties and was part of the basis of the agreement which ultimately resulted in amendment No. 1 in October 1966," and that that method was not commercially feasible within the financial parameters of the contract. We affirm the court's conclusion that the contract was impossible of performance.

* * *

PROBLEMS

1. A-1 Roofing Co. entered into a written contract with Jaffe to put a new roof on the latter's residence for $900 with a specified type of roofing, and to complete the job without unreasonable delay. A-1 undertook the work within a week thereafter, and when all the roofing material was at the site and the labor 50 percent completed, the premises were totally destroyed by fire caused by lighting. A-1 submitted a bill to Jaffe for $600 for materials furnished and labor performed up to the time of the destruction of the premises. Jaffe refused to pay the bill, and A-1 sued Jaffe. Decision?

2. By contract dated January 5, 1985, A agreed to sell to B and B agreed to buy from A a certain parcel of land then zoned commercial. The specific intent of B, which was known to A, was to erect a storage plant on the land. The contract stated that the agreement was conditioned upon B's ability to construct a storage plant upon the land. The closing date for the transaction was set for April 1, 1985. On February 15, 1985, the city council

rezoned the land from commercial to residential, which precluded the erection of the storage plant intended by B. As the closing date drew near, B made it known to A that she did not intend to go through with the purchase because the land could no longer be used as intended. On April 1, A tendered the deed to B, who refused to pay A the agreed purchase price. A brought an action against B for breach of their contract. Decision?

3. The Perfection Produce Company entered into a written contract with Hiram Hodges for the purchase of 200 tons of potatoes to be grown on Hodge's farm in Maine at a stipulated price per ton. The land would ordinarily produce 1,000 tons. Although the planting and cultivation were properly done, Hodges was able to deliver only 100 tons because of a partial crop failure owing to an unprecedented drought. Hodges sued the produce company to recover an unpaid balance of the agreed price for 100 tons of potatoes. The produce company, by an appropriate counterclaim against

Hodges, sought damages for his failure to deliver the additional 100 tons. Decision?

4. On November 23, S agreed to sell to B her Pontiac automobile for $7,000, delivery and payment to be made on December 1. On November 26, B informed S that he wished to rescind the contract and would pay S $350 if S agreed. S agreed and took the $350 cash. On December 1, B tendered to S $6,650 and demanded that S deliver the automobile. S refused and B initiated a law suit. Decision?

5. S dealt in automobile accessories at wholesale. Although manufacturing a few items in his own factory, among them windshield wipers, S purchased most of his supplies from a large number of other manufacturers. In January, S entered into a written contract to sell B 2,000 windshield wipers for $3,900, delivery to be made June 1. In April S's factory burned to the ground, and S failed to make delivery on June 1. B, forced to buy windshield wipers elsewhere at a higher price, brings an action against S for breach of contract. Decision?

6. On May 15, the Hughes Electric Company and the Moss Coal Company entered into a written contract whereby the coal company agreed to sell and deliver to the electric company 500 tons of coal at a stipulated price, on or before November 1. By September 1, the market price of coal had increased considerably and, on that date, the coal company notified the electric company that it would not make delivery of the coal. By its reply, mailed on September 2, the electric company notified the coal company that it would expect performance in full by the coal company on November 1. On September 30, the electric company closed its plant temporarily because of a slump in the sales of electric equipment. On November 1, the coal company delivered 500 tons of coal to the electric company. The electric company refused to accept any part of the coal delivered. Thereafter, the coal company sued the electric company for damages for breach of contract. Decision?

7. Green owed White $3,500, which was due and payable on June 1. White owed Brown $3,500, which was due and payable on August 1. On May 25, White received a letter signed by Green stating: "If you will cancel my debt to you, in the amount of $3,500, I will pay, on the due date, the debt you owe Brown, in the amount of $3,500." On

May 28, Green received a letter signed by White stating: "I received your letter and agree to the proposals recited therein. You may consider your debt to me cancelled as of the date of this letter." On June 1, White, needing money to pay his income taxes, made a demand upon Green to pay him the $3,500 due on that date. Is Green obligated to pay the money demanded by White?

8. By written contract Ames agreed to build a house on Bowen's lot for $45,000 commencing within ninety days of the date of the contract. Prior to the date for beginning construction, Ames informed Bowen that he was repudiating the contract and would not perform. Bowen refused to accept the repudiation and demanded fulfillment of the contract. Eighty days after the date of the contract, Bowen entered into a new contract with Curd for $42,000. The next day, without knowledge or notice of Bowen's contract with Curd, Ames began construction, Bowen ordered Ames from the premises and refused to allow him to continue.

Ames sued Bowen for damages. Decision?

9. A agreed in writing to work for B for three years as Superintendent of B's manufacturing establishment and to devote herself entirely to the business, giving it her whole time, attention, and skill, for which she was to receive $24,000 per annum, in monthly installments of $2,000. A worked and was paid for the first twelve months, when through no fault of her own or B's, she was arrested and imprisoned for one month. It became imperative for B to employ another, and he treated the contract with A as breached and abandoned, refusing to permit A to resume work upon her release from jail. What rights, if any, does A have under the contract?

10. The Park Plaza Hotel awarded the valet and laundry concession to Larson for a three-year term. The contract contained the following provision: "It is distinctly understood and agreed that the services to be rendered by Larson shall meet with the approval of the Park Plaza Hotel, which shall be the sole judge of the sufficiency and propriety of the services." After seven months, the hotel gave a month's notice to discontinue services based on the failure of the services to meet its approval. Larson brought an action against the hotel, alleging that its dissatisfaction was unreasonable. The hotel defended upon the ground that subjective or personal satisfaction may be the sole justification for termination of the contract. Decision?

Chapter 16

REMEDIES

T O revert to the Restatement's definition of a contract, it is, in part, "a promise or a set of promises for the breach of which the law gives a remedy." A remedy is the means by which a violation of a right is redressed, compensated, or prevented. There are several classes of remedies, but by far the most important are judicial remedies. A judicial remedy is one which is effected by an action or suit in court.

When one party to a contract breaches the contract by failing to perform his contractual duties, the law provides a remedy for the injured party. The primary objective of contract remedies is to compensate the injured party for the loss resulting from the breach. However, it is impossible for any remedy to equal the promised performance. The only relief that any court can give the injured party is what it regards as an equivalent of the promised performance. Even a decree of *specific performance* (a court order

requiring the breaching party to perform his contractual duties) does not give the injured party what he was entitled to receive by the terms of the contract because the remedy comes at the end of a lawsuit many months or even years after the performance was due.

This chapter will examine the most common judicial remedies available for breach of contract: (1) monetary damages; (2) the equitable remedies of specific performance and injunction; and (3) restitution. Sales of goods are governed by Article 2 of the Uniform Commercial Code which provides specialized remedies that are discussed in Chapter 23.

MONETARY DAMAGES

Compensatory Damages

The right to recover compensatory money damages for breach of contract is always available to the injured party. Restatement, Section 346. As previously mentioned, the purpose in allowing damages is to provide compensation to the injured party which will, to the extent possible, place him in as good a position as if the other party had performed under the contract. The amount of damages is generally the loss of value to the injured party caused by the other party's failure to perform or deficient performance. Damages are not recoverable for loss beyond an amount that the injured party can establish with reasonable certainty. Restatement, Section 352.

In general, the **loss of value** is the *difference between the value of the promised performance* of the breaching party *and the value of the actual performance* rendered by the breaching party. If no performance is rendered at all, then the loss of value is the value of the promised performance. If defective or partial performance is rendered, the loss of value is the difference between the value that the performance would have had if there had been no breach and the value of the performance actually rendered. Thus, where there has been a breach of warranty, the injured party may recover the difference between the value of the goods if they had been as warranted and the value of the goods in their actual condition when received by the buyer. To illustrate, A sells an automobile to B and expressly warrants that it will get forty-five miles per gallon, but the automobile only gets twenty miles per gallon. The automobile would have been worth $8,000 if as warranted but is worth only $6,000 as delivered. B would recover $2,000 in damages for loss of value.

The injured party may *also* recover for all other loss actually suffered, subject to the limitation of foreseeability discussed below. These damages include incidental and consequential damages. **Incidental damages** are damages that arise directly out of the breach, such as costs incurred to arrange for the acquisition of the non-delivered performance from some other source. For example, A employs B for nine months for $20,000 to supervise construction of a factory. A fires B

without cause after three weeks. B spends $350 in reasonable fees attempting to find comparable employment. B may recover $350 in incidental damages in addition to any other actual loss suffered. **Consequential damages** include lost profits and injury to person or property resulting from defective performance. Thus, if A leases to B a machine which is defective and causes $4,000 in property damage and $12,000 in personal injuries, B may recover, in addition to damages for loss of value and incidental damages, $16,000 as consequential damages.

The recovery by the injured party, however, is reduced by any cost or loss she has avoided by not having to perform. For example, A agrees to build a hotel for B for $1,250,000 by September 1. A breaches by not completing construction until October 1. As a consequence, B loses revenues for one month in the amount of $10,000 but saves operating expenses of $6,000. B may recover damages for $4,000. Similarly, in a contract in which the injured party has not fully performed, the injured party's recovery is reduced by the value to the injured party of the performance promised by the injured party but not rendered. For example, A agrees to convey land to B in return for B's promise to work for A for two years. B repudiates the contract before A has conveyed the land to B. A's recovery for loss from B is reduced by the value to A of the land.

To summarize, the amount of **compensatory damages** an injured party may recover for breach of contract is computed as follows:

Value of performance of party in default
+ Incidental damages
+ Consequential damages
− Loss or cost avoided by injured party
―――――――――――――――――――――
Compensatory damages

An action to recover damages for breach of contract may be maintained even though the plaintiff has not sustained or cannot prove any injury or loss resulting from the breach. Restatement, Section 346. In such case he will be permitted to recover **nominal damages**—a small sum fixed without regard to the amount of loss. Such a judgment may also include an award of court costs. For example, A contracts to sell and deliver goods to B for $1,000. A refuses to deliver the goods as agreed, and so breaks the contract. B, however, is able to purchase goods of the same kind and quality elsewhere for $1,000. As a result, although A has violated B's rights under the contract, B has suffered no actual loss. Consequently, if B, as he may, should sue A for breach of contract, he would recover a judgment for nominal damages only. Nominal damages are also available where loss is actually sustained but cannot be proved with reasonable certainty.

Reliance Damages

As an alternative to compensatory damages the injured party may seek reimbursement for loss caused by his reliance upon the contract. This remedy results in placing the injured party in as good a position as he would have been in had the contract *not been made*. Damages for reliance include expenses incurred in preparing to perform, in actually performing, or in foregoing opportunities to enter into other contracts. An injured party may prefer damages for reliance rather than compensatory damages when he is unable to establish his lost profits with reasonable certainty or when the contract is itself unprofitable. For example, A agrees to sell his retail store to B. B spends $50,000 in acquiring inventory and fixtures. A then repudiates the contract, and B sells the inventory and fixtures for $35,000. Neither party can establish with reasonable certainty what profit B would have made. B may recover from A as damages the loss of $15,000 he sustained on the sale of the inventory and fixtures plus any other costs he incurred in entering into the contract.

Foreseeability of Damages

A contracting party is generally expected to consider those risks that are foreseeable at the time he entered into the contract. Therefore, compensatory or reliance damages are only recoverable for loss that the party in breach had reason to foresee as a *probable* result of such breach when the contract was made. The breaching party is not liable in the event of a breach for loss that was not foreseeable at the time of entering into the contract. The test of foreseeability is an **objective** test based upon what the breaching party had reason to foresee. Loss may be foreseeable as a probable result of a breach because it follows from the breach (a) in the ordinary course of events, or (b) as a result of special circumstances, beyond the ordinary course of events, that the party in breach had reason to know. Restatement, Section 351(2). Moreover, "a court may limit damages for foreseeable loss by excluding recovery for loss of profits, by allowing recovery only for loss incurred in reliance, or otherwise if it concludes that in the circumstances justice so requires in order to avoid disproportionate compensation." Restatement, Section 351(3).

A leading case on the subject of foreseeability of damages is *Hadley v. Baxendale*, decided in England in 1854. In this case the plaintiffs operated a flour mill at Gloucester. Their mill was compelled to cease operating because of a broken crankshaft attached to the steam engine which furnished power to the mill. It was necessary to send the broken shaft to a foundry located at Greenwich so that a new shaft could be made. The plaintiffs delivered the broken shaft to the defendants, who were common carriers, for immediate transportation from Gloucester to Greenwich, but did not inform the defendants that operation of the mill had ceased because of the nonfunctioning crankshaft. The defendants received the shaft, collected the freight charges in advance, and promised the plaintiffs to deliver the shaft at Greenwich the following day. The defendants neglected to make prompt delivery as promised, and as a result the resumption of the operation of the mill was delayed for several days, causing the plaintiffs to lose profits which they otherwise would have received. The defendants contended that the loss of profits was too remote, and therefore unforeseeable, to be recoverable. In awarding damages to the plaintiffs, the jury was permitted to take into consideration the loss of these profits. The appellate court reversed the decision and ordered a new trial on the ground that the special circumstances which caused the loss of profits, namely, the continued stoppage of the mill while awaiting the return of the repaired crankshaft, had never been communicated by the plaintiffs to the defendants. A common carrier would not reasonably foresee that the plaintiff's mill would be shut down as a result of delay in transporting the broken crankshaft.

On the other hand, if the defendant in *Hadley v. Baxendale* had been informed that the shaft was necessary for the operation of the mill, or otherwise had reason to know this fact, he would be liable to the plaintiffs for loss of profit during the period of shutdown caused by his delay. Under these circumstances the loss would be the "foreseeable" and "natural" result of the breach in accordance with common experience. The plaintiff's loss of profit would be the probable result of defendant's delay in transporting the shaft and would be recoverable from the defendant.

But what if the plaintiff's expected profit should be extraordinarily large? The general rule, as stated above, is that the breaching party will only be liable for such extraordinary loss if he had reason to know of the special loss. In any event the plaintiff may recover for any ordinary loss resulting from the breach. Thus, if A breaches a contract with B, causing B, due to special circumstances, $10,000 in damages where ordinarily such a breach would only result in $6,000 of damages, A would be liable to B for $6,000, not $10,000, so long as A was unaware of the special circumstances causing B the unusually large loss.

Damages for Misrepresentation

Fraud A party who has been induced to enter into a contract by fraud may recover damages in a tort action. The minority of States allow the injured party to recover only **"out-of-pocket"** damages equal to the difference between the value of what she has received and the value of what she has given for it. The great majority of States, however, permit the intentionally defrauded party to recover damages under the **"benefit-of-the-bargain"** rule which is equal to the difference between the value of what she has received and the value of the fraudulent party's performance as represented. The Restatement of Torts provides the fraudulently injured party with the option of either out-of-pocket or benefit-of-the-bargain damages. Section 549. To illustrate, A intentionally misrepresents the capabilities of a printing press which induces B to purchase the machine for $20,000. The value of the press as delivered is $14,000, but if the machine performed as represented, it would be worth $24,000. Under the out-of-pocket rule B would recover $6,000, while under the benefit-of-the-bargain rule she would recover $10,000.

Non-fraudulent Misrepresentation Where the misrepresentation is not fraudulent, the Restatement of Torts permits out-of-pocket damages but expressly excludes recovery of benefit-of-the-bargain damages. Sections 552B and 552C.

Punitive Damages

Punitive damages are monetary damages in addition to compensatory damages awarded a plaintiff in certain situations involving willful, wanton, or malicious conduct in order to punish the defendant and thus discourage him and others from similar wrongful conduct. The purpose of allowing contract damages, on the other hand, is to compensate the plaintiff for the loss which he has sustained by reason of the defendant's breach of contract. In a case in which the plaintiff has established a breach of contract and evidence of loss or damage, the court will award him a judgment in an amount it deems sufficient to place him in the position in which he would have been had the defendant not breached the contract. Accordingly, the Restatement provides that punitive damages are not recoverable for a breach of contract unless the conduct constituting the breach is also a tort for which punitive damages are recoverable. Restatement, Section 355.

Liquidated Damages

A contract may contain a provision by which the parties agree in advance to the damages to be paid in event of breach. Such a liquidated damages provision will be enforced if it amounts to a reasonable forecast of the loss which may result from the breach. If, however, the sum agreed upon as liquidated damages does not bear a reasonable relationship to the amount of probable loss which may result from breach, it is unenforceable as an invalid penalty. Restatement, Section 356, Comment a states:

The parties to a contract may effectively provide in advance the damages that are to be payable in the event of breach as long as the provision does not disregard the principle of compensation. The enforcement of such provisions for liquidated damages saves the time of courts, juries, parties and witnesses and reduces the expense of litigation. This is especially important if the amount in controversy is small. However, the parties to a contract are not free to provide a penalty for its breach. The central objective behind the system of contract remedies is compensatory, not punitive.

The law will look at the substance of the provision, the nature of the contract, and the extent of probable harm to the promisee which may reasonably be expected to be caused by a breach in order to determine whether the agreed amount is proper as liquidated damages or unenforceable as a penalty. It is immaterial what name or label the parties to the contract attach to the provision. If a liquidated damage provision is not enforceable, the injured party is nevertheless entitled to the ordinary remedies for breach of contract. *See City of Rye v. Public Service Mutual Insurance Co.*

To illustrate, A contracts with B to build a grandstand at B's race course at a cost of $1,330,000, to have it completed by a certain date, and to pay B, as liquidated damages, $1,000 per day for every day's delay beyond that date in completing the grandstand. The stipulated sum for delay is liquidated damages and not a penalty, because the amount is reasonable. If, instead, the sum stipulated had been $10,000 per day, it would obviously have been unreasonable and therefore a penalty. Provisions for liquidated damages are sometimes found in contracts for the sale of a business, in which the seller agrees not to re-enter the same business within a reasonable geographic area and time period. Actual damages resulting from the seller's breach of his agreement would ordinarily be difficult to ascertain, and the sum stipulated, if reasonable, would be held to be liquidated damages.

Mitigation of Damages

Where a breach of contract occurs, the injured party is required to take such steps as may be reasonably calculated to lessen or mitigate the damages that he may sustain. Damages are not recoverable for loss that the injured party could have avoided without undue risk, burden, or humiliation. Restatement, Section 350. *See Copenhaver v. Berryman.* Thus, where A is under a contract to manufacture goods for B who repudiates the contract after A has commenced performance, A will not be allowed to recover for losses he sustains by continuing to manufacture the goods, if to do so would increase the amount of damages. The amount of loss that could reasonably have been avoided is deducted from the amount that would otherwise be recoverable as damages. On the other hand, if the goods were almost completed when B repudiated, the completion of the goods might mitigate the damages, as the finished goods may be resalable whereas the unfinished goods may not. U.C.C. Section 2-704(2).

Similarly, a buyer who does not receive goods or services promised to him under a contract cannot recover damages resulting from his doing without such goods or services where it is possible for him to substitute other goods or services which he can obtain elsewhere. Likewise, if A contracts to work for B for one year for a weekly salary and after two months is wrongfully discharged by B, A must use reasonable efforts to mitigate his damages by seeking other employment. If he cannot obtain other employment of the same general character, he is entitled to recover full pay for the contract period that he is unemployed. He is not obliged to accept a radically different type of employment or to accept work at a distant place. A person who is employed as a school teacher or accountant and is wrongfully discharged is not obliged, in order to mitigate damages, to accept available employment as a chauffeur or truck driver. *See Parker v. Twentieth Century-Fox Film Corp.* in Chapter 2.

REMEDIES IN EQUITY

The remedies of specific performance and injunction are forms of equitable relief that may be available as alternatives to the award of damages as means of enforcing contracts. The remedies of specific performance and injunction are not a matter of right but rest largely in the discretion of the court. It must appear clearly that the equities are with the party seeking these remedies. Consequently, they will not be granted where there is an adequate remedy at law; where it is impossible

to enforce them, as where the seller has already conveyed the subject matter of the contract to an innocent third person; where the contract is without consideration; where the consideration is grossly inadequate; or where the contract is tainted with fraud, duress, undue influence or other defect. It must appear also that the plaintiff is ready and able to perform in full on his part. This can usually be shown by a tender of the full purchase price into court.

Specific Performance

It is said that a contract creates enforceable rights, that courts will enforce contracts, and that a remedy is the means of enforcing rights. These statements are substantially correct, but as to the vast majority of contracts they are not literally correct. Ordinarily, a contract will not be enforced by courts in the sense that they will require the breaching party literally to carry out his contractual obligations. The usual remedy for breach of contract, it has been seen, is an action at law for money damages by way of compensation for the loss. As the term "remedy" is used here, the emphasis is on a remedy as a means of redressing a violation of a right, rather than the specific or literal enforcement of the right. Suppose, for example, that A contracts to sell and deliver coal to B, and that A wrongfully refuses to deliver the coal to B. No court, at B's suit, will force A to deliver the coal to B. B can buy the coal elsewhere. However, if B suffers a loss by having to pay a higher price than the contract price, he has his remedy at law: an action against A for money damages to compensate B for his loss. A judgment for money damages is the only remedy that a court of law can award. And, in most cases, it is a just and adequate remedy. Cases, however, occasionally arise where the circumstances are such that an award of money damages is wholly inadequate as a remedy. Since this is the only remedy a court of law can grant, the injured party is without an adequate remedy at law. In any such case, his remedy is a suit in equity for specific performance of the contract. *See Tamarind Lithography Workshop v. Sanders.*

Specific performance, in one sense, is the actual performance by the defaulting party of his contractual obligations as decreed by a court of equity. Primarily, the term is used to indicate the equitable remedy which compels the performance of a contract according to its terms. Ordinarily, as has been seen, in case of breach by the seller of his contract for the sale of personal property, the buyer has a sufficient remedy at law. Where, however, the article contracted for is rare or *unique*, this remedy is inadequate. Examples of such articles are a famous painting or statue, the original manuscript or a rare edition of a book, a patent, a copyright, shares of stock in a close corporation, a relic or an heirloom. Articles of this character obviously cannot be purchased elsewhere, nor do they have a market value. Clearly, on breach by the seller of his contract for the sale of any such article, money damages will not adequately or completely compensate the buyer. Consequently, in any such case, he may avail himself of the equitable remedy of specific performance.

While it is only in exceptional circumstances that courts of equity will grant specific performance in connection with contracts for the sale of personal property, they will always grant it in case of breach of contract for the sale of *real property*. The reason for this is that any particular parcel of land is regarded as unique and as differing from any other parcel. Consequently, if the seller refuses to convey title to the real estate contracted for, the buyer may seek the aid of a court of equity to compel the seller to convey the title. As to real estate contracts, the remedy is mutual. Courts of equity will likewise compel the buyer to perform at the suit of the seller.

Courts of equity will not grant specific performance of contracts for personal services. In the first place, there is the practical difficulty, if not impossibility, of enforcing a decree in any such case. In the second place, it is against the policy of the courts to force one person to work for or serve another against his will, even though he has contracted to do so. Such enforcement would probably amount to involuntary servitude. For example, if A, an accomplished concert pianist, agrees to appear at a certain time and place to play a specified program for B, upon A's refusal to appear a court would not issue a decree of specific performance.

Injunctions

The injunction, as used as a contract remedy, is a formal order of the court commanding a person to refrain from doing a specific act or engaging in specified conduct. A person who violates an injunctive order may be held guilty of contempt of court and fined or imprisoned until released by court.

A court of equity, at its discretion, may grant an injunction against breach of a contractual duty where damages for a breach would be inadequate. For example, A enters into a written agreement to give B the right of first refusal on a tract of land owned by A. A subsequently offers the land to C without first offering it to B. A court of equity may properly enjoin A from selling the land to C. Similarly, valid covenants not to compete may be enforced by an injunction.

A promise of exclusive personal services may be enforced by an injunction against serving another employer as long as the probable result will not be to leave the employee without other reasonable means of making a living. Restatement, Section 367. Suppose, for example, that A makes a contract with B, a famous singer, under which B agrees to sing at A's theater on certain dates for an agreed fee. Before the date of the first performance, B makes a contract with C to sing for C at his theater on the same dates. A cannot secure specific performance by B of his contract, as already discussed. A court of equity will, however, on suit by A against B, issue an injunction against B, ordering B not to sing for C. This may or may not have the effect of inducing B to perform his contract with A, but it is as far as a court of equity will go in such a case. *See Madison Square Garden Corp., Ill. v. Carnera.* Where the services contracted for are not unusual or extraordinary in character, the injured party cannot get injunctive relief. His only remedy is an action at law for damages.

RESTITUTION

One of the remedies which may be available to a party to a contract is restitution. Restitution is a return to the aggrieved party of the consideration, or its value, which he gave to the other party. The object of restitution is to restore the injured party to the position he was in before the contract was made. Therefore, the party seeking restitution must return what he has received from the other party.

Restitution is available in several contractual situations: (1) as an alternative remedy for a party injured by breach; (2) for a party in default; (3) for a party who may not enforce the contract because of the Statute of Frauds; and (4) upon avoidance of a voidable contract.

Party Injured by Breach

A party is entitled to restitution if the other party totally breaches the contract by non-performance or repudiation. Restatement, Section 373. For example, A agrees to sell land to B for $60,000. B makes a part payment of $15,000. A wrongfully refuses to transfer title. As an alternative to damages or specific performance, B may recover the $15,000 in restitution.

Comment b to Restatement Section 373 provides:

If, after one party has fully performed his part of the contract, the other party then refuses to pay

a definite sum of money that has been fixed as the price for that performance, the injured party is barred from recovery of a greater sum as restitution under the rule stated in Subsection (2). Since he is entitled to recover the price in full together with interest, he has a remedy that protects his expectation interest by giving him the very thing that he was promised. Even if he asserts that the benefit he conferred on the other party exceeds the price fixed by the contract, justice does not require that he have the right to recover this larger sum in restitution.

Thus, A contracts to work for B for one month for $2,000. After A has fully performed, B repudiates the contract and refuses to pay the $2,000. A can get damages against B for $2,000, together with interest, but cannot recover more than that sum even if he can show that the benefit to B from the services was greater than $2,000.

Party in Default

Where a party, after having partly performed, commits a breach by non-performance or repudiation that discharges the other party's duty to perform, the party in default is entitled to restitution for any benefit she has conferred in excess of the loss she has caused by her breach. Restatement, Section 374. For example, A agrees to sell land to B for $60,000, and B makes a part payment of $15,000. B then repudiates the contract. A sells the land to C in good faith for $55,000. B may recover from A in restitution the part payment of the $15,000 *less* the $5,000 damages A sustained because of B's breach, which equals $10,000.

Statute of Frauds

Parties to a contract which is unenforceable because of the Statute of Frauds may have, nonetheless, acted in reliance upon the contract. In such a case each party may recover in restitution the benefits conferred upon the other in relying upon their unenforceable contract. Thus, if A makes an oral contract to furnish services to B that are not to be performed within a year and B discharges A after three months, A may recover as restitution the value of the services rendered during the three months.

Voidable Contracts

A party who has avoided a contract for lack of capacity, duress, undue influence, fraud, misrepresentation, or mistake is entitled to restitution for any benefit he has conferred upon the party. Restatement, Section 376. For example, A fraudulently induces B to sell land for $60,000. A pays the purchase price, and B conveys the land. B then discovers the fraud. B may disaffirm the contract and recover as restitution the land. Generally, the party seeking restitution must return any benefit that he has received under the agreement; however, this is not always the case as discussed in Chapter 12 dealing with contractual capacity.

LIMITATIONS ON REMEDIES

Election of Remedies

If a party is injured by a breach of contract and has more than one remedy available to him, his manifestation of a choice of one of them by bringing suit or otherwise is not a bar to another remedy unless the remedies are inconsistent and the other party materially changes his position in reliance on the manifestation. Restatement, Section 378. For example, a party who seeks specific performance, an injunction, or restitution may be entitled to incidental damages, for delay in performance. *See Billy Williams Builders & Development Inc. v. Hillerich.* However, damages for total breach are inconsistent with the remedies of specific performance and injunction, or restitution. Likewise, the rem-

edy of specific performance or an injunction is inconsistent with that of restitution.

The Code liberalizes the common law with respect to contracts for the sale of goods by not restricting a defrauded party to an election of remedies. U.C.C. Section 2-721 states:

Remedies for material misrepresentation or fraud include all remedies available under this Article for non-fraudulent breach. Neither rescission or a claim for rescission of the contract for sale nor rejection or return of the goods shall bar or be deemed inconsistent with a claim for damages or other remedy.

Thus, the injured party may both rescind the contract by restoring the status quo and, in addition, recover damages or obtain any other remedy available under the Code.

Loss of Power of Avoidance

A party with a power of avoidance for lack of capacity, duress, undue influence, fraud, misrepresentation, or mistake may lose that power if (1) she affirms the contract; (2) she delays unreasonably in exercising the power of disaffirmance; or (3) the rights of third parties intervene.

Affirmance A party who has the power to avoid a contract for lack of capacity, duress, undue influence, fraud, misrepresentation, or mistake will lose that power by affirming the contract. Affirmance occurs where the party, with full knowledge of the facts, either declares his intention to proceed with the contract or takes some other action from which such intention may reasonably be inferred. Thus, suppose that A was induced to purchase a ring from B through the latter's fraudulent misrepresentation. If, after learning the truth, A undertakes to sell the ring to C or otherwise does something which is consistent only with his ownership of the ring, he may no longer rescind the transaction. In the case of incapacity, duress, or undue influence, affirmance is effective only after the circumstances that made the contract voidable cease to exist. Where there has been fraudulent misrepresentation, the defrauded party may affirm only after he knows of the misrepresentation. If the misrepresentation is non-fraudulent or there is a mistake, the defrauded or mistaken party may affirm only after he knows or should know of the misrepresentation or mistake.

Delay The power of avoidance may be lost if the party who has the power does not rescind within a reasonable time. What is a reasonable time depends upon all the circumstances, including the extent to which the delay enables the party with the power of avoidance to speculate at the other party's risk. To illustrate, a defrauded purchaser of stock cannot wait unduly to see if the market price or value of the stock appreciates sufficiently to justify retaining the stock. A reasonable time does not begin until the circumstances that made the contract voidable have ceased to exist.

Rights of Third Parties The power of avoidance and the accompanying right to restitution are further limited by the intervening rights of third parties. If A transfers property to B in a transaction that is voidable by A, but before A exercises her power of avoidance, B sells the property to C, a good faith purchaser for value, A will lose the right to recover the property.

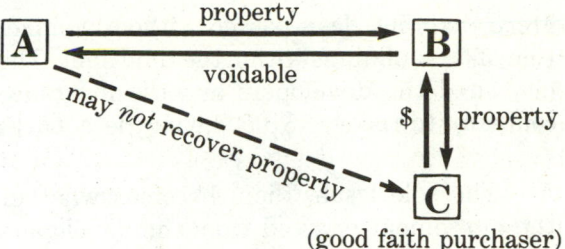

(good faith purchaser)

Thus, if, C, a third party who is a good faith purchaser, acquires an interest in the subject matter of the contract before A has elected to rescind, no rescission is permitted. Because the transaction is voidable, B acquires a voidable title to the property. Upon a sale of the property by him to C, who is a purchaser in good faith and for value, C obtains good title and is allowed to retain the property. Since both A and C are innocent, the law will not disturb the title in C, the good faith purchaser. In this case, as in all cases where rescission is not available, A's only recourse is against B.

The one notable exception to this rule is the situation involving a sale by a minor who subsequently wishes to avoid a transaction, _other than for a sale of goods,_ from a good faith purchaser. Under this special rule a good faith purchaser is deprived of the protection generally provided. Therefore, the third party in a transaction not involving goods is no more protected from the minor's disaffirmance than is the person dealing directly with the minor.

CASES

Liquidated Damages

CITY OF RYE v. PUBLIC SERVICE MUTUAL INSURANCE CO.

Court of Appeals of New York, 1974.
34 N.Y.2d 470, 358 N.Y.S. 2d 391, 315 N.E.2d 458.

BREITEL, C. J.
[Developers under a plan approved by the city of Rye had constructed six luxury

cooperative apartment buildings and were to construct six more. In order to obtain certificates of occupancy for the six completed buildings, the developers were required to post a bond with the city to insure completion of the remaining buildings. The developers posted a $100,000 bond upon which the defendant, Public Service Mutual Insurance Company, as guarantor or surety, agreed to pay $200 for each day after April 1, 1971 that the remaining buildings were not completed.

More than 500 days passed without completion of the buildings within the time limit. The city sued the developers and the insurance company to recover $100,000 on the bond.]

* * *

The sole issue, then, becomes whether the agreement exacted from the developers and the conditional bond supplied provide for a penalty or for liquidated damages. If the agreement provides for a penalty or forfeiture . . . it is unenforceable. Where, however, damages flowing from a breach are difficult to ascertain, a provision fixing the damages in advance will be upheld if the amount is a reasonable measure of the anticipated probable harm. [Citations.] If, on the other hand, the amount fixed is grossly disproportionate to the anticipated probable harm or if there were no anticipatable harm, the provision will not be enforced.

The harm which the city contends it would suffer by delay in construction is minimal, speculative, or simply not cognizable. The city urges that its inspectors and employees will be required to devote more time to the project than anticipated because it has taken extra years to complete. It also urges that it will lose tax revenues for the years the buildings are not completed. It contends, too, that it is harmed by a continuing violation of the height restrictions of its zoning ordinance. * * * Only after all of the structures in the complex are built will the project comply with the average height requirement of the ordinance.

The most serious disappointments in expectation suffered by the city are not pecuniary in nature and therefore not measurable in monetary damages. The effect on increased inspectorial services or on tax revenue are not likely to be substantial and, in any event, are not developed in the record on summary judgment. There is nothing to show that either the sum of $200 per day or the aggregate amount of the bond bear any reasonable relationship to the pecuniary harm likely to be suffered or in fact suffered.

* * *

[Judgment for the developers and the insurance company affirmed.]

Mitigation of Damages

COPENHAVER v. BERRYMAN

Court of Civil Appeals of Texas, Corpus Christi, 1980.
602 S.W. 2d 540.

NYE, C. J.

[Copenhaver (plaintiff), the owner of a laundry business, contracted with Berryman (defendant), the owner of a large apartment complex, to allow Copenhaver to own and operate the laundry facilities within the apartment complex. Berryman terminated the contract with Copenhaver when forty-seven months remained in the five-year contract. Within six months Copenhaver placed the equipment into use in other locations. Copenhaver filed suit, claiming that he was entitled to conduct the laundry operations for an additional forty-seven months and, by such, would have earned a profit of $13,886.58, after deducting Berryman's share of the gross receipts and other operating expenses. The trial court awarded Copenhaver $3,525.84. Copenhaver appealed.]

* * *

Before addressing the merits of plaintiffs' specific points, however, a brief review of some of the principles relating to damages and mitigation of damages is necessary to gain the proper appellate perspective of the contentions advanced by the respective parties. As a general rule, damages for breach of contract seek to allow the injured party to have just compensation for the damages or loss actually sustained. [Citations.] The burden is upon the complaining party to establish his right to recover compensatory damages by proving he suffered a pecuniary loss as a result of the breach. [Citations.]

Here plaintiffs sought to recover damages measured by loss of profits they sustained due to defendants' breach of the contract. As a general rule, where it is shown that a loss of profit is a natural and probable consequence of the act or omission complained of, and the amount is shown with sufficient certainty, recovery of lost profits is permitted. Anticipated profits, however, cannot be recovered where they are dependent upon uncertain and changing conditions, such as market fluctuations or a change of business, or where there is no evidence from which they may be intelligently estimated. Evidence to establish profits must not be uncertain or speculative. It is not necessary that profits should be susceptible of exact calculation. It is sufficient that there be data from which they may be ascertained with a reasonable degree of certainty and exactness. [Citations.] The term, "net profits" is, " 'to a large degree, self-explanatory and implies, generally speaking, what remains in the conduct of a business after deducting from its total receipts all of the expenses incurred in carrying on the business.' " [Citations.] In the calculation of net profits, allowance should be made for expenditures that the plaintiff would have been compelled to make, and also for the value of the plaintiff's time. [Citation.]

* * *

While the defendant is liable for the pecuniary loss sustained by the party injured by the breach, the party so injured must exercise, as a general rule, reasonable efforts in an attempt to minimize his damages. As stated by our Supreme Court in *Walker v. Salt Flat Water Co.*, [Citation]:

Where a party is entitled to the benefits of a contract and can save himself from the damages resulting from its breach at a trifling expense or with reasonable exertions, it is his duty to incur such expense and make such exertions.

Although the injured party has a duty to minimize his loss, the burden of proof as to the extent to which the damages were or could have been mitigated lies with the party who has breached the contract.

* * *

We are of the opinion that there is evidence in the record to support the finding of fact that the plaintiffs suffered no damage from September 10, 1977, to the date of trial. After September 10, all of the equipment was in use in other locations. There is also some evidence * * * that plaintiffs were generating at least as much income, if not more, from the operation of the machines in question after September 10, 1977.

* * *

Plaintiffs, however, apparently contend the case before us is different because of the nature of their over-all business. In effect, plaintiffs contend the proof established, as a matter of law, that they were capable of performing a number of concurrent laundry facility contracts which performance is limited solely by the availability of facilities for the placement of such equipment. Implicit in this contention is the assumption that, when defendants breached the contract in question, the expansion of plaintiffs' business was thereby limited because they were forced to place the equipment in question into a location they would have acquired anyway.

The testimony concerning the plaintiff's over-all business is vague, speculative, and conclusory. The only evidence we can find to substantiate this contention is some general testimony to the effect that plaintiffs acquired some 14 to 15 new locations after the breach. Plaintiffs admitted they did not even know where the machines in question were ultimately placed. Nor, did the plaintiffs introduce evidence from which it could be reasonably concluded that they would have expanded to each new location even had defendants not breached the contract in question and that defendants' breach somehow limited their expansion.

We are of the opinion that the trial judge could reach no reasonable conclusion other than to find plaintiffs had not proved they were damaged beyond the six-month period, after which all the machines were in use in other locations.

* * *

[The judgment of the trial court awarding Copenhaver $3,525.84 is affirmed.]

Specific Performance

TAMARIND LITHOGRAPHY WORKSHOP v. SANDERS

Court of Appeal of California, Second Distict, 1983.
143 Cal.App.3d 571, 193 Cal.Rptr. 409.

STEPHENS, J.

The essence of this appeal concerns the question of whether an award of damages is an adequate remedy at law in lieu of specific performance for the breach of an agreement to give screen credits. Our saga traces its origin to March of 1969, at which time appellant, and cross-complainant below, Terry Sanders (hereinafter "Sanders" or "appellant"), agreed in writing to write, direct and produce a motion picture on the subject of lithography for respondent, Tamarind Lithography Workshop, Inc. (hereinafter referred to as "Tamarind" or "respondent").

Pursuant to the terms of the agreement, the film was shot during the summer of 1969, wherein Sanders directed the film according to an outline/treatment of his authorship, and acted as production manager by personally hiring and supervising personnel comprising the film crew. Additionally, Sanders exercised both artistic control over the mixing of the sound track and overall editing of the picture.

After completion, the film, now titled the "Four Stones for Kanemitsu," was screened by Tamarind at its tenth anniversary celebration on April 28, 1970. Thereafter, a dispute arose between the parties concerning their respective rights and obligations under the original 1969 agreement. Litigation ensued and in January 1973 the matter went to trial. Prior to the entry of judgment, the parties entered into a written settlement agreement, which became the premise for the instant action. Specifically, this April 30, 1973, agreement provided that Sanders would be entitled to a screen credit entitled "A Film by Terry Sanders."

Tamarind did not comply with its expressed obligation pursuant to that agreement, in that it failed to include Sanders' screen credits in the prints it distributed. As a result a situation developed wherein Tamarind and co-defendant Wayne filed suit for declaratory relief, damages due to breach of contract, emotional distress, defamation and fraud.

Sanders cross-complained, seeking damages for Tamarind's breach of contract, declaratory relief, specific performance of the contract to give Sanders screen credits, and defamation. Both causes were consolidated and brought to trial on May 31, 1977. A jury was impaneled for purposes of determining damage issues and decided that Tamarind had breached the agreement and awarded Sanders $25,000 in damages

The remaining claims for declaratory and injunctive relief were tried by the court. The court made findings that Tamarind had sole ownership rights in the film, that "both June Wayne and Terry Sanders were each creative producers of the film, that Sanders shall have the right to modify the prints in his personal possession to include his credits." All other prayers for relief were denied.

It is from the denial of appellant's request for specific performance upon which appellant predicates this appeal.

* * *

The availability of the remedy of specific performance is premised upon well established requisites. These requisites include: A showing by plaintiff of (1) the inadequacy of his legal remedy; (2) an underlying contract that is both reasonable and supported by adequate consideration; (3) the existence of a mutuality of remedies; (4) contractual terms which are sufficiently definite to enable the court to know what it is to enforce; and (5) a substantial similarity of the requested performance to that promised in the contract. [Citation.]

It is manifest that the legal remedies available to Sanders for harm resulting from the future exhibition of the film are inadequate as a matter of law. The primary reasons are twofold: (1) that an accurate assessment of damages would be far too difficult and require much speculation, and (2) that any future exhibitions might be deemed to be a continuous breach of contract and thereby create the danger of an untold number of lawsuits.

There is no doubt that the exhibition of a film, which is favorably received by its critics and the public at large, can result in valuable advertising or publicity for the artists responsible for that film's making. Likewise, it is unquestionable that the nonappearance of an artist's name or likeness in the form of screen credit on a successful film can result in a loss of that valuable publicity. However, whether that loss of publicity is measurable dollar wise is quite another matter.

By its very nature, public acclaim is unique and very difficult, if not sometimes impossible, to quantify in monetary terms. Indeed, courts confronted with the dilemma of estimating damages in this area have been less than uniform in their disposition of same. Nevertheless, it is clear that any award of damages for the loss of publicity is contingent upon those damages being reasonably certain, specific, and unspeculative. [Citation.]

*   *   *

Accordingly, where the jury in the matter sub judice was fully apprised of the favorable recognition Sanders' film received from the Academy of Motion Picture Arts and Sciences, the Los Angeles International Film Festival, and public television, and further, where they were made privy to an assessment of the value of said exposure by three experts, it was resonable for the jury to award monetary damages for that ascertainable loss of publicity. However, pecuniary compensation for Sanders' future harm is not a fully adequate remedy. [Citation.]

We return to the remaining requisites for Sanders' entitlement to specific performance. The need for our finding the contract to be reasonable and supported by adequate consideration is obviated by the jury's determination of respondent's breach of that contract. The requisite of mutuality of remedy has been satisfied in that Sanders had fully performed his obligations pursuant to the agreement (i.e., release of all claims of copyright to the film and dismissal of his then pending action against respondents). [Citation.] Similarly, we find the terms of the agreement sufficiently definite to permit enforcement of the respondent's performance as promised.

In the present case it should be obvious that specific performance through injunctive relief can remedy the dilemma posed by the somewhat ambiguous jury verdict. The injunction disposes of the problem of future damages, in that full compliance by Tamarind moots the issue. Of course, violation of the injunction by Tamarind would raise new problems, but the court has numerous options for dealing with the situation and should choose the one best suited to the particular violation.

In conclusion, the record shows that the appellant is entitled to relief consisting of the damages recovered, and an injunction against future injury.

Injunctions

MADISON SQUARE GARDEN CORP., ILL. v. CARNERA

Circuit Court of Appeals, Second Circuit, 1931.
52 F.2d 47.

CHASE, J.

Suit by plaintiff, Madison Square Garden Corporation, against Primo Carnera, defendant. From an order granting an injunction against defendant, defendant appeals.

On January 13, 1931, the plaintiff and defendant by their duly authorized agents entered into the following agreement in writing:

1. Carnera agrees that he will render services as a boxer in his next contest (which contest, hereinafter called the "First Contest," shall be with the winner of the proposed Schmeling-Stribling contest, or, if the same is drawn, shall be with Schmeling, and shall be deemed to be a contest for the heavyweight championship title; provided, however, that, in the event of the inability of the Garden to cause Schmeling or Stribling, as the case may be, to perform the terms of his agreement with the Garden calling for such contest, the Garden shall be without further liability to Carnera,) exclusively under the auspices of the Garden, in the United States of America, or the Dominion of Canada, at such time, not, however, later than midnight of September 30, 1931, as the Garden may direct. * * *

9. Carnera shall not, pending the holding of the First Contest, render services as a boxer in any major boxing contest, without the written permission of the Garden in each case had and obtained. A major contest is understood to be one with Sharkey, Baer, Campolo, Godfrey, or like grade heavyweights, or heavyweights who shall have beaten any of the above subsequent to the date hereof. If in any boxing contest engaged in by Carnera prior to the holding of the First Contest, he shall lose the same, the Garden shall at its option, to be exercised by a two weeks' notice to Carnera in writing, be without further liability under the terms of this agreement to Carnera. Carnera shall not render services during the continuance of the option referred to in paragraph 8 hereof for any person, firm or corporation other than the Garden. Carnera shall, however, at all times be permitted to engage in sparring exhibitions in which no decision is rendered and in which the heavyweight championship title is not at stake, and in which Carnera boxes not more than four rounds with any one opponent. * * *

Thereafter the defendant, without the permission of the plaintiff, written or otherwise, made a contract to engage in a boxing contest with the Sharkey mentioned in paragraph 9 of the agreement above quoted, and by the terms thereof the contest was to take place before the first contest mentioned in the defendant's contract with the plaintiff was to be held.

The plaintiff then brought this suit to restrain the defendant from carrying out his contract to box Sharkey, and obtained the preliminary injunction order, from which this appeal was taken. Jurisdiction is based on diversity of citizenship and the required amount is involved.

The District Court has found on affidavits which adequately show it that the defendant's services are unique and extraordinary. A negative covenant in a contract for such personal services is enforceable by injunction where the damages for a breach are incapable of ascertainment. [Citations.]

The defendant points to what is claimed to be lack of consideration for his negative promise, in that the contract is inequitable and contains no agreement to employ him. It is true that there is no promise in so many words to employ the defendant to box in a contest with Stribling or Schmeling, but the agreement read as a whole binds the plaintiff to do just that, providing either Stribling or Schmeling becomes the contestant as the result of the match between them and can be induced to box the defendant. The defendant has agreed to "render services as a boxer" for the plaintiff exclusively, and the plaintiff has agreed to pay him a definite percentage of the gate receipts as his compensation for so doing. The promise to employ the defendant to enable him to earn the compensation agreed upon is implied to the same force and effect as though expressly stated. * * * [Citations.]

As we have seen, the contract is valid and enforceable. It contains a restrictive covenant which may be given effect. Whether a preliminary injunction shall be issued under such circumstances rests in the sound discretion of the court. [Citations.] The District Court, in its discretion, did issue the preliminary injunction and required the plaintiff as a condition upon its issuance to secure its own performance of the contract in suit with a bond for $25,000 and to give a bond in the sum of $35,000 to pay the defendant such damages as he may sustain by reason of the injunction. Such an order is clearly not an abuse of discretion.

Order affirmed.

Election of Remedies

BILLY WILLIAMS BUILDERS & DEVELOP. INC. v. HILLERICH

Supreme Court of Kentucky, 1969.
446 S.W.2d 280.

HILL, J.

Appellees (hereinafter Hillerich) sued appellant (hereinafter Williams) for specific performance of a contract to convey a house and a lot, for damages growing out of the defective construction of the house, and for damages due to delay in performance.

* * *

The main thrust of Williams' argument concerns the right of the buyer to have two remedies (1) specific performance of a contract to purchase real estate (a house and a lot) and (2) damages for defective construction and for delay in performance. Williams argues that by complying with the judgment for specific performance and by accepting the deed to the property, Hillerich elected to have one of two inconsistent remedies; and by so doing, he cannot back up to the "forks of the road" and take a road different from the one on which he "first embarked."

In a proper case there can be little doubt that one may be entitled to the specific performance of a contract to purchase real estate and damages for delay in performance. [Citation.] But damages for deficiency of quantity or quality present a more complex question, on which there is some conflict among the authorities.

* * *

We find in Thompson on Real Property, [citation], the remedies available to both vendor and purchaser clearly defined in this fashion:

Whether the vendor or purchaser is the plaintiff there are three alternatives presented when the vendor is able to give only a performance nonconforming in quantity, *quality* or value: (1) to refuse the remedy of specific performance; (2) to enforce the contract without any regard to the partial failure; (3) to decree a conveyance and allow the vendee an abatement from price equal to the value of the deficiency in the performance. If the vendor cannot convey the agreed quantity of the estate the vendee may have specific performance with pro tanto abatement of purchase price. (Emphasis ours.)

In Pomeroy's Specific Performance of Contracts, [citation], it is said:

The general doctrine is firmly settled, both in England and in this country, that a vendor whose estate is less than or different from that which he agreed to sell, or who cannot give the exact subject-matter embraced in his contract, will not be allowed to set up his inability as a defense against the demand of a purchaser who is willing to take what he can get with a compensation. The vendee may, if he so elect (sic), enforce a specific performance to the extent of the vendor's ability to comply with the terms of the agreement, and may compel a conveyance of the vendor's deficient estate, or defective title or partial subject-matter, and have compensation for the difference between the actual performance, and the performance which would have been an exact fulfillment of the terms of their contract.

* * *

We can see no reason for a distinction between a deficiency in quantity (short acreage or lack of title) and deficiency of quality (defective construction).

We conclude that appellees' remedies were not inconsistent so as to require an election of remedies and that the chancellor did not err in granting specific performance and directing that damages be ascertained by the common law division of the court.

* * *

Judgment affirmed.

PROBLEMS

1. A contracted to buy and B to sell to A, 1,000 barrels of sugar. B failed to deliver, and A could not buy any sugar in the market, so that he was compelled to shut down his candy factory.

    (a) What damages is A entitled to recover?

    (b) Would it make any difference if B had been told by A that he wanted the sugar to make candies for the Christmas trade and that he had accepted contracts for the delivery by certain dates?

2. A agreed to erect an apartment building for B for $750,000, A to suffer deduction of $1,000 per day for every day of delay. A was twenty days late in finishing the job, losing ten days because of a strike and ten days by reason of delay on the part of the material suppliers in furnishing A with materials. A claims that he is entitled to payment in full (a) because the agreement as to $1,000 a day is a penalty; (b) because B had not shown that he has sustained any damage. Discuss each contention and decide.

3. A contracted with B, a shirtmaker, for 1,000 shirts for men. B manufactured and delivered 500 shirts which were paid for by A, who at the same time notified B that she could not use or dispose of the other 500 shirts and directed B not to manufacture any more under the contract. B proceeded to make up the other 500 shirts, tendered them to A who refused to accept, and B then sued for the purchase price. Decision?

4. A contracts to act in a comedy for B and to comply with all theater regulations for four seasons. B promises to pay A $800 for each performance and to allow A one benefit performance each season. It is expressly agreed that "A shall not be employed in any other production for the period of the contract." A and B, during the first year of the contract, engaged in a terrible quarrel. Thereafter, A signed a contract to perform in C's production and ceased performing for B. B seeks (a) to prevent A from performing for C and (b) to require A to perform his contract with B. What result?

5. A leases a building to B for five years at a rental of $1,000 per month, commencing July 1, 1983, B depositing $10,000 as security for performance of all her promises in the lease, to be retained by A

in case of any breach on B's part, otherwise to be applied in payment of rent for the last ten months of the term of the lease. B defaulted in the payment of rent for the months of May and June 1984. After proper notice to B of the termination of the lease for nonpayment of rent, A sued B for possession of the building and recovered a judgment for possession. Thereafter, B sues A to recover the $10,000 less the amount of rent due A for May and June 1984. Decision?

6. (a) A and B enter into a written agreement under which A agrees to sell and B agrees to buy 100 shares of the 300 shares outstanding of the capital stock of the Infinitesimal Steel Corporation, whose shares are not listed on any exchange and are closely held, for ten dollars per share. A refused to deliver when tendered the $1,000, and B sues in equity for specific performance, tendering the $1,000. Decision?

    (b) Modifying (a) above, assume that the subject matter of the agreement is stock of the United States Steel Corporation, which is traded on the New York Stock Exchange. Decision?

    (c) Modifying (a) above, assume that the subject matter of the agreement is undeveloped farm land of little commercial value. Decision?

7. On March 1, A sold to B fifty acres of land in Oregon which A at the time represented to be fine, black loam, high and dry, and free of stumps. B paid A the agreed price of $40,000 and took from A a deed to the land which B subsequently discovered to be low, swampy, and not entirely free of stumps. B, nevertheless, undertook to convert the greater part of the land into cranberry bogs. After one year of cranberry culture, B became entirely dissatisfied, tendered the land back to A, and demanded from A the return of the $40,000. Upon A's refusal to repay the money, B brings an action against him to recover the $40,000. What judgment?

8. A contracts to make repairs to B's building in return for B's promise to pay $12,000 upon completion of the repairs. After partially completing the repairs, A is unable to continue. B hires another builder who completes the repairs for $5,000. The building's value to B has increased by $10,000 as a result of the repairs, but B has lost $500 in rents because of the delay caused by A's breach. A sues B. How much, if any, may A recover in restitution from B?

9. L induced S to enter into a purchase of a stereo amplifier by intentionally misrepresenting the power output to be sixty watts R.M.S. at rated distortion when in fact it only delivers twenty watts. S paid $450 for the amplifier. Amplifiers producing twenty watts generally sell for $200. Amplifiers producing sixty watts generally sell for $550. S decides to keep the amplifier and sue for damages. How much may S recover in damages from L?

10. M induced N to sell N's boat to M by misrepresentation of material fact upon which N reasonably relied. M promptly sold the boat to P who paid fair value for it and knew nothing concerning the transaction between M and N. Upon discovering the misrepresentation, N seeks to recover the boat. What are N's rights against M and P?

PART THREE

Agency

PUBLIC POLICY, SOCIAL ISSUES AND BUSINESS ETHICS

IN considering Part Three, Agency, the reader should keep in mind the importance of the agency relationship in permitting business enterprises—proprietorships, partnerships, and corporations—to expand their business activities. Agency, as will be fully explored in the next two chapters, is a relationship between two persons whereby one of them (the agent) is authorized to act for and on behalf of the other (the principal). Within the scope of the authority granted to her by her principal, the agent may negotiate the terms of contracts with others and bind her principal to such contracts. An agent may be an employee of the principal, but this is not necessary to the existence of the relationship.

If the law were to require each party to a business transaction to participate personally and directly in effecting the transaction, the ability of any person to conduct a business enterprise would be limited by the number of transactions that he could *personally* negotiate. This would severely curtail the size and operation of every business unit and practically paralyze commercial activity. Furthermore, it would make impossible the conduct of business by a corporation, which as an artificial legal entity can act only through its agents, officers, and employees. Moreover, it would radically change the fundamental rule of the law of partnership that every partner is an agent of the partnership with respect to the conduct of its business. The agency concept is therefore indispensable to modern trade and commerce. Through the use of agents, one person may enter into any number of business transactions with the same effect as if done by him personally, and in no more time than he would normally require to negotiate a single contract. A person may thus multiply and expand his business activities.

Given the enormous economic significance of agency it is important to consider the social costs that may be imposed by the use of agents and the public policy considerations that determine the allocation of these costs among those who use agents, the agents themselves, third parties with whom they deal, and society at large.

Because of the power an agent has to bind her principal in contracts the law imposes a number of obligations upon the agent, including the duties of loyalty, diligence and obedience. For example, the duty of loyalty requires an agent to devote her actions exclusively to her principal and to promote the interests of her principal. However, what if her principal is engaged in unlawful conduct such as selling adulterated food or polluting a stream? Should the agent's duty of loyalty to her principal control, or is there a higher duty owed to society which requires the agent to disclose the criminal activities? If the agent does disclose publicly may the principal discharge the agent? The longstanding rule has been that if the agency or employment relationship is not for a definite term, the principal or employer is free to terminate the relationship for cause, no cause or "bad" cause. Some courts, however, have carved out an exception to this rule when the agent's disclosure protects the public interest, especially where there is a definite violation of a criminal statute by the principal or employer.

What if an agent, while pursuing her principal's business, tortiously injures a third party? Who should bear the responsibility for the loss? The principal would argue that he did not cause the harm and the responsibility is solely the agent's. The third party would assert that the agent would not have caused the harm had she not been engaged in carrying on the principal's business. The law has imposed civil liability for the loss upon the agent *and*, when the agent was acting within the scope of her employment, *also* upon the principal. The liability of the principal is vicarious and called *respondeat superior*. William Prosser and W. Page Keeton, eminent authorities on the law of torts, have explained the policy reasons for this doctrine:

What has emerged as the modern justification for vicarious liability is a rule of policy, a deliberate allocation of a risk. The losses caused by the torts of employees, which as a practical matter are sure to occur in the conduct of the employer's enterprise, are placed upon that enterprise itself, as a required cost of doing business. They are placed upon the employer because, having engaged in an enterprise, which will on the basis of all past experience involve harm to others through the torts of employees, and sought to profit by it, it is just that he, rather than the innocent injured plaintiff, should bear them; and because he is better able to absorb them, and to distribute them, through prices, rates or liability insurance, to the public, and so to shift them to society, to the community at large. Added to this is the makeweight argument that an employer who is held strictly liable is under the greatest incentive to be careful in the selection, instruction and supervision of his servants, and to take every precaution to see that the enterprise is conducted safely. Notwithstanding the occasional condemnation of the entire doctrine which used to appear in the past, the tendency is clearly to justify it on such grounds, and gradually to extend it. Keeton, *Prosser and Keeton on Torts* (5th ed.) 500–501 (footnotes omitted).

Similar, but not identical, issues are raised by the question of whether a principal should be held *criminally* liable for an agent's violation of the criminal law. When the principal has actually authorized the agent to commit the crime the answer is simple: both the principal and the agent are criminally liable. But when the principal has not expressly authorized the criminal act the question is much more difficult because the imposition of vicarious criminal liability raises distinctly different policy considerations than imposing vicarious civil liability. The purposes of the criminal law are to punish and deter offensive conduct while the tort law attempts to compensate injured parties and redistribute loss. Accordingly, as a general rule a principal is not ordinarily liable for the unauthorized criminal acts of his agents. However, there has been a trend to impose a criminal penalty upon an employer where the criminal act is that of an advisory or managerial person acting in the scope of employment. Moreover, where a crime does not require intent, a principal may be held subject to a penalty for acts of agents acting within the scope of their employment.

Finally, to what extent should an agent be empowered to bind his principal contractually to third parties? The answer to this question constitutes the keystone of the law of agency and is addressed in detail in Chapter 18. The competing policy interests are clear: the principal wishes to be bound only to those contracts he actually authorized the agent to form, whereas third parties want the principal bound to all contracts that the agent negotiates on the principal's behalf. The law of agency has chosen an intermediate outcome—the principal is bound to those contracts he actually authorized *plus* those the principal has by word or conduct *apparently* authorized the agent to negotiate.

Chapter 17

RELATIONSHIP OF PRINCIPAL AND AGENT

THE law of agency, like the law of contracts, is basic to almost every other branch of business law. Practically every form of contract or business transaction can be created or conducted through an agent. Accordingly, the place and importance of agency in the practical conduct and operation of business cannot be overemphasized. This is particularly and necessarily true in the case of businesses conducted by partnerships and corporations. Partnership is founded on the agency of the partners, as each partner is an agent of the partnership and, as such, has the authority to represent and bind the partnership in all usual transactions pertaining to the partnership business. A corporation, being an artificial legal entity, must of necessity function through the agency of natural persons such as its officers and employees. Thus, practically and legally, agency is an integral part of partnerships and corporations. Agency, however, is not limited to these business associations. Numerous sole proprietors find it necessary to employ agents in the operation of their business. Business, in other words, is very largely conducted, not by the proprietors of business, but by their representatives or agents.

In short, agency is as essential to the operation of modern business as electrical power is to the operation of modern society. Through the use of agents, one person (the principal) may enter into any number of business transactions with the same effect as if done by him personally. A person may thus multiply and expand his business activities. While there is some overlapping, the law of agency divides broadly into two main parts: the internal and external parts. As will be seen shortly, an agent can function as an agent only by dealing with third persons. It is in this way that legal relations are established between the principal and third persons. These relations constitute the general subject matter of the external part of agency law and are discussed in the next chapter. However, in order to understand more clearly the purpose of agency, which is to establish legal contact between the principal and third persons, it will be helpful to consider first the nature and function of agency, as well as other topics of the internal part of the law of agency. This chapter will cover the internal relationship between principal and agent, including the nature of agency, how an agency is created, the duties of agent to principal, the duties of principal to agent, and the termination of agency.

Agency is primarily governed by State common law. An orderly presentation of this law is found in the Restatements of the Law of Agency. The first Restatement was adopted and promulgated on June 30, 1933, by the American Law Institute. On April 11, 1958, the Institute adopted and promulgated a revised edition of the Restatement, the Restatement, Second, Agency, which will be referred to as the Restatement. The Restatements have been regarded as a valuable authoritative reference work and extensively cited and quoted in reported judicial opinions. Selected provisions of the Restatement cited in the text are included in Appendix B of this book.

In addition to the law of agency, the relationship between employer and employee is also governed by a number of Federal and State statutes addressing specific aspects of the employment relationship, including concerted activities by employees, discrimination by employers, and employee safety. Chapter 43 will examine the law regulating the employment relationship.

NATURE OF AGENCY

Agency is the relation existing between two persons known as **principal** and **agent** by vir-

tue of which the agent is the business representative of the principal. An agent, accordingly, is one who represents another, the principal, in business dealings with third persons. Agency in operation necessarily presupposes three persons: the principal, agent, and third person. In his dealings with a third person, the agent acts for and in the name and place of the principal. The parties to the transaction, usually contractual, if properly entered into, are the principal and the third person. The agent is not a party but simply an intermediary. The result of the agent's functioning is exactly the same as if the principal had dealt directly with the third person and without the intervention of an agent. When the agent is dealing with the third person, the principal, in legal effect, is present in the person of the agent.

Definition

Agency is a relationship between two persons whereby one of them (the agent) is authorized to act for and on behalf of the other (the principal). Restatement, Section 1. Within the scope of the authority granted to her by her principal, the agent may negotiate the terms of contracts with others and bind her principal to such contracts. Moreover, the negligence of an agent in conducting the business of her principal exposes the principal to tort liability for injury and loss to third persons. A duly authorized agent may effect a transfer of her principal's title to real estate or personal property. The old maxim "*Qui facet per alium, facet per se*" (Who acts through another, acts himself) accurately describes the relationship of principal and agent.

See Murphy v. Holiday Inns, Inc.

Scope of Agency Purposes

As a general rule, whatever business activity a person may accomplish personally, he may do through an agent. Conversely, whatever he cannot legally do himself, he cannot authorize another to do for him. Thus, a person may not validly authorize another to commit on his behalf an illegal act or crime. Any such agreement is illegal and therefore unenforceable. Restatement, Section 19. Also, a person may not appoint an agent to perform acts which are so personal that their performance may not be delegated to another, as in the case of a contract for personal services. Restatement, Section 17. For example, P, a painter, contracts to paint a portrait of Y. P has one of his students execute the painting and tenders it to Y. This is not a valid tender as the duty to paint Y's portrait is not delegable.

Other Legal Relations

Two other legal relationships are closely related to agency: employer-employee and principal-independent contractor. In the **employment** relationship (historically referred to as the master-servant relationship), the employer has the right to *control* the physical conduct of the employee. Restatement, Section 2. In contrast, a person who engages an **independent contractor** to do a specific job does *not* have the right to control the conduct and activities of the independent contractor in the performance of his contract. Restatement, Section 2(3). The latter simply contracts to do a job and is free to choose the method and manner to perform the job. For example, a full-time chauffeur is an employee, while a taxicab driver hired to carry a person to the airport is an independent contractor of the passenger.

This distinction is extremely important in that a person, as discussed in the next chapter, is liable for the torts committed by an employee within the scope of his employment but ordinarily is not liable for torts committed by an independent contractor. *See Massey v. Tube Art Display, Inc.*

To illustrate: A, owner, and B, a building contractor, enter into a contract under which B agrees to build a house for A in accordance with certain plans and specifications, at an agreed cost. If in the course of the work one of B's workers, C, should injure T, a third person, T cannot recover damages from A since C is not an employee of A. T may, however, recover from C, since one is always liable for his own torts, whether he commits them in the capacity of an employee, agent, or otherwise. T could, of course, trace liability through C to B, because of the relationship of employer and employee between B and C. Since, however, B is neither the agent nor employee of A, T cannot trace liability through B to A. B, as an independent contractor, insulates A from liability, as it were.

CREATION OF AGENCY

Agency is a **consensual** relationship that may arise by contract or agreement between the principal and agent. The Restatement provides that "an agency relation exists only if there has been a manifestation by the principal to the agent that the agent may act on his account, and consent by the agent so to act." Section 15. If the principal requests another to act for him with respect to a matter, and indicates that the other is to act without further communication and the other consents to act, the relation of principal and agent exists. For example, P writes to A, a factor whose business is purchasing goods for others, telling him to select described goods and ship them at once to P. Before answering P's letter, A does as directed, charging the goods to P. A is authorized to do this as there is an agency relationship between P and A.

Because the relationship of principal and agent is consensual and not necessarily contractual, it may exist although the element of consideration is lacking. Restatement, Section 16. Comment b to Section 16 states:

Where the agency relation is created without consideration, it can ordinarily be terminated without liability on the part of either party. However, during the existence of the relation a gratuitous agent has the same power to affect the principal's relations with third persons as if he were paid, and his liabilities to and rights against third persons are the same. Further, he may be liable to the principal for failing to perform a promise on which the principal has relied, or for harm caused by his careless performance, and he is subject to all the paid agent's duties of loyalty.

Nonetheless, agency by contract is the most usual method of creating the relationship and must satisfy all of the requirements of a contract.

Formalities

As a general rule, no particular formality is required in a contract of agency. In many cases, if not most, the contract may be made orally. In some cases, however, the contract is required to be in writing. The appointment of an agent for a period of more than a year comes within the one year clause of the statute of frauds, and so is required to be in writing. In some States, the authority of an agent to sell land must be in writing and signed by the principal. Where the authority of an agent will require him to execute an instrument under seal, such authority must be granted in an instrument executed under seal by the principal. Restatement, Section 28.

A power of attorney is a formal appointment of an agent, who is known as an attorney in fact. Under a power of attorney, for example, a principal may appoint an agent not only to execute a contract for the sale of the principal's real estate, but also to execute the deed conveying title to the real estate to the third party. In such cases, the agent executes the contract, deed, or other instrument in the following manner: John Preston, by Patricia Ames, his attorney in fact.

Capacity

Capacity to Be a Principal The capacity to act through an agent depends upon the capacity of the principal to do the act herself. For example, contracts entered into by a minor or an incompetent not under a guardianship are voidable. Consequently, the appointment of an agent by a minor or an incompetent not under a guardianship—and any resulting contracts—are voidable, regardless of the agent's contractual capacity. See *Goldfinger v. Doherty* in Chapter 18.

Capacity to Be an Agent As the act of the agent is considered the act of the principal, the incapacity of an agent to bind himself by contract does *not* disqualify him from making a contract which is binding on his principal. Thus, minors and incompetents not under a guardianship may act as agents. Although the contract of agency may be voidable, the contract between the principal and the third person who dealt with the agent is valid. Nonetheless, some mental capacity is necessary in an agent; therefore, minors of tender years and mental incompetents, under certain fact situations, may not have the capacity to act as agents.

DUTIES OF AGENT TO PRINCIPAL

Since the relation of principal and agent is ordinarily created by contract, the duties of the agent to the principal will be determined by the provisions of the contract. In addition to the contractual duties assumed by the agent, he is subject to various other duties imposed by law. Normally, a principal selects an agent because of his reliance on the agent's ability, skill, and integrity. Moreover, the principal not only authorizes and empowers the agent to bind him on contracts with third persons, but in many cases he places the agent in possession of his money and other property. As a result, the agent is in a position, either because of his negligence or dishonesty, to injure the principal by involving him in detrimental liabilities or obligations to third persons or by wrongfully using or disposing of the property committed to his care. Accordingly, an agent owes his principal the duties of obedience, diligence, providing information, providing an accounting, and loyalty as a **fiduciary**. In addition, the agent "is subject to liability for loss caused to the principal for any breach of duty." Restatement, Section 401.

Duty of Obedience

The duty of obedience requires the agent to act in the principal's affairs only as authorized by the principal and to obey all reasonable instructions and directions of the principal. Restatement, Sections 383 and 385. The agent may be subject to liability to his principal (1) because he entered into an unauthorized contract for which his principal is liable, (2) because he has improperly delegated his authority, or (3) because he has committed a tort for which the principal is liable. Thus, if an agent sells on credit in violation of the explicit instructions of the principal, the agent has breached the duty of obedience and is liable to the principal for any amounts not paid by the purchaser.

Duty of Diligence

An agent must act with reasonable care and skill in the performance of the work for which she is employed. She must also exercise any special skill that she may have. Restatement, Section 379. If an agent does not exercise the required care and skill she is liable to the principal for any resulting loss.

    Comment c to Restatement, Section 379 provides:

The paid agent is subject to a duty to exercise at least the skill which he represents himself as having. Unless the circumstances indicate otherwise, a paid agent represents that he has at least the skill and undertakes to exercise the care which is standard for that kind of employment in the community. A business agent represents that he understands the usages of the business and undertakes to conduct transactions in accordance with them; one undertaking a matter involving special knowledge represents that he has the special knowledge required.

For example, P appoints A as his agent to sell goods in markets where the highest price can be obtained. A sells goods in a market which is glutted and obtains a low price, although a higher price would have been obtained in a nearby market if A had used care in obtaining information which was available to him. A is subject to liability to P for breach of the duty of diligence.

    See *Bicknell, Inc. v. Havlin*.

Duty to Inform

An agent must use reasonable efforts to give the principal information which is relevant to the affairs entrusted to her and which, as the agent knows or should know, the principal would desire to have. Restatement, Section 381. This duty is made imperative by the rule of agency that provides that notice to an agent is notice to his principal. Some examples of information which an agent has been held under a duty to communicate to his principal are: that a customer of the principal has become insolvent; that a debtor of the principal has become insolvent; that one of the partners of a firm with which the principal has previously dealt, and with which the principal or agent is about to deal, has withdrawn from the firm; or that the principal's property which the principal has authorized the agent to sell at a specified price can be sold at a higher price.

Duty to Account

The agent is under a duty to maintain and provide the principal with a true and complete account of money or other property which the agent has received or expended on behalf of the principal. Restatement, Section 382. An agent must also keep the principal's property separate from his own.

Fiduciary Duty

A fiduciary duty is one which arises out of a relationship of trust and confidence. It is a duty imposed by law and is owed by a trustee to a beneficiary of a trust, an officer or director of a corporation to the corporation and its shareholders, a lawyer to his clients, an employee to his employer, and an agent to his principal. Fiduciary duties are not limited to these situations but exist in every relationship where the law authorizes one person to repose trust and confidence in another.

The fiduciary duty is one of **utmost loyalty and good faith.** An agent must act solely in the interest of his principal and not in his own interest or in the interest of another. An agent may not represent his principal in any transaction in which he has a personal interest. An agent may not take a position in conflict with the interest of his principal, unless the principal, with full knowledge of all of the facts, consents. For example, A, an agent of P who desires to purchase land, agrees with C, who represents B, a seller of land, that A and C will endeavor to effect a transaction between their principals and will pool their commissions. A and C have committed a breach of fiduciary duty to P and B. In addition, the agent owes his principal at all times the duty of full disclosure. He does not deal with his principal at arm's length.

The fiduciary duty of an agent prevents him from competing with his principal or acting on behalf of a competitor or for persons whose interests conflict with those of the principal. Moreover, an agent who is employed to buy may not buy from himself without the principal's consent. Restatement, Section 389. Thus, P employs A to purchase for her a site suitable for a shopping center. A owns one which is suitable and sells it to P at the fair market value. A does not disclose to P that A had owned the land. P may rescind the transaction. An agent who is employed to sell may not become the purchaser nor may he act as agent for the purchaser. The agent's loyalty must be undivided, and his actions devoted exclusively to represent and promote the interests of his principal.

An agent may not use for his own benefit, and contrary to the interest of his principal,

information obtained in the course of the agency. For example, if an agent in the course of his employment discovers a defect in his principal's title to certain property, he may not use the information to acquire the title for himself. Or, if an employee prior to the expiration of his employer's lease secretly obtains a lease of the property for his own benefit, he may be compelled to transfer it to his employer.

An agent is not permitted to make a secret profit out of the subject matter of the agency. All such profits belong to the principal to whom the agent must account. Thus, if an agent authorized to sell certain property of his principal for $1,000 sells it for $1,500, he may not secretly pocket the additional $500. Further, suppose A employs real estate broker B to sell his land for a commission of six percent of the sale price. B, knowing that A is willing to sell for $20,000, agrees secretly with a prospective buyer who is willing to pay $22,000 for the land that he will endeavor to obtain the consent of A to sell for $20,000 in which event the buyer will pay B $1,000, or one-half of the amount which the buyer believes she is saving on the price. The broker has violated his fiduciary duty and would not be allowed to retain the secret profit of $1,000 but must pay it to A. Furthermore, B loses the right to any commission on the transaction. Restatement, Section 469. The result is that the seller, who willingly sold the land for $20,000 expecting to pay a commission of $1,200 and net $18,800, receives $21,000 free of commission. B's breach of fiduciary duty produces an unexpected windfall for A. However, this is incidental to the deterrent effect of the rule requiring a faithless fiduciary to account for any gain or profit from his acts of disloyalty. *See Sierra Pacific Industries v. Carter.*

DUTIES OF PRINCIPAL TO AGENT

With respect to the mutual rights and duties of principal and agent, the emphasis is largely on the duties of the agent. This is necessarily so because of the nature of the agency relationship. In the first place, the acts and services to be performed, both under the agency contract and as may be required by law, are to be performed mostly by the agent. In the second place, the agent is a fiduciary, and so is subject to the several duties of loyalty and good faith, as discussed earlier. Nonetheless, an agent has certain rights against the principal, both under the contract and by the operation of the law. Correlative to these rights are certain duties which the principal owes to the agent. The duties are based in contract and tort law.

Contractual Duties

As in the case of any party to a contract, a principal is under a duty to perform his part of the contract according to its terms. The most important duty of the principal, from the standpoint of the agent, is to compensate the agent as specified in the contract. As will be seen, the duty to compensate, if not expressed, will be implied. It is also the duty of the principal not to terminate wrongfully the agency. Whether the principal must furnish the means of employment or opportunity for work will depend upon the particular case. A bank, upon employing a teller, must obviously furnish the opportunity and usual facilities for work by which the teller can carry on the employment. A principal who employs an agent to sell his goods must supply the agent with such goods. If the contract specifies the quality of the goods, the principal must not furnish inferior or defective goods. In other cases, the agent must create his own opportunity for work, as in the case of a broker employed to procure a buyer for his principal's house. How far, if at all, the principal must assist or cooperate with the agent will depend on the particular agency. Usually, cooperation on the part of the principal is more necessary where the agent's compensation is contingent upon the success of his efforts than where the agent is paid a fixed salary regularly over a period of permanent employment.

Compensation A principal has a duty to compensate her agent unless the agent has agreed to serve gratuitously. If the agreement does not specify a definite amount or rate of compensation, a principal is under a duty to pay the reasonable value of authorized services performed for her by her agent. Restatement, Section 443. A principal also has a duty to maintain and provide the agent a true and complete account of money or property due from her to the agent.

Reimbursement A principal is under a duty to reimburse his agent for authorized payments made by the agent on behalf of the principal and for authorized expenses incurred by the agent. Restatement, Section 438. For example, an agent who reasonably and properly pays a fire insurance premium for the protection of her principal's property is entitled to reimbursement for the payment. "The authority to pay money to third persons on account of the principal or to incur liabilities in the course of the principal's business may be created by specific directions or may be the result of the course of business between the principal and the agent, or of the customs of the business in which the agent is engaged for the principal." Section 439, Comment c.

Indemnification The principal is under a duty to indemnify the agent for losses incurred or suffered while acting as directed by the principal in a transaction which is not illegal or not known by the agent to be wrongful. Restatement, Sections 438 and 439. To indemnify is to make good or pay a loss, as in insurance. Suppose that P, the principal, has in his possession goods belonging to X. P directs A, his agent, to sell these goods. A, believing P to be the owner, sells the goods to T. X then sues A for the conversion of his goods and recovers a judgment which A pays to X. A is entitled to payment from P for his loss, including the amount reasonably expended by A in defense of the action brought by X.

Tort Duties

In addition to her contractual duties, an employer owes certain tort duties to her employees. Among these is the duty to provide an employee with reasonably safe conditions of employment and to warn the employee of any unreasonable risk involved in the employment. An employer is also liable to her employees for injury caused by the negligence of other employees and of other agents doing work for her. These duties are discussed more fully in Chapter 43.

TERMINATION OF AGENCY

Since the authority of an agent is based upon the consent of the principal, when such consent is withdrawn or otherwise ceases to exist, the agency is terminated. Upon revocation by the principal, the power of the agent to bind the principal to contracts with third persons with whom the agent has previously dealt will continue until such persons have been notified or have knowledge of the revocation. Upon termination of the agency the agent's actual authority ends, and he is not entitled to compensation for services subsequently rendered, although the agent's fiduciary duties may continue. Termination of his authority may take place by acts of the parties or by operation of law.

Acts of the Parties

Termination by the acts of the parties may be by the acts of both principal and agent or by the act of either one of them. The methods of termination by acts of the parties are as follows:

Lapse of Time Authority conferred upon an agent for a specified time terminates at the expiration of that period. If no time is specified, authority terminates at the end of a reasonable period. Restatement, Section 105. For example, P authorizes A to sell a tract of land for him. Ten years pass without communication between P and A. A purports to sell

the tract. A's authorization has terminated due to lapse of time and the purported sale is not binding upon P.

Mutual Agreement of the Parties The agency relationship is created by agreement and may be terminated at any time by mutual agreement of the principal and the agent.

Fulfillment of Purpose The authority of an agent to perform a specific act or to accomplish a particular result is terminated when the act is performed or the result is accomplished by the agent. Restatement, Section 106. Thus, if A authorizes B to sell or lease A's land, and B leases the land to C, B's authority is terminated and he may not thereafter sell or lease the land without receiving new authorization.

Revocation of Authority A principal may revoke an agent's authority at any time. Restatement, Section 119. Moreover, the principal may manifest her termination of consent either expressly or implicitly, that is by conduct which is inconsistent with its continuance. Examples include where the principal indicates that the agent is to do an act different from that originally authorized, retakes the goods which she had authorized the agent to sell, sells or disposes of the goods, or voluntarily causes their loss or destruction. Restatement, Section 119, Comment b.

However, if such revocation constitutes a breach of contract by the principal, the agent may recover damages from the principal. For example, P, in consideration of A's agreement to advertise and give his best energies to the sale of P's property, Blackacre, grants to A "a power of attorney, irrevocable for one year." A advertises and spends time trying to sell Blackacre. At the end of three months P informs A that he revokes the power of attorney. A's authority is terminated but A may recover damages from P. Restatement, Section 118, Illustration 1. *See Hilgendorf v. Hague.*

Renunciation by the Agent The agent also has the power to put an end to the agency by notice to the principal that she renounces the authority given her by the principal. However, if the parties have contracted that the agency continue for a specified time, an unjustified renunciation prior to the expiration of the time is a breach of contract.

Operation of Law

In contrast with termination by the acts of the parties, the agency relationship may be terminated by the operation of law. Although, in any such case, one of the parties may suffer a loss, he has no rights against the other in respect of such loss, since the agency was terminated by law. Thus, where the agency is terminated by the death of the principal, the agent has no claim against the deceased principal's estate for any loss occasioned to him by the termination of the agency. As a matter of law, agency is ordinarily terminated by the occurrence of any of the following events.

Bankruptcy Bankruptcy is a proceeding in a Federal court affording relief to financially distressed debtors. The filing of the petition in bankruptcy, which initiates the proceedings, also usually terminates all the debtor's existing agency relationships. Moreover, if the credit standing of the agent is important to the agency relationship, then it will be terminated by the bankruptcy of the agent. Restatement, Section 113. Thus, A is appointed by P, an investment house, to act as its agent in advising P's local clients as to investments. A becomes bankrupt. A is no longer authorized to act for P.

Death The death of the principal terminates the authority of the agent. For example, P employs A to sell P's line of goods under a contract which specifies A's commission and that the employment is to continue for a year even if P should die before then. Without A's knowledge P dies. A has no authority to sell P's goods, even though the contract specified that A would be employed for one year. The death of P, the principal, terminated the au-

thority of the agent and voided the contract. Similarly, the authority given to an agent by a principal is strictly personal, and the agent's death terminates the agency.

Incapacity Incapacity of the principal which occurs after the formation of the agency terminates the agent's authority. To illustrate, P authorizes A to sell in the next 10 months an apartment complex for not less than $2 million. P is adjudicated incompetent two months later without A's knowledge. A's authority to sell the apartment complex is terminated. Likewise, subsequent incapacity of an agent to perform the acts authorized by the principal terminates the agent's authority.

Change in Business Conditions The authority of an agent is terminated by notice or knowledge of a change in the value of the subject matter, or of a change in business conditions from which the agent should reasonably infer that the principal would not consent to an exercise of the authority given him. Restatement, Section 109. Thus, P authorizes A to sell her eighty acres of farm land for $800 per acre. Subsequently, oil is discovered on nearby land which causes P's land to increase substantially in value. A knows of this, but P does not. A's authority to sell the land is terminated.

Loss or Destruction of the Subject Matter Where the authority of the agent relates to a specific subject matter which becomes lost or destroyed, such authority is thereby terminated. This is analogous to the rule that loss or destruction of the subject matter of an offer terminates the offer. For example, P authorizes A to make a contract for the sale of P's residence. The next week the residence burns completely, as A is aware. A's authority is terminated.

Loss of Qualification of Principal or Agent When the authority given the agent relates to the conduct of a certain business, the operation of which requires a license from the government or a regulatory agency, the failure to acquire or the loss of such license terminates the authority of the agent. Restatement, Section 111. Thus, A, who holds a retail liquor license, employs B to sell liquor at retail in A's store. A's license is revoked. B's authority to sell A's liquor at retail is terminated.

Disloyalty of Agent If an agent, without the knowledge of her principal, acquires interests which are adverse to those of the principal or otherwise breaches her duty of loyalty to the principal, her authority to act on behalf of the principal is terminated. Restatement, Section 112. Thus, A employs B, a realtor, to sell A's land. Unknown to A, B has been authorized by C to purchase this land from A. B is not authorized to sell the land to C.

Change of Law Subsequent to the employment of the agent, a change in the law may cause the performance of the authorized act to be illegal or criminal. Such a change in the law terminates the authority of the agent. Restatement, Section 116. Thus, A directs his agent B to ship young elm trees from State X to State Y. In order to control elm disease, a quarantine is established by State X upon the shipment into any other State of elm trees, and any such shipment is punishable by fine. B's authority to ship the elm trees is terminated.

Outbreak of War Where the outbreak of war places the principal and agent in the position of alien enemies, the authority of the agent is terminated because its exercise is illegal.

Where the principal and agent are citizens of the same country and the outbreak of war or a revolution makes the originally authorized transaction unexpectedly hazardous or impracticable, the agent's authority is terminated.

Irrevocable Agencies

In the foregoing discussion of the various ways in which the authority of an agent may be terminated, the agency relationship was assumed to be the ordinary one in which the agent does not have a security interest in the power conferred upon him by the principal. Where the **agency is coupled with an interest** of the agent in the subject matter, as where the agent has advanced funds on behalf of the principal and his power to act is given as security for the loan, the authority of the agent may *not* be revoked by the principal. In addition, neither the death, incapacity, or bankruptcy of the principal terminates the authority or the power of the agent. Restatement, Section 139. Illustration 4 to that section provides the following example:

P desires to borrow money from A, who requires security. P delivers to A certain chattels [personal property] and gives to A a writing by which he gives A the power, in case of nonpayment of the money, to sell the chattels as P's agent at a public or private sale for the best price that can be obtained, and out of the proceeds to retain the amount of the loan, paying the surplus to P. Having obtained the money upon these terms, P tells A that he revokes the power to sell. The power is not revoked. P dies. The power is not affected.

CASES

Definition of Agency

MURPHY v. HOLIDAY INNS, INC.

Supreme Court of Virginia, 1975.
216 Va. 490, 219 S.E.2d 874.

POFF, J.

     On August 21, 1973, Kyran Murphy (plaintiff) filed a motion for judgment against

Holiday Inns, Inc. (defendant), a Tennessee Corporation, seeking damages for personal injuries sustained on August 24, 1971, while she was a guest at a motel in Danville. Plaintiff alleged that "Defendant owned and operated" the motel; that "Defendant, its agents and employees, so carelessly, recklessly, and negligently maintained the premises of the motel that Plaintiff did slip and fall on an area of a walk where water draining from an air conditioner had been allowed to accumulate"; and that as a proximate result of such negligence, plaintiff sustained serious and permanent injuries.

Defendant filed grounds of defense and a motion for summary judgment "on the grounds that it has no relationship with regard to the operator of the premises . . . other than a license agreement permitting the operator of a motel on the same premises to use the name 'Holiday Inns' subject to all the terms and conditions of such license agreement." That agreement, filed as an exhibit with defendant's motion for summary judgment, identifies defendant's license as Betsy-Len Motor Corporation (Betsy-Len).

Upon a finding that defendant did not own the premises upon which the accident occurred and that "there exists no principal-agent or master-servant relationship between the defendant corporation and Betsy-Len Motor Hotel Corporation," the trial court entered a final order on April 25, 1974, granting summary judgment in favor of defendant.

Plaintiff's sole assignment of error is that the trial court erred "in holding that no principal-agent or master-servant relationship exists."

* * *

Actual agency is a consensual relationship.

Agency is the fiduciary relation which results from the manifestation of consent by one person to another that the other shall act on his behalf and subject to his control, and consent by the other so to act. Restatement (Second) of Agency § 1 (1958).

* * *

It is the element of continuous subjection to the will of the principal which distinguishes the agent from other fiduciaries and the agency agreement from other agreements. Id., comment (b).

When an agreement, considered as a whole, establishes an agency relationship, the parties cannot effectively disclaim it by formal "consent." "[T]he relationship of the parties does not depend upon what the parties themselves call it, but rather in law what it actually is." [Citations.] Here, plaintiff and defendant agree that, if the license agreement is sufficient to establish an agency relationship, the disclaimer clause does not defeat it.

Plaintiff and defendant also agree that, in determining whether a contract establishes an agency relationship, the critical test is the nature and extent of the control agreed upon.

The subject matter of the license defendant granted Betsy-Len is a "system." As defined in the agreement, the system is one "providing to the public . . . an inn service . . . of distinctive nature, of high quality, and of other distinguishing characteristics." Those characteristics include trade names using the words "Holiday Inn" and certain variations and combinations of those words, trade marks, architectural designs, insignia, patterns, color schemes, styles, furnishings, equipment, advertising services, and methods of operation.

In consideration of the license to use the "system," the licensee agreed to pay an initial sum of $5,000; to construct one or more inns in accordance with plans approved by the licensor; to make monthly payments of 15 cents per room per day (5 cents of which was to be earmarked for national advertising expenditures); and "to conduct the operation of inns . . . . in accordance with the terms and provisions of this license and of the Rules of operation of said System."

Plaintiff points to several provisions and rules which he says satisfy the control test and establish the principal-agent relationship. These include requirements

That licensee construct its motel according to plans, specifications, feasibility studies, and locations approved by licensor;

That licensee employ the trade name, signs, and other symbols of the "system" designated by licensor;

That licensee pay a continuing fee for use of the license and a fee for national advertising of the "system";

That licensee solicit applications for credit cards for the benefit of other licensees;

That licensee protect and promote the trade name and not engage in any competitive motel business or associate itself with any trade association designed to establish standards for motels;

That licensee not raise funds by sale of corporate stock or dispose of a controlling interest in its motel without licensor's approval;

That training for licensee's manager, housekeeper, and restaurant manager be provided by licensor at licensee's expense;

That licensee not employ a person contemporaneously engaged in a competitive motel or hotel business; and

That licensee conduct its business under the "system," observe the rules of operation, make quarterly reports to licensor concerning operations, and submit to periodic inspections of facilities and procedures conducted by licensor's representatives.

The license agreement of which these requirements were made a part is a franchise contract. In the business world, franchising is a crescent phenomenon of billion-dollar proportions.

[Franchising is] a system for the selective distribution of good and/or services under a brand name through outlets owned by independent businessmen, called "franchisees." Although the franchisor supplies the franchisee with know-how and brand identification on a continuing basis, the franchisee enjoys the right to profit and runs the risk of loss. The franchisor controls the distribution of his goods and/or services through a contract which regulates the activities of the franchisee, in order to achieve standardization. R. Rosenberg, *Profits From Franchising* 41 (1969). (Italics omitted.)

The fact that an agreement is a franchise contract does not insulate the contracting parties from an agency relationship. If a franchise contract so "regulates the activities of the franchisee" as to vest the franchisor with control within the definition of agency, the agency relationship arises even though the parties expressly deny it.

* * *

Here, the license agreement contains the principal features of the typical franchise contract, including regulatory provisions. Defendant owned the "brand name," the trade mark, and the other assets associated with the "system." Betsy-Len owned the sales "outlet." Defendant agreed to allow Betsy-Len to use its assets. Betsy-Len agreed to pay a fee for that privilege. Betsy-Len retained the "right to profit" and bore the "risk of loss." With respect to the manner in which defendant's trade mark and other assets were to be used, both parties agreed to certain regulatory rules of operation.

Having carefully considered all of the regulatory provisions in the agreement, we are of opinion that they gave defendant no "control or right to control the methods or details of doing the work," [citation], and, therefore, agree with the trial court that no principal-agent or master-servant relationship was created. As appears from the face of the document, the purpose of those provisions was to achieve system-wide standardization of business identity, uniformity of commercial service, and optimum public good will, all for the benefit of both contracting parties. The regulatory provisions did not give defendant control over the day-to-day operation of Betsy-Len's motel. While defendant was empowered to regulate the architectural style of the buildings and the type and style of furnishings and equipment, defendant was given no power to control daily maintenance of the premises. Defendant was given no power to control Betsy-Len's current business expenditures, fix customer rates, or demand a share of the profits. Defendant was given no power to hire or fire Betsy-Len's employees, determine employee wages or working conditions, set standards for employee skills or productivity, supervise employee work routine, or discipline employees for nonfeasance or misfeasance. All such powers and other management controls and responsibilities customarily exercised by an owner and operator of an on-going business were retained by Betsy-Len.

We hold that the regulatory provisions of the franchise contract did not constitute control within the definition of agency, and the judgment is affirmed.

Other Legal Relations:
Independent Contractor

MASSEY v. TUBE ART DISPLAY, INC.

Court of Appeals of Washington, Division 1, 1976.
15 Wn.App. 782, 551 P.2d 1387.

SWANSON, J.

Tube Art Display, Inc. (Tube Art) appeals from a judgment entered on a jury verdict awarding $143,000 in damages to John Massey, doing business as Olympic Research & Design Associates (Massey). Tube Art also appeals from an order denying a motion for judgment n. o. v. or for an new trial.

The facts leading to the initiation of this action are not in substantial dispute. A recently opened branch office of McPherson's Realty Company desired to move a reader board sign from its previous location to a site adjacent to its new quarters in a combination commercial-apartment building. An agreement was reached with Tube Art, the owner of the sign, to transport and re-install it on the northwest corner of the building's parking lot. On February 15, 1972, Tube Art obtained a permit from the City of Seattle for installation of the sign. On the following morning Tube Art's service manager and another employee went to the proposed site and took photographs and meausurements. Later, a Tube Art employee laid out the exact size and location for the excavation by marking a 4 by 4 foot square on the asphalt surface with yellow paint. The dimensions of the hole, including its depth of 6 feet, were indicated with spray paint inside the square. After the layout was painted on the asphalt, Tube Art engaged a backhoe operator, defendant Richard F. Redford, to dig the hole.

In response to Tube Art's desire that the job be completed on the 16th of February,

1972, Redford began digging in the early evening hours at the location designated by Tube Art. At approximately 9:30 p.m. the bucket of Redford's backhoe struck a small natural gas pipeline. After examining the pipe and finding no indication of a break or leak, he concluded that the line was not in use and left the site. Shortly before 2 a.m. on the following morning, an explosion and fire occurred in the building serviced by that gas pipeline. As a result, two people in the building were killed and most of its contents were destroyed.

Massey and his associates, as tenants of the building, brought an action against Tube Art, Richard Redford and others, alleging the total destruction of drawings, plans, sketches, prototype machine components, castings, and other work products. * * * The jury rendered its verdict on the liability issue in favor of plaintiffs and against both defendants, Tube Art and Redford. * * * A verdict in favor of Massey was returned, motions for judgment n. o. v. or for a new trial were denied, and judgment on the verdict was entered. Tube Art now appeals.

Tube Art's appeal presents two issues: (1) whether the trial court erred in declaring as a matter of law that an agency relationship existed between Tube Art and Redford, the person it chose to excavate the hole; and (2) whether the trial court erred in instructing the jury on the issue of damages.

* * *

Traditionally, servants and non-servant agents have been looked upon as persons employed to perform services in the affairs of others under an express or implied agreement, and who, with respect to physical conduct in the performance of those services, is subject to the other's control or right of control. [Citations.]

An independent contractor, on the other hand, is generally defined as one who contracts to perform services for another, but who is not controlled by the other nor subject to the other's right to control with respect to his physical conduct in performing the services. [Citations], Restatement (Second) of *Agency* § 2(3) (1958).

In determining whether one acting for another is a servant or independent contractor, several factors must be taken into consideration. These are listed in Restatement (Second) of *Agency* § 220(2) (1958), as follows:

(a) the extent of control which, by the agreement, the master may exercise over the details of the work;

(b) whether or not the one employed is engaged in a distinct occupation or business;

(c) the kind of occupation, with reference to whether, in the locality, the work is usually done under the direction of the employer or by a specialist without supervision;

(d) the skill required in the particular occupation;

(e) whether the employer or the workman supplies the instrumentalities, tools, and the place of work for the person doing the work;

(f) the length of time for which the person is employed;

(g) the method of payment, whether by the time or by the job;

(h) whether or not the work is a part of the regular business of the employer;

(i) whether or not the parties believe they are creating the relation of master and servant; and

(j) whether the principal is or is not in business.

All of these factors are of varying importance in determining the type of relationship involved and, with the exception of the element of control, not all the elements need be present. [Citation.] It is the right to control another's physical conduct that is the essential and oftentimes decisive factor in establishing vicarious liability whether the person controlled is a servant or a non-servant agent. [Citation.]

In discussing the actual extent to which the element of control must be exercised, we pointed out in [citation], that the plaintiff need not show that the principal controlled or had the right to control every aspect of the agent's operation in order to incur vicarious liability. Rather,

[i]t should be sufficient that plaintiff present substantial evidence of . . . control or right to control over those activities from whence the actionable negligence flowed. If the rule were otherwise, then a person wishing to accomplish a certain result through another could declare the other to be an independent contractor generally, and yet retain control over a particularly hazardous part of the undertaking without incurring liability for acts arising out of that part. Such a result would effectively thwart the purpose of the rule of vicarious liability. [Citations.]

In the recent case of [citation], we stated:

In this regard, it may be emphasized that it is not de facto control nor actual exercise of a right to interfere with or direct the work which constitutes the test, but rather, the *right to control* the negligent actor's physical conduct in the performance of the service. (Citations omitted.)

In making his ruling that Tube Art was responsible as a matter of law for Redford's actions the trial judge stated,

I think that under the undisputed evidence in this case they not only had the right to control, but they did control. They controlled the location of the spot to dig. They controlled the dimensions. They controlled the excavation and they got the building permits. They did all of the discretionary work that was necessary before he started to operate. They knew that the method of excavation was going to be by use of a backhoe rather than a pick and shovel which might have made a little difference on the exposure in this situation. They in effect created the whole atmosphere in which he worked. And the fact that even though he did not work for them all of the time and they paid him on a piece-work basis for the individual job didn't impress me particularly when they used him the number of times they did. Most of the time they used him for this type of work. So I am holding as a matter of law that Redford's activities are the responsibility of Tube Art.

Our review of the evidence supports the trial court's evaluation of both the right and exercise of control even though Redford had been essentially self-employed for about 5 years at the time of trial, was free to work for other contractors, selected the time of day to perform the work assigned, paid his own income and business taxes and did not participate in any of Tube Art's employee programs. The testimony advanced at trial, which we find determinative, established that during the previous 3 years Redford had worked exclusively for sign companies and 90 percent of his time for Tube Art. He had no employees, was not registered as a contractor or subcontractor, was not bonded, did not himself obtain permits or licenses for his jobs, and dug the holes at locations and in dimensions in exact accordance with the instructions of his employer. In fact, Redford was left no discretion with regard to the placement of the excavations that he dug. Rather, it was his skill in digging holes pursuant to the exact dimensions prescribed that caused him to be preferred over other backhoe operators. We therefore find no disputed evidence of the essential factor—the right to control, nor is there any dispute that control was exercised over the most significant decisions—the size and location of the hole. Consequently, only one conclusion could reasonably be drawn from the facts presented. In such a circumstance, the nature of the relationship becomes a question of law. [Citation.] We find no error.

* * *

[The court held that the trial court had not erred in giving its instructions on the issue of damages.]

Affirmed.

Duty of Diligence

BICKNELL, INC. v. HAVLIN

Massachusetts Court of Appeals, 1980.
9 Mass. App. Ct. 497, 402 N.E.2d 116.

NOLAN, J.

The plaintiff (Bicknell) claims to be aggrieved by the direction of verdicts for the defendants John J. Havlin and Corcoran & Havlin Insurance Agency, Inc. (Corcoran and Havlin), on counts one and three of its complaint alleging negligence in failing to place proper insurance coverage on two buildings leased to Bicknell and located in Middleton. As to count two, which alleges a breach of contract, the trial judge ordered judgment notwithstanding a verdict for the plaintiff in the amount of $40,000.00. At oral argument, the parties stipulated that the damages assessed by the jury on count two constitute the only recoverable damages under all counts. We reverse the judgment on count two.

* * * Bicknell had been in the business of distributing swimming pools and their accessories and supplies since 1957. Havlin, treasurer of Corcoran & Havlin, and Corcoran & Havlin were independent insurance agents. Bicknell had been doing business with an insurance agency which was purchased by Corcoran & Havlin in 1969. At that time, Havlin met with the principals of Bicknell with a view toward a continuation of business with Bicknell. Havlin described himself as experienced in the insurance business. He told the representatives of Bicknell that he wanted "to handle [the Bicknell] account in a highly professional manner." Bicknell decided to retain Corcoran & Havlin and, thereafter, Havlin devoted himself to the Bicknell account. He procured from various insurance carriers all the insurance required by Bicknell—casualty, liability, automobile, surety, fidelity bonds, workmen's compensation and other coverages, except life insurance. Havlin made recommendations for particular types of coverage and gave advice freely to Bicknell. One of the earliest recommendations which was adopted was for the purchase of a multiperil policy for Bicknell's commercial stock. At the end of each month, Bicknell sent Corcoran & Havlin a report disclosing the value of commercial stock at each warehouse location. Corcoran & Havlin would then review the report to make sure that Bicknell was reporting in accordance with the policy. If the report was in order, Corcoran & Havlin would transmit it to the carrier.

* * *

When Bicknell submitted its monthly report of inventory and its value on March 6, 1974, Havlin took notice that the value of the commercial stock at the warehouse in Middleton was $758,600.00. The limit of insurance coverage at that time for stock at this location was $540,000.00. Havlin telephoned Smith [who represented Bicknell] to inquire about new limits, and Smith agreed that new limits should be purchased. As a result, Havlin increased the coverage at Middleton to $750,000.00, effective immediately. During this telephone conversation, Smith told Havlin that two new warehouses, in the style of Quonset huts, were then under construction in Middleton and that Bicknell would lease them from the owner of the Middleton real estate.

Approximately ten days later, Havlin called Smith and discussed the insurance provisions of the draft of the lease. Smith informed Havlin that the two new warehouses in Middleton were just about ready for use. After Smith told Havlin the value of certain heaters which would be stored in the new warehouses, Havlin asked Smith if he thought that $50,000.00 would cover the stock in each building. When Smith indicated that this would be sufficient "at this point," Havlin said, "Let's slap fifty thousand on each building." Havlin did not indicate that he meant specific coverage. Smith thought that the total limits of coverage were being increased by $100,000.00, consistent with the blanket type of coverage in force on the commercial stock in both Framingham and Middleton. Havlin placed specific, limited coverage of $50,000.00 on the stock in each building, effective April 4, 1974. Corcoran & Havlin on May 8, 1974, submitted its invoice to Bicknell for several changes in coverage on the two buildings in Middleton. The language of the invoice did not distinguish the specific coverage on the contents of the two new buildings from the blanket coverage lately purchased for the contents of the other building in Middleton.

Bicknell transmitted to Corcoran & Havlin on May 6, 1974, its monthly report of stock for April, 1974. The report revealed the value at Middleton to be $839,000.00. Without Bicknell's knowledge, Havlin assigned $739,000.00 in value to the old warehouses. He sent the report to the carrier.

A fire broke out on June 3, 1974, in one of the two new warehouses in Middleton. The fire loss to the commercial stock amounted to $103,275.91. The carrier paid Bicknell $50,000.00, the amount of the endorsement of April 4, 1974.

In a letter dated June 10, 1974, from Havlin to the carrier concerning Bicknell, Havlin admitted making "a technical error of judgment due to unfamiliarity with the advantage of blanket, versus specific, coverage on contents." In the same letter Havlin confessed to "an obvious element of confusion" regarding the different types of coverage.

The evidence warranted a finding that Havlin was the agent of Bicknell. [Citation.] An agent is bound to use due care in the implementation of the agency, [citation], and in carrying out the instructions of the principal-client. [Citation.] See also Restatement (Second) of Agency § 379(1) (1958). The nature and extent of the duty of care owed by an indpendent insurance agent to his client depends in part, at least, upon the degree of skill which he represents himself to possess.

If he holds himself out to the world as possessing certain skill, or if his business is such as to carry with it an implication that he possesses particular skill in effecting insurances, as in [the] case of an insurance broker, then his principal is justified in relying upon the knowledge which he professes to possess, and he is bound to exercise the skill and to use the knowledge which the business requires. . . . 3 Couch, Insurance § 25:37 at 335–336 (2d ed. 1960).

Havlin undertook to advise Bicknell and to make recommendations. It was Havlin, not Smith, who suggested "slapping" $50,000.00 on each building. The jury could find that this was one of many recommendations made by Havlin over a considerable period of time and that these were "special circumstances of assertion, representation and reliance" for which Havlin may be liable. [Citation.]

There is no merit to Havlin's argument that the issue of his failure to use due care required the introduction of expert testimony. Havlin's admission of "a technical error of judgment" was sufficient to raise an inference of negligence. [Citation.]

The judgment on count two is reversed, and judgment is to be entered for the plantiff on the verdict returned by the jury on that count.

So ordered.

Fiduciary Duty

SIERRA PACIFIC INDUSTRIES v. CARTER

Court of Appeal, First District, Division 3, 1980.
104 Cal.App.3d 579, 163 Cal.Rptr. 764.

RHODES, J.

Joseph H. Carter, a licensed California real estate broker for the past 26 years, appeals an order of the trial court granting respondent Sierra Pacific Industries' motion for a new trial in an action involving the sale of real property.

During the fall of 1975, Sierra Pacific purchased, for a lump sum, various timberlands and six other pieces of real property, including the subject of this dispute, a ten-acre parcel in Willow Creek on which five duplexes and two single family units are located.

After the acquisition, Sierra Pacific requested Carter's assistance in selling the non-timberland properties, including the Willow Creek parcel. Carter was familiar with the property, having participated in efforts to sell it to others prior to its purchase by Sierra Pacific. Acting in reliance on Carter's representation as to the value of the Willow Creek parcel, Sierra Pacific commissioned him to sell it for an asking price of $85,000, of which Sierra Pacific would receive $80,000 and Carter, $5,000. The trial testimony was in conflict over whether, if Carter were able to find a buyer willing to pay more than $85,000, the excess was to be equally divided or whether

it would go entirely to Carter under a net listing agreement.

* * *

Pursuant to the agreement, appellant showed the Willow Creek property to several prospective buyers but was for a time unable to secure a sale at the asking price of $85,000. Finally, in June of 1976, Carter sold the property for that amount to his daughter and son-in-law, Debbie and David Benson and, by his own admission, retained a $5,000 commission without informing respondent of his relationship to the buyers.

Sierra Pacific instituted a fraud action against Carter based on the foregoing facts. The jury impaneled to hear the matter returned a general verdict in Carter's favor. Judgment was entered accordingly. Thereafter Sierra Pacific moved for a new trial. The motion was granted as to all issues and on all grounds asserted: inadequacy of damages, insufficient evidence and verdict against the law. Carter appeals, claiming that the order granting the new trial cannot be sustained on any of the grounds enumerated.

We begin with a review of the substantive law. An agent bears a fiduciary relationship to his or her principal which requires, among other things, disclosure of all information in the agent's possession relevant to the subject matter of the agency [citation]. An agent may not compete with the principal, nor may he or she act as agent for another whose interests conflict with those of the principal. [Citation.]

In the context of an agreement to sell land on another's behalf, the general duties inherent in every agency become more specific. A real estate agent must refrain from dual representation in a sale transaction unless he or she obtains the consent of both principals after full disclosure. [Citation.] This means under most circumstances that if the agent is related to the buyer in a way which suggests a reasonable possibility that the agent him or herself could indirectly be acquiring an interest in the subject property, the relationship is a "material fact" which must be disclosed. [Citation.]

There is no question that Carter concealed information material to this transaction from his principal, Sierra Pacific. * * *

It thus is evident that Carter owed a duty of disclosure to his principal, Sierra Pacific. It is equally evident that the duty was breached. Given duty and breach, a minimum of $5,000 in damages to Sierra Pacific flows automatically. Apart from any actual and proximately caused loss on the price it received for its property, Sierra Pacific was entitled to recover the commission it paid to Carter. ". . . [A] real estate broker must act in good faith in the discharge of his duties as agent . . . [B]y misconduct, breach of conduct [sic] or wilful disregard, in a material respect, of an obligation imposed upon him by the law of agency he may forfeit his right to compensation." [Citation.] In a case closely analogous to the one at bar, for example, breach of the duty of full disclosure was held to deprive respondent real estate brokers of their right to a commission. [Citation.] See also Rest.2d Agency (1958) § 469.

We thus are led to the inescapable conclusion that Carter is liable to Sierra Pacific as a matter of law for a minimum of $5,000 and that the jury's verdict to the contrary was in error. * * *

The order granting a new trial is therefore affirmed with instructions to the court below to direct a verdict against defendant as to both duty and breach. The only triable issue remaining concerns the extent of plaintiff's damages.

Termination of Agency by Revocation

HILGENDORF v. HAGUE

Supreme Court of Iowa, 1980.
293 N.W.2d 272.

UHLENHOPP, J.

[Harvey Hilgendorf was a licensed real estate broker acting as the agent of the Hagues in the sale of eighty acres of farmland. The Hagues, however, terminated Hilgendorf's agency before the expiration of the listing contract when they encountered financial difficulties and decided to liquidate their entire holdings of land at one time. Hilgendorf brought this action for breach of the listing contract. The Hagues maintain that Hilgendorf's duty of loyalty requires him to give up the listing contract.]

* * *

I. Right to terminate listing. Since agency is a consensual relationship, a principal has *power* to terminate an agency which is not coupled with an interest [where the agent has an ownership interest in the subject matter of the agency], although the contract is for a period which has not expired. Ordinarily the agent's authority thereupon ceases. Absent some legal ground, however, the principal does not have a *right* to terminate an unexpired agency contract, and may subject himself to damages by doing so. [Citations.].

The whole question regarding liability here turns on whether the Hagues had a legal ground for terminating Hilgendorf's agency before the expiration of the year. All agree that they had power to terminate, but they contend they also had a right to do so. They say PCA [Hagues' principal creditor] would not renew their loan, they had to sell the 80 acres in addition to their other land, and the best way to sell the 80 acres was with the 160 acres. Did these circumstances give them a "right" to terminate the listing contract they had signed and cast on Hilgendorf a "duty" to give up his listing contract as a matter of an agent's loyalty to his principal?

The Hagues appear to confuse the two roles an agent occupies. In performing agency functions for the principal an agent does indeed occupy a fiduciary position, and his duty of loyalty requires him to place the principal's interest first. Restatement (Second) of Agency § 387. But in the contract of agency itself between the agent and principal, neither of the parties is acting for the other; each is acting for himself.

This case involves the latter role. * * *

* * *

Several circumstances are given in the texts as grounds for terminating fixed-term agencies, but coming upon hard times is not among them. [Citations.] We agree with the trial court that the Hagues did not have a right to terminate the one-year listing contract . . . and that Hilgendorf did not have a duty to give up his listing contract.

II. Damages. Hague terminated the listing on August 13, 1976. Since Hague had the power to do so, Hilgendorf no longer had authority to sell the . . . parcel. For that reason, he cannot recover a commission *as such*, although he thereafter and within the year produced a ready, willing, and able buyer for the price in the listing. Nonetheless, since Hague breached the listing agreement by terminating it, Hilgendorf can recover damages. [Citation.]

The question here relates to the *measure* of damages Hilgendorf is entitled to *recover*. The editors state the measure thus in [citation]:

The courts generally support the principle that a broker whose employment or authority is wrongfully revoked may consider his contract of employment as rescinded and sue for damages, in which event he is entitled to have his recovery include the value of the services he has already rendered, his disbursements, and *such prospective profits as he can establish would have been his but for such revocation.* . . .

* * *

Where as here the principal terminates an exclusive listing within the term, the agent may endeavor to show that he would, but for the termination have sold the property within

the unexpired period at the listed price. If he is successful in his proof, his lost profits are ordinarily measured by the commission he would have earned. He does not recover the commission itself, but his damages are measured by the commission. As stated in section 445 of the Restatement, Comment *a*:

If the principal, in breach of contract, prevents the agent from accomplishing the result upon which the agreed compensation is conditioned, the agent is entitled to damages for such breach or, as an alternative, the fair value of his services in attempting to accomplish it. The amount of recovery for damages in such a case is not the specified compensation as such, but the damages which the agent suffers by reason of the breach of contract. *Such damages may coincide in amount with the agreed compensation*; if, however, the agent would have had to incur further expense in order to earn such compensation, and these expenses have been saved to him, he is entitled only to a sum equal to the agreed compensation minus the expenses he has thereby saved.

(Emphasis added.)

* * *

Here Hilgendorf proceeded on the damage issue by showing "the gains prevented" by Hague's breach of the listing contract. He established beyond question that he would have sold the . . . parcel for the full asking price within the listing period. His lost profit was the offered price times the six percent commission rate, and this is the amount the trial court allowed him.

We agree with the trial court's decision. Affirmed.

PROBLEMS

1. A, the owner of certain unimproved real estate in Chicago, employed B, a real estate agent, to sell the property for a price of $25,000 or more and agreed to pay B a commission of six percent for making a sale. B negotiated with C who was interested in the property and willing to pay as

much as $28,000 for it. B made an agreement with C that if B could obtain A's signature to a contract to sell the property to C for $25,000, C would pay B a bonus of $1,000. B prepared and A and C signed a contract for the sale of the property to C for $25,000. C refuses to pay B the $1,000 as promised. A refuses to pay B the six percent commission. In an action by B against A and C, what judgment?

2. P employed A to sell a parcel of real estate at a fixed price without knowledge that D had previously employed A to purchase the same property for him. P gave A no discretion as to price or terms, and A entered into a contract of sale with D upon the exact terms authorized by P. After accepting a partial payment, P discovered that A was employed by D and brought an action to rescind. D resisted on the ground that admittedly P had suffered no damage for the reason that A had been given no discretion and the sale was made upon the exact basis authorized by P. Decision?

3. P owned and operated a fruit cannery in Southton, Illinois. He stored a substantial amount of finished canned goods in a warehouse in East St. Louis, Illinois, owned and operated by A, in order to have goods readily available for the St. Louis market. On March 1, he had 10,000 cans of peaches and 5,000 cans of apples on storage with A. On the day named, he borrowed $5,000 from A, giving A his promissory note for this amount due June 1 together with a letter authorizing A, in the event the note was not paid at maturity, to sell any or all of his goods on storage, pay the indebtedness, and account to him for any surplus. P died on June 2 without having paid the note. On June 8, A told T, a wholesale food distributor, that he had for sale as agent of the owner 10,000 cans of peaches and 5,000 cans of apples. T said he would take the peaches and would decide later about the apples. A contract for the sale of 10,000 cans of peaches for $6,000 was thereupon signed. "A, agent for P, seller; T, buyer." Both A and T knew of the death of P. Delivery of the peaches and payment were made on June 10. On June 11, A and T signed a similar contract covering the 5,000 cans of apples, delivery and payment to be made June 30. On June 23, P's executor, having learned of these contracts, wrote A and T stating that A had no authority to make the contracts, demanding that T return the peaches, and directing A not to deliver the apples. Discuss the correctness of the contentions of P's executor.

4. Green, a licensed real estate broker in Illinois, and Jones, also an Illinois resident, while both were in New York, signed a contract whereby Green agreed to endeavor to find a buyer for certain real estate located in Illinois owned by Jones

who agreed to pay Green a commission of $10,000 in the event of a sale. Green found a buyer, a resident of New York, to whom the land was sold. Thereafter, Jones refused to pay the commission. Green commenced an action in Illinois to recover the commission. Jones defended on the sole ground that the brokerage contract was unenforceable because Green was not a licensed real estate broker in New York.

Relevant provisions of the applicable New York statute forbid any person from holding himself out or acting temporarily as a real estate broker or salesman without first procuring a license. A violation is declared to be a misdemeanor, and the commission of a single prohibited act is a violation for which the statute provides a penalty. For whom should judgment be rendered?

5. B made a valid contract with A under which A was to sell B's goods on commission during the period from January 1 to June 30. A made satisfactory sales up to May 15 and was then about to close an unusually large order when B suddenly and without notice revoked A's authority to sell. Can A continue to sell B's goods during the unexpired term of her contract?

6. A Electric Co. gave a list of delinquent accounts to B, an employee, with instructions to discontinue electric service to delinquent customers. Among those listed was C Hatchery, which was then in the process of hatching chickens in a large, electrically heated incubator. C Hatchery told B that it did not consider its account delinquent, but B nevertheless cut the wires leading to the hatchery. Subsequently, C Hatchery recovered a judgment of $5,000 against B in an action brought against B for the loss resulting from the interruption of the incubation process. B has paid the judgment and brings a cause of action against A Electric Co. Decision?

7. In October 1980, Black, the owner of the Grand Opera House, and Harvey entered into a written agreement leasing the Opera House to Harvey for five years at a rental of $30,000 a year. Harvey engaged Day as manager of the theatre at a salary of $175 per week plus 10 percent of the profits. One of the duties of Day was to determine each night the amount of money taken in and, after deducting expenses, to divide the profits between Harvey and the manager of the particular attraction which was playing at the theatre. In September 1985, Day went to Black and offered to rent

the Opera House from Black at a rental of $37,500 per year, whereupon Black entered into a lease with Day for five years at this figure. When Harvey learned of and objected to this transaction, Day offered to assign the lease to him for $60,000 per year. Harvey refused and brought an appropriate action seeking to have Day declared a trustee of the Opera House on behalf of Harvey. Decision?

Chapter 18

RELATIONSHIP WITH THIRD PARTIES

THE purpose of an agency relationship is to allow the principal to extend his business activities by authorizing agents to enter into contracts with third persons on the principal's behalf. So long as the agent operates within his authority, actual or apparent, the principal and third party become bound to each other, each acquiring contractual rights and liabilities, while the agent assumes neither. In some circumstances, however, the agent will himself have contractually created obligations or rights or both. Moreover, in the course of an agency, third parties may suffer injuries from the tortious conduct of the agent. As a consequence, the principal and agent may incur tort liability to these injured parties.

RELATIONSHIP OF PRINCIPAL AND THIRD PERSONS

This section will first consider the contract liability of the principal; then it will examine the principal's potential tort liability.

CONTRACT LIABILITY OF THE PRINCIPAL

The **authority** of an agent is his power or capacity to change the legal status of his principal. Thus, whenever an agent, acting within his authority, makes a contract for his principal, he thereby creates new rights or liabilities or both as to his principal and so effects a change in his principal's legal status. This authority of an agent to act for his principal in business transactions is the basic factor in agency. Without it the agency relation could not exist.

It is fundamental that a principal is liable on contracts made for her by her agent acting with actual or apparent authority, including those contracts in which her identity is not disclosed. Conversely, she is not liable in contract upon unauthorized acts of an agent unless she subsequently ratifies them. The other party to a contract made by an agent for a disclosed or partially disclosed principal, acting within his actual or apparent authority, is liable to the principal as if he had contracted directly with the principal. Restatement, Section 292.

Types of Authority

There are two basic types of authority: actual and apparent. **Actual authority** depends upon consent manifested by the principal to the agent. It may be either express or implied. In either case it is binding and confers upon the agent both the power and the right to create or affect legal relations of the principal with third persons. **Apparent authority** is based upon acts or conduct of the principal which manifests to a third person that actual authority of the agent exists and upon which the third person *justifiably* relies. Such manifestation can consist of words or actions of the principal as well as other facts and circumstances which induce in the third person reasonable reliance upon the existence of an agency relationship. To the extent that things are as represented, there is both actual and apparent authority. Whether the authority of an agent is actual (express or implied) or apparent, it is effective to bind the principal in contract by acts of the agent or supposed agent within its scope. See Figure 18-1.

Actual Express Authority The express authority of an agent is found in the words of the principal, spoken or written, and communicated to the agent. It is actual authority embodied in language directing or instructing the agent to do something specific. Thus, if A orally or in writing requests his agent B to sell A's automobile for $6,500, B's authority to sell the car for this sum is actual and express.

Actual Implied Authority Implied authority is not found in express or explicit words of the principal, but is inferred from words or conduct manifested to the agent by the principal. Authority granted to an agent to accomplish a particular purpose necessarily includes authority to employ means reasonably required for its accomplishment. Restatement, Section 35. For example, A authorizes B to manage her eighty-two-unit apartment complex. Nothing is said by A about expenses. In order to manage the building, however, B must employ a janitor, purchase fuel for heating, and arrange for ordinary maintenance. The authority to incur these expenses, while not expressly granted, is implied from the express authority to manage the building, as they are required for its proper management. Whatever may be reasonably necessary to complete the task assigned to the agent is impliedly authorized.

Unless otherwise agreed, authority to make a contract is inferred from authority to conduct a transaction, if the making of such a contract is incidental to the transaction, usually accompanies such a transaction, or is reasonably necessary to accomplish it. Restatement, Section 50. Thus, P appoints A as the general manager of P's manufacturing business. A's authority is interpreted as including authority to make contracts for the employment of necessary employees. On the other hand, suppose P employs A, a real estate broker, to find a purchaser for her residence at a stated price. A has no authority to contract for its sale.

Certain rules have been developed with reference to what authority is implied in particular types of agencies. Unless otherwise agreed, authority to buy or to sell property for the principal includes authority to agree upon the terms, to demand or make the usual representations and warranties, to receive or execute the instruments usually required, to pay or receive so much of the purchase price as is to be paid at the time of the transfer, and to receive possession of the goods if a buying agent, or to surrender possession of them if a selling agent.

General authority to manage or operate a business for a principal impliedly confers authority upon the agent to buy and sell property for the principal to the extent usual and customary in such operation. The authority of an agent employed to manage a business is set forth in the Restatement, Section 73, as follows:

Unless otherwise agreed, authority to manage a business includes authority:

(a) to make contracts which are incidental to such business, are usually made in it, or are reasonably necessary in conducting it;

(b) to procure equipment and supplies and to make repairs reasonably necessary for the proper conduct of the business;

(c) to employ, supervise, or discharge employees as the course of business may reasonably require;

(d) to sell or otherwise dispose of goods or other things in accordance with the purposes for which the business is operated;

(e) to receive payment of sums due the principal and to pay debts due from the principal arising out of the business enterprise; and

(f) to direct the ordinary operations of the business.

Seems if P really isn't.

Apparent Authority Apparent authority is authority which arises out of words or conduct of a **disclosed** principal manifested to third persons by which they are reasonably induced to rely upon the assumption that actual authority exists. Restatement, Section 27. Apparent authority confers upon the agent or supposed agent the **power** to bind the principal in contracts with third persons and precludes the principal from denying the existence of actual authority.

Comment *a* to Section 27 compares apparent and actual authority as follows:

Apparent authority is created by the same method as that which creates [actual] authority, except that the manifestation of the principal is to the third person rather than to the agent. For apparent authority there is the basic requirement that the principal be responsible for the information which comes to the mind of the third person, similar to the requirement for the creation of [actual] authority that the principal be responsible for the information which comes to the agent. Thus, either the principal must intend to cause the third person to believe that the agent is authorized to act for him, or he should realize that his conduct is likely to create such belief. The information received by the third person may come directly from the principal by letter or word of mouth, from authorized statements of the agent, from documents or other indicia of authority given by the principal to the agent, or from third persons who have heard of the agent's authority through authorized or permitted channels of communication. Likewise, as in the case of [actual] authority, apparent authority can be created by appointing a person to a position, such as that of manager or treasurer, which carries with it generally recognized duties; to those who know of the appointment there is apparent authority to do the things ordinarily entrusted to one occupying such a position, regardless of unknown limitations which are imposed upon the particular agent. So, too, a person who permits another to do an act in such a way as to establish in a community a reputation for having authority to act, either by directing the agent so to represent, or by directing him to act and doing nothing to prevent the spread of such information by the agent or by others, creates apparent authority with respect to those who learn of the reputation. Third persons who are aware of what a continuously employed agent has done are normally entitled to believe that he will continue to have such authority for at least a limited period in the future, and this apparent authority continues until the third person has been notified or learns facts which should lead him to believe that the agent is no longer authorized.

In addition, there may be apparent authority created by the principal's acquiescence in the agent's conduct when this is known to the third party. Likewise, if the principal manifests to the third person that the agent is authorized to conduct a transaction, there is apparent authority in the agent to conduct it in accordance with the ordinary usages of business, unless the third person has notice that the agent's authority is limited.

For example, A writes a letter to B authorizing her to sell his automobile and sends a copy of the letter to C, a prospective purchaser. On the following day, A writes a letter to B revoking the authority to sell the car, but does not send a copy of the second letter to C, who is not otherwise informed of the revocation. Although B has no actual author-

ity to sell the car, as to C she continues to have apparent authority. Or, suppose that B, in the presence of A, tells C that B is A's agent to buy lumber. Although this statement is not true, A does not deny it, as he could easily have done. C, in reliance upon the statement, ships lumber to A on B's order. A is obligated to pay for the lumber because B had apparent authority to act on A's behalf. However, this apparent authority of B exists only with respect to C. If B were to give D an order for a shipment of lumber to A, D would not be able to hold A liable. No actual authority existed, and as to D there was no apparent authority.

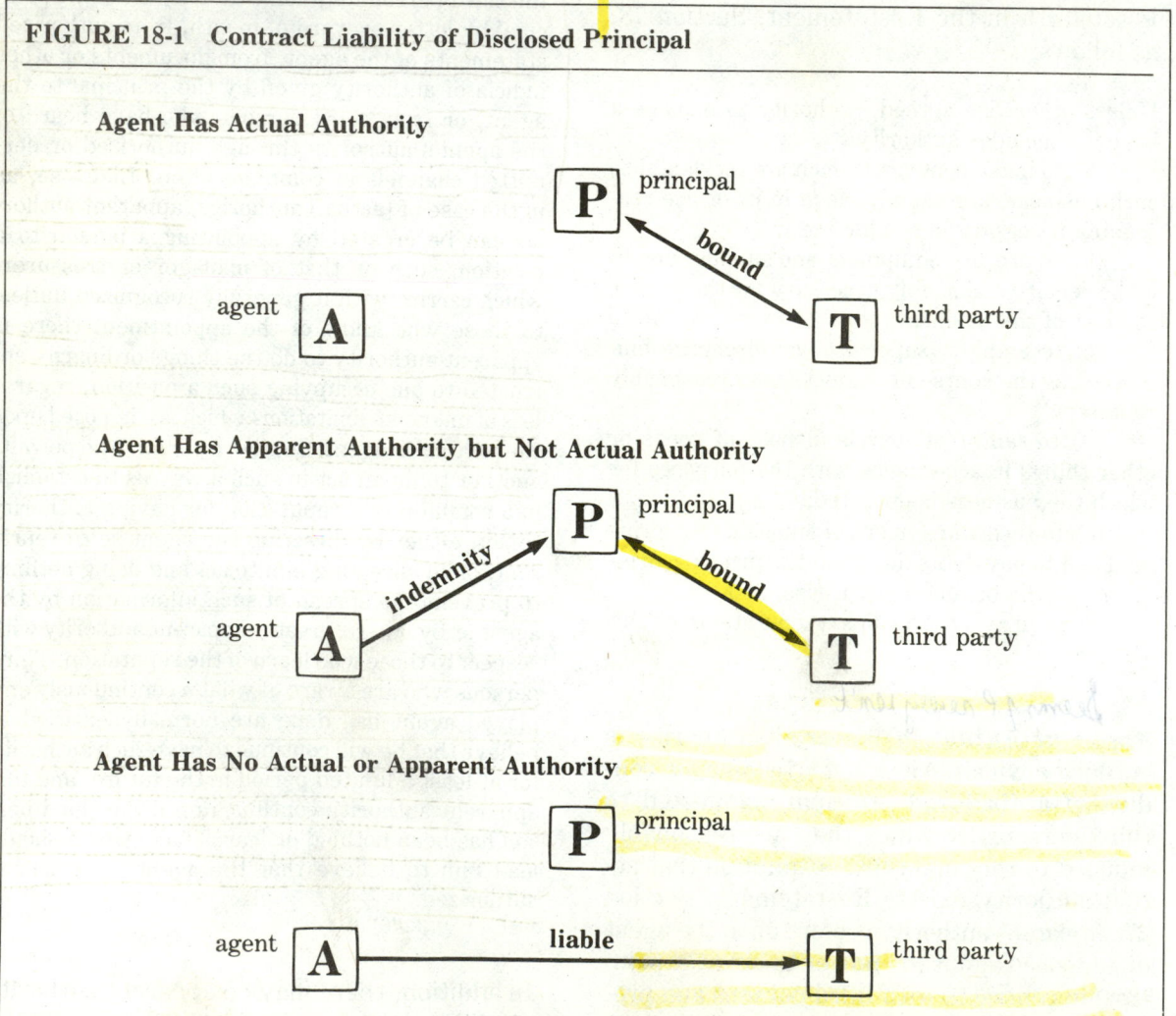

FIGURE 18-1   Contract Liability of Disclosed Principal

Agent Has Actual Authority

Agent Has Apparent Authority but Not Actual Authority

Agent Has No Actual or Apparent Authority

Thus, when there is apparent authority but not actual authority, the principal is nonetheless bound by the act of the agent. However, by exceeding his actual authority the agent has violated his duty of obedience and is liable to the principal for any loss sustained as a result of his acting in excess of his actual authority.

See Schoenberger v. Chicago Transit Authority.

Delegation of Authority

The appointment of an agent reflects confidence and reliance of the principal upon the agent's personal skill, integrity, and other qualifications. The agent has been selected because of her fitness to perform the task assigned to her and, therefore, ordinarily has no power to delegate her authority or to appoint a subagent. Restatement, Section 18. Thus, A employs B to collect her accounts. B may not delegate this authority to C, as A reposed trust and confidence in B and not in C.

However, in certain situations it is clear that the principal intended to permit the agent to delegate the authority granted to her. Such an intention may be gathered from the express authorization of the principal, the character of the business, the usages of trade, or the prior conduct of the parties. Restatement, Sections 78–81. For example, if a check is deposited in a bank for collection at a distant place, the bank is impliedly authorized to employ another bank at the place of payment.

If an agent is authorized to appoint or select other persons, called **subagents,** to perform or assist in the performance of the agent's duties, the acts of the subagent are binding on the principal to the same extent as if they had been done by the agent. The subagent is an agent of both the principal and the agent and owes a fiduciary duty to each.

If no authorization exists to delegate the agent's authority, but the agent nevertheless does so, the acts of the subagent do not impose any obligations or liability upon the principal to third persons. Likewise, the principal acquires no rights against such third persons.

Effect of Termination of Agency Upon Authority

Upon the termination of an agency, the agent's actual authority ceases. When the termination is by death or incapacity of the principal or agent, the agent's apparent authority also expires as notice of such termination to third persons is *not* required. Thus, in a case where T, a tenant of the principal P, paid rent to P's agent A in ignorance of P's death, and A failed to account for the payment, T is liable to P's estate for payment of the amount of the rent. The same holds where an authorized transaction is made impossible of performance.

In other cases, apparent authority continues with respect to third parties (1) with whom the agent had previously dealt on credit, (2) to whom the agent has been specially accredited, or (3) with whom the agent has begun to deal, until such third parties receive **actual notice.** Restatement, Section 136(2). Actual notice requires a communication to the third party, either oral or written. If notice is given by mail it is effective as actual notice upon delivery not upon dispatch. All other third parties as to whom there was apparent authority need only be given **constructive notice** such as publication in a newspaper of general circulation in the area where the agency is regularly carried on. Restatement, Section 136(3). To illustrate: A is the general agent of P, who carries on business in Chicago. X knows of the agency but has never dealt with A. Y sells goods on credit to A, as agent of P. P revokes A's authority and publishes a statement to that effect in a newspaper of general circulation published in Chicago. X does not see the statement and deals with A in accordance with and in reliance upon the former agency. Y also does not see the statement and has no knowledge of the revocation. Y sells more goods to A, as the agent of P. P has given sufficient notice of revocation as to X and, therefore, A's apparent authority has terminated with respect to X. On the other hand, P has not given sufficient notice of revocation as to Y, and P is bound to Y by the contract of sale made on P's behalf by A.

See *Zukaitis v. Aetna Casualty and Surety Co.*

Ratification

Ratification is the confirmation or affirmance by one person of a prior act which another, without authority, has done as his agent. The ratification of such act or contract binds the principal and the third party as if the agent had been initially authorized. As defined in the Restatement, Section 82:

Ratification is the affirmance by a person of a prior act which did not bind him but which was done or professedly done on his account, whereby the act, as to some or all persons, is given effect as if originally authorized by him.

Ratification may relate to the acts of an agent which have exceeded the authority granted to him, as well as to acts of a person who is without any authority but made on behalf of an alleged principal. The act, however, must have indicated to the third person that it was on behalf of the alleged principal in order that it may be ratified. There can be no ratification by a principal who is undisclosed. Thus, A without any authority, contracts to sell to T an automobile belonging to P. A states to T that the auto is A's. T promises to pay $5,500 for the automobile. P affirms. There is *no* ratification and P is not a party to the contract because A did not purport to act on P's behalf.

To effect a ratification the principal must manifest an intent to do so with knowledge of all material facts concerning the transaction. Restatement, Section 91. However, it is not necessary that such intent be communicated either to the purported agent or to the third person. It may be manifested by express language or implied from conduct of the principal. Thus, if A, without authority, contracts in P's name for the purchase of goods from T on credit, and P, having learned of A's unauthorized act, accepts the goods from T, she thereby impliedly ratifies the contract and is bound on the contract. Express ratification consists in the giving of notice of affirmance of the unauthorized act by the supposed principal to the third person. In any event, the principal must ratify the entire act or contract. Restatement, Section 96.

A ratification relates back to the time of performance of the unauthorized act. For example, B, without authority from A, represents to C that he is A's agent and on June 1 enters into a bilateral executory contract with C on behalf of A. Since B acted without authority, neither A nor C is bound to the supposed contract. On June 15, A ratifies the act of B. Both A and C thereupon become bound to the contract, effective as of June 1, to which date the ratification relates back. However, suppose that on June 12, C learned of B's lack of authority and notified A that he withdrew from the contract. A's ratification on June 15 would not cause a contract to be formed. To be effective ratification must occur before the third person gives notice to the principal or agent of his withdrawal. Restatement, Section 88.

If the affirmance of a transaction occurs at a time when the situation has so materially changed that it would be inequitable to subject the third party to liability on the transaction, the third party may elect to avoid liability. For example, A has no authority but, purporting to act for P, A contracts to sell P's house to T. The next day the house burns down. P then affirms. T is not bound.

Finally, for ratification to be effective the purported principal must have been in existence when the act was done. For example, a promoter of a corporation not yet in existence may enter into contracts on behalf of the corporation. In the vast majority of States these acts cannot be *ratified* by the corporation because it had not been in existence when the contracts were made.

A valid ratification once made is irrevocable. Ratification is equivalent to prior authority, which means that the effect of ratification is substantially the same as though the purported agent had been a duly authorized agent when she performed the act in question. As between P and T, their respective rights, duties, and remedies are the same as if A had originally possessed due authority. As between P and A, both are in the same position as they would have been if the act had been originally authorized by P. A is entitled to her due compensation, and is freed from liability to P for acting as his agent without authority or for exceeding her authority, as the case may be. As between A and T, A is released from any liability she may have been under to T by reason of her having induced T to enter into the contract without P's authority. If, however, in the course of her dealings with T, A committed a tort against T, A remains liable on the tort to T, regardless of whether P ratified the tort or not. *See David v. Serges.*

TORT LIABILITY OF THE PRINCIPAL

In addition to contract liability to third persons, a principal may be liable in tort to third persons as a consequence of the acts of her agent. Tort liability may arise directly or indirectly from authorized or unauthorized acts of the agent.

Direct Liability of Principal

All individuals are liable for their own tortious conduct. Consequently, a principal may be held liable in damages for his own negligence or recklessness in carrying on an activity by means of employees or agents. The Restatement, Section 213 provides:

A person conducting an activity through servants or other agents is subject to liability for harm resulting from his conduct if he is negligent or reckless:

(a) in giving improper or ambiguous orders or in failing to make proper regulations; or

(b) in the employment of improper persons or instrumentalities in work involving risk of harm to others:

(i) in the supervision of the activity; or

(ii) permitting, or failing to prevent, negligent or other tortious conduct by persons, whether or not his servants or agents, upon premises or with instrumentalities under his control.

For example, if A lends to her employee, B, a company car to run a business errand knowing that B is incapable of driving the vehicle, A would be liable for her own negligence to anyone injured by B's negligent driving.

Indirect Vicarious Liability of Principal for **Authorized** Acts of Agent

A principal who authorizes his agent to commit a tortious act with respect to the property or person of another is liable for the injury or loss sustained by such person. Restatement, Section 212. The authorized act is that of the principal. Thus, if A directs his agent, B, to enter upon C's land and cut timber which neither A nor B has any right to do, the cutting of the timber is a trespass, and A is liable to C. Or, suppose A instructs his agent B to make certain representations as to A's property which B is authorized to sell. A knows these representations are false, but B does not. Such representations by B to C who buys the property in reliance on them is a deceit for which A is liable to C.

Indirect Vicarious Liability of Principal for **Unauthorized** Acts of Agent

A principal may be liable for a tort committed by his agent which he did not authorize, even one which is in flagrant disobedience of his instructions to the agent, where the tort was committed by the agent in the course of his employment. Restatement, Sections 216 and 219. This is a form of liability without fault and is based upon the doctrine of *respondeat superior,* i.e., let the superior respond. The rationale of this doctrine is that one who carries out his business activities through the use of agents and employees should be liable for their negligence in carrying out the business purposes for which they were employed. It is the price which the employer pays for thus enlarging the scope of his business activities. It does not matter how carefully the employer selected the employee, if in fact the latter negligently injured a third person while engaged in the business of the employer. Consequently, an undisclosed principal is liable for the torts committed by her agent within the scope of the agent's employment. Restatement, Section 222. Also, a principal is liable for the torts committed by an unauthorized agent in connection with a transaction which the purported principal, with full knowledge of the tort, subsequently ratifies. Restatement, Section 218. Needless to say, cases involving unauthorized but ratified torts are rare.

The Doctrine of **Respondeat Superior** The liability of the principal under *respondeat superior* is vicarious or derivative and depends upon proof of wrongdoing by the agent *in the course of his employment.* Restatement, Section 219. Frequently both principal and agent are joined as defendants in the same suit. If the agent is not held liable, the principal is not liable. A principal who is held liable for her agent's tort has a right of **indemnification** against the agent, which is the right to be reimbursed for the amount that she was required to pay by reason of the agent's wrongful act. However, frequently an agent is not sufficiently solvent to reimburse his employer, resulting in the principal's bearing the brunt of the liability.

The wrongful act of the agent or employee must be connected with his employment and within its scope in order that the principal be held liable for resulting injuries or damage to third persons. Section 228 of the Restatement provides a general rule for determining whether the conduct of an employee ("servant") is within the scope of employment:

(1) Conduct of a servant is within the scope of employment if, but only if:

(a) it is of the kind he is employed to perform;

(b) it occurs substantially within the authorized time and space limits;

(c) it is actuated, at least in part, by a purpose to serve the master, and

(d) if force is intentionally used by the servant against another, the use of force is not unexpectable by the master.

(2) Conduct of a servant is not within the scope of employment if it is different in kind from that authorized, far beyond the authorized time or space limits, or too little actuated by a purpose to serve the master.

A servant or employee is an agent employed to perform services for the principal ("master") whose physical conduct in the performance of the service is controlled or subject to the right to control by the master. *See Austen v. Sherwood.*

For example, A is delivering gasoline for P. He lights his pipe and negligently throws the blazing match into a pool of gasoline which has dripped upon the ground during the delivery and which ignites. For the resulting harm, P is subject to liability because the negligence of the employee delivering the gasoline relates directly to the manner in which he is handling the goods in his custody. However, if a chauffeur while driving his employer's car on an errand for his employer suddenly decided to use his pistol and shoot at pedestrians on the sidewalk for target practice, the employer would not be liable to the pedestrians. This willful and intentional misconduct is not related to the performance of the services for which the chauffeur was employed nor is it expectable by the employer.

If A employs B to deliver merchandise in a given city to A's customers, and while driving a delivery truck in going to or returning from a place of delivery B negligently causes the truck to hit and injure C, A is liable to C for injuries sustained. But if, after making the scheduled deliveries, B drives the truck to a neighboring city to visit a friend and while so doing negligently causes the truck to hit and injure D, A is not liable. In such case, B is said to be on a "frolic of his own." He has deviated from the purpose of his employment and was using A's truck to accomplish purposes of his own and not the business of his employer. Of course, in all of these situations the wrongdoing agent is personally liable to the injured persons as a tortfeasor.

A principal may be held liable for the intentional torts of his agent if the commission of the tort is so reasonably connected with the employment as to be within its scope. For example, a principal would be liable if his agent makes fraudulent statements about the products she is selling or defames a competitor or disparages the competitor's product.

The tort liability of principal and agent is illustrated in Figure 18–2.

Torts of Independent Contractor An independent contractor is not the employee of the person for whom he is performing work or rendering services. Hence, the doctrine of *respondeat superior* does not apply to torts committed by an independent contractor, such as an attorney, broker, or rental agent. For example, P authorizes B, his broker, to sell land for him. P, T, and B meet in T's office. B arranges the sale to T. While B is preparing a deed for P to sign, he negligently knocks over an inkstand and ruins a valuable rug belonging to T. B but *not* P is liable to T. Similarly, P employs R, a roofer, as an in-

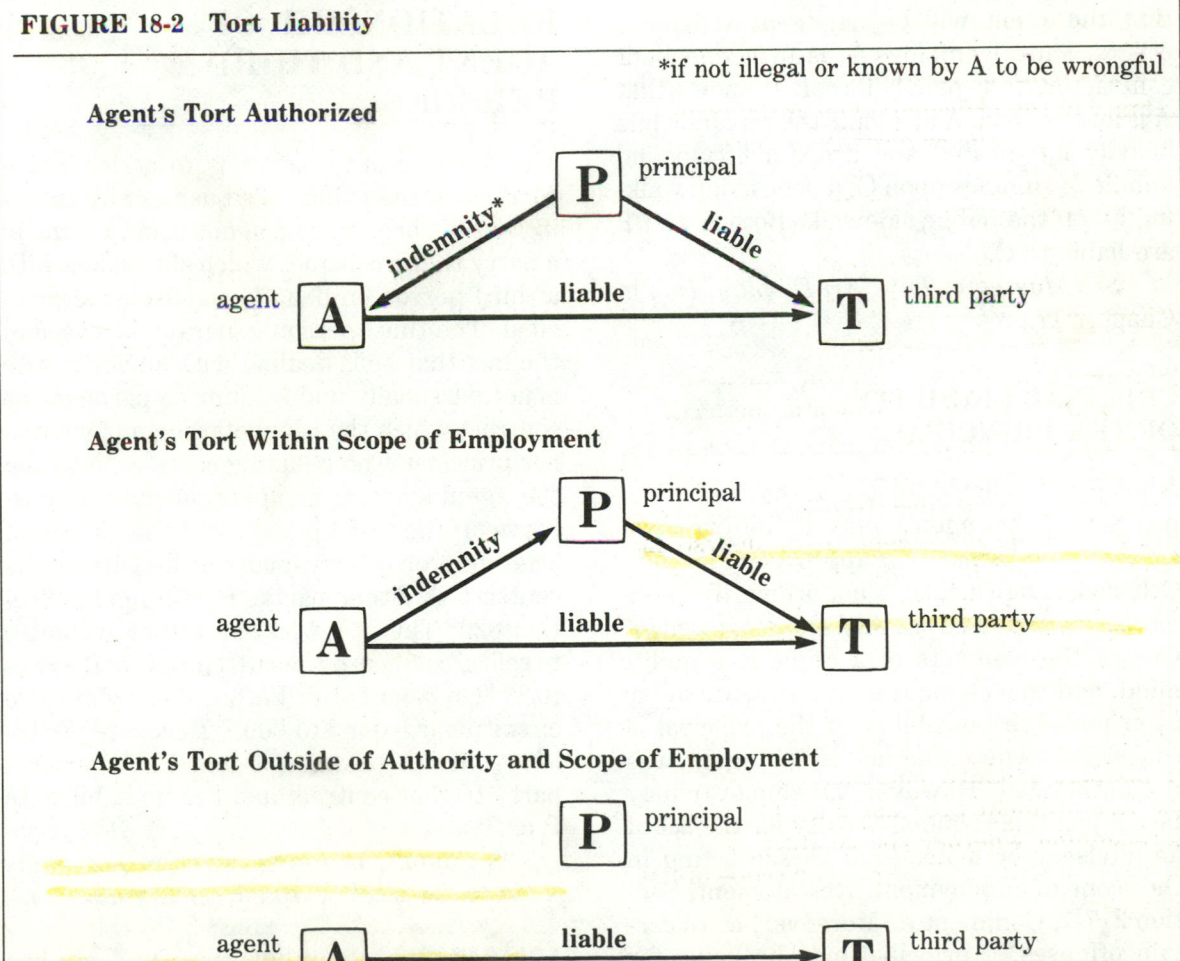

FIGURE 18-2   Tort Liability

*if not illegal or known by A to be wrongful

Agent's Tort Authorized

principal P — liable → T third party
agent A — liable → T
A ← indemnity* — P

Agent's Tort Within Scope of Employment

principal P — liable → T third party
agent A — liable → T
A — indemnity → P

Agent's Tort Outside of Authority and Scope of Employment

principal P
agent A — liable → T third party

dependent contractor to repair P's roof. R drops a hammer upon W, a pedestrian walking by on the public sidewalk. R but not P is liable to W.

Nevertheless, certain duties imposed by law are non-delegable, and a person may not escape the consequences of their non-performance by contracting with an independent contractor. For example, a landowner who permits an independent contractor to maintain a dangerous condition on his premises, such as an excavation adjoining a public sidewalk which is unprotected by a guard rail or by lights at night, is liable to a member of the public who is injured as a result of falling into the excavation.

Moreover, the principal may be liable if she should know that there is an undue risk that the agent will be negligent and harm others. Thus, P employs A, as an independent contractor, to repair her roof. P knows that A is an alcoholic. A attempts the repairs while heavily intoxicated and drops a fifty-pound bundle of shingles upon C, a pedestrian walking by on the public sidewalk. Both A and P are liable to C.

See *Massey v. Tube Art Display, Inc.* in Chapter 17.

CRIMINAL LIABILITY OF THE PRINCIPAL

A principal is liable for the authorized criminal acts of his agents only if the principal directed, participated or approved of the act. Otherwise, a principal is not ordinarily liable for the unauthorized criminal acts of his agents. One of the elements of a crime is a guilty mind, and this element is not present, so far as criminal responsibility of the principal is concerned, where the act of the agent was not authorized. However, an employer may be subject to a criminal penalty for the act of an advisory or managerial person acting in the scope of employment. Restatement, Section 217D, Comment d. Moreover, as to certain offenses, a principal may be liable for penalties under criminal law for the unau-

thorized acts of his agent whether the agent is managerial or not. Even under the common law some crimes do not require intent. In addition, many regulatory statutes do not require intent to violate them, or even knowledge of the act which causes the conduct to be illegal. In such cases, a principal may be held subject to a penalty for conduct of agents acting on his behalf in doing acts or in conducting transactions of the kind for which they are employed. Examples include the publication of a criminal libel in a newspaper, the sale of liquor to minors or to intoxicated persons, or the sale of unwholesome or adulterated food.

K Now

RELATIONSHIP OF AGENT AND THIRD PERSONS

The function of an agent is to assist in the conduct of the principal's business by carrying out his orders. The agent is not normally a party to the contract which she makes with a third person on behalf of a **disclosed** principal. The third person generally is aware of the fact that he is dealing with an agent who is not personally undertaking to perform the contract which she is negotiating on behalf of her principal. The resulting contract, if within the agent's actual or apparent authority, is between the third person and the principal. The agent ordinarily incurs no liability on the contract to either party. Restatement, Section 320. Thus, A who has actual authority to sell circuit boards manufactured by P writes to T: "On behalf of P, I offer to sell you 5,000 circuit boards for $15,000." T accepts. There is a contract between T and P. A is not a party to that contract and has no liability to P or T.

An agent, however, may be personally liable to the third person in certain situations:

1. by acting without authority or exceeding the scope of the authority granted;

2. upon entering into a contract on behalf of an undisclosed or partially disclosed principal;

3. upon knowingly entering into a contract on behalf of a non-existent principal;

4. by guaranteeing performance of a contract by the principal; or

5. by committing a tortious or wrongful act.

These five situations involving personal liability of an agent will be covered in this section as well as the circumstances under which an agent may acquire rights against third persons.

CONTRACT LIABILITY OF AGENT

Unauthorized Contracts

If an agent exceeds his actual and apparent authority, the principal is not bound. However, the fact that the principal is not bound does not of itself make the agent a party to the contract. The agent's liability, if any, arises from express or implied representations made by the agent to the third party concerning the agent's authority.

Agent's Implied Warranty of Authority A person who undertakes to contract as agent impliedly warrants that he is in fact authorized to make the contract on behalf of the party whom he purports to represent. If the agent does not have authority to bind the principal, the agent is liable to the third party for damages unless the principal ratifies the contract. However, no implied warranty exists if the contract expressly provides that the agent shall not be responsible for any lack of authority, or if the agent, acting in good faith, discloses to the third person all of the facts upon which his authority rests. For example, agent B has received a letter of instruction from his principal A which is ambiguous. B shows it to C stating that it represents all of the authority that he has to act, and both B and C rely upon its sufficiency.

In this case there is no implied or express warranty by B to C of his authority.

See *Goldfinger v. Doherty.*

Misrepresentation If a purported agent falsely represents to a third person that he has authority to make a contract on behalf of a principal whom he has no power to bind, he is liable in a tort action to the third person for the loss sustained in reliance upon such misrepresentation.

Undisclosed or Partially Disclosed Principal

An agent acts for an undisclosed principal when she appears to be acting in her own behalf and the third person with whom she is dealing has no knowledge that she is acting as an agent. Restatement, Section 4(3). The instructions of the principal to the agent are not only to conceal the identity of the principal but also not to disclose the agency relationship. Ostensibly, the third person is dealing with the agent as though she were a principal. A partially disclosed principal is one whose existence is known but whose identity is unknown. Restatement, Section 4(2). Thus, the third person is aware that the agent is acting on behalf of another, but he is not informed of the name or identity of the partially disclosed principal. The use of undisclosed or partially disclosed principals may be helpful where the third party might inflate the price of property he was selling if he knew the identity of the principal.

Liability of the Parties The agent is personally liable upon a contract which she enters into with a third person on behalf of an undisclosed principal or a partially disclosed principal, unless the third person after discovery of the existence and identity of such principal elects to hold the principal to the contract. The reason for the liability of the agent is that the third person has placed reliance upon the agent individually and has accepted the agent's personal undertaking to perform the contract. Obviously, where the principal is wholly undisclosed, the third person does not know of the interest of anyone in the contract other than himself and the agent. The reason for the liability of the undisclosed or partially disclosed principal is that the concealment by the agent is pursuant to the instructions of the principal, and having received the benefits of the agent's acts, she should also assume and be responsible for the burdens.

After the third person has become informed of the identity of the undisclosed or partially disclosed principal, he may hold either the principal or the agent to performance of the contract, but not both. Having once made an election, he is irrevocably bound by it. After the third person has demanded performance by both the agent and the principal, he may bring suit against both, as he does not wish to incur the risk that upon a trial the evidence may fail to establish the agency relationship. In most States bringing suit and proceeding to trial against both is not an election, but before the entry of any judgment the third person is compelled to make an election, as

he is not entitled to a judgment against both. If the agent is held liable by the third party the agent has the right to be reimbursed by the principal.

See Van D. Costas, Inc. v. Rosenberg.

Rights of Undisclosed or Partially Disclosed Principal

An undisclosed or partially disclosed principal acquires rights and may maintain an action in his own name against the third person with whom the agent entered into a contract in the agent's name. See Figure 18-3. However, an undisclosed principal does not become liable upon a contract which provides that he or any undisclosed principal shall not be a party to it. Restatement, Section 189.

Liability of Agent Where Principal Is Non-Existent

A person who professes to act as agent for a fictitious or non-existent principal is personally liable on a contract entered into with a third person on behalf of such a principal. Restatement, Section 326. A promoter of a

---

FIGURE 18-3 Contract Liability of Undisclosed or Partially Disclosed Principal

Contract Within Actual Authority

Contract Outside Actual Authority

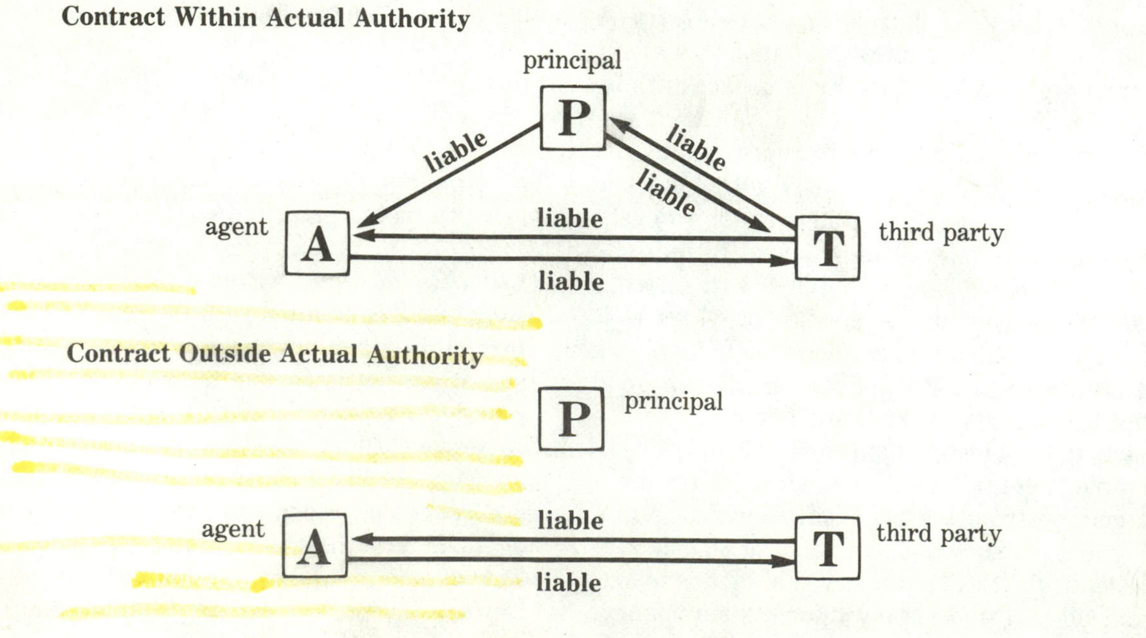

corporation who enters into contracts with third persons in the name of a corporation to be organized is personally liable on such contracts. The corporation is not liable as it did not authorize the contracts. If the corporation after coming into existence affirmatively adopts a pre-incorporation contract made on its behalf, it becomes bound along with the promoter. However, if the corporation enters into a new contract with such a third person, the prior contract between the promoter and the third person is discharged, and the liability of the promoter is terminated. This is a novation.

Where an agent enters into a contract with a third person on behalf of a principal who, unknown to both the agent and the third person, had died prior to the making of the contract, it is generally held that the existence of the principal at the time of the making of the contract is an implied condition precedent to the contract, and that neither the agent, the third person, nor the estate of the decedent principal is liable on it.

Performance Guaranteed by Agent

An agent who guarantees that the principal will perform the contract between the third party and the principal will be liable to the third party if the principal fails to perform. The agent in this situation is acting as a surety and would have a right of reimbursement from the principal. For a more complete discussion of suretyship see Chapter 38.

TORT LIABILITY OF AGENT

An agent is personally liable for his tortious acts which injure third persons, whether or not such acts are authorized by the principal and whether or not the principal may also be liable. Restatement, Section 343.

An agent who commits a wrong at the direction or under instructions of his principal is also personally liable. Restatement, Section 344. For example, an agent is personally liable if he converts the goods of a third person to this principal's use. An agent is also liable for making representations which he knows to be fraudulent to a third person who in reliance sustains a loss.

RIGHTS OF AGENT AGAINST THIRD PERSON

An agent who makes a contract with a third person on behalf of a disclosed principal has no right of action against the third person for breach of contract. Restatement, Section 363. The agent is not a party to the contract. However, an agent for an undisclosed principal or partially disclosed principal may maintain in her own name an action against the third person for breach of contract. Restatement, Section 364. In such case the agent is also individually liable on the contract.

CASES

Types of Authority

SCHOENBERGER v. CHICAGO TRANSIT AUTHORITY

Appellate Court of Illinois, First District, First Division, 1980.
84 Ill.App.3d 1132, 39 Ill.Dec. 941, 405 N.E.2d 1076.

CAMPBELL, J.

The plaintiff, James Schoenberger, brought a small claims action pro se in the

Municipal Department of the circuit court of Cook County against the defendant, Chicago Transit Authority (hereinafter C.T.A.) to recover contract damages. The trial court ruled in favor of the defendant and against the plaintiff. The plaintiff appeals from this judgment. At issue is whether the C.T.A. may be held liable under agency principles of a promise allegedly made by an employee of the C.T.A. to the plaintiff at the time that he was hired to the effect that he would receive a

$500 increase in salary within a specified period of time. We affirm.

Schoenberger was employed by the C.T.A. from August 16, 1976, to October, 1976, at a salary of $19,300. The facts surrounding his employment with the C.T.A. are controverted. The plaintiff's position at the trial was that he took the job with the C.T.A. at a salary of $19,300 upon the condition that he would receive a $500 salary increase, above and beyond any merit raises, within a year. Schoenberger testified at trial that, after filling out a job application and undergoing an initial interview with a C.T.A. Placement Department interviewer, he met several times with Frank ZuChristian, who was in charge of recruiting for the Data Center. At one of the meetings with ZuChristian, the Director of Data Center Operations, John Bonner, was present. At the third meeting held between ZuChristian and the plaintiff, ZuChristian informed the plaintiff that he desired to employ him at $19,800 and that he was making a recommendation to this effect. Schoenberger told ZuChristian that he would accept the offer. ZuChristian informed him that a formal offer would come from the Placement Department within a few days. However, when the offer was made, the salary was stated at $19,300. Schoenberger did not accept the offer immediately. Rather, he called ZuChristian for an explanation of the salary difference. After making inquiries, ZuChristian informed Schoenberger that a clerical error had been made and that it would take a number of weeks to have the necessary paperwork reapproved because several people were on vacation. To expedite matters, ZuChristian suggested Schoenberger take the job at the $19,300 figure and that he would see that the $500 would be made up to him at the April, 1976, October, 1976, or at the latest, the April, 1977, performance and salary review. The $500 increase was to be prospective and not retroactive in nature. John Hogan, the head of the Data Center, was aware of this promise, ZuChristian informed Schoenberger. Because the defendant was found to be ineligible

for the October, 1976 performance evaluation and the April, 1976 review was cancelled, the April, 1977 evaluation was the first evaluation at which the issue of the salary increase was raised. When the increase was not given at that time, the plaintiff resigned and filed this suit.

* * *

The trial court, after hearing the evidence and reviewing the exhibits, ruled in favor of the defendant. The trial court ruled: (1) that it was inconceivable that the plaintiff thought ZuChristian had final authority in regard to employment contracts; and (2) that it was not shown that a commitment or promise was made to the plaintiff by an authorized agent of the C.T.A.

* * *

The main question before us is whether ZuChristian, acting as an agent of the C.T.A., orally contracted with Schoenberger for $500 in compensation in addition to his $19,300 salary. The authority of an agent may only come from the principal and it is therefore necessary to trace the source of an agent's authority to some word or act of the alleged principal. [Citations.] The authority to bind a principal will not be presumed, but rather, the person alleging authority must prove its source unless the act of the agent has been ratified. [Citations.] Moreover, the authority must be founded upon some word or act of the principal, not on the acts or words of the agent. [Citations.]

* * * Both Hogan and Bonner, ZuChristian's superiors, testified that ZuChristian had no actual authority to either make an offer of a specific salary to Schoenberger or to make any promise of additional compensation. Furthermore, ZuChristian's testimony corroborated the testimony that he lacked the authority to make formal offers. From this evidence, it is clear that the trial court properly determined that ZuChristian lacked the actual authority to bind the C.T.A. for the additional $500 in compensation to Schoenberger.

Nor can it be said that the C.T.A. clothed ZuChristian with the apparent authority to make Schoenberger a promise of compensation over and above that formally offered by the Placement Department. The general rule to consider in determining whether an agent is acting within the apparent authority of his principal was stated in [citation] in this way:

Apparent authority in an agent is such authority as the principal knowingly permits the agent to assume or which he holds his agent out as possessing—it is such authority as a reasonably prudent man, exercising diligence and discretion, in view of the principal's conduct, would naturally suppose the agent to possess.

* * *

Here, Schoenberger's initial contact with the C.T.A. was with the Placement Department where he filled out an application and had his first interview. There is no evidence that the C.T.A. did anything to permit ZuChristian to assume authority nor did they do anything to hold him out as having the authority to hire and set salaries. ZuChristian was not at a management level in the C.T.A. nor did his job title of Principal Communications Analyst suggest otherwise. The mere fact that he was allowed to interview prospective employees does not establish that the C.T.A. held him out as possessing the authority to hire employees or set salaries. Moreover, ZuChristian did inform Schoenberger that the formal offer of employment would be made by the Placement Department.

* * *

Our final inquiry concerns the plaintiff's contention that irrespective of ZuChristian's actual or apparent authority, the C.T.A. is bound by ZuChristian's promise because it ratified his acts. Ratification may be express or inferred and occurs where "the principal, with knowledge of the material facts of the unauthorized transaction, takes a position inconsistent with nonaffirmation of the transaction." [Citations.] Ratification is the equivalent to an original authorization and confirms that which was originally unauthorized. [Citation.] Ratification occurs where a principal attempts to seek or retain the benefits of the transaction. [Citations.]

Upon review of the evidence, we are not convinced that the C.T.A. acted to ratify ZuChristian's promise. According to Bonner's testimony, when he took over the supervision of ZuChristian's group in the fall of 1976 and was told of the promise, he immediately informed ZuChristian that the promise was unauthorized and consequently would not be honored. Subsequently, he informed Schoenberger of this same fact. Mere delay in telling Schoenberger does not, as the plaintiff contends, establish the C.T.A.'s intent to ratify. [Citations.]

* * *

For the reasons we have indicated, the judgment of the circuit court of Cook County granting judgment in favor of the defendant, C.T.A., is affirmed.

Effect of Termination of Agency Upon Authority

ZUKAITIS v. AETNA CASUALTY AND SURETY CO.

Supreme Court of Nebraska, 1975.
195 Neb. 59, 236 N.W.2d 819.

BLUE, J.

This is an action for a declaratory judgment brought to determine whether defendant-appellee, the Aetna Casualty and Surety Company, was obligated under its professional liability insurance policy to defend plaintiff-appellant, Raymond R. Zukaitis, in a medical malpractice suit.

The case was tried to the court under a stipulation of facts which can be summarized as follows: Raymond R. Zukaitis was a physician practicing medicine in Douglas County, Nebraska. Aetna issued Dr. Zukaitis a policy of professional liability insurance through its agent, the Ed Larsen Insurance Agency, Inc.

This policy was for a period from August 31, 1969, to August 31, 1970.

On August 7, 1971, Dr. Zukaitis received a written notification of a claim for malpractice which allegedly occurred on September 27, 1969. On August 10, 1971, Dr. Zukaitis telephoned the Ed Larsen Insurance Agency. At the request of the agency the written claim was forwarded to it by Dr. Zukaitis. This was received on August 11, 1971, and was erroneously referred to the St. Paul Fire and Marine Insurance Company on that date by the agency.

Dr. Zukaitis was insured with St. Paul Fire and Marine Insurance Company from August 31, 1970, to August 31, 1971. But on the date of the alleged malpractice, he was insured with Aetna. Apparently without notice to Dr. Zukaitis, the agency contract between Ed Larsen Insurance Agency and Aetna had been canceled effective August 1, 1970. At that time the agency placed Dr. Zukaitis' insurance with St. Paul.

On November 22, 1971, a malpractice action was brought against Dr. Zukaitis based on the alleged malpractice of September 27, 1969. Attorneys for St. Paul undertook the defense of the lawsuit. On January 25, 1974, St. Paul discovered that it was not the insurance carrier for Dr. Zukaitis on September 27, 1969, the date of the alleged malpractice, and advised Aetna of this at that time. Dr. Zukaitis was also advised of this, and the attorney retained for St. Paul to represent Dr. Zukaitis withdrew. Dr. Zukaitis made demand upon Aetna on May 28, 1974, for it to undertake the defense of Dr. Zukaitis, but this demand was refused.

Dr. Zukaitis retained his own attorney to represent him in the malpractice case. A motion for summary judgment was filed by Dr. Zukaitis in that case, which motion was sustained. This action for a declaratory judgment against Aetna therefore resolved itself into an effort to recover attorney's fees and costs. The District Court found for Aetna. Dr. Zukaitis' motion for new trial was overruled, and this appeal followed.

Aetna contends that it is relieved from its obligation to Dr. Zukaitis since notice was not given as required by paragraph 4(b) of the policy which provides: "If claim is made or suit is brought against the insured, the insured shall immediately forward to the company every demand, notice, summons or other process received by him or his representative."

Dr. Zukaitis contends that under the circumstances, notice to Aetna was given within a reasonable period in that the agent who wrote the policy was given notice, and further that a delay in giving notice does not defeat policy obligations unless the insurer is prejudiced by the delay.

* * *

Ordinarily notice to a soliciting agent who countersigns and issues policies of insurance is notice to the insurance company. [Citations.] This is also true even if the agent forwards the notice to the wrong company. * * *

* * *

The question then is whether this is true after the agency contract between the insurance company and the agent has been terminated as it was in this case. To answer this, it is necessary to refer to the general law of agency.

The rule is that a revocation [by agreement of the principal and agent] of the agent's authority does not become effective as between the principal and third persons until they receive [actual] notice of the termination. [Citations.]

Here, Dr. Zukaitis did what most reasonable persons would do in this situation; he notified the agent who sold him the policy. There is no evidence that notice of the termination was sent to him or that he knew the agency contract has been canceled.

"When the insurer terminates the agency contract, it is its duty to notify third persons, such as the insureds with whom the agent dealt, and inform them of such termination. If it does not so notify and such third persons or insureds deal with the agent without notice or knowledge of the termination, and in reliance on the apparently continuing authority of the agent, the insurer is bound by the acts of the former agent." [Citation.]

"The principle of the carrying over of the authority of an agent after termination with respect to third persons having no notice or knowledge thereof has been applied so as to bind the insurer when the third person dealt with the apparent agent by contracting with him, or by forwarding or delivering to him suit papers and proofs of loss." [Citation.]

* * *

Reversed and remanded with directions.

Ratification

DAVID v. SERGES

Supreme Court of Michigan, 1964.
373 Mich. 442, 129 N.W.2d 882.

SOURIS, J.

[Serges is the owner of a retail meat marketing business. His managing agent borrowed $3,500 from David on Serges's behalf and for use in Serges's business. Serges paid $200 on the alleged loan and on several other occasions told David that the full balance owed would eventually be paid. He then disclaimed liability on the debt, asserting that he had not authorized his agent to enter into the loan agreement. David brought this action to collect on the loan.]

When an agent purporting to act for his principal exceeds his actual or apparent authority, the act of the agent still may bind the principal if he ratifies it. The Restatement of Agency 2d, § 82, defines ratification thusly:

Ratification is the affirmance by a person of a prior act which did not bind him but which was done or professedly done on his account, whereby the act, as to some or all persons, is given effect as if originally authorized by him.

"Affirmance" is defined in § 83 of the Restatement:

Affirmance is either

(a) a manifestation of an election by one on whose account an unauthorized act has been done to treat the act as authorized, or

(b) conduct by him justifiable only if there were such an election.

* * * Paragraph (d) of the comment to § 82 of the Restatement, supra, discusses the matter in these terms:

That the doctrine of ratification may at times operate unfairly must be admitted, since it gives to the purported principal an election to blow hot or cold upon a transaction to which, in contract cases, the other party normally believes himself to be bound. But this hardship is minimized by denying a power to ratify when it would obviously be unfair. * * * Further, if the transaction is not ratified normally the pseudoagent is responsible; if not, it is because the third party knew, or agreed to take the risk, of lack of authority by the agent. In many cases, the third person is a distinct gainer as where the purported principal ratifies a tort or a loan for which he was not liable and for which he receives nothing. This result is not, however, unjust, since although the creation of liability against the ratifier may run counter to established tort or contract principles, the liability is self-imposed. Even one who ratifies to protect his business reputation or who retains unwanted goods rather than defend a law suit, chooses ratification as preferable to the alternative. * * *

In this case the only testimony taken was plaintiff's, who testified that defendant's managing agent had borrowed from him $3,500 upon defendant's behalf and for use in defendant's business, a retail meat market. Plaintiff further testified that defendant subsequently had paid to him $200 on the alleged loan and had upon several occasions stated to plaintiff that the full sum would eventually be paid. With this testimony in the record plaintiff rested his case and defendant, without likewise resting, moved for a judgment of no cause on the theory that plaintiff had failed to prove a *prima facie* case.

The trial court erred in granting defendant's motion. * * *

Even if borrowing money were not within the agent's actual or apparent authority, plaintiff's evidence, viewed favorably, was legally sufficient to establish defendant's liability for the alleged loan upon a theory of ratification. Thus, plaintiff's evidence was sufficient to require defendant to be put to his proofs.

[Judgment for defendant reversed and remanded.]

Respondeat Superior

AUSTEN v. SHERWOOD

Court of Appeal of Louisiana, Fifth Circuit, 1983.
425 So.2d 818.

GRISBAUM, J.

Plaintiff/appellee, Kathleen Austen, filed suit against Wallace Sherwood and Cavalier Insurance Company, Sherwood's automobile liability insurer, seeking to recover for injuries and damages sustained in an automobile accident. She later joined as defendants Mississippi Press Register, Inc., Sherwood's employer, and its insurer, Liberty Mutual Insurance Company, who appeal the judgment of the trial court which found Sherwood was in the course and scope of his employment at the time of the accident. We reverse.

Sherwood was employed as an advertising accounts executive by Mississippi Press Register which publishes a newspaper in Pascagoula, Mississippi. He also held a position as "arts editor" for which he wrote a column about various events in the world of art, theater, and general entertainment. As arts editor, Sherwood was invited to attend the Louis Armstrong concert which was a part of the annual New Orleans Jazz and Heritage Festival. He attended the concert and left with a friend who offered him a place to spend the night in the New Orleans area. He planned to make the trip back to Pascagoula early in the morning in a fresh condition. Sherwood was driving to his friend's house on the Westbank Expressway in Jefferson Parish. He testified his attention was distracted from the road by his friend who was attempting to give him directions. He rear-ended the appellee who had stopped for a traffic light.

The collision occurred on April 11, 1978, and plaintiff filed suit on September 27, 1978. The trial was held on February 23, 1981, and judgment was rendered on August 18, 1981, in favor of appellee and against defendants in the amount of $116,059.30. This judgment was subsequently amended to cast Sherwood and Cavalier Insurance Company for $10,000, the limits of Cavalier's policy, and to cast Mississippi Press and Liberty Mutual for the balance of $106,059.30. Neither Sherwood nor Cavalier Insurance Company appealed the judgment. Mississippi Press and Liberty Mutual appealed * * *.

The issue on appeal is whether Sherwood was acting within the course and scope of his employment with Mississippi Press Register at the time of the collision. The trial judge, in his reasons for judgment, was satisfied by the testimony at trial and by the depositions introduced into evidence that the defendant, Wallace Sherwood, was acting within the course and scope of his employment. The trial judge stated that although Mr. Sherwood did attend the concert partly for personal reasons, that fact did not mean his attendance was not in the course and scope of his employment.

However, although Mr. Sherwood may have attended the concert within the scope of his employment, the accident occurred on his way to a friend's house to sleep for the night. The negligent acts of an employee on his way to or from work are not generally imputable to an employer under [Louisiana law]. [Citation.] The inquiry is whether the employee's tortious conduct was so closely connected in time, place and causation to his employment duties as to be regarded a risk of harm fairly attributable to the employer's business, as compared with conduct motivated be purely personal considerations entirely extraneous to the employer's interests. [Citation.] In the instant case Sherwood was clearly on his own time which in no way benefited his employer nor was related to the service of his employer. [Citation.] The accident did not occur within the course and scope of Sherwood's employment. Therefore, the judgment in favor of appellee Austen and against the Mississippi Press Register, Inc. must be reversed.

[Judgment for Austen against Sherwood for $116,059.30; Mississippi Press Register not liable].

Agent's Implied Warranty of Authority

GOLDFINGER v. DOHERTY

Supreme Court, Appellate Term, First Department, 1934.
153 Misc. 826, 276 N.Y.S. 289.

SHIENTAG, J.

The plaintiff sued the defendant Doherty, disaffirming certain purchases of stock, made in her behalf by her duly authorized agent, alleging that she was an infant at the time of the transactions, and that she now elected to rescind and offered to return the stock, together with the stock and cash dividends received thereon. The defendant Doherty thereupon obtained an order permitting him to serve a supplemental summons and complaint on the agent Samuel Goldfinger. * * * The supplemental pleading alleged, in substance, that the agent purchased the stock from Doherty on behalf of the alleged infant "without disclosing the infancy of his principal." It further alleged that, if plaintiff should recover against Doherty, then the defendant Goldfinger, plaintiff's agent, will be liable to defendant Doherty for damages sustained through the rescission of the contracts by plaintiff, "on the ground that defendant Samuel Goldfinger has breached his implied warranty that he was authorized to enter into binding contracts for the plaintiff."

* * *

An infant's appointment of an agent is not void; it is merely voidable, like any other contract he makes. * * *

There is, therefore, no basis for the contention of the appellant that disaffirmance by the infant of a contract entered into on his behalf by his agent renders the transaction void ab initio, so that the agent is deemed to have acted without any authority. The infant, without questioning the authority of his agent, may disaffirm the contract entered into on his behalf, in the same manner as if he had made the contract directly. The infant may disaffirm the contract of agency; he may disaffirm the contract entered into by his agent. Either contract is voidable; neither is void.

* * *

"The agent does not warrant the capacity of the principal." [Citation.] "An agent does not warrant that his principal has full contractual capacity, any more than he warrants that his principal is solvent. Thus an agent for one not of legal age is not necessarily liable if the infant avoids the obligation of the contract made on his account." Comment (a) on section 332, Restatement of the Law of Agency. An agent who misrepresents the capacity of his principal to contract is liable as for any other misrepresentation, and this whether he misrepresents tortiously or innocently.

In the absence of misrepresentation, under what circumstances, if any, is an agent acting for an infant, who subsequently disaffirms, not the agency, but the transaction of the agent, liable to the other contracting party? It must appear that the agent knew or had reason to know of his principal's lack of full capacity, and it must further appear that the other contracting party was in ignorance thereof. The theory of breach of warranty of authority is that one dealing with an agent has been misled by him. * * *

Assuming that the agent knows or has reason to know of his principal's lack of full capacity, and of the other party's ignorance thereof, what, if any, is the agent's liability? * * *

The basis of the liability of an agent in a situation such as we are here considering, is that he has produced "a false impression upon the mind of the other party; and, if this result is accomplished, it is unimportant whether the means of accomplishing it are words or acts of the defendant, or his concealment or suppression of material facts not equally within the knowledge or reach of the plaintiff." [Citation.] We believe that the correct rule is that set forth in the Restatement of the Law of Agency as follows:

par. 332. Agent of partially incompetent principal. An agent making a contract for a disclosed principal whose contracts are voidable because of lack of full capacity to contract, or for a principal who, although having capacity to contract generally, is incompetent to enter into the particular transaction, is not thereby liable to the other party. He does not become liable by reason of the failure of the principal to perform, unless he contracts or represents that the principal has capacity or unless he has reason to know of the principal's lack of capacity and of the other party's ignorance thereof. * * *

If, therefore, the liability of the agent is to be based on his failure to disclose facts in connection with his principal's lack of full capacity to the other contracting party, it must appear (1) that the agent knew or had reason to know the facts indicating his principal's lack of full capacity; (2) that the other contracting party was in ignorance thereof and the agent had reason so to believe; (3) that the transaction is one in which lack of full capacity was a material fact.

* * *

The order dismissing the supplemental complaint is affirmed. * * *

Undisclosed or Partially Disclosed Principal

VAN D. COSTAS, INC. v. ROSENBERG

District Court of Appeal of Florida, Second District, 1983.
432 So.2d 656.

GRIMES, J.

This is an appeal from a final judgment denying appellant's claims for mechanic's lien foreclosure and breach of contract.

Gilbert Rosenberg owned a parcel of real property on Siesta Key upon which the Magic Moment Restaurant was located. Seascape Restaurants, Inc., operated the restaurant and paid a monthly rental to Rosenberg for use of the property. Gilbert Rosenberg, his son Jeff Rosenberg, and Chris Moore each owned one third of Seascape. Jeff was president of Seascape and Moore was vice president, and the two of them operated the restaurant. Gilbert was not an officer of the corporation and was not actively involved in the management of the restaurant.

In November of 1980, appellant's president, Van D. Costas, met with Gilbert and Jeff to discuss the creation of a "magical entrance" for the restaurant. The following month, appellant entered into a contract to remodel the entrance. Jeff Rosenberg signed the contract on a line under which appeared "Jeff Rosenberg, The Magic Moment." After the work commenced, the parties became involved in a dispute over performance and payment, and appellant filed a claim of lien on the real estate. Appellant thereafter sued Gilbert to foreclose the lien and in a second count of the complaint sued Jeff Rosenberg for breach of contract. Jeff counterclaimed for damages for faulty performance and other relief. Following a trial, the court entered a final judgment against the appellant which stated in pertinent part:

* * * On the claim against Jeff Rosenberg, individually, the contract was addressed to "The Magic Moment Restaurant." It was drawn on plaintiff's stationery and referred to "Subject: Design and Creation of Mystical Entrance to 'The Magic Moment Restaurant.'" Under the prepared signature line for defendant's signature was typed "Jeff Rosenberg, The Magic Moment." Jeff Rosenberg signed his name on the line provided. Obviously he signed for "The Magic Moment," and there is no dispute that the plaintiff knew he was contracting with "The Magic Moment Restaurant." Plaintiff did testify that he thought the Rosenbergs owned the restaurant. However, there is also no dispute that the business was owned by Seascape Restaurants, Inc. who were doing business under the trade name of "The Magic Moment Restaurant." Under all these circumstances, there is no individual responsibility and the proper party

to this suit, as to both claims and counterclaims, is Seascape Restaurants, Inc.

*   *   *

Appellant bases its claim against Jeff upon the contention that he signed the contract as agent for an undisclosed principal. It is well settled that where one enters into a contract as agent for an undisclosed principal, he may be held individually liable on the contract. [Citations.] The extent to which an agent must make disclosure of his principal in order to avoid personal liability is explained in 3 Am.Jur.2d *Agency* § 320 (1962):

In order for an agent to avoid personal liability on a contract negotiated in his principal's behalf, he must disclose not only that he is an agent but also the identity of his principal, regardless of whether the third person might have known that the agent was acting in a representative capacity. It is not the third person's duty to seek out the identity of the principal; rather, the duty to disclose the identity of the principal is on the agent. The disclosure of an agency is not complete for the purpose of relieving the agent from personal liability unless it embraces the name of the principal; without that, the party dealing with the agent may understand that he intended to pledge his personal liability and responsibility in support of the contract and for its performance. Furthermore, the use of a tradename is not necessarily a sufficient disclosure of the identity of the principal and the fact of agency so as to protect the agent against personal liability.

Section 321 of the Restatement (Second) of the Law of Agency (1957) discusses the liability of the agent under circumstances in which it appears that he is acting for someone else but the identity of his principal is unknown to the other party.

§ 321. Principal Partially Disclosed
Unless otherwise agreed, a person purporting to make a contract with another for a partially disclosed principal is a party to the contract.
Comment:
    a. A principal is a partially disclosed principal when, at the time of making the contract in question, the other party thereto has notice that

the agent is acting for a principal but has no notice of the principal's identity. See § 4. The fact that, to the knowledge of the agent, the other party does not know the identity of the principal is of great weight in ascribing to the other party the intention to hold the agent liable either solely, or as a surety or co-promisor with the principal. The inference of an understanding that the agent is a party to the contract exists unless the agent gives such complete information concerning his principal's identity that he can be readily distinguished. If the other party has no reasonable means of ascertaining the principal, the inference is almost irresistible and prevails in the absence of an agreement to the contrary.

Restatement (Second) of Agency § 321, at 70.

In view of the contractual reference to the Magic Moment trade name, the annotation at 150 A.L.R. 1303 (1944) entitled "Use of trade name in connection with contract executed by agent as sufficient disclosure of agency or principal to protect agent against personal liability" is directly on point. The annotator points out that with the possible exception of a single decision, all of the prior cases on the subject have held that the use of a trade name is not a sufficient disclosure of the identity of the principal so as to eliminate the liability of the agent.

*   *   *

Of course, if the contracting party knows the identity of the principal for whom the agent purports to act, the principal is deemed to be disclosed. [Citation.] A dispute concerning such knowledge presents an issue of fact. [Citation.] Here, however, nothing indicates that appellant had ever heard of Seascape at the time the contract was signed. Subsequent knowledge of the true principal is irrelevant where performance of an indivisible contract has commenced. [Citation.] The trial court emphasized that Costas drafted the contract. However, it was not incumbent upon him to ferret out the record ownership of the Magic Moment when he had every reason to believe that one of the owners was signing the contract. Jeff knew that the owner was Seascape, and he had it within his power to avoid personal liability by properly disclosing his principal. Since there is no evidence that the appellant knew or should have known the true principal, the law holds Jeff legally responsible.

That portion of the judgment exonerating Jeff Rosenberg from liability is reversed, and the case is remanded for further proceedings. Since Jeff's counterclaim was also dismissed on the premise that only Seascape was bound on the contract, this ruling must also be reversed. If Jeff can be held personally liable on the contract, he also has a right to prosecute a claim for breach of that contract or for other relief which relates to the contract. In all other respects, the judgment is affirmed.

PROBLEMS

1. A was P's traveling salesperson and was also authorized to collect accounts. Prior to the agreed termination of the agency, P wrongfully discharged A. A then called on T, an old customer, and collected an account from T. He also called on X, a new prospect, as P's agent, secured a large order, collected the price of the order, sent the order to P, and disappeared with the collections. P delivered the goods to X as per the order.

(a) P sues T for his account. Decision?

(b) P sues X for the agreed price of the goods. Decision?

2. P instructed A, her agent, to purchase a quantity of hides. A bought the hides from T in his own (A's) name and delivered the hides to P. T, learning later that P was the principal, sends the bill to P, who refuses to pay T. T sues P and A. Decision?

3. A sold goods to B in good faith, believing him to be a principal. B in fact was acting as agent for C and within the scope of his authority. The goods were charged to B, and on his refusal to pay, A sued B for the purchase price. While this action was pending, A learned of B's relationship with C. Nevertheless, thirty days after learning of that relationship, A obtained judgment against B and had an execution issued which was never satisfied. Three months after rendition of the judgment, A sued C for the purchase price of the goods. Decision?

4. X Grocery Company employed Jones as its manager. Jones was given authority by X Company to purchase supplies and goods for resale and had conducted business for several years with Brown Distributing Company. Purchases by Jones from Brown Distributing Company had been limited to groceries. Jones then contacted Brown Distributing Company and had it deliver a color television set to her house, informing Brown Company the set was to be used in promotional advertising, the object of which was to increase X Grocery Company's business. The advertising did not develop. Jones disappeared from the area, taking the television set with her. Brown Company sued X Company for the purchase price of the set. Decision?

5. Stone was the authorized agent to sell stock of the X Company at $10 per share and was authorized in case of sale to fill in the blanks in the certificates with the name of the purchaser, the number of shares, and the date of sale. He sold 100 shares to Barrie, and without the knowledge or consent of the company and without reporting to the company, he indorsed on the back of the certificate the following:

"It is hereby agreed that X Company shall, at the end of three years after the date, repurchase the stock at $11.00 per share on thirty days' notice. X Company, by Stone."

After three years, demand was made on X Company to repurchase, which was refused, and the company repudiated the agreement on the ground that the agent had no authority to make the agreement for repurchase. Barrie sued X Company. Decision?

6. Helper, a delivery boy for Gunn, delivered two heavy packages of groceries to Reed's porch, and, as instructed by Gunn, Helper rang the bell to let Reed know the groceries had arrived. Mrs. Reed came to the door and asked Helper if he would deliver the groceries into the kitchen as the bags were heavy. Helper did so, and upon leaving he observed Mrs. Reed having difficulty in moving a

Moving car was not in scope of job

cabinet in the dining room. He undertook to assist her, but being more interested in watching Mrs. Reed than the cabinet, he failed to observe a small, valuable antique table which he smashed into with the cabinet and totally destroyed.

Does Reed have a cause of action against Gunn for the value of the destroyed antique?

7. Driver picked up Friend to accompany him on an out-of-town delivery for his employer, Speedy Service. A "No Riders" sign was prominently displayed on the windshield of the truck, and Driver violated specific instructions of his employer by permitting an unauthorized person to ride in the vehicle.

While discussing a planned fishing trip with Friend, Driver ran a red light and collided with an automobile driven by Motorist. Both Friend and Motorist were injured. Is Speedy Service liable to either Friend or Motorist for the injuries they sustained?

8. X Department Store advertises *subcont* that it maintains a barber shop in its store managed by Y. Actually, Y is not an employee of the store but merely rents space in the store. Y, while shaving Z in the barber shop, negligently puts a deep gash, into one of Z's ears, requiring ten stitches. Z sues X Department Store for damages. Decision?

9. The following contract was executed on August 22:

Ray agrees to sell and Shaw, the representative of Todd and acting on his behalf, agrees to buy 10,000 pounds of 0.32 × 1⅝ stainless steel strip type 410.

(Signed) Ray
(Signed) Shaw

On August 26, Ray informs Shaw and Todd that the contract was in reality signed by him as agent for Upson. What are the rights of Ray, Shaw, Todd, and Upson, in the event of a breach of the contract?

10. Harris, owner of certain land known as Red Bank, mailed a letter to Byron, a real estate broker in City X, stating: "I have been thinking of selling Red Bank. I have never met you, but a friend has advised that you are an industrious and honest real estate broker. I, therefore, employ you to find a purchaser for Red Bank at a price of $35,000." Ten days after receiving the letter, Byron mailed the following reply to Harris: "Acting pursuant to your recent letter requesting me to find a purchaser for Red Bank, this is to advise that I have sold the property to Sims for $35,000. I enclose your copy of the contract of sale signed by Sims. Your name was signed to the contract by me as your agent."

Is Harris obligated to convey Red Bank to Sims?

PART FOUR

Sales

PUBLIC POLICY, SOCIAL ISSUES AND BUSINESS ETHICS

P ART Four of the text deals with Sales— the most common and important of all commercial transactions. In an exchange economy such as ours, sales are the essential means by which the various units of production exchange their outputs, thereby providing the opportunity for specialization and enhanced productivity. An advanced, complex, industrialized economy with highly coordinated manufacturing and distribution systems requires a reliable mechanism for assuring that *future* exchanges can be entered into today and fulfilled at a later time. The critical role of the law of sales is to establish a framework in which these essential present and future exchanges may take place in a predictable, certain and orderly fashion with a minimum of transaction costs.

Until the early 1900's sales transactions were completely governed by general contract law. In 1906 the Uniform Sales Act was promulgated and eventually adopted by thirty-six States. By the end of the 1930's, however, dissatisfaction with this and other uniform commercial statutes brought about the development of the Uniform Commercial Code with Article Two dealing with transactions in sales. Nevertheless, the law of sales still remains in large measure a part of general contract law:

> The law of sales is a branch of the more general law of contracts. Therefore, rules of law applicable to contracts generally are applicable to contracts for the sale of goods unless those rules have been displaced by the Code. Nordstrom, *Law of Sales*, 80–81.

One of the most significant ways in which the Code has displaced common law is the Code's movement away from formalistic rules to an emphasis upon the intent of the parties. Under the common law parties intending to enter into a binding sale were too often disappointed to discover that they had not done so due to an inadvertent failure to comply with one or another formality. Such an outcome is much less likely under the Code because the rules for contract information have been greatly relaxed by the Code thus making it far easier for parties to form a binding sales contract. This approach achieves several important policies of sales law: to add predictability to the use of sales contracts by recognizing contracts where the parties intend to be bound, and to reduce the transaction costs of sales. It also promotes a third objective of modernizing the law governing business transactions. Accordingly, the Code not only responds more closely than the common law to the intention of the parties but it also reflects the needs, practices and usages of the market place. As Section 1–102 states, one of the underlying purposes and policies of the Code is "to permit the continued expansion of commercial practices through custom, usage and agreement of the parties."

The Code has also modified general contract law by providing that an agreement of the parties does not fail merely because it does not state all the material terms of the contract. The drafters of the Code realized that the parties may intentionally omit a term—such as price—in order to insure themselves of a contract while at the same time not binding themselves to a specific price in a widely fluctuating market. The Code has explicitly adopted the policy of permitting the parties to a sales contract to use such "open terms" by the Code's systematically supplying its own terms to fill the omitted terms. The Code does so on the assumption that the parties intended to be bound by terms that are commercially reasonable.

To counterbalance the relaxed rules of contract formation the Code has statutorily established two overriding regulatory requirements upon all sales transactions—unconscionability and good faith. Under the doctrine of unconscionability, courts may invalidate a contract, or any part of a contract, that is so one-sided as to be unconscionable. This doctrine recognizes that the parties to a contract may not be of relatively equal bargaining power and, therefore, that the laissez-faire principle of freedom of contract must be modified to reflect this reality of the modern world. For example, standardized contracts are widely used today but usually they are non-negotiable and frequently are incomprehensible to the typical consumer. Therefore, the Code has provided the potent device of unconscionability to prevent oppression and unfair surprise.

The other policing device established by the Code is the obligation imposed upon all parties to contracts formed under the Code that they act in good faith. The significance of this provision to business ethics has been explained by Professor Summers:

* * * It is natural for two parties to assume that each will act in good faith toward the other throughout the course of their contractual dealings. Moreover, morals obligate them to act this way. Yet, in one sense their interests will remain essentially antagonistic, for each will be expecting to get something from the other on advantageous terms. And, in a given case, misunderstandings may arise, unforeseen events occur, expected gains disappear or dislikes develop which may motivate one party to act in bad faith. If, however, such a party is legally as well as morally obligated to act in good faith, he will be significantly less likely to break faith. Summers, " 'Good Faith' in General Contract Law and the Sales Pro-

visions of the Uniform Commercial Code," 54 *Va.L.Rev.* 195 (1968).

The Uniform Commercial Code continues, and expands upon, the public policy of contract law to place the aggrieved party in as good a position as if the other party had fully performed. The Code accomplishes this by providing an impressive array of cumulative remedies for both the buyer and seller. At the same time the Code deplores economic waste and requires commercially reasonable actions by the aggrieved party to mitigate damages.

Intertwined with the Code's enhanced remedies is its strengthened warranty provisions. As Professor Kessler stated, "Modern sales law, in its desire to protect the buyer and his expectations as to quality, is adopting the position that the seller is responsible for the qualities which the buyer is entitled to expect in the light of all surroundings circumstances, including the purchase price. * * * Indeed, the conviction is gaining ground that the function of warranty law is to establish a 'subjective' equivalence between price and quality." Kessler, "The Protection of the Consumer Under Modern Sales Law," 74 *Yale L.J.* 262 (1964). Since information is one sided and frequently not available to the consumer, it is important to insure a certain minimum level of quality and safety, an objective which has been greatly furthered by both the warranty provisions in sales law and strict liability in tort law.

While reading the next five chapters that comprise Sales it is important to consider the overall purpose and policy of the law governing sales: to provide a predictable, certain, and orderly system by which exchanges of goods may take place in a complex, highly interdependent exchange economy. General contract law supplies the greater part of this system but Article Two has refined it considerably by simplifying, clarifying, and modernizing the law governing sales transactions.

Chapter 19

INTRODUCTION TO SALES

OF all business and legal transactions, the sale is without question the most common. The manufacture and distribution of goods involve numerous sales transactions and practically everyone in our economy is a purchaser of both durable and consumable goods. In 1983 the total dollar value of final sales was $1,366.5 *billion. Federal Reserve Bulletin* (July 1984). Originally part of the Law Merchant, the law of sales was absorbed into the common law and codified in Article 2 of the Uniform Commercial Code, which has been adopted in all States, except Louisiana, plus the District of Columbia and the Virgin Islands. The Uniform Commercial Code appears in Appendix C.

This chapter will discuss the nature and formation of sales contracts.

NATURE OF SALES CONTRACTS

The law of sales, which governs contracts involving the sale of goods, is a specialized branch of both the law of contracts (discussed previously in Chapters 7–16) and the law of personal property (discussed later in Chapter 46). This section will cover the definition of a sales contract and the fundamentals of Article Two.

DEFINITION

The Code defines a sale as the transfer of title to goods from seller to buyer for a price. Section 2-106. The price can be money, other goods, real estate, or services. **Goods** are essentially defined as **movable, tangible personal property.** For example, the purchase of a bicycle, stereo set, or this textbook is considered a sale of goods. "Goods" also include the unborn young of animals, growing crops, and, if removed by the seller, timber, minerals, or a building attached to real property. Section 2-105(1).

Governing Law

All such sales transactions are governed by Article 2 of the Code, but, where general contract law has not been specifically modified by the Code, contract law continues to apply. In other words, the law of sales is a specialized part of the general law of contracts, and the law of contracts continues to govern unless specifically displaced by the Code.

General contract law also continues to govern all contracts outside the scope of the Code. Transactions not within the scope of Article 2 include employment contracts, service contracts, insurance contracts, contracts involving real property, and contracts for the sale of intangibles such as stocks, bonds, patents, and copyrights. For an illustration of this relationship, refer to Figure 7-1 in Chapter 7.

See Osterholt v. St. Charles Drilling Co.; Helvey v. Wabash County REMC; and Navarro County Electric Co-op, Inc. v. Prince.

Nonsales Transactions in Goods

There are a number of transactions that are not sales yet significantly affect goods. For example, a **bailment** is a transfer of the possession of personal property by the owner or rightful possessor **(bailor)** to another **(bailee)** for a determinable period of time *without* a transfer of title. To illustrate, A, the bailor creates a bailment when he delivers his soiled laundry to the XYZ Laundry Company, the bailee, for cleaning. Other examples of bailments include delivery of goods to a repairman, carrier, or warehouseman. In contrast, transfer of title is essential to a sale, although transfer of possession is not.

A **lease** of goods is a contract whereby the owner of the goods (the **lessor**) agrees with another person (the **lessee**) that she will transfer to the lessee the possession and right to use the goods for a period of time in consideration of a specified payment. A lease of goods does not involve a transfer of title to the goods.

A **gift** is a transfer of property from one person to another without consideration. The lack of any consideration is the basic distinction between a gift and a sale. Since a gift involves no consideration or compensation, to be effective it must be completed by delivery of the gift. A gratuitous promise to make a gift is not binding. In addition, there must be intent on the part of the maker (the **donor**) of the gift to make a present transfer, and there must be acceptance by the recipient (the **donee**) of the gift. Delivery of the property is not necessary in order to pass title by way of sale.

A sale is distinguished from a **security agreement** in that a sale transfers to the buyer all of the ownership rights of the seller in the goods, while under a security agreement both the **creditor** and the **debtor** have ownership rights in the goods. The right of the secured creditor in the goods is to take possession of the goods in the event of default by the debtor.

See Figure 19-1.

Although Article 2 governs sales, the drafters of the Article have invited the courts to extend Code principles to nonsale transactions in goods. To date a number of courts have accepted this invitation and have applied Code provisions by analogy to other transactions in goods not expressly included within the act, most frequently to leases and bailments. The Code has also greatly influenced the revision of the Restatement, Second, Contracts which, as previously discussed, has great effect upon all contracts. In these ways the policies and principles of the Code have been extended to nonsales transactions.

FIGURE 19-1　Transactions in Goods			
	Transfer of Title	Transfer of Possession	Governing Law
Sale	Yes	Usually, but not necessarily	Article 2
Gift	Yes	Yes	Common Law
Bailment	No	Yes	Common Law
Lease	No	Yes	Common Law
Non-possessory Security Interest	No	No	Article 9

FUNDAMENTAL PRINCIPLES OF ARTICLE 2

The purpose of Article 2 is to modernize, clarify, simplify, and make uniform the law of sales. Furthermore, the Article is to be interpreted in accordance with these underlying principles and not according to some abstraction such as the passage of title. The Code "is drawn to provide flexibility so that, since it is intended to be a semi-permanent piece of legislation, it will provide its own machinery for expansion of commercial practices. It is intended to make it possible for the law embodied in this Act to be developed by the courts in the light of unforeseen and new circumstances and practices. However, the proper construction of the Act requires that its interpretation and application be limited to its reason." Section 1-102, Comment 1. This open-ended drafting includes the following fundamental concepts.

Good Faith

All parties who enter into a contract or duty within the scope of the Code must perform their obligations in good faith. The Code defines good faith as "honesty in fact in the conduct or transaction concerned." Section 1-201(19). In the case of a merchant (defined below), good faith also requires the observance of reasonable commercial standards of fair dealing in the trade. Section 2-103(1)(b). For instance, if the parties agree that the seller is to set the price term, the seller must establish the price in good faith. In most instances such good faith would require that the price set be the fair market value.

Unconscionability

Every contract of sale may be scrutinized by the court to determine whether in its commercial setting, purpose, and effect it is unconscionable. The court may refuse to enforce an unconscionable contract or any part of it found to be unconscionable. Section 2-302(1) provides:

If the court as a matter of law finds the contract or any clause of the contract to have been unconscionable at the time it was made the court may refuse to enforce the contract, or it may enforce the remainder of the contract without the unconscionable clause, or it may so limit the application of any unconscionable clause as to avoid any unconscionable result.

The Code does not define "unconscionable;" however, the Oxford Universal Dictionary (3rd ed.) definition is: "Monstrously extortionate, harsh, showing no regard for conscience."

The Code denies or limits enforcement of an unconscionable contract for the sale of goods in the interest of fairness and decency, and to correct harshness or oppression in contracts resulting from inequality in the bargaining positions of the parties. Although the principle is not novel, its embodiment in a statute dealing with commercial transactions is.

In many cases a contract between a necessitous buyer in an unequal bargaining position with the seller has been held unconscionable by reason of the exorbitant price of the goods. A price of $749 ($920 on time) for a vacuum cleaner which cost the seller $140 was held unconscionable. In another case, the buyers, welfare recipients, purchased by time payment contract a home freezer unit for $900 plus time credit charges, credit life insurance, credit property insurance and sales tax for a total price of $1,235. The purchase resulted from a visit to the buyer's home by a salesman representing Your Shop At Home Service, Inc., and the maximum retail value of the freezer unit at time of purchase was $300. The court held the contract unconscionable, and reformed it by changing the price to the total payment ($620) made by the buyers. *Jones v. Star Credit Corp.*, 59 Misc.2d 189, 298 N.Y.S.2d 264 (1969).

See *Frank's Maintenance and Engineering, Inc. v. C. A. Roberts Co.; and Williams v. Walker-Thomas Furniture Co.* in Chapter 11.

Expansion of Commercial Practices

An underlying policy of the Code is "to permit the continued expansion of commercial practices through custom, usage and agreement of the parties." Section 1-102(2)(b). In particular, the Code places great emphasis upon course of dealings and usage of trade in interpreting agreements.

A **course of dealing** is a sequence of previous conduct between the parties which may fairly be regarded as establishing a common basis of understanding for interpreting their expressions and agreement. Section 1-205(1). For example, A, a sugar company, enters into a written agreement with B, a grower of sugar beets, by which B agrees to raise and deliver

and A to purchase specified quantities of beets during the coming season. No price is fixed. The agreement is on a standard form used by A for B and many other growers in prior years. A's practice is to pay all growers uniformly on a formula based on A's established accounting system. Unless otherwise agreed, the established pricing pattern is part of the agreement between A and B as a course of dealing.

A **usage of trade** is a practice or method of dealing regularly observed and followed in a place, vocation, or trade. Section 1-205(2). To illustrate: A contracts to sell B 1,000 feet of San Domingo mahogany. By usage of dealers in mahogany, known to A and B, good figured mahogany of a certain density is known as San Domingo mahogany, though it does not come from San Domingo. Unless otherwise agreed, the usage is part of the contract.

Sales By and Between Merchants

A novel feature of the Code is the establishment of separate rules which apply to transactions between merchants or involving a merchant as a party. A "merchant" is defined as a person who (1) is a dealer in the goods, (2) by his occupation holds himself out as having knowledge or skill peculiar to the goods or practices involved, or (3) employs an agent or broker whom he holds out as having such knowledge or skill. Section 2-104(1).

Various sections of the Code contain special rules which apply solely to transactions between merchants or in which a merchant is a party. These rules exact a higher standard of conduct from merchants because of their knowledge of trade and commerce, and because merchants as a class generally set the standards. The rules are as follows:

1. Good faith in the case of a merchant means honesty in fact plus the observance of reasonable commercial standards of fair dealing in the trade. Section 2-103(1)(b).

2. A contract for the sale of goods for the price of $500 or more requires a writing to be enforceable (Statute of Frauds). Where such a contract between merchants is oral, a confirmatory writing by one to the other satisfies the statute unless the recipient within 10 days objects in writing. Section 2-201(2).

3. A written offer by a merchant to buy or sell goods is irrevocable without consideration during the period of time it is stated to remain open, or if no time is stated, for a reasonable time, not to exceed 3 months. Section 2-205.

4. Between merchants, terms contained in an offeree's acceptance which add to or differ from those in the offer become part of the contract unless (a) the offer expressly limits acceptance to the terms of the offer; (b) the different terms materially alter the offer; or (c) the offeror objects to such additional or different terms within a reasonable time. Section 2-207(2).

5. A signed agreement cannot be modified or rescinded except by a signed writing where it expressly so requires. However, where the signed agreement is not between two merchants such requirement on a form supplied by a merchant party must be separately signed by the non-merchant party. Where the signed agreement is between merchants such requirement on a form supplied by one of them need not be separately signed by the other. Section 2-209(2).

6. A seller who is a merchant impliedly warrants that goods of the kind in which he regularly deals shall be delivered free of any rightful claim of any third person by way of infringement. Section 2-312(3).

7. A seller who is a merchant impliedly warrants the merchantability of the goods that he sells, unless such warranty is expressly excluded or modified. Section 2-314(1).

8. Where goods are delivered for sale to a merchant who maintains a place of business where he deals in goods of the kind involved, under a name other than the name of the person making delivery, the goods are deemed to be on sale or return with respect to creditors of the merchant. Section 2-326(3).

9. Under a sale on approval unless otherwise agreed, a merchant-buyer after giving notice of his election to return the goods must follow any reasonable instructions of the seller in order that the return be at the seller's risk and expense. Section 2-327(1)(c).

10. Where retention of possession of goods by the seller would be fraudulent as to creditors of the seller under any rule of law, such retention by a merchant-seller in good faith and in the current course of trade for a commercially reasonable time is not fraudulent. Section 2-402(2).

11. Any entrusting of the possession of goods to a merchant who deals in goods of that kind gives him power to transfer all rights of the entruster to a buyer in the ordinary course of business. Section 2-403(2).

12. Except where the contract requires or authorizes the seller to ship the goods by carrier, and except where the goods are held by a bailee to be delivered to the buyer without being moved, the risk of loss passes to the buyer upon his receipt of the goods if the seller is a merchant. In such case, if the seller is not a merchant, the risk of loss passes to the buyer on tender of delivery. Section 2-509(3).

13. Where a merchant-buyer has rightfully rejected goods in his possession, and the seller has no agent or place of business at the market of rejection, the merchant-buyer is under a duty to follow any reasonable instructions of the seller with respect to the goods, and in the absence of such instructions to make reasonable efforts to sell them for the seller's account if they are perishable. Section 2-603(1).

14. When a merchant-buyer sells goods pursuant to section 2-603(1), he is entitled to a selling commission and to reimbursement of his reasonable expenses out of the proceeds. Section 2-603(2).

15. Between merchants, a buyer who has rejected goods is precluded from relying upon any unstated defect to justify such rejection or to establish a breach by the seller where the seller has made a request in writing for a full and final written statement of all defects upon which the buyer proposes to rely. Section 2-605(1)(b).

16. When reasonable grounds for insecurity arise with respect to the performance of either party to a contract for the sale of goods, the other party may in writing demand adequate assurance of due performance and may suspend performance until such assurance is received. Between merchants, the reasonableness of grounds for insecurity and the adequacy of any assurance offered is determined according to commercial standards. Section 2-609(1)(2).

Liberal Administration of Remedies

Section 1-106 of the Code provides that its remedies shall be liberally administered in order to place the aggrieved party in as good a position as if the defaulting party had fully performed. However, the Code does make it clear that remedies are limited to compensation and do not include consequential or punitive damages, unless specifically provided by the Code. Nevertheless, the Code provides that even in cases where the Code does not expressly provide a remedy for a right or obligation, the courts should provide an appropriate remedy.

Freedom of Contract

Most of the Code's provisions are not mandatory but permit the parties to vary or displace them altogether. The effect of provisions of the Code may be varied by agreement, except as otherwise provided and except that the obligations of good faith, diligence, reasonableness, and care prescribed by the Code may not be disclaimed by agreement, although the parties may by agreement determine the standards by which the performance of such obligations is to be measured so long as such standards are not manifestly unreasonable. Section 1-102(3). This approach of the Code not only maximizes freedom of contract but also permits the continued expansion of commercial practices through private agreement.

Validation and Preservation of Sales Contracts

One of the requirements of commercial law is the establishment of rules that determine when an agreement is valid. The Code's approach to this is to reduce formal requisites to the bare minimum and attempt to preserve agreements whenever the parties manifest an intent to enter into a contract.

FORMATION OF A SALES CONTRACT

The Code's basic approach to validation is to recognize contracts whenever the parties manifest such an *intent*. This is so regardless of whether a precise moment can be identified as to the point in time at which the contract was formed. Section 2-204(2).

As already noted, the law of sales is a subset of the general law of contracts and is governed by general contract law unless particular provisions of the Code displace the general law. Although the Code leaves the great majority of issues of contract formation to general contract law, it has modified the general law of contract formation in several significant respects. These modifications were made in order to modernize contract law, to relax the validation requirements of contract formation, and to promote fairness.

MANIFESTATION OF MUTUAL ASSENT

Definiteness of an Offer

The Code provides that even though one or more terms to a contract may have been omitted, a contract need not fail for indefiniteness. Section 2-204(3). Standards are provided by which omitted essential terms may be ascertained and supplied provided the parties intended to enter into a binding agreement. The more terms left open, however, the more likely the parties did not intend to enter into a binding contract.

Open Price The parties may enter into a contract for the sale of goods even though they have reached no agreement on the price. Under the Code the price is a reasonable one at the time for delivery where the agreement (1) says nothing as to price, (2) provides that the parties shall agree later as to the price and they fail to so agree, or (3) fixes the price in terms of some agreed market or other standard or as set by a third person or agency and the price is not so set. Section 2-305(1).

An agreement that the price is to be fixed by the seller or buyer means that it must be fixed in good faith. If the price is to be fixed otherwise than by agreement and is not so fixed through the fault of one of the parties, the other party has an option to treat the contract as canceled or to fix a reasonable price in good faith for the goods. However, where the parties intend not to be bound unless the price is fixed or agreed upon as provided in the agreement, and it is not so fixed or agreed upon, the Code in accordance with the parties' intent provides that there is no contract. Section 2-305(4).

Open Delivery Unless otherwise agreed the place of delivery is the seller's place of business. Moreover, the delivery, if unspecified, must be made within a reasonable time period and in a single delivery.

Open Quantity: Output and Requirement Contracts An agreement of a buyer to purchase the entire output of a seller for a stated period, or an agreement of a seller to supply a buyer with all her requirements of certain goods used in her business operations, may appear to lack definiteness and mutuality of obligation. In either case the exact quantity of goods is not specified, and the seller may have some degree of control over his output, and the buyer over her requirements. Nonetheless, such agreements are enforceable by the application of an objective standard based upon the good faith of both parties, and the quantities may not be disproportionate to any stated estimate or the prior output or requirements. Section 2-306(1). For example, the seller cannot operate his factory twenty-four hours a day and insist upon the buyer's taking all of the output when the seller operated the factory only eight hours a day at the time the agreement was made. Nor can the buyer unilaterally triple the size of her business and insist that the seller supply all of her requirements.

Other Open Terms The Code further provides rules, where the parties do not agree, as to the terms of payment, duration, and the particulars of performance.

Firm Offers

The Code provides that a merchant is bound to keep an offer open, for a maximum of three months, if the merchant gives assurance in a signed writing that it will be held open. Section 2-205 states:

An offer by a merchant to buy or sell goods in a signed writing which by its terms gives assurance that it will be held open is not revocable, for lack of consideration, during the time stated or if no time is stated for a reasonable time, but in no event may such period of irrevocability exceed three months; but any such term of assurance on a form supplied by the offeree must be separately signed by the offeror.

The Code, therefore, makes a merchant's written promise not to revoke an offer for a stated period of time enforceable even though no consideration is given the merchant-offeror for that promise.

Variant Acceptances

The common law **"mirror image"** rule, by which the acceptance cannot vary or deviate from the terms of the offer, is modified by the Code. This modification is necessitated by the realities of modern business practices. A vast number of business transactions utilize standardized business forms. For example, a buyer sends to the seller on the buyer's order form a purchase order for 1,000 dozen cotton shirts at sixty dollars per dozen with delivery by October 1 at the buyer's place of business. On the reverse side of this standard form are twenty-five numbered paragraphs containing provisions generally favorable to the buyer. When the seller receives the buyer's order, he sends to the buyer on his acceptance form an unequivocal acceptance of the offer. However, despite the fact that the seller agrees to the buyer's quantity, price, and delivery terms, on the back of his acceptance form the seller has thirty-two numbered paragraphs generally favorable to himself and in significant conflict with the buyer's form. Under the common law's "mirror image" rule no contract would exist, for there has not been an unequivocal acceptance of all of the material terms of the buyer's offer.

Section 2-207 provides:

(1) A definite and seasonable expression of acceptance or a written confirmation which is sent within a reasonable time operates as an acceptance even though it states terms additional to or different from those offered or agreed upon, unless acceptance is expressly made conditional on assent to the additional or different terms.

(2) The additional terms are to be construed as proposals for addition to the contract. Between merchants such terms become part of the contract unless:

    (a) the offer expressly limits acceptance to the terms of the offer;

    (b) they materially alter it; or

    (c) notification of objection to them has already been given or is given within a reasonable time after notice of them is received.

(3) Conduct by both parties which recognizes the existence of a contract is sufficient to establish a contract for sale although the writings of the parties do not otherwise establish a contract. In such case the terms of the particular contract consist of those terms on which the writings of the parties agree, together with any supplementary terms incorporated under any other provisions of this Act.

Thus, the Code addresses this **Battle of the Forms** problem by focusing upon the intent of the parties. If the seller definitely and seasonably expresses his acceptance of the offer and does not expressly make his acceptance conditional upon the buyer's assent to the additional or different terms, a contract is formed. The issue then becomes whether the seller's different or additional terms become part of the contract. If both buyer and seller are merchants, **additional** terms will be part of the contract provided they do not materially alter the agreement and are not objected to either in the offer itself or within a reasonable period of time. If both of the parties are not merchants, or if the terms materially alter the offer, then the additional terms are merely construed as proposals for addition to the contract. **Different** terms proposed by the offeree **also** will not become part of the contract unless specifically accepted by the offeror.

See Dorton v. Collins & Aikman Corp.

Manner of Acceptance

The Code provides that where the language in the offer or the circumstances do not otherwise clearly indicate, an offer to make a contract invites acceptance in any manner and by any medium reasonable in the circumstances. Section 2-206(1)(a). The Code, therefore, allows flexibility of response and the ability to keep pace with new modes of communication.

An offer to buy goods for prompt or current shipment may be accepted either by a prompt promise to ship or by prompt shipment. Section 2-206(1)(b). However, acceptance by performance requires notice within a reasonable time, or the offer may be treated as lapsed.

Auctions

The Code provides that if an auction sale is advertised or announced in explicit terms to be **without reserve,** the auctioneer may not withdraw the article put up for sale unless no bid is made within a reasonable time. Unless the sale is advertised as being without reserve, the sale is **with reserve,** and the auctioneer may withdraw the goods at any time until he announces completion of the sale. Whether with or without reserve, a bidder may retract his bid at any time prior to acceptance by the auctioneer. Such retraction, however, does not revive any previous bid. Section 2-328.

If the auctioneer knowingly receives a bid by or on behalf of the seller, and notice has not been given that the seller reserves the right to bid at the auction sale, the bidder to whom the goods are sold can either avoid the sale or take the goods at the price of the last good faith bid before the sale. For example, A advertises a sale of his household furniture without reserve. An article of furniture is put up for sale without a contrary announcement and B is the highest *bona fide* bidder. A, however, is dissatisfied with the bidding and accepts a higher, fictitious bid from an agent employed for that purpose. A is obligated to sell the article to B at the price B bid.

CONSIDERATION

Contractual Modifications

The Code has abandoned the common law rule requiring that a modification of an existing contract be supported by consideration in order to be valid. The Code provides that a contract for the sale of goods can be effectively modified without new consideration

provided the modification is made in good faith. Section 2-209.

Discharge of Claim after Breach

Any claim of right arising out of an alleged breach can be discharged in whole or in part without consideration by a written waiver or renunciation signed and delivered by the aggrieved party. Section 1-107.

Firm Offers

As previously noted, a firm offer is not revocable for lack of consideration.

FORM OF THE CONTRACT

Statute of Frauds

Section 17 of the original Statute of Frauds applied to contracts for the sale of goods and has been used as a prototype for the Article 2 Statute of Frauds provision (Section 2-201) which applies to a contract for the sale of goods costing **$500 or more.**

Modification of Contracts Within the Statute of Frauds An agreement modifying a contract must be in writing if the resulting contract is within the Statute of Frauds. Section 2-209(3). Conversely, if a contract that was previously within the Statute of Frauds is modified so as to no longer fall within it, the modification is enforceable even if it is oral. Thus, if the parties enter into an oral contract to sell a dining room table for $450 to be delivered to the buyer and later, prior to delivery, *orally* agree that the seller shall stain the table and the buyer pay a price of $550, the modified contract is unenforceable. In contrast, if the parties have a written contract for the sale of 150 bushels of wheat at a price of $4.50 per bushel and later, upon oral agreement, decrease the quantity to 100 bushels at the same price per bushel, the agreement, as modified, is enforceable.

Written Compliance The Statute of Frauds compliance provisions under the Code are more liberal than the rules under general contract law. The Code requires merely some writing (1) sufficient to indicate that a contract has been made between the parties, (2) signed by the party against whom enforcement is sought or by her authorized agent or broker, and (3) includes a term specifying the quantity. Its non-insistence that the writing contain all of the terms, other than quantity, is consistent with other provisions of the Code that contracts may be enforced, even though material terms are omitted. Nevertheless, the contract is enforceable only to the extent of the quantity stated. Given proof that a contract was intended and a signed writing describing the goods, the quantity of goods, and the names of the parties, under the Code the court can supply omitted terms such as price and particulars of performance. Moreover, several related documents may satisfy the writing requirement.

As between merchants, if within a reasonable time a writing in confirmation of the contract is received, the written confirmation, if sufficient against the sender, is also sufficient against the recipient of the confirmation unless the recipient gives written notice of his objection within ten days after receiving the confirmation. Section 2-201(2).

Alternative Methods of Compliance A contract which does not satisfy the writing requirement but is otherwise valid is enforceable in the following instances:

The Code permits an oral contract for the sale of goods to be enforced against a party who in his pleading, testimony, or otherwise in court **admits** that a contract was made, but the Code limits enforcement to the quantity of goods so admitted. Section 2-201(3)(b). This provision recognizes that the policy behind the Statute of Frauds does not apply when the party seeking to avoid the oral contract admits under oath the existence of the contract.

The Code also permits enforcement of an oral contract for goods **specially manufactured** for the buyer. Section 2-201(3)(a). Nevertheless, if the goods, although manufactured on special order, are readily marketable in the ordinary course of the seller's business, the contract is not enforceable unless in writing.

In most States, prior to the Code, delivery and acceptance of part of the goods or payment of part of the price and acceptance of the payment made the entire oral contract enforceable against the buyer who had received part delivery or against the seller who had received part payment. Under the Code such "partial performance" validates the contract only for the goods which have been **delivered and accepted** or for which **payment** has been **accepted.** Section 2-201(3)(c). Receipt and acceptance either of the goods or of the price constitutes an admission by both parties that some contract exists between them. If the court can make a just apportionment, the agreed price of any goods delivered under an oral contract can be recovered, or, if the price has been paid, the seller can be forced to deliver an apportionable part of the goods.

Parol Evidence

Contractual terms which are set forth in a writing intended by the parties as a final expression of their agreement may not be contradicted by evidence of any prior agreement or of a contemporaneous oral agreement but may be explained or supplemented by (1) course of dealing, usage of trade, or course of performance; and (2) evidence of consistent additional terms unless the writing was intended as the complete and exclusive statement of the terms of the agreement. Section 2-202.

Seal

The Uniform Commercial Code makes seals inoperative with respect to contracts for the sale of goods or an offer to buy or sell goods. Section 2-203.

CASES

Definition of Sale of Goods

OSTERHOLT v. ST. CHARLES DRILLING CO.

United States District Court, E.D. Missouri, 1980.
500 F.Supp. 529.

FILIPPINE, J.

[St. Charles Drilling Co. (defendant) contracted with Osterholt (plaintiff) to install a well and water system which would produce a specified quantity of water. The water system failed to meet its warranted capacity and Osterholt sued for breach of contract.]

* * *

The parties have not addressed the possibility that the Uniform Commerical Code, as adopted by Illinois, governs this case. The Court has given strong consideration to that possibility, but has concluded that the contract at issue was primarily a service contract, with a sale of goods incidental thereto, rather than vice versa. [Citation.] At least one Illinois appellate court has adopted a "predominant factor in the contract" test, [citation] to determine the applicability of the U.C.C. [Citation.] *Bonebrake v. Cox* [citation] involved a contract to sell and install specified items of used equipment in a bowling alley that had been damaged by fire. The Court held that the contract fell within the (Iowa) Uniform Commercial Code, rejecting the decision below that because the contract was "mixed" (for goods and services), the U.C.C. did not govern. The Court held that the U.C.C. did apply because the items to be installed fell within the U.C.C.'s definition of "goods" and because the language of the contract was essentially that of a sales contract. The Court formulated the following general test of the U.C.C.'s applicability: "The test for inclusion or exclusion is not whether [contracts] are mixed, but, granting that they are mixed, whether their predominant factor, their

thrust, their purpose, reasonably stated, is the rendition of service, with goods incidentally involved (e.g., contract with artist for painting) or is a transaction of sale, with labor incidentally involved (e.g., installation of a water heater in a bathroom)." [Citation.] The Seventh Circuit, in a case governed by Illinois law, approved the *Bonebrake* test and held that a contract for the construction of a one-million-gallon water tank fell within the U.C.C. [Citation.]

This Court finds that the transaction between the parties in the instant case falls on the "service" side of the *Bonebrake* test, for two reasons: with two exceptions discussed below, the parties had no agreement specifying the various component parts of the "water system" which were to be installed. The defendant was not bound to use specified items of "goods" in the water system. Neither party has suggested that the estimate sheet . . . prepared by defendant the day before the contract was signed, was a part of the parties' contract. Essentially, defendant undertook to install a "water system" of indefinite description but with a certain warranted capacity, rather than to install a detailed list of specific "goods." Therefore, not only was the contract essentially for defendant's services, but the component parts did not become identified to the contract until they were actually installed on plaintiff's property, and thus it is doubtful that they fell within the definition of "goods" contained in [U.C.C.] 2-105.

Secondly, the language of the instant contract is unmistakably that of service rather than of sale. Defendant is identified as the "contractor," and the contract acknowledges "an express mechanics lien . . . to secure the amount of contract or repairs."

Thus, the Court concludes that the U.C.C. does not, strictly speaking, govern this case.

* * *

[Judgment for plaintiff.]

Definition of Sale of Goods

HELVEY v. WABASH COUNTY REMC

Court of Appeals of Indiana, First District, 1972.
151 Ind.App. 176, 278 N.E.2d 608.

ROBERTSON, J.

Appellant Helvey filed an action against appellee REMC, based upon a breach of implied and express warranties, for damages caused to certain 110 volt household appliances. The damage was a result of REMC furnishing electicity of 135 or more volts. REMC filed an answer in denial as well as the special defense that more than four years had accrued since the incident occurred. REMC then filed a motion for summary judgment, predicated upon the statute of limitations. * * *

A hearing on the summary judgment was held, Helvey's deposition being published in the meantime, and the court subsequently granted REMC's motion for summary judgment. * * *

The first issue to be resolved is which statute of limitations applies to the facts of this case. REMC says the following applies:

An action for breach of any contract for sale must be commenced within four years after the cause of action has accrued. [U.C.C. § 2–725.]

Helvey recollected that the incident in question was corrected the cold night the damage occurred. The incident was identified because of the presence of Bill Yentes. Yentes' affidavit shows the date to be the 10th of January, 1966. The cause was filed on the 4th of March, 1970.

In order for the Uniform Commercial Code statute of limitations to apply, electicity must possess the following qualities:

(1) "Goods" means all things (including specially manufactured goods) which are movable at the time of identification to the contract for sale other than the money in which the price is to be paid, investment securities (Article 8) and things in action. . . .

(2) Goods must be both existing and identified before any interest in them can pass. . . .
[U.C.C. § 2–105.]

Helvey is of the opinion that electrical energy is not a transaction in goods but rather a furnishing of a service, which would make the following statute of limitations applicable:

The following actions shall be commenced within six [6] years after the cause of action has accrued, and not afterwards.

First. On Accounts and contracts not in writing. [Citation.]

Helvey concedes that electricity is legally considered to be personal property, that it is subject to ownership, and that it may be bartered and sold. [Citations.] We further note that electricity may be stolen; [citations].

It is necessary for goods to be (1) a thing; (2) existing; and (3) movable; with (2) and (3) existing simultaneously. We are of the opinion that electricity qualifies in each respect. Helvey says it is not movable and in this respect we do not agree, if for no other reason than the monthly reminder from the electric company of how much current has passed through the meter. Logic would indicate that whatever can be measured in order to establish the price to be paid would be indicative of fulfilling both the existing and movable requirements of goods.

We further take note that one of the principle [sic] underlying purposes in adoption of the Uniform Commercial Code is "to make uniform the law among the various jurisdictions." [U.C.C. § 1–102(2)(c).] With this in mind, we rely upon the authority of [citation], wherein natural gas was determined to be goods within the scope of the Uniform Commercial Code, therefore, the four year statute of limitations was applicable.

Judgment affirmed.

Definition of Sale of Goods

NAVARRO COUNTY ELECTRIC CO-OP, INC. v. PRINCE

Court of Appeals of Texas, 1982.
640 S.W.2d 398.

CHASE, J.

*   *   *

The record reflects that the Appellee lived in a mobile home located adjacent to a children's home he was constructing in Freestone County, Texas.

Located above the mobile home was a high voltage electrical transmission line carrying some 7200 volts of electricity. This was not the line which served the mobile home, since there were other wires leading from a transformer to the mobile home.

While adjusting a television antenna beside the mobile home and underneath the high voltage electric transmission line, Appellee received an electric shock from which he received injuries and brought suit against the Appellant in Freestone County, Texas.

*   *   *

Article 2.314 of the Texas Business and Commerce Code provides:

(a) Unless excluded or modified (Section 2.316), a warranty that the goods shall be merchantable is implied in a contract for their sale if the seller is a merchant with respect to goods of that kind. . . .

(b) Goods to be merchantable must be at least such as

(1) pass without objection in the trade under the contract description; and

(2) in the case of fungible goods, are of fair average quality within the description; and

(3) are fit for the ordinary purpose for which such goods are used; and

(4) run, within the variations permitted by the agreement, of even kind, quality, and quantity within each unit and among all units involved; and

(5) are adequately contained, packaged, and labeled as the agreement may require; and

(6) conform to the promises or affirmations of fact made on the container or label if any . . .

Appellee alleged that by virtue of Section 2.314 of the Business and Commerce Code there arose in connection with the purchase of electricity by Appellee, an implied warranty that the electricity was fit for the purpose for which it was to be used. More specifically that the implied warranty of merchantability extended to the container of the product, the wiring, in that it was unfit for the purpose of transporting electricity from the Appellant to the Appellee's property. Appellee testified that he did not believe he hit the wire and that the electric current jumped from the transmission line to the aerial.

It is Appellant's contention that Section 2.314 is not applicable because there was no transaction or sale involved and that the electricity with which the plaintiff allegedly came in contact was not being sold to the Appellee but was being transmitted along its high voltage lines to later be distributed through a transformer to various outlets. In support of this position Appellant cites *Hedges v. Public Service Company of Indiana, Inc.*, 396 N.E.2d 933 (Ct. App. Indiana 1979) in which the Indiana Court held inapplicable a similar section of the U.C.C. where the injury was produced by coming in contact with a 7200 volt power line which was used to transmit high voltage electricity and not used for the purpose of metering the electricity in making a sale thereof.

Section 2.102 of the Business and Commerce Code setting forth the scope of the chapter on sales states "Unless the context otherwise requires, this chapter applies to transactions in goods. . . ."

Section 2.105 defines goods:

(a) "Goods" means all things (including specifically manufactured goods) which are movable at the time of identification to the contract for sale other than the money in which the price is to be paid, investment securities, . . . and things in action . . .

The wording of the requirements for merchantable goods are set forth in Section 2.314 would indicate that it was the intention of the Legislature in passing this act to confine its applicability to tangible manufactured or produced products which might normally be found in bulk quantity or in packaged goods. When applying those requirements to electrical energy it certainly could not be classified as fungible goods nor is there any way to adequately package or label electrical energy. Rather than be classified as goods the sale of electric energy would more fittingly be termed the rendition of a service.

* * *

No Texas authority has been cited and we have found none. However, the following cases from other jurisdictions hold the sale of electricity to be the rendition of a service rather than the sale of goods. [Citations.]

We therefore hold that the transmission of electrical energy along high tension power lines which eventually leads into a transformer is not goods within the meaning of Section 2.314 of the Business and Commerce Code.

Furthermore, we hold that the 7200 volts of electricity being transmitted along Appellant's high tension line was not the subject of a sale of electricity to Appellee. Appellee was purchasing 110 volts being carried to his mobile home by other wires. *Hedges v. Public Service Co. of Indiana, Inc.,* supra; *Helvey v. Wabash County REMC,* 151 Ind. App. 176, 278 N.E.2d 608 (Ct.App. Indiana 1972); *Genaust v. Illinois Power Co.,* 62 Ill.2d 456, 343 N.E.2d 465 (S.Ct.Ill.1979).

Appellee has not proved a cause of action within the meaning of [citation].

Unconscionability

FRANK'S MAINTENANCE AND ENGINEERING, INC. v. C. A. ROBERTS CO.

Appellate Court of Illinois, First District, Fourth Division, 1980.
86 Ill.App.3d 980, 42 Ill.Dec. 25, 408 N.E.2d 403.

ROMITI, J.

[The plaintiff, Frank's Maintenance and Engineering, Inc., orally ordered steel tubing from the defendant C. A. Roberts Co. for use in the manufacture of motorcycle front fork tubes. Since these front fork tubes bear the bulk of the weight of a motorcycle, the steel used must be of high quality. The defendant sent an acknowledgement with conditions of sale including paragraph 11 which limited consequential damages and restricted remedies available upon breach by requiring claims for defective equipment to be promptly made upon receipt. The conditions were located on the back of the acknowledgement. The legend "conditions of sale on reverse side" was stamped over so that on first appearance it read "No conditions of sale on reverse side." The defendants delivered the order in December, 1975. The steel had no visible defects. However, when the plaintiff began using the steel in its manufacture in the summer of 1976, it discovered that the steel was pitted and cracked beyond repair. Plaintiff informed defendant of the defects and revoked its acceptance of the steel. Plaintiff sued defendant for breach of warranty of merchantibility.]

* * *

The Uniform Commercial Code [citation], provides that consequential damages may be limited or excluded unless the limitation or exclusion is unconscionable and such clauses have been upheld in many cases. [Citations.] The Code provides that such limitation is prima facie unconscionable where personal injuries are involved, but not where the loss is commercial. Nevertheless, the existence of a commercial setting is not of itself sufficient insulation against a charge of unconscionability. [Citation.] While under the Code [U.C.C. § 2–302], the question of the unconscionability of a clause is for the court to decide, the court before making this determination must give the parties a reasonable opportunity to present evidence as to its commercial setting, purpose and effect. Generally a full hearing on the issue is required. [Citations.]

Unconscionability can be either procedural or substantive or a combination of both. [Citations.] Procedural unconscionability consists of some impropriety during the process of forming the contract depriving a party of a meaningful choice. [Citation.] Factors to be considered are all the circumstances surrounding the transaction including the manner in which the contract was entered into, whether each party had a reasonable opportunity to understand the terms of the contract, and whether important terms were hidden in a maze of fine print; both the conspicuousness of the clause and the negotiations relating to it are important, albeit not conclusive factors in determining the issue of unconscionability. [Citation.] To be a part of the bargain, a provision limiting the defendant's liability must, unless incorporated into the contract through prior course of dealings or trade usage, have been bargained for, brought to the purchaser's attention or be conspicuous. [Citation.] If not, the seller has no reasonable expectation that the remedy was being so restricted and the restriction cannot be said to be part of the agreement of the parties. [Citation.] Nor does the mere fact that both parties are businessmen justify the utilization of unfair surprise to the detriment of one of the parties since the Code specifically provides for the recovery of consequential damages and an individual should be able to rely on their existence in the absence of being informed to the contrary either directly or constructively through prior course of dealings or trade usage. [Citation.] This requirement that the seller obtain the knowing assent of the buyer "does not detract from

the freedom to contract, unless that phrase denotes the freedom to impose the onerous terms of one's carefully-drawn printed document on an unsuspecting contractual partner. Rather, freedom to contract is enhanced by a requirement that both parties be aware of the burdens they are assuming. The notion of free will has little meaning as applied to one who is ignorant of the consequences of his acts." [Citation.]

Substantive unconscionability concerns the question whether the terms themselves are commercially reasonable. [Citation.] While the Code permits the limitation of remedies, it must be remembered that it disfavors them [sic] and specifically provides for their deletion if they would act to deprive a contracting party of reasonable protection against a breach. [Citations.] The Code [U.C.C.] 1–106(1), specifically provides that the remedies provided by it shall be liberally construed to the end that the aggrieved party may be put in as good a position as if the other party had fully performed. [Citations.] And as specifically stated in [the comments to the U.C.C.], if the parties intend to conclude a contract for sale within the scope of the Uniform Commercial Code-Sales, they must accept the legal consequence that there be at least a fair quantum of remedy for breach of the obligations or duties outlined in the contract. Reasonable agreements which limit or modify remedies will be given effect but the parties are not free to shape their remedies in an unreasonable or unconscionable way. [Citations.] It is for this reason that courts have tended to strike down clauses barring the recovery of consequential damages or otherwise limiting recovery when the defect was latent. [Citations.]

In the present case, the evidence produced by the plaintiff discloses that the limiting clause was not conspicuous and was not known to the plaintiff at the time the contract was made. Indeed, the clause directing the plaintiff's attention to conditions on the reverse side of the acknowledgment was stamped over, indicating that legend was irrelevant.

In addition, the plaintiff was directed to check to see if the order as acknowledged conformed to the terms of the order as the seller otherwise could not be responsible for mistakes in the execution of the order. Thus by implication plaintiff was informed that there was nothing else in the acknowledgment to be checked. Furthermore the defects in the steel allegedly were latent. Absent evidence produced by the defendants tending to refute this evidence or tending to show the paragraph had been negotiated by the parties and agreed to, or that prior contracts between the parties had established a consistently adhered to policy of excluding consequential damages, or whether a recognized trade practice, reasonable as applied to the plaintiff, had established such a policy [citation], we do not believe that the court could reasonably find the clause to be conscionable.

* * *

[Judgment for plaintiff.]

Variant Acceptances: Battle of the Forms

DORTON v. COLLINS & AIKMAN CORP.

United States Court of Appeals, Sixth Circuit, 1972.
453 F.2d 1161.

CELEBREZZE, J.

[Plaintiffs-Appellees, Frank E. Dorton and J. A. Castle] (hereinafter The Carpet Mart), carpet retailers in Kingsport, Tennessee, purchased carpets from Defendant-Appellant (hereinafter Collins & Aikman), incorporated under the laws of the State of Delaware, with its principal place of business in New York, New York, and owner of a carpet manufacturing plant (formerly the Painter Carpet Mills, Inc.) located in Dalton, Georgia. The Carpet Mart originally brought this action in a Tennessee state trial court, seeking compensatory and punitive damages in the amount of $450,000 from Collins & Aikman for the latter's alleged fraud, deceit, and mis-

representation in the sale of what were supposedly carpets manufactured from 100% Kodel polyester fiber. The Carpet Mart maintains that in May, 1970, in response to a customer complaint, it learned that not all of the carpets were manufactured from 100% Kodel polyester fiber but rather some were composed of a cheaper and inferior carpet fiber. After the cause was removed to the District Court on the basis of diversity of citizenship, Collins & Aikman moved for a stay pending arbitration, asserting that The Carpet Mart was bound to an arbitration agreement which appeared on the reverse side of Collins & Aikman's printed sales acknowledgment forms. Holding that there existed no binding arbitration agreement between the parties, the District Court denied the stay. For the reasons set forth below, we remand the case to the District Court for further findings.

* * *

The primary question before us on appeal is whether the District Court, in denying Collins & Aikman's motion for a stay pending arbitration, erred in holding that The Carpet Mart was not bound by the arbitration agreement appearing on the back of Collins & Aikman's acknowledgment forms. * * *

* * * Under the common law, an acceptance or a confirmation which contained terms additional to or different from those of the offer or oral agreement constituted a rejection of the offer or agreement and thus became a counter-offer. The terms of the counter-offer were said to have been accepted by the original offeror when he proceeded to perform under the contract without objecting to the counter-offer. Thus, a buyer was deemed to have accepted the seller's counter-offer if he took receipt of the goods and paid for them without objection.

Under Section 2–207 the result is different. This section of the Code recognizes that in current commercial transactions, the terms of the offer and those of the acceptance will seldom be identical. Rather, under the current "battle of the forms," each party typically has a printed form drafted by his attorney and containing as many terms as could be envisioned to favor that party in his sales transactions. Whereas under common law the disparity between the fine-print terms in the parties' forms would have prevented the consummation of a contract when these forms are exchanged, Section 2–207 recognizes that in many, but not all, cases the parties do not impart such significance to the terms on the printed forms. [Citation.] Subsection 2–207(1) therefore provides that "[a] definite and seasonable expression of acceptance or a written confirmation . . . operates as an acceptance even though it states terms additional to or different from those offered or agreed upon, unless acceptance is expressly made conditional on assent to the additional or different terms." Thus, under Subsection (1), a contract is recognized notwithstanding the fact that an acceptance or confirmation contains terms additional to or different from those of the offer or prior agreement, provided that the offeree's intent to accept the offer is definitely expressed, *see* Sections 2–204 and 2–206, and provided that the offeree's acceptance is not expressly conditioned on the offeror's assent to the additional or different terms. When a contract is recognized under Subsection (1), the additional terms are treated as "proposals for addition to the contract" under Subsection (2), which contains special provisions under which such additional terms are deemed to have been accepted when the transaction is between merchants. Conversely, when no contract is recognized under Subsection 2–207(1)—either because no definite expression of acceptance exists or, more specifically, because the offeree's acceptance is expressly conditioned on the offeror's assent to the additional or different terms—the entire transaction aborts at this point. If, however, the subsequent conduct of the parties—particularly, performance by both parties under what they apparently believe to be a contract—recognizes the existence of a contract, under Subsection 2–207(3) such conduct by both parties is sufficient to establish a contract, notwithstanding the fact that no

contract would have been recognized on the basis of their writings alone. Subsection 2–207(3) further provides how the terms of contracts recognized thereunder shall be determined.

* * *

Assuming, for purposes of analysis, that the arbitration provision was an addition to the terms of The Carpet Mart's oral offers, we must next determine whether or not Collins & Aikman's acceptances were "expressly made conditional on assent to the additional . . . terms" therein, within the proviso of Subsection 2–207(1). * * * [T]he provision appearing on the face of Collins & Aikman's acknowledgment forms stated that the acceptances (or orders) were "subject to all of the terms and conditions on the face and reverse side thereof, including arbitration, all of which are accepted by buyer." * * * Although Collins & Aikman's use of the words "subject to" suggests that the acceptances were conditional to some extent, we do not believe the acceptances were "expressly made conditional on [the buyer's] assent to the additional or different terms," as specifically required under the Subsection 2–207(1) proviso. In order to fall within this proviso, it is not enough that an acceptance is expressly conditional on additional or different terms; rather, an acceptance must be *expressly* conditional on the offeror's *assent* to those terms. Viewing the Subsection (1) proviso within the context of the rest of that Subsection and within the policies of Section 2–207 itself, we believe that it was intended to apply only to an acceptance which clearly reveals that the offeree is unwilling to proceed with the transaction unless he is assured of the offeror's assent to the additional or different terms therein.

* * *

Because Collins & Aikman's acceptances were not expressly conditional on the buyer's assent to the additional terms within the proviso of Subsection 2–207(1), a contract is recognized under Subsection (1), and the additional terms are treated as "proposals" for addition to the contract under Subsection 2–207(2). Since both Collins & Aikman and The Carpet Mart are clearly "merchants" as that term is defined in Subsection 2–104(1), the arbitration provision will be deemed to have been accepted by The Carpet Mart under Subsection 2–207(2) unless it materially altered the terms of The Carpet Mart's oral offers. [UCC § 2–207(2)(b)]. We believe that the question of whether the arbitration provision materially altered the oral offer under Subsection 2–207(2)(b) is one which can be resolved only by the District Court on further findings of fact in the present case. If the arbitration provision did in fact materially al-ter The Carpet Mart's offer, it could not become a part of the contract "unless expressly agreed to" by The Carpet Mart. [UCC § 2–207], Official Comment No. 3.

We therefore conclude that if on remand the District Court finds that Collins & Aikman's acknowledgments were in fact acceptances and that the arbitration provision was additional to the terms of The Carpet Mart's oral orders, contracts will be recognized under Subsection 2–207(1). The arbitration clause will then be viewed as a "proposal" under Subsection 2–207(2) which will be deemed to have been accepted by The Carpet Mart unless it materially altered the oral offers.

PROBLEMS

1. A orders 1,000 widgets at five dollars per widget from International Widget to be delivered within sixty days. After the contract is consummated and signed, A requests that International deliver the widgets within thirty days rather than sixty days. International agrees. Is the contractual modification binding?

2. In question 1 what affect, if any, would the following telegram have:

International Widget:

In accordance with our agreement of this date you will deliver the 1,000 previously ordered widgets within thirty days. Thank you for your cooperation in this matter.

(signed) A

3. A, a San Francisco company, orders from U.S. Electronics, a New York company, 10,000 electronic units. A's order form provides that any dispute would be resolved by an arbitration panel located in San Francisco. U.S. Electronics executes and delivers to A its acknowledgment form which accepts the order and contains the following provision: "All disputes will be resolved by the State courts of New York." A dispute arose concerning the workmanship of the parts, and A wishes the case to be arbitrated in San Francisco. What result?

4. Would the result change in problem 3 if the U.S. Electronics' form contained any of the following provisions:

(a) "The seller's acceptance of the purchase order to which this acknowledgment responds is expressly made conditional on the buyer's assent to any or different terms contained in this acknowledgment"?

(b) "The seller's acceptance of the purchase order is subject to the terms and conditions on the face and reverse side hereof and which the buyer accepts by accepting the goods described herein"?

(c) "The seller's terms govern this agreement—this acknowledgment merely constitutes a counter-offer"?

5. A executed a written contract with B to purchase an assorted collection of shoes for $3,000. A week before the agreed shipment date, B called A and said, "We cannot deliver at $3,000; unless you agree to pay $4,000, we will cancel the order." After considerable discussion, A agreed to pay $4,000 if B would ship as agreed in the contract. After the shoes had been delivered and accepted by A, A refused to pay $4,000 and insisted on paying only $3,000. Decision?

6. On November 23, A, a dress manufacturer, mailed to B a written and signed offer to sell 1,000 sun dresses at fifty dollars per dress. The offer stated that "it would remain open for ten days and that it could not be withdrawn prior to that date."

Two days later, A, noting a sudden increase in the price of sun dresses changed his mind. A therefore sent B a letter revoking the offer. The letter was sent on November 25 and received by B on November 28.

B chose to disregard the letter of November 25; instead, she happily continued to watch the price of sun dresses rise. On December 1, B sent a letter accepting the original offer. The letter, however, was not received by A until December 9, due to a delay in the mails.

B has demanded delivery of the goods according to the terms of the offer of November 23, but A has refused. Decision?

7. H and W, an elderly immigrant couple, agree to purchase from B a refrigerator with fair market value of $450 for twenty-five monthly installments of sixty dollars per month. H and W now wish to void the contract asserting that they did not realize the exorbitant price they were paying. Result?

Chapter 20

TRANSFER OF TITLE AND RISK OF LOSS

HISTORICALLY, title governed nearly every aspect of the rights and duties of the buyer and seller arising out of a sales contract. The Code, on the other hand, in an attempt to add greater precision and certainty has abandoned the common law's reliance upon title. Instead, the Code approaches each legal issue arising out of a sales contract on its own merits and provides separate and specific rules to control the various transactional situations. This chapter covers the Code's approach to the transfer of title and other property rights, the passage of risk of loss, and the transfer of goods sold in bulk.

TRANSFER OF TITLE AND OTHER PROPERTY RIGHTS

In addition to de-emphasizing the significance of the passage of title the Code utilizes other property rights in its transactional approach to the law of sales. These other property rights include the newly created special property as well as insurable interests and security interests. Nevertheless, the determination of who has title to the goods does retain some significance. This section will explore these topics in addition to the circumstances under which the seller has the right or power to transfer title to the buyer.

PASSAGE OF TITLE

A sale of goods is defined as the transfer of title from the seller to the buyer for a consideration known as the price. Section 2-106. Transfer of title is, therefore, fundamental to the existence of a sale of goods. *See Meinhard-Commercial Corp. v. Hargo Woolen Mills.*

Title passes when the parties *intend* it to pass, but in many cases such intention is difficult to ascertain by reason of conflicting testimony, or because the negotiations between the parties leading up to formation of the contract involved no discussion or mention of title. Where the parties have no explicit agreement as to transfer of title, the Code provides, in Section 2-401, rules that determine when title passes to the buyer.

Physical Movement of the Goods

When delivery is to be made by moving the goods, title passes at the time and place at which the seller completes his performance with reference to delivery of the goods. Section 2-401(2).

Shipment Contracts A "shipment contract" requires or authorizes the seller to send the goods to the buyer but does not require the seller to deliver them to a particular destination. Under a shipment contract, title passes to the buyer at the time and place that the seller delivers the goods to the carrier for shipment to the buyer.

Destination Contracts A "destination contract" requires the seller to deliver the goods to a particular destination, and title passes to the buyer upon tender of the goods at that destination. For example, title passes under a destination contract which specifies the destination as the buyer's place of business at the time the goods are tendered to the buyer at her place of business.

No Movement of the Goods

When delivery is to be made without moving the goods, title passes: (1) upon delivery of a document of title where the contract calls for delivery of such document (documents of title are documents which evidence a right to receive specified goods—they are discussed more fully in Chapter 47); or (2) at the time and place of contracting where the goods at that time are identified to the contract and no documents are to be delivered. Section 2-401(3).

OTHER PROPERTY RIGHTS

Special Property

The Code creates a new property interest in goods which did not exist at common law. It is described as a "special property" right which the buyer obtains by the *identification* of existing goods as goods to which the contract of sale refers. Sections 2-401(1), 2-501(1). After formation of the contract it is normal for the seller to take steps to obtain, manufacture, prepare, or select goods with which to fulfill her obligation under the contract. At some stage in the process the seller will have identified the goods which she intends to ship, deliver, or hold for the buyer. These goods may or may not conform to the contract but in either case the identification of goods to the contract immediately creates for the buyer a special property right in the goods identified.

This Code created interest, designated as a special property in goods identified to the contract, has specific incidents which give rise to the following rights in the buyer:

1. The buyer has an insurable interest in the goods. Section 2-501.
2. Where the buyer has paid all or part of the price of goods he may reclaim them from the seller who has become insolvent within 10 days after receiving the first installment on the price. If the identification creating the special property was made by the buyer alone he may reclaim the goods only if they conform to the contract of sale. Section 2-502.
3. The buyer has the right to inspect identified goods at any reasonable time and place. Section 2-513(1).
4. The buyer has the right to replevin goods identified to the contract if he is unable to effect cover for such goods. Section 2-716.
5. The buyer may maintain an action and recover damages against a third party for conversion of identified goods or for loss or injury

to the goods caused by a third party. Section 2-722.

Identification may be made by either the seller or the buyer and can be made at any time and in any manner agreed upon by the parties. In the absence of explicit agreement, identification takes place as provided in Section 2-501(1):

1. upon the making of the contract if it is for goods already existing and identified;
2. if the contract is for crops to be grown within twelve months or the next normal harvest, or for the offspring of animals to be born within twelve months, when the crops are planted or become growing, or when the young animals are conceived; or
3. if the contract is one for all other future goods, when the seller ships, marks, or otherwise designates the goods as those to which the contract refers.

Where the goods have been identified to the contract by the seller alone he may substitute other goods for those so identified until such time as he (1) defaults, (2) becomes insolvent, or (3) notifies the buyer that the identification is final. Section 2-501(2).

Insurable Interest

In order for a contract or policy of insurance to be valid, the insured must have an insurable interest in the subject matter. At common law only a person with title or a lien could insure his interest in specific goods. The Code, as previously noted, extends this right to a buyer's interest in goods which have been identified as goods to which the contract of sale refers. Section 2-501(1). This interest enables the buyer to purchase insurance protection on goods which he does not presently own but which he may own upon delivery by the seller.

The seller also has an insurable interest in the goods so long as he has title to them or any security interest in them. Section 2-501(2). There is nothing to prevent both seller and buyer at the same time from carrying insurance on goods in which they both have a property interest, whether it be title, a security interest, or a special property.

Security Interest

A "security interest" is defined in the Code as an interest in personal property or fixtures which secures payment or performance of an obligation. Section 1-201(37). Any reservation by the seller of title to goods delivered to the buyer is limited in effect to a reservation of a security interest. Section 2-401(1). Security interests in goods are governed by Article 9 of the Code (discussed in Chapter 37), except that so long as the buyer does not have or lawfully obtain possession of the goods (1) no security agreement is necessary, (2) no filing is required, and (3) the rights of the seller on default by the buyer are governed by Article 2. Section 9-113.

The special property in the goods created by Sections 2-401(1) and 2-501(1) is not a security interest, but the buyer may acquire a security interest by complying with Article 9.

POWER TO TRANSFER TITLE

Having discussed when title and other property rights pass from the seller to the buyer, it is crucial to understand under what circumstances a seller has the right or power to transfer these property rights to the buyer. If the seller is the rightful owner of goods or is authorized to sell the goods for the rightful owner, then the seller has the **right** to transfer title. But when a seller is in possession of goods which he neither owns nor has authority to sell, then the sale is not rightful. However, in some situations these non-owner sellers may have the **power** to transfer good title to certain buyers. This section pertains to such sales by a person in possession of goods which he neither owns nor has authority to sell.

The venerable rule of property law protecting existing ownership of goods is the starting point and background in any discussion of a sale of goods by a non-owner. It is elementary that a purchaser of goods obtains such title as his transferor had or had power to transfer, and the Code expressly so states. Section 2-403. Likewise, the purchaser of a limited interest in goods acquires rights only to the extent of the interest which he purchased. By the same token, no one can transfer what he does not have. A purported sale by a thief or finder or ordinary bailee of goods does not transfer title to the purchaser.

The reasons underlying the policy of the law in protecting existing ownership of goods are obvious. A person should not be required to retain possession at all times of all the goods that he owns in order to maintain his ownership of them. One of the valuable incidents of ownership of goods is the freedom of the owner to make a bailment of his goods as he pleases, and the mere possession of goods by a bailee does not authorize the bailee to sell them.

A policy of the law in competition with that which protects existing ownership is protection of the good faith purchaser based upon the needs of trade and commerce in protecting the security of good faith transactions in goods. In order to encourage and make secure good faith acquisitions of goods it is necessary that *bona fide* (good faith) purchasers for value under certain circumstances be protected. A **good faith purchaser** is defined as one who acts honestly, gives value, and takes the goods without notice or knowledge of any defect in the title of his transferor.

The problems presented in this section and the rules for their solution should be considered in the light of these two competing policies of the law. Both policies are sound, beneficial, and worthy of enforcement. One protects existing property rights; the other protects the stability of good faith transactions in the market place. In the area of sales of goods by a non-owner, these policies come into conflict. In every such conflict only one

may prevail. As between these two innocent parties, the law must either protect existing ownership and defeat the interest of the *bona fide* purchaser for value, or vice versa.

Void and Voidable Title to Goods

A void title is no title. A person claiming ownership of goods by an agreement that is void obtains no title to the goods. Thus, a person who acquires goods by physical duress or from someone under guardianship as well as a thief or a finder of goods has no title to them and can transfer none.

A voidable title is one acquired under circumstances which permit the former owner to rescind the transfer and revest herself with title, as in the case of mistake, common duress, undue influence, fraud in the inducement, or sale by a person without contractual capacity (other than an individual under guardianship). In these situations, the buyer has acquired legal title to the goods of which he may be divested by action taken by the seller. However, if, before the seller has rescinded the transfer of title, the buyer should resell the goods to a *bona fide* purchaser for value and without notice of any infirmity in his title, the right of rescission in the seller is cut off, and the *bona fide* purchaser acquires good title.

The distinction between a void and voidable title is, therefore, extremely important in determining the rights of *bona fide* purchasers of goods. The *bona fide* purchaser always believes that she is buying the goods from the owner or from one with authority to sell. Otherwise she would not be acting in good faith. In each situation the party selling the goods appears to be the owner whether his title is valid, void, or voidable. As between two innocent persons, the true owner who has done nothing wrong and the *bona fide* purchaser who has done nothing wrong, the law will not disturb the legal title but will rule in favor of the one who has it. Thus, where A transfers possession of goods to B under such circumstances that B acquires no

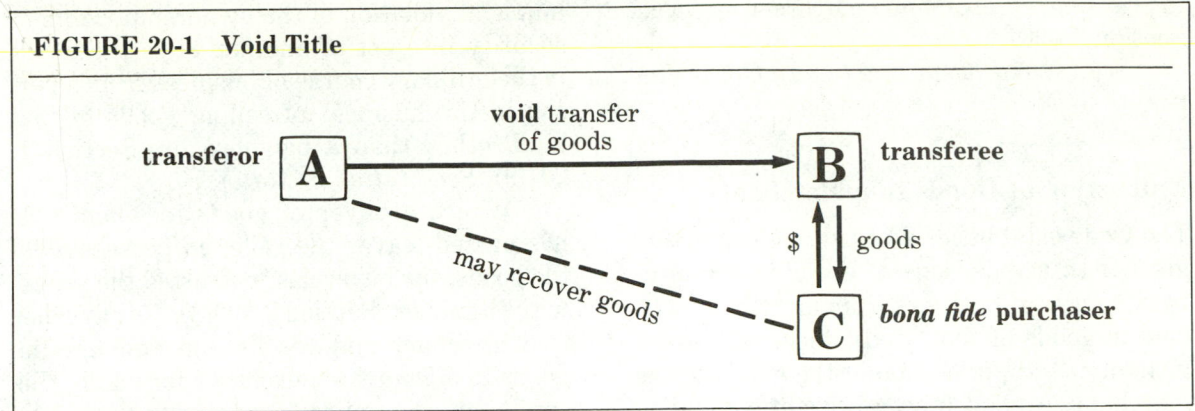

FIGURE 20-1   Void Title

title or a void title, and B thereafter sells the goods to C, a *bona fide* purchaser for value, B has nothing except possession to transfer to C. In a lawsuit between A and C involving the right to the goods, A will win because she has the legal title. C's only recourse is against B for breach of warranty of title discussed in Chapter 21. See Figure 20-1.

However, if B acquired a voidable title from A and resold the goods to C, in a suit between A and C over the goods, C would win. In this case, B had title, although it was voidable, which she transferred to the *bona fide* purchaser. The title thus acquired by C will be protected. The voidable title in B is title until it has been avoided. After transfer to a *bona fide* purchaser, it may not be avoided. A's only recourse is against B for restitution or damages. See Figure 20-2.

The Code enlarges this doctrine by providing that a good faith purchaser for value obtains valid title from one possessing voidable title even if that person's voidable title was obtained by (1) fraud as to his identity, (2) delivery of a subsequently dishonored check, (3) an agreement that the transaction was to be a cash sale and the sale price has not been paid, or (4) criminal fraud punishable as larceny. Section 2-403(1).

Another way in which the Code has expanded the rights of *bona fide* purchasers is with respect to sales by **minors.** The common law permitted a minor seller of goods to disaffirm the sale and to recover the goods from a third person who had purchased them in good faith from the party who acquired the goods from the minor. The Code has changed this rule and does not permit a minor seller

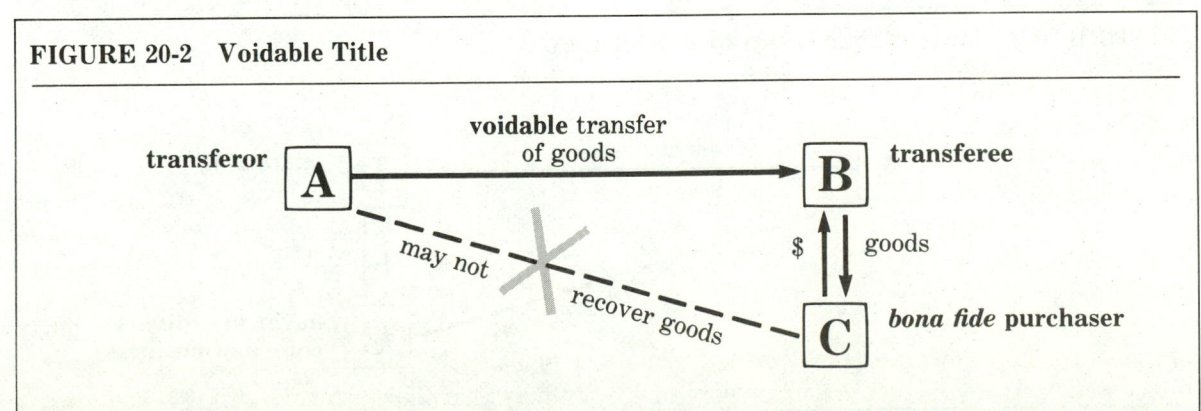

FIGURE 20-2   Voidable Title

to prevail over a *bona fide* purchaser for value. Section 2-403.

See *United Road Machinery Co. v. Jasper.*

Entrusting of Goods to a Merchant

The Code establishes a broad rule protecting good faith acquisitions of goods in the ordinary course of business from merchants who deal in goods of that kind, where the owner has entrusted possession of the goods to the merchant. Any such entrusting of possession bestows upon the merchant the power to transfer all rights of the entruster to a buyer in the ordinary course of business. Section 2-403(2). For example, A brings her stereo for repair to B, who also sells both new and used stereo equipment. C purchases A's stereo from B in good faith and in the ordinary course of business. The Code protects the rights of C and defeats the rights of A. A's only recourse is against B. See Figure 20-3.

The Code, however, does not go so far as to protect the *bona fide* purchaser from a merchant to whom the goods have been entrusted by a thief or finder or by a completely unauthorized person. It merely grants the good faith buyer in the ordinary course of business the rights of the entruster.

The Code defines **buyer in ordinary course of business** as a person who in good faith and without knowledge that the sale to him is in violation of the ownership rights or security interest of another buys the goods in the ordinary course of business from a person in the business of selling goods of that kind, other than a pawnbroker. Section 1-201(9). *See Mattek v. Malofsky.*

Where a buyer of goods to whom title has passed leaves the seller in possession of the goods, the buyer has "entrusted the goods" with the seller. Section 2-403(3). If that seller is a merchant and resells and delivers the goods to a *bona fide* purchaser for value, this second buyer acquires good title to the goods. Thus, A sells certain goods to B who pays the price but allows possession to remain with A. A thereafter sells the same goods to C, a *bona fide* purchaser for value without notice of the prior sale to B. C takes delivery of the goods. B does not have any rights against C or to the goods. B's only remedy is against A.

The Code treats more favorably the rights of *bona fide* purchasers under Section 2-403 than the rights of attaching creditors under Section 2-402 which deals with the rights of creditors of the seller in goods sold but left in the possession of the seller. Section 2-402(2) provides:

A creditor of the seller may treat a sale or an identification of goods to a contract for sale as void if as against him a retention of possession by the seller is fraudulent under any rule of law of the state where the goods are situated, except that

---

FIGURE 20-3   Entrusting of Goods to a Merchant

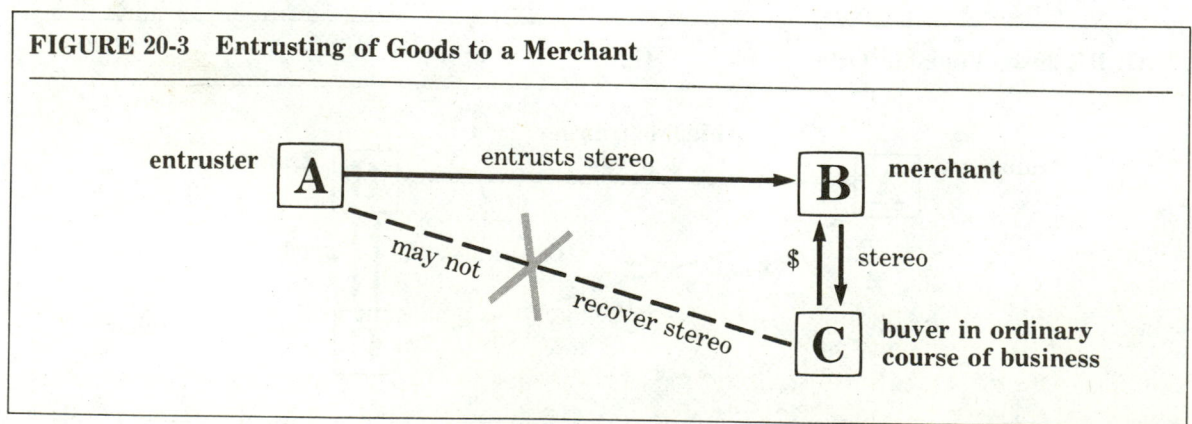

retention of possession in good faith and current course of trade by a merchant-seller for a commercially reasonable time after a sale or identification is not fraudulent.

It is the purpose of the Code *not* to change the local law as to the rights of creditors with respect to goods sold but left in the possession of the seller. The statutes in the various States contain different provisions regarding the fraudulent effect of retention of possession by the seller or a transfer of both title and possession with intent to defraud, and each State has well-settled rules on this subject embodied in its court decisions. These various rules of local State law are not changed by the Code.

RISK OF LOSS

Risk of loss, as the term is used in the law of sales, means the placement of the loss between seller and buyer where the goods have been damaged, destroyed, or lost *without the fault* of either the seller or the buyer. If placed upon the buyer, he is under a duty to pay the price for the goods even though they were damaged or he never received them. If placed upon the seller, he has no right to recover the purchase price from the buyer and is usually liable to the buyer for damages for nondelivery unless he tenders a performance in replacement for the lost or destroyed goods.

In determining the location of risk of loss the Code provides definite rules for specific situations, a sharp departure from the common law concept of risk of loss, which was determined by ownership of the goods and depended upon whether title had been transferred. In its transactional approach the Code is necessarily detailed and for this reason is probably more understandable and meaningful than the common law's reliance upon the abstract concept of title.

For the most part, the Code attempts to place the risk of loss upon the party who is more likely to have greater control over the goods, is more likely to insure the goods, or

is better able to prevent the loss. However, this approach is not followed where one party has breached the contract. Accordingly, the Code has adopted separate rules for determining the risk of loss in the absence of breach from those that apply where there has been a breach of the sales contract.

RISK OF LOSS IN ABSENCE OF A BREACH

Agreement of the Parties

The parties by agreement may not only shift the allocation of risk of loss but may also divide the risk between them. Section 2-303. Such agreement is controlling. Thus, the parties may agree that a seller shall retain the risk of loss even though the buyer is in possession of the goods or has title to them. Or, the agreement may provide that the buyer bears 60 percent of the risk and the seller bears 40 percent.

Trial Sales

Sale on Approval In a sale on approval, possession, but not title to the goods, is transferred to the buyer for a stated period of time or, if none is stated, for a reasonable time, during which period the buyer may use the goods to determine whether she wishes to buy them. Both title and risk of loss remain with the *seller* until "approval" or acceptance of the goods by the buyer. Section 2-327(1)(a).

Use of the goods consistent with the purpose of approval by the buyer is not acceptance, but failure of the buyer within a reasonable period of time to notify the seller of her election to return the goods is an acceptance. The buyer's approval may also be manifested by exercising any dominion or control over the goods inconsistent with the seller's ownership. Upon approval, risk of loss and title passes to the buyer who then becomes liable to the seller for the purchase price of the goods. If the buyer elects to return the goods and notifies the seller, the return is at the seller's risk and expense.

Sale or Return

Sale or Return In a sale or return, the goods are sold and delivered to the buyer with an option to return them to the seller. The risk of loss is on the *buyer* who also has title until she revests it in the seller by a return of the goods. The return of the goods is at the buyer's risk and expense.

It is frequently difficult to determine from the facts of a particular transaction whether the parties intended a sale on approval or a sale or return. The consequences are drastically different with respect to transfer of title and risk of loss. The Code provides a test which is neat, sensible, and easily applied: unless otherwise agreed, if the goods are delivered primarily for the buyer's use, the transaction is a sale on approval; if they are delivered primarily for resale by the buyer, it is a sale or return. Section 2-236(1).

Consignment A consignment is a delivery of possession of personal property to an agent for sale by the agent. Under the Code, a sale on consignment is regarded as a sale or return. Therefore, creditors of the consignee (the agent who receives the merchandise for sale) prevail over the consignor and may obtain possession of the consigned goods, provided the consignee maintains a place of business where he deals in goods of the kind involved under a name other than the name of the consignor. Nevertheless, under Section 2-326(3) the consignor will prevail if he

(a) complies with an applicable law providing for a consignor's interest or the like to be evidenced by a sign, or

(b) establishes that the person conducting the business is generally known by his creditors to be substantially engaged in selling the goods of others, or

(c) complies with the filing provisions of the Article on Secured Transactions (Article 9).

Contracts Involving Carriers

If the contract does not require the seller to deliver the goods at a particular destination but merely to the carrier (**a shipment contract**), risk of loss passes to the buyer upon delivery of the goods to the carrier. If the seller is required to deliver them to a particular destination (**a destination contract**), risk of loss passes to the buyer at destination upon tender of the goods to the buyer. Section 2-509(1).

Sales contracts frequently contain terms which indicate the agreement of the parties as to delivery. These terms designate whether the contract is a shipment contract or a destination contract and, by implication, when the risk of loss passes.

Shipment Contracts The initials *"F.O.B."* mean "free on board" and *"F.A.S."* mean "free alongside." Under the Code these are delivery terms even though used only in connection with the stated price. Section 2-319(1)(a). When the contract provides that the sale is **F.O.B. place of shipment** or **F.A.S. port of shipment**, then the contract is a shipment contract. For example, A whose place of business is in New York enters into a contract with B, the buyer, who is located in San Francisco. The contract calls for delivery of the goods F.O.B. New York. This would be a shipment contract.

The initials **"C.I.F."** mean "cost, insurance, and freight" and **"C. & F."** mean simply "cost and freight." Under a C.I.F. contract, in consideration for an agreed unit price for the goods, the seller pays all costs of transportation, insurance, and freight to the destination. The amount of the agreed unit price of the goods will, of course, reflect these costs. The unit price in a C. & F. contract is understandably less than in a C.I.F. contract as it does not include the cost of insurance. Under the Code, *both* C.I.F. and C. & F. contracts are regarded as shipment, and not destination, contracts.

Under any of these shipment contracts, when the seller has delivered the goods to the carrier under a proper contract of shipment, title and risk of loss pass to the buyer. For example, in *Ninth Street East, Limited v. Harrison*, 5 Conn. Cir. 597, 259 A.2d 772 (1968), Harrison, a men's clothing retailer located in Westport, Connecticut, ordered merchandise from Ninth Street East, Ltd., a Los Angeles-based clothing manufacturer. Ninth Street delivered the merchandise to Denver Chicago Trucking Company in Los Angeles, and then sent four invoices to Harrison that bore the notation "F.O.B. Los Angeles." Denver subsequently transferred the merchandise to a connecting carrier, Old Colony Transportation Company, for final delivery to Harrison's Westport store. When Old Colony tried to deliver the merchandise, Harrison's wife asked the truck driver to deliver the boxes inside the store, but the driver refused. The dispute remained unresolved, and the truck departed with Old Colony still in possession of the goods. Harrison then notified Ninth Street by letter of the nondelivery, but Ninth Street was unable to locate the shipment. Ninth Street then sought to recover the contract purchase price from Harrison. Harrison refused, however, contending that risk of loss remained with Ninth Street because of its refusal to deliver the merchandise to Harrison's place of business. Judgment for Ninth Street. The agreement provided for F.O.B. shipment, and thus risk of loss passed to Harrison after Ninth Street placed the goods in possession of the carrier Denver, made a reasonable contract for their transportation, and notified Harrison of the shipment, including the F.O.B. provision. Harrison, therefore, is liable for the entire purchase price of the merchandise.

The initials "C.O.D." mean "Collect on Delivery" and are instructions to the carrier not to deliver the goods at the destination until it has collected the price and transportation charges from the buyer. In this manner the seller retains control over possession of the goods by preventing the buyer from ob-

taining delivery unless he pays the price. A C.O.D. contract is generally a shipment contract, and title and risk of loss pass to the buyer upon delivery to the carrier.

See *Pestana v. Karinol Corporation.*

Destination Contracts Where the contract provides that the sale is **F.O.B. place of destination,** the seller must at his own expense and risk transport the goods to that place and there tender delivery of them to the buyer. Section 2-319(1)(b). These are destination contracts. For example, if the buyer is in Boston and the seller in Chicago, a contract providing F.O.B. Boston would be a destination contract under which the seller is obligated at his own expense and risk to deliver the goods to the designated place in Boston.

Where the contract provides for delivery **"ex-ship,"** or from the ship, it is not only a destination contract but risk of loss does not pass to the buyer until the goods are unloaded from the carrier at destination.

Finally, where the contract contains terms **"no arrival, no sale,"** the title and risk of loss do not pass to the buyer until the seller makes a tender of the goods after their arrival at destination. The major significance of the "no arrival, no sale" term is that it excuses the seller from any liability to the buyer for failure of the goods to arrive, unless the seller has caused their nonarrival.

Goods in Possession of Bailee

In some sales the goods at the time of the contract are held by a bailee and are to be delivered without being moved. For instance, a seller may contract with a buyer to sell grain which is located in a grain elevator and which the buyer intends to leave in the same elevator. In such situations Section 2-509(2) provides that the risk of loss passes to the buyer upon the occurrence of one of the following:

1. If a negotiable document of title (discussed in Chapter 47) is involved, upon the buyer's *receipt* of the document.

2. If a non-negotiable document of title is utilized by the bailee as a receipt for the seller's goods being stored, upon the tender of the document to the buyer, unless the buyer seasonably objects.

3. If no documents of title are employed, upon either (a) the seller's tender to the buyer of written directions to the bailee to deliver the goods to the buyer, unless the buyer seasonably objects or (b) an acknowledgment by the bailee of the buyer's right to possession of the goods.

All Other Sales

If the goods are in the possession of the buyer at the time of the making of the contract, risk of loss passes to the buyer at that time. Section 2-509(3).

However, if the contract of sale is not on approval and does not provide expressly for the passage of risk of loss and, if at the time the contract was formed, the goods were not in the possession of the buyer, were not to be shipped by carrier, and were not in the possession of a bailee, the situation is one of frequent occurrence in which a seller is required to tender or deliver the goods to the buyer. In such case risk of loss depends upon whether the seller is a merchant. If the seller is a **merchant,** risk of loss passes to the buyer upon the buyer's receipt of the goods. If the seller is **not a merchant,** it passes on tender of the goods from the seller to the buyer. Section 2-509(3).

Suppose B goes to A's furniture store, selects a particular set of dining room furniture, and pays A the agreed price of $800 for it upon A's agreement to stain the set a darker color and deliver it. A stains the furniture and notifies B that she may pick up the furniture. That night it is accidentally destroyed by fire. B can recover from A the $800 payment. The risk of loss is on seller A as he is a merchant and the goods were not received by B but were only tendered to her.

On the other hand, suppose X, an accountant, upon moving to a different city contracts to sell his household furniture to Y for $3,000 by a written agreement signed by Y, and notifies Y that the furniture is available for Y to pick up. Y delays picking up the furniture several days and in the interim the furniture is stolen from X's residence without X's fault. X may recover from Y the $3,000 purchase price. The risk of loss is on buyer Y as the seller is not a merchant and tender is sufficient to transfer the risk.

See Martin v. Melland's Inc.

RISK OF LOSS
WHERE THERE IS A BREACH

Breach by the Seller

If the seller ships non-conforming goods to the buyer, the risk of loss remains on the seller until the buyer has accepted the goods or the seller has remedied the defect. Section 2-510(1).

Where the buyer has accepted non-conforming goods, and thereafter by timely notice to the seller rightfully revokes his acceptance (discussed in Chapter 22), he may treat the risk of loss as resting on the seller from the beginning to the extent of any deficiency in the buyer's effective insurance coverage. Section 2-510(2). For example, S delivers to B non-conforming goods which B accepts. Subsequently, B discovers a hidden defect in the goods and rightfully revokes his prior acceptance. If the goods are destroyed through no fault of either party, and B has insured the goods for 60 percent of their fair market value of $10,000, then the insurance company will cover $6,000 of the loss and S will bear the loss of $4,000. If the buyer's insurance coverage had been $10,000, then the seller would not bear any of the loss.

Breach by the Buyer

Where conforming goods have been identified to a contract which the buyer repudiates or breaches before risk of loss has passed to him, the seller may treat the risk of loss as resting on the buyer "for a commercially reasonable time" to the extent of any deficiency in the seller's effective insurance coverage. Section 2-510(3). For example, S agrees to sell 40,000 pounds of plastic resin to B, F.O.B. B's factory, delivery by March 1. On February 1, B wrongfully repudiates the contract by telephoning S and telling her that he does not want the resin. S immediately seeks out another buyer, but before she is able to locate one, and within a commercially reasonable time, the resin is destroyed by a fire through no fault of S. The fair market value of the resin is $35,000. S's insurance only covers $15,000 of the loss. B is liable for $20,000.

In a case involving the question of a commercially reasonable time, the seller had manufactured 40,000 pounds of plastic resin pellets specially for the buyer who agreed to accept them at the rate of 1,000 pounds per day upon his issuance of shipping instructions. Despite numerous requests by the seller, the buyer issued no such instructions. On August 18, the seller, after warehousing the goods for 40 days, demanded by letter that the buyer issue instructions. The buyer agreed to issue them beginning August 20 but never did. On September 22, a fire destroyed the seller's plant containing the goods which were not covered by insurance. The court fixed the date of the breach as August 20, and held that since the goods were conforming and manufactured for the buyer, it was reasonable for the seller to believe that the buyer would soon take them off his hands, so as to forego obtaining insurance. The court held that from August 20 until September 22 was, therefore, a commercially reasonable time for the risk of loss to rest on the buyer. Judgment for the seller for the contract price was affirmed. *Multiplastics, Inc. v. Arch Industries, Inc.*, 166 Conn. 280, 348 A.2d 618 (1974).

SALES OF GOODS IN BULK

Creditors have an obvious interest in a merchant's disposal of the bulk of his merchandise not in the ordinary course of business. The danger to creditors is that the debtor may secretly liquidate all or a major part of his tangible assets by a bulk sale and conceal or divert the proceeds of the sale without paying his creditors. The central purpose of bulk sales law is to deal with two common forms of commercial fraud, namely: (1) the merchant, owing debts, who sells out his stock in trade to a friend for a low price, pays his creditors less than he owes them, and hopes to come back into the business through the back door some time in the future; and (2) the merchant, owing debts, who sells out his stock in trade to any one for any price, pockets the proceeds, and disappears without paying his creditors.

Article 6 of the Code applies to such sales and defines a bulk transfer as "any transfer in bulk and not in the ordinary course of the transferor's business of a major part of the materials, supplies, merchandise, or other inventory." Section 6-102. The transfer of a substantial part of equipment is a bulk transfer only if made in connection with a bulk transfer of inventory. The enterprises subject to Article 6 of the Code are those whose principal business is the sale of merchandise from stock, including those who manufacture what they sell.

REQUIREMENTS OF ARTICLE 6

The Code provides that a bulk transfer of assets is ineffective against any creditor of the transferor, unless four requirements are met, namely:

1. The transferor furnishes to the transferee a sworn list of his existing creditors, including those whose claims are disputed, stating names, business addresses, and amounts due and owing when known. Section 6-104(1)(a).
2. The transferor and transferee prepare a schedule or list of the property being transferred. Section 6-104(1)(b).
3. The transferee preserves the list of creditors and schedule of property for six months and permits inspection by any creditor of the transferor. Section 6-104(1)(c).

4. The transferee gives the notice of the proposed transfer in bulk to each creditor of the transferor at least ten days before the transferee takes possession of the goods or makes payment for them. Section 6-105. Notice must specify: (a) that a bulk transfer is about to be made; (b) the names and business addresses of the transferor in bulk and transferee in bulk; and (c) whether all debts of the transferor in bulk are to be paid in full as a result of the transaction, and if so, the address to which creditors should send their bills. Section 6-107(1).

If all of the above steps are taken, the transfer in bulk complies with the statute and the transferee acquires the goods free of all claims of creditors of the transferor. The transferor is responsible for the completeness and accuracy of the sworn list of his creditors. Errors or omissions in this list do not impair the validity of the bulk transfer unless the transferee has knowledge of such errors or omissions. Section 6-104(3).

EXEMPTED BULK TRANSFERS

Certain transfers in bulk are exempt and need not comply with Article 6 of the Code, such as:

1. transfers by way of security;
2. general assignments for the benefit of all the creditors of the transferor in bulk;
3. transfers in settlement or realization of a lien or security interest;
4. sales by executors, administrators, receivers, trustees in bankruptcy, or any public officer under judicial process;
5. sales in the course of proceedings for the dissolution or reorganization of a corporation in a court proceeding where notice is given to creditors;
6. transfers to a person who maintains a known place of business in the State who agrees to become bound to pay in full the debts of the transferor in bulk, gives public notice of that fact, and who is solvent after becoming so bound;

7. transfers to a new business enterprise organized to take over and continue the business of the transferor in bulk if public notice is given and the new enterprise assumes the debts of the transferor in bulk who receives nothing from the transaction except an interest in the new enterprise which is junior to the claims of creditors; and
8. transfers of property which is exempt from execution under exemption statutes.

EFFECT OF FAILURE
TO COMPLY WITH ARTICLE 6

The effect of a failure to comply with the requirements of Article 6 of the Code is that the goods in the possession of the transferee continue to be subject to the claims of unpaid creditors of the transferor. These creditors may proceed against the goods by levy or attachment and by sheriff's sale, or by causing the involuntary bankruptcy of the transferor and the appointment of a trustee in bankruptcy to take over the goods from the transferee.

Where the title of the transferee is subject to the defect of non-compliance with the Code, a *bona fide* purchaser of the goods from the transferee who pays value in good faith and takes the property without notice of such defect acquires the goods free of any claim of creditors of the transferor. A purchaser of the property from the transferee who pays no value or who takes with notice of non-compliance acquires the goods subject to the claims of creditors of the transferor.

APPLICATION
OF THE PROCEEDS

In the case of bulk transfers for which new consideration is payable, except those made at auction sales, the Code imposes in an optional section a personal duty upon the transferee to apply the new consideration to the payment of the debts of the transferor and, if it is insufficient to pay them in full, to make distribution to creditors *pro rata*. Section 6-106.

In Code States which do not adopt the optional section, there is no duty on the transferee owing to the creditors of the transferor. In the event of non-compliance with Code, except for sales at auction, the creditors merely proceed to enforce their claims against the property transferred as though it belonged to the transferor. This is what is meant by the language of the Code that the bulk transfer "is ineffective against any creditor of the transferor." The transferee loses the property but does not assume any obligation to pay the debts of the transferor.

Optional subsection (4) of Section 6-106 provides that the transferee may discharge her duty to pay the creditors of the transferor out of the proceeds by payment of the consideration into court within ten days after taking possession of the goods, and by giving notice to all of the creditors that such payment has been made and that they should file their claims with the court.

AUCTION SALES

The Code has special provisions with respect to auction sales of goods which represent a transfer in bulk not in the ordinary course of the transferor's business where the goods offered for sale are a major part of the materials, supplies, merchandise, or inventory used in the business. In such an auction sale Section 6-108 requires that:

1. The transferor furnish the auctioneer a sworn list of his creditors and assist in the preparation of a schedule of the property to be sold.
2. The auctioneer receive and retain the list of creditors and schedule of property for six months and permit inspection thereof by any creditor.
3. The auctioneer give notice by registered or certified mail at least 10 days before the auction to all creditors named in the list as well as all other persons known to him to have any claims against the transferor.
4. The auctioneer apply the net proceeds of the auction sale to payment of all debts of the transferor as provided in Section 6-106.

A failure of the auctioneer to perform his duties does not affect the validity of the sale or the title of the purchasers of the goods at the auction sale. The auctioneer is personally liable to creditors of the transferor as a class to the extent of the net proceeds of the auction.

CASES

Passage of Title

MEINHARD-COMMERCIAL CORP. v. HARGO WOOLEN MILLS

Supreme Court of New Hampshire, 1972.
112 N.H. 500, 300 A.2d 321.

GRIMES, J.

[Shabry Trading Company shipped twenty-four bales of card waste to Hargo, a manufacturer of woolen cloth. Although Shabry had supplied card waste to Hargo for many years, Hargo had not ordered the present shipment, nor did it wish to purchase it. Hargo intended to return the card waste, but Shabry, in order to avoid the cost of warehouse storage, offered to let Hargo retain possession of the bales with the option to buy as much as Hargo would give notice that it intended to use. Hargo agreed and accordingly marked and stored Shabry's card waste separately from its other goods. On one occasion Hargo notified Shabry that it would use eight bales of waste, and Shabry invoiced the goods to Hargo accordingly. The sixteen remaining bales were kept separately stored until a receiver appointed for Hargo took possession of them. Shabry claimed that it was the owner of the bales and requested their return.]

* * *

The utilization of the concept of title in sales transactions is not novel, nor is the misconception and the misuse of it. Learned Hand has said: " '[T]itle' is a formal word for a purely conceptual notion; I do not know what it means and I question whether anybody does, except perhaps legal historians." [Citation.] Prior to the Uniform Commercial Code, the Uniform Sales Act accepted the common-law notion that title determination was the main solvent of sales problems. The U.C.C. deliberately deemphasizes this view. 2–101, Uniform Law Comments. The code supplants many title-determined issues with specific code provisions to determine the rights and duties of the buyer and seller, such as risk of loss (2–509, 2–510), insurable interest (2–501), suit of third parties (2–722), buyer's rights on seller's insolvency (2–709), and buyer's right to replevy identified goods (2–716). Despite its minimization of the title concept, the code does recognize situations where the lack of any other legal tool requires the courts to fall back on the eternal title question of mine or thine. The code therefore provides a catch-basin rule (2–401) that applies only when the more specific code provisions fail to deal with the issue. The case before us was decided below with resort to this catch-basin rule, the pertinent portion of which reads as follows: "Any retention or reservation by the seller of the title (property) in goods shipped or delivered to the buyer is limited in effect to a reservation of a security interest. *Subject to these provisions * * *,* title to goods passes from the seller to the buyer in any manner and on any conditions explicitly agreed on by the parties." 2–401(1) (emphasis added).

* * *

However, since 2–401 speaks only in terms of buyers and sellers, we believe it does not apply to the transaction between these parties. 2–103(1)(d) defines seller as "unless the context otherwise requires * * * (1)(d) 'Seller' means a person who sells or contracts to sell goods." A buyer is defined in 2–103(1)(a) as "unless the context otherwise requires * * *, (a) 'Buyer' means a person who buys or contracts to buy goods." To determine the meaning of these sections, we refer to the definition of sale and contract for sale in 2–106(1). " 'Contract for sale' includes both a present sale of goods and a contract to sell goods at a future time. A 'sale' consists in the passing of title from the seller to the buyer for a price. (See 2–401)." For 2–401(1) to apply, we must therefore first find that the transaction between the supplier, Shabry, and the manufacturer, Hargo, was a sale. [Citation.]

Whether this transaction was a sale or some other type of transaction is a question of the intent of the parties, which is a question for the trier of fact to determine. [Citation.] Under the code, there must still be a meeting of minds between the parties before there is a contract. [Citation.] The master found in the parties' requests for findings and rulings that the factual understanding between Hargo and Shabry contemplated no passage of title until Shabry was notified of Hargo's intention to use the goods and Shabry thereafter invoiced the goods to Hargo. The master also found that Hargo was never obligated to purchase and Shabry could have sold the goods to other buyers.

Given these findings, it is clear that the parties' agreement concerning the delivered card waste created no contract for sale by the passage of title for a price. The parties showed no intent to pass title. No title may pass for a price without commitment of the buyer to pay the price. [Citations.] The mere fact that goods are delivered to the premises of a prospective buyer does not in and of itself create a sale, where neither party considered it a sale. [Citation.]

* * *

We find from the master's finding of the express terms of the parties' agreement, from the parties' course of dealing, and from the parties' course of performance, that the parties agreed only as to storage of the goods with Hargo for their mutual benefit. No sale was made until Shabry's offer was accepted by Hargo through notification of intent to use. No such acceptance occurred with respect to the sixteen bales at issue here.

* * *

We therefore hold that, since there was no sale, title to these goods cannot be determined by 2–401 and, since no other provisions of the code apply, the rights of the parties are determined by the law of contracts. *See* 2–102, 1–103.

The master found the parties' stated intentions to be that title to these sixteen bales never passed to Hargo. We therefore hold that title remained in Shabry and that the receiver wrongfully withheld return of the sixteen bales to Shabry.

[Judgment for Shabry.]

Voidable Title to Goods

UNITED ROAD MACHINERY CO. v. JASPER

Court of Appeals of Kentucky, 1978.
568 S.W.2d 242.

WHITE, J.

Appellant seeks reversal of a Laurel Circuit Court order dismissing the complaint against appellees Ethard Jasper individually and d/b/a Jasper Wrecking or Junk Yard, Jasper & Jasper Coal Co., Inc. and Clyde Jasper. * * *

Appellant United Road Machinery Co. is a dealer in heavy road equipment, including truck scales, with its principal place of business in Memphis, Tennessee. Its supplier for such truck scales is Thurman Scale Company in Columbus, Ohio. Appellant received a phone call on July 21, 1975, from James R. Durham, an officer of Consolidated Coal Co., seeking acquisition of truck scales for his coal-mining operation. A lease-purchase agreement was entered into by the parties at this time providing for monthly payments of $608 over a 24-month period with an option to purchase for one dollar consideration, exercisable at the termination of the lease. * * *

Appellant subsequently notified its supplier, Thurman Scale Company, that Consolidated Coal would take possession of the scales from the supplier. Appellant paid for the machinery at that time. On July 28, 1975, Consolidated Coal obtained the scales without signing a contract with appellant at that time; rather, the contract papers were forwarded to Consolidated by appellant but never returned. The scales were taken to Consolidated's place of business in Laurel County where decking was added, increasing the value of the scales to approximately $16,000. Appellant has never received any consideration, either in rental payments or purchase price, on this equipment.

On September 20, 1975, Consolidated Coal, through its agent and officer J. R. Durham, sold the truck scales to Kentucky Mobile Homes, whose president is Ethard Jasper, for a purchase price of $8,500. Before purchase, Ethard Jasper checked Laurel and Pulaski County records for any possible lien, mortgage, or other encumbrance on the property. Such search revealed no encumbrance of any kind. Ethard Jasper contends that Consolidated Coal appeared to have good title to the scales and he further denies any knowledge of the dispute between appellant and Consolidated Coal.

On September 22, 1975, Kentucky Mobile Homes sold the truck scales to Clyde Jasper, individually, for $8,500 in cash. Before purchasing the equipment, Clyde Jasper also conducted a search of Laurel and Pulaski County records, which revealed no evidence of any lien, mortgage, or encumbrance on said machinery. Clyde Jasper also denies any knowledge of the dispute between appellant and Consolidated Coal Company or appellant and Kentucky Mobile Homes. The scales are presently in the possession of Clyde Jasper. * * *

[Several] possible situations exist under which appellees [Jasper] received possession of the scales, any one and/or all * * * of the possibilities conferring good title in appellees.

The first possibility is that Consolidated Coal Company had good title to the truck scales. Under both Common Law and the Uniform Commercial Code, a purchaser acquires all title the seller had or, if a limited interest is transferred, all title to the extent of that interest. [U.C.C. 2–403(1)]. Thus if Consolidated Coal possessed good title to the truck scales, appellees in turn gained good title upon transfer.

The second possibility occurs if Consolidated Coal had voidable title. [U.C.C.] 2–403(1) provides: "A person with voidable title has power to transfer a good title to a good faith purchaser for value." Assuming that Consolidated Coal had voidable title, appellees, to obtain good title, must be found to be good faith purchasers for value. [U.C.C.] 1–201(19) defines "good faith" as ".   .   . honesty in fact in the conduct or transaction concerned." "Purchaser" is defined as ".   .   . a person who takes by purchase." [U.C.C.] 1–201(33). "Purchase" in turn ".   .   . includes taking by sale, discount, negotiation, mortgage, pledge, lien, issue or reissue, gift or any other voluntary transaction creating an interest in property." [U.C.C.] 1–201(32). Lastly, ".   .   . a person gives 'value' for rights if he acquires them (d) generally, in return for any consideration sufficient to support a simple contract." [U.C.C.] 1–201(44)(d). As the circuit court aptly put it: "A 'good faith purchaser for value' can be defined as one who takes by purchase getting sufficient consideration to support a simple contract, and who is honest in the transaction of the purchase." It is the opinion of this court that appellees meet this criteria.

Concerning voidable title, [U.C.C.] 2–403(1) goes on to state that good title may be transferred under certain circumstances:

When goods have been delivered under a transaction of purchase the purchaser has such power even though (a) the transferor was deceived as to the identity of the purchaser, or (b) the delivery was in exchange for a check which is later dishonored, or (c) it was agreed that the transaction was to be a "cash sale," or (d) the delivery was procured through fraud punishable as larcenous under the criminal law.

Assuming that Consolidated Coal's actions toward appellant [United] fall within one of the four enumerated circumstances, a "transaction of purchase" is still requisite before the statute becomes operative allowing transfer of good title. Appellant argues that no transaction of purchase occurred, that the agreement between appellant and Consolidated Coal was not a purchase transaction but merely a lease, and that the law concerning landlord-tenant, and not the Uniform Commercial Code, governs. Therefore the concept of voidable title has no application in this case.

This court feels there was a "transaction of purchase" per the code definition (see above). "The purpose, rather than the name given a contract by the parties controls, and the court will give effect to the real and dominant intention of the parties when definitely ascertained." [Citation.]

*   *   *

For the foregoing reasons, the judgment is affirmed.

Entrusting of Goods to a Merchant

MATTEK v. MALOFSKY

Supreme Court of Wisconsin, 1969.
42 Wisc.2d 16, 165 N.W.2d 406.

HALLOWS, C. J.

[Mattek entrusted a car to Frakes, a used car dealer. Malofsky, another automobile dealer, subsequently purchased the car from Frakes without obtaining or inquiring about the certificate of title to the car. Although Frakes did not have to secure a certificate of title for cars held in stock or acquired for stock purposes, he did have a duty under State law to deliver the certificate on the subsequent sale to Malofsky. Mattek brought suit against Malofsky to recover the car.]

Two issues are presented on this appeal: (1) Whether the provisions of [U.C.C.] 2.403 are applicable to sales between merchants; and (2) whether an automobile dealer who buys a used car from another automobile dealer, who has lawful possession of the car, without obtaining or inquiring about the certificate of title to the used car is a "buyer in the ordinary course of business" within the meaning of [U.C.C.] 2.403.

We think the provisions of [U.C.C.] 2.403 are applicable to sales between merchants. We come to this conclusion because the purpose of [U.C.C.] 2.403(2) and (3) is to protect a person from a third-party interest in goods purchased from the general inventory of a merchant regardless of that merchant's actual authority to sell those goods. This section does not expressly or by implication restrict such protection of a sale by a merchant to a member of the consumer public. If the policy of negotiability of goods held in the inventory of a mechant is to be promoted, it would seem to apply between merchants where merchants buy from one another in the ordinary course of business. The protection is afforded to "a buyer in the ordinary course of business," and by other provisions of the Uniform Commercial Code the term "buyer" includes a merchant.

In [U.C.C.] 1.201(9) a buyer in the ordinary course of business is defined as "a person who in good faith and without knowledge that the sale to him is in violation of the ownership rights or security interest of a third party in the goods buys in ordinary course from a person in the business of selling goods of that kind but does not include a pawn broker." Good faith is defined in [U.C.C.] 1.201(19) to mean "honesty in fact in the conduct or transaction concerned." This definition applies to a member of the consumer public only, because in [U.C.C.] 2.103(1)(b) " 'good faith' in the case of a merchant" is defined to mean "honesty in fact and the observance of rea-

sonable commercial standards of fair dealing in the trade." In addition, [U.C.C.] 2.104(3), relating to the general standard applicable to transactions between merchants charges each merchant with the "knowledge or skill of merchants."

Consequently, a merchant may be a buyer in the ordinary course of business under [U.C.C.] 2.403 from another merchant if he meets four elements: (1) be honest in fact, (2) be without knowledge of any defects of title in the goods, (3) pay value, and (4) observe reasonable commercial standards. In the observance of reasonable commercial standards, however, a merchant is chargeable with the knowledge or skill of a merchant.

We think Malofsky was not the buyer in the ordinary course of business within the meaning of [U.C.C.] 2.403. Although the delivery of the automobile to Frakes, a used-car dealer, constituted an entrustment, Frakes could by subsequent sale pass title to a buyer in the ordinary course of business. However, Malofsky as a merchant was not a buyer in the ordinary course of business because he was chargeable with the knowledge that the registration law, [citation], which provides that while a dealer need not apply for a certificate of title for a vehicle in stock or acquired for stock purposes, he shall upon the transfer of such vehicle give the transferee evidence of title, and in the case of a vehicle which has a certificate of title, the certificate of title shall be reassigned and delivered to the transferee. Malofsky should have known the used automobile had a certificate of title outstanding and that Frakes was required to give him such certificate of title. Under the standards set forth in [U.C.C.] 2.104(3) applicable to transactions between merchants, Malofsky is chargeable with this knowledge and his failure to procure a certificate of title or some evidence of title was unreasonable as a matter of law. Evidence of custom or usage of automobile dealers contrary to the statute cannot be used to defeat the rights of a third party whatever the value of such evidence may be in adjusting disputes between dealers.

* * *

[Judgment for Mattek affirmed.]

Shipment Contracts

PESTANA v. KARINOL CORP.

District Court of Appeals of Florida, Third
District, 1979.
367 So.2d 1096.

Hubbart, J.

This is an action for damages based on a contract for the sale of goods. The defendant seller and others prevailed in this action after a non-jury trial in the Circuit Court for the Eleventh Judicial Circuit of Florida. The plaintiff buyer appeals.

The central issue presented for review is whether a contract for the sale of goods, which stipulates the place where the goods sold are to be sent by carrier but contains (a) no explicit provisions allocating the risk of loss while the goods are in the possession of the carrier and (b) no delivery terms such as F.O.B. place of destination, is a shipment contract or a destination contract under the Uniform Commercial Code. We hold that such a contract, without more, constitutes a shipment contract wherein the risk of loss passes to the buyer when the seller duly delivers the goods to the carrier under a reasonable contract of carriage for shipment to the buyer. Accordingly, we affirm.

The critical facts of this case are substantially undisputed. On March 4, 1975, Nahim Amar B. (the plaintiff Pedro P. Pestana's decedent herein) who was a resident of Mexico entered into a contract through his authorized representative with the Karinol Corporation (the defendant herein) which is an exporting company licensed to do business in Florida and operating out of Miami. The terms of this contract were embodied in a one-page invoice written in Spanish and prepared by the defendant Karinol. By the terms of this contract, the plaintiff's Amar agreed to pur-

chase 64 electronic watches from the defendant Karinol for $6,006. A notation was printed at the bottom of the contract which, translated into English, reads as follows: "Please send the merchandise in cardboard boxes duly strapped with metal bands via air parcel post to Chetumal. Documents to Banco de Commercio De Quintano Roo S.A." There were no provisions in the contract which specifically allocated the risk of loss on the goods sold while in the possession of the carrier; there were also no F.O.B., F.A.S., C.I.F. or C. & F. terms contained in the contract. See [U.C.C. §§ 2–319, 2–320]. A 25% downpayment on the purchase price of the goods sold was made prior to shipment.

On April 11, 1975, there is sufficient evidence, although disputed, that the defendant Karinol delivered the watches in two cartons to its agent American International Freight Forwarders, Inc. (the second defendant herein) for forwarding to the plaintiff's decedent Amar. The defendant American insured the two cartons with Fidelity & Casualty Company of New York (the third defendant herein) naming the defendant Karinol as the insured. The defendant American as freight forwarder strapped the cartons in question with metal bands and delivered them to TACA International Airlines consigned to one Bernard Smith, a representative of the plaintiff's decedent, in Belize City, Belize, Central America. The shipment was arranged by Karinol in this manner in accord with a prior understanding between the parties as there were no direct flights from Miami, Florida to Chetumal, Mexico. Mr. Smith was to take custody of the goods on behalf of the plaintiff's decedent in Belize and arrange for their transport by truck to the plaintiff's decedent Amar in Chetumal, Mexico.

On April 15, 1975, the cartons arrived by air in Belize City and were stored by the airline in the customs and air freight cargo room. Mr. Smith was duly notified and thereupon the plaintiff's decedent made payment on the balance due under the contract to the defendant Karinol. On May 2, 1975, Mr. Smith took custody of the cartons after a certain delay was experienced in transferring the cartons to a customs warehouse. Either on that day or shortly thereafter, the cartons were opened by Mr. Smith and customs officials as was required for clearance prior to the truck shipment to Chetumal, Mexico. There were no watches contained in the cartons. The defendant Karinol and its insurance carrier the defendant Fidelity were duly notified, but both eventually refused to make good on the loss.

* * *

There are two types of sales contracts under Florida's Uniform Commercial Code wherein a carrier is used to transport the goods sold: a shipment contract and a destination contract. A shipment contract is considered the normal contract in which the seller is required to send the subject goods by carrier to the buyer but is not required to guarantee delivery thereof at a particular destination. Under a shipment contract, the seller, unless otherwise agreed, must: (1) put the goods sold in the possession of a carrier and make a contract for their transportation as may be reasonable having regard for the nature of the goods and other attendant circumstances, (2) obtain and promptly deliver or tender in due form any document necessary to enable the buyer to obtain possession of the goods or otherwise required by the agreement or by usage of the trade, and (3) promptly notify the buyer of the shipment. On a shipment contract, the risk of loss passes to the buyer when the goods sold are duly delivered to the carrier for shipment to the buyer. [Citations.]

A destination contract, on the other hand, is considered the variant contract in which the seller specifically agrees to deliver the goods sold to the buyer at a particular destination and to bear the risk of loss of the goods until tender of delivery. This can be accomplished by express provision in the sales contract to that effect or by the use of delivery terms such as F.O.B. (place of destination). Under a destination contract, the seller is required to tender delivery of the goods

sold to the buyer at the place of destination. The risk of loss under such a contract passes to the buyer when the goods sold are duly tendered to the buyer at the place of destination while in the possession of the carrier so as to enable the buyer to take delivery. The parties must explicitly agree to a destination contract; otherwise the contract will be considered a shipment contract. [Citations.]

Where the risk of loss falls on the seller at the time the goods sold are lost or destroyed, the seller is liable in damages to the buyer for non-delivery unless the seller tenders a performance in replacement for the lost or destroyed goods. On the other hand, where the risk of loss falls on the buyer at the time the goods sold are lost or destroyed, the buyer is liable to the seller for the purchase price of the goods sold. [Citation.]

In the instant case, we deal with the normal shipment contract involving the sale of goods. The defendant Karinol pursuant to this contract agreed to send the goods sold, a shipment of watches, to the plaintiff's decedent in Chetumal, Mexico. There was no specific provision in the contract between the parties which allocated the risk of loss on the goods sold while in transit. In addition, there were no delivery terms such as F.O.B. Chetumal contained in the contract.

All agree that there is sufficient evidence that the defendant Karinol performed its obligations as a seller under the Uniform Commercial Code if this contract is considered a shipment contract. Karinol put the goods sold in the possession of a carrier and made a contract for the goods [sic] safe transportation to the plaintiff's decedent; Karinol also promptly notified the plaintiff's decedent of the shipment and tendered to said party the necessary documents to obtain possession of the goods sold.

The plaintiff Pestana contends, however, that the contract herein is a destination contract in which the risk of loss on the goods sold did not pass until delivery on such goods had been tendered to him at Chetumal, Mexico—an event which never occurred. He relies for this position on the notation at the bottom of the contract between the parties which provides that the goods were to be sent to Chetumal, Mexico. We cannot agree. A "send to" or "ship to" term is a part of every contract involving the sale of goods where carriage is contemplated and has no significance in determining whether the contract is a shipment or destination contract for risk of loss purposes. [Citations.] As such, the "send to" term contained in this contract cannot, without more, convert this into a destination contract.

It therefore follows that the risk of loss in this case shifted to the plaintiff's decedent as buyer when the defendant Karinol as seller duly delivered the goods to the defendant freight forwarder American under a reasonable contract of carriage for shipment to the plaintiff's decedent in Chetumal, Mexico. The defendant Karinol, its agent the defendant American, and its insurer the defendant Fidelity could not be held liable to the plaintiff in this action. The trial court properly entered judgment in favor of all the defendants herein.

Affirmed.

Risk of Loss: Seller Not a Merchant

MARTIN v. MELLAND'S INC.

Supreme Court of North Dakota, 1979.
283 N.W.2d 76.

ERICKSTAD, C. J.

The narrow issue on this appeal is who should bear the loss of a truck and an attached haystack mover that was destroyed by fire while in the possession of the plaintiff, Israel Martin (Martin), but after certificate of title had been delivered to the defendant, Melland's Inc. (Melland's). The destroyed haymoving unit was to be used as a trade-in for a new haymoving unit that Martin ultimately purchased from Melland's. Martin appeals from a district court judgment dated September 28, 1978, that dismissed his action on the mer-

its after it found that at the time of its destruction Martin was the owner of the unit pursuant to [Section 2–401 U.C.C.]. We hold that Section 2–401 is inapplicable to this case, but we affirm the district court judgment on the grounds that risk of loss had not passed to Melland's pursuant to [Section 2–509 U.C.C.].

On June 11, 1974, Martin entered into a written agreement with Melland's, a farm implement dealer, to purchase a truck and attached haystack mover for the total purchase price of $35,389. Martin was given a trade-in allowance of $17,389 on his old unit, leaving a balance owing of $18,000 plus sales tax of $720 or a total balance of $18,720. The agreement provided that Martin "mail or bring title" to the old unit to Melland's "this week." Martin mailed the certificate of title to Melland's pursuant to the agreement, but he was allowed to retain the use and possession of the old unit "until they had the new one ready." The new unit was not expected to be ready for two to three months because it required certain modifications. During this interim period, Melland's performed minor repairs to the trade-in unit on two occasions without charging Martin for the repairs.

Fire destroyed the truck and the haymoving unit in early August, 1974, while Martin was moving hay. The parties did not have any agreement regarding insurance or risk of loss on the unit and Martin's insurance on the trade-in unit had lapsed. Melland's refused Martin's demand for his new unit and Martin brought this suit. The parties subsequently entered into an agreement by which Martin purchased the new unit, but they reserved their rights in any lawsuit arising out of the prior incident.

The district court found "that although the Plaintiff [Martin] executed the title to the . . . [haymoving unit], he did not relinquish possession of the same and therefore the Plaintiff was the owner of said truck at the time the fire occurred pursuant to Section 2–401."

Martin argues that the district court erroneously applied Section 2–401 regarding passage of title, to this case and that Section 2–509, which deals with risk of loss in the absence of breach, should have been applied instead. Martin argues further that title (apparently pursuant to Section 2–401) and risk of loss passed to Melland's and the property was then merely bailed back to Martin who held it as a bailee. Martin submits that this is supported by the fact that Melland's performed minor repairs on the old unit following the passage of title without charging Martin for the repairs. Melland's responds that Section 2–401(2), governs this case and that the district court's determination of the issue should be affirmed.

One of the hallmarks of the pre-Code law of sales was its emphasis on the concept of title. The location of title was used to determine, among other things, risk of loss, insurable interest, place and time for measuring damages, and the applicable law in an interstate transaction. This single title or "lump" title concept proved unsatisfactory because of the different policy considerations involved in each of the situations that title was made to govern. Furthermore, the concept of single title did not reflect modern commercial practices, *i.e.* although the single title concept worked well for "cash-on-the-barrelhead sales," the introduction of deferred payments, security agreements, financing from third parties, or delivery by carrier required a fluid concept of title with bits and pieces held by all parties to the transaction.

Thus the concept of title under the U.C.C. is of decreased importance. The official comment to Section 2–101 U.C.C. provides in part:

The arrangement of the present Article is in terms of contract for sale and the various steps of its performance. The legal consequences are stated as following directly from the contract and action taken under it without resorting to the idea of when property or title passed or was to pass as being the determining factor. The purpose is to avoid making practical issues between practical

men turn upon the location of an intangible something, the passing of which no man can prove by evidence and to substitute for such abstractions proof of words and actions of a tangible character.

[§ 2–401 U.C.C.], which the district court applied in this case, provides in relevant part:

Each provision of this chapter with regard to the rights, obligations and remedies of the seller, the buyer, purchasers or other third parties applies irrespective of title to the goods except where the provision refers to such title. Insofar as situations are not covered by the other provisions of this chapter and matters concerning title become material the following rules apply . . .

[§ 2–509 U.C.C.], is an "other provision of this chapter" and is applicable to this case without regard to the location of title. Comment one to Section 2–509 U.C.C. provides that "the underlying theory of these sections on risk of loss is the adoption of the contractual approach rather than an arbitrary shifting of the risk with the 'property' in the goods."

The position that the Code has taken, divorcing the question of risk of loss from a determination of title, is summed up by Professor Nordstrom in his hornbook on sales:

No longer is the question of title of any importance in determining whether a buyer or seller bears the risk of loss. It is true that the person with title will also (and incidentally) often bear the risk that the goods may be destroyed or lost; but the seller may have title and the buyer the risk, or the seller may have the risk and the buyer the title. In short, title is not a relevant consideration in deciding whether the risk has shifted to the buyer. R. Nordstrom, Handbook of the Law of Sales, 393 (1970).

* * *

Thus, the question in this case is not answered by a determination of the location of title, but by the risk of loss provisions in [§ 2–509 U.C.C.]. Before addressing the risk of loss question in conjunction with [§ 2–509 U.C.C.], it is necessary to determine the posture of the parties with regard to the trade-in unit, *i.e.* who is the buyer and the seller and how are the responsibilities allocated. It is clear that a barter or trade-in is considered a sale and is therefore subject to the Uniform Commercial Code. [Citations.] It is also clear that the party who owns the trade-in is considered the seller. [§ 2–304 U.C.C.], provides that the "price can be made payable in money or otherwise. If it is payable in whole or in part in goods each party is a seller of the goods which he is to transfer." [Citations.]

Martin argues that he had already sold the trade-in unit to Melland's and, although he retained possession, he did so in the capacity of a bailee (apparently pursuant to [§ 2–509(2) U.C.C.]). White and Summers in their hornbook on the Uniform Commercial Code argue that the seller who retains possession should not be considered bailee within Section 2–509.

* * *

The courts that have addressed this issue have agreed with White and Summers. [Citations.]

It is undisputed that the contract did not require or authorize shipment by carrier pursuant to Section [2–509(1)] therefore, the residue section, subsection 3, is applicable:

In any case not within subsection 1 or 2, the risk of loss passes to the buyer on his receipt of the goods if the seller is a merchant; otherwise the risk passes to the buyer on tender of delivery.

Martin admits that he is not a merchant; therefore, it is necessary to determine if Martin tendered delivery of the trade-in unit to Melland's. Tender is defined in [§ 2–503 U.C.C.], as follows:

Manner of seller's tender of delivery.—1. Tender of delivery requires that the seller put and hold conforming goods at the buyer's disposition and give the buyer any notification reasonably necessary to enable him to take delivery. The manner, time and place for tender are determined by the agreement and this chapter, and in particular

a. tender must be at a reasonable hour, and if it is of goods they must be kept available for the period reasonably necessary to enable the buyer to take possession; but

b. unless otherwise agreed the buyer must furnish facilities reasonably suited to the receipt of the goods.

It is clear that the trade-in unit was not tendered to Melland's in this case. The parties agreed that Martin would keep the old unit "until they had the new one ready."

* * *

We hold that Martin did not tender delivery of the trade-in truck and haystack mover to Melland's pursuant to [§ 2–509 U.C.C.]; consequently, Martin must bear the loss.

We affirm the district court judgment.

PROBLEMS

1. Stein, a mechanic, and Beal, a life insurance agent, entered into a written contract for the sale of Stein's tractor to Beal for $2,800 cash. It was agreed that Stein would tune the motor on the tractor. Stein fulfilled this obligation and on the night of July 1 telephoned Beal that the tractor was ready to be picked up upon making payment. Beal responded, "I'll be there in the morning with the money." On the next morning, however, Beal was approached by an insurance prospect and decided to get the tractor at a later date. On the night of July 2, the tractor was destroyed by fire of unknown origin. Neither Stein nor Beal had any fire insurance. Who must bear the loss?

2. Regan received a letter from Chase, the material portion of which stated: "Chase hereby places an order with you for fifty cases of Red Top Tomatoes, ship them C.O.D." Promptly upon receipt of the letter Regan shipped the tomatoes to Chase. While en route, the railroad car carrying the tomatoes was wrecked. Upon Chase's refusal to pay for the tomatoes, Regan commenced an action to recover the purchase price. Chase defended on the

ground that as the shipment was C.O.D., neither title to the tomatoes nor risk of loss passed until their delivery to Chase. Decision?

3. On May 10, the A Company, acting through one Brown, entered into a contract with C for the installation of a milking machine at C's farm. Following the enumeration of the articles to be furnished, together with the price of each article, the written contract provided: "This outfit is subject to thirty-days free trial and is to be installed about June 1." Within thirty days after installation the entire outfit, excepting the double utility unit, was destroyed by fire through no fault of C. The A Company sued C to recover the value of the articles destroyed. Decision?

4. A, located in Knoxville, contracted to buy sixty cases of X Brand canned corn from B in Toledo at a contract price of $600. Pursuant to the contract, B selected and set aside sixty cases of X Brand canned corn and tagged them "For A." The contract required B to ship the corn to A via T Railroad, F.O.B. Toledo. Before B delivered the corn to the railroad the sixty cases were stolen from B's warehouse.

(a) Who is liable for the loss of the sixty cases of corn, A or B?

(b) Suppose B had delivered the corn to the railroad in Toledo. After the corn had been loaded on a freight car, but before the train left the yard, the car was broken open and its contents, including the corn, stolen. As between A and B, who is liable for the loss?

(c) Would your answer in question (b) be the same if this was an F.O.B. Knoxville contract, all other facts remaining the same?

5. A owned a quantity of corn which was contained in a corn crib located on A's farm. On March 12, A wrote a letter to B stating that he would sell to B all of the corn in this crib, which he estimated at between 900 and 1,000 bushels, for $3.60 per bushel. B received this letter on March 13 and immediately wrote and mailed on the same day a letter to A stating that he would buy the corn. The corn crib and its contents were accidentally destroyed by fire which broke out about 3 o'clock a.m. on March 14.

What are the rights of the parties?

What difference, if any, in result if A were a merchant?

6. A, a New York dealer, purchased twenty-five barrels of specially graded and packed apples from a producer at Hood River, Oregon. These apples he afterwards resold to B under a contract which specified an agreed price on delivery at B's place of business in New York. The apples were shipped to A from Oregon but, through no fault of either A or B, were totally destroyed before reaching New York. Is there any liability resting upon A?

7. Smith was approached by a man who introduced himself as Brown of Brown and Co. Brown was not known to Smith, but Smith asked Dun & Bradstreet for a credit report and obtained a very favorable report on Brown. He thereupon sold Brown some expensive gems and billed Brown & Co. "Brown" turned out to be a clever jewel thief, who later sold the gems to Brown & Co. for valuable consideration. Brown & Co. was unaware of "Brown's" transaction with Smith. Smith sued Brown & Co. for the return of the gems or the price as billed to Brown & Co. Decision?

8. Z, the owner of a new Cadillac automobile, agreed to loan the car to Y for the month of February while she (Z) went to Florida for a winter vacation. It was understood that Y, who was a small town Cadillac dealer, would merely place Z's car in his showroom for exhibition and sales promotion purposes. While Z was away, Y sold the car to B. Upon Z's return from Florida, she sued to recover the car from B. Decision?

9. A offered to sell his used automobile to B for $2,600 cash. B agreed to buy the car, gave A a check for $2,600, and drove away in the car. The next day B sold the car for $3,000 to C, a *bona fide* purchaser. The $2,600 check was returned to A by the bank in which he had deposited it for the reason that were insufficient funds in B's account. A brings an action against C to recover the automobile. What judgment?

10. B told S he wished to buy S's automobile. He drove the car for about ten minutes, returned to S, stated he wanted to take the automobile to show it to his wife, and then left with the automobile and never returned. B sold the automobile in another State to T and gave him a bill of sale. S sued T to recover the automobile. Decision?

Chapter 21

PRODUCTS LIABILITY: WARRANTIES AND STRICT LIABILITY IN TORT

THIS chapter considers the liability of manufacturers and sellers of goods to buyers, users, consumers, and bystanders for damages caused by defective products. The rapid and expanding development of case law has established products liability as a separate and distinct field of law, combining and enforcing rules and principles of contracts, sales, negligence, torts, and statutory law.

An impetus to the expansion of such liability has been the modern practice whereby the retailer serves principally as a conduit of prepackaged goods in sealed containers which are widely advertised by the manufacturer or distributor. This has hastened the extension of product liability coverage to include manufacturers and other parties within the chain of distribution. The extension of products liability to manufacturers, however, has not appreciably lessened the exposure of a seller to liability to his immediate purchaser. Rather, it has broadened and extended the base of liability by the development and application of new principles of law.

Currently, the liability of manufacturers and sellers of goods for a defective product, or its failure to perform adequately, may be based upon one or more of the following: (1) negligence, (2) misrepresentation, (3) violation of statutory duty, (4) warranty, and (5) strict liability in tort. The first three of these causes of actions have been covered in Chapters 6 and 9. This chapter will explore the last two.

WARRANTIES

The concept of warranty as an obligation of the seller to the buyer with respect to the title, quality, quantity, condition, or performability of goods sold or to be sold is an ancient one. Historically, the remedy of the buyer for breach of warranty was an action in tort for deceit. However, today the liability of a seller for breach of warranty is universally recognized as contractual and has been codified by the Uniform Commerical Code.

The liability of a seller for the quality of goods he sells has long presented numerous legal problems. The traditional concept of *caveat emptor*—let the buyer beware—was premised upon the principle that the buyer and seller were each attempting to obtain the best bargain possible. Since each wielded relatively equal bargaining power, the law did not interfere. Today, however, this is not the case; the consumer generally possesses far less bargaining power. Consequently, the law of sales has abandoned the doctrine of *caveat emptor* and employs warranties to protect the buyer.

A warranty creates a duty on the part of the seller that the goods he sells will conform to certain qualities, characteristics, or conditions. A warranty may arise out of any affirmation of fact or promise to the buyer (an express warranty) or the circumstances under which the sale is made (an implied warranty). If the seller breaches his warranty, the buyer may recover a judgment against the seller for damages. In addition, by timely notice, the buyer may reject or revoke acceptance of the goods.

A seller is not required to warrant the goods, and in general she may, by appropriate words, disclaim, exclude, negate, or modify a particular warranty or even all warranties. Moreover, she may carefully refrain from making an express warranty. With respect to implied warranties, she must act affirmatively and in the manner prescribed by the Code in order to effectively disclaim liability.

This section will examine the various types of warranties as well as the obstacles to a cause of action for breach of warranty.

TYPES OF WARRANTIES

Express Warranties

Under Section 2-313 of the Code, express warranties of the seller are that: (1) The goods shall conform to any affirmation of fact or promise made by the seller to the buyer which relates to the goods and becomes part of the basis of the bargain. (2) The goods shall conform to any description of them which is made part of the basis of the bargain. (3) The whole of the goods shall conform to any sample or model of the goods which is made part of the basis of the bargain.

An express warranty is an explicit undertaking by the seller with respect to the quality, description, condition, or performability of the goods. The undertaking may consist of **affirmations** or **statements of fact** or **promises.** For example, a statement made by the seller of an automobile that it would get 42 miles to the gallon of gasoline is an express warranty. The Code does not require that the affirmations by the seller be relied upon by the buyer but only that they constitute a part of the *basis of the bargain.* If it is basic to the bargain, reliance by the buyer is implicit.

In order to create an express warranty it is not necessary that the seller have a specific intention to make a warranty or use formal words such as "warrant" or "guarantee." Moreover, it is not necessary that a seller have knowledge of the falsity of a statement made by her in order to be liable for breach of express warranty; the seller may be acting in good faith. To be liable for fraud, on the other hand, a person must make a misrepresentation of fact with knowledge of its falsity.

Affirmations of fact by the seller with respect to the goods are frequently a part of the **description** of the goods. If so the seller expressly warrants that the goods shall conform to the description. The use of a **sample** or model is a means of describing the goods, and the seller expressly warrants that the entire lot of goods sold shall conform to the sample or model.

Statements or promises made by the seller to the buyer prior to the sale may be express warranties, as they may form a part of the basis of the bargain just as much as statements made at the time of the sale. Therefore, statements in advertisements, catalogs, and the like may constitute an express warranty. Under the Code, statements or promises made by the seller subsequent to the contract of sale may become express warranties even though no new consideration is given. Section 2-209(1) provides that "An Agreement modifying a contract within this Article needs no consideration to be binding." Thus, a statement or promise or assurance with respect to the goods made by the seller to the buyer at the time of delivery may be a binding modification of the prior contract of sale and held to be an express warranty as basic to the bargain.

The Code further provides that a mere affirmation of the value of the goods or a statement purporting merely to be the seller's *opinion* or commendation of the goods does *not* create a warranty. Section 2-313(2). Such statements are not factual and do not deceive the ordinary buyer. They are accepted merely as opinions or as puffing statements. If the seller genuinely believes the goods to be more valuable than the price at which she is willing to sell them, she probably would not sell. However, a statement of *value* may be an express warranty where the seller states the price at which the goods were purchased from a former owner, or where she gives market figures relating to sales of similar goods. These are affirmations of facts. They are statements of events and not mere opinions, and the seller is liable for breach of warranty if they are untrue.

While ordinarily a statement of opinion by the seller is not a warranty, if the seller is an *expert* and gives her opinion as such, she may be liable for breach of warranty. Thus, if an art expert states that a certain painting is a genuine Rembrandt, and this becomes part of the basis of the bargain, then the expert warrants the accuracy of her professional opinion. A seller may also be liable if she misrepresents her opinion. A seller may say, "This car is in excellent mechanical condition," or she may say, "In my opinion, this car is in excellent mechanical condition." In the first instance she has made an express warranty of the mechanical soundness of the car. In the second, she has made no warranty as to the mechanical soundness of the car but has warranted that she believes the car to be mechanically sound. Thus, if she knew that the car was mechanically unsound at the time of stating her opinion, she has misrepresented her opinion as a factual matter. This is not only fraud, but also a breach of warranty.

Warranty of Title

Under the early English common law, there was no implied warranty of title by the seller. The principle applied was that of *caveat emptor*. A seller was held liable for fraud where he knew that he did not have title and concealed this fact from the buyer, but otherwise he assumed no risk as to title unless he made an express warranty. The law subsequently developed to the point where a seller impliedly warranted title.

Under the Code the seller implicitly warrants that (1) the title conveyed is good and its transfer rightful, and (2) the goods are not encumbered by any security interest or other lien of which the buyer had no knowledge at the time of contracting. Section 2-312.

For example, S acquires goods from A in a transaction that is void and then sells the goods to B. A brings an action against B and recovers the goods. S has breached the warranty of title due to the fact that S did not have good title to the goods and his transfer of the goods to B was not rightful. Accordingly, S is liable to B for damages.

The Code, however, does not label the warranty of title as an implied warranty, despite the fact that it arises out of the sale and not from any particular words or conduct. This is done in order to make the Code's general disclaimer provision for implied warranties inapplicable and instead have the warranty of title subject to its own disclaimer provision. Nevertheless, a seller of goods does impliedly warrant title to those goods.

A seller who is a merchant makes an additional warranty in sales of goods of the kind in which he regularly deals that such goods shall be delivered free of the rightful claim of any third person by way of infringement of any existing patent. Section 2-312(3).

Implied Warranties

An implied warranty, unlike an express warranty, is not a specific affirmation or promise by the seller; it is not found in the language of the sales contract. An implied warranty is, instead, brought into existence by operation of law. An implied warranty arises out of the circumstances under which the parties enter into their contract and depends upon such factors as the type of contract or sale entered into, whether the seller is a merchant, the conduct of the parties, and the applicability of other Federal or State statutes. Implied warranties have been developed by the law, not as something to which the parties have agreed, but as a departure from the early rule of *caveat emptor.* In its early formative period of development the law of sales was influenced more by the pressures and demands of sellers as a class rather than by those of buyers as a class. However, the law has developed a greater solicitude for buyers and has imposed implied warranties upon the seller unless expressly disclaimed.

Merchantability At early common law a seller was not held to any implied warranty as to the quality of the goods. However, under the Code a **merchant seller** impliedly warrants the merchantability of goods that are of the kind in which she deals. The implied warranty of merchantability is an obligation of the merchant seller that the goods are reasonably fit for the **ordinary** purposes for which they are manufactured and sold, and also that they are of fair, average quality. Under Section 2-314 of the Code, the minimum requirements of merchantability are that the goods must:

1. pass without objection in the trade under the contract description;
2. in the case of fungible goods, be of fair, average quality within the description;
3. be fit for the ordinary purposes for which the goods are used;
4. run, within variations permitted by the agreement, of even kind, quality, and quantity within each unit and among all units involved;
5. be adequately contained, packaged, and labeled as the agreement may require; and
6. conform to the promises or affirmations of fact made on the container or label, if any.

The Code in Section 2-314(3) expressly provides that implied warranties may arise from course of dealing or usage of trade. Thus, where the seller of a new automobile failed to lubricate it before delivery to the buyer, and the evidence established that it was the regular custom and usage of new car dealers to do so, the seller was held liable to the buyer for the resulting damages to the automobile in an action for breach of implied warranty. *See Sheeskin v. Giant Food, Inc.*

The official Comments to the Code further provide that a contract for the sale of secondhand goods "involves only such obligation as is appropriate to such goods for that is their description." It has been held that "such obligation" includes an implied warranty of merchantability. In defining this warranty the price, age, and condition of the goods are factors that are considered. For example, the defendant purchased in June, 1970, a used 1965 model automobile from plaintiff retail dealer. The day after the purchase, the transmission fell out of the car while being driven by defendant on an expressway. A week after repairs were made, the brakes went out completely on another expressway. The court held that any car without adequate transmission and proper brakes is not fit for the ordinary purpose of driving, that the implied warranty of merchantability was therefore breached, and that defendant had justifiably revoked his acceptance of the car. *Overland Bond & Investment Corp. v. Howard*, 9 Ill.App.3d 348, 292 N.E.2d 168 (1972).

Fitness for Particular Purpose **Any** seller, whether or not he is a merchant, impliedly warrants that the goods sold are reasonably fit for the **particular** purpose of the buyer for which the goods are required, if at the time of sale the seller has reason to know such particular purpose and that the buyer is relying upon the seller's skill and judgment to select suitable goods. Section 2-315 provides:

Where the seller at the time of contracting has reason to know any particular purpose for which the goods are required and that the buyer is relying on the seller's skill or judgment to select or furnish suitable goods, there is unless excluded or modified under the next section an implied warranty that the goods shall be fit for such purpose.

As contrasted with the implied warranty of merchantability, the implied warranty of fitness for a particular purpose pertains to a specific purpose, rather than the ordinary purpose, of the goods. A particular purpose may be a specific use or relate to a special situation in which the buyer intends to use the goods. Thus, if the seller has reason to know that the buyer is purchasing a pair of shoes for mountain climbing and that the buyer is relying upon the seller's judgment to furnish suitable shoes for this purpose, a sale of shoes suitable only for ordinary walking purposes would be a breach of this implied warranty.

The buyer need not specifically inform the seller of her particular purpose. It is sufficient if the seller has reason to know. However, the buyer must rely upon the seller's skill or judgment to select or furnish suitable goods in order that this implied warranty exist.

The Code provides that the serving for value of food or drink to be consumed on the premises or elsewhere is a sale. Section 2-314(1). Where injuries have been caused by a nonedible substance in food, however, an implied warranty may not exist if the substance is natural to the food. A minority of jurisdictions distinguish between natural objects in food, such as fish bones in fish, and objects which are foreign, as a pebble, piece of wire, or glass. For example, a person injured by a fish bone becoming lodged in her throat while eating fish chowder served in a restaurant was denied recovery on the ground that fish bones are a proper ingredient of fish chowder and therefore are to be reasonably expected. *Webster v. Blue Ship Tea Room, Inc.*, 347 Mass. 421, 198 N.E.2d 309 (1964). Nonetheless, under this test, damages are recoverable for a broken tooth and lacerated gums caused by a piece of metal in a serving of maple walnut ice cream.

The modern and majority test is not the natural relation of the injurious substance to the food, but the reasonable expectation of the consumer upon eating it. A substance natural to a product in one stage of preparation does not necessarily imply that the consumer will reasonably anticipate or expect it to be in the final product served. In one case the plaintiff, upon being served a martini cocktail, removed the olive, observed that it had a hole in the end, and bit down upon it thereby breaking a tooth upon the olive pit. The court held it was a question of fact for the jury to determine whether he had acted reasonably in expecting that the olive contained no pit. If this was a reasonable expectation, he was entitled to recover damages. *Hochberg v. O'Donnell's Restaurant, Inc.*, 272 A.2d 846 (D.C.App. 1971).

OBSTACLES TO WARRANTY ACTIONS

Disclaimer or Modification of Warranties

Section 2-316(4) provides that remedies and recovery of damages for breach of warranty may be contractually limited. Nonetheless the Code calls for a reasonable construction of words or conduct tending to negate or limit warranties, Section 2-316(1), and makes clear that the seller should not rely upon a time-honored formula of words and expect to obtain a disclaimer which may go unnoticed by the buyer. To be effective, disclaimers should be positive, explicit, unequivocal, and conspicuous.

Express Exclusions A **warranty of title** may be excluded or modified only by specific language or by certain circumstances, including a judicial sale or sales by sheriffs, executors, or foreclosing lienors. Section 2-312(2). In such latter cases the seller is manifestly offering to sell only such right or title as he or a third person might have in the goods, as it is apparent that the goods are not the property of the person selling them.

Express warranties may be excluded by the seller's carefully refraining from making any promise or affirmation of fact relating to the goods, or description of the goods, or a sale by means of a sample or model. Section 2-313. The seller may also negate an express warranty by *clear, specific, unambiguous* language. The Code, nevertheless, provides that words or conduct relevant to the creation of an express warranty and words or conduct tending to negate or limit a warranty shall be construed wherever reasonable as consistent with each other and that a negation or limitation is inoperative to the extent that such construction is unreasonable. Thus, seller and buyer enter into a written contract in which the seller warrants that the camera which it is selling to the buyer is free of defects. This express warranty renders inoperative another provision in the contract which attempts to disclaim liability for any repairs required by any defects in the camera. The inconsistency between the two contractual provisions makes the disclaimer ineffective. Moreover, if the seller's disclaimer attempts to negate "all express warranties" this general disclaimer would be ineffective against the specific express warranty providing that the camera is free of all defects. Finally, oral warranties made prior to the execution of a written agreement which contains an express disclaimer are subject to the parol evidence rule. Thus, as discussed in Chapter 13, if the written contract is intended to be the final and *complete* statement of the agreement between the parties, parol evidence of warranties which *contradict* the terms of the written contract is inadmissible.

To exclude or to modify an **implied warranty of merchantability,** the language of disclaimer or modification must mention *merchantability* and, in the case of a writing, must be *conspicuous.* Section 2-316(2).

To exclude or to modify an **implied warranty of fitness** for the particular purpose of the buyer, the disclaimer must be in *writing* and *conspicuous.* Section 2-316(2) subject to Section 2-316(3).

All implied warranties, unless the circumstances indicate otherwise, are excluded by expressions like **as is, with all faults,** or other language plainly calling the buyer's attention to the exclusion of warranties. Section 2-316(3)(a). Implied warranties may also be excluded by course of dealing, course of performance, or usage of trade.

See O'Neil v. International Harvester Co.

Buyer's Examination or Refusal to Examine If the buyer inspects the goods, **implied** warranties do not apply to obvious defects which are apparent upon examination. Moreover, not only is there no implied warranty as to defects which an examination ought to have revealed where the buyer has examined the goods as fully as she desired, but also where the buyer has *refused* to examine the goods. Section 2-316(3)(b).

A mere failure or omission to examine the goods is not a refusal to examine them. It is not enough that the goods were available for inspection and the buyer did not see fit to inspect them. In order for the buyer to have "refused to examine the goods," the seller *must* have first made a demand upon the buyer that she examine them.

Cumulation and Conflict of Warranties In a contract for the sale of goods it is possible to have both express and implied warranties. All warranties are to be construed as consistent with each other and cumulative, unless such construction is unreasonable. When warranties conflict, the *intention* of the parties is controlling, and in ascertaining that intention the Code sets forth the following rules: (1) exact or technical specifications displace an inconsistent sample, model, or general language of description; (2) a sample displaces inconsistent general descriptive language; and (3) express warranties displace inconsistent implied warranties other than an implied warranty of fitness for a particular purpose. Section 2-317.

Federal Legislation Relating to Warranties of Consumer Products

In order to afford protection to purchasers of **consumer products** (defined as "tangible personal property normally used for personal, family, or household purposes"), the Congress enacted the **Magnuson-Moss Warranty Act.** The purpose of the Act is to make available to consumer purchasers adequate information with respect to warranties and to prevent deception.

Administration and enforcement of the Act is by the Federal Trade Commission. The statutory guidelines for rules and regulations of the Commission with respect to the type of information required to be set forth in warranties of consumer products are aimed at providing the consumer with clear and useful information. More significantly, the Act provides that a seller who makes a written warranty cannot disclaim *any* implied warranty. For a more complete discussion of the Act see Chapter 42.

Privity of Contract

By reason of association of warranties with contracts, a principle of law became established in the nineteenth century whereby recovery for breach of warranty would not be allowed unless the plaintiff was in a contractual relationship with the defendant. This relationship is known as privity of contract.

Under this rule a warranty by seller A to buyer B who resells the goods to purchaser C under a similar warranty gives C no rights against A. There is no privity of contract between A and C. In the event of breach of warranty, C may recover only from his seller B who in turn may recover from A.

Horizontal Privity

Horizontal privity pertains to non-contracting parties who are injured by the defective goods; this group would include users, consumers, and bystanders who are not the contracting purchaser. Horizontal privity concerns who benefits from a warranty and may, therefore, sue for its breach. See Figure 21-1.

The Code relaxes the requirement of horizontal privity of contract to the extent of permitting recovery on a seller's warranty to, at a minimum, members of the family or household of the buyer or guests in his home. The Code, Section 2-318, provides three alternative sections from which the States may select. *Alternative A*, the least comprehensive and most widely adopted of these legislative alternatives, provides: a seller's warranty whether express or implied extends to any natural person who is in the family or household of his buyer or who is a guest in his home if it is reasonable to expect that such person may use, consume, or be affected by the goods and who is injured in person by breach of the warranty. A seller may not exclude or limit the operation of this section. *Alternative B* extends Alternative A to "any natural person who may reasonably be expected to use, consume, or be affected by the goods." *Alternative C* further expands the coverage of the section to any person, not just natural persons, and to property damage as well as personal injury.

However, the Code was not intended to establish outer boundaries as to which third parties may recover for injuries caused by defective goods, but rather it sets a minimum beyond which the States may expand through case law. Most States have judicially accepted the Code's invitation to relax the requirements of horizontal privity and, for all practical purposes, have *eliminated* horizontal privity in warranty cases.

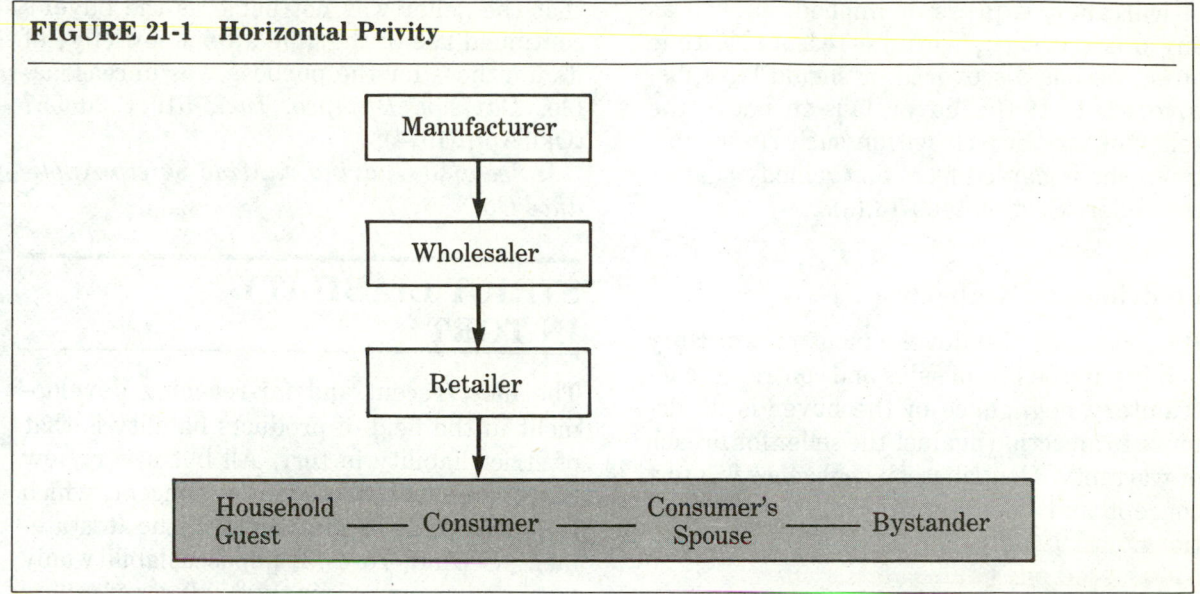

FIGURE 21-1 Horizontal Privity

Vertical Privity Vertical privity pertains to remote sellers within the chain of distribution, such as manufacturers and wholesalers, with whom the consumer purchaser has not dealt. (See Figure 21-2.) Thus, vertical privity determines who is liable upon a warranty. The Code adopts a neutral position regarding vertical privity; nevertheless, the courts in the great majority of the States have elimi-

nated the requirement of vertical privity in warranty actions. *See Sheeskin v. Giant Food, Inc.*

Notice of Breach

Where the buyer has accepted a tender of goods which are not as warranted by the seller, he is required to notify the seller of any breach

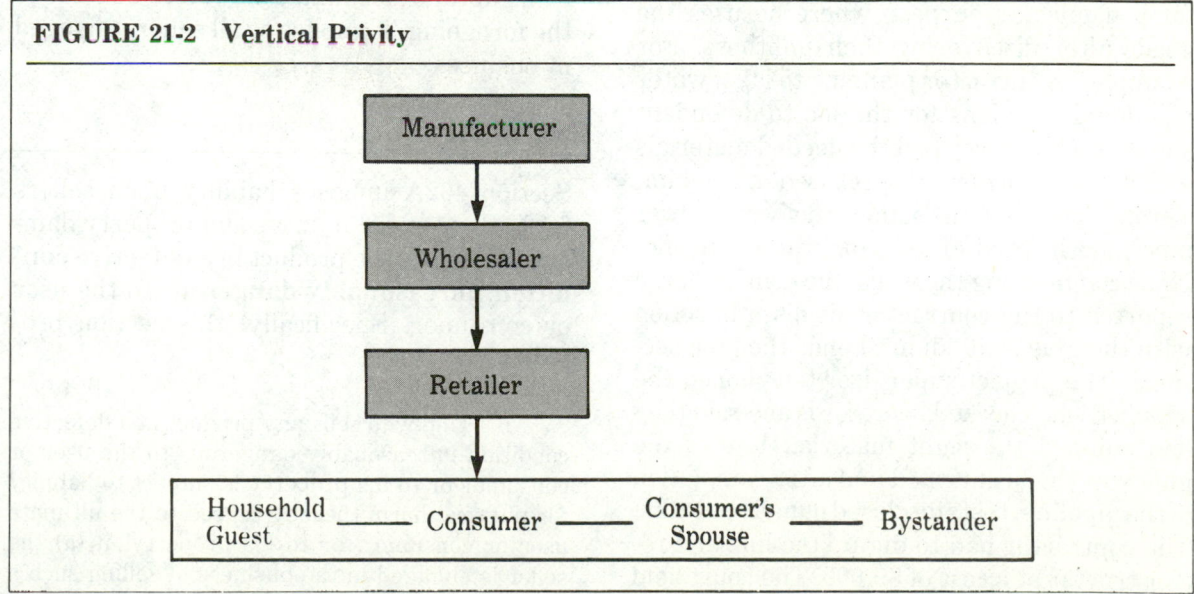

FIGURE 21-2 Vertical Privity

of warranty, express or implied, as well as any other breach, within a reasonable time after she has discovered or should have discovered it. If the buyer fails to notify the seller of any breach within such reasonable time, she is barred from any remedy against the seller. Section 2-607(3)(a).

Contributory Negligence

By reason of the development of warranty liability in the law of sales and contracts, contributory negligence of the buyer is *no* defense to an action against the seller for breach of warranty. Contributory negligence is a tort concept and does *not* apply to contract actions.

Voluntary Assumption of Risk

If the buyer after discovering a defect in the goods which may cause injury and being aware of the danger nevertheless proceeds to make use of the goods, he will not be permitted to recover damages from the seller for loss or injuries caused by such use. This is not contributory negligence, but voluntary assumption of a known risk.

Thus, a buyer may not recover damages for breach of an implied warranty of fitness for a particular purpose where he uses the goods after discovering their unfitness. For example, a contractor planning to lay a water pipeline gave plans for the job to defendant supplier who prescribed the needed materials which the contractor purchased from him. Through an error, the supplier delivered sewer pipe glue instead of glue for water pipeline. Upon commencing the work, the man in charge reported to the contractor his dissatisfaction with the glue as it "didn't bond" the pipe sections. The project supervisor telephoned the supplier who checked his records and said they had shipped the right material. Use of the glue was then continued and after completion of the pipeline, tests disclosed numerous leaks. The contractor had to dig up the line and reconstruct it at a cost of $9,000. The court held

that the seller was not liable as the buyer's continued use of the glue after knowledge of its unfitness for the purpose was unreasonable. *Davis v. Pumpco, Inc.*, 519 P.2d 557 (Okl. App. 1974).

See also Guarino v. Mine Safety Appliance Co.

STRICT LIABILITY IN TORT

The most recent and far-reaching development in the field of products liability is that of strict liability in tort. All but a very few States have now accepted the concept, which is embodied in **Section 402A** of the Restatement, Second, Torts. It imposes liability only upon a person who is in the *business* of selling the product involved. It does not apply to an occasional seller who is not in the business of selling the product, such as a person who trades in his used car or who sells his lawn mower to a neighbor. It is similar in this respect to the implied warranty of merchantability which applies only to sales by a merchant with respect to goods of the type in which he deals. It also does not apply to sales of the stock of merchants not in the usual course of business such as execution sales, bankruptcy sales, and bulk sales. Subject to the foregoing, it applies to all sellers engaged in business.

NATURE

Section 402A imposes liability upon sellers for both personal injuries and property damage for selling the product in **a defective condition unreasonably dangerous** to the user or consumer. Specifically, this section provides:

1. One who sells any product in a defective condition unreasonably dangerous to the user or consumer or to his property is subject to liability for physical harm thereby caused to the ultimate user or consumer, or to his property, if (a) the seller is engaged in the business of selling such a

product, and (b) it is expected to and does reach the user or consumer without substantial change in the condition in which it is sold.

2.   The rule stated in Subsection (1) applies although (a) the seller has exercised all possible care in the preparation and sale of his products, and (b) the user or consumer has not bought the product from or entered into any contractual relation with the seller.

It is to be emphasized that negligence is not the basis of this liability; it applies even though "the seller has exercised all possible care in the preparation and sale of his product." However, the seller is not an insurer of the goods which he manufactures or sells, and the essential requirements for this type of liability are that: (1) the defendant sold the product in a defective condition; (2) the defendant was engaged in the business of selling such a product; (3) the defective condition was one which made the product unreasonably dangerous to the user or consumer or to his property; (4) the defect in the product existed at the time it left the hands of the defendant; (5) the plaintiff sustained physical harm or property damage by use or consumption of the product; and (6) the defective condition was the proximate cause of such injury or damage.

This liability is imposed by law as a matter of public policy and does not depend upon contract, either express or implied. It does not require reliance by the injured user or consumer upon any statements made by the manufacturer or seller. The liability is not limited to persons in a relationship of buyer and seller; thus neither vertical nor horizontal privity is required. No notice of defect is required to have been given by the injured user or consumer. The liability, furthermore, is generally not subject to disclaimer, exclusion, or modification by contractual agreement. The liability is strictly in tort and arises out of the common law. It is not governed by the provisions of the Uniform Commercial Code. The majority of courts considering the question, however, have held that Section 402A imposes liability only for injury to person and

damage to property but not for commercial loss (such as loss of bargain or profits), which loss is recoverable in an action for breach of warranty.

The reasons asserted in support of imposing strict liability in tort upon manufacturers and assemblers of products are: (1) maximum protection should be given consumers against dangerous defects in products; (2) manufacturers are in the best position to prevent or reduce the hazards to life and health in defective products; (3) manufacturers realize the most profit from the total sales of their goods and are best able to carry the financial burden of such liability by distributing it among the public as a cost of doing business; (4) manufacturers utilize wholesalers and retailers merely as conduits in the marketing of their products and should not be permitted to avoid liability simply because they have no contract with the user or consumer; and (5) since the manufacturer is liable to his vendee who may be a wholesaler who in turn is liable to the retailer who in turn is liable to the ultimate purchaser, time and expense would be saved by making the liability a direct one rather than a chain reaction.

Although liability for personal injuries caused by the defective condition of goods which makes them unreasonably dangerous is usually associated with sales of goods, such liability also exists with respect to **leases** and **bailments** of such goods. The extension of liability to lessors and bailors of goods is not surprising in view of the rationale developed by the courts in imposing strict liability in tort upon manufacturers and sellers of products. The danger to which the public is exposed by defectively manufactured cars and trucks traveling on the highways is not greatly different from the hazards of defectively maintained cars and trucks leased to operators.

Defective Condition

In an action against a defendant manufacturer or seller to recover damages under the rule of strict liability in tort, the plaintiff must prove a defective condition in the product, but she is not required to prove how or why or in what manner the product became defective. On the issue of liability, the reason or cause of the defect is not material as it would be in an action based upon negligence. The plaintiff, however, must show that at the time she was injured the condition of the product was not substantially changed from what it was at the time it was sold by the defendant manufacturer or seller. The defect may arise through faulty manufacturing, through faulty product design, or through inadequate warning, labeling, or instructions.

Manufacturing Defect A manufacturing defect occurs when the product is not properly made, such as failing to meet its own manufacturing specifications. For instance, suppose a chair is manufactured with legs designed to be attached by four screws and glue. If such a chair were produced without inserting the appropriate screws, this would constitute a manufacturing defect.

Design Defect A product contains a design defect when it is produced as specified but is dangerous or hazardous because its design is inadequate. Design defects can result from a number of causes, including poor engineering and poor choice of materials. An example of a design defect that received great notoriety was the Ford Pinto. A number of courts found the car to be inadequately designed in that its fuel tank had been placed too close to its rear axle, causing the fuel tank to rupture upon impact from the rear. *See also Heckman v. Federal Press Co. and Kennedy v. Custom Ice Equipment Co., Inc.*

Inadequate Warning or Instructions A seller is under a duty to provide adequate warning of danger and to provide appropriate directions for safe use. Nevertheless, inadequate and dangerous products, regardless of their warning, will be held to be defective, especially if there are superior, alternative designs or manufacturing procedures. Typically, warning or instructions are needed to insure that appropriately designed and manufactured products are properly utilized. Comment j to Section 402A provides that in some instances "in order to prevent the product from being unreasonably dangerous, the seller may be required to give directions or warning, on the container, as to its use." For example, in one case a drug company was found liable for inadequately warning of the dangerous and not infrequent side-effects of one of its drugs (MER 29). *Toole v. Richardson-Merrell, Inc.*, 251 Cal.App.2d 689, 60 Cal.Rptr. 398 (1967).

Almost any product may be used or misused in a manner which involves danger of physical harm. The blow of a poorly aimed hammer may crush a thumb. The inhaling of a feather may damage a lung. The use of a sled on a busy street may endanger the child using it. The excessive drinking of liquor is dangerous. Allowing children to play with firearms is also dangerous. These hazards arise out of the use of products in a manner or to the extent that they were not intended by the supplier to be used, and generally no duty is imposed upon the manufacturer or seller to give warning against the possible dangers that might arise from such misuse of the product.

The duty to give a warning arises out of a foreseeable danger of physical harm arising out of the normal or probable use of the product and the likelihood that unless warned, the user or consumer will not ordinarily be aware of such danger or hazard.

In *Spruill v. Boyle-Midway Incorporated*, 308 F.2d 79 (1962), the defendants were manufacturers and distributors of furniture polish, containing 98% mineral seal oil, the remaining ingredients consisted of cedar oil, a trace of turpentine, and some red dye. The label on the bottle in which the product was sold stated in red letters about ⅛ inch in height "CAUTION, COMBUSTIBLE MATERIAL." Beneath this in red letters 1/16 inch in height were the words "DO NOT USE NEAR FIRE OR FLAME." This warning was followed by seven lines of directions printed in letters about ⅟₃₂ inch in height following which was a statement in letters of the same height: "Contents refined petroleum distillate, may be harmful if swallowed, especially by children." A baby, 14 months old, died as the result of chemical pneumonia caused by swallowing a small quantity of this furniture polish. The defendants were held liable for failure to give adequate notice of its poisonous nature. Mineral seal oil is extremely toxic, and the warning against combustibility overshadowed and made more inconspicuous the toxicity warning in smaller print.

In addition to warning of dangers, the seller must provide adequate directions for the safe and efficient use of the product. Furthermore, whenever a deviation from the directions may give rise to a serious danger to the user, it is incumbent upon the seller to provide warning of this danger.

Unreasonably Dangerous

Section 402A liability only applies if the defective product is unreasonably dangerous to the user or consumer. An unreasonably dangerous product is one which contains a danger beyond that which would be contemplated by the ordinary consumer who purchases it with the common knowledge of its characteristics. Thus, "good whiskey is not unreasonably dangerous merely because it will make some people drunk, and is especially dangerous to alcoholics; but bad whiskey, containing a dangerous amount of fuel oil, is unreasonably dangerous. Good tobacco is not unreasonably dangerous merely because the effects of smoking may be harmful; but tobacco containing something like marijuana may be unreasonably dangerous. Good butter is not unreasonably dangerous merely because, if such be the case, it deposits cholesterol in the arteries and leads to heart attacks; but bad butter, contaminated with poisonous fish oil, is unreasonably dangerous." Comment i to Section 402A. Most courts have left the question of what a consumer reasonably expects to find

to the jury. *See Kennedy v. Custom Ice Equipment Co., Inc.*

OBSTACLES TO RECOVERY

Disclaimers and Notice

Comment m to Section 402A provides that the basis of strict liability rests solely in tort and, therefore, is not subject to contractual defenses. The comment specifically states that strict product liability is not governed by the Code, that it is not affected by contractual limitations or disclaimers, and that it is not subject to any requirement that notice be given to the seller by the injured party within a reasonable time. Nevertheless, most courts have *allowed* clear and specific disclaimers of Section 402A liability in commercial transactions between merchants of relatively equal economic power.

Privity

Horizontal Privity The strict liability in tort of manufacturers and other sellers extends not only to buyers, users, and consumers, but also to injured bystanders. Illustrative cases are: occupants of automobile injured in collision with another car due to the other car having defective brakes; golfer killed by runaway golf cart which started due to faulty transmission system; bystander injured by runaway truck started by short circuit; bystander injured by explosion of defective beer keg; neighbor injured by explosion of propane gas tank; and bystander injured by explosion of shotgun barrel caused by defective shell.

Vertical Privity The rule of strict liability in tort, as formulated in Section 402A, imposes liability upon the seller for physical harm to the ultimate user or consumer of the defective product. Such liability extends to any seller who is engaged in the business of selling the product, including a wholesaler or distributor as well as the manufacturer and retailer. *See*

Embs v. Pepsi-Cola Bottling Co. of Lexington, Kentucky, Inc.

The rule of strict liability in tort also applies to the manufacturer of a defective component part which has been incorporated into the larger product where no essential change has been made in it by the manufacturer of the finished product, and such manufacturer is not excused from liability by reason of the failure of the manufacturer of the finished product to discover the defect by testing or inspection. The manufacturer of the finished product is also liable for damages caused by a defective condition of the goods resulting exclusively from a defective component part.

Finally, there are a growing number of jurisdictions which recognize the applicability of strict liability in tort to merchant-sellers of used goods. One court has stated in a case involving the sale of a used automobile: "The safety of the general public demands that when a used motor vehicle, for example, is sold for use as a *serviceable motor vehicle* (and not as junk parts), absent special circumstances, the seller be responsible for safety defects whether known or unknown at the time of sale, present while the machine was under his control."

Plaintiff's Conduct

Contributory Negligence At common law in an action based on negligence, contributory negligence of the plaintiff completely barred recovery. Contributory negligence generally is immaterial in an action based upon strict liability in tort, although a few States have held contributory negligence to be a valid defense. The minority view, however, totally bars the plaintiff from recovery, is contrary to the principle of strict liability, and is contrary to Comment n to Section 402A.

Comparative Negligence A great number of States have adopted the rule of comparative negligence in negligence actions. This rule diminishes the amount of a plaintiff's recovery in proportion to his fault. In response to the doctrinal difficulties and inequities of applying contributory negligence to strict liability in tort, a growing number of courts and legislatures have applied the principle of comparative negligence to strict liability in tort.

Voluntary Assumption of the Risk Assumption of risk is a defense in an action based on strict liability in tort. The user or consumer who voluntarily uses the goods in an unusual, inappropriate, or improper manner for which they were not intended, and which under the circumstances is unreasonable, assumes the risk of injuries which result from such use.

To establish such defense the burden is on the defendant to show that (1) the plaintiff actually knew and appreciated the particular risk or danger created by the defect, (2) the plaintiff voluntarily encountered the risk while realizing the danger, and (3) the plaintiff's decision to encounter the known risk was unreasonable.

Misuse or Abuse of the Product Closely connected to voluntary assumption of the risk is the valid defense of misuse or abuse of the product by the injured party. The major difference is that misuse or abuse includes actions which the injured party does not know to be dangerous, while assumption of the risk does not include such conduct. The courts, however, have significantly limited this defense by requiring that the misuse or abuse not be foreseeable by the seller. If a use is foreseeable, then the seller must take measures to guard against it. Thus, a manufacturer has been held liable for injuries to a stevedore who was injured while walking on cargo for failing to package its cargo so as to avoid such injury. It was foreseeable that stevedores would indeed walk on the cargo.

Subsequent Alteration

Section 402A provides that liability only exists if the product reaches "the user or consumer without substantial change in the condition in which it is sold." Accordingly, most, but not all, courts would not hold a manufacturer liable for a faulty carburetor if the retailer were to remove the part and make significant changes in it prior to reinserting it into the automobile.

For a summary on products liability, see Figure 21-3.

FIGURE 21-3   Products Liability

	Warranty of Merchantability	Strict Liability in Tort
Condition of goods	Not merchantable	Defective condition, unreasonably dangerous
Character of defendant	Seller who is a merchant with respect to the goods sold	Seller who is engaged in the business of selling such a product
Disclaimer	Permitted if: 1) specific 2) conspicuous 3) conscionable subject to Magnuson-Moss Act	None possible in consumer transaction; most courts allow in commercial transactions
Notice	Within reasonable time	None required
Causation	Required	Required
Protected Harm	Alt. A: To person of buyer, family or guests in home. Alt. B: To person of anyone reasonably to be expected to use product. Alt. C: To person reasonably to be expected to use product or to his property	Physical harm to person or property of the ultimate user or consumer; judicial trend towards including bystanders
Type of Transaction	Sales; some courts apply to leases and bailments	Sales, leases, and bailments

---

CASES

Implied Waranties/Privity

SHEESKIN v. GIANT FOOD, INC.

Court of Special Appeals of Maryland, 1974.
20 Md.App. 611, 318 A.2d 874.

DAVIDSON, J.

[Seigel, a 73-year-old man, was injured at one of Giant Foods' retail food stores when a bottle of Coca Cola exploded as he was placing a six-pack of Coke into his shopping cart. The explosion caused him to lose his balance and fall, with injuries resulting. Seigel brought suit against Giant Foods and Washington Coca Cola Bottling Company for damages allegedly caused by their breach of the implied warranty of merchantability. The trial court granted judgment in favor of Giant and Washington, Seigel (appellant) brought this appeal.]

* * *

The retailer, Giant Food, Inc., contends that appellant failed to prove that an implied warranty existed between himself and the retailer because he failed to prove that there was a sale by the retailer to him or a contract of sale between the two. The retailer maintains that there was no sale or contract of sale because at the time the bottles exploded Mr. Seigel had not yet paid for them. We do not agree.

Code § 2–314(1) states in pertinent part:

Unless excluded or modified (§ 2–316), a warranty that the goods shall be merchantable is implied *in a contract for their sale* if the seller is a merchant with respect to goods of that kind (emphasis added).

Thus, in order for the implied warranties of § 2–314 to be applicable there must be a "contract for sale." In Maryland it has been recognized that neither a completed "sale" nor a fully executed contract for sale is required. It is enough that there be in existence an executory contract for sale. [Citation.]

* * *

Here, the plaintiff has the burden of showing the existence of the warranty by establishing that at the time the bottles exploded there was a contract for their sale existing between himself and the Giant. [Citations.] Mr. Titus, the manager of the Giant, testified that the retailer is a "self-service" store in which "the only way a customer can buy anything is to select it himself and take it to the checkout counter." He stated that there are occasions when a customer may select an item in the store and then change his mind and put the item back. There was no evidence to show that the retailer ever refused to sell an item to a customer once it had been selected by him or that the retailer did not consider himself bound to sell an item to the customer after the item had been selected. Finally, Mr. Titus said that an employee of Giant placed the six-pack of Coca Cola selected by Mr. Seigel on the shelf with the purchase price already stamped upon it. Mr. Seigel testified that he picked up the six-pack with the intent to purchase it.

We think that there is sufficient evidence to show that the retailer's act of placing the bottles upon the shelf with the price stamped upon the six-pack in which they were contained manifested an intent to offer them for sale, the terms of the offer being that it would pass title to the goods when Mr. Seigel presented them at the check-out counter and paid the stated price in cash. We also think that the evidence is sufficient to show that Mr. Seigel's act of taking physical possession of the goods with the intent to purchase them manifested an intent to accept the offer and a promise to take them to the check-out counter and pay for them there.

* * *

Appellant [Seigel] contends that the evidence was sufficient to show that the retailer breached an implied warranty of merchantability and that he suffered loss as a result of that breach. We agree.

It is axiomatic that a buyer may recover for breach of warranty without proving negligence on the part of the seller. [Citations.] In order to recover on a warranty, the plaintiff need show only that the article sold did not conform to the representation of the warranty at the time it left the control of the defendant. [Citations.]

Here Mr. Seigel testified that all of the circumstances surrounding his selection of the bottles were normal; that the carton in which the bottles came was not defective; that in lifting the carton from the shelf and moving it toward his basket the bottles neither touched nor were touched by anything other than his hand; that they exploded almost instantaneously after he removed them from the shelf; and that as a result of the explosion he fell, injuring himself. It is obvious that Coca Cola bottles which would break under normal handling are not fit for the ordinary use for which they were intended and that the relinquishment of physical control of such a defective bottle to a consumer constitutes a breach of warranty. Thus the evidence was sufficient to show that when the bottles left the retailer's control they did not conform to the representations of the warranty of merchantability, and that this breach of the warranty was the cause of the loss sustained. * * *

Appellant contends that the bottler also breached the implied warranties of merchantability found in Code § 2–314. The bottler concedes that an implied warranty of merchantability exists with respect to appellant, the ultimate consumer, but asserts that appellant failed to prove that the warranty was broken because he failed to prove that a defect existed in the bottles at the time of their delivery to the retailer. We agree with the bottler.

* * *

Effective 1 July 1969, § 2–314 was amended so as to include within the meaning of the term "seller" the "manufacturer, distributor, dealer, wholesaler, or other middleman and/or the retailer." The section was also amended to provide, in pertinent part, that "any previous requirement of privity is abolished as between the buyer and any of the aforementioned parties in any action brought by the buyer." In addition, § 2–318 was amended to extend a "seller's" express or implied warranty not only to any natural person who is in the family or household of his buyer or a guest in his home, but also to "any other ultimate consumer or user of the goods or person affected thereby if it is reasonable to expect that such person may use, consume, or be affected by the goods and who is injured in person by breach of the warranty."

These amendments establish that protection under the implied warranty of merchantability provided in § 2–314 extends not only to the person buying for resale to the ultimate consumer (that is, the retailer) but also to the ultimate consumer. [Citation.]

While privity between the bottler and the ultimate consumer is not required, a "sale" or "contract for sale" is required in order to make the warranty implied by § 2–314 applicable. Thus, there must be a sale or contract for sale from the bottler to some individual in the distributive chain in order for the implied warranties to arise in favor of the ultimate consumer. Here there was evidence that prior to Mr. Seigel's injuries, the bottler sold the bottles of Coca Cola selected by Mr. Seigel to the retailer, Giant Food, Inc. This evidence was sufficient to show that there was a warranty in existence which extended from the bottler to Mr. Seigel, the ultimate consumer [,but not sufficient to show that the defect existed at the time of the sale from the bottler to Giant.]

* * *

Disclaimer or Modification of Warranties

O'NEIL v. INTERNATIONAL HARVESTER CO.

Colorado Court of Appeals, 1978.
40 Colo.App. 369, 575 P.2d 862.

RULAND, J.

The plaintiff, Albert M. O'Neil, appeals from a summary judgment dismissing his complaint against the defendants, International Harvester Company and International Harvester Credit Corporation, and from a summary judgment in favor of the defendants on their first counterclaim. * * * We affirm in part, reverse in part, and remand for further proceedings.

The pleadings, interrogatories, and depositions in this case disclose the following pertinent facts. On August 22, 1975, O'Neil entered into a "Retail Installment Contract" with the defendant, International Harvester Company, for the purchase of a used diesel tractor and trailer. International Harvester Company assigned its interest in the contract to the defendant, International Harvester Credit Corporation. The contract provided:

Each USED motor vehicle covered by this contract is sold AS IS WITHOUT WARRANTY OF ANY CHARACTER expressed or implied, unless purchaser has received from seller a separate written warranty executed by seller.

No written warranties were received by O'Neil. The contract also provided:

Purchaser agrees that this contract . . . which he has read and to which he agrees contains the entire agreement relating to the installment sale of said property and supersedes all previous contracts and agreements between purchaser and seller relating to the order or sale of said property except as to any written agreements between purchaser and seller concerning warranty.

Pursuant to the contract, O'Neil paid $1,700 as a down payment, but failed to make any of the required monthly payments.

According to O'Neil's deposition, shortly after the purchase his employee drove the truck to a location in the mountains for the purpose of hauling firewood to Denver. He had numerous problems with the truck, causing delays which resulted in the loss of his permit to cut and remove firewood, as well as loss of business. A representative of International Harvester agreed to pay one-half of the cost of certain repairs. After several attempts to have the defendants repair the truck during the next month, O'Neil returned it to the defendants, but the defendants refused to rescind the sale.

O'Neil admitted reading the contract, including the warranty exclusion provision. He stated, however, that he understood the provision to mean that the tractor and trailer would be in the condition represented by the defendant's salesman. According to O'Neil, the salesman represented that the truck had been recently overhauled and would be suitable for operation in the mountains; later, when he returned the truck, O'Neil overheard another employee of the defendant International Harvester Company say to the salesman, "I told you not to sell him Inman's truck— Inman took every piece of used equipment off his other fleet of trucks and stuck it on that one."

In his complaint O'Neil sought both rescission of the contract and damages, alleging that International Harvester was liable for breach of express warranties, an implied warranty of fitness for a particular purpose, and fraud. Defendants answered denying that any warranties were made to O'Neil or that any fraud was committed in the sale and, insofar as pertinent here, defendants counterclaimed for the balance due under the contracts.

O'Neil first contends that the trial court improperly granted summary judgment against him on his claim that the defendants breached an implied warranty of fitness for a particular purpose relative to the capability of the truck. In response, the defendants assert that summary judgment was proper because this warranty was effectively disclaimed in the contract. We agree with the defendants.

Pursuant to the Uniform Commercial Code, one way an implied warranty of fitness for a particular purpose can be excluded is by a conspicuous writing which states generally that there are no warranties extending beyond the description in the contract. § 2–316(2). O'Neil admits reading the warranty disclaimer provision. * * * And, we hold that the language "AS IS WITHOUT WARRANTY OF ANY CHARACTER expressed or implied" was sufficient to inform O'Neil that there was no implied warranty in effect for the truck. See § 2–316(2). [Citation.]

Even though express warranties are also included in the above quoted language, still O'Neil asserts that summary judgment was improvidently granted against him on his claim that International Harvester breached the express warranties. The defendants argue that the trial court's ruling was correct. We agree with O'Neil.

Section 2–316 provides that "[w]ords or conduct relevant to the creation of an express warranty *and* words or conduct tending to negate or limit warranty shall be construed wherever reasonable as consistent with each other . . . ." Here, the oral warranties relied upon by O'Neil are totally inconsistent with the warranty exclusion clause of the contract. Section 2–316 further provides that, under these circumstances (but subject to the provisions of the Code governing the admission of parol evidence), a provision limiting an express warranty is inoperative.

Turning to the applicable parol evidence rule as set forth in § 2–202, one finds that:

terms with respect to which the confirmatory memoranda of the parties agree or which are otherwise set forth in writing intended by the parties as a final expression of their agreement with respect to such terms as are included therein, may not be contradicted by evidence of any prior agreement or of a contemporaneous oral agreement. . . . .

Various commentators have noted the difficulty in applying §§ 2–316 and 2–202 when, as here, the buyer alleges oral warranties by the seller, but the written contract contains both a warranty disclaimer clause and an "integration" provision. [Citations.] While the courts divide on whether testimony as to the oral warranties may be admitted under these circumstances, [citations] we do not reach that issue in this case.

Where, as here, the buyer alleges the existence of oral warranties prior to execution of the written contract, as well as conduct following the sale (such as a commitment to pay for certain repairs) which tends to show that warranties were in fact made, there is a material issue of fact for resolution. That issue is whether the parties intended the written contract to be a final expression of their agreement, and if not, of what the terms actually agreed upon by the parties consisted. Further, we hold that, under such circumstances, evidence of both oral warranties and the conduct of the parties subsequent to signing the contract is admissible for purpose of resolving this issue. Thus, entry of summary judgment on this issue was in error. [Citations.]

* * *

That part of the judgment dismissing O'Neil's claim for breach of implied warranty is affirmed. The balance of the judgment is reversed and the cause remanded for further proceedings consistent with this opinion.

Voluntary Assumption of the Risk

GUARINO v. MINE SAFETY APPLIANCE CO.

Court of Appeals of New York, 1969.
25 N.Y.2d 460, 306 N.Y.S.2d 942, 255 N.E.2d 173.

JASEN, J.

These consolidated actions arose out of an accident wherein three men died and five others were injured.

On October 2, 1957, one John J. Rooney, an engineer employed by the Bureau of Sewage Disposal of the City of New York, died of gas asphyxiation after descending into an interceptor sewer located 30 or 40 feet below the ground in the Borough of Queens to ascertain the source of water in the bulkhead. At the time of the accident, he was wearing an oxygen-type protective mask manufactured by the defendant herein. The estate of John J. Rooney recovered a judgment against the defendant on a theory of breach of implied warranty of merchantability, in "that the mask did not work because the plunger was defective." [Citation.]

The two other decedents, and the surviving plaintiffs, were all sewage treatment workers and members of Rooney's work team at the time of the accident. Plaintiff Fattore entered the sewer tunnel with Rooney after testing for gas and finding none. Decedent Guarino was stationed at the bottom level of the shaft, decedent Messina was at the next level, and a survivor, Mirabile, was at the upper level. After correcting the water leakage problem, Rooney and Fattore began to recross the tunnel and return to the shaft, at which time Fattore felt Rooney slump behind him. He attempted to drag Rooney from the sewer tunnel, but finding himself having difficulty breathing, he released Rooney, ripped off his own mask, and hollered for help. Guarino and Messina were fatally stricken by the lethal gas present in the sewer when they left their posts in the sewer shaft and entered the sewer tunnel without masks in answer to Fattore's call for help. The other surviving plaintiffs were injured as they also descended into the sewer in response to Rooney's plight.

This appeal presents for our review the "danger invites rescue" doctrine.

In New York the rescue doctrine had its historical genesis in *Eckert v. Long Is. R. R. Co.* [citation] which stated that the plaintiff's intestate, who was killed while attempting to rescue a child on the railroad tracks was not to be found contributorily negligent unless acting rashly or recklessly. The purpose of the doctrine, we said, was to prevent a plaintiff from being found contributorily negligent, as a matter of law, when he voluntarily placed himself in a perilous situation to prevent another from suffering serious injury.

The doctrine has been most frequently applied when a defendant through his negligence either injured or imperilled another and a third person was injured in attempting to rescue the person in jeopardy. [Citations.]
* * *

In these actions plaintiffs seek application of the "danger invites rescue" doctrine to a situation where a breach of warranty endangers a person so as to invite rescue by a third party. It is significant to note that all of the cases that have invoked the rescue doctrine since it was first promulgated by this court have been negligence actions. This is, we believe, the first instance in which the doctrine has been invoked in an action where the gravamen of the wrong complained of has been breach of warranty.

We do not believe that the theory of the action, whether it be negligence or breach of warranty, is significant where the doctrine of "danger invites rescue" applies. A breach of warranty and an act of negligence are each clearly wrongful acts. Both terms are synonymous as regards fixation of liability, differing primarily in their requirements of proof.

As we recently held in *Provenzo v. Sam* [citation], the rescue doctrine should be applied when "one party *by his culpable act* has placed another person in a position of imminent peril which invites a third person, the rescuing plaintiff, to come to his aid."

* * *

Here the defendant committed a culpable act against the decedent Rooney, by manufacturing and distributing a defective oxygen-producing mask, for which it has been held accountable in damages. [Citation.] By virtue of this defendant's culpable act, Rooney was placed in peril, thus inviting his rescue by the plaintiffs who were all members of Rooney's sewage treatment crew. There was no time for reflection when it became known that Rooney was in need of immediate assistance in the dark tunnel some 30 to 40 feet below the street level. These plaintiffs responded to the cries for help in a manner which was reasonable and consistent with their concern for each other as members of a crew. To require that a rescuer answering the cry for help make inquiry as to the nature of the culpable act that imperils someone's life would defy all logic.

As Judge Cardozo so eloquently stated in *Wagner v. International Ry. Co.*: "Danger invites rescue. The cry of distress is the summons to relief. * * * The *wrong* that imperils life is a wrong to the imperilled victim; it is a wrong also to his rescuer." [Citation.]

* * *

We conclude that a person who by his culpable act whether it stems from negligence or breach of warranty places another person in a position of imminent peril, may be held liable for any damages sustained by a rescuer in his attempt to aid the imperilled victim.

* * *

Design Defect

HECKMAN v. FEDERAL PRESS CO.

United States Court of Appeals, Third Circuit, 1979.
587 F.2d 612.

WEIS, J.

In this products liability case, a jury found that a power press manufactured by defendant without a guarding device was unreasonably dangerous, and awarded plaintiff damages for the injuries he sustained while operating the machine. Although the question of liability was for the jury, the judgment must be vacated because of error in permitting expert testimony that included a "growth factor" in projecting future loss of earnings. Admission of such evidence being impermissible under applicable Pennsylvania law, we grant a new trial.

Plaintiff's left hand was severely injured when it was caught in a power press he was operating in the course of his employment with the Clark Equipment Company. He brought suit against The Federal Press Company, the manufacturer of the machine, alleging defective design because of the lack of an adequate safety device. A jury returned a verdict in favor of the plaintiff in the amount of $750,000 against Federal, with a verdict over [for Federal] against the employer Clark, joined [sued] by Federal on a claim for contribution.

The accident occurred on September 24, 1972, at the Clark factory in Reading, Pennsylvania as Heckman was using a foot pedal to operate the press. The machine functions by dropping a heavy ram onto a die, cutting or shaping the metal which resets on the lower surface. As plaintiff placed a piece of metal in the machine to be cut, the ram came down on his hand, resulting in the amputation of several fingers and other damage.

The press had been purchased by Clark in 1970. It could be operated in two different ways: with hand controls requiring the use of both hands on switches away from the point of operation, or, alternatively, by the use of a foot pedal, an optional item ordered by Clark. When the manual operation was used, the employee's hands necessarily were protected. However, when the foot pedal was utilized without a guard, there was nothing to prevent the hands from being placed in the operating area directly under the descending ram.

Federal did not provide safety appliances other than the dual buttons for manual op-

eration except upon the customer's specific request and at its expense. When ordered, the guards were secured from other sources and attached by Federal. On delivery of the equipment to Clark, Federal sent a letter suggesting that the customer "obtain, install, and use 'point of operation' guarding for greater operator safety." In addition, the press itself had a warning plate with similar instructions for use.

Various types of safeguards designed to protect the operator were available on the market, including some designed to accommodate specific uses of the multi-purpose machine. Clark did in fact purchase a point-of-operation guard for $100, but it was not on the press at the time the injury occurred, and, in any event, its efficacy was challenged. Plaintiff produced expert testimony to establish that at least one type of appliance would be effective in about 95% of the customary uses of the press, and that the failure to supply such a device made the press defective within the meaning of Restatement (Second) of Torts § 402A (1965).

Federal contended it was not customary in the trade to furnish guards except upon request, and the multitude of uses to which the machine could be put made it impracticable to designate any one device as standard equipment. Moreover, Clark's failure to heed Federal's warning was said to be a superseding cause absolving defendant from all liability. Finally, Federal relied upon state regulations placing responsibility for the safe operation of presses upon employers and employees.

* * *

* * * [T]he jury found that Federal had sold a press in a defective condition . . . and plaintiff Heckman had not assumed a risk. It awarded Heckman damages of $750,000. [Citation.]

* * * In *Webb v. Zern*, [citation] Pennsylvania adopted the strict liability provisions of § 402A of the Restatement (Second) of Torts. Cases interpreting this section have held that lack of proper safety devices can constitute a defective design which may subject the manufacturer of machinery to liability. [Citations.]

We find the present case quite similar on its facts to *Capasso v. Minster Machine Co.*, [citation], which also discussed a power press injury. There, as here, a two-button system provided protection in manual operation, but no guard was provided when the optional foot control pedal was used. The manufacturer failed to provide any proposals for a safety guard and a device of the customer's own design proved to be ineffective. We held that since the original purchase included the optional foot switch, its use did not as a matter of law constitute a "substantial change" in the machinery within the scope of § 402(A)(1)(b) absolving the manufacturer; nor did the use of the inadequate shield act as a superseding cause as a matter of law. [Citations.] We concluded that the issue of a defect in the press at delivery was for the jury.

Similarly here, plaintiff's expert maintained that the defendant should have provided safeguards to be used in connection with the foot pedal operation, and that effective implements were available at a reasonable cost. [Citation.]

Federal asserts that the bolster plate which Clark had installed blocked the operator's view of the machine's warning plate, and that this screening constituted a superseding cause insulating the manufacturer from liability. Thus, Federal's theory is that when Clark obscured the warning sign it effected a substantial change that became a superseding cause of the accident. But it cannot be said that as a matter of law the decreased visibility of the plaque was such a major departure from the original design of the machine as to cut off the manufacturer's obligations. [Citation.] Particularly is this so when the sign was addressed to a condition that was not latent. We are unwilling to accept the proposition that the warning plate in and of itself absolved Federal as a matter of law.

As we observed in *Schell v. AMF, Inc.*, [citation]:

[A]s a matter of policy, it is questionable whether a manufacturer which produces a machine without minimal available safeguards is entitled to escape liability by warning of a dangerous condition which could reasonably have been avoided by a better design.

In the circumstances here, the warning issue was for the jury as was the defense of assumption of the risk. [Citation.]

Federal also maintains that it was exculpated as a matter of law because regulations of the Pennsylvania Department of Labor and Industry requiring the use of point-of-operation devices placed the responsibility upon the employer and employee. We do not accept this premise. Whatever effect the regulations might have as between employer and employee does not extend to relieve the manufacturer of its liability under § 402A as a matter of law. If a manufacturer fails to provide reasonable safety devices for a product and thus creates an unreasonable risk of harm to the user, the fact that the manufacturer may expect the user to provide a protective appliance is not sufficient to preclude liability in most circumstances. [Citations.] The issue is one which should be decided by a jury in light of such matters as the feasibility of incorporating safety features during manufacture of the machine, the likelihood that users will not secure adequate devices, whether the machinery is of a standard make or built to the customer's specifications, the relative expertise of manufacturer and customer, the extent of risk to the user, and the seriousness of injury which may be anticipated.

* * *

We conclude that the questions of liability were for the jury's consideration and it was not error to deny Federal's motion for judgment n.o.v.

[A new trial is granted due to a reversible error in the award of damages.]

Design Defect/Unreasonably Dangerous

KENNEDY v. CUSTOM ICE EQUIPMENT CO., INC.

Supreme Court of South Carolina, 1978.
271 S.C. 171, 246 S.E.2d 176.

GREGORY, J.

Respondent Odell C. Kennedy brought this action by his guardian *ad litem* [a person appointed to bring the suit] against appellant Custom Ice Equipment Company, Inc. [Custom] to recover damages he sustained when his left arm was amputated by machinery designed and installed by appellant. The jury returned a verdict for respondent [for $208,000].

* * *

On July 15, 1976, the day of the accident, Odell Kennedy had been employed at Georgetown Ice Company [Georgetown] for three days. He was fifteen years old and this was his first job.

Georgetown is in the business of manufacturing and distributing crushed or "party" ice.

Custom designed and installed the machinery used by Georgetown to manufacture ice.

Odell was instructed to enter the cold storage room at Georgetown and empty the ice storage bins. These storage bins are fed by an overhead Archimedean screw conveyor which carries the ice from the ice making machine to the bins. The ice is removed from an opening in the underside of each bin through which the ice falls when a trap door is opened. It is common for the ice in these bins to freeze up or solidify and not fall out of the bins through the trap doors. When this freezing up of the ice, or "bridging" as the condition is called, occurs, the ice has to be physically dislodged.

To this purpose, Goergetown constructed a wooden catwalk alongside the storage bins from which its employees could reach into the bins and break up the frozen ice with a garden hoe.

On the morning of the accident Odell mounted the catwalk for the first time and proceeded to dislodge the frozen ice with a garden hoe. He was drawn into the overhead conveyor by his left arm when the hoe made contact with the conveyor. Odell's left arm was torn off and he suffered disfiguring scars to his left shoulder.

It is undisputed that all machinery involved in the accident was designed and installed by appellant [Custom] and that the wooden catwalk was constructed by respondent's [Odell Kennedy's] employer, Georgetown.

Respondent's complaint alleges two causes of action against appellant: one for negligent design of the overhead screw conveyor and one based on strict liability in tort.

* * *

Appellant * * * contends it was entitled to a directed verdict as to respondent's second cause of action for strict liability in tort. Appellant alleged the screw conveyor was not defective when installed because of the insulation provided by height and argued Georgetown modified the conveyor when it constructed the catwalk and thereby created the defect.

Respondent admitted the catwalk was constructed by Georgetown, but offered evidence that appellant had actual knowledge of the construction and use of similar catwalks in other ice plants and should have foreseen the use of a catwalk by Georgetown. Respondent argued the failure to anticipate the foreseeable use of a catwalk by placing protective shields on the conveyor rendered the design of the conveyor defective. [Citation.]

The test of whether a product is defective when sold is whether the product is unreasonably dangerous to the consumer or user given the conditions and circumstances that will foreseeably attend the use of the product. Under this test, the jury could have determined that the construction of the catwalk by Georgetown was a foreseeable circumstance that required the incorporation of protective shields in the design of the conveyor. [Citation.]

The evidence created a factual question of whether respondent's injuries were proximately caused by a defect in the product as designed or by a defect created by an unforeseeable modification by a third party. [Citation.]

In Young v. Tide Craft, Inc., [citation], we held the question of proximate cause was improperly submitted to the jury where the only reasonable inference to be drawn from the evidence was that the product was not defective as designed. Since the evidence here is susceptible of the inference that the product was defective as designed, the trial judge did not err by submitting the question of proximate cause to the jury. [Citations.]

*   *   *

Affirmed.

Defective Condition—Privity

EMBS v. PEPSI-COLA BOTTLING CO. OF LEXINGTON, KENTUCKY, INC.

Court of Appeals of Kentucky, 1975.
528 S.W.2d 703.

Lukowsky, J.

This is an appeal from a judgment entered by the Clark Circuit Court dismissing the claim of plaintiff-appellant pursuant to a directed verdict granted at the completion of her proof. We reverse and remand.

On the afternoon of July 25, 1970, plaintiff-appellant entered the self-service retail store operated by the defendant-appellee, Stamper's Cash Market, Inc., for the purpose of "buying soft drinks for the kids." She went to an upright soft drink cooler, removed five bottles and placed them in a carton. Unnoticed by her, a carton of Seven-Up was sitting on the floor at the edge of the produce counter about one foot from where she was standing. As she turned away from the cooler she heard an explosion that sounded "like a shotgun."

When she looked down she saw a gash in her leg, pop on her leg, green pieces of a bottle on the floor and the Seven-Up carton in the midst of the debris. She did not kick or otherwise come into contact with the carton of Seven-Up prior to the explosion. Her son, who was with her, recognized the green pieces of glass as part of a Seven-Up bottle.

She was immediately taken to the hospital by Mrs. Stamper, a managing agent of the store. Mrs. Stamper told her that a Seven-Up bottle had exploded and that several bottles had exploded that week. Before leaving the store Mrs. Stamper instructed one of her children to clean up the mess. Apparently, all of the physical evidence went out with the trash. The location of the Seven-Up carton immediately before the explosion was not a place where such items were ordinarily kept.

The defendant-appellee, Arnold Lee Vice, was the distributor of Seven-Up in the Clark County area. As such, he supplied Stamper's Cash Market, Inc. with its entire stock of Seven-Up. He would deliver it with his truck to the store and place it in the store and the cooler. Employees of the store would also place Seven-Up in the cooler from other locations in the store. His truck was loaded with Seven-Up by the bottler at the plant.

The defendant-appellee, Pepsi-Cola Bottling Co. of Lexington, Kentucky, Inc., was the bottler who produced and supplied Vice with his entire stock of Seven-Up.

*   *   *

In *Dealers Transport Co. v. Battery Distributing Co., Ky.*, [citation] we adopted the view of strict product liability in tort expressed in Section 402A of the American Law Institute's Restatement, Second, Torts.

*   *   *

Our expressed public policy will be furthered if we minimize the risk of personal injury and property damage by charging the costs of injuries against the manufacturer who can procure liability insurance and distribute its expense among the public as a cost of doing business; and since the risk of harm from defective products exists for mere bystanders and passersby as well as for the purchaser or user, there is no substantial reason for protecting one class of persons and not the other. The same policy requires us to maximize protection for the injured third party and promote the public interest in discouraging the marketing of products having defects that are a menace to the public by imposing strict liability upon retailers and wholesalers in the distributive chain responsible for marketing the defective product which injures the bystander. The imposition of strict liability places no unreasonable burden upon sellers because they can adjust the cost of insurance protection among themselves in the course of their continuing business relationship. [Citation.]

We must not shirk from extending the rule to the manufacturer for fear that the retailer or middleman will be impaled on the sword of liability without regard to fault. Their liability was already established under Section 402A of the Restatement of Torts 2d. As a matter of public policy the retailer or middleman as well as the manufacturer should be liable since the loss for injuries resulting from defective products should be placed on those members of the marketing chain best able to pay the loss, who can then distribute such risk among themselves by means of insurance and indemnity agreements. [Citation.]

* * *

The result which we reach does not give the bystander a "free ride." When products and consumers are considered in the aggregate, bystanders, as a class, purchase most of the same products to which they are exposed as bystanders. Thus, as a class, they indirectly subsidize the liability of the manufacturer, middleman, and retailer and in this sense do pay for the insurance policy tied to the product.

Public policy is adequately served if parameters are placed upon the extension of the rule so that it is limited to bystanders whose injury from the defect is reasonably foreseeable. [Citation.]

For the sake of clarity we restate the extension of the rule. The protections of Section 402A of the Restatement, Second, Torts extend to bystanders whose injury from the defective product is reasonably foreseeable.

* * *

In cases involving multiple defendants the better reasoned view places the onus of tracing the defect on the shoulders of the dealers and the manufacturer as a policy matter, seeking to compensate the plaintiff and to require the defendants to fight out the question of responsibility among themselves. [Citation.]

The motions for a directed verdict should have been denied.

Judgment reversed, and cause remanded.

PROBLEMS

1. At the advent of the social season Aunt Lavinia purchased a hula skirt in Sadie's dress shop. The saleslady told her: "This superior garment will do things for a person." Aunt Lavinia's house guest, her niece, Florabelle, asked and obtained her aunt's permission to wear the skirt to a masquerade ball. In the midst of the festivity at which there was much dancing, drinking, and smoking, the long skirt brushed against a glimmering cigarette butt. Unknown to Aunt Lavinia and Florabelle, its wearer, the garment was made of a fine unwoven fiber which is highly flammable. It burst into flames, and Florabelle suffered severe burns. Aunt Lavinia notified Sadie of the accident and of Florabelle's intention to recover from Sadie. Florabelle seeks to recover damages in an action against Sadie, the proprietor of the dress shop, and Exotic Clothes, Inc., the manufacturer from which Sadie purchased the skirt. Decision?

2. The X Company, manufacturer of a widely advertised and expensive perfume, sold a quantity of this product to Y, a retail druggist. A and B visited the store of Y, and A, desiring to make a gift to B, purchased from Y a bottle of this perfume, asking for it by its trade name. Y wrapped up the bottle and handed it directly to B. The perfume contained an injurious foreign chemical substance which, upon the first use of the perfume by B, severely burned her face and caused a permanent facial disfigurement. What are the rights of B, if any, against A, Y, and the X Company, respectively?

3. Jane Doe, a housewife, purchased a bottle of "Bleach-All," a well-known brand, from Roe's combination service station and grocery store. When Jane Doe used the "Bleach-All," the clothes severely deteriorated due to an error made in mixing the chemicals during manufacture of "Bleach-All." Jane Doe brings an action against Roe to recover damages. Decision?

4. A route salesman for Ideal Milk Company delivered a one-half gallon glass jug of milk to Allen's home. The next day when Allen grasped the milk container by its neck to take it out of his refrigerator, it shattered in his hand and caused serious injury. Allen paid Ideal on a monthly basis for the regular delivery of milk. Ideal's milk bottles each contained the legend "Property of Ideal—to be returned," and the route salesman would pick up the empty bottles when he delivered milk. Allen brought an action against Ideal Milk Company. Decision?

5. While Butler and his wife Wanda were browsing through Sloan's used car lot, Butler told Sloan that he was looking for a safe but cheap family car. Sloan said, "That old Cadillac hearse ain't hurt at all, and I'll sell it to you for $3,950." Butler said, "I'll have to take your word for it because I don't know a thing about cars." Butler asked Sloan whether he would guarantee the car, and Sloan replied, "I don't guarantee used cars." Then Sloan added, "But I have checked that Caddy over, and it will run another 10,000 miles without needing any repairs." Butler replied, "It has to because I won't have an extra dime for any repairs." Butler made a downpayment of $400 and signed a printed form contract furnished by Sloan which contained a provision, "Seller does not warrant the merchandise's condition or performance of any used automobile described herein."

As Butler drove the car out of Sloan's lot, the left rear wheel fell off, and Butler lost control

of the vehicle. It veered over an embankment, causing serious injuries to Wanda. What is Sloan's liability to Butler and Wanda?

6. John purchased for cash a Revenge automobile manufactured by Japanese Motors, Ltd., from an authorized franchised dealer in the United States. The dealer told John that the car had a "24 months— 24,000 miles warranty." Two days after John accepted delivery of the car, he received an eighty-page fine print manual which stated, among other things, on page 72:

The warranties herein are expressly in lieu of any other express or implied warranty, including any implied warranty of merchantability or fitness, and of any other obligation on the part of the company or the selling dealer.

Japanese Motors, Ltd. and the selling dealer warrant to the owner each part of this vehicle to be free under use and service from defects in material and workmanship for a period of twenty-four months from the date of original retail delivery of first use, or until it has been driven for 24,000 miles, whichever first occurs.

Within nine months after the purchase, John has been forced to return the car for repairs to the dealer on thirty different occasions, and the car has been in the dealer's custody for over seventy days during these nine months. The dealer has been forced to make major repairs of the engine, transmission, and steering assembly. The car is now in the custody of the dealer for further major repairs, and John has demanded that it keep the car and refund his entire purchase price. The dealer has refused on the ground that it has not breached its contract and is willing to continue repairing the car during the remainder of the "24–24" period. What are the rights and liabilities of the dealer and John?

7. Fred Lyon of New York, while on vacation in California, rented a 1984 model Home Run automobile from Hart's Drive-A-Car. The car was manufactured by the X Motor Company and was purchased by Hart's from Jammer, Inc., an automobile importer. Lyon was driving the car on a street in San Jose when, due to a defect in the steering mechanism, it suddenly became impossible to steer. The speed of the car at the time was thirty miles per hour, but before Lyon could bring it to a stop, the car jumped a low curb and struck Peter Wolf standing on the sidewalk, breaking both of his legs and causing other inju-

ries. Wolf sues Hart's Drive-A-Car, the X Motor Company, Jammer, Inc., and Lyon. Decisions?

8. Plaintiff brings this cause of action against a manufacturer for the loss of one leg below the hip. The leg was lost when caught in the gears of a screw auger machine sold and installed by the defendant. Shortly before the accident, plaintiff's co-employees had removed a covering panel from the machine by use of sledgehammers and crowbars in order to do repair work. When finished, they replaced the panel with a single piece of cardboard instead of restoring the equipment to its original condition. The plaintiff stepped on the cardboard in the course of his work and fell, catching his leg in the moving parts. Decision?

9. The plaintiff, while driving a van manufactured by the defendant, was struck in the rear by another motor vehicle. Upon impact, the plaintiff's head was jarred backward against the rear window of the cab, causing the plaintiff serious injury. The van was not equipped with a headrest, and none was required at the time. Should the plaintiff prevail on a cause of action based upon strict liability in tort? Why?

10. Plaintiff, while dining at defendant's restaurant, ordered a chicken pot pie. While she was eating the food, she swallowed a sliver of chicken bone which became lodged in her throat, causing her serious injury. Plaintiff brings a cause of action. Should she prevail? Why?

Chapter 22

PERFORMANCE

PERFORMANCE of a contract is a realization of the expectations of the parties and a discharge of the duties created by the contract. The basic obligation of the seller in a contract for the sale of goods is to transfer and deliver the goods, and that of the buyer is to accept and pay for the goods in accordance with the contract.

The obligations of the parties are determined by their contractual agreement. Thus, the contract of sale may expressly provide whether the seller must deliver the goods before receiving payment of the price or whether the buyer must pay the price before receiving the goods. If the contract does not sufficiently cover the particulars of performance, these terms will be supplied by the Code, common law, course of dealings, usage of trade, and course of performance. In all events, both parties to the sales contract must perform their contractual obligations in good faith.

In order for either party to maintain against the other an action for non-performance of the contract, he must first put the other party in default. This is accomplished either by his (a) performance according to the contract, (b) tender of performance according to the contract, or (c) being excused from tender of performance. This chapter will examine the performance obligations of the seller and the buyer as well as the circumstances under which they may be excused from performance of their contractual obligations.

PERFORMANCE BY THE SELLER

Unless the parties have agreed otherwise, the Code is explicit in requiring a tender of performance by one party as a condition to performance by the other party. Section 2-507(1). Tender of conforming goods by the seller entitles him to acceptance of them by the buyer and to payment of the price according to the contract. The rights of the parties are fixed by the terms of the contract. For example, if the seller has agreed to sell goods on sixty or ninety-days' credit, he is required to perform his part of the contract in advance of performance of the buyer.

Tender of delivery requires that the seller put and hold goods which conform to the contract at the buyer's disposition and that he give the buyer reasonable notification to enable him to take delivery. Section 2-503. For example, A agrees to sell B a stereo system composed of a turntable, receiver, tape deck, and two speakers. Each component is specified by manufacturer and model number, and delivery is to be at A's store. A obtains the ordered equipment in accordance with the contractual specifications and notifies B that she may pick the system up at her convenience. A has now tendered and thus performed his obligations under the sales contract: he holds goods which conform to the contract, he has placed them at the buyer's disposition, and he has notified the buyer of their readiness.

Time and Manner of Delivery

Tender must be at a **reasonable** time, and the goods tendered must be kept available for the period reasonably necessary to enable the buyer to take possession of them. Unless otherwise agreed the buyer must furnish facilities reasonably suited to the receipt of the goods. Section 2-503.

If no definite time for delivery is fixed by the terms of the contract, the seller is allowed a reasonable time after the making of the contract within which to deliver the goods to the buyer. Likewise, the buyer has a reasonable time within which to accept delivery. What length of time is reasonable depends upon the facts and circumstances of each case. If the goods are capable of immediate delivery, a reasonable time would be very short. Where

the goods must be constructed or manufactured, a reasonable time would be longer and would depend upon all the circumstances including the usual length of time required to make the goods.

A contract is not performable piecemeal or in installments unless the parties so agree. All of the goods called for by a contract must be tendered in a single delivery, and payment is due on such tender. However, where the circumstances give either party the right to make or demand delivery in lots, the price if it can be apportioned may be demanded for each lot. Section 2-307.

Place of Tender

If the contract is silent as to the place for delivery of the goods, the place for delivery is the *seller's place of business;* or if he has none, his residence. If the contract is for the sale of identified goods which the parties know at the time of making the contract are located elsewhere than the seller's place of business or residence, the *location* of the goods is then the place for delivery. Section 2-308. For example, A, a boat builder in Chicago, contracts to sell to B a certain yacht which both parties know is anchored at Milwaukee. The place of delivery would be Milwaukee. On the other hand, if the contract provides that A shall overhaul the motor at A's shipyard in Chicago, A would have to return the yacht to Chicago, and the place of delivery would be A's Chicago shipyard.

As discussed previously in Chapter 20, the parties frequently agree expressly upon the place of delivery, typically by use of one of the various *delivery terms.* Such agreements determine the place where the seller must tender delivery of the goods.

Shipment Contracts The delivery terms F.O.B. place of shipment, F.A.S. seller's port, C.I.F., C. & F., and C.O.D. are all "shipment contracts." Under a shipment contract the seller is required or authorized to send the goods to the buyer, but the contract does not obligate her to deliver them at a particular destination. In these cases the seller's tender of performance occurs at the **point of shipment,** provided the seller meets certain specified conditions which are designed to protect the interests of the absent buyer.

Under a shipment contract the seller is required to: (1) deliver the goods to a carrier; (2) make a contract for their transportation which is reasonable according to the nature of the goods and other circumstances of the case; (3) obtain and promptly deliver or tender to the buyer any document necessary to enable the buyer to obtain possession of the goods from the carrier; and (4) promptly notify the buyer of the shipment. Section 2-504.

Destination Contracts The delivery terms "F.O.B. at city of buyer," "ex-ship," and "no arrival, no sale" are destination contracts. Since a destination contract requires the seller to tender *delivery* of conforming goods at a **specified destination,** the seller must place the goods at the buyer's disposition and give the buyer reasonable notice to enable him to take delivery. In addition, if the destination contract involves documents of title, the seller must tender the necessary documents. Section 2-503.

Goods Held by Bailee Where goods are in the possession of a bailee and are to be delivered without being moved, in most instances the seller may either tender a document of title or obtain an acknowledgment by the bailee of the buyer's right to possess the goods. Section 2-503(4).

For a summary of performance by the seller, see Figure 22–1.

Quality of Tender

The Code's perfect tender rule requires that the seller's tender conform exactly to the requirements of the contract. However, there are three basic modifications of the buyer's right to reject the goods upon the seller's failure to comply with the perfect tender rule:

(1) agreement between the parties limiting the buyer's right to reject non-conforming goods, (2) cure by the seller, and (3) installment contracts.

Perfect Tender Rule The Code imposes upon the seller the obligation that her tender of goods conform *exactly* to the requirements of the contract. The seller's tender cannot deviate in any way from the terms of the contract. If the goods or the tender of delivery fail in any respect to conform to the contract, the buyer may (1) reject the whole lot, (2) accept the whole lot, or (3) accept any commercial unit or units and reject the rest. Section 2-601. A commercial unit means such a unit of goods as by commercial usage is a single unit and which, if divided, would materially impair its character or value. Section 2-105(6). Thus, a buyer may rightfully reject the delivery of 110 dozen shirts under an agreement calling for delivery of 100 dozen shirts. The size or extent of the breach does *not* affect the right to reject. *See Moulton Cavity & Mold Inc. v. Lyn-Flex Ind.*

Agreement by the Parties The parties may contractually agree to limit the operation of the perfect tender rule. For example, they may agree that the seller shall have the right to repair or replace any defective parts or goods. Such contractual limitations are discussed in Chapter 23.

Cure by the Seller Where the buyer refuses to accept a tender of goods which do not conform to the contract, the seller by acting promptly and within the time allowed for performance may make a proper tender or delivery of conforming goods and "cure" his defective tender or performance. Section 2-508. For example, A is to deliver to B twenty-five blue shirts and fifty white shirts by October 15. On October 1, A delivers twenty-nine blue shirts and forty-six white shirts which B rejects as not conforming to the contract. B notifies A of her rejection and the reasons for it. A has until October 15 to cure the defect

FIGURE 22-1 Tender of Performance by Seller

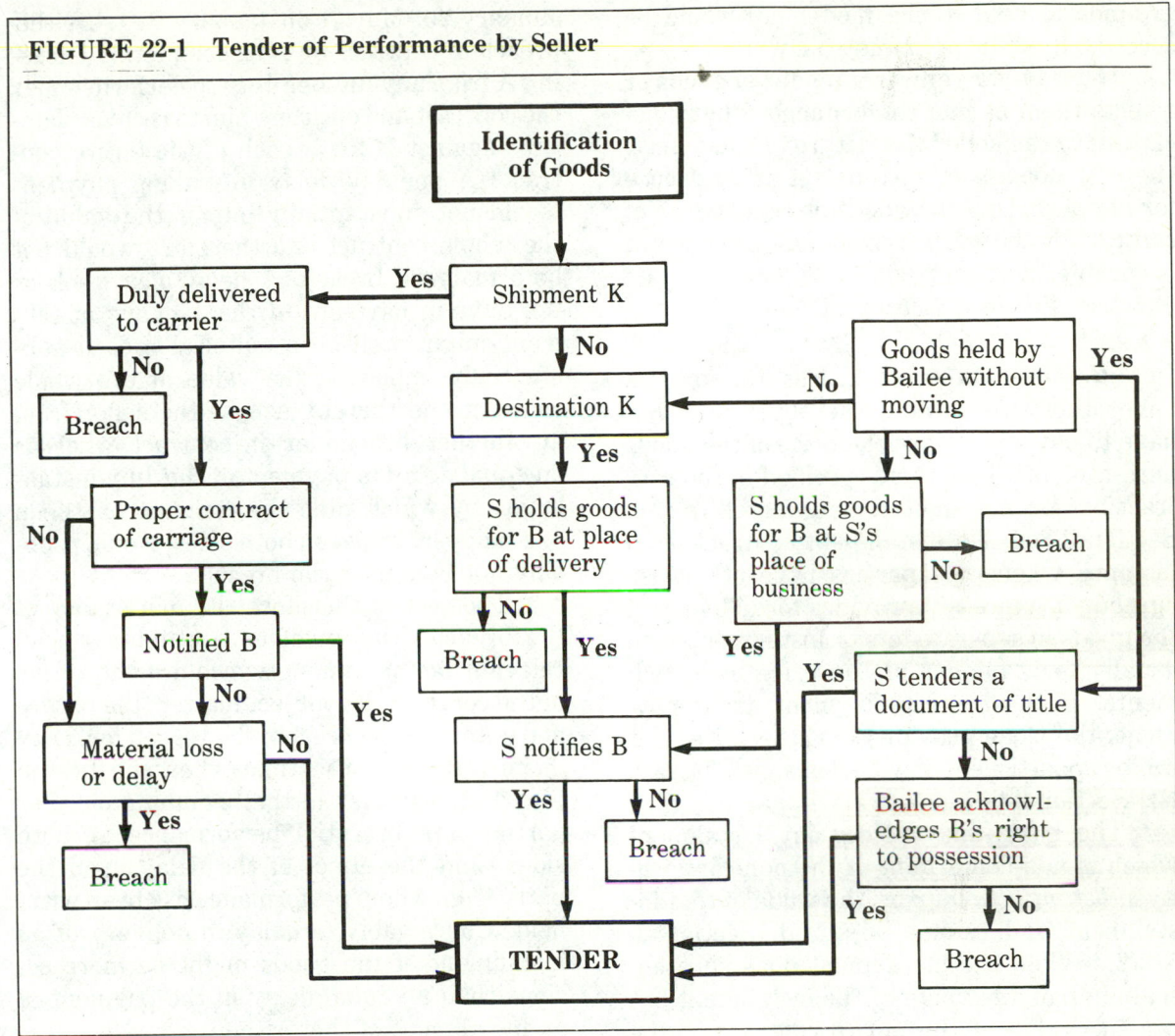

by making a perfect tender if he seasonably notifies B of his intention to do so.

The Code also provides the seller an opportunity to cure a non-conforming tender which the seller had reasonable grounds to believe would be acceptable with or without money allowance. Section 2-508(2) states:

Where the buyer rejects a non-conforming tender which the seller had reasonable grounds to believe would be acceptable with or without money allowance the seller may if he seasonably notifies the buyer have a further reasonable time to substitute a conforming tender.

For example, A orders from B a model 110X S.C.A. television to be delivered on January 20. The 110X is unavailable, but B can obtain a model 110, which is last year's model of the same television and lists for five percent less than the 110X. On January 20, B delivers to A the 110 at a discount price of ten percent less than the contract price for the 110X. A rejects the substituted television set. B promptly notifies A that he will obtain and deliver a model 110X. B will have a reasonable time beyond the January 20 deadline in which to deliver the 110X television set to A because under these facts B had reasonable grounds to believe the model 110 would be acceptable with the money allowance.

If the buyer refuses a tender of goods or rejects them as non-conforming without disclosing to the seller the nature of the defect, she may not assert such defect as an excuse for not accepting the goods or as a breach of contract by the seller if the defect is one which is curable. Section 2-605.

See Wilson v. Scampoli.

Installment Contracts Unless the parties have otherwise agreed, the buyer does not have to pay any part of the price of the goods until the entire quantity specified in the contract has been delivered or tendered to her. Section 2-307. An installment contract is an instance where the parties have otherwise agreed. It expressly provides for delivery of the goods in separate lots or installments and usually for payment of the price in installments. If the contract is silent about payment, the Code provides that the price, if it can be apportioned, may be demanded for each lot. Section 2-307.

The buyer may reject any installment which is non-conforming if the non-conformity *substantially* impairs the value of that installment and cannot be cured. Section 2-612(2). When the installment does substantially impair the value of the installment but not the value of the entire contract, if the seller gives adequate assurance of the installment's cure, then the buyer cannot reject the installment. Section 2-612(2). Whenever the non-conformity or default with respect to one or more of the installments substantially impairs the value of the whole contract, the buyer can treat the breach as a breach of the whole contract. Section 2-612(3).

For example, A makes a contract to deliver to B 50 tons of coal each month for one year, delivery to be made on the first day of each month commencing with January; B agrees to pay a certain price for each installment on the twentieth day of the month of delivery. A delivers to B 50 tons of coal on January 1. B does not pay for this coal on January 20. May A on January 21 treat this breach of contract by B as completely excusing A from any further duty to perform under the contract and entitling him to recover damages against B for breach of the entire contract? A one-day delay in making payment would not substantially impair the value of the whole contract and therefore would not be a material breach. A delay of a week or ten days in payment of the January installment might well be a material breach substantially impairing the value of the whole contract and thereby excuse the seller from any further duty under the contract, whereas an equal delay in payment of the July installment, by which time the contract has been one-half performed on both sides, would probably not be a material breach.

The test is therefore the materiality of the breach. This involves a weighing of all relevant factors among which are the terms of the contract, its subject matter, the nature and extent of the breach, the reason for delay in performance, the time when the breach occurred, whether in the beginning or after partial or substantial performance on both sides, and the effect of the delay upon the party from whom performance has been withheld. Conceivably, a delay in delivery of an installment of the goods might be more serious than an equal delay in the payment of an installment of the price.

PERFORMANCE BY THE BUYER

The obligation of the buyer is to accept conforming goods and to pay for them according to the contract terms. Tender of payment or payments by the buyer, unless otherwise agreed, is a condition to the seller's duty to tender and to complete any delivery. Thus, if the buyer has agreed to pay for the goods in advance of delivery either to the seller or to a carrier, his duty to perform is not conditional upon performance or a tender of performance by the seller. Tender of payment in the form of a check in the ordinary course of business is sufficient unless the seller demands cash and allows the buyer a reasonable time within which to obtain it. However, payment by personal check is defeated as between seller and buyer by dishonor of the check on due presentment. Section 2-511(3).

Inspection

Unless otherwise agreed between the parties, the buyer has a right to inspect the goods before payment or acceptance. Section 2-513(1). This enables him to satisfy himself that the goods tendered or delivered conform to the contract. If the contract requires payment before acceptance, such as where the contract provides for shipment C.O.D., payment must be made prior to inspection unless the non-conformity appears without inspection. Section 2-512. However, payment in such case is *not* an acceptance of the goods.

The buyer is allowed a reasonable time to inspect the goods and may lose the right to reject or revoke acceptance of non-conforming goods by failing to inspect them within a reasonable time. For example, in one case the defendant, a plumbing contractor, entered into a contract with the plaintiff, a supplier, to purchase four kitchen units per specifications. They were to be installed by the defendant in a building under construction. The plaintiff delivered the units enclosed in shipping crates to the construction site where the defendant stored them without opening the crates or inspecting the contents. Three months later the crates were opened and the units installed, when they were then found to be of defective quality and not to comply with the contract specifications. The defendant notified the plaintiff that he rejected the goods and shipped them back to the plaintiff who refused to accept them. A dismissal of plaintiff's action for the price was reversed on appeal upon the ground that the defendant had lost his right to reject or revoke acceptance as three months was not a reasonable time within which to inspect the goods and notify the seller that they were non-conforming. The case was remanded with directions to enter judgment in favor of the plaintiff for the price, subject to defendant's right to damages for breach of contract. *Cervitor Kitchens Inc. v. Chapman*, 7 Wash.App. 520, 500 P.2d 783 (1972).

The expenses of inspection must be borne by the buyer but may be recovered from the seller if the goods do not conform and are rejected. Section 2-513(2).

The buyer is not obliged to accept a tender or delivery of goods which do not conform to the contract. Upon such non-conforming tender or delivery the buyer has the choice of three alternatives. As previously noted, he may (1) reject all of the goods, (2) accept all of the goods, or (3) accept any commercial unit or units of the goods and reject the rest. Section 2-601. The buyer must pay at the contract rate for the commercial units he accepts.

Rejection

Rejection is a manifestation by the buyer of his unwillingness to become owner of the goods. It must be made within a reasonable time after the goods have been tendered or delivered. It is not effective unless the buyer seasonably notifies the seller. Section 2-602(1). *See Can-Key Industries, Inc. v. Industrial Leasing Corp.*

Rejection of the goods may be rightful or wrongful, depending on whether the goods tendered or delivered conform to the contract. The buyer's rejection of non-conforming goods or tender is rightful under the perfect tender rule.

After the buyer has rejected the goods, any exercise of ownership of the goods by her is wrongful as against the seller. If the buyer has possession of the rejected goods but no security interest in them, she is obliged to hold them with reasonable care for a time sufficient to permit the seller to remove them. The buyer who is not a merchant is under no further obligation with regard to goods rightfully rejected. Section 2-602(2).

A merchant buyer of goods who has rightfully rejected them is obligated to follow reasonable instructions from the seller with respect to the disposition of the goods in her possession or control, when the seller has no agent or business at the place of rejection. Section 2-603(1). If the merchant buyer receives no instructions from the seller within a reasonable time after notice of the rejection, and the rejected goods are perishable or threaten to decline in value speedily, she is obligated to make reasonable efforts to sell them for the seller's account. Otherwise, she may (1) store the goods for the seller's account, (2) reship them to the seller, or (3) resell them for the seller's account. Such action is not an acceptance or conversion of the goods. Section 2-604.

When the buyer sells the rejected goods, she is entitled to reimbursement from the seller or out of the proceeds for the reasonable expenses of caring for and selling them and a reasonable selling commission not to exceed ten percent of the gross proceeds. Section 2-603(2).

Acceptance

Acceptance of goods means a willingness by the buyer to become the owner of the goods tendered or delivered to him by the seller. Acceptance of the goods precludes any rejection of the goods accepted. Section 2-607(2). It includes overt acts or conduct which manifest such willingness. Acceptance may be indicated by express words, by the presumed intention of the buyer through his failure to act, or by conduct of the buyer inconsistent with the seller's ownership of the goods. More specifically, acceptance occurs when the buyer, after a reasonable opportunity to inspect the goods, (1) signifies to the seller that the goods conform to the contract, (2) signifies to the seller that he will take the goods or retain them in spite of their non-conformity to the contract, or (3) fails to make an effective rejection of the goods. Section 2-606(1). *See Import Traders, Inc. v. Frederick Manufacturing Corp.*

To illustrate: Lang Company purchased an ice cream freezer and refrigeration compressor unit from Fleet for $2,160. Although the parties agreed to a written installment contract providing for an $850 down payment and eighteen installments payments, Lang made only one $200 payment upon receipt of the goods. One year later Lang moved to a new location and took the equipment along without notifying Fleet. Then, another year later Lang disconnected the compressor from the freezer and used it to operate an air conditioner. Lang continued to use the compressor for that purpose until the sheriff seized the equipment and returned it to Fleet pursuant to a court order. Fleet then sold the equipment for $500 in what both parties conceded was a fair sale. Lang then brought an action charging that the equipment was defective and unusable for the intended purpose and sought to recover the down payment and expenses incurred in repairing the equipment. Fleet counterclaimed for the balance due under the installment contract less the proceeds from the sale. Judgment for Fleet. In order effectively to reject goods the buyer must reject the goods within a reasonable time after their delivery or tender and then seasonably notify the buyer of the rejection. The alleged rejection was not effective in that Lang failed to notify Fleet of the rejection, kept the equipment for his own use, moved it to a new location without notifying Fleet, and then used it to operate an air conditioner. These acts were inconsistent with Fleet's ownership of the goods and therefore constituted an acceptance. *F. W. Lang Co. v. Fleet*, 193 Pa.Super. 365, 165 A.2d 258 (1960).

Acceptance of any part of a commercial unit is acceptance of the entire unit. Section 2-606(2). **Commercial unit** is defined in Section 2-106(6):

"Commercial unit" means such a unit of goods as by commercial usage is a single whole for purposes of sale and division of which materially impairs its character or value on the market or in use. A commercial unit may be a single article (as a machine) or a set of articles (as a suite of furniture or an assortment of sizes) or a quantity (as a bale, gross, or carload) or any other unit treated in use or in the relevant market as a single whole.

The buyer must pay at the contract rate for such commercial units as he accepts. However, after giving the seller timely notice of the breach, he is entitled to recover from the seller or deduct from the purchase price the amount of damages for non-conformity of the commercial units accepted and for non-delivery of the commercial units rejected. Sections 2-714 and 2-717. For example, A agrees to deliver to B 500 light bulbs of 100 watts each for $300 and 100 light bulbs of 60 watts each for $500. A delivers on time but the shipment contains only 400 of the 100-watt bulbs and 750 of the 60-watt bulbs. If B accepts the shipment he must pay A $240 for the 100-watt bulbs accepted and $375 for the 60-watt bulbs accepted less the amount of damages caused B by A's non-conforming delivery.

With regard to goods rejected by the buyer, the burden is on the seller to establish their conformity to the contract; but the burden is on the buyer to establish any breach of contract or warranty with regard to goods accepted. Section 2-607(4).

Revocation of Acceptance

The buyer may revoke his acceptance of goods which do not conform to the contract and such non-conformity *substantially* impairs the value of the goods to him, provided that his acceptance was: (1) premised on the reasonable assumption that the non-conformity would be cured by the seller, and it was not seasonably cured; or (2) made without discovery of the non-conformity, and such acceptance was reasonably induced by the difficulty of discovery before acceptance or by assurances of the seller.

The test of substantial impairment of the value to the buyer of non-conforming goods is subjective rather than objective. Section 2-608(1). For example, the plaintiffs, buyers of a new mobile home on an installment contract, after moving in discovered water and air leaks and defects in doors, cabinets, vents, and walls. The defendant seller repaired some of the defects, but leakage continued creating other problems. After giving notice of revocation of acceptance, the plaintiffs continued to live in the mobile home for approximately one year. The revocation was upheld on the grounds (1) that substantial impairment of value to the buyers justifying revocation of acceptance was not to be measured objectively by the relatively small cost of repairs, but subjectively by plaintiffs' deprivation of a home for a substantial period of time; and (2) that continued occupancy of the home was not inconsistent with revocation as plaintiffs had a security interest for the down payment, and occupancy was a feasible method of preserving their collateral. *Jorgensen v. Pressnall*, 274 Or. 285, 545 P.2d 1382 (1976).

Revocation of acceptance is not effective until notification is given to the seller which must be within a reasonable time after the buyer discovers or should have discovered the grounds for revocation and before the goods have undergone any substantial change which was not caused by their own defects. Section 2-608(2). *See Peckham v. Larsen Chevrolet.* Upon revocation of acceptance, the buyer is in the same position with respect to the goods and has the same rights and duties with regard to them as if she had rejected them. Section 2-608(3).

Obligation of Payment

The terms of the contract may expressly state the time and place that the buyer is obligated to pay for the goods. If so, these terms are controlling. In the absence of agreement, payment is due at the time and place at which the buyer is to receive the goods even though the place of shipment is the place of delivery. Section 2-310(a). This rule is understandable in view of the right of the buyer to inspect the goods before being obliged to pay for them in the absence of agreement to the contrary.

Where the sale is on credit, the buyer is not obligated to pay for the goods when he receives them. The credit provision in the contract will control the time of payment. Unless the contract specifies the time when the credit period commences to run, the time commences on the date of the shipment of the goods. However, post-dating the invoice or delaying its dispatch will correspondingly delay the starting of the credit period. Section 2-310(d).

EXCUSES FOR NONPERFORMANCE

Contracts for the sale of goods necessarily involve risks that future events may or may not occur. In some instances the parties explicitly allocate these risks; in most instances they do not. The Code contains three sections that allocate these risks when the parties fail to do so themselves. Each provision, when applicable, relieves the parties from the obligation of full performance under the sales contract. The first section deals with casualty to identified goods, the second with the non-happening of presupposed conditions, and the third with substituted performance.

Casualty to Identified Goods

If goods are destroyed before an offer to sell or buy them is accepted, the offer is terminated by general contract law. But what if the goods are destroyed after the sales contract is formed? With one exception the rules for the passage of risk of loss apply. The exception is: if the contract is for goods which are identified when the contract was made, and these goods are totally lost or damaged without fault of either party and before the risk of loss passes to the buyer, the contract is avoided. Section 2-613(a). This means that the seller is no longer obligated to deliver and the buyer need not pay the price. Each party

is excused from his performance obligation under the contract.

In the case of a partial destruction or deterioration of the goods, the buyer has the option to avoid the contract or to accept the goods with due allowance or deduction from the contract price for the deterioration or deficiency in quantity. Section 2-613(b). Thus, A agrees to sell to B a specific lot of wheat containing 1,000 bushels at a price of four dollars per bushel. Without the fault of A or B fire destroys 300 bushels of the wheat. B does not have to take the remaining 700 bushels of wheat, but he has the option to do so upon paying $2,800, the price of 700 bushels.

If the destruction or casualty to the goods, whether total or partial, occurs after risk of loss has passed to the buyer, the buyer has no option but must pay the entire contract price of the goods.

Non-Happening of Presupposed Condition

The ability to perform a contract for the sale of goods is subject to a number of possible hazards, such as strikes, lockouts, unforeseen shutdown of sources of supply, or loss of plant or machinery by fire or other casualty. Ordinarily these do not operate as an excuse on the ground of impossibility of performance, unless the contract expressly so provides. However, both parties may have understood at the time the contract was made that its performance depended upon the existence of certain facilities, or that the purpose of the contract and the value of performance depended entirely upon the happening of a specific future contemplated event. In such a case the seller is excused from her duty of performance upon the non-occurrence of presupposed conditions which were a basic assumption of the contract, unless the seller has expressly assumed the risk. Section 2-615(a).

Increased production cost alone does not excuse performance by the seller, nor does a collapse of the market for the goods excuse the buyer. However, a contract for the sale of programs for a scheduled yacht regatta which is called off, or for the sale of tin horns for export which become subject to embargo, or for the production of goods at a designated factory which becomes damaged or destroyed by fire would be an excuse for non-performance.

Although the seller may be relieved of her contractual duty by the non-happening of presupposed conditions, if the contingency affects only a part of the seller's capacity to perform, she must to the extent of her remaining capacity allocate delivery and production among her customers. Section 2-615(b).

Substituted Performance

The Code provides that where neither party is at fault and the agreed manner of delivery of the goods becomes commercially impracticable, as by reason of the failure of loading or unloading facilities or unavailability of an agreed type of carrier, a substituted manner of performance, if commercially reasonable, must be tendered and accepted. Section 2-614(1). Neither seller nor buyer is excused on the ground that delivery in the express manner provided in the contract is impossible where a practical alternative or substitute exists.

If the means or manner in which the buyer is to make payment becomes impossible by reason of supervening governmental regulation, the seller may withhold or stop delivery of the goods unless the buyer provides payment which is commercially a substantial equivalent to that required by the contract. If delivery has already been made, payment as provided by the governmental regulation discharges the buyer unless the regulation is discriminatory, oppressive, or predatory. Section 2-614(2).

CASES

Perfect Tender Rule

MOULTON CAVITY & MOLD INC. v. LYN-FLEX IND.

Supreme Court of Maine, 1979.
396 A.2d 1024.

DELAHANTY, J.

Defendant, Lyn-Flex Industries, Inc., appeals from a judgment entered after a jury trial by the Superior Court, York County, in favor of plaintiff, Moulton Cavity & Mold, Inc. The case concerns itself with an oral contract for the sale of goods which, as both parties agree, is governed by Article 2 of the Uniform Commercial Code * * *. For the reasons set forth below, we agree with defendant that the presiding Justice committed reversible error by instructing the jury that the doctrine of substantial performance applied to a contract for the sale of goods.

* * *

An examination of the record discloses the following sequence of events: On March 19, 1975, Lynwood Moulton, president of plaintiff, and Ernest Sturman, president of defendant, orally agreed that plaintiff would produce, and defendant purchase, twenty-six innersole molds capable of producing saleable innersoles. The price was fixed at $600.00 per mold. Whether or not a time for delivery had been established was open to question. In his testimony at trial, Mr. Moulton admitted that he was fully aware that defendant was in immediate need of the molds, and he stated that he had estimated that he could provide suitable molds in about five weeks' time. * * *

In apparent conformity with standard practice in the industry, plaintiff set about constructing a sample mold and began a lengthy series of tests. These tests consisted of bringing the sample mold to defendant's plant, fitting the mold to one of defendant's plastic-injecting machines, and checking the innersole thus derived from the plaintiff's mold to determine if it met the specifications imposed by defendant. After about thirty such tests over a ten-week period, several problems remained unsolved. * * *

It was plaintiff's contention at trial, supported by credible evidence, that at one point during the testing period officials of defendant signified that in their judgment plaintiff's sample mold was turning out innersoles correctly configured so as to fit the model last supplied by defendant's customer. Allegedly relying on this approval, plaintiff went ahead and constructed the full run of twenty-six molds.

For its part, defendant introduced credible evidence to rebut the assertion that it had approved the fit of the molds. It also noted that Moulton's allegation of approval extended only to the fit of the mold; as Moulton conceded, defendant had never given full approval since it considered the flashing problem, among others, unacceptable.

* * *

At trial, plaintiff's basic theory of recovery was that it had received approval with regard to the fit of the sample mold, that in reliance on that approval it had constructed a full run of twenty-six molds, and that defendant had, in effect, committed an anticipatory breach of contract within the meaning of Section 2–610 by demanding that the fit of the molds be completely redesigned. On its counterclaim, and in response to plaintiff's position, defendant advanced the theory that plaintiff had breached the contract by failing to tender conforming goods within the five-week period mentioned by both parties.

After the presiding Justice had charged the jury, counsel for plaintiff requested at side bar that the jury be instructed on the doctrine of substantial performance. Counsel for defendant entered a timely objection to the proposed charge which objection was overruled. The court then supplemented its charge as follows:

The only point of clarification that I'll make, ladies and gentlemen, is that I've referred a couple of times to performance of a contract and you, obviously, have to determine no matter which way

you view the contract to be, and there might even be a possible third way that I haven't even considered, whether the contract whatever it is has been performed and there is a doctrine that you should be aware of in considering that. That is the doctrine of substantial performance.

It is not required that performance be in any case one hundred percent complete in order to entitle a party to enforcement of their contractual rights. That is not to say within the confines of this case that the existence of flashing would be excused or not be excused. It is just a recognition on the part of the law when we talk about performance, probably if we took any contract you could always find something of no substance that was not completed one hundred percent. It is for you to determine that whether it has been substantially performed or not and what in fact constitutes substantial performance.

In your consideration, and as I say in this case, that's not to intimate that something like flashing is to be disregarded or to be considered. It's up to you based upon facts.

The jury returned a verdict in favor of plaintiff in the amount of $14,480.82.

In *Smith, Fitzmaurice Co. v. Harris*, [citation], a case decided under the common law, we recognized the then-settled rule that with respect to contracts for the sale of goods the buyer has the right to reject the seller's tender if in any way it fails to conform to the specifications of the contract. We held that "[t]he vendor has the duty to comply with his order in kind, quality and amount." [Citation.] Thus, in *Smith*, we ruled that a buyer who had contracted to purchase twelve dozen union suits could lawfully refuse a tender of sixteen dozen union suits. Various provisions of the Uniform Sales Act, enacted in Maine in 1923, codified the common-law approach. [Citation.] The so-called "perfect tender" rule came under considerable fire around the time the Uniform Commercial Code was drafted. No less an authority than Karl Llewellyn, recognized as the primum mobile of the Code's tender provisions, [citations] attacked the rule principally on the ground that it allowed a dishonest buyer to avoid an unfavorable contract on the basis of an insubstantial defect in the seller's tender. Llewellyn, *On Warranty of Quality and Society*, 37 Colum. L. Rev. 341, 389 (1937). Although Llewellyn's views are represented in many Code sections governing tender, the basic tender provision, Section 2–601, represents a rejection of Llewellyn's approach and a continuation of the perfect tender policy developed by the common law and carried forward by the draftsmen of the Uniform Sales Act. [Citations.] Thus, Section 2–601 states that, with certain exceptions not here applicable, the buyer has the right to reject "if the goods or the tender of delivery fail *in any respect* to conform to the contract . . . " (emphasis supplied). Those few courts that have considered the question agree that the perfect tender rule has survived the enactment of the Code. [Citations.] We, too, are convinced of the soundness of this position.

In light of the foregoing discussion, it is clear that the presiding Justice's charge was erroneous and, under the circumstances, reversibly so.

*   *   *

Appeal sustained. New trial ordered.

Cure by the Seller

WILSON v. SCAMPOLI

District of Columbia Court of Appeals, 1967.
228 A.2d 848.

MYERS, J.

This is an appeal from an order of the trial court granting rescission of a sales contract for a color television set and directing the return of the purchase price plus interest and costs.

Appellee purchased the set in question on November 4, 1965, paying the total purchase price in cash. The transaction was evidenced by a sales ticket showing the price paid and guaranteeing ninety days' free service and replacement of any defective tube and parts for a period of one year. Two days after purchase the set was delivered and uncrated, the antennae adjusted and the set

plugged into an electrical outlet to "cook out." When the set was turned on, however, it did not function properly, the picture having a reddish tinge. Appellant's delivery man advised the buyer's daughter, Mrs. Kolley, that it was not his duty to tune in or adjust the color but that a service representative would shortly call at her house for that purpose. After the departure of the delivery men, Mrs. Kolley unplugged the set and did not use it.

On November 8, 1965, a service representative arrived, and after spending an hour in an effort to eliminate the red cast from the picture advised Mrs. Kolley that he would have to remove the chassis from the cabinet and take it to the shop as he could not determine the cause of the difficulty from his examination at the house. He also made a written memorandum of his service call, noting that the television "Needs Shop Work (Red Screen)." Mrs. Kolley refused to allow the chassis to be removed, asserting she did not want a "repaired" set but another "brand new" set. Later she demanded the return of the purchase price, although retaining the set. Appellant refused to refund the purchase price, but renewed his offer to adjust, repair, or, if the set could not be made to function properly, to replace it. Ultimately, appellee instituted this suit against appellant seeking a refund of the purchase price. After a trial, the court ruled that "under the facts and circumstances the complaint is justified. Under the equity powers of the Court I will order the parties put back in their original status, let the $675 be returned, and the set returned to the defendant."

Appellant does not contest the jurisdiction of the trial court to order rescission in a proper case, but contends the trial judge erred in holding that rescission here was appropriate. He argues that he was always willing to comply with the terms of the sale either by correcting the malfunction by minor repairs or, in the event the set could not be made thereby properly operative, by replacement; that as he was denied the opportunity to try to correct the difficulty, he did not breach the contract of sale or any warranty thereunder, expressed or implied.

[U.C.C.] 2–508 provides:

(1) Where any tender or delivery by the seller is rejected because non-conforming and the time for performance has not yet expired, the seller may seasonably notify the buyer of his intention to cure and may then within the contract time make a conforming delivery.

(2) Where the buyer rejects a non-conforming tender which the seller had reasonable grounds to believe would be acceptable with or without money allowance the seller may if he seasonably notifies the buyer have a further reasonable time to substitute a conforming tender.

A retail dealer would certainly expect and have reasonable grounds to believe that merchandise like color television sets, new and delivered as crated at the factory, would be acceptable as delivered and that, if defective in some way, he would have the right to substitute a conforming tender. The question then resolves itself to whether the dealer may conform his tender by adjustment or minor repair or whether he must conform by substituting brand new merchandise. The problem seems to be one of first impression in other jurisdictions adopting the Uniform Commercial Code as well as in the District of Columbia.

* * *

While these cases provide no mandate to require the buyer to accept patchwork goods or substantially repaired articles in lieu of flawless merchandise, they do indicate that minor repairs or reasonable adjustments are frequently the means by which an imperfect tender may be cured. In discussing the analogous question of defective title, it has been stated that:

The seller, then, should be able to cure [the defect] under subsection 2–508(2) in those cases in which he can do so without subjecting the buyer to any great inconvenience, risk, or loss. [Citations.]

Removal of a television chassis for a short period of time in order to determine the cause of color malfunction and ascertain the extent of adjustment or correction needed to effect full operational efficiency presents no great inconvenience to the buyer. In the instant case, [Scampoli's] expert witness testified that this was not infrequently necessary with new televisions. Should the set be defective in workmanship or parts, the loss would be upon the manufacturer who warranted it free from mechanical defect. Here the adamant refusal of Mrs. Kolley . . . to allow inspection essential to the determination of the cause of the excessive red tinge to the picture defeated any effort by the seller to provide timely repair or even replacement of the set if the difficulty could not be corrected. The cause of the defect might have been minor and easily adjusted or it may have been substantial and required replacement by another new set—but the seller was never given an adequate opportunity to make a determination.

We do not hold that appellant [Scampoli] has no liability to appellee [Wilson], but as he was denied access and a reasonable opportunity to repair, appellee has not shown a breach of warranty entitling him either to a brand new set or to rescission. We therefore reverse the judgment of the trial court granting rescission and directing the return of the purchase price of the set.

Reversed.

Rejection

CAN-KEY INDUSTRIES, INC. v. INDUSTRIAL LEASING CORP.

Supreme Court of Oregon, 1979.
286 Or. 173, 593 P.2d 1125.

HOWELL, J.

This is an action at law on a contract for the sale of goods. Plaintiff Can-Key Industries, Inc., manufactured a turkey hatching unit which it sold to defendant Industrial Leasing Corporation (ILC) which in turn leased it to Rose-A-Linda Turkey Farms, a California corporation. ILC's purchase order conditioned its final acceptance on Rose-A-Linda's willingness to accept the equipment. When Rose-A-Linda indicated that it was dissatisfied with the equipment, defendant refused to proceed with the contract of sale and plaintiff brought this action against ILC. From a judgment for plaintiff, defendant appeals.

*   *   *

The sole issue in this case is whether defendant "accepted" the equipment manufactured by plaintiff. The contract between plaintiff and defendant provided that defendant's obligation to pay would be conditioned upon acceptance of the equipment by its lessee. Consequently, the trial court could properly find that defendant accepted the equipment only if there is evidence that Rose-A-Linda, the lessee, accepted the equipment.

*   *   *

[U.C.C. § 2–606(1)] provides:

Acceptance of goods occurs when the buyer:
    (a) After a reasonable opportunity to inspect the goods signifies to the seller that the goods are conforming or that he will take or retain them in spite of their nonconformity; or
    (b) Fails to make an effective rejection as provided in subsection (1) of [U.C.C. § 2–602], but such acceptance does not occur until the buyer has had a reasonable opportunity to inspect them; or
    (c) Does any act inconsistent with the seller's ownership; but if such act is wrongful as against the seller it is an acceptance only if ratified by him.

No contention is made that [U.C.C. § 2–606(1)(a)] is applicable in this case. There is absolutely no evidence that Rose-A-Linda ever signified that the turkey-hatching equipment was conforming or that it would retain the equipment in spite of its nonconformity. Plaintiff does contend, however, that the trial court could have found that there was an acceptance under the terms of [U.C.C. § 2–

606(1)(b) or (c).] The applicability of these subsections will be considered separately.

Plaintiff argues that the trial court "could have found" that defendant failed to make an effective rejection and that acceptance therefore occurred under the terms of [U.C.C. § 2–606(1)(b).] Plaintiff notes that the equipment was first in use on March 3, 1976, and it was still in use as late as May 6, 1977. Plaintiff concludes that the trial court "could readily have found that 15 months was an unreasonable time to make a rejection."

Plaintiff's position can only be sustained if we ignore the uncontradicted testimony of Mr. Gibson, Rose-A-Linda's president. As noted above, Gibson testified that he twice notified plaintiff that the equipment was unacceptable and asked that it be removed.

*   *   *

In these particular circumstances, we hold that the uncontradicted testimony of Gibson is conclusive of the facts involved in this issue. [Citation.] We further hold that Gibson's statements constituted an "effective rejection" as that term is used in [U.C.C. § 2–606(1)(b).] Plaintiff's evidence that Rose-A-Linda accepted the equipment is therefore sufficient only if it shows that Rose-A-Linda performed acts inconsistent with the seller's ownership under the terms of [U.C.C. § 2–606(1)(c).]

What constitutes "any act inconsistent with the seller's ownership" has proved to be one of the trouble areas under Article 2 of the Uniform Commercial Code. Courts that have applied the provision have reached inconsistent results and commentators have termed the provision an "obstreperous" one. [Citations.] It has been suggested that "courts are first deciding upon the merits of the buyer's claim and then reasoning backwards to the determination of whether there has been an acceptance because of an inconsistent act." [Citation.]

A reasoned application of the section requires that the court recognize the existence of two competing policies. A buyer who verbally rejects goods should not in all cases be allowed to use the goods as if he were the owner and effectively "have it both ways." On the other hand, there are many cases in which use of the goods after rejection is not only reasonable in that it minimizes economic waste, but may be required under the buyer's statutory duty to mitigate consequential damages. *See* [U.C.C. § 2–715(2)(a).] The court must consider both policies when defining the scope of "any act inconsistent with the seller's ownership."

* * *

Nearly all the evidence plaintiff relies upon to demonstate that Rose-A-Linda performed acts inconsistent with plaintiff's ownership was provided by Gibson, Rose-A-Linda's president. Plaintiff did introduce testimony that Rose-A-Linda used the equipment in March and April of 1976, but it is clear from the record that these uses related to Rose-A-Linda's initial inspection of the equipment and plaintiff's efforts to solve the "problems" with the equipment that it recognized in its April letter to Rose-A-Linda. Neither of these uses was inconsistent with plaintiff's ownership of the equipment. Rose-A-Linda's initial inspection cannot be considered inconsistent with plaintiff's ownership because [U.C.C. § 2–606(1)(b)] assures a buyer of goods a "reasonable opportunity to inspect them." Nor can the use of the equipment during April be considered inconsistent, because that use was approved by plaintiff, which was attempting to solve the problems with the equipment.

Plaintiff's primary reliance is on the modifications and alterations performed by Rose-A-Linda "after the equipment was installed and functioning." These acts all occurred after Gibson notified plaintiff that the equipment was unacceptable and asked that it be removed. The only testimony concerning these acts is Gibson's. That testimony shows that Rose-A-Linda employed the original developer of the equipment in an attempt to remedy the defects. It used the equipment

four times during 1977. Three of those uses followed modifications or suggestions for modifications by the developer, and the final use was for the purpose of conducting a comparative test. Although the equipment apparently remains in Rose-A-Linda's possession, it has not been used since May of 1977.

We hold that this evidence does not demonstrate a use inconsistent with the seller's ownership under the terms of [U.C.C. § 2–606(1)(c).] To hold otherwise would have the effect of penalizing Rose-A-Linda for its apparent good faith efforts to cure the defects in the equipment. We do not believe such a holding is compelled by the language of [U.C.C. § 2–606(1)(c).] On the contrary, we think such a holding might be inconsistent with other provisions of the Code, specifically the statutory duty to mitigate consequential damages and the statutory obligation of good faith. [U.C.C. §§ 2–715(2)(a), 1–203.]

It must be remembered that this transaction involved a newly developed product, the first of its kind manufactured by plaintiff. All parties to the transaction undoubtedly expected that the equipment would have some initial "bugs." After an initial test, Rose-A-Linda found the equipment unsatisfactory and notified plaintiff to that effect. Plaintiff then attempted to remedy the problems, and Rose-A-Linda again found the equipment unsatisfactory. Rose-A-Linda asked plaintiff to remove the equipment and plaintiff refused. Plaintiff did not instruct Rose-A-Linda to refrain from using the equipment, and plaintiff has not demonstrated that Rose-A-Linda's testing and modifications damaged the equipment in any way.

* * * Viewing the evidence in the present case in a light most favorable to the plaintiff, we nevertheless conclude that, as a matter of law, Rose-A-Linda did not perform any act inconsistent with plaintiff's ownership within the meaning of [U.C.C. § 2–606(1)(c).] * * *

Because there is no evidence that Rose-A-Linda ever accepted the equipment in this case, the judgment against the defendant Industrial Leasing must be reversed.

Reversed.

Acceptance

IMPORT TRADERS, INC. v. FREDERICK MANUFACTURING CORP.

Civil Court of the City of New York, Kings County, 1983.
117 Misc.2d 305, 457 N.Y.S.2d 742.

DIAMOND, J.

* * *

Defendant-buyer ordered the goods in question on August 7, 1981 after earlier conversations with plaintiff-seller. It was clear that buyer wanted a relatively "soft" pad. The agreed purchase price was $2,580 for 500 dozen units (43¢ per unit). The goods were delivered on November 19, 1981. They were not paid for. Demand for payment was made in a timely manner. Buyer still has the goods.

Both parties knew there would be a question about exactly how soft the pads would be, when delivered.

Buyer had two samples (# 221 and # 222). His order indicated that he wanted a pad "as soft as possible—like the sample no. 222 . . . ."

Both buyer and seller could have waited for an exact sample before ordering, or confirming the order. Neither did so. Buyer's order asked for delivery "as soon as possible."

The # 221 and # 222 samples were not in evidence, but the delivered pads were harder than what buyer really wanted.

Buyer did not inspect the goods in a timely manner, especially since he was aware that there was a question about how "soft" the pads would be at the time he ordered them, and during earlier discussions.

Buyer did not advise seller of his disapproval of merchandise until April, 1982—and only then after seller contacted him at that time about payment.

Buyer desired the imported pads from Taiwan because they would be less expensive than comparable pads manufactured in the United States.

* * *

The remedies available to a seller for the breach of a sales contract, by a buyer, are provided in UCC § 2–703. In the present case, the seller has brought an action for the price pursuant to UCC § 2–709. The contract price may be recovered by seller when buyer accepts the goods. UCC § 2–709(1)(a). Acceptance occurred when buyer failed to make an effective rejection [UCC § 2–602(1)] after having had a reasonable opportunity to inspect the goods. UCC § 2–606(1)(b). Official Comment 1 to this section states, "Under this Article 'acceptance' as applied to goods means that the buyer takes particular goods which have been appropriated to the contract as his own, whether or not he is obligated to do so, and whether he does so by words, action or silence when it is time to speak." The goods were delivered to buyer in November, 1981 and it was not until April, 1982, when seller contacted buyer about payment, did buyer first complain about the non-conformity of the rubber pads. Buyer had a reasonable opportunity to inspect and reject the goods. It was his silence for five months that constituted the acceptance.

The acceptance of goods precludes their subsequent rejection. UCC § 2–607(2). Once accepted, return of the goods can only be made by way of revocation of acceptance. UCC § 2–608. "Revocation of acceptance must occur within a reasonable time after the buyer discovers or should have discovered the ground for it. . . . It is not effective until the buyer notifies the seller of it." UCC § 2–608(2). Although this assertion was not made by defendant, he failed to act within a reasonable time to revoke acceptance of the goods.

* * *

Judgment for plaintiff-seller in the amount of $2,580, plus interest from January 1, 1982, plus costs.

Revocation of Acceptance

PECKHAM v. LARSEN CHEVROLET

Supreme Court of Idaho, 1978.
99 Idaho 675, 587 P.2d 816.

SHEPARD, C. J.

This is an appeal from a summary judgment in an action by plaintiff-appellant John Peckham seeking a rescission of a contract under which he had purchased a new automobile from the defendant-respondents Larsen Chevrolet and General Motors. Summary judgment was entered in favor of defendants. We reverse on the basis that genuine issues of material fact remain for resolution.

Although the action was brought for "rescission," we treat it as one for revocation of acceptance under the Uniform Commercial Code. Peckham asserts that the action is not one for rejection of goods pursuant to [U.C.C. §§ 2–601 and 2–602], and hence we decline to discuss the potential application of the remedy of rejection to a factual situation similar to that presented here.

On March 17, 1976, Peckham purchased a new automobile for the sum of $6,400.85, by entering into an installment sale and security agreement with Larsen Chevrolet.

* * *

During the first month and one-half after the purchase of the automobile, Peckham discovered that there was a dent in the hood, the gas tank contained no baffles, the emergency brake was inoperable, that the automobile did not contain a jack or spare tire, and that the clock and speedometer were inoperable. He asserts that despite repeated attempts to have those defects repaired, they were not finally completed until June 11, 1976. Larsen Chevrolet, on the other hand, argues that all of the alleged defects were known by Peckham at the time of purchase.

On July 15, 1976, a fire occurred in the dashboard of the automobile, resulting in damage to it and the carpeting, and also rendering the vehicle inoperable. Peckham has stated in an affidavit in opposition to the motion for summary judgment that the automobile was thereafter returned to Larsen Chevrolet and he informed Larsen Chevrolet that they had the responsibility of repairing the vehicle at their expense and otherwise he would either rescind the contract or demand a new automobile. There appears to have ensued a discussion relating to the damage from the fire being the responsibility of Peckham's insurance company. Peckham contends that at the conclusion of that discussion he orally informed Larsen Chevrolet that he was electing to rescind the contract and was demanding the return of the purchase price. Larsen Chevrolet denies having received that alleged oral notice of rescission.

* * *

On October 12, 1976, Peckham's written notice of rescission was sent to Larsen Chevrolet and General Motors and Peckham's complaint was filed on January 26, 1977. * * *

Sale of the automobile here is a sale of goods governed by Article 2 of the Uniform Commercial Code. [U.C.C.] 2–711 sets forth in general a buyer's remedies. It is provided therein that a buyer may cancel the contract if the seller's delivery is such that it gives the buyer a right to reject or a right to revoke acceptance of the goods.

* * * The principal issue in this case is whether Peckham has sufficiently established the elements necessary for a revocation of acceptance under [U.C.C.] 2–608, so as to avoid a summary judgment in favor of the defendants.

Before a buyer may revoke acceptance under [U.C.C.] 2–608, he must first show that the goods are nonconforming and that the nonconformity substantially impairs the value of the goods to the buyer * * *.

Thereafter, if the buyer knew of the nonconformity when he accepted the goods, it is necessary that he show he acted with a reasonable assumption that the nonconformity would be cured, but that it was not seasonably cured. [U.C.C.] 2–608(1)(a). If the buyer did not know of the nonconformity when he accepted, he must show that his acceptance was reasonably induced, either by the difficulty of discovering the nonconformity before acceptance or by the seller's assurances. [U.C.C.] 2–608(1)(b); [citation.] Finally, the revocation of acceptance by the buyer must occur within a reasonable time after the buyer discovers the defect or should have discovered it, and before any substantial change in condition of the goods which is not caused by their own defects. Such revocation of acceptance is not effective until the buyer notifies the seller. [U.C.C.] 2–608(2).

* * *

Considering the requisite elements for a revocation of acceptance and the facts construed most favorably toward Peckham, a factual dispute exists as to whether Peckham orally notified Larsen Chevrolet of his desire to cancel or rescind the contract (revocation of acceptance) immediately following the fire. Such is denied by Larsen Chevrolet. Depending upon the resolution of that disputed fact, also unresolved is whether Peckham's alleged oral or written notice of cancellation of the contract took place within a reasonable time.

As explained by comment 4 to § 2–608(2) of the Uniform Commercial Code, revocation of acceptance is required within . . . a reasonable time after discovery of the grounds for such revocation. Since this remedy will be generally resorted to only after attempts at adjustment have failed, the reasonable time period should extend in most cases beyond the time in which notification of breach must be given, beyond the time for discovery of non-conformity after acceptance and beyond the time for rejection after tender.

It would appear that no particular form or content of notice of revocation of acceptance is required if the notice is sufficient to inform the seller that the buyer has revoked and identify the particular goods as to which he has revoked. [Citations.]

A further factual issue appears to remain regarding the conformity of the goods. Here there appears to be a dispute as to whether the goods were accepted by Peckham in a defective nonconforming condition or whether he accepted the goods upon assurance by the seller that the defects would be remedied.

* * *

The cause is reversed and remanded for further proceedings consistent with this opinion.

PROBLEMS

1. A contracted with B to manufacture, sell, and deliver to B and put in running order a certain machine. A set up the machine and put it in running order. B found it unsatisfactory and notified A that she rejected the machine. She continued to use it for three months, but continually complained of its defective condition. At the end of the three months she notified A to come and get it. Has B lost her right (a) to reject the machine? (b) to revoke acceptance of the machine?

2. Smith, having contracted to sell to Beyer thirty tons of described fertilizer, shipped to Beyer by carrier thirty tons of fertilizer which he stated conformed to the contract. Nothing was stated in the contract as to time of payment, but Smith demanded payment as a condition of handing over to Beyer the fertilizer. Beyer refused to pay unless he were given the opportunity to inspect the fertilizer. Smith sues Beyer for breach of contract. Decision?

3. A and B entered into a contract for the sale of 100 barrels of flour. No mention was made of any place of delivery. Thereafter, B demanded that A deliver the flour at B's place of business, and A demanded that B come and take the flour from A's place of business. Neither party acceded to the demand of the other. Has either one a right of action against the other?

4. A, a manufacturer of air conditioning units, makes a written contract with B to sell and deliver to B forty units at a price of $200 each and to

deliver them at a certain apartment building owned by B for installation by B. Upon the arrival of A's truck for delivery at the apartment building, B examines the units on the truck, counts only thirty units, and asks the driver if this is the total delivery. The driver replies that it is as far as he knows. B tells the driver that she will not accept delivery of the units. The next day A telephones B and inquires why delivery was refused. B states that the units on the truck were not what she ordered in that she ordered forty units and that only thirty were tendered, and that she was going to buy air conditioning units elsewhere. In an action by A against B for breach of contract, B defends upon the ground that the tender of thirty units was improper as the contract called for delivery of forty units. Is this a valid defense?

5. S sells a sofa to B for $800. S and B both know that the sofa is in S's warehouse located approximately ten miles from B's home. The contract did not specify the place of delivery, and B insists that the place of delivery is either B's house or S's store. Is B correct?

6. On November 4, S contracted to sell to B 500 sacks of flour at four dollars each to be shipped in November to B in X City. On November 27, S shipped the flour. By December 5, when the car arrived, containing only 450 sacks, the market price of flour had fallen. The usual time required for shipment was five to twelve days. B refused to accept delivery or to pay. S shipped fifty more sacks of flour which arrived December 10. B refused delivery. S resold the flour for three dollars per sack. What are S's rights against B?

7. A and B enter into a written contract whereby A agrees to sell and B to buy 6,000 bushels of wheat at $3.75 per bushel, deliverable at the rate of 1,000 bushels a month commencing June 1, the price for each installment being payable ten days after delivery thereof. A delivered and received payment for the June installment. A defaulted by failing to deliver the July and August installments. By August 15, the market price of wheat had increased to four dollars per bushel. B thereupon entered into a contract with C to purchase 5,000 bushels of wheat at four dollars per bushel deliverable over the ensuing four months. In late September, the market price of wheat commenced to decline and by December 1 was $3.25 per bushel. B brings an action against A for breach of contract. Decision?

8. Bain ordered from Marcum a carload of lumber which he intended to use in the construction of small boats for the U.S. Navy pursuant to contract. The order specified that the lumber was to be free from knots, wormholes, and defects. The lumber was shipped, and immediately upon receipt Bain looked into the door of the fully loaded car, ascertained that there was a full carload of lumber, and acknowledged to Marcum that the carload had been received. On the same day Bain moved the car to his private siding and sent to Marcum full payment in accordance with the terms of the order.

A day later the car was moved to the work area and unloaded in the presence of the Navy inspector, who refused to allow three-fourths of it to be used because of excessive knots and wormholes in the lumber. Bain then informed Marcum that he was rejecting the order and requested refund of the payment and directions as to disposition of the lumber. Marcum replied that since Bain had accepted the order and unloaded it, he was not entitled to return of the purchase price. Bain thereupon brought an action against Marcum to recover the purchase price. Decision?

Chapter 23

REMEDIES

THE performance of a contract for the sale of goods may require total performance at one point or part performance in stages, and at any stage one of the parties may breach or repudiate the contract, or insolvency of one of the parties may occur. Breach may occur when the goods are in the possession of the seller while identified to the contract, or in the possession of a bailee of the buyer, or in transit to the buyer, or in the possession of the buyer. Moreover, the goods may be conforming or non-conforming to the contract. The buyer may have justifiably or unjustifiably rejected the goods on tender or delivery or revoked his acceptance of them. Remedies, therefore, are necessary to address not only the type of breach of contract but also the factual situation with respect to the goods. Consequently, the Code provides separate and distinct remedies for the seller and for the buyer, each specifically keyed to the factual situation.

In all events, the purpose of the Code is to put the aggrieved party in as good a position as if the other party had fully performed. This purpose has been furthered by the Code's rejection of the doctrine of election of remedies. Essentially, the Code provides that remedies for breach are cumulative in nature. Whether one remedy bars another depends entirely on the facts of the individual case.

REMEDIES OF THE SELLER

When a buyer defaults in any of his contractual obligations, the seller has been deprived of the rights for which he bargained. The buyer's default may consist of any of the following acts: the buyer wrongfully rejects the goods, the buyer wrongfully revokes acceptance of the goods, the buyer fails to make a payment due on or before delivery, or the buyer repudiates the contract in whole or in part. Section 2-703 of the Code catalogs the seller's remedies for each of these defaults. These remedies are:

1. to withhold delivery of the goods;
2. to stop delivery of the goods by a carrier or other bailee;
3. to identify conforming goods to the contract not already identified;
4. to resell the goods and recover damages;
5. to recover damages for non-acceptance of the goods or repudiation of the contract;
6. to recover the price;
7. to recover incidental damages;
8. to cancel the contract; and
9. to reclaim the goods upon the buyer's insolvency.

It is useful to note that the first three and the ninth remedies indexed above are **goods oriented** in that they relate to the seller's exercising control over the goods. The fourth through seventh remedies are **money oriented** because they provide the seller with the opportunity to recover monetary damages. The eighth remedy is **obligation oriented** as it allows the seller to avoid his obligation under the contract.

Moreover, it should be observed that if the seller delivers goods on credit and the buyer fails to pay the price as it comes due, the seller's sole remedy, unless the buyer is insolvent, is to sue for the unpaid price. If, however, the buyer received the goods on credit while insolvent, the seller may be able to reclaim the goods. **Insolvency** is defined by the Code to include both its equity meaning and its bankruptcy meaning. Section 1-201(23). The **equity** meaning of insolvency is the inability of a person to pay his debts in the ordinary course of business or as they become due. The **bankruptcy** meaning is that total liabilities exceed the total value of all assets.

As noted above, the Code's remedies are **cumulative.** Thus, by way of example, an aggrieved seller may (1) identify goods to the contract; *and* (2) withhold delivery; *and* (3) resell or recover damages for non-acceptance or recover the price; *and* (4) recover incidental damages; *and* (5) cancel the contract.

To Withhold Delivery of the Goods

A seller may withhold delivery of the goods to a buyer who has wrongfully rejected or revoked acceptance of the goods, or has failed to make a payment due on or before delivery, or has repudiated the contract. Section 2-703. This right is essentially that of a seller to withhold or discontinue performance of her side of the contract by reason of the buyer's breach.

Where the contract calls for installments, any breach of an installment which impairs the value of the *whole* contract will permit the seller to withhold the entire undelivered balance of the goods. In addition, upon discovery of the buyer's insolvency, the seller may refuse to deliver the goods except for cash, including payment for all goods previously delivered under the contract. Section 2-702.

To Stop Delivery of the Goods

An extension of the right to withhold delivery is the right of an aggrieved seller to stop delivery of the goods in transit to the buyer or in the possession of a bailee. The seller accomplishes this by timely notification to the carrier or other bailee to stop delivery of the goods. After such notification the carrier or bailee must hold and deliver the goods according to the directions of the seller who is liable to the carrier or bailee for any charges or damages incurred. Section 2-705(3).

If the seller discovers the buyer to be insolvent, then the seller may stop *any* delivery. If the buyer is not insolvent but repudiates or otherwise breaches the contract, the seller may stop carload, truckload, planeload, or larger shipments.

The right of the seller to stop delivery ceases when (1) the buyer receives the goods; or (2) the bailee of the goods, except a carrier, acknowledges to the buyer that he holds them for the buyer; or (3) the carrier acknowledges to the buyer that he holds them for the buyer by reshipment or as warehouseman; or (4) a negotiable document of title covering the goods is negotiated to the buyer. Section 2-705(2).

To Identify Goods to the Contract

Upon a breach of the contract by the buyer, the seller may proceed to identify to the contract conforming goods in her possession or control which were not so identified at the time she learned of the breach. Section 2-704(1). Furthermore, the seller may resell any unfinished goods which have demonstrably been intended for fulfillment of the particular contract. With respect to such unfinished goods, the seller may either complete their manufacture and identify them to the contract or cease their manufacture and resell the unfinished goods for scrap or salvage value. Section 2-704(2). In so deciding, the seller must exercise reasonable judgment in order to minimize her loss.

For example, if at the time of the buyer's breach or repudiation the goods in the process of manufacture are 90% finished, in order to avoid loss and obtain maximum realization of value a seller may be justified in completing their manufacture and reselling them as finished goods. On the other hand, if at the time of breach the manufacturing process has only just commenced, sound business judgment may require that the manufacture be halted in order to mitigate loss and damage.

To Resell the Goods
and Recover Damages

Under the same circumstances which permit the seller to withhold delivery of goods to the buyer (i.e., wrongful rejection or revocation, repudiation, or failure to make timely payment), the seller may resell the goods concerned or the undelivered balance of the goods.

If the resale is made in good faith and in a commercially reasonable manner, the seller may recover from the buyer the **difference between the resale price and the contract price,** *together* with any incidental damages (discussed below), *less* expenses saved in consequence of the buyer's breach. Section 2-706(1). For example, A agrees to sell goods to B for a contract price of $8,000 due on delivery. B wrongfully rejects the goods and refuses to pay A anything. A resells the goods in strict compliance with the Code for $6,000 and incurs incidental damages for sales commissions of $500 but saves $200 in transportation costs. A would recover from B the contract price ($8,000) minus the resale price ($6,000) plus incidental damages ($500) minus expenses saved ($200) which equals $2,300.

The resale may be a public or private sale, and the goods may be sold as a unit or in parcels. The goods resold must be identified as those related to the contract, but it is not necessary that the goods be in existence or that they have been identified to the contract before the buyer's breach. Section 2-706(2).

Where the resale is a private sale, the seller must give the buyer reasonable notice of his intention to resell. Section 2-706(3).

Where the resale is at a public sale, only identified goods can be sold except where there is a recognized market for a public sale of future goods of the kind involved. The public sale must be made at a usual place or market for public sale if one is reasonably available. The seller must give the buyer reasonable notice of the time and place of the resale unless the goods are perishable or threaten to decline in value speedily. Prospective bidders at the sale must be given an opportunity for reasonable inspection of the goods before the sale. The seller may be a purchaser of the goods at the public sale. Section 2-706(4).

The seller is not accountable to the buyer for any profit made on any resale of the goods. Moreover, a *bona fide* purchaser at a resale takes the goods free of any rights of the original buyer, even though the seller has failed to comply with one or more of the requirements of the Code with respect to making the resale. Section 2-706(5).

To Recover Damages for Non-Acceptance or Repudiation

The seller, in the event of the buyer's repudiation, failure to make timely payment, or wrongful rejection or revocation, may recover damages from the buyer measured by the **difference between the market price** at the time and place of tender of the goods **and the unpaid contract price,** *plus* incidental damages, *less* expenses saved in consequence of the buyer's breach. Section 2-708(1). This remedy is an alternative to the remedy of reselling the goods.

For example, A in Seattle agrees to sell goods to B in Chicago for $20,000 F.O.B. Chicago, delivery on June 15. B wrongfully rejects the goods. The market price would be ascertained as of June 15 in Chicago because F.O.B. Chicago is a destination contract in which the place of tender would be Chicago. The market price of the goods on June 15 in Chicago is $15,000. A incurred $1,000 in incidental expenses while saving $500 in expenses. A's recovery from B would be the contract price ($20,000), minus the market price ($15,000), plus incidental damages ($1,000), minus expenses saved ($500), which equals $5,500.

If the difference between the market price and the contract price is inadequate to place the seller in as good a position as performance would have done, then the measure of damages is the profit, including reasonable overhead, which the seller would have realized from full performance by the buyer, plus any incidental damages less expenses saved in consequence of the buyer's breach. Section 2-708(2). For example, A, an automobile dealer, enters into a contract to sell a large, luxury, fuel-inefficient car to B for $22,000. The price of gasoline increases 20 percent, and B repudiates. The market value of the car is still $22,000, but because A cannot sell as many cars as he can obtain, A's sales volume has decreased by one due to B's breach. Therefore, A would be permitted to recover the profits he lost on the sale to B (computed as the contract price minus what the car costs A plus an allocation of overhead) plus any incidental damages. *See Teradyne, Inc. v. Teledyne Industries, Inc.*

To Recover the Price

Under the common law an action by the seller to recover the price depended upon a transfer of title to the buyer. The Code permits the seller to recover the price in three situations: (1) where the buyer has accepted the goods; (2) where conforming goods have been lost or damaged after the risk of loss has passed to the buyer; and (3) where the goods have been identified to the contract and there is no ready market available for their resale at a reasonable price. Section 2-709(1). *See French v. Sotheby & Co.*

A seller who sues for the price must hold for the buyer any goods which have been identified to the contract and are still in her control. If resale becomes possible, the seller may resell the goods at any time prior to the collection of the judgment, and the net proceeds of such resale must be credited to the buyer. Payment of the judgment entitles the buyer to any goods not resold. Section 2-709(2).

If the buyer has wrongfully rejected or revoked acceptance of the goods or has repudiated or failed to make a payment due, a seller who is held not entitled to recover the price shall be awarded damages for non-acceptance of the goods. Section 2-709(3).

To Recover Incidental Damages

In addition to recovering damages for the difference between the resale price and the contract price, or recovering damages for non-acceptance or repudiation, or recovering the price, the seller may also recover in the same action her incidental damages. Incidental damages are defined by Section 2-710 as follows:

Incidental damages to an aggrieved seller include any commercially reasonable charges, expenses or commissions incurred in stopping delivery, in the transportation, care and custody of goods after the buyer's breach, in connection with return or resale of the goods or otherwise resulting from the breach.

To Cancel the Contract

Where the buyer wrongfully rejects or revokes acceptance of the goods, or fails to make a payment due on or before delivery, or repudiates the contract in whole or in part, the seller may cancel the contract with respect to the goods directly affected. If the breach is of an installment contract and it substantially impairs the whole contract, the seller may cancel the entire contract. Section 2-703(f).

The Code defines cancellation as the putting an end to the contract by one party by reason of a breach by the other. Section 2-106. The obligation of the canceling party for any future performance under the contract is discharged, although she retains any remedy for breach of the whole contract or any unperformed balance. Thus, if the seller has the right to cancel, she may recover damages for breach without having to tender any further performance.

To Reclaim the Goods
Upon Buyer's Insolvency

In addition to the right of an unpaid seller to withhold and stop delivery of the goods, he may reclaim them from an insolvent buyer by demand upon the buyer within ten days after the buyer has received the goods. Section 2-702(2). Moreover, where the buyer has committed fraud by a misrepresentation of her solvency made to the seller in writing within three months prior to delivery of the goods, the ten-day limitation does not apply.

The seller's right to reclaim, however, is subject to the rights of a purchaser of the goods from the buyer in ordinary course or other good faith purchaser. Upon a successful reclamation of the goods from an insolvent buyer, the seller is excluded from all other remedies with respect to them. Section 2-702(3).

REMEDIES OF THE BUYER

There are basically three different ways in which a seller may default: he may repudiate; he may fail to deliver the goods without repudiation; or he may deliver or tender goods that do not conform to the contract. The Code provides remedies for each of these breaches. Some remedies are available for all of these types of breaches, while others are only available for certain types. Moreover, some remedies must be triggered by certain actions taken by the buyer. For example, if the seller tenders non-conforming goods, the buyer may reject or accept them. If the buyer rejects them, he will have a number of remedies from which to choose. On the other hand, if the buyer accepts the non-conforming goods and does not justifiably revoke his acceptance, he will limit himself to recovering damages.

Where the seller fails to make delivery or repudiates, or the buyer rightfully rejects or justifiably revokes acceptance, the buyer may with respect to any goods involved, or with respect to the whole if the breach goes to the whole contract, (1) cancel, *and* (2) recover payments made. In addition, the buyer may (3) "cover" and have damages, *or* (4) recover damages for non-delivery. Where the seller fails to deliver or repudiates, the buyer where appropriate may also (5) recover identified goods if the seller is insolvent, *or* (6) replevy the goods, *or* (7) obtain specific performance. Moreover, upon rightful rejection or justifiable revocation of acceptance, the buyer (8) has a security interest in the goods. Where the buyer has accepted goods and given notification to the seller of their non-conformity, the buyer may (9) recover damages for breach of warranty. Finally, in addition to the remedies listed above, the buyer may, where appropriate, (10) recover incidental damages, and (11) recover consequential damages.

It may be observed that the first remedy catalogued above is **obligation oriented;** the second through fourth and ninth through eleventh are **money oriented;** while the fifth through eighth are **goods oriented.**

To Cancel the Contract

Where the seller fails to make delivery or repudiates the contract, or where the buyer rightfully rejects or justifiably revokes acceptance of goods tendered or delivered to him, the buyer may cancel the contract with respect to any goods involved, and if the breach by the seller goes to the whole contract, the buyer may cancel the entire contract. Section 2-711(1).

The buyer must give the seller notice of his cancellation of the contract and is not only excused from further performance or tender on his part but also may "cover" and have damages or recover damages from the seller for non-delivery of the goods. Section 2-711(1).

To Recover Payments Made

The buyer, upon the seller's breach, may also recover so much of the price as has been paid. Section 2-711(1). For example, A and B enter into a contract for a sale of goods for a contract price of $3,000, and B, the buyer, has made a down payment of $600. A delivers non-conforming goods to B who rightfully rejects them. B may cancel the contract and recover the $600 plus whatever other damages he may prove.

To Cover

Upon the seller's breach the buyer may protect himself by obtaining "cover." This means that the buyer may in good faith and without unreasonable delay proceed to purchase goods

or make a contract to purchase goods in substitution for those due under the contract from the seller. Section 2-712(1). This right enables the buyer to assure himself of the needed goods.

Upon making a reasonable contract of cover the buyer may recover from the seller the **difference between the cost of cover and the contract price,** *plus* any incidental and consequential damages *less* expenses saved in consequence of the seller's breach. Section 2-712(2). For example, A, whose factory is in Oakland, agrees to sell goods to B, in Atlanta, for $22,000 F.O.B. Oakland. A fails to deliver and B covers by purchasing substitute goods for $25,000, incurring $700 in sales commissions. B suffered no other damages as a consequence of A's breach. Shipping costs from Oakland to Atlanta for the goods are $1,300. B would recover the cost of cover ($25,000), less the contract price ($22,000), plus incidental damages ($700 in sales commissions), minus expenses saved ($1,300 in shipping costs B need not pay under the contract of cover), which equals $2,400. *See Bigelow-Sanford, Inc. v. Gunny Corp.*

The buyer is not required to effect "cover," and his failure to do so does not bar him from any other remedy provided by the Code. Section 2-712(3). However, the buyer may not recover consequential damages which he could have prevented by cover. Section 2-715(2)(a). To illustrate: a farmer who made a contract in April to sell to a grain dealer 40,000 bushels of corn deliverable in October, unequivocally informed the buyer on June 3 that he was not going to plant any corn, that he would not fulfill the contract, and that if the buyer had commitments to resell the corn he should make other arrangements. This was an anticipatory repudiation of the contract. Under Section 2-610(a) the aggrieved party may await performance for a commercially reasonable time, or under 2-610(b) resort to any remedy for breach. The court held that a commercially reasonable time expired on June 3, as the buyer had no reasonable expectation of performance by the seller, and "cover" was available. The buyer was therefore denied under Section 2–715(2) the consequential damages that he could have prevented by cover, and was allowed to recover from the seller only the difference between the contract price and the June 3 futures market price for corn to be delivered for October. This was substantially less than the actual loss sustained by the grain dealer who in vain had awaited performance of the repudiated contract until October and then had to buy corn at a greatly increased price on the market in order to fulfill commitments to his purchasers. *Oloffson v. Coomer*, 11 Ill.App.3d 918, 296 N.E.2d 871 (1973).

To Recover Damages for Non-Delivery or Repudiation

In the event that the seller repudiates the contract or fails to deliver the goods, or the buyer rightfully rejects or justifiably revokes acceptance of the goods, the buyer is entitled to recover damages from the seller measured by the **difference between the market price** at the time when the buyer learned of the breach **and the contract price,** together *with* incidental and consequential damages, *less* expenses saved in consequence of the seller's breach. Section 2-713(1). The market price is to be determined as of the place for tender, or, in the event that the buyer has rightfully rejected the goods or has justifiably revoked his acceptance of them, the market price is to be determined as of the place of arrival. Section 2-713(2).

For example, A agrees to sell goods to B for $7,000 C.O.D. delivery by November 15. A fails to deliver. As a consequence B suffered incidental damages of $1,500 and consequential damages of $1,000. In the case of non-delivery or repudiation, market price is determined as of the place of tender. Since C.O.D. is a shipment contract, the place of tender would be the seller's city. Therefore, the market price must be determined in the seller's city and on November 15, the date when B learned of the breach. At this time

and place the market price is $8,000. B would recover the market price ($8,000), minus the contract price ($7,000), plus incidental damages ($1,500), plus consequential damages ($1,000), less expenses saved ($0 in this example), which equals $3,500.

In the example above, if A had instead delivered non-conforming goods which B rejected, then the market price would be determined at B's place of business; if instead A repudiated the contract on November 1, then the market price would be determined on that date.

To Recover Identified Goods Upon the Seller's Insolvency

Where existing goods are identified to the contract of sale, the buyer acquires a **special property** in the goods. Section 2-501. This special property exists even though the goods are non-conforming and the buyer has the right to return or reject them. Identification of the goods to the contract may be made either by the buyer or by the seller.

The Code gives the buyer a right, which does not exist at common law, to recover from an insolvent seller the goods in which the buyer has a special property and for which he has paid a part or all of the price. This right exists where the seller, who is in possession or control of the goods, becomes insolvent within ten days after receipt of the first installment of the price. To exercise it the buyer must tender to the seller any unpaid portion of the price. If the special property exists by reason of an identification made by the buyer, he may recover the goods only if they conform to the contract for sale. Section 2-502.

To Sue for Replevin

Replevin is a form of action at law to recover specific goods in the possession of a defendant which are being unlawfully withheld from the plaintiff. The buyer may maintain against the seller an action for replevin for goods which have been identified to the contract where the seller has repudiated or breached the contract, if (1) the buyer after a reasonable effort is unable to effect cover for such goods, or (2) the goods have been shipped under reservation of a security interest in the seller and satisfaction of this security interest has been made or tendered. Section 2-716(3).

To Sue for Specific Performance

Other than the limited right of replevin, in an action at law the buyer may recover only a money judgment against a seller who refuses or fails to perform. Ordinarily, compensatory money damages are an adequate remedy. However, where the contract is for the purchase of a unique item such as a work of art, a famous racehorse, or an heirloom, money damages may not be an adequate remedy, and in such case a court of equity has jurisdiction to order the seller specifically to deliver to the buyer the goods described in the contract upon payment of the price. Section 2-716(1). In addition, the Code provides that a decree for specific performance may include terms and conditions as to payment of the price, damages, or other relief. Section 2-716(2).

To Enforce a Security Interest in the Goods

A buyer who has rightfully rejected or justifiably revoked his acceptance of goods which remain in his possession or control has a security interest in these goods to the extent of any payment of the price which he has made and for any expenses reasonably incurred in their inspection, receipt, transportation, care, and custody. The buyer may hold such goods and resell them in the same manner as an aggrieved seller may resell goods. Section 2-711(3). In the event of resale the buyer is required to account to the seller for any excess of the net proceeds of the resale over the amount of his security interest. Section 2–706(6).

To Recover Damages for Breach in Regard to Accepted Goods

Where the buyer has accepted non-conforming goods and has given timely notification to the seller of the breach of contract, the buyer is entitled to maintain an action at law to recover from the seller the damages resulting in the ordinary course of events from the seller's breach. Section 2-714(1). In a proper case incidental and consequential damages may also be recovered. Section 2-714(3).

In the event of breach of warranty, the measure of damages is the **difference** at the time and place of acceptance **between the value of the goods which have been accepted and the value** that the goods would have had if they had been **as warranted**, unless special circumstances show proximate damages of a different amount. Section 2-714(2). In addition, incidental and consequential damages, where appropriate, may also be recovered.

The contract price of the goods does not figure in this computation, as the buyer is entitled to the benefit of his bargain, which is to receive goods that are as warranted. For example, A agrees to sell goods to B for $1,000. The value of the goods accepted is $800, but if they had been as warranted, their value would have been $1,200. The buyer's damages for breach of warranty are $400, which he may deduct from any unpaid balance due on the purchase price upon notice to the seller of his intention to do so. Section 2-717.

To Recover Incidental Damages

In addition to such remedies as covering, recovering damages for non-delivery or repudiation, or recovering damages for breach of warranty, the buyer may recover incidental damages. Section 2-715(1) of the Code defines the buyer's incidental damages as follows:

Incidental damages resulting from the seller's breach include expenses reasonably incurred in inspection, receipt, transportation and care and custody of goods rightfully rejected, any commercially reasonable charges, expenses or commissions in connection with effecting cover and any other reasonable expense incident to the delay or other breach.

For example, the buyer of a racehorse justifiably revokes acceptance because the horse does not conform to the contract. The buyer will be allowed to recover as incidental damages the cost of caring for the horse from the date the horse was delivered until it is returned to the seller.

It should be noted that the incidental damages listed in Section 2-715(1) are not intended to be exhaustive but merely illustrative of typical kinds of incidental damages. Comment 1 to Section 2-715.

To Recover Consequential Damages

In many cases the remedies discussed above will not fully compensate the aggrieved buyer for her losses. For example, non-conforming goods that are accepted may explode and destroy the buyer's warehouse and its contents. Goods that are not delivered may have been the subject of a lucrative contract of resale, the profits from which are lost. The Code responds to this problem by providing the buyer with the opportunity to recover consequential damages resulting from the seller's breach including (1) any loss resulting from the buyer's requirements and needs of which the seller at the time of contracting had reason to know and which could not reasonably be prevented by cover or otherwise; and (2) injury to person or property proximately resulting from any breach of warranty. Section 2-715(2).

An illustration of the first type of consequential damage is: A, a manufacturer, contracts to sell B, a dealer in used machinery, a used machine that B plans to resell. A repudiates and B is unable to obtain a similar machine elsewhere. B's damages include the net profit that he would have made on resale of the machine. On the other hand, consider

the following: A contracts to sell B a used machine to be delivered at B's factory by June 1, for $10,000. A repudiates the contract on May 1. By reasonable efforts B could buy a similar machine from C for $11,000 in time to be delivered by June 1. B fails to do so and loses a profit of $5,000 that he would have made from the resale of the machine. B's damages do *not* include the loss of the $5,000 profit, but he can recover $1,000 from A. Sections 2-713(1), 2-715(2)(a).

An example of the second type of consequential damage is: A sells a machine to B, warranting its suitability for B's purpose. The machine is not suitable for B's purpose and causes $10,000 in damage to B's property and $15,000 in personal injuries. B can recover the $25,000 consequential loss in addition to any other loss suffered.

For a summary of the remedies available to both the buyer and the seller for breach of a sales contract, see Figure 23-1.

CONTRACTUAL PROVISIONS AFFECTING REMEDIES

Within specified limits, the Code permits the parties to a sales contract to modify, exclude, or limit by agreement the remedies or damages that will be available for breach of that contract. There are two basic types of contractual provisions that affect remedies: (1) liquidation or limitation of damages and (2) modification or limitation of remedy.

Liquidation or Limitation of Damages

The parties may provide in their contract for liquidated damages by specifying the amount or measure of damages which either party may recover in the event of a breach by the other party. The amount of such damages must be reasonable and commensurate with the anticipated or actual loss resulting from

---

FIGURE 23-1   Remedies for Breach

Buyer's Breach	Seller's Breach
1) B wrongfully rejects	1) B rightfully rejects
2) B wrongfully revokes acceptance	2) B justifiably revokes acceptance
3) B fails to make payment	3) S fails to deliver
4) B repudiates	4) S repudiates
	5) B accepts non-conforming goods

Seller's Remedy   **Buyer's Remedy**

Obligation Oriented

(1–4)	Cancel	Cancel	(1–4)

Goods Oriented

(1–4)	Withhold delivery of goods	Recover payments made	(1–4)
(3)	Reclaim goods upon B's insolvency	Recover identified goods if S is insolvent	(3,4)
(1–4)	Stop delivery of goods by carrier or bailee	Have security interest	(1,2)
(1–4)	Identify conforming goods to contract		

Money Oriented

(1–4)	Resell and recover damages	Cover and recover damages	(1–4)
(1–4)	Recover damages for non-acceptance	Recover damages for non-delivery	(1–4)
		Recover damages for breach of warranty	(5)

Specific Performance

(1–4)	Recover price	Replevy goods	(3,4)
		Obtain specific performance	(3,4)

---

a breach. A provision in a contract fixing unreasonably large liquidated damages is void as a penalty. Section 2-718(1).

Modification or Limitation of Remedy by Agreement

The contract between the seller and buyer may expressly provide for remedies in addition to or in lieu of those provided in the Code and may limit or change the measure of damages recoverable in the event of breach. Section 2-719(1). For instance, the contract may validly limit the remedy of the buyer to a return of the goods and a refund of the price, or to the replacement of non-conforming goods or parts.

A remedy provided by the contract, however, is deemed optional unless it is expressly agreed to be exclusive of other remedies, in which event it is the sole remedy. Moreover, where circumstances cause an exclusive or limited remedy to fail of its essential purpose, resort may be had to the remedies provided by the Code. Section 2-719(2). *See Wilson Trading Corp. v. David Ferguson, Limited.*

The contract may expressly limit or exclude consequential damages unless such limitation or exclusion would be unconscionable. Limitation of consequential damages for personal injuries resulting from breach of warranty in the sale of consumer goods is *prima facie* unconscionable, whereas limitation of such damages where the loss is commercial is not. Section 2-719(3).

CASES

Seller's Damages for Non-acceptance or Repudiation

TERADYNE, INC. v. TELEDYNE INDUSTRIES, INC.

United States Court of Appeals, First Circuit, 1982.
676 F.2d 865.

WYZANSKI, J.

* * *

The following facts, derived from the master's report, are undisputed.

On July 30, 1976 Teradyne, Inc. ("the seller"), a Massachusetts corporation, entered into a Quantity Purchase Contract ("the contract") which, though made with a subsidiary, binds Teledyne Industries, Inc., a California corporation ("the buyer"). That contract governed an earlier contract resulting from the seller's acceptance of the buyer's July 23, 1976 purchase order to buy at the list price of $98,400 (which was also its fair market value) a T-347A transistor test system ("the T-347A"). One consequence of such governance was that the buyer was entitled to a $984 discount from the $98,400 price.

The buyer canceled its order for the T-347A when it was packed ready for shipment scheduled to occur two days later. The seller refused to accept the cancellation.

The buyer offered to purchase instead of the T-347A a $65,000 Field Effects Transistor System ("the FET") which would also have been governed by "the contract." The seller refused the offer.

After dismantling, testing, and reassembling at an estimated cost of $614 the T-347A, the seller, pursuant to an order that was on hand prior to the cancellation, sold it for $98,400 to another purchaser (hereafter "resale purchaser").

Teradyne would have made the sale to the resale purchaser even if Teledyne had not broken its contract. Thus if there had been no breach, Teradyne would have made two sales and earned two profits rather than one.

The seller was a volume seller of the equipment covered by the July 23, 1976 purchase order. The equipment represented standard products of the seller and the seller had the means and capacity to duplicate the equipment for a second sale had the buyer honored its purchase order.

* * *

The parties are agreed that § 2–708(2) applies to the case at bar. Inasmuch as this conclusion is not plain from the text, we explain the reasons why we concur in that agreement.

Section 2–708(2) applies only if the damages provided by § 2–708(1) are inadequate to put the seller in as good a position as performance would have done. Under § 2–708(1) the measure of damages is the difference between unpaid contract price and market price. Here the unpaid contract price was $97,416 and the market price was $98,400. Hence no damages would be recoverable under § 2–708(1). On the other hand, if the buyer had performed, the seller (1) would have had the proceeds of two contracts, one with the buyer Teledyne and the other with the "resale purchaser" and (2) *it seems* would have had in 1976–7 one more T-347A sale.

A literal reading of the last sentence of § 2–708(2)—providing for "due credit for payments or proceeds of resale"—would indicate that Teradyne recovers nothing because the proceeds of the resale exceeded the price set in the Teledyne-Teradyne contract. However, in light of the statutory history of the subsection, it is universally agreed that in a case where after the buyer's default a seller resells the goods, the proceeds of the resale are not to be credited to the buyer if the seller is a lost volume seller—that is, one who had there been no breach by the buyer, could and would have had the benefit of both the original contract and the resale contract.

Thus, despite the resale of the T-347A, Teradyne is entitled to recover from Teledyne what § 2–708(2) calls its expected "profit (including reasonable overhead)" on the broken Teledyne contract.

Teledyne not only "does not dispute that damages are to be calculated pursuant to § 2–708(2)" but concedes that the formula used in Jericho Sash & Door Co. v. Building Erectors Inc., [citation], for determining lost profit including overhead—that is, the formula under which direct costs of producing and selling manufactured goods are deducted from the contract price in order to arrive at "profit (including reasonable overhead)" as that term is used in § 2–708(2)—"is permissible provided all variable expenses are identified."

* * *

Teledyne's more significant objection to Teradyne's and the master's application of the Jericho formula in the case at bar is that neither of them made deductions on account of the wages paid to testers, shippers, installers, and other Teradyne employees who directly handled the T-347A, or on account of the fringe benefits amounting in the case of the fringe benefits amounting in the case of those and other employees to 12 per cent of wages. Teradyne gave as the reason for that those wages would not have been affected if each of the testers, etc. handled one product more or less. However, the work of those employees entered as directly into producing and supplying the T-347A as did the work of a fabricator of a T-347A. Surely no one would regard as "reasonable overhead" within § 2–708(2) the wages of a fabricator of a T-347A even if his wages were the same whether he made one product more or less. We conclude that the wages of the testers, etc. likewise are not part of overhead and as a "direct cost" should have been deducted from the contract price. A fortiori fringe benefits amounting to 12 per cent of wages should also have been deducted as direct costs. Taken together we cannot view these omitted items

as what Jericho called "relatively insignificant items." We, therefore, must vacate the district court's judgment. [Citations.] [We] remand this case so that with respect to the omitted direct labor costs specified above the parties may offer further evidence and the court may make the findings "with whatever definiteness and accuracy the facts permit, but no more." [Citation.]

* * *

The district court's judgment is vacated and the case is remanded to the district court to proceed in accordance with this opinion.

Seller's Right to Recover Price

FRENCH v. SOTHEBY & CO.
Supreme Court of Oklahoma, 1970.
470 P.2d 318.

DAVISON, J.

* * *

Plaintiff is located in London, England. Defendant is a resident of Ardmore, Oklahoma, but was in Europe most of the time, where her children were in school.

Plaintiff's petition (filed July 19, 1965) and amendment thereto alleged that defendant was indebted to plaintiff on open account in the sum of $24,886.27 for merchandise purchased by defendant on March 22, 1965, and March 25, 1965. The attached statement of account stated Sotheby & Co. were Auctioneers of Works of Art in London, England, and showed that the merchandise consisted of eight ancient or antique guns bought (bid in) for 10,480 pounds, on which there had been credited on May 6, 1965, the amount of 1,571 pounds, 2 shillings, and 3 pence, leaving a balance due of 8,908 pounds, 17 shillings, and 9 pence. It was alleged that the value of the British pound at the time the debt was made was $2.7937.

* * *

Defendant contends that regardless of all other questions, it was error of law to render judgment for the price of the guns. It is defendant's position that under the circumstances reflected by the record the defendant's liability, if any, would be only for the difference between the market price and the upaid contract price.

Sec. 2–703, of Uniform Commercial Code, provides in part that where the buyer wrongfully rejects acceptance of goods, the aggrieved seller may: "(d) resell and recover damages as hereafter provided (Section 2–706); (e) recover damages for non-acceptance (Section 2–708) or in a proper case the price (Section 2–709); "

* * * Plaintiff did not proceed under Subd. (d) and elected to seek recovery of the price.

Sec. 2–708 referred to in Subd. (d) * * * provides that the measure of damages for non-acceptance or repudiation by the buyer is the difference between the market price at the time and place for tender and the unpaid contract price together with any incidental damages, but less expenses saved in consequence of the buyer's breach.

Defendant did not accept the guns, they are still in the possession of plaintiff. The remedy provided by Sec. 2–708 and Subd. (e) of Sec. 2–703, is clearly and distinctly described therein. * * * This remedy was available to plaintiff, but plaintiff sought recovery of the price.

This leaves for consideration the statutory provisions governing actions to recover the price of goods.

Sec. 2–709 states in part as follows:

(1) When the buyer fails to pay the price as it becomes due the seller may recover, together with any incidental damages under the next section, the price:

(a) of goods accepted or of conforming goods lost or damaged within a commercially reasonable time after risk of their loss has passed to the buyer; and

(b) of goods identified to the contract if the seller is unable after reasonable effort to resell them at a reasonable price or the circumstances reasonably indicate that such effort will be unavailing.

* * *

Applying the provisions of Sec. 2–709 to the present situation, there is nothing in the record to show that the goods were accepted, or that they were lost after risk thereof has passed to defendant, or that plaintiff was unable to resell them at a reasonable price. The record lacked an essential fact, the presence of which was necessary to entitle plaintiff to recover the balance of the price of the goods.

* * *

[Judgment for French; Sotheby may not recover the price but is limited to recovery of damages for non-acceptance.]

Buyer's Remedy of Cover

BIGELOW-SANFORD, INC. v. GUNNY CORP.

United States Court of Appeals, Fifth Circuit,
Unit B, 1981.
649 F.2d 1060.

KRAVITCH, J.

[The plaintiff, Bigelow-Sanford, Inc., contracted with defendant Gunny Corp. for the purchase of 100,000 linear yards of jute at $.64 per yard. Gunny delivered 22,228 linear yards in January 1979. The February and March deliveries required under the contract were not made, and 8 rolls (each roll containing 66.7 linear yards) were delivered in April. With 72,265 linear yards undelivered Gunny told Bigelow-Sanford that no more would be delivered. In mid-March Bigelow-Sanford then turned to the jute spot market to replace the balance of the order at a price of $1.21 per linear yard. Since several other companies had also defaulted on their jute contracts with Bigelow-Sanford, the plaintiff purchased a total of 164,503 linear yards on the spot market. Plaintiff sues defendant to recover losses sustained as a result of the breach of contract.]

* * *

Gunny contends that appellee's [Bigelow-Sanford] alleged cover purchases should not have been used to measure damages in that they were not made in substitution for the contract purchases, were not made seasonably or in good faith and were not shown to be due to Gunny's breach. [W]e disagree. Again, we quote UCC § 2–711 providing in part for cover damages where the seller fails to make delivery or repudiates the contract:

(1) Where the seller fails to make delivery or repudiates or the buyer rightfully rejects or justifiably revokes acceptance then with respect to any goods involved, and with respect to the whole if the breach goes to the whole contract (2–612), the buyer may cancel and whether or not he has done so may in addition to recovering so much of the price as has been paid

(a) "cover" and have damages under the next section as to all the goods affected whether or not they have been identified to the contract; or

(b) recover damages for non-delivery as provided in this Article (2–713).

UCC § 2–712 defines cover:

(1) After a breach within the preceding section the buyer may "cover" by making in good faith and without unreasonable delay any reasonable purchase of or contract to purchase goods in substitution for those due from the seller.

(2) The buyer may recover from the seller as damages the difference between the cost of cover and the contract price together with any incidental or consequential damages as hereinafter defined (2–715), but less expenses saved in consequence of the seller's breach.

(3) Failure of the buyer to effect cover within this section does not bar him from any other remedy.

In addition, the purchaser may recover under 2–713:

(1) Subject to the provisions of this Article with respect to proof of market price (2–723), the measure of damages for non-delivery or repudiation by the seller is the difference between the market price at the time when the buyer learned of the breach and the contract price together with any incidental and consequential damages provided in this Article (2–715), but less expenses saved in consequence of the seller's breach.

(2) Market price is to be determined as of the place for tender or, in cases of rejection after arrival or revocation of acceptance, as of the place of arrival.

Most importantly, "whether a plaintiff has made his cover purchases in a reasonable manner poses a classic jury issue." [Citation.] The district court thus acted properly in submitting the question of cover damages to the jury, which found that Gunny had breached, appellee had covered, and had done so in good faith without unreasonable delay by making reasonable purchases, and was therefore entitled to damages under § 2–712. Gunny argues Bigelow is not entitled to such damages on the ground that it failed to make cover purchases without undue delay and that the jury should not have been permitted to average the cost of Bigelow's spot market purchases totalling 164,503 linear yards in order to arrive at the cost of cover for the 72,265 linear yards Gunny failed to deliver. Both arguments fail. Gunny notified Bigelow in February that no more jute would be forthcoming. Bigelow made its first spot market purchases in mid-March. Given that it is within the jury's province to decide the reasonableness of the manner in which cover purchases were made, we believe the jury could reasonably decide such purchases, made one month after the date the jury assigned to Gunny's breach, were made without undue delay. The same is true with respect to Gunny's second argument: Bigelow's spot market purchases were made to replace several vendors' shipments. Bigelow did not specifically allocate the spot market replacements to individual vendors' accounts, however, nor was there a requirement that they do so. The jury's method of averaging such costs and assigning them to Gunny in proportion to the amount of jute if [sic] failed to deliver would, therefore, seem not only fair but well within the jury's permissible bounds.

Gunny also argues that the court erroneously charged the jury regarding damages under both §§ 2–712 and 2–713. We disagree.

Whether Bigelow covered was a question of fact submitted to the jury. In the event that it had not, alternative damages were available to Bigelow under § 2–713. [Citation.] The jury found that Bigelow had covered and awarded damages under § 2–712; § 2–713 then became irrelevant. Since either was applicable until that time, the court's charge as to both sections was not error.

*   *   *

[Judgment for Bigelow is affirmed.]

Limitation of Remedies

WILSON TRADING CORP. v. DAVID FERGUSON, LIMITED

Court of Appeals of New York, 1968.
23 N.Y.2d 398, 297 N.Y.S.2d 108, 244 N.E.2d 685.

JASEN, J.

The plaintiff, Wilson Trading Corporation, entered into a contract with the defendant, David Ferguson, Ltd., for the sale of a specified quantity of yarn. After the yarn was delivered, cut, and knitted into sweaters, the finished product was washed. It was during this washing that it was discovered that the color of the yarn had "shaded"—that is, "there was a variation in color from piece to piece and within the pieces." This defect, the defendant claims, rendered the sweaters "unmarketable."

This action for the contract price of the yarn was commenced after the defendant refused payment. As a defense to the action and as a counterclaim for damages, the defendant alleges that "[p]laintiff has failed to perform all of the conditions of the contract on its part required to be performed, and has delivered *   *   * defective and unworkmanlike goods."

The sales contract provides in pertinent part:

2. No claims relating to excessive moisture content, short weight, count variations, twist, quality or shade shall be allowed *if made after weaving, knitting, or processing*, or more than 10 days after receipt of shipment. *   *   * The buyer shall within 10 days of the receipt of the merchandise by himself or agent examine the merchandise for any and all defects. (Emphasis supplied.)

*   *   *

Special Term granted plaintiff summary judgment for the contract price of the yarn sold on the ground that "notice of the alleged breach of warranty for defect in shading was not given within the time expressly limited and is not now available by way of defense or counterclaim." The Appellate Division affirmed, without opinion.

The defendant on this appeal urges that the time limitation provision on claims in the contract was unreasonable since the defect in the color of the yarn was latent and could not be discovered until after the yarn was processed and the finished product washed.

Defendant's affidavits allege that its sweaters were rendered unsaleable because of latent defects in the yarn which caused "variation in color from piece to piece and within the pieces." *   *   * Indeed, the plaintiff does not seriously dispute the fact that its yarn was unmerchantable, but instead, like Special Term, relies upon the failure of defendant to give notice of the breach of warranty within the time limits prescribed by paragraph 2 of the contract.

Subdivision (3) (par.[a]) of section 2–607 of the Uniform Commercial Code expressly provides that a buyer who accepts goods has a reasonable time after he discovers or should have discovered a breach to notify the seller of such breach. *   *   * Defendant's affidavits allege that a claim was made immediately upon discovery of the breach of warranty after the yarn was knitted and washed, and that this was the earliest possible moment at which the defects could reasonably be discovered in the normal manufacturing process. *   *   *

However, the Uniform Commercial Code allows the parties, within limits established by the code, to modify or exclude warranties and to limit remedies for breach of warranty. *   *   *

We are, therefore, confronted with the effect to be given the time limitation provision in * * * the contract. * * *

Parties to a contract are given broad latitude within which to fashion their own remedies for breach of contract (Uniform Commercial Code, § 2–316, subd. [4]; §§ 2–718–2–719). Nevertheless, it is clear from the official comments to section 2–719 of the Uniform Commercial Code that it is the very essence of a sales contract that at least minimum adequate remedies be available for its breach. "If the parties intend to conclude a contract for sale within this Article they must accept the legal consequence that there be at least a fair quantum of remedy for breach of the obligations or duties outlined in the contract. Thus any clause purporting to modify or limit the remedial provisions of this Article in an *unconscionable manner* is subject to deletion and in that event the remedies made available by this Article are applicable as if the stricken clause had never existed." [Citation.]

It follows that contractual limitations upon remedies are generally to be enforced unless unconscionable. * * *

However, it is unnecessary to decide the issue of whether the time limitation is unconscionable on this appeal for section 2–719 (subd. [2]) of the Uniform Commercial Code provides that the general remedy provisions of the code apply when "circumstances cause an exclusive or limited remedy to fail of its essential purpose." As explained by the official comments to this section: "where an apparently fair and reasonable clause because of circumstances fails in its purpose or operates to deprive either party of the substantial value of the bargain, it must give way to the general remedy provisions of this article." [Citation.] Here * * * the contract bars all claims for shade and other specified defects made after knitting and processing. Its effect is to eliminate any remedy for shade defects not reasonably discoverable within the time limitation period. It is true that parties may set by agreement any time not manifestly unreasonable whenever the code "requires any action to be taken within a reasonable time" [citation], but here the time provision eliminates all remedy for defects not discoverable before knitting and processing and section 2–719 (subd. [2]) of the Uniform Commercial Code therefore applies.

* * * The time limitation clause of the contract, therefore, insofar as it applies to defects not reasonably discoverable within the time limits established by the contract, must give way to the general code rule that a buyer has a reasonable time to notify the seller of breach of contract after he discovers or should have discovered the defect. [Citation.]

* * *

The order of the Appellate Division should be reversed, with costs, and plaintiff's motion for summary judgment should be denied.

PROBLEMS

1. A contracts to sell 1,000 bushels of wheat to B at four dollars per bushel. Just prior to the time A was to deliver the wheat, B notified her that he would not receive or accept the wheat. A sold the wheat for $3.60 per bushel, the market price, and later sued B for the difference of $400. B claims he was not notified by A of the resale and, hence, not liable. Decision?

2. On December 15, 1984, A wrote a letter to B stating that he would sell to B all of the mine run coal that B might wish to buy during the calendar year 1985 for use at B's factory, delivered at the factory at a price of forty dollars per ton. B immediately replied by letter to A stating that he accepted the offer, that he would purchase all of his mine run coal from A, and that he would need 200 tons of coal during the first week in January 1985. During the months of January, February, and March, A delivered to B a total of 700 tons of coal, for all of which B made payment to A at the rate of forty dollars per ton. On April 10, B ordered 200 tons of mine run coal from A who replied to B on April 11 that he could not supply A with

any more coal except at a price of forty-eight dollars per ton delivered. B thereafter purchased elsewhere at the market price, namely forty-eight dollars per ton, all of the requirements of his factory of mine run coal for the remainder of the year amounting to a total of 2,000 tons of coal. B now brings an action against A to recover damages at the rate of eight dollars per ton for the coal thus purchased amounting to $16,000. Decision?

3. On January 10, B, of Emanon, Missouri, visited the show rooms of the X Piano Company in St. Louis and selected a piano. A sales memorandum of the transaction signed both by B and by the salesman of the X Piano Company read as follows: "Sold to B one new Andover piano, factory number 46832, price $3,300 to be shipped to the buyer at Emanon, Missouri, freight prepaid, before February 1. Prior to shipment seller will stain the case a darker color in accordance with buyer's directions and will make the tone more brilliant." On January 15, B repudiated the contract by letter to the X Piano Company. The Company subsequently stained the case, made the tone more brilliant, and offered to ship the piano to B on January 26. B persisted in her refusal to accept the piano. In an action by the X Piano Company against B to recover the contract price, what judgment?

4. Sims contracted in writing to sell Blake 100 electric motors at a price of $100 each, freight prepaid to Blake's warehouse. By the contract of sale Sims expressly warranted that each motor would develop twenty-five brake horsepower. The contract provided that the motors would be delivered in lots of twenty-five per week beginning January 2, that Blake should pay for each lot of twenty-five motors as delivered, but that Blake was to have right of inspection upon delivery.

Immediately upon delivery of the first lot of twenty-five motors on January 2, Blake forwarded Sims a check for $2,500, but upon testing each of the twenty-five motors Blake determined that none of the twenty-five motors would develop more than fifteen brake horsepower.

State all of the remedies available to Blake.

5. A and B entered into a written contract whereby A agreed to sell and B agreed to buy a certain automobile for $3,500. A drove the car to B's residence and properly parked it on the street in front of B's house where he tendered it to B and requested payment of the price. B refused to take the car or pay the price. A informed B that he would hold him to the contract; but before A had time to enter the car and drive it away, a fire truck, answering a fire alarm and traveling at a high speed, crashed into the car and demolished it. A brings an action against B to recover the price of the car. Who is entitled to judgment? Would there be any difference in result if A were a dealer in automobiles?

6. A sells and delivers to B on June 1 certain goods and receives from B at the time of delivery B's check in the amount of $900 for the goods. The following day B is petitioned into bankruptcy, and the check is dishonored by B's bank. On June 5, A serves notice upon B and the trustee in bankruptcy that she reclaims the goods. The trustee is in possession of the goods and refuses to deliver them to A. What are the rights of the parties?

7. The ABC Company, located in Chicago, contracted to sell a carload of television sets to Dodd in St. Louis, Missouri, on sixty-days' credit. ABC Company shipped the carload to Dodd. Upon arrival of the car at St. Louis, Dodd paid the freight charges, and reshipped the car to Hines of Little Rock, Arkansas, to whom he had previously contracted to sell the television sets. While the car was in transit to Little Rock, Dodd was adjudged bankrupt. ABC Company was informed of this at once and immediately telegraphed XYZ Railroad Company to withhold delivery of the television sets. What should the XYZ Railroad Company do?

8. S in Chicago entered into a contract to sell certain machines to B in New York. The machines were to be manufactured by S and shipped F.O.B. Chicago not later than March 25. On March 24, when S is about to ship the machines, he receives a telegram from B wrongfully repudiating the contract. The machines cannot readily be resold for a reasonable price being of a special kind used only in B's manufacturing processes. S sues B to recover the agreed price of the machines. What are the rights of the parties?

Commercial Paper

PUBLIC POLICY, SOCIAL ISSUES AND BUSINESS ETHICS

COMMERCIAL paper includes checks, promissory notes, drafts, and certificates of deposit. These instruments are crucial to the sale of goods and services as well as the financing of most businesses. The use of commercial paper has increased to such an extent that payments made with these instruments, in particular checks, are now many times greater than payments made with cash. In fact, the use of currency has been primarily relegated to smaller transactions. Accordingly, the vital importance of commercial paper as a method of payment cannot be overstated:

A reliable payment system is crucial to the economic growth and stability of the nation. The smooth functioning of markets for virtually every good and service is dependent upon the smooth functioning of banking and financial markets, which in turn is dependent upon the integrity of the nation's payment mechanism. History tells us—all too vividly—that fragility of a country's payment system can precipitate or intensify a general economic crisis. *Federal Reserve Bulletin*, September 1984 at p. 708.

To accomplish these social and economic objectives the payment system must be quick, sure, and efficient. The use of cash can never satisfy all of these requirements because (1) it is inconvenient to maintain large quantities of cash, (2) the risk of loss or theft is far too great, (3) the risk in sending cash is likewise too high as is the cost of postage and insurance in shipping cash over long distances, and (4) the costs to the Federal government of maintaining an adequate supply of currency would be prohibitive. In addition, commercial paper used for payment provides a convenient receipt as well as a record for accounting and tax purposes. Although commercial paper acts as a very close approximation of cash for the purpose of payment, it is not the exact equivalent of cash because, for example, commercial paper may be forged, it may be drawn on insufficient funds, payment may be stopped, or the instrument may be materially altered. Nevertheless, these risks (which are real but very infrequent as over 99 percent of all checks are paid), assume small proportions compared to the advantages that commercial paper provides for payment. Consequently, a major policy objective of the law of commercial paper and the bank collection process is to reduce these risks by increasing the safety, soundness, and operating efficiency of the entire payment system.

Given the central role of commercial paper in the payment system, it is important to be aware of the social and ethical issues arising out of the use of commercial paper. A number of these issues involve the relationship between a customer and his bank. For instance, should a customer have the right to stop payment on a check? If so, under what conditions? At whose expense? How long should a stop payment order be effective? What effect do stop payment orders have upon public confidence in the payment system? With regard to the risks of forgeries, who should bear the loss: the bank or the customer? Given the enormous volume of checks written daily can a bank be expected to "know" the signatures of all of its customers? These are just some of the public policy questions concerning customer/bank relations that the reader should consider in studying this part of the text.

Equally important are the ethical issues concerning the forthrightness of banks in informing their customers of their rights as depositors. What obligations should a financial institution have to inform its customers of their rights? What responsibility should the customer have to inform himself of his rights? Should the State or Federal governments be involved in resolving these issues?

Closely related is the ethical question regarding what essential services should financial institutions provide and how much they should charge for the services. It has been argued that with the deregulation of the financial services industry current customer services fees greatly favor large customers at heavy financial cost to lower income households. Testimony of Professor Nicholas M. Didow before the Committee on Banking, Finance and Urban Affairs, United States House of Representatives, April 12, 1984. Should such disparate treatment be permitted? Who should be responsible for monitoring such developments?

Another significant ethical question that various legislative and administrative bodies are now addressing concerns the right of banks to "hold" deposited checks before making the funds available to its depositors. Some banks hold checks for up to fifteen days prior to permitting the customer to use funds to enable the bank to determine the validity of the check. Such delay permits the banks to use the funds while at the same time requires the depositor to cover its checks with other funds. Some States are now restricting the time period for which financial institutions may hold checks.

The current payment system has transformed the United States into a virtually "cashless" society. The advent and technological advances of computers make it likely that in the foreseeable future electronic fund transfer systems will bring about a "checkless" society. Such a system could increase the speed and efficiency of the payment system by eliminating the cumbersome process of moving paper. However, there are important, and to date unanswered questions, regarding the safety of electronic fund transfer systems. Moreover, it is not yet determined how, if at all, such a system would be able to perform all of the various functions now accomplished by checks.

Commercial paper also serves an equally important role in facilitating the creation and transfer of debt. One of the most significant policy issues regarding commercial paper as a credit device is the *negotiability* of commercial paper. Negotiability confers upon those transferees who qualify as holders in due course greater rights against parties liable upon the instrument than the payee possessed.

In 1975 the Federal Trade Commission intervened by promulgating a rule which sharply limits the rights of a holder in due course of an instrument which evidences a debt arising out of a consumer credit contract which includes commercial paper. The rule preserves claims and defenses of consumer buyers and borrowers against holders in due course. The rule raises a number of policy questions. Is it desirable? What will its impact be upon the availability and cost of consumer credit? Should its application be extended to all credit transactions? Should it be administratively imposed. Should it be promulgated by the Federal government.

While studying Part Five the reader should consider these and other social, ethical, and policy issues in order to determine the reasonableness, appropriateness and, above all, the fairness of the legal principles of commercial paper.

Chapter 24

FORM AND CONTENT

JUST as no business could be operated without the law of contracts, modern business could not be conducted without the use of commercial paper—checks, drafts, promissory notes, and certificates of deposit. A tremendous number of transactions involve the writing of one or more checks. Drafts, of which checks are a specialized form, provide an important monetary and credit function in the business world, both within and without the banking system. Promissory notes serve an important business purpose, not only in areas of high finance, but at the level of the small businessperson and consumer as well. In recent years certificates of deposit have been used increasingly by individuals instead of savings accounts. The various forms of commercial paper, commonly referred to as instruments, may or may not possess the unique characteristic of negotiability, al-

though the term "commercial paper" is generally used to refer to instruments that are negotiable. The manner in which rights and obligations are acquired in commercial paper is important because of the huge volume of daily transactions in promissory notes, certificates of deposit, drafts, and checks.

NEGOTIABILITY

The quality of negotiability is imparted to commercial paper by law. It was devised by the law to meet the needs of traders, merchants, and businesspeople who wanted promises and orders to pay money to circulate freely in the marketplace, not as money, but as a ready substitute for money in business transactions. The concept of negotiability applies not only to commercial paper, which is governed by Article 3 of the Code, but also to documents of title (governed by Article 7 and discussed in Chapter 47) and investment securities (governed by Article 8 and discussed in Chapter 34).

The starting point for an understanding of negotiable instruments is to recognize that four or five centuries ago in England a contract right to the payment of money was not assignable. The reason was that a contractual promise ran to the promisee and required that performance be rendered to him and to no one else. This was a hardship on the owner of the right as it prevented him from selling or disposing of it. Development of the law ultimately permitted recovery upon an assignment by the assignee against the obligor, although the assignee acquired no new rights but only those of his assignor.

In an action by an innocent assignee against the obligor he was subject to all defenses available to the obligor. Such an action would result in the same outcome regardless of whether it was brought by the assignee or assignor. Thus, a contract right became assignable but not very marketable, as merchants had no interest in buying into a possible lawsuit. That is still the law of assignments: that the **assignee stands in the shoes of his assignor.**

With the flourishing of trade and commerce it became essential that a means would be developed to exchange contractual rights for money. A merchant who sells goods for cash may use the cash to buy more goods for resale. If he makes a sale on credit in exchange for a promise to pay money, why should he not be permitted to sell that promise to someone else for cash with which to carry on his business. One difficulty was that the buyer of the goods gave the seller only a promise to pay money to him. He was the only person to whom performance or payment was promised. However, if the seller obtained from the buyer a promise in writing to pay money to anyone in possession (**bearer**) of the writing (**paper** or **instrument**) or to anyone the seller (*payee*) designated, then the duty of performance would run directly to the bearer of the paper or to the person to whom the payee ordered payment to be made. This is one of the essential distinctions between negotiable and non-negotiable instruments. There are other formal requirements of a negotiable instrument, but this particular one eliminates the limitations of a promise to pay money only to a named promisee.

Moreover, if the promise to pay were not subject to all of the defenses available against the assignor, then a transferee such as the bearer, or the person to whom the payee *ordered* payment to be made, would not only be more willing to acquire the promise but would also pay more for it. The law of negotiable instruments accordingly developed the concept of **holder in due course** whereby certain good faith transferees who gave value acquired the right to be paid free of most of the defenses to which an assignee would be subject. Thus, by reason of this doctrine such a transferee of a negotiable instrument acquires *greater* rights than his transferor had, whereas an assignee would acquire *only* the rights of his assignor.

With these two basic innovations, negotiable instruments enabled merchants to sell their contractual rights more readily and thereby keep their capital working.

Negotiability invests commercial paper with a high degree of marketability and commercial utility by allowing it to be freely transferable and enforceable by a person with the rights of a holder in due course against any person obligated on the paper, subject only to a limited number of defenses. To illustrate, let it be assumed that A sells and delivers goods to B for $500 on sixty days' credit, and that, a few days later, A assigns this account to C. Unless B is duly notified of this assignment, he may safely pay the $500 to A on the due date without incurring any liability to C, the assignee. Assume next that the goods were defective and that B, accordingly, has a defense against A to the extent of $200. Assume also that C duly notified B of the assignment. The result is that C can recover only $300 from B and not $500, for the reason that B's defense against A is equally available against A's assignee, C. In other words, an assignee of contractual rights merely "steps into the shoes" of his assignor and, hence, acquires only the same rights as his assignor had—and no greater.

Assume instead, that upon the sale by A to B, B executed and delivered his negotiable note to A for $500 payable to A's order in sixty days, and that, a short time later, A duly negotiates the note to C. In the first place, C is not required to notify B that he has acquired the note from A. One who issues a negotiable instrument is charged with knowledge that the instrument may be negotiated from hand to hand and is obligated to pay the holder of the instrument. In the second place, and assuming that C acquired the note in good faith and for value and had no knowledge of B's defense against A, B's defense is not available against C. C, therefore, is entitled to hold B at maturity for the full face amount of the note, namely, $500. In other words, C, by the negotiation of the note to him acquired greater rights than A had, since A, had he kept the note, could have recovered only $300 thereon because B could have successfully asserted the defense to the amount of $200 against A.

To have the full benefit of negotiability, commercial paper must not only meet the requirements of negotiability under the Code, but must also be acquired by a "holder in due course." This chapter and the three chapters that follow discuss in order: (1) form and content, (2) transfer and negotiation, (3) holder in due course, and (4) liability of the parties.

TYPES OF COMMERCIAL PAPER

There are four types of commercial paper: drafts, checks, notes, and certificates of deposit. U.C.C., Section 3–104(2). The first two each contain **orders** to pay money, while the last two involve **promises** to pay money.

Order to Pay

Drafts A draft involves three parties, each in a distinctly different capacity. One party, the **drawer, orders** a second party, the **drawee**, to pay a sum certain in money to a third party, the **payee.** See sample in Figure 24-1. The same party may appear in more than one capacity; for instance, the drawer may also be the payee.

Drafts may be either "time" or "sight." A **time** draft is one payable at a specified future date, while a **sight** draft is payable immediately upon presentation to the drawee.

A form of time draft, known as a trade acceptance, is frequently used as a credit device in a commercial transaction. For example, Ben Buyer wishes to purchase goods from Sam Seller. Seller needs cash immediately,

---

FIGURE 24-1   Draft

St. Louis, Missouri
May 1, 1985

Two years from date pay to the order of Smith & Associates
$50,000 Fifty Thousand . . . Dollars

(Signed) Donald Drawer
DONALD DRAWER

To: DEBRA DRAWEE
50 Main St.
Louisville, Kentucky

but Buyer cannot pay for the goods until he has resold them, or processed and sold them, which will require time. Therefore, Seller draws a draft on Buyer ordering Buyer to pay the amount of the purchase price to the order of Seller at a specified future date. Seller presents this draft to Buyer, who "accepts" it thereby agreeing to make payment according to its terms, and returns the accepted draft to Seller, who can then sell the draft to a third party.

A sight draft, sometimes called customer's draft, is used by the seller of goods who desires immediate payment for the goods upon delivery of a bill of lading. Upon shipment of the goods, the seller would obtain from the carrier an order bill of lading which he would attach to a customer's draft drawn on the buyer and would send to his local bank for handling. The local bank would send the paper to a bank located in the city where the goods were to be delivered. That bank would then notify the buyer upon arrival of the goods. In order to obtain the bill of lading and thus the goods, the buyer would pay the amount of the seller's draft, which would be forwarded to the seller's bank and there credited to his account.

Checks A check is a specialized form of draft, namely, an order to pay money drawn on a **bank** and payable on **demand.** Once again, there are parties involved in three distinct capacities: the **drawer,** who orders the **drawee,** a bank, to pay the **payee** on demand. See Figure 24-2.

A *cashier's check* is a check drawn by a bank upon itself to the order of the named payee. It is accepted in advance by the act of its issuance, and upon presentment for payment by the payee the bank must honor the check.

Promises to Pay

Negotiable instruments containing promises to pay money are either notes or certificates of deposit. The most frequently used and in greater volume are notes.

Notes A promissory note is an instrument involving two parties in two capacities. One party, the **maker, promises** to pay to the order of a second party, the **payee,** a stated sum of money, either on demand or at a stated future date. The note may range from a sim-

---

FIGURE 24-2   Check

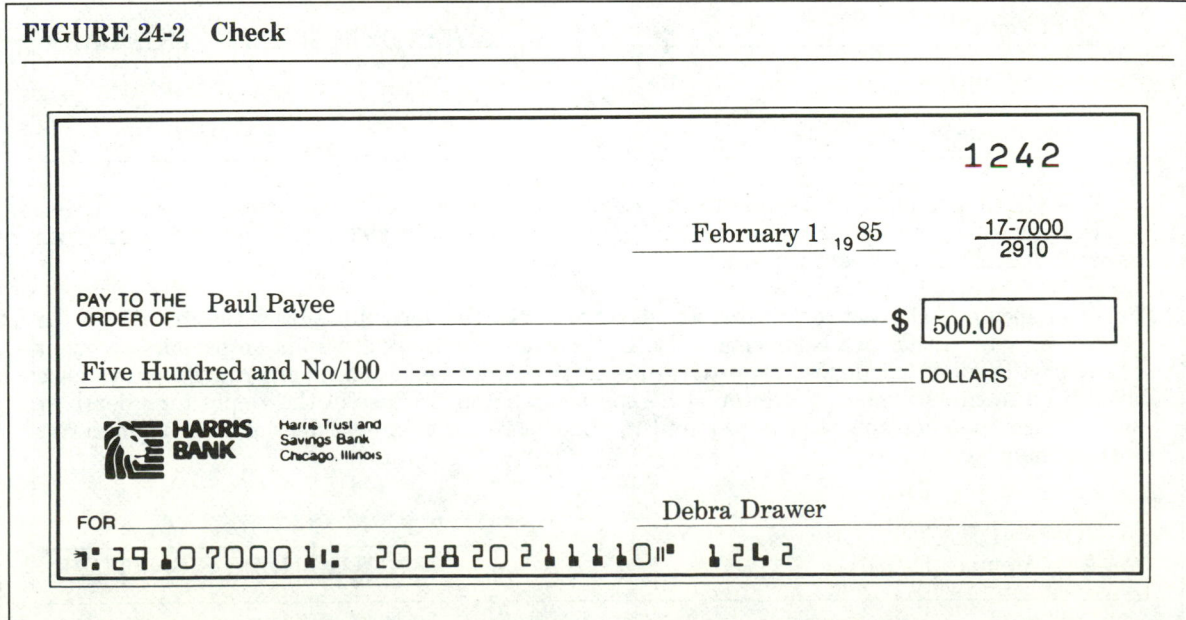

FIGURE 24-3 Note

$10,000   Albany, N.Y.   April 7, 1985

Six months from date I promise to pay to the order of Pat Payee ten thousand dollars.

(signed) Matthew Maker

---

ple, "I promise to pay $X to the order of Y," form to more complex legal instruments such as installment notes, collateral notes, mortgage notes, and judgment notes. See Figure 24-3 for a sample note.

Certificates of Deposit A certificate of deposit is a specialized form of *promise* to pay money given by **a bank** or thrift association. It is a written acknowledgment by a bank of the receipt of a specific sum of money which it engages to pay on demand or at a stated

future date, with interest at a stated rate, to a person named in the certificate, and upon the terms stated in the certificate. The issuing party, the **maker,** which is always a bank or thrift association, promises to pay a second party, the **payee.** See Figure 24-4.

FORM OF COMMERCIAL PAPER

In order for commercial paper to perform its function in the business community effectively, it must be capable of passing from

---

FIGURE 24-4 Certificate of Deposit

CERTIFICATE OF DEPOSIT

The Mountain Bank
1200 Central Avenue, Mountain, Illinois 70040   Date August 3, 1984   Soc. Sec. No. 123-5-7809   No. 13900

.... John Payee .... HAS DEPOSITED IN THIS BANK

.... One Thousand .... DOLLARS $ 1,000 ....

This Certificate shall be payable to the Registered Holder(s) or to the survivor(s) in current funds upon surrender property endorsed by the Registered Holder(s) on August 3, 1985 with interest at ____14____ per cent per annum.

This Certificate of Deposit constitutes a contract whereby the depositor agrees that no part of the deposit may be withdrawn before maturity. In the event the Bank at its option permits payment of any part or all of this deposit prior to the maturity thereof Federal laws and regulations require that three month/six months of interest hereon be forfeited. In case of the Depositor's death or mental incompetency the bank is required to honor a request for withdrawal prior to maturity without penalty.

Bill Bank

NOT SUBJECT TO CHECK
Member F.D.I.C.   AUTHORIZED SIGNATURE

hand to hand freely. This is made possible because **negotiability** is wholly a matter of form. Within the four corners of the instrument must be all the information required to determine whether it is negotiable. No reference to any other source is required or permitted. For this reason a negotiable instrument is called a "courier without luggage."

The formal requirements which an instrument must satisfy if it is to be negotiable are as follows:

1. it must be in writing,
2. it must be signed,
3. it must contain a promise or order to pay,
4. it must be unconditional,
5. it must be for a sum certain in money,
6. it must contain no other promise or order,
7. it must be payable on demand or at a definite time, and
8. it must be payable to order or to bearer.

U.C.C. Section 3-104(1). See *First State Bank at Gallup v. Clark*. If these requirements are not met, the instrument is not negotiable, and the rights of the parties are governed by the law of assignment discussed in Chapter 14.

Writing

The requirement that the instrument be a writing is broadly construed. Printing, typewriting, or any other intentional reduction to tangible form is sufficient to satisfy the requirement. U.C.C., Section 1–201(46). Most negotiable instruments, of course, are written on paper, but this is not required.

Signed

A note or certificate of deposit must be signed by the maker; a draft or check must be signed by the drawer. As in the case of a writing, extreme latitude is granted in determining what constitutes a signature. Any symbol executed or adopted by a party with the present intention to authenticate a writing is sufficient. U.C.C., Section 1–201(39). Moreover,

it may consist of any word or mark used in place of a written signature, U.C.C., Section 3–401(2), such as initials, an X, or a thumb print. It may be a trade name or assumed name. U.C.C., Section 3–401(2). Even the location of the signature on the document is unimportant. Normally, a maker or drawer signs in the lower right-hand corner of the instrument, but this is not required.

Promise or Order to Pay

A negotiable instrument must contain a promise to pay money, in the case of a note or certificate of deposit, or an order to pay, in the case of a draft or check.

A promise is an undertaking and must be more than the mere acknowledgment or recognition of the existing obligation. U.C.C., Section 3–102(1)(c). The so-called "due bill" or "I.O.U." is not a promise, but a mere acknowledgment of indebtedness. Accordingly, an instrument reciting, "due Adam Brown $100" or "I.O.U., Adam Brown, $100" is not negotiable because it does not contain a promise to pay.

An order is a direction to pay which must be more than an authorization or request and must identify the person to pay with reasonable certainty. U.C.C., Section 3–102(1)(b). The usual way to express an order is by use of the word "pay:" "*Pay* to the order of John Jones" or "*Pay* bearer."

Unconditional

The requirement that the promise or order be unconditional is to prevent the inclusion of any provision that could diminish the obligation. The currency and credit functions of negotiable instruments would be defeated by conditions limiting the promise, since costly and time-consuming investigations would become necessary to ascertain the degree of risk imposed by the condition. Moreover, if the **holder** (transferee) had to take an instrument subject to certain conditions, her risk factor would be substantial, and this would lead to limited transferability. Substitutes for money must be capable of rapid circulation at minimum risks.

A promise or order is conditional if (a) the instrument states that it is subject to or governed by any other agreement, or (b) the instrument states that it is to be paid only out of a particular fund or source. U.C.C., Section 3–105(2).

Reference to Other Agreements

The restriction against reference to another agreement is to enable any person to determine the right to payment provided by the instrument without having to look beyond its four corners. If such right is made subject to the terms of another agreement, the instrument is non-negotiable. See *Holly Hill Acres, Ltd. v. Charter Bank of Gainesville*. However, it may be clear from the reference that the other agreement is one which does not impair the obligation. For instance, an instrument may refer to a mortgage securing its payment without affecting its negotiability.

A distinction is to be made between a mere recital of the *existence* of a separate agreement (this does not destroy negotiability) and a recital which makes the instrument *subject* to the terms of another agreement (this does destroy negotiability).

A statement in a note such as

This note is given in partial payment for a color T.V. set to be delivered two weeks from date in accordance with a contract of this date between the payee and the maker

does not impair negotiability. It merely is a description of the transaction giving rise to the note and describes the consideration. It does not place any restriction or condition on the maker's obligation to pay. The promise is not made subject to any implied or constructive condition. Added words which *would* impair negotiability are:

and in the event such set is not delivered, then the maker's obligation hereunder shall be null and void.

These added words make the promise to pay conditional upon delivery of the television set and thus render the instrument non-negotiable.

The Particular Fund Doctrine

An order or promise to pay out of a particular fund is conditional and destroys negotiability because payment is made dependent upon the existence and sufficiency of the particular fund. On the other hand, a promise or order to pay, coupled with a mere indication of a particular fund out of which reimbursement is to be made or a particular account to be debited with the amount, does not impair negotiability since the drawer's or maker's general credit is relied upon; charging a particular account is merely a bookkeeping entry to be followed after payment.

Thus, there is a difference between an instrument which says, "Sixty days after date pay to the order of John Jones $500 out of the proceeds of the sale of the contents of freight car No. 1234" and one which states, "Sixty days after date pay to the order of John Jones $500 and charge to proceeds of sale of the contents of freight car No. 1234." In the first case, payment would be made only if such contents were sold and then only to the extent of the proceeds. In the second case, the instrument contains an unqualified order to pay with merely bookkeeping instructions to the drawee of the draft.

The U.C.C. creates two exceptions to the particular fund rule, however, in the interest of promoting marketability of instruments. The first exception permits governmental agencies to draw short-term commercial paper in which payment is restricted to a particular fund. Statutes in many States and ordinances in municipalities may authorize the issuance of instruments to pay for public improvements, and these instruments are generally payable only out of funds raised from special assessments levied against the property benefited. To aid municipalities and States, and to prevent investors from disappointment, Section 3–105(1)(g) provides that an instrument is not rendered non-negotiable solely because payable out of a particular fund "if the instrument is issued by a government or governmental agency or unit."

The other exception is in favor of persons and organizations generally regarded in commercial circles as business entities. Trustees, executors, and administrators commonly limit payment to the assets of the trust or estate they are administering. Partners tend to limit payment to the assets of the partnership. Other unincorporated organizations such as associations, joint stock companies, and Massachusetts Trusts or business trusts issue instruments limited to payment from the entire assets of the organization, expressly providing that the members are not to be personally liable. Section 3–105(1)(h) of the U.C.C. specifies that none of these limitations impair negotiability of an instrument despite the fact that its payment is limited to a particular fund. In fact, the limitation is no more than that present in the case of a corporate promissory note. A corporation's note does not lack negotiability because payable only from its assets which is true of all its obligations.

Sum Certain in Money

The holder must be able to determine from the face of the instrument the amount which he is entitled to receive in any event, so that he can ascertain the present and future value of the instrument.

Money The term "money" means a medium of exchange authorized or adopted by a domestic or foreign government as part of its currency. U.C.C., Section 1–201(24). Consequently, even though local custom may make gold dust or uncut diamonds a medium of exchange, an instrument payable in such commodities would be non-negotiable because of the lack of governmental sanction of such media as legal tender. On the other hand, a sum certain payable in French francs, German marks, Italian lira, Japanese yen, or other foreign currency would not impair its negotiability.

Sum Certain The requirement that payment be of a "sum certain" must be considered from the point of view of the holder, not the maker or drawer. The holder must be assured of a determinable minimum payment, although provisions of the instrument may increase the recovery under certain circumstances. Thus, a frequent provision of a note is that the maker will pay, in addition to the face amount and specified interest, costs of collection and attorney's fees upon default in payment. Such provision is designed to make the paper more attractive without lessening the certainty of the amount due.

An instrument payable at a stated rate of interest is an obligation for a sum certain. The rates may be different before and after default, or before and after a specified date. However, if interest is payable "at the current rate" (which means current banking rate), it is non-negotiable because this is *not* a matter that can be determined without reference to any outside source.

Where no date is specified from which interest is to run, interest accrues from the date of the instrument, and if the instrument is undated, from the time the possession of it is first transferred to the payee or the first holder.

In addition, a sum payable is a sum certain even though it is payable in installments, or with a fixed discount if paid before maturity, or a fixed addition if paid after maturity. This is because it is always possible to make the necessary computations from the face of the instrument to determine the amount due at any given time.

The U.C.C., however, does not render any of these provisions legal where they would otherwise be illegal under State law, such as a statute with respect to usury. It merely provides that any such provision does not affect negotiability.

No Other Promise or Order

A negotiable instrument must contain a promise or order to pay money, but it may not contain any other promise, order, obligation or power given by the maker or drawer, except as otherwise specifically authorized under the Code. U.C.C., Section 3–104(1)(b). Accordingly, if an instrument contains an order or promise to do an act in addition to the payment of money, it is not negotiable. For example, a promise to pay $100 "and a ton of coal" would be non-negotiable. The concept of negotiability requires that an instrument be made payable in money because this makes it possible to determine its present value. Where the promise requires something in addition to money, its present value is more difficult to compute, and such promises, therefore, are not suitable in instruments which must be highly certain as to present value to serve the credit and currency functions for which they are created.

The U.C.C. sets out a list of terms and provisions which may be included in instruments without adversely affecting negotiability. Among these are: a promise or power to maintain, protect, or increase collateral and to sell it in case of a default in payment of the instrument; a term authorizing confession of judgment (written authority by the debtor to allow the holder to enter judgment against the debtor in favor of the holder) on the instrument if it is not paid when due; a term purporting to waive the benefit of any law intended for the advantage or protection of any obligor; and a term in a draft providing that the payee, by endorsing or cashing it acknowledges full satisfaction of an obligation of the drawer. It is important to note that the U.C.C. does not render any of these terms legal or effective; it merely provides that their inclusion will not affect negotiability.

The rule that the instrument may contain no promise, order, obligation or power other than for the payment of money does not prevent incorporation of such matters into a separate agreement, so long as the instrument is not made subject to such agreement. The terms of such other agreement, however, while binding on the parties to it, cannot limit the rights of a holder in due course who takes without notice of the limitation. Section 3–119.

Payable on Demand or at a Definite Time

A negotiable instrument must "be payable on demand or at a definite time." U.C.C., Section 3–104(1)(c). This requirement, like the other formal requisites of negotiability, is designed to promote certainty in ascertaining the present value of a negotiable instrument.

Demand paper always has been considered sufficiently certain as to time of payment to satisfy the requirements of negotiability, because it is the holder who makes the demand and thus sets the time for payment. An instrument such as a check in which no time for payment is stated is payable on demand. An instrument qualifies as being payable on demand if it is payable "at sight" or "on presentation." U.C.C., Section 3–108.

Instruments payable at a definite time, other than on demand, are called **time paper.** U.C.C. Section 3–109(2) provides that an instrument which by its terms is otherwise payable only upon an act or event uncertain as to time of occurrence is *not* payable at a definite time even though the act or event has occurred. Familiar examples include notes providing for payment to the payee or order "thirty days after my marriage" or "when he (payee) is twenty-one years old." Such promises in instruments otherwise negotiable in form destroy the negotiable character of the paper. The notes are not payable at a definite time. Nor does the fact that the maker of the note may marry or the payee becomes twenty-one years of age after the execution of the notes change the result. Negotiability is determined from the face of the instrument.

If an instrument provides: "Upon the sale of my house, I promise to pay * * * ," a holder would have no certainty as to whether it would ever become payable. If it provides: "Six weeks after the death of my Uncle George Doe, I promise to pay * * *" the holder would be sure that the note would become payable, but the time when payment would become due could not be ascertained with sufficient definiteness. Hence, each instrument is non-negotiable.

Various types of provisions which are regarded as fixing a definite time for payment of an instrument are detailed in Section 3–109(1) and will now be considered.

"On or before" Clauses An instrument is payable at a definite time if it is payable "on or before a stated date." Section 3–109(1)(a). Obligors, with bargaining strength, frequently insist on the use of the "on or before" clause. For example, in 1984 a person desires to borrow money and have five years within which to repay the loan. There is a possibility that he might be able to repay it sooner, and he would like to have the legal right to do so in order to reduce interest payments if there should be a drastic decline in rates. He therefore insists that the promissory language of the note take the following form: "On or before September 1, 1989, I promise to pay to the order of * * *." The holder is thus assured that she will have her money, at the latest by the maturity date, although she may receive it sooner. This right of prepayment enables the obligor, at his option, to pay in advance of the stated maturity date and thereby stop the further accrual of interest or, in the event of a decline in interest rates, to refinance at a lower rate of interest. Nevertheless, it constitutes sufficient certainty so as not to impair negotiability.

At a Fixed Period after a Stated Date Frequently, instruments are made payable at a fixed period after a stated date. For example, the instrument may be made payable "thirty days after date." This means it is payable thirty days after the date of issuance which is recited on the instrument. Such an instrument is payable at a definite time, for its exact maturity date can be determined by simple arithmetic.

An undated instrument payable "thirty days after date" is not payable at a definite

time, since the date of payment cannot be determined from its face. It is therefore non-negotiable until it is completed.

At a Fixed Period after Sight This clause is frequently used in drafts. An instrument payable in a fixed period after sight is negotiable, for it means a fixed period after acceptance, and therefore a slight mathematical calculation makes the maturity date certain.

At a Definite Time Subject to Acceleration An instrument payable at a fixed time subject to acceleration by the holder satisfies the requirement of being payable at a definite time. Indeed, such an instrument would seem to have a more certain maturity date than a demand instrument because it at least states a definite maturity date.

At a Definite Time Subject to Extension A provision permitting the obligor of an instrument to extend the maturity date to a further *definite* time does not affect negotiability. U.C.C., Section 3–109(1)(d). For example, a provision in a note, payable one year from date, that the maker may extend the maturity date six months does not impair negotiability. However, if the obligor is given an option to extend the maturity of the instrument for an *indefinite* period of time, his promise is illusory, and there is no certainty of time of payment. Such an instrument is non-negotiable. If the obligor's right to extend is limited to a definite time, the extension clause is no more indefinite than an acceleration clause with a time limitation. Moreover, a provision in an instrument granting the *holder* an option to extend the maturity of the instrument for a definite or indefinite period does not impair its negotiability.

In addition, extension may be made automatic upon or after a specified act or event, provided a definite time limit is stated. An example of such an extension clause is, "I promise to pay to the order of John Doe the sum of $2,000 on December 1, 1985, but it is agreed that if the crop of sections 25 and 26 of Twp. 145 is below eight bushels per acre for the 1985 season, this note shall be extended for one year."

Payable to Order or to Bearer

A negotiable instrument must contain words indicating that the maker or drawer intends that it may pass into the hands of someone other than the payee. The "magic words" of negotiability are thus *"to the order of"* or *"to bearer,"* but other words which are clearly equivalent to these may be regarded as fulfilling this requirement. The use of synonyms, however, only invites trouble.

This requirement should not be confused with the requirement that the instrument contain an order or promise to pay. An order to pay is a direction to a third party to pay the instrument as drawn. An "order instrument," on the other hand, pertains to the transferability of the instrument rather than specifying which party is to pay.

See In Re Levine.

Payable to Order In addition to the eminently correct "Pay to the order of Jane Jones," the maker or drawer may state: "Pay to Jane Jones or her order"; or "Pay to Jane Jones or her assigns." U.C.C., Section 3–110. Moreover, in every instance the person to whose order the instrument is payable must be designated with reasonable certainty. Within this limitation a broad range of payees is possible, including an individual, the maker or drawer, the drawee, two or more payees, an office, an estate, trust or fund, a partnership or unincorporated association, and a corporation.

Payable to Bearer Section 3–111 of the Code states that an instrument fulfills the requirements of being payable to bearer if by its terms it is payable (1) to bearer or the order of bearer; (2) to a specified person or "bearer"; or (3) to "cash" or to the order of "cash" or any other indication which does not purport to designate a specific payee. It should be noted, however, that an instrument made payable both to order and to bearer is payable

to order unless the bearer words are handwritten or typewritten. U.C.C., Section 3–110(3).

See Broadway Management Corp. v. Briggs.

Terms and Omissions and Their Effect on Negotiability

Frequently the negotiability of an instrument is questioned because of an omission of certain provisions or ambiguity of language. Problems may also arise in connection with interpretation of instruments whether or not negotiability is called into question. Section 3–118 of the Code contains rules of construction which apply to every instrument.

Absence of Statement of Consideration Consideration is required to support a contract. However, as stated in *In Re Levine*, the negotiability of an instrument is *not* affected by the omission of a statement of consideration. U.C.C., Section 3–112(1)(a).

Absence of Statement of Where the Instrument is Drawn or Payable To determine what law applies to the issuance and form of an instrument, the place of issue must be known. To determine the law applicable to matters of payment, the place of payment must be known. But the omission of a statement of either of these on the face of the instrument does not affect its negotiability. U.C.C., Section 3–112(1)(a).

Sealed Instruments The fact that an instrument is under seal has no effect on its negotiability, whatever other effect the seal might have under common law. U.C.C., Section 3–113.

Dating of the Instrument The negotiability of an instrument is not affected by the fact that it is *antedated, postdated,* or *undated.* U.C.C., Section 3–114.

If the instrument is *antedated,* that is, carries a date prior to its actual issue, the stated date controls. Hence, a note dated October 1, 1985, payable thirty days after date, and issued on November 1, 1985, is due and payable the day before its issue.

If the instrument is *postdated*, that is, carries a date later than the day on which it was issued, the date stated on the instrument is conclusive. A demand instrument, therefore, by postdating becomes a time instrument. For example, if on January 2, 1985, the drawer issues a check and dates it January 21, 1985, the drawer's bank is not authorized to pay the instrument until January 21.

An *undated* instrument payable at a fixed time "after date" is uncertain as to time of payment and therefore non-negotiable, subject to the special rules applicable to incomplete instruments.

Incomplete Instruments On occasion a party will sign a paper the contents of which show that it is intended to become an instrument, but which, either by intention or through oversight, is incomplete in some necessary respect, such as the omission of a promise or order, designation of the payee, amount payable, or time for payment. Section 3–115 provides that such an instrument is not negotiable until completed.

If an undated instrument is delivered on November 1, 1985, payable "thirty days after date," the payee has implied authority to fill in "November 1, 1985." Until he does so, however, the instrument is not negotiable because it is not payable at a definite time. If the payee completes the instrument by inserting an erroneous date, such date will control, unless the maker or drawer in a lawsuit establishes the correct date.

Ambiguous Instruments Rather than commit the parties to the use of parol evidence to establish the interpretation of an instrument, the Code establishes rules to resolve common ambiguities. This tends to promote negotiability by providing a degree of certainty to the holder which would otherwise be lacking.

Where it is doubtful whether the instrument is a draft or note, the holder may treat it as either and present it for payment to the drawee or the person signing it. For example, an instrument reading

To X: On demand I promise to pay $500 to the order of Y.

/s/Z

may be presented for payment to X as a draft or to Z as a note.

An instrument naming no drawee but stating

On demand, pay $500 to the order of Y
/s/Z

although in the form of a draft, may be treated as a note and presented to Z for payment.

If a printed form of note or draft is used and the party signing it inserts handwritten or typewritten language which is inconsistent with the printed words, the handwritten words control the typewritten and the printed words, and the typewritten words control the printed.

If the amount payable is set forth on the face of the instrument in both figures and words which differ, the words control the figures. It is presumed that the maker or drawer would be more careful with words.

If an instrument omits to provide for any interest, no interest accrues until after maturity, at which time the unpaid principal will begin to bear interest at the rate that applies to unpaid money judgments under the law of the place where the instrument is payable. If an instrument states that it is payable "with interest" but does not designate any rate, the judgment rate under the law at the place of payment applies from the date of the instrument.

The U.C.C., Section 3–118(c), provides: "Unless the instrument otherwise specifies, two or more persons who sign as maker, acceptor or drawer or endorser and as part of the same transaction are jointly and severally liable even though the instrument contains such words as 'I promise to pay.'"

CASES

Form of Commercial Paper

FIRST STATE BANK AT GALLUP v. CLARK

Supreme Court of New Mexico, 1977.
91 N.M. 117, 570 P.2d 1144.

EASLEY, J.

First State Bank of Gallup (First State), Plaintiff-Appellee sued M. S. Horne (Horne), Defendant-Appellant on a promissory note. The trial court granted summary judgment against defendant and we affirm.

Facts. Horne had executed a $100,000 note in favor of R. C. Clark which contained a restriction that the note could not be transferred, pledged or assigned without the written consent of Horne. As part of the transaction between Horne and Clark, Horne gave Clark a separate letter authorizing Clark to pledge the note as collateral for a loan of $50,000 which Clark anticipated making with First State. Clark did make the loan and pledged the note, which was accompanied by Horne's letter authorizing the note to be used as collateral. First State also called Horne to verify that he was in agreement that his note could be accepted as collateral. First State attempted to collect from Horne on Horne's note to Clark which had been pledged as collateral. Horne refused to pay and this suit resulted.

Issues. The issues raised on appeal include (1) whether the note was a negotiable instrument for purposes of Article 3 of the Uniform Commercial Code (U.C.C.) * * *. Article 3 of the U.C.C. defines a certain type of readily transferable instrument and lays down certain rules for the treatment of that instrument and rules concerning the rights, remedies and defenses of persons dealing with it.

In order to be a "negotiable instrument" for Article 3 purposes the paper must pre-cisely meet the definition set out in § 3–104, since § 3–104 itself states that, to be a negotiable instrument, a writing "must" meet the definition therein set out. Moreover, it is clear that in order to determine whether an instrument meets that definition *only the instrument itself* may be looked to, *not* other documents, even when other documents are referred to in the instrument. [Citations.] As [citation] points out in its text and in footnote 3:

The applicability of Article 3 must be determined from the instrument itself, without reference to other documents or oral agreements. The "four-corners test" is still applicable: the determination of negotiability under Article 3 must be made by inspecting only the instrument itself. . . .

This is clear from the mandatory language of U.C.C. § 3–104, and from the following language from the Official Comment to U.C.C. § 3–105 found under the heading "Purposes of Changes": "The section is intended to make it clear that, so far as negotiability is affected, the conditional or unconditional character of the promise or order is to be determined by what is expressed in the instrument itself. . . .

We recognize the Official Comments to the U.C.C. as persuasive, though they are not controlling authority. [Citation.]

Section 3–104 thus requires that, in order to be a negotiable instrument for Article 3 purposes, one must be able to ascertain without reference to other documents that the instrument:

(a) [is] signed by the maker or drawer; and (b) contain[s] an unconditional promise or order to pay a sum certain in money and no other promise, order, obligation or power given by the maker or drawer except as authorized by [Article 3]; and (c) [is] payable on demand or at a definite time; and (d) [is] payable to order or to bearer.

The note in question here failed to meet the requirements of § 3–104, since the promise to pay contained in the note was not unconditional. Moreover, the note was expressly drafted to be non-negotiable since it stated:

This note may not be transferred, pledged, or otherwise assigned without the written consent of M. S. Horne.

These words, even though they appeared on the back of the note, effectively cancelled any implication of negotiability provided by the words "Pay to the order of" on the face of the note. Notations and terms on the back of a note, made contemporaneously with the execution of the note and intended to be part of the note's contract of payment, constitute as much a part of the note as if they were incorporated on its face. [Citation.]

* * *

The whole purpose of the concept of a negotiable instrument under Article 3 is to declare that transferees in the ordinary course of business are only to be held liable for information appearing in the instrument itself and will not be expected to know of any limitations on negotiability or changes in terms, etc., contained in any separate documents. The whole idea of the facilitation of easy transfer of notes and instruments requires that a transferee be able to trust what the instrument says, and be able to determine the validity of the note and its negotiability from the language in the note itself. [Citation.] * * *

Since the note in question is not negotiable for Article 3 purposes, First State cannot be a holder in due course under Article 3, and we need not discuss that issue.

* * *

The summary judgment of the district court is hereby affirmed for the stated reasons * * *.

Reference to Other Agreements

HOLLY HILL ACRES, LTD. v. CHARTER BANK OF GAINESVILLE

Court of Appeals of Florida, 1975.
314 So.2d 209.

SCHEB, J.

* * *

Appellant/defendant appeals from a summary judgment in favor of appellee/plaintiff Bank in a suit wherein the appellee sought to foreclose a note and mortgage given by appellant.

The appellee Bank was the assignee from appellees Rogers and Blythe of a promissory note and purchase money mortgage executed and delivered by the appellant. The note, executed April 28, 1972, contains the following stipulation:

This note with interest is secured by a mortgage on real estate, of even date herewith, made by the maker hereof in favor of the said payee, and shall be construed and enforced according to the laws of the State of Florida. *The terms of said mortgage are by this reference made a part hereof.* (Emphasis supplied.)

* * *

The note having incorporated the terms of the purchase money mortgage was not negotiable. * * *

The note, incorporating by reference the terms of the mortgage, did not contain the unconditional promise to pay required by [U.C.C. §] 3–104(1)(b). Rather, the note falls within the scope of [U.C.C. §] 3–105(2)(a). Although negotiability is now governed by the Uniform Commercial Code, this was the Florida view even before the U.C.C. was adopted. * * *

Appellee Bank relies upon *Scott v. Taylor*, [Citation], as authority for the proposition that its note is negotiable. *Scott*, however, involved a note which stated: "this note secured by mortgage." Mere reference to a note being secured by mortgage is a common commercial practice and such reference in itself does not impede the negotiability of the note. There is, however, a significant difference in a note stating that it is "secured by a mortgage" from one which provides, "the terms of said mortgage are by this reference made a part hereof." In the former instance the note merely refers to a separate agreement which does not impede its negotiability, while in the latter instance the note is rendered non-negotiable. *See* [U.C.C. §] 3–105(2)(a); [U.C.C. §] 3–119.[4]

As a general rule the assignee of a mortgage securing a non-negotiable note, even though a bona fide purchaser for value, takes subject to all defenses available as against the mortgagee. [Citation.] Appellant raised the issue of fraud as between himself and other parties to the note, therefore, it was incumbent on the appellee Bank, as movant for a summary judgment, to prove the non-existence of any genuinely triable issue. [Citation.]

Accordingly, the entry of a summary final judgment is reversed and the cause remanded for further proceedings.

Payable to Order or to Bearer

IN RE LEVINE

United States Bankruptcy Court, S.D. New York, 1982.
23 B.R. 410.

SCHWARTZBERG, J.

[On September 2, 1976 Barbara Levine executed a mortgage bond under which she promised to pay the Mykoffs a pre-existing obligation of $54,000. On October 14, 1979, the Mykoffs transferred the mortgage to Bankers Trust Co., endorsing the instrument with the words "Pay to the Order of Bankers Trust Company Without Recourse." The plaintiff Lincoln First Bank, N.A., brought this action asserting that the Mykoffs' mortgage is a non-negotiable instrument because it is not payable to order or bearer and thus is subject to Lincoln's defense that the mortgage was not supported by consideration in that an antecedent debt is not consideration.]

* * *

If the bond in question were a negotiable instrument, the lack of legal consideration supporting it would not affect Bankers Trust's secured status as assignee of the mortgage. New York's Uniform Commercial Code (U.C.C.) § 3–408 states in pertinent part:

§ 3–408. Consideration.

Want or failure of consideration is a defense as against any person not having the rights of a holder in due course (Section 3–305), except that no consideration is necessary for an instrument or obligation thereon given in payment of or as security for an antecedent obligation of any kind.

The use of the word "instrument" in the statute means a negotiable instrument. U.C.C. § 3–102(1)(e). Thus, an antecedent debt is sufficient consideration for the execution of a *negotiable instrument*, even if the holder of the instrument does not have the rights of a holder in due course. Here, the assignee does not have the rights of a holder in due course and therefore would ordinarily be subject to the defense of want or failure of consideration [U.C.C. § 3–306(c)]; however, if the bond is a negotiable instrument, U.C.C. § 3–408 would resolve any problem

---

4. Official Comment 5 to [U.C.C.] § 3–119 provides: Subsection (2) rejects decisions which have carried the rule that contemporaneous writings must be read together to the length of holding that a clause in a mortgage affecting a note destroyed the negotiability of the note. The negotiability of an instrument is always to be determined by what appears on the face of the instrument alone, and if it is negotiable in itself a purchaser without notice of a separate writing is in no way affected

by it. *If the instrument itself states that it is subject to or governed by any other agreement, it is not negotiable under this Article;* but if it merely refers to a separate agreement or states that it arises out of such an agreement, it is negotiable. (Emphasis supplied.)

regarding the consideration. In light of the foregoing, it is crucial to determine the character of the mortgage bond which was endorsed over and assigned to Bankers Trust.

A negotiable instrument is one that meets the standards set out in U.C.C. § 3–104. It is § 3–104(1)(d) that is of concern here, a writing, to be negotiable, must "be payable to order or to bearer" [see U.C.C. § 3–110 and § 3–111]. The mortgage bond in question does not contain such language and therefore cannot be a negotiable instrument. In the case of *In re Deveson's Estate*, [citation], the court addressed the issue of whether an ordinary mortgage bond, payable to the obligee, his executors, administrators, or assigns, accompanied by real estate security, is a negotiable instrument. (This language is identical to that used in the subject mortgage bond). Citing the former Negotiable Instruments Law, § 20(4) (now incorporated in the U.C.C.), which was in accord with the U.C.C. requirement that the instrument be payable to order or bearer, the court concluded, "[t]hus, by statute, a mortgage bond, as in the instant case, becomes nonnegotiable." [Citation.]

* * *

The fact that the Mykoffs endorsed the bond with the words "payable to the order of Bankers Trust Company without recourse" does not change the inherent character of the bond. "[N]o intention, no agreement, may make negotiable an instrument which the statute declares to be nonnegotiable."

Accordingly, it must be concluded that the subject mortgage bond is not a negotiable instrument, and that U.C.C. § 3–408 cannot operate to excuse the lack of legal consideration. The bond which the Levines executed and gave to the Mykoffs, evidencing their promise to pay an antecedent debt is unenforceable, and therefore the accompanying mortgage falls with it. Since the assignee, Bankers Trust, holds an unenforceable bond and mortgage (its position can be no better than that of its assignor), its claim is rendered unsecured.

Payable to Bearer

BROADWAY MANAGEMENT CORP. v. BRIGGS

Court of Appeals of Illinois, 1975.
30 Ill. App. 3d 403, 332 N.E. 2d 131.

CRAVEN, J.

Conan Briggs appeals from a circuit court's refusal to vacate an allegedly void judgment by confession against him, * * *.

The note on which the confession of judgment was based reads in part: "Ninety Days after date, I, we, or either of us, promise to pay to the order of Three Thousand Four Hundred Ninety Eight and 45/100 . . . . Dollars." (The underlined words and symbols have been typed in; the remainder is printed.) There are no blanks on the face of the instrument, any unused space having been filled in with hyphens. The note contains clauses permitting acceleration in the event the holder deems itself insecure and authorizes confession of judgment "if this note is not paid at any stated or accelerated maturity."

The trial court determined this instrument to be non-negotiable paper, yet applied certain elements of the law of negotiable instruments in arriving at its conclusion. We believe the instrument to be negotiable. Uniform Commercial Code, section 3–109 establishes that an acceleration clause does not affect negotiability; neither, under Uniform Commercial Code, section 3–112(d) is negotiability impaired by a clause confessing judgment on an instrument "if it is not paid when due." Since the operation of the acceleration clause would have made the note due (that is, mature) as of the time of its operation, [citation] the note does not, as suggested by the trial court, authorize confession of judgment prior to maturity.

Thus, the critical question of whether this is order or bearer paper is to be determined by section [Article] 3 of the Uniform Commercial Code, which governs negotiable instruments. If this is bearer paper, the plaintiff's possession was sufficient to make it a holder (Uniform Commercial Code, section 1–201(20)) and this note on its face authorizes the holder to confess judgment against the maker.

On the other hand, if the instrument is order paper, it becomes apparent that the payee cannot be determined upon the face of the instrument. The power to confess judgment must be clearly given and strictly pursued. [Citation.] The warrant of authority having been given in favor of a named person, that warrant may be exercised only by the person named. [Citation.] If the warrant in this case cannot be read to extend to "bearer", then it may not be exercised, since the strict construction mandated by Illinois decisions will not allow a court to guess in whose name such a power may be exercised.

Under the Code, an instrument is payable to bearer only when by its terms it is payable to:

(a) bearer or the order of bearer; or (b) a specified person or bearer; or (c) 'cash' or the order of 'cash', or any other indication which does not purport to designate a specific payee. (U.C.C., § 3–111.)

The official comments to the section note that an instrument made payable "to the order of _____ " is not bearer paper, but an incomplete order instrument unenforceable until completed in accordance with authority. U.C.C., § 3–115.

The instrument here is not bearer paper. We cannot say that it "does not purport to designate a specific payee." Rather, we believe the wording of the instrument is clear in its implication that the payee's name is to be inserted between the promise and the amount, so that the literal absence of blanks is legally insignificant.

Since the holder could not be determined from the face of the instrument, the trial court was in error in allowing plaintiff Broadway Management Corporation to exercise the warrant of attorney granted by this instrument to its holder. The judgment by confession therefore must be vacated.

*   *   *

Reversed and remanded with directions to allow the motion to vacate the confession of judgment * * *

PROBLEMS

1. State whether the following provisions impair or preclude negotiability, the instrument in each instance being otherwise in proper form. Answer each statement with either the word "Negotiable" or "Non-negotiable," and explain why.

(a) A note for $2,000 payable in twenty monthly installments of $100 each, providing: "In case of death of maker all payments not due at date of death are canceled."

(b) A note stating, "this note is secured by a mortgage of even date herewith on personal property located at 351 Maple Street, Smithton, Illinois."

(c) A certificate of deposit reciting, "John Jones has deposited in the Citizens Bank of Emanon, Illinois, Two Thousand Dollars, to the credit of himself, payable upon the return of this instru-

ment properly indorsed, with interest at the rate of 12¾ percent per annum from date of issue upon ninety days written notice."

(d) An instrument reciting "I.O.U., Mark Noble, $1,000.00."

(e) A note stating "In accordance with our contract of December 13, 1984, I promise to pay to the order of Sam Stone $100 on March 13, 1985."

(f) A draft drawn by Brown on the Acme Publishing Company for $500, payable to the order of the Sixth National Bank of Erehwon, directing the bank to "Charge this draft to my royalty account."

(g) A note executed by Pierre Janvier, a resident of Chicago, for $2,000, payable in Swiss francs.

(h) An undated note for $1,000 payable "six months after date."

(i) A note for $500 payable to the order of Ray Rodes six months after the death of Albert Olds.

(j) A note of $500 payable to the assigns of Levi Lee.

2. State whether the following provisions in a note impair or preclude negotiability, the instrument in each instance being otherwise in proper form. Answer each statement with either the word "Negotiable" or "Non-negotiable" and explain why.

(a) A note signed by Henry Brown in the trade name of the Quality Store.

(b) A note for $450, payable to the order of TV Products Company, "If, but only if, the color television set for which this note is given proves entirely satisfactory to me."

(c) A note executed by Adams, Burton, and Cady Company, a partnership, for $1,000, payable to the order of Davis, payable only out of the assets of the partnership.

(d) A note promising to pay $500 to the order of Leigh and to deliver ten tons of coal to Leigh.

(e) A note for $10,000 executed by Eaton payable to the order of the First National Bank of Emanon in which Eaton promises to give additional collateral if the bank deems itself insecure and demands additional security.

(f) A note reading, "I promise to pay to the order of Richard Roe $2,000 on January 31, 1985, but it is agreed that if the crop of Blackacre falls below ten bushels per acre for the 1984 season, this note shall be extended indefinitely."

(g) A note payable to the order of Ray Rogers fifty years from date but providing that payment shall be accelerated by the death of Silas Hughes to a point of time four months after his death.

(h) A note for $4,000 calling for payments of installments of $250 each and stating, "In the event any installment hereof is not paid when due this note shall immediately become due at the holder's option."

(i) An instrument dated September 17, 1985, in the handwriting of John Henry Brown which reads in full: "Sixty days after date, I, John Henry Brown, promise to pay to the order of William Jones $500."

(j) A note reciting; "I promise to pay Ray Reed $100 on December 24, 1985."

3. On March 10, Tolliver Tolles, also known as Thomas Towle, delivered to Alonzo Craig and Abigail Craig the following instrument, written by him in pencil:

For value received, I, Thomas Towle, promise to pay to the order of Alonzo Craig or Abigail Craig One Thousand Seventy-Five ($1,000.75) Dollars six months after my mother, Alma Tolles, dies with interest at the rate of 12 percent from date to maturity and after maturity at the rate of 14 percent. I hereby waive the benefit of all laws exempting real or personal property from levy or sale.

Is this instrument negotiable? Explain.

4. Henry Hughes, who operates a department store, executed the following instrument:

$2,600   Chicago, March 5, 1985
On July 1, 1985, I promise to pay Daniel Dalziel, or order, the sum of Twenty-Six Hundred Dollars for the privilege of one framed advertising sign, size 24 × 36 inches, at one end of each of two hundred sixty motor coaches of the New Omnibus Company for a term of three months from May 15, 1985.

                              Henry Hughes.

Is this instrument negotiable? Explain.

5. P agreed to lend M $500. Thereupon M made and delivered his note for $500 payable to P or order "ten days after my marriage." Shortly thereafter M was married. Is the instrument negotiable? Explain.

6. On June 1, A executed a note for $1,000 payable to the order of B, which contained the clause: "This note is payable when this year's corn crop is harvested." Is the instrument negotiable? Explain.

7. M employs A to work for her for one year from January 1, 1985, to December 31, 1985, at a salary of $800 a month payable monthly. On January 2, M delivers to A twelve promissory notes in otherwise negotiable form, maturing respectively on the last day of successive calendar months throughout the year 1985. On the first note there is the statement "For January 1985 salary"; on the second note "For February 1985 salary"; and so on for each note. On January 3, 1985, A sold and endorsed the twelve notes to XYZ Bank and on January 4, 1985, quit work. Are these notes negotiable? Explain.

8. For the balance due on the purchase of a tractor Henry Brown executed and delivered to Jane Jones

his promissory note containing the following language:

January 1, 1985, I promise to pay to the order of Jane Jones the sum of $7,000 to be paid only out of my checking account at the XYZ National Bank in Pinckard, Illinois, in two installments of $3,500 each, payable on May 1, 1985, and on July 1, 1985, provided that if I fail to pay the first installment on the due date, the entire sum shall become immediately due. (Signed) Henry Brown.

Is the note negotiable? Explain.

9. Sam Sharpe executed and delivered to Don Dole the following instrument:

Knoxville, Tennessee
May 29, 1985

Thirty days after date I promise to pay Don Dole or order, Five Thousand Dollars. The holder of this instrument shall have the election to require the assignment and delivery to him of my 100 shares of Brookside Iron Works Corporation stock in lieu of the payment of Five Thousand Dollars in money.

(Signed) Sam Sharpe.

Is this instrument negotiable? Explain.

TRANSFER

THE essential utility of commercial paper is in the ease of its transferability. Both negotiable and non-negotiable instruments are transferable by assignment, but only negotiable instruments can result in the transferee becoming a holder. This distinction is highly significant. If the transferee of a negotiable instrument is by its terms entitled to payment, he is a holder of the instrument. Only holders may be holders in due course and thus entitled to greater rights in the instrument than the transferor may have possessed. These rights are discussed in the next chapter and are the reason why negotiable instruments move freely in the marketplace. The transfer of a non-negotiable instrument and of a negotiable instrument otherwise than by a means which renders the transferee a holder operates as an assignment. This chapter discusses the methods by which commercial paper may be transferred.

TRANSFER AND NEGOTIATION

Whether a transfer is by *assignment* or *negotiation*, the transferee acquires the rights his transferor had. Section 3–201(1). The transfer need not be for value: if the instrument is transferred as a gift, the donee acquires all the rights of the donor. If the transferor was a holder in due course, the transferee acquires the rights of a holder in due course, which rights he in turn may transfer. This rule, which is sometimes referred to as the **shelter rule,** existed at common law and exists under the U.C.C., Section 3–201(1).

Negotiation is the transfer of a negotiable instrument in such a manner that the transferee becomes a holder of it. Section 3–202(1). A **holder** however is broadly defined as "a person who is in possession of an instrument drawn, issued or indorsed to him or to his order or to bearer or in blank." Section 1–201(20). Accordingly, to qualify as a holder a person must have possession of an instrument that runs to him. Since **bearer paper** (an instrument payable to bearer) runs to whoever is in possession of it, a finder or a thief of bearer paper would be a holder even though he did not receive possession by voluntary transfer. For example, an instrument payable to bearer and issued to P is lost by P. It is found by F who sells and delivers it to B, who thus receives it by negotiation and is a holder. F also qualifies as a holder because he is in possession of bearer paper. Section 1–201(20). As a holder, F has the power to negotiate the instrument (Section 3–301), and the transferee may be a holder in due course if he meets the Code's requirements for such a holder. See Figure 25-1.

Thus, a bearer instrument is transferred by mere *possession* and is therefore comparable to cash. On the other hand, if the instrument is **order paper** (an instrument payable to order), both *possession* and *indorsement* by the appropriate parties are necessary for the transferee to become a holder. See Figure 25-2.

Any transfer for value of an instrument not payable to bearer gives the transferee the specifically enforceable right to have the un-qualified indorsement of the transferor, unless the parties otherwise agreed. Section 3–201(3). The parties may agree that the transfer is to be an assignment rather than a negotiation, in which case no indorsement is required. Absent such agreement, it is presumed when value is given that negotiation was intended, and if the instrument is not payable to bearer, the right of the transferee to an unqualified indorsement is enforceable by court order. Where a transfer is not for value, the transaction is normally not commercial in nature, and such presumption is not appropriate.

Until the necessary indorsement has been supplied, the transferee has nothing more than the contract rights of an assignee. Negotiation takes effect only when a proper indorsement is made, as it is not until then, notwithstanding possession, that the transferee becomes a holder of the instrument.

INDORSEMENTS

An indorsement is the signature of a payee, drawee, accommodation indorser, or holder of an instrument. An indorsement must be written on the instrument or on a paper, called an allonge, so firmly affixed to the instrument as to become a part of it. The use of an allonge is required when there are so many indorsements that there is no room for additional signatures. A purported indorsement on a separate piece of paper, clipped or pinned to

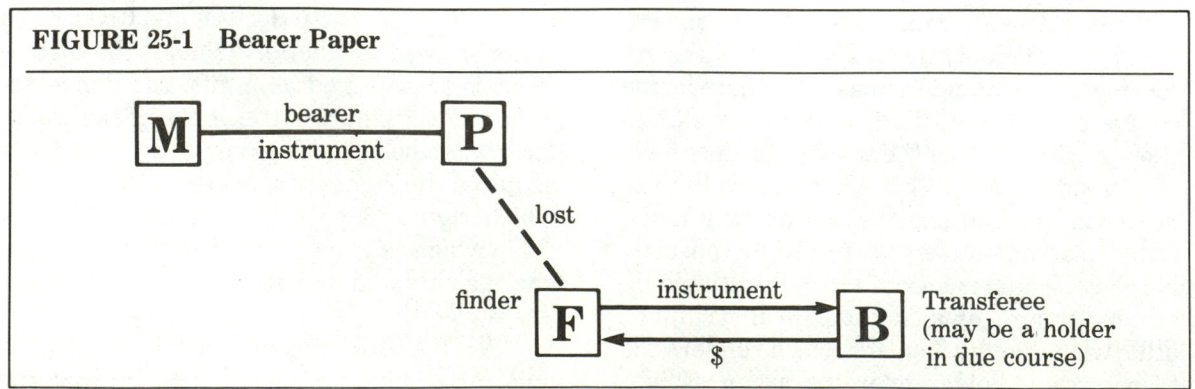

FIGURE 25-1   Bearer Paper

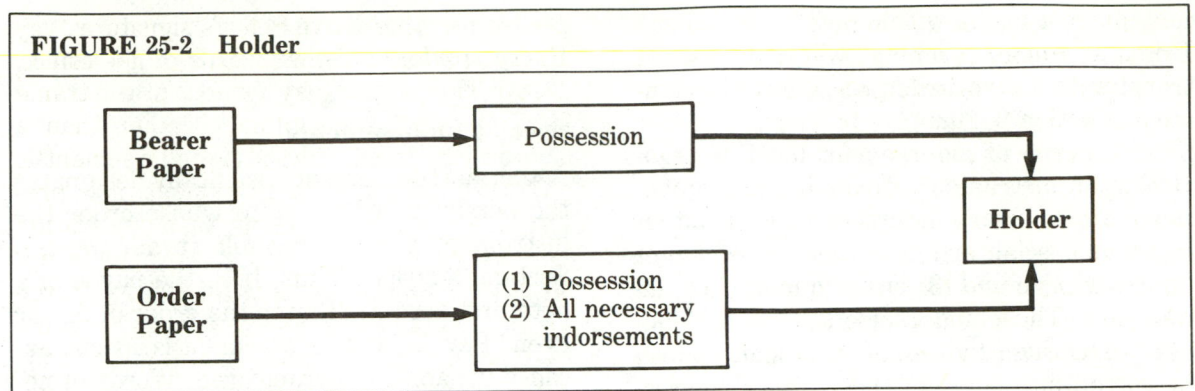

FIGURE 25-2   Holder

the instrument, is not valid. *See Lamson v. Commercial Credit Corp.*

Customarily, indorsements are made on the back or reverse side of the instrument, starting at the top and continuing down the back. The order of the indorsement and the liability of indorsers, unless otherwise agreed, is presumed to be the order in which their signatures appear. Section 3–414(2). Occasionally, however, a signature may appear on an instrument in such a way that it is impossible to tell with certainty the nature of the liability undertaken by the signer. In such an event, Section 3–402 specifies that signer is to be treated as an indorser. In keeping with the rule that a transferee must be able to determine her rights from the face of the instrument, the person who signed in an ambiguous capacity may not introduce parol evidence to establish that she intended to be something other than an indorser.

An indorsement which shows that it is not in the chain of title is notice of its **accommodation** character. Section 3–415(4). An accommodation indorser receives no money or value for her indorsement but signs in order to add her liability and thereby accommodate, or assist, another party who might otherwise be unable to obtain funds.

An indorsement may be complex or simple. It may be dated and may indicate where it is made, but neither date nor place is required to be shown. The simplest type is merely the signature of the indorser. Since

the indorser undertakes certain obligations, as explained later, an indorsement consisting of merely a signature may be said to be the shortest contract known to the law. A forged or otherwise unauthorized signature necessary to negotiation is inoperative and thus breaks the chain of title to the instrument. Section 3–404(1).

If the name of the payee or indorsee is misspelled, or is a name different from the holder, as for example, a trade name, he may indorse the instrument in that name or in his own or both. Section 3–203. A check payable to "Crescent Pizza Palace," a sole proprietorship, may be quite properly indorsed by the owner in either his own name, John Doe, or in that of his business, Crescent Pizza Palace. To assure the highest degree of security and to facilitate subsequent negotiation, a person paying or giving value for such an instrument may require indorsement in both names. Section 3–203.

An indorsement which conveys less than the entire instrument or any unpaid balance is ineffective as a negotiation. Section, 3–202(3). For example, an indorsement containing a direction to pay A "one-half of the note" or "$500 of the note," or to pay "two-thirds to A, one-third to B" constitutes only an assignment and neither A nor B becomes a holder. But an indorsement "to A and B" is effective as a negotiation because it transfers the entire interest to A and B. Words such as "I hereby assign all my right, title, and interest in the within note" are also sufficient as a negotiation and will not cause the transfer to be regarded as a mere assignment. Section 3–202(4).

The type of indorsement used in negotiating an instrument affects its subsequent negotiation. Every indorsement is (1) either blank or special, and (2) either restrictive or nonrestrictive and (3) either qualified or unqualified. These indorsements are not mutually exclusive. Indeed, all indorsements may be sorted into three of these six categories. This is true because all indorsements disclose three things: (1) The method to be employed in making subsequent negotiations. This depends upon whether the indorsement is blank or special. (2) The kind of interest that is being transferred. This depends upon whether the indorsement is restrictive or nonrestrictive. (3) The liability of the indorser. This depends upon whether the indorsement is qualified or unqualified. For instance, an indorser who merely signs her name on the back of an instrument is making a blank, nonrestrictive, unqualified indorsement.

Blank Indorsements

A blank indorsement is one specifying no indorsee and may consist of merely the signature of the indorser. Section 3–204(2). A blank indorsement converts order paper into **bearer paper.** Thus, an instrument indorsed in blank may be negotiated by delivery alone without further indorsement. Hence, the holder should treat it with the same care as cash. *See Palmer & Ray Dental Supply of Abilene, Inc. v. First Nat'l. Bank.* He may protect himself, however, by converting the blank indorsement to a special indorsement by writing over the signature of the indorser any contract consistent with the character of the indorsement. For example, on the back of a negotiable instrument appears the blank indorsement "Sally Seller." Harry Holder, who received the instrument from Seller, may convert this bearer instrument into order paper by inserting above Seller's signature "Pay Harry Holder" or other words of like effect.

Special Indorsements

A special indorsement specifically designates the person to whom or to whose order the instrument is to be payable (**order paper**). Section 3–204(1). Thus, if P, the payee of a note, indorses it, "Pay to the order of A," or even "Pay A," the indorsement is special because it names the transferee. Words of negotiability are not required in an indorsement and any further negotiation of the instrument requires A's indorsement. *See Tubin v. Rabin.*

Restrictive Indorsements

As the term implies, a restrictive indorsement attempts to restrict the rights of the indorsee in some fashion. The U.C.C. defines four types of indorsements as restrictive: conditional indorsements, indorsements prohibiting further transfer, indorsements for deposit or collection, and indorsements in trust.

Conditional Indorsements A conditional indorsement is one by which the indorser makes the rights of the indorsee subject to the happening or non-happening of a specified event. Suppose M makes a note payable to P's order. P indorses it "Pay A, but only if the good ship Jolly Jack arrives in Chicago harbor by November 15, 1985." If M had used this language in the instrument, it would be non-negotiable, because her promise to pay must be unconditional to satisfy the formal requisites of negotiability. But indorsers *are* permitted to condition the rights of their indorsees without destroying negotiability.

If the good ship Jolly Jack does not arrive in Chicago harbor by November 15, 1985, A has no rights in the instrument. If he presents the instrument to M for payment, M must dishonor the instrument or be required to pay it again to P. M is not discharged when she pays an instrument which has been restrictively indorsed, unless she pays in a manner consistent with the indorsement. Section 3–603(1)(b).

Indorsements Prohibiting Further Transfer To be negotiable, an instrument not payable to bearer must be payable to the order of a payee. Section 3–104(1)(d). If the instrument reads merely "Pay A," it is not negotiable, and the only method of transfer would be by assignment. The requirements of negotiability, however, are not imposed upon indorsements. An indorsement reading "Pay A" or even "Pay A only" is interpreted as meaning "Pay to the order of A." Such indorsements, or any other purporting to prohibit further transfer, are designed to be a restriction on the rights of the indorsee. To remove any doubt as to the effect of such a provision, the Code provides that *no* restrictive indorsement prevents further transfer or negotiation of the instrument. Section 3–206(1). The net result of this provision is that an indorsement which purports to prohibit further transfer of the instrument is given the same effect as an unrestricted indorsement.

Indorsements for Deposit or Collection The most frequently used form of restrictive indorsement is that designed to lodge the instrument in the banking system for deposit or collection. Indorsements of this type include those "for collection," "for deposit," and "pay any bank." Such indorsements *effectively limit* further negotiation to those consistent with its limitation and put all nonbanking persons on notice as to who has a valid interest in the paper. *See Fultz v. First Nat'l Bank in Graham.*

Indorsements in Trust Another common kind of restrictive indorsement is that in which the indorser creates a trust for the benefit of himself or others. If an instrument is indorsed "Pay T in trust for B" or "Pay T for B" or "Pay T for account of B" or "Pay T as agent for B," T is a fiduciary, subject to liability for any breach of his obligation. Trustees commonly and legitimately sell trust assets, and as a consequence, a trustee has power to negotiate an instrument. The first taker under an indorsement to him in trust (T in the above examples) is under the duty to pay or apply all funds given by him consistently with the indorsement or risk having to pay twice. Section 3–206(4). Subsequent indorsees or transferees are not bound by such indorsement unless they have knowledge that the negotiation to the first taker was in breach of fiduciary duty.

Qualified Indorsements

Indorsers, except those indorsing without recourse, engage that they will pay the instrument according to its tenor at the time of their indorsement to the holder or to any subsequent indorser who takes it up. Section 3–414(1). In short, an **unqualified** indorser guarantees payment of the instrument if certain conditions are met.

An indorser may disclaim her liability on the contract of indorsement, but only if the indorsement so declares and the disclaimer is written on the instrument. The customary manner of disclaiming an indorser's liability is to add the words **"without recourse,"** either before or after her signature. A "without recourse" indorsement is called a **qualified** indorsement. A qualified indorsement and delivery is a negotiation and transfers legal title to the indorsee, but the indorser does *not* guarantee payment of the instrument. A qualified indorsement does not destroy negotiability nor prevent further negotiation of the instrument. For example, assume that an attorney receives a check payable to her order in payment of a client's claim. She may indorse the check to the client without recourse, thereby disclaiming liability as a guarantor of payment of the check. The qualified indorsement plus delivery would transfer title to the client.

See Figure 25-3.

FIGURE 25-3 Indorsements

Indorsement	Type of Indorsement	Interest Transferred	Liability of Indorser
1. "John Doe"	Blank	Non-restrictive	Unqualified
2. "Pay to Richard Roe, John Doe"	Special	Non-restrictive	Unqualified
3. "Without recourse, John Doe"	Blank	Non-restrictive	Qualified
4. "Pay to Richard Roe, without recourse, John Doe"	Special	Non-restrictive	Qualified
5. "For collection only, without recourse, John Doe"	Blank	Restrictive	Qualified
6. "Pay to XYZ Bank, for collection only, John Doe"	Special	Restrictive	Unqualified

CASES

Indorsements

LAMSON v. COMMERCIAL CREDIT CORP.

Supreme Court of Colorado, 1975.
187 Colo. 382, 531 P.2d 966.

DAY, J.

Plaintiff Lamson possessed two checks issued by the defendant Commercial Credit Corporation. He sued the defendant for the face value of the checks, plus interest. The trial court found for Lamson, but the Court of Appeals reversed. * * *

I

A chronology of the transactions and the subsequent court trial and appeal draws the issues into focus. Originally, the drawer Commercial Credit Corporation ("the Corporation") issued the two checks payable to Rauch Motor Company ("Rauch"). Rauch indorsed the checks in blank, deposited them to its account in University National Bank ("the Bank"), and received a corresponding amount

of money. The Bank stamped the checks "pay any bank," and initiated collection. However, the checks were dishonored and returned to the Bank with the notation "payment stopped." Rauch was obliged to return the money advanced. Its account with the Bank was then overdrawn, but through subsequent deposits Rauch regained a credit balance, which the Bank used to repay itself.

Some months later, to compromise a lawsuit, the Bank executed a special two-page indorsement of the two checks to the plaintiff Lamson. Lamson sued the defendant drawer Corporation on the checks.

* * *

In reversing the trial court the Court of Appeals held as a matter of law that the plaintiff Lamson was not a holder of the checks. It arrived at the decision by ruling that the Bank's indorsement to Lamson was not in conformance with the Uniform Commercial Code because it was stapled to the checks. It was this interpretation of section 3–202(2) which prompted us to grant *certiorari*. It is that holding of the Court of Appeals which we expressly reverse.

II

When Rauch deposited the checks, it indorsed them in blank, transforming them into bearer paper. Sections 1–201(5) and 3–204(2). The Bank in turn indorsed the checks "pay any bank." That is a restrictive indorsement. Section 3–205(c). After a check has been restrictively indorsed, "only a bank may acquire the rights of a holder . . . [u]ntil the item has been specially indorsed by a bank to a person who is not a bank." Section 4–201(2)(b).

There is no question that the checks were indorsed to Lamson by name, thus qualifying as a special indorsement. Section 3–204(1). The problem is whether the special indorsement was correctly and properly affixed to the checks under section 3–202(2). It provides that "[a]n indorsement must be written . . . on behalf of the holder and on the instrument or on a paper so firmly affixed thereto as to become a part thereof."

The subject indorsement was typed on two legal size sheets of paper. It would have been physically impossible to place all of the language on the two small checks. Therefore, the indorsement had to be "affixed" to them in some way. Such a paper is called an allonge. In this case the allonge was affixed by stapling it to the checks.

We agree with the Court of Appeals' statement that a separate paper pinned or paper-clipped to an instrument is not sufficient for negotiation. Section 3–202(2), comment 3. However, we hold, *contra* to its decision, that the section does permit stapling as an adequate method of firmly affixing the indorsement. Stapling is the modern equivalent of gluing or pasting. Certainly as a physical matter it is just as easy to cut by scissors a document pasted or glued to another as it is to detach the two by unstapling. Therefore we hold that under the circumstances described, stapling an indorsement to a negotiable instrument is a permanent attachment to the checks so that it becomes "a part thereof."

Section 1–201(20) defines a holder as "a person who is in possession of . . . an instrument . . . indorsed to him . . . ." The Bank's special indorsement, stapled to the two checks, effectively made Lamson a holder, although not a holder in due course.

III

Once signatures are proven, Lamson, as a holder was entitled to payment by mere production of the instrument unless the Corporation established a defense. Sections 3–301 and 3–307(2).

* * *

V

Since we decide that Lamson became a holder by special indorsement, we do not have to consider whether he acquired rights as an assignee.

The judgment is reversed, and the cause remanded with directions to reinstate the judgment of the trial court.

Blank Indorsements

PALMER & RAY DENTAL SUPPLY OF ABILENE, INC. v. FIRST NAT'L BANK

Court of Civil Appeals of Texas, 1972.
477 S.W.2d 954.

WALTER, J.

* * * Palmer and Ray Dental Supply Company of Abilene, Inc. filed suit against First National Bank of Abilene for conversion of the proceeds of thirty-five checks presented to the Bank by its bookkeeper Mrs. Wilson on which she received cash. The court granted the Bank's motion for summary judgment and Palmer and Ray Dental Supply have appealed.

* * *

James Frank Ray, President and manager of the dental supply company testified substantially as follows: Mrs. Wilson was employed as our office manager. In February 1970, our auditor found a discrepancy in our inventory and we started looking for the leak. After we had worked on it for about two weeks, Mrs. Wilson called me one Saturday night and told me she would like to talk to me. I met her at the office and she told me she had been stealing by cashing checks that she was supposed to deposit. She was employed to answer the phone, take orders, invoice merchandise, order merchandise and to perform the general office duties. She also made deliveries and looked after the internal workings of the office. We do a credit business and the customers pay by check. I generally take the checks from the mail and place them in Mrs. Wilson's desk and she deposited them. We try to do our banking business everyday. She made out the deposit slips in our office. At the time Mrs. Wilson was working for us we had a rubberstamp which we used to endorse our checks. The stamp read:

Palmer & Ray Dental Supply
Inc. of Abilene
Box 2894
3110 B N. 1st
Abilene, Texas 79603

I authorized and directed Mrs. Wilson to endorse the checks with this rubber stamp. During the time Mrs. Wilson worked for us this was the only endorsement stamp we used. We had no stamp which read "for deposit only".

Most of the time she would go to the bank in our van. All deposits were made at the First National Bank and she would bring the deposit slips back to the office. She made the deposits about 75% of the time.

* * *

In its trial petition appellant alleges that Mrs. Wilson made the deposits for it at First National Bank but instead of depositing the thirty-five checks which are listed in appellant's petition as she was instructed to do, she drew cash on them and did not account

to the company for such money. It further alleged: "and by means of an unauthorized endorsement by said Dinah Wilson, the defendant First National paid cash to the *plaintiff* (Mrs. Wilson?) for the amount of the checks". It further alleged that by giving Mrs. Wilson cash instead of depositing the checks to its account the Bank converted its funds. Its cause of action against the Bank was predicated on the theory of wrongful conversion.

Section 3–204, Tex. Uniform Commercial Code, defines a blank endorsement as one that specifies no particular endorsee and may consist of a mere signature. Section 3–205 of the U.C.C. defines a restrictive endorsement to include one that uses the words "for deposit". Section 1.201(43), U.C.C., defines an unauthorized signature or endorsement as one made without actual implied or apparent authority and includes a forgery.

The summary judgment proof establishes that each of the checks has affixed thereto the blank rubber stamp endorsement of the appellant. We hold that such blank endorsement constitutes an authorized endorsement. When the Bank delivered cash to Mrs. Wilson instead of depositing the proceeds from the checks to appellant's account, the Bank was not guilty of conversion [wrongdoing]. [Citation].

The judgment is affirmed.

Special Indorsements

TUBIN v. RABIN

United States Court of Appeals, Fifth Circuit,
1976.
533 F.2d 255.

PER CURIAM:

This is a diversity of citizenship claim predicated on the Uniform Commercial Code (U.C.C.). Max Triplett sought to acquire a $2,850,000 loan for the acquisition and development of a New Mexico ghost town. Triplett attempted to arrange the financing through Meyer Rabin and Consumers Investment Company (CIC). CIC issued a commitment letter conditioned on the payment of a $14,250 commitment fee and the personal guarantee of C. D. Wyche. Because Triplett lacked the personal resources to fund the commitment fee, he sought to secure an additional loan. Melvin Rueckhaus, a New Mexico attorney, arranged a meeting between Triplett and E. S. Tubin to discuss the transaction. Tubin agreed to provide the $14,250 if the money would be "safe" pending the closing of the $2,850,000 loan and if he would receive $4,500 for the use of his money. Triplett agreed and Tubin purchased a $14,250 cashier's check from First National Bank of Albuquerque payable to Rueckhaus.

Rueckhaus typed the following restrictive endorsement on the back of the check:

PAY TO THE ORDER—CONSUMERS INVESTMENT CO. and CHARLES D. WYCHE, SR., of 1631 Rachelle Road, Irving, Texas, the same C. D. WYCHE mentioned in commitment letter 11/6/67 by CONSUMERS to Max Triplett. Endorsement constitutes acknowledgement by endorsees that the money represented by this check is the only remaining condition to funding the loan committee (sic commitment) and that endorsees will return the $14,250.00 to Melvin E. Rueckhaus, Attorney for E. S. Tubin, within 30 days if the loan is not funded as per agreement before that time.

Rabin presented the check to Fair Park National Bank for deposit and immediate credit to CIC's account. Wyche's signature was forged, but Fair Park National Bank was unaware of the forgery and immediately credited $14,250 to CIC and Rabin's account. Rabin depleted the CIC account, including the $14,250 attributable to the credit for Tubin's cashier's check.

The loan was never closed, but the $14,250 was never returned to Tubin or Rueckhaus.

Tubin sued Fair Park National Bank for breach of warranty and conversion of the cashier's check. After a non-jury trial, Judge Taylor filed two opinions in favor of Tubin.

[Citations.] Essentially, in his memorandum opinion Judge Taylor held:

Under § 3.202 [of the U.C.C.], negotiation of an 'order' instrument occurs when delivery, together with any necessary endorsements, is accomplished so that the tranferee becomes a qualified 'holder' of that instrument. In the present case, Fair Park could not stand in the shoes of either a 'holder' or a 'holder in due course' because C. D. Wyche's special endorsement was forged. According to § 3.204(a) a special endorsement is one which specifies the person to whose order the instrument is made payable, Reuckhaus, in endorsing the check as the original payee, required that in order for further negotiation of the check to occur, a collecting bank should 'pay to the order of Consumers Investment Company and Charles D. Wyche, Sr.' Thus, the $14,250.00 cashier's check became a specially endorsed instrument and could only be negotiated by both Wyche's and C.I.C.'s special endorsements together. The forgery of Wyche's signature rendered both special endorsements inoperative under § 3–404(a) and insofar as § 3–204(a) is concerned prevented the attempted negotiation.

By specially endorsing the check, the payee Reuckhaus in effect was saying that he desired only his enumerated endorsees or those persons who they desired by further negotiation, to receive the proceeds of the check. When the defendant collecting bank [Fair Park National Bank] paid the proceeds to a forger, the payee's [Reuckhaus] specific wishes were not carried out and under § 3–419(1)(c) it converted the payee's funds. Placing the funds received into the C.I.C. account, an account owned by one of its customers, does not alter this conclusion insofar as the collecting bank is concerned. When a payee specially endorses a check, he remains the rightful and deserving owner until his designated special endorsees—in this case, Wyche and C.I.C.—endorse.

The Court is of the opinion that Fair Park National Bank is liable to plaintiff upon the conversion theory. [Citation.]

* * *

Finding no reversible error, we affirm the judgment of the district court.

Indorsements for Deposit or
Collection

FULTZ v. FIRST NAT'L BANK IN GRAHAM

Supreme Court of Texas, 1965.
338 S.W.2d 405.

STEAKLEY, J.

This suit was brought by W. B. Fultz, Petitioner here, against the First National Bank in Graham, Respondent, to recover the sum of $13,060.00 representing "less cash" sums, in amounts ranging between $50.00 and $300.00, paid by the bank to Mrs. Fern McCoy, an employee of Fultz, in "for deposit only" transactions to the account of Fultz over a period of time between February, 1960, and April, 1963. The sums so paid to Mrs. McCoy were misappropriated to her personal use. Mrs. McCoy had not signed a signature card at the bank and was not authorized by Fultz either to check on his account or to withhold cash amounts from the deposits made for him. The full endorsement which was stamped on each of the checks read: "Pay to the order of the First National Bank, Graham, Texas— For deposit only—W. B. Fultz."

Both parties moved for summary judgment and the trial court granted the motion of Fultz. The Court of Civil Appeals held that the alleged negligence on the part of Fultz in not examining his bank statements and other records and discovering the defalcations so as to notify the bank would, if found to be true, constitute a defense to his suit against the bank. Consequently, that Court held that in these respects there were issues of fact to be determined by the trier of facts and the summary judgment for Fultz was improper. * * * We reverse the judgment of the Court of Civil Appeals and affirm that of the trial court.

The key to the first problem is the undisputed fact that the bank violated the written instructions of Fultz, and hence breached its deposit contract with him in each deposit transaction. In the exercise of care by Fultz, all of the checks which were deposited were endorsed "For Deposit Only." This was an unqualified direction to the bank to place the full amount of the checks to the account of Fultz. This instruction was violated when part of the amount of the checks was paid to Mrs. McCoy in cash. The bank had knowledge of its acts in violation of the instruction. Fultz as a depositor had the right to rely on the bank to honor the "For Deposit Only" instructions he had established as the regular deposit routine for his employee and the bank to follow; he was under no duty to exercise further care to ascertain if the bank had followed his instructions, and it is not asserted that Fultz had actual knowledge that the bank had not done so. The instruction carried in the restricted endorsement, "For Deposit Only," if followed, afforded absolute protection to both the bank and the depositor in the check deposit transactions and would have rendered the misappropriations impossible. The bank was in no way misled. Fultz had not filed a signature card for his defalcating employee and had not authorized his employee to sign checks on his account or make cash withdrawals in connection with deposits to his account. The "For Deposit Only" endorsements in the latter transactions were positively to the contrary. The decisions which consider the question of the liability of a bank for the payment of forged checks recognize the principle stated by the Supreme Court of the United States * * * that "If the bank's officers, before paying forged or altered checks, could by proper care and skill have detected the forgeries, then it cannot receive a credit for the amount of these checks, even if the depositor omitted all examination of his account."

So it is here. The Respondent bank had only to exercise proper care by following the specific instructions of Fultz, the depositor, the doing of this required no skill. Its course of action in failing to do so resulted in liability to Fultz "even if" he "omitted all examination of his account." This distinguishes the decisions in the cases which are premised upon a duty of the depositor to examine his statements from the bank, which examination would have revealed the defalcations. [Citations.]

* * *

Since Fultz owed no duty to the bank to examine his bank statements and other records, he was, for that reason, not guilty of negligence in not doing so, and in not discov-

ering the defalcations of his employee. For the same reason he is not estopped to assert the liability of the bank. There existed no genuine issue of fact between the parties in such respects.

The judgment of the Court of Civil Appeals is reversed and that of the trial court is affirmed.

PROBLEMS

1. Roy Rand executed and delivered to Sue Sims the following note: "Chicago, Illinois, June 1, 1985, I promise to pay to the order of Sue Sims or bearer, on or before July 1, 1985, the sum of $7,000. This note is given in consideration of Sim's transferring to the undersigned title to her 1982 Buick automobile. (signed) Roy Rand." Rand and Sims agreed that delivery of the car be deferred to July 1, 1985. On June 15, Sims sold and delivered the note, without indorsement, to Karl Kaye for $6,200. What rights, if any, has Kaye acquired?

2. Lavinia Lane received a check from Wilmore Enterprises, Inc., drawn on the Citizens Bank of Erehwon, in the sum of $10,000. Mrs. Lane indorsed the check "Mrs. Lavinia Lane for deposit only, Account of Lavinia Lane," placed it in a "Bank by Mail" envelope addressed to the First National Bank of Emanon, where she maintained a checking account, and placed the envelope over a tier of mailboxes in her apartment building along with other letters to be picked up by the postman the next day.

Flora Fain stole the check, went to the Bank of X, where Mrs. Lane was unknown, represented herself to be Lavinia Lane, and cashed the check. Has Bank X taken the check by negotiation? Why or why not?

3. What types of indorsements are the following:
  (a) "Pay to M without recourse."
  (b) "Pay to A for collection."
  (c) "I hereby assign all my rights, title, and interest in this note to F in full."
  (d) "Pay to the Southern Trust Company."
  (e) "Pay to the order of the Farmers Bank of Nicholasville for deposit only."

Indicate whether the indorsement is (1) blank or special, (2) restrictive or nonrestrictive, and (3) qualified or unqualified.

4. Explain whether the following transactions result in a valid negotiation:
  (a) A gives a negotiable check payable to bearer to B without indorsing it.
  (b) G indorses a negotiable, promissory note payable to the order of G, "Pay to M and N, (signed) G."
  (c) X lost a negotiable check payable to his order. Y found it and indorsed the back of the check: "Pay to Z, (signed) Y."
  (d) C indorsed a negotiable promissory note payable to the order of C, "(signed) C," and delivered it to D. D then wrote above C's signature, "Pay to D."

5. Alpha issues a negotiable check to Beta payable to the order of Beta in payment of an obligation Alpha owed Beta. Beta delivers the check to Gamma without indorsing it in exchange for 100 shares of General Motors stock owned by Gamma. How has Beta transferred the check? What rights, if any, does Gamma have against Beta?

6. M executed and delivered to P a negotiable promissory note payable to the order of P as payment for 100 bushels of wheat P had sold to M. P indorsed the note "Pay to R only, (signed) P" and sold it to R. R then sold the note to S after indorsing it "Pay to S, (signed) R." What rights, if any, does S acquire in the instrument?

7. Simon Sharpe executed and delivered to Ben Bates a negotiable promissory note payable to the order of Ben Bates for $500. Bates indorsed the note, "Pay to Carl Cady upon his satisfactorily repairing the roof of my house, (signed) Ben Bates," and delivered it to Cady as a downpayment on the contract price of the roofing job. Cady then indorsed the note and sold it to Timothy Tate for $450. What rights, if any, does Tate acquire in the promissory note?

8. Debbie Dean issued a check to Betty Brown payable to the order of Cathy Cain and Betty Brown. Betty indorsed the check "Payable to Elizabeth East, (signed) Betty Brown." What rights, if any, does Elizabeth acquire in the check?

Chapter 26

HOLDER IN DUE COURSE

THE unique and most significant aspect of negotiability is the concept of the holder in due course. While a mere holder acquires a negotiable instrument subject to all claims and defenses to it, a holder in due course, except in *consumer* credit transactions, takes the instrument free of all claims of other parties and free of all defenses to the instrument except for a very limited number specifically set forth in the Code. The law has conferred this preferred position upon the holder in due course in order to encourage the free negotiability of commercial paper by minimizing the risks assumed by an innocent purchaser of the instrument. This chapter discusses what the law requires of a transferee to become a holder in due course and the benefits conferred upon a holder in due course.

REQUIREMENTS OF A HOLDER IN DUE COURSE

To acquire the preferential rights of a holder in due course, a person must meet the requirements of Section 3–302 of the Code or she must "inherit" these rights under the shelter provision, Section 3–201. To satisfy the requirements of Section 3–302, a holder in due course must:

1. be a holder of a negotiable instrument;
2. take it for value;
3. take it in good faith; and
4. take it without notice
   (a) that it is overdue or has been dishonored, or
   (b) of any defense against or claim to it on the part of any person.

535

FIGURE 26-1   Rights of Transferees

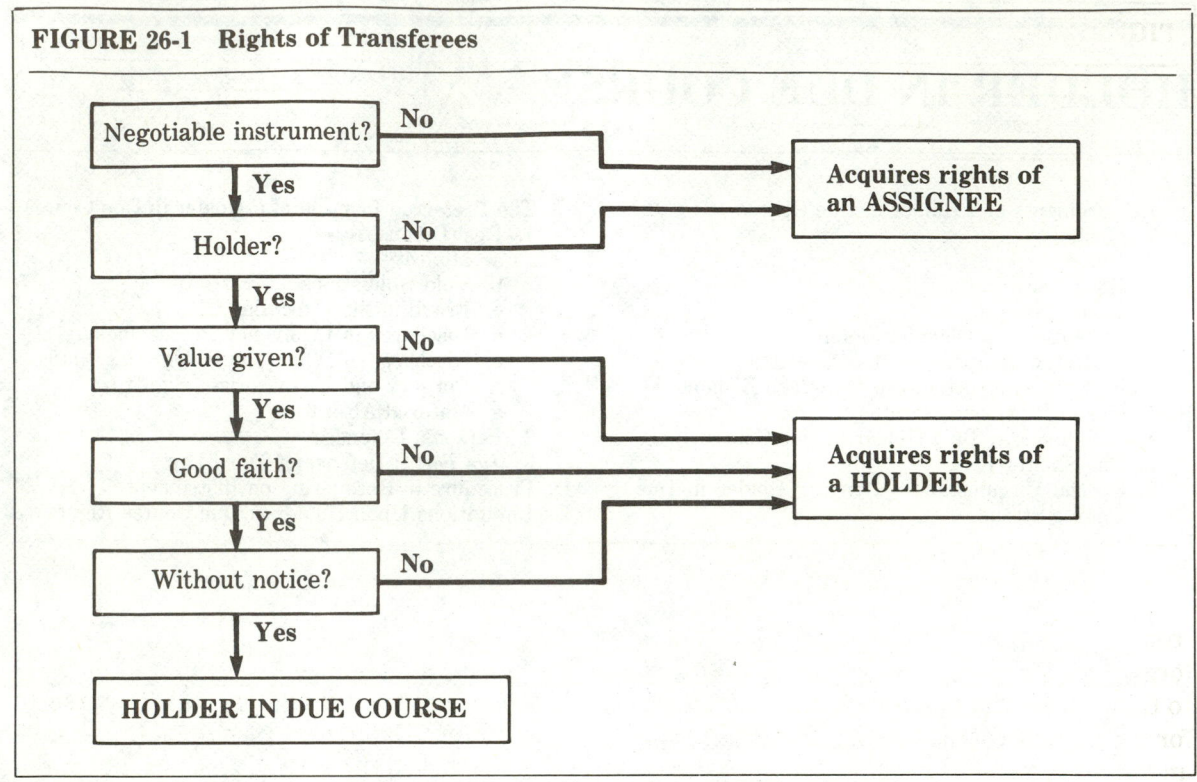

Holder

In order to become a holder in due course, the transferee must first be a holder. A "holder" is a person who is in possession of a negotiable instrument drawn or issued to his order or to bearer, or indorsed to him or in blank. He is, therefore, a person in possession who by the terms of the instrument is entitled to payment. Whether or not the holder is the owner of the instrument, he may transfer it, negotiate it, discharge it (with certain exceptions specified in Section 3–603), or enforce payment in his own name.

The significance of being a holder is brought out in the following factual situation. Poe indorsed her paycheck in blank and cashed it at a tavern where she was a well-known customer. Shortly thereafter, a burglar stole the check from the tavern. The tavernkeeper immediately notified Poe's employer who gave the drawee bank a stop payment order. The burglar indorsed the check in a false name and passed it to a grocer who took it in good faith and for value. The check was dishonored upon presentment to the drawee. The paycheck became bearer paper when Poe indorsed it in blank. It retained this character in the hands of the tavernkeeper, in the hands of the burglar, and in the hands of the grocer, who became a holder in due course even though he had received it from a thief who had indorsed it with a false name. An indorsement is not necessary to the negotiation of bearer paper. The forged indorsement was therefore immaterial. The thief was a "holder" of the check within the definition of Section 1–201(20) and under Section 3–301 a holder may negotiate a check "whether or not he is the owner." Accordingly, one who, like the grocer, takes from a holder for value, in good faith, and without notice becomes a holder in due course. See Figure 26-2.

This rule does not apply to a stolen order instrument. In the preceding example assume that the thief had stolen the paycheck

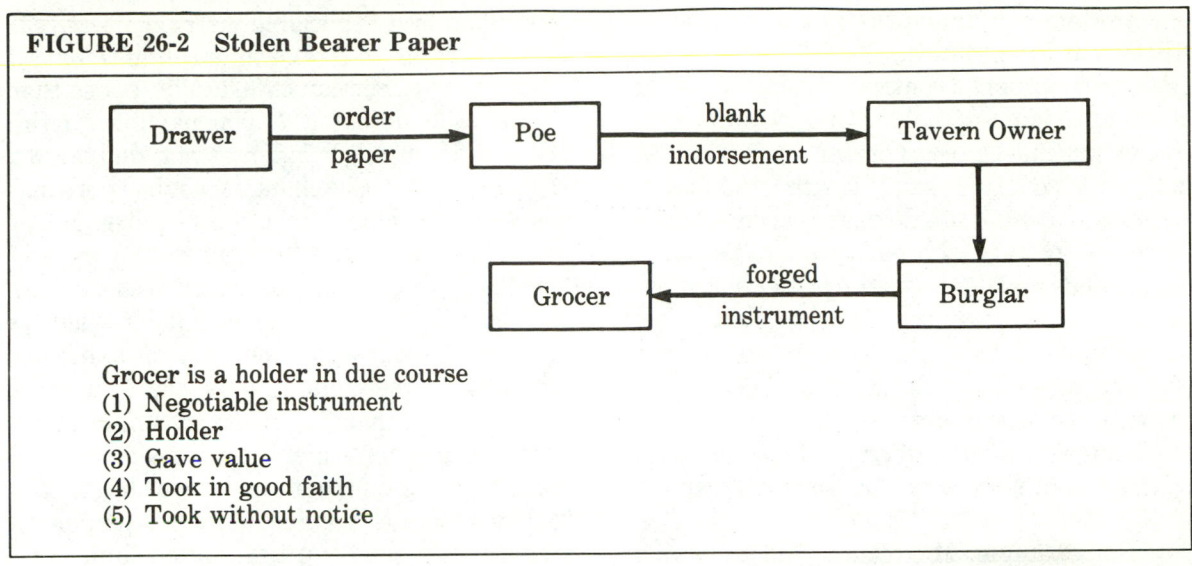

FIGURE 26-2   Stolen Bearer Paper

Grocer is a holder in due course
(1) Negotiable instrument
(2) Holder
(3) Gave value
(4) Took in good faith
(5) Took without notice

from Poe prior to indorsement. The thief then forged Poe's signature and passed the check to the grocer who again took it in good faith, for value, and without notice. Negotiation of an order instrument requires a valid indorsement by the person to whose order the instrument is payable, in this case Poe. Since the forged indorsement is not effective as Poe's, there has been no valid indorsement by Poe. Consequently, the grocer has not taken the instrument with all necessary indorsements, and, therefore, he could not be a holder nor a holder in due course. See Figure 26-3.

Value

The law requires a holder in due course to give value. An obvious case of failure to give value is where the holder makes a gift of the instrument to a third person. For example, assume M executes a note payable to the order of P, who indorses the note and gives it to his fiancee, W. Since W had not given value for the note, she cannot be a holder in due course.

The concept of value in the law of negotiable instruments is not the same as that

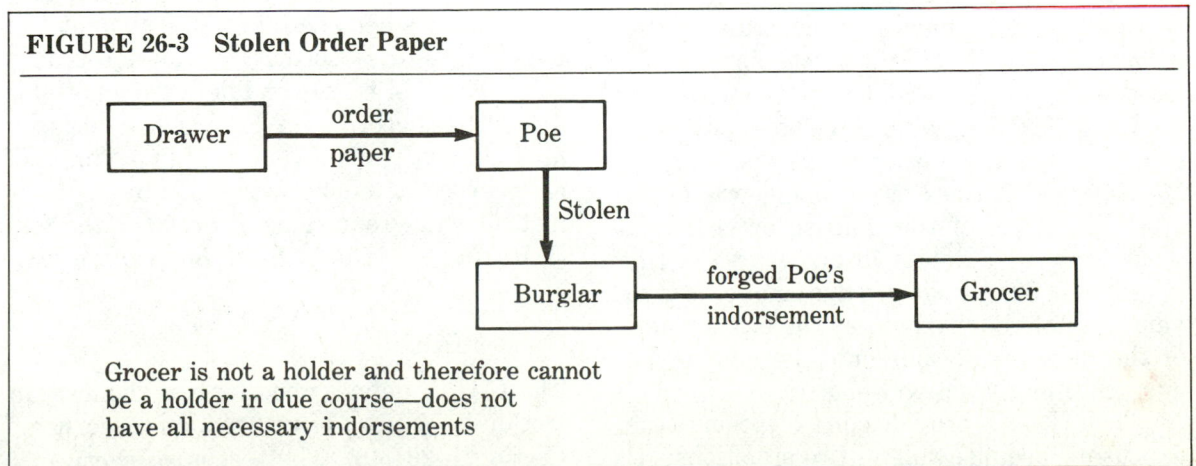

FIGURE 26-3   Stolen Order Paper

Grocer is not a holder and therefore cannot
be a holder in due course—does not
have all necessary indorsements

of consideration under the law of contracts. An executory promise, clearly valid consideration to support a contract, is not the giving of value to support holder in due course status. A purchaser of a note or draft who has not yet given value may rescind the transaction and avoid it if a defense becomes known to her. A person who has given value, however, needs and deserves the protection given to a holder in due course. Thus, a holder takes an instrument for value only to the extent that the agreed consideration has been *given*, provided the consideration was given prior to the holder's learning of any defense or claim to the instrument. *See Korzenik v. Supreme Radio, Inc.*

For example, M executes and delivers a $1,000 note payable to the order of P, who negotiates it to H who promises to pay P for it a month later. During the month, H learns that M has a defense against P. H can rescind the agreement with P and return or tender the note back to P. This makes him whole. He has no need to cut off M's defense. Assume, on the other hand, that H has paid P for the note before he learns of M's defense. It may not be possible for H to recover his money from P. H then needs the holder-in-due-course protection which permits him to recover on the instrument from M. Further, assume that H had agreed to pay P $850 for the note. If H had paid P $600, he could be a holder in due course only to the extent of $600, and if a defense were available, it would be valid against him only to the extent of the balance. When H paid the $250 balance to P, he would become a holder in due course as to the full $1,000 face value of the note, provided payment was made prior to H's discovery of M's defense. If the $250 payment was made after discovery of the defense or claim, H would only be a holder in due course to the extent of $600. A holder in due course, to give value, is not required to pay the face amount of the instrument, but only the amount he agreed to pay. Section 3–303(a).

The U.C.C. provides an exception to the executory promise rule in two situations: (1) the giving of a negotiable instrument and (2) the making of an irrevocable commitment to a third party. Section 3–303(c). Suppose that M makes a note for $1,000 payable to the order of P, which P indorses and delivers to H, who gives P in exchange for it her personal check for $1,000. H met the requirement of giving value for the note when she gave P her check, not when the check was paid by the drawee bank. Value would likewise be given if H made any other irrevocable commitment, if the commitment was to a *third party* rather than to P. An example of an irrevocable commitment is the issuance by a bank of a letter of credit, under which it agrees to pay amounts advanced to the person to whom it is issued, up to a stated limit. The bank has no way of stopping payment on such a letter of credit.

Where an instrument is given as security for an obligation the lender is regarded as having given value to the extent of his security interest. Sections 3–302(4) and 3–303(a). For example, P is the holder of a $1,000 note payable to his order, executed by M, and due in twelve months. P uses the note as security for a $700 loan made to him by H. Since H has advanced $700, he has met the requirement of value to this extent.

Finally, under general contract law an **antecedent debt** is not sufficient consideration to support a promise to pay the debt or a lesser amount in full satisfaction. However, under Section 3–303(b) of the Code a holder gives value when she takes an instrument in payment of or as security for an antecedent debt. Thus, M makes and delivers a note for $1,000 to the order of P, which P sells by indorsement and delivery to H in payment of or security for a debt owing to H by P. H has met the value requirement. *See St. Paul Fire & Marine Ins. Co. v. State Bank of Salem.*

Good Faith

The U.C.C. defines good faith as "honesty in fact in the conduct or transaction concerned." Section 1–201(19). The test is **subjective:** it measures good faith by what the purchaser knows or believes. He may be empty-headed, but if his heart is pure, he can pass muster on good faith grounds. Under this test, if the purchaser was actually innocent, he is held to have bought the paper in good faith, even though a prudent man under the circumstances would have known that something was wrong.

Lack of Notice

To become a holder in due course, a holder must also take the instrument without notice that it is overdue, dishonored, or subject to any defense or claim. Notice of any of these matters should alert the purchaser that she may be buying a lawsuit and, therefore, should refuse to take the instrument. "Notice" is defined in Section 1–201(25) as follows: "A person has 'notice' of a fact when (a) he has actual knowledge of it; or (b) he has received a notice or notification of it; or (c) from all the facts and circumstances known to him at the time in question he has reason to know that it exists." The first two clauses of this definition impose a wholly subjective standard. The last clause provides a partially objective one: the fact that suspicious circumstances are present does not adversely affect the purchaser, unless he has reason to recognize them as suspicious.

Section 3–304(6) deals with the issue of the timing of the notice, that is, the question of a prospective holder learning of a defense before he has purchased the instrument, but the knowledge comes too late for him to act upon it. Suppose that the bank upon which a check is drawn is notified one minute before the teller cashes it that payment is stopped because of fraud. The acquisition of this notice does not prevent the bank from being a holder in due course. Section 3–304(6) provides:

To be effective, notice must be received at such time and in such manner as to give a reasonable opportunity to act on it.

Of course, notice acquired *after* the holder has purchased an instrument does not impair his status as a holder in due course.

Notice of a Claim or Defense A purchaser has notice of a claim or defense if the instrument is so incomplete, bears visible evidence of forgery or alteration, or is otherwise so irregular as to call into question its validity. Section 3–304(1)(a). For example, D draws a check on the XYZ Bank for $100, payable to the order of P. P crudely raises the amount of the check to $1,000 and negotiates it to H. H cannot be a holder in due course. He is charged with information which he can learn from the face of the instrument. The instrument is irregular, and the alteration is so manifest on its face that H would be held to have notice of it.

Suppose, however, there is an obvious change on the face of the instrument which would not indicate wrongdoing. For instance, the date is changed from January 2, 1984 to January 2, 1985, and thus it might be reasonable to assume that the drawer, out of force of habit, wrote "1984" rather than "1985." This would not be considered a material alteration that would give notice of a defense or claim. *See St. Paul Fire & Marine Ins. Co. v. State Bank of Salem.*

Additionally, a purchaser has notice of a claim or defense if the purchaser has notice that the obligation of any party is *voidable* or that *all* parties to the instrument have been discharged. Section 3–304(1)(b). The fact that the holder knows that one or more but not all the parties have been discharged, however, does not prevent the holder from being a holder in due course with respect to the non-discharged parties. For example, M issues a negotiable promissory note to P, who indorses it in blank and delivers it to A. The instrument then passes by blank indorsements to B, C, and D. D strikes out C's indorsement and negotiates it for value to H. H would have notice that C's liability had been discharged. This would not prevent H from being a holder in due course with respect to

M, P, A, B, and D because their liability is not discharged. Section 3–304(1) applies only when a purchaser has notice that all the parties have been discharged.

Section 3–304(4) provides a listing of facts the knowledge of which does not of itself give the purchaser notice of a defense or claim. Subparagraph (4)(a) provides that knowledge of the fact that the instrument is antedated or postdated does not of itself give the purchaser notice of a defense or claim. This accords with Section 3–114(1) that antedating or postdating does not affect negotiability. Subparagraph (b) of Section 3–304(4) provides that the mere fact that the purchaser of an instrument knows that it was originally given or negotiated for an executory promise or was accompanied by a separate agreement does not impair his good faith, unless he knows that the promise has not been kept. Suppose M makes and delivers a note to the order of P which recites that it was given "As per our contract of even date." This recital does not impair negotiability because it does not burden the note with the extraneous contract. Section 3–105(1)(b). The recital notifies prospective purchasers that the note was given pursuant to a contract which may or may not have been performed. Subparagraph (c) states that mere knowledge of the fact that one party has signed for the accommodation of another does not give the purchaser notice of any claim or defense. Suppose that M makes a note payable to the order of P and W also signs as maker to accommodate M. If a purchaser of the note from P knows the relationship between M and W, he has knowledge of the possibility of a defense by W based upon some conduct by P, but if he does not know of any such defense he is not deprived of the status of holder in due course. Subparagraph (d) provides that knowledge of the fact that an incomplete instrument has been completed does not of itself constitute notice of a defense or claim unless the purchaser also has knowledge that the completion was improper.

Notice an Instrument Is Overdue To be a holder in due course the purchaser must take the instrument without notice that it is overdue. This requirement is based on the idea that overdue paper conveys a suspicion that something is wrong. Thus, if an instrument is payable on July 1, a purchaser cannot become a holder in due course by buying it on July 2, provided that July 1 was a business day.

In the case of an installment note, or of several notes issued as part of the same transaction with successive maturity dates, there is a natural question as to the effect of notice of default in payment of an installment or of a note in the same series. Section 3–304(3)(a) answers this by providing that the purchaser has notice that an instrument is overdue if he has reason to know that any part of the principal amount is overdue or that there is an uncured default in payment of another instrument of the same series.

Demand paper is not overdue for purposes of preventing one from becoming a holder in due course unless the purchaser has notice that she is taking it after demand has been made, or until it has been outstanding an unreasonable length of time. Section 3–304(3)(c). The U.C.C. does not state what constitutes a reasonable time. Usually, in the case of a demand note, this means about sixty days. The time is somewhat shorter for drafts, and with regard to checks a reasonable time is presumed to be thirty days. However, the particular situation, business custom, and other relevant factors must be considered in making the determination, and no hard-and-fast rules are possible.

Acceleration clauses have also caused trouble. If an instrument's maturity date has been accelerated, the holder may be unaware that it is past due. A prospective purchaser may similarly be unaware of this fact and may qualify as a holder in due course, unless she has reason to know that the acceleration has occurred. Section 3–304(3)(b).

Notice an Instrument Has Been Dishonored If a transferee has notice that an instrument has been dishonored by the refusal of a party to pay or accept it, he cannot become a holder in due course. He knows the instrument may not be paid.

HOLDER IN DUE COURSE STATUS

A Payee May Be a Holder in Due Course

The Code provides that a payee may be a holder in due course. Section 3–302(2). This does not mean that the payee will always be a holder in due course but merely that he *may* if he satisfies all the requirements for a holder to become a holder in due course. For example, if a seller delivers goods to a buyer and accepts a current check in payment, the seller will be a holder in due course if he acted in good faith and had no notice of defenses or claims. However, the seller takes the check *subject* to all claims and defenses because a holder in due course takes free of defenses only as to persons with whom he had *not* dealt. Section 3–305(2).

There are a number of situations, however, in which the payee is not an immediate party to the transaction and, therefore, if he meets the requirements of a holder in due course will not be subject to claims and most defenses. For example, R, upon purchasing goods from P, fraudulently obtains a check from C payable to the order of P and forwards it to P. P takes it for value and without any knowledge that R had defrauded C into issuing the check. In such a case, the payee, P, is held to be a holder in due course, and, take the instrument free and clear of C's defense of fraud in the inducement. There are a number of other ways in which a payee may be a holder in due course, but they are rather infrequent. In every instance there are three parties involved in the transaction, and the defense exists between the parties other than the payee. *See Eldon's Super Fresh Stores, Inc. v. Merrill Lynch, Pierce, Fenner & Smith, Inc.*

The Shelter Rule

The transferee of an instrument, as previously noted, acquires such rights in the instrument as the transferor had. Section 3–201. Therefore, even if a holder does not comply with all the requirements for being a holder in due course, she, nevertheless, acquires all the rights of that status if some previous holder of the instrument had been a holder in due course. Thus, P induces M by fraud to make a note payable to her order and then negotiates it to A, a holder in due course. After the note is overdue, A gives it to B, who has notice of the fraud. B is not a holder in due course, since he has taken the instrument when overdue, did not pay value, and has notice of M's defense. Nonetheless, through the operation of the shelter rule B acquires A's rights as a holder in due course, and M cannot successfully assert his defense against B. The purpose of the shelter provision is not to benefit the transferee but to assure the holder in due course of a free market for commercial paper he acquires.

The rule, however, provides that a person who is not a holder in due course cannot wash the paper clean in her hands by later re-acquiring it from a subsequent holder in due course or person having the rights of one. For example, P induces M by fraud to make an instrument payable to the order of P. P subsequently negotiates the instrument to H, a holder in due course, and later reacquires it from H. P does not succeed to H's rights as a holder in due course and remains subject to the defense of fraud.

Special Circumstances Denying Holder in Due Course Status

In keeping with the theory that the purpose of negotiability is to facilitate the flow of commerce, when an instrument is acquired in a way other than the ordinary flow of commerce, there is no reason to accord the transferee holder in due course status. Section 3–302(3) defines the situations to which this rule applies:

A holder does not become a holder in due course of an instrument:

(a) by purchase of it at judicial sale or by taking it under legal process; or

(b) by acquiring it in taking over an estate; or

(c) by purchasing it as a part of a bulk transaction not in regular course of business of the transferor.

In each of these situations, the transferee takes under unusual circumstances which indicate she is merely a successor in interest to the prior holder. As such, she should acquire no better rights. But if her transferor was a holder in due course, under the shelter provision of Section 3–201, the transferee acquires the rights of a holder in due course.

THE PREFERRED POSITION OF A HOLDER IN DUE COURSE

A holder in due course, in a *non-consumer* transaction, takes the instrument free from all claims on the part of any person and free from all defenses of any party with whom he has not dealt except for a limited number of defenses which are available against anyone, including a holder in due course. Such defenses are referred to as **real** defenses, as opposed to defenses which may not be asserted against a holder in due course and which are referred to as **personal** or **contractual** defenses.

Real Defenses

The real defense available against **all** holders, including holders in due course, are:

1. minority to the extent that it is a defense to a simple contract, Section 3–305(2)(a);
2. such other incapacity or duress or illegality of the transaction as renders the obligation of the party void, Section 3–305(2)(b);
3. fraud in the execution, Section 3–305(2)(c);
4. discharge in insolvency proceedings, Section 3–305(2)(d);

5. any other discharge of which the holder has notice when he takes the instrument, Section 3–305(2)(e);
6. forgery, Section 3–404; and
7. material alteration, Section 3–407.

Minority All States have a firmly entrenched public policy of protecting minors from persons who might take advantage of them through contractual dealings. The U.C.C. does not state when minority is available as a defense or the conditions under which it may be asserted. Rather, it provides that minority is a defense available against a holder in due course to the extent that it is a defense to a simple contract under the laws of the State involved.

Void Obligations Where the obligation on an instrument originates in such a way that under the law of the State involved it is *void*, the U.C.C. authorizes the use of this defense against a holder in due course. This follows from the fact that where the party was never obligated, it is unreasonable to permit an event over which he has no control—negotiation to a holder in due course—to convert a nullity into a valid claim against him.

Incapacity, duress, and illegality of the transaction are defenses which may render the obligation of a party voidable or void, depending upon the law of the State involved as applied to the facts of a transaction. To the extent the obligation is rendered void, the defense may be asserted against a holder in due course. To the extent it is voidable, which is generally the case, the defense (other than minority) is not available against a holder in due course.

Fraud in the Execution Fraud in the execution of the instrument renders the instrument void and therefore is a defense valid against a holder in due course. The Code describes this type of fraud as such misrepresentation as has induced the party to sign the instrument with neither knowledge nor reasonable opportunity to obtain knowledge of its character or its essential terms. For example, M is asked to sign a receipt and does so without realizing or having the opportunity of learning that her signature is going on a form of promissory note cleverly concealed under the receipt. M's signature has been obtained by fraud in the execution, and M would have a valid defense against a holder in due course. *See Exchange International Leasing Corp. v. Consolidated Business Forms Co.*

Discharge in Insolvency Proceedings

If a party's obligation on an instrument is discharged in a bankruptcy proceeding, he has a defense that is valid in any action brought against him on the instrument, including one by a holder in due course.

Discharge of Which the Holder Has Notice

Any holder, including a holder in due course, takes the instrument subject to *any* discharge of which she has notice when she takes the instrument. As previously noted, if a holder acquires an instrument with notice that *all* prior parties have been discharged, she cannot become a holder in due course. Section 3–304(1)(b). However, if only some, but not all, of the parties to the instrument have been discharged, this fact does not preclude a purchaser from being a holder in due course. Those parties of whose discharge the holder in due course had notice, however, possess a real defense.

Forgery and Unauthorized Signature

A party's signature to an instrument is a forgery when it is made without actual, implied or apparent authority. A person whose signature is forged cannot be held liable on the instrument in the absence of estoppel or ratification, even if the instrument is negotiated to a holder in due course. He has not made a contract. Similarly, if A's signature were forged on the back of an instrument, A could not be held as an indorser. A has not made a contract. Thus, any unauthorized signature is wholly inoperative as that of the person whose name is signed unless he ratifies it or is precluded from denying it; the unauthorized signature operates only as the signature of the unauthorized signer. Section 3–404(1).

It is well settled that a person may be **estopped** or precluded from asserting a defense because his conduct in the matter has caused reliance by a third party to his loss or damage. Suppose D's son forges D's name to a check which the drawee bank cashes. When the returned check reaches D, he learns of the forgery. Rather than subject his son to trouble, possibly criminal prosecution, D says nothing. Thereafter, D's son continues to forge checks and cashes them at the drawee bank. The bank may be suspicious of the signature, but the fact that D has not complained may induce it to believe that the signatures are proper. Finally, D does complain, seeking to compel the bank to recredit his account for all the forged checks. D will not succeed, as he is estopped by his conduct from denying that his son had authority to sign his name.

A party is similarly precluded from denying the validity of his signature if his negligence substantially contributes to the making of the unauthorized signature. The most obvious case is that of the drawer who makes use of a mechanized or other automatic signing device and is negligent in looking after it. In such an instance the drawer would not be permitted to assert the unauthorized signature as a defense against a holder in due course.

An unauthorized signature may be *ratified* and thereby become valid so far as its effect as a signature. Thus, A forges B's indorsement on a promissory note and negotiates it to C. B subsequently ratifies A's act. As a result A is no longer liable to C on the note although B is liable. Nonetheless, B's ratification does *not* relieve A from civil liability to B nor does it in any way affect A's criminal liability for the forgery.

Material Alteration

Any alteration is material which changes the contract of any party to the instrument in any respect. As against any person *other* than a subsequent holder in due course

  (a) alteration by the holder which is *both* fraudulent and material discharges any party whose contract is thereby changed, unless that party assents or is precluded from asserting the defense;

  (b) no other alteration discharges any party, and the instrument may be enforced according to its original tenor or as to incomplete instruments according to the authority given. Section 3–407(2).

A subsequent holder in due course may always enforce the instrument according to its original tenor, and when an incomplete instrument has been completed, she may enforce it as completed. Section 3–407(3).

  Since an alteration is material only as it may change the contract of a party to the instrument, the addition or deletion of words which do not in any way affect the contract of any previous signer is not material. For example, where there is a discrepancy between words and figures on a check, the words being "twenty-five hundred dollars" and the figures "$25," a change of the figures to $2,500 is not a material change. But even a slight change in the contract of a party is a material alteration; the addition of one cent to the amount payable or an advance of one day in the date of payment will operate as a discharge if it is fraudulent.

  Where an instrument contains blanks or is otherwise incomplete, it may be completed in accordance with the authority given and is then valid and effective as completed. If, however, the completion is unauthorized and has the effect of changing the contract of any previous signer, it is considered a material alteration.

  A material alteration does not discharge any party unless it is made for a fraudulent purpose. Thus, there is no discharge where a blank is filled in the honest belief that it is as authorized. Likewise, if the alteration is not material there is no discharge, and the instrument may be enforced according to its

original tenor. Where blanks are filled or an incomplete instrument is otherwise completed, there is no original tenor, but the instrument may be enforced according to the authority actually given.

  Thus, a party is discharged from liability on a negotiable instrument to any holder other than a holder in due course by an alteration if the alteration is (1) made by a holder (2) with fraudulent intent and (3) is material. If any of these requirements is not met, no party is discharged, and a holder may recover the original tenor of the altered instrument or the authorized amount where the instrument was incomplete. In keeping with the preferential position accorded a holder in due course, he may enforce any altered instrument according to its original terms and may enforce an incomplete instrument as completed. See Figure 26-4.

  Material alterations frequently are made possible by the *negligent* manner in which the instrument is drawn or made. Suppose that M makes a note, writing it out in lead pencil. A party raises the amount. M will be precluded from raising the defense of material alteration due to his own negligence which allowed the alteration. Section 3–406. Assent to an alteration given before or after it is made also prevents the party from asserting the defense.

The following illustrations may explain the operation of these rules.

1. M executes and delivers a note to P for $2,000 which P subsequently indorses and transfers to A for $1900. A intentionally and skillfully raises the note to $20,000 and then negotiates it to B who takes it in good faith and without notice of any wrongdoing for $19,000. B is a holder in due course and, therefore, can collect the amount of the original tenor ($2,000) from M or P and the full amount ($20,000) from A, less the amount paid by the other parties.

2. Assume the facts in (1) except that B is not a holder in due course, M and P are both discharged by A's fraudulent and material al-

FIGURE 26-4   Effects of Alterations

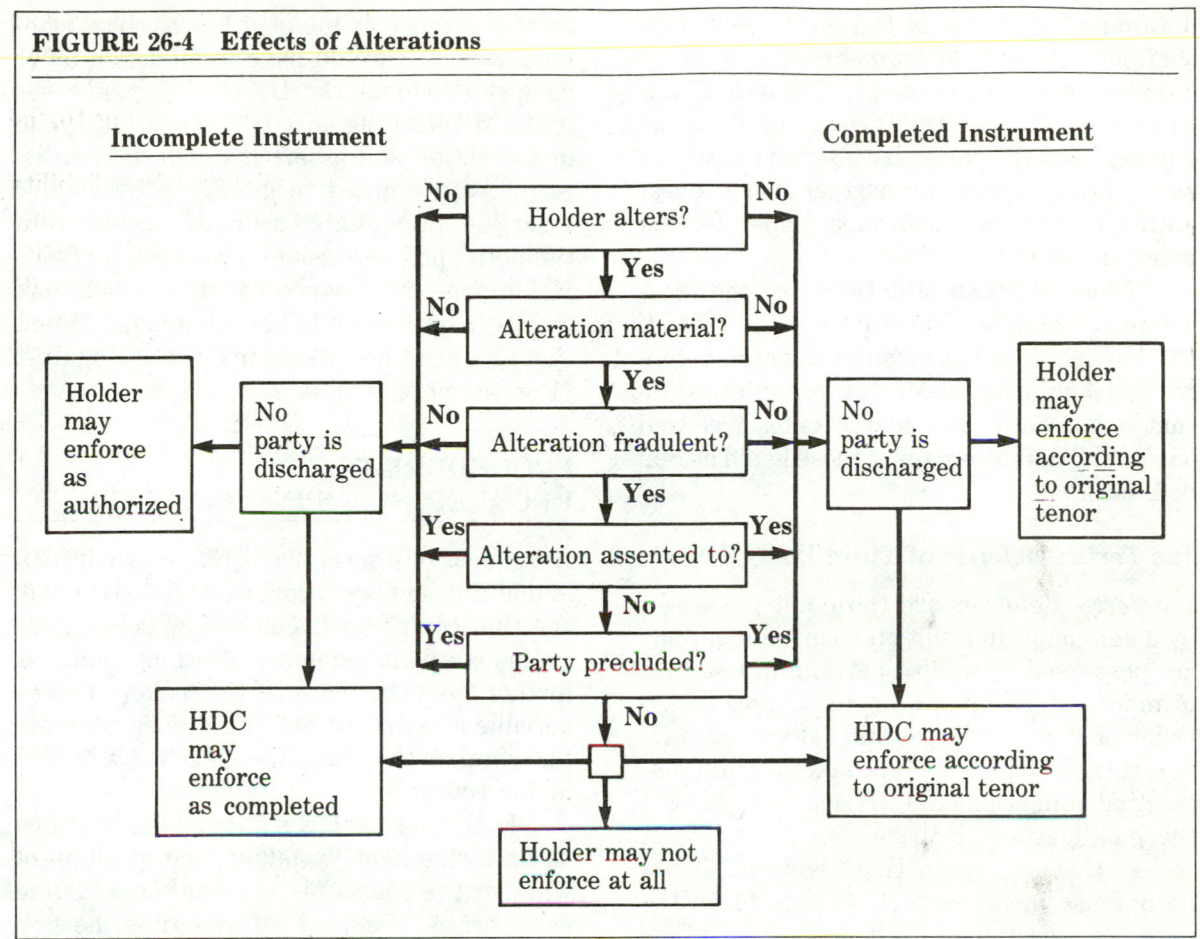

teration. B's only recourse is against A for the full amount ($20,000).

3. M issues his blank check to P who is to complete it when the exact amount is determined. P wrongfully fills in $4,000 when the correct amount should be $2,000. P then negotiates the check to H. If H is a holder in due course, she can collect the amount as completed ($4,000) from either M or P. However, if H is not a holder in due course, she has no recourse against M but may recover the full amount ($4,000) from P.

Personal Defenses

Defenses to an instrument may arise in many ways, either at the time of its issuance or later. In general, defenses to liability on a negotiable instrument are of the kind which may be raised in the case of any action for breach of contract. They are numerous and are available against any holder of the instrument unless he has the rights of a holder in due course. Among the personal defenses are: (1) lack of consideration; (2) failure of consideration; (3) breach of contract; (4) fraud in the inducement; (5) illegality which does not render the transaction a nullity; (6) duress, undue influence, mistake, misrepresentation, or incapacity which does not render the transaction void; (7) set-off or counterclaim; (8) discharge of which the holder in due course does not have notice; (9) non-delivery of an instrument, whether complete or incomplete; (10) unauthorized completion of an incomplete instrument; (11) payment without obtaining surrender of the instrument; (12) theft of a bearer instrument or a properly indorsed order instrument; (13) lack of authority of a corporate officer or an agent or partner as to the particular instrument, where such officer, agent, or partner had general authority to issue negotiable paper for his principal or firm.

These thirteen situations are the most common examples, but others exist. Indeed, the U.C.C. does not attempt to detail defenses which may be cut off. It is content to state that a holder in due course takes free and clear of all defenses except those listed as real defenses.

Jus Tertii: Defense of Third Party

Jus tertii defenses are those not possessed by a defendant in a suit on an instrument but are possessed by a third party. Suppose that M makes and delivers a note payable to the order of P who indorses and delivers it to H, in return for which H undertakes certain contractual obligations to P. H does not perform these obligations. P thereupon directs M not to pay the note when H presents it. M has no defense of his own. If H sues M on the note M's assertion of P's defense is called *jus tertii*. Section 3–306(d) denies the right of *jus tertii*, except where the instrument has been stolen or restrictively indorsed by providing:

Unless he has the rights of a holder in due course any person takes the instrument subject to * * * (d) the defense that he or a person through whom he holds the instrument acquired it by theft, or that payment or satisfaction to such holder would be inconsistent with the terms of a restrictive indorsement. The claim of any third party to the instrument is not otherwise available as a defense to any party liable thereon unless the third person himself defends the action for such party.

The *jus tertii* situation seldom arises where the plaintiff is a holder in due course as the defense is a personal one and not available against such a holder. Where H is not a holder in due course, he may nevertheless be able to recover against M, where M does not

have a defense of his own but asserts a defense which P would have in an action by H against P. Under the U.C.C., M cannot set up P's defenses against H. P must intervene in the action and assert his own defense. P might be prompted to intervene by way of asserting an equitable claim of ownership to the note upon rescission of his contract with H for non-performance by H. P would ask that H take nothing in his suit against M and that judgment be entered in favor of P against M on the note.

PROCEDURE IN RECOVERING ON INSTRUMENT

A frequent misconception is that only a holder in due course may recover on an instrument and that the plaintiff's lack of holder-in-due-course status is a defense. Nothing could be further from the truth. If the maker of a negotiable note has no defense it does not matter whether the plaintiff is or is not a holder in due course.

In the normal law suit in which recovery on an instrument is sought, the question of whether the plaintiff is a holder in due course never arises. Section 3–307 describes the step by step procedure.

When the holder brings an action to collect, he relies upon Section 3–301, which provides that the holder of an instrument, whether or not he is a holder in due course, may, among other things, enforce payment in his own name. Upon filing of suit, it is assumed that all signatures are valid and effective unless the defendant denies this. At this point it is not pertinent whether the plaintiff is a holder in due course, since the defense of unauthorized signature is valid against any holder.

If the signatures are admitted, or proved valid, the plaintiff is entitled to recover merely upon production of the instrument and proof of the amount of the unpaid principal due. Up to this point there has been no occasion for the plaintiff to allege that he is a holder in due course. If no defense is asserted, he obtains judgment without more. If the de-

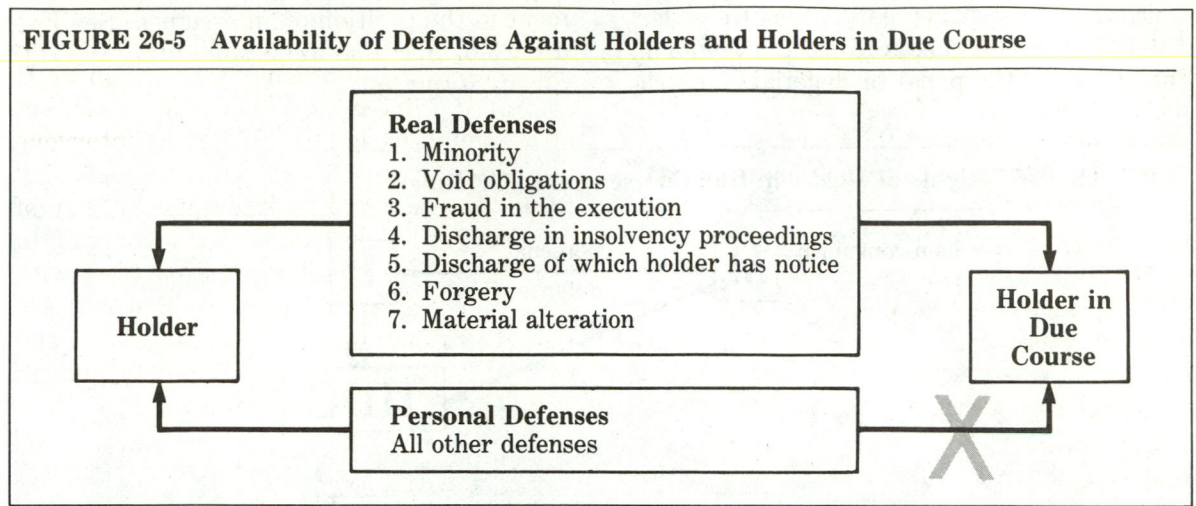

FIGURE 26-5   Availability of Defenses Against Holders and Holders in Due Course

fense asserted is a real defense, it is effective against a holder in due course. However, a party claiming to be a holder in due course has the burden of proof to show by evidence the facts necessary to establish his holder in due course status. Section 3–307(3).

LIMITATIONS UPON HOLDER IN DUE COURSE RIGHTS

The preferential position enjoyed by a holder in due course has been severely circumscribed by a Federal Trade Commission rule limiting the rights out of a **consumer credit contract,** which includes negotiable instruments. The rule, entitled "Preservation of Consumers' Claims and Defenses," applies to sellers and lessors of consumer goods, which are goods for personal, household or family use. It also applies to lenders who advance money to finance the consumer's purchase of consumer goods or services. The rule is intended to prevent situations in which consumer purchase transactions have been financed in such manner that the purchaser is legally obligated to make full payment of the price to a third party, although the dealer from whom she bought the goods had committed fraud or the goods were defective. This occurs when the purchaser executes and delivers to the seller her negotiable instrument

which the seller negotiates to a holder in due course. The buyer's defense that the goods were defective or that the seller had committed fraud, although valid against the seller, is not valid against a holder in due course of the instrument.

In order to correct this situation the Federal Trade Commission rule preserves claims and defenses of consumer buyers and borrowers against holders in due course. The rule states that no seller or creditor can take or receive a consumer credit contract unless the contract contains this conspicuous (ten point, boldface type) provision:

This credit contract finances a purchase. All legal rights which the buyer has against the seller arising out of this transaction, including all claims and defenses, are also valid against any holder of this contract. The right to recover money from the holder under this provision is limited to the amount paid by the buyer under this contract.

A claim is a legally valid reason for suing the seller. A defense is a legally valid reason for not paying the seller. A holder is anyone trying to collect for the purchase.

The purpose of this conspicuous notice is to inform any holder that he takes the instrument subject to all claims and defenses which the buyer could assert against the seller. The effect of the rule is to place a holder in due course of the paper or negotiable instru- ment in the position of an assignee. See Figure 26-6. *See also Jefferson Bank & Trust Co. v. Stamatiou.*

FIGURE 26-6   Rights of Holder in Due Course under FTC Rule

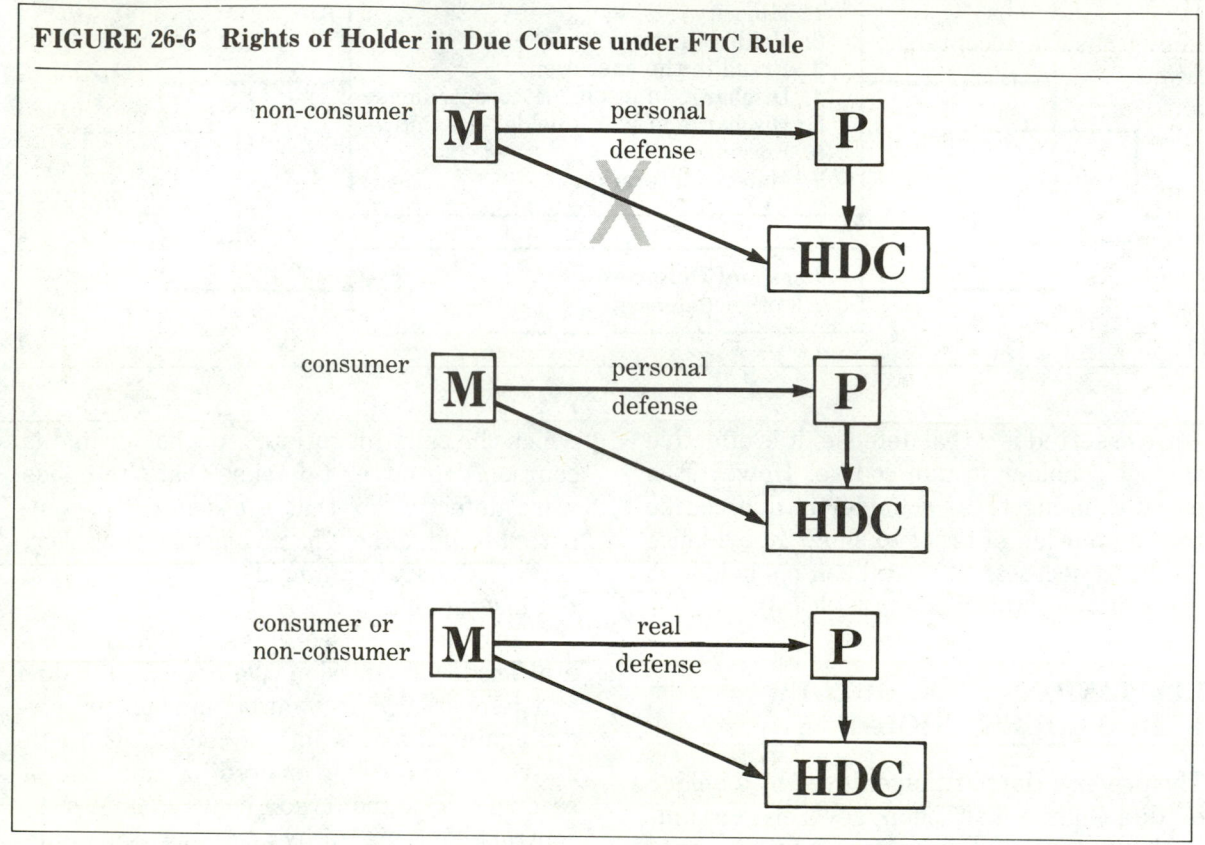

CASES

Value

KORZENIK v. SUPREME RADIO, INC.

Supreme Judicial Court of Massachusetts, 1964.
347 Mass. 309, 197 N.E.2d 702.

WHITTEMORE, J.

The plaintiffs, as indorsees, brought an action in the District Court of Western Hampden to recover $1,900 on two "note[s] in the form of * * * trade acceptance[s]" given by Supreme Radio, Inc. (Supreme), to Southern New England Distributing Corpo- ration (Southern), dated October 16, 1961, and due, respectively, on November 1, 1961, and December 1, 1961. The plaintiffs are partners in the practice of law. The trade acceptances in suit and others, all of a total face value of about $15,000, were transferred to them on October 31, 1961, by their client Southern "as as retainer for services to be performed" by the plaintiff Korzenik. The trade acceptances in suit and two others given by Supreme had been obtained by fraud. Southern had re- tained Korzenik on October 25, 1961, in con- nection with certain anti-trust litigation. Korzenik did some legal work between October 25 and October 31, but there was no testimony as to the value of the services and the trial judge was unable to determine their value. He found for the defendant. Korzenik did not know that the acceptances were obtained by fraud. "He has paid co-counsel retained in the antitrust case part of the money he has collected" on the assigned items.

The Appellate Division dismissed the report of the trial judge.

Decisive of the case, as the Appellate Division held, is the correct ruling that the plaintiffs are not holders in due course under * * * § 3–302; they have not shown to what extent they took for value under § 3–303. That section provides: "A holder takes the instrument for value (a) to the extent that the agreed consideration has been performed or that he acquires a security interest in or a lien on the instrument otherwise than by legal process; or (b) when he takes the instrument in payment of or as security for an antecedent claim against any person whether or not the claim is due; or (c) when he gives a negotiable instrument for it or makes an irrevocable commitment to a third person."

Under clause (a) of § 3–303 the "agreed consideration" was the performance of legal services. It is often said that a lawyer is "retained" when he is engaged to perform services, and we hold that the judge spoke of "retainer" in this sense. The phrase that the judge used, "retainer *for services*" (emphasis supplied), shows his meaning as does the finding as to services already performed by Korzenik at the time of the assignments. Even if the retainer had been only a fee to insure the attorney's availability to perform future services [citation] there is no basis in the record for determining the value of this commitment for one week.

The Uniform [U.C.C.] Laws Comment to § 3–303 points out that in this article "value is divorced from consideration" and that except as provided in paragraph (c) "[a]n executory promise to give value is not * * * value. * * * The underlying reason of pol-

icy is that when the purchaser learns of a defense * * * he is not required to enforce the instrument, but is free to rescind the transaction for breach of the transferor's warranty."

[U.C.C.] § 3–307(3), provides: "After it is shown that a defense exists a person claiming the rights of a holder in due course has the burden of establishing that he or some person under whom he claims is in all respects a holder in due course." The defense of fraud having been established this section puts the burden on the plaintiffs. The plaintiffs have failed to show "the extent * * * [to which] the agreed consideration * * * [had] been performed."

*   *   *

Order dismissing report affirmed.

Value/Notice

ST. PAUL FIRE AND MARINE INSURANCE CO. v. STATE BANK OF SALEM

Court of Appeals of Indiana, First District, 1980. 412 N.E.2d 103.

NEAL, J.

*   *   *

On November 26, 1975, Stephens, a farmer, delivered and sold 184 bushels of corn to Aubrey for $478.23. Aubrey was engaged at the time in the sale and distribution of feed and grain in Louisville, Kentucky, under the name of Aubrey Feed Mills, Inc. The following day, Aubrey prepared its check payable to Stephens in payment for the corn and mailed it to Stephens. The check was prepared in the following fashion: the amount "478.23" was typewritten upon the line customarily used to express the amount of the check in numbers, abutting the printed dollar sign. On the line customarily used to express the amount in words there appeared "The sum of $100478 and 23 cts," which was imprinted in red by a checkwriting machine; the line ended with the printed word "Dollars."

On December 9, 1975, Stephens appeared at the Bank's branch in Hardinsburg, Indiana, and presented the Aubrey check and two other items totalling $5,604.51 to the branch manager Charles Anderson. Stephens told Anderson that he wished to apply these funds to the amount of his indebtedness to the Bank, to withdraw $2,000.00 in cash, and to deposit the balance in his checking account. During the interval between November 27, 1975, and December 9, 1975, someone had typed on the check the figures "100" immediately before the typed figures "478.23." This was rather crudely done, and involved typing the "100" in an uneven line; the second "0" was typed directly over the printed dollar sign on the check.

Anderson questioned Stephens about the Aubrey check since Stephens's prior dealings with the Bank had not involved transactions in the amount represented by the Aubrey check. Anderson also knew that Stephens had filed a voluntary petition in bankruptcy several months prior, but had subsequently reaffirmed his obligations to the Bank. Stephens explained that he had purchased a large quantity of corn in Northern Indiana and had sold it in Kentucky at a higher price. Evidently satisfied with his explanation, Anderson stamped nine promissory notes, of which Stephens was maker, "paid" and returned them to Stephens. Anderson then directed a teller at the Bank to fill out a deposit slip for the transaction. At that point, neither Anderson nor the teller noticed the typewritten modification on the check. The transaction consisted of applying the funds represented by the three items in the deposit ($106,082.74) to Stephens's debt represented by the nine promissory notes ($31,851.81), an installment payment of which Stephens was a joint obligor, of $27,559.27, accrued interest owed the Bank by Stephens in the amount of $5,265.65, and the $2,000 cash given to Stephens. The balance was credited to Stephens's account. Stephens then left the Bank

Later that afternoon, Anderson began thinking about the transaction and examined the items in the deposit. He noted that Aubrey's check bore signs of possible tampering and contacted Aubrey's office in Louisville to inquire about the validity of the check. An Aubrey representative told Anderson that a check in that amount was suspicious, and Anderson then "froze" the transaction. The next day, Aubrey stopped payment on the check.

Thereafter, the Bank attempted to recover possession of the nine promissory notes from Stephens but was unsuccessful. Stephens subsequently left Hardinsburg and his present whereabouts are unknown.

After freezing Stephens's account, the Bank reversed the December 9, 1979, transaction by applying the $5,604.51 then on deposit in Stephens's account (said sum representing the amount of the two checks deposited on December 9, 1979 with Aubrey's check) against the $2,000 paid to Stephens in cash on December 9, 1979, and crediting the remaining $3,604.51 against the aggregate principal balance of the nine promissory notes delivered to Stephens on that date. As a result, the Bank claimed a loss of $28,193.91 and made demand therefor upon Aubrey * * *.

* * *

We think the only issue dispositive of Aubrey's appeal is whether the trial court could rightfully have found on the evidence that the Bank was a holder in due course of the Aubrey check under the Uniform Commercial Code (UCC) as adopted in Indiana. * * *

The Bank's right to recover on the check is conditioned upon its status as a holder in due course of the check. Section 3–305 states in part:

To the extent that a holder is a holder in due course he takes the instrument free from
    (1) all claims to it on the part of any person; and
    (2) all defenses of any party to the instrument with whom the holder has not dealt except
. . .

Assuming without presently deciding, that Aubrey showed the existence of a defense, the burden was on the Bank to prove by a preponderance of the evidence that it was in all respects a holder in due course of the check § 3–307(3).

* * *

There is no contention on appeal, and there was none at trial, that the Bank did not take the Aubrey check in good faith, which means honesty in fact in the transaction concerned. [Citation.] There is also no question that the Bank was a holder of the instrument, as it was in possession of the check indorsed by the payee Stephens in blank. See § 1–204(20).

We initially consider whether the Bank took the Aubrey check for value. The Bank contends that it gave value for the check to the extent that it (a) acquired a security interest in the instrument under §§ 3–303(a), 4–208, and 4–209; and (b) took the check in payment of an antecedent claim under § 3–303(b). Aubrey contends that the Bank did not take the check for value since it immediately froze Stephens's account upon apprisal that the validity of the check was suspect and cancelled the amounts it had credited against Stephens's debt. Aubrey considers that the Bank's action in crediting Stephens's debt on the notes merely constituted a bookkeeping procedure and the Bank did not change its position by doing so, particularly since the Bank could still maintain an action against Stephens on the notes. Finally, Aubrey maintains that general principles of law and equity render the UCC provisions relied on by the Bank inapplicable.

We are of the opinion that the Bank took the check for value. The issue is most readily resolved by § 3–303(b) which states in part:

A holder takes the instrument for value

* * *

(b) when he takes the instrument in payment of or as security for an antecedent claim against any person whether or not the claim is due; . . .

The statute [U.C.C.] plainly states that value is given for an instrument when the instru-

ment is taken in payment for an antecedent debt not yet due. The statute contains no provision precluding application of the rule when fraud is exercised by the presenter of the instrument, as Aubrey would have us find.

While this section has not been construed in Indiana, an examination of authorities from other jurisdictions lends support to the Bank's position that the application of funds made available by the Aubrey check to Stephens's indebtedness and the surrender of the notes constituted taking the instrument for value.

Further, we believe that the Bank gave value for the check under §§ 4–208(1) and 4–209, in that it acquired a security interest in the check to the extent funds represented thereby were applied to Stephens's debt. Section 4–208(1)(a) states in part:

(1) A bank has a security interest in an item and any accompanying documents or the proceeds of either
(a) in case of an item deposited in an account to the extent to which credit given for the item has been withdrawn or applied; . . .

Section 4–209 provides:

For the purposes of determining its status as a holder in due course, the bank has given value to the extent that it has a security interest in an item provided that the bank otherwise complies with the requirements of § 3–302 on what constitutes a holder in due course.

We find no support for Aubrey's argument that the Bank did not give value since it did not change its position vis-a-vis Stephens and made a bookkeeping entry only of the credit given Stephens. * * * Official Comment 3 to § 3–303 states that it is not necessary to give holder in due course status to one who has not actually paid value, and cites as illustration "the bank credit not drawn upon, which can be and is revoked when a claim or defense appears." [Citation.] When the credit is drawn upon, however, value is given to that extent § 4–208(1)(a). Further, if the depositor's account is overdrawn at the time the check is taken, and funds represented thereby are applied to the overdrawal by way of set-off, value is given to that extent if the check is later dishonored. [Citation.]

* * *

Aubrey vigorously contends the Bank was not a holder in due course of the check because, under the objective standard imposed upon the Bank by § 3–304(1), the Bank took the check with notice of a defense to the check on the part of Aubrey. Aubrey argues the evidence of alteration on the face of the check and the irregular circumstances attending the transaction were such as to put a reasonably prudent banker, exercising normal commercial standards, on notice. The circumstances alleged to have imparted notice to Bank include the small size of Stephens's farming operations, Stephens's banking history including frequent indebtedness and overdrawals, the Bank's knowledge of Stephens's petition in bankruptcy, the size of the Aubrey check in relation to typical transactions undertaken by the Bank, and the implausibility of Stephens's explanation to Anderson, himself familiar with farming, of the transaction underlying Stephens's receipt of the check. The Bank concedes the UCC imposed an objective standard of conduct upon it in the transaction. The essence of the Bank's contention is that the matter of the Bank's notice is a question of fact, and the trial court's implicit finding that the Bank took the check without notice of Aubrey's defense was not erroneous.

The general notice provision of the UCC is stated in § 1–201(25), which provides in part:

A person has 'notice' of a fact when (a) he has actual knowledge of it; or (b) he has received a notice or notification of it; or (c) from all the facts and circumstances known to him at the time in question he has reason to know that it exists.

Section 3–304, titled "Notice to Purchasers," states in part:

(1) The purchaser has notice of a claim or defense if

    (a) the instrument is so incomplete, bears such visible evidence of forgery or alteration, or is otherwise so irregular as to call into question its validity, terms or ownership or to create an ambiguity as to the party to pay; . . .

The Bank is a "purchaser" within the meaning of § 3–304. [Citation.]

Section 1–201(25) imposes subjective and quasi-objective standards; § 3–304 imposes an objective standard. [Citation.] An irregularity on the face of an instrument is sufficient to import notice under § 3–304(1)(a) where,

A reasonably prudent person exercising normal commercial standards would immediately be put on notice that there was something very irregular about the terms of the [instrument.]

[Citation.]

The gist of Aubrey's argument is that the alleged "alteration" on the face of the check, i.e., the typed figure "100," was "such visible evidence" of alteration as to call into question its validity or terms.

We do not think that the trial court erred as a matter of law in finding that the Bank took the Aubrey check without notice of a defense.

The Bank's branch manager, Anderson, with whom Stephens dealt in the transaction, admitted that he took the check without comparing the amount expressed in typewritten figures; indeed, he testified that he did not even look at the figures. He relied, instead, upon the amount expressed by the check-writer that was entered upon the line generally used to express the amount of a check in words.

Section 3–118, captioned "Ambiguous terms and rules of construction," states in part:

The following rules apply to every instrument:

* * *

    (b) Handwritten terms control typewritten and printed terms, and typewritten control printed.

    (c) Words control figures except that if the words are ambiguous figures control.

* * *

As the section makes clear, in the event of an ambiguity between printed terms and typewritten terms, the latter would control. We do not consider the impressions made by the check imprinter to be "printed" terms under this section. [Citation.]

A conflict between the two amounts on a check would be resolved by § 3–118(c) which states that words control figures. Arguably, the amount imprinted by the checkwriting machine upon the line customarily expressing the amount in words, is expressed in figures. (Recall that the entry reads: "The sum of $100478 and 23 cts.") We think, however, that the purposes of the U.C.C. are best served by considering an amount imprinted by a checkwriting machine as "words" for the purpose of resolving an ambiguity between that amount and an amount entered upon the line usually used to express the amount in figures.

*   *   *

We cannot say as a matter of law that the bank acted unreasonably in relying upon the amount expressed by the checkwriting machine. Aubrey presented no evidence that customary banking standards require a bank to closely examine and compare the two amounts on the check, and it was Aubrey's burden to prove the existence of such custom. [Citation.] The issue of the Bank's constructive knowledge of any defense Aubrey may have had to the check, based on the alleged irregularity on the face of the check, was a question of fact for the trial court to determine. It was not error for the court to have determined that the Bank acted reasonably in relying on the amount imprinted by the checkwriting machine and took the check without notice, actual or constructive, of a defense thereto.

Aubrey further argues that the circumstances surrounding the transaction were so irregular as to put a reaosnably prudent banker on notice of a defense to Aubrey's check. Aubrey directs us to no cases in which a holder was denied holder in due course status because of its knowledge of the questionable general financial position of the presenter of the instrument. Our research reveals such

knowledge is not sufficient in itself to defeat holder in due course status. *   *   *

The only knowledge the Bank had concerning the transaction underlying the issue of the Aubrey check to Stephens, and thus the only knowledge relevant to the issue of Bank's notice of a possible defense to the check, grew out of Stephens's explanation to Anderson of how the check came into his hands. This was not sufficient to call into question the integrity of the Aubrey check.

We therefore hold that the evidence supports the trial court's determination that the Bank was a holder in due course of the Aubrey check. Since Aubrey has not shown a "real defense" under § 3–305(2) the Bank may enforce the check against Aubrey to the extent it gave value therefor, and we shall not disturb the trial court's award of that amount.

*   *   *

Payee May be a Holder in Due Course

ELDON'S SUPER FRESH STORES, INC. v. MERRILL LYNCH, PIERCE, FENNER & SMITH, INC.

Supreme Court of Minnesota, 1973.
296 Minn. 130, 207 N.W.2d 282.

OLSON, J.

Plaintiff, drawer of a check payable to defendant Merrill Lynch, Pierce, Fenner & Smith, Inc., appeals from a summary judgment entered in favor of defendant. The appeal raises the issue of whether the payee was, as a matter of law, a holder in due course and thus not subject to the drawer's claim that the check, possession of which it gave to its agent, was wrongfully delivered to defendant-payee in payment of the agent's own personal obligation to defendant rather than for the benefit of plaintiff-drawer.

Elson's Super Fresh Stores, Inc. (hereafter Eldon's) is a closely held corporation headquartered in Faribault, Minnesota, and engaged in the retail grocery business. Merrill Lynch, Pierce, Fenner & Smith, Inc. (hereafter Merrill Lynch) is a national stock brokerage firm with offices in St. Paul, Minnesota. William E. Drexler was the attorney for and corporate secretary of Eldon's and the personal attorney of Eldon Prinzing, the corporation's president and sole shareholder.

The relevant facts are not in dispute. From January 1968 through January 1970, Drexler maintained a trading account in his name with Merrill Lynch by which he purchased and sold stock at various times. Eldon's, on the other hand, maintained no trading account with Merrill Lynch at any time relevant herein. On August 12, 1969, Drexler purchased 100 shares of Clark Oil & Refining Company stock through his stockbroker at Merrill Lynch for $41.50 per share. A confirmation statement was mailed to Drexler by the stockbroker, and Drexler then mailed the $4,150 check here involved, together with the confirmation statement, to Merrill Lynch in payment for the stock purchase. The check was drawn by the corporation, Eldon's Super Fresh Stores, Inc., on the Security National Bank and Trust Company of Faribault, Minnesota, and contained corporate identification. * * * The check, in the exact amount of the purchase price of the 100 shares of stock (not including commission charge of $39.75) and payable to Merrill Lynch, was dated August 12, 1969, and signed for the corporation by E. C. Prinzing, its president. The check contained no other designation or directive as to its use. On August 15, 1969, Merrill Lynch accepted the check in payment of Drexler's stock purchase, treating Drexler as the remitter. * * * There was no communication between Drexler and Merrill Lynch except the stock purchase order for Drexler's personal account on August 12, the mailing of the confirmation statement to Drexler, and the receipt by Merrill Lynch on August 15 of the check and confirmation statement. * * * There was no communication between Eldon's and Merrill Lynch until November 1970, 15 months after the issuance of the check, at which time Eldon's inquired of Merrill Lynch relative to the stock certificate and asserted a claim to its ownership.

* * *

The narrow issue * * * is whether under the recited factual circumstances Merrill Lynch, as payee of the check, was a holder in due course. Since defendant, as payee, took as a holder and obviously took for full value, decision turns on whether the payee, which received the check from the drawer's agent who in turn had received possession with the drawer's consent, took it "without notice * * * of any defense against or claim to it on the part of any person," [U.C.C.] 3–302 (1)(c), and thus became a holder in due course free of any claim of the drawer that the delivery to the payee was wrongful.

* * *

Section 3–102(1)(a) defines "issue" as "the first delivery of an instrument to a holder or a remitter." Section 1–201(20), which contains general definitions for the U.C.C., defines "holder" as "a person who is in possession of * * * an instrument * * * drawn, issued or endorsed to him or to his order or to bearer or in blank." The facts in this case are undisputed that Eldon's, the drawer of the check, placed the check in the hands of its agent, Drexler, for the purpose of delivery to the payee, Merrill Lynch.

It follows from those facts and those two code definitions (while somewhat circular) of "issue" and "holder" that Merrill Lynch was a holder of the instrument. * * * For the purposes of this case then, we treat the instrument as "issued" to Merrill Lynch, the payee and the holder * * *

We next consider the requirements for a "holder" to become a "holder in due course" (hereafter HDC).

[U.C.C.] 3–302 sets out the requirements for being a HDC of negotiable instruments as follows:

(1) A holder in due course is a holder who takes the instrument (a) for value; and (b) in good faith; and (c) *without notice* that it is overdue or has been dishonored or *of any defense against or claim to it on the part of any person.*

(2) A payee may be a holder in due course. (Italics supplied.)

The U.C.C. has thus made it clear that a payee may be a HDC. 3–302(2). A payee who fulfills the requirements of 3–302(1) acquires the rights of a HDC as set forth in § 3–305 with respect to the unknown claims or defenses of parties with whom he has not dealt even though he has become a holder as payee by delivery from a remitter or the drawer's agent rather than by negotiation from a prior holder.

* * *

It is the third and critical requirement— taking "without notice * * * of any defense against or claim to it on the part of a person"—with which we must deal.

The holder of an instrument has the burden of proving that he is a HDC when defenses or claims are shown. [Citations.]

"Notice" is defined in § 1–201(25) as follows:

A person has 'notice' of a fact when (a) he has *actual knowledge* of it; or (b) he has received a notice or notification of it; or (c) from all the facts and circumstances known to him at the time in question he has *reason to know* that it exists.

A person 'knows' or has 'knowledge' of a fact when he has actual knowledge of it. (Italics supplied.)

The Minnesota Code Comment to [U.C.C.] 1–201(25), points out that "notice" (as with "notice" in other recited uniform acts) is restricted—

* * * to actual knowledge of the fact, receipt of notification of it, or knowledge of facts from which the fact in question is inferable; and they all exclude the situation in which a person does not have actual or inferable knowledge but merely *could discover* the fact by reasonable investigation. In the latter situation it is sometimes said that when a person has a duty to another to investigate a matter he has 'notice' of what he could have discovered, but the U.C.C. does not employ 'notice' in that sense under this definition except in the case covered by paragraph (b) where one

has *received notification* but may not have read or understood it.

The knowledge which a person has that constitutes "notice" according to § 1–201(25) could, then, be termed "inferable" knowledge.

Facts or circumstances from which a purchaser could infer that a claim exists on the part of any person are referred to in Minnesota as "danger signals" and knowledge of such facts is the "red light" test. * * * We have in Minnesota several cases applying this test to facts similar to the case at hand. In applying the test, this court has rather consistently held that having notice by way of the "inferable knowledge" test is something more than failure to make inquiry about an unknown fact. Failure to make such inquiry may be negligence and lack of diligence, but it is not "notice" of what he might discover. [Citations.]

* * *

Applying the "inferable knowledge" test to the instant case, this court concludes that Merrill Lynch did not have notice of any claim of the drawer, Eldon's, simply by virtue of its receipt of the check and confirmation notice from Drexler. The fact that Merrill Lynch was the named payee on the check drawn by Eldon's did not in and of itself constitute "notice" that Drexler was using the check improperly. Significantly, there were no other identification or designation marks on the check to indicate or give notice that it was drawn in payment for stock for Eldon's. Furthermore, and equally as significant, Eldon's had no account with Merrill Lynch. The designation on the check that the corporate maker was doing business as Prinzing's Market is not by itself sufficient to constitute such "notice." Merrill Lynch was entitled to conclude that Drexler, known to be an attorney, had lawfully obtained and was delivering the instrument to discharge the debt incurred by his own stock purchase. Merrill Lynch was not required to surmise that the check, rather than being a payment for Drexler's legal services, was being misused.

* * *

Under the circumstances of this case, namely, where (1) a bank check was delivered to the payee by the drawer's agent with the drawer's consent and knowledge, (2) the check itself contained no restrictions or designations as to its use, and (3) the payee, a stock brokerage firm, had no trading account with, or indebtedness to, the drawer, we hold that the payee took the check without notice of the drawer's claims. Thus, the payee became a holder in due course of the instrument.

* * *

[Judgment for Merrill Lynch affirmed.]

Real Defense: Fraud in the Execution

EXCHANGE INTERNATIONAL LEASING CORP. v. CONSOLIDATED BUSINESS FORMS CO.

United States District Court, W.D. Pennsylvania, 1978.
462 F. Supp. 626.

DIAMOND, J.

[Consolidated Business Forms leased a Phillips business computer from Benchmark. Benchmark subsequently transferred the lease and promissory note to Exchange International Leasing Corporation. Consolidated stopped making rental payments when the computer malfunctioned, and Exchange International brought this suit to recover the payments due on the promissory note. Consolidated defends on the grounds that Benchmark prevented its agent, Mr. Spohn, from examining the contents of the agreement between the two companies and further represented that the computer would be removed with a complete refund if it failed to operate properly.]

* * *

It has been established * * * that the aforesaid assignment conferred upon plaintiff [Exchange International] the status of a holder in due course under § 3–302 of the Uniform Commercial Code (hereinafter U.C.C.), and

that the defendant's [Consolidated's] only plausible defense was misrepresentation under § 3–305(2)(c) of the U.C.C. The matter now before the court is plaintiff's * * * motion for summary judgment in which it claims that no genuine issue of misrepresentation exists. For the reasons set forth below, we conclude that there is no genuine issue of a material fact regarding the misrepresentations defense and that the defendant was not the victim of misrepresentation within the meaning of § 3–305(2)(c) and, therefore, grant the [plaintiff's] motion.

In order to rule on the instant motion we must consider (1) the meaning of "misrepresentation" under § 3–305(2)(c); (2) the factual basis in support of the allegations of misrepresentation relied on by Consolidated; and (3) whether or not there exists a genuine issue of a material fact which if true would constitute a defense.

Turning first to the meaning of "misrepresentation," § 3–305(2)(c) states:

To the extent that a holder is a holder in due course he takes the instruments free from

. . . . .

(2) all defenses of any party to the instrument with whom the holder has not dealt except

. . . . .

(c) such misrepresentation as has induced the party to sign the instrument with neither knowledge nor reasonable opportunity to obtain knowledge of its character or its essential terms . . .

Thus, to establish the defense, one must not only have had no knowledge of a document's character or essential terms, but also have had no "reasonable opportunity" to acquire such knowledge. Comment 7 to § 3–305 elaborates by stating that in determining what constitutes a "reasonable opportunity" factors such as the age, intelligence, and business experience of the signator, his ability to read English, and the representations made to him and his reason to rely on them are to be considered.

The reported Pennsylvania decisions interpreting § 3–305(2)(c) while few in number are nonetheless uniform in holding that only fraud in the [execution] as opposed to fraud in the inducement, is a defense under § 3–305. [Citations.] This view is in accord with comment 7 and also the view expressed by certain scholars in the area. [Citations.]

As comment 7 notes, the classic example of fraud in the [execution] is that of a person who is tricked into signing a note on the pretense that it is a mere receipt of some sort. Pennsylvania is apparently hesitant to expand the defense and afford relief to less obvious victims. For example, in [citation], defendants agreed to permit a company to install and demonstrate a water softening machine in defendants' home in order to promote sales to defendants' neighbors. The defendants signed a document which was represented by the company to be a bond securing against damage to the equipment. In reality, the document was a note securing the purchase price of the equipment. The court refused to hold that defendants had been the victims of misrepresentation within the purview of § 3–305(2)(c), for the reason that defendants had established no basis from which it could be concluded that they had reason to rely on the statements of the company's representative and, that they had the opportunity, time, and ability to read the document before signing it. * * *

With the foregoing in mind we consider the specific misrepresentations relied on by Consolidated. In its brief Consolidated contends that "Mr. Spohn was precluded from examining the contents of the agreement by the representations made to him" by employees of Phillips and Benchmark. Although defendant's brief does not disclose the specifics of those representations, Spohn's deposition indicates that they were in the nature of assurances that the computer would be removed with a complete refund if it failed to function properly. * * *

Assuming without deciding that the statements referred to by Spohn could form the basis of a misrepresentation, nevertheless the court is of the opinion that no genuine issue exists as to the presence of a § 3–305(2)(c) defense. For, even if it be true that Spohn

did not have actual knowledge of the essential terms of the lease, it can hardly be said that he lacked a "reasonable opportunity" to acquire that knowledge—an essential element of a § 3–305(2)(c) defense. Spohn testified unequivocally that O'Connor in no way prevented him from reading the instrument before he signed it, that he could have read the document in its entirety had he so desired, and that he was not busy or otherwise distracted at the time of execution. Spohn further testified that he read part of the lease but simply chose not to read the "fine print" because he had trust in O'Connor.

Consolidated argues for a contrary result by emphasizing that portion of comment 7 which states that in determining what constitutes a "reasonable opportunity" one is to consider the representations made to the signator and "his reason to rely on them or to have confidence in the person making them." The court does not find this argument persuasive because it simply ignores the other facts to be considered in determining whether one had reasonable opportunity to obtain knowledge of the instrument's character and essential terms. When these other factors; viz., age, intelligence, business experience, ability to read the document, necessity for acting speedily, are considered in the light of Spohn's deposition it is clear that there is no legal justification for the blind reliance which Spohn contends he had on the statements of O'Connor.

An appropriate Order will be entered granting plaintiff's motion for summary judgment.

*Limitations Upon Holder in
Due Course Rights*

JEFFERSON BANK & TRUST CO. v. STAMATIOU

Supreme Court of Louisiana, 1980.
384 So.2d 388.

CALOGERO, J.

Defendant's [answer] asserting a defense to plaintiff's suit on a promissory note given plaintiff's assignor for the purchase of a truck was dismissed. The trial judge held in favor of the plaintiff bank, granting its exception of no cause of action upon finding the bank to be a holder in due course. The Court of Appeal affirmed the trial court judgment. [Citation.] We granted writs upon application of defendant, vendee and maker of the promissory note.

Defendant, Christos G. Stamatiou, purchased a truck from Key Dodge, Inc. At the time of purchase, defendant and an agent of Key Dodge signed an instrument designated Sale and Chattel Mortgage. The instrument or contract is on a single sheet of paper, front and back. It consists of provisions relative to the Sale and Chattel Mortgage with a promissory note at the bottom of this same page. The note portion of the contract bears language indicating that it is an unconditional promise to pay $10,774.44 on prescribed terms. The preceding Sale and Chattel Mortgage portion of the instrument has numerous provisions including the following which preserves for the purchaser his defenses against a future holder:

NOTICE: ANY HOLDER OF THIS CONSUMER CREDIT CONTRACT IS SUBJECT TO ALL CLAIMS AND DEFENSES WHICH THE DEBTOR COULD ASSERT AGAINST THE SELLER OF GOODS OR SERVICES OBTAINED PURSUANT HERETO OR WITH THE PROCEEDS HEREOF. RECOVERY HEREUNDER SHALL NOT EXCEED AMOUNTS PAID BY THE DEBTOR HEREUNDER.

Defendant's signature appears twice on the instrument, once following the sale and chattel mortgage and once at the conclusion of the promissory note. The purchaser is shown on the contract as "Christos G. Stamatiou" and no provision of the sale and chattel mortgage/promissory note indicates the purpose of the purchase, or the use to which the truck is to be put. Nor does any provision of the instrument indicate that Stamatiou purchased anything other than an ordinary truck. Near the top of the contract there is a "Disclosure Statement" by which "Buyer acknowledges

that the Promissory Note secured by Sale and Chattel Mortgage will be assigned to JEFFERSON BANK, as Assignee and CREDITOR within the meaning of the Federal Truth-In-Lending Act."

Key Dodge assigned this contract to plaintiff, Jefferson Bank and Trust Co., as comtemplated. Defendant alleges that the truck became inoperable and unusable a short time after purchase and that he notified Key Dodge and Jefferson Bank of the problem and demanded rescission of the sale. * * * Later, Jefferson Bank filed an ordinary petition against Stamatiou for the unpaid balance on the note (after separating or cutting the note off from the remainder of the contract).

Defendant answered the suit * * * seeking rescission of the sale and judgment for return of the purchase price.

Plaintiff bank filed an exception of no cause of action * * * contending that because defendant purchased the truck for use in his tow truck business, the instrument is not a "consumer credit contract" and that therefore the above quoted language of the contract is not applicable.

* * *

Our [decision to review this case] requires that we determine whether the inclusion of the preservation of defenses language (federally required in all "consumer credit contracts") in a contract which is not a consumer credit contract, allows the defendant to present his defense against a party who would otherwise be a holder in due course; in effect, whether the language, specifically countering the primary effect of holder in due course status is applicable to this holder, Jefferson Bank.

Under authority of [Federal statute], the Federal Trade Commission, a United States regulatory agency, requires the inclusion of the exact same language as was included in the present contract in all "consumer credit contracts" for the sale of goods or services. [Citation.] The federal regulations define a consumer as "a natural person who seeks or acquires goods or services for *personal, family or household use*." Therefore in any contract for the sale of goods or services where credit is being extended to the purchaser, and the purchaser is acquiring the item for personal, family, or household use, * * * language identical to that language used in the contract and quoted above, must be contained in the contract.

* * *

The express purpose of the FTC regulation is to prevent the seller, in a consumer credit transaction, from separating the buyer's duty to pay from the seller's duty to perform as promised, by the seller's assigning the buyer's promissory note to a financing institution, as against whom, because of holder in due course status, defenses would otherwise not be available.

Plaintiff makes the following argument: that the preservation of defenses language is included in all credit contracts to insure compliance with federal regulations but is only intended to apply to the appropriate transactions even though there is no notation to the effect that the clause is possibly inapplicable; absent inclusion in all credit contracts, the vendor and/or finance company would be required to have two different forms and to hire a staff attorney to instruct them each time which to use; and that the sale of the truck to defendant for use in his tow truck business takes the transaction out of the consumer credit contract category as defined by the FTC, and thus the provision, although there in the contract, was not applicable to this transaction and should be ignored.

Defendant on the other hand claims that the preservation of defenses language (whether federally required in this contract

or not) was included in the contract and as such becomes a part of that contract.

* * *

We conclude that defendant's argument is the more persuasive and is more supported by the law. . . . , parties are free to govern their relationships through their contracts, and the contractural provisions have the effect of law on the parties. The contract between Stamatiou and Key Dodge, as assigned to plaintiff, provided "Any holder of this . . . contract is subject to all claims and defenses which the debtor could assert against the seller." That the parties to the contract mistakenly asserted that it was a consumer credit contract ("any holder of this consumer credit contract") is of little consequence. In looking at the contract, there was nothing on the face of the instrument to indicate that this was not a "consumer contract." The assignee/holder was put on notice that all defenses were available to the buyer against him at the time he acquired the instrument. In looking at the face of the instrument, plaintiff could not have expected to be a holder in due course, and is not now entitled to be so treated. At best the contract is ambiguous and is surely not to be construed against the purchaser who did not confect it. [Citations.]

* * *

For these reasons we conclude that the preservation of defenses language is applicable to the contract. Plaintiff bank is subject to defendant purchaser's claims or defenses and the contract provision takes precedence over the right plaintiff would otherwise have been legally entitled to under [U.C.C.] 3–305 as a holder in due course.

REVERSED; remanded to District Court.

PROBLEMS

1. On November 1, P installed a burglar alarm system in M's store. M executed and delivered to P a negotiable promissory note payable to the order of P for $1,100, the purchase price, due on December 1. On November 8, P returned to M's store and told M that he needed money and would accept $1,000 as payment in full. M immediately paid P $1,000 but forgot to obtain the note from P.

On November 10, P indorsed the note in blank and transferred it to H for value. Two days later, H learned that M had already paid P for the note, whereupon he gave the note to X, his mother-in-law, as a going away present without further indorsement. X was not aware of M's prior payment of the note.

What are the rights of X, if any, against M? Explain.

2. M issues a negotiable promissory note payable to the order of P for the amount of $3,000. P raises the amount to $13,000 and negotiates it to H for $12,000.

(a) If H is a holder in due course, how much can she recover from M? How much from P? If M's negligence substantially contributed to the making of the alteration, how much can H recover from M and P, respectively?

(b) If H is not a holder in due course, how much can she recover from M? How much from P? If M's negligence substantially contributed to the making of the alteration, how much can H recover from M and P, respectively?

3. On December 2, 1984, Miles executed and delivered to Proctor a negotiable promissory note for $1,000, payable to Proctor or order, due March 2, 1985, with interest at 14 percent from maturity, in partial payment of a printing press. On January 3, 1985, Proctor, in need of ready cash, indorsed and sold the note to Hughes for $800. Hughes paid $600 in cash to Proctor on January 3 and agreed to pay the balance of $200 one week later, namely, on January 10. On January 6, Hughes learned that Miles claimed a breach of warranty by Proctor and, for this reason, intended to refuse to pay the note when it matured. On January 10, Hughes paid Proctor $200, in conformity with their agreement of January 3. Following Miles's refusal to pay the note on March 2, 1985, Hughes sues Miles for $1,000. Decision?

4. X fraudulently represented to D that he would obtain for her a new car to be used in D's business for $7,800 from P Motor Company. D thereupon executed her personal check for $7,800, payable to the order of P Motor Company, and delivered the check to X, who immediately delivered it to the Motor Company in payment of his own prior indebtedness. The Motor Company had no knowledge of the representations made by X to D. P Motor Company now brings an action on the check against D, who defends on the ground of failure of consideration. Decision?

5. Adams reads with difficulty. He arranged to borrow $200 from Bell. Bell prepared a note which Adams read laboriously. As Adams was about to sign it, Bell diverted Adams's attention and substituted the following paper, which was identical with the note Adams had read except that the amounts were different:

On June 1, 1985, I promise to pay Ben Bell or order Two Thousand Dollars with interest from date at 16 percent. This note is secured by certificate No. 13 for 100 shares of stock of Brookside Mills, Inc.

Adams did not detect the substitution, signed as maker, handed the note and stock certificate to Bell, and received from Bell $200. Bell indorsed and sold the paper to Fore, a holder in due course, who paid him $1,800. Fore presented the note at maturity to Adams who refused to pay. What are Fore's rights, if any, against Adams?

6. On January 2, 1985, Martin, seventeen years of age, as a result of Dealer's fradulent misrepresentation bought a used motorboat to use in his fishing business for $2,000 from Dealer, signed an installment contract for $1,500, and gave Dealer the following instrument as down payment:

Dated: _____ 1985
I promise to pay to the order of Dealer, six months after date, the sum of $500 without interest. This is given as a down payment on an installment contract for a motorboat.

(signed) Martin

Dealer, on July 1, sold his business to Henry and included this note in the transaction. Dealer wrote on the back of the note the following: "Collection guaranteed. (signed) Dealer" and handed it to Henry. Henry left the note in his office safe. On July 10, Sharpie, an employee of Henry, without authority stole the note and sold it to Bert for $300, indorsing the note "Sharpie." At the time, in Bert's presence, Sharpie filled in the date on the note as February 2, 1985. Bert demanded payment from Martin, who refused to pay.

What are Bert's rights against Martin? Please discuss.

7. M borrowed $1,000 from A. A, disturbed about M's ability to pay, demanded security. M indorsed

and delivered to A a negotiable promissory note executed by T for $1,200 payable to M's order in twelve equal monthly installments. The note did not contain an acceleration clause, but it recited that the consideration for the note was M's promise to paint and shingle T's barn. At the time M transferred the note to A, the first installment was overdue and unpaid. A was unaware that the installment had not been paid. T did not pay any of the installments on the note. When the last installment became due, A presented the note to T for payment. T refused upon the ground that M had not painted or reshingled her barn.

What are A's rights, if any, against T on the note?

8. M purchased a refrigerator for his home from P Appliance Store for $700. M paid $200 in cash and signed an installment contract for $500, which in its entirety stated:

> January 15, 1985
>
> I promise to pay to the order of P Appliance Store the sum of $500 in ten equal monthly installments.
>
> (Signed) M

P negotiated the installment contract to H, who took the instrument for value, in good faith, and without notice of any claim or defense of any party. After paying two installments, the refrigerator ceased operating, and M wishes to recover his down payment, his first two monthly payments, and to discontinue further payments. What outcome?

9. Joseph Higbee executed and delivered to Robert Dudley, the following instrument:

> On September 19, 1985, I promise to pay $15,000 to Robert Dudley.
>
> (signed) Joseph Higbee.

This note was secured by a mortgage on Higbee's real property. Dudley altered the note and mortgage by changing the amount to $25,000 and the date to September 17, 1985. Dudley then sold the note and mortgage for $25,000 less 2 percent discount to Citizens Bank which was unaware of the alterations. Dudley assigned the mortgage to Citizens Bank and signed the reverse side of the note as follows:

> I hereby assign this note to the order of Citizens Bank. (signed) Robert Dudley.

On September 8, 1985, Citizens Bank demanded payment of the note form Higbee. Higbee refused. On September 22, Citizens Bank notified Higbee that the note was in default and demanded payment from him. Higbee again refused. Citizens Bank thereupon brought an action against Higbee to recover $25,000 on the note. No action was taken by Citizens Bank to foreclose the mortgage.

What defenses, if any, may Higbee properly assert in this action?

10. Adams, by fraudulent representations, induced Barton to purchase 100 shares of the capital stock of the Evermore Oil Company. The shares were worthless. Barton executed and delivered to Adams a negotiable promissory note for $5,000 dated May 5, in full payment for the shares, due six months after date. On May 20, Adams indorsed and sold the note to Cooper for $4,800. On October 21, Barton, having learned that Cooper now held the note, notified Cooper of the fraud and stated he would not pay the note. On December 1, Cooper negotiated the note to Davis who, while not a party, had full knowledge of the fraud perpetrated on Barton. Upon refusal of Barton to pay the note, Davis sues Barton for $5,000. Decision?

LIABILITY OF PARTIES

THE preceding chapters discussed the negotiability of commercial paper, the transfer of negotiable instruments, and the preferred position of a holder in due course. This chapter examines the liability of parties arising out of negotiable instruments and the ways in which liability may be terminated.

There are two types of potential liability associated with commercial paper: contractual liability and warranty liability. The basis for contract liability, as provided in Section 3–401(1), is that "[n]o person is liable on an instrument unless his signature appears thereon." **Contractual liability** is imposed by the operation of law upon those who **sign** a negotiable instrument. Some parties to a negotiable instrument never sign it and consequently never assume contractual liability.

Warranty liability, on the other hand, does not depend upon a party's signing the instrument and thus may be imposed upon both signers and non-signers. Warranty liability applies: (1) to persons who transfer an instrument, and (2) to persons who receive payment or acceptance of an instrument.

CONTRACTUAL LIABILITY

All parties whose **signatures** appear on a negotiable instrument, unless they disclaim liability, incur certain contractual obligations. The *maker* of a promissory note and the *acceptor* of a draft assume an absolute obligation (**primary liability**) to pay according to the tenor of the signed instrument at the time of their engagement. *Drawers* of drafts and checks and *indorsers* incur **secondary liability** in the event of nonpayment. A *drawee* assumes **no** liability on the instrument until he *accepts* it. The contractual obligations of the maker, drawer, drawee, indorser, and acceptor are codified by the U.C.C. as illustrated by Figure 27-1.

FIGURE 27-1   Contractual Liability

	Maker	Drawee	Acceptor	Drawer	Indorser
Primary Liability	●		●		
Secondary Liability				●	●

SIGNATURE

The word "signature" is broadly defined to include any name, word, or mark, whether handwritten, typed, printed, or made in any other manner, if it is done with the present intention of authenticating the instrument. Sections 3–401(2) and 1–201(39). The signature may be signed by the individual herself or on her behalf by the individual's authorized agent.

Authorized Signatures

Negotiable instruments are frequently executed by authorized agents with a view to binding their principals only. Where the execution is done properly (e.g., "P, principal, by A, agent") and the agent is authorized to execute the instrument, the principal is liable, and the agent is not liable. Occasionally, however, the agent, although fully authorized, uses an inappropriate form of signature, and holders or prospective holders may be misled as to the identity of the obligor. (For a comprehensive discussion of the principal agent relationship see Chapters 22 and 23.)

Incorrect forms of signatures by agents are numerous, but they can be conveniently sorted into three groups. The first is where the agent signs his own name to an instrument intending to bind his principal, but neither the fact that the agent is signing in a representative capacity nor the name of the principal is revealed. For example, Adams, the agent of Prince, makes a note on behalf of Prince but signs it "Adams." The signature does not indicate that Adams has signed in a representative capacity nor that he has made the instrument on behalf of Prince. In this situation the agent alone is liable on the in-

strument. Prince may be liable to Adams or to a third party, but not on the instrument because his name does not appear on it.

The second type is that in which the authorized agent indicates that he is signing in a representative capacity but does not disclose the name of his principal. For example, Adams, executing an instrument on behalf of Prince, merely signs it "Adams, agent." As between the immediate parties to the instrument, if the payee knows that Adams represents Prince, Prince is liable. As to any subsequent party, and to the payee if he does not know that Adams represents Prince, Prince is not liable, and Adams alone is personally liable.

The third type of inappropriate signature involves signatures by agents which reveal their principal's name, but do not indicate that the agent has signed in a representative capacity. For example, Adams, signing an instrument on behalf of Prince, signs it "Adams and Prince." A holder might well think that Adams and Prince were co-makers, and it would be unfair to let Adams avoid liability to remote parties. Consequently, he is fully liable to them. If the party who dealt with Adams knew he was acting on behalf of Prince without intending to incur personal liability, Adams may prove this fact by parol evidence and avoid liability to this immediate party. *See Valley National Bank, Sunnymead v. Cook.*

Unauthorized Signatures

An unauthorized signature includes both a forgery and a signature made by an agent exceeding her actual or apparent authority. The unauthorized signature is generally not binding on the person whose name appears on the instrument, but is binding upon the unauthorized signer whether or not her own name appears on the instrument. Section 3–404(1). Thus, if Adams, without authority, signed Prince's name to an instrument, Adams, and not Prince, would be liable on the instrument. The rule represents, therefore, an exception to the principle that only those whose names appear on a negotiable instrument can be liable on it.

There is an important exception to this principle that an unauthorized signature does not bind the person whose name is signed: any person who by his **negligence** substantially contributes to the making of an unauthorized signature may not assert the lack of authority as a defense against a holder in due course or a person who pays for the instrument in good faith and in accordance with reasonable commercial standards. Section 3–406. For example, A employs a signature stamp to sign his checks and carelessly leaves it accessible to third parties. B discovers the stamp and uses it to write a number of checks without A's authorization. H, a subsequent holder in due course of one of the checks, will *not* be subject to A's defense of unauthorized signature and will be able to recover the amount of the check from A due to A's negligence in storing the signature stamp.

In addition, an unauthorized signature may be ratified by the person whose name appears on the instrument. Section 3–404(2). However, the ratification does not of itself affect any rights of the person ratifying against the actual signer.

LIABILITY OF PRIMARY PARTIES

There is a primary party on every note: the *maker*. The maker's commitment is unconditional. No one, however, is primarily liable on a draft or check as issued. The *drawee* is *not* liable on the instrument unless he accepts it. He is free to pay or accept it as he sees fit, although by refusing to accept or pay it he may be liable to the drawer for breach of contract. For example, a bank is not obligated to pay any check drawn upon it. To do so would be to obligate a bank to pay an instrument regardless of whether the drawer had an account at that bank or sufficient funds in his account. On the other hand, if the drawer does have sufficient funds to cover the check, the drawee may, nevertheless, refuse to honor the instrument, but such dishonor will constitute a breach of its contract of deposit with the drawer.

The refusal of the drawee to pay or accept the draft causes the *drawer* to become liable on the instrument upon receiving proper notice of dishonor. If, on the other hand, the drawee accepts the draft, after which he is known as the *acceptor*, he becomes primarily liable on the instrument. **Acceptance,** or in the case of a check, **certification,** is the drawee's signed engagement to honor the draft as presented to him.

Since the maker of a note and the acceptor of a draft are primarily liable, presentment (that is, a demand for payment) is not a condition to the right of the holder to recover from them. While the holder usually makes a demand, there is no such requirement, nor need one be timely, and he may prefer to hold onto a "good" instrument for a period of time, possibly accumulating interest. Unless the maker knows the identity and address of the holder, or the note specifies a place of payment, he has no way to pay or tender payment of the instrument so as to avoid liability for any accruing interest. Unlike parties who are secondarily liable, such as indorsers, he cannot claim discharge or excuse by the failure of the holder to present, because presentment and demand for payment is not a condition precedent to his liability. He is liable absolutely.

Makers

Makers engage that they will pay the instrument according to its tenor at the time of their engagement or as completed if an incomplete instrument.

Acceptors

A drawee has no liability on the instrument until she accepts it, at which time she becomes an acceptor and, like a maker, primarily liable. Upon acceptance the acceptor becomes liable on the draft according to its terms at the time of the acceptance or as completed if an incomplete instrument. Section 3–413(1).

An acceptance must be written on the draft. Section 3–410(1). No writing separate from the draft and no oral statement or conduct of the drawee will convert the drawee into an acceptor. The acceptance may take many forms. It may be printed on the face of the draft, ready for the drawee's signature. It may consist of a rubber stamp, with the signature of the drawee added. It may be the drawee's signature, preceded by a word or phrase such as "Accepted," "Certified," or "Good." It may consist of nothing more than the drawee's signature. Normally, but by no means necessarily, an acceptance is written vertically across the face of the draft. It must not, however, bear any words indicating an intent to refuse to honor the draft. Checks, when accepted, are said to be certified. **Certification** is the drawee bank's promise to honor the check when subsequently presented for payment. The bank, however, has no obligation to certify a check. Section 3–411(2). The order upon the bank is to *pay* the check, and if the bank is willing to pay, refusal to certify is not dishonor of the check.

Where a check is certified at the request of the holder, the drawer and all prior indorsers are discharged. The liability of indorsers subsequent to certification is not affected. Upon certification the bank should withhold from the drawer's account sufficient funds to pay the check. Since the bank is primarily liable on its certification and has the funds and the drawer does not, the discharge is reasonable.

Certification at the request of the drawer does not, however, relieve the drawee of secondary liability on the instrument. For example, the drawer may have a check certified before using it to close a business transaction, such as the purchase of a house. Since the drawer is then obtaining the benefit of the transaction, she should bear the risk of the bank's credit, rather than the payee.

Assume that Moe, a depositor in the Last National Bank, had $3,000 on deposit when the bank ceased operations because of insolvency. The bank proved to be 60% solvent. Two weeks prior to the bank's closing, Hume received two checks for $1,000 each from Moe drawn on the bank. Check no. 1 was certified by the bank at the request of Moe prior to Moe's delivery of the check to Hume. Check no. 2 was taken by Hume to the bank which certified it at Hume's request. When the bank went into receivership, Hume was the holder of both checks.

Since check no. 1 was certified at the request of Moe, the drawer, he remains secondarily liable on the instrument. The bank having certified the instrument is primarily liable. Hume may recover judgment against Moe for $1,000. Either Hume or Moe, or both, may file a claim in the insolvency proceedings against the bank for $1,000 upon which $600 is ultimately distributable. If Moe pays the judgment he is entitled to the $600 distribution. If he fails to do so, Hume will receive it and credit the amount against the unpaid judgment.

Since Hume, the holder, obtained the bank's certification of check no. 2, the drawer, Moe, is released from liability on that check. The bank is primarily liable. Hume is a general creditor of the bank to the extent of $1,000 and his only right is to file a claim and receive through the insolvency proceedings 60% ($600).

LIABILITY OF SECONDARY PARTIES

The drawer, the payee (if he indorses), and other indorsers are secondarily liable. This is because their liability is subject to the conditions of presentment, dishonor, and notice of dishonor. They do not unconditionally promise to pay the instrument, but expect the drawee-acceptor or maker to pay.

Indorsers and Drawers

If the instrument is not paid by a primary party and the conditions precedent to the liability of secondary parties are satisfied, a secondary party who is not a qualified drawer or qualified indorser is liable. The drawer engages that she will pay the amount of the draft to the holder, or any indorser who takes it up, unless she has disclaimed this liability by drawing without recourse. Section 3–413(2). *See also Davis v. Watson Brothers Plumbing, Inc.* Unless the indorsement otherwise specifies, as by using such words as "without recourse," every indorser engages that she will pay the instrument according to its tenor at the time of her indorsement to the holder or any subsequent indorser who takes it up. Section 3–414(1).

Conditions Precedent to Liability

Conditions precedent to the liability of secondary parties are presentment, dishonor, prompt notice of dishonor, and, in some situations, protest. The consequences of failing to comply with the conditions precedent, however, vary greatly between indorsers and drawers.

Presentment Presentment is a demand for acceptance or payment made by the holder upon the maker, acceptor, or drawee. Section 3–504(1). If there are two or more makers, acceptors, or drawees, presentment to one is sufficient.

Presentment may be made in any reasonable manner. The only specific requirement is that an accepted draft or a note made payable at a bank in the United States must be presented at such bank. Section 3–504(4). Otherwise, presentment may be made by mail, through a clearing house in a proper case, or at the place specified in the instrument, or if none is specified, at the place of business or residence of the acceptor or payor. Section 3–504(2).

The date when presentment is to be made is set forth in detail in Section 3–503. An instrument with a specified maturity date is due for presentment on that date. In any other case presentment is due within "a reasonable time." The definition of "a reasonable time" depends upon all the facts of the particular case, including the nature of the instrument and any usage of banking or trade. *See Hane v. Exten.*

In the case of an uncertified check, Section 3–503(2) is specific: a reasonable time for presentment for payment or to initiate the bank collection process is *presumed* to be:

(a) with respect to the liability of the drawer, thirty days after date or issue, whichever is later; and (b) with respect to the liability of an indorser, seven days after his indorsement.

A delay in presentment discharges the indorser; however, the drawer is discharged only to the extent of any loss suffered by reason of the delay. The difference in treatment between indorsers and drawers is based upon the simple fact that the drawer always expects to have to pay the check, and the indorser has no reason to expect that he will ever be called upon to do so. Consequently, the latter should be given prompt notice of dishonor so that he may take immediate steps to assert his rights against other parties that he may charge with liability.

Nonetheless, the discharge of one indorser does not mean that all are discharged. Assume that D draws a check payable to the order of P on March 1. P indorses it to A on March 3, and A indorses it to B on March 6. B must present the check by the 10th to hold P liable on the instrument, but if he presents by the 13th, he can hold A liable on the check. If he waits until after the 13th, both indorsers are discharged unless B can show that the presentment was within a reasonable time. B, nevertheless, has thirty days within which to present the check in order to hold D liable, this period being presumptively reasonable as to the drawer. If he did not present the check for payment until after March 31, D would be discharged *only* to the extent of any loss he might have suffered as the result of the delay, but not otherwise. The indorsers P and A, however, would be competely discharged by B's failure to make presentment within a reasonable time, irrespective of any showing of loss.

Presentments are of two types: presentment for acceptance and presentment for payment.

Presentment of a draft for **acceptance** is necessary to charge secondary parties where the draft so provides, or is payable elsewhere than at the residence or place of business of the drawee, or its date of payment depends on such presentment, as in the case of a draft providing: "Seven days after acceptance pay * * * ." Presentment for acceptance is also authorized in the case of any other time draft, although it is not required.

Presentment of any instrument for **payment** is necessary to charge any indorser, although an exception exists in the case of an instrument indorsed after maturity. Failure to present for payment does not discharge the drawer, however, except to the extent, as indicated above, that there was unreasonable delay in presenting a draft to a bank where funds were available for its payment and the bank became insolvent in the interim.

Although the drawee may be willing to accept the draft in strict accordance with its terms, he nevertheless has certain rights which he is entitled to exercise before he commits himself. These rights, the exercise of which in no sense constitutes a dishonor, are set out in Sections 3–505 and 3–506. He may require exhibition of the instrument, its production at a proper place, reasonable identification of the person making presentment, and upon payment, a signed receipt, with surrender of the instrument if it is paid in full. Failure to comply with any of these requests invalidates the presentment, and consequently there can be no dishonor. The person making present-

ment is entitled to a reasonable opportunity to comply with any such requests, and the time for making presentment is extended accordingly.

Acceptance may be deferred until the close of the next business day following a proper presentment, thereby giving the drawee the opportunity to check back with the drawer or to take any other steps he may desire to assure himself of the propriety of acceptance. Conversely, the holder is authorized to allow postponement of acceptance for an additional business day in a good faith effort to obtain acceptance. For example, the drawee may refuse to accept without verification from the drawer and be unable to get in touch with him. He would either have to dishonor the instrument or ask the holder for an additional day. If the holder grants it, there is no dishonor.

Payment of an instrument may be deferred without dishonor pending reasonable examination to determine whether the instrument is properly payable, but payment must be made in any event before the close of business on the day of presentment.

Notice of Dishonor An instrument is dishonored when: (1) presentment has been duly made, and acceptance or payment is refused or cannot be obtained within the prescribed time, or (2) presentment is excused and the instrument is not duly accepted or paid. Section 3–507(1). Return for lack of a proper indorsement is not dishonor. *See First National Bank of Allentown v. Montgomery.*

Upon proper presentment and dishonor, and subject to any necessary notice of protest, the holder has an immediate right of recourse against drawers and indorsers upon giving them seasonable notice of presentment and dishonor. Such notice is necessary to charge any indorser. Notice is also necessary with respect to any drawer, the acceptor of a draft payable at a bank or the maker of a note payable at a bank, but failure to give such notice discharges these parties only if the insolvency of the bank deprives them of funds which they maintained at the bank to cover the instrument. Section 3–502(1)(b).

Notice of dishonor is normally given by the holder or by an indorser who has himself recieved notice. For example, M makes a note payable to the order of P; P indorses it to A; A indorses it to B; B indorses it to H, the last holder; H timely presents it to M, who refuses payment. H may give notice of dishonor to all secondary parties: P, A, and B. If he is satisfied that B will pay him, he may only notify B. B then must see to it that A or P is notified, or B will have no recourse. B may notify either or both. If he notifies A only, A will have to see to it that P is notified, or A will have no recourse.

If, in this hypothetical problem, H notifies P alone, A and B are discharged. P cannot complain, because he has no claim against A or B who indorsed subsequent to him. It cannot matter to P that he is compelled to pay H rather than A, and therefore subsequent parties are permitted to skip intermediate indorsers if they want to discharge them and are willing to look solely to prior indorsers for recourse.

Any necessary notice must be given by a *bank* before midnight on the *next* banking day following the banking day on which it receives notice of dishonor. Any *nonbank* must give notice before midnight of the third business day after dishonor or receipt of notice of dishonor. Section 3–508. *See Hane v. Exten.* Written notice is effective when sent regardless of whether it is received. For instance, D draws a check on Y bank payable to the order of P; P indorses it to A; A deposits it to her account in X bank; X bank properly presents it to Y bank, the drawee; Y bank dishonors it because the drawer, D, has insufficient funds on deposit to cover it. Y bank has until midnight of the following day to notify X bank, A, P, or D of the dishonor. X bank has until midnight of the day after receipt of notice of dishonor to notify A, P, or D of the dishonor. That is, if X received the notice of dishonor on Monday, it would have until midnight of Tuesday to notify A,

P, or D. If it failed to notify A, it could not charge the item back to her. But A has until midnight of the third business day after receipt of notice of dishonor to notify P or D. If she received notice on Tuesday, she would have until midnight on Friday to notify P or D. P would also have three business days in which to notify D.

Parties other than banks are given additional time to give notice of dishonor because they are normally not in the business of handling commercial paper. Consequently, they are given additional time to find out what they need to do, and under most circumstances they will have time to take care of the matter by an ordinary business letter.

Frequently, notice of dishonor is given by returning the unpaid instrument with a stamp, ticket, or memorandum attached stating that the item was not paid and requesting that the recipient make good on it. But since the purpose of notice is to give knowledge of dishonor and to inform the secondary party that he may be held liable on the instrument, any kind of notice which informs the recipient of his potential liability is sufficient. No formal requisites are imposed—notice may be given in any reasonable manner. An oral notice is sufficient, but is inadvisable because it may be difficult to prove. Consequently, one is not advised to use it, and oral notification has little place in the business world, except as a mere preliminary to be followed by a more formal statement in writing.

If the person notified is not misled, a misdescription of the instrument does not defeat the notice. Section 3–508(3). Thus, if a payee of a promissory note executed on January 3 by Mike Maker is told that the "note of January 5 made by Mike Maker" has been dishonored, this would constitute a sufficient notice if the recipient knew that the dishonor related to Mike Maker's note dated January 3. Furthermore, notice operates for the benefit of all parties who have rights against the party notified. Section 3–508(8). For example, M makes a note payable to the order of P; P indorses it to A; A indorses it to H.

H duly presents the note to M who dishonors it. H notifies both P and A of the dishonor, and then asks A to pay him. A does so. Can A now hold P? The answer is yes. A does not have to notify P of the dishonor. P already has been notified of it by H.

Protest A protest is a certificate of dishonor made under the hand and seal of a United States consul or vice-consul or a notary public or other person authorized to certify to a dishonor by the law of the place where the dishonor occurred. It must identify the instrument and certify either that due presentment has been made or the reason why it is excused and that the instrument has been dishonored by non-acceptance or non-payment. The protest may also certify that notice of dishonor has been given to all parties or to specified parties. Protest, or the noting for protest, must be made within the time allowed for giving notice of dishonor. Protest is only required where the draft is drawn or payable outside the United States.

Delay in Presentment, Notice, or Protest Excused The Code excuses *a delay* in presentment, notice, or protest in two situations. Section 3–511(1). The first excuses a delay where the holder does not have notice that the instrument is due; for example, an instrument may provide that its maturity shall be automatically accelerated upon the happening of a particular event. If the holder does not know that this event has happened, she is excused from presentment until she learns of the acceleration, and secondary parties are not discharged because of the delay. Once the holder learns that the event has occurred she must present the note within a reasonable time and give prompt notice of dishonor to hold the indorsers liable.

The second situation excuses the holder's delay where it is caused by circumstances beyond his control. For example, suppose the holder cannot present the instrument to the primary party because a storm has disrupted all means of communication and transporta-

tion. The circumstances need not make presentment impossible. It is enough if they are of the degree and character which would deter persons of ordinary prudence, energy, and courage from encountering them in the pursuit of business.

Presentment, Notice, or Protest Excused The Code *entirely* excuses the holder from presentment, notice, or protest if the party to be charged has himself dishonored the instrument or has countermanded payment, or if the holder otherwise has no reason to expect the instrument to be accepted or paid. Section 3–511(2)(b). If, for example, D draws a check on a bank with which he has no account, or has closed his account, or has stopped payment on the check, he is not entitled to a due presentment and notice of dishonor. These matters are entirely excused so far as he is concerned. But they would not be excused as to intermediate indorsers who did not have any reason to expect that the instrument would not be accepted or paid.

Section 3–511(2)(c) also entirely excuses a presentment, notice, or protest, as the case may be, if these things cannot be accomplished by reasonable diligence. For example, if the maker of a note has "departed for places unknown" and cannot be located by reasonable diligence, the holder has no way of making a presentment to him. In such case, presentment is entirely excused, and the holder should treat the instrument as dishonored and give prompt notice of dishonor to the indorsers. Likewise, if one of the indorsers cannot be located by reasonable diligence, notice of dishonor would not have to be given to him— it would be entirely excused.

Presentment Excused The Code sets out some specific situations in which presentment is *entirely* excused. These situations, which do not excuse notice or protest, include the following: (1) the maker, acceptor, or drawee is dead or in insolvency proceedings; or (2) payment or acceptance is refused for reasons not relating to proper presentment, making it clear that a subsequent presentment would be a useless ceremony. Section 3–511(3).

Waiver of Presentment, Notice, or Protest Presentment, notice, or protest may also be waived either before or after it is due. Section 3–511(2)(a). Waivers are of two types, express and implied. Express waivers have not caused much difficulty. Usually, they are stated in terms such as "Presentment, notice, and protest waived" or "Protest waived." Where such language appears on the face of the instrument, it is deemed to bind all parties. Where it is written above the signature of an indorser, it binds her only. Section 3–511(6).

It is possible to waive all conditions or only some conditions. For example, an indorser could waive notice of dishonor, but require the holder to make a due presentment to hold her liable. However, under the Code a waiver of protest is also a waiver of presentment and of notice of dishonor even though protest is not required.

Under Section 3–511(5) it is provided that a waiver of protest is also a waiver of presentment and of notice of dishonor even though protest is not required. This rule is based upon common commercial understanding of the term "protest waived."

Disclaimer by Secondary Parties

Both drawers and indorsers *may* disclaim their normal secondary liability by drawing or indorsing instruments **"without recourse."** Sections 3–413(2) and 3–414(1). The use of the qualifying words "without recourse" is understood in commercial circles to place purchasers on notice that they may not rely on the credit of the person using this language, but may look only to the other parties to the instrument. A person drawing or indorsing an instrument in this manner does not incur the normal contractual liability of a drawer or indorser to pay the instrument, but he may

nonetheless be liable for breach of warranty under certain circumstances.

LIABILITY OF ACCOMMODATION PARTIES

Accommodation parties are those who sign a negotiable instrument for the purpose of lending their credit to another party to it. They may be makers or co-makers, drawers or co-drawers, or indorsers. An indorsement which shows that it is not in the chain of title is notice of its accommodation character. *See First National Bank of Allentown v. Montgomery.*

Frequently, one or more persons indorse an instrument to accommodate another party, rather than sign as maker or drawer. Suppose M wants to borrow money from P, and P insists that M procure the signatures of A, B, C, and D before the loan is made. M asks these parties to accommodate him; and, pursuant to the agreement with P, M makes the note, and A, B, C, and D sign their names on the back of it in that order. A, B, C, and D by reason of signing on the back are liable to P as indorsers. M is liable to P and to A, B, C, and D, if these accommodating parties pay the instrument.

Suppose M becomes insolvent so that the reimbursement rights that A, B, C, and D have against him are meaningless. Suppose further that P enforces the note against D. Can D pass the loss on to C? May C shift it to B? Would A ultimately be out-of-pocket simply because she signed first? Parol evidence would be admissible to show that the indorsers had agreed to share the loss equally or in some other proportion, if that is the case. If they made no agreement among themselves, the rule that indorsers are liable in the order in which they signed should *not* apply. The law of suretyship, which applies to accommodation parties, is based upon concepts of equity and fairness which would not be consistent with having the rights of these sureties among themselves depend upon the accidental or fortuitous order in which they signed the instrument. Although each is liable to the holder for the full amount, they should share the loss equally, and one who is required to pay more than his share is entitled to recover ratably from the others. See Chapter 36 for a further discussion of suretyship.

LIABILITY FOR CONVERSION

Conversion is a tort whereby a person becomes liable in damages by reason of his wrongful exercise of dominion over the personal property of another. The Code provides that a conversion occurs in three situations: (1) when a drawee to whom a draft is delivered for acceptance refuses to return it on demand; (2) when any person to whom an instrument is delivered for payment refuses on demand either to pay or to return it; and (3) when an instrument is paid on a forged indorsement. Section 3–419(1). Situations (1) and (2) involve willful action on the part of the party guilty of the conversion, whereas in situation (3) the payor's action was in all probability completely innocent as his dominion over the instrument resulted from an unrecognized break in the chain of title. Nevertheless, the liability is the same in all three cases, as good faith is completely immaterial and the person wrongfully exercising dominion over the instrument is liable for damages.

SPECIAL SITUATIONS AFFECTING LIABILITY

If a drawee of a draft or check pays it, the drawer is generally under a duty to make reimbursement. Usually the drawer has funds in the hands of the drawee, and the drawee, honoring a draft or check, reimburses itself immediately by charging the drawer's account or her funds. The drawee can be reimbursed, however, only if it acts in accordance with the drawer's *order* as it appears on the

instrument. Thus, if Davis draws a check to the order of Jones, the drawee bank to whom the instrument is addressed acquires no right of reimbursement by paying Roe, unless Jones has indorsed the check to Roe. In short, it is up to the drawee to determine whether the one presenting the item for payment or acceptance has rights in it, for if it pays the wrong party, it is the drawee's loss and not the drawer's. Two situations involving these principles have been especially troublesome and have been specifically addressed by the Code.

The Impostor Rule

Usually, this rule comes into play in situations involving a confidence man who impersonates a respected citizen and who deceives a third party into delivering a negotiable instrument to the impostor in the name of the respected citizen. For instance, John Doe, falsely representing himself as Richard Roe, a creditor of Ray Davis, induces Davis to draw a check payable to the order of Richard Roe and to deliver it to him. Doe then forges Roe's name to the check and presents it to the drawee for payment. The drawee pays it. Subsequently, the drawer denies the drawee's right of reimbursement upon the ground that the drawee did not pay in accordance with his order: the drawer ordered payment to Roe or to Roe's order. Roe did not order payment to anyone; therefore, the drawee would not acquire a right of reimbursement against the drawer Davis. This is the argument in favor of the drawer and is supported by the general rule governing unauthorized signatures.

Nevertheless, Section 3–405(1)(a) provides that the indorsement of the impostor or of any other person in the name of the named payee is **effective** if the impostor has induced the maker or drawer to issue the instrument to him or his confederate using the name of the payee. It is as if the named payee had indorsed the instrument. The reason for this rule is that the drawer or maker is to blame for failing to detect the impersonation by the impostor. Thus, in the above example, the drawee would be able to debit the drawer's account. *See also Philadelphia Title Ins. Co. v. Fidelity-Philadelphia Trust Co.*

The Fictitious Payee Rule

The second situation is similar, only it involves a faithless agent rather than an impostor. For instance, the drawer's agent falsely tells the drawer that money is owed to X, and the drawer draws a check payable to the order of X and hands it to the agent for delivery to X. The agent forges X's name to the check and obtains payment from the drawee bank. The drawer then denies the bank's claim to reimbursement upon the ground that the latter did not comply with her order; that the drawer had ordered payment to X or order; that the drawee did not make payment either to X or as ordered by X, inasmuch as the forgery of X's signature is wholly inoperative; that the drawee paid in accordance with the scheme of the faithless agent and not in compliance with the drawer's order.

Once again, the drawee bank will be able to debit the drawer's account. "An indorsement by any person in the name of a named payee is **effective** if * * * an agent or employee of the maker or drawer has supplied him with the name of the payee intending the latter to have no such interest." Section 3–405(1)(c). (Emphasis supplied.) The risk of employee fraud presents business risks which the Code imposes upon the party employing the agent.

The same rule also applies to the analogous situation in which a person signs as or on behalf of a maker or drawer intending the payee to have no interest in the instrument. Section 3–405(1)(b). In such situations any person's indorsement in the name of the named payee is **effective.** For instance, P gives A, her employee, authority to write checks in order to pay P's debts. A writes a check for $2,000 to F, a fictitious payee, which A takes

and indorses in F's name to A. A cashes the check at P's bank. P's bank can debit P's account. P should bear the risk of her unscrupulous employees.

LIABILITY BASED ON WARRANTY

A negotiable instrument is not only the written evidence of contract liability, but it is also a special kind of property intended for trading and having marketability. Just as certain implied warranties under the Code attach to the sale of goods, certain warranties imposed by the Code attach to the *sale* of commercial paper. These warranties are effective whether or *not* the transferor or presenter signs the instrument although, as will be seen, the extent of the warranty to subsequent holders does depend upon whether they have indorsed the instrument. There are two types of warranties: (a) transferor's warranties and (b) presenter's warranties. Like other warranties, these may be disclaimed by agreement between immediate parties. In the case of an indorser, his disclaimer of transfer warranties must appear in the indorsement itself.

WARRANTIES ON TRANSFER

Any person who transfers an instrument, whether by negotiation or assignment, and receives consideration makes certain warranties. Section 3–417(2). *See First National Bank of Allentown v. Montgomery.* Warranties on transfer run to the immediate transferee only if transfer is by delivery alone, but if the transfer is made by indorsement, whether qualified or unqualified, the warranties run to "any subsequent holder who takes the instrument in good faith." The warranties of the transferor are as follows.

Good Title

The first warranty imposed by the Code upon a transferor is that the transferor has good title to the instrument or is authorized to obtain payment or acceptance on behalf of one who has good title, and the transfer is otherwise rightful. Section 3–417(2)(a). Under this rule, if M makes a note payable to the order of P which is stolen from the latter and the thief forges P's indorsement and sells the instrument to A, A does not have good title. The break in the indorsement chain prevents him from acquiring title. If A indorses the instrument over to B for value, B can hold A liable for breach of warranty. The warranty action is important to B, because it enables him to hold A liable, even if A has indorsed the note "without recourse."

Signatures Genuine

In the foregoing situation the second warranty imposed by the Code, that **all** signatures are genuine or authorized, would also be breached. Section 3–417(2)(b). However, if the signature of a maker, drawer, drawee, acceptor, or indorser not in the chain of title is unauthorized, there is a breach of this warranty but no breach of the warranty of good title.

No Material Alteration

A third warranty is the warranty against material alteration. Section 3–417(2)(c). Suppose that M makes a note payable to the order of the payee in the amount of $100. The payee, without authority, raises the note so that it appears to be drawn for $1,000 and negotiates the instrument to A, who buys it innocent of the alteration. A, indorsing "without recourse," negotiates the instrument to B for value. B presents the instrument to M, who refuses to pay more than $100 on it. B can collect the difference from A. While A is not liable to B on the indorsement contract due to her qualified indorsement, she is liable to him upon the breach of warranty. If A had not qualified her indorsement, B would be able to recover against A on either the basis of warranty or the indorsement contract.

No Defenses

The fourth transferor's warranty imposed by the Code is that *no defense* of any party is good against the transferor. Section 3–417(2)(d). Under this warranty a transferor who indorses "without recourse" stands in a better position than an unqualified indorser. His warranty is only that he has *no knowledge* of any such defense. Section 3–417(3). Suppose that M, a minor, a resident of a State where minors' contracts for non-necessaries are void, in payment of a motorcycle makes a note payable to bearer; P, the first holder, negotiates it to A by mere delivery; A indorses it "without recourse" (qualified indorsement) and negotiates it to B; B unqualifiedly indorses it to H. H cannot recover upon the instrument against M because of M's minority (a real defense). H, therefore, recovers against B on either the breach of warranty that no valid defenses exist to the instrument or the indorsement contract, provided H gave B prompt notice of dishonor. B cannot recover against A upon A's qualified indorsement. Can B hold A for breach of warranty? Since A indorsed without recourse, he does not warrant that the instrument is without defense; he only warrants that he knows of no defense which is good against him. Assuming that A did not know that M was a minor, B cannot hold A for breach of warranty. Can B hold P? P is not liable as an indorser, because he did not indorse the instrument. Although P as a transferor warrants that there are no defenses good against him, this warranty only extends to his immediate transferee, A. Therefore, B cannot hold P. This illustration shows the interplay between indorsement and warranty liability and the relationship between the liability imposed under the various warranties and the individuals who can or cannot claim protection under a particular warranty.

No Knowledge of Insolvency

Any person who transfers a negotiable instrument warrants that he has no knowledge of any insolvency proceedings instituted with respect to the maker or acceptor or the drawer of an unaccepted instrument. Section 3–417(2)(e). Thus, if M makes a note payable to bearer, and the first holder, P, negotiates it without indorsement to A, who then negotiates it by qualified indorsement to B, both P and A make a warranty that they do not know that M is in bankruptcy. However, B could not hold P for breach of warranty, since P's warranty runs only in favor of her immediate transferee, A. If B should hold A liable on her warranty, A could thereupon hold P, her immediate transferor, liable.

Figure 27-2 summarizes liabilities on transfer.

WARRANTIES ON PRESENTMENT

All parties called upon to pay or accept an instrument must do so strictly in compliance with the order given. The drawee bank agrees to pay checks as ordered by the drawer so long as his account is sufficient to cover them. If the bank pays other than pursuant to the drawer's order, it cannot charge the payment to the drawer's account.

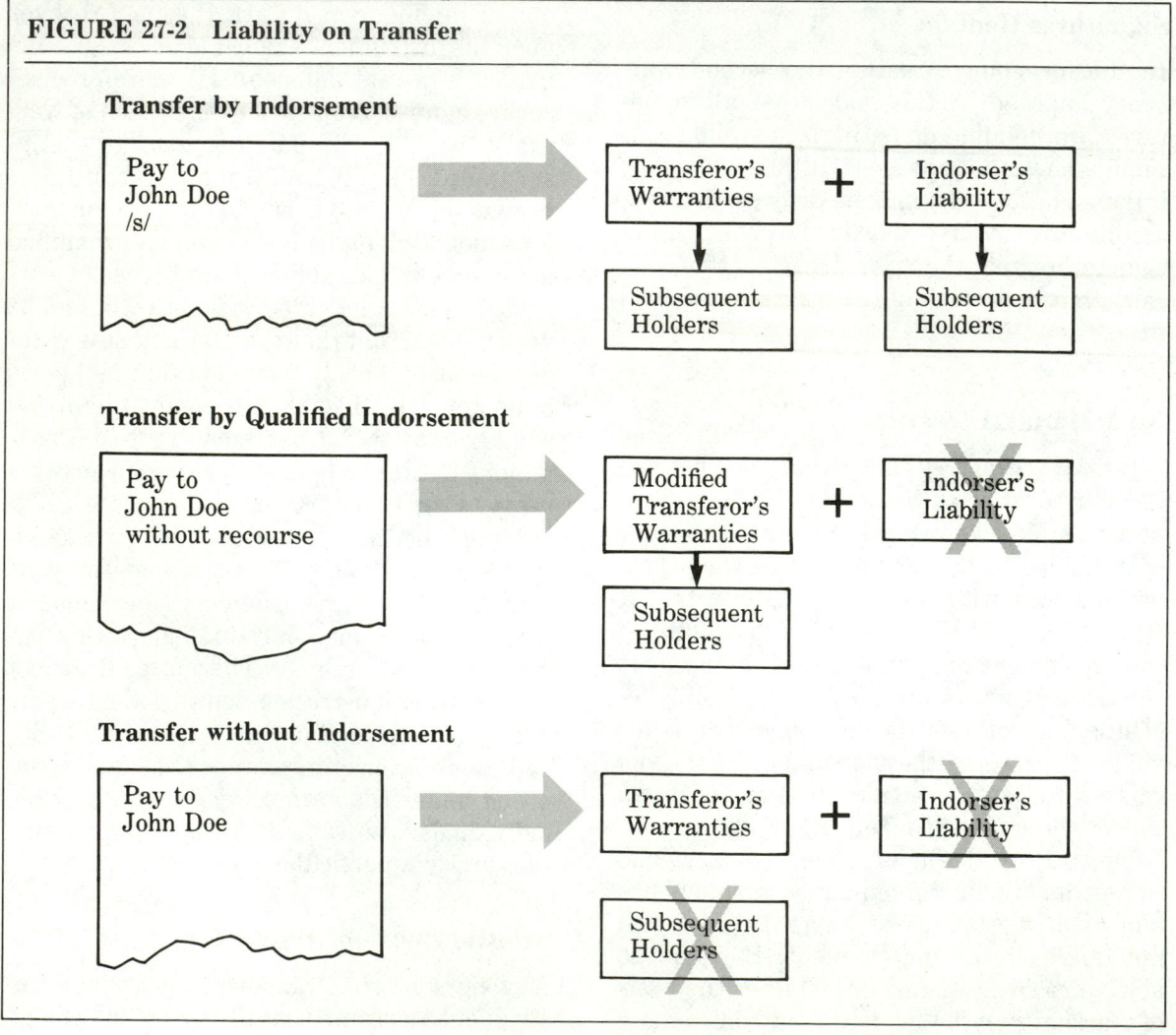

FIGURE 27-2   Liability on Transfer

Transfer by Indorsement

Pay to
John Doe
/s/

→ Transferor's Warranties + Indorser's Liability

Transferor's Warranties → Subsequent Holders

Indorser's Liability → Subsequent Holders

Transfer by Qualified Indorsement

Pay to
John Doe
without recourse

→ Modified Transferor's Warranties + Indorser's Liability ✗

Modified Transferor's Warranties → Subsequent Holders

Transfer without Indorsement

Pay to
John Doe

→ Transferor's Warranties + Indorser's Liability ✗

Subsequent Holders ✗

If a drawee pays an instrument which has been forged or altered, he has the initial loss, for he cannot charge this amount to the drawer. May the drawee shift this loss to the person who received the payment? With respect to instruments on which the drawer's signature has been forged, the general answer is "no." The drawee can, however, recover from a person to whom he made payment for any loss incurred because of a forged indorsement or an alteration of the instrument.

For example, suppose D's (drawer's) name is forged to a check so as to make it appear that it was drawn by her. If the bank pays this check, it cannot charge D's account nor recover from a *holder in due course*, or a person who in *good faith* has changed his position in reliance, to whom it made the payment. Similarly, if a drawee pays a draft purportedly drawn by D, it cannot seek reimbursement from D if D's signature is forged. The justification for the rule is that the drawee is supposed to know the drawer's signature. On the other hand, if D draws a check to P or order, and P's indorsement is forged, the bank does not follow D's order in paying such an item, and hence cannot charge her account (except in the impostor or faithless employee situations discussed above). The bank, however, can recover from the person who obtained payment of the check from it. The bank should not be required to bear this loss, because it should not be expected to know the signature of payees of checks although it should know the signatures of its own customers.

The same rationale applies to raised instruments. If D makes a check to P's order in the amount of $3 and it is raised so as to appear to be in the amount of $300, the bank cannot charge the $300 it pays out on such an item to the drawer's account. It can only charge the account to the extent of $3, because that is all the drawer ordered it to pay. On the other hand, the bank can charge back the difference against the presenting party who received payment from it.

The examples to this point have involved drawees. The maker of a note, obviously, cannot recover payment he made on a forged maker's signature to a holder in the course or a good faith taker who changed his position in reliance; he should know his own signature. But, suppose that the maker of a note pays on a forged indorsement or an altered item. The maker, like the drawee, cannot know everyone's signature, and where the indorser's signature is forged, the maker can recover any money paid to the presenting party. The situation is different where the amount of the note has been raised. Suppose that the maker makes a note in the amount of $300, and it is raised to $3,000. If he pays this note, he is not permitted to recover from an innocent presenting party, because the maker—unlike a drawee—has a way of knowing the original principal amount of the instrument. Similarly, suppose that a check or draft is raised *after* it has been accepted or certified by the drawee. If the acceptor pays the raised amount to an innocent presenting party, the acceptor is not entitled to recover the amount by which the instrument was raised because it has no way of knowing the proper amount of this item.

Presenter's warranties run not only *from* the person who obtains payment or acceptance, but also from *any* prior transferor. These presentment warranties are now codified in Section 3–417(1) and are as follows.

Good Title

Presenters give the same warranty of good title to persons who pay or accept as is granted to transferees under the transferor's warranty. More significantly, the warranty extends to the genuineness of the indorser's signatures, but *not* to the signature of the drawer or maker.

Genuineness of
Signature of Maker and Drawer

The presenter warrants that he has no *knowledge* that the signature of the maker or drawer is unauthorized. To protect a person who takes an instrument in good faith and later learns it was forged, certain exceptions to this warranty are specified in the Code. A holder in due course acting in good faith does not give such a warranty to: (1) the maker with respect to his own signature; (2) the drawer with respect to his own signature; and (3) an acceptor of a draft with respect to the drawer's signature if such holder took the draft after acceptance or obtained the acceptance without knowledge of the unauthorized signature. Only a holder in due course can avail himself of these exceptions.

No Material Alteration

A warranty is also given against material alteration, but again it is not given by a holder in due course acting in good faith to a maker or drawer, whether or not the drawer is also the drawee. Further, the holder in due course does not give this warranty to the acceptor of a draft or check with respect to an alteration made prior to acceptance if such holder took after acceptance, even though the acceptance included a term such as "payable as originally drawn." The acceptor had the first opportunity to detect the alteration. To permit the acceptor to shift the responsibility for a prior material alteration to a subsequent party would defeat the entire purpose of acceptance and certification. An acceptance or certification must constitute a definite commitment to honor a definite instrument.

This rule should not be confused with that which applies where the alteration is made *after* the acceptance or certification. In such a situation the drawee knows the amount of the original acceptance or certification, and she should not be able to charge back against an innocent party if she pays out more than that amount. Hence, a holder in due course does not warrant against post-acceptance or post-certification alterations.

Figure 27-3 recaps liability based on warranty.

TERMINATION OF LIABILITY

Sooner or later, every commercial transaction must come to rest, with the potential liabilities of the parties to the instrument terminated. Except for the presentment warranties, a holder in due course has no further liability to an acceptor or payor after acceptance or payment: the payment or acceptance is *final*. The payor or acceptor cannot subsequently recover even though she discovers she has paid or accepted an instrument with a forged drawer's or maker's signature, or she has paid a check over a stop order. These provisions, as previously noted, also run in favor of a person who in good faith has changed her position in reliance on the payment or acceptance.

The Code specifies the various methods and extent by which the liability of any party, primary or secondary, and of all parties is discharged. Section 3-601. However, no discharge of a party is effective against a subsequent holder in due course unless she has knowledge of the discharge when she takes the instrument. Section 3-602.

PAYMENT OR SATISFACTION

The most obvious way for a party to discharge his liability on an instrument is to pay the holder. Section 3-603. Such a payment results in a discharge even though it is made with knowledge of the claim of another person to the instrument, unless such other person either supplies adequate indemnity or obtains an injunction in a proceeding to which the holder is made a party. The person making payment is not required to decide at his peril whether the claim to the instrument is valid or not. Such a claim may arise, for example, where the prior holder contends the instrument was stolen from him.

The person making payment should, of course, take the instrument or have it can-

FIGURE 27-3   Liability Based on Warranty

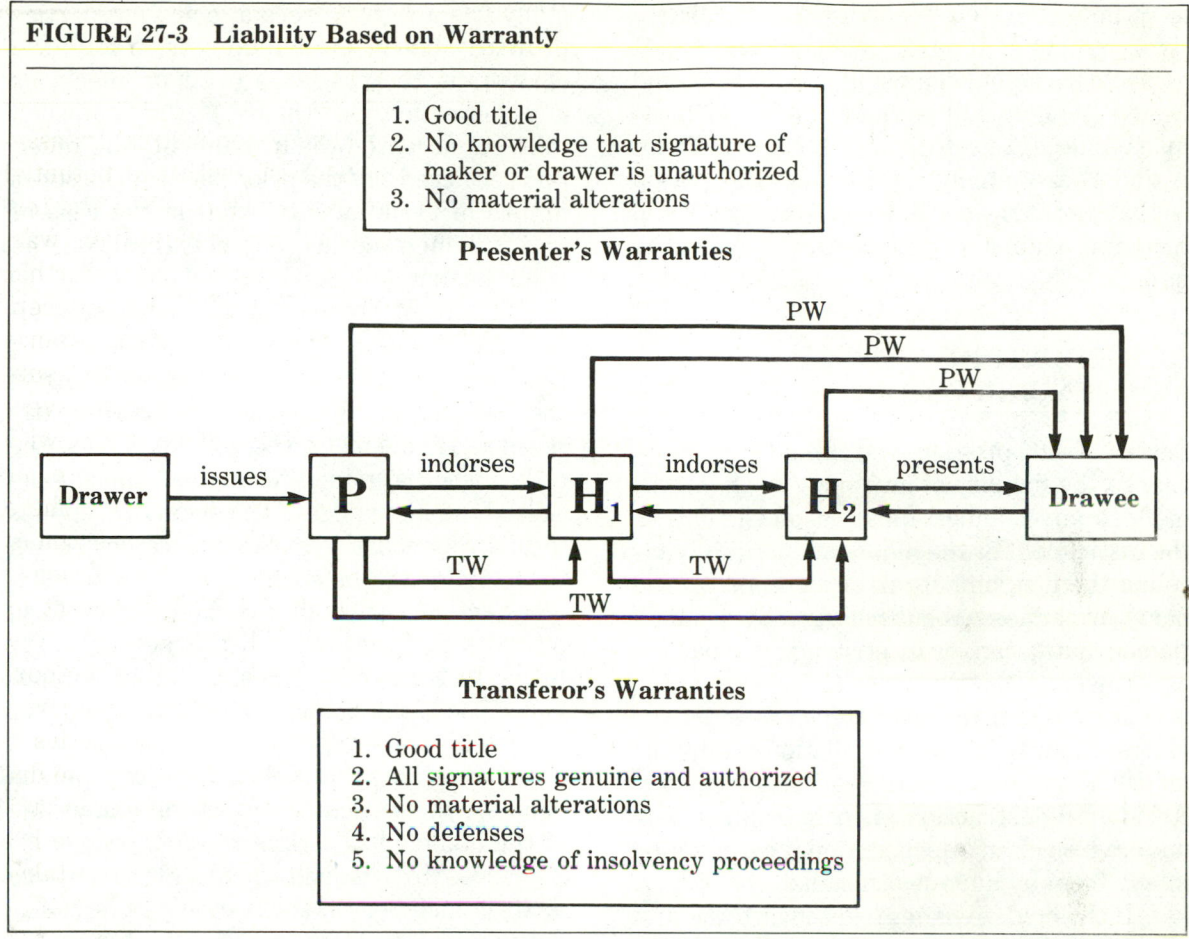

1. Good title
2. No knowledge that signature of maker or drawer is unauthorized
3. No material alterations

Presenter's Warranties

Transferor's Warranties

1. Good title
2. All signatures genuine and authorized
3. No material alterations
4. No defenses
5. No knowledge of insolvency proceedings

celed so that it cannot pass into the hands of a subsequent holder in due course against whom his discharge would not be effective.

TENDER OF PAYMENT

Any party liable on an instrument who makes tender of full payment to a holder when or after payment is due is discharged to the extent of all subsequent liability for interest, costs, and attorney's fees. Section 3–604(1). However, her tender does not relieve her of liability for the face amount of the instrument or any interest accrued until that time. The maker or acceptor may, however, have no way of seeking out a holder so as to make tender to stop the running of interest. Sub-

section (3) of Section 3–604 solves this problem by providing that if such party is ready and able to pay a time instrument when it is due at the place of payment specified in the instrument, it is the equivalent of tender. This remedy is not available in the case of demand paper or paper which does not specify a place of payment.

Occasionally a holder will refuse a tender of payment for reasons known only to himself. It may be that he believes he has rights over and beyond the amount of the tender, or because he desires to enforce payment against another party. In any event, his refusal of the tender has the effect of wholly discharging every party who has a right of recourse against the party making tender. Section 3–604(2). For example, a note executed by M in favor of P is negotiated by indorsement successively to A, B, and H. M defaults, and H perfects his rights against indorsers P, A, and B. If P tenders full payment to H and H refuses to accept it, desiring to collect from M, A and B are wholly discharged. The reason is that both A and B would have rights of recourse against P if they were required to pay.

CANCELLATION AND RENUNCIATION

Section 3–605 provides that a holder may discharge the liability of any party to an instrument in any manner apparent on the face of the instrument or the indorsement, as by canceling the instrument or the signature of the party or parties to be discharged by destruction or mutilation, or by striking out a party's signature.

Since the instrument itself constitutes the obligation, intentional cancellation of it by the holder results in a discharge of all parties. Accidental destruction of an instrument does not have such an effect, nor does cancellation in any form by anyone other than the holder.

If the holder wishes to discharge one, but not all parties, he may merely strike out that party's signature. He must be careful, however, that he does not discharge other parties as well by impairing their rights of recourse, as discussed below.

A holder may also renounce his rights by a writing, signed and delivered, or by surrendering the instrument to the party to be discharged. As in the case of other discharges, however, a written renunciation is of no effect against a subsequent holder in due course who takes without knowledge of it.

Cancellation or renunciation is effective even without consideration.

IMPAIRMENT OF RECOURSE OR COLLATERAL

If the holder collects the amount of an instrument from an indorser, the latter nor-

mally has a right of recourse against parties primarily liable, prior indorsers, if any, the drawer, in the case of a draft or check, or any one or more of them. At the time such indorser accepted the instrument, she relied upon the credit of the prior parties, the strict nature of their liability, and, in the case of an instrument secured by collateral, on the value of that collateral.

If any of these rights is adversely affected by the action or inaction of the holder, the indorser should not be required to pay the instrument; for when she subsequently seeks reimbursement, she will not possess the rights, she bargained for at the time she accepted the instrument. The same rule applies to an accommodation maker or acceptor known to the holder to be such.

Section 3–606 of the Code, therefore, provides that the holder discharges any party to the instrument to the extent that without her consent the holder:

1. releases or agrees not to sue any person against whom such party, to the knowledge of the holder, has a right of recourse;
2. agrees to suspend the right to enforce against such person the instrument or collateral;
3. otherwise discharges such person; or
4. unjustifiably impairs any collateral for the instrument given by or on behalf of the party or any person against whom such party has a right of recourse.

As indicated above striking out the signature of a prior indorser discharges subsequent indorsers who have a right of recourse against the indorser discharged.

Similarly, if the holder suspends the right to enforce the instrument, as by granting an unauthorized extension of time to pay, the subsequent indorsers are discharged. Their undertaking is only to pay if the maker or drawee does not pay on demand or on the date specified in a time instrument. They have not contracted for any extension of time for payment. The discharge of the indorser is based upon principles of suretyship law.

The holder may, however, take any of the first three steps indicated above without discharging a party with a right of recourse if at the same time he expressly reserves his rights against such party. In so doing, he cannot, of course, impair any rights of recourse which such party may possess against others.

OTHER METHODS OF DISCHARGE

As discussed earlier, other methods by which a party's liability may be discharged include:

1. fraudulent and material alteration. Section 3–407.

2. discharge of the drawer and prior indorsers by certification of a check procured by a holder. Section 3–411.

3. unexcused delay in presentment, notice of dishonor, or protest. Section 3–502.

4. Any party may also be discharged as against another party by an act or agreement with such party which would discharge a simple contract for the payment of money. Section 3–601(2).

CASES

Signature

VALLEY NATIONAL BANK, SUNNYMEAD v. COOK

Arizona Court of Appeals, Division One, 1983.
136 Ariz. 232, 665 P.2d 576.

CORCORAN, J.

The issue raised in this appeal is whether an individual who signs a check without indicating her representative capacity is personally liable on the obligation evidenced by the check when the check has the name of the corporate principal printed on it. We adopt the minority rule and hold that the individual is not personally liable. [Citation.]

On October 21, 1977, appellee J. M. Cook (Cook), the treasurer of Arizona Auto Auction and R.V. Center, Inc., (Arizona Auto Auction, Inc.) issued three corporate checks to Central Motors Company. Central Motors deposited these checks in its corporate account which was held by appellant Valley National Bank, Sunnymead, a California corporation (Bank). The Bank then sent each of these checks for payment to Arizona Auto Auction, Inc.'s, drawee bank, First National Bank of Arizona. However, a stop payment order had been put on these checks, and the First National Bank dishonored each of the checks. The checks were returned to the Bank, and the account of Central Motors was charged

back for the amount of the checks which totaled $9,795. The bank was unable to recover this amount from Central Motors. The Bank demanded payment from Arizona Auto Auction, Inc., but the demand was not honored. On March 27, 1978, the Bank commenced suit against Arizona Auto Auction, Inc., and J. M. Cook and her spouse.

The case was tried to the court on August 1, 1979. After trial the court found that the Bank was a holder in due course and that the Arizona Auto Auction, Inc., was obligated as drawer for the face amount of the checks, $9,795. However, the judgment provided that Cook was not personally liable on the checks.
* * *

The question of whether Cook signed in her individual or representative capacity is governed by § 3–403 of the Uniform Commercial Code (UCC) as adopted in this state. [§ 3–403] provides:

(1) A signature may be made by an agent or other representative, and his authority to make it may be established as in other cases of representation. No particular form of appointment is necessary to establish such authority.
(2) An authorized representative who signs his own name to an instrument:
    (a) Is personally obligated if the instrument neither names the person represented nor shows

that the representative signed in a representative capacity;

(b) Except as otherwise established between the immediate parties, is personally obligated if the instrument names the person represented but does not show that the representative signed in a representative capacity, or if the instrument does not name the person represented but does show that the representative signed in a representative capacity.

(3) Except as otherwise established the name of an organization preceded or followed by the name and office of an authorized individual is a signature made in a representative capacity.

The Bank argues that this section conclusively establishes Cook's personal liability on the checks. We do not agree. Admittedly, the checks fail to specifically show the office held by Cook. However, we do not find that this fact conclusively establishes liability, since [§ 3–403(2)(b)] imposes personal liability on an agent who signs his or her own name to an instrument only "if the instrument . . . does not show that the representative signed in a representative capacity." Thus, we must look to the entire instrument for evidence of the capacity of the signer. [Citations.]

The checks are in evidence and are boldly imprinted at the top "Arizona Auto Auction, Inc." and also "Arizona Auto Auction, Inc." is imprinted above a signature line appearing at the lower right-hand corner. Under the imprinted name of the corporate defendant appears the signature of appellee Cook without any designation of office or capacity on each of the checks before us on appeal. Appellee Cook did not endorse the checks on the back. The record does not reflect appellee Cook made any personal guaranty of these checks or any other corporate obligation.

*   *   *

The Superior Court of Pennsylvania was confronted with a similar situation in *Pollin v. Mindy Mfg. Co., Inc.* There the court denied recovery by a third party endorsee against one who affixed his signature to a payroll check directly beneath the printed corporate name without indicating his representative capac-

ity. In Pollin the checks were boldly imprinted at the top with the corporate name, address, and appropriate check number. The printed name of the drawee bank appeared in the lower lefthand corner of the instrument and the corporate name was imprinted in the lower righthand corner. Directly beneath the corporate name were two blank lines. The defendant-appellant had signed the top line without any designation of office or capacity. Pointing out that the code imposes liability on the individual only when the instrument controverts any showing of representative capacity, the court considered the instrument in its entirety. The court in Pollin held that disclosure on the face of the instrument that the checks were payable from a special payroll account of the corporation over which the appellant had no control as an individual negated any contention that appellant intended to make the instrument his own order to pay money to the payee.

The difference in outcome in the Pollin case and the cases cited by the Bank in which corporate agents were held liable for failing to show a corporate title reflects the Pollin court's emphasis on *business expectations*, an emphasis which is proper and entirely consistent with the spirit of UCC § 3–403. [Citation.] In determining what these expectations might be, it is important to draw a distinction between a check and a note:

The payee of a corporate check with the corporate name imprinted on its face probably expects less from the individual drawer than the payee of a corporate note may, where both the corporate name and the maker's name may be either handwritten or typewritten. Further, it is common for creditors to demand the individual promise of officers on corporate promissory notes, specially in the case of small corporations. Thus, we think a court should be more reluctant to find an agent personally liable who has signed a corporate check than in the case of a similar indorsement of a corporate note. This does not mean that the drawer of a corporate check will never be personally liable; indeed, more than a few have been stuck. Rather, we hope that courts will be more conscious of differences in business practices with respect to different types of instruments when they evaluate the extrinsic evidence presented by the parties.

[Citation.] Thus, while it may be common for creditors of small corporations to demand that corporate officers personally obligate themselves on corporate notes, it would be most unusual to demand the individual obligation of an officer on corporate checks.

*   *   *

The judgment of the trial court and the award of attorneys' fees are affirmed.

Drawer's Liability

DAVIS v. WATSON BROTHERS PLUMBING, INC.

Court of Civil Appeals of Texas, Dallas, 1981.
615 S.W.2d 844.

AKIN, J.

*   *   *

Defendant was the drawer of a check for $152.38 payable to its employee Arnett Lee. Lee, in turn, endorsed the check over to plaintiff, who operated a liquor store. After Lee endorsed the check to plaintiff and after plaintiff had placed cash on the counter, Lee stated that he wanted to buy a six-pack of beer and a bottle of scotch. When plaintiff turned to obtain the requested merchandise, a thief grabbed approximately $110.00 of the $150.88 ($152.38 less a $1.50 check cashing fee) for which plaintiff cashed the check. Lee took the remainder of the $150.88, approximately $40.88, and notified defendant of the theft. Defendant issued Lee a second check for $152.38 and stopped payment on the first check. Plaintiff sued defendant based on the dishonor of the first check.

The county court rendered judgment for plaintiff for the $40.88 that Lee actually received from plaintiff [after the robbery]. Plaintiff, as appellant, asserts that since he proved that he was the holder of the check and since defendant failed to raise any valid

defenses, defendant was liable to him for the full face value of the check, $152.38. We agree.

"Holder" is defined in *Tex Bus & Com Code Ann* [U.C.C.] § 1.201(20) as: "[A] *person who is in possession of* a document of title or *an instrument* or an investment security drawn, issued or *indorsed to him* or to his order or to brearer or *in blank*." Under the undisputed facts, Lee, the payee endorsed the check in blank to plaintiff, who is now in possession of the check. Thus, as a matter of law, plaintiff is a "holder" under the code [U.C.C.] § 3.413(b), which sets forth the rights of a holder, provides, in pertinent part, that: "The drawer engages that upon dishonor of the draft . . . *he will pay the amount of the draft to the holder* or to any indorser who takes it up." Thus, the defendant is liable to the holder of the dishonored check unless the defendant has raised a valid defense against the holder.

The rights of a holder not in due course are subject to the defenses specified in § 3.306, which provides:

Unless he has the rights of a holder in due course any person takes the instrument subject to

(1) all valid claims to it on the part of any person; and

(2) all defenses of any party which would be available in an action on a simple contract; and

(3) *the defenses of want or failure of consideration*, non-performance of any condition precedent, non-delivery, or delivery for a special purpose (Section 3.408); and

(4) the defense that he or a person through whom he holds the instrument acquired it by theft, or that payment or satisfaction to such holder would be inconsistent with the terms of a restrictive indorsement. *The claim of any third person to the instrument is not otherwise available as a defense to any party liable thereon unless the third person himself defends the action for such party.*

Defendant here asserts that it may raise want or failure of consideration in the transaction between *plaintiff and Lee*, its payee, as a defense to plaintiff's enforcement of the instrument against it. We disagree.

[U.C.C.] § 3.408 provides, in pertinent part that: "Want or failure of consideration is a defense against any person not having the rights of a holder in due course . . ." The comments to § 3.408 provide that: " 'Consideration' refers to what the obligor has received for his obligation, and is important only on the question of whether his obligation can be enforced against him." Thus, any holder can enforce the obligation of a draft against the drawer regardless of whether the holder gave anything in consideration for the draft to his endorser. The drawer can assert as a defense to enforcement of the draft want or failure of consideration only to the extent such defense lies against the payee of the draft. Thus, the fact that a holder remote to the drawer's transaction with the payee did not give full consideration for the draft is not a defense available to the drawer. [Citation.]

This is true because the drawer's sole obligation on the check is to pay it according to its tenor. Consequently, the fact that the transfer of the check by the payee to the transferee is without consideration is immaterial to the drawer's obligation and is not a defense available to the drawer against the holder. A similar conclusion was reached in [Citation]. In that case the court held that a defendant maker was not the proper party to raise as a defense that the transfer of the note to the holder was void. Consequently, that court concluded that the maker could not assert the defense that the equitable ownership of the instrument was in someone other than the holder-plaintiff.

The rationale of this, and other decisions, reaching the same conclusion, is that the maker or drawer of an instrument admittedly owes the money and he should not be permitted to bring into the controversy equities of parties with which he has no connection. [Citation.] Furthermore, if the drawer or maker is permitted to assert the defense of another party such as the payee, the judgment on that issue would not be binding on the third party claimant who is not a party to the suit. [Citation.]

Because defendant here may not assert want or failure of consideration in the trans-action between plaintiff and Lee, and because defendant has asserted no other defense against plaintiff, plaintiff is entitled to recover the full face value of the check under § 3.413(b) of the Texas Uniform Commercial Code. Accordingly, the judgment of the trial court is reversed and judgment is rendered that plaintiff recover judgment against defendant for $152.38 and all costs.

Conditions Precedent to Liability

HANE v. EXTEN

Court of Appeals of Maryland, 1969.
255 Md. 668, 259 A.2d 290.

SINGLEY, J.

John B. Hane is the assignee of the note of Theta Electronic Laboratories, Inc. (Theta) in the stated amount of $15,377.07, with interest at six per cent per annum. The note was dated 10 August 1964; stipulated that the first monthly payment of $320.47 would be due five months from date, or on 10 January 1965; and that "In the event of the failure to pay the interest or principal, as the same becomes due on this Note the entire debt represented hereby shall at the end of thirty (30) days become due and demandable * * *." The note was assigned without recourse to Hane by George B. and Marguerite F. Thomson, the original payees, on 26 November 1965. A default having occurred in the making of the monthly payments, Hane took judgments by confession in the Circuit Court for Montgomery County on 7 June 1967 against Theta and three individuals, Gerald M. Exten, Emil L. O'Neal, and James W. Hane, and their wives, who had endorsed Theta's note. On motion of the Extens, the judgment was vacated as to them and the case came on for trial on the merits before the court without a jury. From a judgment for the Extens for costs, Hane has appealed.

This case raises the familiar question: Must Hane show that the Extens were given notice of presentment and dishonor before he can hold them on their indorsement?

The court below, in finding for the Extens, relied on the provisions of Uniform Commercial Code (the U.C.C.), § 3–414(1) of the U.C.C. provides:

"Unless the indorsement otherwise specifies (as by such words as 'without recourse') every indorser engages that upon dishonor and any necessary notice of dishonor and protest he will pay the instrument according to its tenor at the time of his indorsement to the holder or to any subsequent indorser who takes it up, even though the indorser who takes it up was not obligated to do so."

§ 3–501(1)(b) provides that "Presentment for payment is necessary to charge any indorser" and § 3–501(2)(a) that "Notice of any dishonor is necessary to charge any indorser," in each case subject, however, to the provisions of § 3–511 which recite the circumstances under which notice of dishonor may be waived or excused, none of which is here present. § 3–502(1)(a) makes it clear that unless presentment or notice of dishonor is waived or excused, unreasonable delay will discharge an indorser. [Citations.]

There was testimony from which the trier of facts could find as he did that presentment and notice of dishonor were unduly delayed.

It is clear that Hane held the note from November 1965, until some time in April 1967 before he made demand for payment. U.C.C. § 3–503(1)(d) provides that "Where an instrument is accelerated presentment for payment is due within a reasonable time after the acceleration." "Reasonable time" is not defined in § 3–503, except that § 3–503(2) provides "A reasonable time for presentment is determined by the nature of the instrument, any usage of banking or trade and the facts of the particular case." But § 1–204(2) characterizes it. "What is a reasonable time for taking any action depends on the nature, purpose and circumstances of such action."

Reasonableness is primarily a question for the fact finder. [Citations.] We see no reason to disturb the lower court's finding that Hane's delay of almost 18 months in presenting the note "was unreasonable from any viewpoint." [Citation.]

As regards notice of dishonor, § 3–508(2) requires that notice be given by persons other than banks "before midnight of the third business day after dishonor or receipt of notice of dishonor." Exten, called as an adverse witness by Hane, testified that his first notice that the note had not been paid was . . . on 7 June 1967. Hane's brother testified that demand had been made about 15 April 1967. He was uncertain as to when he had given Exten notice of dishonor, but finally conceded that it was "within a week." The lower court found that the ambiguity of this testimony, coupled with Exten's denial that he had received *any* notice before 7 June fell short of meeting the three day notice requirement of the U.C.C. The date of giving notice of dishonor is a question of fact, solely for determination by the trier of facts. [Citation.] We cannot say that the court erred in its finding.

In the absence of evidence that presentment and notice of dishonor were waived or excused, Hane's unreasonable delay discharged the Extens, § 3–501(1)(a).

*   *   *

Whether Hane was or was not a holder in due course has no relevance to the issue here presented. In either case timely presentment and notice of dishonor were required to hold the Extens. Whether Hane was or was not a holder in due course is of no significance unless there was a defense which could have been asserted against the payee. [Citations.]

Judgment affirmed, *   *   *.

The Imposter Rule

PHILADELPHIA TITLE INSURANCE CO. v. FIDELITY-PHILADELPHIA TRUST CO.

Supreme Court of Pennsylvania, 1965.
419 Pa. 78, 212 A.2d 222.

Cohen, J.

[Edmund Jezemski, estranged and living apart from his wife, Paula, was administrator and sole heir-at-law of his deceased mother's estate, one asset of which was real estate in

Philadelphia. Without Edmund's knowledge or consent, and with the assistance of John M. McAllister, an attorney, and Anthony DiBenedetto, a real estate broker, Paula arranged for a mortgage on the property through Philadelphia Title Insurance Company. Shortly before settlement, Paula represented to McAllister and DiBenedetto that her husband would be unable to attend the closing on the mortgage. She appeared at McAllister's office in advance of the closing, accompanied by a man, whom she introduced to McAllister and DiBenedetto as her husband. She and this man, in the presence of McAllister and DiBenedetto, executed a deed conveying the property from the estate to her husband and herself as tenants by the entireties and also executed the mortgage. McAllister and DiBenedetto were witnesses. Thereafter, McAllister, DiBenedetto, and Paula met at the office of the Title Company on the closing date, produced the signed deed and mortgage, and Paula obtained from Title Company its check for the mortgage loan proceeds of $15,640.82, payable to the order of Edmund Jezemski and Paul Jezemski, individually, and to Edmund as administrator.

Paula cashed the check, bearing the purported indorsements of all the payees, at Penns Grove National Bank and Trust Company. Edmund received none of the proceeds, either individually or as administrator. His purported indorsements were forgeries. In the collection process the check was presented to and paid by the drawee bank, Fidelity-Philadelphia Trust Company and charged against the drawer Title Company's account. Upon discovery of the existence of the mortgage, Edmund brought an action which resulted in the setting aside of the deed and mortgage and the repayment of the amount advanced by the mortgagee. Title Company thereupon sued the drawee bank (Fidelity) to recover the amount of the check, $15,640.82.]

*   *   *

The complaint alleged that the endorsement of one of the payees had been forged and that, therefore, Fidelity should not have paid the check. *   *   * By way of defense all of the banks asserted that none of them were liable because the issuance of the check by the Title Company was induced by an impostor and delivered by the Title Company to a confederate of the impostor thereby making the forged endorsement effective.

*   *   * Judgment was entered against the Title Company and in favor of the banks.

*   *   *

"There is no question that the man whom Mrs. Jezemski introduced to McAllister and DiBenedetto was not Edmund Jezemski, her husband. It was sometime later that Edmund Jezemski, when he tried to convey the real estate, discovered the existence of the mortgage. When he did so he instituted an action in equity which resulted in the setting aside of the deed and mortgage and the repayment of the fund advanced by the mortgagee."

The parties do not dispute the proposition that as between the [drawee] bank (Fidelity-Philadelphia) and its customer (Title Company), ordinarily, the former must bear the loss occasioned by the forgery of a payee's endorsement (Edmund Jezemski) upon a check drawn by its customer and paid by it. Uniform Commercial Code § 3–404. The latter provides . . . that "(1) Any unauthorized signature [Edmund Jezemski's] is wholly inoperative as that of the person whose name is signed unless he ratifies it or is precluded from denying *   *   *."

However, the banks argue that this case falls within an exception to the above rule, making the forged indorsement of Edmund Jezemski's name effective so that Fidelity-Philadelphia was entitled to charge the account of its customer, the Title Company, who was the drawer of the check. The exception asserted by the banks is found in § 3–405(1)(a) of the Uniform Commercial Code—Commercial Paper which provides:

"An indorsement by any person in the name of a named payee is effective if (a) an impostor by use of the mails, or otherwise has induced the maker or drawer to issue the instrument to him or his confederate in the name of the payee; * * *."

The lower court found and the Title Company does not dispute that an impostor appeared before McAllister and DiBenedetto, impersonated Mr. Jezemski, and, in their presence, signed Mr. Jezemski's name to the deed, bond, and mortgage; that Mrs. Jezemski was a confederate of the impostor; that the drawer, Title Company, issued the check to Mrs. Jezemski naming her and Mr. Jezemski as payees; and that some person other than Mr. Jezemski indorsed his name on the check. In effect, the only argument made by the Title Company to prevent the applicability of Section 3–405(1)(a) is that the impostor, who admittedly played a part in the swindle, *did not "by the mails or otherwise" induce the Title Company* to issue the check within the meaning of Section 3–405(1)(a). The argument must fail.

* * *

Both the words of Section 3–405(1)(a) and the official Comment thereto leave no doubt that the impostor can induce the drawer to issue him or his confederate a check within the meaning of the section even though he does not carry out his impersonation before the very eyes of the drawer. Section 3–405(1)(a) says the inducement might be by "the mails or otherwise."

* * * For purposes of imposing the loss on one of two "innocent" parties, either the drawer who was defrauded or the drawee bank which paid out on a forged indorsement, we see no reason for distinguishing between the drawer who is duped by an impersonator communicating directly with him through the mails and a drawer who is duped by an impersonator communicating indirectly with him through third persons. Thus, both the language of the Code and common sense dictate that the drawer must suffer the loss in both instances.

* * *

Judgment affirmed.

Warranties on Transfer/
Accommodation Parties/
Dishonor

FIRST NATIONAL BANK OF ALLENTOWN v. MONTGOMERY

Court of Common Pleas, 1979.
9 Pa. D. & C. 3d 491.

Davison, J.

This case is before the court on plaintiff's motion for summary judgment, pursuant to which the parties filed a stipulation of facts.

The parties have stipulated that on July 14, 1975, the Georgia Farm Bureau Mutual Insurance Company (maker) [(sic) drawer] issued a check in the amount of $658.28, payable through the First National Bank and Trust Company in Macon, to the order of Willie Mincey, Jr. and MIC. Without indorsing it, MIC forwarded the check to Mincey for his indorsement. Mincey placed his indorsement on the check and endeavored to cash it at one of plaintiff's branches which declined to do so because Mincey was not known to bank personnel. Thereafter, Mincey returned to the bank with his uncle, defendant, and both men were told by plaintiff's branch manager that since defendant was a known depositor, the check would be cashed if defendant added his indorsement. Whereupon, defendant indorsed and plaintiff cashed the check. The funds were turned over to Mincey.

Subsequently, after plaintiff forwarded the check for collection, the maker returned the check to the Macon bank due to the lack of MIC's indorsement. The check was eventually returned to plaintiff. Since the facts are not in dispute, the litigation is ripe for summary judgment.

In order to determine defendant's liability, we must first ascertain the capacity in which he indorsed. Section 3–415(1) of the Uniform Commercial Code (UCC) provides that: "An accommodation party is one who signs the instrument in any capacity for the purpose of lending his name to another party to it." Commentaries on this section indicate that where a person receives no direct benefit from the execution of the paper it is likely he will be regarded as an accommodation party [citation]. Further, it has been held in similar situations where a bank refused to cash a check unless a stranger payee obtained the indorsement of someone known to the bank, that the second indorsement constitutes an accommodation indorsement. [Citation.] We thus conclude, under the facts stipulated, that defendant was an accommodation indorser in that he received no benefit from the negotiation of the paper and that he indorsed the check solely to assist the payee.

Plaintiff's contention that defendant is liable on his indorsement is grounded on UCC § 3–417. That section provides, in part that:

(1) Any person who obtains payment or acceptance and any prior transferor warrants to a person who in good faith pays or accepts that (a) he has a good title to the instrument or is authorized to obtain payment or acceptance on behalf of one who has a good title; . . . (2) Any person who transfers an instrument and receives consideration warrants to his transferee and if the transfer is by indorsement to any subsequent holder who takes the instrument in good faith that (a) he has a good title to the instrument or is authorized to obtain payment or acceptance on behalf of one who has a good title and the transfer is otherwise rightful; . . . .

However, § 3–417 warranties are not applicable in this case, and they do not apply to accommodation indorsers generally: [citation.] Section 3–417(1) sets forth warranties which run only to a party who "pays or accepts" an instrument. The only parties who "pay" an instrument are a payor bank or a maker, and the only parties who "accept" an instrument are a drawee bank or a maker: [citation.] UCC §§ 3–410, 4–105(b). Here plaintiff is neither payor nor drawee; it is a mere transferee, and thus garners no benefit from § 3–417(1).

Section 3–417(2) creates warranties which run to all transferees, but these warranties are given only by transferors who receive consideration. The stipulated facts clearly indicate that defendant received no consideration for his indorsement, and, in addition, it has generally been held that an accommodation indorser does not transfer the instrument. [Citation.]

* * *

Defendant's liability is, thus, not pursuant to any warranty, but is governed solely by his indorser's contract under § 3–414. That section provides: "(1) Unless the indorsement otherwise specifies . . . every indorser engages that upon dishonor and any necessary notice of dishonor and protest he will pay the instrument . . . to the holder or to any subsequent indorser who takes it up, . . ." Although plaintiff is not and was not a holder: [citations] it is a subsequent indorser. However, to hold defendant under this section it would be necessary to show that the check was "dishonored" and § 3–507(3) specifically provides that the return of an instrument for lack of proper indorsement is *not* dishonor: [citation.] The result is the same even if the check in question here is deemed a "payable through" instrument.

Finally, we are constrained to observe that, as between the litigants before us, the equities do not favor plaintiff. While § 3–417 requires only that a collecting bank act in "good faith" in taking up an instrument, and does not require comportment with reasonable commercial standards, it is apparent that a modicum of care on plaintiff's part in noticing MIC's lack of indorsement would have avoided this series of events.

The facts having been stipulated and the law being clear, we are obliged to enter summary judgment, not, however, for the moving party, but rather in favor of the nonmoving defendant. [Citations.]

* * *

Now January 4, 1979, for the reasons set forth in the foregoing opinion it is ordered that judgment be and it is here entered in favor of defendant.

PROBLEMS

1.

$800.00   Smalltown, Illinois
                                              November 15, 1985

The undersigned promises to pay to the order of John Doe, Nine Hundred Dollars with interest from date of note. Payment to be made in five monthly installments of One Hundred Eighty Dollars, plus accrued interest beginning on December 1, 1985. In the event of default in the payment of any installment or interest on installment date, the holder of this instrument may declare the entire obligation due and owing and proceed forthwith to collect the balance due on this instrument.

                                              (Signed) Acton, agent.

On December 18, no payment having been made on the note, Doe indorsed and delivered the instrument to Todd to secure a pre-existing debt in the amount of $800.

On January 18, 1986, Todd brought an action against Acton and Phi Corporation, Acton's principal, to collect the full amount of the instrument with interest. Acton defended on the basis that he signed the instrument in a representative capacity and that Doe had failed to deliver the consideration for which the instrument had been issued. Phi Corporation defended on the basis that it did not sign the instrument and that its name does not appear on the instrument.

For what amount if any, are Acton and Phi Corporation liable?

2. Cole was supervisor of the shipping department of Machine Mfg. Inc. In February, Cole found herself in need of funds and, at the end of that month, submitted to Ames, the treasurer of the corporation, a payroll listing which showed as an employee, among others, "Ben Day," to whom was allegedly owed $800 for services rendered during February. Actually, there was no employee named Day. Relying upon the word of Cole, Ames drew and delivered to her a series of corporate payroll checks, drawn upon the corporate account in the Capital Bank, one of which was made payable to the order of "Ben Day" for $800. Cole took the check, indorsed on its back "Ben Day," cashed it at the Capital Bank, and pocketed the proceeds. She repeated the same procedure at the end of March, April, and May. In mid-June, Machine Mfg. Inc. learned of Cole's fraudulent conduct, fired her,

and brought an appropriate action against Capital Bank seeking a judgment for $3,200. Decision?

3. While employed as a night watchman at the place of business of A. B. Cate Trucking Company, Fred Fain observed that the office safe had been left unlocked. It contained fifty payroll checks which were ready for distribution to employees two days later. The checks had all been signed by the sole proprietor, Cate. Fain removed five of these checks and took two blank checks which were also in the safe. Fain forged the indorsements of the payees on the five payroll checks and cashed them at local supermarkets. He then filled out one of the blank checks, making himself payee, and forged Cate's signature as drawer. After cashing that check at a supermarket, Fain departed by airplane to Jamaica. The six checks were promptly presented for payment to the drawee bank, the Bank of Emanon, which paid each of the checks. Shortly thereafter Cate learned about the missing payroll checks and forgeries, and demanded that the Bank of Emanon credit his account with the amount of the six checks.

Must the Bank comply with Cate's demand? What are the Bank's rights, if any, against the supermarkets? You may assume that the supermarkets cashed all of the checks in good faith.

4. A negotiable promissory note executed and delivered by B to C passed in due course to and was indorsed in blank by C, D, E, and F. G, the present holder, strikes out D's indorsement. What is the liability of C, D, E, and F on their respective indorsements?

5. On June 15, 1980, J, for consideration, executed a negotiable promissory note for $10,000 payable to R on or before June 15, 1985. J subsequently suffered financial reverses. In January of 1985, R on two occasions told J that he knew that J was having a difficult time and that he, R, did not need the money and the debt should be considered as completely canceled with no other act or payment being required. These conversations were witnessed by three persons, including L. On March 15, 1985, R changed his mind and indorsed the note for value to L. The note was not paid by June 15, 1985, and L sued J for the amount of the note.

J defended upon the ground that R had canceled the debt and renounced all rights against J and that L had notice of this fact. Decision?

6. Tate and Fitch were longtime friends. Tate was a man of considerable means; Fitch had encountered financial difficulties. In order to bolster his failing business, Fitch desired to borrow $6,000 from Farmers Bank of Erehwon. To accomplish this, he persuaded Tate to aid him in the making of a promissory note by which it would appear that Tate had the responsibility of maker, but with Fitch agreeing to pay the instrument when due. Accordingly, they executed the following instrument:

December 1, 1984

Thirty days after date and for value received, I promise to pay to the order of Frank Fitch the sum of $6,600.

/s/ Timothy Tate

On the back of the note, Fitch indorsed, "Pay to the order of Farmers Bank of Erehwon /s/ Frank Fitch" and delivered it to the Bank in exchange for $6,000.

The note not having been paid at maturity, the Bank, without first demanding payment by Fitch, brought an action on the note against Tate. (a) Decision? (b) If Tate voluntarily pays the note to the Bank, may he then recover on the note against Fitch who appears as an indorser?

7. Alpha orally appointed Omega as his agent to find and purchase for him a 1930 Dodge automobile in good condition. Omega located such a car. The car's owner, Roe, agreed to sell and deliver the car on January 10, 1985, for $9,000. To evidence the purchase price, Omega mailed to Roe the following instrument:

December 1, 1984

$9,000.00

We promise to pay to the order of bearer Nine Thousand Dollars with interest from date of this instrument on or before January 10, 1985. This note is given in consideration of John Roe's transferring title to and possession of his 1930 Dodge automobile.

(Signed) Omega, agent.

Smith stole the note from Roe's mailbox, indorsed Roe's name on the note, and promptly discounted it with Sunset Bank for $8,700. Not having received the note, Roe sold the car to a third party. On January 10, 1985, the bank having discovered all the facts demanded payment of the note from Alpha and Omega. Payment was refused by both.

What are Sunset Bank's rights with regard to Omega; its rights with regard to Roe and Smith?

8. In payment of the purchase price of a used motorboat which had been fraudulently misrepresented, Y signed and delivered to A his negotiable note in the amount of $2,000 due October 1, with S as an accommodation co-maker. Y intended to use the boat for his fishing business. A indorsed the note in blank preparatory to discounting it. T stole the note from A and delivered it to M on July 1 in payment of a past due debt owing by T to M in the amount of $600, with M making up the difference by giving T his check for $800 and an oral promise to pay T an additonal $600 on October 1.

When M demanded payment of the note on December 1, both Y and S refused to pay the note because it had not been presented for payment on its due date and because A had fraudulently misrepresented the motorboat for which the note had been executed.

What are M's rights, if any, against Y; S; T; and A, respectively?

9. On July 1 A sold D, who is a jeweler, a necklace containing imitation gems which A fraudulently represented to be diamonds. In payment for the necklace D executed and delivered to A her promissory note for $25,000 dated July 1 and payable on December 1 to A's order with interest at 14 percent per annum.

The note was thereafter successively indorsed in blank and delivered by A to B, B to C, and by C to S, who became a holder in due course on August 10. On November 1, D discovered A's fraud and immediately notified A, B, C, and S that she would not pay the note when it became due. B, a friend of S, requested that S release him from liability on the note, and S, as a favor to B and for no other consideration, struck out B's indorsement.

On November 15, S, who was solvent and had no creditors, indorsed the note to the order of F, his father, and delivered it to F as a gift. At the same time, S told F of D's statement that D would not pay the note when it became due. F presented the note to D for payment on December 1, but D refused to pay. Thereafter F gave due notice of dishonor to A, B, and C.

What are F's rights, if any, against A, B, C, and D on the note?

Chapter 28

BANK DEPOSITS AND COLLECTIONS

IN our society, goods and services are in substantial measure sold and paid for with some form of credit and without a physical transfer of "money." The wide acceptance of credit cards, charge accounts, and various deferred payment plans have made the cash sale increasingly rare. But even credit sales must ultimately be settled, and a check, rather than cash, is the vehicle by which payment is usually made. If the parties to a sales transaction happen to have accounts at the same bank, a transfer of credit is easily accomplished. In the vast majority of cases, however, the parties do business at different banks. Then the buyer's check must journey from the seller-payee's bank (**depositary** bank), where the check is deposited by the seller for credit to his account, to the buyer-drawer's bank (**payor** bank) for payment. In this collection process the check frequently passes through one or more other banks (**intermediary** banks) so

that it may be collected and the appropriate entries recorded. Any bank handling the item for collection other than the payor bank (i.e., any intermediary or depositary bank) is also referred to as a **collecting** bank.

Our banking system has developed a network to handle the collection of checks and other instruments. Article 4 of the U.C.C., entitled "Bank Deposits and Collections," provides the principal rules which govern the bank collection process. Since items in the bank collection process are essentially those covered by Article 3, "Commercial Paper," and to a lesser extent by Article 8, "Investment Securities," these Articles may have application to a bank collection problem.

COLLECTION OF ITEMS

Upon the deposit of a check by the payee or holder in his bank, his account is given a credit in the amount of the check which is characterized as **provisional.** Normally, a bank will not permit a customer to draw against a provisional credit, but if it does permit its customer to draw against the credit it has given value and may be a holder in due course. Under the payee's contract with his bank, the depository bank, the bank is obligated to make a reasonable effort to obtain payment of all checks deposited for collection. When the amount of the check has been collected from the payor bank (drawee), the credit becomes **final.**

If the check is not paid for any reason, such as a stop payment order or insufficient funds in the drawer's account, the provisional credit to the payee's or holder's account is reversed, his account is debited for that amount, and the check is returned to him with a statement of the reason for non-payment. If, in the meantime, he has been permitted to draw against the provisional credit, the bank may recover the payment from him.

In some cases the bank involved is both the "depository bank"—the bank in which the payee or holder deposited the check for credit to his account—and the "payor bank"—the bank on which the drawer wrote his check. In most cases, however, the depository and payor banks are different in which event the bank collection aspects of Article 4 come into play. Where the depository and payor banks are different, it is necessary for the item to pass from one to the other, either directly through a clearing-house or through one or more "intermediary banks" as illustrated in Figure 28-1.

Collecting Banks

In the usual situation where the depository and payor banks are different, the depository bank gives a provisional credit to its customer, transfers the item to the next bank in the chain, receiving a provisional credit or "settlement" from it, and so on to the payor bank which gives a provisional settlement to its transferor. When the item is paid, all the provisional settlements given by the respective banks in the chain become final, and the particular transaction has been completed. No adjustment is necessary on the books of any

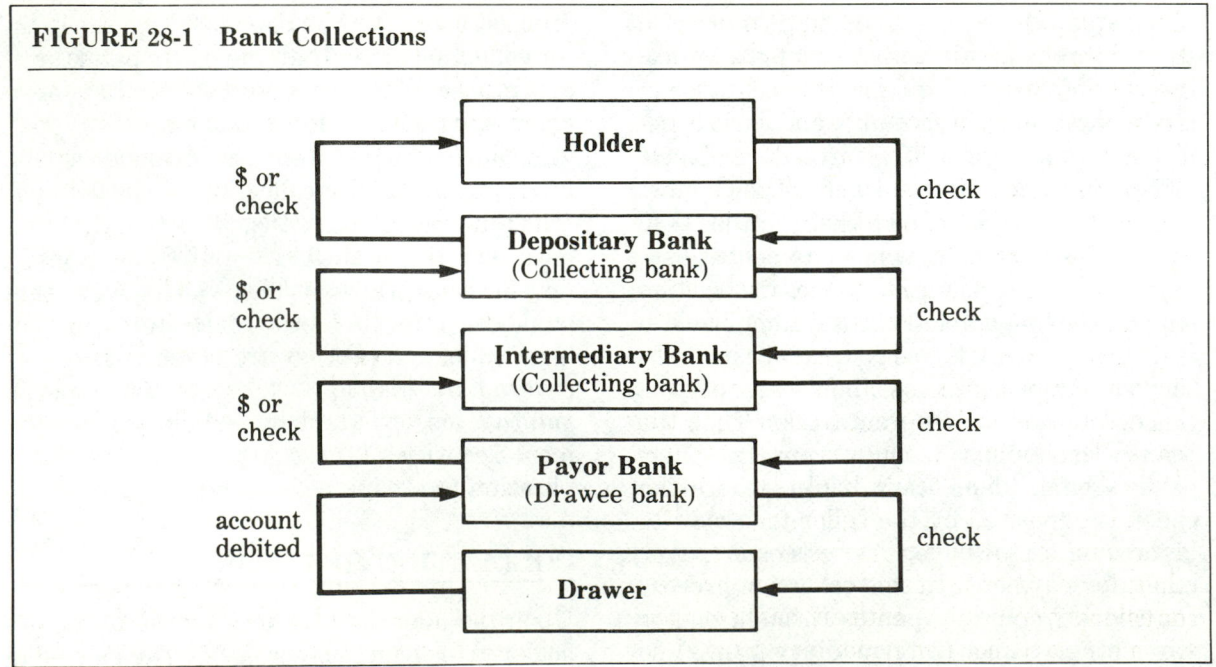

FIGURE 28-1   Bank Collections

of the banks involved. This procedure simplifies the bookkeeping processes of all the banks involved because only one entry is necessary if the item is paid.

If an item is not paid by the payor, it is returned and each intermediary or collecting bank reverses the provisional settlement or credit previously given by it to its forwarding bank. Ultimately, the depositary bank will charge the account of its customer that deposited the item, and he must seek recovery from the indorsers or the drawer.

A collecting bank, Section 4–105(d), is an **agent** or subagent of the owner of the item until the settlement which it gave the owner becomes final. Section 4–201(1). Clearly, then, unless otherwise provided, any credit given for the item initially is provisional. Once it is finally settled, the agency relationship changes to one of debtor-creditor. The effect of this agency rule is that the risk of loss remains with the owner and any chargebacks go to her, not to the collecting bank.

All collecting banks have certain responsibilities and duties in collecting an item. These will now be discussed.

Duty of Care A collecting bank must use ordinary care in handling an item transferred to it for collection. Section 4–202(1). Of particular importance are the steps it takes in presenting an item or sending it for presentment. It must act within a reasonable time after receipt of the item and must choose a reasonable method of forwarding the item for presentment. It is also responsible for using care with respect to routing and in the selection of intermediary banks or other agents.

The proper method of presenting an item drawn on or payable by a non-bank payor is in person by a representative of the collecting bank. To simplify procedures and save time, it is specified by Section 4–210 that unless otherwise instructed, the collecting bank may send a written notice to the drawee or maker that the bank holds the item for acceptance or payment. When presentment has been made by notice and neither honor nor request for

compliance with a requirement under Section 3–505—such as exhibiting the item or establishing its authority to present it—is received by the close of business on the day after maturity in the case of a time item, or by the close of business on the third banking day after notice was sent in the case of a demand item, the presenting bank may treat the item as dishonored and charge secondary parties by sending appropriate notice.

Duty to Act Seasonably Closely related to the collecting bank's duty of care is its duty to act seasonably. A collecting bank acts seasonably in any event if it takes proper action, such as forwarding or presenting an item before its "midnight deadline" following receipt of the item, notice, or payment. If the bank adheres to this standard, the timeliness of its action cannot be challenged. Nonetheless, a reasonably longer time may be seasonable, but the bank bears the burden of proof. The **midnight deadline** means midnight of a bank's next banking day following the banking day on which it receives the relevant item or notice or from which the time for taking action commences to run, whichever is later. Section 4–104(1)(h). Thus, if the time for a bank to take action of some sort commences to run on a Monday, the midnight deadline applicable is midnight of the next banking day, or Tuesday. A banking day means that part of any day on which a bank is open to the public for carrying on substantially all of its banking functions. Section 4–104(1)(c).

The midnight deadline presents a problem in that it necessarily takes time to process an item through a bank, whether it be the depositary, intermediary, or payor bank. If the various steps in connection with a day's transaction are to be completed without overtime work, either the bank must close early or it must fix an earlier cutoff time for the day's work. Recognizing this problem, Section 4–107 of the Code provides that for the purpose of allowing time to process items, prove balances, and make the necessary entries on its books to determine its position for the day, a bank may fix an afternoon hour of 2:00 P.M. or later as a cutoff hour for the handling of money and items and the making of entries on its books. Items received after the cutoff hour so fixed or after the close of the banking day may be treated as having been received at the opening of the next banking day, and the time for taking action and for determining the bank's midnight deadline with respect to the item involved begins to run from that point.

Recognizing that if an item is not paid everyone involved will be greatly inconvenienced, Section 4–108 provides that unless otherwise instructed a collecting bank in a good faith effort to secure payment may, in the case of specific items, waive, modify, or extend the time limits, but not in excess of one additional banking day. Such an extension may be made without the approval of the parties involved and without discharging secondary parties. Delay is also authorized in the case of interruption of communications, as by blizzard, flood, hurricane, or other disaster or "Act of God," suspension of payments by another bank, war, emergency conditions, or other circumstances beyond the control of the bank. Delay for such causes will be excused only if the bank exercises such diligence as the circumstances require.

A collecting bank acts seasonably in any event if it takes proper action, such as forwarding or presenting an item before its midnight deadline following receipt of the item, notice or payment, as the case may be. Section 4–202(2). If the bank adheres to this standard, the timeliness of its action cannot be challenged.

Indorsements When an item is restrictively indorsed with words such as "pay any bank," it is locked into the bank collection system, and only a bank may acquire the rights of a holder. When a bank forwards an item for collection, it normally indorses it "pay any bank," irrespective of the type of indorsement, if any, which the item carried at the

time of receipt. This serves to protect the collecting bank by making it impossible for the item to stray from regular collection channels.

If the item had no indorsement when received by the depositary bank, it may supply any indorsement of its customer which is necessary to title unless the item contains the words "payee's indorsement required" or the like, as is the case with certain government, pension, and insurance checks. Section 4–205(1). This rule speeds up the collection process by eliminating the necessity of returning checks for indorsement when the depositary bank knows they came from its customers. The usual form of such an indorsement reads "Deposited to the account of the within named payee." This will be followed by the bank's own "pay any bank" indorsement. Each intermediary bank will in turn place a similar restrictive indorsement on the item, since no bank in the collection chain other than a depositary bank is given notice or otherwise affected by the restrictive indorsement of any person except its immediate transferor. Sections 4–205(2) and 3–206. This rule is necessary to keep the collection process moving smoothly and rapidly. The depositary bank has the responsibility of examining the item for prior restrictive indorsements. Subsequent intermediary banks and the payor bank need check only one indorsement, and may rely on the fact that the depositary bank performed its required function. It would be unnecessarily time consuming to require each bank to examine all the indorsements on each item.

Warranties Customers and collecting banks give substantially the same warranties as those given by parties under Article 3 upon presentment and transfer, which are discussed in Chapter 27. Section 4–207. Each customer or collecting bank who **transfers** an item and receives a settlement or consideration warrants to his transferee and subsequent transferees that: (1) he has good title (i.e., the transferor is the true owner or is an authorized agent of the owner); (2) *all* signatures are genuine or authorized; (3) the item has not been materially altered; (4) no defense of any party is good against him; and (5) he has no knowledge of any insolvency proceeding involving the maker or acceptor or the drawer of an unaccepted instrument. Moreover, each customer or collecting bank who obtains payment or acceptance, as well as all prior customers and collecting banks, warrants to the *payor* bank upon **presentment** that: (1) she has good title or is authorized to obtain payment; (2) she has no knowledge that the signature of the maker or drawer is unauthorized; and (3) the item has not been materially altered.

See *Birmingham Trust National Bank v. Central Bank & Trust Co.*

Final Payment The provisional settlements made in the collection chain are all pointed toward final payment of the item by the payor bank. This is one terminus of the collection process—the turn-around point from which the proceeds of the item begin the return flow and the initiation of the process of firming provisional settlements into final ones. For example, a customer of the California Country State Bank may deposit a check drawn on the State of Maine Country National Bank. The check may then take a course such as follows: from the California Country State Bank to a correspondent bank in San Francisco, to the Federal Reserve Bank of San Francisco, to the Federal Reserve Bank of Boston, to the payor bank. At each step, provisional settlements were made. When the payor bank finally paid the item, the proceeds began a return flow over the same course.

The critical question, then, is the point in time when the item has been **paid** by the payor bank, since this not only commences the payment process but also has a bearing on questions of priority between the item on the one hand and actions such as the filing of a stop payment order against the item. It is clear that final payment occurs at some moment during the processing of the item by the payor bank; however, this moment may be difficult to ascertain. An item may be received by a bank in many ways: over the counter, through the mail from a customer, in a collection letter from another bank, or through a clearing house. Under some of these circumstances a receipt may be given or an entry made in a passbook. The item then normally moves through the sorting and proving departments. Still later it goes to the bookkeeping department, where it is examined for form and signature. It is then matched against the ledger for the customer's account to see if funds are sufficient or whether there is a stop order or some other reason why the item should not be paid. If everything is in good order, the item will be posted to the drawer's account either then or later. The item will be stamped or punched "Paid" and filed with the other items paid from the customer's account. When did final payment occur? Section 4–213 establishes rules for determining when that point in time has been reached.

Traditionally, when a bank pays an item in cash, it is deemed to have made a final payment. This rule is reaffirmed in subsection (1)(a) of Section 4–213. Equivalent to cash payment in making final payment is a final settlement of the item. If the payor bank has not reserved the right to revoke the settlement, or does not have such right through agreement, statute, or clearing house rule, final payment has been made. Section 4–213(1)(b).

A provisional settlement also becomes a final payment if the payor bank does not revoke it in the time and manner permitted by statute, clearing house rule, or agreement. Section 4–213(1)(d).

More importantly, however, final payment is made when the payor bank has completed the process of posting the item to the account of the drawer or maker. Section 4–213(1)(c). Essentially, this means the point in time when the decision is made to pay the item. The question then arises: when is the process of posting completed?

To clarify the steps legitimately involved in posting an item, Section 4–109 provides as follows:

The "process of posting" means the usual procedure followed by a payor bank in determining to pay an item and in recording the payment including one or more of the following or other steps as determined by the bank:

    (a) verification of any signature;

    (b) ascertaining that sufficient funds are available;

    (c) affixing a "paid" or other stamp;

    (d) entering a charge or entry to a customer's account;

    (e) correcting or reversing an entry or erroneous action with respect to the item.

Normally, all of these steps must be taken before the "process of posting" is completed, and an item may be regarded as finally paid.

Payor Banks

The payor or drawee, under its contract of deposit with the drawer, agrees to pay to the payee or his order checks issued by the drawer provided the order is not countermanded and that there are sufficient funds in the drawer's account.

Due to the tremendous increase in volume of bank collections as well as the improved methods of processing items by payor banks, it has become necessary to adopt production line methods for handling checks to assure an even flow of items on a day-to-day basis. This is necessary if work is to be conducted without abnormal peak loads and overtime. The solution has been the institution of deferred posting procedures whereby items are sorted and proved on the day of receipt, but are not posted to customers' accounts or returned until the next banking day. The U.C.C. not only gives approval to this procedure but sets up specific standards to govern its application to the actions of payor banks.

When a payor bank, which is not a depositary bank, receives a demand item other than for immediate payment over the counter, it must either return the item or give its transferor a provisional settlement before midnight of the banking day on which the item is received. Otherwise it becomes liable to its tranferor for the amount of the item unless it has a valid defense. Section 4–302(a).

If it gives the provisional settlement as required, it then has until its midnight deadline to return the item or, if it is held for protest or is otherwise unavailable for return, to send written notice of dishonor or nonpayment. Section 4–301(1). Upon so doing, it is entitled to revoke the settlement and recover any payment made. If the payor bank fails to return the item or send notice before its midnight deadline, it becomes accountable for the amount of the item unless it has a valid defense for its inaction.

There are innumerable reasons why a bank may dishonor an item and return it or send notice where appropriate. Among these are that the drawer or maker either has no account or has insufficient funds to cover the item; that a signature on the item is forged; or that payment of the item has been stopped by the drawer or maker.

As to the priority between items, where the customer's account is not sufficient to pay them all, the bank may charge them against the account in any order it deems convenient. Items against an account may reach the bank in several different ways on the same day. It would be unreasonable to require the bank to determine their order of arrival. Items received at the same time but passing through different channels may be posted to the customer's account hours apart. Consequently, a person presenting an item to a payor bank may not object that the bank paid other items received the same day and left his unpaid. He is properly relegated to seeking his remedy against the maker, drawer, or other secondary parties. The owner of the account from which the item was payable also has no basis for complaint that one item, rather than another, was paid. It is his responsibility to have enough funds on deposit to pay all items chargeable to his account at any time.

PAYOR BANK AND ITS CUSTOMER

Payment of an Item

When a payor bank receives an item properly payable from a customer's account, but there are insufficient funds in the account to pay it, the bank may: (1) dishonor the item and return it or (2) pay the item and charge its customer's account even though an overdraft is created as a result. The item authorizes or directs the bank to make the payment and hence carries with it an enforceable implied promise to reimburse the bank. Further, the customer may be liable to the bank to pay a service charge for the bank's handling of the overdraft or may be liable to pay interest on the amount of the overdraft.

A check or draft, however, is not an assignment of funds in the hands of the drawee available for its payment, and the drawee is not liable on an instrument until it is accepted. Section 3–409(1). The holder of a check has no right to require the drawee bank to pay it, whether or not there are sufficient funds in the drawer's account. But if an item is presented to a payor bank and the bank improperly refuses payment, it will incur a liability to its customer from whose account the item should have been paid. Section 4–402. If the item is not more than six months old and regular in form and if the customer had adequate funds on deposit and there is no other valid basis for the refusal to pay, the bank is liable to its customer for any reasonably expectable damages which the customer incurs.

A payor bank is under no obligation to its customer to pay an uncertified check which is over six months old. Section 4–404. This rule reflects the usual banking practice of consulting a depositor before paying a stale item on her account. The bank is not required to dishonor such an item, however, and if payment is made in good faith, it may charge the amount of the item to its customer's account. *See Advanced Alloys, Inc. v. Sergeant Steel Corp.*

Stop Payment Orders

A check drawn on a bank is an order to pay a sum of money and an authorization to charge the amount to the drawer's account. The drawer may countermand this order, however, by means of a stop payment order. Section 4–403. If such order does not come too late, the bank is bound by it. If the bank inadvertently pays a check over a valid stop order, it is *prima facie* liable to the customer, but only to the extent of the customer's loss resulting from the payment. The burden of establishing the fact and amount of loss is on the customer.

A stop payment order to be effective must be received by the bank in time to give it a reasonable opportunity to act on it. Section 4–403(1). *See Siniscalchi v. Valley Bank of New York*. An oral stop order is binding on the bank for only fourteen calendar days. Section 4–403(2). Therefore, the normal practice is for a customer to confirm an oral stop order in writing, and such an order is effective for six months and may be renewed in writing.

The fact that a drawer has filed a stop payment order does not automatically relieve her of liability. If the bank honors the stop payment order and returns the check, the holder may bring an action against the drawer. If the holder qualifies as a holder in due course, personal defenses that the drawer might have to such an action would be of no avail.

Customer's Death or Incompetence

The general rule is that death or incompetence revokes all agency agreements. Furthermore, adjudication of incompetency by a court is regarded as notice to the world of that fact. Actual notice is not required. Section 4–405 of the Code modifies these stringent rules with respect to bank deposits and collections in several ways.

First, a payor or collecting bank's authority to accept, pay, or collect an item or to account for proceeds of its collection is not rendered ineffective by the incompetence of a customer of either bank at the time the item is issued or its collection undertaken if the bank does not in fact know of the adjudication of incompetence. The item may be paid without the bank's incurring any liability.

Second, neither death nor adjudication of incompetence of a customer revokes a payor or collecting bank's authority to accept, pay, or collect an item until the bank knows of it and has a reasonable opportunity to act on such knowledge.

Finally, even though a bank knows of the death of its customer, it may for ten days after the date of his death pay or certify checks drawn by the customer unless a person claiming an interest in the account, such as an heir, executor, or administrator, orders the bank to stop making such payments. Section 4–405(2). This rule facilitates matters for all concerned. There is almost never any reason why such checks should not be paid, and if there is, the personal representative of the deceased customer would have a claim against the person receiving payment. If the check is not paid, the holder will be required to file a claim in the probate proceeding, and the personal representative will have the duty of processing it for payment.

Customer's Duties

The Code imposes certain affirmative duties on bank customers and fixes time limits within which they must assert their rights. Section 4–406. The duties arise and the time starts to run from the time the bank either sends or makes available to its customer a statement of account accompanied by the items paid against the account. The customer is required to exercise reasonable care and promptness to examine the bank statement and items to discover his unauthorized signature or any alteration on an item. Since he is not presumed to know the signatures of payees or indorsers, this duty of prompt and careful examination applies only to the customer's own signature and alterations, both of which he should be able to detect immediately. If he discovers an unauthorized signature or an alteration, he must notify the bank promptly.

If the customer fails to discharge these duties of prompt examination and notice, he is precluded from asserting against the bank his unauthorized signature or any alteration if the bank establishes that it suffered a loss by reason of such failure. Section 4–406(2).

Furthermore, he will lose his rights in a potentially more important situation. Occasionally a forger will embark upon a series of transactions involving the account of the same individual. Perhaps he is an employee who has access to his employer's check book. He may forge one or more checks each month until he is finally detected. The bank, on the other hand, having paid one or more of the customer's checks bearing such signatures without objection, may be lulled into a false sense of security. Suddenly the forgery is detected by the customer after many months or even years. The bank, under Section 4–406(2) of the Code, however, is not held liable for all such items. Once the statement and items become available to him, the customer must examine them within a reasonable period, which in no event may exceed fourteen calendar days, but may, under the circumstances, be less, and notify the bank. Any alterations or unauthorized signatures on instruments by the same wrongdoer and paid by the bank during that period will still be the responsibility of the bank, but any paid thereafter but before the customer notifies the bank may not be asserted against it. This rule is based on the concept that the loss involved is directly traceable to the customer's negligence and, as a result, he should stand the loss.

These rules, however, depend on the bank's exercising ordinary care in paying the items involved. If it does not, it properly loses its right to require prompt action on the part of its customer. But whether the bank exercised due care or not, the customer must in all events report an alteration or his unauthorized signature within one year from the time the statement and items were made available to him or be precluded from asserting them against the bank. Any unauthorized indorsement must be asserted within three years from the time the bank statements and items containing such indorsements are made available to the customer.

See *Tally v. American Security Bank*.

ELECTRONIC FUND TRANSFER

As previously discussed, the use of commercial paper for payment has transformed the United States into a virtually "cashless" society. The advent and technological advances of computers make it likely that in the foreseeable future electronic fund transfer systems (EFTS) will bring about a "checkless" society. There are two principal reasons that financial institutions seek to substitute EFTS for checks. The first is to eliminate the ever-increasing paper work involved in processing the billions of checks that are issued annually. The second is to eliminate the "float" that a drawer of a check currently enjoys as a result of maintaining the use of his funds during the check processing period between issuance of the check and final payment.

An EFT has been defined as "any transfer of funds, other than a transaction originated by check, draft, or similar paper instrument, which is initiated through an electronic terminal, telephonic instrument, or computer or magnetic tape so as to order, instruct or authorize a financial institution to debit or credit an account." For example, with an EFT, A in New York would be able to pay a debt owed to B in Illinois by A's entering into his computer an order to his bank to pay B the amount of the debt owed. The drawee bank would then instantly debit A's account in the amount of the debt and transfer the credit to B's bank where B's account would immediately be credited in that amount. The entire transaction would be completed in minutes.

To date the use of EFTS is still in its beginning stages. Nonetheless, these systems have generated considerable confusion concerning the legal rights of customers and financial institutions. A partial solution to these legal issues was provided in 1978 by Congress when it enacted the Electronic Fund Transfer Act discussed below. However, significant and numerous legal problems remain. Currently, a committee of the Permanent Editorial Board of the Uniform Commercial Code is in the process of drafting a New Payments Code to deal with EFTS.

Types of Electronic Fund Transfers

Although it is highly probable that a number of new EFTS will appear in the coming years, at the moment there are principally four types of EFTS in use: (1) automated teller machines, (2) point-of-sale systems, (3) direct deposit and withdrawal of funds, and (4) pay-by-phone systems.

Automated Teller Machines Automated Teller Machines (ATMs) are a form of electronic fund transfer which are rapidly becoming available throughout the country. ATMs permit customers to conduct various transactions with their bank through the use of electronic terminals. Once activated by a plastic identification card and secret number, the ATMs allow customers to deposit and withdraw funds from their accounts, to transfer funds between accounts, to obtain cash advances from bank credit card accounts, and to make payments on loan accounts.

Point-of-Sale Systems Point-of-Sale (POS) systems permit consumers to automatically transfer funds from their bank account to a merchant. The POS machines are located within the merchant's store and are activated by the consumer's identification card and code. The computer will then instantaneously debit the consumer's account while at the same time crediting the merchant's account.

Direct Deposits and Withdrawals Another type of EFT involves direct deposits made to a customer's account through an electronic terminal when the deposit has been authorized in advance by the consumer. Examples include direct payroll deposits, deposits of Social Security payments, and deposits of pension payments. Conversely, automatic withdrawals are preauthorized electronic fund transfers from the customer's account to pay at regularly recurring intervals obligations of the customer to some party other than the financial institution at which the funds are deposited. Automatic withdrawals to pay insurance premiums, utility bills, or automobile loan payments are common examples of this type of EFT.

Pay-by-Phone Systems Recently some financial institutions have instituted a service which permits customers to pay bills by telephoning the bank's computer system and directing transfer of funds to a designated third party. This service also permits customers to transfer funds between accounts.

Electronic Fund Transfer Act

In 1978 Congress determined that the use of electronic systems to transfer funds provided the potential for substantial benefits to consumers but, due to the unique characteristics of such systems, the application of existing consumer protection legislation was unclear, leaving the rights and obligations of consumers and financial institutions undefined. Accordingly, Congress enacted the Electronic Fund Transfer Act to "provide a basic framework establishing the rights, liabilities, and responsibilities of participants in electronic fund transfers" with primary emphasis upon "the provision of individual consumer rights." The Act is similar in many respects to the Fair Credit Billing Act (see Chapter 40) which applies to credit card transactions. The Act is administered by the Board of Governors of the Federal Reserve System which is mandated to prescribe regulations to carry out the purposes of the Act.

Disclosure The Act requires that the terms and conditions of electronic fund transfers involving a consumer's account be disclosed at the time the consumer contracts for such services in readily understandable language. Included among the required disclosure are the consumer's liability for unauthorized transfers, the types of EFTs allowed, any charges for transfers or the right to make transfers, the consumer's right to stop payment of preauthorized EFTs, the consumer's right to receive documentation of EFTs, and the financial institution's liability to the consumer under the Act.

Documentation and Periodic Statements The Act requires the financial institution to provide the consumer with written documentation of each transfer made from an electronic terminal at the time of transfer. The documentation must clearly state the amount involved, the date, the type of transfer, the identity of the consumer's accounts involved, the identity of any third party involved, and the location of the terminal involved. In addition, the financial institution must provide each consumer with a periodic statement for each account of the consumer that may be accessed by means of an EFT.

Preauthorized Transfers A preauthorized transfer *from* a consumer's account must be authorized in advance by the consumer in *writing* and a copy of the authorization must be provided to the consumer when made. A consumer may stop payment of a preauthorized EFT by notifying the financial institution orally or in writing at any time up to three business days preceding the scheduled date of such transfer. The financial institution may require written confirmation to be provided within fourteen days of an oral notification.

Error Resolution The consumer has sixty days after the financial institution sends a periodic statement in which to notify the financial institution of any errors that appear on that statement. The financial institution is required to investigate and report the results within ten business days. If the financial institution needs more than ten days to investigate, it may take up to forty-five days provided it recredits the consumer's account for the amount alleged to be in error. If it determines that an error did occur, it must properly correct the error. Failure to investigate in good faith makes the financial institution liable to the consumer for treble damages.

Consumer Liability A consumer's liability for unauthorized electronic fund transfer is limited to a maximum of $50 if the consumer notifies the financial institution within *two days* after he learns of the loss or theft. If the consumer does not report the loss or theft within two days, he is liable for losses up to $500. If the consumer fails to report the unauthorized use within *sixty days* of transmittal of a periodic statement, he is liable for losses resulting from *any* unauthorized EFT which appeared on the statement if the financial institution can show that the loss would not have occurred but for the failure of the consumer to report the loss within sixty days.

Liability of Financial Institution A financial institution is liable to a consumer for all damages proximately caused by its failure to make an EFT in accordance with the terms and conditions of an account, in the correct amount, or in a timely manner when properly instructed to do so by the consumer. However, there are some exceptions. The financial institution will not be liable if

1. the consumer's account has insufficient funds through no fault of the financial institution,
2. the funds are subject to legal process,
3. such transfer would exceed an established credit limit,
4. an electronic terminal has insufficient cash, or
5. circumstances beyond the financial institution's control prevents the transfer.

The financial institution is also liable for failure to stop payment of a pre-authorized transfer from a consumer's account when instructed to do so in accordance with the terms and conditions of the account.

CASES

Warranties

BIRMINGHAM TRUST NATIONAL BANK v. CENTRAL BANK & TRUST CO.

Court of Civil Appeals of Alabama, 1973.
49 Ala.App. 630, 275 So.2d 148.

WRIGHT, P. J.

The Birmingham Trust National Bank brought suit for breach of warranty against Central Bank & Trust Company.

The facts out of which the suit arose are briefly as follows: On July 21, 1969, one Boehmer, a customer of Birmingham Trust, secured a loan from Birmingham Trust for the principal sum of $5,500.00. The loan was granted for the purchase of a boat allegedly being manufactured for Boehmer by A. C. Manufacturing Company, Inc., of Florida. Upon signing of a note and security instruments by Boehmer granting them a mortgage upon the boat, Birmingham Trust issued its cashier's check to Boehmer and A. C. Manufacturing Company as payees. The check was given into the possession of Boehmer.

Apparently Boehmer immediately went to Central Bank and deposited the check in an account which he had established there and to which he was the only authorized signatory. It is stipulated that the endorsement of A. C. Manufacturing Company on the check was a forgery and was upon the check when it was presented to Central Bank. The account of Boehmer was credited with the amount of the check. Central placed its legend "P.E.G." meaning in the banking business "Prior Endorsements Guaranteed" on the check on July 21, 1969, and it was received by Birmingham Trust and paid by them on July 22, 1969, to Central.

After some difficulty in collecting payments on the loan, and after it ultimately became delinquent, Birmingham Trust in the latter part of March, 1970 contacted A. C. Manufacturing Company in Florida, attempting to learn the location of the boat. They learned at that time that the boat had never been purchased by Boehmer. At about the same time it was learned that Boehmer had died or killed himself on January 24, 1970.

* * *

On May 1, 1970, Birmingham Trust called upon Central for reimbursement under its warranty of prior endorsements. Central refused repayment. Thus, this suit.

* * *

The cause of action brought here by Birmingham Trust arose under the provisions of § 4–207 which in pertinent part are as follows:

§ 4–207. Warranties of customer and collecting bank on transfer or presentment of items; time for claims.—(1) Each customer or collecting bank who obtains payment or acceptance of an item and each prior customer and collecting bank warrants to the payor bank or other payor who in good faith pays or accepts the item that (a) he has a good title to the item or is authorized to obtain payment or acceptance on behalf of one who has a good title; and * * * (3) The warranties and the engagement to honor set forth in the two preceding subsections arise notwithstanding the absence of indorsement or words of guaranty or warranty in the transfer or presentment and a collecting bank remains liable for their breach despite remittance to its transferor. Damages for breach of such warranties or engagement to honor shall not exceed the consideration received by the customer or collecting bank responsible plus finance charges and expenses related to the item, if any. (4) Unless a claim for breach of warranty under this section is made within a reasonable time after the person claiming learns of the breach, the person liable is discharged to the extent of any loss caused by the delay in making claim. (1965, No. 549, effective midnight Dec. 31, 1966).

The above quoted provisions of the Uniform Commercial Code codifies the theory of implied warranty of the genuineness of prior endorsements which was the accepted general rule as to transactions between collecting banks and drawee banks prior to the Uniform Commercial Code. This provision of the Code places the burden directly upon the first bank in the collection chain to make sure that endorsements on a check are valid. The reason for such requirement is that the first bank is in a better position to insure that the one presenting the check has good title than subsequent banks or the payor bank. [Citation.]

This is different from the rule of Price v. Neal, [Citation], which is that the drawee bank is presumed to know the signature of his customer, the drawer. This is the principle contended for by appellee in brief—that is, that in spite of the warranty of the collecting bank (Central), that it had good title to the check and all signatures and endorsements thereon were genuine and authorized, there yet remained a duty on the payor or drawee (Birmingham Trust National), to check or verify the genuineness of all endorsements before it paid the check.

Such principle does not apply to endorsements on a check as it may to a drawer's signature or to the drawees' signature. There is no duty either under law merchant or under Uniform Commercial Code for a drawee bank to verify the endorsement of a payee on a check which comes to it from a collecting bank under a warranty of endorsement. [Citations.]

It is stated in the *Clearfield Trust* case that the drawee's right to recover from the collecting bank accrues when the drawee makes payment. The warranty of the endorsements is breached at that time. The court said in *Clearfield* "there is no other barrier to the maintenance of the cause of action."

It was the payment of the check to Central, who had no legal right to collect it, (because of the forged endorsement) which constituted Birmingham Trust's loss. It was the responsibility of Central to determine that the endorser and the payee were one and the same. Central's warranty, and the requirement of § 4–207, even in the absence of such express warranty, were designed to protect Birmingham Trust from the failure of Central to fulfill its responsibility. [Citations.]

It is clear that there was no duty upon Birmingham Trust to discover the forgery of the endorsement, either prior or subsequent to payment of the check to Central. A plea or evidence of negligence in that respect is no defense to the action on the breach of warranty.

Appellee attempted to plead that the failure of Birmingham Trust to promptly, or within a reasonable time after discovery of the forgery, notify Central of the forged endorsement was a defense of contributory negligence and a bar to recovery by Birmingham Trust. The trial court gave written charges requested by appellee to that effect. Such defense is not available as a bar to recovery.

* * *

[Judgment for collecting bank and against drawee bank reversed and cause remanded.]

Payment of an Item

ADVANCED ALLOYS, INC. v. SERGEANT STEEL CORP.

Civil Court of the City of New York, Queens County, 1973.
72 Misc.2d 614, 340 N.Y.S.2d 266.

COHEN, J.

[Advanced Alloys, Inc., issued a check in the amount of $2,500 to Sergeant Steel Corporation. The check was presented for payment fourteen months later to the Chase Manhattan Bank. Chase Manhattan made payment on the check and charged Advanced Alloy's account. Advanced Alloy (plaintiff) now seeks to recover the payment made on the check.]

The question presented is whether a bank has a duty of inquiry before paying a check which is stale in that it was presented for payment 14 months after issuance. Prior to the enactment of the Uniform Commercial Code, such a duty existed. [Citation.] However, U.C.C. 4–404 states that:

A bank is under no obligation to a customer having a checking account to pay a check, other than a certified check, which is presented more than six months after its date, but it may charge its customer's account for a payment made thereafter in good faith.

* * *

Under this statute, it must be determined whether this payment was made "in good faith." Since no evidence was presented on this point and since both plaintiff and defendant The Chase Manhattan Bank, N.A. agree that there are no issues of fact—the case having been presented to the Court on affidavits prepared for a summary judgment motion—the Court must simply decide whether a payment of a check by a drawee bank 14 months after issuance is a payment "in good faith" when made without inquiry of the depositor. U.C.C. 1–201(19) defines "good faith" as "honesty in fact in the conduct or transaction concerned." Under this definition, to which the Official Comment to U.C.C. 4–404 makes reference, it appears that the payment of the stale check, without making such inquiry constitutes a payment "in good faith." [Citation.]

Apparently, when the Code intends to apply a concept of "good faith" beyond "honesty in fact," a broader definition is provided. Thus, with respect to dealings of merchants, U.C.C. 2–103(1)(b) states:

Good faith in the case of a merchant means honesty in fact and the observance of reasonable commercial standards of fair dealing in the trade.

Presumably, if it were intended to place a duty of inquiry upon a bank before it could safely pay a stale check, a broader definition of "good faith" would have been made applicable to this situation. It may very well be that in enacting the Code consideration was given, as defendant [Chase] argues, to the vast number of checks being issued and the requirement that a bank accept or refuse to honor a check within a short, prescribed time limit (U.C.C. 4–301, 302), leading to the conclusion that a bank should not be liable for paying stale checks as long as the bank was honest in fact. * * *

The court realizes that a determination that there is no duty of inquiry puts a substantial burden upon one who issues a check, and then, even for a good reason—as in this case—does not want it to be paid. Since a stop payment order is good for only six months (U.C.C. 4–403(2)), it means that the issuer must, in order to protect himself, either continue to renew the stop payment order every six months or close the account. Apparently, in balancing the problems of the issuer and the bank in this situation, the Code resolved the matter in favor of the bank.

The court notes the statement in the Official Comment [citation] that normally a bank will not pay a stale check without consulting the depositor and, further that U.C.C. 4–404 does not require a bank to pay a stale check but the bank " * * * is given the option to pay because it may be in a position to know, as in the case of dividend checks, that the drawer wants payment made." Plaintiff argues that this option to pay is given only when the drawee bank is in a position to know that the drawer wants the check to be paid; and in this case the bank could only know this if it made inquiry—something it did not do. However, the language of the Code itself, as indicated above, does not support this argument and does not impose a duty of inquiry upon the bank in the situation presented herein.

Judgment is directed in favor of the defendant the Chase Manhattan Bank, N.A. against plaintiff; * * *.

Judgment is directed in favor of plaintiff against defendant Sergeant Steel Corpora-

tion, the payee of the check, in the amount of $2,500 with interest thereon from April 5, 1971, plus cost.

Stop Payment Order

SINISCALCHI v. VALLEY BANK OF NEW YORK

District Court, Nassau County, Second District, 1974.
79 Misc.2d 64, 359 N.Y.S.2d 173.

MELLAN, J.

This action was tried before me in a Small Claims Part of this Court and involved a claim by the plaintiff against the defendant bank for the sum of $200 based upon the fact that he had issued a check dated June 11, 1974, which incidentally was a Tuesday, and that on Monday following, namely, on June 17, 1974, bright and early as he testified, at 9 A.M. he appeared at the bank and asked them to place a stop payment on the check. The plaintiff testified that in speaking to the employee of the bank when he appeared in person as stated, the bank's employee detained the plaintiff for approximately 25 minutes or more while she checked the records to see if in fact this instrument had cleared the bank and, thereafter, at 9:45 A.M. gave him a printed notice confirming his request to stop payment and charging his account $5 for this stop payment * * *.

Nevertheless, it appears from the testimony in this matter that this bank has evening hours on Fridays and morning hours on Saturdays so that on June 14, 1974, Friday evening the bank was open for business, received deposits, made payments on checks and similarly on Saturday morning June 15, 1974. The bank transacted such business, but those transactions were not recorded or processed through the bookkeeping system of the bank until Monday June 17, 1974, the date on which the plaintiff appeared to stop payment the first thing in the morning. Thus, although the bank employee checked early that morning, the activities of Saturday morning had not yet been reflected and it appeared at that time that the check had not yet cleared.

The testimony shows that on Saturday morning, June 15, 1974, the check had been cashed so that the cashing of the check preceded the actual stop order. It is significant that the check was outstanding for nearly a full week before the stop order payment came in.

Section 4–403 of the Uniform Commercial Code provides for the customer's right to stop payment on a check, but specifically provides that the stop payment order must be received at such time and in such manner as to afford the bank a reasonable opportunity to act on the stop payment order prior to other action normally taken by the bank as described in Section 4–303 of the Uniform Commercial Code. Furthermore, the law thus provides that the burden is upon the depositor or customer of the bank to establish the amount of loss which may result from the payment by the bank of an item contrary to a binding stop payment order.

A payment in violation of an effective direction to stop payment is an improper payment even though it is made by mistake or inadvertence. This, however, does not appear to have been the case in this instance since the payment actually anteceded the stop payment order.

It may have been difficult for most depositors without special knowledge of banking practices to realize the multiple details involved in the handling of checks and other banking instruments, but it is clear that the bank must have a reasonable opportunity to act upon stop payment orders. [Citation.] In the case of knowledge, notice and stop orders the effective time for determining whether they were received too late to affect the payment of an item and a charge to the customer's account by reason of such payment is receipt plus a reasonable time for the bank to act on any of these communications. Usually a relatively short time is required to communicate to the bookkeeping department advice of these specific notices, but certainly some time is necessary. In the instant case with the weekend activities all being reflected on the records on the Monday following, the bank certainly did not have a reasonable time to act upon the plaintiff's stop payment order. [Citation.]

Under Section 4–303 of the Uniform Commercial Code a stop payment order comes too late to modify the bank's right or duty to pay a check after the bank has already paid the item in cash. Such is the case in the instant matter and for these reasons I find that the defendant is entitled to judgment.

Customer's Duties

TALLY v. AMERICAN SECURITY BANK

United States District Court, District of Columbia, 1982.
355 U.C.C.R.S. 215.

GREENE, J.

In this breach of contract action a customer sues his bank to recover money allegedly paid to a forger out of three accounts maintained or controlled by the plaintiff. Before the court is a motion by the bank for partial summary judgment * * *.

The background of the case is straightforward. The plaintiff contends that he was swindled out of $52,825 by the once-trusted personal secretary who managed his Washington, D.C. law office. Her job and his trust were lost to the secretary when he discovered, sometime after the employee's confession in February, 1980, that * * * in seven instances she had signed his name on savings account withdrawal slips that she then presented to the defendant American Security Bank. As custodian of the plaintiff's passbook, and recipient of his bank statements, the secretary had avoided detection for some four years.

* * *

§ 4–406(1) * * * establishes the duty of a bank customer to review promptly a "statement and items" sent to him or made available to him "in a reasonable manner." Subsection (4) provides that "a customer who does not within one year from the time the statement and items are made available to the customer (subsection (1)) discover and report his unauthorized signature . . . on the face or back of the item . . . is precluded from asserting against the bank such unauthorized signature. . . ." The issue is whether subsection (4) applies when the "item," here a savings withdrawal order, is made available to the customer not through the mail but upon the customer's request.

The U.S. Court of Appeals for this Circuit recently decided that § 4–406 applies to savings as well as checking accounts. *Boutros v. Riggs National Bank* [citation.] Boutros also held that savings withdrawal slips are "items" within the meaning of § 4-406. Subsection (4), however, was not in issue in Boutros, and the plaintiff urges first, that it is not applicable to savings accounts even if the other subsections are, and second, if the subsection is applicable, the one-year time bar attaches only when the savings statements sent to the customer are accompanied by the negotiated items supporting the statement's entries. The court rejects both contentions.

In order to hold that subsections (2) and (3) were applicable to allegedly unauthorized savings withdrawal orders, the Court of Appeals in Boutros necessarily had to find that when banks send periodic statements to savings customers while keeping the withdrawal orders on file they are "mak[ing] the statement and items available to the customer" within the meaning of § 4–406(1). No reason is apparent from the face of § 4–406 or from the comments to it to suspect that subsection (1) and subsection (4) apply to different kinds of banking transactions. Indeed, subsection (4) expressly incorporates subsection (1) by reference. It is not illogical to suppose that the drafters of the UCC expected a customer to make inquiries of his bank if his savings account balance, as stated on the mailed statement, appeared inexplicably low. Upon these inquiries, the savings withdrawal slips would then be "made available."

It is not necessary now to decide whether the one year should run from the time the customer receives his statement, or from the time the slips are made available for inspection. If the appropriate starting point were the latter, the law would have to require that the request for the items be made reasonably promptly after issuance of the statement, or the objective of finality would be undermined. In the instant case, the last allegedly wrongful savings withdrawal took place over three years before the plaintiff notified the bank that his account was awry. It is unclear whether he asked to see the withdrawal orders at this time, but even if he did so, it was too late to fall within a reasonable interpretation of § 4–406(4).

The court is mindful that § 4–406 should not be interpreted so as to give banks more protection than was intended by the drafters of the UCC or by Congress when it adopted the provision for the District of Columbia. [Citation.] It is this court's view, however, that if § 4–406 is to be segmented into subsections that apply to checking accounts and subsections that apply to savings accounts, it is for the legislating body to do. The court holds, therefore, that subsection (4) bars assertion of the savings account claims as the bank was not notified of the irregularities until over three years after the last withdrawal was effected.

Therefore, upon consideration of the defendant's motion for partial summary judgment, it is this 14th day of December, 1982,

Ordered That said motion be and it is hereby granted. The court dismisses with prejudice that portion of the plaintiff's claim based on allegedly forged * * * savings withdrawal orders paid by defendant * * *.

PROBLEMS

1. On December 9, Jane Jones writes a check for $500 payable to Ralph Rodgers in payment for goods to be received later in the month. Before the close of business on the 9th Jane notifies the bank by telephone to stop payment on the check. On the 19th of December Ralph gives the check to Bill Briggs for value and without notice. On the 20th Bill deposits the check in his account at Bank A. On the 21st Bank A sends the check to its correspondent Bank B. On the 22nd Bank B presents the check through the clearing house to Bank C. On the 23rd Bank C presents the check to Bank P, the payor bank. On the 28th of December the payor bank makes payment of the check final. John Jones sues the payor bank. Decision?

2. Howard Harrison, a long-time customer of Western Bank, operates a small department store, Harrison's Store. Since his store has few experienced employees, Harrison frequently travels throughout the United States on buying trips, although he also runs the financial operations of the business. On one of his buying trips Harrison purchased a gross of sport shirts from Well-Made Shirt Company and paid for the transaction with a check on his store account with Western Bank in the amount of $1,000. Adams, an employee of Well-Made who deposits its checks in Security Bank, sloppily raised the amount of the check to $10,000 and indorsed the check, "Pay to the order of Adams from Pension Plan Benefits, Well-Made Shirt Company by Adams." He cashes the check and cannot be found. The check is processed and paid by the Western Bank and is sent to Harrison's Store with the monthly statement. After brief examination of the statement, Harrison leaves on another buying trip for three weeks.

(a) Assuming the bank acted in good faith and the alteration is not discovered and reported to the bank until an audit conducted thirteen months after the statement was received by Harrison's Store, who must bear the loss on the raised check?

(b) Assuming that Harrison, because he was unable to examine his statement promptly due to his buying trips, left instructions with the bank to carefully examine and to notify him of any item over $5,000 to be charged to his account and the bank paid the item anyway in his absence, who bears the loss if the alteration is discovered one month after the statement was received by Harrison's Store?

3. Tom Jones owed Bank Y $10,000 on a note due November 17, with 1 percent interest due the bank for each day delinquent in payment. Tom Jones issued a $10,000 check to Bank Y and delivered it *via* night vault the evening of November 17. Several days later he received a letter saying he owed

one day's interest on the payment because of one-day delinquency in payment. Jones refused because he said he had put it in the vault on the 17th of November. Decision?

4. Assume that D draws a check on Y Bank payable to the order of P; that P indorses it to A; that A deposits it to her account in X Bank; that X Bank presents it to Y Bank, the drawee; that Y Bank dishonors it because of insufficient funds. X Bank receives notification of the dishonor on Monday. X Bank, because of an interruption of communication facilities, fails to notify A until Wednesday. What result?

5. Jones, a food wholesaler whose company carries an account with B Bank in New York City, is traveling in California on business. He comes upon a particularly attractive offer and decides to buy a carload of oranges for delivery in New York. He gives S, the seller, his company's check for $25,000 to pay for the purchase. S deposits the check, with others he received that day, with his bank, the C Bank. C Banks sends the check to D Bank in Los Angeles which, in turn, deposits it with the Los Angeles Federal Reserve Bank. The L.A. Fed sends the check, with others, to the N.Y. Fed. The N.Y. Fed forwards the check to B Bank, Jones's bank, for collection.

(a) Is B Bank a depository bank? A collecting bank? A payor bank?

(b) Is C Bank a depository bank? A presenting bank?

(c) Is the N.Y. Fed. an intermediary bank?

(d) Is D Bank a collecting bank?
Explain.

6. On April 1, M gave P a check properly drawn by M on Z Bank for $500 in payment of a painting to be framed and delivered the next day. P immediately indorsed the check and gave it to Y Bank as payment in full of his indebtedness to the Bank on a note he previously had signed. Y Bank canceled the note and returned it to P.

On April 2, upon learning that the painting had been destroyed in a fire at P's studio, M promptly went to Z Bank, signed a printed form of stop payment order, and gave it to the cashier.

Z Bank refused payment on the check upon proper presentment by Y Bank.

(a) What are the rights of Y Bank against Z Bank?

(b) What are the rights of Y Bank against M?

(c) Assuming that Z Bank by inadvertence had paid the amount of the check to Y Bank and debited M's account, what are the rights of M against Z Bank?

7. As payment in advance for services to be performed, Acton signed and delivered the following instrument:

December 1, 1985

LAST NATIONAL BANK
MONEYVILLE, STATE X

Pay to the order of Olaf Owen $1,500.00 _____
Fifteen Hundred Dollars _____ For services to be performed by Olaf Owen starting on December 6, 1985, (signed) Arthur Acton

Owen requested and received Last National Bank's certification of the check even though Acton had only $900 on deposit. Owen indorsed the check in blank and delivered it to Dan Doty in payment of a pre-existing debt.

When Owen failed to appear for work, Acton gave a written stop payment order to the bank ordering the bank not to pay the check. Doty presented the check to Last National Bank for payment. The bank refused payment.

What are the Bank's rights and liabilities relating to the transactions described?

8. Jones drew a check for $1,000 on The First Bank and mailed it to the payee, T, Inc. C stole the check from T, Inc., chemically erased the name of the payee, and inserted the name of H as payee. C also increased the amount of the check to $10,000 and, by using the name of H, negotiated the check to W. W then took the check to The First Bank and obtained its certification on the check. W then negotiated the check to G who deposited the check in The Second National Bank for collection. The Second National Bank forwarded the check to the D Trust Company for collection from The First Bank which honored the check. G exhausted her account in the Second National Bank, and the account was closed. Shortly thereafter, The First Bank learned that it had paid an altered check.

What are the rights of each of the parties? Assume that all parties (except C) are respectively holders in due course.

PART SIX

Partnerships

PUBLIC POLICY, SOCIAL ISSUES AND BUSINESS ETHICS

OWNERS of a business frequently decide to join forces with one or more associates, usually to gain additional and otherwise unavailable capital or expertise. Once this decision has been made a second, and just as significant, decision must be reached—what form of business organization should be used? Presently there are two general types of business associations: unincorporated and incorporated. Part Six discusses the three most commonly utilized forms of unincorporated business associations, which are: general partnerships, joint ventures and limited partnerships. Part Seven covers incorporated business associations which are usually referred to simply as corporations.

Although corporations today outnumber unincorporated business associations by almost two to one and generate greater revenues by twenty-two to one, there are a number of areas in which unincorporated business associations are widely used. General partnerships have been used principally in finance, insurance, accounting, real estate, wholesale and retail trade, law, and other services. Joint ventures have enjoyed popularity among major corporations planning to engage in cooperative research; in the exploitation of land and mineral rights; in the development, promotion and sale of patents, trade names and copyrights; and in manufacturing operations in foreign countries. Limited partnerships have been widely utilized for enterprises such as real estate investment and development, motion picture and legitimate theater productions, oil and gas ventures, and purchases of a single depreciable asset such as railroad rolling stock.

Regardless of the particular form of business organization, there are three sets of basic policy issues which affect their use. First, what should be the rights and responsibilities of the owners and managers of the business among themselves? Second, what should the rights and responsibilities of the business unit and its members be with respect to the rest of society including suppliers, customers, and creditors? Third, what should be the rights and responsibilities between the business organization and its employees? Unlike the first two policy issues which vary considerably with the form of business organization, employee relations is independent of the type of business entity and is discussed in Chapter 43.

The first issue—the relationship of the owners and managers among themselves—involves a host of policy questions. For example, with respect to formation of the organization, what limitations, if any, should be placed upon the number or type of associates, the name they may use for the business, the purposes for which the business may be formed, the size of the entity, the powers it may exercise or the property it may own? In addition, to what extent should the associates be allowed to vary by contract their rights and responsibilities? Conversely, how much automatic protection should the law provide for business associates who fail to make their own arrangements?

Regarding the operation of the business, to what extent may the associates exert control over the management of the enterprise? How far may the majority go in advancing their own interests? May the minority have veto power over the will of the majority? What remedies should be available to the minority and to the majority? How should the financial gains and losses be divided among the owners?

Concerning changes in the organization, should all the owners have control over choosing new associates and making fundamental changes in the business? Should a member be permitted to transfer his interest to outsiders or to withdraw his capital contribution? How long should the enterprise be permitted to exist and who may bring about the termination of its existence?

The other important set of policy issues involves the relationship of the business unit and its members with respect to the rest of society including suppliers, customers, creditors, parties injured by civil wrongs committed by members, employees and agents of the business, and society at large in the event the enterprise or its members commit a crime. How these issues of external liability are resolved affect the ease by which capital is raised and the extent to which financially risky enterprises utilize a particular form of business organization. External liability for a business arises in a variety of ways, but for most enterprises the crucial and most commonly occurring causes of loss consist of tort and contract liability. The first results from some act or omission that falls below the standard of care that society demands of all its members. Losses from contract liability can occur as a result of incorrect judgments about market conditions, constrictions in cash flow that render the firm unable to meet its debt service, as well as any number of other problems.

A critical social issue is whether a person with a tort or contract claim should be limited to proceeding against the property of the enterprise or may he seek satisfaction of his court judgment from property of the individual members of the business organization. Another issue—one that arises less frequently but is of great consequence—is the extent to which the organization and its members should be held accountable for the criminal conduct of the business' employees, members and agents.

As indicated above, the resolution of these questions varies considerably among the different types of business organizations. Consequently, when business associates are choosing which form is most appropriate, these factors as well as questions of taxation should be considered. This decision, however, cannot be made in any general way but rather depends entirely upon the particular circumstances of the given group of associates:

Apart from the ever changing problems of taxation, * * * there are certain ponderables and imponderables which must be weighed in the choice of a business association. Continuity of existence of the business, centralization of control, legitimate devices to obtain and keep control, limited or unlimited liability of the associates, the possibility of death, bankruptcy, insanity, inadequate performance or poor health and old age of the associates, probability of expansion and the necessity of obtaining capital from outside sources, the ease or difficulty of holding and disposing of property both personal and real, of bringing suit and defending the same, of the use of authority or the abuse of it by the associates, of the amount of "red tape" involved in making reports to governmental agencies, of complying with state and federal securities acts, and of the expense involved in setting up the particular business association, should be analyzed and weighed before determining what business form should be recommended. N. Lattin, *The Law of Corporations* 3–4 (1971).

Part Six of the text examines the law's resolution of these public policy issues with regard to unincorporated business associations. This resolution impacts significantly upon business persons in organizing, financing, operating and dissolving their business organizations.

NATURE AND FORMATION

A business enterprise may be operated or conducted by a sole proprietor, a general partnership, a limited partnership, a corporation, or by some other form of business organization. The selection of the particular form of business unit to be employed is a matter for the owner or owners of the enterprise to determine. When a new enterprise is started, various factors will affect the decision to use one medium rather than another, not the least of which will be Federal and State income tax laws. Other factors include ease of formation, capital requirements, flexibility of management and control, extent of external liability, and the duties imposed by law upon management. For a concise comparison of general partnerships, limited partnerships and corporations, see Figure 33-1 in Chapter 33.

This and the following two chapters will examine general partnerships, commonly called simply partnerships; Chapter 32 discusses limited partnerships and other types of unincorporated business associations. Part Seven covers corporations. The three chapters dealing with general partnerships will make frequent reference to the Uniform Partnership Act (U.P.A.), which, since its promulgation in 1914 has been adopted by all States except Georgia and Louisiana, and also by the District of Columbia, the Virgin Islands, and Guam. The U.P.A. is reprinted in Appendix D.

NATURE OF PARTNERSHIP

Definition

A partnership, or copartnership as it is sometimes called, has been variously defined, although the standard definition is that contained in the Uniform Partnership Act

(U.P.A.): "A partnership is an association of two or more persons to carry on as co-owners a business for profit." Section 6.

The U.P.A. broadly defines "person" to include "individuals, partnerships, corporations, and other associations." Section 2. A business is defined by the U.P.A. to include every trade, occupation, or profession. Section 2.

Entity Theory

An entity is anything which possesses the quality of oneness and may, therefore, be regarded as a single unit. A legal person or legal entity is such a unit which has the recognized capacity of possessing legal rights and being subject to legal duties. A legal entity may acquire, own, and dispose of property. It may enter into contracts, commit wrongs, sue, and be sued. Each human being is a legal entity of natural origin. Each business corporation is a legal entity having a distinct legal existence separate from its members.

A partnership is an association of persons which has the quality of oneness but was regarded by the common law, not as an entity, but as an aggregation of individuals. The U.P.A., however, has basically, but not totally, rejected the common law view of partnerships. The U.P.A. treats partnerships as a legal entity for most purposes, although for some purposes it still treats them as an aggregate. *See Washington v. Birch.*

Partnership as a Legal Entity A partnership is recognized as a legal entity in the following respects:

1. The assets, liabilities, and business transactions of the firm are treated as those of a business unit and are considered separate and distinct from the individual assets, liabilities, and non-partnership business transactions of its members. Section 25.
2. In the marshaling of assets, the assets and liabilities of the firm and those of the respective individual members are considered separate and distinct. Partnership creditors have a prior right to partnership assets, while creditors of the individual members have a prior right, respectively, to the separate assets of their individual debtors. Section 40(h).
3. Title to real estate may be acquired by a partnership in the partnership name and, if so acquired, can be conveyed only in the partnership name. Section 8(3).
4. Every partner is considered an agent of the partnership. Section 9(1).
5. In certain States and in the Federal courts, a partnership may sue and be sued in the partnership name.
6. A partnership is defined as a person in such statutes as the Uniform Commercial Code (Sections 1–201(28), (30)) and the Bankruptcy Reform Act. Section 101(30)).

This listing is by no means exhaustive. It may, therefore, be observed that a partnership is a unit and in most transactions is regarded as a business entity distinct from each of its component members. It is manifest that a partnership could be endowed by the law with full legal personality and thereby become a full legal entity. It is so regarded by the law of Louisiana and of certain foreign countries.

Partnership as a Legal Aggregate As a result of the legal characterization of a partnership as an aggregate for some purposes, a partnership can neither sue nor be sued in the firm name in the absence of a permissive statute. Similarly, the debts of the partnership are ultimately the debts of the individual partners, and any one partner may be held liable for the partnership's entire indebtedness. Section 15. Thus, if A and B enter into a partnership which becomes insolvent, as does A, B is fully liable for the debts of the partnership.

In addition, a partnership lacks continuity of existence: whenever any partner ceases to be associated with the partnership, it is dissolved. Section 29. However, the U.P.A. does grant partnership continuity of existence in certain circumstances.

Finally, the Internal Revenue Code treats a partnership as an aggregate. A partnership is not required to pay Federal income tax but must file an information return setting forth the name of each partner and the amount of income derived from the partnership. It is the responsibility of each partner to include his share of partnership income in his individual tax return and to pay the tax on his share. Partnership income is taxed to the individual partners regardless of whether the income is actually distributed.

Types of Partners

A **general partner** is a partner whose liability for partnership indebtedness is unlimited, who has full management powers, and who shares in the profits.

A **special or limited partner** is one who, as a member of a limited partnership, is liable for firm indebtedness only to the extent of the capital which he has contributed or agreed to contribute. Limited partners are discussed in Chapter 32.

A **silent partner** is a partner who has no voice and takes no part in the partnership business.

A **secret partner** is a partner whose membership in the firm is not disclosed to the public.

A **dormant partner** is a partner who is both a silent and a secret partner.

An **ostensible partner** is one who has consented to be held out as a partner whether he is a real partner or not. The term is more commonly applied to one who is a partner by estoppel: although not an actual partner, he is liable to those who, in good faith, have extended credit on the reasonable assumption that he was a partner.

A **subpartner** is one who is not a partner at all but has a contractual arrangement with a partner which entitles him to a share of the profits realized by such partner. The relationship calls for no continuous acts or the performance of any duty by the subpartner.

FORMATION OF A PARTNERSHIP

Association

The formation of a partnership is relatively simple and may be done consciously or unconsciously. A partnership may result from an oral or written agreement between the parties, from an informal arrangement, or from the conduct of the parties. Persons become partners by associating themselves in business together as co-owners. Whether their agreement is simple or elaborate, definite or indefinite, fully understood and fair or obscure and inequitable is of importance principally to the partners. The legal existence of the relationship depends upon the parties' explicit or implicit agreement and their association in business as co-owners, and not upon the degree of care, intelligence, study, or investigation which preceded its formation.

Articles of Partnership In the interest of achieving a more clear, definite, and complete understanding between the partners, it is preferable, although not usually required, that their partnership agreement be reduced to writing. A written agreement creating a partnership is referred to as the partnership agreement or articles of partnership and should include:

1. The firm name and the identity of the partners;
2. The nature and scope of the partnership business;
3. The duration of the partnership;
4. The capital contributions of each partner;
5. The division of profits and sharing of losses;
6. The duties of each partner in the management;
7. A provision for salaries if desired;
8. Restrictions, if any, upon the authority of particular partners to bind the firm;
9. The right, if desired, of a partner to withdraw from the firm, and the terms, condi-

tions, and required notice in the event of such withdrawal; and

10. A provision for continuation of the business by the remaining partners, if desired, in the event of the death of a partner or other dissolution, and a statement of the method or formula for appraisal and payment of the interest of the deceased or former partner.

When a well-drawn agreement is used, it can provide almost any conceivable arrangement of capital investment, control sharing and profit distribution that the partners desire. In addition, it can provide for continuity of the partnership in the event of one member's death or retirement.

Figure 29-1 shows a sample partnership agreement.

Who May Become Partners Any natural person having full *capacity* may enter into a partnership. Nonetheless, no person may become a member of a partnership without the consent of all the partners. Section 18(g). To the extent that a minor has capacity to act as a principal or agent, she may become a partner, although she has the right both to disaffirm the partnership agreement at any time before reaching majority and to avoid personal liability to partnership creditors. Upon disaffirmance and withdrawal from the partnership, a minor is entitled to the return of her capital contribution and her accrued and unpaid share of the profits except to the extent that such funds are necessary to pay partnership creditors.

The position of a non-adjudicated incompetent is substantially the same as that of a minor except that his incompetency may afford his co-partners a ground for seeking dissolution by court decree. Section 32. Since all contracts of an adjudicated incompetent are void, not voidable, a partnership agreement entered into by such an individual is null and void.

A corporation is defined as a "person" by Section 2 of the U.P.A. and is, therefore, legally capable of entering into a partnership in those States whose incorporation statutes authorize a corporation to do so.

Incidence of Statute of Frauds The Statute of Frauds does not expressly apply to a contract for the formation of a partnership, and therefore no writing is required in order to create the relationship. The promise of an incoming partner to assume existing debts incurred in the prior operation of the business is likewise not within the Statute of Frauds. It is not a promise to answer for the debt or default of another because such a promise is made not to the creditors but to the partners who are the debtors.

However, a contract to form a partnership to continue for a period longer than one year is **within** the Statute and requires a writing in order to be enforceable. Moreover, a contract for the transfer of an interest in real estate to or by a partnership is governed by the Statute of Frauds and requires a writing to be enforceable.

Firm Name In the interest of acquiring and retaining good will a partnership should have a firm name. The name selected by the partners should not be identical with or deceptively similar to the name of any other existing business concern. It may be the name of the partners or of any one of them, or the partners may decide to operate the business under a fictitious or assumed name, such as "Peachtree Restaurant" or "Globe Theater" or "Paradise Laundry." A partnership may not use a name which would be likely to indicate to the public that it is a corporation.

Nearly all of the States have enacted statutes which require any person or persons conducting or transacting any business under an assumed or fictitious name to file in a designated public office a certificate setting forth the name under which the business is conducted and the real names and addresses of all persons conducting the business as partners or proprietors. The purpose of such a statute is to disclose and make available to the public the real names of all parties who choose to deal with the public under an assumed or fictitious name. The statutes generally provide penalties of a fine or imprisonment, or both, for violations. Some statutes provide that no action upon any contract can be maintained by an individual or a partnership which has failed to comply with the statute. Other statutes provide that the failure to file the required certificate may be cured, with respect to the right to institute a suit,

---

FIGURE 29-1 Sample Partnership Agreement

PARTNERSHIP AGREEMENT

This agreement, made and entered into as of the [*Date*], by and among [*Names*] (hereinafter collectively sometimes referred to as "Partners").

WITNESSETH:

Whereas, the Parties hereto desire to form a General Partnership (hereinafter referred to as the "Partnership"), for the term and upon the conditions hereinafter set forth;

Now, therefore, in consideration of the mutual covenants hereinafter contained, it is agreed by and among the Parties hereto as follows:

Article I
BASIC STRUCTURE

§ 1.1 Form

The Parties hereby form a General Partnership pursuant to the Laws of [*Name of State*].

§ 1.2 Name

The business of the Partnership shall be conducted under the name of [*Name*].

§ 1.3 Place of Business

The principal office and place of business of the Partnership shall be located at [*Describe*], or such other place as the Partners may from time to time designate.

§ 1.4 Term

The Partnership shall commence on [*Date*], and shall continue for [*Number*] years, unless earlier terminated in the following manner:

(a) By the completion of the purpose intended, or

(b) Pursuant to this Agreement, or

(c) By applicable [*State*] law, or

(d) By death, insanity, bankruptcy, retirement, withdrawal, resignation, expulsion, or disability of all of the then Partners.

§ 1.5 Purpose—General

The purpose for which the Partnership is organized is _____ .

FIGURE 29-1   Sample Partnership Agreement (cont'd.)

Article II

FINANCIAL ARRANGEMENTS

§ 2.1   Initial Contributions of Partners

Each Partner has contributed to the initial capital of the Partnership property in the amount and form indicated on Schedule A attached hereto and made a part hereof. Capital contributions to the Partnership shall not earn interest. An individual capital account shall be maintained for each Partner.

§ 2.2   Additional Capital Contribution

If at any time during the existence of the Partnership it shall become necessary to increase the capital with which the said Partnership is doing business, then (upon the vote of the Managing Partner(s)):

Each party to this Agreement shall contribute to the capital of this Partnership within _____ days notice of such need in an amount according to his then Percentage Share of Capital as called for by the Managing Partner(s).

§ 2.3   Percentage Share of Profits and Capital

(a) The Percentage Share of Profits and Capital of each Partner shall be (unless otherwise modified by the terms of this Agreement) as follows:

Names   **Initial Percentage Share of Profits and Capital**

§ 2.4   Interest

No interest shall be paid on any contribution to the capital of the Partnership.

§ 2.5   Return of Capital Contributions

No Partner shall have the right to demand the return of his capital contributions except as herein provided.

§ 2.6   Rights of Priority

Except as herein provided, the individual Partners shall have no right to any priority over each other as to the return of capital contributions except as herein provided.

§ 2.7   Distributions

Distributions to the Partners of net operating profits of the Partnership, as hereinafter defined, shall be made at (*least monthly/at such times as the Managing Partners(s) shall reasonably agree.*) Such distributions shall be made to the Partners simultaneously.

For the purpose of this Agreement, net operating profit for any accounting period shall mean the gross receipts of the Partnership for such period, less the sum of all cash expenses of operation of the Partnership, and such sums as may be necessary to establish a reserve for operating expenses.

§ 2.8   Compensation

No Partner shall be entitled to receive any compensation from the Partnership, nor shall any Partner receive any drawing account from the Partnership.

FIGURE 29-1   Sample Partnership Agreement (cont'd.)

Article III

MANAGEMENT

§ 3.1   Managing Partners

The Managing Partner(s) shall be [*Names*] [*or* "all partners"].

§ 3.2   Voting

The Managing Partner(s) shall have the right to vote as to the management and conduct of the business of the Partnership as follows:

Names   **Vote**

Article IV

DISSOLUTION

§ 4.1   Dissolution

In the event that the Partnership shall hereafter be dissolved for any reason whatsoever, a full and general account of its assets, liabilities, and transactions shall at once be taken. Such assets may be sold and turned into cash as soon as possible and all debts and other amounts due the Partnership collected. The proceeds thereof shall thereupon be applied as follows:

(a) To discharge the debts and liabilities of the Partnership and the expenses of liquidation.

(b) To pay each Partner or his legal representative any unpaid salary, drawing account, interest or profits to which he shall then be entitled and in addition, to repay to any Partner his capital contributions in excess of his original capital contribution.

(c) To divide the surplus, if any, among the Partners or their representatives as follows:

(1) First (to the extent of each Partner's then capital account) in proportion to their then capital accounts.

(2) Then according to each Partner's then Percentage Share of *Capital/Income*.

§ 4.2   Right To Demand Property

No Partner shall have the right to demand and receive property in kind for his distribution.

Witnesses   **Partners**

_____   _____

_____   _____

Dated: _____ .

SOURCE: Adapted from *West's Legal Forms*, 2d ed. by Paul Lieberman. Copyright © 1981 by West Publishing Co. Reprinted with permission.

provided that the certificate is filed prior to the institution of suit even though it was not filed at the time the cause of action arose.

When a person ceases to be a member of a partnership operating under an assumed name or a new member is added, and the partnership continues to use the assumed name, a new certificate must be filed.

Tests of Partnership Existence

Partnerships can be formed without the slightest formality. Consequently, if two or more individuals share the control and profits of a business, the law may deem them partners irrespective of how they might characterize their relationship. Thus, associates frequently discover, to their chagrin, that they have inadvertently formed a partnership and have thereby subjected themselves to the duties and liabilities of partners. The existence of a common interest for business purposes is the fundamental test of the existence of a partnership. By this it is meant that there exists a common interest in profits and losses, and a common authority to conduct the business operations. In short, there must be **co-ownership of a business.**

Business Element The Uniform Partnership Act provides that co-ownership, whether it be joint tenancy, tenancy in common, tenancy by the entireties, joint property, common property, or part-ownership, does not of itself establish a partnership, even though the co-owners share the profits derived from use of the property. Section 7(2). In order for there to be a partnership, in addition to the mere co-ownership of property, there must also be a business. An intention to acquire profits being essential to the conduct of a business enterprise, it is clear that an unincorporated nonprofit association, such as a social club, literary society, or fraternal or political organization, is not a business and therefore not a partnership. Where persons are associated together for mutual financial gain on a temporary or limited basis involving a single transaction or relatively few isolated transactions, no partnership results because the parties are not engaged in a continuous series of commercial activities necessary to constitute a business. Co-ownership of the means or instrumentality of accomplishing a single business transaction or a limited series of transactions may result in a joint venture but not a general partnership. Joint ventures are discussed in Chapter 32.

To illustrate: A and B are joint owners of shares of the capital stock of a corporation, have a joint bank account, and have inherited or purchased real estate as joint tenants or tenants in common. They share the dividends paid on the stock, the interest on the bank account, and the net proceeds from the sale or lease of the real estate. A and B are not partners. Although they are co-owners and share profits, they are not engaged in the carrying on of a business, and hence no partnership results. On the other hand, if A and B were engaged in continuous transactions of buying and selling real estate over a period of time and were carrying on a business of trading in real estate, a partnership relation would exist between them, irrespective of whether they regarded one another as partners.

To illustrate further: A, B, and C each inherit an undivided one-third interest in a hotel and, instead of selling the property, decide by an informal and incomplete agreement to continue operation of the hotel. The operation of a hotel is a business, and, as co-owners of a hotel business, A, B, and C are partners and are subject to all of the rights, duties, and incidents arising from the partnership relation.

Co-ownership Although co-ownership of *property* used in a business is neither a necessary nor a sufficient condition for the existence of a partnership, the co-ownership of a *business* is essential. In determining the element of co-ownership of a business, factors such as the sharing of profits, the sharing of losses, and the right to manage and control the business are important.

The receipt by a person of a share of the **profits** of a business is *prima facie* evidence that he is a partner in the business. However, Section 7(4) of the Uniform Partnership Act provides that no inference of the existence of a partnership relation shall be drawn where such profits are received in payment:

1. of a debt by installments or otherwise;
2. of wages of an employee or rent to a landlord;
3. of an annuity to a widow or representative of a deceased partner;
4. of interest on a loan, though the amount of payment may vary with the profits of the business; or
5. as consideration for the sale of the good will of a business or other property by installments, or otherwise.

These transactions do not give rise to a presumption that the party is a partner because the law assumes it more likely that the creditor, employee, landlord, or other recipient of a share of the profits is not a co-owner. However, it is possible to establish that such a person was a partner by proof of other facts and circumstances. For example, the payment of money or the transfer of title to property in exchange for a share of the profits may be either the capital contribution of a partner or a loan or sale on credit by a creditor. Outside of the usual incidents of a loan or a sale on credit, the test most frequently employed in doubtful situations is whether an obligation has been created to pay for the property received or to repay the money advanced in any event. If the party sought to be charged as a partner is entitled at some time to receive payment for the money or property which he advanced, he is generally not a partner but a creditor. Moreover, the sharing of *gross returns*, in contrast to profits, does *not* of itself establish a partnership. Section 7(3). This is so whether or not the persons sharing the gross returns have a joint or common interest in any property from which the returns are derived.

An agreement to share in or contribute to the *losses* of a business, however, affords strong evidence of an ownership interest. Few jurisdictions insist upon an express agreement of loss sharing for a partnership to exist, but all consider such an agreement compelling proof of the existence of a partnership.

Evidence as to participation in the *management* or **control** of a business, standing alone, does not constitute conclusive proof of a partnership relation. A voice in management and control of a business may be accorded, in a limited degree, to an employee, a landlord, or a creditor. On the other hand, one who is actually a partner may take no active part in the affairs of the firm and, indeed, may, by agreement with his co-partners, forego all right to exercise any control over the ordinary affairs of the business. In any event, the right to participate in control is an important factor considered by the courts in conjunction with other factors, in particular, profit sharing. Figure 29-2 illustrates the tests for the existence of a partnership.

See Chaiken v. Employment Security Commission and Cutler v. Bowen.

Partnership Capital

The sum total of the money and property contributed by the partners and dedicated to permanent use in the enterprise is the **partnership capital.** Unlike a corporation, there is no legal requirement that a partnership have a minimum amount of capitalization before commencing business. Nonetheless, except upon dissolution no partner may withdraw any part of his capital contribution without the consent of all the partners.

Partnership property, on the other hand, is the sum of all of the partnership assets including capital contributions and may vary in amount, while partnership capital is a fixed amount, changed only by an amendment to the articles of partnership. All property originally brought into the partnership or subsequently acquired by purchase, or other-

FIGURE 29-2   Tests for Existence of a Partnership

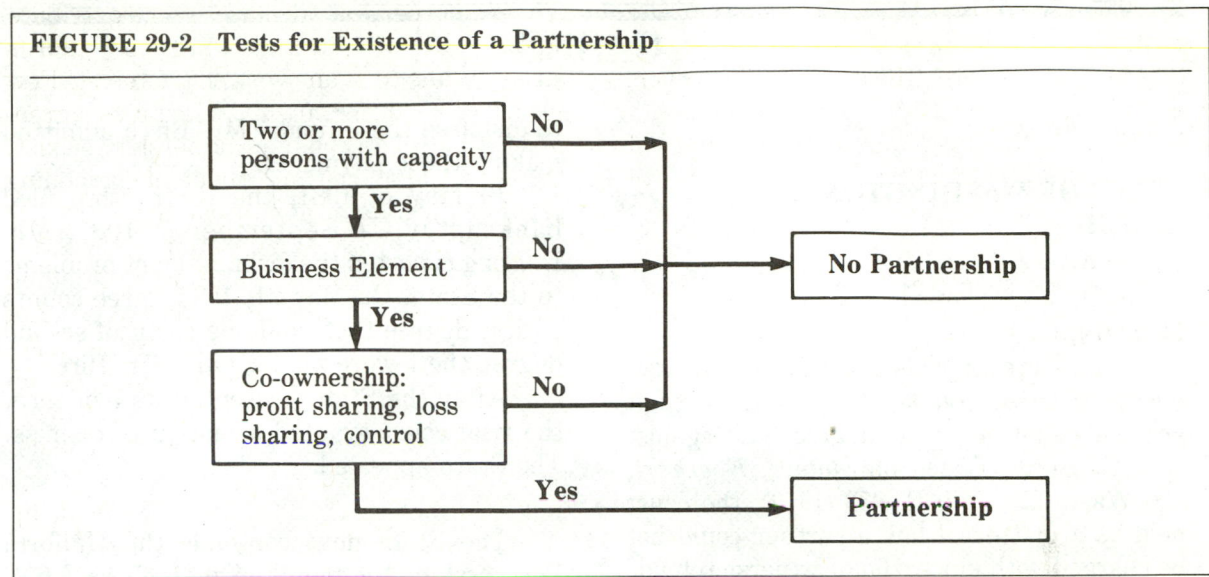

wise, on account of the partnership, is partnership property. Section 8(1). Unless the contrary intention appears, property acquired with partnership funds is also partnership property. Section 8(2).

A partner, by the terms of the agreement, may contribute no capital but only his skill and services, or a partner may contribute the use of certain property rather than the property itself. For example, a partner who owns a store building may contribute to the partnership the use of the building but not the building itself. The building is, therefore, not partnership property, and the amount of capital contributed by this partner is the reasonable value of the rental of the building.

Although in accounting practice partnership profits are frequently included in the capital amount, a clear differentiation should be made between capital and profits. Likewise, a loan by a partner to the firm should be distinguished from capital. A partner is entitled to her share of the profits and to repayment of money advanced as a loan without any new agreement with her copartners, but a withdrawal of capital requires a new agreement. Furthermore, upon dissolution, a debt owing to a partner by the partnership has priority over the rights of partners to return of capital.

Title to real estate which is properly a partnership asset, as where purchased with partnership funds or specifically made a capital contribution, may stand in the name of the partnership, an individual partner, or a third party. The U.P.A. alters the common law by permitting title to real estate to be conveyed to a partnership in the partnership name. Section 8(3). Title so acquired may be conveyed only in the partnership name.

A question may arise whether property owned by a partner before formation of the partnership and used in the partnership business is a capital contribution and an asset of the partnership. Whether it is a partnership asset determines the rights of creditors and partners in the property. The fact that legal title to the property remains unchanged is not conclusive evidence that it has not become a partnership asset. An intention that property is partnership property may be inferred from any of the following facts: (1) the property was improved with partnership funds; (2) the property was carried on the books of the partnership as an asset; (3) taxes, liens, or expenses, such as insurance, were paid by the partnership; (4) income or proceeds of the property were treated as partnership funds; or (5) admissions or declarations by the partners. *See Gauldin v. Corn.*

CASES

Entity Theory

STATE OF WASHINGTON v. BIRCH

Court of Appeals of Washington, 1984.
36 Wn.App. 405, 675 P.2d 246.

MUNSON, C. J.

The State appeals the trial court's dismissal of three counts of first degree theft and one count of second degree theft against Ken E. Birch. Based on *State v. Eberhart*, 106 Wash. 222, 179 P. 853 (1919), the court held as a matter of law a partner could not be charged with embezzling partnership funds because the partner would not be exerting unauthorized control over the property of another. We affirm, believing this issue is better left to the Legislature.

The facts are relatively simple. Richard DeLong and Ken Birch formed Birch-DeLong Construction Company in 1972 as a joint adventure. In their contract, they agreed to the following term:

All proceeds received by the joint venture from the sale of any houses or other buildings shall be deposited in a bank as the parties mutually decide and shall be disbursed only on mutual agreement or authorization.

Initially, Mr. Birch and Mr. DeLong signed all checks. After 2 years, however, Mr. Birch took over all business accounting and disbursed funds solely on his signature. Mr. DeLong agreed to this change because it was inconvenient for him to find time to sign the checks.

The business began well, but in 1979 fell on hard times. The partnership borrowed $60,000 to weather the recession; about 1980, Mr. DeLong began to question disbursements. He received copies of bills and checks and realized Mr. Birch was paying some personal expenses out of partnership funds. Mr. DeLong had not given Mr. Birch permission to disburse these funds. Mr. Birch admitted making these payments.

In May of 1981, the partnership filed bankruptcy. In September of 1981, Mr. DeLong reported the disbursement problems to the State. On May 21, 1982, three counts of first degree theft and one count of second degree theft were filed against Mr. Birch.

After the State presented its evidence, the trial court granted a motion to dismiss. The State appealed.

* * *

The State next contends the Uniform Partnership Act, adopted in 1945 as RCW 25.04, has changed both the relationship of a partner to the partnership and the relationship of each partner to other partners.

Under both the common law and the Uniform Partnership Act, partnerships are treated both as aggregates of individuals and entities distinct from the people involved in the partnership. [Citations.] At the time *Eberhart* was decided, the common law indicated each partner's interest in the property of a partnership was as a joint tenant. [Citation.] This is an aggregate theory because it does not recognize the partnership as a separate entity.

The State contends the entity approach is apparent in RCW 25.04.210 [U.P.A. § 21], which states in pertinent part:

(1) Every partner must account to the partnership for any benefit, and hold as *trustee* for it any profits derived by him without the consent of the other partners from any transaction connected with the formation, conduct, or liquidation of the partnership or from any use by him of its property.

(Italics ours.)

* * *

Although RCW 25.04.210 speaks of the partnership as a separate entity, the issue is whether "the title to the property would be in another." The title would not be in another;

the statute still retains the aggregate approach under which partners own all partnership property as joint tenants. RCW 25.04.210 is therefore inapplicable. [Citation.]

The State contends RCW 25.04.250 [U.P.A. § 25] imposes limitations upon partners' use of partnership property. RCW 25.04.250 states in pertinent part:

Nature of a partner's right in specific partnership property. (1) A partner is co-owner with his partners of specific partnership property holding as a tenant in partnership.

(2) The incidents of this tenancy are such that:

(a) A partner, subject to the provisions of this chapter and to any agreement between the partners, has an equal right with his partners to possess specific partnership property for partnership purposes; but he has no right to possess such property for any other purpose without the consent of his partners.

The theory of tenancy in partnership was developed by the draftsman of the Uniform Partnership Act to deal with problems created by the joint tenancy theory. [Citation.] Under RCW 25.04.250(2)(c), each partner retains his "right in specific partnership property". The partner's interest, however, is subordinated to partnership use of the property for partnership purposes, and the partner gives up the uncontrolled "right to possess such property for any other purpose without the consent of his partners." The State correctly contends RCW 25.04.250 modifies the definition of property of another as it relates to partnership property.

We are loathe to take such a nebulous concept and reduce it, by judicial opinion, to a criminal rule. "[E]xplicit standards are necessary in order to guard against arbitrary enforcement of the laws." [Citation.] Otherwise, a citizen does not have fair notice of proscribed conduct.

A statute relating to larceny by a partner was repealed in 1909. The statute construed in *Eberhart* remains substantially the same today, even though our Legislature made

sweeping revisions in the criminal code in 1976. The Legislature is presumed to be aware of both *Eberhart* and the adoption of the Uniform Partnership Act. The Legislature had the opportunity, therefore, to make theft of partnership funds a crime if it wished by adding "partners" to the list in [the statute for theft]. It did not do so. The trial court did not err in dismissing the four theft charges.

We affirm.

Test of Partnership Existence

CHAIKEN v. EMPLOYMENT SECURITY COMMISSION

Superior Court of Delaware, 1971.
274 A.2d 707.

Storey, J.

[Chaiken entered into separate but nearly identical agreements with Strazella and Spitzer to operate a barber shop. Under the terms of the "partnership" agreements, Chaiken would provide barber chairs, supplies, and licenses, while the other two would provide tools of the trade. The agreements also stated that gross returns from the partnership were to be divided on a percentage basis among the three men and that Chaiken would decide all matters of partnership policy. Finally, the agreements stated hours of work and holidays for Strazella and Spitzer and required Chaiken to hold and distribute all receipts. The Delaware Employment Security Commission, however, determined that Strazella and Spitzer were not partners of Chaiken but rather were his employees. The commission then brought this action to assess unemployment compensation contributions against Chaiken for the two barbers. Chaiken contends that they are not employees but partners pursuant to written partnership agreements. As partners, Chaiken would not be liable for unemployment compensation contributions.]

*   *   *

Chaiken contends that he and his "partners":

(1) properly registered the partnership name and names of partners in the Prothonotary's office, in accordance with [citation],

(2) properly filed federal partnership information returns and paid federal taxes quarterly on an estimated basis, and

(3) duly executed partnership agreements.

Of the three factors, the last is most important. Agreements of "partnership" were executed between Chaiken and Mr. Strazella, a barber in the shop, and between Chaiken and Mr. Spitzer, similarly situated. The agreements were nearly identical. The first paragraph declared the creation of a partnership and the location of business. The second provided that Chaiken would provide barber chair, supplies, and licenses, while the other partner would provide tools of the trade. The paragraph also declared that upon dissolution of the partnership, ownership of items would revert to the party providing them. The third paragraph declared that the income of the partnership would be divided 30% for Chaiken, 70% for Strazella; 20% for Chaiken and 80% for Spitzer. The fourth paragraph declared that all partnership policy would be decided by Chaiken, whose decision was final. The fifth paragraph forbade assignment of the agreement without permission of Chaiken. The sixth paragraph required Chaiken to hold and distribute all receipts. The final paragraph stated hours of work for Strazella and Spitzer and holidays.

The mere existence of an agreement labeled "partnership" agreement and the characterization of signatories as "partners" does not conclusively prove the existence of a partnership. Rather, the intention of the parties, as explained by the wording of the agreement, is paramount. [Citation.]

A partnership is defined as an association of two or more persons to carry on as co-owners a business for profit. [Citation.] As co-owners of a business, partners have an equal right in the decision making process. [Citation.] But this right may be abrogated by agreement of the parties without destroying the partnership concept, provided other partnership elements are present. [Citation.]

Thus, while paragraph four reserves for Chaiken all right to determine partnership policy, it is not standing alone, fatal to the partnership concept. Co-owners should also contribute valuable consideration for the creation of the business. Under paragraph two, however, Chaiken provides the barber chair (and implicitly the barber shop itself), mirror, licenses, and linen, while the other partners merely provide their tools and labor—nothing more than any barber-employee would furnish. Standing alone, however, mere contribution of work and skill can be valuable consideration for a partnership agreement. [Citations.]

Partnership interests may be assignable, although it is not a violation of partnership law to prohibit assignment in a partnership agreement. [Citation.] Therefore, paragraph five on assignment of partnership interests does not violate the partnership concept. On the other hand, distribution of partnership assets to the partners upon dissolution is only allowed after all partnership liabilities are satisfied. [Citation.] But paragraph two of the agreement, in stating the ground rules for dissolution, makes no declaration that the partnership assets will be utilized to pay partnership expenses before reversion to their original owners. This deficiency militates against a finding in favor of partnership intent since it is assumed Chaiken would have inserted such provision had he thought his lesser partners would accept such liability. Partners do accept such liability, employees do not.

Most importantly, co-owners carry on "a business for profit." The phrase has been interpreted to mean that partners share in the profits and the losses of the business. The intent to divide the profits is an indispensable requisite of partnership. [Citations.] Paragraph three of the agreement declares that each partner shall share in the income of the business. There is no sharing of the profits, and as the agreement is drafted, there are no profits. Merely sharing the gross returns does not establish a partnership. [Citation.] Nor is the sharing of profits prima facie evidence of a partnership where the profits received are in payment of wages. [Citation.]

The failure to share profits therefore, is fatal to the partnership concept here.

Evaluating Chaiken's agreement in the light of the elements implicit in a partnership, no partnership intent can be found. The absence of the important right of decision making or the important duty to share liabilities upon dissolution individually may not be fatal to a partnership. But when both are absent, coupled with the absence of profit sharing, they become strong factors in discrediting the partnership argument. * * *

In addition, the total circumstances of the case taken together indicate the employer-employee relationship between Chaiken and his barbers. The agreement set forth the hours of work and days off—unusual subjects for partnership agreements. The barbers brought into the relationship only the equipment required of all barber shop operators. And each barber had his own individual "partnership" with Chaiken. Furthermore, Chaiken conducted all transactions with suppliers, and purchased licenses, insurance, and the lease for the business property in his own name. Finally, the name "Richard's Barber Shop" continued to be used after the execution of the so-called partnership agreements.

* * *

[Judgment for Commission.]

Test of Partnership Existence

CUTLER v. BOWEN

Supreme Court of Utah, 1975.
543 P.2d 1349.

CROCKETT, J.

Plaintiff, alleging a partnership with defendant, sued to recover half of $10,000 paid by the Salt Lake City Redevelopment Agency as compensation for the disruption of their tavern business known as The Havana Club at the corner of Second South and West Tem-

ple Streets. The district court made findings and entered judgment in favor of the plaintiff. Defendant appeals.

The Havana Club had been operated for some years at the location mentioned under a lease running to defendant Dale Bowen, who owned the equipment, furnishings and inventory. He did not himself work in operating the club. In June, 1968, he discussed with the plaintiff Frances Cutler, who had been working for him as a bartender, that she take over the management of the club. They arrived at an oral agreement which included these conditions: that the plaintiff was to have the authority and the responsibility for the entire active management and operation; to purchase the supplies, pay the bills, keep the books, to hire and fire employees; and do whatever else was necessary to run the business. As to compensation, the arrangement was for a down-the-middle split; each was to receive $100 per week, plus one half of the net profits.

The business was operated under this arrangement for four years, until the lessor's building was taken over by the Redevelopment Agency in 1972. * * * On the basis of the regulations it was ascertained that for such displacement the Havana Club should be entitled to the maximum allowable amount of $10,000. The parties made some effort to find a suitable new location for the Havana Club, but failing to do so, decided to terminate that business in April, 1972.

The dispute giving rise to this lawsuit arose because the defendant contended that he was the sole owner of the entire business; and that the plaintiff's status was merely that of an employee, so defendant was entitled to the whole $10,000. Whereas, plaintiff took the position that, conceding the defendant was the owner of the physical assets of the business as above stated, insofar as the going concern and goodwill value, as a partner in the business, she was entitled to one half of the relocation fund.

One of the primary matters to consider in determining whether a partnership exists is the nature of the contribution each party makes to the enterprise. It need not be in the form of tangible assets or capital, but, as is frequently done, one partner may make such a contribution, and this may be balanced by the other's performance of services and the shouldering of responsibility.

When parties join in an enterprise, it is usually in contemplation of success and making profits, and is often without much concern about who will bear losses. However, when they so engage in a venture for their mutual benefit or profit, that is generally held to be a partnership, in which the law imposes upon them both liability for debts or losses that may occur. This basic principle of partnership law is set forth in our Uniform Partnership Act, [Section 7]:

Rules for determining the existence of a partnership.—In determining whether a partnership exists these rules shall apply:

* * *

(4) The receipt by a person of a share of the profits of a business is prima facie evidence that he is a partner in the business, but no such inference shall be drawn if such profits were received in payment:

* * *

(b) As wages of an employee or rent to a landlord.

On the question whether profits shared should be regarded simply as wages, it is important to consider the degree to which a party participates in the management of the enterprise and whether the relationship is such that the party shares generally in the potential profits or advantages and thus should be held responsible for losses or liability incurred therein.

* * *

It is not shown here that any occasion arose where the plaintiff's responsibility for debts or other liabilities of the business was tested. However, throughout the four years in which she operated and managed the Club, apparently with competence and efficiency, it was her responsibility to see that all bills were paid, including the rental on the lease, employees' salaries, the costs of all purchases, licenses and other expenses of the business. During that time she saw the defendant Bowen only infrequently for the purpose of rendering an accounting and dividing the profits. It is further pertinent that the parties reported their income tax as a partnership.

Under the arrangement as shown and as found by the trial court, a good case can be made out that it was largely through the capability, experience, and efforts of the plaintiff that, in addition to the physical plant, there existed a separate asset in the value of the "going concern and goodwill" of the business, which was being lost by its displacement. On the basis of what has been said above, we see nothing to persuade us to disagree with the view taken by the trial court: that the plaintiff's involvement in this business was such that she would have been liable for any losses that might have occurred in its operation; and that, concomitantly, she was entitled to participate in any profits or advantages that inured to it.

* * *

From the circumstances shown in evidence as discussed herein, there appears to be a reasonable basis for the trial court's view that, except for the physical assets, which belonged to the defendant and to which the plaintiff makes no claim, the further asset of the business: that is, the value of what is called going concern and goodwill belonged to the two of them as partners in the enterprise; and that when the business could not be relocated, the $10,000 should properly be regarded as compensation for the loss by the forced relocation (which turned out to be a termination) of the business; and that the partners having lost their respective equal shares in the going business operation, they should also share equally in the compensation for its loss.

* * *

[Judgment for Cutler affirmed.]

Partnership Property

GAULDIN v. CORN

Court of Appeals of Missouri, Southern District,
Division One, 1980.
595 S.W.2d 329.

GREENE, J.

* * *

The following evidence was presented to the trial court. Defendant Joe Corn, testified that in October, 1966, he entered into a 50–50 partnership with plaintiff Claude Gauldin for the purpose of raising cattle and hogs. Defendant and plaintiff contributed equally to getting the business started. The partnership business was carried out on approximately 25 acres of an 83 acre tract of land owned, at the beginning of the partnership, by defendant's parents and later acquired by defendant and his wife.

The bulk of the partnership profits were put back into the business. Some of the profits were used to improve the 25 acres on which the cattle and hogs were raised. Partnership money was used to fence in 10–15 acres and to repair already existing fence. Top dressing and seed, costing $2,000.00, was placed on some of the land. A machine shed, or barn, was built on the land while it was still owned by defendant's father. Defendant testified that the barn cost either $2,487.50 or $2,400.00. He said that a Cargill unit was built on the property in 1975 at a cost of either $8,000.00 or $7,995.00.

At time of trial, both the barn and the Cargill unit were still on the property. Neither could be removed from the land. Defendant testified that neither building could be used for anything other than the raising of cattle and hogs, that he was no longer in the business because of his health, and that the buildings were therefore useless to him and had no value. Defendant admitted, however, that the land was put into better shape by the labors of the partners and that the value of the land was increased thereby.

The partnership never paid any rent on this property either before or after defendant owned it. Nor did plaintiff pay any rent after the partnership was dissolved. However, no rent was ever requested. * * *

* * *

Upon completion of all of the testimony, the case was taken under advisement by the court. On June 13, 1978, the trial court issued its findings of fact and conclusions of law. The court found that the parties had entered into an oral partnership agreement to share costs, labor, losses, and profits equally; that the business was started on land owned by defendant's parents and acquired by defendant and his wife in February, 1971; that no rent was paid for the use of the land and no agreement existed to consider the use of the land as a contribution by defendant; that the machine shed/barn was built in 1970 at a cost of $2,487.50; that the Cargill unit was built in 1975 at a cost of $8,000.00; that $1,167.83 was paid out of partnership funds to seed and fertilize the land between 1969–1975; that fences were improved and new ones built with partnership money; that partnership funds were used to clear or bulldoze the land; that all improvements to the land were made for and used by the partnership; that the partnership was dissolved in January, 1976; that in March, 1977, plaintiff paid defendant $7,500.00 and took a receipt for all "removable assets"; and that plaintiff and defendant had no agreement regarding the distribution of fixed assets upon dissolution of the partnership. The court found for defendant and against plaintiff, who took nothing. This decision was based on reasoning that defendant did not own the land during the period of the partnership, since it was owned either by defendant's parents or by defendant and his wife as an estate by the entirety, and defendant's wife was not made a party to the suit, and by the fact that plaintiff knew that the improvements could not be removed at the time they were constructed.

On appeal, plaintiff's sole point is that the trial court erred, as a matter of law, in awarding judgment against plaintiff in the light of its findings of fact. He contends that since the trial court found that fixed partnership assets were erected on land owned by the defendant after formation of the partnership, which assets were acquired with partnership funds and were used by the partnership, and that there was no agreement regarding the disposition of the fixed assets upon dissolution of the partnership, he was entitled to a judgment, as a matter of law, in the sum of $5,750.00, which he contends is one-half the value of the Cargill unit ($8,000.00) and the barn ($3,500.00).

* * *

We agree that the rule is "well-established" that improvements made upon lands owned by one partner, if made with partnership funds for purposes of partnership business, are the personal property of the partnership, and the non-landowning partner is entitled to his proportionate share of their value. * * * [U.P.A. § 8] states, in part:

1. *All property* originally brought into the partnership stock or *subsequently acquired by purchase or otherwise, on account of the partnership is partnership property.*

2. *Unless the contrary intention appears,* property acquired with partnership funds is partnership property. (emphasis added)

It is clear * * * that the general rule, governing the disposition of improvements upon dissolution of a partnership, is activated only where, as here, there is no agreement between the partners which controls such disposition. It matters not that the landowning partner contributed the use of his land to the partnership, that the non-landowning partner knew that the improvements, when made, could not be removed from the land, or that a joint owner with the landowning partner was not joined in the suit for dissolution and accounting of the partnership. Thus the trial court, after finding that the partners had no agreement regarding the disposition of fixed assets upon dissolution of the partnership, should have applied the rule that we have approved here, and should have awarded plaintiff his proportionate share of the value of the improvements at the time of dissolution of the partnership.

We therefore reverse the judgment of the trial court awarding plaintiff nothing, and remand with directions to the trial court to determine, from the record, the value of the Cargill unit and the barn at the time of dissolution of the partnership, that the trial court reopen the record for the purpose of hearing testimony on that issue only, and to thereafter enter a judgment awarding plaintiff his proportionate share (one-half) of their value.

PROBLEMS

1. A and B are joint owners of shares of stock of a corporation, have a joint bank account, and have purchased and own as tenants in common a piece of real estate. They share equally the dividends paid on the stock, the interest on the bank account, and the rent from the real estate. Without the knowledge of A, B makes a trip to inspect the real estate and on his way runs over X. X sues A and B for his personal injuries, joining A as defendant on the theory that A was B's partner. Is A liable as a partner of B?

2. Smith, Jones, and Brown were creditors of White who operated a grain elevator known as White's

Elevator. White was heavily involved and was about to fail when the three creditors mentioned agreed to take title to his elevator property and pay all the debts. It was also agreed that White should continue as manager of the business at a salary of $1,500 per month and that all profits of the business were to be paid to Smith, Jones, and Brown. It was further agreed that they could dispense with White's services at any time, and he was also at liberty to quit when he pleased. White accepted the proposition and continued to operate the business as before, buying and selling grain, incurring obligations, and borrowing money at the bank in his own name for the business. He did, however, tell the banker of the transaction with Smith, Jones, and Brown, and other former creditors of the business knew of it. It worked successfully and for several years paid substantial profits, enough so that Smith, Jones, and Brown had received back nearly all that they had originally advanced. Explain whether Smith, Jones, and Brown were partners.

3. A and B engaged in the grocery business as partners. In one year they earned considerable money, and at the end of the year, after due deliberation, they decided to and did invest a part of the profits in oil land. Title to the land was taken in their names as tenants in common. The investment was fortunate, for oil was discovered near the land, and its value increased many times. A died, leaving a wife and one child. At the time of A's death both he and the partnership were heavily involved financially, and there was a contest between his creditors and the partnership creditors for a prior claim against the oil land. Critical to determining the rights of the creditors is deciding whether the oil land is partnership property. Is the oil land partnership property? Why?

4. A owned an old roadside building which she believed could be easily converted into an antique shop. She talked to her friend B, an antique fancier, and they executed the following written agreement:

　(a) A would supply the building, all utilities, and $10,000 capital for purchasing antiques.

　(b) B would supply $3,000 for purchasing antiques, A to repay her at the time the business terminates.

　(c) B would manage the shop, make all purchases, and receive a salary of $100 per week plus 5 percent of the gross receipts.

　(d) Fifty percent of the net profits would go into the purchase of new stock. The balance of the net profits would go to A.

　(e) The business would operate under the name "Roadside Antiques."

Business went poorly, and the result after one year is a debt of $4,000 owing to Old Fashioned, Inc., the principal supplier of antiques purchased by B in the name of "Roadside Antiques." Old Fashioned, Inc., sues "Roadside Antiques," and A and B as partners. Decision?

5. Clark owned a vacant lot. Bird was engaged in building houses. An oral agreement was entered into between Clark and Bird by which Bird was to erect a house on the lot. Upon the sale of the house and lot, Bird was to have his money first. Clark was then to have the agreed value of the lot, and the profits were to be equally divided. Did a partnership exist?

6. X, Y, and Z formed a partnership for the purpose of betting on boxing matches. X and Y would become friendly with various boxers and offer them bribes to lose certain bouts. Z would then place large bets, using money contributed by all three, and would collect the winnings. After Z had accumulated a large sum of money, X and Y demanded their share, but Z refused to make any split. X and Y then brought suit in a court of equity to compel Z to account for the profits of the partnership. What decision?

7. A, B, C, and D, residents of the State of X, were partners doing business under the trade name of Morning Glory Nursery. A owned a one-third interest and B, C, and D, two-ninths each. The partners acquired three tracts of land in the State of X for the purpose of the partnership. Two of the tracts were acquired in the names of the four partners, "trading and doing business as Morning Glory Nursery." The third tract was acquired in the names of the individuals, the trade name not appearing in the deed. This third tract was acquired by the partnership out of partnership funds and for partnership purposes. Who owns each of the three tracts? Why?

Chapter 30

RIGHTS AND DUTIES

THE operation and management of a partnership involves numerous interactions among the partners as well as with third persons. This chapter will consider both of these relationships. The first part of the chapter focuses on the rights and duties of the partners among themselves, which are determined by the partnership agreement, the common law, and the U.P.A. The relations of partners to third persons dealing with the partnership are governed by the law of agency and the U.P.A. and will be covered in the second portion of this chapter.

RELATIONSHIPS OF PARTNERS TO ONE ANOTHER

When parties enter into a partnership or other business association, the law imposes certain obligations upon the parties as well as providing them with specific rights. So long as the rights of third parties are not affected and standards of fairness are maintained, the parties may by agreement vary these rights and obligations.

The legal duties imposed upon partners *vis à vis* one another are (1) the duty of loyalty (the fiduciary duty), (2) the duty of obedience, and (3) the duty of care. These duties correspond precisely with those duties owed by an agent to his principal and reflect the fact that a large part of the law of partnership is the law of agency.

Likewise, the law provides partners with certain rights which include: (1) rights in specific partnership property; (2) their interest in the partnership; (3) the right to share in distributions; (4) the right to participate in management; (5) the right to choose associates; and (6) enforcement rights.

These rights and duties of the partners among themselves remain in force until the actual termination of the partnership.

DUTIES AMONG PARTNERS

Fiduciary Duty

A fiduciary relationship exists among the members of a partnership based upon the high standard of trust and confidence which they have a right to place in one another. Each partner owes a duty of absolute and **utmost good faith** and **loyalty** to his partners. It is only upon such basis that so intimate a business relationship can function.

The law of partnership has adopted as part of the fiduciary duty the requirement of the law of agency that a partner shall not make a profit other than his agreed compensation, shall not compete with the partnership, and shall not otherwise profit from the relationship at the expense of the partnership. The U.P.A. provides that every partner must account to the partnership for any benefit and hold as trustee for it any profits derived by him without the consent of the other partners from any transaction connected with the formation, conduct, or liquidation of the partnership or from any use by him of its property. Section 21. A partner may not deal at arm's length with his partners. He may not prefer himself over the firm. His duty is one of undivided and continuous loyalty to his partners. Thus, it constituted a breach of duty for a partner to retain a secret discount on purchases of petroleum which he obtained through acquisition of a bulk plant, and the partnership was entitled to the entire amount of the discount. *Liggett v. Lester*, 237 Or. 52, 390 P.2d 351 (1964). Moreover, where an equal partner received $3,500,000 from the sale of a partnership asset, he was entitled to assume that the selling partner had sold the asset for $7,000,000, and the selling partner was under an obligation to account for the discrepancy

if this was not the case. *Vogel v. Brewer*, 176 F.Supp. 892 (E.D.Ark. 1959).

The extent of this fiduciary duty, which binds all fiduciaries and not just partners, has been most eloquently expressed by the often quoted words of Judge (later Justice) Cardozo:

Joint adventurers, like copartners, owe to one another, while the enterprise continues, the duty of the *finest loyalty*. Many forms of conduct permissible in a workaday world for those acting at arm's length, are forbidden to those bound by fiduciary ties. A trustee is held to something stricter than the morals of the market place. *Not honesty alone, but the punctilio of an honor the most sensitive, is then the standard of behavior*. As to this there has developed a tradition that is unbending and inveterate. Uncompromising rigidity has been the attitude of courts of equity when petitioned to undermine the rule of undivided loyalty by the "disintegrating erosion" of particular exceptions. Only thus has the level of conduct for fiduciaries been kept at a level higher than that trodden by the crowd. It will not consciously be lowered by any judgment of this court. *Meinhard v. Salmon*, 249 N.Y. 458, 459, 164 N.E. 545, 546 (1928) [emphasis added].

A partner cannot, without the permission of his partners, engage in any other business within the scope of the partnership enterprise. Any profit acquired from a competing or similar business must be disgorged by the disloyal partner together with compensation for any damage suffered by the existing partnership as a result of the competititon. However, a partner may enter into any business not in competition with nor within the scope of the partnership's business. For example, a partner in a law firm may, without violating his fiduciary duty, act as an executor or administrator of an estate, and need not account for his fees where it cannot be shown that his partnership suffered by his service in this other capacity such as by his lack of attention. This is so even if the partner uses information obtained in the course of his partnership business to benefit his new business.

See Clement v. Clement.

Duty of Obedience

A partner owes his partners a duty to act in obedience to the partnership agreement and to any business decisions properly made by the partnership. Any partner violating this duty will be individually liable for any resulting loss. Thus, a partner who, in violation of an express agreement not to extend credit to relatives, advanced money from partnership funds and sold goods on credit to an insolvent relative, was held personally liable to his partners for the unpaid debt.

Duty of Care

Whereas a partner "is held to something stricter than the morals of the market place," he is held to something less than the skill of the market place. Each partner owes a duty to the partnership of faithful service to the best of his ability. Nonetheless, he need not possess the degree of knowledge and skill of an ordinary paid agent.

A partner must manage the partnership affairs without culpable negligence. **Culpable negligence** is something more than ordinary negligence, yet short of gross negligence. Thus, a partner does not breach her duty of care if she makes honest errors of judgment or fails to use ordinary skill in transacting partnership business so long as she is not culpably negligent. For example, a partner assigned to keep the partnership books utilizes a complicated system of bookkeeping which produces numerous mistakes. Since these errors result simply from poor judgment rather than fraud and are neither intended to, nor do they, operate to the personal advantage of the bookkeeping partner, the negligent partner is *not* liable to her copartners for any resulting loss.

RIGHTS AMONG PARTNERS

Rights in Specific Partnership Property

A partner's ownership interest in any specific item of partnership property is that of a **tenant in partnership.** Section 25. This species of ownership exists only in a partnership, and the principal characteristics of a tenancy in partnership are:

1. Each partner has an equal right with his copartners to possess partnership property for partnership purposes, but he has no right to possess it for any other purpose without the consent of his copartners.
2. A partner may not make an individual assignment of his right in specific partnership property.
3. A partner's interest in specific partnership property is not subject to attachment or execution by his individual creditors. It is subject to attachment or execution only on a claim against the partnership.
4. Upon the death of a partner, his right in specific partnership property vests in the surviving partner or partners. Upon the death of the last surviving partner, his right in such property vests in his legal representative.

Partner's Interest in the Partnership

In addition to owning as a tenant in partnership every specific item of partnership property, each partner has an interest in the partnership which is defined as his share of the **profits** and **surplus** and is expressly stated to be personal property. Section 26.

Assignability A partner may sell or assign her interest in the partnership, but this does not cause dissolution. The new owner does *not* become a partner, does not succeed to the partner's rights to participate in the management, and does not have access to the information available to a member of the firm as a matter of right. She is merely entitled to receive the share of profits and rights upon liquidation to which the assigning partner would otherwise be entitled. Section 27. The assigning partner remains a partner with all the other rights and duties of a partner.

Creditors' Rights A partner's interest is subject to the claims of that partner's creditors who may obtain a charging order (a type of judicial lien) against the partner's interest. Section 28. A creditor who has charged the interest of a partner with a judgment debt may apply for the appointment of a receiver. The court may appoint a receiver for the partner's interest who will receive and hold for the benefit of the creditor the share of profits which ordinarily would be paid to the partner. Neither the judgment creditor nor the receiver becomes a partner nor is entitled to participate in the management or to have access to information. *See Bohonus v. Amerco.*

Right to Distributions

A distribution is a transfer of partnership property from the partnership to a partner. Distributions include a division of profits, a return of capital contributions, a repayment of a loan or advance made by a partner to the partnership, and a payment made to compensate a partner for services rendered to the partnership.

Right to Share in Profits As a partnership is an association to carry on a business for profit, each partner is entitled, unless otherwise agreed, to a share of the profits and, conversely, must contribute toward the losses. Section 18(a). In the absence of an agreement among the partners with regard to division of profits, the partners share the profits *equally*, regardless of the ratio of their financial contributions or the degree of their participation in the management. Unless the partnership agreement provides otherwise, the partners bear losses in the *same proportion* in which they share profits. The agreement may, however, validly provide for bearing losses in some different proportion than that in which profits are shared.

Right to Return of Capital Subject to the rights of the partnership creditors, upon termination of the firm each partner is entitled to be repaid his capital contribution. Section 18(a). Unless otherwise agreed, a partner is not entitled to interest on his capital contribution. His share of the profits of the partnership may be considered as earnings on his investment of capital. However, if there is a delay in return of his capital contribution, he is entitled to interest at the legal rate from the date when it should have been repaid. Section 18(d).

Right to Return of Advances If a partner makes advances (loans) over and above his agreed capital contribution, he is entitled to repayment of the advance plus interest on it. Section 18(c). His position as a creditor of the firm, however, is subordinate to the claims of creditors who are not partners. In addition, a partner who has reasonably and necessarily incurred personal liabilities in the ordinary and proper conduct of the business of the firm

---

FIGURE 30-1   Partnership Property Compared with Partner's Interest

	Partnership Property	Partner's Interest
Definition	Tenant in Partnership	Share of profits and surplus
Possession	For partnership purposes and not for individual purposes	Intangible, personal property right
Assignability	NO: unless all other partners assign their rights in the property	YES: but the assignee does not become a partner
Attachment	YES: but only for a claim against the partnership	YES: by a charging order
Inheritance	NO: goes to surviving partner(s)	YES: passes to the personal representative

or who has made payments on behalf of the partnership is entitled to indemnification or repayment. Section 18(b).

Right to Compensation The U.P.A. provides that, unless otherwise agreed, *no* partner is entitled to remuneration for acting in the partnership business. Section 18(f). This represents the common law viewpoint that whatever a partner does for the partnership, he is doing for himself. If the partnership agreement contemplates that one partner shall perform a substantial or disproportionate share of the work of conducting the business, such partner may, by agreement among all of the partners, receive a salary or, in lieu of salary, an increased percentage of the profits. In the absence of agreement, he is entitled to no salary but only his share of the profits. The only exception to the rule is that a surviving partner is entitled to reasonable compensation for his services in winding up the partnership affairs. Section 18(f).

Right to Participate in Management

Although each of the partners may carve out for himself, or have delegated to him, a certain sphere of activity within the business, each of them, unless otherwise agreed, has an *equal* voice in its management. Section 18(e). The majority generally governs the actions and decisions of the partnership except that acts in contravention of the partnership agreement require the consent of *all* the partners. Section 18(h). There is conflict, however, among the authorities as to what should be done in the event of an equal division of opinion resulting in a stalemate. Some courts hold that, in such case, a partner may go ahead and deal with third parties with impunity. Others hold to the contrary. For example, in *National Biscuit v. Stroud*, 249 N.C. 467, 106 S.E.2d 692 (1959), Stroud and Freeman were general partners in Stroud's Food Center, a grocery store. Nothing in the articles of partnership restricted the power or authority of either partner to act in respect to the ordinary and legitimate business of the

Food Center. In late 1955, however, Stroud informed National Biscuit that he would not be personally responsible for any more bread sold to the partnership. Then, in February 1956, at the request of Freeman, National Biscuit sold and delivered more bread to the Food Center. When payment was refused, National Biscuit brought an action against the partner Stroud and the partnership to recover the value of the bread delivered to the Food Center. Judgment for National Biscuit. Freeman's purchase bound both the partnership and his copartner Stroud. Freeman is a general partner with no restrictions on his authority to act within the scope of partnership business. Under the U.P.A., then, he had "equal rights in the management and conduct of the partnership business." Stroud could not restrict the power and authority of Freeman to buy bread for the partnership as a going concern, for such a purchase was an "ordinary matter connected with the partnership business," for the purpose of its business and within its scope. Such a restriction on Freeman's powers could only be implemented by a majority of the partners, which Stroud was not.

Right to Choose Associates

No partner may be forced to accept any person as a partner whom she does not choose. This is because of the fiduciary relationship between the parties, and because each partner has a right to take part in the management of the business, to handle the partnership assets for partnership purposes, and to act as agent of the partnership. Accordingly, a partner, by her negligence, injudiciousness, or dishonesty, may bring financial loss or ruin to her co-partners. Because of the close relationship involved, partnerships must necessarily be founded on mutual trust and confidence. All this finds expression in the term *delectus personae,* which means, literally, choice of the person and indicates the right one has to choose or select her partners. This principle is embodied in Section 18(g) of the U.P.A. which provides: "No person can become a member of a partnership without the consent of **all** the partners." [Emphasis added.]

When a partner sells her interest to another, the purchaser does not become a partner and is not entitled to participate in the management. He is entitled only to receive the profits and rights upon liquidation accruing to the share which he has bought. Section 27. If the purchaser is admitted to the firm as a partner by agreement of all of the parties, the old partnership is ended, and a new one has been formed.

Enforcement Rights

As discussed, the partnership relationship creates a number of duties and rights among the partners. Accordingly, partnership law provides the partners with the means to enforce these rights and duties. First, each partner is given access to all information concerning the partnership and its books. Second, under certain circumstances, a partner may obtain a judicially ordered and supervised accounting (a detailed statement of financial transactions including a balance owed) in an action brought in a court of equity against the partnership or his partners.

Right to Information and Inspection of the Books Each partner is entitled to full information as to all partnership matters upon demand at any time, and each has a duty to supply such information as he may possess. Section 20. The right to demand information extends also to the legal representative of a deceased partner for a reasonable time following the dissolution of the partnership.

Unless the partners agree otherwise, the books of the partnership are to be kept at the principal place of business at all times, and each partner has an absolute right to have access to them, to inspect them, and to copy any of them. Section 19. This right may be exercised by a duly authorized attorney or accountant on behalf of a partner.

Right to an Accounting At common law and under the U.P.A., a partner is entitled to an accounting which is an equitable proceeding for a comprehensive and effective settlement of all partnership affairs. An accounting is designed to produce and evaluate all testimony relevant to the various claims of the partners. A partner may invoke the power of a court of equity to decree an accounting whenever (1) he is wrongfully excluded from the partnership business or possession of its property by his copartners, (2) the partnership agreement provides, (3) a partner makes a profit in violation of his fiduciary duty, or (4) other circumstances render it just and reasonable. Section 22. A partner may not be permitted to sue the partnership at law, as he would be suing himself, but he may sue in equity in an action for an accounting. *See Central Trust & Safe Co. v. Respass.*

RELATIONSHIP BETWEEN PARTNERS AND THIRD PARTIES

In addition to the partners' rights and duties among themselves, in the course of transacting business partners may also acquire rights and incur duties to third parties. Under the law of **agency** a principal is liable upon contracts made on his behalf by his duly authorized agents and is liable in tort for the wrongful acts of his agents committed in the course of their employment. A large part of the law of partnership is the law of agency, and most problems arising between partners and third persons require the application of principles of agency law. This relationship is made explicit by the U.P.A. which states that "The law of agency shall apply under this act," and that "Every partner is an agent of the partnership for the purpose of its business." Sections 4(3) and 9(1).

CONTRACTS OF PARTNERSHIP

Contract Liability of Partners

The act of every partner binds the partnership with respect to transactions *within* the scope of the partnership business unless the partner does not have actual or apparent authority to so act. If the partnership is bound, then each partner has **unlimited, personal liability** for that partnership obligation. The U.P.A. provides that partners are jointly liable on all debts and contract obligations of the partnership. Section 15(b). The consequences of joint liability are as follows:

1. In a suit upon a joint obligation, each living joint obligor must be made a party defendant in the action.
2. A judgment based upon a joint obligation must be against all of the obligors or none.
3. The death of an obligor terminates his liability.
4. A release of one joint obligor releases all.
5. A convenant not to sue may be given to one of several joint obligors and will have the effect of releasing that one while preserving rights against the others.

Therefore, any suit in contract against the partners must name all the partners as defendants.

Authority to Bind Partnership

A partner may bind the partnership by her act (1) if she has actual authority, express or implied, to perform the act; or (2) if she has apparent authority to perform the act. If the act is not apparently within the scope of the partnership business, then the partnership is bound only where the partner has actual authority, and the third person dealing with the partner assumes the risk of the existence of such actual authority. Section 9(2). See Figure 30-2. *See Hodge v. Garrett.*

Actual Express Authority This authority may be specifically set forth in the partnership agreement or in a collateral agreement between the partners and may be written or oral. In addition, it may arise from decisions made by a majority of the partners regarding ordinary matters connected with the partnership business. Section 18(h).

Section 9(3) of the U.P.A. provides that the following acts do **not** bind the partnership unless authorized by **all** of the partners:

1. assignment of partnership property for the benefit of its creditors;
2. disposal of the good will of the business;
3. any act which would make it impossible to carry on the ordinary business of the partnership;
4. confession of a judgment;
5. submission of a partnership claim or liability to arbitration or reference.

In addition, a partner who does not have actual authority from all of her partners may not bind the partnership by any of the following acts inasmuch as they are clearly outside of the scope of the partnership under ordinary circumstances: (1) execution of contracts of guaranty and suretyship in the firm name; (2) sale of partnership property not held for sale in the usual course of business; and (3) payment of individual debts out of partnership assets.

Actual Implied Authority This authority includes authority which is neither expressly granted nor expressly denied but is reasonably deduced from the nature of the partnership, the terms of the partnership agreement, or the relations of the partners. For example, a partner has implied authority to hire and fire employees whose services are necessary to carry on the business of the partnership. In addition, a partner has implied authority to purchase property necessary for the business.

Apparent Authority Apparent authority, which may or may not be actual, is such authority as may, in view of the circumstances and the conduct of the parties, be reasonably considered to exist by a third person who has no knowledge or notice of the lack of actual authority. For example, a partner has apparent authority to indorse checks and notes, to make representations and warranties in selling goods, and to enter into contracts for

FIGURE 30-2   Contract Liability

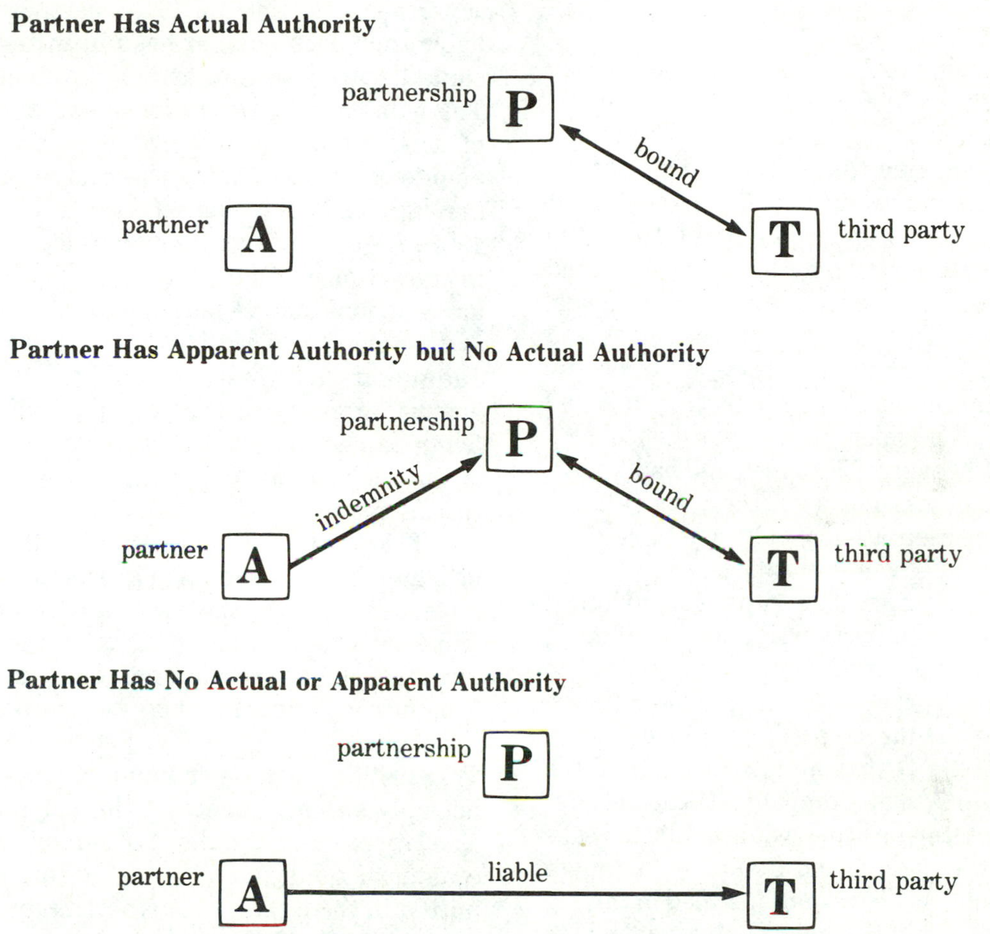

Partner Has Actual Authority

partnership [P]

[A] partner

P ← *bound* → T   third party

Partner Has Apparent Authority but No Actual Authority

partnership [P]

partner [A] — *indemnity* → [P]

[P] ← *bound* → [T] third party

Partner Has No Actual or Apparent Authority

partnership [P]

partner [A] — *liable* → [T] third party

advertising. A third person may not rely upon apparent authority in any situation where he is put on notice or has knowledge that the partner does not, or may not, have actual authority. Sections 9(1) and 9(4). In such case, the third person must ascertain the actual authority of the partner or assume the risk of the absence of such authority.

Partnership by Estoppel

Partnership by estoppel imposes partnership duties and liabilities upon a person who is not a partner in an existing partnership by reason of his making or consenting to a representation that he is a partner. It extends to a third person to whom such representation is made and who gives credit to the partnership in justifiable reliance upon the representation. It existed at common law, and is codified in the U.P.A. Section 16(1) as follows:

When a person, by words spoken or written or by conduct, represents himself, or consents to another representing him to anyone, as a partner in an existing partnership or with one or more persons not actual partners, he is liable to any such person to whom such representation has been made, who has, on the faith of such representation, given credit to the actual or apparent partnership, and if he has made such representation or consented to its being made in a public manner he is liable to such person, whether the representation has or has not been made or communicated to such person so giving credit by or with the knowledge of the apparent partner making the representation or consenting to its being made.

For example, A and B are partners doing business as A and Company. A introduces C to T, describing C as a member of the partnership. Believing that C is a member of the partnership and relying upon C's good credit standing, T sells goods on credit to A and Company. In an action by T against A, B, and C as partners to recover the price of the goods, C is liable although not a partner in A and Company. T had justifiably relied upon the representation that C was a partner in A and Company, to which C by his silence consented. However, if T at the time had knowledge that C was not a partner, his reliance on the representation would not have been justified, and C would not be liable.

Except where the representation of membership in a partnership has been made in a public manner, no person is entitled to rely upon a representation of partnership unless it is made directly to him. For example, C falsely tells D that he is a member of the partnership A and Company. D casually relays this statement to T who in reliance sells goods on credit to A and Company. T cannot hold C liable, as he was not justified in relying on the representation made privately by C to D which C did not consent to have repeated to T.

However, where C knowingly permits his name to appear publicly in the firm name or a list of partners, or used in public announcements or advertisements in a manner which indicates that he is a partner in the firm, C is liable to any member of the public dealing with the partnership whether or not the representations have been made or communicated to such person by or with the knowledge of C. Section 16(1).

TORTS OF PARTNERSHIP

The U.P.A. provides that a partnership is liable for loss or injury caused by any wrong-

ful act or omission of any partner while acting within the ordinary course of the business of the partnership or with the authority of his copartners. Section 13. If the partnership is liable then each partner has **unlimited, personal liability** for the partnership obligation. The liability of partners for a tort or breach of trust committed by any partner or by an employee of the firm in the course of partnership business is joint and several. Section 15(a). All of the partners may be sued jointly in one action based upon tort liability, or separate actions may be maintained against each of them and separate judgments obtained. Judgments obtained are enforceable only against property of the defendant or defendants named in the suit. However, payment of any one of the judgments operates as a satisfaction of all of them.

This liability is comparable to the vicarious liability imposed upon a principal for the torts of an agent by the doctrine of *respondeat superior*. The partner committing the tort is directly liable to the third party and must also **indemnify** the partnership for any damages it pays to the third party. See Figure 30-3. Tort liability of the partnership may include not only the negligence of the partners but also trespass, fraud, defamation, and breach of fiduciary duty, so long as the tort is committed in the course of partnership business. Moreover, the fact that a tort is intentional does not necessarily remove it from the course of business, but it is a factor to be considered. *See Phillips v. Cook.*

ADMISSIONS OF AND
NOTICE TO A PARTNER

An admission or representation by any partner concerning partnership affairs, within the scope of his authority, is evidence against the partnership. Section 11. An admission by one person that a partnership exists does not prove its existence. But once the partnership is established by competent evidence, the admission of one partner may be used against the partnership, provided the partner is acting within the scope of the partnership business.

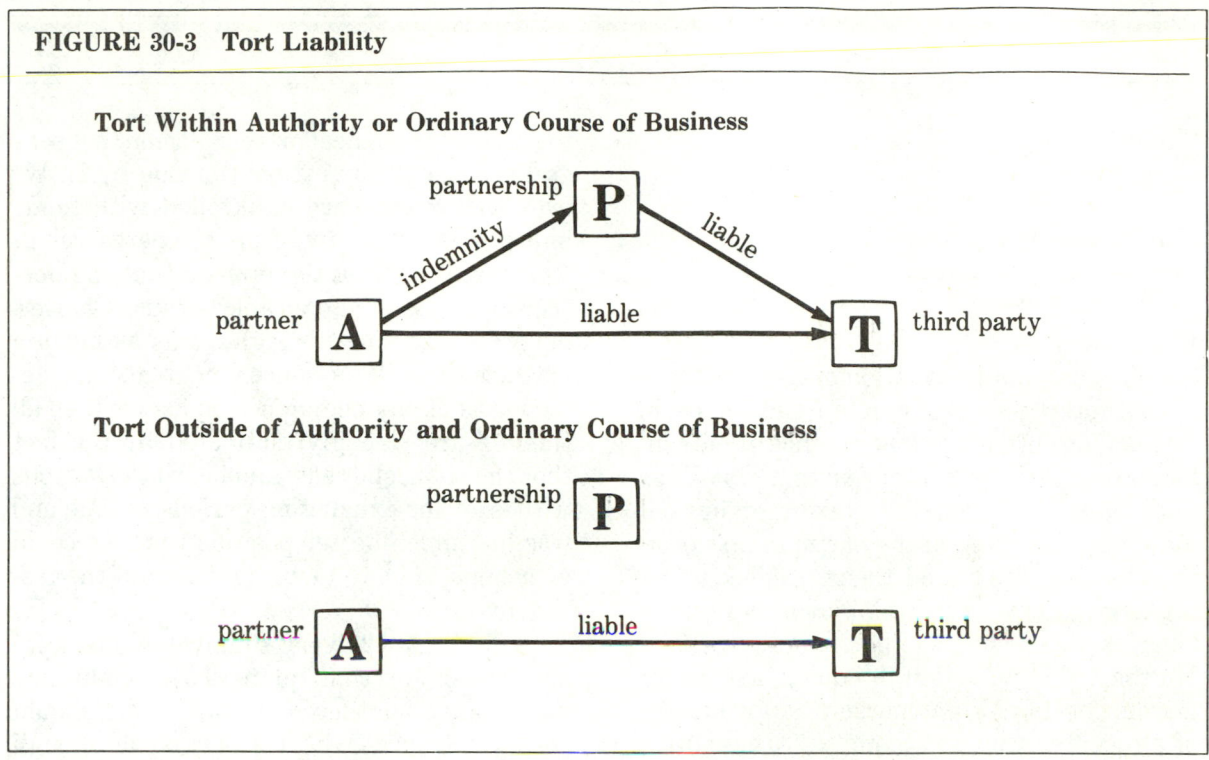

FIGURE 30-3   Tort Liability

Tort Within Authority or Ordinary Course of Business

Tort Outside of Authority and Ordinary Course of Business

A partnership is bound (1) by notice to any partner of any matter relating to partnership affairs, (2) by the knowledge of the partner acting in a particular matter acquired while he was a partner or then present in his mind, and (3) by the knowledge of any other partner who reasonably could and should have communicated it to the acting partner. Section 12. If the knowledge was then present in the mind of the acting partner or other partner, it is immaterial when either one acquired it.

A demand upon one partner as representative of the firm constitutes a demand upon the partnership.

LIABILITY OF INCOMING PARTNER

A person admitted as a partner into an existing partnership is liable for **all** of the obligations of the partnership arising before his admission as though he had been a partner when such obligations were incurred, although this liability may be satisfied **only** out of partnership property. Section 17. In substance, the liability of an incoming partner for antecedent debts and obligations of the firm is limited to his capital contribution. This restriction does not apply, of course, to obligations arising subsequent to his admission into the partnership as to which his liability is *unlimited*. For example, Nash is admitted to Higgins, Cooke, and White Co., a partnership. Nash's capital contribution is $7,500 which was paid in cash upon her admission to the partnership. A year later the partnership is dissolved when liabilities of the firm exceed its assets by $40,000. Porter had lent the firm $15,000 eight months before Nash was admitted; Skinner lent the firm $20,000 two months after Nash was admitted. Nash has no liability to Porter *except* to the extent of her capital contribution. Nash is *personally* liable to Skinner.

CASES

Fiduciary Duty

CLEMENT v. CLEMENT

Supreme Court of Pennsylvania, 1970.
436 Pa. 466, 260 A.2d 728.

ROBERTS, J.

Charles and L. W. Clement are brothers whose forty year partnership had ended in acrimonious litigation. The essence of the conflict lies in Charles' contention that L. W. has over the years wrongfully taken for himself more than his share of the partnership's profits. Charles discovered these misdeeds during negotiations with L. W. over the sale of Charles' interest in the partnership in 1964. He then filed an action in equity, asking for dissolution of the partnership, appointment of a receiver, and an accounting. Dissolution was ordered and a receiver appointed. After lengthy hearings on the issue of the accounting the chancellor decided that L. W., who was the brighter of the two and who kept the partnership books, had diverted partnership funds. The chancellor awarded Charles a one-half interest in several pieces of property owned by L. W. and in several insurance policies on L. W.'s life on the ground that these had been purchased with partnership assets.

The court en banc then heard the case and reversed the chancellor's decree in several material respects. The reversal was grounded on two propositions: that Charles' recovery could only be premised on a showing of fraud and that this burden was not met, and that the doctrine of laches [unreasonable delay] foreclosed Charles' right to complain about the bulk of the alleged misdeeds.

We disagree with the court en banc's statement of the applicable law and therefore reverse. Our theory is simple. There is a fiduciary relationship between partners. Where such a relationship exists actual fraud need not be shown. There was ample evidence of self-dealing and diversion of partnership assets on the part of L. W.—more than enough

to sustain the chancellor's conclusion that several substantial investments made by L. W. over the years were bankrolled with funds improperly withdrawn from the partnership. Further, we are of the opinion that the doctrine of laches is inapplicable because Charles' delay in asserting his rights was as much a product of L. W.'s concealment and misbehavior as of any negligence on his part. In all this we are strongly motivated by the fact that the chancellor saw and heard the various witnesses for exhausting periods of time and was in a much better position than we could ever hope to be to taste the flavor of the testimony.

[U.P.A.] § 21 very simply and unambiguously provides that partners owe a fiduciary duty one to another. [Citation.] One should not have to deal with his partner as though he were the opposite party in an arms-length transaction. One should be allowed to trust his partner, to expect that he is pursuing a common goal and not working at cross-purposes. * * *

It would be unduly harsh to require that one must prove actual fraud before he can recover for a partner's derelictions. Where one partner has so dealt with the partnership as to raise the probability of wrongdoing it ought to be his responsibility to negate that inference. It has been held that "where a partner fails to keep a record of partnership transactions, and is unable to account for them, every presumption will be made against him." [Citation.] Likewise, where a partner commingles partnership funds with his own assets he ought to have to shoulder the task of demonstrating the probity of his conduct.

In the instant case L. W. dealt loosely with partnership funds. At various times he made substantial investments in his own name. He was totally unable to explain where he got the funds to make these investments. The court en banc held that Charles had no claim on the fruits of these investments because he could not trace the money that was invested therein dollar for dollar from the partnership. Charles should not have had this burden. He did show that his brother diverted substantial sums from the partnership funds under his control. The inference that these funds provided L. W. with the wherewithal to make his investments was a perfectly reasonable one for the chancellor to make and his decision should have been allowed to stand.

* * *

The decree is vacated and the case remanded for further proceedings consistent with this opinion.

Partner's Interest in Partnership Property

BOHONUS v. AMERCO
Supreme Court of Arizona, 1979.
124 Ariz. 88, 602 P.2d 469.

HAYS, J.

[Amerco secured a personal judgment against Bohonus. The company now seeks to enforce that judgment by requesting a judicial sale of the assets and property of a partnership of which Bohonus is a member and in which he has an interest.]

* * *

The first issue before us is: *May the trial court order the sale of partnership property to satisfy the individual debt of a partner?*

The appellee, Amerco, after it secured a judgment against the appellant, Bohonus, sought a charging order from the court pursuant to a provision embodied in the Uniform Partnership Act [§ 28]. The court granted the request for a charging order and as a part of that order mandated the sale of appellant's interest in the assets and property of the partnership business, including a spiritous liquor license. The sheriff proceeded with the sale and filed his return.

We now look at the partnership statute. [U.P.A. § 25] says:

A partner's right in specific partnership property is not subject to attachment or execution, except on a claim against the partnership. * * *

[U.P.A. § 24] sets forth the extent of the property rights of the partner:

The property rights of a partner are:
    1. His rights in specific partnership property.
    2. His interest in the partnership.
    3. His right to participate in the management.

[U.P.A. § 26] defines "a partner's interest":

A partner's interest in the partnership is his share of the profits and surplus, and the same is personal property.

[U.P.A. § 28] reads, in pertinent part, as follows:

A. On due application to a competent court by any judgment creditor of a partner, the court which entered the judgment, order, or decree, or any other court, may charge the interest of the debtor partner with payment of the unsatisfied amount of such judgment debt with interest thereon; and may then or later appoint a receiver of his share of the profits, and of any other money due or to fall due to him in respect of the partnership, and make all other orders, directions, accounts and inquiries which the debtor partner might have made, or which the circumstances of the case may require.

With the foregoing statutes in mind, we note that it is only a partner's interest in the partnership which may be charged and, in some jurisdictions, sold. It cannot be overemphasized that "interest in the partnership" has a special limited meaning in the context of the Uniform Partnership Act and hence in the Arizona statutes.

The appellee urges that somehow [U.P.A. § 28(1)] authorizes the sale of partnership assets and property. We note that the record reflects that pursuant to the provisions of the same statute a receiver was appointed in this case. The fact of the receivership provision enforces the conclusion that only the "interest in the partnership" may be charged and we find no provision therein for sale of assets or property of the partnership.

* * *

For the foregoing reasons, we reverse and remand to the trial court for proceedings consistent with this opinion.

Right to an Accounting

CENTRAL TRUST & SAFE DEPOSIT CO. v. RESPASS

Court of Appeals of Kentucky, 1902.
112 Ky. 606, 66 S.W. 421.

DURELLE, J.

[Action for the settlement of partnership accounts by J. B. Respass against the trust company, as executor of the will of his deceased partner, S. L. Sharp. The partners owned and managed a racing stable and, in addition, were engaged in bookmaking, or accepting wagers on race horses. At the time Sharp died, $4,724, representing the undistributed profits of the bookmaking business, was on deposit in Sharp's personal bank account. The trial court held that Respass was entitled to one-half of the profits from the bookmaking business and the executor appeals.]

* * *

A closer question is presented by the claim for a division of the "bank roll." This $4,724 was, as found by the chancellor, earned by the firm composed of Respass and Sharp in carrying on an illegal business—that of "bookmaking"—in the State of Illinois. But though this amount had been won upon horse races in Chicago, it is claimed that, though secured illegally, "the transaction has been closed, and the appellee Respass is only seeking his share from the realized profits from the illegal contracts, if they are illegal." On the other hand, it is claimed for appellant, the executor, that, as to the bank roll, this proceeding is a bill for an accounting of profits from the business of gambling.

It does not seem to be seriously contended that the business of "bookmaking," whether carried on in Chicago or in this Commonwealth, was legal, for by the common law

of this country all wagers are illegal. [Citation.] One of the most interesting cases upon this subject is that of Everet v. Williams—the celebrated Highwaymen's Case—an account of which is given in 9 Law Quart. Rev., 197 [England]. That was a bill for an accounting of a partnership in the business of highwaymen, though the true nature of the partnership was veiled in ambiguous language. The bill set up the partnership between defendant and plaintiff, who was "skilled in dealing in several sorts of commodities," that they "proceeded jointly in the said dealing with good success on Hounslow Heath, where they dealt with a gentleman for a gold watch," that defendant had informed plaintiff that Finchley "was a good and convenient place to deal in," such commodities being "very plenty" there, and if they were to deal there "it would be almost all gain to them"; that they accordingly "dealt with several gentlemen for divers watches, rings, swords, canes, hats, cloaks, horses, bridles, saddles, and other things, to the value of £2,000 and upwards"; that a gentleman of Blackheath had several articles which defendant thought "might be had for a little or no money in case they could prevail on the said gentleman to part with the same things," and that, "after some small discourse with the said gentleman," the said things were dealt for "at a very cheap rate." The dealings were alleged to have amounted to £2,000 and upward. This case, while interesting, from the views it gives of the audacity of the parties and their solicitors, sheds little light upon the legal questions involved, for the bill was condemned for scandal and impertinence; the solicitors were taken into custody, and "fyned" £50 each for "reflecting upon the honor and dignity of this court"; the counsel whose name was signed to the bill was required to pay the costs; and both the litigants were subsequently hanged, at Tyburn and Maidstone, respectively, while one of the solicitors was transported. [Citations.] * * *

In Watson v. Fletcher, [citation], the business of the firm had been the operation of a faro bank. One of the partners having died, the survivor sought an accounting of profits earned. The syllabus reads: "A court of equity will not lend its aid for the settlement and adjustment of the transactions of a partnership for gambling. Nor will it give relief to either partner against the other, founded on transactions arising out of such partnership, whether for profits, losses, expenses, contribution, or reimbursement. * * * "

We conclude that in this country, in the case of a partnership in a business confessedly illegal, whatever may be the doctrine where there has been a new contract in relation to, or a new investment of, the profits of such illegal business, and whatever may be the doctrine as to the rights or liabilities of a third person who assumes obligations with respect to such profits, or by law becomes responsible therefor, the decided weight of authority is that a court of equity will not entertain a bill for an accounting.

The judgment of the chancellor is therefore reversed, and the cause remanded, with directions to enter a judgment in accordance with this opinion.

Authority to Bind Partnership

HODGE v. GARRETT

Supreme Court of Idaho, 1980.
101 Idaho 397, 614 P.2d 420.

BRISTLINE, J.

Following a non-jury trial the court below granted specific performance to the plaintiff-respondent Bill Hodge. All defendants joined in a single notice of appeal, and all defendants joined in a single brief filed in this Court. * * *

Hodge and defendant-appellant Rex E. Voeller, the managing partner of the Pay-Ont Drive-In Theatre, signed a contract for the sale of a small parcel of land belonging to the partnership. That parcel, although adjacent to the theater, was not used in theater operations except insofar as the east 20 feet were necessary for the operation of the theater's driveway. The agreement for the sale of

land stated that it was between Hodge and the Pay-Ont Drive-In Theatre, a partnership. Voeller signed the agreement for the partnership, and written changes as to the footage and price were initialed by Voeller.

Voeller testified that he had told Hodge prior to signing that Hodge would have to present him with a plat plan which would have to be approved by the partners before the property could be sold. Hodge denied that a plat plan had ever been mentioned to him, and he testified that Voeller did not tell him that the approval of the other partners was needed until after the contract was signed. Hodge also testified that he offered to pay Voeller the full purchase price when he signed the contract, but Voeller told him that that was not necessary.

The trial court found that Voeller had actual and apparent authority to execute the contract on behalf of the partnership, and that the contract should be specifically enforced. The partners of the Pay-Ont Drive-In Theatre appeal, arguing that Voeller did not have authority to sell the property and that Hodge knew that he did not have that authority.

At common law one partner could not, "without the concurrence of his copartners, convey away the real estate of the partnership, bind his partners by a deed, or transfer the title and interest of his copartners in the firm real estate." [Citation.] This rule was changed by the adoption of the Uniform Partnership Act. The relevant provisions are currently embodied in [U.P.A. § § 9(1) and 10(1)] as follows:

[U.P.A. § 10(1)]: Where title to real property is in the partnership name, any partner may convey title to such property by a conveyance executed in the partnership name; but the partnership may recover such property unless the partner's act binds the partnership under the provisions of paragraph 1 of section [9] unless such property has been conveyed by the grantee or a person claiming through such grantee to a holder for value without knowledge that the partner, in making the conveyance, has exceeded his authority.

[U.P.A. § 9(1)]: Every partner is an agent of the partnership for the purpose of its business, and the act of every partner, including the execution in the partnership name of any instrument, for apparently carrying on in the usual way the business of the partnership of which he is a member binds the partnership, unless the partner so acting has in fact no authority to act for the partnership in the particular matter, and the person with whom he is dealing has knowledge of the fact that he has no such authority.

The meaning of these provisions was stated in one text as follows:

If record title is in the partnership and a partner conveys in the partnership name, legal title passes. But the partnership may recover the property (except from a bona fide purchaser from the grantee) if it can show (A) that the conveying partner was not apparently carrying on business in the usual way or (B) that he had in fact no authority and the grantee had knowledge of that fact. The burden of proof with respect to authority is thus on the partnership. Crane and Bromburg [sic] on Partnership § 50A (1968) (footnotes omitted).

Thus this contract is enforceable if Voeller had the actual authority to sell the property, or, even if Voeller did not have such authority, the contract is still enforceable if the sale was in the usual way of carrying on the business and Hodge did not know that Voeller did not have this authority.

As to the question of actual authority, such authority must affirmatively appear, "for the authority of one partner to make and acknowledge a deed for the firm will not be presumed . . . ." [Citation.] Although such authority may be implied from the nature of the business, *id.*, or from similar past transactions, [citation], nothing in the record in this case indicates that Voeller had express or implied authority to sell real property belonging to the partnership. There is no evidence that Voeller had sold property belonging to the partnership in the past, and obviously the partnership was not engaged in the business of buying and selling real estate.

The next question, since actual authority has not been shown, is whether Voeller was conducting the partnership business in the usual way in selling this parcel of land such that the contract is binding under [U.P.A. § § 10(1) and 9(1)], *i.e.*, whether Voeller had apparent authority. Here the evidence showed, and the trial court found:

* * *

That at the inception of the partnership, and at all times thereafter, Rex E. Voeller was the exclusive, managing partner of the partnership and had the full authority to make all decisions pertaining to the partnership affairs, including paying the bills, preparing profit and loss statements, income tax returns and the ordering of any goods or services necessary to the operation of the business.

The court made no finding that it was customary for Voeller to sell real property, or even personal property, belonging to the partnership. Nor was there any evidence to this effect. Nor did the court discuss whether it was in the usual course of business for the managing partner of a theater to sell real property. Yet the trial court found that Voeller had apparent authority to sell the property. From this it must be inferred that the trial court believed it to be in the usual course of business for a partner who has exclusive control of the partnership business to sell real property belonging to the partnership, where that property is not being used in the partnership business. We cannot agree with this conclusion. For a theater, "carrying on in the usual way the business of the partnership," [U.P.A. § 9(1)], means running the operations of the theater; it does not mean selling a parcel of property adjacent to the theater. Here the contract of sale stated that the land belonged to the partnership, and, even if Hodge believed that Voeller as the exclusive manager had authority to transact all business for the firm, Voeller still could not bind the partnership through a unilateral act which was not in the usual business of the partnership. We therefore hold that the trial court erred in holding that this contract was binding on the partnership.

Judgment reversed. Costs to appellant.

Torts of Partnership

PHILLIPS v. COOK

Supreme Court of Maryland, 1965.
239 Md. 215, 210 A.2d 743.

MARBURY, J.

This is an appeal by Daniel Phillips individually, and trading as "Dan's Used Cars", one of the defendants below, from a judgment in favor of Delores Cook and Marshall Cook, her husband, plaintiffs below, entered upon the verdict of a jury in favor of the plaintiffs against the defendants, Isadore Harris and Daniel Phillips, individually and as co-partners trading as Dan's Used Cars, in the Superior Court of Baltimore City. The verdict was rendered in an action by the Cooks to recover damages for injuries sustained by them as a result of a collision involving a partnership automobile operated by Harris and bearing dealer plates issued to Dan's Used Cars by the Department of Motor Vehicles.

The Cooks sued Harris and Phillips, individually, and as co-partners trading as Dan's Used Cars. The accident in question occurred on January 7, 1960, at about 6:50 p.m., when a partnership automobile operated by Harris struck the rear of a vehicle driven by one Smith, which in turn hit an automobile operated by Delores Cook, at the intersection of Reisterstown Road and Quantico Avenue in Baltimore. Harris was on his way home from the used car lot when the accident occurred. He was using the most direct route from the partnership lot and was only five blocks from his home at the time of the incident.

In October 1959, Harris and Phillips entered into a partnership on an equal basis under the name of "Dan's Used Cars" for the purpose of buying and selling used automobiles. * * * This partnership agreement was oral and it was agreed between the partners that each would have an equal voice in the conduct and management of the business.

Neither of the partners owned a personal automobile or had one titled in his individual name. It was agreed as a part of the partnership arrangement that Harris would use a partnership vehicle for transportation to and from his home. Under this agreement, he was authorized to demonstrate and sell such automobiles, call on dealers for the purpose of seeing and purchasing used cars, or go to the Department of Motor Vehicles on partnership business after leaving the lot in the evening and before returning the next day. Both Harris and Phillips could use a partnership automobile as desired. Such vehicles were for sale at any time during the day or night and at various times and places they had "for sale" signs on the windshields. Harris had no regular hours to report to the used car lot but could come and go as he saw fit. Phillips testified that it was essential that Harris have a partnership automobile for his transportation to and from his home, and that it was the most practical way to operate. * * *

* * * It is clear that the partnership is bound by the partner's wrongful act if done within the scope of the partnership's business. [U.P.A.] Section 13 provides:

Where, by any wrongful act or omission of any partner acting in the ordinary course of the business of the partnership, or with the authority of his copartners, loss or injury is caused to any person, not being a partner in the partnership, or any penalty is incurred, the partnership is liable therefor to the same extent as the partner so acting or omitting to act.

The test of the liability of the partnership and of its members for the torts of any one partner is whether the wrongful act was done within what may reasonably be found to be the scope of the business of the partnership and for its benefit. The extent of the authority of a partner is determined essentially by the same principles as those which measure the scope of an agent's authority. [Citation.]

* * *

Here, the fact that the defendant partners were in the used car business; that the very vehicle involved in the accident was one of the partnership assets for sale at all times, day or night, at any location; that Harris was on call by Phillips or customers at his home—he went back to the lot two or three times after going home; that he had no set time and worked irregular hours, coupled with the fact that he frequently stopped to conduct partnership business on the way to and from the lot; that he drove partnership vehicles to the Department of Motor Vehicles, and to dealers in Baltimore to view and buy used cars while on his way to or from his home; that one of the elements of the partnership arrangement was that each partner could have full use of the vehicles; that the uses of the automobile by Harris for transportation to and from his home was admittedly "essential" to the partnership arrangement and the most practical and convenient way to operate; and that Harris conducted partnership business both at the used car lot and from his home requires that the question of whether the use of the automobile at the time of the accident was in the partnership interest and for its benefit be submitted to the jury. * * *

Judgment affirmed.

PROBLEMS

1. A, B, and C own and operate the Roy Lumber Company, each contributing one-third of the capital and sharing equally in the profits and losses. Their agreement provides that all firm purchases over $500 must be authorized in advance by two partners and that only A is authorized to draw checks. Unknown to A or C, B purchases on the firm account a $2,500 diamond bracelet and a $5,000 fork lift truck and orders $2,000 worth of logs, all from D who operates a jewelry store and is engaged in various activities connected with the lumber business. A has told D prior to these purchases that B is not the log buyer. A refuses to pay D for these purchases. D calls at the mill to collect, and A again refuses to pay him. D calls A an unprintable name, and A then punches D in the nose. While D is lying unconscious on the ground, an employee of Roy Lumber Company negligently drops a log on D's leg, breaking three bones. The firm and the three partners are completely solvent.

What are the rights of D?

2. A, B, and C agree that A and B will form and conduct a partnership business and that C will become a partner in two years. C agrees to lend the firm $5,000 and take 10 percent of the profits in lieu of interest. Without C's knowledge, A and B tell X that C is a partner, and X, relying on C's sound financial status, gives the firm credit. Later the firm becomes insolvent, and X seeks to hold C liable as a partner. Should X succeed?

3. X and Y had been partners for many years in a mercantile business. Their relationship deteriorated, however, to the point where X threatened to bring an action for an accounting and dissolution of the firm. Thereupon, Y offered to buy X's interest in the partnership for $25,000. X refused the offer and told Y that she would take no less than $36,000. Shortly thereafter, Z approached Y and informed him he had inside information that a proposed street change would greatly benefit the business and that he, Z, would buy the entire business for $100,000 or buy a one-half interest for $50,000. Y made a final offer of $35,000 to X for her interest. X accepted this offer, and the transaction was completed. Thereafter, Y sold the one-half interest to Z for $50,000. Several months later, X learned for the first time of the transaction between Y and Z.

What rights, if any, does X have against Y?

4. A and B were partners doing business as the Petite Garment Company. C owned a dye plant which did much of the processing for the Company. A and B decided to offer C an interest in their Company in consideration for which C would contribute his dye plant to the partnership. C accepted the offer and was duly admitted as a partner.

Unknown to C at the time he was admitted as a partner was the fact that the partnership was on the verge of insolvency. Numerous debts had been incurred which A and B had been unable to meet. About three months after C was admitted to the partnership, a textile firm obtained a judgment against the partnership in the amount of $50,000. This debt represented an unpaid balance which had existed before C was admitted as a partner.

The textile firm brought an action to subject the partnership property, including the dye plant, to the satisfaction of its judgment. The complaint also requested that, in the event the judgment was unsatisfied by sale of the partnership property, C's home be sold and the proceeds applied to the balance of the judgment. A and B owned nothing but their interest in the partnership property.

What should be the result (a) with regard to the dye plant, and (b) with regard to C's home?

5. Jones and Ray formed a partnership in October 1983 known as JR Construction Co. to engage in the construction business, each partner owning a one-half interest. On December 27, 1983, while conducting partnership business, Jones negligently injured Ware who brought an action against Jones, Ray, and JR Construction Co., and obtained judgment for $25,000 against them on March 1, 1984. On April 15, 1984, Muir joined the partnership by contributing $10,000 cash, and by agreement each partner was entitled to a one-third interest. In July 1984, the partners agreed to purchase new construction equipment for the partnership, and Muir was authorized to obtain a loan from XYZ Bank in the partnership name for $20,000 to finance the purchase. On July 10, 1984, Muir signed a $20,000 note on behalf of the partnership, and the equipment was purchased.

In November 1984 the partnership was in financial difficulty, its total assets amounting to $5,000. The note was in default, with a balance of $15,000 owing to XYZ Bank. Muir has substantial resources, while Jones and Ray each individually have assets of $2,000.

What is the extent of Muir's personal liability and the personal liability of Jones and Ray as to (a) the judgment obtained by Ware, and (b) the debt owing to XYZ Bank?

6. A, B, and C were partners under a written agreement made in 1977 that it should continue for ten years. During 1984, C, being indebted to X, sold and conveyed his interest in the partnership to X. A and B paid X $5,000 as C's share of the profits for the year 1984 but refused X permission to inspect the books or to come into the managing office of the partnership. X brings an action setting forth the above facts and asks for an account of partnership transactions and an order to inspect the books and to participate in the management of the partnership business.

(a) Does C's action dissolve the partnership?

(b) To what is X entitled with respect to (1) partnership profits, (2) inspection of partnership books, (3) account of partnership transactions, and (4) participation in the partnership management?

7. Adams, a consulting engineer, entered into a partnership with three others for the practice of their profession. The only written partnership agreement is a brief document specifying that Adams is entitled to 55 percent of the profits and the others to 15 percent each. The venture is a total failure. Creditors are pressing for payment, and some have filed suit. The partners are in fundamental disagreement as to the future course of action.

How many of the partners must agree to achieve each of the following objectives:

(a) To add Jones, also an engineer, as a partner, Jones being willing to contribute a substantial amount of new capital.

(b) To sell a vacant lot held in the partnership name, which had been acquired as the site of a future office for the partnership.

(c) To move the offices of the partnership to less expensive quarters.

(d) To demand a formal accounting.

(e) To dissolve the partnership.

(f) To agree to submit certain disputed claims to arbitration which Adams believes will prove less expensive than litigation.

(g) To sell all of the partnership personal property, Adams having what he believes to be a good offer for the property from a newly formed engineering firm.

(h) To alter the respective interests of the parties in the profits and losses by decreasing Adams' share to 40 percent and increasing the others accordingly.

(i) To assign all the assets to a bank in trust for the benefit of creditors, hoping to work out satisfactory arrangements without formal bankruptcy.

8. A and B orally agreed to become partners in a small tool and die business. A, who had experience in tool and die work, was to operate the business. B was to take no active part but was to contribute the entire $50,000 capitalization. A worked ten hours a day at the plant for which he was paid nothing. Despite A's best efforts, the business failed. The $50,000 capital was depleted, and the partnership owed $50,000 in debts. Prior to the failure of the partnership business B became personally insolvent so that the creditors of the partnership collected the entire $50,000 indebtedness from A, who was forced to sell his home and farm to satisfy the indebtedness. Subsequently, B regained his financial responsibility, and A brought an appropriate action against B for (a) one-half of the $50,000 he had paid to partnership creditors; and (b) one-half of $18,000, the reasonable value of his (A's) services during the operation of the partnership. Decision?

9. S refuses an invitation to become a partner of P and R in the retail grocery business. Nevertheless, P inserts an advertisement in the local newspaper representing S as their partner. S takes no steps to deny the existence of a partnership between them. X, who extended credit to the firm, seeks to hold S liable as a partner. Decision?

10. Hanover leased a portion of his farm to Brown and Black, doing business as the "Colorite Hatchery." Brown went upon the premises to remove certain chicken sheds which they had placed there for hatchery purposes. Hanover thought Brown intended to remove certain other sheds which were his property, and an altercation occurred between them. Brown willfully struck Hanover and knocked him down. Thereafter, Brown ran to the Colorite truck which he had previously loaded with chicken coops and proceeded to drive back to the hatchery. Upon his return trip, he picked up George, who was hitchhiking to the city to look for a job. Brown was in a hurry and was driving at seventy miles per hour down the highway. At an open intersection with another highway, Brown ran a stop sign, striking another vehicle at the intersection, the collision causing severe injuries to George. Immediately thereafter, the partnership was dissolved; Brown was insolvent. Hanover and George each bring separate actions against Black as copartner for the alleged tort committed by Brown against each.

    What judgments as to each?

Chapter 31

DISSOLUTION, WINDING UP, AND TERMINATION

THERE are three stages in the extinguishment of a partnership: (1) dissolution, (2) winding up or liquidation, and (3) termination. The Uniform Partnership Act defines dissolution as the change in the relation of the partners caused by any partner's ceasing to be associated in the carrying on, as distinguished from the winding up, of the business. Upon dissolution, the partnership is not terminated but continues until the winding up of the partnership affairs is completed, during which the business affairs are put in order, receivables collected, payments made to creditors, and distribution of the remaining assets made to the partners. Termination occurs upon the completion of the process of winding up.

DISSOLUTION

Causes of Dissolution

Dissolution may be brought about by (1) an act of the partners, (2) operation of law, or (3) court order. Section 31. It should be noted that a number of events that the common law considered causes of dissolution are no longer so under the U.P.A. For example, the assignment of a partner's interest, a creditor's charging order on a partner's interest, and an accounting do *not* cause a dissolution.

Dissolution by Act of the Partners As a partnership is a personal relationship, a partner always has the *power* to dissolve it, but whether he has the *right* to do so is determined by the partnership agreement. A partner who has withdrawn in violation of the partnership agreement is liable to the remaining partners for damages resulting from the wrongful dissolution.

A partnership is **rightfully dissolved**, that is, without violation of the agreement between the partners, by the act of the parties:

1. when they expressly agree to dissolve the partnership;
2. upon expiration of the period of time provided in the agreement or accomplishment of the purpose for which the partnership was formed;
3. when a partner withdraws from a partnership at will; or
4. by the expulsion of a partner in accordance with a power to expel conferred by the partnership agreement.

See Box v. Crowther.

Dissolution by Operation of Law A partnership is dissolved by operation of law upon (1) the death of a partner; (2) the bankruptcy of a partner or of the partnership; or (3) the subsequent illegality of the partnership, which includes any event which makes it unlawful for the business of the partnership to be carried on or for the members to carry on such business in partnership form. Section 31. For example, a partnership formed to manufacture liquor would be dissolved by a law prohibiting the production and sale of alcoholic beverages. A partnership of lawyers would be dissolved if one of its members was disbarred from the practice of law.

Dissolution by Court Order Upon application by a partner, a court will order a dissolution if it finds that (1) a partner is incompetent or suffers some other incapacity preventing him from functioning as a partner; (2) a partner is guilty of conduct prejudicial to the business or has willfully and persistently breached the partnership agreement; (3) the business can only be carried on at a

loss; or (4) other circumstances render a dissolution equitable. Section 32.

An assignee of a partner's interest or a partner's personal creditor who has obtained a charging order against the partner's interest may petition the court to dissolve a partnership. Application for a court-ordered dissolution may be made at any time if the partnership was at will when the interest was assigned or the charging order was issued but, if the partnership was not at will, only after the end of the specified term or particular undertaking.

Effects of Dissolution

On dissolution the partnership is *not* terminated but continues until the winding up of partnership affairs is completed. Section 30. Moreover, dissolution does *not* of itself discharge the existing liability of any partner. However, dissolution *does* bring about restrictions upon the authority of partners to act for the partnership.

On Authority Upon dissolution, the *actual authority* of a partner to act for the partnership terminates, except so far as may be necessary to wind up partnership affairs. Section 33. Actual authority to wind up includes completing existing contracts, reducing partnership assets to cash, and paying partnership obligations.

Although actual authority terminates upon dissolution, *apparent authority* persists and binds the partnership for acts within the scope of the partnership business unless notice of the dissolution is given to the third party. Section 35. A third party who had extended credit to the partnership prior to dissolution may hold the partnership liable for any transaction which would bind the partnership if dissolution had not taken place unless the third party has knowledge or actual notice of the dissolution. **Actual notice** requires a verbal statement to the third party or actual delivery of a written statement. Section 3(2). On the other hand, a third party, who prior to dissolution had not extended credit to the partnership but nevertheless knew of the partnership, can hold the partnership liable unless he has knowledge, actual notice, or constructive notice of dissolution. **Constructive notice** consists of advertising a notice of dissolution in a newspaper of general circulation in the places at which partnership business was regularly conducted. Section 35(1)(b)(II).

On Existing Liability The dissolution of the partnership does not of itself discharge the existing liability of any partner. Section 36(1). But in some instances the cause of dissolution may result in discharging an executory contract. For example, if the contract called for the personal services of one of the partners, the death of that partner usually will discharge the contract as well as bring about the dissolution of the partnership.

A retiring partner may be discharged from his existing liabilities by a **novation** entered into with the continuing partners and the creditors. A creditor must agree to the novation, although such consent may be inferred from his course of dealing with the partnership after dissolution. Section 36(2). Whether such dealings with the continuing partnership constitutes an implied novation is a factual question of intent.

WINDING UP

Whenever a dissolved partnership is not to be continued, the partnership must be liquidated. The process of **liquidation** is called winding up and involves completing unfinished business, collecting debts, reducing assets to cash, taking inventory, auditing the partnership books, paying creditors, and distributing the remaining assets to the partners. During this period the fiduciary duties of the partners continue in effect.

The Right to Wind Up

Upon dissolution any partner has the right to insist upon the winding up of the partnership unless the partnership agreement provides otherwise. *See Stark v. Utica Screw Products, Inc.* However, a partner who has wrongfully dissolved the partnership or who has been expelled pursuant to the partnership agreement cannot force the liquidation of the partnership. Unless otherwise agreed, all non-bankrupt partners who have not wrongfully dissolved the partnership have the right to wind up the partnership affairs. Section 37. A court, upon the petition of a partner, may appoint a receiver of all of the property and assets of the partnership with authority to operate the business subject to the direction of the court for such time as may be reasonably necessary. The appointment of a receiver is discretionary with the court, and its discretion may be exercised upon such grounds as dissension among the partners or waste, fraud, mental incompetence, misconduct, or other breach of duty by a partner.

Distribution of Assets

After all the partnership assets have been collected and reduced to cash, they are then distributed to the creditors and partners. When the partnership has been profitable, the order of distribution is not critical; however, when liabilities are greater than assets, the order assumes great importance.

Section 40 of the U.P.A. sets forth the rules to be observed in settling accounts between the parties after dissolution and provides the order in which the liabilities of a partnership are ranked for payment out of partnership assets:

1. Amounts owing to creditors other than partners;
2. Amounts owing to partners other than for capital and profits;
3. Amounts owing to partners in respect of capital;
4. Amounts owing to partners in respect of profits.

The partners may by agreement change the internal priorities of distribution (Nos. 2, 3, and 4) but not the preferred position of third parties (1). *See Petersen v. Petersen.* The U.P.A. defines partnership assets to include all partnership property as well as the contributions necessary for the payment of all partnership liabilities, which consists of 1, 2, and 3. Section 40(a).

In addition, the U.P.A. provides that, in the absence of any contrary agreement, each partner shall share equally in the profits and surplus remaining after all liabilities (Nos. 1, 2, and 3) are satisfied and must contribute towards the losses, whether capital or otherwise, sustained by the partnership according to his share in the profits. Section 18(a). Thus, the proportion in which the partners bear losses, whether capital or otherwise, does not depend upon their relative capital contributions. Rather, it is determined by their agreement, and absent agreement, losses are borne in the same proportion in which profits are shared.

If the partnership is insolvent, the partners individually must contribute their respective share of the losses in order to make the creditors whole. Furthermore, if one or more of the partners is insolvent or bankrupt or, being out of the jurisdiction, refuses to contribute, the other partners must contribute the additional amount necessary to pay the firm's liabilities, in the relative proportions in which they share the profits. Section 40(d). When any partner has paid an amount in excess of his proper share of the losses, he has a right of contribution against the other partners who have not paid their share. Section 40(f).

To illustrate the operation of these rules, consider the following examples.

Solvent Partnership Assume that A, B, and C form the ABC Company, a partnership, with A contributing $6,000 capital, B contributing $4,000 capital, and C contributing services but no capital. A also loaned the partnership $3,000 which has not been repaid. There is no agreement as to the proportions in which profits and losses are to be shared. After a few years of operation, the partnership is liquidated. At this time the assets of ABC Company are $54,000, and its liabilities to creditors are $26,000. The partnership is thus solvent and has enjoyed a profit of $15,000 which is calculated by subtracting from the total assets ($54,000) the total liabilities ($39,000), which represents the sum of the amounts owed to creditors ($26,000) plus amounts owed to partners other than for capital and profits ($3,000 owed to A for his loan) plus the amounts owed to partners in respect of capital ($6,000 to A and $4,000 to B). Since A, B, and C have not explicitly agreed upon a profit sharing ratio, they share equally, in this case $15,000 ÷ 3 = $5,000. After the creditors have been paid in full, A will receive $14,000 ($3,000 for repayment of the loan, $6,000 for capital, and $5,000 for share of profits); B will receive $9,000 ($4,000 for capital and $5,000 for share of profits); and C will receive $5,000 (for share of profits).

Insolvent Partnership Assume the same partnership had, instead, experienced financial adversity. While still owing creditors $26,000, its total assets only amount to $12,000. In this case the partnership has sustained an aggregate loss of $27,000, which is calculated by subtracting from the total assets ($12,000) the total liabilities ($39,000), calculated in the same manner as the solvent partnership example. In the absence of an agreement, the losses are shared as the profits are, which in this case is equally. Accordingly, each partner's share of the loss will be $9,000 ($27,000 ÷ 3 = $9,000). After the creditors are paid ($26,000), A will receive nothing ($3,000 owed for the loan plus $6,000 for capital *minus* $9,000 for his share of losses); B must make an additional *contribution* of $5,000 to make good his share of the loss ($4,000 owed for capital *minus* $9,000 for his share of losses); and C must contribute $9,000 (his share of losses).

Contribution of Partner upon Insolvency In the insolvent partnership example above, if A were individually insolvent, the results would not be changed, since A was not required to contribute any additional moneys.

However, if A and B were solvent and C were individually insolvent, C would be unable to pay any of his share of the loss. Then A and B must contribute equally, since that is the relative proportion in which they share profits, in order to make good the amount of C's share. As C's share of the loss is $9,000, A and B are each required to contribute an additional $4,500. This means that in total A will have to contribute $4,500 and B $9,500 in order to satisfy the unpaid claims of partnership creditors. Suppose further that A and C individually are insolvent while B is solvent. B would be required to pay the entire balance of $14,000 due to partnership creditors, representing his unpaid share of the loss plus a contribution of the full amount of C's unpaid share of the loss.

Marshaling of Assets

The doctrine of marshaling of assets is applicable *only* where the assets of a partnership and of its members are being administered by a court of equity. Marshaling means segregating and considering separately the assets and liabilities of the partnership from the respective assets and liabilities of the individual partners. Partnership creditors are entitled to be satisfied first out of partnership assets. They have a right to recover any deficiency out of the individually owned assets of the partners, subordinate however to the rights of nonpartnership creditors to those assets.

Conversely, the non-partnership creditors have first claim to the individually owned assets of their respective debtors and a claim junior to that of partnership creditors to participate in partnership assets.

When the partnership and several or all of the partners are insolvent, the partnership creditors are entitled to prior participation in the partnership assets and nonpartnership creditors are entitled to prior participation in the individually owned assets of their respective debtors. When a partner is insolvent, the order of distribution of his assets is as follows: (1) debts and liabilities owing to nonpartnership creditors; (2) debts and liabilities owing to partnership creditors; and (3) contributions owing to other partners by reason of payments by them to partnership creditors in excess of their respective share of the liabilities of the firm. Section 40(i).

This rule, however, is *no longer* followed if the partnership is a debtor under the Bankruptcy Reform Act of 1978. In a proceeding under the Federal bankruptcy law, a trustee is appointed to administer the estate of the debtor. If the partnership property is insufficient to pay all the claims against the partnership, then the trustee is directed by the Act to seek recovery of the deficiency first from the general partners who are not bankrupt. Then, the trustee may seek recovery against the estates of bankrupt partners on the same basis as other creditors of the bankrupt partner. Bankruptcy Reform Act, Section 723. This provision, although contrary to the U.P.A.'s doctrine of marshaling of assets, governs whenever the assets of a partnership are being administered by a bankruptcy court.

CONTINUATION OF PARTNERSHIP AFTER DISSOLUTION

After a partnership has been dissolved one of two outcomes must ensue: either the partnership is liquidated or the remaining partners continue the partnership. However, when a partnership is liquidated after dissolution, the value of a going concern is sacrificed. On the other hand, continuation of the partnership after dissolution avoids this loss. The U.P.A., nonetheless, gives each partner the right to have the partnership liquidated except in a limited number of instances where the partners have the right to continue the partnership. Section 37.

Partners' Right to Continue Partnership

After dissolution the remaining partners have the right to continue the partnership (1) when the partnership has been dissolved in contravention of the partnership agreement, (2) when a partner has been expelled in accordance with the partnership agreement, or (3) when all the partners agree to continue the business.

Continuation after Wrongful Dissolution

Because of the personal element in a partnership, courts will not decree specific performance of a partnership agreement. However, a partner who wrongfully withdraws cannot force the liquidation of the firm. The aggrieved partners have the option of either liquidating the firm and recovering damages for the breach of the partnership agreement or continuing the partnership by buying out the withdrawing partner. The withdrawing partner is entitled to realize his interest in the partnership less the amount of the damages which the other partners have sustained as the result of his breach. However, his interest is computed without reference to the good will of the business. In addition, the remaining partners are entitled, if they so desire, to use the capital contributions of the wrongdoing partner for the unexpired period of the partnership agreement. They must, however, indemnify the former partner against all present and future partnership liabilities. Section 38(2).

Continuation after Expulsion

A partner expelled pursuant to the partnership agreement also cannot force the liquidation of the partnership. He is only entitled to be discharged from all partnership liabilities by either payment or a novation with the creditors and to receive in cash the net amount due him from the partnership. Section 38(1).

Continuation per Agreement of the Parties

By far the best and most reliable way of assuring the preservation of a partnership business after dissolution is a continuation agreement. Professor Bromberg clearly explains the reasons for this:

Without an agreement, the alternatives at dissolution may be bleak. If the business is liquidated, there is typically a sacrifice of economic values in a going concern, not to mention the livelihood of the other partners. Recognizing this, an outgoing partner may demand an exorbitant price to forego his liquidation right. If the business is continued too long after dissolution pending negotiations for an agreement, the continuing partners are at the mercy of the outgoing interest's election to be paid its full value at dissolution, plus either profits or interest on that amount until final settlement. On the other hand, if the outgoing partner is ill or dead, it is in practice all too easy for the other partners to take advantage of the situation. Bromberg, *Crane and Bromberg on Partnership*, Section 90A, p. 509.

Continuation agreements are frequently used to insure continuity in the event of death or retirement of one of the partners. A continuation agreement permits the remaining partners to keep the partnership property and carry on its business while providing a specified settlement with the outgoing partners. Otherwise, when a partner dies or retires and the business is continued by the surviving partners, the retired partner or legal representative of the deceased partner is entitled to be paid the value of his interest as of the date of the dissolution as an ordinary creditor of the partnership. In addition, he is entitled to receive interest on this amount or, at his option, in lieu of interest, the profits of the business attributable to the use of his right in the property of the dissolved partnership. His rights, however, are subordinate to those of creditors of the dissolved partnership. Section 42.

See *McClennen v. Commissioner of Internal Revenue.*

Rights of Creditors

Whenever a partnership undergoes any change in membership, it is dissolved, and a new partnership is formed even though a majority of the old partners are present in the new combination. This is true whether the change consists in dropping one or more members, adding one or more members, or both. The creditors of the old partnership have claims against the new partnership and may also proceed to hold personally liable all of the members of the dissolved partnership. Section 41. If a withdrawing partner has made arrangements with those who continue the business whereby they assume and pay all debts and obligations of the firm, the withdrawing partner is, nevertheless, liable to creditors whose claims arose prior to the dissolution. Upon being compelled to pay such debts, she immediately has a right of indemnity against her former partners who had agreed to pay the debts but failed to do so.

A withdrawing partner may protect herself against liability upon contracts which were entered into by the firm subsequent to her withdrawal by giving notice that she is no longer a member of the firm. Otherwise, she is liable for debts thus incurred to a creditor who had no notice or knowledge of the partner's having withdrawn from the firm. Actual notice is required to be given to the persons with whom the partnership regularly does business, while notice by newspaper publication will be sufficient for the general business community. Section 35.

Figure 31-1 summarizes dissolution and its causes and effects.

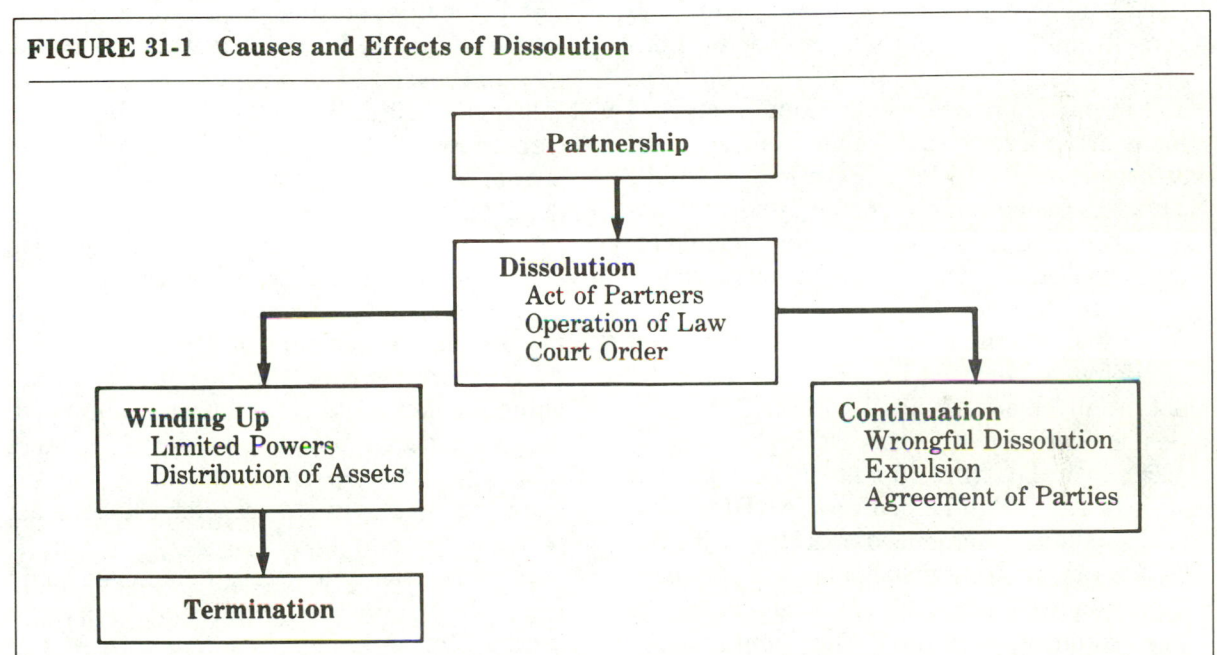

FIGURE 31-1 Causes and Effects of Dissolution

CASES

Dissolution by Act of the Partners

BOX v. CROWTHER

Court of Appeals of Washington, Division Two, 1970.
3 Wash.App. 67, 473 P.2d 417.

PEARSON, J.
Action was instituted by plaintiffs against defendants for the purpose of recovering damages and for an accounting. The parties had formed two business associations in the fall of 1967. Their relationship commenced disintegrating by late January, 1968, and this action was commenced in April, 1968.

* * *

The cause was tried to the court, sitting with a jury, and resulted in a verdict favorable to the plaintiffs in the total sum of $10,500, with interest at 6 per cent per annum. Plaintiffs were awarded $4,500 for loss of net profits to the partnership and $6,000 for loss of net profits to the corporation. * * *

Defendants are appealing from the damage judgment rendered against them. * * *

Prior to September 15, 1967, both Box and Crowther were engaged separately in the air freight business. Box's operation, Kitsap Delivery, Inc. (KDI) was strictly a trucking operation, carrying air freight between Sea-Tac Airport and the Kitsap Peninsula. Crowther, on the other hand, was engaged in an air operation, Bremerton Air Taxi, Inc. (BAT) involving carriage of passengers and some freight between the same points. Both were seeking to expand their freight business and in particular were separately interested in securing a large air freight contract with an organization entitled Air Cargo, Inc. (ACI). This was a corporation created by several major airlines to arrange local pickup and delivery services of freight from various airports to points of destination.

Realizing the need for both trucking and air delivery services in order to obtain the potentially lucrative ACI contract, the parties decided to join forces. On September 15, 1967, an oral partnership under the name and style of Air Cargo Expediters (ACE) was established and commenced operating with the ACI contract as its principal asset. This contract required the carriage of air freight at fixed rates between the Kitsap Peninsula and ACI's Sea-Tac Airport facilities.

All seemed to be going well with performances of the ACI contract and Box and Crowther decided to incorporate. Both parties agreed that they would put all their non-ACI contract freight business into the "pot" (the corporate income), along with the income from such contract.

When the corporation, Air Cargo Expediters, Inc., was formed on November 4, 1967, it is clear that both parties intended the corporation to succeed the partnership. There were three directors of the corporation, namely the defendant, Robert L. Crowther, and the plaintiffs, Harold L. and Jane L. Box, husband and wife. Crowther was elected president.

The testimony is somewhat confusing as to the extent of the corporate participation in the venture. The ACI contract was not formally transferred to the corporation, and there was a provision in that contract which would have prohibited such assignment without the consent of ACI. It seems clear, however, that the corporation did function for a short period of time, and the parties did contribute income from their operations into the corporate "pot" along with revenues from the ACI contract.

Difficulties soon began to overwhelm the corporation, and for all intents and purposes, the men ceased to do business together after February, 1968. Crowther considered the corporation had terminated after he was voted out of the presidency by the Boxes on January 29, 1968.

The parties themselves were confused over their technical business relationship. Box at one point in testimony refers to Crowther as "one of the partners of the corporation." ACI never regarded the corporation as existing insofar as its contract was concerned. ACI considered that it was doing business with a partnership and received no request from the "partners" to transfer the contract to the corporation.

There was undisputed evidence that in April, 1968 Crowther negotiated a separate contract for air freight handling with ACI at reduced rates and in direct competition with the partnership or the corporation. He did this on behalf of his own corporation, the defendant, Bremerton Air Taxi, Inc. In April, 1968 and thereafter the latter corporation also commenced serving some independent air freight forwarders who had given a substantial volume of business to plaintiff's corporation, Kitsap Delivery, Inc., prior to September 15, 1967.

* * *

Summarizing these instructions, the jury was, in effect, told that both a partnership and a corporation existed, and that either or both were entitled to recover for net profits lost as a direct result of any wrongful acts of the defendants. At the close of the plaintiff's evidence, the trial court decided that as a matter of law a partnership existed between September 15, 1967 and September 15, 1968. This ruling was based on the testimony of both Box and Crowther that they believed the partnership continued to exist after the formation of the corporation.

* * *

Depending on the circumstances of the case and the intention of the parties, when members of a partnership organize a corporation to succeed it and to carry on the business of the partnership, the partnership may cease to exist. [Citations.] However, incorporation without further action to transfer some or all the partnership assets and business to the corporation will not terminate the existence of the preceding partnership. [Citation.] The two organizations remain distinct entities and the rights and liabilities of the one are not the same as those of the other. [Citation.] There is no evidence in this case of a transfer of partnership assets other than certain income to the corporation. We think that the trial court correctly ruled as a matter of law that the partnership continued to exist during the year for which the original ACI contract was applicable.

* * *

In this case, exact damages were difficult to prove, due to the novelty of the ventures and the early disagreements which disrupted their operations. There was, however, substantial evidence upon which a jury could make an estimation of damages. The first problem the jury faced was to segregate damages between the partnership and the corporation, since the instructions and interrogatories indicated that either or both might recover. An apportionment could be made based on the evidence before the jury. The partnership had the rights to the ACI contract until September 15, 1968, the last day for which the jury might award damages. * * * There was testimony that the defendants entered into a contract with ACI in April of 1968 for the carrying of freight between Sea-Tac and Kitsap County. The jury could have awarded damages to the partnership by determining the amount of net profits earned by Crowther in the ACI contract up to September 15, 1968. These damages directly resulted from his obtaining that account from the partnership in breach of his fiduciary duty.

* * *

However, with reference to the partnership, the jury was not specifically instructed to allow plaintiffs, Box, damages only for their 50 per cent interest in the partnership, nor was a full partnership accounting submitted to the jury. The damages awarded for breach of Crowther's fiduciary duty to his partner must, therfore, be presumed to establish the loss of profits *to the partnership* as distinguished from the net loss to Box for his partnership interest. Our consideration of the exhibits offered in support of the damage award convince us that the jury, in fact, estimated the loss to the partnership and not to the individual partners, Box.

Since the judgment entered is crucial to the partnership accounting and corporate dissolution which must now take place, the judgment should be clarified by providing that the $4,500 verdict inures to the partnership and should be used to satisfy the obligations of that entity before distribution to the partners in accordance with their respective interests in the partnership. *See* RCW 25.04.380 [U.P.A. §38], which provides that a partner who has wrongfully caused a dissolution of the partnership continues to have his rights of a partner on dissolution after responding in damages for breach of the partnership agreement.

We think, also, that the accounting provision of the final judgment is too narrow and such order should have provided for a full accounting of the partnership assets and obligations and distribution of any remaining assets or liabilities to the partners in accordance with their interests in the partnership. RCW 25.04.380 [U.P.A. §38].

Judgment is affirmed as modified and remanded for completion of the partnership and corporate dissolutions, in a manner consistent with this opinion.

The Right to Wind Up

STARK v. UTICA SCREW PRODUCTS, INC.

City Court of Utica, 1980.
103 Misc.2d 163, 425 N.Y.S.2d 750.

HYMES, J.

Stark, Henning & Co. is a partnership formed by Karol Stark and Ronald Henning for the purpose of acting as sales representatives for various firms in upstate New York. Individually, they had been representing such businesses but because they resided in different parts of the state, they formed a partnership to limit the extent of their travel. The partnership was formed by oral agreement.

On June 19, 1975, the partnership entered into a contract with the defendant, Utica Screw Products, Inc., to act as its sales representative for all of New York State, excluding New York City and the area below Kingston.

Because Ronald Henning lived in the Buffalo area, he assumed responsibility for calling on the accounts in the western half of the state. Karol Stark, who lived in Oneida County, attended the accounts in the eastern half of the state. The contract was to remain in force for one year and continued thereafter unless terminated by either party upon written 60-day notice before its expiration date, or before each succeeding anniversary date. No notice of termination was given on its first anniversary date and the contract was continued into its second year of operation.

On October 21, 1976 Karol Stark and Ronald Henning met with Gerald Williams, president of the Utica Screw Products, Inc. There was a dispute between the partners concerning the accounting for commissions. As a result of this meeting, Stark sent a letter dated October 22, 1976, to Ronald Henning, terminating the partnership. In the letter,

Stark stated that each would return to his previous status as individual salesman for the companies that he had been representing. As to those companies with whom they had made agreements as a partnership, each would make a separate agreement. Utica Screw Products, Inc. was one of the accounts with whom they had made an agreement as a partnership.

A copy of this letter of dissolution of the partnership was sent to the president of the defendant corporation. * * *

The defendant corporation retained Ronald Henning as sales representative for another eleven months. However, it did not retain Stark. Plaintiff Stark now claims that there are commissions still due from the defendant to the partnership for orders that were received by the defendant corporation between February 10, 1976 and * * * October 20, 1976.

The defendant contends that plaintiff Stark has no standing in this action because he has not received authority from his co-partner to institute this action. This defense is without merit.

Upon dissolution of a partnership, any partner has the right to participate in the winding up of a partnership. He needs no authority from his co-partners. An unilateral letter of dissolution does not cut off the partnership relationship. On dissolution the partnership continues until the winding up of the partnership affairs is completed. [Citation.] The only way in which a partnership is wound up is through an accounting. [Citations.]

The duty imposed upon the partner who is engaged in winding up the partnership business is one of agency. [Citations.] The general agency of one partner . . . ceases, but each partner then has the equal duty and power to do whatever is necessary to collect the debts of the partnership. [Citations.]

After the dissolution of a partnership, a partner may bind the partnership by any appropriate action necessary to wind up the partnership affairs or to complete transactions unfinished at the time of dissolution. [Citation.] While a partner would not be entitled to remuneration for winding up the partnership affairs, he would be allowed reasonable expenses incurred in performing these services. [Citations.]

* * *

A partner cannot bar his co-partner from suing to collect debts due the partnership. Any judgment recovered by Stark would be for the benefit of the partnership and not for himself individually. It would then be up to the partners to wind up the partnership through an accounting.

* * *

The defendant [Utica] was incorrect in assuming that the dissolution of the partnership voided the contract with the plaintiff [Stark.] The dissolution of a partnership operates only with respect to future transactions. All past transactions and obligations of the partnership continue until all pre-existing matters are terminated. The partnership continues to be responsible for its obligations and debts, and third parties are responsible to the partnership for obligations which they owe said partnership.

* * *

Under the terms of the agreement, both written and oral, the plaintiff had performed all that was required of him. * * *

"Where the major consideration in the earning of commissions is procurement of orders for the defendant, the employee is entitled to commissions on the sales he obtained during the period of employment." [Citations.]

* * *

[Judgment for Stark on behalf of the partnership.]

Distribution of Assets

PETERSEN v. PETERSEN

Supreme Court of Minnesota, 1969.
284 Minn. 61, 169 N.W.2d 228.

GALLAGHER, J.

Appeal by defendant from a judgment in favor of plaintiff entered in the district court following a trial before the court without a jury.

This case arose out of a dispute between the estate of a deceased partner and the surviving partner over the distribution of the assets of the partnership following dissolution on the death of the deceased partner.

Donald Petersen returned home from the service in 1946 and in May of that year joined his father, William Petersen, in a chicken hatchery business. Prior to that time, William had operated the business as a sole proprietorship. When the partnership was formed, William contributed the assets of the proprietorship, which included cash, machinery, and equipment, inventory, and accounts receivable, having a total value of $41,000. Donald contributed nothing. From that time until Donald's death on October 2, 1964, the business continued to operate as a partnership. Donald in effect took over the operation of the hatchery, and William played a decreasing role in the business, simply helping out when called upon.

During the intervening years the taxes, upkeep, and improvements on the property contributed by William were paid out of partnership funds. The depreciation on the building and equipment was deducted on the partnership tax returns and the net income was split 50–50 between William and Donald. However, the property contributed by William remained in his name. William testified at trial that he had made a will in which he left all of the property used in the partnership to Donald.

* * *

Following Donald's death, William went to Maylon Muir, who had been the attorney for the hatchery and was probating the estate. He asked Muir to prepare a letter to be sent out by the hatchery in order to get the accounts receivable paid up and indicated that half of them belonged to Donald. William hired a girl to work with him in getting copies of this letter out. The letter stated that the law required that all accounts be paid in order to wind up the affairs of Donald's estate. Muir testified that after most of the collections had been made, William indicated that he was not going to give any of the assets to plaintiff as he needed the money to meet bills in connection with his wife's illness. As a result of this refusal, plaintiff brought the present action to compel a division of the partnership assets.

The total value of the partnership property at the time of Donald's death, as established by testimony or stipulation, was $18,572.89. William based his claim to the full amount on the theory that he was entitled to the return of his capital investment before Donald's estate could recover anything. Since he had contributed $41,000 in capital, this obviously included all the partnership assets. Plaintiff contended, and the trial court found, that the conduct of the parties established an agreement for an equal division of the total assets of the partnership without a prior return of capital to William. It is from the judgment entered on the basis of this finding that William appeals.

* * *

The law in Minnesota on the distribution of partnership property upon dissolution of the partnership is governed by [§ 40] of the Uniform Partnership Act, which establishes the following priority: (1) Payment of debts to creditors other than partners; (2) payment of debts to partners for other than capital contributions; (3) payment to partners for capital contributions; and (4) payment to partners of their share of the profit. It is established beyond question in this state, as elsewhere, that the capital contributed by a partner is a debt of the partnership which must be paid after the outside creditors but before there is any division of the profits. [Citations.] However, the above-cited authorities, including § [40], make it equally clear that the right of a partner to receive back the capital he contributed is subject to a contrary agreement among the partners. Before setting out the rules for distribution of assets, § [40] provides:

In settling accounts between the partners after dissolution, the following rules shall be observed, *subject to any agreement to the contrary* * * *. (Italics supplied.)

It is also clear from past cases that a contrary agreement of the type referred to above need not be in writing. Where it is not written it is in effect an implied-in-fact contract and may be established in the same manner as any other such contract. [Citation.]

* * *

While the deceased did not contribute any capital to the business, for all but the very early years of the partnership, he operated it with very little help from his father. Although contributing nothing more than occasional assistance during this period, William continued to receive half of the income. The conduct of the parties makes it entirely reasonable to infer that William put up the capital and Donald provided the labor under an agreement by which each was to own half of the business, including both capital and profits.

Affirmed.

Continuation per Agreement of the Parties

McCLENNEN v. COMMISSIONER OF INTERNAL REVENUE

United States Court of Appeals, First Circuit, 1943.
131 F.2d 165.

MAGRUDER, J.

[George Nutter was a partner in the law firm of Nutter, McClennen & Fish. The partnership agreement provided that he was entitled to receive 8 percent of the firm's net profits and that on his death or retirement payments in the same percentage of net profits would continue to be made to Nutter or his estate for a period of eighteen months. The agreement expressly stated that the payments would be in full satisfaction of the deceased or retiring partner's interest in the capital, the assets, the receivables, and the good will of the firm.

When Nutter died in 1937, his partners continued the business and made the required payments totaling $34,070 to Nutter's estate, but the Federal estate tax return filed for the estate did not include an amount representing the value of Nutter's interest in the partnership. As a result the Commissioner of Internal Revenue filed this notice of deficiency for taxes due on $34,070, the value of Nutter's partnership interest.]

* * *

In his notice of deficiency the Commissioner determined that $34,069.99 should have been included in the gross estate as the value of decedent's "interest in partnership Nutter, McClennen & Fish." The Board has upheld the Commissioner in this determination. We think the Board was right.

In the absence of a controlling agreement in the partnership articles the death of a partner dissolves the partnership. The survivors have the right and duty, with reasonable dispatch, to wind up the partnership affairs, to complete transactions begun but not then finished, to collect the accounts receivable, to pay the firm debts, to convert the remaining firm assets into cash, and to pay in cash to the partners and the legal representative of the deceased partner the net amounts shown by the accounts to be owing to each of them in respect of capital contributions and in respect of their shares of profits and surplus. The representative of a deceased partner does not succeed to any right to specific partnership property. In substance the deceased partner's interest, to which his representative succeeds, is a chose in action, a right to receive in cash the sum of money shown to be due him upon a liquidation and accounting. These substantive results may be rationalized upon a theory of the partnership "entity." [Citation.] The same substantive results are reached under the Uniform Partnership Act which, in form at least, proceeds on the aggregate theory. [Citation.] That act, which is law in Massachusetts, conceives of the partner as a "co-owner with his partners of specific partnership property holding as a tenant in partnership;" but provides that on the death of a partner "his right in specific partnership

property vests in the surviving partner or partners." Another enumerated property right of a partner, "his interest in the partnership," is described as "his share of the profits and surplus, and the same is personal property," regardless of whether the firm holds real estate or personalty or both. [Citations.] * * *

In the case at bar, if there had not been the controlling provision in the partnership articles, above quoted, or if the survivors had not come to some agreement otherwise with the executors of Mr. Nutter, the survivors would have had to proceed to wind up the affairs of the partnership, to conclude all unfinished legal business on hand at the date of the death, or realize upon all of the assets of the firm, tangible or intangible, to pay the debts, to return to Mr. Nutter's estate his contribution of capital, if any, and to pay to his estate in cash the amount shown to be due in respect of his "interest in the partnership," that is, his "share of the profits and surplus", as determined upon an accounting. Among other things to be taken into account, "the earned proportion of the unfinished business" would have had "to be valued to determine the decedent's interest in the partnership assets." [Citations.]

To obviate the necessity of a liquidation, or to eliminate accounting difficulties in determining the value of the deceased partner's interest, partners often make specific provision in the partnership articles.

* * *

In the case at bar the partnership agreement contains another familiar arrangement, whereby no liquidation and final accounting will ever be necessary in order to satisfy the claim of the deceased partner. In place of the chose in action to which Mr. Nutter's executor would have succeeded in the absence of specific provision in the partnership articles, that is, a right to receive payment in cash of the amount shown to be due the deceased partner upon a complete liquidation and accounting, a different right is substituted, a right of the estate to receive a share of the net profits of the firm for 18 calendar months after the partner's death.

The language of the partnership agreement in the present case is couched in terms of a purchase of the deceased partner's interest. What the estate is to receive "shall be in full of the retiring or deceasing member's interest in the capital, the assets, the receivables, the possibilities and the good will of the Firm." There is to be an extinguishment of the decedent's interest in the totality of the firm assets, tangible and intangible, as they stood at the moment of death, and the interests therein of the surviving partners are to be correspondingly augmented. Decision in the estate tax case now before us does not turn on the question whether the effect of the partnership agreement may be characterized with entire accuracy as a "purchase" and "sale" of the deceased partner's interest in the partnership.

[Judgment in favor of the Commissioner is affirmed.]

PROBLEMS

1. Simmons, Hoffman, and Murray were partners doing business under the firm name of Simmons & Co. The firm borrowed money from a bank and gave the bank the firm's note for the loan. In addition, each partner guaranteed the note individually. The firm became insolvent, and a receiver was appointed. The bank claims that it has a right to file its claim as a firm debt and also that it has a right to participate in the distribution of the assets of the individual partners before partnership creditors receive any payment from such assets.

    (a) Explain the principle involved in this case.

    (b) Is the bank correct?

2. A, B, and C form a partnership, A contributing $10,000; B, $5,000; and C his time and skill. Nothing was said as to the division of profits. The firm becomes insolvent, and after payment of all firm debts $6,000 is left. A claims that she is entitled to the entire $6,000. B contends that the distribution should be $4,000 to A and $2,000 to B. C claims the $6,000 should be divided equally among the partners. Who is correct? Explain.

3. Martin, Mark, and Marvin formed a retail clothing partnership by the name of "M" Clothiers and conducted a business for many years, buying most of their clothing from Hill, a wholesaler. On January 15 Marvin retired from the business, but Martin and Mark decided to continue it. As part of the retirement agreement, Martin and Mark agreed in writing with Marvin that Marvin would not be responsible for any of the partnership debts, either past or future. A news item concerning Marvin's retirement appeared in the local newspaper on January 15.

Prior to January 15, Hill was a creditor of "M" Clothiers to the extent of $10,000 and, on January 30, extended additional credit of $5,000. Hill was not advised and did not, in fact, know of Marvin's retirement and the change of the partnership. On January 30, Ray, a competitor of Hill, extended credit for the first time to "M" Clothiers in the amount of $3,000.

On February 1, Martin and Mark left for parts unknown and left no partnership assets with which to pay the described debts. What is Marvin's liability, if any, (a) to Hill, and (b) to Ray?

4. A, B, and C were partners sharing profits in proportions of one-fourth, one-third, and five-twelfths, respectively. Their business failed, and the firm was dissolved. At the time of dissolution no financial adjustments between the partners were necessary with reference to their respective capital contributions, but the firm's liabilities to creditors exceed its assets by $24,000. Without contributing any amount toward the payment of the liabilities, B has moved to a destination unknown. A and C are financially responsible. How much must each contribute?

5. Indicate which of the following statements are true and which are false:

    (a) Creditors having claims based upon torts committed by partners in the course of business of the partnership are preferred over creditors with claims based upon contracts.

    (b) Partners who wish to continue the business have a prior right to purchase the assets.

    (c) In the absence of a contract providing otherwise, the distribution to partners of accrued profits should be in equal parts regardless of the fact that the partners had contributed to the firm unequally.

(d) Advances in the nature of loans made by the various partners to the partnership share in the firm assets on the same basis as debts due other creditors.

(e) As between the partners, the assets of the partnership must be applied to pay the claims of partners in respect of capital ahead of the claims of partners in respect to profits.

(f) Debts owing to partners (other than for the capital and profits) rank ahead of debts owing to partners in respect to capital and profits.

6. Ames, Bell, and Cole were equal partners in the ABC Construction Company. They had no formal or written partnership agreement. Cole died on June 30, 1984, and his widow, Cora Cole, qualified as executor of his will.

Ames and Bell continued the business of the partnership until December 31, 1984, when they sold all of the assets of the partnership. After paying all partnership debts, they distributed the balance equally among themselves and Mrs. Cole as executor.

Subsequently, Mrs. Cole learned that Ames and Bell had made and withdrawn a net profit of $20,000 during the period July 1 to December 31, 1984. The profit was made through new contracts using the partnership name and assets. Ames and Bell had concealed from Mrs. Cole the fact of such contracts and profit, and she learned about it from other sources. Immediately upon acquiring this information, Mrs. Cole made demand upon Ames and Bell for one-third of the profit of $20,000. They rejected her demand.

What are the rights and remedies, if any, of Cora Cole as executor?

7. A and B were partners in Miami. C, a traveling salesman for D, called on them and on January 14 received from them an order for merchandise. The order was forwarded by C to D in New York on January 15; the partnership of A and B was dissolved by agreement between the partners on January 18. On January 19, D, without knowledge of the dissolution, acknowledged receipt of the order, accepted it, and shipped the goods the next day. B received them on January 23. On January 25, notice of dissolution of the partnership of A and B was duly published. D sues A and B for the purchase price of the merchandise sold. Decision?

8. The articles of partnership of the firm of Wilson and Company provide:

William Smith to contribute $50,000; to receive interest thereon at 13 percent per annum and to devote such time as he may be able to give; to receive 30 percent of the profits.

John Jones to contribute $50,000; to receive interest on same at 13 percent per annum; to give all of his time to the business and to receive 30 percent of the profits.

Henry Wilson to contribute all of his time to the business and to receive 20 percent of the profits.

James Brown to contribute all of his time to the business and to receive 20 percent of the profits.

There is no provision for sharing losses. After six years of operations, the firm has assets of $400,000 and liabilities to creditors of $420,000. Upon dissolution and winding up, what are the rights and liabilities of the respective parties?

9. Harold Fuller, Mary Warner, and Tom Clardy were co-partners in the operation of a cattle raising partnership. Fuller and Clardy were both killed as the result of a common disaster. Mary Warner took charge of the partnership business and spent considerable time and effort in winding up the partnership business. In a suit brought for an accounting, Mary Warner made a claim for a reasonable allowance for services rendered in winding up the affairs of the partnership. The partnership agreement contained no provision for payment for services rendered in connection with the winding up of partnership affairs. What decision?

Chapter 32

LIMITED PARTNERSHIPS

T HIS chapter will consider limited partnerships and other types of unincorporated business associations including joint ventures and business trusts. These forms of organizations have developed to meet special business and investment needs. Each has its own set of characteristics that make it most appropriate for certain purposes.

LIMITED PARTNERSHIPS

The limited partnership has proved itself to be an attractive vehicle for a variety of investments as a result of its tax advantages and the limited liability it confers upon the limited partners. Prior to 1976 the governing statute in all States except Louisiana was the Uniform Limited Partnership Act (U.L.P.A.), which was promulgated in 1916. At that time the typical limited partnership was decidedly small scale with a mere handful of limited partners. Today it has been replaced by a much larger organization typically involving a small number of major investors and a relatively large group of widely distributed investors who purchase limited partnership interests. This type of limited partnership has evolved to attract substantial amounts of investment capital. However, the large scale and multistate operations of the modern limited partnership have severely burdened the framework established by the Uniform Limited Partnership Act. These shortcomings prompted the National Conference of Commissioners on Uniform State Laws to develop a Revised Uniform Limited Partnership Act (R.U.L.P.A.), which was promulgated in 1976. According to its preface, the R.U.L.P.A. is "intended to modernize the prior uniform law while retaining the special character of limited partnerships as compared with corporations." Both the U.L.P.A. and R.U.L.P.A. are supplemented by the U.P.A. which applies to limited partnership except to the extent it is inconsistent with either Act. U.P.A. Section 6(2). For a concise comparison of general and limited partnerships, see Figure 33-1 in Chapter 33.

In addition, limited partnership interests are considered to be securities, and their sale is subject to State and Federal regulation as discussed in Chapter 44.

Definition

A limited partnership is one composed of one or more general partners and one or more limited partners. It differs from a general partnership in several respects, three of which are basic:

1. there must be a statute in effect providing for the formation of limited partnerships;
2. the limited partnership must fully comply with the requirements of such statute; and
3. the **liability** of a *limited* partner for partnership debts or obligations is **limited** to the extent of the capital which he has contributed or agreed to contribute.

Formation

While the formation of a *general* partnership may be accomplished without formality, the formation of a *limited* partnership requires substantial compliance with the U.L.P.A. or R.U.L.P.A. Failure to do so may result in the limited partners' loss of limited liability.

Filing of Certificate The U.L.P.A. provides that two or more persons desiring to form a limited partnership shall sign and swear to a certificate, which shall contain the name of the partnership; the character of the business; the location of the principal place of business; the name and place of residence of each general and limited partner; the term for which the partnership is to exist; the

amount of cash and any other property contributed by each limited partner; the additional contributions, if any, agreed to be made by each limited partner and the times at which or events on the happening of which they shall be made; the time, if agreed upon, when the contribution of each limited partner is to be returned; and the share of the profits or the other compensation by way of income which each limited partner is entitled to receive. Section 2.

The certificate must be filed in the office of a designated public official, usually in the county in which the principal office of the limited partnership is located. In some States there is the further requirement that a copy of the certificate shall also be filed with the Secretary of State. Under the R.U.L.P.A., the certificate need only be filed in the office of the Secretary of State of the State in which the limited partnership has its principal office. Section 201.

Figure 32-1 shows a sample certificate.

Name The inclusion of the surname of a limited partner in the partnership name is prohibited unless it is also the surname of a general partner or the business had been carried on under that name before the admission of that limited partner. A violation of this provision renders the limited partner liable as a general partner to any creditor who did not know that he was a limited partner. The R.U.L.P.A. further prohibits a name that is deceptively similar to any corporation or other limited partnership. Section 102. In addition, the name of the limited partnership must contain without abbreviation the words "limited partnership."

Contributions Under the U.L.P.A. the contribution of a limited partner may be cash or other property but *not* services. Section 4. The R.U.L.P.A., on the other hand, explicitly authorizes the contribution of a partner to be in cash, property, or services rendered or a promissory note or other obligation to contribute cash or property or to perform ser-

FIGURE 32-1 Sample Limited Partnership Certificate

CERTIFICATE OF LIMITED PARTNERSHIP

The undersigned, desiring to form a Limited Partnership under the Uniform Limited Partnership Act of the State of _____ , make this certificate for that purpose.

§ 1. **Name.** The name of the Partnership shall be " _____ _____ " .

§ 2. **Purpose.** The purpose of the Partnership shall be to [*describe*].

§ 3. **Location.** The location of the Partnership's principal place of business is _____ County, _____ .

§ 4. **Members and Designation.** The names and places of residence of the members, and their designation as General or Limited Partners are:

_____	[*Address*]	General Partner
_____	[*Address*]	General Partner
_____	[*Address*]	Limited Partner
_____	[*Address*]	Limited Partner

§ 5. **Term.** The term for which the Partnership is to exist is indefinite.

§ 6. **Initial Contributions of Limited Partners.** The amount of cash and a description of the agreed value of the other property contributed by each Limited Partner are:

[*Name*]	[*Describe*]
[*Name*]	[*Describe*]

§ 7. **Subsequent Contributions of Limited Partners.** Each Limited Partner may (but shall not be obliged to) make such additional contributions to the capital of the Partnership as may from time to time be agreed upon by the General Partners.

§ 8. **Profit Shares of Limited Partners.** The share of the profits which each Limited Partner shall receive by reason of his contribution is:

[*Name*]	_____ %
[*Name*]	_____ %

Signed _____ , 19 _____

_____

_____

_____

Signed and sworn before me, the undersigned authority, this _____ _____ , 19 _____ .
Notary Public

_____ County _____

SOURCE: Reprinted with permission from Edmund O. Belsheim's "Modern Legal Forms." Copyright © 1971 by West Publishing Co.

vices. Section 501. A limited partner is liable to the partnership for the difference between her contribution as actually made and that stated in the certificate as having been made.

Defective Formation The U.L.P.A. states that a person who has contributed to the capital of a business (an "equity participant"), erroneously believing that he has become a limited partner in a limited partnership, is not liable as a general partner provided that on ascertaining the mistake he promptly renounces his interest in the profits of the business. Section 11. For example, in *Vidricksen v. Grover*, 363 F.2d 372 (9th Cir. 1966), Dr. Vidricksen contributed $25,000 to become a limited partner in a Chevrolet car agency business with Thom, the general partner. Articles of limited partnership were drawn up, but no effort was made to comply with the State's statutory requirement of recording the certificate of limited partnership. In March 1961, Vidricksen learned that he may not have the status of a limited partner because of the failure to file. At this time the business developed financial difficulties and went into bankruptcy on September 11, 1961. Eight days later Vidricksen filed a renunciation of the business's profits. The trustee in bankruptcy sought to have Dr. Vidricksen adjudged a general partner for bankruptcy purposes. Judgment for the trustee in bankruptcy. Vidricksen was a general partner with Thom in so far as their relationship with third party creditors is concerned. A person who has contributed to the capital of a business erroneously believing that he has become a limited partner will not be considered a general partner if, upon ascertainment of the mistake, he promptly renounces his interst in the business's profits. Although Vidricksen had filed a renunciation, his renunciation was not prompt because it was filed six months after he first learned that something was wrong with the organizational setup.

It is unclear whether the profits that must be renounced include past, current, or future profits. The R.U.L.P.A. clarifies this ambi-guity by requiring the equity participant to either withdraw from the business and re-nounce *future* profits or to file an amendment curing the defect. Section 304. In any event, the R.U.L.P.A. provides that the equity participant will be liable to any third party who transacted business with the enterprise before the withdrawal or amendment and in good faith believed that the equity participant was a general partner at the time of the transaction.

Foreign Limited Partnerships A limited partnership is considered "foreign" in any State in which it has not been formed. The U.L.P.A. does not address the fundamental issue of whether a limited partnership must qualify in foreign States in order to be recognized as a limited partnership and to maintain the limited liability of its limited partners. As a result many limited partnerships with multi-state operations must form new partnerships in each State of operation.

The R.U.L.P.A. clearly establishes that the laws of the State under which a foreign limited partnership is organized govern its organization, its internal affairs, and the lia-bililty of its limited partners. Section 901. At the same time it requires all foreign limited partnerships to register with the Secretary of State before transacting any business in the State. Section 902. Any foreign limited partnership transacting business without so registering may not bring enforcement actions in the State's courts until it registers, although it may defend itself in the State's courts. Section 907.

Rights

Since limited partnerships are organized pursuant to statute, the rights of the parties usually are set forth with relative clarity in the articles of limited partnership. In addition, a general partner of a limited partnership has all the rights and powers of a partner in a partnership without limited partners.

Control The general partners of a limited partnership are vested with almost exclusive control and management over the limited partnership. A limited partner, on the other hand, cannot share in the management or control of the association; if he does so, he forfeits his limited liability. U.L.P.A. Section 7. However, the U.L.P.A. does not define what constitutes "taking part in control." In the landmark case of *Holzman v. De Escamilla*, 86 Cal.App.2d 858, 195 P.2d 833 (1948), the following was held to be taking part in control: Early in 1943, Hacienda Farms, Limited, was organized as a limited partnership with de Escamilla as the general partner and Russell and Andrews as limited partners. De Escamilla was raising beans on farm lands near Escondido at the time the partnership was formed. The limited partnership continued raising vegetable and truck crops which were marketed principally through a produce concern controlled by Andrews. The two limited partners visited the farm about twice a week and were active in dictating the crops to be planted, in some instances against the wishes of the general partner. The bank accounts of Hacienda Farms, Limited were set up such that checks could be drawn upon the signatures of any two of the three partners. Money had been withdrawn on twenty checks signed by the limited partners, Russell and Andrews. In October, 1943, the limited partners requested that de Escamilla resign as manager, and they selected his successor.

See also Weil v. Diversified Properties, Inc.

Section 303 of the R.U.L.P.A. specifies a number of activities in which a limited partner may engage without losing limited liability:

1. being a contractor for, an agent or employee of the limited partnership or of a general partner;
2. consulting with and advising a general partner with respect to the business of the limited partnership;
3. acting as surety for the limited partnership;
4. approving or disapproving an amendment to the partnership agreement; and
5. voting on one or more of the following matters:

   a. the dissolution and winding up of the partnership;
   b. the sale, exchange, lease, mortgage, pledge, or other transfer of all or substantially all of the assets of the limited partnership other than in the ordinary course of its business;
   c. the incurrence of indebtedness by the limited partnership other than in the ordinary course of its business;
   d. a change in the nature of the business; or
   e. the removal of a general partner.

More significantly, the R.U.L.P.A. restricts the liability of a limited partner, whose participation is not substantially the same as the exercise of the powers of a general partner, to persons who transact business with the limited partnership with actual knowledge of his participation in control. Section 303(a).

Choice of Associates No person may be added as a general partner or a limited partner without the consent of **all** partners. After the formation of a limited partnership the admission of additional limited partners requires the written consent of all partners unless the partnership agreement provides otherwise. U.L.P.A., Sections 8 and 9; R.U.L.P.A. Section 301. The admission of the new limited partner is effective only upon the amendment of the certificate of limited partnership reflecting that fact. After the formation of a limited partnership new general partners may be admitted *only* with the specific written consent of each partner. U.L.P.A., Section 9(1)(e); R.U.L.P.A., Section 401.

Assignment of Interest A limited partner may assign her interest. If she does so, the assignee may become a substituted limited partner if all the other partners consent, or if the assigning partner, having such power provided in the certificate, grants the assignee this right. Upon the death of a limited partner, her executor or administrator has all the rights of such partner for the purpose of settling her estate, and such power as the deceased partner had to constitute her assignee a substituted limited partner.

Profit Sharing Unless otherwise agreed, a limited partner is entitled to his share of the profits as stipulated in the certificate before the general partners receive their share of the profits. A limited partner does not share in the losses of the partnership beyond his capital contribution.

Under the R.U.L.P.A., the profits and losses are allocated among the partners as provided in the partnership agreement. If the partnership agreement does not make such a provision, then the profits and losses are allocated on the basis of the value of contributions actually made by each partner. Section 503. Nonetheless, limited partners are not liable for losses beyond their capital contribution.

Return of Contribution A limited partner may rightfully demand the return of his contribution upon dissolution of the limited partnership, upon the date specified in the certificate for its return, or upon six-months' written demand if no time is specified in the certificate for the return of the contribution or for dissolution. In all cases, a limited partner may not receive his capital contribution unless there are sufficient partnership assets to pay all liabilities owed to third party creditors and limited partners, other than their capital contributions. U.L.P.A. Section 16 and R.U.L.P.A. Section 607. *See Kramer v. McDonald's System, Inc.*

Loans Under the U.L.P.A. limited partners may make unsecured loans to the partnership

and are entitled to repayment of the loan on a *pro rata* basis with creditors of the partnership. The U.L.P.A., however, prohibits limited partners from receiving or holding any partnership property as security for a loan made to the partnership. Section 13. General partners also may make unsecured loans to the partnership but are subordinated to all claims of limited partners and outside creditors. Section 23.

Under the R.U.L.P.A. both general and limited partners may be secured or unsecured creditors of the partnership with the same rights as a person who is not a partner, subject to applicable State and Federal bankruptcy and fraudulent conveyance statutes. Section 107.

Information The U.L.P.A., Section 10 provides that:

(1) A limited partner shall have the same rights as a general partner to
(a) Have the partnership books kept at the principal place of business of the partnership, and at all times to inspect and copy any of them
(b) Have on demand true and full information of all things affecting the partnership, and a formal account of partnership affairs whenever circumstances render it just and reasonable, * * *

The R.U.L.P.A. has a similar provision which also specifically grants a limited partner the right to obtain a copy of the limited partnership's Federal, State, and local income tax returns for each year. Section 305.

Duties and Liabilities

The duties and liabilities of general partners in a limited partnership are quite different from those of a limited partner. A general partner is subject to all the duties and restrictions of a partner in a partnership without limited partners, while a limited partner is subject to few, if any, duties and enjoys limited liability.

Duties A *general partner* of a limited partnership occupies a **fiduciary** relation with respect to her limited partners. This fiduciary duty imposed upon the general partner has extreme importance to the limited partners due to the circumscribed role that a limited partner may play in the control and management of the business enterprise. *See Riviera Congress Associates v. Yassky*. Conversely, it remains unclear whether a limited partner stands in a fiduciary relation to his general partners or the limited partnership. Very limited judicial authority on this question exists, but it seems to point towards not placing such a duty on the limited partner.

As with fiduciary duty, the law does not distinguish between the duty of care owed by a general partner to a general partnership and that owed by a general partner to a limited partnership. This results in part from the U.P.A. which provides that the act will apply to limited partnerships except insofar as it is inconsistent with the statutes relating to such partnerships. Section 6(2). On the other hand, a limited partner owes no duty of care to a limited partnership as long as she remains a limited partner.

Liabilities One of the most appealing features of a limited partnership is the **limited personal liability** it offers to limited partners. Limited liability means that once a limited partner has paid her contribution she has no further liability to the limited partnership nor its creditors. Thus, if a limited partner buys a 25 percent share of a limited partnership for $50,000 and does not forfeit her limited liability, her liability is limited to the $50,000 contributed even if the limited partnership suffers losses of $500,000. However, this protection is subject to three conditions:

1. that there is substantial compliance in good faith with the requirement that a certificate of limited partnership be filed;
2. that the surname of the limited partner does not appear in the partnership name; and

3. that the limited partner does not take part in control of the business.

In addition, if the certificate contains a false statement, any one who suffers loss by reliance on such statement may hold liable any party to the certificate who knew the statement to be false. U.L.P.A. Section 6 and R.U.L.P.A. Section 207. As long as the limited partner abides by these conditions, his liability for any and all obligations of the partnership is limited to his capital contribution. At the same time, the general partners of a limited partnership have unlimited external liability.

Dissolution

As with a general partnership there are three steps involved in the extinguishment of a limited partnership: (1) dissolution, (2) winding up or liquidation, and (3) termination. The causes of dissolution and the priorities in the distribution of the assets, however, are somewhat different than in a general partnership.

Causes In a limited partnership the limited partners do *not* have the right nor the power to dissolve the partnership, except by decree of the court. The death or bankruptcy of a limited partner does not dissolve the partnership. However, the retirement, death, or insanity of a general partner dissolves the partnership unless the business is continued by the remaining general partners under a right to do so stated in the certificate or with the consent of all members. In addition, the U.L.P.A. grants a limited partner the right to have the partnership dissolved and its affairs wound up whenever he rightfully but unsuccessfully demands the return of his contribution. Section 16(4). This rather drastic remedy has been eliminated by the R.U.L.P.A. which specifies more precisely those events that will trigger a dissolution, after which the affairs of the partnership must be liquidated. Section 801. These events are:

1. at the time, or upon the happening of the events, specified in the certificate;
2. upon the unanimous written consent of all the partners;
3. the withdrawal of a general partner unless all partners agree to continue the business; or
4. a decree of judicial dissolution which may be granted whenever it is not reasonably practicable to carry on the business in conformity with the partnership agreement.

Distribution of Assets The priorities in distributing the assets of a limited partnership are set forth in Section 23 of the U.L.P.A.:

1. To creditors, in the order of priority as provided by law, except those to limited partners on account of their contributions, and to general partners;
2. To limited partners in respect to their share of the profits and other compensation by way of income on their contributions;
3. To limited partners in respect to the capital of their contributions;
4. To general partners other than for capital and profits;
5. To general partners in respect to profits;
6. To general partners in respect to capital.

A limited partner shares *pro rata* with general creditors with respect to advances beyond her capital contribution. Section 13. Where there are several limited partners the members may agree that one or more of the limited partners shall have a priority over other limited partners as to the return of their contributions, as to their compensation by way of income, or as to any other matter. If such an agreement is made it shall be stated in the certificate, and in the absence of such a statement all the limited partners shall stand upon equal footing. Section 14.

The U.L.P.A.'s provisions for dissolution and liquidation are unclear, incomplete, and contrary to the normal expectations of partners. The R.U.L.P.A. not only remedies these deficiencies but also introduces greater flexibility by explicitly authorizing the partners to vary by agreement the internal priorities in distributing the assets of the partnership. The R.U.L.P.A. makes it clear that, to the extent that both general and limited partners are also creditors (other than in respect of their interests in the partnership), they share *pro rata* with other creditors. Section 107. In addition, once the partnership's obligation to make a distribution to partners has accrued, it must be paid after monies owed to creditors but before any other distributions of an equity nature. Finally, general and limited partners rank on the same level (except as otherwise provided in the partnership agreement) in sharing the return of their capital contributions and profits, in that order. Section 804.

Figure 32-2 compares general and limited partners.

OTHER TYPES OF UNINCORPORATED BUSINESS ASSOCIATIONS

Joint Venture

A joint venture or joint adventure is a form of temporary partnership organized to carry out a *single* or isolated business enterprise for profit and usually, although not necessarily, of short duration. It is an association of persons who combine their property, money, efforts, skill, and knowledge for the purpose of carrying out a single business operation for profit. An example is a securities underwritings syndicate. Another is a syndicate formed to acquire a certain tract of land for subdivision and resale. A joint venture differs from a partnership which is formed to carry on a business over a considerable or indefinite period of time. A joint venturer, as such, is *not* an agent of her co-venturers and does not necessarily have authority to bind them, although in a given case a joint venturer may have actual or apparent authority

---

FIGURE 32-2   Comparison of General and Limited Partners

	General Partner	Limited Partner
Control	Has all the rights and powers of a partner in a partnership without limited partners	Has no right to take part in management or control
Liability	Unlimited	Limited, unless takes part in control or name used
Agency	Is an agent of the partnership	Is not an agent of the partnership
Fiduciary Duty	Yes	No
Duty of Care	Yes	No

---

to bind her co-venturers. Usually the management and operation of the enterprise is placed by agreement in the hands of one member designated as manager. The death of a partner dissolves the partnership, while the death of a joint venturer does not necessarily dissolve the joint venture. A partner cannot sue a copartner or the firm at law, but must go into equity for relief. On the other hand, a court of law will take jurisdiction over disputes between joint venturers. Except for these principal differences, a joint venture is generally governed by the law of partnerships.

Joint Stock Company

A joint stock company, or joint stock association as it is sometimes called, is technically a form of general partnership having some of the attributes of a corporation yet differing in several important respects from the ordinary partnership. It is dissimilar to a partnership in that:

1. its capital is divided into shares represented by certificates which are transferable;
2. its business and affairs are managed by directors or managers elected by the members, who alone have the authority to represent and bind it;

3. its members as such are not its agents; and
4. a transfer of shares by a member, or his death, insanity, or other incapacity, does not dissolve it or afford a ground for dissolution

It is similar to a partnership, but unlike a corporation, in that it is formed by contract and not by State authority.

Mining Partnerships

A mining partnership is an association of the several owners of the mineral rights in land for the purpose of operating a mine and extracting minerals of economic value for their mutual profit. Although mining partnerships are governed to a considerable extent by the law of general partnerships, there are certain important differences between them. For example, a mining partner has the right to sell his interest in the partnership, and the death of a partner does not dissolve a mining partnership.

Limited Partnership Associations

This form of business unit is permitted by statute in certain States. It is a legal hybrid. Although called a partnership association, it closely resembles a corporation. It is a legal entity separate and distinct from its members who are not personally responsible for its debts, their liabilities being limited to their capital contribution, except in the event of violation of some statutory provision. An important difference between this type of association and a corporation pertains to the transfer of shares. Although the shares in a limited partnership association are freely transferable, the transferee does not, however, become a member in the association unless so elected by the other members. If membership is refused, he may recover the value of his shares from the association.

Business Trusts

A trust is a transfer of the legal title to certain specific property to one person for the use and benefit of another. Where an express trust results from contract, the agreement is commonly known as a declaration of trust which customarily sets forth a designation of the property or trust *res*, the duration of the trust, the exact functions and duties of the trustees with respect to the management of the property, the persons to whom the income of the trust is to be paid and the share to be received by each, the method of winding up the trust, and the person or persons entitled to share in the trust property upon termination. See Chapter 50 for a more complete discussion of trusts.

Although trusts are almost as old as the law of equity itself, it was not until late in the nineteenth century that lawyers and business perceived that the trust concept was capable of being utilized as a method of conducting a commercial enterprise. The business trust, sometimes called a Massachusetts trust, was devised to avoid the burdens of corporate regulation and particularly the formerly widespread prohibition denying to corporations the power to own and deal in real estate. Like an ordinary trust between natural persons, a business trust may be created by a voluntary

agreement without the necessity of any authorization or consent of the State.

There are three distinguishing characteristics of a business trust: (1) the trust estate is devoted to the conduct of a business; (2) by the terms of the agreement each beneficiary is entitled to a certificate evidencing his ownership of a beneficial interest in the trust which he is free to sell or otherwise transfer; and (3) the trustees must have the exclusive right to manage and control the business free from control of the beneficiaries, otherwise the trust may fail, and the beneficiaries become personally liable for the obligations of the business as partners.

The trustees are personally liable for the debts of the business unless, in entering into contractual relations with others, it is expressly stipulated or definitely understood between the parties that the obligation is incurred solely upon the responsibility of the trust estate. The trustee, in order to escape personal liability on the contractual obligations of the business, must obtain the agreement or consent of the other contracting party to look solely to the assets of the trust. The personal liability of the trustees for their own torts or the torts of their agents and servants employed in the operation of the business stands on a different footing. While this liability cannot be avoided, the risk involved may be reduced substantially or eliminated altogether by insurance.

Unincorporated Associations

With regard to contracts of an unincorporated association and torts committed by its agents, members of the association who have not authorized the contract or participated in commission of the tort are not personally liable. However, managers of the association entering into contracts on its behalf are personally liable on such contracts; and managers who negligently supervise or conduct an association affair or social event are liable in tort for injuries caused by such negligence.

CASES

Control

WEIL v. DIVERSIFIED PROPERTIES, INC.

United States District Court, District of Columbia, 1970.
319 F.Supp. 778.

GESELL, J.

This is an equitable action brought by the general partner of a limited partnership asking the Court to declare the limited partners general partners and for the appointment of a receiver and an accounting. The case raises some factual issues and presents legal questions under the Uniform Limited Partnership Act, 41 D.C.Code § 401, *et seq.*, apparently not previously determined in this jurisdiction. Testimony was taken on the issue whether the defendant limited partners became general partners and on the merits of two counterclaims filed by different limited partners.

Diversified Properties is a limited partnership organized effective January 2, 1967, with varying degrees of ownership in several garden-type apartments and other real estate located mostly in Maryland. A formal written agreement was signed in July 1967, and the partnership was duly registered in the District of Columbia under the provisions of the Code. The origins of the partnership are not in dispute. Weil had been managing and dealing in real estate and had varying participations in several properties. He needed capital and approached defendant Baer with a view to placing some of his real estate interests in a limited partnership to be formed. Baer, a CPA, had several clients looking for tax shelter and mainly through his auspices a group of limited partners was assembled and the agreement signed by all parties on the advice of various attorneys and backdated to January in order to get maximum depreciation and

loss carry-over tax deductions. Weil was the only general partner.

All parties agree the limited partners remained strictly in that status until about May 1, 1968. By April, however, the partnership was hard pressed for cash, various mortgage obligations had to be satisfied or refinanced and the projected cash flow was very inadequate. Weil, who had been managing the properties from a partnership office at one of the apartment projects, looked for other employment and at a meeting of the partners on April 24 offered to discontinue his salary and close up the partnership office, steps which would effect a saving of something in the neighborhood of $75,000. This was a gloomy and revealing meeting. Weil's proposal was accepted with little consideration of what, if anything, Weil would do in the future. By the time of the next partnership meeting a week later, two individuals—Rubenstein and Tempchin—had been selected to manage one or more of the properties on a commission basis in accordance with a general proposal Weil had advanced. The partnership books and records had been transferred to Baer's office, the official business address of the partnership, and Weil commenced working for another real estate company as vice president. From then on the partners were involved in refinancing and meeting further capital demands. Although they put more money into the venture money pressures increased and the partnership remained very short of cash with early foreclosures threatening. All partners hoped to sell some properties and thus keep others afloat. Weil's name still appeared on various obligations which in fact had been assigned to the partnership. As general partner he had also naturally made numerous business commitments for the partnership. Creditors therefore turned to him with persistent demands for payment which could not be met. The limited partners had no obligation or willingness to come forward with still more capital sufficient to meet these demands.

It is against this general background that the activities and relationships of the partners must be analyzed in more detail. Weil argues that the limited partners took control of the enterprise within the meaning of [U.L.P.A. § 7], which provides:

A limited partner shall not become liable as a general partner unless, in addition to the exercise of his rights and powers as a limited partner, he takes part in the control of the business.

Weil contends that after his withdrawal from a salaried position on May 1, 1968, he was supposed to continue as general partner, keeping an eye on the business, but that he was ignored. He claims that meetings of the other partners were held in his absence and without notice, and that Rubenstein and Tempchin not only refused to follow his instructions but took orders from the limited partners, particularly Baer, Kaye, Steinberg and Jerome Snider. He points to various isolated episodes suggesting interference by certain individual limited partners with matters Weil contends he should have handled as general partner. The limited partners by categorical testimony strenuously deny these charges and the over-all inferences that Weil seeks to draw from various incidents.

*   *   *

Cases relating to whether or not limited partners have taken part in control of the business and are thus to be treated as general partners involve claims by creditors against the partners. [Citations.] No case has been found where a general partner has invoked Section 7 of the [Uniform Limited Partnership] Act against his own limited partners. The purpose of Section 7 is to protect creditors:

The Act proceeds on the assumption that no public policy requires a person who contributes to the capital of a business, acquires an interest in its profits, and some degree of control over the conduct of the business to become bound for the obligations of the business, provided creditors have no reason to believe that when their credits were extended that such persons were so bound. [Citations.]

*   *   *

The remedy of a general partner who faces interference from his limited partners is to dissolve the partnership under Section 31 of the Uniform Partnership Act. So long as the partnership continues, he is in a relationship of trust with his colleagues. [Citation.] He may not invoke the provisions of the Act to enlarge the liability of his partners.

Even if a general partner might hold his limited partners to account as general partners under certain circumstances, Weil cannot do so on the facts of this case. Weil considers himself still a general partner and recognizes that the written partnership agreement by its terms is a bona fide limited partnership under the [U.L.P.A.] As between themselves, partners may make any agreement they wish which is not barred by prohibitory provisions of statutes, by common law, or by considerations of public policy. [Citation.] Whatever may be the obligations of the limited partners as against creditors or third parties, Weil may not prevail against them if they have not breached the terms of the agreement. *   *   * Accordingly, the initial inquiry must be to determine whether the limited partners have in any way violated the terms of the written agreement.

*   *   *

A limited partner under the [U.P.L.A.] has the right to require that the books and records be kept at a designated place for inspection and copying and he may at any time demand "true and full information of all things affecting the partnership". It is well established that just because a man is a limited partner in an enterprise he is not by reason of that status precluded from continuing to have an interest in the affairs of the partnership, from giving advice and suggestions to the general partner or his nominees, and from interesting himself in specific aspects of the business. Such casual advice as limited partners may have given to Rubenstein and Tempchin can hardly be said to be interference in day-to-day management. Certainly common sense dictates that in times of severe financial crisis all partners in such an enterprise, limited or general, will become actively interested in any effort to keep the enterprise afloat and many abnormal problems will arise that are not under any stretch of the imagination mere day-to-day matters of managing the partnership business. This is all that occurred in this instance.

* * *

Weil has not by a preponderance of the evidence established any violation by the limited partners of terms of the agreement with him, which at the very most is all that Weil can complain of in his effort to have the limited partners declared general partners. Since the partnership agreement was not violated by the limited partners, Weil has no cause of action and his request for the appointment of a receiver and an accounting will be denied. The provisions of the Limited Partnership Act were primarily designed to protect creditors. So long as the provisions of the agreement were followed, no partner can complain. Weil's complaint is dismissed.

[Judgment for limited partners.]

Return of Contribution

KRAMER v. McDONALD'S SYSTEM, INC.

Supreme Court of Illinois, 1979.
77 Ill. 2d 323, 33 Ill. Dec. 115, 396 N.E.2d 504.

CLARK, J.

This cause was brought in the circuit court of Cook County by Arnold I. Kramer, plaintiff, as a declaratory judgment action seeking a declaration of the rights of the parties in certain equipment, inventory, accounts receivable, fixtures and furniture incidental to the operation of a McDonald's restaurant in Midland, Texas. Moreover, Kramer sought a determination that the defendants, McDonald's System, Inc., McDonald's Corporation and a subsidiary, Franchise Realty Interstate Corporation (McDonald's), the defendants, had converted property in which Kramer had a security interest when McDonald's permitted the Bank of River Oaks (the bank) to sell the equipment at public sale and when McDonald's leased the premises to a second franchisee.

The circuit court denied McDonald's motions to dismiss and for summary judgment and granted Kramer's motion for summary judgment against McDonald's for $104,784.41. On appeal, the appellate court of Illinois affirmed that part of the lower court's judgment denying McDonald's motion to dismiss the complaint, reversed the order granting Kramer summary judgment, and rendered summary judgment in favor of McDonald's. [Citation.] We thereafter granted Kramer's petition for leave to appeal. We affirm the judgment of the appellate court, though we base our decision on different reasons.

On December 9, 1974, Ralph Baker entered into a franchise license agreement and a lease agreement with McDonald's. Under the terms of the agreements Baker was given a 20-year leasehold interest in a McDonald's hamburger restaurant in Midland, Texas. Prior to commencing operation of the restaurant, Baker obtained a loan from the bank for $107,000. Baker granted a security interest in the restaurant equipment he had purchased to the bank. * * *

On January 17, 1975, Baker, in order to obtain additonal working capital, entered into several agreements with Arnold Kramer. On that day the following documents were executed: (1) a limited partnership agreement creating the B/K Limited Partnership, with Baker and his wife as general partners, and Kramer and four others as limited partners; * * * and (6) a note and security agreement evidencing a principal debt of $90,000 and a finance charge for interest over the life of the note of $85,823.80. The security agreement granted a security interest in the restaurant equipment to Kramer, subject to the prior security interest of the bank in the same collateral. * * *

* * *

The certificate of limited partnership filed with the recorder of deeds of Cook County, Illinois, on February 3, 1975, reveals in paragraph 7 that the amount of cash "contributed" by the limited partners totaled $90,000, with Kramer contributing $54,000 and each of the other four limited partners contributing $9,000. Paragraph 8 states: "No additional contributions are to be made by any Limited Partner."

Baker commenced business in March 1975, and closed the business in January 1976. He sent a telegram to McDonald's on January 22, 1976, informing it he would abandon the restaurant January 24, 1976, at 12:01 a.m. On the same day he sent a telegram to Kramer and the other limited partners informing them they had until 11:59 p.m. on January 23, 1976, to take over the restaurant. Kramer did not reply. McDonald's delivered a letter to Baker on January 23, 1976, stating it would take over the restaurant, sell it and distribute the proceeds to Baker and his creditors.

Baker did not turn over the restaurant to McDonald's but did cease to operate it. On January 26, 1976, McDonald's notified Baker he was in default under the license and lease agreements. McDonald's eventually took possession of the restaurant. Kramer then notified McDonald's that Baker was in default and demanded payment of the February installment from McDonald's. McDonald's subsequently entered into a franchise and lease agreement with Victor Moore, who began to operate the restaurant in April 1976.

Kramer filed the instant action in the circuit court of Cook County on April 12, 1976, seeking a declaratory judgment concerning his rights in the property in the restaurant and alleging that the defendant McDonald's unlawfully converted his property.

* * *

But the issue herein is not whether a limited partner may secure a loan but whether a limited partner may secure his capital contribution. We conclude that the answer is that he may not. Since there are no genuine issues of material fact, we decide as a matter of law that the appellate court properly entered summary judgment in favor of McDonald's.

We think that the pleadings, depositions, affidavits and documents on record clearly evince that the $90,000 was intended as a contribution to the capital of the limited partnership. The word "contributions" as it is used in the ULPA is limited to the contribution made by a limited partner at the time of the formation of the partnership for the benefit of the partnership's creditors. [Citation.]

Kramer's transfer to Baker of $90,000 was made at the time of the formation of the limited partnership. This is revealed in the limited partnership agreement executed on January 17, 1975, the certificate of limited partnership, as well as in the mutual agreement indemnifying the limited partners, signed on January 22, 1975.

The important distinction between the initial capital contribution and subsequent transfers of funds to the partnership has been noted elsewhere by courts which have been asked to decide whether limited partners may take collateral security for loans made to the partnership. Those courts had been careful to note that the initial contribution had been made previously, and that it was subsequent advances of money over which issue was joined. [Citations.]

Additionally, after the limited partnership was formed and, indeed, even after the instant action was commenced, Kramer still continued to treat the $90,000 as a capital contribution. The partnership income return for 1975 (IRS Form 1065) was signed by Kramer on June 12, 1976, two months after filing this action. On schedule K–1 of form 1065 Kramer stated that his deductible share of the partnership's loss for 1975 of $91,364.47 was $43,067.00. He also claimed a share in the investment tax credit on partnership property taken by the partnership. Clearly then, the $90,000 payment from Kramer to Baker was intended to be, was treated by the parties as, and must be considered to be, an initial capital contribution to the limited partnership. [Citation.]

A limited partner is prohibited from taking collateral to secure repayment of his capital contribution. [Citation.] To do so would give him an unfair priority over the creditors of the partnership contrary to the express provisions of section 16(1) of the ULPA:

(1) A limited partner shall not receive from a general partner or out of partnership property any part of his contribution until

(a) All liabilities of the partnership, except liabilities to general partners and to limited partners on account of their contributions, have been paid or there remains property of the partnership sufficient to pay them,

(b) The consent of all members is had, unless the return of the contribution may be rightfully demanded under the provision of paragraph (2), and

(c) The certificate is cancelled or so amended as to set forth the withdrawal or reduction. [Citation.]

A limited partnership interest is in the nature of an investment [Citation.] Through his contribution, the limited partner becomes entitled to share in the profits and losses of the partnership, though his share of the losses will not exceed the amount of capital initially contributed to the enterprise. [Citation.] However, when the limited partner makes the contribution, he is placing that amount at risk. He is not permitted to insure that risk or to guarantee a return to himself by taking some form of security. He may not vie with creditors for the assets available to pay the partnership's obligations. "[The ULPA] was designed to prevent illegal competition between the limited partner and creditors of the partnership for the assets of the partnership." [Citation.] It would therefore defeat the purpose of the ULPA to permit Kramer to enforce a security interest against the property purchased by the partnership to operate the restaurant.

We therefore hold that Kramer is prohibited by the express provisions of section 16 of the ULPA from accepting collateral as security for his capital contribution.

* * *

Accordingly, for the reasons given, the judgment of the appellate court granting summary judgment in favor of McDonald's and denying summary judgment to Kramer is affirmed.

Judgment affirmed.

Duties of General Partner

RIVIERA CONGRESS ASSOCIATES v. YASSKY

Court of Appeals of New York, 1966.
18 N.Y.2d 540, 277 N.Y.S.2d 386, 223 N.E.2d 876.

FULD, J.

* * *

The plaintiffs are five out of approximately 350 limited partners in Riviera Congress Associates (hereafter referred to as the Syndicate), a real estate syndicate which is the owner in fee of the Riviera Congress Motel in New York City. The individual defendants are the general partners who organized the Syndicate in 1961 pursuant to a prospectus which recited that the land was acquired "for investment" and that the Syndicate would not "operate the property" but would lease it instead to the defendant Yassky Corporation for 20 years at a fixed annual net rental of $179,500. The prospectus also stated that the general partners were "the sole principals of The Yassky Corporation" and that they would not only "contribute to (that company) $50,000 to be used for working capital, utility deposits and advertising" but would also pay, "out of their own funds, the sum of $125,000" in order to obtain for the corporation a motel franchise from Congress Enterprises, Inc. Finally, it was asserted that the lease was "non-cancellable" but could be assigned "with the written consent of the General Partners * * * provided the assignee assumes all obligations of the tenant". In the partnership agreement, each limited partner acknowledged that "he received and examined a copy of the offering Prospectus * * * and that he is relying solely upon the information contained therein and in the agreements and instruments referred to therein".

Yassky Corporation was given the lease in 1961 and, in 1962, with the consent of the general partners of the Syndicate, it assigned its interest in the lease to Riviera Corporation of Manhattan, another company wholly owned and operated by the four individual defendants. In September, Riviera Corporation of Manhattan assigned its interest to Mid-Manhattan Associates, a limited partnership consisting of the four individual defendants as general partners and 19 limited partners. Mid-Manhattan Associates simultaneously subleased the premises back to Riviera Corporation. At this point, then, the motel was being operated by a corporation (Riviera) but both the landlord and tenant were limited partnerships of which the same persons, the four individual defendants, were general partners.

On March 29, 1963, after sustaining $170,000 in operating losses, Mid-Manhattan Associates, with the consent of the general partners of the Syndicate, assigned its interest in the lease to Mid-Manhattan Hotel Associates, Inc., another corporation wholly owned by the individual defendants. Later that same day, the lease was reassigned to Riviera Congress Associates, Inc., a corporate subsidiary of the Syndicate. Riviera Corporation then assigned its sublease to Riviera Congress Associates, Inc., thus putting the Syndicate in full possession of the motel without a tenant. The general partners advised the limited partners that, "due to current financial losses suffered by the operating lessee, the General Partners on behalf of the partnership have accepted a surrender of the operating lease". The limited partners who

had previously shared in the fixed rental derived from the property thereafter ceased to receive any return on their investments. About 250 of the 350 limited partners met together and selected an "Investors' Committee" to protect their interests.

Five of the limited partners, some of whom were on the Investors' Committee, brought * * * a claim against the four individual defendants, not in their capacity as the general partners of the Syndicate, but rather in their capacity as general partners of the other real estate syndicate, Mid-Manhattan Associates, for nearly a half million dollars in *rent* said to be due and owing since April 1, 1963 to the Syndicate from Mid-Manhattan Associates. * * *

In their amended answer, the defendants attacked the plaintiffs' right to maintain the action in the name of the partnership and set up, as an affirmative defense to the cause of action for rent, a release given by the general partners of the Syndicate when they consented to the assignment of the lease by Mid-Manhattan Associates to a corporation. In short, the cause of action is for rent; the defense is release; and the plaintiffs counter with a claim that the release is invalid because it was given by the defendants, as general partners of the Syndicate, to themselves, as general partners of Mid-Manhattan Associates—it being urged that such self-dealing is a breach of fiduciary obligations.

* * *

* * * In the case before us, a reading of the complaint demonstrates that the plaintiffs instituted, and properly so, a *derivative* suit on behalf of the partnership, rather than a class action on behalf of their fellow limited partners. The cause of action asserted is for the payment of rent, an obligation which Mid-Manhattan Associates expressly assumed when it accepted the assignment of the lease from Riviera Corporation. That obligation, it is clear, runs to the Syndicate, as landlord, not to its limited partners who are, for all intents and purposes, strangers to the contract. Accordingly, a suit for rent must be

brought by the Syndicate or by someone who is entitled to act on its behalf. [Citations.]

* * * We hold that the plaintiffs are authorized to sue as limited partners on behalf of the partnership entity to enforce a partnership claim when those in control of the business wrongfully decline to do so.

* * *

There can be no question that a managing or general partner of a limited partnership is bound in a fiduciary relationship with the limited partners [citations.] * * * In the case before us, the cause of action for rent belongs to the Syndicate alone. Since its general partners will not sue because they are the very persons who would be liable for payment of the rent, the limited partners, as *cestuis que trustent*, should be permitted to initiate the necessary legal proceedings on behalf of the Syndicate. [Citations.]

On the remaining issue in this appeal—whether the plaintiffs have made out a case for summary judgment—we agree with the Appellate Division that disputed questions of fact are presented which require a trial. The plaintiffs charge a breach of fiduciary duty by the general partners in that they were assertedly guilty of self-dealing and, on the surface, it is difficult to dispute the fact of such self-dealing since they leased the motel to their own thinly capitalized corporation and then consented to successive assignments of the lease to other business entities which they owned or controlled. Ordinarily, such self-dealing would render the defendants incapable, as general partners of the Syndicate, from releasing themselves from liability on the lease, as general partners of Mid-Manhattan Associates. [Citation.] However, partners may include in the partnership articles practically "any agreement they wish" [citation] and, if the asserted self-dealing was actually contemplated and authorized, it would not, *ipso facto*, be impermissible and deemed wrongful. [Citations.] As bearing on this, it seems clear that the limited partners were fully apprised in the prospectus that the defendant general partners intended to lease the premises to their own corporation and that such tenant would be capitalized at only $50,000. This clear statement of purpose has the effect of "exonerating" the defendants, at least in part, " 'from adverse inferences which might otherwise be drawn against them' " simply from the fact that they dealt with themselves. [Citation.] Since the papers before us disclose an issue of fact whether the defendants acted "honestly and in good faith" [citation], determination of that question may only be resolved upon a trial.

The order of the Appellate Division denying the plaintiffs motion for summary judgment should be affirmed, without costs, and the certified question answered in the affirmative.

PROBLEMS

1. John Palmer and Henry Morrison formed the partnership of Palmer & Morrison for the management of the Huntington Hotel and filed an appropriate certificate in compliance with the limited partnership statute. The partnership agreement provided that Palmer would contribute $40,000 and be a general partner and Morrison would contribute $30,000 and be a limited partner. Palmer was to manage the dining and cocktail rooms, and Morrison was to manage the rest of the hotel. Nanette, a popular French singer, who knew nothing of the partnership affairs, appeared for four weeks in the Blue Room at the hotel and was not paid her salary of $8,000. Subsequently, Palmer and Morrison had a difference of opinion, and Palmer bought Morrison's interest in the partnership for $20,000. Palmer later went into bankruptcy. Nanette sued Morrison for $8,000. For how much, if anything, is Morrison liable?

2. A limited partnership was formed consisting of Webster as the general partner and Stevens and

Stewart as the limited partners. The limited partnership was organized in strict compliance with the limited partnership statute. Stevens was employed by the partnership as a purchasing agent. Stewart personally guaranteed a loan made to the partnership. Both Stevens and Stewart consulted with Webster with respect to partnership business, voted on a change in the nature of the partnership business, and disapproved an amendment to the partnership agreement proposed by Webster. The partnership experienced serious financial difficulties and its creditors seek to hold Webster, Stevens, and Stewart personally liable for the debts of the partnership. Decision?

3. Fox, Dodge, and Gilbey agreed to become limited partners in Palatine Ventures, a limited partnership. The certificate of limited partnership stated that each would contribute $20,000. Fox's contribution consisted entirely of cash; Dodge contributed $12,000 in cash and gave the partnership her promissory note for $8,000; and Gilbey's contribution was his promise to perform 500 hours of legal services to the partnership. What liability, if any, do Fox, Dodge, and Gilbey have to the partnership by way of capital contribution?

4. Madison and Tilson agree to form a limited partnership with Madison as general partner and Tilson as the limited partner, each to contribute $12,500 as capital. No papers were ever filed, and after ten months the enterprise fails with liabilities exceeding assets by $30,000. Creditors of the partnership seek to hold Madison and Tilson personally liable for the $30,000. Decision?

5. Kraft is a limited partner of Johnson Enterprises, a limited partnership. As provided in the limited partnership agreement, Kraft decided to leave the partnership and demanded that her capital contribution of $20,000 be returned. At this time the partnership assets were $150,000 and liabilities to all creditors totaled $140,000. The partnership returned to Kraft her capital contribution of $20,000. What liability, if any, does Kraft have to the creditors of Johnson Enterprises?

6. Gordon is the only limited partner in a limited partnership whose general partners are Daniels and McKenna. Gordon contributed $10,000 for his limited partnership interest and loaned the partnership $7,500. Daniels and McKenna each contributed $5,000 by way of capital. After a year the partnership is dissolved, at which time it owes $12,500 to its only creditor, Dickel, and has assets of $30,000. How should these assets be distributed?

7. A limited partner has which of the following rights or powers: (a) to assign his interest in the limited partnership, (b) to receive repayment of loans made to the partnership on a *pro rata* basis with general creditors, (c) to manage the affairs of the limited partnership, (d) to receive his share of the profits before the general partners receive their shares of the profits, (e) to dissolve the partnership upon his withdrawing from the partnership.

PUBLIC POLICY, SOCIAL ISSUES
AND BUSINESS ETHICS

PART Seven covers corporations which are without question the dominant type of business organization: corporate assets currently exceed $5 trillion, corporate revenues now exceed $4 trillion annually, the number of persons directly owning shares in corporations is approximately 30 million with 100 million additional persons owning shares indirectly through institutional investors such as banks, insurance companies, pension funds and investment companies. Moreover, corporations employ three-fourths of the nation's labor force. H. Henn and J. Alexander, *Laws of Corporations* 5 (1983).

There are two basic types of corporations—closely held and publicly-held.

The closely-held corporation desires to function and does function very differently from the larger corporations with public shareholders. In the closely-held corporation, there are usually no public investors; its shareholders are active in the conduct and management of the business (with resulting coincidence of control and management); the insiders want to keep out outsiders (delectus personae), and the emphasis is on simplified and informal procedures with all participating, with attendant possible risk of deadlock. In short, its member or members desire to gain certain corporate advantages, such as limited liability and certain corporate tax consequences (with minimization of double taxation), at the same time preserving many of the internal attributes of an individual proprietorship or partnership.

In contrast with the closely-held corporation, larger corporations with public shareholders and other investors necessarily involve substantial separation of ownership and control, have a form of representative government-by-the-majority, with management delegated to a board of directors, following rather formal procedures, and operate in a relatively institutionalized and depersonalized manner, which is not susceptible to deadlock. The transfer of its shares is usually not only free from transfer restrictions but is facilitated by securities exchange listing or an active over-the-counter market. H. Henn and J. Alexander, *Laws of Corporations* 696 (1983).

Closely held corporations comprise the large majority of incorporated business entities in the United States. Nonetheless, their special needs, which in many instances differ from those of the public issue corporation, have not until very recently received any specific statutory attention. One of the difficulties in drafting such legislation is the great diversity of close corporations. Nevertheless, close corporations do share one problem in common: minority shareholders in a close corporation are especially in need of protection from oppression exerted by other shareholders. Given that the typical shareholder has a relatively large investment of his time and financial assets committed to the closely held corporation, the need to protect his reasonable expectations is greater than the needs of a shareholder in a publicly held corporation. While the precise contours and details of unfair treatment are infinitely varied, there are two basic types of oppression in a close corporation. First, and probably most widespread, is the oppression of the minority shareholders by the majority shareholders. In the absence of specific legal protection, the minority shareholders are essentially subject to the goodwill of the majority. The second type is oppression exercised by the minority upon the majority shareholders which can occur when minority shareholders have a veto power over action desired by the majority and misuse the power. Under these circumstances the majority needs an adequate remedy to resolve the deadlock. In the absence of special close corporation statutes (only a dozen States have such legislation) the shareholders must provide their own protection through carefully drawn shareholder agreements and bylaws. While studying the corporate legal norms in the next four chapters, the reader should be alert to their failure to address the special requirements of the most common of corporations, the closely held corporation.

Whereas the shareholders of a closely held corporation need protection from oppression by other *shareholders*, those who own shares in a publicly-held corporation need protection from unfair treatment by *management;* that is, the officers of the corporation who are ostensibly selected by the board of directors who are elected by the shareholders. "In reality, this legal image is virtually a myth. In nearly every large American business corporation, there exists a management autocracy. One man—variously titled the President, or the Chairman of the Board, or the Chief Executive Officer—or a small coterie of men rule the corporation. Far from being chosen by the directors to run the corporation, this chief executive or executive clique chooses the board of directors and, with the acquiescence of the board, controls the corporation." R. Nader, M. Green, and J. Seligman, *Taming the Giant Corporation* 75–76 (1976). In a classic study published in 1932, Adolf Berle and Gardner Means concluded that great amounts of economic power had been concentrated in a relatively few large corporations, that the ownership of these corporations had become widely dispersed, and that the shareholders of these corporations had become far removed from active participation in management. Since their original study these trends have steadily continued and in 1981 the 500 largest U.S. industrial corporations had sales of $1,773.4 billion, profits of $84.2 billion, assets of $1,282.8 billion and 15,600,000 employees. *Fortune*, May 3, 1982 at 258.

Thus, vast amounts of wealth and power are now controlled by a small number of corporations which are in turn controlled by a small group of corporate officers. In fact, the separation of ownership and control has widened so far that Myles Mace, a leading scholar in this area, has stated that board of directors are so reluctant to discharge ineffective management that they only fire a chief executive when "the leadership of the [chief executive] was so unsatisfactory that even his mother thought he ought [to be removed] for the good of the company *   *   * before the board [of directors] reluctantly moved." Testimony before the SEC, September 30, 1977.

These developments raise a large number of social, policy, and ethical issues regarding the governance of the large, publicly-owned corporations. These issues include: who is actually running these corporations, who should run them, to whom are they accountable, to whom should they be accountable, what role should employees and shareholders be accorded in corporate governance, should the existing system of governance be changed, if so, how, and, is chartering by the States effective or should these corporations be Federally chartered? The resolution of these and other issues is critical to dealing with a number of national policy issues affecting business such as long term economic prospects, employment policies, health and safety in the work place, the quality of products, the effects of overseas operations, and environmental decisions. In reading the chapters on corporations the student should keep in mind the social, policy, and ethical concerns that impact upon the operations of the large, publicly-held American business corporation.

Chapter 33

NATURE, FORMATION, AND POWERS

A corporation is an entity created by law and existing separate and distinct from the individuals whose contributions of initiative, property, and control make it possible for it to function. In the opinion of the Supreme Court in *Dartmouth College v. Woodward*, 4 U.S. (Wheat.) 518, 4 L.Ed. 629 (1819), Chief Justice Marshall stated:

A corporation is an artificial being, invisible, intangible, and existing only in contemplation of law. Being the mere creature of law, it possesses only those properties which the charter of its creation confers upon it, either expressly or as incidental to its very existence. These are such as are supposed best calculated to effect the object for which it was created. Among the most important are immortality, and, if the expression may be allowed, individuality; properties by which a perpetual succession of many persons are considered as the same, so that they may act as a single in-

dividual. A corporation manages its own affairs, and holds property without the hazardous and endless necessity of perpetual conveyances for the purpose of transmitting it from hand to hand. It is chiefly for the purpose of clothing bodies of men, in succession, with these qualities and capacities, that corporations were invented, and are in use. By these means, a perpetual succession of individuals are capable of acting for the promotion of the particular object, like one immortal being.

The corporation is the dominant form of business organization in the United States, accounting for eighty-eight percent of the gross receipt of all business entities. Domestic corporations currently doing business in the United States number well over two million with annual revenues and assets in the trillions of dollars. Moreover, approximately thirty million Americans own shares of stock while an additional one hundred million people own stock indirectly through institutional investors such as banks, insurance companies, pension funds, and investment companies. Use of the corporation as an instrument of commercial enterprise has made possible the vast concentrations of wealth and capital which have largely transformed this country from an agrarian to an industrial economy. Due to its size, power, and impact, the business corporation is a key institution not only in the American economy but also in the world power structure.

In 1946 a committee of the American Bar Association after careful study and research submitted a draft of a Model State Business Corporation Act. The Model Act has been amended frequently since then and a completely revised act has been drafted and distributed for comment in 1983. The provisions of the Model Act do not become law until enacted by a State, but its influence has been widespread, and it has been adopted in whole or in part by a majority of the States. As a recommended model statute, it sets a standard for the statutory law of business corporations. It will be used throughout the chapters on corporations in this text and referred to as the Model Act or the MBCA. Because a number of States have not amended their versions of the MBCA, the text will discuss the Model Act in both its amended and unamended forms. Appendix G of this text contains the MBCA as amended.

In 1983 a major revision of the Model Act was completed and distributed for comment. In 1984 it was approved by the Committee on Corporate Laws of the Section of Corporation, Banking, and Business Law of the American Bar Association. It is "designed to be a convenient guide for revision of state business corporation statutes, reflecting current views as to the appropriate accommodation of the various commercial and social interest involved in modern business corporations." The Revised Act is the first complete revision of the Model Act in over 30 years, although there had been numerous statutory amendments to it since it was first

published. One of the tasks of the revision was to reorganize the provisions of the Model Act more logically and to revise the language to make the Act more consistent. In addition, substantive changes were made in a number of areas. This text will discuss those provisions of the Revised Act that have made significant changes in the Model Act as amended. The revision will be referred to as the Revised Act or the RMBCA. Appendix H of this text contains those provisions of the RMBCA cited in this book.

NATURE OF CORPORATIONS

The nature of corporations is most readily understood by examining the common attributes and the various types of corporations. Both of these topics will be discussed in this section.

CORPORATE ATTRIBUTES

The principal attributes of a corporation are that (1) it is a legal entity; (2) it owes its existence to a State which also regulates it; (3) it provides limited liability to its shareholders; (4) its shares of stock are freely transferable; (5) it may have perpetual existence; (6) its management is centralized; and it is considered, for some purposes, (7) a person and (8) a citizen.

Legal Entity

A corporation is a legal entity separate and apart from its shareholders, with rights and liabilities entirely distinct from theirs. It may sue or be sued by, as well as contract with, any other party including any one of its shareholders. A transfer of stock in the corporation from one individual to another has no effect upon the legal existence of the corporation. Title to corporate property belongs not to the shareholders but to the corporation. Even where a single individual owns all of the stock of the corporation, the shareholder and the corporation are not the same but have separate and distinct existences.

Creature of the State

A corporation may only be formed by compliance with a State incorporation statute. In order to obtain the advantages of conducting a business enterprise in corporate form, a charter or franchise granted by the legislative branch of the government is required. Prior to the middle of the nineteenth century, it was not uncommon for the legislatures of the several States to pass special Acts creating corporations. In order to avoid a special privileged class of corporations, State legislatures began enacting during the nineteenth century general statutes authorizing the Secretary of State to issue a certificate of incorporation or charter upon compliance with its provisions. Presently, all States have such general incorporation statutes.

A corporation's charter and the provisions of the statute under which it is formed constitute a contract between it and the State. Article I, Section 10, of the United States Constitution provides that no State shall pass any law "impairing the obligation of contracts," and this prohibition applies to contracts between a State and a corporation. See Chapter 3.

To avoid the impact of this provision, incorporation statutes reserve to the State the power to prescribe such regulations, provisions, and limitations as it shall deem advisable and to amend, repeal, or modify the statute at its pleasure. MBCA Section 149. As such reservation is a material part of the contract between the State and a corporation formed under the statute, amendments or modifications regulating or altering the structure of the corporation do not impair the obligation of contract because they are expressly permitted by the contract.

Limited Liability

A corporation is a legal entity and as such is liable out of its own assets for its debts. The shareholders generally are *not personally liable* for the corporation's debts beyond the amount of their investment. The circumstances under which a shareholder may be personally liable are discussed later in this chapter. By the same token, the corporation is not liable for the personal obligations of its shareholders.

Free Transferability of Corporate Shares

In the absence of contractual restrictions, shares in a corporation may be freely transferred by way of sale, gift, or pledge. The ability to transfer shares is a valuable right and may enhance their market value. Transfers of shares of stock are governed by Article 8 of the Uniform Commercial Code, Investment Securities, and are discussed in Chapter 34.

Perpetual Existence

A corporation has perpetual existence unless a limited period of duration is stated in its articles of incorporation. Section 4(a). As a consequence, the death or withdrawal of a shareholder, director, or officer does not terminate the existence of a corporation.

Centralized Management

The shareholders of a corporation elect the **board of directors** which manages the business affairs of the corporation. It is then incumbent upon the board to appoint **officers** to run the day-to-day operations of the business. Since neither the directors nor the officers (collectively referred to as "management") need be shareholders, it is entirely possible, and in large corporations quite typical, for the ownership of the corporation to be separated from the management of the corporation. The management structure of corporations is further discussed in Chapter 35.

As a Person

Whether a corporation is a "person" within the meaning of a constitution or statute is a matter of construction based upon the intent of the lawmakers in using the word. For example, a corporation is considered a person within the provision in the Fifth and Fourteenth Amendments to the Federal Constitution that no "person" shall be "deprived of life, liberty, or property without due process of law"; and the provision in the Fourteenth Amendment that no State shall "deny to any person within its jurisdiction the equal protection of the laws." A corporation also enjoys the right of a person to be secure against unreasonable searches and seizures as provided for in the Fourth Amendment. On the other hand, a corporation is not considered to be a person within the clause of the Fifth Amendment which protects a "person" against self-incrimination.

As a Citizen

A corporation is considered a citizen for some purposes but not for others. A corporation is not deemed to be a citizen as that term is used in the Fourteenth Amendment which provides "No State shall make or enforce any law which shall abridge the privileges or immunities of citizens of the United States."

A corporation, however, is regarded as a citizen of the State of its incorporation and of the State in which it has its principal office for the purpose of determining whether diversity of citizenship exists between the parties to a lawsuit as a basis for jurisdiction of the Federal courts.

CLASSIFICATION OF CORPORATIONS

Corporations may be classified as public or private, profit or non-profit, domestic or foreign, closely held, and professional. As will be seen, these classifications are not mutually exclusive. For example, a corporation may be a closely held, professional, private, profit, domestic corporation.

Public or Private

A public corporation is one which is created to administer a unit of local civil government, such as a county, city, town, village, school district or park district, or one created by the United States to conduct public business, such as the Tennessee Valley Authority or the Federal Deposit Insurance Corporation. Many public corporations are also referred to as municipal corporations.

A private corporation is one organized to conduct either a privately owned business enterprise for profit or a non-profit corporation organized for community benefit or enjoyment.

Profit or Non-profit

A profit corporation is one founded for the purpose of operating a business for profit from which payments are made to its shareholders in the form of dividends.

Although a non-profit (or not-for-profit) corporation may make a profit, the profit may not be distributed to its members, directors, or officers but must be used exclusively for the charitable, educational, or scientific purpose for which it was organized. Examples of non-profit corporations include private schools, library clubs, athletic clubs, fraternities, sororities, and hospitals.

Domestic or Foreign

A corporation is domestic in the State in which it is incorporated. It is foreign in every other State or jurisdiction. A corporation may not do business, except for acts in interstate commerce, in a State other than the State of its incorporation without the permission and authorization of such other State. Every State, however, provides for the issuance to foreign corporations of a certificate to do business within its borders and for the taxation of such foreign businesses. Obtaining a certificate (called "qualifying") usually involves filing certain information with the Secretary of State, the payment of prescribed fees, and designation of a resident agent. The doing or transacting of business within a particular State is a determinant of whether that State's courts have jurisdiction over a foreign corporation.

What may constitute doing sufficient business in the State to subject a foreign corporation to valid service of process may not be sufficient to require the foreign corporation to obtain a certificate of authority from the State. Furthermore, the qualifying statutes are limited in their application by the constitutional provision that the regulation of commerce between the States is within the power of the Congress of the United States. See Chapter 3.

For example, in *Terral v. Burke Construction Co.*, 257 U.S. 529 (1922), an Arkansas statute provided that if any foreign corporation authorized to do business in the State should remove to the Federal court any suit brought against it by a citizen of Arkansas or initiate any suit in the Federal court against a local citizen, without the consent of the other party, Arkansas's Secretary of State should revoke all authority of the corporation to do business in the State. The Burke Construction Company, a Missouri Corporation authorized to do business in Arkansas, brought a suit in and removed a State suit brought against it to the Federal court. Burke sought to enjoin the Secretary of State from revoking its authority to do business in Arkansas, contending that the Arkansas statute is unconstitutional. Judgment for Burke on grounds that the statute is unconstitutional. The right to resort to the Federal courts is guaranteed by the Federal Constitution, and the surrender of a constitutional right may not be imposed as a condition to a foreign corporation's doing business in a State.

The Model Act does not attempt to formulate an inclusive definition of what constitutes the transaction of business. Instead, it is defined in a negative manner by stating that certain activities do *not* constitute the transaction of business. Section 106. Generally, any conduct more regular, systematic, or extensive than that described in this section constitutes the transaction of business and requires the corporation to obtain a certificate of authority. Conduct typically requiring a certificate of authority includes maintaining an office to conduct local intrastate business, selling personal property not in interstate commerce, entering into contracts relating to local business or sales, and owning or using real estate for general corporate purposes. RMBCA Section 15.01, Comment.

The Model Act, as stated, provides a non-exclusive list of activities in which a foreign corporation may engage without being considered to have transacted intrastate business:

(a) Maintaining, defending, or settling any action or suit or any administrative or arbitration proceeding.

(b) Holding meetings of its directors or shareholders to carry on other activities concerning its internal affairs.

(c) Maintaining bank accounts.

(d) Maintaining offices or agencies for the transfer, exchange, and registration of its securities, or appointing and maintaining trustees or depositaries with relation to its securities.

(e) Effecting sales through independent contractors.

(f) Soliciting or obtaining orders, whether by mail or through employees or agents or otherwise, where such orders require acceptance outside this State before becoming binding contracts.

(g) Creating or acquiring evidences of debt, mortgages, liens or security interests in real or personal property.

(h) Securing or collecting debts or enforcing any rights in property securing the debts.

(i) Transacting any business in interstate commerce.

(j) Conducting an isolated transaction that is completed within a period of thirty days and that is not in the course of a number of repeated transactions of like nature. *See also* RMBCA Section 15.01.

See Reisman v. Martori, Meyer, Hendricks, & Victor.

It is a common and accepted principle that local courts will not interfere with the internal affairs of a foreign corporation. The Model Act states that "nothing in this Act contained shall be construed to authorize this State to regulate the organization or internal affairs of [a foreign] corporation." Section 106.

A foreign corporation that transacts business without having first qualified may be subject to a number of penalties. Most statutes provide that an unlicensed foreign corporation doing business in the State shall not be entitled to maintain a suit in the State courts until such corporation shall have obtained a certificate of authority. However, a failure to obtain a certificate of authority to transact business in the State does not impair the validity of a contract entered into by the corporation nor prevent such corporation from defending any action or proceeding brought against it in the State. Section 124. In addition, many States impose fines upon the corporation, while a few States also impose fines upon the corporation's officers and directors as well as holding them personally liable on contracts made within the State.

A State may also specify conditions under which a license or certificate of authority shall be revoked. In general, the statutes provide that a failure to pay taxes, file reports, or maintain a registered agent or registered office in the State will justify revocation of a license.

Closely Held

A corporation is described as closely held when its outstanding shares of stock are held by a small number of persons, frequently family relatives or friends. In most closely held corporations the shareholders are active in the management and control of the business. Accordingly, the shareholders are concerned with who are their fellow shareholders and therefore they typically enter into a buy-sell agreement with one another at the time of incorporation in order to prevent the stock from getting into the hands of persons outside the original group of shareholders. *See Galler v. Galler in Chapter 35.* Closely held corporations comprise the majority of all corporations in the United States but account for only a small fraction of corporate revenues and assets.

In most States closely held corporations are subject to the general incorporation statute which governs all corporations. The 1969 Amendments to the MBCA included a number of liberalizing provisions for closely held corporations. The end of Appendix E contains a concise summary of these provisions and some of the ways they may be adapted to closely held corporations. Some States, however, have enacted special legislation to accommodate the needs of closely held corporations. Moreover, a Statutory Close Corporation Supplement to the MBCA has been recently promulgated.

Professional Corporations

All of the States have a "professional association act" which permits the practice of professions by duly licensed individuals under corporate form. Some statutes apply to all professions licensed to practice within the State while others apply only to specified professions. The purpose of the statute in authorizing the formation of this type of corporation under specified limitations is to permit duly licensed professionals to obtain tax advantages not allowable to individuals or partnerships. Nonetheless, as a result of the Tax Equity and Fiscal Responsibility Act of 1982 (effective 1984), these tax advantages of the corporate form have in the main been eliminated.

FIGURE 33-1   General Partnership, Limited Partnership, and Corporation Compared

	Partnership	Limited Partnership*	Corporation
Creation	By agreement of the parties	By statutory authorization	By statutory authorization
Entity	A legal entity for some but not all purposes	A legal entity for some but not all purposes	A legal entity
Duration	Dissolved by death, bankruptcy, or withdrawal of a partner	Limited partner may dissolve partnership only by decree of court	May be perpetual
Liability	Partners are subject to unlimited liability upon the contracts, debts, and torts of the partnership	Limited partners are not generally liable for the contracts, debts or torts of the partnership	Shareholders are not generally liable for the contracts, debts, or torts of the corporation
Transferability	Interest of a partner in a partnership may be assigned but the assignee does not become a partner	Interest of a limited partner may be assigned and assignee may become a substituted limited partner if all members consent	Shares of stock in a corporation are freely transferable
Management	Each partner is entitled to an equal voice in the management and control of the business	Limited partner may not take part in control of the business	The business of the corporation is managed by a board of directors elected by the shareholders
Agency	Each partner is an agent of the partnership	Limited partner is not an agent of the partnership	A shareholder is neither a principal nor an agent of the corporation
Suits	In actions brought by or against the partnership all partners are generally necessary parties	Limited partners are not a necessary party except where suit is to enforce their rights against or liability to the partnership	The corporation may sue and be sued in its own name

*A general partner of a limited partnership has all the rights, powers and liabilities of a partner in a general partnership.

FORMATION OF A CORPORATION

Incorporation involves greater expense and formality than the formation of any other form of business organization. The formation of a corporation under a general incorporation statute requires the performance of several acts by various groups, individuals, and State officials. The procedure to organize a corporation begins with the promotion of the proposed corporation by its organizers, also known as **promoters,** who procure offers by interested persons known as **subscribers** to buy stock in the corporation when created and who also prepare the necessary incorporation papers. The articles of incorporation are then executed by the **incorporators** and filed with the Secretary of State who issues the charter or certificate of incorporation. Finally, an organizational meeting is held by the incorporators and shareholders or by the directors.

ORGANIZING THE CORPORATION

Promoters

A promoter is a person who brings about the "birth" of a corporation. The promoter arranges for the capital and financing of the corporation as well as assembling the necessary assets, equipment, licenses, personnel, leases, and services. He will also attend to the actual legal formation of the corporation. Upon incorporation, the promoter's organizational task is finished.

Promoters' Contracts In addition to procuring subscriptions and preparing the incorporation papers, promoters often enter into contracts in anticipation of the creation of the corporation. The contracts may be ordinary agreements necessary for the eventual operation of the business, such as leases, purchase orders, employment contracts, sales contracts, or franchises. If these contracts are executed by the promoter in her own name and there is no further action, the promoter is liable on such contracts, and the corporation, when created, is not liable. Moreover, a pre-incorporation contract made by promoters in the name of the corporation and on its behalf does not bind the corporation, except where so provided by statute. The promoter, in executing such contracts, may do so in the corporate name although incorporation has not yet taken place. Prior to its formation a corporation has no capacity to enter into contracts or to employ agents or representatives. Upon being formed it is not liable at common law upon any prior contract, even one made in its name, unless it adopts or ratifies the contract expressly, impliedly, or by knowingly accepting benefits under it.

A promoter who enters into a pre-incorporation contract in the name of the corporation usually remains liable on that contract even if the corporation adopts or ratifies the contract. This results from the rule of agency law that a principal must be in existence at the time a contract is made in order to ratify it. A promoter will be relieved of liability, however, if the contract itself provides that adoption shall terminate the promoter's liability or if the promoter, the third party, and the corporation enter into a novation substituting the corporation for the promoter. See Figure 33-2.

Promoters' Fiduciary Duty The promoters of a corporation occupy a fiduciary relationship among themselves as well as to the corporation, to its subscribers, and to its initial shareholders. This duty requires good faith, fair dealing, and full disclosure. Accordingly, the promoters are under a duty to account for any secret profit realized by them at the expense of those to whom such duty is owing. *See Golden v. Oahe Enterprises, Inc.* Failure to disclose may also constitute a violation of Federal or State securities laws discussed in Chapter 44.

Subscribers

A **pre-incorporation subscription** is an offer to purchase capital stock in a corporation yet to be formed. The offeror is called a "subscriber." Courts have traditionally viewed subscriptions in two ways. The majority regards a subscription as a continuing offer to purchase stock from a nonexisting entity, which is incapable of accepting the offer until created. Under this view a subscription may be revoked at any time prior to its acceptance. A minority of jurisdictions treat a sub-

FIGURE 33-2   Promoters' Pre-incorporation Contracts

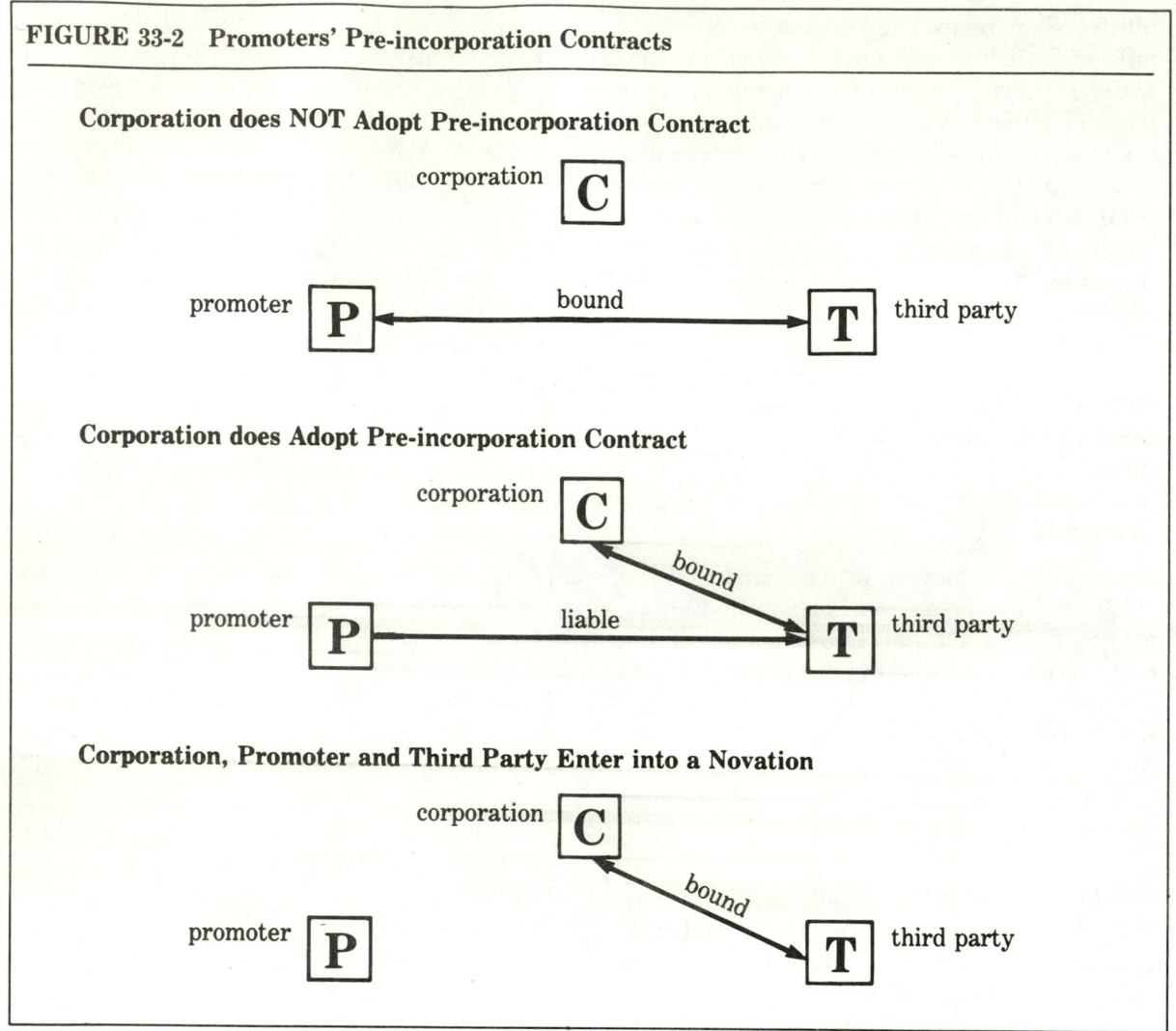

scription as a contract among the various subscribers and, therefore, irrevocable except with the consent of all of the subscribers. Modern incorporation statutes, however, have taken an intermediate position in resolving this issue. The MBCA provides that a subscription is irrevocable for a period of six months, unless otherwise provided in the subscription agreement or unless all of the subscribers consent to the revocation of the subscription. Section 17. If the corporation accepts the subscription during the period of irrevocability, the subscription becomes a contract binding on both the subscriber and the corporation.

Selection of State for Incorporation

A corporation is usually incorporated in the State in which it is intended to be located and transact all or the principal part of its business. However, a corporation may be formed in one State and have its principal place of business and conduct all or most of its operations in another State or States by duly qualifying and obtaining a certificate of authority to transact business in such other States. The principal criteria useful in selecting a State for incorporation include the flexibility accorded management, the rights granted to shareholders, the limitations imposed upon the issuance of shares, the restrictions placed upon the payment of dividends, and the organizational costs such as fees and taxes.

FORMALITIES OF INCORPORATION

Although the procedure involved in organizing a corporation varies to some extent under the different State incorporation laws, typically the incorporators execute and deliver to the Secretary of State, or other designated official, articles of incorporation in duplicate, which in effect are an application for a charter. The Model Act provides that after issuance of the certificate of incorporation, an organization meeting of the board of directors named in the articles of incorporation shall be held for the purpose of adopting bylaws, electing officers, and transacting such other business as may come before the meeting. Section 57. Upon completion of these organizational details the life of the corporation is in the hands of its shareholders, and its business and affairs are managed by its board of directors and by its officers.

Selection of Name

Most general incorporation laws require that the name contain a word or words which clearly indicate that it is a corporation, such as "corporation," "company," "incorporated," "limited," "Corp.," "Co.," "Inc.," or "Ltd." Section 8. Practically every incorporation statute provides that no corporate name shall be the same as, or deceptively similar to, the name of an existing corporation doing business within the State.

Incorporators

The incorporators are the persons who sign the articles of incorporation which are filed with the Secretary of State of the State of incorporation. Although they perform a necessary function, their services as incorporators are perfunctory and short-lived, ending with the organizational meeting of the initial board of directors following the issuance of the certificate of incorporation. Accordingly, modern statutes have greatly relaxed the qualifications of incorporators and reduced the number required. The Model Act, for example, provides that one or more persons or a domestic or foreign corporation may act as incorporators. Section 53.

Articles of Incorporation

The articles of incorporation or **charter** is generally a rather simple document which includes:

1. the name of the corporation,
2. the location and address of the corporation,
3. the purpose for which the corporation is organized,
4. the period of duration which may be perpetual,
5. the number of authorized shares and designations of classes of shares,
6. the number and names of the initial directors,
7. the name and address of each incorporator, and
8. any other provision consistent with the incorporation statute and other law.

After the charter is drawn up it must be signed and filed with the Secretary of State in order to form a corporation. Section 55. The articles of incorporation then become the basic governing document of the corporation, so long as its provisions are consistent with State and Federal law. See Figure 33-3.

Organization Meeting

The Model Act requires that an organization meeting be held to adopt the bylaws, elect

FIGURE 33-3   Sample Articles of Incorporation

ARTICLES OF INCORPORATION OF [CORPORATE NAME]

The undersigned, acting as incorporator(s) of a corporation under the _____ Business Corporation Act, adopt(s) the following Articles of Incorporation for such corporation:

First: The name of the corporation is _____

_____

Second: The period of its duration is _____

Third: The purpose or purposes for which the corporation is organized are: _____

_____

Fourth: The aggregate number of shares which the corporation shall have authority to issue is _____

_____

Fifth: Provisions granting preemptive rights are:

Sixth: Provisions for the regulation of the internal affairs of the corporation are:

Seventh: The address of the initial registered office of the corporation is _____ ,
and the name of its initial registered agent at such address is _____

_____

Eighth: The number of directors constituting the initial board of directors of the corporation is _____ , and the names and addresses of the persons who are to serve as directors until the first annual meeting of shareholders or until their successors are elected and shall qualify are:

Name	Address
_____	_____
_____	_____
_____	_____

Ninth: The name and address of each incorporator is:

Name	Address
_____	_____
_____	_____
_____	_____

Dated _____ , 19 __ .

_____

_____

_____

Incorporator(s)

Source: Reprinted with permission from Henn & Alexander, Corporations, 3rd ed. Copyright © 1983 by West Publishing Co.

officers, and transact "such other business as may come before the meeting." Section 57. Such business typically includes authorization to issue shares of stock, approval of preincorporation contracts made by promoters, selection of a bank as well as approval of a corporate seal and the form of stock certificate.

Bylaws

The bylaws of a corporation are the rules and regulations which govern its internal management. They are necessary to its organization, and the adoption of bylaws is one of the first items of business at the organization meeting held promptly after incorporation. Section 57. Under the Revised Act either the incorporators or the initial directors adopt the bylaws. RMBCA Section 2.06.

Under the Model Business Corporation Act, the bylaws may provide for:

1. penalties for failure to pay installments or calls on subscriptions for shares (Section 17);
2. the place of shareholders' meetings (Section 28);
3. the calling of special meetings of shareholders (Section 28);
4. the qualifications of directors (Section 35);
5. an increase or decrease in the number of directors (Section 36);
6. the number of directors necessary for a quorum, not less than a majority (Section 40);
7. an executive committee of the board of directors (Section 42);
8. the notice to be given for meetings of the board of directors (Section 43); and
9. the duties of each of the officers (Section 50).

The bylaws may contain provisions other than those just enumerated. However, nothing contained in the bylaws may be contrary to or inconsistent with any provision in the statute or in the articles of incorporation, and nothing in the articles may be repugnant to the statute. Section 27. In contrast to the certificate of incorporation which embodies the articles of incorporation, the bylaws do not have to be publicly filed and may be changed without shareholder approval: "The power to alter, amend, or repeal the by-laws or adopt new by-laws, subject to repeal or change by action of the shareholders, shall be vested in the board of directors unless reserved to the shareholders by the articles of incorporation." Section 27.

RECOGNITION AND DISREGARD OF CORPORATENESS

Business associates choose to incorporate in order to obtain one or more of the corporate attributes, primarily limited liability and perpetual existence. Since a corporation is a creature of the State, such corporate attributes are recognized when the enterprise complies with the State's requirements for incorporation. Although the formal procedures are relatively simple, it is possible for errors or omissions to occur. In some cases the mistakes may be trivial, such as an incorrect address of an incorporator; in other instances the error may be more significant, such as a complete failure to file the articles of incorporation. The consequences of noncompliance with the statutory incorporation procedure depend upon the seriousness of the error. Conversely, even when a corporation has been formed in strict compliance with the incorporation statute, a court may disregard the corporateness of the enterprise if justice requires. This section addresses these two complementary issues.

RECOGNITION OF CORPORATENESS

Corporation *de Jure*

A corporation *de jure* is one which is not defectively organized but formed in strict compliance with the incorporation statute and the required organizational procedure. Once formed, the existence of a *de jure* corporation may not be challenged by anyone, even the State in a direct proceeding for this purpose.

Corporation *de Facto*

A *de facto* corporation is a corporation which is not *de jure* due to a failure to comply substantially with the incorporation statute but nevertheless is recognized for most purposes as a corporation. A failure to form a *de jure* corporation may result in the formation of a *de facto* corporation if the following requirements are met: (1) the existence of a general corporation statute; (2) a *bona fide* attempt to comply with that law in organizing a corporation under the statute; and (3) the actual exercise of corporate power by conducting a business in the belief that a corporation has been formed. The existence of a *de facto* corporation can be challenged only by the State. If such corporation sues to collect a debt, it is no defense to such suit that the plaintiff corporation is not *de jure*. Not even the State can collaterally (in a proceeding involving some other issue) question the *de facto* corporation's existence. The State must bring an independent suit against the corporation for this express purpose, known as an action of *quo warranto* (by what right).

The MBCA provides that a "certificate of incorporation shall be conclusive evidence that all conditions precedent required to be performed by the incorporators have been complied with and that the corporation has been incorporated under this Act, except as against this State." Section 56.

Corporation by Estoppel

A person who has dealt with a defectively organized corporation may be precluded or estopped from denying its corporate existence where the necessary elements of holding out and reliance are present. The doctrine of corporation by estoppel is separate and distinct from that of corporation *de facto*. Estoppel does not create a corporation. It only operates to prevent a person or persons under the facts and circumstances of a particular case from raising the question of a corporation's existence or its capacity to act or to own property. The doctrine can be applied not only to third parties but also to the purported corporation as well as the associates who held themselves out as a corporation. *See*

Cranson v. International Business Machines Corp.

Defective Corporation

If the associates who purported to form a corporation fail to comply with the requirements of the incorporation statute to such an extent that neither a *de jure* nor a *de facto* corporation is formed and the circumstances do not justify the application of the corporation by estoppel doctrine, then the courts generally deny the associates the benefits of incorporation. With respect to the attribute of limited liability, the Model Act provides that all persons who assume to act as a corporation without authority to do so shall have joint and several unlimited liability for all debts and liabilities incurred as a result of so acting. Section 146.

The Revised Act imposes liability only on persons who act as or on behalf of a corporation, *knowing that there was no incorporation*. RMBCA Section 2.04. This provision is analogous to U.L.P.A. Section 12 and R.U.L.P.A. Section 3.04 discussed in Chapter 32. Consider the following two illustrations: First, A had been shown executed articles of incorporation some months before he invested in the corporation and became an officer and director. He was also told by the corporation's attorney that the articles had been filed, but in fact they had not been filed because of confusion in the attorney's office. Under the Revised Act and many court decisions, A would not be held liable for the obligations of the defective corporation. Second, B represents that a corporation exists and enters into a contract in the corporate name when she knows that no corporation has been formed because no attempt has been made to file articles of incorporation. B would be held liable for the obligations of the defective corporations under the Model Act, the Revised Act, and most court decisions involving similar situations. RMBCA Section 2.04 and Comment.

Figure 33-4 illustrates the recognition of corporate attributes.

DISREGARD OF CORPORATENESS

If a corporation is formed by substantial compliance with the incorporation statute so that a *de jure* or *de facto* corporation results, the general rule is that corporateness and its attendant attributes including limited liability will be recognized. However, the courts will disregard the corporation entity when it is used to defeat public convenience, commit wrongdoing, protect fraud, or circumvent the law. Going behind the corporate entity in order to prevent its use by individuals seeking to insulate themselves from personal accountability and the consequences of their wrongdoing is referred to as **piercing the corporate veil.** Courts will pierce the corporate veil where deemed necessary to remedy wrongdoing and have done so most frequently with closely held corporations and in parent-subsidiary relationships.

Closely Held Corporations

The joint and active management by all the shareholders of closely held corporations frequently results in a tendency to forgo adherence to all of the niceties of corporate formalities, such as holding meetings of the board and shareholders, while the small size of close corporations often results in creditors who are unable to satisfy fully their claims against the corporation. Accordingly, the frustrated creditor will likely invoke the court to disregard the organization's corporateness and impose personal liability for the corporate obligations upon the shareholders. Courts have responded by piercing the corporate veil where the shareholders (1) have not conducted the business on a corporate basis, (2) have not provided an adequate financial basis for the business, or (3) have used the corporation to defraud. For example, in *D. I. Felsenthal Co. v. Northern Assurance Co.*, 284 Ill. 343, 120 N.E. 268 (1918), Felsenthal Company sued the Northern Assurance Company to collect on its fire insurance policy. Northern claimed that it was not liable under the policy because

---

FIGURE 33-4   Recognition of Corporate Attributes

Requirements		Result
Strict compliance with incorporation statute	**Corporation *de Jure***	Corporate attributes, insulation from collateral and direct suits
• *Bona fide* attempt to comply with incorporation statute • Exercise of corporate powers	**Corporation *de Facto***	Corporate attributes, insulation from collateral suits
• Holding out • Reliance • Equitable considerations	**Corporation by Estoppel**	Corporate existence may not be denied by the parties
Serious failure to comply with incorporation statute	**Defective Corporation**	Unlimited personal liability for associates

Felsenthal's property had been destroyed by a fire instigated by Fox, the president, director, creditor, and principal shareholder of Felsenthal. Judgment for Northern Assurance. The instigator of the fire, Fox, is the beneficial owner of almost all of the corporation's stock as well as the corporation's president and director. Under these circumstances the corporation cannot recover because to allow such a recovery would allow a wrongdoer to benefit from his own illegal act. The corporate form cannot be used in this case to protect Fox and to aid him in his plan to defraud the insurance company.

Conducting the business on a corporate basis involves maintaining the corporation's funds separate from the shareholders' funds, maintaining separate financial records, holding regular directors' meetings, and generally observing corporate formalities. Adequate capitalization requires that the shareholders invest sufficient capital to meet the reasonably anticipated requirements of the enterprise. *See United States v. Healthwin-Midtown Convalescent Hospital.*

Parent-Subsidiary

A corporation may choose to risk only a portion of its assets in a particular enterprise by forming a subsidiary corporation. A **subsidiary corporation** is one in which another corporation, **the parent corporation,** owns at least a majority of the subsidiary's shares and therefore has control over the subsidiary corporation. Courts will pierce the corporate veil and hold the parent liable for the debts of its subsidiary if

1. both corporations are not adequately capitalized, *or*
2. the formalities of separate corporate procedures are not observed, *or*
3. each corporation is not held out to the public as separate enterprises, *or*
4. the funds of the two corporations are commingled, *or*

5. the parent corporation completely dominates the operation of the subsidiary to advance solely the parent's own interests.

So long as these pitfalls are avoided, the courts will generally recognize the separateness of the subsidiary even though the parent owns all the stock of the subsidiary and the two corporations have common directors and officers. *See Berger v. Columbia Broadcasting System, Inc.*

CORPORATE POWERS

A corporation derives its existence and all of its powers from the State of incorporation and, therefore, has only such powers as the State has conferred upon it. These powers are those expressly set forth in the statute and articles of incorporation and powers reasonably implied from them.

SOURCES OF CORPORATE POWERS

Statutory Powers

Typical of the general powers granted by incorporation statutes are those provided by Sections 4 and 5 of the Model Act, which include the following:

1. To have perpetual succession.
2. To sue and be sued in its corporate name.
3. To acquire, own, mortgage, and dispose of real and personal property.
4. To lend money and use its credit to assist its employees.
5. To acquire, own, vote, and dispose of shares or obligations of other business entities.
6. To make contracts, incur liabilities, and issue notes, bonds, or other obligations.
7. To invest surplus funds and acquire its own shares.

8. To conduct its business and carry on its operations within or without the State of incorporation.

9. To elect or appoint officers and agents, define their duties, and fix their compensation.

10. To make and alter bylaws for the administration and regulation of its affairs.

11. To make donations for the public welfare or for charitable, scientific, or educational purposes.

12. To establish pension, profit sharing, and other incentive plans for its directors, officers, and employees.

13. To be a promoter, partner, member, associate, or manager of any partnership, joint venture, trust, or other enterprise.

14. To amend its articles of incorporation.

15. To effect a merger or consolidation with one or more other corporations.

16. To indemnify against personal liability officers, directors, employees, and agents of the corporation who act on behalf of the corporation in good faith and without negligence.

Express Charter Powers

The objects or purposes for which a corporation is formed are stated in its articles of incorporation, which delineate in general language the type of business activities in which the corporation proposes to engage. This serves (1) to advise the shareholders of the nature and kind of particular business activity in which their investment is being risked; (2) to guide the officers, directors, and management as to the extent of the corporation's authority to act; and (3) to inform any person who may contemplate dealing with the corporation of the extent of its legally authorized power.

The express powers must relate to a legitimate business activity or industry within the purview of the general statute. Thus, a State may provide that a bank, savings and loan association, insurance company, or railroad company may not be organized under its general corporation law but may be organized under a separate statute. In such case, the power to engage in any of these businesses is not granted to a corporation formed under the general statute.

Implied Powers

A corporation has the authority to do any act which is necessary or convenient to and consistent with the execution of any of its express powers and the operation of the business which it was formed to conduct. This power exists by implication and does not depend upon express language in the charter or statute but upon reasonable inference as to the proper scope and content of such language, taking into consideration the facts and circumstances of the particular case.

The express powers of a corporation may and should be stated in general language, and it is not necessary to set forth in detail every particular type of act which the corporation is empowered to perform. A general statement of corporate purpose or object is sufficient to give rise to all of the powers necessary, incidental, or convenient to accomplish that purpose. Section 4(q). For instance, a corporation organized "to buy and sell goods, wares, and merchandise" has implied power to (a) purchase or lease store premises, (b) employ salesmen, (c) buy or rent trucks, (d) spend money for advertising, (e) open and manage a bank account, (f) employ buyers and pay their salaries and traveling expenses, and (g) purchase insurance on the lives of officers, as well as other powers necessary or incidental to such stated purpose.

ULTRA VIRES ACTS

Since a corporation has authority to act only within the limitation of its express and implied powers, any action taken or contract made by it which goes beyond these powers is *ultra vires*. *Ultra vires* does not mean without power or capability, but rather without legal authorization because the act is not within the scope and type of acts which the corporation is legally empowered to perform.

The doctrine of *ultra vires* is of less significance today because modern statutes permit incorporation for any lawful purpose and most articles of incorporation do not limit the powers of the corporation. As a consequence, far fewer acts are *ultra vires*.

Effect of *Ultra Vires* Acts

Traditionally, *ultra vires* contracts were unenforceable as null and void. Under the modern approach courts allow the *ultra vires* defense where the contract is wholly executory on both sides. A corporation having received full performance from the other party to the contract is not permitted to escape liability by a plea of *ultra vires*. Conversely, where a corporation is suing for breach of a contract which has been fully performed on its side, the defense of *ultra vires* is unavailing. In any event, an illegal contract, whether *ultra vires* or not, is unenforceable on the basis of illegality.

Most statutes now have abolished the defense of *ultra vires* in an action by or against a corporation. The MBCA provides that "no act of a corporation and no conveyance or transfer of real or personal property to or by a corporation shall be invalid by reason of the fact that the corporation was without capacity or power to do such act or to make or receive such conveyance or transfer." Section 7. This section extends beyond contract actions and includes any corporate action including conveyances of property. Thus, under this section it is not necessary for persons dealing with a corporation to examine its articles of incorporation to discover any limitations upon its purposes or powers that may appear there. The section does not, however, validate illegal corporate actions.

Remedies for *Ultra Vires* Acts

While *ultra vires* under modern statutes may no longer be used defensively as a shield against liability, corporate activities which are *ultra vires* may be redressed in any of the three following ways, as provided by Section 7 of the Model Act:

1. In an injunction proceeding brought by a shareholder against the corporation to restrain and enjoin the commission of the *ultra vires* act if equitable and if all affected persons are party to the proceeding.
2. In a suit by the corporation or through shareholders in a representative suit against the officers or directors of the corporation for causing the corporation to engage in an *ultra vires* act.
3. In a proceeding by the Attorney General of the State of incorporation to dissolve the corporation or to enjoin it from the transaction of unauthorized business.

LIABILITY FOR TORTS AND CRIMES

A corporation is liable for the torts and crimes committed by its agents in the course of their employment. The doctrine of *ultra vires*, even in those jurisdictions where it is permitted as a defense, has no application to wrongdoing by the corporation. The doctrine of **respondeat superior** imposes full liability upon a corporation for the torts committed by its agents and employees during the course of their employment. For example, X, a truck driver employed by the ABC Corporation, while on a business errand, negligently runs over Y, a pedestrian. Both X and the ABC Corporation are liable to Y in an action by her to recover damages for the injuries sustained. A corporation may also be found liable for fraud, false imprisonment, malicious prosecution, libel, and other torts, but some States hold the corporation liable for *punitive* damages only if it authorized or ratified the act of the agent.

One of the essential elements of most crimes is a guilty mind or criminal intent, and it has been argued that since a corporation is artificial, intangible, and incorporeal, it cannot have either a mind or a soul and is therefore incapable of committing a crime. This is a tenuous argument and overlooks the fact that corporations do transgress the laws of man which exist for the welfare and safety of the community and the State. The modern trend is to make corporations criminally responsible for the criminal conduct of their agents, if the conduct is attributable to the corporation. The Model Penal Code provides that a corporation may be convicted of a criminal offense for the conduct of its employees if:

1. the legislative purpose of the statute defining the offense is to impose liability on corporations and the conduct is within the scope of the agent's office or employment;
2. the offense consists of an omission to discharge a specific, affirmative duty imposed upon corporations by law; *or*
3. the offense was authorized, requested, commanded, performed or recklessly tolerated by the board of directors or by a high managerial agent of the corporation.

The punishment necessarily is by fine and not imprisonment.

CASES

Foreign Corporation

REISMAN v. MARTORI, MEYER, HENDRICKS, & VICTOR

Court of Appeals of Georgia, 1980.
155 Ga.App. 551, 271 S.E.2d 685.

BANKE, J.

[The plaintiff is an Arizona professional corporation consisting of approximately 18 lawyers. The defendant, Dr. Reisman, is a medical doctor and general surgeon practicing in Georgia. In November of 1977, Dr. Reisman engaged Edwin Hendricks, a member of the law firm, to provide legal advice and representation in a dispute between himself and the Floyd County Medical Center. Hendricks flew to Atlanta and hired local counsel with Dr. Reisman's approval. Hendricks represented Dr. Reisman in two hearings before the hospital and one court proceeding as well as negotiating a compromise between Dr. Reisman and the hospital. The total bill for the law firm's travel costs and professional services was $21,438.14 but Dr. Reisman refused to pay $6,438.14 of it. The law firm brought an action against Dr. Reisman for the balance owed and a jury awarded the firm the full amount of the unpaid portion of the bill. Dr. Reisman appealed arguing that

the action should have been dismissed because the law firm failed to register as a foreign corporation in accordance with the Georgia Corporation Statute.]

* * * We do not agree. Assuming, without deciding, that the appellee professional association was required under Code Ann. § 22–1421(a) to procure a certificate of authority from the Secretary of State in order to transact business in Georgia, its activites in this state have not been sufficiently extensive to invoke the statute here. " 'In most jurisdictions it has been held that single or isolated transactions do not constitute doing business within the meaning of such statutes, although they are a part of the very business for [sic] which the corporation is organized to transact, if the action of the corporation in engaging therein indicated no purpose of continuity of conduct in that respect.' [Citation.]" Winston Corp. v. Park Elec. Co. [Citation.]

Winston held that "the question of 'doing business' is to be considered a matter of fact to be resolved on an ad hoc or case-by-case basis * * * [and] * * * the meaning of 'isolated transaction' in our corporation code is to be determined in the same way as the term 'doing business'." [Citation.] Winston also makes it clear that the purpose of Code Ann.

§ 22–1401 is to require registration of foreign corporations which intend to conduct business in Georgia on a continuous basis, not as a temporary matter. Activity related to a single transaction or contract is thus not contemplated.

The evidence here showed that the [law firm's] activities were concentrated in Arizona, although various attorneys in the firm had handled litigation (or "transacted business") outside the state of incorporation. Hendricks had represented clients in Georgia on two prior occasions, but these had nothing to do with his representation of Dr. Reisman. Under these circumstances, there is ample basis for the court's conclusion that the [law firm] had neither extended its business into Georgia on a continuous basis nor engaged "in the course of a number of repeated transactions of like nature" within the state. [Citations.] The trial court correctly held that the [law firm's] representation of Dr. Reisman amounted to an isolated transaction and therefore properly denied the motion for directed verdict.

[Judgment in favor of the law firm affirmed.]

Promoters' Fiduciary Duty

GOLDEN v. OAHE ENTERPRISES, INC.

Supreme Court of South Dakota, 1980.
295 N.W.2d 160.

WOLLMAN, C. J.

* * *

Emmick is the major figure in the story of Oahe. In years past, Emmick has been involved in the sale of industrial chemicals, the promotion of nursing homes, and the management of various farming activities. Emmick approached one J. B. Morris (now deceased) with a plan whereby Morris' Sully County, South Dakota, ranch would be incorporated and through Emmick's managerial skills made to show a profit. At approximately the same time, Emmick approached Golden, who was then operating the Silver Spur Bar in Ft. Pierre, and proposed that Golden contribute some farm machinery and livestock to Oahe. Golden was not, however, present on October 26, 1966, when Oahe was incorporated at a meeting in the office of George Qualley, Emmick's lawyer, in Sioux City, Iowa.

At this meeting, it was concluded that Oahe shares would be given a $50 par value. Officers of the corporation were elected: Chairman and Secretary-Treasurer, J. B. Morris; President, Emmick; and Vice-President, Milton Morris (J. B. Morris' son). An agreement was signed whereby J. B. and Mary Morris transferred their ranch to Oahe Enterprises. It was concluded that the Morris ranch was worth $168,000.00. Of this amount, Morris' equity was determined to be $120,000.00. As his contribution, Emmick transferred 6,315 shares of Colonial Manors, Inc., stock (CM stock) to Oahe.

Colonial Manors, Inc., is an Iowa corporation that is involved in the promotion and management of nursing homes throughout the Midwest. There is serious disagreement concerning the value this stock had at the time Emmick exchanged it for Oahe stock. Emmick represented to the Morrises that the stock was worth $19 per share. At the March 1966 meeting of the CM Corporation, the board of directors set the value of CM stock for internal stock-option purposes at $19 per share. This figure represented $1 for each nursing home the CM Corporation was involved with. At the September 1966 meeting, the value of the CM stock was reduced by the board of directors to $9.50 per share. Emmick knew of the reduction in value of the CM stock prior to the October 26, 1966, meeting at which Oahe was incorporated. There is, however, no evidence that would suggest that this knowledge was disclosed to the Morrises.

* * *

Courts faced with the situation in which a promoter benefits from a violation of his fiduciary duty at the expense of the corporation or its members often characterize the promoter's gain as "secret profit." Such profit is not secret if all interested parties know of and assent to it. But where a promoter through, for example, overvaluation of property exchanged for stock and failure to disclose all material facts regarding such exchange, takes more from the corporation than he transfers in, he is held liable for what courts term secret profit. [Citations.]

As a promoter of Oahe, Emmick stood in a fiduciary relationship to both the corporation and its stockholders and was bound to deal with them in the utmost good faith. "The obtaining of a secret profit by a promoter through the sale of property to a corporation is uniformly held to be a fraud on the corporation and stockholders, and the promoter may be required to account for such profit." [Citation.]

The valuation of the CM stock was based on Emmick's self-serving estimate of matters well known to him as a CM insider and was warped by Emmick's self-interest. Emmick was not trading stock that had an easily ascertainable value; he was not dealing with people experienced in transactions of this type. He failed to make known facts of which he, as an insider of CM, was aware. It is true that Emmick was not the only member on the Oahe board of directors. He was, however, the controlling member and the one in possession of information pertinent to the value of his CM stock not generally available to the public or to the other Oahe board members. In addition to being an insider of CM, he was both a director of and the dominant and controlling force in Oahe. We hold, therefore, that he failed in his duty to the corporation to disclose information regarding stock he intended to transfer into Oahe for Oahe shares and is therefore liable for the shortfall to the corporation therefrom.

* * *

Because the total value of the CM stock Emmick transferred to Oahe was less than the value Emmick received in Oahe stock, the difference can be equalized by canceling the number of Oahe shares held by Emmick that is proportional to the overevaluation. [Citations.] We note that this Court has upheld the cancellation of stock under circumstances where original issue stock was transferred for the worthless stock of another corporation or for services to be performed in the future.

* * *

The judgment is reversed, and the case is remanded to the circuit court with directions to redetermine the fair market value of the CM stock exchanged by Emmick for Oahe stock * * *.

Recognition of Corporateness

CRANSON v. INTERNATIONAL BUSINESS MACHINES CORP.

Court of Appeals of Maryland, 1964.
234 Md. 477, 200 A.2d 33.

HORNEY, J.

* * *

The agreed statement of facts shows that in April 1961, Cranson was asked to invest in a new business corporation which was about to be created. Towards this purpose he met with other interested individuals and an attorney and agreed to purchase stock and become an officer and director. Thereafter, upon being advised by the attorney that the corporation had been formed under the laws of Maryland, he paid for and received a stock certificate evidencing ownership of shares in the corporation, and was shown the corporate seal and minute book. The business of the new venture was conducted as if it were a corporation, through corporate bank accounts, with auditors maintaining corporate books and records, and under a lease entered into by the corporation for the office from which it operated its business. Cranson was elected president and all transactions conducted by him for the corporation, including the dealings with I.B.M., were made as an officer of the corporation. At no time did he assume any personal obligation or pledge his individual credit to I.B.M. Due to an oversight on the part of the attorney, of which Cranson was not aware, the certificate of incorporation, which had been signed and acknowledged prior to May 1, 1961, was not filed until November 24, 1961. Between May 17 and November 8, the Bureau purchased eight typewriters from I.B.M., on account of which partial payments were made, leaving a balance due of $4,333.40, for which this suit was brought.

*   *   *

The fundamental question presented by the appeal is whether an officer of a defectively incorporated association may be subjected to personal liability under the circumstances of this case. We think not.

Traditionally, two doctrines have been used by the courts to clothe an officer of a defectively incorporated association with the corporate attribute of limited liability. The first, often referred to as the doctrine of *de facto* corporations, has been applied in those cases where there are elements showing: (1) the existence of law authorizing incorporation; (2) an effort in good faith to incorporate under the existing law; and (3) actual user or exercise of corporate powers. [Citations.] The second, the doctrine of estoppel to deny the corporate existence, is generally employed where the person seeking to hold the officer personally liable has contracted or otherwise dealt with the association in such a manner as to recognize and in effect admit its existence as a corporate body. [Citations.]

It is not at all clear what Maryland has done with respect to the two doctrines. There have been no recent cases in this State on the subject and some of the seemingly irreconcilable earlier cases offer little to clarify the problem.

In one line of cases, the Court, in determining the rights and liabilities of a defectively organized corporation, or a member or stockholder thereof, seems to have drawn a distinction between those acts or require-

ments which are a condition precedent to corporate existence and those acts prescribed by law to be done after incorporation. In so doing, it has been generally held that where there had been a failure to comply with a requirement which the law declared to be a condition precedent to the existence of the corporation, the corporation was not a legal entity and was therefore precluded from suing or being sued as such. [Citations.] These cases appear to stand for the proposition that substantial compliance with those formalities of the corporation law, which are made a condition precedent to corporate existence, was not only necessary for the creation of a corporation *de jure*, but was also a prerequisite to the existence of a *de facto* corporation or a corporation by estoppel.

*   *   *

On the other hand, where the corporation has obtained legal existence but has failed to comply with a condition subsequent to corporate existence, this Court has held that such nonperformance afforded the State the right to institute proceedings for the forfeiture of the charter, but that such neglect or omission could never be set up by the corporation itself, or by its members and stockholders, as a defense to an action to enforce their liabilities. [Citations.]

*   *   *

*   *   * It seems clear therefore that when a defect in the incorporation process resulted from a failure to comply with a condition subsequent, the doctrine of estoppel may be applied for the benefit of a creditor to estop the corporation, or the members or stockholders thereof, from denying its corporate existence. [Citations.]

In another line of Maryland cases which determined the rights and liabilities of a defectively organized corporation, or a member or stockholder thereof, the Court, apparently disregarding the distinction made between those requirements which are conditions precedent and those which are conditions subsequent to corporate existence, has generally precluded, on the grounds of estoppel or collateral attack, inquiry into the question of corporate existence. [Citations.]

*   *   *

*   *   * From these cases it appears that where the parties have assumed corporate existence and dealt with each other on that basis, the Court will apply the estoppel doctrine on the theory that the parties by recognizing the organization as a corporation were thereafter prevented from raising a question as to its corporate existence.

When summarized, the law in Maryland pertaining to the *de facto* and estoppel doctrines reveals that the cases seem to fall into one or the other of two categories. In one line of cases, the Court, choosing to disregard the nature of the dealings between the parties, refused to recognize both doctrines where there had been a failure to comply with a condition precedent to corporate existence, but, whenever such noncompliance concerned a condition subsequent to incorporation, the Court often applied the estoppel doctrine. In the other line of cases, the Court, choosing to make no distinction between defects which were conditions precedent and those which were conditions subsequent, emphasized the course of conduct between the parties and applied the estoppel doctrine when there had been substantial dealings between them on a corporate basis.

*   *   * There is, as we see it, a wide difference between creating a corporation by means of the *de facto* doctrine and estopping a party, due to his conduct in a particular case, from setting up the claim of no incorporation. Although some cases tend to assimilate the doctrines of incorporation *de facto* and by estoppel, each is a distinct theory and they are not dependent on one another in their application. [Citations.] Where there is a concurrence of the three elements necessary for the application of the *de facto* corporation doctrine, there exists an entity which is a corporation *de jure* against all persons but the

state. On the other hand, the estoppel theory is applied only to the facts of each particular case and may be invoked even where there is no corporation *de facto*. Accordingly, even though one or more of the requisites of a *de facto* corporation are absent, we think that this factor does not preclude the application of the estoppel doctrine in a proper case, such as the one at bar.

I.B.M. contends that the failure of the Bureau to file its certificate of incorporation debarred *all* corporate existence. But, in spite of the fact that the omission might have prevented the Bureau from being either a corporation *de jure* or *de facto*, [citation] supra, we think that I.B.M. having dealt with the Bureau as if it were a corporation and relied on its credit rather than that of Cranson, is estopped to assert that the Bureau was not incorporated at the time the typewriters were purchased. [Citations.] In 1 Clark and Marshall, Private Corporations, § 89, it is stated:

The doctrine in relation to estoppel is based upon the ground that it would generally be inequitable to permit the corporate existence of an association to be denied by persons who have represented it to be a corporation, or held it out as a corporation, or by any persons who have recognized it as a corporation by dealing with it as such; and by the overwhelming weight of authority, therefore, a person may be estopped to deny the legal incorporation of an association which is not even a corporation *de facto*.

In cases similar to the one at bar, involving a failure to file articles of incorporation, the courts of other jurisdictions have held that where one has recognized the corporate existence of an association, he is estopped to assert the contrary with respect to a claim arising out of such dealings. [Citations.]

Since I.B.M. is estopped to deny the corporate existence of the Bureau, we hold that Cranson was not liable for the balance due on account of the typewriters.

Judgment reversed; the appellee to pay the costs.

Disregard of Corporateness:
Closely Held Corporation

UNITED STATES v. HEALTHWIN-MIDTOWN CONVALESCENT HOSPITAL

United States District Court, Central District of
California, 1981.
511 F.Supp. 416.

MALETZ, J.

This is an action by the United States to recover Medicare funds paid to the Healthwin-Midtown Convalescent Hospital and Rehabilitation Center, Inc. (Healthwin). The defendants are Healthwin and Israel Zide, its former president and owner of fifty percent of its stock.

The facts are as follows: On September 14, 1971, Healthwin was organized in California for the purpose of operating a health care facility. From that date, until November 30, 1974, it participated as a provider of services under the Medicare Act, [citation], and received periodic payments from the United States Department of Health, Education and Welfare (HEW). These payments, which were compensation for the services provided Medicare beneficiaries by Healthwin, were only approximations of the exact amount due; the exact amount was determined by periodic audits conducted by Blue Cross of Southern California which was HEW's agent for the purpose of paying Healthwin and auditing its cost reports. It is undisputed that these audits showed that a series of overpayments had been made to Healthwin in 1972, 1973 and 1974 in the total amount of $30,481.55. It is this sum, plus interest, that the United States seeks to recover here.

* * *

Against this background, the issue here is whether defendant Zide is personally liable for the Medicare overpayments to Healthwin. As a basis for such liability, plaintiff [United States] first argues that the corporate entity should be disregarded under the *alter ego* theory of liability. * * *

We note at the outset that plaintiff's *alter ego* claim must be analyzed in accordance with state law. [Citation.] And under California law, "[i]ssues of *alter ego* do not lend themselves to strict rules and *prima facie* cases. Whether the corporate veil should be pierced depends upon the innumerable individual equities of each case." [Citation.] Generally, however, the corporate veil may be pierced when it is shown:

(1) that there . . . [is] such unity of interest and ownership that the separate personalities of the corporation and the individual no longer exist and (2) that if the acts are treated as those of the corporation alone, an inequitable result will follow.

[Citation.]

With regard to the "unity of interest and ownership" test, . . . the evidence at trial showed that at all times relevant here, Zide was a fifty percent shareholder of the Healthwin corporation. In addition, Zide had a fifty percent interest in a partnership which owned both the realty in which Healthwin's health care facility was located and the furnishings used at that facility.

Zide was also president of the Healthwin corporation as well as a member of its board of directors and the administrator of its health care facility. While there were other members of the board, they usually did not attend board meetings. Further, only Zide could sign the corporation's checks without the prior approval of another corporate officer, and virtually all the corporation's checks were in fact signed by him. Thus, Zide alone controlled the corporation's operations. Although not dispositive, substantial ownership of a corporation and dominance of its management, as has been shown here, are factors favoring the piercing of the corporate veil. [Citations.]

Other factors the courts consider in determining whether the corporate veil should be pierced include: the inadequacy of the corporation's capitalization or its insolvency; the failure to observe corporate formalities; the absence of regular board meetings; the nonfunctioning of corporate directors; the commingling of corporate and noncorporate assets; the diversion of assets from the corporation to the detriment of creditors; and the failure of an individual to maintain an arm's length relationship with the corporation. [Citations.]

All these factors are present here. Zide himself testified that the corporation was undercapitalized. This testimony was confirmed by further evidence which established that although Healthwin consistently had outstanding liabilities in excess of $150,000, its initial capitalization was only $10,000. * * * In 1974 and 1975 the liabilities of the corporation continued substantially to exceed its assets.

The evidence also established that Zide exercised his control over Healthwin so as to cause its finances to become inextricably intertwined with both his personal finances and his other business holdings. * * *

* * *

The necessary conclusion from all this is that Zide handled Healthwin's finances so as to accommodate his own business interests. Treatment of corporate assets in this fashion has long been considered a significant factor supporting the piercing of the corporate veil. [Citations.]

Another factor present here is that the operations of Healthwin were marked by an essential disregard of corporate formalities. [Citation.] Thus board meetings were not regularly held and with the exception of the first board meeting Zide and his wife were the only directors or shareholders present.

There is the final consideration that the court should not pierce the corporation's veil unless necessary to prevent an inequitable result. [Citations.] As to this, it is not necessary that plaintiff prove actual fraud; it is enough if the failure to pierce the corporation's veil would result in an injustice. [Citations.] Given the situation present here, the court must conclude that it would be unjust not to pierce the corporate veil. For one thing,

Healthwin's undercapitalization subjected all its creditors, including plaintiff, to inequitable risks regarding Healthwin's obligations to them. [Citations.] Further, the court finds it particularly inequitable that in 1974 Healthwin, though insolvent, paid back to the Zide partnership some $109,000 it had previously borrowed from the partnership leaving a balance due the partnership of only $164.06. What is more, the record indicates that during 1975 Healthwin repaid Zide at least $39,384 on loans he had made to it.

In view of the foregoing considerations, the court holds that Healthwin's corporate entity should be disregarded under the *alter ego* theory of liability.

* * *

For the reasons set forth above, the court holds that Zide is personally liable to plaintiff for the Medicare overpayments to Healthwin. Accordingly, judgment will be entered against defendants in the sum of $30,481.55 plus interest at seven percent from the date of first demand on November 13, 1973.

Disregard of Corporateness: Parent-Subsidiary

BERGER v. COLUMBIA BROADCASTING SYSTEM, INC.

United States Court of Appeals, Fifth Circuit, 1972.
453 F.2d 991.

GOLDBERG, J.

[Berger was planning to produce a fashion show in Las Vegas. In April 1965, Berger entered into a written licensing agreement with CBS Films, Inc., a wholly owned subsidiary of CBS, for presentation of the show. In 1966 Stewart Cowley decided to produce a fashion show similar to Berger's and entered into a contract with CBS. CBS broadcast Cowley's show and not Berger's show, and Berger brought this action against CBS to recover damages for breach of his contract with CBS Films. Berger claims that CBS is liable because CBS Films is its instrumentality or alter ego, and that the court should disregard the parent-subsidiary form. In support of this claim, Berger has shown that CBS Films' directors are employees of CBS, that CBS's organizational chart includes CBS Films, and that all lines of employee authority from CBS Films pass through employees of CBS to the chairman of the board of CBS. CBS, in turn, argues that Berger has failed to justify piercing the corporate veil and disregarding the corporate identity of CBS Films in order to hold CBS liable.]

* * *

It is elemental jurisprudence that a corporation is a creature of the law, endowed with a personality separate and distinct from that of its owners, and that one of the principal purposes for legal sanctioning of a separate corporate personality is to accord stockholders an opportunity to limit their personal liability. There does exist, however, a large class of cases in which the separateness of a corporate entity has been disregarded and a parent corporation held liable for the acts of its subsidiary because the subsidiary's affairs had been so controlled as to render it merely an instrument or agent of its parent. [Citation.] But the dual personality of parent and subsidiary is not lightly disregarded, since application of the instrumentality rule operates to defeat one of the principal purposes for which the law has created the corporation. [Citation.] Therefore, to justify judicial derogation of the separateness of a corporate creature, an aggrieved party must prove something more than a parent's mere ownership of a majority or even all of the capital stock and the parent's use of its power as an incident of its stock ownership to elect officers and directors of the subsidiary. [Citations.]

In formulating a basis for predicating liability of a parent corporation for the acts of its subsidiary, courts have developed various legal theories and descriptive terms to explain the relationship between a subsidiary and its dominating parent. For example, un-

der the "identity" theory the separate corporate entity of the dominated subsidiary is disregarded and the parent and subsidiary are treated as one corporation. [Citation.] Furthermore, a dominated subsidiary has been labeled an instrument, agent, adjunct, branch, dummy, department, or tool of the parent corporation. [Citation.] In Lowendahl v. Baltimore & O.R.R., [citation], a New York court analyzed the various terms and legal theories and concluded that the instrumentality rule furnished the most practical theory for toppling a parent corporation's immunity. The court in *Lowendahl* then postulated the following three elements as the quantum of proof necessary to sustain application of the instrumentality rule:

(1) Control, not mere majority or complete stock control, but complete domination, not only of finances, but of policy and business practice in respect to the transaction attacked so that the corporate entity as to this transaction had at the time no separate mind, will or existence of its own; and (2) Such control must have been used by the defendant to commit fraud or wrong, to perpetrate the violation of a statutory or other positive legal duty, or a dishonest and unjust act in contravention of plaintiff's legal rights; and (3) The aforesaid control and breach of duty must proximately cause the injury or unjust loss complained of.

Applying these three elements to the relationship between the defendant and Films in the case at bar, we first turn to the lower court's factual determinations. The district court held that at all relevant times Films was merely an instrumentality of the defendant based on the following findings: (1) the board of directors of Films consisted solely of employees of the defendant; (2) the organization chart of CBS, Inc. included Films; and (3) all lines of employee authority from Films passed through employees of the defendant and other subsidiaries to the chairman of the board of CBS, Inc. In addition, the trial judge was greatly influenced by the fact that several witnesses, including a comptroller of one of the defendant's subsidiaries, testified that Films was a "division" of CBS, Inc. Comparing these several facts to the requisite quantum of proof necessary to satisfy *Lowendahl's* "control" element, we think it is obvious that these factual determinations, standing alone, are insufficient to sustain application of the instrumentality rule. Moreover, an independent examination of the record in this case convinces us that the evidence adduced below concerning the relationship between the defendant and Films could not sustain any finding that the defendant completely dominated not only the finances, but the policy and business practice of Films.

* * * In our opinion complete stock ownership, common officers and directors, and the use of organizational charts illustrating lines of authority are all business practices common to most parent-subsidiary relationships, and such proof of a parent's potential to dominate its subsidiary is precisely the kind of evidence that New York courts have consistently rejected as insufficient in proving a community of management between corporations. [Citations.] Furthermore, with respect to the testimony concerning Films' status as a division of the defendant, we think this evidence under New York law is equally unpersuasive. Affixing labels to corporate relationships for purposes of showing a parent's complete domination of a subsidiary is a dangerous business. As Justice Cardozo, speaking for the New York Court of Appeals [citation], stated:

Metaphors in law are to be narrowly watched, for starting as devices to liberate thought, they end often by enslaving it. We say at times that the corporate entity will be ignored when the parent corporation operates a business through a subsidiary which is characterized as an "alias" or a "dummy." All this is well enough if the picturesqueness of the epithets does not lead us to forget that the essential term to be defined is the act of operation.

* * * But when a lay witness testifies that one corporation is a division of another,

then individual thought indeed becomes enslaved for a court to assume that the use of a descriptive term, by some process of testimonial osmosis, automatically introduces into evidence a composite of facts tending to show a community of management. Just as siamesing is a biological fact, so must corporate umbilication be anatomically demonstrated under New York Law. For purposes of application of the instrumentality rule, descriptive characterization is simply not an adequate alternative to a factual showing of the essential "act of operation."

Our prerequisition of the record in this case reveals that the evidence concerning the defendant's "act of operation" is totally insufficient to sustain any possible finding that, with respect to the transaction attacked, Films possessed at the time no separate mind, will, or existence of its own.

* * *

Faced with both this testimony and the total absence of any evidence showing the defendant's actual domination of its subsidiary Films during the period in which the plaintiff's contract was executed and allegedly breached, this court has no alternative but to reverse the decision of the district court on the simple basis that plaintiff has failed to prove, in accordance with New York law, that Films was the alter ego of the defendant. We reiterate that under the substantive law of the State of New York a parent's potential to dominate its subsidiary is insufficient to justify application of the instrumentality rule. New York law respects corporate identity, and its destruction by piercing or surrogation requires substantiation of facts, not just organizational charts and labels. The instrumentality referred to in New York cases requires a specific kinetic result, and muscularity to effectuate such result must be demonstrated. Plaintiff's omission in proving such muscularity constitutes his failing.

[The judgment of the district court in favor of Berger is reversed.]

PROBLEMS

1. After part of the shares of a proposed corporation had been successfully subscribed, A, the promoter, hired a carpenter to repair a building. The promoters subsequently secured subscriptions to the balance of the shares and completed the organization, but the corporation declined to use the building or pay the carpenter for the reason that it was not suitable to the purposes of the company. Thus, the carpenter brought suit against the corporation for the amount agreed to be paid him by the promoter. Decision?

2. C. A. Nimocks was a promoter engaged in effecting the organization of the Times Printing Company. On September 12, on behalf of the proposed corporation, he made a contract with McArthur for her services as comptroller for the period of one year beginning October 1. The Times Printing Company was incorporated October 16, and on that date McArthur commenced her duties as comptroller. No formal action with reference to her employment was taken by the board of directors or by any officer, but all the shareholders, directors, and officers knew of the contract made by Nimocks. On December 1, McArthur was discharged without cause. Has she a cause of action against the Times Printing Company?

3. A and B obtained an option on a building which has been used for manufacturing pianos. They acted as the promoters for a corporation and turned over the building to the new corporation for $500,000 worth of stock. As a matter of fact, their option on the building called for a purchase price of only $300,000. The other shareholders desire to have $200,000 of the common stock canceled. Can they succeed in an action to have it canceled?

4. S signed a subscription agreement for ten shares of stock having a par value of $100 per share of the proposed ABC Company. Two weeks later the company was incorporated. A certificate was duly tendered to S, but he refused to accept it. He was notified of all shareholders' meetings, but he never attended. A dividend check was sent to him, but he returned it. ABC Company brings an action against S to recover $1,000. He defends upon the ground that his subscription agreement was an unaccepted offer and that he had done nothing to

ratify it and that he was, therefore, not liable upon it. Decision?

5. A, B, and C petitioned for a corporate charter for the purpose of conducting a retail shoe business. All the statutory provisions were complied with, except that they failed to have their charter recorded. This was an oversight on their part, and they felt that they had fully complied with the law. They operated the business for three years, after which time it became insolvent. The creditors desire to hold the members personally and individually liable. May they do so?

6. A, B, C, and D decided to form a corporation for bottling and selling apple cider. A, B, and C were to operate the business, and D was to supply the necessary capital but was to have no voice in the management. They went to Jane Lawyer who agreed to organize a corporation for them under the name, A-B-C Inc., and sufficient funds were paid to her to accomplish the incorporation. Lawyer promised that the corporation would definitely be formed by May 3. On April 27, A telephoned Lawyer to inquire how the incorporation was progressing, and Lawyer said she had drafted the articles of incorporation and would send them to the Secretary of State that very day. She assured A that A, B, C, and D would be incorporated before May 3.

Relying on Lawyer's assurance, A, with the approval of B and C, on May 4 entered into a written contract with Grower for the latter's entire apple crop. The contract was executed by A in behalf of "A-B-C Inc." Grower delivered the apples as agreed. Unknown to A, B, C, D, or Grower the articles of incorporation were never filed, through Lawyer's negligence. The business subsequently failed.

What are Grower's rights, if any, against A, B, C, and D as individuals?

7. The AB Corporation has outstanding 20,000 shares of common stock without par value, of which 19,000 are owned by Peter B. Arson, 500 shares are owned by Elizabeth Arson, his wife, and 500 shares are owned by Joseph Q. Arson, his brother. These three individuals are the officers and directors of the corporation. The AB Corporation obtained a $250,000 fire insurance policy covering a certain building owned by it. Thereafter, Peter B. Arson set fire to the building which was wholly destroyed by the fire. The corporation now brings an action against the fire insurance company to recover on the $250,000 fire insurance policy. What judgment?

8. A Corporation is formed for the purpose of manufacturing, buying, selling, and dealing in drugs, chemicals, and similar products. The corporation, under authority of its board of directors, contracted to purchase the land and building occupied by it as a factory and store. S, a shareholder, sues in equity to restrain the corporation from completing the contract, claiming that as the certificate of incorporation contained no provision authorizing the corporation to purchase real estate, the contract was *ultra vires*. Decision?

9. X Corporation, organized under the laws of State S, sends traveling salespersons into State M to solicit orders which are accepted only at the Home Office of X Corporation in State S. D, a resident of State M, places an order which is accepted by X Corporation in State S. The Corporation Act of State M provides that "no foreign corporation transacting business in this state without a certificate of authority shall be permitted to maintain an action in any court of this state until such corporation shall have obtained a certificate of authority." D fails to pay for the goods, and when X Corporation sues D in a court of State M, D defends on the ground that X Corporation does not possess a certificate of authority from State M. Result?

Chapter 34

FINANCIAL STRUCTURE

CAPITAL is necessary for any business to function. Two of the principal sources of capital formation in corporations involve debt and equity investment securities. An initial, and often continuing, source of corporate funds derives from the sale of equity securities. **Equity securities** represent an ownership interest in the corporation and include both common and preferred stock. In addition, corporations finance much of their continued operations through debt securities. **Debt securities,** or bonds, do not represent an ownership interest in the corporation but rather create a debtor-creditor relationship between the corporation and the bondholder. The third principal way in which a corporation may meet its financial needs is through retained earnings.

This chapter will discuss debt and equity securities as well as the payment of dividends and other distributions. In addition, the last part of this chapter will examine the manner in which debt and equity investment securities are transferred.

DEBT SECURITIES

Corporations frequently find it advantageous to utilize debt as a source of funds. Debt securities generally involve the corporation's promise to repay the principal amount of the loan at a stated time and to pay interest, usually at a fixed rate, while the debt is outstanding. In addition to bonds a corporation may finance its operations through the use of other forms of debt such as credit extended by its suppliers and short-term commercial paper.

AUTHORITY TO ISSUE DEBT SECURITIES

The Model Act provides that "[e]ach corporation shall have power to . . . borrow money at such rates of interest as the corporation may determine, issue its notes, bonds, and other obligations, and secure any of its obligations by mortgage or pledge of all or any of its property, franchises, and income." Section 4(h). Moreover, the board of directors may do so without the authorization or consent of the shareholders.

TYPES OF DEBT SECURITIES

Debt securities can be classified into various types depending upon their characteristics. However, there are a great number of variants and combinations of each type, limited only by the ingenuity of the corporation. Debt securities are typically issued under an *indenture* or debt agreement, which specifies in great detail the terms of the loan.

Unsecured Bonds

Unsecured bonds, usually called **debentures,** have only the obligation of the corporation behind them. Debenture holders, thus, are unsecured creditors and rank equally with other general creditors. In order to protect the unsecured bondholders, debenture agreements frequently impose limitations upon the corporation's borrowing, payment of dividends, as well as its redemption and reacquisition of its own shares.

Secured Bonds

A secured creditor is one whose claim against the corporation is enforceable not only against the general assets of the corporation but is also a lien upon specific property. Thus, secured bond holders enjoy the security of specific corporate property in addition to the general obligation of the corporation. After exhaustion of the specified security, the holder of secured bonds becomes a general creditor with respect to any unsatisfied amount of the debt.

Income Bonds

Traditionally, debt securities bear a fixed interest rate which is payable without regard to the financial condition of the corporation. Income bonds, on the other hand, condition the payment of interest to some extent upon corporate earnings. This provision lessens the burden of the debt upon the issuer during periods of financial adversity. Nonetheless, some income bonds call for a stated percentage of return regardless of earnings with additional payments dependent upon earnings.

Convertible Bonds

Convertible bonds may be exchanged, usually at the option of the holder, for other securities of the corporation at a specified ratio. For example, a convertible bond may provide that the bondholder shall have the right for a specified time to exchange each bond for twenty shares of common stock.

Callable Bonds

Callable bonds are bonds that are subject to a **redemption** provision which permits the corporation to redeem or call (that is, pay off) all or part of the issue before maturity at a specified redemption price. This provision enables the corporation to reduce fixed costs, to improve its credit rating, to refinance at a lower interest rate, to free mortgaged property, or to reduce its proportion of debt.

EQUITY SECURITIES

The shareholders of a corporation as owners of the equity occupy a position of greater financial risk than creditors and bear in greater measure than any other class of investor the impact of changes in the corporation's fortunes and general economic conditions. The market value of shares of stock should proportionately advance more in times of prosperity and decline more in times of adversity, and do either more speedily, than should the market value of bonds, debentures, or any type of debt security.

Shares are a method of describing a proportionate proprietary interest in a corporate enterprise, but they do not in any way vest their owner with title to any property of the corporation. However, shares do confer on their owner a threefold interest in the corporation: (1) the right to participate in control, (2) the right to participate in the earnings of the corporation, and (3) the right to participate in the residual assets of the corporation upon dissolution. The shareholder's interest is usually evidenced by a certificate of ownership and is recorded by the corporation.

ISSUANCE OF SHARES

Authority to Issue

The amount of shares to be initially issued is determined by the promoters or incorporators and is generally governed by practical business considerations and financial needs. A corporation, however, is limited to selling only the amount of shares that has been authorized in the articles of incorporation. Section 15. Once the amount which the corporation is authorized to issue has been established and specified in the charter, it cannot be increased or decreased without amendment to the charter. Section 58(d). This means that the shareholders have the residual authority over increases or decreases in the amount of authorized capital stock, since they must approve any amendment to the articles of incorporation. Consequently, it is a frequent practice to authorize initially more shares than are immediately to be issued. Un-

authorized shares of stock which are purportedly issued by a corporation are void.

Qualification of Stock

All States now have statutes regulating the issuance and sale of corporate shares and other securities, popularly known as **"Blue Sky Laws."** These statutes all have provisions prohibiting fraud in the sale of securities. In addition, a number of States require the registration of securities, while some States also regulate brokers, dealers, and others who engage in the securities business. In no case, however, does any State, by qualifying an issue of stock or other security for sale, give any endorsement of the merits of the security.

In 1933, Congress passed the first Federal statute providing regulation of securities offered for sale and sold through the use of the mails or instrumentalities of interstate commerce. This statute, often called the **"Truth in Securities Act,"** is administered by the Securities and Exchange Commission (S.E.C.). It is a disclosure type statute: the S.E.C. does not examine the merits of the security proposed to be offered but only the truthfulness, accuracy, and completeness of the information given and required to be given in a registration statement and prospectus. Regulation of the issuance and sale of securities is sanctioned by anti-fraud provisions and by requirements for registration of broker-dealers, agents, and investment advisers, as well as by registration of securities.

An exemption from the requirement of registration under the Blue-Sky Laws of most States and the Securities Act of 1933 may be available under certain conditions upon compliance with the rules and regulations of the appropriate State agency and of the S.E.C. If no exemption is available, a corporation offering for sale or selling its shares of stock or other securities, as well as any person selling such securities, is subject to court injunction, possible criminal prosecution, and civil liability in damages to the persons to whom securities are sold in violation of the regulatory statute. A more detailed discussion of Federal regulation of securities appears in Chapter 44.

Pre-emptive Rights

At common law, a shareholder has the pre-emptive right to purchase a *pro rata* share of every new offering of stock by the corporation in order to preserve his proportionate interest in the equity. Pre-emptive rights do not apply to the re-issue of previously issued shares, shares issued for non-cash consideration, or shares issued in connection with a merger or consolidation. There is a division among the jurisdictions whether pre-emptive rights apply to originally authorized shares. Currently, most States expressly authorize the articles of incorporation to deny or limit pre-emptive rights. In some States pre-emptive rights exist unless denied by the charter while in others they do not exist unless the charter so provides. See Sections 26 and 26A.

In the absence of a pre-emptive right, a shareholder may be unable to prevent a dilution of his ownership interest in the corporation. For example, X owns 200 shares of stock of the ABC Company, which has a total of 1,000 shares outstanding. The company determines to increase its capital stock to 2,000 shares. If X has pre-emptive rights, he and every other shareholder will be offered one share of the newly issued stock for every share they own. Upon accepting the offer and buying the stock, he will have 400 shares out of a total of 2,000 outstanding, and his relative interest in the corporation is unchanged. However, without pre-emptive rights he may have only 200 out of the 2,000 shares outstanding and, instead of owning 20 percent of the stock, would own 10 percent.

Amount of Consideration for Shares

Shares are deemed fully paid and non-assessable when the corporation receives full payment of the lawful consideration for which the shares are issued. Section 19. The amount of that consideration depends upon the type of shares being issued.

Par Value Stock Par value shares may be issued for any amount, not less than par, set by the board of directors or shareholders. The par value of a share of stock can be an arbitrary value selected by the corporation and may or may not reflect either the actual value of the share or the actual price paid to the corporation. It only indicates the *minimum price* which the corporation must receive for it. The par value of stock must be stated in the articles of incorporation.

The consideration received constitutes *stated capital* to the extent of the par value of the shares; any consideration in excess of par value constitutes *capital surplus*.

The 1979 amendments to the MBCA eliminated the concepts of "par values," "stated capital," and "capital surplus." Under the MBCA as amended *all* shares may be issued for such consideration as authorized by the board of directors. Section 18(a).

One court has explained the lack of practical significance between par and no par stock by observing that "if the assets received are one thousand dollars in money, it is of no consequence whether five shares or ten shares, or one thousand shares are given for it. Each share has its one-fifth or one-tenth or one one-thousandth aliquot part of the thousand dollars as the case may be, and no one is damaged because everyone knows that under each share is simply its proportionate part of the total assets, unexpressed in terms of money." *Bodell v. General Gas & Electric Corp.*, 15 Del.Ch. 119, 130, 132 A. 442, 447 (1926).

No Par Value Stock Shares without par value may be issued for any amount set by the board of directors or shareholders. The entire consideration received constitutes *stated capital* unless within sixty days after issuance the board of directors allocates a portion of the consideration to capital surplus. Section

21, repealed in 1979. The directors are free to allocate any or all of the consideration received, unless the no par stock has a liquidation preference. In that event, only the consideration in excess of the amount of liquidation preference may be allocated to capital surplus. For this reason preferred stock is usually issued with a par value. Thus, no par shares provide the directors with great latitude in establishing capital surplus, which can in some jurisdictions provide greater flexibility for subsequent distributions to shareholders.

Treasury Stock Treasury stock are shares that have been issued and subsequently reacquired by the corporation. Treasury shares are *issued but not outstanding*, in contrast to shares owned by shareholders which are deemed issued *and* outstanding. Treasury shares may be disposed of by the corporation for any amount the board of directors determines, even if the shares have a par value that is more than the sale price. Treasury shares may not be voted, nor any dividend be paid upon them, nor do they have any preemptive rights.

The 1979 amendments to the MBCA eliminated the concept of treasury shares. Under the MBCA as amended all shares reacquired by a corporation constitute authorized but unissued shares, unless the articles of incorporation prohibit reissue, in which event the authorized shares are reduced by the number of shares acquired. Section 6.

Figure 34-1 illustrates the issuance of shares.

Payment for Newly Issued Shares

With respect to the issuance of capital stock, there are two paramount questions: (a) What type of consideration may be validly accepted in payment for shares, and (b) who shall determine whether valid consideration has been paid and what limits are placed upon the discretion of those making the decision?

Type of Consideration Consideration for the issuance of capital stock is defined in a more limited fashion than consideration is under contract law. Cash, property, and services actually rendered to the corporation are generally acceptable as valid consideration, but promissory notes and future services are not. Section 19. *See United Steel Industries, Inc. v. Manhart.*

The Revised Act has greatly liberalized this rule by specifically validating contracts for future services and promissory notes as consideration for the issuance of shares. RMBCA Section 6.21(b). To guard against possible abuse, the Revised Act requires that corporations annually inform in writing shareholders of all shares issued during the pervious year for promissory notes or promises of future services. RMBCA Section 16.21.

Valuation of Consideration The determination of the value to be placed on property which is exchanged for shares is the responsibility of the directors. The ultimate consequence of issuing stock for overvalued property may be to impose liability for the amount of the overvaluation upon the shareholder to creditors or to other shareholders even though the stock purports to be fully paid and nonassessable. The majority of jurisdictions hold that valuation is a matter of opinion and that, in the absence of fraud in the transaction, the judgment of the board of directors as to the value of the consideration received for shares shall be conclusive. Section 19.

Liability for Shares

A corporation is said to have issued **watered stock** when it issues fully paid up and nonassessable shares upon receiving consideration worth less than the full, lawful consideration for the shares. The liability of shareholders on watered stock is enforceable by both the corporation and its creditors. For example, assume that the directors of Corporation X authorize the issuance of 2,000

FIGURE 34-1   Issuance of Shares

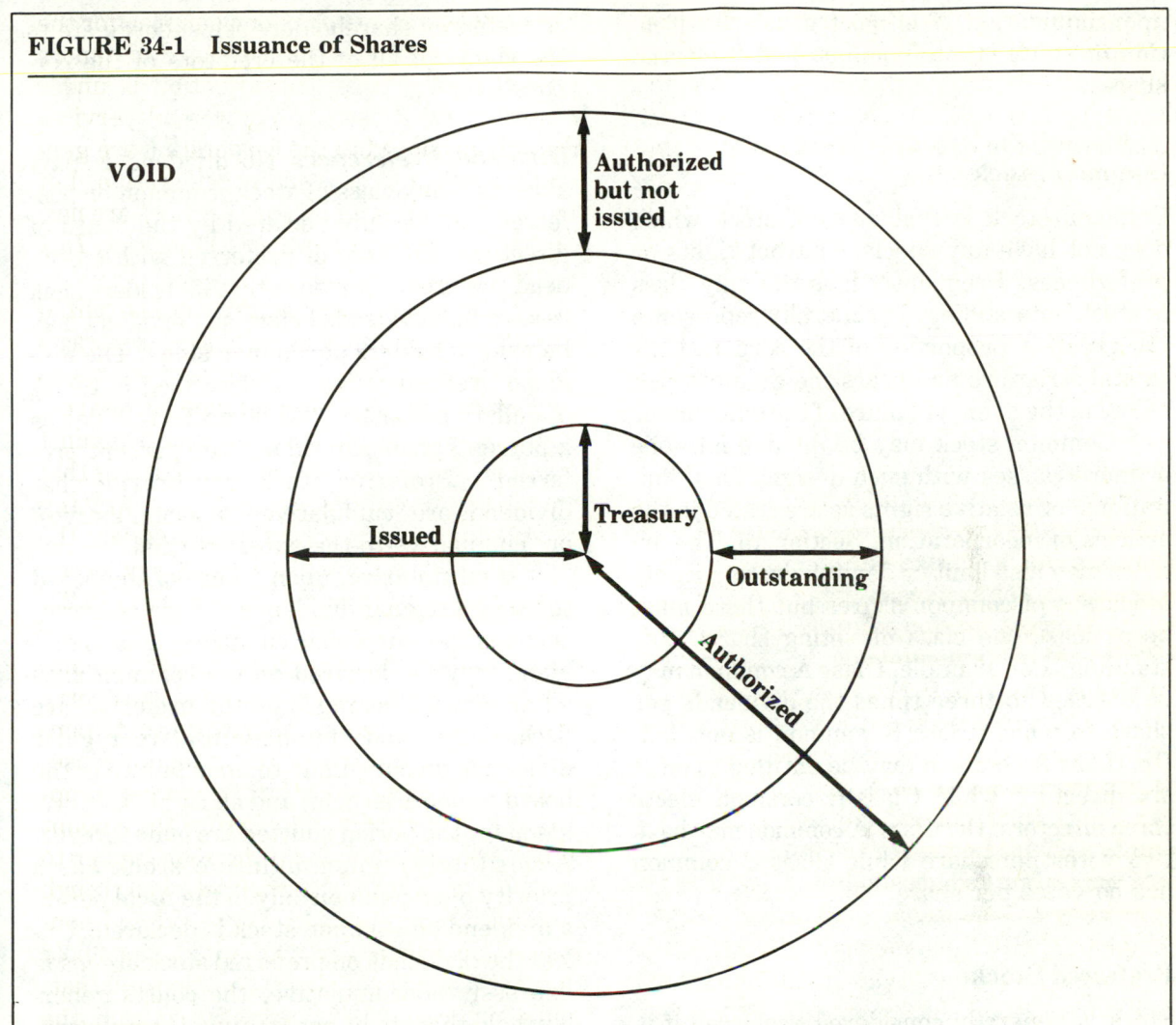

shares of common stock for five dollars per share to A for property which the directors value at $10,000. The valuation is fraudulent and the property is actually worth $5,000. A is liable to Corporation X and its creditors for $5,000. If, on the other hand, the valuation had been made by the directors without fraud and in good faith, then A would not be liable even though the property is actually worth less than $10,000.

A transferee of watered stock is also liable for the balance due on the stock until the par or stated value of the stock has been fully paid, unless the certificate transferred to her recites that it is fully paid and non-assessable or she acquires the shares in good faith and without knowledge or notice that the shares are not fully paid. Section 25.

CLASSES OF SHARES

Corporations are generally authorized by statute to issue two or more classes of stock which may vary with respect to their rights to dividends, their voting rights, and their right to share in the assets of the corporation upon liquidation. The most usual classification of stock is into common and preferred shares.

Common Stock

Common stock is that class of stock which does not have any special contract rights or preferences. Frequently it is the only class of stock outstanding. It generally represents the greatest proportion of the corporation's capital structure and bears the greatest risk of loss in the event of failure of the enterprise.

Common stock may be divided into one or more classes with such designations, limitations, or relative rights as are stated in the articles of incorporation. Section 15. The articles may also limit or deny the voting rights of classes of common shares but there must be at least one class of voting shares outstanding. For example, Class A common may be entitled to three times the dividends per share to which Class B common is entitled. Or, Class A common may be entitled to elect six directors while Class B common elects three directors. Or, Class A common may have two votes per share while Class B common has no votes per share.

Preferred Stock

Stock is generally considered preferred if it has contractual rights superior to common stock with regard to dividends or assets upon liquidation or both. Other types of special rights or privileges are not generally considered as removing a class of stock from the classification of common stock. The contractual rights and preferences of an issue of preferred stock must be provided for in the articles of incorporation. Section 15.

Notwithstanding the special rights and preferences which distinguish preferred from common, both represent a contribution of capital. Preferred stock is no more a debt than common, and until a dividend is declared the holder of preferred shares is not a creditor of the corporation. Furthermore, the rights of preferred shareholders are subordinate to the rights of all of the creditors of the corporation.

Dividend Preferences No dividend is payable upon any class of stock, common or preferred, unless duly declared by the board of directors. An issue of preferred with a dividend preference provides that its holders shall receive full dividends before any dividend may be paid to holders of common stock. The dividend preference may be described in terms of dollars per share ("$3.00 preferred") or as a percentage of par value ("ten percent preferred"). Preferred stock may provide that dividends are "cumulative," "noncumulative," or "cumulative-to-the-extent-earned."

If **cumulative**, upon failure of the board to declare regular dividends on the preferred, such omitted dividends cumulate, and no dividend may be declared on the common until all dividend arrearages on the preferred are declared and paid. If **noncumulative**, regular dividends do not cumulate upon failure of the board to declare them, and all rights to a dividend for the period omitted are gone forever. Accordingly, noncumulative stock has a priority over common only in the fiscal period a dividend on common stock is declared. Unless the dividends on preferred stock are made expressly noncumulative, the courts generally hold them to be cumulative. **Cumulative-to-the-extent-earned** shares cumulate unpaid dividends only to the extent funds were legally available to pay such dividends in that fiscal period.

Preferred stock may also be **participating.** The nature and extent of such participation on a specified basis with the common stock must be stated in the articles of incorporation. For example, a class of participating preferred stock could be entitled to share at the same rate with the common in any additional distribution of earnings for a given year *after* provision has been made for payment of the prior preferred dividend and payment of dividends on the common at a rate equal to the fixed rate of the preferred.

The increased volatility of the capital markets has necessitated not only the development of stock with special provisions but also greater flexibility in designing these provisions. Therefore, the Act permits the articles of incorporation to authorize the board of directors to fix the terms of a series of preferred shares to meet the current financial markets, without holding a shareholders' meeting to amend the articles of incorporation. Section 16.

Liquidation Preferences When a corporation is dissolved, its assets liquidated, and claims of all of its creditors have been satisfied, the remaining assets are distributable *pro rata* among the shareholders according to their priority as provided in the articles of incorporation. In the event that preferred stock does not expressly provide for a preference of any kind upon dissolution and liquidation, the holders of the preferred stock share *pro rata* with the common shareholders.

When a liquidation preference is provided, preferred stock usually has priority over common to the extent of the par value of the stock. *See Rothschild International Corp. v. Liggett Group, Inc.* In addition, if specified, preferred shares may participate beyond the liquidation preference in a stated ratio with other classes of shares. Such shares are called participating preferred with reference to liquidation. If not so specified, preferred shares do not participate beyond the liquidation preference. Thus, in the case of *In re Olympic National Agencies, Inc.*, 74 Wn. 2d 1, 442 P.2d 246 (1968), Olympic National Agencies was organized with an authorized capitalization of preferred stock and common stock. The articles of incorporation provided for a seven percent annual dividend for the preferred stock. The articles further stated that the preferred stock would be given priority interests in the corporation's assets up to the par value of the stock. In 1965 the shareholders voted to dissolve Olympic. Because the assets of Olympic greatly exceeded its liabilities, the liquidating trustee petitioned the court for instructions on the respective rights of the shareholders in the assets of the corporation upon dissolution. The court held that the preferred stockholders should be paid only the par value of their stock before any liquidation dividends are paid to the common stockholders. Where one class of stock is afforded a stated preference as to assets on liquidation and the articles of incorporation are silent as to any further participation, the clear implication is that the rights of the preferred stock are exhausted once the preference has been satisfied.

Additional Rights and Limitations Preferred stock may have additional rights, designations, and limitations. For instance, it may be expressly denied voting rights if permitted by the statute, it may be redeemable by the corporation, or convertible into shares of another class. Sections 15 and 33. Many States and the Model Act prohibit "upstream" conversions; that is, conversions of preferred shares into a class of shares having prior or superior rights and preferences as to dividends or distribution of assets upon liquidation. Section 15(e). Accordingly, preferred stock may be converted into common but common may not be converted into preferred.

Stock Rights and Options

A corporation may create and issue rights or options entitling the holders of them to purchase from the corporation shares of a specified class or classes. Such rights or options shall set forth the terms upon which, the time or times within which, and the price or prices at which such shares may be purchased from the corporation upon the exercise of any such right or option. In the absence of fraud in the transaction, the judgment of the board of directors as to the adequacy of the consideration received for such rights or options shall be conclusive. Section 20. One of the uses of share rights or options is incentive compensation plans for directors, officers, and employees. Another is to assist in raising capital by making one class of securities more attractive by including rights to purchase shares in another class.

DIVIDENDS AND OTHER DISTRIBUTIONS

The objective of every private, for-profit business corporation is to operate profitably, and it is a fundamental desire of most shareholders to share in the profits through the receipt of distributions, in particular dividends. In almost every State the declaration of distributions, including dividends, is within the discretion of the board of directors subject to certain restrictions and limitations.

The conditions under which the earnings of a business may be paid out in the form of dividends or other distributions of corporate assets will depend upon the contractual rights of the holders of the particular shares involved, the provisions in the charter and by-laws of the corporation, and the statute of the State of incorporation which is designed to protect creditors and shareholders from dissipation of corporate assets. More significant protection of creditors is provided by contractual restrictions typically included in their loan agreements, as well as State fraudulent conveyance laws and Federal bankruptcy law.

TYPES OF DIVIDENDS AND OTHER DISTRIBUTIONS

The Model Act defines a distribution as "a direct or indirect transfer of money or other property (except its own shares) or incurrence of indebtedness, by a corporation to or for the benefit of any of its shareholders in respect of any of its shares, whether by dividend or by purchase, redemption or other acquisition of its shares, or otherwise." Section 2(i). In addition to these distributions, stock dividends and stock splits, which are not included in this definition, will also be covered in this section.

Cash Dividends

The most customary type of dividend is the cash dividend declared and paid at regular intervals from legally available funds. These dividends may vary in amount depending upon the policy of the board of directors and the earnings of the enterprise.

Property Dividends

While dividends are almost invariably paid in cash, in a few instances a distribution of earnings has been made to shareholders in the form of property and has been termed a property dividend. On one occasion a distillery declared and paid a dividend in bonded whiskey.

Stock Dividends

A stock or share dividend is a ratable distribution of additional shares of the capital stock of the corporation to its shareholders. The practical and legal significance of a stock dividend differs greatly from a dividend payable in cash or property. Following the payment of a stock dividend, the assets of the corporation are no less than they were before, and the shareholder does not have any greater relative interest in the net worth of the corporation than he had before except possibly where the dividend is paid in shares of a different class. His shares will each represent a smaller proportionate interest in the assets of the corporation, but by reason of the increase in the number of shares his total investment will remain the same. For instance, Shareholder A owns 100 shares of Corporation X's common stock of which 1,000 shares are issued and outstanding. The board of directors declares and pays a 15 percent stock dividend. Prior to the stock dividend A owned 100 out of a total of 1,000 shares, or 10 percent. Subsequent to the stock dividend A owns 115 shares out of 1,150 total shares, or 10 percent. Although A owns more shares, her proportionate ownership of the common stock is unchanged by the stock dividend. Accordingly, a stock dividend is not considered to be a distribution.

Stock Splits

A stock dividend should not be confused with a stock split. By the latter, each of the issued and outstanding shares is simply broken up into a greater number of shares, each representing a proportionately smaller interest in the corporation. The usual purpose of a stock split is to lower the price per share to a more marketable price and thus increase the number of potential shareholders. As with a stock dividend, a stock split is not a distribution.

Liquidating Dividends

While dividends ordinarily are identified with the distribution of profits, a distribution of capital assets to shareholders upon termination of the business is considered a form of dividend and is referred to as a liquidating dividend. A distribution to common shareholders of paid-in surplus or capital surplus is also a liquidating dividend and should be specifically identified as such. Incorporation statutes usually require that the shareholder be informed when a distribution is a liquidating dividend.

Redemption of Shares

Redemption is the repurchase by the corporation of its own shares, usually at its own option. Shares of common stock ordinarily are not subject to redemption. Preferred shares, however, are frequently redeemable by the corporation at a **call** price stated in the stock certificate. This power of redemption must be expressly provided for in the articles of incorporation. Section 15(a).

Acquisition of Shares

A corporation may acquire its own shares by purchase, gift, or otherwise. Such shares, unless canceled, are referred to as treasury shares. Under the MBCA as amended such shares are considered authorized but unissued. Section 6. As with redemptions, acquisition of shares is a distribution to shareholders and has an effect similar to a dividend.

LEGAL RESTRICTIONS ON DIVIDENDS AND OTHER DISTRIBUTIONS

The board of directors in its discretion determines when to declare distributions and dividends and in what amount. The corporation's working capital requirements, expectations of shareholders, tax consequences, and other factors influence the board in its formation of distribution policy. Nonetheless, the board is constrained as to the amount of distributions it may declare by a number of legal restrictions. All States have statutes restricting the funds that are legally available for dividends and other distributions of corporate assets. In many instances contractual restrictions imposed by lenders provide even more stringent limitations upon the declaration of dividends and distributions.

States restrict in one way or another the payment of dividends and other distributions in order to protect creditors. All States impose the **equity insolvency test** which prohibits the payment of any dividend or other distribution when the corporation is insolvent or when the payment of the dividend or distribution would render the corporation insolvent. **"Insolvent"** means the inability of a corporation to pay its debts as they become due in the usual course of its business.

In addition, each State imposes further restrictions as to what funds are legally available to pay dividends and other distributions. Some States permit dividends and other distributions to be paid only out of earned surplus, while others are more permissive by allowing dividends and other distributions to come from any kind of surplus. Moreover, some States permit *dividends* to be paid from current earnings even in the absence of the required surplus. Such dividends are called "nimble dividends."

Definitions

The legal restrictions upon the payment of dividends or other distributions involve the concepts of earned surplus, surplus, net assets, stated capital, and capital surplus. See Figure 34-2.

Earned surplus consists of the undistributed net profits, income, gains, and losses from the date of incorporation.

Surplus means the excess of the net assets of a corporation over its stated capital.

Net assets are the amount by which the total assets of a corporation exceed the total debts of the corporation.

Stated capital is defined as the sum of the consideration received by the corporation for its issued stock, excepting that part of the consideration properly allocated to capital surplus, and including any amount transferred to stated capital upon issuance of shares by way of stock dividend. In the case of par value shares, the amount of stated capital is the aggregate par value of all the issued shares. In the case of no par stock, it is the consideration received by the corporation for all the no par shares which have been issued, except such part as may have been allocated in a manner permitted by law, to an account designated as capital surplus or paid-in surplus.

Capital surplus means the entire surplus of a corporation other than its earned surplus. It may result from an allocation of part of the consideration received for no par shares or from any consideration in excess of par value received for par shares or from a reappraisal upward of certain corporate assets.

Legal Restrictions on Cash Dividends

Earned Surplus Test Unreserved and unrestricted earned surplus is available for dividends in all jurisdictions. Some States permit dividends to be paid *only* from earned surplus; dividends in these jurisdictions may not be paid out of capital surplus or stated capital. Until 1979 the MBCA utilized this test.

FIGURE 34-2   Key Concepts in Legal Restrictions upon Distributions

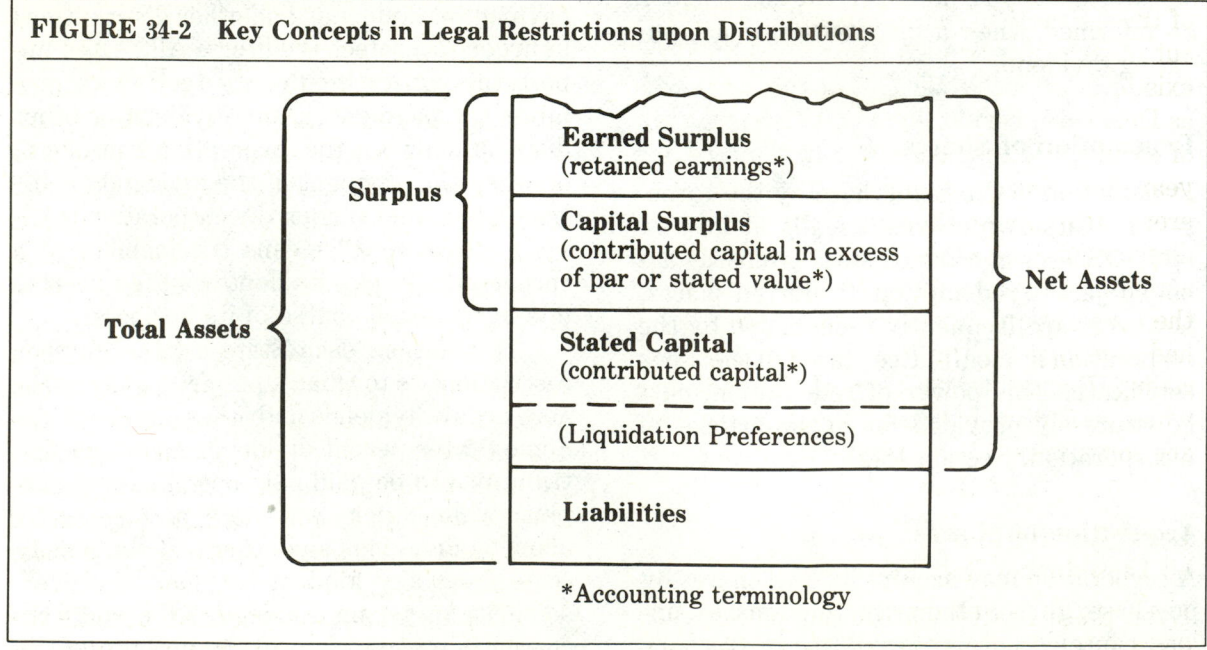

Surplus Test A number of States are less restrictive and permit dividends to be paid out of any surplus—earned or capital. Some of these States express this test by prohibiting dividends that impair stated capital.

Net Asset Test Section 45 of the MBCA as amended states:

Subject to any restrictions in the articles of incorporation, the board of directors may authorize and the corporation may make distributions, except that no distribution may be made if, after giving effect thereto, either:

(a) the corporation would be unable to pay its debts as they become due in the usual course of its business; or

(b) the corporation's total assets would be less than the sum of its total liabilities and (unless the articles of incorporation otherwise permit) the maximum amount that then would be payable, in any liquidation, in respect of all outstanding shares having preferential rights in liquidation.

Nimble Dividends Although dividends in many States are properly payable only out of earnings or earned surplus and are generally not payable when the corporation has an accrued earned deficit, the statutes of a number of these States permit payment of dividends out of current earnings notwithstanding the existence of such deficit. Some States, such as Delaware, permit dividends to be paid out of earnings of the current or next preceding year, but shares having a liquidation preference may not be thus impaired. A board of directors in these States is permitted by timely action to declare a dividend in a year when the corporation has no earnings, provided it had earnings for the year immediately preceding. Because of the time limitation within which such dividends must be declared, they are sometimes called "nimble dividends."

Legal Restrictions on Liquidating Distributions

Even those States that do not permit cash dividends to be paid from capital surplus usu-

ally will permit distributions, or dividends, in partial liquidation from that source. A distribution paid out of such surplus is a return to the shareholders of a part of their investment.

No such distribution may be made, however, when the corporation is insolvent or would be rendered insolvent by the distribution. Distributions from capital surplus are also restricted to protect the liquidation preference of preferred shareholders.

Unless provided for in the articles of incorporation, a liquidating dividend must be authorized not only by the board of directors but also by the affirmative vote of the holders of a majority of the outstanding shares of stock of each class.

The Model Act, as amended, does not distinguish between cash and liquidating dividends but imposes the same limitations discussed above under cash dividends. Section 45.

Legal Restrictions on Redemptions and Acquisition of Shares

To protect creditors and holders of other classes of preferred shares, in most States there are statutory restrictions upon redemption. A corporation may not redeem or purchase its redeemable shares when insolvent or when such redemption or purchase would render it insolvent or reduce its net assets below the aggregate amount payable upon shares having prior or equal rights to the assets of the corporation upon involuntary dissolution.

A corporation may purchase its own shares only out of earned surplus or, if the articles of incorporation permit or if the shareholders approve, out of capital surplus. As with redemption, no purchase of shares may be made at a time when the corporation is insolvent or when such purchase would make it insolvent.

The Model Act, as amended, permits the purchase, redemption, or other acquisition by a corporation of its own shares unless (1) the corporation's total assets after the distribution would be less than the sum of its total liabilities and the maximum amount that then would be payable in respect of all outstanding shares having preferential rights in liquidation, or (2) the corporation would be unable to pay its debts as they become due in the usual course of its business. Section 45.

DECLARATION AND PAYMENT OF DIVIDENDS

The declaration of dividends is within the discretion of the board of directors of the corporation and may not be delegated. However, if the charter clearly and expressly provides for mandatory dividends, the board must comply with the provision. Nonetheless, such provisions are extremely infrequent and any other attempt by shareholders to usurp the power is ineffective, although it is in the shareholders' power to elect a new board. Moreover, it is well settled that there can be no discrimination in the declaration of dividends among shareholders of the same class.

A shareholder may not maintain an action at law against the corporation to recover a dividend until and unless the dividend has been formally declared by resolution of the board of directors. A proper dividend so declared becomes a debt of the corporation and enforceable at law as any other debt.

Where the directors have failed to declare a dividend, a shareholder may bring a suit in equity against them and the corporation seeking a mandatory injunction requiring the directors to declare a dividend. Courts of equity are reluctant to order an injunction of this kind which involves substituting the business judgment of the court for that of the directors elected by the shareholders. A court of equity will, however, grant an injunction and require the directors to declare a dividend where

1. a demand has been made upon the directors before commencement of the suit;
2. corporate earnings or surplus are available out of which a dividend may be legally declared;
3. the earnings or surplus is in the form of available cash; and
4. the directors have acted so unreasonably in withholding a dividend that their conduct clearly amounts to an abuse of discretion.

The existence of a large accumulated surplus will not alone justify compelling the directors to distribute funds which, in their opinion, should be retained for *bona fide* corporate purposes. However, where the evidence shows noncorporate motives or personal animosity as the basis for a refusal to declare dividends, a court may require the directors to distribute what appears to be a reasonable portion of the earnings. *See Dodge v. Ford Motor Co.*

The fact that a preferred shareholder has prior rights with respect to dividends does not make her position different from that of the holder of common shares with respect to the discretion of the directors as to the declaration of dividends. The holders of preferred stock, in the absence of special contractual or statutory rights, must likewise abide by the decision of the directors.

Once lawfully and properly declared, a cash dividend is considered a debt owing by the corporation to the shareholders. It follows from the debtor-creditor relationship created by the declaration of a cash dividend that, once declared, it cannot be rescinded as against nonassenting shareholders. However, a stock dividend may be revoked unless actually distributed.

The time, place, and manner of payment are in the discretion of the directors. It is not uncommon for the resolution declaring a dividend to fix a cutoff date by providing that the dividend shall be paid to the shareholders of record as of the close of business on a specified future date, usually about two weeks earlier than the date fixed for payment. Where the resolution declaring a dividend fixes a cut-off date, the shareholder of record as of that date is entitled to the dividend.

LIABILITY FOR IMPROPER DIVIDENDS AND DISTRIBUTIONS

The Model Act imposes joint and several liability upon the directors of a corporation who vote for or assent to the declaration of a dividend or other distribution of corporate assets contrary to the incorporation statute or the articles of incorporation. Section 48. The measure of damages is the amount of the dividend or distribution in excess of the amount that could have been lawfully paid. The directors may not escape liability by delegation of the power to declare dividends to an executive committee. The directors are not liable, however, if they rely in good faith upon financial statements presented by the corporation's officers, public accountants, or finance committee.

The liability of directors is generally to the corporation or to its creditors. The Model Act expressly provides that the directors who vote for or assent to an illegal dividend or distribution are jointly and severally liable to the corporation. Section 48.

The obligation of a shareholder to repay an illegally declared dividend depends upon a variety of factors which may include the good or bad faith on the part of the shareholder in accepting the dividend, his knowledge of the facts, the solvency or insolvency of the corporation, and, in some instances, special statutory provisions. The existence of statutory liability on the part of directors does not relieve shareholders from the duty to make repayment.

A shareholder who receives illegal dividends either as a result of his own fraudulent act or with knowledge of their unlawful character is under a duty to refund them to the corporation. See Section 48. Where the corporation is insolvent, a dividend may not be retained by the shareholder even though received by him in good faith. The assets of an insolvent corporation are regarded as a trust fund for its creditors. Where an unsuspecting shareholder receives an illegal dividend from a solvent corporation, the majority rule is that he cannot be compelled to make a refund. *See Fried v. Cano.*

TRANSFER OF INVESTMENT SECURITIES

An investor has the right to transfer by way of sale, gift, or pledge her securities just as she has the inherent right to transfer any other properties she may own. The right to transfer securities is a valuable one and the ease with which it may be done adds to their value and marketability. The availability of a ready market for any security affords liquidity and makes the security attractive to investors and useful as collateral.

The statutory rules applicable to transfers of securities are contained in the Uniform Commercial Code, Article 8, Investment Securities, which establishes rules similar to those in Article 3. Article 8 applies not only to shares but also to bonds, debentures, voting trust certificates, certificates of beneficial interest in business trusts, and any other "interest in property of or an enterprise of the issuer or an obligation of the issuer" which is of a "class or series" and "issued or dealt in as a medium for investment." Section 8-102.

A number of aspects of the transfer of securities are also regulated by the Federal securities laws, discussed in Chapter 44.

OWNERSHIP OF SECURITIES

Record Ownership

A security is intangible personal property and exists independently of a certificate. Article 8 permits the issuance and transfer of

"uncertificated securities," which are securities not represented by a certificate, and the transfer of which is registered on books maintained for that purpose by or on behalf of the issuer. Section 8-102(1)(b).

The 1979 amendments to the Model Business Corporation Act provide that "the shares of a corporation shall be represented by certificates or shall be uncertificated shares." Section 23. The rights and obligations of holders of uncertificated shares and certificated shares of the same class and series are identical.

Duty of Issuer to Register Transfer of Security

The issuing corporation is under a duty to register transfer of its certificated securities and issue new certificates to the new owner if:

1. the certificate is indorsed by the appropriate person or persons (Section 8-308);
2. reasonable assurance is given that those endorsements are genuine and effective (Section 8-402);
3. the issuer has no duty as to adverse claims or has discharged the duty (Section 8-403);
4. any applicable law relating to the collection of taxes has been complied with; and
5. the transfer is in fact rightful or is to a *bona fide* purchaser.

The owner or purchaser is entitled to registration in order to vote and to receive dividends, notices, and periodic reports of the corporation and to receive a new certificate, as the only way that he can sell or pledge or dispose of the certificated securities is by a transfer of the certificate.

Lost, Destroyed, or Stolen Certificated Securities

If a certificated security has been lost, destroyed, or wrongfully taken, the owner is entitled to a new certificate to replace the missing one provided she (1) requests it before the issuer has notice that the "missing" certificate has been acquired by a *bona fide* purchaser, (2) files with the issuer a sufficient indemnity bond, and (3) satisfies other reasonable requirements of the issuer such as furnishing a sworn statement of the facts in connection with the loss. Section 8-405(2).

The owner of a lost, destroyed, or stolen certificate may be deprived of the right to a replacement certificate by failing to notify the issuing corporation within a reasonable time after learning of the loss, if the corporation has registered a transfer of the certificate before receiving such notification. Section 8-405(1).

TRANSFER OF SECURITIES

Statute of Frauds

A contract for the sale of securities is not enforceable unless one of the following conditions is satisfied:

1. a writing signed by the party against whom enforcement is sought and indicating that a contract has been made for sale of a stated quantity of described securities at a defined or stated price;
2. performance as evidenced by acceptance of delivery or acceptance of payment, but only to the extent of such delivery or payment;
3. failure to object in writing within ten days to a written confirmation binding on the sender; or
4. an admission in pleading, testimony, or otherwise in court that a contract was made. Section 8-319.

Manner of Transfer

Under the Code, a transfer of certificated securities is made by delivery of the certificate alone if it is in bearer form or indorsed in blank or, if in registered form, which is more usual, by delivery of the certificate with either (1) the indorsement on it by "an appropriate person," or (2) a separate document of assignment and transfer signed by "an appropriate person." The term "appropriate person" includes the person specified in the certificate or entitled to it by special indorsement, their successors in interest, or the authorized agent of a person so specified or so entitled. Section 8–308. A transfer of uncertificated securities occurs at the time the transfer is registered.

Prior to presentment for registration of transfer of a certificated security in registered form, the corporation may treat the registered owner as the person entitled to vote, to receive notices, and otherwise to exercise all of the rights and powers of the owner. Section 8–207.

The delivery of an unindorsed certificate by the owner with the intention of transferring title to the securities represented thereby gives the intended transferee as against the transferor complete rights in the certificate and in the certificated securities, including the right to compel indorsement. He becomes a *bona fide* purchaser of the certificated securities, however, only as of the time the indorsement is supplied. Section 8–307.

Bona Fide Purchasers

A "*bona fide* purchaser" is a purchaser for value in good faith and without notice of any adverse claim who takes delivery of a certificated security in bearer form or in registered form issued to her or indorsed to her or in blank. Section 8–302. The negotiation and transfer of a security to a *bona fide* purchaser passes title to her free of all adverse claims not conspicuously noted on the certificate. Section 8–204. Adverse claims include a claim that a transfer was or would be wrongful or that a particular adverse person is the owner of or has an interest in the security. Section 8–302(2). Thus, the *bona fide* purchaser from

a thief, finder, or other unauthorized person is protected.

Transfer Warranties

As provided by Section 8–306(2), a person by transferring certificated securities to a purchaser for value warrants that

1. the transfer is effective and rightful;
2. the security is genuine and has not been materially altered; and
3. he knows of no fact which might impair the validity of the security.

A person who presents a certificated security for registration of transfer or for payment or exchange warrants to the issuer that he is entitled to the registration, payment, or exchange, but a purchaser for value and without notice of adverse claims who receives a new, reissued, or reregistered certificated security on registration of transfer warrants only that he has no knowledge of any unauthorized signature in a necessary indorsement. Section 8–306(1).

Forged or Unauthorized Indorsement

The owner of securities represented by a certificate is not deprived of his title by a transfer of the certificate bearing a forged or unauthorized indorsement. The purchaser of a security bearing a forged or unauthorized indorsement who resells and transfers it to a *bona fide* purchaser is liable to him for the value of the securities at the time of sale, as he has breached his warranty that the transfer is effective and rightful. Section 8–306(2)(a). Neither party is owner of the securities, as title cannot be transferred through a forged or unauthorized indorsement.

Unless the owner has ratified an unauthorized indorsement or is otherwise precluded from asserting its ineffectiveness, he may assert its ineffectiveness against the issuer and against any purchaser, other than a *bona fide* purchaser who has in good faith received a new, reissued, or reregistered certificated security on registration of transfer. Section 8–311(a). An issuer who registers the transfer of a certificated security upon an unauthorized indorsement is subject to liability for improper registration. Section 8–311(b).

Example: A lost by theft or in some other manner his unindorsed certificate of stock, and within a reasonable time gave notice of the loss to the issuing corporation. X, a thief or finder, forges A's signature on the reverse side of the certificate, or without authority signs A's name by X, as agent. X thereafter sells and delivers the certificate to B, a *bona fide* transferee who pays value and takes the certificate without knowledge of the theft or loss or of the forged or unauthorized indorse-

ment. A is still the owner of the shares, and B is liable to A for their value.

If B surrenders the certificate to the issuing corporation which cancels it and issues a new one in B's name, B is now owner of the shares represented by the certificate registered in his name. Section 8–311. However, A is entitled on demand to receive from the corporation a new certificate for the same number of shares. Section 8–402(2). If all of its authorized shares are outstanding, any additionally issued shares would be illegal as an overissue of stock. The corporation must therefore buy the replacement shares on the market, or if no shares are available for purchase must pay A the price that he or the last purchaser for value paid for the stock, with interest from the date of the demand. Section 8–104.

CASES

Payment for Newly Issued Shares

UNITED STEEL INDUSTRIES, INC. v. MANHART

Court of Civil Appeals of Texas, 1966.
405 S.W.2d 231.

McDONALD, C. J.

This is an appeal by defendants, United Steel Industries, Inc., J. R. Hurt, and W. B. Griffitts, from a judgment declaring void and cancelling 5000 shares of stock in United Steel Industries, Inc. issued to Hurt, and 4000 shares of stock in such corporation issued to Griffitts.

Plaintiffs Manhart filed this suit individually and as major stockholders against defendants United Steel Industries, Inc., Hurt, and Griffitts, alleging the corporation had issued Hurt 5000 shares of its stock in consideration of Hurt agreeing to perform CPA and bookkeeping services for the corporation for one year in the future; and had issued Griffitts 4000 shares of its stock in consideration for

the promised conveyance of a 5 acre tract of land to the Corporation, which land was never conveyed to the Corporation. Plaintiffs assert the 9000 shares of stock were issued in violation of Article 2.16 Business Corporation Act, V.A.T.S. and prayed that such stock be declared void and cancelled.

Trial was before the Court without a jury which, after hearing, entered judgment declaring the 5000 shares of stock issued to Hurt and the 4000 shares issued to Griffitts, issued without valid consideration, void, and decreeing such stock cancelled.

*   *   *

The trial court found (on ample evidence) that the incorporators of the Corporation made an agreement with Hurt to issue him 5000 shares in consideration of Hurt's agreement to perform bookkeeping and accounting services for the Corporation for the first year of its operation. The Corporation minutes reflect the 5000 shares issued to Hurt "in consideration of labor done, services in the incorporation and organization of the Corporation." The trial court found (on ample evidence) that such minutes do not reflect the true consideration agreed upon, and that Hurt performed no services for the Corporation prior to February 1, 1965. The Articles of Incorporation were filed on January 28, 1965, and the 5000 shares were issued to Hurt on May 29,1965. There is evidence that Hurt performed some services for the Corporation between January and May 29, 1965; but Hurt himself testified the "5000 (shares) were issued to me for services rendered or to be rendered for the first year in keeping the books * * *."

The situation is thus one where the stock was issued to Hurt both for services already performed and for services to be rendered in the future.

The trial court concluded the promise of future services was not a valid consideration for the issuance of stock under Article 2.16 Business Corporation Act; that the issuance was void; and that since there was no apportionment of the value of future services from the value of services already rendered, the entire 5000 shares were illegally issued and void.

Article 12, Section 6, Texas Constitution, Vernon's Ann.St. provides: "No corporation shall issue stock * * * except for money paid, labor done, or property actually received * * *." And Article 2.16 Texas Business Corporation Act provides:

Payment for Shares.

A. The consideration paid for the issuance of shares shall consist of money paid, labor done, or property actually received. Shares may not be issued until the full amount of the consideration, fixed as provided by law, has been paid. * * *

B. Neither promissory notes nor the promise of future services shall constitute payment or part payment for shares of a corporation.

C. In the absence of fraud in the transaction, the judgment of the board of directors * * * as to the value of the consideration received for shares shall be conclusive.

* * *

The 5000 shares were issued before the future services were rendered. Such stock was illegally issued and void.

Griffitts was issued 10,000 shares partly in consideration for legal services to the Corporation and partly in exchange for the 5 acres of land. The stock was valued at $1 per share and the land had an agreed value of $4000. The trial court found (upon ample evidence) that the 4000 shares of stock issued to Griffitts was in consideration of his promise to convey the land to the Corporation; that Griffitts never conveyed the land; and the issuance of the stock was illegal and void.

The judgment of the board of directors "as to the value of consideration received for shares" is conclusive, but such does not authorize the board to issue shares contrary to the Constitution, for services to be performed in the future (as in the case of Hurt), or for property not received (as in the case of Griffitts).

The judgment is correct. Defendants' points and contentions are overruled.

Affirmed.

Preferred Stock

ROTHSCHILD INTERNATIONAL CORP. v. LIGGETT GROUP, INC.

Court of Chancery of Delaware, 1983.
463 A.2d 642.

BROWN, Chancellor.

This suit arises out of a combined tender offer and merger whereby GM Sub Corporation, an indirect, wholly-owned subsidiary of Grand Metropolitan Limited, a corporation of England, acquired all outstanding shares of the defendant Liggett Group, Inc., a Delaware corporation. GM Sub Corporation ("GM Sub") was formed as a Delaware corporation for the purpose of carrying out this acquisition. At the time of the tender offer and merger the plaintiff Rothschild International Corporation (hereafter "Rothschild") was the owner of 650 shares of the 7% Cumulative Preferred Stock of Liggett Group, Inc.

Rothschild has brought this suit as a purported class action on behalf of all former owners of the 7% Cumulative Preferred Stock (hereafter "the 7% Preferred"), including both those who voluntarily tendered their preferred shares in response to the tender offer as well as those who were subsequently cashed out under the terms of the merger. It is the position of Rothschild that under the applicable provisions of the restated certificate of incorporation of the Liggett Group, Inc. (hereafter "Liggett") all of the 7% Preferred shareholders were shortchanged $30 per share under the terms of both the tender offer and the merger. Rothschild charges that Liggett initially as well as Grand Metropolitan Limited ("Grand Met") as the emerging majority shareholder of Liggett through GM Sub, breached a fiduciary duty owed to the 7% Preferred shareholders by not causing them to be paid the full contractual value of their preferred shares. Rothschild seeks the recovery of $30 per share on behalf of the class comprised of all former owners of the 7% Preferred.

* * *

Liggett was incorporated originally in 1911 in New Jersey under the name of Liggett & Myers Tobacco Company. Among other things, its certificate of incorporation authorized the issuance of some 153,000 shares of the 7% Preferred stock. This preferred stock had a fixed par value of $100 per share. More importantly for the purposes of the present matter, it also carried with it a liquidation value of $100 per share. In addition, the 7% Preferred contained certain features which are said to be relatively uncommon in today's market. Specifically, it could not be redeemed; it was not convertible; and it was not subject to call. Moreover, it was senior to the other classes of Liggett stock in the event of a liquidation.

In time Liggett was reincorporated in Delaware. However, the original liquidation rights of the 7% Preferred stock were carried over and set forth as follows in Liggett's restated certificate of incorporation:

In the event of any liquidation of the assets of the Corporation (whether voluntary or involuntary) the holders of the 7% Preferred Stock shall be entitled to be paid the par amount ($100) of their 7% Preferred shares and the amount of any dividends accumulated and unpaid thereon before any amount shall be payable or paid to the holders of any other class or series of stock, and after payment to the holders of the 7% Preferred Stock of its par value and the dividends accrued and unpaid thereon, the residue of the assets of the Corporation shall be divided among and paid to the holders of the other classes or series of stock.

It is against this framework of Liggett's corporate charter that we have the acquisition of Liggett by Grand Met through GM Sub and the accompanying birth of Rothschild's class action contentions.

Grand Met, through GM Sub, commenced its tender offer for all of the equity securities of Liggett on April 18, 1980. The initial offer of GM Sub was $67.50 for each share of the 7% Preferred, $114.94 for each share of another series of Liggett preferred stock—the $5.25 Convertible Preferred—and $50 per share for each share of Liggett common stock. At the time of the tender offer the 7% Preferred was listed for trading on the New York Stock Exchange and traded in the range of $60–61 per share.

In its offer to purchase, GM Sub fully disclosed that "in the event of voluntary or involuntary liquidation of [Liggett], the holders of the 7% Preferred Stock are entitled to receive $100 per share, plus any accumulated or unpaid dividends thereon, before any amounts shall be paid to holders of any other class or series of capital stock of [Liggett]."

On May 12, 1980, Standard Brands Incorporated entered the picture as a white knight on behalf of Liggett and commenced a competing tender offer. The offer of Standard Brands was at $70 per share for any and all shares of the 7% Preferred and $65 per share for up to 4 million shares of Liggett's common stock. The offer of Standard Brands was endorsed by the board of directors of Liggett as being fair to Liggett's shareholders.

Thereafter, on May 14, 1980, GM Sub increased its offer to the shareholders of Liggett to $70 per share for the 7% Preferred, to $158.62 for the $5.25 Convertible Preferred, and to $69 for each share of common stock. Standard Brands immediately withdrew its competing offer. Liggett's board of directors correspondingly approved the amended offer of GM Sub as being fair and recommended that it be accepted by Liggett's shareholders. As a result, 39.8% of the outstanding shares of the 7% Preferred was tendered and sold to GM Sub. In addition, GM Sub acquired 87.4% of Liggett's outstanding common stock and 75.9% of the $5.25 Convertible Preferred.

Under the terms of Liggett's charter, the 7% Preferred had no right to vote as a class on a merger proposal. As a consequence, even though less than 40% of the 7% preferred tendered their shares in response to the offer, GM Sub's combined acquisition of an overwhelming majority of both Liggett's common stock and the $5.25 Convertible Preferred gave it sufficient voting power to approve a followup merger proposal whereby all remaining shareholders of Liggett other than GM Sub were eliminated in return for the payment of cash for their shares. This merger was approved on August 7, 1980, and GM Sub became the sole owner of all Liggett shares. Under the terms of the merger those who remained shareholders of Liggett after the tender offer were paid the same consideration for their shares in the merger as had been offered to them in the tender offer. In other words, the remaining owners of the 7% Preferred were merged out of Liggett at $70 per share.

Based upon the foregoing facts it is the position of the plaintiff Rothschild that as a matter of law both Liggett as well as Grand Met, through GM Sub, breached a duty of fair dealing owed to the 7% Preferred shareholders. It is argued that Liggett's board of directors did so by ultimately agreeing to its takeover by Grand Met and by recommending the terms of the tender offer to Liggett's shareholders when it had to know that insofar as the offer pertained to the 7% Preferred shareholders it was in contravention of Liggett's certificate of incorporation. As to GM Sub and Grand Met, it is charged that upon becoming the majority shareholder of Liggett as a result of the tender offer they breached the duty of fairness owed by them to the remaining minority 7% Preferred shareholders by merging them out of the corporation without paying them the stated liquidation value of their shares.

Both of the foregoing contentions—and indeed the entire theory of Rothschild's case—is based upon one premise, namely, that the combined tender offer and merger constituted a liquidation of Liggett insofar as the rights of the 7% Preferred stock were concerned, thus entitling its owners to receive the liquidation preference of $100 per share from Grand Met through its subsidiary, GM Sub. * * *

* * *

Quite simply, no liquidation of Liggett occurred here. It still existed as a corporate entity following the tender offer and merger. It still retained shareholder status even though all shares merged in one owner. What happened was that all of its outstanding shares were acquired by a single owner. The corporation did not sell off all of its assets, pay its obligations, distribute the remaining proceeds to its shareholders, and cease to exist as a corporate entity. The fact that the practical effect of the transaction as to the 7% Preferred shareholders may have been similar to the result that would have followed from a liquidation does not make the transaction a liquidation.

The Delaware General Corporation law recognizes the concept of a merger. It is separate and distinct from a liquidation or a sale of assets. Indeed, the argument that a good faith merger is essentially a sale of assets when it suits a plaintiff to view it as such has long since been put to rest. [Citation.] Moreover, it has been held that preference rights of preferred stock can be eliminated legally through the merger process.

Consequently, in a case where a merger of corporations is permitted by law and is accomplished in accordance with the law, the holder of cumulative preference stock as to which dividends have accumulated may not insist that his right to the dividends is a fixed contractual right in the nature of a debt, in that sense vested and, therefore, secure against attack. Looking at the law which is a part of the corporate charter, and, therefore, a part of the shareholder's contract, he has not been deceived nor lulled into the belief that the right to such dividends is firm and stable. On the contrary, his contract has informed him that the right is defeasible; and with that knowledge the stock was acquired.

So here, the merger provisions of the Delaware General Corporation Law necessarily form a part of Liggett's charter. Thus, the liquidation preference given the 7% Preferred under Liggett's restated certificate of incorporation, * * * was always subject to the possibility of defeasance by merger, and the 7% Preferred shareholders were necessarily charged with knowledge of this at the time that they acquired their shares.

The preferential rights attaching to shares of preferred stock are contractual in nature and are governed by the express provisions of a corporation's charter. [Citations.] Nothing is to be presumed in favor of preferences attached to stock, but rather they must be expressed in clear language. [Citations.]

Under the express language of Liggett's charter the holders of the 7% Preferred were entitled to be paid the $100 par value of the shares only in the event of "any liquidation of the assets of the Corporation (whether voluntary or involuntary)." From this there can be no presumption that they would also be paid the par value under other circumstances.

The total transfer of the ownership of the stock of the corporation through the tender offer and the follow-up merger was not a "liquidation of the assets" of the corporation, and, I think it fair to say, was never intended to be by either Liggett or by GM Sub. Therefore, no contractual liquidation right of the 7% Preferred shareholders was activated by the combined transaction, and thus no contractual right of the 7% Preferred shareholders was violated by either Liggett or by GM Sub as a result of the payment to the 7% Preferred shareholders of something less than $100 per share.

The contractual aspect of the matter highlights, I think, a significant point of distinction to be made. Closely examined, what Rothschild is arguing is that the 7% Preferred shareholders are entitled to be paid the liquidation value of their shares because *their rights* as preferred shareholders were liquidated as a result of GM Sub's acquisition. As stated by Rothschild in its reply brief, "the *interests of the 7% Preferred* Stockholders were forcibly *liquidated* under any fair and reasonable reading of the terms of Liggett's charter." And also, the "acquisition resulted in the liquidation of *their interests* in Liggett." (Emphasis added.)

In other words, Rothschild is arguing that where the preferred shareholders' rights are liquidated—i.e., their shareholder status terminated in return for the payment of cash— then the transaction by which it is accomplished should be viewed as a liquidation of the corporation itself insofar as those preferred shareholders are concerned even though the corporation continues on as an operating legal entity.

Thus, the argument is not that the corporation has liquidated, or that its assets have been liquidated, but rather it is an argument that the interests of the 7% Preferred shareholders have been liquidated. But under the contractual language of Liggett's charter the right to payment of the par value of the shares springs into being only "[i]n the event of any liquidation of the assets of the Corporation."

Thus, as I view Rothschild's argument, it is not based on a right spelled out in the contractual language of the charter.

*   *   *

Finally, I think it significant to note that Rothschild is making no charge that the $70 price offered in the tender offer and merger was inadequate or unfair in any respect other than it did not meet the stated liquidation price set forth in Liggett's charter. Thus, Rothschild's complaint has nothing to do with the fair value of the 7% Preferred as of the time of the tender offer and merger, or with the intrinsic fairness of the price offered and paid. Rather, its complaint is based strictly on the contention that there was a liquidation within the contemplation of those provisions of Liggett's certificate of incorporation which created the preference rights of the 7% Preferred. On the undisputed facts I find as a matter of law that there was none.

Accordingly, the motion of the plaintiff Rothschild for summary judgment will be denied. The motion of the defendants will be granted and summary judgment will be entered in favor of Liggett and GM Sub.

Declaration of Dividends

DODGE v. FORD MOTOR CO.

Supreme Court of Michigan, 1919.
204 Mich. 459, 170 N.W. 668.

OSTRANDER, J.

[Action in equity by John F. and Horace E. Dodge, plaintiffs, against the Ford Motor Company and its directors to compel the declaration of dividends and for an injunction restraining a contemplated expansion of the business. The complaint was filed in November, 1916. Since 1909, the capital stock of the company has been $2,000,000, divided into 20,000 shares of the par value of $100 each of which plaintiffs held 2,000. As of the close of business of July 31, 1916, the end of the company's fiscal year, the surplus above capital was $111,960,907.53 and the assets included cash on hand of $52,550,771.92.

For a number of years the company had paid regularly quarterly dividends equal to sixty percent annually on the capital stock of $2,000,000. In addition, from December, 1911, to October, 1915, inclusive, eleven special dividends totalling $41,000,000 had been paid and in November, 1916, after this action was commenced, a special dividend of $2,000,000 was paid.

Plaintiffs' complaint alleged that Henry Ford, president of the company and a member of its board of directors, had declared it to be the settled policy of the company not to pay any special dividends in the future, but to put back into the business all future earnings in excess of the regular quarterly dividend. Plaintiffs sought an injunction restraining the carrying out of the alleged declared policy of Henry Ford and a decree requiring the directors to pay a dividend of at least seventy-five percent of the accumulated cash surplus.

In December, 1917, the trial court entered a decree requiring the directors to declare and pay a dividend of $19,275,385.96 and enjoining the corporation from using its funds for a proposed smelting plant and certain other planned projects. From this decree, defendants have appealed.]

*   *   *

The case for plaintiffs must rest upon the claim, and the proof in support of it, that the proposed expansion of the business of the corporation involving the further use of profits as capital, ought to be enjoined because inimical to the best interests of the company and its shareholders, and upon the further claim that in any event the withholding of the special dividend asked for by plaintiffs is arbitrary action of the directors requiring judicial interference.

The rule which will govern courts in deciding these questions is not in dispute. * * * In [citation], it is stated:

Profits earned by a corporation may be divided among its shareholders; but it is not a violation of the charter if they are allowed to accumulate and remain invested in the company's business. The managing agents of a corporation are impliedly invested with a discretionary power with regard to the time and manner of distributing its profits. They may apply profits in payment of floating or funded debts, or in development of the company's business; and so long as they do not abuse their discretionary powers, or violate the company's charter, the courts cannot interfere.

But it is clear that the agents of a corporation, and even the majority, cannot arbitrarily withhold profits earned by the company, or apply them to any use which is not authorized by the company's charter. The nominal capital of a company does not necessarily limit the scope of its operations; a corporation may borrow money for the purpose of enlarging its business, and in many instances it may use profits for the same purpose. * * *

When plaintiffs made their complaint and demand for further dividends the Ford Motor Company had concluded its most prosperous year of business. The demand for its cars at the price of the preceding year continued. It could make and could market in the year beginning August 1, 1916, more than 500,000 cars. Sales of parts and repairs would necessarily increase. The cost of materials was likely to advance, and perhaps the price of labor, but it reasonably might have expected a profit for the year of upwards of $60,000,000. It had assets of more than $132,000,000, a surplus of almost $112,000,000, and its cash on hand and municipal bonds were nearly $54,000,000. Its total liabilities, including capital stock, was a little over $20,000,000. It had declared no special dividend during the business year except the October, 1915, dividend. It had been the practice, under similar circumstances, to declare larger dividends. Considering only these facts, a refusal to declare and pay further dividends appears to be not an exercise of discretion on the part of the directors, but an arbitrary refusal to do what the circumstances required to be done. These facts and others call upon the directors to justify their action, or failure or refusal to act. In justification, the defendants have offered testimony tending to prove, and which

does prove, the following facts. It had been the policy of the corporation for a considerable time to annually reduce the selling price of cars, while keeping up, or improving their quality. As early as in June 1915 a general plan for the expansion of the productive capacity of the concern by a practical duplication of its plant had been talked over by the executive officers and directors and agreed upon, not all of the details having been settled and no formal action of directors having been taken. The erection of a smelter was considered, and engineering and other data in connection therewith secured. In consequence, it was determined not to reduce the selling price of cars for the year beginning August 1, 1915, but to maintain the price and to accumulate a large surplus to pay for the proposed expansion of plant and equipment, and perhaps to build a plant for smelting ore. It is hoped, by Mr. Ford, that eventually 1,000,000 cars will be annually produced. The contemplated changes will permit the increased output.

The plan, as affecting the profits of the business for the year beginning August 1, 1916, and thereafter, calls for a reduction in the selling price of cars. * * * In short, the plan does not call for and is not intended to produce immediately a more profitable business but a less profitable one; not only less profitable than formerly but less profitable than it is admitted it might be made. The apparent immediate effect will be to diminish the value of shares and the return to shareholders.

It is the contention of plaintiffs that the apparent effect of the plan is intended to be the continued and continuing effect of it and that it is deliberately proposed, not of record and not by official corporate declaration, but nevertheless proposed, to continue the corporation henceforth as a semi-eleemosynary institution and not as a business institution. In support of this contention they point to the attitude and to the expressions of Mr. Henry Ford.

Mr. Henry Ford is the dominant force in the business of the Ford Motor Company. No plan of operations could be adopted unless he consented, and no board of directors can be elected whom he does not favor. One of the directors of the company has no stock. One share was assigned to him to qualify him for the position, but it is not claimed that he owns it. A business, one of the largest in the world, and one of the most profitable, has been built up. It employs many men, at good pay.

"My ambition," said Mr. Ford, "is to employ still more men, to spread the benefits of this industrial system to the greatest possible number, to help them build up their lives and their homes. To do this we are putting the greatest share of our profits back in the business." * * *

The record, and especially the testimony of Mr. Ford, convinces that he has to some extent the attitude towards shareholders of one who has dispensed and distributed to them large gains and that they should be content to take what he chooses to give. His testimony creates the impression, also, that he thinks the Ford Motor Company has made too much money, has had too large profits, and that although large profits might still be earned, a sharing of them with the public, by reducing the price of the output of the company, ought to be undertaken. We have no doubt that certain sentiments, philanthropic and altruistic, creditable to Mr. Ford, had large influence in determining the policy to be pursued by the Ford Motor Company— the policy which has been herein referred to. * * *

These cases, after all, like all others in which the subject is treated, turn finally upon the point, the question, whether it appears that the directors were not acting for the best interest of the corporation. * * * The difference between an incidental humanitarian expenditure of corporate funds for the benefit of the employees, like the building of a hospital for their use and the employment of agencies for the betterment of their condi-

tion, and a general purpose and plan to benefit mankind at the expense of others, is obvious. * * * A business corporation is organized and carried on primarily for the profit of the stockholders. The powers of the directors are to be employed for that end. The discretion of directors is to be exercised in the choice of means to attain that end and does not extend to a change in the end itself, to the reduction of profits or to the nondistribution of profits among stockholders in order to devote them to other purposes. * * *

We are not, however, persuaded that we should interfere with the proposed expansion of the business of the Ford Motor Company. In view of the fact that the selling price of products may be increased at any time, the ultimate results of the larger business cannot be certainly estimated. The judges are not business experts. It is recognized that plans must often be made for a long future, for expected competition, for a continuing as well as an immediately profitable venture. The experience of the Ford Motor Company is evidence of capable management of its affairs. * * *

Defendants say, and it is true, that a considerable cash balance must be at all times carried by such a concern. But, as has been stated, there was a large daily, weekly, monthly, receipt of cash. The output was practically continuous and was continuously, and within a few days, turned into cash. Moreover, the comtemplated expenditures were not to be immediately made. The large sum appropriated for the smelter plant was payable over a considerable period of time. So that, without going further, it would appear that, accepting and approving the plan of the directors, it was their duty to distribute on or near the first of August, 1916, a very large sum of money to stockholders. * * *

The decree of the court below fixing and determining the specific amount to be distributed to stockholders is affirmed. In other respects, except as to the allowance of costs, the said decree is reversed.

Liability for Improper
Dividends

FRIED v. CANO

United States District Court, Southern District of
New York, 1958.
167 F.Supp. 625.

DAWSON, J.

[International Distributing Export Company (I.D.E.) was organized as a corporation on September 7, 1948 under the laws of New York, and commenced business on November 1, 1948. I.D.E. had formerly been in existence as an individual proprietorship. On October 31, 1948, the newly organized corporation had liabilities of $64,084.00. Its only assets, in the sum of $33,042, were those of the former sole proprietorship. However, the corporation set up an asset on its balance sheet in the amount of $32,000 for goodwill. As a result of this entry, I.D.E. had a surplus at the end of each of its fiscal years from 1949 until 1954. Cano, a shareholder, received $7,144 in dividends from I.D.E. during the period from 1950 to 1955. Fried, the trustee in bankruptcy of I.D.E., brought an action against Cano to recover the amount of these dividends paid to Cano, alleging that they had been paid when I.D.E. was insolvent or when its capital was impaired.]

*   *   *

The Minute Book shows that when dividends were declared the accountant reported that the surplus was sufficient to allow the declaration of the dividend. The income tax returns of the corporation for the years in which dividends were paid showed that the corporation, at least from a book standpoint, had a surplus out of which dividends could be paid. It is true that this might have been a fictitious surplus, if the good will was not of the value attributed to it, or if certain accounts receivable carried on the books were not collectible. However, no proof was offered that the defendant had knowledge at the time that he received the dividends that they were being paid out of capital or that the corporation was insolvent. There was no evidence produced that the corporation was not paying its debts as they matured.

The law is clear that the wrongful declaration of a dividend out of capital, in violation of [the incorporation statute] is a wrong of those committing it and innocent participants are not accomplices to its commission; and in order to hold the stockholder who received the dividend liable it is necessary positively to allege and prove the stockholder's complicity in and knowledge of the wrong. [Citations.]

The Court holds that the plaintiff has not established by a fair preponderance of the evidence that the defendant had knowledge that the dividends received by him were paid out of capital of I.D.E., or that the dividends which were paid impaired the capital of I.D.E. The Court concludes that the plaintiff has not established a cause of action against the defendant, in so far as the defendant received dividends from I.D.E.

[Decision for the shareholder Cano.]

PROBLEMS

1. Frank McAnarney and Joseph Lemon entered into an agreement to promote a corporation to engage in the manufacture of farm implements. Prior to the organization of the corporation McAnarney and Lemon solicited subscriptions to the stock of the corporation and presented a written agreement for signatures of the subscribers.

The agreement provided that subscribers pay $100 per share for stock in the corporation in consideration of McAnarney's and Lemon's agreement to organize the corporation and advance the pre-incorporation expenses. Thomas Jordan signed the agreement making application for 100 shares of stock. Subsequent to the filing of the articles of incorporation with the Secretary of State, but prior to the issuance of a charter to the corporation, Jordan died. The administrator of Jordan's estate notified McAnarney and Lemon that the estate would not honor Jordan's subscription.

After the formation of the corporation, Franklin Adams signed a subscription agreement making application for 100 shares of stock. Before acceptance by the corporation, Adams informed the corporation that he was canceling his subscription.

(a) The corporation brings an appropriate action against Jordan's estate to enforce Jordan's stock subscription. Decision?

(b) The corporation brings an appropriate action to enforce Adams's stock subscription. Decision?

2. The XYZ Corporation was duly organized on July 10. Its certificate of incorporation provides for a total authorized capital of $100,000, consisting of 1,000 shares of common stock, par value $100 per share. The corporation issues for cash a total of fifty certificates, numbered one to fifty inclusive, representing various amounts of shares in the names of various individuals. Payment for the shares having been made in advance, the certificates are all dated and mailed on the same day. The fifty certificates of stock represent a total of 1,050 shares. Certificate No. 49 for thirty shares was issued to Jane Smith. Certificate No. 50 for twenty-five shares was issued to William Jones. Is there any question concerning the validity of any of the stock thus issued? What are the rights of Smith and Jones?

3. D subscribed for 200 shares of 12 percent cumulative, participating, redeemable, convertible, preferred shares of the X Hotel Company with a par value of $100 per share. The subscription agreement provided that she was to receive a bonus of one share of common stock of $100 par value for each share of preferred stock. D fully paid her subscription agreement of $20,000 and received the 200 shares of preferred and the bonus stock of 200 shares of the par value common. Subsequently, the X Hotel Co. becomes insolvent. R, the receiver of the corporation, brings suit for $20,000, the par value of the common stock. What judgment?

4. The X Company has an authorized capital stock of 1,000 shares of par value of $100 per share, of which 900 shares, all fully paid, are outstanding.

Having an ample surplus, the X Company purchases from its shareholders 100 shares at par. Subsequently, the X Company, needing additional working capital, issues the 200 shares in question to S at eighty dollars per share. Two years later the X Company is forced into bankruptcy. The trustee in bankruptcy now sues S for $4,000. Decision?

5. For five years B and C had been engaged as partners in building houses. They owned the necessary equipment to conduct the business and had an excellent reputation for competence. In March, D, who had previously been in the same kind of business, proposed that B, C, and D form a corporation for the purposes of constructing medium-price houses. They engaged attorney A who did all the work required and caused the business to be incorporated under the name of X Corp.

The certificate of incorporation authorized 100 shares of $100 par value stock. At the organization meeting of the incorporators, B, C, and D were elected directors, and X Corp. issued a total of sixty-five shares of its stock. B and C each received twenty shares in consideration of transferring to X Corp. the equipment and good will of their partnership having a value of over $4,000. D received twenty shares in consideration for promising to work for X Corp. in the future, and A received five shares as compensation for the legal services rendered in forming X Corp.

Later that year X Corp. had a number of financial setbacks and in December ceased operations. What rights, if any, does X Corp. have against B, C, D, and A in connection with the original issuance of its shares?

6. Paul Bunyan is the owner of non-cumulative 8 percent preferred stock in the Broadview Corporation which had no earnings or profits in 1982. In 1983 the corporation had large profits and a surplus from which it might properly have declared dividends. The directors refused to do so but used the surplus to purchase goods necessary for their expanding business.

In view of the large profits made in 1983, the directors at the end of 1984 declared a 10 percent dividend on the common stock and an 8 percent dividend on the preferred stock without paying preferred dividends for 1983. The corporation earned a small profit in 1984.

(a) Is Bunyan entitled to dividends for 1982? For 1983?

(b) Is Bunyan entitled to a dividend of 10 percent rather than 8 percent in 1984?

7. A corporation has outstanding 400 shares of $100 par value common stock which has been issued and sold at $105 per share for a total of $42,000. A is incorporated in State X which has adopted the earned surplus test for all distributions. At a time when the assets of the corporation amount to $65,000 and the liabilities to creditors total $10,000, the directors learn that S, who holds 100 of the 400 shares of stock, is planning to sell her shares on the open market for $10,500. Believing that this will not be to the best interest of the corporation, the directors enter into an agreement with S for S to sell to the corporation the shares for $10,500. About six months later, when the assets of the corporation have decreased to $50,000 and its liabilities, exclusive of its liability to S, have increased to $20,000, the directors use $10,000 to pay a dividend to all of the shareholders. Subsequently, the corporation becomes insolvent.

(a) Does S have any liability to the corporation or its creditors in connection with the reacquisition by the corporation of the 100 shares?

(b) Was the payment of the $10,000 dividend proper?

8. Almega Corporation, organized under the laws of State S, has outstanding 20,000 shares of $100 par value non-voting preferred stock calling for non-cumulative dividends of five dollars per year; 10,000 shares of voting preferred fifty dollars par value, calling for cumulative dividends of $2.50 per year; and 10,000 shares of no par common. State S has adopted the earned surplus test for all distributions. In 1980 the corporation had net earnings of $170,000; in 1981, $135,000; in 1982, $60,000; in 1983, $210,000; and 1984, $120,000. The board of directors passed over all dividends during the four years 1980–1983, since the company needed working capital for expansion purposes. In 1984 the directors declared a dividend on the non-cumulative preferred shares of five dollars per share, on the cumulative preferred of $12.50, and on the common a dividend of $30. The board submitted

their declaration to the voting shareholders, and they ratified it. Before the dividends were paid, Payne, the record holder of 500 shares of the non-cumulative preferred stock, brought an appropriate action to restrain any payment to the cumulative preferred or common shareholders until a full dividend for the five years stated were paid to non-cumulative preferred shareholders. Decision?

9. Sayre learned that Adams, Boone, and Chase were planning to form a corporation for the purpose of manufacturing and marketing a line of novelties to wholesale outlets. Sayre had patented a self-lock gas tank cap but lacked the financial backing to market it profitably. He negotiated with Adams, Boone, and Chase who agreed to purchase the patent rights for $5,000 in cash and 200 shares of $100 par value preferred stock in a corporation to be formed.

The corporation was formed and Sayre's stock issued to him, but the corporation has refused to make the cash payment. It has also refused to declare dividends, although the business has been very profitable due to the value of Sayre's patent, and has a substantial earned surplus with a large cash balance on hand. It is selling the remainder of the originally authorized issue of preferred shares, ignoring Sayre's demand to purchase a proportionate share of the stock so sold. What are Sayre's rights, if any?

10. A bylaw of Betma Corporation provides that no shareholder can sell their shares unless they first offer them for sale to the corporation or its directors. The bylaw also states that this restriction shall be printed or stamped upon each stock certificate and binds all present or future owners or holders. Betma Corporation did not comply with this latter provision. Shaw, having knowledge of the bylaw restriction, nevertheless purchased twenty shares of the corporation's stock from Rice, without having Rice first offer them for sale to the corporation or its directors. When Betma Corporation refused to effectuate a transfer of the shares to her, Shaw sued to compel a transfer and the issuance of a new certificate to her. Decision?

Chapter 35

MANAGEMENT STRUCTURE

THE corporate management structure, as designed by State incorporation statutes, is pyramidal. At the base of the pyramid are the **shareholders,** who are the residual owners of the corporation. Basic to their role in controlling the corporation is the right to elect representatives to manage the ordinary business matters of the corporation and the right to approve all extraordinary matters.

The **board of directors,** as the shareholders' elected representatives, are delegated the power to manage the business of the corporation. Directors exercise dominion and control over the corporation, hold positions of trust and confidence, and determine questions of operating policy. Directors are not ordinarily expected to devote full time to the affairs of the corporation and have broad authority to delegate power to officers and agents. The **officers** of the corporation hold their office at the will of the board. The officers, in turn, hire and fire all necessary operating personnel and run the day-to-day affairs of the corporation. The pyramid structure of corporate management is illustrated in Figure 35–1.

ROLE OF SHAREHOLDERS

The role of the shareholders in management is generally restricted to the election of di-

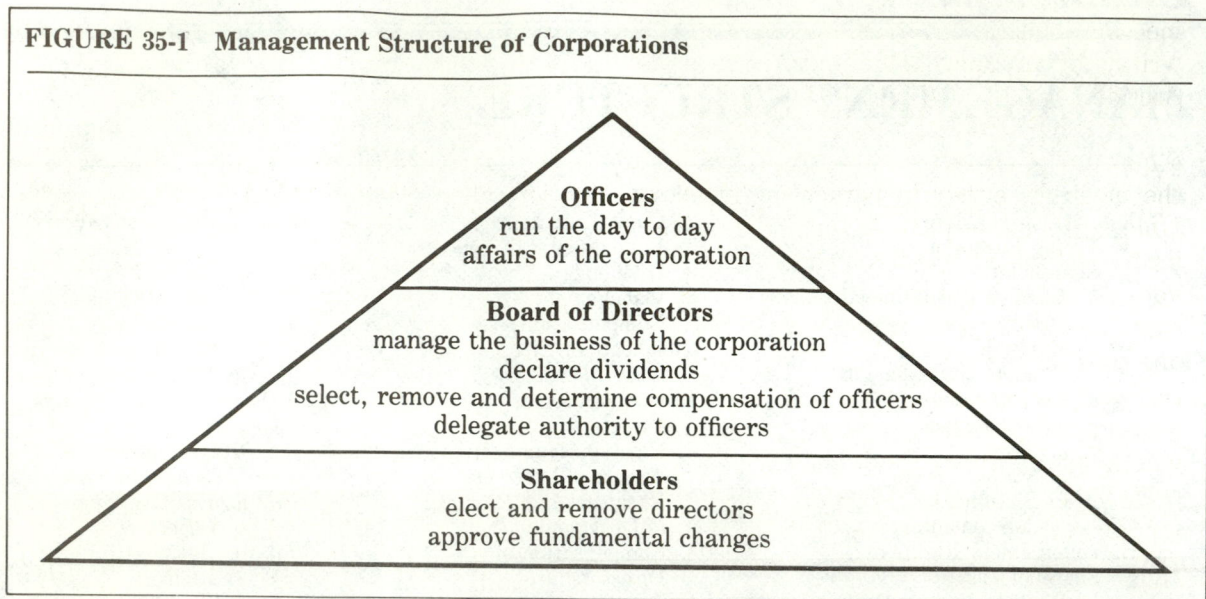

FIGURE 35-1   Management Structure of Corporations

Officers
run the day to day
affairs of the corporation

Board of Directors
manage the business of the corporation
declare dividends
select, remove and determine compensation of officers
delegate authority to officers

Shareholders
elect and remove directors
approve fundamental changes

rectors, approval of certain extraordinary matters, and the right to bring suits to enforce these rights. At the same time, shareholders assume potential personal liability for defective incorporation, disregard of corporateness, and receipt of improper distributions.

VOTING RIGHTS OF SHAREHOLDERS

The shareholder's right to vote is fundamental to the concept of the corporation and its management structure. In most States today a shareholder is entitled to one vote for each share of stock that he owns, unless the articles of incorporation provide otherwise. In addition, incorporation statutes generally permit the issuance of one or more classes of non-voting stock, so long as at least one class of shares has voting rights. Section 33. The articles of incorporation may provide for more or less than one vote for any share. Section 33. For example, in *Providence & Worcester Co. v. Baker*, 378 A.2d 121 (Del. 1977), the articles of incorporation provided that each shareholder was entitled to 1 vote per share for each share owned by him not exceeding

50 shares and 1 vote for every 20 shares in excess of 50, but no shareholder was entitled to vote more than one-fourth of the whole number of outstanding shares.

Shareholders may exercise their voting rights at both annual and special shareholder meetings. **Annual meetings** are required and must be held at a time fixed by the bylaws. If the annual shareholder meeting is not held within a thirteen-month period, any shareholder may petition and obtain a court order requiring such meeting to be held. Section 28. The Revised Act provides this right if the annual meeting is "not held within the earlier of 6 months after the end of the corporation's fiscal year or 15 months after its last annual meeting." RMBCA Section 7.03. The Revised Act further provides that the failure to hold an annual meeting does not affect the validity of any corporate action. RMBCA Section 7.01(c). **Special meetings** may be called by the board of directors, holders of at least 10 percent of the shares, or such other persons authorized in the articles of incorporation. Section 28. Written notice stating the place, day, and hour of the meeting and, in the case of a special meeting, the purposes for which it is called must be given in advance of the meeting. Notice, however, may be waived in writing by any shareholder entitled to notice. Section 144.

In order to effectuate corporate business a quorum of shares must be represented at the meeting, either in person or by proxy. Unless otherwise provided in the articles of incorporation, a majority of shares entitled to vote constitutes a **quorum,** but under no circumstances may a quorum consist of less than one-third of the shares entitled to vote. Section 32. Unissued shares and treasury stock may not be voted nor counted in determining whether a quorum exists. Once a quorum is present at a meeting, it is deemed present for the rest of the meeting despite the withdrawal of shareholders in an effort to break quorum.

Most States require shareholder actions to be approved by a majority of shares represented at the meeting and entitled to vote. Nonetheless, many States permit the articles of incorporation to increase the percentage of shares required to take any action subject to shareholder approval. Section 143. A provision which increases the voting requirements is usually referred to as a "supermajority provision". Section 7.27 of the Revised Act has added an additional requirement to supermajority provisions:

An amendment to the articles of incorporation that adds, changes, or deletes a greater quorum or voting requirement must meet the same quorum requirement and be adopted by the same vote and voting groups required to take action under the quorum and voting requirement then in effect or proposed to be adopted, whichever is greater.

Section 7.27 thus protects a supermajority requirement for shareholder action from elimination by a simple majority vote generally required for amendments. For example, a supermajority provision requiring a 75 percent affirmative vote may not be deleted from the articles of incorporation or reduced except by a 75 percent affirmative vote. A proposal to increase the 75 percent voting requirement to 90 percent must be approved by a 90 percent affirmative vote.

A number of States permit shareholders to conduct business without a meeting if all the shareholders consent in writing to the action taken. Section 145. A few States, including Delaware, have further relaxed the formalities of shareholder action by permitting shareholders to act without a meeting with written consent of only the number of shares required to act on the matter.

Election and Removal of Directors

Directors are elected each year at the annual meeting of the shareholders. Most States provide that where the board consists of nine or more directors, the charter or by-laws may provide for a **classification** of directors, that is, a division into two or three classes to be as nearly equal in number as possible. Section 37. If into two classes, the members of each class are elected once a year in alternate years for a two-year term; if into three classes, for three-year terms. This permits one-half of the board to be elected every two years, or one-third to be elected every three years, thus providing an element of continuity in the membership of the board. Moreover, where there are two or more classes of shares, it has been generally held that each class may elect a specified number of directors if provided for in articles of incorporation. This is made explicit by Section 8.04 of the RMBCA.

Normally, each shareholder has one vote for each share owned and directors are elected by a *plurality* of the votes. However, in certain States, shareholders have the right of cumulative voting for the election of directors of the corporation. In most of these States cumulative voting is permissive and not mandatory. Section 33. **Cumulative voting** entitles each shareholder, who has one vote for each share owned, to cumulate his votes and give one candidate as many votes as the number of directors to be elected multiplied by the number of shares owned, or to distribute such number of votes among as many candidates as he wishes. Cumulative voting permits a minority shareholder, or group of minority shareholders acting together, to obtain minority representation on the board if they own a certain minimum number of shares. Without cumulative voting, the holder or holders of 51 percent of the voting shares can elect all of the members of the board.

The formula for determining how many shares a minority shareholder with cumulative voting rights must own, or have proxies to vote, in order to secure representation on the board is as follows:

$$X = \frac{ac}{b + 1} + 1.$$

a = number of shares voting.

b = number of directors to be elected.

c = number of directors desired to be elected.

X = number of shares necessary to elect the number of directors desired to be elected.

For example, Z corporation has two shareholders, A with 64 shares and B with 36 shares. The board of directors of Z corporation consists of three directors. Under "straight" or noncumulative voting, A could cast 64 votes for each of her three candidates, and B could cast 36 votes for his three candidates. As a result, all three of A's candidates would be elected. On the other hand, if cumulative voting were in force, B could elect one director:

$$X = \frac{ac}{b + 1} + 1$$

$$X = \frac{100\ (1)}{3 + 1} + 1 = 26\ \text{shares}$$

Since B has the right to vote more than 26 shares, he would be able to elect one director. A, of course, with her 64 shares, could elect the remaining two directors:

$$X = \frac{ac}{b + 1} + 1$$

$$X = \frac{100\ (2)}{3 + 1} + 1 = 51\ \text{shares}$$

To elect all three directors, A would need 76 shares ($\frac{100\ (3)}{3 + 1} + 1$).

The effect of cumulative voting for directors may be diluted by classification or staggered election of the board of directors or by reducing the size of the board. For example, if nine directors are each elected annually, only 11 percent of the shares are needed to elect one director; whereas if the nine directors are classified and three are elected annually, 26 percent of the shares are required to elect one director.

Shareholders may by a majority vote remove, with or without cause, any director or the entire board of directors in a meeting called for that purpose. However, in the case of a corporation having cumulative voting, removal of a director requires sufficient votes to prevent his election. Section 39. Removal of directors is discussed more fully later in this chapter.

Approval of Fundamental Changes

The board of directors manages the ordinary business affairs of the corporation. Extraordinary matters involving fundamental changes in the corporation require shareholder approval and include such matters as amendments to the articles of incorporation, a sale or lease of all or substantially all of the corporate assets not in the regular course of business, most mergers, consolidations, compulsory share exchanges, and dissolution. Fundamental changes are discussed in Chapter 36.

Concentrations of Voting Power

Proxies A shareholder may vote either in person or by written proxy. A proxy is simply the authorization by a shareholder to an agent to vote his shares at a particular meeting or on a particular question. Generally, proxies must be in writing to be effective. The duration of proxies are typically limited by statute to no more than eleven months, unless the proxy specifically provides otherwise. Section 33. Since a proxy is the appointment of an agent, it is revocable, as all agencies are, unless coupled with an interest, such as when shares are held as collateral. The solicitation of proxies by publicly held corporations is also regulated by the Securities Exchange Act of 1934 as discussed in Chapter 44.

Voting Trusts Voting trusts are devices designed to concentrate corporate control in one or more persons and have been used in both publicly held and closely held corporations. A voting trust is a device by which one or more shareholders separate the voting rights of their shares from the ownership of them. Under a voting trust, all or part of the stock of a corporation may, by written agreement among the shareholders, be issued to a trustee or trustees who then hold legal title to the stock and have all of the voting rights possessed by the stock. In most States, voting trusts are permitted by statute, but are usually limited in duration to ten years. Section 34.

Shareholder Agreements In most jurisdictions, shareholders may agree in advance to vote in a specified manner for the election or removal of directors or on any other matter subject to shareholder approval. Section 34. Unlike voting trusts, shareholder agreements are not usually limited in duration. Shareholder agreements are used frequently in closely held corporations, especially in conjunction with restrictions on the transfer of shares, in order to provide each of the shareholders with greater control and *delectus personae. See Galler v. Galler.*

ENFORCEMENT RIGHTS OF SHAREHOLDERS

In order to protect a shareholder's interests in the corporation, the law provides share-holders with certain "enforcement" rights including the right to information, the right to sue the corporation directly or on its behalf, and the right to dissent.

Right to Inspect Books and Records

Most States have enacted statutory provisions granting shareholders the right to inspect for a *proper purpose* books and records in person or by agent and to make extracts from them. The Revised Act extends the right to copy records to include, if reasonable, the right to receive copies made by photographic or other means. RMBCA Section 16.03. A number of States, however, limit this right to shareholders who own a minimum number of shares or have been a shareholder for a minimum period of time. For example, the MBCA requires that a shareholder either own five per cent of the outstanding shares or have owned his shares for at least six months, but a *court* may order an inspection even when neither condition is met. Section 52. The Revised Act relaxes this rule and provides that *every* shareholder is entitled to examine specified corporate records upon prior written request if the demand is made in good faith and for a proper purpose. RMBCA Section 16.02.

Proper purpose for inspection means a purpose that is reasonably relevant to that shareholder's interest in the corporation. Proper purpose includes determining the financial condition of the corporation, the value of shares, the existence of mismanagement or improper transactions, or the names of other shareholders in order to communicate with them concerning corporate affairs. The right of inspection is subject to abuse and will be denied a shareholder who is seeking information for an improper purpose, such as use by a competing company, or to obtain a list of the shareholders in order to offer it for sale. *See Application of Lopez.*

Shareholder Suits

The ultimate recourse of a shareholder, short of selling his shares, is to bring suit against or on behalf of the corporation. Shareholder suits are essentially of two types: direct suits or derivative suits.

Direct Suits A direct suit may be brought by a shareholder to enforce a claim that the shareholder has *against* the corporation based upon his ownership of shares. Any recovery in a direct suit goes to the shareholder plaintiff. Examples of direct suits include actions by a shareholder to compel payment of dividends properly declared, to enforce the right to inspect corporate records, to enforce the right to vote, to protect pre-emptive rights, and to compel dissolution.

Derivative Suits A derivative suit is a cause of action brought by one or more shareholders *on behalf* of the corporation to enforce a right belonging to the corporation. It is brought when the board of directors refuses to take such action on behalf of the corporation. Recovery usually goes to the corporate treasury so that all shareholders can benefit proportionately. Examples of a derivative suit are actions to recovery damages from an *ultra vires* act, to recover damages for a breach of duty by management, and to recover improper dividends. In many such situations the board of directors may be hesitant to bring suit against the corporation's officers or directors. Consequently, a shareholder derivative suit is the only recourse. *See McMenomy v. Ryden.*

In most States in order to bring a derivative suit a shareholder must have owned his shares at the time that the transaction complained of occurred. Section 49. In addition, the shareholder must first make demand upon the board of directors to enforce the corporate right. The Revised Act does not require that such demand be made if circumstances indicate that a demand would be useless. RMBCA Section 7.40(b) and Comment.

The Model Act and the statutes of many States require a plaintiff to give security for reasonable expenses, including attorneys' fees, if his holdings of shares are not of a specified size or value—five percent of the outstanding shares or a value of $25,000 in the Model Act. Section 49. The Revised Act has deleted this requirement. Both Acts provide that upon termination of a proceeding the court may require the plaintiff to pay the defendants' reasonable expenses, including attorneys' fees, if it finds that the proceeding was brought without reasonable cause. MBCA Section 49; RMBCA Section 7.40(d). The Revised Act and the statutes of a number of States require that all proposed settlements and discontinuances receive judicial approval. RMBCA Section 7.40(c).

Shareholder's Right to Dissent

A shareholder has the right to dissent from certain corporate actions which require shareholder approval. These actions include most mergers, consolidations, compulsory share exchanges, and a sale or exchange of all or substantially all the assets of the corporation not in the usual and regular course of business. The shareholder's right to dissent is discussed in Chapter 36.

LIABILITY OF SHAREHOLDERS

As a general rule the liability of a shareholder is limited to his investment. However, as discussed in the previous chapter, a shareholder who has not fully paid the required consideration for his shares is liable for the deficiency. In addition, there are several instances in which a shareholder who has fully paid for his shares may, nonetheless, have liability beyond his capital contribution.

Defective Incorporation

If a purported corporation is too defectively formed, shareholders who actively participated may be personally liable for the enterprise's obligations. See Chapter 33.

Disregard of the Corporate Entity

Where justice requires, courts will "pierce the corporate veil" and impose liability upon shareholders even though they have strictly complied with the required incorporation procedures. See Chapter 33.

Illegal Distributions

Shareholders who knowingly receive improperly declared dividends or other distributions are liable to return them to the corporation. Moreover, if the corporation is insolvent, the shareholders who received dividends must return them without regard to knowledge. See Chapter 34.

Controlling Shareholders

Shareholders who own a sufficient number of shares to have effective control over the corporation are termed "controlling shareholders." In some instances controlling shareholders are held to the same duties as directors and officers, which are discussed later in this chapter. Moreover, in close corporations some courts impose upon *all* the shareholders a fiduciary duty similar to that imposed upon partners. *See Pepper v. Litton.*

A special problem arises when controlling shareholders sell their shares in a block because such a sale necessarily and unavoidably conveys control to the purchaser. Such sales are required by the courts to be made with due care. The controlling shareholders must make a reasonable investigation so as not to transfer control to purchasers who wrongfully plan to convert or "loot" the assets of the corporation or to act contrary to the best interests of the corporation.

Additionally, purchasers are frequently willing to pay a premium for a block of shares that also conveys control. Although some courts require this so-called "control premium" to inure to the benefit of the corporation, other courts permit the controlling shareholders to retain the full amount of the control premium. When recoverable, the courts are divided over whether to permit the corporation to retain the premium or to require the corporation to distribute the premium ratably among the shareholders.

ROLE OF DIRECTORS AND OFFICERS

Management of a corporation is vested in its board of directors which determines general corporate policy and appoints officers to execute that policy and to administer the day-to-day operations of the corporation. Both the directors and officers of the corporation owe certain duties to the corporate entity as well as to the corporation's shareholders and are liable for breaching these duties.

The following sections will discuss the role of directors and officers of a corporation, including: the function of the board of directors; qualification, election, and tenure of directors; the exercise of directors' functions; officers; duties of directors and officers; and liabilities of directors and officers.

FUNCTION OF THE BOARD OF DIRECTORS

Although the directors are elected by the shareholders to manage the corporation, they are neither trustees nor agents of the shareholders or the corporation. They are, however, fiduciaries who must perform their duties in good faith, in the best interests of the corporation, and with due care.

The Model Act states that "[a]ll corporate powers shall be exercised by or under authority of, and the business and affairs of a corporation shall be managed under the direction of, a board of directors." Section 35. In some corporations the board is composed of members, all of whom are actively involved in the management of the business. In these cases the corporate powers are exercised *by* the board of directors. On the other hand, in publicly held corporations a majority of the board members frequently are not actively involved in management. Here, the corporate powers are exercised *under* the authority of the board which formulates major management policy but does not involve itself in the day-to-day management.

The board determines corporate policy in a number of areas, including (1) selecting and removing officers, (2) determining the capital structure, (3) initiating fundamental changes, (4) declaring dividends, and (5) setting management compensation.

Under the Revised Act, a corporation having 50 or fewer shareholders may dispense with or limit the authority of a board of directors by describing in its articles of incorporation who will perform some or all of the duties of a board. RMBCA Section 8.01(c). The comment to this section explains:

The persons who perform some or all of the duties of the board may be designated "trustees," "agents," or "managers," and they may be selected in ways other than the traditional election by the shareholders. It is necessary, however, that some person or group perform these duties, and the designated persons, while performing them, are subject to the same duties as directors.

Selection and Removal of Officers

In most States the board of directors has the responsibility to choose the corporate officers and may remove any officer at any time. Sections 50 and 51. Officers are agents of the corporation and are delegated their responsibilities by the board of directors.

Capital Structure

The board of directors determines the capital structure and financial policy of the corporation. For example, the board of directors has the power to:

1. Fix the selling price of newly issued par value shares at not less than par.
2. Fix the stated value and selling price of no par shares, unless the power to do so is reserved to the shareholders by the articles.
3. Determine the value of the consideration in the form of property, or labor or services received by the corporation in payment for shares issued.

4. Purchase, redeem or otherwise acquire shares of the corporation's equity securities.
5. Borrow money; issue notes, bonds and other obligations; and secure any of the corporation's obligations by mortgage or pledge of any or all of the corporation's property.
6. Sell, lease, exchange, or mortgage assets of the corporation in the *usual* and *regular* course of business.

Fundamental Changes

The board of directors has the power to make, alter, amend, or repeal the bylaws, unless this power is reserved to the shareholders by the articles of incorporation. Section 27. In addition, the board initiates a number of actions that are beyond its powers and require shareholder approval. For instance, the board must initiate proceedings to amend the articles of incorporation; to effect a merger, consolidation, compulsory share exchange, or the sale or lease of all or substantially all of the assets of the corporation other than in the usual and regular course of business; and to dissolve the corporation.

Dividends

The board of directors declares the amount and type of dividends, subject to restrictions in the State incorporation statute, the articles of incorporation as well as corporate loan and preferred stock agreements. Section 45. The board also provides for closing of stock transfer books and fixes a record date for the purpose of determining the shareholders who are entitled to receive dividends. Section 30.

Management Compensation

The board of directors usually determines the compensation of officers. Moreover, a number of States empower the board to fix the compensation of board members. In addition to fixed salaries, executive compensation may include: (1) cash bonuses, (2) share bonuses, (3) share options, (4) share purchase plans,

(5) insurance benefits, (6) deferred compensation, (7) retirement plans, and (8) a variety of other fringe benefits.

QUALIFICATION, ELECTION, AND TENURE OF DIRECTORS

Qualification of Directors

The governing incorporation statute, articles of incorporation, and bylaws determine the qualifications which individuals must possess in order to be eligible as directors of the corporation. The statute may require that directors be shareholders or residents of the State of incorporation, although most States have eliminated such requirements.

Election, Number, and Tenure of Directors

The initial board of directors is generally named in the articles of incorporation and serves until the first meeting of the shareholders. Thereafter, directors are elected at annual meetings of the shareholders and hold office for one year or until their successors are duly elected and qualified. As previously mentioned, the terms of members of the board are frequently staggered in order to provide continuity to the board. If the shares represented at a meeting in person or by proxy are not sufficient to constitute a quorum, the incumbent board continues in office as "holdover" directors until a valid election can be held. State statutes traditionally required that each corporation have three or more directors, although the modern trend is to permit the board to consist of one or more members. Section 36.

Moreover, the number of directors may be increased or decreased, within statutory limits, by amendment to the bylaws or charter. The Revised Act permits the board of directors, if it has the power to fix or change the number of directors, to increase or decrease its own size by up to 30 percent without shareholder approval. RMBCA Section 8.03(b). For example, in a board fixed or approved by the shareholders at 15 members, the board may, without shareholder approval, change the size of the board to as few as 11 or as many as 19. A board of 5 may be changed by the board to as few as 4 or as many as 6. Section 8.03(c) of the Revised Act authorizes the articles of incorporation or bylaws to establish a variable range for the size of the board by fixing a minimum and maximum number of directors.

Vacancies and Removal of Directors

The Model Act provides that a vacancy in the board may be filled by the affirmative vote of a majority of the remaining directors, even though they constitute less than a quorum of the board, and the director so elected shall hold office for the unexpired term of his predecessor. A directorship to be filled by reason of an increase in the number of directors may be filled by the board for a term continuing until the next election of directors by the shareholders. Section 38.

Some States have no statutory provision for removal of directors, although a common law rule permits removal for cause by action of the shareholders. The Model Act and an increasing number of other statutes permit removal of one or more of the directors or of the entire board by the shareholders, with or without cause, at a special meeting called for that purpose, subject to cumulative voting rights. Section 39. The Revised Act permits the articles of incorporation to provide that directors may be removed only for cause. RMBCA Section 8.08(a).

Compensation of Directors

Traditionally, directors did not receive salaries for their services as directors, although it was usual for them to be paid a fee or honorarium for attendance at meetings. The Model Act and other incorporation statutes now expressly authorize the board of directors to fix the compensation of directors absent a contrary provision in the articles of incorporation. Section 35.

EXERCISE OF DIRECTORS' FUNCTIONS

Meetings

Directors by reason of their office do not have the power to bind the corporation when acting individually but only when acting as a board. When an individual acts as a director, it is at a meeting with other directors or without a meeting by a written consent signed by all of the directors, provided that this manner of action is authorized by the statute and not contrary to the charter or bylaws.

The board is presumably representative of the shareholders. Its members usually are people of experience in various fields of business and professions, who may represent and speak for diverse interests among the shareholders.

Meetings are held either regularly at a time and place fixed in the bylaws or specially as they may be called. Notice of meetings must be given as prescribed in the bylaws. Attendance of a director at any meeting is a waiver of such notice, unless the director attends for the express purpose of objecting to the transaction of any business on the ground that the meeting is not lawfully called or convened. Most modern statutes provide that meetings of the board may be held either within or without the State of incorporation. Section 43.

Quorum

A majority of the members of the board of directors constitutes a quorum, the minimum number of members necessary to be present at a meeting in order to transact business. The articles of incorporation or bylaws may, however, require a number greater than a simple majority. If a quorum is present at any meeting, the act of a majority of the di-

rectors in attendance at such meeting is the act of the board, unless the act of a greater number is required by the articles of incorporation or bylaws. Section 40.

The Revised Act requires a quorum to be present when "a vote is taken," making it clear that the board may act only when a quorum is present. RMBCA Section 8.24(c) and Comment 2. This rule is in contrast to the rule governing shareholder meetings: once a quorum of shareholders is obtained it *cannot* be broken by the withdrawal of shareholders. In any event, directors may not vote by proxy, although a number of States permit directors to participate in meetings by means of conference telephones.

Action Taken without a Meeting

The Model Act provides that, unless otherwise provided by the articles of incorporation or bylaws, any action required by the statute to be taken at a meeting of the board may be taken without a meeting if a consent in writing is signed by all of the directors. Section 44. Such consent has the same effect as a unanimous vote.

Delegation of Board Powers

If provided for by the articles of incorporation or bylaws, the board of directors may by majority vote of the full board appoint executive and other committees, all of whose members must be directors. The Revised Act provides that the "creation of a committee and appointment of members to it must be approved by the greater of (1) a majority of all the directors in office when the action is taken or (2) the number of directors required by the articles of incorporation or bylaws to take action." RMBCA Section 8.25(b). Committees may exercise all of the authority of the board except for certain matters specified in the incorporation statute such as the declaration of dividends and other distributions, amending the bylaws, recommending fundamental changes to the shareholder, approving a merger not requiring shareholder approval, and authorizing the sale of stock. Section 42. Delegation of authority to a committee does not relieve any board member of his duties to the corporation. Commonly used committees include executive committees, audit committees (recommend and oversee independent public accountants), compensation committees, finance committees, nominating committees, and investment committees. The New York Stock Exchange requires that companies listed on the exchange have audit committees composed exclusively of outside directors. NYSE Company Manual A-29.

Directors' Inspection Rights

Directors have the right to inspect corporate books and records so they can competently and fully perform their duties.

OFFICERS

The officers of a corporation are appointed in most States by the board of directors to hold the offices provided in the bylaws which sets forth the respective duties of each officer. Statutes generally require as a minimum that they consist of a president, one or more vice-presidents as prescribed by the bylaws, a secretary, and a treasurer. Section 50. A person may hold more than one office, except that the same person may not hold the office of president and secretary at the same time.

The Revised Act permits the same individual to hold *all* of the offices of a corporation. RMBCA Section 8.40(d) and Comment.

Selection and Removal of Officers

Most State statutes provide that the officers are appointed by the board of directors and serve at the pleasure of the board. Section 50. Accordingly, officers may be removed by the board with or without cause.

Section 51. For example, in *Stott v. Stott Realty Co.*, 246 Mich. 267, 224 N.W. 623 (1929), the board of directors of Stott Realty Company removed Julia Orloff from her position as corporate secretary when she refused to follow the board's direction to sign certain mortgage papers. Julia brought an action against Stott Realty to enjoin her removal from the post. Judgment for Stott Realty. Directors of private corporations are chosen by the stockholders and, therefore, can be removed only by the stockholders. Officers, however, are selected by the directors and, therefore, generally hold their offices at the will of the board of directors. Since the board is charged with the management of the affairs of the corporation, it may remove any officer at any time without cause except where the officer was elected or employed by the stockholders.

Of course, if the officer has a valid employment contract for a specified period of time, removal of the officer without cause before the contract expires would constitute a breach of the employment contract. The board also determines the compensation of officers.

Role of Officers

The officers are, like the directors, fiduciaries to the corporation. On the other hand, unlike the directors, they are agents of the corporation. The roles of officers are set forth in the corporate bylaws, typical of which is the following description drawn from model bylaws:

President The president is the principal executive officer of the corporation and, subject to the control of the board of directors, in general supervises and controls all of the business and affairs of the corporation. He presides at all meetings of the shareholders and of the board of directors. He may sign for the corporation any deeds, mortgages, bonds, contracts, or other instruments which the board of directors has authorized to be executed.

Vice-President In the absence of the president or in the event of his death, inability, resignation or refusal to act, the vice-president shall perform the duties of the president and, when so acting, shall have all the powers of and be subject to all the restrictions upon the president.

Secretary The secretary keeps the minutes of the proceedings of the shareholders and of the board of directors; sees that all notices are duly given; is custodian of the corporate records and of the seal of the corporation; signs with the president certificates for shares of the corporation, the issuance of which shall have been authorized by resolution of the board of directors; and has general charge of the stock transfer books of the corporation.

Treasurer The treasurer has charge and custody of and is responsible for all funds and securities of the corporation and receives and gives receipts for and deposits moneys due and payable to the corporation.

Authority of Officers

The Model Act provides that all officers of the corporation shall have such authority as may be provided in the bylaws or as may be determined by resolution of the board of directors not inconsistent with the bylaws. Section 50. As with other agents, the authority of an officer to bind the corporation may be (1) actual express, (2) actual implied, or (3) apparent.

Actual Express Authority Actual express authority results from the manifestation of assent by the corporation to the officer that the officer should act on the behalf of the corporation. Actual express authority arises from the incorporation statute, the articles of incorporation, the bylaws, and resolutions of the board of directors. The principal source of actual express authority is the resolutions of the board of directors.

Actual Implied Authority Officers, as agents of the corporation, have implied authority to do what is reasonably necessary to perform their actual, delegated authority. In addition, the question arises whether officers possess implied authority merely by virtue of their positions. The courts have been circumspect in granting such implied or inherent authority. Traditionally, the courts tended to hold that the president had no implied authority by virtue of his office, although the more recent decisions tend to recognize his authority to bind the corporation in ordinary business transactions. However, any act requiring board approval, such as issuing stock, is clearly beyond the implied authority of the president or any other officer. In most jurisdictions, implied authority of position does not extend to any officer other than the president.

Apparent Authority Apparent authority arises from acts of the principal that lead third parties to believe reasonably and in good faith that an officer has the requisite authority. Apparent authority might arise when a third party relies on the fact that an officer has exercised the same authority in the past with the consent of the board of directors.

Ratification A corporation may ratify the unauthorized acts of its officers. Ratification is equivalent to the corporation's having granted the officer prior authority. Ratification relates back to the original transaction and may be express or implied from the corporation's acceptance of the benefits of the contract with full knowledge of the facts.

DUTIES OF
DIRECTORS AND OFFICERS

A corporation may not recover damages from its directors and officers for losses resulting from their poor business judgment or honest mistake of judgment. The directors and officers are not insurers of business success. They are required only to be obedient, reasonably diligent, and completely loyal. These duties of obedience, diligence, and loyalty are for the most part judicially imposed. State statutes supplement the common law by imposing liability upon directors and officers for specific acts, but the common law still remains the most significant source of duties.

Duty of Obedience

Directors and officers must act within their respective authority. For any loss resulting to the corporation from their unauthorized acts, they are held absolutely liable in some jurisdictions, while in others they are held liable only if they intentionally or negligently exceeded their authority.

Duty of Diligence

In the discharge of their duties, directors and officers must exercise ordinary care and prudence. Some States interpret this standard as providing that directors and officers must exercise "the same degree of care and prudence that men promoted by self-interest generally exercise in their own affairs." *Hun v. Cary*, 82 N.Y. 65. Most States, and the MBCA, however, hold that the test requires that "[a] director shall perform his duties as a director . . . in good faith, in a manner he reasonably believes to be in the best interests of the corporation, and with such care as an ordinarily prudent person in a like position would use under similar circumstances." Section 35.

So long as the directors and officers act in good faith and with due care, the courts will not substitute their judgment for the board's or officer's judgment—the so-called **"business judgment rule."** Directors and officers will, nonetheless, be held liable for bad faith or negligent conduct. Moreover, they may be liable for failing to act. For instance, a director of a bank, who in the five-and-a-half years that he had been on the board had never attended a board meeting or made any examination of the books and records, was held liable for the losses resulting from the unsupervised acts of the president and cashier who had made various improper loans and had permitted large overdrafts. *See also Francis v. United Jersey Bank.*

Reliance Upon Others Directors and officers, however, are permitted to entrust important work to others and, if employees have been selected with care, are not personally liable for the negligent acts or willful wrongs of such employees. A reasonable amount of supervision is required, and an officer or director will be held liable for the losses resulting from an employee's carelessness, theft, or embezzlement if he knew or ought to have known or suspected that such losses were being incurred.

Directors may also rely upon information provided them by officers and employees of the corporation. Section 35 of the Model Act provides:

In performing his duties, a director shall be entitled to rely on information, opinions, reports or statements, including financial statements and other financial data, in each case prepared or presented by:

(a) one or more officers or employees of the corporation whom the director reasonably believes to be reliable and competent in the matters presented,

(b) counsel, public accountants or other persons as to matters which the director reasonably believes to be within such person's professional or expert competence, or

(c) a committee of the board upon which he does not serve, duly designated in accordance with a provision of the articles of incorporation or the by-laws, as to matters within its designated authority, which committee the director reasonably believes to merit confidence,

but he shall not be considered to be acting in good faith if he has knowledge concerning the matter in question that would cause such reliance to be unwarranted.

An officer is also entitled to rely upon this information but this right may, in many circumstances, be more limited than a director's because of the officer's greater familiarity with the affairs of the corporation. RMBCA Section 8.42 and Comment.

Business Judgment Rule Directors are continuously called upon to make decisions which require the balancing of benefits and risks for the corporation. Although hindsight may reveal that some of these decisions were less than optimal, the business judgment rule precludes imposing liability upon the directors for honest mistakes of judgment. To benefit from the business judgment rule a director must

1. exercise due care,
2. act in good faith, and
3. act in a manner he reasonably believed to be in the best interests of the corporation.

MBCA Section 35 and RMBCA Section 8.30. This requires that the director make an informed decision, without any conflict of interests and have a rational basis for making it. Moreover, when there is a failure to satisfy this standard of conduct, it must be shown that the directors' action (or inaction) is the proximate cause of damage to the corporation.

In *Neese v. Brown*, 218 Tenn. 686, 405 S.W.2d 577 (1964), Neese, trustee in bankruptcy for First Trust Company, brought an action against the directors of the company for losses sustained by the company as a result of the failure of the directors to use due care and diligence in the discharge of their duties. The specific acts of negligence alleged were: (1) failure to give as much time and attention to the affairs of the company as its business interests required; (2) abdication of their control of the corporation by turning the entire management of the corporation over to its president, Brown; (3) failure to keep informed as to the affairs, condition, and management of the corporation; (4) taking no ac-

tion to direct or control the corporation's affairs; (5) permitting large, open, unsecured loans to affiliated but financially unsound companies that were owned and controlled by Brown; (6) failure to examine financial reports which would have shown illegal diversions and waste of the corporation's funds; and (7) failure to supervise properly the corporation's officers and directors. The court held for Neese. Liability of officers and directors of a corporation is not limited to acts constituting a willful breach of trust or power but also extend to acts that are merely negligent. The directors must be something more than just figureheads. Although they are not responsible for simple errors in judgment, as fiduciaries the directors have the duty of caring for the property of the corporation and the additional duty of managing its affairs honestly and in good faith. The directors must exercise their best judgment and act solely and always with reasonable care to promote the welfare of the corporation. Therefore, the directors here can be held liable for inaction where such inaction was the proximate cause of a loss to the corporation.

The business judgment rule also applies to officers. Section 8.42 of the Revised Act provides:

(a) An officer with discretionary authority shall discharge his duties under that authority:

    (1) in good faith;

    (2) with the care an ordinarily prudent person in a like position would exercise under similar circumstances; and

    (3) in a manner he reasonably believes to be in the best interests of the corporation.

Duty of Loyalty

The officers and directors of a corporation owe a duty of loyalty (**fiduciary duty**) to the corporation and to its shareholders. The essence of a fiduciary duty is the subordination of self-interest to the interest of the person or persons to whom the duty is owing. It requires undeviating loyalty on the part of officers and directors to the corporation which they both serve and control.

An officer or director is required to make full disclosure to the corporation of any financial interest which he may have in any contract or transaction to which the corporation is a party. This is a corollary to the rule which forbids fiduciaries from making secret profits. His business conduct must be insulated from self-interest, and he may not avail himself of opportunities to advance his personal interest at the expense of the corporation. He may not represent conflicting interests, and his duty is one of strict allegiance to the corporation.

The remedy for breach of fiduciary duty is a suit in equity by the corporation, or more often a derivative suit instituted by a shareholder, to require the fiduciary to pay to the corporation the secret profits which he has obtained through breach of his fiduciary duty. It need not be shown that the corporation could otherwise have made the profits which the fiduciary has realized. The object of the rule is to discourage breaches of duty by a fiduciary, and this is achieved by taking from the fiduciary all of the profits he has made. The enforcement of the rule may result in a windfall to the corporation, but this is incidental to the deterrent effect of the rule.

Conflict of Interests A contract between an officer or a director and the corporation is not void, but voidable. A rule which would preclude such a contract would be unreasonable because it would prevent directors from entering into contracts that are beneficial to the corporation. Therefore, if such a contract is honest and fair, it will be upheld.

In the case of contracts between corporations having an interlocking directorate, or having one or more persons who are members of both boards of directors, the courts subject the contracts to the severest scrutiny and are quick to set them aside unless the transaction is shown to have been entirely fair and entered into in good faith.

The Model Act addresses both of these related problems by providing that such transactions are neither void nor voidable if they are approved after full disclosure by either the board of disinterested directors or the shareholders or if they are fair and reasonable to the corporation.

No contract or other transaction between a corporation and one or more of its directors or any other corporation, firm, association or entity in which one or more of its directors are directors or officers or are financially interested, shall be either void or voidable because of such relationship or interest or because such director or directors are present at the meeting of the board of directors or a committee thereof which authorizes, approves or ratifies such contract or transaction or because his or their votes are counted for such purpose, if:

(a) the fact of such relationship or interest is disclosed or known to the board of directors or committee which authorizes, approves or ratifies the contract or transaction by a vote or consent sufficient for the purpose without counting the votes or consents of such interested directors; or

(b) the fact of such relationship or interest is disclosed or known to the shareholders entitled to vote and they authorize, approve or ratify such contract or transaction by vote or written consent; or

(c) the contract or transaction is fair and reasonable to the corporation. Section 41.

The Revised Act continues this approach and clarifies the procedure for obtaining authorization, approval or ratification. See RMBCA Section 8.31.

Loans to Directors The Model Act does not permit a corporation to lend money to its directors without authorization in the particular case by its shareholders. Section 47. The Revised Act permits such loans if the particular loan is approved (1) by a majority of disinterested shareholders or (2) by the board of directors after determining that the loan benefits the corporation. RMBCA Section 8.32.

Corporate Opportunity Directors and officers may not usurp any corporate opportunity that in all fairness should belong to the corporation. A corporate opportunity in an opportunity in which the corporation has a right, property interest, or expectancy and depends upon the facts and circumstances of each case. For instance, a party proposes a business arrangement to X Corporation through its vice-president who personally accepts it without offering it to the corporation. The vice-president has usurped a corporate opportunity. On the other hand, it would not generally include an opportunity which the corporation was unable to accept or one which the corporation expressly rejected by a vote of disinterested directors after full disclosure. In both of these instances a director or officer can take personal advantage of the opportunity.

Transactions in Shares The issuance of shares at favorable prices to management by excluding other shareholders will normally constitute a violation of the fiduciary duty. So might the issuance of shares to a director at a fair price if the purpose of the issuance is to perpetuate corporate control rather than to raise capital or serve some other interest of the corporation.

Officers and directors have access to inside advance information not available to the public which may affect the future market value of the shares of the corporation. Federal statutes have attempted to deal with this trading advantage by prohibiting officers and directors from purchasing or selling shares of stock of their corporation without adequate disclosure of all material facts in their possession that may affect the value or potential value of the stock. Under the Securities Exchange Act of 1934, the Securities and Exchange Commission adopted Rule 10b-5 which requires disclosure in such purchases or sales where use has been made of the mails or an instrumentality of interstate commerce, such as the telephone or telegraph. In addition, Section 16(b) of the same statute requires insiders to disgorge to the corporation any profit realized by their short-swing speculation in its stock. See Chapter 44 for a discussion of these matters.

Although State law has not consistently imposed liability upon officers and directors for secret, profitable use of inside information, the trend is toward holding them liable for breach of fiduciary duty to shareholders from whom they purchase stock without making disclosure to them of facts which give the stock added value potential; and liable to the corporation for profits realized upon a sale of the stock when undisclosed conditions of the corporation make a substantial decline in value practically inevitable.

For example, a shareholders' derivative action was filed in New York against officers and directors of Management Assistance, Inc. (MAI) to compel an accounting to the corporation for profits resulting from their sale of personally held shares of stock of the corporation shortly prior to a severe decline in its market value. MAI was in the business of financing computer installations through sale and lease back arrangements with commercial and industrial users. Lacking the capacity to maintain and repair the computers, MAI engaged IBM, the manufacturer, to service the machines. Due to a sharp increase by IBM of its charges for the service, MAI's expenses in August, 1966, rose and its net earnings declined from $262,000 in July to $66,000 in August, a 75% decrease. This information was not made public until October, 1966, although it was known earlier by the defendants. Prior to public release of the information, the president and chairman of the board of MAI sold 56,500 shares of their MAI stock at the current market price of $28 a share. In October, 1966, after the release, the market price declined to $11 a share. These defendants thus realized $800,000 more for their securities than they could have realized if the inside information had not been available to them. Although MAI sustained no loss nor suffered any damage by this sale of stock, the court in *Diamond v. Oreamuno*, 24 N.Y.2d 494, 301

N.Y.S.2d 78, 248 N.E.2d 910 (1969) held these defendants liable to the corporation for the profits which they had realized, stating:

Just as a trustee has no right to retain for himself the profits yielded by property placed in his possession but must account to his beneficiaries, a corporate fiduciary, who is entrusted with potentially valuable information, may not appropriate that asset for his own use even though, in so doing, he causes no injury to the corporation. The primary concern, in a case such as this, is not to determine whether the corporation has been damaged but to decide, as between the corporation and the defendants, who has a higher claim to the proceeds derived from the exploitation of the information. In our opinion, there can be no justification for permitting officers and directors, such as the defendants, to retain for themselves profits which, it is alleged, they derived solely from exploiting information gained by virtue of their inside position as corporate officials.

Duty Not to Compete As fiduciaries, directors and officers owe to the corporation the duty of undivided loyalty which does not permit them to compete with the corporation. Although directors and officers may engage in their own business interests, courts will closely scrutinize any interest that competes with the business of the corporation. Moreover, an officer or a director may not use corporate personnel, facilities, or funds for his own benefit nor disclose trade secrets of the corporation to others.

LIABILITIES OF DIRECTORS AND OFFICERS

Directors and officers incur personal liability for breaching any of the duties they owe to the corporation and shareholders. As discussed above, most of these duties arise from court-made rules with some supplementation by State and Federal statutory laws. Most of the potential liability applies to both officers and directors.

Under many modern incorporation statutes a corporation may indemnify a director or officer for liability incurred if he acted in good faith and in a manner he reasonably believed to be in the best interests of the corporation, so long as he has not been adjudged negligent or liable for misconduct. A corporation may purchase insurance to indemnify officers and directors for liability arising out of their corporate activities, including liabilities against which the corporation is not empowered to indemnify directly.

Breach of Duties to Corporation

Directors and officers are liable to the corporation for breach of any duty owed the corporation. Where the breach is of the duty of obedience or diligence, the liability is for the loss resulting to the corporation from the *ultra vires*, unauthorized or negligent act. Where the breach is the duty of loyalty, the corporation may avail itself of a number of equitable remedies fashioned to the particular circumstances of the case. For instance, where a corporate opportunity has been usurped, the director or officer will be required to disgorge the profits he has realized on the transaction, and the corporation may avail itself of the usurped opportunity. Where a conflict of interest is involved, the corporation may rescind the contract. A director or officer who breaches his fiduciary duty by competing with the corporation is liable for damages caused to the corporation. Whenever a director or officer breaches his fiduciary duty, he forfeits his rights to compensation during the period he engaged in the breach. *See Wilshire Oil Co. of Texas v. Riffe.*

Defective Incorporation

The MBCA imposes joint and several liability upon those who assume to act as a corporation without authority for all debts and liabilities incurred as a result. Section 146. Some States impose liability upon directors and officers for transacting business before the statutory minimum paid in capital has been received.

Contracts

An officer who binds the corporation to a contract within his apparent authority but beyond his actual authority is liable to the corporation for any resulting loss. An officer who purports to contract with a third party in excess of his actual and apparent authority is personally liable to the third party for breach of implied warranty of authority.

Torts

Although officers and directors are insulated from personal liability on contracts of the corporation, unless outside the scope of their actual authority or *ultra vires*, they are subject to personal liability in tort for their intentional wrongdoing or negligent conduct even while engaged in corporate business activities.

Violation of State and Federal Statutes

Directors and officers may incur civil or criminal liability for violating State and Federal statutes. For example, failure to file required reports (Section 136), denial of shareholders' inspection rights (Section 52, omitted by the Revised Act), violation of antitrust law (Chapter 41), and violation of securities laws (Chapter 44) may result in civil or criminal penalties or both.

Illegal Distributions

Directors are jointly and severally liable for issuing shares of the corporation at a discount and for declaring a dividend which is paid when the corporation is insolvent or in violation of the State incorporation statute. Section 48. They are also liable for voting or assenting to a purchase by the corporation of its own shares in violation of the statute. Section 48.

A director is not liable for any of the acts mentioned in the preceding paragraph if in assenting to them he acted in good faith and in reliance upon information, reports, or financial statements of the corporation represented to him to be correct by an officer or employee of the corporation having charge of its books of account, or public accountant, or by a board committee. Nor is he liable if in good faith he considered the assets of the corporation to be of their book value in determining the amount available for a dividend or other distribution to shareholders. Section 35.

If a director is present at a meeting of the board at which action on any corporate matter is taken, he is presumed to have assented to such action unless in addition to dissenting from it he (1) has his dissent entered in the minutes of the meeting, or (2) files his written dissent to such action with the person acting as secretary before the meeting adjourns, or (3) forwards his written dissent by registered mail to the secretary of the corporation immediately after the adjournment of the meeting. Section 35.

CASES

Shareholder Agreements

GALLER v. GALLER

Supreme Court of Illinois, 1965.
32 Ill.2d 16, 203 N.E.2d 577.

UNDERWOOD, J.

[In 1927, two brothers, Benjamin and Isadore Galler, incorporated the Galler Drug Co., a wholesale drug business that they had operated as equal partners since 1919. The company continued to grow, and in 1955, the two brothers and their wives, Emma and Rose Galler, entered into a written shareholder agreement to leave the corporation in equal control of each family after the death of either brother. Specifically, the agreement provided for the corporation to continue to provide income for the support and maintenance of their immediate families and for the parties to vote for directors so as to give the estate and heirs of a deceased shareholder the same representation as before.

Benjamin died in 1957, and shortly thereafter his widow Emma requested that Isadore, the surviving brother, comply with the terms of the agreement. When he refused and proposed that certain changes be made in the agreement, Emma brought this action seeking specific performance of the agreement. Isadore and his wife, Rose, defend on the ground that the shareholder agreement was against public policy and the State's corporation law. The trial court entered a decree of specific performance in favor of the plaintiff Emma. On appeal, the decree was reversed by the Appellate Court on the ground that the July, 1955, agreement was void as contrary to the Illinois Business Corporation Act and as against public policy.]

*   *   *

At this juncture it should be emphasized that we deal here with a so-called close corporation. Various attempts at definition of the close corporation have been made. [Citation.] For our purposes, a close corporation is one in which the stock is held in a few hands, or in a few families, and wherein it is not at all, or only rarely, dealt in by buying or selling. [Citation.] Moreover, it should be recognized that shareholder agreements similar to that in question here are often, as a practical consideration, quite necessary for the protection of those financially interested in the close corporation. While the shareholder of a public-issue corporation may readily sell his shares on the open market should management fail to use, in his opinion, sound business judgment, his counterpart of the close corporation often has a large total of his entire capital invested in the business and has no ready market for his shares should he desire to sell. He feels, understandably, that he is more than a mere investor and that his voice should be heard concerning all corporate activity. Without a shareholder agreement, specifically enforceable by the courts, insuring him a modicum of control, a large minority shareholder might find himself at the mercy of an oppressive or unknowledgeable majority. Moreover, as in the case at bar, the shareholders of a close corporation are often also the directors and officers thereof. With substantial shareholding interests abiding in each member of the board of directors, it is often quite impossible to secure, as in the large public-issue corporation, independent board judgment free from personal motivations concerning corporate policy. For these and other reasons too voluminous to enumerate here, often the only sound basis for protection is afforded by a lengthy, detailed shareholder agreement securing the rights and obligations of all concerned.

*   *   *

*   *   * While limiting voting trusts in 1947 to a maximum duration of 10 years, the legislature has indicated no similar policy regarding straight voting agreements although these have been common since prior to 1870. In view of the history of decisions of this court generally upholding, in the absence of fraud or prejudice to minority interests or public policy, the right of stockholders to agree among themselves as to the manner in which their stock will be voted, we do not regard the period of time within which this agreement may remain effective as rendering the agreement unenforceable.

The clause that provides for the election of certain persons to specified offices for a period of years likewise does not require invalidation. *   *   *

We turn next to a consideration of the effect of the stated purpose of the agreement upon its validity. The pertinent provision is: "The said Benjamin A. Galler and Isadore A. Galler desire to provide income for the support and maintenance of their immediate families." Obviously, there is no evil inherent in a contract entered into for the reason that the persons originating the terms desired to so arrange their property as to provide post-death support for those dependent upon them. Nor does the fact that the subject property is corporate stock alter the situation so long as there exists no detriment to minority stock interests, creditors or other public injury.

*   *   *

The terms of the dividend agreement require a minimum annual dividend of $50,000, but this duty is limited by the subsequent provision that it shall be operative only so long as an earned surplus of $500,000 is maintained. It may be noted that in 1958, the year prior to commencement of this litigation, the corporation's net earnings after taxes amounted to $202,759 while its earned surplus was $1,543,270, and this was increased in 1958 to $1,680,079 while earnings were $172,964. The minimum earned surplus requirement is designed for the protection of the corporation and its creditors, and we take no exception to the contractual dividend requirements as thus restricted. [Citation.]

The salary continuation agreement is a common feature, in one form or another, of corporate executive employment. It requires that the widow should receive a total benefit, payable monthly over a five-year period, aggregating twice the amount paid her deceased husband in one year. This requirement was likewise limited for the protection of the corporation by being contingent upon the payments being income tax-deductible by the corporation. The charge made in those cases which have considered the validity of payment to the widow of an officer and shareholder in a corporation is that a gift of its property by a noncharitable corporation is in violation of the rights of its shareholders and *ultra vires*. Since there are no shareholders here other than the parties to the contract, this objection is not here applicable, and its effect, as limited, upon the corporation is not so prejudicial as to require its invalidation.

*   *   *

Accordingly, the judgment of the Appellate Court is reversed except insofar as it relates to fees, and is, as to them affirmed.
*   *   *

Affirmed in part and reversed in part, and remanded with directions.

Right to Inspect Books and Records

APPLICATION OF LOPEZ

Supreme Court, Appellate Division, First Department, 1979.
420 N.Y.S.2d 225, 71 A.D.2d 976.

MEMORANDUM DECISION

Order and judgment, Supreme Court, New York County, entered August 30, 1979, denying application for disclosure of respondent's shareholder lists, unanimously reversed on the law and the facts, with costs, and the petition is granted to the extent of disclosure of all record and beneficial ownership of shares as of September 7, 1979.

Respondent [SCM] is currently defending a multimillion dollar lawsuit brought in federal court by one Muller over the latter's unsuccessful negotiations for purchase of SCM assets abroad. Muller formed the "SCM Corporation Shareholders Committee," consisting of himself, his corporation (MacMuller Industries) and two other officers of his corporation, to challenge the position of respondent's management in this controversy. Up until August 6, 1979, this committee controlled 269,900 of the more than 9½ million outstanding shares of SCM stock. In order to wage a proxy battle for management control at the next meeting for election of directors, scheduled for October 25, 1979, the committee was anxious to obtain the list of shareholders eligible to vote as of the record date of September 7, 1979. However, [the incorporation statute] allows for the availability of such information only to shareholders of record in the corporation for at least six months. As of August 5, 1979, Muller's committee consisted of shareholders of record whose longevity of holdings in the corporation ranged from one month to four months and 23 days. On August 6 petitioner [Lopez], a former SCM executive and record holder of 38 shares of stock since 1977, joined the committee. That same day, petitioner, on behalf of the committee, demanded inspection of minutes of respondent's shareholder proceedings, as well as current lists of shareholders' names and addresses, updated by daily transfer sheets to reflect those eligible to vote at the next election of directors. The stated purpose of the demand was to communicate with shareholders for solicitation of proxies in support of the committee's nominees for directors. Respondent's rejection of this request inspired the instant proceeding.

The purpose of petitioner's demand was clearly set forth in his letter of August 6, so there is no procedural basis for respondent's rejection. [Citation.] Further, the inspection of shareholder lists to facilitate a proxy challenge to incumbent directors is a valid purpose. [Citation.] The burden is on respondent to show an improper purpose for the demand. [Citation.] Petitioner's association with Muller is certainly no indication of impropriety, in light of the otherwise valid stated purpose of the demand. Petitioner alleges without challenge that he has independently concluded that change in the management of SCM in the interest of its shareholders is warranted, and that in this respect his views and those of the committee are similar. Where the demand is facially valid, good faith is assumed, obviating the necessity for a hearing on this issue. [Citation.] The mere fact that Muller and his companies are engaged in litigation with SCM does not demonstrate lack of good faith. Nor would there be an improper purpose or bad faith if communications with shareholders discussed such litigation. [Citation.]

Petitioner is entitled to access to available transfer sheets, at his expense, showing the daily status of record and beneficial ownership. [Citation.]

Shareholder Derivative Suits

McMENOMY v. RYDEN

Supreme Court of Minnesota, 1970.
286 Minn. 358, 176 N.W.2d 876.

KNUTSON, C. J.

[Minority shareholders of Midwest Technical Institute Development Corporation, a closed-end investment company owning assets consisting principally of securities of companies in technological fields, brought a shareholder derivative suit against officers and directors of Midwest. The shareholders sought to recover on Midwest's behalf the profits realized by the officers and directors through dealings in stock held in Midwest's portfolio in breach of their fiduciary duty. Approximately three years after commencement of the action a new corporation, Midtex, was organized to acquire Midwest's assets. The shareholders now seek to add Midtex as a party defendant to their suit, but the trial court denied their motion.]

*   *   *

A stockholder's derivative action of the type that we have here is an invention of equity to permit stockholders to seek relief for breach of fiduciary duty by officers or directors when the corporation itself refuses to being such action. In [citation] the court said:

> The stockholder's derivative action * * * is an invention of equity to supply the want of an adequate remedy at law to redress breaches of fiduciary duty by corporate managers. Usually the wrongdoing officers also possess the control which enables them to suppress any effort by the corporate entity to remedy such wrongs. Equity therefore traditionally entertains the derivative or secondary action by which a single stockholder may sue in the corporation's right when he shows that the corporation on proper demand has refused to pursue a remedy, or shows facts that demonstrate the futility of such a request. * * *
>
> The cause of action which such a plaintiff brings before the court is not his own but the corporation's. It is the real party in interest and he is allowed to act in protection of its interest, somewhat as a "next friend" might do for an individual, because it is disabled from protecting itself.

That being so, it should not be possible to frustrate this remedy created by equity by the simple expedient of creating a new corporation and assigning the assets of one for whose benefit suit is brought to the newly created entity. Someone should have the continuing right to seek relief from those guilty of breach of fiduciary duty, if there has been such. The stockholders of Midwest, if there was a breach of fiduciary duty by the managing officers, did not lose the right to recover simply because the assets were transferred to a new corporation.

*   *   *

It has been argued that inasmuch as Midtex, after procuring legal advice from independent attorneys, decided not to continue the suit or to join it, plaintiffs are thereby barred from continuing the suit. *   *   *

*   *   *

Here the members of the board of directors of Midtex, only one of whom was a member of the board of Midwest at the time plaintiffs commenced this action, have exercised their judgment in deciding not to join the lawsuit or to continue with it. This they had a right to do. By refusing to become a party to the lawsuit, they undoubtedly have chosen a course that will eliminate liability on the part of Midtex for the payment of expenses of the litigation. However, this should not preclude the joining of Midtex as an involuntary defendant if it is in fact the real party in interest as the assignee of the cause of action brought for the benefit of Midwest.

It may be possible to determine prior to trial whether it was the intention of the parties to assign this cause of action to Midtex. If so, the action should proceed for the benefit of the corporation that will receive the benefit of the recovery, if there is one. Unless that issue is determined before trial, Midtex should be joined as an involuntary defendant and the case proceed with both Midwest and Midtex named as defendants. If there is a recovery, the question as to who shall receive the benefit of it can then be determined after the trial.

The case is therefore remanded to the trial court for disposition in conformity with this opinion.

Duties of Controlling Shareholders

PEPPER v. LITTON

Supreme Court of the United States, 1939.
308 U.S. 295, 60 S.Ct. 238, 84 L.Ed. 281.

DOUGLAS, J.

[Litton, an officer and the dominant shareholder of Dixie Splint Coal Company, transferred the company's remaining assets to himself when the company came on the verge of bankruptcy. The transfer allegedly was in satisfaction of an accrued salary claim that Litton had not enforced until the company came into financial difficulty. The trustee in bankruptcy seeks to have Litton's claim disallowed. The District Court disallowed the claim. The Court of Appeals for the Fourth Circuit reversed the District Court. Certiorari was granted.]

*   *   *

The mere fact that an officer, director, or stockholder has a claim against his bankrupt corporation or that he has reduced that claim to judgment does not mean the bankruptcy court must accord it pari passu treatment with the claims of other creditors. Its disallowance or subordination may be necessitated by certain cardinal principles of equity jurisprudence. A director is a fiduciary. [Citation.] So is a dominant or controlling stockholder or a group of stockholders. [Citation.] Their powers are powers in trust. [Citation.] Their dealings with the corporation are subjected to rigorous scrutiny and where any of their contracts or engagements with the corporation is challenged the burden is on the director or stockholder not only to prove the good faith of the transaction but also to show its inherent fairness from the viewpoint of the corporation and those interested therein. [Citation.] The essence of the test is whether or not under all the circumstances the transaction carries the earmarks of an arm's length bargain. If it does not, equity will set it aside. While normally that fiduciary obligation is enforceable directly by the corporation, or through a stockholder's derivative action, it is, in the event of bankruptcy of the corporation, enforceable by the trustee. For that standard of fiduciary obligation is designed for the protection of the entire community of interests in the corporation—creditors as well as stockholders.

As we have said, the bankruptcy court in passing on allowance of claims sits as a court of equity. Hence, these rules governing the fiduciary responsibilities of directors and stockholders come into play on allowance of their claims in bankruptcy. In the exercise of its equitable jurisdiction the bankruptcy court has the power to sift the circumstances surrounding any claim to see that injustice or unfairness is not done in administration of the bankrupt estate. And its duty so to do is especially clear when the claim seeking allowance accrues to the benefit of an officer, director, or stockholder. That is clearly the power and duty of the bankruptcy courts under the reorganization sections. * * * Similar results have properly been reached in ordinary bankruptcy proceedings. Thus, salary claims of officers, directors, and stockholders in bankruptcy of "one-man" or family corporations have been disallowed or subordinated where the courts have been satisfied that allowance of the claims would not be fair or equitable to other creditors. And that result may be reached even though the salary claim has been reduced to judgment. It is reached where the claim is void or voidable because the vote of the interested director or stockholder helped bring it into being or where the history of the corporation shows dominancy and exploitation on the part of the claimant. It is also reached where on the facts the bankrupt has been used merely as a corporate pocket of the dominant stockholder, who, with disregard of the substance or form of corporate management, has treated its affairs as his own. And so-called loans or advances by the dominant or controlling stockholder will be subordinated to claims of other creditors

and thus treated in effect as capital contributions by the stockholder not only in the foregoing types of situations but also where paid-in capital is purely nominal, the capital necessary for the scope and mangitude of the operations of the company being furnished by the stockholder as a loan. * * *

On such a test the action of the District Court in disallowing or subordinating Litton's claim was clearly correct. Litton allowed his salary claims to lie dormant for a year and sought to enforce them only when his debtor corporation was in financial difficulty. Then he used them so that the rights of another creditor were impaired. Litton as an insider utilized his strategic position for his own preferment to the damage of Pepper. Litton as the dominant influence over Dixie Splint Coal Company used his power not to deal fairly with the creditors of that company but to manipulate its affairs in such a manner that when one of its creditors came to collect her just debt the bulk of the assets had disappeared into another Litton company. Litton, though a fiduciary, was enabled by astute legal maneuvering to acquire most of the assets of the bankrupt not for cash or other consideration of value to creditors but for bookkeeping entries representing at best merely Litton's appraisal of the worth of Litton's services over the years.

This alone would be a sufficient basis for the exercise by the District Court of its equitable powers in disallowing the Litton claim. But when there is added the existence of a "planned and fraudulent scheme," as found by the District Court, the necessity of equitable relief against that fraud becomes insistent. No matter how technically legal each step in that scheme may have been, once its basic nature was uncovered it was the duty of the bankruptcy court in the exercise of its equity jurisdiction to undo it. Otherwise, the fiduciary duties of dominant or management stockholders would go for naught; exploitation would become a substitute for justice; and equity would be perverted as an instrument for approving what it was designed to thwart.

* * *

[Judgment of the Court of Appeals reversed and that of the District Court affirmed.]

Duty of Diligence

FRANCIS v. UNITED JERSEY BANK

Superior Court of New Jersey, 1978.
162 N.J.Super. 355, 392 A.2d 1233.

STANTON, J.

* * *

Pritchard & Baird was engaged in the business of being a reinsurance broker. Along with three related corporations, it was controlled for many years by Charles H. Pritchard, who died on December 10, 1973. Prior to his death he had taken his sons, Charles, Jr. and William, into the business. During the last few years of the elder Pritchard's life the sons, particularly Charles, Jr., had played an increasingly dominant role in the affairs of Pritchard & Baird. After the father's death the sons took complete control of the business.

Charles, Jr. and William were extremely incompetent businessmen and they were almost totally devoid of any sense of self-restraint or business morality. By the end of 1975 they had plunged Pritchard and Baird and the related corporations into hopeless bankruptcy. I understand from my general knowledge of the bankruptcy proceedings which are under way in the United States District Court for the District of New Jersey that the creditors of the various businesses stand to lose something on the order of $70,000,000. This present action is part of a much larger picture of chicanery and fraud. It deals with more than $10,000,000 in funds transferred unlawfully from Pritchard & Baird to various members of the Pritchard family.

In order to understand what occurred in this case it is necessary to say something about the business of being a reinsurance broker. If an insurer has a very large individual risk on which it has given coverage, it may seek to protect itself from too heavy a loss by shifting the risk to another larger insurer or to a group of insurers. It does this by reinsuring, that is, by purchasing insurance on all or a portion of the underlying risk from one or more other insurers. This approach may be taken with respect to a single very large risk or with respect to a class or category of policies in which there seems to be a dangerously high concentration of risk. An insurance company which has provided underlying coverage and seeks to spread all or part of the risk to one or more other insurers is known as a ceding company. An insurance company which sells protection to a ceding company is a reinsurer.

The function of a reinsurance broker such as Pritchard & Baird is to bring ceding companies and reinsurers together. However, the task of the reinsurance broker is much more complicated and sophisticated than that of the ordinary retail insurance broker with whom we are all familiar in our capacities as owners of automobiles or houses. Very often, scores of insurance companies are involved in a single reinsurance transaction, and it is common for reinsurance transactions to cross national boundaries. There is virtually no governmental regulation at any level of the business of reinsurance. Frequently, the ceding and reinsuring companies involved in a reinsurance transaction do not know each other's identites, and this may be true even after the transaction has been consummated, and even after a substantial loss has been incurred and paid. The insurance companies involved rely to a large extent upon the knowledge, skill, integrity and bookkeeping of the reinsurance broker.

The elder Pritchard was in the reinsurance broker's business for many years, going back to at least 1948. His base of operations was always in downtown Manhattan. He organized Pritchard & Baird in 1959 under the laws of New York. Pritchard & Baird continued operations in Manhattan until shorly after 1970. In the early 1970s Charles, Jr. and William moved the corporation's operations to Morristown, New Jersey, so that their office would be closer to their homes. All, or virtually all, of the unlawful transfers involved in this case took place entirely in New Jersey after the operations had been transferred to Morristown.

All of the income of Pritchard & Baird was derived from commissions earned on reinsurance transactions. All of the funds passing through Pritchard & Baird came from premium payments being sent by ceding companies to reinsurers (out of which Pritchard & Baird was entitled to deduct a commission) or from loss payments being sent by reinsurers to ceding companies. While the elder Pritchard was in control of the brokerage corporation, the corporation commingled all funds. All payments to ceding companies, to reinsurers, and for the operations and profits of Pritchard & Baird were paid out of a single, unsegregated account. To make matters worse, Pritchard & Baird never paid the elder Pritchard funds designated as salary, or commissions, or earnings, during the course of a fiscal year. Instead, the elder Pritchard during the course of a year would take out substantial sums designated as "loans" on the books of the corporation. There were never resolutions of the board of directors authorizing these "loans," and the "loans" were never evidenced by promissory notes.

At the end of the fiscal year the accountant for Pritchard & Baird would calculate how much was paid or owing to ceding corporations with respect to transactions during the fiscal year, how much was paid or owing to reinsurers and how much was attributable to the broker's internal operations and expenses. The remainder was profit. The profit was used first to wipe out "loans" made to the elder Pritchard and the balance was then paid out to him.

* * *

The Pritchard sons started to plunder Pritchard & Baird during the fiscal year ending on January 31, 1970. In that year they caused Pritchard & Baird to pay to Charles, Jr. $230,932 more than he was entitled to receive by way of legitimate salary or other lawful earnings or profits. In that year they also caused the corporation to pay William $207,329 more than he was entitled to receive by way of legitimate salary or other earnings or profits. In succeeding fiscal years withdrawals under the heading of "loans" continued to be made vastly in excess of what might legitimately have been withdrawn by way of salary or other earnings or profits. By the time Pritchard & Baird filed its petition in bankruptcy on December 4, 1975, the total of excessive payments to William from the corporation amounted to $5,483,799.02 and the total of excessive payments to Charles, Jr. amounted to $4,391,133.21.

Between February 1, 1970 and the date of his death, December 10, 1973, the elder Pritchard received from Pritchard & Baird $189,194.17 more than he was entitled to receive by way of legitimate salary or other lawful earning or profits. After the elder Pritchard's death, corporate funds of Pritchard & Baird amounting to $168,454 were improperly used to pay his federal estate taxes. All of the payments mentioned in this paragraph were designated as "loans" on the corporate books.

After the death of Charles H. Pritchard, Pritchard & Baird made periodic "loans" to his widow, Lillian G. Pritchard, totalling $33,000. Defense counsel have suggested that these payments might be treated as proper death benefit payments. It is conceivable that a proper death benefit plan might have been established under which Pritchard & Baird might lawfully have made some payments to Mrs. Pritchard. However, the fact is that no death benefit plan was ever established by appropriate corporate action, and there was not even any contemporaneous attempt to justify the payments as death benefits.

Except for some clerical work which she did many years ago for the corporation, Lillian Overcash never had any connection with

Pritchard & Baird. However, like most people, she could use money. The corporation met that need by making periodic payments designated as "loans" to Mrs. Overcash in the total amount of $123,156.51 between February 12, 1970 and October 14, 1975.

The payments mentioned in the four paragraphs immediately preceding this one total $10,388,736.91. * * *

* * *

Mrs. Lillian G. Pritchard was a member of the board of directors of Pritchard & Baird from the time of its organization on April 1, 1959 until she resigned on December 3, 1975, the day before the corporation filed its petition in the bankruptcy court. Thus, aside from the $33,000 which she personally received, she sat as a director of Pritchard & Baird while $10,355,736.91 was unlawfully paid out by that corporation to other members of the Pritchard family. I will now deal with the question of Mrs. Pritchard's responsibility for those payments.

* * *

Directors are responsible for the general management of the affairs of a corporation. [Citation.] They have particular responsibility with respect to distributions of assets to shareholders and with respect to loans to officers and directors. [Citation.] It is true that in this case the directors were never asked to take explicit and formal action with respect to any of the unlawful payments made to members of the Pritchard family. I am satisfied that, in terms of her actual knowledge, Mrs. Pritchard did not know what her sons were doing to the corporation and she did not know that it was unlawful. She did not intend to cheat anyone or to defraud creditors of the corporation. However, if Mrs. Pritchard had paid the slightest attention to her duties as a director, and if she had paid the slightest attention to the affairs of corporation, she would have known what was happening.

Financial statements were prepared for Pritchard & Baird every year. They were simple statements, typically no longer than three or four pages. The annual financial statements accurately and clearly reflected the payments to members of the Pritchard family, and they clearly reflected the desperate financial condition of the corporation. For example, a brief glance at the statement for the fiscal year ending on January 31, 1970 would have revealed that Charles, Jr. had withdrawn from the corporation $230,932 to which he was not entitled, and William had improperly withdrawn $207,329. A brief glance at the statement for the year ending January 31, 1973 would have shown Charles, Jr. owing the corporation $1,899,288 and William owing it $1,752,318. The same statement showed a working capital deficit of $3,506,460. The statement for the fiscal year ending January 31, 1975, a simple four-page document, showed Charles, Jr. owing the corporation $4,373,928, William owing $5,417,388, and a working capital deficit of $10,176,419. All statements reflected the fact that the corporation had virtually no assets and that liabilities vastly exceeded assets. In short, anyone who took a brief glance at the annual statements at any time after January 31, 1970 and who had the slightest knowledge of the corporation's business activities would know that Charles, Jr. and William were, in simple and blunt terms, stealing money which should have been paid to the corporation's customers.

There are not controlling New Jersey cases in this area, and, in fact, I can find no New Jersey cases which are closely enough in point to be helpful in resolving our case. However, it seems to me that the inherent nature of a corporate director's job necessarily implies that he must have a basic idea of the corporation's activities. He should know what business the corporation is in, and he should have some broad idea of the scope and range of the corporation's affairs. In terms of our case, Mrs. Pritchard should have known that Pritchard & Baird was in the reinsurance business as a broker and that it annually handled millions of dollars belonging to, or owing to, ceding companies and reinsurers. Charged with that knowledge, it seems to me that a director in Mrs. Pritchard's position had, at the bare minimum, an obligation to ask for and read the annual financial statements of the corporation. She would then have the obligation to react appropriately to what a reading of the statements revealed.

It has been urged in this case that Mrs. Pritchard should not be held responsible for what happened while she was a director of Pritchard & Baird because she was a simple housewife who served as a director as an accommodation to her husband and sons. Let me start by saying that I reject the sexism which is unintended but which is implicit in such an argument. There is no reason why the average housewife could not adequately discharge the functions of a director of a corporation such as Pritchard & Baird, despite a lack of business career experience, if she gave some reasonable attention to what she was supposed to be doing. The problem is not that Mrs. Pritchard was a simple housewife. The problem is that she was a person who took a job which necessarily entailed certain responsibilities and she then failed to make any effort whatever to discharge those responsibilities. The ultimate insult to the fundamental dignity and equality of women would be to treat a grown woman as though she were a child not responsible for her acts and omissions.

It has been argued that allowance should be made for the fact that during the last years in question Mrs. Pritchard was old, was grief-stricken at the loss of her husband, sometimes consumed too much alcohol and was psychologically overborne by her sons. I was not impressed by the testimony supporting that argument. There is no proof whatever that Mrs. Pritchard ever ceased to be fully competent. There is no proof that she ever made any effort as a director to question or stop the unlawful activities of Charles, Jr. and William. The actions of the sons were so blatantly wrongful that it is hard to see how they could have resisted any moderately firm objection to what they were doing. The fact is that Mrs. Pritchard never knew what they were doing because she never made the slightest effort to discharge any of her responsibilities as a director of Pritchard & Baird.

* * *

* * * Talk of corporate "figureheads" is not really helpful. If a director actively participates in a wrongful diversion of corporate funds, he is liable on some intentional tort basis. If he does not actively participate in the wrongful diversion, he may or may not be liable. He is not liable merely because he is a director. He is liable if, in the exercise of due care in performing his duties as director, he should have known of the diversion and acted to stop it. In short, the issue is one of negligence. * * *

In legal contemplation there is no such thing as a "figurehead" director. This has been clearly recognized for many years so far as banking corporations are concerned. 3A *Fletcher, Cyclopedia of the Law of Private Corporations*, (rev. perm. ed. 1975), § 1090, has this to say:

It frequently happens that persons become directors of banking houses for the purpose of capitalizing the position in the community where the bank does business, without any intention of watching or participating in the conduct of its affairs. It is a dangerous practice for the director, since such figureheads and rubber stamp are universally held liable on the ground that they have not discharged their duty nor exercised the required amount of diligence exacted of them.

[Citations.] There is no reason why the rule stated by *Fletcher* should be limited to banks. Certainly, there is no reason why the rule should not be extended to a corporation such as Pritchard & Baird which routinely handled millions of dollars belonging to, or owing to, other persons. For a case extending the rule to a nonbanking corporation which handled other persons' money, see [citation.]

I hold that Mrs. Pritchard was negligent in performing her duties as a director of Pritchard & Baird. Had she performed her duties with due care, she would readily have discovered the wrongdoing of Charles, Jr. and William shortly after the close of the fiscal year ending on January 31, 1970, and she could easily have taken effective steps to stop the wrongdoing. Her negligence caused customers and creditors of Pritchard & Baird to suffer losses amounting to $10,355,736.91. There will be a judgment against her estate in that amount.

Liability for Breach of Fiduciary Duty

WILSHIRE OIL CO. OF TEXAS v. RIFFE

United States Court of Appeals, Tenth Circuit, 1969.
406 F.2d 1061.

SETH, C. J.

* * *

This is an appeal by the plaintiff-appellant from a portion of the judgment of the trial court in this action which was commenced by the plaintiff corporation against one of its former corporate officers. The suit was to recover profits made by the corporate officer by participating in competitive enterprises, in receiving personally commissions for corporate construction work, and to recover the compensation paid to the officer by the corporation during the period he was interested in a competitive corporation.

This is the second appeal. This court on the first appeal reversed and remanded the case, holding that the defendant had breached his duty to the corporation and had engaged in activities contrary to the terms of his contract of employment (Wilshire Oil Co. of Texas v. Riffe, 381 F.2d 646). On remand the trial court entered judgment on the claims for recovery of the profits made through participating in a competitive corporation, but denied the corporation recovery of the

compensation it paid to the defendant for this period.

The nature and extent of the fiduciary duties owed by a corporate officer to the corporation he serves have been long established. This matter was considered at some length in the previous opinion in this case as it related to these facts and need not be repeated here. As stated in the first opinion the acts of the appellee also constituted a breach of his contract of employment. On the prior appeal all the basic and determinative issues were thus decided.

When a corporate officer engages in activities which constitute a breach of his duty of loyalty or if it is a wilful breach of his contract of employment, he is not entitled to compensation for services during such a period of time although part of his services may have been properly performed. In the Restatement (Second), Agency § 469 the above doctrine is set forth, and this is followed by the comment which states in part:

"An agent, who, without the acquiescence of his principal, acts for his own benefit or for the benefit of another in antagonism to or in competition with the principal in a transaction is not entitled to compensation which otherwise be due him."

The comment continues and states that the agent is not entitled to compensation although the acts may not actually harm his principal and even if he thinks his actions will benefit the principal or he is otherwise "justified" in "so acting." [Citations.]

This rule is applicable to the case before us, and it is not necessary to again describe the several breaches of duty involved which were clearly established in the record. The record shows, as to one of the principal events, that the failure commenced on or before May 31, 1962, and continued to the end of the year when the officer's employment terminated. It was then also that the particular division which he was responsible for was sold by the corporation. The record thus sets out the period of this violation, and this is sufficient to apply the above doctrine. Thus we hold that the appellee was not entitled to compensation of any kind from May 31, 1962, to December 31, 1962.

The appellee argues that the corporate division he was responsible for made money during the period in question, and that the division was itself sold at a profit to appellant corporation. However, under the authorities or on any other basis, this is no answer to the established violation of duty. The fact that the division may have made money does not prove that no breach took place nor does it excuse one any more than a failure to make money demonstrates a breach of duty. The same may be said about whether the officer considered that he was acting properly or in good faith.

The case is reversed and remanded to the trial court with directions to enter judgment for appellant against appellee in an amount equal to seven-twelfths of all compensation (both salary and bonus) paid to appellee for services during the calendar year 1962. * * *

PROBLEMS

1. Brown was the president and director of a corporation engaged in owning and operating a chain of motels. Brown was advised, upon what seemed to be good authority, that a super-highway was to be constructed through the town of X, which would afford a most desirable location for a motel. Brown presented these facts to the board of directors of the motel corporation and recommended that the corporation build a motel in the town of X at the location described. The board of directors agreed, and the new motel was constructed. It developed that the super-highway plans were changed after the motel was constructed. The highway was never built. Later, a packing house was built on property adjoining the motel, and as a result the corporation sustained a considerable loss.

The shareholders brought an appropriate action against Brown charging that his proposal had caused a substantial loss to the corporation and seeking recovery of that loss from Brown. Decision?

2. A, B, C, D, and E constituted the board of directors of the X Corporation. While D and E were out of town, A, B, and C held a special meeting of the board. Just as the meeting began, C became ill. He then gave a proxy to A and went home. A resolution was then adopted directing and authorizing the purchase by the X Corporation of an adjoining piece of land owned by S as a site for an additional factory building. As was known by S, the purchase required approval by the board of directors. A and B voted for the resolution, and A, as C's proxy, cast C's vote in favor of the resolution. A contract was then made by the X Corporation with S for the purchase of the land. Upon the return of D and E, another special meeting of the board was held with all five directors present. A resolution was then unanimously adopted to cancel the contract with S. S was so notified and now sues X Corporation for damages for breach of contract. Decision?

3. Bernard Koch was president of United Corporation, a closely held corporation. Koch, James Trent, and Henry Phillips comprised the three person board of directors. At a meeting of the board of directors, Trent was elected president, replacing Koch. At the same meeting, Trent attempted to have the salary of the president increased. He was unable to obtain board approval of the increase because, while Phillips voted for the increase, Koch voted against it. Trent was disqualified from voting by the corporation's charter.

As a result the directors, by a two-to-one vote, amended the bylaws to provide for the appointment of an executive committee composed of three reputable business persons to pass upon and fix all matters of salary for employees of the corporation. Subsequently, the executive committee consisting of Jane Jones, James Black, and William Johnson increased the salary of the president.

Koch brought an appropriate action against the corporation, Trent, and Phillips to enjoin them from paying the increased compensation to the president above that fixed by the board of directors. What decision?

4. Zenith Steel Company operated a prosperous business. In January 1985 its president, Roe, who is also a director, was voted a $100,000 bonus by the board of directors for his valuable services he provided to the company in 1984. Roe receives an annual salary of $85,000 from the company. Black, a minority shareholder in Zenith Steel Company, brings an appropriate action to enjoin the payment by the company of the $100,000 bonus. Decision?

5. (a) Smith, a director of the Sample Corporation, sells a piece of vacant land to the Sample Corporation for $25,000, which land cost him $10,000.

(b) Jones, a shareholder of the Sample Corporation, sells a used truck to the Sample Corporation for $2,800, which truck was worth $2,400.

Raphael, a minority shareholder of the Sample Corporation, claims that the above sales are void and should be annulled. Is he correct? Why?

6. The X Corporation manufactures machine tools. The five directors of X Corporation are Black, White, Brown, Green, and Crimson. At a duly called meeting of the board of directors of X Corporation in January, all five directors were present. They transacted the following business and voted as indicated.

A contract for the purchase of $1 million worth of steel from the D Company of which Black, White, and Brown are directors was discussed and approved by a unanimous vote. There was a lengthy discussion about entering into negotiations for the purchase of Q Corporation, which allegedly was about to be sold for around $15 million. By a three-to-two vote it was decided not to open such negotiations.

Three months later Green purchased Q Corporation for $15 million. Shortly thereafter, a new board of directors for X Corporation took office.

X Corporation now brings actions to rescind its contract with D Company and to compel Green to assign to X Corporation his contract for the purchase of Q Corporation. Decisions as to each action?

7. Gore had been the owner of 1 percent of the outstanding shares of the Webster Company, a corporation, since its organization in 1962. Ratliff, the president of the company, was the owner of 70 percent of the outstanding shares. In April, 1985, Ratliff used the shareholders' list to submit to the shareholders an offer of fifty dollars per share for their stock. Gore, upon receiving the offer, called Ratliff and told him that the offer was inadequate and advised that she was willing to offer sixty dollars per share, and for that purpose demanded a shareholders' list. Ratliff knew that Gore was willing and able to supply the funds necessary to purchase the stock, but he nevertheless refused to supply the list to Gore. Further, he did not offer to transmit Gore's offer to the shareholders of record. Gore then brought an action to compel the corporation to make the shareholders' list available to her. Decision?

8. M, N, O, and P, experts in manufacturing baubles, each owned 15 out of 100 authorized shares of Baubles, Inc., a corporation of State X which does not permit cumulative voting. On July 7, 1980, the corporation sold forty shares to Q, an investor, for $1,500,000 which it used to purchase a factory building for $1,500,000. On July 8, 1980, M, N, O, and P contracted as follows:

All parties will act jointly in exercising voting rights as shareholders. In the event of a failure to agree, the question shall be submitted to George Yost, whose decision shall be binding upon all parties.

Until a meeting of shareholders on April 17, 1985, when a dispute arose, all parties to the contract had consistently and regularly voted for N, O, and P as directors.

At that meeting Yost considered the dispute and decided and directed that M, N, O, and P vote their shares for the latter three as directors. N, O, and P so voted. M and Q voted for themselves and Mrs. Q as directors.

(a) Is the contract of July 8, 1980, valid, and, if so, what is its effect?

(b) Who were elected directors of Baubles, Inc. at the meeting of its shareholders on April 17, 1985?

9. X Corporation's articles of incorporation require cumulative voting for the election of its directors. The board of directors of X Corporation consists of nine directors, each elected annually.

(a) A owns 25 percent of the outstanding shares of X Corporation. How many directors can he elect with his votes?

(b) If X Corporation were to classify its board into three classes, each consisting of three directors elected every three years, how many directors would A be able to elect?

Chapter 36

FUNDAMENTAL CHANGES

CERTAIN extraordinary changes affect a corporation in such a fundamental manner that they are outside the ambit of the board of directors and require shareholder approval. Changes, such as charter amendments, sale or lease of all or substantially all the corporation's assets, mergers, consolidations, compulsory share exchanges, and dissolution are fundamental in nature because they alter the basic structure of the corporation. Although each of these actions is authorized by State incorporation statutes which impose specific procedural requirements, they are also subject to equitable limitations imposed by the courts.

Since shareholder approval for fundamental changes usually need not be unanimous, such changes will frequently be approved despite opposition by minority shareholders. Shareholder approval means a majority (or some other specified fraction) of *all* votes entitled to be cast rather than a majority (or other fraction) of votes represented at a shareholders' meeting at which a quorum is present. In some instances minority shareholders are accorded the right to dissent and recover the fair value of their shares if they follow the prescribed procedure. This right is called the **appraisal remedy.** The legal aspects of fundamental changes will be discussed in this chapter.

CHARTER AMENDMENTS

Authority to Amend

Modern statutes permit the articles of incorporation to be amended freely. The amended articles of incorporation, however, may contain only such provisions as might be lawfully contained in the original articles of incorporation. The Model Act is comprehensive in its authorization for amendments and includes very broad powers. Illustrative of these powers granted by Section 58 of the Act are the power to:

1. change its corporate name;
2. change its period of duration;
3. change, enlarge, or diminish its corporate purposes;
4. increase or decrease the number or par value of shares;
5. reclassify shares and change the preferential rights of shares;
6. create new classes of shares; and
7. limit, deny, or grant pre-emptive rights.

Since articles of incorporation now rarely limit the duration or powers of the corporation, the most common amendments relate to changes in the capital structure of the corporation.

Procedure

The typical procedure under modern statutes for amending the articles of incorporation requires the board of directors to adopt a resolution setting forth the proposed amendment, which must then be approved by a majority vote of the shareholders entitled to vote, although some older statutes require a two-thirds shareholder vote. Moreover, a class of shares is entitled to vote as a class on a proposed amendment, whether or not entitled to vote on it by the articles of incorporation, if that amendment would:

(a) Increase or decrease the aggregate number of authorized shares of such class.

(b) Effect an exchange, reclassification or cancellation of all or part of the shares of such class.

(c) Effect an exchange, or create a right of exchange, of all or any part of the shares of another class into the shares of such class.

(d) Change the designations, preferences, limitations or relative rights of the shares of such class.

(e) Change the shares of such class into the same or a different number of shares of the same class or another class or classes.

(f) Create a new class of shares having rights and preferences prior and superior to the shares of such class, or increase the rights and preferences or the number of authorized shares, of any class having rights and preferences prior or superior to the shares of such class.

(g) In the case of a preferred or special class of shares, divide the shares of such class into series and fix and determine the designation of such series and the variations in the relative rights and preferences between the shares of such series, or authorize the board of directors to do so.

(h) Limit or deny any existing preemptive rights of the shares of such class.

(i) Cancel or otherwise affect dividends on the shares of such class which have accrued but have not been declared. Section 60.

The comment to Section 10.04 of the Revised Act provides the following example: "Assume there is a class of preferred shares comprised of three series each with different dividend rights. A proposed amendment would reduce the rate of dividend applicable to Series A preferred and would change the dividend right of Series B preferred from a cumulative to a noncumulative right. The amendment would not affect the dividend right of Series C preferred. Both Series A and B would be entitled to vote as separate classes on the proposed amendment; the holders of Series C preferred, not directly affected by the amendment, would not be entitled to vote at all unless the shares are otherwise voting shares under the articles of incorporation. If the proposed amendment would reduce the dividend right of series A and change the dividend right of both Series B and C from a cumulative to a noncumulative right, the holders of Series A would be entitled to vote as a single class, and the holders of Series B and C would be entitled to vote together as a single separate class."

After the amendment is approved by the shareholders, articles of amendment are executed and filed with the Secretary of State.

The amendment becomes effective upon the issuance of the certificate of amendment by the Secretary of State but does not affect the existing rights of non-shareholders. Sections 59–63.

The Revised Act permits the board of directors to adopt certain amendments without shareholder action unless the articles of incorporation provide otherwise. RMBCA Section 10.02. These amendments include: (1) extension of the duration of the corporation, (2) splitting authorized shares if the corporation has only one class of shares, and (3) making minor name changes.

Under Section 80(a)(4) of the Model Act *dissenting shareholders* are given an appraisal remedy *only* if an amendment materially and adversely affects the rights attached to the shares owned by the dissenting shareholders in that it:

1. alters or abolishes a preferential right of such shares;
2. creates, alters, or abolishes a right involving the redemption of such shares;
3. alters or abolishes a pre-emptive right of the holder of such shares; or
4. excludes or limits the right of the holder of such shares to vote on any matter, or to cumulate his votes.

Under the Revised Act the required shareholder approval for an amendment depends upon the nature of the amendment. If the amendment would give rise to dissenters' rights, the amendment must be approved by a majority of all votes *entitled* to be cast on the amendment unless the Act, the articles of incorporation or the board of directors require a greater vote. All other amendments must be approved by a majority of all votes *cast* on the amendment at a meeting where a quorum exists, unless the Act, the articles of incorporation or the board of directors require a greater vote. RMBCA Sections 10.03, 7.25.

COMBINATIONS

It may be desirable and profitable for a corporation to acquire all or substantially all of the assets of another corporation or corporations. This may be accomplished by (1) purchase or lease of such assets, (2) purchase of a controlling stock interest in such other corporations, (3) merger with such corporations, or (4) consolidation with such corporations.

When any of these methods of combination involves the issuance of shares, proxy solicitations, or tender offers, it may be subject to Federal securities regulation, as discussed in Chapter 44. Moreover, when a combination may have a detrimental effect on competition, the Federal antitrust laws, as discussed in Chapter 41, may apply.

Purchase or Lease of All or Substantially All of the Assets

When one corporation purchases or leases all or substantially all of the assets of another corporation, no change is effected in the legal personality of either corporation. The purchaser or lessee corporation has simply acquired ownership or control of additional physical assets. The selling or lessor corporation, in exchange for its physical properties, has cash, other property, or a stipulated rental. Each corporation continues its separate existence with only the form or extent of its assets altered.

Generally, a corporation which purchases the assets of another corporation does not assume the other's liabilities unless: (1) the purchaser expressly or impliedly agrees to assume the liabilities of the seller; (2) the transaction amounts to a consolidation or merger of the two corporations; (3) the purchaser is a mere continuation of the seller; or (4) the sale is for the fraudulent purpose of avoiding the liabilities of the seller. Some courts recognize a fifth exception (called the "product line" exception) which imposes strict tort liability upon the purchaser for defects in products manufactured and distributed by the seller corporation when the purchaser corporation continues the product line. *See Ray v. Alad Corporation.*

Regular Course of Business If such sale or lease of all or substantially all of its assets is in the **usual and regular** course of business of the selling or lessor corporation, approval by its board of directors is required while shareholder authorization is not. In addition, a mortgage or pledge of any or all property and assets of a corporation—whether or *not* in the usual or regular course of business— also requires approval by just the board of directors. Section 78.

Other Than in Regular Course of Business Shareholder approval is necessary only if such a sale or lease is *not* in the usual and regular course of business. The selling corporation by liquidation of its assets or the lessor corporation by placing its physical assets beyond its control has significantly changed its position and perhaps its ability to carry on the type of business contemplated by its charter. For this reason, such sale or lease must be approved not only by action of the directors but also by the affirmative vote of the holders of a majority of its shares entitled to vote at a meeting of shareholders called for this purpose. Section 79. *Dissenting shareholders* of the selling corporation are given an appraisal remedy in the majority of States. Section 80(2).

Purchase of Shares

An alternative to the purchase of the assets of another corporation is the purchase of its stock. When one corporation acquires all or a controlling interest of the stock of another corporation, there is no change in the legal existence of either corporation. The acquiring corporation acts through its board of directors, while the corporation which becomes a subsidiary does not act at all, as the sale of stock is a decision made by the individual

shareholders. The capital structure of the subsidiary remains unchanged, and that of the parent is usually not altered unless required in connection with financing the acquisition of the stock. Since no formal shareholder approval of either corporation is required, there is *no* appraisal remedy.

Compulsory Share Exchange

The Model Act provides different procedures, however, where the share acquisition is through a compulsory share exchange, which is a transaction by which a corporation becomes the owner of *all* the outstanding shares of one or more classes of another corporation by an exchange which is *compulsory* on *all* owners of the acquired shares. Section 72A. The shares may be acquired with shares, obligations or other securities of the acquiring corporation, or with other consideration. For example, if B corporation acquires all of the outstanding shares of A corporation through a compulsory exchange, then A becomes a wholly owned subsidiary of B. In all compulsory share exchanges the separate existence of both corporate parties to the transaction is not affected by the exchange. Although producing results similar to a merger, as discussed below, compulsory share exchanges are utilized instead of mergers where it is desirable that the acquired corporation does not go out of existence as, for example, in the formation of holding company systems for insurance companies and banks.

A compulsory share exchange requires approval of the board of directors of each corporation and approval by the shareholders of the corporation whose shares are being acquired. Sections 72A and 73. The transaction need *not* be approved by the shareholders of the corporation acquiring the shares. After the compulsory share exchange plan is adopted and approved by the shareholders it is binding on all holders of shares of the class to be acquired. Dissenting shareholders of the corporation whose shares are acquired are given an appraisal remedy. Section 80(a)(3).

Merger

A merger of two or more corporations is the combination of all of their assets, title to which is vested in one of them, known as the **surviving corporation.** The other party or parties to the merger, known as the **merged corporation** or corporations, are merged into the surviving corporation and cease to exist as a separate entity. Thus, if A Corporation and B Corporation combine into the A Corporation, A is the surviving corporation and B the merged corporation. All debts and other liabilities of the merged corporation are assumed by the surviving corporation by operation of law. Section 76. The shareholders of the merged corporation may receive stock or other securities issued by the surviving corporation or other consideration, as provided in the plan of merger. *See Tretter v. Rapid American Corp.*

A merger requires the approval of the board of directors of each corporation, as well as the affirmative vote of the holders of a majority of the shares entitled to vote of each corporation party to the merger. Sections 71 and 73. However, if the number of voting or participating shares of the surviving corporation is increased by no more than 20 percent as a result of the merger, then the approval of the shareholders of the surviving coporation is *not* required. MBCA Section 73(d). Dissenting shareholders of each corporation which is a party to the merger have an appraisal remedy, except for shareholders of the surviving corporation if their votes are not required under Section 73(d).

In a **"short-form merger"** a corporation that owns at least *90 percent* of the outstanding shares of a subsidiary may merge the subsidiary into itself *without* approval by the shareholders of either corporation. Section 75. Requiring the approval of the shareholders or board of directors of the subsidiary is unnecessary because the parent's ninety percent ownership assures that the plan of merger would be approved. All that is required is a resolution by the board of directors of the parent corporation. The dissenting shareholders of the subsidiary have the right to obtain payment from the parent for their shares. Section 80(a)(1). The shareholders of the parent do not have this appraisal remedy because the transaction has not materially changed their rights. Section 80(c). Instead of indirectly owing ninety percent of the subsidiary's assets the parent now directly owns 100 percent of the same assets.

Consolidation

A consolidation of two or more corporations is the combination of all of their assets, title to which is taken by a newly created corporation known as the **consolidated corporation.** Each of the constituent corporations ceases to exist, and all of their debts and liabilities are assumed by the new corporation. Section 76. The shareholders of each of the constituent corporations receive stock or other securities, not necessarily of the same class, issued to them by the new corporation or other consideration pursuant to the plan of consolidation. A consolidation requires the approval of the boards of directors of each constituent corporation as well as the affirmative vote of the holders of a majority of the shares entitled to vote of each constituent corporation. Sections 72 and 73. Dissenting shareholders have an appraisal remedy. Section 80(a)(1).

The Revised Act has deleted all references to consolidations as explained by the comment to RMBCA Section 11.01:

* * * the Model Act also provided for a "consolidation," which was similar to a merger, except that all corporate parties to the transaction disappeared and an entirely new corporation was created. In modern corporate practice consolidation transactions are obsolete since it is nearly always advantageous for one of the parties in the transaction to be the surviving corporation. (If creation of a new entity is considered desirable, a new entity may be created before the merger and the disappearing entities merged into it.)

Dissenting Shareholders

The shareholder's right to dissent is a statutory right to obtain payment for his shares and is accorded to shareholders who object to certain fundamental changes in the corporation. Most States grant a right to dissent to any plan of *merger* or *consolidation* to which the corporation is a party as well as to a *sale or lease* of all or substantially all of the property or assets of the corporation not made in the usual or regular course of business. In addition to these three fundamental changes, the Model Act also provides a right to dissent to: (1) any plan of compulsory share exchange to which the corporation is a party as the corporation the shares of which are to be acquired, (2) any amendment of the articles of incorporation which materially and adversely affects the rights appurtenant to the shares of the dissenting shareholder, and (3) any other corporate action taken pursuant to a shareholder vote with respect to which the articles of incorporation, the bylaws, or a resolution of the board of directors directs that dissenting shareholders shall have a right to obtain payment for their shares. Section 80.

The Introductory Comment to Chapter 13 of the Revised Act explains the purpose of dissenters' rights:

Chapter 13 deals with the tension between the desire of the corporate leadership to be able to enter new fields, acquire new enterprises, and rearrange investor rights and the desire of investors to adhere to the rights and the risks on the basis of which they invested. Most contemporary corporation codes in the United States attempt to resolve this tension through a combination of two devices. On the one hand, the majority is given an almost unlimited power to change the nature and shape of the enterprise and the rights of its members. On the other hand, the members who dissent from these changes are given a right to withdraw their investment at a fair value.

The corporation must notify the shareholders of the existence of dissenters' rights before the vote is taken on the corporate ac-tion. If a shareholder dissents and strictly complies with the provisions of the statute he is entitled to receive the fair value of his shares. In order to perfect his right to payment for his shares, a dissenting shareholder must:

1. File with the corporation a written objection to the proposed corporate action prior to the vote of the shareholders.
2. Refrain from voting in favor of the proposed corporate action either in person or by proxy.
3. Make a written demand upon the corporation on a form provided by that corporation within the time period set by the corporation, which may not be less than thirty days after the corporation mails the form. Section 81.

Unless written demand is made within the prescribed time period, the dissenting shareholder is not entitled to payment for his shares.

A dissenting shareholder who complies with all of these requirements is entitled to an appraisal remedy which is payment by the corporation of the fair value of his shares accrued with interest. The Model Act defines **fair value** to mean their value immediately before the effectuation of the corporate action to which the dissenter objects, excluding any appreciation or depreciation in anticipation of such corporate action unless such exclusion would be inequitable. Section 81(a)(3). *See Endicott Johnson Corp. v. Bade.*

The purpose of the statutory procedure is to fix a reasonable time in which the corporation may be apprised of the number of shares for which it is required to pay cash in order to carry through the proposed corporate action. If dissenting shareholders in sufficient numbers perfect their right to be paid, the lack of sufficient cash or the inability of the surviving or new corporation to raise funds for this purpose may make the proposed corporate acton impracticable at this stage.

A shareholder of a corporation who has a right to obtain payment for his shares shall have no right at law or in equity to attack the validity of the corporate action that gives rise to his right to obtain payment, nor to have the action set aside or rescinded, except when the corporate action is unlawful or fraudulent with regard to the complaining shareholder or to the corporation. MBCA Section 80(d). Where the corporate action is not unlawful or fraudulent the appraisal remedy is exclusive and the shareholder may not challenge the action.

DISSOLUTION

Although a corporation may have perpetual existence, its life may be terminated in a number of ways. Incorporation statutes usually provide both for dissolution without judicial proceedings and for dissolution with judicial proceedings. Dissolution does not terminate the corporation's existence but does require that the corporation **wind up** its affairs and **liquidate** its assets.

Nonjudicial Dissolution

Nonjudicial dissolution may be brought about by:

1. An act of the legislature of the State of incorporation.
2. Expiration of the period of time provided for in the articles of incorporation.
3. Voluntary action on the part of all of the holders of all of the outstanding shares of stock. Section 83.
4. Voluntary action by the corporation, pursuant to a resolution of the board of directors

---

FIGURE 36-1   Fundamental Changes

Change	Board of Director Resolution Required	Shareholder Approval Required	Shareholders' Appraisal Remedy Available
A amends its articles of incorporation	A: Yes	A: Yes	A: No, unless amendment materially and adversely affects rights of shares
A sells its assets in usual and regular course of business to B	A: Yes B: No	A: No B: No	A: No B: No
A sells its assets not in usual and regular course of business to B	A: Yes B: No	A: Yes B: No	A: Yes B: No
A voluntarily purchases shares of B	A: Yes B: No	A: No B: No, individual shareholders decide	A: No B: No
A acquires shares of B through a compulsory exchange	A: Yes B: Yes	A: No B: Yes	A: No B: Yes
A and B merge	A: Yes B: Yes	A: Yes B: Yes	A: Yes B: Yes
A merges its 90% subsidiary B into A	A: Yes B: No	A: No B: No	A: No B: Yes
A and B consolidate	A: Yes B: Yes	A: Yes B: Yes	A: Yes B: Yes
A voluntarily dissolves	A: Yes, unless unanimous shareholder consent	A: Yes	A: Not usually

which is approved by the affirmative vote of the holders of a majority of the shares of the corporation entitled to vote at a meeting of the shareholders duly called for this purpose. Section 84. No right to dissent and recover the fair value of shares is usually provided to shareholders objecting to dissolution. However, the Model Act grants dissenters' rights in connection with a sale or exchange of all or substantially all the assets not made in the usual or regular course of business *including* a sale in dissolution, but *excludes* such rights in sales by court order and sales for cash on terms requiring that all or substantially all of the net proceeds be distributed to the shareholders within one year. Section 80(a)(2).

Judicial Dissolution

Involuntary dissolution by judicial proceeding may be instituted by the State, the shareholders, or the creditors and may occur by:

1. Court action taken at the instance of the attorney general of the State of incorporation when it is established that the corporation has failed to file its annual report with the Secretary of State, failed to pay its annual franchise tax, procured its articles of incorporation through fraud, continued to exceed or abuse the authority conferred upon it by law, failed for thirty days to appoint and maintain a registered agent in the State, or failed for thirty days after a change of its registered office or registered agent to file a statement of such change. Section 94. The Revised Act substitutes administrative dissolutions by the Secretary of State for judicial dissolution except where the corporation obtained its articles of incorporation through fraud or has continued to exceed or abuse the authority conferred upon it by law, in which case judicial proceedings must still be brought by the attorney general. RMBCA Sections 14.20 and 14.30.

2. Court action brought by shareholders when it is established that the directors are deadlocked in the management of the corporate affairs and the shareholders are unable to break the deadlock and that irreparable injury to the corporation is being suffered or is threatened; that the acts of the directors or those in control of the corporation are illegal, oppressive, or fraudulent; that the corporate assets are being misapplied or wasted; or that the shareholders are deadlocked and cannot elect directors. Section 97(a). *See Callier v. Callier.*

3. Court action instituted by a creditor upon a showing that the corporation has become unable to pay its debts and obligations as they mature in the regular course of its business and either (a) the creditor has reduced his claim to a judgment and an execution issued on it has been returned unsatisfied, or (b) that the corporation has admitted in writing that the claim of the creditor is due and owing. Section 97(b).

Liquidation

Dissolution does not terminate the corporation's existence but does require that the corporation devote itself to winding up its affairs and liquidating its assets. After dissolution the corporation must cease carrying on its business except as is necessary to wind up. Section 86. Upon dissolution the assets of a corporation are liquidated and used first to pay the expenses of liquidation and its creditors according to their respective contract or lien rights, and any remainder is distributed to shareholders ratably according to their respective contract rights, stock with a liquidation preference having priority over common. When liquidation is voluntary, it is usually carried out by the board of directors who serve as trustees; but when liquidation is involuntary, it is conducted by a court appointed receiver. Section 98.

Protection of Creditors

The statutory provisions governing dissolution and liquidation usually prescribe procedures to safeguard the interests of creditors of the corporation. Such procedures typically include required mailing of notice to known creditors, general publication of notice, and preservation of claims against the corporation. For example, the Model Act provides that the dissolution of a corporation shall not impair any remedy available to or against the corporation, its directors, officers, or shareholders, for any right or claim existing, or any liability incurred, prior to dissolution if suit is brought within two years after the date of dissolution. Section 105. The Revised Act provides a five-year period for (1) a claimant who did not receive notice, (2) a claimant whose timely claim was not acted on, or (3) a claimant whose claim is contingent on an event occurring after dissolution. RMBCA Section 14.07.

CASES

Purchase of Assets

RAY v. ALAD CORP.

Supreme Court of California, 1977.
19 Cal.3d 22, 136 Cal.Rptr. 574, 560 P.2d 3.

WRIGHT, J.

Claiming damages for injury from a defective ladder, plaintiff asserts strict tort liability against defendant Alad Corporation (Alad II) which neither manufactured nor sold the ladder but prior to plaintiff's injury succeeded to the business of the ladder's manufacturer, the now dissolved "Alad Corporation" (Alad I), through a purchase of Alad I's assets for an adequate cash consideration. Upon acquiring Alad I's plant, equipment, inventory, trade name, and good will, Alad II continued to manufacture the same line of ladders under the "Alad" name, using the same equipment, designs, and personnel, and soliciting Alad I's customers through the same sales representatives with no outward indication of any change in the ownership of the business. The trial court entered summary judgment for Alad II and plaintiff appeals.

*   *   *

Plaintiff alleges in his complaint that on March 24, 1969, he fell from a defective ladder in the laundry room of the University of California at Los Angeles while working for the contracting company by which he was employed. The complaint was served on Alad II as a "Doe" defendant alleged to have manufactured the ladder. [Citation.] The Regents of the University of California (Regents) were named and served as a defendant on the basis of their ownership and control not only of the laundry room but of the ladder itself.

In granting summary judgment to Alad II, the trial court considered not only the supporting and opposing declarations of witnesses with attached exhibits but also excerpts from depositions and answers to interrogatories. [Citation.] It is undisputed that the ladder involved in the accident was not made by Alad II and there was testimony that the ladder was an "old" model manufactured by Alad I. Hence the principal issue addressed by the parties' submissions on the motion for summary judgment was the presence or absence of any factual basis for imposing any liability of Alad I as manufacturer of the ladder upon Alad II as successor to Alad I's manufacturing business.

Prior to the sale of its principal business assets, Alad I was in "the specialty ladder business" and was known among commercial and industrial users of ladders as a "top quality manufacturer" of that product. On July 1, 1968, Alad I sold to Lighting Maintenance Corporation (Lighting) its "stock in trade, fixtures, equipment, trade name, inventory and goodwill" and its interest in the real property used for its manufacturing activities. The sale did not include Alad I's cash, receivables, unexpired insurance, or prepaid expenses. As part of the sale transaction Alad I agreed "to dissolve its corporate existence as soon as practical and [to] assist and cooperate with Lighting in the organization of a new corporation to be formed by Lighting under the name 'ALAD CORPORATION.'" Concurrently with the sale the principal stockholders of Alad I, Mr. and Mrs. William S. Hambly, agreed for a separate consideration not to compete with the purchased business for 42 months and to render nonexclusive consulting services during that period. By separate agreement Mr. Hambly was employed as a salaried consultant for the initial five months. There was ultimately paid to Alad I and the Hamblys "total cash consideration in excess of $207,000.00 plus interest for the assets and goodwill of ALAD [I]."

The only provisions in the sale agreement for any assumption of Alad I's liabilities by Lighting were that Lighting would (1) accept and pay for materials previously ordered by Alad I in the regular course of its business and (2) fill uncompleted orders taken by Alad I in the regular course of its business and hold Alad I harmless from any damages or liability resulting from failure to do so. The possibility of Lighting's or Alad II's being held liable for defects in products manufactured or sold by Alad I was not specifically discussed nor was any provision expressly made therefor.

* * *

The tangible assets acquired by Lighting included Alad I's manufacturing plant, machinery, offices, office fixtures, and equipment, and inventory of raw materials, semifinished goods, and finished goods. These assets were used to continue the manufacturing operations without interruption except for the closing of the plant for about a week "for inventory." The factory personnel remained the same, and identical "extrusion plans" were used for producing the aluminum components of the ladders. The employee of Lighting designated as the enterprise's general manager as well as the other previous employees of Lighting were all without experience in the manufacture of ladders. The former general

manager of Alad I, Mr. Hambly, remained with the business as a paid consultant for about six months after the takeover.

The "Alad" name was used for all ladders produced after the change of management. Besides the name, Lighting and Alad II acquired Alad I's lists of customers, whom they solicited, and continued to employ the salesman and manufacturer's representatives who had sold ladders for Alad I. Aside from a redesign of the logo, or corporate emblem, on the letterheads and labels, there was no indication on any of the printed materials to indicate that a new company was manufacturing Alad ladders, and the manufacturer's representatives were not instructed to notify customers of the change.

Our discussion of the law starts with the rule ordinarily applied to the determination of whether a corporation purchasing the principal assets of another corporation assumes the other's liabilities. As typically formulated the rule states that the purchaser does not assume the seller's liabilities unless (1) there is an express or implied agreement of assumption, (2) the transaction amounts to a consolidation or merger of the two corporations, (3) the purchasing corporation is a mere continuation of the seller, or (4) the transfer of assets to the purchaser is for the fraudulent purpose of escaping liability for the seller's debts. [Citations.]

If this rule were determinative of Alad II's liability to plaintiff it would require us to affirm the summary judgment. None of the rule's four stated grounds for imposing liability on the purchasing corporation is present here. There was no express or implied agreement to assume liability for injury from defective products previously manufactured by Alad I. Nor is there any indication or contention that the transaction was prompted by any fraudulent purpose of escaping liability for Alad I's debts.

With respect to the second stated ground for liability, the purchase of Alad I's assets did not amount to a consolidation or merger.

This exception has been invoked where one corporation takes all of another's assets without providing any consideration that could be made available to meet claims of the other's creditors [citation] or where the consideration consists wholly of shares of the purchaser's stock which are promptly distributed to the seller's shareholders in conjunction with the seller's liquidation [citation]. In the present case the sole consideration given for Alad I's assets was cash in excess of $207,000. Of this amount Alad I was paid $70,000 when the assets were transferred and at the same time a promissory note was given to Alad I for almost $114,000. Shortly before the dissolution of Alad I the note was assigned to the Hamblys, Alad I's principal stockholders, and thereafter the note was paid in full. The remainder of the consideration went for closing expenses or was paid to the Hamblys for consulting services and their agreement not to compete. There is no contention that this consideration was inadequate or that the cash and promissory note given to Alad I were not included in the assets available to meet claims of Alad I's creditors at the time of dissolution. Hence the acquisition of Alad I's assets was not in the nature of a merger or consolidation for purposes of the aforesaid rule.

Plaintiff contends that the rule's third stated ground for liability makes Alad II liable as a mere continuation of Alad I in view of Alad II's acquisition of all Alad I's operating assets, its use of those assets and of Alad I's former employees to manufacture the same line of products, and its holding itself out to customers and the public as a continuation of the same enterprise. However, California decisions holding that a corporation acquiring the assets of another corporation is the latter's mere continuation and therefore liable for its debts have imposed such liability only upon a showing of one or both of the following factual elements: (1) no adequate consideration was given for the predecessor corporation's assets and made available for meeting the claims of its unsecured creditors;

(2) one or more persons were officers, directors, or stockholders of both corporations. [Citations.] There is no showing of either of these elements in the present case.

We therefore conclude that the general rule governing succession to liabilities does not require Alad II to respond to plaintiff's claim. * * * We must decide whether the policies underlying strict tort liability for defective products call for a special exception to the rule that would otherwise insulate the present defendant from plaintiff's claim. [Citations.]

The purpose of the rule of strict tort liability "is to insure that the costs of injuries resulting from defective products are borne by the manufacturers that put such products on the market rather than by the injured persons who are powerless to protect themselves." [Citation.] However, the rule "does not rest on the analysis of the financial strength or bargaining power of the parties to the particular action. It rests, rather, on the proposition that '[t]he cost of an injury and the loss of time or health may be an overwhelming misfortune to the person injured, and a needless one, for the risk of injury can be insured by the manufacturer and distributed among the public as a cost of doing business.' [Citations.]" Thus, "the paramount policy to be promoted by the rule is the protection of otherwise defenseless victims of manufacturing defects and the *spreading throughout society* of the cost of compensating them." (Italics added.) [Citation.] Justification for imposing strict liability upon a *successor* to a manufacturer under the circumstances here presented rests upon (1) the virtual destruction of the plaintiff's remedies against the original manufacturer caused by the successor's acquisition of the business, (2) the successor's ability to assume the original manufacturer's risk-spreading rule, and (3) the fairness of requiring the successor to assume a responsibility for defective products that was a burden necessarily attached to the original manufacturer's good will being enjoyed by the successor in the continued operation of the business. We turn to a consideration of each of these aspects in the context of the present case.

We must assume for purposes of the present proceeding that plaintiff was injured as a result of defects in a ladder manufactured by Alad I and therefore could assert strict tort liability against Alad I under the rule of [Citation.] However, the practical value of this right of recovery against the original manufacturer was vitiated by the purchase of Alad I's tangible assets, trade name and good will on behalf of Alad II and the dissolution of Alad I within two months thereafter in accordance with the purchase agreement. The injury giving rise to plaintiff's claim against Alad I did not occur until more than six months after the filing of the dissolution certificate declaring that Alad I's "known debts and liabilities have been actually paid" and its "known assets have been distributed to its shareholders." This distribution of assets was perfectly proper as there was no requirement that provision be made for claims such as plaintiff's that had not yet come into existence. Thus, even if plaintiff could obtain a judgment on his claim against the dissolved and assetless Alad I he would face formidable and probably insuperable obstacles in attempting to obtain satisfaction of the judgment from former stockholders or directors. [Citations.]

* * *

While depriving plaintiff of redress against the ladder's manufacturer, Alad I, the transaction by which Alad II acquired Alad I's name and operating assets had the further effect of transferring to Alad II the resources that had previously been available to Alad I for meeting its responsibilities to persons injured by defects in ladders it had produced. These resources included not only the physical plant, the manufacturing equipment, and the inventories of raw material, work in process, and finished goods, but also the know-how available through the records of manufacturing designs, the continued employment of the factory personnel, and the consulting services of Alad I's general manager. With these facilities and sources of information, Alad II had virtually the same capacity as Alad I to estimate the risks of claims for injuries from defects in previously manufactured ladders for purposes of obtaining insurance coverage or planning self-insurance. [Citation.] Moreover, the acquisition of the Alad enterprise gave Alad II the opportunity formerly enjoyed by Alad I of passing on to purchasers of new "Alad" products the costs of meeting these risks. Immediately after the takeover it was Alad II, not Alad I, which was in a position to promote the "paramount policy" of the strict products liability rule by "spreading throughout society . . . the cost of compensating (otherwise defenseless victims of manufacturing defects)" [Citation.]

Finally, the imposition upon Alad II of liability for injuries from Alad I's defective products is fair and equitable in view of Alad II's acquisition of Alad I's trade name, good will, and customer lists, its continuing to produce the same line of ladders, and its holding itself out to potential customers as the same enterprise. This deliberate albeit legitimate exploitation of Alad I's established reputation as a going concern manufacturing a specific product line gave Alad II a substantial benefit which its predecessor could not have enjoyed without the burden of potential liability for injuries from previously manufactured units. Imposing this liability upon successor manufacturers in the position of Alad II not only causes the one "who takes the benefit (to) bear the burden" [citation] but precludes any windfall to the predecessor that might otherwise result from (1) the reflection of an absence of such successor liability in an enhanced price paid by the successor for the business assets and (2) the liquidation of the predecessor resulting in avoidance of its responsibility for subsequent injuries from its defective products. [Citations.] By taking over and continuing the established business of producing and distributing Alad ladders, Alad II became "an integral part of the overall producing and marketing enterprise that should bear the cost of injuries resulting from defective products" [Citation.]

We therefore conclude that a party which acquires a manufacturing business and continues the output of its line of products under the circumstances here presented assumes strict tort liability for defects in units of the same product line previously manufactured and distributed by the entity from which the business was acquired. * * *

The judgment is reversed.

Merger

TRETTER v. RAPID AMERICAN CORP.

United States District Court, Eastern District of Missouri, 1981.
514 F.Supp. 1344.

NANGLE, J.

[Tretter alleged that his exposure over the years to asbestos products manufactured by Philip Carey Manufacturing Corporation caused him to contract asbestosis. Tretter brought an action against Rapid American Corporation which was the surviving corporation of a merger between Philip Carey and Rapid American. Rapid American denied liability claiming that imemdiately after the merger it had transferred its asbestos operations to a newly formed subsidiary corporation.]

* * *

The law is clear that "[i]f the parties effect the transfer of a corporate enterprise through a merger, consolidation, or sale of stock, the transferee assumes its predecessor's liabilities, including product liability claims." [Citations.] When [Rapid American] merged with [Philip] Carey, therefore, [Rapid American] assumed the liability for the claim involved in this suit. This fact was recognized in the "General Assignment & Assumption of Liabilities" agreement between [Rapid American] and [its subsidiary.] That document specifically referred to liabilities "to which [Rapid American] became subject as a result of the aforementioned merger [the merger between Rapid American and Philip Carey]." That [Rapid American] subsequently transferred this liability to [its subsidiary] does not defeat plaintiff's cause of action herein; it merely gives [Rapid American] a claim for indemnity * * *

* * *

This Court therefore believes that Rapid American, as the successor corporation to Philip Carey Manufacturing Corporation, may be held liable for the liabilities of its predecessor.

[Judgment for Tretter.]

Dissenting Shareholders

ENDICOTT JOHNSON CORP. v. BADE

Court of Appeals of New York, 1975.
37 N.Y.2d 585, 376 N.Y.S.2d 103, 338 N.E.2d 614.

FUCHSBERG, J.

This proceeding was brought pursuant to section 623 of the Business Corporation Law to fix the fair value of the stock of respondent stockholders, who had dissented from a proposed merger as a result of which petitioner Endicott Johnson Corporation was to become a wholly-owned subsidiary of McDonough Corporation. Special Term, confirming and adopting the report of the appraiser it had appointed, fixed, *inter alia*, the fair value of the common stock at $45.75. The Appellate Division having modified the order of Special Term by reducing the valuation of the stock to $42.77 per share and having increased the amount of fees allowed to one of respondent's counsel, both sides now appeal.

At the heart of the issues involved are the weight required to be given to the market price of the stock * * *.

The general principles applicable here are clear. Dissenting stockholders were entitled to be paid the "fair value" of their Endicott common stock, excluding any appreciation or depreciation due to the merger or its proposal. [Citation.] Although the statute itself is silent as to how fair value is to be determined, it is well established by case law that, in our State, the elements which are to enter into such an appraisal are net asset value, investment value and market value. [Citation.] While, in order to provide the elasticity deemed necessary to reach a just result, all three factors are to be considered, the weight to be accorded to each varies with the facts and circumstances in a particular case. [Citations.]

* * *

It follows that all three elements do not have to influence the result in every valuation proceeding. It suffices if they are all considered. Compelling the consideration of all of them, including those which may turn out to be unreliable in a particular case, has the salutary effect of assuring more complete justification by the appraiser of the conclusion he reaches. It also provides a more concrete basis for court review.

The three elements are not always discrete: definitionally, they may even flow into one another. For instance, in this very case, by their general concurrence that it would here be inappropriate, no estimation of net asset value was attempted by the parties or the appraiser. Since the corporation was not being liquidated, but was to continue to operate as part of the surviving parent McDonough Corporation, that made business and legal sense. For, in cases of nonliquidation, to the extent that the net asset value might include elements such as good will and potential earnings, these are invariably taken into account, in any event, among the numerous tangible and intangible factors that enter into judgment of the investment value of going concerns, whether by experienced appraisers or prudent investors. [Citations.]

Indeed, in this case investment value, for all practical purposes, became the sole determinant of fair value when the appraiser eliminated market value as a meaningful factor by reporting as follows:

My opinion is that little weight should be given to the past history of market value prior to 1969 because I believe that there was a radical enough change in the management of the company so that it had 'turned around', and that the pre-1969 market is not particularly helpful.

I agree with the thinking of the text writers that a dramatic change in leadership for the good may be valid grounds for disregarding company's [sic] past history of weakness.

Subsequent to 1969 I believe the market became so thin because of the control of McDonough and the subsequent delisting that it is fairly meaningless.

Endicott, pointing to an average market price of $26.25 per share in public trading of the stock for the six months immediately preceding the announcement of the merger, argues that market value was required to be given substantial weight and that the lower courts acted contrary to law in adopting that part of the appraiser's report which had failed to do so. In further support of its position, Endicott, among other things, asserts that, during the pre-merger period it regards as relevant McDonough controlled only 31.8% of the common shares, the remainder constituting a large enough public float in the hands of over two thousand stockholders to ensure a free and active market. On the other hand, the stockholders, relying heavily on such facts as the stock's delisting from the New York Stock Exchange, its relegation for a year before the merger to being traded on the over-the-counter market and, by then, the ownership by McDonough of 70% of the stock, claim the marketplace was no longer "a fair reflection of the judgment of the buying and selling public" as to Endicott common. [Citation.]

Under the circumstances, the weight of market value, whether great or small or none, was for the fact-finding tribunals, and there is no reason to disturb the Appellate Division's conclusion, on the facts and in its discretion, that in this case the appraiser was not required to rely "to any large degree" on the market value of Endicott's common stock.

* * *

In addition, the right of dissenting stockholders to obtain fair value rather than market value for their stock protects them from being forced to sell at unfair values arbitrarily and unilaterally fixed by those who may dominate a corporation. The obligation to accept fair value is an accepted risk of public stock ownership for, in some instances, market price at the time of a merger may have been pushed to levels in excess of fair value, and the automatic right to it in a valuation proceeding could bring a windfall. Either way, market price is but an ingredient that must enter into the calculation for what it is worth, no more and no less. [Citation.]

* * *

Accordingly, the order should be affirmed.

Involuntary Judicial Dissolution

CALLIER v. CALLIER

Appellate Court of Illinois, Fifth District, 1978.
61 Ill.App.3d 1011, 18 Ill. Dec. 941, 378 N.E.2d 405.

WINELAND, J.

This is an appeal from a judgment of the Circuit Court of St. Clair County ordering liquidation of the assets and business of All Steel Pipe and Tube, Inc., an Illinois corporation, pursuant to [citation].

* * *

All Steel Pipe and Tube is a close corporation formed in 1969 to engage in the business of selling steel pipes and tubes. The two equal shareholders, plaintiff-appellee Leo Callier and defendant-appellant Scott Callier, each made an initial investment of $500 in the corporation. Scott is Leo's uncle. Defendant-appellant Felix Callier, one of the two directors of the corporation, is Scott's father and Leo's grandfather. It is undisputed that Felix, who is in his 80's, is the "nominee" of Scott on the board of directors, and that he has never taken an active role in the day-to-day management of the business. Leo is the other director, and is president of the corporation. Scott's title is general manager; he was appointed to that position by unanimous reso-

lution of the board, and can only be removed by the board.

Increasingly over the years of their business association, Scott and Leo had differences of opinion about various aspects of the operation of the company. Despite the steady deterioration of the owners' relationship, the company flourished. From about $200,000 in 1970, gross sales had increased to $25,000,000 a year in 1974.

In early 1975, the series of events leading to this litigation took place. Scott was involved in preparing and sending to each employee of the corporation, and each employee's spouse, a letter warning that "social and/or emotional and/or physical relationships between male and female employees for other than business purposes" would thenceforth be grounds for immediate dismissal. This so called "fraternization letter" created a furor within the company, and resulted in Leo's informing Scott that he no longer wanted to be associated with him.

Negotiations looking towards the redemption of Scott's shares by Leo began immediately, but despite the diligent efforts of their attorneys the parties could not reach an agreement. In April 1975, the discussion turned to voluntary dissolution and liquidation of the corporation, but still no agreement could be reached.

On April 30, 1975, Leo sent a telegram to Scott purporting to fire him as general manager. On the next day, without any prior notice, Leo called all the employees together and announced that the business was being closed down immediately. During the next month, Leo began to wind down the business of All Steel. On May 5 he formed a new Delaware corporation, Callier Steel Pipe and Tube, Inc. On May 30, all operations at All Steel ceased. Callier Steel opened for business on June 2, employing about 40 of All Steel's previous employees. On June 11, Leo filed the complaint in the instant cause.

The issue on this appeal is whether the plaintiff sustained his burden of proof under Section 86(a)(1) of the Business Corporation Act. The defendants contend that there was insufficient proof of either a deadlock or irreparable injury within the meaning of the Act to justify dissolution and liquidation of the corporation.

Corporations, which are creatures of statute, can only be dissolved according to statute. [Citation.] As our Supreme Court said in [citation], "Corporate dissolution is a drastic remedy, and the teachings of generations of chancellors admonish us that it must not be lightly invoked." [Citations.]

The statute at issue here is as follows:

Circuit courts have full power to liquidate the assets and business of a corporation:

(a) In an action by a shareholder when it appears:

(1) That the directors are deadlocked in the management of the corporate affairs and the shareholders are unable to break the deadlock, and that irreparable injury to the corporation is suffered or threatened by reason thereof * * *. [Citation.]

[This] section has not been a frequently used basis for dissolution, presumably because of the "substantial problems of interpretation" connected with its provisions. [Citation.] The terms *deadlock* and *irreparable injury* are both undefined and troublesome. It has been said that mere dissension among stockholders is not a ground for dissolution unless it is of such serious proportions as to defeat the end for which the corporation is organized [Citations.] * * *

After a careful review of the entire record, we have concluded that plaintiff's proof was insufficient to show either deadlock in the management of corporate affairs or the threat of irreparable injury to the corporation. What the evidence shows, instead, is two equal shareholders who were unable to get along

and unable to reach agreement within a four-month period as to the redemption of one's shares by the other or to the terms of voluntary dissolution. This is not equivalent to an inability of the corporation to perform the functions for which it was created. Without adopting the position of defendants that the threat of irreparable injury can never be shown under this statute so long as a corporation is making a profit, we must agree with defendants that such a threat was not proved here.

It appears to us that Leo Callier simply decided that he was not going to have anything more to do with Scott Callier, and when their redemption-liquidation negotiations stalled, he made a unilateral decision—without consulting the other director or shareholder—to shut down the corporation. On the day that he informed the employees of the closing of the corporation, corporate affairs were being managed, and quite successfully. In fact, the company appeared on its way to the second best year of its history, despite a general downturn in the pipe industry. Neither Scott nor Felix Callier was interfering with the management of the corporation; Scott had in fact intentionally stayed away from the company and allowed Leo to run things alone while the redemption discussions were going on.

Thus, absent sufficient proof of the jurisdictional facts of deadlock and irreparable injury, the court below erred in ordering liquidation of the corporate assets.

* * *

For the foregoing reasons the judgment of the Circuit Court of St. Clair County is reversed, and this cause is remanded to that court for further proceeding consistent with this opinion.

Reversed and Remanded.

PROBLEMS

1. The stock in Hotel Management, Inc., a hotel management corporation, was divided equally between two families. For several years the two families had been unable to agree or cooperate in the management of the corporation. As a result of this dissension no meeting of shareholders or directors

had been held for five years. There had been no withdrawal of profits for five years, and last year the hotel operated at a loss. While the corporation was not insolvent, such a state was imminent due to the fact that the business was poorly managed and its properties in need of repair. As a result the owners of one-half of the stock brought an action in equity for dissolution of the corporation. What decision?

2. (a) When may a corporation sell, lease, exchange, mortgage, or pledge all or substantially all of its assets in the usual and regular course of its business?

(b) When may a corporation sell, lease, exchange, mortgage, or pledge all or substantially all of its assets otherwise than in the usual and regular course of its business?

(c) What are the rights of a shareholder who dissents from a proposed sale or exchange of all or substantially all of the assets of a corporation otherwise than in the usual and regular course of its business?

3. The X Company was duly merged into the Y Company. S, a shareholder of the former X Company, having paid in only one-half of her subscription, is now sued by the Y Company for the balance of such subscription. S, who took no part in the merger proceedings, denied liability on the ground that, inasmuch as the X Company no longer exists, all her rights and obligations in connection with the X Company have been terminated. Decision?

4. Smith, while in the course of his employment with the Bee Corporation, negligently ran the company's truck into X, injuring him very severely. Subsequently, the Bee Corporation and the Sea Corporation consolidated, forming the SeaBee Corporation. X filed suit against the SeaBee Corporation for damages, and the SeaBee Corporation interposed the defense that the injuries sustained by X were not caused by any of SeaBee's employees, that SeaBee was not even in existence at the time of the injury, and that, therefore, the SeaBee Corporation was not liable. What decision?

5. The Business Corporation Act of the State of X, after prescribing the procedure for the consolidation and/or merger of two or more corporations, provides that "such surviving or new corporation shall thenceforth be responsible and liable for all the liabilities and obligations of each of the corporations so merged or consolidated."

The A Company, a corporation organized under the laws of the State of X, duly authorized by the shareholders sold its entire assets to the B Company, also an X State corporation. T, an unpaid creditor of the A Company, sues the B Company upon her claim. Decision?

6. Zenith Steel Company operates a prosperous business. In January 1985 the board of directors voted to spend $20 million of the surplus funds of the company to purchase a majority of the stock of two other companies—the Green Insurance Company and the Blue Trust Company. The Green Insurance Company is a thriving business whose stock is an excellent investment at the price at which it will be sold to Zenith Steel Company. The principal reasons for the purchase of the Green Insurance stock by the Steel Company are as an investment of surplus funds and as a diversification of its business. The Blue Trust Company owns a controlling interest in Zenith Steel Company. The main purpose for the purchase of the Blue Trust Company stock by Zenith Steel Company is to enable the present management and directors of Zenith Steel Company to perpetuate their management of the company.

Jones, a minority shareholder in Zenith Steel Company, brings an appropriate action to enjoin the purchase by Zenith Steel Company of the stock of either the Green Insurance Company or of the Blue Trust Company. Decision?

7. X, Y, and Z each own one-third of the stock of XYZ Corporation. On Friday, X received an offer to merge XYZ into Buyer Corporation. X agreed to call a shareholders' meeting to discuss the offer on the following Tuesday. X telephoned Y and Z and informed them of the offer and the scheduled meeting. Y agreed to attend. However, Z, unable to attend because he was leaving on a trip on Saturday, asked if the three of them could meet Friday night to discuss the offer. X and Y agreed. The three shareholders met informally Friday night and agreed to accept the offer only if they received preferred stock of Buyer Corporation for their shares. Z then left on his trip. On Tuesday, at the time and place appointed by X, X and Y convened the shareholders' meeting. After discussion, they concluded that the preferred stock payment limitation was unwise and passed a formal resolution to accept Buyer Corporation's offer without any such condition.

Z files suit to enjoin X, Y, and the XYZ Corporation from implementing this resolution. Decision?

PUBLIC POLICY, SOCIAL ISSUES AND BUSINESS ETHICS

PART Eight discusses debtor and creditor relations, an area of business which has assumed great importance. Today our economy literally runs on borrowed funds. In 1983 total net borrowing in the United States was over $600 billion. As of July, 1984 there was $435 billion of consumer installment credit outstanding and almost $2,000 billion of mortgage debt outstanding.

This extensive use of credit has not always been the case. Polonius' often repeated advice to his son Laertes reflects the earlier view of debt: "Neither a borrower nor a lender be; For loan oft loses both itself and friend, And borrowing dulls the edge of husbandry." William Shakespeare, *The Tragedy of Hamlet, Prince of Denmark* Act I, Scene III. Professors Speidel, Summers and White in their text *Teaching Materials on Commercial Transactions* (1969) at pp. 65–66 have explained the longstanding historical opposition to debt:

It was once thought bad for a person to incur debts. In Plato's ideal legal system, debts were not to be incurred at all. It was thought even worse not to repay a debt. In early Rome, debtors who did not repay were dismembered: deprived of arms and legs and more. Not too long ago in Anglo-American law, they were thrown in jail where they might well rot. This was known as body execution on a live body. Even corpses were in jeopardy. Thus on July 7, 1816, Richard Brinsley Sheridan expired at the age of 65. "As his body lay in state in Great George Street, London, a bailiff, disguised as a mourner was admitted to have a last look. Once entered, he served the corpse with a warrant arresting it in the King's name for a debt of five hundred pounds. Only when Mr. Carring and Lord Sidmouth each satisfied the bailiff with a check for two-hundred and fifty pounds did he release the body, so that the funeral could proceed." Harris, The Fine Art of Political Wit 40 (1964).

Over time this attitude has changed dramatically and today under our economic system borrowed funds are absolutely essential and entirely honorable. Without them units of production would be severely restricted in the goods and services they could provide while the consumers of these outputs would be greatly limited in the quantities they could afford to purchase. The public policy and social issues, to which the enormous use of debt gives rise, are essentially fourfold. First, the means by which debt is created and transferred should be as simple and inexpensive as possible. Second, the risks to lenders should be reduced to the minimum level possible. Third, the lenders should have adequate means for collecting unpaid debts. Finally, debtors should have protection from overreaching and deception by lenders and, in some instances, from their own foolhardiness. The legal system's response to these needs constitutes the law of debtor and creditor relations.

The law governing the creation and transfer of debt is designed to make it as expeditious and efficient as possible. For the most part, this area of the law has been discussed elsewhere. For example, Article 3 of the Uniform Commercial Code (discussed in Part Five) deals with debt which is evidenced by commercial paper while Article 8 (discussed in Chapter 34) governs debt evidenced by investment securities such as bonds. The issuance and transfer of investment securities is also subject to State and Federal securities regulation discussed in Chapter 44. In addition, the common law of contracts and sales law under Article 2 of the U.C.C. provide simple methods of creating debt although they do not provide very efficient means by which to transfer such debt. See Chapter 14 for a discussion of the assignment of contract rights.

There are basically two collection risks that a lender incurs. The first is that although the borrower is able to repay the loan he is *unwilling* to do so. The law has provided the lender with a considerable arsenal of collection remedies which reduce significantly this risk although these remedies are by no means costless. A number of these remedies are discussed in Chapter 39.

The law has also sought to deal with the second and more significant collection risk: that the borrower may prove to be *unable* to repay the loan. In addition to the remedies just mentioned, the law has developed several devices to maximize the likelihood that the loan will be repaid. The two most important of these are consensual security interests and sureties. A consensual security interest is an agreement by the borrower granting to the lender the right to reach specified property of the borrower to pay off the debt if the borrower fails to do so. If the property used as collateral is real property then the security is called a mortgage or a deed of trust as discussed in Chapter 49 in the next part of the book. If the property is personal property then the security interest is governed by Article 9 of the Uniform Commercial Code which is covered in this Part.

The Official Comment to U.C.C. Section 9–101 states: "The aim of this Article is to provide a simple and unified structure within which the immense variety of present-day secured financing transactions can go forward with less cost and with greater certainty." Article 9 establishes a comprehensive scheme for the regulation of security interests in personal property that supercedes prior law which, although it had recognized a wide variety of security devices, did not keep pace with new types of collateral and financing that had developed. Moreover, the recognition of so many inconsistent devices had not only increased the costs to both lender and debtor but had also increased the uncertainty as to their rights. Article 9 replaced these distinct and diverse devices with a single, "generic" security interest that applies to all transactions intended to create security interests in personal property. By doing so Article 9 has radically simplified the formal requisites for creating a security interest and has substituted for the multiple filing systems of prior law a more rational system. Both of these changes have reduced the cost of acquiring a security interest in personal property.

The other commonly utilized device to reduce the risk of default is the use of a surety. A surety is a person who promises the creditor that he will pay the debtor's obligation to the creditor if the debtor does not. If the debtor defaults the creditor may proceed directly against the surety. The use of a surety with or without security can significantly reduce the collection risk to the lender.

The last important policy objective of debtor-creditor law is the protection of debtors against the overreaching of creditors as well as from the debtor's own foolhardiness. This problem is most acute where the creditor is a professional and the debtor is a consumer. Special legislation has been enacted at the State and Federal levels designed to address many of the particular problems faced by consumer debtors. These statutes are discussed in Chapter 42.

In some instances debtors of all sorts—wage earners, sole proprietorships, partnerships, and corporations—accumulate debts far in excess of their assets or suffer financial reverses that make it impossible for them to meet their obligations as they become due. In such an event it is an important policy of the law to treat all creditors fairly and equitably. It is also necessary to provide the debtor with relief from these debts so that he may continue to function and contribute to society. These are the two basic purposes of the Federal Bankruptcy law discussed in Chapter 39.

Chapter 37

SECURED TRANSACTIONS IN PERSONAL PROPERTY

A secured transaction includes two elements: (1) a debt or obligation to pay money, and (2) an interest of the creditor in specific property of the debtor which secures performance of the obligation. An obligation or debt needs no security in order to exist; a vast amount of indebtedness is unsecured. The integrity, reputation, and net worth of the debtor are deemed adequate by the creditor.

In many situations, however, businesses or other individuals cannot obtain credit without giving adequate security. Sometimes an unsecured loan can be obtained, but giving security may result in a lower interest rate. Financing transactions involving security in personal property are governed by **Article 9** of the U.C.C., Secured Transactions. The aim of this Article is to provide a simple and unified structure within which the tremendous variety of current secured financing transactions can go forward with less cost and with greater certainty. Moreover, the Article's flexibility and simplified formalities should make it possible for new forms of secured financing to fit comfortably under its provisions. This chapter will discuss secured transactions in personal property. Article 9 does not cover secured transactions involving real property; these transactions are discussed in Chapter 48.

ESSENTIALS OF SECURED TRANSACTIONS

Secured transactions in personal property are governed by Article 9 if the debtor *consents* to provide a security interest in personal property to secure the payment of a debt. Article 9 does *not* apply to non-consensual security interests that arise by operation of law such as a mechanic's or landlord's lien. A common type of consensual secured transaction covered by Article 9 occurs where a person wants to buy goods and does not have either the cash or sufficient credit standing to obtain the goods on open credit. The seller obtains a security interest in the goods to secure payment of all or part of the price. Alternatively, the buyer may borrow the purchase price from a third party and pay the seller in cash. The third party lender may then take a security interest in the goods to secure repayment of the loan.

In every consensual secured transaction there is a debtor, a secured party, collateral, a security agreement, and a security interest. As defined in Section 9–105(1) of the Code, a **debtor** is a person who owes payment or performance of an obligation. A **secured party** is the creditor-lender, seller, or other person who owns the security interest in the collateral. **Collateral** is the property subject to the security interest. **Security agreement** is the agreement that creates or provides for a **security interest**, which, Section 1–201(37) defines as "an interest in personal property or fixtures which secures payment or performance of an obligation." Thus, a security interest is created when an automobile dealer sells and delivers a car to an individual (*debtor*) under a retail installment contract (*security agreement*) that provides that the dealer (*secured party*) obtains a *security interest* in the car (*collateral*) until the price is paid. A security interest in property cannot exist apart from the debt which it secures, and upon a discharge of the debt in any manner, the security interest in the property is terminated. See Figure 37-1.

CLASSIFICATION OF COLLATERAL

The Code classifies collateral as: (a) goods, (b) collateral involving "indispensable paper," and (c) intangibles.

Goods

Goods essentially are tangible personal property which are movable at the time the security interest in them becomes enforceable. Section 9–105(1)(h). Goods are subdivided into (1) consumer goods, (2) equipment, (3) farm products, (4) inventory, and (5) fixtures. An item of goods may fall into different classifications depending on its use or purpose. For example, a refrigerator purchased by a physician to store medicines in his office is classified as equipment, while the same refrigerator would be classified as consumer goods if purchased for use in his home, or as inventory in the hands of a refrigerator dealer or manufacturer.

Consumer Goods Goods are consumer goods if they are used or bought for use primarily for personal, family, or household purposes. Section 9–109(1). Thus, A purchases a refrigerator for use in his house from an appliance dealer under a retail installment contract and

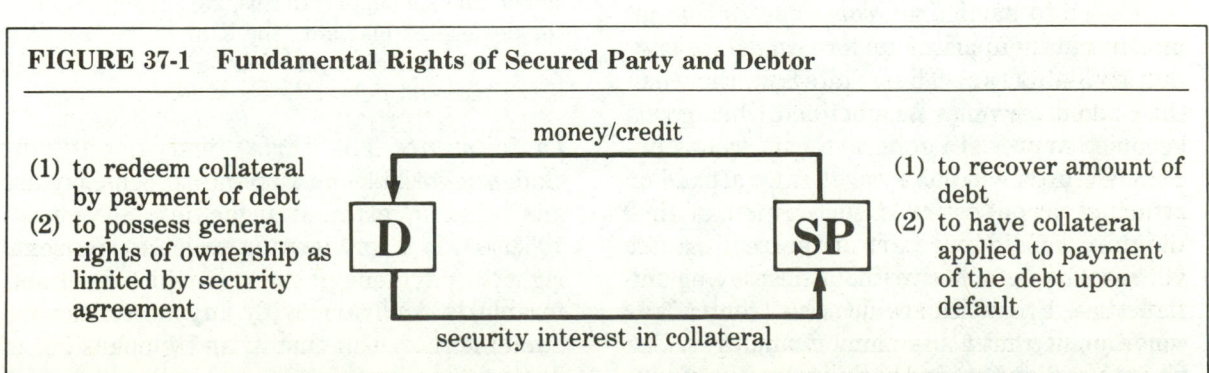

FIGURE 37-1 Fundamental Rights of Secured Party and Debtor

money/credit

(1) to redeem collateral by payment of debt
(2) to possess general rights of ownership as limited by security agreement

D

SP

(1) to recover amount of debt
(2) to have collateral applied to payment of the debt upon default

security interest in collateral

grants the dealer a security interest in the refrigerator, this is an example of consumer goods.

Equipment Goods are classified as equipment if they are used or purchased for use primarily in business (including farming or a profession), provided they are not included in the definition of inventory, farm products, or consumer goods. Section 9–109(2). This category is broad enough to include a lawyer's library, a physician's office furniture, or machinery in a factory.

Farm Products The Code defines farm products as "crops or livestock or supplies used or produced in farming operations or if they are products of crops or livestock in their unmanufactured states. . . ." Section 9–109(3). Thus, farm products would include wheat growing on the farmer's land, the farmer's pigs, cows, hens, and the hens' eggs. When such products come into possession of a person not engaged in farming operations they cease to be farm products.

Inventory The term "inventory" includes goods held for sale or lease as well as raw materials, work in process, or materials used or consumed in a business. Section 9–109(4). Thus, a retailer's or wholesaler's merchandise as well as a manufacturer's materials are inventory.

Fixtures The term "fixtures" refers to personal property or goods which have become so related to particular *real property* that an interest in them arises under real estate law. Section 9–313(1)(a). Thus, State law other than the Code determines whether and when goods become fixtures. In general terms, goods become fixtures when they are firmly affixed or attached to real estate in such a manner that they are considered part of the real estate, yet may be detached without destroying the structure. Examples are furnaces, central air-conditioning units, and plumbing fixtures. See Chapter 46 for a further discussion of fix-

tures. A security interest under Article 9 may be created in goods which are fixtures, and, under certain circumstances, a perfected security interest in fixtures will have priority over a conflicting security interest or mortgage in the real property to which the goods have been attached.

Indispensable Paper

Three kinds of collateral involve rights evidenced by "indispensable paper": (1) chattel paper, (2) instruments, and (3) documents.

Chattel Paper "Chattel paper" is a writing or writings which evidence both a monetary obligation and a security interest in or a lease of specific goods. Frequently, a secured party may borrow against or sell the security agreement of his debtor along with his interest in the collateral. The secured party's collateral in this type of transaction is described by the term "chattel paper." Comment 4 to Section 9–105 of the Code provides the following illustration:

A dealer sells a tractor to a farmer on conditional sales contract or purchase money security interest. The conditional sales contract is a "security agreement," the farmer is the debtor, the dealer is the "secured party" and the tractor is the type of "collateral" defined . . . as "equipment." But now the dealer transfers the contract to his bank either by outright sale or to secure a loan. Since the conditional sales contract is a security agreement relating to specific equipment, the conditional sales contract is now the type of collateral called "chattel paper." In this transaction between the dealer and his bank, the bank is the "secured party," the dealer is the "debtor," and the farmer is the "account debtor."

Instruments The term "instrument" includes negotiable instruments, stocks, bonds, and other investment securities. Section 9–105(1)(i). It is any writing which evidences a right to payment of money, which is transferable by delivery with any necessary indorsement or assignment, and which is not of itself a security agreement or lease.

Documents The term "document" includes documents of title such as bills of lading and warehouse receipts which may be either negotiable or non-negotiable. Sections 9–105(1)(f), 1–201(15). A document of title is negotiable if by its terms the goods it covers are deliverable to bearer or to the order of a named person. Any other document is non-negotiable.

Intangibles

The Code also recognizes two kinds of collateral which are neither goods nor indispensable paper, namely, accounts and general intangibles. These types of intangible collateral are not evidenced by any indispensable paper, such as a stock certificate or a negotiable bill of lading.

Accounts The term "account" or "accounts receivable" refers to the right to payment for goods sold or leased or for services rendered, which is not evidenced by an instrument or chattel paper, whether or not it has been earned by performance. Section 9–106. The 1972 Code deletes the term "contract right" but includes contract rights in its expanded definition of account.

General Intangibles The term "general intangibles" applies to any personal property other than goods, accounts, chattel paper, documents, instruments, and money. Section 9–106. This is a catch-all category for interests not otherwise covered unless they are specifically excluded. It leaves room for the utilization of new kinds of collateral for financing purposes. It includes good will, literary rights, rights to performance of a contract, and interests in patents, trademarks, and copyrights to the extent they are not regulated by Federal statute.

ATTACHMENT

Attachment is the Code's terminology to describe a security interest that is **enforceable** against the debtor. Attachment is also a prerequisite to a security interest's enforceability against parties other than the debtor. Enforceability against third parties is called perfection and is discussed below. Until a security interest "attaches," it is ineffective against the debtor. Under Section 9–203 of the Code, the security interest created by a security agreement attaches to the described collateral once the following events have taken place:

1. the giving of value by the secured party;
2. the debtor's acquiring rights in the collateral; and
3. either the collateral is in the possession of the secured party pursuant to agreement *or* the security agreement is in a writing which contains a reasonable description of the collateral and is signed by the debtor.

Value

The term "value" is broadly defined and includes consideration under contract law, a binding commitment to extend credit, as well as an antecedent debt. Section 1–201(44). For example, Buyer purchases goods from Seller on credit. When Buyer fails to make timely payment, Seller and Buyer enter into a security agreement under which Seller is granted a security interest in the goods. Value has been given by the Seller even though he does not provide any new consideration but instead relies upon an antecedent debt—the original transfer of goods to Buyer. Moreover, Seller is not limited to acquiring a security interest in the goods he sold to Buyer but may also obtain a security interest in other personal property of Buyer.

Debtor's Rights in Collateral

The concept of the debtor's rights in collateral is illusive and not specifically defined by the Code. Prior to 1972, the U.C.C. attempted to provide rules for determining when a debtor acquired rights in certain types of collateral.

The 1972 amendments eliminated these provisions because they were considered unnecessary, arbitrary, and confusing. It was decided that such questions were best left for the courts to determine. As a general rule, the debtor is deemed to have rights in collateral which he owns or is in possession of as well as those items that he is in the process of acquiring from the seller. For example, if A borrows money from B and grants B a security interest in corporate stock that A owns, then A had rights in the collateral prior to entering into the secured transaction. If S sells goods to P on credit and P provides S a security interest in the goods, P will acquire rights in the collateral upon identification of the goods to the contract.

Security Agreement

A security agreement cannot attach unless there is an agreement between the debtor and creditor granting, creating, or providing the creditor a security interest in the debtor's collateral. Moreover, unless the secured party is in possession of the collateral the agreement must be (1) **in writing,** (2) **signed** by the **debtor,** and (3) contain a **reasonable description** of the collateral. Section 9–203(1)(a). *See Matter of Amex-Protein Dev. Corp.* In addition, if the collateral is crops growing or to be grown, or timber to be cut, the agreement must contain a reasonable description of the land.

A sample security agreement is provided as Figure 37-2.

After-Acquired Property "A security agreement may provide that any or all obligations covered by the security agreement are to be secured by after-acquired collateral." Section 9–204(1). After-acquired property is property which the debtor does not own or have rights to but may acquire at some time in the future. For example, after-acquired property clauses in a security agreement may include all present and subsequently acquired inventory, accounts, or equipment of the debtor.

This clause would provide the secured party with a valid security interest not only in the debtor's presently existing typewriter, desk, and file cabinet, but also in a micro-computer subsequently purchased by the debtor. The concept of a "continuing general lien" or a "floating lien" is therefore accepted by Article 9. Nevertheless, it should be noted that no security interest may attach under an after-acquired property clause to consumer goods other than accessions when given as additional security unless the debtor acquires rights in them within ten days after the secured party gives value. Section 9–204(2).

Proceeds A secured party is necessarily interested in the use and disposition of the proceeds from the sale, exchange, collection, or other disposition of the collateral. These proceeds may be in the form of money, checks, deposit accounts, promissory notes, or other types of personal property. Unless otherwise agreed, a security agreement gives the secured party rights to proceeds. Section 9–203(3).

Future Advances The obligations covered by a security agreement may include future advances. Section 9–204(3). Frequently a debtor will obtain a line of credit from a creditor for advances to be made at some later time. For instance, a manufacturer may provide a retailer with a $60,000 line of credit although the retailer only initially utilizes $20,000 of the credit. Nevertheless, the manufacturer may enter into a security agreement with the retailer granting the manufacturer a security interest in the retailer's inventory to secure not only the initial $20,000 advance but also any future advances.

PERFECTION

In order for a security interest to be effective against third parties (including other creditors of the debtor, the debtor's trustee in bankruptcy, and transferees of the debtor), the security interest must be perfected. "A

FIGURE 37-2   Sample Security Agreement

SECURITY AGREEMENT

August 22, 1985

Daniel Debtor of 113 Hillsborough Street, City of Raleigh, County of Wake, State of North Carolina, hereinafter called the "Debtor," does hereby grant to S.P. & Assoc., Inc., of Raleigh, North Carolina, hereinafter called "S.P.," its successors and assigns, a security interest in the following described property, hereinafter called the "Collateral," to-wit:

> One (1) Deluxe Micro-Computer
> Serial number VDL 16794321
> Manufacturer: Apex Mechanical
>   Equipment Co.
> Model 420A

to secure the payment of Debtor's note or notes of even date herewith in the aggregate principal or aggregate face amount of Seven Thousand Five Hundred Dollars ($7,500.00), together with interest and any renewal or extension thereof, in whole or in part, and any and all other debts, obligations, and liabilities of any kind of Debtor to S.P., however created, arising, or evidenced, whether direct or indirect, joint or several, whether as maker, indorser, surety, guarantor or otherwise, whether now or hereafter existing, whether due or not due, and however acquired by S.P. (all hereinafter called the "Obligations").

DEBTOR WARRANTS AND AGREES THAT:

1. Except for the security interest hereby granted, the Debtor will use the proceeds of advances made hereunder, which proceeds may be paid by the S.P. directly to the seller of the Collateral, to become the owner of marketable title to the Collateral free from any prior lien, security interest or encumbrance, and the Debtor will defend the Collateral against all claims and demands of all persons at any time claiming an interest therein.

2. The Collateral is and will be used primarily for personal, family, or household purposes, and the Debtor's residence is that shown at the beginning of this Agreement.

3. The Collateral will be kept at the Debtor's address shown at the beginning of this Agreement.

4. There are no financing statements covering any of the Collateral on file in any public office, and the Debtor has not executed in favor of other secured parties financing statements that could be placed on file prior to any of S.P.'s financing statements.

5. DEBTOR AGREES THAT:
A. He will pay to S.P. all amounts due on the note or notes mentioned above and the other Obligations secured hereby as and when same shall be due and payable, whether by maturity, acceleration, or otherwise, and will pay to S.P. reasonable attorney's fees incurred by S.P. in collection of said Obligations or enforcement of this Security Agreement.
B. He will maintain all mechanical equipment and machinery hereby covered in sound and efficient operating condition, including the procurement and installation of such new parts, attachments, and replacements as may be necessary or desirable to maintain said Collateral in proper operating condition.
C. He will maintain such insurance upon all of the Collateral as S.P. may require, payable to Debtor and S.P. as their interest may appear, in an amount not less than the actual value of the Collateral.
D. He will pay all insurance premiums and taxes, licenses, or other charges assessed against the Collateral or required to be paid in connection with the use and ownership of the Collateral. If Debtor shall fail to pay such insurance premiums, taxes, licenses, or other charges when they are due, S.P. at its opinion, may pay the cost thereof, and the amounts so paid and advanced shall be added to the indebtedness secured hereby and shall bear interest at the maximum rate permitted by Law.

FIGURE 37-2   Sample Security Agreement (cont'd.)

E. He will not (a) permit any liens or security interest to attach to any of the Collateral; (b) permit any of the Collateral to be levied upon under any legal process; (c) sell or dispose of any of the Collateral without prior written consent of S.P.; (d) permit anything to be done that may impair the value of the Collateral or the security intended to be afforded by this Agreement.

F. He will immediately notify S.P. in writing of any change of the Debtor's place or residence, place or places of business, or the location of the Collateral.

G. He will not remove the Collateral from the State of North Carolina without prior written consent by S.P.

6. IT IS FURTHER AGREED THAT THE DEBTOR SHALL BE IN DEFAULT UNDER THIS AGREEMENT:

A. If the Debtor uses any of the Collateral in violation of any statute or ordinance or the Debtor is found to have a record or reputation for violating the laws of the United States or any State relating to liquor or narcotics; or

B. If the Debtor shall fail to perform any covenant or Agreement made by him herein; or

C. If the Debtor shall fail to make due and punctual payment of any of the Obligations secured hereby when and as any part or all of such Obligation becomes due and payable; or

D. If any warranty, representation, or statement made or furnished to S.P. by or on behalf of the Debtor in connection with this Agreement proves to have been false in any material respect when made or furnished; or

E. If the Collateral suffers material damage or destruction; or

F. If any bankruptcy or insolvency proceedings are commenced by or against the Debtor or any guarantor or surety for the Debtor; or

G. If the Debtor dies, becomes incompetent, is dissolved, or the Debtor's existence otherwise terminates.

Upon the happening of any of the above events of default or in the event that S.P., in good faith, deems itself insecure, S.P. may at its option, declare all Obligations secured hereby due and payable immediately and have, in addition to other rights and remedies, the rights and remedies of a secured party upon default under the North Carolina Uniform Commercial Code.

The waiver of any particular default of the Debtor hereunder shall not be a waiver of any other or subsequent default of the Debtor.

Any requirement of the North Carolina Uniform Commercial Code of reasonable notification of time and place of public sale, or the time on or after which private sale may be held, may be met by sending written notice by registered or certified mail to the above address of the Debtor at least five (5) days prior to public sale or the date after which private sale may be made.

The Debtor shall be and remain liable for any deficiency remaining after applying the proceeds of disposition of the Collateral first to the reasonable expenses of re-taking, holding, preparing for sale, selling, and the like, including the reasonable attorney's fees, incurred by S.P. in connection therewith, and then to satisfaction of the Obligations secured hereby.

This Agreement and all rights, remedies, and duties hereunder, including matters of construction, shall be governed by the laws of North Carolina.

This Agreement shall apply to, inure to the benefit of, and be binding upon the heirs, administrators, executors, and assigns of S.P. and the Debtor. This is the entire agreement of the parties, and no amendment, alteration, deletion, or addition hereto shall be effective and binding unless it is in writing and signed by the parties.

Debtor acknowledges that this Agreement is and shall be effective upon execution by the Debtor and delivery hereof to S.P., and it shall not be necessary for S.P. to execute or otherwise signify its acceptance hereof.

Signed and delivered on the day first above written.

                _____ (SEAL)
                Daniel Debtor

                S.P. & Assoc., Inc.
                (Secured Party)
                By: _____

security interest is perfected when it has attached and when all the applicable steps required for perfection have been taken." Section 9–303(1).

A security interest may be perfected:

1. by filing a financial statement signed by the debtor;
2. by the secured party's taking or retaining possession of the collateral; or
3. automatically upon the attachment of the security interest.

Figure 37-3 lists the requisites for enforceability.

Filing a Financing Statement

The filing of a financing statement is the general method of perfecting a security interest under Article 9. Filing may be used to perfect a security interest in any type of collateral. The form of the financing statement, which is filed to give public notice of the security interest, may vary from State to State. The financing statement does not contain details, but must include the names and addresses of the secured party and the debtor, a reasonable description of the collateral, and the signature of the debtor. Section 9–402(1). See Figure 37-4 for a sample financing statement.

In order to ascertain the terms of a secured transaction between the parties, one must look to the security agreement or the collateral note or preferably both. It is possible that the maturity date of the obligation will not appear on the financing statement nor the amount of the obligation secured. The maturity date for a financing statement is *five years* from the date of filing. Section 9–403(2). Moreover, if a **continuation statement** is filed by the secured party within six months prior to expiration, the effectiveness of the filing will be extended for another five-year period. Section 9–403(3).

In most States, security interests in **motor vehicles** must be perfected by a notation on the **certificate of title** rather than by filing a financing statement. Nevertheless, in most States, certificate of title laws do not apply to motor vehicles that are held as inventory for sale by a dealer.

Where to File Section 9–401(1) of the Code provides three alternative provisions regarding the proper place to file a financing statement. The alternatives differ as to which types of collateral are to be filed **locally** (in the county) or **centrally** (with the Secretary of State or other designated State official).

The first alternative, which has been adopted in only a few States, provides that where the collateral is fixtures, timber to be cut, and minerals to be extracted, then the financing statement should be filed locally in the office where a mortgage on real estate would be filed or recorded. All other filings are to be made centrally with the Secretary of State or other designated State official.

FIGURE 37-3 Requisites for Enforceability

I. Attachment
(against Debtor)

A. Agreement
   1) in writing (unless SP has possession)
   2) providing a security interest
   3) in described collateral
   4) signed by debtor,

B. Value given by secured party, and

C. Debtor has rights in collateral

II. Perfection
(against Third Parties)

A. Filing a financing statement, or

B. SP takes possession, or

C. Automatically

FIGURE 37-4   Sample Financing Statement

UNIFORM COMMERCIAL CODE—FINANCING STATEMENT
APPROVED FOR USE IN NORTH CAROLINA AND THE FOLLOWING STATES

Alabama	Delaware	Maine	New Jersey	Tennessee	
Alaska	Hawaii	Maryland	New Mexico	Virginia	
Arkansas	Idaho	Massachusetts	North Dakota	West Virginia	UCC-1
Arizona	Indiana	Mississippi	Ohio	Wyoming	
Colorado	Kansas	Montana	Oklahoma	District of Columbia	
Connecticut	Kentucky	New Hampshire	South Carolina		

This FINANCING STATEMENT is presented to a Filing Officer for filing pursuant to the Uniform Commercial Code.

No. of Additional Sheets Presented:

(1) Debtor(s) (Last Name First) and Address(es):

(2) Secured Party(ies) Name(s) and Address(es):

(3) (a) ☐ Collateral is or includes fixtures.
    (b) ☐ Timber, Minerals or Accounts Subject to G.S. 25·9·103(5) are covered
    (c) ☐ Crops Are Growing Or To Be Grown On Real Property Described in Section (5). If either block 3(a) or block 3(b) applies describe real estate, including record owner(s) in section (5).

(4) Assignee(s) of Secured Party, Address(es):

For Filing Officer

(5) This Financing Statement Covers the Following types [or items] of property.

☐ Products of the Collateral Are Also Covered.

(6) Signatures: Debtor(s)   Secured Party(ies) [or Assignees]

(By) _____

Standard Form Approved by N.C. Sec. of State and other states shown above.

    (1) Filing Officer Copy—Numerical

(By) _____

Signature of Secured Party Permitted in Lieu of Debtor's Signature:

(1) Collateral is subject to Security Interest In Another Jurisdiction and ☐
    ☐ Collateral Is Brought Into This State
    ☐ Debtor's Location Changed To This State

(2) For Other Situations See: G.S. 25·9·402(2)

UCC-1

The second alternative, which is the most widely adopted, stipulates local filing for fixtures, farm products, consumer goods, timber, minerals, and farming equipment. All other filings are to be made in the office of the Secretary of State or other designated State official.

The third alternative is the same as the second except that, where central filing is required, the secured party must *also* file locally if the debtor has a place of business in only one county or if the debtor has no place of business in the State but resides in the State.

Improper Filing If a secured party fails to file the financing statement in the proper location or fails to file it in all the required locations, the filing is *ineffective*, subject to two exceptions. First, if the filing is made in good faith, it is nevertheless effective with regard to any collateral as to which the filing complied with the requirements of Article 9. Section 9–401(2). This exception applies to situations in which the filing covers a number of different types of collateral and is proper with respect to some but not all of the collateral listed. Second, a filing made in good faith is also effective with regard to collateral covered by the financing statement against any person who has knowledge of the contents of that financing statement. Section 9–401(2). *See In Re Mistura, Inc.* This exception has been limited by the 1972 Amendments which give a lien creditor a priority over an unperfected security interest without regard to whether the lien creditor knew of the unperfected security interest. Section 9–30(1)(b).

Subsequent Change of Information After a financing statement has been properly filed by a secured party, the debtor may change the place of his residence or business or the location or use of the collateral and thus render the information in the filing incorrect. Nevertheless, in all the States a change in the *use* of the collateral does not impair the

effectiveness of the original filing. Most States also provide that the original filing made in the proper place continues to be effective despite any change of location provided the change is **intrastate.** Section 9–401(3). A minority of States have adopted a second alternative provided by Section 9–401(3) limiting the effectiveness of a filing which is made in the proper county to a period of four months after the debtor has moved his residence, place of business, or the collateral to another county. Under the second alternative if the secured party does not file a financing statement in the new county within the four-month time period, perfection ceases until a new filing is made. To address this problem most security agreements provide that the debtor shall keep or use the collateral at the location described in the agreement and that the debtor will immediately notify the secured party in writing of any change of the debtor's place of residence, place of business, or location of the collateral. For example, see the sample security agreement, Figure 37-2.

With respect to **interstate** changes, there are two situations which require a new filing: (1) if the collateral is mobile goods, accounts, or general intangibles and the *debtor* moves his residence or place of business to another State or (2) if the *debtor* moves the collateral to another State. Section 9–103. In either case, the security interest perfected in the former State remains in effect until the expiration of four months or until perfection would have ceased under the laws of the first State, whichever occurs first. *See Exchange Bank of Osceola v. Jarrett.* If the security interest is not perfected within the four-month period, it becomes unperfected and such loss of perfection under the 1972 Amendments is retroactive to the time of the change in location of the debtor or collateral. Thus, D purchases goods in Arizona and grants S.P. a security interest in the goods, which S.P. perfects by filing. D then moves to Kansas and immediately sells the goods to B. If S.P. refiles in Kansas within the four-month period, S.P. would have priority over B; however, if S.P.

fails to file within the four-month period, B would prevail since the loss of perfection dates back to the time of D's move from Arizona to Kansas. Under the 1962 provision, the loss is not retroactive and thus any purchase within the four-month grace period is subordinate to the original perfection in Arizona. Most security agreements, in an attempt to avoid this problem, stipulate that the debtor will not remove the collateral from the State of original filing. For example, see sample security agreement, Figure 37-2.

Possession

A **pledge,** or possessory security interest, is the delivery of possession of personal property to a creditor, or to a third party acting as an agent for the creditor, as security for the payment of a debt. Perhaps the most common pledge is that of a borrower who pledges corporate stock by delivery of the certificates to a bank in order to secure a loan. The delivery of the stock certificates (collateral) to the bank (secured party) is the essential element of the pledge. Since *delivery* is made, the security interest is "perfected" without filing. Section 9-302(1)(a). There is no pledge where the debtor retains possession of the collateral. In a pledge it is not legally required that the debtor sign a written security agreement; an oral agreement granting the secured party a security interest will suffice. In any situation other than a pledge a written security agreement is required by the Code. Section 9-203.

Possession by the secured party may be used to perfect a security interest in goods (e.g., pawnbrokers), instruments, negotiable documents, or chattel paper. Section 9-305. A pledge cannot be utilized with respect to items which are completely intangible. Subject to the limited exception of the 21-day temporary period of perfection discussed later in this chapter, possession is the *only* way to perfect a security interest in instruments. Section 9-304. In addition, the usual and advisable method of perfecting a security inter-

est in both negotiable documents and chattel paper is also by possession. Although both of these types of collateral may be perfected by filing, it is not advisable to rely upon filing because: (a) a holder of a negotiable document of title which has been duly negotiated to him takes priority in the goods over an earlier security interest perfected by filing, Section 9-309; and (b) a good faith purchaser in the ordinary course of business of chattel paper take's priority over an earlier security interest perfected by filing. Section 9-308.

One common type of pledge is the **field warehouse.** This is an arrangement which is often used with the financing of inventory in order to provide the debtor with access to the pledged goods while at the same time providing the secured party with control over the pledged property. The field warehousing operation is generally accomplished by a professional warehouseman establishing a warehouse on the debtor's premises—usually by enclosing a portion of the premises and posting appropriate signs—to store the debtor's unsold inventory. Non-negotiable receipts for the goods are then typically issued by the warehouseman to the secured party. The secured party may then authorize the warehouseman to release a portion of the goods to the debtor as the goods are sold, at a specified quantity per week, or at any rate agreed upon by the parties. Thus, the secured party is legally in possession of the goods while allowing the debtor easy access to her inventory.

Automatic Perfection

In some situations a security interest is automatically perfected upon attachment. The two most important situations to which automatic perfection applies are (1) purchase money security interests in consumer goods and (2) temporary perfection with respect to instruments and documents. In addition, a partial assignment of accounts which does not transfer a significant part of the outstanding accounts of the assignor is also automatically perfected. Moreover, a security interest in proceeds is automatically perfected for ten days after receipt of the proceeds if the security interest in the original collateral was perfected.

Purchase Money Security Interest in Consumer Goods A seller of goods retaining a security interest in them by a security agreement has a **purchase money security interest** (PMSI). Similarly, a third party which advances funds to enable the debtor to purchase goods has a purchase money security interest if it has a security agreement and the debtor in fact uses the funds to purchase the goods. A purchase money security interest in consumer goods, with the exception of motor vehicles, is perfected automatically upon attachment without the necessity of filing a financial statement. Section 9–302(1)(d). Thus, D purchases a refrigerator from C on credit for D's own personal, family, or household use. D takes possession of the refrigerator, and then D grants C a security interest in the refrigerator pursuant to a written security agreement. Upon D's granting C the security interest in the refrigerator, C's security in-

terest attaches and is automatically perfected. The same is also true if D purchased the refrigerator for cash but borrowed the money from L, to whom D granted a written security interest in the refrigerator. L's security interest attached and was automatically perfected upon C's receiving the security interest from D.

Temporary Perfection A security interest in *negotiable documents* or *instruments* is automatically perfected without filing or taking possession for **twenty-one days** from the time it attaches to the extent it arises for new value given under a written security agreement. Section 9–304(4). However, the secured party runs the risk of loss or impairment of his security interest during the twenty-one day period, for although his interest is temporarily perfected, a holder in due course of a negotiable instrument or a holder to whom a document has been duly negotiated will take priority over the security interest.

The types of collateral and their applicable methods of perfection are shown in Figure 37-5.

FIGURE 37-5   Methods of Perfecting Security Interests

Collateral	Filing	Possession	Automatic
Goods			
Consumer	●	●	PMSI
Equipment	●	●	
Farm products	●	●	
Inventory	●	●	
Fixtures	●	●	
Indispensable Paper			
Chattel paper	●	●	
Instrument	●	●	21 days
Document	●	●	21 days
Intangibles			
Account	●		●
General Intangibles	●		●

PRIORITIES

As previously noted, in order for a security interest to be effective against other creditors of the debtor, the debtor's trustee in bankruptcy, and transferees of the debtor, the security interest must be perfected. Nonetheless, perfection of a security interest does *not* provide the secured party with a priority over *all* third parties with an interest in the collateral. On the other hand, even an unperfected security interest has priority over a limited number of third parties and is enforceable against the debtor. Article 9 establishes a complex set of rules that determine the relative priorities among these parties.

Against Unsecured Creditors

Once a security interest **attaches,** it has priority over claims of other creditors who do not have a security interest or a lien. This priority does not depend upon perfection. However, an unperfected security interest is subordinate to a representative of unsecured creditors such as an assignee for the benefit of creditors, a trustee in bankruptcy, or a receiver in equity. Section 9–301.

Against Lien Creditors

A **perfected** security interest has priority over lien creditors who acquire their lien after perfection. An **unperfected** security interest is subordinate to the rights of a person who becomes a lien creditor before the security interest is perfected. Section 9–301(1)(b). However, if a secured party files with respect to a *purchase money security interest* within ten days after the debtor receives possession of the collateral, the secured party takes priority over the rights of a lien creditor which arise between the time the security interest attaches and the time of filing. Section 9–301(2). A **lien creditor** means a creditor who has acquired a lien in the property by attachment *and* includes an assignee for the benefit of creditors and a **trustee in bank-**

ruptcy. Section 9–301(3). Nonetheless, a lien securing claims arising from services or materials furnished with respect to goods (an artisan's or mechanic's lien) "takes priority over a perfected security interest unless the lien is statutory and the statute expressly provides otherwise." Section 9–310.

Against Other Secured Creditors

The rights of a secured creditor against other secured creditors depends upon which security interests are perfected, when they are perfected, and the type of collateral. Notwithstanding the rules of priority, it is possible for a secured party entitled to priority to subordinate her interest to that of another secured creditor. This may be done by agreement between the secured parties, and nothing need be filed.

Perfected versus Unperfected A creditor with a **perfected** security interest has greater rights in the collateral than a creditor with an unperfected security interest.

Perfected versus Perfected As between two parties, each with a **perfected** security interest, they rank according to priority in *time of filing or perfection*. This general rule is stated in Section 9–312(5)(a) which provides:

(a) Conflicting security interests rank according to priority in time of filing or perfection. Priority dates from the time a filing is first made covering the collateral or the time the security interest is first perfected, whichever is earlier, provided that there is no period thereafter when there is neither filing nor perfection.

This rule gives special treatment to filing since it can occur prior to attachment and thus grants priority from a time which may precede perfection.

For example, D Store and S Bank enter into a loan agreement under the terms of which S agrees to lend $5,000 upon the security of D's existing store equipment. A financing statement is filed, but no funds are advanced. One week later, D enters into a loan agreement with R Bank, and R Bank agrees to lend $5,000 on the security of the same store equipment. The funds are advanced, and a financing statement is filed. One week later, S Bank advances the agreed sum of $5,000. D Store defaults on both loans. As between S Bank and R Bank, S has priority. When both security interests are perfected by filing, priority is determined in the order of filing. R Bank could have checked the financing statements on file and would have learned that S Bank claimed a security interest in the equipment. Once S's financing statement was on file, with no prior secured party of record, S was not required to check the files prior to advancing funds to D Store in accordance with its loan commitment.

To illustrate further, assume that X grants a security interest in a Chagall painting to S Bank, and in accordance with the loan agreement the Bank advances funds to X. A financing statement is filed. Later X wishes more money and goes to C, an art dealer, who advances funds to X upon a pledge of the painting. X defaults on both loans. As between S and C, S has priority because its security interest was filed prior to C's perfection by possession. By checking the financing statements on file, C could have discovered that S had a prior security interest in the painting.

Where there is a **purchase money security interest** in the collateral, the rules vary depending upon whether the collateral is non-inventory or inventory.

1. A purchase money security interest in **non-inventory** collateral takes priority over a conflicting security interest if the purchase money security interest is perfected at the time the debtor receives possession of the collateral *or* within *ten days* of receipt. Section 9–312(4).

For example, D Manufacturing Co. entered into a loan agreement with S Bank which loaned money to D upon the security of D's existing and future equipment. A financing statement was filed reciting that the collateral is "all equipment presently owned and subsequently acquired" by D. At a later date, D buys new equipment from X Supply Co., paying 25 percent of the purchase price with X retaining a security interest in the equipment to secure the remaining balance. If X files a financing statement within ten days of D's obtaining possession of the equipment, X's purchase money security interest in the new equipment has priority over S's interest. *See Matter of Ultra Precision Industries, Inc.* If X filed on the eleventh day after D received the equipment, X's interest would be subordinate to S's interest.

2. A purchase money security interest in **inventory** has priority over conflicting security interests, provided that the purchase money security holder perfects his interest in the inventory at the time the debtor receives the inventory and notifies, in writing, all holders of conflicting security interests who have filed a financing statement covering the same type of inventory of his acquisition of a purchase money security interest and a description of the secured inventory. Section 9–312(3).

D Store and S Bank enter into a loan agreement under the terms of which S agrees to finance D's entire inventory of stoves, refrigerators, and other kitchen appliances. A financing statement is filed, and S advances funds to D. Subsequently, D enters into an agreement under which R Stove Co. will supply D with stoves, retaining a purchase money security interest in this inventory. R will have priority as to the inventory it supplies to D *provided* that a financing statement is filed and R notifies S that it is going to engage in this purchase money financing of the described stoves. If R fails to give the required notice or fails to file a financing statement, S will have priority over R as to the stoves supplied by R to D. The Code adopts a system of notice filing, and secured parties proceed at their peril in failing to check the financing statement on file.

Unperfected versus Unperfected

If neither security interest is perfected, then the first to attach has priority. Section 9–312(5)(6).

Against Buyers

A security interest continues in collateral even though it is sold, unless the secured party authorizes the sale. Section 9–306(2). However, in some instances buyers of collateral which was sold without the secured party's authorization nonetheless take it free of the security interest. Some of these purchasers take free of even a perfected security interest while others take free of only an unperfected security interest.

Buyers in the Ordinary Course of Business

A buyer in the ordinary course of business "takes free of a security interest created by *his* seller, even though the security interest is perfected and even though the buyer knows of its existence." Section 9–307(1). This rule, however, does not apply to a person buying farm products from a person engaged in farming operations. A buyer in the ordinary course of business is a person who buys in good faith, without knowledge that the sale violates a security interest of a third party, and buys from a person in the business of selling goods of that kind. Section 1–201(9). Thus, this rule applies primarily to purchasers of inventory. For example, a consumer who purchases a sofa from a furniture dealer and the dealer who purchases the sofa from another dealer are both buyers in the ordinary course of business. On the other hand, a person who purchases a sofa from a dentist who used the sofa in his waiting room or from an individual who used the sofa in his home is not a buyer in the ordinary course of business.

To illustrate further: a buyer in the ordinary course of business of an automobile from an automobile dealership will take free and clear of a security interest created by the dealer from whom she purchased the car. However, that same buyer in the ordinary course of business will *not* take clear of a security interest created by any person who owned the automobile prior to the dealer. A leading case on this point is *National Shawmut Bank of Boston v. Jones*, 108 N.H. 386, 236 A.2d 484 (1967). In that case Wever bought a 1964 Dodge Dart from Wentworth Motor Company for his own personal use and granted a security interest in the car to Wentworth. Wentworth later assigned the security interest to National Shawmut Bank who properly perfected it. Without Shawmut's consent, Wever sold the car to Hanson-Rock, another automobile dealer. Hanson-Rock then sold the car to Jones. Even though Jones is a buyer in the ordinary course of business from Hanson-Rock, he took the automobile subject to Shawmut's security interest since that interest had not been created by Jones' seller, Hanson-Rock. *See also Exchange Bank of Osceola v. Jarrett.*

Buyers of Consumer Goods

In the case of consumer goods, a buyer who buys without knowledge of a security interest, for value, and for his own personal, family, or household use takes free of any purchase money security interest **automatically** perfected, but takes the goods subject to a security interest perfected by filing. Section 9–307(2). For example, A purchases on credit a refrigerator from S for use in his home and grants S a security interest in the refrigerator. S does not file a financing statement but has a perfected security interest by attachment. A subsequently sells the refrigerator to his neighbor, N, for use in N's home. N did not have knowledge of S's security interest and, therefore, takes free of S's interest. However, if S had filed a financing statement, S's security interest would continue in the collateral in the hands of N.

Other Buyers

An unperfected security interest is subordinated to the rights (**1**) in the case of goods, instruments, documents, and chattel paper of a purchaser who gives value for the collateral, takes it without knowledge of the existing security interest, and before it is perfected, Section 9–301(1)(c); and (2) in the case of accounts and general intangibles of a purchaser who takes for value, without knowledge of the security interest, and before perfection. Section 9–301(1)(d). If either of these purchasers has knowledge of the unperfected security interest, he takes the collateral subject to the security interest.

A purchaser of chattel paper or an instrument who gives new value and takes possession of it in the ordinary course of his business has priority over a security interest in the chattel paper or instrument which is perfected if he acts without knowledge that the specific paper or instrument is subject to a security interest. Section 9–308. A holder in due course of a negotiable instrument, a holder to whom a negotiable document of title has been duly negotiated, and a *bona fide* purchaser of an investment security take priority over an earlier security interest even though perfected. Filing under Article 9 does *not* constitute notice of the security interest to such holders or purchasers. Section 9–309.

DEFAULT

After default, the rights and remedies of the parties are governed by the security agreement and by the applicable provisions of the Code. In general, the secured party may reduce his claim to judgment, foreclose, or otherwise enforce the security interest by available judicial procedure. Section 9–501. Unless the parties have agreed otherwise, the secured party may take possession of the collateral on default without judicial process if it can be done without a breach of the peace. Without removing it, the secured party may render equipment unusable and dispose of it on the debtor's premises. Section 9–503. Unless the debtor has waived his rights in the collateral after default, he has a right of re-

demption at any time before the secured party has disposed of the collateral or entered into a contract to dispose of it. Section 9–506.

Sale of Collateral

The secured party may sell, lease, or otherwise dispose of any collateral in its condition existing at the time of repossession or following any commercially reasonable preparation or processing. Section 9–504(1). The debtor is entitled to any surplus and is liable for any deficiency, except that in the case of a sale of accounts or chattel paper, he is not entitled to any surplus or liable for a deficiency unless the security agreement so provides. Section 9–504(2).

The collateral may be disposed of at *public* or *private* sale, so long as all aspects of its disposition are "commercially reasonable." *See Eggeman v. Western National Bank*. Unless the collateral is perishable or threatens to decline speedily in value or is of a type customarily sold on a recognized market, reasonable *notice* must be given to the debtor of a public sale or of the time after which a private disposition will be made and, except in the case of consumer goods, to other secured parties who have filed or who are known by the secured party to have security interests in the collateral. The secured party may buy at a public sale and at a private sale if the collateral is customarily sold in a recognized market or is the subject of widely distributed standard price quotations. Section 9–504(3).

Retention of Collateral

The secured party may, after default and repossession, send written notice to the debtor and, except in the case of consumer goods, to other secured parties that he proposes to retain the collateral in satisfaction of the obligation, and if no objection is received within twenty-one days, the secured party may retain the collateral; but if objection is received, the collateral must be disposed of as provided in the Code. Section 9–505(2). In the case of

consumer goods, if the debtor has paid *60 percent* of the obligation and has not, after default, signed a statement renouncing his rights, the secured party who has taken possession of the collateral must dispose of it by sale within ninety days after repossession, or the debtor may recover in conversion or under the Code not less than the credit service charge plus 10 percent of the principal amount of the debt or the time price differential plus 10 percent of the cash price. Sections 9–505(1) and 9–507(1).

CASES

Security Agreement

MATTER OF AMEX-PROTEIN DEVELOPMENT CORP.

United States Court of Appeals, Ninth Circuit, 1974.
504 F.2d 1056.

PER CURIAM:

This is an appeal filed pursuant to § 24 of the Bankruptcy Act [Citation] from a judgment of the district court holding that a valid and enforceable security interest was created under the provisions of the Uniform Commercial Code.

We adopt the following opinion of the Honorable George B. Harris, United States District Judge for the Northern District of California:

"This matter is on review from an Order of the Referee which declared invalid a security interest claimed by petitioner Plant Reclamation, a creditor of the bankrupt, in certain personal property in the possession of the bankrupt.

"Plant Reclamation had sold equipment to the bankrupt on open account, but on October 16, 1972, substituted a promissory note for the open account indebtedness and caused a financing statement to be signed and filed. The parties intended to create a security interest in the property sold as collateral for the note, and the Referee so found.

"The promissory note included the following line: 'This note is secured by a Security Interest in subject personal property as per invoices.' The words 'subject * * * as per invoices' were handwritten in an otherwise typewritten sentence; the testimony before the Referee established that such words were added by an officer of the bankrupt in order to tie the security interest to the personal property that had been sold to the bankrupt by Plant Reclamation. The invoices referred to in the promissory note were the only ones submitted by Plant Reclamation.

"The financing statement named Plant Reclamation as the secured party and recited that it covered the following types or items of property:

1—Door Oliver 100 Sq. Ft. Vacuum Filter
1—Chicago Pheumatic [sic] Vacuum Compression
1—Stainless Steel Augar [sic] and Drive
1—Nichols micro 7″ dryer
1—Tolhurst Centerfuge [sic] 26 inch

Discussion

"I. Did the Promissory Note 'Create or Provide for' a Security Interest?

* * *

"No magic words or precise form are necessary to create or provide for a security interest so long as the minimum formal requirements of the Code are met. [Citations.] This liberal approach is mandated by an expressed purpose of the secured transaction provisions of the Code:

The aim of this Article is to provide a simple and unified structure within which the immense variety of present-day secured financing transactions can go forward with less cost and with greater certainty.

* * *

The Article's flexibility and simplified formalities should make it possible for new forms of secured financing, as they develop, to fit comfortably under its provisions * * *. Comment to U.C.C.

"The court in *In re Center Auto Parts*, [citation] upheld the validity of a promissory note as a security agreement by reading the two together. The promissory note merely recited that, 'This note is secured by a certain financing statement,' and the court found that such was sufficient to 'create or provide for' a security interest within the meaning of § 9–105(1)(h).

* * *

"Accordingly, the promissory note herein qualifies as a security agreement which by its terms 'creates or provides for' a security interest.

"II. Adequacy of Description of the Collateral

"The trustee urges a second ground for sustaining the Order of the Referee complained of here, namely the inadequacy of the description of the collateral in the promissory note and hence the failure to comply with [U.C.C.] § 9–203(1)(b) [citation].

* * *

"Although the promissory note does not describe the collateral within the four corners of the document such description is provided (1) through incorporation by reference of the subject invoices, as well as (2) through reference to the more specific description of the collateral contained in the financing statement.

"The use of such extrinsic aids is clearly permissible to identify the collateral:

Under the Uniform Commercial Code there is no reason why parol evidence may not be admitted in aid of the description of the collateral, even where the collateral has been reasonably and sufficiently identified in the security agreement. In many instances, a description in a security agreement may be in general terms; parol evidence should therefore be admissible to explain or supplement the general description, or to resolve ambiguities.

"The doctrine of incorporation by reference is likewise available in this area:

There is nothing in the Uniform Commercial Code to prevent reference in the security agreement to another writing for particular terms and conditions of the transaction. There is also nothing in the Uniform Commercial Code to prevent reference in the Security Agreement to another writing for a description of the collateral, so long as the reference in the security agreement is sufficient to identify reasonably what it described. In other words, it will at times be expedient to give a general description of the collateral in the security agreement and refer to a list or other writing for more exact description. In addition, the security agreement could itself consist of separate parts, one a general description of the obligation secured and the rights and duties of the parties, and the other a description of the collateral, both such writings being signed by the debtor and stated to comprise a single security agreement or referring to each other.

"Thus there is no requirement that the description of the collateral be complete within the four corners of the security agreement or other single document. The description in the security agreement is sufficient, however, if it provides such information as would lead a reasonable inquirer to the identity of the collateral. [Citations.]

"It is manifest that the reference to the invoices in the subject promissory note, coupled with the existence of a financing statement containing a more specific description, satisfies the requirements of [U.C.C.] §§ 9–203(1)(b) and 9–110.

* * *

Conclusion

"For the reasons stated above, the petition of Plant Reclamation is hereby granted, and the Order of the Referee Declaring Lien Invalid, dated April 10, 1973, is hereby reversed. It is so ordered."

The judgment is affirmed.

Improper Filing

IN RE MISTURA, INC.

United States Court of Appeals, Ninth Circuit, 1983.
705 F.2d 1496.

KILKENNY, J.

[The Marcuses sold a drug store to Mistura, Inc., taking back a security interest in the fixtures and personal property for the upaid balance. They filed a financing statement on June 15, 1977. However, only the lien on fixtures, not the lien on personal property, was perfected because the Marcuses filed the statement with the Maricopa County Recorder, rather than the Arizona Secretary of State as required by Arizona law. Subsequently, Mistura sought additional financing and obtained a loan from McKenon secured by the same collateral. McKenon properly perfected its security interest by filing a financing statement with the Arizona Secretary of State on September 5, 1979. Upon learning of their improper filing, the Marcuses filed a financing statement with the Secretary on September 12, 1980.

Mistura subsequently went into bankruptcy and the trustee in bankruptcy questions which party has priority to the personal property. The Marcuses base their claim upon the contention that their good faith filing with the Maricopa County Recorder was effective against McKenon because McKenon had knowledge of the improperly filed financing statement.]

* * *

[U.C.C. § 9–401(2)] provides a careless creditor with some protection when a filing is made in good faith in an improper place. It provides:

A filing which is made in good faith in an improper place or not in all of the places required by this section is nonetheless effective with regard to any collateral as to which the filing complied with the requirements of this article and is also effective with regard to collateral covered by the financing statement against any person who has *knowledge of the contents of such financing statement.*

No Arizona courts have interpreted the requisite knowledge requirement in the above statute. * * * Other jurisdictions, however, are not in accord as to the meaning or application of the phrase "knowledge of the contents of such financing statement."

Several courts have held knowledge of a creditor's prior security interest to be "knowledge of the contents of such financing statement." [Citations.] This line of cases assumes that knowledge of the security interest provides the subsequent creditor with knowledge of the contents of the financing statement. Other courts, however, have reached the opposite result. [Citation.]

It is clear that the courts have almost universally required actual, rather than constructive, knowledge of the general contents of the financing statement. However, the nature of the actual knowledge required varies substantially across a broad spectrum. To complicate matters, "the Code provides no further guidance as to where on the spectrum from 'should have found out' to 'actually eyeing the maverick [financing statement]' the correct solution lies." [Citation.]

* * *

* * * [W]e hold that given an opportunity the Arizona Supreme Court would follow the line of cases holding that knowledge of the facts contained in a financing statement, even though learned in ignorance of the improperly filed financing statement, satisfies the requisite knowledge requirement of the statute. The statute by its terms requires "knowledge of the contents of such financing statement," but does not require an examination of the financing statement itself.

[Judgment for the Marcuses.]

*Priorities: Purchase Money
Security Interest*

MATTER OF ULTRA PRECISION INDUSTRIES, INC.

United States Court of Appeals, Ninth Circuit, 1974.
503 F.2d 414.

Eᴀsᴛ, J.

The Appeal

National Acceptance Company of California (National) appeals from the two several orders of the District Court denying its Petition for Review and affirming the referee's two several rulings or orders that the security interest held by Community Bank (Bank) and Wolf Machinery Company (Wolf) in three large Rigid Hydro Copy Profiling Machines, numbered 5890 and 5910 (Bank) and machine numbered 5934 (Wolf), respectively, had priority over a conflicting security interest held by National. § 9–312(4) of the Uniform Commercial Code of California (Code). We affirm.

Facts

The pertinent facts are:

National loaned Ultra Precision Industries, Inc. (Ultra) $692,000, and to secure the repayment of that sum, Ultra on or about March 7, 1967, executed in favor of National a Chattel Mortgage Security Agreement covering specifically described equipment of Ultra. National perfected its security interest by timely filing a Financing Statement. The Chattel Mortgage Security Agreement and the Financing Statement contained the usual after-acquired equipment security clauses; however, without reference to any specific property.

Subsequent to the acquisition of National's security interest and during 1967 and 1968, Ultra placed orders with Wolf for two of the machines, later identified as machines numbered 5890 and 5910. It was agreed between Ultra and Wolf that after those machines had

been shipped to Ultra and installed, Ultra would be given an opportunity to test them in their operations during a reasonable testing period, and, further, that arrangements satisfactory to Ultra for outside financing was a condition precedent to the ultimate purchase of those machines. The machines were delivered to Ultra on April 30, 1968 and June 20, 1968, respectivelty, satisfactory testing was accomplished, outside financing obtained, and on July 31, 1968, Ultra and Wolf executed a Purchase Money Security Interest Conditional Sales Agreement (Security Interest Agreement) covering the sale of those two machines by Wolf to Ultra, and as a part of the outside financing arrangement, Wolf in consideration of the payment of $128,122.20 assigned the Security Interest Agreement to Bank. Bank's security interest was perfected by the filing of a Financing Statement on August 5, 1968.

In June, 1968, Ultra placed another order with Wolf for a similar machine, later identified as machine numbered 5934, under identical terms of testing and purchase as those for the purchase of the above numbered machines 5890 and 5910. The machine was delivered to Ultra on August 7, 1968, satisfactory testing was accomplished, outside financing obtained, and on October 23, 1968, Ultra and Wolf executed a similar Security Interest Agreement covering the sale of the machine numbered 5934 by Wolf to Ultra, and as a part of the outside financing arrangement, Wolf, for value received, assigned the Security Interest Agreement to C.I.T. Corporation. C.I.T. Corporation's security interest was perfected by the filing of a Financing Statement on October 30, 1968. On October 7, 1969, C.I.T. Corporation reassigned the Security Interest Agreement to Wolf when Ultra became bankrupt.

Issue

The priorities among the three security interests involved are determined by the application of § 9–312(4), which reads:

A purchase money security interest in collateral other than inventory has priority over a conflicting security interest in the same collateral *if the purchase money security interest is perfected at the time the debtor receives possession of the collateral or within 10 days thereafter. (Emphasis added)*.

The sole issue presented by the facts and the contention of the parties on appeal is: On what dates did Ultra become "the debtor [receiving] possession of the collateral [the three respective machines]" within the meaning of § 9–312(4)?

Discussion

Briefly stated, National contends that Ultra was its "debtor" in "possession of the collateral" at the moment it received physical delivery of the respective three machines, without regard to any agreement to the contrary between Wolf and Ultra as to the terms and conditions of the ultimate sale and purchase of the machines respectively; hence, the machines were within the grasp of the after-acquired property clause. Since the Security Interest Agreements held by Bank and Wolf were not perfected within ten days "thereafter" as commanded by § 9–312(4), they are unenforceable as against National's perfected security interest.

Bank and Wolf each contend that Ultra did not become their "debtor" in "possession of the collateral" (the three respective machines) until the terms and conditions of the proposed sales and the purchases thereof had been met and the Security Interest Agreement had been executed and delivered. We subscribe to that contention.

Section 9–105(1) of the Code provides:

(1) In this division unless the context otherwise requires:

(d) "Debtor" means the person who owes payment or other performance of the obligation secured * * *.

National urges that the term "debtor" as used in § 9–312(4) means the debtor under

its "conflicting security interest." Such an interpretation does violence to the clear language of the section, and such a thesis is inherently rejected under the rationale and holdings in [citation]. To us, the word "debtor" in § 9–312(4) means the debtor of the seller or holder of the "purchase money security interest in collateral" (the thing sold).

It is manifest that Ultra was not a "debtor" of Wolf and did not owe payment or other performance of the obligation secured unto Wolf until the moment of the execution and delivery of the Security Interest Agreements on July 31, 1968, and October 23, 1968, respectively. Suffice to say that prior to those dates, (a) Wolf held no definitive security interest in the machines which could be perfected by the filing of a Financing Statement, and (b) Ultra held no assignable legal interest in the machines which could fall into the grasp of National's after-acquired property security clause.

We hold that Ultra bacame the purchase money security interest "debtor [receiving] possession of the collateral [the three respective machines]" at the instant of the execution and delivery of the Security Interest Agreements, respectively, and not before; and, further, that since each of the Security Interest Agreements were timely perfected, the security interests of Wolf and Bank, respectively, are each prior and superior to the conflicting security interest held by National. [Citation.]

* * *

The record as a whole reveals good faith, above board, uninvolved commercial credit transactions, without any withholding on the part of or secret equities among the parties. National was in no way misled by any acts of Wolf or Bank giving rise to an estoppel, and National advanced no money or credit on the strength of Ultra's pre-Security Interest Agreement possession of the machines. Wolf was entitled to abide with the terms and conditions of the proposed sales and purchases of its machines and to perfect its ultimate

Security Interest Agreements in accordance with § 9–312(4).

Affirmed.

Priorities: Buyer in the
Ordinary Course of Business/
Where to File

EXCHANGE BANK OF OSCEOLA v. JARRETT

Supreme Court of Montana, 1979.
180 Mont. 33, 588 P.2d 1006.

SHEEHY, J.

Plaintiff appeals from an order entered by the District Court, Custer County, granting defendant's motion to dismiss for failure to state a claim upon which relief could be granted. We reverse.

The material facts are not in dispute. On September 8, 1976, Daniel F. Holland purchased a Michigan tractor-scraper through the Exchange Bank of Osceola (bank), located in Kissimmee, Florida. The bank retained a security interest in the tractor to insure full payment of the $13,000.00 purchase price. The bank took the necessary steps to perfect its security interest under Florida's Commercial Code.

On February 1, 1977, Daniel F. Holland, without plaintiff's permission and in violation of the security agreement, sold the tractor-scraper to C. B. and O. Equipment Co. of Council Bluffs, Iowa. C. B. and O., an Iowa merchant dealing in farm implements, transported the tractor-scraper from Florida to Council Bluffs, Iowa. The record shows that the tractor arrived in Iowa on February 7, 1977.

On February 21, 1977, defendant, a Montana contractor, purchased the tractor-scraper from C. B. and O. for a good and valuable consideration. Defendant took possession of the tractor-scraper on or about February 21, 1977 and returned to Montana. The record indicates the tractor-scraper arrived in Miles City, Montana on March 9, 1977.

On April 4, 1977 (within four months from the date the tractor arrived in Iowa) the bank filed a financing statement in Iowa, pursuant to Iowa Code § 9–401. Thereafter, plaintiff filed the same financing statement with the Montana Secretary of State.

When Daniel F. Holland defaulted on his obligation to the bank, the bank instituted this action in the District Court, Custer County, to foreclose its security interest.

On November 4, 1977, the District Court entered the following order, dismissing plaintiff's complaint:

*   *   *

The defendant's motion to dismiss is based upon the following factual premise: An Iowa dealer sold certain equipment to the defendant, a Montana resident. The equipment was supplied to the Iowa dealer by a Florida company, who had given plaintiff a security interest, which was filed in Florida. The security interest agreement of plaintiff was filed in Iowa after the Iowa dealer had sold and delivered the equipment to the Montana purchaser.

The Court agrees with defendant's contention that Sections 9–307(1), 1–201(9) and 2–403(2) control and gives the purchaser title free of the security agreement filed in Iowa.

It is Ordered that defendant's motion to dismiss be granted.

*   *   *

Judgment finalizing the dismissal was signed on November 29, 1977. This appeal followed.

The sole issue for our determination is whether Spencer Jarrett purchased the tractor-scraper "free of" or "subject to" the bank's security interest.

It is agreed that the bank perfected its security interest in the tractor-scraper by filing the financing statement required by [U.C.C.] § 9–302. The Uniform Commercial Code contemplates the continued perfection of a security interest if there has been no intervening period when it was unperfected. [U.C.C.] § 9–303. A perfected security interest is generally not destroyed by the sale, exchange or other disposition of the collateral:

(2) Except where this chapter otherwise provides, a security interest continues in collateral notwithstanding sale, exchange or other disposition thereof by the debtor unless his action was authorized by the secured party in the security agreement or otherwise, and also continues in any identifiable proceeds including collections received by the debtor. [U.C.C.] § 9–306(2).

Since Daniel Holland sold the tractor without plaintiff's permission and in violation of the security agreement, it is clear that C. B. and O. purchased the tractor-scraper "subject to" the bank's security interest.

When C. B. and O. transported the tractor from Florida to Iowa, the continued existence of the bank's security interest was contingent on the provisions of Iowa's Commercial Code. Iowa Code § 9–103, provides:

d. When collateral is brought into and kept in this state while subject to a security interest perfected under the law of the jurisdiction from which the collateral was removed, the security interest remains perfected, but if action is required by Part 3 of this Article to perfect the security interest,

i. if the action is not taken before the expiration of the period of perfection in the other jurisdiction or the end of four months after the collateral is brought into this state, whichever period first expires, the security interest becomes unperfected at the end of that period and is thereafter deemed to have been unperfected as against a person who became a purchaser after removal;

ii. *if the action is taken before the expiration of the period specified in subparagraph (i), the security interest continues perfected thereafter,*

The courts uniformly hold that Section 9–103 gives a secured party a four-month grace period during which his security interest is protected without any further action on his part. * * *

Applying the provisions of Iowa Code § 9–103 to our fact pattern, it is obvious that the bank's security interest was viable at the time defendant purchased the tractor-scraper from C. B. and O. Equipment Company. The bank fully complied with section 9–103 by filing its financing statement in Iowa on April 4, 1977, well within the four-month period. Therefore, plaintiff's security interest continued unless Article 9 provides otherwise.

Defendant contends that Iowa Code § 9–307 allowed him to purchase the tractor-scraper "free of" plaintiff's security interest. Section 9–307 provides:

Protection of buyers of goods. 1. A buyer in ordinary course of business (subsection 9 of Section 1–201) other than a person buying from products from a person engaged in farming operations takes free of a security interest *created by his seller* even though the security interest is perfected and even though the buyer knows of its existence.

In the present case, defendant Jarrett purchased in good faith and without knowledge that the sale to him was in violation of the bank's security interest. Defendant also purchased the tractor in the ordinary course from a person in the business of selling tractors, therefore, he was a "buyer in the ordinary course of business". Iowa Code § 1–201(9).

However, section 9–307 contains the further limitation that the security interest must be "created by his [defendant's] seller". This Court has never interpreted the "created by his seller" limitation. However, the landmark case in this area is *National Shawmut Bank of Boston v. Jones* [citation.]

Shawmut was a replevin action instituted to recover possession of a 1964 Dodge station wagon. The station wagon was originally purchased by a man named Robert Wever. To obtain the car, Wever had secured a loan from the plaintiff bank and had executed a security agreement using the car as collateral. Sometime thereafter, Wever traded or sold the wagon to a reputable dealer engaged in the business of selling new and used cars to the public. The dealer then sold the car to defendant. Neither the dealer nor the defendant knew of plaintiff's security interest.

While the defendant in Shawmut was obviously a "buyer in the ordinary course," the Court nonetheless allowed the bank to recover the automobile from him. The Shawmut Court held:

* * * defendant purchased in good faith without knowledge that the sale was in violation of the security interest of another and bought in the ordinary course from a person in the business of selling automobiles, he was a "buyer in the ordinary course of business" * * *. However, 9–307(1) permits him to take free only of "a security interest created by his seller". The security interest of the plaintiff was not created by * * * the defendant's seller, but by Wentworth Motor Co., Inc. *Defendant, therefore, does not take free of the plaintiff's security interest under this section.* [Citation.]

As in Shawmut, defendant's seller *did not* create plaintiff's security interest, therefore, defendant does not take the tractor "free of" plaintiff's security interest under Iowa Code § 9–307.

* * *

This Court recognizes that this is a harsh result, since the purchaser, on the date of purchase in Iowa, had no means to learn in Iowa that the property he purchased was subject to a security interest. It may be that legislative action is necessary to prevent such results in the future. Since we are bound by the enacted laws, and must give full faith and credit to the laws of our sister states, no other course is open to us here.

For the foregoing reasons, this cause is reversed and remanded to the District Court for further proceedings consistent with this decision.

Default

EGGEMAN v. WESTERN NATIONAL BANK

Supreme Court of Wyoming, 1979.
596 P.2d 318.

ROONEY, J.

This is an appeal from an order denying a motion of appellant-defendant to vacate a sheriff's sale of defendant's real and personal property, which was made pursuant to a foreclosure action brought by appellee-plaintiff. We will reverse and order vacation of the sale.

On January 15, 1973, defendant and his wife gave plaintiff a promissory note in the principal amount of $41,000, and they secured the debt by a mortgage on two adjoining tracts of land near Lovell. The two tracts were purchased at different times. On one was a building, which was used by defendant in his business, known as Lovell Machine. The other tract was vacant.

On April 25, 1975, defendant gave plaintiff another note in the principal amount of $8,625, which was secured by collateral described only as "inventory and accounts receivable" in the note, and as follows in the security agreement:

(a) All of debtor's inventory including all goods, merchandise, raw materials, goods in process, finished goods and all other tangible personal property now owned or hereafter acquired and held for sale or lease or furnished or to be furnished under contracts of service or used or consumed in debtor's business, * * * and in contract rights with respect thereto and proceeds of both. * * *

(b) All accounts, notes, drafts, chattel paper, acceptances and other forms of obligations and receivables now or hereafter received by or belonging to debtor for goods sold by it or for services rendered by it, all guaranties and securities thereof, hereinafter called the "receivables", all right, title and interest of debtor in the merchandise which gave rise thereto including the right of stoppage in transit, and all rights of debtor earned or yet to be earned under contracts to sell goods or render services and in the proceeds thereof, including all accounts receivable listed and described on Exhibit A attached hereto and by this reference made a part hereof.

There was no Exhibit A.

Defendant defaulted in payments on both notes, and plaintiff filed a complaint containing two claims for relief. One was against defendant for judgment on the balance due on the $8,625 note and requesting sale of the collateral in satisfaction thereof. The other was against defendant and his wife on the balance due on the $41,000 note and requesting sale of the mortgaged real property in satisfaction thereof. * * *

The judgment recited that "it appearing to the Court" that defendant and his wife "authorized" their counsel to stipulate to the entry of judgment in the amount of $42,197.04 against them, specifically: (1) in amount of $38,431.05 against defendant and his wife, and that the "premises covered by the mortgage * * * be decreed sold *according to law*; that the proceeds of the sale be brought into the Court and applied * * * [to] the amount due Plaintiff; and that Plaintiff have judgment *and execution* against the Defendants, and each of them, for any deficiency * * *"; and (2) in the amount of $3,765.99 against defendant, and that "the lien represented by the security agreement * * * be foreclosed; that the collateral listed in the security agreement be sold *under and pursuant to the judgment of this Court* and the proceeds of such sale be applied toward the satisfaction and payment of the lien"; and judgment for deficiency to be rendered against defendant. There was no reference to the disposition to be made of any amount received from the sale in excess of the debt.

* * *

A Notice of Foreclosure Sale of defendant's property was duly published. It read in part:

* * * on January 20, 1978, at 11:00 o'clock A.M., at the front door of the courthouse at Basin, Big Horn County, Wyoming, the Sheriff of Big Horn County will sell the above-described real property, inventory and accounts receivable or so much thereof as may be necessary to satisfy Plaintiff Western National Bank's judgment with interest and costs, to the highest bidder.

The two tracts of real property were described separately in this notice—as they were in the mortgage.

At the sale, both tracts of real property and the inventory and the accounts receivable

were offered only as a whole and in one group. They were sold in that fashion for the high bid of James T. Frost in the amount of $67,500.

* * *

The inventory and accounts receivable were never listed or itemized. A list of the items taken into Frost's possession was attached to an affidavit of defendant. Most of the items listed thereon were equipment and supplies rather than inventory and accounts receivable. The term "inventory" does not include "equipment." Section 9–109(2) and (4).

Defendant contends that the remedy taken by plaintiff with reference to the default of the $8,625 note and of the security agreement was not pursuant to law, and he contends that the sale of the real property was illegal inasmuch as each tract was not separately offered for bid. Plaintiff contends that the sale was proper as a *judicial* sale, wherein the several requirements of a sale by execution under a judgment are not applicable.

Sale of Inventory and Accounts Receivable

Under law, there are five principal remedies given to the secured party on default of the terms of a security agreement by the debtor. Since none of the remedies were properly used in this case, the sale of the personal property was not proper. The five remedies are:

1. Use of the real estate mortgage foreclosure procedures if the security agreement covers both real and personal property. [Section 9–501(4).] Although both real and personal property were involved in this action, the security agreement does not cover real property. Therefore, this remedy is not available to plaintiff.
2. With reference to accounts receivable, as here, collect the same from those obligated thereon. [Section 9–502(1).] Plaintiff did not choose to pursue this remedy.
3. Any special remedy provided in the security agreement. [Section 9–501(2).] This security agreement did not set forth any special remedy.

4. Take possession of the collateral without judicial process [Section 9–503] and either accept it in full satisfaction [Section 9–505(2)] or sell it. [Section 9–504(1).] The notice required for acceptance in full satisfaction was not here given. Here possession was not taken without judicial process, and the sale was made before plaintiff took possession. A sale under this remedy must be commercially reasonable. Section 9–504(3). This is the remedy most commonly used. The usual reasons for not using it are: (a) inability to secure peaceable possession of the collateral, and (b) desire to be able to proceed against assets of the debtor, other than the collateral. Plaintiff did not use this remedy.

5. Take a judgment on the underlying obligation, and proceed under the judgment. [Section 9–501(1).] This seems to be the remedy attempted in this case. The procedure for this remedy is not set out in the Uniform Commercial Code, i.e., § 1–101, et seq. The usual procedure for enforcement of judgments for money is set out in [Citation]. Usually the judgment is executed on by issuance of a writ of execution. The sheriff levies the writ upon the goods and chattels of the debtor, taking them actually or constructively into his possession. The various items levied upon are then identified and are subject to valuation and inspection. If necessary, the sheriff then holds an execution sale. Such procedure is anticipated by the Uniform Commercial Code. [Section 9–501(5).]

A writ of execution was not issued or levied in this case. The sheriff did not take possession of the goods, actually or constructively, and they were not otherwise specifically identified or evaluated. The usual execution and levy procedure was not followed.

But plaintiff contends that a judicial sale, as distinguished from an execution sale, was here held. A judicial sale is proper under the Code [Section 9–501(5)] and under the remedy here under discussion. However, the judicial sale attempted in this case was not properly mandated or conducted. Inasmuch as the property to be sold was not definitely or accurately described in the judgment and at the sale; inasmuch as it was not taken into the sheriff's possession prior to the sale or was not otherwise specifically identified or made subject to evaluation as to quantity and quality prior to the sale, a jurisdictional defect existed and the sale was void.

* * *

The judgment in this case only directed that the sale be "pursuant to judgment of this court." It did not prescribe the terms and mode of sale as is required for a fair and proper judicial sale.

The distinctive characteristics of a judicial sale are that it must be the result of a judicial proceeding; it must be based upon an order, decree, or judgment directing that the property be sold, as distinguished from a judicial assent to the sale of property under statutory provisions authorizing certain sales by fiduciaries; and it must be made by the court or by its direction upon the terms and in the mode provided by the decree or order, which of course must conform with any pertinent statutory provisions regulating judicial sales * * *.

* * *

A judicial sale cannot be held in a "grab bag" fashion. Such would not be commercially reasonable. All parties to the sale must have an opportunity to see and evaluate the goods being sold. [Citations.] The judgment can direct that the sale be held at the place where the items are located, or it can direct a time and place before the sale at which the items can be inspected. Some means must be provided by which the items to be sold can be identified specifically, or the items must be identified specifically and not generically in the judgment.

Since this judgment and the sale resulting therefrom were deficient in these respects, the sale of personal property was void and must be vacated.

* * *

Reversed and remanded.

PROBLEMS

1. A sells to B a refrigerator under a conditional sales contract for $600 payable in monthly installments of $30 for twenty months. The refrigerator is installed in the kitchen of B's apartment. There is no filing of any financing statement. Assume that after B has made the first three monthly payments:

(a) B moves from her apartment and sells the refrigerator in place to the new occupant for $350 cash. What are the rights of A?

(b) B is adjudicated bankrupt, and her trustee in bankruptcy claims the refrigerator. What are the rights of the parties?

2. On January 2, Burt asked Logan to loan him money "against my diamond ring." Logan agreed to do so if a credit check proved Burt to be solvent. To guard against intervening liens, Logan received permission to record his interest, and Burt and Logan signed a security agreement giving Logan an interest in the ring. Burt also signed a financing statement which Logan properly filed on January 3. On January 4, Burt borrowed money from Tillo pledging his ring to secure the debt. Tillo took possession of the ring and paid Burt the money on the same day. The next day, January 5, Logan received a favorable credit report on Burt and loaned him the money under the assumption that Burt still had the ring.

Who has priority, Logan or Tillo?

3. A takes a security interest in the equipment in X Store and files a financing statement claiming "equipment and all after-acquired equipment." B later sells X Store a cash register on conditional sale and (a) files nine days after X receives the register, or (b) files fifteen days after X receives the register. If X fails to pay both A and B and they foreclose their security interests, who has priority as to the cash register?

4. X Motor Company sells an automobile to A and retains a security interest in the automobile. The automobile is insured, and X is named beneficiary. The automobile is totally destroyed in an accident, and three days later A files a petition in bankruptcy. As between X and A's trustee in bankruptcy, who is entitled to the insurance proceeds?

5. On September 5, a widow who occasionally teaches piano and organ in her home, purchased an electric organ from M's music store for $4,800, trading in her old organ for $1,200 and promising in writing to pay the balance at $120 per month and granting to M a security interest in the property in terms consistent with and incorporating provisions of the UCC. A financing statement covering the transaction was also properly filled out and signed, and M properly filed it. W did not make the December or January payments, and M went to her home to collect the payments or take the organ. Finding no one home and the door unlocked, he went in and took the organ. Two hours later, T, a third party and the present occupant of the house who had purchased the organ for his own use, stormed into M's store demanding return of the organ, exhibiting a bill of sale from W to T dated December 15, listing the organ and other furnishings in the house.

(a) What are the rights of M, T, and W?

(b) Would your answer change if M did not file a financing statement? Why?

6. On May 1, A lends B $20,000 and receives from B his promissory note for this amount due in two years and takes a security interest in the machinery and equipment in B's factory. A proper financing statement is filed with respect to the security agreement. On August 1, upon A's request, B executes an addendum to the security agreement covering after-acquired machinery and equipment in B's factory. A second financing statement is filed covering the addendum. In September B acquires $5,000 worth of new equipment which he installs in his factory. In December C, a judgment creditor of B, causes an attachment to issue against the new equipment. What are the rights of the parties?

7. A bought a television set from B for her own personal use. B was out of conditional sales contracts and showed A a form B had executed with C, another consumer. A and B orally agreed to the terms of the form. A subsequently defaults on payment, and B seeks to repossess the television. Decision? Would the result differ if B had filed a financing statement?

8. A bought a television set for his own personal use from B. A properly signed a security agreement and paid B twenty-five dollars down as required by their agreement. B did not file, and subsequently A sells the television to C, A's neighbor, for $300 for C to use in her hotel lobby.

(a) When A fails to make the January and February payments, may B repossess the television from C?

(b) What if instead of A's selling the television set to C, a judgment creditor levied (sought possession) of the television? Who would prevail?

9. Jones bought a used car from the A-Herts Car Rental System, who regularly sold its used equipment at the end of its fiscal year. First National Bank of Roxboro had previously obtained a perfected security interest in the car based upon its financing of A-Herts' automobiles. Upon A-Herts failure to pay, First National is seeking to repossess the car from Jones. Decision?

10. On May 1, A purchased on credit a refrigerator for his own personal use from XYZ for $600 and gave XYZ a security interest in the refrigerator. On May 5, A borrowed $500 from the Friendly Finance Company and gave Friendly a security interest in the refrigerator. Friendly properly perfected its security interest by filing. On May 15, one of A's creditors obtained a judgment lien against A and properly recorded the lien. On May 20th, after A had failed to make her payment on the refrigerator, XYZ properly filed a financing statement. On May 30, A sold the refrigerator at a yard sale to one of his neighbors for $200. All are claiming priority to the refrigerator. Who will prevail? Why?

Chapter 38

SURETYSHIP

IT is common in many business transactions involving the extension of credit for the creditor to require that someone in addition to the debtor promise to fulfill the obligation. This promisor generally is known as a surety. Sureties are commonly used in contracts involving minors so that there is a party with full contractual capacity responsible for the obligations arising from the contract. Sureties are often used in *addition to* security to reduce further the risks involved in the extension of credit. Sureties are used *instead* of security interests when security is not available or use of a secured transaction is too expensive or inconvenient. Sureties are also frequently utilized by employers to protect against losses caused by defalcations of employees, as well as in construction contracts for commercial buildings to bond the performance of the contract. Similarly, it is commonly required by statute that many contracts for

work to be done for governmental entities have the added protection of a surety. Premiums for compensated sureties exceed $1 billion annually in the United States.

NATURE AND FORMATION

A **surety** promises to answer for the payment of a debt or the performance of a duty owed to one person (called the **creditor**) by another (the **principal debtor**) upon the *failure* of the principal debtor to make payment or otherwise perform the obligation. Thus, the suretyship relationship involves three parties—the principal debtor, the creditor, and the surety—and three contractual obligations, as illustrated by Figure 38-1. When there is more than one person bound for the same debt of a principal debtor they are **cosureties.**

The creditor's rights against the principal debtor are determined by the contract between them. The creditor may also realize upon any collateral securing the principal debtor's performance that the creditor or the surety holds. In addition, the creditor may proceed against the surety if the principal debtor defaults. If the surety is an **absolute surety,** then the creditor may hold the surety liable as soon as the principal debtor defaults. The creditor need *not* first proceed against the principal debtor. However, if the surety is a **conditional guarantor of collection** he is liable only upon the creditor's *first* exhausting his legal remedies against the principal debtor. Thus, a conditional guarantor of collection is liable if the creditor first obtains a judgment against the principal debtor and is unable to collect under the judgment.

A surety who is required to pay the creditor for the principal debtor's obligation is entitled to be **exonerated** (relieved of liability) and **reimbursed** by the principal debtor. In addition, the surety is **subrogated** to (assumes) the rights of the creditor and has a right of contribution from cosureties. See Figure 38-2. These rights of sureties are discussed more fully below.

Although in theory a distinction is drawn between a surety and a guarantor, the two terms are used almost synonymously in common usage. Strictly speaking, a **surety** is bound with the principal debtor as a primary obligor and usually, although not necessarily, on the same instrument, whereas the **guarantor** is separately or collaterally bound to pay if the principal debtor does not. For convenience, the term "surety" will be used to include both of these terms, as the rights and duties of a surety and a guarantor are almost indistinguishable.

See *United States v. Tilleraas.*

Types of Sureties

A suretyship arrangement is frequently used by creditors seeking to reduce the risk of default by their debtors. For example, PD, a closely held corporation, applies to C, a lending institution, for a loan. After scrutinizing the assets and financial prospects of PD, the lender refuses to extend credit unless S, the sole shareholder of PD, promises to repay the loan if PD does not. S agrees and C makes the loan. S's undertaking is that of a surety. Similarly, PD wishes to purchase goods on credit from C, the seller, who agrees to extend credit to PD only if he obtains an acceptable surety. S agrees to pay C for the goods if PD does not. S is a surety. In each of these examples, the effect of the surety's promise is to give the creditor recourse for payment against two persons—the principal debtor and the surety—instead of one, thereby reducing the creditor's risk of loss.

FIGURE 38-1   Suretyship Relationship

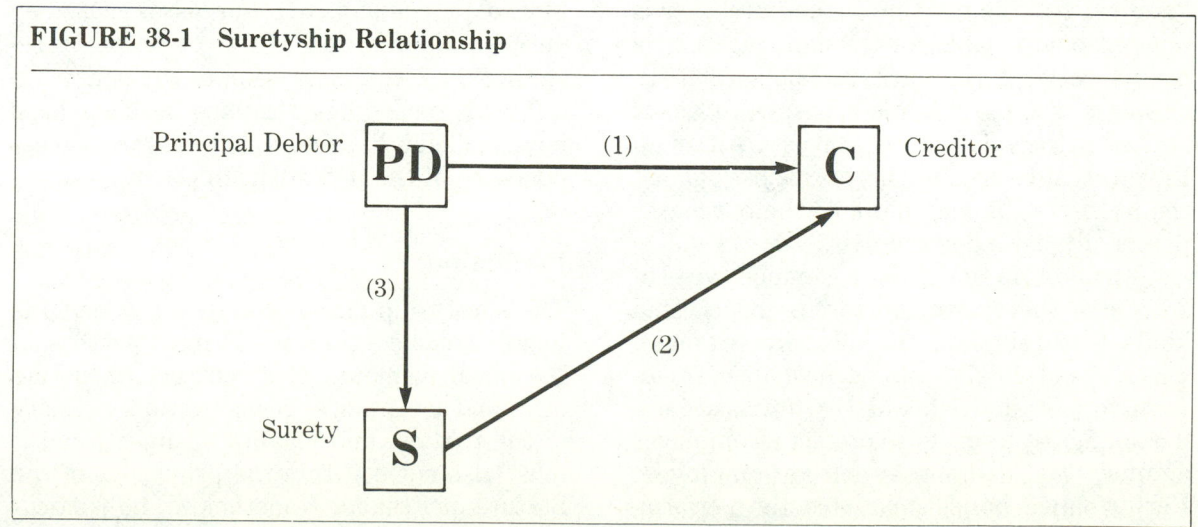

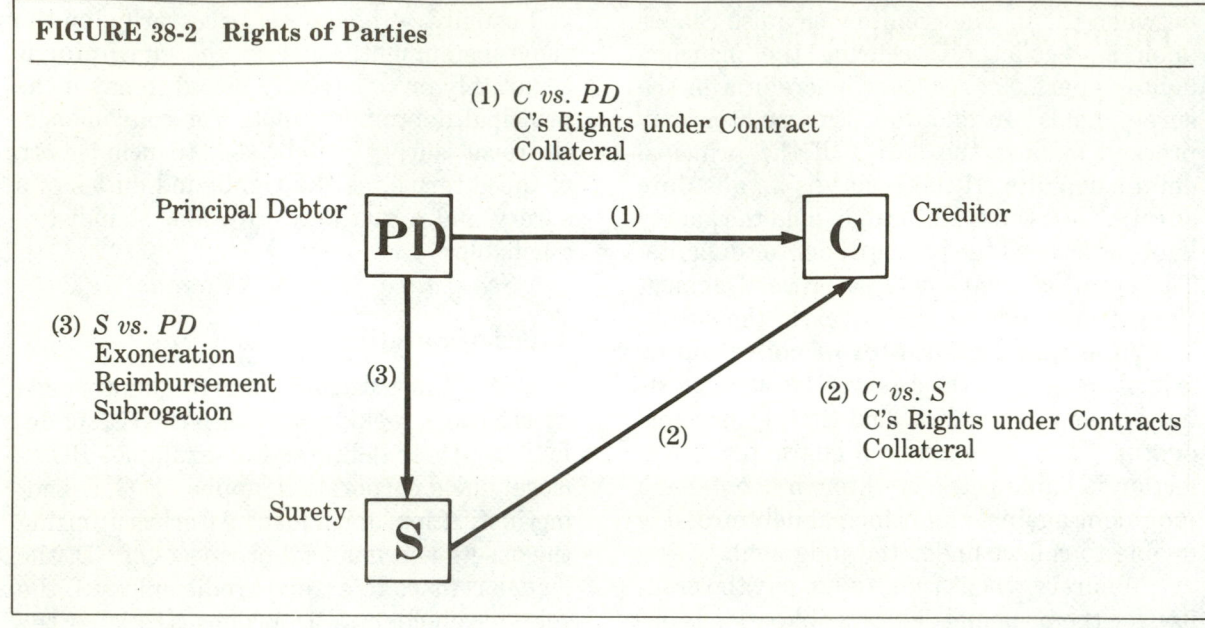

FIGURE 38-2   Rights of Parties

(1) *C vs. PD*
C's Rights under Contract
Collateral

Principal Debtor   **PD** → (1) → **C**   Creditor

(3) *S vs. PD*
Exoneration
Reimbursement
Subrogation

(3)

(2) *C vs. S*
C's Rights under Contracts
Collateral

(2)

Surety   **S**

Another common instance of a surety-ship relation arises when an owner of property subject to a mortgage sells the property to a purchaser who expressly **assumes the mortgage.** By assuming the obligation, the purchaser becomes the principal debtor and is personally obligated to pay the seller's debt to the lender. The seller nevertheless remains liable to the lender and is a surety on the obligation assumed by the purchaser. See Figure 38-3. If the purchaser does *not* assume the mortgage but simply takes the property **"subject to"** the mortgage, the purchaser is *not* personally liable for the mortgage nor is he a surety for the mortgage obligation. In this case, the purchaser's exposure to loss is limited to the value of the property. Although the mortgagee creditor may foreclose against the property, he may not hold the purchaser personally liable for the debt.

In addition to the more common types of sureties, there are numerous specialized kinds of suretyship, the most important of which are (1) fidelity, (2) performance, (3) official, and (4) judicial. **Fidelity bonds** are undertakings by a surety to protect an employer against the dishonesty of an employee. **Performance bonds** guarantee the perform-ance of the terms and conditions of a contract. These bonds are used frequently in the construction industry to protect the owner from losses that may result from the contractor's failure to perform the building contract. Statutes commonly require that a public officer furnish a bond for the faithful performance of her duties. Such bonds are called **official bonds** and obligate the surety for all losses caused by the officer's negligence or non-performance of her duties. **Judicial bonds** are provided on behalf of a party to a judicial proceedings to cover losses caused by delay or deprivation of use of property resulting from the institution of the action. In criminal proceedings, the purpose of a judicial bond, called a **bail bond,** is to assure the appearance of the defendant in court.

Formation

The suretyship and guaranty relationship is founded on a contract which must possess all the usual elements of a contract, including offer and acceptance, consideration, capacity of the parties, and legality of object, and it must also come within the provisions of the Statute of Frauds. Nonetheless, no particu-

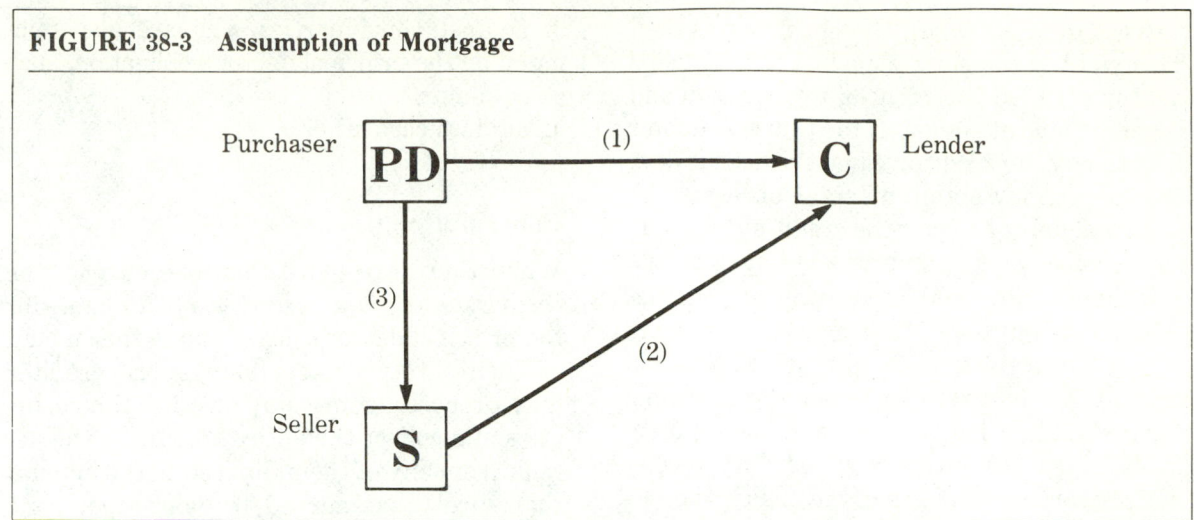

FIGURE 38-3   Assumption of Mortgage

lar words are required to constitute a contract of suretyship or guaranty.

As discussed in Chapter 13, the contractual promise of a surety to the creditor must be in writing to be enforceable under the **Statute of Frauds.** This requirement applies only to collateral promises and is subject to the exception called the *main purpose doctrine.* Under this doctrine, if the leading object of the promisor (surety) is to obtain an economic benefit which he did not previously enjoy, then the promise is *not* within the Statute of Frauds.

The promise of a surety is *not* binding without **consideration.** The surety's promise is usually supported by the same consideration that supports the principal debtor's promise because the surety's promise is generally made to induce the creditor to confer a benefit upon the principal debtor. Thus, if C lends money to PD upon S's promise to act as a surety, PD's extension of credit is the consideration to support not only PD's promise to repay the loan but also S's suretyship undertaking. However, if the surety's promise is made *subsequent* to the principal debtor's receipt of the creditor's consideration, the surety's promise must be supported by new consideration. Accordingly, if C has already sold goods on credit to PD, a subsequent

guaranty by S will not be binding unless new consideration is given.

RIGHTS OF SURETY

Upon the principal debtor's default, the surety has a number of rights against the principal debtor, third parties, and cosureties. These rights include (1) exoneration, (2) reimbursement, (3) subrogation, and (4) contribution. As discussed above, a surety or absolute guarantor has *no* right to compel the creditor to collect from the principal debtor or to realize upon collateral provided by the principal debtor. Unless the contract of suretyship provides otherwise, the creditor is *not* required to give the surety notice of the principal debtor's default. A conditional guarantor of collection, on the other hand, has the right that the creditor first sue the principal debtor and exhaust his legal remedies of collection before resorting to the surety.

Exoneration

The ordinary expectation in a suretyship relation is that the principal debtor will perform the obligation and the surety will therefore not be required to perform. Therefore, the surety has the right that his principal debtor pay the creditor when the obligation is due. This right of the surety against the principal debtor is called the right of exoneration and is enforceable at equity. If the principal debtor fails to pay the creditor when the debt is due, the surety may obtain a decree ordering the principal debtor to pay the creditor. The surety's remedy of exoneration is against the principal debtor and in no way affects the creditor's right to proceed against the surety.

A surety also has a right of exoneration against his cosureties. When the principal debtor's obligation becomes due, each surety owes every other cosurety the duty to pay her proportionate share of the principal debtor's obligation to the creditor. Accordingly, a surety may bring an action in equity against his cosureties for an order requiring them to pay their share.

Reimbursement

When a surety pays the creditor upon the default of the principal debtor, the surety has the right of reimbursement against the principal debtor. The surety, however, has no right to reimbursement until he actually has made payment, and then only to the extent of the payment. Thus, a surety, who makes an advantageous negotiation of a defaulted obligation and settles it at a compromise figure less than the original sum, may not recover from the principal debtor any more than he had to pay.

Subrogation

Upon the surety's payment of the principal debtor's *entire* obligation, the surety "steps into the shoes" of the creditor. This is called subrogation and confers upon the surety all the rights the creditor has against or through the principal debtor. These include the creditor's rights

1. against the principal debtor, including the creditor's priorities in a bankruptcy proceeding;
2. in security of the principal debtor;

3. against third parties who are also obligated on the principal debtor's obligation, such as co-makers; and
4. against cosureties.

Contribution

When there are more than one surety, the cosureties are *jointly and severally* liable for the principal debtor's default up to the amount of each surety's undertaking. The creditor may proceed against any or all of the cosureties and collect the entire amount of the default from any of them, limited to the amount that surety has agreed to guarantee. As a result, it is possible that one cosurety may pay the creditor the entire amount of the principal debtor's obligation.

When a surety pays her principal debtor's obligation, she is entitled to have her cosureties pay to her their proportionate share of the obligation paid. This right of contribution arises when a surety has paid more than her proportionate share of the debt even though the cosureties originally were not aware of each other or were bound on separate instruments. All that is required is that they are sureties for the same principal debtor and the same obligation. The right and extent of contribution can be determined by contractual agreement among the cosureties. In the absence of such agreement, sureties obligated for equal amounts share equally; where they are obligated for varying amounts, the proportion of the debt that each surety must contribute is determined by proration according to each surety's undertaking. For example, if X, Y, and Z are cosureties for PD to C in the amounts of $5,000, $10,000, and $15,000 respectively, then X's contributive share is one-sixth $\left(\dfrac{\$5,000}{\$5,000+\$10,000+\$15,000}\right)$, Y's share is one-third $\left(\dfrac{\$10,000}{\$30,000}\right)$, and Z's share is one-half $\left(\dfrac{\$15,000}{\$30,000}\right)$.

See Collins v. Throckmorton.

DEFENSES OF SURETY

The obligations owed to the creditor by the principal debtor and the surety both arise out of contracts. Accordingly, the usual contractual defenses are applicable, such of those which result from (1) the non-existence of the principal debtor's obligation, (2) a discharge of the principal debtor's obligation, (3) a modification of the principal debtor's contract, or (4) a variation of the surety's risk. Some of these defenses are available only to the principal debtor, some only to the surety, while others are available to both parties. See Figure 38-4.

Personal Defenses of Principal Debtor

Some defenses that a principal debtor may assert against the creditor are available *only*

to him and thus are called personal defenses of the principal debtor. The principal debtor's **incapacity** due to infancy or mental incompetency is a defense for the principal debtor but may *not* be used by the surety. However, if the principal debtor disaffirms the contract *and* returns the consideration he received from the creditor, then the surety is discharged from his liability. A discharge of the principal debtor's obligation in **bankruptcy** also does not discharge the surety's liability to the creditor on that obligation. In addition, the surety may not use as a **set-off** any claim that the principal debtor has against the creditor.

Personal Defenses of Surety

Those defenses that only the surety may assert are called personal defenses of the sur-

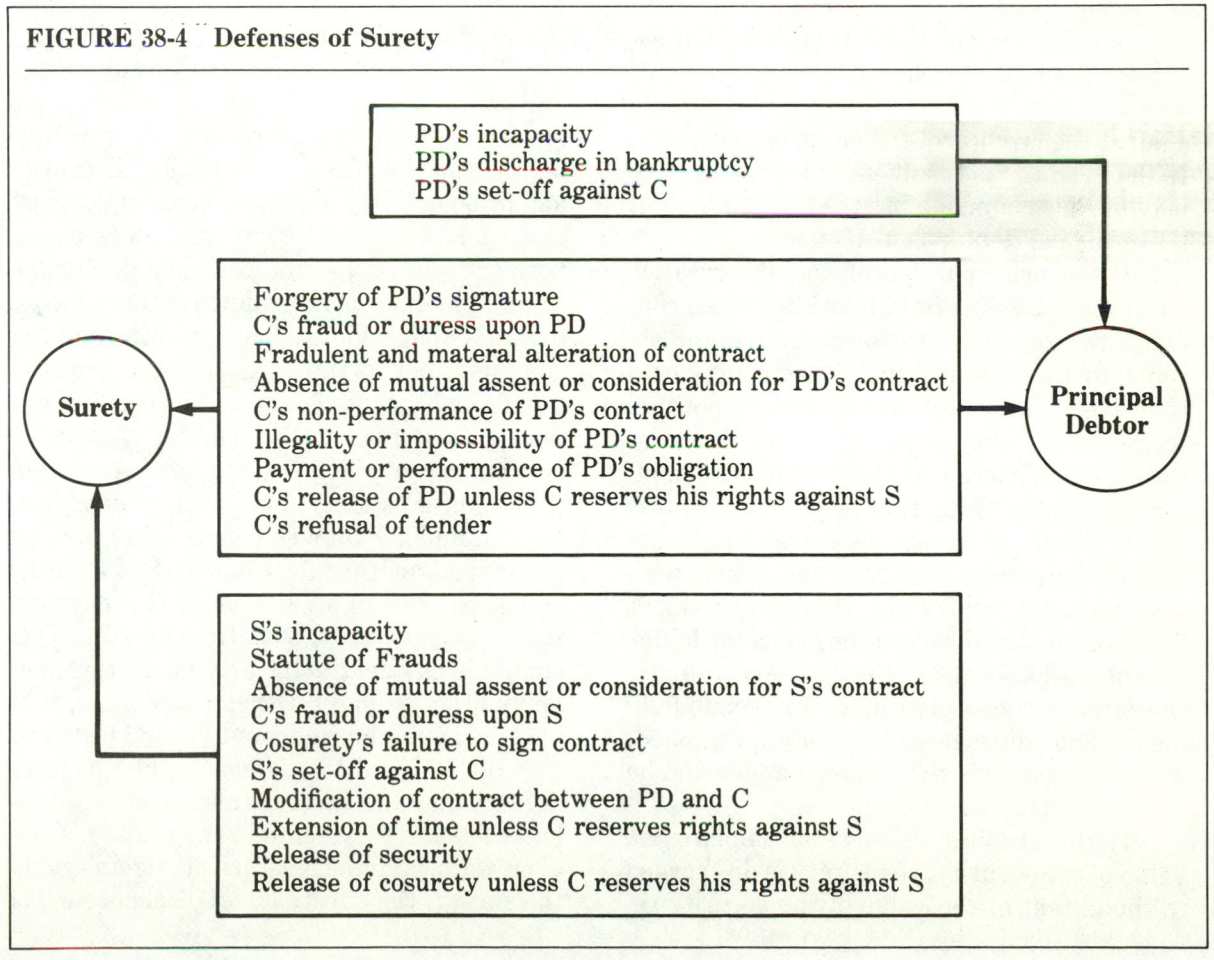

FIGURE 38-4   Defenses of Surety

PD's incapacity
PD's discharge in bankruptcy
PD's set-off against C

Forgery of PD's signature
C's fraud or duress upon PD
Fradulent and materal alteration of contract
Absence of mutual assent or consideration for PD's contract
C's non-performance of PD's contract
Illegality or impossibility of PD's contract
Payment or performance of PD's obligation
C's release of PD unless C reserves his rights against S
C's refusal of tender

Surety   **Principal Debtor**

S's incapacity
Statute of Frauds
Absence of mutual assent or consideration for S's contract
C's fraud or duress upon S
Cosurety's failure to sign contract
S's set-off against C
Modification of contract between PD and C
Extension of time unless C reserves rights against S
Release of security
Release of cosurety unless C reserves his rights against S

ety. The surety may use his own **incapacity** as a defense as well as assert non-compliance with the **Statute of Frauds** or the absence of mutual assent and/or consideration. **Fraud** or **duress** practiced by the creditor upon the surety is a defense for the surety. Although, as a general rule, non-disclosure of material facts by the creditor to the surety is not fraud, there are two important exceptions. If the prospective surety requests information, the creditor must disclose it, and concealment of material facts will constitute fraud. Second, if the creditor knows, or should know, that the surety is being deceived, the creditor is under a duty to disclose, and non-disclosure is considered fraud upon the surety. Fraud on the part of the principal debtor may *not* be asserted against the creditor if the creditor is unaware of the fraud. Similarly, duress exerted by the principal debtor upon the surety is not a defense against the creditor.

A surety is not liable if an intended cosurety, as shown by the contract instrument, does not sign. A surety may set off his claims against the creditor if the creditor is solvent. If the creditor is insolvent, then the surety may use his claim against the creditor only if the principal debtor is also insolvent.

If the principal debtor and the creditor enter into a binding **modification** of their contract, the surety is discharged unless he assents to the modification. Most courts hold that even a modification which does not materially affect the surety's risk will discharge the surety. This rule applies to valid and binding extensions of the time of payment *unless* the creditor expressly reserves his rights against the surety. An extension of time with reservation is construed as only an agreement by the creditor not to sue the principal debtor for the period of the extension. Accordingly, the surety's rights of exoneration, reimbursement, and subrogation are *not* postponed. Thus, the surety's risk is not changed and he is not discharged.

If the creditor releases or impairs the value of the security, the surety is discharged to the extent of the value of the security re-

leased or impaired. Similarly, if the creditor releases a cosurety, the other cosureties are discharged to the extent of the contributive share of the surety released. However, if the creditor reserves his rights against the remaining cosureties, the release is considered a promise not to sue. As a result, the remaining cosureties are not discharged.

Defenses of Both Surety and Principal Debtor

A number of defenses are available to both the surety and the principal debtor. Where the principal debtor's signature on an instrument is **forged** or the creditor has exerted **fraud** or **duress** upon the principal debtor, both the principal debtor and the surety are not liable. Likewise, if the contract instrument is fraudulently and **materially altered** by the creditor, both the principal debtor and the surety are discharged.

The absence of mutual assent or consideration to support the principal debtor's obligation is a defense for both the principal debtor and the surety. In addition, **illegality** and **impossibility** of performance of the principal debtor's contract are also defenses to both the surety and the principal debtor.

Payment or **performance** of the principal debtor's obligation discharges both the principal debtor and the surety. If the principal debtor owes several debts to the creditor and makes a payment to the creditor without directions as to which debt to apply payment, the creditor is free to apply it to any debt. For example, PD owes C two debts, one for $5,000 and another for $10,000. S is a surety on the $10,000 debt. PD sends C a payment in the amount of $3,500. If PD directs C to apply the payment to the $10,000 debt, C must apply it accordingly. Otherwise C may, if he pleases, apply the payment to the $5,000 debt.

If the creditor releases the principal debtor, then the surety is also discharged unless the surety consents to the release. However, if the creditor reserves his rights against the surety, the surety is *not* discharged. The release with reservation is construed as a promise not to sue which leaves the surety's rights against the principal debtor unimpaired. Therefore, the surety is not discharged. This rule has been well explained in *Dean v. Rice*, 63 Kan. 691, 66 P. 992 (1901):

As a general rule an agreement between the creditor and principal for an extension of time to the principal in which to pay the debt, without the knowledge or consent of the surety will operate as a release of the surety. An important exception to the rule is that if the creditor, at the time of the extension, reserves his remedies against the surety the latter will not be discharged from liability.

The principal reason for the release of sureties in such cases is that the postponement of payment varies the contract relation and deprives the surety of the right to pay the debt when it becomes due and to have the immediate recourse on the principal. When a creditor ties his own hands and grants an indulgence which prevents a surety from obtaining that indemnity against a principal which the law gives him, the surety is necessarily prejudiced and should be released. If, however, a creditor explicitly reserves all remedies against the surety, it rebuts the presumption of a purpose to release the surety, and, in effect, it is an agreement between creditor and principal that the creditor may sue the surety, who in turn may then proceed against the principal. If the surety is not deprived of the protection and indemnity which the law affords him against a principal he is not prejudiced and is not entitled to be released from the obligation which he has undertaken.

The creditor's release or impairment of collateral of the principal debtor releases the surety to the extent of the value of the security released or impaired. This rule protects the surety's right of subrogation. *See Langeveld v. L.R.Z.H. Corp.*

The creditor's refusal to accept tender of payment or performance by either the principal debtor or the surety completely discharges the surety. However, tender of payment by the principal debtor refused by the creditor does *not* discharge the principal debtor. The effect of such refusal is to stop further accrual of interest on the debt and to deprive the creditor of court costs on a subsequent suit by him to recover the amount due.

CASES

Nature and Formation

UNITED STATES v. TILLERAAS

United States Court of Appeals, Sixth Circuit, 1983.
709 F.2d 1088.

WELLFORD, J.

Defendant-appellant, Elizabeth Tilleraas, applied for and received three student loans totalling $3,500.00 under the Federal Insured Student Loan Program (FISLP) of the Higher Education Act of 1965, 20 U.S.C. § 1071, *et seq*. These loans were secured by three promissory notes executed, respectively, on September 4, 1969, June 18, 1970, and October 5, 1970, in favor of Dakota National Bank & Trust Co., Fargo, North Dakota. Under terms of these student loans, periodic payments were required commencing twelve months after Tilleraas ceased to carry at least one-half of a full-time academic workload at an eligible institution. 20 U.S.C. § 1077(a)(2)(B). Her student status terminated on January 28, 1971, and the first installment payment thus became due January 28, 1972. Appellant never made any payment on any of her loans. The United States insured to the lender bank the repayment in event of any failure to pay by the borrower under the terms of the FISLP.

Under 20 U.S.C. § 1080(e)(2)(B), it is provided:

the term "default" includes only such defaults as have existed for . . .

(B) one hundred eighty days in the case of a loan which is repayable in less frequent [than monthly] installments.

The first payment due on the loans was in "default" within the meaning of the law on or about July 27, 1972, one hundred and eighty days after the failure to make the first installment payment had continued to exist. It was not until December 17, 1973, that the Dakota National Bank sent notice of its election under the provisions of the loan to accelerate the maturity of the note. The Bank demanded payment in full of the full principal due by December 27, 1973. It then filed FISLP insurance claims against the United States on May 6, 1974, and assigned the three Tilleraas notes to the United States on May 10, 1974. The government, in turn, paid the Bank's claim in full on July 5, 1974. It was not until June 4, 1980, that the appellee government filed suit in Cleveland, Ohio, against the original borrower-recipient of this largess intended to assist students in obtaining a higher education.

The government's suit was met in the trial court by defendant-appellant's motion for a summary judgment based on her contention that the action of the United States was barred by the six year statute of limitations set forth in 28 U.S.C. § 2514(a). The complaint in the cause alleged that the government paid the Bank's insurance claim and was assigned title to the notes after default on the loan and payment by the government pursuant to 45 C.F.R. § 177.48.

* * *

* * * The government argues, however, that it is not limited to assignee status, since it may also rely on its common law right as a surety to bring an action against the principal for reimbursement. Since a surety's or guarantor's cause of action for indemnity does not accrue until payment of the principal's liability [citations], the government claims that it *also* has a cause of action which accrued on the date it paid the lender, July 6, 1974, a cause which was timely when this action was filed.

* * *

The use of the word "insurance" in the statute is not determinative in light of the realities existing between the relevant parties. The nature of the substantive rights and duties among the parties clearly reflects a surety-principal-lender relationship. Insurance is a contract where one undertakes to indemnify another against loss, damage or liability caused by an unknown or contingent event. Since the insured pays the insurer for the promise of indemnity, the insurer benefits to the extent that a contingency never occurs. Where a contingency does occur, the insurer can still be made whole, by virtue of subrogation, to the extent that the insured would be able to recover damages from a third party. Despite the presence of this right of subrogation it is clear that *when the contract is formed* all legal rights and obligations flow between the insurer and the insured. At this initial stage, there is no legal obligation owing from the third party to the insurer. In fact, it is unknown at that stage whether such a third party obligation will ever arise and, if so, who that third party will be.

A surety, on the other hand, promises to assume the responsibility for the payment of a debt incurred by another should he or she fail to repay the creditor. The arrangement is made to induce the creditor to deal with the borrower where there might otherwise be a reluctance to do so. Under this arrangement, the nature, size, and source of the possible loss to the creditor is known from the start. In additon, there is no payment from the creditor to the surety or guarantor for this "insured" payment. Rather, a kind of tripartite relationship is formed. The consideration running from the creditor to the debtor is deemed sufficient to support the surety's promise to make the debt good. In turn, the benefit flowing to the debtor by virtue of the surety's promise places that debtor under an implied legal obligation to make good any loss incurred by any payment the surety must ultimately make to the creditor. [Citation.] It is clear then that the two contracts are materially distinguishable, as are the rights and duties of the parties involved. [Citations.]

Under the FISLP the student contracts to borrow money with no collateral and upon favorable interest and repayment terms. The lender, in turn, contracts with the Department of Education to insure repayment should the student default. This has consistently been interpreted as creating a third-party surety contract, despite its nomenclature. [Citations.] The only possible "contingency" from which the government protects the lending institution is the possibility that the named student (in this case Tilleraas) may ultimately default on all or part of the designated loan amount. The interdependencies between the three parties, in this case the Dakota National Bank & Trust Co., Tilleraas, and the United States government, "are a situational adaptation of long-recognized principles of guaranty." [Citation.] At common law the nature of the relationship would have undoubtedly given rise to an implied obligation on the part of Tilleraas to make good the loss incurred by the government when forced to satisfy her debt, a loss arising when the monies were paid to the Dakota National Bank & Trust Co.

The courts which have found a surety relationship in the student loan program have, either explicitly or impliedly, determined that § 1080(b) did not prevent the government from enforcing its rights at common law. Changes in or abrogation of the common law must be clearly expressed by the legislature. [Citations.] Even where such an intention is explicit, the scope of the common law will be altered no further than is necessary to give effect to the language of the statute. [Citations.] Where the issue raised is whether or not a given statutory provision is intended to abrogate the common law rights of the government, the presumption against such a reading of the statute is even stronger. The

conclusion that the sovereign is to be denied rights which the realities of the relationship would otherwise allow it to exercise is only justified where the language of, and clear implications from, the statute itself command such a construction. [Citations.]

* * *

We conclude, therefore, that the United States in this instance stands in the position of a surety-guarantor, and therefore it may pursue its rights as a surety under FISLP. As pointed out, it was not until July of 1974 that the government paid the Bank's claim and obtained its right to sue the defaulting appellant on the underlying loan. Under the realities of the FISLP, the government is a surety of the borrower and is entitled to its rights as such. This is the position supported by the other Courts of Appeals that have considered the same issue under this law. [Citations.]

* * *

Accordingly, we affirm the thoughtful decision of the district court, concluding that the United States, as surety-guarantor, has six years after paying a claim under FISLP in which to institute suit against a defaulting borrower.

Right of Contribution

COLLINS v. THROCKMORTON

Supreme Court of Delaware, 1980.
425 A.2d 146.

McNEILLY, J.

The defendants below appeal from a money judgment for the plaintiff entered by the Superior Court after a non-jury trial. The basic facts underlying the controversy are as follows:

Plaintiff Philip Throckmorton and defendant Robert Collins were the sole stockholders (as well as the officers and directors) in Central Ceilings, Inc. (hereinafter referred to as "Central"). On March 26, 1973, Central borrowed $10,000 from the Wilmington Trust

Company ("the bank"); a demand note therefor was executed by the corporate officers. On the back of the note, the plaintiff, his wife and the defendants (then husband and wife) signed a provision unconditionally guaranteeing payment of the note on behalf of Central. Subsequent to this transaction, relations between Mr. Throckmorton and Mr. Collins deteriorated to the point where, in August, 1973, Mr. Collins left the employ of Central and ceased to be actively involved in the management of the company. Although the Central stockholders discussed terms whereby Mr. Collins was to completely sever his relationship with the company, no agreement was ever reached.

After Mr. Collins' departure from Central, the plaintiff continued to operate the business. However, by Mid-1975, Central had become insolvent and simply ceased to do business. The record clearly shows that Central's financial woes, particularly certain problems with the Internal Revenue Service, began before Mr. Collins' departure from the company and continued more or less unabated until the company went out of business.

Apparently Central made no payments on the demand note after 1973. By May, 1975, the bank had become sufficiently concerned about Central's ability to pay the note to institute certain protective actions. Central's assets on deposit with the bank were frozen and demand made on the Throckmortons to satisfy various debts owed by Central to the bank, including the balance on the 1973 note which they and the defendants had guaranteed. On May 30, 1975, pursuant to negotiations between the Throckmortons and the bank, the plaintiff and his wife took out a loan in the amount of $15,402. All of these proceeds were used to satisfy Central's debts to the bank. Of the total, $9,668.73 was paid to satisfy the 1973 note, *i.e.*, $8,800 in unpaid principal plus $868.73 in interest at eight and three-quarters percent per year as specified in the note. In return, the bank assigned its rights under the 1973 note to the plaintiff, individually.

On June 4, 1975, the plaintiff demanded that the defendants reimburse him in full for the amounts he paid in satisfaction of the 1973 note; the defendants refused. The plaintiff subsequently, in his complaint and at trial, reduced his claims against each defendant to one-quarter of the amounts thus paid by him. The Superior court entered judgment against each defendant in the amount of $3,492.86 allocated as follows: $2,417.18 representing the proportionate one-quarter share of each defendant on the demand note as paid by the plaintiff on May 30, 1975; $909.35 representing interest on such proportionate shares at the rate of eight and three-quarters percent per year from June 15, 1975 to November 1, 1979 (the Trial Court order was entered in November, 1979); and $166.33 representing awards of attorney fees at the rate of five percent of the amounts otherwise assessed against each defendant.

* * *

In order to understand the defendants' * * * argument, it is necessary to state the general rule governing contribution rights among co-guarantors. The Restatement of the Law of Security, *supra*, § 154 provides in pertinent part:

(1) A surety who has discharged more than his proportionate share of the principal's duty is entitled to contribution from a co-surety.

(a) who has consented to the surety's becoming bound, in the proportionate amount of the net outlay property expended . . . . .

[Citations.]

The undisputed facts show that the 1973 note was guaranteed by four persons. Consequently, each was potentially liable for one-quarter of Central's default on the note. See Restatement of the Law of Restitution § 85, Comment (e) (1937). Although the complaint alleged the plaintiff personally satisfied Central's default by paying the entirety of the principal and interest owed on the note in May, 1975, the defendants argue that the trial proofs show that the plaintiff's wife, the fourth co-guarantor, contributed equally with the plaintiff to this satisfaction. Thus, of the $9,668.73 paid to satisfy the 1973 note, the defendants claim the plaintiff contributed only half ($4,834.36). Of that amount the plaintiff was personally liable for half, which constituted one-quarter of Central's total default ($2,417.18). Thus argue the defendants, the maximum amount of contribution which the plaintiff could recover from the two defendants was $2,417.18, *i.e.* the amount in excess of his share of Central's default which the plaintiff personally paid to satisfy the 1973 note. Therefore, the defendants argue that the Trial Court's decision, which was premised on the assumption that the plaintiff satisfied the entire default by Central (or at least three-quarters thereof), erroneously awarded judgment against each defendant in the amount of $2,417.18, double the excess amount which the plaintiff allegedly paid in satisfaction of the note and, thus, double the total amount of contribution which he was entitled to recover from the defendants collectively.

* * *

Even considering the evidentiary aspect of the argument on the merits, we are not persuaded that the defendants are entitled to appellate relief. Although there was no direct testimony concerning the respective amounts which the plaintiff and his wife contributed to satisfaction of the 1973 note, the bank's assignment of the note to the plaintiff, individually, gives rise to a reasonable inference that, as between the plaintiff and his wife, the plaintiff alone was entitled to seek contribution from the defendants. While it would obviously be desirable to have a more detailed and explicit factual record on this point, the failure to so develop the record must be laid at the defendants' doorstep. Therefore, we will not disturb that portion of the Trial Court's judgment which requires each defendant to pay the plaintiff $2,417.18 for their contributive shares on the demand note as satisfied.

* * *

In conclusion, we modify the judgment below to eliminate the awards of interest and attorney fees, and we affirm the judgment as so modified.

AFFIRMED, as modified.

Defenses

LANGEVELD v. L.R.Z.H. CORP.

Supreme Court of New Jersey, 1977.
74 N.J. 45, 376 A.2d 931.

MOUNTAIN, J.

[On March 10, 1972, L.R.Z.H. Corporation made and delivered to plaintiff, Langeveld, its promissory note in the sum of $57,500. The indebtedness evidenced by the note was secured by a mortgage in the same amount on real property owned by the corporation. By an instrument of guaranty set forth at the bottom of the note, the defendant, Higgins, guaranteed performance of all obligations of the corporation under the note. The note became due on February 15, 1973 and was not paid. At this time Higgins discovered that Langeveld had never recorded the mortgage securing the note. Langeveld then recorded the mortgage on March 1, 1973. In the intervening year between execution of the mortgage and recordation, another mortgage and two liens in substantial amounts had been filed. When Langeveld instituted suit against Higgins on the guaranty. Higgins defended on the ground that the creditor, Langeveld, owed a duty to him as surety for the debt to protect the security and allow nothing to occur to impair its value. Higgins argued that he should be released from all liability on his guaranty because Langeveld failed to fulfill this duty.]

* * *

On March 8, 1973 plaintiff instituted this suit on the guaranty. In defense of the claim thus asserted against him, defendant pointed out that there existed here the tripartite arrangement typical of a suretyship relationship. L.R.Z.H. Corporation was principal debtor. Plaintiff was its creditor; defendant stood in the position of a guarantor or surety. He further called attention to the fact that plaintiff, as such creditor, held the mortgage from L.R.Z.H. Corporation as collateral security for the corporate obligation and that it owed a duty to him, as surety for the same debt, to protect this security and allow nothing to occur to impair its value and worth that reasonable effort and foresight on plaintiff's part could prevent or avoid. Failure to record the mortgage for about a year, predictably followed by the intervention of recorded liens in substantial amounts, constituted, he argued, a failure on plaintiff's part to fulfill this duty. Accordingly, concluded defendant, he should be *released from all liability* on his guaranty.

* * *

It is a well-recognized principle of the law of suretyship that a release of collateral held by a creditor, or its impairment by improper action or inaction on his part, will extinguish the obligation of the surety, at least to the extent of the value of the security released or impaired. This rule has come to be accepted as the law of our State. [Citations.]
* * *

The doctrine is an equitable one, designed to protect the surety's right of subrogation. Upon paying the debt, the surety is, as a matter of law, subrogated to all the creditor's rights against the principal debtor and is entitled to all benefits derivable from any security of the principal debtor that may be in the creditor's hands. The rule forbidding impairment of collateral has as its chief aim the protection of these potential benefits made available through subrogation.

Defendant has made out a prima facie case to support his contention that he comes within the favor of the rule. * * * A failure to record a mortgage held as collateral security—absent waiver, estoppel, or the like—seems clearly to be an instance of unjustifiable impairment. Common law authorities so held, almost without exception. [Citations.]

* * *

The point is that defendant appears to have been deprived of the opportunity effectively to exploit his right of subrogation to unimpaired collateral by the failure of plaintiff to record the mortgage given him by L.R.Z.H. Corporation.

* * *

* * * If the impairment of collateral can be measured in monetary terms, then the calculated amount of the impairment will ordinarily measure the extent of the surety's discharge. But there are factual situations—this may or may not be one of them—where a surety may be able to establish that he has sustained prejudice, but be unable to measure the extent of the prejudice in terms of monetary loss. Where such a situation is presented the surety will normally be completely discharged.

* * * The effect of the impairment upon one secondarily liable may or may not be translatable into dollars. There may be clear prejudice without precisely calculable loss. This will normally result in the discharge of the surety. To the extent that such impairment is found, defendant Higgins will stand discharged of his obligation as guarantor.

[Judgment for Higgins.]

PROBLEMS

1. Allen, Barker, and Cooper are cosureties on a $750,000 loan by Durham National Bank to Kingston Manufacturing Co., Inc. The maximum liability of the sureties is as follows: Allen—$750,000, Barker—$300,000, and Cooper—$150,000. If Kingston defaults on the entire $750,000 loan, what is the liability of Allen, Barker, and Cooper?

2. Peter Diamond owes Carter $500,000 secured by a first mortgage on Diamond's plant and land. Stephens is a surety on this obligation in the amount of $250,000. After Diamond defaulted on the debt, Carter made demand upon and received payment of $250,000 from Stephens. Carter then foreclosed upon the mortgage and sold the property for

$375,000. What rights, if any, does Stephens have in the proceeds from the sale of the property?

3. Adams sold his house to Baldwin for $80,000 with Baldwin expressly assuming a mortgage held by Evans on the property in the amount of $60,000. The property has a fair market value of $140,000. Sixth months later Baldwin defaulted in his payments to Evans on the mortgage.

    (a) What are Evans' rights, if any, against Baldwin?

    (b) What are Evans' rights, if any, against Adams?

    (c) What are Adams' rights, if any, against Baldwin?

4. Paula Daniels purchased an automobile from Carey on credit. At the time of the sale Scott agreed to be a surety for Paula, who is sixteen years old. The automobile's odometer stated 52,000 miles but Carey had turned it back from 72,000 miles. Paula refuses to make any payments due on the car. Carey proceeds against Paula and Scott. What defenses, if any, are available to (a) Paula and (b) Scott?

5. Stafford Surety Co. agreed to act as the conditional guarantor of collection on a debt owed by Preston Decker to Cole. Stafford was paid a premium by Preston to serve as surety. Preston defaults on the obligation. What are Cole's rights against Stafford Surety Co?

6. Campbell loaned Perry Dixon $7,000 which was secured by a possessory security interest in stock owned by Perry. The stock had a market value of $4,000. In addition, Campbell insisted that Perry obtain a surety. For a premium, Sutton Surety Co. agreed to act as a surety for the full amount of the loan. Prior to the due date of the loan Perry convinced Campbell to return the stock because its value had increased and he wished to sell it in order to realize the gain. Campbell released the stock and Perry subsequently defaulted. Campbell proceeds against Sutton. Decision?

7. Pamela Darden owed Clark $5,000 on an unsecured loan. On May 1, Pamela approached Clark for an additional loan of $3,000. Clark agreed to make the loan only if Pamela could obtain a surety. On May 5, Simpson agreed to be a surety on the $3,000 loan which was granted that day. Both loans were due on October 1. On June 15, Pamela sent $1,000 to Clark but did not provide any instructions.

    (a) What are Clark's rights?

    (b) What are Simpson's rights?

8. Patrick Dillon applied for a $10,000 loan from Carlton Savings & Loan. Carlton required him to obtain a surety. Patrick approached Sinclair Surety Co. which insisted that Patrick provide it with a financial statement. Patrick did so but the statement was materially false. In reliance upon the financial statement and in return for a premium, Sinclair agreed to act as surety. Upon Sinclair's commitment to act as surety Carlton loaned Patrick the $10,000. After one payment of $400 Patrick defaulted. Patrick then filed a voluntary petition in bankruptcy. Carlton proceeds against Sinclair. Decision?

9. On June 1, Smith contracted with Martin d/b/a Martin Publishing Company to distribute Martin's newspapers and to account for the proceeds. As part of the contract Smith agreed to furnish Martin a bond in the amount of $10,000 guaranteeing the payment of the proceeds. At the time the contract was executed and the credit extended the bond was not furnished and no mention was made as to the prospective sureties. On July 1, Smith signed the bond with Black and Blue signing as sureties. The bond recited the awarding of the contract for distribution of the newspapers as consideration for the bond.

    On December 1, there was due from Smith to Martin the sum of $3,600 under the distributor's contract. Demand for payment was made but Smith failed to make payment. As a result, Martin brought an appropriate action against Black and Blue to recover the $3,600.

    What decision?

10. Diggitt Construction Company was the low bidder on a well digging job for the Village of Drytown. On April 15, Diggitt signed a contract with Drytown for the job at a price of $40,000. At the same time, pursuant to the notice of bidding, Diggitt prevailed upon Ace Surety Company to execute a performance bond indemnifying Drytown on the contract. On May 1, after having put in three days on the job, the president of Diggitt refigured his bid and realized that if his company were to complete the job it would lose $10,000. Accordingly, Diggitt notified Drytown that it was cancelling the contract, effective immediately. What are the rights and duties of Ace Surety Company?

Chapter 39

BANKRUPTCY AND RELIEF OF DEBTORS

A debt is an obligation to pay money owing by a person referred to as a "debtor" to a person referred to as a "creditor." Debts are created daily in countless instances by purchases of goods at the consumer level; by retailers of goods in buying merchandise from a manufacturer, wholesaler, or distributor; and through the issuance and sale of debentures, corporate mortgage bonds, and other types of debt securities. An enormous volume of business transactions is entered into daily on a credit basis. Commercial activity would be restricted and greatly diminished if credit were not readily obtainable or needed funds not available for lending.

Fortunately, most debts are paid when due, thus justifying the extension of credit and encouraging its continuation. Defaults may create credit and collection problems, but normally the total amount in default repre-

sents a very small percentage of the total amount of outstanding indebtedness. Nevertheless, both individuals and corporations encounter financial crises and business misfortune. An individual or a business unit may be confronted by an accumulation of debts which exceeds total assets, or, although having assets in excess of total indebtedness, may have the assets in such non-liquid form that the debtor is unable to pay his debts as they mature. Relief from pressing debt and from the threat of impending lawsuits by creditors is frequently necessary for economic survival.

Out of the conflict between creditor rights and debtor relief various solutions have developed, such as voluntary adjustments and compromises requiring payment in installments to creditors over a period of time during which they agree to withhold legal action. Other voluntary methods include compositions and assignments of assets by a debtor to a trustee or assignee for the benefit of creditors. Equity receiverships or insolvency proceedings are sometimes filed by creditors in a State court pursuant to statute. Nonetheless, the most adaptable and frequently employed method of debtor relief—one which also affords protection to creditors—is by a proceeding in a Federal court under the Bankruptcy Act.

FEDERAL BANKRUPTCY LAW

The most important method of protecting creditor rights and granting debtor relief is Federal Bankruptcy law, which is largely statutory and involves court supervision. The word "bankrupt" is derived from the Latin *banque*, meaning bench or table, and *ruptus*, meaning broken. There is some authority for the legend that, upon bankruptcy, the customary place of business of a merchant in medieval times, his bench or table, was literally broken. In any event, it was figuratively broken since bankruptcy meant commercial failure.

Bankruptcy legislation serves a dual purpose: (1) to effect an **equitable distribution** of the debtor's property among her creditors, and (2) to **discharge** the debtor from her debts and enable her to rehabilitate herself and start afresh. Other subsidiary purposes are to provide uniform treatment of creditors, preserve existing business relations, stabilize commercial usages, and effect a speedy, as well as equitable, distribution of the debtor's assets.

The Constitution of the United States provides that "The Congress shall have power . . . to establish . . . uniform Laws on the subject of Bankruptcies throughout the United States." Article I, Section 8, clause 4. Under this power Congress has enacted or substantially revised Bankruptcy Acts in 1800, 1841, 1867, 1898, and 1938. Federal bankruptcy law has generally superseded State insolvency laws.

In 1978 Congress again enacted a major revision of the Bankruptcy Act. The **Bankruptcy Reform Act of 1978** became effective on October 1, 1979, and will be discussed in the first part of this chapter. It will be referred to as the Bankruptcy Act. It was amended in several important respects by the Bankruptcy Amendments and Federal Judgeship Act of 1984.

The Bankruptcy Act consists of eight odd-numbered chapters:

CHAPTER	TITLE
1	General Provisions
3	Case Administration
5	Creditors, the Debtor, and the Estate
7	Liquidation
9	Adjustment of Debts of a Municipality
11	Reorganization
13	Adjustment of Debts of an Individual with Regular Income
15	United States Trustees

Chapters 7, 9, 11, and 13 provide four different types of proceedings, while Chapters 1, 3, and 5 apply to all four proceedings. **Straight,** or ordinary, **bankruptcy** (Chapter 7) provides for liquidation and termination of the business of the debtor, whereas the other proceedings provide for **reorganization** and continuance of the business of the debtor.

Chapter 7 applies to *all* debtors with the exception of railroads, insurance companies, banks, savings and loan associations, homestead associations, and credit unions. Moreover, Chapter 7 has special provisions for the liquidation of the estates of stockbrokers and commodity brokers. Any person that may be a debtor under Chapter 7 (except stockbrokers and commodity brokers) as well as railroads may be a debtor under Chapter 11. Chapter 9, however, applies only to a municipality that is generally authorized to be a debtor under that chapter, is insolvent, and desires to effect a plan to adjust its debts.

Chapter 13 applies to individuals with regular income who owe liquidated unsecured debts of less than $100,000 and secured debts of less than $350,000.

The Act had established a new bankruptcy court system which was held by the United States Supreme Court to have been granted powers in violation of Article III of the U.S. Constitution. *Northern Pipeline Co. v. Marathon Pipe Line Co.*, 458 U.S. 50 (1982). The Bankruptcy Amendments Act of 1984 restructured the bankruptcy court system in an attempt to satisfy the constitutional considerations raised by the *Marathon* case. As amended, the Bankruptcy Act grants to U.S. district courts original and exclusive jurisdiction over all bankruptcy cases and original, but not exclusive, jurisdiction over civil proceedings arising under bankruptcy cases. The district court must abstain from related matters that, but for bankruptcy, could not have been brought in a Federal court. The district court in which a bankruptcy case is commenced has exclusive jurisdiction of all of the debtor's property. In addition, a bankruptcy court staffed by bankruptcy judges is established as a unit of each Federal district court. Bankruptcy courts are authorized to hear certain matters specified by the Act and to enter appropriate orders and judgments subject to review by the district court, or where established, a panel of three bankruptcy judges. The Circuit Court of Appeals has jurisdiction over appeals from the district court or panel. In all other matters, unless the parties assent, only the district court may issue a final order or judgment that is based upon proposed findings of fact and conclusions of law submitted to the district court by the bankruptcy judge.

CASE ADMINISTRATION— CHAPTER 3

Chapter 3 of the Bankruptcy Act contains provisions dealing with the commencement of the case, the officers that administer the case, the meetings of creditors, and the administrative powers of the various officers.

Commencement of the Case

The jurisdiction of the bankruptcy court and the operation of the bankruptcy laws are commenced by the filing of a voluntary or involuntary petition.

Voluntary Petitions The great majority of petitions are voluntarily filed. Any person eligible to be a debtor under a given bankruptcy proceeding may file a voluntary petition under that chapter. Moreover, the debtor need *not* be insolvent to file the petition. The commencement of a voluntary case constitutes an automatic **order for relief.** A voluntary petition includes a list of all creditors both secured and unsecured, a list of all property owned by the debtor, a list of property claimed by the debtor to be exempt, and a statement of the debtor's affairs.

Involuntary Petitions An involuntary petition in bankruptcy may be filed only under Chapter 7 or 11. It may be filed by (1) three or more creditors who have unsecured claims which total $5,000 or more, or (2) if all of the creditors of the debtor are fewer than twelve in number, then by one or more creditors whose total claims equal $5,000 or more. Section 303(b). However, an involuntary petition may not be filed against a farmer or a banking, insurance, or nonprofit corporation. Section 303(a).

If the debtor does not contest the involuntary petition, the court will enter an order for relief against the debtor. However, if the debtor opposes the petition, the court may enter an order of relief only if (1) the debtor is generally not paying his undisputed debts as they become due, or (2) within 120 days before the filing of the petition a custodian or receiver took possession of substantially all of the debtor's property to enforce a lien against that property. Section 303(h).

If an involuntary petition is contested successfully by the debtor and dismissed by the court, Section 303(i) empowers the court to grant a judgment in favor of the debtor against the petitioning creditors for (1) costs, (2) reasonable attorney's fees, and (3) damages proximately caused by the trustee's taking possession of the debtor's property. Moreover, if the petition was filed in bad faith the court may award damages proximately caused by the filing or punitive damages.

If the court orders relief the debtor must provide the court with the same schedules as those provided by a voluntary petitioner.

Automatic Stays

The filing of a voluntary or involuntary petition operates as a stay against (prevents) attempts by creditors to begin or continue to recover claims against the debtor, to enforce judgments against the debtor, or to create or enforce liens against property of the debtor. Section 362. This stay applies to both secured and unsecured creditors, although a secured creditor may petition the court to terminate the stay as to her security upon showing that she lacks adequate protection in the secured property.

Trustees

The trustee is the representative of the estate and has the capacity to sue and be sued. In proceedings under Chapter 7, trustees are selected by a vote of the creditors; in all other proceedings the trustee is appointed by the court. The trustee is responsible for collecting, liquidating, and distributing the debtor's estate. The duties and powers of the trustee include:

1. After notice and a hearing, to use, sell, or lease, other than in the ordinary course of business, property of the estate (Section 363(b));
2. If the business of the debtor is authorized to be operated and unless the court orders otherwise, to use, sell, or lease the property of the estate and to obtain credit in the ordinary course of business (Sections 363(c)(1) and 364);
3. To deposit or invest the money of the estate so as to yield the maximum reasonable net return, taking into account the safety of such deposit or investment (Section 345);

4. Subject to court approval to employ disinterested professionals such as attorneys, accountants, appraisers, or auctioneers and to act himself as attorney or accountant for the estate (Section 327); and
5. Subject to the court's approval, to assume or reject any executory contract or unexpired lease of the debtor (Section 365).

Meetings of Creditors

Within a reasonable time after relief is ordered, a meeting of creditors must be held. The court may not attend this meeting. The debtor must appear and submit to an examination by creditors and the trustee with respect to his financial situation. In a proceeding under Chapter 7, qualified creditors at this meeting elect the permanent trustee.

CREDITORS, THE DEBTOR, AND THE ESTATE—CHAPTER 5

Creditors

The Bankruptcy Act defines creditors to include any entity that has a claim against the debtor that arose at the time of or before the order for relief. A **claim** means a "right to payment whether or not such right is reduced to judgment, liquidated, unliquidated, fixed, contingent, matured, unmatured, disputed, undisputed, legal, equitable, secured, or unsecured." Section 101(4).

Proof of Claims Creditors may file a proof of claim. If a creditor does not do so in a timely manner, then the debtor or trustee may file a proof of such claim. Claims that are filed are allowed unless a party in interest objects. If an objection to a claim is made, the court determines after a hearing the amount and validity of the claim. The court may not allow any claim that (1) is unenforceable against the debtor or his property, (2) is for unmatured interest, or (3) is for services of an insider or attorney in excess of the reasonable value of such services. Section 502. An **insider** includes a relative or general partner of a debtor as well as a partnership in which the debtor is a general partner or a corporation of which the debtor is a director, officer, or person in control. Section 101(28).

Secured Claims An allowed claim of a creditor who has a lien on property of the estate is a secured claim to the extent of the value of the creditor's interest in the property. The creditor's claim is unsecured to the extent the value of his interest is less than the allowed amount of his claim. Thus, if A has an allowed claim of $5,000 against the estate of debtor B and has a security interest in property of the estate that is valued at $3,000, A has a secured claim in the amount of $3,000 and an unsecured claim for $2,000.

Priority of Claims After secured claims have been satisfied the remaining assets are distributed among creditors with unsecured claims. However, certain classes of unsecured claims have a **priority,** which means that they must be paid in full before any distribution is made to claims of lesser rank. The claims having a priority and the order of their priority, as provided in Section 507, are:

1. **Expenses of administration** of the debtor's estate, including the filing fees paid by creditors in involuntary cases; the expenses of creditors in recovering concealed assets for the benefit of the bankrupt's estate; the trustee's necessary expenses; and reasonable compensation to receivers, trustees, and their attorneys as allowed by the court.
2. Unsecured claims in an involuntary case arising in the ordinary course of the debtor's business after the commencement of the case but before the earlier of the appointment of the trustee or the order for relief. Such claimants are referred to as **"gap" creditors.**
3. Allowed, unsecured claims up to $2,000 for **wages, salaries, or commissions** earned within ninety days before the filing of the petition or the date of cessation of the debtor's business, whichever comes first.
4. Allowed, unsecured claims for contributions to **employee benefit plans** arising from services rendered within 180 days before the filing of the petition or the cessation of the debtor's business, whichever occurs first, but limited to $2,000 multiplied by the number of employees covered by the plan.
5. Allowed, unsecured claims up to $2,000 for **grain** or **fish producers** against a storage facility.
6. Allowed, unsecured claims up to $900 for **consumer deposits,** that is, moneys deposited in connection with the purchase, lease, or rental of property or the purchase of services for personal, family, or household use.
7. Specified **taxes** owed to governmental units for specified income, property, employment, or excise taxes.

After creditors with secured claims and creditors with claims having a priority have been satisfied, creditors with allowed, unsecured claims share proportionately in any remaining assets.

Subordination of Claims In addition to statutory and contract priorities, the bankruptcy court itself can, under Section 510, in its discretion in proper cases, apply equitable priorities. This is accomplished through the doctrine of subordination of claims, whereby, assuming two claims of equal statutory priority, the bankruptcy court declares that one claim must be paid in full before the other claim can be paid anything. Subordination is applied in cases where allowing a claim in full would be unfair and inequitable to other creditors, such as to allow the inflated salary claims of officers in closely held corporations. In such cases, the court does not disallow the claim but merely orders it paid after all other claims are paid in full.

The claim of a parent corporation against its bankrupt subsidiary corporation may be subordinated to the claims of other creditors of the subsidiary in cases where the parent has been guilty of mismanaging the subsidiary to the detriment of its innocent creditors in a manner so unconscionable as to preclude the parent from seeking the aid of a bankruptcy court. For example, assume that corporation ABC owns all of the capital stock of corporation XYZ. Assume further that whenever XYZ shows a profit, such profit is taken out of XYZ and transferred to ABC by means of questionable intercorporate transactions; whenever XYZ shows a loss and ABC is required to put some money back into XYZ, it does so by "lending" the money to XYZ. Over a period of time, ABC takes $500,000 out of XYZ and puts $100,000 back. When XYZ goes into bankruptcy, ABC has a claim of $100,000, while outside creditors have claims aggregating $100,000. If the assets total $100,000, ABC will receive $50,000 and the other creditors $50,000. Since ABC has already received $500,000, it is clearly unfair for it to receive an additional $50,000 at the expense of the other creditors. The bankruptcy court can exercise its equity power of subordinating claims and subordinate ABC's claim to that of the other creditors. Thereupon, the other creditors will receive the entire $100,000 and ABC will receive nothing until the prior claims are paid in full.

Debtors

As indicated, the purpose of the Bankruptcy Act is to effect an equitable distribution of the debtor's assets and to provide a discharge to the debtor. Accordingly, the Act explicitly subjects the debtor to specified duties while exempting some of the debtor's property and discharging most of his debts.

Debtor's Duties Under the Bankruptcy Act the debtor must file a list of creditors, a schedule of assets and liabilities, and a statement of her financial affairs. In any case in which a trustee is serving, the debtor must cooperate with the trustee and surrender to the trustee all property of the estate and all records relating to property of the estate.

Debtor's Exemptions Section 522 of the Bankruptcy Act exempts specified property of an individual debtor from the bankruptcy proceedings including the following:

1. Up to $7,500 in equity in property used as a residence or burial plot.

2. Up to $1,200 in equity in one motor vehicle.

3. Up to $200 for any particular item, and not to exceed $4,000 in aggregate value, of household furnishings, household goods, wearing apparel, appliances, books, animals, crops, or musical instruments that are held primarily for personal, family, or household use.

4. Up to $500 in jewelry.

5. Any property up to $400 plus up to $3,750 of any unused amount of the first exemption.

6. Up to $750 in implements, professional books or tools of the debtor's trade.

7. Unmatured life insurance contracts owned by debtor other than a credit life insurance contract.

8. Professionally prescribed health aids.

9. Social security, veterans, and disability benefits.

10. Unemployment compensation.

11. Alimony and support payments including child support.

12. Payments from pension, profit sharing, and annuity plans.

13. Payments from an award under a crime victim's reparation law, a wrongful death award, and up to $7,500, not including pain and suffering or compensation for actual pecuniary loss, from a personal injury award.

The debtor has the option of using either the exemptions provided by the Bankruptcy Act or those available under State law. Nevertheless, a State may by specific legislative action deny to its citizens the use of the Federal exemptions and limit them to the exemptions provided by State law. More than two-thirds of the States have enacted such legislation.

Discharge Discharge is the termination of all dischargeable debts of the debtor for allowed claims. Certain debts, however, are non-dischargeable under the Act. A discharge of a debt voids any judgment obtained at any time with respect to that debt and operates as an injunction against the commencement or continuation of any action to recover that debt.

A discharge does not, however, affect a secured creditor to the extent of his security.

No private employer may terminate the employment of, or discriminate with respect to employment against, an individual who is or has been a debtor under the Bankruptcy Act solely because such debtor (1) is or has been a debtor under the Bankruptcy Act; (2) has been insolvent before the commencement of a case or during the case; or (3) has not paid a debt that is dischargeable in a case under the Bankruptcy Act. Section 525(b).

An agreement between a debtor and a creditor permitting the creditor to enforce a discharged debt is enforceable to the extent State law permits but only if (1) the agreement was made before the discharge has been granted; (2) the agreement contains a clear and conspicuous statement which advises the debtor that the agreement may be rescinded; (3) the agreement has been filed with the court and, if applicable, accompanied by a declaration or an affidavit of the attorney that represented the debtor during the course of negotiating the agreement, which states that such agreement represents a fully informed and voluntary agreement by the debtor, and does not impose an undue hardship on the debtor; (4) the debtor has not rescinded the agreement at any time prior to discharge or within sixty days after the agreement is filed with the court, whichever occurs later; (5) the court has informed a debtor who is an individual that he is not required to enter into such an agreement and explains the legal effect of the agreement; and (6) in a case concerning an individual who was not represented by an attorney during the course of negotiating the agreement, the court approves such agreement as not imposing an undue hardship on the debtor and in the best interests of the debtor. Section 524.

Section 523 provides that the following debts are **not dischargeable** in bankruptcy:

1. Certain taxes and customs duties;
2. Legal liabilities for obtaining money or property by false pretenses, false representations, or actual fraud;
3. Legal liability for willful and malicious injuries to the person or property of another;
4. Alimony and support of spouse or child;
5. Debts not scheduled, unless the creditor knew of the bankruptcy;
6. Debts created by the fraud or defalcation of the debtor while acting in a fiduciary capacity, embezzlement, or larceny;
7. Student loans which became first due less than five years before the filing of the petition;
8. Debts that were or could have been listed in a previous bankruptcy in which the debtor waived or was denied a discharge;
9. Consumer debts for luxury goods in excess of $500 per creditor if incurred by an individual debtor on or within forty days before the order for relief;
10. Cash advances aggregating more than $1,000 obtained by an individual debtor under an open end credit plan within twenty days before the order for relief; and
11. Liability for a court judgment based upon the debtor's operation of a motor vehicle while legally intoxicated.

To illustrate: D files a petition in bankruptcy. D owes A $1,500, B $2,500, and C $3,000. A's claim is not dischargeable in bankruptcy while B's and C's claims are. A receives $180 from the liquidation of D's bankruptcy estate, B receives $300, and C receives $360. If D receives a bankruptcy discharge, B and C will be precluded from pursuing D for the remainder of their claims ($2,200 and $2,640 respectively). A, on the other hand, because his debt is not dischargeable, may pursue D for the remaining $1,320 subject to the applicable statute of limitations. If D does *not* receive a discharge, A, B and C may all pursue D for the unpaid portion of their claims.

The Estate

The commencement of a bankruptcy case creates an estate consisting of all legal and equitable interests of the debtor in non-exempt property at the time of commencement of the case. The estate also includes property that the debtor acquires within 180 days after the commencement of the case by inheritance or as a beneficiary of a life insurance policy and any interest in property that the *estate* acquires after the commencement of the case. In addition the estate includes property that the trustee recovers under her powers (1) as a lien creditor, (2) to avoid voidable preferences, (3) to avoid fraudulent transfers, and (4) to avoid statutory liens.

Trustee as Lien Creditor The trustee has, as of the commencement of the case, the rights and powers of any creditor with a judicial lien against the debtor or an execution that is returned unsatisfied, whether or not such creditor exists. Section 544(a). A **judicial lien** is a charge or interest in property to secure payment of a debt or performance of an obligation that is obtained by judgment, levy, or other legal or equitable process. The trustee is made an ideal creditor possessing every right and power conferred by the law of the State upon its most favored creditor who has acquired a lien by legal or equitable proceedings. The trustee need not locate an actual existing lien creditor, for the trustee assumes the rights and powers of a purely hypothetical lien creditor.

For example, A, the debtor, grants a security interest in goods purchased on credit to B, the seller. B fails to perfect the security interest before A files a voluntary petition. C, the trustee, would assume the status of a lien creditor who has priority over an unperfected security interest. U.C.C. Section 9–301. As a consequence, A would be denied standing as a secured creditor and be relegated to the ranks of the unsecured creditors.

Voidable Preferences The Bankruptcy Act invalidates certain preferential transfers from the debtor to favored creditors before the date of bankruptcy. Under Section 547 the trustee may recover any transfer of property of the debtor—

1. to or for the benefit of a creditor;
2. for or on account of an antecedent debt

owed by the debtor before such transfer was made;

3. made while the debtor was insolvent;
4. made on or within ninety days before the date of the filing of the petition, or, if the creditor was an "insider" as previously defined, within one year of the date of the filing of the petition; and
5. that enables such creditor to receive more than he would have received under Chapter 7.

A transfer is any mode, direct or indirect, voluntary or involuntary, of disposing of property or an interest in property including the retention of title as a security interest. Section 101(48). It is presumed that the debtor has been insolvent on and during the ninety days immediately preceding the date of the filing of the petition. **Insolvency** is a financial condition of a debtor such that the sum of its debts is greater than all of its property at fair valuation.

The policy behind the voidable preference provision is explained by the House report as follows:

The purpose of the preference section is two-fold. First, by permitting the trustee to avoid pre-bankruptcy transfers that occur within a short period before bankruptcy, creditors are discouraged from racing to the courthouse to dismember the debtor during his slide into bankruptcy. The protection thus afforded the debtor often enables him to work his way out of a difficult financial situation through cooperation with all of his creditors. Second, and more important, the preference provisions facilitate the prime bankruptcy policy of equality of distribution among creditors of the debtor. Any creditor that received a greater payment than others of his class is required to disgorge so that all may share equally. *House of Representatives Report* 95–595 at 177–78 (1977).

It should be noted that not all transfers made within ninety days of bankruptcy are voidable. For example, if sixty days before the petition is filed the debtor purchases an automobile for $9,000, this transfer of property (i.e., the $9,000) is *not* voidable because it was not made for an antecedent debt but rather as a contemporaneous exchange for new value. Similarly, if within ninety days of the filing of the petition the debtor purchases a refrigerator on credit and grants the seller a security interest in the refrigerator, the transfer of that interest is not voidable if the secured party perfects within ten days after the security interest attaches. In addition; the trustee may *not* avoid a transfer (1) in payment of a debt incurred in the ordinary course of business or financial affairs of the debtor and the transferee, (2) made in the ordinary course of business or financial affairs of the debtor and transferee, and (3) according to ordinary business terms. Section 547(c).

    See In Re Conn.

Fraudulent Transfers The trustee may avoid fraudulent transfers made on or within one year before the date of the filing of the petition. Section 548. One type of fraudulent transfer consists of the debtor's tranferring property with the actual intent to hinder, delay, or defraud any of her creditors. Another type of a fraudulent transfer is the transfer by the debtor of property for less than a reasonably equivalent consideration while she is insolvent or would become insolvent because of the transfer. For example, A, who is in debt, transfers title to her house to B, her father, without any payment by B to A and with the understanding that when the house is no longer in danger of seizure by creditors, B will reconvey it to A. The transfer of the house by A to B is a fraudulent transfer.

Statutory Liens The trustee may avoid a statutory lien on property of the debtor if the lien (1) first becomes effective when the debtor becomes insolvent *or* (2) is not perfected or enforceable on the date of the time of the commencement of the case against a *bona fide* purchaser. Section 545. A statutory lien is a lien arising solely by force of a statute but does *not* include a security interest or judicial lien. Section 101(45).

LIQUIDATION—CHAPTER 7

In order to accomplish its dual goals of an equitable distribution of the debtor's property and providing the debtor with a fresh start, the Bankruptcy Act has established two approaches: liquidation and adjustment of debts. Chapter 7 utilizes the first approach of liquidation while Chapters 11 and 13, discussed below, take the second approach. Liquidation involves the termination of the business of the debtor, distribution of his nonexempt assets, and usually a discharge of all dischargeable debts of the debtor.

Proceedings

Proceedings under Chapter 7 apply to all debtors except railroads, insurance companies, banks, savings and loan associations, homestead associations, and credit unions. Once a voluntary or involuntary petition has been filed, the court must determine whether to enter an order for relief. If an order is entered the court appoints an interim trustee who serves until a permanent trustee is selected by the creditors. Under Chapter 7, the trustee performs the following duties:

1. collect and reduce to money the property of the estate for which such trustee serves, and close up such estate as expeditiously as is compatible with the best interests of parties in interest;
2. be accountable for all property received;
3. investigate the financial affairs of the debtor;
4. if a purpose would be served, examine proofs of claims and object to the allowance of any claim that is improper;
5. if advisable, oppose the discharge of the debtor;
6. unless the court orders otherwise, furnish such information concerning the estate and the estate's administration as is requested by a party in interest;
7. if the business of the debtor is authorized to be operated, file with the court and with any governmental unit charged with respon-

sibility for collection or determination of any tax arising out of such operation periodic reports and summaries of the operation of such business; and

8. make a final report and file a final account of the administration of the estate with the court. Section 704.

The creditors may also elect a committee of not fewer than three nor more than eleven unsecured creditors which committee may consult with the trustee, make recommendations to him, and submit questions to the court.

After notice and a hearing, the court on its motion may dismiss a case filed by an individual debtor whose debts are primarily consumer debts if the court finds that granting relief would be a substantial abuse of the provisions of Chapter 7. Section 707(b).

Distribution of the Estate

After the trustee has collected all the assets of the debtor's estate, she distributes them to the creditors and, if any assets remain, to the debtor in the following order:

1. Secured creditors collect on their security interests.
2. Creditors entitled to a priority receive payment in the order provided.
3. Payment is made to unsecured creditors who filed their claims on time.
4. Payment is made to unsecured creditors who filed their claims tardily.
5. Claims for multiple, exemplary, or punitive damages are paid.
6. Interest at the legal rate from the date of the filing of the petition is paid to all of the above claimants.
7. Whatever property remains is distributed to the debtor.

Claims of the same rank are paid *pro rata*. For example: D has filed a petition for a Chapter 7 proceeding. The total value of D's estate *after* paying the expenses of administration

is $25,000. E, who is owed $15,000, has a security interest in property valued at $10,000. F has an unsecured claim of $6,000, which is entitled to a priority of $2,000. The United States has a claim for income taxes of $4,000. G has an unsecured claim of $9,000 that was filed on time. H has an unsecured claim of $12,000 that was filed on time. J has a claim of $8,000 that was not filed on time even though J was aware of the bankruptcy proceedings. The distribution would be as follows:

1. E receives $11,500
2. F receives $3,200
3. United States receives $4,000
4. G receives $2,700
5. H receives $3,600
6. J receives $0

E receives $10,000 as a secured creditor and has an unsecured claim of $5,000. F receives $2,000 on the portion of his claim entitled to a priority and has an unsecured claim of $4,000. The United States has a priority of $4,000. After paying $10,000 to E, $2,000 to F, and $4,000 to the United States, there remains $9,000 ($25,000—$10,000—$2,000—$4,000) to be distributed *pro rata* to unsecured creditors who filed on time. Their claims total $30,000 (E = $5,000, F = $4,000, G = $9,000 and H = $12,000). Therefore, each will receive $\frac{\$9,000}{\$30,000}$ or 30¢ on the dollar. Accordingly, E receives an additional $1,500, F receives an additional $1,200, G receives $2,700, and H receives $3,600. Because there were insufficient assets to pay all unsecured claimants who filed on time, J, who filed tardily, receives nothing.

See Figure 39-1.

Discharge

Upon distribution of the estate, the court will grant the debtor a discharge unless the debtor:

1. Is not an individual;
2. Has destroyed, falsified, concealed, or failed to keep books of account and records;

FIGURE 39-1   Collection and Distribution of the Debtor's Estate

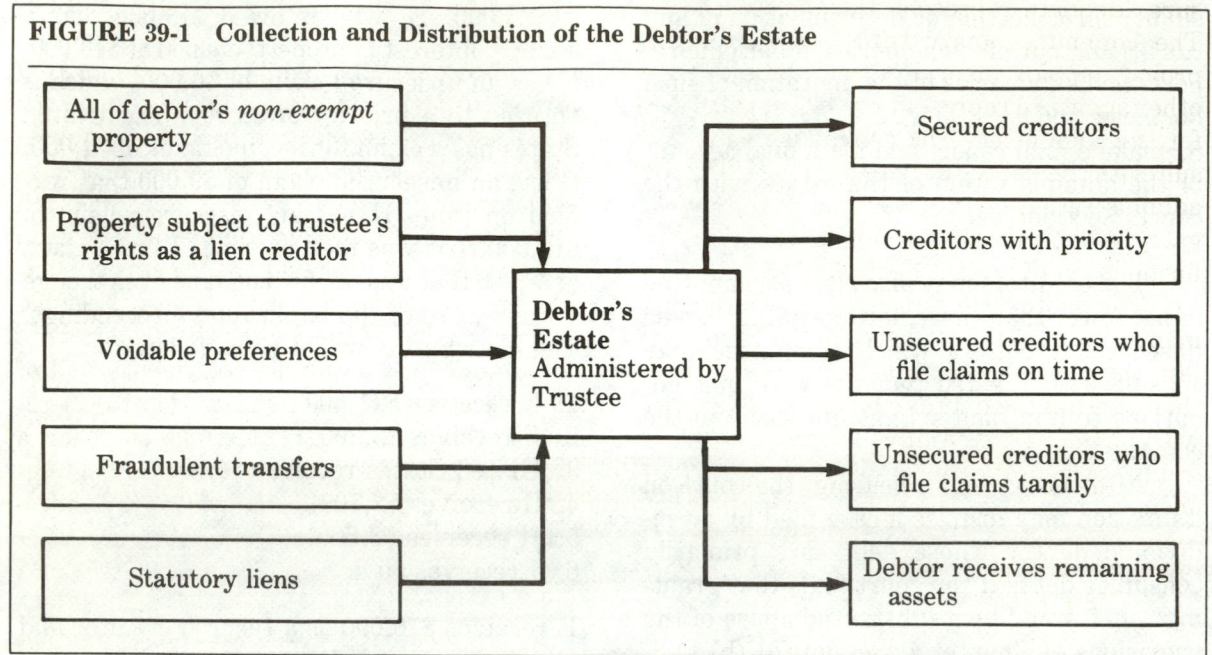

3. Has knowingly and fraudulently made a false oath or account, presented or used a false claim, or given or received bribes;

4. Transferred, removed, destroyed, or concealed any of (a) *his* property with intent to hinder, delay, or defraud his creditors within twelve months preceding the filing of the bankruptcy petition, or, (b) property of the *estate* after the date of filing of the petition;

5. Has within six years prior to bankruptcy been granted a discharge;

6. Refused to obey any lawful order of the court or to answer any question approved by the court;

7. Has failed to explain satisfactorily any losses of assets or deficiency of assets to meet his liabilities; or

8. Has executed a written waiver of discharge approved by the court.

Upon the request of the trustee or a creditor and after notice and a hearing, the court may revoke a discharge within one year if it was obtained through the fraud of the debtor.

REORGANIZATION—CHAPTER 11

Reorganization is the means by which a distressed business enterprise and its value as a going concern are preserved through the correction or elimination of those factors that brought about its distress. Chapter 11 of the Bankruptcy Act governs reorganization of eligible debtors, including partnerships and corporations, and permits restructuring of their capital structure. The main objective of a reorganization proceeding is to develop and consummate a fair, equitable, and feasible plan of reorganization. After a plan has been prepared and filed, a hearing is held before the court to determine whether or not it shall be confirmed.

Proceedings

Any person that may be a debtor under Chapter 7 (except stockbrokers and commodity brokers) and railroads may be a debtor under Chapter 11. Petitions may be voluntary or involuntary.

As soon as practicable after the order for relief, the court will appoint a committee of unsecured creditors ordinarily consisting of persons that hold the seven largest claims against the debtor. In addition, the court may appoint additional committees of creditors or of equity security holders if necessary to assure adequate representation. Section 1102. The committee may, with the court's approval, employ attorneys, accountants, and other agents to represent or perform services for the committee. The committee may consult with the debtor or trustee concerning the administration of the case and may investigate the debtor's affairs and participate in the formulation of a plan. Section 1103.

The debtor will remain in possession and management of the property of the estate unless the court appoints a trustee, who may then operate the debtor's business. The court will appoint a trustee only for cause (including fraud, dishonesty, incompetence, or gross mismanagement of the debtor's affairs) or if such appointment is in the interests of creditors or equity security holders. Section 1104. If the court does not appoint a trustee, upon the request of a party in interest the court will appoint an examiner to conduct investigations into any allegations of fraud, dishonesty, incompetence, misconduct, or mismanagement if (1) such appointment is in the interests of creditors or equity security holders or (2) the debtor's fixed, liquidated, unsecured debts exceed $5,000,000.

The duties of a trustee in a case under Chapter 11 include:

1. to be accountable for all property received;
2. to examine proof of claims;
3. to furnish information to all parties in interest;
4. to provide the court and taxing authorities with financial reports of the business operations;
5. to make a final report and account of the administration of the estate;
6. to investigate the financial condition of the debtor and the desirability of the continuance of the debtor's business; and
7. to file a plan or a report as to why there will be no plan or to recommend conversion of the case to Chapter 7.

At any time before confirmation of a plan, the court may terminate the trustee's apointment and restore the debtor to possession and management of the property of the estate and operation of the debtor's business. Section 1105.

The Bankruptcy Amendments Act added a new provision (Section 1113) dealing with the rejection of collective bargaining agreements. Subsection (b)(1) provides that subsequent to filing and prior to seeking such rejection, the trustee or debtor-in-possession must make a proposal for the necessary modifications of the labor contract that will enable reorganization of the debtor and also provide for the fair and equitable treatment of all of the parties concerned. Subsection (b)(2) requires that good faith meetings to reach a mutually satisfactory agreement be held between management and the union. Subsection (c) authorizes the court to approve rejection of the collective bargaining agreement only if the court finds that the proposal was made in accordance with these conditions, that the union refused the proposal without good cause, and that the balance of equities clearly favors rejection of such agreement.

Plan of Reorganization

The debtor may file a plan at any time and has the exclusive right to file a plan during the 120 days after the order for relief, unless a trustee has been appointed. Then other parties in interest including the trustee or a creditors' committee may file a plan, if the debtor has not filed a plan within 120 days or the plan has not been accepted within 180 days. Section 1121.

A plan of reorganization must divide creditors' claims and shareholders' interests into classes, specify how each class will be treated, and deal with each class equally. After a plan has been filed, the plan and a written disclosure statement approved by the court as containing adequate information must be transmitted to each holder of a claim before soliciting acceptance or rejection of the plan. "Adequate information" means information of a kind and in sufficient detail that would enable a hypothetical reasonable investor to make an informed judgment about the plan. Section 1125.

Acceptance of Plan

Each class of claims and interests has the opportunity to accept or reject the proposed plan. A **class of claims** has accepted a plan if it has been accepted by creditors that hold at least two-thirds in amount and more than one-half of the allowed claims of such class. Acceptance of a plan by a **class of interests**, such as shareholders, requires acceptance by holders of at least two-thirds in amount of the allowed interests of such class.

A class that is not impaired under a plan is conclusively presumed to have accepted the plan. Basically, a class is not impaired if the plan leaves unaltered the legal, equitable, and contractual rights to which such claim or interest entitles the holder of that claim or right. Section 1124.

Confirmation of Plan

A plan must be confirmed, after notice and a hearing, by the court before the plan is binding upon any parties. A court may confirm a plan only if it meets all of the requirements of Section 1129 of the Bankruptcy Act. The most important of these requirements are the following.

Good Faith The plan must have been proposed in good faith and not by any means forbidden by law. Section 1129(a)(3).

Feasibility The court must find that confirmation of the plan is not likely to be followed by the liquidation or the need for further financial reorganization of the debtor. Section 1129(a)(11). The essence of feasibility is that the reorganization entity will be able to operate economically and efficiently, will be able to compete upon fairly equal terms with other companies within the industry, and is not likely to require liquidation or a second reorganization within the foreseeable future.

Cash Payments Certain classes of creditors must have their allowed claims paid in full in cash immediately or, in some instances, upon a deferred basis. Section 1129(a)(9). These classes include the expenses of administration, gap creditors, claims for wages and salaries, and employee benefits and consumer deposits.

Acceptance by Creditors To be confirmed, the plan must be accepted by at least *one* class of claims, and with respect to *each* class each holder must either accept the plan *or* receive not less than the amount he would have received under Chapter 7. In addition, each class must accept the plan or be unimpaired by the plan. Nonetheless, under certain circumstances the court may confirm a plan that is not accepted by all impaired classes. The court must determine that the plan does not discriminate unfairly and that it is fair and equitable. Section 1129(b)(1). Under these circumstances a class of claims or interests may, over its objections, be involuntarily subjected to the provisions of a plan.

"Fair and equitable" with respect to secured creditors requires that they either retain their security interest and receive deferred cash payments at least equal to their claims or that they realize the "indubitable equivalent" of their claims. Fair and equitable with respect to unsecured creditors means that such creditors receive property of value equivalent to the full amount of their claim *or* that no junior claim or interest receive anything at all. With respect to a class of interests, a plan is fair and equitable if the holders receive full value or if no junior interest receives anything at all.

See *Matter of Landmark at Plaza Park Ltd.*

Effect of Reorganization

The reorganized debtor or the new entity succeeding to the debtor's properties emerges from the proceedings and begins life anew with only such obligations as are imposed upon it by the plan. The plan binds the debtor and any creditor, equity security holder, or general partner of the debtor. Upon the entry of a final decree closing the proceedings, the debtor is discharged from all of its debts and liabilities except those that are not dischargeable. Sections 523 and 1141. All persons who are entitled to participate in the plan of reorganization have a period of not less than five years from the date of the final decree within which to exchange their old securities for the new, as provided in the plan.

ADJUSTMENT OF DEBTS OF INDIVIDUALS—CHAPTER 13

In order to encourage debtors to pay their debts wherever possible, Congress enacted Chapter 13 of the Bankruptcy Act. The chapter permits an individual debtor to file a repayment plan which, if confirmed by the court, will provide him with a discharge from almost all of his debts upon his completion of payments under the plan.

Proceedings

Chapter 13 provides a procedure for the adjustment of debts of an *individual* with regular income who owes liquidated, unsecured debts of less than $100,000 and secured debts of less than $350,000. So long as the debt limitations are met, sole proprietorships are also eligible. A case under Chapter 13 may *only* be initiated by a voluntary petition. The court appoints a trustee in every Chapter 13 case.

The Plan

The debtor files the plan and may modify it at any time before confirmation. The plan must meet three requirements under Section 1322:

1. It must provide for submission of all or any portion of future earnings or income of the debtor, as is necessary for the execution of the plan, to the supervision and control of the trustee.

2. It must provide for full payment on a deferred basis of all claims entitled to a priority unless a holder of a claim agrees to a different treatment of such claim.

3. If the plan classifies claims, it must provide the same treatment for each claim in the same class.

In addition, the plan *may* modify the rights of unsecured creditors and the rights of secured creditors except those secured only by a security interest in the debtor's principal residence. A plan may provide for payments on any unsecured claim to be made concurrently with payments on any secured claim.

The plan may *not* provide for payments over a period that is longer than three years, unless the court approves for cause a longer period not to exceed five years.

Confirmation

The plan will be confirmed by the court if certain requirements have been met. First, the plan must comply with applicable law and be proposed in good faith. Second, the value of the property to be distributed to unsecured creditors must be not less than the amount that would be paid them under Chapter 7. Third, either the secured creditors must accept the plan *or* the plan must provide that the debtor will surrender to the secured creditors the collateral *or* the plan must permit the secured creditors to retain their security interest and the value of property to be distributed to them is not less than the allowed amount of their claim. Fourth, the debtor must be able to make all payments and comply with the plan. Moreover, while a debtor who receives a discharge under Chapter 7 cannot obtain a discharge again under that chapter for six years, a debtor discharged under Chapter 13 is not always subject to that bar. *See In Re Jonson.*

Discharge

After a debtor completes all payments under the plan, the court will grant him a discharge of all debts except long-term debts whose maturity extends beyond the expiration of the plan and non-dischargeable debts for alimony, maintenance, and support. This discharge is considerably more extensive than that granted under Chapter 7.

Even if all payments have *not* been made, the court may, after a hearing, grant a discharge if the debtor's failure to complete such payments is due to circumstances for which the debtor should not justly be held accountable, the value of property actually distributed is not less than what would have been received under Chapter 7, and modification of the plan is not practicable. Section 1328(b).

CREDITORS' RIGHTS AND DEBTOR RELIEF OUTSIDE OF BANKRUPTCY

The rights and remedies of debtors and creditors outside of bankruptcy are principally governed by State law. Because of the expense and notoriety associated with bankruptcy it is often in the best interests of both debtor and creditor to resolve their claims outside of a bankruptcy proceeding. Accordingly, bankruptcy is usually viewed as the last resort.

The rights and remedies of creditors outside of bankruptcy are varied. The first part of this section examines the basic right of *all* creditors to pursue their overdue claims to judgment and to satisfy that judgment out of property belonging to the debtor. Other rights and remedies are discussed elsewhere in this book. The rights under Article 2 of the Uniform Commercial Code of an unpaid credit seller to reclaim the goods sold are covered in Chapter 23. The right of a secured creditor to enforce a security interest in personal property is the subject of Chapter 37. Likewise, the right of a creditor to foreclose a mortgage on real property is discussed in Chapter 49. In addition, the right of a cred-

itor to proceed against a surety on the debt is addressed in Chapter 38.

At the same time, the law attempts to protect debtors against overreaching by creditors. This goal has been pursued by a number of means. States have enacted usury laws as discussed in Chapter 11. The Federal Trade Commission has limited the rights of a holder in due course against consumer debtors as explained in Chapter 26. Congress has prohibited abusive, deceptive, and unfair debt collection practices employed by debt collection agencies as discussed in Chapter 42. That chapter also covers other legal protection offered to *consumer* debtors. The second part of this section describes the various forms of non-bankruptcy compromises that have developed to provide relief to debtors who have become overextended and are unable to pay all of their creditors.

CREDITORS' RIGHTS

When a debtor fails to pay a debt, the creditor may file suit to collect the debt owed. The ultimate objective is to obtain a judgment against the debtor and then to collect on that judgment.

Pre-judgment Remedies

Because litigation takes time, a creditor attempting to collect on a claim through the judicial process will almost always experience delay in obtaining judgment. To protect against the debtor's disposing of his assets the creditor may utilize, when available, certain pre-judgment remedies. The most important of these is **attachment** which is the process of seizing property, by virtue of a writ, summons, or other judicial order, and bringing the property into the custody of the court for the purpose of securing satisfaction of the judgment ultimately to be entered in the action. At common law the main objective was to coerce the defendant debtor to appear in court; today the writ of attachment is statutory and used primarily to seize the debtor's property in the event a judgment is rendered. Most States limit attachment to specified grounds and require the opportunity for a hearing before a judge prior to the issuance of a writ of execution. Generally, attachment is limited to situations in which (a) the defendant cannot be personally served; (b) the claim is based upon fraud or the equivalent; or (c) the defendant has or is likely to transfer away his property. In addition, the plaintiff must generally post a bond to compensate the defendant for loss should the plaintiff not prevail in the cause of action.

Similar in purpose is the remedy of prejudgment **garnishment** which is a statutory proceeding directed at a third person who owes a debt to the debtor or has property belonging to the debtor. Garnishment is most commonly used against the employer of the debtor and the bank in which the debtor has a savings or checking account. Property garnished remains in the hands of the third party pending the outcome of the suit. For example, C brings an action against B to collect a debt that is past due. A has property belonging to B. C might garnish this property so that if C is successful in his action against B, C's judgment could be satisfied out of that property held by A. If A no longer had the property when C obtained judgment, C could recover from A.

Post-judgment Remedies

If the debtor still has not paid the claim, the creditor may proceed to trial and try to obtain a court judgment against the debtor. Obtaining a judgment, however, is only the first, although necessary, step in collecting the debt. If the debtor does not voluntarily pay the judgment the creditor will have to take additional steps to collect on the judgment. These steps are called "post-judgment remedies."

First, the judgment creditor will have the clerk issue a **writ of execution** which is served by the sheriff upon the defendant/debtor demanding payment of the judgment.

Upon return of the writ "unsatisfied," the judgment creditor may post bond or other security and order a levy on and sale of specified nonexempt property belonging to the defendant/debtor which is then seized by the sheriff, advertised for sale, and sold at public sale under the writ of execution.

The writ of execution is limited to property of the debtor that is not exempt. All States restrict creditors from recourse to certain property the type and amount of which varies greatly from State to State.

If the proceeds of the sale do not produce sufficient funds to pay the judgment, the creditor may institute a **supplementary proceeding** in an attempt to locate money or other property belonging to the defendant. He may also proceed by **garnishment** against the debtor's employer or a bank in which the debtor has an account in an attempt to collect the judgment.

DEBTOR'S RELIEF

In the area of creditors' rights and debtor relief, there are several inherent conflicts: (1) The right of diligent creditors to pursue their claims to judgment and to satisfy their judgment by sale of property of the debtor; (2) The right of unsecured creditors who have refrained from suing the debtor; and (3) The social policy of affording relief to a debtor who has contracted debts beyond his ability to pay and who may be confronted by a lifetime burden. A resolution of these conflicts necessarily involves a compromise under which the debtor will disclose and surrender all his assets to a trustee or other person for the benefit of his creditors, and the creditors will receive fair and equal treatment.

Various forms of non-bankruptcy compromises have been developed to provide relief to debtors, some of which are less formal, such as those effected by credit agencies and adjustment bureaus. Some are founded in common law and involve simple contract and trust principles, such as compositions and assignments; others are statutory, such as statutory assignments. Some involve the intervention of a court and its officers, such as equity receiverships, while others do not.

Compositions

A common law or non-statutory composition is an ordinary contract or agreement between the debtor on the one hand and her creditors on the other, under which the creditors receive *pro rata* a part of their claims, and the debtor is discharged from the balance of the claims. As a contract it requires the formalities of a contract, such as offer, acceptance, and consideration. For example, debtor D owing debts of $5,000 to A, $2,000 to B, and $1,000 to C offers to settle these claims by paying $4,000 to A, B, and C. If A, B, and C accept the offer, a composition results with A receiving $2,500, B $1,000, and C $500. The consideration for the promise of A to forgive the balance of his claim consists of the promises of B and C, respectively, to forgive the balance of their claims. All the creditors benefit since a race among creditors to obtain the debtor's limited assets is avoided.

It should be noted, however, that the debtor in a composition is discharged from liability only upon the claims of creditors who voluntarily consent to the composition. If, in the illustration above, C had refused to accept the offer of composition and had refused to take the $500, he could attempt to collect the full $1,000 claim. Likewise, if D owed additional debts to X, Y, and Z, these creditors would not be bound by the agreement between D and A, B, and C. Another disadvantage of the composition is the fact that any creditor can attach the assets of the debtor during the usual period of bargaining and negotiation which precedes the execution of the composition agreement. For instance, once D advised A, B and C that he was offering to compose the claims, any one of the creditors could seize D's property.

A variation of the composition is an extension agreement worked out by the debtor with her creditors providing for payment of her debts either in full or proportionately scaled down over a period of time.

Assignments for Benefit of Creditors

A common law or non-statutory assignment for the benefit of creditors, or general assignment as it is sometimes called, is a voluntary transfer by the debtor of some or all of his property to a trustee who applies the property to the payment of all of the debtor's debts. For instance, debtor D transfers title to his property to trustee T, who converts the property into money and pays it to all of the creditors on a *pro rata* basis.

The advantage of the assignment over the composition is that it immunizes the debtor's assets from attachment and execution, and it halts the race of diligent creditors to attach. On the other hand, the common-law assignment does not require the consent of the creditors and payment by the trustee of part of the claims does not discharge the debtor from the balance of them. Thus, even after T pays A $2,500, B $1,000, and C $500 (and appropriate payments to all other creditors), nevertheless A, B, and C and the other creditors may still attempt to collect the balance of their claims.

Statutory Assignments

Because assignments benefit creditors by immunizing the debtor's assets from attachment, there have been many statutory attempts to combine the idea of the assignment with a corresponding benefit to the debtor by discharging him from the balance of his debts. Since the United States Constitution prohibits a State from impairing the obligation of a contract between private citizens, it is impossible for a State to force all creditors to discharge a debtor upon a *pro rata* distribution of assets, although, as previously discussed, the Federal government *does* have such power and exercises it in the Bankruptcy Act. Accordingly, the States have generally enacted assignment statutes permitting the debtor to exact *voluntary* releases of the balance of claims from creditors who accept part payments, thus combining the advantages of common law compositions and assignments.

Equity Receiverships

One of the oldest remedies in equity is the appointment of a receiver by the court. The receiver is a disinterested person who collects and preserves the debtor's assets and income and disposes of them at the direction of the court which appointed her. The court may instruct her either (1) to liquidate the assets by public or private sale; (2) to operate the business as a going concern temporarily; or (3) to conserve the assets until final disposition of the matter before the court.

A receiver will be appointed upon the petition (1) of a secured creditor seeking foreclosure of his security; (2) of a judgment creditor after exhausting legal remedies to satisfy the judgment; or (3) of a shareholder of a corporate debtor where it appears that the assets of the corporation will be dissipated by fraud or mismanagement. The appointment of a receiver always rests within the sound discretion of the court. Insolvency, in the equity sense of inability by the debtor to pay his debts as they mature, is one of the factors considered by the court in appointing a receiver.

CASES

Voidable Preferences

IN RE CONN

United States Bankruptcy Court, Northern
District of Ohio, 1981.
9 B.R. 431.

WHITE, BKRTCY, J.

A complaint to recover property transferred pursuant to an avoided preference was filed by Marc P. Gertz, trustee of the estate of Freelin Alva Conn, debtor herein, against BancOhio National Bank, hereinafter referred to as creditor, on December 9, 1980.

An answer admitting that the disputed transfers of property of the debtor to the creditor amounting to $439.17 were made within 90 days preceding the filing of debtor's petition, on account of an antecedent debt, while the debtor was insolvent and denying the remaining allegations of the complaint was filed by creditor on January 12, 1981.

A trial on said complaint was held on February 19, 1981. From the testimony of the debtor and the exhibits admitted into evidence, the court makes the following finding of fact and law.

Finding of Fact

1. A voluntary petition under Chapter 7 of the Bankruptcy Code was filed by Freelin Alva Conn on September 30, 1980.

2. Marc P. Gertz was appointed interim trustee of debtor's estate on September 30, 1980 and became trustee, pursuant to 11 U.S.C. § 702(d), subsequent to the meeting of creditors on November 4, 1980.

3. BancOhio National Bank was listed by debtor on his Schedule A-2 as having a claim incurred in October of 1979, in the amount of $4,000.00 secured by a 1978 Oldsmobile Omega having a market value of $3,500.00.

4. During the period from June 30, 1980 to September 30, 1980 the following payments were made by debtor to creditor:

August 9, 1980	$148.39
August 22, 1980	$145.39
September 10, 1980	$145.39

* * *

5. The net payoff balance on creditor's installment loan to debtor was $4,015.91 at the time debtor's bankruptcy petition was filed on September 30, 1980. * * *

6. The debtor was insolvent with liabilities of $19,775.00 and assets of $6,010.00 for the entire period in question.

7. The debtor was granted a discharge on January 20, 1981.

Issue

Do the transfers of property of the debtor to the creditor constitute voidable preferences under 11 U.S.C. § 547(b)?

Discussion of Law

A trustee may avoid a transfer of property of the debtor to a creditor as a preference if the trustee proves that the five elements of a preference under 11 U.S.C. § 547(b) are met. 11 U.S.C. § 547(b) provides that:

the trustee may avoid any transfer of property of the debtor—

(1) to or for the benefit of a creditor;

(2) for or on account of an antecedent debt owed by the debtor before such transfer was made;

(3) made while the debtor was insolvent;

(4) made—

(A) on or within 90 days before the date of the filing of the petition; or

(B) between 90 days and one year before the date of the filing of the petition, if such creditor at the time of such transfer—

(i) was an insider; *   *   * and

(5) that enables such creditor to receive more than such creditor would receive if—

(A) the case were a case under chapter 7 of this title;

(B) the transfer had not been made; and

(C) such creditor received payment of such debt to the extent provided by the provisions of this title.

In the instant case, debtor, during the period from June 30, 1980 to September 30, 1980, made three transfers of property to creditor. Creditor admits that said transfers meet the first four elements of a preference under § 547(b).

The existence of the fifth and final element of a preferential transfer is denied by creditor. *   *   *

In order to determine whether a transfer allows a creditor to receive a greater percentage of his claim than otherwise receivable under the distributive provisions of the Code, the court must determine the status of the creditor's claim; i.e., whether the creditor's claim is a secured claim or an undersecured claim. The Court must also consider the classes of creditors as provided for under Sections 507 and 506. The provision of the Bankruptcy Code that governs the determination of secured status is 11 U.S.C. § 506(a). Under § 506(a), a creditor's claim is secured to the extent of the value of his collateral. If the amount of a creditor's claim is greater than the value of his collateral, the creditor is undersecured and his claim is broken down into two parts: he has a secured claim to the extent of the value of his collateral; and he has an unsecured claim for the balance of his claim. [Citations.]

The claim of the creditor herein was secured by a 1978 Oldsmobile Omega automobile. The amount of creditor's claim on the date of the filing of debtor's petition was $4,015.91. The market value of creditor's collateral was listed by debtor on his Schedule A-2 at $3,500.00. At the trial upon the instant matter, debtor testified that he did not believe that $3,500.00 was a fair value of what the car was worth at the time he filed bankruptcy.

Debtor testified that the car was in excellent condition, except for a few stone marks around the rear wheel wells, at the time he filed his petition in bankruptcy. Debtor had purchased the car in October of 1979 for $4,250.00.

Trustee failed to carry his burden of establishing what the value of the collateral car was on the date of the filing of debtor's petition. There was no evidence presented by the trustee to prove that the amount of creditor's claim was greater than the value of creditor's collateral. Therefore, the court finds that the amount of creditor's claim was equivalent to the value of the collateral car and thus, creditor had a fully secured claim.

A trustee may only avoid as a preference a pre-bankruptcy transfer which enables one creditor to recover more on his claim than other creditors of the same class. The greater percentage test under § 547(b)(5) serves the prime bankruptcy policy of equality of distribution among creditors of the debtor.

Trustee, herein, has failed to carry his burden of proving that the effect of the payments was to enable creditor to obtain a greater percentage of its debt than it would receive under the distributive provisions of the Code. If any one of the elements of a preference under § 547(b), is wanting, a preference has not been established. [Citation.]

Therefore, it is the conclusion of this Court that the transfers of property of the debtor to the creditor do not constitute voidable preferences under 11 U.S.C. § 547(b) as the trustee failed to prove that the effect of the transfers was to enable the creditor to obtain a greater percentage of its debt than it would receive under the distributive provisions of the Code. Trustee's complaint to recover the amount of the August 9, 1980, August 22, 1980, and September 10, 1980 payments in the total sum of $439.17 should be denied as said payments do not meet all five elements necessary for a preference under 11 U.S.C. § 547(b).

Confirmation of Plan of Reorganization

MATTER OF LANDMARK AT PLAZA PARK LIMITED

United States Bankruptcy Court, District of New Jersey, 1980.
7 B.R. 653.

HILL, BKRTCY, J.

This opinion constitutes the Court's findings of fact and conclusions of law with respect to a Chapter 11 confirmation hearing held on debtor's plan of reorganization, as modified. The opinion explains the November 3, 1980, letter decision of the Court.

Debtor, Landmark at Plaza Park, Ltd., is a limited partnership whose only substantial asset is a 200-unit garden apartment complex located in Morrisville, Pennsylvania. City Federal (hereafter City) holds a first mortgage on this property in the face amount of $2,250,000. The mortgage bears an interest rate of 9.5% and is due and payable on October 1, 1986. * * * This opinion deals with debtor's plan as it affects City, the only objecting class of creditors. As to all other classes of creditors, there is no dispute and the Court is satisfied that the confirmation standards specified in 11 U.S.C. Section 1129 have been met.

* * *

The Plan as Modified

Crucial to an understanding of the Court's decision is a discussion of the plan and how it affects City. Contractually, City is a first mortgagee without recourse. It has possession of the property and is collecting the rents pursuant to a rent assignment agreement. The mortgage has been in default since at least December, 1979. City is undersecured and wants to complete its foreclosure action.

The debtor has proposed in substance the following plan:

1. City is to redeliver possession of the property to the debtor.
2. On the 16th month after the effective date of the plan and through the 36th month debtor will commence monthly interest payments at the rate of 12.5% computed on the value of the property—$2,260,000.
3. Debtor will deliver to City a non-recourse note, payable in three years in the face amount of $2,705,820.31, in substitution of all existing liabilities.
4. The existing mortgage will secure the note set forth in paragraph 3, except to the extent that it is inconsistent with or modified by the plan.
5. City is the only member of the class of creditors to which it has been assigned.

The face amount of the note is derived as follows:

a. Current value of collateral	$2,260,000.00
b. Unpaid interest: months 1–15 @ 12.5%	353,125.00
c. Interest on unpaid interest: 21 months @ 15%	92,695.31
Face amount of note	$2,705,820.31

The debtor's principal theory is that the note will be paid off at the end of 36 months by a combination of refinancing and accumulation of cash from the project, all of which will subsequently be discussed at length. The key to the debtor's plan is a proposal to obtain a new first mortgage in three years in the face amount of $2,400,000.

It is undisputed that pursuant to this plan City is impaired within the meaning of Section 1124 of the Code. City has rejected the plan.

The Issues

Confirmation standards under the Code are set forth in Section 1129. Clearly, the debtor has complied with all provisions of that section except for the following subsections: * * * (a)(11), (b)(1) and (b)(2). Subsection (a)(11) of Section 1129 is the feasibility requirement and, in a general sense, deals with whether the debtor can and will accomplish what it has proposed. Subsection (b) of Section 1129 is the "cram-down" provision of the Code. It describes those circumstances in which a class of creditors or interests may over its objection be involuntarily subjected to the provisions of a plan. Each of these sections will be discussed at length. The provisions of subsection (b) will be discussed first because certain determinations made there bear on the feasibility determination required by subsection (a)(11).

The Requirements of Section 1129(b)(1) and (2)

The provisions of Section 1129(b) specify the circumstances under which a class of creditors or interests may be involuntarily subjected to a plan of reorganization.

* * *

Given the present posture of this case the Court is satisfied that the factors set forth in Section 1129(b)(2)(A)(i), dealing with the cram down of a secured creditor, adequately deal with the question of whether the plan, as to City, is fair and equitable, and the Court will limit its consideration to those factors.

To meet the requirements of Section 1129(b)(2)(A)(i) the debtor's plan must do three things. First, it must provide for retention by the creditor of its lien. Second, the total stream of deferred cash payments proposed by the plan must at least total the amount of the secured claim. Third, the total stream of payments must have a value equal to the value of the property. The plan before the Court satisfies the first two requirements, but may not satisfy the third.

* * *

Conceptually, the modified plan seeks to force City to make a $2,260,000 loan, repayable in three years, with the first 15 months of interest deferred. There is no amortization over the term of the loan. Since there is currently no equity in the property the debtor is asking City to make a 100% loan. The rate of interest of a loan of this type should correspond to the rate of interest which would be charged or obtained by a creditor making a loan to a third party with similar terms, duration, collateral and risk. [Citation.] Although the rate of interest may be identical to the market rate of interest, this will often not be the case because of the particular risk involved. [Citation.]

It appears clear to the Court that the forced loan proposed by the debtor includes terms less favorable to City than would typically be found in the market and that any confirmable plan must compensate City for this deficiency. * * * Thus, if a note and interest payments were offered to City by debtor at a 15% rate debtor would appear to meet the requirement that the discounted stream of payments equal the value of the property. Because the 12.5% rate proposed by debtor is below the 15% minimum rate established by the Court the plan as presented does not comply with Section 1129(b)(2)(A)(i)(II) and, therefore, cannot be confirmed. Since the plan can be readily modified, however, the Court must determine whether the plan is feasible if funded at a 15% rate. * * *

The Requirements of Section 1129(a)(11)

* * *

Section 1129(a)(11) of the Code * * * requires the Court to scrutinize the plan proposed by a debtor to determine whether it offers a reasonable prospect of success and whether it is workable. Specifically Section 1129(a)(11) requires the court to find that:

Confirmation of the plan is not likely to be followed by the liquidation, or the need for further financial reorganization, of the debtor or any successor to the debtor under the plan, unless such liquidation or reorganization is proposed in the plan. [Citation.]

[Citation] states that the purpose of Section 1129(a)(11) is to prevent confirmation of visionary schemes that promise creditors and equity security holders more under a proposed plan than the debtor could possibly attain after confirmation. [Citation.] Thus, if the facts indicate that the plan will ultimately lead to liquidation, it is not feasible and cannot be confirmed even if the debtor is sincere and has made a best effort to perform according to the terms of the plan. [Citation.] The factors courts should generally consider in making the above determination are (1) the adequacy of the capital structure; (2) the earning power of the business; (3) economic conditions; (4) the ability of management; (5) the probability of the continuation of the same management; and (6) any other related matters which determine the prospects of a sufficiently successful operation to enable performance of the provisions of the plan. [Citation.]

* * *

It is clear, then, that debtor's projections of income and expense are not realistic. In response to this conclusion the Court has formulated its own judgment as to what income and expenses should properly be over a three-year period. * * * Given these figures and the 15% interest factor previously derived the final question for the Court is whether debtor can realistically carry out its plan, as required by 1129(a)(11).

Fulfillment of the Plan

As stated earlier, fulfillment of the plan contemplates the ability of the debtor to cure certain deferred maintenance items, to make certain interest payments to City, and to pay off a note to City in three years. * * *

* * *

The Court has discussed the cost of curing deferred maintenance and the income and expenses of the project over the next three years. In the Court's opinion fulfillment of the plan by the debtor is not possible if its "best judgment" figures are utilized. Furthermore, even assuming a 10% income increase, fulfillment of the plan's conditions is highly doubtful. In the Court's judgment it is more probable than not that confirmation of a plan would likely be followed either by a liquidation or further reorganization proceedings. Thus, the debtor has not fulfilled the requirements of Section 1129(a)(11) and confirmation of the debtor's plan, as modified, must be denied.

Confirmation of Chapter 13 Plan

IN RE JONSON

United States Bankruptcy Court, Southern District of Indiana, 1981.
17 B.R. 78

Bayt, Bkrtcy. J.

[The debtor, Jonson, is a single, thirty-five year old male with no dependents. He works as an administrative assistant for a medical doctor and has a net income of $755.00 per month. Jonson received a Master of Music degree from Indiana University and is only 2 courses short of receiving his doctorate. His only indebtedness is a student loan in the amount of $10,250.00 from Indiana University. Jonson has made no payments on this loan which became due and payable two years ago with monthly payments of $98.98. Jonson filed an amended plan under Chapter 13 in which he proposes to make payments to the Trustee of $140.00 per month for 36 months. Jonson's proposed plan would result in a total payment of $4,036.00 to Indiana University for a $10,250.00 loan. The plaintiff, Indiana University, objected to the confirmation of Jonson's Chapter 13 plan, raising the question of "good faith" on the part of Jonson.]

* * *

Before a bankruptcy court can confirm a Chapter 13 plan it must make certain findings. *See* 11 U.S.C. § 1325(a)(3). "In this respect, Chapter 13 differs markedly from Chapter 7 [since] [t]he court has virtually no role to play in straight bankruptcy or liquidation under Chapter 7." [Citation.]

One of the findings that the court must make is whether the "plan has been proposed in good faith. . . ." 11 U.S.C. § 1325(a)(3). The term "good faith", as used in 11 U.S.C. § 1325(a)(3), is not defined in the Code, nor can one look to the legislative history for a definition or a clarification of that term. Therefore, it is the court's duty "to fashion the meaning of that term." [Citation.]

This court is of the opinion that the major purpose of the court's discretion under § 1325 to scrutinize a Chapter 13 plan prior to confirmation, is to prevent debtor abuse of Chapter 13, and to insure that the distinction between Chapter 7 and Chapter 13, as well as the basic and underlying purpose of Chapter 13, is maintained. [Citation.]

A review of the legislative history unmistakably leads to the conclusion that the purpose of a Chapter 13 plan is to enable a debtor to pay either in full or in part, "debts which have become too burdensome to meet without the help of the bankruptcy laws." [Ci-

tations.] The purpose of Chapter 13 is not to allow a debtor to discharge a debt or debts which would not be dischargeable under Chapter 7, [citation], without substantial payment by the debtor to the creditor or creditors. To be sure, "the drafters [of the Code] did not intend the liberal provisions of Chapter 13 to be used as a disguised Chapter 7 liquidation. The drafters intended debtors to deal fairly and justly with their creditors." [Citation.] If a debtor is not dealing in such a manner, the court cannot find that the plan was proposed in good faith.

It is the court's opinion that the debtor's plan was not proposed in good faith. It appears that the debtor's sole purpose is to avoid the provisions of Chapter 7 which would not allow a discharge of the debtor's only debt, a student loan. [Citation.] This court does not mean to say, however, that a debtor's use of the liberal discharge provisions of Chapter 13 is *per se* bad faith. [Citation.] "But it may be bad faith to utilize these provisions without a corresponding attempt to repay creditors a meaningful [or substantial] amount." [Citation.] To allow confirmation of debtor's plan would in effect sanction "an abuse of the provisions, purpose and spirit of Chapter 13." [Citation.]

According to the terms of his plan, debtor would pay $140.00 per month for 36 months. At the end of 36 months debtor would have paid approximately $4,036.00 on a $10,250.00 student loan. The court notes that debtor's proposed payment is $41.00 more than the monthly payment of the sudent loan itself. Debtor's proposed payment is not a meaningful or substantial one. If he is able to pay more under the plan for three years than is required under the terms of his agreement with Indiana University, the court wonders why he should not continue to pay until the entire amount is paid off, particularly in view of the fact that he will earn more money as time passes.

In his Response, debtor maintains that a 39% dividend is a substantial payment, thus warranting confirmation of his plan. Such a dividend may well be substantial in other situations, but it is not so in the instant one, in which the debtor has only one debt and that debt is a student loan.

Given the nature of the debt, public policy should demand that the plan not be confirmed. Student loans serve an important and useful purpose. If a debtor fails to repay a student loan, a loan used to better oneself through higher education, such action by the debtor diminishes the amount that others may borrow.

The court CONCLUDES that debtor's Chapter 13 plan was not filed in good faith and, therefore, should not be confirmed by the court.

PROBLEMS

1. (a) B goes into bankruptcy. His estate has no assets. Are B's taxes discharged by the proceedings? Why?

(b) B obtains property from A on credit by representing that he is solvent when, in fact, he knows he is insolvent. Is B's debt to A discharged by B's discharge in bankruptcy?

2. B goes into bankruptcy owing $5,000 as wages to his four employees. There is enough in his estate to pay all costs of administration and enough to pay his employees, but nothing will then be left for general creditors. Do the employees take all the estate? Under what conditions? If the general creditors received nothing at all, would these debts be discharged?

3. A sold goods to B for $2,500 and retained a security interest in them. Three months later B filed a petition in bankruptcy under Chapter 7. At this time B still owed A $2,000 for the purchase price of the goods whose value was $1,500.

(a) May the trustee invalidate A's security interest. If so, under what provision?

(b) If the security interest is invalidated, what is A's status in the bankruptcy proceeding?

(c) If the security interest is *not* invalidated, what is A's status in the bankruptcy proceeding?

4. A debtor went through bankruptcy and received his discharge. Which of the following debts were completely discharged, and which remain debts against him in the future:

(a) Claims of $900 each by X and Y for wages earned within three months immediately prior to bankruptcy.

(b) A judgment of $3,000 against the debtor by C for breach of contract.

(c) Sales taxes of $1,800.

(d) $1,000 in past alimony and support money owed to his divorced wife for herself and their child.

(e) A judgment of $4,000 for injuries received because of the debtor's negligent operation of an automobile.

5. Rosinoff and his wife, who were business partners, entered bankruptcy. Objection was made to their discharge in bankruptcy by a creditor, Baldwin, on the grounds that:

(a) The partners had obtained credit from Baldwin on the basis of a false financial statement;

(b) The partners had failed to keep books of account and records from which their financial condition could be ascertained;

(c) Rosinoff had falsely sworn that he had taken seventy dollars from the partnership account when the correct amount was $700.

Were the debtors entitled to a discharge?

6. X Corporation is a debtor in reorganization proceeding under Chapter 11 of the Bankruptcy Reform Act. By fair and proper valuation its assets are worth $100,000. The indebtedness of the corporation is $105,000, it has outstanding $100 par value preferred stock in the amount of $20,000, and $30 par value common stock in the amount of $75,000. The plan of reorganization submitted by the trustees would give nothing to the common shareholders, bonds of the face amount of $5,000 to the creditors, and common stock in the ratio of 84 percent to the creditors and 16 percent to the preferred shareholders. Should this plan be confirmed?

7. A is a wage earner with a regular income. She has unsecured debts of $42,000 and secured debts owing to B, C, D, and E totaling $120,000. E's debt is secured only by a mortgage on A's house. A files a petition under Chapter 13 and a plan providing payment as follows: (a) 60 percent of all taxes owed, (b) 35 percent of all unsecured debts, and (c) $100,000 in total to B, C, D, and E. Should the court confirm the plan? If not, how must the plan be modified and/or what other conditions must be satisfied?

8. John Bunker has assets of $130,000 and liabilities of $185,000 owed to nine creditors. Nonetheless, his cash flow is positive and he is making payment on all of his obligations as they become due. I. M. Flintheart, who is owed $22,000 by Bunker, files an involuntary petition in bank-ruptcy against Bunker. Bunker contests the petition. Decision?

9. D has filed a petition for a Chapter 7 proceeding. The total value of D's estate is $35,000. V, who is owed $18,000 has a security interest in property valued at $12,000. X has an unsecured claim of $9,000, which is entitled to a priority of $2,000. The United States has a claim for income taxes of $7,000. Y has an unsecured claim of $10,000 that was filed on time. Z has an unsecured claim of $17,000 that was filed on time. W has a claim of $14,000 that was not filed on time even though J was aware of the bankruptcy proceedings.

What should each of the creditors receive in a distribution under Chapter 7?

Part Nine—Regulation of Business

PUBLIC POLICY, SOCIAL ISSUES AND BUSINESS ETHICS

PART Nine addresses the role of government in regulating business, a role that has grown in this country to far greater proportions during the twentieth century. It is theoretically possible to have an economic system in which government plays no part at all; it is also conceivable to have an economy in which government exercises a totally dominant role by owning all productive property as well as deciding what is produced, where it is produced, who shall produce it and who shall consume it. In practice, however, economic systems fall in between these two extremes: our economy has less governmental involvement than the Soviet Union's or China's but greater than Hong Kong's.

Our ecomomic system is thus a "mixed economy" which has evolved from capitalism. As explained and justified by Adam Smith in his book, *The Wealth of Nations* (1776), the capitalistic system is composed of six "institutions": economic motivation, private productive property, free enterprise, free markets, competition, and limited government. Economic motivation assumes that a person will work harder if he receives an economic return for his effort; therefore the economic system should provide greater economic rewards for those who work harder. Private property (as discussed in Part Ten of this book) is the means by which economic motivation is exercised. It permits individuals to innovate and produce while securing to them the fruits of their efforts. Professor Behrman has described how the four other institutions combine with these two to bring about industrialized capitalism:

* * * Free enterprise permits the combination of properties so people can do things together that they can't do alone. Free enterprise means a capitalistic combination of factors of production under decisions of free individuals. Free enterprise is the group expression of the use of private property, and it permits greater efficiency in an industrial setting through variation in the levels and kinds of production.

* * * The free market operates to equate supply and demand—supply reflecting the ability and willingness to offer certain goods or services, and demand reflecting the consumers' *ability* and *willingness* to pay. Price is adjusted to include the maximum number of *both* bids and offers. The market, therefore, is *the* decision-making mechanism outside of the firm. It is the *means* by which basic decisions are made about the use of resources, and all factors are supposed to respond to it, however they wish. * * *

Just in case it doesn't work out that way, there is one more institution—the *Government*—which is supposed to set rules and provide protection for the society and its members. That's all, said Smith, that it should do: it should set the rules, enforce them, and stand aside. J. Behrman, *Discourses on Ethics and Business* 25–29 (1981).

So long as all these constituent institutions continued to exist and operate in a balanced manner the factors of production—land, capital, and labor—would combine to produce an efficient allocation of resources for individual consumers and for the economy as a whole. For this outcome to obtain, however, Smith's model required that a number of conditions be satisfied: "standardized products, numerous firms in markets, each firm with a small share and unable by its actions alone to exert significant influence over price, no barriers to entry, and output carried to the point where each seller's marginal cost equals the going market price." E. Singer, *Antitrust Economics and Legal Analysis* 2 (1981).

History has demonstrated that virtually all of these assumptions have *not* been satisfied by the actual operation of the economy.

More specifically, the actual competitive process falls considerably short of the assumptions of classical economic's model of perfect competition:

Competitive industries are never perfectly competitive in this sense. Many of the resources they employ cannot be shifted to other employments without substantial cost and delay. The allocation of those resources, as between industries or as to relative proportions within a single industry, is unlikely to have been made in a way that affords the best possible expenditure of economic effort. Information is incomplete, motivation confused, and decision therefore ill informed and often unwise. Variations in efficiency are not directly reflected in variations of profit. Success is derived in large part from competitive selling efforts, which in the aggregate may be wasteful, and from differentiation of products, which may be undertaken partly by methods designed to impair the opportunity of the buyer to compare quality and price. Profit is sought not only in producing or distributing goods but also in a wide variety of fianancial manipulations that have no fixed relationship to the productive process. Rivalry is often between a few concerns that strike at one another in a conscious effort to do injury rather than between a large number of concerns that compete anonymously and impersonally. Incentives to limit production and maintain prices are often dominant in spite of this rivalry. C. Edwards, *Maintaining Competition* 7(1964).

In addition to capitalism's failure to accomplish its objective of efficient resource allocation, it cannot be relied upon to achieve all of the social and public policy objectives required by a pluralistic democracy. For example, equitable distribution of wealth, national defense, conservation of natural resources, full employment, stability in economic cycles, protection against economic dislocations, health and safety, social security and other important social and economic goals are simply not comprehended nor addressed by

the free enterprise model. As a consequence, increased governmental intervention has occurred not only to preserve the competitive process in our mixed economic system but also to achieve social goals extrinsic to the efficient allocation of resources. Such intervention attempts (1) to regulate both "legal" monopolies such as those conferred by law through copyrights, patents and trade symbols and "natural" monopolies such as utilities, transportation and communications; (2) to correct imperfections in the market system in order to preserve competition; (3) to protect specific groups from failures of the market place, the most important example being labor; and (4) to promote other social goals. Successful government regulation involves a delicate balance between regulations that attempt to preserve competition and those advancing other social objectives. The latter must not undermine the basic competitive processes that are relied upon to bring about an efficient allocation of economic resources.

Part Nine examines a number of critical areas of governmental intervention. The chapters on Unfair Competition and Antitrust address the ways in which the government has sought to preserve a free and fair competitive system. The chapter on Consumer Protection deals with the attempts by government to ensure that, as Adam Smith said, "the consumer is King". The chapter on Employment Law covers the various regulatory efforts protecting one of the productive factors in capitalism: labor. Governmental regulation of another key factor—capital—is discussed in the chapters on Securities Regulation and Accountants' Legal Liability. (The third factor—land—is discussed in Part Ten.) In studying these chapters the reader should keep in mind the goals and objectives of the capitalistic system, the failures of the system in actual operation, the abuses of the system, and the economic and social reasons underlying government's intervention.

Chapter 40

UNFAIR COMPETITION AND BUSINESS TORTS

THE economic system in the United States is based upon free and fair competition. The law of unfair competition and antitrust attempt to preserve fairness and to protect freedom of competition by preventing businesses from taking unfair advantage of their competitors. Antitrust is the subject of Chapter 41. This chapter covers the law of unfair competition which can be divided into two broad categories: business torts and intellectual property. The first part of the law of unfair competition is part of the common law of torts. It provides businesses with a remedy against various forms of unauthorized interference with protected economic interests. The first part of this chapter will discuss this type of unfair competition.

The second category of unfair competition is primarily statutory and protects business' interest in intellectual property. The term "intellectual property" includes (1) trade-marks and other trade symbols (protection for devices indicating the origin of goods and services); (2) copyrights (protection for original expressions of ideas); (3) patents (protection for useful, novel, and nonobvious applications of ideas); and (4) trade secrets (protection for unpatented but undisclosed processes or methods). Trade symbols, copyrights, and patents are protected by specific Federal statutes while trade secrets receive protection under State common law. Infringement—the unauthorized interference with protected interests in intellectual property—is considered unfair competition and is discussed in the second part of this chapter.

BUSINESS TORTS

The law of torts, as previously discussed in Chapter 5, protects a person from interference with legally protected interests, among which are economic interests. Economic or pecuniary interests include a person's existing and prospective contractual relations, a person's business reputation, a person's name and likeness, and a person's freedom from deception. Business torts—those torts that protect a person's economic interests—are discussed in this section under the following headings: (1) Interference with Contractual Relations, (2) Defamation, (3) Disparagement, (4) Appropriation, and (5) Misrepresentation.

Interference with Contractual Relations

In order to conduct business it is necessary to establish trade relations with employees, suppliers, and customers. These relations may or may not be contractual but those that are, or are capable of being established by contract, receive legal protection against interference. Section 766 of the Restatement provides:

One who intentionally and improperly interferes with the performance of a contract (except a contract to marry) between another and a third person by inducing or otherwise causing the third person not to perform the contract, is subject to liability to the other for the pecuniary loss resulting to the other from the failure of the third person to perform the contract.

Similar liability is imposed for intentional and improper interference with another's prospective contractual relation. Restatement, Section 766B.

In either case, the rule applies whenever a person acts with the purpose or motive of interfering with another's contract or with the knowledge that such interference is substantially certain to occur as a natural consequence of her actions. The interference may be by prevention through the use of physical force or by threats to frighten away employees or customers. In some instances a conditional refusal to deal will constitute a threat.

The Restatement provides the following illustrations.

1. Upon hearing of B's contract with C, A ceases to buy from B. When asked by B to explain his conduct, A replies that his reason is B's contract with C. Thereupon B breaks his contract with C in order to regain A's business. A has not induced the breach and is not subject to liability to C under the rule stated in this Section.

2. Upon hearing of B's contract with C, A writes to B as follows: "I cannot tolerate your contract with C. You must call it off. I am sure that our continued relations will more than compensate you for any payment you may have to make to C. If you do not advise me within ten days that your contract with C is at an end, you may never expect further business from me." Thereupon B breaks his contract with C. A has induced the breach and is subject to liability under the rule stated in this Section.

Frequently, the interference is accomplished by inducement such as the offer of a better contract. For instance, A may offer B, an employee of C, a yearly salary of $5,000 per year more than the contractual arrangement between B and C. If A is aware of the contract between B and C and that his offer to B interferes with that contract, then A is liable to C for intentional interference with contractual relations.

To be distinguished is the situation where the contract may be terminated at will or there is only the prospect of a contractual relation. In these cases competition is a proper basis for interference, for if one party is pursuing a contractual relation, others are also free to pursue a similar arrangement. Section 768 of the Restatement provides:

(1) One who intentionally causes a third person not to enter into a prospective contractual relation with another who is his competitor or not to continue an existing contract terminable at will does not interfere improperly with the other's relation if

(a) the relation concerns a matter involved in the competition between the actor and the other and

(b) the actor does not employ wrongful means and

(c) his action does not create or continue an unlawful restraint of trade and

(d) his purpose is at least in part to advance his interest in competing with the other.

(2) The fact that one is a competitor of another for the business of a third person does not prevent his causing a breach of an existing contract with the other from being an improper interference if the contract is not terminable at will.

For example, A and B are competing distributors of transistors. A induces C, a prospective customer of B, to buy the transistors from A instead of B. A has no liability to B because A's interference with B's prospective contract with C is justified on the basis of competition, so long as A does not use predatory means such as physical violence, fraud, civil suits, or criminal prosecution to persuade C to deal with A.

With respect to damages, Section 774A of the Restatement provides:

One who is liable to another for interference with a contract or prospective contractual relation is liable for damages for

(a) the pecuniary loss of the benefits of the contract or the prospective relation;

(b) consequential losses for which the interference is a legal cause; and

(c) emotional distress or actual harm to reputation, if they are reasonably to be expected to result from the interference.

In addition, sinced this tort is intentional, punitive damages may be awarded where the defendant's conduct is outrageous or his motive is evil. Restatement, Section 908. Moreover, in appropriate circumstances, injunctive relief may be granted.

Defamation

The tort of defamation is a communication which injures a person's reputation by disgracing him and diminishing the respect in which he is held. An example would be the publication of a statement that a person had committed a crime or had a loathsome disease.

If the defamatory communication is handwritten, typewritten, printed, pictorical, or by other means with like communicative power, such as television or radio, it is designated **libel**. If it is spoken or oral, it is designated **slander**. In either case it must be communicated to another person or persons. This is referred to as its *publication*. If A writes a defamatory letter about B's character which he hands or mails to B, this is not a publication as it is intended only for B.

Privilege and truth are defenses to defamation. There are three types of privileges: (1) absolute, (2) conditional, and (3) constitutional. In most States, **truth** is a complete defense without regard to the purpose or intent in publishing the defamation.

As with the defense of truth, **absolute privilege** protects the defendant regardless of his motive or intent. Absolute privilege has been confined to those few situations where public policy clearly favors complete freedom of speech and includes: (1) statements made regarding a judicial proceeding; (2) statements made by members of Congress on the floor of Congress; (3) statements made by certain executive officers in the discharge of their governmental duty; and (4) statements made between spouses when they are alone.

Conditional or qualified privilege is conditioned upon proper use of the privilege. A person has conditional privilege to publish defamatory matter to protect his own legitimate interests, or in some cases the interests of another. Conditional privilege also extends to many cases where the publisher and the recipient have a common interest as with letters of reference. Conditional privilege, however, is forfeited by the publisher if she acts in an excessive manner, without probable cause, or for an improper purpose.

The First Amendment to the United States Constitution guarantees freedom of speech and freedom of press. The courts have applied these rights to the law of defamation by extending a form of **constitutional privilege** to comment regarding public officials or public figures so long as it is done without malice. Restatement, Section 580A. For these purposes "malice" is not ill will but proof of the publisher's knowledge of falsity or reckless disregard of the truth. *See Hutchinson v. Proxmire in Chapter 5.*

False statements that disparage another in the conduct of his business, trade or profession give rise to liability without proof of special damages as harm is inferred from the publication of the defamatory statements. Restatement, Section 573. This rule applies to artisans, mechanics, merchants, agents, and officers of corporations as well as members of the various professions. For instance, A in the presence of B, charges C, a merchant, with using false weights and measures as a result of which C's business falls off appreciably. C may recover damages from A for defamation without proving loss of trade. In addition, C may recover damages for the loss of business that he can establish with reasonable certainty.

Disparagement

The tort of disparagement or injurious falsehood imposes liability for the *publication* of a false statement that results in harm to another's interests which have pecuniary value if the publisher knows that the statement is false or acts in reckless disregard of its truth or falsity. Restatement, Section 623A. This tort most commonly involves false statements intended by the party making them to cast doubt upon the title or quality of another's property or products. Restatement, Section 626. Thus A, while contemplating the purchase of a stock of merchandise that belongs to B, reads an advertisement in a newspaper in which C falsely asserts he owns the merchandise. C has disparaged B's property in the goods. Similarly, A, knowing her statement to be false, tells C that B, an importer of wood, does not deal in mahogany. As a result C, who had intended to buy mahogany

from B, buys it elsewhere. A is liable to B for disparagement.

The torts of defamation and disparagement are similar in a number of respects and may overlap in some situations. Both torts involve the imposition of liability for injuries sustained through publication of false statements. Moreover, the defense of **truth** as well as absolute, conditional, and constitutional **privilege** apply to the same extent to the tort of disparagement as they do to defamation. Nevertheless, the torts protect two different interests. Defamation protects the *reputation* of the injured party while disparagement protects the *economic interests* of the injured party. Therefore, if the statement reflects solely upon the quality of the product sold by the plaintiff, then there is only disparagement. For example, A knowingly states to B that C manufactures and sells soap that is gritty. Although C's soap is not gritty, her sales of soap fall off as a consequence. A is liable to C for disparagement but not defamation. If, on the other hand, the statement implies that the plaintiff lacks integrity or is dishonest, there may also be personal defamation. For instance, A falsely states to a number of people that B knowingly sells pork that is diseased. A is liable to B for both defamation and disparagement.

A person who publishes disparaging matter is liable for loss sustained by the owner of the property disparaged as a result of repetition of the disparaging matter by a third person if the repetition was either authorized or reasonably foreseeable. For instance, Jones makes an offer to purchase Smith's farm which has been represented free and clear of encumbrances. Tattle tells Mrs. Jones that the farm is mortgaged up to its full value. Mrs. Jones, as she is privileged to do, repeats this to her husband who withdraws his offer for the farm. Tattle is liable to Smith.

The pecuniary loss which may be recovered by an injured person is that which directly and immediately results from impairment of the marketability of the property disparaged. Thus, A publishes an untrue statement in a magazine that cranberries grown during the current season in a particular area are unwholesome. B is a jobber who has contracted to buy the entire output of cranberries grown in this area. B's business falls off 50%. If there are no other facts which account for this falling off of B's business, B is entitled to recover the amount of his loss from A.

Appropriation

Appropriation is the use of the plaintiff's name or likeness for the benefit of the defendant, as for example in promoting or advertising a product or service. Restatement, Section 652 C. The tort of appropriation seeks to protect the individual's right to the exclusive use of his identity and is also known as the "right of publicity." For example, A is a well-known actress. In promoting his line of diet foods, B publishes a photograph of A above a caption stating "Keep That Youthful Figure by Eating B's Diet Foods." B is liable to A for appropriation.

In order for there to be liability for appropriation—

* * * the defendant must have appropriated to his own use or benefit the reputation, prestige, social or commercial standing, public interest or other values of the plaintiff's name or likeness. It is not enough that the defendant has adopted for himself a name that is the same as that of the plaintiff, so long as he does not pass himself off as the plaintiff or otherwise seek to obtain for himself the values or benefits of the plaintiff's name or identity. Unless there is such an appropriation, the defendant is free to call himself by any name he likes, whether there is only one person or a thousand others of the same name. Until the value of the name has in some way been appropriated, there is no tort. Restatement, Section 652 C, Comment C.

In *Hirsch v. S. C. Johnson & Son, Inc.,* 90 Wis.2d 379, 280 N.W.2d 129 (1979), the court held that use by defendant of the name "Crazylegs" on a shaving gel for women violated plaintiff's right of publicity. Plaintiff,

Elroy Hirsch, a famous football player, had been known by this nickname. The court said:

The fact that the name, "Crazylegs," used by Johnson, was a nickname rather than Hirsch's actual name does not preclude a cause of action. All that is required is that the name clearly identify the wronged person. In the instant case, it is not disputed at this juncture of the case that the nickname identified the plaintiff Hirsch. It is argued that there were others who were known by the same name. This, however, does not vitiate the existence of a cause of action. It may, however, if sufficient proof were adduced, affect the quantum of damages should the jury impose liability or it might preclude liability altogether. Prosser points out "that a stage or other fictitious name can be so identified with the plaintiff that he is entitled to protection against its use." [Citation.] He writes that it would be absurd to say that Samuel L. Clemens would have a cause of action if that name had been used in advertising, but he would not have one for the use of "Mark Twain." If a fictitious name is used in a context which tends to indicate that the name is that of the plaintiff, the factual case for identity is strengthened.

See *Carson v. Here's Johnny Portable Toilets, Inc.* and *Factors Etc., Inc. v. Creative Card Co.*

Misrepresentation

Section 525 of the Restatement provides:

One who fraudulently makes a misrepresentation of fact, opinion, intention, or law for the purpose of inducing another to act or to refrain from action in reliance upon it, is subject to liability to the other in deceit for pecuniary loss caused to him by his justifiable reliance upon the misrepresentation.

For example, A misrepresents to B that a tract of land in Texas is located in an area where drilling for oil had recently commenced. A made this statement knowing it was not true. In reliance upon the statement B purchased the land from A. A is liable to B for fraudulent misrepresentation.

The requisite elements of fraudulent mis-representation are:

1. a false representation
2. of a fact
3. that is material
4. and made with knowledge of its falsity and the intention to deceive
5. which is justifiably relied upon.

A basic element of fraud is a false representation. There must be some positive statement or conduct that misleads. There is generally no obligation on the part of a seller to tell a purchaser everything he knows about the subject of the sale, although if there is a latent (hidden) defect of a substantial character, one that would not be discovered by an ordinary examination, the seller is obliged to reveal it.

Another basic element of fraud is the misrepresentation of a material fact: actionable fraud can rarely be predicated upon what is merely a statement of **opinion**. A representation is one of opinion if it expresses only the belief of the representor as to the existence of a fact or his judgment as to quality, value, authenticity, or other matters of judgment. Restatement, Section 538 A. The line between fact and opinion is not an easy one to draw. Suppose that A induces B to purchase shares in a company unknown to B at a price of $100 per share by representing that she had the preceding year paid $150 per share for them, when in fact she had paid $50. This is a representation of a past event, definitely ascertainable, verifiable, and fraudulent. If, on the other hand, A said to B that the shares were "a good investment," she is merely stating her opinion, and in the usual case B ought to regard it as no more than that.

In addition to the requirement that the misrepresentation be one of fact, it is necessary that it be material. Restatement, Section 538. It must relate to something of sufficient substance to induce reliance. In the sale of a race horse it may not be material whether the horse was ridden in its most re-cent race by a certain jockey, but its running time for the race probably would be.

To establish fraud the misrepresentation must have been known by the one making it to be false and must be made with an intention to deceive. Knowledge of falsity can consist of (a) actual knowledge, (b) lack of belief in the statement's truthfulness, or (c) reckless indifference as to its truthfulness. Restatement, Sections 526 and 527. In addition, a majority of courts now permit a rescission for negligent or innocent (non-negligent) misrepresentation, provided, of course, that all of the remaining elements of fraud are present.

A person is not entitled to relief unless he has justifiably relied upon the misrepresentation to his detriment or injury. Restatement, Section 537. If the complaining party's decision was in no way influenced by the misrepresentation, he must abide by the terms of the contract. He is not deceived if he does not rely. Moreover, if the complaining party knew or should have known that the representation of the defendant was untrue, but still entered into the contract, he has not justifiably relied. Restatement, Section 541. For example, A, seeking to purchase a six-passenger car, was told by the salesman that a two-seat sports car was appropriate and took A for a test drive. If A, nevertheless, relied on the salesman's statement, such reliance would not be justified, and A would not have been legally defrauded.

A party who has been induced to enter into a contract by fraud may recover damages in a tort action. The minority of States allow the injured party to recover only **"out-of-pocket"** damages equal to the difference between the value of what she has received and the value of what she has given for it. The great majority of States, however, permit the intentionally defrauded party to recover damages under the **"benefit-of-the-bargain"** rule which is equal to the difference between the value of what she has received and the value of the fraudulent party's performance as represented. The Restatement of Torts provides the fraudulently injured party with the option of either the out-of-pocket or the benefit-of-the-bargain damages. Section 549. To illustrate, A intentionally misrepresents the capabilities of a printing press which induces B to purchase the machine for $20,000. The value of the press as delivered is $14,000, but if the machine performed as represented, it would be worth $24,000. Under the out-of-pocket rule B would recover $6,000, while under the benefit-of-the-bargain rule she would recover $10,000.

Where the misrepresentation is not fraudulent, the Restatement of Torts permits out-of-pocket damages but expressly excludes recovery of benefit-of-the-bargain damages. Sections 552 B and 552 C.

INTELLECTUAL PROPERTY

Intellectual property includes trade secrets, trade symbols, copyrights, and patents. These interests are protected from infringement or unauthorized use by others. Such protection is essential to the conduct of business. For example, business would be far less willing to invest considerable resources in research and development unless the resulting discoveries, inventions, and processes were protected by patents and trade secrets. Similarly, business would not be secure in devoting time and money to the marketing of its products and services if its trade symbols and trade names were not protected. Moreover, without copyright protection, the publishing, entertainment, and computer software industries would be vulnerable to having their efforts pirated by competition. This section will discuss the law protecting (1) Trade Secrets; (2) Trade Symbols including Trademarks, Service Marks, Certification Marks, Collective Marks and Trade Names; (3) Copyrights, and (4) Patents.

Trade Secrets

Every business has secret information including lists of customers as well as contracts with suppliers and customers. Some have se-

cret formulas, processes, and methods used in the production of goods that are vital to successful operation of the business. These are sometimes designated as "trade secrets", involving information received and held in confidence by employees which they are required to have in order to perform their duties.

An employee is under a duty of loyalty to his employer which includes the nondisclosure of trade secrets to competitors. It is wrongful for a competitor to obtain vital secret trade information of this type from an employee by bribery or otherwise. The faithless employee also commits a tort by divulging secret trade information. Contracts of employment frequently contain restrictive covenants whereby the employee agrees that for a stated period of time and within a specific territory he will not directly or indirectly engage in competition with his former employer, or become employed by a competitor of his former employer. These restrictive agreements, if reasonable with respect to time and area limitations, are enforced by the courts, although in some jurisdictions enforcement depends upon the employee having acquired trade secrets of his employer during the course of his employment.

In the absence of contract restriction, an employee is under no duty upon termination of his employment to refrain from competing or working for a competitor of his former employer. During the period of employment he is under such a duty whether or not provided by contract. An example of unfair competition would be the inducement by one company of employees of another company possessed of certain unique technical skills and secret knowledge acquired by them in the course of such employment, to terminate their employment and to use such skills and secret information for its benefit. Thus, A and B, who have been employees of the X Company for 15 years, have developed in the course of their employment highly specialized knowledge and skills in the manufacture of space suits for astronauts. There are few, if any, persons who have equivalent skill and knowledge. Y Company, desirous of obtaining a contract with the government for the manufacture of space suits, approaches A and B and offers them employment. There is no contract which prohibits A and B from leaving the X Company and going to work for the Y Company. However, if they do so, the X Company is entitled to an injunction restraining A, B, and the Y Company from the use of trade secrets and methods for manufacturing space suits which were developed by A and B while in the employ of the X Company.

Another improper method of acquiring trade secrets is industrial espionage such as electronic surveillance or spies. In the broadest sense, discovery of another's trade secrets by any means other than one's own independent research efforts or inspection of the finished product is improper unless the other party voluntarily discloses the secret or fails to take reasonable precautions to protect its secrecy. *E.I. du Pont de Nemours & Co. v. Christopher*, 431 F.2d 1012 (5th Cir. 1970). To illustrate: Plaintiff and defendant were competitors in the business of dehairing raw cashmere, the fleece of certain Asiatic goats. Dehairing is the process of separating the commercially valuable soft down from the matted mass of raw fleece which also contains long coarse guard hairs and other impurities. Machinery for this process is not readily available on the open market. Each company in the business designed and built its own machinery and kept the nature of its process secret. Plaintiff contracted with one Lawton, owner of a small machine shop, to build and install new improved dehairing machinery of increased efficiency for which plaintiff furnished designs, drawings, and instructions. Lawton knew that the design of the machinery was confidential, and agreed that he would manufacture the machinery exclusively for plaintiff and that he would not reproduce the machinery or any of its essential parts for any one else. Defendant purchased from Lawton a copy of the dehairing machinery which plaintiff had thus specially de-

signed. Defendant was held liable to plaintiff for the tort of appropriation of plaintiff's trade secrets, despite the nonpatentability of the machinery. *Atlantic Wool Combing Co. v. Norfolk Mills, Inc.*, 357 F.2d 866 (1st Cir. 1966).

Trade Symbols

One of the earliest forms of unfair competition is the fraudulent marketing of one person's goods as those of another. This unlawful practice is sometimes referred to as "passing off" or "palming off." It is basically a "cashing in" on the good will, good name, and reputation of a competitor and of his products. It results in deception of the public and loss of trade by honest businesses. A statutory descendant of "palming off" protects certain forms of good will which have become identified by trade symbols: trademarks, service marks, certification marks, collective marks, and trade names. These trade symbols are protected against misuse or infringement by injunctive relief and a right of action for damages against the infringer. An infringement is a form of passing off one's goods or services as those of the owner of the mark, is deceptive of the public, and constitutes unfair competition.

Trademarks A trademark is a *distinctive* mark, word, letter, number, design, picture, or combination in any form of arrangement which is affixed to goods and is adopted or used by a person identifying goods which he manufactures or sells. Generic and descriptive designations cannot be used as trademarks. Thus, a word which is descriptive of the ingredients, quality, purpose, function, or uses of a product may not be monopolized by a person as his proprietary trademark. The word "Plow" cannot be a trademark for plows, although it may be a trademark for shoes.

At common law a trademark was required to be affixed to the goods it identified. The Federal trademark statute, the Lanham Act, relaxes this requirement by permitting trademark registration and protection of a mark placed "on the goods of their containers or the displays associated therewith or on the tags or labels affixed thereto."

Trademarks may be registered in the United States Patent Office. If infringed, the owner is entitled to injunctive relief and damages.

Service Marks Similar in function to the trademark which identifies tangible goods and products, a service mark is used to identify and distinguish the services of one person from those of others. A service mark need not be affixed to goods and when registered is entitled to the same protection as a registered trademark. Service marks were not registerable prior to the Lanham Act.

For example, plaintiff in 1954 registered its service mark "Holiday Inn" in the U.S. Patent Office. In 1961 defendant commenced operating a 16-room motel under the name "Holiday Inn" at Charlotte Amalie, St. Thomas, Virgin Islands. Plaintiff did not have a motel in the Virgin Islands, and its nearest motel was at San Juan, Puerto Rico, approximately 70 miles distant. The Virgin Islands are over 1,000 miles east of the U.S. Mainland and travel to them is only by ship or plane. Plaintiff had a national reputation, a public image created and maintained by national advertising and promotional campaigns, and approximately 830 motels, either directly owned or franchised. It had received two applications for a franchise to operate a Holiday Inn in the U.S. Virgin islands, but had reserved making a decision pending the outcome of this suit to enjoin defendant from the use of the name. The Court held that plaintiff had a superior right to the name Holiday Inn, but that defendant's use of the name for its motel, by reason of its isolated geographic location, would not be competitively injurious to the plaintiff until plaintiff should actually begin the development or construction of a motel in the U.S. Virgin Islands. Accordingly, the injunctive order of the lower court was modified so that it would be effective only upon plaintiff making such a showing. *Holiday Inns of*

America, Inc. v. B & B Corp., 409 F.2d 614 (3d Cir. 1969).

Certification Marks A certification mark is a mark used upon or in connection with goods or services to certify regional or other origin, material, mode of manufacture, quality, accuracy, or other characteristics of the goods or services, or that the work or labor in the goods or services were performed by members of a union or other organization. The owner of the certification mark may *not* be the producer or provider of the goods or services with which the mark is used.

Collective Marks A collective mark is a distinctive mark or symbol used to indicate either membership in a trade union, trade association, fraternal society, or other organization, or that the goods or services are produced by members of a collective group.

Trade Names A trade name, like a trademark, is serviceable as an identification of the product of a particular manufacturer or distributor. It may also designate a service or be the name under which a business is conducted. Trade names, therefore, have broader scope than trademarks which only identify goods. A trade name for a product may be coined, such as "Kodak" or "Nylon," or it may be a popularly accepted nickname as "Coke."

Descriptive and generic words, and personal and generic names, although not proper trademarks, may become protected as trade names upon acquiring a special significance in the trade. This special significance is frequently referred to as a "secondary meaning" of the name acquired as the result of continuing and extended use in connection with specific goods or services whereby the name has lost its primary meaning to a substantial number of purchasers or users of the goods or services.

For example, plaintiff operated an apartment-hotel known as "Forest Park Hotel" located one block east of Forest Park, a large and well known municipal park in St. Louis,

Mo., which was established by the Missouri Legislature in 1874 and was the site of the St. Louis World's Fair in 1904. It is the second largest municipal park in the United States and contains numerous educational and recreational facilities. Plaintiff's hotel building was constructed in 1923 and acquired by plaintiff in 1954. Defendant in 1964 constructed a building across the street from Forest Park, but 11 blocks south and 13 blocks east of plaintiff's hotel in which defendant conducted a convalescent and nursing home under the name of "Forest Park Manor". In an action to enjoin defendant from the use of this name as unfair competition on the ground that plaintiff and defendant were both operating a place of accommodations for elderly persons and that the similarity in names was deceptive to the public, defendant prevailed. The court concluded from the evidence that the conduct of defendant's business had no tendency or effect to deceive the public that it was the Forest Park Hotel. *Pan American Realty Corp. v. Forest Park Manor, Inc.*, 431 S.W.2d 144 (Mo.1968).

Although trade names may *not* be federally registered under the Lanham Act, trade names are protected, and a person who palms off his goods or services by using the trade name of another is liable in damages and also may be enjoined from doing so.

Copyrights

Copyright is a form of protection provided by Federal law to authors of original works, which under Section 102 of the Copyright Act includes literary works, musical works, dramatic works, pantomimes, choreographic works, pictorial, graphic and sculptural works, motion picture and other audiovisual works, and sound recordings. This listing is illustrative and not exhaustive as the Act extends copyright protection to "original works of authorship in any tangible medium of expression, now known or later developed." Moreover, in 1980 the Copyright Act was amended to extend copyright protection to computer programs.

In no case does copyright protection for an original work of authorship include any idea, procedure, process, system, method of operation, concept, principle, or discovery, regardless of the form in which it is described, explained, illustrated, or embodied in such work. Section 102(b).

Copyright protection subsists in most instances for a period of the author's life plus an additional fifty years. Section 106 of the Copyright Act gives the owner of the copyright the exclusive right to do, and to authorize others to do, the following:

1. to reproduce the copyrighted work in copies or phonorecords;
2. to prepare derivative works based upon the copyrighted work;
3. to distribute copies or phonorecords of the copyrighted work to the public by sale or other transfer of ownership, or by rental, lease, or lending;
4. to perform the copyrighted work publicly in the case of literary, musical, dramatic, choreographic, pantomime, motion picture, and other audiovisual works; and
5. to display the copyrighted work publicly in the case of literary, musical, dramatic, and choreographic works, pantomimes, and pictorial, graphic, or sculptural works, including the individual images of a motion picture or other audiovisual work.

These broad rights are subject, however, to several limitations, the most important of which are "compulsory licenses" and "fair use". **Compulsory licenses** permit certain limited uses of copyrighted material upon the payment of specified royalties and compliance with statutory conditions. Section 107 codifies the common law doctrine of **fair use** as follows:

Notwithstanding the provisions of section 106, the fair use of a copyrighted work, including such use by reproduction in copies or phonorecords or by any other means specified by that section, for purposes such as criticism, comment, news reporting, teaching (including multiple copies for classroom use), scholarship, or research, is not an infringement of copyright. In determining whether the use made of a work in any particular case is a fair use the factors to be considered shall include—

(1) the purpose and character of the use, including whether such use is of a commercial nature or is for nonprofit educational purposes;

(2) the nature of the copyrighted work;

(3) the amount and substantiality of the portion used in relation to the copyrighted work as a whole; and

(4) the effect of the use upon the potential market for or value of the copyrighted work.

See Sony Corporation of America v. Universal City Studios, Inc.

Applications for copyright are filed with the Register of Copyrights, Copyright Office, Library of Congress, Washington, D.C. Registration of the copyright is not required, as copyright protection begins as soon as the work is fixed in a tangible medium. Registration is, nonetheless, advisable as it is a condition of certain remedies for copyright infringement and some rights can be permanently lost by failure to register soon enough. When a work is published, a notice of copyright should be placed on all publicly distributed copies so as to give reasonable notice of the claim of copyright. Section 401.

The ownership of a copyright may be transferred in whole or in part by conveyance, will, or intestate succession. Section 201. A transfer of copyright ownership, other than by operation of law, is not valid unless a note or memorandum of the transfer is in writing and signed by the owner of the rights conveyed or the owner's duly authorized agent. Section 204.

Ownership of a copyright, or of any of the exclusive rights under a copyright, is distinct from ownership of any material object in which the work is embodied. Transfer of ownership of any material object, including the copy or phonorecord in which the work is first fixed, does not of itself convey any rights in the copyrighted work embodied in the object; nor, in the absence of an agreement, does transfer of ownership of a copyright or of any exclusive rights under a copy-

right convey property rights in any material object. Section 202. Thus, the purchase of this textbook does not affect the publisher's copyright nor does it authorize the purchaser to make and sell copies of the book.

Infringement occurs whenever somebody exercises the rights exclusively reserved for the copyright owner without authorization. Infringement need *not* be intentional. *See Bright Tunes Music Corp. v. Harrisongs Music, Ltd.* In order to sue for infringement, the copyright must be registered with the Copyright Office. If an infringement occurs *after* registration the following remedies are available:

1. injunction,
2. impoundment and possible destruction of infringing articles,
3. actual damages plus profits made by the infringer that are additional to those damages *or* statutory damages of at least $250 but no more than $10,000 according to what the court determines to be just,
4. costs and, in the court's discretion, reasonable attorney's fees to the prevailing party,
5. criminal penalties of a fine of up to $10,000 or up to one year's imprisonment for willful infringement for purposes of commercial advantage or private gain. The Piracy and Counterfeiting Amendments Act of 1982 imposes harsher punishments for large scale piracy: $250,000 fine and five years for pirating 1,000 phonorecords or 65 films within 180 days.

Patents

A patent is a grant by the Federal government of a monopoly right to an inventor to make, use, or sell the invention to the absolute exclusion of others for the period of the patent which currently is 17 years. The owner of the patent may also profit by licensing others to use the patent on a royalty basis. The patent may not be renewed and upon expiration the invention enters the "public domain" and anyone may then use it.

The Patent Act specifies those inventions that may be patented. Section 101 provides:

Whoever invents or discovers any new and useful process, machine, manufacture, or composition of matter, or any new and useful improvement thereof, may obtain a patent therefor, subject to the conditions and requirements of this title.

Thus, naturally occurring substances are not patentable as the invention must be made or modified by humans. For example, the discovery of an existing bacteria with useful properties is *not* patentable, whereas the manufacture of a human-made, genetically engineered bacterium is patentable. *See Diamond, Commissioner of Patents and Trademarks v. Chakrabarty.* By the same token, laws of nature, principles, systems of bookkeeping, fundamental truths, methods of calculation, and ideas are not patentable. Accordingly, Einstein could not patent his law that $E = mc^2$, nor could Newton have patented the law of gravity. *Funk Brothers Seed Co. v. Kalo Inoculant Co.*, 333 U.S. 127, 130 (1948). Similarly, isolated computer programs are not patentable although, as mentioned above, they may be copyrighted.

To be patentable the process, machine, manufacture, or composition of matter must meet three criteria:

1. novelty,
2. utility, and
3. nonobviousness.

A patent is issued by the United States Patent Office upon the basis of an application containing specific claims relating to the invention, process, product, or design. Before granting a patent, the Patent Office makes a careful and thorough examination of the prior art and determines whether the submitted invention has novelty (does not conflict with a prior pending application or a previously issued patent), utility, and is nonobvious. An application for a patent is confidential and its contents will not be divulged by the Patent Office. This confidentiality ends upon the granting of the patent.

Anyone who, without permission, makes, uses, or sells a patented invention is a direct infringer. The remedies for infringement under the Patent Act are (1) injunctive relief (Section 283); (2) damages, adequate to compensate the plaintiff but "in no event less than a reasonable royalty for the use made of the invention by the infringer" (Section 284); (3) treble damages when appropriate (Section 284); (4) attorney's fees in exceptional cases such as knowing infringement (Section 285); and (5) costs (Section 284).

CASES

Appropriation

CARSON v. HERE'S JOHNNY PORTABLE TOILETS, INC.

United States Court of Appeals, Sixth Circuit, 1983.
698 F.2d 831.

Brown, J.

This case involves claims of unfair competition and invasion of the right of privacy and the right of publicity arising from appellee's adoption of a phrase generally associated with a popular entertainer.

Appellant, John W. Carson (Carson), is the host and star of "The Tonight Show," a well-known television program broadcast five nights a week by the National Braodcasting Company. Carson also appears as an entertainer in night clubs and theaters around the country. From the time he began hosting "The Tonight Show" in 1962, he has been introduced on the show each night with the phrase "Here's Johnny." This method of introduction was first used for Carson in 1957 when he hosted a daily television program for the American Broadcasting Company. The phrase

"Here's Johnny" is generally associated with Carson by a substantial segment of the television viewing public. In 1967, Carson first authorized use of this phrase by an outside business venture, permitting it to be used by a chain of restaurants called "Here's Johnny Restaurants."

Appellant Johnny Carson Apparel, Inc. (Apparel), formed in 1970, manufactures and markets men's clothing to retail stores. Carson, the president of Apparel and owner of 20% of its stock, has licensed Apparel to use his name and picture, which appear on virtually all of Apparel's products and promotional material. Apparel has also used, with Carson's consent, the phrase "Here's Johnny" on labels for clothing and in advertising campaigns. In 1977, Apparel granted a license to Marcy Laboratories to use "Here's Johnny" as the name of a line of men's toiletries. The phrase "Here's Johnny" has never been registered by appellants as a trademark or service mark.

Appellee, Here's Johnny Portable Toilets, Inc., is a Michigan corporation engaged in the business of renting and selling "Here's Johnny" portable toilets. Appellee's founder was aware at the time he formed the corporation that "Here's Johnny" was the introductory slogan for Carson on "The Tonight Show." He indicated that he coupled the phrase with a second one, "The World's Foremost Commodian," to make "a good play on a phrase."

Shortly after appellee went into business in 1976, appellants brought this action alleging unfair competition, trademark infringement, under federal and state law, and invasion of privacy and publicity rights. They sought damages and an injunction prohibiting appellee's further use of the phrase "Here's Johnny" as a corporate name or in connection with the sale or rental of its portable toilets.

* * *

Appellants' first claim alleges unfair competition from appellee's business activities in violation of § 43(a) of the Lanham Act, [citation], and of Michigan common law. The district court correctly noted that the test for

equitable relief under both § 43(a) and Michigan common law is the "likelihood of confusion" standard. [Citations.]

* * *

The district court first found that "Here's Johnny" was not such a strong mark that its use for other goods should be entirely foreclosed. [Citation.] Although the appellee had intended to capitalize on the phrase popularized by Carson, the court concluded that appellee had not intended to deceive the public into believing Carson was connected with the product. [Citation.] The court noted that there was little evidence of actual confusion and no evidence that appellee's use of the phrase had damaged appellants. For these reasons, the court determined that appellee's use of the phrase "Here's Johnny" did not present a likelihood of confusion, mistake, or deception. [Citation.]

* * *

The facts as found by the district court do not implicate such likelihood of confusion, and we affirm the district court on this issue.

The appellants also claim that the appellee's use of the phrase "Here's Johnny" violates the common law right of privacy and right of publicity. The confusion in this area of the law requires a brief analysis of the relationship between these two rights.

In an influential article, Dean Prosser delineated four distinct types of the right of privacy: (1) intrusion upon one's seclusion or solitude, (2) public disclosure of embarrassing private facts, (3) publicity which places one in a false light, and (4) appropriation of one's name or likeness for the defendant's advantage. Prosser, *Privacy*, 48 Calif.L.Rev. 383, 389 (1960). This fourth type has become known as the "right of publicity." [Citations.] Henceforth we will refer to Prosser's last, or fourth, category as the "right of publicity."

* * *

The right of publicity has developed to protect the commercial interest of celebrities in their identities. The theory of the right is that a celebrity's identity can be valuable in the promotion of products, and the celebrity has an interest that may be protected from the unauthorized commercial exploitation of that identity. In [citation], we stated: "The famous have an exclusive legal right during life to control and profit from the commercial use of their name and personality." [Citation.]

The district court dismissed appellants' claim based on the right of publicity because appellee does not use Carson's name or likeness. [Citation.] It held that it "would not be prudent to allow recovery for a right of publicity claim which does not more specifically identify Johnny Carson." [Citation.] We believe that, on the contrary, the district court's conception of the right of publicity is too narrow. The right of publicity, as we have stated, is that a celebrity has a protected pecuniary interest in the commercial exploitation of his identity. If the celebrity's identity is commercially exploited, there has been an invasion of his right whether or not his "name or likeness" is used. Carson's identity may be exploited even if his name, John W. Carson, or his picture is not used.

In *Motschenbacher v. R. J. Reynolds Tobacco Co.*, [citation], the court held that the unauthorized use of a picture of a distinctive race car of a well known professional race car driver, whose name or likeness were not used, violated his right of publicity. * * *

In *Ali v. Playgirl, Inc.*, [citation], Muhammad Ali, former heavyweight champion, sued Playgirl magazine under the New York "right of privacy" statute and also alleged a violation of his common law right of publicity. The magazine published a drawing of a nude, black male sitting on a stool in a corner of a boxing ring with hands taped and arms outstretched on the ropes. The district court concluded that Ali's right of publicity was invaded because the drawing sufficiently identified him in spite of the fact that the drawing was captioned "Mystery Man." The district court found that the identification of Ali was made certain because of an accompanying verse that identified the figure as "The Greatest." The district court took judicial notice of

the fact that "Ali has regularly claimed that appellation for himself." [Citation.]

* * *

In this case, Earl Braxton, president and owner of Here's Johnny Portable Toilets, Inc., admitted that he knew that the phrase "Here's Johnny" had been used for years to introduce Carson. * * *

* * *

* * * It is our view that, under the existing authorities, a celebrity's legal right of publicity is invaded whenever his identity is intentionally appropriated for commercial purposes. * * * It is not fatal to appellant's claim that appellee did not use his "name." Indeed, there would have been no violation of his right of publicity even if appellee had used his name, such as "J. William Carson Portable Toilet" or the "John William Carson Portable Toilet" or the "J. W. Carson Portable Toilet." The reason is that, though literally using appellant's "name," the appellee would not have appropriated Carson's identity as a celebrity. Here there was an appropriation of Carson's identity without using his "name."

* * *

The judgment of the district court is vacated and the case remanded for further proceedings consistent with this opinion.

Appropriation

FACTORS ETC., INC. v. CREATIVE CARD COMPANY

United States District Court, Southern District of New York, 1977.
444 F.Supp. 279.

TENNEY, J.

Plaintiffs have moved this Court for a preliminary injunction pursuant to Rule 65 of the Federal Rules of Civil Procedure ("Rules") to restrain defendant Creative Card Company from the manufacture, distribution and sale of any poster or other commercially exploitive souvenir merchandise bearing the likeness of the late entertainer Elvis Presley. Plaintiffs claim possession of an exclusive right to that activity, based on a "right of publicity" assigned by Elvis Presley in life. Defendant Creative Card Company, an Illinois corporation, disputes the existence and assignment of this right, and has also moved for dismissal * * *. [B]y the tests for preliminary relief articulated in this circuit, I conclude that plaintiffs have made "a clear showing of . . . probable success on the merits *and* possible irreparable injury." [Citations.] * * *

THE FACTS

On August 16, 1977, Elvis Presley, without doubt a world famous celebrity-entertainer, died at the age of forty-two. During life his professional career and the commercial exploitation of his person were managed exclusively by "Colonel" Tom Parker, as demonstrated by the deposition of Col. Parker begun on September 30, 1977 and continued on October 1, 1977, and the documents appended thereto. On March 26, 1956, Presley and Parker entered into a written management contract which, although it does not specifically allude to souvenir merchandise, authorizes Parker to act exclusively for Presley "in any and all fields of public and private entertainment . . . embracing any and all branches thereof now known or hereafter coming into existence." * * * However, that items of merchandise were clearly contemplated by the parties becomes apparent in later agreements including, inter alia, one concluded a few months later among Parker, Presley and a Mr. Saperstein of Special Projects, Inc., a merchandising company. The Special Projects organization was made "exclusive agent" for a period of time to license other firms "in connection with the sale, marketing and exploitation of consumer items."

* * *

Plaintiff Boxcar Enterprises, Inc. ("Boxcar") entered into the Presley-Parker relationship as a corporation formed in January 1974. The Court does not have before it the certificate of incorporation, but Col. Parker has testified that he owned 56% of the shares and that Presley and one Tom Diskin, President of Boxcar, each owned 22%. There is, from this point on, some confusion as to which entity—Boxcar or Col. Parker doing business as All Star—handled merchandising, but there are numerous exhibits of checks issued from Boxcar to Elvis Presley bearing such notations as "For Royalty Earnings From Sales of Elvis Presley Souvenir Material On Tour June 25th through July 5th, 1976 as per contractual agreement." (Further checks and royalty statements from Boxcar to the Elvis Presley Estate have also been submitted.) On August 18, 1977, two days after the entertainer's death, plaintiff Boxcar entered into an agreement with plaintiff Factors Etc., Inc. ("Factors") which purported to afford the latter an exclusive license to use the Presley likeness in connection with all souvenir merchandise. On August 24, 1977, Vernon Presley, father of the deceased and executor of his estate, agreed to a royalty arrangement with Boxcar as "Merchandising Representatives for the Elvis Presley Estate." Vernon Presley also wrote to Col. Parker on August 23, 1977 asking Col. Parker to "carry on according to the same terms and conditions as stated in the contractual agreement you had with Elvis dated January 22, 1976."

DEFENDANT'S POSITION

Defendant argues along several lines, the most germane of which are: (1) that plaintiff Boxcar never acquired the exclusive right to merchandise the Presley name and image; (2) that even if Boxcar did have such a right in Presley's lifetime, that right died with the entertainer; * * *.

THE MERITS

* * *

The Right of Publicity

By far the most interesting issue in this case is whether Boxcar had anything to transfer to Factors when it entered into the August 18, 1977 "exclusive licensing" contract. After consulting the case law and certain commentaries in this field, [citations], I have concluded that it did. It appears that a recognized property right, the "right of publicity," inhered in and was exercised by Elvis Presley in his lifetime, that it was assignable by him and was so assigned, that it survived his death and was capable of further assignment.

The "right of publicity" is not a new concept, but, to the detriment of legal clarity, it has often been discussed only under the rubric "right of privacy." It is said that the right of privacy embraces "four distinct kinds of invasion of four different interests of the plaintiff, which are tied together by the common name, but otherwise have almost nothing in common *except that each represents an interference with the right of the plaintiff 'to be let alone.'*" W. Prosser, *Torts* 804 (4th ed. 1971) (emphasis added). It is this language which is at the root of the conceptual difficulty in the "right of publicity" area. Dean Prosser recognized that the fourth species of right of privacy tort, *i. e.*, the appropriation of plaintiff's name or likeness for defendant's benefit, is distinct from "intrusion upon the plaintiff's physical solitude or seclusion," "public disclosure of private facts," or "false light in the public eye," *id.* at 807, 809, 812, in that "appropriation" is the only one which "involves a use for the defendant's advantage." *Id.* at 814. However, Prosser has failed to discuss the fact that appropriation of plaintiff's name and likeness for defendant's financial advantage has different consequences in a case where the celebrity himself has attempted to commercialize his own name and face. It is evident that courts address intrusions on feelings, reputation and privacy only when an individual has elected not to engage in personal commercialization. By contrast, when a "persona" is in effect a product, and when that product has already been marketed to good advantage, the appropriation by another of that valuable property has more to do with unfair competition than it does with the right to be left alone. [Citations.]

* * *

Price v. Hal Roach Studios, Inc., supra, a case decided in this district, is particularly interesting because it is the only reported decision known to this Court where the right of publicity was deemed descendible. In that case the widows of Stan Laurel and Oliver Hardy and another party claiming the right to exploit the Laurel and Hardy image through merchandise sued to restrain defendants from infringing on that right. Plaintiffs set up the exclusivity of a prior contract covering commercial merchandise which had been entered into by Stan Laurel, Hardy's widow, and the plaintiff licensee. Although there was no evidence to show that the comedians had ever exploited their own personalities through merchandising efforts, the *Price* court, relying on the distinction between a personal right of privacy which is extinguished at death and a valuable, alienable property right in name and image, *i. e.*, the "right of publicity," asked "what policy should operate to cut off this [latter] right at death?" [Citation.] The *Price* court could find none, and on the much stronger facts here presented, this Court adopts that view. There is no reason why the valuable right of publicity—*clearly exercised by and financially benefiting Elvis Presley in life*—should not descend at death like any other intangible property right.

* * *

On the basis of the foregoing, the Court concludes that the facts of the instant case demonstrate a strong likelihood that plaintiffs will prevail on the merits at trial.

Irreparable Harm

Having satisfied one of the *Sonesta* mandates, *i. e.*, that a preliminary injunction may not issue absent probable success on the merits, the Court must address the second aspect of that test: whether plaintiff is exposed to possible irreparable injury. * * *

However, the Court need not determine possible irreparable damage by speculating on the caprice of the consumer market. Plaintiff Factors claims that its licensing program for articles other than posters is jeopardized by its inability to grant exclusive rights. * * * The Court concludes that there is a rush to capitalize on the Presley image in this postmortem period, and that if Factors has exclusive property rights in the manufacture and marketing of Presley souvenir merchandise, as it so appears, then it must be protected at this time.

* * *

* * * Defendant Creative Card Company will be enjoined from manufacturing, distributing, selling or by any other means profiting from souvenir merchandise bearing the name or likeness of the late Elvis Presley until the merits of the case are determined.

Order is being filed simultaneously herewith.

Copyright

SONY CORP. OF AMERICA v. UNIVERSAL CITY STUDIOS, INC.

Supreme Court of the United States, 1984.
— U.S.—, 104 S.Ct. 774, 78 L.Ed.2d 574.

STEVENS, J.

Petitioners manufacture and sell home video tape recorders. Respondents own the copyrights on some of the television programs that are broadcast on the public airwaves. Some members of the general public use video tape recorders sold by petitioners to record some of these broadcasts, as well as a large number of other broadcasts. The question presented is whether the sale of petitioners' copying equipment to the general public violates any of the rights conferred upon respondents by the Copyright Act.

Respondents commenced this copyright infringement action against petitioners in the United States District Court for the Central District of California in 1976. Respondents alleged that some individuals had used Betamax video tape recorders (VTR's) to record some of respondents' copyrighted works which had been exhibited on commercially sponsored television and contended that these individuals had thereby infringed respon-

dents' copyrights. Respondents further maintained that petitioners were liable for the copyright infringement allegedly committed by Betamax consumers because of petitioners' marketing of the Betamax VTR's. Respondents sought no relief against any Betamax consumer. Instead, they sought money damages and an equitable accounting of profits from petitioners, as well as an injunction against the manufacture and marketing of Betamax VTR's.

After a lengthy trial, the District Court denied respondents all the relief they sought and entered judgment for petitioners. [Citation.] The United States Court of Appeals for the Ninth Circuit reversed the District Court's judgment on respondent's copyright claim, holding petitioners liable for contributory infringement and ordering the District Court to fashion appropriate relief. [Citation.] We now reverse.

* * *

Article I, Sec 8 of the Constitution provides that:

The Congress shall have Power . . . to Promote the Progress of Science and useful Arts, by securing for limited Times to Authors and Inventors the exclusive Right to their respective Writings and Discoveries.

The monopoly privileges that Congress may authorize are neither unlimited nor primarily designed to provide a special private benefit. Rather, the limited grant is a means by which an important public purpose may be achieved. It is intended to motivate the creative activity of authors and inventors by the provision of a special reward, and to allow the public access to the products of their genius after the limited period of exclusive control has expired.

* * *

As the text of the Constitution makes plain, it is Congress that has been assigned the task of defining the scope of the limited monopoly that should be granted to authors or to inventors in order to give the public appropriate access to their work product. * * *

* * *

The judiciary's reluctance to expand the protections afforded by the copyright without explicit legislative guidance is a recurring theme. [Citations.] * * *

In a case like this, in which Congress has not plainly marked our course, we must be circumspect in construing the scope of rights created by a legislative enactment which never contemplated such a calculus of interests. * * *

Copyright protection "subsists . . . in original works of authorship fixed in any tangible medium of expression." [Citation.] This protection has never accorded the copyright owner complete control over all possible uses of his work. Rather, the Copyright Act grants the copyright holder "exclusive" rights to use and to authorize the use of his work in five qualified ways, including reproduction of the copyrighted work in copies. Id., § 106. All reproductions of the work, however, are not within the exclusive domain of the copyright owner; some are in the public domain. Any individual may reproduce a copyrighted work for a "fair use;" the copyright owner does not possess the exclusive right to such a use. [Citation.]

"Anyone who violates any of the exclusive rights of the coyright owner," that is, anyone who trespasses into his exclusive domain by using or authorizing the use of the copyrighted work in one of the five ways set forth in the statute, "is an infringer of the copyright." Id., § 501(a). Conversely, anyone who is authorized by the copyright owner to use the copyrighted work in a way specified in the statute or who makes a fair use of the work is not an infringer of the copyright with respect to such use.

The Copyright Act provides the owner of a copyright with a potent arsenal of remedies against an infringer of his work, including an injunction to restrain the infringer from violating his rights, the impoundment and destruction of all reproductions of his work made in violation of his rights, a recovery of his actual damages and any additional profits realized by the infringer or a recovery of statutory damages, and attorney's fees. Id., §§ 502–505.

The two respondents in this case do not seek relief against the Betamax users who have allegedly infringed their copyrights. * * * It is, however, the taping of respondents' own copyrighted programs that provides them with standing to charge Sony with contributory infringement. To prevail, they have the burden of proving that users of the Betamax have infringed their copyrights and that Sony should be held responsible for that infringement.

The Copyright Act does not expressly render anyone liable for infringement committed by another. * * * The absence of such express language in the copyright statute does not preclude the imposition of liability for copyright infringements on certain parties who have not themselves engaged in the infringing activity. For vicarious liability is imposed in virtually all areas of the law, and the concept of contributory infringement is merely a species of the broader problem of identifying the circumstances in which it is just to hold one individual accountable for the actions of another.

* * *

* * * [A]nd the label "contributory infringement" has been applied in a number of lower court copyright cases involving an ongoing relationship between the direct infringer and the contributory infringer at the time the infringing conduct occurred. In such cases, as in other situations in which the imposition of vicarious liability is manifestly just, the "contributory" infringer was in a position to control the use of copyrighted works by others and had authorized the use without permission from the copyright owner. This case, however, plainly does not fall in that category. The only contact between Sony and the users of the Betamax that is disclosed by this record occurred at the moment of sale. * * *

If vicarious liability is to be imposed on petitioners in this case, it must rest on the fact that they have sold equipment with constructive knowledge of the fact that their customers may use that equipment to make unauthorized copies of copyrighted material. There is no precedent in the law of copyright for the imposition of vicarious liability on such a theory. * * *

* * *

* * * Accordingly, the sale of copying equipment, like the sale of other articles of commerce, does not constitute contributory infringement if the product is widely used for legitimate, unobjectionable purposes. Indeed, it need merely be capable of substantial noninfringing uses.

* * *

* * * In this case, the record makes it perfectly clear that there are many important producers of national and local television programs who find nothing objectionable about the enlargement in the size of the television audience that results from the practice of time-shifting for private home use.

Even unauthorized uses of a copyrighted work are not necessarily infringing. An unlicensed use of the copyright is not an infringement unless it conflicts with one of the specific exclusive rights conferred by the copyright statute. [Citation.] Moreover, the definition of exclusive rights in § 106 of the present Act is prefaced by the words "subject to sections 107 through 118." Those sections describe a variety of uses of copyrighted material that "are not infringements of copyright notwithstanding the provisions of § 106." The most pertinent in this case is § 107, the legislative endorsement of the doctrine of "fair use."

That section identifies various factors that enable a Court to apply an "equitable rule of reason" analysis to particular claims of infringement. * * *

* * *

* * * A challenge to a noncommercial use of a copyrighted work requires proof either that the particular use is harmful, or that if it should become widespread, it would adversely affect the potential market for the copyrighted work.

* * *

When these factors are all weighed in the "equitable rule of reason" balance, we must conclude that this record amply supports the District Court's conclusion that home time-shifting is fair use. In light of the findings of the District Court regarding the state of the empirical data, it is clear that the Court of Appeals erred in holding that the statute as presently written bars such conduct.

In summary, the record and findings of the District Court lead us to two conclusions. First, Sony demonstrated a significant likelihood that substantial numbers of copyright holders who license their works for broadcast on free television would not object to having their broadcasts time-shifted by private viewers. And second, respondents failed to demonstrate that time-shifting would cause any likelihood of non-minimal harm to the potential market for, or the value of, their copyrighted works. The Betamax is, therefore, capable of substantial noninfringing uses. Sony's sale of such equipment to the general public does not constitute contributory infringement of respondent's copyrights.

The direction of Art I is that *Congress* shall have the power to promote the progress of science and the useful arts. When, as here, the Constitution is permissive, the sign of how far Congress has chosen to go can come only from Congress. Deepsouth Packing Co. v. Laitram Corp., [citation.]

One may search the Copyright Act in vain for any sign that the elected representatives of the millions of people who watch television every day have made it unlawful to copy a program for later viewing at home, or have enacted a flat prohibition against the sale of machines that make such copying possible.

It may well be that Congress will take a fresh look at this new technology, just as it so often has examined other innovations in the past. But it is not our job to apply laws that have not yet been written. Applying the copyright statute, as it now reads, to the facts as they have been developed in this case, the judgment of the Court of Appeals must be reversed.

It is so ordered.

Copyright Infringement

BRIGHT TUNES MUSIC CORP. v. HARRISONGS MUSIC, LTD.

United States District Court, Southern District of New York, 1976.
420 F.Supp. 177.

OWEN, J.

This is an action in which it is claimed that a successful song, My Sweet Lord, listing George Harrison as the composer, is plagiarized from an earlier successful song, He's So Fine, composed by Ronald Mack, recorded by a singing group called the "Chiffons," the copyright of which is owned by plaintiff, Bright Tunes Music Corp.

He's So Fine, recorded in 1962, is a catchy tune consisting essentially of four repetitions of a very short basic musical phrase, "sol-mi-re," (hereinafter motif A), altered as necessary to fit the words, followed by four repetitions of another short basic musical phrase, "sol-la-do-la-do," (hereinafter motif B). While neither motif is novel, the four repetitions of A, followed by four repetitions of B, is a highly unique pattern. In addition, in the second use of the motif B series, there is a grace note inserted making the phrase go "sol-la-do-la-re-do."

My Sweet Lord, recorded first in 1970, also uses the same motif A (modified to suit the words) four times, followed by motif B, repeated three times, not four. In place of He's So Fine's fourth repetition of motif B, My Sweet Lord has a transitional passage of musical attractiveness of the same approximate length, with the identical grace note in the identical second repetition. The harmonies of both songs are identical.

George Harrison, a former member of The Beatles, was aware of He's So Fine. In the United States, it was No. 1 on the billboard charts for five weeks; in England, Harrison's home country, it was No. 12 on the charts on June 1, 1963, a date upon which one of the Beatle songs was, in fact, in first position. For seven weeks in 1963, He's So Fine was one of the top hits in England.

According to Harrison, the circumstances of the composition of My Sweet Lord were as follows. Harrison and his group, which include an American black gospel singer named Billy Preston, were in Copenhagen, Denmark, on a singing engagement. There was a press conference involving the group going on backstage. Harrison slipped away from the press conference and went to a room upstairs and began "vamping" some guitar chords, fitting on to the chords he was playing the words, "Hallelujah" and "Hare Krishna" in various ways. During the course of this vamping, he was alternating between what musicians call a Minor II chord and a Major V chord.

At some point, germinating started and he went down to meet with others of the group, asking them to listen, which they did, and everyone began to join in, taking first "Hallelujah" and then "Hare Krishna" and putting them into four part harmony. Harrison obviously started using the "Hallelujah," etc., as repeated sounds, and from there developed the lyrics, to wit, "My Sweet Lord," "Dear, Dear Lord," etc. In any event, from this very free-flowing exchange of ideas, with Harrison playing his two chords and everybody singing "Hallelujah" and "Hare Krishna," there began to emerge the My Sweet Lord text idea, which Harrison sought to develop a little bit further during the following week as he was playing it on his guitar. Thus developed motif A and its words interspersed with "Hallelujah" and "Hare Krishna."

Approximately one week after the idea first began to germinate, the entire group flew back to London because they had earlier booked time to go to a recording studio with Billy Preston to make an album. In the studio,

Preston was the principal musician. Harrison did not play in the session. He had given Preston his basic motif A with the idea that it be turned into a song, and was back and forth from the studio to the engineer's recording booth, supervising the recording "takes." Under circumstances that Harrison was utterly unable to recall, while everybody was working toward a finished song, in the recording studio, somehow or other the essential three notes of motif A reached polished form.

* * *

Similarly, it appears that motif B emerged in some fashion at the recording session as did motif A. This is also true of the unique grace note in the second repetition of motif B. * * * The Billy Preston recording, listing George Harrison as the composer, was thereafter issued by Apple Records. The music was then reduced to paper by someone who prepared a "lead sheet" containing the melody, the words and the harmony for the United States copyright application.

Seeking the wellsprings of musical composition—why a composer chooses the succession of notes and the harmonies he does—whether it be George Harrison or Richard Wagner—is a fascinating inquiry. It is apparent from the extensive colloquy between the Court and Harrison covering forty pages in the transcript that neither Harrison nor Preston were conscious of the fact that they were utilizing the He's So Fine theme. However, they in fact were, for it is perfectly obvious to the listener that in musical terms, the two songs are virtually identical except for one phrase. There is motif A used four times, followed by motif B, four times in one case, and three times in the other, with the same grace note in the second repetition of motif B.

What happened? I conclude that the composer, in seeking musical materials to clothe his thoughts, was working with various possibilities. As he tried this possibility and that, there came to the surface of his mind a particular combination that pleased him as being one he felt would be appealing to a prospec-

tive listener; in other words, that this combination of sounds would work. Why? Because his subconscious knew it already had worked in a song his conscious mind did not remember. Having arrived at this pleasing combination of sounds, the recording was made, the lead sheet prepared for copyright and the song became an enormous success. Did Harrison deliberately use the music of He's So Fine? I do not believe he did so deliberately. Nevertheless, it is clear that My Sweet Lord is the very same song as He's So Fine with different words, and Harrison had access to He's So Fine. This is, under the law, infringement of copyright, and is no less so even though subconsciously accomplished. [Citations.]

Given the foregoing, I find for the plaintiff on the issue of plagiarism, and set the action down for trial on November 8, 1976 on the issue of damages and other relief as to which the plaintiff may be entitled. The foregoing constitutes the Court's findings of fact and conclusions of law.

So ordered.

Patents

DIAMOND, COMMISSIONER OF PATENTS AND TRADEMARKS v. CHAKRABARTY

Supreme Court of the United States, 1980.
447 U.S. 303, 100 S.Ct. 2204, 65 L.Ed.2d 144.

BURGER, C. J.

We granted certiorari to determine whether a live, human-made micro-organism is patentable subject matter under § 101 [of the Patent Act].

I

In 1972, respondent Chakrabarty, a microbiologist, filed a patent application, assigned to the General Electric Co. The application asserted 36 claims related to Chakrabarty's invention of "a bacterium from the genus *Pseudomonas* containing therein at least two stable energy-generating plasmids, each of said plasmids providing a separate hydrocarbon degradative pathway." This human-made, genetically engineered bacterium is capable of breaking down multiple components of crude oil. Because of this property, which is possessed by no naturally occurring bacteria, Chakrabarty's invention is believed to have significant value for the treatment of oil spills.

Chakrabarty's patent claims were of three types: first, process claims for the method of producing the bacteria; second, claims for an inoculum comprised of a carrier material floating on water, such as straw, and the new bacteria; and third, claims to the bacteria themselves. The patent examiner allowed the claims falling into the first two categories, but rejected claims for the bacteria. His decision rested on two grounds: (1) that micro-organisms are "products of nature," and (2) that as living things they are not patentable subject matter under § 101 [of the Patent Act].

Chakrabarty appealed the rejection of these claims to the Patent Office Board of Appeals, and the Board affirmed the examiner on the second ground. Relying on the legislative history of the 1930 Plant Patent Act, in which Congress extended patent protection to certain asexually reproduced plants, the Board concluded that § 101 was not intended to cover living things such as these laboratory created micro-organisms.

The Court of Customs and Patent Appeals, by a divided vote, reversed on the authority of [citation], which held that "the fact that micro-organisms . . . are alive . . . [is] without legal significance" for purposes of the patent law. * * *

II

The Constitution grants Congress broad power to legislate to "promote the Progress of Science and useful Arts, by securing for limited Times to Authors and Inventors the exclusive Right to their respective Writings and Discoveries." Art. I, § 8, cl. 8. The patent laws promote this progress by offering inventors exclusive rights for a limited period as an incentive for their inventiveness and research efforts. [Citations.] The authority of Congress is exercised in the hope that "[t]he productive effort thereby fostered will have a positive effect on society through the introduction of new products and processes of manufacture into the economy, and the emanations by way of increased employment and better lives for our citizens." [Citation.]

The question before us in this case is a narrow one of statutory interpretation requiring us to construe § 101 [of the Patent Act], which provides:

Whoever invents or discovers any new and useful process, machine, manufacture, or composition of matter, or any new and useful improvement thereof, may obtain a patent therefor, subject to the conditions and requirements of this title.

Specifically, we must determine whether respondent's micro-organism constitutes a "manufacture" or "composition of matter" within the meaning of the statute.

III

In cases of statutory construction we begin, of course, with the language of the statute. [Citation.] And "unless otherwise defined, words will be interpreted as taking their ordinary, contemporary, common meaning." [Citation.] We have also cautioned that courts "should not read into the patent laws limitations and conditions which the legislature has not expressed." [Citation.]

Guided by these canons of construction, this Court has read the term "manufacture" in § 101 in accordance with its dictionary definition to mean "the production of articles for use from raw or prepared materials by giving to these materials new forms, qualities, properties, or combinations, whether by hand-labor or by machinery." [Citation.] Similarly, "composition of matter" has been construed consistent with its common usage to include "all compositions of two or more substances and . . . all composite articles, whether they be the results of chemical union, or of mechanical mixture, or whether they be gases, fluids, powders or solids." [Citation.] In choosing such expansive terms as "manufacture" and "composition of matter," modified by the comprehensive "any," Congress plainly contemplated that the patent laws would be given wide scope.

* * *

This is not to suggest that § 101 has no limits or that it embraces every discovery. The laws of nature, physical phenomena, and abstract ideas have been held not patentable. [Citations.] Thus, a new mineral discovered in the earth or a new plant found in the wild is not patentable subject matter. Likewise, Einstein could not patent his celebrated law that $E = mc^2$; nor could Newton have patented the law of gravity. Such discoveries are "manifestations of . . . nature, free to all men and reserved exclusively to none." [Citation.]

Judged in this light, respondent's microorganism plainly qualifies as patentable subject matter. His claim is not to a hitherto unknown natural phenomenon, but to a nonnaturally occurring manufacture or composition of matter—a product of human ingenuity "having a distinctive name, character [and] use." [Citation.] The point is underscored dramatically by comparison of the invention here with that in *Funk*. There, the patentee had discovered that there existed in nature certain species of root-nodule bacteria which did not exert a mutually inhibitive effect on each other. He used that discovery to produce a mixed culture capable of inoculating the seeds of leguminous plants. Concluding that the patentee had discovered "only some of the handiwork of nature," the Court ruled the product nonpatentable:

Each of the species of root-nodule bacteria contained in the package infects the same group of leguminous plants which it always infected. No species acquires a different use. The combination of species produces no new bacteria, no change in the six species of bacteria, and no enlargement of the range of their utility. Each species has the same effect it always had. The bacteria perform in their natural way. Their use in combination does not improve in any way their natural functioning. They serve the ends nature originally provided and act quite independently of any effort of the patentee." [Citation.]

Here, by contrast, the patentee has produced a new bacterium with markedly different characteristics from any found in nature and one having the potential for significant utility. His discovery is not nature's handiwork, but his own; accordingly it is patentable subject matter under § 101.

* * *

We have emphasized in the recent past that "[o]ur individual appraisal of the wisdom or unwisdom of a particular [legislative] course . . . is to be put aside in the process of interpreting a statute." [Citation.] Our task, rather, is the narrow one of determining what Congress meant by the words it used in the statute; once that is done our powers are exhausted. Congress is free to amend § 101 so as to exclude from patent protection organisms produced by genetic engineering. Cf. 42 U.S.C. § 2181 (a), exempting from patent protection inventions "useful solely in the utilization of special nuclear material or atomic energy in an atomic weapon." Or it may choose to craft a statute specifically designed for such living things. But, until Congress takes such action, this Court must construe the language of § 101 as it is. The language of that section fairly embraces respondent's invention.

Accordingly, the judgment of the Court of Customs and Patent Appeals is

Affirmed.

PROBLEMS

1. Keller, a professor of legal studies at Rhodes University, is a diligent instructor. Late one night while reading a newly published, copyrighted treatise of 1800 pages written by Gilbert, he came across a three-page section discussing the subject matter he was going to cover in class the next day.

Keller considered the treatment to be illuminating and therefore photocopied the three pages and distributed the copies to his class. One of Keller's students is a second cousin of Gilbert, the author of the treatise, and she showed Gilbert the copies. Instead of being flattered, Gilbert sued Keller for copyright infringement. Decision?

2. A conceived a secret process for the continuous freeze drying of food stuffs and related products and constructed a small pilot plant which practiced the process. A lacked the financing necessary to develop the commercial potential of the process and in hopes of obtaining a contract for its development and the payment of royalties, disclosed it in confidence to B, a coffee manufacturer, who signed an agreement not to disclose it to anyone else. At the same time, A signed an agreement not to disclose the process to any other person as long as A and B were considering a contract for its development. Upon disclosure, B became extremely interested and offered to pay A the sum of $1,750,000 if, upon further development, the process proved to be commercially feasible. While negotiations between A and B were in progress, C, a competitor of B, learned of the existence of the process and requested a disclosure from A who informed C that the process could not be disclosed to anyone unless negotiations with B were broken off. C offered to pay A $2,500,000 for the process provided it met certain defined objective performance criteria. A contract was prepared and executed between A and C on this basis without any prior disclosure of the process to C. Upon the making of this contract, A rejected the offer of B. The process was thereupon disclosed to C and demonstration runs of the pilot plant in the presence of representatives of C were conducted under varying conditions. After three weeks of experimental demonstrations, compiling of data and analyses of results, C informed A that the process did not meet the performance criteria in the contract and that for this reason C was rejecting the process. Two years later C placed on the market freeze-dried coffee which resembled in color, appearance, and texture the product of A's pilot plant. What are the rights of the parties?

3. B, a chemist, was employed by A, a manufacturer, to work on a secret process for A's product under an exclusive three-year contract. C, a salesman, was employed by A on a week-to-week basis. B and C resigned the employment with A and accepted employment in their respective capacities with D, a rival manufacturer. C began soliciting patronage from A's former customers whose names he had memorized. What are the rights of the parties in (a) a suit by A to enjoin B from working for D; and (b) a suit by A to enjoin C from soliciting A's customers?

4. Martin is employed by Reynold's Co. York Insurance Co. insures Reynolds for its liability under the worker's compensation plan required by the laws of State X. Martin is injured in the course of his employment and files a claim with York. York offers to settle the claim at an amount that Martin considers wholly inadequate. Upon Martin's rejection of the offer York informs Martin that unless he accepts the settlement Martin will lose his job with Reynolds. Martin still refuses the settlement offer and York causes Reynolds to discharge Martin by threatening to cancel all of Reynold's insurance with York. Martin brings suit against York for causing his dismissal. Decision?

5. X, having filed locally an affidavit required under the "Assumed Name" statute, has been operating and advertising his exclusive toy store for 20 years in Centerville, Illinois. His advertising has consisted of large signs on his premises reading "The Toy Mart". B, after operating a store in Chicago under the name of "The Chicago Toy Mart" relocated in Centerville, Illinois, and erected a large sign reading "TOY MART" with the word "Centerville" being written underneath in substantially smaller letters. Thereafter, the sales of X declined, and many of X's customers patronized B's store thinking it to be a branch of B's business. What are the rights of the parties?

6. Adams tells Bennett, whom he knows to be contemplating the purchase of a home in Greenacre Estates, that Cobb's parcel of land, which is located there, is subject to a right of way granted to the owner of a neighboring quarry entitling the latter to haul stone from the quarry to the highway across a part of Cobb's land. This statement is untrue but causes Bennett to cease considering the purchase of Cobb's property. Cobb brings an action against Adams. Decision?

7. George McCoy of Florida has been manufacturing and distributing a cheese cake for over five years, labeling his product with a picture of a cheese cake which serves as a background for a Florida bathing beauty under which is written the slogan "McCoy All Spice Florida Cheese Cake." George

McCoy has not registered his trademark. Subsequently, Leo McCoy of California begins manufacturing a similar product on the West coast using a label in appearance similar to that of George McCoy, containing a picture of a Hollywood star, and the words "McCoy's All Spice Cheese Cake."

Leo McCoy begins marketing his products in the Eastern United States, using labels with the word "Florida" added as in George McCoy's label. Leo McCoy has registered his product under the Federal Trademark Act. To what relief, if any, is George McCoy entitled?

ANTITRUST

THE economic community is best served in normal times by free competition in trade and industry. It is in the public interest that quality, price, and service in an open, competitive market for goods and services be determining factors in the business rivalry for the customer's dollar. The law of trade regulation attempts to assure such free and fair competition.

The common law has traditionally favored free and open competition in the market place and has held illegal and unenforceable agreements and contracts in restraint of trade. In addition, some States had enacted antitrust statutes but in the latter half of the nineteenth century it became apparent that concentrations of economic power in the form of "trusts" and "combinations" were too powerful and widespread to be effectively curbed and controlled by State action. This prompted the Congress in 1890 to enact the first Federal statute in this field known as the Sherman Antitrust Act. Since then, Congress has enacted other antitrust statutes including the Clayton Act, the Robinson-Patman Act, and the Federal Trade Commission Act. These statutes prohibit anti-competitive practices and seek to prevent unreasonable aggregation of economic power which would stifle or weaken competition.

SHERMAN ANTITRUST ACT

Section 1 of the Sherman Act prohibits contracts, combinations, and conspiracies in restraint of trade, while Section 2 proscribes monopolization and attempts to monopolize violations. Violations of either section are criminal felonies and subject the offender to fine or imprisonment, or both. Individual offenders are subject to imprisonment up to three years and fines up to $100,000, while corporate offenders are subject to fines up to $1,000,000. Moreover, the Federal district courts are empowered to issue injunctions restraining violations, and anyone injured by a violation is entitled to recover in a civil action **treble damages,** that is, three times the amount of the actual loss sustained. In addition, State Attorney Generals may bring suit for treble damages on behalf of citizens of their state. It is the duty of the United States Justice Department and of the Federal Trade Commission to institute appropriate enforcement proceedings other than treble damage actions.

The Supreme Court stated the purpose of the Sherman Act as follows:

The Sherman Act was designed to be a comprehensive charter of economic liberty aimed at preserving free and unfettered competition as the rule of trade. It rests on the premise that the unrestrained interaction of competitive forces will yield the best allocation of our economic resources, the lowest prices, the highest quality and the greatest material progress, while at the same time providing an environment conducive to the preservation of our democratic political and social institutions. *Northern Pacific Railway Co. v. United States,* 356 U.S. 1 (1958).

Restraint of Trade

Section 1 of the Sherman Act provides that "[e]very contract, combination in the form of trust or otherwise, or conspiracy, in restraint of trade or commerce among the several states, or with foreign nations is hereby declared to be illegal." Taken literally, this prohibition would invalidate every unperformed contract. In order to avoid such a broad and impractical application, the courts have interpreted this section to invalidate only *unreasonable* restraints of trade:

The true test of legality is whether the restraint imposed is such as merely regulates and perhaps thereby promotes competition or whether it is such as may suppress or even destroy competition. To determine that question the courts must ordinarily consider the facts peculiar to the business to which the restraint is applied; its condition before and after the restraint was imposed; the nature of the restraint and its effect, actual or probable. The history of the restraint, the evil believed to exist, the reason for adopting the particular remedy, the purpose or end sought to be attained, are all relevant facts. This is not because a good intention will save an otherwise objectionable regulation or the reverse; but because knowledge of intent may help the court to interpret facts and to predict consequences. *Chicago Board of Trade v. United States,* 246 U.S. 231 (1918).

This standard, known as the **rule of reason test,** however, presented several problems of its own. By mandating that courts balance the *anticompetitive* effects against the *procompetitive* effects of every questioned restraint, this standard placed a substantial burden upon the judicial system. The United States Supreme Court accordingly responded by declaring certain categories of restraints to be unreasonable by their very nature and thus **illegal per se:**

[T]here are certain agreements or practices which because of their pernicious effect on competition and lack of any redeeming virtue are conclusivly presumed to be unreasonable and therefore illegal without elaborate inquiry as to the precise harm they have caused or the business excuse for their use. This principle of *per se* unreasonableness not only makes the type of restraints which are proscribed by the Sherman Act more certain to the benefit of everyone concerned, but it also avoids the necessity for an incredibly complicated and prolonged economic investigation into the entire history of the industry involved, as well as related industries, in an effort to determine at large whether a particular restraint has been unreasonable—an inquiry so often wholly fruitless when undertaken. *Northern Pacific Railway Co. v. United States,* 356 U.S. 1 (1958).

Those restraints not categorized as *per se* illegal are judged by the rule of reason test.

In addition, restraints may be classified as either horizontal or vertical. A restraint is **horizontal** if it involves collaboration among

FIGURE 41-1   Horizontal Restraints

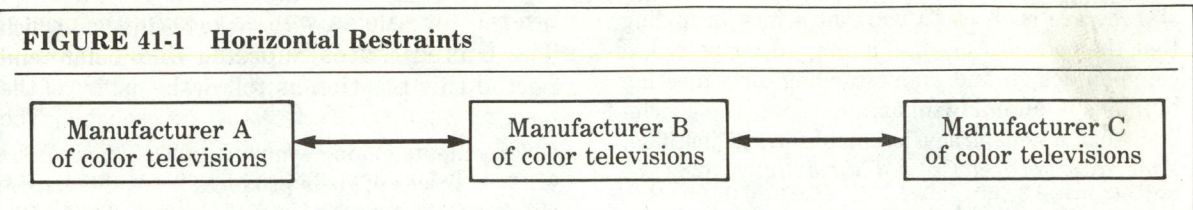

competitors at the same level in the chain of distribution. For example, an agreement among manufacturers or among wholesalers or among retailers would be horizontal. See Figure 41-1.

On the other hand, an agreement is **vertical** if made by parties not in direct competition at the same level of distribution. Thus, an agreement between a manufacturer and a wholesaler is vertical. Although the distinction between horizontal and vertical restraints can become blurred, it is often determinative of whether a restraint is illegal *per se* or judged by the rule of reason. For instance, horizontal market allocations are illegal *per se*, whereas vertical market allocations are not *per se* illegal but are subject to the rule of reason test. See Figure 41-2.

Finally, Section 1 does not prohibit **unilateral** conduct; rather, it forbids **concerted** action. Thus, one person or business cannot violate the section alone. Although concerted action usually takes the form of explicit agreements, combinations, or conspiracies, less overt conduct has on occasion been found to violate Section 1 where there is sufficient circumstantial evidence to warrant such a finding.

It is not the form of the combination or the particular means used but the result to be achieved that the statute condemns. It is not of importance whether the means used to accomplish the unlawful objective are in themselves lawful or unlawful. Acts done to give effect to the conspiracy may be in themselves wholly innocent acts.

Yet, if they are part of the sum of the acts which are relied upon to effectuate the conspiracy which the statute forbids, they come within its prohibition. No formal agreement is necessary to constitute an unlawful conspiracy. Often crimes are a matter of inference deduced from the acts of the person accused and done in pursuance of a criminal purpose. Where the conspiracy is proved, as here, from the evidence of the action taken in concert by the parties to it, it is all the more convincing proof of an intent to exercise the power of exclusion acquired through the conspiracy. The essential combination or conspiracy in violation of the Sherman Act may be found in a course of dealings or other circumstances as well as in any exchange of words. * * * Where the circum-

FIGURE 41-2   Vertical Restraints

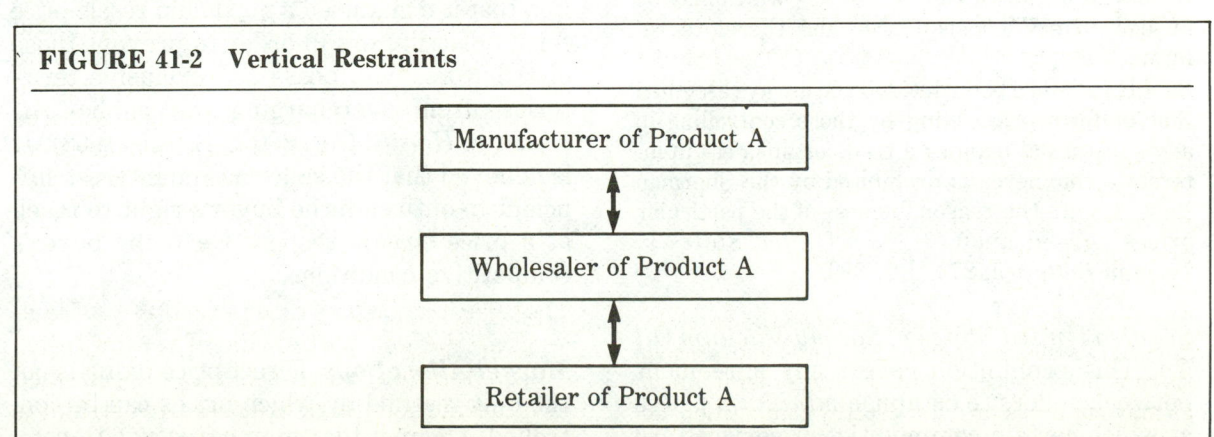

stances are such as to warrant a jury in finding that the conspirators had a unity of purpose or a common design and understanding, or a meeting of minds in an unlawful arrangement, the conclusion that a conspiracy is established is justified. *American Tobacco Co. v. United States*, 328 U.S. 781 (1946).

Price Fixing Price fixing is the primary and most serious example of a *per se* violation under the Sherman Act. *All* **horizontal** price fixing agreements are considered illegal *per se*.

The aim and result of every price-fixing agreement, if effective, is the elimination of one form of competition. The power to fix prices, whether reasonably exercised or not, involves power to control the market and to fix arbitrary and unreasonable prices. The reasonable price fixed today may through economic and business changes become the unreasonable price of tomorrow. Once established, it may be maintained unchanged because of the absence of competition secured by the agreement for a price reasonable when fixed. Agreements which create such potential power may well be held to be in themselves unreasonable or unlawful restraints, without the necessity of minute inquiry whether a particular price is reasonable or unreasonable as fixed and without placing on the Government in enforcing the Sherman Law the burden of ascertaining from day to day whether it has become unreasonable through the mere variation of economic conditions. * * * Thus viewed, the Sherman Law is not only a prohibition against the infliction of a particular type of public injury. It "is a limitation of rights, * * * which may be pushed to evil consequences and therefore restrained. * * *"

It has since been decided and always assumed that uniform price-fixing by those controlling in any substantial manner a trade or business in interstate commerce is prohibited by the Sherman Law, despite the reasonableness of the particular prices agreed upon. * * * *United States v. Trenton Potteries*, 273 U.S. 392.

See also United States v. Socony-Vacuum Oil Co. This prohibition covers any agreement between sellers to establish *minimum* prices at which certain commodities or services are offered for sale as well as *maximum* prices. The United States Supreme Court has supported this position as follows:

[A]greements among competitors to fix maximum * * * prices of their products * * * , cripple the freedom of traders and thereby restrain their ability to sell in accordance with their own judgment. We affirm what we said in United States v. Socony: "Under the Sherman Act a combination formed for the purpose and with the effect of raising, depressing, fixing, pegging, or stabilizing the price of a commodity in interstate or foreign commerce is illegal per se." *Kiefer-Stewart Co. v. Joseph E. Seagram & Sons*, 340 U.S. 211 (1951).

The law also prohibits sellers' agreements to change simultaneously the prices of certain commodities or services or not to advertise their prices.

Similarly, it is illegal *per se* for a seller to fix the price at which its purchasers must resell the product. This **vertical** form of price fixing—usually called retail price maintenance—was allowed in some States under the "Fair Trade Laws." However, in 1975 Congress repealed the statute authorizing these laws, and now minimum and maximum resale price maintenance is considered a *per se* violation of Section 1. The United States Supreme Court has been extremely reluctant to approve any form of restraint involving the "heart" of the competitive free market—the pricing mechanism. Accordingly, the Court has rejected a newspaper publisher's assertion that it maintained a maximum resale price for its distributors in order to prevent these distributors, who possessed exclusive territories, from overcharging the public. *Albrecht v. Herald Co.*, 390 U.S. 145 (1968). It is believed that the seller has no interest sufficient to outweigh the buyer's right to resell at a price that is responsive to the buyer's competitive conditions.

Market Allocations Direct price fixing is not the only method by which prices can be controlled. Competitors may agree not to compete with each other in specific markets, which may be defined by geographic area, type of customer, or class of product. Because their effects are similar to price fixing, all **horizontal** agreements to divide markets have been declared illegal *per se*. Thus, if A and B, both manufacturers of color televisions, agree that A shall have the exclusive right to sell color televisions in Illinois and Iowa and that B shall have the exclusive right in Minnesota and Wisconsin, A and B have committed a *per se* violation of Section 1 of the Sherman Act. Likewise, if A and B agree that A shall have the exclusive right to sell color televisions to Sears and B to J.C. Penney, or that A shall have exclusive rights to manufacture 19 inch color televisions and B to manufacture 15 inch sets, they are also in *per se* violation of Section 1 of the Sherman Antitrust Act. Horizontal market allocations may be found not only on the manufacturing level but also on the wholesale or retail level.

Vertical territorial and customer restrictions are no longer illegal *per se* but are now judged by the rule of reason. This change in approach has resulted from a 1977 United States Supreme Court decision, *see Continental T.V. v. GTE Sylvania*, which mandated the lower Federal courts to balance the positive effect of vertical market restrictions upon interbrand competition against the negative effects upon intrabrand competition. Consequently, in some situations vertical market restrictions will be found legitimate if they, on balance, increase competition.

Boycotts Section 1 of the Sherman Act, as previously noted, does not apply to unilateral action but only to agreements or combinations. Accordingly, the refusal of a seller to deal with any particular buyer does not violate the Act. Thus, a manufacturer can refuse to sell to a retailer who persists in selling below the manufacturer's suggested retail price. On the other hand, **concerted refusals to deal**—group boycotts—are prohibited. Therefore, a manufacturer would violate Section 1 if it were to induce wholesalers to re-fuse to deal with retailers that disobeyed a suggested retail price.

Thus, manufacturer A, who wishes to establish set prices for the resale of its products by both wholesalers and retailers, indicates that it will cease to deal with any wholesaler who resells at a different price. Manufacturer A has *not* violated the Sherman Act in that it has merely exercised its right to deal with whomever it pleases. On the other hand, if A requires that its wholesalers refuse to deal with any retailer who does not follow A's pricing policy, A and the wholesalers have entered into an illegal, concerted refusal to deal as well as an illegal vertical price fixing scheme. Moreover, the illegality of the conduct does not depend upon the express agreement of A and its wholesalers but may be implied from the conduct of the parties. Finally, it should be noted that A would violate the Sherman Act by engaging in vertical price fixing if it obtained an agreement from the wholesalers that they will sell at prices established by A or that they will report to A any violations of A's pricing policy.

Tying Arrangements A seller of a product, service, or intangible (the "tying" product) may condition its sale upon the buyer's purchasing a second product, service, or intangible (the "tied" product) from the seller. For example, A, a major manufacturer of photocopying equipment, requires that all purchasers of its photocopiers must also purchase from A all of the paper they use with the copier. A has tied the sale of its photocopier—the *tying* product—to the sale of paper—the *tied* product. Because tying arrangements limit the freedom of choice of buyers and may exclude competitors, the law closely scrutinizes such agreements. When the seller has considerable economic power in the tying product *or* when a not insubstantial amount of interstate commerce is affected in the tied product, the tying arrangement will be *per se* illegal. Otherwise, tying arrangements are judged by the rule of reason.

Monopolies

Economic analysis indicates that a monopolist will utilize its power to limit production and increase prices. Accordingly, a monopolistic market will produce fewer goods at a higher price than a competitive market. In order to address the problem of monopolization, Section 2 of the Sherman Act prohibits monopolies, attempts to monopolize, and conspiracies to monopolize. Thus, Section 2 prohibits both agreements among businesses and, unlike Section 1, unilateral conduct by one firm.

Monopolization Although the language of Section 2 appears to prohibit *all* monopolization, the courts have declined to interpret it in that manner. Rather, they have required that in addition to the mere possession of market power there also be either the unfair attainment of the monopoly power or the abusive use of that power once attained.

It is extremely rare to find an unregulated industry with only one firm, so the issue of monopoly power involves defining what degree of market dominance constitutes monopoly power. **Monopoly power** is the ability to control prices or to exclude competitors from the market place. The courts have grappled with this question of monopoly power and have developed a number of approaches, but the prevalent test is market share. A market share greater than 75 percent generally indicates monopoly power, a share less than 50 percent does not, while a 50 to 75 percent share is inconclusive.

Market share is the fractional share possessed by a firm of the total relevant product and geographic markets. Nonetheless, defining the relevant markets is often a difficult and subjective project for the courts. The relevant *product market* includes products that are substitutable for the firm's product on the basis of price, quality, and cross-elasticity. For example, although brick and wood siding are both used in buildings as exteriors it is not likely that they would be considered as part of the same product market. On the other

hand, Coca-Cola and Seven-Up are both soft drinks and would be considered part of the same product market. *See United States v. E. I. duPont De Nemours & Co.*

The relevant *geographic market* is that territory in which the firm makes sales of its products or services. This may be at the local, regional, or national level. For instance, the relevant geographic market for the manufacture and sale of aluminum might be national while that of a taxicab operating company would be local. The scope of the relevant geographic market will depend upon such factors as transportation costs, the type of product or services, and the location of competitors and customers.

Assuming sufficient monopoly power has been proved, it must then be shown that the firm has engaged in **unfair conduct**. The courts have not yet agreed upon what constitutes unfair conduct. One judicial approach is that a firm possessing monopoly power has the burden of proving that it acquired such power passively or that it had the power "thrust" upon it. An alternative view is that monopoly power, when coupled with conduct designed to exclude competitors, violates Section 1. A third approach requires monopoly power plus some type of predatory practice, such as pricing below marginal costs. For example, one case that adopted the third approach held that a firm does not violate Section 2 of the Sherman Act if it attained its market share by either (1) research, technical innovation, or a superior product, or (2) ordinary marketing methods available to all. *Telex Corp. v. IBM*, 510 F.2d 894 (10th Cir. 1975).

To date, however, the United States Supreme Court has not provided a definitive answer to the basic question of exactly what conduct, beyond the mere possession of monopoly power, violates Section 2. To do so, the Court must resolve the complex and conflicting policies involved. On the one hand, condemning fairly acquired monopoly power—that acquired "merely by virtue of superior skill, foresight, and industry"—penalizes firms that compete effectively. On the other hand, permitting firms with monopoly power to continue provides them the opportunity to lower output and raise prices, thereby injuring consumers.

Attempts to Monopolize Section 2 also prohibits attempts to monopolize. As with monopolization, the courts have experienced difficulty in developing a standard that distinguishes undesirable conduct likely to lead to monopoly from healthy competitive conduct. The standard test applied by the courts requires proof of a specific intent to monopolize plus a dangerous probability of success. This standard leaves unanswered numerous questions, such as what conduct constitutes an attempt and how much power must be achieved. Recent cases suggest that the greater the power acquired, the less flagrant the conduct must be to constitute an attempt. These cases, however, do not specify any threshold level of market power.

CLAYTON ACT

In 1914 Congress strengthened the Sherman Act by adopting the Clayton Act which was expressly designed "to supplement existing laws against unlawful restraints and monopolies." The Clayton Act does not provide for criminal penalties but only for civil actions. Civil actions may be brought by private parties in Federal court for *treble* damages and attorney fees. In addition, the Justice Department and the Federal Trade Commission are authorized to bring civil actions including proceedings in equity to prevent and restrict violations of the Act.

The substantive provisions of the Clayton Act deal with price discrimination, tying contracts, exclusive dealing, mergers, and interlocking directorates. Section 2, which deals with price discrimination, was amended and rewritten by the Robinson-Patman Act, discussed below. In addition, the Clayton Act exempts labor, agricultural, and horticultural organizations from all antitrust laws.

Tying Contracts and Exclusive Dealing

Section 3 of the Clayton Act prohibits tying arrangements and exclusive dealing, selling, or leasing arrangements which prevent purchasers from dealing with the seller's competitors, where the effect **may** be substantially to lessen competition or **tend** to create a monopoly. This section is intended to attack anticompetitive practices in their incipiency before they ripen into violations of Section 1 or 2 of the Sherman Act. Unlike the Sherman Act, however, Section 3 only applies to leases or sales of goods, wares, merchandise, machinery, supplies, or other commodities.

Tying arrangements, which have already been discussed under the Sherman Act, have been labeled by the Supreme Court as serving "hardly any purpose beyond the suppression of competition." Exclusive dealing arrangements are agreements by which the seller or lessor of a product conditions the agreement upon the buyer or lessor's promise not to deal in the goods of a competitor. For example, a manufacturer of razors might require that retailers wishing to sell its line of shaving equipment agree not to carry competing merchandise. Such conduct, although treated more leniently than tying arrangements, will violate Section 3 if it tends to create a monopoly or may substantially lessen competition.

Mergers

Section 7 of the Clayton Act, as amended, prohibits the merger or acquisition by a corporation of stock in another corporation or assets of another corporation where the effect may be to lessen substantially competition or tend to create a monopoly.

Section 7 of the Clayton Act was intended to arrest the anticompetitive effects of market power in their incipiency. The core question is whether a merger may substantially lessen competition, and necessarily requires a prediction of the merger's impact on competition, present and future. The section can deal only with probabilities, not with certainties. And there is certainly no requirement that the anticompetitive power manifest itself in anticompetitive action before § 7 can be called into play. If the enforcement of § 7 turned on the existence of actual anticompetitive practices, the congressional policy of thwarting such practices in their incipiency would be frustrated. *F.T.C. v. Procter & Gamble Co.*, 386 U.S. 568 (1967).

The current state of the law regarding horizontal, vertical, and conglomerate mergers is, particularly with respect to the last two, in a state of flux. A **horizontal merger** involves the acquisition by a company of all or part of the stock or assets of a competing company. For example, if IBM were to acquire Apple this would be a horizontal merger. A **vertical merger** is the acquisition of a company of one of its customers or suppliers. A vertical merger is a *forward* merger if the acquiring company purchases a *customer* such as the purchase of Revco Discount Drug Stores by Procter & Gamble. A vertical merger is a *backward* merger if the acquiring company purchases a supplier; for example, the purchase of a manufacturer of micro-chips by IBM. The third type of merger, the **conglomerate merger,** is a catchall category which covers all other mergers.

The principal objective of antitrust law governing mergers is to maintain competition. Accordingly, horizontal mergers are scrutinized most stringently. Factors which are considered in reviewing the legality of a horizontal merger include the market share of each of the merging firms, degree of industry concentration, number of firms in the industry, entry barriers, market trends, vigor and strength of other competitors in the industry, character and history of the merging firms, market demand, and extent of industry price competition. *See United States v. Von's Grocery Co.* Vertical mergers, which are far less likely to be challenged by the Justice Department or the FTC, will be attacked if the merger is likely to raise entry barriers in the industry or is likely to foreclose other firms

in the industry of the acquiring firm from competitively significant customers or suppliers. Finally, conglomerate mergers have only been challenged (1) where one of the merging firms is a highly likely entrant into the market of the other firm, or (2) where the merged company would be disproportionately large as compared with the largest competitors in its industry.

In 1982, the Justice Department and the FTC both indicated that they will be primarily concerned with horizontal mergers in highly or moderately concentrated industries and that they question the benefits of challenging vertical and conglomerate mergers. Both the Justice Department and the FTC have justified this policy on the basis that the latter two types of mergers are necessary to transfer assets to their most productive use and that any challenge to them would impose costs upon consumers without corresponding benefits.

Interlocking Directorates

Section 8 prohibits interlocking directorates in competing corporations engaged in interstate commerce (except banks, banking associations, trust companies, and common carriers) where the aggregate capitalization is a million dollars or more.

The broad purposes of Congress are unmistakably clear. Section 8 was but one of a series of measures which finally emerged as the Clayton Act, all intended to strengthen the Sherman Act, which, through the years, had not proved entirely effective. Congress had been aroused by the concentration of control by a few individuals or groups over many gigantic corporations which in the normal course of events should have been in active and unrestrained competition. Instead, and because of such control, the healthy competition of the free enterprise system had been stifled or eliminated. Interlocking directorships on rival corporations had been the instrumentality of defeating the purpose of the antitrust laws. They had tended to suppress competition or to foster joint action against third party competitors. The continued potential threat to the competitive system resulting from these conflicting directorships was the evil aimed at. Viewed against this background, a fair reading of the legislative debates leaves little room for doubt that, in its efforts to strengthen the antitrust laws, what Congress intended by § 8 was to nip in the bud incipient violations of the antitrust laws by removing the opportunity or temptation to such violations through interlocking directorates. The legislation was essentially preventative. *United States v. Sears, Roebuck & Co.*, 111 F. Supp. 14 (S.D.N.Y. 1953).

ROBINSON-PATMAN ACT

In an attempt to limit the power of large purchasers, the Congress amended Section 2 of the Clayton Act by adopting the Robinson-Patman Act which prohibits **price discrimination** in interstate commerce of commodities of like grade and quality. In order to constitute a violation, the price discrimination must substantially lessen competition or tend to create a monopoly.

Under this Act sellers of goods are prevented from granting discounts to buyers, including allowances for advertisements, counter displays, and samples, unless offered to all other purchasers on proportionately equal terms. The Act also prohibits other types of discounts, rebates, and allowances and makes it unlawful to sell goods at unreasonably low prices for the purpose of destroying competition or eliminating a competitor. The Act makes it unlawful for a person knowingly to "induce or receive" an illegal discrimination in price, thus imposing liability upon the buyer as well as the seller. Violation of the Robinson-Patman Act, with limited exceptions, is civil and not criminal in nature.

Price differentials are permitted when justified by proof of either a cost savings to the seller or a good faith price reduction to meet the lawful price of a competitor.

Cost Justification

If a seller can show that it costs less to sell a product to a particular buyer, the seller may lawfully pass along the cost savings. Sec-

tion 2(a) provides that the Act does not "prevent differentials which make only due allowance for differences in the cost of manufacture, sale, or delivery resulting from the differing methods or quantities in which * * * commodities are * * * sold or delivered." Thus, if retailer A orders goods from Seller X by the carload while retailer B orders in small quantities from Seller X, Seller X, who delivers F.O.B. buyer's warehouse, may pass along the transportation savings to buyer A. Nonetheless, although it is possible to pass along transportation savings, it is extremely difficult to pass along alleged savings in manufacturing or distribution because of the complexity involved in calculating and proving such savings. Therefore, sellers rarely rely upon the defense of cost justification.

Meeting Competition

A seller may lower his price in a good faith attempt to meet competition. To illustrate:

1. Manufacturer X sells its motor oil to retail outlets for 65 cents per can. Manufacturer Y approaches A, one of Manufacturer X's customers, and offers to sell a comparable type of motor oil for 60 cents per can. Manufacturer X will be permitted to lower its price to A to sixty cents per can and need not lower its price to its other retail customers—B, C, and D. Manufacturer X, however, may *not* lower its price to A to 55 cents unless it also lowers its price to B, C, and D.

2. Manufacturer X will not be permitted to lower its price to A without also lowering its price to B, C, and D, in order to allow A to meet the lower price charged by A's competitor N selling Manufacturer Y's oil. The meeting competition defense is available only to meet the competition of the seller and does not extend to the price of a competitor of a specific, individual *purchaser*. See Figure 41-3.

However, as illustrated in *Great Atlantic & Pacific Tea Co. v. Federal Trade Commission*, a seller may beat its competitor's

FIGURE 41-3 Meeting Competition Defense

Illustration One

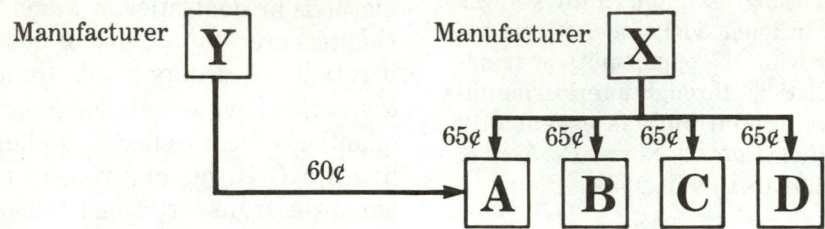

Result:

Manufacturer X may lower its price to A to 60¢ without lowering its price to B, C, and D.

Illustration Two

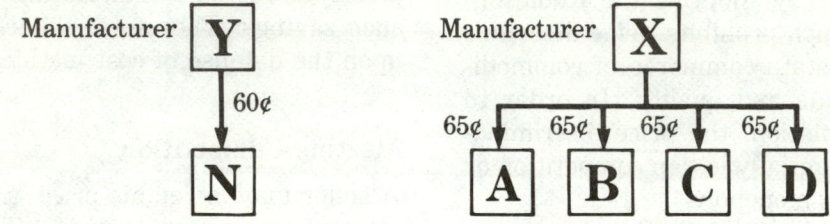

Result:

Manufacturer X may *not* lower its price to A without also lowering its price to B, C, and D.

price if it does not know the competitor's price, cannot reasonably determine the competitor's price, and acts reasonably in setting its own price.

FEDERAL TRADE COMMISSION ACT

In 1914 Congress enacted the Federal Trade Commission Act creating the Federal Trade Commission and charging it with the duty to prevent "unfair methods of competition in commerce, and unfair or deceptive acts or practices in commerce." To this end the five-member Commission is empowered to conduct appropriate investigations and hearings. It may issue "cease and desist" orders against violators enforceable in the Federal courts.

Its broad power has been described as follows by the United States Supreme Court:

The "unfair methods of competition," which are condemned by . . . the Act, are not confined to those that were illegal at common law or that were condemned by the Sherman Act . . . . It is also clear that the Federal Trade Commission Act was designed to supplement and bolster the Sherman Act and the Clayton Act * * * *to stop in their incipiency acts and practices which, when full blown, would violate those Acts. F.T.C. v. Motion Picture Advertising Service Co.,* 344 U.S. 392, (1953). (Emphasis supplied.)

Complaints may be instituted by the Commission which after a hearing "has wide latitude for judgment and the courts will not interfere except where the remedy selected has no reasonable relation to the unlawful practices found to exist." Although the Commission most frequently enters a cease and desist order having the effect of an injunction, it may order other relief such as affirmative disclosure, corrective advertising, and the granting of licenses to patents on a reasonable royalty basis. *See Warner-Lambert Co. v. Federal Trade Commission* in Chapter 42. Appeals may be taken from orders of the Commission to the United States Courts of Appeals which have exclusive jurisdiction to enforce, set aside, or modify orders of the Commission.

The work of the Federal Trade Commission includes not only investigation of possible violations of the antitrust laws but also unfair methods of competition, such as false and misleading advertisements, false or inadequate labeling of products, passing or palming off goods as those of a competitor, lotteries, gambling schemes, discriminatory offers of rebates and discounts, false disparagement of a competitor's goods, false or misleading descriptive names of products, use of false testimonials, and other unfair trade practices.

CASES

Horizontal Price Fixing

UNITED STATES v. SOCONY-VACUUM OIL CO.

Supreme Court of the United States, 1940.
310 U.S. 150, 60 S.Ct. 811, 84 L.Ed. 1129.

DOUGLAS, J.

Respondents were convicted by a jury under an indictment charging violations of § 1 of the Sherman Anti-Trust Act. The Circuit Court of Appeals reversed and remanded for a new trial. * * *

The Indictment

* * *

The methods of marketing and selling gasoline in the Mid-Western area are set forth in the indictment in some detail. * * * Each defendant major oil company owns, operates or leases retail service stations in this area. It supplies those stations, as well as independent retail stations, with gasoline from its bulk storage plants. All but one sell large quantities of gasoline to jobbers in tank car lots under term contracts. In this area these jobbers exceed 4,000 in number and distribute about 50% of all gasoline distributed to retail service stations therein, the bulk of the jobbers' purchases being made from the defendant companies. The price to the jobbers under those contracts with defendant companies is made dependent on the spot market price, pursuant to a formula. * * * And the spot market tank car prices of gasoline directly and substantially influence the retail prices in the area. In sum, it is alleged that defendants by raising and fixing the tank car prices of gasoline in these spot markets could and did increase the tank car prices and the retail prices of gasoline sold in the Mid-Western area. * * *

Background of the Alleged Conspiracy

Evidence was introduced (or respondents made offers of proof) showing or tending to show the following conditions preceding the commencement of the alleged conspiracy in February 1935. * * *

Beginning about 1926 there commenced a period of production of crude oil in such quantities as seriously to affect crude oil and gasoline markets throughout the United States. Overproduction was wasteful, reduced the productive capacity of the oil fields and drove the price of oil down to levels below the cost of production from pumping and stripper wells. When the price falls below such cost, those wells must be abandoned. Once abandoned, subsurface changes make it difficult or impossible to bring those wells back into production. Since such wells constitute about 40% of the country's known oil reserves, conservation requires that the price of crude oil be maintained at a level which will permit such wells to be operated. As Oklahoma and Kansas were attempting to remedy the situation through their proration laws, the largest oil field in history was discovered in East Texas. That was in 1930. The supply of oil from this field was so great that at one time crude oil sank to 10 to 15 cents a barrel, and gasoline was sold in the East Texas field for 2⅛¢ a gallon. Enforcement by Texas of its proration law was extremely difficult. Orders restricting production were violated, the oil unlawfully produced being known as "hot oil" and the gasoline manufactured therefrom, "hot gasoline." Hot oil sold for substantially lower prices than those posted for legal oil. Hot gasoline therefore cost less and at times could be sold for less than it cost to manufacture legal gasoline. The latter, deprived of its normal outlets, had to be sold at distress prices. The condition of many independent refiners using legal crude oil was precarious. In spite of their unprofitable operations they could not afford to shut down, for if they did so they would be apt to lose their oil connections in the field and their regular customers. Having little storage capacity they had to sell their gasoline as fast as they made it. As a result their gasoline became "distress" gasoline—gasoline which the refiner could not store, for which he had no regular sales outlets and which therefore he had to sell for whatever price it would bring. Such sales drove the market down.

In the spring of 1933 conditions were acute. The wholesale market was below the cost of manufacture. As the market became flooded with cheap gasoline, gasoline was dumped at whatever price it would bring. On June 1, 1933, the price of crude oil was 25¢ a barrel; the tank car price of regular gasoline was 2⅝¢ a gallon. * * *

Meanwhile the retail markets had been swept by a series of price wars. These price wars affected all markets—service station, tank wagon, and tank car. Early in 1934 the Petroleum Administrative Board tried to deal with them—by negotiating agreements between marketing companies and persuading individual companies to raise the price level for a period. * * *

The Alleged Conspiracy

* * *

It was estimated that there would be between 600 and 700 tank cars of distress gasoline produced in the Mid-Continent oil field every month by about 17 independent refiners. These refiners, not having regular outlets for the gasoline, would be unable to dispose of it except at distress prices. Accordingly, it was proposed and decided that certain major companies (including the corporate respondents) would purchase gasoline from these refiners. The Committee would assemble each month information as to the quantity and location of this distress gasoline. Each of the major companies was to select one (or more) of the independent refiners having distress gasoline as its "dancing partner," and would assume responsibility for purchasing its distress supply. In this manner buying power would be coordinated, purchases would be effectively placed, and the results would be much superior to the previous haphazard purchasing. There were to be no formal contractual commitments to purchase this gasoline, either between the major companies or between the majors and the independents. Rather it was an informal gentlemen's agreement or understanding whereby each undertook to perform his share of the joint undertaking. Purchases were to be made at the "fair going market price." * * *

Application of the Sherman Act

The [trial] court charged the jury that it was a violation of the Sherman Act for a group of individuals or corporations to act together to raise the prices to be charged for the commodity which they manufactured where they controlled a substantial part of the interstate trade and commerce in that commodity. The court stated that where the members of a combination had the power to raise prices and acted together for that purpose, the combination was illegal; and that it was immaterial how reasonable or unreasonable those prices were or to what extent they had been affected by the combination. It further charged that if such illegal combination existed, it did not matter that there may also have been other factors which contributed to the raising of the prices. * * * The court then charged that, unless the jury found beyond a reasonable doubt that the price rise and its continuance were "caused" by the combination and not caused by those other factors, verdicts of "not guilty" should be returned. It also charged that there was no evidence of governmental approval which would exempt the buying programs from the prohibitions of the Sherman Act; and that knowledge or acquiescence of officers of the government or the good intentions of the members of the combination would not give immunity from prosecution under that Act.

The Circuit Court of Appeals held this charge to be reversible error, since it was based upon the theory that such a combination was illegal per se. In its view respondents' activities were not unlawful unless they constituted an unreasonable restraint of trade.

* * *

In United States v. Trenton Potteries Co., [citation], this Court sustained a conviction under the Sherman Act where the jury was charged that an agreement on the part of the members of a combination, controlling a substantial part of an industry, upon the prices which the members are to charge for their commodity is in itself an unreasonable restraint of trade without regard to the reasonableness of the prices or the good intentions of the combining units.

* * *

Therefore the sole remaining question of this phase of the case is the applicability of the rule of the Trenton Potteries case to these facts. Respondents seek to distinguish the Trenton Potteries case from the instant one.

* * *

But we do not deem those distinctions material. In the first place, there was abundant evidence that the combination had the purpose to raise prices. And likewise, there was ample evidence that the buying programs at least contributed to the price rise and the stability of the spot markets, and to increases in the price of gasoline sold in the Mid-Western area during the indictment period. That other factors also may have contributed to that rise and stability of the markets is immaterial. * * *

Secondly, the fact that sales on the spot markets were still governed by some competition is of no consequence. For it is indisputable that the competition was restricted through the removal by respondents of a part of the supply which but for the buying programs would have been a factor in determining the going prices on those markets. * * *

The elimination of so-called competitive evils is not legal justification for such buying programs. The elimination of such conditions was sought primarily for its effect on the price structures. Fairer competitive prices, it is claimed, resulted when distress gasoline was removed from the market. But such defense is typical of the protestations usually made in price-fixing cases. Ruinous competition, financial disaster, evils of price cutting and the like appear throughout our history as ostensible justifications for price-fixing. If the so-called competitive abuses were to be appraised here, the reasonableness of prices would necessarily become an issue in every price-fixing case. In that event the Sherman Act would soon be emasculated; its philosophy would be supplanted by one which is wholly alien to a system of free competition; it would not be the charter of freedom which its framers intended.

The reasonableness of prices has no constancy due to the dynamic quality of the business facts underlying price structures. Those who fixed reasonable prices today would perpetuate unreasonable prices tomorrow, since those prices would not be subject to continuous administrative supervision and readjustment in light of changed conditions. Those who controlled the prices would control or effectively dominate the market. And those who were in that strategic position would have it in their power to destroy or drastically impair the competitive system. But the thrust of the rule is deeper and reaches more than monopoly power. Any combination which tampers with price structures is engaged in an unlawful activity. Even though the members of the price-fixing group were in no position to control the market, to the extent that they raised, lowered, or stabilized prices they would be directly interfering with the free play of market forces. The Act places all such schemes beyond the pale and protects the vital part of our economy against any degree of interference. Congress has not left us the determination of whether or not particular price-fixing schemes are wise or unwise, healthy or destructive. It has not permitted the age-old cry of ruinous competition and competitive evils to be a defense to price-fixing conspiracies. * * *

Nor is it important that the prices paid by the combination were not fixed in the sense that they were uniform and inflexible. * * * That price-fixing includes more than the mere establishment of uniform prices is clearly evident from the Trenton Potteries case itself, where this Court noted with approval Swift & Co. v. United States, [citation], in which a decree was affirmed which restrained a combination from "raising or lowering prices or fixing uniform prices" at which meats will be sold. Hence prices are fixed within the meaning of the Trenton Potteries case if the range within which purchases or sales will be made is agreed upon, if the prices paid or charges are to be at a certain level or on ascending or descending scales, if they are to be uniform, or if by various forumulae they are related to the market prices. They are fixed because they are agreed upon.

* * *

Under the Sherman Act a combination formed for the purpose and with the effect of raising, depressing, fixing pegging, or stabilizing the price of a commodity in interstate or foreign commerce is illegal per se. Where the machinery for price-fixing is an agreement on the prices to be charged or paid for the commodity in the interstate or foreign channels of trade, the power to fix prices exists if the combination had control of a substantial part of the commerce in that commodity.

* * *

Accordingly, we conclude that the Circuit Court of Appeals erred in reversing the judgments on this ground. A fortiori the position taken by respondents in their cross petition that they were entitled to directed verdicts of acquittal is untenable. * * *

Reversed.

Vertical Market Allocation

CONTINENTAL T.V. v. GTE SYLVANIA

Supreme Court of the United States, 1977.
433 U.S. 36, 97 S.Ct. 2549, 53 L.Ed.2d 568.

POWELL, J.

Franchise agreements between manufacturers and retailers frequently include provisions barring the retailers from selling franchised products from locations other than those specified in the agreements. This case presents important questions concerning the appropriate antitrust analysis of these restrictions under § 1 of the Sherman Act and the Court's decision in United States v. Arnold, Schwinn & Co., 388 U.S. 365 (1967).

I.

Respondent GTE Sylvania, Inc. (Sylvania) manufactures and sells television sets through its Home Entertainment Products Division. Prior to 1962, like most other television manufacturers, Sylvania sold its televisions to independent or company-owned distributors who in turn resold to a large and diverse group of retailers. Prompted by a decline in its market share to a relatively insignificant 1 to 2% of national television sales Sylvania conducted an intensive reassessment of its marketing strategy, and in 1962 adopted the franchise plan challenged here. Sylvania phased out its wholesale distributors and began to sell its televisions directly to a smaller and more select group of franchised retailers. An acknowledged purpose of the change was to decrease the number of competing Sylvania retailers in the hope of attracting the more aggressive and competent retailers thought necessary to the improvement of the company's market position. To this end, Sylvania limited the number of franchises granted for any given area and required each franchisee to sell his Sylvania products only from the location or locations at which he was franchised. A franchise did not constitute an exclusive territory, and Sylvania retained sole discretion to increase the number of retailers in an area in light of the success or failure of existing retailers in developing their market. The revised marketing strategy appears to have been successful during the period at issue here, for by 1965, Sylvania's share of national television sales had increased to approximately 5%, and the company ranked as the Nation's eighth largest manufacturer of color television sets.

This suit is the result of the rupture of a franchisor-franchisee relationship that had previously prospered under the revised Sylvania plan. Dissatisfied with its sales in the city of San Francisco, Sylvania decided in the spring of 1965 to franchise Young Brothers, an established San Francisco retailer of televisions, as an additional San Francisco retailer. The proposed location of the new franchise was approximately a mile from a retail outlet operated by petitioner Continental T.V., Inc. (Continental), one of the most successful Sylvania franchisees. Continental protested that the location of the new franchise violated Sylvania's marketing policy, but Sylvania persisted in its plans. Continental then cancelled a large Sylvania order and placed a large order with Phillips, one of Sylvania's competitors.

During this same period, Continental expressed a desire to open a store in Sacramento, Cal., a desire Sylvania attributed at least in part to Continental's displeasure over the Young Brothers decision. Sylvania believed that the Sacramento market was adequately served by the existing Sylvania retailers and denied the request. In the face of this denial, Continental advised Sylvania in early September 1965, that it was in the process of moving Sylvania merchandise from its San Jose, Cal., warehouse to a new retail location that it had leased in Sacramento. Two weeks later, allegedly for unrelated reasons, Sylvania's credit department reduced Continental's credit line from $300,000 to $50,000. In response to the reduction in credit and the generally deteriorating relations with Sylvania, Continental withheld all payments owed to John P. Maguire & Co., Inc. (Maguire), the finance company that handled the credit arrangements between Sylvania and its retailers. Shortly thereafter, Sylvania terminated Continental's franchises, and Maguire filed this diversity action in the United States District Court for the Northern District of California seeking recovery of money owed and of secured merchandise held by Continental.

The antitrust issues before us originated in cross-claims brought by Continental against Sylvania and Maguire. Most important for our purposes was the claim that Sylvania had violated § 1 of the Sherman Act by entering into and enforcing franchise agreements that prohibited the sale of Sylvania products other than from specified locations. At the close of evidence in the jury trial of Continental's claims, Sylvania requested the District Court to instruct the jury that its location restriction was illegal only if it unreasonably restrained or suppressed competition. Relying on this Court's decision in United Stated v. Arnold, Schwinn & Co., the District Court rejected the proffered instruction in favor of the following one: "Therefore, if you find by a preponderance of the evidence that Sylvania entered into a contract, combination or conspiracy with one or more of its dealers pursuant to which Sylvania exercised dominion or control over the products sold to the dealer, after having parted with title and risk to the products, you must find any effort thereafter to restrict outlets or store locations from whch its dealers resold the merchandise which they had purchased from Sylvania to be a violation of Section 1 of the Sherman Act, regardless of the reasonableness of the location restrictions." In answers to special interrogatories, the jury found that Sylvania had engaged "in a contract, combination or conspiracy in restraint of trade in violation of the antitrust laws with respect to location restrictions alone," and assessed Continental's damages at $591,505, which was trebled. * * *

On appeal, the Court of Appeals for the Ninth Circuit, sitting en banc, reversed by a divided vote. * * * Contrasting the nature of the restrictions, their competitive impact, and the market shares of the franchisors in the two cases, the court concluded that Sylvania's location restriction had less potential for competitive harm than the restrictions invalidated in Schwinn and thus should be judged under the "rule of reason" rather than the per se rule stated in Schwinn. * * *

II.
A

We turn first to Continental's contention that Sylvania's restriction on retail locations is a per se violation of § 1 of the Sherman Act as interpreted in Schwinn.

* * *

Schwinn produced sharply contrasting results depending upon the role played by the distributor in the distribution system. With respect to that portion of Schwinn's sales for which the distributors acted as ordinary wholesalers, buying and reselling Schwinn bicycles, the Court held that the territorial and customer restrictions challenged by the Government were per se illegal. But, with respect to that larger portion of Schwinn's sales in which the distributors functioned under the Schwinn Plan [manufacturer's representa-

tives or sales agents] and under the less common consignment and agency arrangements, the Court held that the same restrictions should be judged under the rule of reason. * * *

B

In the present case, it is undisputed that title to the televisions passed from Sylvania to Continental. Thus, the Schwinn per se rule applies unless Sylvania's restriction on locations falls outside Schwinn's prohibition against a manufacturer attempting to restrict a "retailer's freedom as to where and to whom it will resell the products." As the Court of Appeals concluded, the language of Schwinn is clearly broad enough to apply to the present case. Unlike the Court of Appeals, however, we are unable to find a principled basis for distinguishing Schwinn from the case now before us.

* * *

III.

Sylvania argues that if Schwinn cannot be distinguished, it should be reconsidered. Although Schwinn is supported by the principle of stare decisis [citation] we are convinced that the need for clarification of the law in this area justifies reconsideration. Schwinn itself was an abrupt and largely unexplained departure from White Motor Co. v. United States, 372 U.S. 253 (1963), where only four years earlier the Court had refused to endorse a per se rule for vertical restrictions. Since its announcement, Schwinn has been the subject of continuing controversy and confusion, both in the scholarly journals and in the federal courts. The great weight of scholarly opinion has been critical of the decision, and a number of the federal courts confronted with analogous vertical restrictions have sought to limit its reach. In our view, the experience of the past 10 years should be brought to bear on this subject of considerable commercial importance.

The traditional framework of analysis under § 1 of the Sherman Act is familiar and does not require extended discussion. * * *

[The "rule of reason" is] the prevailing standard of analysis. [Citation.] Under this rule, the factfinder weighs all of the circumstances of a case in deciding whether a restrictive practice should be prohibited as imposing an unreasonable restraint on competition. Per se rules of illegality are appropriate only when they relate to conduct that is manifestly anticompetitive. As the Court explained in Northern Pac. R. Co. v. United States, 356 U.S. 1, 5 (1958), "there are certain agreements or practices which because of their pernicious effect on competition and lack of redeeming virtue are conclusively presumed to be unreasonable and therefore illegal without elaborate inquiry as to the precise harm they have caused or the business excuse for their use."

In essence, the issue before us is whether Schwinn's per se rule can be justified under the demanding standards of Northern Pac. R. Co. The Court's refusal to endorse a per se rule in White Motor Co. was based on its uncertainty as to whether vertical restrictions satisfied those standards. Addressing this question for the first time, the Court stated: "We need to know more than we do about the actual impact of these arrangements on competition to decide whether they have such a 'pernicious effect on competition and lack * * * any redeeming virtue' [citation] and therefore should be classified as per se violations of the Sherman Act." Only four years later the Court in Schwinn announced its sweeping per se rule without even a reference to Northern Pac. R. Co. and with no explanation of its sudden change in position. We turn now to consider Schwinn in light of Northern Pac. R. Co.

The market impact of vertical restrictions is complex because of their potential for a simultaneous reduction of intrabrand competition and stimulation of interbrand competition. Significantly, the Court in Schwinn did not distinguish among the challenged restrictions on the basis of their individual potential for intrabrand harm or interbrand benefit. Restrictions that completely eliminated intrabrand competition among Schwinn distributors were analyzed no differently than those that merely moderated intrabrand competition among retailers. The pivotal factor was the passage of title: All restrictions were held to be per se illegal where title had passed, and all were evaluated and sustained under the rule of reason where it had not. The location restriction at issue here would be subject to the same pattern of analysis under Schwinn.

*   *   *

Vertical restrictions reduce intrabrand competition by limiting the number of sellers of a particular product competing for the business of a given group of buyers. Location restrictions have this effect because of practical constraints on the effective marketing area of retail outlets. Although intrabrand competition may be reduced, the ability of retailers to exploit the resulting market may be limited both by the ability of consumers to travel to other franchised locations and, perhaps more importantly, to purchase the competing products of other manufacturers.

*   *   *

Vertical restrictions promote interbrand competition by allowing the manufacturer to achieve certain efficiencies in the distribution of his products. These "redeeming virtues" are implicit in every decision sustaining vertical restrictions under the rule of reason. Economists have identified a number of ways in which manufacturers can use such restrictions to compete more effectively against other manufacturers. [Citation.] For example, new manufacturers and manufacturers entering new markets can use the restrictions in order to induce competent and aggressive retailers to make the kind of investment of capital and labor that is often required in the distribution of products unknown to the consumer. Established manufacturers can use them to induce retailers to engage in promotional activities or to provide service and repair facilities necessary to the efficient marketing of their products. Service and repair are vital for many products, such as automobiles and major household appliances. The availability and quality of such services affect a manufacturer's good will and the competitiveness of his product. Because of market imperfections such as the so-called "free rider" effect, these services might not be provided by retailers in a purely competitive situation, despite the fact that each retailer's benefit would be greater if all provided the services than if none did. [Citation.]

* * *

Certainly, there has been no showing in this case, either generally or with respect to Sylvania's agreements, that vertical restrictions have or are likely to have a "pernicious effect on competition" or that they "lack * * * any redeeming virtue." Accordingly, we conclude that the per se rule stated in Schwinn must be overruled. In so holding we do not foreclose the possibility that particular applications of vertical restrictions might justify per se prohibition under Northern Pac. R. Co. But we do make clear that departure from the rule of reason standard must be based upon demonstrable economic effect rather than—as in Schwinn—upon formalistic line drawing.

In sum, we conclude that the appropriate decision is to return to the rule of reason that governed vertical restrictions prior to Schwinn. When anticompetitive effects are shown to result from particular vertical restrictions they can be adequately policed under the rule of reason, the standard traditionally applied for the majority of anticompetitive practices challenged under § 1 of the Act. Accordingly, the decision of the Court of Appeals is affirmed.

Monopolization

UNITED STATES v. E. I. du PONT De NEMOURS & CO.

Supreme Court of the United States, 1956.
351 U.S. 377, 76 S.Ct. 994, 100 L.Ed. 1264.

REED, J.

[In 1923, du Pont was granted the exclusive right to make and sell cellophane in North America. In 1927, the company introduced a moistureproof brand of cellophane that was ideal for various wrapping needs. Although more expensive than most competing wrapping, it was favored for many uses because it offered a desired combination of transparency, strength, and cost. Except as to permeability to gases, however, cellophane had no qualities that were not possessed by a number of competing materials. Cellophane sales increased dramatically, and by 1950, du Pont produced almost 75 percent of the cellophane sold in the United States. Nevertheless, sales of the material constituted less than 20 percent of the sales of "flexible packaging materials."

The United States brought this action contending that by so dominating cellophane production, du Pont had monopolized a part of trade or commerce in violation of the Sherman Act because it did not have the power to control the price of cellophane or to exclude competitors from the market for flexible wrapping materials.]

* * *

III.   THE SHERMAN ACT, § 2— MONOPOLIZATION . . .

Our cases determine that a party has monopoly power if it has, over "any part of the trade or commerce among the several states," a power of controlling prices or unreasonably restricting competition. * * *

If cellophane is the "market" that du Pont is found to dominate, it may be assumed it does have monopoly power over that "market." Monopoly power is the power to control prices or exclude competition. It seems apparent that du Pont's power to set the price of cellophane has been limited only by the competition afforded by other flexible packaging materials.

* * *

Determination of the competitive market for commodities depends on how different from one another are the offered commodities in character or use, how far buyers will go to substitute one commodity for another. For example, one can think of building materials as in commodity competition but one could hardly say that brick competed with steel or wood or cement or stone in the meaning of Sherman Act litigation; the products are too different. This is the interindustry competition emphasized by some economist. * * * On the other hand, there are certain differences in the formulae for soft drinks but one can hardly say that each one is an illegal monopoly. Whatever the market may be, we hold that control of price or competition establishes the existence of monopoly power under § 2. Section 2 requires the application of a reasonable approach in determining the existence of monopoly power just as surely as did § 1. This of course does not mean that there can be a reasonable monopoly. Our next step is to determine whether du Pont has monopoly power over cellophane: that is, power over its price in relation to or competition with other commodities. The charge was monopolization of cellophane. The defense, that cellophane was merely a part of the relevant market for flexible packaging materials.

IV. THE RELEVANT MARKET

When a product is controlled by one interest, without substitutes available in the market, there is monopoly power. Because most products have possible substitutes, we cannot * * * give "that infinite range" to the definition of substitutes. Nor is it a proper interpretation of the Sherman Act to require that products be fungible to be considered in the relevant market.

* * *

But where there are market alternatives that buyers may readily use for their purposes, illegal monopoly does not exist merely because the product said to be monopolized differs from others. If it were not so, only physically identical products would be a part of the market. To accept the Government's argument, we would have to conclude that the manufacturers of plain as well as mois-

tureproof cellophane were monopolists, and so with films such as Pliofilm, foil, glassine, polyethylene, and Saran, for each of these wrapping materials is distinguishable. These were all exhibits in the case. New wrappings appear, generally similar to cellophane: is each a monopoly? What is called for is an appraisal of the "cross-elasticity" of demand in the trade. * * * In considering what is the relevant market for determining the control of price and competition, no more definite rule can be declared than that commodities reasonably interchangeable by consumers for the same purposes make up that "part of the trade or commerce," monopolization of which may be illegal. As respects flexible packaging materials, the market geographically is nationwide.

* * *

Cellophane differs from other flexible packaging materials. From some it differs more than from others. The basic materials from which the wrappings are made * * * are aluminum, cellulose acetate, chlorides, wood pulp, rubber hydrochloride, and ethylene gas. * * *

* * *

An element for consideration as to cross-elasticity of demand between products is the responsiveness of the sales of one product to price changes of the other. If a slight decrease in the price of cellophane causes a considerable number of customers of other flexible wrappings to switch to cellophane, it would be an indication that a high cross-elasticity of demand exists between them; that the products compete in the same market. The court below held that the "[g]reat sensitivity of customers in the flexible packaging markets to price or quality changes" prevented du Pont from possessing monopoly control over price. The record sustains these findings.

We conclude that cellophane's interchangeability with the other materials mentioned suffices to make it a part of this flexible packaging material market.

The Government stresses the fact that the variation in price between cellophane and other materials demonstrates they are non-competitive. * * *

[The district court concluded that] "The record establishes plain cellophane and moistureproof cellophane are each flexible packaging materials which are functionally interchangeable with other flexible packaging materials and sold at same time to same customers for same purpose at competitive prices; there is no cellophane market distinct and separate from the market for flexible packaging materials; the market for flexible packaging materials is the relevant market for determining nature and extent of du Pont's market control; and du Pont has at all times competed with other cellophane producers and manufacturers of other flexible packaging materials in all aspects of its cellophane business." * * *

[T]he trial court found that du Pont could not exclude competitors even from the manufacture of cellophane, an immaterial matter if the market is flexible packaging material. Nor can we say that du Pont's profits, while liberal (according to the Government 15.9% net after taxes on the 1937–1947 average), demonstrate the existence of a monopoly without proof of lack of comparable profits during those years in other prosperous industries. Cellophane was a leader, over 17%, in the flexible packaging materials market. There is no showing that du Pont's rate of return was greater or less than that of other producers of flexible packaging materials.

The "market" which one must study to determine when a producer has monopoly power will vary with the part of commerce under consideration. The tests are constant. That market is composed of products that have reasonable interchangeability for the purposes for which they are produced—prices, use and qualities considered. While the application of the tests remains uncertain, it seems to us that du Pont should not be found to monopolize cellophane when that product

has the competition and interchangeability with other wrappings that this record shows.

Affirmed.

Horizontal Merger

UNITED STATES v. VON'S GROCERY CO.

Supreme Court of the United States, 1966.
384 U.S. 270, 86 S.Ct. 1478, 16 L.Ed.2d 555.

BLACK, J.

On March 25, 1960, the United States brought this action charging that the acquisition by Von's Grocery Company of its direct competitor Shopping Bag Food Stores, both large retail grocery companies in Los Angeles, California, violated § 7 of the Clayton Act which, as amended in 1950 by the Celler-Kefauver Anti-Merger Act, provides in relevant part:

That no corporation engaged in commerce . . . shall acquire the whole or any part of the assets of another corporation engaged also in commerce, where in any line of commerce in any section of the country, the effect of such acquisition may be substantially to lessen competition, or to tend to create a monopoly.

On March 28, 1960, three days later, the District Court refused to grant the Government's motion for a temporary restraining order and immediately Von's took over all of Shopping Bag's capital stock and assets including 36 grocery stores in the Los Angeles area. After hearing evidence on both sides, the District Court made findings of fact and concluded as a matter of law that there was "not a reasonable probability" that the merger would tend "substantially to lessen competition" or "create a monopoly" in violation of § 7. For this reason the District Court entered judgment for the defendants. [Citation.] The Government appealed directly to this Court * * *. The sole question here is whether the District Court properly concluded on the facts before it that the Government had failed to prove a violation of § 7.

The record shows the following facts relevant to our decision. The market involved here is the retail grocery market in the Los Angeles area. In 1958 Von's retail sales ranked third in the area and Shopping Bag's ranked sixth. In 1960 their sales together were 7.5% of the total two and one-half billion dollars of retail groceries sold in the Los Angeles market each year. For many years before the merger both companies had enjoyed great success as rapidly growing companies. From 1948 to 1958 the number of Von's stores in the Los Angeles area practically doubled from 14 to 27, while at the same time the number of Shopping Bag's stores jumped from 15 to 34. During that same decade, Von's sales increased fourfold and its share of the market almost doubled while Shopping Bag's sales multiplied seven times and its share of the market tripled. The merger of these two highly successful, expanding and aggressive competitors created the second largest grocery chain in Los Angeles with sales of almost $172,488,000 annually. In addition the findings of the District Court show that the number of owners operating single stores in the Los Angeles retail grocery market decreased from 5,365 in 1950 to 3,818 in 1961. By 1963, three years after the merger, the number of single-store owners had dropped still further to 3,590. During roughly the same period, from 1953 to 1962, the number of chains with two or more grocery stores increased from 96 to 150. While the grocery business was being concentrated into the hands of fewer and fewer owners, the small companies were continually being absorbed by the larger firms through mergers. According to an exhibit prepared by one of the Government's expert witnesses, in the period from 1949 to 1958 nine of the top 20 chains acquired 126 stores from their smaller competitors. * * *

From this country's beginning there has been an abiding and widespread fear of the evils which flow from monopoly—that is the concentration of economic power in the hands of a few. On the basis of this fear, Congress in 1890, when many of the Nation's industries were already concentrated into what it deemed too few hands, passed the Sherman Act in an attempt to prevent further concentration and to preserve competition among a large number of sellers. Several years later, in 1897, this Court emphasized this policy of the Sherman Act by calling attention to the tendency of powerful business combinations to restrain competition "by driving out of business the small dealers and worthy men whose lives have been spent therein, and who might be unable to readjust themselves in their altered surroundings." *United States v. Trans-Missouri Freight Assn.*, [citation]. The Sherman Act failed to protect the smaller businessmen from elimination through the monopolistic pressures of large combinations which used mergers to grow ever more powerful. As a result in 1914 Congress, viewing mergers as a continuous, pervasive threat to small business, passed § 7 of the Clayton Act which prohibited corporations under most circumstances from merging by purchasing the stock of their competitors. Ingenious businessmen, however, soon found a way to avoid § 7 and corporations began to merge simply by purchasing their rivals' assets. This Court in 1926, over the dissent of Justice Brandeis, joined by Chief Justice Taft and Justices Holmes and Stone approved this device for avoiding § 7 and mergers continued to concentrate economic power into fewer and fewer hands until 1950 when Congress passed the Celler-Kefauver Anti-Merger Act now before us.

Like the Sherman Act in 1890 and the Clayton Act in 1914, the basic purpose of the 1950 Celler-Kefauver Act was to prevent economic concentration in the American economy by keeping a large number of small competitors in business. In stating the purposes of their bill, both of its sponsors, Representative Celler and Senator Kefauver, emphasized their fear, widely shared by other members of Congress, that this concentration was rapidly driving the small businessman out of the market. The period from 1940 to 1947, which was at the center of attention throughout the hearings and debates on the Celler-Kefauver bill, had been characterized by a series of mergers between large corporations and their smaller competitors resulting in the steady erosion of the small independent business in our economy. As we said in *Brown Shoe Co. v. United States*, [citation], "The dominant theme pervading congressional consideration of the 1950 amendments was a fear of what was considered to be a rising tide of economic concentration in the American economy." To arrest this "rising tide" toward concentration into too few hands and to halt the gradual demise of the small businessman, Congress decided to clamp down with vigor on mergers. It both revitalized § 7 of the Clayton Act by "plugging its loophole" and broadened its scope so as not only to prohibit mergers between competitors, the effect of which "may be substantially to lessen competition, or to tend to create a monopoly" but to prohibit all mergers having that effect. By using these terms in § 7 which look not merely to the actual present effect of a merger but instead to its effect upon future competition, Congress sought to preserve competition among many small businesses by arresting a trend toward concentration in its incipiency before that trend developed to the point that a market was left in the grip of a few big companies. Thus, where concentration is gaining momentum in a market, we must be alert to carry out Congress' intent to protect competition against ever-increasing concentration through mergers.

The facts of this case present exactly the threatening trend toward concentration which Congress wanted to halt. The number of small grocery companies in the Los Angeles retail grocery market had been declining rapidly before the merger and continued to decline rapidly afterwards. This rapid decline in the number of grocery store owners moved hand in hand with a large number of significant absorptions of the small companies by the larger ones. In the midst of this steadfast trend toward concentration, Von's and Shop-

ping Bag, two of the most successful and largest companies in the area, jointly owning 66 grocery stores merged to become the second largest chain in Los Angeles. This merger cannot be defended on the ground that one of the companies was about to fail or that the two had to merge to save themselves from destruction by some larger and more powerful competitor. What we have on the contrary is simply the case of two already powerful companies merging in a way which makes them even more powerful than they were before. If ever such a merger would not violate § 7, certainly it does when it takes place in a market characterized by a long and continuous trend toward fewer and fewer owner-competitors which is exactly the sort of trend which Congress, with power to do so, declared must be arrested.

Appellees' primary argument is that the merger between Von's and Shopping Bag is not prohibited by § 7 because the Los Angeles grocery market was competitive before the merger, has been since, and may continue to be in the future. Even so, § 7 "requires not merely an appraisal of the immediate impact of the merger upon competition, but a prediction of its impact upon competitive conditions in the future; this is what is meant when it is said that the amended § 7 was intended to arrest anticompetitive tendencies in their 'incipiency.' " *U.S. v. Philadelphia Nat. Bank*, 374 U.S. 321, 362. It is enough for us that Congress feared that a market marked at the same time by both a continuous decline in the number of small businesses and a large number of mergers would slowly but inevitably gravitate from a market of many small competitors to one dominated by one or a few giants, and competition would thereby be destroyed. Congress passed the Celler-Kefauver Act to prevent such a destruction of competition. Our cases since the passage of that Act have faithfully endeavored to enforce this congressional command. We adhere to them now.

* * *

Reversed and remanded.

Robinson-Patman Act

GREAT ATLANTIC & PACIFIC TEA CO. v. FEDERAL TRADE COMMISSION

Supreme Court of the United States, 1979.
440 U.S. 69, 99 S.Ct. 925, 59 L.Ed.2d 153.

STEWART, J.

[Great Atlantic and Pacific Tea Company desired to achieve cost savings by switching to the sale of "private label" milk. A&P asked Borden Company, its longtime supplier of "brand label" milk to submit a bid to supply certain of A&P's private label dairy products. A&P was not satisfied with Borden's bid, however, and it solicited other offers. Bowman Dairy, a competitor of Borden's, submitted a lower bid. At this point, A&P contacted Borden and asked it to rebid on the private label contract. A&P included a warning that Borden would have to substantially lower its original bid in order to undercut Bowman's bid. Borden offered a bid that doubled A&P's potential annual cost savings. A&P accepted Borden's bid. The Federal Trade Commission then brought this action charging that A&P had violated the Robinson-Patman Act by knowingly inducing or receiving illegal price discriminations from Borden.]

* * *

[T]he Court of Appeals for the Second Circuit * * * held that * * * as a matter of law A&P could not successfully assert a meeting competition defense because it, unlike Borden, had known that Borden's offer was better than Bowman's. * * *

Liability under § 2(f) [inducing an illegal price concession] * * * is limited to situations where the price discrimination is one "which is prohibited by this section." While the phrase "this section" refers to the entire § 2 of the Act, only subsections (a) and (b) dealing with seller-liability involve discriminations in price. Under the plain meaning of § 2(f), therefore, a buyer cannot be liable if a prima facie case could not be established against a seller or if the seller has an affirmative defense. In either situation, there is no

price discrimination "prohibited by this section." The legislative history of § 2(f) fully confirms the conclusion that buyer liability under § 2(f) is dependent on seller liability under § 2(a). * * *

III.

The petitioner [A&P], relying on this plain meaning of § 2(f) * * * argues that it cannot be liable under § 2(f) if Borden had a valid meeting competition defense. The respondent [FTC], on the other hand, argues that the petitioner may be liable even assuming that Borden had such a defense. The meeting competition defense, the respondent contends, must in these circumstances be judged from the point of view of the buyer. Since A&P knew for a fact that the final Borden bid beat the Bowman bid, it was not entitled to assert the meeting competition defense even though Borden may have honestly believed that it was simply meeting competition. Recognition of a meeting competition defense for the buyer in this situation, the respondent argues, would be contrary to the basic purpose of the Robinson-Patman Act to curtail abuses by large buyers.

The short answer to these contentions of the respondent is that Congress did not provide in § 2(f) that a buyer can be liable even if the seller has a valid defense. The clear language of § 2(f) states that a buyer can be liable only if he receives a price discrimination "prohibited by this section." If a seller has a valid meeting competition defense, there is simply no prohibited price discrimination. * * *

* * *

In a competitive market, uncertainty among sellers will cause them to compete for business by offering buyers lower prices. Because of the evils of collusive action, the Court has held that the exchange of price information by competitors violates the Sherman Act. [Citation.] Under the view advanced by the respondent, however, a buyer, to avoid liability, must either refuse a seller's bid or at least inform him that his bid had beaten competition. Such a duty of affirmative disclosure would almost inevitably frustrate competitive bidding and, by reducing uncertainty, lead to price matching and anticompetitive cooperation among sellers.

* * *

[W]e decline to adopt a construction of § 2(f) that is contrary to its plain meaning and would lead to anticompetitive results. Accordingly, we hold that a buyer who had done

no more than accept the lower of two prices competitively offered does not violate § 2(f) provided the seller has a meeting competition defense.

* * *

Since Borden had a meeting competition defense and thus could not be liable under § 2(b) the petitioner who did no more than accept that offer cannot be liable under § 2(f).

Accordingly, the judgment is reversed.

PROBLEMS

1. Discuss the validity and effect of each of the following:

(a) A, B, and C, manufacturers of radios, orally agree that due to the disastrous, cutthroat competition in the market, they would establish a reasonable price to charge their purchasers.

(b) A, B, C, and D, newspaper publishers, agree not to charge their customers more than thirty cents per newspaper.

(c) A, a distiller of liquor, and B, A's retail distributor, agree that B should charge a price of five dollars per bottle.

2. Discuss the validity of the following:

(a) An agreement between two manufacturers of the same type of products to allocate territories whereby neither will sell its products in the area allocated to the other.

(b) An agreement between manufacturer and distributor not to sell a dealer a particular product or parts necessary for repair of the product.

3. Universal Video sells $40 million worth of video recording equipment in the United States. The total sales of such equipment in the United States is $100 million. One-half of Universal's sales is to Giant Retailer, a company which possesses 50 percent of the retail market. Giant is presently seeking (1) to obtain an exclusive dealing arrangement with Universal, or (2) to acquire Universal. Please advise Giant as to the validity of its alternatives.

4. Z sells cameras to A, B, C, and D for sixty dollars per camera. Y, one of Z's competitor's, sells a comparable camera to A for $58.50. Z, in response to this competitive pressure from Y, lowers its price to A to $58.50. B, C, and D insist that Z lowers its price to them to $58.50, but Z refuses. B, C, and D sue Z for unlawful price discrimina-

tion. Decision? Would your answer differ if Z reduced its price to A to $58?

5. Discount is a discount appliance chain store that continually sells goods at a price below the manufacturers' suggested retail prices. A, B, and C, the three largest manufacturers of appliances, agree that unless Discount ceases from its discount pricing, they will no longer sell to Discount. Discount refuses, and A, B, and C refuse to sell to Discount. Discount sues A, B, and C. Decision?

6. Company X produces 77 percent of all the coal utilized in the United States. Coal provides 25 percent of all of the energy used in the United States. In a suit brought by the United States against X for violation of the antitrust laws, what result?

7. Justin Manufacturing Company sells high fashion clothing under the prestigious "Justin" label. The company has a firm policy that it will not deal with any company that sells below its suggested retail price. Justin is informed by one of its customers, XYZ, that its competitor, Duplex, is selling the "Justin" line at a great discount. Justin now demands that Duplex comply with their agreement that they will not sell the "Justin" line below the suggested retail price. Discuss the implications of this situation.

8. Jay Corporation, the largest manufacturer of bicycles in the United States with 40 percent of the market, has recently entered into an agreement with Retail Bike, the largest retailer of bicycles in the United States with 37% of the market, under which Jay will furnish its bicycles only to Retail and Retail will sell only Jay's bicycles. The government is now questioning this agreement. Discuss.

Chapter 42

CONSUMER PROTECTION

THE volume of consumer transactions has increased enormously since World War II and now amounts to hundreds of billions of dollars. Although the definition of a consumer transaction varies, it is generally considered one which involves goods, credit, services, or land acquired for personal, household, or family purposes. Historically, consumers were subject to the rule of *caveat emptor*— let the buyer beware. However, in recent years the law has abandoned this principle in most consumer transactions and has afforded greater protection to consumers. Most of this protection has taken the form of statutory enactments at both the State and Federal levels with a wide variety of governmental agencies charged with enforcement of these statutes.

This chapter examines consumer protection statutes that regulate (a) unfair and deceptive trade practices; (b) consumer purchases of goods, services, and land; (c) consumer credit obligations; and (d) consumer health and safety.

UNFAIR AND DECEPTIVE TRADE PRACTICES

In 1914 Congress enacted the **Federal Trade Commission Act** creating the Federal Trade Commission, which is charged with the duty to prevent "unfair methods of competition in or affecting commerce, and unfair or deceptive acts or practices in or affecting commerce." To this end the five-member Commission is empowered to issue substantive rules and to conduct appropriate investigations and hearings. Complaints may be instituted by the Commission which after a hearing may enter appropriate relief, including cease and desist orders, and, under certain circumstances, recovery of civil penalties and damages for persons injured by unfair or deceptive acts or practices. Appeals may be taken from orders of the Commission to the United States Courts of Appeals which have exclusive jurisdiction to enforce, set aside, or modify orders of the Commission.

The Commission has established a Bureau of Consumer Protection which investigates unfair methods of competition such as false and misleading advertisements, false or inadequate labeling of products, passing or palming off goods as those of a competitor, lotteries, gambling schemes, discriminatory offers of rebates and discounts, disparagement of a competitor's goods, false or misleading descriptions of products, use of false testimonials, and other unfair trade practices.

The Federal Trade Commission is the principal Federal agency concerned with the regulation of **advertising.** The Commission is concerned with providing purchasers with a sufficient supply of accurate information and thus attempts to regulate misleading or deceptive advertising. Deception may occur by either false representation or material omission. The FTC Act lends some guidance by defining false advertising as it relates to foods, drugs, devices, and cosmetics:

The term "false advertisement" means an advertisement, other than labeling which is misleading in a material respect; and in determining whether any advertisement is misleading, there shall be taken into account (among other things) not only representations made or suggested by statement, word, design, device, sound, or any combination thereof, but also the extent to which the advertisement fails to reveal facts material in the light of such representations or material with respect to consequences which may result from the use of the commodity to which the advertisement relates under the conditions prescribed in said advertisement, or under such conditions as are customary or usual. Section 55(a)(1).

The Commission need not prove that there was actual deception; it merely must show that the material misrepresentation or material omission has the "tendency or capacity" to deceive a significant number of consumers. Representations can be either expressed or implied and the determination of what representations have been made rests with the expertise of the Commission. Thus, a cereal advertisement which states that "no cereal has fewer calories than ours" might be considered deceptive if other cereals have equally few calories. It is unclear whether the standard for determining that an advertisement has the capacity to deceive is based upon "the average man," "the ignorant, unthinking, and the credulous," "the least-sophisticated reader," or some other standard. Nevertheless, the Commission has stated:

True * * * the Commission's responsibility is to prevent deception of the gullible and credulous, as well as the cautious and knowledgeable. . . . [T]his principle loses its validity, however, if it is applied uncritically or pushed to an absurd extreme. An advertiser cannot be charged with liability with respect of every conceivable misconception, however outlandish, to which his representations might be subject among the foolish or feeble-minded * * *. A representation does not become "false and deceptive" merely because it will be unreasonably misunderstood by an insignificant and unrepresentative segment of the class of persons to whom the representation is addressed. *Kirchner v. Federal Trade Commission,* 63 F.T.C. 1282, *aff'd,* 337 F.2d 751.

Examples of deceptive practices include advertising that a certain product will save the consumer 25 percent on their automotive motor oil where the product simply replaced a quart of oil in the engine (which normally contains four quarts of oil) and was more expensive than the replaced motor oil; placing marbles in a bowl of vegetable soup in order to displace the vegetables from the bottom of the soup and therefore make it appear that the soup had more vegetables; and claiming that a drug provides greater pain relief than another named drug when there was insufficient evidence to prove the claim to the medical community.

In addition to the remedies discussed above the FTC has recently employed three other potent remedies: (1) affirmative disclosure, (2) corrective advertising, and (3) multiple product orders. **Affirmative disclosure** is frequently employed by the FTC and requires the offender to provide certain information in its advertisement in order for the advertisement not to be considered deceptive. In ordering such remedial action, however, the Commission must be careful not to infringe upon the advertiser's constitutional rights. For instance, the National Commission on Egg Nutrition (NCEN), an egg producers' trade association, was organized in an attempt to combat the damage being done to the egg industry by the anti-cholesterol forces. The Federal Trade Commission alleged that in its attempt to achieve this goal the NCEN had made several false and misleading statements in its advertising campaign. Principally, the FTC contended and subsequently ruled that it was an unfair trade practice for NCEN to represent "that there is no scientific evidence that eating eggs increases the risk of * * * heart and [circulatory] disease * * * ." In addition to ordering the NCEN to cease and desist from this and other representations the FTC also ordered that (1) any reference made to the relationship between cholesterol (and hence eggs) and circulatory disease be accompanied by a conspicuous statement that many medical authorities believe that eating cholesterol might increase the risk of heart or circulatory disease, and (2) any representation disparaging the scientific evidence connecting cholesterol and heart and circulatory disease is forbidden. However, the United States Court of Appeals for the Seventh Circuit amended the FTC's affirmative disclosure order on the ground that the order was an overly broad remedial decree. It held that the First Amendment prohibited a remedy "broader than that which is necessary." And, since the order directed NCEN to argue the other side of the issue rather than merely acknowledge the existence of the controversy, the order

unduly infringed upon NCEN's freedom of speech. The Court, nevertheless, held that: (1) the NCEN cannot disseminate any advertisement that represents that the consumption of eggs or cholesterol does not enhance the risk of heart or circulatory disease unless it conspicuously discloses that a controversy exists surrounding this contention and that the advertisement is merely stating its position and (2) that NCEN cannot disseminate any advertisement that presents scientific evidence supporting the position that the consumption of eggs and/or cholesterol does not increase the consumer's risk of heart or circulatory disease unless it conspicuously discloses that many medical authorities are of the belief that the eating of eggs (cholesterol) does, based on scientific evidence, increase one's risk of heart or circulatory ailment. *National Commission on Egg Nutrition v. FTC*, 570 F.2d 157 (7th Cir. 1977).

Corrective advertising goes beyond affirmative disclosure and requires that the advertiser of a deceptive claim disclose in future advertisements that the deceptive claims made in the prior advertisements are in fact not true. For a full discussion of this remedy *see Warner-Lambert Co. v. FTC* at the end of this Chapter.

Multiple product orders require that the deceptive advertisers cease and desist from any future deception in regard to the product in question but also to all products sold by the company. *See Sears, Roebuck and Co. v. FTC* at the end of this chapter. This remedy is particularly useful in dealing with companies that are repeated violators of the law.

Numerous States have consumer protection statutes that are similar to the Federal Trade Commission Act and prohibit unfair and deceptive trade practices.

CONSUMER PURCHASES

A number of State and Federal regulations protect the consumer in his purchases of goods, services, and real property for personal, household, or family use. The Uniform Commercial Code, discussed more fully in Chapters 19–23, prohibits unconscionable contractual terms and imposes implied warranties for the protection of the purchaser.

Federal Warranty Protection

In order to provide protection to buyers of consumer products by making available to them adequate information with respect to warranties of such products and to prevent deception, Congress in 1974 enacted the Magnuson-Moss Warranty Act. Administration and enforcement of the Act is by the Federal Trade Commission.

The **Magnuson-Moss Warranty Act** was enacted in order to alleviate certain reported warranty problems: (1) most warranties were not understandable; (2) most warranties disclaimed implied warranties; (3) most warranties were unfair; and (4) in some instances the warrantors did not live up to their warranties. The Act was Congress's attempt to make consumer product warranties more easily understood and to facilitate the consumer in satisfactorily enforcing her remedies. In order to accomplish this purpose the Act provides for:

1. disclosure in clear and understandable language of the warranty that is to be offered;
2. a description of the warranty as either "full" or "limited";
3. a prohibition against disclaiming implied warranties if a written warranty is given; and
4. an optional informal settlement mechanism.

The Act is applicable when a **consumer** product containing a **written warranty** is marketed. A consumer product is defined as any item of tangible personal property which is *normally* used for family, household, or personal use and which is distributed in commerce. The exclusion of commercial purchasers from the Act's protection is to some degree based on the notion that such persons are sufficiently knowledgeable in contracting,

are able to employ their own attorneys to protect themselves, and are able to spread the cost of their injuries in the marketplace.

The Act contains *pre-sale disclosure* provisions, which are calculated to avert confusion and deception and to enable purchasers to make educated product comparisons. A warrantor must, "to the extent required by the rules of the Commission [Federal Trade Commission], fully and conspicuously disclose in simple and readily understood language the terms and conditions of such warranty."

The second major part of the Act pertains to the *labeling* requirement. The Act divides written warranties into two categories, "limited" and "full," one of which, for any product costing more than ten dollars must be designated on the written warranty itself. The purpose of this provision is to alert the consumer to the legal rights under a certain warranty for purposes of initial comparison. In order to designate the warranty as *full*, the warrantor must agree to repair the product without charge to conform with the warranty, no limitation may be placed on the duration of any implied warranty, the consumer must be given the option of a refund or replacement if repair is unsuccessful, and consequential damages may be excluded only if conspicuously noted.

Most significantly, the Act provides that a *written* warranty, whether full or limited, can **not** *disclaim any implied* warranty. This provision strikes at the heart of the problem, for as revealed in an earlier Presidential task force report, most written warranties gave limited protection but in return took away the more valuable implied warranties. Hence, consumers were lulled into believing that the warranties they received and the warranty registration cards they promptly returned to the manufacturer were to their benefit. The Act, on the other hand, provides that a "full" warranty must not disclaim, modify, or limit any implied warranty, while a "limited" warranty cannot disclaim or modify any implied warranty but can limit its duration to that of the written warranty, provided that such limitation is reasonable, conscionable, and conspicuously displayed.

For example, A sells consumer goods to B for $150 and provides a written warranty regarding the quality of the goods. A must designate the warranty as full or limited, depending upon the characteristics of the warranty, and cannot disclaim or modify any implied warranty. On the other hand, if A had not provided B with a written warranty, then the Magnuson-Moss Act would not apply, and A could disclaim any and all implied warranties.

Finally, the Act also contains a part dealing with *remedies* and the establishment, at the option of the warrantor, of an informal settlement procedure. However, the Act does not provide any new or expanded remedies. See Figure 42-1.

Consumer Right of Rescission

In most cases once a consumer has signed a contract, he is legally obligated. In many States, however, a consumer has by statute a brief period of time—generally two or three days—during which he may rescind an otherwise binding credit obligation if the solicitation of the sale occurred in his home. Moreover, the Federal Trade Commission has also promulgated a Trade Regulation applicable to door-to-door sales of goods and services for twenty-five dollars or more, whether the sale is for cash or on credit. The regulation permits a consumer to rescind the contract within *three days* of signing.

A consumer also has a right of rescission under the **Federal Consumer Credit Protection Act,** which allows a consumer three days during which he may withdraw from any credit obligation secured by a mortgage on his home, unless the extension of credit was made to acquire the dwelling. After the consumer rescinds, the creditor has twenty days to return any money or property he has received from the consumer.

The **Interstate Land Sales Full Disclosure Act** applies to sales or leases of 100 or more lots of unimproved land as part of a common promotional plan in interstate commerce. The Act requires the filing of a detailed "statement of record" containing specified information about the subdivision and the developer with the Department of Housing and Urban Development before offering the lots for sale or lease. The developer must provide a property report, which is a condensed version of the statement of record, to each prospective purchaser or lessee. The Act provides that any contract or agreement for sale or lease may be revoked at the option of the purchaser or lessee within seven days of signing the contract, and the contract must clearly provide this right. If the property report has not been given to the purchaser or lessee in advance of signing the contract, the

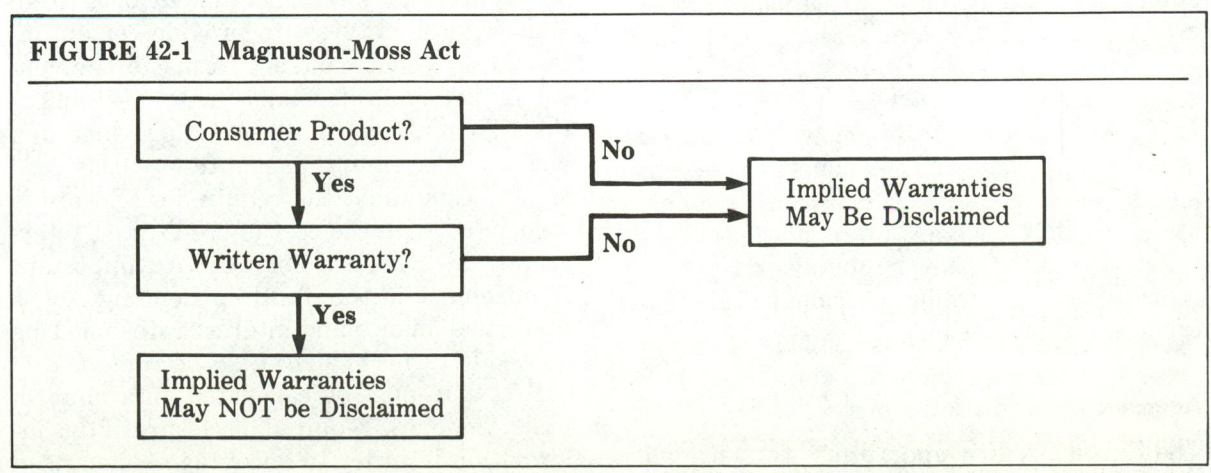

FIGURE 42-1   Magnuson-Moss Act

contract may be revoked within two years from the date of signing.

CONSUMER CREDIT OBLIGATIONS

In the absence of special regulation, consumer credit transactions are governed by laws regulating commercial transactions generally. A consumer credit transaction is customarily defined as any transaction the subject matter of which is to be used by one of the parties for personal, household, or family purposes. The following are illustrative: A borrows $600 from a bank to pay a dentist bill or to take a vacation; B buys a refrigerator for her home from a department store and agrees to pay the purchase price in twelve equal monthly installments; C has a credit card with an oil company which he uses to purchase gasoline and tires for his family car.

Two significant developments have accelerated the legislative trend toward regulating consumer sales credit: (1) the enactment in 1968 of the **Federal Consumer Credit Protection Act** (FCCPA), and (2) the promulgation of the **Uniform Consumer Credit Code** (UCCC) in the same year. The FCCPA deals with effective disclosure of interest and finance charges, credit extension charges, and garnishment proceedings. The UCCC integrates into one document the regulation of all consumer credit transactions and gives substantially similar regulatory treatment to both credit sales and loan transactions.

Consumer credit protection has broadened considerably since the passage of the FCCPA and includes the following areas: (1) access by creditors and consumers to the consumer credit market, (2) disclosure of information to the consumer, (3) regulation of contract terms, (4) fair reportage of credit information concerning consumers, and (5) creditors' remedies.

Access to the Market

The **Equal Credit Opportunity Act,** enacted by Congress in 1974, prohibits all businesses that regularly extend credit from discriminating in extending credit on the basis of sex, marital status, race, color, religion, national origin, or age. The Act requires the creditor within thirty days after receipt of an application for credit to notify the applicant of action taken and to provide specific reasons for a denial of credit. The Act is administered and enforced by several Federal agencies with overall enforcement authority given to the Federal Trade Commission. Credit applicants who are aggrieved by a violation of the Act may recover actual and punitive damages, including attorney's fees.

Disclosure Requirements

Title One of the FCCPA, also known as the **Truth-in-Lending Act,** has superseded State disclosure requirements relating to credit terms for both consumer loans and credit sales. Federal disclosure standards must be complied with in every State except those specifically exempted by the Federal Reserve Board. Such an exemption is only made if the State disclosure requirements are substantially the same as the Federal requirements and enforcement is assured. The FCCPA does not eliminate the necessity for creditor compliance with State requirements not covered by, or more stringent than, the requirements of the FCCPA, so long as the State required disclosure is not inconsistent with the FCCPA.

A creditor is required, under both State and Federal statutes, to provide certain information about contract terms to the consumer before he formally incurs the obligation. This information must be provided in a written statement presented to the consumer. Generally, the required disclosure is associated with the cost of credit, i.e., interest or sales finance charges. An important requirement in the Truth-in-Lending Act is that sales finance and interest rates must be quoted in terms of an *annual percentage rate* (**APR**) and must be calculated on a uniform basis. Congress required disclosure of this information in order to encourage comparison of credit terms by consumers, increase competition among financial institutions, and facilitate economic stability. Enforcement and interpretation of the Truth-in-Lending Act was assigned to the Federal Reserve Board, which issued **Regulation Z** to carry out this responsibility.

In addition to the cost of the credit, under the Truth-in-Lending Act a creditor must inform the consumer who is opening a revolving or open-ended credit account as to when the finance charge is imposed and how it is computed, what other charges may be imposed, and whether a security interest is retained or acquired by the creditor. An **open-ended** credit account is one which permits the debtor to enter into a series of credit transactions which he may pay off in installments or in a lump sum. Examples of this type of credit include most department store credit cards, many gasoline credit cards, VISA, and MASTERCARD. With this type of credit the creditor is also required to provide a statement of account for each billing period.

As to non-revolving or closed end credit, the creditor must provide the consumer with information about the total amount financed; the cash price; the number, amount, and due date of installments; delinquency charges; and a description of the security, if any. **Closed end** credit is credit extended for a specified period of time during which periodic payments are generally made in an amount and at a time agreed upon in advance. Examples of this type of transaction include most automobile financing agreements, most real estate purchases, and numerous other major purchases. *See Chapman v. Miller.*

In 1975 the **Fair Credit Billing Act** went into effect to relieve some of the problems and abuses associated with billing errors. The Act establishes procedures for the consumer to follow in making complaints about specified errors in billing and requires the creditor to explain or correct such errors. Billing errors are defined to include: (1) extensions of credit that were never made or were not made in the amount indicated on the billing statement; (2) undelivered or unaccepted goods or services; (3) incorrect recordation of payments

or credits; and (4) accounting or computational errors. Until the creditor responds to the complaint, it may not (1) take any action to collect the disputed amount, (2) restrict the use of an open-ended credit account because the disputed amount is unpaid, or (3) report the disputed amount as delinquent.

In 1974 Congress enacted the **Real Estate Settlement Procedures Act** (RESPA) in order to provide consumers who purchase a home with greater and more timely information on the nature and costs of the settlement process and with protection from unnecessarily high settlement charges. The Act applies to all Federally related mortgage loans and requires advance disclosure to home buyers and sellers of all settlement costs including attorney's fees, credit reports, and title insurance. Nearly all first mortgage loans fall within the scope of the Act. RESPA prohibits kickbacks and referral fees and limits the amount home buyers are required to place in escrow accounts to insure payment of real estate taxes and insurance. The Act is administered and enforced by the Secretary of Housing and Urban Development.

Contract Terms

Consumer credit is marketed on a mass basis. Contract documents are frequently printed forms containing blank spaces to be filled in by the creditor. These blank spaces relate to matters usually negotiated at the time of the extension of credit. Standardization and uniformity of contract terms facilitate transfer of the rights of the creditor, in most situations a seller, to a third party which is usually a bank or finance company.

Practically all of the States impose statutory ceilings on the amount that may be charged for the extension of consumer credit. Statutes regulating rates also specify what other charges may be made. For example, charges for insurance, official fees, and taxes are usually not considered part of the finance charge. Charges that are incidental to the extension of credit are usually considered part of the finance charge, e.g., a service charge or commission for extending credit. Any charge that does not qualify as an authorized additional charge is treated as part of the finance charge and subject to the statutory rate ceiling. Other special permitted charges include delinquency and default charges, charges incurred in connection with storing and repairing repossessed goods for sale, reasonable attorney's fees for a lawyer who is not a salaried employee of the creditor and court costs.

Most statutes require a creditor to permit the debtor to pay her obligation in full at any time prior to the maturity date of the final installment. In case the interest charge over the period of the loan was computed in advance and added to the principal of the loan, upon making pre-payment in full the debtor is entitled to a refund of an amount representing the interest portion of the loan that is unearned by reason of the pre-payment.

Aside from provisions relating to cost, the balance of a credit contract deals with the terms of repayment and the remedies of the creditor if payments are delinquent. Usually, payments must be periodic and substantially equal in amount. Balloon payments (e.g., where the monthly installments are $50 and the final installment is $1,000) may be prohibited, or, if not prohibited, the creditor may be required to refinance the loan at the same rate and with installments in the same amount as the original loan without penalty to the borrower.

Situations have arisen in which consumer purchase transactions have been financed in such manner that the purchaser is legally obligated to make full payment of the price to a third party, although the dealer from whom she bought the goods had committed fraud or the goods were defective. This occurred when the purchaser executed and deliverd to the seller her negotiable promissory note which the seller negotiated to a holder in due course, a third party who purchased the note for value, in good faith, and without notice that it was overdue or of any defenses or claims to it. The buyer's defense that the goods were defective or that the seller had committed fraud,

although valid against the seller, were not valid against a holder in due course of the note. The Federal Trade Commission, in order to correct this situation by preserving and making available claims and defenses of consumer buyers and borrowers against holders in due course, adopted a rule which limits the rights of a holder in due course of an instrument which evidences a debt arising out of a *consumer credit contract*. The rule applies to sellers and lessors of goods and defines consumer credit contracts in terms which include negotiable instruments. A discussion of the rule is in Chapter 26.

A similar rule applies to credit card issuers under the **Fair Credit Billing Act.** The Act preserves consumers' defenses against the issuer provided the consumer has made a good faith attempt to resolve the dispute with the seller, but only if (1) the seller is controlled by the issuer or under common control with the issuer; or (2) the card issuer included the seller's promotional literature in the monthly billing statement sent to the card holder; or (3) the sale involves more than fifty dollars and the consumer's billing address is in the same State as or within 100 miles of the seller's place of business.

Moreover, the FCCPA limits the card holder's liability for unauthorized use of a credit card to fifty dollars. The card issuer may collect up to that amount for unauthorized use only if (1) the card has been accepted; (2) the issuer has furnished adequate notice of potential liability to the card holder; (3) the issuer has provided the card holder with a statement of the means by which the card issuer may be notified of the loss or theft of the credit card; (4) the unauthorized use occurs before the card holder has notified the card issuer of the loss or theft; and (5) the card issuer has provided a method by which the user can be identified as the person authorized to use the card.

Fair Reportage

Since the extension of credit to consumers is usually made only after an investigation into the consumer's credit worthiness, it is essential that the information upon which such decisions are made is accurate and current. To this end, Congress enacted the **Fair Credit Reporting Act** in 1970, which applies to consumer reports used for purposes of securing employment, insurance, and credit. The Act prohibits the inclusion in consumer reports of inaccurate or obsolete information specifically listed in the statute. The Act requires that a consumer be notified in writing in advance that an investigative report may be made. The consumer may request information regarding the nature and substance of all information in the consumer reporting agency's files, the source of the information, and the names of all recipients of the consumer reports furnished for employment purposes within the preceding two years and for other purposes within the preceding six months.

If the consumer notifies the reporting agency of disagreement with the accuracy and completeness of information in the file, the agency must then re-investigate the matter within a reasonable period of time unless the complaint is frivolous or irrelevant. If re-investigation proves that the information is inaccurate, it must be promptly deleted. If after re-investigation the dispute remains unresolved, the consumer may submit a brief statement setting forth the nature of the dispute which must be incorporated into the report.

Creditors' Remedies

Of primary concern to creditors, once credit is granted, are their rights if the debtor defaults or is tardy in payment. When the credit charge is precomputed, the creditor may impose a delinquency charge for late payments, subject to statutory limits for such charges. If instead of being delinquent, the consumer defaults, the creditor may declare the entire balance of the debt immediately due and payable and sue on the debt. What other courses of action are open to him depend upon his security. Various security provisions included in consumer credit contracts are: a cosigner, an assignment of wages, a security interest in the goods sold, a security interest in other real or personal property of the debtor, and a confession of judgment clause.

However, wage assignments are prohibited by some States. In most States and under the FCCPA, a limitation is imposed on the amount that may be deducted from an individual's wages during any pay period. In addition, the FCCPA prohibits an employer from discharging an employee solely because of a creditor's exercise of an assignment of wages in connection with any one debt.

Even where assignments of wages are prohibited, the creditor may still reach the wages of the consumer through garnishment. However, garnishment is only available in a court proceeding to enforce the collection of a judgment. The FCCPA and State statutes contain exemption provisions which limit the amount of wages subject to garnishment.

In the case of credit sales, the seller may retain a security interest in the goods sold. Many States impose restrictions on other security the creditor may obtain. Where the debt is secured by property as collateral, the creditor, upon default by the debtor, may take possession of the property and, subject to the provisions of the U.C.C., either retain it in full satisfaction of the debt or sell it and, if the proceeds are less than the outstanding debt, sue the debtor for the balance and obtain a deficiency judgment. The U.C.C. provides that where the buyer of goods has paid 60 percent of the purchase price of the goods or 60 percent of a loan secured by consumer goods, the secured creditor may not retain the property in full satisfaction but must sell the goods and pay to the buyer that part of the sale proceeds in excess of the balance due. Secured transactions are discussed in Chapter 37.

In 1977 Congress enacted the **Fair Debt Collection Practices Act** in order to eliminate abusive, deceptive, and unfair practices employed in collecting consumer debts by debt collection agencies. The Act does not apply to the creditors themselves. The Act provides that any debt collector who communicates with a person other than the consumer for the purpose of acquiring information about the location of the consumer may not state that the consumer owes any debt. Moreover, the Act prohibits a number of abusive collection practices including: (1) communication with the consumer at unusual or inconvenient hours; (2) communication with the consumer if she is represented by an attorney; (3) conduct that is harrassing, oppressive, or abusive such as threats of violence or obscene language; (4) false, deceptive, or misleading representation or means; and (5) any unfair or unconscionable means to collect any debt. The Act is enforced by the Federal Trade Commission, and consumers may recover damages from the collection agency for violations of the Act.

CONSUMER HEALTH AND SAFETY

In 1972 Congress enacted the **Consumer Product Safety Act,** the purposes of which are:

1. to protect the public against unreasonable risks of injury associated with consumer products;

2. to assist consumers in evaluating the comparative safety of consumer products;
3. to develop uniform safety standards for consumer products and to minimize conflicting State and local regulations; and
4. to promote research and investigation into the causes and prevention of product-related deaths, illnesses, and injuries.

The Act creates an independent regulatory Federal agency, the Consumer Product Safety Commission, consisting of five commissioners, to carry out the Act's mandate.

There are also a number of Federal statutes that impose labeling and packaging requirements designed to provide the consumer with accurate information and adequate warnings about specific products. Such statutes include the Fair Packaging and Labeling Act; the Food, Drugs, and Cosmetic Act; the Fur Products Labeling Act; the Wholesome Meat Act; the Flammable Fabrics Act; the Cigarette Labeling and Advertising Act; the Wool Products Labeling Act; the Wholesome Poultry Products Act; the Special Packaging of Household Substances for the Protection of Children Act; and the Refrigerator Safety Act.

CASES

FTC: Corrective Advertising

WARNER-LAMBERT CO. v. FEDERAL TRADE COMMISSION

United States Court of Appeals, District of Columbia Circuit, 1977.
562 F.2d 749.

WRIGHT, J.

The Warner-Lambert Company petitions for review of an order of the Federal Trade Commission requiring it to cease and desist from advertising that its product, Listerine Antiseptic mouthwash, prevents, cures,

or alleviates the common cold. The FTC order further requires Warner-Lambert to disclose in future Listerine advertisements that: "Contrary to prior advertising, Listerine will not help prevent colds or sore throats or lessen their severity." We affirm but modify the order to delete from the required disclosure the phrase "Contrary to prior advertising."

Background
The order under review represents the culmination of a proceeding begun in 1972, when the FTC issued a complaint charging peti-

tioner with violation of Section 5(a)(1) of the Federal Trade Commission Act by misrepresenting the efficacy of Listerine against the common cold.

Listerine has been on the market since 1879. Its formula has never changed. Ever since its introduction it has been represented as being beneficial in certain respects for colds, cold symptoms, and sore throats. Direct advertising to the consumer, including the cold claims as well as others, began in 1921.

* * *

The Commission's Power

Petitioner [Warner-Lambert] contends that even if its advertising claims in the past were false, the portion of the Commission's order requiring "corrective advertising" exceeds the Commission's statutory power. The argument is based upon a literal reading of Section 5 of the Federal Trade Commission Act, which authorizes the Commission to issue "cease and desist" orders against violators and does not expressly mention any other remedies. The Commission's position, on the other hand, is that the affirmative disclosure that Listerine will not prevent colds or lessen their severity is absolutely necessary to give effect to the prospective cease and desist order; a hundred years of false cold claims have built up a large reservoir of erroneous consumer belief which would persist, unless corrected, long after petitioner ceased making the claims.

The need for the corrective advertising remedy and its appropriateness in this case are important issues which we will explore. But the threshold question is whether the Commission has the authority to issue such an order. We hold that it does.

Petitioner's narrow reading of Section 5 was at one time shared by the Supreme Court. In *FTC v. Eastman Kodak Co.* the Court held that the Commission's athority did not exceed that expressly conferred by statute. The Commission has not, the Court said, "been delegated the authority of a court of equity." But the modern view is very different.

* * *

"[W]here the problem lies within the purview of the [Commission], * * * Congress must have intended to give it authority that was ample to deal with the evil at hand. * * * Authority to mold administrative decrees is indeed like the authority of courts to frame injunctive decrees * * *."

* * *

Thus it is clear that the Commission has the power to shape remedies which go beyond the simple cease and desist order. Our next inquiry must be whether a corrective advertising order is for any reason outside the range of permissible remedies. Petitioner * * * argue(s) that it is because (1) legislative history precludes it, (2) it impinges on the First Amendment, and (3) it has never been approved by any court.

Legislative History. Petitioner relies on the legislative history of the 1914 Federal Trade Commission Act and the Wheeler-Lea amendments to it in 1938 for the proposition that corrective advertising was not contemplated. In 1914 and in 1938 Congress chose not to authorize such remedies as criminal penalties, treble damages, or civil penalties, but that fact does not dispose of the question of corrective advertising.

Petitioner's reliance on the legislative history of the 1975 amendments to the Act is also misplaced. The amendments added a new Section 19 to the Act authorizing the Commission to bring suits in federal District Courts to redress injury to consumers resulting from a deceptive practice. The section authorizes the court to grant such relief as it "finds necessary to redress injury to consumers or other persons, partnerships, and corporations resulting from the rule violation or the unfair or deceptive act or practice," including, but not limited to, rescission or reformation of contracts, the refund of money or return of property, the payment of damages, and public notification respecting the rule violation or the unfair or deceptive act or practice * * *.

* * *

The First Amendment. Petitioner * * * further contends that corrective advertising is not a permissible remedy because it trenches on the First Amendment. Petitioner is correct that this triggers a special responsibility on the Commission to order corrective advertising only if the restriction inherent in its order is no greater than necessary to serve the interest involved. But this goes to the appropriateness of the order in this case.

* * *

The Supreme Court [has] expressly noted that the First Amendment presents "no obstacle" to government regulation of false or misleading advertising. The First Amendment, the Court said, as we construe it today, does not prohibit the State from insuring that the stream of commercial information flow[s] cleanly as well as freely.

* * *

Precedents. According to petitioner, "The first reference to corrective advertising in Commission decisions occurred in 1970, nearly fifty years and untold number of false advertising cases after passage of the Act." In petitioner's view, the late emergence of this "newly discovered" remedy is itself evidence that it is beyond the Commission's authority. This argument fails on two counts. First the fact that an agency has not asserted a power over a period of years is not proof that the agency lacks such power. Second, and more importantly, we are not convinced that the corrective advertising remedy is really such an innovation. The label may be newly coined, but the concept is well established. It is simply that under certain circumstances an advertiser may be required to make affirmative disclosure of unfavorable facts.

* * *

The Remedy

Having established that the Commission does have the power to order corrective advertising in appropriate cases, it remains to consider whether use of the remedy against Listerine is warranted and equitable. We have

concluded that the order should be modified to delete the phrase "Contrary to prior advertising." With that modification we approve the order.

Our role in reviewing the remedy is limited. The Supreme Court has set forth the standard:

The Commission is the expert body to determine what remedy is necessary to eliminate the unfair or deceptive trade practices which have been disclosed. It has wide latitude for judgment and the courts will no interfere except where the remedy selected has no reasonable relation to the unlawful practices found to exist.

The Commission has adopted the following standard for the imposition of corrective advertising:

[I]f a deceptive advertisement has played a substantial role in creating or reinforcing in the public's mind a false and material belief which lives on after the false advertising ceases, there is clear and continuing injury to competition and to the consuming public as consumers continue to make purchasing decisions based on the false belief. Since this injury cannot be averted by merely requiring respondent to cease disseminating the advertisement, we may appropriately order respondent to take affirmative action designed to terminate the otherwise continuing ill effects of the advertisement.

We think this standard is entirely reasonable.

* * *

Accordingly, the order, as modified, is Affirmed.

FTC: Multiple Product Orders

SEARS, ROEBUCK AND CO. v. F.T.C.

United States Court of Appeals, Ninth Circuit, 1982.
676 F.2d 385.

REINHARDT, J.

Petitioner Sears, Roebuck and Co. is the largest retailer of general merchandise in the United States. As such, it is also one of the country's largest advertisers. This case presents a number of questions relating to the validity of a multi-product order issued by the Federal Trade Commission (the Commission) as the result of Sears' use of certain unfair and deceptive advertising practices to sell one of the products in the product group. We enforce the order.

I

THE ADVERTISEMENTS AND THE COMMISSION PROCEEDINGS

The material facts are undisputed. In the early 1970's Sears formulated a plan to increase sales of its top of the line "Lady Kenmore" brand dishwasher. The plan did not call for reengineering of the dishwasher or any mechanical improvement. Rather, it contemplated changing the image of the Lady Kenmore, or, in the jargon, it sought a "repositioning" of the machine. The objective was to:

transform the consumer image [of the Lady Kenmore] from a "price" brand to a superior product at a reasonable price. Eventually, the brand should move from market leadership to market dominance as the market share increases.

To achieve this objective, the company needed a sales strategy. Like any good merchant, Sears knew its market. It knew that a machine that would actually perform the entire job of washing dishes and would eliminate the need for people to pre-rinse and pre-scrape their dishes would attract new customers and command a premium price. It also knew that a machine's ability to clean dishes on the upper rack as thoroughly as those on the bottom rack would be an effective inducement to the consumer.

Acting on this knowledge, Sears prepared advertisements claiming that the Lady Kenmore "completely eliminated" the need for pre-scraping and pre-rinsing, and characterized the machine as the "Freedom Maker." Advertisements stated:

SEARS LADY KENMORE. THE DO-IT-YOURSELF DISHWASHER. No scraping. No pre-rinsing. Lady Kenmore has 6 powerful hot water jets for the bottom rack, surging hot water with enough force to scrub every dish, pot and pan *really* clean. Even baked-on food comes off. And the dishes on top get as clean as those on the bottom.

* * * * * *

. . . With a Kenmore you'll never have to scrape or rinse again. Even dishes crusty with leftover good. Kenmore's 14 powerful hot water jets scour every dish clean . . . with no scraping or rinsing.

* * * * * *

It's great! You'll like the way it makes pre-rinsing and soaking of heavily soiled dishes, pots and pans a thing of the past.

* * * * * *

Gets even the messiest baking dishes and roasting pans spotlessly clean . . . without pre-rinsing!

* * * * * *

Wouldn't the woman in your life love a Kenmore Dishwasher for Mother's Day. A Kenmore dishwasher from Sears means no more dishpan hands, she'll never have to touch dishwater again! Egg, lipstick, peanut butter, jelly, even spaghetti sauce come right off with no pre-rinsing.

Rendered in various forms, these themes appeared in print and electronic advertisements throughout the country over a four year period at a cost to Sears of roughly $8 million. During the first three years of the promotion (1971–1973), Lady Kenmore unit sales rose 300%, from 35,029 units in 1971 to 105,570 units in 1973. These figures represent the Lady Kenmore's rise from only 10% of total Sears dishwasher sales in 1971 to 23% of total Sears' dishwasher sales in 1973. The value of the company's total dishwasher sales rose from $73,470,000 in 1971 to $94,500,000 in 1973.

Unfortunately, the "no scraping, no pre-rinsing" claim was not true. Sears had no reasonable basis for asserting the claim, and the instructions in the Owner's Manual which customers received *after* they purchased the dishwasher contradicted the claim. In addition, a 1973 survey conducted for Sears showed that more than half of recent Lady Kenmore purchasers either disagreed, or would not "completely agree" with the proposition that the Lady Kenmore "does not require pre-rinsing".

The Commission began an investigation of the advertisements in July of 1975. A complaint issued on November 20, 1977, charging petitioner and its advertising agency, J. Walter Thompson Co., with disseminating deceptive and unfair advertisements in violation of section 5 of the Federal Trade Commission Act (The Act) [citation].

After extensive administrative proceedings, the administrative law judge (ALJ) made elaborate findings of fact and held Sears liable on all charges in the complaint. He entered a proposed order. The company appealed.

Before the Commission, Sears challenged * * * several aspects of the remedial order. It did not dispute the ALJ's findings (1) that the no pre-rinsing or scraping claim was false and unsubstantiated; (2) that the "upper rack gets as clean as those on the bottom rack" claim was unsubstantiated; (3) that demonstrations purporting to prove these cleaning claims were false; (4) that its own tests showed a need for pre-scraping and rinsing and that its surveys showed that consumers found it necesssary to pre-scrape and rinse; and (5) that the Owner's Manual provided with each dishwasher contradicted the advertisements. Nor did Sears contest the order's provisions covering these findings. It did quarrel with * * * the order's coverage of products other than dishwashers, including the proscription against false and unsubstantiated performance claims * * * .

* * *

The final order requires Sears to cease and desist from making the "no pre-rinsing or scraping" and "top rack as clean as the bottom rack" claims. It also prevents Sears from (1) making any "performance claims" for "major home appliances" without first possessing a reasonable basis consisting of "[c]ompetent and reliable tests" or other evidence that substantiates such claims; (2) misrepresenting any test, survey or demonstration regarding "major home appliances"; and (3) making any advertising statements not

consistent with statements in post-purchase materials supplied to purchasers of "major home appliances."

* * *

II
STATUTORY POWER AND THE RATIONALITY OF THE REMEDY

1. *Statutory Power.* Sears argues first that the language and legislative history of section 5(b) of the Act, [citation], require the Commission to direct its cease and desist orders only to those specific violations alleged in the complaint since only those violations have been litigated in the manner contemplated by the statute. From this doctrine, Sears seems to reason that since the complaint here describes dishwasher advertising, the Commission lacks the power to issue an order covering any product except dishwashers. Sears' conclusion is that to the extent that the order covers products other than dishwashers, it is invalid as a matter of law. We disagree.

It is too late to argue that when the Commission establishes a violation only as to one product, its power under the Act is limited to the issuance of a single product order. As the Second Circuit said in [citation] "[C]ourts have often upheld FTC orders encompassing all products or all products in a broad category, based on violations involving only a single product or group of products * * * ." (Citations omitted). The Supreme Court rendered this doctrine metaphorically in [citation]. There, the Court reminded the companies that objected to the breadth of the Commission's order that "those caught violating the Act must expect some *fencing in.*" [Citation] (emphasis added). Allowance of this "fencing in" authority is based in part on our deference to the FTC's accumulated expertise in striking the proper relationship between violations found and effective orders, [citation], and in part on necessity since "there is no limit to human inventiveness in this field." [Citation.]

Accordingly, we reject Sears' argument here.

2. *Rationality of the Remedy.* Sears' next argument can be separated into * * * elements. First, the company says there is no reasonable relationship between the multi-product portion of the order and the violation found; second, that a multi-product order covering "performance claims" is unreasonably broad. . . .

* * *

The general principles governing objections to FTC orders are well known.

The Commission is the expert body to determine what remedy is necessary to eliminate the unfair or deceptive trade practices which have been disclosed. It has wide latitude for judgment and the courts will not interfere except where the remedy selected has no reasonable relation to the unlawful practices found to exist.

[Citation.]

In addition,

Congress has placed the primary responsibility for fashioning orders on the Commission. *Federal Trade Comm'n v. National Lead Co.*, 352 U.S. 419, 429. For these reasons the courts should not "lightly modify" the Commission's orders. *Federal Trade Comm'n v. Cement Institute*, 333 U.S. 683, 726. However, this Court has also warned that an order's prohibitions "should be clear and precise in order that they may be understood by those against whom they are directed," *Federal Trade Comm'n v. Cement Institute*, *supra*, at 726 * * *.

[Citation.]

A judgment regarding "reasonable relation" in multi-product order cases "depends upon the specific circumstances of the case." [Citation.] "[T]he ultimate question is the likelihood of the petitioner committing the sort of unfair practices [the order] prohibit[s]," [citation]. We answer that question by first examining the specific circumstances present in a particular case. Then, giving due deference to the Commission's expertise and judgment, we determine whether there is a "reasonable relation" between those circumstances and the concern regarding future violations manifested by the Commission's order.

Where a fair assessment of an advertiser's conduct shows a ready willingness to flout the law, sufficient cause for concern regarding further, additional violations exists. Two factors or elements frequently influence our decision—the deliberateness and seriousness of the present violation, and the violator's past record with respect to unfair advertising practices. [Citation.] Other circumstances may be weighed, including the adaptability or transferability of the unfair practice to other products. [Citation.] The weight given a particular factor or element will vary. The more egregious the facts with respect to a particular element, the less important it is that another negative factor be present. In the final analysis, we look to the circumstances as a whole and not to the presence or absence of any single factor. [Citations.]

* * *

We now consider the Commission's order in light of the specific circumstances of this case. This advertising campaign cost $8 million, ran for four years, and appeared in magazines, newspapers and on television throughout the country. The Commission found, and Sears does not dispute, that the campaign's central claim was false. Sears had no reasonable basis for making the claim, and the tests which Sears purportedly relied on showed, if anything, that the claim was false. Moreover, the Owner's Manual, which Sears furnished its customers after they purchased the Lady Kenmore, implicitly acknowledged the falsity of the claim and establishes that Sears knew it was false at all times. Under these circumstances, Sears' advertising campaign demonstrates "blatant and utter disregard" for the law. [Citation.] The Commission also considered petitioner's compliance record and concluded that it was "a wash." [Citation.] We see no reason to find otherwise.

Sears' advertisements were no accident or "isolated instance." [Citation] Rather, they were part of an advertising strategy, with attendant slogans, adopted without regard to the actual performance of the advertised machines. As the Commission pointed out, the covered machines are major ticket items generally purchased infrequently by any particular person. For that reason, their profitability does not depend on repeat purchases as is the case with frequently purchased, low-cost items. A selling strategy based on this purchasing fact, *e.g.*, the making of false and unsubstantiated performance claims as to a major ticket item, would be effective for a considerable period of time, with great benefit to the merchant but at great cost to consumers. This selling strategy could readily be transferred to the marketing of other machines in the home appliance category.

* * *

To prevent the false and unsubstantiated performance claims strategy from being used in connection with another major home appliance or from becoming Sears' general practice with respect to such appliances, the Commission deemed a broad order necessary. A judgment of this nature depends on detailed knowledge of the major home appliances business and its related advertising techniques. "[D]eceptive advertising cases necessarily require 'inference and pragmatic judgment.'" [Citations.] This sort of knowledge of the commercial world and the ability to make the type of judgment required lie in the realm of the Commission's greatest expertise.

* * *

In light of the flagrant and egregious nature of the violation found and the other circumstances present here, and giving the Commission's conclusions the required "great weight," [citations], we find no basis for substituting our judgment for the Commission's regarding the necessity for this multi-product order. We hold that the multi-product order is reasonably related to the petitioner's conduct, that a multi-product order is appropriate, and that the inclusion of the "performance claims" provision in that order is

supported by the record before us and does not render the order overbroad.

* * *

Federal Truth in Lending Act

CHAPMAN v. MILLER
Court of Civil Appeals of Texas, 1978.
575 S.W.2d 581.

KEITH, J.

Defendant below appeals from an adverse judgment rendered in a bench trial of a suit brought under * * * the Federal Truth in Lending Act and Regulation Z promulgated thereunder.

Plaintiff entered into a retail installment contract with Don Chapman Motor Sales for the purchase of a used automobile. The contract provided for a down payment of $200, six weekly payments of $25, and eighteen monthly payments of $70.47. Plaintiff made the down payment and the six weekly payments without too much difficulty. The next five monthly installments were accepted even though they were late; but, when the March 1975 payment became overdue, defendant repossessed the car notifying plaintiff that the entire balance was then due and payable. When plaintiff did not pay the balance due, defendant sold the car and determined that plaintiff was entitled to a refund of $19.69. Before the refund was made, plaintiff brought this suit alleging several violations of the cited statute and regulation. The trial court agreed and awarded damages, plus attorney's fees, and the appeal is predicated upon nineteen points of error.

Violation of Federal Regulation. * * * defendant complains that the trial court erred * * * by holding that his contract violated Regulation Z because the description of the security interest is not on the same side of the paper as the buyer's signature.

The cited section requires that all disclosures which must be made thereunder be made together on:

(1) The note or other instrument evidencing the obligation on the same side of the page and above or adjacent to the place for the customer's signature; or (2) One side of a separate statement which identifies the transaction.

Defendant chose to make his disclosures on the retail credit contract. However, he failed to put all the required disclosures on one side of the contract above plaintiff's signature, *i.e.*, the description of his retained security interest is located on the reverse side of the contract. Relying upon the language found in [citation], we are of the opinion that the trial court correctly found a violation of Regulation Z.

Defendant claims that he did not have to make all required disclosures on the front side because of the Interpretive Ruling of the Federal Reserve Board, [citation], which allows the required disclosures to be made on both sides of a combination contract and security agreement. This interpretation, however, has a caveat:

Provided, That the amount of the finance charge and the annual percentage rate shall appear on the face of the document, and, if the reverse side is used, the printing on both sides of the document shall be equally clear and conspicuous, both sides shall contain the statement, "NOTICE: See other side for important information," *and the place for the customer's signature shall be provided following the full content of the document.*

The space provided for the plaintiff's signature is on the front page of the contract only and does not follow "the full content of the document." Therefore, defendant has violated [this] Section. [Citation.]

Defendant rationalizes that his notices at the top and bottom of the front side allow him to incorporate by reference all disclosures and conditions from the reverse side into the front side above the signature. The notice at the top of the page provides:

BUYER HAS ELECTED TO PURCHASE FROM SELLER SUBJECT TO THE TERMS AND CONDITIONS AS SET FORTH BELOW AND UPON THE REVERSE SIDE HEREOF, THE FOLLOWING DESCRIBED MOTOR VEHICLE, WHICH BUYER HAS THOROUGHLY INSPECTED AND WHICH MEETS WITH BUYER'S APPROVAL IN ALL RESPECTS:

The notice at the bottom of the page provides: "NOTICE: SEE REVERSE SIDE FOR IMPORTANT INFORMATION, ALL TERMS OF WHICH ARE HEREBY INCORPORATED BY REFERENCE." However, this notice was below plaintiff's signature.

The Truth in Lending Act was enacted and Regulation Z was issued "to assure a meaningful disclosure of credit terms so that the consumer will be able to compare more readily the various credit terms available to him and avoid the uninformed use of credit * * *." [Citations.] Their provisions are detailed and explicit.

As noted in [citation]:

Moreover, liability flows from even minute deviations from the requirements of the statute and of Regulation Z. The statute aims to assure a meaningful disclosure of credit terms so that consumers may shop comparatively for credit * * *. [Citations.] Therefore, the defendant may not escape liability by means of incorporation by reference. The line provided for plaintiff's signature should have been at the end of the contract; her signature so located would show that she knew to read the entire contract—front and back—for all important provisions before signing it. The fact that she did not read any of the contract is immaterial. * * *

Finance Charge and Statutory Penalty. * * * both parties contend that the trial court erred . . . by holding that the finance charge in this transaction was $326.99. Defendant claims the finance charge was $199.99, while plaintiff claims it was $423.46. We disagree with both parties.

[Regulation Z] gives instructions on how to determine a finance charge. Applying these rules to the contract before us, we hold that the finance charge is the sum of the time price differential and the official fees, or $249.04. We are not required to include the premiums for property insurance, credit life insurance, or health and accident insurance in the finance charge * * *.

The applicable statutory penalty . . . includes twice the amount of the finance charge, plus court costs and reasonable attorney's fees. [Citations.] In the present case, the proper statutory penalty would have been twice of $249.04 or $498.08, plus court costs and reasonable attorney's fees.

* * *

The judgment of the trial court is reformed so that the plaintiff will recover of and from the defendant the sum of $498.08 for the violation of Regulation Z instead of the excessive amount of $652.98 mistakenly awarded by the trial court; and, as reformed, the judgment is Affirmed.

PROBLEMS

1. The Federal Trade Commission brings a deceptive trade practice action against Beneficial Finance Company based on Beneficial's use of its "instant tax refund" slogan. The FTC argues that Beneficial's advertising a tax refund loan or instant tax refund is deceptive in that the loan is not in any way connected with a tax refund but is merely Beneficial's everyday loan based on the applicant's creditworthiness. Decision?

2. B borrows $1000 from L for one year. B agreed to pay L $200 in interest on the loan and to repay the loan in twelve monthly installments of $100. The contract which L provides and B signs specifies that the annual percentage rate is 20 percent. B now contends that the contract violates the FCCPA. Decision?

3. A consumer entered into an agreement with Rent-It Corporation for the rental of a television set at a charge of seventeen dollars per week. The agreement also provided that if the renter chooses to rent the set for seventy-eight consecutive weeks, title would be transferred. The consumer now contends that the agreement was really a sales agreement and not a lease and, therefore, was a credit sale subject to the Truth-in-Lending Act. Decision?

4. Central Adjustment Bureau allegedly threatened Consumer with a lawsuit, service at his office, and attachment and sale of his property in order to collect a debt when it did not intend to do so and when it did not have the authority to commence litigation. On some notices sent to Consumer, Central failed to disclose that it was attempting to collect a debt. In addition, Central, it is charged, sent notices demanding payment that purported to be from attorneys but were written, signed, and sent by Central. Decision?

5. The Giant Development Company undertakes a massive real estate venture to sell 9,000 one-acre unimproved lots in Utah. The company advertises the project nationally. A, a resident of New York, learns of the opportunity and requests information about the project. The company provides A with a small advertising brochure that is devoid of information about the developer and the land. The brochure consists of vague descriptions of the joys of home ownership and nothing else. A purchases a lot. Two weeks after entering into the agreement, A wishes to rescind the contract. Will A prevail?

6. Jane Jones, a married woman, applies for a credit card from Exxon but is refused credit. Jane is bewildered as to why she was turned down. What are her legal rights in this situation?

7. On a beautiful Saturday in October, A decides to take the twenty-mile ride from her home in New Jersey into New York City in order to do some shopping. A finds that B Retail Sales, Inc., has a terrific sale on television sets and decides to surprise her husband with a new color T.V. She purchases the set from B on her American Express credit card for $450. When the set is delivered, A discovers that it does not work. B refuses to repair or replace it or to refund the money. A, therefore, refuses to pay American Express for the television. American Express brings this suit against A. Decision?

8. F finds A's wallet which contains numerous credit cards and A's identification. By using A's identification and Visa Card, F goes on a shopping spree and runs up $5,000 in charges. A does not discover that he has lost his wallet until the following day when he promptly notifies his Visa bank. How much can Visa collect from A?

9. B applies to N National Bank for a loan. Prior to granting the loan, N requests that C Credit Agency provide it with a credit report on B. C reports that three years previously B had embezzled money from his employer. Based on this report, N rejects B's loan application.

(a) B demands to know why, but N refuses to divulge the information arguing that it is privileged. Is B entitled to the information?

(b) Assume that B obtains the information and alleges that it is inaccurate. What recourse does B have?

10. A owed B $400, which was long overdue. B decided to hire the C Collection Agency to collect the debt. After writing several letters to A, C began a campaign of calling A every hour on the hour between the hours of 8 A.M. and 8 P.M., both at work and at home. A brings suit against C and B for harassment. Decision?

EMPLOYMENT LAW

THE common law governed the relationship between employer and employee in terms of tort and contract duties. These rules are a part of the law of agency and are discussed in Chapter 17—Relationship of Principal and Agent. This common law has been supplemented—and in some instances replaced—by statutory enactments, principally at the Federal level. In fact, the balance and working relationship between employers and employees are now greatly affected by government regulation. First, the general framework in which management and labor negotiate and bargain over the terms of employment is regulated by Federal statutes designed to promote both labor-management harmony and the welfare of society at large. Second, Federal law has been enacted to prohibit discrimination in employment based upon race, sex, religion, age, handicap, or national origin. Finally, Congress, in response to the changing nature of American industry and the tremendous number of industrial accidents, has intervened by mandating that employers provide their employees with a safe and healthy work environment. Moreover, all of the States have adopted Worker's Compensation Acts to provide compensation to employees injured during the course of employment.

This chapter will focus upon these three categories of government regulation of the employment relationship: (1) labor law, (2) employment discrimination law, and (3) employee safety. These topics will be discussed in that order.

LABOR LAW

Traditionally, labor law did not favor concerted activities by workers (such as strikes, picketing, and refusals to deal with certain employers) to obtain higher wages and better working conditions. These concerted activities, at various times, were found to constitute criminal conspiracy, tortious conduct, and violation of antitrust law. As early as 1806 one judge stated that "a combination of workers to raise wages may be considered in a twofold point of view: one is to benefit themselves, the other is to injure those who do not join their society. The rule of [criminal] law condemns both." *Commonwealth v. Pullis.* Subjecting union workers to criminal sanctions, however, became publicly unpopular so employers resorted to civil remedies in an attempt to halt unionization. The primary tool in this campaign was the injunction. Eventually public pressure in response to the adverse treatment accorded labor forced Congress to intervene.

Norris-La Guardia Act

The Norris-LaGuardia Act, which was enacted in 1932, withdrew from the Federal courts the power to issue injunctions in non-violent labor disputes. Section 1. The term **labor dispute** was broadly defined to include any controversy concerning terms or conditions of employment or union representation regardless of whether the parties stood in an employer-employee relationship. Section 13(c). More significantly, the Act declared it to be the policy of the United States that labor was to have full freedom to form labor unions without interference by the employer. Section 2.

National Labor Relations Act

The National Labor Relations Act (NLRA), or **Wagner Act,** was enacted in 1935 and marked an affirmative effort by the Federal government to support collective bargaining and unionization. The Act was upheld against constitutional challenge by the Supreme Court in *NLRB v. Jones & Laughlin Steel Corp.*:

[Employees right to bargain collectively] is a fundamental right. Employees have as clear a right

to organize and select their representatives for lawful purposes as the respondent [employer] has to organize its business and select its own officers and agents. Discrimination and coercion to prevent the free exercise of the right of employees to self-organization and representation is a proper subject for condemnation by competent legislative authority. Long ago we stated the reason for labor organizations. We said that they were organized out of the necessities of the situation; that a single employee was helpless in dealing with an employer; that he was dependent ordinarily on his daily wage for the maintenance of himself and family; that if the employer refused to pay him the wages that he thought fair, he was nevertheless unable to leave the employ and resist arbitrary and unfair treatment; that union was essential to give laborers opportunity to deal on an equality with their employer * * *. Fully recognizing the legality of collective action on the part of employees in order to safeguard their proper interests, we said that Congress was not required to ignore this right but could safeguard it. Congress could seek to make appropriate collective action of employees an instrument of peace rather than of strife. We said that such collective action would be a mockery if representation were made futile by interference with freedom of choice. Hence the prohibition by Congress of interference with the selection of representatives for the purpose of negotiation and conference between employers and employees, "instead of being an invasion of the constitutional right of either, was based on the recognition of the rights of both." *NLRB v. Jones & Laughlin Steel Corp.*, 301 U.S. 1 (1937).

The Act provides that "the right to self-organization, to form, join or assist labor organizations, to bargain collectively through representatives of their own choosing, and to engage in concerted activities for the purpose of collective bargaining or other mutual aid or protection" is a Federally protected right. Section 7. Moreover, the Act seeks to enforce this right by prohibiting certain conduct by employers as **unfair labor practices.** Under the Act, the following activities by employers are unfair labor practices: (1) to interfere with the employees' rights to unionize and bargain collectively; (2) to dominate the union; (3) to discriminate against union members; (4) to discriminate against an employee because he has filed charges or testified under the NLRA; and (5) to refuse to bargain in good faith with the duly established representatives of the employees. Section 8(a). *See National Labor Relations Board v. Berger Transfer & Storage.*

The United States Supreme Court has interpreted Section 8(a)(1) to include as an unfair employer practice conduct by the employer which improves employment conditions or benefits that are being criticized by the union as part of its organizing drive:

The danger inherent in well-timed increases in benefits is the suggestion of a fist inside the velvet glove. Employees are not likely to miss the inference that the source of benefits now conferred is also the source from which future benefits must flow and which may dry up if it is not obliged. *NLRB v. Exchange Parts Co.*, 375 U.S. 405 (1964).

The Act further established the **National Labor Relations Board** (NLRB) to monitor and administer these employee rights. The NLRB is empowered to order employers to remedy their unfair labor practices and to supervise elections by secret ballot so that employees can freely select a representative organization.

Labor-Management Relations Act

Following the passage of the National Labor Relations Act, the country underwent a tremendous increase in union membership and labor unrest. In response to this trend Congress in 1947 passed the Labor-Management Relations Act **(Taft-Hartley Act)** which prohibits certain **unfair union practices** as well as separates the NLRB's prosecutorial and adjudicative functions. More specifically, the Act amended the NLRA by forbidding secondary boycotts, jurisdictional strikes over work assignments, refusal to bargain in good faith, causing an employer to pay for work not performed (featherbedding), and strikes to force an employer to discharge or discriminate against a non-union employee. NLRA Section 8(b). *See In the Matter of Sailor's*

Union of the Pacific, AFL and Moore Dry Dock Company. In addition, the Act established "employer free speech" by declaring that no *employer* unfair labor practice could be based upon any statement of opinion or argument which contained no threat of reprisal. NLRA Section 8(c).

[W]e do note that an employer's free speech right to communicate his views to his employees is firmly established and cannot be infringed by a union or the Board. Thus, § 8(c) * * * merely implements the First Amendment by requiring that the expression of "any views, argument, or opinion" shall not be "evidence of an unfair labor practice," so long as such expression contains "no threat of reprisal or force or promise of benefit" in violation of § 8(a)(1). Section 8(a)(1), in turn, prohibits interference, restraint or coercion of employees in the exercise of their right to self-organization. *NLRB v. Gissel Packing Co.*, 395 U.S. 575 (1969).

Finally, the Act reinstated the availability of civil injunctions in labor disputes, but only against an unfair labor practice and at the request of the NLRB.

Labor-Management Reporting and Disclosure Act

This Act, also known as the **Landrum-Griffin Act,** was aimed at eliminating corruption in labor unions. Section 2(b) of the Act provides the following statement in support of the passage of the Act:

The Congress further finds, from recent investigations in the labor and managment fields, that there have been a number of instances of breach of trust, corruption, disregard of the rights of individual employees, and other failures to observe high standards of responsibility and ethical conduct which require further and supplementary legislation that will afford necessary protection of the rights and interests of employees and the public generally as they relate to the activities of labor organizations, employers, labor relations consultants, and their officers and representatives.

The Act, which was passed in 1959, attempts to deal with the problem of corruption through the mechanism of establishing an elaborate reporting system and the enactment of a union "bill of rights" designed to make unions more democratic. Section 101. The latter provides union members with the right to nominate candidates for union offices, to vote in elections, to attend membership meetings, to participate in union business, to have free expression at union meetings and conventions, and to be accorded a full and fair hearing before any disciplinary action is taken by the union against them.

EMPLOYMENT DISCRIMINATION LAW

A number of Federal statutes prohibit discrimination in employment on the basis of race, sex, religion, national origin, age, and handicap. The cornerstone of Federal employment discrimination law is Title VII of the 1964 Civil Rights Act, but also of significance are the Equal Pay Act, the Age Discrimination in Employment Act of 1967, the Rehabilitation Act of 1973, and various Executive Orders. In addition, most States have enacted similar laws prohibiting discrimination based on race, sex, religion, national origin, and handicap.

Equal Pay Act

The Equal Pay Act prohibits an employer from discriminating between employees on the basis of **sex** by paying unequal wages for the same work. The Act forbids an employer from paying wages at a rate less than the rate at which he pays wages to employees of the opposite sex for equal work at the same establishment. Once the employee has demonstrated that the employer pays unequal wages for *equal* work to members of the opposite sex, the burden shifts to the employer to prove that the pay differential is based on:

1. A seniority system;
2. A merit system;
3. A system which measures earnings by quantity or quality of production; or
4. Any factor except sex.

Remedies include recovery of back pay and enjoining the employer from further unlawful conduct. The Department of Labor is the Federal agency designated by the statute to interpret and enforce the Act. In 1979 these functions were transferred to the Equal Employment Opportunity Commission.

Civil Rights Act of 1964

Title VII of the Civil Rights Act of 1964 prohibits **discrimination** on the basis of race, color, sex, religion, or national origin in hiring, firing, compensating, promoting, training, or otherwise. The Act applies to employers which are engaged in an industry affecting commerce and have fifteen or more employees.

Each of the following constitutes discriminatory conduct prohibited by the Act:

1. An individual shows that an employer utilized a proscribed criteria in making an employment decision. The Supreme Court held in *McDonnell Douglas Corp. v. Green*, 411 U.S. 792 (1973), that a *prima facie* case of discrimination would be shown if the plaintiff (a) is within a protected class, (b) applied for an open position, (c) was qualified for the position, (d) was denied the job, and (e) the employer continued to try to fill the position. Once the plaintiff establishes a *prima facie* case the burden shifts to the defendant to "articulate legitimate and non-discriminatory reasons for the plaintiff's rejection."

2. An employer engages in conduct which on its face is "neutral", that is non-discriminatory, but nonetheless continues to perpetuate past discriminatory practices. For example, it has been held illegal for a union that had previously limited membership to whites to adopt a requirement that new members be related to or recommended by existing members. *Local 53 of International Association of Heat and Frost Insulators and Asbestos Workers v. Vogler*, 407 F.2d 104 (5th Cir. 1969).

3. An employer adopts "neutral" rules which have an adverse impact on a protected class

and which are not justified as being necessary to the business. *See Griggs v. Duke Power Co.*

The enforcement agency is the **Equal Employment Opportunity Commission** (EEOC). The EEOC is charged with the responsibility and empowered to (1) file legal actions in its own name or to intervene in actions filed by third parties; (2) to attempt to resolve alleged violations through informal means prior to bringing suit; (3) to investigate all charges of discrimination; and (4) to issue guidelines and regulations concerning enforcement policy.

The Act provides three basic defenses: (1) a *bona fide* seniority or merit system; (2) a professionally developed ability test; and (3) a *bona fide* occupational qualification. Remedies for violation of the Act include enjoining the employer from engaging in the unlawful behavior, appropriate affirmative action, and reinstatement of employees and award of back pay from a date not more than two years prior to the filing of the charge with the EEOC. **Affirmative action** generally means the active recruitment of minority applicants, although courts have utilized the remedy of affirmative action to impose numerical hiring ratios and hiring goals based on race and sex. *See United Steelworkers of America v. Weber* for a discussion of **reverse discrimination.**

Age Discrimination in Employment Act of 1967

The Age Discrimination in Employment Act prohibits discriminating in hiring, firing, salaries, or otherwise on the basis of age. It applies the substantive language of Title VII to benefit individuals between the ages of forty and seventy years. The Act applies to private employers having 20 or more employees and to all governmental units regardless of size. The Act also prohibits the mandatory retirement of most employees under the age of seventy.

The major statutory defenses include: (1) a *bona fide* occupational qualification; (2) a *bona fide* seniority system; and (3) any other reasonable action. Remedies include back pay, injunctive relief, and affirmative action.

Rehabilitation Act of 1973

The Rehabilitation Act of 1973 attempts to provide assistance to the handicapped in obtaining rehabilitation training, access to public facilities, and employment. Concerning the last of these, the Act requires Federal contractors and Federal agencies to take affirmative action to hire qualified handicapped persons as well as prohibiting discrimination on the basis of handicap in Federal programs and programs receiving Federal financial assistance.

Executive Order

In 1965 President Johnson issued an Executive Order which prohibited discrimination by Federal contractors on the basis of race, color, sex, religion, or national origin in employment on *any work* performed by the contractor during the period of the Federal contract. Federal contractors are also required to take affirmative action in recruiting. The Secretary of Labor, **Office of Federal Contract Compliance Programs** (OFCCP) administers enforcement of the program.

The program applies to all contractors who enter into a contract to be performed in the United States with the Federal government and all of their subcontractors in excess of $10,000. Compliance with the affirmative action requirement differs for construction and non-construction contractors. All **non-construction** contractors with fifty or more employees or with contracts for more than $50,000 must have a written affirmative action plan in order to be in compliance. The plan must include a work force analysis, planned corrective action, if necessary, with specific goals and timetables, and procedures for auditing and reporting. The Director of the OFCCP periodically issues goals and timetables for each segment of the **construction** industry for each region of the country. As a condition precedent to bidding on the Federal contract, the contractor must agree to make a good faith effort to achieve current published goals.

EMPLOYEE SAFETY

Occupational Safety and Health Act

In 1970 Congress enacted the Occupational Safety and Health Act to assure, as far as possible, every worker a safe and healthful working environment. The Act established the **Occupational Safety and Health Administration** (OSHA) to develop standards, conduct inspections, monitor compliance, and institute enforcement actions against those who are not in compliance.

The Act imposes upon each employer a general duty to provide a work environment that is "free from recognized hazards that are causing or likely to cause death or serious physical harm to his employees." Section 119. In addition to this general duty the employer is required to comply with specific safety risks promulgated by OSHA. The Act also requires employees to comply with all OSHA rules and regulations. Finally, the Act prohibits any employer from discharging or discriminating against an employee who exercises his rights under the Act. Section 11(c)(1). For example, in *Whirlpool Corp. v. Marshall*, the Supreme Court held that two employees were improperly discriminated against when they were reprimanded for refusing to perform assigned work which they reasonably believed was life threatening.

The enforcement of the Act generally involves OSHA inspections and citations of employers, if appropriate, for: (1) breach of the general duty obligation; (2) breach of specific safety and health standards; or (3) failure to keep records, make reports, or post notices required by the Act.

When a violation is discovered, a written citation, proposed penalty, and correction date are given to the employer. Citations may be contested, and in such cases, administrative law judges are assigned by the Occupational Safety and Health Review Commission to hold hearings. The Commission, at its discretion, may grant review of an administrative law judge's decision; review is not a matter of right. If Commission review is not undertaken, then the judge's decision becomes the final order of the Commission thirty days after receipt and the order may be appealed by the aggrieved party to the appropriate United States Circuit Court of Appeals.

Penalties for violations are both civil and criminal and may be as high as $1,000 per violation per day, while a $10,000 criminal penalty may be imposed for certain willful violations. In cases involving civil penalties, serious violations require that a penalty be proposed, while in nonserious violation cases penalties are rarely proposed. The Secretary of Labor is further empowered by the Act to obtain temporary restraining orders in situations where regular OSHA procedures cannot be effective to shut down business operations that create imminent dangers of death or serious injury.

Worker's Compensation

At common law the basis of most actions by an injured employee against his employer is the failure of the employer to use reasonable care under the circumstances for the safety of the employee. However, in such an action the employer has several well-established defenses available to him at common law. These include the defense of the fellow servant rule; contributory negligence on the part of the employee; and the doctrine of assumption of risk by the employee.

The **fellow servant rule** is that an employer is not liable for injuries sustained by an employee caused by the negligence of a fellow employee. Another common law defense is **contributory negligence**. If an employer establishes that the negligence of an injured employee contributed to the injury he sustained in the course of his employment, in many jurisdictions the employee cannot recover damages from the employer. At common law an employer is not liable to an employee for harm or injury caused by the unsafe condition of the premises if the employee, with knowledge of the facts and understanding the risks involved, voluntarily enters into or continues in the employment. This is regarded as a **voluntary assumption of risk** by the employee.

In order to provide speedier and more certain relief to injured employees, all States have adopted Worker's Compensation Acts. These statutes create commissions or boards which determine whether an injured employee is entitled to receive compensation and, if so, how much. The common law defenses discussed above are *not* available to employers in proceedings under these statutes. Such defenses are abolished, and the only requirement is that the employee be injured and that the injury arise out of and in the course of his employment. The amounts recoverable are fixed by statute for each type of injury and are on a scale which is less than a court or jury would probably award in an action at common law. However, actions at law are not permitted against employers to injured employees who come within the Worker's Compensation Acts. The courts do not have jurisdiction over such cases except to review decisions of the board or commission, and then only to determine whether such decisions are in accordance with the statute. However, if a third party causes the injury, the employee may bring a tort action against that third party.

Social Security and Unemployment Insurance

Social Security was enacted in 1935 in an attempt to provide limited retirement and death benefits to certain employees. Since then the Federal Social Security system has expanded to cover almost all employees and to increase greatly the benefits offered. The system now contains four major benefit programs: (1) Old-Age and Survivors Insurance (OASI) (providing retirement and survivor benefits); (2) Disability Insurance (DI); (3) Hospitalization Insurance (Medicare); and (4) Supplemental Security Income (SSI).

The system is financed by contributions (taxes) paid by employers, employees, and self-employed individuals. Employees and employers pay matching contributions. These contributions are calculated by multiplying the social security tax (a fixed percentage) times the employee's wages up to a specified maximum. Both the base tax rate and the maximum dollar amount are subject to change by Congress. It is the employer's responsibility to withhold the employee's contribution and to forward the full amount of the tax to the Internal Revenue Service. Contributions made by the employee are not tax deductible by the employee, while those made by the employer are tax deductible.

Self-employed persons are also required to report their own taxable income and pay the Social Security tax. Currently, the tax paid by self-employed individuals is greater than that paid by either the employer or employee, but less than the combined employer/employee contribution.

Benefits vary greatly depending upon the particular program and whether the beneficiary is "fully" insured, "currently" insured, or a dependent. To be **fully insured** a person must be credited with forty quarters of coverage: a quarter of coverage is received for each $370 of earnings in a year up to a maximum of four quarters per year. An individual is **currently insured** if they have been credited with at least six quarters of coverage in the last three years. In addition, dependents (spouses and children) are also eligible for certain Social Security benefits. Finally, benefits received are tax-free unless the individual receiving benefits under OASI has income in excess of a specified amount, which in 1984 was $25,000 for single persons and $32,000 for married couples.

The Federal **unemployment insurance** system was initially created by Title IX of the Social Security Act of 1935. Subsequently, Title IX was supplemented by the Federal Unemployment Tax Act as well as numerous other Federal statutes. This complex system depends upon the cooperation of State and Federal programs. Federal law provides the general guidelines, standards, and requirements, while the States handle the administration of the program under their own employment laws. The system is funded by taxes imposed on employers with Federal taxes generally paying the administrative costs of the program and State contributions paying for the actual benefits.

Under the Federal Unemployment Tax Act an employer must pay unemployment tax if (1) he employs one or more persons for some portion of a day in each of twenty weeks in the current or preceding calendar year or (2) he pays $1,500 or more in wages in any calendar quarter. The employee does not pay any unemployment tax. The tax, like the Social Security tax, is calculated as a fixed percentage of an employee's salary up to a stated maximum. The purpose of the tax is to provide unemployment compensation to workers who have lost their jobs and cannot find other employment. Payments generally are made weekly and are based on the particular State's formula.

Fair Labor Standards Act

The Fair Labor Standards Act (FLSA) regulates the employment of child labor outside of agriculture. The Act prohibits the employment of anyone under fourteen years in non-farm work except for newspaper deliverers and child actors. Fourteen and fifteen year olds may be employed for a limited number of hours outside of school hours, under specific conditions, in certain *nonhazardous* occupations. Sixteen and seventeen year olds may work in any *nonhazardous* job while persons eighteen years old or older may work in *any* job whether it is hazardous or not. The Secretary of Labor determines which occupations are considered hazardous.

In addition, the FLSA imposes wage and hour requirements upon covered employers. The Act provides for a minimum hourly wage (currently $3.35) and overtime pay of time-and-a-half for hours worked in excess of forty hours per week. Certain jobs are exempted from both the FLSA's minimum wage and overtime provisions including the following: professionals, managers, and outside sales persons.

CASES

Unfair Labor Practices

NATIONAL LABOR RELATIONS BOARD v. BERGER TRANSFER & STORAGE

United States Court of Appeals, Seventh Circuit, 1982.
678 F.2d 679.

BAKER, J.

[The defendant, Berger Transfer and Storage, operates a national moving and transfer business employing approximately 40 persons. In May and June of 1979, Local 705 of the International Brotherhood of the Teamsters Union spoke with a number of Berger Employees, obtaining 28 cards signed in support of the Union. The management of Berger, unwilling to work with the Union, attempted to prevent it from representing its employees. The company first assigned all work to those with high seniority, in effect temporarily laying off low seniority employees. The management then threatened permanently to lay off those with low seniority and threatened all employees with a total close down of the plant. The management interrogated several employees about their union involvement and attempted to extract information about other employees' activities. When the Union presented the company the signed cards and Recognition Agreement, Berger refused to acknowledge the Union's existence or right to bargain on behalf of the employees. The Union then called a strike with employees picketing the warehouse. During the picketing, the Company threatened to discharge the picketers if they did not return to work. Later, one manager on two occasions recklessly drove a truck through the picket line, striking employees. Finally, the company contacted several of the employees and offered them the "grievance procedures and job security" the Union would provide. The employees refused the offer. On June 15, the strike ended with most of the picketers returning to work. Local 705 of the International Brotherhood of Teamsters filed a complaint with the National Labor Relations Board that the defendant is guilty of unfair labor practices by violating Sections 8(a)(1), (3) and (5) of the National Labor Relations Act.]

* * *

SECTIONS 8(A)(1), (3) and (5) VIOLATIONS.

The Board adopted the ALJ's [Administrative Law Judge] findings and conclusions that the Company had violated sections 8(a)(1), (3) and (5) of the Act. These findings must be enforced if they are supported by substantial evidence based upon the record as a whole. [Citations.]

(A) Section 8(a)(1) Violations.

The Board found the Company had committed eighteen independent 8(a)(1) violations which can be divided into six basic categories: (1) interrogating employees about union activities; (2) threatening employees with discharge, layoff and plant closure; (3) creating the impression of surveillance; (4) making promises to redress employees' complaints; (5) assaulting employees; and (6) actual layoff and discharge of employees.

Section 8(a)(1) makes it an unfair labor practice for an employer to interfere with, restrain, or coerce employees in the exercise of their rights to organize and bargain collectively through representatives of their own choosing. [Citation.] The test of interference with the right of self-organization is not whether an attempt at coercion has succeeded or failed, but whether the employer engaged in conduct which reasonably tends to interfere with, restrain, or coerce employees in the free exercise of their section 7 rights. [Citation.]

(1) Interrogation of employees. Section 8(a)(1) does not prohibit all employer questioning of employees about union activities. However, when the questions asked "viewed and interpreted as the employee must have understood the questioning and its ramifications, could reasonably coerce or intimidate the employee with regard to union activities," a violation has been established. [Citation.] An analysis of the employer's conduct should consider: (1) the background of the employer-employee relationship; (2) the questioner's identity; (3) the nature of the information sought; (4) the place and method of the interrogation; and (5) the truthfulness of the reply. [Citations.]

* * *

Applying the[se] consideration[s] * * * it is apparent that the findings of the Board are supported by substantial evidence. * * *

(2) Threats to close the plant, discharge and layoff employees. An employer violates section 8(a)(1) when he threatens employees with reprisals or other unfavorable consequences as a result of their union activities. [Citation.] Here the evidence shows that the Company began a campaign of threatened reprisals immediately following the Union's organizational drive. In particular, the Company: (1) informed the employees that if the Union succeeded there would be less work, smaller crews; (2) told the employees that no work would be booked for Mondays and Tuesdays; (3) emphasized that layoffs would be controlled by seniority; (4) threatened to dis-

charge employees if they continued to participate in the strike; and (5) threatened to close the warehouse if employees continued to support the Union.

Threats to cut back available work in response to employees' exercise of their section 7 rights are classic section 8(a)(1) violations, [citation], as are threats to discharge those employees. [Citation.]

Whether or not threats of plant closure are threats or predictions of the economic consequences of union organization, which fall outside the ambit of section 8(a)(1), turn on the nature of the employer's statement. * * * Here the Company failed to articulate any objective facts to support its "prediction" that the unionization would have dire economic consequences. Instead the record supports the finding that the employees understood the message as a threat of reprisal.

(3)Impressions of surveillance. An employer violates section 8(a)(1) when it conveys to employees the impression that it is engaged in surveillance of their union activities. [Citation.] Here the Company: (1) made it known to employees that the Company was aware of employees signing authorization cards, (2) made notes on a list of employees during an interrogation, and (3) suggested that York and Roesecke [two employees] were the instigators. This course of conduct supports the Board's finding that the Company violated section 8(a)(1) by creating an impression of surveillance.

(4) Solicitation of grievances, implied promises or redress. An employer violates section 8(a)(1) of the Act by soliciting grievances when such solicitation is " 'accompanied by an express or implied promise of benefits specifically aimed at interfering with, restraining, and coercing employees in their organizational effort.' " [Citation.] Here the Company repeatedly approached employees to determine how differences could be reconciled. On one occasion, Vice-President Goodwin told employee Overton that the Company would give him "basically the same thing" as the Union, and suggested a meeting with the "top guys." Such employer initiated conduct supports a finding that the Company violated section 8(a)(1) by soliciting grievances and impliedly promising redress.

(5) Assaults. The evidence shows that on two occasions, Manager Harris recklessly drove his truck through the picket line. The first incident occurred on May 23, when Harris drove a Company truck through the picket line striking picketers Most and Gocha. He later stated that he hit the picketers both "intentionally and unintentionally." A similar incident occurred on June 6. Although there was testimony that the picketers were inebriated and blocking the Company driveway on that occasion, the Board found that the assaults were connected to the employees' union activity. Considering the active anti-union stand taken by the Company as evidenced in the record, there is substantial support for the Board's finding.

(B) Section 8(a)(3) Violations—Layoffs, Demotions & Discharges.
Section 8(a)(3) of the Act makes it an unfair labor practice for an employer to discriminate against an employee "in regard to hire or tenure of employment or any term or condition of employment to encourage or discourage membership in any labor organization * * * ." [Citation.] For example, an employer violates section 8(a)(3) when it discharges an employee because of his union activities. [Citation.]

The critical issue in a section 8(a)(3) claim is whether the employer's actions are motivated by anti-union considerations. [Citation.] * * * If a causal relationship between the discharge and protected activity is established, the employer is responsible under the Act unless he sustains his burden of proof. Furthermore, an employer's explanation need not be accepted if there is a reasonable basis for believing the explanation is a pretext for the retaliatory action. [Citation.]

The evidence shows that Company officials made numerous unlawful threats of discharge, layoff, plant shutdown, together with unlawful interrogations, solicitation of grievances, promises of redress and assaults. Such conduct is a significant factor in determining motive. [Citation.] * * *

(1) Discharges. One of the protected rights of employees under section 7 of the Act is the right to strike. The strike began on May 23 as a recognitional strike. However, after Maierhofer threatened strikers with discharge, the strike was converted to an unfair labor practices strike entitling strikers to unconditional reinstatement. [Citation.] That evening the Company sent the following telegram to striking employees:

We are asking you to report to work at our terminal 2N225 Grace St., Lombard, Illinois at 8 A.M. Thursday, May 24, 1979. If you do not report, we will take this to mean that you have voluntarily terminated your employment with Berger Transfer and Storage, Inc. If you terminate your employment, your hospitalization will be terminated at midnight May 31, 1979. If you contact us, we will advise the procedure to convert your personal policy.

> Berger Transfer & Storage, Inc.
> 2N225 Grace Street
> Lombard, Illinois

The Board concluded that the employees were discharged for their union activities and that the Company's follow-up telegram of May 28 did not cure the violation but instead was a factor to consider in any remedial order. Although the Company asserts that the employees "quit," the total atmosphere of hostility promoted by the Company supports the inference of a section 8(a)(3) violation and discredits the Company's argument about the second telegram.

(2) Layoffs. Where anti-union considerations result in the layoff of employees, the employer has violated section 8(a)(3) of the Act.

[Citation.] The testimony before the ALJ established that during the week of May 21, several employees were laid off when the Company failed to book jobs on Mondays and Tuesdays. Furthermore employee Redman testified that he overheard Manager Harris state that he had work for "thirty guys" but was not using them because of the organizational drive. The record therefore supports the finding that the motivation for the threats and actual layoffs was anti-union animus and not economic compulsion.

(3) Demotion of Gocha. The demotion of an employee for engaging in protected union activities is a violation of section 8(a)(3) of the Act. [Citation.] Although there was testimony that Gocha was demoted because of customer complaints, the Board found the claimed justification to be a pretext, citing Harris' explanation that Gocha was no longer warehouse foreman because of his union sympathy. There is substantial evidence in the record to support this finding, particularly since no evidence was introduced that Gocha was aware of the customer complaints or the Company's displeasure with his work.

Section 8(a)(5) Violation.
The evidence shows that on May 23 the Union had collected signed authorization cards from twenty-eight employees. The Board found that the appropriate unit consisted of forty-two employees, giving the Union majority status. It is well established that the National Labor Relations Act authorized two methods for the confirmation of a binding bargaining relationship between an employer and a labor union. Generally, Board certification of a union's election success is the prevalent and preferred practice, but it is not the only one; and employer may voluntarily recognize the union upon some demonstrable showing of majority status, i.e., union authorization cards.

Although an employer generally has the right to refuse to recognize a card based majority and to demand an election, an employer who engages in unfair labor practices "likely to destroy the union's majority and seriously impede the election" may not insist that before it bargains an election be held. [Citation.] Therefore, when a union requests recognition and bargaining from an employer which has been presented with cards showing a majority support for the union, and the employer subsequently engages in unfair labor practices which destroy the "laboratory conditions" needed for a fair election, the employer forfeits any right to an election and must bargain with the union or violate section 8(a)(5) of the Act. Whether or not the union maintains majority status in the face of the employer's unfair labor practices is irrelevant to such a violation finding. [Citation.]

The evidence is clear that the Union had valid authorization cards from twenty-eight of the forty-two employees within the bargaining unit and properly requested recognition by the Company. The Company's response was an onslaught of flagrant, unfair labor practices. Under these circumstances there is substantial evidence to support the finding of a section 8(a)(5) violation.

* * *

For the reasons advanced, the order of the National Labor Relations Board is enforced.

Unfair Union Practices

IN THE MATTER OF SAILORS' UNION OF THE PACIFIC, AFL *AND* MOORE DRY DOCK COMPANY

92 NLRB No. 93, 1950.

DECISION AND ORDER

On May 26, 1950, Trial Examiner Arthur Leff issued his Intermediate Report in the above-entitled proceeding, finding that the Respondent had not engaged in the unfair labor practices [unfair union practice under Section 8(b)] alleged in the complaint and recommending that the complaint be dismissed

in its entirety, as set forth in the copy of the Intermediate Report attached hereto. Thereafter, the General Counsel and Moore Dry Dock Company, the charging party, filed exceptions to the Intermediate Report and supporting briefs.

The Board has reviewed the rulings made by the Trial Examiner at the hearing and finds that no prejudicial error was committed. The rulings are hereby affirmed. The Board has considered the Intermediate Report, the exceptions and briefs, and the entire record in the case, and hereby adopts the findings,[1] conclusions, and recommendations of the Trial Examiner with the following clarification.

Section 8(b)(4)(A) is aimed at secondary boycotts and secondary strike activities. It was not intended to proscribe primary action by a union having a legitimate labor dispute with an employer. Picketing at the premises of a primary employer is traditionally recognized as primary action even though it is "necessarily designed to induce and encourage third persons to cease doing business with the picketed employer." As we said in 1949,

(Section 8(b)(4)(A)) * * * was intended only to outlaw certain *secondary* boycotts, whereby unions sought to enlarge the economic battleground beyond the premises of the primary Employer. When picketing is wholly at the premises of the employer with whom the union is engaged in a labor dispute, it cannot be called "secondary" even though, as is virtually always the case, an object of the picketing is to dissuade all persons from entering such premises for business reasons. * * *

Hence, if Samsoc, the owner of the S. S. *Phopho*, had had a dock of its own in California

---

1. With respect to the unfair labor practices, the complaint alleged in substance that since on or about February 17, 1950, the Respondent induced and encouraged employees of Moore to engage in a strike or concerted refusal in the course of their employment to perform services for Moore in connection with the conversion into a bulk gypsum carrier of the S. S. *Phopho*, a vessel owned by Compania Maritima Samsoc, Limitada, S. A., herein, called Samsoc, an object thereof being to force or require Moore to cease doing business with Samsoc.

to which the *Phopho* had been tied up while undergoing conversion by Moore Dry Dock employees, picketing by the Respondent at the dock site would unquestionably have constituted *primary* action, even though the Respondent might have expected that the picketing would be more effective in persuading Moore employees not to work on the ship than to persuade the seamen aboard the *Phopho* to quit that vessel. The difficulty in the present case arises therefore, not because of any difference in picketing objectives, but from the fact that the *Phopho* was not tied up at its own dock, but at that of Moore, while the picketing was going on in front of the Moore premises.

In the usual case, the *situs* of a labor dispute is the premises of the primary employer. * * * But in some cases the *situs* of the dispute may not be limited to a fixed location; it may be ambulatory. Thus in the *Schultz* case, a majority of the Board held that the truck upon which a truck driver worked was the *situs* of a labor dispute between him and the owner of the truck. Similarly, we hold in the present case that, as the *Phopho* was the place of employment of the seamen, it was the *situs* of the dispute between Samsoc and the Respondent over working conditions aboard that vessel.

When the *situs* is ambulatory, it may come to rest temporarily at the premises of another employer. The perplexing question is: Does the right to picket follow the *situs* while it is stationed at the premises of a secondary employer, when the only way to picket that *situs* is in front of the secondary employer's premises? Admittedly, no easy answer is possible. Essentially, the problem is one of balancing the right of a union to picket at the site of its dispute as against the right of a secondary employer to be free from picketing in a controversy in which it is not directly involved.

When a secondary employer is harboring the *situs* of a dispute between a union and a primary employer, the right of neither the union to picket nor of the secondary employer to be free from picketing can be absolute. The enmeshing of premises and *situs* qualifies both rights. In the kind of situation that exists in this case, we believe that picketing of the premises of a secondary employer is primary if it meets the following conditions: (a) The picketing is strictly limited to times when the *situs* of dispute is located on the secondary employer's premises; (b) at the time of the picketing the primary employer is engaged in its normal business at the *situs*; (c) the picketing is limited to places reasonably close to the location of the *situs*; and (d) the picketing discloses clearly that the dispute is with the primary employer. All these conditions were met in the present case.

* * *

We believe that our dissenting colleagues' expressions of alarm are based on a misunderstanding of our decision. We are not holding, as the dissenters seem to think, that a union which has a dispute with a shipowner over working conditions of seamen aboard a ship may lawfully picket the premises of an independent shipyard to which the shipowner has delivered his vessel for overhaul and repair. We are only holding that, if a shipyard permits the owner of a vessel to use its dock for the purpose of readying the ship for its regular voyage by hiring and training a crew and putting stores aboard ship, a union representing seamen may then, within the careful limitations laid down in this decision, lawfully picket in front of the shipyard premises to advertise its dispute with the shipowner.

It is true, of course, that the *Phopho* was delivered to the Moore yard for conversion into a bulk gypsum carrier. But Moore in its contract agreed that "During the last two weeks, . . . [the *Phopho's*] Owner shall have the right to put a crew on board the vessel for training purposes, provided, however, that such crew shall not interfere in any way with the work of conversion." Samsoc (the *Phopho's* owner) availed itself of this contract privilege. When it did, Moore and Samsoc were simultaneously engaged in their separate businesses in the Moore yard.

*   *   *

Under the circumstances of this case, we therfore find that the picketing practice followed by the Respondent was primary and not secondary and therefore did not violate Section 8(b)(4)(A) of the Act.

*   *   *

Civil Rights Act of 1964:
Adverse Impact

GRIGGS v. DUKE POWER CO.

Supreme Court of the United States, 1971.
401 U.S. 424, 91 S.Ct. 849, 28 L.Ed.2d 158.

BURGER, C. J.

We granted the writ in this case to resolve the question whether an employer is prohibited by the Civil Rights Act of 1964, Title VII, from requiring a high school education or passing of a standardized general intelligence test as a condition of employment in or transfer to jobs when (a) neither standard is shown to be significantly related to successful job performance, (b) both requirements operate to disqualify Negroes at a substantially higher rate than white applicants, and (c) the jobs in question formerly had been filled only by white employees as part of a longstanding practice of giving preference to whites.

*   *   *

The District Court found that prior to July 2, 1965, the effective date of the Civil Rights Act of 1964, the Company openly discriminated on the basis of race in the hiring and assigning of employees at its Dan River plant. The plant was organized into five operating departments: (1) Labor, (2) Coal Handling, (3) Operations, (4) Maintenance, and (5) Laboratory and Test. Negroes were employed only in the Labor Department where the highest paying jobs paid less than the lowest paying jobs in the other four "operating" departments in which only whites were employed. Promotions were normally made within each department on the basis of job seniority. Transferees into a department usually began in the lowest position.

In 1955 the Company instituted a policy of requiring a high school education for initial assignment to any department except Labor, and for transfer from the Coal Handling to any "inside" department (Operations, Maintenance, or Laboratory). When the Company abandoned its policy of restricting Negroes to the Labor Department in 1965, completion of high school also was made a prerequisite to transfer from Labor to any other department. From the time the high school requirement was instituted to the time of trial, however, white employees hired before the time of the high school education requirement continued to perform satisfactorily and achieve promotions in the "operating" departments. Findings on this score are not challenged.

The Company added a further requirement for new employees on July 2, 1965, the date on which Title VII became effective. To qualify for placement in any but the Labor Department it became necessary to register satisfactory scores on two professionally prepared aptitude tests, as well as to have a high school education. Completion of high school alone continued to render employees eligible for transfer to the four desirable departments from which Negroes had been excluded if the incumbent had been employed prior to the time of the new requirement. In September 1965 the Company began to permit incumbent employees who lacked a high school education to qualify for transfer from Labor or Coal Handling to an "inside" job by passing two tests—the Wonderlic Personnel Test, which purports to measure general intelligence, and the Bennett Mechanical Comprehension Test. Neither was directed or intended to measure the ability to learn to perform a particular job or category of jobs. The requisite scores used for both initial hiring and transfer approximated the national median for high school graduates.

The objective of Congress in the enactment of Title VII is plain from the language of the statute. It was to achieve equality of employment opportunities and remove barriers that have operated in the past to favor an identifiable group of white employees over other employees. Under the Act, practices, procedures, or tests neutral on their face, and even neutral in terms of intent, cannot be maintained if they operate to "freeze" the status quo of prior discriminatory employment practices.

The Court of Appeals' opinion, and the partial dissent, agreed that, on the record in the present case, "whites register far better on the Company's alternative requirements" than Negroes.[6] This consequence would appear to be directly traceable to race. Basic intelligence must have the means of articulation to manifest itself fairly in a testing process. Because they are Negroes, petitioners have long received inferior education in segregated schools and this Court expressly recognized these differences in [citation]. There, because of the inferior education received by Negroes in North Carolina, this Court barred the institution of a literacy test for voter registration on the ground that the test would abridge the right to vote indirectly on account of race. Congress did not intend by Title VII, however, to guarantee a job to every person regardless of qualifications. In short, the Act does not command that any person be hired simply because he was formerly the subject of discrimination, or because he is a member of a minority group. Discriminatory preference for any group, minority or majority, is precisely and only what Congress has proscribed. What is required by Congress is the removal of artificial, arbitrary, and unnecessary barriers to employment when the barriers operate invidiously to discriminate on

the basis of racial or other impermissible classification.

* * *

The Act proscribes not only overt discrimination but also practices that are fair in form, but discriminatory in operation. The touchstone is business necessity. If an employment practice which operates to exclude Negroes cannot be shown to be related to job performance, the practice is prohibited.

On the record before us, neither the high school completion requirement nor the general intelligence test is shown to bear a demonstrable relationship to successful performance of the jobs for which it was used. Both were adopted, as the Court of Appeals noted, without meaningful study of their relationship to job-performance ability. * * *

The evidence, however, shows that employees who have not completed high school or taken the tests have continued to perform satisfactorily and make progress in departments for which the high school and test criteria are now used.

* * *

The facts of this case demonstrate the inadequacy of broad and general testing devices as well as the infirmity of using diplomas or degrees as fixed measures of capability. History is filled with examples of men and women who rendered highly effective performance without the conventional badges of accomplishment in terms of certificates, diplomas, or degrees. Diplomas and tests are useful servants, but Congress has mandated the commonsense proposition that they are not to become masters of reality.

* * *

Nothing in the Act precludes the use of testing or measuring procedures; obviously they are useful. What Congress has forbidden is giving these devices and mechanisms controlling force unless they are demonstrably a reasonable measure of job performance. Congress has not commanded that the less qualified be preferred over the better qualified simply because of minority origins. Far from

---

6. In North Carolina, 1960 census statistics show that, while 34% of white males had completed high school, only 12% of Negro males had done so. Similarly, with respect to standardized tests, the EEOC in one case found that use of a battery of tests, including the Wonderlic and Bennett tests used by the Company in the instant case, resulted in 58% of whites passing the tests, as compared with only 6% of the blacks. [Citations.]

disparaging job qualifications as such, Congress has made such qualifications the controlling factor, so that race, religion, nationality, and sex become irrelevant. What Congress has commanded is that any tests used must measure the person for the job and not the person in the abstract.

* * *

Civil Rights Act of 1964:
Reverse Discrimination

UNITED STEELWORKERS OF AMERICA v. WEBER

Supreme Court of the United States, 1979.
443 U.S. 193, 99 S.Ct. 2721, 61 L.Ed.2d 480.

BRENNAN, J.

Challenged here is the legality of an affirmative action plan—collectively bargained by an employer and a union—that reserves for black employees 50% of the openings in an in-plant craft training program until the percentage of black craft workers in the plant is commensurate with the percentage of blacks in the local labor force. The question for decision is whether Congress, in Title VII of the Civil Rights Act of 1964 [citation], left employers and unions in the private sector free to take such race-conscious steps to eliminate manifest racial imbalances in traditionally segregated job categories. We hold that Title VII does not prohibit such race-conscious affirmative action plans.

I

In 1974 petitioner United Steelworkers of America (USWA) and petitioner Kaiser Aluminum & Chemical Corporation (Kaiser) entered into a master collective-bargaining agreement covering terms and conditions of employment at 15 Kaiser plants. The agreement contained an affirmative action plan designed to eliminate conspicuous racial imbalances in Kaiser's then almost exclusively white craftwork forces. Black craft-hiring goals were set for each Kaiser plant equal to the percentage of blacks in the respective local labor

forces. To enable plants to meet these goals, on-the-job training programs were established to teach unskilled production workers—black and white—the skills necessary to become craftworkers. The plan reserved for black employees 50% of the openings in these newly created in-plant training programs.

This case arose from the operation of the plan at Kaiser's plant in Gramercy, La. Until 1974, Kaiser hired as craftworkers for that plant only persons who had had prior craft experience. Because blacks had long been excluded from craft unions, few were able to present such credentials. As a consequence, prior to 1974 only 1.83% (5 out of 273) of the skilled craftworkers at the Gramercy plant were black, even though the work force in the Gramercy area was approximately 39% black.

Pursuant to the national agreement Kaiser altered its craft-hiring practice in the Gramercy plant. Rather than hiring already trained outsiders, Kaiser established a training program to train its production workers to fill craft openings. Selection of craft trainees was made on the basis of seniority, with the proviso that at least 50% of the new trainees were to be black until the percentage of black skilled craftworkers in the Gramercy plant approximated the percentage of blacks in the local labor force. [Citation].

During 1974, the first year of the operation of the Kaiser-USWA affirmative action plan, 13 craft trainees were selected from Gramercy's production work force. Of these, seven were black and six white. The most senior black selected into the program had less seniority than several white production workers whose bids for admission were rejected. Thereafter one of those white production workers, respondent Brain Weber (hereafter respondent), instituted this * * * action * * *.

The complaint alleged that the filling of craft trainee positions at the Gramercy plant pursuant to the affirmative action program had resulted in junior black employees' receiving training in preference to senior white employees, thus discriminating against respondent and other similarly situated white employees in violation of * * * Title VII.

* * *

II

We emphasize at the outset the narrowness of our inquiry. Since the Kaiser-USWA plan does not involve state action, this case does not present an alleged violation of the Equal Protection Clause of the Fourteenth Amendment. Further, since the Kaiser-USWA plan was adopted voluntarily, we are not concerned with what Title VII requires or with what a court might order to remedy a past proved violation of the Act. The only question before us is the narrow statutory issue of whether Title VII *forbids* private employers and unions from voluntarily agreeing upon *bona fide* affirmative action plans that accord racial preferences in the manner and for the purpose provided in the Kaiser-USWA plan. That question was expressly left open in *McDonald v. Santa Fe Trail Transp. Co.*, [citation], which held, in a case not involving affirmative action, that Title VII protects whites as well as blacks from certain forms of racial discrimination.

Respondent argues that Congress intended in Title VII to prohibit all race-conscious affirmative action plans. Respondent's argument rests upon a literal interpretation of [two sections] of the Act. Those sections make it unlawful to "discriminate * * * because of * * * race" in hiring and in the selection of apprentices for training programs. Since, the argument runs, *McDonald v. Santa Fe Trail Transp. Co.* settled that Title VII forbids discrimination against whites as well as blacks, and since the Kaiser-USWA affirmative action plan operates to discriminate against white employees solely because they are white, it follows that the Kaiser-USWA plan violates Title VII.

Respondent's argument is not without force. But it overlooks the significance of the fact that the Kaiser-USWA plan is an affirmative action plan voluntarily adopted by private parties to eliminate traditional patterns of racial segregation. * * *

Congress' primary concern in enacting the prohibition against racial discrimination in Title VII of the Civil Rights Act of 1964 was with "the plight of the Negro in our economy." [Citation.] Before 1964, blacks were largely relegated to "unskilled and semi-skilled jobs." [And, the situation was worsening.] "In 1947 the nonwhite unemployment rate was only 64 percent higher than the white rate; in 1962 it was 124 percent higher" (remarks of Sen. Humphrey). [Citation.] Congress considered this a serious social problem. As Senator Clark told the Senate:

The rate of Negro unemployment has gone up consistently as compared with white unemployment for the past 15 years. This is a social malaise and a social situation which we should not tolerate. That is one of the principal reasons why the bill should pass. [Citation.]

Congress feared that the goals of the Civil Rights Act—the integration of blacks into the mainstream of American society—could not be achieved unless this trend were reversed. And Congress recognized that that would not be possible unless blacks were able to secure jobs "which have a future."

* * *

Accordingly, it was clear to Congress that "[t]he crux of the problem [was] to open employment opportunities for Negroes in occupations which have been traditionally closed to them," [citation], and it was to this problem that Title VII's prohibition against racial discrimination in employment was primarily addressed.

* * *

Given this legislative history, we cannot agree with respondent that Congress intended to prohibit the private sector from taking effective steps to accomplish the goal that Congress designed Title VII to achieve. The very statutory words intended as a spur or catalyst to cause "employers and unions to self-examine and to self-evaluate their employment practices and to endeavor to eliminate, so far as possible, the last vestiges of an unfortunate and ignominious page in this country's history," [citation], cannot be interpreted as an absolute prohibition against all private, voluntary, race-conscious affirmative action efforts to hasten the elimination of such vestiges. It would be ironic indeed if a law triggered by a Nation's concern over centuries of racial injustice and intended to improve the lot of those who had "been excluded from the American dream for so long," [citation], constituted the first legislative prohibition of all voluntary, private, race-conscious efforts to abolish traditional patterns of racial segregation and hierarchy.

* * *

We need not today define in detail the line of demarcation between permissible and impermissible affirmative action plans. It suffices to hold that the challenged Kaiser-USWA affirmative action plan falls on the permissible side of the line. The purposes of the plan mirror those of the statute. Both were designed to break down old patterns of racial segregation and hierarchy. Both were structured to "open employment opportunities for Negroes in occupations which have been traditionally closed to them." [Citation.]

At the same time, the plan does not unnecessarily trammel the interests of the white employees. The plan does not require the discharge of white workers and their replacement with new black hirees. [Citation.] Nor does the plan create an absolute bar to the advancement of white employees; half of those trained in the program will be white. Moreover, the plan is a temporary measure; it is not intended to maintain racial balance, but simply to eliminate a manifest racial imbalance. Preferential selection of craft trainees at the Gramercy plant will end as soon as the percentage of black skilled craftworkers in the Gramercy plant approximates the percentage of blacks in the local labor force. [Citation.]

We conclude, therefore, that the adoption of the Kaiser-USWA plan for the Gra-

mercy plant falls within the area of discretion left by Title VII to the private sector voluntarily to adopt affirmative action plans designed to eliminate conspicuous racial imbalance in traditionally segregated job categories. Accordingly, the judgment of the Court of Appeals for the Fifth Circuit is *Reversed.*

Occupational Safety and
Health Act

WHIRLPOOL CORP. v. MARSHALL

Supreme Court of the United States, 1980.
445 U.S. 1, 100 S.Ct. 883, 63 L.Ed.2d 154.

STEWART, J.

The Occupational Safety and Health Act of 1970 (Act) prohibits an employer from discharging or discriminating against any employee who exercises "any right afforded by" the Act. The Secretary of Labor (Secretary) has promulgated a regulation providing that, among the rights that the Act so protects, is the right of an employee to choose not to perform his assigned task because of a reasonable apprehension of death or serious injury coupled with a reasonable belief that no less drastic alternative is available. The question presented in the case before us is whether this regulation is consistent with the Act.

The petitioner company [Whirlpool Corporation] maintains a manufacturing plant in Marion, Ohio, for the production of household appliances. Overhead conveyors transport appliance components throughout the plant. To protect employees from objects that occasionally fall from these conveyors, the petitioner has installed a horizontal wire-mesh guard screen approximately 20 feet above the plant floor. This mesh screen is welded to angle-iron frames suspended from the building's structural steel skeleton.

Maintenance employees of the petitioner spend several hours each week removing objects from the screen, replacing paper spread on the screen to catch grease drippings from the material on the conveyors, and performing occasional maintenance work on the conveyors themselves. To perform these duties, maintenance employees usually are able to stand on the iron frames, but sometimes find it necessary to step onto the steel mesh screen itself.

In 1973, the company began to install heavier wire in the screen because its safety had been drawn into question. Several employees had fallen partly through the old screen, and on one occasion an employee had fallen completely through to the plant floor below but had survived. A number of maintenance employees had reacted to these incidents by bringing the unsafe screen conditions to the attention of their foremen. The petitioner company's contemporaneous safety instructions admonished employees to step only on the angle-iron frames.

On June 28, 1974, a maintenance employee fell to his death through the guard screen in an area where the newer, stronger mesh had not yet been installed. Following this incident, the petitioner effectuated some repairs and issued an order strictly forbidding maintenance employees from stepping on either the screens or the angle-iron supporting structure. An alternative but somewhat more cumbersome and less satisfactory method was developed for removing objects from the screen. This procedure required employees to stand on power-raised mobile platforms and use hooks to recover the material.

On July 7, 1974, two of the petitioner's maintenance employees, Virgil Deemer and Thomas Cornwell, met with the plant maintenance superintendent to voice their concern about the safety of the screen. The superintendent disagreed with their view, but permitted the two men to inspect the screen with their foreman and to point out dangerous areas needing repair. Unsatisfied with the petitioner's response to the results of this inspection, Deemer and Cornwell met on July 9 with the plant safety director. At that meeting, they requested the name, address, and telephone number of a representative of the local office of the Occupational Safety and Health Administration (OSHA). Although the safety direc-

tor told the men that they "had better stop and think about what [they] were doing," he furnished the men with the information they requested. Later that same day, Deemer contacted an official of the regional OSHA office and discussed the guard screen.

The next day, Deemer and Cornwell reported for the night shift at 10:45 p.m. Their foreman, after himself walking on some of the angle-iron frames, directed the two men to perform their usual maintenance duties on a section of the old screen. Claiming that the screen was unsafe, they refused to carry out this directive. The foreman then sent them to the personnel office, where they were ordered to punch out without working or being paid for the remaining six hours of the shift. The two men subsequently received written reprimands, which were placed in their employment files.

A little over a month later, the Secretary filed suit in the United States District Court for the Northern District of Ohio, alleging that the petitioner's actions against Deemer and Cornwell constituted discrimination in violation of § 11(c)(1) of the Act.

* * *

The Act itself creates an express mechanism for protecting workers from employment conditions believed to pose an emergent threat of death or serious injury. Upon receipt of an employee inspection request stating reasonable grounds to believe that an imminent danger is present in a workplace, OSHA must conduct an inspection. [Citation.] In the event this inspection reveals workplace conditions or practices that "could reasonably be expected to cause death or serious physical harm immediately or before the imminence of such danger can be eliminated through the enforcement procedures otherwise provided by" the Act, [citation], the OSHA inspector must inform the affected employees and the employer of the danger and notify them that he is recommending to the Secretary that injunctive relief be sought. [Citation.] At this juncture, the Secretary can petition a federal court to restrain the conditions or practices giving rise to the imminent danger. By means of a temporary restraining order or preliminary injunction, the court may then require the employer to avoid, correct, or remove the danger or to prohibit employees from working in the area. [Citation.]

To ensure that this process functions effectively, the Act expressly accords to every employee several rights, the exercise of which may not subject him to discharge or discrimination. An employee is given the right to inform OSHA of an imminently dangerous workplace condition or practice and request that OSHA inspect that condition or practice. [Citation.] He is given a limited right to assist the OSHA inspector in inspecting the workplace, [citation], and the right to aid a court in determining whether or not a risk of imminent danger in fact exists. [Citation.] Finally, an affected employee is given the right to bring an action to compel the Secretary to seek injunctive relief if he believes the Secretary has wrongfully declined to do so. [Citation.]

In the light of this detailed statutory scheme, the Secretary is obviously correct when he acknowledges in his regulation that, "as a general matter, there is no right afforded by the Act which would entitle employees to walk off the job because of potential unsafe conditions at the workplace." By providing for prompt notice to the employer of an inspector's intention to seek an injunction against an imminently dangerous condition, the legislation obviously contemplates that the employer will normally respond by voluntarily and speedily eliminating the danger. And in the few instances where this does not occur, the legislative provisions authorizing prompt judicial action are designed to give employees full protection in most situations from the risk of injury or death resulting from an imminently dangerous condition at the worksite.

As this case illustrates, however, circumstances may sometimes exist in which the employee justifiably believes that the express statutory arrangement does not sufficiently protect him from death or serious injury. Such circumstances will probably not often occur, but such a situation may arise when (1) the employee is ordered by his employer to work under conditions that the employee reasonably believes pose an imminent risk of death or serious bodily injury, and (2) the employee has reason to believe that there is not sufficient time or opportunity either to seek effective redress from his employer or to apprise OSHA of the danger.

Nothing in the Act suggests that those few employees who have to face this dilemma must rely exclusively on the remedies expressly set forth in the Act at the risk of their own safety. But nothing in the Act explicitly provides otherwise. Against this background of legislative silence, the Secretary has exercised his rulemaking power [citation] and has determined that, when an employee in good faith finds himself in such a predicament, he may refuse to expose himself to the dangerous condition, without being subjected to "subsequent discrimination" by the employer.

* * *

The regulation clearly conforms to the fundamental objective of the Act—to prevent occupational deaths and serious injuries. The Act, in its preamble, declares that its purpose and policy is "to assure so far as possible every working man and woman in the Nation safe and healthful working conditions and to *preserve* our human resources . * * *" [Citation.]

To accomplish this basic purpose, the legislation's remedial orientation is prophylactic in nature. [Citation]. The Act does not wait for an employee to die or become injured. It authorizes the promulgation of health and safety standards and the issuance of citations in the hope that these will act to prevent deaths or injuries from ever occurring. It would seem anomalous to construe an Act so directed and constructed as prohibiting an employee, with no other reasonable alternative, the freedom to withdraw from a workplace environment that he reasonably believes is highly dangerous.

Moreover, the Secretary's regulation can be viewed as an appropriate aid to the full effectuation of the Act's "general duty" clause. That clause provides that "[e]ach employer . . . shall furnish to each of his employees employment and a place of employment which are free from recognized hazards that are causing or are likely to cause death or serious physical harm to his employees." [Citation.] As the legislative history of this provision reflects, it was intended itself to deter the oc-currence of occupational deaths and serious injuries by placing on employers a mandatory obligation independent of the specific health and safety standards to be promulgated by the Secretary. Since OSHA inspectors cannot be present around the clock in every workplace, the Secretary's regulation ensures that employees will in all circumstances enjoy the rights afforded them by the "general duty" clause.

The regulation thus on its face appears to further the overriding purpose of the Act, and rationally to complement its remedial scheme.

PROBLEMS

1. Gooddecade manufactures and sells automobile parts throughout the Eastern part of the United States. Among its full-time employees are 220 fourteen and fifteen year-olds. These teenagers are employed throughout the company and are paid at an hourly wage rate of $3.00 per hour. Discuss the legality of this arrangement.

2. Janet, a twenty year-old woman, applied for a position driving a truck for Federal Trucking, Inc. Janet, who is 5'4" tall and weighs 135 lbs., was denied the job because the company requires that all employees be at least 5'6" tall and weigh at least 150 lbs. Federal justified this requirement on the basis that its drivers frequently were forced to move heavy loads in order to make pick-ups and deliveries. Janet brings a cause of action. Decision?

3. N.I.S. promoted John, a forty-two year-old employee, to a foreman's position while passing over James, a 58-year-old employee. N.I.S. told James he was too old for the job and preferred a younger man. James brings a cause of action. Decision?

4. Anthony was employed as a forklift operator for Blackburn Construction Company. While on the job Anthony carelessly, and in direct violation of Blackburn's procedure manual, operated the forklift and caused himself severe injury. Blackburn now denies liability based on Anthony's (a) gross negligence, (b) disobedience of the procedural manual, and (c) written waiver of liability. Anthony now brings a cause of action. Decision?

5. Hazelwood School District is located in Sleepy Hollow Township. It is being sued by applicants who applied for teaching positions with the school but were rejected. The plaintiffs are all black and produce the following evidence:

(a) 1.8% of the Hazelwood School districts teachers are black whereas 15.4% of the teachers in Sleepy Hollow Township are black, and

(b) the hiring decisions by Hazelwood School District are based solely on subjective criteria.

6. T.W.E., a large manufacturer, prohibited its employees from distributing union leaflets to other employees while on the compnay's property. Richard, an employee of T.W.E., disregarded the prohibition and passed out the leaflets before his work shift began. T.W.E. discharged Richard for his actions. Has T.W.E. committed an unfair labor practice?

7. Erwick was dismissed from her job at the C&T Steel Company because she was "an unsatisfactory employee." At the time Erwick was active in an effort to organize a union at C&T. Is the dismissal valid?

8. Johnson, president of the First National Bank of A, believes that it is only appropriate to employ female tellers. Hence, First National refuses to employ Ken Baker as a teller but does make him an offer to be a maintenance man at the same salary. Baker brings a cause of action against First National Bank. Decision?

SECURITIES REGULATION

THE primary purpose of Federal securities regulation is to prevent fraudulent practices in the sale of securities and thereby maintain public confidence in the securities market. Federal securities law consists principally of two statutes: the Securities Act of 1933, which focuses on the issuance of securities, and the Securities Exchange Act of 1934, which deals mainly with trading in issued securities. Both Acts are administered by the Securities and Exchange Commission (SEC), an independent, quasi-judicial agency. The SEC is empowered to seek civil injunctions against violations of the Acts, to recommend that the Justice Department bring criminal prosecution and to issue orders suspending or expelling broker-dealers.

The 1933 Act has two basic objectives: (1) to provide investors with material information concerning securities offered for sale to the public; and (2) to prohibit misrepresentation, deceit, and other fraudulent acts and practices in the sale of securities generally, whether or not they are required to be registered.

The 1934 Act extends protection for investors to trading in securities that are already issued and outstanding. The 1934 Act also imposes disclosure requirements on publicly held corporations and regulates tender offers and proxy solicitations.

In addition to the Federal laws regulating the sale of securities, the States have their own laws regulating such sales within the State, commonly called "Blue-Sky" laws. These statutes all have provisions prohibiting fraud in the sale of securities. In addition, a number of States require the registration of securities while some States also regulate brokers and dealers.

Any person selling securities must comply with the Federal securities laws as well as those of each State in which he intends to offer his securities. Because of the diversity among the State securities laws, this chapter will discuss only the 1933 Act and the 1934 Act.

THE SECURITIES ACT OF 1933

The 1933 Act requires that a registration statement be filed with the Securities and Exchange Commission (SEC) and become effective before any securities may be offered for sale to the public, unless either the securities or the transaction in which they are offered is exempt from registration. The purpose of registration is to provide disclosure of financial and other information about the issuer and those in control of it, on the basis of which potential investors may appraise the merits of the securities. The Act provides that such investors must be furnished with a prospectus containing the important data set forth in the registration statement.

Regardless of whether the securities are exempt from the registration and disclosure requirements of the Act, the antifraud provisions of the Act apply to all sales of securities involving interstate commerce or the mails. Civil and criminal liability may be imposed for violations of the provisions of the Act.

Definition of a Security

Section 2(1) of the 1933 Act defines the term security to mean:

any note, stock, treasury stock, bond, debenture, evidence of indebtedness, certificate of interest or participation in any profit-sharing agreement, collateral-trust certificate, preorganization certificate or subscription, transferable share, investment contract, voting-trust certificate, certificate of deposit for a security, fractional undivided interest in oil, gas, or other mineral rights, any put, call, straddle, option, or privilege on any security * * * or, in general, any interest or instrument commonly known as a "security,"or any certificate of interest or participation in, temporary or in-

terim certificate for, receipt for, guarantee of, or warrant or right to subscribe to or purchase, any of the foregoing.

This definition expansively incorporates the numerous types of instruments that fall within the ordinary concept of a security. Nevertheless, even though a transaction is evidenced by an instrument labeled "stock," it may not be considered a security under the Securities Act. For example, the Supreme Court has held that shares of stock entitling a purchaser to lease an apartment in a State subsidized and supervised non-profit housing cooperative are not securities. *United Housing Foundation, Inc. v. Forman*, 421 U.S. 837, 95 S.Ct. 2051, 44 L.Ed.2d 621 (1975). Accordingly, the ultimate task of determining which of the numerous financial transactions constitutes a security has fallen to the SEC and the Federal courts.

The courts have generally interpreted the statutory definition so as to expand its coverage to non-traditional forms of investments. For the purpose of the securities laws, a security is an investment of money, property, or other valuable consideration made in expectation of receiving a financial return solely from the efforts of others. The basic test enunciated by the Supreme Court for determining the existence of a security involves three elements: (1) an investment in a common venture, (2) premised on a reasonable expectation of profit, (3) to be derived from the entrepreneurial or managerial efforts of others. *United Housing Foundation, Inc. v. Forman.* Under this test, such investments as the sale of limited partnership interests, citrus groves, whiskey warehouse receipts, real estate condominiums, cattle, franchises, and pyramid schemes have been held in certain circumstances to be securities. *See Securities and Exchange Commission v. W. J. Howey Co.*

Registration of Securities

The 1933 Act prohibits the offer or sale through the use of the mails or any means of interstate commerce of any security, unless a registration statement is in effect as to that security or an exemption from registration is secured. Section 5. The purpose of registration is to provide **disclosure** of financial and other information upon which investors may appraise the merits of the securities. Registration does not insure investors against loss, as the SEC does *not* pass on the financial merits of any security nor does it guarantee the accuracy of the facts presented in the registration statement.

In general, registration calls for disclosure of such information as (1) a description of the registrant's properties and business, (2) a description of the significant provisions of the security to be offered for sale and its relationship to the registrant's other capital securities, (3) information about the management of the registrant, and (4) financial statements certified by independent public accountants.

The registration statement and prospectus become public immediately on filing with the Commission, but it is unlawful to sell the securities until the effective date. However, after the filing of the registration statement, the securities may be offered orally or by certain summaries of the information in the registration statement as permitted by rules of the SEC. The effective date of a registration statement is the twentieth day after filing, although the Commission, at its discretion, may advance the effective date.

The SEC has acted to make permanent **Rule 415** governing "shelf registrations." **Shelf registrations** permit certain qualified issuers to register securities that are to be offered and sold "off the shelf" on a delayed or continuous basis in the future. This rule is a departure from the requirement that an issuer must file a registration for *every* new distribution of non-exempt securities. Rule 415 requires that the information in the original registration is kept accurate and current by updates. The use of shelf registrations allows an issuer to respond more quickly to market conditions such as changes in stock prices and interest rates. A company issuing securities for the first time does not qualify for shelf registrations.

Exempt Securities

The 1933 Act exempts a number of specific securities from the registration requirements of the Act. These exempt securities include (1) those sold under Regulation A, (2) those sold in intrastate transactions, and (3) those that are short-term commercial paper. Since these exemptions apply to the securities themselves, the securities may be resold without registration.

Regulation A This regulation permits an issuer to offer up to $1.5 million of securities in any twelve-month period without registering them provided that the issuer files a notification and an offering circular with the SEC's regional office prior to the sale of the securities. The circular must also be provided to offerees and purchasers. Regulation A filings are less detailed and time consuming than full registration statements, and the required financial statements are simpler and need not be audited. Because each purchaser must be supplied with an offering circular, securities sold under Regulation A may be freely traded after issuance.

Intrastate Issues The 1933 Act exempts from registration any security which is a part of an issue offered and sold *only* to persons resident within a single state where the issuer of such security is resident and doing business within such state. Section 3(a)(11). This exemption is intended to apply to issues local in character representing local financing by local persons and carried out through local investments. The exemption is inapplicable if merely one offeree, who need not be a purchaser, is not a resident of the State in which the issuer is resident.

Rule 147, promulgated by the SEC, provides a "non-exclusive safe harbor" for securing the intrastate exemption. Satisfying the rule assures the exemption, but there is no presumption that the exemption is not available for transactions which do not comply with the rule. Rule 147 requires that:

1. the issuer is incorporated or organized in the State in which the issuance occurs;
2. the issuer is principally doing business in that State, which means that 80 percent of its gross revenues must be derived from that State, 80 percent of its assets must be located in that State, and 80 percent of the net proceeds from the issue must be used in that State;
3. all of the *offerees* and purchasers are residents of that State;
4. during the period of sale and for nine months after the last sale, no resales to non-residents are made; and
5. precautions are taken against interstate distributions which include placing on the certificate evidencing the security a legend which states that the securities have not been registered and that resales can only be made to persons resident within the state as well as obtaining from each purchaser a written statement as to his residence.

Short-term Commercial Paper The Act exempts any note, draft, or bankers' acceptance issued for working capital which has a maturity at the time of issuance of not more than nine months. Section 3(a)(3). The exemption is not available if the proceeds are to be used for permanent purposes, such as the acquisition of a plant, or if the paper is sold in relatively small denominations to the public.

Other Exempt Securities Section 3 of the 1933 Act also exempts from registration the following types of securities:

1. Securities of domestic governments.
2. Securities of domestic banks and savings and loans associations.
3. Securities of not-for-profit, charitable organizations.
4. Securities of issuers where the issuance is regulated by the Interstate Commerce Commission.

5. Certificates issued by a receiver or trustee in bankruptcy with court approval.
6. Insurance policies and annuity contracts issued by regulated insurance companies.
7. Securities issued solely for exchange by the issuer with its existing security holders where no commission is paid.
8. Reorganization securities issued and exchanged with court or other governmental approval.

Exempt Transactions

In addition to the exemptions provided for specific types of securities, the 1933 Act also provides issuers with an exemption from the registration requirements for certain kinds of transactions. These transactions include (1) private placements, (2) limited offers not exceeding $5 million, (3) limited offers not exceeding $500,000, and (4) limited offers solely to accredited investors. These exemptions from registration apply only to the transaction in which the securities are issued and not to the securities themselves. Securities sold pursuant to these exemptions are considered **restricted securities** and may be resold only by registration or in another transaction exempt from registration.

An issuer utilizing these exemptions must take reasonable care to assure against nonexempt, unregistered resales of restricted securities. Reasonable care includes, but is not limited to, the following: (a) making a reasonable inquiry to determine if the purchaser is acquiring the securities for herself or for other persons; (b) providing written disclosure prior to the sale to each purchaser that the securities have not been registered and, therefore, cannot be resold unless they are registered or an exemption from registration is available; and (c) placing a legend on the securities certificate stating that the securities have not been registered and that they are restricted securities.

Private Placements The most important exemption for issuers wishing to raise money without registration is the so-called "private placement" provision of the Act (Section 4(2)) which exempts "transactions by an issuer not involving any public offering." **Rule 506** of the SEC establishes a non-exclusive, safe harbor for limited offers and sales without regard to the dollar amount of the offering. Securities sold under this exemption are restricted securities and may be resold only by registration or in a transaction exempt from registration. General advertising or general solicitation is not permitted. The issue may be purchased by an unlimited number of "accredited investors" and by no more than thirty-five other purchasers. The term **"accredited investor"** includes banks, insurance companies, investment companies, executive officers or directors of the issuer, any person who purchases at least $150,000 of the securities being offered so long as the total purchase price does not exceed 20 percent of the investor's net worth, any person whose net worth exceeds $1 million and any person with an income over $200,000 in each of the last two years and reasonably expects an income in excess of $200,000 in the current year. If the sale involves any non-accredited investors, *all* purchasers must be furnished prior to the sale with information material to an understanding of the issuer, its business, and the securities being offered; otherwise such information is not required to be disclosed. The issuer must reasonably believe that each purchaser who is not an accredited investor has such knowledge and experience in financial and business matters that he is capable of evaluating the merits and risks of the investment or has the services of a representative who has the requisite knowledge and experience to make such an evaluation. The issuer must take precautions against non-exempt, unregistered resales and must notify the SEC of sales made pursuant to the exemption.

Limited Offers Not Exceeding $5 Million

In order to facilitate small business capital formation, the SEC has promulgated **Rule 505** which exempts from registration offerings by non-investment company issuers that do not

exceed $5 million over twelve months. Securities sold under this exemption are restricted securities and may be resold only by registration or in a transaction exempt from registration. General advertising or general solicitation is not permitted. The issue may be purchased by an unlimited number of "accredited investors" and by no more than thirty-five other purchasers. If the sale involves any non-accredited investors, *all* purchasers must be furnished prior to the sale with information material to an understanding of the issuer, its business, and the securities being offered; otherwise, such information is not required to be disclosed. However, unlike Rule 506, the issuer is *not* required to believe reasonably that each non-accredited investor, either alone or with his representative, has such knowledge and experience in financial matters that he is capable of evaluating the merits and risks of the investment. The issuer must take precautions against non-exempt, unregistered resales and must notify the SEC of sales made pursuant to the exemption.

Limited Offers Not Exceeding $500,000

The SEC's **Rule 504** provides private, non-investment company issuers with an exemption from registration for small issues. The rule permits sales to an unlimited number of investors and does not require any information to be furnished to them. The exemption requires that:

1. the securities are offered and sold without general advertising;
2. the aggregate offering price within twelve months does not exceed $500,000;
3. the issuer takes precautions against non-exempt, unregistered resales; and
4. the issuer notifies the SEC of sales under the rule.

However, the limitations upon general advertising do not apply and unregistered resales are permitted if (1) the offering is made exclusively in States which provide for the registration of the securities and require the delivery of a disclosure document before sale, and (2) the securities are sold in compliance with those State provisions.

Limited Offers Solely to Accredited Investors In 1980 Congress added **Section 4(6)** which provides an exemption for offers and sales by an issuer made *solely* to accredited investors if not in excess of five million dollars. General advertising or public solicitation is not permitted. Like Rules 505 and 506, an unlimited number of accredited investors may purchase the issue; however, unlike these rules, *no* unaccredited investors may purchase at all. No information is required to be furnished to the purchasers. Securities sold under this exemption are restricted securities and may be resold only by registration or in a transaction exempt from registration. The issuer must take precautions against non-exempt, unregistered resales and must notify the SEC of sales made pursuant to the exemption.

Resales of Restricted Securities The transaction-based exemptions from registration do not necessarily exempt a subsequent transaction in the same securities. Rather, those who acquire securities under Rule 506, Rule 505, Rule 504, or Section 4(6) must register any resales or find an exemption from registration, subject to the limited exception provided for some issuances under Rule 504.

Rule 144 of the SEC sets forth conditions, which if met by any person selling restricted securities, exempts her from registering them. The rule requires that there must be adequate current public information with respect to the issuer, that the person selling under the rule must have owned the securities for at least two years, that she sell them only in limited amounts in unsolicited brokers' transactions, and that notice of the sale must be provided to the SEC. However, a person who is *not* an affiliate of the issuer at the time of sale of the restricted securities and has owned the securities for at least three years may sell them in unlimited amounts and is not subject to *any* of the other requirements of Rule 144.

Moreover, **Regulation A,** in addition to providing an exemption for issuers from registration for securities up to $1.5 million also provides an exemption of up to $300,000 in any twelve-month period for all investors with a $100,000 limit for any one investor. Use of this exemption requires compliance with all of the conditions imposed upon issuers by Regulation A, as discussed above.

Exemptions under the 1933 Act are summarized in Figure 44-1.

Liability

In order to implement the statutory objectives of providing full disclosure and preventing fraud in the sale of securities, the 1933 Act imposes a number of sanctions for non-compliance with its requirements. The sanctions include administrative remedies by the SEC, civil liability to injured investors, and criminal penalties.

Unregistered Sales The Act imposes civil liability for the sale of an unregistered security which is required to be registered, the sale of a registered security without delivery of a prospectus, the sale of a security by use of a non-current prospectus, or the offer of a sale prior to the filing of the registration statement. Section 12(1). Liability is absolute as there are no defenses. The person who purchases a security sold in violation of this provision of the Act has the right to tender it back to the seller and recover the purchase price. If the purchaser no longer owns the security, he may recover monetary damages from the seller.

False Registration Statements When securities have been sold subject to a registration statement, the Act imposes liability for the inclusion in the registration statement of any untrue statement or omission of material fact. Section 11. **Material** refers to those matters to which there is a substantial likelihood that a reasonable investor would attach importance in determining whether to purchase the security registered. SEC Rule 405. Liability is imposed upon (1) the issuer; (2) all

FIGURE 44–1   Exemptions under the 1933 Act

Exemption	Requirements	Result
Regulation A	1. Limited to $1.5 million of securities sold within 12 months 2. Proper notification and offering circular provided to SEC and offerees	Unrestricted resales
Intrastate sales Rule 147	1. Issuer incorporated or organized in that State 2. Issuer principally doing business within that State 3. All offerees and purchasers are residents of that State 4. No resale for 9 months to non-residents	Freely transferable to residents; transferable to non-residents after 9 months
Private placement Section 4(2) Rule 506	1. No dollar limitation 2. Unlimited number of accredited purchasers 3. No more than 35 unaccredited but "sophisticated" purchasers 4. If any unaccredited investors must disclose material information 5. Sold without advertising 6. Notify SEC of sale	Restricted security
Limited offers not exceeding $5 million Rule 505	1. Not exceed $5 million over 12 months 2. Unlimited number of accredited purchasers 3. No more than 35 unaccredited purchasers 4. If any unaccredited investors must disclose material information 5. Sold without advertising 6. Notify SEC of sale	Restricted security
Limited offers not exceeding $500,000 Rule 504	1. Not exceed $500,000 over 12 months 2. Sold without advertising 3. Notify SEC of sale	Restricted security
Limited offers solely to accredited investors Section 4(6)	1. Not exceed $5 million 2. Unlimited number of accredited purchasers 3. No unaccredited investors 4. No information required 5. Sold without advertising 6. Notify SEC of sale	Restricted security

persons who signed the registration statement; (3) every person who was a director or partner; (4) every accountant, engineer, appraiser, or expert who prepared or certified any part of the registration statement; and (5) all underwriters. These persons are jointly and severally liable to any person who acquires the security without knowledge of the untruth or omission for the amount paid for the security less either its value at the time of suit or the price for which it was sold.

However, an expert is only liable for misstatements or omissions in the portion of the registration that he prepared or certified. Moreover, any defendant, other than the issuer, may assert the affirmative defense of **due diligence.** This defense generally requires a showing that the defendant had reasonable grounds to believe that there were no untrue statements or material omissions. In some instances due diligence requires that a reasonable investigation be made. In determining what constitutes a reasonable investigation and reasonable ground for belief, the standard of reasonableness is that required of a prudent man in the management of his own property. Section 11(c). *See Escott v. BarChris Const. Corp.* SEC Rule 176 provides:

In determining whether or not the conduct of a person constitutes a reasonable investigation or a reasonable ground for belief meeting the standard set forth in section 11(c), relevant circumstances include, with respect to a person other than the issuer.

    (a) The type of issuer;
    (b) The type of security;
    (c) The type of person;
    (d) The office held when the person is an officer;
    (e) The presence or absence of another relationship to the issuer when the person is a director or proposed director;
    (f) Reasonable reliance on officers, employees, and others whose duties should have given them knowledge of the particular facts (in the light of the functions and responsibilities of the particular person with respect to the issuer and the filing);
    (g) When the person is an underwriter, the type of underwriting arrangement, the role of the particular person as an underwriter and the availability of information with respect to the registrant; and
    (h) Whether, with respect to a fact or document incorporated by reference, the particular person had any responsibility for the fact or document at the time of the filing from which it was incorporated.

Antifraud Provisions The Act also contains two broad anti-fraud provisions which apply to *all* securities, whether registered or exempt. The first, **Section 12(2),** imposes liability upon any person who offers or sells a security by means of a prospectus or oral communication which includes an untrue statement of material fact or an omission of a material fact. Liability extends only to the immediate purchaser provided she did not know of the untruth or omission. The seller may avoid liability by proving that he did not know, and in the exercise of reasonable care could not have known, of the untrue statement or omission. The seller is liable to the purchaser for the amount paid upon tender of the security. If the purchaser no longer owns the security, she may recover damages from the seller.

The second provision, **Section 17(a),** makes it unlawful for any person in the offer or sale of any securities by the use of any means of transportation or communication in interstate commerce or by the use of the mails, directly or indirectly—

1. to employ any device, scheme, or artifice to defraud, or
2. to obtain money or property by means of any untrue statement of a material fact or any omission to state a material fact necessary in order to make the statements made not misleading, or
3. to engage in any transaction, practice, or course of business that operates or would operate as a fraud or deceit upon the purchaser.

There is some doubt whether the courts may imply a private right of action for persons injured by violations of this section. The Supreme Court has reserved this question and the lower courts are divided on the issue. The SEC may, however, bring enforcement actions under Section 17(a).

Criminal Sanctions The 1933 Act imposes criminal sanctions upon any person who willfully violates any of the provisions of the Act or the rules and regulations promulgated by

FIGURE 44-2   Registration and Exemptions under the 1933 Act

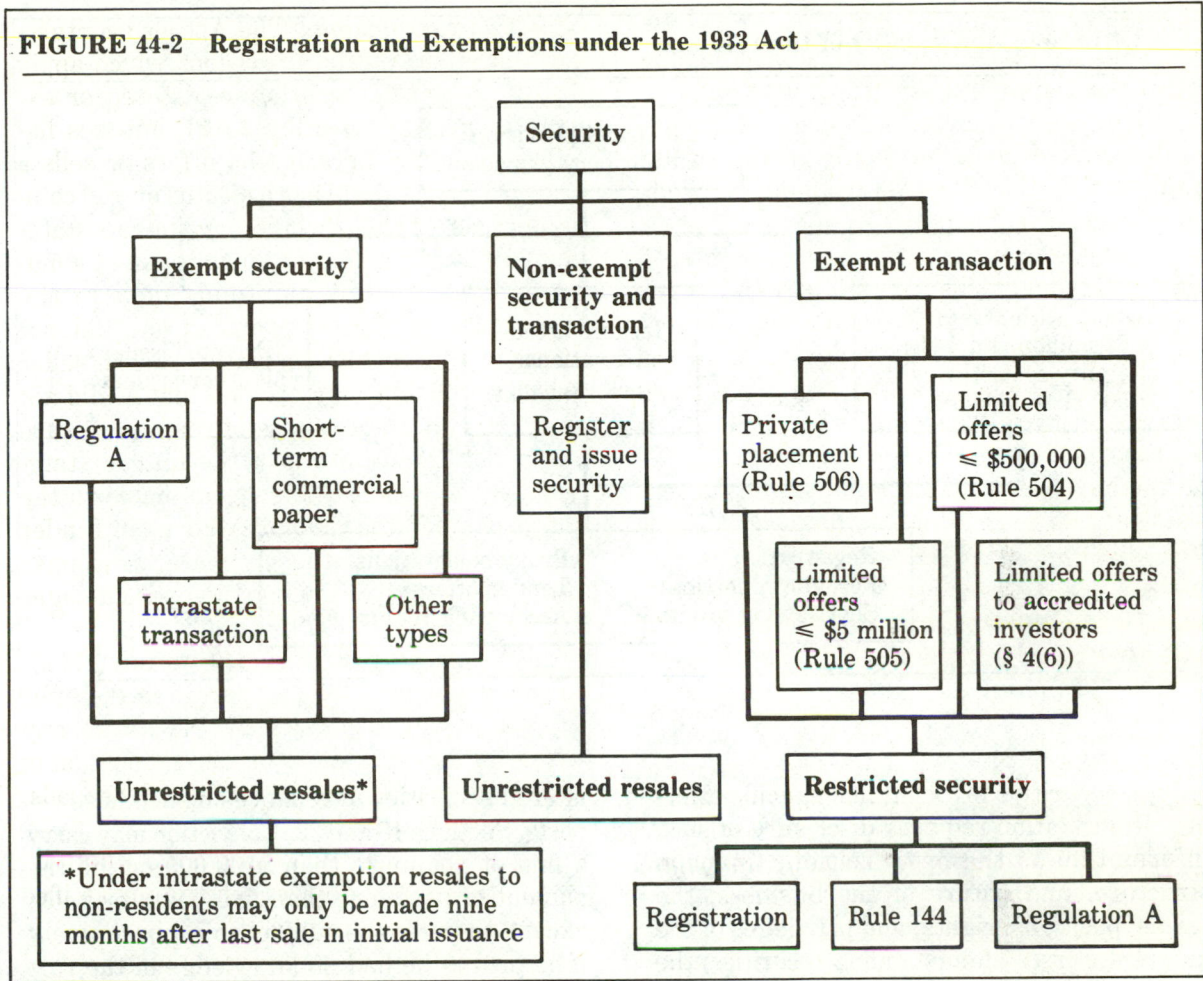

the SEC pursuant to the Act. Section 24. Conviction may carry a fine of not more than $10,000 or imprisonment of not more than five years or both.

THE SECURITIES EXCHANGE ACT OF 1934

The Securities Exchange Act of 1934 deals principally with the secondary distribution of securities. It provides protection for the holders of securities listed on national exchanges as well as equity securities of companies traded over the counter if their assets exceed $3 million and they have a class of equity securities with 500 or more shareholders. Companies must register such securities and are also subject to the Act's periodic reporting re-

quirements, the short swing profits provision, the tender offer provisions, the proxy solicitation provisions, and the internal control and record keeping requirements of the Foreign Corrupt Practices Act. In addition, issuers of securities, whether registered under the 1934 Act or not, must comply with the antifraud and the antibribery provisions of the Act. See Figure 44-3.

Registration and Periodic Reporting Requirements

The 1934 Act requires all regulated publicly held companies to register with the SEC. Section 12. These registrations are one-time registrations which apply to an entire class of securities and differ from registrations under the Securities Act of 1933 which relate

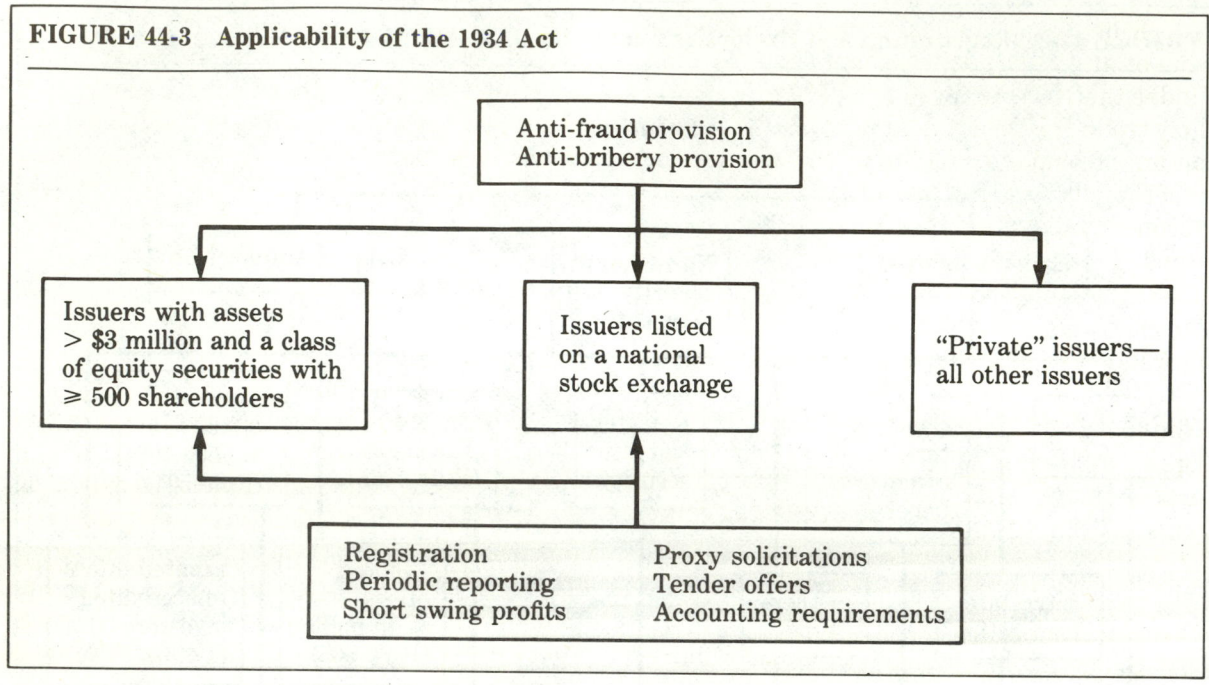

FIGURE 44-3   Applicability of the 1934 Act

Anti-fraud provision
Anti-bribery provision

Issuers with assets > $3 million and a class of equity securities with ≥ 500 shareholders

Issuers listed on a national stock exchange

"Private" issuers— all other issuers

Registration
Periodic reporting
Short swing profits

Proxy solicitations
Tender offers
Accounting requirements

only to securities involved in a specific offering. Registration requires disclosure of such information as the organization, financial structure, and nature of the business; the terms, positions, rights, and privileges of the different classes of outstanding securities; the names of the directors, officers, underwriters, and each security holder owning more than ten percent of any class of non-exempt equity security; bonus and profit-sharing arrangements; and balance sheets and profit and loss statements for the three preceding fiscal years. Following registration, an issuer must file specified annual and periodic reports to update the information contained in the original registration. The Act also requires that each director, officer and any person who owns ten percent or more of a registered equity security file with the SEC monthly reports stating any changes in his ownership of such equity securities.

The 1934 Act imposes penalties for filing false statements and reports with the SEC as well as providing liability to investors who suffer losses in the purchase or sale of reg-

istered securities in reliance on such false reports. Sections 18 and 32. Conviction may carry a fine of not more than $100,000 or imprisonment of not more than five years or both, except no person is subject to *imprisonment* if he proves he had no knowledge of the rule or regulation.

Antifraud Provision

Section 10(b) of the 1934 Act and SEC **Rule 10b-5** make it unlawful for any person by use of the mails or facilities of interstate commerce in connection with the purchase or sale of any security:

1. to employ any device, scheme, or artifice to defraud;
2. to make any untrue statement of a material fact;
3. to omit to state a material fact necessary in order to make the statements made not misleading; or
4. to engage in any act, practice, or course of business which operates or would operate as a fraud or deceit upon any person.

Rule 10b-5 applies to any purchase or sale of **any** security, whether it is registered under the 1934 Act or not, whether it is publicly traded or closely held, whether it is listed on an exchange or sold over the counter, or whether it is part of an initial issuance or a secondary distribution. There are **no** exemptions. Unlike the liability provisions of the 1933 Act, Rule 10b-5 applies to misconduct of purchasers as well as sellers and allows both defrauded sellers and buyers to recover.

Requisites of Rule 10b-5 Recovery of damages under Rule 10b-5 requires proof of several elements including (1) a misstatement or omission, (2) that is material, (3) made with *scienter*, and (4) relied upon (5) in connection with the purchase or sale of a security. Unlike common law fraud, the rule imposes an affirmative duty of disclosure. A misstatement or omission is **material** if there is a substantial likelihood that a reasonable investor would consider it important in deciding whether to purchase or sell the security. In an action for damages under Rule 10b-5, it must be shown that the violation was committed with **scienter,** which is intentional misconduct. Negligence is not sufficient.

Insider Trading Rule 10b-5 applies to sales or purchases of securities made by an "insider" who possesses material information which is non-public. An insider will be liable under Rule 10b-5 if he fails to disclose the material non-public information before trading on the information unless he waits until the information becomes public. **Insiders** for the purpose of Rule 10b-5 include directors, officers, employees, and agents of the issuer of the security as well as those with whom the issuer has entrusted information solely for corporate purposes, such as underwriters, accountants, lawyers, and consultants. In some instances, persons who receive material, non-public information from insiders—"**tippees**"—are also precluded from trading on that information. A tippee is under a duty not to trade on inside information when the insider has breached his fiduciary duty to the shareholders by disclosing the information to the tippee who knows or should know that there has been such a breach. *See Securities and Exchange Comm'n v. Texas Gulf Sulphur Co. and Dirks v. Securities and Exchange Commission.*

Short Swing Profits

Section 16(b) of the 1934 Act imposes liability upon insiders—directors, officers, and any person owning 10 percent or more of the stock of the corporation which is listed upon a national stock exchange or registered with the SEC—for all profits resulting from their "short swing" trading in such stock. If any of the above described "insiders" sells such stock within six months from the date of its purchase or purchases such stock within six months from the date of a sale of the stock, the corporation is entitled to recover any and all profit realized by the insider from such transactions. The "profit" recoverable is calculated by matching the highest sale price against the lowest purchase price within six months of each other. Losses cannot be offset against profits.

Section 16(b) states:

For the purpose of preventing the unfair use of information which may have been obtained by such beneficial owner, director, or officer by reason of his relationship to the issuer, any profit realized by him from any purchase and sale, or any sale and purchase, of any equity security of such issuer (other than an exempted security) within any period of less than six months, unless such security was acquired in good faith in connection with a debt previously contracted, shall inure to and be recoverable by the issuer, irrespective of any intention on the part of such beneficial owner, director, or officer in entering into such transaction of holding the security purchased or of not repurchasing the security sold for a period exceeding six months. Suit to recover such profit may be instituted at law or in equity in any court of competent jurisdiction by the issuer, or by the owner of any security of the issuer in the name and in behalf of the issuer if the issuer shall fail or refuse to bring such suit within sixty days after request or shall fail diligently to prosecute the same thereafter; but no such suit shall be brought more than two years after the date such profit was realized. This subsection shall not be construed to cover any transaction where such beneficial owner was not such both at the time of the purchase and sale, or the sale and purchase, of the security involved, or any transactions or transactions which the Commission by rules and regulations may exempt as not comprehended within the purpose of this subsection.

Although both Section 16(b) and Rule 10b-5 address the problem of "insider trading" and both may apply to the same transaction, they differ in a number of respects. First, Section 16(b) only applies to transactions involving registered equity securities while Rule 10b-5 applies to all securities. Second, the term "insider" is much broader under Rule 10b-5 and may extend beyond directors, officers, and ten percent owners whereas Section 16(b) is limited to these persons. Third, Section 16(b) does *not* require that the insider possess material non-public information; Rule 10b-5 only applies to insider trading where such information is not disclosed. Fourth, Section 16(b) only applies to transactions within six months of each other; Rule 10b-5 has no such limitation. Finally, under Rule 10b-5 injured investors may recover damages on their own behalf while under Section 16(b), although shareholders may bring suit, any recovery is on behalf of the corporation.

Insider Trading Sanctions Act

In addition to the remedies discussed above, the SEC is authorized by the Insider Trading Sanctions Act of 1984 to bring an action in a U.S. district court to have a civil penalty imposed upon any person who purchases or sells a security while in possession of material non-public information. Liability also extends to any person who aids and abets a violation by such person. The transaction must be on or through the facilities of a national securities exchange or from or through a broker or dealer. Purchases which are part of a public offering by an issuer of securities are not subject to this provision. The amount of the civil penalty is determined by the court in light of the facts and circumstances, but may not exceed three times the profit gained or loss avoided as a result of the unlawful purchase or sale. The penalty is payable into the Treasury of the United States. For the purpose of this provision, "profit gained" or "loss avoided" is "the difference between the purchase or sale price of the security and the value of that security as measured by the trading price of the security a reasonable period after public dissemination of the non-public information." Section 21(2)(C). An action must be brought within five years after the date of the purchase or sale.

Proxy Solicitations

A proxy is a writing signed by a shareholder of a corporation authorizing a named person to vote his shares of stock at a specified meeting of the shareholders. The 1934 Act makes it unlawful for any person to solicit any proxy with respect to any registered security "in contravention of such rules and regulations as the Commission may prescribe." Section 14. The rules of the SEC require the issuer to furnish security holders with a *proxy statement* describing all material facts concerning the matters being submitted to their vote together with a *proxy form* on which the security holders can indicate their approval or disapproval of each proposal to be presented. Even if a company does not solicit proxies from its shareholders but submits a matter to a shareholder vote, it must provide them with information substantially equivalent to that which would appear in a proxy statement.

Where management makes a solicitation, any security holder entitled to vote has the opportunity to communicate with other security holders. Upon written request, the corporation must mail the communication or, at its option, promptly furnish to that security holder a current list of security holders.

If an eligible security holder entitled to vote timely submits a proposal for action at a forthcoming meeting, management must include the proposal in its proxy statement and provide security holders with an opportunity to vote for or against it. To be eligible, the holder must own at least one percent or $1,000 in market value of the security for at least one year prior to submitting the proposal. If management opposes the proposal, it must include in its proxy materials a supporting statement by the security holder. The aggregate length of the proposal and the supporting statement is limited to a total of 500 words. A security holder is limited to submitting one proposal to an issuer each year.

Management may omit a proposal if, among other things, it (1) is under State law not a proper subject for shareholder action, (2) is not significantly related to the business of the issuer or is beyond the issuer's power to effectuate, or (3) relates to the conduct of the ordinary business operations of the issuer.

An issuer who distributes a false or misleading proxy statement to its security holders may be liable to any person who suffers a loss caused by purchasing or selling a security in reliance upon the statement.

Tender Offers

In 1968 Congress amended the 1934 Act to extend reporting and disclosure requirements to tender offers and other block acquisitions. A tender offer is a general invitation to all of the shareholders of a company to purchase their shares at a specified price.

The Act requires any person or group that acquires, or makes a tender offer that would result in the acquisition of, more than **5 percent** of a class of registered equity securities to file with the SEC a statement containing (1) the person's background; (2) the source of the funds used to acquire the securities; (3) the purpose of the acquisition; (4) the number of shares owned; and (5) any relevant contracts, arrangements, or under-

standings. Sections 13(d) and 14(d). A copy of the statement must be furnished to each offeree and sent to the issuer. It is unlawful for any person to make any untrue statement of material fact or omit to state any material fact or to engage in any fraudulent, deceptive, or manipulative practices in connection with any tender offer. Section 14(e).

Shareholders who tender their shares may withdraw them during the first seven days of a tender offer and, if the offeror has not yet purchased their shares, at any time after sixty days from the commencement of the offer. Moreover, all shares tendered must be purchased for the same price; if an offering price is increased, those who have already tendered receive the benefit of the increase. A tender offeror who offers to purchase less than all of the outstanding securities of the target must accept on a *pro rata* basis securities tendered during the offer.

Foreign Corrupt Practices Act

In 1977 Congress enacted the Foreign Corrupt Practices Act as an amendment to the 1934 Act. The Act imposes internal control requirements upon companies with securities registered under the 1934 Act and prohibits all domestic concerns from bribing foreign governmental or political officials.

Accounting Requirements The Act requires every issuer which has a class of registered securities to:

1. make and keep books which, in reasonable detail, accurately and fairly reflect the transactions and disposition of the assets of the issuer, and
2. devise and maintain internal controls to assure that transactions are executed as authorized and recorded in conformity with generally accepted accounting principles so as to provide accountability for assets and that access to assets is permitted only in accordance with management's authorization. Section 13(b).

Antibribery Provisions The Foreign Corrupt Practices Act makes it unlawful for *any* domestic concern or any of its officers, directors, employees, or agents to offer or give directly or indirectly anything of value to any foreign official, political party, or political official for the purpose of (1) influencing any act or decision of such person or party in his or its official capacity, or (2) inducing such person or party to use his or its influence to affect a decision of a foreign government in order to assist such domestic concern in obtaining or retaining business. Section 30A of the 1934 Act. An offer or promise to make a prohibited payment is a violation even if the offer is not accepted or the promise is not performed. Violations can result in fines of up to $1 million for companies; individuals may be fined a maximum of $10,000 and imprisoned up to five years or both. Section 32(c). Fines imposed upon individuals may not be paid directly or indirectly by the issuer.

CASES

Definition of a Security

SECURITIES AND EXCHANGE COMMISSION v. W. J. HOWEY CO.

Supreme Court of the United States, 1946.
328 U.S. 293, 66 S.Ct. 1100, 90 L.Ed. 1244.

MURPHY, J.

This case involves the application of § 2(1) of the Securities Act of 1933 to an offering of units of a citrus grove development coupled with a contract for cultivating, marketing and remitting the net proceeds to the investor.

The Securities and Exchange Commission instituted this action to restrain the respondents from using the mails and instrumentalities of interstate commerce in the offer and sale of unregistered and non-exempt securities in violation of § 5(a) of the Act. The District Court denied the injunction, * * * and the Fifth Circuit Court of Appeals affirmed the judgment * * *.

* * *

Most of the facts are stipulated. The respondents, W. J. Howey Company and Howey-in-the-Hills Service, Inc., are Florida corporations under direct common control and management. The Howey Company owns large tracts of citrus acreage in Lake County, Florida. During the past several years it has planted about 500 acres annually, keeping half of the groves itself and offering the other half to the public "to help us finance additional development." Howey-in-the-Hills Service, Inc., is a service company engaged in cultivating and developing many of these groves, including the harvesting and marketing of the crops.

Each prospective customer is offered both a land sales contract and a service contract, after having been told that it is not feasible to invest in a grove unless service arrangements are made. While the purchaser is free to make arrangements with other service companies, the superiority of Howey-in-the-Hills Service, Inc., is stressed. Indeed, 85% of the acreage sold during the 3-year period ending May 31, 1943, was covered by service contracts with Howey-in-the-Hills Service, Inc.

The land sales contract with the Howey Company provides for a uniform purchase price per acre or fraction thereof, varying in amount only in accordance with the number of years the particular plot has been planted with citrus trees. Upon full payment of the purchase price the land is conveyed to the purchaser by warranty deed. Purchases are usually made in narrow strips of land arranged so that an acre consists of a row of 48 trees. During the period between February 1, 1941, and May 31, 1943, 31 of the 42 persons making purchases bought less than 5 acres each. The average holding of these 31 persons was 1.33 acres and sales of as little as 0.65, 0.7 and

0.73 of an acre were made. These tracts are not separately fenced and the sole indication of several ownership is found in small land marks intelligible only through a plat book record.

The service contract, generally of a 10-year duration without option of cancellation, gives Howey-in-the-Hills Service, Inc., a leasehold interest and "full and complete" possession of the acreage. For a specified fee plus the cost of labor and materials, the company is given full discretion and authority over the cultivation of the groves and the harvest and marketing of the crops. The company is well established in the citrus business and maintains a large force of skilled personnel and a great deal of equipment, including 75 tractors, sprayer wagons, fertilizer trucks and the like. Without the consent of the company, the land owner or purchaser has no right of entry to market the crop; thus there is ordinarily no right to specific fruit. The company is accountable only for an allocation of the net profits based upon a check made at the time of picking. All the produce is pooled by the respondent companies, which do business under their own names.

The purchasers for the most part are non-residents of Florida. They are predominantly business and professional people who lack the knowledge, skill and equipment necessary for the care and cultivation of citrus trees. They are attracted by the expectation of substantial profits.

*   *   *

Section 2(1) of the Act defines the term "security" to include the commonly known documents traded for speculation or investment. This definition also includes "securities" of a more variable character, designated by such descriptive terms as "certificate of interest or participation in any profit-sharing agreement," "investment contract" and "in general, any interest or instrument commonly known as a 'security.' " The legal issue in this case turns upon a determination of whether, under the circumstances, the land sales contract, the warranty deed and the service contract together constitute an "investment contract" within the meaning of § 2(1). An affirmative answer brings into operation the registration requirements of § 5(a), unless the security is granted an exemption under § 3(b). *   *   *

The term "investment contract" is undefined by the Securities Act or by relevant legislative reports. But the term was common in many state "blue sky" laws in existence prior to the adoption of the federal statute *   *   *.

By including an investment contract within the scope of § 2(1) of the Securities Act, Congress was using a term the meaning of which had been crystallized by this prior judicial interpretation. It is therefore reasonable to attach that meaning to the term as used by Congress, especially since such a definition is consistent with the statutory aims. In other words, an investment contract for purposes of the Securities Act means a contract, transaction or scheme whereby a person invests his money in a common enterprise and is led to expect profits solely from the efforts of the promoter or a third party, it being immaterial whether the shares in the enterprise are evidenced by formal certificates or by nominal interests in the physical assets employed in the enterprise. Such a definition *   *   * permits the fulfillment of the statutory purpose of compelling full and fair disclosure relative to the issuance of "the many types of instruments that in our commercial world fall within the ordinary concept of a security." [Citation.] It embodies a flexible rather than a static principle, one that is capable of adaptation to meet the countless and variable schemes devised by those who seek the use of the money of others on the promise of profits.

The transactions in this case clearly involve investment contracts as so defined. The respondent companies are offering something more than fee simple interests in land, something different from a farm or orchard coupled with management services. They are offering an opportunity to contribute money and to share in the profits of a large citrus fruit enterprise managed and partly owned by respondents. They are offering this opportunity to persons who reside in distant localities and who lack the equipment and experience requisite to the cultivation, harvesting and marketing of the citrus products. Such persons have no desire to occupy the land or to develop it themselves; they are attracted solely by the prospects of a return on their investment. Indeed, individual development of the plots of land that are offered and sold would seldom be economically feasible due to their small size. Such tracts gain utility as citrus groves only when cultivated and developed as component parts of a larger area. A common enterprise managed by respondents or third parties with adequate personnel and equipment is therefore essential if the investors are to achieve their paramount aim of a return on their investments. Their respective shares in this enterprise are evidenced by land sales contracts and warranty deeds, which serve as a convenient method of determining the investors' allocable shares of the profits. The resulting transfer of rights in land is purely incidental.

Thus all the elements of a profit-seeking business venture are present here. The investors provide the capital and share in the earnings and profits; the promoters manage, control and operate the enterprise. It follows that the arrangements whereby the investors' interests are made manifest involve investment contracts, regardless of the legal terminology in which such contracts are clothed. The investment contracts in this instance take the form of land sales contracts, warranty deeds and service contracts which respondents offer to prospective investors. And respondents' failure to abide by the statutory and administrative rules in making such offerings, even though the failure result from a bona fide mistake as to the law, cannot be sanctioned under the Act.

This conclusion is unaffected by the fact that some purchasers choose not to accept the full offer of an investment contract by declining to enter into a service contract with the respondents. The Securities Act prohibits the offer as well as the sale of unregistered, nonexempt securities. Hence it is enough that the respondents merely offer the essential ingredients of an investment contract.

* * *

Reversed.

Liability for False Registration Statements

ESCOTT v. BARCHRIS CONSTRUCTION CORP.

United States District Court, Southern District of New York, 1968.
283 F.Supp. 643.

McLean, J.

This is an action by purchasers of 5½ per cent convertible subordinated fifteen year debentures of BarChris Construction Corporation (BarChris). * * *

The action is brought under Section 11 of the Securities Act of 1933. Plaintiffs allege that the registration statement with respect to these debentures filed with the Securities and Exchange Commission, which became effective on May 16, 1961, contained material false statements and material omissions.

Defendants fall into three categories: (1) the persons who signed the registration statement; (2) the underwriters, consisting of eight investment banking firms, led by Drexel & Co. (Drexel); and (3) BarChris's auditors, Peat, Marwick, Mitchell & Co. (Peat, Marwick).

The signers, in addition to BarChris itself, were the nine directors of BarChris, plus its controller, defendant Trilling, who was not a director. Of the nine directors, five were officers of BarChris, *i.e.*, defendants Vitolo, president; Russo, executive vice president; Pugliese, vice president; Kircher, treasurer; and Birnbaum, secretary. Of the remaining four, defendant Grant was a member of the firm of Perkins, Daniels, McCormack & Collins, BarChris' attorneys. He became a director on April 17, 1961, as did the other two,

Auslander and Rose, who were not otherwise connected with BarChris.

Defendants, in addition to denying that the registration statement was false, have pleaded the defense open to them under Section 11 of the Act, * * *. On the main issue of liability, the questions to be decided are (1) did the registration statement contain false statements of fact, or did it omit to state facts which should have been stated in order to prevent it from being misleading; (2) if so, were the facts which were falsely stated or omitted "material" within the meaning of the Act; (3) if so, have defendants established their affirmative defenses?

* * *

In December 1959, BarChris sold 560,000 shares of common stock to the public at $3.00 per share. This issue was underwritten by Peter Morgan & Company, one of the present defendants.

By early 1961, BarChris needed additional working capital. The proceeds of the sale of the debentures involved in this action were to be devoted, in part at least, to fill that need.

The registration statement of the debentures, in preliminary form, was filed with the Securities and Exchange Commission on March 30, 1961. A first amendment was filed on May 11 and a second on May 16. The registration statement became effective on May 16. The closing of the financing took place on May 24. On that day BarChris received the net proceeds of the financing.

By that time BarChris was experiencing difficulties in collecting amounts due from some of its customers. Some of them were in arrears in payments due to factors on their discounted notes. As time went on those difficulties increased. Although BarChris continued to build [bowling] alleys in 1961 and 1962, it became increasingly apparent that the industry was overbuilt. Operators of alleys, often inadequately financed, began to fail. Precisely when the tide turned is a matter of dispute, but at any rate, it was painfully apparent in 1962.

In May of that year BarChris made an abortive attempt to raise more money by the sale of common stock. It filed with the Securities and Exchange Commission a registration statement for the stock issue which it later withdrew. In October 1962 BarChris came to the end of the road. On October 29, 1962, it filed in this court a petition for an arrangement under Chapter XI of the Bankruptcy Act.

[The court found that the registration statement contained material false statements.]

* * *

The "Due Diligence" Defenses

Section 11(b) of the Act provides that:

"* * * no person, other than the issuer, shall be liable * * * who shall sustain the burden of proof—

* * *

"(3) that (A) as regards any part of the registration statement not purporting to be made on the authority of an expert * * * he had, after reasonable investigation, reasonable ground to believe and did believe, at the time such part of the registration statement became effective, that the statements therein were true and that there was no omission to state a material fact required to be stated therein or necessary to make the statements therein not misleading; * * * and (C) as regards any part of the registration statement purporting to be made on the authority of an expert (other than himself) * * * he had no reasonable ground to believe and did not believe, at the time such part of the registration statement became effective, that the statements therein were untrue or that there was an omission to state a material fact required to be stated therein or necessary to make the statements therein not misleading. * * *"

Section 11(c) defines "reasonable investigation" as follows:

In determining, for the purposes of paragraph (3) of subsection (b) of this section, what constitutes reasonable investigation and reasonable ground for belief, the standard of reasonableness shall be that required of a prudent man in the management of his own property.

Every defendant, except BarChris itself, to whom, as the issuer, these defenses are not available, and except Peat, Marwick, whose position rests on a different statutory provision, has pleaded these affirmative defenses. Each claims that (1) as to the part of the registration statement purporting to be made on the authority of an expert (which, for convenience, I shall refer to as the "expertised portion"), he had no reasonable ground to believe and did not believe that there were any untrue statements or material omissions, and (2) as to the other parts of the registration statement, he made a reasonable investigation, as a result of which he had reasonable ground to believe and did believe that the registration statement was true and that no material fact was omitted. As to each defendant, the question is whether he has sustained the burden of proving these defenses. Surprising enough, there is little or no judicial authority on this question. No decisions directly in point under Section 11 have been found.

Before considering the evidence, a preliminary matter should be disposed of. The defendants do not agree among themselves as to who the "experts" were or as to the parts of the registration statement which were expertised.

* * *

* * * Neither the lawyer for the company nor the lawyer for the underwriters is an expert within the meaning of Section 11. The only expert, in the statutory sense, was Peat, Marwick, and the only parts of the registration statement which purported to be made upon the authority of an expert were the portions which purported to be made on Peat, Marwick's authority.

* * *

I turn now to the question of whether defendants have proved their due diligence defenses. The position of each defendant will be separately considered.

* * *

Kircher

Kircher was treasurer of BarChris and its chief financial officer. He is a certified public accountant and an intelligent man. He was thoroughly familiar with BarChris's financial affairs. * * *

Moreover, as a member of the executive committee, Kircher was kept informed as to those branches of the business of which he did not have direct charge.

* * *

Knowing the facts, Kircher had reason to believe that the expertised portion of the prospectus, *i.e.*, the 1960 figures, was in part incorrect. He could not shut his eyes to the facts and rely on Peat, Marwick for that portion.

As to the rest of the prospectus, knowing the facts, he did not have a reasonable ground to believe it to be true. On the contrary, he must have known that in part it was untrue. Under these circumstances, he was not entitled to sit back and place the blame on the lawyers for not advising him about it.

Kircher has not proved his due diligence defenses.

* * *

Birnbaum

Birnbaum was a young lawyer, admitted to the bar in 1957, who, after brief periods of employment by two different law firms and an equally brief period of practicing in his own firm, was employed by BarChris as house counsel and assistant secretary in October 1960. Unfortunately for him, he became secretary and a director of BarChris on April 17, 1961, after the first version of the registration statement had been filed with the Securities and Exchange Commission. He signed the later amendments, thereby becoming responsible for the accuracy of the prospectus in its final form.

Although the prospectus, in its description of "management," lists Birnbaum among the "executive officers" and devotes several sentences to a recital of his career, the fact seems to be that he was not an executive officer in any real sense. He did not participate in the management of the company. As house counsel, he attended to legal matters of a routine nature.

* * *

One of Birnbaums' more important duties, first as assistant secretary and later as fullfledged secretary, was to keep the corporate minutes of BarChris and its subsidiaries. This necessarily informed him to a considerable extent about the company's affairs.
* * *

It seems probable that Birnbaum did not know of many of the inaccuracies in the prospectus. He must, however, have appreciated some of them. In any case, he made no investigation and relied on the others to get it right. * * * As a lawyer, he should have known his obligations under the statute. He should have known that he was required to make a reasonable investigation of the truth of all the statements in the unexpertised portion of the document which he signed. Having failed to make such an investigation, he did not have reasonable ground to believe that all these statements were true. Birnbaum has not established his due diligence defenses except as to the audited 1960 figures.

Auslander

Auslander was an "outside" director, *i.e.*, one who was not an officer of BarChris. He was chairman of the board of Valley Stream National Bank * * *.

* * *

In considering Auslander's due diligence defenses, a distinction is to be drawn between the expertised and non-expertised portions of the prospectus. As to the former, Auslander knew that Peat, Marwick had audited the 1960 figures. He believed them to be correct because he had confidence in Peat, Marwick. He

had no reasonable ground to believe otherwise.

As to the non-expertised portions, however, Auslander is in a different position. He seems to have been under the impression that Peat, Marwick was responsible for all the figures. This impression was not correct, as he would have realized if he had read the prospectus carefully. Auslander made no investigation of the accuracy of the prospectus.
* * *

It is true that Auslander became a director on the eve of the financing. He had little opportunity to familiarize himself with the company's affairs. The question is whether, under such circumstances, Auslander did enough to establish his due diligence defense with respect to the nonexpertised portions of the prospectus.

* * *

Section 11 imposes liability in the first instance upon a director, no matter how new he is. He is presumed to know his responsibility when he becomes a director. He can escape liability only by using that reasonable care to investigate the facts which a prudent man would employ in the management of his own property. In my opinion, a prudent man would not act in an important matter without any knowledge of the relevant facts, in sole reliance upon representations of persons who are comparative strangers and upon general information which does not purport to cover the particular case. To say that such minimal conduct measures up to the statutory standard would to all intents and purposes, absolve new directors from responsibility merely because they are new. This is not a sensible construction of Section 11, when one bears in mind its fundamental purpose of requiring full and truthful disclosures for the protection of investors.

* * *

Grant

Grant became a director BarChris in October 1960. His law firm was counsel to BarChris in matters pertaining to the registration of securities. Grant drafted the registration statement for the stock issue in 1959 and for the warrants in January 1961. He also drafted the registration statement for the debentures. In the preliminary division of work between him and Ballard, the underwriters' counsel, Grant took initial responsibility for preparing the registration statement, while Ballard devoted his efforts in the first instance to preparing the indenture.

Grant is sued as a director and as a signer of the registration statement. This is not an action against him for malpractice in his capacity as a lawyer. Nevertheless, in considering Grant's due diligence defenses, the unique position which he occupied cannot be disregarded. As the director most directly concerned with writing the registration statement and assuring its accuracy, more was required of him in the way of reasonable investigation than could fairly be expected of a director who had no connection with this work.

*   *   *

Grant was entitled to rely on Peat, Marwick for the 1960 figures. He had no reasonable ground to believe them to be inaccurate. But the matters which *   *   * were not within the expertised portion of the prospectus *   *   * Grant was obliged to make a reasonable investigation. I am forced to find that he did not make one. *   *   *

The Underwriters

The underwriters other than Drexel made no investigation of the accuracy of the prospectus. *   *   * They all relied upon Drexel as the "lead" underwriter.

Drexel did make an investigation. The work was in charge of Coleman, a partner of the firm, assisted by Casperson, an associate. Drexel's attorneys acted as attorneys for the entire group of underwriters. Ballard did the work, assisted by Stanton.

*   *   *

The underwriters say that the prospectus is the company's prospectus, not theirs.

Doubtless this is the way they customarily regard it. But the Securities Act makes no such distinction. The underwriters are just as responsible as the company if the prospectus is false. And prospective investors rely upon the reputation of the underwriters in deciding whether to purchase the securities.

*   *   *

The purpose of Section 11 is to protect investors. To that end the underwriters are made responsible for the truth of the prospectus. If they may escape that responsibility by taking at face value representations made to them by the company's management, then the inclusion of underwriters among those liable under Section 11 affords the investors no additional protection. To effectuate the statute's purpose, the phrase "reasonable investigation" must be construed to require more effort on the part of the underwriters than the mere accurate reporting in the prospectus of "data presented" to them by the company. It should make no difference that this data is elicited by questions addressed to the company officers by the underwriters, or that the underwriters at the time believe that the company's officers are truthful and reliable. In order to make the underwriters' participation in this enterprise of any value to the investors, the underwriters must make some reasonable attempt to verify the data submitted to them. They may not rely solely on the company's officers or on the company's counsel. A prudent man in the management of his own property would not rely on them.

It is impossible to lay down a rigid rule suitable for every case defining the extent to which such verification must go. It is a question of degree, a matter of judgment in each case. In the present case, the underwriters' counsel made almost no attempt to verify management's representations. I hold that that was insufficient.

On the evidence in this case, I find that the underwriters' counsel did not make a reasonable investigation of the truth of those portions of the prospectus which were not made on the authority of Peat, Marwick as an expert. Drexel is bound by their failure. It is not a matter of relying upon counsel for legal advice. Here the attorneys were dealing with matters of fact. Drexel delegated to them, as its agent, the business of examining the corporate minutes and contracts. It must bear the consequences of their failure to make an adequate examination.

The other underwriters, who did nothing and relied solely on Drexel and on the lawyers, are also bound by it. It follows that although Drexel and the other underwriters believed that those portions of the prospectus were true, they had no reasonable ground for that belief, within the meaning of the statute. Hence, they have not established their due diligence defense, except as to the 1960 audited figures.

[The decision with respect to the auditors Peat, Marwick is presented in the next chapter.]

*   *   *

Defendants' motions to dismiss this action, upon which decision was reserved at the trial, are denied. *   *   *

Pursuant to Rule 52(a), this opinion constitutes the court's findings of fact and conclusions of law with respect to the issues determined herein.

So ordered.

Insider Trading

SECURITIES AND EXCHANGE COMMISSION v. TEXAS GULF SULPHUR CO.

United States Court of Appeals, Second Circuit, 1968.
401 F.2d 833, *cert. denied* 394 U.S. 976, 89 S.Ct. 1454, 22 L.Ed.2d 756 (1969).

WATERMAN, J.

This action was commenced in the United States District Court for the Southern District of New York by the Securities and Exchange Commission (the SEC) pursuant to Sec. 21(e) of the Securities Exchange Act of 1934 (the Act) against Texas Gulf Sulphur Company (TGS) and several of its officers,

directors and employees, to enjoin certain conduct by TGS and the individual defendants said to violate Section 10(b) of the Act and Rule 10b–5 (the Rule), promulgated thereunder, and to compel the rescission by the individual defendants of securities transactions assertedly conducted contrary to law. The complaint alleged (1) that defendants Fogarty, Mollison, Darke, Murray, Huntington, O'Neill, Clayton, Crawford, and Coates had either personally or through agents purchased TGS stock or calls thereon from November 12, 1963 through April 16, 1964 on the basis of material inside information concerning the results of TGS drilling in Timmins, Ontario, while such information remained undisclosed to the investing public generally or to the particular sellers; (2) that defendants Darke and Coates had divulged such information to others for use in purchasing TGS stock or calls or recommended its purchase while the information was undisclosed to the public or to the sellers; (3) that defendants Stephens, Fogarty, Mollison, Holyk, and Kline had accepted options to purchase TGS stock on February 20, 1964, without disclosing the material information as to the drilling progress to either the Stock Option Committee or the TGS Board of Directors; and (4) that TGS issued a deceptive press release on April 12, 1964. The case was tried at length before Judge Bonsal of the Southern District of New York, sitting without a jury. Judge Bonsal in a detailed opinion decided, *inter alia*, that the insider activity prior to April 9, 1964 was not illegal because the drilling results were not "material" until then; that Clayton and Crawford had traded in violation of law because they traded after that date; that Coates had committed no violation as he did not trade before disclosure was made; and that the issuance of the press release was not unlawful because it was not issued for the purpose of benefiting the corporation, there was no evidence that any insider used the release to his personal advantage and it was not "misleading, or deceptive on the basis of the facts then known." Defendants Clayton and Crawford appeal from that part of the decision below which held that they had violated Sec. 10(b) and Rule 10b–5 and the SEC appeals from the remainder of the decision which dismissed the complaint against defendants TGS, Fogarty, Mollison, Holyk, Darke, Stephens, Kline, Murray, and Coates.

* * *

The Factual Setting

This action derives from the exploratory activities of TGS begun in 1957 on the Canadian Shield in eastern Canada.

* * *

On October 29 and 30, 1963, Clayton conducted a ground geophysical survey on the northeast portion of the Kidd 55 segment which confirmed the presence of an anomaly and indicated the necessity of diamond core drilling for further evaluation. Drilling of the initial hole, K–1, at the strongest part of the anomaly was commenced on November 8 and terminated on November 12 at a depth of 655 feet. Visual estimates by Holyk of the core of K–55–1 indicated an average copper content of 1.15% and an average zinc content of 8.64% over a length of 599 feet. This visual estimate convinced TGS that it was desirable to acquire the remainder of the Kidd 55 segment, and in order to facilitate this acquisition TGS President Stephens instructed the exploration group to keep the results of K–55–1 confidential and undisclosed even as to other officers, directors, and employees of TGS. The hole was concealed and a barren core was intentionally drilled off the anomaly. Meanwhile, the core of K–55–1 had been shipped to Utah for chemical assay which, when received in early December, revealed an average mineral content of 1.18% copper, 8.26% zinc, and 3.94% ounces of silver per ton over a length of 602 feet. These results were so remarkable that neither Clayton, an experienced geophysicist, nor four other TGS expert witnesses, had ever seen or heard of a comparable initial exploratory drill hole in a base metal deposit. So, the trial court concluded, "There is no doubt that the drill core of K–55–1 was unusually good and that it excited the interest and speculation of those who knew about it." By March 27, 1964, TGS decided that the land acquisition program had advanced to such a point that the company might well resume drilling, and drilling was resumed on March 31.

During this period, from November 12, 1963 when K–55–1 was completed, to March 31, 1964 when drilling was resumed, certain of the individual defendants * * * and persons * * * said to have received "tips" from them, purchased TGS stock or calls thereon. Prior to these transactions these persons had owned 1135 shares of TGS stock and possessed no calls; thereafter they owned a total of 8235 shares and possessed 12,300 calls.

On February 20, 1964, also during this period, TGS issued stock options to 26 of its officers and employees whose salaries exceeded a specified amount, five of whom were the individual defendants Stephens, Fogarty, Mollison, Holyk, and Kline. Of these, only Kline was unaware of the detailed results of K–55–1, but he, too, knew that a hole containing favorable bodies of copper and zinc ore had been drilled in Timmins. At this time, neither the TGS Stock Option Committee nor its Board of Directors had been informed of the results of K–55–1, presumably because of the pending land acquisition program which required confidentiality. All of the foregoing defendants accepted the options granted them.

* * *

Meanwhile, rumors that a major ore strike was in the making had been circulating throughout Canada. On the morning of Saturday, April 11, Stephens at his home in Greenwich, Conn. read in the New York Herald Tribune and in the New York Times unauthorized reports of the TGS drilling which seemed to infer a rich strike from the fact that the drill cores had been flown to the United States for chemical assay. * * * With the aid of one Carroll, a public relations consultant, Fogarty drafted a press release designed to quell the rumors which release, after having been channeled through Stephens and Huntington, a TGS attorney, was issued at 3:00 P.M. on Sunday, April 12, and which appeared in the morning newspapers of general circulation on Monday, April 13. It read in pertinent part as follows:

NEW YORK, April 12—The following statement was made today by Dr. Charles F. Fogarty, executive vice president of Texas Gulf Sulphur Company, in regard to the company's drilling operations near Timmins, Ontario, Canada. Dr. Fogarty said:

During the past few days, the exploration activities of Texas Gulf Sulphur in the area of Timmins, Ontario, have been widely reported in the press, coupled with rumors of a substantial copper discovery there. These reports exaggerate the scale of operations, and mention plans and statistics of size and grade of ore that are without factual basis and have evidently originated by speculation of people not connected with TGS.

The facts are as follows: TGS has been exploring in the Timmins area for six years as part of its overall search in Canada and elsewhere for various minerals—lead, copper, zinc, etc. During the course of this work, in Timmins as well as in Eastern Canada, TGS has conducted exploration entirely on its own, without the participation by others. Numerous prospects have been investigated by geophysical means and a large number of selected ones have been core-drilled. These cores are sent to the United States for assay and detailed examination as a matter of routine and on advice of expert Canadian legal counsel. No inferences as to grade can be drawn from this procedure.

Most of the areas drilled in Eastern Canada have revealed either barren pyrite or graphite without value; a few have resulted in discoveries of small or marginal sulphide ore bodies.

Recent drilling on one property near Timmins has led to preliminary indications that more drilling would be required for proper evaluation of this prospect. The drilling done to date has not been conclusive, but the statements made by many outside quarters are unreliable and include information and figures that are not available to TGS.

The work done to date has not been sufficient to reach definite conclusions and any statement as to size and grade of ore would be premature and possibly misleading. When we have progressed to the point where reasonable and logical conclusions can be made, TGS will issue a definite statement to its stockholders and to the public in order to clarify the Timmins project.

*   *   *

The release purported to give the Timmins drilling results as of the release date, April 12. From Mollison Fogarty had been told of the developments through 7:00 P.M. on April 10, and of the remarkable discoveries made up to that time, detailed supra, which discoveries, according to the calculations of the experts who testified for the SEC at the hearing, demonstrated that TGS had already discovered 6.2 to 8.3 million tons of proven ore having gross assay values from $26 to $29 per ton. TGS experts, on the other hand, denied at the hearing that proven or probable ore could have been calculated on April 11 or 12 because there was then no assurance of continuity in the mineralized zone.

The evidence as to the effect of this release on the investing public was equivocal and less than abundant. *   *   * The trial court stated only that "While, in retrospect, the press release may appear gloomy or incomplete, this does not make it misleading or deceptive on the basis of the facts then known."

*   *   *

While drilling activity ensued to completion, TGS officials were taking steps toward ultimate disclosure of the discovery. On April 13, a previously-invited reporter for The Northern Miner, a Canadian mining industry journal, visited the drillsite, interviewed Mollison, Holyk and Darke, and prepared an article which confirmed a 10 million ton ore strike. This report, after having been submitted to Mollison and returned to the reporter unamended on April 15, was published in the April 16 issue. A statement relative to the extent of the discovery, in substantial part drafted by Mollison, was given to the Ontario Minister of Mines for release to the Canadian media. Mollison and Holyk expected it to be released over the airways at 11 P.M. on April

15th, but, for undisclosed reasons, it was not released until 9:40 A.M. on the 16th. An official detailed statement, announcing a strike of at least 25 million tons of ore, based on the drilling data set forth above, was read to representatives of American financial media from 10:00 A.M. to 10:10 or 10:15 A.M. on April 16, and appeared over Merrill Lynch's private wire at 10:29 A.M. and, somewhat later than expected, over the Dow Jones ticker tape at 10:54 A.M.

Between the time the first press release was issued on April 12 and the dissemination of the TGS official announcement on the morning of April 16, the only defendants before us on appeal who engaged in market activity were Clayton and Crawford and TGS director Coates.

* * *

During the period of drilling in Timmins, the market price of TGS stock fluctuated but steadily gained overall. On Friday, November 8, when the drilling began, the stock closed at 17⅜; on Friday, November 15, after K–55–1 had been completed, it closed at 18. After a slight decline to 16⅜ by Friday, November 22, the price rose to 20⅞ by December 13, when the chemical assay results of K–55–1 were received, and closed at a high of 24⅛ on February 21, the day after the stock options had been issued. It had reached a price of 26 by March 31, after the land acquisition program had been completed and drilling had been resumed, and continued to ascend to 30⅛ by the close of trading on April 10, at which time the drilling progress up to then was evaluated for the April 12th press release. On April 13, the day on which the April 12 release was disseminated, TGS opened at 30⅛, rose immediately to a high of 32 and gradually tapered off to close at 30⅞. It closed at 30¼ the next day, and at 29⅜ on April 15. On April 16, the day of the official announcement of the Timmins discovery, the price climbed to a high of 37 and closed at 36⅜. By May 15, TGS stock was selling at 58¼.

The Individual Defendants

* * *

Rule 10b–5 was promulgated pursuant to the grant of authority given the SEC by Congress in Section 10(b) of the Securities Exchange Act of 1934. By that Act Congress purposed to prevent inequitable and unfair practices and to insure fairness in securities transactions generally, whether conducted face-to-face, over the counter, or on exchanges. The Act and the Rule apply to the transactions here, all of which were consummated on exchanges. Whether predicated on traditional fiduciary concepts or on the "special facts" doctrine . . . the Rule is based in policy on the justifiable expectation of the securities marketplace that all investors trading on impersonal exchanges have relatively equal access to material information. The essence of the Rule is that anyone who, trading for his own account in the securities of a corporation has "access, directly or indirectly, to information intended to be available only for a corporate purpose and not for the personal benefit of anyone" may not take "advantage of such information knowing it is unavailable to those with whom he is dealing," i.e., the investing public. Insiders, as directors or management officers are, of course, by this Rule, precluded from so unfairly dealing, but the Rule is also applicable to one possessing the information who may not be strictly termed an "insider" within the meaning of Sec. 16(b) of the Act. Thus, anyone in possession of material inside information must either disclose it to the investing public, or, if he is disabled from disclosing it in order to protect a corporate confidence, or he chooses not to do so, must abstain from trading in or recommending the securities concerned while such inside information remains undisclosed. So, it is here no justification for insider activity that disclosure was forbidden by the legitimate corporate objective of acquiring options to purchase the land surrounding the exploration site; if the information was, as the SEC contends, material, its possessors should have kept out of the market until disclosure was accomplished.

Material Inside Information. An insider is not, of course, always foreclosed from investing in his own company merely because he may be more familiar with company operations than are outside investors. An insider's duty to disclose information or his duty to abstain from dealing in his company's securities arises only in "those situations which are essentially extraordinary in nature and which are reasonably certain to have a substantial effect on the market price of the security if [the extraordinary situation is] disclosed."

Nor is an insider obligated to confer upon outside investors the benefit of his superior financial or other expert analysis by disclosing his educated guesses or predictions. The only regulatory objective is that access to material information be enjoyed equally, but this objective requires nothing more than the disclosure of basic facts so that outsiders may draw upon their own evaluative expertise in reaching their own investment decisions with knowledge equal to that of the insiders.

* * * As we stated in List v. Fashion Park, Inc., "The basic test of materiality * * * is whether a *reasonable* man would attach importance * * * in determining his choice of action in the transaction in question. (Emphasis supplied.) This, of course, encompasses any fact " * * * which in reasonable and objective contemplation *might* affect the value of the corporation's stock or securities * * *." [Citation.] Such a fact is a material fact and must be effectively disclosed to the investing public prior to the commencement of insider trading in the corporation's securities. The speculators and chartists of Wall and Bay Streets are also "reasonable" investors entitled to the same legal protection afforded conservative traders. Thus, material facts include not only information disclosing the earnings and distributions of a company but also those facts which affect the probable future of the company and those which may affect the desire of investors to buy, sell, or hold the company's securities.

In each case, then, whether facts are material within Rule 10b–5 when the facts relate to a particular event and are undisclosed by those persons who are knowledgeable thereof will depend at any given time upon a balancing of both the indicated probability that the event will occur and the anticipated magnitude of the event in light of the totality of the company activity. Here, * * * knowledge of the possibility, which surely was more than marginal, of the existence of a mine of the vast magnitude indicated by the remarkably rich drill core located rather close to the surface (suggesting mineability by the less expensive open-pit method) within the confines of a large anomaly (suggesting an extensive region of mineralization) might well have affected the price of TGS stock and would certainly have been an important fact to a reasonable, if speculative, investor in deciding whether he should buy, sell, or hold. After all, this first drill core was "unusually good and * * * excited the interest and speculation of those who knew about it."

* * *

When May Insiders Act?

* * *

Before insiders may act upon material information, such information must have been effectively disclosed in a manner sufficient to insure its availability to the investing public. Particularly here, where a formal announcement to the entire financial news media had been promised in a prior official release known to the media, all insider activity must await dissemination of the promised official announcement.

* * *

The Corporate Defendant

At 3:00 P.M. on April 12, 1964, evidently believing it desirable to comment upon the rumors concerning the Timmins project, TGS issued the press release . . . The SEC argued below and maintains on this appeal that this release painted a misleading and deceptive picture of the drilling progress at the time of its issuance, and hence violated Rule 10b-5(2).

* * *

* * * Congress intended to protect the investing public in connection with their purchases or sales on Exchanges from being misled by misleading statements promulgated for or on behalf of corporations irrespective of whether the insiders contemporaneously trade in the securities of that corporation and irrespective of whether the corporation or its management have an ulterior purpose or purposes in making an official public release. Indeed, the Commission has been charged by Congress with the responsibility of policing all misleading corporate statements from those contained in an initial prospectus to those contained in a notice to stockholders relative to the need or desirability of terminating the existence of a corporation or of merging it with another. To render the Congressional purpose ineffective by inserting into the statutory words the need of proving, not only that the public may have been misled by the release, but also that those responsible were actuated by a wrongful purpose when they issued the release, is to handicap unreasonably the Commission in its work. * * *

As was pointed out by the trial court, the intent of the Securities Exchange Act of 1934 is the protection of investors against fraud. Therefore, it would seem elementary that the Commission has a duty to police management so as to prevent corporate practices which are reasonably likely fraudulently to injure investors. And, of course, as we have already emphasized, a corporation's misleading material statement may injure an investor irrespective of whether the corporation itself, or those individuals managing it, are contemporaneously buying or selling the stock of the corporation. Therefore, when materially misleading corporate statements or deceptive

insider activities have been uncovered, the courts, as they should, have broadly construed the statutory phrase "in connection with the purchase or sale of any security." The court below found: "There is no evidence that TGS derived any direct benefit from the issuance of the press release or that any of the defendants who participated in its preparation used it to their personal advantage." The requirement that a statement may not be found misleading unless its issuance is actuated by a "wrongful purpose" might well have the effect of permitting the issuers of misleading statements to seek an advantage but to escape liability if the advantage fails to materialize to the degree contemplated, or cannot be demonstrated.

* * *

We conclude, then, that having established that the release was issued in a manner reasonably calculated to affect the market price of TGS stock and to influence the investing public, we must remand to the district court to decide whether the release was misleading to the reasonable investor and if found to be misleading, whether the court in its discretion should issue the injunction the SEC seeks.

Insider Trading

DIRKS v. SECURITIES AND EXCHANGE COMMISSION

Supreme Court of the United States, 1983.
— U.S. —, 103 S.Ct. 3255, 77 L.Ed.2d 911.

POWELL, J.

Petitioner Raymond Dirks received material nonpublic information from "insiders" of a corporation with which he had no connection. He disclosed this information to investors who relied on it in trading in the shares of the corporation. The question is whether Dirks violated the antifraud provisions of the federal securities laws by this disclosure.

I

In 1973, Dirks was an officer of a New York broker-dealer firm who specialized in providing investment analysis of insurance company securities to institutional investors. On March 6, Dirks received information from Ronald Secrist, a former officer of Equity Funding of America. Secrist alleged that the assets of Equity Funding, a diversified corporation primarily engaged in selling life insurance and mutual funds, were vastly overstated as the result of fraudulent corporate practices. Secrist also stated that various regulatory agencies had failed to act on similar charges made by Equity Funding employees. He urged Dirks to verify the fraud and disclose it publicly.

Dirks decided to investigate the allegations. He visited Equity Funding's headquarters in Los Angeles and interviewed several officers and employees of the corporation. The senior management denied any wrongdoing, but certain corporation employees corroborated the charges of fraud. Neither Dirks nor his firm owned or traded any Equity Funding stock, but throughout his investigation he openly discussed the information he had obtained with a number of clients and investors. Some of these persons sold their holdings of Equity Funding securities, including five investment advisers who liquidated holdings of more than $16 million.

While Dirks was in Los Angeles, he was in touch regularly with William Blundell, the *Wall Street Journal's* Los Angeles bureau chief. Dirks urged Blundell to write a story on the fraud allegations. Blundell did not believe, however that such a massive fraud could go undetected and declined to write the story. He feared that publishing such damaging hearsay might be libelous.

During the two-week period in which Dirks pursued his investigation and spread word of Secrist's charges, the price of Equity Funding stock fell from $26 per share to less than $15 per share. This led the New York Stock Exchange to halt trading on March 27. Shortly thereafter California insurance authorities impounded Equity Funding's records and uncovered evidence of the fraud. Only then did the Securities and Exchange Commission (SEC) file a complaint against Equity Funding and only then, on April 2, did the *Wall Street Journal* publish a front-page story based largely on information assembled by Dirks. Equity Funding immediately went into receivership.

The SEC began an investigation into Dirks' role in the exposure of the fraud. After a hearing by an administrative law judge, the SEC found that Dirks had aided and abetted violations of § 17(a) of the Securities Act of 1933, [citation], § 10(b) of the Securities Exchange Act of 1934, [citation], and SEC Rule 10b–5, [citation], by repeating the allegations of fraud to members of the investment community who later sold their Equity Funding stock. The SEC concluded: "Where 'tippees'—regardless of their motivation or occupation—come into possession of material 'information that they know is confidential and know or should know came from a corporate insider,' they must either publicly disclose that information or refrain from trading." [Citation.] Recognizing, however, that Dirks "played an important role in bringing (Equity Funding's) massive fraud to light," [citation] the SEC only censured him.

Dirks sought review in the Court of Appeals for the District of Columbia Circuit. The court entered judgment against Dirks * * *

* * *

In the seminal case of In re Cady, Roberts & Co., [citation], the SEC recognized that the common law in some jurisdictions imposes on "corporate 'insiders,' particularly officers, directors, or controlling stockholders" an "affirmative duty of disclosure * * * when dealing in securities." [Citation.] The SEC found that not only did breach of this common-law duty also establish the elements of a Rule 10b-5 violation, but that individuals other than corporate insiders could be obligated either to disclose material nonpublic information before trading or to abstain from trading altogether. [Citation.] In *Chiarella*, e accepted the two elements set out in *Cady, Roberts* for establishing a Rule 10b-5 violation: "(i) the existence of a relationship affording access to inside information intended to be available only for a corporate purpose, and (ii) the unfairness of allowing a corporate insider to take advantage of that information by trading without disclosure." [Citation.] In examining whether Chiarella had an obligation to disclose or abstain, the Court found that there is no general duty to disclose before trading on material nonpublic information, and held that "a duty to disclose under § 10(b) does not arise from the mere possession of nonpublic market information." [Citation.] Such a duty arises rather from the existence of a fiduciary relationship. [Citation.]

Not "all breaches of fiduciary duty in connection with a securities transaction," however, come within the ambit of Rule 10b-5. [Citation.] There must also be "manipulation or deception." [Citation.] In an inside-trading case this fraud derives from the "inherent unfairness involved where one takes advantage" of "information intended to be available only for a corporate purpose and not for the personal benefit of anyone." [Citation.] Thus, an insider will be liable under Rule 10b-5 for inside trading only where he fails to disclose material nonpublic information before trading on it and thus makes "secret profits." *Cady, Roberts,* [citation.]

We were explicit in *Chiarella* in saying that there can be no duty to disclose where the person who has traded on inside information "was not (the corporation's) agent, * * * was not a fiduciary, (or) was not a person in whom the sellers (of the securities) had placed their trust and confidence." [Citation.] Not to require such a fiduciary relationship, we recognized, would "depar[t] radically from the established doctrine that duty arises from a specific relationship between two parties" and would amount to "recognizing a general duty between all participants in market transactions to forgo actions based on material, nonpublic information." [Citation.] This requirement of a specific relationship between the shareholders and the individual trading on inside information has created an-

alytical difficulties for the SEC and courts in policing tippees who trade on inside information. Unlike insiders who have independent fiduciary duties to both the corporation and its shareholders, the typical tippee has no such relationships. In view of this absence, it has been unclear how a tippee acquires the *Cady, Roberts* duty to refrain from trading on inside information.

* * *

In effect, the SEC's theory of tippee liability . . . appears rooted in the idea that the antifraud provisions require equal information among all traders. This conflicts with the principle set forth in *Chiarella* that only some persons, under some circumstances, will be barred from trading while in possession of material nonpublic information. Judge Wright correctly read our opinion in *Chiarella* as repudiating any notion that all traders must enjoy equal information before trading: "[T]he 'information' theory is rejected. Because the disclose-or-refrain duty is extraordinary, it attaches only when a party has legal obligations other than a mere duty to comply with the general antifraud proscriptions in the federal securities laws." [Citation.] We reaffirm today that "[a] duty (to disclose) arises from the relationship between parties * * * and not merely from one's ability to acquire information because of his position in the market." [Citation.]

Imposing a duty to disclose or abstain solely because a person knowingly receives material nonpublic information from an insider and trades on it could have an inhibiting influence on the role of market analysts, which the SEC itself recognizes is necessary to the preservation of a healthy market. It is commonplace for analysis to "ferret out and analyze information," and this often is done by meeting with and questioning corporate officers and others who are insiders. And information that the analysts obtain normally may be the basis for judgments as to the market worth of a corporation's securities. The analyst's judgment in this respect is made available in market letters or otherwise to clients of the firm. It is the nature of this type of information, and indeed of the markets themselves, that such information cannot be made simultaneously available to all of the corporation's stockholders or the public generally.

The conclusion that recipients of inside information do not invariably acquire a duty to disclose or abstain does not mean that such tippees always are free to trade on the information. The need for a ban on some tippee trading is clear. Not only are insiders forbidden by their fiduciary relationship from personally using undisclosed corporate information to their advantage, but they may not give such information to an outsider for the same improper purpose of exploiting the information for their personal gain. * * *

Thus, some tippees must asssume an insider's duty to the shareholders not because they receive inside information, but rather because it has been made available to them *improperly.* * * * Thus, a tippee assumes a fiduciary duty to the shareholders of a corporation not to trade on material nonpublic information only when the insider has breached his fiduciary duty to the shareholders by disclosing the information to the tippee and the tippee knows or should know that there has been a breach. * * *

* * * Whether disclosure is a breach of duty therefore depends in large part on the purpose of the disclosure. This standard was identified by the SEC itself in *Cady, Roberts*: a purpose of the securities laws was to eliminate "use of inside information for personal advantage." [Citation.] Thus, the test is whether the insider personally will benefit, directly or indirectly, from his disclosure. Absent some personal gain, there has been no breach of duty to stockholders. And absent a breach by the insider, there is no derivative breach.

* * *

Under the inside-trading and tipping rules set forth above, we find that there was no actionable violation by Dirks. It is undisputed that Dirks himself was a stranger to Equity Funding, with no pre-existing fiduciary duty to its shareholders. He took no action, directly or indirectly, that induced the shareholders or officers of Equity Funding to repose trust or confidence in him. There was no expectation by Dirks' sources that he would keep their information in confidence. Nor did Dirks misappropriate or illegally obtain the information about Equity Funding. Unless the insiders breached their *Cady, Roberts* duty to shareholders in disclosing the nonpublic information to Dirks, he breached no duty when he passed it on to investors * * *.

It is clear that neither Secrist nor the other Equity Funding employees violated their *Cady, Roberts* duty to the corporation's shareholders by providing information to Dirks. The tippers received no monetary or personal benefit for revealing Equity Funding's secrets, nor was their purpose to make a gift of valuable information to Dirks. As the facts of this case clearly indicate, the tippers were motivated by a desire to expose the fraud. In the absence of a breach of duty to shareholders by the insiders, there was no derivative breach by Dirks. * * *

We conclude that Dirks, in the circumstances of this case, had no duty to abstain from use of the inside information that he obtained. The judgment of the Court of Appeals therefore is

Reversed.

PROBLEMS

1. Acme Realty, a real estate development company, is a limited partnership organized in Georgia. It is planning to develop a 200-acre parcel of land for a regional shopping center and needs to raise $1,250,000. As part of its financing, Acme plans to offer $1,250,000 worth of limited partnership interests to about 100 prospective investors in the southeastern United States. It anticipates that about forty to fifty private investors will purchase the limited partnership interests.

(a) Must Acme register this offering? Why or why not?

(b) If Acme must register but fails to do so, what are the legal consequences?

2. Bigelow Corporation has total assets of $850,000, sales of $1,350,000, one class of common stock with 375 shareholders, and a class of preferred stock with 250 shareholders, both of which are traded over-the-counter. Which provisions of the Securities Exchange Act of 1934 apply to Bigelow Corporation?

3. Capricorn, Inc., is planning to "go public" by offering its common stock which had been previously owned by only three shareholders. The company intends to limit the number of purchasers to twenty-five persons resident in the State of its incorporation. All of Capricorn's business and all of its assets are located in the State of incorporation. Based upon these facts, what exemptions from registration, if any, are available to Capricorn, and what conditions would each of these available exemptions impose upon the terms of the offer?

4. The boards of directors of DuMont Corp. and Epsot, Inc., agreed to enter into a friendly merger with DuMont Corp. to be the surviving entity. The stock of both corporations was listed on a national stock exchange. In connection with the merger both corporations distributed to their shareholders proxy statements seeking approval of the proposed merger. The shareholders of both corporations voted to approve the merger. About three weeks after the merger was consummated, the price of DuMont Corp. stock fell from $25 to $13 as a result of the discovery that Epsot, Inc., had entered into several unprofitable long term contracts two months before the merger had been proposed. The contracts will result in substantial losses from Epsot's operations for at least the next four years. The existence and effect of these contracts, although known to both corporations at the time of the proposed merger, were not disclosed in the proxy statements of either corporation. Shareholders of DuMont Corp. bring suit against DuMont Corp. under the 1934 Act. Decision?

5. Farthing is a director and vice-president of Garp, Inc., whose common stock is listed on the New York Stock Exchange. Farthing engaged in the following transactions in 1985: on January 1, Farthing sold 500 shares at thirty dollars per share; on January 15 she purchased 300 shares at thirty dollars per share; on February 1, she purchased 200 shares at forty-five dollars per share; on March 1, she purchased 300 shares at sixty dollars per share; on March 15 she sold 200 shares at fifty-five dollars per share; on April 1, she sold 100 shares at forty dollars per share. Howell brings suit on behalf of Garp alleging that Farthing has violated the Securities Exchange Act of 1934. Farthing defends on the ground that she lost money on the transactions in question. Decision?

6. Intercontinental Widgets, Inc., had applied for a patent for a new state-of-the-art widget which, if patented, would increase significantly the value of Intercontinental's shares. On September 1 the Patent Office notified Jackson, attorney for Intercontinental, that the patent application had been approved. After informing Kingsley, the president of Intercontinental, of the good news, Jackson called his broker and purchased 1,000 shares of Intercontinental at eighteen dollars per share. He also told his partner, Lucas, who immediately proceeded to purchase 500 shares at nineteen dollars per share. Lucas then called his brother-in-law, Mammon, and told him the news. On September 3 Mammon bought 4,000 shares at twenty-one dollars per share. On September 4 Kingsley issued a press release which accurately reported that a patent had been granted to Intercontinental. On the next day Intercontinental's stock soared to thirty-eight dollars per share. A class action suit is brought against Jackson, Lucas, Mammon, and Intercontinental for violations of Rule 10b-5. Who, if anyone, is liable?

7. Nova, Inc., sought to sell a new issue of common stock. It registered the issue with the Securities and Exchange Commission but included false information in both the registration statement and the prospectus. The issue was underwritten by Omega & Sons and was sold in its entirety by Periwinkle, Rameses, and Sheffield, Inc., a securities broker-dealer. Telford purchased 500 shares at six dollars per share. Three months later the falsity of the information contained in the prospectus was made public and the price of the shares fell to one dollar per share. The following week

Telford brought suit under the Securities Act of 1933.

   (a) Who is liable, if anyone, under the Act?

   (b) What defenses, if any, are available to the various defendants?

8. T, a director and officer of Deep Hole Oil Company, approached R for the purpose of buying 200 shares of Deep Hole Company stock owned by R. During the period of negotiations, T concealed his identity and did not disclose the fact that earlier in the day he had received a report of two rich oil "strikes" on the oil company's property. R sold his 200 shares to T for ten dollars per share. Taking into consideration the new strikes, the fair value of the stock was approximately twenty dollars per share. R sues T to recover damages. Decision?

9. Venable Corporation has 750,000 shares of common stock outstanding which is owned by 640 shareholders. The assets of Venable Corporation are valued at over $5 million dollars. In March, Underhill began purchasing shares of Venable's common stock in the open market. By April he had acquired 40,000 shares at prices ranging from $12 to $14. Upon discovering Underhill's activities in late April, the directors of Venable had the corporation purchase the 40,000 shares from Underhill for $18 per share. Which provisions of the 1934 Act, if any, have been violated?

Chapter 45

ACCOUNTANTS' LEGAL LIABILITY

ACCOUNTANTS perform a number of important roles in our business society. One of them is providing reliable financial information to facilitate the effective and efficient allocation of resources in the economy. As Harold M. Williams, former Chairman of the Securities and Exchange Commission, stated: "Obviously, if users of financial data, who often may have little or no contact with the business in question, could not trust in its financial statements, capital formation and lending could not be carried on as they are today."

An accountant is subject to potential civil liability arising from the professional services he provides to his clients and third parties. This legal liability is imposed by both the common law at the State level as well as the Federal securities laws. In addition, an accountant may violate Federal or State criminal law in connection with the performance of his professional activities. This chapter will deal with accountants' legal liability under both State and Federal law.

COMMON LAW

An accountant's legal responsibility under State law may be predicated upon (1) contract law, (2) tort law, or (3) criminal law. In addition, the common law provides accountants with certain rights and privileges; in particular, ownership of their working papers and, in some States, a limited accountant-client privilege.

Contract Liability

The employment contract between the accountant and her client is subject to the general principles of contract law. All of the requisites of a common law contract must be present for the contract to be binding, including: offer and acceptance, capacity, consideration, legality, and a writing if, as is often the case, the agreement falls within the one-year provision of the Statute of Frauds.

Upon entering into a binding contract the accountant is bound to perform all the duties she **explicitly** agrees to render under the contract. For example, if an accountant agrees to complete her audit of the client by October 15 to enable the client to release its annual report on time, the accountant is under a contractual obligation to so perform. Likewise, if an accountant contractually promises to conduct an audit for the client so as to detect possible defalcations, the accountant is under a contractual obligation to audit the client *beyond* Generally Accepted Auditing Standards (GAAS) and must conduct an expanded audit.

By entering into a contract an accountant also **implicitly** agrees to perform the contract in a competent and professional manner. By agreeing to render professional services, an accountant is held to those standards which are generally accepted by the accounting profession.

If an accountant breaches his contract he will incur liability not only to his client but also to certain third party beneficiaries. A **third party beneficiary** is a non-contracting party whom the contracting parties *intended* to receive the *primary* benefit under the contract. For example, X Manufacturing Co. hires A, an accountant, to prepare X's financial statement for X to use in order to obtain a loan from Chemical Bank. Chemical is a third party beneficiary of the contract between X and A.

Pursuant to general contract principles, an accountant will not be entitled to any compensation if he *materially breaches* his contract. Thus, if an accountant does not perform his audit on time when time is of the essence, or the accountant completes only sixty percent of the audit, he has materially breached the contract. On the other hand, if the accountant *substantially performs* his contractual duties he is generally entitled to be com-pensated for the contractually agreed upon fee less any damages or loss his non-material breach has caused the client.

Tort Liability

An accountant in performing his professional services may incur tort liability to his client or third parties for negligence or fraud. A tort, as discussed in Chapters 5 and 6, is a private or civil wrong or injury, other than a breach of contract, for which the courts will provide a remedy in the form of an action for damages.

An accountant is **negligent** if she does not exercise the degree of care a reasonably competent accountant would exercise under the circumstances. *See Rhode Island Hospital Trust National Bank v. Swartz, Bresenoff, Yavner & Jacobs.* For example, A, an accountant, is engaged to audit the books of Z Corporation. During the course of A's investigation A is notified by O, an officer of Z, that O suspects that T, Z's Treasurer, is engaged in a scheme to embezzle from the corporation. A does not pursue the matter since she was previously informed that O and T are on bad terms with each other. T, in fact, was engaged in a commonly used scheme of embezzlement. A is negligent for failing to conduct a reasonable investigation of the alleged defalcation. Nonetheless, an accountant is *not* liable for honest inaccuracies or errors of judgment so long as she exercised reasonable care in performing her duties. Moreover, an accountant is *not an insurer* of the accuracy of her reports provided she acted in a reasonably competent and professional manner.

Historically, an accountant's liability for negligence extended only to the client and third party beneficiaries. Under this view **privity** of contract was a requirement to a cause of action based upon negligence. This approach was established in 1931 by the landmark case of *Ultramares Corporation v. Touche*, which appears at the end of this chapter. In recent years the *Ultramares* doctrine has been eroded by some courts which have in general extended the class of protected persons to include foreseeable plaintiffs. For example, in *Rusch Factor, Inc. v. Levin,* a Federal district court stated that "[t]he wisdom of the decision in *Ultramares* has been doubted and this Court shares the doubt. Why should an innocent reliant party be forced to carry the weighty burden of an accountant's professional malpractice? Isn't the risk of loss more easily distributed and fairly spread by imposing it on the accounting profession which can pass the cost of insuring against the risk on to its customers, who can then pass the cost onto the entire consuming public?"

This approach has also been adopted by the Restatement of Torts. Section 552 provides:

(1) One who, in the course of his business, profession or employment, or in any other transaction in which he has a pecuniary interest, supplies false information for the guidance of others in their business transactions, is subject to liability for pecuniary loss caused to them by their justifiable reliance upon the information, if he fails to exercise reasonable care or competence in obtaining or cummunicating the information.

(2) Except as stated in Subsection (3), the liability stated in Subsection (1) is limited to loss suffered

(a) by the person or one of a limited group of persons for whose benefit and guidance he intends to supply the information or knows that the recipient intends to supply it; and

(b) through reliance upon it in a transaction that he intends the information to influence or knows that the recipient so intends or in a substantially similar transaction.

(3) The liability of one who is under a public duty to give the information extends to loss suffered by any of the class of persons for whose benefit the duty is created, in any of the transactions in which it is intended to protect them.

Foreseeable third parties are individuals who are members of a class that is known to the accountant or auditor to be intended recipients of the information provided or certified by the accountant. This class does not, however, include potential investors and the general public.

An accountant who commits a **fraudulent act** is liable to any person who the accountant *should have* reasonably foreseen would be injured by the misrepresentation and who justifiably relied upon it. The requisite elements of fraud, which are more fully discussed in Chapter 9, are: (1) a false representation (2) of fact (3) that is material (4) and made with knowledge of its falsity and with the intention to deceive (5) which is justifiably relied upon. An accountant who commits fraud may be held liable for *both* compensatory and punitive damages.

Criminal Liability

An accountant's potential criminal liability in rendering professional services is primarily founded upon the Federal law of securities regulation (discussed below) and taxation. Nonetheless, an accountant would violate State criminal law if she knowingly and willfully certified false documents, altered or tampered with accounting records, used false financial reports, gave false testimony under oath, or otherwise committed forgery.

Criminal sanctions may be imposed under the Internal Revenue Code for knowingly preparing false or fraudulent tax returns or documents used in connection with a tax return. Such liability also extends to willfully assisting or advising a client or others to prepare a false return. Penalties may be a fine not to exceed $5,000 or three years imprisonment or both.

Client Information

In providing services for his client an accountant necessarily obtains information concerning the client's business affairs. Two legal issues arise concerning this client information: (1) who owns the working papers generated by the accountant and (2) is the client information privileged.

Working Papers Audit working papers include the records kept by the auditor of the procedures followed, the tests performed, the information obtained, and the conclusions reached pertaining to the audit. All relevant information obtained in connection with the examination should be included in the working papers. An accountant is held to be the owner of his working papers and thus need not surrender them to his client. Nevertheless, the accountant may not disclose the contents of these papers unless: (1) the client consents or (2) a court orders the disclosure.

Accountant—Client Privilege The issue of confidentiality of communication between the accountant and his client is important for, if such information is considered to be privileged, it may not be admitted into evidence over the objection of the person possessing the privilege. The question of a possible accountant—client privilege frequently arises in tax disputes, criminal prosecution, and civil litigation.

Neither the common law nor Federal law recognizes such a privilege. Nevertheless, some States have adopted statutes granting some form of accountant—client privilege. Most of these statutes grant the privilege to the client, although a few extend the privilege to the accountant. Regardless of whether the privilege exists, it is generally considered to be professionally unethical for an accountant to disclose confidential communications from his client unless the disclosure is in accordance with (1) American Institute of Certified Public Accountants (AICPA) or GAAS requirements, (2) a court order, or (3) the client's request.

FEDERAL SECURITIES LAW

Accountants may be both civilly and criminally liable under provisions of the Securities Act of 1933 and the Securities Exchange Act of 1934. Such liability is more extensive and subject to fewer limitations than liability under the common law.

Securities Act of 1933

Accountants are subject to express **civil** liability under Section 11 if the financial statements they prepare or certify for inclusion in a registration statement contain any untrue statement or omission of material fact. Liability extends to anyone who acquires the security without knowledge of the untruth or omission. Not only is there no requirement of privity between the accountant and the purchasers, but proof of reliance upon the financial statements is also usually not required under Section 11. However, an accountant will not be liable if he can prove his "due diligence defense." **Due diligence** requires that the accountant had, after reasonable investigation, reasonable ground to believe and did believe, at the *time* the registration statement became *effective*, that the financial statements were true, complete, and accurate. The standard of reasonableness is that required of a prudent man in the management of his own property. Thus, Section 11 imposes liability upon accountants for **negligence** in the conduct of the audit or the presentation of the information in the financial statements. *See Escott v. BarChris Construction Corp.*

Moreover, if an accountant *willfully* violates this section, he may be held **criminally** liable for a fine of not more than $10,000 or imprisonment of not more than five years or both. Section 24.

Securities Exchange Act of 1934

Section 18 imposes express **civil** liability upon an accountant if she makes or causes to be made any false or misleading statement with respect to any material fact in any application, report, document, or registration filed with the SEC under the 1934 Act. Liability extends to any person who purchased or sold a security in reliance upon that false or misleading statement and without knowing that it was false or misleading. An accountant is not liable, however, if she proves that she acted in good faith and had no knowledge that such statement was false or misleading.

Accountants may also be held **civilly** liable for violations of **Rule 10b-5.** Their liability may be for direct participation in a violation of the rule or for indirect participation resulting from their aiding and abetting others. Rule 10b-5, as previously discussed in Chapter 44, is extremely broad in that it applies to *both* oral and written misstatement or omissions of material fact, and to *all* securities. Liability runs to purchasers and sellers who rely upon the misstatement or omis-

sion of material fact in connection with the purchase or sale of a security. However, liability is only imposed if the accountant acted with **scienter** which is intentional or knowing conduct. Therefore, accountants are not liable under Rule 10b-5 for mere negligence although reckless disregard of the truth *may* constitute *scienter. See Ernst & Ernst v. Hochfelder.*

Accountants may also be held **criminally** liable for any willful violation of Section 18 or Rule 10b-5. Conviction may carry a fine of not more than $100,000 or imprisonment for not more than five years, or both. Section 32.

CASES

Tort Liability

ULTRAMARES CORP. v. TOUCHE

Court of Appeals of New York, 1931.
255 N.Y. 170, 174 N.E. 441.

CARDOZO, C. J.

The action is in tort for damages suffered through the misrepresentations of accountants, the first cause of action being for misrepresentations that were merely negligent, and the second for misrepresentations charged to have been fraudulent.

In January, 1924, the defendants, a firm of public accountants, were employed by Fred Stern & Co., Inc., to prepare and certify a balance sheet exhibiting the condition of its business as of December 31, 1923. They had been employed at the end of each of the three years preceding to render a like service. Fred Stern & Co., Inc., which was in substance Stern himself, was engaged in the importation and sale of rubber. To finance its operations, it required extensive credit and borrowed large sums of money from banks and other lenders. All this was known to the defendants. The defendants knew also that in the usual course of business the balance sheet when certified would be exhibited by the Stern Company to banks, creditors, stockholders, pruchasers or sellers, according to the needs of the occasion, as the basis of financial deal-

ings. Accordingly, when the balance sheet was made up, the defendants supplied the Stern Company with thirty-two copies certified with serial numbers as counterpart originals. Nothing was said as to the persons to whom these counterparts would be shown or the extent or number of the transactions in which they would be used. In particular there was no mention of the plaintiff, a corporation doing business chiefly as a factor, which till then had never made advances to the Stern Company, though it had sold merchandise in small amounts. The range of the transactions in which a certificate of audit might be expected to play a part was as indefinite and wide as the possibilities of the business that was mirrored in the summary.

By February 26, 1924, the audit was finished and the balance sheet made up. It stated assets in the sum of $2,550,671.88 and liabilities other than capital and surplus in the sum of $1,479,956.62, thus showing a net worth of $1,070,715.26. Attached to the balance sheet was a certificate as follows:

Touche, Niven & Co.
Public Accountants
Eighty Maiden Lane
New York
February 26, 1924.
Certificate of Auditors

We have examined the accounts of Fred Stern & Co., Inc., for the year ending December 31, 1923, and hereby certify that the annexed balance sheet is in acordance therewith and with the information and explanations given us. We further certify that, subject to provision for federal taxes on income, the said statement, in our opinion, presents a true and correct view of the financial condition of Fred Stern & Co., Inc., as at December 31, 1923.

Touche, Niven & Co.
Public Accountants.

Capital and surplus were intact if the balance sheet was accurate. In reality both had been wiped out, and the corporation was insolvent. The books had been falsified by those in charge of the business so as to set forth accounts receivable and other assets which turned out to be fictitious. * * *

The plaintiff, a corporation engaged in business as a factor, was approached by Stern in March, 1924, with a request for loans of money to finance the sales of rubber. Up to that time the dealings between the two houses were on a cash basis and trifling in amount. As a condition of any loans the plaintiff insisted that it receive a balance sheet certified by public accountants, and in response to that demand it was given one of the certificates signed by the defendants and then in Stern's possession. On the faith of that certificate the plaintiff made a loan which was followed by many others. * * *

This action, brought against the accountants in November, 1926, to recover the loss suffered by the plaintiff in reliance upon the audit, was in its inception one for negligence. On the trial there was added a second cause of action asserting fraud also. The trial judge dismissed the second cause of action without submitting it to the jury. As to the first cause of action, he reserved his decision on the defendants' motion to dismiss, and took the jury's verdict. They were told that the defendants might be held liable if with knowledge that the results of the audit would be communicated to creditors they did the work negligently, and that negligence was the omission to use reasonable and ordinary care. The ver-

dict was in favor of the plaintiff for $187,576.32. On the coming in of the verdict, the judge granted the reserved motion. The Appellate Division [citation] affirmed the dismissal of the cause of action for fraud, but reversed the dismissal of the cause of action for negligence, and reinstated the verdict. The case is here on cross-appeals.

The two causes of action will be considered in sucession, first the one for negligence and second that for fraud.

1. We think the evidence supports a finding that the audit was negligently made, though in so saying we put aside for the moment the question whether negligence, even if it existed, was a wrong to the plaintiff. To explain fully or adequately how the defendants were at fault would carry this opinion beyond reasonable bounds. A sketch, however, there must be, at least in respect of some features of the audit, for the nature of the fault, when understood, is helpful in defining the ambit of the duty.

We begin with the item of accounts receivable. At the start of the defendant's audit, there had been no posting of the general ledger since April, 1923. Siess, a junior accountant, was assigned by the defendants to the performance of that work. On Sunday, February 3, 1924, he had finished the task of posting, and was ready the next day to begin with his associates the preparation of the balance sheet and the audit of its items. The total of the accounts receivable for December, 1923, as thus posted by Siess from the entries in the journal, was $644,758.17. At some time on February 3, Romberg, an employee of the Stern Company, who had general charge of its accounts, placed below that total another item to represent additional accounts receivable growing out of the transactions of the month. This new item, $706,843.07, Romberg entered in his own handwriting. The sales that it represented were, each and all, fictitious. Opposite the entry were placed other figures (12–29), indicating or supposed to indicate a reference to the journal. Siess when he resumed his work saw the entries thus added, and included the new item in making up his footings, with the result of an apparent increase of over $700,000 in the assets of the business. He says that in doing this he supposed the entries to be correct, and that, his task at the moment being merely to post the books, he thought the work of audit or verification might come later, and put it off accordingly.

* * *

The December entry of accounts receivable was not the only item that a careful and skillful auditor would have desired to investigate. There was ground for suspicion as to an item of $113,199.60, included in the accounts payable as due from the Baltic Corporation. As to this the defendants received an explanation, not very convincing, from Stern and Romberg. A cautious auditor might have been dissatisfied and have uncovered what was wrong. There was ground for suspicion also because of the inflation of the inventory. The inventory as it was given to the auditors, was totaled at $347,219.08. The defendants discovered errors in the sum of $303,863.20, and adjusted the balance sheet accordingly. Both the extent of the discrepancy and its causes might have been found to cast discredit upon the business and the books. There was ground for suspicion again in the record of assigned accounts. Inquiry of the creditors gave notice to the defendants that the same accounts had been pledged to two, three, and four banks at the same time. The pledges did not diminish the value of the assets, but made in sum circumstances they might well evoke a doubt as to the solvency of a business where such conduct was permitted. There was an explanation by Romberg which the defendants accepted as sufficient. Caution and diligence might have pressed investigation farther.

If the defendants owed a duty to the plaintiff to act with the same care that would have been due under a contract of employment, a jury was at liberty to find a verdict of negligence upon a showing of a scrutiny so imperfect and perfunctory. * * *

We are brought to the question of duty, its origin and measure.

The defendants owed to their employer a duty imposed by law to make their certificate without fraud, and a duty growing out of contract to make it with the care and caution proper to their calling. Fraud includes the pretense of knowledge when knowledge there is none. To creditors and investors to whom the employer exhibited the certificate, the defendants owed a like duty to make it without fraud, since there was notice in the circumstances of its making that the employer did not intend to keep it to himself. [Citations.] A different question develops when we ask whether they owed a duty to these to make it without negligence. If liability for negligence exists, a thoughtless slip or blunder, the failure to detect a theft or forgery beneath the cover of deceptive entries, may expose accountants to a liability in an indeterminate amount for an indeterminate time to an indeterminate class. The hazards of a business conducted on these terms are so extreme as to enkindle doubt whether a flaw may not exist in the implication of a duty that exposes to these consequences. We put aside for the moment any statement in the certificate which involves the representation of a fact as true to the knowledge of the auditors. If such a statement was made, whether believed to be true or not, the defendants are liable for deceit in the event that it was false. The plaintiff does not need the invention of novel doctrine to help it out in such conditions. The case was submitted to the jury, and the verdict was returned upon the theory that, even in the absence of a misstatement of a fact, there is a liability also for erroneous opinion. The expression of an opinion is to be subject to a warranty implied by law. What, then, is the warranty, as yet unformulated, to be? Is it merely that the opinion is honestly conceived and that the preliminary inquiry has been honestly pursued, that a halt has not been made without a genuine belief that the search has been reasonably adequate to bring disclosure of the truth? Or does it go farther and involve the assumption of a liability for any blunder or inattention that could fairly be spoken of as negligence if the controversy were one between accountant and employer for breach of a contract to render services for pay?

The assault upon the citadel of privity is proceeding in these days apace. How far the inroads shall extend is now a favorite subject of juridical discussion. [Citations.] In the field of the law of contract there has been a gradual widening of the doctrine of [third party] beneficiary of a promise, clearly designated as such, [such that he] is seldom left without a remedy. [Citation.] Even in that field, however, the remedy is narrower where the beneficiaries of the promise are indeterminate or general. Something more must then appear than an intention that the promise shall redound to the benefit of the public or to that of a class of indefinite extension. The promise must be such as to "bespeak the assumption of a duty to make reparation directly to the individual members of the public if the benefit is lost." [Citations.] In the field of the law of torts a manufacturer who is negligent in the manufacture of a chattel in circumstances pointing to an unreasonable risk of serious bodily harm to those using it thereafter may be liable for negligence though privity is lacking between manufacturer and user. [Citations.] A force or instrument of harm having been launched with potentialities of danger manifest to the eye of prudence, the one who launches it is under a duty to keep it within bounds. [Citation.] Even so, the question is still open whether the potentialities of danger that will charge with liability are confined to harm to the person or include injury to property. [Citation.] In either view, however, what is released or set in motion is a physical force. We are now asked to say that a like liability attaches to the circulation of a thought or a release of the explosive power resident in words.

* * *

From the foregoing analysis the conclusion is, we think, inevitable that nothing in our previous decisions commits us to a holding of liability for negligence in the circumstances of the case at hand, and that such liability, if recognized, will be an extension of the principle of those decisions to different conditions, even if more or less analogous. The question then is whether such an extension shall be made.

The extension, if made, will so expand the field of liability for negligent speech as to make it nearly, if not quite, coterminous with that of liability for fraud. Again and again, in decisions of this court, the bounds of this latter liability have been set up, with futility the fate of every endeavor to dislodge them. Scienter has been declared to be an indispensable element, except where the representation has been put forward as true of one's own knowledge [citation], or in circumstances where the expression of opinion was a dishonorable pretense. [Citations.] Even an opinion, especially an opinion by an expert, may be found to be fraudulent if the grounds supporting it are so flimsy as to lead to the conclusion that there was no genuine belief back of it. Further than that this court has never gone.

* * *

We have said that the duty to refrain from negligent representation would become coincident or nearly so with the duty to refrain from fraud if this action could be maintained. A representation, even though knowingly false, does not constitute ground for an action of deceit unless made with the intent to be communicated to the persons or class of persons who act upon it to their prejudice. Affirmance of this judgment would require us to hold that all or nearly all the persons so situated would suffer an impairment of an interest legally protected if the representation had been negligent. We speak of all "or nearly all," for cases can be imagined where a casual response, made in circumstances insufficient to indicate that care should be expected, would permit recovery for fraud if willfully deceitful. Cases of fraud between persons so circumstanced are, however, too infrequent and exceptional to make the radii greatly different if the fields of liability for negligence and deceit be figured as concentric circles. The like may be said of the possibility that the negligence of the injured party, contributing to the result, may avail to overcome the one remedy, though unavailing to defeat the other.

* * *

Liability for negligence if adjudged in this case will extend to many callings other than an auditor's. Lawyers who certify their opinion as to the validity of municipal or corporate bonds, with knowledge that the opinion will be brought to the notice of the public, will become liable to the investors, if they have overlooked a statute or a decision, to the same extent as if the controversy were one between client and adviser. Title companies insuring titles to a tract of land, with knowledge that at an approaching auction the fact that they have insured will be stated to the bidders, will become liable to purchasers who may wish the benefit of a policy without payment of a premium. These illustrations may seem to be extreme, but they go little, if any, farther than we are invited to go now.

* * *

Our holding does not emancipate accountants from the consequences of fraud. It does not relieve them if their audit has been so negligent as to justify a finding that they had no genuine belief in its adequacy, for this again is fraud. It does no more than say that, if less than this is proved, if there has been neither reckless misstatement nor insincere profession of an opinion, but only honest blunder, the ensuing liability for negligence is one that is bounded by the contract and is to be enforced between the parties by whom the contract has been made. We doubt whether the average business man receiving a certificate without paying for it, and receiving it merely as one among a multitude of possible investors, would look for anything more.

* * *

Tort Liability

RHODE ISLAND HOSPITAL TRUST NATIONAL BANK v. SWARTZ, BRESENOFF, YAVNER & JACOBS.

United States Court of Appeals, Fourth Circuit, 1972.
455 F.2d 847.

WINTER, J.

Rhode Island Hospital Trust National Bank ("Bank") sued Swartz, Bresenoff, Yavner & Jacobs, a firm of certified public accountants ("Accountants"), each of the partners of the firm and the estate of a deceased partner, alleging that Accountants had negligently audited the financial statements of International Trading Corporation and related companies ("Borrower") in consequence of which Bank had made loans to Borrower which was unable to repay them and Bank sustained a loss in excess of $100,000.00. The district court, sitting nonjury, concluded that the evidence failed to establish "fraud or collusion on the part of Accountants, any lack of good faith, misrepresentation, breach of duty, negligence, or failure to use reasonable care in the preparation and issuance of the financial statements," and it dismissed the complaint. We disagree with the district court's conclusions with regard to negligence. We, therefore, reverse and remand for further proceedings.

Borrower, an importer of cement, became a customer of Bank in 1962 when it expanded its operations to New England and opened leased pier facilities at Fall River, Massachusetts, and at Providence, Rhode Island. Borrower obtained a line of credit from Bank, to be secured by a pledge of inventories and accounts receivable, in the amount of 75% of collateral but not to exceed $200,000.00. At approximately the same time, Borrower undertook to change its method of loading and unloading cement imports from handling in bags to handling in bulk.

This change in method necessitated a modification of facilities and the expenditure of considerable sums for leasehold improvements. In 1962 in excess of $155,000.00 was spent to improve Borrower's facilities, principally at Fort Lauderdale, Florida; and, since long-term financing was not sought, this tended to deplete working capital.

In 1963 Borrower sought long-term financing of leasehold improvements from Bank, but Bank was unwilling to lend on this basis. Bank, however, did accede to Borrower's request that the maximum amount of its line of credit be exceeded upon Borrower's assurance that economies from savings on labor costs expected to result from bulk handling would enable Borrower to operate more profitably and to meet greater loan obligations.

In June 1964 Borrower represented to Bank that during 1963 it had expended $212,000.00 for leasehold improvements to its facilities at Palm Beach, Florida, Brunswick, Georgia, and Providence, Rhode Island. The work was purportedly done by Borrower, using its own labor and materials. *In fact, the claimed 1963 leasehold improvements were totally fictitious*. The labor expenses claimed to have been incurred were incurred as operating expenses of handling and storing cement. No materials were purchased. An inspection in 1964 of all three of the facilities disclosed that they were in the same condition as they were at the end of 1962.

In accordance with the loan agreement establishing the line of credit, Borrower was obligated to furnish Bank with financial statements for each year, ending December 31; and, beginning March 27, 1964, Bank pressed to obtain the statements for the year 1963. They were not forthcoming until June 24, 1964. The income statement showed that total operating expenses, amounting to $609,956.42, were reduced by $212,000.00, designated "Estimated Expenses Contained in Operating Expenses Representing Cost of Lease-

hold Improvements," with the net effect that Borrower had a net profit after taxes of $9,257.60. The balance sheet similarly capitalized this sum on the asset side, together with other leasehold improvements, and showed a net worth of $339,427.48. If the $212,000.00 had not been capitalized, the income statement would have shown a substantial loss from operations and the balance sheet would have shown a substantial depletion of net worth (both of approximately $200,000.00).

When Accountants transmitted the financial statements to their client they wrote a covering letter expressing certain reservations about the "fairness of the accompanying statements." * * *

The letter then discussed the crucial item concerned in this litigation—the leasehold improvements—and set forth the following:

Additions to fixed assets in 1963 *were found* to include principally warehouse improvements and installation of machinery and equipment in Providence, Rhode Island, Brunswick, Georgia, and Palm Beach, Florida. Practically *all of this work was done by company employees and materials and overhead was borne by the International Trading Corporation and its affiliates.* Unfortunately, fully complete detailed cost records were not kept of these capital improvements and no exact determination could be made as to the actual cost of said improvements. (emphasis added)

* * *

As of the date of receipt of its copies of the financial statements, Bank had lent Borrower $220,000.00. There was testimony, not disputed, that if it had known on the date that $212,000.00 of leasehold improvements were fictitious, it would have refused further loans and immediately begun efforts to effect collection of the amount outstanding. Since Bank claimed that it did not know this crucial fact, the loan balance was allowed to increase during the summer of 1964 until it reached the level of $336,685.61 on September 24, 1964, the date of the adverse report of Bank's analysis department. Thought was given to taking additional collateral, but this was not done because additional property which could be pledged was in other jurisdictions and would be impractical to service. After the analysis department reported critically on Borrower's financial statements, no further loans or commitments were made. After that date, collections were effected from collateral pledges, and they were routinely applied to the oldest loan standing on Bank's books. Total collections reduced the unpaid balance to $116,685.61, and this sum has become uncollectible.

* * *

As stated by the district court, the liability, if any, of Accountants for negligence is to be determined by the rule that "[a]ccountants owe a duty to their employer, and others whom they know or expect to rely on the report, to make the report in good faith without fraud or collusion and with care and caution of experts." While the Rhode Island Supreme Court has not spoken on the problem, a district court, analyzing Rhode Island decisions, concluded, in full accord with the trial court here, that "an accountant should be liable in negligence for careless financial misrepresentations relied upon by actually foreseen and limited classes of persons." [Citation.] Since the evidence here is uncontroverted that Accountants not only knew but acknowledged that Bank sought Borrower's financial statements in connection with loans, that is the rule which will be applied. [Citations.]

* * *

By application of the rule stated, we think that Accountants are liable for negligence on either of alternate theories.

From the Accountants' work papers and the other evidence in the case, either of two inferences may be drawn. First, Accountants, having identifed some of the purported labor costs of the purported leasehold improvements, failed, from pressure of work or other reason, to search for material costs. Second, Accountants, having identified some of the purported labor costs of the purported leasehold improvements, searched for mate-

rial costs and, not finding any, failed to conduct any independent investigation of the existence of the leasehold improvements and their value and failed to disclose that there was no verification that the leasehold improvements were in being. In either event, Accountants, certified the financial statements, saying overall only that they could not express an opinion with regard to their fairness. This disclaimer, however, followed other reference to the purported leasehold improvements which expressed no reservation about their existence but only about their precise value. We think that a fair reading of Accountants' covering letter and disclaimer indicates that while the leasehold improvements may have had a value of more or less than $212,000.00, there was no question but that they existed and that they had substantial value. Whether Acountants failed to look or, having looked, failed to find, they were guilty of actionable negligence if Bank, in reliance on the statements, made further loans.

Our conclusions with respect to the report and disclosure are reinforced by reference to industry standards of what should have been done in these circumstances. While industry standards may not always be the maximum test of liability, certainly they should be deemed the minimum standard by which liability should be determined.

* * *

Liability Under the 1933 Act:
Section 11

ESCOTT v. BARCHRIS CONSTRUCTION CORP.

United States District Court, Southern District of New York, 1968.
283 F.Supp. 643.

McLEAN, J.

This is an action by purchasers of 5½ per cent convertible subordinated fifteen year debentures of BarChris Construction Corporation (BarChris). * * *

The action is brought under Section 11 of the Securities Act of 1933. Plaintiffs allege that the registration statement with respect to these debentures filed with the Securities and Exchange Commission, which became effective on May 16, 1961, contained material false statements and material omissions.

Defendants fall into three categories: (1) the persons who signed the registration statement; (2) the underwriters, consisting of eight investment banking firms, led by Drexel & Co. (Drexel); and (3) BarChris's auditors, Peat, Marwick, Mitchell & Co. (Peat, Marwick).

[The case against the first two categories was presented in Chapter 44.]

* * *

Defendants, in addition to denying that the registration statement was false, have pleaded the defenses open to them under Section 11 of the Act, * * *. On the main issue of liability, the questions to be decided are (1) did the registration statement contain false statements of fact, or did it omit to state facts which should have been stated in order to prevent it from being misleading; (2) if so, were the facts which were falsely stated or omitted "material" within the meaning of the Act; (3) if so, have defendants established their affirmative defenses?

* * *

In December 1959, BarChris sold 560,000 shares of common stock to the public at $3.00 per share. This issue was underwritten by Peter Morgan & Company, one of the present defendants.

By early 1961, BarChris needed additional working capital. The proceeds of the sale of the debentures involved in this action were to be devoted, in part at least, to fill that need.

The registration statement of the debentures, in preliminary form, was filed with the Securities and Exchange Commission on March 30, 1961. A first amendment was filed on May 11 and a second on May 16. The registration statement became effective on May 16. The closing of the financing took place on May 24. On that day BarChris received the net proceeds of the financing.

By that time BarChris was experiencing difficulties in collecting amounts due from some of its customers. Some of them were in arrears in payments due to factors on their discounted notes. As time went on those difficulties increased. Although BarChris continued to build [bowling] alleys in 1961 and 1962, it became increasingly apparent that the industry was overbuilt. Operators of alleys, often inadequately financed, began to fail. Precisely when the tide turned is a matter of dispute, but at any rate, it was painfully apparent in 1962.

In May of that year BarChris made an abortive attempt to raise more money by the sale of common stock. It filed with the Securities and Exchange Commission a registration statement for the stock issue which it later withdrew. In October 1962 BarChris came to the end of the road. On October 29, 1962, it filed in this court a petition for an arrangement under Chapter XI of the Bankruptcy Act.

* * *

Summary

For convenience, the various falsities and omissions which I have discussed in the preceding pages are recapitulated here. They were as follows:

1. *1960 Earnings*
   (a) *Sales*

As per prospectus	$9,165,320
Correct figure	8,511,420
Overstatement	$ 653,900

   (b) *Net Operating Income*

As per prospectus	$1,742,801
Correct figure	1,496,196
Overstatement	$ 246,605

   (c) *Earnings per Share*

As per prospectus	$.75
Correct figure	.65
Overstatement	$.10

2. *1960 Balance Sheet*
   Current Assets

As per prospectus	$4,524,021
Correct figure	3,914,332
Overstatement	$ 609,689

3. *Contingent Liabilities as of December 31, 1960 on Alternative Method of Financing*

As per prospectus	$ 750,000
Correct figure	1,125,795
Understatement	$ 375,795
Capitol Lanes should have been shown as a direct liability	$ 325,000

4. *Contingent Liabilities as of April 30, 1961*

As per prospectus	$ 825,000
Correct figure	1,443,853
Understatement	$ 618,853
Capitol Lanes should have been shown as a direct liability	$ 314,166

5. *Earnings Figures for Quarter ending March 31, 1961*
   (a) *Sales*

As per prospectus	$2,138,455
Correct figure	1,618,645
Overstatement	$ 519,810

   (b) *Gross Profit*

As per prospectus	$ 483,121
Correct figure	252,366
Overstatement	$ 230,755

6. *Backlog as of March 31, 1961*

As per prospectus	$6,905,000
Correct figure	2,415,000
Overstatement	$4,490,000

7. *Failure to Disclose Officers' Loans Outstanding and Unpaid on May 16, 1961* $ 386,615

8. *Failure to Disclose Use of Proceeds in Manner not Revealed in Prospectus*

Approximately	$1,160,000

9. *Failure to Disclose Customers' Delinquencies In May 1961 and BarChris's Potential Liability with Respect Thereto*   Over $1,350,000

10. *Failure to Disclose the Fact that BarChris was Already Engaged and was about to be More Heavily Engaged, in the Operation of Bowling Alleys*

*   *   *

Peat Marwick

Section 11(b) provides:

"Notwithstanding the provisions of subsection (a) no person * * * shall be liable as provided therein who shall sustain the burden of proof—

*   *   *

"(3) that * * * (B) as regards any part of the registration statement purporting to be made upon his authority as an expert * * * (i) he had, after reasonable investigation, reasonable ground to believe and did believe, at the time such part of the registration statement became effective, that the statements therein were true and that there was no omission to state a material fact required to be stated therein or necessary to make the statements therein not misleading * * *."

This defines the due diligence defense for an expert. Peat, Marwick has pleaded it.

The part of the registration statement purporting to be made upon the authority of Peat, Marwick as an expert was, as we have seen, the 1960 figures. But because the statute requires the court to determine Peat, Marwick's belief, and the grounds thereof, "at the time such part of the registration statement became effective," for the purposes of this affirmative defense the matter must be viewed as of May 16, 1961, and the question is whether at that time Peat, Marwick, after reasonable investigation, had reasonable ground to believe and did believe that the

1960 figures were true and that no material fact had been omitted from the registration statement which should have been included in order to make the 1960 figures not misleading. In deciding this issue, the court must consider not only what Peat, Marwick did in its 1960 audit, but also what it did in its subsequent "S–1 review."

*   *   *

The 1960 Audit. Peat, Marwick's work was in general charge of a member of the firm, Cummings, and more immediately in charge of Peat, Marwick's manager, Logan. Most of the actual work was performed by a senior accountant, Berardi, who had junior assistants, one of whom was Kennedy.

Berardi was then about thirty years old. He was not yet a C.P.A. He had had no previous experience with the bowling industry. This was his first job as a senior accountant. He could hardly have been given a more difficult assignment.

After obtaining a little background information on BarChris by talking to Logan and reviewing Peat, Marwick's work papers on its 1959 audit, Berardi examined the results of test checks of BarChris's accounting procedures which one of the junior accountants had made, and he prepared an "internal control questionnaire" and an "audit program." Thereafter, for a few days subsequent to December 30, 1960, he inspected BarChris's inventories and examined certain alley construction. Finally, on January 13, 1961, he began his auditing work which he carried on substantially continuously until it was completed on February 24, 1961. Toward the close of the work, Logan reviewed it and made various comments and suggestions to Berardi. It is unnecessary to recount everything that Berardi did in the course of the audit. We are concerned only with the evidence relating to what Berardi did or did not do with respect to those items which I have found to have been incorrectly reported in the 1960 figures in the prospectus. More narrowly, we are directly concerned only with such of those items as I have found to be material.

Capitol Lanes. First and foremost is Berardi's failure to discover that Capitol Lanes had not been sold. The error affected both the sales figure and the liability side of the balance sheet. Fundamentally, the error stemmed from the fact that Berardi never realized that Heavenly Lanes and Capitol were two different names for the same alley.

*   *   *

In any case, he never identified this mysterious Capitol with the Heavenly Lanes which he had included in his sales and profit figures. The vital question is whether he failed to make a reasonable investigation which, if he had made it, would have revealed the truth.

Certain accounting records of BarChris, which Berardi testified he did not see, would have put him on inquiry. One was a job cost ledger card for job no. 6036, the job number which Berardi put on his own sheet for Heavenly Lanes. This card read "Capitol Theatre (Heavenly)." In addition, two accounts receivable cards each showed both names on the same card, Capitol and Heavenly. Berardi testified that he looked at the accounts receivable records but that he did not see these particular cards. He testified that he did not look on the job cost ledger cards because he took the costs from another record, the costs register.

The burden of proof on this issue is on Peat, Marwick. Although the question is a rather close one, I find that Peat, Marwick has not sustained that burden. Peat, Marwick has not proved that Berardi made a reasonable investigation as far as Capitol Lanes was concerned and that his ignorance of the true facts was justified.

Howard Lanes Annex. Berardi also failed to discover that this alley was not sold. Here the evidence is much scantier. Berardi saw a contract for this alley in the contract file. No one told him that it was to be leased rather than sold. There is no evidence to indicate that any record existed which would have put him on notice. I find that his investigation was reasonable as to this item.

*   *   *

The S–1 Review

The purpose of reviewing events subsequent to the date of a certified balance sheet (referred to as an S–1 review when made with reference to a registration statement) is to ascertain whether any material change has occurred in the company's financial position which should be disclosed in order to prevent the balance sheet figures from being misleading. The scope of such a review, under generally accepted auditing standards, is limited. It does not amount to a complete audit.

Peat, Marwick prepared a written program for such a review. I find that this program conformed to generally accepted auditing standards.

* * *

Berardi made the S–1 review in May 1961. He devoted a little over two days to it, a total of 20½ hours. He did not discover any of the errors or omissions pertaining to the state of affairs in 1961 * * *, all of which were material. The question is whether, despite his failure to find out anything, his investigation was reasonable within the meaning of the statute.

What Berardi did was to look at a consolidating trial balance as of March 31, 1961, which had been prepared by BarChris, compare it with the audited December 31, 1960, figures, discuss with Trilling [controller of BarChris] certain unfavorable developments which the comparison disclosed, and read certain minutes. He did not examine any "important financial records" other than the trial balance. As to minutes, he read only what minutes Birnbaum [BarChris's house counsel and secretary] gave him, which consisted only of the board of directors' minutes of BarChris. He did not read such minutes as there were of the executive committee. He did not know that there was an executive committee, hence he did not discover that Kircher [BarChris's treasurer] had notes of executive committee minutes which had not been written up. He did not read the minutes of any subsidiary.

In substance, what Berardi did [was to ask] questions, he got answers which he considered satisfactory, and he did nothing to verify them.

* * *

Accountants should not be held to a standard higher than that recognized in their profession. I do not do so here. Berardi's review did not come up to that standard. He did not take some of the steps which Peat, Marwick's written program prescribed. He did not spend an adequate amount of time on a task of this magnitude. Most important of all, he was too easily satisfied with glib answers to his inquiries.

This is not to say that he should have made a complete audit. But there were enough danger signals in the materials which he did examine to require some futher investigation on his part. Generally accepted accounting standards required such further investigation under these circumstances. It is not always sufficient merely to ask questions.

Here again, the burden of proof is on Peat, Marwick. I find that that burden has not been satisfied. I conclude that Peat, Marwick has not established its due diligence defense.

* * *

Defendants' motions to dismiss this action, upon which decision was reserved at the trial, are denied. * * *

Pursuant to Rule 52(a), this opinion constitutes the court's findings of fact and conclusions of law with respect to the issues determined herein.

So ordered.

Liability Under the 1934 Act: Rule 10b-5

ERNST & ERNST v. HOCHFELDER

Supreme Court of the United States, 1976.
425 U.S. 185, 96 S.Ct. 1375, 47 L.Ed.2d 668.

POWELL, J.

The issue in this case is whether an action for civil damages may lie under § 10(b) of the Securities Exchange Act of 1934 (1934 Act), * * *, and Securities and Exchange Commission Rule 10b–5, * * * in the absence of an allegation of intent to deceive, manipulate, or defraud on the part of the defendant.

Petitioner, Ernst & Ernst, is an accounting firm. From 1946 through 1967 it was retained by First Securities Company of Chicago (First Securities), a small brokerage firm and member of the Midwest Stock Exchange and of the National Association of Securities Dealers, to perform periodic audits of the firm's books and records. In connection with these audits Ernst & Ernst prepared for filing with the Securities and Exchange Commission (Commission) the annual reports required of First Securities under § 17(a) of the 1934 Act. It also prepared for First Securities responses to the financial questionnaires of the Midwest Stock Exchange (Exchange).

Respondents were customers of First Securities who invested in a fraudulent securities scheme perpetrated by Leston B. Nay, president of the firm and owner of 92% of its stock. * * *

This fraud came to light in 1968 when Nay committed suicide, leaving a note that described First Securities as bankrupt and the escrow accounts as "spurious." Respondents subsequently filed this action for damages against Ernst & Ernst in the United States District Court for the Northern District of Illinois under § 10(b) of the 1934 Act. The complaint charged that Nay's escrow scheme violated § 10(b) and Commission Rule 10b–5, and that Ernst & Ernst had "aided and abetted" Nay's violations by its "failure" to conduct proper audits of First Securities. As revealed through discovery, respondents' cause of action rested on a theory of negligent nonfeasance. The premise was that Ernst & Ernst had failed to utilize "appropriate auditing procedures" in its audits of First Securities, thereby failing to discover internal practices of the firm said to prevent an effective audit.

* * *

Federal regulation of transactions in securities emerged as part of the aftermath of the market crash in 1929. The Securities Act of 1933 (1933 Act), [citation] was designed to provide investors with full disclosure of material information concerning public offerings of securities in commerce, to protect investors against fraud and, through the imposition of specified civil liabilities, to promote ethical standards of honesty and fair dealing. [Citation.] The 1934 Act was intended principally to protect investors against manipulation of stock prices through regulation of transactions upon securities exchanges and in over-the-counter markets, and to impose regular reporting requirements on companies whose stock is listed on national securities exchanges. [Citation.] Although the Acts contain numerous carefully drawn express civil remedies and criminal penalties, Congress recognized that efficient regulation of securities trading could not be accomplished under a rigid statutory program. As part of the 1934 Act Congress created the Commission, which is provided with an arsenal of flexible enforcement powers. [Citations.]

Section 10 of the 1934 Act makes it "unlawful for any person * * * (b) [t]o use or employ, in connection with the purchase or sale of any security * * * any manipulative or deceptive device or contrivance in contravention of such rules and regulations as the Commission may prescribe as necessary or appropriate in the public interest or for the protection of investors." [Citation.] In 1942, acting pursuant to the power conferred by § 10(b), the Commission promulgated Rule 10b–5.

* * *

Although § 10(b) does not by its terms create an express civil remedy for its violation, and there is no indication that Congress, or the Commission when adopting Rule 10b–5, contemplated such a remedy, the existence of a private cause of action for violations of the statute and the Rule is now well established. [Citation.] During the 30-year period since a private cause of action was first implied under § 10(b) and Rule 10b–5, a substantial body of case law and commentary has developed as to its elements. Courts and commentators long have differed with regard to whether scienter is a necessary element of such a cause of action, or whether negligent conduct alone is sufficient.

* * *

Although the extensive legislative history of the 1934 Act is bereft of any explicit explanation of Congress' intent, we think the relevant portions of that history support our conclusion that § 10(b) was addressed to practices that involve some element of scienter and cannot be read to impose liability for negligent conduct alone.

* * *

The section was described rightly as a "catchall" clause to enable the Commission "to deal with new manipulative [or cunning] devices." It is difficult to believe that any lawyer, legislative draftsman, or legislator would use these words if the intent was to create liability for merely negligent acts of omissions. Neither the legislative history nor the briefs supporting respondents identify any usage or authority for construing "manipulative [or cunning] devices" to include negligence.

* * *

The Commission argues that Congress has been explicit in requiring willful conduct when that was the standard of fault intended, * * *.

* * *

The structure of the Acts does not support the Commission's argument. In each instance that Congress created express civil liability in favor of purchasers or sellers of securities it clearly specified whether recovery was to be premised on knowing or intentional conduct, negligence, or entirely innocent mistake. [Citations.] For example, § 11 of the 1933 Act unambiguously creates a private action for damages when a registration statement includes untrue statements of material facts or fails to state material facts necessary to make the statements therein not misleading. Within the limits specified by § 11(e), the issuer of the securities is held absolutely liable for any damages resulting from such misstatement or omission. But ex-

perts such as accountants who have prepared portions of the registration statement are accorded a "due diligence" defense. In effect, this is a negligence standard. An expert may avoid civil liability with respect to the portions of the registration statement for which he was responsible by showing that "after reasonable investigation" he had "reasonable ground[s] to believe" that the statements for which he was responsible were true and there was no omission of a material fact. § 11(b)(3)(B)(i). See e.g., Escott v. BarChris Const. Corp. [citation.] The express recognition of a cause of action premised on negligent behavior in § 11 stands in sharp contrast to the language of § 10(b), and significantly undercuts the Commission's argument.

We also consider it significant that each of the express civil remedies in the 1933 Act allowing recovery for negligent conduct, see §§ 11, 12(2), 15, [citations] is subject to significant procedural restrictions not applicable under § 10(b). * * *

* * *

We have addressed, to this point, primarily the language and history of § 10(b). The Commission contends, however, that subsections (b) and (c) of Rule 10b-5 are cast in language which—if standing alone— could encompass both intentional and negligent behavior. These subsections respectively provide that it is unlawful "[t]o make any untrue statement of a material fact or to omit to state a material fact necessary in order to make the statements made, in the light of the circumstances under which they were made, not misleading * * *" and "[t]o engage in any act, practice, or course of business which operates or would operate as a fraud or deceit upon any person * * *."

Viewed in isolation the language of subsection (b), and arguably that of subsection (c), could be read as proscribing, respectively, any type of material misstatement or omission, and any course of conduct, that has the effect of defrauding investors, whether the wrongdoing was intentional or not.

We note first that such a reading cannot be harmonized with the administrative history of the Rule, a history making clear that when the Commission adopted the Rule it was intended to apply only to activities that involved scienter. More importantly, Rule 10b-5 was adopted pursuant to authority granted the Commission under § 10(b). The rulemaking power granted to an administrative agency charged with the administration of a federal statute is not the power to make law. Rather, it is " 'the power to adopt regulations to carry into effect the will of Congress as expressed by the statute.' " [Citations.] * * * When a statute speaks so specifically in terms of manipulation and deception, and of implementing devices and contrivances—the commonly understood terminology of intentional wrongdoing—and when its history reflects no more expansive intent, we are quite unwilling to extend the scope of the statute to negligent conduct.

* * *

The judgment of the Court of Appeals is Reversed.

PROBLEMS

1. Baldwin Corporation made a public offering of $25,000,000 of convertible debentures. It registered the offering with the SEC. The registration statement contained financial statements certified by Adams and Allen, CPAs. The financial statements overstated Baldwin's net income and assets by 20 percent while it understated the company's liability by 15 percent. Because Adams and Allen did not carefully follow GAAS it failed to detect these inaccuracies, the discovery of which has caused the bond prices to drop from their original selling price of $1,000 per bond to $720. Conrad, who purchased $10,000 of the debentures, has brought suit against Adams and Allen. Decision?

2. Ingram is a CPA employed by Jordan, Keller and Lane, CPA's, to audit Martin Enterprises, Inc., a fast-growing service firm that had gone public two years earlier. The financial statements that were audited by Ingram were included in a proxy statement proposing a merger with several other firms. The proxy statement was filed with the SEC and included several inaccuracies. First, approximately $1 million, or more than 20%, of the previous year's "net sales originally reported" had proven nonexistent by the time the proxy statement was filed and had been written off on Martin's own books. This was not disclosed in the proxy statement in violation of Accounting Board Opinion Number 9. Second, net sales of Martin for the current year were stated as $11,300,000 when they were less than $10,500,000. Third, net profits of Martin for the current year were reported as $700,000 when it had no earnings at all.

(a) What civil liability, if any, does Ingram have?

(b) What criminal liability, if any, does Ingram have?

3. Girard & Company, CPAs, audited the financial statements included in the annual report submitted by PMG Enterprises, Inc., to the SEC. The audit failed to detect numerous false and misleading statements contained in the financial statements.

(a) Investors who subsequently purchased PMG stock have brought suit against Girard under Section 18 of the 1934 Act. What defenses, if any, are available to Girard?

(b) The SEC has initiated criminal proceedings under the 1934 Act against Girard. What must be proven for Girard to be held criminally liable?

4. Dryden, a CPA, audited the books of Elixir, Inc., and certified incorrect financial statements in Form 10-K which were filed with the SEC. Shortly thereafter Elixer, Inc., went bankrupt. Investigation into the bankruptcy disclosed that Kraft, the president of Elixir, had engaged in an intricate and clever embezzlement scheme that siphoned off substantial sums of money which now supports Kraft in a luxurious lifestyle in South America. Investors who purchased shares of Elixir have brought suit against Dryden under Rule 10b-5. At trial Dryden produces evidence which demonstrates that his failure to discover the embezzlements resulted merely from negligence on his part and that he had no knowledge of the fraudulent conduct. Decision?

5. Johnson Enterprises, Inc. contracted with the accounting firm of P, A. & E. to perform an audit of Johnson. The accounting firm performed its duty in a non-negligent, competent manner but failed to discover a novel embezzlement scheme perpetrated by Johnson's treasurer. Shortly thereafter Johnson's treasurer disappeared with $75,000 of the company's money. Johnson now refuses to pay P, A. & E. its $20,000 audit fee and is seeking to recover $75,000 from P, A. & E.

(a) What are the rights and liabilities of P, A. & E. and Johnson? Explain.

(b) Would you answer to (a) differ if the scheme was a common-place embezzlement scheme which GAAS should have disclosed? Explain.

6. The accounting firm of T, W & S was engaged to perform an audit of Progate Manufacturing Company. During the course of its investigation T, W & S discovered that the inventory was overvalued by the company in that it was carried on the books at last year's prices which were significantly higher than current prices. When T, W & S approached Progate's president, Lehman, about the improper valuation of inventory, Lehman became enraged and told T, W & S that unless the firm accepted the valuation Progate would sue T, W & S. Although T, W & S knew that Progate's suit was frivolous and unfounded it wished to avoid the negative publicity that would arise from any suit brought against it. Therefore, on the assumption that the overvaluation would not harm anybody T, W & S accepted Progate's inflated valuation of inventory, Progate subsequently went bankrupt and T, W & S is now being sued (1) by First National Bank, a bank that relied upon T, W & S's statement to loan money to Progate, and (2) by Thomas, an investor who purchased 20% of Progate's stock after receiving T, W & S's statement. What are the rights and liabilities of First National Bank, Thomas and T, W & S?

7. J, B, and J, CPAs, has audited the Highcredit Corporation for the past five years. Recently the SEC has commenced an investigation against Highcredit for possible violations of the Federal securities law. The SEC has subpoenaed all of J, B, and J's working papers pertinent to the audit of Highcredit. Highcredit insists that J, B, and J not turn over the documents to the SEC. What action should J, B, and J take? Why?

8. On February 1, 1985, the Gazette Corporation hired Susan Sharp to conduct an audit of its books and to prepare financial statements for the corporation's annual meeting on July 1. Sharp made every reasonable attempt to comply with the deadline but could not finish the report on time due to delays in receiving needed information from Gazette. Gazette now refused to pay Sharp for her audit and is threatening to bring a cause of action against Sharp. What course of action should Sharp pursue? Why?

PUBLIC POLICY, SOCIAL ISSUES AND BUSINESS ETHICS

PART Ten deals with property, a concept that is fundamental to our economic system based as it is upon exchanges between units of production and consumption. Even beyond its immeasurable economic importance, "[t]here is nothing which so generally strikes the imagination, and engages the affections of mankind, as the right of property; or that sole and despotic dominion which one man claims and exercises over the external things of the world, in total exclusion of the right of any other individual in the universe." Blackstone, *Commentaries on the Law of England* 2 (15th ed. 1809).

Before inquiring further into the social and public policy issues concerning the private and public ownership of property, it is necessary first to arrive at a definition of property. Jeremy Bentham, in explaining the advantages of law stated: "Property is nothing but a basis of expectation; the expectation of deriving certain advantages from a thing which we are said to possess, in consequence of the relation in which we stand towards it. * * * Property and law are born together, and die together. Before laws were made there was no property; take away laws, and property ceases." Bentham, *Theory of Legislation* 111-13 (1864). More specifically, property consists of a set of *rights* entitling one person to use and enjoy exclusively some item:

By property we mean an exclusive right to control an economic good.

By private property we mean the exclusive right of a private person to control an economic good.

By public property we mean the exclusive right of a political unit (city, state, nation, etc.) to control an economic good.

* * *

* * * Speaking accurately, then, property is not a thing but the rights which extend over a thing. A less strict use of the word property makes property include the things over which the right extends. We say of a farm, this is my property, meaning the land and improvements on it and not merely the right, or rather, the land and its improvements together with the right. But, strictly speaking, property is the right, and not the object over which the right extends. R. Ely, *Property and Contract in their Relation to the Distribution of Wealth* 101–02, 08 (1914).

In either sense of the word—the right over the object or the object itself—there is an enormous quantity of property in the United States today. It has been estimated that as of 1980 in the United States there was $4,247 billion of real estate, $1,381 billion of stock owned, $1,112 billion of bonds and other fixed income assets, $973 billion of durables and $373 billion of cash. R. Ibbotson and L. Siegel, "The World Wealth Portfolio," *Journal of Portfolio Management* (1980).

The most obvious, but at the same time most important, question regarding all of this wealth is, who should own it? This question has been answered quite differently at various times in history and today is answered just as diversely in different places. Our economic and political system has provided for both private and public ownership of property. Moreover, it has established constitutional protections for the private ownership of property. As a result, private ownership is accepted as the norm in this country and those who own property may assert: " 'To the world: Keep off unless you have my permission, which I may grant or withhold. Signed: Private citizen. Endorsed: The state.' " F. Cohen, "Dialogue on Private Property," 9 *Rutgers L. Review* 357, 374 (1954). Of course, there are other views regarding the propriety of private property. For example, Karl Marx and Friedrich Engels in *The Communist Manifesto* maintain that "The proletarians cannot become masters of the productive forces of society, except by abolishing their own previous mode of appropriation, and thereby also every other previous mode of appropriation. They have nothing of their own to secure and to fortify; their mission is to destroy all previous securities for, and insurances of, individual property."

Economists have propounded numerous arguments supporting the notion of privately owned property. The basic one is that by allowing private property the capitalistic system creates incentives for the efficient use and allocation of resources. The right to exclusive ownership of property encourages individuals to incur costs to make efficient use of their property, while the right to transfer ownership in their property provides an incentive for them to shift resources from less productive uses to more productive uses. Professor Behrman has explained this concept as follows:

An individual must have something to be creative with. Private property can be used for private benefit, but the society as a whole should benefit, too. Each individual will greedily use property for his greatest economic benefit: he would not use it as efficiently if someone else owned it and paid him part of the fruits of his labor. Private productive property assures that each person reaps the benefit of his own efforts. If everybody works for one man, who alone has all the property, he is the only one with the ability to create. The feudal lord who owned all of the land, the cattle, stables, and so forth—he told the serfs what to do. He could be creative. But the serf who was greedy— what happened to him? He got his hands cuffed! Private productive property is a necessary complement to individual economic motivation. It is necessary for individuals to work effectively, doing the best they can with it, responsibly, and thereby

improving the whole society. J. Behrman, *Discourses on Ethics and Business* 23 (1981).

Even in our society which constitutionally recognizes the private ownership of property, such ownership is by no means absolute. The government imposes limitations upon a number of the rights embodied in ownership:

* * * Our students of property law need, therefore, to be reminded that not only has the whole law since the industrial revolution shown a steady growth in ever new restrictions upon the use of private property, but that the ideal of absolute *laissez faire* has never in fact been completely operative.

         * * *

* * * There must be restrictions on the use of property not only in the interests of other property owners but also in the interests of the health, safety, religion, morals, and general welfare of the whole community. No community can view with indifference the exploitation of the needy by commercial greed. As under the conditions of crowded life the reckless or unconscionable use of one's property is becoming more and more dangerous, enlightened jurists find new doctrines to limit the abuse of ancient rights. M. Cohen, "Property and Sovereignty", 13 *Cornell L. Q.* 8 (1927).

The next six chapters will explore our legal system's answers to such questions of public policy regarding the private ownership of property as (1) how freely should property rights be transferable, (2) should the government be permitted to seize privately owned property, (3) to what extent should the government control the use of private property, and (4) should individuals be allowed to restrict the use of property which they have transferred.

Chapter 46

INTRODUCTION TO REAL AND PERSONAL PROPERTY

IN a democratic and enterprising society such as the United States the concept of "property" has an importance second only to the idea of "liberty." While a large part of our rules of property stems directly from English law, property in America occupies a unique status because of the protection expressly granted it by the Federal constitution as well as by most State constitutions. The Fifth Amendment to the Federal constitution provides, in part, that "No person shall be * * * deprived of life, liberty, or property, without due process of law; nor shall private property be taken for public use, without just compensation." A similar injunction is contained in the Fourteenth Amendment: "No State shall * * * deprive any person of life, liberty, or property, without due process of law." This protection afforded to property owners is subject, however, to police power regulation for the public good. In addition, the private ownership of property is an essential component of the economic system of the United States. This chapter will begin with a general introduction to the law governing real and personal property. The second part of this chapter deals specifically with personal property.

INTRODUCTION TO PROPERTY

In spite of the unique place accorded property, uncertainties arise because the term "property" is not easily defined. This should not be surprising, as the term "property" includes almost every **right,** exclusive of personal liberty, that the law will protect. Property is valuable only because our law provides that certain consequences follow from the ownership of it. The right to use the property, sell it, and control to whom it shall pass on the death of the owner are all included within the term "property." Accordingly, property is an interest or group of interests that is legally protected.

Thus, when a person speaks of "owning property" he may have two separate ideas in mind: (1) the *physical thing* itself, as when a home owner says, "I just bought a piece of property in Oakland," meaning complete ownership of a physically identifiable parcel of land; or (2) a *right* or *interest* in the physical object, as, for example, with respect to land, a tenant under a lease has a property interest in the leased land, although he does not "own" the land.

KINDS OF PROPERTY

Property may be classified as (1) tangible or intangible property and (2) real or personal property. See Figure 46-1. As will be seen, these classifications are not mutually exclusive.

Tangible and Intangible

A forty-acre farm, a chair, and a household pet are *tangible* property. The group of rights or interests referred to as "title" or "ownership" are embodied in each of these *physical* objects. On the other hand, *intangible* property is property that does *not* exist in a physical form. For example, a stock certificate, a promissory note, and a deed granting X a right-of-way over the land of Y are intangible property. Each represents and stands for certain rights that are not capable of reduction to physical possession, but have a legal reality in the sense that they will be protected.

The same item may be the object of both tangible and intangible property rights. Suppose A purchases a book published by B. On the first page, there is the statement "Copyright 1985 by B." A owns the volume he purchased. He has the right to exclusive physical possession and use of that particular copy. It is a tangible piece of property of which he is the owner. B, however, has the exclusive right to publish copies of the book. This is a right granted him by the copyright laws. The courts will protect this intangible property of B's as well as A's right to the particular volume.

Real and Personal

The most significant practical distinction between types of property is the classification into real and personal property. A simple definition would be to say that land and all interests in it are *real* property, and every other thing or interest identified as property is *personal*. For most purposes this easy description is adequate although certain physical objects that are personal property under most

---

FIGURE 46-1   Kinds of Property

	Personal	Real
Tangible	goods	land buildings fixtures
Intangible	commercial paper stock certificates contract rights copyrights patents	leases easements mortgages

circumstances may, because of their attachment to land or their use in connection with land, become a form of real property called *fixtures*.

Fixtures

A fixture is an article or piece of personal property which has been attached in some manner to land or a building so that an interest in it arises under *real* property law. For example, materials for a building are clearly personal property; but when worked into a building as its construction progresses, they become real property because buildings are part of the land. Thus, clay in its natural state is, of course, real property; when made into bricks it becomes personal property and, if the bricks are then built into the wall of a house the "clay" once again becomes real property.

However, it is frequently rather difficult to determine whether a particular item of personal property becomes a fixture. Consider the following list which, at one stage, are clearly personal property but which are used in connection with buildings: heating, lighting, and air conditioning systems; appliances; television antennae; cabinets; fireplaces; door mirrors; venetian blinds; shades; window screens; awnings; storm windows; window boxes; storm doors; screen doors; and mail boxes. These items may be so firmly affixed to the land or building that they become an actual part of the real property, or they may be annexed in such a way as to retain their character as personal property.

While the question whether these various items are personal property or real property may in certain instances be difficult to answer, it is only by obtaining the answer that conflicting claims to their ownership may be determined. Unless otherwise provided by agreement, personal property remains the property of the person who placed it on the real estate. On the other hand, if the property has been affixed so as to become a fixture, an actual part of the real estate, it becomes the property of the owner of the real estate.

These questions affect many persons. The apartment dweller who puts a new chandelier or a bathroom cabinet in his landlord's apartment and the shoe repairman who attaches equipment to the floor of his leased premises will not be entitled to remove them at the expiration of the lease *if* they are held to have become part of the real estate. The seller of real estate who leaves screens on the premises will learn to his surprise that the buyer is entitled to them as part of the real estate even though they were not expressly mentioned in the deed.

In determining whether personal property becomes a fixture, the intention of the parties with conflicting claims to the property as expressed in their agreement will control. Absent the binding force of an agreement, the following guides are helpful in determining whether any particular item is a fixture:

1. the physical relationship of the item to the land or building;
2. the intention of the person who attaches the item to the land or building;
3. the purpose served by the item in relation to the land or building and in relation to the person who brought it there; and
4. the interest of that person in the land or building at the time of the attachment of the item.

Although physical attachment is significant, a more important test is whether the item can be removed without material injury to the land or building on the land. If it *cannot* be so removed, it is generally held that the item has become part of the realty. The converse is also true but to a lesser degree. Where the item may be removed without material injury to the land or building, it is generally held that it has not become part of the realty. This test, however, is not conclusive.

Rather, the courts have searched for the answer in the intention of the person who attached the item to the realty. The tests of intention are objective. One of the tests developed has been to inquire into the purpose or use of the item in relation to the land and in relation to the person who brought it there. If the use or purpose of the item is unusual for the type of realty involved (e.g., a small crane in the backyard of a country house) or peculiar to the particular individual who brought it there, then it may be reasonably concluded that the individual intended to remove the item when he leaves.

However, an item is not regarded as part of the realty merely because its use or purpose is usual for the type of realty involved. For example, it is usual to have beds and dressers in bedrooms and dining tables in dining rooms, but these items are not ordinarily part of the realty. The test of purpose or use applies only if the item both (1) is affixed to the realty in some way and (2) can be removed without material injury to the realty. In such a situation, if the use or purpose of the item is peculiar to the particular owner or occupant of the premises, the courts will tend to let him remove the item when he leaves. Accordingly, in the law of landlord and tenant, it is settled that the tenant may remove **trade fixtures**, i.e., items used in connection with his trade, provided that this can be done without material injury to the realty. On the other hand, doors may be removed without injury to the structure, yet because they are necessary to the ordinary use of the building and not peculiar to the use of the occupant, they are considered fixtures and thus part of the real property. *See Sears, Roebuck, and Co. v. Seven Palms Motor Inn, Inc.*

INCIDENTS OF PROPERTY OWNERSHIP

The importance of the distinction between real and personal property stems primarily from very practical legal consequences that follow from the distinction. Some of these consequences are:

Transfer of Property During Life

As will be explained in Chapter 49, the transfer of real property during life can only be accomplished by certain formalities, including the execution and delivery of a written instrument known as a deed. Personal property, on the other hand, may be transferred with relative simplicity and informality.

Devolution of Title on Death of Owner

In many States, if a person dies without a will, title to her real property passes directly to whomever the law declares to be her heirs, while title to her personal property passes to her personal representative who, in turn, must distribute it as the law directs. For a more detailed discussion of this topic see Chapter 50.

Taxation

Most States levy taxes on the ownership of both real property and personal property. However, the applicable tax rate will be dependent on whether the property is classified as real property or personal property.

PERSONAL PROPERTY

The law pertaining to personal property has been largely codified. The Uniform Commercial Code includes the law of sales of goods (Article 2) as well as the law governing the transfer and negotiation of commercial paper (Article 3) and of investment securities (Article 8). Nonetheless, a number of aspects pertaining to the ownership and transfer of title to personal property are not covered by the Code. The remainder of this chapter will address these issues.

TRANSFER OF TITLE

We shall see that the acquisition or transfer of title to real property is generally a formal affair accompanied by ritual that may have little but historical significance today. In contrast, title to personal property may be acquired and transferred with relative ease and with a minimum of formality. The facility with which personal property may be transferred is required by the demands of a society whose trade and industry is principally based upon transactions in personal property. Stocks, bonds, merchandise, and even ideas must be sold with a minimum of delay in a free economy. It is only natural that the law will reflect these mercantile needs. If the sale of a share of stock or a suit of clothes required the ritual of a sale of land, our conception of commerce would be impossible.

By Sale

By definition, a sale of *tangible* personal property (goods) is a transfer of title to specified existing goods for a consideration known as the price. Title passes when the parties intend it to pass, and transfer of possession is not requisite to a transfer of title. For a discussion of this manner of transfer of title, refer to Chapter 20.

Sales of *intangible* personal property also involve the transfer of title. These sales are also governed by provisions of the U.C.C. except for copyrights and patents which are governed by specialized Federal legislation.

By Gift

A gift is a transfer of property from one person to another without consideration. The lack of any consideration is the basic distinction between a gift and a sale. Since a gift involves no consideration or compensation, to be effective it must be completed by delivery of the gift. A gratuitous promise to make a gift is not binding. In addition, there must be intent on the part of the maker (the **donor**) of the gift to make a present transfer, and there must be acceptance by the recipient (the **donee**) of the gift.

Delivery Delivery is absolutely necessary to a valid gift. The term "delivery" has a very special meaning including, but not limited to,

manual transfer of the item to the donee. There can be "delivery" of a gift sufficient to make it irrevocable if the item is turned over to a third person with instructions to give it to the donee. Frequently, an item, because of its size or location or because it is intangible, is incapable of immediate manual delivery. In such cases an irrevocable gift may be effected by delivery of something symbolic of dominion over the item. This is referred to as **constructive delivery**. For example, if A declares that she gives an antique desk and all its contents to B and hands B the key to the desk, in many States a valid gift has been made.

Intent The law is also clear that there must be an intent on the part of the donor to make a present gift of the property. Thus, if A leaves a packet of stocks and bonds with B, B may or may not acquire good title to them, depending upon whether A intended to make a gift of them or simply to place them in B's hands for safekeeping. A voluntary, uncompensated delivery with intent to give the recipient title constitutes a gift upon the donee's acceptance of it. If these conditions are met, the donor has no further claim to the property. *See Cohen v. Bayside Federal Savings and Loan Association.*

Acceptance The final requirement of a valid gift is acceptance by the donee. In most instances, of course, the donee will accept the gift with gratitude. Accordingly, the law usually presumes that the donee has accepted. However, there are situations where a donee does not wish to accept a gift, such as when the gift imposes a burden upon the donee. In such cases the law will not require the recipient to accept an unwanted gift. For example, a gift of an elephant or a wrecked car in need of extensive repairs may be prudently rejected by a donee.

By Will or Descent

Title to personal property is frequently acquired by inheritance from a person who dies, either with or without a will. This method of acquiring title is discussed in Chapter 50.

By Accession

Many of the practical problems surrounding the title to personal property stem from its principal characteristic—movability. One of these problems is identified by the phrase "title by accession." "*Accession*," in its strict sense, means the right of the owner of property to any increase in it, whether caused by natural or man-made means. For example, the owner of a cow acquires title by accession to any calves born to that cow.

Problems arise, however, if A attaches an item of personal property to B's property without B's consent or if A improves by his labor the property of B without B's consent. For example, A takes lumber belonging to B and without B's consent builds it into a wagon. Or, A takes a silver cup belonging to B and without B's consent melts it down into a tray. To whom does the "new" product belong? The material, or part of it, was originally the property of B. The labor and skill necessary to create the new product were A's. B, the owner of the property converted, will be entitled to one of two forms of relief. He will either be entitled to a return of the item or to damages. Which of these two forms of relief he can claim will depend upon the facts of the case. If the taking was deliberate and with knowledge that the item was the property of another, the general rule is that the original owner can have the improved property returned to him.

The more difficult and frequent problem arises where the person making the improvement mistakenly believes that the property belongs to him. In this case the law is not aided by a sense of punishing a wrongdoer. The law must attempt to reconcile the competing interests of two innocent parties. If there is an innocent taking and the identity of the converted item has changed or the value of the labor is greater than the value of the converted material in its original form, then title passes to the person who applied the labor. In such a case, the original owner will not be entitled to the new item; his only remedy will be an award of money damages for the value of the original article. Otherwise, the original owner may recover the property but must compensate the other party for the reasonable value of the benefits conferred by the improvements.

By Confusion

The basic problem of confusion is somewhat similar to the case of title by accession. It arises when identical goods belonging to different people are so *commingled* that the owners cannot identify their own property. For example, Hereford cattle belonging to B are mixed with Hereford cattle belonging to A, and neither person's herd can be specifically identified; or grain owned by X is combined with similar grain owned by Y. Confusion may result from accident, mistake, willful act, or agreement of the parties. If the goods can be apportioned, each owner proving his proportion of the whole is entitled to receive his share. If, however, the confusion results from the willful and wrongful act of one of the parties, he will lose his entire interest if he cannot prove his share. Frequently, the problem arises not because the original interest cannot be proved but because there is not enough left to distribute a full share to each owner. In such a case, if the confusion was due to mistake, accident, or agreement, the loss will be borne by each in proportion to his share. If caused by an intentional and unauthorized act, the wrongdoer will first bear any loss.

By Possession

In some instances a person may acquire title to movable personal property by taking possession of it. The general rule is that a **finder** is entitled to lost property as against everyone except the true owner. Suppose X, the owner of an apartment complex, leases a kitchenette apartment to Y. One night, Z, Y's mother-in-law, is invited to sleep in the convertible bed in the living room. In the course of preparing the bed, Z finds an emerald ring caught on the springs under the mattress. The ring is turned over to the police, but diligent inquiry does not turn up the true owner. Z will be entitled to the ring because she is considered the "finder."

A different rule applies when the lost property is in the ground. Here, the owner of the land has a claim superior to that of the finder. For example, X employs Y to excavate a lateral sewer. Y uncovers old Indian relics. X, not Y, has the superior claim.

There is a further exception to the rule giving the "finder" first claim against all but the true owner. Most decisions hold that if property has been **mislaid,** not lost, then the owner of the premises, not the "finder," has first claim if the true owner is not discovered. This doctrine is involved frequently in cases where items are found on trains, buses, airplanes, and in restaurants. The true owner, it is said, did not lose the property, she simply mislaid it.

Many States now have statutes which provide a means of vesting title to lost property in the "finder" where a prescribed search for the owner proves fruitless. These statutes generally do not determine the right to possession against any party other than the true owner.

See Paset v. Old Orchard Bank and Trust Co.

CONCURRENT OWNERSHIP

The ownership of real or personal property may be held by one individual or, concurrently, by two or more persons. If title is concurrently in two or more persons, they are generally referred to as **co-tenants,** each entitled to an undivided interest in the entire item and neither having a claim to any specific portion of it. Each may have equal undivided interests or one may have a larger undivided share than the other.

There are four ways in which personal property may be owned concurrently: (1) joint tenancy, (2) tenancy in common, (3) tenancy by the entireties, and (4) community property. The forms of concurrent ownership are discussed in Chapter 48.

CASES

Fixtures

**SEARS, ROEBUCK, AND CO. v.
SEVEN PALMS MOTOR INN, INC.**

Supreme Court of Missouri, 1975.
530 S.W.2d 695.

HENLEY, J.

* * *

It involves a claim by Sears, Roebuck, and Company (respondent) to recover $8,357.49 with interest, and to establish a merchanic's lien, for materials and labor including, among other items, drapes and bedspreads furnished Seven Palms Motor Inn (defendant) in connection with the construc-

tion of a motel on land then owned by it. The case was submitted on a stipulation in which * * * the only issue to be decided is whether respondent is entitled to a mechanic's lien. The trial court decided this issue for respondent and entered judgment accordingly. The court of appeals affirmed the money judgment but reversed that portion of the judgment imposing the lien, holding that the bedspreads were not lienable items and their inclusion in the statement vitiated the entire lien. While we determine the case the same as on original appeal, Mo.Const. Art. V, § 10, we ordered the transfer primarily to review the questions presented by the holding that the whole lien was vitiated. We decide that it was not.

* * *

[Missouri law] provides in part: "Every mechanic or other person, who shall do or perform any work or labor upon, or furnish any material [or], fixtures * * * for any building * * * under or by virtue of any contract with the owner * * * shall have for his work or labor done, or materials [or], fixtures * * * furnished, a lien upon such building * * * and upon the land * * *."

Characterization of an item as a fixture, something otherwise personal but attached to realty under such circumstances as to become part of it, depends upon the finding of three elements: annexation to the realty, adaption to the use to which the realty is devoted, and intent of the annexor that the object become a permanent accession to the freehold [realty]. Missouri cases are uniform in requiring each of these elements to be present in some degree, however slight, before an item may be considered a fixture. [Citations.]

Appellants [Seven Palms] contend that neither the drapes nor the bedspreads are fixtures * * * and therefore not lienable, because they are not annexed or attached to the building.

The purpose of attaching the traverse rods to the realty was to hang drapes therefrom which could be opened or drawn across a window by the motel's guest to control the light in his room or secure his privacy. Of itself, the traverse rod attached to the wall above the window in the room did not accomplish this purpose. To serve this purpose it was essential that the drapes be provided and attached to the rod. They were provided and attached, and became an integral part of the instrument designed for use in connection with the window in the guest's room. As such, the drapes were as much a fixture as the traverse rod itself. It is obvious that the rod and drapes, as a unit, were adapted to the proper use of rooms in a motel and were placed therein with the intent they would form a part of the special purpose for which the building was designed to be used.

Not so the bedspreads. Respondent [Sears] admits that those items are not physically attached to the realty in any way but insists that they have been "constructively annexed." In support of this proposition, respondent argues: the rods are physically fastened to the building; the drapes are affixed to the rods by hooks; the bedspreads match the drapes; a fortiori, the bedspreads "are at least 'constructively annexed' to the rooms * * * by their relationship with the drapes."

The doctrine of constructive annexation recognizes that a particular article, not physically attached to the land, "may be so adapted to the use to which the land is put that it may be considered an integral part of the land" and "constructively annexed" thereto. [Citation.] * * * The rule has not been applied to establishments such as hotels, restaurants, bars, and apartment buildings. Thus, movable furniture, tableware, and similar equipment, although necessary to the operation of a hotel, are generally not considered fixtures. [Citations.]

The bedspreads are not essential to the use of what is clearly a fixture, nor has it been shown that they cannot readily be used independently elsewhere. Respondent asserts that because the bedspreads "were designed to match and to coexist with the drapes" they must be considered part of a matched set which is essential to the use of rods which are clearly fixtures. Respondent seeks support for this contention in cases that have held easily removable parts of machines and other fixtures may not be considered as separate items. [Citations.] However, in each of these cases, the fixture would have been rendered absolutely useless by removal of the items in question, and such items could not readily be used independently elsewhere. There is no indication that the unit of rod and drapes could not serve its function, which respondent says is to "regulate the flow of light and serve the need for privacy," if the bedspreads were removed. That the decor of a guest room in a motel may be more aesthetically pleasing when bedspreads are made of the same material as drapes, falls far short of the functional relationship needed to justify "constructive annexation." Since the bedspreads were not annexed, physically or constructively, they cannot be characterized as fixtures and are, therefore, nonlienable items.

* * *

* * * Respondent's argument that both were lienable was not without some substance, even though we have determined that one, the bedspreads, was not a fixture and not lienable. In these circumstances, the inclusion in the lien statement of the nonlienable item, separable as it is from the lienable items, does not vitiate the entire lien.

Appellants do not question the money judgment in favor of respondent and against defendant, Seven Palms Motor Inn. Accordingly, that part of the judgment is affirmed. That part of the judgment imposing a lien on the property for the full amount of the money judgment is reversed and the cause is remanded with directions that the trial court enter judgment in favor of respondent imposing a lien for the amount of the balance due according to the statement after deducting therefrom the amount charged for the bedspreads.

Transfer of Title by Gift

COHEN v. BAYSIDE FEDERAL SAVINGS AND LOAN ASSOCIATION

Supreme Court of New York, Term, 1970.
62 Misc.2d 738, 309 N.Y.S.2d 980.

TESSLER, J.

The fundamental question presented to this court in an agreed statement of facts submitted by the parties is:

Can an engagement ring, given in contemplation of marriage, be recovered from a "donee", by the estate of the "donor", when the contemplated marriage fails to occur because of the death of the "donor"?

The undisputed facts can be summarized as follows: Richard Alan Rothchild became en-

gaged to be married to Carol Sue Cohen, the defendant in this action. Both were over 21 years of age. Richard gave Carol a diamond "engagement" ring which is valued at $1,000. Shortly before the wedding date, Richard was killed in an automobile accident and his estate has instituted this action to recover the ring. The sole question for determination by this court is: "Who is entitled to the ring?"

Actions for return of engagement rings have had an interesting and confusing history in New York. These actions were permitted at common law prior to 1935. However, in 1935 the Legislature of this State enacted * * * (the heart balm statute) which was later interpreted by the courts so as to bar actions for the return of engagement rings in most instances. [Citations.] These results were widely criticized. [Citations.] In response to this criticism, in 1965 the Legislature amended * * * the Civil Rights Law to permit recovery of engagement rings where "justice so requires."

In Lowe v. Quinn, [citation] the Appellate Division, First Department, held that the common law rules formulated before 1935 would again be applicable. * * *

However, reference to these common law rules formulated prior to 1935 is of little help in the present instance since this case appears to be one of first impression in this State. In the absence of any controlling authority, this court has sought help by looking to applicable decisional law in other jurisdictions, the general principles underlying engagement ring cases in general and, finally, to what justice requires in this situation.

An examination of the relevant authorities in other states indicates that they are split. * * *

* * *

Nor does an examination of the principles underlying the gift of engagement ring cases in general clearly point the way to a particular result. The results set forth in the decisions in gift of engagement ring cases are usually predictable and understandable. However, the legal principles and rationales relied upon by the courts are often divergent and muddled. For example, it is settled that where a fiancee breaks an engagement without the fault of the donor, she must return the ring. [Citation.] It is also well settled that where the donor breaks the engagement, the ring may be kept by the donee [citation] and, generally, where the engagement is broken by mutual consent, the ring also goes back to the donor. [Citation.]

While these results are equitable, the various legal theories asserted are not always logical and persuasive. Some courts have propounded a pledge theory. [Citation.] Other courts state that principles of unjust enrichment govern [citation] and the most popular rationale is that the ring is given as a gift on condition subsequent. [Citation.] It is not always clear, however, whether it is the actual marriage of the parties or the donee's not performing any act what would prevent the marriage that is the actual condition of the "transaction."

Thus, a confusing body of law has grown up around the engagement ring and, after careful consideration of these principles, this court has decided that Carol should keep the ring because that result is equitable and because "justice so requires" for the following reasons:

While the engagement ring to some people in the "mod" world of today is just another material possession and while it has not been unknown in some circles for recipients of these rings to flaunt them, to compare their luster, number of carats, etc., with the rings of their friends, for the vast majority the ring still remains a hallowed symbol of the love and devotion that a prospective husband and wife bear for each other. In my judgment, no gift given during a lifetime can approach the meaningfulness and significance of the engagement ring. When Richard gave the ring to Carol, he obviously intended that she have it and keep it unless she affirmatively did something to prevent the marriage of the parties. While it is improbable that at the time of the gift either gave a thought to the consequences that would arise in the event of the death of one of the parties, I firmly believe that had Richard thought of these consequences he would have intended that in the event of his untimely death Carol should keep the ring as a symbol of his love and affection. There appears to be no reason, in logic or morals, to prevent such a result.

This court frankly acknowledges that implicit in this determination is a recognition that the gift of an engagement ring is a special occasion interwoven with romance and mutual love. It is a meaningful act symbolic of much more than the ordinary and usual business transaction. I am convinced that it is time for a change in our approach to this area. The traditional approach of applying the sound and settled principles of business law and the law of gifts to the giving of an engagement ring has resulted in a myriad of decisional law in this area, which is, to say the least, in much confusion and determinative of little.

I cannot believe that the age-old ritual of giving an engagement ring to bind the mutual premarital vows can be or is intended to be treated as an exchange of consideration as practiced in the everyday market place. Can it be seriously urged that the giving of this ring by the decedent "groom" to his loved one and bride-to-be can be treated as the ordinary commercial or business transaction requiring the ultimate in consideration and payment? I think not. To treat this special and usually once in a lifetime occasion, one as requiring quid pro quo, is a mistake and unrealistic.

Accordingly, the ring shall remain with Carol and judgment shall be entered.

Title to Lost or Misplaced
Personal Property

PASET v. OLD ORCHARD BANK AND TRUST CO.

Appellate Court of Illinois, First District, 1978.
62 Ill.App.3d 534, 19 Ill.Dec. 389, 378 N.E.2d 1264.

SIMON, J.

On May 8, 1974, the plaintiff, Bernice Paset, a safety deposit box subscriber at the defendant Old Orchard Bank (the bank), found $6,325 in currency on the seat of a chair in an examination booth in the safety deposit vault. The chair was partially under a table. The plaintiff notified officers of the bank and turned the money over to them. She then was told by bank officials that the bank would try to locate the owner, and that she could have the money if the owner was not located within 1 year.

The bank wrote to everyone who had been in the safety deposit vault area either on the day of, or on the day preceding, the discovery, stating that some property had been found and inviting the customers to describe any property they might have lost. No one reported the loss of currency, and the money remained unclaimed a year after it had been found. However, when the plaintiff requested the money, the bank refused to deliver it to her, explaining that it was obligated to hold the currency for the owner.

The safety deposit vault area of the bank was located on a lower floor of the bank. This area was separated from a lobby by a gate, and * * * entrance to the safety deposit vault area was restricted to bank employees and customers maintaining safety deposit boxes in the vault. * * * The plaintiff sought a declaratory judgment that the Illinois estray statute [citation] was applicable to her discovery and granted her ownership of the $6,325. The circuit court judge, however, found that the money was "deemed mislaid," and concluded that despite the plaintiff's compliance with the requirements of the estray statute, that statute was not applicable.

This appeal, then, requires a determination of whether a finder of cash in an examining booth in a safety deposit vault may be a keeper under the Illinois estray statute and an analysis of the extent to which the common law concepts of lost and mislaid property apply to the statute. * * * The Illinois estray statute's principle purposes are to encourage and facilitate the return of property to the true owner, and then to reward a finder for his honesty if the property remains un-

claimed. The statute provides an incentive for finders to report their discoveries by making it possible for them, after the passage of the requisite time, to acquire legal title to the property they have found. [Citation.] By directing the county clerk to publicize and advertise the property, the statute further enhances the opportunity of the owner to recover what he has lost.

Traditionally, the common law has treated lost and mislaid property differently for the purposes of determining ownership of property someone has found. Mislaid property is that which is intentionally put in a certain place and later forgotten; at common law a finder acquires no rights to mislaid property. The element of intentional deposit present in the case of mislaid property is absent in the case of lost property, for property is deemed lost when it is unintentionally separated from the dominion of its owner. The general rule is that the finder is entitled to possession of lost property against everyone except the true owner. We are not concerned in this case with abandoned property where the owner, intending to relinquish all rights to his property, leaves it free to be appropriated by any other person. Although at common law the finder is entitled to keep abandoned property, the plaintiff has not taken the position that the money here was abandoned. [Citation.]

As is usual in cases involving a determination of whether property is lost or mislaid, this court is not here assisted by direct evidence, for, obviously, the true owner is not available to state what his intent was. Also, because all the evidence here has been presented by affidavit or stipulation, this court is in as advantageous a position as the trial judge to determine whether the money was lost or mislaid. Our conclusion is that the estray statute should be applied, and ownership of the money vested in the plaintiff finder.

Thus, we do not accept the bank's argument that the money was mislaid rather than lost. It is complete speculation to infer, as the bank urges, that the money was deliberately placed by its owner on the chair located partially under a table in the examining booth, and then forgotten. If the money was intentionally placed on the chair by someone who forgot where he left it, the bank's notice to safety deposit box subscribers should have alerted the owner. The failure of an owner to appear to claim the money in the interval since its discovery is affirmative evidence that the property was not mislaid. [Citations.]

Because the evidence, though ambiguous, tends to indicate that the money probably was not mislaid, and because neither party contends that the money was abandoned, we conclude that the ambiguity should, as a matter of public policy, be resolved in favor of the presumption that the money was lost. This conclusion is in harmony with the above mentioned purposes of the estray statute, for it construes the statute liberally rather than technically, with the result that the statute

is brought into play rather than rejected. Such an application of the statute better effectuates the legislature's goal of restoring property to a true owner, it provides incentive for a finder to report his discovery by rewarding him if the true owner does not appear within the statutorily-determined time limit.

* * *

Further, whether the property was discovered in a public or private place should not be permitted to preclude the application of the estray statute. The statute itself makes no distinction between "public" and "private" places of finding. * * *

Accordingly, the judgment of the circuit court is reversed and the case is remanded with directions to enter judgment in favor of the plaintiff finder.

Judgment reversed and remanded with directions.

PROBLEMS

1. In January, Roger Burke loaned his favorite nephew, Jimmy White, his valuable painting by Picasso. Knowing that on May 15, Jimmy would celebrate his twenty-first birthday, Burke, on April 14, sent a letter to Jimmy stating:

Dear Jimmy,

Tomorrow I leave on my annual trip to Europe, and I want to make you a fitting birthday gift which I do by sending you my enclosed promissory note. Also I want you to keep the Picasso which I loaned you last January, and you may now consider it yours. Happy birthday!

Affectionately,
/s/ Uncle Roger

The negotiable promissory note for $5,000 sent with the letter was signed by Roger Burke, payable to Jimmy White or bearer, and dated May 15. On May 21, Burke was killed in an automobile accident while motoring in France.

First Bank was appointed administrator of Burke's estate. Jimmy presented the note to the administrator and demanded payment, which was refused. Jimmy brought an action against First

Bank as administrator seeking recovery on the note. The administrator brought an action against Jimmy seeking return of the painting by Picasso.

(a) What decision in the action on the note?

(b) What decision in the action to recover the painting?

2. Several years ago P purchased a tract of land on which there was an old, vacant house. Recently, P employed F, a carpenter, to repair and remodel the house. While F was tearing out a partition for the purpose of enlarging one of the rooms, he discovered a metal box hidden in the wall of the house. F broke open the box and discovered that it contained $2,000 in gold and silver coins and old-style bills. F then took the box and its contents to P and told her where he had found it. When F handed the box and the money over to P, he said, "If you do not find the owner, I claim the money." P placed the money in an envelope and deposited it in her safe deposit box where it is at present. No one has ever claimed the money, but P refuses to give it to F.

F brings an action against P to recover the money. Decision?

3. Gable, the owner of a lumber company, was cutting trees over the boundary line of his property and property owned by Lane. Although he realized he had crossed onto Lane's property, Gable cut trees on Lane's property of the same kind as those he had cut on his own land. While on Lane's property, he found a diamond ring on the ground, which he took home. All of the timber cut that day by Gable was commingled.

What are Lane's rights, if any, (a) in the timber; and (b) in the ring?

4. Decide each of the following problems.

(a) A chimney sweep found a jewel and took it to a goldsmith whose apprentice took the stone out and refused to return it. The chimney sweep sues the goldsmith.

(b) One of several boys walking along a railroad track found an old stocking. All started playing with it until it burst in the hands of its discoverer, revealing several hundred dollars. The original discoverer claims it all; the other boys claim it should be divided equally.

(c) A traveling salesman notices a parcel of bank notes on the floor of a store as he is leaving. He picks them up and gives them to the owner of the store to keep for the true owner. After three years they have not been reclaimed, and the salesman sues the storekeeper.

(d) F is hired to clean out the swimming pool at the country club. He finds a diamond ring on the bottom of the pool. The true owner cannot be found. The country club sues F for possession of the ring.

(e) A customer found a pocketbook lying on a barber's table. He gave it to the barber to hold for the true owner who failed to appear. The customer sues the barber.

5. Jones had fifty crates of oranges about equally divided between grades A, B, and C, grade A being the highest quality and C the lowest quality. Smith had 1,000 crates of oranges, about 90 percent of which were of grade A but some of them grades B and C, the exact quantity of each being unknown. Smith willfully mixed Jones's crates with his own so that it was impossible to identify any particular crate. Jones seized the whole lot. Smith demanded 900 crates of grade A and fifty each of grades B and C. Jones refused to give them up unless Smith could identify particular crates. This Smith could not do. Smith brought an action against Jones to recover what he demanded or its value. Judgment for whom, and why?

6. A, the owner and operator of Blackacre, decided to cease farming operations and liquidate his holdings. A sold fifty head of yearling Merino sheep to B and then sold Blackacre to C. He executed and delivered to B a bill of sale for the sheep and was paid for the fifty sheep. It was understood that B would send a truck for the sheep within a few days. At the same time, A executed a warranty deed conveying Blackacre to C. C took possession of the farm and brought along 100 head of his yearling Merino sheep and turned them into the pasture, not knowing the sheep A sold B were still in the pasture. After the sheep were mixed, it was impossible to identify the fifty head belonging to B. After proper demand, B sued C to recover the fifty head of sheep. Decision?

7. O permitted S to take her very old grandfather clock on the basis of S's representations that he was skilled at repairing such clocks and restoring them to their original condition and could do the job for sixty dollars. The clock had been badly damaged for years. S immediately sold it to Fixit Shop for thirty dollars. Fixit Shop was in the business of repairing a large variety of items and also sold used articles. Three months later, O was in the Fixit Shop and clearly established that a grandfather clock Fixit Shop had for sale was the one she had given S to repair. Fixit Shop has replaced more than half of the moving parts by having exact duplicates custom made; the clock's exterior had been restored by a skilled cabinet maker; and the clock's face had been replaced by a duplicate. All materials belonged to Fixit Shop, and the work was accomplished by its employees. Fixit Shop asserts it bought the clock in the normal course of business from S who represented that it belonged to him. The fair market value of the clock in its damaged condition was thirty dollars, and the value of repairs made is $220.

O sued Fixit Shop for return of the clock. Fixit Shop defended that it now had title to the clock, and, in the alternative, that O must pay the value of the repairs if she is entitled to regain possession. Decision?

8. A rented a vacant lot from B for a filling station under an oral agreement and placed on it a lightly constructed building bolted to a concrete slab and storage tanks laid on the ground in a shallow excavation. Later, a lease was prepared by A, providing that A might remove the equipment at the termination of the lease. This lease was not executed, having been rejected by B because of a

renewal clause it contained, but several years later another lease was prepared which A and B signed. This lease did not mention removal of the equipment. At the termination of this lease A removed the equipment, and B brought an action to recover possession of the equipment. What judgment?

9. A sold a parcel of real estate, describing it by its legal description and making no mention of any improvements or fixtures on it. The land had upon it a residence, a barn, a rail fence, a stack of hay, some growing corn, and a wind mill; and the residence had a mirror built into the panel, a heating system consisting of a furnace, steam pipes and coils; in the house were chairs, beds, tables, and other furniture. On the house was a lightning rod. In the basement were screens for the windows. State which of these things passed by the deed and which did not.

10. John Swan rented a safety deposit box at the Tenth Citizens Bank of Emanon, State of X. On December 17, 1984, Swan went to the Bank with stock certificates for placing in the safety deposit box. After admittance to the vault and having placed the stock certificates in the box, Swan found lying on the floor of the vault a $5,000 negotiable bearer bond issued by the State of Wisconsin with coupons attached, due June 30, 1990. Swan picked up the bond and, observing that it did not recite the name of the owner, left the vault and went to the office of the President of the Bank. He told the President what had occurred and delivered the bond to the President only after obtaining his promise that, should the owner not call for the bond or become known to the Bank by June 30, 1985, the Bank would redeliver the bond to Swan. On July 1, Swan learned that the owner of the bond had not called for it, nor was his identity known to the Bank. Swan then asked that the bond be returned to him. The Bank refused, stating that it would continue to hold the bond until claimed by the owner. Swan brings an action against the Bank to recover possession of the bond. Decision?

Chapter 47

BAILMENTS AND DOCUMENTS OF TITLE

A bailment is the relationship created by the transfer by delivery of possession of personal property, without transfer of title, by one person called the **bailor,** to another called the **bailee** for the accomplishment of a certain purpose, after which the property is to be returned by the bailee to the bailor or disposed of according to the bailor's directions. Unlike such well-known legal terms as contract, agent, sale, partnership, corporation, and insurance, the term "bailment" has not passed into common usage, and so is not familiar to the average person. Nonetheless, the word "bailment" denotes a transaction which is not only of considerable antiquity but which is also one of the most common occurrences in everyday life. It is not an exaggeration to say that practically every person, whether carrying on a business or not, becomes a party to a bailment. This will be readily understood from the following common ex-

amples of bailments: keeping a car in a public garage; leaving a car, watch, or any other article to be repaired; renting a car or truck; checking a hat or coat at a theater or restaurant; leaving wearing apparel to be laundered, pressed, cleaned, or dyed; delivery of jewelry or other valuables or of stocks or bonds to secure the payment of a debt; storage of goods in a warehouse; and the shipment of goods by any mode of public or private transportation.

Not only are bailments of common occurrence but they are also of great commercial importance in their own right. As the above examples indicate, bailments encompass the transportation, storage, repairing, and renting of goods, which together involve billions of dollars' worth of transactions each year.

Documents of title are commonly used in bailment transactions. The most frequently used documents of title are warehouse receipts issued by warehousemen and bills of lading issued by carriers.

BAILMENTS

The benefit of a bailment may, by its terms, accrue solely to the bailor or solely to the bailee, or may accrue to both parties. A bailment may be with or without compensation. On this basis, bailments are classified as follows:

1. **Bailments for the bailor's sole benefit** include the gratuitous custody of personal property and the gratuitous services which involve personal property such as repairs or transportation. For example, if B stores, repairs, or transports A's goods without compensation, this is a bailment for the sole benefit of the bailor, A.

2. **Bailments for the bailee's sole benefit** are usually limited to the gratuitous loan of personal property for use by the bailee, as where A, without compensation, lends his car, lawn mower, or book to B for B's use.

3. **Bailments for the mutual benefit of both parties** include the ordinary commercial bailments such as when goods are delivered to a repairman, jewels to a pawnbroker, or an automobile delivered to a parking lot attendant.

ESSENTIAL ELEMENTS OF A BAILMENT

The basic and essential elements of a bailment are (1) the parties, known respectively as bailor and bailee; (2) the subject matter, which must be personal property and not real property; (3) possession of the property, but without ownership, by the bailee; and (4) an absolute duty on the bailee to return the property to the bailor or to dispose of it according to the bailor's directions.

In the great majority of cases, there are two simple tests by which the existence of a bailment can be determined, namely (1) a sep-

aration of ownership and possession of the property (possession without ownership) and (2) a duty on the party in possession to redeliver the identical property to the owner or to dispose of it according to his directions.

Delivery of Possession

The term "bailment" is derived from the French word *bailler*, which means to deliver. Possession by a bailee in a bailment relationship involves: (1) the bailee's power to control, and (2) either an intention to control or an awareness on the part of the bailee that the rightful possessor has given up physical control of the personal property. Thus, where a customer in a restaurant hangs her hat or coat on a hook furnished for that purpose, the hat or coat is within an area which is under the physical control of the restaurant owner. However, the restaurant owner is not a bailee of the hat or coat unless he clearly signifies that he intends to exercise the power to control the hat or coat. On the other hand, where a clerk in a store helps a customer remove her coat in order to try on a new one, it is generally held that the owner of the store becomes a bailee of the old coat through the clerk, his employee. Here, the clerk has signified an intention to exercise control over the coat by taking it from the customer and a bailment results.

Traditionally, the courts have analyzed the "possession" question by seeking to determine whether there has been a delivery. They have said that the customer in the restaurant does not "deliver" the coat or hat to the restaurant owner when he hangs it on a hook, while the customer in the store "delivers" his coat to the clerk. This concept of delivery, however, does not account for many cases where a bailment is said to exist. For example, suppose that the customer in the restuarant hangs his hat on a hook and then forgets and leaves it behind. If the restaurant owner then notices the hat and realizes that it has been left behind by one of his customers, he becomes a bailee of the hat. What has happened is not that some mysterious delivery has suddenly taken place, but that the restaurant owner, having physical control of the area in which the hat is found, becomes aware that the rightful possessor has relinquished the power to control it, that he now has both the power to control and the intent to control, and therefore possession of the hat. This is similar to the position of all finders of personal property. *See Laval v. Leopold.*

The "parking lot cases" fall generally into three categories: (1) where an owner parks his car in a parking lot, pays a charge, and receives a claim check, but locks the car and takes the keys away; (2) where an owner leaves his car with an attendant who assumes control of the car and parks it, and the owner pays a charge and receives a ticket as a means of identifying the car on redelivery; and (3) where the status of the parties falls in between the above two categories and is controlled by the nature of the circumstances.

The first class of cases is generally held to be a lease or license, whereas the second class is held to be a bailment. The third class covers cases where, even though the owner parks his car and keeps the keys, the parking lot operator maintains sufficient control to constitute a bailment. In analyzing this third class of cases, the amount of free access permitted by the parking lot operator is crucial. The question is how much control does the parking lot operator hold himself out to the public to be exercising? *See Sewall v. Fitz-Inn Auto Parks, Inc.*

Personal Property

The bailment relation can only exist with respect to personal property. The delivery of possession of real property by the owner to another is covered by real property law. It is not necessary that the bailed property be tangible. Intangible property such as promissory notes, corporate bonds, shares of stock and life insurance policies being evidenced by written instruments and thus capable of delivery, may be and frequently are the subject matter of bailments. This is also true of such documents of title as warehouse receipts and bills of lading.

Possession for a Determinable Time

To establish a bailment relationship the person receiving possession must be under a duty to return the personal property and must not obtain title to it. This brings us to a discussion of the distinction between bailments and transactions involving transfers of title, such as sales.

Sales Whether a particular transaction constitutes a bailment or a sale must be determined by the particular factual situation presented. A sale always involves a transfer to the buyer of *title* to specific property. If the identical property transferred is to be returned, even though in altered form, the transaction is a bailment; however, if other property of equal value or the money value may be returned, there is a transfer of title, and the transaction is a sale.

Conditional Sales In a conditional sale the seller reserves title to the goods until the purchase price is paid in full. However, title is reserved in the seller for security purposes only. For all other purposes, including risk of loss, beneficial ownership is in the buyer. The position of the buyer under a conditional sales contract is not the same as that of a bailee in any respect. He has no option to return the goods but must pay the contract price. On the other hand, a bailee *must* return the goods or be liable to the bailor for their value. The fact that the goods are damaged or destroyed without his fault will not relieve the buyer from payment of the contract price because the goods are at his risk. In contrast, a bailee is not liable for goods destroyed without his fault.

Other Transfers of Title Whenever a person intentionally abandons all her interest in certain personal property, the relation between her and the person who takes possession of the property will not be that of bailor and bailee. On the other hand, a loser and finder are bailor and bailee because, although the loser may abandon hope that she will ever find the property, she does not abandon her interest in it. One who intentionally throws her property away, however, cannot be a bailor because she has abandoned her interest in it. Likewise, one who gives her property to another is not a bailor because she has transferred title to the donee. Thus, the finder of intentionally abandoned property and the donee of a gift are not bailees.

Restoration of Possession to the Bailor

The bailee is legally obligated to restore possession of the property when the period of the bailment has come to an end. A bailment for the mutual benefit of both parties ordinarily terminates when the purpose of the bailment is fully accomplished or when the time expires for which the bailment was created. The bailment may, of course, be terminated earlier by mutual consent of the parties. A breach by the bailee of any of his obligations gives the bailor the privilege of terminating the bailment. A bailment is also terminated by destruction of the bailed property because there can be no bailment without personal property.

Bailments for the benefit of the bailee alone or for the benefit of the bailor alone are ordinarily for a definite time or purpose. Such bailments do not terminate until the specified time expires or the purpose is accomplished. In practice, however, such bailments are often terminated at will. For example, one who has gratuitously undertaken to store his neighbor's piano for six months will most likely be able to return the piano before the expiration of that period without liability.

Normally, the bailee is required to return the identical goods bailed although the goods may be in a changed condition due to the work which the bailee was required to

perform upon them. An exception to this rule obtains in the case of **fungible goods,** such as grain, where, for all practical purposes, every particle is the equivalent of every other particle, and which the bailee is expected to mingle with other like goods during the bailment. In such a case, obviously the bailee cannot be required to return the identical goods bailed. His obligation is simply to return goods of the same quality and quantity.

The very nature of a bailment requires a bailee to return the property when the purpose of the bailment has been accomplished to the bailor or to a person designated by the bailor at the proper time or place. The bailee has a strict duty to return the property to the correct person.

RIGHTS AND DUTIES OF BAILOR AND BAILEE

The bailment relationship creates rights and duties on the part of the bailor and the bailee. The bailee is under a duty to exercise due care for the safety of the property and to return it to the right person. The bailee has the exclusive right to possess the property for the term of the bailment. Depending upon the nature of the transaction, a bailee may have the right to compensation and reimbursement of expenses.

The law does not permit certain bailees—namely, common carriers, public warehousemen, and innkeepers—to limit their liability for breach of their duties to the bailor, except as provided by statute. Other bailees, however, may vary their duties and liabilities by contract with the bailor. Where liability is limited by contract, the law requires that any such limitation be properly brought to the attention of the bailor before the property is bailed by her. This is especially true in the case of "professional bailees," such as repair garages, who make it their business to act as bailees and who deal with the public on a uniform rather than an individual basis. Thus, a variation or limitation in writing contained in a check or stub given to the bailor or posted on the walls of the bailee's place of business will *not* ordinarily bind the bailor unless (a) the bailee draws her attention to the writing and (b) informs her that it contains a limitation or variation of liability.

Bailee's Duty to Exercise Due Care

The bailee must exercise due care not to permit injury to or destruction of the property by himself or third parties. The degree of care depends upon the nature of the bailment relationship and the character of the property. *See Mieske v. Bartell Drug Co.*

Ordinarily, a bailee is *not* an insurer of the subject of the bailment. Since the failure to exercise due care for the property or intentional wrongdoing is the basis of his liability, in the absence of fault, the bailee is not liable where the property is lost, stolen, or destroyed.

In the context of a **commercial bailment,** from which both parties derive a mutual benefit, the law requires the bailee to exercise the care which a reasonably prudent person would exercise under the same circumstances. Where the bailment is one which benefits the bailee alone, as in the case of one who gratuitously borrows a truck from another, the law requires more than reasonable care of him. On the other hand, where the bailee accepts the property for the sole benefit of the bailor, the law requires a lesser degree of care. See Figure 47-1.

It should be remembered, however, that the amount of care required to satisfy any of the standards will vary with the character of the property. A bailee required to take only slight care under the foregoing general rules may be liable if he does not take greater care of a $1,000 bracelet than he would have of a $20 watch. In practice, therefore, the distinctions are blurred by the fact that whatever degree of care is required in the abstract, a bailee must respond to the magnitude of the consequences which reasonably ought to have been foreseen if the property were lost or destroyed.

When the property is lost, damaged, or destroyed while in the possession of the bailee, it is often impossible for the bailor to obtain enough information to show that the loss or damage was due to the bailee's failure to exercise the required care. The law aids the bailor in this respect by setting up a *presumption* that the bailee was at fault. The bailor is merely required to show that certain property was delivered by way of bailment and that the bailee has failed to return them or that they were returned in damaged condition. The burden then rests upon the bailee to prove that he exercised the degree of care required of him.

Bailee's Absolute Liability

As just discussed, the bailee is free from liability if she has exercised the degree of care required of her under the particular bailment, while the property was within her control. To this general rule there are certain important exceptions that impose an absolute duty upon the bailee to return the property undamaged to the proper person.

Where the bailee has an obligation by express *agreement* with the bailor or by *custom* to insure the property against certain risks, but fails to do so and the property is

---

FIGURE 47-1   Bailee's Duty of Care

Type of Bailment	Duty of Care	Liability For
For sole benefit of bailor	Relaxed	Gross negligence
For sole benefit of bailee	Utmost	Slight negligence
For mutual benefit	Ordinary	Ordinary negligence

destroyed or damaged through such risks, she is liable for the damage or non-delivery, even though she has exercised due care.

Where the bailee uses the bailed property in a manner *not* authorized by the bailor or by the character of the bailment, and during the course of such use the property is damaged or destroyed, without fault on the part of the bailee, the bailee is absolutely liable for the damage or destruction. The reason for this is that wrongful use by the bailee automatically terminates her lawful possession, and she becomes a trespasser as to the property. To illustrate, suppose a garage mechanic, after repairing A's car, takes it out for a road test, and the car is damaged in an accident which is solely the fault of someone other than the mechanic. The proprietor of the garage will not be liable as bailee for such damage, because a road test is a normal incident to this type of bailment. However, where the mechanic takes A's car for a joy ride or on independent business, and the car is damaged solely through the fault of someone other than the mechanic, the proprietor will be absolutely liable as bailee for such damage.

A bailee has a duty to return the property to the right person. She is not excused by delivering the property to the wrong person by mistake, even where such mistake was induced by negligence on the part of the bailor. If the bailee, by mistake or intentionally, *misdelivers* the property to someone other than the bailor, someone who has no right to its possession, she is guilty of conversion and is liable to the bailor.

Bailee's Right to Compensation

A bailee, who by express or implied agreement undertakes to perform work upon or render services in connection with the bailed goods, is entitled to reasonable compensation for those services or work. In most cases, the agreement between bailor and bailee fixes the amount of compensation and provides how it shall be paid. In the absence of a contrary

agreement, the compensation is payable upon completion of the work or the performance of the services by the bailee. If, after such completion or performance, and before the goods are redelivered to the bailor, the goods are lost or damaged without fault on the part of the bailee, the bailee is still entitled to compensation for his work and services.

Most bailees who are entitled to compensation for work and services performed in connection with bailed goods acquire a lien upon the goods to secure the payment of such compensation. By statute in most jurisdictions the bailee is given the right to obtain a judicial foreclosure of his lien and sale of the goods. A substantial number of statutes provide also that the bailee does not lose his lien upon redelivery of the goods to the bailor, as was the case at common law. Instead, the lien continues for a specified period after redelivery by timely recording with the proper authorities an instrument claiming such lien.

SPECIAL KINDS OF BAILMENTS

While pledgees, warehousemen, and safe deposit companies are ordinarily bailees and are subject to the general principles applicable to all ordinary bailees, there are some special features about the transactions in which they respectively engage which make it desirable they be given some further consideration. In addition, innkeepers and common carriers are known as *"extraordinary"* bailees, while all other bailees are known as *"ordinary"* bailees. This distinction is based upon the character and extent of the liability of these two classes of bailees for loss of or injury to the bailed goods. As has been seen, an ordinary bailee is liable for such loss or injury only where it resulted from his failure to exercise ordinary or reasonable care. The liability of the extraordinary bailee, on the other hand, is, in general, **absolute.** In other words, the extraordinary bailee is liable to the bailor for any loss or injury to the goods without regard to the question of his care of negligence as to their safety. As it is frequently put, an extraordinary bailee is an insurer of the safety of the goods. This simply means that just as an insurer, in general, becomes automatically liable to the insured upon the happening of the hazard insured against, regardless of the cause, so likewise does the extraordinary bailee become liable to the bailor for any loss or injury to the goods, regardless of the cause.

Pledges

A pledge is a bailment for security in which the owner gives possession of her personal property to another (the secured party) to secure a debt or the performance of some obligation. The secured party does not have title to the property involved but merely a possessory interest to secure a debt or some other obligation. The secured party can usually transfer and assign his special interest in the property to others, even without the consent of the debtor. Pledges of most types of personal property for security purposes are governed by Article 9 of the Uniform Commercial Code, which is discussed in Chapter 37. In most respects the secured party's duties and liabilities are the same as those of a bailee for compensation.

Warehousing

A warehouseman is a bailee who receives goods to be stored in his warehouse for compensation. His duties and liabilities under the common law were in all respects the same as those of the ordinary bailee for compensation. Today, because the activities of warehousemen are affected by a strong public interest, they are subject to extensive regulation by State and Federal authorities. Warehousemen must also be distinguished from ordinary bailees in that the receipts they issue for storage have acquired a special status in commerce. These receipts are regarded as "documents of title" and are governed by Article 7 of the Uniform Commercial Code, discussed later in this chapter.

Carriers of Goods

In the broadest sense of the term, anyone is a carrier who transports goods from one place to another, either gratuitously or for compensation. Normally, however, a carrier engages in the business of transportation for hire or reward. The delivery of goods to a carrier for shipment creates a bailment; the carrier has the exclusive possession of the goods without ownership, and is under a duty to deliver them to the person designated by the shipper. The carrier of goods is by far the most important of all bailees. Not only are his transactions the most numerous and the largest in volume, but his function in the movement of raw materials and the distribution of manufactured and other goods of every description is of enormous importance in our economic system.

Carriers are classified primarily as common carriers and private carriers. A **common carrier** offers its services and facilities to the public upon terms and under circumstances which indicate that the offering is made to all persons. Common carriers of goods include railroad, steamship, aircraft, public trucking, and pipe line companies. One who carries the goods of another on isolated occasions or who serves a limited number of customers under individual contracts without offering the same or similar contracts to the public at large, is a **private or contract carrier**—not a common carrier. Stated somewhat differently, the criteria for determining whether a carrier is subject to the rules applicable to common carriers are: (1) the carriage must be part of its business; (2) the carriage must be for remuneration; and (3) the carrier must represent to the general public that it is willing to serve the public in the transportation of property.

The person who delivers goods to a carrier for shipment is known as the **consignor or shipper.** The person to whom the goods are to be delivered by the carrier is known as the **consignee.** The instrument containing the terms of the contract of transportation, which the carrier issues to the shipper, is called a **bill of lading.**

Duty to Carry A common carrier is under a duty to serve the public to the limits of its capacity and, within those limits, to accept for carriage goods of the kind which it normally transports. A private carrier has no duty to accept goods for carriage except where it agrees to do so by contract.

Liability for Loss or Damage A private carrier, in the absence of special contract terms, is liable as a bailee with respect to the goods it undertakes to carry. The common carrier, on the other hand, is under a stricter liability which approaches that of an insurer of the safety of the goods, except where loss or damage is caused by an act of God, an act of a public enemy, the acts or fault of the shipper, the inherent nature or defect of the goods, or an act of the public authority.

In most jurisdictions the carrier is permitted to limit its liability by contract with the shipper. However, a carrier may not absolve itself of liability for its own negligence. U.C.C., Section 7–309.

Duty to Deliver to the Right Person The carrier is under an absolute duty to deliver the goods to the person to whom they are consigned by the shipper. This duty is not peculiar to common carriers but applies also to private carriers. Essentially, this is the duty which renders an ordinary bailee liable for misdelivery. The person to whom delivery must be made is controlled by the form of the bill of lading or other contract of carriage, as discussed later in this chapter.

Innkeepers

At common law, innkeepers (today better known as hotel owners or operators) are held to the same **strict liability** with regard to their guests' belongings as are common carriers with regard to the goods they carry. This rule of strict liability applies only to those who furnish lodging to the public for compensation as a regular business, and such liability extends only to the belongings of lodgers who are "guests." To qualify as a "guest," within this rule, a person must be a "transient"; thus persons who intend to become and are accepted as permanent lodgers are not guests.

Today, in almost all jurisdictions, the old common law strict liability of the innkeeper has been substantially modified by case law and statute. The statutes vary as to detail, but they all have certain features in common. They provide that the innkeeper may avoid strict liability for loss of his guests' valuables or money by providing a safe where they may be kept and by posting adequate notice of its availability. With regard to articles which are not placed in a safe provided for this purpose, or which are not articles of the kind normally kept in a safe, the statutes often limit recovery to a maximum figure which, while it differs from State to State, is generally insubstantial. However, these statutory limitations do not apply where the loss is due to the fault of the innkeeper or his employees, in which event the innkeeper is liable for the full value of the lost property.

DOCUMENTS OF TITLE

A document of title is a warehouse receipt, bill of lading, or other document which evidences a right to receive, hold, and dispose of the document *and* the goods it covers. To be a document of title a document must be issued by or addressed to a bailee and cover goods in the bailee's possession which are either identified or are fungible portions of an identified mass.

Briefly, a document of title is a symbol of ownership of the goods it describes. Because of the legal characteristics of a document of title, its ownership is equivalent to the ownership or control of the goods it represents, without the necessity of the actual or physical possession of the goods. Likewise, its transfer is a transfer of the ownership or control of the goods without the necessity or inconvenience of the physical transfer of the goods themselves. For these reasons, documents of title afford a convenient way of dealing with the billions of dollars' worth of goods which are transported by carriers or are stored with warehousemen. Documents of title also serve a very important function in facilitating the transfer of title to goods and the creation of a security interest in goods. Article 7 of the U.C.C. has consolidated and revised the Uniform Warehouse Receipts Act and the Uniform Bills of Lading Act and now governs the negotiation of documents of title.

TYPES OF DOCUMENTS OF TITLE

Section 1–201(15) of the U.C.C. defines document of title as follows:

(15) "Document of title" includes bill of lading, dock warrant, dock receipt, warehouse receipt or order for the delivery of goods, and also any other document which in the regular course of business or financing is treated as adequately evidencing that the person in possession of it is entitled to receive, hold and dispose of the document and the goods it covers. To be a document of title a document must purport to be issued by or addressed to a bailee and purport to cover goods in the bailee's possession which are either identified or are fungible portions of an identified mass.

Warehouse Receipts

A warehouse receipt is a receipt issued by a person engaged in the business of **storing** goods for hire. Section 1–201(45).

Duties of Warehouseman A warehouseman is liable for damages for loss or injury to the goods caused by his failure to exercise such care in regard to them as a reasonably careful man would exercise under the circumstances. Section 7–204(1). The warehouseman must deliver the goods to the person entitled to receive them under the terms of the warehouse receipt. If he has already delivered the goods to another, the burden is on him to establish that such delivery was rightful as

against the holder of the document. Similarly, if the goods have become damaged, lost, or destroyed, the burden is on the warehouseman to prove by evidence the facts and circumstances which establish her non-liability. Section 7–403(1). *See I.C.C. Metals, Inc. v. Municipal Warehouse Co.*

The extent of the liability of a warehouseman, however, *may* be limited by a provision in the warehouse receipt fixing a specific maximum liability per article or item or unit of weight. This limitation does not apply in the event of a conversion of the goods by the warehouseman to his own use. Section 7–204(2).

A warehouseman is not required to keep the goods indefinitely. At the termination of the period of storage stated in the document, the warehouseman may notify the person on whose account the goods are held to pay storage charges and remove the goods. If no period of time is stated in the document, the warehouseman is required to give thirty days' notice to pay charges and remove the goods. A shorter time, which must be reasonable, is permitted if the goods are about to deteriorate or decline in value to less than the amount of the warehouseman's lien, or if the quality or condition of the goods cause them to be a hazard to other property or to persons. Section 7–206.

Lien of Warehouseman To enforce the payment of his charges and necessary expenses in connection with keeping and handling the goods, a warehouseman has a lien on the goods which enables him to sell them at public or private sale after notice and to apply the net proceeds of the sale to the amount of his charges. The Code, moreover, provides a definite procedure for enforcement of the lien of a warehouseman against the goods stored and in his possession. Section 2–710.

As against the holder of a negotiable warehouse receipt to whom it has been duly negotiated, this lien is limited to charges at the rate specified in the receipt, and if none are specified, to a reasonable charge for storage of the goods subsequent to the date of the receipt. Section 7–209(1).

Bills of Lading

A bill of lading is a document issued by a carrier upon receipt of goods for **transportation.** It serves a threefold function: (1) as a receipt for the goods, (2) as evidence of the contract of carriage, and (3) as a document of title. A bill of lading is negotiable if by its terms the goods are deliverable to bearer or to the order of a named person. Any other document is non-negotiable. Section 7–104.

Under the Code, bills of lading may be issued not only by common carriers but also by contract carriers, freight forwarders, or any person engaged in the business of transporting or forwarding goods. Section 1–201(6).

Duties of Issuer of Bill of Lading The carrier must deliver the goods to the person entitled to receive them under the terms of the bill of lading. The carrier's duty in this respect is similar to that of the warehouseman. However, common carriers of goods are extraordinary bailees under the law and subject to a greater degree of liability than an ordinary bailee such as a warehouseman. See Section 7–309(1).

The Code allows a carrier to limit its liability by contract in all cases where its rates are dependent upon value and the shipper is given an opportunity to declare a higher value. The limitation does not apply to a conversion of the goods by the carrier to its own use. Section 7–309(2).

Through Bills of Lading A bill of lading may provide that the issuer deliver the goods to a *connecting* carrier for further transportation to destination. A bill of lading which specifies one or more connecting carriers is called a "through bill of lading."

The initial or *originating* carrier, which receives the goods from the shipper and issues a through bill of lading, is liable to the holder of the document for loss or damage to the goods caused by any connecting or delivering carrier. Section 7–302(1). The initial carrier has a right of reimbursement from the connecting or delivering carrier in possession of the goods when the loss or damage occurred. A carrier, however, is not required to issue through bills of lading.

Unlike the initial carrier, the liability of a connecting carrier is limited to the period while the goods are in its possession.

Lien of Carrier The carrier has a lien upon goods in its possession covered by a bill of lading for its charges and expenses necessary for preservation of the goods. As against a purchaser for value of a negotiable bill of lading, this lien is limited to charges stated in the bill or in the applicable published tariff, and if no charges are so stated, to a reasonable charge. Section 7–307(1).

The enforcement of the lien of the carrier is by public or private sale of the goods after notice to all persons known to the carrier to claim an interest in them. The sale must be on terms which are "commercially reasonable," and must be conducted in a "commercially reasonable manner." Section 7–308(1).

A purchaser in good faith of goods sold to enforce the lien takes free of any rights of persons against whom the lien was valid, even though the enforcement of the lien does not comply with the requirements of the Code. This rule applies to both carrier's and warehouseman's liens. Section 7–308(4), 7–310(5).

NEGOTIABILITY OF DOCUMENTS OF TITLE

The concept of negotiability has long been established in law. It is important not only in connection with documents of title but also in commercial paper and investment securities treated in other chapters of this book.

Negotiability is a characteristic which the law confers upon instruments and documents which comply with the requisite statutory form. The magic words are "bearer" or "order." A promise to deliver goods to a named person is manifestly different from a promise to deliver the goods to bearer or to the order of a named person. The first promise may be safely performed by the promisor by delivery of the goods to the person named in the promise. This is typical of a straight bill of lading, i.e, one issued by a carrier which undertakes to deliver the goods at destination to a named consignee. In such case it is not necessary for the carrier to obtain surrender of the bill of lading upon delivery of the goods at destination. The only concern of the carrier is to make sure that the person to whom it delivers the goods at destination is the person named in the straight bill of lading as consignee. Such a bill of lading is **non-negotiable.**

If, on the other hand, the promise of the carrier in the bill of lading is to deliver the goods to **bearer** or to the **order** of a person named in the bill, the carrier may not safely deliver the goods to anyone at destination without obtaining surrender of the original bill of lading. Anyone in possession of a bearer form document is entitled to receive the goods from the carrier. Anyone in possession of an order form document, properly indorsed, is likewise entitled to receive possession of the goods from the carrier. A bearer or order form document of title is **negotiable.** By the terms of the promise contained on its face it was intended to go to market, to pass from hand to hand, and to circulate freely on the channels of commerce.

The Code provides that a warehouse receipt, bill of lading, or other document of title is negotiable if by its terms the goods are to be delivered to bearer or to the order of a named person or where, in overseas trade, it runs to a named person or assigns. *Any* other document is non-negotiable. Section 7–104.

A non-negotiable document, such as a straight bill of lading or a warehouse receipt under which the goods are deliverable to a person named in the bill and not to the order of any person or to bearer, may be transferred by assignment but may not be negotiated. Only a negotiable document or instrument may be negotiated.

Due Negotiation

The manner in which a negotiable document of title may be negotiated and the requirements of "due negotiation" are set forth in Section 7–501 of the Code. An order form negotiable document of title running to the order of a named person is negotiated by her indorsement and delivery. After such indorsement in blank or to bearer, the document may be negotiated by delivery alone. A special indorsement by which the document is indorsed over to a specified person requires the indorsement of the special indorsee as well as delivery in order to accomplish a further negotiation.

The naming in a negotiable document of a person to be notified upon the arrival of the goods does not limit the negotiabiliy of the bill of lading nor serve as notice to any purchaser of the document that such person has any interest in the goods.

"Due negotiation" is a term peculiar to Article 7 and requires not only that the purchaser of the negotiable document must take it in good faith without notice of any adverse claim or defense and pay value, but also that she must take it in the regular course of business or financing, and not in settlement or payment of a money obligation. Thus, a transfer for value of a negotiable document of title to a non-business person or non-banker, such as a college professor or student, would not be a due negotiation.

Rights Acquired by Due Negotiation

Negotiation is a form of transfer which the transferee acquires not only the rights which the transferor had but also direct rights based upon the language of the promise contained in the instrument or document. Where a property right is merely assigned, the assignee takes only such rights as the assignor had. He stands in the shoes of the assignor, and his rights are subject to all defects and infirmities in the title of the assignor. However, where a document is negotiable and is transferred by due negotiation, the transferee is one to whom the promise of the issuer runs, and he thereby acquires the direct obligation of the issuer. Thus, if A issues a warehouse receipt to B wherein he promises to deliver the goods to bearer, and subsequently X presents the document to A and demands the goods, X is the bearer and therefore the very person to whom A promised to deliver the goods. The same is true with respect to a properly indorsed order form warehouse receipt or bill of lading.

The effect of due negotiation is that it creates new rights in the holder of the document. Upon due negotiation the transferee does not stand in the shoes of his transferor. Defects and defenses available against the transferor are not available against the new holder. His rights are newly created by the negotiation and free of such defects and defenses. This enables bankers and business persons to extend credit upon documents of title without concern about possible adverse claims or the rights of third parties.

The rights of a holder of a negotiable document of title to whom it has been duly negotiated are that he has (1) title to the document; (2) title to the goods; (3) all rights accruing under the law of agency or estoppel including rights to goods delivered to the bailee after the document was issued; and (4) the direct obligation of the issuer to hold or deliver the goods according to the terms of the document. Section 7–502.

If an order form document of title is transferred without a requisite indorsement, the transferee has the right to compel his transferor to supply any necessary indorsement. This right is specifically enforceable in a court of equity. The transfer becomes a negotiation only as of the time the indorsement is supplied. Section 7–506.

Rights Acquired in the Absence of Due Negotiation

If a non-negotiable document is transferred or a negotiable document is transferred without due negotiation, the transferee of the document acquires all of the title and rights

which the transferor had or had actual authority to convey. Prior to notification received by the bailee of the transfer, the rights of the transferee may be defeated (1) by the creditors of the transferor who could treat the sale as void; or (2) by a buyer from the transferor in the ordinary course of business, if the bailee has delivered the goods to the buyer; or (3) as against the bailee by good faith dealings of the bailee with the transferor. Section 7–504.

Warranties

A person who either negotiates or transfers a document of title for value other than a collecting bank or other intermediary incurs certain warranty obligations unless otherwise agreed. Section 7–507. Such transferor warrants to her immediate purchaser: (1) that the document is genuine; (2) that she had no knowledge of any fact that would impair its validity or worth; and (3) that her negotiation or transfer is rightful and fully effective with respect to the title to the document and the goods it represents.

Ineffective Documents of Title

It is fundamental that a thief or finder of goods may not by delivery of them to a warehouseman or carrier in return for the issuance to the thief or finder of a negotiable document of title defeat the rights of the owner by a negotiation of the document. While such document would be genuine and its indorsement by the thief or finder not a forgery, it would in such case not represent title to the goods.

In order that a person obtain title to goods by a negotiation to him of a document, the goods must have been delivered to the issuer of the document by the owner of the goods or by one to whom the owner has delivered or entrusted them with actual or apparent authority to ship, store, or sell them. Section 7–503(1).

A warehouseman or carrier may deliver goods according to the terms of the document which it has issued or otherwise dispose of the goods as provided in the Code without incurring liability even though the document did not represent title to the goods. It must have acted in good faith and complied with reasonable commercial standards in both the receipt and delivery or other disposition of the goods. The bailee has no liability even though the person from whom it received the goods had no authority to obtain the issuance of the document or dispose of the goods, and even though the person to whom it delivered the goods had no authority to receive them. Section 7–404.

Thus, a carrier or warehouseman who receives goods from a thief or finder and later delivers them to a person to whom the thief or finder ordered them to be delivered is not liable to the true owner of the goods. Even a sale of the goods by the carrier or warehouseman to enforce a lien for transportation or storage charges and expenses would not subject it to liability.

Warehousemen and carriers are regarded as furnishing a service necessary to trade and commerce. They are not a link in the chain of title and do not purport to represent the owner in transactions affecting title to the goods. Consequently, it is a sound rule which relieves them from liability upon delivery of the goods pursuant to their contract under the document of title even though the document is ineffective against the true owner of the goods.

Lost or Missing Documents of Title

If a document has been lost, stolen, or destroyed, a claimant of the goods may apply to a court for an order directing delivery of the goods or the issuance of a substitute document. Compliance of the carrier or warehouseman with the order of court relieves it of liability. Section 7–601(1). The claimant must provide security approved by the court if the missing document is negotiable.

If the carrier or warehouseman without a court order delivers goods to a person claiming them under a missing negotiable document, it is liable to any person who is thereby injured. Delivery to such person in good faith is not a conversion of the goods if security is posted in an amount at least double the value of the goods to indemnify any person injured by the delivery who files notice of claim within one year. Section 7–601(2).

CASES

Bailment: Delivery of Possession

LAVAL v. LEOPOLD

Civil Court of City of New York, Special Term, 1965.
47 Misc.2d 624, 262 N.Y.S.2d 820.

NADEL, J.

Plaintiff brings this action to recover $1,725, the value of plaintiff's coat, which she claims she delivered into defendant's care and custody and which was not returned.

Defendant moves for summary judgment, asserting that there are no triable issues of fact and that plaintiff, as a matter of law, was guilty of contributory negligence and therefore may not have a recover against him. Plaintiff cross-moves for summary judgment in her favor.

Defendant is a practicing psychiatrist, who, at the time, when plaintiff was his patient, maintained his office with two associates or colleagues, also practicing in the same field. No receptionist or other employee attended the office.

Plaintiff claims that on one of her professional visits to defendant's office, in accordance with her usual custom she deposited her coat in a clothes closet in the office reception room. When plaintiff's professional consultation was complete and she was ready to leave defendant's office, her coat was missing.

The maintenance of the closet in defendant's office created an implied invitation to plaintiff to deposit her coat there.

In Webster v. Lane, [citation], which involved the loss of a coat in a dentist's office, the court took judicial notice of the fact that patients of a dentist are not placed in a dental chair with their wraps on. This court likewise takes judicial notice that it is not custom for a patient to lie on the couch or sit in the chair in a psychiatrist's office wrapped in her fur coat.

The plaintiff cannot be said to be contributorily negligent as a matter of law because she placed her coat in a clothes closet in defendant's reception room.

Implicit in the relationship between the parties, the defendant became a bailee of plaintiff's coat, and it is for the trier of the facts to determine whether under the circumstances then prevailing at the time and place of this happening, reasonable care was exercised by the defendant with reference to plaintiff's coat which was temporarily deposited in the reception room closet preliminary to treatment by the defendant.

Accordingly, the motion and cross-motion are denied.

Bailment: Delivery of Possession

SEWALL v. FITZ-INN AUTO PARKS, INC.

Court of Appeals of Massachusetts, 1975.
3 Mass.App.Ct. 380, 330 N.E.2d 853.

ARMSTRONG, J.

The plaintiff seeks recovery of the value of his automobile, which was left by him on the defendant's parking lot early on the morning of April 15, 1970, and was gone when he returned for it early that evening, having apparently been stolen by an unidentified third person. The declaration is in two counts, one based on a theory of breach of the defendant's contractual duty to safeguard the automobile and the other based on principles of ordinary negligence. At the conclusion of the evidence the trial judge directed verdicts for the defendant on both counts. The propriety of that action is the sole issue raised by the plaintiff's bill of exceptions.

The facts do not appear to be in dispute. The defendant's parking lot was approximately 100 by 200 feet in size. A chain link fence had been erected along its rear boundary, separating the lot from a facility of the Massachusetts Bay Transportation Authority. The normal entrance and exit to the lot were located at the front, but it was also possible to leave the lot from the sides, each of which bordered on a small street. Upon entering the lot on the morning of April 15, the plaintiff paid the attendant on duty a fee of twenty-five cents, a flat rate for which he was permitted to park all day or for a shorter period, as he chose. He parked his car in a space designated by the attendant, locked it and took the keys with him. The attendant remained on duty until 10:30 or 11:00 A.M. on April 15, after which time the lot was unattended, apparently pursuant to a practice followed by the defendant. The plaintiff had never been expressly informed of that practice, but he had regularly parked in the lot for several years and had never seen an attendant when he returned for his car in the evening.

The case turns on whether the facts warranted a finding that the transaction between the parties constituted a bailment for hire of the plaintiff's automobile, rather than a mere letting of parking space. [Citations.] The existence of a bailment is a prerequisite to the plaintiff's right to recover, either in contract or in tort, as the defendant would not otherwise be under any duty to safeguard the plaintiff's car against theft. [Citations.] We are of the opinion that no bailment has been shown and that the trial judge was correct in directing verdicts [in favor of Fitz-Inn Auto Parks.]

A bailment, by definition, arises only upon delivery of possession of the property sought to be bailed, and at least some degree of control over that property, to the putative bailee. [Citations.] Once possession and control of an automobile have been transferred to the operator of a parking facility for a fee, the owner (in the absence of any warning or understanding to the contrary) is justified in concluding that the operator has assumed responsibility to safeguard the automobile, and the operator has a legally enforceable duty to exercise reasonable care in the fulfillment of that responsibility. [Citation.] But if there has been no such delivery of possession or control to the operator, nor any acceptance thereof by him, he cannot, without more, be regarded as having undertaken to protect the car and owes the owner no duty to do so. [Citation.]

It has long been held that the surrender of the car keys to the parking facility attendant is a sufficient delivery of possession and control to create a bailment for hire, whether the keys are left at the attendant's request [citation] or with his knowledge and acquiescence in the absence of such a request. [Citation.] The same result has recently been reached where the owner parked and locked his car, without surrendering the keys, in an enclosed parking facility whose sole means of egress was manned by an attendant responsible for stopping and checking each car leaving the facility. [Citation.] * * *

The plaintiff in effect is asking us to extend the principle applied in [citations]. In those cases the garage, while not exercising the degree of control possible through possession of the keys, did exercise (or purport to exercise) control over the departure of vehicles from its facility. In the present case neither type of control was actually or apparently exercised or asserted by the defendant. The role of the attendant, so far as known to the plaintiff, was confined to collecting a uniform twenty-five cent fee from motorists as they entered the lot and directing them to parking spaces. The plaintiff knew that he could remove his car from the lot at any time without interference by any employee of the defendant. Indeed, it should have been obvious to him, because of the open character of the lot and the absence of any attendant on all the evenings when he had removed his car, that any control exercised by the defendant over his car, and any correlative responsibility assumed with respect thereto, came to an end once he had paid the fee and parked the car. [Citation.]

Exceptions overruled.

Bailee's Duty to Return Bailed Property

MIESKE v. BARTELL DRUG CO.

Supreme Court of Washington, 1979.
92 Wn.2d 40, 593 P.2d 1308.

BRACHTENBACH, J.

This case determines the measure of damages for personal property, developed movie film, which is destroyed, and which cannot be replaced or reproduced. It also decides the legal effect of a clause which purports to limit the responsibility of a film processor to replacement of film.

We will detail the facts later, but the heart of the matter is that plaintiffs delivered already developed movie film to a retail store for the sole purpose of having the film spliced onto larger reels. The film was lost or destroyed by the retailer's processing agent. A jury verdict of $7,500 was returned against the retailer and the agent-processor. Those defendants appeal. We affirm.

The facts are that over a period of years the plaintiffs had taken movie films of their family activities. The films started with the plaintiffs' wedding and honeymoon and continued through vacations in Mexico, Hawaii and other places, Christmas gatherings, birthdays, Little League participation by their son, family pets, building of their home and irreplaceable pictures of members of their family, such as the husband's brother, who are now deceased.

Plaintiffs had 32 50-foot reels of such developed film which they wanted spliced together into four reels for convenience of viewing. Plaintiff wife visited defendant Bartell's camera department, with which she had dealt as a customer for at least 10 years. She was told that such service could be performed.

The films were put in the order which plaintiffs desired them to be spliced and so marked. They were then placed in four separate paper bags which in turn were placed in one large bag and delivered to the manager of Bartell. The plaintiff wife explained the desired service and the manner in which the films were assembled in the various bags. The manager placed a film processing packet on the bag and gave plaintiff wife a receipt which contained this language: "We assume no responsibility beyond retail cost of film unless otherwise agreed to in writing." There was no discussion about the language on the receipt. Rather, plaintiff wife told the manager, "Don't lose these. They are my life."

There was no discussion or agreement about who was going to perform the splicing service.

Bartell sent the film package to defendant GAF Corporation, which intended to send them to another processing lab for splicing. Plaintiffs assumed that Bartell did this service and were unaware of the involvement of two other firms.

The bag of films arrived at the processing lab of GAF. The manager of the GAF lab described the service ordered and the packaging as very unusual. Yet it is undisputed that the film was in the GAF lab at the end of one day and gone the next morning. The manager immediately searched the garbage disposal dumpster which already had been emptied. The best guess is that the plaintiff's film went from GAF's lab to the garbage dumpster to a truck to a barge to an up-Sound landfill where it may yet repose.

After several inquiries to Bartell, plaintiff wife was advised to call GAF. Not surprisingly, after being advised of the complete absence and apparent fatality of plaintiffs' films, this lawsuit ensued.

At trial defendants Bartell and GAF denied liability. The janitorial service company which aparently removed the film was a de-

fendant. The verdict was against Bartell and GAF but not against the janitorial service company. It is not a party to the appeal. For purposes of appeal, Bartell and GAF admit liability for negligence.

Two main issues are raised: (1) the measure of damages and (2) the effect of the exclusionary clause appearing on the film receipt.

On damages, the defendants assign error to (a) the court's damages instruction and (b) the court's failure to give their proposed damages instruction.

The standard of recovery for destruction of personal property was summarized in *McCurdy v. Union Pac. R.R.*, [citation]. We recognized in *McCurdy* that (1) personal property which is destroyed may have a market value, in which case that market value is the measure of damages; (2) if destroyed property has no market value but can be replaced or reproduced, then the measure is the cost of replacement or reproduction; (3) if the destroyed property has no market value and cannot be replaced or reproduced, then the value to the owner is to be the proper measure of damages. However, while not stated in *McCurdy*, we have held that in the third *McCurdy* situation, damages are not recoverable for the sentimental value which the owner places on the property. [Citations.]

The defendants argue that plaintiffs' property comes within the second rule of *McCurdy*, i.e., the film could be replaced and that their liability is limited to the cost of replacement film. Their position is not well taken. Defendants' proposal would award the plaintiffs the cost of acquiring film without pictures imposed thereon. That is not what plaintiffs lost. Plaintiffs lost not merely film able to capture images by exposure but rather film upon which was recorded a multitude of frames depicting many significant events in their lives. Awarding plaintiffs the funds to purchase 32 rolls of blank film is hardly a replacement of the 32 rolls of image which they had recorded over the years. Therefore the third rule of *McCurdy* is the appropriate measure of damages, i.e., the property has no market value and cannot be replaced or reproduced.

The law, in those circumstances, decrees that the measure of damages is to be determined by the value to the owner, often referred to as the intrinsic value of the property. Restatement of Torts § 911 (1939).

Necessarily the measure of damages in these circumstances is the most imprecise of the three categories. Yet difficulty of assessment is not cause to deny damages to a plaintiff whose property has no market value and cannot be replaced or reproduced. [Citations.]

The fact that damages are difficult to ascertain and measure does not diminish the loss to the person whose property has been destroyed. Indeed, the very statement of the rule suggests the opposite. If one's destroyed property has a market value, presumably its equivalent is available on the market and the owner can acquire that equivalent property. However, if the owner cannot acquire the property in the market or by replacement or reproduction, then he simply cannot be made whole.

The problem is to establish the value to the owner. Market and replacement values are relatively ascertainable by appropriate proof. Recognizing that value to the owner encompasses a subjective element, the rule has been established that compensation for sentimental or fanciful values will not be allowed. [Citations.] That restriction was placed upon the jury in this case by the court's damages instruction.

*   *   *

Under these rules, the court's damages instruction was correct. In essence it allowed recovery for the actual or intrinsic value to the plaintiffs but denied recovery for any unusual sentimental value of the film to the plaintiffs or a fanciful price which plaintiffs for their own special reasons, might place thereon.

*   *   *

The next issue is to determine the legal effect of the exclusionary clause which was on the film receipt given plaintiff wife by Bartell. As noted above, it read: "We assume no responsibility beyond retail cost of film unless otherwise agreed to in writing."

Is the exclusionary clause valid? Defendants rely upon 2–719(3), a section of the Uniform Commercial Code, which authorizes a limitation or exclusion of consequential damages unless the limitation is unconscionable.

Plaintiffs, on the other hand, argue that the Uniform Commercial Code is not applicable to this transaction. Their theory is that article 2 applies only to sales and not to a bailment as was present in this case. Plaintiffs read article 2 too narrowly. While article 2 is entitled "Sales," the declared scope is more comprehensive. 2–102 sets the parameters of the article by its declaration that it applies to *transactions in goods*, excluding security transactions. If article 2 were limited to sales it would not be directly applicable to this bailment transaction as 2–106(1) defines "Sales" as the passing of title from a seller to a buyer, a factor not present here. Obviously "transactions in goods"—the scope of article 2—is broader than "sales." Had the drafters of the code intended to limit article 2 to sales they could have easily so stated. They did not.

Our analysis seems commonly accepted. See for example [citation] which states:

It is now clearly established that the reach of Article 2 goes considerably beyond the confines of that type transaction which the Code itself defines to be a "sale"; namely, the passing of title from a party called the seller to one denominated a buyer for a price. Chief opportunity for this expansion is found in Section 2–102, which states that the article applies to "transactions in goods." Article 2 sections are finding their way into more and more decisions involving transactions which are not sales, but which are used as substitutes for a sale or which to a court appear to have attributes to which sales principles—or at least some of them— seem appropriate for application. . . .

 . . . . Most important of these is the application of the Article's warranty provisions to leases, *bailments*, or construction contracts. Of growing importance is the tendency of courts to find the

Section on unconscionability, Section 2–302, appropriate to nonsales deals.

[Citations.]

While there are cases to the contrary, [citations] we do not find them persuasive. In fact we have held already that article 2 declares a public policy as to disclaimers and, at least by analogy, applied it to a bailment. *Baker v. Seattle*, 79 Wn.2d 198, 484 P.2d 405 (1971). (Article 2's provisions apply to lease of golf cart.)

We do not think that a distinction can be drawn between a bailment arising from a service transaction, as is the case here, and one arising from a leasing transaction, as was the case in *Baker*, [Citation.] Nor do we think, for this purpose, that a proper distinction can be drawn between the lease or rental of a chattel and the sale of a chattel.

*   *   *

In determining conscionability, the parties are to be provided "a reasonable opportunity to present evidence as to its commercial setting, purpose and effect to aid the court in making the determination." RCW 62A.2–302(2). Defendants concede that there was adequate compliance with that requirement in this case. The court had before it testimony and documents as to each element it was required to consider. *   *   *

Judgment affirmed.

Duties of Warehousemen

I.C.C. METALS, INC. v. MUNICIPAL WAREHOUSE CO.

Court of Appeals of New York, 1980.
50 N.Y.2d 657, 431 N.Y.S.2d 372, 409 N.E.2d 849.

GABRIELLI, J.

[In the fall of 1974, I.C.C. Metals, Inc., delivered three lots of indium, an industrial metal, to Municipal Warehouse Company for safekeeping. The indium had an aggregate weight of 845 pounds and was worth $100,000. The Warehouse supplied I.C.C. with receipts for each lot. Printed on the back of these receipts were the terms and conditions of the bailment including an exculpatory clause limiting the liability of the Warehouse to a maximum of $50.00. For two years, the Warehouse billed I.C.C. for storage of the indium, and I.C.C. paid each invoice. In 1976, I.C.C. requested the return of the indium. For the first time, the Warehouse told I.C.C. it was unable to locate any of the indium. I.C.C. brought an action in conversion to recover the full value of the indium. The Warehouse defended on the ground that the metal had been stolen through no fault of its own; and that its liability was limited to $50.00 in accordance with the terms of the Warehouse receipts.]

Absent an agreement to the contrary, a warehouse is not an insurer of goods and may not be held liable for any injury to or loss of stored property not due to some fault upon its part (Uniform Commercial Code, § 7–204, subd. [1]). As a bailee, however, a warehouse is required both to exercise reasonable care so as to prevent loss of or damage to the property [citation] and, a fortiori, to refrain from itself converting materials left in its care [citation.] If a warehouse does not convert the goods to its own use and does exercise reasonable care, it may not be held liable for any loss of or damage to the property unless it specifically agrees to accept a higher burden. If, however, the property is lost or damaged as a result of negligence upon the part of the warehouse, it will be liable in negligence. Similarly, should a warehouse actually convert stored property to its own use, it will be liable in conversion. Hence, a warehouse which fails to redeliver goods to the person entitled to their return upon a proper demand, may be liable for either neglience or conversion, depending upon the circumstances. [Citation.]

A warehouse unable to return bailed property either because it has lost the property as a result of its negligence or because it has converted the property will be liable for the full value of the goods at the time of the loss or conversion [citations], unless the parties have agreed to limit the warehouse's potential liability. It has long been the law in this State that a warehouse, like a common carrier, may limit its liability for loss of or damage to stored goods even if the injury or loss is the result of the warehouse's negligence, so long as it provides the bailor with an opportunity to increase that potential liability by payment of a higher storage fee. [Citations.] If the warehouse converts the goods, however, strong policy considerations bar enforcement of any such limitation upon its liability. [Citations.] This rule, which has now been codified in subdivision (2) of section 7–204 of the Uniform Commercial Code, is premised on the distinction between an intentional and an unintentional tort. Although public policy will in many situations countenance voluntary prior limitations upon that liability which the law would otherwise impose upon one who acts carelessly [citations], such prior limitations may not properly be applied so as to diminish one's liability for injuries resulting from an affirmative and intentional act of misconduct (see, generally, Restatement, Torts 2d, § 500; Restatement, Contracts 2d, Tent Draft No. 12, § 337) such as a conversion. Any other rule would encourage wrongdoing by allowing the converter to retain the difference between the value of the converted property and the limited amount of liability provided in the agreement of storage. That result would be absurd. To avoid such an anomaly, the law provides that when a warehouse converts bailed property, it thereby ceases to function as a warehouse and thus loses its entitlement to the protections afforded by the agreement of storage. [Citation.] In short, although the merely careless bailee remains a bailee and is entitled to whatever limitations of liability the bailor has agreed to, the converter forsakes his status as bailee completely and accordingly forfeits the protections of such limitations. Hence, in the instant case, whether defendant is entitled to the benefit of the liability limiting provision of the warehouse receipt turns upon whether plaintiff has proven conversion or merely negligence.

Plaintiff [I.C.C.] has proffered uncontroverted proof of delivery of the indium to defendant [Warehouse], of a proper demand for its return, and of defendant's failure to honor that demand. Defendant has failed to make a sufficient showing in support of its suggested explanation of the loss. * * * [Defendant's] unsupported claim that the metal was stolen does not suffice to raise any issue of fact on this point. Upon this record, it is beyond cavil that plaintiff would be entitled to judgment had it elected to sue defendant in negligence. [Citations]. We now hold that such a record also suffices to sustain plaintiff's action in conversion, thereby rendering inapplicable the contractual limitation upon defendant's liability.

[Judgment for I.C.C.]

PROBLEMS

1. A was the owner of a herd of twenty highly bred dairy cows. He was a prosperous farmer, but his health was very poor. On the advice of his doctor, A decided to winter in Arizona. Before he left, he made an agreement with Y under which Y was to keep the cows on Y's farm through the winter, pay A the sum of $800, and return to A the twenty cows at the close of the winter. For reasons that Y thought were good farming, Y sold six of the cows and replaced them with six other cows. After the winter was over, A returned from Arizona. When he saw that Y had replaced six cows out of the twenty originally given, he sued Y for the conversion of the original six cows. Decision?

2. Hines stored her furniture, including a grand piano, in Arnett's warehouse. Needing more space, Arnett stored Hines's piano in Butler's warehouse next door. As a result of a fire, which occurred without any fault of Arnett or Butler, both warehouses and contents were destroyed. Hines sues

Arnett for the value of her piano and furniture. Decision?

3. B rented a safe deposit box from X Safe Deposit Company in which he deposited valuable securities and $4,000 in currency. Subsequently, B went to the box and found that $1,000 was missing. B brought an action against X, and at the trial the company showed that its customary procedure was as follows: that there were two keys for each box furnished to each renter; that if the key was lost, the lock was changed; also, that new keys were provided for each lock each time a box was rented; that there were two clerks in charge of the vault; and that one of the clerks was always present to open the box. X Safe Deposit Company also proved two keys were given to B at the time he rented his box; that his box could not be opened without the use of one of the keys in his possession, and the company had issued no other keys to B's box. Decision?

4. A, B, and C each stored 5,000 bushels of yellow corn in the same bin in X's warehouse. X wrongfully sold 10,000 bushels of this corn to Y. A contends that inasmuch as his 5,000 bushels of corn were placed in the bin first, the remaining 5,000 bushels belong to him. What are the rights of the parties?

5. (a) On April 1, Mary Rich, at the solicitation of Super Fur Company, delivered a $3,000 mink coat to the company at its place of business for storage in its vaults until November 1. On the same day, she paid the company its customary charge of twenty dollars for such storage. After Mary left the store, the general manager of the company, upon finding that its storage vaults were already filled to capacity, delivered Mary's coat to Swift Trucking Company for shipment to Fur Storage Company. En route, the truck in which Mary's coat was being transported was totally damaged by fire caused by negligence on the part of the driver of the truck, and Mary's coat was totally destroyed. Is Super Fur Company liable to Mary for the value of her coat? Why?

(b) Would your answer be the same if Mary's coat had been safely delivered to Fur Storage Company and had been stolen from its storage vaults without negligence on its part? Why?

6. Rich, a club member, left his golf clubs with Bogan, the pro at the Happy Hours Country Club, to be refinished at Bogan's pro shop. The refinisher

employed by Bogan suddenly left town taking Rich's clubs with him. The refinisher had previously been above suspicion, although Bogan had never checked on the man's character references. A valuable sand wedge which Bogan had borrowed from another member, Smith, for his own use in an important tournament match was also stolen by the refinisher, as well as several pairs of golf shoes which Bogan had checked for members without charge as an accommodation. The concerned club members each made claims against Bogan for their losses. Can (a) Rich, (b) Smith, and (c) the other members compel Bogan to make good their respective losses?

7. B left his automobile at T's garage in order for T to repair the auto at an agreed upon charge of $125. B never returned to reclaim the automobile, and two months later C saw it in T's garage. C claimed it as his own and asserted that it had been stolen from him. T told C that he could have the automobile upon paying for the repairs and storage. C paid him, took the automobile, and disappeared. A week later O appeared and proved that the automobile was hers, that it had been stolen from her, and that neither B nor C had any rights in it.

O brings an action against T for conversion of the automobile. Decision?

8. On June 1, Cain delivered his 1978 automobile to Barr, operator of a repair shop, for necessary repairs. Barr put the car in his lot on Main Street which is fenced on all sides except that along Main Street. The lot accommodates 100 cars and is unguarded at night although the police make periodic checks. The lot is well illuminated. The cars do not have the keys in them when left out overnight. Some time during the night of June 4, the hood, starter, alternator, and gear shift were removed by theft from Cain's car. The car remained on the lot, and during the evening of June 5 the transmission was stolen from the car. The cost of replacement of the parts stolen in the first theft was $600 and in the second theft $500.

Cain sued Barr to recover $1,100. Decision?

9. A, in Phoenix, pursuant to a contract with B in New York, ships to B goods conforming to the contract and takes from the carrier a shipper's order bill of lading. A indorses the bill of lading in blank and forwards it by mail to C, his agent in New York, with instructions to deliver the bill of lading to B upon receipt of payment of the price for the goods. X, a thief, steals the bill of lading from C and transfers it for value to Y, a *bona fide* purchaser. Before the goods arrive in New York, B is petitioned into bankruptcy. What are the rights of the parties?

10. A, a Philadelphia merchant, purchased merchandise from B in Chicago. The contract of sale provided that the merchandise was sold F.O.B., Chicago, payment to be made sixty days after delivery. B delivered the goods to the railroad carrier in Chicago, took an order bill of lading in the name of A, and forwarded it to A. Before the goods arrived in Philadelphia, B learned that A had become insolvent and exercised a right of stoppage in transit by proper notice to the railroad company. Thereafter, and before the shipment reached Philadelphia, A indorsed and delivered the bill of lading to C, an innocent purchaser for value. C claimed the goods by reason of holding the bill of lading. To whom should the goods be awarded?

Chapter 48

INTERESTS IN REAL PROPERTY

INTERESTS in real property may be divided into ownership, possessory, and nonpossessory interests. Rights of ownership in real property are called estates and are classified to indicate the quantity, nature, and extent of the rights. The two major categories are freehold estates (those existing for an indefinite time or for the life of a person) and estates less than freehold (those which exist for a predetermined time), called leasehold estates.

The ownership of property may be held by one individual or, concurrently, in two or more persons, each entitled to an undivided interest in the entire property.

Both freehold estates and leasehold estates are regarded as possessory interests in property. In addition, there are several non-possessory interests in property including easements, *profits a prendre*, and licenses.

This chapter will consider these topics in the following order: (1) freehold estates, (2) leasehold estates, (3) concurrent ownership, and (4) nonpossessory interests.

FREEHOLD ESTATES

Among all the variety of estates in real property the most valuable, generally speaking, are those which combine the enjoyment of immediate possession with ownership at least for life. These estates are either fee estates in one form or another, or estates for life. In addition, it is possible that either type of estate may be created without immediate right to possession, called a future interest. Each of these types of possessory freehold estates in land will be discussed in this section of the chapter.

FEE ESTATES

Fee estates include both fee simple and qualified fee estates.

Fee Simple

When a person says that he has "bought" a house or a corporation informs its shareholders that it has "purchased" an industrial site, the property is generally held in fee simple. That is, the property is owned absolutely (possibly subject to a mortgage) and it can be sold or passed on at will to heirs or successors. The absolute right of transferability and of transmitting by inheritance are basic characteristics of a fee simple estate. The estate signifies full control over the property which is *owned absolutely* and can be sold or disposed of as desired.

A fee simple is created by any words which indicate an intent to convey absolute ownership. "To B in fee simple" will accomplish just that as will "To B forever." The general presumption is that a conveyance is intended to convey full and absolute title in the absence of a clear intent to the contrary.

A practical consequence of a fee simple title is that it may not only be voluntarily transferred, but it also may be levied upon and sold at the instance of judgment creditors of the fee simple holder (owner).

Base or Qualified Fee

It is possible to convey or will property to a person to enjoy it absolutely, *subject to* its being taken away at a later date if a certain event takes place. The estate thus created is known as a base fee, qualified fee, conditional fee, or fee simple defeasible. For example, A may provide in his will that his widow is to have his house and lot in "fee simple forever

so long as she does not remarry." If his widow dies without remarrying, the property is transferred to her heirs as though she owned it absolutely since the condition did not take place. However, if A's widow remarries or sells the land to B and then remarries, the widow and B would respectively lose their title to the land, and it would revert to the heirs of A.

LIFE ESTATES

By tradition, life estates are divided into two major classes: (1) conventional life estates or those created by voluntary act, and (2) those established by law, the most significant example of which is a wife's dower right in the property of her husband.

Conventional Life Estates

A grant or a devise "to A for life" creates in A an estate which terminates on his death. Such a provision may stand alone, in which case the property will revert to the grantor and his heirs or, as is more likely, it will be followed by a subsequent grant to another party such as "to A for life and then to B and his heirs." A is the **life tenant,** and B is generally described as the **remainderman.** A's life, however, may not be the measure of his life estate, as where an estate is granted "to A for the life of B." Upon B's death, A's interest terminates, and, if A dies before B, A's interest passes to his heirs or as he directs in his will for the remainder of B's life.

No particular words are necessary to create a life estate. It is always a matter of determining the intent of the grantor. Life estates arise most frequently in connection with the creation of trusts, a subject considered in Chapter 50.

Generally, a life tenant may make such reasonable use of the property as long as he does not commit "waste." Any act or omission which does permanent injury to the realty or unreasonably changes its characteristics or value will constitute **waste.** For example, the failure to make repairs on a building, the unreasonable cutting of timber, or the neglect of an adequate conservation policy may subject the life tenant to an action by the remainderman to recover damages for waste.

A conveyance by the life tenant passes only his interest. The life tenant and the remainderman may, however, join in a conveyance to pass the entire fee to the property, or the life tenant may terminate his interest by conveying it to the remainderman.

Life Estates Established by Law

Dower Under common law, dower is a life estate which a **wife** surviving her husband has in one-third of all the real property the husband owned during the marriage. It arises by operation of law and exists irrespective of the intent or wishes of the parties. By statute the common law has been generally modified so as to provide the wife with a one-third interest in such real estate, rather than just a life estate in the real property.

Until the death of the husband, the wife's dower is contingent or **inchoate.** During his life she cannot transfer or sell her dower interest. Dower can only exist in fee simple estates or in an estate that, for practical purposes, is equivalent to a fee simple estate. There is no dower in a life estate since it is not an estate of inheritance.

Although the widow does not realize her dower unless she survives her husband, her right in this respect is protected during the marriage. If the husband sells his property after he marries, the purchaser takes subject to the inchoate right of dower even though the purchaser did not know the seller was married. Dower also takes precedence over any claims against the husband's estate which were not reduced to judgment or made a lien against his property before marriage. Generally, to bar dower during marriage, it is necessary that the wife expressly waive her dower, and, since dower is an interest in land, such a release must be in writing. Generally, the husband is required to join in the release.

In most jurisdictions the wife can relinquish her dower simply by joining in a conveyance with her husband.

The incidents of dower at common law have been substantially modified by statute in most jurisdictions. In some States the widow may elect whether to take common law dower or an alternative amount given her by statute, the widow being given a period of time within which to elect between dower and her statutory portion. In many jurisdictions, dower has been abolished, and a statutory share of the husband's property, generally including both real and personal, is substituted in lieu of it.

Curtesy The surviving **husband,** at common law, had a life estate in the real property of his wife similar to, if not identical with, the widow's dower. This estate, known as curtesy, required a valid marriage and the death of the wife before the husband. As with dower, it existed only in estates of inheritance, and there was no curtesy in a life estate. Unlike dower, curtesy did not exist unless a child were born of the marriage. The child need not, however, survive the wife. But, like dower, the wife could not alienate the husband's claim to curtesy without his written waiver. In most States the estate of curtesy has been substantially modified or entirely abolished, and in lieu of it the husband in some States is given a statutory share in the estate of his deceased wife.

FUTURE INTERESTS

Not all interests in property are subject to immediate use and possession even though the right and title to the interest are absolute. Thus, where property is conveyed or devised by will "to A during her life and then to B and her heirs," B has a definite present *interest* in the property, but she is not entitled to immediate *possession.* Such and similar rights are generically referred to as future interests.

Reversions

If A conveys property "to B for life" and makes no disposition of the remainder of the estate, A holds the reversion—the grantor's right to the property upon the death of the life tenant. Thus, upon B's death A would regain ownership to the property. This result is not as apparent when A conveys property "to B for life and then to my heirs." It is arguable that there is a remainder in the grantor's next-of-kin. The common law doctrine, however, was that such a reference to the heirs of the grantor placed a reversion in *him*, and his heirs took nothing except as they might inherit the reversion.

A **possibility of reverter,** as the phrase suggests, exists where property may return to the grantor or his successor in interest because of the happening of an event upon which a fee simple estate was to terminate. It is the possibility of a reversion that is present in the grant of a base or qualified fee as previously discussed in this chapter. Thus, A has a possibility of reverter if she dedicates property to a public use "so long as it is used as a park." If, in one hundred years, the city ceases to use the property for a park, the persons who are the heirs of A will be entitled to the property. Unlike a reversion, which is a present estate to be enjoyed in the future, a possibility of reverter is simply an expectancy.

Remainders

A remainder is an estate in property which, like a reversion, will take effect in possession, if at all, upon the termination of a prior estate created by the *same instrument*. Unlike the reversion, a remainder is held by a person other than the grantor or his successors. A grant from G to "A for his life and then to B and his heirs" creates a remainder in B. Upon the termination of the life estate, B will be entitled to possession as remainderman. B takes his title not from A but from the original grantor, G.

The two kinds of remainders, vested remainders and contingent remainders, are discussed below.

Vested Remainders A remainder is vested when the only contingency to the possession by the remainderman is the termination of the preceding estate. When B has a remainder in fee, subject only to a life estate in A, the only obstacle to the right of immediate possession by B or his heirs is A's life. A's death, no more, no less, is sufficient and necessary to place B in possession. The law considers this vested remainder as a fixed *present* interest to be enjoyed in the future. It is an interest in property which is transferable just as much as the preceding life estate, and it is characteristic of a vested remainder that the owner of the preceding estate can do nothing to defeat the remainder. *See Griffin v. Moon.*

By his will X devised certain property, "to my wife Y for her life, and then to my daughter Z for her life, and then to my nephew, A, and his heirs." Upon the death of X, A has at that instant a vested remainder although it may be many years before he or his heirs will enjoy possession. If the remainder is vested in fee simple the vesting does not depend upon the named remainderman surviving the owner of the intervening estate.

Contingent Remainders A remainder is contingent if the right to possession is dependent or conditional upon the happening of some event *in addition to* the termination of the preceding estate. The remainder may be conditioned upon the existence of some person not yet in being or upon the happening of an event which may never occur. A contingent remainder, by definition and unlike a vested remainder, is *not* ready to take immediate possession simply upon the termination of the preceding estate. A provision in a will "to A for life and then to his children but if he has no children then to B" creates contingent remainders both as to the children and as to B. If A marries and has a child, the remainder then vests in that child, and B's expectancy is closed out. If A dies without having fathered a child, then and only then will an estate vest in B. It is, of course, possible for a contingent remainder to become vested while possession is still in the preceding life estate, as evidenced by the birth of a child to A in the foregoing illustration.

A remainder may be contingent until the termination of the preceding estate. "To A for life and upon A's death to B and his heirs if B then be living in Chattanooga" will give B an estate only if he meets the condition. In such case, it is impossible to determine whether the remainder will be vested until the death of A. A gift to X "until Y returns from Mexico, and then to Z" is another illustration of a remainder (to Z) contingent upon an event which may never take place.

It is not always easy to decide whether a remainder is contingent or is actually "vested" subject to being divested by a condition subsequent. If X, by his will, leaves his property to his wife for her life with the power to dispose of it by her will but, in the absence of such disposition, to their children, he creates a vested remainder in the children upon the death of X, subject to being divested by the exercise of the power.

In one sense, both vested and contingent remainders are contingent but there is an important distinction in the nature of the contingency. The grant "to A for life and then to B and his heirs" is contingent only as to the exact time when B will be entitled to possession. A grant "to A for life and then to B and his heirs if B is then a bachelor" is contingent upon the qualification of B, not just upon the death of A. *See Strickland v. Jackson.*

Rule Against Perpetuities A contingent estate is void unless, by the terms of its creation, it must vest within a life or lives in being plus twenty-one years. The purpose of this rule is to encourage the easy transfer of property by prohibiting the clouding of the title with future interests dependent upon uncertain contingencies which may not take place for a long period of time. A gift in a will by C to the first son of B who reaches the age of thirty years is void if B had no son at the death of C because a son might be born who would not reach the age of thirty until longer than twenty-one years after B's death, B being

the "life in being" under the rule. If, on the other hand, the gift had been to the first child of B who reaches twenty-one years of age the gift is valid since such an event must take place, if at all, within twenty-one years of B's death. A "life in being" may be anyone named by the donor and need not be connected in any way with the property. Any number of persons may be the lives in being as long as the death of the last survivor can be determined. Thus, a gift to the children of B who are living upon the death of the last survivor of the present living descendents of Queen Victoria is valid. The fact that it is probable the contingent gift will vest, if at all, within the required period is not enough to avoid the rule. The rule is a strict rule which is not always governed by what appears reasonable in view of general human experience. For example, if property is deeded to A for life, remainder to his wife for life, remainder to such of his children as survive his wife, the rule requires the assumption that A's wife may die, that he may marry another woman who was not living at the date of the deed, that A may have more children by her, that she may live for more than twenty-one years after A's death and that the children's interests thus may not vest in quantity and quality within the limits of time.

Vested interests are not within the rule against perpetuities. If a future interest is vested, it is not prohibited by the rule against perpetuities no matter how long it may be before the possession will be enjoyed. A grant to X for 999 years and then to Z and his heirs creates a present vested interest in Z and his interest is not therefore subject to the rule.

LEASEHOLD ESTATES

No part of the law of real property affects so many persons in their daily affairs as does the law of landlord and tenant. A tenant, by virtue of his lease, has an estate in land, an interest in real property, the primary characteristic of which is the right to possession. If A, the owner of a house and lot, rents it to B for a year, A, of course, still holds title to the property but he has sold the right to occupy the property to B. B's right to occupy the property is superior to that of A and, as long as B occupies in accordance with the terms of the lease contract, he does, as a practical matter, have exclusive possession against all the world as though he were the actual owner.

CREATION AND DURATION

A lease is both a contract and a grant of an estate in land. It is a contract by which the owner of the land, the **landlord,** grants to another, the **tenant**, an exclusive right to use and possession of the land for a definite or ascertainable period of time or term. The possessory term thus granted is an estate in land called a **leasehold**. The landlord retains an interest in the property called a **reversion**. The principal characteristics of the leasehold estate are that it continues for a definite or ascertainable term and that it carries with it the obligation upon the part of the tenant to pay rent to the landlord.

By statute, in most jurisdictions, leases for a term longer than a specified period of time must be in writing. The period is fixed generally at either one or three years.

Definite Term

A lease for a definite term automatically expires at the end of the term by virtue of its own limitation. Such leases are frequently termed an **"estate for years"** even though the duration may be for one year or shorter. No notice to terminate is required.

Periodic Tenancy

A periodic tenancy is a definite term lease of specified duration that is to be held over and over in the same length of time in indefinite succession. To illustrate, a lease "to T from month to month" or "from year to year" creates a periodic tenancy. Periodic tenancies arise frequently by implication. L leases to T without stating any term in the lease. This creates a tenancy at will. If T pays rent to L at the beginning of each month and L accepts such payments, most courts hold that the tenancy at will has been transformed into a tenancy from month to month.

A periodic tenancy may be terminated by either party at the expiration of any one period but only upon adequate notice to the other party. In the absence of an express agreement in the lease, the common law requires six months' notice in tenancies from year to year. However, this period has been shortened in most jurisdictions by statute to periods ranging between thirty and ninety days. In periodic tenancies involving periods of less than one year, the notice required at common law is one full period in advance, but, again, this may be subject to regulation by statute.

Tenancy at Will

A lease containing a provision that either party may terminate at any time creates a tenancy at will. A lease which does not specify any duration likewise creates a tenancy at will. At common law such tenancies were terminable without any prior notice, but many jurisdictions now have statutes requiring a notice to terminate, usually thirty days.

Tenancy at Sufferance

One who is in possession without a valid lease is a tenant at sufferance. A tenant at sufferance is technically a trespasser, and the landlord owes him no duties except to the extent that, under the common law, no landowner has a right wilfully to injure a trespasser.

The most common case of a tenancy at sufferance arises when a tenant fails to vacate the premises at the expiration of the lease. The common law gives the landlord the right to elect either to dispossess such tenant or to hold him for another term. Until the landlord makes this election, a tenancy at sufferance exists.

TRANSFER OF INTERESTS

Both the tenant's interest in the leasehold and the landlord's reversionary interest in the property may be freely transferred in the absence of contractual or statutory prohibition. This general rule is subject to one major exception: the tenancy at will. Any attempt by either party to transfer her interest is usually considered as an expression of the intent to terminate the tenancy.

Transfers by Landlord

After conveying the leasehold interest, a landlord is left with a reversionary interest in the property plus the right to rent and other benefits acquired under the lease. The landlord may transfer either or both of these interests. A party to whom the reversion is transferred takes the property subject to the tenant's leasehold interest if the transferee has actual or constructive notice of the lease. For example, L leases Whiteacre to T for five years, and T records the lease with the Register of Deeds. L then sells Whiteacre to A. T's lease is still valid and enforceable against A whose right to possession of Whiteacre begins only after the expiration of the lease.

Transfers by Tenant

A tenant may dispose of his interest either by (1) assignment or (2) sublease. In the absence of a provision in his lease, both of these rights are available to him. As a consequence, most standard leases expressly require the consent of the landlord to an assignment or subletting of the premises.

Assignment If a tenant transfers *all* his interest in the leasehold so that he has no reversionary rights he has made an assignment. This complete transfer means not simply the length of the time involved in the transfer. A transfer of the entire remaining period may not involve an assignment if the tenant retains any control over the premises. An as-

signment depends on the quantity of the interest assigned not the length of time involved. Absent specific restrictions in the lease, leases are freely assignable. Many leases, however, prohibit assignment without the landlord's written consent. If the tenant assigns without such written consent, the assignment is not void, but it may be avoided by the landlord. In other words, the prohibition of assignment in a lease is only for the benefit of the landlord and cannot be relied upon by the assignor to terminate an otherwise valid assignment on the ground that the landlord did not consent. If, however, the landlord accepts rent from the assignee, he will be held to have waived the restriction.

The agreement to pay rent and certain other contractual **covenants** (express promises) pass to and obligate the assignee of the lease so long as he remains in possession of the leasehold estate. Although the assignee of the lease is thus bound to pay rent, the original tenant is *not* relieved of his contractual obligation to pay rent. Should the assignee fail to pay the stipulated rent, the original tenant will have to pay it. He will, of course, have a right to be reimbursed by the assignee. Thus, after an assignment of a tenant's interest, *both* the original tenant and the assignee are primarily liable to the landlord for failure to pay rent.

Sublease A sublease differs from an assignment in that it involves the transfer by the tenant to another of *less* than all the tenant's rights in the lease. For example, T, is a tenant under a lease from L which is to terminate on December 31, 1985. If T leases the premises to SL for a shorter period than that covered by her own lease, e.g., until November 30, 1985, T has subleased the premises because she has transferred less than her whole interest in the lease.

The legal effects of a sublease are entirely different from those of an assignment. In a sublease the sublessee, SL in the example above, has no obligation to T's landlord, L. SL's obligations run solely to T, the original tenant; T is not relieved of any of her obligations under the lease. Thus, L has no right of action against T's sublessee SL under any covenants contained in the original lease between him and T, because that lease has not been assigned to SL. T, of course, remains liable to L for the rent reserved and upon all of the other covenants in the original lease between her and L. Under the majority view a covenant against assignment of a lease does not prohibit the tenant from subleasing the premises. Conversely, a prohibition against subleasing is not considered a restriction upon the right to assign the lease. See Figure 48-1.

TENANT'S OBLIGATIONS

While the leasehold estate carries with it an implied obligation upon the part of the tenant to pay reasonable rent, the contract of lease almost always contains an express promise, or a covenant by the tenant to pay rent in specified amounts at specified times. In the absence of such express covenant providing the amount of rental and the times for payment, the rent is a *reasonable* amount and is *payable only at the end of the term.*

Most leases contain a provision to the effect that breach by the tenant of any of his covenants in the lease will entitle the landlord to declare the lease at an end and will give him the right to regain possession of the premises. The tenant's express undertaking to pay rent thus becomes one of the covenants upon which this provision can operate. Where there is no such provision in the lease, at common law the tenant's failure to pay rent when due gives the landlord only the right to recover a judgment for the amount of such rent; it gives him *no* right to oust the tenant from the premises. In most jurisdictions today the foregoing rule has been changed by statute to the extent that the landlord is given a right to dispossess the tenant for non-payment of rent, even though there is no provision for this in the lease.

A tenant is under *no* duty to make any repairs to the leased premises, unless the lease expressly so provides. He is not obliged to

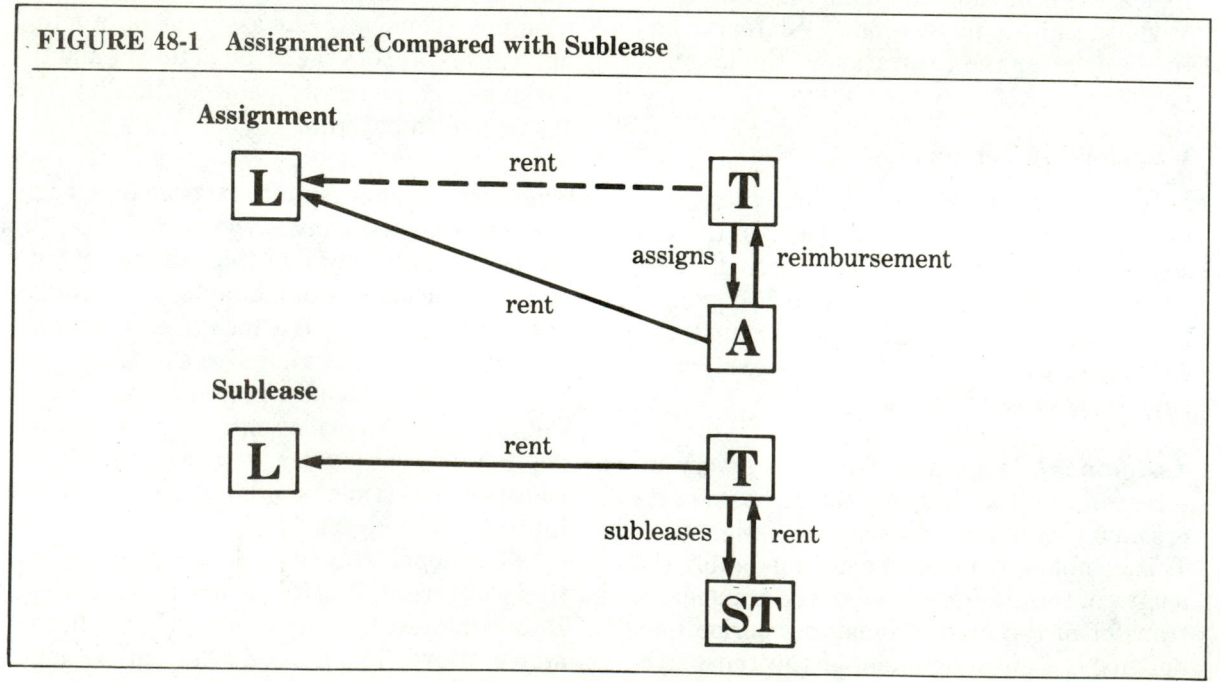

FIGURE 48-1   Assignment Compared with Sublease

repair or restore substantial or extraordinary damage occurring without his fault, nor to repair damage caused by ordinary wear and tear. The tenant is obliged to so use the premises that no substantial injury is caused them. The law imposes this duty upon him even though it is not expressly stipulated in the lease. A tenant who overloads a barn causing it to fall is liable to the landlord and the overloading of an electric connection that causes damage to a wiring system will entitle a landlord to maintain an action for damages.

Effect of Destruction of the Premises

The dual character of a lease as a contract and as a grant of an estate in land is particularly evident when considering the common law rule governing the destruction of the premises by fire or other cause. Where the tenant leases land together with a building and the building is destroyed by fire or other fortuitous cause, the common law does not relieve him of his obligation to pay rent nor does it permit him to terminate the lease. The common law rule has been modified in some States by statute, and in most States it is not applied to tenants who occupy only a portion of the building and have no interest in the building as a whole, such as apartment tenants. Most courts take the view that it would be stretching the concept of an "estate" too far to say that a tenant occupying a few rooms in a house is left with his "estate" in return for which he must pay rent, despite the total destruction of the building or his rooms.

Most leases contain clauses covering the fortuitous destruction of the premises. A typical clause provides that, upon damage by fire or other fortuitous cause, the landlord will repair and restore, and that, if the premises are wholly untenantable, the tenant's obligation to pay rent will be suspended until the premises are restored, but that if the landlord decides to demolish and reconstruct the premises, the lease will terminate.

Effect of Eviction or Abandonment

The tenant's obligations are further dependent upon whether (1) the landlord rightfully evicts the tenants, (2) the tenant wrongfully abandons the premises, and (3) the landlord wrongfully evicts the tenant. These factors will be discussed in this section.

Dispossession by Landlord for Breach of Covenant When the tenant breaches one of the covenants in her lease, such as the covenant to pay rent, and the landlord evicts or dispossesses her pursuant to an express provision in the lease or under statute authorizing her to do so, the lease is terminated. Because the breach of the covenant to pay rent does not involve any injury to the premises and because the landlord's action in evicting the tenant terminates the lease, the tenant is not liable to the landlord for any future installments of the rent after such eviction. However, most long term leases contain a **"survival clause"** providing that the eviction of the tenant for non-payment of rent will not relieve her of liability for damages measured by the difference between the rent reserved in the lease and the rent the landlord is able to obtain upon a reletting.

Wrongful Abandonment by Tenant If the tenant wrongfully abandons the premises before the expiration of the term of the lease and the landlord reenters the premises or relets them to another, a majority of the courts hold that the tenant's obligation to pay rent after reentry terminates. The landlord, if he desires to hold the tenant to his obligation to pay rent, must either leave the premises vacant, or he must have available in the lease another "survival clause" covering this situation.

Wrongful Eviction by Landlord If the tenant is wrongfully evicted by the landlord, the tenant's obligations under the lease are terminated, and, as discussed below, the landlord is liable for breach of the tenant's right of quiet enjoyment.

LANDLORD'S OBLIGATIONS

Absent express provisions in the lease, the landlord, under the common law, has few obligations to her tenant. At the beginning of the lease she must give the tenant a right to possession, but, under the majority rule, she is not required to give the tenant actual possession. Thus, if the previous tenant wrongfully holds over and refuses to move out, the landlord must bring dispossession proceedings to oust him, but she is not responsible to the new tenant for the delay thus occasioned, and the new tenant is not relieved of the obligation to pay rent from the inception of her lease.

Quiet Enjoyment

The landlord may not interfere with the tenant's right to physical possession, use, and enjoyment of the premises. The landlord is bound to provide the tenant with quiet and peaceful enjoyment. This duty arises by implication and is known as the landlord's covenant of "quiet enjoyment." The landlord breaches this covenant whenever he wrongfully evicts the tenant. He is also regarded as having breached this covenant if the tenant is evicted by someone having a better title than the landlord. The landlord is not responsible, however, for the wrongful acts of third parties unless they are done with his assent and under his direction.

Fitness for Use

Unless there is a specific undertaking in the lease, the landlord, under the common law, is under *no* obligation to maintain the premises in a tenantable condition or to make them fit for any purpose. Some courts, however, have abandoned this rule in residential leases by imposing an implied warranty that the leased premises are habitable, that is, fit for

ordinary residential purposes. These courts have also held that the covenant to pay rent is conditioned upon the landlord's performance of the **implied warranty of habitability**. Courts reaching these results have emphasized the contractual aspects of a lease, although some have limited the warranty to leases of units in multiple-unit apartment buildings. *See Javins v. First National Realty Corp.* Moreover, where the lease is of a furnished apartment, the majority of the courts hold that the landlord must maintain it in a tenantable condition.

In a few States there are statutes requiring landlords, specifically apartment landlords, to keep the premises fit for occupation. Zoning ordinances and health and safety regulations may also impose certain duties upon the landlord.

Repair

In the absence of an express provision in the lease or statutory duty, *no* obligation rests upon the landlord to repair or restore the premises. The landlord does have, however, a duty to maintain, repair, and keep in safe condition those portions of the premises which remain under her control. For example, an apartment house owner who controls the stairways, elevators, and other common areas is liable for their maintenance and repair and is responsible for injuries occurring as a result of her failure to do so. In respect to apartment buildings, the presumption obtains that any portion of the premises which is not expressly leased to the tenants remains under the landlord's control. Thus, the landlord, in such cases, is liable to make external repairs, including repairs to the roof.

While at common law the landlord is under no duty to repair, restore, or keep the premises in a tenantable condition, she may and often does assume those duties in the lease. When she does, the question presents itself whether breach by her of any of her undertakings under the lease entitles the tenant to abandon the premises and refuse to pay rent. Unless an express provision in the lease gives the tenant this right, the common law gives him only an action for damages.

Under the doctrine of **constructive eviction**, however, a failure by the landlord in any of her undertakings under the lease, which causes a substantial and lasting injury to the tenant's beneficial enjoyment of the premises, is regarded as being, in effect, an eviction of the tenant. Under such circumstances the courts permit the tenant to abandon the premises and terminate the lease. The tenant must abandon possession within a reasonable time in order to claim that there was a constructive eviction.

CONCURRENT OWNERSHIP

The ownership of property may be held by one individual or, concurrently, by two or more persons. If title is concurrently in two or more persons, they are generally referred to as **co-tenants**, each entitled to an undivided interest in the entire property and neither having a claim to any specific portion of it. Each may have equal undivided interests, or one may have a larger undivided share than the other. Regardless of the particular relationships between the co-tenants, this form of ownership must be carefully distinguished from the separate ownership of specific parts of property by different persons. Thus, it is possible, for example, for A, B, and C to each own distinct and separate parts of Blackstone Manor, or they may each own, as co-tenants, an undivided one-third interest in all of Blackstone Manor. Whether they are co-tenants or owners of specific portions will depend upon the manner and form in which they acquire their interests.

The two major types of concurrent ownership are tenancy in common and joint tenancy. They have in common the characteristic of undivided interest in the whole, a right in both tenants to possession, and the right of either to sell his interest during life thereby terminating the original relationship. Other forms of co-ownership of real estate are tenancy by the entireties, community property, condominiums, and cooperatives.

JOINT TENANCY

The most significant incident of joint tenancy is the right of **survivorship**. Upon the death of one of the joint tenants, title to the entire property passes by operation of law to the survivor or survivors. The heirs-at-law of the deceased joint tenant have no claim to his interest nor do his general creditors; nor can a joint tenant transfer his interest by executing a will. However, any joint tenant may sever the joint tenancy by conveying or mortgaging his interest to a third party. Further, the interest of either cotenant is subject to levy and sale upon execution. **"Sever"** means the right of survivorship is lost, and the tenancy becomes a tenancy in common between the remaining joint tenants and the transferee. *See Hendrickson v. Minneapolis Federal Savings & Loan Association.*

By statute in most States, certain words must be used to create a joint tenancy in real property. Some of those statutes provide that a grant of an estate to two or more persons in their own right shall be a tenancy in common unless expressly declared to be in joint tenancy. Thus, if a deed of conveyance is not drafted properly, the resulting ownership would be a tenancy in common.

To sustain a joint tenancy, the common law requires the presence of what is known as the **"four unities"** of time, title, interest, and possession.

1. The unity of time means that the interest of all tenants must vest at the same time;
2. the unity of title means that all tenants must acquire title by the same instrument;
3. the unity of interest means that all tenants must have identical interests as to duration and scope;
4. the unity of possession means that all the tenants have the same right of possession and enjoyment.

The absence of any one of these four unities will prevent the creation of a joint tenancy. Failure of any one of the first three unities will result in the creation of a tenancy in common, as the only unity required of a tenancy in common is the unity of possession.

Thus, a deed conveying title to H to ¾ and W to ¼ as joint tenants would result in a tenancy in common and not a joint tenancy. However, two separate groups of joint tenants may hold a parcel of real estate as tenants in common with the interests of the two groups being unequal. For example, assume that H and W, as joint tenants, own an undivided ¾ interest in Blackacre, and A and B, as joint tenants, own the other ¼ interest in the property. The right of survivorship would exist between H and W only with respect to their joint tenancy, and between A and B in their joint tenancy, and the two groups would hold as tenants in common toward one another. Accordingly, if A and B should both die in a common disaster, H and W would not acquire any interest in their one-fourth, which would pass to the heirs of A and B.

TENANCY IN COMMON

Tenants in common, like joint tenants, are persons who hold undivided interests in the same property, each having the right to possession but neither claiming any specific portion of the property. Unlike joint tenants, there is no right of survivorship, and, also unlike joint tenants, the only pre-requisite is the unity of possession. By statute in many States a conveyance to two or more persons will be presumed to create a tenancy in common.

Tenancy in common may be terminated either by transfer of all co-interests to one person or by partition of the property among the tenants, making each the exclusive owner of a specific part of the entire property. **Partition** is a device recognized and regulated by law for changing undivided interests into several and exclusive interests proportionate to the former undivided shares.

TENANCY BY THE ENTIRETIES

This form of concurrent ownership, less common today than formerly, is created only by a conveyance to a **husband and wife.** It is distinguished from joint tenancy by the inability of either spouse to convey separately his or her interest during life and thus destroy the right of survivorship. Likewise, the interest of either spouse can not be attached by creditors. By the nature of the tenancy, a divorce terminates the relationship, and partition would then be available as a method of creating separate interests in the property.

COMMUNITY PROPERTY

In Arizona, California, Idaho, Louisiana, Nevada, New Mexico, Texas, and Washington, any property acquired by the efforts of either

---

FIGURE 48-2 Rights of Concurrent Owners

	Undivided Interest	Right to Possession	Right to Sell	Right to Mortgage	Levy by Creditors	Right to Will	Right of Survivorship
Joint Tenancy	YES	YES	YES	YES	YES	NO	YES
Tenancy in Common	YES	YES	YES	YES	YES	YES	NO
Tenancy by Entireties	YES	YES	NO	NO	NO	NO	YES

the husband or wife belongs one-half to each spouse. This system known as "community property" originated in the civil law of continental Europe, but it has been modified and affected by the common law as well as by statutes in this country.

In most instances the only property which belongs separately to either spouse is that acquired prior to the marriage or subsequent to it by gift or devise. Upon the death of either spouse, one-half of the community property belongs outright to the survivor, and the interest of the deceased spouse in the other half may go to the heirs of the decedent or as directed by will, although, under some conditions in a few jurisdictions, the surviving spouse may also claim an interest in the decedent's one-half share of the property.

CONDOMINIUMS

A form of co-ownership called "condominium" has recently gained extensive use in the United States. All States have enacted statutes authorizing the use of this form of ownership. The purchaser of a condominium acquires separate ownership to the unit and becomes a tenant in common in the common facilities such as the land upon which the project is built, recreational facilities, hallways, parking areas, and spaces between the units. The common elements are maintained by a condominium association funded by assessments levied on each unit. The transfer of a condominium conveys both the separate ownership of the unit and the share in the common elements.

COOPERATIVES

Cooperatives involve an indirect form of common ownership. A cooperative, usually a corporation, purchases or constructs the dwelling units. The cooperative then leases the units to its shareholders as tenants who acquire the right to use and occupy their units.

NONPOSSESSORY INTERESTS

Nonpossessory interests include easements, *profits a prendre*, and licenses. These three types of nonpossessory interests are discussed in the remainder of the chapter.

EASEMENTS

An easement may be defined as a *limited right* to make use of the land of another in a specific manner, created by the acts of the parties or by operation of law, and having all the attributes of an estate in the land itself. A typical easement exists where A sells a part of his land to B and expressly provides in the same or a separate document that B, as the adjoining landowner, shall have a right-of-way over a strip of A's remaining parcel of land. B's land is said to be the **dominant** parcel, and A's land, which is subject to the easement, is the **servient** parcel. Easements may, of course, include a multitude of different types of uses as, for example, a right to run a ditch across another's land, to lay pipe under the surface, to erect power lines, or, in the case of adjacent buildings, to use a stairway or a common or "party" wall.

Since the title to the servient parcel remains in the owner of the entire servient tract, he may make any use of or allow others the use of the tract which does not interfere with the easement. Thus, crops may be grown over an easement for a pipe line, but livestock could not be pastured on an easement for a driveway. Although it is the duty of the owner of the servient parcel not to interfere with the use of the easement, it is generally the responsibility of the owner of the dominant parcel to maintain and keep in repair the easement.

Types of Easements

Easements fall into two classes, easements appurtenant and easements in gross. **Appurtenant** easements are by far the more common type, and, as the name indicates, the rights and duties created by such easements pertain to the land itself and not to the particular individuals who may have created them. Thus, in the foregoing illustration, if A conveys his servient parcel to C who has actual notice of the easement for the benefit of B's land or constructive notice by means of the local recording act, C takes the parcel subject to the easement. Likewise, if B conveys his dominant parcel to D, it is not necessary to refer specifically to the easement in the deed from B to D in order to give to D, as the new owner of the dominant parcel, the right to use the right-of-way over the servient parcel. Since B does not then own the dominant parcel, he has no further right to use the right-of-way. B could not, however, transfer the benefit of the easement to a party who did not acquire an interest in the dominant parcel of land. Most frequently, a deed conveying the land "together with all appurtenances" is sufficient to transfer the easement. This characteristic of an appurtenant easement is described by the statement that both the burden and the benefit of an appurtenant easement pass with the land.

The second class of easements are those which are said to be **in gross** or personal to the particular individual who received the right. They do not depend upon the ownership of land and, in effect, amount to little more than an irrevocable personal right to use.

Creation of Easements

Easements may be created in a number of different ways, by: (1) express grant or reservation, (2) implied grant or reservation, (3) necessity, (4) dedication, and (5) prescription.

Express Grant or Reservation The most common way to create an easement is to convey it by deed. For example, when A conveys part of her land to B, she may, in the same deed, expressly grant an easement to B over A's remaining property. Alternatively, A may grant an easement to B in a separate docu-

ment. This document must comply with all the formalities of a deed. An easement is an interest in land subject to the Statute of Frauds.

In other instances, when an owner of land transfers it, she may wish to retain certain rights in it. In the example given, A may want to "reserve" an easement in favor of the land retained by herself over the land granted to B. A may do this by express words reserving that right to herself in the deed of conveyance to B.

Implied Grant or Reservation Easements by implied grant or implied reservation arise whenever an owner of adjacent properties establishes an *apparent* and *permanent* use, in the nature of an easement, and then conveys one of the properties without mention of any easement. Suppose A owns two adjacent lots, Nos. 1 and 2. There is a house on each lot. Behind each house is a garage. A has constructed a driveway along the medial line between the two lots, partly on lot 1 and partly on lot 2, which leads from the street in front of the houses to the two garages in the rear. A conveys lot 2 to B without any mention of the driveway. A is held to have *impliedly granted* an easement to B over that portion of the driveway which lies on A's lot 1, and she is held to have *impliedly reserved* an easement over that portion of the driveway which lies on B's lot 2.

Necessity If A conveys part of his land to B and the part conveyed to B is so situated that B would have no access to it except across A's remaining land, the law implies a grant by A to B of an easement by necessity across A's remaining land. A way by necessity will not usually arise if an alternative but circuitous approach to B's land is available.

A way by necessity may also arise by implied reservation. This would be the case where A conveys part of his land to B, and A's remaining property would be wholly landlocked unless he is given a right-of-way across the land conveyed to B.

Dedication When an owner of land subdivides it into lots and records the plan or plat of the subdivision, she is held, both by common law and now more frequently by statute, to have dedicated *to the public* all of the streets, alleys, parks, playgrounds, and beaches shown on the plat. In addition, when the subdivider sells the lots by reference to the plat, it is now generally recognized that the purchasers acquire easements by implication over the areas shown dedicated to the public.

Prescription An easement may arise by prescription in most States if certain required conditions are met. To obtain an easement by prescription, a person must use a portion of land owned by another in a way (1) that is adverse to the rightful owner's use, (2) that is open and notorious, and (3) that is continuous and uninterrupted for a specific period of time which varies from State to State. If the owner gives the claimant permission to use the land, no easement by prescription is acquired.

PROFITS A PRENDRE

A *profit a prendre* is a right to remove the produce of another's land. An example would be the grant by B to A, an adjoining landowner, of the right to remove coal or fish or timber from B's land or to graze his cattle on B's land. Like an easement, a profit may arise by prescription, but, if by act of the parties, it must be created with all the formalities of a grant of an estate in real property. Unless the right is clearly designated as exclusive, it is always subject to a similar use by the owner of the land. The right to take profits is frequently held independent of the ownership of other land. Thus, A may have a right to remove crushed gravel from B's acreage even though A lives in another part of the county.

LICENSES

It is not always easy to distinguish such real interests in property as easements or *profits a prendre* from an equally common right of use designated as a license. Permission to make use of one's land generally constitutes a license which creates no interest in the property and is, in most circumstances, exercised only at the will of and subject to revocation by the owner at any time. If A tells B she may cut across A's land to pick hickory nuts, B has nothing but a license subject to revocation at any time. It is possible that, upon the basis of a license, B may expend funds to exercise the right, and the courts may prevent A from revoking the license simply because, under the circumstances, it would be unfair to penalize B. In such a case, B's interest is practicably indistinguishable from an easement. *See Bunn v. Offutt.*

The usual illustration of a typical license is a theater ticket or the use of a hotel room. No interest is acquired in the premises; simply a right of use for a given length of time, subject to good behavior. No formality is required to create a license; a shopkeeper licenses persons to enter his establishment merely by being open for business.

CASES

Vested Remainders

GRIFFIN v. MOON

Supreme Court of Arkansas, 1965.
238 Ark. 692, 384 S.W.2d 243.

HOLT, J.

This case requires the interpretation of a will. The appellees instituted an action against the appellants seeking specific performance of their written agreement to purchase certain realty. The appellants' refusal to purchase was based upon their assertion that appellees did not have a merchantable title because of the ambiguous terms in a will devising the property to the appellees. The chancellor decreed specific performance of appellants' contract to purchase the lands. On appeal appellants' sole contention is that the trial court erred in finding that appellees' title to the land in question is marketable.

The appellants argue that the correctness of the decision of the chancellor depends upon the construction of a portion of the will which reads as follows:

"I give all the residue of my estate comprising a farm of twenty-four (24) acres and one lot, where I now reside, in Miller County, State of Arkansas, after fulfilling the foregoing legacies, to my wife, with the remainder thereof on her decease or marriage, to my said children and their children, respectively, share and share alike."

The testator was survived only by his widow, Maggie J. Moon, and his four sons, Ivor, Erbert, Loy, and Fred Moon. These parties and the wives of the four sons are the appellees. The testator's widow is living and has never remarried. Each of his sons now has children; however, his sons had no children when the testator died. The appellants reject the title as unmarketable upon the contention that the remainder interest does not finally vest in the testator's children until the death or remarriage of the life tenant, the testator's widow. Further, that the testator's grandchildren, born and unborn, eventually would be entitled to an interest as remaindermen. We do not agree with the appellants and find no merit in either contention.

The real issue to be determined is whether the testator's four sons, the appellees, took a vested or contingent remainder upon the death of their father. If they took a vested remainder, then they can join with their mother, the life tenant, and convey a merchantable title; if they took only a contingent remainder, then they cannot. [Citation.] We are of the view that the questioned provisions of the will created a vested remainder in the testator's sons upon his death.

* * *

In McKinney v. Dillard & Coffin Co., [citation], the devise involved principles applicable to the case at bar. In that case the father devised realty to his daughter for her natural life and at her death the lands were devised to her children in equal portions and if at the time of her death "any of her children be dead, leaving children, then such child or children is to have the same interest in said lands that said parent would have had, if alive." In that case we held that the remainder vested in the daughter's children as soon as born and before the death of the daughter. Further, that such vested interest, upon partition of the lands by the consent of the life tenant and vested remaindermen, was subject to a valid and enforceable mortgage. [Citations.]

In the very recent case of Gibson v. Lowry, [citation], we held that where a will gave a life estate to the testator's mother and stepfather and provided that at their death the farm should vest absolutely in the testator's brother, a vested remainder and not a contingent remainder was created in the brother. There we said that the interest vested "at the same instant and by the same grant as the life estate" and that although "the enjoyment of the possession of this interest was postponed until the termination of the life estate, still this right, * * * was presently fixed, and was in no wise dependent upon the happening of any event." [Citation.]

Thus, in the case at bar, appellants' contention that under the terms of the will the remainder is not vested in the testator's four sons until the death or remarriage of the life tenant is without merit. We hold that the testator's four sons now have a vested remainder and it is not subject to the happening of any future event. Their remainder interest vested at the same time that the life estate vested. [Citations.]

It is well settled that where both the life tenant and vested remaindermen join in a deed the entire estate in fee is passed to the grantee. Therefore, it follows that in the case at bar a deed by the appellees conveys a merchantable title.

The decree of the chancellor ordering specific performance of the contract is affirmed.

Remainders

STRICKLAND v. JACKSON

Supreme Court of North Carolina, 1963.
259 N.C. 81, 130 S.E.2d 22.

RODMAN, J.

[In 1905 a deed for land in Pitt County was executed and delivered by Joel and Louisa Tyson "unto M. H. Jackson and wife Maggie Jackson, for and during the term of their natural lives and after their death to the children of the said M. H. Jackson and Maggie Jackson that shall be born to their inter-marriage as shall survive them to them and their heirs and assigns in fee simple forever." Thelma Jackson Vester, a daughter of M. H. Jackson and Maggie Jackson, died in 1957, survived by three children. M. H. Jackson, who survived his wife Maggie Jackson, died in 1958, survived by four sons. The children of Thelma Jackson Vester brought this action against M. P. Jackson, a son of and executor of the will of M. H. Jackson. The children of Vester contended that through their deceased mother they were entitled to a 1/5 interest in the land conveyed by the deed of 1905. The executor contended that the deed conveyed a contingent remainder and only those children who survived the parents took an interest in the land.]

*   *   *

The distinction between a vested and a contingent remainder is the capacity to take upon the termination of the preceding estate. Where those who are to take in remainder cannot be determined until the happening of a stated event, the remainder is contingent. Only those who can answer the roll immediately upon the happening of the event acquire any estate in the properties granted. [Citations.]

Here the estate in remainder was not given to the children of M. H. Jackson and Maggie Jackson, but by clear and express language to those children and only those who survived their parents. Since Mrs. Vester did not survive her parents, there was nothing for her children, plaintiffs, to inherit. [Citations.]

It affirmatively appears from the complaint that plaintiffs acquired no interest in the land by virtue of the deed from Tyson and wife to M. H. Jackson and others.

[Judgment in favor of defendant/executor affirmed.]

Warranty of Habitability

JAVINS v. FIRST NATIONAL REALTY CORP.

United States Court of Appeals, District of Columbia Circuit, 1970.
428 F.2d 1071.

WRIGHT, J.

These cases present the question whether housing code violations which arise during the term of a lease have any effect upon the tenant's obligation to pay rent. The Landlord and Tenant Branch of the District of Columbia Court of General Sessions ruled proof of such violations inadmissible when proffered as a defense to an eviction action for nonpayment of rent. The District of Columbia Court of Appeals upheld this ruling. [Citation.]

Because of the importance of the question presented, we granted appellants' petitions for leave to appeal. We now reverse and hold that a warranty of habitability, measured by the standards set out in the Housing Regulations for the District of Columbia, is implied by operation of law into leases of urban dwelling units covered by those Regulations and that breach of this warranty gives rise to the usual remedies for breach of contract.

I

The facts revealed by the record are simple. By separate written leases, each of the appellants rented an apartment in a three-building apartment complex in Northwest Washington known as Clifton Terrace. The landlord, First National Realty Corporation, filed separate actions in the Landlord and Tenant Branch of the Court of General Sessions on April 8, 1966, seeking possession on the ground that each of the appellants had defaulted in the payment of rent due for the month of April. The tenants, appellants here, admitted that they had not paid the landlord any rent for April. However, they alleged numerous violations of the Housing Regulations as "an equitable defense or [a] claim by way of recoupment or set-off in an amount equal to the rent claim," as provided in the rules of the Court of General Sessions. They offered to prove

[t]hat there are approximately 1500 violations of the Housing Regulations of the District of Columbia in the building at Clifton Terrace, where Defendant resides some affecting the premises of this Defendant directly, others indirectly, and all tending to establish a course of conduct of violation of the Housing Regulations to the damage of Defendants * * *.

[Citation.] Appellants conceded at trial, however, that this offer of proof reached only violations which had arisen since the term of the lease had commenced.

* * *

II

Since, in traditional analysis, a lease was the conveyance of an interest in land, courts have usually utilized the special rules governing real property transactions to resolve controversies involving leases. However, as the Supreme Court has noted in another context, "the body of private property law * * *, more than almost any other branch of law, has been shaped by distinctions whose validity is largely historical." Courts have a duty to reappraise old doctrines in the light of the facts and values of contemporary life—particularly old common law doctrines which the courts themselves created and developed. As we have said before, "[T]he continued vitality of the common law * * * depends upon its ability to reflect contemporary community values and ethics."

The assumption of landlord-tenant law, derived from feudal property law, that a lease primarily conveyed to the tenant an interest in land may have been reasonable in a rural,

agrarian society; it may continue to be reasonable in some leases involving farming or commercial land. In these cases, the value of the lease to the tenant is the land itself. But in the case of the modern apartment dweller, the value of the lease is that it gives him a place to live. The city dweller who seeks to lease an apartment on the third floor of a tenement has little interest in the land 30 or 40 feet below, or even in the bare right to possession within the four walls of his apartment. When American city dwellers, both rich and poor, seek "shelter" today, they seek a well known package of goods and services—a package which includes not merely walls and ceilings, but also adequate heat, light and ventilation, serviceable plumbing facilities, secure windows and doors, proper sanitation, and proper maintenance.

* * *

Ironically, however, the rules governing the construction and interpretation of "predominantly contractual" obligations in leases have too often remained rooted in old property law.

Some courts have realized that certain of the old rules of property law governing leases are inappropriate for today's transactions. In order to reach results more in accord with the legitimate expectations of the parties and the standard of the community, courts have been gradually introducing more modern precepts of contract law in interpreting leases. Proceeding piecemeal has, however, led to confusion where "decisions are frequently conflicting, not because of a healthy disagreement on social policy, but because of the lingering impact of rules whose policies are long since dead."

In our judgment the trend toward treating leases as contracts is wise and well considered. Our holding in this case reflects a belief that leases of urban dwelling units should be interpreted and construed like any other contract.

III

Modern contract law has recognized that the buyer of goods and services in an industrialized society must rely upon the skill and honesty of the supplier to assure that goods and services purchased are of adequate quality. In interpreting most contracts, courts have sought to protect the legitimate expectations of the buyer and have steadily widened the seller's responsibility for the quality of goods and services through implied warranties of fitness and merchantability.

* * *

The rigid doctrines of real property law have tended to inhibit the application of implied warranties to transactions involving real estate. Now, however, courts have begun to hold sellers and developers of real property responsible for the quality of their product. For example, builders of new homes have recently been held liable to purchasers for improper construction on the ground that the builders had breached an implied warranty of fitness. In other cases courts have held builders of new homes liable for breach of an implied warranty that all local building regulations had been complied with. And following the developments in other areas, very recent decisions and commentary suggest the possible extension of liability to parties other than the immediate seller for improper construction of residential real estate.

Despite this trend in the sale of real estate, many courts have been unwilling to imply warranties of quality, specifically a warranty of habitability, into leases of apartments. Recent decisions have offered no convincing explanation for their refusal; rather they have relied without discussion upon the old common law rule that the lessor is not obligated to repair unless he covenants to do so in the written lease contract. However, the Supreme Courts of at least two states, in recent and well reasoned opinions, have held landlords to implied warranties of quality in housing leases. [Citations.] In our judgment, the old no-repair rule cannot coexist with the obligations imposed on the landlord by a typical modern housing code, and must be abandoned in favor of an implied warranty of habitability. In the District of Columbia, the standards

of this warranty are set out in the Housing Regulations.

IV

A. In our judgment the common law itself must recognize the landlord's obligation to keep his premises in a habitable condition. This conclusion is compelled by three separate considerations. First, we believe that the old rule was based on certain factual assumptions which are no longer true; on its own terms, it can no longer be justified. Second, we believe that the comsumer protection cases discussed above require that the old rule be abandoned in order to bring residential landlord-tenant law into harmony with the principles on which those cases rest. Third, we think that the nature of today's urban housing market also dictates abandonment of the old rule.

* * *

Today's urban tenants, the vast majority of whom live in multiple dwelling houses, are interested, not in the land, but solely in "a house suitable for occupation." Furthermore, today's city dweller usually has a single, specialized skill unrelated to maintenance work; he is unable to make repairs, like the "jack-of-all-trades" farmer who was the common law's model of the lessee. Further, unlike his agrarian predecessor who often remained on one piece of land for his entire life, urban tenants today are more mobile than ever before. A tenant's tenure in a specific apartment will often not be sufficient to justify efforts at repairs. In addition, the increasing complexity of today's dwellings renders them much more difficult to repair than the structures of earlier times. In a multiple dwelling repair may require access to equipment and areas in control of the landlord. Low and middle income tenants, even if they were interested in making repairs, would be unable to obtain any financing for major repairs since they have no long-term interest in the property.

* * *

Since a lease contract specifies a particular period of time during which the tenant has a right to use his apartment for shelter, he may legitimately expect that the apartment will be fit for habitation for the time period for which it is rented. We point out that in the present cases there is no allegation that appellants' [lessees'] apartments were in poor condition or in violation of the housing code at the commencement of the leases. Since the lessees continue to pay the same rent, they were entitled to expect that the landlord would continue to keep the premises in their beginning condition during the lease term. It is precisely such expectations that the law now recognizes as deserving of formal, legal protection.

* * *

We follow the Illinois court in holding that the housing code must be read into housing contracts—a holding also required by the purposes and the structure of the code itself. The duties imposed by the Housing Regulations may not be waived or shifted by agreement if the Regulations specifically place the duty upon the lessor.

* * *

V

In the present cases, the landlord sued for possession for nonpayment of rent. Under contract principles, however, the tenant's obligation to pay rent is dependent upon the landlord's performance of his obligations, including his warranty to maintain the premises in habitable condition.

* * *

The judgment of the District of Columbia Court of Appeals is reversed and the cases are remanded for further proceedings consistent with this opinion.

Concurrent Ownership

HENDRICKSON v. MINNEAPOLIS FEDERAL SAVINGS & LOAN ASSOCIATION

Supreme Court of Minnesota, 1968.
281 Minn. 462, 161 N.W.2d 688.

SHERAN, J.

Appeal from an order and decree of registration of the district court.

The Facts

On June 30, 1956, Martin Hendrickson and Solveig Hendrickson were married, and on January 3, 1957, a home previously owned by him was so conveyed as to make them owners of it as joint tenants and not as tenants in common. No part of the consideration for the premises was paid by Mrs. Hendrickson and there is no evidence to show that the creation of the joint tenancy was pursuant to an enforceable agreement.

On August 3, 1964, Martin Hendrickson duly executed a Declaration of Election to Sever Survivorship of Joint Tenancy by which he endeavored to preserve an interest in the premises for Ruth Halbert, his daughter by a previous marriage, appellant in this court. On the same day, he executed his last will and testament, by the terms of which he directed that his wife, Solveig M. Hendrickson, receive the minimum amount to which she was entitled under the laws of the State of Minnesota.

Mr. Hendrickson died testate on October 9, 1964. Thereafter, Solveig M. Hendrickson made application to register title to the premises here involved in her name as fee owner. Ruth Halbert appeared and asserted claim to the interest in the realty to which she would be entitled if the declaration was effective to make Martin Hendrickson and Solveig M. Hendrickson owners of the realty as tenants in common, i.e., an undivided one-half interest subject to the widow's life estate.[1]

Upon reference, the referee found that Martin Hendrickson did not terminate the joint tenancy by his declaration, and that Solveig M. Hendrickson became the owner of an estate in fee simple in the whole of said property as surviving joint tenant. The district court ratified the report of the referee. A decree was entered accordingly and this appeal followed.

---

1. Mrs. Hendrickson would be the owner in fee of the other undivided one-half interest in this realty because if the joint tenancy was severed she became with respect to it a tenant in common and owner in fee of an undivided one-half interest therein.

The Issue

The issue for decision is this: Did the declaration have the effect of severing the joint tenancy, creating a tenancy in common? If it did, Ruth Halbert is the owner of an undivided one-half interest in said real estate subject to the life estate therein of Solveig M. Hendrickson. If it did not, Solveig M. Hendrickson owns the realty in fee simple absolute.

The Decision

Under the common law, there were three types of concurrent ownership: Tenancy in common, joint tenancy, and tenancy by the entirety. A joint tenancy is distinguished from a tenancy in common by the fact that a surviving joint tenant succeeds to the person with whom he shared the joint tenancy. A tenancy by the entirety, which can exist only between husband and wife, is like a joint tenancy in that survivorship exists, but is distinguished from the joint tenancy by the fact that there can be no partition, and it cannot be converted into a tenancy in common. [Citations.]

As the common law of property developed during feudal times, there was a presumption in favor of joint tenancy due to reasons related to feudalism. As the age of feudalism ended, the reasons for this presumption also ended and survivorship came to be regarded "as an 'odious thing' that too often deprived a man's heirs of their rightful inheritance." [Citations.]

In Minnesota, the original presumption in favor of joint tenancy has been reversed by Minn.St. 500.19, subd. 2, which provides: "All grants and devises of lands, made to two or more persons, shall be construed to create estates in common, and not in joint tenancy, unless expressly declared to be in joint tenancy." Disfavor for survivorship in Minnesota is also shown by the fact that in this state the estate of tenancy by the entirety, with its indestructible survivorship, is not recognized. [Citations.]

For a joint tenancy to exist, unity of time, title, interest, and possession must concur. [Citations.] Traditionally, the survivorship

feature could be destroyed and the joint tenancy converted into a tenancy in common if one of the unities was destroyed. [Citations.] This would result, for example, if one of the joint tenants conveyed his interest to a third party. [Citation.] The common-law lawyer used this principle to enable one joint tenant to unilaterally eliminate the survivorship feature and yet retain ownership in the property. A conveyance would be made to a third party or strawman, thus destroying the joint tenancy. Immediately thereafter the property would be reconveyed to the original owner. A tenancy in common would thus be created because the unities of time and interest would no longer be present. More recently the courts have come to allow joint tenants to convert their estate into a tenancy in common without the ritual of conveyance and reconveyance. It is only necessary for the joint tenants to mutually agree to sever the joint tenancy. [Citations.] We are now asked to allow one joint tenant to do unilaterally that which we allow joint tenants acting in concert to do, i.e., terminate the joint tenancy by declaration without being required to go through the ceremony of a conveyance to a strawman and a reconveyance back again.

* * *

We hold that the method chosen here is sufficient to sever a joint tenancy. Had the property involved been any property other than a homestead, the decedent could have unilaterally severed the joint tenancy. Minn.St. 507.02 and 525.145(1)(b)[7] establish a public policy to protect for the wife the continued occupancy of the place of joint abode. However, this public policy does not neces-

---

7. Minn.St. 525.145(1) provides: "Where there is a surviving spouse the homestead shall descend free from any testamentary or other disposition thereof to which such spouse has not consented in writing or by election to take under the will as provided by law, as follows:

* * *

"(b) If there be children or issue of deceased children surviving, then to the spouse for the term of his natural life and the remainder in equal shares to such children and the issue of deceased children by right of representation."

sarily apply to the remainder interest, which can be disposed of without adversely affecting the right of the surviving spouse to continue in possession and enjoyment for so long as she might live. Putting the property into joint tenancy was apparently an estate-planning device. If the decedent had kept title to this real estate in his own name and executed a will by the terms of which it was devised to his wife in fee simple absolute, he would have been free at any time to revoke the will unilaterally. His wife would nevertheless have the right to a life estate in the homestead upon his death, but her right would be based on the statute and not the will. § 525.145(1)(b).
* * *

If the survivor had taken some irrevocable action in reliance upon the creation or existence of the joint tenancy, or if some consideration was given or received when the joint tenancy was created, it would seem reasonable to insist that unilateral action would not be effective to deprive the passive joint tenant of the rights so created. But this is not such a case.

Our conclusion is that the trial court should be reversed.

Licenses

BUNN v. OFFUTT

Supreme Court of Virginia, 1976.
216 Va. 681, 222 S.E.2d 522.

HARRISON, J.

* * *

On July 9, 1962, Temco, Inc. conveyed to Harvey W. Wynn and Rosabelle G. Wynn property known as 900 South Wakefield Street in Arlington. Prior thereto, on January 26, 1962, the Wynns had signed a contract of purchase prepared by the seller's agent. in this contract is found the following provision: "Use of apartment swimming pool to be available to purchaser and his family." The Wynns testified that the agent, Willis L. Lawrence, told them that the use of the pool went with the

ownership of the home being purchased, and that subsequent purchasers would have the right to use the pool. The pool is located in an adjoining apartment complex which was being developed by appellees at the time. The Wynns said the sales agent emphasized that use of this pool would be a desirable feature in the event they subsequently decided to sell the property. No reference was made to the pool in the deed from Temco to the Wynns.

On May 31, 1969, the Bunns contracted in writing to buy the property from the Wynns through the latter's agent, Sonnett Realty Co., Inc. While no reference to the pool was made in the contract, the Wynns and a representative of Sonnett told the Bunns that the use of the pool went with the purchase of the property. However, the deed, dated July 18, 1969, conveying the property from the Wynns to the Bunns contains no reference to the pool. After the purchase was effected, and when the Bunns requested passes from appellees showing their entitlement to the use of the pool, their request was refused.

Appellants attach significance to the close relationship which they allege existed between Offutt, Temco, Dittmar, and Sonnett. The appellees all have their offices in the same room of a building situated on the property where the pool is located, and Sonnett, which in 1969 was the exclusive sales agency for the appellees, has its office in the same building. Furthermore, the Wynns had agreed to purchase another house, then under construction, from appellees provided Sonnett could sell their Wakefield home. The Bunns testified that as an inducement for them to increase by $750 their offering price for the Wynn property, Sonnett stressed the value of using the swimming pool, and represented that pool membership in a club elsewhere would cost them an initial $300 fee plus annual dues.

Representatives of Sonnett attempted to persuade the appellees to grant pool privileges to appellants, but without success. Ultimately, on November 14, 1969, Sonnett wrote Mr. Bunn a letter advising that it had been unable to secure from appellees passes for the swimming pool, and that since the situation was beyond its control, Sonnett "would be only too happy to assume your existing trust and give you the cash you have invested in the property." This offer was refused.

We agree with the trial judge that the rights of the parties depend upon the nature of the transaction in 1962 between appellees [Temco and Offutt] as seller, and Mr. and Mrs. Wynn, as purchasers.

The dispositive issue in this case is whether the language in the contract, "Use of apartment swimming pool to be available to purchaser and his family," amounted to a grant of a mere license to the Wynns and their family; or whether the Wynns acquired thereby a private easement across the land of appellees to the swimming pool and to the use of the pool, which easement was thereafter transferred to the Bunns.

A license has been described as "a right, given by some competent authority to do an act which without such authority would be illegal, a tort, or a trespass." [Citation.] A license is personal between the licensor and the licensee and cannot be assigned. * * * [A] grant which creates any interest or estate in land is not a license. Such a grant creates an easement. * * *

An easement has been described as " 'a privilege without profit, which the owner of one tenement has a right to enjoy in respect of that tenement in or over the tenement of another person; by reason whereof the latter is obliged to suffer, or refrain from doing something in his own tenement to the advantage of the former'." Stevenson v. Wallace, [citation].

* * *

Easements may be created by express grant or reservation, by implication, by estoppel or by prescription. The only rights acquired by the Wynns in the property of ap-

pellees were acquired by deed from Temco. The provisions of the contract were merged in this deed. However, the deed is silent as to the pool, and the contract made the use of the pool available only to "purchaser and his family." The trial court found this language consistent with appellees' theory that a mere license only was granted to the purchasers and their families, and not an interest in land or an estate of inheritance; that the absence of any provision regarding the swimming pool in the deed to the Wynns was sufficient to preclude any easement by grant or reservation; and that the evidence and exhibits failed to show that an easement was created by estoppel, necessity or prescription. The trial court further found that no easement had been created by implication for there was neither a showing of a preexisting use of the easement prior to the conveyance by Temco to the Wynns, nor any showing that the use of the swimming pool was essential to the beneficial enjoyment of the land conveyed.

* * *

In Hamlin v. Pandapas, [citation], the court held:

> In the construction of language contained in a deed the grantor must generally be considered as having intended to convey all that the language he employed is capable of passing to the grantee, and where the description admits of two constructions, it will be construed most favorably to the grantee. * * *

However, the deed from Temco to the Wynns did not purport to convey an easement to the swimming pool, and the language in the sales contract between the parties is not sufficient to create an express easement. The Wynns and their family were given a mere license to use the swimming pool. It was not an interest running with the land that could subsequently be tranferred by them.

The decree of the lower court under review is affirmed.

PROBLEMS

1. X conveyed a farm to Y to have and to hold for and during his life and upon his death to Z. Some years thereafter, oil was discovered in the vicinity. Y thereupon made an oil and gas lease, and the oil company set up its machinery to commence drilling operations. Z thereupon filed suit to enjoin the operations. Assuming an injunction to be the proper form of remedy, what decision?

2. S owned Blackacre in fee simple. In section 3 of a properly executed will, S devised Blackacre as follows: "I devise my farm Blackacre to my son D so long as it is used as a farm." Sections 5 and 6 made testamentary gifts to persons other than D. The last and residuary clause of S's will provided: "All the residue of my real and personal property not disposed of heretofore in this will, I devise and bequeath to the A B C University."

S died in 1985, survived by her son D. S's estate has been administered. D has been offered $100,000 for Blackacre if he can convey title to it in fee simple.

What interests in Blackacre were created by S's will?

3. A leased to B for a term of ten years beginning May 1, certain premises located at 527–529 Main Street in the city of X. The premises were improved with a three-story building, the first floor being occupied by stores and the upper stories by apartments. On May 1 of the following year B leased one of the apartments to C for one year. On July 5, a fire destroyed the second and third floors of the building. The first floor was not burned but was rendered untenantable. Neither the lease from A to B, nor the lease from B to C contained any provision in regard to the fire loss. Discuss the liability of B and C to continue to pay rent.

4. Ames leased an apartment to Boor at $200 a month payable the last day of each month. The term of the written lease was from January 1, 1984 through April 30, 1985. On March 15, 1984 Boor moved out, telling Ames that he disliked all the other tenants. Ames replied: "Well, you are no prize as a tenant; I probably can get more rent from someone more agreeable than you." Ames and Boor then had a minor physical altercation in which neither was injured. Boor sent the keys to the apartment to Ames by mail. Ames wrote Boor, "It will be my pleasure to hold you for every penny

you owe me. I am renting the apartment on your behalf to Clay until April 30, 1985, at $175 a month." Boor had paid his rent through February 28, 1984. Clay entered the premises on April 1, 1984.

How much rent, if any, may Ames recover from Boor?

5. Jay signed a two-year lease which contained a clause which expressly prohibited subletting. After six months Jay asked the landlord for permission to sublet the apartment for one year. The landlord refused. This angered Jay, and he immediately assigned his right under the lease to Kay. Kay was a distinguished gentleman, and Jay knew that everyone would consider him a desirable tenant. Is Jay's assignment of his lease to Kay valid?

6. In 1975 Roy Martin and his wife, Alice, their son, Hiram, and the latter's wife, Myrna, acquired title to a 240-acre farm. The deed ran to Roy Martin and Alice Martin, the father and mother, as joint tenants with the right of survivorship and to Hiram Martin and Myrna Martin, the son and his wife, as joint tenants with the right of survivorship. Alice Martin died in 1980, and in 1983 Roy Martin married Agnes Martin. By his will, Roy Martin bequeathed and devised his entire estate to Agnes Martin. When Roy Martin died in 1985, Hiram and Myrna Martin assumed complete control of the farm.

State the interest in the farm, if any, of Agnes, Hiram, and Myrna Martin immediately upon the death of Roy Martin.

7. T, through her will, granted a life estate to A in certain real estate, with remainder to B and C in joint tenancy. All the residue of T's estate was left to the X College. While going to T's funeral, the car in which A, B, and C were driving was wrecked. B was killed instantly, C died a few minutes later, and A died on his way to the hospital. Who is entitled to the real estate in question?

8. Otis Olson, the owner of two adjoining city lots, A and B, built a house on each. He laid a drainpipe from lot B across lot A to the main sewer pipe under the alley beyond lot A. Olson then sold and conveyed lot A to Fred Ford. The deed, which made no mention of the drainpipe, was promptly recorded. Ford had no actual knowledge or notice of the drainpipe although it would have been apparent to anyone making an inspection of the premises, having been only partially imbedded. Later, Olson sold and conveyed lot B to Luke Lane. This deed, which likewise made no reference to the drainpipe, was also promptly recorded.

A few weeks thereafter Ford discovered the drainpipe across lot A and removed it. Did he have the right to do so?

9. At the time of his marriage to Ann, Robert owned several parcels of real estate in joint tenancy with his brother, Sam. During his marriage, Robert purchased a house, title to which he put in his name and his wife's name as joint tenants and not as tenants in common. Robert died; within a month of his death, Smith obtained a judgment against the estate of Robert. What are the relative rights of Sam, the judgment creditor, and Ann?

10. In 1959, Ogle was the owner of two adjoining lots numbered 6 and 7 fronting at the north on a city street. In that year she laid out and built a concrete driveway along and two feet in from what she erroneously believed to be the west boundary of lot 7. Ogle used the driveway for access to buildings situated at the southern end of both lots. Later, in 1959 she conveyed lot 7 to Dale, and thereafter in the same year she conveyed lot 6 to Pace. Neither deed made any reference to the driveway, and after the conveyance Dale used it exclusively for access to lot 7. In 1985 a survey by Pace established that the driveway encroached six inches on lot 6, and he brought an appropriate action to establish his lawful ownership of the strip upon which the driveway approaches, to enjoin its use by Dale, and to require Dale to remove the overlap. Decision?

Chapter 49

TRANSFER AND CONTROL OF REAL PROPERTY

THE law has always been and is today extremely cautious with respect to the transfer of title to real estate. Personal property may, for the most part, be readily and informally passed from owner to owner but real property, occupying a position of uniqueness and singularity, can only be transferred in compliance with a variety of formalities. This tendency is apparent in the transfer of real property at death where the strict formalities are relaxed only with respect to personal property and this attitude of care and formality reaches its zenith in a transfer of land during the lifetime of the owner.

There are three principal ways in which title to land may be transferred: (1) by deed (2) by will or by the law of descent upon the death of the owner; and (3) by open, continuous, and adverse possession by a non-owner for a statutorily prescribed period of years. This chapter will discuss the first method—transfer by deeds as well as the third method of transfer—adverse possession. The second method is covered in Chapter 50.

In addition to the legal restrictions placed upon the transfer of real property, the use of privately owned property is also subject to a number of other controls. Some of these are imposed by governmental units and include zoning and eminent domain. Others are imposed by private parties through restrictive covenants. These three controls are considered in the second part of this chapter.

TRANSFER OF REAL PROPERTY

The most common way in which real property is transferred is by deed. Such transfers usually involve a contract for the sale of the land and the subsequent delivery of the deed and payment of the agreed consideration. In most cases the purchase of real estate requires borrowing a part of the purchase price secured by the real property. This section will discuss these matters under the headings of (1) contract of sale, (2) deeds, and (3) secured transactions. This section will also consider the uncommon method of transfer called adverse possession.

CONTRACT OF SALE

Formation

Since an oral agreement for the sale of an interest in land will not be enforceable under the Statute of Frauds, the parties must reduce the agreement to *writing* and have it signed by the other party in order to be able to enforce the agreement against that party. The simplest agreement should contain (1) the names and addresses of the parties; (2) a description of the property to be conveyed; (3) the time for the conveyance; (4) the type of deed to be given; and (5) the price and manner of payment. To avoid dispute and to assure adequate protection of the rights of both parties, there are many other points which should be covered by a properly drawn contract for the sale of land. For example, the contract should contain carefully written provisions as to any and all fixtures intended to be included in the sale.

The great majority of the jurisdictions adhere to the common law rule that, after the contract is formed, the risk of loss or destruction of the property is upon the purchaser. The contract of sale may, of course, provide that the risk of loss or destruction shall remain upon the seller until conveyance of the deed to the purchaser, or it may provide that the seller shall restore any structures destroyed before closing, or that the seller must obtain insurance for the benefit of the purchaser, or any other allocation of risk agreed upon by the parties.

Marketable Title

It is firmly established in the law of conveyancing that a contract for the sale of land carries with it an *implied* obligation upon the part of the seller to transfer marketable title. A marketable title is one which is free from (a) encumbrances, such as mortgages, easements, liens, leases, and restrictive covenants; (b) defects in the chain of title appearing in the land records such as a prior recorded conveyance of the same property by the seller; (c) any defects which, while they are not sufficient to amount to encumbrances, may subject the purchaser to the inconvenience of having to defend his title in court. The significance of the seller's obligation to convey marketable title is that if the title search reveals any flaw which has not been made an *express* exception to that obligation, the purchaser may refuse to take the conveyance on the date set for closing and may sue and recover damages from the seller unless the defect in title is promptly remedied.

Two important exceptions to this rule should be noted. (1) Most courts hold that the seller's implied or express obligation to convey marketable title does not require him to convey free from existing zoning restrictions. (2) Some courts also hold that the seller's implied or express obligation to convey marketable title does not require him to convey free from open and visible public rights of way or easements such as public roads and sewers.

Except in those two instances, however, the purchaser's *knowledge* or constructive knowledge of an encumbrance or other title defect *never* operates to diminish the vendor's obligation to convey marketable title. In all such cases, it is conclusively presumed that by the contract of sale the vendor has undertaken to remove such defects before the date set for delivery of the deed and payment of the price known as the "closing date."

DEEDS

Types of Deeds

The modern deed as authorized in American jurisdictions is a somewhat simplified version of an early English deed known as a "grant."

Originally, a grant was used to transfer intangible interests in land but its use was gradually expanded to include transfers of any type of interest in land.

Warranty By a warranty deed, the **grantor** (seller) promises the **grantee** (buyer) that she has a valid title to the property. In addition, under such a deed the grantor, expressly or impliedly, obliges herself to make the grantee whole if the latter suffers any damage because the grantor's title was defective. Aside from the liability of the grantor for any defects in her title, a distinct characteristic of the general warranty deed is that it will convey after-acquired title. For example, on January 30, A conveys Blackacre by warranty deed to B. On January 30, A's title to Blackacre is defective, but by February 14, A has acquired a good title. Without more, B has acquired A's good title under the January 30 warranty deed.

Special Warranty Whereas a warranty deed contains a general warranty of title, a special warranty deed is one which warrants only that the title has not been impaired, encumbered, or rendered defective by reason of any act or omission *of the grantor*. The grantor merely warrants the title so far as acts or omissions of the grantor are concerned. He does *not* warrant that the title may not be defective by reason of the acts or omissions of others.

Quitclaim By a quitclaim deed, the grantor says no more, in effect, than "I make no promise as to what interest I do have in this land, but whatever it be I convey it to you." Quitclaim deeds are used most frequently when it is desired to have persons who appear to have an interest in land release their interest.

Formal Requirements

As previously noted, any transfer of an interest in land is within the Statute of Frauds if it is an interest of more than a limited du-

ration and must, therefore, be in writing. Nearly all deeds, whatever the type, follow substantially the same pattern. The statutory forms of deeds prescribed by statute in most States suggest certain operative words of conveyance. The words used will vary depending upon whether the instrument is a warranty deed, general or special, or a quitclaim deed. A common phrase for a warranty deed is "convey and warrant," although in a number of States the phrase "grant, bargain, and sell" is used together with a covenant by the seller later in the deed that she will "warrant and defend the title." A quitclaim deed will generally provide that the grantor "conveys and quitclaims" or, more simply, "quitclaims all interest" in the property.

Consideration In most instances the law does not require consideration for a valid deed. A grantor may be bound by his gift of land if the deed is properly executed and delivered.

Description of the Land The primary requirement of any description is that it be sufficiently clear and certain to permit identification of the property conveyed. The test is frequently applied in terms of whether a subsequent purchaser or a surveyor employed by him could mark off the land from the description. This does not mean that any particular method is necessary to a valid conveyance. There is a great variety to be found in legal descriptions of property. A conveyance of "all my land in McHenry County" is sufficient, provided all the grantor's land is determinable from other records. The conveyance of "my house" will pass title to the lot although a description in a conveyance by street number is risky because of the chance of revisions in the street numbers.

Such informal descriptions may be sufficiently definite to convey property; this is not, however, the usual method. Customary descriptions generally fall into three major classes: (a) description by reference to monuments and courses, (b) description by reference to Rectangular Survey System, and (c) description by reference to recorded plat.

Quantity of the Estate After the property has been described, the deed will generally proceed to describe the quantity of estate conveyed to the grantee. Thus, either "to have and to hold to himself and his heirs forever" or "to have and to hold in fee simple" would vest the grantee with absolute title to the land. A deed conveying title to "X for life and to Y upon X's death" would grant a life estate to X and a remainder interest to Y.

Covenants of Title It is the practice in deeds for the grantor to make certain promises concerning her title to the land. If any one of these promises or covenants is breached, the grantee is entitled to be indemnified. There are a number of these convenants, the most usual of which are of **title, against incumbrances,** of **quiet enjoyment,** and of **warranty.** These various covenants add up to an assurance that the grantee will have undisturbed possession and will, in turn, be able to transfer the land without adverse claims of third parties. In many States, these covenants or many of them are implied from the words of conveyance themselves such as "warrants" or "grant, bargain, and sell."

Execution Deeds are generally concluded by the signature of the grantor, a seal, and an acknowledgment before a notary public or other official authorized to attest to the authenticity of documents. The signature can be made by a person other than the grantor herself as her agent if such party has written authority from the grantor in a form required by law. The seal today has lost a great deal of its former significance, and in those jurisdictions where it is required, the seal is sufficient if the word "Seal" or the letters "L. S." appear next to the signature.

Although the acknowledgment may not be required to bind the parties to the deed, it is generally a prerequisite to recording the deed, and without an acknowledgment a deed may not be effective against third parties. In most jurisdictions a special form of acknowledgment for deeds is specified by statute.

Delivery of Deeds

A deed does not transfer title to land until it is delivered. "Delivery" means an **intent** that the deed shall take effect and is evidenced by the acts or statements of the grantor. Manual or physical transfer of the deed is usually the best evidence of this intent but is not necessary to effect "delivery." Thus, the act of the grantor in placing a deed in a safe deposit box may or may not constitute delivery depending upon many facts such as whether the grantee did or did not have access to the box and whether the grantor acts as if the property were the grantee's. A deed conceivably may be "delivered" even when kept in the possession of the grantor, just as it would be possible that physical delivery of the deed to the grantee would not transfer title. *See Parramore v. Parramore.* A deed is frequently turned over to a third party to hold until the performance of certain conditions by the grantee. This is spoken of as an **escrow,** and the third party is the escrow agent. Upon the performance of the condition, the escrow agent, is obliged to turn the deed over to the grantee.

In one case, the grantors, H and W, husband and wife, executed quitclaim deeds conveying their house to their granddaughters. After execution, the deeds were placed in a strongbox under the control of the grantors' son. The grantors continued to live in the house and pay taxes on the property. Further, they continuously made statements that they wanted the house to go to the girls. W died the year following execution of the deeds. H died fifteen years later. In an action by the granddaughters for a declaration that they had title to the property, the court found that there was no intent to make a present conveyance. The granddaughters did not have that dominion of the incidents of ownership requisite to a finding of transfer of title.

Haasjes v. Woldring, 10 Mich.App. 100, 158 N.W.2d 777 (1968).

This case illustrates the uncertainties which arise when the intent of a deceased person is the deciding factor. It is indispensable to the delivery of a deed that the grantor should part with control over it with the intention that it will immediately become operative to convey the estate described. If the grantor retains dominion and control over the deed it is ineffectual as a conveyance. In this case, the court felt that the grantors did not intend a present conveyance as evidenced by their expressed wishes and subsequent acts of ownership.

Recordation

In almost all States it is not necessary to record deeds in order to pass title from grantor to grantee. However, unless the grantee has the deed recorded, a subsequent good faith purchaser of the property will acquire superior title to the grantee. Recordation consists of delivery of a duly executed and acknowledged deed to the recorder's office in the county where the property is located. There a copy of the instrument is made and inserted in the current deed book and indexed.

In some States, **notice** States, unrecorded instruments are invalid against any subsequent purchaser without notice. In other States, **notice-race** States, an unrecorded deed is invalid against any subsequent purchaser without notice who records first. Finally, in a few States, **race** States, an unrecorded deed is invalid against any deed recorded before it.

SECURED TRANSACTIONS

The purchase of real estate usually involves a relatively large outlay of money so that few people pay cash for a house or business real estate. It is then necessary to borrow a part of the purchase price or defer payment over a period of time. In such case, the real estate

itself is used to secure the obligation evidenced by a note and mortgage or trust deed. The debtor is referred to as the **mortgagor** and the creditor as the **mortgagee**.

A secured transaction includes two elements: (1) a debt or obligation to pay money, and (2) an interest of the creditor in specific property which secures performance of the obligation. However, a security interest in property cannot exist apart from the debt which it secures, and upon a discharge of the debt in any manner, the security interest in the property is terminated. Transactions involving the use of real estate as security for a debt are subject to real estate law consisting of statutes and rules developed by the common law relating to mortgages and trust deeds. The Uniform Commercial Code does **not** apply to real estate mortgages or trust deeds.

Form of Mortgages

The instrument creating a mortgage is in the form of a conveyance from the *mortgagor* to the *mortgagee* with all the necessary requirements for such documents, namely, in writing, adequate description of the property, seal and acknowledgment, and delivery. The usual mortgage, however, will differ from an outright conveyance of the property by virtue of a provision in the instrument that, upon the performance of the promise by the mortgagor, the conveyance is void and of no effect. This condition is referred to as the "defeasance," and, while normally it appears on the face of the mortgage, it may be in a separate document.

The concept of a mortgage as a lien upon real property as security for the payment of a debt applies with equal force to transactions having the same purpose but under a different name and form. A **trust deed** is fundamentally identical with a mortgage, the most striking difference being that, under a trust deed, the property is conveyed not to the creditor as security but to a third person as trustee for the benefit of the creditor. The trust deed creates rights substantially similar to those created by a mortgage. In some States it is customary to use a trust deed in lieu of the ordinary form of mortgage.

As with all interests in realty, the mortgage or deed of trust should be promptly recorded to protect the mortgagee's rights against persons who acquire an interest in the mortgaged property without knowledge of the mortgage.

Rights and Duties

The correlative rights and duties of the parties to a mortgage may depend upon whether it is viewed as creating a lien or as transferring legal title to the mortgagee. In the majority of States, the **"lien"** theory has been adopted. The mortgagor retains title and, even in the absence of any stipulation in the mortgage, is entitled to possession of the premises to the exclusion of the mortgagee even in the event of default by the mortgagor. Only by foreclosure or sale or court appointment of a receiver can the right of possession be taken from the mortgagor. The minority of States have adopted the common law **"title"** theory which gives the right of ownership and possession to the mortgagee. In most cases, as a practical matter, the mortgagor retains possession because the mortgagee has little interest in possession until default occurs.

If the mortgagor is in possession, he is entitled to the rents and profits from the land. His obligation to the mortgagee is to pay the interest and principal when due. It is occasionally stipulated, however, that rents and profits shall be assigned to the mortgagee as additional security for the debt.

Even though the mortgagor is generally entitled to possession and to many of the attributes of unrestricted ownership, he has a responsibility to deal with the property in such a manner as not to impair the security. In most instances, *"waste"* (impairment of the security) results from failure of the mortgagor to prevent the action or threatened action of third parties against the land. Thus, a failure by the debtor to pay taxes or to discharge

a prior lien may seriously impair the security of the creditor. In such cases the creditor is generally permitted to pay the obligation and add it to his claim against the mortgagor.

The mortgagor has the right to relieve his mortgaged property from the lien of a mortgage by payment of the indebtedness which it secures. This right of **redemption** is characteristic of a mortgage and cannot be extinguished except by operation of law. The right to redeem carries with it the obligation to pay the debt, and payment in full with interest is prerequisite to redemption.

Transfer of Mortgage Interests

The interests of the original mortgagor and mortgagee are capable of being transferred, and the rights and obligations of the assignees will depend primarily upon (1) the agreement of the parties to the assignment, and (2) the rules of law protecting the interest of the one who is party to the mortgage but not to the transfer.

If the mortgagor conveys the land, the purchaser is *not* personally liable for the mortgage debt unless she expressly **assumes** the mortgage. If she assumes it, she is personally obligated to pay the mortgagor's debt owing to the mortgagee who can also hold the mortgagor on his promise to pay. A transfer of mortgaged property **"subject to"** the mortgage does *not* personally obligate the transferee to pay the mortgage debt. In such case the grantee's exposure to loss is limited to the realty.

A mortgagee has the right to assign the mortgage to another person without the consent of the mortgagor. An assignee of a mortgage is well advised to obtain the assignment in writing duly executed by the mortgagee and to record it promptly with the proper public official. This will protect her rights against persons who subsequently acquire an interest in the mortgaged property without knowledge of the assignment. Failure to record an assignment may cause an assignee of a mortgage note to lose her security. For example, A buys land from B, relying upon a release executed and recorded by the mortgagee, C. C, however, had previously assigned the mortgage to D who had failed to have her assignment recorded. In the absence of actual knowledge on the part of A of the assignment by C, D has no claim against the property.

Foreclosure

Usually, the right to foreclose arises when the mortgagor fails to pay the debt. However, the mortgagor's default by non-performance of other promises in the mortgage may also give the mortgagee this right. Thus, a mortgage may provide that failure of the mortgagor to pay taxes is a default which permits foreclosure. It is also a common provision in mortgages that default in payment of an installment of the debt makes the entire unpaid balance of the indebtedness immediately due and payable, permitting foreclosure for the entire amount.

The most general method of terminating the right to redeem is by a suit in equity to obtain a judicial decree directing the sale of the property by an officer of the court, the debt being paid out of the proceeds of the sale and the excess, if any, paid to the mortgagor. In some jurisdictions the mortgagor is given a statutory right to redeem from the foreclosure sale within a specified period of time after the sale. This right, in effect, is a second "right of redemption" and should not be confused with the customary right of redemption before foreclosure. In most jurisdictions a foreclosure sale is subject to approval by the court.

In States where foreclosure is not limited to a sale under judicial decree, a clause may be inserted in mortgages permitting the mortgagee to foreclose by a sale without obtaining an order of court. This power of sale in a trust deed form of mortgage is considerably more expedient than a judicial proceeding. The power of sale usually provides for a public auction with published notice, and not infrequently the mortgagee is forbidden by statute to purchase at the sale on the theory that he occupies a fiduciary relation to the mortgagor which would be breached by his buying in the property at a sale conducted by himself.

Whether foreclosure is by sale under judicial proceeding or by grant of power in the mortgage itself, the transaction retains its character of a procedure to obtain satisfaction of a debt. If the proceeds are insufficient to satisfy the debt in full, the debtor-mortgagor remains liable for payment of the balance of the debt. Generally, the mortgagee will obtain a *deficiency judgment* for any unsatisfied balance of the debt and may proceed to enforce payment of this amount out of other assets of the mortgagor.

ADVERSE POSSESSION

It is a possible, although very rare, event that title to land may be transferred **involuntarily** without any deed or other formality. Such an occurrence results from what the law calls "adverse possession." In most States, if a person openly and continuously occupies the land of another for a statutorily prescribed period of time, typically twenty years, that person will gain title to the land. The possession must be actual and not merely constructive. Living on land, farming it, building on it, or maintaining structures on it have been held sufficient to constitute possession. It is necessary, however, that the possession be adverse. By this, it is meant that any act of dominion by the true owner will stop the period from running. Her entry on the land or the assertion of ownership by her will break the period. In such event the period will have to commence anew from that time. *See Gerwitz v. Gelsomin.*

In some jurisdictions, shorter periods of adverse possession have been established by statute where there is not only possession but also some other claim such as the payment of taxes for seven years and at least a colorable claim of title.

PUBLIC AND PRIVATE CONTROLS

In the exercise of its police power, the State can and does place controls upon the use of privately owned land for the benefit of the community. For loss or damage sustained by the owner by reason of such legitimate controls, the State does not pay the owner any compensation. The enforcement of zoning laws, which is a proper exercise of the police power, is not a taking of property but a regulation of its use. However, the taking of private property for a public use or purpose under the State's power of eminent domain is not an exercise of the police power, and the owners of the property so taken are entitled to be paid its fair and reasonable value.

There are also private controls of the use of privately owned property by means of restrictive covenants, which will also be considered in this section.

ZONING

Zoning is the principal method of public control over *land use*. The validity of zoning is based upon the police power of the State. The police power to provide for the public health, safety, morals, and welfare is one of the inherent powers of government. Police power can be used only to **regulate** private property, never to "take" it. It is firmly established that regulation which has no reasonable relation to public health, safety, morals, or welfare is unconstitutional as being contrary to due process of law.

Enabling Acts and Zoning Ordinances

The power to zone is generally delegated to local city and village authorities by statutes known as "enabling" statutes. A typical enabling statute grants the following powers to municipalities: (1) to regulate and limit the height and bulk of buildings to be erected; (2)

to establish, regulate, and limit the building or setback lines on or along any street, traffic way, drive or parkway; (3) to regulate and limit the intensity of the use of lot areas and to regulate and determine the area of open spaces, within and surrounding buildings; (4) to classify, regulate, and restrict the location of trades and industries and the location of buildings designated for specified industrial, business, residential, and other uses; (5) to divide the entire municipality into districts of such number, shape, area, and such different classes as may be deemed best suited to carry out the purposes of the statute; and (6) to fix standards to which buildings or structures shall conform.

Under these powers the local authorities may enact zoning ordinances which consist of a map and a text. The map divides the municipality into districts which are designated principally as industrial, commercial, or residential, with possible subclassifications. A well drafted zoning ordinance will carefully define the uses permitted in each area.

Variance

All enabling statutes provide that the zoning authorities shall have power to grant variances in cases of "particular hardship." Mere failure to make a profit is not enough. It must affirmatively appear that the property as presently zoned cannot yield a reasonable return upon the owner's investment.

Non-Conforming Uses

A zoning ordinance may not immediately terminate a lawful use existing prior to its enactment. Such use must be permitted to continue as a non-conforming use—at least for a reasonable time. Most ordinances provide for the elimination of non-conforming uses (1) when the use is discontinued, (2) when a nonconforming structure is destroyed or substantially damaged, or (3) when a non-conforming structure has been permitted to exist for the period of its useful life as fixed by municipal authorities. *See Franklin Planning & Zoning Commission v. Simpson County Lumber Co.*

Judicial Review of Zoning

Although the zoning process is traditionally viewed as legislative in nature, it is subject to judicial review on a number of grounds, including: (1) invalidity of the zoning ordinance, (2) unreasonable application of the zoning ordinance, and (3) zoning ordinance amounts to a confiscation or taking of property.

Invalidity of Zoning Ordinance A zoning ordinance may be invalid as a whole either because it bears no reasonable relation to public health, safety, morals, or welfare, or because it involves an exercise of powers not granted to the municipality by the enabling act.

Unreasonable Application of Zoning Ordinance A property owner may be able to show that classification of his property as "residential" is unreasonable in the light of the character and use of the area immediately contiguous to his property. He may argue that the classification of property located on one side of the street as "residential", while property located on the other side is classified and built up as "industrial", is unreasonable. Part of his argument would be that the classification deprives him of any beneficial use of the property because there is very little incentive to build or purchase a residence opposite a factory. In most cases, the contrast and its effects are not so obvious.

Zoning Amounts to a Taking Another form of attack is to show that the restrictions amount to confiscation or a "taking." For this purpose, it is not sufficient for the owner to show that he will sustain a financial loss if the restriction is not lifted. In this connection, the courts have stated that what is good for the entire community cannot be bad for a particular owner. Other courts merely say that the

private interest must give way to the public good. But when the property owner can show that the restriction makes it impracticable for him to use the property for any beneficial purpose, he should be entitled to prevail. Deprivation of all beneficial use is confiscation.

Suppose A owns a small lot in a residential area. The city adopts an official map which locates a proposed street through the middle of A's lot. The Official Map Statute provides that one who builds in the bed of a proposed street will not be entitled to compensation for such building when his property is condemned for a street. The street may never be built. Meanwhile, A is effectively prevented from making any use of his property for residential purposes. This is confiscation.

Subdivision Master Plans

A growing municipality has a special interest in regulating new housing developments so that they will harmonize with the rest of the community; that streets within the development are integrated with existing streets or planned roads; that adequate provision is made for open spaces for traffic, recreation, light, and air; and that adequate provision is made for water, drainage, and sanitary facilities. Accordingly, in most States there is legislation enabling local authorities to require municipality approval of every land subdivision plat. These enabling statutes provide penalties for failure to secure such approval where required by local ordinance. Some statutes make it a criminal offense to sell lots by reference to unrecorded plats and provide that such plats may not be recorded unless approved by the local planning board. Other statutes provide that building permits will not be issued unless the plat is approved and recorded.

EMINENT DOMAIN

The power to take private property for public use, known as the power of eminent domain, is recognized as one of the inherent powers of government in the Federal constitution and in the constitutions of the States. At the same time, however, the power is carefully circumscribed and controlled. The Fifth Amendment to the Federal constitution provides: "Nor shall private property be taken for public use without just compensation." Similar or identical provisions are to be found in the constitutions of the States. There is, therefore, a direct constitutional prohibition against taking private property without just compensation and an implicit prohibition against taking private property for other than public use. Moreover, under both Federal and State constitutions, the individual is entitled to due process of law in connection with the taking.

Public Use

As noted, there is an implicit constitutional prohibition against taking private property for other than public use. "Public use," here, has been interpreted to mean the same thing as "public purpose." Thus, it was early established that the power of eminent domain may be delegated to railroad and public utility companies. The reasonable exercise of this power by such companies to enable them to offer continued and improved service to the public is upheld as being for a public purpose.

As society grows more complex, other public purposes are accepted as legitimate grounds for exercise of the power of eminent domain. One is in the area of urban renewal. Most States have legislation permitting the establishment of housing authorities with power to condemn slum, blighted, and vacant areas and to finance, construct, and maintain housing projects.

Just Compensation

When the power of eminent domain is exercised, just compensation must be made to the owners of the property taken. The measure of compensation is the fair market value of the property as of the time of taking. *See Urban Renewal Agency v. Gospel Mission Church*. The compensation award goes to holders of vested interests in the condemned property. Future contingent interests are not compensable. For example, a wife is not entitled to compensation for her inchoate dower interest in her husband's land since she may predecease her husband.

PRIVATE RESTRICTIONS UPON LAND USE

The owners of lots are subject to restrictive convenants which, if actually brought to the attention of subsequent purchasers or recorded by original deed, or by means of a recorded plat or separate agreement, bind purchasers of lots in the subdivision as though the restriction had been inserted in their own deed.

Suppose X owns a lot in a residential subdivision of a suburban community. On the lot are a house and a garage, and the remainder of the subdivision is either similarly improved or vacant. X decides to enlarge his living room and to extend the front of the house to within twenty feet of the front line of the lot. He knows that this is not prohibited by the zoning ordinance and that there is no limitation in the deed from his seller limiting the area of the house. He will, indeed, be astounded when a neighbor, observing the excavation, informs him that he cannot build to within twenty feet of the front line. He will be only slightly less surprised to hear that the reason he cannot do so is because of a provision in the recorded deed from the original subdivider to the original purchasers of lots in the subdivision requiring front yards of at least thirty-foot depth.

X will discover upon further investigation that the entire subdivision has been subjected to a general building plan designed to benefit all the lots, and any lot owner in the subdivision has the right to enforce the restriction against a purchaser whose title descends from a common grantor.

Nature of Restrictive Covenants

Restrictive covenants of the foregoing type are, in a sense, easements—or at least *negative* easements—to the extent that they impose a limitation on the use of the land. Yet, unlike most easements they are not directly based upon any formal grant, and the ability of any number of property owners to enforce them does not suggest the usual easement that normally is enforceable by an adjoining landowner.

If there is a clear intent that a restriction is intended to benefit an entire tract, the fact that the covenant is not formally executed will not prevent it being enforced against a subsequent purchaser of one of the lots in the tract. As long as two requirements are met, the restriction will be enforced: first, that it is apparent that the restriction was intended to benefit the purchaser of any lot in the tract, and second, that the restriction appears somewhere in the chain of title to which the lot is subject.

Type and Construction of Restrictive Covenants

There are many types of restrictive covenants. The more common types limit the use of property to residential purposes or restrict the area of the lot on which a structure can be built or provide for a special type of architecture. Frequently a subdivider will specify a minimum size for each house, attempting thereby to maintain a minimum standard in the neighborhood. *See John J. Walker v. Robert V. Gross.*

Termination of Restrictive Covenants

The principal reason for not enforcing private restrictions is long *acquiescence* by neighbors to numerous violations in the past. Evidence of *changed conditions* may be found either within the tract covered by the original covenant or in the area adjacent to or surrounding the tract. Acquiescence with respect to one or two isolated violations in the entire tract will not, however, be a defense to a complaint for violation. In the example of X and his desire to enlarge his living room, if he is advised to proceed with his plans, it may be that the character of the neighborhood has so changed that the original purpose of the covenant (in this case, to provide front yards not less than thirty feet in depth) has no further application. If, during the preceding decade, houses, apartment buildings, and even stores have been constructed in disregard of the building line restriction, X may successfully maintain that the character of the area has so changed as no longer to justify enforcement of the covenant against him. To succeed, he must convince the court that the circumstances which gave rise to the covenant no longer exist.

Validity of Restrictive Covenants

Although restrictions upon the use of land have never been popular in the law, if it appears that the restriction will operate to the general benefit of the owners of all the land intended to be affected, the restriction will be enforced. The usual method of enforcing such agreements is by injunction to restrain a violation.

For many decades the United States Supreme Court took the position that **private** racial restrictive agreements, regardless of their moral status, did not deny any right guaranteed by the Federal constitution. It has been the law for many years, however, that a State or municipality could not, under the Fourteenth Amendment to the Federal constitution, impose any such restrictions by statute or ordinance. In 1947, the United States Supreme Court held that private racial restrictive covenants could not be enforced by State courts since the courts were an arm of the State government. This effectively invalidated private racial restrictive covenants.

CASES

Delivery of Deeds

PARRAMORE v. PARRAMORE

Court of Appeals of Florida, 1978.
371 So.2d 123.

SMITH, ACTING C. J.

Appellant Alney Parramore and his brother and sisters, appellees Eudell, Bernice, and Iris, are the four surviving children of Fred Parramore of Gadsden County, who died there in November 1974. Fred Parramore's estate was almost entirely in Gadsden County lands, and his plan was to parcel and convey those lands to his children at his death. He implemented that plan by inter vivos deeds purporting to convey life estates to himself and his wife with remainder interests to his children. In May 1963, the deeds were executed and acknowledged, but not delivered to the grantees. Fred placed the deeds with his will in a safe deposit box of a Quincy bank and instructed his children to pick up their deeds at his death. Fred survived his wife, later delivered Alney's deed to him, and, six months before his death, made another conveyance to Alney, the apparent effect of which was to release Fred's life estate and merge the fee in Alney. But Fred's deeds conveying remainder interests to appellees Eudell, Bernice, and Iris were never handed over to them during Fred's lifetime.

Appellant Alney, whose parcel is securely vested in him, urges that the inter vivos deeds of remainder interests to his brother and sisters failed for want of delivery, and that the affected lands pass to all four children equally by the residuary clause of Fred's will. After a trial in which the decedent's later years were explored for evidence of his intent, the circuit court held that Fred Parramore's words and acts accomplished a symbolic and constructive delivery of the deeds during his lifetime, and that the remainder estates were vested in Eudell,

Bernice, and Iris before their father's death. Alney appeals. We affirm.

Delivery is "the life of a deed"; without it no deed is good, though "the intent to deliver is clear and failure to deliver due to accident." [Citation.] Yet delivery is not an exact ceremony, to be done invariably in a particular way. The clearest delivery is by "a manual tradition of the prepared deed with accompanying words or circumstances showing an appropriate intent." [Citation.] But a grantor may fully relinquish a deed, signifying a conveyance, otherwise than by placing it in the grantee's hands. The grantor may hand his deed to a person not the grantee, with directions to deliver it; and, if an intent to relinquish the deed is shown, and the grantor's directions eventually are carried out, delivery is regarded as having been accomplished even though it cannot be proved absolutely that the grantor could never have retrieved the deed. [Citations.]

* * *

We believe there is substantial competent evidence to support the trial court's decision that Fred Parramore, during his life, vested remainder interests in his children [Eudell, Bernice, and Iris] by conduct recognizable as delivery of the deeds. * * * It is enough that Fred Parramore, unsophisticated in such matters, signed deeds creating remainder interests in his several children and put the deeds beyond his immediate reach in a place which he understandably regarded and verbally identified as the appropriate depository for instruments having practical effect at life's end; that he invariably spoke and acted to indicate that he considered the children's remainder interests vested, even to the point of declaring to a prospective buyer that he could not convey the land because it had been deeded away; and that he did not again take the deeds into his more immediate possession or otherwise disturb them. There is no reason why the grantor's evident intent, as discerned by the trial court, should not be regarded as effectuated by his conduct; nor any reason to doubt that his deeds were thereby delivered by all ceremonies that the law may sensibly require.

Affirmed.

Adverse Possession

GERWITZ v. GELSOMIN

Supreme Court, Appellate Division, Fourth
Department, 1979.
69 A.D.2d 992, 416 N.Y.S.2d 127.

MEMORANDUM:

Plaintiffs reside at 317 Rita Drive, Clay, New York, property known also as Lot #24 of the Belleville Tract. They acquired the premises in 1957 and shortly thereafter they began to use the adjacent vacant Lot #25, now owned by defendant Gelsomin. At various times they have planted grass seed, flowers and shrubs on the land and used it for picnics or cookouts. In 1977 defendant Gelsomin acquired Lot #25. He constructed a foundation on it on which he attempted to move a house. Plaintiffs thereupon commenced this action claiming title to Lot #25 by adverse possession.

Before a claimant may acquire land by adverse possession, he must prove by clear and convincing evidence that his possession of the premises has been (1) hostile and under a claim of right, (2) actual, (3) open and notorious, (4) exclusive, and (5) continuous. [Citations.] The trial court found that plaintiffs had failed to prove that their occupation of these premises had been exclusive or continuous. We affirm because the possession was not hostile to the owner and under a claim of right.

The reasonable inference to be drawn from the evidence is that plaintiffs knew in 1957 that they did not own Lot #25 and they never intended to claim ownership of it. They entered the land to remedy an eyesore next to their home and use the land as they could.

Thus, the proof establishes that plaintiffs had clear knowledge of the boundaries of their land by map and deed and because the other lots on the street were the same size. At the time of purchase, plaintiffs' Lot #24 was graded and improved by the contractor, but he did not grade or improve lot #25. Plaintiffs were satisfied with this grading which established a clear boundary line between their improved property and the unimproved Lot #25 next door which was covered with debris. Plaintiffs paid the taxes on their own property regularly and received receipts for those payments. They have never paid or attempted to pay the taxes on Lot #25, even after defendant started his construction. While the failure to pay taxes is not conclusive evidence, it is a significant circumstance which weakens plaintiffs' claim that occupation of the land was under a claim of title, particularly when the failure continued for 20 years. [Citation.]

Finally, the proof establishes that at various times during the prospective period "For sale" signs were placed upon the vacant premises by the owner without objection or inquiry by plaintiffs. Upon this evidence, plaintiffs have failed to sustain their burden of proof that they occupied Lot #25 or any part of it under a claim of right.

Judgment unanimously affirmed with costs.

Zoning: Non-conforming Uses

FRANKLIN PLANNING & ZONING COMMISSION v. SIMPSON COUNTY LUMBER CO.

Supreme Court of Kentucky, 1965.
394 S.W.2d 593.

HILL, J.

This appeal concerns the propriety of a judgment interpreting the rights of these litigants under a planning and zoning ordinance of the City of Franklin.

Appellee Desford Potts for about seve.. years owned a six-acre tract of land within the corporate limits of Franklin. It lies between Railroad and Morris Streets. During this period, Potts maintained a livestock barn on the tract in which was stored lumber and other building materials. Outside, and mostly to the rear of the barn, brick was stored in stacks four or five feet high. In 1959 the City of Franklin passed a zoning ordinance by virtue of which Potts' lot was classified as residential (R-2) property.

Shortly before this suit was instituted, Potts moved some saw logs onto his lot back of the barn where he had recently had a bulldozer level the lot. The city complained. Potts sued to enjoin interference by the city. The chancellor decided in favor of Potts.

The city contends the continued use by Potts of his property for storage of building materials is a "nonconforming" use, and under the law cannot be enlarged by storing saw logs thereon. Potts contends it is not an enlargement of the "nonconforming" use and therfore not in violation of the zoning ordinance. We should say here that a "nonconforming use" means simply a use which does not conform to the classification provided for in the ordinance, residential in this instance.

The applicable portion of the ordinance is as follows:

Section 33, Continuance of Non-Conforming Uses. Any use of land or structure existing at the time of enactment or subsequent amendment of this ordinance, but not in conformity with its use provisions may be continued * * *

Regardless of our sadness at seeing the elimination of the "spreading chestnut tree," and the village smith, it must be admitted that in the interest of progress the law favors the gradual elimination of "nonconforming" uses of property in our cities. [Citation.] It naturally follows that such nonconforming uses as are tolerated under the law cannot be enlarged. [Citations.]

So, our question is whether the storage of saw logs in Potts' lot is an enlargement of the "nonconforming use" he enjoyed previously. The chancellor found as a matter of fact the use was not enlarged. We have numerous photographs of the stored logs, and they appear to be stacked higher than the brick, perhaps eight feet high; but it cannot be said they are unsightly, obnoxious, or a health hazard.

Admitting the saw logs were stacked higher than the brick and not so symmetrically, unless they obstruct the view or impede the natural flow of air we cannot see wherein their storage in back of the barn is materially different from the storage of the stacks of brick. Accordingly, we agree with the chancellor that the "nonconforming use" by Potts of his property has not been enlarged by the storage of saw logs on the property. There is no contention Potts plans a sawmill. It goes without saying that a sawmill in such a residential community would be such an enlargement as appellants oppose.

The judgment is affirmed.

Just Compensation for Property Taken by Eminent Domain

URBAN RENEWAL AGENCY v. GOSPEL MISSION CHURCH

Court of Appeals of Kansas, 1979.
4 Kan.App.2d 101, 603 P.2d 209.

SPENCER, J.

At issue in this case is the proper measure of compensation for the taking by condemnation of property owned and operated exclusively for religious and educational purposes on a nonprofit basis.

The Gospel Mission Church and School was located at 1545 North Wabash in Wichita. The property taken consisted of land, a dwelling house, and a structure housing the church sanctuary and a gymnasium. There is no issue in this court as to the land or the dwelling house. The sanctuary and gymnasium consisted of a large concrete block building which had been erected in two stages. The sanctuary portion was built to accommodate approximately 200 worshipers and contained separate rooms for the church office, choir, and restrooms. The gymnasium portion was equipped with kitchen facilities, restrooms, a storage deck, and basketball goals. The gymnasium was used on a regular basis for basketball games and served as a fellowship and banquet hall.

* * *

The sole issue on appeal is whether the trial court erred in applying the "substitute facilities" measure of compensation, i.e., the amount needed to provide an equivalent necessary replacement facility undiminished by depreciation or functional obsolescence. The Agency contends that the proper measure is the "depreciated replacement cost" approach, i.e., the cost to build an equivalent facility less depreciation as of the date of taking.

It is fundamental that private property shall not be taken or damaged for public use without just compensation. U.S. Const. Amend. 5th; K.S.A. 26–513(a). It is also the law of this state that, if the entire tract of land or interest therein is taken, the measure of compensation is the value of the property or interest at the time of the taking. K.S.A. 26–513(b).

The three generally accepted methods of valuing real property for purposes of condemnation are: (1) The market data approach based upon what comparable properties within the area have sold for at or near the time of taking; (2) the depreciated replacement cost or cost approach based upon what it would cost to acquire the land and to erect equivalent improvements, less depreciation; and (3) the income approach or capitalization of income based upon what the property taken is producing or is capable of producing in income at the time of the taking. [Citations.] As stated in [citation] the market data approach is by far the most commonly used method of appraisal and is the method which should be used when there have been sales of comparable properties in the same locale near the time of the taking. When, however, the property is so unique that it has no ascertainable market and there are no sales of reasonably

similar or comparable property, the other methods—depreciated replacement cost or capitalization of income—may be used. [Citation.]

It is agreed that the value of the church sanctuary and gymnasium could not, in this instance, be determined by the traditional market data approach. Obviously, the capitalization of income method is inappropriate. However, there would appear to be no obstacle to determining value under the depreciated replacement approach advocated by the Agency. Despite this, the Church contends and the trial court ruled that when a condemnee is a "private owner of a non-profit public facility devoted to a special purpose," "just compensation" requires departure from the value standard and application of the substitute facilities method.

* * *

The rationale for departing from value as the measure of compensation in the case of a public condemnee was stated as follows:

The status of a school district deprived by condemnation of its property differs radically from that of a private condemnee. A school district exists to further the educational process, and when its school property has been condemned, it may not take its money and liquidate its operations. The district remains charged with the same public duty of providing educational facilities for its children as it had before its property was taken. And the cost of constructing substitute facilities is equally great whether those condemned were new or ancient. [Citation.]

* * *

Even though it was established that the church facilities consisted of properties not ordinarily traded on the market and the market data approach was not therefore available, the fact remains that here we are concerned with private property for which the Church is entitled to just compensation based on the value of the property at the time of the taking. K.S.A. 26–513. It may be noted that for the Church to continue to serve its congregation and community in the same manner as before the taking, a comparable facility may be necessary. However, there is no requirement beyond good intentions that it do so.

*   *   *

The substitute facilities approach applied to public condemnees is based on the condemnee's legal or factual obligation to replace the facilities. It does not apply to a private condemnee which is "free to allocate its resources to serve its own institutional objectives, which may or may not correspond with community needs." Awarding replacement cost on the theory that the condemnee would continue to operate for a public purpose as before the taking would provide a windfall if substitute facilities were never acquired or, if acquired, were later sold or converted to another use.
*   *   *

Having determined that this case must be reversed on the issue of measure of compensation, we turn to the disposition of the matter on remand. *   *   *

We find no justification for a new trial on all issues, but rather that the trial court should receive and consider evidence on the limited issues of depreciation and functional obsolescence of the church property, if any, and reduce the jury's award of compensation accordingly.

Reversed and remanded for new trial on the limited issues of depreciation and functional obsolescence.

Restrictive Covenants

WALKER v. GROSS

Supreme Court of Massachusetts, 1972.
362 Mass. 703, 290 N.E.2d 543.

WILKINS, J.

The plaintiffs seek a determination, under G.L. c. 240, § 10A, that a deed restriction providing that no part of their premises in Waltham shall be "used for any business purpose" does not prevent the use of their premises for an apartment house. The plaintiffs' land is subject to a restriction, imposed by a

1947 deed to a predecessor in title, which reads as follows: "The premises are conveyed with the benefit of and subject to any easements of record and subject to a permanent restriction that no part of the premises shall be used for any business purpose except for raising, growing and selling live bait and for the sale at retail of fishing tackle and sporting goods, and the grantees for themselves, their heirs, executors, administrators and assigns, covenant and agree with the grantor, his heirs and assigns, not to use the premises or any part thereof in violation of the above restriction, and it is agreed that this covenant shall run with the land."

The plaintiffs contemplate the construction of an apartment building with eighty-three family units and a store. Building permits have been issued for the apartment house by the building inspector of Waltham. The defendants, landowners in the neighborhood of the plaintiffs' premises, are entitled to the benefit of the restriction by which the plaintiffs' premises are burdened.

The restriction itself gives no significant guidance on the question whether an apartment house use is a use for a business purpose. No extrinsic evidence has been presented to assist us in interpreting the intent of the parties in light of the material circumstances and pertinent facts known to the parties to the deed at the time it was executed. We know only that the retail sale of fishing tackle and sporting goods was regarded as a business purpose because those activities were expressly excluded from the prohibition of the restriction. In these circumstances we are guided in reaching our conclusion by the general rule that restrictions in a deed are to be strictly construed against the party seeking to enforce those restrictions. [Citation.] Thus any doubt should be "resolved in favor of the freedom of land from servitude." [Citation.]

We hold that the use of the plaintiffs' premises for apartment house purposes does not violate the deed restriction against the use of those premises for any business purpose. The plaintiffs' apartment building will be used by its occupants for residential purposes. The fact that the apartment house may be owned for income producing purposes does not make the *use* of the premises a use for a business purpose. If we were to accept the view asserted by the defendants, the renting of a single family house and the construction of such a house for sale would seemingly be in violation of this restriction as well. We think that the language of the restriction is concerned with the physical activity carried on upon the premises and not with the presence or absence of a profit making motive on the part of the landowner.

Authority in other jurisdictions supports our view that the use of premises for apartment house purposes does not violate a deed restriction against the use of premises for any business purpose. [Citations.]

The defendants basically object to the construction of an apartment house instead of single family houses. The restriction, however, does not speak in terms of allowing only single family houses, but rather it speaks in words of exclusion to prevent any use for business purposes. If use of an apartment house is, as we hold under the language of the deed restriction, not a use for a business purpose, the scope of the limitation contained in the deed obviously fails to reach the proposed apartment house use. What the grantor might have done if he had anticipated present circumstances need not concern us. Construed, as it must be, strictly against the parties asserting the applicability of the restriction, the restriction simply fails to do what the defendants assert.

Decree affirmed.

PROBLEMS

1. A was the father of B, C, and D and the owner of Redacre, Blackacre, and Greenacre.

A made and executed his warranty deed to B conveying Redacre. The deed provided that "this deed shall only become effective upon the death of the grantor." A retained possession of the deed and died leaving the deed in his safe deposit box.

A made and executed his warranty deed to C conveying Blackacre. The deed provided "this deed shall only become effective upon the death of the grantor." A delivered the deed to C. A died, and after A's death, C recorded the deed.

A made and executed his warranty deed to D conveying Greenacre. The deed was delivered by A to X with specific instructions to deliver the deed to D upon A's death. Upon the death of A, X delivered the deed to D.

    (a) What is the interest of B in Redacre, if any?

    (b) What is the interest of C in Blackacre, if any?

    (c) What is the interest of D in Greenacre, if any?

2. A, the owner of Redacre, executed a real estate mortgage to the Shawnee Bank and Trust Company for $10,000. After the execution and record-

ing of the mortgage, A constructed a dwelling on the premises and planted a corn crop. After default in the payment of the mortgage debt, the bank proceeded to foreclose the mortgage. At the time of the foreclosure sale, the corn crop was mature and unharvested. A contends: (a) the value of the dwelling should be credited to him, and (b) he is entitled to the corn crop. Decision?

3. Robert and Stanley held legal title of record to adjacent tracts of land, each consisting of eighty acres. Stanley fenced his eighty acres in 1960. He placed his east fence fifteen feet onto Robert's property. Thereafter, he was in possession of this fifteen-foot strip of land and kept it fenced and cultivated continuously until possession thereof was delivered by him to Nathan on March 1, 1966. Nathan took possession under deed from Stanley. Nathan continued possession and cultivation of the fifteen-foot strip until May 27, 1985, when Robert, having on several occasions strenuously objected to Nathan's possession, brought suit against Nathan for trespass.

What decision?

4. A executed a mortgage of Blackacre to secure her indebtedness to Ajax Savings and Loan As-

sociation in the amount of $25,000. Later A sold Blackacre to B. The deed contained the following, "this deed is subject to the mortgage executed by the Grantor herein to Ajax Savings and Loan Association."

The sale price of Blackacre to B was $50,000. B paid $25,000 in cash, deducting the $25,000 mortgage debt from the purchase price. Upon default in the payment of the mortgage debt, Ajax brings an action against A and B to recover a judgment for the amount of the mortgage debt and to foreclose the mortgage. Decision?

5. On January 1, 1984, A and B owned Blackacre as tenants in common. On July 1, 1984, A made a written contract to sell Blackacre to C for $25,000. Pursuant to this contract, C paid A $25,000 on August 1, 1984, and A executed and delivered to C a warranty deed to Blackacre. On May 1, 1985, B quitclaimed his interest in Blackacre to A. C brings an action against A for breach of warranty of title. What judgment?

6. John Doe, for valuable consideration, agreed to convey to Richard Roe eighty acres of land. He delivered a deed, the material portions of which read:

"I, John Doe, grant and convey to Richard Roe eighty acres of land [legal description]: To have and to hold unto Richard Roe, his heirs, and assigns forever.

"I, John Doe, covenant to warrant and defend the premises hereby conveyed against all persons claiming the same or any part thereof by or through me."

Thereafter, Roe conveyed "all my right, title and interest" in the eighty acres to Paul Poe. It develops that Doe had no title to the land when he conveyed to Roe. Subsequently, Doe inherited an undivided one-half interest in the property.

What rights, if any, does Poe have against Doe and Roe?

7. B operated a retail bakery, D a drugstore, F a food store, G a gift shop, and H a hardware store in adjoining locations along one side of a single suburban village block. As the population grew, the business section developed at the other end of the village, and the establishments of B, D, F, G,

and H were surrounded for at least a mile in each direction solely by residences. A zoning ordinance with the usual provisions was adopted by the village, and the area including the five stores was declared to be a "residential district for single-family dwellings." Thereafter, B tore down the frame building which housed the bakery and commenced to construct a modern brick bakery. D found her business increasing to such an extent that she began to build an addition upon the drugstore in order to extend it to the rear alley. F's building was destroyed by fire, and he started to reconstruct it in order to restore it to its former condition. G changed the gift shop into a sporting goods store and after six months of operation has decided to go back into the gift shop business. H sold his hardware store to X.

The village building commissioner brings an action under the zoning ordinance to enjoin the construction work of B, D, and F and to enjoin the carrying on of any business by G and X. Assume the ordinance is valid. What result?

8. A and B are residents of Unit I of Chimney Hills Subdivision. The lots owned by A and B are subject to the following restrictive covenant: "Lots shall be for single-family residence purposes only." A intends to convert the interior of her carport into a beauty shop, and B brings suit against A to enjoin her from doing so. A argues that the covenant restricts only the type of building that can be constructed, not the incidental use to which residential structures are put. Decision?

9. The City of Boston sought to condemn land in fee simple for use in constructing an entrance to an underground terminal for a subway. The owners of the land contend that no more than surface and subsurface easements are necessary for the terminal entrance and seek to retain air rights above thirty-six feet. The city argues that any building utilizing this airspace would require structural supports that would interfere with the city's plan for the terminal. The city concedes that the properties around the condemned property could be assembled and structures could be designed to span over the condemned property, in which case the air rights would be quite valuable. Decision?

Chapter 50

TRUSTS AND WILLS

IN previous chapters we have seen that real and personal property may be transferred in a number of ways including by sale and by gift. Another important way in which a person may convey property or allow others to use or benefit from it is through the utilization of trusts and wills. Trusts may take effect during the transferor's lifetime or, when used in a will, they may become effective upon his death. Wills enable individuals to control the transfer of their property at their death. Upon a person's death his or her property must pass to someone. It is almost always the best policy for individuals to decide how their property should be distributed and, except for the limitations of dower and curtesy, the law permits individuals to do so by sale, gift, trust, and will. If, however, an individual dies without a will—that is, *intestate*—State law prescribes who shall be entitled to the property owned by that individual at death. This chapter will examine both trusts and wills as well as the manner in which property descends when a person dies without leaving a will.

TRUSTS

The legal title to property may be held by one or more persons, while its use, enjoyment, and benefit belong to another. This situation may arise by agreement of the parties, by testamentary bequest, or by decree of court. However created, the relationship is known as a "trust." The party creating the trust is the **creator** or **settlor**, the party holding the legal title to the property is the **trustee** of the trust, and the beneficial owner of the trust is the **beneficiary**. See Figure 50-1.

TYPES OF TRUSTS

Although there are many varieties of trusts, all trusts may be divided into two major groups, express and implied.

FIGURE 50-1 Trusts

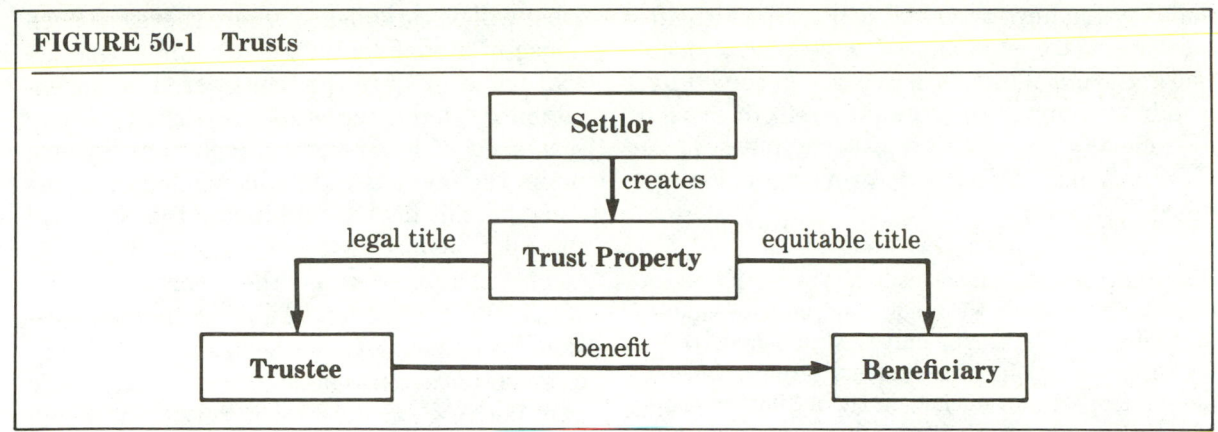

Express Trusts

The express trust is, as the name indicates, a trust established by voluntary action and is represented by a written document or, under some conditions, an oral statement. In a majority of jurisdictions, an express trust of real property must be in writing to meet the requirements of the Statute of Frauds. No particular words are necessary to create a trust, provided that the intent of the settlor to establish a trust is unmistakable. It is not always easy to tell whether a settlor really intended to create a trust. Sometimes, words of request or recommendation are used in connection with a gift implying or hoping that the gift will be used for the purpose stated. Thus, instead of leaving property "to X for the benefit and use of Y," a settlor may leave property to X "in full confidence and with hope that he will care for Y." Such a **"precatory expression"** may be so definite and certain as to impose a trust upon the property for the benefit of Y. Whether it creates a trust or is nothing more than a gratuitous wish will depend on whether the court believes from all the facts that the settlor genuinely intended a trust. More frequently, courts are viewing words such as "request," "hope," and "rely" as creating no legal obligation upon the recipient of the gift and therefore do not create a trust.

Charitable Trusts Almost any trust which has for its purpose the improvement of mankind or a class of mankind will be classified as charitable, provided it is not so vague and indefinite as to be incapable of enforcement. Gifts for public museums, upkeep of parks, propagation of a particular political doctrine or religious belief have been upheld as "charitable" in character.

There are practical differences in the law depending upon whether a trust is for charitable or private purposes. In general, the rule against perpetuities does not apply to charitable trusts. For example, it is valid to provide for a gift in trust to the Middlesex Hospital, a nonprofit corporation, with a provision that if the Hospital ceased to maintain free wards the property should go to the Town of Middlesex for care of the poor. If the trust had been noncharitable the contingent gift to the town would have violated the rule against perpetuities.

Spendthrift Trusts A settlor frequently does not believe that a beneficiary can be relied upon to preserve even the limited rights granted her as beneficiary. He may then provide that the beneficiary cannot, by assignment or otherwise, impair her rights to receive principal or income and that creditors of the beneficiary cannot attach the fund or the income. The term "spendthrift," as used in connection with spendthrift trusts, refers to a provision in a trust instrument under which the trust estate is removed from the beneficiary's control and disposition and from liability for her individual debts. Spendthrift provisions are generally valid. Of course, once income from the trust is actually received by the beneficiary, creditors may seize it or the beneficiary may do with it as she pleases.

A typical spendthrift provision is as follows:

Payments and distributions to all the beneficiaries hereunder, except to minors and persons under disability, shall be made only to such beneficiaries in person or upon their personal receipt, and no interest of any beneficiary in the income or principal of the Trust Estate shall be assignable in anticipation of payment, either by the voluntary or involuntary act of such beneficiary or by operation of law, or be liable in any way for the debts of such beneficiary.

Totten Trusts A totten trust involves a joint bank account opened by the settlor of the trust. Typically, A deposits a sum of money in a savings account in a bank in the name of "A, in trust for B." A may make additional deposits in the account from time to time and may withdraw money from it whenever she pleases. The courts have held this to be a tentative trust which the depositor may revoke by withdrawing the fund or changing the form of the account. The transfer of ownership becomes complete only upon the depositor's death.

Implied Trusts

In some cases the courts, in the absence of any expressed trust intent to create a trust, will impose a trust upon property because the acts of the parties appear to call for such a construction. An implied trust owes its existence to the law. Customarily, implied trusts are divided into two classes, constructive trusts and resulting trusts.

Constructive Trusts A constructive trust covers those instances where a court will impose a trust upon property to rectify fraud or to prevent unjust enrichment. A constructive trust will be established where there has been abuse of a confidential relation or where actual fraud or duress is considered as an equitable ground for creating the trust. The mere existence of a confidential relationship prohibits the one trusted from seeking any personal benefit for himself during the course of the relationship. Justice Cardozo referred to a constructive trust as "the formula through which the conscience of equity finds expression. When property has been acquired in such circumstances that the holder of the legal title may not in good conscience retain the beneficial interest, equity converts him into a trustee." *Beatty v. Guggenheim Exploration Co.*, 225 N.Y. 380, 122 N.E. 378, (1919).

In general, a fiduciary or confidential relation exists where trust and confidence are reposed by one person in another, who, as a result gains an influence and superiority over the first. Specifically, a confidential relation exists where, by reason of kinship, business or association, disparity in age, physical or mental condition, or other reason, the grantee occupies an especially intimate position with regard to the grantor and the latter reposes a high degree of trust and confidence in the former. Where a fiduciary relation exists, the burden rests upon the grantee or beneficiary of an instrument executed during the existence of such relationship to prove, by clear and convincing proof, the fairness of the transaction, that it was equitable and just, that it did not proceed from undue influence, and that he exercised good faith and did not betray the confidence reposed in him, irrespective of whether he was instrumental in causing the conveyance to be made. It is not essential that the undue influence vitiating the transfer be deemed fraudulent. It is sufficient if the influence arises out of the fiduciary or confidential relation. *See Sharp v. Kosmalski.*

Business and personal affairs provide many examples of constructive trusts. A director of a corporation who takes advantage of a "corporate opportunity" or who makes an undisclosed profit in a deal with the corporation will be treated as a trustee for the corporation with respect to the property thus acquired by him, or to the extent of the profit realized by him. A trustee under an express trust who permits a lease held by the trust to expire and then acquires a new lease of the property in his individual capacity will be required to hold the new lease in trust for the beneficiary. If an agent who is given money by his principal to purchase property in the name of the principal instead uses the funds to acquire title in himself, courts will treat him as a trustee for the principal.

Resulting Trusts A resulting trust is distinguished from a constructive trust in that, while the latter is designed to rectify fraud, duress, or a breach of confidence, the former serves to carry out the true *intent* of the parties in those cases where the intent was inadequately expressed. The most common example of a resulting trust is where A pays the purchase price for property and title is taken in the name of B. The presumption here is that the parties intended B to hold the property for the benefit of A, and B will be treated as a trustee. The difficulty is that, in many cases, it may be equally reasonable to presume that A intended to make a gift to B.

A resulting trust does not depend on contract or agreement but is founded on a presumed intent which arises out of the acts of the parties. Since a resulting trust is created by implication and operation of law, it need not be evidenced in writing. However, if a reasonable explanation of the evidence may be made upon any theory other than the existence of a resulting trust, a trust will not be declared and enforced.

CREATION OF TRUSTS

Each trust has (1) a creator or "settlor," (2) a "corpus" or trust property, (3) a trustee, and (4) a beneficiary. A may convey property in trust to B for the benefit of C; or A may declare himself trustee for the benefit of C; or A may convey in trust to B for the benefit of himself, A.

No particular words are necessary to create a trust, provided that the intent of the settlor to establish a trust is unmistakable. Consideration is not essential to an enforceable trust. In this respect, a trust is more akin to a conveyance than a contract. Trusts employed in wills are known as **testamentary trusts** because they become effective after the death of the settlor. Frequently, individuals establish trusts during their lifetime, in which case they are referred to as *inter vivos* or **"living" trusts**.

The Settlor

Any person legally capable of making a contract can create a trust. However, if the settlor's conveyance would be voidable or void because of infancy, incompetency, or other reason, a declaration of trust is likewise voidable or void.

Subject Matter

One of the principal characteristics which sets a trust apart from other relationships, such as a debtor-creditor relationship, is the requirement of a trust corpus or *res* which must be property that is definite and specific. A trust cannot be effective immediately with respect to property not yet in existence or to be acquired at a later date. For example, S organizes a corporation and executes a trust instrument declaring that he holds all future dividends in trust for his children. When dividends are subsequently declared, S may keep them or set them aside as trust property. His prior declaration does not oblige him to hold the *future* unrealized profits in trust. In each succeeding year, a declaration and segregation of dividends received is necessary in order to impose the character of a trust upon them.

The requirement of a definite and certain subject matter is satisfied by the creation of a testamentary trust in A's will which provides that she leaves to B, as trustee, sufficient funds to pay $300 a month to C. The will takes effect upon the death of A.

The Trustee

Anyone legally capable of holding title to and dealing with property may be a trustee. The lack of a trustee will not destroy the trust. If the settlor neglects to appoint one, or if a named trustee does not qualify, or if a named trustee declines to serve, the court, upon request, will appoint an individual or institution to act as trustee.

A trustee can, of course, decline to serve, and before the property will vest in him it is necessary that he accept the trust. Acceptance is often inferred from the acts of the trustee indicative of an intent to exercise dominion over the trust estate. It is a common statutory requirement that a court appointed trustee must post a bond for the honest administration of his duties. A bond is not required of a trustee appointed by the settlor.

Duties of the Trustee The three primary duties of any trustee are to:

1. carry out the purposes of the trust,
2. act with prudence and care in the administration of the trust, and
3. exercise a high degree of loyalty toward the beneficiary.

No special skills are required of a trustee under ordinary circumstances. He is required to act with the same degree of care that a **prudent man** would exercise with respect to his personal affairs. What constitutes the care of a "prudent man" is, of course, not easy to classify in any particular case. One court has spoken as follows of this responsibility:

* * * trustees are bound in the management of all matters of the trust to act in good faith and employ such vigilance, sagacity, diligence, and prudence as in general prudent men of discretion and intelligence in like matters employ in their affairs. The law does not hold a trustee, acting in accord with such rule, responsible for errors of judgment. *Costello v. Costello*, 209 N.Y. 252, 103 N.E. 148 [1913].

See also Witmer v. Blair.

The duty of loyalty arises out of and illustrates the fiduciary character of the relationship between the trustee and the beneficiary. The trustee in all his dealings with the trust property, the beneficiary, and third parties must always act in the exclusive interest of the beneficiary. Lack of loyalty may arise from palpable self-dealing, or it may be entirely innocent; in either event the trustee can be charged with lack of loyalty. The sale of his own property to a trust or the purchase of trust property at a sale conducted by himself as trustee are common instances of a violation of this fiduciary duty. The loan of trust funds by a trustee to himself or the loan of such funds to a corporation of which he is a principal shareholder, director, or officer, would constitute a breach of this duty. The fact that the transaction is carried on through a "dummy" will not prevent a court from setting aside such a transaction. The fact that no harm may be done to the trust does not excuse the transaction. It is a prophylactic rule designed to discourage temptation regardless of the outcome of any particular transaction.

Powers of the Trustee The powers of a trustee are determined by (1) the rules of law in the jurisdiction in which the trust is established, and (2) the authority granted him by the settlor in the instrument creating the trust. State laws affecting the powers of trustees have their greatest impact upon the investments a trustee may make with trust funds. Most States prescribe a list of types of securities qualified for trust investment. In some jurisdictions this list is permissive; in others it is mandatory. If the list is permissive, the trustee may invest in types of securities not listed although he carries the burden of showing that he made a prudent choice. The trust instrument may give the trustee wide discretion as to investments, and in such an event the trustee is not bound to adhere to the list deemed advisable under the statute.

Allocation of Principal and Income Trusts often settle a life estate in the trust corpus upon one beneficiary and a remainder interest upon another beneficiary. For example, a man leaves his property upon death to trustees who are instructed to pay the income from the property to his widow during her life, and upon her death to distribute the property to his children. In these instances the trustee must distribute the principal to one party (the remainderman) and the income to another (the life tenant or income beneficiary). The trustee must also allocate receipts and charge expenses between the income beneficiary and the remainderman. If the trust agreement does not specify how the funds should be allocated, the trustee is provided guidance by statute, which in most States is the **Uniform Principal and Income Act.** A failure of the trustee to comply with the trust agreement or the statute will render him personally liable for any loss.

The general rule in allocating benefits and burdens between income beneficiaries and remaindermen is that *ordinary* or current receipts and expenses are chargeable to the income beneficiary while *extraordinary* receipts and expense are allocated to the remainderman. Figure 50-2 provides illustrations of these four types of allocations.

The Beneficiary

There are very few restrictions on who (or what) may be a beneficiary. Dogs, cats, horses, and a multitude of pets have at one time or another been held to be the proper objects of a settlor's bounty. Charitable uses are a common purpose of trusts, and if the settlor's object does not outrage public policy or morals, almost any purpose which happens to strike the fancy of a settlor will be upheld.

In the absence of restrictive provisions in the trust instrument such as a spendthrift clause, a beneficiary's interest may be reached by his creditors, or the beneficiary may sell or dispose of his interest. If he held more than a life estate in the trust, his interest upon his death, unless disposed of by his will, passes to his heirs or personal representatives.

TERMINATION OF A TRUST

Unless a power of revocation is reserved by the settlor, the general rule is that a trust, once validly created, is *irrevocable*. If so reserved, the trust may be terminated at the discretion of the settlor.

Normally, a trust has a termination date in the instrument, and the trust terminates at the time stated without complication. A period of years may be specified, or the settlor may provide that the trust shall continue during the life of a named individual. The death of the trustee or beneficiary does not terminate the trust if neither of their lives is the measure of the duration of the trust.

FIGURE 50-2   Allocation of Principal and Income

	Receipts	Expenses
Ordinary— **Income Beneficiary**	Rents Royalties Cash dividends (regular and extraordinary) Interest	Interest payments Insurance Ordinary taxes Ordinary repairs
Extraordinary— **Remainderman**	Stock dividends Stock splits Proceeds for sale or exchange of corpus Settlement of claims for injury to corpus	Extraordinary repairs Long-term improvements Principal amortization Costs incurred in the sale or purchase of corpus Depreciation

Occasionally, the purpose for which a trust has been established may be regarded as fulfilled before the specified termination date. In such a case, a court upon petition by the trustee or beneficiary may decree a termination of the trust. A court will usually decree a trust terminated if the beneficiary acquires legal title to the trust assets, but courts will not order the termination of a trust simply because all of the beneficiaries petition the court to do so. The court will be governed by the purposes set forth in the trust instrument by the settlor, not by the wishes of the beneficiaries.

DECEDENT'S ESTATES

The assets of a person who dies leaving a valid will are to be distributed according to the directions contained in the will. If she dies without leaving a will, her property will pass to her heirs and next of kin in the proportions provided in the applicable State statute. This is known as **intestate** (dying without a will) succession. If a person dies without a will and leaves no heirs or next of kin, her property *escheats* (reverts) to the State.

WILLS

There is one major characteristic of a will which sets it apart from other transactions such as deeds and contracts: a will is revocable at any time during life. There is no such thing as an irrevocable will. A document binding during life may be a contract (such as a promise to make a will) or a deed (conveying a vested remainder after a life estate in the grantor), but it is not a will. A will takes effect only upon and not until the death of the testator.

In August, 1969, the National Conference of Commissioners on Uniform State Laws and the American Bar Association approved the Uniform Probate Code (U.P.C.), an extraordinary attempt to encourage throughout the United States—in the face of wide-spread criticism of the present American probate institution—the adoption of a uniform, flexible, speedy, efficient, and, in most cases, less expensive system of settling a decedent's estate. The U.P.C. is based on the major premise that the probate court's appropriate role is to be available to assist in the settlement of an estate when assistance is requested or required rather than to impose its unsolicited supervision to enforce every detailed formality upon completely non-contentious settlements.

In the following discussion of decedents' estates, principles and procedures are summarized generally with a notation of the parallel principles and procedures under the U.P.C.

Mental Capacity

Testamentary Capacity and Power In order to make a valid will, the testator must have both the "power" and the "capacity" to do so. The *power* to make a will is granted by the State to persons who are of a class believed generally able to handle their affairs without regard to personal limitations. Thus, in most States, children under a certain age cannot make valid wills.

The *capacity* to make a will refers to the limits placed upon particular persons in the class generally granted the power to make wills because of personal mental deficiencies. Underlying the notion of capacity is the premise that, in order to be valid, a testator must *intend* a document to be his will. This requisite intent will be lacking if he is incompetent or suffers from delusions. Nevertheless, since capacity is a personal matter it is not easy to set down any test which will, in all cases, measure this qualification. A person adjudicated incompetent can, in a lucid period, make a valid will. An aged and enfeebled octogenarian may have the capacity to execute a will. If one rule appears clear, it is that it takes less in the way of mental qualities to meet the test of capacity to make a will than is required for the independent management of one's affairs during lifetime. A deed from X to Y may be set aside because of the incompetence of X, although X may validly leave the same property to Y by will. Proof that the testator held beliefs not accepted by society in general will not impinge upon his capacity.

Under the U.P.C. any person eighteen or more years of age who is of sound mind may make a will. Section 2–501.

Conduct Invalidating a Will The requisite testamentary intent must always be present in order to create a valid will. Any document purporting to be a will that reflects an intent other than the testator's is not a valid will. This is the basis for the rule that a will which transmits property as a result of *duress, undue influence* or *fraud* is no will at all.

The great difficulty in this area is what constitutes "undue influence" cannot be generally defined. Certainly, a wife can urge her husband to leave all his property to her and, out of love and affection, he will probably accede. This influence is not "undue." Nor is a general influence over the testator sufficient to make a case of improper pressure. The influence must be directed specifically to the act of making the will. Most frequently, the charge of undue influence is made when a testator leaves his property to a person who is not a blood relative, such as a friend who took care of the testator in his last illness or during his last years. If the evidence demonstrates that the beneficiary under the will was in close contact with the testator and that natural objects of his bounty are ignored in the will, there is a suggestion of undue influence. *See In Re Estate of Peterson.*

The charge of fraud is similar. For example, A dies leaving all his property to B upon the representation by B that he is A's long lost son. B in fact is not A's son. In such a case, the will may be set aside because the misrepresentation was made with the intent to deceive and that A rely upon it.

The law is generally not as ready to invalidate or partially revise a will because of *mistake* as it is to adjust a contract based on an error. Nonetheless, a mistake as to the identity of the instrument voids a will and a stenographic error or a mistake in drafting may be corrected by clear evidence of the testator's intent.

Formal Requirements of a Will

By statute in all jurisdictions a will, to be valid, must comply with certain formalities. These are necessary not only to indicate that the testator understood what she was doing but also to help prevent fraud.

Writing A basic requirement to a valid will is that it be in writing. U.P.C., Section 2–502. The writing may be informal so long as the basic formalities required by the statute are substantially met. Pencil, ink, and mimeograph are equally valid methods, and valid wills have been made on scratch paper and on an envelope.

It is also valid to incorporate into a will by reference another document which in itself is not a will for lack of proper execution. To incorporate a memorandum in a will by reference, the following four conditions must exist: (1) the memorandum must be in writing; (2) it must be in existence when the will is executed; (3) it must be adequately described in the will; and (4) it must be described in the will as being in existence. U.P.C., Section 2–510.

Signature A will must be signed by the testator. U.P.C., Section 2–502. The signature verifies that the will has been executed and is a fundamental requirement in almost all jurisdictions. The initials "A. H." or "father" at the end of a will in the handwriting of the testator are adequate if intended as an execution.

Most statutes require the signature to be at the end of the will, and, even in jurisdictions where this is not specified, careful draftsmanship will so provide to avoid the charge that the portions of a will coming after a signature were written subsequent to the execution and, therefore, without the necessary formality of a signature.

Attestation With the exception of a few isolated types of wills noted later that are valid in a limited number of jurisdictions, a written will must be attested by witnesses. The number and qualification of witnesses and the manner of attestation are generally set out by statute. Usually two or three witnesses are required. Section 2–502 of the U.P.C. requires that at least two persons, each of whom witnessed either the signing or the testator's acknowledgement of the will, act as witnesses to the will. Nevertheless, it is good practice to have a will attested by one more than the legal minimum number to increase the likelihood that at least the minimum will be available when the will is offered for probate. However, the signature of a witness who has predeceased the testator may be proved by a competent witness. Although a witness generally need not be a resident of or domiciled in the jurisdiction of the testator, it is expedient to have witnesses who may be easily available. Age is no barrier to a witness, provided he is generally competent, although for obvious reasons an elderly person may be a risky witness from an actuarial point of view.

The function of witnesses is to acknowledge that the testator did execute the will and that she had the requisite intent and capacity. It is important that the testator sign first in the presence of all the witnesses, and it is usually essential that each witness sign in her presence and in the presence of one another.

The most common restriction is that a witness must not have any interest under the will. This requirement takes at least two forms under statutes. One type of statute disqualifies a witness who is also a beneficiary under the will. The other type voids the bequest or devise to the interested witness, thus making

him a disinterested and qualified witness. What constitutes an "interest" sufficient to disqualify a witness is not always easily defined. The spouse of a beneficiary under a will has been held to be "interested" and thus not qualified. Generally, a person is not disqualified simply because he is named as executor in the will. The attorney who drafts the will is generally a qualified witness. A member of a church named as a beneficiary or a shareholder of a corporate executor or trustee under a will is not so "interested" as to be disqualified. In all cases, however, caution should dictate that the witnesses have no connection with persons or institutions entitled to share under a will.

Under the U.P.C. no will or any provision thereof is invalid because the will was attested by an interested witness. Section 2–505.

Revocation of a Will

By definition, a will is revocable by the testator. Under certain circumstances a will may be revoked by operation of law. This does not mean that certain formalities are not necessary to effect a revocation. In most jurisdictions the methods by which a will is revoked are specified by statute.

Destruction or Alteration Tearing, burning or otherwise destroying a will is a strong sign that the testator intended to revoke it and, in the absence of a showing that the destruction was inadvertent, is an effective way of revoking a will. U.P.C., Section 2–507. *See also Barksdale v. Pendergrass.* In some States, partial revocation of a will may be accomplished by erasure or obliteration of a part of the will. In no case, however, will a substituted or additional bequest by interlineation be effective without reexecution and reattestation.

Subsequent Will The execution of a second will does not in itself constitute a revocation of an earlier will. To the extent that the second will is inconsistent with the former will, the first will is revoked. U.P.C., Section 2–507. The most certain manner of revocation is the execution of a later will which contains a declaration that all former wills are revoked. In some but not all jurisdictions, a will may be revoked by a written declaration to this effect in a subsequent document, such as a letter, even though the document does not meet the formal requirements of a will.

Operation of Law A *marriage* generally revokes a will executed prior to the marriage. *Divorce*, on the other hand, under the general rule, does *not* revoke a provision in the will of one of the parties for the benefit of the other party.

The *birth* of a child after execution of a will may revoke a will at least as far as that child is concerned if it appears that the testator omitted to make a provision for the child. In some jurisdictions the subsequent birth of a child will not revoke the will, but the child is entitled to the same share as though the testator died without a will unless it appears from the will that the omission was intentional. U.P.C., Section 2–302.

Section 2–508 of the U.P.C. takes a different position and provides that a divorce or annulment which occurs after the execution of a will revokes any disposition of property made by the will to the former spouse. No change of circumstances other than divorce or annulment revokes a will. Thus, a subsequent marriage or marriage plus the birth of issue does not revoke a will. However, a spouse who marries the testator after the execution of the will and a child born subsequent to the will are entitled to the same share as though the testator died without a will. U.P.C., Sections 2–301 and 2–302.

Renunciation by the Surviving Spouse Statutes generally provide for a right of renunciation of the will by a surviving spouse and set forth the method of accomplishing it. The purpose of such statutory provisions is to enable the spouse to elect which method of taking—under the will or under intestate succession—would be more advantageous to him or her. Where a spouse dies owning real and personal property, the surviving spouse has an interest in the decedent's estate which cannot be divested by will without the surviving spouse's consent. The right to renounce a will may be exercised only by persons designated by the statute, and the right conferred on the surviving spouse is personal. Upon renunciation of the will, the law of intestate succession determines the share of the estate taken by the surviving spouse.

Abatement and Ademption of a Bequest In his will, A leaves $5,000 to B, $5,000 to C, and "my faithful collie, Rex" to D. At the time of A's death, after payment of his debts, there is only $5,000 in his estate and a Siamese cat by the name of Queenie, faithful Rex having been disposed of after biting his master. B and C will each receive $2,500, and D will receive nothing, Queenie going to whomever takes the residue of A's estate. The gifts to B and C are said to have abated, while the gift to D, not being in existence at the time of A's death, has "adeemed."

Abatement generally results from a reduction in the value of the estate of the testator after the execution of his will. It can have serious implications. The first items which abate in a will are all the *residue* or remainder after provisions for *specific devises* and legacies. Specific gifts must be satisfied first. Thus, if John, a widower, after making specific gifts, leaves "all the rest, residue, and remainder of my estate to my daughter, Mary," Mary may receive a great deal less than her deceased father intended. For example, suppose at the time John executes his will he estimates his worth at $150,000. He leaves $20,000 to his church and $20,000 to the Salvation Army and assumes that Mary will receive approximately $110,000. John dies five years later without changing his will but having suffered substantial business and market reverses. His executor reports that there is only $50,000 in the estate. Mary will receive $10,000.

Ademption may not be as serious as abatement, but the consequences may be regretable. It occurs when a testator neglects to change his will after changed circumstances have rendered impossible the performance of a provision in the will. For example, X buys a farm "Blackacre" and wants it to go on his death to a favorite nephew who is studying agriculture at college. After so providing in his will, he sells "Blackacre" and, with the purchase price, buys "Greenacre." The general rule is that the nephew will not be entitled to Greenacre. *See In Re Estate of Wolfe.*

Special Types of Wills

There are a number of special types of wills, these include nuncupative wills, holographic wills, soldiers' and sailors' wills, conditional wills, and joint and reciprocal wills.

Nuncupative Wills A nuncupative will is an oral declaration made before witnesses without any writing. In the few jurisdictions where authorized, it can usually only be made when the testator is in his last illness. Under most statutes permitting nuncupative wills only limited amounts of personal property, generally under $1,000, may be passed by such a will. Under the U.P.C., all wills must be in writing. Section 2–502.

Holographic Wills In some jurisdictions a signed will entirely in the handwriting of the testator is a valid testamentary document notwithstanding the fact that the will is *not* witnessed. U.P.C., Section 2–503. Such an instrument is referred to as a holographic will. A holographic will must comply strictly with the statutory requirements for such wills.

Soldiers' and Sailors' Wills In the case of soldiers on active service and sailors while at sea, most statutes relax the formal requirements and permit a valid testamentary disposition regardless of the informality of the

document. In most jurisdictions, however, such a will cannot pass title to real estate.

Conditional Wills A contingent or conditional will is one which takes effect as a will only on the happening of a specified contingency which is a *condition precedent* to the operation of the will.

Joint and Mutual or Reciprocal Wills A joint will is one where the same instrument is made the will of two or more persons and is signed by them jointly. Mutual or reciprocal wills are separate instruments of two or more persons, the terms being reciprocal and by which each testator makes testamentary disposition in favor of the other.

Codicil to a Will

A codicil is an addition to or revision of a will, generally by a separate instrument, in which the will is expressly referred to and, in effect, incorporated into the codicil by reference. Codicils must be executed with all the formal requirements of a will. The most frequent problem raised by codicils is the extent to which their terms, if not absolutely clear, revoke or alter provisions in the will. For the purpose of determining the testator's intent, the codicil and the will are regarded as a single instrument.

INTESTATE SUCCESSION

When a person dies, the title to her property must pass to someone. If the decedent leaves a valid will, property will pass as she directs, subject only to certain limitations imposed by the State, such as the widow's right to dower discussed in Chapter 48. If, however, no valid will has been executed, the decedent is said to have died "intestate," and the State prescribes who shall be entitled to the property.

The rules set forth in statutes for determining, in case of intestacy, to whom the decedent's property shall be distributed not only assure an orderly transfer of title to property but also purport to carry out what would probably be the wishes of the decedent.

Property which Descends

All vested property interest will descend to the heirs. For instance, a vested remainder following a life estate will pass to the heirs of the remainderman upon his death and may be possessed by his heirs upon the death of the life tenant.

Course of Descent

The rules of descent vary widely from State to State, but, as a general rule and excepting the specific statutory or dower rights of the widow, the intestate property passes in equal shares to each child of the decedent living at the time of his death, with the share of any predeceased child to be divided equally among the children of such predeceased child. For example, if A dies intestate leaving a widow and children, the widow generally will receive one-third of his real estate and personal property, and the remainder passes to his children in the manner stated above. If the wife does not survive A, his entire estate

passes to the children. If A dies leaving two surviving children, B and C, and grandchildren, D_1 and D_2, the children of a predeceased child D, the estate will go one-third to B, one-third to C, and one-sixth each to D_1 and D_2, the grandchildren dividing equally their parent's one-third share. This result is legally described by the statement that *lineal* descendants of predeceased children take **per stirpes**, or by representation of their parent. If A had executed a will, he may have provided that all his lineal descendants, regardless of generation, would share equally. In such case A's estate would be divided into four equal parts, and his descendants would be said to take **per capita**. See Figure 50-3.

If no children but only the widow and other relatives survive the decedent, a larger share is generally allotted the widow. She may receive all the personal property and one-half the real estate or, in some States, the entire estate.

At common law, property could not lineally ascend; parents of an intestate decedent did not share in his estate. Today, in many States, if there are no lineal descendants, the statute provides that parents are the next to share.

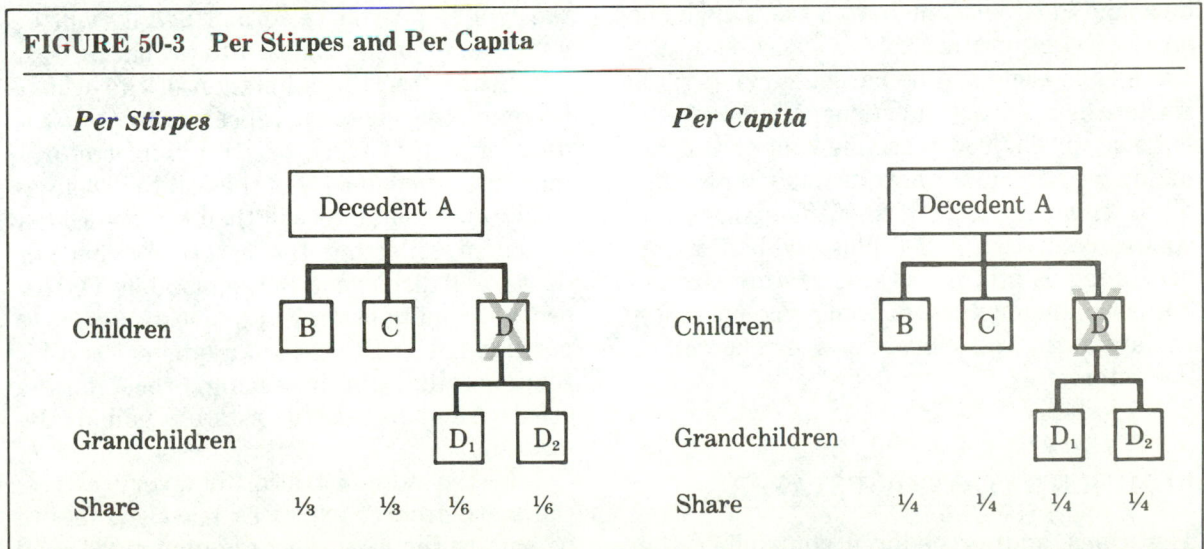

FIGURE 50-3   Per Stirpes and Per Capita

Most statutes make some provision for brothers and sisters in the event no spouse, parents, or children survive the decedent. Brothers and sisters, together with nieces, nephews, aunts, and uncles are termed *collateral* heirs. Beyond these limits most statutes provide that, if there are no survivors of the named classes, the property shall be distributed equally among the next of kin in equal degree.

The common law did not consider a *stepchild* as an heir or next of kin, that is, as one to whom property would descend by operation of law, and this rule prevails today. Legally *adopted* children are, however, recognized as lawful heirs of their adopting parents.

These generalities should be accepted as such; few fields of the law of property are so strictly a matter of statute, and the rights of heirs cannot be reasonably predicted without a knowledge of the exact terms of the applicable statute.

Under the U.P.C., the surviving spouse is entitled to (1) a homestead allowance of $5,000, (2) exempt household and personal effects of a value not to exceed $3,500, and (3) a family allowance to provide for one year after death not to exceed $6,000. Sections 2–401, 2–402, 2–403 and 2–404.

Furthermore under the U.P.C., if the decedent dies without a will, the surviving spouse (1) is entitled to the entire estate if there is no issue and no parent surviving; (2) if there is a parent surviving, the spouse is entitled to $50,000 plus one-half of the remaining estate; (3) if there are surviving issue all of whom are issue also of the spouse, the spouse receives $50,000 plus one-half of the remaining estate; and (4) if there are surviving issue one or more of whom are not issue of the spouse, the spouse receives one-half of the estate.

ADMINISTRATION OF ESTATES

The rules and procedures controlling the management of the estate of a deceased are statutory and, therefore, vary in some respect from State to State. In all jurisdictions the estate is managed and finally disbursed under the supervision of a court. The procedure of managing the estates of decedents is referred to as **probate**, and not infrequently the court which supervises the procedure is designated as the Probate Court.

The first legal step after death is usually to determine whether or not the deceased left a will. If a will exists, it is probable that in it the testator named her executor.

If there is no will or if there is a will which fails to name an executor, the court will, upon petition, appoint an administrator. The closest adult relative who is a resident of the State is entitled to such appointment.

Once approved or appointed by the court, it is the **executor** or **administrator** who holds title to all the personal property of the deceased and who accounts to the creditors and the beneficiaries. The estate is his responsibility.

If there is a will, it must be proved before the court by the witnesses. They will testify to the signing of the will by all signatories and as to the mental condition of the testator at the time of the execution of the will. If the witnesses are dead, proof of their handwriting is necessary. If the court is satisfied that the will is proved, a formal decree will be entered admitting the will to probate.

Soon after the admission of the will to probate, the personal representative of the decedent—the executor or administrator—must file an inventory of the estate. The personal representative will then commence her duties of collecting the assets, paying the debts, and disbursing the remainder. The executor or administrator occupies a *fiduciary* position not unlike that of a trustee, and his responsibility for investing proceeds and otherwise managing the estate is equally demanding.

In the administration of every estate, there are probate expenses as well as fees to be paid to the executor or administrator and the attorney who handles the estate. In addition, taxes are imposed at death by both the Federal and State governments. The Federal government imposes an **estate tax** which is on the transfer of property at death. Most State governments impose an **inherit-** **ance tax** which is on the privilege of an heir or beneficiary to receive the property. These taxes are separate and apart from the basic income tax which the estate must pay on income received during estate administration.

CASES

Constructive Trusts

SHARP v. KOSMALSKI

Court of Appeals of New York, 1976.
40 N.Y.2d 119, 386 N.Y.S.2d 72, 351 N.E.2d 721.

GABRIELLI, J.

Plaintiff commenced this action to impose a constructive trust upon property transferred to defendant on the ground that the retention of the property and the subsequent ejection of the plaintiff therefrom was in violation of a relationship of trust and confidence and constituted unjust enrichment. The Trial Judge dismissed plaintiff's complaint and his decision was affirmed without opinion by the Appellate Division.

Upon the death of his wife of 32 years, plaintiff, a 56-year-old dairy farmer whose education did not go beyond the eighth grade, developed a very close relationship with defendant, a school teacher and a woman 16 years his junior. Defendant assisted plaintiff in disposing of his wife's belongings, performed certain domestic tasks for him such as ironing his shirts and was a frequent companion of the plaintiff. Plaintiff came to depend upon defendant's companionship and, eventually, declared his love for her, proposing marriage to her. Notwithstanding her refusal of his proposal of marriage, defendant continued her association with plaintiff and permitted him to shower her with many gifts, fanning his hope that he could induce defendant to alter her decision concerning his marriage proposal. Defendant was given access to plaintiff's bank account, from which it is not denied that she withdrew substantial amounts of money. Eventually, plaintiff made a will naming defendant as his sole beneficiary and executed a deed naming her a joint owner of his farm. The record reveals that numerous alterations in the way of modernization were made to plaintiff's farmhouse in alleged furtherance of "domestic plans" made by plaintiff and defendant.

In September 1971 while the renovations were still in progress, plaintiff transferred his remaining joint interest to defendant. At the time of the conveyance, a farm liability policy was issued to plaintiff naming defendant and her daughter as additional insureds. Furthermore, the insurance agent was requested by plaintiff, in the presence of defendant, to change the policy to read "J. Rodney Sharp, life tenant. Jean C. Kosmalski, owner." In February 1973 the liaison between the parties was abruptly severed as defendant ordered plaintiff to move out of his home and vacate the farm. Defendant took possession of the home, the farm, and all the equipment thereon, leaving plaintiff with assets of $300.

Generally, a constructive trust may be imposed "[w]hen property has been acquired in such circumstances that the holder of the legal title may not in good conscience retain the beneficial interest" [citation]. In the development of the doctrine of constructive trust as a remedy available to courts of equity, the following four requirements were posited: (1) a confidential or fiduciary relation, (2) a promise, (3) a transfer in reliance thereon and (4) unjust enrichment. [Citations.]

Most frequently, it is the existence of a confidential relationship which triggers the equitable considerations leading to the imposition of a constructive trust. [Citation.] Although no marital or other family relationship is present in this case, such is not essential for the existence of a confidential relation. [Citations.] The record in this case clearly indicates that a relationship of trust and confidence did exist between the parties and, hence, the defendant must be charged with an obligation not to abuse the trust and confidence placed in her by the plaintiff. The disparity in education between the plaintiff and defendant highlights the degree of dependence of the plaintiff upon the trust and honor of the defendant.

Unquestionably, there is a transfer of property here, but the Trial Judge found that the transfer was made "without a promise or understanding of any kind." Even without an express promise, however, courts of equity have imposed a constructive trust upon property transferred in reliance upon a confidential relationship. In such a situation, a promise may be implied or inferred from the very transaction itself. As Judge Cardozo so eloquently observed: "Though a promise in words was lacking, the whole transaction, it might be found, was 'instinct with an obligation' imperfectly expressed." [Citations.] In deciding that a formal writing or express promise was not essential to the application of the doctrine of constructive trust, Judge Cardozo further observed in language that is most fitting in the instant case:

"Here was a man transferring to his sister the only property he had in the world. . . . He was doing this, as she admits, in reliance upon her honor. Even if we were to accept her statement that there was no distinct promise to hold for his benefit, the exaction of such a promise, in view of the relation, might well have seemed to be superfluous" [citation].

* * *

Indeed in the case before us, it is inconceivable that plaintiff would convey all of his interest in property which was not only his abode but the very means of his livelihood without at least tacit consent upon the part of the defendant that she would permit him to continue to live on and operate the farm. I would therefore reject the Trial Judge's conclusion, erroneously termed a finding of fact, that no agreement or limitation may, as a matter of law, be implied from the circumstances surrounding the transfer of plaintiff's farm.

The statutory purpose of the constructive trust remedy is to prevent unjust enrichment and it is to this requirement that I now turn. The Trial Judge in his findings of fact, concluded that the transfer did not constitute unjust enrichment. In this instance also, a legal conclusion was mistakenly labeled a finding of fact. A person may be deemed to be unjustly enriched if he (or she) has received a benefit, the retention of which would be unjust (Restatement, Restitution, § 1, Comment a). A conclusion that one has been unjustly enriched is essentially a legal inference drawn from the circumstances surrounding the transfer of property and the relationship of the parties. It is a conclusion reached through the application of principles of equity. Having determined that the relationship between plaintiff and defendant in this case is of such a nature as to invoke consideration of the equitable remedy of constructive trust, it remains to be determined whether defendant's conduct following the transfer of plaintiff's farm was in violation of that relationship and, consequently, resulted in the unjust enrichment of the defendant. This must be determined from the circumstances of the transfer since there is no express promise concerning plaintiff's continued use of the land. Therefore, the case should be remitted to the Appellate Division for a review of the facts. In so doing I would emphasize that the conveyance herein should be interpreted "not literally or irrespective of its setting, but sensibly and broadly with all its human implications." [Citation.] This case seems to present the classic example of a situation where equity should intervene to scrutinize a transaction pregnant with opportunity for abuse and unfairness. It was for just this type of case that there evolved equitable principles and remedies to prevent injustices. Equity still lives. To suffer the hands of equity to be bound by misnamed "findings of fact" which are actually conclusions of law and legal inferences drawn from the facts is to ignore and render impotent the rich and vital impact of equity on the common law and, perforce, permit injustice. Universality of law requires equity.

Accordingly, the order of the Appellate Division should be reversed and the case remitted to that court for a review of the facts, or, if it be so advised, in its discretion, to order a new trial in the interests of justice.

Duties of the Trustee

WITMER v. BLAIR

Missouri Court of Appeals, Western District, 1979.
588 S.W.2d 222.

WELBORN, J.

Plaintiffs, beneficiaries of a testamentary trust, filed a two-count action against defendant trustee, seeking an accounting, removal of the trustee, and actual and punitive damages for breach of fiduciary duties. After trial to the court, the court ordered an accounting and removal of the defendant as trustee and entered judgment against defendant for $309 for unaccounted-for funds but found against plaintiffs on their claim for damages for breach of fiduciary duties. Plaintiffs appeal from this portion of the decree.

By his Last Will and Testament, Henry F. Nussbaum made a residual bequest and devise of his estate to his niece, Jane Ann Blair, as trustee, "in Trust however, for the education of my grandchildren (children of my daughter, Dorothy Janice Witmer) living at the time of my decease, or born within a period of nine months thereafter." In the event that none of his grandchildren survived to inherit the estate, the residue would revert to plaintiff Dorothy Janice Witmer, his daughter and first cousin of defendant trustee.

Nussbaum died in 1960. The trust estate came into the hands of the trustee in 1961. It consisted of $1,905 in checking and savings accounts, $5,700 in certificates of deposit, and a house valued at $6,000.00. The house was sold in 1962, netting $4,467 to the trust estate. That amount was deposited in a trust checking account. In 1963, $2,000 in certificates of deposit were acquired by the trust and $500 was so invested in 1964. As of December 31, 1970, the trust fund assets consisted of $5,847 in checking account, $506 in savings account, and $8,200 in certificates of deposit. In 1971 and 1972, the checking account balance was reduced by transfers to the savings account and on December 31, 1975, the trust assets consisted of $2,741 checking account, $5,474 savings account, and $8,200 certificates of deposit.

Plaintiff-appellant Marguerite Janice Witmer was the only grandchild of the testator who became a beneficiary of the trust. She was born September 3, 1953. At the time of the trial, she was 23 years of age. She had not attended a college or university. However, various sums of money had been expended from the trust for her benefit, including a typewriter, clothes, glasses, modeling school tuition and expenses, and a tonsillectomy. These expenditures totalled some $1,225.00. The trust also provided $350 for dentures for the mother, Dorothy Witmer.

The trust was handled by appellant rather informally. She kept no books for the trust. The expenditures above mentioned were in most cases advanced by her from her personal account and she reimbursed herself from the trust income. In 1965, the bank erroneously credited the trust account with $560 which should have gone to the trustee's personal account. The mistake was not corrected and that amount remained in the trust account. The trustee received no compensation for her services. Asked at the trial whether she had ever been a trustee before, she responded negatively, adding: "And never again." She explained the large checking account balances in the trust account by the fact that college for Janice "was talked about all the way through high school. * * * [I]n my opinion it was the sensible way to keep the money where I could get it to her without any problems at all in case she needed it quickly."

An accountant testified for plaintiffs that if the sum of $800 had been kept in the checking and savings accounts (the $800 was based upon the maximum disbursement in any year) and the balance of the trust placed in one-year certificates of deposit, $9,138 more interest would have been earned as of September 30, 1976, from the trust estate than had been received under respondent's handling of the trust.

* * *

In this court, appellants contend that the respondent as trustee was bound to comply with the directions of the trust that she "invest the principal and reinvest the same" and that her failure to invest the trust corpus constituted a breach of her fiduciary duty for which she is liable. The respondent answers that inasmuch as the will failed to specify when and what investments were to be made, such matters were left to the discretion of the trustee and that she exercised such discretion honestly, with ordinary prudence and within the limits of the trust and is not liable for damages.

A concise summary of the law applicable in this situation appears in [citation]:

"It is a general power and duty of a trustee, implied if not expressed, at least in the case of an ordinary trust, to keep trust funds properly invested. Having uninvested funds in his hands, it is his duty to make investments of them, where at least they are not soon to be applied to the purposes and objects or turned over to the beneficiaries of the trust. Generally, he cannot permit trust funds to lie dormant or on deposit for a prolonged period, but he may keep on hand a fund sufficient to meet expenses, including contingent expenses, and he need not invest a sum too small to be prudently invested. A trustee ordinarily may not say in excuse of a failure to invest that he kept the funds on hand to pay the beneficiaries on demand."

"The trustee is under a duty to the beneficiary to use reasonable care and skill to make the trust property productive." Restatement (Second) of Trusts § 181 (1959). Comment c to this section states:

"*Money.* In the case of money, it is normally the duty of the trustee to invest it so that it will produce an income. The trustee is liable if he fails to invest trust funds which it is his duty to invest for a period which is under all the circumstances unreasonably long. If, however, the delay is not unreasonable, he is not liable."

"A breach of trust is a violation by the trustee of any duty which as trustee he owes to the beneficiary." Restatement (Second) of Trusts § 201 (1959). Comment b to this section states:

"*Mistake of law as to existence of duties and powers.* A trustee commits a breach of trust not only where he violates a duty in bad faith, or intentionally although in good faith, or negligently, but also where he violates a duty because of a mistake as to the extent of his duties and powers. This is true not only where his mistake is in regard to a rule of law, whether a statutory or common-law rule, but also where he interprets the trust instrument as authorizing him to do acts which the court determines he is not authorized by the instrument to do. In such case, he is not protected from liability merely because he acts in good faith, nor is he protected merely because he relies upon the advice of counsel. [Citation.] If he is in doubt as to the interpretation of the instrument, he can protect himself by obtaining instructions from the court. The extent of his duties and powers is determined by the trust instrument and the rules of law which are applicable, and not by his own interpretation of the instrument or his own belief as to the rules of law."

Under the above rules, there has been a breach of trust by the trustee in this case and her good faith is not a defense to appellants' claim.

* * *

The accountant who testified for appellants calculated that between the opening of the Trust and 1971, when college for Marguerite would have been a realistic possibility, had the trust funds, in excess of $100 checking account and approximately $800–1,000 savings account, been invested in one-year certificates of deposit, the trust would have earned additional interest of $2,840.00. In view of the trustee's transfer of a substantial portion of the checking account balance to savings in 1971 and 1972 and in view of the relatively small difference between the return from savings and what might have been earned from certificates of deposit (½% to 1½%), no damages should be assessed against the trustee for the handling of the estate during that period. However, the trustee should be held liable for the $2,840 which, according to the measure of damages, invoked by appellants, might have been earned by investment of the trust between 1962 and 1971.

Conduct Invalidating a Will

IN RE ESTATE OF PETERSON

Supreme Court of Minnesota, 1969.
283 Minn. 446, 168 N.W.2d 502.

ROGOSHESKE, J.

Appeal from a judgment affirming an order of the probate court of Hennepin County denying admission of a purported will of Grace V. Peterson, decedent, to probate.

The sole question presented for review is whether the evidence sustains the determination by the district court that a purported will of decedent, dated October 21, 1964, was procured by undue influence exerted upon the testatrix by appellant, the named executor and the attorney who drafted it and supervised its execution. We hold that it does.

In April 1961, decedent, Grace V. Peterson, a spinster then aged 74, asked Chester G. W. Gustafson, a Minneapolis attorney, to draw a will for her. Gustafson, who had probated her sister's estate, drew this first as well as six subsequent wills and codicil free of charge because, as he testified, she had no money to pay for his services. The benefi-

ciaries of this first will were various cousins and close friends. In this will, as well as in all subsequent wills except the last, decedent bequeathed to each beneficiary specifically described household goods, wearing apparel, or personal effects, and named Howard Rhedin, a cousin, as the residual beneficiary. On December 11, 1962, and on January 14, 1963, Gustafson drew new wills for decedent, each containing several changes in her bequests and in the beneficiaries. On May 19, 1964, Gustafson drew a fourth will for decedent. In this will, decedent for the first time included Gustafson's children, Chester G. W. Jr., then aged 20 or 21, and Jo H., then aged 18, as beneficiaries. She left each a diamond ring and also left a watch and a coffee table to Jo. Gustafson testified that the only contacts decedent ever had with his children were several chance encounters between 5 and 10 years before in the offices where she worked, when the children delivered some produce to one of decedent's employers. There is no claim that she ever saw the children after that time. They neither attended her funeral nor appeared or testified in probate or district court.

Subsequent to this fourth will, Gustafson drew two more wills and a codicil, each will increasing the specific bequests of household articles to his children. On October 21, 1964, he drew a seventh will in which decedent left all of her property, which at her death included a homestead valued at $10,000 (encumbered by a $1,000 mortgage) and personal property valued, as the court found, at $1,459, to the Gustafson children. This will was drawn and executed under Gustafson's supervision within a one-hour period. It was witnessed by two attorneys from a nearby office. Despite the radical changes in the will, its contents were never discussed with the witnesses, and they did not read its dispositive provisions. Gustafson immediately took possession of the will. Except for the testimony of Gustafson, no evidence was submitted that decedent knew she had named the Gustafson children as sole beneficiaries.

As the trial court found, during the last 5 years of her life decedent often visited Gustafson in his office, where he joshed, kidded, and flattered her. He sent her flowers, brought her vegetables, visited in her home but never entertained her in his, was given a key to her house, and arranged a $1,000 loan for her (secured by a mortgage on her home) from a trust of which he was the trustee. Gustafson had himself appointed decedent's guardian in November 1965 following her incapacitating stroke without consulting with the relatives who arranged for her hospitalization.

Grace V. Peterson died on February 1, 1966, without ever changing the will of October 21, 1964. Gustafson, who, as in prior wills, was named as executor, sought to have it admitted to probate. The probate court refused on the ground that the will was "executed by decedent as a result of undue influence exercised upon her by * * * Chester G. W. Gustafson." Gustafson, as proponent of the will, appealed this decision to the district court. After a trial de novo, the district court found that the will was procured as the result of Gustafson's "exercising undue influence over and upon Testatrix" and affirmed the order of the probate court. Gustafson appeals.

* * *

Undue influence has been defined as influence—

"* * * such as to substitute the will of the person exercising it for that of the testator, thereby making the written result express the purpose and intent of such person, not those of the testator. It must be equivalent to moral coercion or constraint overpowering the will of the testator. *It must operate at the very time the will is made and dominate and control its making.*" [Citation.]

By its very nature, undue influence can usually be shown only by circumstantial evidence. [Citations.] Among the factors which should be considered in determining whether the circumstantial evidence clearly and convincingly supports a finding of undue influence are whether the evidence shows (1) an opportunity to exercise undue influence; (2) a confidential relationship between the person making the will and the party allegedly ex-

ercising the undue influence; (3) active participation in the preparation of the will by the party alleged to have exercised it; (4) disinheritance of those whom the decedent would have been expected to remember in his will; (5) a singularity of the provisions of the will; and (6) the exercise of either influence or persuasion to induce decedent to make the will in question. [Citation.]

The evidence clearly shows that each one of these factors was in some degree present in this case. Gustafson had the opportunity to exert undue influence; and developed a confidential relationship with decedent; and had himself controlled the drafting of each of the series of wills which progressively disinherited all of her relatives and friends, with whom she had maintained close relationships, until finally her entire estate was left to his children, whom she had met only briefly a few times at least 4 years before she executed her final will. While the presence of any one of these facts standing alone might not have been enough to establish undue influence, taken together they clearly permit an inference of undue influence, furnish adequate evidentiary support for the court's determination, and most certainly answer the argument that the evidence is conclusive against the determination.

Once undue influence, however exerted, is established, a proffered will may not be admitted to probate even though the named beneficiaries are innocent of any wrongdoing, for such an instrument cannot thereafter be regarded as a free and voluntary declaration of the testator's intentions. [Citation]

* * *

While it was the children of decedent's attorney who were the sole beneficiaries of the will rather than the attorney himself, under the circumstances of this case surely the same must apply. * * * Appellant could easily have avoided the effects of this rule by referring decedent to another attorney for a discussion of her wishes, independent advice, and preparation of her will. Such adherence to what we view as a proper standard of professional conduct would have provided disinterested testimony that decedent did in fact intend his children to inherit her estate and quite probably would have avoided placing of the will in jeopardy. * * *

Affirmed.

Revocation of a Will

BARKSDALE v. PENDERGRASS

Supreme Court of Alabama, 1975.
294 Ala. 526, 319 So.2d 267.

MERRILL, J.

Mrs. Mamie C. Henry, a widow, died on October 18, 1972. She had no children, but was survived by a number of nieces and nephews.

No duly executed will was found and Joe Barksdale, a nephew of Mrs. Henry, was appointed administrator of her estate.

Later, Rita Jan Pendergrass, formerly Rita Jan Gray, filed a petiton in the Probate Court of DeKalb County to probate an alleged lost or destroyed will of Mamie C. Henry. A copy of the will was made an exhibit to the petition. According to its terms, Mrs. Henry left all of her property to Rita Jan Gray and appointed her as executrix.

Joe Barksdale and Olen Barksdale filed a contest and the case was transferred to the circuit court, where it was tried before a jury. The grounds of the contest were that the purported will was never duly executed, or, that if executed, was destroyed by Mrs. Henry prior to her death.

The jury found in favor of the proponent, Rita Jan Gray Pendergrass. Judgment was entered ordering the will admitted to probate. * * *

* * *

In a proceeding to probate an alleged lost or destroyed will, the burden is on the proponent to establish, to the reasonable satisfaction of the judge or jury trying the facts:

(1) The existence of a will—an instrument in writing, signed by the testator or some person in his presence, and by his direction, and attested by at least two witnesses, who must subscribe their names thereto in the presence of the testator. [Citations.]

* * *

(3) The nonrevocation of the instrument by the testator. [Citations.]

(4) The contents of the will in substance and effect. [Citations.]

The first question then is whether there was a validly executed will. It is not necessary that the attestation be at the personal request of the testator. It is sufficient if done in testator's presence with his knowledge and consent expressed or implied. [Citations.]

The testator does not have to tell the subscribing witnesses that the instrument is his will, or to inform them of its contents. [Citations.]

It is not necessary for the witnesses to actually see the testator sign his name. [Citations.] The testator may acknowledge to the subscribing witnesses that it is his signature on the instrument by his express words or by implication from his conduct and from the surrounding circumstances. [Citations.]

* * *

The evidence produced at trial showed that Charles M. Scott, a Ft. Payne attorney, prepared a will for Mrs. Henry in November of 1963. She did not execute the will in Scott's office because she wanted to "get her own witnesses" in Collinsville where she lived. Scott subsequently made several minor changes in the will and mailed her a final version in January of 1964. Rita Jan Gray [Pendergrass] was named a beneficiary in every version of the will.

The evidence also showed that sometime around 1964, Bill Cook, Jack Farmer and Cecil Sharp met at Sharp's funeral home and witnessed Mrs. Henry's signature on a document. The testimony adduced at trial indicated that there was some doubt as to whether each of the witnesses knew that the document was a will. Jack Farmer was deceased at the time of the trial. Witness Bill Cook thought that Mrs. Henry mentioned that the document was a will at some time, but Cecil Sharp could only say that Mrs. Henry wanted him to witness a signature. Nevertheless it is apparent that the requirements of [citation], were met since both Cook and Sharp witnessed a signature which Mrs. Henry acknowledged as her own.

The second thing which the proponent must prove is the loss or destruction of the instrument. Billy McDowell, who rented an apartment from Mrs. Henry between 1967 and 1969, testified that Mrs. Henry showed him a will; that she said Charles M. Scott prepared it, that Cecil Sharp's name was on the will as a witness, and that Rita Jan Gray [Pendergrass] was the sole beneficiary. He also said that Mrs. Henry kept the will in a purse under a mattress in a spare room. Floyd Gray, the father of the beneficiary, testified that he saw one of Mrs. Henry's nephews at her house shortly after her death. Willard Reaves, an employee of the funeral home, testified that several of Mrs. Henry's relatives visited her house that day after she died. There was also an abundance of testimony that the will might have been lost or destroyed by accident. Finally, attorney Scott testified that several weeks after Mrs. Henry's death he searched the house himself. Proponent Rita Jan Gray Pendergrass subsequently filed an application to compel production of the will. Appellant Barksdale responded "That the said purported will, if executed, has been destroyed prior to the death of the Testatrix, and was not found in her possession nor among has [sic] effects at the time of her death, and is presumed, if ever executed, to have been destroyed in accordance with law."

The third element of proof involved the presumption of revocation. When the will is shown to have been in the possession of the testator, and is not found at his death, the presumption arises that he destroyed it for the purpose of revocation; but the presumption may be rebutted, and the burden of rebutting it is on the proponent. [Citations.]

Billy McDowell, attorney Scott, and Mildred Johnson, a former neighbor of Mrs. Henry, testified that Mrs. Henry said that she did not want her nieces and nephews to have anything she had; that she had always made it abundantly clear that she wanted to select somebody other than her nieces and nephews; that she was afraid they were going to get her property; that she knew that her nieces and nephews would get her property if she died intestate; that she wanted Rita to have it, and that this was her fixed opinion.

Finally, proponent offered the copy of the will in evidence as proof of its contents.

A jury question was adequately presented * * * and the jury found for the proponent.

* * *

In the instant case, Billy McDowell testified that Mrs. Henry showed him her will; that he remembered seeing Cecil Sharp's signature; and that Mrs. Henry told him that attorney Scott had written the will, and that Rita Jan Gray was her sole beneficiary. It would appear that there was sufficient evidence from which to identify the copy.

* * *

Affirmed.

Ademption

IN RE ESTATE OF WOLFE

Supreme Court of Iowa, 1973.
208 N.W.2d 923.

LeGrand, J.

On June 6, 1971, the decedent, Leonard Allen Wolfe, was involved in a fatal automobile accident while driving his 1969 Buick Electra automobile. The car was rendered a total loss and subsequently decedent's insurance carrier paid his executor $3,550.00 for damage to the vehicle.

This litigation involves a dispute between decedent's daughter, Carol Lynn Wolfe, (the residuary legatee under his will) and his brother, David Wolfe, (to whom he left the automobile) over who shall have this money.

The case submitted on stipulated facts raising this one legal issue: Was the testamentary gift to David Wolfe adeemed by the virtual destruction of the automobile in the accident which caused decedent's death? The trial court held there was no ademption and we affirm.

The decedent's will included this provision:

Item III. To my brother, David Wolfe, * * *, I will the sum of $1,000.00 and any automobile which I may own at the time of my death to be his absolutely and forever, if he survives me, and if not this bequest shall lapse.

Put as briefly as possible, ademption means a taking away. It occurs when property which has been specifically given under a will is later destroyed or disposed of so that it does not exist as part of the estate at the testator's death. The general rule is that nothing else may be substituted for that which was originally given, and the gift is then said to have adeemed. [Citations.]

There is a split of authority over the part intent should play in resolving ademption problems. The minority view adheres to a rigid "identity" theory, concerning itself solely with the presence of the property in the estate at the time of death. If it is not among the decedent's assets, there has been an ademption, regardless of the reason for its absence. Intent is immaterial under this view. [Citations.]

The majority rule gives consideration and effect to circumstances which explain why the property is not among the decedent's assets at the time of his death. This rule, like the minority, finds there has been an ademption when there has been a *voluntary* sale or other disposal of specifically devised property by the testator during his lifetime. However, when the property in question is missing from the estate because of some act or event *involuntary* as to him, there is no ademption. This is the rule we follow.

It is clear the difference in the two rules is based upon the importance attached to the testator's intent. We have referred to our rule as the "modified intention theory." In re Estate of Bierstedt, [citation]. There we put it this way,

Where the testator is competent and disposes of the subject of the gift, the gift is adeemed; where the testator is incompetent and the subject of the gift is sold by a guardian with court approval, the gift is only adeemed to the extent the proceeds are used for care and maintenance of the ward. The only question of intention involved is the opportunity of the testator to change the will. This opportunity is denied the incompetent testator. No question of his intentions other than expressed in the will is involved. Where, as here, the testator is incompetent and under guardianship, a sale by the guardian does not work an ademption so far as the proceeds are traceable. This is the majority view in this country.

Both the Bierstedt case and Stake v. Cole, [citation], deal with judicial sales made under court order, one by an executor, the other by a guardian. We have never faced the precise problem now presented. However, we believe those two decisions clearly point the way to the proper result here.

The accident which cost decedent his life and caused destruction of the devised car was, it seems unnecessary to point out, an involuntary disposition of the automobile indicating no intention to change the terms of the will. Furthermore, like the incompetent testator mentioned in Bierstedt, decedent was denied by death any opportunity to change his will after the event occurred. The argument against ademption under these circumstances is at least as persuasive as in the Bierstedt and Stake cases.

We find surprisingly little authority from other states. Under almost identical facts the California appellate court ruled, as we do here, in favor of the specific legatee of the destroyed vehicle, basing its decision on the obvious intent of the testator. [Citation.]

In Reading v. Dixon, [citation], the specific legatee again prevailed over the objection a testamentary gift of silverware had adeemed by reason of its loss or theft at a time when the testator was mentally unable to change his will. The insurance proceeds were awarded to the specific legatee of the silverware, again on a finding of testamentary intent.

We have already referred to several cases holding to the strict identity theory. In re Wright's Will and In re Barry's Estate, both supra. It is interesting to note, however, New York has refused to follow its own pronouncements in the Wright case on at least two occasions. See [citation] (insurance proceeds awarded to specific devisee of damaged real estate over objection fire had worked an ademption); [citation] (gift of car was not adeemed by accident resulting in death of testator and destruction of vehicle).

* * *

An interesting discussion of the question appears in Walsh v. Gillespie, [citation]. We also believe this quotation from Wilmerton v. Wilmerton, [citation] 900 expresses quite well the right rule,

[W]e think that the rule, that legacies are adeemed only where such an intention appears on the part of the testator himself, ought to be followed. The question, in our judgment, is not whether, as a mere matter of accident, * * *, the thing set apart as the corpus of a special bequest has been changed in specie. The real question is whether, all things considered, the testator's testamentary disposition did, or did not, remain, with reference to the particular thing embodied in the specific bequest or its proceeds, the same as it was the last moment he was able to exercise a testamentary disposition. In that way, and in that way only, we think, can the right of the man to dispose of his property according to his own wishes, exempt from the interference, caprice or interest of others, be fully carried out. In that way only can his intention, as embodied in his will, be truly administered.

We approve that statement and adopt its rationale in holding the gift to David Wolfe was not adeemed by the accident in question.

Affirmed.

PROBLEMS

1. In each of the following situations state whether or not a trust is created.

    (a) A declares herself trustee of "the bulk of my securities" in trust for B.

    (b) A, the owner of Blackacre, purports to convey to B in trust for C "a small part" of Blackacre.

    (c) A orders B, a stockbroker, to buy 2,000 shares of American Steel or any part thereof at $20. After the broker has brought 500 shares but before A knows whether any shares have been bought for him, A declares himself trustee for C of such shares of American Steel as B has bought.

    (d) A owns ten bonds. He declared himself trustee for B of such five of the bonds as B may select at any time within a month.

    (e) A deposits $1,000 in a savings bank. He declares himself trustee of the deposit in trust to pay B $500 out of the deposit, reserving the power to withdraw from the deposit any amounts not in excess of $500.

2. Testator gives property to T in trust for B's benefit, providing that B cannot anticipate the income by assignment or pledge. B borrows money from L, assigning his future income under the trust for a stated period. Can L obtain any judicial relief to prevent B from collecting this income?

3. Collins was trustee for Indolent under the will of Indolent's father. Indolent, a middle-aged doctor, gave little concern to the management of the trust fund, contenting himself with receiving the income paid him by the trustee. Among the assets of the trust were 100 shares of ABC Corporation and 100 shares of XYZ Corporation. About two years before the termination of the trust Collins, at a fair price and after full explanation to Indolent, purchased from the trust the ABC stock. At the same time but without saying anything to Indolent, he purchased the XYZ stock at a price in excess of its then market value. At the termination of the trust both stocks had advanced in market value well beyond the prices paid by Collins, and Indolent demanded that Collins either account for this advance in the value of both stocks or replace the stocks. What are Indolent's rights?

4. Joe Brown on September 1, 1974, furnished to his wife, Mary Brown, $35,000 with which to buy real property. It was orally agreed between them that title to the real property should be taken in the name of Mary Brown but that she should hold the same in trust for Joe Brown. There were two witnesses to the oral agreement, both of whom are now living. On the following day the property was purchased, and a deed to it with Mary Brown as the grantee was delivered.

Mary died on October 5, 1985, without a will. The real property is now worth $100,000. Joe Brown is claiming the property as the beneficiary of a trust. Mary's children are claiming that the property belongs to Mary's estate and have pleaded the Statute of Limitations and the Statute of Frauds as defenses to the claim of Joe. There is no evidence one way or the other as to whether Mary would have conveyed the property to Joe during her lifetime if she had been requested to do so.

What are Joe's ownership rights to this particular real property?

5. John Carver executed his will on March 10, 1985, which was witnessed by William Hobson and Sam Witt. By his will Carver devised his farm, Stonecrest, to his nephew Roy White. The residue of his estate was given to his sister, Florence Carver.

A codicil to his will executed April 15, 1985, provided that $5,000 be given to Carver's niece, Mary Jordan, and $5,000 to Wanda White, Roy White's wife. The codicil was witnessed by Roy White and Harold Brown. John Carver died September 1, 1985, and the will and codicil were admitted to probate.

How should Carver's estate be distributed?

6. Edwin Fuller, a bachelor, prepared his will in his office. The will, which contained no residuary clause, provided that one-third of his estate would go to his nephew, Tom Fuller, one-third to the City of Emanon to be used for park improvements, and one-third to his brother Kurt.

He signed the will in his office and then went to the office of his nephew Tom Fuller who, at Edwin's request, signed the will as a witness. Since no other persons were available in Tom's office, Edwin then went to the bank where Frank Cash,

the cashier, at Edwin's request, also signed as a witness. In each instance Edwin stated that he had signed the document but did not state that it was his will.

Edwin returned to his office where he placed the will in his safe. Subsequently, Edwin died, survived by Kurt, his only heir-at-law. How should the estate be distributed?

7. A executed a one-page will, wherein she devised her farm to B. Later, as the result of a quarrel with B, A wrote the words, "I hereby cancel and revoke this will /s/A," in the margin of the will but did not destroy the will. A then executed a deed to the property, naming C as grantee, and placed the deed and will in her safe. Shortly afterwards, A married D, by whom she had one child, E. Thereafter, A died, and the deed and will were found in her safe. B, C, and E claim the farm, and D claims dower. Discuss the validity of each claim.

8. John Walker, a widower, died testate. His will, in part, provided:

"I give and bequeath my piano to my daugher Nancy. I give and bequeath to my daughter Jennifer the sum of $1,000. I give and bequeath to my son John the sum of $1,000 to be paid out of my account at the Tenth National Bank in the city of Erehwon. All the rest and residue of my estate I give to Nancy, Jennifer, and John, share and share alike."

Subsequent to the execution of his will Walker sold his piano for $2,300 and deposited the proceeds in the Citizens Bank of Erehwon. He withdrew the money he had on deposit in the Tenth National Bank and purchased a new automobile.

At the time of his death, Walker had no debts. The account in the Citizens Bank of Erehwon had a balance of $2,300 which constituted his entire net estate after all expenses of administration were paid. How should Walker's estate be distributed?

9. The validly executed will of John Dane contained the following provision: "I give and devise to my daughter, Mary, Redacre for and during her natural life and, at her death, the remainder to go to Wilmore College." The will also provided that the residue of his estate should go to Wilmore College. Thereafter, Dane sold Redacre and then added a validly executed codicil to his will, "Due to the fact that I have sold Redacre which I previously gave to my daughter, Mary, I now give

and devise Blackacre to Mary in place and instead of Redacre."

Another clause of the codicil provided: "I give my one-half interest in the oil business which I own in common with William Steele to my son, Henry." Subsequently, Dane acquired all of the interest in the oil business from his partner, Steele, and at the time of his death Dane owned the entire oil business. The will and codicil have been admitted to probate.

(a) What interest, if any, does Mary acquire in Blackacre?

(b) What is the interest, if any, of Henry in the oil business?

Chapter 51

INSURANCE

INSURANCE covers a vast range of contracts each of which distributes risk among a large number of members (the **insured**) through an insurance company (the **insurer**). It is a contractual undertaking by the insurer to pay a sum of money or give something of value to the insured or a beneficiary upon the happening of a contingency or fortuitous event which is beyond the control of the contracting parties.

It is literally impossible to name a commercial activity which is not affected by insurance coverage of one form or other. Tangible assets of a business can be the subject of insurance protecting it against almost any form of damage or destruction, whether from natural causes or from the accidental or improper actions of another. Insurance may also protect a business from virtually any type of liability that may be asserted against it through the negligent or intentional act of any of its representatives which, in any way, might be deemed to be the act of the business. A business may procure credit insurance to protect against losses from poor credit risks and fidelity bonds to protect it against losses incurred through defalcations of employees. If a business hires a famous pianist, it may insure the latter's hands; if it decides to present an outdoor concert, it may insure against the possibility of rain. A business may purchase life insurance on its key executives to reimburse it for the financial loss arising from their deaths, or it may purchase such life insurance payable to the families of the executives as part of an incentive compensation. An additional development of growing importance is the use of insurance to carry out pension commitments arising from bargaining agreements with unions.

The McCarran-Ferguson Act, enacted in 1945, left the regulation of insurance to the

States. Each State has its own statutes regulating its domestic insurance companies as well as setting forth standards which foreign insurance companies must meet in order to do business within the State. Most of the State legislation relates to the incorporation, licensing, supervision, and liquidation of insurers and to licensing and supervision of agents and brokers.

Because the insurance relationship arises from a contract of insurance between the insurer and the insured, the law of insurance is a branch of contract law. For this reason, the doctrines of offer and acceptance, consideration, and other rules applicable to contracts in general are equally applicable to insurance contracts. Beyond that, however, insurance law, like the law of sales, bailments, negotiable instruments, or other specialized types of contracts, contains numerous modifications and ramifications of fundamental contract law with which this chapter will be concerned.

KINDS OF INSURANCE

There are many kinds of insurance and many kinds of insurance policies. While the listing which follows does not pretend to be complete, it contains the most commonly utilized kinds of insurance.

Life Insurance

Life insurance might be more accurately called "death insurance," since it is a contract by the terms of which the insurer will pay a specified sum of money upon the death of the insured, provided the required premiums have been paid. The payment is made either to a named beneficiary, ordinarily a third-party donee or creditor, or to the estate of the deceased. The naming of a beneficiary is a privilege of the *owner* of the policy, but unless the right to do so is reserved in the policy, the owner has no right to change the beneficiary. Most modern policies as part of the standard form reserve to the owner of the

policy the express right to change beneficiaries. One person may occupy one or more of these three roles (insured, owner, and beneficiary) or each may be held by a different party.

Ordinary Life This type of life insurance is often considered a form of savings or investment, since the insured has a right to borrow from the insurer an amount not to exceed the **cash surrender value** of the policy, which value increases the longer the policy is in force. Such a loan generally bears a low interest rate and is secured by an assignment to the insurer of the policy proceeds to the extent necessary to pay the loan in the event of death, with the remainder going to the beneficiary.

Ordinary life or **whole-life** insurance is designed to run for the entire life of the insured and generally, under a **straight-life** policy, requires the payment of premiums until the insured's death. **Limited-payment** life policies require the payment of premiums only for a fixed number of years, thus eliminating the duty of paying premiums through the later years of life when such payments may be burdensome. With **single premium** life insurance the entire premium is pre-paid in one lump sum.

Term Life Term life insurance is issued for a limited period of time with premiums payable during the period of coverage. The insurance proceeds are only paid if the insured dies within the specified time period. Term insurance, moreover, does not build up any cash surrender value or loan value, and thus the insurer may not be obligated to pay out anything on the policy. Frequently, this type of life insurance carries with it a provision to renew the policy without regard to the state of the insured's health.

Endowment and Annuity Contracts

An endowment contract is basically an agreement by the insurer to pay a lump sum of money to the insured when she reaches a certain age or to a beneficiary in the event of premature death, while an annuity contract is an agreement by the insurer to pay fixed sums to the insured at periodic intervals after the insured reaches a designated age. Strictly speaking, endowment and annuity policies are not insurance contracts; but numerous endowment and annuity contracts contain various provisions which are customarily found in life insurance contracts and are therefore subject to regulation by State insurance departments.

Accident and Health Insurance

Accident and health insurance is really insurance against losses due to accidents and sickness and provides for the payment of certain benefits or the reimbursement of specified expenses in the event of illness or accidental injury, within the limits set forth in the policies.

Fire Insurance

Fire insurance protects the owner, or other person with an insurable interest such as a secured creditor or mortgagee, of real or personal property against loss resulting from damage to or destruction of the property by fire and certain related perils.

Fire insurance policies are standardized in the United States, either by statute or by order of the State insurance departments, but their coverage is frequently enlarged by an "endorsement" or "rider" to include other perils or to benefit the insured in ways not provided in the standard form. These policies are normally written for periods of one or three years.

Co-insurance is common in property insurance and is a means of sharing the risk between insurer and insured. For example, under the typical 80 percent co-insurance clause, the insured may recover the full amount of loss not to exceed the face amount of the policy, provided the policy is for an amount not less than 80 percent of the insurable value

of the property. If the policy is less than such 80 percent the insured recovers that proportion of the loss which the amount of the policy bears to 80 percent of the insurable value. The applicable formula is as follows:

$$\text{Recovery} = \frac{\text{Fair Value of Policy}}{\text{Fair Market Value of Property} \times \text{Co-insurance \%}} \times \text{Loss}$$

Thus, if the co-insurance percentage is 80 percent, the value of the property is $100,000, and the policy is for $80,000 or more, the insured is protected against loss not to exceed the amount of the policy. However, if the amount of the policy is less than 80 percent, the insured does not receive the full amount of loss but only the above stated proportion. Thus, in the above example, if the fire policy was in the amount of $60,000 and the property 50 percent destroyed, the loss would be $50,000, of which the insurer would pay $37,500, which is 60,000/80,000 of $50,000. On a total loss the recovery could not, of course, exceed the face amount of the policy.

Recovery under non-life insurance policies is typically also limited by "other insurance" clauses. These clauses generally require that liability be distributed *pro rata* among the various insurers. Thus, X insures his $120,000 building with A Insurance Co. for $60,000 and B Insurance Co. for $90,000. X's building is partially destroyed by fire causing X $20,000 in damages. X will collect $\frac{2}{5}\left(\dfrac{60,000}{150,000}\right)$ of his damages from A ($8,000) and $\frac{3}{5}\left(\dfrac{90,000}{150,000}\right)$ from B ($12,000).

Casualty Insurance

The term casualty insurance is broad in scope but usually covers loss due to the damage or destruction of personal property by various causes other than fire or the elements, and is sometimes applied to personal injury or death or property loss due to accident.

Collision Insurance

Collision insurance protects the owner of an automobile against the risk of loss or damage due to contact with other vehicles or objects, usually subject to a deductability clause.

Liability Insurance

Liability insurance provides indemnification against loss by reason of liability of the insured for damages resulting from injuries to another's person or property. While this kind of insurance is most generally thought of in connection with automobiles, where it is often of greater interest to the injured person than to the driver who caused the injury, it is customarily carried by owners and lessees of real property to protect against public liability for injuries arising on the premises owned or leased.

No-Fault Insurance

A number of States have legislatively adopted a system of compensating victims of automobile accidents regardless of liability. Generally, coverage is provided for personal injury to the named insured, members of his household, authorized operators of the vehicle, passengers, and pedestrians caused by a motor vehicle accident involving the insured's vehicle.

Credit Insurance

Credit insurance protects creditors against loss due to the insolvency of their debtors. Credit life insurance protects the creditor and the debtor by providing for the payment of an indebtedness of the insured in the event of her death before the indebtedness has been fully paid.

Fidelity Insurance

Fidelity insurance protects an employer against loss due to the dishonesty or defalcation of employees.

Group Insurance

Group insurance covers a number of individuals, having some common interest, under a blanket or single policy. This insurance is usually either life or accident and health insurance. The term "group" insurance simply refers to the method of selling standard types of insurance.

Marine Insurance

Marine insurance originally was restricted to destruction of vessels or cargo due to perils of the sea. Now it is a comprehensive form of all-risk insurance covering ship and cargo against the "perils of the sea." While it is sometimes divided into ocean marine and inland marine, the distinction is not always made, and marine insurance covers transportation risks generally as well as personal property risks and other personal property coverages of almost all kinds.

Title Insurance

Title insurance provides indemnity against loss arising from defects in the title to real estate or due to liens or encumbrances on the property. An owner's title insurance policy is issued in the amount of the purchase price of the property and guarantees the owner against any loss due to defects in the title to the property or due to liens or encumbrances, except for those stated in the policy as existing at the time the policy is issued. Such policies may also be issued to mortgagees or to tenants of property to protect their interests.

NATURE OF INSURANCE CONTRACTS

The basic principles of **contract** law are applicable to insurance policies. However, insurance companies engage in a large volume of business over wide areas, and therefore their policies are standardized. In some States standardization is required by statute. This usually means that the insured must accept a given policy or do without the desired insurance.

Offer and Acceptance

No matter how aggressively a life insurance agent has solicited a person to take out a policy, it is generally true that it is the applicant who makes the offer, and the contract is created when that offer is accepted by the company. The company's acceptance may be conditioned, for instance, upon payment of the premium or delivery of the policy while the insured is in good health. If the company writes a policy which differs from the application, then it is the company which makes a counteroffer which the applicant may or may not choose to accept. This situation arises more frequently where the company is unwilling to write the policy which the agent proposed, because of the results of a physical examination of the applicant, but is willing to write a different policy based on the particular risk involved.

Life insurance agents, therefore, cannot generally bind the company to a contract with the insured, although on occasion a **binding receipt** may be issued by an authorized agent, acknowledging payment of the premium and providing for the issuance of a standard policy effective from the date of the medical examination so long as the company has no *bona fide* reason to reject the application. In fire and casualty insurance, agents often have authority to make the insurance effective immediately, when needed, by means of a **"binder."** In the event of a loss before the company has actually issued a policy, the binder will be effective on the same terms and conditions the policy would have had if it had been issued.

Insurable Interest

The concept of insurable interest has been developed over many years, primarily to eliminate gambling and to lessen the moral hazard. If a person could obtain an enforce-able insurance policy on the life of anyone or a fire insurance policy on property that he did not own or in which he had no interest, he would be in a position to profit by the death of a stranger or the destruction of property which represented no loss to him. An insurable interest is such relationship which a person has to another person or with respect to certain property that the happening of a possible, specific, damage-causing contingency would result in direct loss or injury to him. The purpose of insurance is protection against the risk of loss resulting from such happening, not the realization of gain or profit.

Property Insurance Ownership, obviously, creates an insurable interest in the property, whether the ownership is sole or concurrent. Moreover, a right deriving from a contract concerning the property also gives rise to an insurable interest. *See Scarola v. Insurance Co. of North America.* For instance, shareholders in a closely held corporation have been held to have an insurable interest in the corporation's property. Lessees of property have interests which are insurable as do holders of security interests, such as mortgagees or conditional sellers. The insurable interest must exist at the time the property *loss* occurs. Property insurance policies are not assignable before loss occurs but are freely assignable after the loss.

Life Insurance Those who may take out insurance on another's life are limited to close relatives, creditors, and business associates or employers, depending generally on the particular facts involved. *See New York Life Insurance Co. v. Baum.* An insured, however, may take out a policy on her own life and name anyone she chooses as beneficiary, although that particular beneficiary may have no insurable interest in the insured's life. The insurable interest must exist at the time the *policy* is taken out and need not exist at the time of death.

An insured, as indicated in the preceding paragraph, may assign the life policy proceeds to a third person who has no insurable interest. In the leading case on the assignability of a life insurance policy the United States Supreme Court stated:

[L]ife insurance has become in our days one of the best recognized forms of investment and self-compelled saving. So far as reasonable safety permits, it is desirable to give to life policies the ordinary characteristics of property. This is recognized by the bankruptcy law, § 70, which provides that unless the cash surrender value of a policy like the one before us is secured to the trustee within thirty days after it has been stated, the policy shall pass to the trustee as assets. Of course the trustee may have no interest in the bankrupt's life. To deny the right to sell except to persons having such an interest is to diminish appreciably the value of the contract in the owner's hands. The collateral difficulty that arose from regarding life insurance as a contract of indemnity only, long has disappeared. And cases in which a person having an interest lends himself to one without any, as a cloak to what is, in its inception, a wager, have no similarity to those where an honest contract is sold in good faith. *Grigsby v. Russell*, 222 U.S. 149 (1911).

Premiums

Life insurance companies usually receive premiums from their insureds over periods of years. These premiums are fixed in amount and are such that the company will be able to pay the principal sum when the policy matures upon the death of the insured through the accumulation of reserves. Life insurance premiums are calculated on the basis of (1) mortality rates, (2) interest, and (3) expense.

Casualty insurance policies are written only for periods of a few years at most. Long, continued liability on this type of policy is the exception rather than the rule. The rates which may be charged for fire and various kinds of casualty insurance are regulated by State law. The regulatory authorities are under a duty to require that the companies' rates be reasonable, not unfairly discriminatory, and neither excessively high nor inadequately low.

Double Indemnity

A provision found in some life insurance contracts provides for the recovery of "double indemnity," or twice the face amount of the policy, in the event of accidental death or death which results "directly and independently of all other causes from bodily injuries sustained solely from external, violent, and accidental means." These accidental death provisions are worded in various ways and have given rise to much litigation, frequently involving the question whether a death which resulted from the unexpected consequences of an intentional act was an accidental death. The cases cannot be reconciled, but it has been held that death resulting from an infection following the intentional pulling of a hair from the nose was accidental death, whereas death resulting from sunstroke, due to voluntary but unintentional overexposure to the sun, was not. Death as a result of playing Russian roulette has been held not to be accidental, under a double indemnity clause.

Defenses of the Insurer

In addition to the ordinary defenses to a contract, the insurer may assert the closely related defenses of misrepresentation, breach of warranty, and concealment.

Misrepresentation A representation is a statement made by or on behalf of an applicant for insurance to induce an insurer to enter into a contract. The representation is not a part of the insurance contract, but if the application containing the representation is incorporated by reference into the contract, as in liability or burglary insurance, the representation becomes a warranty. For a representation to have legal consequences, it must have been relied upon by the insurer as an inducement to enter into the contract, and it must have been substantially false when made or it must have become so, to the insured's knowledge, before the contract was created. *See Hawkeye-Security Insurance Co. v. Gov-*

ernment Employees Insurance Co. The principal remedy of the insurer on discovery of the material misrepresentation is rescission of the contract. To rescind the contract, the insurer must tender to the insured all premiums which have been paid, since a rescission restores the parties to the position they were in before the contract was made. To be effective, rescission must be made as soon as possible after discovery of the misrepresentation.

Rescission may or may not be available to the life insurer, however, because of the **incontestability clause** which generally makes the policy incontestable by the insurer after a specified period of time, generally two years, after the policy has been in effect. The incontestability clause, however, does not prevent the insurer from contesting the policy for failure to pay the premiums, for misrepresentation of age, for lack of an insurable interest by the policy owner, and for false impersonation as when the physical examination is taken by another. If the applicant for insurance **misstates his age,** the amount of insurance is simply reduced to that sum which the premiums paid would have purchased at the insured's correct age.

An innocent misrepresentation of a material fact (not opinion) prior to the running of the incontestability clause is a sufficient ground for avoidance of a policy by the insurer. Whether the fact is material or not depends generally upon whether the policy would have been issued had the truth been known. An immaterial misrepresentation, even though fraudulently made, is not a ground for avoidance of the policy.

Breach of Warranty Warranties are of great importance in insurance contracts because they operate as conditions which *must* exist before the contract is effective or before the insurer's promise to pay is enforceable. Failure of the condition to exist or to occur relieves the insurer from any obligation to perform its promise. Broadly speaking, a condition is simply an event the happening of which or its

failure to happen precedes the existence of a legal relationship or terminates one previously existing. Conditions are either precedent or subsequent; for example, payment of the premium is a condition precedent to the enforcement of the insurer's promise, as is the happening of the insured event. A condition subsequent is an operative event the happening of which terminates an existing matured legal obligation. A provision in a policy to the effect that the insured shall not be liable unless suit is brought within twelve months from the date of the occurrence of the loss operates as a condition subsequent.

Usually, those statements in policies which the insurer looks upon as express warranties can be identified by the use of the words "warrant" or "on condition that" or "provided that" or words of similar import. Other statements which are important to the risk assumed, such as the building address in the case where personal property at a particular location is insured against fire, are sometimes held to be informal warranties. Generally, the trend is away from allowing an insurer to avoid liability on the policy for *any* breach of a warranty by an insured; the breach must usually be material to have such an effect.

Concealment While rarely relied upon in life insurance, the doctrine of concealment has vitality in other fields of insurance. Concealment is simply the failure of an applicant for insurance to disclose material facts which the insurer does not know. The non-disclosure must normally be fraudulent as well as material to invalidate the policy; that is, (1) did the applicant have reason to believe the fact was material, and (2) would its disclosure have affected the acceptance of the risk by the insurer? The rationale behind the defense of concealment was well expressed by Lord Mansfield in 1766:

The special facts, upon which the contingent chance is to be computed, lie most commonly in the knowledge of the *insured* only: the under-writer trusts to his representation, and proceeds upon confidence that he does not keep back any circumstance in his knowledge, to mislead the under-writer into a belief that the circumstance does not exist, and to induce him to estimate the risque, as if it did not exist.

The keeping back such circumstance is a *fraud*, and therefore the policy is void. *Carter v. Boehm*, 1766, 3 Burrows 1905.

Waiver and Estoppel

There are instances when an insurer would normally be entitled to deny liability under a policy because of a misrepresentation, breach of condition or concealment, but because of other facts, the insurer is said to be "estopped" from taking advantage of the defense or else to have "waived" the right to rely on it.

"Waiver" and "estoppel" are terms used interchangeably, although by definition they are not synonymous. As generally defined, waiver is the intentional relinquishment of a known right, and estoppel means that a person is prevented by his own conduct from asserting a position which is inconsistent with his acts which have been relied upon by another with justification.

Since a corporation such as an insurance company can act only by agents, situations involving waiver invariably find root in an agent's conduct. The higher the agent's position in the company's organization, the more likely is his conduct to bind the company, since an agent acting within the scope of his authority binds the principal. Insureds have the right to rely on representations made by the insurer's employees, and where such representations reasonably induce or cause a change of position by the insured or prevent the insured from causing a condition to occur, the insurer may not assert the failure of the condition to occur whether the term applied to his situation be waiver or estoppel. Companies have tried in many ways to limit the authority of local selling agents to bind the company through waiver or estoppel, but this is difficult to do effectively. *See Marlowe v. Reserve Life Insurance Co.*

As a general rule, when a local agent delivers a policy with knowledge of the non-occurrence of a condition precedent to the company's liability which would make the policy void or voidable at the company's option, the condition is waived. While there is always a question whether the agent had authority to waive the condition, most courts will find an effective waiver even though the condition is a delivery-in-good-health clause or the medical-treatment clause in a life insurance policy. Such clauses provide that a life insurance policy shall not take effect unless delivered to the applicant while his insurability or good health continues and that the policy shall not take effect if the applicant has been treated by a physician or has been hospitalized between the date of the application and the date of delivery of the policy.

Performance and Termination

Most contracts of insurance are performed according to their terms, and due performance terminates the insurer's obligation. In insurance contracts the insurer pays the principal sum due and the contract is thereby performed and discharged.

Cancellation Cancellation of an insurance contract by mutual consent is one way of terminating it. Cancellation by the insurer alone means that the insurer is liable according to the terms of the policy until such time as the cancellation is effective. This is not always a right which is available to insurers, but where available, it is sometimes mistakenly used where rescission is preferable from the insurer's point of view. If an insurer under an accident policy elects to cancel after the occurrence of an insured event, where a right of rescission existed because of material misrepresentation, this will be taken as an admission of liability for events occurring before cancellation. To cancel a policy, the insurer must tender the unearned portion of the premium to the insured. To effect a rescission, all premiums received by the insurer must be returned to the insured.

Notice After the occurrence of the insured event, the owner of the policy or the insured is required to give notice to the insurer and, in the case of property insurance, proof of loss within a specified time, such as sixty days for fire insurance. In liability policies the requirement of immediate notice is construed by the courts as notice within a "reasonable" time.

Automobile liability policies require that the insured immediately notify the insurer of any accident or occurrence which may involve liability. Notice requirements are conditions precedent to the insurer's contractual liability but may be waived by the insurer.

CASES

Insurable Interest: Property

SCAROLA v. INSURANCE CO. OF NORTH AMERICA

Court of Appeals of New York, 1972.
31 N.Y.2d 411, 340 N.Y.S.2d 630, 292 N.E.2d 776.

BERGAN, J.

The finding of fact that plaintiff purchased the automobile insured by defendant for value and without knowledge it was stolen has been affirmed, both by the Appellate Term, 67 Misc.2d 437, 323 N.Y.S.2d 1001, and by the Appellate Division, 38 A.D.2d 1012, 331 N.Y.S.2d 340, and is not an open question here. Thus the issue of plaintiff's insurable interest must be examined on the assumption he was an innocent buyer of the vehicle insured by defendant, and subsequently stolen.

Plaintiff had a right to possession of the car against any contrary assertion except that of the true owner. This right, under general principles, ought to be regarded as an insurable interest. The New York rule was laid down by Judge Finch in National Filtering Oil Co. v. Citizen's Ins. Co. of Mo., [citation]. He noted that the cases he cited, [citation], "decided that an interest, legal or equitable, in the property burned, is not necessary to support an insurance upon it; that it is enough if the assured is so situated as to be liable to loss if it be destroyed by the peril insured against; that such an interest in property connected with its safety and situation as will cause the insured to sustain a direct loss from its destruction, is an insurable interest; that if there be a right in or against the property which some court will enforce upon the property, a right so closely connected with it and so much dependent for value upon the continued existence of it alone as that a loss of the property will cause pecuniary damage to the holder of the right against it, he has an insurable interest." [Citation]

This decision was followed in Riggs v. Commercial Mut. Ins. Co., [citation], in which Judge Andrews observed that although a stockholder of a corporation had neither title to corporate property nor equitable title which he could convert to a legal title, he has a sufficient interest in such property to insure it. For example, its loss might affect dividends. If the law recognizes the right of a purchaser of a car in good faith and for value to possession, it would seem to follow that this right to possession, limited though it may be, is insurable.

* * *

Two states (New Jersey and Washington) have held under similar circumstances to those now here that the purchaser in good faith of a car has an insurable interest. [Citation.]

In the latter case the court observed: "The car covered by the policy upon which the action is based was purchased by the respondent in good faith, used by him, the insurance policy issued to him and the premium paid. Even though the automobile may have been originally stolen from the rightful owner, the respondent had the title and the right to possession of it as against all the world, except the rightful owner, assuming that the car had been stolen from him" [citation].

In a recent case in the Second Department [citation] the court treated as decisive on insurable interest whether plaintiff was "an innocent purchaser of the automobile." Holding that he was not, the court held he had no insurable interest.

* * *

The order should be affirmed.

Insurable Interest: Life

NEW YORK LIFE INSURANCE CO. v. BAUM

United States Court of Appeals, Fifth Circuit, 1983.
700 F.2d 928.

THORNBERRY, J.

[In 1973, Baum and Cook began discussing a joint business venture in media advertising. Cook was to furnish the experience for setting up the corporation, while Baum was to furnish the capital. Cook, nevertheless, in the interim, agreed with Cutler to start a partnership in Texas, doing business as Media Sales. Baum extended at least $16,500 worth of credit to Cook for starting the business and decided to procure key man life insurance on Cook, to protect his investment. On December 8, 1973 Baum purchased an insurance policy on the life of Cook from New York Life Insurance Company. The named beneficiary was Media Sales, because Baum was an agent of New York Life and the company did not allow agents to be named as the beneficiaries in policies issued on the lives of persons other than family members. Twelve days after the policy was issued Cutler and Cook incorporated their business, Media Sales, and excluded Baum. Baum paid the premiums on Cook's policy, because he was the principal financier of the proposed Media Sales Corporation. Media Sales also filed a claim, as-

serting that it was the named corporate beneficiary.]

* * *

N.Y.Ins. Law * * * Section 146 defines an insurable interest in the case of persons not related by blood or by law as follows:

[I]n the case of other persons, a lawful and substantial economic interest in having the life, health or bodily safety of the person insured continue, as distinguished from an interest which would arise only by, or would be enhanced in value by, the death, disablement or injury, as the case may be, of the persons insured. [Citation.]

"It may be generally stated that the reasoning behind legislation requiring an insurable interest . . . is in furtherance of the public policy against wagering or gambling on human lives. This policy has been adopted in most jurisdictions to prevent speculation in human life, since the incentive to shorten the life of the insured would be increased." [Citation.] While discussing the subject of insurable interest between creditors and their debtors another New York court held as follows:

It is now well settled that the bank had an insurable interest in the life of the plaintiff's intestate at the time it made the loan to him and under such circumstances the bank had the right to enter into any agreement with the insurance company so that it would receive a sum of money as indemnity in case its interest in the subject matter should suffer diminution of value by reason of certain specified causes or contingencies. [Citation.] The bank with such an insurable interest in the borrower clearly had the right to secure itself against the death of the borrower. [Citations.] It may be stated generally, however, to be such an [insurable] interest, arising from the relations of the party obtaining the insurance, either as *creditor* of or surety for the assured . . . . as will justify a reasonable expectation of advantage of benefit from the continuance of his life." [Citations.]

* * *

Applying these principles to our case, we hold that, under New York law, Baum had an insurable interest in the life of Cook, his debtor, as a matter of law. A creditor-debtor relationship existed between Baum and Cook at the time the policy was executed and Baum loaned the majority of the funds to Cook *after* the policy went into effect. The facts fail to show that the policy was taken as a wager. As creditor, Baum had a reasonable ground to expect some benefit or advantage from the continuation of Cook's life, namely, repayment of the loan. Furthermore, there are compelling arguments against allowing the insurer to escape its obligation.

It is surely not a sound policy to permit insurers to contract to insure the lives of persons, receive premiums therefor as long as the * * * beneficiary * * * will continue to pay, and then, when the time comes for the insurers to pay what they agreed to pay, allow them to escape their contract on the ground of want of insurable interest in the life insured, unless it clearly appears that such contracts are pernicious and dangerous to society. [Citation.]

* * *

Regarding Media [Sales], the situation is less clear. While it is true that, as a general rule, a corporation has an insurable interest in the life of its key employees "the record clearly demonstrates that Media Sales (Texas) was nothing more than a nonfunctioning corporate shell."

[Judgment in favor of Baum.]

Misrepresentation

HAWKEYE-SECURITY INSURANCE CO. v. GOVERNMENT EMPLOYEES INSURANCE CO.

Supreme Court of Virginia, 1967.
207 Va. 944, 154 S.E.2d 173.

SNEAD, J.

On August 18, 1962, Einer Carl Mattson, Jr. was operating an automobile owned by and with consent of his father, Einer Carl Mattson, Sr. It became involved in a collision with another vehicle operated by William Henry Droughn who received personal injuries. Mattson, Sr. reported the accident to Government Employees Insurance Company, appellee, which had issued to him a liability insurance policy on his car involved in the mishap. Under the terms of the policy, Mattson, Jr. was an additional insured. On November 20, 1962, after some investigation, Government Employees wrote Mattson, Sr. advising "[W]e hereby declare the captioned policy null and void and of no effect as of its inception date" because of a material misrepresentation made in his application for the insurance coverage, and it enclosed a check for a refund of premiums paid.

On September 22, 1964, Droughn recovered a judgment in the sum of $2,000 against Mattson, Jr., and on the same day Droughn assigned it to Hawkeye-Security Insurance Company, appellant, for a valuable consideration. Execution on the judgment was returned "unsatisfied."

* * *

Hawkeye, assignee, instituted an action against Government Employees seeking a judgment for $2,000 against it. In its answer and grounds of defense, Government Employees denied that the Mattson vehicle was insured by it, and denied that it was liable to Hawkeye in any amount. A trial by jury was waived, and after hearing all the evidence, the court found that Mattson, Sr. had made a material misrepresentation in his application to Government Employees for the insurance policy and on November 3, 1965, rendered judgment in its behalf. We granted Hawkeye a writ of error.

* * *

* * * The crucial issue presented in this appeal is whether the insurance policy issued to Mattson, Sr. by Government Employees was in full force and effect on August 18, 1962, the date Droughn was injured, or whether it was void *ab initio* because of an alleged material misrepresentation made by Mattson, Sr. in the procurement of the policy.

The record shows that Mattson, Sr. was insured under an automobile liability policy issued by State Farm Mutual Insurance Company from January 29, 1959, until it was cancelled by the Company on August 5, 1959. Douglas R. Mays, an underwriter for State Farm, testified that the policy was cancelled for "general underwriting reasons" and that Mattson, Sr. was notified of the Company's action by registered mail.

Thereafter, Mattson, Sr. obtained another policy from Home Indemnity Insurance Company which he retained until October 20, 1960 when he was issued the policy here involved by Government Employees. This policy was twice renewed with coverage extending through October 20, 1963. All premiums were duly paid.

Mattson, Sr. testified that he contacted Government Employees by mail for the insurance and was mailed an application for him to complete and return. Above the space for his signature and the questions to be answered the application read:

"I understand and agree that if the answers to questions 7, 8, 9, or 10, or any of them are other than 'No,' the insurance requested will not be effective until approved by the Company. * * * The Company agrees that * * * if the true answers to questions 7, 8, 9, and 10 are 'No', the insurance applied for will be effective as of: postmarked time and date * * *

"IMPORTANT ISSUANCE OF A VALID POLICY IS DEPENDENT UPON YOUR TRUE ANSWERS."

We are here concerned only with question No. 7, which follows:

"7. Has any insurance company (including this Company) ever refused, concelled, refused to renew, or given notice of intention to cancel or refuse, any automobile insurance for you or any member of your household? * * * If 'yes,' see above (the quoted statement) (Give full information on separate sheet)"

The application which Mattson, Sr. admitted that he himself completed and signed, contained a "No" answer in response to question No. 7. * * *

Gerald T. Jackson, underwriting manager for Government Employees, testified that he had the responsibility of deciding whether a policy should or should not be issued by his Company to an applicant. He said that if question No. 7 had been answered "yes" without elaboration, the application of Mattson, Sr. would have been rejected; * * *.

Jackson, on the other hand, testified that when an application contained a "No" answer to question No. 7, and the rest of the application showed no accidents or violations, the answer would be accepted as true and no investigation would be made.

Hawkeye concedes that the answer "No" to question No. 7 was untrue, but contends Government Employees did not clearly prove that such answer was material to the risk when assumed.

"A fact is material to the risk to be assumed by an insurance company if the fact would reasonably influence the company's decision whether or not to issue a policy." [Citations.]

* * *

We have repeatedly held that a misrepresentation of a fact material to the risk when assumed renders an insurance contract void. [Citations.]

Here, Government Employees carried its burden of clearly proving that the untrue answer to question No. 7 in the application for insurance made by Mattson, Sr. was material to the risk when assumed. * * *

Government Employees was entitled to know the whole truth. The false answer ("No") to question No. 7 caused the Company to forego an opportunity to investigate why the State Farm policy was cancelled and to determine whether or not the risk should be assumed as well as the premium rate applicable to the risk in the event the policy was issued. [Citation.]

* * *

Under the evidence adduced, the trial court properly held that the misrepresentation was material to the risk when assumed and that the policy was null and void *ab initio* for that reason.

Accordingly, the judgment appealed from is

Affirmed.

Waiver and Estoppel

MARLOWE v. RESERVE LIFE INSURANCE CO.

Supreme Court of South Carolina, 1973.
261 S.C. 23, 198 S.E.2d 267.

Moss, C. J.

The appellant, Reserve Life Insurance Company, on January 15, 1970, issued a hospital insurance policy to Helen S. Marlowe, the respondent herein. By the terms of said policy, appellant agreed to pay to the insured certain hospital expenses incurred by her.

The respondent instituted this action alleging that while the aforesaid policy was in full force and effect she was hospitalized in Duke Hospital, in Durham, North Carolina, there receiving medical treatment from May 19, 1970, until May 28, 1970. She alleges that she has filed a claim for the benefits due her under said policy and the appellant has refused to pay said claim.

The appellant, by answer, * * * refused to pay the claim upon the ground that there were misrepresentations in the application of the respondent as to her medical history, which was relied upon by it, such being material to the risk involved and had the truth been known the policy would not have been issued and it has elected to rescind said policy of insurance and declare same null and void from its inception.

The facts in this case are undisputed. The respondent contacted an agent of New York Life Insurance Company for the purpose of purchasing hospital insurance coverage for herself and her children. This agent informed her that his company could not insure her in view of her medical history, but he agreed to contact an agent of another company which might possibly provide coverage. Shortly thereafter, one John Rouse, an agent of the appellant, contacted her by telephone and made an appointment with her for January 7, 1970, at her home. * * * The application

was filled out by the agent himself while asking the respondent questions with respect to the medical history portion of the application. She told the agent that her medical history was so long that she could not remember it all but if he would inquire of Dr. Shingleton at Duke Hospital and Dr. Smith of Conway, South Carolina, they could make such history available to him.

The respondent testified that her application for hospital insurance was filled out by the agent of the appellant and that she made no entries thereon except the affixation of her signature on the bottom line thereof. She was then asked, "Did you read the application as completed before you signed it?", and her answer thereto was, "No sir, he didn't offer it to me. He just asked me to sign it, and he asked me for a check, and I told him I felt sure he was wasting his time."

The policy in question was delivered to the respondent by mail and when asked if she read it she replied, "No sir, because he (the agent) told me what it would be and I can tell you now."

* * *

The general rule is that the knowledge of an agent acquired within the scope of his agency is imputable to his principal, and if an insurance company, at the inception of the contract of insurance has knowledge of facts which render the policy void at its option, and the company delivers the policy as a valid policy, it is estopped to assert such ground of forfeiture. * * * [Citations.]

The appellant admits that if the foregoing rule was applicable it would be estopped to rescind the contract by reason of misrepresentations in the application. However, the appellant contends that the soliciting agent, Rouse, had no authority to waive any of the appellant's rights by reason of the above quoted limitation contained in the application and that the insured was bound by such.

The rule in this State is that an insurance company cannot set up forfeiture on account of facts known by the agent of the company to be existing at the time of the making of the contract. A provision limiting the power of an agent has no sacrosanct character over any other provision, and like all of them is itself subject to waiver by the company. [Citation.]

* * *

When an agent of an insurance company, who fills out an application for an insurance policy, is duly informed of the facts and fails to state them in the application, the actual knowledge of the agent will be held to be the knowledge of the company, where there is good faith on the part of the applicant. [Citation.]

* * *

We conclude that where the insured, acting in good faith, makes truthful answers to the application questions, but those answers are incorrectly transcribed by reason of the fraud, mistake, or negligence of the insurer's soliciting agent, the insurer is estopped to set up the omissions in or the falsity of such answers, even though there is a limitation on such agent's authority in the application.

* * *

Affirmed.

PROBLEMS

1. Lile, an insurance broker, handled all insurance for X Co. Lile purchased a fire policy from Insurance Company insuring X Co.'s factory against fire in the amount of $150,000. Before the policy was delivered to X Co. and while it was in Lile's hands, X Co. advised Lile to cancel the policy. Prior to cancellation, X Co. suffered a loss and makes claim against Insurance Company on the policy. The premium had been billed to Lile but was unpaid at the time of loss. In an action by X Co. against Insurance Company, what judgment?

2. On July 15, A purchased in Chicago a Buick Sedan intending to drive it that day to St. Louis, Missouri. He telephoned a friend X who was in the insurance business and told him that he wished liability insurance on the automobile, limited in amount to $50,000 for injuries to one person and $100,000 for any one accident. X took the order and told A over the telephone that he was covered and that his policy would be written by the Y Insurance Company. Later that same day and before X had informed the Y Insurance Company of A's application, A negligently operated the automobile and seriously injured B who brings suit against A. Is A covered by liability insurance?

3. A owns a building having a fair market value of $120,000. She takes out a fire insurance policy from the B Insurance Company for $72,000, the policy contains an 80 percent co-insurance clause. The building is damaged by fire to the extent of $48,000. How much insurance is A entitled to collect?

4. The B Automobile Insurance Company issues to A, owner of a Mercury automobile, a liability policy, $30,000–$60,000 limits. On April 3, as the result of A's negligent operation of his car, C, D, and E are injured in a collision. C, D, and E sue A and recover judgments of $45,000, $9,000, and $6,000, respectively. To what extent is the B Company liable?

5. Arthur Heartburn, having knowledge of a bad heart condition, arranges to have his friend, Ira Impostor, represent himself as Heartburn to the medical examiner of the Taken Life Insurance Company. Impostor, posing as Heartburn, is found to be physically sound, and the Insurance Company issues a $75,000 life insurance policy to Heartburn. The policy contains a two-year incontestable clause. Twenty-six months after the issuance of the policy Heartburn suffers a heart attack and dies. Before paying off the claim of Heartburn's widow, the beneficiary under the policy, the Insurance Company learns about Impostor's actions in helping Heartburn procure the policy. When the Taken Insurance Company refuses to pay the claim, the widow files suit on the policy. Decision?

6. Wiley, an insurance salesman, induces Glutz to purchase a $60,000 life insurance policy on the life of his best friend Doe and at the same time sells a policy to Doe insuring Glutz's life. After ten years Doe dies, and on due proof of death the insurance company denies liability. Glutz sues the company. Decision?

7. Kay was issued a $30,000 life insurance policy by Atlantic Bell Life Insurance Company. In her application Kay truthfully warranted that she was a professional actress and that she was not engaged in the employ of a railroad company or an airplane company. The policy provided that the company insured "the life of Kay so long as she engaged solely in the business of a professional actress." The policy also provided:

This policy shall be incontestable for any cause after it shall have been in force during the life of the insured for two years from its date.

After the policy had been in effect for three years, Kay was killed while employed as a brakeman by a railroad company. Kay was so employed without the knowledge and consent of the insurance company. The beneficiary of the policy sued the company to recover the face amount of the policy. The company defended, denying liability on the ground that Kay was employed by a railroad company at the time of her death and had been so employed for six months previously. Decision?

8. Paul Poe purchased a life insurance policy in the sum of $100,000. The policy provided: "The proceeds of this policy are payable upon the death of the insured to Penelope Poe, wife of the in-

sured." The policy also provided that Poe had the right to change the name of the beneficiary. Four years after the policy had been purchased, Poe obtained a divorce from his wife, Penelope. One year later, Poe married Dora Doe, and this marriage continued until Poe's death two years later. At Poe's death the policy remained in its original form. Penelope demanded that the insurance company pay her the proceeds of the policy. Upon its refusal, she brought an action against the company to recover $100,000. Decision?

9. Day had for some time been seeking out Short to "teach him a lesson" for taking out Day's girlfriend, and Day carried a pistol for this purpose. Eventually, Day caught up with Short at a local beer parlor and without warning, fired a shot at Short. Day's aim was not too good, for the shot only creased Short's head. Short dove at Day, and a scuffle ensued. During the scuffle Day fell to the floor, hitting his head upon the bar railing. As a direct result of this blow to his head, Day died. At the time of his death, Day had in effect a policy of accidental death insurance in which the insurance company had agreed to pay the named beneficiary, Day's mother, $70,000 upon the death of Day if the death were "effected solely through external, violent, and accidental means." The insurance company refused to pay the beneficiary. What are the beneficiary's rights, if any?

Appendix A

THE CONSTITUTION OF THE UNITED STATES OF AMERICA

We the People of the United States, in Order to form a more perfect Union, establish Justice, insure domestic Tranquility, provide for the common defense, promote the general Welfare, and secure the Blessings of Liberty to ourselves and our Posterity, do ordain and establish this Constitution for the United States of America.

Article I

Section 1

All legislative Powers herein granted shall be vested in a Congress of the United States, which shall consist of a Senate and House of Representatives.

Section 2

The House of Representatives shall be composed of Members chosen every second Year by the People of the several States, and the Electors in each State shall have the Qualifications requisite for Electors of the most numerous Branch of the State Legislature.

No Person shall be a Representative who shall not have attained to the Age of twenty five Years, and been seven Years a Citizen of the United States, and who shall not, when elected, be an Inhabitant of that State in which he shall be chosen.

Representatives and direct Taxes shall be apportioned among the several States which may be included within this Union, according to their respective Numbers, which shall be determined by adding to the whole Number of free Persons, including those bound to Service for a Term of Years, and excluding Indians not taxed, three fifths of all other Persons. The actual Enumeration shall be made within three Years after the first Meeting of the Congress of the United States, and within every subsequent Term of ten Years, in such Manner as they shall by Law direct. The number of Representatives shall not exceed one for every thirty Thousand, but each State shall have at Least one Representative; and until such enumeration shall be made, the State of New Hampshire shall be entitled to chuse three, Massachusetts eight, Rhode Island and Povidence Plantations one, Connecticut five, New-York six, New Jersey four, Pennsylvania eight, Delaware one, Maryland six, Virginia ten, North Carolina five, South Craolina five, and Georgia three.

When vacancies happen in the Representation from any State, the Executive Authority thereof shall issue Writs of Election to fill such vacancies.

The House of Representatives shall chuse their Speaker and other Officers; and shall have the sole Power of Impeachment.

Section 3

The Senate of the United States shall be composed of two Senators from each State, chosen by the Legislature thereof, for six Years; and each Senator shall have one Vote.

Immediately after they shall be assembled in Consequence of the first Election, they shall be divided as equally as may be into three Classes. The Seats of the Senators of the first Class shall be vacated at the Expiration of the second Year, of the second Class at the Expiration of the fourth Year, and of the third Class at the Expiration of the sixth Year, so that one third may be chosen every second Year; and if Vacancies happen by Resignation, or otherwise, during the Recess of the Legislature of any State, the Executive thereof may make temporary Appointments until the next Meeting of the Legislature, which shall then fill such Vacancies.

No Person shall be a Senator who shall not have attained to the Age of thirty Years, and been nine Years a Citizen of the United States, and who shall not, when elected, be an Inhabitant of that State for which he shall be chosen.

The Vice President of the United States shall be President of the Senate, but shall have no Vote, unless they be equally divided.

The Senate shall chuse their other Officers, and also a President pro tempore, in the Absence of the Vice President, or when he shall exercise the Office of President of the United States.

The Senate shall have the sole power to try all Impeachments. When sitting for that Purpose, they shall be an Oath or Affirmation. When the President of the United States is tried, the Chief Justice shall preside: And no Person shall be convicted without the Concurrence of two thirds of the Members present.

Judgment in Cases of Impeachment shall not extend further than to removal from Office, and disqualification to hold and enjoy any Office of honor, Trust or Profit under the United States: but the Party convicted shall nevertheless be liable and subject to Indictment, Trial, Judgment and Punishment, according to Law.

Section 4

The Times, Places and Manner of holding Elections for Senators and Representatives, shall be prescribed in each State by the Legislature thereof: but the Congress may at any time by Law make or alter such Regulations, except as to the Places of chusing Senators.

The Congress shall assemble at least once in every Year, and such Meeting shall be on the first Monday in December, unless they shall by Law appoint a different Day.

Section 5

Each House shall be the Judge of the Elections, Returns and Qualifications of its own Members, and a Majority of each shall constitute a Quorum to do Business; but a smaller Number may adjourn from day to day, and may be authorized to compel the Attendance of absent Members, in such Manner, and under such Penalties as each House may provide.

Each House may determine the Rules of its Proceedings, punish its Members for disorderly Behaviour, and, with the Concurrence of two thirds, expel a Member.

Each House shall keep a Journal of its Proceedings, and from time to time publish the same, excepting such Parts as may in their Judgment require Secrecy; and the Yeas and Nays of the Members of either House on any question shall, at the Desire of one fifth of those Present, be entered on the Journal.

Neither House, during the Session of Congress, shall, without the Consent of the other, adjourn for more than three days, nor to any other Place than that in which the two Houses shall be sitting.

Section 6

The Senators and Representatives shall receive a Compensation for their Services, to be ascertained by Law, and paid out of the Treasury of the United States. They shall in all Cases, except Treason, Felony and Breach of the Peace, be privileged from Arrest during their Attendance at the Session of their respective Houses, and in going to and returning from the same; and for any Speech or Debate in either House, they shall not be questioned in any other Place.

No Senator or Representative shall, during the Time for which he was elected, be appointed to any civil Office under the Authority of the United States, which shall have been created, or the Emoluments whereof shall have been encreased during such time; and no Person holding any Office under the United States, shall be a Member of either House during his Continuance in Office.

Section 7

All Bills for raising Revenue shall originate in the House of Representatives; but the Senate may propose or concur with Amendments as on other Bills.

Every Bill which shall have passed the House of Representatives and the Senate, shall, before it become a Law, be presented to the President of the United States; If he approve he shall sign it, but if not he shall return it, with his Objections to that House in which it shall have originated, who shall enter the Objections at large on their Journal, and proceed to reconsider it. If after such Reconsideration two thirds of that House shall agree to pass the Bill, it shall be sent, together with the Objections, to the other House, by which it shall likewise be reconsidered, and if approved by two thirds of that House, it shall become a Law. But in all such Cases the Votes of both Houses shall be determined by Yeas and Nays, and the Names of the Persons voting for and against the Bill shall be entered on the Journal of each House respectively. If any Bill shall not be returned by the President within ten Days (Sundays excepted) after it shall have been presented to him, the Same shall be a Law, in like Manner as if he had signed it, unless the Congress by their Adjournment prevent its Return, in which Case it shall not be a Law.

Every Order, Resolution, or Vote to which the Concurrence of the Senate and House of Representatives may be necessary (except on a question of Adjournment) shall be presented to the President of the United States; and before the Same shall take Effect, shall be approved by him, or being disapproved by him, shall be repassed by two thirds of the Senate and House of Representatives, according to the Rules and Limitations prescribed in the Case of a Bill.

Section 8

The Congress shall have Power to lay and collect Taxes, Duties, Imposts and Excises, to pay the Debts and provide for the common Defence and general Welfare of the United States; but all Duties, Imposts and Excises shall be uniform throughout the United States;

To borrow Money on the credit of the United States;

To regulate Commerce with foreign Nations, and among the several States, and with the Indian Tribes;

To establish an uniform Rule of Naturalization, and uniform Laws on the subject of Bankruptcies throughout the United States;

To coin Money, regulate the Value thereof, and of foreign Coin, and fix the Standard of Weights and Measures;

To provide for the Punishment of counterfeiting the Securities and current Coin of the United States;

To establish Post Offices and post Roads;

To promote the Progress of Science and useful Arts, by securing for limited Times to Authors and Inventors the exclusive Right to their respective Writings and Discoveries;

To constitute Tribunals inferior to the supreme Court;

To define and punish Piracies and Felonies committed on the high Seas, and Offenses against the Law of Nations;

To declare War, grant Letters of Marque and Reprisal, and make Rules concerning Captures on Land and Water;

To raise and support Armies, but no Appropriation of Money to that Use shall be for a longer Term than two Years;

To provide and maintain a Navy;

To make Rules for the Government and Regulation of the land and naval Forces;

To provide for calling forth the Militia to execute the Laws of the Union, suppress Insurrections and repel Invasions;

To provide for organizing, arming, and disciplining, the Militia, and for governing such Part of them as may be employed in the Service of the United States, reserving to the States respectively, the Appointment of the Officers, and the Authority of training the Militia according to the discipline described by Congress;

To exercise exclusive Legislation in all Cases whatsoever, over such District (not exceeding ten Miles square) as may, by Cession of particular States, and the Acceptance of Congress, become the Seat of the Government of the United States, and to exercise like Authority over all Places purchased by the Consent of the Legislature of the State in which the Same shall be, for the Erection of Forts, Magazines, Arsenals, dock-Yards, and other needful Buildings;—And

To make all Laws which shall be necessary and proper for carrying into Execution the foregoing Powers, and all other Powers vested by this Constitution in the Government of the United States, or in any Department or Officer thereof.

Section 9

The Migration or Importation of such Persons as any of the States now existing shall think proper to admit, shall not be prohibited by the Congress prior to the Year one thousand eight hundred and eight, but a Tax or Duty may be imposed on such Importation, not exceeding ten dollars for each Person.

The Privilege of the Writ of Habeas Corpus shall not be suspended, unless when in Cases of Rebellion or Invasion the public Safety may require it.

No Bill of Attainder or ex post facto Law shall be passed.

No Capitation, or other direct, Tax shall be laid, unless in Proportion to the Census or Enumeration herein before directed to be taken.

No Tax or Duty shall be laid on Articles exported from any State.

No Preference shall be given by any Regulation of Commerce or Revenue to the Ports of one State over those of another; nor shall Vessels bound to, or from, one State, be obliged to enter, clear, or pay Duties in another.

No Money shall be drawn from the Treasury, but in Consequence of Appropriations made by Laws; and a regular Statement and Account of the Receipts and Expenditures of all public Money shall be published from time to time.

No Title of Nobility shall be granted by the United States: And no Person holding any Office of Profit or Trust under them, shall, without the Consent of the Congress, accept of any present, Emolument, Office, or Title, of any kind whatever, from any King, Prince, or foreign State.

Section 10

No State shall enter into any Treaty, Alliance, or Confederation; grant Letters of Marque and Reprisal; coin Money; emit Bills of Credit; make any Thing but gold and silver Coin a Tender in Payment of Debts; pass any Bill of Attainder, ex post facto Law, or Law impairing the Obligation of Contracts, or grant any Title of Nobility.

No State shall, without the Consent of the Congress, lay any Imposts or Duties on Imports or Exports, except what may be absolutely necessary for executing its inspection Laws: and the net Produce of all Duties and Imposts, laid by any State on Imports or Exports, shall be for the Use of the Treasury of the United States; and all such Laws shall be subject to the Revision and Controul of the Congress.

No State shall, without the Consent of Congress, lay any Duty of Tonnage, keep Troops, or Ships of War in time of Peace, enter into any Agreement or Compact with another State, or with a foreign Power, or engage in War, unless actually invaded, or in such imminent Danger as will not admit of delay.

Article II

Section 1

The executive Power shall be vested in a President of the United States of America. He shall hold his Office during the Term of four Years, and, together with the Vice President, chosen for the same Term, be elected, as follows:

Each State shall appoint, in such Manner as the Legislature thereof may direct, a Number of Electors, equal to the whole Number of Senators and Representatives to which the State may be entitled in the Congress: but no Senator or Representative, or Person holding an Office of Trust or Profit under the United States, shall be appointed an Elector.

The Electors shall meet in their respective States, and vote by Ballot for two Persons, of whom one at least shall not be an Inhabitant of the same State with themselves. And they shall make a list of all the Persons voted for, and of the Number of Votes for each; which List they shall sign and certify, and transmit sealed to the Seat of the Government of the United States, directed to the President of the Senate. The President of the Senate shall, in the presence of the Senate and House of Representatives, open all the Certificates, and the Votes shall be counted. The Person having the greatest Number of Votes shall be the President, if such Number be a Majority of the whole Number of Electors appointed; and if there be more than one who have such Majority, and have an equal Number of Votes, then the House of Representatives shall immediately chuse by Ballot one of them for President; and if no Person have a Majority, then from the five highest on the List the said House shall in like Manner chuse the President. But in chusing the President, the Votes shall be taken by States, the Representation from each State having one Vote; A quorum for this Purpose shall consist of a Member or Members from two thirds of the States, and a Majority of all the States shall be necessary to a Choice. In every Case, after the Choice of the President, the Person having the greatest Number of Votes of the Electors shall be the Vice President. But if there should remain two or more who have equal Votes, the Senate shall chuse from them by Ballot the Vice President.

The Congress may determine the Time of Chusing the Electors, and the Day on which they shall give their Votes; which Day shall be the same throughout the United States.

No Person except a natural born Citizen, or a Citizen of the United States, at the time of the Adoption of this Constitution, shall be eligible to the Office of President; neither shall any Person be eligible to that Office who shall not have attained to the Age of thirty five Years, and been fourteen Years a Resident within the United States.

In Case of the Removal of the President from Office, or of his Death, Resignation, or Inability to discharge the Powers and Duties of the said Office, the Same shall devolve on the Vice President, and the Congress may by Law provide for the Case of Removal, Death, Resignation or Inability, both of the President and Vice President, declaring what Officer shall then act as President, and such Officer shall act accordingly, until the Disability be removed, or a President shall be elected.

The President shall, at stated Times, receive for his Services, a Compensation, which shall neither be encreased nor diminished during the Period for which he shall have been elected, and he shall not receive within that Period any other Emolument from the United States, or any of them.

Before he enter on the Execution of his Office, he shall take the following Oath or Affirmation:—"I do solemnly swear (or affirm) that I will faithfully execute the Office of President of the United States, and will to the best of my Ability, preserve, protect and defend the Constitution of the United States."

Section 2

The President shall be Commander in Chief of the Army and Navy of the United States, and of the Militia of the several States, when called into the actual Service of the United States; he may require the Opinion, in writing, of the principal Officer in each of the executive Departments, upon any Subject relating to the Duties of their respective Offices, and he shall have Power to grant Reprieves and Pardons for Offences against the United States, except in Cases of Impeachment.

He shall have Power, by and with the Advice and Consent of the Senate, to make Treaties, providing two thirds of the Senators present concur; and he shall nominate, and by and with the Advice and Consent of the Senate, shall appoint Ambassadors, other public Ministers and Consuls, Judges of the supreme Court, and all other Officers of the United States, whose Appointments are not herein otherwise provided for, and which shall be established by Law: but the Congress may by Law vest the Appointment of such inferior Officers, as they think proper, in the President alone, in the Courts of Law, or in the Heads of Departments.

The President shall have Power to fill up all Vacancies that may happen during the Recess of the Senate, by granting Commissions which shall expire at the End of their next Session.

Section 3

He shall from time to time give to the Congress Information of the State of the Union, and recommend to their Consideration such Measures as he shall judge necessary and expedient; he may, on extraordinary Occasions, convene both Houses, or either of them, and in Case of Disagreement between them, with Respect to the Time of Adjournment, he may adjourn them to such Time as he shall think proper, he shall receive Ambassadors and other public Ministers; he shall take Care that the Laws be faithfully executed, and shall Commission all the Offices of the United States.

Section 4

The President, Vice President and all civil Officers of the United States, shall be removed from Office on Impeachment for, and Conviction of, Treason, Bribery, or other high Crimes and Misdemeanors.

Article III

Section 1

The judicial Power of the United States, shall be vested in one supreme Court, and in such inferior Courts as the Congress may from time to time ordain and establish. The Judges, both of the supreme and inferior Courts, shall hold their Offices during good Behaviour, and shall, at Times, receive for their Services, a Compensation, which shall not be diminished during their Continuance in Office.

Section 2

The judicial Power shall extend to all Cases, in Law and Equity, arising under this Constitution, the Laws of the United States, and Treaties made, or which shall be made, under their Authority;—to all Cases affecting Ambassadors, other public Ministers and Consuls;—to all Cases of admirality and maritime Jurisdiction;—to Controversies to which the United States shall be a Party;—to Controversies between two or more States;—between a State and Citizens of another State;—between Citizens of different States;—between Citizens of the same State claiming Lands under Grants of different States; and between a State, or the Citizens thereof, and foreign States, Citizens or Subjects.

In all Cases affecting Ambassadors, other public Ministers and Consuls, and those in which a State shall be Party, the supreme Court shall have original Jurisdiction. In all the other Cases before mentioned, the supreme Court shall have appellate Jurisdiction, both as to Law and Fact, with such Exceptions, and under such Regulations as the Congress shall make.

The Trial of all Crimes, except in Cases of Impeachment, shall be by Jury; and such Trial shall be held in the State where the said Crimes shall have been committed; but when not committed within any State, the Trial shall be at such Place or Places as the Congress may by Law have directed.

Section 3

Treason against the United States, shall consist only in levying War against them, or in adhering to their Enemies, giving them Aid and Comfort. No Person shall be convicted of Treason unless on the Testimony of two Witnesses to the same overt Act, or on Confession in open Court.

The Congress shall have Power to declare the Punishment of Treason, but no Attainder of Treason shall work Corruption of Blood, or Forfeiture except during the Life of the Person attainted.

Article IV

Section 1

Full Faith and Credit shall be given in each State to the public Acts, Records, and judicial Proceedings of every other State. And the Congress may by general Laws prescribe the Manner in which such Arts, Records and Proceedings shall be proved, and the Effect thereof.

Section 2

The Citizens of each State shall be entitled to all Privileges and Immunities of Citizens in the several States.

A Person charged in any State with Treason, Felony, or other Crime, who shall flee from Justice, and be found in another State, shall on Demand of the executive Authority of the State from which he fled, be delivered up, to be removed to the State having Jurisdiction of the Crime.

No Person held to Service or Labour in one State, under the Laws thereof, escaping into another, shall, in Consequence of any Law or Regulation therein, be discharged from such Service or Labour, but shall be delivered up on Claim of the Party to whom such Service or Labour may be due.

Section 3

New States may be admitted by the Congress into this Union; but no new State shall be formed or erected within the Jurisdiction of any other State; nor any State be formed by the Junction of two or more States, or Parts of States, without the Consent of the Legislatures of the States concerned as well as the Congress.

The Congress shall have Power to dispose of and make all needful Rules and Regulations respecting the Territory or other Property belonging to the United States; and nothing in this Constitution shall be so construed as to Prejudice any Claims of the United States, or of any particular State.

Section 4

The United States shall guarantee to every State in this Union a Republican Form of Government, and shall protect each of them against Invasion; and on Application of the Legislature, or of the Executive (when the Legislature cannot be convened) against domestic Violence.

Article V

The Congress, whenever two thirds of both Houses shall deem it necessary, shall propose Amendments to this Constitution, or, on the Application of the Legislatures of two thirds of the several States, shall call a Convention for proposing Amendments, which, in either Case, shall be valid to all Intents and Purposes, as Part of this Constitution, when ratified by the Legislatures of three fourths of the several States, or by Conventions in three fourths thereof, as the one or the other Mode of Ratification may be proposed by the Congress; Provided that no Amendment which may be made prior to the Year One thousand eight hundred and eight shall in any Manner affect the first and fourth Clauses in the Ninth Section of the first Article; and that no State, without its Consent, shall be deprived of its equal Suffrage in the Senate.

Article VI

All Debts contracted and Engagements entered into, before the Adoption of this Constitution, shall be as valid against the United States under this Constitution, as under the Confederation.

This Constitution, and the Laws of the United States which shall be made in Pursuance thereof; and all Treaties made, or which shall be made, under the Authority of the United States, shall be the supreme Law of the Land; and the Judges in every State shall be bound thereby, any Thing in the Constitution or Laws of any State to the Contrary notwithstanding.

The Senators and Representatives before mentioned, and the Members of the several State Legislatures, and all executive and judicial Officers, both of the United States and of the Several States, shall be bound by Oath or Affirmation, to support this Constitution; but no religious Test shall ever be required as a Qualification to any Office or public Trust under the United States.

Article VII

The Ratification of the Conventions of nine States, shall be sufficient for the Establishment of this Constitution between the States so ratifying the Same.

Amendment I [1791]

Congress shall make no law respecting an establishment of religion, or prohibiting the free exercise thereof; or abridging the freedom of speech, or the press; or the right of the people peaceably to assemble, and to petition the Government for a redress of grievances.

Amendment II [1791]

A well regulated Militia, being necessary to the security for a free State, the right of the people to keep and bear Arms, shall not be infringed.

Amendment III [1791]

No Soldier shall, in time of peace be quartered in any house, without the consent of the Owner, nor in time of war, but in a manner to be prescribed by law.

Amendment IV [1791]

The right of the people to be secure in their persons, houses, papers, and effects, against unreasonable searches and seizures, shall not be violated, and no Warrants shall issue, but upon probable cause, supported by Oath or affirmation, and particularly describing the place to be searched, and the persons or things to be seized.

Amendment V [1791]

No person shall be held to answer for a capital, or otherwise infamous crime, unless on a presentment or indictment of a Grand Jury, except in cases arising in the land or naval forces, or in the Militia, when in actual service in time of War or public danger; nor shall any person be subject for the same offense to be twice put in jeopardy of life or limb; nor shall be compelled in any criminal case to be a witness against himself, nor be deprived of life, liberty, or property, without due process of law; nor shall private property be taken for public use, without just compensation.

Amendment VI [1791]

In all criminal prosecutions, the accused shall enjoy the right to a speedy and public trial, by an impartial jury of the State and district wherein the crime shall have been committed, which district shall have been previously ascertained by law, and to be informed of the nature and cause of the accusation; to be confronted with the Witnesses against him; to have compulsory process for obtaining witnesses in his favor, and to have the Assistance of counsel for his defence.

Amendment VII [1791]

In suits at common law, where the value in controversy shall exceed twenty dollars, the right of trial by jury shall be preserved, and no fact tried by a jury, shall be otherwise re-examined in any Court of the United States, than according to the rules of the common law.

Amendment VIII [1791]

Excessive bail shall not be required, no excessive fines imposed, nor cruel and unusual punishments inflicted.

Amendment IX [1791]

The enumeration in the Constitution, of certain rights, shall not be construed to deny or disparage others retained by the people.

Amendment X [1791]

The powers not delegated to the United States by the Constitution, nor prohibited by it to the States, are reserved to the States respectively, or to the people.

Amendment XI [1798]

The judicial power of the United States shall not be construed to extend to any suit in law or equity, commenced or prosecuted against one of the United States by Citizens of another State, or by Citizens or Subjects of any Foreign State.

Amendment XII [1804]

The Electors shall meet in their respective states and vote by ballot for President and Vice-Presi-

dent, one of whom, at least, shall not be an inhabitant of the same state with themselves; they shall name in their ballots the person voted for as President, and in distinct ballots the person voted for as Vice-President, and they shall make distinct lists of all persons voted for as President, and of all persons voted for as Vice-President, and of the number of votes for each, which lists they shall sign and certify, and transmit sealed to the seat of the government of the United States, directed to the President of the Senate;—The President of the Senate shall, in the presence of the Senate and House of Representatives, open all the certificates and the votes shall then be counted;—The person having the greatest number of votes for President, shall be the President, if such number be a majority of the whole number of Electors appointed; and if no person have such majority, then from the persons having the highest numbers not exceeding three on the list of those voted for as President, the House of Representatives shall choose immediately, by ballot, the President. But in choosing the President, the votes shall be taken by states, the representation from each state having one vote; a quorum for this purpose shall consist of a member or members from two-thirds of the states, and a majority of all the states shall be necessary to a choice. And if the House of Representatives shall not choose a President whenever the right of choice shall devolve upon them, before the fourth day of March next following, then the Vice-President shall act as President, as in the case of the death of other constitutional disability of the President. The person having the greatest number of votes as Vice-President, shall be the Vice-President, if such number be a majority of the whole number of Electors appointed, and if no person have a majority, then from the two highest numbers on the list, the Senate shall choose the Vice-President; a quorum for the purpose shall consist of two-thirds of the whole number of Senators, and a majority of the whole number shall be necessary to a choice. But no person constitutionally ineligible to the office of President shall be eligible to that of the Vice-President of the United States.

Amendment XIII [1865]

Section 1

Neither slavery nor involuntary servitude, except as a punishment for crime whereof the party shall have been duly convicted, shall exist within the United States, or any place subject to their jurisdiction.

Section 2

Congress shall have power to enforce this article by appropriate legislation.

Amendment XIV [1868]

All persons born or naturalized in the United States, and subject to the jurisdiction thereof, are citizens of the United States and of the State wherein they reside. No State shall make or enforce any law which shall abridge the privileges or immunities of citizens of the United States; nor shall any State deprive any person of life, liberty, or property, without due process of law; nor deny to any person within its jurisdiction the equal protection of the laws.

Section 2

Representatives shall be appointed among the several States according to their respective numbers, counting the whole number of persons in each State, excluding Indians not taxed. But when the right to vote at any election for the choice of electors for President and Vice President of the United States, Representatives in Congress, the Executive and Judicial officers of a State, or the members of the Legislature thereof, is denied to any of the male inhabitants of such State, being twenty-one years of age, and citizens of the United States, or in any way abridged, except for participation in rebellion, or other crime, the basis of representation therein shall be reduced in the proportion which the number of such male citizens shall bear the whole number of male citizens twenty-one years of age in such State.

Section 3

No person shall be a Senator or Representative in Congress, or elector of President and Vice President, or hold any office, civil or military, under the United States, or under any State, who, having previously taken an oath, as a member of Congress, or as an officer of the United States, or as a member of any State legislature, or as an executive or judicial officer of any State, to support the Constitution of the United States, shall have engaged in insurrection or rebellion against the same, or given aid or comfort to the enemies thereof. But Congress may by a vote of two-thirds of each House, remove such disability.

Section 4

The validity of the public debt of the United States, authorized by law, including debts incurred for payment of pensions and bounties for services in suppressing insurrection or rebellion, shall not be questioned. But neither the United States nor any State shall assume or pay any debt or obligation incurred in aid of insurrection of rebellion against the United States, or any claim for the loss or emancipation of any slave; but all such debts, obligations and claims shall be held illegal and void.

Section 5

The Congress shall have power to enforce, by appropriate legislation, the provisions of this article.

Amendment XV [1870]

Section 1

The right of citizens of the United States to vote shall not be denied or abridged by the United States or by any State on account of race, color, or previous condition of servitude.

Section 2

The Congress shall have power to enforce this article by appropriate legislation.

Amendment XVI [1913]

The Congress shall have power to lay and collect taxes on incomes, from whatever source derived, without apportionment among the several States, and without regard to any census or enumeration.

Amendment XVII [1913]

The Senate of the United States shall be composed of two Senators from each State, elected by the people thereof, for six years; and each Senator shall have one vote. The electors in each State shall have the qualifications requisite for electors of the most numerous branch of the State legislatures.

When vacancies happen in the representation of any State in the Senate, the executive authority of each State shall issue writs of election to fill such vacancies; *Provided*, That the legislature of any State may empower the executive thereof to make temporary appointments until the people fill the vacancies by election as the legislature may direct.

This amendment shall not be construed as to affect the election or term of any Senator chosen before it becomes valid as part of the Constitution.

Amendment XVIII [1919]

Section 1

After one year from the ratification of this article the manufacture, sale, or transportation of intoxicating liquors within, the importation thereof into, or the exportation thereof from the United States and all territory subject to the jurisdiction thereof for beverage purposes is hereby prohibited.

Section 2

The Congress and the several States shall have concurrent power to enforce this article by appropriate legislation.

Section 3

This article shall be inoperative unless it shall have been ratified as an amendment to the Constitution by the legislatures of the several States, as provided in the Constitution, within seven years from the date of the submission hereof to the States by the Congress.

Amendment XIX [1920]

The right of citizens of the United States to vote shall not be denied or abridged by the United States or by any State on account of sex.

Congress shall have power to enforce this article by appropriate legislation.

Amendment XX [1933]

Section 1

The terms of the President and Vice President shall end at noon on the 20th day of January, and the terms of Senators and Representatives at noon on the 3d day of January, of the years in which such terms would have ended if this article had not been ratified; and the terms of their successors shall then begin.

Section 2

The Congress shall assemble at least once in every year, and such meeting shall begin at noon on the 3d day of January, unless they shall by law appoint a different day.

Section 3

If, at the time fixed for the beginning of the term of the President, the President elect shall have died, the Vice President elect shall become President. If a President shall not have been chosen before the time fixed for the beginning of his term, or if the President elect shall have failed to qualify, then the Vice President elect shall act as President until a President shall have qualified; and the Congress may by law provide for the case wherein neither a President elect nor a Vice President elect shall have qualified, declaring who shall then act as President, or the manner in which one who is to act shall be selected, and such person shall act accordingly until a President or Vice President shall have qualified.

Section 4

The Congress may by law provide for the case of the death of any of the persons from whom the House of Representatives may choose a President whenever the right of choice shall have devolved upon them, and for the case of the death of any of the persons from whom the Senate may choose a Vice President whenever the right of choice shall have devolved upon them.

Section 5

Sections 1 and 2 shall take effect on the 15th day of October following the ratification of this article.

Section 6

This article shall be inoperative unless it shall have been ratified as an amendment to the Constitution by the legislatures of three-fourths of the several States within seven years from the date of its submission.

Amendment XXI [1933]

Section 1

The eighteenth article of amendment to the Constitution of the United States is hereby repealed.

Section 2

The transportation or importation into any State, Territory, or possession of the United States for delivery or use therein of intoxicating liquors, in violation of the laws thereof, is hereby prohibited.

Section 3

This article shall be inoperative unless it shall have been ratified as an amendment to the Constitution by conventions in the several States, as provided in the Constitution, within seven years from the date of the submission hereof to the States by the Congress.

Amendment XXII [1951]

Section 1

No person shall be elected to the office of the President more than twice, and no person who has held the office of President, or acted as President, for more than two years of a term to which some other person was elected President shall be elected to the office of the President more than once. But this Article shall not apply to any person holding the office of President when this Article was proposed by the Congress, and shall not prevent any person who may be holding the office of President, or acting as President, during the term within which this Article becomes operative from holding the office of President or acting as President during the remainder of such term.

Section 2

This article shall be inoperative unless it shall have been ratified as an amendment to the Constitution by the legislatures of three-fourths of the several States within seven years from the date of its submission to the States by the Congress.

Amendment XXIII [1961]

Section 1

The District constituting the seat of Government of the United States shall appoint in such manner as the Congress may direct:

A number of electors of President and Vice President equal to the whole number of Senators and Representatives in Congress to which the District would be entitled if it were a State, but in no event more than the least populous State; they shall be in addition to those appointed by the States, but they shall be considered, for the purposes of the election of President and Vice President, to be electors appointed by a State; and they shall meet in the District and perform such duties as provided by the twelfth article of amendment.

Section 2

The Congress shall have power to enforce this article by appropriate legislation.

Amendment XXIV [1964]

Section 1

The right of citizens of the United States to vote in any primary or other election for President or Vice President, for electors for President or Vice President, or for Sentor or Representative in Congress, shall not be denied or abridged by the United States or any State by reason of failure to pay any poll tax or other tax.

Section 2

The Congress shall have power to enforce this article by appropriate legislation.

Amendment XXV [1967]

Section 1

In case of the removal of the President from office or of his death or resignation, the Vice President shall become President.

Section 2

Whenever there is a vacancy in the office of the Vice President, the President shall nominate a Vice President who shall take office upon confirmation by a majority vote of both Houses of Congress.

Section 3

Whenever the President transmits to the President pro tempore of the Senate and the Speaker of the House of Representatives his written declaration that he is unable to discharge the powers and duties of his office, and until he transmits to them a written declaration to the contrary, such powers and duties shall be discharged by the Vice President as Acting President.

Section 4

Whenever the Vice President and a majority of either the principal officers of the executive departments or of such other body as Congress may by law provide, transmit to the President pro tempore of the Senate and the Speaker of the House of Representatives their written declaration that the President is unable to discharge the powers and duties of his office, the Vice President shall immediately assume the powers and duties of the office as Acting President.

Thereafter, when the President transmits to the President pro tempore of the Senate and the Speaker of the House of Representatives his written declaration that no inability exists, he shall resume the powers and duties of his office unless the Vice President and a majority of either the principal officers of the executive department or of such other body as Congress may by law provide, transmit within four days to the President pro tempore of the Senate and the Speaker of the House of Representatives their written declaration that the President is unable to discharge the powers and duties of his office. Thereupon Congress shall decide the issue, assembling within forty-eight hours for that purpose if not in session. If the Congress, within twenty-one days after receipt of the latter written declaration, or, if Congress is not in session, within twenty-one days after Congress is required to assemble, determines by two-thirds vote of both Houses that the President shall continue to discharge the same as Acting President; otherwise, the President shall resume the powers and duties of his office.

Amendment XXVI [1971]

Section 1

The right of citizens of the United States, who are eighteen years of age or older, to vote shall not be denied or abridged by the United States or by any State on account of age.

Section 2

The Congress shall have power to enforce this article by appropriate legislation.

Appendix B

SELECTED PROVISIONS
OF RESTATEMENTS

Restatement, Second, of Torts [13]
Restatement, Second, of Contracts [15]
Restatement, Second, of Agency [18]

RESTATEMENT, SECOND, OF TORTS*

* * *

§ 8A. Intent

The word "intent" is used throughout the Restatement of this Subject to denote that the actor desires to cause consequences of his act, or that he believes that the consequences are substantially certain to result from it.

* * *

§ 218. Liability to Person in Possession

One who commits a trespass to a chattel is subject to liability to the possessor of the chattel if, but only if,

(a) he dispossesses the other of the chattel, or

(b) the chattel is impaired as to its condition, quality, or value, or

(c) the possessor is deprived of the use of the chattel for a substantial time, or

(d) bodily harm is caused to the possessor, or harm is caused to some person or thing in which the possessor has a legally protected interest.

* * *

* Copyright 1965 by The American Law Institute. Reprinted with the permission of The American Law Institute.

§ 282. Negligence Defined

In the Restatement of this Subject, negligence is conduct which falls below the standard established by law for the protection of others against unreasonable risk of harm. It does not include conduct recklessly disregardful of an interest of others.

* * *

§ 283A. Children

If the actor is a child, the standard of conduct to which he must conform to avoid being negligent is that of a reasonable person of like age, intelligence, and experience under like circumstances.

* * *

§ 314A. Special Relations Giving Rise to Duty to Aid or Protect

(1) A common carrier is under a duty to its passengers to take reasonable action

(a) to protect them against unreasonable risk of physical harm, and

(b) to give them first aid after it knows or has reason to know that they are ill or injured, and to care for them until they can be cared for by others.

(2) An innkeeper is under a similar duty to his guests.

(3) A possessor of land who holds it open to the public is under a similar duty to members of the public who enter in response to his invitation.

(4) One who is required by law to take or who voluntarily takes the custody of another under circumstances such as to deprive the other of his

normal opportunities for protection is under a similar duty to the other.

* * *

§ 342. Dangerous Conditions Known to Possessor

A possessor of land is subject to liability for physical harm caused to licensees by a condition on the land if, but only if,

(a) the possessor knows or has reason to know of the condition and should realize that it involves an unreasonable risk of harm to such licensees, and should expect that they will not discover or realize the danger, and

(b) he fails to exercise reasonable care to make the condition safe, or to warn the licensees of the condition and the risk involved, and

(c) the licensees do not know or have reason to know of the condition and the risk involved.

§ 343. Dangerous Conditions Known to or Discoverable by Possessor

A possessor of land is subject to liability for physical harm caused to his invitees by a condition on the land if, but only if, he

(a) knows or by the exercise of reasonable care would discover the condition, and should realize that it involves an unreasonable risk of harm to such invitees, and

(b) should expect that they will not discover or realize the danger, or will fail to protect themselves against it, and

(c) fails to exercise reasonable care to protect them against the danger.

* * *

§ 431. What Constitutes Legal Cause

The actor's negligent conduct is a legal cause of harm to another if

(a) his conduct is a substantial factor in bringing about the harm, and

(b) there is no rule of law relieving the actor from liability because of the manner in which his negligence has resulted in the harm.

* * *

§ 463. Contributory Negligence Defined

Contributory negligence is conduct on the part of the plaintiff which falls below the standard to which he should conform for his own protection, and which is a legally contributing cause co-operating with the negligence of the defendant in bringing about the plaintiff's harm.

* * *

§ 496A. General Principle

A plaintiff who voluntarily assumes a risk of harm arising from the negligent or reckless conduct of the defendant cannot recover for such harm.

* * *

§ 568. Libel and Slander Distinguished

(1) Libel consists of the publication of defamatory matter by written or printed words, by its embodiment in physical form or by any other form of communication that has the potentially harmful qualities characteristic of written or printed words.

(2) Slander consists of the publication of defamatory matter by spoken words, transitory gestures or by any form of communication other than those stated in Subsection (1).

(3) The area of dissemination, the deliberate and premeditated character of its publication and the persistence of the defamation are factors to be considered in determining whether a publication is a libel rather than a slander.

* * *

§ 580A. Defamation of Public Official or Public Figure

One who publishes a false and defamatory communication concerning a public official or public figure in regard to his conduct, fitness or role in that capacity is subject to liability, if, but only if, he

(a) knows that the statement is false and that it defames the other person, or

(b) acts in reckless disregard of these matters.

* * *

§ 623A. Liability for Publication of Injurious Falsehood—General Principle

One who publishes a false statement harmful to the interests of another is subject to liability for pecuniary loss resulting to the other if

(a) he intends for publication of the statement to result in harm to interests of the other having a pecuniary value, or either recognizes or should recognize that it is likely to do so, and

(b) he knows that the statement is false or acts in reckless disregard of its truth or falsity.

* * *

§ 652A. General Principle

(1) One who invades the right of privacy of another is subject to liability for the resulting harm to the interests of the other.

(2) The right of privacy is invaded by

(a) unreasonable intrusion upon the seclusion of another, as stated in § 652B; or

(b) appropriation of the other's name or likeliness, as stated in § 652C; or

(c) unreasonable publicity given to the other's private life, as stated in § 652D; or

(d) publicity that unreasonably places the other in a false light before the public, as stated in § 652E.

§ 652B. Intrusion upon Seclusion

One who intentionally intrudes, physically or otherwise, upon the solitude or seclusion of another or his private affairs or concerns, is subject to liability to the other for invasion of his privacy, if the intrusion would be highly offensive to a reasonable person.

§ 652C. Appropriation of Name or Likeness

One who appropriates to his own use or benefit the name or likeness of another is subject to liability to the other for invasion of his privacy.

* * *

§ 652E. Publicity Placing Person in False Light

One who gives publicity to a matter concerning another that places the other before the public in a false light is subject to liability to the other for invasion of his privacy, if

(a) the false light in which the other was placed would be highly offensive to a reasonable person, and

(b) the actor had knowledge of or acted in reckless disregard as to the falsity of the publicized matter and the false light in which the other would be placed.

* * *

§ 766B. Intentional Interference with Prospective Contractual Relation

One who intentionally and improperly interferes with another's prospective contractual relation (except a contract to marry) is subject to liability to the other for the pecuniary harm resulting from loss of the benefits of the relation, whether the interference consists of

(a) inducing or otherwise causing a third person not to enter into or continue the prospective relation or

(b) preventing the other from acquiring or continuing the prospective relation.

* * *

§ 908. Punitive Damages

(1) Punitive damages are damages, other than compensatory or nominal damages, awarded against a person to punish him for his outrageous conduct and to deter him and others like him from similar conduct in the future.

(2) Punitive damages may be awarded for conduct that is outrageous, because of the defendant's evil motive or his reckless indifference to the rights of others. In assessing punitive damages, the trier of fact can properly consider the character of the defendant's act, the nature and extent of the harm to the plaintiff that the defendant caused or intended to cause and the wealth of the defendant.

* * *

RESTATEMENT, SECOND, OF CONTRACTS*

* * *

§ 13. Persons Affected by Guardianship

A person has no capacity to incur contractual duties if his property is under guardianship by reason of an adjudication of mental illness or defect.

§ 14. Infants

Unless a statute provides otherwise, a natural person has the capacity to incur only voidable contractual duties until the beginning of the day before the person's eighteenth birthday.

* * *

§ 30. Form of Acceptance Invited

(1) An offer may invite or require acceptance to be made by an affirmative answer in words, or by performing or refraining from performing a specified act, or may empower the offeree to make a selection of terms in his acceptance.

(2) Unless otherwise indicated by the language or the circumstances, an offer invites acceptance in any manner and by any medium reasonable in the circumstances.

* * *

§ 41. Lapse of Time

(1) An offeree's power of acceptance is terminated at the time specified in the offer, or, if no time is specified, at the end of a reasonable time.

(2) What is a reasonable time is a question of fact, depending on all the circumstances existing when the offer and attempted acceptance are made.

---

* Copyright 1981 by The American Law Institute. Reprinted with the permission of The American Law Institute.

(3) Unless otherwise indicated by the language or the circumstances, and subject to the rule stated in § 49, an offer sent by mail is seasonably accepted if an acceptance is mailed at any time before midnight on the day on which the offer is received.

* * *

§ 67. Effect of Receipt of Acceptance Improperly Dispatched

Where an acceptance is seasonably dispatched but the offeree uses means of transmission not invited by the offer or fails to exercise reasonable diligence to insure safe transmission, it is treated as operative upon dispatch if received within the time in which a properly dispatched acceptance would normally have arrived.

* * *

§ 77. Illusory and Alternative Promises

A promise or apparent promise is not consideration if by its terms the promisor or purported promisor reserves a choice of alternative performances unless

(a) each of the alternative performances would have been consideration if it alone had been bargained for; or

(b) one of the alternative performances would have been consideration and there is or appears to the parties to be a substantial possibility that before the promisor exercises his choice events may eliminate the alternatives which would not have been consideration.

* * *

§ 79. Adequacy of Consideration; Mutuality of Obligation

If the requirement of consideration is met, there is no additional requirement of

(a) a gain, advantage, or benefit to the promisor or a loss, disadvantage, or detriment to the promisee; or

(b) equivalence in the values exchanged; or

(c) "mutuality of obligation."

* * *

§ 89. Modification of Executory Contract

A promise modifying a duty under a contract not fully performed on either side is binding

(a) if the modification is fair and equitable in view of circumstances not anticipated by the parties when the contract was made; or

(b) to the extent provided by statute; or

(c) to the extent that justice requires enforcement in view of material change of position in reliance on the promise.

* * *

§ 116. Main Purpose; Advantage to Surety

A contract that all or part of a duty of a third person to the promisee shall be satisfied is not within the Statute of Frauds as a promise to answer for the duty of another if the consideration for the promise is in fact or apparently desired by the promisor mainly for his own economic advantage, rather than in order to benefit the third person. If, however, the consideration is merely a premium for insurance, the contract is within the Statute.

* * *

§ 130. Contract Not to Be Performed Within a Year

(1) Where any promise in a contract cannot be fully performed within a year from the time the contract is made, all promises in the contract are within the Statute of Frauds until one party to the contract completes his performance.

(2) When one party to a contract has completed his performance, the one-year provision of the Statute does not prevent enforcement of the promises of other parties.

* * *

§ 157. Effect of Fault of Party Seeking Relief

A mistaken party's fault in failing to know or discover the facts before making the contract does not bar him from avoidance or reformation under the rules stated in this Chapter, unless his fault amounts to a failure to act in good faith and in accordance with reasonable standards of fair dealing.

* * *

§ 174. When Duress by Physical Compulsion Prevents Formation of a Contract

If conduct that appears to be a manifestation of assent by a party who does not intend to engage in that conduct is physically compelled by duress, the conduct is not effective as a manifestation of assent.

§ 175. When Duress by Threat Makes a Contract Voidable

(1) If a party's manifestation of assent is induced by an improper threat by the other party that leaves the victim no reasonable alternative, the contract is voidable by the victim.

(2) If a party's manifestation of assent is induced by one who is not a party to the transaction, the contract is voidable by the victim unless the other party to the transaction in good faith and without reason to know of the duress either gives value or relies materially on the transaction.

* * *

§ 195. Term Exempting from Liability for Harm Caused Intentionally, Recklessly or Negligently

(1) A term exempting a party from tort liability for harm caused intentionally or recklessly is unenforceable on grounds of public policy.

(2) A term exempting a party from tort liability for harm caused negligently is unenforceable on grounds of public policy if

    (a) the term exempts an employer from liability to an employee for injury in the course of his employment;

    (b) the term exempts one charged with a duty of public service from liability to one to whom that duty is owed for compensation for breach of that duty, or

    (c) the other party is similarly a member of a class protected against the class to which the first party belongs.

(3) A term exempting a seller of a product from his special tort liability for physical harm to a user or consumer is unenforceable on grounds of public policy unless the term is fairly bargained for and is consistent with the policy underlying that liability.

* * *

§ 213. Effect of Integrated Agreement on Prior Agreements (Parol Evidence Rule)

(1) A binding integrated agreement discharges prior agreements to the extent that it is inconsistent with them.

(2) A binding completely integrated agreement discharges prior agreements to the extent that they are within its scope.

(3) An integrated agreement that is not binding or that is voidable and avoided does not discharge a prior agreement. But an integrated agreement, even though not binding, may be effective to render inoperative a term which would have been part of the agreement if it had not been integrated.

* * *

§ 261. Discharge by Supervening Impracticability

Where, after a contract is made, a party's performance is made impracticable without his fault by the occurrence of an event the non-occurrence of which was a basic assumption on which the contract was made, his duty to render that performance is discharged, unless the language or the circumstances indicate the contrary.

* * *

§ 280. Novation

A novation is a substituted contract that includes as a party one who was neither the obligor nor the obligee of the original duty.

§ 281. Accord and Satisfaction

(1) An accord is a contract under which an obligee promises to accept a stated performance in satisfaction of the obligor's existing duty. Performance of the accord discharges the original duty.

(2) Until performance of the accord, the original duty is suspended unless there is such a breach of the accord by the obligor as discharges the new duty of the obligee to accept the performance in satisfaction. If there is such a breach, the obligee may enforce either the original duty or any duty under the accord.

(3) Breach of the accord by the obligee does not discharge the original duty, but the obligor may maintain a suit for specific performance of the accord, in addition to any claim for damages for partial breach.

* * *

§ 322. Contractual Prohibition of Assignment

(1) Unless the circumstances indicate the contrary, a contract term prohibiting assignment of "the contract" bars only the delegation to an assignee of the performance by the assignor of a duty or condition.

(2) A contract term prohibiting assignment of rights under the contract, unless a different intention is manifested,

    (a) does not forbid assignment of a right to damages for breach of the whole contract or a right arising out of the assignor's due performance of his entire obligation;

    (b) gives the obligor a right to damages for breach of the terms forbidding assignment but does not render the assignment ineffective;

    (c) is for the benefit of the obligor, and does not prevent the assignee from acquiring rights against the assignor or the obligor from discharging his duty as if there were no such prohibition.

* * *

§ 333. Warranties of an Assignor

(1) Unless a contrary intention is manifested, one who assigns or purports to assign a right by assignment under seal or for value warrants to the assignee

(a) that he will do nothing to defeat or impair the value of the assignment and has no knowledge of any fact which would do so;

(b) that the right, as assigned, actually exists and is subject to no limitations or defenses good against the assignor other than those stated or apparent at the time of the assignment;

(c) that any writing evidencing the right which is delivered to the assignee or exhibited to him to induce him to accept the assignment is genuine and what it purports to be.

(2) An assignment does not of itself operate as a warranty that the obligor is solvent or that he will perform his obligation.

(3) An assignor is bound by affirmations and promises to the assignee with reference to the right assigned in the same way and to the same extent that one who transfers goods is bound in like circumstances.

(4) An assignment of a right to a sub-assignee does not operate as an assignment of the assignee's rights under his assignor's warranties unless an intention is manifested to assign the rights under the warranties.

* * *

§ 342. Successive Assignees from the Same Assignor

Except as otherwise provided by statute, the right of an assignee is superior to that of a subsequent assignee of the same right from the same assignor, unless

(a) the first assignment is ineffective or revocable or is voidable by the assignor or by the subsequent assignee; or

(b) the subsequent assignee in good faith and without knowledge or reason to know of the prior assignment gives value and obtains

(i) payment or satisfaction of the obligation,

(ii) judgment against the obligor,

(iii) a new contract with the obligor by novation, or

(iv) possession of a writing of a type customarily accepted as a symbol or as evidence of the right assigned.

* * *

§ 378. Election Among Remedies

If a party has more than one remedy under the rules stated in this Chapter, his manifestation of a choice of one of them by bringing suit or otherwise is not a bar to another remedy unless the remedies are inconsistent and the other party materially changes his position in reliance on the manifestation.

* * *

RESTATEMENT, SECOND, OF AGENCY*

§ 1. Agency; Principal; Agent

(1) Agency is the fiduciary relation which results from the manifestation of consent by one person to another that the other shall act on his behalf and subject to his control, and consent by the other so to act.

(2) The one for whom action is to be taken is the principal.

(3) The one who is to act is the agent.

§ 2. Master; Servant; Independent Contractor

(1) A master is a principal who employs an agent to perform service in his affairs and who controls or has the right to control the physical conduct of the other in the performance of the service.

(2) A servant is an agent employed by a master to perform service in his affairs whose physical conduct in the performance of the service is controlled or is subject to the right to control by the master.

(3) An independent contractor is a person who contracts with another to do something for him but who is not controlled by the other nor subject to the other's right to control with respect to his physical conduct in the performance of the undertaking. He may or may not be an agent.

* * *

§ 4. Disclosed Principal; Partially Disclosed Principal; Undisclosed Principal

(1) If, at the time of a transaction conducted by an agent, the other party thereto has notice that the agent is acting for a principal and of the prin-

* Copyright 1958 by The American Law Institute. Reprinted with the permission of The American Law Institute.

cipal's identity, the principal is a disclosed principal.

(2) If the other party has notice that the agent is or may be acting for a principal but has no notice of the principal's identity, the principal for whom the agent is acting is a partially disclosed principal.

(3) If the other party has no notice that the agent is acting for a principal, the one for whom he acts is an undisclosed principal.

* * *

§ 18. Delegation of Powers Held by Agent

Unless otherwise agreed, an agent cannot properly delegate to another the exercise of discretion in the use of a power held for the benefit of the principal.

* * *

§ 27. Creation of Apparent Authority: General Rule

Except for the execution of instruments under seal or for the conduct of transactions required by statute to be authorized in a particular way, apparent authority to do an act is created as to a third person by written or spoken words or any other conduct of the principal which, reasonably interpreted, causes the third person to believe that the principal consents to have the act done on his behalf by the person purporting to act for him.

* * *

§ 50. When Authority to Contract Inferred

Unless otherwise agreed, authority to make a contract is inferred from authority to conduct a transaction, if the making of such a contract is incidental to the transaction, usually accompanies such a transaction, or is reasonably necessary to accomplish it.

* * *

§ 88. Affirmance after Withdrawal of Other Party or Other Termination of Original Transaction

To constitute ratification, the affirmance of a transaction must occur before the other party has manifested his withdrawal from it either to the purported principal or to the agent, and before the offer or agreement has otherwise terminated or been discharged.

* * *

§ 91. Knowledge of Principal at Time of Affirmance

(1) If, at the time of affirmance, the purported principal is ignorant of material facts involved in the original transaction, and is unaware of his ignorance, he can thereafter avoid the effect of the affirmance.

(2) Material facts are those which substantially affect the existence or extent of the obligations involved in the transaction, as distinguished from those which affect the values or inducements involved in the transaction.

* * *

§ 136. Notification Terminating Apparent Authority

(1) Unless otherwise agreed, there is a notification by the principal to the third person of revocation of an agent's authority or other other fact indicating its termination:

(a) when the principal states such fact to the third person; or

(b) when a reasonable time has elapsed after a writing stating such fact has been delivered by the principal

(i) to the other personally;

(ii) to the other's place of business;

(iii) to a place designated by the other as one in which business communications are received; or

(iv) to a place which, in view of the business customs or relations between the parties is reasonably believed to be the place for the receipt of such communications by the other.

(2) Unless otherwise agreed, a notification to be effective in terminating apparent authority must be given by the means stated in Subsection (1) with respect to a third person:

(a) who has previously extended credit to or received credit from the principal through the agent in reliance upon a manifestation from the principal of continuing authority in the agent;

(b) to whom the agent has been specially accredited;

(c) with whom the agent has begun to deal, as the principal should know; or

(d) who relies upon the possession by the agent of indicia of authority entrusted to him by the principal.

(3) Except as to the persons included in Subsection (2), the principal can properly give notification of the termination of the agent's authority by:

(a) advertising the fact in a newspaper of general circulation in the place where the agency is regularly carried on; or

(b) giving publicity by some other method reasonably adapted to give the information to such third person.

* * *

§ 189. Contracts Specifically Excluding Principal

An undisclosed principal does not become liable upon a contract which provides that he or any undisclosed principal shall not be a party to it.

* * *

§ 216. Unauthorized Tortious Conduct

A master or other principal may be liable to another whose interests have been invaded by the tortious conduct of a servant or other agent, although the principal does not personally violate a duty to such other or authorize the conduct of the agent causing the invasion.

* * *

§ 219. When Master is Liable for Torts of His Servants

(1) A master is subject to liability for the torts of his servants committed while acting in the scope of their employment.

(2) A master is not subject to liability for the torts of his servants acting outside the scope of their employment, unless:

(a) the master intended the conduct or the consequences, or

(b) the master was negligent or reckless, or

(c) the conduct violated a non-delegable duty of the master, or

(d) the servant purported to act or to speak on behalf of the principal and there was reliance upon apparent authority, or he was aided in accomplishing the tort by the existence of the agency relation.

* * *

§ 292. General Rule

The other party to a contract made by an agent for a disclosed or partially disclosed principal, acting within his authority, apparent authority or other agency power, is liable to the principal as if he had contracted directly with the principal, unless the principal is excluded as a party by the form or terms of the contract.

* * *

§ 343. General Rule

An agent who does an act otherwise a tort is not relieved from liability by the fact that he acted at the command of the principal or on account of the principal, except where he is exercising a privilege of the principal, or a privilege held by him for the protection of the principal's interests, or where the principal owes no duty or less than the normal duty of care to the person harmed.

§ 344. Liability for Directed Conduct or Consequences

An agent is subject to liability, as he would be for his own personal conduct, for the consequences of another's conduct which results from his directions if, with knowledge of the circumstances, he intends the conduct, or its consequences, except where the agent or the one acting has a privilege or immunity not available to the other.

* * *

§ 363. Contracts; General Rule

An agent who makes a contract on behalf of a principal cannot maintain an action in his own name on behalf of the principal although authorized by the principal to bring suit, unless the agent is a promisee or transferee.

§ 364. Contracts; Agent a Party Promisee

A person with whom an agent makes a contract on behalf of a principal is subject to liability in an action brought thereon by the agent in his own name on behalf of the principal if the agent is a party promisee.

* * *

§ 379. Duty of Care and Skill

(1) Unless otherwise agreed, a paid agent is subject to a duty to the principal to act with standard care and with the skill which is standard in the locality for the kind of work which he is employed to perform and, in addition, to exercise any special skill that he has.

(2) Unless otherwise agreed, a gratuitous agent is under a duty to the principal to act with the care and skill which is required of persons not agents performing similar gratuitous undertakings for others.

* * *

§ 383. Duty to Act Only as Authorized

Except when he is privileged to protect his own or another's interests, an agent is subject to a duty to the principal not to act in the principal's affairs except in accordance with the principal's manifestation of consent.

*   *   *

§ 385. Duty to Obey

(1) Unless otherwise agreed, an agent is subject to a duty to obey all reasonable directions in regard to the manner of performing a service that he has contracted to perform.

(2) Unless he is privileged to protect his own or another's interests, an agent is subject to a duty not to act in manners entrusted to him on account of the principal contrary to the directions of the principal, even though the terms of the employment prescribe that such directions shall not be given.

*   *   *

§ 438. Duty of Indemnity; the Principle

(1) A principal is under a duty to indemnify the agent in accordance with the terms of the agreement with him.

(2) In the absence of terms to the contrary in the agreement of employment, the principal has a duty to indemnify the agent where the agent

    (a) makes a payment authorized or made necessary in executing the principal's affairs or,

unless he is officious, one beneficial to the principal, or

    (b) suffers a loss which, because of their relation, it is fair that the principal should bear.

§ 439. When Duty of Indemnity Exists

Unless otherwise agreed, a principal is subject to a duty to exonerate an agent who is not barred by the illegality of his conduct to indemnify him for:

    (a) authorized payments made by the agent on behalf of the principal;

    (b) payments upon contracts upon which the agent is authorized to make himself liable, and upon obligations arising from the possession or ownership of things which he is authorized to hold on account of the principal;

    (c) payments of damages to third persons which he is required to make on account of the authorized performance of an act which constitutes a tort or a breach of contract;

    (d) expenses of defending actions by third persons brought because of the agent's authorized conduct, such actions being unfounded but not brought in bad faith; and

    (e) payments resulting in benefit to the principal, made by the agent under such circumstances that it would be inequitable for indemnity not to be made.

*   *   *

THE UNIFORM COMMERCIAL CODE

(Adopted in 52 jurisdictions; all 50 States, although Louisiana has adopted only Articles 1, 3, 4, and 5; the District of Columbia, and the Virgin Islands.)

The Code consists of 10 Articles as follows:

Art.

1. GENERAL PROVISIONS

2. Sales.

3. Commercial Paper

4. Bank Deposits and Collections

5. Letters of Credit

6. Bulk Transfers

7. Warehouse Receipts, Bills of Lading and Other Documents of Title

8. Investment Securities

9. Secured Transactions: Sales of Accounts, Contract Rights and Chattel Paper

10. Effective Date and Repealer

Article 1
GENERAL PROVISIONS

Part 1 Short Title, Construction, Application and Subject Matter of the Act

§ 1—101. **Short Title.**

This Act shall be known and may be cited as Uniform Commercial Code.

§ 1—102. **Purposes; Rules of Construction; Variation by Agreement.**

(1) This Act shall be liberally construed and applied to promote its underlying purposes and policies.

(2) Underlying purposes and policies of this Act are

(a) to simplify, clarify and modernize the law governing commercial transactions;

(b) to permit the continued expansion of commercial practices through custom, usage and agreement of the parties;

(c) to make uniform the law among the various jurisdictions.

(3) The effect of provisions of this Act may be varied by agreement, except as otherwise provided in this Act and except that the obligations of good faith, diligence, reasonableness and care prescribed by this Act may not be disclaimed by agreement but the parties may by agreement determine the standards by which the performance of such obligations is to be measured if such standards are not manifestly unreasonable.

(4) The presence in certain provisions of this Act of the words "unless otherwise agreed" or words of similar import does not imply that the effect of other provisions may not be varied by agreement under subsection (3).

(5) In this Act unless the context otherwise requires

(a) words in the singular number include the plural, and in the plural include the singular;

(b) words of the masculine gender include the feminine and the neuter, and when the sense so indicates words of the neuter gender may refer to any gender.

§ 1—103. Supplementary General Principles of Law Applicable.

Unless displaced by the particular provisions of this Act, the principles of law and equity, including the law merchant and the law relative to capacity to contract, principal and agent, estoppel, fraud, misrepresentation, duress, coercion, mistake, bankruptcy, or other validating or invalidating cause shall supplement its provisions.

§ 1—104. Construction Against Implicit Repeal.

This Act being a general act intended as a unified coverage of its subject matter, no part of it shall be deemed to be impliedly repealed by subsequent legislation if such construction can reasonably be avoided.

§ 1—105. Territorial Application of the Act; Parties' Power to Choose Applicable Law.

(1) Except as provided hereafter in this section, when a transaction bears a reasonable relation to this state and also to another state or nation the parties may agree that the law either of this state or of such other state or nation shall govern their rights and duties. Failing such agreement this Act applies to transactions bearing an appropriate relation to this state.

(2) Where one of the following provisions of this Act specifies the applicable law, that provision governs and a contrary agreement is effective only to the extent permitted by the law (including the conflict of laws rules) so specified:

Rights of creditors against sold goods. Section 2—402.

Applicability of the Article on Bank Deposits and Collections. Section 4—102.

Bulk transfers subject to the Article on Bulk Transfers. Section 6—102.

Applicability of the Article on Investment Securities. Section 8—106.

Perfection provisions of the Article on Secured Transactions. Section 9—103.

§ 1—106. Remedies to Be Liberally Administered.

(1) The remedies provided by this Act shall be liberally administered to the end that the aggrieved party may be put in as good a position as if the other party had fully performed but neither consequential or special nor penal damages may be had except as specifically provided in this Act or by other rule of law.

(2) Any right or obligation declared by this Act is enforceable by action unless the provision declaring it specifies a different and limited effect.

§ 1—107. Waiver or Renunciation of Claim or Right After Breach.

Any claim or right arising out of an alleged breach can be discharged in whole or in part without consideration by a written waiver or renunciation signed and delivered by the aggrieved party.

§ 1—108. Severability.

If any provision or clause of this Act or application thereof to any person or circumstances is held invalid, such invalidity shall not affect other provisions or applications of the Act which can be given effect without the invalid provision or application, and to this end the provisions of this Act are declared to be severable.

§ 1—109. Section Captions.

Section captions are parts of this Act.

Part 2 General Definitions and Principles of Interpretation

§ 1—201. General Definitions

Subject to additional definitions contained in the subsequent Articles of this Act which are applicable to specific Articles or Parts thereof, and unless the context otherwise requires, in this Act:

(1) "Action" in the sense of a judicial proceeding includes recoupment, counterclaim, set-off, suit in equity and any other proceedings in which rights are determined.

(2) "Aggrieved party" means a party entitled to resort to a remedy.

(3) "Agreement" means the bargain of the parties in fact as found in their language or by implication from other circumstances including course of dealing or usage of trade or course of performance as provided in this Act (Sections 1—205 and 2—208). Whether an agreement has legal consequences is determined by the provisions of this Act, if applicable; otherwise by the law of contracts (Section 1—103). (Compare "Contract".)

(4) "Bank" means any person engaged in the business of banking.

(5) "Bearer" means the person in possession of an instrument, document of title, or certificated security payable to bearer or indorsed in blank.

(6) "Bill of lading" means a document evidencing the receipt of goods for shipment issued by a person engaged in the business of transporting or forwarding goods, and includes an airbill. "Airbill" means a document serving for air transportation as a bill of lading does for marine or rail transportation, and includes an air consignment note or air waybill.

(7) "Branch" includes a separately incorporated foreign branch of a bank.

(8) "Burden of establishing" a fact means the burden of persuading the triers of fact that the existence of the fact is more probable than its non-existence.

(9) "Buyer in ordinary course of business" means a person who in good faith and without knowledge that the sale to him is in violation of the ownership rights or security interest of a third party in the goods buys in ordinary course from a person in the business of selling goods of that kind but does not include a pawnbroker. All persons who sell minerals or the like (including oil and gas) at wellhead or minehead shall be deemed to be persons in the business of selling goods of that kind. "Buying" may be for cash or by exchange of other property or on secured or unsecured credit and includes receiving goods or documents of title under a pre-existing contract for sale but does not include a transfer in bulk or as security for or in total or partial satisfaction of a money debt.

(10) "Conspicuous": A term or clause is conspicuous when it is so written that a reasonable person against whom it is to operate ought to have noticed it. A printed heading in capitals (as: NON-NEGOTIABLE BILL OF LADING) is conspicuous. Language in the body of a form is "conspicuous" if it is in larger or other contrasting type or color. But in a telegram any stated term is "conspicuous". Whether a term or clause is "conspicuous" or not is for decision by the court.

(11) "Contract" means the total legal obligation which results from the parties' agreement as affected by this Act and any other applicable rules of law. (Compare "Agreement".)

(12) "Creditor" includes a general creditor, a secured creditor, a lien creditor and any representative of creditors, including an assignee for the benefit of creditors, a trustee in bankruptcy, a receiver in equity and an executor or administrator of an insolvent debtor's or assignor's estate.

(13) "Defendant" includes a person in the position of defendant in a cross-action or counterclaim.

(14) "Delivery" with respect to instruments, documents of title, chattel paper, or certificated securities means voluntary transfer of possession.

(15) "Document of title" includes bill of lading, dock warrant, dock receipt, warehouse receipt or order for the delivery of goods, and also any other document which in the regular course of business or financing is treated as adequately evidencing that the person in possession of it is entitled to receive, hold and dispose of the document and the goods it covers. To be a document of title a document must purport to be issued by or addressed to a bailee and purport to cover goods in the bailee's possession which are either identified or are fungible portions of an identified mass.

(16) "Fault" means wrongful act, omission or breach.

(17) "Fungible" with respect to goods or securities means goods or securities of which any unit is, by nature or usage of trade, the equivalent of any other like unit. Goods which are not fungible shall be deemed fungible for the purposes of this Act to the extent that under a particular agreement or document unlike units are treated as equivalents.

(18) "Genuine" means free of forgery or counterfeiting.

(19) "Good faith" means honesty in fact in the conduct or transaction concerned.

(20) "Holder" means a person who is in possession of a document of title or an instrument or a certificated investment security drawn, issued, or indorsed to him or his order or to bearer or in blank.

(21) To "honor" is to pay or to accept and pay, or where a credit so engages to purchase or discount a draft complying with the terms of the credit.

(22) "Insolvency proceedings" includes any assignment for the benefit of creditors or other proceedings intended to liquidate or rehabilitate the estate of the person involved.

(23) A person is "insolvent" who either has ceased to pay his debts in the ordinary course of business or cannot pay his debts as they become due or is insolvent within the meaning of the federal bankruptcy law.

(24) "Money" means a medium of exchange authorized or adopted by a domestic or foreign government as a part of its currency.

(25) A person has "notice" of a fact when

(a) he has actual knowledge of it; or

(b) he has received a notice or notification of it; or

(c) from all the facts and circumstances known to him at the time in question he has reason to know that it exists.

A person "knows" or has "knowledge" of a fact when he has actual knowledge of it. "Discover" or "learn" or a word or phrase of similar import refers to knowledge rather than to reason to know. The time and circumstances under which a notice or notification may cease to be effective are not determined by this Act.

(26) A person "notifies" or "gives" a notice or notification to another by taking such steps as may be reasonably required to inform the other in ordinary course whether or not such other actually comes to know of it. A person "receives" a notice or notification when

(a) it comes to his attention; or

(b) it is duly delivered at the place of business through which the contract was made or at any other place held out by him as the place for receipt of such communications.

(27) Notice, knowledge or a notice or notification received by an organization is effective for a particular transaction from the time when it is brought to the attention of the individual conducting that transaction, and in any event from the time when it would have been brought to his attention if the organization had exercised due diligence. An organization exercises due diligence if it maintains reasonable routines for communicating significant information to the person conducting the transaction and there is reasonable compliance with the routines. Due diligence does not require an individual acting for the organization to communicate information unless such communication is part of his regular duties or unless he has reason to know of the transaction and that the transaction would be materially affected by the information.

(28) "Organization" includes a corporation, government or governmental subdivision or agency, business trust, estate, trust, partnership or association, two or more persons having a joint or common interest, or any other legal or commercial entity.

(29) "Party", as distinct from "third party", means a person who has engaged in a transaction or made an agreement within this Act.

(30) "Person" includes an individual or an organization (See Section 1—102).

(31) "Presumption" or "presumed" means that the trier of fact must find the existence of the fact presumed unless and until evidence is introduced which would support a finding of its non-existence.

(32) "Purchase" includes taking by sale, discount, negotiation, mortgage, pledge, lien, issue or re-issue, gift or any other voluntary transaction creating an interest in property.

(33) "Purchaser" means a person who takes by purchase.

(34) "Remedy" means any remedial right to which an aggrieved party is entitled with or without resort to a tribunal.

(35) "Representative" includes an agent, an officer of a corporation or association, and a trustee, executor or administrator of an estate, or any other person empowered to act for another.

(36) "Rights" includes remedies.

(37) "Security interest" means an interest in personal property or fixtures which secures payment or performance of an obligation. The retention or reservation of title by a seller of goods notwithstanding shipment or delivery to the buyer (Section 2—401) is limited in effect to a reservation of a "security interest". The term also includes any interest of a buyer of accounts or chattel paper which is subject to Article 9. The special property interest of a buyer of goods on identification of such goods to a contract for sale under Section 2—401 is not a "security interest", but a buyer may also acquire a "security interest" by complying with Article 9. Unless a lease or consignment is intended as security, reservation of title thereunder is not a "security interest" but a consignment is in any event subject to the provisions on consignment sales (Section 2—326). Whether a lease is intended as security is to be determined by the facts of each case; however, (a) the inclusion of an option to purchase does not of itself make the lease one intended for security, and (b) an agreement that upon compliance with the terms of the lease the lessee shall become or has the option to become the owner of the property for no additional consideration or for a nominal consideration does make the lease one intended for security.

(38) "Send" in connection with any writing or notice means to deposit in the mail or deliver for transmission by any other usual means of communication with postage or cost of transmission provided for and properly addressed and in the case of an instrument to an address specified thereon or otherwise agreed, or if there be none to any address reasonable under the circumstances. The receipt of any writing or notice

within the time at which it would have arrived if properly sent has the effect of a proper sending.

(39) "Signed" includes any symbol executed or adopted by a party with present intention to authenticate a writing.

(40) "Surety" includes guarantor.

(41) "Telegram" includes a message transmitted by radio, teletype, cable, any mechanical method of transmission, or the like.

(42) "Term" means that portion of an agreement which relates to a particular matter.

(43) "Unauthorized" signature or indorsement means one made without actual, implied or apparent authority and includes a forgery.

(44) "Value". Except as otherwise provided with respect to negotiable instruments and bank collections (Sections 3—303, 4—208 and 4—209) a person gives "value" for rights if he acquires them

(a) in return for a binding commitment to extend credit or for the extension of immediately available credit whether or not drawn upon and whether or not a chargeback is provided for in the event of difficulties in collection; or

(b) as security for or in total or partial satisfaction of a pre-existing claim; or

(c) by accepting delivery pursuant to a pre-existing contract for purchase; or

(d) generally, in return for any consideration sufficient to support a simple contract.

(45) "Warehouse receipt" means a receipt issued by a person engaged in the business of storing goods for hire.

(46) "Written" or "writing" includes printing, typewriting or any other intentional reduction to tangible form.
Amended in 1962, 1972 and 1977.

§ 1—202. Prima Facie Evidence by Third Party Documents.

A document in due form purporting to be a bill of lading, policy or certificate of insurance, official weigher's or inspector's certificate, consular invoice, or any other document authorized or required by the contract to be issued by a third party shall be prima facie evidence of its own authenticity and genuineness and of the facts stated in the document by the third party.

§ 1—203. Obligation of Good Faith.

Every contract or duty within this Act imposes an obligation of good faith in its performance or enforcement.

§ 1—204. Time; Reasonable Time; "Seasonably".

(1) Whenever this Act requires any action to be taken within a reasonable time, any time which is not manifestly unreasonable may be fixed by agreement.

(2) What is a reasonable time for taking any action depends on the nature, purpose and circumstances of such action.

(3) An action is taken "seasonably" when it is taken at or within the time agreed or if no time is agreed at or within a reasonable time.

§ 1—205. Course of Dealing and Usage of Trade.

(1) A course of dealing is a sequence of previous conduct between the parties to a particular transaction which is fairly to be regarded as establishing a common basis of understanding for interpreting their expressions and other conduct.

(2) A usage of trade is any practice or method of dealing having such regularity of observance in a place, vocation or trade as to justify an expectation that it will be observed with respect to the transaction in question. The existence and scope of such a usage are to be proved as facts. If it is established that such a usage is embodied in a written trade code or similar writing the interpretation of the writing is for the court.

(3) A course of dealing between parties and any usage of trade in the vocation or trade in which they are engaged or of which they are or should be aware give particular meaning to and supplement or qualify terms of an agreement.

(4) The express terms of an agreement and an applicable course of dealing or usage of trade shall be construed wherever reasonable as consistent with each other; but when such construction is unreasonable express terms control both course of dealing and usage of trade and course of dealing controls usage of trade.

(5) An applicable usage of trade in the place where any part of performance is to occur shall be used in interpreting the agreement as to that part of the performance.

(6) Evidence of a relevant usage of trade offered by one party is not admissible unless and until he has given the other party such notice as the court finds sufficient to prevent unfair surprise to the latter.

§ 1—206. Statute of Frauds for Kinds of Personal Property Not Otherwise Covered.

(1) Except in the cases described in subsection (2) of this section a contract for the sale of personal property

is not enforceable by way of action or defense beyond five thousand dollars in amount or value of remedy unless there is some writing which indicates that a contract for sale has been made between the parties at a defined or stated price, reasonably identifies the subject matter, and is signed by the party against whom enforcement is sought or by his authorized agent.

(2) Subsection (1) of this section does not apply to contracts for the sale of goods (Section 2—201) nor of securities (Section 8—319) nor to security agreements (Section 9—203).

§ 1—207. Performance or Acceptance Under Reservation of Rights.

A party who with explicit reservation of rights performs or promises performance or assents to performance in a manner demanded or offered by the other party does not thereby prejudice the rights reserved. Such words as "without prejudice", "under protest" or the like are sufficient.

§ 1—208. Option to Accelerate at Will.

A term providing that one party or his successor in interest may accelerate payment or performance or require collateral or additional collateral "at will" or "when he deems himself insecure" or in words of similar import shall be construed to mean that he shall have power to do so only if he in good faith believes that the prospect of payment or performance is impaired. The burden of establishing lack of good faith is on the party against whom the power has been exercised.

§ 1—209. Subordinated Obligations

An obligation may be issued as subordinated to payment of another obligation of the person obligated, or a creditor may subordinate his right to payment of an obligation by agreement with either the person obligated or another creditor of the person obligated. Such a subordination does not create a security interest as against either the common debtor or a subordinated creditor. This section shall be construed as declaring the law as it existed prior to the enactment of this section and not as modifying it. Added 1966.

Note: *This new section is proposed as an optional provision to make it clear that a subordination agreement does not create a security interest unless so intended.*

Article 2
SALES

Part 1
Short Title, Construction and Subject Matter

§ 2—101. Short Title.

This Article shall be known and may be cited as Uniform Commercial Code—Sales.

§ 2—102. Scope; Certain Security and Other Transactions Excluded From This Article.

Unless the context otherwise requires, this Article applies to transactions in goods; it does not apply to any transaction which although in the form of an unconditional contract to sell or present sale is intended to operate only as a security transaction nor does this Article impair or repeal any statute regulating sales to consumers, farmers or other specified classes of buyers.

§ 2—103. Definitions and Index of Definitions.

(1) In this Article unless the context otherwise requires

(a) "Buyer" means a person who buys or contracts to buy goods.

(b) "Good faith" in the case of a merchant means honesty in fact and the observance of reasonable commercial standards of fair dealing in the trade.

(c) "Receipt" of goods means taking physical possession of them.

(d) "Seller" means a person who sells or contracts to sell goods.

(2) Other definitions applying to this Article or to specified Parts thereof, and the sections in which they appear are:

"Acceptance". Section 2—606.
"Banker's credit". Section 2—325.
"Between merchants". Section 2—104.
"Cancellation". Section 2—106(4).
"Commercial unit". Section 2—105.
"Confirmed credit". Section 2—325.
"Conforming to contract". Section 2—106.
"Contract for sale". Section 2—106.
"Cover". Section 2—712.
"Entrusting". Section 2—403.
"Financing agency". Section 2—104.
"Future goods". Section 2—105.
"Goods". Section 2—105.
"Identification". Section 2—501.

"Installment contract". Section 2—612.
"Letter of Credit". Section 2—325.
"Lot". Section 2—105.
"Merchant". Section 2—104.
"Overseas". Section 2—323.
"Person in position of seller". Section 2—707.
"Present sale". Section 2—106.
"Sale". Section 2—106.
"Sale on approval". Section 2—326.
"Sale or return". Section 2—326.
"Termination". Section 2—106.

(3) The following definitions in other Articles apply to this Article:
"Check". Section 3—104.
"Consignee". Section 7—102.
"Consignor". Section 7—102.
"Consumer goods". Section 9—109.
"Dishonor". Section 3—507.
"Draft". Section 3—104.

(4) In addition Article 1 contains general definitions and principles of construction and interpretation applicable throughout this Article.

§ 2—104. Definitions: "Merchant"; "Between Merchants"; "Financing Agency".

(1) "Merchant" means a person who deals in goods of the kind or otherwise by his occupation holds himself out as having knowledge or skill peculiar to the practices or goods involved in the transaction or to whom such knowledge or skill may be attributed by his employment of an agent or broker or other intermediary who by his occupation holds himself out as having such knowledge or skill.

(2) "Financing agency" means a bank, finance company or other person who in the ordinary course of business makes advances against goods or documents of title or who by arrangement with either the seller or the buyer intervenes in ordinary course to make or collect payment due or claimed under the contract for sale, as by purchasing or paying the seller's draft or making advances against it or by merely taking it for collection whether or not documents of title accompany the draft. "Financing agency" includes also a bank or other person who similarly intervenes between persons who are in the position of seller and buyer in respect to the goods (Section 2—707).

(3) "Between merchants" means in any transaction with respect to which both parties are chargeable with the knowledge or skill of merchants.

§ 2—105. Definitions: Transferability; "Goods"; "Future" Goods; "Lot"; "Commercial Unit".

(1) "Goods" means all things (including specially manufactured goods) which are movable at the time of identification to the contract for sale other than the money in which the price is to be paid, investment securities (Article 8) and things in action. "Goods" also includes the unborn young of animals and growing crops and other identified things attached to realty as described in the section on goods to be severed from realty (Section 2—107).

(2) Goods must be both existing and identified before any interest in them can pass. Goods which are not both existing and identified are "future" goods. A purported present sale of future goods or of any interest therein operates as a contract to sell.

(3) There may be a sale of a part interest in existing identified goods.

(4) An undivided share in an identified bulk of fungible goods is sufficiently identified to be sold although the quantity of the bulk is not determined. Any agreed proportion of such a bulk or any quantity thereof agreed upon by number, weight or other measure may to the extent of the seller's interest in the bulk be sold to the buyer who then becomes an owner in common.

(5) "Lot" means a parcel or a single article which is the subject matter of a separate sale or delivery, whether or not it is sufficient to perform the contract.

(6) "Commercial unit" means such a unit of goods as by commercial usage is a single whole for purposes of sale and division of which materially impairs its character or value on the market or in use. A commercial unit may be a single article (as a machine) or a set of articles (as a suite of furniture or an assortment of sizes) or a quantity (as a bale, gross, or carload) or any other unit treated in use or in the relevant market as a single whole.

§ 2—106. Definitions: "Contract"; "Agreement"; "Contract for Sale"; "Sale"; "Present Sale"; "Conforming" to Contract; "Termination"; "Cancellation".

(1) In this Article unless the context otherwise requires "contract" and "agreement" are limited to those relating to the present or future sale of goods. "Contract for sale" includes both a present sale of goods and a contract to sell goods at a future time. A "sale" consists in the passing of title from the seller to the buyer for a price (Section 2—401). A "present

sale" means a sale which is accomplished by the making of the contract.

(2) Goods or conduct including any part of a performance are "conforming" or conform to the contract when they are in accordance with the obligations under the contract.

(3) "Termination" occurs when either party pursuant to a power created by agreement or law puts an end to the contract otherwise than for its breach. On "termination" all obligations which are still executory on both sides are discharged but any right based on prior breach or performance survives.

(4) "Cancellation" occurs when either party puts an end to the contract for breach by the other and its effect is the same as that of "termination" except that the cancelling party also retains any remedy for breach of the whole contract or any unperformed balance.

§ 2—107. **Goods to Be Severed From Realty: Recording.**

(1) A contract for the sale of minerals or the like (including oil and gas) or a structure or its materials to be removed from realty is a contract for the sale of goods within this Article if they are to be severed by the seller but until severance a purported present sale thereof which is not effective as a transfer of an interest in land is effective only as a contract to sell.

(2) A contract for the sale apart from the land of growing crops or other things attached to realty and capable of severance without material harm thereto but not described in subsection (1) or of timber to be cut is a contract for the sale of goods within this Article whether the subject matter is to be severed by the buyer or by the seller even though it forms part of the realty at the time of contracting, and the parties can by identification effect a present sale before severance.

(3) The provisions of this section are subject to any third party rights provided by the law relating to realty records, and the contract for sale may be executed and recorded as a document transferring an interest in land and shall then constitute notice to third parties of the buyer's rights under the contract for sale.

Part 2 **Form, Formation and Readjustment of Contract**

§ 2—201. **Formal Requirements; Statute of Frauds.**

(1) Except as otherwise provided in this section a contract for the sale of goods for the price of $500 or more is not enforceable by way of action or defense unless there is some writing sufficient to indicate that a contract for sale has been made between the parties and signed by the party against whom enforcement is sought or by his authorized agent or broker. A writing is not insufficient because it omits or incorrectly states a term agreed upon but the contract is not enforceable under this paragraph beyond the quantity of goods shown in such writing.

(2) Between merchants if within a reasonable time a writing in confirmation of the contract and sufficient against the sender is received and the party receiving it has reason to know its contents, it satisfies the requirements of subsection (1) against such party unless written notice of objection to its contents is given within ten days after it is received.

(3) A contract which does not satisfy the requirements of subsection (1) but which is valid in other respects is enforceable

(a) if the goods are to be specially manufactured for the buyer and are not suitable for sale to others in the ordinary course of the seller's business and the seller, before notice of repudiation is received and under circumstances which reasonably indicate that the goods are for the buyer, has made either a substantial beginning of their manufacture or commitments for their procurement; or

(b) if the party against whom enforcement is sought admits in his pleading, testimony or otherwise in court that a contract for sale was made, but the contract is not enforceable under this provision beyond the quantity of goods admitted; or

(c) with respect to goods for which payment has been made and accepted or which have been received and accepted (Sec. 2—606).

§ 2—202. **Final Written Expression: Parol or Extrinsic Evidence.**

Terms with respect to which the confirmatory memoranda of the parties agree or which are otherwise set forth in a writing intended by the parties as a final expression of their agreement with respect to such terms as are included therein may not be contradicted by evidence of any prior agreement or of a contemporaneous oral agreement but may be explained or supplemented

(a) by course of dealing or usage of trade (Section 1—205) or by course of performance (Section 2—208); and

(b) by evidence of consistent additional terms unless the court finds the writing to have been intended also as a complete and exclusive statement of the terms of the agreement.

§ 2—203. **Seals Inoperative.**

The affixing of a seal to a writing evidencing a contract for sale or an offer to buy or sell goods does not constitute the writing a sealed instrument and the law with respect to sealed instruments does not apply to such a contract or offer.

§ 2—204. **Formation in General.**

(1) A contract for sale of goods may be made in any manner sufficient to show agreement, including conduct by both parties which recognizes the existence of such a contract.

(2) An agreement sufficient to constitute a contract for sale may be found even though the moment of its making is undetermined.

(3) Even though one or more terms are left open a contract for sale does not fail for indefiniteness if the parties have intended to make a contract and there is a reasonably certain basis for giving an appropriate remedy.

§ 2—205. **Firm Offers.**

An offer by a merchant to buy or sell goods in a signed writing which by its terms gives assurance that it will be held open is not revocable, for lack of consideration, during the time stated or if no time is stated for a reasonable time, but in no event may such period of irrevocability exceed three months; but any such term of assurance on a form supplied by the offeree must be separately signed by the offeror.

§ 2—206. **Offer and Acceptance in Formation of Contract.**

(1) Unless other unambiguously indicated by the language or circumstances

(a) an offer to make a contract shall be construed as inviting acceptance in any manner and by any medium reasonable in the circumstances;

(b) an order or other offer to buy goods for prompt or current shipment shall be construed as inviting acceptance either by a prompt promise to ship or by the prompt or current shipment of conforming or nonconforming goods, but such a shipment of non-conforming goods does not constitute an acceptance if the seller seasonably notifies the buyer that the shipment is offered only as an accommodation to the buyer.

(2) Where the beginning of a requested performance is a reasonable mode of acceptance an offeror who is not notified of acceptance within a reasonable time may treat the offer as having lapsed before acceptance.

§ 2—207. **Additional Terms in Acceptance or Confirmation.**

(1) A definite and seasonable expression of acceptance or a written confirmation which is sent within a reasonable time operates as an acceptance even though it states terms additional to or different from those offered or agreed upon, unless acceptance is expressly made conditional on assent to the additional or different terms.

(2) The additional terms are to be construed as proposals for addition to the contract. Between merchants such terms become part of the contract unless:

(a) the offer expressly limits acceptance to the terms of the offer;

(b) they materially alter it; or

(c) notification of objection to them has already been given or is given within a reasonable time after notice of them is received.

(3) Conduct by both parties which recognizes the existence of a contract is sufficient to establish a contract for sale although the writings of the parties do not otherwise establish a contract. In such case the terms of the particular contract consist of those terms on which the writings of the parties agree, together with any supplementary terms incorporated under any other provisions of this Act.

§ 2—208. **Course of Performance or Practical Construction.**

(1) Where the contract for sale involves repeated occasions for performance by either party with knowledge of the nature of the performance and opportunity for objection to it by the other, any course of performance accepted or acquiesced in without objection shall be relevant to determine the meaning of the agreement.

(2) The express terms of the agreement and any such course of performance, as well as any course of dealing and usage of trade, shall be construed whenever reasonable as consistent with each other; but when such construction is unreasonable, express terms shall control course of performance and course of performance shall control both course of dealing and usage of trade (Section 1—205).

(3) Subject to the provisions of the next section on modification and waiver, such course of performance shall be relevant to show a waiver or modification of any term inconsistent with such course of performance.

§ 2—209. **Modification, Rescission and Waiver.**

(1) An agreement modifying a contract within this Article needs no consideration to be binding.

(2) A signed agreement which excludes modification or rescission except by a signed writing cannot be otherwise modified or rescinded, but except as between merchants such a requirement on a form supplied by the merchant must be separately signed by the other party.

(3) The requirements of the statute of frauds section of this Article (Section 2—201) must be satisfied if the contract as modifed is within its provisions.

(4) Although an attempt at modification or rescission does not satisfy the requirements of subsection (2) or (3) it can operate as a waiver.

(5) A party who has made a waiver affecting an executory portion of the contract may retract the waiver by reasonable notification received by the other party that strict performance will be required of any term waived, unless the retraction would be unjust in view of a material change of position in reliance on the waiver.

§ 2—210. **Delegation of Performance; Assignment of Rights.**

(1) A party may perform his duty through a delegate unless otherwise agreed or unless the other party has a substantial interest in having his original promisor perform or control the acts required by the contract. No delegation of performance relieves the party delegating of any duty to perform or any liability for breach.

(2) Unless otherwise agreed all rights of either seller or buyer can be assigned except where the assignment would materially change the duty of the other party, or increase materially the burden or risk imposed on him by his contract, or impair materially his chance of obtaining return performance. A right to damages for breach of the whole contract or a right arising out of the assignor's due performance of his entire obligation can be assigned despite agreement otherwise.

(3) Unless the circumstances indicate the contrary a prohibition of assignment of "the contract" is to be construed as barring only the delegation to the assignee of the assignor's performance.

(4) An assignment of "the contract" or of "all my rights under the contract" or an assignment in similar general terms is an assignment of rights and unless the language or the circumstances (as in an assignment for security) indicate the contrary, it is a delegation of performance of the duties of the assign-or and its acceptance by the assignee constitutes a promise by him to perform those duties. This promise is enforceable by either the assignor or the other party to the original contract.

(5) The other party may treat any assignment which delegates performance as creating reasonable grounds for insecurity and may without prejudice to his rights against the assignor demand assurances from the assignee (Section 2—609).

Part 3 **General Obligation and Construction of Contract**

§ 2—301. **General Obligations of Parties.**

The obligation of the seller is to transfer and deliver and that of the buyer is to accept and pay in accordance with the contract.

§ 2—302. **Unconscionable Contract or Clause.**

(1) If the court as a matter of law finds the contract or any clause of the contract to have been unconscionable at the time it was made the court may refuse to enforce the contract, or it may enforce the remainder of the contract without the unconscionable clause, or it may so limit the application of any unconscionable clause as to avoid any unconscionable result.

(2) When it is claimed or appears to the court that the contract or any clause thereof may be unconscionable the parties shall be afforded a reasonable opportunity to present evidence as to its commercial setting, purpose and effect to aid the court in making the determination.

§ 2—303. **Allocation or Division of Risks.**

Where this Article allocates a risk or a burden as between the parties "unless otherwise agreed", the agreement may not only shift the allocation but may also divide the risk or burden.

§ 2—304. **Price Payable in Money, Goods, Realty, or Otherwise.**

(1) The price can be made payable in money or otherwise. If it is payable in whole or in part in goods each party is a seller of the goods which he is to transfer.

(2) Even though all or part of the price is payable in an interest in realty the transfer of the goods and the seller's obligations with reference to them are subject to this Article, but not the transfer of the interest in realty or the transferor's obligations in connection therewith.

§ 2—305. **Open Price Term.**

(1) The parties if they so intend can conclude a contract for sale even though the price is not settled. In such a case the price is a reasonable price at the time for delivery if

(a) nothing is said as to price; or

(b) the price is left to be agreed by the parties and they fail to agree; or

(c) the price is to be fixed in terms of some agreed market or other standard as set or recorded by a third person or agency and it is not so set or recorded.

(2) A price to be fixed by the seller or by the buyer means a price for him to fix in good faith.

(3) When a price left to be fixed otherwise than by agreement of the parties fails to be fixed through fault of one party the other may at his option treat the contract as cancelled or himself fix a reasonable price.

(4) Where, however, the parties intend not to be bound unless the price be fixed or agreed and it is not fixed or agreed there is no contract. In such a case the buyer must return any goods already received or if unable so to do must pay their reasonable value at the time of delivery and the seller must return any portion of the price paid on account.

§ 2—306. **Output, Requirements and Exclusive Dealings.**

(1) A term which measures the quantity by the output of the seller or the requirements of the buyer means such actual output or requirements as may occur in good faith, except that no quantity unreasonably disproportionate to any stated estimate or in the absence of a stated estimate to any normal or otherwise comparable prior output or requirements may be tendered or demanded.

(2) A lawful agreement by either the seller or the buyer for exclusive dealing in the kind of goods concerned imposes unless otherwise agreed an obligation by the seller to use best efforts to supply the goods and by the buyer to use best efforts to promote their sale.

§ 2—307. **Delivery in Single Lot or Several Lots.**

Unless otherwise agreed all goods called for by a contract for sale must be tendered in a single delivery and payment is due only on such tender but where the circumstances give either party the right to make or demand delivery in lots the price if it can be apportioned may be demanded for each lot.

§ 2—308. **Absence of Specified Place for Delivery.**

Unless otherwise agreed

(a) the place for delivery of goods is the seller's place of business or if he has none his residence; but

(b) in a contract for sale of identified goods which to the knowledge of the parties at the time of contracting are in some other place, that place is the place for their delivery; and

(c) documents of title may be delivered through customary banking channels.

§ 2—309. **Absence of Specific Time Provisions; Notice of Termination.**

(1) The time for shipment or delivery or any other action under a contract if not provided in this Article or agreed upon shall be a reasonable time.

(2) Where the contract provides for successive performances but is indefinite in duration it is valid for a reasonable time but unless otherwise agreed may be terminated at any time by either party.

(3) Termination of a contract by one party except on the happening of an agreed event requires that reasonable notification be received by the other party and an agreement dispensing with notification is invalid if its operation would be unconscionable.

§ 2—310. **Open Time for Payment or Running of Credit; Authority to Ship Under Reservation.**

Unless otherwise agreed

(a) payment is due at the time and place at which the buyer is to receive the goods even though the place of shipment is the place of delivery; and

(b) if the seller is authorized to send the goods he may ship them under reservation, and may tender the documents of title, but the buyer may inspect the goods after their arrival before payment is due unless such inspection is inconsistent with the terms of the contract (Section 2—513); and

(c) if delivery is authorized and made by way of documents of title otherwise than by subsection (b) then payment is due at the time and place at which the buyer is to receive the documents regardless of where the goods are to be received; and

(d) where the seller is required or authorized to ship the goods on credit the credit period runs from the time of shipment but post-dating the invoice or delaying its dispatch will correspondingly delay the starting of the credit period.

§ 2—311. **Options and Cooperation Respecting Performance.**

(1) An agreement for sale which is otherwise sufficiently definite (subsection (3) of Section 2—204) to be a contract is not made invalid by the fact that it leaves particulars of performance to be specified by one of the parties. Any such specification must be made in good faith and within limits set by commercial reasonableness.

(2) Unless otherwise agreed specifications relating to assortment of the goods are at the buyer's option and except as otherwise provided in subsections (1) (c) and (3) of Section 2—319 specifications or arrangements relating to shipment are at the seller's option.

(3) Where such specification would materially affect the other party's performance but is not seasonably made or where one party's cooperation is necessary to the agreed performance of the other but is not seasonably forthcoming, the other party in addition to all other remedies

(a) is excused for any resulting delay in his own performance; and

(b) may also either proceed to perform in any reasonable manner or after the time for a material part of his own performance treat the failure to specify or to cooperate as a breach by failure to deliver or accept the goods.

§ 2—312. **Warranty of Title and Against Infringement; Buyer's Obligation Against Infringement.**

(1) Subject to subsection (2) there is in a contract for sale a warranty by the seller that

(a) the title conveyed shall be good, and its transfer rightful; and

(b) the goods shall be delivered free from any security interest or other lien or encumbrance of which the buyer at the time of contracting has no knowledge.

(2) A warranty under subsection (1) will be excluded or modified only by specific language or by circumstances which give the buyer reason to know that the person selling does not claim title in himself or that he is purporting to sell only such right or title as he or a third person may have.

(3) Unless otherwise agreed a seller who is a merchant regularly dealing in goods of the kind warrants that the goods shall be delivered free of the rightful claim of any third person by way of infringement or the like but a buyer who furnishes specifications to the seller must hold the seller harmless against any such claim which arises out of compliance with the specifications.

§ 2—313. **Express Warranties by Affirmation, Promise, Description, Sample.**

(1) Express warranties by the seller are created as follows:

(a) Any affirmation of fact or promise made by the seller to the buyer which relates to the goods and becomes part of the basis of the bargain creates an express warranty that the goods shall conform to the affirmation or promise.

(b) Any description of the goods which is made part of the basis of the bargain creates an express warranty that the goods shall conform to the description.

(c) Any sample or model which is made part of the basis of the bargain creates an express warranty that the whole of the goods shall conform to the sample or model.

(2) It is not necessary to the creation of an express warranty that the seller use formal words such as "warrant" or "guarantee" or that he have a specific intention to make a warranty, but an affirmation merely of the value of the goods or a statement purporting to be merely the seller's opinion or commendation of the goods does not create a warranty.

§ 2—314. **Implied Warranty: Merchantability; Usage of Trade.**

(1) Unless excluded or modified (Section 2—316), a warranty that the goods shall be merchantable is implied in a contract for their sale if the seller is a merchant with respect to goods of that kind. Under this section the serving for value of food or drink to be consumed either on the premises or elsewhere is a sale.

(2) Goods to be merchantable must be at least such as

(a) pass without objection in the trade under the contract description; and

(b) in the case of fungible goods, are of fair average quality within the description; and

(c) are fit for the ordinary purposes for which such goods are used; and

(d) run, within the variations permitted by the agreement, of even kind, quality and quantity within each unit and among all units involved; and

(e) are adequately contained, packaged, and labeled as the agreement may require; and

(f) conform to the promises or affirmations of fact made on the container or label if any.

(3) Unless excluded or modified (Section 2—316) other implied warranties may arise from course of dealing or usage of trade.

§ 2—315. **Implied Warranty: Fitness for Particular Purpose.**

Where the seller at the time of contracting has reason to know any particular purpose for which the goods are required and that the buyer is relying on the seller's skill or judgment to select or furnish suitable goods, there is unless excluded or modified under the next section an implied warranty that the goods shall be fit for such purpose.

§ 2—316. **Exclusion or Modification of Warranties.**

(1) Words or conduct relevant to the creation of an express warranty and words or conduct tending to negate or limit warranty shall be construed wherever reasonable as consistent with each other; but subject to the provisions of this Article on parol or extrinsic evidence (Section 2—202) negation or limitation is inoperative to the extent that such construction is unreasonable.

(2) Subject to subsection (3), to exclude or modify the implied warranty of merchantability or any part of it the language must mention merchantability and in case of a writing must be conspicuous, and to exclude or modify any implied warranty of fitness the exclusion must be by a writing and conspicuous. Language to exclude all implied warranties of fitness is sufficient if it states, for example, that "There are no warranties which extend beyond the description on the face hereof."

(3) Notwithstanding subsection (2)

(a) unless the circumstances indicate otherwise, all implied warranties are excluded by expressions like "as is", "with all faults" or other language which in common understanding calls the buyer's attention to the exclusion of warranties and makes plain that there is no implied warranty; and

(b) when the buyer before entering into the contract has examined the goods or the sample or model as fully as he desired or has refused to examine the goods there is no implied warranty with regard to defects which an examination ought in the circumstances to have revealed to him; and

(c) an implied warranty can also be excluded or modified by course of dealing or course of performance or usage of trade.

(4) Remedies for breach of warranty can be limited in accordance with the provisions of this Article on liquidation or limitation of damages and on contractual modification of remedy (Sections 2—718 and 2—719).

§ 2—317. **Cumulation and Conflict of Warranties Express or Implied.**

Warranties whether express or implied shall be construed as consistent with each other and as cumulative, but if such construction is unreasonable the intention of the parties shall determine which warranty is dominant. In ascertaining that intention the following rules apply:

(a) Exact or technical specifications displace an inconsistent sample or model or general language of description.

(b) A sample from an existing bulk displaces inconsistent general language of description.

(c) Express warranties displace inconsistent implied warranties other than an implied warranty of fitness for a particular purpose.

§ 2—318. **Third Party Beneficiaries of Warranties Express or Implied.**

Note: If this Act is introduced in the Congress of the United States this section should be omitted. (States to select one alternative.)

Alternative A

A seller's warranty whether express or implied extends to any natural person who is in the family or household of his buyer or who is a guest in his home if it is reasonable to expect that such person may use, consume or be affected by the goods and who is injured in person by breach of the warranty. A seller may not exclude or limit the operation of this section.

Alternative B

A seller's warranty whether express or implied extends to any natural person who may reasonably be expected to use, consume or be affected by the goods and who is injured in person by breach of the warranty. A seller may not exclude or limit the operation of this section.

Alternative C

A seller's warranty whether express or implied extends to any person who may reasonably be expected to use, consume or be affected by the goods and who is injured by breach of the warranty. A seller may not exclude or limit the operation of this section with respect to injury to the person of an individual to whom the warranty extends. As amended 1966.

§ 2—319. **F.O.B. and F.A.S. Terms.**

(1) Unless otherwise agreed the term F.O.B. (which means "free on board") at a named place, even though used only in connection with the stated price, is a delivery term under which

 (a) when the term is F.O.B. the place of shipment, the seller must at that place ship the goods in the manner provided in this Article (Section 2—504) and bear the expense and risk of putting them into the possession of the carrier; or

 (b) when the term is F.O.B. the place of destination, the seller must at his own expense and risk transport the goods to that place and there tender delivery of them in the manner provided in this Article (Section 2—503);

 (c) when under either (a) or (b) the term is also F.O.B. vessel, car or other vehicle, the seller must in addition at his own expense and risk load the goods on board. If the term is F.O.B. vessel the buyer must name the vessel and in an appropriate case the seller must comply with the provisions of this Article on the form of bill of lading (Section 2—323).

(2) Unless otherwise agreed the term F.A.S. vessel (which means "free alongside") at a named port, even though used only in connection with the stated price, is a delivery term under which the seller must

 (a) at his own expense and risk deliver the goods alongside the vessel in the manner usual in that port or on a dock designated and provided by the buyer; and

 (b) obtain and tender a receipt for the goods in exchange for which the carrier is under a duty to issue a bill of lading.

(3) Unless otherwise agreed in any case falling within subsection (1) (a) or (c) or subsection (2) the buyer must seasonably give any needed instructions for making delivery, including when the term is F.A.S. or F.O.B. the loading berth of the vessel and in an appropriate case its name and sailing date. The seller may treat the failure of needed instructions as a failure of cooperation under this Article (Section 2—311). He may also at his option move the goods in any reasonable manner preparatory to delivery or shipment.

(4) Under the term F.O.B. vessel or F.A.S. unless otherwise agreed the buyer must make payment against tender of the required documents and the seller may not tender nor the buyer demand delivery of the goods in substitution for the documents.

§ 2—320. **C.I.F. and C. & F. Terms.**

(1) The term C.I.F. means that the price includes in a lump sum the cost of the goods and the insurance and freight to the named destination. The term C. & F. or C.F. means that the price so includes cost and freight to the named destination.

(2) Unless otherwise agreed and even though used only in connection with the stated price and destination, the term C.I.F. destination or its equivalent requires the seller at his own expense and risk to

 (a) put the goods into the possession of a carrier at the port for shipment and obtain a negotiable bill or bills of lading covering the entire transportation to the named destination; and

 (b) load the goods and obtain a receipt from the carrier (which may be contained in the bill of lading) showing that the freight has been paid or provided for; and

 (c) obtain a policy or certificate of insurance, including any war risk insurance, of a kind and on terms then current at the port of shipment in the usual amount, in the currency of the contract, shown to cover the same goods covered by the bill of lading and providing for payment of loss to the order of the buyer or for the account of whom it may concern; but the seller may add to the price the amount of the premium for any such war risk insurance; and

 (d) prepare an invoice of the goods and procure any other documents required to effect shipment or to comply with the contract; and

 (e) forward and tender with commercial promptness all the documents in due form and with any indorsement necessary to perfect the buyer's rights.

(3) Unless otherwise agreed the term C. & F. or its equivalent has the same effect and imposes upon the seller the same obligations and risks as a C.I.F. term except the obligation as to insurance.

(4) Under the term C.I.F. or C. & F. unless otherwise agreed the buyer must make payment against tender of the required documents and the seller may not tender nor the buyer demand delivery of the goods in substitution for the documents.

§ 2—321. **C.I.F. or C. & F.: "Net Landed Weights"; "Payment on Arrival"; Warranty of Condition on Arrival.**

Under a contract containing a term C.I.F. or C. & F.

(1) Where the price is based on or is to be adjusted according to "net landed weights", "delivered

weights", "out turn" quantity or quality or the like, unless otherwise agreed the seller must reasonably estimate the price. The payment due on tender of the documents called for by the contract is the amount so estimated, but after final adjustment of the price a settlement must be made with commercial promptness.

(2) An agreement described in subsection (1) or any warranty of quality or condition of the goods on arrival places upon the seller the risk of ordinary deterioration, shrinkage and the like in transportation but has no effect on the place or time of identification to the contract for sale or delivery or on the passing of the risk of loss.

(3) Unless otherwise agreed where the contract provides for payment on or after arrival of the goods the seller must before payment allow such preliminary inspection as is feasible; but if the goods are lost delivery of the documents and payment are due when the goods should have arrived.

§ 2—322. **Delivery "Ex-Ship".**

(1) Unless otherwise agreed a term for delivery of goods "ex-ship" (which means from the carrying vessel) or in equivalent language is not restricted to a particular ship and requires delivery from a ship which has reached a place at the named port of destination where goods of the kind are usually discharged.

(2) Under such a term unless otherwise agreed

(a) the seller must discharge all liens arising out of the carriage and furnish the buyer with a direction which puts the carrier under a duty to deliver the goods; and

(b) the risk of loss does not pass to the buyer until the goods leave the ship's tackle or are otherwise properly unloaded.

§ 2—323. **Form of Bill of Lading Required in Overseas Shipment; "Overseas".**

(1) Where the contract contemplates overseas shipment and contains a term C.I.F. or C. & F. or F.O.B. vessel, the seller unless otherwise agreed must obtain a negotiable bill of lading stating that the goods have been loaded on board or, in the case of a term C.I.F. or C. & F., received for shipment.

(2) Where in a case within subsection (1) a bill of lading has been issued in a set of parts, unless otherwise agreed if the documents are not to be sent from abroad the buyer may demand tender of the full set; otherwise only one part of the bill of lading need be tendered. Even if the agreement expressly requires a full set

(a) due tender of a single part is acceptable within the provisions of this Article on cure of improper delivery (subsection (1) of Section 2—508); and

(b) even though the full set is demanded, if the documents are sent from abroad the person tendering an incomplete set may nevertheless require payment upon furnishing an indemnity which the buyer in good faith deems adequate.

(3) A shipment by water or by air or a contract contemplating such shipment is "overseas" insofar as by usage of trade or agreement it is subject to the commercial, financing or shipping practices characteristic of international deep water commerce.

§ 2—324. **"No Arrival, No Sale" Term.**

Under a term "no arrival, no sale" or terms of like meaning, unless otherwise agreed,

(a) the seller must properly ship conforming goods and if they arrive by any means he must tender them on arrival but he assumes no obligation that the goods will arrive unless he has caused the non-arrival; and

(b) where without fault of the seller the goods are in part lost or have so deteriorated as no longer to conform to the contract or arrive after the contract time, the buyer may proceed as if there had been casualty to identified goods (Section 2—613).

§ 2—325. **"Letter of Credit" Term; "Confirmed Credit".**

(1) Failure of the buyer seasonably to furnish an agreed letter of credit is a breach of the contract for sale.

(2) The delivery to seller of a proper letter of credit suspends the buyer's obligation to pay. If the letter of credit is dishonored, the seller may on seasonable notification to the buyer require payment directly from him.

(3) Unless otherwise agreed the term "letter of credit" or "banker's credit" in a contract for sale means an irrevocable credit issued by a financing agency of good repute and, where the shipment is overseas, of good international repute. The term "confirmed credit" means that the credit must also carry the direct obligation of such an agency which does business in the seller's financial market.

§ 2—326. **Sale on Approval and Sale or Return; Consignment Sales and Rights of Creditors.**

(1) Unless otherwise agreed, if delivered goods may

be returned by the buyer even though they conform to the contract, the transaction is

   (a) a "sale on approval" if the goods are delivered primarily for use, and

   (b) a "sale or return" if the goods are delivered primarily for resale.

(2) Except as provided in subsection (3), goods held on approval are not subject to the claims of the buyer's creditors until acceptance; goods held on sale or return are subject to such claims while in the buyer's possession.

(3) Where goods are delivered to a person for sale and such person maintains a place of business at which he deals in goods of the kind involved, under a name other than the name of the person making delivery, then with respect to claims of creditors of the person conducting the business the goods are deemed to be on sale or return. The provisions of this subsection are applicable even though an agreement purports to reserve title to the person making delivery until payment or resale or uses such words as "on consignment" or "on memorandum". However, this subsection is not applicable if the person making delivery

   (a) complies with an applicable law providing for a consignor's interest or the like to be evidenced by a sign, or

   (b) establishes that the person conducting the business is generally known by his creditors to be substantially engaged in selling the goods of others, or

   (c) complies with the filing provisions of the Article on Secured Transactions (Article 9).

(4) Any "or return" term of a contract for sale is to be treated as a separate contract for sale within the statute of frauds section of this Article (Section 2—201) and as contradicting the sale aspect of the contract within the provisions of this Article on parol or extrinsic evidence (Section 2—202).

§ 2—327. **Special Incidents of Sale on Approval and Sale or Return.**

(1) Under a sale on approval unless otherwise agreed

   (a) although the goods are identified to the contract the risk of loss and the title do not pass to the buyer until acceptance; and

   (b) use of the goods consistent with the purpose of trial is not acceptance but failure seasonably to notify the seller of election to return the goods is acceptance, and if the goods conform to the contract acceptance of any part is acceptance of the whole; and

   (c) after due notification of election to return, the return is at the seller's risk and expense but a merchant buyer must follow any reasonable instructions.

(2) Under a sale or return unless otherwise agreed

   (a) the option to return extends to the whole or any commercial unit of the goods while in substantially their original condition, but must be exercised seasonably; and

   (b) the return is at the buyer's risk and expense.

§ 2—328. **Sale by Auction.**

(1) In a sale by auction if goods are put up in lots each lot is the subject of a separate sale.

(2) A sale by auction is complete when the auctioneer so announces by the fall of the hammer or in other customary manner. Where a bid is made while the hammer is falling in acceptance of a prior bid the auctioneer may in his discretion reopen the bidding or declare the goods sold under the bid on which the hammer was falling.

(3) Such a sale is with reserve unless the goods are in explicit terms put up without reserve. In an auction with reserve the auctioneer may withdraw the goods at any time until he announces completion of the sale. In an auction without reserve, after the auctioneer calls for bids on an article or lot, that article or lot cannot be withdrawn unless no bid is made within a reasonable time. In either case a bidder may retract his bid until the auctioneer's announcement of completion of the sale, but a bidder's retraction does not revive any previous bid.

(4) If the auctioneer knowingly receives a bid on the seller's behalf or the seller makes or procures such a bid, and notice has not been given that liberty for such bidding is reserved, the buyer may at his option avoid the sale or take the goods at the price of the last good faith bid prior to the completion of the sale. This subsection shall not apply to any bid at a forced sale.

Part 4 Title, Creditors and Good Faith Purchasers

§ 2—401. **Passing of Title; Reservation for Security; Limited Application of This Section.**

Each provision of this Article with regard to the rights, obligations and remedies of the seller, the buyer, purchasers or other third parties applies irrespective of title to the goods except where the provision refers to such title. Insofar as situations are not covered by the other provisions of this Article and matters concerning title became material the following rules apply:

(1) Title to goods cannot pass under a contract for sale prior to their identification to the contract (Section 2—501), and unless otherwise explicitly agreed the buyer acquires by their identification a special property as limited by this Act. Any retention or reservation by the seller of the title (property) in goods shipped or delivered to the buyer is limited in effect to a reservation of a security interest. Subject to these provisions and to the provisions of the Article on Secured Transactions (Article 9), title to goods passes from the seller to the buyer in any manner and on any conditions explicitly agreed on by the parties.

(2) Unless otherwise explicitly agreed title passes to the buyer at the time and place at which the seller completes his performance with reference to the physical delivery of the goods, despite any reservation of a security interest and even though a document of title is to be delivered at a different time or place; and in particular and despite any reservation of a security interest by the bill of lading

(a) if the contract requires or authorizes the seller to send the goods to the buyer but does not require him to deliver them at destination, title passes to the buyer at the time and place of shipment; but

(b) if the contract requires delivery at destination, title passes on tender there.

(3) Unless otherwise explicitly agreed where delivery is to be made without moving the goods,

(a) if the seller is to deliver a document of title, title passes at the time when and the place where he delivers such documents; or

(b) if the goods are at the time of contracting already identified and no documents are to be delivered, title passes at the time and place of contracting.

(4) A rejection or other refusal by the buyer to receive or retain the goods, whether or not justified, or a justified revocation of acceptance revests title to the goods in the seller. Such revesting occurs by operation of law and is not a "sale".

§ 2—402. **Rights of Seller's Creditors Against Sold Goods.**

(1) Except as provided in subsections (2) and (3), rights of unsecured creditors of the seller with respect to goods which have been identified to a contract for sale are subject to the buyer's rights to recover the goods under this Article (Sections 2—502 and 2—716).

(2) A creditor of the seller may treat a sale or an identification of goods to a contract for sale as void if as against him a retention of possession by the seller is fraudulent under any rule of law of the state where the goods are situated, except that retention of possession in good faith and current course of trade by a merchant-seller for a commercially reasonable time after a sale or identification is not fraudulent.

(3) Nothing in this Article shall be deemed to impair the rights of creditors of the seller

(a) under the provisions of the Article on Secured Transactions (Article 9); or

(b) where identification to the contract or delivery is made not in current course of trade but in satisfaction of or as security for a pre-existing claim for money, security or the like and is made under circumstances which under any rule of law of the state where the goods are situated would apart from this Article constitute the transaction a fraudulent transfer or voidable preference.

§ 2—403. **Power to Transfer; Good Faith Purchase of Goods; "Entrusting".**

(1) A purchaser of goods acquires all title which his transferor had or had power to transfer except that a purchaser of a limited interest acquires rights only to the extent of the interest purchased. A person with voidable title has power to transfer a good title to a good faith purchaser for value. When goods have been delivered under a transaction of purchase the purchaser has such power even though

(a) the transferor was deceived as to the identity of the purchaser, or

(b) the delivery was in exchange for a check which is later dishonored, or

(c) it was agreed that the transaction was to be a "cash sale", or

(d) the delivery was procured through fraud punishable as larcenous under the criminal law.

(2) Any entrusting of possession of goods to a merchant who deals in goods of that kind gives him power to transfer all rights of the entruster to a buyer in ordinary course of business.

(3) "Entrusting" includes any delivery and any acquiescence in retention of possession regardless of any condition expressed between the parties to the delivery or acquiescence and regardless of whether the procurement of the entrusting or the possessor's disposition of the goods have been such as to be larcenous under the criminal law.

(4) The rights of other purchasers of goods and of lien creditors are governed by the Articles on Secured

Transactions (Article 9), Bulk Transfers (Article 6) and Documents of Title (Article 7).

Part 5 Performance

§ 2—501. Insurable Interest in Goods; Manner of Identification of Goods.

(1) The buyer obtains a special property and an insurable interest in goods by identification of existing goods as goods to which the contract refers even though the goods so identified are non-conforming and he has an option to return or reject them. Such identification can be made at any time and in any manner explicitly agreed to by the parties. In the absence of explicit agreement identification occurs

(a) when the contract is made if it is for the sale of goods already existing and identified;

(b) if the contract is for the sale of future goods other than those described in paragraph (c), when goods are shipped, marked or otherwise designated by the seller as goods to which the contract refers;

(c) when the crops are planted or otherwise become growing crops or the young are conceived if the contract is for the sale of unborn young to be born within twelve months after contracting or for the sale of crops to be harvested within twelve months or the next normal harvest season after contracting whichever is longer.

(2) The seller retains an insurable interest in goods so long as title to or any security interest in the goods remains in him and where the identification is by the seller alone he may until default or insolvency or notification to the buyer that the identification is final substitute other goods for those identified.

(3) Nothing in this section impairs any insurable interest recognized under any other statute or rule of law.

§ 2—502. Buyer's Right to Goods on Seller's Insolvency.

(1) Subject to subsection (2) and even though the goods have not been shipped a buyer who has paid a part or all of the price of goods in which he has a special property under the provisions of the immediately preceding section may on making and keeping good a tender of any unpaid portion of their price recover them from the seller if the seller becomes insolvent within ten days after receipt of the first installment on their price.

(2) If the identification creating his special property has been made by the buyer he acquires the right to recover the goods only if they conform to the contract for sale.

§ 2—503. Manner of Seller's Tender of Delivery.

(1) Tender of delivery requires that the seller put and hold conforming goods at the buyer's disposition and give the buyer any notification reasonably necessary to enable him to take delivery. The manner, time and place for tender are determined by the agreement and this Article, and in particular

(a) tender must be at a reasonable hour, and if it is of goods they must be kept available for the period reasonably necessary to enable the buyer to take possession; but

(b) unless otherwise agreed the buyer must furnish facilities reasonably suited to the receipt of the goods.

(2) Where the case is within the next section respecting shipment tender requires that the seller comply with its provisions.

(3) Where the seller is required to deliver at a particular destination tender requires that he comply with subsection (1) and also in any appropriate case tender documents as described in subsections (4) and (5) of this section.

(4) Where goods are in the possession of a bailee and are to be delivered without being moved

(a) tender requires that the seller either tender a negotiable document of title covering such goods or procure acknowledgment by the bailee of the buyer's right to possession of the goods; but

(b) tender to the buyer of a non-negotiable document of title or of a written direction to the bailee to deliver is sufficient tender unless the buyer seasonably objects, and receipt by the bailee of notification of the buyer's rights fixes those rights as against the bailee and all third persons; but risk of loss of the goods and of any failure by the bailee to honor the non-negotiable document of title or to obey the direction remains on the seller until the buyer has had a reasonable time to present the document or direction, and a refusal by the bailee to honor the document or to obey the direction defeats the tender.

(5) Where the contract requires the seller to deliver documents

(a) he must tender all such documents in correct form, except as provided in this Article with respect to bills of lading in a set (subsection (2) of Section 2—323); and

(b) tender through customary banking channels is sufficient and dishonor of a draft accompanying the documents constitutes non-acceptance or rejection.

§ 2—504. Shipment by Seller.

Where the seller is required or authorized to send the goods to the buyer and the contract does not require him to deliver them at a particular destination, then unless otherwise agreed he must

(a) put the goods in the possession of such a carrier and make such a contract for their transportation as may be reasonable having regard to the nature of the goods and other circumstances of the case; and

(b) obtain and promptly deliver or tender in due form any document necessary to enable the buyer to obtain possession of the goods or otherwise required by the agreement or by usage of trade; and

(c) promptly notify the buyer of the shipment.

Failure to notify the buyer under paragraph (c) or to make a proper contract under paragraph (a) is a ground for rejection only if material delay or loss ensues.

§ 2—505. Seller's Shipment Under Reservation.

(1) Where the seller has identified goods to the contract by or before shipment:

(a) his procurement of a negotiable bill of lading to his own order or otherwise reserves in him a security interest in the goods. His procurement of the bill to the order of a financing agency or of the buyer indicates in addition only the seller's expectation of transferring that interest to the person named.

(b) a non-negotiable bill of lading to himself or his nominee reserves possession of the goods as security but except in a case of conditional delivery (subsection (2) of Section 2—507) a non-negotiable bill of lading naming the buyer as consignee reserves no security interest even though the seller retains possession of the bill of lading.

(2) When shipment by the seller with reservation of a security interest is in violation of the contract for sale it constitutes an improper contract for transportation within the preceding section but impairs neither the rights given to the buyer by shipment and identification of the goods to the contract nor the seller's powers as a holder of a negotiable document.

§ 2—506. Rights of Financing Agency.

(1) A financing agency by paying or purchasing for value a draft which relates to a shipment of goods acquires to the extent of the payment or purchase and in addition to its own rights under the draft and any document of title securing it any rights of the shipper in the goods including the right to stop delivery and the shipper's right to have the draft honored by the buyer.

(2) The right to reimbursement of a financing agency which has in good faith honored or purchased the draft under commitment to or authority from the buyer is not impaired by subsequent discovery of defects with reference to any relevant document which was apparently regular on its face.

§ 2—507. Effect of Seller's Tender; Delivery on Condition.

(1) Tender of delivery is a condition to the buyer's duty to accept the goods and, unless otherwise agreed, to his duty to pay for them. Tender entitles the seller to acceptance of the goods and to payment according to the contract.

(2) Where payment is due and demanded on the delivery to the buyer of goods or documents of title, his right as against the seller to retain or dispose of them is conditional upon his making the payment due.

§ 2—508. Cure by Seller of Improper Tender or Delivery; Replacement.

(1) Where any tender or delivery by the seller is rejected because non-conforming and the time for performance has not yet expired, the seller may seasonably notify the buyer of his intention to cure and may then within the contract time make a conforming delivery.

(2) Where the buyer rejects a non-conforming tender which the seller had reasonable grounds to believe would be acceptable with or without money allowance the seller may if he seasonably notifies the buyer have a further reasonable time to substitute a conforming tender.

§ 2—509. Risk of Loss in the Absence of Breach.

(1) Where the contract requires or authorizes the seller to ship the goods by carrier

(a) if it does not require him to deliver them at a particular destination, the risk of loss passes to the buyer when the goods are duly delivered to the carrier even though the shipment is under reservation (Section 2—505); but

(b) if it does require him to deliver them at a particular destination and the goods are there duly tendered while in the possession of the carrier, the risk of loss passes to the buyer when the goods are there duly so tendered as to enable the buyer to take delivery.

(2) Where the goods are held by a bailee to be delivered without being moved, the risk of loss passes to the buyer

    (a) on his receipt of a negotiable document of title covering the goods; or

    (b) on acknowledgment by the bailee of the buyer's right to possession of the goods; or

    (c) after his receipt of a non-negotiable document of title or other written direction to deliver, as provided in subsection (4) (b) of Section 2—503.

(3) In any case not within subsection (1) or (2), the risk of loss passes to the buyer on his receipt of the goods if the seller is a merchant; otherwise, the risk passes to the buyer on tender of delivery.

(4) The provisions of this section are subject to contrary agreement of the parties and to the provisions of this Article on sale on approval (Section 2—327) and on effect of breach on risk of loss (Section 2—510).

§ 2—510. **Effect of Breach on Risk of Loss.**

(1) Where a tender or delivery of goods so fails to conform to the contract as to give a right of rejection the risk of their loss remains on the seller until cure or acceptance.

(2) Where the buyer rightfully revokes acceptance he may to the extent of any deficiency in his effective insurance coverage treat the risk of loss as having rested on the seller from the beginning.

(3) Where the buyer as to conforming goods already identified to the contract for sale repudiates or is otherwise in breach before risk of their loss has passed to him, the seller may to the extent of any deficiency in his effective insurance coverage treat the risk of loss as resting on the buyer for a commercially reasonable time.

§ 2—511. **Tender of Payment by Buyer; Payment by Check.**

(1) Unless otherwise agreed tender of payment is a condition to the seller's duty to tender and complete any delivery.

(2) Tender of payment is sufficient when made by any means or in any manner current in the ordinary course of business unless the seller demands payment in legal tender and gives any extension of time reasonably necessary to procure it.

(3) Subject to the provisions of this Act on the effect of an instrument on an obligation (Section 3—802),

payment by check is conditional and is defeated as between the parties by dishonor of the check on due presentment.

§ 2—512. **Payment by Buyer Before Inspection.**

(1) Where the contract requires payment before inspection non-conformity of the goods does not excuse the buyer from so making payment unless

    (a) the non-conformity appears without inspection; or

    (b) despite tender of the required documents the circumstances would justify injunction against honor under the provisions of this Act (Section 5—114).

(2) Payment pursuant to subsection (1) does not constitute an acceptance of goods or impair the buyer's right to inspect or any of his remedies.

§ 2—513. **Buyer's Right to Inspection of Goods.**

(1) Unless otherwise agreed and subject to subsection (3), where goods are tendered or delivered or identified to the contract for sale, the buyer has a right before payment or acceptance to inspect them at any reasonable place and time and in any reasonable manner. When the seller is required or authorized to send the goods to the buyer, the inspection may be after their arrival.

(2) Expenses of inspection must be borne by the buyer but may be recovered from the seller if the goods do not conform and are rejected.

(3) Unless otherwise agreed and subject to the provisions of this Article on C.I.F. contracts (subsection (3) of Section 2—321), the buyer is not entitled to inspect the goods before payment of the price when the contract provides

    (a) for delivery "C.O.D." or on other like terms; or

    (b) for payment against documents of title, except where such payment is due only after the goods are to become available for inspection.

(4) A place or method of inspection fixed by the parties is presumed to be exclusive but unless otherwise expressly agreed it does not postpone identification or shift the place for delivery or for passing the risk of loss. If compliance becomes impossible, inspection shall be as provided in this section unless the place or method fixed was clearly intended as an indispensable condition failure of which avoids the contract.

§ 2—514. **When Documents Deliverable on Acceptance; When on Payment.**

Unless otherwise agreed documents against which a draft is drawn are to be delivered to the drawee on acceptance of the draft if it is payable more than three days after presentment; otherwise, only on payment.

§ 2—515. **Preserving Evidence of Goods in Dispute.**

In furtherance of the adjustment of any claim or dispute

(a) either party on reasonable notification to the other and for the purpose of ascertaining the facts and preserving evidence has the right to inspect, test and sample the goods including such of them as may be in the possession or control of the other; and

(b) the parties may agree to a third party inspection or survey to determine the conformity or condition of the goods and may agree that the findings shall be binding upon them in any subsequent litigation or adjustment.

Part 6 Breach, Repudiation and Excuse

§ 2—601. **Buyer's Rights on Improper Delivery.**

Subject to the provisions of this Article on breach in installment contracts (Section 2—612) and unless otherwise agreed under the sections on contractual limitations of remedy (Sections 2—718 and 2—719), if the goods or the tender of delivery fail in any respect to conform to the contract, the buyer may

(a) reject the whole; or

(b) accept the whole; or

(c) accept any commercial unit or units and reject the rest.

§ 2—602. Manner and Effect of Rightful Rejection.

(1) Rejection of goods must be within a reasonable time after their delivery or tender. It is ineffective unless the buyer seasonably notifies the seller.

(2) Subject to the provisions of the two following sections on rejected goods (Sections 2—603 and 2—604),

(a) after rejection any exercise of ownership by the buyer with respect to any commercial unit is wrongful as against the seller; and

(b) if the buyer has before rejection taken physical possession of goods in which he does not have a security interest under the provisions of this

Article (subsection (3) of Section 2—711), he is under a duty after rejection to hold them with reasonable care at the seller's disposition for a time sufficient to permit the seller to remove them; but

(c) the buyer has no further obligations with regard to goods rightfully rejected.

(3) The seller's rights with respect to goods wrongfully rejected are governed by the provisions of this Article on seller's remedies in general (Section 2—703).

§ 2—603. **Merchant Buyer's Duties as to Rightfully Rejected Goods.**

(1) Subject to any security interest in the buyer (subsection (3) of Section 2—711), when the seller has no agent or place of business at the market of rejection a merchant buyer is under a duty after rejection of goods in his possession or control to follow any reasonable instructions received from the seller with respect to the goods and in the absence of such instructions to make reasonable efforts to sell them for the seller's account if they are perishable or threaten to decline in value speedily. Instructions are not reasonable if on demand indemnity for expenses is not forthcoming.

(2) When the buyer sells goods under subsection (1), he is entitled to reimbursement from the seller or out of the proceeds for reasonable expenses of caring for and selling them, and if the expenses include no selling commission then to such commission as is usual in the trade or if there is none to a reasonable sum not exceeding ten per cent on the gross proceeds.

(3) In complying with this section the buyer is held only to good faith and good faith conduct hereunder is neither acceptance nor conversion nor the basis of an action for damages.

§ 2—604. **Buyer's Options as to Salvage of Rightfully Rejected Goods.**

Subject to the provisions of the immediately preceding section on perishables if the seller gives no instructions within a reasonable time after notification of rejection the buyer may store the rejected goods for the seller's account or reship them to him or resell them for the seller's account with reimbursement as provided in the preceding section. Such action is not acceptance or conversion.

§ 2—605. **Waiver of Buyer's Objections by Failure to Particularize.**

(1) The buyer's failure to state in connection with rejection a particular defect which is ascertainable by

reasonable inspection precludes him from relying on the unstated defect to justify rejection or to establish breach

(a) where the seller could have cured it if stated seasonally; or

(b) between merchants when the seller has after rejection made a request in writing for a full and final written statement of all defects on which the buyer proposes to rely.

(2) Payment against documents made without reservation of rights precludes recovery of the payment for defects apparent on the face of the documents.

§ 2—606. What Constitutes Acceptance of Goods.

(1) Acceptance of goods occurs when the buyer

(a) after a reasonable opportunity to inspect the goods signifies to the seller that the goods are conforming or that he will take or retain them in spite of their nonconformity; or

(b) fails to make an effective rejection (subsection (1) of Section 2—602), but such acceptance does not occur until the buyer has had a reasonable opportunity to inspect them; or

(c) does any act inconsistent with the seller's ownership; but if such act is wrongful as against the seller it is an acceptance only if ratified by him.

(2) Acceptance of a part of any commercial unit is acceptance of that entire unit.

§ 2—607. Effect of Acceptance; Notice of Breach; Burden of Establishing Breach After Acceptance; Notice of Claim or Litigation to Person Answerable Over.

(1) The buyer must pay at the contract rate for any goods accepted.

(2) Acceptance of goods by the buyer precludes rejection of the goods accepted and if made with knowledge of a non-conformity cannot be revoked because of it unless the acceptance was on the reasonable assumption that the non-conformity would be seasonably cured but acceptance does not of itself impair any other remedy provided by this Article for non-conformity.

(3) Where a tender has been accepted

(a) the buyer must within a reasonable time after he discovers or should have discovered any breach notify the seller of breach or be barred from any remedy; and

(b) if the claim is one for infringement or the like (subsection (3) of Section 2—312) and the buyer is

sued as a result of such a breach he must so notify the seller within a reasonable time after he receives notice of the litigation or be barred from any remedy over for liability established by the litigation.

(4) The burden is on the buyer to establish any breach with respect to the goods accepted.

(5) Where the buyer is sued for breach of a warranty or other obligation for which his seller is answerable over

(a) he may give his seller written notice of the litigation. If the notice states that the seller may come in and defend and that if the seller does not do so he will be bound in any action against him by his buyer by any determination of fact common to the two litigations, then unless the seller after seasonable receipt of the notice does come in and defend he is so bound.

(b) if the claim is one for infringement or the like (subsection (3) of Section 2—312) the original seller may demand in writing that his buyer turn over to him control of the litigation including settlement or else be barred from any remedy over and if he also agrees to bear all expense and to satisfy any adverse judgment, then unless the buyer after seasonable receipt of the demand does turn over control the buyer is so barred.

(6) The provisions of subsections (3), (4) and (5) apply to any obligation of a buyer to hold the seller harmless against infringement or the like (subsection (3) of Section 2—312).

§ 2—608. Revocation of Acceptance in Whole or in Part.

(1) The buyer may revoke his acceptance of a lot or commercial unit whose non-conformity substantially impairs its value to him if he has accepted it

(a) on the reasonable assumption that its non-conformity would be cured and it has not been seasonably cured; or

(b) without discovery of such non-conformity if his acceptance was reasonably induced either by the difficulty of discovery before acceptance or by the seller's assurances.

(2) Revocation of acceptance must occur within a reasonable time after the buyer discovers or should have discovered the ground for it and before any substantial change in condition of the goods which is not caused by their own defects. It is not effective until the buyer notifies the seller of it.

(3) A buyer who so revokes has the same rights and

duties with regard to the goods involved as if he had rejected them.

§ 2—609. **Right to Adequate Assurance of Performance.**

(1) A contract for sale imposes an obligation on each party that the other's expectation of receiving due performance will not be impaired. When reasonable grounds for insecurity arise with respect to the performance of either party the other may in writing demand adequate assurance of due performance and until he receives such assurance may if commercially reasonable suspend any performance for which he has not already received the agreed return.

(2) Between merchants the reasonableness of grounds for insecurity and the adequacy of any assurance offered shall be determined according to commercial standards.

(3) Acceptance of any improper delivery or payment does not prejudice the aggrieved party's right to demand adequate assurance of future performance.

(4) After receipt of a justified demand failure to provide within a reasonable time not exceeding thirty days such assurance of due performance as is adequate under the circumstances of the particular case is a repudiation of the contract.

§ 2—610. **Anticipatory Repudiation.**

When either party repudiates the contract with respect to a performance not yet due the loss of which will substantially impair the value of the contract to the other, the aggrieved party may

(a) for a commercially reasonable time await performance by the repudiating party; or

(b) resort to any remedy for breach (Section 2—703 or Section 2—711), even though he has notified the repudiating party that he would await the latter's performance and has urged retraction; and

(c) in either case suspend his own performance or proceed in accordance with the provisions of this Article on the seller's right to identify goods to the contract notwithstanding breach or to salvage unfinished goods (Section 2—704).

§ 2—611. **Retraction of Anticipatory Repudiation.**

(1) Until the repudiating party's next performance is due he can retract his repudiation unless the aggrieved party has since the repudiation cancelled or materially changed his position or otherwise indicated that he considers the repudiation final.

(2) Retraction may be by any method which clearly indicates to the aggrieved party that the repudiating party intends to perform, but must include any assurance justifiably demanded under the provisions of this Article (Section 2—609).

(3) Retraction reinstates the repudiating party's rights under the contract with due excuse and allowance to the aggrieved party for any delay occasioned by the repudiation.

§ 2—612. **"Installment Contract"; Breach.**

(1) An "installment contract" is one which requires or authorizes the delivery of goods in separate lots to be separately accepted, even though the contract contains a clause "each delivery is a separate contract" or its equivalent.

(2) The buyer may reject any installment which is non-conforming if the non-conformity substantially impairs the value of that installment and cannot be cured or if the non-conformity is a defect in the required documents; but if the non-conformity does not fall within subsection (3) and the seller gives adequate assurance of its cure the buyer must accept that installment.

(3) Whenever non-conformity or default with respect to one or more installments substantially impairs the value of the whole contract there is a breach of the whole. But the aggrieved party reinstates the contract if he accepts a non-conforming installment without seasonably notifying of cancellation or if he brings an action with respect only to past installments or demands performance as to future installments.

§ 2—613. **Casualty to Identified Goods.**

Where the contract requires for its performance goods identified when the contract is made, and the goods suffer casualty without fault of either party before the risk of loss passes to the buyer, or in a proper case under a "no arrival, no sale" term (Section 2—324) then

(a) if the loss is total the contract is avoided; and

(b) if the loss is partial or the goods have so deteriorated as no longer to conform to the contract the buyer may nevertheless demand inspection and at his option either treat the contract as avoided or accept the goods with due allowance from the contract price for the deterioration or the deficiency in quantity but without further right against the seller.

§ 2—614. **Substituted Performance.**

(1) Where without fault of either party the agreed berthing, loading, or unloading facilities fail or an agreed type of carrier becomes unavailable or the agreed manner of delivery otherwise becomes com-

mercially impracticable but a commercially reasonable substitute is available, such substitute performance must be tendered and accepted.

(2) If the agreed means or manner of payment fails because of domestic or foreign governmental regulation, the seller may withhold or stop delivery unless the buyer provides a means or manner of payment which is commercially a substantial equivalent. If delivery has already been taken, payment by the means or in the manner provided by the regulation discharges the buyer's obligation unless the regulation is discriminatory, oppressive or predatory.

§ 2—615. Excuse by Failure of Presupposed Conditions.

Except so far as a seller may have assumed a greater obligation and subject to the preceding section on substituted performance:

(a) Delay in delivery or non-delivery in whole or in part by a seller who complies with paragraphs (b) and (c) is not a breach of his duty under a contract for sale if performance as agreed has been made impracticable by the occurrence of a contingency the non-occurrence of which was a basic assumption on which the contract was made or by compliance in good faith with any applicable foreign or domestic governmental regulation or order whether or not it later proves to be invalid.

(b) Where the causes mentioned in paragraph (a) affect only a part of the seller's capacity to perform, he must allocate production and deliveries among his customers but may at his option include regular customers not then under contract as well as his own requirements for further manufacture. He may so allocate in any manner which is fair and reasonable.

(c) The seller must notify the buyer seasonably that there will be delay or non-delivery and, when allocation is required under paragraph (b), of the estimated quota thus made available for the buyer.

§ 2—616. Procedure on Notice Claiming Excuse.

(1) Where the buyer receives notification of a material or indefinite delay or an allocation justified under the preceding section he may by written notification to the seller as to any delivery concerned, and where the prospective deficiency substantially impairs the value of the whole contract under the provisions of this Article relating to breach of installment contracts (Section 2—612), then also as to the whole,

    (a) terminate and thereby discharge any unexecuted portion of the contract; or

    (b) modify the contract by agreeing to take his available quota in substitution.

(2) If after receipt of such notification from the seller the buyer fails so to modify the contract within a reasonable time not exceeding thirty days the contract lapses with respect to any deliveries affected.

(3) The provisions of this section may not be negated by agreement except in so far as the seller has assumed a greater obligation under the preceding section.

Part 7 Remedies

§ 2—701. Remedies for Breach of Collateral Contracts Not Impaired.

Remedies for breach of any obligation or promise collateral or ancillary to a contract for sale are not impaired by the provisions of this Article.

§ 2—702. Seller's Remedies on Discovery of Buyer's Insolvency.

(1) Where the seller discovers the buyer to be insolvent he may refuse delivery except for cash including payment for all goods theretofore delivered under the contract, and stop delivery under this Article (Section 2—705).

(2) Where the seller discovers that the buyer has received goods on credit while insolvent he may reclaim the goods upon demand made within ten days after the receipt, but if misrepresentation of solvency has been made to the particular seller in writing within three months before delivery the ten day limitation does not apply. Except as provided in this subsection the seller may not base a right to reclaim goods on the buyer's fraudulent or innocent misrepresentation of solvency or of intent to pay.

(3) The seller's right to reclaim under subsection (2) is subject to the rights of a buyer in ordinary course or other good faith purchaser under this Article (Section 2—403). Successful reclamation of goods excludes all other remedies with respect to them.

§ 2—703. Seller's Remedies in General.

Where the buyer wrongfully rejects or revokes acceptance of goods or fails to make a payment due on or before delivery or repudiates with respect to a part or the whole, then with respect to any goods directly affected and, if the breach is of the whole contract (Section 2—612), then also with respect to the whole undelivered balance, the aggrieved seller may

(a) withhold delivery of such goods;

(b) stop delivery by any bailee as hereafter provided (Section 2—705);

(c) proceed under the next section respecting goods still unidentified to the contract;

(d) resell and recover damages as hereafter provided (Section 2—706);

(e) recover damages for non-acceptance (Section 2—708) or in a proper case the price (Section 2—709);

(f) cancel.

§ 2—704. Seller's Right to Identify Goods to the Contract Notwithstanding Breach or to Salvage Unfinished Goods.

(1) An aggrieved seller under the preceding section may

(a) identify to the contract conforming goods not already identified if at the time he learned of the breach they are in his possession or control;

(b) treat as the subject of resale goods which have demonstrably been intended for the particular contract even though those goods are unfinished.

(2) Where the goods are unfinished an aggrieved seller may in the exercise of reasonable commercial judgment for the purposes of avoiding loss and of effective realization either complete the manufacture and wholly identify the goods to the contract or cease manufacture and resell for scrap or salvage value or proceed in any other reasonable manner.

§ 2—705. Seller's Stoppage of Delivery in Transit or Otherwise.

(1) The seller may stop delivery of goods in the possession of a carrier or other bailee when he discovers the buyer to be insolvent (Section 2—702) and may stop delivery of carload, truckload, plane-load or larger shipments of express or freight when the buyer repudiates or fails to make a payment due before delivery or if for any other reason the seller has a right to withhold or reclaim the goods.

(2) As against such buyer the seller may stop delivery until

(a) receipt of the goods by the buyer; or

(b) acknowledgment to the buyer by any bailee of the goods except a carrier that the bailee holds the goods for the buyer; or

(c) such acknowledgment to the buyer by a carrier by reshipment or as warehouseman; or

(d) negotiation to the buyer of any negotiable document of title covering the goods.

(3) (a) To stop delivery the seller must so notify as to enable the bailee by reasonable diligence to prevent delivery of the goods.

(b) After such notification the bailee must hold and deliver the goods according to the directions of the seller but the seller is liable to the bailee for any ensuing charges or damages.

(c) If a negotiable document of title has been issued for goods the bailee is not obliged to obey a notification to stop unitl surrender of the document.

(d) A carrier who has issued a non-negotiable bill of lading is not obliged to obey a notification to stop received from a person other than the consignor.

§ 2—706. Seller's Resale Including Contract for Resale.

(1) Under the conditions stated in Section 2—703 on seller's remedies, the seller may resell the goods concerned or the undelivered balance thereof. Where the resale is made in good faith and in a commercially reasonable manner the seller may recover the difference between the resale price and the contract price together with any incidental damages allowed under the provisions of this Article (Section 2—710), but less expenses saved in consequence of the buyer's breach.

(2) Except as otherwise provided in subsection (3) or unless otherwise agreed resale may be at public or private sale including sale by way of one or more contracts to sell or of identification to an existing contract of the seller. Sale may be as a unit or in parcels and at any time and place and on any terms but every aspect of the sale including the method, manner, time, place and terms must be commercially reasonable. The resale must be reasonably identified as referring to the broken contract, but it is not necessary that the goods be in existence or that any or all of them have been identified to the contract before the breach.

(3) Where the resale is at private sale the seller must give the buyer reasonable notification of his intention to resell.

(4) Where the resale is at public sale

(a) only identified goods can be sold except where there is a recognized market for a public sale of futures in goods of the kind; and

(b) it must be made at a usual place or market for public sale if one is reasonably available and except in the case of goods which are perishable or threaten to decline in value speedily the seller must give the buyer reasonable notice of the time and place of the resale; and

(c) if the goods are not to be within the view of those attending the sale the notification of sale must state the place where the goods are located and provide for their reasonable inspection by prospective bidders; and

(d) the seller may buy.

(5) A purchaser who buys in good faith at a resale takes the goods free of any rights of the original buyer even though the seller fails to comply with one or more of the requirements of this section.

(6) The seller is not accountable to the buyer for any profit made on any resale. A person in the position of a seller (Section 2—707) or a buyer who has rightfully rejected or justifiably revoked acceptance must account for any excess over the amount of his security interest, as hereinafter defined (subsection (3) of Section 2—711).

§ 2—707. **"Person in the Position of a Seller".**

(1) A "person in the position of a seller" includes as against a principal an agent who has paid or become responsible for the price of goods on behalf of his principal or anyone who otherwise holds a security interest or other right in goods similar to that of a seller.

(2) A person in the position of a seller may as provided in this Article withhold or stop delivery (Section 2—705) and resell (Section 2—706) and recover incidental damages (Section 2—710).

§ 2—708. **Seller's Damages for Non-Acceptance or Repudiation.**

(1) Subject to subsection (2) and to the provisions of this Article with respect to proof of market price (Section 2—723), the measure of damages for non-acceptance or repudiation by the buyer is the difference between the market price at the time and place for tender and the unpaid contract price together with any incidental damages provided in this Article (Section 2—710), but less expenses saved in consequence of the buyer's breach.

(2) If the measure of damages provided in subsection (1) is inadequate to put the seller in as good a position as performance would have done then the measure of damages is the profit (including reasonable overhead) which the seller would have made from full performance by the buyer, together with any incidental damages provided in this Article (Section 2—710), due allowance for costs reasonably incurred and due credit for payments or proceeds of resale.

§ 2—709. **Action for the Price.**

(1) When the buyer fails to pay the price as it becomes due the seller may recover, together with any incidental damages under the next section, the price

(a) of goods accepted or of conforming goods lost or damaged within a commercially reasonable time after risk of their loss has passed to the buyer; and

(b) of goods identified to the contract if the seller is unable after reasonable effort to resell them at a reasonable price or the circumstances reasonably indicate that such effort will be unavailing.

(2) Where the seller sues for the price he must hold for the buyer any goods which have been identified to the contract and are still in his control except that if resale becomes possible he may resell them at any time prior to the collection of the judgment. The net proceeds of any such resale must be credited to the buyer and payment of the judgment entitles him to any goods not resold.

(3) After the buyer has wrongfully rejected or revoked acceptance of the goods or has failed to make a payment due or has repudiated (Section 2—610), a seller who is held not entitled to the price under this section shall nevertheless be awarded damages for non-acceptance under the preceding section.

§ 2—710. **Seller's Incidental Damages.**

Incidental damages to an aggrieved seller include any commercially reasonable charges, expenses or commissions incurred in stopping delivery, in the transportation, care and custody of goods after the buyer's breach, in connection with return or resale of the goods or otherwise resulting from the breach.

§ 2—711. **Buyer's Remedies in General; Buyer's Security Interest in Rejected Goods.**

(1) Where the seller fails to make delivery or repudiates or the buyer rightfully rejects or justifiably revokes acceptance then with respect to any goods involved, and with respect to the whole if the breach goes to the whole contract (Section 2—612), the buyer may cancel and whether or not he has done so may in addition to recovering so much of the price as has been paid

(a) "cover" and have damages under the next section as to all the goods affected whether or not they have been identified to the contract; or

(b) recover damages for non-delivery as provided in this Article (Section 2—713).

(2) Where the seller fails to deliver or repudiates the buyer may also

(a) if the goods have been identified recover them as provided in this Article (Section 2—502); or

(b) in a proper case obtain specific performance or replevy the goods as provided in this Article (Section 2—716).

(3) On rightful rejection or justifiable revocation of acceptance a buyer has a security interest in goods in his possession or control for any payments made on their price and any expenses reasonably incurred in their inspection, receipt, transportation, care and custody and may hold such goods and resell them in like manner as an aggrieved seller (Section 2—706).

§ 2—712. "Cover"; Buyer's Procurement of Substitute Goods.

(1) After a breach within the preceding section the buyer may "cover" by making in good faith and without unreasonable delay any reasonable purchase of or contract to purchase goods in substitution for those due from the seller.

(2) The buyer may recover from the seller as damages the difference between the cost of cover and the contract price together with any incidental or consequential damages as hereinafter defined (Section 2—715), but less expenses saved in consequence of the seller's breach.

(3) Failure of the buyer to effect cover within this section does not bar him from any other remedy.

§ 2—713. Buyer's Damages for Non-Delivery or Repudiation.

(1) Subject to the provisions of this Article with respect to proof of market price (Section 2—723), the measure of damages for non-delivery or repudiation by the seller is the difference between the market price at the time when the buyer learned of the breach and the contract price together with any incidental and consequential damages provided in this Article (Section 2—715), but less expenses saved in consequence of the seller's breach.

(2) Market price is to be determined as of the place for tender or, in cases of rejection after arrival or revocation of acceptance, as of the place of arrival.

§ 2—714. Buyer's Damages for Breach in Regard to Accepted Goods.

(1) Where the buyer has accepted goods and given notification (subsection (3) of Section 2—607) he may recover as damages for any non-conformity of tender the loss resulting in the ordinary course of events from the seller's breach as determined in any manner which is reasonable.

(2) The measure of damages for breach of warranty is the difference at the time and place of acceptance

between the value of the goods accepted and the value they would have had if they had been as warranted, unless special circumstances show proximate damages of a different amount.

(3) In a proper case any incidental and consequential damages under the next section may also be recovered.

§ 2—715. Buyer's Incidental and Consequential Damages.

(1) Incidental damages resulting from the seller's breach include expenses reasonably incurred in inspection, receipt, transportation and care and custody of goods rightfully rejected, any commercially reasonable charges, expenses or commissions in connection with effecting cover and any other reasonable expense incident to the delay or other breach.

(2) Consequential damages resulting from the seller's breach include

(a) any loss resulting from general or particular requirements and needs of which the seller at the time of contracting had reason to know and which could not reasonably be prevented by cover or otherwise; and

(b) injury to person or property proximately resulting from any breach of warranty.

§ 2—716 Buyer's Right to Specific Performance or Replevin.

(1) Specific performance may be decreed where the goods are unique or in other proper circumstances.

(2) The decree for specific performance may include such terms and conditions as to payment of the price, damages, or other relief as the court may deem just.

(3) The buyer has a right of replevin for goods identified to the contract if after reasonable effort he is unable to effect cover for such goods or the circumstances reasonably indicate that such effort will be unavailing or if the goods have been shipped under reservation and satisfaction of the security interest in them has been made or tendered.

§ 2—717. Deduction of Damages From the Price.

The buyer on notifying the seller of his intention to do so may deduct all or any part of the damages resulting from any breach of the contract from any part of the price still due under the same contract.

§ 2—718. Liquidation or Limitation of Damages; Deposits.

(1) Damages for breach by either party may be liquidated in the agreement but only at an amount which is reasonable in the light of the anticipated or actual harm caused by the breach, the difficulties of proof of loss, and the inconvenience or nonfeasibility of otherwise obtaining an adequate remedy. A term fixing unreasonably large liquidated damages is void as a penalty.

(2) Where the seller justifiably withholds delivery of goods because of the buyer's breach, the buyer is entitled to restitution of any amount by which the sum of his payments exceeds

    (a) the amount to which the seller is entitled by virtue of terms liquidating the seller's damages in accordance with subsection (1), or

    (b) in the absence of such terms, twenty per cent of the value of the total performance for which the buyer is obligated under the contract or $500, whichever is smaller.

(3) The buyer's right to restitution under subsection (2) is subject to offset to the extent that the seller establishes

    (a) a right to recover damages under the provisions of this Article other than subsection (1), and

    (b) the amount or value of any benefits received by the buyer directly or indirectly by reason of the contract.

(4) Where a seller has received payment in goods their reasonable value or the proceeds of their resale shall be treated as payments for the purposes of subsection (2); but if the seller has notice of the buyer's breach before reselling goods received in part performance, his resale is subject to the conditions laid down in this Article on resale by an aggrieved seller (Section 2—706).

§ 2—719. Contractual Modification or Limitation of Remedy.

(1) Subject to the provisions of subsections (2) and (3) of this section and of the preceding section on liquidation and limitation of damages,

    (a) the agreement may provide for remedies in addition to or in substitution for those provided in this Article and may limit or alter the measure of damages recoverable under this Article, as by limiting the buyer's remedies to return of the goods and repayment of the price or to repair and replacement of non-conforming goods or parts; and

    (b) resort to a remedy as provided is optional unless the remedy is expressly agreed to be exclusive, in which case it is the sole remedy.

(2) Where circumstances cause an exclusive or limited remedy to fail of its essential purpose, remedy may be had as provided in this Act.

(3) Consequential damages may be limited or excluded unless the limitation or exclusion is unconscionable. Limitation of consequential damages for injury to the person in the case of consumer goods is prima facie unconscionable but limitation of damages where the loss is commercial is not.

§ 2—720. Effect of "Cancellation" or "Rescission" on Claims for Antecedent Breach.

Unless the contrary intention clearly appears, expressions of "cancellation" or "rescission" of the contract or the like shall not be construed as a renunciation or discharge of any claim in damages for an antecedent breach.

§ 2—721. Remedies for Fraud.

Remedies for material misrepresentation or fraud include all remedies available under this Article for non-fraudulent breach. Neither rescission or a claim for rescission of the contract for sale nor rejection or return of the goods shall bar or be deemed inconsistent with a claim for damages or other remedy.

§ 2—722. Who Can Sue Third Parties for Injury to Goods.

Where a third party so deals with goods which have been identified to a contract for sale as to cause actionable injury to a party to that contract

    (a) a right of action against the third party is in either party to the contract for sale who has title to or a security interest or a special property or an insurable interest in the goods; and if the goods have been destroyed or converted a right of action is also in the party who either bore the risk of loss under the contract for sale or has since the injury assumed that risk as against the other;

    (b) if at the time of the injury the party plaintiff did not bear the risk of loss as against the other party to the contract for sale and there is no arrangement between them for disposition of the recovery, his suit or settlement is, subject to his own interest, as a fiduciary for the other party to the contract;

    (c) either party may with the consent of the other sue for the benefit of whom it may concern.

§ 2—723. **Proof of Market Price: Time and Place.**

(1) If an action based on anticipatory repudiation comes to trial before the time for performance with respect to some or all of the goods, any damages based on market price (Section 2—708 or Section 2—713) shall be determined according to the price of such goods prevailing at the time when the aggrieved party learned of the repudiation.

(2) If evidence of a price prevailing at the times or places described in this Article is not readily available the price prevailing within any reasonable time before or after the time described or at any other place which in commercial judgment or under usage of trade would serve as a reasonable substitute for the one described may be used, making any proper allowance for the cost of transporting the goods to or from such other place.

(3) Evidence of a relevant price prevailing at a time or place other than the one described in this Article offered by one party is not admissible unless and until he has given the other party such notice as the court finds sufficient to prevent unfair surprise.

§ 2—724. **Admissibility of Market Quotations.**

Whenever the prevailing price or value of any goods regularly bought and sold in any established commodity market is in issue, reports in official publications or trade journals or in newspapers or periodicals of general circulation published as the reports of such market shall be admissible in evidence. The circumstances of the preparation of such a report may be shown to affect its weight but not its admissibility.

§ 2—725. **Statute of Limitations in Contracts for Sale.**

(1) An action for breach of any contract for sale must be commenced within four years after the cause of action has accrued. By the original agreement the parties may reduce the period of limitation to not less than one year but may not extend it.

(2) A cause of action accrues when the breach occurs, regardless of the aggrieved party's lack of knowledge of the breach. A breach of warranty occurs when tender of delivery is made, except that where a warranty explicitly extends to future performance of the goods and discovery of the breach must await the time of such performance the cause of action accrues when the breach is or should have been discovered.

(3) Where an action commenced within the time limited by subsection (1) is so terminated as to leave available a remedy by another action for the same breach such other action may be commenced after the expiration of the time limited and within six months after the termination of the first action unless the termination resulted from voluntary discontinuance or from dismissal for failure or neglect to prosecute.

(4) This section does not alter the law on tolling of the statute of limitations nor does it apply to causes of action which have accrued before this Act becomes effective.

Article 3
COMMERCIAL PAPER

Part 1 Short Title, Form and Interpretation

§ 3—101. **Short Title.**

This Article shall be known and may be cited as Uniform Commercial Code—Commercial Paper.

§ 3—102. **Definitions and Index of Definitions.**

(1) In this Article unless the context otherwise requires

(a) "Issue" means the first delivery of an instrument to a holder or a remitter.

(b) An "order" is a direction to pay and must be more than an authorization or request. It must identify the person to pay with reasonable certainty. It may be addressed to one or more such persons jointly or in the alternative but not in succession.

(c) A "promise" is an undertaking to pay and must be more than an acknowledgment of an obligation.

(d) "Secondary party" means a drawer or endorser.

(e) "Instrument" means a negotiable instrument.

(2) Other definitions applying to this Article and the sections in which they appear are:
"Acceptance". Section 3—410.
"Accommodation party". Section 3—415.
"Alteration". Section 3—407.
"Certificate of deposit". Section 3—104.
"Certification". Section 3—411.
"Check". Section 3—104.
"Definite time". Section 3—109.
"Dishonor". Section 3—507.
"Draft". Section 3—104.
"Holder in due course". Section 3—302.

"Negotiation". Section 3—202.

"Note". Section 3—104.

"Notice of dishonor". Section 3—508.

"On demand". Section 3—108.

"Presentment". Section 3—504.

"Protest". Section 3—509.

"Restrictive Indorsement". Section 3—205.

"Signature". Section 3—401.

(3) The following definitions in other Articles apply to this Article:

"Account". Section 4—104.

"Banking Day". Section 4—104.

"Clearing House". Section 4—104.

"Collecting Bank". Section 4—105.

"Customer". Section 4—104.

"Depositary Bank". Section 4—105.

"Documentary Draft". Section 4—104.

"Intermediary Bank". Section 4—105.

"Item". Section 4—104.

"Midnight deadline". Section 4—104.

"Payor Bank". Section 4—105.

(4) In addition Article 1 contains general definitions and principles of construction and interpretation applicable throughout this Article.

§ 3—103. **Limitations on Scope of Article.**

(1) This Article does not apply to money, documents of title or investment securities.

(2) The provisions of this Article are subject to the provisions of the Article on Bank Deposits and Collections (Article 4) and Secured Transactions (Article 9).

§ 3—104. **Form of Negotiable Instruments; "Draft"; "Check"; "Certificate of Deposit"; "Note".**

(1) Any writing to be a negotiable instrument within this Article must

(a) be signed by the maker or drawer; and

(b) contain an unconditional promise or order to pay a sum certain in money and no other promise, order, obligation or power given by the maker or drawer except as authorized by this Article; and

(c) be payable on demand or at a definite time; and

(d) be payable to order or to bearer.

(2) A writing which complies with the requirements of this section is

(a) a "draft" ("bill of exchange") if it is an order;

(b) a "check" if it is a draft drawn on a bank and payable on demand;

(c) a "certificate of deposit" if it is an acknowledgment by a bank of receipt of money with an engagement to repay it;

(d) a "note" if it is a promise other than a certificate of deposit.

(3) As used in other Articles of this Act, and as the context may require, the terms "draft", "check", "certificate of deposit" and "note" may refer to instruments which are not negotiable within this Article as well as to instruments which are so negotiable.

§ 3—105. **When Promise or Order Unconditional.**

(1) A promise or order otherwise unconditional is not made conditional by the fact that the instrument

(a) is subject to implied or constructive conditions; or

(b) states its consideration, whether performed or promised, or the transaction which gave rise to the instrument, or that the promise or order is made or the instrument matures in accordance with or "as per" such transaction; or

(c) refers to or states that it arises out of a separate agreement or refers to a separate agreement for rights as to prepayment or acceleration; or

(d) states that it is drawn under a letter of credit; or

(e) states that it is secured, whether by mortgage, reservation of title or otherwise; or

(f) indicates a particular account to be debited or any other fund or source from which reimbursement is expected; or

(g) is limited to payment out of a particular fund or the proceeds of a particular source, if the instrument is issued by a government or governmental agency or unit; or

(h) is limited to payment out of the entire assets of a partnership, unincorporated association, trust or estate by or on behalf of which the instrument is issued.

(2) A promise or order is not unconditional if the instrument

(a) states that it is subject to or governed by any other agreement; or

(b) states that it is to be paid only out of a particular fund or source except as provided in this section.

§ 3—106. Sum Certain.

(1) The sum payable is a sum certain even though it is to be paid

(a) with stated interest or by stated installments; or

(b) with stated different rates of interest before and after default or a specified date; or

(c) with a stated discount or addition if paid before or after the date fixed for payment; or

(d) with exchange or less exchange, whether at a fixed rate or at the current rate; or

(e) with costs of collection or an attorney's fee or both upon default.

(2) Nothing in this section shall validate any term which is otherwise illegal.

§ 3—107. Money.

(1) An instrument is payable in money if the medium of exchange in which it is payable is money at the time the instrument is made. An instrument payable in "currency" or "current funds" is payable in money.

(2) A promise or order to pay a sum stated in a foreign currency is for a sum certain in money and, unless a different medium of payment is specified in the instrument, may be satisfied by payment of that number of dollars which the stated foreign currency will purchase at the buying sight rate for that currency on the day on which the instrument is payable or, if payable on demand, on the day of demand. If such an instrument specifies a foreign currency as the medium of payment the instrument is payable in that currency.

§ 3—108. Payable on Demand.

Instruments payable on demand include those payable at sight or on presentation and those in which no time for payment is stated.

§ 3—109. Definite Time.

(1) An instrument is payable at a definite time if by its terms it is payable

(a) on or before a stated date or at a fixed period after a stated date; or

(b) at a fixed period after sight; or

(c) at a definite time subject to any acceleration; or

(d) at a definite time subject to extension at the option of the holder, or to extension to a further definite time at the option of the maker or acceptor or automatically upon or after a specified act or event.

(2) An instrument which by its terms is otherwise payable only upon an act or event uncertain as to time of occurrence is not payable at a definite time even though the act or event has occurred.

§ 3—110. Payable to Order.

(1) An instrument is payable to order when by its terms it is payable to the order or assigns of any person therein specified with reasonable certainty, or to him or his order, or when it is conspicuously designated on its face as "exchange" or the like and names a payee. It may be payable to the order of

(a) the maker or drawer; or

(b) the drawee; or

(c) a payee who is not maker, drawer or drawee; or

(d) two or more payees together or in the alternative; or

(e) an estate, trust or fund, in which case it is payable to the order of the representative of such estate, trust or fund or his successors; or

(f) an office, or an officer by his title as such in which case it is payable to the principal but the incumbent of the office or his successors may act as if he or they were the holder; or

(g) a partnership or unincorporated association, in which case it is payable to the partnership or association and may be indorsed or transferred by any person thereto authorized.

(2) An instrument not payable to order is not made so payable by such words as "payable upon return of this instrument properly indorsed."

(3) An instrument made payable both to order and to bearer is payable to order unless the bearer words are handwritten or typewritten.

§ 3—111. Payable to Bearer.

An instrument is payable to bearer when by its terms it is payable to

(a) bearer or the order of bearer; or

(b) a specified person or bearer; or

(c) "cash" or the order of "cash", or any other indication which does not purport to designate a specific payee.

§ 3—112. Terms and Omissions Not Affecting Negotiability.

(1) The negotiability of an instrument is not affected by

(a) the omission of a statement of any consideration or of the place where the instrument is drawn or payable; or

(b) a statement that collateral has been given to secure obligations either on the instrument or otherwise of an obligor on the instrument or that in case of default on those obligations the holder may realize on or dispose of the collateral; or

(c) a promise or power to maintain or protect collateral or to give additional collateral; or

(d) a term authorizing a confession of judgment on the instrument if it is not paid when due; or

(e) a term purporting to waive the benefit of any law intended for the advantage or protection of any obligor; or

(f) a term in a draft providing that the payee by indorsing or cashing it acknowledges full satisfaction of an obligation of the drawer; or

(g) a statement in a draft drawn in a set of parts (Section 3—801) to the effect that the order is effective only if no other part has been honored.

(2) Nothing in this section shall validate any term which is otherwise illegal.

§ 3—113. **Seal.**

An instrument otherwise negotiable is within this Article even though it is under a seal.

§ 3—114. **Date, Antedating, Postdating.**

(1) The negotiability of an instrument is not affected by the fact that it is undated, antedated or postdated.

(2) Where an instrument is antedated or postdated the time when it is payable is determined by the stated date if the instrument is payable on demand or at a fixed period after date.

(3) Where the instrument or any signature thereon is dated, the date is presumed to be correct.

§ 3—115. **Incomplete Instruments.**

(1) When a paper whose contents at the time of signing show that it is intended to become an instrument is signed while still incomplete in any necessary respect it cannot be enforced until completed, but when it is completed in accordance with authority given it is effective as completed.

(2) If the completion is unauthorized the rules as to material alteration apply (Section 3—407), even though the paper was not delivered by the maker or drawer; but the burden of establishing that any completion is unauthorized is on the party so asserting.

§ 3—116. **Instruments Payable to Two or More Persons.**

An instrument payable to the order of two or more persons

(a) if in the alternative is payable to any one of them and may be negotiated, discharged or enforced by any of them who has possession of it;

(b) if not in the alternative is payable to all of them and may be negotiated, discharged or enforced only by all of them.

§ 3—117. **Instruments Payable With Words of Description.**

An instrument made payable to a named person with the addition of words describing him

(a) as agent or officer of a specified person is payable to his principal but the agent or officer may act as if he were the holder;

(b) as any other fiduciary for a specified person or purpose is payable to the payee and may be negotiated, discharged or enforced by him;

(c) in any other manner is payable to the payee unconditionally and the additional words are without effect on subsequent parties.

§ 3—118. **Ambiguous Terms and Rules of Construction.**

The following rules apply to every instrument:

(a) Where there is doubt whether the instrument is a draft or a note the holder may treat it as either. A draft drawn on the drawer is effective as a note.

(b) Handwritten terms control typewritten and printed terms, and typewritten control printed.

(c) Words control figures except that if the words are ambiguous figures control.

(d) Unless otherwise specified a provision for interest means interest at the judgment rate at the place of payment from the date of the instrument, or if it is undated from the date of issue.

(e) Unless the instrument otherwise specifies two or more persons who sign as maker, acceptor or drawer or indorser and as a part of the same transaction are jointly and severally liable even though the instrument contains such words as "I promise to pay."

(f) Unless otherwise specified consent to extension authorizes a single extension for not longer than the original period. A consent to extension, expressed in the instrument, is binding on secondary parties and accommodation makers. A holder may not exercise his option to extend an instrument over the objection of a maker or acceptor or other party who in accordance with Section 3—604 tenders full payment when the instrument is due.

§ 3—119. Other Writings Affecting Instrument.

(1) As between the obligor and his immediate obligee or any transferee the terms of an instrument may be modified or affected by any other written agreement executed as a part of the same transaction, except that a holder in due course in not affected by any limitation of his rights arising out of the separate written agreement if he had no notice of the limitation when he took the instrument.

(2) A separate agreement does not affect the negotiability of an instrument.

§ 3—120. Instruments "Payable Through" Bank.

An instrument which states that it is "payable through" a bank or the like designates that bank as a collecting bank to make presentment but does not of itself authorize the bank to pay the instrument.

§ 3—121. Instruments Payable at Bank.

Note: If this Act is introduced in the Congress of the United States this section should be omitted.
(States to select either alternative)

Alternative A—

A note or acceptance which states that it is payable at a bank is the equivalent of a draft drawn on the bank payable when it falls due out of any funds of the maker or acceptor in current account or otherwise available for such payment.

Alternative B—

A note or acceptance which states that it is payable at a bank is not of itself an order or authorization to the bank to pay it.

§ 3—122. Accrual of Cause of Action.

(1) A cause of action against a maker or an acceptor accrues

(a) in the case of a time instrument on the day after maturity;

(b) in the case of a demand instrument upon its date or, if no date is stated, on the date of issue.

(2) A cause of action against the obligor of a demand or time certificate of deposit accrues upon demand, but demand on a time certificate may not be made until on or after the date of maturity.

(3) A cause of action against a drawer of a draft or an indorser of any instrument accrues upon demand following dishonor of the instrument. Notice of dishonor is a demand.

(4) Unless an instrument provides otherwise, interest runs at the rate provided by law for a judgment

(a) in the case of a maker, acceptor or other primary obligor of a demand instrument, from the date of demand;

(b) in all other cases from the date of accrual of the cause of action.

Part 2 Transfer and Negotiation

§ 3—201. Transfer: Right to Indorsement.

(1) Transfer of an instrument vests in the transferee such rights as the transferor has therein, except that a transferee who has himself been a party to any fraud or illegality affecting the instrument or who as a prior holder had notice of a defense or claim against it cannot improve his position by taking from a later holder in due course.

(2) A transfer of a security interest in an instrument vests the foregoing rights in the transferee to the extent of the interest transferred.

(3) Unless otherwise agreed any transfer for value of an instrument not then payable to bearer gives the transferee the specifically enforceable right to have the unqualified indorsement of the transferor. Negotiation takes effect only when the indorsement is made and until that time there is no presumption that the transferee is the owner.

§ 3—202. Negotiation.

(1) Negotiation is the transfer of an instrument in such form that the transferee becomes a holder. If the instrument is payable to order it is negotiated by delivery with any necessary indorsement; if payable to bearer it is negotiated by delivery.

(2) An indorsement must be written by or on behalf of the holder and on the instrument or on a paper so firmly affixed thereto as to become a part thereof.

(3) An indorsement is effective for negotiation only when it conveys the entire instrument or any unpaid residue. If it purports to be of less it operates only as a partial assignment.

(4) Words of assignment, condition, waiver, guaranty, limitation or disclaimer of liability and the like accompanying an indorsement do not affect its character as an indorsement.

§ 3—203. **Wrong or Misspelled Name.**

Where an instrument is made payable to a person under a misspelled name or one other than his own he may indorse in that name or his own or both; but signature in both names may be required by a person paying or giving value for the instrument.

§ 3—204. **Special Indorsement; Blank Indorsement.**

(1) A special indorsement specifies the person to whom or to whose order it makes the instrument payable. Any instrument specially indorsed becomes payable to the order of the special indorsee and may be further negotiated only by his indorsement.

(2) An indorsement in blank specifies no particular indorsee and may consist of a mere signature. An instrument payable to order and indorsed in blank becomes payable to bearer and may be negotiated by delivery alone until specially indorsed.

(3) The holder may convert a blank indorsement into a special indorsement by writing over the signature of the indorser in blank any contract consistent with the character of the indorsement.

§ 3—205. **Restrictive Indorsements.**

An indorsement is restrictive which either

(a) is conditional; or

(b) purports to prohibit further transfer of the instrument; or

(c) includes the words "for collection", "for deposit", "pay any bank", or like terms signifying a purpose of deposit or collection; or

(d) otherwise states that it is for the benefit or use of the indorser or of another person.

§ 3—206. **Effect of Restrictive Indorsement.**

(1) No restrictive indorsement prevents further transfer or negotiation of the instrument.

(2) An intermediary bank, or a payor bank which is not the depositary bank, is neither given notice nor otherwise affected by a restrictive indorsement of any person except the bank's immediate transferor or the person presenting for payment.

(3) Except for an intermediary bank, any transferee under an indorsement which is conditional or includes the words "for collection", "for deposit", "pay any bank", or like terms (subparagraphs (a) and (c) of Section 3—205) must pay or apply any value given by him for or on the security of the instrument consistently with the indorsement and to the extent that he does so he becomes a holder for value. In addition such transferee is a holder in due course if he otherwise complies with the requirements of Section 3—302 on what constitutes a holder in due course.

(4) The first taker under an indorsement for the benefit of the indorser or another person (subparagraph (d) of Section 3—205) must pay or apply any value given by him for or on the security of the instrument consistently with the indorsement and to the extent that he does so he becomes a holder for value. In addition such taker is a holder in due course if he otherwise complies with the requirements of Section 3—302 on what constitutes a holder in due course. A later holder for value is neither given notice nor otherwise affected by such restrictive indorsement unless he has knowledge that a fiduciary or other person has negotiated the instrument in any transaction for his own benefit or otherwise in breach of duty (subsection (2) of Section 3—304).

§ 3—207. **Negotiation Effective Although It May Be Rescinded.**

(1) Negotiation is effective to transfer the instrument although the negotiation is

(a) made by an infant, a corporation exceeding its powers, or any other person without capacity; or

(b) obtained by fraud, duress or mistake of any kind; or

(c) part of an illegal transaction; or

(d) made in breach of duty.

(2) Except as against a subsequent holder in due course such negotiation is in an appropriate case subject to rescission, the declaration of a constructive trust or any other remedy permitted by law.

§ 3—208. **Reacquisition.**

Where an instrument is returned to or reacquired by a prior party he may cancel any indorsement which is not necessary to his title and reissue or further negotiate the instrument, but any intervening party is discharged as against the reacquiring party and subsequent holders not in due course and if his indorsement has been cancelled is discharged as against subsequent holders in due course as well.

Part 3 **Rights of a Holder**

§ 3—301. **Rights of a Holder.**

The holder of an instrument whether or not he is the owner may transfer or negotiate it and, except as otherwise provided in Section 3—603 on payment or satisfaction, discharge it or enforce payment in his own name.

§ 3—302. **Holder in Due Course.**

(1) A holder in due course is a holder who takes the instrument

    (a) for value; and

    (b) in good faith; and

    (c) without notice that it is overdue or has been dishonored or of any defense against or claim to it on the part of any person.

(2) A payee may be a holder in due course.

(3) A holder does not become a holder in due course of an instrument:

    (a) by purchase of it at judicial sale or by taking it under legal process; or

    (b) by acquiring it in taking over an estate; or

    (c) by purchasing it as part of a bulk transaction not in regular course of business of the transferor.

(4) A purchaser of a limited interest can be a holder in due course only to the extent of the interest purchased.

§ 3—303. **Taking for Value.**

A holder takes the instrument for value

(a) to the extent that the agreed consideration has been performed or that he acquires a security interest in or a lien on the instrument otherwise than by legal process; or

(b) when he takes the instrument in payment of or as security for an antecedent claim against any person whether or not the claim is due; or

(c) when he gives a negotiable instrument for it or makes an irrevocable commitment to a third person.

§ 3—304. **Notice to Purchaser.**

(1) The purchaser has notice of a claim or defense if

    (a) the instrument is so incomplete, bears such visible evidence of forgery or alteration, or is otherwise so irregular as to call into question its validity, terms or ownership or to create an ambiguity as to the party to pay; or

    (b) the purchaser has notice that the obligation of any party is voidable in whole or in part, or that all parties have been discharged.

(2) The purchaser has notice of a claim against the instrument when he has knowledge that a fiduciary has negotiated the instrument in payment of or as security for his own debt or in any transaction for his own benefit or otherwise in breach of duty.

(3) The purchaser has notice that an instrument is overdue if he has reason to know

    (a) that any part of the principal amount is overdue or that there is an uncured default in payment of another instrument of the same series; or

    (b) that acceleration of the instrument has been made; or

    (c) that he is taking a demand instrument after demand has been made or more than a reasonable length of time after its issue. A reasonable time for a check drawn and payable within the states and territories of the United States and the District of Columbia is presumed to be thirty days.

(4) Knowledge of the following facts does not of itself give the purchaser notice of a defense or claim

    (a) that the instrument is antedated or postdated;

    (b) that it was issued or negotiated in return for an executory promise or accompanied by a separate agreement, unless the purchaser has notice that a defense or claim has arisen from the terms thereof;

    (c) that any party has signed for accommodation;

    (d) that an incomplete instrument has been completed, unless the purchaser has notice of any improper completion;

    (e) that any person negotiating the instrument is or was a fiduciary;

    (f) that there has been default in payment of interest on the instrument or in payment of any other instrument, except one of the same series.

(5) The filing or recording of a document does not of itself constitute notice within the provisions of this Article to a person who would otherwise be a holder in due course.

(6) To be effective notice must be received at such time and in such manner as to give a reasonable opportunity to act on it.

§ 3—305. **Rights of a Holder in Due Course.**

To the extent that a holder is a holder in due course he takes the instrument free from

(1) all claims to it on the part of any person; and

(2) all defenses of any party to the instrument with whom the holder has not dealt except

    (a) infancy, to the extent that it is a defense to a simple contract; and

    (b) such other incapacity, or duress, or illegality of the transaction, as renders the obligation of the party a nullity; and

    (c) such misrepresentation as has induced the party to sign the instrument with neither knowledge nor reasonable opportunity to obtain knowledge of its character or its essential terms; and

(d) discharge in insolvency proceedings; and

(e) any other discharge of which the holder has notice when he takes the instrument.

§ 3—306. Rights of One Not Holder in Due Course.

Unless he has the rights of a holder in due course any person takes the instrument subject to

(a) all valid claims to it on the part of any person; and

(b) all defenses of any party which would be available in an action on a simple contract; and

(c) the defenses of want or failure of consideration, nonperformance of any condition precedent, nondelivery, or delivery for a special purpose (Section 3—408); and

(d) the defense that he or a person through whom he holds the instrument acquired it by theft, or that payment or satisfaction to such holder would be inconsistent with the terms of a restrictive indorsement. The claim of any third person to the instrument is not otherwise available as a defense to any party liable thereon unless the third person himself defends the action for such party.

§ 3—307. Burden of Establishing Signatures, Defenses and Due Course.

(1) Unless specifically denied in the pleadings each signature on an instrument is admitted. When the effectiveness of a signature is put in issue

(a) the burden of establishing it is on the party claiming under the signature; but

(b) the signature is presumed to be genuine or authorized except where the action is to enforce the obligation of a purported signer who has died or become incompetent before proof is required.

(2) When signatures are admitted or established, production of the instrument entitles a holder to recover on it unless the defendant establishes a defense.

(3) After it is shown that a defense exists a person claiming the rights of a holder in due course has the burden of establishing that he or some person under whom he claims is in all respects a holder in due course.

Part 4 Liability of Parties

§ 3—401. Signature.

(1) No person is liable on an instrument unless his signature appears thereon.

(2) A signature is made by use of any name, including any trade or assumed name, upon an instrument, or by any word or mark used in lieu of a written signature.

§ 3—402. Signature in Ambiguous Capacity.

Unless the instrument clearly indicates that a signature is made in some other capacity it is an indorsement.

§ 3—403. Signature by Authorized Representative.

(1) A signature may be made by an agent or other representative, and his authority to make it may be established as in other cases of representation. No particular form of appointment is necessary to establish such authority.

(2) An authorized representative who signs his own name to an instrument

(a) is personally obligated if the instrument neither names the person represented nor shows that the representative signed in a representative capacity;

(b) except as otherwise established between the immediate parties, is personally obligated if the instrument names the person represented but does not show that the representative signed in a representative capacity, or if the instrument does not name the person represented but does show that the representative signed in a representative capacity.

(3) Except as otherwise established the name of an organization preceded or followed by the name and office of an authorized individual is a signature made in a representative capacity.

§ 3—404. Unauthorized Signatures.

(1) Any unauthorized signature is wholly inoperative as that of the person whose name is signed unless he ratifies it or is precluded from denying it; but it operates as the signature of the unauthorized signer in favor of any person who in good faith pays the instrument or takes it for value.

(2) Any unauthorized signature may be ratified for all purposes of this Article. Such ratification does not of itself affect any rights of the person ratifying against the actual signer.

§ 3—405. Impostors; Signature in Name of Payee.

(1) An indorsement by any person in the name of a named payee is effective if

(a) an impostor by use of the mails or otherwise has induced the maker or drawer to issue the instrument to him or his confederate in the name of the payee; or

(b) a person signing as or on behalf of a maker or drawer intends the payee to have no interest in the instrument; or

(c) an agent or employee of the maker or drawer has supplied him with the name of the payee intending the latter to have no such interest.

(2) Nothing in this section shall affect the criminal or civil liability of the person so indorsing.

§ 3—406. Negligence Contributing to Alteration or Unauthorized Signature.

Any person who by his negligence substantially contributes to a material alteration of the instrument or to the making of an unauthorized signature is precluded from asserting the alteration or lack of authority against a holder in due course or against a drawee or other payor who pays the instrument in good faith and in accordance with the reasonable commercial standards of the drawee's or payor's business.

§ 3—407. Alteration.

(1) Any alteration of an instrument is material which changes the contract of any party thereto in any respect, including any such change in

(a) the number or relations of the parties; or

(b) an incomplete instrument, by completing it otherwise than as authorized; or

(c) the writing as signed, by adding to it or by removing any part of it.

(2) As against any person other than a subsequent holder in due course

(a) alteration by the holder which is both fraudulent and material discharges any party whose contract is thereby changed unless that party assents or is precluded from asserting the defense;

(b) no other alteration discharges any party and the instrument may be enforced according to its original tenor, or as to incomplete instruments according to the authority given.

(3) A subsequent holder in due course may in all cases enforce the instrument according to its original tenor, and when an incomplete instrument has been completed, he may enforce it as completed.

§ 3—408. Consideration.

Want or failure of consideration is a defense as against any person not having the rights of a holder in due course (Section 3—305), except that no consideration is necessary for an instrument or obligation thereon given in payment of or as security for an antecedent obligation of any kind. Nothing in this section shall be taken to displace any statute outside this Act under which a promise is enforceable notwithstanding lack or failure of consideration. Partial failure of consideration is a defense pro tanto whether or not the failure is in an ascertained or liquidated amount.

§ 3—409. Draft Not an Assignment.

(1) A check or other draft does not of itself operate as an assignment of any funds in the hands of the drawee available for its payment, and the drawee is not liable on the instrument until he accepts it.

(2) Nothing in this section shall affect any liability in contract, tort or otherwise arising from any letter of credit or other obligation or representation which is not an acceptance.

§ 3—410. Definition and Operation of Acceptance.

(1) Acceptance is the drawee's signed engagement to honor the draft as presented. It must be written on the draft, and may consist of his signature alone. It becomes operative when completed by delivery or notification.

(2) A draft may be accepted although it has not been signed by the drawer or is otherwise incomplete or is overdue or has been dishonored.

(3) Where the draft is payable at a fixed period after sight and the acceptor fails to date his acceptance the holder may complete it by supplying a date in good faith.

§ 3—411. Certification of a Check.

(1) Certification of a check is acceptance. Where a holder procures certification the drawer and all prior indorsers are discharged.

(2) Unless otherwise agreed a bank has no obligation to certify a check.

(3) A bank may certify a check before returning it for lack of proper indorsement. If it does so the drawer is discharged.

§ 3—412. Acceptance Varying Draft.

(1) Where the drawee's proffered acceptance in any manner varies the draft as presented the holder may refuse the acceptance and treat the draft as dishonored in which case the drawee is entitled to have his acceptance cancelled.

(2) The terms of the draft are not varied by an acceptance to pay at any particular bank or place in the United States, unless the acceptance states that the draft is to be paid only at such bank or place.

(3) Where the holder assents to an acceptance varying the terms of the draft each drawer and indorser who does not affirmatively assent is discharged.

§ 3—413. **Contract of Maker, Drawer and Acceptor.**

(1) The maker or acceptor engages that he will pay the instrument according to its tenor at the time of his engagement or as completed pursuant to Section 3—115 on incomplete instruments.

(2) The drawer engages that upon dishonor of the draft and any necessary notice of dishonor or protest he will pay the amount of the draft to the holder or to any indorser who takes it up. The drawer may disclaim this liability by drawing without recourse.

(3) By making, drawing or accepting the party admits as against all subsequent parties including the drawee the existence of the payee and his then capacity to indorse.

§ 3—414. **Contract of Indorser; Order of Liability.**

(1) Unless the indorsement otherwise specifies (as by such words as "without recourse") every indorser engages that upon dishonor and any necessary notice of dishonor and protest he will pay the instrument according to its tenor at the time of his indorsement to the holder or to any subsequent indorser who takes it up, even though the indorser who takes it up was not obligated to do so.

(2) Unless they otherwise agree indorsers are liable to one another in the order in which they indorse, which is presumed to be the order in which their signatures appear on the instrument.

§ 3—415. **Contract of Accommodation Party.**

(1) An accommodation party is one who signs the instrument in any capacity for the purpose of lending his name to another party to it.

(2) When the instrument has been taken for value before it is due the accommodation party is liable in the capacity in which he has signed even though the taker knows of the accommodation.

(3) As against a holder in due course and without notice of the accommodation oral proof of the accommodation is not admissible to give the accommodation party the benefit of discharges dependent on his character as such. In other cases the accommodation character may be shown by oral proof.

(4) An indorsement which shows that it is not in the chain of title is notice of its accommodation character.

(5) An accommodation party is not liable to the party accommodated, and if he pays the instrument has a right of recourse on the instrument against such party.

§ 3—416. **Contract of Guarantor.**

(1) "Payment guaranteed" or equivalent words added to a signature mean that the signer engages that if the instrument is not paid when due he will pay it according to its tenor without resort by the holder to any other party.

(2) "Collection guaranteed" or equivalent words added to a signature mean that the signer engages that if the instrument is not paid when due he will pay it according to its tenor, but only after the holder has reduced his claim against the maker or acceptor to judgment and execution has been returned unsatisfied, or after the maker or acceptor has become insolvent or it is otherwise apparent that it is useless to proceed against him.

(3) Words of guaranty which do not otherwise specify guarantee payment.

(4) No words of guaranty added to the signature of a sole maker or acceptor affect his liability on the instrument. Such words added to the signature of one of two or more makers or acceptors create a presumption that the signature is for the accommodation of the others.

(5) When words of guaranty are used presentment, notice of dishonor and protest are not necessary to charge the user.

(6) Any guaranty written on the instrument is enforcible notwithstanding any statute of frauds.

§ 3—417. **Warranties on Presentment and Transfer.**

(1) Any person who obtains payment or acceptance and any prior transferor warrants to a person who in good faith pays or accepts that

   (a) he has a good title to the instrument or is authorized to obtain payment or acceptance on behalf of one who has a good title; and

   (b) he has no knowledge that the signature of the maker or drawer is unauthorized, except that this warranty is not given by a holder in due course acting in good faith

      (i) to a maker with respect to the maker's own signature; or

(ii) to a drawer with respect to the drawer's own signature, whether or not the drawer is also the drawee; or

(iii) to an acceptor of a draft if the holder in due course took the draft after the acceptance or obtained the acceptance without knowledge that the drawer's signature was unauthorized; and

(c) the instrument has not been materially altered, except that this warranty is not given by a holder in due course acting in good faith

(i) to the maker of a note; or

(ii) to the drawer of a draft whether or not the drawer is also the drawee; or

(iii) to the acceptor of a draft with respect to an alteration made prior to the acceptance if the holder in due course took the draft after the acceptance, even though the acceptance provided "payable as originally drawn" or equivalent terms; or

(iv) to the acceptor of a draft with respect to an alteration made after the acceptance.

(2) Any person who transfers an instrument and receives consideration warrants to his transferee and if the transfer is by indorsement to any subsequent holder who takes the instrument in good faith that

(a) he has a good title to the instrument or is authorized to obtain payment or acceptance on behalf of one who has a good title and the transfer is otherwise rightful; and

(b) all signatures are genuine or authorized; and

(c) the instrument has not been materially altered; and

(d) no defense of any party is good against him; and

(e) he has no knowledge of any insolvency proceeding instituted with respect to the maker or acceptor or the drawer of an unaccepted instrument.

(3) By transferring "without recourse" the transferor limits the obligation stated in subsection (2) (d) to a warranty that he has no knowledge of such a defense.

(4) A selling agent or broker who does not disclose the fact that he is acting only as such gives the warranties provided in this section, but if he makes such disclosure warrants only his good faith and authority.

§ 3—418. Finality of Payment or Acceptance.

Except for recovery of bank payments as provided in the Article on Bank Deposits and Collections (Article

4) and except for liability for breach of warranty on presentment under the preceding section, payment or acceptance of any instrument is final in favor of a holder in due course, or a person who has in good faith changed his position in reliance on the payment.

§ 3—419. Conversion of Instrument; Innocent Representative.

(1) An instrument is converted when

(a) a drawee to whom it is delivered for acceptance refuses to return it on demand; or

(b) any person to whom it is delivered for payment refuses on demand either to pay or to return it; or

(c) it is paid on a forged indorsement.

(2) In an action against a drawee under subsection (1) the measure of the drawee's liability is the face amount of the instrument. In any other action under subsection (1) the measure of liability is presumed to be the face amount of the instrument.

(3) Subject to the provisions of this Act concerning restrictive indorsements a representative, including a depositary or collecting bank, who has in good faith and in accordance with the reasonable commercial standards applicable to the business of such representative dealt with an instrument or its proceeds on behalf of one who was not the true owner is not liable in conversion or otherwise to the true owner beyond the amount of any proceeds remaining in his hands.

(4) An intermediary bank or payor bank which is not a depositary bank is not liable in conversion solely by reason of the fact that proceeds of an item indorsed restrictively (Sections 3—205 and 3—206) are not paid or applied consistently with the restrictive indorsement of an indorser other than its immediate transferor.

Part 5 Presentment, Notice of Dishonor and Protest

§ 3—501. When Presentment, Notice of Dishonor, and Protest Necessary or Permissible.

(1) Unless excused (Section 3—511) presentment is necessary to charge secondary parties as follows:

(a) presentment for acceptance is necessary to charge the drawer and indorsers of a draft where the draft so provides, or is payable elsewhere than at the residence or place of business of the drawee, or its date of payment depends upon such presentment. The holder may at his option present for acceptance any other draft payable at a stated date;

(b) presentment for payment is necessary to charge any indorser;

(c) in the case of any drawer, the acceptor of a draft payable at a bank or the maker of a note payable at a bank, presentment for payment is necessary, but failure to make presentment discharges such drawer, acceptor or maker only as stated in Section 3—502(1) (b).

(2) Unless excused (Section 3—511)

(a) notice of any dishonor is necessary to charge any indorser;

(b) in the case of any drawer, the acceptor of a draft payable at a bank or the maker of a note payable at a bank, notice of any dishonor is necessary, but failure to give such notice discharges such drawer, acceptor or maker only as stated in Section 3—502(1) (b).

(3) Unless excused (Section 3—511) protest of any dishonor is necessary to charge the drawer and indorsers of any draft which on its face appears to be drawn or payable outside of the states, territories, dependencies, and possessions of the United States, the District of Columbia and the Commonwealth of Puerto Rico. The holder may at his option make protest of any dishonor of any other instrument and in the case of a foreign draft may on insolvency of the acceptor before maturity make protest for better security.

(4) Notwithstanding any provision of this section, neither presentment nor notice of dishonor nor protest is necessary to charge an indorser who has indorsed an instrument after maturity.

§ 3—502. Unexcused Delay; Discharge.

(1) Where without excuse any necessary presentment or notice of dishonor is delayed beyond the time when it is due

(a) any indorser is discharged; and

(b) any drawer or the acceptor of a draft payable at a bank or the maker of a note payable at a bank who because the drawee or payor bank becomes insolvent during the delay is deprived of funds maintained with the drawee or payor bank to cover the instrument may discharge his liability by written assignment to the holder of his rights against the drawee or payor bank in respect of such funds, but such drawer, acceptor or maker is not otherwise discharged.

(2) Where without excuse a necessary protest is delayed beyond the time when it is due any drawer or indorser is discharged.

§ 3—503. Time of Presentment.

(1) Unless a different time is expressed in the instrument the time for any presentment is determined as follows:

(a) where an instrument is payable at or a fixed period after a stated date any presentment for acceptance must be made on or before the date it is payable;

(b) where an instrument is payable after sight it must either be presented for acceptance or negotiated within a reasonable time after date or issue whichever is later;

(c) where an instrument shows the date on which it is payable presentment for payment is due on that date;

(d) where an instrument is accelerated presentment for payment is due within a reasonable time after the acceleration;

(e) with respect to the liability of any secondary party presentment for acceptance or payment of any other instrument is due within a reasonable time after such party becomes liable thereon.

(2) A reasonable time for presentment is determined by the nature of the instrument, any usage of banking or trade and the facts of the particular case. In the case of an uncertified check which is drawn and payable within the United States and which is not a draft drawn by a bank the following are presumed to be reasonable periods within which to present for payment or to initiate bank collection:

(a) with respect to the liability of the drawer, thirty days after date or issue whichever is later; and

(b) with respect to the liability of an indorser, seven days after his indorsement.

(3) Where any presentment is due on a day which is not a full business day for either the person making presentment or the party to pay or accept, presentment is due on the next following day which is a full business day for both parties.

(4) Presentment to be sufficient must be made at a reasonable hour, and if at a bank during its banking day.

§ 3—504. How Presentment Made.

(1) Presentment is a demand for acceptance or payment made upon the maker, acceptor, drawee or other payor by or on behalf of the holder.

(2) Presentment may be made

(a) by mail, in which event the time of presentment is determined by the time of receipt of the
mail; or

(b) through a clearing house; or

(c) at the place of acceptance or payment specified
in the instrument or if there be none at the place of
business or residence of the party to accept or pay.
If neither the party to accept or pay nor anyone
authorized to act for him is present or accessible at
such place presentment is excused.

(3) It may be made

(a) to any one of two or more makers, acceptors,
drawees or other payors; or

(b) to any person who has authority to make or
refuse the acceptance or payment.

(4) A draft accepted or a note made payable at a bank
in the United States must be presented at such bank.

(5) In the cases described in Section 4—210 presentment may be made in the manner and with the result
stated in that section.

§ 3—505. Rights of Party to Whom Presentment Is Made.

(1) The party to whom presentment is made may
without dishonor require

(a) exhibition of the instrument; and

(b) reasonable identification of the person making presentment and evidence of his authority to
make it if made for another; and

(c) that the instrument be produced for acceptance or payment at a place specified in it, or if
there be none at any place reasonable in the
circumstances; and

(d) a signed receipt on the instrument for any
partial or full payment and its surrender upon full
payment.

(2) Failure to comply with any such requirement
invalidates the presentment but the person presenting has a reasonable time in which to comply and the
time for acceptance or payment runs from the time of
compliance.

§ 3—506. Time Allowed for Acceptance or Payment.

(1) Acceptance may be deferred without dishonor
until the close of the next business day following
presentment. The holder may also in a good faith
effort to obtain acceptance and without either
dishonor of the instrument or discharge of secondary
parties allow postponement of acceptance for an
additional business day.

(2) Except as a longer time is allowed in the case of
documentary drafts drawn under a letter of credit,
and unless an earlier time is agreed to by the party to
pay, payment of an instrument may be deferred
without dishonor pending reasonable examination to
determine whether it is properly payable, but
payment must be made in any event before the close
of business on the day of presentment.

§ 3—507. Dishonor; Holder's Right of Recourse; Term Allowing Re-Presentment.

(1) An instrument is dishonored when

(a) a necessary or optional presentment is duly
made and due acceptance or payment is refused or
cannot be obtained within the prescribed time or in
case of bank collections the instrument is seasonably returned by the midnight deadline (Section
4—301); or

(b) presentment is excused and the instrument is
not duly accepted or paid.

(2) Subject to any necessary notice of dishonor and
protest, the holder has upon dishonor an immediate
right of recourse against the drawers and indorsers.

(3) Return of an instrument for lack of proper
indorsement is not dishonor.

(4) A term in a draft or an indorsement thereof
allowing a stated time for re-presentment in the event
of any dishonor of the draft by nonacceptance if a time
draft or by nonpayment if a sight draft gives the
holder as against any secondary party bound by the
term an option to waive the dishonor without
affecting the liability of the secondary party and he
may present again up to the end of the stated time.

§ 3—508. Notice of Dishonor.

(1) Notice of dishonor may be given to any person
who may be liable on the instrument by or on behalf of
the holder or any party who has himself received
notice, or any other party who can be compelled to pay
the instrument. In addition an agent or bank in whose
hands the instrument is dishonored may give notice to
his principal or customer or to another agent or bank
from which the instrument was received.

(2) Any necessary notice must be given by a bank
before its midnight deadline and by any other person
before midnight of the third business day after
dishonor or receipt of notice of dishonor.

(3) Notice may be given in any reasonable manner. It
may be oral or written and in any terms which identify
the instrument and state that it has been dishonored.
A misdescription which does not mislead the party
notified does not vitiate the notice. Sending the
instrument bearing a stamp, ticket or writing stating

that acceptance or payment has been refused or sending a notice of debit with respect to the instrument is sufficient.

(4) Written notice is given when sent although it is not received.

(5) Notice to one partner is notice to each although the firm has been dissolved.

(6) When any party is in insolvency proceedings instituted after the issue of the instrument notice may be given either to the party or to the representative of his estate.

(7) When any party is dead or incompetent notice may be sent to his last known address or given to his personal representative.

(8) Notice operates for the benefit of all parties who have rights on the instrument against the party notified.

§ 3—509. **Protest; Noting for Protest.**

(1) A protest is a certificate of dishonor made under the hand and seal of a United States consul or vice consul or a notary public or other person authorized to certify dishonor by the law of the place where dishonor occurs. It may be made upon information satisfactory to such person.

(2) The protest must identify the instrument and certify either that due presentment has been made or the reason why it is excused and that the instrument has been dishonored by nonacceptance or nonpayment.

(3) The protest may also certify that notice of dishonor has been given to all parties or to specified parties.

(4) Subject to subsection (5) any necessary protest is due by the time that notice of dishonor is due.

(5) If, before protest is due, an instrument has been noted for protest by the officer to make protest, the protest may be made at any time thereafter as of the date of the noting.

§ 3—510. **Evidence of Dishonor and Notice of Dishonor.**

The following are admissible as evidence and create a presumption of dishonor and of any notice of dishonor therein shown:

(a) a document regular in form as provided in the preceding section which purports to be a protest;

(b) the purported stamp or writing of the drawee, payor bank or presenting bank on the instrument or accompanying it stating that acceptance or payment has been refused for reasons conconsistent with dishonor;

(c) any book or record of the drawee, payor bank, or any collecting bank kept in the usual course of business which shows dishonor, even though there is no evidence of who made the entry.

§ 3—511. **Waived or Excused Presentment, Protest or Notice of Dishonor or Delay Therein.**

(1) Delay in presentment, protest or notice of dishonor is excused when the party is without notice that it is due or when the delay is caused by circumstances beyond his control and he exercises reasonable diligence after the cause of the delay ceases to operate.

(2) Presentment or notice or protest as the case may be is entirely excused when

(a) the party to be charged has waived it expressly or by implication either before or after it is due; or

(b) such party has himself dishonored the instrument or has countermanded payment or otherwise has no reason to expect or right to require that the instrument be accepted or paid; or

(c) by reasonable diligence the presentment or protest cannot be made or the notice given.

(3) Presentment is also entirely excused when

(a) the maker, acceptor or drawee of any instrument except a documentary draft is dead or in insolvency proceedings instituted after the issue of the instrument; or

(b) acceptance or payment is refused but not for want of proper presentment.

(4) Where a draft has been dishonored by nonacceptance a later presentment for payment and any notice of dishonor and protest for nonpayment are excused unless in the meantime the instrument has been accepted.

(5) A waiver of protest is also a waiver of presentment and of notice of dishonor even though protest is not required.

(6) Where a waiver of presentment or notice or protest is embodied in the instrument itself it is binding upon all parties; but where it is written above the signature of an indorser it binds him only.

Part 6 Discharge

§ 3—601. **Discharge of Parties.**

(1) The extent of the discharge of any party from

liability on an instrument is governed by the sections on

    (a) payment or satisfaction (Section 3—603); or

    (b) tender of payment (Section 3—604); or

    (c) cancellation or renunciation (Section 3—605); or

    (d) impairment of right of recourse or of collateral (Section 3—606); or

    (e) reacquisition of the instrument by a prior party (Section 3—208); or

    (f) fraudulent and material alteration (Section 3—407); or

    (g) certification of a check (Section 3—411); or

    (h) acceptance varying a draft (Section 3—412); or

    (i) unexcused delay in presentment or notice of dishonor or protest (Section 3—502).

(2) Any party is also discharged from his liability on an instrument to another party by any other act or agreement with such party which would discharge his simple contract for the payment of money.

(3) The liability of all parties is discharged when any party who has himself no right of action or recourse on the instrument

    (a) reacquires the instrument in his own right; or

    (b) is discharged under any provision of this Article, except as otherwise provided with respect to discharge for impairment of recourse or of collateral (Section 3—606).

§ 3—602. Effect of Discharge Against Holder in Due Course.

No discharge of any party provided by this Article is effective against a subsequent holder in due course unless he has notice thereof when he takes the instrument.

§ 3—603. Payment or Satisfaction.

(1) The liability of any party is discharged to the extent of his payment or satisfaction to the holder even though it is made with knowledge of a claim of another person to the instrument unless prior to such payment or satisfaction the person making the claim either supplies indemnity deemed adequate by the party seeking the discharge or enjoins payment or satisfaction by order of a court of competent jurisdiction in an action in which the adverse claimant and the holder are parties. This subsection does not, however, result in the discharge of the liability

    (a) of a party who in bad faith pays or satisfies a holder who acquired the instrument by theft or who (unless having the rights of a holder in due course) holds through one who so acquired it; or

    (b) of a party (other than an intermediary bank or a payor bank which is not a depositary bank) who pays or satisfies the holder of an instrument which has been restrictively indorsed in a manner not consistent with the terms of such restrictive indorsement.

(2) Payment or satisfaction may be made with the consent of the holder by any person including a stranger to the instrument. Surrender of the instrument to such a person gives him the rights of a transferee (Section 3—201).

§ 3—604. Tender of Payment.

(1) Any party making tender of full payment to a holder when or after it is due is discharged to the extent of all subsequent liability for interest, costs and attorney's fees.

(2) The holder's refusal of such tender wholly discharges any party who has a right of recourse against the party making the tender.

(3) Where the maker or acceptor of an instrument payable otherwise than on demand is able and ready to pay at every place of payment specified in the instrument when it is due, it is equivalent to tender.

§ 3—605. Cancellation and Renunciation.

(1) The holder of an instrument may even without consideration discharge any party

    (a) in any manner apparent on the face of the instrument or the indorsement, as by intentionally cancelling the instrument or the party's signature by destruction or mutilation, or by striking out the party's signature; or

    (b) by renouncing his rights by a writing signed and delivered or by surrender of the instrument to the party to be discharged.

(2) Neither cancellation nor renunciation without surrender of the instrument affects the title thereto.

§ 3—606. Impairment of Recourse or of Collateral.

(1) The holder discharges any party to the instrument to the extent that without such party's consent the holder

    (a) without express reservation of rights releases or agrees not to sue any person against whom the party has to the knowledge of the holder a right of recourse or agrees to suspend the right to enforce against such person the instrument or collateral or otherwise discharges such person, except that failure or delay in effecting any required presentment, protest or notice of dishonor with respect to any such person does not discharge any party as to whom presentment, protest or notice of dishonor is effective or unnecessary; or

(b) unjustifiably impairs any collateral for the instrument given by or on behalf of the party or any person against whom he has a right of recourse.

(2) By express reservation of rights against a party with a right of recourse the holder preserves

(a) all his rights against such party as of the time when the instrument was originally due; and

(b) the right of the party to pay the instrument as of that time; and

(c) all rights of such party to recourse against others.

Part 7 Advice of International Sight Draft

§ 3—701. Letter of Advice of International Sight Draft.

(1) A "letter of advice" is a drawer's communication to the drawee that a described draft has been drawn.

(2) Unless otherwise agreed when a bank receives from another bank a letter of advice of an international sight draft the drawee bank may immediately debit the drawer's account and stop the running of interest pro tanto. Such a debit and any resulting credit to any account covering outstanding drafts leaves in the drawer full power to stop payment or otherwise dispose of the amount and creates no trust or interest in favor of the holder.

(3) Unless otherwise agreed and except where a draft is drawn under a credit issued by the drawee, the drawee of an international sight draft owes the drawer no duty to pay an unadvised draft but if it does so and the draft is genuine, may appropriately debit the drawer's account.

Part 8
Miscellaneous

§ 3—801. Drafts in a Set.

(1) Where a draft is drawn in a set of parts, each of which is numbered and expressed to be an order only if no other part has been honored, the whole of the parts constitutes one draft but a taker of any part may become a holder in due course of the draft.

(2) Any person who negotiates, indorses or accepts a single part of a draft drawn in a set thereby becomes liable to any holder in due course of that part as if it were the whole set, but as between different holders in due course to whom different parts have been negotiated the holder whose title first accrues has all rights to the draft and its proceeds.

(3) As against the drawee the first presented part of a draft drawn in a set is the part entitled to payment, or if a time draft to acceptance and payment. Acceptance of any subsequently presented part renders the drawee liable thereon under subsection (2). With respect both to a holder and to the drawer payment of a subsequently presented part of a draft payable at sight has the same effect as payment of a check notwithstanding an effective stop order (Section 4—407).

(4) Except as otherwise provided in this section, where any part of a draft in a set is discharged by payment or otherwise the whole draft is discharged.

§ 3—802. Effect of Instrument on Obligation for Which It Is Given.

(1) Unless otherwise agreed where an instrument is taken for an underlying obligation

(a) the obligation is pro tanto discharged if a bank is drawer, maker or acceptor of the instrument and there is no recourse on the instrument against the underlying obligor; and

(b) in any other case the obligation is suspended pro tanto until the instrument is due or if it is payable on demand until its presentment. If the instrument is dishonored action may be maintained on either the instrument or the obligation; discharge of the underlying obligor on the instrument also discharges him on the obligation.

(2) The taking in good faith of a check which is not postdated does not of itself so extend the time on the original obligation as to discharge a surety.

§ 3—803. Notice to Third Party.

Where a defendant is sued for breach of an obligation for which a third person is answerable over under this Article he may give the third person written notice of the litigation, and the person notified may then give similar notice to any other person who is answerable over to him under this Article. If the notice states that the person notified may come in and defend and that if the person notified does not do so he will in any action against him by the person giving the notice be bound by any determination of fact common to the two litigations, then unless after seasonable receipt of the notice the person notified does come in and defend he is so bound.

§ 3—804. **Lost, Destroyed or Stolen Instruments.**

The owner of an instrument which is lost, whether by destruction, theft or otherwise, may maintain an action in his own name and recover from any party liable thereon upon due proof of his ownership, the facts which prevent his production of the instrument and its terms. The court may require security indemnifying the defendant against loss by reason of further claims on the instrument.

§ 3—805. **Instruments Not Payable to Order or to Bearer.**

This Article applies to any instrument whose terms do not preclude transfer and which is otherwise negotiable within this Article but which is not payable to order or to bearer, except that there can be no holder in due course of such an instrument.

Article 4
BANK DEPOSITS AND COLLECTIONS

Part 1 **General Provisions and Definitions**

§ 4—101. **Short Title.**

This Article shall be known and may be cited as Uniform Commercial Code—Bank Deposits and Collections.

§ 4—102. **Applicability.**

(1) To the extent that items within this Article are also within the scope of Articles 3 and 8, they are subject to the provisions of those Articles. In the event of conflict the provisions of this Article govern those of Article 3 but the provisions of Article 8 govern those of this Article.

(2) The liability of a bank for action or non-action with respect to any item handled by it for purposes of presentment, payment or collection is governed by the law of the place where the bank is located. In the case of action or non-action by or at a branch or separate office of a bank, its liability is governed by the law of the place where the branch or separate office is located.

§ 4—103. **Variation by Agreement; Measure of Damages; Certain Action Constituting Ordinary Care.**

(1) The effect of the provisions of this Article may be varied by agreement except that no agreement can disclaim a bank's responsibility for its own lack of good faith or failure to exercise ordinary care or can limit the measure of damages for such lack or failure; but the parties may by agreement determine the standards by which such responsibility is to be measured if such standards are not manifestly unreasonable.

(2) Federal Reserve regulations and operating letters, clearing house rules, and the like, have the effect of agreements under subsection (1), whether or not specifically assented to by all parties interested in items handled.

(3) Action or non-action approved by this Article or pursuant to Federal Reserve regulations or operating letters constitutes the exercise of ordinary care and, in the absence of special instructions, action or non-action consistent with clearing house rules and the like or with a general banking usage not disapproved by this Article, prima facie constitutes the exercise of ordinary care.

(4) The specification or approval of certain procedures by this Article does not constitute disapproval of other procedures which may be reasonable under the circumstances.

(5) The measure of damages for failure to exercise ordinary care in handling an item is the amount of the item reduced by an amount which could not have been realized by the use of ordinary care, and where there is bad faith it includes other damages, if any, suffered by the party as a proximate consequence.

§ 4—104. **Definitions and Index of Definitions.**

(1) In this Article unless the context otherwise requires

　(a) "Account" means any account with a bank and includes a checking, time, interest or savings account;

　(b) "Afternoon" means the period of a day between noon and midnight;

　(c) "Banking day" means that part of any day on which a bank is open to the public for carrying on substantially all of its banking functions;

　(d) "Clearing house" means any association of banks or other payors regularly clearing items;

(e) "Customer" means any person having an account with a bank or for whom a bank has agreed to collect items and includes a bank carrying an account with another bank;

(f) "Documentary draft" means any negotiable or nonnegotiable draft with accompanying documents, securities or other papers to be delivered against honor of the draft;

(g) "Item" means any instrument for the payment of money even though it is not negotiable but does not include money;

(h) "Midnight deadline" with respect to a bank is midnight on its next banking day following the banking day on which it receives the relevant item or notice or from which the time for taking action commences to run, whichever is later;

(i) "Properly payable" includes the availability of funds for payment at the time of decision to pay or dishonor;

(j) "Settle" means to pay in cash, by clearing house settlement, in a charge or credit or by remittance, or otherwise as instructed. A settlement may be either provisional or final;

(k) "Suspends payments" with respect to a bank means that it has been closed by order of the supervisory authorities, that a public officer has been appointed to take it over or that it ceases or refuses to make payments in the ordinary course of business.

(2) Other definitions applying to this Article and the sections in which they appear are:

"Collecting bank" Section 4—105.
"Depositary bank" Section 4—105.
"Intermediary bank" Section 4—105.
"Payor bank" Section 4—105.
"Presenting bank" Section 4—105.
"Remitting bank" Section 4—105.

(3) The following definitions in other Articles apply to this Article:

"Acceptance" Section 3—410.
"Certificate of deposit" Section 3—104.
"Certification" Section 3—411.
"Check" Section 3—104.
"Draft" Section 3—104.
"Holder in due course" Section 3—302.
"Notice of dishonor" Section 3—508.
"Presentment" Section 3—504.
"Protest" Section 3—509.
"Secondary party" Section 3—102.

(4) In addition Article 1 contains general definitions and principles of construction and interpretation applicable throughout this Article.

§ 4—105. "Depositary Bank"; "Intermediary Bank"; "Collecting Bank"; "Payor Bank"; "Presenting Bank"; "Remitting Bank".

In this Article unless the context otherwise requires:

(a) "Depositary bank" means the first bank to which an item is transferred for collection even though it is also the payor bank;

(b) "Payor bank" means a bank by which an item is payable as drawn or accepted;

(c) "Intermediary bank" means any bank to which an item is transferred in course of collection except the depositary or payor bank;

(d) "Collecting bank" means any bank handling the item for collection except the payor bank;

(e) "Presenting bank" means any bank presenting an item except a payor bank;

(f) "Remitting bank" means any payor or intermediary bank remitting for an item.

§ 4—106. Separate Office of a Bank.

A branch or separate office of a bank [maintaining its own deposit ledgers] is a separate bank for the purpose of computing the time within which and determining the place at or to which action may be taken or notices or orders shall be given under this Article and under Article 3.

Note: *The brackets are to make it optional with the several states whether to require a branch to maintain its own deposit ledgers in order to be considered to be a separate bank for certain purposes under Article 4. In some states "maintaining its own deposit ledgers" is a satisfactory test. In others branch banking practices are such that this test would not be suitable.*

§ 4—107. Time of Receipt of Items.

(1) For the purpose of allowing time to process items, prove balances and make the necessary entries on its books to determine its position for the day, a bank may fix an afternoon hour of two P.M. or later as a cut-off hour for the handling of money and items and the making of entries on its books.

(2) Any item or deposit of money received on any day after a cut-off hour so fixed or after the close of the banking day may be treated as being received at the opening of the next banking day.

§ 4—108. Delays.

(1) Unless otherwise instructed, a collecting bank in a good faith effort to secure payment may, in the case of specific items and with or without the approval of any person involved, waive, modify or extend time limits imposed or permitted by this Act for a period not in excess of an additional banking day without

discharge of secondary parties and without liability to its transferor or any prior party.

(2) Delay by a collecting bank or payor bank beyond time limits prescribed or permitted by this Act or by instructions is excused if caused by interruption of communication facilities, suspension of payments by another bank, war, emergency conditions or other circumstances beyond the control of the bank provided it exercises such diligence as the circumstances require.

§ 4—109. Process of Posting.

The "process of posting" means the usual procedure followed by a payor bank in determining to pay an item and in recording the payment including one or more of the following or other steps as determined by the bank:

(a) verification of any signature;

(b) ascertaining that sufficient funds are available;

(c) affixing a "paid" or other stamp;

(d) entering a charge or entry to a customer's account;

(e) correcting or reversing an entry or erroneous action with respect to the item.

Part 2 Collection of Items: Depositary and Collecting Banks

§ 4—201. Presumption and Duration of Agency Status of Collecting Banks and Provisional Status of Credits; Applicability of Article; Item Indorsed "Pay Any Bank".

(1) Unless a contrary intent clearly appears and prior to the time that a settlement given by a collecting bank for an item is or becomes final (subsection (3) of Section 4—211 and Sections 4—212 and 4—213) the bank is an agent or sub-agent of the owner of the item and any settlement given for the item is provisional. This provision applies regardless of the form of indorsement or lack of indorsement and even though credit given for the item is subject to immediate withdrawal as of right or is in fact withdrawn; but the continuance of ownership of an item by its owner and any rights of the owner to proceeds of the item are subject to rights of a collecting bank such as those resulting from outstanding advances on the item and valid rights of setoff. When an item is handled by banks for purposes of presentment, payment and collection, the relevant provisions of this Article apply even though action of parties clearly establishes that a particular bank has purchased the item and is the owner of it.

(2) After an item has been indorsed with the words "pay any bank" or the like, only a bank may acquire the rights of a holder

(a) until the item has been returned to the customer initiating collection; or

(b) until the item has been specially indorsed by a bank to a person who is not a bank.

§ 4—202. Responsibility for Collection; When Action Seasonable.

(1) A collecting bank must use ordinary care in

(a) presenting an item or sending it for presentment; and

(b) sending notice of dishonor or non-payment or returning an item other than a documentary draft to the bank's transferor [or directly to the depositary bank under subsection (2) of Section 4—212] (see note to Section 4—212) after learning that the item has not been paid or accepted as the case may be; and

(c) settling for an item when the bank receives final settlement; and

(d) making or providing for any necessary protest; and

(e) notifying its transferor of any loss or delay in transit within a reasonable time after discovery thereof.

(2) A collecting bank taking proper action before its midnight deadline following receipt of an item, notice or payment acts seasonably; taking proper action within a reasonably longer time may be seasonable but the bank has the burden of so establishing.

(3) Subject to subsection (1) (a), a bank is not liable for the insolvency, neglect, misconduct, mistake or default of another bank or person or for loss or destruction of an item in transit or in the possession of others.

§ 4—203. Effect of Instructions.

Subject to the provisions of Article 3 concerning conversion of instruments (Section 3—419) and the provisions of both Article 3 and this Article concerning restrictive indorsements only a collecting bank's transferor can give instructions which affect the bank or constitute notice to it and a collecting bank is not liable to prior parties for any action taken pursuant to such instructions or in accordance with any agreement with its transferor.

§ 4—204. Methods of Sending and Presenting; Sending Direct to Payor Bank.

(1) A collecting bank must send items by reasonably prompt method taking into consideration any relevant instructions, the nature of the item, the number of such items on hand, and the cost of collection involved and the method generally used by it or others to present such items.

(2) A collecting bank may send

(a) any item direct to the payor bank;

(b) any item to any non-bank payor if authorized by its transferor; and

(c) any item other than documentary drafts to any non-bank payor, if authorized by Federal Reserve regulation or operating letter, clearing house rule or the like.

(3) Presentment may be made by a presenting bank at a place where the payor bank has requested that presentment be made.

§ 4—205. Supplying Missing Indorsement; No Notice from Prior Indorsement.

(1) A depositary bank which has taken an item for collection may supply any indorsement of the customer which is necessary to title unless the item contains the words "payee's indorsement required" or the like. In the absence of such a requirement a statement placed on the item by the depositary bank to the effect that the item was deposited by a customer or credited to his account is effective as the customer's indorsement.

(2) An intermediary bank, or payor bank which is not a depositary bank, is neither given notice nor otherwise affected by a restrictive indorsement of any person except the bank's immediate transferor.

§ 4—206. Transfer Between Banks.

Any agreed method which identifies the transferor bank is sufficient for the item's further transfer to another bank.

§ 4—207. Warranties of Customer and Collecting Bank on Transfer or Presentment of Items; Time for Claims.

(1) Each customer or collecting bank who obtains payment or acceptance of an item and each prior customer and collecting bank warrants to the payor bank or other payor who in good faith pays or accepts the item that

(a) he has a good title to the item or is authorized to obtain payment or acceptance on behalf of one who has a good title; and

(b) he has no knowledge that the signature of the maker or drawer is unauthorized, except that this warranty is not given by any customer or collecting bank that is a holder in due course and acts in good faith

(i) to a maker with respect to the maker's own signature; or

(ii) to a drawer with respect to the drawer's own signature, whether or not the drawer is also the drawee; or

(iii) to an acceptor of an item if the holder in due course took the item after the acceptance or obtained the acceptance without knowledge that the drawer's signature was unauthorized; and

(c) the item has not been materially altered, except that this warranty is not given by any customer or collecting bank that is a holder in due course and acts in good faith

(i) to the maker of a note; or

(ii) to the drawer of a draft whether or not the drawer is also the drawee; or

(iii) to the acceptor of an item with respect to an alteration made prior to the acceptance if the holder in due course took the item after the acceptance, even though the acceptance provided "payable as originally drawn" or equivalent terms; or

(iv) to the acceptor of an item with respect to an alteration made after the acceptance.

(2) Each customer and collecting bank who transfers an item and receives a settlement or other consideration for it warrants to his transferee and to any subsequent collecting bank who takes the item in good faith that

(a) he has a good title to the item or is authorized to obtain payment or acceptance on behalf of one who has a good title and the transfer is otherwise rightful; and

(b) all signatures are genuine or authorized; and

(c) the item has not been materially altered; and

(d) no defense of any party is good against him; and

(e) he has no knowledge of any insolvency proceeding instituted with respect to the maker or acceptor or the drawer of an unaccepted item.

In addition each customer and collecting bank so transferring an item and receiving a settlement or other consideration engages that upon dishonor and any necessary notice of dishonor and protest he will take up the item.

(3) The warranties and the engagement to honor set forth in the two preceding subsections arise notwithstanding the absence of indorsement or words of guaranty or warranty in the transfer or presentment and a collecting bank remains liable for their breach despite remittance to its transferor. Damages for breach of such warranties or engagement to honor shall not exceed the consideration received by the customer or collecting bank responsible plus finance charges and expenses related to the item, if any.

(4) Unless a claim for breach of warranty under this section is made within a reasonable time after the person claiming learns of the breach, the person liable is discharged to the extent of any loss caused by the delay in making claim.

§ 4—208. **Security Interest of Collecting Bank in Items, Accompanying Documents and Proceeds.**

(1) A bank has a security interest in an item and any accompanying documents or the proceeds of either

(a) in case of an item deposited in an account to the extent to which credit given for the item has been withdrawn or applied;

(b) in case of an item for which it has given credit available for withdrawal as of right, to the extent of the credit given whether or not the credit is drawn upon and whether or not there is a right of charge-back; or

(c) if it makes an advance on or against the item.

(2) When credit which has been given for several items received at one time or pursuant to a single agreement is withdrawn or applied in part the security interest remains upon all the items, any accompanying documents or the proceeds of either. For the purpose of this section, credits first given are first withdrawn.

(3) Receipt by a collecting bank of a final settlement for an item is a realization on its security interest in the item, accompanying documents and proceeds. To the extent and so long as the bank does not receive final settlement for the item or give up possession of the item or accompanying documents for purposes other than collection, the security interest continues and is subject to the provisions of Article 9 except that

(a) no security agreement is necessary to make the security interest enforceable (subsection (1) (b) of Section 9—203); and

(b) no filing is required to perfect the security interest; and

(c) the security interest has priority over conflicting perfected security interests in the item, accompanying documents or proceeds.

§ 4—209. **When Bank Gives Value for Purposes of Holder in Due Course.**

For purposes of determining its status as a holder in due course, the bank has given value to the extent that it has a security interest in an item provided that the bank otherwise complies with the requirements of Section 3—302 on what constitutes a holder in due course.

§ 4—210. **Presentment by Notice of Item Not Payable by, Through or at a Bank; Liability of Secondary Parties.**

(1) Unless otherwise instructed, a collecting bank may present an item not payable by, through or at a bank by sending to the party to accept or pay a written notice that the bank holds the item for acceptance or payment. The notice must be sent in time to be received on or before the day when presentment is due and the bank must meet any requirement of the party to accept or pay under Section 3—505 by the close of the bank's next banking day after it knows of the requirement.

(2) Where presentment is made by notice and neither honor nor request for compliance with a requirement under Section 3—505 is received by the close of business on the day after maturity or in the case of demand items by the close of business on the third banking day after notice was sent, the presenting bank may treat the item as dishonored and charge any secondary party by sending him notice of the facts.

§ 4—211. **Media of Remittance; Provisional and Final Settlement in Remittance Cases.**

(1) A collecting bank may take in settlement of an item

(a) a check of the remitting bank or of another bank on any bank except the remitting bank; or

(b) a cashier's check or similar primary obligation of a remitting bank which is a member of or clears through a member of the same clearing house or group as the collecting bank; or

(c) appropriate authority to charge an account of the remitting bank or of another bank with the collecting bank; or

(d) if the item is drawn upon or payable by a person other than a bank, a cashier's check, certified check or other bank check or obligation.

(2) If before its midnight deadline the collecting bank properly dishonors a remittance check or authoriza-

tion to charge on itself or presents or forwards for collection a remittance instrument of or on another bank which is of a kind approved by subsection (1) or has not been authorized by it, the collecting bank is not liable to prior parties in the event of the dishonor of such check, instrument or authorization.

(3) A settlement for an item by means of a remittance instrument or authorization to charge is or becomes a final settlement as to both the person making and the person receiving the settlement

    (a) if the remittance instrument or authorization to charge is of a kind approved by subsection (1) or has not been authorized by the person receiving the settlement and in either case the person receiving the settlement acts seasonably before its midnight deadline in presenting, forwarding for collection or paying the instrument or authorization,—at the time the remittance instrument or authorization is finally paid by the payor by which it is payable;

    (b) if the person receiving the settlement has authorized remittance by a non-bank check or obligation or by a cashier's check or similar primary obligation of or a check upon the payor or other remitting bank which is not of a kind approved by subsection (1) (b),—at the time of the receipt of such remittance check or obligation; or

    (c) if in a case not covered by sub-paragraphs (a) or (b) the person receiving the settlement fails to seasonably present, forward for collection, pay or return a remittance instrument or authorization to it to charge before its midnight deadline,—at such midnight deadline.

§ 4—212. Right of Charge-Back or Refund.

(1) If a collecting bank has made provisional settlement with its customer for an item and itself fails by reason of dishonor, suspension of payments by a bank or otherwise to receive a settlement for the item which is or becomes final, the bank may revoke the settlement given by it, charge back the amount of any credit given for the item to its customer's account or obtain refund from its customer whether or not it is able to return the items if by its midnight deadline or within a longer reasonable time after it learns the facts it returns the item or sends notification of the facts. These rights to revoke, charge-back and obtain refund terminate if and when a settlement for the item received by the bank is or becomes final (subsection (3) of Section 4—211 and subsections (2) and (3) of Section 4—213).

[(2) Within the time and manner prescribed by this section and Section 4—301, an intermediary or payor

bank, as the case may be, may return an unpaid item directly to the depositary bank and may send for collection a draft on the depositary bank and obtain reimbursement. In such case, if the depositary bank has received provisional settlement for the item, it must reimburse the bank drawing the draft and any provisional credits for the item between banks shall become and remain final.]

Note: *Direct returns is recognized as an innovation that is not yet established bank practice, and therefore, Paragraph 2 has been bracketed. Some lawyers have doubts whether it should be included in legislation or left to development by agreement.*

(3) A depositary bank which is also the payor may charge-back the amount of an item to its customer's account or obtain refund in accordance with the section governing return of an item received by a payor bank for credit on its books (Section 4—301).

(4) The right to charge-back is not affected by

    (a) prior use of the credit given for the item; or
    (b) failure by any bank to exercise ordinary care with respect to the item but any bank so failing remains liable.

(5) A failure to charge-back or claim refund does not affect other rights of the bank against the customer or any other party.

(6) If credit is given in dollars as the equivalent of the value of an item payable in a foreign currency the dollar amount of any charge-back or refund shall be calculated on the basis of the buying sight rate for the foreign currency prevailing on the day when the person entitled to the charge-back or refund learns that it will not receive payment in ordinary course.

§ 4—213. Final Payment of Item by Payor Bank; When Provisional Debits and Credits Become Final; When Certain Credits Become Available for Withdrawal.

(1) An item is finally paid by a payor bank when the bank has done any of the following, whichever happens first:

    (a) paid the item in cash; or

    (b) settled for the item without reserving a right to revoke the settlement and without having such right under statute, clearing house rule or agreement; or

    (c) completed the process of posting the item to the indicated account of the drawer, maker or other person to be charged therewith; or

    (d) made a provisional settlement for the item and failed to revoke the settlement in the time and manner permitted by statute, clearing house rule or agreement.

Upon a final payment under subparagraphs (b), (c) or (d) the payor bank shall be accountable for the amount of the item.

(2) If provisional settlement for an item between the presenting and payor banks is made through a clearing house or by debits or credits in an account between them, then to the extent that provisional debits or credits for the item are entered in accounts between the presenting and payor banks or between the presenting and successive prior collecting banks seriatim, they become final upon final payment of the item by the payor bank.

(3) If a collecting bank receives a settlement for an item which is or becomes final (subsection (3) of Section 4—211, subsection (2) of Section 4—213) the bank is accountable to its customer for the amount of the item and any provisional credit given for the item in an account with its customer becomes final.

(4) Subject to any right of the bank to apply the credit to an obligation of the customer, credit given by a bank for an item in an account with its customer becomes available for withdrawal as of right

    (a) in any case where the bank has received a provisional settlement for the item,—when such settlement becomes final and the bank has had a reasonable time to learn that the settlement is final;

    (b) in any case where the bank is both a depositary bank and a payor bank and the item is finally paid,—at the opening of the bank's second banking day following receipt of the item.

(5) A deposit of money in a bank is final when made but, subject to any right of the bank to apply the deposit to an obligation of the customer, the deposit becomes available for withdrawal as of right at the opening of the bank's next banking day following receipt of the deposit.

§ 4—214. **Insolvency and Preference.**

(1) Any item in or coming into the possession of a payor or collecting bank which suspends payment and which item is not finally paid shall be returned by the receiver, trustee or agent in charge of the closed bank to the presenting bank or the closed bank's customer.

(2) If a payor bank finally pays an item and suspends payments without making a settlement for the item with its customer or the presenting bank which settlement is or becomes final, the owner of the item has a preferred claim against the payor bank.

(3) If a payor bank gives or a collecting bank gives or receives a provisional settlement for an item and thereafter suspends payments, the suspension does not prevent or interfere with the settlement becoming final if such finality occurs automatically upon the lapse of certain time or the happening of certain events (subsection (3) of Section 4—211, subsections (1) (d), (2) and (3) of Section 4—213).

(4) If a collecting bank receives from subsequent parties settlement for an item which settlement is or becomes final and suspends payments without making a settlement for the item with its customer which is or becomes final, the owner of the item has a preferred claim against such collecting bank.

Part 3 **Collection of Items: Payor Banks**

§ 4—301. **Deferred Posting; Recovery of Payment by Return of Items; Time of Dishonor.**

(1) Where an authorized settlement for a demand item (other than a documentary draft) received by a payor bank otherwise than for immediate payment over the counter has been made before midnight of the banking day of receipt the payor bank may revoke the settlement and recover any payment if before it has made final payment (subsection (1) of Section 4—213) and before its midnight deadline it

    (a) returns the item; or

    (b) sends written notice of dishonor or nonpayment if the item is held for protest or is otherwise unavailable for return.

(2) If a demand item is received by a payor bank for credit on its books it may return such item or send notice of dishonor and may revoke any credit given or recover the amount thereof withdrawn by its customer, if it acts within the time limit and in the manner specified in the preceding subsection.

(3) Unless previous notice of dishonor has been sent an item is dishonored at the time when for purposes of dishonor it is returned or notice sent in accordance with this section.

(4) An item is returned:

    (a) as to an item received through a clearing house, when it is delivered to the presenting or last collecting bank or to the clearing house or is sent or delivered in accordance with its rules; or

    (b) in all other cases, when it is sent or delivered to the bank's customer or transferor or pursuant to his instructions.

§ 4—302. Payor Bank's Responsibility for Late Return of Item.

In the absence of a valid defense such as breach of a presentment warranty (subsection (1) of Section 4—207), settlement effected or the like, if an item is presented on and received by a payor bank the bank is accountable for the amount of

(a) a demand item other than a documentary draft whether properly payable or not if the bank, in any case where it is not also the depositary bank, retains the item beyond midnight of the banking day of receipt without settling for it or, regardless of whether it is also the depositary bank, does not pay or return the item or send notice of dishonor until after its midnight deadline; or

(b) any other properly payable item unless within the time allowed for acceptance or payment of that item the bank either accepts or pays the item or returns it and accompanying documents.

§ 4—303. When Items Subject to Notice, Stop-Order, Legal Process or Setoff; Order in Which Items May Be Charged or Certified.

(1) Any knowledge, notice or stop-order received by, legal process served upon or setoff exercised by a payor bank, whether or not effective under other rules of law to terminate, suspend or modify the bank's right or duty to pay an item or to charge its customer's account for the item, comes too late to so terminate, suspend or modify such right or duty if the knowledge, notice, stop-order or legal process is received or served and a reasonable time for the bank to act thereon expires or the setoff is exercised after the bank has done any of the following:

(a) accepted or certified the item;

(b) paid the item in cash;

(c) settled for the item without reserving a right to revoke the settlement and without having such right under statute, clearing house rule or agreement;

(d) completed the process of posting the item to the indicated account of the drawer, maker or other person to be charged therewith or otherwise has evidenced by examination of such indicated account and by action its decision to pay the item; or

(e) become accountable for the amount of the item under subsection (1) (d) of Section 4—213 and Section 4—302 dealing with the payor bank's responsibility for late return of items.

(2) Subject to the provisions of subsection (1) items may be accepted, paid, certified or charged to the indicated account of its customer in any order convenient to the bank.

Part 4 Relationship Between Payor Bank and Its Customer

§ 4—401. When Bank May Charge Customer's Account.

(1) As against its customer, a bank may charge against his account any item which is otherwise properly payable from that account even though the charge creates an overdraft.

(2) A bank which in good faith makes payment to a holder may charge the indicated account of its customer according to

(a) the original tenor of his altered item; or

(b) the tenor of his completed item, even though the bank knows the item has been completed unless the bank has notice that the completion was improper.

§ 4—402. Bank's Liability to Customer for Wrongful Dishonor.

A payor bank is liable to its customer for damages proximately caused by the wrongful dishonor of an item. When the dishonor occurs through mistake liability is limited to actual damages proved. If so proximately caused and proved damages may include damages for an arrest or prosecution of the customer or other consequential damages. Whether any consequential damages are proximately caused by the wrongful dishonor is a question of fact to be determined in each case.

§ 4—403. Customer's Right to Stop Payment; Burden of Proof of Loss.

(1) A customer may by order to his bank stop payment of any item payable for his account but the order must be received at such time and in such manner as to afford the bank a reasonable opportunity to act on it prior to any action by the bank with respect to the item described in Section 4—303.

(2) An oral order is binding upon the bank only for fourteen calendar days unless confirmed in writing within that period. A written order is effective for only six months unless renewed in writing.

(3) The burden of establishing the fact and amount of loss resulting from the payment of an item contrary to a binding stop payment order is on the customer.

§ 4—404. Bank Not Obligated to Pay Check More Than Six Months Old.

A bank is under no obligation to a customer having a checking account to pay a check, other than a certified check, which is presented more than six months after its date, but it may charge its customer's account for a payment made thereafter in good faith.

§ 4—405. Death or Incompetence of Customer.

(1) A payor or collecting bank's authority to accept, pay or collect an item or to account for proceeds of its collection if otherwise effective is not rendered ineffective by incompetence of a customer of either bank existing at the time the item is issued or its collection is undertaken if the bank does not know of an adjudication of incompetence. Neither death nor incompetence of a customer revokes such authority to accept, pay, collect or account until the bank knows of the fact of death or of an adjudication of incompetence and has reasonable opportunity to act on it.

(2) Even with knowledge a bank may for ten days after the date of death pay or certify checks drawn on or prior to that date unless ordered to stop payment by a person claiming an interest in the account.

§ 4—406. Customer's Duty to Discover and Report Unauthorized Signature or Alteration.

(1) When a bank sends to its customer a statement of account accompanied by items paid in good faith in support of the debit entries or holds the statement and items pursuant to a request or instructions of its customer or otherwise in a reasonable manner makes the statement and items available to the customer, the customer must exercise reasonable care and promptness to examine the statement and items to discover his unauthorized signature or any alteration on an item and must notify the bank promptly after discovery thereof.

(2) If the bank establishes that the customer failed with respect to an item to comply with the duties imposed on the customer by subsection (1) the customer is precluded from asserting against the bank

(a) his unauthorized signature or any alteration on the item if the bank also establishes that it suffered a loss by reason of such failure; and

(b) an unauthorized signature or alteration by the same wrongdoer on any other item paid in good faith by the bank after the first item and statement was available to the customer for a reasonable period not exceeding fourteen calendar days and

before the bank receives notification from the customer of any such unauthorized signature or alteration.

(3) The preclusion under subsection (2) does not apply if the customer establishes lack of ordinary care on the part of the bank in paying the item(s).

(4) Without regard to care or lack of care of either the customer or the bank a customer who does not within one year from the time the statement and items are made available to the customer (subsection (1)) discover and report his unauthorized signature or any alteration on the face or back of the item or does not within three years from that time discover and report any unauthorized indorsement is precluded from asserting against the bank such unauthorized signature or indorsement or such alteration.

(5) If under this section a payor bank has a valid defense against a claim of a customer upon or resulting from payment of an item and waives or fails upon request to assert the defense the bank may not assert against any collecting bank or other prior party presenting or transferring the item a claim based upon the unauthorized signature or alteration giving rise to the customer's claim.

§ 4—407. Payor Bank's Right to Subrogation on Improper Payment.

If a payor bank has paid an item over the stop payment order of the drawer or maker or otherwise under circumstances giving a basis for objection by the drawer or maker, to prevent unjust enrichment and only to the extent necessary to prevent loss to the bank by reason of its payment of the item, the payor bank shall be subrogated to the rights

(a) of any holder in due course on the item against the drawer or maker; and

(b) of the payee or any other holder of the item against the drawer or maker either on the item or under the transaction out of which the item arose; and

(c) of the drawer or maker against the payee or any other holder of the item with respect to the transaction out of which the item arose.

Part 5 Collection of Documentary Drafts

§ 4—501. Handling of Documentary Drafts; Duty to Send for Presentment and to Notify Customer of Dishonor.

A bank which takes a documentary draft for collection must present or send the draft and accompanying documents for presentment and upon learning that the draft has not been paid or accepted in due course must seasonably notify its customer of such fact even though it may have discounted or bought the draft or extended credit available for withdrawal as of right.

§ 4—502. Presentment of "On Arrival" Drafts.

When a draft or the relevant instructions require presentment "on arrival", "when goods arrive" or the like, the collecting bank need not present until in its judgment a reasonable time for arrival of the goods has expired. Refusal to pay or accept because the goods have not arrived is not dishonor; the bank must notify its transferor of such refusal but need not present the draft again until it is instructed to do so or learns of the arrival of the goods.

§ 4—503. Responsibility of Presenting Bank for Documents and Goods; Report of Reasons for Dishonor; Referee in Case of Need.

Unless otherwise instructed and except as provided in Article 5 a bank presenting a documentary draft

(a) must deliver the documents to the drawee on acceptance of the draft if it is payable more than three days after presentment; otherwise, only on payment; and

(b) upon dishonor, either in the case of presentment for acceptance or presentment for payment, may seek and follow instructions from any referee in case of need designated in the draft or if the presenting bank does not choose to utilize his services it must use diligence and good faith to ascertain the reason for dishonor, must notify its transferor of the dishonor and of the results of its effort to ascertain the reasons therefor and must request instructions.

But the presenting bank is under no obligation with respect to goods represented by the documents except to follow any reasonable instructions seasonably received; it has a right to reimbursement for any expense incurred in following instructions and to prepayment of or indemnity for such expenses.

§ 4—504. Privilege of Presenting Bank to Deal With Goods; Security Interest for Expenses.

(1) A presenting bank which, following the dishonor of a documentary draft, has seasonably requested instructions but does not receive them within a reasonable time may store, sell, or otherwise deal with the goods in any reasonable manner.

(2) For its reasonable expenses incurred by action under subsection (1) the presenting bank has a lien upon the goods or their proceeds, which may be foreclosed in the same manner as an unpaid seller's lien.

Article 5
LETTERS OF CREDIT

§ 5—101. Short Title.

This Article shall be known and may be cited as Uniform Commercial Code—Letters of Credit.

§ 5—102. Scope.

(1) This Article applies

(a) to a credit issued by a bank if the credit requires a documentary draft or a documentary demand for payment; and

(b) to a credit issued by a person other than a bank if the credit requires that the draft or demand for payment be accompanied by a document of title; and

(c) to a credit issued by a bank or other person if the credit is not within subparagraphs (a) or (b) but conspicuously states that it is a letter of credit or is conspicuously so entitled.

(2) Unless the engagement meets the requirements of subsection (1), this Article does not apply to engagements to make advances or to honor drafts or demands for payment, to authorities to pay or purchase, to guarantees or to general agreements.

(3) This Article deals with some but not all of the rules and concepts of letters of credit as such rules or concepts have developed prior to this act or may hereafter develop. The fact that this Article states a rule does not by itself require, imply or negate application of the same or a converse rule to a situation not provided for or to a person not specified by this Article.

§ 5—103. Definitions.

(1) In this Article unless the context otherwise requires

(a) "Credit" or "letter of credit" means an engagement by a bank or other person made at the request of a customer and of a kind within the scope of this Article (Section 5—102) that the issuer will honor drafts or other demands for payment upon compliance with the conditions specified in the credit. A credit may be either revocable or irrevocable. The engagement may be either an agreement to honor or a statement that the bank or other person is authorized to honor.

(b) A "documentary draft" or a "documentary demand for payment" is one honor of which is conditioned upon the presentation of a document or documents. "Document" means any paper including document of title, security, invoice, certificate, notice of default and the like.

(c) An "issuer" is a bank or other person issuing a credit.

(d) A "beneficiary" of a credit is a person who is entitled under its terms to draw or demand payment.

(e) An "advising bank" is a bank which gives notification of the issuance of a credit by another bank.

(f) A "confirming bank" is a bank which engages either that it will itself honor a credit already issued by another bank or that such a credit will be honored by the issuer or a third bank.

(g) A "customer" is a buyer or other person who causes an issuer to issue a credit. The term also includes a bank which procures issuance or confirmation on behalf of that bank's customer.

(2) Other definitions applying to this Article and the sections in which they appear are:

"Notation of Credit". Section 5—108.
"Presenter". Section 5—112(3).

(3) Definitions in other Articles applying to this Article and the sections in which they appear are:

"Accept" or "Acceptance". Section 3—410.
"Contract for sale". Section 2—106.
"Draft". Section 3—104.
"Holder in due course". Section 3—302.
"Midnight deadline". Section 4—104.
"Security". Section 8—102.

(4) In addition, Article 1 contains general definitions and principles of construction and interpretation applicable throughout this Article.

§ 5—104. Formal Requirements; Signing.

(1) Except as otherwise required in subsection (1) (c) of Section 5—102 on scope, no particular form of phrasing is required for a credit. A credit must be in writing and signed by the issuer and a confirmation must be in writing and signed by the confirming bank. A modification of the terms of a credit or confirmation must be signed by the issuer or confirming bank.

(2) A telegram may be a sufficient signed writing if it identifies its sender by an authorized authentication. The authentication may be in code and the authorized naming of the issuer in an advice of credit is a sufficient signing.

§ 5—105. Consideration.

No consideration is necessary to establish a credit or to enlarge or otherwise modify its terms.

§ 5—106. Time and Effect of Establishment of Credit.

(1) Unless otherwise agreed a credit is established

(a) as regards the customer as soon as a letter of credit is sent to him or the letter of credit or an authorized written advice of its issuance is sent to the beneficiary; and

(b) as regards the beneficiary when he receives a letter of credit or an authorized written advice of its issuance.

(2) Unless otherwise agreed once an irrevocable credit is established as regards the customer it can be modified or revoked only with the consent of the customer and once it is established as regards the beneficiary it can be modified or revoked only with his consent.

(3) Unless otherwise agreed after a revocable credit is established it may be modified or revoked by the issuer without notice to or consent from the customer or beneficiary.

(4) Notwithstanding any modification or revocation of a revocable credit any person authorized to honor or negotiate under the terms of the original credit is entitled to reimbursement for or honor of any draft or demand for payment duty honored or negotiated before receipt of notice of the modification or revocation and the issuer in turn is entitled to reimbursement from its customer.

§ 5—107. Advice of Credit; Confirmation; Error in Statement of Terms.

(1) Unless otherwise specified an advising bank by advising a credit issued by another bank does not assume any obligation to honor drafts drawn or demands for payment made under the credit but it does assume obligation for the accuracy of its own statement.

(2) A confirming bank by confirming a credit becomes directly obligated on the credit to the extent of its confirmation as though it were its issuer and acquires the rights of an issuer.

(3) Even though an advising bank incorrectly advises the terms of a credit it has been authorized to advise the credit is established as against the issuer to the extent of its original terms.

(4) Unless otherwise specified the customer bears as against the issuer all risks of transmission and

reasonable translation or interpretation of any message relating to a credit.

§ 5—108. "Notation Credit"; Exhaustion of Credit.

(1) A credit which specifies that any person purchasing or paying drafts drawn or demands for payment made under it must note the amount of the draft or demand on the letter or advice of credit is a "notation credit".

(2) Under a notation credit

(a) a person paying the beneficiary or purchasing a draft or demand for payment from him acquires a right to honor only if the appropriate notation is made and by transferring or forwarding for honor the documents under the credit such a person warrants to the issuer that the notation has been made; and

(b) unless the credit or a signed statement that an appropriate notation has been made accompanies the draft or demand for payment the issuer may delay honor until evidence of notation has been procured which is satisfactory to it but its obligation and that of its customer continue for a reasonable time not exceeding thirty days to obtain such evidence.

(3) If the credit is not a notation credit

(a) the issuer may honor complying drafts or demands for payment presented to it in the order in which they are presented and is discharged pro tanto by honor of any such draft or demand;

(b) as between competing good faith purchasers of complying drafts or demands the person first purchasing has priority over a subsequent purchaser even though the later purchased draft or demand has been first honored.

§ 5—109. Issuer's Obligation to Its Customer.

(1) An issuer's obligation to its customer includes good faith and observance of any general banking usage but unless otherwise agreed does not include liability or responsibility

(a) for performance of the underlying contract for sale or other transaction between the customer and the beneficiary; or

(b) for any act or omission of any person other than itself or its own branch or for loss or destruction of a draft, demand or document in transit or in the possession of others; or

(c) based on knowledge or lack of knowledge of any usage of any particular trade.

(2) An issuer must examine documents with care so as to ascertain that on their face they appear to comply with the terms of the credit but unless otherwise agreed assumes no liability or responsibility for the genuineness, falsification or effect of any document which appears on such examination to be regular on its face.

(3) A non-bank issuer is not bound by any banking usage of which it has no knowledge.

§ 5—110. Availability of Credit in Portions; Presenter's Reservation of Lien or Claim.

(1) Unless otherwise specified a credit may be used in portions in the discretion of the beneficiary.

(2) Unless otherwise specified a person by presenting a documentary draft or demand for payment under a credit relinquishes upon its honor all claims to the documents and a person by transferring such draft or demand or causing such presentment authorizes such relinquishment. An explicit reservation of claim makes the draft or demand non-complying.

§ 5—111. Warranties on Transfer and Presentment.

(1) Unless otherwise agreed the beneficiary by transferring or presenting a documentary draft or demand for payment warrants to all interested parties that the necessary conditions of the credit have been complied with. This is in addition to any warranties arising under Articles 3, 4, 7 and 8.

(2) Unless otherwise agreed a negotiating, advising, confirming, collecting or issuing bank presenting or transferring a draft or demand for payment under a credit warrants only the matters warranted by a collecting bank under Article 4 and any such bank transferring a document warrants only the matters warranted by an intermediary under Articles 7 and 8.

§ 5—112. Time Allowed for Honor or Rejection; Withholding Honor or Rejection by Consent; "Presenter".

(1) A bank to which a documentary draft or demand for payment is presented under a credit may without dishonor of the draft, demand or credit

(a) defer honor until the close of the third banking day following receipt of the documents; and

(b) further defer honor if the presenter has expressly or impliedly consented thereto.

Failure to honor within the time here specified constitutes dishonor of the draft or demand and of the credit [except as otherwise provided in subsection (4) of Section 5—114 on conditional payment].

Note: *The bracketed language in the last sentence of subsection (1) should be included only if the optional provisions of Section 5—114(4) and (5) are included.*

(2) Upon dishonor the bank may unless otherwise instructed fulfill its duty to return the draft or demand and the documents by holding them at the disposal of the presenter and sending him an advice to that effect.

(3) "Presenter" means any person presenting a draft or demand for payment for honor under a credit even though that person is a confirming bank or other correspondent which is acting under an issuer's authorization.

§ 5—113. **Indemnities.**

(1) A bank seeking to obtain (whether for itself or another) honor, negotiation or reimbursement under a credit may give an indemnity to induce such honor, negotiation or reimbursement.

(2) An indemnity agreement inducing honor, negotiation or reimbursement

(a) unless otherwise explicitly agreed applies to defects in the documents but not in the goods; and

(b) unless a longer time is explicitly agreed expires at the end of ten business days following receipt of the documents by, the ultimate customer unless notice of objection is sent before such expiration date. The ultimate customer may send notice of objection to the person from whom he received the documents and any bank receiving such notice is under a duty to send notice to its transferor before its midnight deadline.

§ 5—114. **Issuer's Duty and Privilege to Honor; Right to Reimbursement.**

(1) An issuer must honor a draft or demand for payment which complies with the terms of the relevant credit regardless of whether the goods or documents conform to the underlying contract for sale or other contract between the customer and the beneficiary. The issuer is not excused from honor of such a draft or demand by reason of an additional general term that all documents must be satisfactory to the issuer, but an issuer may require that specified documents must be satisfactory to it.

(2) Unless otherwise agreed when documents appear on their face to comply with the terms of a credit but a required document does not in fact conform to the warranties made on negotiation or transfer of a document of title (Section 7—507) or of a certificated security (Section 8—306) or is forged or fraudulent or there is fraud in the transaction:

(a) the issuer must honor the draft or demand for payment if honor is demanded by a negotiating bank or other holder of the draft or demand which has taken the draft or demand under the credit and under circumstances which would make it a holder in due course (Section 3—302) and in an appropriate case would make it a person to whom a document of title has been duly negotiated (Section 7—502) or a bona fide purchaser of a certificated security (Section 8—302); and

(b) in all other cases as against its customer, an issuer acting in good faith may honor the draft or demand for payment despite notification from the customer of fraud, forgery or other defect not apparent on the face of the documents but a court of appropriate jurisdiction may enjoin such honor.

(3) Unless otherwise agreed an issuer which has duly honored a draft or demand for payment is entitled to immediate reimbursement of any payment made under the credit and to be put in effectively available funds not later than the day before maturity of any acceptance made under the credit.

[(4) When a credit provides for payment by the issuer on receipt of notice that the required documents are in the possession of a correspondent or other agent of the issuer

(a) any payment made on receipt of such notice is conditional; and

(b) the issuer may reject documents which do not comply with the credit if it does so within three banking days following its receipt of the documents; and

(c) in the event of such rejection, the issuer is entitled by charge back or otherwise to return of the payment made.]

[(5) In the case covered by subsection (4) failure to reject documents within the time specified in sub-paragraph (b) constitutes acceptance of the documents and makes the payment final in favor of the beneficiary.]

Amended in 1977.

Note: *Subsections (4) and (5) are bracketed as optional. If they are included the bracketed language in the last sentence of Section 5—112(1) should also be included.*

§ 5—115. **Remedy for Improper Dishonor or Anticipatory Repudiation.**

(1) When an issuer wrongfully dishonors a draft or demand for payment presented under a credit the person entitled to honor has with respect to any documents the rights of a person in the position of a

seller (Section 2—707) and may recover from the issuer the face amount of the draft or demand together with incidental damages under Section 2—710 on seller's incidental damages and interest but less any amount realized by resale or other use or disposition of the subject matter of the transaction. In the event no resale or other utilization is made the documents, goods or other subject matter involved in the transaction must be turned over to the issuer on payment of judgment.

(2) When an issuer wrongfully cancels or otherwise repudiates a credit before presentment of a draft or demand for payment drawn under it the beneficiary has the rights of a seller after anticipatory repudiation by the buyer under Section 2—610 if he learns of the repudiation in time reasonably to avoid procurement of the required documents. Otherwise the beneficiary has an immediate right of action for wrongful dishonor.

§ 5—116. **Transfer and Assignment.**

(1) The right to draw under a credit can be transferred or assigned only when the credit is expressly designated as transferable or assignable.

(2) Even though the credit specifically states that it is nontransferable or nonassignable the beneficiary may before performance of the conditions of the credit assign his right to proceeds. Such an assignment is an assignment of an account under Article 9 on Secured Transactions and is governed by that Article except that

 (a) the assignment is ineffective until the letter of credit or advice of credit is delivered to the assignee which delivery constitutes perfection of the security interest under Article 9; and

 (b) the issuer may honor drafts or demands for payment drawn under the credit until it receives a notification of the assignment signed by the beneficiary which reasonably identifies the credit involved in the assignment and contains a request to pay the assignee; and

 (c) after what reasonably appears to be such a notification has been received the issuer may without dishonor refuse to accept or pay even to a person otherwise entitled to honor until the letter of credit or advice of credit is exhibited to the issuer.

(3) Except where the beneficiary has effectively assigned his right to draw or his right to proceeds, nothing in this section limits his right to transfer or negotiate drafts or demands drawn under the credit.

§ 5—117. **Insolvency of Bank Holding Funds for Documentary Credit.**

(1) Where an issuer or an advising or confirming bank or a bank which has for a customer procured issuance of a credit by another bank becomes insolvent before final payment under the credit and the credit is one to which this Article is made applicable by paragraphs (a) or (b) of Section 5—102(1) on scope, the receipt or allocation of funds or collateral to secure or meet obligations under the credit shall have the following results:

 (a) to the extent of any funds or collateral turned over after or before the insolvency as indemnity against or specifically for the purpose of payment of drafts or demands for payment drawn under the designated credit, the drafts or demands are entitled to payment in preference over depositors or other general creditors of the issuer or bank; and

 (b) on expiration of the credit or surrender of the beneficiary's rights under it unused any person who has given such funds or collateral is similarly entitled to return thereof; and

 (c) a charge to a general or current account with a bank if specifically consented to for the purpose of indemnity against or payment of drafts or demands for payment drawn under the designated credit falls under the same rules as if the funds had been drawn out in cash and then turned over with specific instructions.

(2) After honor or reimbursement under this section the customer or other person for whose account the insolvent bank has acted is entitled to receive the documents involved.

Article 6
BULK TRANSFERS

§ 6—101. **Short Title.**

This Article shall be known and may be cited as Uniform Commercial Code—Bulk Transfers.

§ 6—102. **"Bulk Transfer"; Transfers of Equipment; Enterprises Subject to This Article; Bulk Transfers Subject to This Article.**

(1) A "bulk transfer" is any transfer in bulk and not in the ordinary course of the transferor's business of a major part of the materials, supplies, merchandise or

other inventory (Section 9—109) of an enterprise subject to this Article.

(2) A transfer of a substantial part of the equipment (Section 9—109) of such an enterprise is a bulk transfer if it is made in connection with a bulk transfer of inventory, but not otherwise.

(3) The enterprises subject to this Article are all those whose principal business is the sale of merchandise from stock, including those who manufacture what they sell.

(4) Except as limited by the following section all bulk transfers of goods located within this state are subject to this Article.

§ 6—103. Transfers Excepted From This Article.

The following transfers are not subject to this Article:

(1) Those made to give security for the performance of an obligation;

(2) General assignments for the benefit of all the creditors of the transferor, and subsequent transfers by the assignee thereunder;

(3) Transfers in settlement or realization of a lien or other security interest;

(4) Sales by executors, administrators, receivers, trustees in bankruptcy, or any public officer under judicial process;

(5) Sales made in the course of judicial or administrative proceedings for the dissolution or reorganization of a corporation and of which notice is sent to the creditors of the corporation pursuant to order of the court or administrative agency;

(6) Transfers to a person maintaining a known place of business in this State who becomes bound to pay the debts of the transferor in full and gives public notice of that fact, and who is solvent after becoming so bound;

(7) A transfer to a new business enterprise organized to take over and continue the business, if public notice of the transaction is given and the new enterprise assumes the debts of the transferor and he receives nothing from the transaction except an interest in the new enterprise junior to the claims of creditors;

(8) Transfers of property which is exempt from execution.

Public notice under subsection (6) or subsection (7) may be given by publishing once a week for two consecutive weeks in a newspaper of general circulation where the transferor had its principal place of business in this state an advertisement including the names and addresses of the transferor and transferee and the effective date of the transfer.

§ 6—104. Schedule of Property, List of Creditors.

(1) Except as provided with respect to auction sales (Section 6—108), a bulk transfer subject to this Article is ineffective against any creditor of the transferor unless:

(a) The transferee requires the transferor to furnish a list of his existing creditors prepared as stated in this section; and

(b) The parties prepare a schedule of the property transferred sufficient to identify it; and

(c) The transferee preserves the list and schedule for six months next following the transfer and permits inspection of either or both and copying therefrom at all reasonable hours by any creditor of the transferor, or files the list and schedule in (a public office to be here identified).

(2) The list of creditors must be signed and sworn to or affirmed by the transferor or his agent. It must contain the names and business addresses of all creditors of the transferor, with the amounts when known, and also the names of all persons who are known to the transferor to assert claims against him even though such claims are disputed. If the transferor is the obligor of an outstanding issue of bonds, debentures or the like as to which there is an indenture trustee, the list of creditors need include only the name and address of the indenture trustee and the aggregate outstanding principal amount of the issue.

(3) Responsibility for the completeness and accuracy of the list of creditors rests on the transferor, and the transfer is not rendered ineffective by errors or omissions therein unless the transferee is shown to have had knowledge.

§ 6—105. Notice to Creditors.

In addition to the requirements of the preceding section, any bulk transfer subject to this Article except one made by auction sale (Section 6—108) is ineffective against any creditor of the transferor unless at least ten days before he takes possession of the goods or pays for them, whichever happens first, the transferee gives notice of the transfer in the manner and to the persons hereafter provided (Section 6—107).

[§ 6—106. Application of the Proceeds.

In addition to the requirements of the two preceding sections:

(1) Upon every bulk transfer subject to this Article for which new consideration becomes payable except those made by sale at auction it is the duty of the transferee to assure that such consideration is applied so far as necessary to pay those debts of the transferor which are either shown on the list furnished by the transferor (Section 6—104) or filed in writing in the place stated in the notice (Section 6—107) within thirty days after the mailing of such notice. This duty of the transferee runs to all the holders of such debts, and may be enforced by any of them for the benefit of all.

(2) If any of said debts are in dispute the necessary sum may be withheld from distribution until the dispute is settled or adjudicated.

(3) If the consideration payable is not enough to pay all of the said debts in full distribution shall be made pro rata.]

Note: *This section is bracketed to indicate division of opinion as to whether or not it is a wise provision, and to suggest that this is a point on which State enactments may differ without serious damage to the principle of uniformity. In any State where this section is omitted, the following parts of sections, also bracketed in the text, should also be omitted, namely:*
Section 6—107(2)(c).
    6—108(3)(c).
    6—109(2).

In any State where this section is enacted, these other provisions should be also.

Optional Subsection (4)

[(4) The transferee may within ten days after he takes possession of the goods pay the consideration into the (specify court) in the county where the transferor had its principal place of business in this state and thereafter may discharge his duty under this section by giving notice by registered or certified mail to all the persons to whom the duty runs that the consideration has been paid into that court and that they should file their claims there. On motion of any interested party, the court may order the distribution of the consideration to the persons entitled to it.]

Note: *Optional subsection (4) is recommended for those states which do not have a general statute providing for payment of money into court.*

§ 6—107. **The Notice.**

(1) The notice to creditors (Section 6—105) shall state:

(a) that a bulk transfer is about to be made; and

(b) the names and business addresses of the transferor and transferee, and all other business names and addresses used by the transferor within three years last past so far as known to the transferee; and

(c) whether or not all the debts of the transferor are to be paid in full as they fall due as a result of the transaction, and if so, the address to which creditors should send their bills.

(2) If the debts of the transferor are not to be paid in full as they fall due or if the transferee is in doubt on that point then the notice shall state further:

(a) the location and general description of the property to be transferred and the estimated total of the transferor's debts;

(b) the address where the schedule of property and list of creditors (Section 6—104) may be inspected;

(c) whether the transfer is to pay existing debts and if so the amount of such debts and to whom owing;

(d) whether the transfer is for new consideration and if so the amount of such consideration and the time and place of payment; [and]

[(e) if for new consideration the time and place where creditors of the transferor are to file their claims.]

(3) The notice in any case shall be delivered personally or sent by registered or certified mail to all the persons shown on the list of creditors furnished by the transferor (Section 6—104) and to all other persons who are known to the transferee to hold or assert claims against the transferor.

§ 6—108. **Auction Sales; "Auctioneer".**

(1) A bulk transfer is subject to this Article even though it is by sale at auction, but only in the manner and with the results stated in this section.

(2) The transferor shall furnish a list of his creditors and assist in the preparation of a schedule of the property to be sold, both prepared as before stated (Section 6—104).

(3) The person or persons other than the transferor who direct, control or are responsible for the auction are collectively called the "auctioneer". The auctioneer shall:

(a) receive and retain the list of creditors and prepare and retain the schedule of property for the period stated in this Article (Section 6—104);

(b) give notice of the auction personally or by registered or certified mail at least ten days before it occurs to all persons shown on the list of creditors and to all other persons who are known to him to hold or assert claims against the transferor; [and]

[(c) assure that the net proceeds of the auction are applied as provided in this Article (Section 6—106).]

(4) Failure of the auctioneer to perform any of these duties does not affect the validity of the sale or the title of the purchasers, but if the auctioneer knows that the auction constitutes a bulk transfer such failure renders the auctioneer liable to the creditors of the transferor as a class for the sums owing to them from the transferor up to but not exceeding the net proceeds of the auction. If the auctioneer consists of several persons their liability is joint and several.

§ 6—109. **What Creditors Protected; [Credit for Payment to Particular Creditors].**

(1) The creditors of the transferor mentioned in this Article are those holding claims based on transactions or events occurring before the bulk transfer, but creditors who become such after notice to creditors is given (Sections 6—105 and 6—107) are not entitled to notice.

[(2) Against the aggregate obligation imposed by the provisions of this Article concerning the application of the proceeds (Section 6—106 and subsection (3) (c) of 6—108) the transferee or auctioneer is entitled to credit for sums paid to particular creditors of the transferor, not exceeding the sums believed in good faith at the time of the payment to be properly payable to such creditors.]

§ 6—110. **Subsequent Transfers.**

When the title of a transferee to property is subject to a defect by reason of his non-compliance with the requirements of this Article, then:

(1) a purchaser of any of such property from such transferee who pays no value or who takes with notice of such non-compliance takes subject to such defect, but

(2) a purchaser for value in good faith and without such notice takes free of such defect.

§ 6—111. **Limitation of Actions and Levies.**

No action under this Article shall be brought nor levy made more than six months after the date on which the transferee took possession of the goods unless the transfer has been concealed. If the transfer has been concealed, actions may be brought or levies made within six months after its discovery.

Note to Article 6: *Section 6—106 is bracketed to indicate division of opinion as to whether or not it is a wise provision, and to suggest that this is a point on which State enactments may differ without serious damage to the principle of uniformity.*

In any State where Section 6—106 is not enacted, the following parts of sections, also bracketed in the text, should also be omitted, namely:
Sec. 6—107(2)(e).
    6—108(3)(c).
    6—109(2).
In any State where Section 6—106 is enacted, these other provisions should be also.

Article 7
Warehouse Receipts, Bills of Lading and Other Documents of Title

Part 1 General

§ 7—101. **Short Title.**

This Article shall be known and may be cited as Uniform Commercial Code—Documents of Title.

§ 7—102. **Definitions and Index of Definitions.**

(1) In this Article, unless the context otherwise requires:

(a) "Bailee" means the person who by a warehouse receipt, bill of lading or other document of title acknowledges possession of goods and contracts to deliver them.

(b) "Consignee" means the person named in a bill to whom or to whose order the bill promises delivery.

(c) "Consignor" means the person named in a bill as the person from whom the goods have been received for shipment.

(d) "Delivery order" means a written order to deliver goods directed to a warehouseman, carrier or other person who in the ordinary course of business issues warehouse receipts or bills of lading.

(e) "Document" means document of title as defined in the general definitions in Article 1 (Section 1—201).

(f) "Goods" means all things which are treated as movable for the purposes of a contract of storage or transportation.

(g) "Issuer" means a bailee who issues a document except that in relation to an unaccepted delivery order it means the person who orders the possessor of goods to deliver. Issuer includes any person for whom an agent or employee purports to act in issuing a document if the agent or employee has real or apparent authority to issue documents, notwithstanding that the issuer received no goods or that the goods were misdescribed or that in any other respect the agent or employee violated his instructions.

(h) "Warehouseman" is a person engaged in the business of storing goods for hire.

(2) Other definitions applying to this Article or to specified Parts thereof, and the sections in which they appear are:
"Duly negotiate". Section 7—501.
"Person entitled under the document". Section 7—403(4).

(3) Definitions in other Articles applying to this Article and the sections in which they appear are:
"Contract for sale". Section 2—106.
"Overseas". Section 2—323.
"Receipt" of goods. Section 2—103.

(4) In addition Article 1 contains general definitions and principles of construction and interpretation applicable throughout this Article.

§ 7—103. **Relation of Article to Treaty, Statute, Tariff, Classification or Regulation.**

To the extent that any treaty or statute of the United States, regulatory statute of this State or tariff, classification or regulation filed or issued pursuant thereto is applicable, the provisions of this Article are subject thereto.

§ 7—104. **Negotiable and Non-Negotiable Warehouse Receipt, Bill of Lading or Other Document of Title.**

(1) A warehouse receipt, bill of lading or other document of title is negotiable

(a) if by its terms the goods are to be delivered to bearer or to the order of a named person; or

(b) where recognized in overseas trade, if it runs to a named person or assigns.

(2) Any other document is non-negotiable. A bill of lading in which it is stated that the goods are consigned to a named person is not made negotiable by a provision that the goods are to be delivered only against a written order signed by the same or another named person.

§ 7—105. **Construction Against Negative Implication.**
The omission from either Part 2 or Part 3 of this Article of a provision corresponding to a provision

made in the other Part does not imply that a corresponding rule of law is not applicable.

Part 2 **Warehouse Receipts: Special Provisions**

§ 7—201. **Who May Issue a Warehouse Receipt; Storage Under Government Bond.**

(1) A warehouse receipt may be issued by any warehouseman.

(2) Where goods including distilled spirits and agricultural commodities are stored under a statute requiring a bond against withdrawal or a license for the issuance of receipts in the nature of warehouse receipts, a receipt issued for the goods has like effect as a warehouse receipt even though issued by a person who is the owner of the goods and is not a warehouseman.

§ 7—202. **Form of Warehouse Receipt; Essential Terms; Optional Terms.**

(1) A warehouse receipt need not be in any particular form.

(2) Unless a warehouse receipt embodies within its written or printed terms each of the following, the warehouseman is liable for damages caused by the omission to a person injured thereby:

(a) the location of the warehouse where the goods are stored;

(b) the date of issue of the receipt;

(c) the consecutive number of the receipt;

(d) a statement whether the goods received will be delivered to the bearer, to a specified person, or to a specified person or his order;

(e) the rate of storage and handling charges, except that where goods are stored under a field warehousing arrangement a statement of that fact is sufficient on a non-negotiable receipt;

(f) a description of the goods or of the packages containing them;

(g) the signature of the warehouseman, which may be made by his authorized agent;

(h) if the receipt is issued for goods of which the warehouseman is owner, either solely or jointly or in common with others, the fact of such ownership; and

(i) a statement of the amount of advances made and of liabilities incurred for which the warehouseman claims a lien or security interest (Section 7—209). If the precise amount of such advances made or of such liabilities incurred is, at the time of the issue of the receipt, unknown to the warehouseman or to his agent who issues it, a statement of the fact that advances have been made or liabilities incurred and the purpose thereof is sufficient.

(3) A warehouseman may insert in his receipt any other terms which are not contrary to the provisions of this Act and do not impair his obligation of delivery (Section 7—403) or his duty of care (Section 7—204). Any contrary provisions shall be ineffective.

§ 7—203. **Liability for Non-Receipt or Misdescription.**

A party to or purchaser for value in good faith of a document of title other than a bill of lading relying in either case upon the description therein of the goods may recover from the issuer damages caused by the non-receipt or misdescription of the goods, except to the extent that the document conspicuously indicates that the issuer does not know whether any part or all of the goods in fact were received or conform to the description, as where the description is in terms of marks or labels or kind, quantity or condition, or the receipt or description is qualified by "contents, condition and quality unknown", "said to contain" or the like, if such indication be true, or the party or purchaser otherwise has notice.

§ 7—204. **Duty of Care; Contractual Limitation of Warehouseman's Liability.**

(1) A warehouseman is liable for damages for loss of or injury to the goods caused by his failure to exercise such care in regard to them as a reasonably careful man would exercise under like circumstances but unless otherwise agreed he is not liable for damages which could not have been avoided by the exercise of such care.

(2) Damages may be limited by a term in the warehouse receipt or storage agreement limiting the amount of liability in case of loss or damage, and setting forth a specific liability per article or item, or value per unit of weight, beyond which the warehouseman shall not be liable; provided, however, that such liability may on written request of the bailor at the time of signing such storage agreement or within a reasonable time after receipt of the warehouse receipt be increased on part or all of the goods thereunder, in which event increased rates may be charged based on such increased valuation, but that no such increase shall be permitted contrary to a lawful limitation of liability contained in the warehouseman's tariff, if any. No such limitation is effective with respect to the warehouseman's liability for conversion to his own use.

(3) Reasonable provisions as to the time and manner of presenting claims and instituting actions based on the bailment may be included in the warehouse receipt or tariff.

(4) This section does not impair or repeal . . .

Note: *Insert in subsection (4) a reference to any statute which imposes a higher responsibility upon the warehouseman or invalidates contractual limitations which would be permissible under this Article.*

§ 7—205. **Title Under Warehouse Receipt Defeated in Certain Cases.**

A buyer in the ordinary course of business of fungible goods sold and delivered by a warehouseman who is also in the business of buying and selling such goods takes free of any claim under a warehouse receipt even though it has been duly negotiated.

§ 7—206. **Termination of Storage at Warehouseman's Option.**

(1) A warehouseman may on notifying the person on whose account the goods are held and any other person known to claim an interest in the goods require payment of any charges and removal of the goods from the warehouse at the termination of the period of storage fixed by the document, or, if no period is fixed, within a stated period not less than thirty days after the notification. If the goods are not removed before the date specified in the notification, the warehouseman may sell them in accordance with the provisions of the section on enforcement of a warehouseman's lien (Section 7—210).

(2) If a warehouseman in good faith believes that the goods are about to deteriorate or decline in value to less than the amount of his lien within the time prescribed in subsection (1) for notification, advertisement and sale, the warehouseman may specify in the notification any reasonable shorter time for removal of the goods and in case the goods are not removed, may sell them at public sale held not less than one week after a single advertisement or posting.

(3) If as a result of a quality or condition of the goods of which the warehouseman had no notice at the time of deposit the goods are a hazard to other property or to the warehouse or to persons, the warehouseman may sell the goods at public or private sale without advertisement on reasonable notification to all persons known to claim an interest in the goods. If the warehouseman after a reasonable effort is unable to sell the goods he may dispose of them in any lawful manner and shall incur no liability by reason of such disposition.

(4) The warehouseman must deliver the goods to any person entitled to them under this Article upon due demand made at any time prior to sale or other disposition under this section.

(5) The warehouseman may satisfy his lien from the proceeds of any sale or disposition under this section but must hold the balance for delivery on the demand of any person to whom he would have been bound to deliver the goods.

§ 7—207. **Goods Must Be Kept Separate; Fungible Goods.**

(1) Unless the warehouse receipt otherwise provides, a warehouseman must keep separate the goods covered by each receipt so as to permit at all times identification and delivery of those goods except that different lots of fungible goods may be commingled.

(2) Fungible goods so commingled are owned in common by the persons entitled thereto and the warehouseman is severally liable to each owner for that owner's share. Where because of overissue a mass of fungible goods is insufficient to meet all the receipts which the warehouseman has issued against it, the persons entitled include all holders to whom overissued receipts have been duly negotiated.

§ 7—208. **Altered Warehouse Receipts.**

Where a blank in a negotiable warehouse receipt has been filled in without authority, a purchaser for value and without notice of the want of authority may treat the insertion as authorized. Any other unauthorized alteration leaves any receipt enforceable against the issuer according to its original tenor.

§ 7—209. **Lien of Warehouseman.**

(1) A warehouseman has a lien against the bailor on the goods covered by a warehouse receipt or on the proceeds thereof in his possession for charges for storage or transportation (including demurrage and terminal charges), insurance, labor, or charges present or future in relation to the goods, and for expenses necessary for preservation of the goods or reasonably incurred in their sale pursuant to law. If the person on whose account the goods are held is liable for like charges or expenses in relation to other goods whenever deposited and it is stated in the receipt that a lien is claimed for charges and expenses in relation to other goods, the warehouseman also has a lien against him for such charges and expenses whether or not the other goods have been delivered by the warehouseman. But against a person to whom a negotiable warehouse receipt is duly negotiated a warehouseman's lien is limited to charges in an amount or at a rate specified on the receipt or if no

charges are so specified then to a reasonable charge for storage of the goods covered by the receipt subsequent to the date of the receipt.

(2) The warehouseman may also reserve a security interest against the bailor for a maximum amount specified on the receipt for charges other than those specified in subsection (1), such as for money advanced and interest. Such a security interest is governed by the Article on Secured Transactions (Article 9).

(3) (a) A warehouseman's lien for charges and expenses under subsection (1) or a security interest under subsection (2) is also effective against any person who so entrusted the bailor with possession of the goods that a pledge of them by him to a good faith purchaser for value would have been valid but is not effective against a person as to whom the document confers no right in the goods covered by it under Section 7—503.

(b) A warehouseman's lien on household goods for charges and expenses in relation to the goods under subsection (1) is also effective against all persons if the depositor was the legal possessor of the goods at the time of deposit. "Household goods" means furniture, furnishings and personal effects used by the depositor in a dwelling.

(4) A warehouseman loses his lien on any goods which he voluntarily delivers or which he unjustifiably refuses to deliver.

§ 7—210. **Enforcement of Warehouseman's Lien.**

(1) Except as provided in subsection (2), a warehouseman's lien may be enforced by public or private sale of the goods in bloc or in parcels, at any time or place and on any terms which are commercially reasonable, after notifying all persons known to claim an interest in the goods. Such notification must include a statement of the amount due, the nature of the proposed sale and the time and place of any public sale. The fact that a better price could have been obtained by a sale at a different time or in a different method from that selected by the warehouseman is not of itself sufficient to establish that the sale was not made in a commercially reasonable manner. If the warehouseman either sells the goods in the usual manner in any recognized market therefor, or if he sells at the price current in such market at the time of his sale, or if he has otherwise sold in conformity with commercially reasonable practices among dealers in the type of goods sold, he has sold in a commercially reasonable manner. A sale of more goods than apparently necessary to be offered to insure satisfac-

tion of the obligation is not commercially reasonable except in cases covered by the preceding sentence.

(2) A warehouseman's lien on goods other than goods stored by a merchant in the course of his business may be enforced only as follows:

(a) All persons known to claim an interest in the goods must be notified.

(b) The notification must be delivered in person or sent by registered or certified letter to the last known address of any person to be notified.

(c) The notification must include an itemized statement of the claim, a description of the goods subject to the lien, a demand for payment within a specified time not less than ten days after receipt of the notification, and a conspicuous statement that unless the claim is paid within the time the goods will be advertised for sale and sold by auction at a specified time and place.

(d) The sale must conform to the terms of the notification.

(e) The sale must be held at the nearest suitable place to that where the goods are held or stored.

(f) After the expiration of the time given in the notification, an advertisement of the sale must be published once a week for two weeks consecutively in a newspaper of general circulation where the sale is to be held. The advertisement must include a description of the goods, the name of the person on whose account they are being held, and the time and place of the sale. The sale must take place at least fifteen days after the first publication. If there is no newspaper of general circulation where the sale is to be held, the advertisement must be posted at least ten days before the sale in not less than six conspicuous places in the neighborhood of the proposed sale.

(3) Before any sale pursuant to this section any person claiming a right in the goods may pay the amount necessary to satisfy the lien and the reasonable expenses incurred under this section. In that event the goods must not be sold, but must be retained by the warehouseman subject to the terms of the receipt and this Article.

(4) The warehouseman may buy at any public sale pursuant to this section.

(5) A purchaser in good faith of goods sold to enforce a warehouseman's lien takes the goods free of any rights of persons against whom the lien was valid, despite noncompliance by the warehouseman with the requirements of this section.

(6) The warehouseman may satisfy his lien from the proceeds of any sale pursuant to this section but must hold the balance, if any, for delivery on demand to any person to whom he would have been bound to deliver the goods.

(7) The rights provided by this section shall be in addition to all other rights allowed by law to a creditor against his debtor.

(8) Where a lien is on goods stored by a merchant in the course of his business the lien may be enforced in accordance with either subsection (1) or (2).

(9) The warehouseman is liable for damages caused by failure to comply with the requirements for sale under this section and in case of willful violation is liable for conversion.

Part 3 **Bills of Lading: Special Provisions**

§ 7—301. **Liability for Non-Receipt or Misdescription; "Said to Contain"; "Shipper's Load and Count"; Improper Handling.**

(1) A consignee of a non-negotiable bill who has given value in good faith or a holder to whom a negotiable bill has been duly negotiated relying in either case upon the description therein of the goods, or upon the date therein shown, may recover from the issuer damages caused by the misdating of the bill or the non-receipt or misdescription of the goods, except to the extent that the document indicates that the issuer does not know whether any part of all of the goods in fact were received or conform to the description, as where the description is in terms of marks or labels or kind, quantity, or condition or the receipt or description is qualified by "contents or condition of contents of packages unknown", "said to contain", "shipper's weight, load and count" or the like, if such indication be true.

(2) When goods are loaded by an issuer who is a common carrier, the issuer must count the packages of goods if package freight and ascertain the kind and quantity if bulk freight. In such cases "shipper's weight, load and count" or other words indicating that the description was made by the shipper are ineffective except as to freight concealed by packages.

(3) When bulk freight is loaded by a shipper who makes available to the issuer adequate facilities for weighing such freight, an issuer who is a common carrier must ascertain the kind and quantity within a reasonable time after receiving the written request of

the shipper to do so. In such cases "shipper's weight" or other words of like purport are ineffective.

(4) The issuer may by inserting in the bill the words "shipper's weight, load and count" or other words of like purport indicate that the goods were loaded by the shipper; and if such statement be true the issuer shall not be liable for damages caused by the improper loading. But their omission does not imply liability for such damages.

(5) The shipper shall be deemed to have guaranteed to the issuer the accuracy at the time of shipment of the description, marks, labels, number, kind, quantity, condition and weight, as furnished by him; and the shipper shall indemnify the issuer against damage caused by inaccuracies in such particulars. The right of the issuer to such indemnity shall in no way limit his responsibility and liability under the contract of carriage to any person other than the shipper.

§ 7—302. **Through Bills of Lading and Similar Documents.**

(1) The issuer of a through bill of lading or other document embodying an undertaking to be performed in part by persons acting as its agents or by connecting carriers is liable to anyone entitled to recover on the document for any breach by such other persons or by a connecting carrier of its obligation under the document but to the extent that the bill covers an undertaking to be performed overseas or in territory not contiguous to the continental United States or an undertaking including matters other than transportation this liability may be varied by agreement of the parties.

(2) Where goods covered by a through bill of lading or other document embodying an undertaking to be performed in part by persons other than the issuer are received by any such person, he is subject with respect to his own performance while the goods are in his possession to the obligation of the issuer. His obligation is discharged by delivery of the goods to another such person pursuant to the document, and does not include liability for breach by any other such persons or by the issuer.

(3) The issuer of such through bill of lading or other document shall be entitled to recover from the connecting carrier or such other person in possession of the goods when the breach of the obligation under the document occurred, the amount it may be required to pay to anyone entitled to recover on the document therefor, as may be evidenced by any receipt, judgment, or transcript thereof, and the amount of any expense reasonably incurred by it in defending any action brought by anyone entitled to recover on the document therefor.

§ 7—303. **Diversion; Reconsignment; Change of Instructions.**

(1) Unless the bill of lading otherwise provides, the carrier may deliver the goods to a person or destination other than that stated in the bill or may otherwise dispose of the goods on instructions from

(a) the holder of a negotiable bill; or

(b) the consignor on a non-negotiable bill notwithstanding contrary instructions from the consignee; or

(c) the consignee on a non-negotiable bill in the absence of contrary instructions from the consignor, if the goods have arrived at the billed destination or if the consignee is in possession of the bill; or

(d) the consignee on a non-negotiable bill if he is entitled as against the consignor to dispose of them.

(2) Unless such instructions are noted on a negotiable bill of lading, a person to whom the bill is duly negotiated can hold the bailee according to the original terms.

§ 7—304. **Bills of Lading in a Set.**

(1) Except where customary in overseas transportation, a bill of lading must not be issued in a set of parts. The issuer is liable for damages caused by violation of this subsection.

(2) Where a bill of lading is lawfully drawn in a set of parts, each of which is numbered and expressed to be valid only if the goods have not been delivered against any other part, the whole of the parts constitute one bill.

(3) Where a bill of lading is lawfully issued in a set of parts and different parts are negotiated to different persons, the title of the holder to whom the first due negotiation is made prevails as to both the document and the goods even though any later holder may have received the goods from the carrier in good faith and discharged the carrier's obligation by surrender of his part.

(4) Any person who negotiates or transfers a single part of a bill of lading drawn in a set is liable to holders of that part as if it were the whole set.

(5) The bailee is obliged to deliver in accordance with Part 4 of this Article against the first presented part of a bill of lading lawfully drawn in a set. Such delivery discharges the bailee's obligation on the whole bill.

§ 7—305. **Destination Bills.**

(1) Instead of issuing a bill of lading to the consignor at the place of shipment a carrier may at the request

of the consignor procure the bill to be issued at destination or at any other place designated in the request.

(2) Upon request of anyone entitled as against the carrier to control the goods while in transit and on surrender of any outstanding bill of lading or other receipt covering such goods, the issuer may procure a substitute bill to be issued at any place designated in the request.

§ 7—306. **Altered Bills of Lading.**

An unauthorized alteration or filling in of a blank in a bill of lading leaves the bill enforceable according to its original tenor.

§ 7—307. **Lien of Carrier.**

(1) A carrier has a lien on the goods covered by a bill of lading for charges subsequent to the date of its receipt of the goods for storage or transportation (including demurrage and terminal charges) and for expenses necessary for preservation of the goods incident to their transportation or reasonably incurred in their sale pursuant to law. But against a purchaser for value of a negotiable bill of lading a carrier's lien is limited to charges stated in the bill or the applicable tariffs, or if no charges are stated then to a reasonable charge.

(2) A lien for charges and expenses under subsection (1) on goods which the carrier was required by law to receive for transportation is effective against the consignor or any person entitled to the goods unless the carrier had notice that the consignor lacked authority to subject the goods to such charges and expenses. Any other lien under subsection (1) is effective against the consignor and any person who permitted the bailor to have control or possession of the goods unless the carrier had notice that the bailor lacked such authority.

(3) A carrier loses his lien on any goods which he voluntarily delivers or which he unjustifiably refuses to deliver.

§ 7—308. **Enforcement of Carrier's Lien.**

(1) A carrier's lien may be enforced by public or private sale of the goods, in bloc or in parcels, at any time or place and on any terms which are commercially reasonable, after notifying all persons known to claim an interest in the goods. Such notification must include a statement of the amount due, the nature of the proposed sale and the time and place of any public sale. The fact that a better price could have been obtained by a sale at a different time or in a different method from that selected by the carrier is not of itself sufficient to establish that the sale was not made in a commercially reasonable manner. If the carrier either sells the goods in the usual manner in any recognized market therefor or if he sells at the price current in such market at the time of his sale or if he has otherwise sold in conformity with commercially reasonable practices among dealers in the type of goods sold he has sold in a commercially reasonable manner. A sale of more goods than apparently necessary to be offered to ensure satisfaction of the obligation is not commercially reasonable except in cases covered by the preceding sentence.

(2) Before any sale pursuant to this section any person claiming a right in the goods may pay the amount necessary to satisfy the lien and the reasonable expenses incurred under this section. In that event the goods must not be sold, but must be retained by the carrier subject to the terms of the bill and this Article.

(3) The carrier may buy at any public sale pursuant to this section.

(4) A purchaser in good faith of goods sold to enforce a carrier's lien takes the goods free of any rights of persons against whom the lien was valid, despite noncompliance by the carrier with the requirements of this section.

(5) The carrier may satisfy his lien from the proceeds of any sale pursuant to this section but must hold the balance, if any, for delivery on demand to any person to whom he would have been bound to deliver the goods.

(6) The rights provided by this section shall be in addition to all other rights allowed by law to a creditor against his debtor.

(7) A carrier's lien may be enforced in accordance with either subsection (1) or the procedure set forth in subsection (2) of Section 7—210.

(8) The carrier is liable for damages caused by failure to comply with the requirements for sale under this section and in case of willful violation is liable for conversion.

§ 7—309. **Duty of Care; Contractual Limitation of Carrier's Liability.**

(1) A carrier who issues a bill of lading whether negotiable or non-negotiable must exercise the degree of care in relation to the goods which a reasonably careful man would exercise under like circumstances. This subsection does not repeal or change any law or rule of law which imposes liability upon a common carrier for damages not caused by its negligence.

(2) Damages may be limited by a provision that the carrier's liability shall not exceed a value stated in the

document if the carrier's rates are dependent upon value and the consignor by the carrier's tariff is afforded an opportunity to declare a higher value or a value as lawfully provided in the tariff, or where no tariff is filed he is otherwise advised of such opportunity; but no such limitation is effective with respect to the carrier's liability for conversion to its own use.

(3) Reasonable provisions as to the time and manner of presenting claims and instituting actions based on the shipment may be included in a bill of lading or tariff.

Part 4 Warehouse Receipts and Bills of Lading: General Obligations

§ 7—401. Irregularities in Issue of Receipt or Bill or Conduct of Issuer.

The obligations imposed by this Article on an issuer apply to a document of title regardless of the fact that

(a) the document may not comply with the requirements of this Article or of any other law or regulation regarding its issue, form or content; or

(b) the issuer may have violated laws regulating the conduct of his business; or

(c) the goods covered by the document were owned by the bailee at the time the document was issued; or

(d) the person issuing the document does not come within the definition of warehouseman if it purports to be a warehouse receipt.

§ 7—402. Duplicate Receipt or Bill; Overissue.

Neither a duplicate nor any other document of title purporting to cover goods already represented by an outstanding document of the same issuer confers any right in the goods, except as provided in the case of bills in a set, overissue of documents for fungible goods and substitutes for lost, stolen or destroyed documents. But the issuer is liable for damages caused by his overissue or failure to identify a duplicate document as such by conspicuous notation on its face.

§ 7—403. Obligation of Warehouseman or Carrier to Deliver; Excuse.

(1) The bailee must deliver the goods to a person entitled under the document who complies with subsections (2) and (3), unless and to the extent that the bailee establishes any of the following:

(a) delivery of the goods to a person whose receipt was rightful as against the claimant;

(b) damage to or delay, loss or destruction of the goods for which the bailee is not liable [, but the burden of establishing negligence in such cases is on the person entitled under the document];

Note: The brackets in (1)(b) indicate that State enactments may differ on this point without serious damage to the principle of uniformity.

(c) previous sale or other disposition of the goods in lawful enforcement of a lien or on warehouseman's lawful termination of storage;

(d) the exercise by a seller of his right to stop delivery pursuant to the provisions of the Article on Sales (Section 2—705);

(e) a diversion, reconsignment or other disposition pursuant to the provisions of this Article (Section 7—303) or tariff regulating such right;

(f) release, satisfaction or any other fact affording a personal defense against the claimant;

(g) any other lawful excuse.

(2) A person claiming goods covered by a document of title must satisfy the bailee's lien where the bailee so requests or where the bailee is prohibited by law from delivering the goods until the charges are paid.

(3) Unless the person claiming is one against whom the document confers no right under Sec. 7—503(1), he must surrender for cancellation or notation of partial deliveries any outstanding negotiable document covering the goods, and the bailee must cancel the document or conspicuously note the partial delivery thereon or be liable to any person to whom the document is duly negotiated.

(4) "Person entitled under the document" means holder in the case of a negotiable document, or the person to whom delivery is to be made by the terms of or pursuant to written instructions under a non-negotiable document.

§ 7—404. No Liability for Good Faith Delivery Pursuant to Receipt or Bill.

A bailee who in good faith including observance of reasonable commercial standards has received goods and delivered or otherwise disposed of them according to the terms of the document of title or pursuant to this Article is not liable therefor. This rule applies even though the person from whom he received the goods had no authority to procure the document or to dispose of the goods and even though the person to whom he delivered the goods had no authority to receive them.

Part 5 Warehouse Receipts and Bills of Lading: Negotiation and Transfer

§ 7—501. Form of Negotiation and Requirements of "Due Negotiation".

(1) A negotiable document of title running to the order of a named person is negotiated by his indorsement and delivery. After his indorsement in blank or to bearer any person can negotiate it by delivery alone.

(2) (a) A negotiable document of title is also negotiated by delivery alone when by its original terms it runs to bearer.

(b) When a document running to the order of a named person is delivered to him the effect is the same as if the document had been negotiated.

(3) Negotiation of a negotiable document of title after it has been indorsed to a specified person requires indorsement by the special indorsee as well as delivery.

(4) A negotiable document of title is "duly negotiated" when it is negotiated in the manner stated in this section to a holder who purchases it in good faith without notice of any defense against or claim to it on the part of any person and for value, unless it is established that the negotiation is not in the regular course of business or financing or involves receiving the document in settlement or payment of a money obligation.

(5) Indorsement of a non-negotiable document neither makes it negotiable nor adds to the transferee's rights.

(6) The naming in a negotiable bill of a person to be notified of the arrival of the goods does not limit the negotiability of the bill nor constitute notice to a purchaser thereof of any interest of such person in the goods.

§ 7—502. Rights Acquired by Due Negotiation.

(1) Subject to the following section and to the provisions of Section 7—205 on fungible goods, a holder to whom a negotiable document of title has been duly negotiated acquires thereby:

(a) title to the document;

(b) title to the goods;

(c) all rights accruing under the law of agency or estoppel, including rights to goods delivered to the bailee after the document was issued; and

(d) the direct obligation of the issuer to hold or deliver the goods according to the terms of the document free of any defense or claim by him

except those arising under the terms of the document or under this Article. In the case of a delivery order the bailee's obligation accrues only upon acceptance and the obligation acquired by the holder is that the issuer and any indorser will procure the acceptance of the bailee.

(2) Subject to the following section, title and rights so acquired are not defeated by any stoppage of the goods represented by the document or by surrender of such goods by the bailee, and are not impaired even though the negotiation or any prior negotiation constituted a breach of duty or even though any person has been deprived of possession of the document by misrepresentation, fraud, accident, mistake, duress, loss, theft or conversion, or even though a previous sale or other transfer of the goods or document has been made to a third person.

§ 7—503. Document of Title to Goods Defeated in Certain Cases.

(1) A document of title confers no right in goods against a person who before issuance of the document had a legal interest or a perfected security interest in them and who neither

(a) delivered or entrusted them or any document of title covering them to the bailor or his nominee with actual or apparent authority to ship, store or sell or with power to obtain delivery under this Article (Section 7—403) or with power of disposition under this Act (Sections 2—403 and 9—307) or other statute or rule of law; nor

(b) acquiesced in the procurement by the bailor or his nominee of any document of title.

(2) Title to goods based upon an unaccepted delivery order is subject to the rights of anyone to whom a negotiable warehouse receipt or bill of lading covering the goods has been duly negotiated. Such a title may be defeated under the next section to the same extent as the rights of the issuer or a transferee from the issuer.

(3) Title to goods based upon a bill of lading issued to a freight forwarder is subject to the rights of anyone to whom a bill issued by the freight forwarder is duly negotiated; but delivery by the carrier in accordance with Part 4 of this Article pursuant to its own bill of lading discharges the carrier's obligation to deliver.

§ 7—504. Rights Acquired in the Absence of Due Negotiation; Effect of Diversion; Seller's Stoppage of Delivery.

(1) A transferee of a document, whether negotiable or non-negotiable, to whom the document has been delivered but not duly negotiated, acquires the title

and rights which his transferor had or had actual authority to convey.

(2) In the case of a non-negotiable document, until but not after the bailee receives notification of the transfer, the rights of the transferee may be defeated

    (a) by those creditors of the transferor who could treat the sale as void under Section 2—402; or

    (b) by a buyer from the transferor in ordinary course of business if the bailee has delivered the goods to the buyer or received notification of his rights; or

    (c) as against the bailee by good faith dealings of the bailee with the transferor.

(3) A diversion or other change of shipping instructions by the consignor in a non-negotiable bill of lading which causes the bailee not to deliver to the consignee defeats the consignee's title to the goods if they have been delivered to a buyer in ordinary course of business and in any event defeats the consignee's rights against the bailee.

(4) Delivery pursuant to a non-negotiable document may be stopped by a seller under Section 2—705, and subject to the requirement of due notification there provided. A bailee honoring the seller's instructions is entitled to be indemnified by the seller against any resulting loss or expense.

§ 7—505. Indorser Not a Guarantor for Other Parties.

The indorsement of a document of title issued by a bailee does not make the indorser liable for any default by the bailee or by previous indorsers.

§ 7—506. Delivery Without Indorsement: Right to Compel Indorsement.

The transferee of a negotiable document of title has a specifically enforceable right to have his transferor supply any necessary indorsement but the transfer becomes a negotiation only as of the time the indorsement is supplied.

§ 7—507. Warranties on Negotiation or Transfer of Receipt or Bill.

Where a person negotiates or transfers a document of title for value otherwise than as a mere intermediary under the next following section, then unless otherwise agreed he warrants to his immediate purchaser only in addition to any warranty made in selling the goods

(a) that the document is genuine; and

(b) that he has no knowledge of any fact which would impair its validity or worth; and

(c) that his negotiation or transfer is rightful and fully effective with respect to the title to the document and the goods it represents.

§ 7—508. Warranties of Collecting Bank as to Documents.

A collecting bank or other intermediary known to be entrusted with documents on behalf of another or with collection of a draft or other claim against delivery of documents warrants by such delivery of the documents only its own good faith and authority. This rule applies even though the intermediary has purchased or made advances against the claim or draft to be collected.

§ 7—509. Receipt or Bill: When Adequate Compliance With Commercial Contract.

The question whether a document is adequate to fulfill the obligations of a contract for sale or the conditions of a credit is governed by the Articles on Sales (Article 2) and on Letters of Credit (Article 5).

Part 6 Warehouse Receipts and Bills of Lading: Miscellaneous Provisions

§ 7—601. Lost and Missing Documents.

(1) If a document has been lost, stolen or destroyed, a court may order delivery of the goods or issuance of a substitute document and the bailee may without liability to any person comply with such order. If the document was negotiable the claimant must post security approved by the court to indemnify any person who may suffer loss as a result of non-surrender of the document. If the document was not negotiable, such security may be required at the discretion of the court. The court may also in its discretion order payment of the bailee's reasonable costs and counsel fees.

(2) A bailee who without court order delivers goods to a person claiming under a missing negotiable document is liable to any person injured thereby, and if the delivery is not in good faith becomes liable for conversion. Delivery in good faith is not conversion if made in accordance with a filed classification or tariff or, where no classification or tariff is filed, if the claimant posts security with the bailee in an amount at least double the value of the goods at the time of posting to indemnify any person injured by the delivery who files a notice of claim within one year after the delivery.

§ 7—602. Attachment of Goods Covered by a Negotiable Document.

Except where the document was originally issued upon delivery of the goods by a person who had no power to dispose of them, no lien attaches by virtue of any judicial process to goods in the possession of a bailee for which a negotiable document of title is outstanding unless the document be first surrendered to the bailee or its negotiation enjoined, and the bailee shall not be compelled to deliver the goods pursuant to process until the document is surrendered to him or impounded by the court. One who purchases the document for value without notice of the process or injunction takes free of the lien imposed by judicial process.

§ 7—603. Conflicting Claims; Interpleader.

If more than one person claims title or possession of the goods, the bailee is excused from delivery until he has had a reasonable time to ascertain the validity of the adverse claims or to bring an action to compel all claimants to interplead and may compel such interpleader, either in defending an action for non-delivery of the goods, or by original action, whichever is appropriate.

Article 8
INVESTMENT SECURITIES

Part 1 Short Title and General Matters

§ 8—101. Short Title.

This Article shall be known and may be cited as Uniform Commercial Code—Investment Securities.

§ 8—102. Definitions and Index of Definitions.

(1) In this Article, unless the context otherwise requires:

(a) A "certificated security" is a share, participation, or other interest in property of or an enterprise of the issuer or an obligation of the issuer which is

(i) represented by an instrument issued in bearer or registered form;

(ii) of a type commonly dealt in on securities exchanges or markets or commonly recognized in any area in which it is issued or dealt in as a medium for investment; and

(iii) either one of a class or series or by its terms divisible into a class or series of shares, participations, interests, or obligations.

(b) An "uncertificated security" is a share, participation, or other interest in property or an enterprise of the issuer or an obligation of the issuer which is

(i) not represented by an instrument and the transfer of which is registered upon books maintained for that purpose by or on behalf of the issuer;

(ii) of a type commonly dealt in on securities exchanges or markets; and

(iii) either one of a class or series or by its terms divisible into a class or series of shares, participations, interests, or obligations.

(c) A "security" is either a certificated or an uncertificated security. If a security is certificated, the terms "security" and "certificated security" may mean either the intangible interest, the instrument representing that interest, or both, as the context requires. A writing that is a certificated security is governed by this Article and not by Article 3, even though it also meets the requirements of that Article. This Article does not apply to money. If a certificated security has been retained by or surrendered to the issuer or its transfer agent for reasons other than registration of transfer, other temporary purpose, payment, exchange, or acquisition by the issuer, that security shall be treated as an uncertificated security for purposes of this Article.

(d) A certificated security is in "registered form" if

(i) it specifies a person entitled to the security or the rights it represents; and

(ii) its transfer may be registered upon books maintained for that purpose by or on behalf of the issuer, or the security so states.

(e) A certificated security is in "bearer form" if it runs to bearer according to its terms and not by reason of any indorsement.

(2) A "subsequent purchaser" is a person who takes other than by original issue.

(3) A "clearing corporation" is a corporation registered as a "clearing agency" under the federal securities laws or a corporation:

(a) at least 90 percent of whose capital stock is held by or for one or more organizations, none of which, other than a national securities exchange or association, holds in excess of 20 percent of the capital stock of the corporation, and each of which is

(i) subject to supervision or regulation pursuant to the provisions of federal or state banking laws or state insurance laws,

(ii) a broker or dealer or investment company registered under the federal securities laws, or

(iii) a national securities exchange or association registered under the federal securities laws; and

(b) any remaining capital stock of which is held by individuals who have purchased it at or prior to the time of their taking office as directors of the corporation and who have purchased only so much of the capital stock as is necessary to permit them to qualify as directors.

(4) A "custodian bank" is a bank or trust company that is supervised and examined by state or federal authority having supervision over banks and is acting as custodian for a clearing corporation.

(5) Other definitions applying to this Article or to specified Parts thereof and the sections in which they appear are:

"Adverse claim". Section 8—302.
"Bona fide purchaser". Section 8—302.
"Broker". Section 8—303.
"Debtor". Section 9—105.
"Financial intermediary". Section 8—313.
"Guarantee of the signature". Section 8—402.
"Initial transaction statement". Section 8—408.
"Instruction". Section 8—308.
"Intermediary bank". Section 4—105.
"Issuer". Section 8—201.
"Overissue". Section 8—104.
"Secured Party". Section 9—105.
"Security Agreement". Section 9—105.

(6) In addition, Article 1 contains general definitions and principles of construction and interpretation applicable throughout this Article.

Amended in 1962, 1973 and 1977.

§ 8—103. **Issuer's Lien.**

A lien upon a security in favor of an issuer thereof is valid against a purchaser only if:

(a) the security is certificated and the right of the issuer to the lien is noted conspicuously thereon; or

(b) the security is uncertificated and a notation of the right of the issuer to the lien is contained in the initial transaction statement sent to the purchaser or, if his interest is transferred to him other than by registration of transfer, pledge, or release, the initial transaction statement sent to the registered owner or the registered pledgee.

Amended in 1977.

§ 8—104. **Effect of Overissue; "Overissue".**

(1) The provisions of this Article which validate a security or compel its issue or reissue do not apply to the extent that validation, issue, or reissue would result in overissue; but if:

(a) an identical security which does not constitute an overissue is reasonably available for purchase, the person entitled to issue or validation may compel the issuer to purchase the security for him and either to deliver a certificated security or to register the transfer of an uncertificated security to him, against surrender of any certificated security he holds; or

(b) a security is not so available for purchase, the person entitled to issue or validation may recover from the issuer the price he or the last purchaser for value paid for it with interest from the date of his demand.

(2) "Overissue" means the issue of securities in excess of the amount the issuer has corporate power to issue.

Amended in 1977.

§ 8—105. **Certificated Securities Negotiable; Statements and Instructions Not Negotiable; Presumptions.**

(1) Certificated securities governed by this Article are negotiable instruments.

(2) Statements (Section 8—408), notices, or the like, sent by the issuer of uncertificated securities and instructions (Section 8—308) are neither negotiable instruments nor certificated securities.

(3) In any action on a security:

(a) unless specifically denied in the pleadings, each signature on a certificated security, in a necessary indorsement, on an initial transaction statement, or on an instruction, is admitted;

(b) if the effectiveness of a signature is put in issue, the burden of establishing it is on the party claiming under the signature, but the signature is presumed to be genuine or authorized;

(c) if signatures on a certificated security are admitted or established, production of the security entitles a holder to recover on it unless the defendant establishes a defense or a defect going to the validity of the security;

(d) if signatures on an initial transaction statement are admitted or established, the facts stated in the statement are presumed to be true as of the time of its issuance; and

(e) after it is shown that a defense or defect exists, the plaintiff has the burden of establishing that he or some person under whom he claims is a person against whom the defense or defect is ineffective (Section 8—202).

Amended in 1977.

§ 8—106. **Applicability.**

The law (including the conflict of laws rules) of the jurisdiction of organization of the issuer governs the validity of a security, the effectiveness of registration by the issuer, and the rights and duties of the issuer with respect to:

(a) registration of transfer of a certificated security;

(b) registration of transfer, pledge, or release of an uncertificated security; and

(c) sending of statements of uncertificated securities.

Amended in 1977.

§ 8—107. **Securities Transferable; Action for Price.**

(1) Unless otherwise agreed and subject to any applicable law or regulation respecting short sales, a person obligated to transfer securities may transfer any certificated security of the specified issue in bearer form or registered in the name of the transferee, or indorsed to him or in blank, or he may transfer an equivalent uncertificated security to the transferee or a person designated by the transferee.

(2) If the buyer fails to pay the price as it comes due under a contract of sale, the seller may recover the price of:

(a) certificated securities accepted by the buyer;

(b) uncertificated securities that have been transferred to the buyer or a person designated by the buyer; and

(c) other securities if efforts at their resale would be unduly burdensome or if there is no readily available market for their resale.

Amended in 1977.

§ 8—108. **Registration of Pledge and Release of Uncertificated Securities.**

A security interest in an uncertificated security may be evidenced by the registration of pledge to the secured party or a person designated by him. There can be no more than one registered pledge of an uncertificated security at any time. The registered owner of an uncertificated security is the person in

whose name the security is registered, even if the security is subject to a registered pledge. The rights of a registered pledgee of an uncertificated security under this Article are terminated by the registration of release.

Added in 1977.

Part 2 **Issue—Issuer**

§ 8—201. **"Issuer"**

(1) With respect to obligations on or defenses to a security, "issuer" includes a person who:

(a) places or authorizes the placing of his name on a certificated security (otherwise than as authenticating trustee, registrar, transfer agent, or the like) to evidence that it represents a share, participation, or other interest in his property or in an enterprise, or to evidence his duty to perform an obligation represented by the certificated security;

(b) creates shares, participations, or other interests in his property or in an enterprise or undertakes obligations, which shares, participations, interests, or obligations are uncertificated securities;

(c) directly or indirectly creates fractional interests in his rights or property, which fractional interests are represented by certificated securities; or

(d) becomes responsible for or in place of any other person described as an issuer in this section.

(2) With respect to obligations on or defenses to a security, a guarantor is an issuer to the extent of his guaranty, whether or not his obligation is noted on a certificated security or on statements of uncertificated securities sent pursuant to Section 8—408.

(3) With respect to registration of transfer, pledge, or release (Part 4 of this Article), "issuer" means a person on whose behalf transfer books are maintained.

Amended in 1977.

§ 8—202. **Issuer's Responsibility and Defenses; Notice of Defect or Defense.**

(1) Even against a purchaser for value and without notice, the terms of a security include:

(a) if the security is certificated, those stated on the security;

(b) if the security is uncertificated, those contained in the initial transaction statement sent to such purchaser or, if his interest is transferred to him other than by registration of transfer, pledge, or release, the initial transaction statement sent to the registered owner or registered pledgee; and

(c) those made part of the security by reference, on the certificated security or in the initial transaction statement, to another instrument, indenture, or document or to a constitution, statute, ordinance, rule, regulation, order or the like, to the extent that the terms referred to do not conflict with the terms stated on the certificated security or contained in the statement. A reference under this paragraph does not of itself charge a purchaser for value with notice of a defect going to the validity of the security, even though the certificated security or statement expressly states that a person accepting it admits notice.

(2) A certificated security in the hands of a purchaser for value or an uncertificated security as to which an initial transaction statement has been sent to a purchaser for value, other than a security issued by a government or governmental agency or unit, even though issued with a defect going to its validity, is valid with respect to the purchaser if he is without notice of the particular defect unless the defect involves a violation of constitutional provisions, in which case the security is valid with respect to a subsequent purchaser for value and without notice of the defect. This subsection applies to an issuer that is a government or governmental agency or unit only if either there has been substantial compliance with the legal requirements governing the issue or the issuer has received a substantial consideration for the issue as a whole or for the particular security and a stated purpose of the issue is one for which the issuer has power to borrow money or issue the security.

(3) Except as provided in the case of certain unauthorized signatures (Section 8—205), lack of genuineness of a certificated security or an initial transaction statement is a complete defense, even against a purchaser for value and without notice.

(4) All other defenses of the issuer of a certificated or uncertificated security, including nondelivery and conditional delivery of a certificated security, are ineffective against a purchaser for value who has taken without notice of the particular defense.

(5) Nothing in this section shall be construed to affect the right of a party to a "when, as and if issued" or a "when distributed" contract to cancel the contract in the event of a material change in the character of the security that is the subject of the contract or in the plan or arrangement pursuant to which the security is to be issued or distributed.

Amended in 1977.

§ 8—203. **Staleness as Notice of Defects or Defenses.**

(1) After an act or event creating a right to immediate performance of the principal obligation represented by a certificated security or that sets a date on or after which the security is to be presented or surrendered for redemption or exchange, a purchaser is charged with notice of any defect in its issue or defense of the issuer if:

(a) the act or event is one requiring the payment of money, the delivery of certificated securities, the registration of transfer of uncertificated securities, or any of these on presentation or surrender of the certificated security, the funds or securities are available on the date set for payment or exchange, and he takes the security more than one year after that date; and

(b) the act or event is not covered by paragraph (a) and he takes the security more than 2 years after the date set for surrender or presentation or the date on which performance became due.

(2) A call that has been revoked is not within subsection (1).

Amended in 1977.

§ 8—204. **Effect of Issuer's Restrictions on Transfer.**

A restriction on transfer of a security imposed by the issuer, even if otherwise lawful, is ineffective against any person without actual knowledge of it unless:

(a) the security is certificated and the restriction is noted conspicuously thereon; or

(b) the security is uncertificated and a notation of the restriction is contained in the initial transaction statement sent to the person or, if his interest is transferred to him other than by registration of transfer, pledge, or release, the initial transaction statement sent to the registered owner or the registered pledgee.

Amended in 1977.

§ 8—205. **Effect of Unauthorized Signature on Certificated Security or Initial Transaction Statement.**

An unauthorized signature placed on a certificated security prior to or in the course of issue or placed on an initial transaction statement is ineffective, but the signature is effective in favor of a purchaser for value of the certificated security or a purchaser for value of an uncertificated security to whom the initial transaction statement has been sent, if the purchaser is without notice of the lack of authority and the signing has been done by:

(a) an authenticating trustee, registrar, transfer agent, or other person entrusted by the issuer with the signing of the security, of similar securities, or of initial transaction statements or the immediate preparation for signing of any of them; or

(b) an employee of the issuer, or of any of the foregoing, entrusted with responsible handling of the security or initial transaction statement.

Amended in 1977.

§ 8—206. Completion or Alteration of Certificated Security or Initial Transaction Statement.

(1) If a certificated security contains the signatures necessary to its issue or transfer but is incomplete in any other respect:

(a) any person may complete it by filling in the blanks as authorized; and

(b) even though the blanks are incorrectly filled in, the security as completed is enforceable by a purchaser who took it for value and without notice of the incorrectness.

(2) A complete certificated security that has been improperly altered, even though fraudulently, remains enforceable, but only according to its original terms.

(3) If an initial transaction statement contains the signatures necessary to its validity, but is incomplete in any other respect:

(a) any person may complete it by filling in the blanks as authorized; and

(b) even though the blanks are incorrectly filled in, the statement as completed is effective in favor of the person to whom it is sent if he purchased the security referred to therein for value and without notice of the incorrectness.

(4) A complete initial transaction statement that has been improperly altered, even though fraudulently, is effective in favor of a purchaser to whom it has been sent, but only according to its original terms.

Amended in 1977.

§ 8—207. Rights and Duties of Issuer With Respect to Registered Owners and Registered Pledgees.

(1) Prior to due presentment for registration of transfer of a certificated security in registered form, the issuer or indenture trustee may treat the regis-

tered owner as the person exclusively entitled to vote, to receive notifications, and otherwise to exercise all the rights and powers of an owner.

(2) Subject to the provisions of subsections (3), (4), and (6), the issuer or indenture trustee may treat the registered owner of an uncertificated security as the person exclusively entitled to vote, to receive notifications, and otherwise to exercise all the rights and powers of an owner.

(3) The registered owner of an uncertificated security that is subject to a registered pledge is not entitled to registration of transfer prior to the due presentment to the issuer of a release instruction. The exercise of conversion rights with respect to a convertible uncertificated security is a transfer within the meaning of this section.

(4) Upon due presentment of a transfer instruction from the registered pledgee of an uncertificated security, the issuer shall:

(a) register the transfer of the security to the new owner free of pledge, if the instruction specifies a new owner (who may be the registered pledgee) and does not specify a pledgee;

(b) register the transfer of the security to the new owner subject to the interest of the existing pledgee, if the instruction specifies a new owner and the existing pledgee; or

(c) register the release of the security from the existing pledge and register the pledge of the security to the other pledgee, if the instruction specifies the existing owner and another pledgee.

(5) Continuity of perfection of a security interest is not broken by registration of transfer under subsection (4)(b) or by registration of release and pledge under subsection (4)(c), if the security interest is assigned.

(6) If an uncertificated security is subject to a registered pledge:

(a) any uncertificated securities issued in exchange for or distributed with respect to the pledged security shall be registered subject to the pledge;

(b) any certificated securities issued in exchange for or distributed with respect to the pledged security shall be delivered to the registered pledgee; and

(c) any money paid in exchange for or in redemption of part or all of the security shall be paid to the registered pledgee.

(7) Nothing in this Article shall be construed to affect

the liability of the registered owner of a security for calls, assessments, or the like.

Amended in 1977.

§ 8—208. Effect of Signature of Authenticating Trustee, Registrar, or Transfer Agent.

(1) A person placing his signature upon a certificated security or an initial transaction statement as authenticating trustee, registrar, transfer agent, or the like, warrants to a purchaser for value of the certificated security or a purchaser for value of an uncertificated security to whom the initial transaction statement has been sent, if the purchaser is without notice of the particular defect, that:

(a) the certificated security or initial transaction statement is genuine;

(b) his own participation in the issue or registration of the transfer, pledge, or release of the security is within his capacity and within the scope of the authority received by him from the issuer; and

(c) he has reasonable grounds to believe the security is in the form and within the amount the issuer is authorized to issue.

(2) Unless otherwise agreed, a person by so placing his signature does not assume responsibility for the validity of the security in other respects.

Amended in 1962 and 1977.

Part 3 Transfer

§ 8—301. Rights Acquired by Purchaser.

(1) Upon transfer of a security to a purchaser (Section 8—313), the purchaser acquires the rights in the security which his transferor had or had actual authority to convey unless the purchaser's rights are limited by Section 8—302(4).

(2) A transferee of a limited interest acquires rights only to the extent of the interest transferred. The creation or release of a security interest in a security is the transfer of a limited interest in that security.

Amended in 1977.

§ 8—302. "Bona Fide Purchaser"; "Adverse Claim"; Title Acquired by Bona Fide Purchaser.

(1) A "bona fide purchaser" is a purchaser for value in good faith and without notice of any adverse claim:

(a) who takes delivery of a certificated security in bearer form or in registered form, issued or indorsed to him or in blank;

(b) to whom the transfer, pledge, or release of an uncertificated security is registered on the books of the issuer; or

(c) to whom a security is transferred under the provisions of paragraph (c), (d)(i), or (g) of Section 8—313(1).

(2) "Adverse claim" includes a claim that a transfer was or would be wrongful or that a particular adverse person is the owner of or has an interest in the security.

(3) A bona fide purchaser in addition to acquiring the rights of a purchaser (Section 8—301) also acquires his interest in the security free of any adverse claim.

(4) Notwithstanding Section 8—301(1), the transferee of a particular certificated security who has been a party to any fraud or illegality affecting the security, or who as a prior holder of that certificated security had notice of an adverse claim, cannot improve his position by taking from a bona fide purchaser.

Amended in 1977.

§ 8—303. "Broker".

"Broker" means a person engaged for all or part of his time in the business of buying and selling securities, who in the transaction concerned acts for, buys a security from, or sells a security to, a customer. Nothing in this Article determines the capacity in which a person acts for purposes of any other statute or rule to which the person is subject.

§ 8—304. Notice to Purchaser of Adverse Claims.

(1) A purchaser (including a broker for the seller or buyer, but excluding an intermediary bank) of a certificated security is charged with notice of adverse claims if:

(a) the security, whether in bearer or registered form, has been indorsed "for collection" or "for surrender" or for some other purpose not involving transfer; or

(b) the security is in bearer form and has on it an unambiguous statement that it is the property of a person other than the transferor. The mere writing of a name on a security is not such a statement.

(2) A purchaser (including a broker for the seller or buyer, but excluding an intermediary bank) to whom the transfer, pledge, or release of an uncertificated security is registered is charged with notice of adverse claims as to which the issuer has a duty under Section 8—403(4) at the time of registration and which are noted in the initial transaction statement sent to the purchaser or, if his interest is transferred to him other

than by registration of transfer, pledge, or release, the initial transaction statement sent to the registered owner or the registered pledgee.

(3) The fact that the purchaser (including a broker for the seller or buyer) of a certificated or uncertificated security has notice that the security is held for a third person or is registered in the name of or indorsed by a fiduciary does not create a duty of inquiry into the rightfulness of the transfer or constitute constructive notice of adverse claims. However, if the purchaser (excluding an intermediary bank) has knowledge that the proceeds are being used or the transaction is for the individual benefit of the fiduciary or otherwise in breach of duty, the purchaser is charged with notice of adverse claims.

Amended in 1977.

§ 8—305. Staleness as Notice of Adverse Claims.

An act or event that creates a right to immediate performance of the principal obligation represented by a certificated security or sets a date on or after which a certificated security is to be presented or surrendered for redemption or exchange does not itself constitute any notice of adverse claims except in the case of a transfer:

(a) after one year from any date set for presentment or surrender for redemption or exchange; or

(b) after 6 months from any date set for payment of money against presentation or surrender of the security if funds are available for payment on that date.

Amended in 1977.

§ 8—306. Warranties on Presentment and Transfer of Certificated Securities; Warranties of Originators of Instructions.

(1) A person who presents a certificated security for registration of transfer or for payment or exchange warrants to the issuer that he is entitled to the registration, payment, or exchange. But, a purchaser for value and without notice of adverse claims who receives a new, reissued, or re-registered certificated security on registration of transfer or receives an initial transaction statement confirming the registration of transfer of an equivalent uncertificated security to him warrants only that he has no knowledge of any unauthorized signature (Section 8—311) in a necessary indorsement.

(2) A person by transferring a certificated security to a purchaser for value warrants only that:

(a) his transfer is effective and rightful;

(b) the security is genuine and has not been materially altered; and

(c) he knows of no fact which might impair the validity of the security.

(3) If a certificated security is delivered by an intermediary known to be entrusted with delivery of the security on behalf of another or with collection of a draft or other claim against delivery, the intermediary by delivery warrants only his own good faith and authority, even though he has purchased or made advances against the claim to be collected against the delivery.

(4) A pledgee or other holder for security who redelivers a certificated security received, or after payment and on order of the debtor delivers that security to a third person, makes only the warranties of an intermediary under subsection (3).

(5) A person who originates an instruction warrants to the issuer that:

(a) he is an appropriate person to originate the instruction; and

(b) at the time the instruction is presented to the issuer he will be entitled to the registration of transfer, pledge, or release.

(6) A person who originates an instruction warrants to any person specially guaranteeing his signature (subsection 8—312(3)) that:

(a) he is an appropriate person to originate the instruction; and

(b) at the time the instruction is presented to the issuer

(i) he will be entitled to the registration of transfer, pledge, or release; and

(ii) the transfer, pledge, or release requested in the instruction will be registered by the issuer free from all liens, security interests, restrictions, and claims other than those specified in the instruction.

(7) A person who originates an instruction warrants to a purchaser for value and to any person guaranteeing the instruction (Section 8—312(6)) that:

(a) he is an appropriate person to originate the instruction;

(b) the uncertificated security referred to therein is valid; and

(c) at the time the instruction is presented to the issuer

(i) the transferor will be entitled to the registration of transfer, pledge, or release;

(ii) the transfer, pledge, or release requested in the instruction will be registered by the issuer free from all liens, security interests, restrictions, and claims other than those specified in the instruction; and

(iii) the requested transfer, pledge, or release will be rightful.

(8) If a secured party is the registered pledgee or the registered owner of an uncertificated security, a person who originates an instruction of release or transfer to the debtor or, after payment and on order of the debtor, a transfer instruction to a third person, warrants to the debtor or the third person only that he is an appropriate person to originate the instruction and, at the time the instruction is presented to the issuer, the transferor will be entitled to the registration of release or transfer. If a transfer instruction to a third person who is a purchaser for value is originated on order of the debtor, the debtor makes to the purchaser the warranties of paragraphs (b), (c)(ii) and (c)(iii) of subsection (7).

(9) A person who transfers an uncertificated security to a purchaser for value and does not originate an instruction in connection with the transfer warrants only that:

(a) his transfer is effective and rightful; and

(b) the uncertificated security is valid.

(10) A broker gives to his customer and to the issuer and a purchaser the applicable warranties provided in this section and has the rights and privileges of a purchaser under this section. The warranties of and in favor of the broker, acting as an agent are in addition to applicable warranties given by and in favor of his customer.

Amended in 1962 and 1977.

§ 8—307. **Effect of Delivery Without Indorsement; Right to Compel Indorsement.**

If a certificated security in registered form has been delivered to a purchaser without a necessary indorsement he may become a bona fide purchaser only as of the time the indorsement is supplied; but against the transferor, the transfer is complete upon delivery and the purchaser has a specifically enforceable right to have any necessary indorsement supplied.
Amended in 1977.

§ 8—308. **Indorsements; Instructions.**

(1) An indorsement of a certificated security in registered form is made when an appropriate person signs on it or on a separate document an assignment or transfer of the security or a power to assign or transfer

it or his signature is written without more upon the back of the security.

(2) An indorsement may be in blank or special. An indorsement in blank includes an indorsement to bearer. A special indorsement specifies to whom the security is to be transferred, or who has power to transfer it. A holder may convert a blank indorsement into a special indorsement.

(3) An indorsement purporting to be only of part of a certificated security representing units intended by the issuer to be separately transferable is effective to the extent of the indorsement.

(4) An "instruction" is an order to the issuer of an uncertificated security requesting that the transfer, pledge, or release from pledge of the uncertificated security specified therein be registered.

(5) An instruction originated by an appropriate person is:

(a) a writing signed by an appropriate person; or

(b) a communication to the issuer in any form agreed upon in a writing signed by the issuer and an appropriate person.

If an instruction has been originated by an appropriate person but is incomplete in any other respect, any person may complete it as authorized and the issuer may rely on it as completed even though it has been completed incorrectly.

(6) "An appropriate person" in subsection (1) means the person specified by the certificated security or by special indorsement to be entitled to the security.

(7) "An appropriate person" in subsection (5) means:

(a) for an instruction to transfer or pledge an uncertificated security which is then not subject to a registered pledge, the registered owner; or

(b) for an instruction to transfer or release an uncertificated security which is then subject to a registered pledge, the registered pledgee.

(8) In addition to the persons designated in subsections (6) and (7), "an appropriate person" in subsections (1) and (5) includes:

(a) if the person designated is described as a fiduciary but is no longer serving in the described capacity, either that person or his successor;

(b) if the persons designated are descirbed as more than one person as fiduciaries and one or more are no longer serving in the described capacity, the remaining fiduciary or fiduciaries, whether or not a successor has been appointed or qualified;

(c) if the person designated is an individual and is

without capacity to act by virtue of death, incompetence, infancy, or otherwise, his executor, administrator, guardian, or like fiduciary;

(d) if the persons designated are described as more than one person as tenants by the entirety or with right of survivorship and by reason of death all cannot sign, the survivor or survivors;

(e) a person having power to sign under applicable law or controlling instrument; and

(f) to the extent that the person designated or any of the foregoing persons may act through an agent, his authorized agent.

(9) Unless otherwise agreed, the indorser of a certificated security by his indorsement or the originator of an instruction by his origination assumes no obligation that the security will be honored by the issuer but only the obligations provided in Section 8—306.

(10) Whether the person signing is appropriate is determined as of the date of signing and an indorsement made by or an instruction originated by him does not become unauthorized for the purposes of this Article by virtue of any subsequent change of circumstances.

(11) Failure of a fiduciary to comply with a controlling instrument or with the law of the state having jurisdiction of the fiduciary relationship, including any law requiring the fiduciary to obtain court approval of the transfer, pledge, or release, does not render his indorsement or an instruction originated by him unauthorized for the purposes of this Article.

Amended in 1962 and 1977.

§ 8—309. **Effect of Indorsement Without Delivery.**

An indorsement of a certificated security, whether special or in blank, does not constitute a transfer until delivery of the certificated security on which it appears or, if the indorsement is on a separate document, until delivery of both the document and the certificated security.

Amended in 1977.

§ 8—310. **Indorsement of Certificated Security in Bearer Form.**

An indorsement of a certificated security in bearer form may give notice of adverse claims (Section 8—304) but does not otherwise affect any right to registration the holder possesses.

Amended in 1977.

§ 8—311. **Effect of Unauthorized Indorsement or Instruction.**

Unless the owner or pledgee has ratified an unauthorized indorsement or instruction or is otherwise precluded from asserting its ineffectiveness:

(a) he may assert its ineffectiveness against the issuer or any purchaser, other than a purchaser for value and without notice of adverse claims, who has in good faith received a new, reissued, or re-registered certificated security on registration of transfer or received an initial transaction statement confirming the registration of transfer, pledge, or release of an equivalent uncertificated security to him; and

(b) an issuer who registers the transfer of a certificated security upon the unauthorized indorsement or who registers the transfer, pledge, or release of an uncertificated security upon the unauthorized instruction is subject to liability for improper registration (Section 8—404).

Amended in 1977.

§ 8—312. **Effect of Guaranteeing Signature, Indorsement or Instruction.**

(1) Any person guaranteeing a signature of an indorser of a certificated security warrants that at the time of signing:

(a) the signature was genuine;

(b) the signer was an appropriate person to indorse (Section 8—308); and

(c) the signer had legal capacity to sign.

(2) Any person guaranteeing a signature of the originator of an instruction warrants that at the time of signing:

(a) the signature was genuine;

(b) the signer was an appropriate person to originate the instruction (Section 8—308) if the person specified in the instruction as the registered owner or registered pledgee of the uncertificated security was, in fact, the registered owner or registered pledgee of the security, as to which fact the signature guarantor makes no warranty;

(c) the signer had legal capacity to sign; and

(d) the taxpayer identification number, if any, appearing on the instruction as that of the registered owner or registered pledgee was the taxpayer identification number of the signer or of the owner or pledgee for whom the signer was acting.

(3) Any person specially guaranteeing the signature of the originator of an instruction makes not only the warranties of a signature guarantor (subsection (2))

but also warrants that at the time the instruction is presented to the issuer:

(a) the person specified in the instruction as the registered owner or registered pledgee of the uncertificated security will be the registered owner or registered pledgee; and

(b) the transfer, pledge, or release of the uncertificated security requested in the instruction will be registered by the issuer free from all liens, security interests, restrictions, and claims other than those specified in the instruction.

(4) The guarantor under subsections (1) and (2) or the special guarantor under subsection (3) does not otherwise warrant the rightfulness of the particular transfer, pledge, or release.

(5) Any person guaranteeing an indorsement of a certificated security makes not only the warranties of a signature guarantor under subsection (1) but also warrants the rightfulness of the particular transfer in all respects.

(6) Any person guaranteeing an instruction requesting the transfer, pledge, or release of an uncertificated security makes not only the warranties of a special signature guarantor under subsection (3) but also warrants the rightfulness of the particular transfer, pledge, or release in all respects.

(7) No issuer may require a special guarantee of signature (subsection (3)), a guarantee of indorsement (subsection (5)), or a guarantee of instruction (subsection (6)) as a condition to registration of transfer, pledge, or release.

(8) The foregoing warranties are made to any person taking or dealing with the security in reliance on the guarantee, and the guarantor is liable to the person for any loss resulting from breach of the warranties.

Amended in 1977.

§ 8—313. When Transfer to Purchaser Occurs; Financial Intermediary as Bona Fide Purchaser; "Financial Intermediary".

(1) Transfer of a security or a limited interest (including a security interest) therein to a purchaser occurs only:

(a) at the time he or a person designated by him acquires possession of a certificated security;

(b) at the time the transfer, pledge, or release of an uncertificated security is registered to him or a person designated by him;

(c) at the time his financial intermediary acquires possession of a certificated security specially indorsed to or issued in the name of the purchaser;

(d) at the time a financial intermediary, not a clearing corporation, sends him confirmation of the purchase and also by book entry or otherwise identifies as belonging to the purchaser

(i) a specific certificated security in the financial intermediary's possession;

(ii) a quantity of securities that constitute or are part of a fungible bulk of certificated securities in the financial intermediary's possession or of uncertificated securities registered in the name of the financial intermediary; or

(iii) a quantity of securities that constitute or are part of a fungible bulk of securities shown on the account of the financial intermediary on the books of another financial intermediary;

(e) with respect to an identified certificated security to be delivered while still in the possession of a third person, not a financial intermediary, at the time that person acknowledges that he holds for the purchaser;

(f) with respect to a specific uncertificated security the pledge or transfer of which has been registered to a third person, not a financial intermediary, at the time that person acknowledges that he holds for the purchaser;

(g) at the time appropriate entries to the account of the purchaser or a person designated by him on the books of a clearing corporation are made under Section 8—320;

(h) with respect to the transfer of a security interest where the debtor has signed a security agreement containing a description of the security, at the time a written notification, which, in the case of the creation of the security interest, is signed by the debtor (which may be a copy of the security agreement) or which, in the case of the release or assignment of the security interest created pursuant to this paragraph, is signed by the secured party, is received by

(i) a financial intermediary on whose books the interest of the transferor in the security appears;

(ii) a third person, not a financial intermediary, in possession of the security, if it is certificated;

(iii) a third person, not a financial intermediary, who is the registered owner of the security, if it is uncertificated and not subject to a registered pledge; or

(iv) a third person, not a financial intermediary, who is the registered pledgee of the security, if it is uncertificated and subject to a registered pledge;

(i) with respect to the transfer of a security interest where the transferor has signed a security agreement containing a description of the security, at the time new value is given by the secured party; or

(j) with respect to the transfer of a security interest where the secured party is a financial intermediary and the security has already been transferred to the financial intermediary under paragraphs (a), (b), (c), (d), or (g), at the time the transferor has signed a security agreement containing a description of the security and value is given by the secured party.

(2) The purchaser is the owner of a security held for him by a financial intermediary, but cannot be a bona fide purchaser of a security so held except in the circumstances specified in paragraphs (c), (d)(i), and (g) of subsection (1). If a security so held is part of a fungible bulk, as in the circumstances specified in paragraphs (d)(ii) and (d)(iii) of subsection (1), the purchaser is the owner of a proportionate property interest in the fungible bulk.

(3) Notice of an adverse claim received by the financial intermediary or by the purchaser after the financial intermediary takes delivery of a certificated security as a holder for value or after the transfer, pledge, or release of an uncertificated security has been registered free of the claim to a financial intermediary who has given value is not effective either as to the financial intermediary or as to the purchaser. However, as between the financial intermediary and the purchaser the purchaser may demand transfer of an equivalent security as to which no notice of adverse claim has been received.

(4) A "financial intermediary" is a bank, broker, clearing corporation, or other person (or the nominee of any of them) which in the ordinary course of its business maintains security accounts for its customers and is acting in that capacity. A financial intermediary may have a security interest in securities held in account for its customer.

Amended in 1962 and 1977.

§ 8—314. Duty to Transfer, When Completed

(1) Unless otherwise agreed, if a sale of a security is made on an exchange or otherwise through brokers:

(a) the selling customer fulfills his duty to transfer at the time he:

(i) places a certificated security in the possession of the selling broker or a person designated by the broker;

(ii) causes an uncertificated security to be registered in the name of the selling broker or a person designated by the broker;

(iii) if requested, causes an acknowledgment to be made to the selling broker that a certificated or uncertificated security is held for the broker; or

(iv) places in the possession of the selling broker or of a person designated by the broker a transfer instruction for an uncertificated security, providing the issuer does not refuse to register the requested transfer if the instruction is presented to the issuer for registration within 30 days thereafter; and

(b) the selling broker, including a correspondent broker acting for a selling customer, fulfills his duty to transfer at the time he:

(i) places a certificated security in the possession of the buying broker or a person designated by the buying broker;

(ii) causes an uncertificated security to be registered in the name of the buying broker or a person designated by the buying broker;

(iii) places in the possession of the buying broker or of a person designated by the buying broker a transfer instruction for an uncertificated security, providing the issuer does not refuse to register the requested transfer if the instruction is presented to the issuer for registration within 30 days thereafter; or

(iv) effects clearance of the sale in accordance with the rules of the exchange on which the transaction took place.

(2) Except as provided in this section or unless otherwise agreed, a transferor's duty to transfer a security under a contract of purchase is not fulfilled until he:

(a) places a certificated security in form to be negotiated by the purchaser in the possession of the purchaser or of a person designated by the purchaser;

(b) causes an uncertificated security to be registered in the name of the purchaser or a person designated by the purchaser; or

(c) if the purchaser requests, causes an acknowledgment to be made to the purchaser that a certificated or uncertificated security is held for the purchaser.

(3) Unless made on an exchange, a sale to a broker purchasing for his own account is within subsection (2) and not within subsection (1).

Amended in 1977.

§ 8—315. Action Against Transferee Based Upon Wrongful Transfer

(1) Any person against whom the transfer of a security is wrongful for any reason, including his incapacity, as against anyone except a bona fide purchaser, may:

    (a) reclaim possession of the certificated security wrongfully transferred;

    (b) obtain possession of any new certificated security representing all or part of the same rights;

    (c) compel the origination of an instruction to transfer to him or a person designated by him an uncertificated security constituting all or part of the same rights; or

    (d) have damages.

(2) If the transfer is wrongful because of an unauthorized indorsement of a certificated security, the owner may also reclaim or obtain possession of the security or a new certificated security, even from a bona fide purchaser, if the ineffectiveness of the purported indorsement can be asserted against him under the provisions of this Article on unauthorized indorsements (Section 8—311).

(3) The right to obtain or reclaim possession of a certificated security or to compel the origination of a transfer instruction may be specifically enforced and the transfer of a certificated or uncertificated security enjoined and a certificated security impounded pending the litigation.

Amended in 1977.

§ 8—316. Purchaser's Right to Requisites for Registration of Transfer, Pledge, or Release on Books

Unless otherwise agreed, the transferor of a certificated security or the transferor, pledgor, or pledgee of an uncertificated security on due demand must supply his purchaser with any proof of his authority to transfer, pledge, or release or with any other requisite necessary to obtain registration of the transfer, pledge, or release of the security; but if the transfer, pledge, or release is not for value, a transferor, pledgor, or pledgee need not do so unless the purchaser furnishes the necessary expenses. Failure within a reasonable time to comply with a demand made gives the purchaser the right to reject or rescind the transfer, pledge, or release.

Amended in 1977.

§ 8—317. Creditors' Rights

(1) Subject to the exceptions in subsections (3) and (4), no attachment or levy upon a certificated security or any share or other interest represented thereby which is outstanding is valid until the security is actually seized by the officer making the attachment or levy, but a certificated security which has been surrendered to the issuer may be reached by a creditor by legal process at the issuer's chief executive office in the United States.

(2) An uncertificated security registered in the name of the debtor may not be reached by a creditor except by legal process at the issuer's chief executive office in the United States.

(3) The interest of a debtor in a certificated security that is in the possession of a secured party not a financial intermediary or in an uncertificated security registered in the name of a secured party not a financial intermediary (or in the name of a nominee of the secured party) may be reached by a creditor by legal process upon the secured party.

(4) The interest of a debtor in a certificated security that is in the possession of or registered in the name of a financial intermediary or in an uncertificated security registered in the name of a financial intermediary may be reached by a creditor by legal process upon the financial intermediary on whose books the interest of the debtor appears.

(5) Unless otherwise provided by law, a creditor's lien upon the interest of a debtor in a security obtained pursuant to subsection (3) or (4) is not a restraint on the transfer of the security, free of the lien, to a third party for new value; but in the event of a transfer, the lien applies to the proceeds of the transfer in the hands of the secured party or financial intermediary, subject to any claims having priority.

(6) A creditor whose debtor is the owner of a security is entitled to aid from courts of appropriate jurisdiction, by injunction or otherwise, in reaching the security or in satisfying the claim by means allowed at law or in equity in regard to property that cannot readily be reached by ordinary legal process.

Amended in 1977.

§ 8—318. No Conversion by Good Faith Conduct

An agent or bailee who in good faith (including observance of reasonable commercial standards if he is in the business of buying, selling, or otherwise dealing with securities) has received certificated securities and sold, pledged, or delivered them or has sold or caused the transfer or pledge of uncertificated securities over which he had control according to the

instructions of his principal, is not liable for conversion or for participation in breach of fiduciary duty although the principal had no right so to deal with the securities.
Amended in 1977.

§ 8—319. Statute of Frauds

A contract for the sale of securities is not enforceable by way of action or defense unless:

(a) there is some writing signed by the party against whom enforcement is sought or by his authorized agent or broker, sufficient to indicate that a contract has been made for sale of a stated quantity of described securities at a defined or stated price;

(b) delivery of a certificated security or transfer instruction has been accepted, or transfer of an uncertificated security has been registered and the transferee has failed to send written objection to the issuer within 10 days after receipt of the initial transaction statement confirming the registration, or payment has been made, but the contract is enforceable under this provision only to the extent of the delivery, registration, or payment;

(c) within a reasonable time a writing in confirmation of the sale or purchase and sufficient against the sender under paragraph (a) has been received by the party against whom enforcement is sought and he has failed to send written objection to its contents within 10 days after its receipt; or

(d) the party against whom enforcement is sought admits in his pleading, testimony, or otherwise in court that a contract was made for the sale of a stated quantity of described securities at a defined or stated price.

Amended in 1977.

§ 8—320. Transfer or Pledge Within Central Depository System

(1) In addition to other methods, a transfer, pledge, or release of a security or any interest therein may be effected by the making of appropriate entries on the books of a clearing corporation reducing the account of the transferor, pledgor, or pledgee and increasing the account of the transferee, pledgee, or pledgor by the amount of the obligation or the number of shares or rights transferred, pledged, or released, if the security is shown on the account of a transferor, pledgor, or pledgee on the books of the clearing corporation; is subject to the control of the clearing corporation; and

(a) if certificated,

(i) is in the custody of the clearing corporation, another clearing corporation, a custodian bank,

or a nominee of any of them; and

(ii) is in bearer form or indorsed in blank by an appropriate person or registered in the name of the clearing corporation, a custodian bank, or a nominee of any of them; or

(b) if uncertificated, is registered in the name of the clearing corporation, another clearing corporation, a custodian bank, or a nominee of any of them.

(2) Under this section entries may be made with respect to like securities or interests therein as a part of a fungible bulk and may refer merely to a quantity of a particular security without reference to the name of the registered owner, certificate or bond number, or the like, and, in appropriate cases, may be on a net basis taking into account other transfers, pledges, or releases of the same security.

(3) A transfer under this section is effective (Section 8—313) and the purchaser acquires the rights of the transferor (Section 8—301). A pledge or release under this section is the transfer of a limited interest. If a pledge or the creation of a security interest is intended, the security interest is perfected at the time when both value is given by the pledgee and the appropriate entries are made (Section 8—321). A transferee or pledgee under this section may be a bona fide purchaser (Section 8—302).

(4) A transfer or pledge under this section is not a registration of transfer under Part 4.

(5) That entries made on the books of the clearing corporation as provided in subsection (1) are not appropriate does not affect the validity or effect of the entries or the liabilities or obligations of the clearing corporation to any person adversely affected thereby.

Added in 1962; amended in 1977.

§ 8—321. Enforceability, Attachment, Perfection and Termination of Security Interests

(1) A security interest in a security is enforceable and can attach only if it is transferred to the secured party or a person designated by him pursuant to a provision of Section 8—313(1).

(2) A security interest so transferred pursuant to agreement by a transferor who has rights in the security to a transferee who has given value is a perfected security interest, but a security interest that has been transferred solely under paragraph (i) of Section 8—313(1) becomes unperfected after 21 days unless, within that time, the requirements for transfer under any other provision of Section 8—313(1) are satisfied.

(3) A security interest in a security is subject to the provisions of Article 9, but:

(a) no filing is required to perfect the security interest; and

(b) no written security agreement signed by the debtor is necessary to make the security interest enforceable, except as provided in paragraph (h), (i), or (j) of Section 8—313(1). The secured party has the rights and duties provided under Section 9—207, to the extent they are applicable, whether or not the security is certificated, and, if certificated, whether or not it is in his possession.

(4) Unless otherwise agreed, a security interest in a security is terminated by transfer to the debtor or a person designated by him pursuant to a provision of Section 8—313(1). If a security is thus transferred, the security interest, if not terminated, becomes unperfected unless the security is certificated and is delivered to the debtor for the purpose of ultimate sale or exchange or presentation, collection, renewal, or registration of transfer. In that case, the security interest becomes unperfected after 21 days unless, within that time, the security (or securities for which it has been exchanged) is transferred to the secured party or a person designated by him pursuant to a provision of Section 8—313(1).

Added in 1977.

Part 4 **Registration**

§ 8—401. **Duty of Issuer to Register Transfer, Pledge, or Release**

(1) If a certificated security in registered form is presented to the issuer with a request to register transfer or an instruction is presented to the issuer with a request to register transfer, pledge, or release, the issuer shall register the transfer, pledge, or release as requested if:

(a) the security is indorsed or the instruction was originated by the appropriate person or persons (Section 8—308);

(b) reasonable assurance is given that those indorsements or instructions are genuine and effective (Section 8—402);

(c) the issuer has no duty as to adverse claims or has discharged the duty (Section 8—403);

(d) any applicable law relating to the collection of taxes has been complied with; and

(e) the transfer, pledge, or release is in fact rightful or is to a bona fide purchaser.

(2) If an issuer is under a duty to register a transfer, pledge, or release of a security, the issuer is also liable to the person presenting a certificated security or an instruction for registration or his principal for loss resulting from any unreasonable delay in registration or from failure or refusal to register the transfer, pledge, or release.

Amended in 1977.

§ 8—402. **Assurance that Indorsements and Instructions Are Effective**

(1) The issuer may require the following assurance that each necessary indorsement of a certificated security or each instruction (Section 8—308) is genuine and effective:

(a) in all cases, a guarantee of the signature (Section 8—312(1) or (2)) of the person indorsing a certificated security or originating an instruction including, in the case of an instruction, a warranty of the taxpayer identification number or, in the absence thereof, other reasonable assurance of identity;

(b) if the indorsement is made or the instruction is originated by an agent, appropriate assurance of authority to sign;

(c) if the indorsement is made or the instruction is originated by a fiduciary, appropriate evidence of appointment or incumbency;

(d) if there is more than one fiduciary, reasonable assurance that all who are required to sign have done so; and

(e) if the indorsement is made or the instruction is originated by a person not covered by any of the foregoing, assurance appropriate to the case corresponding as nearly as may be to the foregoing.

(2) A "guarantee of the signature" in subsection (1) means a guarantee signed by or on behalf of a person reasonably believed by the issuer to be responsible. The issuer may adopt standards with respect to responsibility if they are not manifestly unreasonable.

(3) "Appropriate evidence of appointment or incumbency" in subsection (1) means:

(a) in the case of a fiduciary appointed or qualified by a court, a certificate issued by or under the direction or supervision of that court or an officer thereof and dated within 60 days before the date of presentation for transfer, pledge, or release; or

(b) in any other case, a copy of a document showing the appointment or a certificate issued by or on behalf of a person reasonably believed by the issuer to be responsible or, in the absence of that document or certificate, other evidence reasonably deemed by the issuer to be appropriate. The issuer may adopt standards with respect to the evidence if they are not manifestly unreasonable. The issuer is not charged with notice of the contents of any document obtained pursuant to this paragraph (b) except to the extent that the contents relate directly to the appointment or incumbency.

(4) The issuer may elect to require reasonable assurance beyond that specified in this section, but if it does so and, for a purpose other than that specified in subsection (3)(b), both requires and obtains a copy of a will, trust, indenture, articles of co-partnership, by-laws, or other controlling instrument, it is charged with notice of all matters contained therein affecting the transfer, pledge, or release.

Amended in 1977.

§ 8—403. Issuer's Duty as to Adverse Claims

(1) An issuer to whom a certificated security is presented for registration shall inquire into adverse claims if:

(a) a written notification of an adverse claim is received at a time and in a manner affording the issuer a reasonable opportunity to act on it prior to the issuance of a new, reissued, or re-registered certificated security, and the notification identifies the claimant, the registered owner, and the issue of which the security is a part, and provides an address for communications directed to the claimant; or

(b) the issuer is charged with notice of an adverse claim from a controlling instrument it has elected to require under Section 8—402(4).

(2) The issuer may discharge any duty of inquiry by any reasonable means, including notifying an adverse claimant by registered or certified mail at the address furnished by him or, if there be no such address, at his residence or regular place of business that the certificated security has been presented for registration of transfer by a named person, and that the transfer will be registered unless within 30 days from the date of mailing the notification, either:

(a) an appropriate restraining order, injunction, or other process issues from a court of competent jurisdiction; or

(b) there is filed with the issuer an indemnity bond, sufficient in the issuer's judgment to protect the issuer and any transfer agent, registrar, or other agent of the issuer involved from any loss it or they may suffer by complying with the adverse claim.

(3) Unless an issuer is charged with notice of an adverse claim from a controlling instrument which it has elected to require under Section 8—402(4) or receives notification of an adverse claim under subsection (1), if a certificated security presented for registration is indorsed by the appropriate person or persons the issuer is under no duty to inquire into adverse claims. In particular:

(a) an issuer registering a certificated security in the name of a person who is a fiduciary or who is described as a fiduciary is not bound to inquire into the existence, extent, or correct description of the fiduciary relationship; and thereafter the issuer may assume without inquiry that the newly registered owner continues to be the fiduciary until the issuer receives written notice that the fiduciary is no longer acting as such with respect to the particular security;

(b) an issuer registering transfer on an indorsement by a fiduciary is not bound to inquire whether the transfer is made in compliance with a controlling instrument or with the law of the state having jurisdiction of the fiduciary relationship, including any law requiring the fiduciary to obtain court approval of the transfer; and

(c) the issuer is not charged with notice of the contents of any court record or file or other recorded or unrecorded document even though the document is in its possession and even though the transfer is made on the indorsement of a fiduciary to the fiduciary himself or to his nominee.

(4) An issuer is under no duty as to adverse claims with respect to an uncertificated security except:

(a) claims embodied in a restraining order, injunction, or other legal process served upon the issuer if the process was served at a time and in a manner affording the issuer a reasonable opportunity to act on it in accordance with the requirements of subsection (5);

(b) claims of which the issuer has received a written notification from the registered owner or the registered pledgee if the notification was received at a time and in a manner affording the issuer a reasonable opportunity to act on it in accordance with the requirements of subsection (5);

(c) claims (including restrictions on transfer not imposed by the issuer) to which the registration of transfer to the present registered owner was subject and were so noted in the initial transaction statement sent to him; and

(d) claims as to which an issuer is charged with

notice from a controlling instrument it has elected to require under Section 8—402(4).

(5) If the issuer of an uncertificated security is under a duty as to an adverse claim, he discharges that duty by:

(a) including a notation of the claim in any statements sent with respect to the security under Sections 8—408(3), (6), and (7); and

(b) refusing to register the transfer or pledge of the security unless the nature of the claim does not preclude transfer or pledge subject thereto.

(6) If the transfer or pledge of the security is registered subject to an adverse claim, a notation of the claim must be included in the initial transaction statement and all subsequent statements sent to the transferee and pledgee under Section 8—408.

(7) Notwithstanding subsections (4) and (5), if an uncertificated security was subject to a registered pledge at the time the issuer first came under a duty as to a particular adverse claim, the issuer has no duty as to that claim if transfer of the security is requested by the registered pledgee or an appropriate person acting for the registered pledgee unless:

(a) the claim was embodied in legal process which expressly provides otherwise;

(b) the claim was asserted in a written notification from the registered pledgee;

(c) the claim was one as to which the issuer was charged with notice from a controlling instrument it required under Section 8—402(4) in connection with the pledgee's request for transfer; or

(d) the transfer requested is to the registered owner.

Amended in 1977.

§ 8—404. Liability and Non-Liability for Registration

(1) Except as provided in any law relating to the collection of taxes, the issuer is not liable to the owner, pledgee, or any other person suffering loss as a result of the registration of a transfer, pledge, or release of a security if:

(a) there were on or with a certificated security the necessary indorsements or the issuer had received an instruction originated by an appropriate person (Section 8—308); and

(b) the issuer had no duty as to adverse claims or has discharged the duty (Section 8—403).

(2) If an issuer has registered a transfer of a certificated security to a person not entitled to it, the issuer on demand shall deliver a like security to the true owner unless:

(a) the registration was pursuant to subsection (1);

(b) the owner is precluded from asserting any claim for registering the transfer under Section 8—405(1); or

(c) the delivery would result in overissue, in which case the issuer's liability is governed by Section 8—104.

(3) If an issuer has improperly registered a transfer, pledge, or release of an uncertificated security, the issuer on demand from the injured party shall restore the records as to the injured party to the condition that would have obtained if the improper registration had not been made unless:

(a) the registration was pursuant to subsection (1); or

(b) the registration would result in overissue, in which case the issuer's liability is governed by Section 8—104.

Amended in 1977.

§ 8—405. Lost, Destroyed, and Stolen Certificated Securities

(1) If a certificated security has been lost, apparently destroyed, or wrongfully taken, and the owner fails to notify the issuer of that fact within a reasonable time after he has notice of it and the issuer registers a transfer of the security before receiving notification, the owner is precluded from asserting against the issuer any claim for registering the transfer under Section 8—404 or any claim to a new security under this section.

(2) If the owner of a certificated security claims that the security has been lost, destroyed, or wrongfully taken, the issuer shall issue a new certificated security or, at the option of the issuer, an equivalent uncertificated security in place of the original security if the owner:

(a) so requests before the issuer has notice that the security has been acquired by a bona fide purchaser;

(b) files with the issuer a sufficient indemnity bond; and

(c) satisfies any other reasonable requirements imposed by the issuer.

(3) If, after the issue of a new certificated or uncertificated security, a bona fide purchaser of the original certificated security presents it for registration of transfer, the issuer shall register the transfer unless

registration would result in overissue, in which event the issuer's liability is governed by Section 8—104. In addition to any rights on the indemnity bond, the issuer may recover the new certificated security from the person to whom it was issued or any person taking under him except a bona fide purchaser or may cancel the uncertificated security unless a bona fide purchaser or any person taking under a bona fide purchaser is then the registered owner or registered pledgee thereof.

Amended in 1977.

§ 8—406. Duty of Authenticating Trustee, Transfer Agent, or Registrar

(1) If a person acts as authenticating trustee, transfer agent, registrar, or other agent for an issuer in the registration of transfers of its certificated securities or in the registration of transfers, pledges, and releases of its uncertificated securities, in the issue of new securities, or in the cancellation of surrendered securities:

(a) he is under a duty to the issuer to exercise good faith and due diligence in performing his functions; and

(b) with regard to the particular functions he performs, he has the same obligation to the holder or owner of a certificated security or to the owner or pledgee of an uncertificated security and has the same rights and privileges as the issuer has in regard to those functions.

(2) Notice to an authenticating trustee, transfer agent, registrar or other agent is notice to the issuer with respect to the functions performed by the agent.

Amended in 1977.

§ 8—407. Exchangeability of Securities

(1) No issuer is subject to the requirements of this section unless it regularly maintains a system for issuing the class of securities involved under which both certificated and uncertificated securities are regularly issued to the category of owners, which includes the person in whose name the new security is to be registered.

(2) Upon surrender of a certificated security with all necessary indorsements and presentation of a written request by the person surrendering the security, the issuer, if he has no duty as to adverse claims or has discharged the duty (Section 8—403), shall issue to the person or a person designated by him an equivalent uncertificated security subject to all liens, restrictions, and claims that were noted on the certificated security.

(3) Upon receipt of a transfer instruction originated by an appropriate person who so requests, the issuer of an uncertificated security shall cancel the uncertificated security and issue an equivalent certificated security on which must be noted conspicuously any liens and restrictions of the issuer and any adverse claims (as to which the issuer has a duty under Section 8—403(4)) to which the uncertificated security was subject. The certificated security shall be registered in the name of and delivered to:

(a) the registered owner, if the uncertificated security was not subject to a registered pledge; or

(b) the registered pledgee, if the uncertificated security was subject to a registered pledge.

Added in 1977.

§ 8—408. Statements of Uncertificated Securities

(1) Within 2 business days after the transfer of an uncertificated security has been registered, the issuer shall send to the new registered owner and, if the security has been transferred subject to a registered pledge, to the registered pledgee a written statement containing:

(a) a description of the issue of which the uncertificated security is a part;

(b) the number of shares or units transferred;

(c) the name and address and any taxpayer identification number of the new registered owner and, if the security has been transferred subject to a registered pledge, the name and address and any taxpayer identification number of the registered pledgee;

(d) a notation of any liens and restrictions of the issuer and any adverse claims (as to which the issuer has a duty under Section 8—403(4)) to which the uncertificated security is or may be subject at the time of registration or a statement that there are none of those liens, restrictions, or adverse claims; and

(e) the date the transfer was registered.

(2) Within 2 business days after the pledge of an uncertificated security has been registered, the issuer shall send to the registered owner and the registered pledgee a written statement containing:

(a) a description of the issue of which the uncertificated security is a part;

(b) the number of shares or units pledged;

(c) the name and address and any taxpayer identification number of the registered owner and the registered pledgee;

(d) a notation of any liens and restrictions of the issuer and any adverse claims (as to which the issuer has a duty under Section 8—403(4)) to which the uncertificated security is or may be subject at the time of registration or a statement that there are none of those liens, restrictions, or adverse claims; and

(e) the date the pledge was registered.

(3) Within 2 business days after the release from pledge of an uncertificated security has been registered, the issuer shall send to the registered owner and the pledgee whose interest was released a written statement containing:

(a) a description of the issue of which the uncertificated security is a part;

(b) the number of shares or units released from pledge;

(c) the name and address and any taxpayer identification number of the registered owner and the pledgee whose interest was released;

(d) a notation of any liens and restrictions of the issuer and any adverse claims (as to which the issuer has a duty under Section 8—403(4)) to which the uncertificated security is or may be subject at the time of registration or a statement that there are none of those liens, restrictions, or adverse claims; and

(e) the date the release was registered.

(4) An "initial transaction statement" is the statement sent to:

(a) the new registered owner and, if applicable, to the registered pledgee pursuant to subsection (1);

(b) the registered pledgee pursuant to subsection (2); or

(c) the registered owner pursuant to subsection (3).

Each initial transaction statement shall be signed by or on behalf of the issuer and must be identified as "Initial Transaction Statement".

(5) Within 2 business days after the transfer of an uncertificated security has been registered, the issuer shall send to the former registered owner and the former registered pledgee, if any, a written statement containing:

(a) a description of the issue of which the uncertificated security is a part;

(b) the number of shares or units transferred;

(c) the name and address and any taxpayer identification number of the former registered owner and of any former registered pledgee; and

(d) the date the transfer was registered.

(6) At periodic intervals no less frequent than annually and at any time upon the reasonable written request of the registered owner, the issuer shall send to the registered owner of each uncertificated security a dated written statement containing:

(a) a description of the issue of which the uncertificated security is a part;

(b) the name and address and any taxpayer identification number of the registered owner;

(c) the number of shares or units of the uncertificated security registered in the name of the registered owner on the date of the statement;

(d) the name and address and any taxpayer identification number of any registered pledgee and the number of shares or units subject to the pledge; and

(e) a notation of any liens and restrictions of the issuer and any adverse claims (as to which the issuer has a duty under Section 8—403(4)) to which the uncertificated security is or may be subject or a statement that there are none of those liens, restrictions, or adverse claims.

(7) At periodic intervals no less frequent than annually and at any time upon the reasonable written request of the registered pledgee, the issuer shall send to the registered pledgee of each uncertificated security a dated written statement containing:

(a) a description of the issue of which the uncertificated security is a part;

(b) the name and address and any taxpayer identification number of the registered owner;

(c) the name and address and any taxpayer identification number of the registered pledgee;

(d) the number of shares or units subject to the pledge; and

(e) a notation of any liens and restrictions of the issuer and any adverse claims (as to which the issuer has a duty under Section 8—403(4)) to which the uncertificated security is or may be subject or a statement that there are none of those liens, restrictions, or adverse claims.

(8) If the issuer sends the statements described in subsections (6) and (7) at periodic intervals no less frequent than quarterly, the issuer is not obliged to send additional statements upon request unless the owner or pledgee requesting them pays to the issuer the reasonable cost of furnishing them.

(9) Each statement sent pursuant to this section must bear a conspicuous legend reading substantially as follows: "This statement is merely a record of the rights of the addressee as of the time of its issuance.

Delivery of this statement, of itself, confers no rights on the recipient. This statement is neither a negotiable instrument nor a security."

Added in 1977.

Article 9
Secured Transactions; Sales of Accounts and Chattel Paper

Note: *The adoption of this Article should be accompanied by the repeal of existing statutes dealing with conditional sales, trust receipts, factor's liens where the factor is given a non-possessory lien, chattel mortgages, crop mortgages, mortgages on railroad equipment, assignment of accounts and generally statutes regulating security interests in personal property.*

Where the state has a retail installment selling act or small loan act, that legislation should be carefully examined to determine what changes in those acts are needed to conform them to this Article. This Article primarily sets out rules defining rights of a secured party against persons dealing with the debtor; it does not prescribe regulations and controls which may be necessary to curb abuses arising in the small loan business or in the financing of consumer purchases on credit. Accordingly there is no intention to repeal existing regulatory acts in those fields by enactment or re-enactment of Article 9. See Section 9—203(4) and the Note thereto.

Part 1 Short Title, Applicability and Definitions

§ 9—101. **Short Title.**

This Article shall be known and may be cited as Uniform Commercial Code—Secured Transactions.

§ 9—102. **Policy and Subject Matter of Article.**

(1) Except as otherwise provided in Section 9—104 on excluded transactions, this Article applies

  (a) to any transaction (regardless of its form) which is intended to create a security interest in personal property or fixtures including goods, documents, instruments, general intangibles, chattel paper or accounts; and also

  (b) to any sale of accounts or chattel paper.

(2) This Article applies to security interests created by contract including pledge, assignment, chattel mortgage, chattel trust, trust deed, factor's lien, equipment trust, conditional sale, trust receipt, other lien or title retention contract and lease or consign-

ment intended as security. This Article does not apply to statutory liens except as provided in Section 9—310.

(3) The application of this Article to a security interest in a secured obligation is not affected by the fact that the obligation is itself secured by a transaction or interest to which this Article does not apply. Amended in 1972.

§ 9—103. **Perfection of Security Interest in Multiple State Transactions**

(1) Documents, instruments and ordinary goods.

  (a) This subsection applies to documents and instruments and to goods other than those covered by a certificate of title described in subsection (2), mobile goods described in subsection (3), and minerals described in subsection (5).

  (b) Except as otherwise provided in this subsection, perfection and the effect of perfection or non-perfection of a security interest in collateral are governed by the law of the jurisdiction where the collateral is when the last event occurs on which is based the assertion that the security interest is perfected or unperfected.

  (c) If the parties to a transaction creating a purchase money security interest in goods in one jurisdiction understand at the time that the security interest attaches that the goods will be kept in another jurisdiction, then the law of the other jurisdiction governs the perfection and the effect of perfection or non-perfection of the security interest from the time it attaches until thirty days after the debtor receives possession of the goods and thereafter if the goods are taken to the other jurisdiction before the end of the thirty-day period.

  (d) When collateral is brought into and kept in this state while subject to a security interest perfected under the law of the jurisdiction from which the collateral was removed, the security interest remains perfected, but if action is required by Part 3 of this Article to perfect the security interest,

    (i) if the action is not taken before the expiration of the period of perfection in the other jurisdiction or the end of four months after the collateral is brought into this state, whichever period first expires, the security interest becomes unperfected at the end of that period and is thereafter deemed to have been unperfected as against a person who became a purchaser after removal;

(ii) if the action is taken before the expiration of the period specified in subparagraph (i), the security interest continues perfected thereafter;

(iii) for the purpose of priority over a buyer of consumer goods (subsection (2) of Section 9—307), the period of the effectiveness of a filing in the jurisdiction from which the collateral is removed is governed by the rules with respect to perfection in subparagraphs (i) and (ii).

(2) Certificate of title.

(a) This subsection applies to goods covered by a certificate of title issued under a statute of this state or of another jurisdiction under the law of which indication of a security interest on the certificate is required as a condition of perfection.

(b) Except as otherwise provided in this subsection, perfection and the effect of perfection or non-perfection of the security interest are governed by the law (including the conflict of laws rules) of the jurisdiction issuing the certificate until four months after the goods are removed from that jurisdiction and thereafter until the goods are registered in another jurisdiction, but in any event not beyond surrender of the certificate. After the expiration of that period, the goods are not covered by the certificate of title within the meaning of this section.

(c) Except with respect to the rights of a buyer described in the next paragraph, a security interest, perfected in another jurisdiction otherwise than by notation on a certificate of title, in goods brought into this state and thereafter covered by a certificate of title issued by this state is subject to the rules stated in paragraph (d) of subsection (1).

(d) If goods are brought into this state while a security interest therein is perfected in any manner under the law of the jurisdiction from which the goods are removed and a certificate of title is issued by this state and the certificate does not show that the goods are subject to the security interest or that they may be subject to security interests not shown on the certificate, the security interest is subordinate to the rights of a buyer of the goods who is not in the business of selling goods of that kind to the extent that he gives value and receives delivery of the goods after issuance of the certificate and without knowledge of the security interest.

(3) Accounts, general intangibles and mobile goods.

(a) This subsection applies to accounts (other than an account described in subsection (5) on minerals) and general intangibles (other than uncertificated securities) and to goods which are mobile and which are of a type normally used in more than one jurisdiction, such as motor vehicles, trailers, rolling stock, airplanes, shipping containers, road building and construction machinery and commercial harvesting machinery and the like, if the goods are equipment or are inventory leased or held for lease by the debtor to others, and are not covered by a certificate of title described in subsection (2).

(b) The law (including the conflict of laws rules) of the jurisdiction in which the debtor is located governs the perfection and the effect of perfection or non-perfection of the security interest.

(c) If, however, the debtor is located in a jurisdiction which is not a part of the United States, and which does not provide for perfection of the security interest by filing or recording in that jurisdiction, the law of the jurisdiction in the United States in which the debtor has its major executive office in the United States governs the perfection and the effect of perfection or non-perfection of the security interest through filing. In the alternative, if the debtor is located in a jurisdiction which is not a part of the United States or Canada and the collateral is accounts or general intangibles for money due or to become due, the security interest may be perfected by notification to the account debtor. As used in this paragraph, "United States" includes its territories and possessions and the Commonwealth of Puerto Rico.

(d) A debtor shall be deemed located at his place of business if he has one, at his chief executive office if he has more than one place of business, otherwise at his residence. If, however, the debtor is a foreign air carrier under the Federal Aviation Act of 1958, as amended, it shall be deemed located at the designated office of the agent upon whom service of process may be made on behalf of the foreign air carrier.

(e) A security interest perfected under the law of the jurisdiction of the location of the debtor is perfected until the expiration of four months after a change of the debtor's location to another jurisdiction, or until perfection would have ceased by the law of the first jurisdiction, whichever period first expires. Unless perfected in the new jurisdiction before the end of that period, it becomes unperfected thereafter and is deemed to have been unperfected as against a person who became a purchaser after the change.

(4) Chattel paper.

The rules stated for goods in subsection (1) apply to a possessory security interest in chattel paper. The rules stated for accounts in subsection (3) apply to a non-possessory security interest in chattel paper, but the security interest may not be perfected by notification to the account debtor.

(5) Minerals.

Perfection and the effect of perfection or non-perfection of a security interest which is created by a debtor who has an interest in minerals or the like (including oil and gas) before extraction and which attaches thereto as extracted, or which attaches to an account resulting from the sale thereof at the wellhead or minehead are governed by the law (including the conflict of laws rules) of the jurisdiction wherein the wellhead or minehead is located.

(6) Uncertificated securities.

The law (including the conflict of laws rules) of the jurisdiction of organization of the issuer governs the perfection and the effect of perfection or non-perfection of a security interest in uncertificated securities.

Amended in 1972 and 1977.

§ 9—104. **Transactions Excluded From Article.**

This Article does not apply

(a) to a security interest subject to any statute of the United States, to the extent that such statute governs the rights of parties to and third parties affected by transactions in particular types of property; or

(b) to a landlord's lien; or

(c) to a lien given by statute or other rule of law for services or materials except as provided in Section 9—310 on priority of such liens; or

(d) to a transfer of a claim for wages, salary or other compensation of an employee; or

(e) to a transfer by a government or governmental subdivision or agency; or

(f) to a sale of accounts or chattel paper as part of a sale of the business out of which they arose, or an assignment of accounts or chattel paper which is for the purpose of collection only, or a transfer of a right to payment under a contract to an assignee who is also to do the performance under the contract or a transfer of a single account to an assignee in whole or partial satisfaction of a preexisting indebtedness; or

(g) to a transfer of an interest in or claim in or under any policy of insurance, except as provided with respect to proceeds (Section 9—306) and priorities in proceeds (Section 9—312); or

(h) to a right represented by a judgment (other than a judgment taken on a right to payment which was collateral); or

(i) to any right of set-off; or

(j) except to the extent that provision is made for fixtures in Section 9—313, to the creation or transfer of an interest in or lien on real estate, including a lease or rents thereunder; or

(k) to a transfer in whole or in part of any claim arising out of tort; or

(l) to a transfer of an interest in any deposit account (subsection (1) of Section 9—105), except as provided with respect to proceeds (Section 9—306) and priorities in proceeds (Section 9—312).

Amended in 1972.

§ 9—105. **Definitions and Index of Definitions**

(1) In this Article unless the context otherwise requires:

(a) "Account debtor" means the person who is obligated on an account, chattel paper or general intangible;

(b) "Chattel paper" means a writing or writings which evidence both a monetary obligation and a security interest in or a lease of specific goods, but a charter or other contract involving the use or hire of a vessel is not chattel paper. When a transaction is evidenced both by such a security agreement or a lease and by an instrument or a series of instruments, the group of writings taken together constitutes chattel paper;

(c) "Collateral" means the property subject to a security interest, and includes accounts and chattel paper which have been sold;

(d) "Debtor" means the person who owes payment or other performance of the obligation secured, whether or not he owns or has rights in the collateral, and includes the seller of accounts or chattel paper. Where the debtor and the owner of the collateral are not the same person, the term "debtor" means the owner of the collateral in any provision of the Article dealing with the collateral, the obligor in any provision dealing with the obligation, and may include both where the context so requires;

(e) "Deposit account" means a demand, time, savings, passbook or like account maintained with a bank, savings and loan association, credit union or like organization, other than an account evidenced by a certificate of deposit;

(f) "Document" means document of title as defined in the general definitions of Article 1 (Section 1—201), and a receipt of the kind described in subsection (2) of Section 7—201;

(g) "Encumbrance" includes real estate mortgages and other liens on real estate and all other rights in real estate that are not ownership interests;

(h) "Goods" includes all things which are movable at the time the security interest attaches or which are fixtures (Section 9—313), but does not include money, documents, instruments, accounts, chattel paper, general intangibles, or minerals or the like (including oil and gas) before extraction. "Goods" also includes standing timber which is to be cut and removed under a conveyance or contract for sale, the unborn young of animals, and growing crops;

(i) "Instrument" means a negotiable instrument (defined in Section 3—104), or a certificated security (defined in Section 8—102) or any other writing which evidences a right to the payment of money and is not itself a security agreement or lease and is of a type which is in ordinary course of business transferred by delivery with any necessary indorsement or assignment;

(j) "Mortgage" means a consensual interest created by a real estate mortgage, a trust deed on real estate, or the like;

(k) An advance is made "pursuant to commitment" if the secured party has bound himself to make it, whether or not a subsequent event of default or other event not within his control has relieved or may relieve him from his obligation;

(l) "Security agreement" means an agreement which creates or provides for a security interest;

(m) "Secured party" means a lender, seller or other person in whose favor there is a security interest, including a person to whom accounts or chattel paper have been sold. When the holders of obligations issued under an indenture of trust, equipment trust agreement or the like are represented by a trustee or other person, the representative is the secured party;

(n) "Transmitting utility" means any person primarily engaged in the railroad, street railway or trolley bus business, the electric or electronics communications transmission business, the transmission of goods by pipeline, or the transmission or the production and transmission of electricity, steam, gas or water, or the provision of sewer service.

(2) Other definitions applying to this Article and the sections in which they appear are:

"Account". Section 9—106.
"Attach". Section 9—203.
"Construction mortgage". Section 9—313(1).
"Consumer goods". Section 9—109(1).
"Equipment". Section 9—109(2).
"Farm products". Section 9—109(3).
"Fixture". Section 9—313(1).
"Fixture filing". Section 9—313(1).
"General intangibles". Section 9—106.
"Inventory". Section 9—109(4).
"Lien creditor". Section 9—301(3).
"Proceeds". Section 9—306(1).
"Purchase money security interest". Section 9—107.
"United States". Section 9—103.

(3) The following definitions in other Articles apply to this Article:

"Check". Section 3—104.
"Contract for sale". Section 2—106.
"Holder in due course". Section 3—302.
"Note". Section 3—104.
"Sale". Section 2—106.

(4) In addition Article 1 contains general definitions and principles of construction and interpretation applicable throughout this Article.

Amended in 1966, 1972 and 1977.

§ 9—106. Definitions: "Account"; "General Intangibles".

"Account" means any right to payment for goods sold or leased or for services rendered which is not evidenced by an instrument or chattel paper, whether or not it has been earned by performance. "General intangibles" means any personal property (including things in action) other than goods, accounts, chattel paper, documents, instruments, and money. All rights to payment earned or unearned under a charter or other contract involving the use or hire of a vessel and all rights incident to the charter or contract are accounts. Amended in 1966, 1972.

§ 9—107. Definitions: "Purchase Money Security Interest".

A security interest is a "purchase money security interest" to the extent that it is

(a) taken or retained by the seller of the collateral to secure all or part of its price; or

(b) taken by a person who by making advances or incurring an obligation gives value to enable the debtor to acquire rights in or the use of collateral if such value is in fact so used.

§ 9—108. When After-Acquired Collateral Not Security for Antecedent Debt.

Where a secured party makes an advance, incurs an obligation, releases a perfected security interest, or otherwise gives new value which is to be secured in whole or in part by after-acquired property his security interest in the after-acquired collateral shall be deemed to be taken for new value and not as security for an antecedent debt if the debtor acquires his rights in such collateral either in the ordinary course of his business or under a contract of purchase made pursuant to the security agreement within a reasonable time after new value is given.

§ 9—109. Classification of Goods; "Consumer Goods"; "Equipment"; "Farm Products"; "Inventory".

Goods are

(1) "consumer goods" if they are used or bought for use primarily for personal, family or household purposes;

(2) "equipment" if they are used or bought for use primarily in business (including farming or a profession) or by a debtor who is a non-profit organization or a governmental subdivision or agency or if the goods are not included in the definitions of inventory, farm products or consumer goods;

(3) "farm products" if they are crops or livestock or supplies used or produced in farming operations or if they are products of crops or livestock in their unmanufactured states (such as ginned cotton, wool-clip, maple syrup, milk and eggs), and if they are in the possession of a debtor engaged in raising, fattening, grazing or other farming operations. If goods are farm products they are neither equipment nor inventory;

(4) "inventory" if they are held by a person who holds them for sale or lease or to be furnished under contracts of service or if he has so furnished them, or if they are raw materials, work in process or materials used or consumed in a business. Inventory of a person is not to be classified as his equipment.

§ 9—110. Sufficiency of Description.

For purposes of this Article any description of personal property or real estate is sufficient whether or not it is specific if it reasonably identifies what is described.

§ 9—111. Applicability of Bulk Transfer Laws.

The creation of a security interest is not a bulk transfer under Article 6 (see Section 6—103).

§ 9—112. Where Collateral Is Not Owned by Debtor.

Unless otherwise agreed, when a secured party knows that collateral is owned by a person who is not the debtor, the owner of the collateral is entitled to receive from the secured party any surplus under Section 9—502(2) or under Section 9—504(1), and is not liable for the debt or for any deficiency after resale, and he has the same right as the debtor

(a) to receive statements under Section 9—208;

(b) to receive notice of and to object to a secured party's proposal to retain the collateral in satisfaction of the indebtedness under Section 9—505;

(c) to redeem the collateral under Section 9—506;

(d) to obtain injunctive or other relief under Section 9—507(1); and

(e) to recover losses caused to him under Section 9—208(2).

§ 9—113. Security Interests Arising Under Article on Sales.

A security interest arising solely under the Article on Sales (Article 2) is subject to the provisions of this Article except that to the extent that and so long as the debtor does not have or does not lawfully obtain possession of the goods

(a) no security agreement is necessary to make the security interest enforceable; and

(b) no filing is required to perfect the security interest; and

(c) the rights of the secured party on default by the debtor are governed by the Article on Sales (Article 2).

§ 9—114. Consignment.

(1) A person who delivers goods under a consignment which is not a security interest and who would be required to file under this Article by paragraph (3)(c) of Section 2—326 has priority over a secured party who is or becomes a creditor of the consignee and who would have a perfected security interest in the goods if they were the property of the consignee, and also has priority with respect to identifiable cash proceeds received on or before delivery of the goods to a buyer, if

(a) the consignor complies with the filing provision of the Article on Sales with respect to consignments (paragraph (3) (c) of Section 2—326) before the consignee receives possession of the goods; and

(b) the consignor gives notification in writing to the holder of the security interest if the holder has filed a financing statement covering the same types of goods before the date of the filing made by the consignor; and

(c) the holder of the security interest receives the notification within five years before the consignee receives possession of the goods; and

(d) the notification states that the consignor expects to deliver goods on consignment to the consignee, describing the goods by item or type.

(2) In the case of a consignment which is not a security interest and in which the requirements of the preceding subsection have not been met, a person who delivers goods to another is subordinate to a person who would have a perfected security interest in the goods if they were the property of the debtor. Added in 1972.

Part 2 Validity of Security Agreement and Rights of Parties Thereto

§ 9—201. General Validity of Security Agreement.

Except as otherwise provided by this Act a security agreement is effective according to its terms between the parties, against purchasers of the collateral and against creditors. Nothing in this Article validates any charge or practice illegal under any statute or regulation thereunder governing usury, small loans, retail installment sales, or the like, or extends the application of any such statute or regulation to any transaction not otherwise subject thereto.

§ 9—202. Title to Collateral Immaterial.

Each provision of this Article with regard to rights, obligations and remedies applies whether title to collateral is in the secured party or in the debtor.

§ 9—203. Attachment and Enforceability of Security Interest; Proceeds; Formal Requisites

(1) Subject to the provisions of Section 4—208 on the security interest of a collecting bank, Section 8—321 on security interests in securities and Section 9—113 on a security interest arising under the Article on Sales, a security interest is not enforceable against the debtor or third parties with respect to the collateral and does not attach unless:

(a) the collateral is in the possession of the secured party pursuant to agreement, or the debtor has signed a security agreement which contains a description of the collateral and in addition, when the security interest covers crops growing or to be grown or timber to be cut, a description of the land concerned;

(b) value has been given; and

(c) the debtor has rights in the collateral.

(2) A security interest attaches when it becomes enforceable against the debtor with respect to the collateral. Attachment occurs as soon as all of the events specified in subsection (1) have taken place unless explicit agreement postpones the time of attaching.

(3) Unless otherwise agreed a security agreement gives the secured party the rights to proceeds provided by Section 9—306.

(4) A transaction, although subject to this Article, is also subject to . . . . *, and in the case of conflict between the provisions of this Article and any such statute, the provisions of such statute control. Failure to comply with any applicable statute has only the effect which is specified therein.

Amended in 1972 and 1977.

Note: *At * in subsection (4) insert reference to any local statute regulating small loans, retail installment sales and the like.*

The foregoing subsection (4) is designed to make it clear that certain transactions, although subject to this Article, must also comply with other applicable legislation.

This Article is designed to regulate all the "security" aspects of transactions within its scope. There is, however, much regulatory legislation, particularly in the consumer field, which supplements this Article and should not be repealed by its enactment. Examples are small loan acts, retail installment selling acts and the like. Such acts may provide for licensing and rate regulation and may prescribe particular forms of contract. Such provisions should remain in force despite the enactment of this Article. On the other hand if a retail installment selling act contains provisions on filing, rights on default, etc., such provisions should be repealed as inconsistent with this Article except that inconsistent provisions as to deficiencies, penalties, etc., in the Uniform Consumer Credit Code and other recent related legislation should remain because those statutes were drafted after the substantial enactment of the Article and with the intention of modifying certain provisions of this Article as to consumer credit.

§ 9—204. After-Acquired Property; Future Advances.

(1) Except as provided in subsection (2), a security agreement may provide that any or all obligations covered by the security agreement are to be secured by after-acquired collateral.

(2) No security interest attaches under an after-acquired property clause to consumer goods other than accessions (Section 9—314) when given as additional security unless the debtor acquires rights in them within ten days after the secured party gives value.

(3) Obligations covered by a security agreement may include future advances or other value whether or not the advances or value are given pursuant to commitment (subsection (1) of Section 9—105). Amended in 1972.

§ 9—205. Use or Disposition of Collateral Without Accounting Permissible.

A security interest is not invalid or fraudulent against creditors by reason of liberty in the debtor to use, commingle or dispose of all or part of the collateral (including returned or repossessed goods) or to collect or compromise accounts or chattel paper, or to accept the return of goods or make repossessions, or to use, commingle or dispose of proceeds, or by reason of the failure of the secured party to require the debtor to account for proceeds or replace collateral. This section does not relax the requirements of possession where perfection of a security interest depends upon possession of the collateral by the secured party or by a bailee. Amended in 1972.

§ 9—206. Agreement Not to Assert Defenses Against Assignee; Modification of Sales Warranties Where Security Agreement Exists.

(1) Subject to any statute or decision which establishes a different rule for buyers or lessees of consumer goods, an agreement by a buyer or lessee that he will not assert against an assignee any claim or defense which he may have against the seller or lessor is enforceable by an assignee who takes his assignment for value, in good faith and without notice of a claim or defense, except as to defenses of a type which may be asserted against a holder in due course of a negotiable instrument under the Article on Commercial Paper (Article 3). A buyer who as part of one transaction signs both a negotiable instrument and a security agreement makes such an agreement.

(2) When a seller retains a purchase money security interest in goods the Article on Sales (Article 2) governs the sale and any disclaimer, limitation or modification of the seller's warranties. Amended in 1962.

§ 9—207. Rights and Duties When Collateral is in Secured Party's Possession.

(1) A secured party must use reasonable care in the custody and preservation of collateral in his possession. In the case of an instrument or chattel paper reasonable care includes taking necessary steps to preserve rights against prior parties unless otherwise agreed.

(2) Unless otherwise agreed, when collateral is in the secured party's possession

(a) reasonable expenses (including the cost of any insurance and payment of taxes or other charges) incurred in the custody, preservation, use or operation of the collateral are chargeable to the debtor and are secured by the collateral;

(b) the risk of accidental loss or damage is on the debtor to the extent of any deficiency in any effective insurance coverage;

(c) the secured party may hold as additional security any increase or profits (except money) received from the collateral, but money so received, unless remitted to the debtor, shall be applied in reduction of the secured obligation;

(d) the secured party must keep the collateral identifiable but fungible collateral may be commingled;

(e) the secured party may repledge the collateral upon terms which do not impair the debtor's right to redeem it.

(3) A secured party is liable for any loss caused by his failure to meet any obligation imposed by the preceding subsections but does not lose his security interest.

(4) A secured party may use or operate the collateral for the purpose of preserving the collateral or its value or pursuant to the order of a court of appropriate jurisdiction or, except in the case of consumer goods, in the manner and to the extent provided in the security agreement.

§ 9—208. Request for Statement of Account or List of Collateral.

(1) A debtor may sign a statement indicating what he believes to be the aggregate amount of unpaid indebtedness as of a specified date and may send it to the secured party with a request that the statement be approved or corrected and returned to the debtor. When the security agreement or any other record kept

by the secured party identifies the collateral a debtor may similarly request the secured party to approve or correct a list of the collateral.

(2) The secured party must comply with such a request within two weeks after receipt by sending a written correction or approval. If the secured party claims a security interest in all of a particular type of collateral owned by the debtor he may indicate that fact in his reply and need not approve or correct an itemized list of such collateral. If the secured party without reasonable excuse fails to comply he is liable for any loss caused to the debtor thereby; and if the debtor has properly included in his request a good faith statement of the obligation or a list of the collateral or both the secured party may claim a security interest only as shown in the statement against persons misled by his failure to comply. If he no longer has an interest in the obligation or collateral at the time the request is received he must disclose the name and address of any successor in interest known to him and he is liable for any loss caused to the debtor as a result of failure to disclose. A successor in interest is not subject to this section until a request is received by him.

(3) A debtor is entitled to such a statement once every six months without charge. The secured party may require payment of a charge not exceeding $10 for each additional statement furnished.

Part 3 Rights of Third Parties; Perfected and Unperfected Security Interests; Rules of Priority

§ 9—301. Persons Who Take Priority Over Unperfected Security Interests; Rights of "Lien Creditor".

(1) Except as otherwise provided in subsection (2), an unperfected security interest is subordinate to the rights of

    (a) persons entitled to priority under Section 9—312;

    (b) a person who becomes a lien creditor before the security interest is perfected;

    (c) in the case of goods, instruments, documents, and chattel paper, a person who is not a secured party and who is a transferee in bulk or other buyer not in ordinary course of business or is a buyer of farm products in ordinary course of business, to the extent that he gives value and receives delivery of the collateral without knowledge of the security interest and before it is perfected;

    (d) in the case of accounts and general intangibles, a person who is not a secured party and who is a transferee to the extent that he gives value without knowledge of the security interest and before it is perfected.

(2) If the secured party files with respect to a purchase money security interest before or within ten days after the debtor receives possession of the collateral, he takes priority over the rights of a transferee in bulk or of a lien creditor which arise between the time the security interest attaches and the time of filing.

(3) A "lien creditor" means a creditor who has acquired a lien on the property involved by attachment, levy or the like and includes an assignee for benefit of creditors from the time of assignment, and a trustee in bankruptcy from the date of the filing of the petition or a receiver in equity from the time of appointment.

(4) A person who becomes a lien creditor while a security interest is perfected takes subject to the security interest only to the extent that it secures advances made before he becomes a lien creditor or within 45 days thereafter or made without knowledge of the lien or pursuant to a commitment entered into without knowledge of the lien. Amended in 1972.

§ 9—302. When Filing Is Required to Perfect Security Interest; Security Interests to Which Filing Provisions of This Article Do Not Apply

(1) A financing statement must be filed to perfect all security interests except the following:

    (a) a security interest in collateral in possession of the secured party under Section 9—305;

    (b) a security interest temporarily perfected in instruments or documents without delivery under Section 9—304 or in proceeds for a 10 day period under Section 9—306;

    (c) a security interest created by an assignment of a beneficial interest in a trust or a decedent's estate;

    (d) a purchase money security interest in consumer goods; but filing is required for a motor vehicle required to be registered; and fixture filing is required for priority over conflicting interests in fixtures to the extent provided in Section 9—313;

    (e) an assignment of accounts which does not alone or in conjunction with other assignments to the same assignee transfer a significant part of the outstanding accounts of the assignor;

(f) a security interest of a collecting bank (Section 4—208) or in securities (Section 8—321) or arising under the Article on Sales (see Section 9—113) or covered in subsection (3) of this section;

(g) an assignment for the benefit of all the creditors of the transferor, and subsequent transfers by the assignee thereunder.

(2) If a secured party assigns a perfected security interest, no filing under this Article is required in order to continue the perfected status of the security interest against creditors of and transferees from the original debtor.

(3) The filing of a financing statement otherwise required by this Article is not necessary or effective to perfect a security interest in property subject to

(a) a statute or treaty of the United States which provides for a national or international registration or a national or international certificate of title or which specifies a place of filing different from that specified in this Article for filing of the security interest; or

(b) the following statutes of this state; [list any certificate of title statute covering automobiles, trailers, mobile homes, boats, farm tractors, or the like, and any central filing statute.]; but during any period in which collateral is inventory held for sale by a person who is in the business of selling goods of that kind, the filing provisions of this Article (Part 4) apply to a security interest in that collateral created by him as debtor; or

(c) a certificate of title statute of another jurisdiction under the law of which indication of a security interest on the certificate is required as a condition of perfection (subsection (2) of Section 9—103).

(4) Compliance with a statute or treaty described in subsection (3) is equivalent to the filing of a financing statement under this Article, and a security interest in property subject to the statute or treaty can be perfected only by compliance therewith except as provided in Section 9—103 on multiple state transactions. Duration and renewal of perfection of a security interest perfected by compliance with the statute or treaty are governed by the provisions of the statute or treaty; in other respects the security interest is subject to this Article.

Amended in 1972 and 1977.

§ 9—303. When Security Interest Is Perfected; Continuity of Perfection.

(1) A security interest is perfected when it has attached and when all of the applicable steps required for perfection have been taken. Such steps are specified in Sections 9—302, 9—304, 9—305 and 9—306. If such steps are taken before the security interest attaches, it is perfected at the time when it attaches.

(2) If a security interest is originally perfected in any way permitted under this Article and is subsequently perfected in some other way under this Article, without an intermediate period when it was unperfected, the security interest shall be deemed to be perfected continuously for the purposes of this Article.

§ 9—304. Perfection of Security Interest in Instruments, Documents, and Goods Covered by Documents; Perfection by Permissive Filing; Temporary Perfection Without Filing or Transfer of Possession

(1) A security interest in chattel paper or negotiable documents may be perfected by filing. A security interest in money or instruments (other than certificated securities or instruments which constitute part of chattel paper) can be perfected only by the secured party's taking possession, except as provided in subsections (4) and (5) of this section and subsections (2) and (3) of Section 9—306 on proceeds.

(2) During the period that goods are in the possession of the issuer of a negotiable document therefor, a security interest in the goods is perfected by perfecting a security interest in the document, and any security interest in the goods otherwise perfected during such period is subject thereto.

(3) A security interest in goods in the possession of a bailee other than one who has issued a negotiable document therefor is perfected by issuance of a document in the name of the secured party or by the bailee's receipt of notification of the secured party's interest or by filing as to the goods.

(4) A security interest in instruments (other than certificated securities) or negotiable documents is perfected without filing or the taking of possession for a period of 21 days from the time it attaches to the extent that it arises for new value given under a written security agreement.

(5) A security interest remains perfected for a period of 21 days without filing where a secured party having a perfected security interest in an instrument (other than a certificated security), a negotiable document or goods in possession of a bailee other than one who has issued a negotiable document therefor

(a) makes available to the debtor the goods or documents representing the goods for the purpose of ultimate sale or exchange or for the purpose of loading, unloading, storing, shipping, transshipping, manufacturing, processing or otherwise dealing with them in a manner preliminary to their sale or exchange, but priority between conflicting security interests in the goods is subject to subsection (3) of Section 9—312; or

(b) delivers the instrument to the debtor for the purpose of ultimate sale or exchange or of presentation, collection, renewal or registration of transfer.

(6) After the 21 day period in subsections (4) and (5) perfection depends upon compliance with applicable provisions of this Article.

Amended in 1972 and 1977.

§ 9—305. When Possession by Secured Party Perfects Security Interest Without Filing

A security interest in letters of credit and advices of credit (subsection (2) (a) of Section 5—116), goods, instruments (other than certificated securities), money, negotiable documents, or chattel paper may be perfected by the secured party's taking possession of the collateral. If such collateral other than goods covered by a negotiable document is held by a bailee, the secured party is deemed to have possession from the time the bailee receives notification of the secured party's interest. A security interest is perfected by possession from the time possession is taken without a relation back and continues only so long as possession is retained, unless otherwise specified in this Article. The security interest may be otherwise perfected as provided in this Article before or after the period of possession by the secured party.

Amended in 1972 and 1977.

§ 9—306. "Proceeds"; Secured Party's Rights on Disposition of Collateral.

(1) "Proceeds" includes whatever is received upon the sale, exchange, collection or other disposition of collateral or proceeds. Insurance payable by reason of loss or damage to the collateral is proceeds, except to the extent that it is payable to a person other than a party to the security agreement. Money, checks, deposit accounts, and the like are "cash proceeds". All other proceeds are "non-cash proceeds".

(2) Except where this Article otherwise provides, a security interest continues in collateral notwithstanding sale, exchange or other disposition thereof unless the disposition was authorized by the secured party in the security agreement or otherwise, and also continues in any identifiable proceeds including collections received by the debtor.

(3) The security interest in proceeds is a continuously perfected security interest if the interest in the original collateral was perfected but it ceases to be a perfected security interest and becomes unperfected ten days after receipt of the proceeds by the debtor unless

(a) a filed financing statement covers the original collateral and the proceeds are collateral in which a security interest may be perfected by filing in the office or offices where the financing statement has been filed and, if the proceeds are acquired with cash proceeds, the description of collateral in the financing statement indicates the types of property constituting the proceeds; or

(b) a filed financing statement covers the original collateral and the proceeds are identifiable cash proceeds; or

(c) the security interest in the proceeds is perfected before the expiration of the ten day period.

Except as provided in this section, a security interest in proceeds can be perfected only by the methods or under the circumstances permitted in this Article for original collateral of the same type.

(4) In the event of insolvency proceedings instituted by or against a debtor, a secured party with a perfected security interest in proceeds has a perfected security interest only in the following proceeds:

(a) in identifiable non-cash proceeds and in separate deposit accounts containing only proceeds;

(b) in identifiable cash proceeds in the form of money which is neither commingled with other money nor deposited in a deposit account prior to the insolvency proceedings;

(c) in identifiable cash proceeds in the form of checks and the like which are not deposited in a deposit account prior to the insolvency proceedings; and

(d) in all cash and deposit accounts of the debtor in which proceeds have been commingled with other funds, but the perfected security interest under this paragraph (d) is

(i) subject to any right to set-off; and

(ii) limited to an amount not greater than the amount of any cash proceeds received by the debtor within ten days before the institution of the insolvency proceedings less the sum of (I) the payments to the secured party on account of cash proceeds received by the debtor during such period and (II) the cash proceeds received by the debtor during such period to which the secured party is entitled under paragraphs (a) through (c) of this subsection (4).

(5) If a sale of goods results in an account or chattel paper which is transferred by the seller to a secured party, and if the goods are returned to or are repossessed by the seller or the secured party, the following rules determine priorities:

(a) If the goods were collateral at the time of sale, for an indebtedness of the seller which is still unpaid, the original security interest attaches again to the goods and continues as a perfected security interest if it was perfected at the time when the goods were sold. If the security interest was originally perfected by a filing which is still effective, nothing further is required to continue the perfected status; in any other case, the secured party must take possession of the returned or repossessed goods or must file.

(b) An unpaid transferee of the chattel paper has a security interest in the goods against the transferor. Such security interest is prior to a security interest asserted under paragraph (a) to the extent that the transferee of the chattel paper was entitled to priority under Section 9—308.

(c) An unpaid transferee of the account has a security interest in the goods against the transferor. Such security interest is subordinate to a security interest asserted under paragraph (a).

(d) A security interest of an unpaid transferee asserted under paragraph (b) or (c) must be perfected for protection against creditors of the transferor and purchasers of the returned or repossessed goods.

Amended in 1972.

§ 9—307. **Protection of Buyers of Goods.**

(1) A buyer in ordinary course of business (subsection (9) of Section 1—201) other than a person buying farm products from a person engaged in farming operations takes free of a security interest created by his seller even though the security interest is perfected and even though the buyer knows of its existence.

(2) In the case of consumer goods, a buyer takes free of a security interest even though perfected if he buys without knowledge of the security interest, for value and for his own personal, family or household purposes unless prior to the purchase the secured party has filed a financing statement covering such goods.

(3) A buyer other than a buyer in ordinary course of business (subsection (1) of this section) takes free of a

security interest to the extent that it secures future advances made after the secured party acquires knowledge of the purchase, or more than 45 days after the purchase, whichever first occurs, unless made pursuant to a commitment entered into without knowledge of the purchase and before the expiration of the 45 day period. Amended in 1972.

§ 9—308. **Purchase of Chattel Paper and Instruments.**

A purchaser of chattel paper or an instrument who gives new value and takes possession of it in the ordinary course of his business has priority over a security interest in the chattel paper or instrument

(a) which is perfected under Section 9—304 (permissive filing and temporary perfection) or under Section 9—306 (perfection as to proceeds) if he acts without knowledge that the specific paper or instrument is subject to a security interest; or

(b) which is claimed merely as proceeds of inventory subject to a security interest (Section 9—306) even though he knows that the specific paper or instrument is subject to the security interest.

Amended in 1972.

§ 9—309. **Protection of Purchasers of Instruments, Documents and Securities**

Nothing in this Article limits the rights of a holder in due course of a negotiable instrument (Section 3—302) or a holder to whom a negotiable document of title has been duly negotiated (Section 7—501) or a bona fide purchaser of a security (Section 8—302) and the holders or purchasers take priority over an earlier security interest even though perfected. Filing under this Article does not constitute notice of the security interest to such holders or purchasers.
Amended in 1977.

§ 9—310. **Priority of Certain Liens Arising by Operation of Law.**

When a person in the ordinary course of his business furnishes services or materials with respect to goods subject to a security interest, a lien upon goods in the possession of such person given by statute or rule of law for such materials or services takes priority over a perfected security interest unless the lien is statutory and the statute expressly provides otherwise.

§ 9—311. **Alienability of Debtor's Rights: Judicial Process.**

The debtor's rights in collateral may be voluntarily or involuntarily transferred (by way of sale, creation of a security interest, attachment, levy, garnishment or other judicial process) notwithstanding a provision in the security agreement prohibiting any transfer or making the transfer constitute a default.

§ 9—312. Priorities Among Conflicting Security Interests in the Same Collateral

(1) The rules of priority stated in other sections of this Part and in the following sections shall govern when applicable: Section 4—208 with respect to the security interests of collecting banks in items being collected, accompanying documents and proceeds; Section 9—103 on security interests related to other jurisdictions; Section 9—114 on consignments.

(2) A perfected security interest in crops for new value given to enable the debtor to produce the crops during the production season and given not more than three months before the crops become growing crops by planting or otherwise takes priority over an earlier perfected security interest to the extent that such earlier interest secures obligations due more than six months before the crops become growing crops by planting or otherwise, even though the person giving new value had knowledge of the earlier security interest.

(3) A perfected purchase money security interest in inventory has priority over a conflicting security interest in the same inventory and also has priority in identifiable cash proceeds received on or before the delivery of the inventory to a buyer if

(a) the purchase money security interest is perfected at the time the debtor receives possession of the inventory; and

(b) the purchase money secured party gives notification in writing to the holder of the conflicting security interest if the holder had filed a financing statement covering the same types of inventory (i) before the date of the filing made by the purchase money secured party, or (ii) before the beginning of the 21 day period where the purchase money security interest is temporarily perfected without filing or possession (subsection (5) of Section 9—304); and

(c) the holder of the conflicting security interest receives the notification within five years before the debtor receives possession of the inventory; and

(d) the notification states that the person giving the notice has or expects to acquire a purchase money security interest in inventory of the debtor, describing such inventory by item or type.

(4) A purchase money security interest in collateral other than inventory has priority over a conflicting security interest in the same collateral or its proceeds if the purchase money security interest is perfected at the time the debtor receives possession of the collateral or within ten days thereafter.

(5) In all cases not governed by other rules stated in this section (including cases of purchase money security interests which do not qualify for the special priorities set forth in subsections (3) and (4) of this section), priority between conflicting security interests in the same collateral shall be determined according to the following rules:

(a) Conflicting security interests rank according to priority in time of filing or perfection. Priority dates from the time a filing is first made covering the collateral or the time the security interest is first perfected, whichever is earlier, provided that there is no period thereafter when there is neither filing nor perfection.

(b) So long as conflicting security interests are unperfected, the first to attach has priority.

(6) For the purposes of subsection (5) a date of filing or perfection as to collateral is also a date of filing or perfection as to proceeds.

(7) If future advances are made while a security interest is perfected by filing, the taking of possession, or under Section 8—321 on securities, the security interest has the same priority for the purposes of subsection (5) with respect to the future advances as it does with respect to the first advance. If a commitment is made before or while the security interest is so perfected, the security interest has the same priority with respect to advances made pursuant thereto. In other cases a perfected security interest has priority from the date the advance is made.

Amended in 1972 and 1977.

§ 9—313. Priority of Security Interests in Fixtures.

(1) In this section and in the provisions of Part 4 of this Article referring to fixture filing, unless the context otherwise requires

(a) goods are "fixtures" when they become so related to particular real estate that an interest in them arises under real estate law

(b) a "fixture filing" is the filing in the office where a mortgage on the real estate would be filed or recorded of a financing statement covering goods which are or are to become fixtures and conforming to the requirements of subsection (5) of Section 9—402

(c) a mortgage is a "construction mortgage" to the extent that it secures an obligation incurred for the construction of an improvement on land including the acquisition cost of the land, if the recorded writing so indicates.

(2) A security interest under this Article may be created in goods which are fixtures or may continue in goods which become fixtures, but no security interest exists under this Article in ordinary building materials incorporated into an improvement on land.

(3) This Article does not prevent creation of an encumbrance upon fixtures pursuant to real estate law.

(4) A perfected security interest in fixtures has priority over the conflicting interest of an encumbrancer or owner of the real estate where

(a) the security interest is a purchase money security interest, the interest of the encumbrancer or owner arises before the goods become fixtures, the security interest is perfected by a fixture filing before the goods become fixtures or within ten days thereafter, and the debtor has an interest of record in the real estate or is in possession of the real estate; or

(b) the security interest is perfected by a fixture filing before the interest of the encumbrancer or owner is of record, the security interest has priority over any conflicting interest of a predecessor in title of the encumbrancer or owner, and the debtor has an interest of record in the real estate or is in possession of the real estate; or

(c) the fixtures are readily removable factory or office machines or readily removable replacements of domestic applicances which are consumer goods, and before the goods become fixtures the security interest is perfected by any method permitted by this Article; or

(d) the conflicting interest is a lien on the real estate obtained by legal or equitable proceedings after the security interest was perfected by any method permitted by this Article.

(5) A security interest in fixtures, whether or not perfected, has priority over the conflicting interest of an encumbrancer or owner of the real estate where

(a) the encumbrancer or owner has consented in writing to the security interest or has disclaimed an interest in the goods as fixtures; or

(b) the debtor has a right to remove the goods as against the encumbrancer or owner. If the debtor's right terminates, the priority of the security interest continues for a reasonable time.

(6) Notwithstanding paragraph (a) of subsection (4) but otherwise subject to subsections (4) and (5), a security interest in fixtures is subordinate to a construction mortgage recorded before the goods become fixtures if the goods become fixtures before the completion of the construction. To the extent that it is given to refinance a construction mortgage, a mortgage has this priority to the same extent as the construction mortgage.

(7) In cases not within the preceding subsections, a security interest in fixtures is subordinate to the conflicting interest of an encumbrancer or owner of the related real estate who is not the debtor.

(8) When the secured party has priority over all owners and encumbrancers of the real estate, he may, on default, subject to the provisions of Part 5, remove his collateral from the real estate but he must reimburse any encumbrancer or owner of the real estate who is not the debtor and who has not otherwise agreed for the cost of repair of any physical injury, but not for any diminution in value of the real estate caused by the absence of the goods removed or by any necessity of replacing them. A person entitled to reimbursement may refuse permission to remove until the secured party gives adequate security for the performance of this obligation. Amended in 1972.

§ 9—314. **Accessions.**

(1) A security interest in goods which attaches before they are installed in or affixed to other goods takes priority as to the goods installed or affixed (called in this section "accessions") over the claims of all persons to the whole except as stated in subsection (3) and subject to Section 9—315(1).

(2) A security interest which attaches to goods after they become part of a whole is valid against all persons subsequently acquiring interests in the whole except as stated in subsection (3) but is invalid against any person with an interest in the whole at the time the security interest attaches to the goods who has not in writing consented to the security interest or disclaimed an interest in the goods as part of the whole.

(3) The security interests described in subsections (1) and (2) do not take priority over

(a) a subsequent purchaser for value of any interest in the whole; or

(b) a creditor with a lien on the whole subsequently obtained by judicial proceedings; or

(c) a creditor with a prior perfected security interest in the whole to the extent that he makes subsequent advances

if the subsequent purchase is made, the lien by judicial proceedings obtained or the subsequent advance under the prior perfected security interest is made or contracted for without knowledge of the security interest and before it is perfected. A purchaser of the whole at a foreclosure sale other than the holder of a perfected security interest purchasing at his own foreclosure sale is a subsequent purchaser within this section.

(4) When under subsections (1) or (2) and (3) a secured party has an interest in accessions which has priority over the claims of all persons who have interests in the whole, he may on default subject to the provisions of Part 5 remove his collateral from the whole but he must reimburse any encumbrancer or owner of the whole who is not the debtor and who has not otherwise agreed for the cost of repair of any physical injury but not for any diminution in value of the whole caused by the absence of the goods removed or by any necessity for replacing them. A person entitled to reimbursement may refuse permission to remove until the secured party gives adequate security for the performance of this obligation.

§ 9—315. Priority When Goods Are Commingled or Processed.

(1) If a security interest in goods was perfected and subsequently the goods or a part thereof have become part of a product or mass, the security interest continues in the product or mass if

(a) the goods are so manufactured, processed, assembled or commingled that their identity is lost in the product or mass; or

(b) a financing statement covering the original goods also covers the product into which the goods have been manufactured, processed or assembled.

In a case to which paragraph (b) applies, no separate security interest in that part of the original goods which has been manufactured, processed or assembled into the product may be claimed under Section 9—314.

(2) When under subsection (1) more than one security interest attaches to the product or mass, they rank equally according to the ratio that the cost of the goods to which each interest originally attached bears to the cost of the total product or mass.

§ 9—316. Priority Subject to Subordination.

Nothing in this Article prevents subordination by agreement by any person entitled to priority.

§ 9—317. Secured Party Not Obligated on Contract of Debtor.

The mere existence of a security interest or authority given to the debtor to dispose of or use collateral does not impose contract or tort liability upon the secured party for the debtor's acts or omissions.

§ 9—318. Defenses Against Assignee; Modification of Contract After Notification of Assignment; Term Prohibiting Assignment Ineffective; Identification and Proof of Assignment.

(1) Unless an account debtor has made an enforceable agreement not to assert defenses or claims arising out of a sale as provided in Section 9—206 the rights of an assignee are subject to

(a) all the terms of the contract between the account debtor and assignor and any defense or claim arising therefrom; and

(b) any other defense or claim of the account debtor against the assignor which accrues before the account debtor receives notification of the assignment.

(2) So far as the right to payment or a part thereof under an assigned contract has not been fully earned by performance, and notwithstanding notification of the assignment, any modification of or substitution for the contract made in good faith and in accordance with reasonable commercial standards is effective against an assignee unless the account debtor has otherwise agreed but the assignee acquires corresponding rights under the modified or substituted contract. The assignment may provide that such modification or substitution is a breach by the assignor.

(3) The account debtor is authorized to pay the assignor until the account debtor receives notification that the amount due or to become due has been assigned and that payment is to be made to the assignee. A notification which does not reasonably identify the rights assigned is ineffective. If requested by the account debtor, the assignee must seasonably furnish reasonable proof that the assignment has been made and unless he does so the account debtor may pay the assignor.

(4) A term in any contract between an account debtor and an assignor is ineffective if it prohibits assignment of an account or prohibits creation of a security interest in a general intangible for money due or to become due or requires the account debtor's consent to such assignment or security interest. Amended in 1972.

Part 4 Filing

§ 9—401. Place of Filing; Erroneous Filing; Removal of Collateral.

First Alternative Subsection (1)

(1) The proper place to file in order to perfect a security interest is as follows:

(a) when the collateral is timber to be cut or is minerals or the like (including oil and gas) or accounts subject to subsection (5) of Section 9—103, or when the financing statement is filed as a fixture filing (Section 9—313) and the collateral is goods which are or are to become fixtures, then in the office where a mortgage on the real estate would be filed or recorded;

(b) in all other cases, in the office of the [Secretary of State].

Second Alternative Subsection (1)

(1) The proper place to file in order to perfect a security interest is as follows:

(a) when the collateral is equipment used in farming operations, or farm products, or accounts or general intangibles arising from or relating to the sale of farm products by a farmer, or consumer goods, then in the office of the . . . . in the county of the debtor's residence or if the debtor is not a resident of this state then in the office of the . . . . in the county where the goods are kept, and in addition when the collateral is crops growing or to be grown in the office of the . . . . in the county where the land is located;

(b) when the collateral is timber to be cut or is minerals or the like (including oil and gas) or accounts subject to subsection (5) of Section 9—103, or when the financing statement is filed as a fixture filing (Section 9—313) and the collateral is goods which are or are to become fixtures, then in the office where a mortgage on the real estate would be filed or recorded;

(c) in all other cases, in the office of the [Secretary of State].

Third Alternative Subsection (1)

(1) The proper place to file in order to perfect a security interest is as follows:

(a) when the collateral is equipment used in farming operations, or farm products, or accounts or general intangibles arising from or relating to the sale of farm products by a farmer, or consumer goods, then in the office of the . . . . in the county of the debtor's residence or if the debtor is not a resident of this state then in the office of the . . . . in the county where the goods are kept, and in addition when the collateral is crops growing or to be grown in the office of the . . . . in the county where the land is located;

(b) when the collateral is timber to be cut or is minerals or the like (including oil and gas) or accounts subject to subsection (5) of Section

9—103, or when the financing statement is filed as a fixture filing (Section 9—313) and the collateral is goods which are or are to become fixtures, then in the office where a mortgage on the real estate would be filed or recorded;

(c) in all other cases, in the office of the [Secretary of State] and in addition, if the debtor has a place of business in only one county of this state, also in the office of . . . . of such county, or, if the debtor has no place of business in this state, but resides in the state, also in the office of . . . . of the county in which he resides.

Note: *One of the three alternatives should be selected as subsection (1).*

(2) A filing which is made in good faith in an improper place or not in all of the places required by this section is nevertheless effective with regard to any collateral as to which the filing complied with the requirements of this Article and is also effective with regard to collateral covered by the financing statement against any person who has knowledge of the contents of such financing statement.

(3) A filing which is made in the proper place in this state continues effective even though the debtor's residence or place of business or the location of the collateral or its use, whichever controlled the original filing, is thereafter changed.

Alternative Subsection (3)

[(3) A filing which is made in the proper county continues effective for four months after a change to another county of the debtor's residence or place of business or the location of the collateral, whichever controlled the original filing. It becomes ineffective thereafter unless a copy of the financing statement signed by the secured party is filed in the new county within said period. The security interest may also be perfected in the new county after the expiration of the four-month period; in such case perfection dates from the time of perfection in the new county. A change in the use of the collateral does not impair the effectiveness of the original filing.]

(4) The rules stated in Section 9—103 determine whether filing is necessary in this state.

(5) Notwithstanding the preceding subsections, and subject to subsection (3) of Section 9—302, the proper place to file in order to perfect a security interest in collateral, including fixtures, of a transmitting utility is the office of the [Secretary of State]. This filing constitutes a fixture filing (Section 9—313) as to the collateral described therein which is or is to become fixtures.

(6) For the purposes of this section, the residence of an organization is its place of business if it has one or its chief executive office if it has more than one place of business. Amended in 1962 and 1972.

Note: *Subsection (6) should be used only if the state chooses the Second or Third Alternative Subsection (1).*

§ 9—402. Formal Requisites of Financing Statement; Amendments; Mortgage as Financing Statement.

(1) A financing statement is sufficient if it gives the names of the debtor and the secured party, is signed by the debtor, gives an address of the secured party from which information concerning the security interest may be obtained, gives a mailing address of the debtor and contains a statement indicating the types, or describing the items, of collateral. A financing statement may be filed before a security agreement is made or a security interest otherwise attaches. When the financing statement covers crops growing or to be grown, the statement must also contain a description of the real estate concerned. When the financing statement covers timber to be cut or covers minerals or the like (including oil and gas) or accounts subject to subsection (5) of Section 9—103, or when the financing statement is filed as a fixture filing (Section 9—313) and the collateral is goods which are or are to become fixtures, the statement must also comply with subsection (5). A copy of the security agreement is sufficient as a financing statement if it contains the above information and is signed by the debtor. A carbon, photographic or other reproduction of a security agreement or a financing statement is sufficient as a financing statement if the security agreement so provides or if the original has been filed in this state.

(2) A financing statement which otherwise complies with subsection (1) is sufficient when it is signed by the secured party instead of the debtor if it is filed to perfect a security interest in

    (a) collateral already subject to a security interest in another jurisdiction when it is brought into this state, or when the debtor's location is changed to this state. Such a financing statement must state that the collateral was brought into this state or that the debtor's location was changed to this state under such circumstances; or

    (b) proceeds under Section 9—306 if the security interest in the original collateral was perfected. Such a financing statement must describe the original collateral; or

    (c) collateral as to which the filing has lapsed; or

    (d) collateral acquired after a change of name, identity or corporate structure of the debtor (subsection (7)).

(3) A form substantially as follows is sufficient to comply with subsection (1):

Name of debtor (or assignor) ....
Address ....
Name of secured party (assignee) ....
Address ....

1. This financing statement covers the following types (or items) of property:
    (Describe) ....

2. (If collateral is crops) The above described crops are growing or are to be grown on:
    (Describe Real Estate) ....

3. (If applicable) The above goods are to become fixtures on *

*Where appropriate substitute either "The above timber is standing on . . . . " or "The above minerals or the like (including oil and gas) or accounts will be financed at the wellhead or minehead of the well or mine located on . . . . ."

    (Describe Real Estate) ....

and this financing statement is to be filed [for record] in the real estate records. (If the debtor does not have an interest of record) The name of a record owner

is ....

4. (If products of collateral are claimed) Products of the collateral are also covered.

(use   ....
whichever   Signature of Debtor (or Assignor)
is   ....
applicable)   Signature of Secured Party
                   (or Assignee)

(4) A financing statement may be amended by filing a writing signed by both the debtor and the secured party. An amendment does not extend the period of effectiveness of a financing statement. If any amendment adds collateral, it is effective as to the added collateral only from the filing date of the amendment. In this Article, unless the context otherwise requires, the term "financing statement" means the original financing statement and any amendments.

(5) A financing statement covering timber to be cut or covering minerals or the like (including oil and gas) or accounts subject to subsection (5) of Section 9—103, or a financing statement filed as a fixture filing (Section 9—313) where the debtor is not a transmit-

ting utility, must show that it covers this type of collateral, must recite that it is to be filed [for record] in the real estate records, and the financing statement must contain a description of the real estate [sufficient if it were contained in a mortgage of the real estate to give constructive notice of the mortgage under the law of this state]. If the debtor does not have an interest of record in the real estate, the financing statement must show the name of a record owner.

(6) A mortgage is effective as a financing statement filed as a fixture filing from the date of its recording if

(a) the goods are described in the mortgage by item or type; and

(b) the goods are or are to become fixtures related to the real estate described in the mortgage; and

(c) the mortgage complies with the requirements for a financing statement in this section other than a recital that it is to be filed in the real estate records; and

(d) the mortgage is duly recorded.

No fee with reference to the financing statement is required other than the regular recording and satisfaction fees with respect to the mortgage.

(7) A financing statement sufficiently shows the name of the debtor if it gives the individual, partnership or corporate name of the debtor, whether or not it adds other trade names or names of partners. Where the debtor so changes his name or in the case of an organization its name, identity or corporate structure that a filed financing statement becomes seriously misleading, the filing is not effective to perfect a security interest in collateral acquired by the debtor more than four months after the change, unless a new appropriate financing statement is filed before the expiration of that time. A filed financing statement remains effective with respect to collateral transferred by the debtor even though the secured party knows of or consents to the transfer.

(8) A financing statement substantially complying with the requirements of this section is effective even though it contains minor errors which are not seriously misleading. Amended in 1972.

Note: *Language in brackets is optional.*

Note: *Where the state has any special recording system for real estate other than the usual grantor-grantee index (as, for instance, a tract system or a title registration or Torrens system) local adaptations of subsection (5) and Section 9—403(7) may be necessary. See Mass.Gen.Laws Chapter 106, Section 9—409.*

§ 9—403. What Constitutes Filing; Duration of Filing; Effect of Lapsed Filing; Duties of Filing Officer.

(1) Presentation for filing of a financing statement and tender of the filing fee or acceptance of the statement by the filing officer constitutes filing under this Article.

(2) Except as provided in subsection (6) a filed financing statement is effective for a period of five years from the date of filing. The effectiveness of a filed financing statement lapses on the expiration of the five year period unless a continuation statement is filed prior to the lapse. If a security interest perfected by filing exists at the time insolvency proceedings are commenced by or against the debtor, the security interest remains perfected until termination of the insolvency proceedings and thereafter for a period of sixty days or until expiration of the five year period, whichever occurs later. Upon lapse the security interest becomes unperfected, unless it is perfected without filing. If the security interest becomes unperfected upon lapse, it is deemed to have been unperfected as against a person who became a purchaser or lien creditor before lapse.

(3) A continuation statement may be filed by the secured party within six months prior to the expiration of the five year period specified in subsection (2). Any such continuation statement must be signed by the secured party, identify the original statement by file number and state that the original statement is still effective. A continuation statement signed by a person other than the secured party of record must be accompanied by a separate written statement of assignment signed by the secured party of record and complying with subsection (2) of Section 9—405, including payment of the required fee. Upon timely filing of the continuation statement, the effectiveness of the original statement is continued for five years after the last date to which the filing was effective whereupon it lapses in the same manner as provided in subsection (2) unless another continuation statement is filed prior to such lapse. Succeeding continuation statements may be filed in the same manner to continue the effectiveness of the original statement. Unless a statute on disposition of public records provides otherwise, the filing officer may remove a lapsed statement from the files and destroy it immediately if he has retained a microfilm or other photographic record, or in other cases after one year after the lapse. The filing officer shall so arrange matters by physical annexation of financing statements to continuation statements or other related

filings, or by other means, that if he physically destroys the financing statements of a period more than five years past, those which have been continued by a continuation statement or which are still effective under subsection (6) shall be retained.

(4) Except as provided in subsection (7) a filing officer shall mark each statement with a file number and with the date and hour of filing and shall hold the statement or a microfilm or other photographic copy thereof for public inspection. In addition the filing officer shall index the statement according to the name of the debtor and shall note in the index the file number and the address of the debtor given in the statement.

(5) The uniform fee for filing and indexing and for stamping a copy furnished by the secured party to show the date and place of filing for an original financing statement or for a continuation statement shall be $.......... if the statement is in the standard form prescribed by the [Secretary of State] and otherwise shall be $.........., plus in each case, if the financing statement is subject to subsection (5) of Section 9—402, $........... The uniform fee for each name more than one required to be indexed shall be $........... The secured party may at his option show a trade name for any person and an extra uniform indexing fee of $.......... shall be paid with respect thereto.

(6) If the debtor is a transmitting utility (subsection (5) of Section 9—401) and a filed financing statement so states, it is effective until a termination statement is filed. A real estate mortgage which is effective as a fixture filing under subsection (6) of Section 9—402 remains effective as a fixture filing until the mortgage is released or satisfied of record or its effectiveness otherwise terminates as to the real estate.

(7) When a financing statement covers timber to be cut or covers minerals or the like (including oil and gas) or accounts subject to subsection (5) of Section 9—103, or is filed as a fixture filing, [it shall be filed for record and] the filing officer shall index it under the names of the debtor and any owner of record shown on the financing statement in the same fashion as if they were the mortgagors in a mortgage of the real estate described, and, to the extent that the law of this state provides for indexing of mortgages under the name of the mortgagee, under the name of the secured party as if he were the mortgagee thereunder, or where indexing is by description in the same fashion as if the financing statement were a mortgage of the real estate described. Amended in 1972.

Note: *In states in which writings will not appear in the real estate records and indices unless actually recorded the* *bracketed language in subsection (7) should be used.*

§ 9—404. **Termination Statement.**

(1) If a financing statement covering consumer goods is filed on or after ...., then within one month or within ten days following written demand by the debtor after there is no outstanding secured obligation and no commitment to make advances, incur obligations or otherwise give value, the secured party must file with each filing officer with whom the financing statement was filed, a termination statement to the effect that he no longer claims a security interest under the financing statement, which shall be identified by file number. In other cases whenever there is no outstanding secured obligation and no commitment to make advances, incur obligations or otherwise give value, the secured party must on written demand by the debtor send the debtor, for each filing officer with whom the financing statement was filed, a termination statement to the effect that he no longer claims a security interest under the financing statement, which shall be identified by file number. A termination statement signed by a person other than the secured party of record must be accompanied by a separate written statement of assignment signed by the secured party of record complying with subsection (2) of Section 9—405, including payment of the required fee. If the affected secured party fails to file such a termination statement as required by this subsection, or to send such a termination statement within ten days after proper demand therefor, he shall be liable to the debtor for one hundred dollars, and in addition for any loss caused to the debtor by such failure.

(2) On presentation to the filing officer of such a termination statement he must note it in the index. If he has received the termination statement in duplicate, he shall return one copy of the termination statement to the secured party stamped to show the time of receipt thereof. If the filing officer has a microfilm or other photographic record of the financing statement, and of any related continuation statement, statement of assignment and statement of release, he may remove the originals from the files at any time after receipt of the termination statement, or if he has no such record, he may remove them from the files at any time after one year after receipt of the termination statement.

(3) If the termination statement is in the standard form prescribed by the [Secretary of State], the uniform fee for filing and indexing the termination statement shall be $......, and otherwise shall be $......, plus in each case an additional fee of $...... for each

name more than one against which the termination statement is required to be indexed. Amended in 1972.

Note: *The date to be inserted should be the effective date of the revised Article 9.*

§ 9—405. **Assignment of Security Interest; Duties of Filing Officer; Fees.**

(1) A financing statement may disclose an assignment of a security interest in the collateral described in the financing statement by indication in the financing statement of the name and address of the assignee or by an assignment itself or a copy thereof on the face or back of the statement. On presentation to the filing officer of such a financing statement the filing officer shall mark the same as provided in Section 9—403(4). The uniform fee for filing, indexing and furnishing filing data for a financing statement so indicating an assignment shall be $...... if the statement is in the standard form prescribed by the [Secretary of State] and otherwise shall be $......, plus in each case an additional fee of $...... for each name more than one against which the financing statement is required to be indexed.

(2) A secured party may assign of record all or part of his rights under a financing statement by the filing in the place where the original financing statement was filed of a separate written statement of assignment signed by the secured party of record and setting forth the name of the secured party of record and the debtor, the file number and the date of filing of the financing statement and the name and address of the assignee and containing a description of the collateral assigned. A copy of the assignment is sufficient as a separate statement if it complies with the preceding sentence. On presentation to the filing officer of such a separate statement, the filing officer shall mark such separate statement with the date and hour of the filing. He shall note the assignment on the index of the financing statement, or in the case of a fixture filing, or a filing covering timber to be cut, or covering minerals or the like (including oil and gas) or accounts subject to subsection (5) of Section 9—103, he shall index the assignment under the name of the assignor as grantor and, to the extent that the law of this state provides for indexing the assignment of a mortgage under the name of the assignee, he shall index the assignment of the financing statement under the name of the assignee. The uniform fee for filing, indexing and furnishing filing data about such a separate statement of assignment shall be $...... if the statement is in the standard form prescribed by the [Secretary of State] and otherwise shall be $......, plus in each case an additional fee of $...... for each name

more than one against which the statement of assignment is required to be indexed. Notwithstanding the provisions of this subsection, an assignment of record of a security interest in a fixture contained in a mortgage effective as a fixture filing (subsection (6) of Section 9—402) may be made only by an assignment of the mortgage in the manner provided by the law of this state other than this Act.

(3) After the disclosure or filing of an assignment under this section, the assignee is the secured party of record. Amended in 1972.

§ 9—406. **Release of Collateral; Duties of Filing Officer; Fees.**

A secured party of record may by his signed statement release all or a part of any collateral described in a filed financing statement. The statement of release is sufficient if it contains a description of the collateral being released, the name and address of the debtor, the name and address of the secured party, and the file number of the financing statement. A statement of release signed by a person other than the secured party of record must be accompanied by a separate written statement of assignment signed by the secured party of record and complying with subsection (2) of Section 9—405, including payment of the required fee. Upon presentation of such a statement of release to the filing officer he shall mark the statement with the hour and date of filing and shall note the same upon the margin of the index of the filing of the financing statement. The uniform fee for filing and noting such a statement of release shall be $...... if the statement is in the standard form prescribed by the [Secretary of State] and otherwise shall be $......, plus in each case an additional fee of $...... for each name more than one against which the statement of release is required to be indexed. Amended in 1972.

[§ 9—407. **Information From Filing Officer**].

[(1) If the person filing any financing statement, termination statement, statement of assignment, or statement of release, furnishes the filing officer a copy thereof, the filing officer shall upon request note upon the copy the file number and date and hour of the filing of the original and deliver or send the copy to such person.]

[(2) Upon request of any person, the filing officer shall issue his certificate showing whether there is on file on the date and hour stated therein, any presently effective financing statement naming a particular debtor and any statement of assignment thereof and if there is, giving the date and hour of filing of each such statement and the names and addresses of each secured party therein. The uniform fee for such a certificate shall be $...... if the request for the certificate is in the standard form prescribed by the [Secretary of State] and otherwise shall be $....... Upon request the filing officer shall furnish a copy of any filed financing statement or statement of assignment for a uniform fee of $...... per page.] Amended in 1972.

Note: *This section is proposed as an optional provision to require filing officers to furnish certificates. Local law and practices should be consulted with regard to the advisability of adoption.*

§ 9—408. Financing Statements Covering Consigned or Leased Goods.

A consignor or lessor of goods may file a financing statement using the terms "consignor," "consignee," "lessor," "lessee" or the like instead of the terms specified in Section 9—402. The provisions of this Part shall apply as appropriate to such a financing statement but its filing shall not of itself be a factor in determining whether or not the consignment or lease is intended as security (Section 1—201(37)). However, if it is determined for other reasons that the consignment or lease is so intended, a security interest of the consignor or lessor which attaches to the consigned or leased goods is perfected by such filing. Added in 1972.

Part 5 Default

§ 9—501. Default; Procedure When Security Agreement Covers Both Real and Personal Property.

(1) When a debtor is in default under a security agreement, a secured party has the rights and remedies provided in this Part and except as limited by subsection (3) those provided in the security agreement. He may reduce his claim to judgment, foreclose or otherwise enforce the security interest by any available judicial procedure. If the collateral is documents the secured party may proceed either as to the documents or as to the goods covered thereby. A secured party in possession has the rights, remedies and duties provided in Section 9—207. The rights and remedies referred to in this subsection are cumulative.

(2) After default, the debtor has the rights and remedies provided in this Part, those provided in the security agreement and those provided in Section 9—207.

(3) To the extent that they give rights to the debtor and impose duties on the secured party, the rules stated in the subsections referred to below may not be waived or varied except as provided with respect to compulsory disposition of collateral (subsection (3) of Section 9—504 and Section 9—505) and with respect to redemption of collateral (Section 9—506) but the parties may by agreement determine the standards by which the fulfillment of these rights and duties is to be measured if such standards are not manifestly unreasonable:

(a) subsection (2) of Section 9—502 and subsection (2) of Section 9—504 insofar as they require accounting for surplus proceeds of collateral;

(b) subsection (3) of Section 9—504 and subsection (1) of Section 9—505 which deal with disposition of collateral;

(c) subsection (2) of Section 9—505 which deals with acceptance of collateral as discharge of obligation;

(d) Section 9—506 which deals with redemption of collateral; and

(e) subsection (1) of Section 9—507 which deals with the secured party's liability for failure to comply with this Part.

(4) If the security agreement covers both real and personal property, the secured party may proceed under this Part as to the personal property or he may proceed as to both the real and the personal property in accordance with his rights and remedies in respect of the real property in which case the provisions of this Part do not apply.

(5) When a secured party has reduced his claim to judgment the lien of any levy which may be made upon his collateral by virtue of any execution based upon the judgment shall relate back to the date of the perfection of the security interest in such collateral. A judicial sale, pursuant to such execution, is a foreclosure of the security interest by judicial procedure within the meaning of this section, and the secured party may purchase at the sale and thereafter hold the collateral free of any other requirements of this Article. Amended in 1972.

§ 9—502. Collection Rights of Secured Party.

(1) When so agreed and in any event on default the secured party is entitled to notify an account debtor or the obligor on an instrument to make payment to him whether or not the assignor was theretofore making collections on the collateral, and also to take control of any proceeds to which he is entitled under Section 9—306.

(2) A secured party who by agreement is entitled to charge back uncollected collateral or otherwise to full

or limited recourse against the debtor and who undertakes to collect from the account debtors or obligors must proceed in a commercially reasonable manner and may deduct his reasonable expenses of realization from the collections. If the security agreement secures an indebtedness, the secured party must account to the debtor for any surplus, and unless otherwise agreed, the debtor is liable for any deficiency. But, if the underlying transaction was a sale of accounts or chattel paper, the debtor is entitled to any surplus or is liable for any deficiency only if the security agreement so provides. Amended in 1972.

§ 9—503. **Secured Party's Right to Take Possession After Default.**

Unless otherwise agreed a secured party has on default the right to take possession of the collateral. In taking possession a secured party may proceed without judicial process if this can be done without breach of the peace or may proceed by action. If the security agreement so provides the secured party may require the debtor to assemble the collateral and make it available to the secured party at a place to be designated by the secured party which is reasonably convenient to both parties. Without removal a secured party may render equipment unusable, and may dispose of collateral on the debtor's premises under Section 9—504.

§ 9—504. **Secured Party's Right to Dispose of Collateral After Default; Effect of Disposition.**

(1) A secured party after default may sell, lease or otherwise dispose of any or all of the collateral in its then condition or following any commercially reasonable preparation or processing. Any sale of goods is subject to the Article on Sales (Article 2). The proceeds of disposition shall be applied in the order following to

(a) the reasonable expenses of retaking, holding, preparing for sale or lease, selling, leasing and the like and, to the extent provided for in the agreement and not prohibited by law, the reasonable attorneys' fees and legal expenses incurred by the secured party;

(b) the satisfaction of indebtedness secured by the security interest under which the disposition is made;

(c) the satisfaction of indebtedness secured by any subordinate security interest in the collateral if written notification of demand therefor is received before distribution of the proceeds is completed. If requested by the secured party, the holder of a subordinate security interest must

seasonably furnish reasonable proof of his interest, and unless he does so, the secured party need not comply with his demand.

(2) If the security interest secures an indebtedness, the secured party must account to the debtor for any surplus, and, unless otherwise agreed, the debtor is liable for any deficiency. But if the underlying transaction was a sale of accounts or chattel paper, the debtor is entitled to any surplus or is liable for any deficiency only if the security agreement so provides.

(3) Disposition of the collateral may be by public or private proceedings and may be made by way of one or more contracts. Sale or other disposition may be as a unit or in parcels and at any time and place and on any terms but every aspect of the disposition including the method, manner, time, place and terms must be commercially reasonable. Unless collateral is perishable or threatens to decline speedily in value or is of a type customarily sold on a recognized market, reasonable notification of the time and place of any public sale or reasonable notification of the time after which any private sale or other intended disposition is to be made shall be sent by the secured party to the debtor, if he has not signed after default a statement renouncing or modifying his right to notification of sale. In the case of consumer goods no other notification need be sent. In other cases notification shall be sent to any other secured party from whom the secured party has received (before sending his notification to the debtor or before the debtor's renunciation of his rights) written notice of a claim of an interest in the collateral. The secured party may buy at any public sale and if the collateral is of a type customarily sold in a recognized market or is of a type which is the subject of widely distributed standard price quotations he may buy at private sale.

(4) When collateral is disposed of by a secured party after default, the disposition transfers to a purchaser for value all of the debtor's rights therein, discharges the security interest under which it is made and any security interest or lien subordinate thereto. The purchaser takes free of all such rights and interests even though the secured party fails to comply with the requirements of this Part or of any judicial proceedings

(a) in the case of a public sale, if the purchaser has no knowledge of any defects in the sale and if he does not buy in collusion with the secured party, other bidders or the person conducting the sale; or

(b) in any other case, if the purchaser acts in good faith.

(5) A person who is liable to a secured party under a guaranty, indorsement, repurchase agreement or the

like and who receives a transfer of collateral from the secured party or is subrogated to his rights has thereafter the rights and duties of the secured party. Such a transfer of collateral is not a sale or disposition of the collateral under this Article. Amended in 1972.

§ 9—505. Compulsory Disposition of Collateral; Acceptance of the Collateral as Discharge of Obligation.

(1) If the debtor has paid sixty per cent of the cash price in the case of a purchase money security interest in consumer goods or sixty per cent of the loan in the case of another security interest in consumer goods, and has not signed after default a statement renouncing or modifying his rights under this Part a secured party who has taken possession of collateral must dispose of it under Section 9—504 and if he fails to do so within ninety days after he takes possession the debtor at his option may recover in conversion or under Section 9—507(1) on secured party's liability.

(2) In any other case involving consumer goods or any other collateral a secured party in possession may, after default, propose to retain the collateral in satisfaction of the obligation. Written notice of such proposal shall be sent to the debtor if he has not signed after default a statement renouncing or modifying his rights under this subsection. In the case of consumer goods no other notice need be given. In other cases notice shall be sent to any other secured party from whom the secured party has received (before sending his notice to the debtor or before the debtor's renunciation of his rights) written notice of a claim of an interest in the collateral. If the secured party receives objection in writing from a person entitled to receive notification within twenty-one days after the notice was sent, the secured party must dispose of the collateral under Section 9—504. In the absence of such written objection the secured party may retain the collateral in satisfaction of the debtor's obligation. Amended in 1972.

§ 9—506. Debtor's Right to Redeem Collateral.

At any time before the secured party has disposed of collateral or entered into a contract for its disposition under Section 9—504 or before the obligation has been discharged under Section 9—505(2) the debtor or any other secured party may unless otherwise agreed in writing after default redeem the collateral by tendering fulfillment of all obligations secured by the collateral as well as the expenses reasonably incurred by the secured party in retaking, holding and preparing the collateral for disposition, in arranging for the sale, and to the extent provided in the agreement and not prohibited by law, his reasonable attorneys' fees and legal expenses.

§ 9—507. Secured Party's Liability for Failure to Comply With This Part.

(1) If it is established that the secured party is not proceeding in accordance with the provisions of this Part disposition may be ordered or restrained on appropriate terms and conditions. If the disposition has occurred the debtor or any person entitled to notification or whose security interest has been made known to the secured party prior to the disposition has a right to recover from the secured party any loss caused by a failure to comply with the provisions of this Part. If the collateral is consumer goods, the debtor has a right to recover in any event an amount not less than the credit service charge plus ten per cent of the principal amount of the debt or the time price differential plus 10 per cent of the cash price.

(2) The fact that a better price could have been obtained by a sale at a different time or in a different method from that selected by the secured party is not of itself sufficient to establish that the sale was not made in a commercially reasonable manner. If the secured party either sells the collateral in the usual manner in any recognized market therefor or if he sells at the price current in such market at the time of his sale or if he has otherwise sold in conformity with reasonable commercial practices among dealers in the type of property sold he has sold in a commercially reasonable manner. The principles stated in the two preceding sentences with respect to sales also apply as may be appropriate to other types of disposition. A disposition which has been approved in any judicial proceeding or by any bona fide creditors' committee or representative of creditors shall conclusively be deemed to be commercially reasonable, but this sentence does not indicate that any such approval must be obtained in any case nor does it indicate that any disposition not so approved is not commercially reasonable.

Article 10
EFFECTIVE DATE AND REPEALER

§ 10—101. Effective Date.

This Act shall become effective at midnight on December 31st following its enactment. It applies to transactions entered into and events occurring after that date.

§ 10—102. **Specific Repealer; Provision for Transition.**

(1) The following acts and all other acts and parts of acts inconsistent herewith are hereby repealed: (Here should follow the acts to be specifically repealed including the following:

    Uniform Negotiable Instruments Act
    Uniform Warehouse Receipts Act
    Uniform Sales Act
    Uniform Bills of Lading Act
    Uniform Stock Transfer Act
    Uniform Conditional Sales Act
    Uniform Trust Receipts Act
       Also any acts regulating:
    Bank collections
    Bulk sales
    Chattel mortgages
    Conditional sales
    Factor's lien acts
    Farm storage of grain and similar acts
    Assignment of accounts receivable)

(2) Transactions validly entered into before the effective date specified in Section 10—101 and the rights, duties and interests flowing from them remain valid thereafter and may be terminated, completed, consummated or enforced as required or permitted by any statute or other law amended or repealed by this Act as though such repeal or amendment had not occurred.

Note: *Subsection (1) should be separately prepared for each state. The foregoing is a list of statutes to be checked.*

§ 10—103. **General Repealer.**

Except as provided in the following section, all acts and parts of acts inconsistent with this Act are hereby repealed.

§ 10—104. **Laws Not Repealed.**

(1) The Article on Documents of Title (Article 7) does not repeal or modify any laws prescribing the form or contents of documents of title or the services or facilities to be afforded by bailees, or otherwise regulating bailees' businesses in respects not specifically dealt with herein; but the fact that such laws are violated does not affect the status of a document of title which otherwise complies with the definition of a document of title (Section 1—201).

[(2) This Act does not repeal . . . . *, cited as the Uniform Act for the Simplification of

Fiduciary Security Transfers, and if in any respect there is any inconsistency between that Act and the Article of this Act on investment securities (Article 8) the provisions of the former Act shall control.]

Note: *At * in subsection (2) insert the statutory reference to the Uniform Act for the Simplification of Fiduciary Security Transfers if such Act has previously been enacted. If it has not been enacted, omit subsection (2).*

Article 11

(REPORTERS' DRAFT) EFFECTIVE DATE AND TRANSITION PROVISIONS

This material has been numbered Article 11 to distinguish it from Article 10, the transition provision of the 1962 Code, which may still remain in effect in some states to cover transition problems from pre-Code law to the original Uniform Commercial Code. Adaptation may be necessary in particular states. The terms "[old Code]" and "[new Code]" and "[old U.C.C.]" and "[new U.C.C.]" are used herein, and should be suitably changed in each state.

Note: This draft was prepared by the Reporters and has not been passed upon by the Review Committee, the Permanent Editorial Board, the American Law Institute, or the National Conference of Commissioners on Uniform State Laws. It is submitted as a working draft which may be adapted as appropriate in each state.

§ 11—101. **Effective Date.**

This Act shall become effective at 12:01 A.M. on ———, 19——.

§ 11—102. **Preservation of Old Transition Provision.**

The provisions of [here insert reference to the original transition provision in the particular state] shall continue to apply to [the new U.C.C.] and for this purpose the [old U.C.C. and new U.C.C.] shall be considered one continuous statute.

§ 11—103. **Transition to [New Code]—General Rule.**

Transactions validly entered into after [effective date of old U.C.C.] and before [effective date of new U.C.C.], and which were subject to the provisions of [old U.C.C.] and which would be subject to this Act as amended if they had been entered into after the effective date of [new U.C.C.] and the rights, duties and interests flowing from such transactions remain valid after the latter date and may be terminated, completed, consummated or enforced as required or permitted by the [new U.C.C.]. Security interests arising out of such transactions which are perfected when [new U.C.C.] becomes effective shall remain perfected until they lapse as provided in [new U.C.C.], and may be continued as permitted by [new U.C.C.], except as stated in Section 11—105.

§ 11—104. Transition Provision on Change of Requirement of Filing.

A security interest for the perfection of which filing or the taking of possession was required under [old U.C.C.] and which attached prior to the effective date of [new U.C.C.] but was not perfected shall be deemed perfected on the effective date of [new U.C.C.] if [new U.C.C.] permits perfection without filing or authorizes filing in the office or offices where a prior ineffective filing was made.

§ 11—105. Transition Provision on Change of Place of Filing.

(1) A financing statement or continuation statement filed prior to [effective date of new U.C.C.] which shall not have lapsed prior to [the effective date of new U.C.C.] shall remain effective for the period provided in the [old Code], but not less than five years after the filing.

(2) With respect to any collateral acquired by the debtor subsequent to the effective date of [new U.C.C.], any effective financing statement or continuation statement described in this section shall apply only if the filing or filings are in the office or offices that would be appropriate to perfect the security interests in the new collateral under [new U.C.C.].

(3) The effectiveness of any financing statement or continuation statement filed prior to [effective date of new U.C.C.] may be continued by a continuation statement as permitted by [new U.C.C.], except that if [new U.C.C.] requires a filing in an office where there was no previous financing statement, a new financing statement conforming to Section 11—106 shall be filed in that office.

(4) If the record of a mortgage of real estate would have been effective as a fixture filing of goods described therein if [new U.C.C.] had been in effect on the date of recording the mortgage, the mortgage shall be deemed effective as a fixture filing as to such goods under subsection (6) of Section 9—402 of the [new U.C.C.] on the effective date of [new U.C.C.].

§ 11—106. Required Refilings.

(1) If a security interest is perfected or has priority when this Act takes effect as to all persons or as to certain persons without any filing or recording, and if the filing of a financing statement would be required for the perfection or priority of the security interest against those persons under [new U.C.C.], the perfection and priority rights of the security interest continue until 3 years after the effective date of [new U.C.C.]. The perfection will then lapse unless a financing statement is filed as provided in subsection (4) or unless the security interest is perfected otherwise than by filing.

(2) If a security interest is perfected when [new U.C.C.] takes effect under a law other than [U.C.C.] which requires no further filing, refiling or recording to continue its perfection, perfection continues until and will lapse 3 years after [new U.C.C.] takes effect, unless a financing statement is filed as provided in subsection (4) or unless the security interest is perfected otherwise than by filing, or unless under subsection (3) of Section 9—302 the other law continues to govern filing.

(3) If a security interest is perfected by a filing, refiling or recording under a law repealed by this Act which required further filing, refiling or recording to continue its perfection, perfection continues and will lapse on the date provided by the law so repealed for such further filing, refiling or recording unless a financing statement is filed as provided in subsection (4) or unless the security interest is perfected otherwise than by filing.

(4) A financing statement may be filed within six months before the perfection of a security interest would otherwise lapse. Any such financing statement may be signed by either the debtor or the secured party. It must identify the security agreement, statement or notice (however denominated in any statute or other law repealed or modified by this Act), state the office where and the date when the last filing, refiling or recording, if any, was made with respect thereto, and the filing number, if any, or book and page, if any, of recording and further state that the security agreement, statement or notice, however denominated, in another filing office under the [U.C.C.] or under any statute or other law repealed or modified by this Act is still effective. Section 9—401 and Section 9—103 determine the proper place to file such a financing statement. Except as specified in this subsection, the provisions of Section 9—403(3) for continuation statements apply to such a financing statement.

§ 11—107. **Transition Provisions as to Priorities.**

Except as otherwise provided in [Article 11], [old U.C.C.] shall apply to any questions of priority if the positions of the parties were fixed prior to the effective date of [new U.C.C.]. In other cases questions of priority shall be determined by [new U.C.C.].

§ 11—108. **Presumption that Rule of Law Continues Unchanged.**

Unless a change in law has clearly been made, the provisions of [new U.C.C.] shall be deemed declaratory of the meaning of the [old U.C.C.]

Appendix D

THE UNIFORM PARTNERSHIP ACT

(Adopted in 48 States, all except Georgia and Louisiana; the District of Columbia, the Virgin Islands, and Guam. The adoptions by Alabama and Nebraska do not follow the official text in every respect, but are substantially similar, with local variations.)

The Act consists of 7 Parts as follows:

I. Preliminary Provisions

II. Nature of Partnership

III. Relations of Partners to Persons Dealing with the Partnership

IV. Relations of Partners to One Another

V. Property Rights of a Partner

VI. Dissolution and Winding Up

VII. Miscellaneous Provisions

An Act to make uniform the Law of Partnerships Be it enacted, etc.:

Part I Preliminary Provisions

Sec. 1. Name of Act.

This act may be cited as Uniform Partnership Act.

Sec. 2. Definition of Terms.

In this act, "Court" includes every court and judge having jurisdiction in the case.

"Business" includes every trade, occupation, or profession.

"Person" includes individuals, partnerships, corporations, and other associations.

"Bankrupt" includes bankrupt under the Federal Bankruptcy Act or insolvent under any state insolvent act.

"Conveyance" includes every assignment, lease, mortgage, or encumbrance.

"Real property" includes land and any interest or estate in land.

Sec. 3. Interpretation of Knowledge and Notice.

(1) A person has "knowledge" of a fact within the meaning of this act not only when he has actual knowledge thereof, but also when he has knowledge of such other facts as in the circumstances shows bad faith.

(2) A person has "notice" of a fact within the meaning of this act when the person who claims the benefit of the notice

(a) States the fact to such person, or

(b) Delivers through the mail, or by other means of communication, a written statement of the fact to such person or to a proper person at his place of business or residence.

Sec. 4. Rules of Construction.

(1) The rule that statutes in derogation of the common law are to be strictly construed shall have no application to this act.

(2) The law of estoppel shall apply under this act.

(3) The law of agency shall apply under this act.

(4) This act shall be so interpreted and construed as to effect its general purpose to make uniform the law of those states which enact it.

(5) This act shall not be construed so as to impair the obligations of any contract existing when the act goes into effect, nor to affect any action or proceedings begun or right accrued before this act takes effect.

Sec. 5. **Rules for Cases Not Provided for in this Act.**

In any case not provided for in this act the rules of law and equity, including the law merchant, shall govern.

Part II **Nature of Partnership**

Sec. 6. **Partnership Defined.**

(1) A partnership is an association of two or more persons to carry on as co-owners a business for profit.

(2) But any association formed under any other statute of this state, or any statute adopted by authority, other than the authority of this state, is not a partnership under this act, unless such association would have been a partnership in this state prior to the adoption of this act; but this act shall apply to limited partnerships except in so far as the statutes relating to such partnerships are inconsistent herewith.

Sec. 7. **Rules for Determining the Existence of a Partnership.**

In determining whether a partnership exists, these rules shall apply:

(1) Except as provided by Section 16 persons who are not partners as to each other are not partners as to third persons.

(2) Joint tenancy, tenancy in common, tenancy by the entireties, joint property, common property, or part ownership does not of itself establish a partnership, whether such co-owners do or do not share any profits made by the use of the property.

(3) The sharing of gross returns does not of itself establish a partnership, whether or not the persons sharing them have a joint or common right or interest in any property from which the returns are derived.

(4) The receipt by a person of a share of the profits of a business is prima facie evidence that he is a partner in the business, but no such inference shall be drawn if such profits were received in payment:

(a) As a debt by installments or otherwise,

(b) As wages of an employee or rent to a landlord,

(c) As an annuity to a widow or representative of a deceased partner,

(d) As interest on a loan, though the amount of payment vary with the profits of the business.

(e) As the consideration for the sale of a good-will of a business or other property by installments or otherwise.

Sec. 8. **Partnership Property.**

(1) All property originally brought into the partnership stock or subsequently acquired by purchase or otherwise, on account of the partnership, is partnership property.

(2) Unless the contrary intention appears, property acquired with partnership funds is partnership property.

(3) Any estate in real property may be acquired in the partnership name. Title so acquired can be conveyed only in the partnership name.

(4) A conveyance to a partnership in the partnership name, though without words of inheritance, passes the entire estate of the grantor unless a contrary intent appears.

Part III **Relations of Partners to Persons Dealing with the Partnership**

Sec. 9. **Partner Agent of Partnership as to Partnership Business.**

(1) Every partner is an agent of the partnership for the purpose of its business, and the act of every partner, including the execution in the partnership name of any instrument, for apparently carrying on in the usual way the business of the partnership of which he is a member binds the partnership, unless the partner so acting has in fact no authority to act for the partnership in the particular matter, and the person with whom he is dealing has knowledge of the fact that he has no such authority.

(2) An act of a partner which is not apparently for the carrying on of the business of the partnership in the usual way does not bind the partnership unless authorized by the other partners.

(3) Unless authorized by the other partners or unless they have abandoned the business, one or more but less than all the partners have no authority to:

(a) Assign the partnership property in trust for creditors or on the assignee's promise to pay the debts of the partnership,

(b) Dispose of the good-will of the business,

(c) Do any other act which would make it impossible to carry on the ordinary business of a partnership,

(d) Confess a judgment,

(e) Submit a partnership claim or liability to arbitration or reference.

(4) No act of a partner in contravention of a restriction on authority shall bind the partnership to persons having knowledge of the restriction.

Sec. 10. Conveyance of Real Property of the Partnership.

(1) Where title to real property is in the partnership name, any partner may convey title to such property by a conveyance executed in the partnership name; but the partnership may recover such property unless the partner's act binds the partnership under the provisions of paragraph (1) of section 9 or unless such property has been conveyed by the grantee or a person claiming through such grantee to a holder for value without knowledge that the partner, in making the conveyance, has exceeded his authority.

(2) Where title to real property is in the name of the partnership, a conveyance executed by a partner, in his own name, passes the equitable interest of the partnership, provided the act is one within the authority of the partner under the provisions of paragraph (1) of section 9.

(3) Where title to real property is in the name of one or more but not all the partners, and the record does not disclose the right of the partnership, the partners in whose name the title stands may convey title to such property, but the partnership may recover such property if the partners' act does not bind the partnership under the provisions of paragraph (1) of section 9, unless the purchaser or his assignee, is a holder for value, without knowledge.

(4) Where the title to real property is in the name of one or more or all the partners, or in a third person in trust for the partnership, a conveyance executed by a partner in the partnership name, or in his own name, passes the equitable interest of the partnership, provided the act is one within the authority of the partner under the provisions of paragraph (1) of section 9.

(5) Where the title to real property is in the names of all the partners a conveyance executed by all the partners passes all their rights in such property.

Sec. 11. Partnership Bound by Admission of Partner.

An admission or representation made by any partner concerning partnership affairs within the scope of his authority as conferred by this act is evidence against the partnership.

Sec. 12. Partnership Charged with Knowledge of or Notice to Partner.

Notice to any partner of any matter relating to partnership affairs, and the knowledge of the partner acting in the particular matter, acquired while a partner or then present to his mind, and the knowledge of any other partner who reasonably could and should have communicated it to the acting partner, operate as notice to or knowledge of the partnership, except in the case of a fraud on the partnership committed by or with the consent of that partner.

Sec. 13. Partnership Bound by Partner's Wrongful Act.

Where, by any wrongful act or omission of any partner acting in the ordinary course of the business of the partnership or with the authority of his co-partners, loss or injury is caused to any person, not being a partner in the partnership, or any penalty is incurred, the partnership is liable therefor to the same extent as the partner so acting or omitting to act.

Sec. 14. Partnership Bound by Partner's Breach of Trust.

The partnership is bound to make good the loss:

(a) Where one partner acting within the scope of his apparent authority receives money or property of a third person and misapplies it; and

(b) Where the partnership in the course of its business receives money or property of a third person and the money or property so received is misapplied by any partner while it is in the custody of the partnership.

Sec. 15. Nature of Partner's Liability.

All partners are liable

(a) Jointly and severally for everything chargeable to the partnership under sections 13 and 14.

(b) Jointly for all other debts and obligations of the partnership; but any partner may enter into a separate obligation to perform a partnership contract.

Sec. 16. Partner by Estoppel.

(1) When a person, by words spoken or written or by conduct, represents himself, or consents to another representing him to any one, as a partner in an existing partnership or with one or more persons not actual partners, he is liable to any such person to whom such representation has been made, who has, on the faith of such representation, given credit to the actual or

apparent partnership, and if he has made such representation or consented to its being made in a public manner he is liable to such person, whether the representation has or has not been made or communicated to such person so giving credit by or with the knowledge of the apparent partner making the representation or consenting to its being made.

(a) When a partnership liability results, he is liable as though he were an actual member of the partnership.

(b) When no partnership liability results, he is liable jointly with the other persons, if any, so consenting to the contract or representation as to incur liability, otherwise separately.

(2) When a person has been thus represented to be a partner in an existing partnership, or with one or more persons not actual partners, he is an agent of the persons consenting to such representation to bind them to the same extent and in the same manner as though he were a partner in fact, with respect to persons who rely upon the representation. Where all the members of the existing partnership consent to the representation, a partnership act or obligation results; but in all other cases it is the joint act or obligation of the person acting and the persons consenting to the representation.

Sec. 17. **Liability of Incoming Partner.**

A person admitted as a partner into an existing partnership is liable for all the obligations of the partnership arising before his admission as though he had been a partner when such obligations were incurred, except that this liability shall be satisfied only out of partnership property.

Part IV **Relations of Partners to One Another**

Sec. 18. **Rules Determining Rights and Duties of Partners.**

The rights and duties of the partners in relation to the partnership shall be determined, subject to any agreement between them, by the following rules:

(a) Each partner shall be repaid his contributions, whether by way of capital or advances to the partnership property and share equally in the profits and surplus remaining after all liabilities, including those to partners, are satisfied; and must contribute towards the losses, whether of capital or otherwise, sustained by the partnership according to his share in the profits.

(b) The partnership must indemnify every partner in respect of payments made and personal liabilities reasonably incurred by him in the ordinary and proper conduct of its business, or for the preservation of its business or property.

(c) A partner, who in aid of the partnership makes any payment or advance beyond the amount of capital which he agreed to contribute, shall be paid interest from the date of the payment or advance.

(d) A partner shall receive interest on the capital contributed by him only from the date when repayment should be made.

(e) All partners have equal rights in the management and conduct of the partnership business.

(f) No partner is entitled to remuneration for acting in the partnership business, except that a surviving partner is entitled to reasonable compensation for his services in winding up the partnership affairs.

(g) No person can become a member of a partnership without the consent of all the partners.

(h) Any difference arising as to ordinary matters connected with the partnership business may be decided by a majority of the partners; but no act in contravention of any agreement between the partners may be done rightfully without the consent of all the partners.

Sec. 19. **Partnership Books.**

The partnership books shall be kept, subject to any agreement between the partners, at the principal place of business of the partnership, and every partner shall at all times have access to and may inspect and copy any of them.

Sec. 20. **Duty of Partners to Render Information.**

Partners shall render on demand true and full information of all things affecting the partnership to any partner or the legal representative of any deceased partner or partner under legal disability.

Sec. 21. **Partner Accountable as a Fiduciary.**

(1) Every partner must account to the partnership for any benefit, and hold as trustee for it any profits derived by him without the consent of the other partners from any transaction connected with the formation, conduct, or liquidation of the partnership or from any use by him of its property.

(2) This section applies also to the representatives of a deceased partner engaged in the liquidation of the affairs of the partnership as the personal representatives of the last surviving partner.

Sec. 22. **Right to an Account.**

Any partner shall have the right to a formal account as to partnership affairs:

(a) If he is wrongfully excluded from the partnership business or possession of its property by his co-partners,

(b) If the right exists under the terms of any agreement,

(c) As provided by section 21,

(d) Whenever other circumstances render it just and reasonable.

Sec. 23. **Continuation of Partnership Beyond Fixed Term.**

(1) When a partnership for a fixed term or particular undertaking is continued after the termination of such term or particular undertaking without any express agreement, the rights and duties of the partners remain the same as they were at such termination, so far as is consistent with a partnership at will.

(2) A continuation of the business by the partners or such of them as habitually acted therein during the term, without any settlement or liquidation of the partnership affairs, is prima facie evidence of a continuation of the partnership.

Part V **Property Rights of a Partner**

Sec. 24. **Extent of Property Rights of a Partner.**

The property rights of a partner are (1) his rights in specific partnership property, (2) his interest in the partnership, and (3) his right to participate in the management.

Sec. 25. **Nature of a Partner's Right in Specific Partnership Property.**

(1) A partner is co-owner with his partners of specific partnership property holding as a tenant in partnership.

(2) The incidents of this tenancy are such that:

(a) A partner, subject to the provisions of this act and to any agreement between the partners, has an equal right with his partners to possess specific partnership property for partnership purposes; but he has no right to possess such property for any other purpose without the consent of his partners.

(b) A partner's right in specific partnership property is not assignable except in connection with the assignment of rights of all the partners in the same property.

(c) A partner's right in specific partnership property is not subject to attachment or execution, except on a claim against the partnership. When partnership property is attached for a partnership debt the partners, or any of them, or the representatives of a deceased partner, cannot claim any right under the homestead or exemption laws.

(d) On the death of a partner his right in specific partnership property vests in the surviving partner or partners, except where the deceased was the last surviving partner, when his right in such property vests in his legal representative. Such surviving partner or partners, or the legal representative of the last surviving partner, has no right to possess the partnership property for any but a partnership purpose.

(e) A partner's right in specific partnership property is not subject to dower, curtesy, or allowances to widows, heirs, or next of kin.

Sec. 26. **Nature of Partner's Interest in the Partnership.**

A partner's interest in the partnership is his share of the profits and surplus, and the same is personal property.

Sec. 27. **Assignment of Partner's Interest.**

(1) A conveyance by a partner of his interest in the partnership does not of itself dissolve the partnership, nor, as against the other partners in the absence of agreement, entitle the assignee, during the continuance of the partnership to interfere in the management or administration of the partnership business or affairs, or to require any information or account of partnership transactions, or to inspect the partnership books; but it merely entitles the assignee to receive in accordance with his contract the profits to which the assigning partner would otherwise be entitled.

(2) In case of a dissolution of the partnership, the assignee is entitled to receive his assignor's interest and may require an account from the date only of the last account agreed to by all the partners.

Sec. 28. **Partner's Interest Subject to Charging Order.**

(1) On due application to a competent court by any judgment creditor of a partner, the court which entered the judgment, order, or decree, or any other court, may charge the interest of the debtor partner with payment of the unsatisfied amount of such judgment debt with interest thereon; and may then or later appoint a receiver of his share of the profits, and of any other money due or to fall due to him in respect

of the partnership, and make all other orders, directions, accounts and inquiries which the debtor partner might have made, or which the circumstances of the case may require.

(2) The interest charged may be redeemed at any time before foreclosure, or in case of a sale being directed by the court may be purchased without thereby causing a dissolution:

(a) With separate property, by any one or more of the partners, or

(b) With partnership property, by any one or more of the partners with the consent of all the partners whose interests are not so charged or sold.

(3) Nothing in this act shall be held to deprive a partner of his right, if any, under the exemption laws, as regards his interest in the partnership.

Part VI Dissolution and Winding up

Sec. 29. Dissolution Defined.

The dissolution of a partnership is the change in the relation of the partners caused by any partner ceasing to be associated in the carrying on as distinguished from the winding up of the business.

Sec. 30. Partnership Not Terminated by Dissolution.

On dissolution the partnership is not terminated, but continues until the winding up of partnership affairs is completed.

Sec. 31. Causes of Dissolution.

Dissolution is caused:

(1) Without violation of the agreement between the partners,

(a) By the termination of the definite term or particular undertaking specified in the agreement,

(b) By the express will of any partner when no definite term or particular undertaking is specified,

(c) By the express will of all the partners who have not assigned their interests or suffered them to be charged for their separate debts, either before or after the termination of any specified term or particular undertaking.

(d) By the explusion of any partner from the business bona fide in accordance with such a power conferred by the agreement between the partners;

(2) In contravention of the agreement between the partners, where the circumstances do not permit a dissolution under any other provision of this section, by the express will of any partner at any time;

(3) By any event which makes it unlawful for the business of the partnership to be carried on or for the members to carry it on in partnership;

(4) By the death of any partner;

(5) By the bankruptcy of any partner or the partnership;

(6) By decree of court under section 32.

Sec. 32. Dissolution by Decree of Court.

(1) On application by or for a partner the court shall decree a dissolution whenever:

(a) A partner has been declared a lunatic in any judicial proceeding or is shown to be of unsound mind,

(b) A partner becomes in any other way incapable of performing his part of the partnership contract,

(c) A partner has been guilty of such conduct as tends to affect prejudicially the carrying on of the business,

(d) A partner wilfully or persistently commits a breach of the partnership agreement, or otherwise so conducts himself in matters relating to the partnership business that it is not reasonably practicable to carry on the business in partnership with him,

(e) The business of the partnership can only be carried on at a loss,

(f) Other circumstances render a dissolution equitable.

(2) On the application of the purchaser of a partner's interest under sections 27 or 28:

(a) After the termination of the specified term or particular undertaking,

(b) At any time if the partnership was a partnership at will when the interest was assigned or when the charging order was issued.

Sec. 33. General Effect of Dissolution on Authority of Partner.

Except so far as may be necessary to wind up partnership affairs or to complete transactions begun but not then finished, dissolution terminates all authority of any partner to act for the partnership,

(1) With respect to the partners,

(a) When the dissolution is not by the act, bankruptcy or death of a partner; or

(b) When the dissolution is by such act, bankruptcy or death of a partner, in cases where section 34 so requires.

(2) With respect to persons not partners, as declared in section 35.

Sec. 34. **Right of Partner to Contribution From Copartners After Dissolution.**

Where the dissolution is caused by the act, death or bankruptcy of a partner, each partner is liable to his copartners for his share of any liability created by any partner acting for the partnership as if the partnership had not been dissolved unless

(a) The dissolution being by act of any partner, the partner acting for the partnership had knowledge of the dissolution, or

(b) The dissolution being by the death or bankruptcy of a partner, the partner acting for the partnership had knowledge or notice of the death or bankruptcy.

Sec. 35. **Power of Partner to Bind Partnership to Third Persons After Dissolution.**

(1) After dissolution a partner can bind the partnership except as provided in Paragraph (3)

(a) By any act appropriate for winding up partnership affairs or completing transactions unfinished at dissolution;

(b) By any transaction which would bind the partnership if dissolution had not taken place, provided the other party to the transaction

(I) Had extended credit to the partnership prior to dissolution and had no knowledge or notice of the dissolution; or

(II) Though he had not so extended credit, had nevertheless known of the partnership prior to dissolution, and, having no knowledge or notice of dissolution, the fact of dissolution had not been advertised in a newspaper of general circulation in the place (or in each place if more than one) at which the partnership business was regularly carried on.

(2) The liability of a partner under paragraph (1b) shall be satisfied out of partnership assets alone when such partner had been prior to dissolution

(a) Unknown as a partner to the person with whom the contract is made; and

(b) So far unknown and inactive in partnership affairs that the business reputation of the partnership could not be said to have been in any degree due to his connection with it.

(3) The partnership is in no case bound by any act of a partner after dissolution

(a) Where the partnership is dissolved because it is unlawful to carry on the business, unless the act is appropriate for winding up partnership affairs; or

(b) Where the partner has become bankrupt; or

(c) Where the partner has no authority to wind up partnership affairs; except by a transaction with one who

(I) Had extended credit to the partnership prior to dissolution and had no knowledge or notice of his want of authority; or

(II) Had not extended credit to the partnership prior to dissolution, and, having no knowledge or notice of his want of authority, the fact of his want of authority has not been advertised in the manner provided for advertising the fact of dissolution in paragraph (1bII).

(4) Nothing in this section shall affect the liability under section 16 of any person who after dissolution represents himself or consents to another representing him as a partner in a partnership engaged in carrying on business.

Sec. 36. **Effect of Dissolution on Partner's Existing Liability.**

(1) The dissolution of the partnership does not of itself discharge the existing liability of any partner.

(2) A partner is discharged from any existing liability upon dissolution of the partnership by an agreement to that effect between himself, the partnership creditor and the person or partnership continuing the business; and such agreement may be inferred from the course of dealing between the creditor having knowledge of the dissolution and the person or partnership continuing the business.

(3) Where a person agrees to assume the existing obligations of a dissolved partnership, the partners whose obligations have been assumed shall be discharged from any liability to any creditor of the partnership who, knowing of the agreement, consents to a material alteration in the nature or time of payment of such obligations.

(4) The individual property of a deceased partner shall be liable for all obligations of the partnership incurred while he was a partner but subject to the prior payment of his separate debts.

Sec. 37. **Right to Wind Up.**

Unless otherwise agreed the partners who have not wrongfully dissolved the partnership or the legal representative of the last surviving partner, not bankrupt, has the right to wind up the partnership affairs; provided, however, that any partner, his legal representative or his assignee, upon cause shown, may obtain winding up by the court.

Sec. 38. Rights of Partners to Application of Partnership Property.

(1) When dissolution is caused in any way, except in contravention of the partnership agreement, each partner as against his co-partners and all persons claiming through them in respect of their interests in the partnership, unless otherwise agreed, may have the partnership property applied to discharge its liabilities, and the surplus applied to pay in cash the net amount owing to the respective partners. But if dissolution is caused by expulsion of a partner, bona fide under the partnership agreement and if the expelled partner is discharged from all partnership liabilities, either by payment or agreement under section 36(2), he shall receive in cash only the net amount due him from the partnership.

(2) When dissolution is caused in contravention of the partnership agreement the rights of the partners shall be as follows:

(a) Each partner who has not caused dissolution wrongfully shall have,

(I) All the rights specified in paragraph (1) of this section, and

(II) The right, as against each partner who has caused the dissolution wrongfully, to damages for breach of the agreement.

(b) The partners who have not caused the dissolution wrongfully, if they all desire to continue the business in the same name, either by themselves or jointly with others, may do so, during the agreed term for the partnership and for that purpose may possess the partnership property, provided they secure the payment by bond approved by the court, or pay to any partner who has caused the dissolution wrongfully, the value of his interest in the partnership at the dissolution, less any damages recoverable under clause (2aII) of the section, and in like manner indemnify him against all present or future partnership liabilities.

(c) A partner who has caused the dissolution wrongfully shall have:

(I) If the business is not continued under the provisions of paragraph (2b) all the rights of a partner under paragraph (1), subject to clause (2aII), of this section,

(II) If the business is continued under paragraph (2b) of this section the right as against his co-partners and all claiming through them in respect of their interests in the partnership, to have the value of his interest in the partnership, less any damages caused to his co-partners by the dissolution, ascertained and paid to him in cash, or the payment secured by bond approved by the court, and to be released from all existing liabilities of the partnership; but in ascertaining the value of the partner's interest the value of the good-will of the business shall not be considered.

Sec. 39. Rights Where Partnership is Dissolved for Fraud or Misrepresentation.

Where a partnership contract is rescinded on the ground of the fraud or misrepresentation of one of the parties thereto, the party entitled to rescind is, without prejudice to any other right, entitled,

(a) To a lien on, or right of retention of, the surplus of the partnership property after satisfying the partnership liabilities to third persons for any sum of money paid by him for the purchase of an interest in the partnership and for any capital or advances contributed by him; and

(b) To stand, after all liabilities to third persons have been satisfied, in the place of the creditors of the partnership for any payments made by him in respect of the partnership liabilities; and

(c) To be indemnified by the person guilty of the fraud or making the representation against all debts and liabilities of the partnership.

Sec. 40. Rules for Distribution.

In settling accounts between the partners after dissolution, the following rules shall be observed, subject to any agreement to the contrary:

(a) The assets of the partnership are:

(I) The partnership property,

(II) The contributions of the partners necessary for the payment of all the liabilities specified in clause (b) of this paragraph.

(b) The liabilities of the partnership shall rank in order of payment, as follows:

(I) Those owing to creditors other than partners,

(II) Those owing to partners other than for capital and profits,

(III) Those owing to partners in respect of capital,

(IV) Those owing to partners in respect of profits.

(c) The assets shall be applied in the order of their declaration in clause (a) of this paragraph to the satisfaction of the liabilities.

(d) The partners shall contribute, as provided by section 18(a) the amount necessary to satisfy the liabilities; but if any, but not all, of the partners are insolvent, or, not being subject to process, refuse to contribute, the other parties shall contribute their share of the liabilities, and, in the relative proportions in which they share the profits, the additional amount necessary to pay the liabilities.

(e) An assignee for the benefit of creditors or any person appointed by the court shall have the right to enforce the contributions specified in clause (d) of this paragraph.

(f) Any partner or his legal representative shall have the right to enforce the contributions specified in clause (d) of this paragraph, to the extent of the amount which he has paid in excess of his share of the liability.

(g) The individual property of a deceased partner shall be liable for the contributions specified in clause (d) of this paragraph.

(h) When partnership property and the individual properties of the partners are in possession of a court for distribution, partnership creditors shall have priority on partnership property and separate creditors on individual property, saving the rights of lien or secured creditors as heretofore.

(i) Where a partner has become bankrupt or his estate is insolvent the claims against his separate property shall rank in the following order:

(I) Those owing to separate creditors,

(II) Those owing to partnership creditors,

(III) Those owing to partners by way of contribution.

Sec. 41. Liability of Persons Continuing the Business in Certain Cases.

(1) When any new partner is admitted into an existing partnership, or when any partner retires and assigns (or the representative of the deceased partner assigns) his rights in partnership property to two or more of the partners, or to one or more of the partners and one or more third persons, if the business is continued without liquidation of the partnership affairs, creditors of the first or dissolved partnership are also creditors of the partnership so continuing the business.

(2) When all but one partner retire and assign (or the representative of a deceased partner assigns) their rights in partnership property to the remaining partner, who continues the business without liquidation of partnership affairs, either alone or with others, creditors of the dissolved partnership are also creditors of the person or partnership so continuing the business.

(3) When any partner retires or dies and the business of the dissolved partnership is continued as set forth in paragraphs (1) and (2) of this section, with the consent of the retired partners or the representative of the deceased partner, but without any assignment of his right in partnership property, rights of creditors of the dissolved partnership and of the creditors of the person or partnership continuing the business shall be as if such assignment had been made.

(4) When all the partners or their representatives assign their rights in partnership property to one or more third persons who promise to pay the debts and who continue the business of the dissolved partnership, creditors of the dissolved partnership are also creditors of the person or partnership continuing the business.

(5) When any partner wrongfully causes a dissolution and the remaining partners continue the business under the provisions of section 38(2b), either alone or with others, and without liquidation of the partnership affairs, creditors of the dissolved partnership are also creditors of the person or partnership continuing the business.

(6) When a partner is expelled and the remaining partners continue the business either alone or with others, without liquidation of the partnership affairs, creditors of the dissolved partnership are also creditors of the person or partnership continuing the business.

(7) The liability of a third person becoming a partner in the partnership continuing the business, under this section, to the creditors of the dissolved partnership shall be satisfied out of partnership property only.

(8) When the business of a partnership after dissolution is continued under any conditions set forth in this section the creditors of the dissolved partnership, as against the separate creditors of the retiring or deceased partner or the representative of the deceased partner, have a prior right to any claim of the retired partner or the representative of the deceased partner against the person or partnership continuing the business, on account of the retired or deceased partner's interest in the dissolved partnership or on account of any consideration promised for such interest or for his right in partnership property.

(9) Nothing in this section shall be held to modify any

right of creditors to set aside any assignment on the ground of fraud.

(10) The use by the person or partnership continuing the business of the partnership name, or the name of a deceased partner as part thereof, shall not of itself make the individual property of the deceased partner liable for any debts contracted by such person or partnership.

Sec. 42. **Rights of Retiring or Estate of Deceased Partner When the Business is Continued.**

When any partner retires or dies, and the business is continued under any of the conditions set forth in section 41 (1, 2, 3, 5, 6), or section 38(2b), without any settlement of accounts as between him or his estate and the person or partnership continuing the business, unless otherwise agreed, he or his legal representative as against such persons or partnership may have the value of his interest at the date of dissolution ascertained, and shall receive as an ordinary creditor an amount equal to the value of his interest in the dissolved partnership with interest, or, at his option or at the option of his legal representative, in lieu of interest, the profits attributable to the use of his right in the property of the dissolved partnership; provided that the creditors of the dissolved partnership as against the separate creditors, or the representative of the retired or deceased partner, shall have priority on any claim arising under this section, as provided by section 41(8) of this act.

Sec. 43. **Accrual of Actions.**

The right to an account of his interest shall accrue to any partner, or his legal representative, as against the winding up partners or the surviving partners or the person or partnership continuing the business, at the date of dissolution, in the absence of any agreement to the contrary.

Part VII **Miscellaneous Provisions**

Sec. 44. **When Act Takes Effect.**

This act shall take effect on the _____ day of _____ one thousand nine hundred and _____.

Sec. 45. **Legislation Repealed.**

All acts or parts of acts inconsistent with this act are hereby repealed.

Appendix E

THE UNIFORM LIMITED PARTNERSHIP ACT

(Adopted in 39 States, all except Arkansas, Colorado, Connecticut, Louisiana, Maryland, Minnesota, Montana, Nebraska, Washington, West Virginia, and Wyoming. Also adopted in the District of Columbia, and the Virgin Islands.)

Sec. 1. Limited Partnership Defined.

A limited partnership is a partnership formed by two or more persons under the provisions of Section 2, having as members one or more general partners and one or more limited partners. The limited partners as such shall not be bound by the obligations of the partnership.

Sec. 2. Formation.

(1) Two or more persons desiring to form a limited partnership shall

(a) Sign and swear to a certificate, which shall state

I. The name of the partnership,

II. The character of the business,

III. The location of the principal place of business,

IV. The name and place of residence of each member; general and limited partners being respectively designated,

V. The term for which the partnership is to exist,

VI. The amount of cash and a description of and the agreed value of the other property contributed by each limited partner,

VII. The additional contributions, if any, agreed to be made by each limited partner and the times at which or events on the happening of which they shall be made,

VIII. The time, if agreed upon, when the contribution of each limited partner is to be returned,

IX. The share of the profits or the other compensation by way of income which each limited partner shall receive by reason of his contribution,

X. The right, if given, of a limited partner to substitute an assignee as contributor in his place, and the terms and conditions of the substitution,

XI. The right, if given, of the partners to admit additional limited partners,

XII. The right, if given, of one or more of the limited partners to priority over other limited partners, as to contributions or as to compensation by way of income, and the nature of such priority,

XIII. The right, if given, of the remaining general partner or partners to continue the business on the death, retirement or insanity of a general partner, and

XIV. The right, if given, of a limited partner to demand and receive property other than cash in return for his contribution.

(b) File for record the certificate in the office of [here designate the proper office].

(2) A limited partnership is formed if there has been substantial compliance in good faith with the requirements of paragraph (1).

Sec. 3. Business Which May Be Carried On.

A limited partnership may carry on any business which a partnership without limited partners may carry on, except [here designate the business to be prohibited].

Sec. 4. Character of Limited Partner's Contribution.

The contributions of a limited partner may be cash or other property, but not services.

Sec. 5. A Name Not to Contain Surname of Limited Partner; Exceptions.

(1) The surname of a limited partner shall not appear in the partnership name, unless

(a) It is also the surname of a general partner, or

(b) Prior to the time when the limited partner became such the business had been carried on under a name in which his surname appeared.

(2) A limited partner whose name appears in a partnership name contrary to the provisions of paragraph (1) is liable as a general partner to partnership creditors who extend credit to the partnership without actual knowledge that he is not a general partner.

Sec. 6. Liability for False Statements in Certificate.

If the certificate contains a false statement, one who suffers loss by reliance on such statement may hold liable any party to the certificate who knew the statement to be false.

(a) At the time he signed the certificate, or

(b) Subsequently, but within a sufficient time before the statement was relied upon to enable him to cancel or amend the certificate, or to file a petition for its cancellation or amendment as provided in Section 25(3).

Sec. 7. Limited Partner Not Liable to Creditors.

A limited partner shall not become liable as a general partner unless, in addition to the exercise of his rights and powers as a limited partner, he takes part in the control of the business.

Sec. 8. Admission of Additional Limited Partners.

After the formation of a limited partnership, additional limited partners may be admitted upon filing an amendment to the original certificate in accordance with the requirements of Section 25.

Sec. 9. Rights, Powers and Liabilities of a General Partner.

(1) A general partner shall have all the rights and powers and be subject to all the restrictions and liabilities of a partner in a partnership without limited partners, except that without the written consent or ratification of the specific act by all the limited partners, a general partner or all of the general partners have no authority to

(a) Do any act in contravention of the certificate,

(b) Do any act which would make it impossible to carry on the ordinary business of the partnership,

(c) Confess a judgment against the partnership,

(d) Possess partnership property, or assign their rights in specific partnership property, for other than a partnership purpose,

(e) Admit a person as a general partner,

(f) Admit a person as a limited partner, unless the right so to do is given in the certificate,

(g) Continue the business with partnership property on the death, retirement or insanity of a general partner, unless the right so to do is given in the certificate.

Sec. 10 Rights of a Limited Partner.

(1) A limited partner shall have the same rights as a general partner to

(a) Have the partnership books kept at the principal place of business of the partnership, and at all times to inspect and copy any of them,

(b) Have on demand true and full information of all things affecting the partnership, and a formal account of partnership affairs, whenever circumstances render it just and reasonable, and

(c) Have dissolution and winding up by decree of court.

(2) A limited partner shall have the right to receive a share of the profits or other compensation by way of income, and to the return of his contribution as provided in Sections 15 and 16.

Sec. 11. Status of Person Erroneously Believing Himself a Limited Partner.

A person who has contributed to the capital of a business conducted by a person or partnership erroneously believing that he has become a limited partner in a limited partnership, is not, by reason of his exercise of the rights of a limited partner, a general partner with the person or in the partnership carrying on the business, or bound by the obligations of such person or partnership; provided that on ascertaining the mistake he promptly renounces his interest in the profits of the business, or other compensation by way of income.

Sec. 12. One Person Both General and Limited Partner.

(1) A person may be a general partner and a limited partner in the same partnership at the same time.

(2) A person who is a general, and also at the same time a limited partner, shall have all the rights and powers and be subject to all the restrictions of a general partner; except that, in respect to his contribution, he shall have the rights against the other members which he would have had if he were not also a general partner.

Sec. 13. Loans and Other Business Transactions with Limited Partner.

(1) A limited partner also may loan money to and transact other business with the partnership, and, unless he is also a general partner, receive on account of resulting claims against the partnership, with general creditors, a pro rata share of the assets. No limited partner shall in respect to any such claim

 (a) Receive or hold as collateral security any partnership property, or

 (b) Receive from a general partner or the partnership any payment, conveyance, or release from liability, if at the time the assets of the partnership are not sufficient to discharge partnership liabilities to persons not claiming as general or limited partners.

(2) The receiving of collateral security, or a payment, conveyance, or release in violation of the provisions of paragraph (1) is a fraud on the creditors of the partnership.

Sec. 14. Relation of Limited Partners Inter Se.

Where there are several limited partners the members may agree that one or more of the limited partners shall have a priority over other limited partners as to the return of their contributions, as to their compensation by way of income, or as to any other matter. If such an agreement is made it shall be stated in the certificate, and in the absence of such a statement all the limited partners shall stand upon equal footing.

Sec. 15. Compensation of Limited Partner.

A limited partner may receive from the partnership the share of the profits or the compensation by way of income stipulated for in the certificate; provided, that after such payment is made, whether from the property of the partnership or that of a general partner, the partnership assets are in excess of all liabilities of the partnership except liabilities to limited partners on account of their contributions and to general partners.

Sec. 16. Withdrawal or Reduction of Limited Partner's Contribution.

(1) A limited partner shall not receive from a general partner or out of partnership property any part of his contribution until

 (a) All liabilities of the partnership, except liabilities to general partners and to limited partners on account of their contributions, have been paid or there remains property of the partnership sufficient to pay them,

 (b) The consent of all members is had, unless the return of the contribution may be rightfully demanded under the provisions of paragraph (2), and

 (c) The certificate is cancelled or so amended as to set forth the withdrawal or reduction.

(2) Subject to the provisions of paragraph (1) a limited partner may rightfully demand the return of his contribution

 (a) On the dissolution of a partnership, or

 (b) When the date specified in the certificate for its return has arrived, or

 (c) After he has given six months' notice in writing to all other members, if no time is specified in the certificate either for the return of the contribution or for the dissolution of the partnership.

(3) In the absence of any statement in the certificate to the contrary or the consent of all members, a limited partner, irrespective of the nature of his contribution, has only the right to demand and receive cash in return for his contribution.

(4) A limited partner may have the partnership dissolved and its affairs wound up when

 (a) He rightfully but unsuccessfully demands the return of his contribution, or

(b) The other liabilities of the partnership have not been paid, or the partnership property is insufficient for their payment as required by paragraph (1a) and the limited partner would otherwise be entitled to the return of his contribution.

Sec. 17. Liability of Limited Partner to Partnership.

(1) A limited partner is liable to the partnership

(a) For the difference between his contribution as actually made and that stated in the certificate as having been made, and

(b) For any unpaid contribution which he agreed in the certificate to make in the future at the time and on the conditions stated in the certificate.

(2) A limited partner holds as trustee for the partnership

(a) Specific property stated in the certificate as contributed by him, but which was not contributed or which has been wrongfully returned, and

(b) Money or other property wrongfully paid or conveyed to him on account of his contribution.

(3) The liabilities of a limited partner as set forth in this section can be waived or compromised only by the consent of all members; but a waiver or compromise shall not affect the right of a creditor of a partnership, who extended credit or whose claim arose after the filing and before a cancellation or amendment of the certificate, to enforce such liabilities.

(4) When a contributor has rightfully received the return in whole or in part of the capital of his contribution, he is nevertheless liable to the partnership for any sum, not in excess of such return with interest, necessary to discharge its liabilities to all creditors who extended credit or whose claims arose before such return.

Sec. 18. Nature of Limited Partner's Interest in Partnership.

A limited partner's interest in the partnership is personal property.

Sec. 19. Assignment of Limited Partner's Interest.

(1) A limited partner's interest is assignable.

(2) A substituted limited partner is a person admitted to all the rights of a limited partner who has died or has assigned his interest in a partnership.

(3) An assignee, who does not become a substituted limited partner, has no right to require any information or account of the partnership transactions or to inspect the partnership books; he is only entitled to receive the share of the profits or other compensation by way of income, or the return of his contribution, to which his assignor would otherwise be entitled.

(4) An assignee shall have the right to become a substituted limited partner if all the members (except the assignor) consent thereto or if the assignor, being thereunto empowered by the certificate, gives the assignee that right.

(5) An assignee becomes a substituted limited partner when the certificate is appropriately amended in accordance with Section 25.

(6) The substituted limited partner has all the rights and powers, and is subject to all the restrictions and liabilities of his assignor, except those liabilities of which he was ignorant at the time he became a limited partner and which could not be ascertained from the certificate.

(7) The substitution of the assignee as a limited partner does not release the assignor from liability to the partnership under Sections 6 and 17.

Sec. 20. Effect of Retirement, Death or Insanity of a General Partner.

The retirement, death or insanity of a general partner dissolves the partnership, unless the business is continued by the remaining general partners

(a) Under a right so to do stated in the certificate, or

(b) With the consent of all members.

Sec. 21. Death of Limited Partner.

(1) On the death of a limited partner his executor or administrator shall have all the rights of a limited partner for the purpose of settling his estate, and such power as the deceased had to constitute his assignee a substituted limited partner.

(2) The estate of a deceased limited partner shall be liable for all his liabilities as a limited partner.

Sec. 22. Rights of Creditors of Limited Partner.

(1) On due application to a court of competent jurisdiction by any judgment creditor of a limited partner, the court may charge the interest of the indebted limited partner with payment of the unsatisfied amount of the judgment debt; and may appoint a receiver, and make all other orders, directions, and inquiries which the circumstances of the case may require.

In those states where a creditor on beginning an action can attach debts due the defendant before he has obtained a judgment against the defendant it is recommended that paragraph (1) of this section read as follows:

On due application to a court of competent jurisdiction by any creditor of a limited partner, the court may charge the interest of the indebted limited partner with payment of the unsatisfied amount of such claim; and may appoint a receiver, and make all other orders, directions, and inquiries which the circumstances of the case may require.

(2) The interest may be redeemed with the separate property of any general partner, but may not be redeemed with partnership property.

(3) The remedies conferred by paragraph (1) shall not be deemed exclusive of others which may exist.

(4) Nothing in this act shall be held to deprive a limited partner of his statutory exemption.

Sec. 23. Distribution of Assets.

(1) In settling accounts after dissolution the liabilities of the partnership shall be entitled to payment in the following order:

(a) Those to creditors, in the order of priority as provided by law, except those to limited partners on account of their contributions, and to general partners,

(b) Those to limited partners in respect to their share of the profits and other compensation by way of income on their contributions,

(c) Those to limited partners in respect to the capital of their contributions,

(d) Those to general partners other than for capital and profits,

(e) Those to general partners in respect to profits,

(f) Those to general partners in respect to capital.

(2) Subject to any statement in the certificate or to subsequent agreement, limited partners share in the partnership assets in respect to their claims for capital, and in respect to their claims for profits or for compensation by way of income on their contributions respectively, in proportion to the respective amounts of such claims.

Sec. 24. When Certificate Shall be Cancelled or Amended.

(1) The certificate shall be cancelled when the partnership is dissolved or all limited partners cease to be such.

(2) A certificate shall be amended when

(a) There is a change in the name of the partnership or in the amount or character of the contribution of any limited partner,

(b) A person is substituted as a limited partner,

(c) An additional limited partner is admitted,

(d) A person is admitted as a general partner,

(e) A general partner retires, dies or becomes insane, and the business is continued under section 20,

(f) There is a change in the character of the business of the partnership,

(g) There is a false or erroneous statement in the certificate,

(h) There is a change in the time as stated in the certificate for the dissolution of the partnership or for the return of a contribution,

(i) A time is fixed for the dissolution of the partnership, or the return of a contribution, no time having been specified in the certificate, or

(j) The members desire to make a change in any other statement in the certificate in order that it shall accurately represent the agreement between them.

Sec. 25. Requirements for Amendment and for Cancellation of Certificate.

(1) The writing to amend a certificate shall

(a) Conform to the requirements of Section 2(1a) as far as necessary to set forth clearly the change in the certificate which it is desired to make, and

(b) Be signed and sworn to by all members, and an amendment substituting a limited partner or adding a limited or general partner shall be signed also by the member to be substituted or added, and when a limited partner is to be substituted, the amendment shall also be signed by the assigning limited partner.

(2) The writing to cancel a certificate shall be signed by all members.

(3) A person desiring the cancellation or amendment of a certificate, if any person designated in paragraphs (1) and (2) as a person who must execute the writing refuses to do so, may petition the [here designate the proper court] to direct a cancellation or amendment thereof.

(4) If the court finds that the petitioner has a right to have the writing executed by a person who refuses to do so, it shall order the [here designate the responsible official in the office designated in Section 2] in the office where the certificate is recorded to record the cancellation or amendment of the certificate; and where the certificate is to be amended, the court shall also cause to be filed for record in said office a certified copy of its decree setting forth the amendment.

(5) A certificate is amended or cancelled when there is filed for record in the office [here designate the office designated in Section 2] where the certificate is recorded

(a) A writing in accordance with the provisions of paragraph (1), or (2) or

(b) A certified copy of the order of court in accordance with the provisions of paragraph (4).

(6) After the certificate is duly amended in accordance with this section, the amended certificate shall thereafter be for all purposes the certificate provided for by this act.

Sec. 26. **Parties to Actions.**

A contributor, unless he is a general partner, is not a proper party to proceedings by or against a partnership, except where the object is to enforce a limited partner's right against or liability to the partnership.

Sec. 27. **Name of Act.**

This act may be cited as The Uniform Limited Partnership Act.

Sec. 28. **Rules of Construction.**

(1) The rule that statutes in derogation of the common law are to be strictly construed shall have no application to this act.

(2) This act shall be so interpreted and construed as to effect its general purpose to make uniform the law of those states which enact it.

(3) This act shall not be so construed as to impair the obligations of any contract existing when the act goes into effect, nor to affect any action on proceedings begun or right accrued before this act takes effect.

Sec. 29. **Rules for Cases Not Provided for in this Act.**

In any case not provided for in this act the rules of law and equity, including the law merchant, shall govern.

Sec. 30.[1] **Provisions for Existing Limited Partnerships.**

(1) A limited partnership formed under any statute of this state prior to the adoption of this act, may become a limited partnership under this act by complying with the provisions of Section 2; provided the certificate sets forth

(a) The amount of the original contribution of each limited partner, and the time when the contribution was made, and

(b) That the property of the partnership exceeds the amount sufficient to discharge its liabilities to persons not claiming as general or limited partners by an amount greater than the sum of the contributions of its limited partners.

(2) A limited partnership formed under any statute of this state prior to the adoption of this act, until or unless it becomes a limited partnership under this act, shall continue to be governed by the provisions of [here insert proper reference to the existing limited partnership act or acts], except that such partnership shall not be renewed unless so provided in the original agreement.

Sec. 31.[1] **Act [Acts] Repealed.**

Except as affecting existing limited partnerships to the extent set forth in Section 30, the act (acts) of [here designate the existing limited partnership act or acts] is (are) hereby repealed.

[1]Sections 30, 31, will be omitted in any state which has not a limited partnership act.

THE REVISED UNIFORM LIMITED PARTNERSHIP ACT

(Adopted August 5, 1976, by the National Conference of Commissioners on Uniform State Laws, subject to style changes; it is intended that it will replace the existing Uniform Limited Partnership Act (Appendix C); as of publication, it has been adopted in Arkansas, Colorado, Connecticut, Maryland, Minnesota, Montana, Nebraska, Washington, West Virginia, and Wyoming.

The Act consists of 11 Articles as follows:

1. General Provisions
2. Formation; Certificate of Limited Partnership
3. Limited Partners
4. General Partners
5. Finance
6. Distribution and Withdrawal
7. Assignment of Partnership Interests
8. Dissolution
9. Foreign Limited Partnerships
10. Derivative Actions
11. Miscellaneous

Article 1
GENERAL PROVISIONS

Sec. 101. **Definitions.**

As used in this Act:

(1) "Certificate of limited partnership" means the certificate referred to in Section 201, as that certificate is amended from time to time.

(2) "Contribution" means any cash, property, or services rendered, or a promissory note or other binding obligation to contribute cash or property or to perform services, which a partner contributes to a limited partnership in his capacity as a partner.

(3) "Event of withdrawal of a general partner" means an event that causes a person to cease to be a general partner as provided in Section 402.

(4) "Foreign limited partnership" means a partnership formed under the laws of any state other than this State and having as partners one or more general partners and one or more limited partners.

(5) "General partner" means a person who has been admitted to a limited partnership as a general partner in accordance with the partnership agreement and who is named in the certificate of limited partnership as a general partner.

(6) "Limited partner" means a person who has been admitted to a limited partnership as a limited partner in accordance with the partnership agreement and who is named in the certificate of limited partnership as a limited partner.

(7) "Limited partnership" and "domestic limited partnership" mean a partnership formed by 2 or more persons under the laws of this State and having one or more general partners and one or more limited partners.

(8) "Partner" means any limited partner or general partner.

(9) "Partnership agreement" means the agreement, written or, to the extent not prohibited by law, oral or both, of the partners as to the affairs of a limited partnership and the conduct of its business.

(10) "Partnership interest" has the meaning specified in Section 701.

(11) "Person" means a natural person, partnership, limited partnership (domestic or foreign), trust, estate, association, or corporation.

(12) "State" means a state, territory, or possession of the United States, the District of Columbia, or the Commonwealth of Puerto Rico.

Sec. 102. **Name.**

The name of each limited partnership as set forth in its certificate of limited partnership:

(1) shall contain the words "limited partnership" in full;

(2) may not contain the name of a limited partner unless (i) it is also the name of a general partner or (ii) the business of the limited partnership had been carried on under that name before the admission of that limited partner;

(3) may not contain any word or phrase indicating or implying that it is organized other than for a purpose stated in its certificate of limited partnership;

(4) may not be the same as, or deceptively similar to, the name of any corporation or limited partnership organized under the laws of this State or licensed or registered as a foreign corporation or limited partnership in this State; and

(5) may not contain the following words [here insert prohibited words].

Sec. 103. **Reservation of Name.**

(a) The exclusive right to the use of a name may be reserved by:

(1) any person intending to organize a limited partnership under this Act and to adopt that name;

(2) any domestic limited partnership or any foreign limited partnership registered in this State which, in either case, intends to adopt that name;

(3) any foreign limited partnership intending to register in this State and to adopt that name; and

(4) any person intending to organize a foreign limited partnership and intending to have it registered in this State and to adopt that name.

(b) The reservation shall be made by filing with the Secretary of State an application, executed by the applicant, to reserve a specified name. If the Secretary of State finds that the name is available for use by a domestic or foreign limited partnership, he shall reserve the name for the exclusive use of the applicant for a period of 120 days. Once having reserved a name, the same applicant may not again reserve the same name until more than 60 days after the expiration of the last 120-day period for which that applicant had reserved that name. The right to the exclusive use of a name so reserved may be transferred to any other person by filing in the office of the Secretary of State a notice of the transfer, executed by the applicant for whom the name was reserved and specifying the name and address of the transferee.

Sec. 104. **Specified Office and Agent.**

Each limited partnership shall continuously maintain in this State:

(1) an office, which may but need not be a place of its business in this State, at which shall be kept the records required to be maintained by Section 105; and

(2) an agent for service of process on the limited partnership, which agent must be an individual resident of this State, a domestic corporation, or a foreign corporation authorized to do business in this State.

Sec. 105. **Records to be Kept.**

Each limited partnership shall keep at the office referred to in Section 104(1) the following: (1) a current list of the full name and last-known business address of each partner set forth in alphabetical order, (2) a copy of the certificate of limited partnership and all certificates of amendment thereto, together with executed copies of any powers of attorney pursuant to which any certificate has been executed, (3) copies of the limited partnership's federal, state, and local income tax returns and reports, if any, for the 3 most recent years, and (4) copies of any then effective written partnership agreements and of any financial statements of the limited partnership for the 3 most recent years. These records shall be available for inspection and copying at the reasonable request, and at the expense, of any partner during ordinary business hours.

Sec. 106. **Nature of Business.**

A limited partnership may carry on any business that a partnership without limited partners may carry on except [here designate prohibited activities].

Sec. 107. **Business Transactions of Partner with the Partnership.**

Except as otherwise provided in the partnership agreement, a partner may lend money to and transact other business with the limited partnership and, subject to other applicable provisions of law, has the same rights and obligations with respect thereto as a person who is not a partner.

Article 2
FORMATION; CERTIFICATE OF LIMITED PARTNERSHIP

Sec. 201. **Certificate of Limited Partnership.**

(a) Two or more persons desiring to form a limited partnership shall execute a certificate of limited partnership. The certificate shall be filed in the office of the Secretary of State and shall set forth:

(1) the name of the limited partnership;

(2) the general character of its business;

(3) the address of the office and the name and address of the agent for service of process required to be maintained by Section 104;

(4) the name and the business address of each partner (specifying the general partners and limited partners separately);

(5) the amount of cash and a description and statement of the agreed value of the other property or services contributed by each partner and which each partner has agreed to contribute in the future;

(6) the times at which or events on the happening of which any additional contributions agreed to be made by each partner are to be made;

(7) any power of a limited partner to grant an assignee of any part of his partnership interest the right to become a limited partner, and the terms and conditions of the power;

(8) if agreed upon, the time at which or the events on the happening of which a partner may terminate his membership in the limited partnership and the amount of, or the method of determining, the distribution to which he may be entitled respecting his partnership interest, and the terms and conditions of the termination and distribution;

(9) any right of a partner to receive distributions of property including cash from the limited partnership;

(10) any right of a partner to receive, or of a general partner to make, distributions to a partner which include a return of all or any part of the partner's contribution;

(11) any time at which or events upon the happening of which the limited partnership is to be dissolved and its affairs wound up;

(12) any right of the remaining general partners to continue the business on the happening of an event of withdrawal of a general partner; and

(13) any other matters the partners, in their sole discretion, determine to include therein.

(b) A limited partnership is formed at the time of the filing of the certificate of limited partnership in the office of the Secretary of State or at any later time specified in the certificate of limited partnership if, in each case, there has been substantial compliance with the requirements of this section.

Sec. 202. **Amendments to Certificate.**

(a) A certificate of limited partnership is amended by filing a certificate of amendment thereto in the office of the Secretary of State. The certificate shall set forth:

(1) the name of the limited partnership;

(2) the date of filing of the certificate; and

(3) the amendments to the certificate.

(b) Within 30 days after the happening of any of the following events an amendment to a certificate of limited partnership reflecting the occurrence of the event or events shall be filed:

(1) a change in the amount or character of the contribution of any partner, or in any partner's obligation to make a contribution;

(2) the admission of a new partner;

(3) the withdrawal of a partner; and

(4) the continuation of the business under Section 801 after an event of withdrawal of a general partner.

(c) A certificate of limited partnership must be amended promptly by any general partner upon becoming aware that any statement therein was false when made or that any arrangements or other facts described have changed, making the certificate inaccurate in any respect, but amendments to show changes of addresses of limited partners need be filed only once every 12 months.

(d) A certificate of limited partnership may be amended at any time for any other proper purpose the general partners may determine.

(e) No person shall have any liability because an amendment to a certificate of limited partnership has not been filed to reflect the occurrence of any event referred to in subsection (b) of this section if the amendment is filed within the 30-day period specified in subsection (b).

Sec. 203. **Cancellation of Certificate.**

A certificate of limited partnership shall be cancelled upon the dissolution and the commencement of winding up of the limited partnership and at any other time there are no remaining limited partners. A certificate of cancellation shall be filed in the office of the Secretary of State and shall set forth:

(1) the name of the limited partnership;

(2) the date of filing of its certificate of limited partnership;

(3) the reason for filing the certificate of cancellation;

(4) the effective date (which shall be a date certain) of cancellation if it is not to be effective upon the filing of the certificate; and

(5) any other information the general partners filing the certificate may determine.

Sec. 204. **Execution of Certificates.**

(a) Each certificate required by this Article to be filed in the office of the Secretary of State shall be executed in the following manner:

(1) each original certificate of limited partnership must be signed by each partner named therein;

(2) each certificate of amendment must be signed by at least one general partner and by each other partner who is designated in the certificate as a new partner or whose contribution is described as having been increased; and

(3) each certificate of cancellation must be signed by each general partner.

(b) Any person may sign a certificate by an attorney-in-fact, but any power of attorney to sign a certificate relating to the admission or increased contribution of a partner must specifically describe the admission or increase.

(c) The execution of a certificate by a general partner constitutes an affirmation under the penalties of perjury that the facts stated therein are true.

Sec. 205. **Amendment or Cancellation by Judicial Act.**

If the persons required by Section 204 to execute any certificate of amendment or cancellation fail or refuse to do so, any other partner, and any assignee of a partnership interest, who is adversely affected by the failure or refusal, may petition the [here designate the proper court] to direct the amendment or cancellation. If the court finds that the amendment or cancellation is proper and that the persons so designated have failed or refused to execute the certificate, it shall order the Secretary of State to record an appropriate certificate of amendment or cancellation.

Sec. 206. **Filing in the Office of the Secretary of State.**

(a) Two signed copies of the certificate of limited partnership and of any certificates of amendment or cancellation (or of any judicial decree of amendment or cancellation) shall be delivered to the Secretary of State. A person who executes a certificate as an agent or fiduciary need not exhibit evidence of his authority as a prerequisite to filing. Unless the Secretary of State finds that any certificate does not conform to law, upon receipt of all filing fees required by law the Secretary of State shall:

(1) endorse on each duplicate original the word "Filed" and the day, month, and year of the filing thereof;

(2) file one duplicate original in his office; and

(3) return the other duplicate original to the person who filed it or his representative.

(b) Upon the filing of a certificate of amendment (or judicial decree of amendment) in the office of the Secretary of State, the certificate of limited partnership shall be amended as set forth therein, and upon the effective date of a certificate of cancellation (or a judicial decree thereof), the certificate of limited partnership shall be cancelled.

Sec. 207. **Liability for False Statement in Certificate.**

If any certificate of limited partnership or certificate of amendment or cancellation contains a false statement, one who suffers loss by reliance on the statement may recover damages for the loss from:

(1) any person actually executing, or causing another to execute on his behalf, the certificate who knew, and any general partner who knew or should have known, the statement to be false at the time the certificate was executed; and

(2) any general partner who thereafter knew or should have known that any arrangements or other facts described in the certificate have changed, making the statement inaccurate in any respect, within a sufficient time before the statement was relied upon to have reasonably enabled that general

partner to cancel or amend the certificate, or to file a petition for its cancellation or amendment under Section 205.

Sec. 208. Constructive Notice.

The fact that a certificate of limited partnership is on file in the office of the Secretary of State is constructive notice that the partnership is a limited partnership and that the persons designated therein as limited partners are limited partners, but is not constructive notice of any other fact.

Sec. 209. Delivery of Certificates to Limited Partners.

Upon the return by the Secretary of State pursuant to Section 206 of any certificate marked "Filed," the general partners shall promptly deliver or mail a copy of the certificate to each limited partner unless the partnership agreement provides otherwise.

Article 3
LIMITED PARTNERS

Sec. 301. Admission of Additional Limited Partners.

(a) After the filing of a limited partnership's original certificate of limited partnership, a person may be admitted as a new limited partner:

(1) in the case of a person acquiring a partnership interest directly from the limited partnership, upon compliance with the partnership agreement or, if the partnership agreement does not so provide, upon the written consent of all partners; and

(2) in the case of an assignee of a partnership interest of a partner who has the power, as provided in Section 704, to grant the assignee the right to become a limited partner, upon the exercise of that power and compliance with any conditions limiting the grant or exercise of the power.

(b) In each case under subsection (a), the person acquiring the partnership interest becomes a limited partner only upon amendment of the certificate of limited partnership reflecting that fact.

Sec. 302. Voting.

Subject to the provisions of Section 303, the partnership agreement may grant to all or a specified group of the limited partners the right to vote (on a per capita or any other basis) upon any matter.

Sec. 303. Liability to Third Parties.

(a) Except as provided in subsection (d), a limited partner as such is not liable for the obligations of a limited partnership unless, in addition to the exercise of his rights and powers as a limited partner, he takes part in the control of the business. But the limited partner's participation in the control of the business is not substantially the same as the exercise of the powers of a general partner, he is liable only to persons who transact business with the limited partnership with actual knowledge of his participation in control.

(b) A limited partner does not participate in the control of the business within the meaning of subsection (a) solely by doing one or more of the following:

(1) being a contractor for or an agent or employee of the limited partnership or of a general partner;

(2) consulting with and advising a general partner with respect to the business of the limited partnership;

(3) acting as surety for the limited partnership;

(4) approving or disapproving an amendment to the partnership agreement; and

(5) voting on one or more of the following matters:

(i) the dissolution and winding up of the limited partnership;

(ii) the sale, exchange, lease, mortgage, pledge, or other transfer of all or substantially all of the assets of the limited partnership other than in the ordinary course of its business;

(iii) the incurrence of indebtedness by the limited partnership other than in the ordinary course of its business;

(iv) a change in the nature of the business; or

(v) the removal of a general partner.

(c) The enumeration in subsection (b) shall not be construed to mean that the possession or exercise of any other powers by a limited partner constitutes participation by him in the business of the limited partnership.

(d) A limited partner who knowingly permits his name to be used in the name of the limited partnership, except under circumstances permitted by Section 102(2)(i), is liable to creditors who extend credit to the limited partnership without actual knowledge that the limited partner is not a general partner.

Sec. 304. Person Erroneously Believing Himself a Limited Partner.

(a) Except as provided in subsection (b) a person who makes a contribution to a business enterprise and erroneously and in good faith believes that he has become a limited partner in the enterprise is not a general partner in the enterprise and is not bound by its obligations by reason of making the contribution, receiving distributions from the enterprise, or exercising any rights of a limited partner, if, on ascertaining the mistake, he:

(1) causes an appropriate certificate of limited partnership or a certificate of amendment to be executed and filed; or

(2) withdraws from future equity participation in the enterprise.

(b) Any person who makes a contribution of the kind described in subsection (a) is liable as a general partner to any third party who transacts business with the enterprise (i) before the person withdraws and an appropriate certificate if any is filed to show the withdrawal, or (ii) before an appropriate certificate is filed to show his status as a limited partner and, in the case of an amendment, after expiration of the 30-day period for filing an amendment relating to the person as a limited partner under Section 202, but in each case only if the third party actually believed in good faith that the person was a general partner at the time of the transaction.

Sec. 305. Information.

Each limited partner has the right to:

(1) inspect and copy any of the partnership records required to be maintained by Section 105; and

(2) obtain from the general partners from time to time upon reasonable demand (i) true and full information regarding the state of the business and financial condition of the limited partnership, (ii) promptly after becoming available, a copy of the limited partnership's federal, state, and local income tax return for each year, and (iii) any other information regarding the affairs of the limited partnership as is just and reasonable.

Article 4
GENERAL PARTNERS

Sec. 401. Admission.

After the filing of a limited partnership's original certificate of limited partnership, new general partners may be admitted only with the specific written consent of each partner.

Sec. 402. Events of Withdrawal.

Except as otherwise approved by the specific written consent at the time of all partners, a person ceases to be a general partner of a limited partnership upon the happening of any of the following events:

(1) the general partner withdraws from the limited partnership as provided in Section 602;

(2) the general partner ceases to be a member of the limited partnership as provided in Section 702;

(3) the general partner is removed as a general partner in accordance with the partnership agreement;

(4) unless otherwise provided in the certificate of limited partnership, the general partner: makes an assignment for the benefit of creditors; files a voluntary petition in bankruptcy; is adjudicated a bankrupt or insolvent; files any petition or answer seeking for himself any reorganization, arrangement, composition, readjustment, liquidation, dissolution, or similar relief under any statute, law, or regulation; files any answer or other pleading admitting or failing to contest the material allegations of a petition filed against him in any proceeding of this nature; or seeks, consents to, or acquiesces in the appointment of any trustee, receiver, or liquidator of the general partner or of all or any substantial part of his properties;

(5) unless otherwise provided in the certificate of limited partnership, [120] days after the commencement of any proceeding against the general partner seeking any reorganization, arrangement, composition, readjustment, liquidation, dissolution, or similar relief under any statute, law, or regulation, the proceeding has not been dismissed, or if, within [90] days after the appointment without his consent or acquiescence of any trustee, receiver, or liquidator of the general partner or of all or any substantial part of his properties, the appointment is not vacated or stayed, or if, within [90] days after the expiration of any stay, the appointment is not vacated;

(6) in the case of a general partner who is a natural person

(i) his death; or

(ii) the entry by a court of competent jurisdiction adjudicating him incompetent to manage his person or his property;

(7) in the case of a general partner who is acting as such in the capacity of a trustee of a trust, the

termination of the trust (but not merely the substitution of a new trustee);

(8) in the case of a general partner that is a partnership, the dissolution and commencement of winding up of the partnership;

(9) in the case of a general partner that is a corporation, the filing of a certificate of dissolution, or its equivalent, for the corporation or the revocation of its charter; and

(10) in the case of an estate, the distribution by the fiduciary of all the estate's interest in the partnership.

Sec. 403. General Powers and Liabilities.

Except as otherwise provided in this Act and in the partnership agreement, a general partner of a limited partnership has all the rights and powers and is subject to all the restrictions and liabilities of a partner in a partnership without limited partners.

Sec. 404. Contributions by a General Partner.

A general partner may make contributions to a limited partnership and share in the profits and losses of, and in distributions from, the limited partnership as a general partner. A general partner may also make contributions to and share in profits, losses, and distributions as a limited partner. A person who is both a general partner and a limited partner has all the rights and powers, and is subject to all the restrictions and liabilities, of a general partner and also has, except as otherwise provided in the partnership agreement, all powers, and is subject to the restrictions, of a limited partner to the extent he is participating in the partnership as a limited partner.

Sec. 405. Voting.

The partnership agreement may grant to all or a specified group of general partners the right to vote (on a per capita or any other basis), separately or with all or any class of the limited partners, on any matter.

Article 5
FINANCE

Sec. 501. Form of Contributions.

The contribution of a partner may be in cash, property, or services rendered, or a promissory note or other obligation to contribute cash or property or to perform services.

Sec. 502. Liability for Contributions.

(a) Except as otherwise provided in the certificate of limited partnership, a partner is obligated to the limited partnership to perform any promise to contribute cash or property or to perform services regardless of whether he is unable to perform because of death, disability or any other reason. If a partner does not make the required contribution of property or services, he is obligated at the option of the limited partnership to contribute cash equal to that portion of the value (as stated in the certificate of limited partnership) of the stated contribution that has not been made.

(b) Unless otherwise provided in the partnership agreement, the obligation of a partner to make a contribution or return money or other property paid or distributed in violation of this Act may be compromised only by consent of all of the partners. Notwithstanding a compromise so authorized, a creditor of a limited partnership who extends credit, or whose claim arises, after the filing of the certificate of limited partnership or an amendment thereto which, in either case, reflects the obligation and before the amendment or cancellation thereof to reflect the compromise may enforce the precompromise obligation.

Sec. 503. Sharing of Profits and Losses.

The profits and losses of a limited partnership shall be allocated among the partners, and among classes of partners, in the manner provided in the partnership agreement. If the partnership agreement does not so provide, profits and losses shall be allocated on the basis of the value (as stated in the certificate of limited partnership) of the contributions actually made by each partner to the extent they have not been returned.

Sec. 504. Sharing of Distributions.

Distributions of cash or other assets of a limited partnership shall be allocated among the partners, and among classes of partners, in the manner provided in the partnership agreement. If the partnership agreement does not so provide, distributions shall be made on the basis of the value (as stated in the certificate of limited partnership) of the contributions actually made by each partner to the extent they have not been returned.

Article 6
DISTRIBUTIONS AND WITHDRAWAL

Sec. 601. **Interim Distributions.**

Except as otherwise provided in this Article, a partner is entitled to receive distributions from a limited partnership before his withdrawal from the limited partnership and before the dissolution and winding up thereof:

(1) to the extent and at the times or upon the happening of the events specified in the partnership agreement; and

(2) if any distribution constitutes a return of any part of his contribution under Section 608(b), to the extent and at the times or upon the happening of the events specified in the certificate of limited partnership.

Sec. 602. **Withdrawal of General Partner.**

A general partner may withdraw from a limited partnership at any time by giving written notice to the other partners, but if the withdrawal violates the partnership agreement, the limited partnership may recover from the withdrawing general partner damages for breach of the partnership agreement and offset the damages against the amount otherwise distributable to him.

Sec. 603. **Withdrawal of Limited Partner.**

A limited partner may withdraw from a limited partnership at the time or upon the happening of the events specified in the certificate of limited partnership and in accordance with any procedures provided in the partnership agreement. If the certificate of limited partnership does not specify the time or the events upon the happening of which a limited partner may withdraw from the limited partnership or a definite time for the dissolution and winding up of the limited partnership, a limited partner may withdraw from the limited partnership upon not less than 6 months' prior written notice to each general partner at his address on the books of the limited partnership at its office in this State.

Sec. 604. **Distributions Upon Withdrawal.**

Except as provided in this Article, upon withdrawal any withdrawing partner is entitled to receive any distributions to which he is entitled under the partnership agreement and, if not provided, he is entitled to receive, within a reasonable time after withdrawal, the fair value of his interest in the limited partnership as of the date of withdrawal, based upon his right to share in distributions from the limited partnership.

Sec. 605. **Distributions in Kind.**

Except as provided in the certificate of limited partnership, a partner, regardless of the nature of his contribution, has no right to demand and receive any distribution from a limited partnership in any form other than cash. Except as provided in the partnership agreement, a partner may not be compelled to accept a distribution of any asset in kind from a limited partnership to the extent that the percentage of the asset distributed to him exceeds a percentage of that asset which is equal to the percentage in which he shares in distributions from the limited partnership.

Sec. 606. **Right to Distributions.**

At the time a partner becomes entitled to receive a distribution, he has the status of, and is entitled to all of the remedies available to, a creditor of the limited partnership with respect to the distribution.

Sec. 607. **Limitations on Distributions.**

A partner may not receive a distribution from a limited partnership to the extent that, after giving effect to the distribution, all liabilities of the limited partnership other than liabilities to partners on account of their partnership interests, exceed the fair value of the partnership's assets.

Sec. 608. **Liability Upon Return of Contributions.**

(a) If a partner has received the return of any part of his contribution without violation of the partnership agreement or this Act, for a period of one year thereafter he is liable to the limited partnership for the amount of his contribution returned, but only to the extent necessary to discharge the limited partnership's liabilities to creditors who extended credit to the limited partnership during the period the contribution was held by the partnership.

(b) If a partner has received the return of any part of his contribution in violation of the partnership agreement or this Act, for a period of 6 years thereafter he is liable to the limited partnership for the amount of the contribution wrongfully returned.

(c) A partner has received a return of his contribution to the extent that a distribution to him reduces his share of the fair value of the net assets of the limited partnership below the value (as set forth in the certificate of limited partnership) of his contributions which have not theretofore been distributed to him.

Article 7
ASSIGNMENT OF PARTNERSHIP INTERESTS

Sec. 701. **Nature of Partnership Interest.**

A partnership interest is a partner's share of the profits and losses of a limited partnership and the right to receive distributions of partnership assets. A partnership interest is personal property.

Sec. 702. **Assignment of Partnership Interest.**

Except as otherwise provided in the partnership agreement, a partnership interest is assignable in whole or in part. An assignment of a partnership interest does not dissolve a limited partnership nor entitle the assignee to become a partner or to exercise any of the rights thereof. An assignment only entitles the assignee to receive, to the extent assigned, any distributions to which the assignor would be entitled. Except as otherwise provided in the partnership agreement, a partner ceases to be a partner upon assignment of all his partnership interest.

Sec. 703. **Rights of Creditors.**

On due application to a court of competent jurisdiction by any judgment creditor of a partner, the court may charge the partnership interest of the partner with payment of the unsatisfied amount of the judgment debt with interest thereon. To the extent so charged, the judgment creditor has only the rights of an assignee of the partnership interest. This Act shall not be construed to deprive any partner of the benefit of any exemption laws applicable to his partnership interest.

Sec. 704. **Right of Assignee to Become Limited Partner.**

(a) An assignee of a partnership interest, including an assignee of a general partner, may become a limited partner if and to the extent that (1) the assignor gives the assignee that right in accordance with authority described in the certificate of limited partnership or, (2) in the absence of that authority, all other partners consent.

(b) An assignee who has become a limited partner has, to the extent assigned, all the rights and powers, and is subject to all the restrictions and liabilities, of a limited partner under the partnership agreement and this Act. An assignee who becomes a limited partner is also liable for the obligations of his assignor to make and return contributions as provided in Article 6, but the assignee is not obligated for liabilities unknown to the assignee at the time he became a limited partner and which could not be ascertained from the certificate of limited partnership.

(c) If an assignee of a partnership interest becomes a limited partner, the assignor is not released from the liability to the limited partnership under Sections 207 and 502.

Sec. 705. **Power of Estate of Deceased or Incompetent Partner.**

If a partner who is a natural person dies or a court of competent jurisdiction adjudges him to be incompetent to manage his person or his property, the partner's executor, administrator, guardian, conservator, or other legal representative may exercise all of the partner's rights for the purpose of settling his estate or administering his property, including any power the partner had to give an assignee the right to become a limited partner. If a partner that is a corporation, trust, or other entity other than a natural person is dissolved or terminated, those powers may be exercised by the legal representative or successor of the partner.

Article 8
DISSOLUTION

Sec. 801. **Nonjudicial Dissolution.**

A limited partnership is dissolved and its affairs shall be wound up upon the happening of the first to occur of the following:

(1) at the time or upon the happening of the events specified in the certificate of limited partnership;

(2) upon the unanimous written consent of all partners;

(3) upon the happening of an event of withdrawal of a general partner unless at the time there is at least one other general partner and the certificate of limited partnership permits the business of the limited partnership to be carried on by the remaining general partner and he does so, but the limited partnership shall not be dissolved or wound up by reason of any event of withdrawal if, within 90 days after the withdrawal, all partners agree in writing to continue the business of the limited partnership and to the appointment of one or more new general partners if necessary or desired; or

(4) upon entry of a decree of judicial dissolution in accordance with Section 802.

Sec. 802. **Dissolution by Decree of Court.**

On application by or for a partner the [here designate the proper court] court may decree a dissolution of a limited partnership whenever it is not reasonably practicable to carry on the business in conformity with the partnership agreement.

Sec. 803. **Winding Up.**

Unless otherwise provided in the partnership agreement, the general partners who have not wrongfully dissolved the limited partnership or, if none, the limited partners, may wind up the limited partnership's affairs; but any partner, his legal representative or his assignee, upon cause shown, may obtain winding up by the [here designate the proper court] court.

Sec. 804. **Distribution of Assets.**

Upon the winding up of a limited partnership, the assets shall be distributed as follows:

(1) to creditors, including partners who are creditors (to the extent otherwise permitted by law), in satisfaction of liabilities of the limited partnership other than liabilities for distributions to partners pursuant to Section 601 or 604;

(2) except as otherwise provided in the partnership agreement, to partners and ex-partners in satisfaction of liabilities for distributions pursuant to Section 601 or 604; and

(3) except as otherwise provided in the partnership agreement, to partners *first* for the return of their contributions and *second* respecting their partnership interests, in the proportions in which the partners share in distributions.

Article 9
FOREIGN LIMITED PARTNERSHIPS

Sec. 901. **Law Governing.**

Subject to the constitution and public policy of this State, the laws of the state under which a foreign limited partnership is organized govern its organization and internal affairs and the liability of its limited partners, and a foreign limited partnership may not be denied registration by reason of any difference between those laws and the laws of this State.

Sec. 902. **Registration.**

Before transacting business in this State, a foreign limited partnership shall register with the Secretary of State. In order to register, a foreign limited partnership shall submit to the Secretary of State in duplicate an application for registration as a foreign limited partnership, signed and sworn to by a general partner and setting forth:

(1) the name of the foreign limited partnership and, if different, the name under which it proposes to transact business and register in this State;

(2) the state and date of its formation;

(3) the general character of the business it proposes to transact in this State;

(4) the name and address of any agent for service of process on the foreign limited partnership whom the foreign limited partnership desires to appoint, which agent must be an individual resident of this State, a domestic corporation, or a foreign corporation authorized to do business in this State; and with a place of business in this State;

(5) a statement that the Secretary of State is appointed the agent of the foreign limited partnership for service of process if no agent has been appointed pursuant to paragraph (4) or, if appointed the agent's authority has been revoked or the agent cannot be found or served with the exercise of reasonable diligence;

(6) the address of the office required to be maintained in the state of its organization by the laws of that state or, if not so required, of the principal office of the foreign limited partnership; and

(7) if the certificate of limited partnership filed in the foreign limited partnership's state of organization is not required to include the names and business addresses of the partners, a list of the names and addresses.

Sec. 903. **Issuance of Registration.**

(a) If the Secretary of State finds that an application for registration conforms to law and all requisite fees have been paid, he shall:

(1) endorse on the application the word "Filed", and the month, day, and year of the filing thereof;

(2) file in his office one of the duplicate originals of the application; and

(3) issue a certificate of registration to transact business in this State.

(b) The certificate of registration, together with one duplicate original of the application, shall be returned to the person who filed the application or his representative.

Sec. 904. **Name.**

A foreign limited partnership may register with the Secretary of State under any name (whether or not it is the name under which it is registered in its state of organization) that includes the words "limited partnership" and that could be registered by a domestic limited partnership.

Sec. 905. **Changes and Amendments.**

If any statement in a foreign limited partnership's application for registration was false when made or any arrangements or other facts described have changed, making the application inaccurate in any respect, the foreign limited partnership shall promptly file in the office of the Secretary of State a certificate, signed and sworn to by a general partner, correcting the statement.

Sec. 906. **Cancellation of Registration.**

A foreign limited partnership may cancel its registration by filing with the Secretary of State a certificate of cancellation signed and sworn to by a general partner. A cancellation does not terminate the authority of the Secretary of State to accept service of process on the foreign limited partnership with respect to [claims for relief] [causes of action] arising out of the transaction of business in this State.

Sec. 907. **Transaction of Business Without Registration.**

(a) A foreign limited partnership transacting business in this State without registration may not maintain any action, suit, or proceeding in any court of this State until it has registered.

(b) The failure of a foreign limited partnership to register in this State does not impair the validity of any contract or act of the foreign limited partnership, and does not prevent the foreign limited partnership from defending any action, suit, or proceeding in any court of this State.

(c) A limited partner of a foreign limited partnership is not liable as a general partner of the foreign limited partnership solely by reason of the foreign limited partnership's transacting business in this State without registration.

(d) A foreign limited partnership, by transacting business in this State without registration, appoints the Secretary of State as its agent for service of process with respect to [claims for relief] [causes of action] arising out of the transaction of business in this State.

Sec. 908. **Action by [Appropriate Official].**

The [appropriate official] may bring an action to restrain a foreign limited partnership from transacting business in this State in violation of this Article.

Article 10
DERIVATIVE ACTIONS

Sec. 1001. **Right of Action.**

A limited partner may bring an action in the right of a limited partnership to recover a judgment in its favor if the general partners having authority to do so have refused to bring the action or an effort to cause those general partners to bring the action is not likely to succeed.

Sec. 1002. **Proper Plaintiff.**

In a derivative action, the plaintiff must be a partner at (1) the time of bringing the action, and (2) at the time of the transaction of which he complains or his status as a partner must have devolved upon him by operation of law or pursuant to the terms of the partnership agreement from a person who was a partner at the time of the transaction.

Sec. 1003. **Pleading.**

In any derivative action, the complaint shall set forth with particularity the effort of the plaintiff to secure initiation of the action by a general partner having authority to do so or the reasons for not making the effort.

Sec. 1004. **Expenses.**

If a derivative action is successful, in whole or in part, or anything is received by the plaintiff as a result of a judgment, compromise, or settlement of an action or claim, the court may award the plaintiff reasonable expenses, including reasonable attorney's fees, and shall direct him to account to the limited partnership for the remainder of the proceeds so received by him.

Article 11
MISCELLANEOUS

Sec. 1101. **Savings Clause.**

Sec. 1102. **Name of Act.**

This Act may be cited as the Uniform Limited Partnership Act.

Sec. 1103. **Construction and Application.**

This Act shall be so construed and applied to effect its

general purpose to make uniform the law with respect to the subject of this Act among states enacting it.

Sec. 1104. **Rules for Cases Not Provided for in This Act.** In any case not provided for in this Act the provisions of the Uniform Partnership Act govern.

Sec. 1105. **Act Repealed.**

Except as affecting existing limited partnerships to the extent set forth in Section _____, the Act of [here designate the existing limited partnership act or acts] is hereby repealed.

Appendix G

THE MODEL BUSINESS CORPORATION ACT

§ 1. **Short Title***

This Act shall be known and may be cited as the
".....† Business Corporation Act."

§ 2. **Definitions**

As used in this Act, unless the context otherwise
requires, the term:

(a) "Corporation" or "domestic corporation" means
a corporation for profit subject to the provisions of
this Act, except a foreign corporation.

(b) "Foreign corporation" means a corporation for
profit organized under laws other than the laws of this
State for a purpose or purposes for which a corporation may be organized under this Act.

(c) "Articles of incorporation" means the original or
restated articles of incorporation or articles of
consolidation and all amendments thereto including
articles of merger.

(d) "Shares" means the units into which the proprietary interests in a corporation are divided.

(e) "Subscriber" means one who subscribes for
shares in a corporation, whether before or after
incorporation.

(f) "Shareholder" means one who is a holder of record
of shares in a corporation. If the articles of incorporation or the by-laws so provide, the board of directors
may adopt by resolution a procedure whereby a
shareholder of the corporation may certify in writing
to the corporation that all or a portion of the shares
registered in the name of such shareholder are held for
the account of a specified person or persons. The
resolution shall set forth (1) the classification of
shareholder who may certify, (2) the purpose or
purposes for which the certification may be made, (3)
the form of certification and information to be
contained therein, (4) if the certification is with
respect to a record date or closing of the stock transfer
books within which the certification must be received
by the corporation and (5) such other provisions with
respect to the procedure as are deemed necessary or
desirable. Upon receipt by the corporation of a

---

*[By the Editor] The Model Business Corporation Act prepared by the
Committee on Corporate Laws (Section of Corporation, Banking and Business
Law) of the American Bar Association was originally patterned after the Illinois
Business Corporation Act of 1933. It was first published as a complete act in 1950.
In subsequent years several revisions, addenda and optional or alternative
provisions were added. The Act was substantially revised and renumbered in
1979.
This Act should be distinguished from the Model Business Corporation Act
promulgated in 1928 by the Commissioners on Uniform State Laws under the
name "Uniform Business Corporation Act" and renamed Model Business

Corporation Act in 1943. This Uniform Act was withdrawn in 1957.
The Model Business Corporation Act has been influential in the codification of
corporation statutes in more than 35 states. However, there is no state that has
totally adopted it in its current form. Moreover, since the Model Act itself has
been substantially modified from time to time, there is considerable variation
among the statutes of the states that used this Act as a model.

†Supply name of State.

certification complying with the procedure, the persons specified in the certification shall be deemed, for the purpose or purposes set forth in the certification, to be the holders of record of the number of shares specified in place of the shareholder making the certification.

(g) "Authorized shares" means the shares of all classes which the corporation is authorized to issue.

(h) "Employee" includes officers but not directors. A director may accept duties which make him also an employee.

(i) "Distribution" means a direct or indirect transfer of money or other property (except its own shares) or incurrence of indebtedness, by a corporation to or for the benefit of any of its shareholders in respect of any of its shares, whether by dividend or by purchase, redemption or other acquisition of its shares, or otherwise.

(j) "Stated capital" means, at any particular time, the sum of (1) the par value of all shares of the corporation having a par value that have been issued, (2) the amount of the consideration received by the corporation for all shares of the corporation without par value that have been issued, except such part of the consideration therefor as may have been allocated to capital surplus in a manner permitted by law, and (3) such amounts not included in clauses (1) and (2) of this paragraph as have been transferred to stated capital of the corporation, whether upon the issue of shares as a share dividend or otherwise, minus all reductions from such sum as have been effected in a manner permitted by law. Irrespective of the manner of designation thereof by the laws under which a foreign corporation is organized, the stated capital of a foreign corporation shall be determined on the same basis and in the same manner as the stated capital of a domestic corporation, for the purpose of computing fees, franchise taxes and other charges imposed by this Act.

(k) "Surplus" means the excess of the net assets of a corporation over its stated capital.

(l) "Earned surplus" means the portion of the surplus of a corporation equal to the balance of its net profits, income, gains and losses from the date of incorporation, or from the latest date when a deficit was eliminated by an application of its capital surplus or stated capital or otherwise, after deducting subsequent distributions to shareholders and transfers to stated capital and capital surplus to the extent such distributions and transfers are made out of earned surplus. Earned surplus shall include also any portion of surplus allocated to earned surplus in mergers, consolidations or acquisitions of all or substantially

all of the outstanding shares or of the property and assets of another corporation, domestic or foreign.

(m) "Capital surplus" means the entire surplus of a corporation other than its earned surplus.

(n) "Insolvent" means inability of a corporation to pay its debts as they become due in the usual course of its business.

(o) "Employee" includes officers but not directors. A director may accept duties which make him also an employee.

§ 3. Purposes

Corporations may be organized under this Act for any lawful purpose or purposes, except for the purpose of banking or insurance.

§ 4. General Powers

Each corporation shall have power:

(a) To have perpetual succession by its corporate name unless a limited period of duration is stated in its articles of incorporation.

(b) To sue and be sued, complain and defend, in its corporate name.

(c) To have a corporate seal which may be altered at pleasure, and to use the same by causing it, or a facsimile thereof, to be impressed or affixed or in any other manner reproduced.

(d) To purchase, take, receive, lease, or otherwise acquire, own, hold, improve, use and otherwise deal in and with, real or personal property, or any interest therein, wherever situated.

(e) To sell, convey, mortgage, pledge, lease, exchange, transfer and otherwise dispose of all or any part of its property and assets.

(f) To lend money and use its credit to assist its employees.

(g) To purchase, take, receive, subscribe for, or otherwise acquire, own, hold, vote, use, employ, sell, mortgage, lend, pledge, or otherwise dispose of, and otherwise use and deal in and with, shares or other interests in, or obligations of, other domestic or foreign corporations, associations, partnerships or individuals, or direct or indirect obligations of the United States or of any other government, state, territory, governmental district or municipality or of any instrumentality thereof.

(h) To make contracts and guarantees and incur liabilities, borrow money at such rates of interest as the corporation may determine, issue its notes, bonds, and other obligations, and secure any of its obligations by mortgage or pledge of all or any of its property, franchises and income.

(i) To lend money for its corporate purposes, invest and reinvest its funds, and take and hold real and personal property as security for the payment of funds so loaned or invested.

(j) To conduct its business, carry on its operations and have offices and exercise the powers granted by this Act, within or without this State.

(k) To elect or appoint officers and agents of the corporation, and define their duties and fix their compensation.

(l) To make and alter by-laws, not inconsistent with its articles of incorporation or with the laws of this State, for the administration and regulation of the affairs of the corporation.

(m) To make donations for the public welfare or for charitable, scientific or educational purposes.

(n) To transact any lawful business which the board of directors shall find will be in aid of governmental policy.

(o) To pay pensions and establish pension plans, pension trusts, profit sharing plans, stock bonus plans, stock option plans and other incentive plans for any or all of its directors, officers and employees.

(p) To be a promoter, partner, member, associate, or manager of any partnership, joint venture, trust or other enterprise.

(q) To have and exercise all powers necessary or convenient to effect its purposes.

§ 5. Indemnification of Officers, Directors, Employees and Agents

(a) A corporation shall have power to indemnify any person who was or is a party or is threatened to be made a party to any threatened, pending or completed action, suit or proceeding, whether civil, criminal, administrative or investigative (other than an action by or in the right of the corporation) by reason of the fact that he is or was a director, officer, employee or agent of the corporation, or is or was serving at the request of the corporation as a director, officer, employee or agent of another corporation, partnership, joint venture, trust or other enterprise, against expenses (including attorneys' fees), judgments, fines and amounts paid in settlement actually and reasonably incurred by him in connection with such action, suit or proceeding if he acted in good faith and in a manner he reasonably believed to be in or not opposed to the best interests of the corporation, and, with respect to any criminal action or proceeding, had no reasonable cause to believe his conduct was unlawful. The termination of any action, suit or proceeding by judgment, order, settlement, conviction, or upon a plea of nolo contendere or its equivalent, shall not, of itself, create a presumption that the person did not act in good faith and in a manner which he reasonably believed to be in or not opposed to the best interest of the corporation, and, with respect to any criminal action or proceeding, had reasonable cause to believe that his conduct was unlawful.

(b) A corporation shall have power to indemnify any person who was or is a party or is threatened to be made a party to any threatened, pending or completed action or suit by or in the right of the corporation to procure a judgment in its favor by reason of the fact that he is or was a director, officer, employee or agent of the corporation, or is or was serving at the request of the corporation as a director, officer, employee or agent of another corporation, partnership, joint venture, trust or other enterprise against expenses (including attorneys' fees) actually and reasonably incurred by him in connection with the defense or settlement of such action or suit if he acted in good faith and in a manner he reasonably believed to be in or not opposed to the best interests of the corporation and except that no indemnification shall be made in respect of any claim, issue or matter as to which such person shall have been adjudged to be liable for negligence or misconduct in the performance of his duty to the corporation unless and only to the extent that the court in which such action or suit was brought shall determine upon application that, despite the adjudication of liability but in view of all circumstances of the case, such person is fairly and reasonably entitled to indemnity for such expenses which such court shall deem proper.

(c) To the extent that a director, officer, employee or agent of a corporation has been successful on the merits or otherwise in defense of any action, suit or proceeding referred to in subsections (a) or (b), or in defense of any claim, issue or matter therein, he shall be indemnified against expenses (including attorneys' fees) actually and reasonably incurred by him in connection therewith.

(d) Any indemnification under subsections (a) or (b) (unless ordered by a court) shall be made by the corporation only as authorized in the specific case upon a determination that indemnification of the director, officer, employee or agent is proper in the circumstances because he has met the applicable standard of conduct set forth in subsections (a) or (b). Such determination shall be made (1) by the board of directors by a majority vote of a quorum consisting of directors who were not parties to such action, suit or proceeding, or (2) if such a quorum is not obtainable, or, even if obtainable a quorum of disinterested directors so directs, by independent legal counsel in a written opinion, or (3) by the shareholders.

(e) Expenses (including attorneys' fees) incurred in defending a civil or criminal action, suit or proceeding may be paid by the corporation in advance of the final disposition of such action, suit or proceeding as authorized in the manner provided in subsection (d) upon receipt of an undertaking by or on behalf of the director, officer, employee or agent to repay such amount unless it shall ultimately be determined that he is entitled to be indemnified by the corporation as authorized in this section.

(f) The indemnification provided by this section shall not be deemed exclusive of any other rights to which those indemnified may be entitled under any by-law, agreement, vote of shareholders or disinterested directors or otherwise, both as to action in his official capacity and as to action in another capacity while holding such office, and shall continue as to a person who has ceased to be a director, officer, employee or agent and shall inure to the benefit of the heirs, executors and administrators of such a person.

(g) A corporation shall have power to purchase and maintain insurance on behalf of any person who is or was a director, officer, employee or agent of the corporation, or is or was serving at the request of the corporation as a director, officer, employee or agent of another corporation, partnership, joint venture, trust or other enterprise against any liability asserted against him and incurred by him in any such capacity or arising out of his status as such, whether or not the corporation would have the power to indemnify him against such liability under the provisions of this section.

§ 6. Power of Corporation to Acquire Its Own Shares

A corporation shall have the power to acquire its own shares. All of its own shares acquired by a corporation shall, upon acquisition, constitute authorized but unissued shares, unless the articles of incorporation provide that they shall not be reissued, in which case the authorized shares shall be reduced by the number of shares acquired.

If the number of authorized shares is reduced by an acquisition, the corporation shall, not later than the time it files its next annual report under this Act with the Secretary of State, file a statement of cancellation showing the reduction in the authorized shares. The statement of cancellation shall be executed in duplicate by the corporation by its president or a vice president and by its secretary or an

assistant secretary, and verified by one of the officers signing such statement, and shall set forth:

(a) The name of the corporation.

(b) The number of acquired shares cancelled, itemized by classes and series.

(c) The aggregate number of authorized shares, itemized by classes and series, after giving effect to such cancellation.

Duplicate originals of such statement shall be delivered to the Secretary of State. If the Secretary of State finds that such statement conforms to law, he shall, when all fees and franchise taxes have been paid as in this Act prescribed:

(1) Endorse on each of such duplicate originals the word "Filed", and the month, day and year of the filing thereof.

(2) File one of such duplicate originals in his office.

(3) Return the other duplicate original to the corporation or its representative.

§ 7. Defense of Ultra Vires

No act of a corporation and no conveyance or transfer of real or personal property to or by a corporation shall be invalid by reason of the fact that the corporation was without capacity or power to do such act or to make or receive such conveyance or transfer, but such lack of capacity or power may be asserted:

(a) In a proceeding by a shareholder against the corporation to enjoin the doing of any act or the transfer of real or personal property by or to the corporation. If the unauthorized act or transfer sought to be enjoined is being, or is to be, performed or made pursuant to a contract to which the corporation is a party, the court may, if all of the parties to the contract are parties to the proceeding and if it deems the same to be equitable, set aside and enjoin the performance of such contract, and in so doing may allow to the corporation or to the other parties to the contract, as the case may be, compensation for the loss or damage sustained by either of them which may result from the action of the court in setting aside and enjoining the performance of such contract, but anticipated profits to be derived from the performance of the contract shall not be awarded by the court as a loss or damage sustained.

(b) In a proceeding by the corporation, whether acting directly or through a receiver, trustee, or other legal representative, or through shareholders in a representative suit, against the incumbent or former officers or directors of the corporation.

(c) In a proceeding by the Attorney General, as provided in this Act, to dissolve the corporation, or in a proceeding by the Attorney General to enjoin the corporation from the transaction of unauthorized business.

§ 8. Corporate Name

The corporate name:

(a) Shall contain the word "corporation," "company," "incorporated" or "limited," or shall contain an abbreviation of one of such words.

(b) Shall not contain any word or phrase which indicates or implies that it is organized for any purpose other than one or more of the purposes contained in its articles of incorporation.

(c) Shall not be the same as, or deceptively similar to, the name of any domestic corporation existing under the laws of this State or any foreign corporation authorized to transact business in this State, or a name the exclusive right to which is, at the time, reserved in the manner provided in this Act, or the name of a corporation which has in effect a registration of its corporate name as provided in this Act, except that this provision shall not apply if the applicant files with the Secretary of State either of the following: (1) the written consent of such other corporation or holder of a reserved or registered name to use the same or deceptively similar name and one or more words are added to make such name distinguishable from such other name, or (2) a certified copy of a final decree of a court of competent jurisdiction establishing the prior right of the applicant to the use of such name in this State.

A corporation with which another corporation, domestic or foreign, is merged, or which is formed by the reorganization or consolidation of one or more domestic or foreign corporations or upon a sale, lease or other disposition to or exchange with, a domestic corporation of all or substantially all the assets of another corporation, domestic or foreign, including its name, may have the same name as that used in this State by any of such corporations if such other corporation was organized under the laws of, or is authorized to transact business in, this State.

§ 9. Reserved Name

The exclusive right to the use of a corporate name may be reserved by:

(a) Any person intending to organize a corporation under this Act.

(b) Any domestic corporation intending to change its name.

(c) Any foreign corporation intending to make application for a certificate of authority to transact business in this State.

(d) Any foreign corporation authorized to transact business in this State and intending to change its name.

(e) Any person intending to organize a foreign corporation and intending to have such corporation make application for a certificate of authority to transact business in this State.

The reservation shall be made by filing with the Secretary of State an application to reserve a specified corporate name, executed by the applicant. If the Secretary of State finds that the name is available for corporate use, he shall reserve the same for the exclusive use of the applicant for a period of one hundred and twenty days.

The right to the exclusive use of a specified corporate name so reserved may be transferred to any person or corporation by filing in the office of the Secretary of State a notice of such transfer, executed by the applicant for whom the name was reserved, and specifying the name and address of the transferee.

§ 10. Registered Name

Any corporation organized and existing under the laws of any state or territory of the United States may register its corporate name under this Act, provided its corporate name is not the same as, or deceptively similar to, the name of any domestic corporation existing under the laws of this State, or the name of any foreign corporation authorized to transact business in this State, or any corporate name reserved or registered under this Act.

Such registration shall be made by:

(a) Filing with the Secretary of State (1) an application for registration executed by the corporation by an officer thereof, setting forth the name of the corporation, the state or territory under the laws of which it is incorporated, the date of its incorporation, a statement that it is carrying on or doing business, and a brief statement of the business in which it is engaged, and (2) a certificate setting forth that such corporation is in good standing under the laws of the state or territory wherein it is organized, executed by the Secretary of State of such state or territory or by such other official as may have custody of the records pertaining to corporations, and

(b) Paying to the Secretary of State a registration fee in the amount of . . . . for each month, or fraction thereof, between the date of filing such application and December 31st of the calendar year in which such application is filed.

Such registration shall be effective until the close of

the calendar year in which the application for registration is filed.

§ 11. Renewal of Registered Name

A corporation which has in effect a registration of its corporate name, may renew such registration from year to year by annually filing an application for renewal setting forth the facts required to be set forth in an original application for registration and a certificate of good standing as required for the original registration and by paying a fee of .... A renewal application may be filed between the first day of October and the thirty-first day of December in each year, and shall extend the registration for the following calendar year.

§ 12. Registered Office and Registered Agent

Each corporation shall have and continuously maintain in this State:

(a) A registered office which may be, but need not be, the same as its place of business.

(b) A registered agent, which agent may be either an individual resident in this State whose business office is identical with such registered office, or a domestic corporation, or a foreign corporation authorized to transact business in this State, having a business office identical with such registered office.

§ 13. Change of Registered Office or Registered Agent

A corporation may change its registered office or change its registered agent, or both, upon filing in the office of the Secretary of State a statement setting forth:

(a) The name of the corporation.

(b) The address of its then registered office.

(c) If the address of its registered office is to be changed, the address to which the registered office is to be changed.

(d) The name of its then registered agent.

(e) If its registered agent is to be changed, the name of its successor registered agent.

(f) That the address of its registered office and the address of the business office of its registered agent, as changed, will be identical.

(g) That such change was authorized by resolution duly adopted by its board of directors.

Such statement shall be executed by the corporation by its president, or a vice president, and verified by him, and delivered to the Secretary of State. If the Secretary of State finds that such statement conforms to the provisions of this Act, he shall file such statement in his office, and upon such filing the change of address of the registered office, or the appointment of a new registered agent, or both, as the case may be, shall become effective.

Any registered agent of a corporation may resign as such agent upon filing a written notice thereof, executed in duplicate, with the Secretary of State, who shall forthwith mail a copy thereof to the corporation at its registered office. The appointment of such agent shall terminate upon the expiration of thirty days after receipt of such notice by the Secretary of State.

If a registered agent changes his or its business address to another place within the same ....,* he or it may change such address and the address of the registered office of any corporation of which he or it is registered agent by filing a statement as required above except that it need be signed only by the registered agent and need not be responsive to (e) or (g) and must recite that a copy of the statement has been mailed to the corporation.

*Supply designation of jurisdiction, such as county, etc., in accordance with local practice.

§ 14. Service of Process on Corporation

The registered agent so appointed by a corporation shall be an agent of such corporation upon whom any process, notice or demand required or permitted by law to be served upon the corporation may be served.

Whenever a corporation shall fail to appoint or maintain a registered agent in this State, or whenever its registered agent cannot with reasonable diligence be found at the registered office, then the Secretary of State shall be an agent of such corporation upon whom any such process, notice, or demand may be served. Service on the Secretary of State of any such process, notice, or demand shall be made by delivering to and leaving with him, or with any clerk having charge of the corporation department of his office, duplicate copies of such process, notice or demand. In the event any such process, notice or demand is served on the Secretary of State, he shall immediately cause one of the copies thereof to be forwarded by registered mail, addressed to the corporation at its registered office. Any service so had on the Secretary of State shall be returnable in not less than thirty days.

The Secretary of State shall keep a record of all processes, notices and demands served upon him under this section, and shall record therein the time of such service and his action with reference thereto.

Nothing herein contained shall limit or affect the right to serve any process, notice or demand required or permitted by law to be served upon a corporation in any other manner now or hereafter permitted by law.

§ 15. Authorized Shares

Each corporation shall have power to create and issue the number of shares stated in its articles of incorporation. Such shares may be divided into one or more classes with such designations, preferences, limitations, and relative rights as shall be stated in the articles of incorporation. The articles of incorporation may limit or deny the voting rights of or provide special voting rights for the shares of any class to the extent not inconsistent with the provisions of this Act.

Without limiting the authority herein contained, a corporation, when so provided in its articles of incorporation, may issue shares of preferred or special classes:

(a) Subject to the right of the corporation to redeem any of such shares at the price fixed by the articles of incorporation for the redemption thereof.

(b) Entitling the holders thereof to cumulative, noncumulative or partially cumulative dividends.

(c) Having preference over any other class or classes of shares as to the payment of dividends.

(d) Having preference in the assets of the corporation over any other class or classes of shares upon the voluntary or involuntary liquidation of the corporation.

(e) Convertible into shares of any other class or into shares of any series of the same or any other class, except a class having prior or superior rights and preferences as to dividends or distribution of assets upon liquidation.

§ 16. Issuance of Shares of Preferred or Special Classes in Series

If the articles of incorporation so provide, the shares of any preferred or special class may be divided into and issued in series. If the shares of any such class are to be issued in series, then each series shall be so designated as to distinguish the shares thereof from the shares of all other series and classes. Any or all of the series of any such class and the variations in the relative rights and preferences as between different series may be fixed and determined by the articles of incorporation, but all shares of the same class shall be identical except as to the following relative rights and preferences, as to which there may be variations between different series:

(A) The rate of dividend.

(B) Whether shares may be redeemed and, if so, the redemption price and the terms and conditions of redemption.

(C) The amount payable upon shares in the event of voluntary and involuntary liquidation.

(D) Sinking fund provisions, if any, for the redemption or purchase of shares.

(E) The terms and conditions, if any, on which shares may be converted.

(F) Voting rights, if any.

If the articles of incorporation shall expressly vest authority in the board of directors, then, to the extent that the articles of incorporation shall not have established series and fixed and determined the variations in the relative rights and preferences as between series, the board of directors shall have authority to divide any or all of such classes into series and, within the limitations set forth in this section and in the articles of incorporation, fix and determine the relative rights and preferences of the shares of any series so established.

In order for the board of directors to establish a series, where authority so to do is contained in the articles of incorporation, the board of directors shall adopt a resolution setting forth the designation of the series and fixing and determining the relative rights and preferences thereof, or so much thereof as shall not be fixed and determined by the articles of incorporation.

Prior to the issue of any shares of a series established by resolution adopted by the board of directors, the corporation shall file in the office of the Secretary of State a statement setting forth:

(a) The name of the corporation.

(b) A copy of the resolution establishing and designating the series, and fixing and determining the relative rights and preferences thereof.

(c) The date of adoption of such resolution.

(d) That such resolution was duly adopted by the board of directors.

Such statement shall be executed in duplicate by the corporation by its president or a vice president and by its secretary or an assistant secretary, and verified by one of the officers signing such statement, and shall be delivered to the Secretary of State. If the Secretary of State finds that such statement conforms to law, he shall, when all franchise taxes and fees have been paid as in this Act prescribed:

(1) Endorse on each of such duplicate originals the word "Filed," and the month, day, and year of the filing thereof.

(2) File one of such duplicate originals in his office.

(3) Return the other duplicate original to the corporation or its representative.

Upon the filing of such statement by the Secretary of State, the resolution establishing and designating the series and fixing and determining the relative rights and preferences thereof shall become effective and shall constitute an amendment of the articles of incorporation.

§ 17. Subscriptions for Shares

A subscription for shares of a corporation to be organized shall be irrevocable for a period of six months, unless otherwise provided by the terms of the subscription agreement or unless all of the subscribers consent to the revocation of such subscription.

Unless otherwise provided in the subscription agreement, subscriptions for shares, whether made before or after the organization of a corporation, shall be paid in full at such time, or in such installments and at such times, as shall be determined by the board of directors. Any call made by the board of directors for payment on subscriptions shall be uniform as to all shares of the same class or as to all shares of the same series, as the case may be. In case of default in the payment of any installment or call when such payment is due, the corporation may proceed to collect the amount due in the same manner as any debt due the corporation. The by-laws may prescribe other penalties for failure to pay installments or calls that may become due, but no penalty working a forfeiture of a subscription, or of the amounts paid thereon, shall be declared as against any subscriber unless the amount due thereon shall remain unpaid for a period of twenty days after written demand has been made therefor. If mailed, such written demand shall be deemed to be made when deposited in the United States mail in a sealed envelope addressed to the subscriber at his last post-office address known to the corporation, with postage thereon prepaid. In the event of the sale of any shares by reason of any forfeiture, the excess of proceeds realized over the amount due and unpaid on such shares shall be paid to the delinquent subscriber or to his legal representative.

§ 18. Issuance for Shares

Subject to any restrictions in the articles of incorporation:

(a) Shares may be issued for such consideration as shall be authorized by the board of directors establishing a price (in money or other consideration) or a minimum price or general formula or method by which the price will be determined; and

(b) Upon authorization by the board of directors, the corporation may issue its own shares in exchange for or in conversion of its outstanding shares, or distribute its own shares, pro rata to its shareholders or the shareholders of one or more classes or series, to effectuate stock dividends or splits, and any such transaction shall not require consideration; provided, that no such issuance of shares of any class or series shall be made to the holders of shares of any other class or series unless it is either expressly provided for in the articles of incorporation, or is authorized by an affirmative vote or the written consent of the holders of at least a majority of the outstanding shares of the class or series in which the distribution is to be made.

§ 19. Payment for Shares

The consideration for the issuance of shares may be paid, in whole or in part, in cash, in other property, tangible or intangible, or in labor or services actually performed for the corporation. When payment of the consideration for which shares are to be issued shall have been received by the corporation, such shares shall be nonassessable.

Neither promissory notes nor future services shall constitute payment or part payment for the issuance of shares of a corporation.

In the absence of fraud in the transaction, the judgment of the board of directors or the shareholders, as the case may be, as to the value of the consideration received for shares shall be conclusive.

§ 20. Stock Rights and Options

Subject to any provisions in respect thereof set forth in its articles of incorporation, a corporation may create and issue, whether or not in connection with the issuance and sale of any of its shares or other securities, rights or options entitling the holders thereof to purchase from the corporation shares of any class or classes. Such rights or options shall be evidenced in such manner as the board of directors shall approve and, subject to the provisions of the articles of incorporation, shall set forth the terms upon which, the time or times within which and the price or prices at which such shares may be purchased from the corporation upon the exercise of any such right or option. If such rights or options are to be issued to directors, officers or employees as such of the corporation or of any subsidiary thereof, and not to the shareholders generally, their issuance shall be approved by the affirmative vote of the holders of a majority of the shares entitled to vote thereon or shall be authorized by and consistent with a plan approved or ratified by such a vote of shareholders. In the absence of fraud in the transaction, the judgment of the board of directors as to the adequacy of the consideration received for such rights or options shall be conclusive.

§ 21. Determination of Amount of Stated Capital [Repealed]

§ 22. Expenses of Organization, Reorganization and Financing

The reasonable charges and expenses of organization or reorganization of a corporation, and the reasonable expenses of and compensation for the sale or underwriting of its shares, may be paid or allowed by such corporation out of the consideration received by it in payment for its shares without thereby rendering such shares not fully paid or assessable.

§ 23. Shares Represented by Certificates and Uncertified Shares

The shares of a corporation shall be represented by certificates or shall be uncertificated shares. Certificates shall be signed by the chairman or vice-chairman of the board of directors or the president or a vice president and by the treasurer or an assistant treasurer or the secretary or an assistant secretary of the corporation, and may be sealed with the seal of the corporation or a facsimile thereof. Any of or all the signatures [of the president or vice president and the secretary of assistant secretary] upon a certificate may be a facsimile. [s if the certificate is manually signed on behalf of a transfer agent or a registrar, other than the corporation itself or an employee of the corporation.] In case any officer, transfer agent or registrar who has signed or whose facsimile signature has been placed upon such certificate shall have ceased to be such officer, transfer agent or registrar before such certificate is issued, it may be issued by the corporation with the same effect as if he were such officer, transfer agent or registrar at the date of its issue.

Every certificate representing shares issued by a corporation which is authorized to issue shares of more than one class shall set forth upon the face or back of the certificate, or shall state that the corporation will furnish to any shareholder upon request and without charge, a full statement of the designations, preferences, limitations, and relative rights of the shares of each class authorized to be issued, and if the corporation is authorized to issue any preferred or special class in series, the variations in the relative rights and preferences between the shares of each such series so far as the same have been fixed and determined and the authority of the board of directors to fix and determine the relative rights and preferences of subsequent series.

Each certificate representing shares shall state upon the face thereof:

(a) That the corporation is organized under the laws of this State.

(b) The name of the person to whom issued.

(c) The number and class of shares, and the designation of the series, if any, which such certificate represents.

(d) The par value of each share represented by such certificate, or a statement that the shares are without par value.

No certificate shall be issued for any share until such share is fully paid.

Unless otherwise provided by the articles of incorporation or by-laws, the board of directors of a corporation may provide by resolution that some or all of any or all classes and series of its shares shall be uncertificated shares, provided that such resolution shall not apply to shares represented by a certificate until such certificate is surrendered to the corporation. Within a reasonable time after the issuance or transfer of uncertificated shares, the corporation shall send to the registered owner thereof a written notice containing the information required to be set forth or stated on certificates pursuant to the second and third paragraphs of this section. Except as otherwise expressly provided by law, the rights and obligations of the holders of uncertificated shares and the rights and obligations of the holders of certificates representing shares of the same class and series shall be identical.

§ 24. Fractional Shares

A corporation may (1) issue fractions of a share, either represented by a certificate or uncertificated, (2) arrange for the disposition of fractional interests by those entitled thereto, (3) pay in money the fair value of fractions of a share as of a time when those entitled to receive such fractions are determined, or (4) issue scrip in registered or bearer form which shall entitle the holder to receive a certificate for a full share or an uncertificated full share upon the surrender of such scrip aggregating a full share. A certificate for a fractional share or an uncertificated fractional share shall, but scrip shall not unless otherwise provided therein, entitle the holder to exercise voting rights, to receive dividends thereon, and to participate in any of the assets of the corporation in the event of liquidation. The board of directors may cause scrip to be issued subject to the condition that it shall become void if not exchanged for certificates representing full shares or uncertificated full shares before a specified date, or subject to the condition that the shares for which scrip is exchangeable may be sold by the corporation and the proceeds thereof distributed to the holders of scrip, or subject to any other conditions which the board of directors may deem advisable.

§ 25. Liability of Subscribers and Shareholders

A holder of or subscriber to shares of a corporation shall be under no obligation to the corporation or its creditors with respect to such shares other than the obligation to pay to the corporation the full consideration for which such shares were issued or to be issued.

Any person becoming an assignee or transferee of shares or of a subscription for shares in good faith and without knowledge or notice that the full consideration therefor has not been paid shall not be personally liable to the corporation or its creditors for any unpaid portion of such consideration.

An executor, administrator, conservator, guardian, trustee, assignee for the benefit of creditors, or receiver shall not be personally liable to the corporation as a holder of or subscriber to shares of a corporation but the estate and funds in his hands shall be so liable.

No pledgee or other holder of shares as collateral security shall be personally liable as a shareholder.

§ 26. Shareholders' Preemptive Rights

The shareholders of a corporation shall have no preemptive right to acquire unissued shares of the corporation, or securities of the corporation convertible into or carrying a right to subscribe to or acquire shares, except to the extent, if any, that such right is provided in the articles of incorporation.

§ 26A. Shareholders' Preemptive Rights [Alternative]

Except to the extent limited or denied by this section or by the articles of incorporation, shareholders shall have a preemptive right to acquire unissued shares or securities convertible into such shares or carrying a right to subscribe to or acquire shares.

Unless otherwise provided in the articles of incorporation,

(a) No preemptive right shall exist

(1) to acquire any shares issued to directors, officers or employees pursuant to approval by the affirmative vote of the holders of a majority of the shares entitled to vote thereon or when authorized by and consistent with a plan theretofore approved by such a vote of shareholders; or

(2) to acquire any shares sold otherwise than for money.

(b) Holders of shares of any class that is preferred or limited as to dividends or assets shall not be entitled to any preemptive right.

(c) Holders of shares of common stock shall not be entitled to any preemptive right to shares of any class that is preferred or limited as to dividends or assets or to any obligations, unless convertible into shares of common stock or carrying a right to subscribe to or acquire shares of common stock.

(d) Holders of common stock without voting power shall have no preemptive right to shares of common stock with voting power.

(e) The preemptive right shall be only an opportunity to acquire shares or other securities under such terms and conditions as the board of directors may fix for the purpose of providing a fair and reasonable opportunity for the exercise of such right.

§ 27. By-Laws

The initial by-laws of a corporation shall be adopted by its board of directors. The power to alter, amend or repeal the by-laws or adopt new by-laws, subject to repeal or change by action of the shareholders, shall be vested in the board of directors unless reserved to the shareholders by the articles of incorporation. The by-laws may contain any provisions for the regulation and management of the affairs of the corporation not inconsistent with law or the articles of incorporation.

§ 27A. By-Laws and Other Powers in Emergency [Optional]

The board of directors of any corporation may adopt emergency by-laws, subject to repeal or change by action of the shareholders, which shall, notwithstanding any different provision elsewhere in this Act or in the articles of incorporation or by-laws, be operative during any emergency in the conduct of the business of the corporation resulting from an attack on the United States or any nuclear or atomic disaster. The emergency by-laws may make any provision that may be practical and necessary for the circumstances of the emergency, including provisions that:

(a) A meeting of the board of directors may be called by any officer or director in such manner and under such conditions as shall be prescribed in the emergency by-laws;

(b) The director or directors in attendance at the meeting, or any greater number fixed by the emergency by-laws, shall constitute a quorum; and

(c) The officers or other persons designated on a list approved by the board of directors before the emergency, all in such order of priority and subject to such conditions, and for such period of time (not longer than reasonably necessary after the termination of the emergency) as may be provided in the emergency by-laws or in the resolution approving the list shall, to the extent required to provide a quorum at any meeting of the board of directors, be deemed directors for such meeting.

The board of directors, either before or during any such emergency, may provide, and from time to time modify, lines of succession in the event that during such an emergency any or all officers or agents of the corporation shall for any reason be rendered incapable of discharging their duties.

The board of directors, either before or during any such emergency, may, effective in the emergency, change the head office or designate several alternative head offices or regional offices, or authorize the officers so to do.

To the extent not inconsistent with any emergency by-laws so adopted, the by-laws of the corporation shall remain in effect during any such emergency and upon its termination the emergency by-laws shall cease to be operative.

Unless otherwise provided in emergency by-laws, notice of any meeting of the board of directors during any such emergency may be given only to such of the directors as it may be feasible to reach at the time and by such means as may be feasible at the time, including publication or radio.

To the extent required to constitute a quorum at any meeting of the board of directors during any such emergency, the officers of the corporation who are present shall, unless otherwise provided in emergency by-laws, be deemed, in order of rank and within the same rank in order of seniority, directors for such meeting.

No officer, director or employee acting in accordance with any emergency by-laws shall be liable except for willful misconduct. No officer, director or employee shall be liable for any action taken by him in good faith in such an emergency in furtherance of the ordinary business affairs of the corporation even though not authorized by the by-laws then in effect.

§ 28. Meetings of Shareholders

Meetings of shareholders may be held at such place within or without this State as may be stated in or fixed in accordance with the by-laws. If no other place is stated or so fixed, meetings shall be held at the registered office of the corporation.

An annual meeting of the shareholders shall be held at such time as may be stated in or fixed in accordance with the by-laws. If the annual meeting is not held within any thirteen-month period the Court

of . . . . may, on the application of any shareholder, summarily order a meeting to be held.

A special meeting of the shareholders may be called by the board of directors, the holders of not less than one-tenth of all the shares entitled to vote at the meeting, or such other persons as may be authorized in the articles of incorporation or the by-laws.

§ 29. Notice of Shareholders' Meetings

Written notice stating the place, day and hour of the meeting and, in case of a special meeting, the purpose or purposes for which the meeting is called, shall be delivered not less than ten nor more than fifty days before the date of the meeting, either personally or by mail, by or at the direction of the president, the secretary, or the officer or persons calling the meeting, to each shareholder of record entitled to vote at such meeting. If mailed, such notice shall be deemed to be delivered when deposited in the United States mail addressed to the shareholder at his address as it appears on the stock transfer books of the corporation, with postage thereon prepaid.

§ 30. Closing of Transfer Books and Fixing Record Date

For the purpose of determining shareholders entitled to notice of or to vote at any meeting of shareholders or any adjournment thereof, or entitled to receive payment of any dividend, or in order to make a determination of shareholders for any other proper purpose, the board of directors of a corporation may provide that the stock transfer books shall be closed for a stated period but not to exceed, in any case, fifty days. If the stock transfer books shall be closed for the purpose of determining shareholders entitled to notice of or to vote at a meeting of shareholders, such books shall be closed for at least ten days immediately preceding such meeting. In lieu of closing the stock transfer books, the by-laws, or in the absence of an applicable by-law the board of directors, may fix in advance a date as the record date for any such determination of shareholders, such date in any case to be not more than fifty days and, in case of a meeting of shareholders, not less than ten days prior to the date on which the particular action, requiring such determination of shareholders, is to be taken. If the stock transfer books are not closed and no record date is fixed for the determination of shareholders entitled to notice of or to vote at a meeting of shareholders, or shareholders entitled to receive payment of a dividend, the date on which notice of the meeting is mailed or the date on which the resolution of the board of directors declaring such dividend is adopted, as the case may be, shall be the record date for such determination of shareholders. When a determination of shareholders entitled to vote at any meeting of shareholders has been made as provided in this section, such determination shall apply to any adjournment thereof.

§ 31. Voting Record

The officer or agent having charge of the stock transfer books for shares of a corporation shall make a complete record of the shareholders entitled to vote at such meeting or any adjournment thereof, arranged in alphabetical order, with the address of and the number of shares held by each. Such record shall be produced and kept open at the time and place of the meeting and shall be subject to the inspection of any shareholder during the whole time of the meeting for the purposes thereof.

Failure to comply with the requirements of this section shall not affect the validity of any action taken at such meeting.

An officer or agent having charge of the stock transfer books who shall fail to prepare the record of shareholders, or produce and keep it open for inspection at the meeting, as provided in this section, shall be liable to any shareholder suffering damage on account of such failure, to the extent of such damage.

§ 32. Quorum of Shareholders

Unless otherwise provided in the articles of incorporation, a majority of the shares entitled to vote, represented in person or by proxy, shall constitute a quorum at a meeting of shareholders, but in no event shall a quorum consist of less than one-third of the shares entitled to vote at the meeting. If a quorum is present, the affirmative vote of the majority of the shares represented at the meeting and entitled to vote on the subject matter shall be the act of the shareholders, unless the vote of a greater number or voting by classes is required by this Act or the articles of incorporation or by-laws.

§ 33. Voting of Shares

Each outstanding share, regardless of class, shall be entitled to one vote on each matter submitted to a vote at a meeting of shareholders, except as may be otherwise provided in the articles of incorporation. If the articles of incorporation provide for more or less than one vote for any share, on any matter, every reference in this Act to a majority or other proportion of shares shall refer to such a majority or other proportion of votes entitled to be cast.

Shares held by another corporation if a majority of the shares entitled to vote for the election of directors of such other corporation is held by the corporation, shall not be voted at any meeting or counted in determining the total number of outstanding shares at any given time.

A shareholder may vote either in person or by proxy executed in writing by the shareholder or by his duly authorized attorney-in-fact. No proxy shall be valid after eleven months from the date of its execution, unless otherwise provided in the proxy.

[Either of the following prefatory phrases may be inserted here: "The articles of incorporation may provide that" or "Unless the articles of incorporation otherwise provide"] . . . at each election for directors every shareholder entitled to vote at such election shall have the right to vote, in person or by proxy, the number of shares owned by him for as many persons as there are directors to be elected and for whose election he has a right to vote, or to cumulate his votes by giving one candidate as many votes as the number of such directors multiplied by the number of his shares shall equal, or by distributing such votes on the same principle among any number of such candidates.

Shares standing in the name of another corporation, domestic or foreign, may be voted by such officer, agent or proxy as the by-laws of such other corporation may prescribe, or, in the absence of such provision, as the board of directors of such other corporation may determine.

Shares held by an administrator, executor, guardian or conservator may be voted by him, either in person or by proxy, without a transfer of such shares into his name. Shares standing in the name of a trustee may be voted by him, either in person or by proxy, but no trustee shall be entitled to vote shares held by him without a transfer of such shares into his name.

Shares standing in the name of a receiver may be voted by such receiver, and shares held by or under the control of a receiver may be voted by such receiver without the transfer thereof into his name if authority so to do be contained in an appropriate order of the court by which such receiver was appointed.

A shareholder whose shares are pledged shall be entitled to vote such shares until the shares have been transferred into the name of the pledgee, and thereafter the pledgee shall be entitled to vote the shares so transferred.

On and after the date on which written notice of redemption of redeemable shares has been mailed to the holders thereof and a sum sufficient to redeem such shares has been deposited with a bank or trust company with irrevocable instruction and authority to pay the redemption price to the holders thereof upon surrender of certificates therefor, such shares shall not be entitled to vote on any matter and shall not be deemed to be outstanding shares.

§ 34. Voting Trusts and Agreements Among Shareholders

Any number of shareholders of a corporation may create a voting trust for the purpose of conferring upon a trustee or trustees the right to vote or otherwise represent their shares, for a period of not to exceed ten years, by entering into a written voting trust agreement specifying the terms and conditions of the voting trust, by depositing a counterpart of the agreement with the corporation at its registered office, and by transferring their shares to such trustee or trustees for the purposes of the agreement. Such trustee or trustees shall keep a record of the holders of voting trust certificates evidencing a beneficial interest in the voting trust, giving the names and addresses of all such holders and the number and class of the shares in respect of which the voting trust certificates held by each are issued, and shall deposit a copy of such record with the corporation at its registered office. The counterpart of the voting trust agreement and the copy of such record so deposited with the corporation shall be subject to the same right of examination by a shareholder of the corporation, in person or by agent or attorney, as are the books and records of the corporation, and such counterpart and such copy of such record shall be subject to examination by any holder of record of voting trust certificates, either in person or by agent or attorney, at any reasonable time for any proper purpose.

Agreements among shareholders regarding the voting of their shares shall be valid and enforceable in accordance with their terms. Such agreements shall not be subject to the provisions of this section regarding voting trusts.

§ 35. Board of Directors

All corporate powers shall be exercised by or under authority of, and the business and affairs of a corporation shall be managed under the direction of, a board of directors except as may be otherwise provided in this Act or the articles of incorporation. If any such provision is made in the articles of incorporation, the powers and duties conferred or imposed upon the board of directors by this Act shall be exercised or performed to such extent and by such person or persons as shall be provided in the articles of incorporation. Directors need not be residents of this State or shareholders of the corporation unless the articles of incorporation or by-laws so require. The articles of incorporation or by-laws may prescribe other qualifications for directors. The board of directors shall have authority to fix the compensation of directors unless otherwise provided in the articles of incorporation.

A director shall perform his duties as a director, including his duties as a member of any committee of the board upon which he may serve, in good faith, in a manner he reasonably believes to be in the best interests of the corporation, and with such care as an ordinarily prudent person in a like position would use under similar circumstances. In performing his duties, a director shall be entitled to rely on information, opinions, reports or statements, including financial statements and other financial data, in each case prepared or presented by:

(a) one or more officers or employees of the corporation whom the director reasonably believes to be reliable and competent in the matters presented,

(b) counsel, public accountants or other persons as to matters which the director reasonably believes to be within such person's professional or expert competence, or

(c) a committee of the board upon which he does not serve, duly designated in accordance with a provision of the articles of incorporation or the by-laws, as to matters within its designated authority, which committee the director reasonably believes to merit confidence,

but he shall not be considered to be acting in good faith if he has knowledge concerning the matter in question that would cause such reliance to be unwarranted. A person who so performs his duties shall have no liability by reason of being or having been a director of the corporation.

A director of a corporation who is present at a meeting of its board of directors at which action on any corporate matter is taken shall be presumed to have assented to the action taken unless his dissent shall be entered in the minutes of the meeting or unless he shall file his written dissent to such action with the secretary of the meeting before the adjournment thereof or shall forward such dissent by registered mail to the secretary of the corporation immediately after the adjournment of the meeting. Such right to dissent shall not apply to a director who voted in favor of such action.

§ 36. Number and Election of Directors

The board of directors of a corporation shall consist of one or more members. The number of directors shall be fixed by, or in the manner provided in, the articles of incorporation or the by-laws, except as to the number constituting the initial board of directors, which number shall be fixed by the articles of incorporation. The number of directors may be increased or decreased from time to time by amendment to, or in the manner provided in, the articles of incorporation or the by-laws, but no decrease shall have the effect of shortening the term of any incumbent director. In the absence of a by-law providing for the number of directors, the number shall be the same as that provided for in the articles of incorporation. The names and addresses of the members of the first board of directors shall be stated in the articles of incorporation. Such persons shall hold office until the first annual meeting of shareholders, and until their successors shall have been elected and qualified. At the first annual meeting of shareholders and at each annual meeting thereafter the shareholders shall elect directors to hold office until the next succeeding annual meeting, except in case of the classification of directors as permitted by this Act. Each director shall hold office for the term for which he is elected and until his successor shall have been elected and qualified.

§ 37. Classification of Directors

When the board of directors shall consist of nine or more members, in lieu of electing the whole number of directors annually, the articles of incorporation may provide that the directors be divided into either two or three classes, each class to be as nearly equal in number as possible, the term of office of directors of the first class to expire at the first annual meeting of shareholders after their election, that of the second class to expire at the second annual meeting after their election, and that of the third class, if any, to expire at the third annual meeting after their election. At each annual meeting after such classification the number of directors equal to the number of the class whose term expires at the time of such meeting shall be elected to hold office until the second succeeding annual meeting, if there be two classes, or until the third succeeding annual meeting, if there be three classes. No classification of directors shall be effective prior to the first annual meeting of shareholders.

§ 38. Vacancies

Any vacancy occurring in the board of directors may be filled by the affirmative vote of a majority of the remaining directors though less than a quorum of the board of directors. A director elected to fill a vacancy shall be elected for the unexpired term of his predecessor in office. Any directorship to be filled by reason of an increase in the number of directors may be filled by the board of directors for a term of office continuing only until the next election of directors by the shareholders.

§ 39. Removal of Directors

At a meeting of shareholders called expressly for that purpose, directors may be removed in the manner provided in this section. Any director or the entire board of directors may be removed, with or without cause, by a vote of the holders of a majority of the shares then entitled to vote at an election of directors.

In the case of a corporation having cumulative voting, if less than the entire board is to be removed, no one of the directors may be removed if the votes cast against his removal would be sufficient to elect him if then cumulatively voted at an election of the entire board of directors, or, if there be classes of directors, at an election of the class of directors of which he is a part.

Whenever the holders of the shares of any class are entitled to elect one or more directors by the provisions of the articles of incorporation, the provisions of this section shall apply, in respect to the removal of a director or directors so elected, to the vote of the holders of the outstanding shares of that class and not to the vote of the outstanding shares as a whole.

§ 40. Quorum of Directors

A majority of the number of directors fixed by or in the manner provided in the by-laws or in the absence of a by-law fixing or providing for the number of directors, then of the number stated in the articles of incorporation, shall constitute a quorum for the transaction of business unless a greater number is required by the articles of incorporation or the by-laws. The act of the majority of the directors present at a meeting at which a quorum is present shall be the act of the board of directors, unless the act of a greater number is required by the articles of incorporation or the by-laws.

§ 41. Director Conflicts of Interest

No contract or other transaction between a corporation and one or more of its directors or any other corporation, firm, association or entity in which one or more of its directors are directors or officers or are financially interested, shall be either void or voidable because of such relationship or interest or because such director or directors are present at the meeting of the board of directors or a committee thereof which authorizes, approves or ratifies such contract or transaction or because his or their votes are counted for such purpose, if:

(a) the fact of such relationship or interest is disclosed or known to the board of directors or committee which authorizes, approves or ratifies the contract or transaction by a vote or consent sufficient for the purpose without counting the votes or consents of such interested directors; or

(b) the fact of such relationship or interest is disclosed or known to the shareholders entitled to vote and they authorize, approve or ratify such contract or transaction by vote or written consent; or

(c) the contract or transaction is fair and reasonable to the corporation.

Common or interested directors may be counted in determining the presence of a quorum at a meeting of the board of directors or a committee thereof which authorizes, approves or ratifies such contract or transaction.

§ 42. Executive and Other Committees

If the articles of incorporation or the by-laws so provide, the board of directors, by resolution adopted by a majority of the full board of directors, may designate from among its members an executive committee and one or more other committees each of which, to the extent provided in such resolution or in the articles of incorporation or the by-laws of the corporation, shall have and may exercise all the authority of the board of directors, except that no such committee shall have authority to (i) authorize distributions, (ii) approve or recommend to shareholders actions or proposals required by this Act to be approved by shareholders, (iii) designate candidates for the office of director, for purposes of proxy solicitation or otherwise, or fill vacancies on the board of directors or any committee thereof, (iv) amend the by-laws, (v) approve a plan of merger not requiring shareholder approval, (vi) authorize or approve the reacquisition of shares unless pursuant to a general formula or method specified by the board of directors, or authorize or approve the issuance or sale of, or any contract to issue or sell, shares or designate the terms of a series of a class of shares, provided that the board of directors, having acted regarding general authorization for the issuance or sale of shares, or any contract, therefor, and, in the case of a series, the designation thereof, may, pursuant to a general formula or method specified by the board by resolution or by adoption of a stock option or other plan, authorize a committee to fix the terms of any contract for the sale of the shares and to fix the terms upon which such shares may be issued or sold, including, without limitation, the price, the dividend rate, provisions for redemption, sinking fund, conversion, voting or preferential rights, and provisions for other features of a class of shares, or a series of a class of shares, with full power in such committee to adopt any final resolution setting forth all the terms thereof and

to authorize the statement of the terms of a series for filing with the Secretary of State under this Act.

Neither the designation of any such committee, the delegation thereto of authority, nor action by such committee pursuant to such authority shall alone constitute compliance by any member of the board of directors, not a member of the committee in question, with his responsibility to act in good faith, in a manner he reasonably believes to be in the best interests of the corporation, and with such care as an ordinarily prudent person in a like position would use under similar circumstances.

§ 43. Place and Notice of Directors' Meetings; Committee Meetings

Meetings of the board of directors, regular or special, may be held either within or without this State.

Regular meetings of the board of directors or any committee designated thereby may be held with or without notice as prescribed in the by-laws. Special meetings of the board of directors or any committee designated thereby shall be held upon such notice as is prescribed in the by-laws. Attendance of a director at a meeting shall constitute a waiver of notice of such meeting, except where a director attends a meeting for the express purpose of objecting to the transaction of any business because the meeting is not lawfully called or convened. Neither the business to be transacted at, nor the purpose of, any regular or special meeting of the board of directors or any committee designated thereby need be specified in the notice or waiver of notice of such meeting unless required by the by-laws.

Except as may be otherwise restricted by the articles of incorporation or by-laws, members of the board of directors or any committee designated thereby may participate in a meeting of such board or committee by means of a conference telephone or similar communications equipment by means of which all persons participating in the meeting can hear each other at the same time and participation by such means shall constitute presence in person at a meeting.

§ 44. Action by Directors Without a Meeting

Unless otherwise provided by the articles of incorporation or by-laws, any action required by this Act to be taken at a meeting of the directors of a corporation, or any action which may be taken at a meeting of the directors or of a committee, may be taken without a meeting if a consent in writing, setting forth the action so taken, shall be signed by all of the directors, or all of the members of the committee, as the case may be. Such consent shall have the same effect as a unanimous vote.

§ 45. Distributions to Shareholders

Subject to any restrictions in the articles of incorporation, the board of directors may authorize and the corporation may make distributions, except that no distribution may be made if, after giving effect thereto, either:

(a) the corporation would be unable to pay its debts as they become due in the usual course of its business; or

(b) the corporation's total assets would be less than the sum of its total liabilities and (unless the articles of incorporation otherwise permit) the maximum amount that then would be payable, in any liquidation, in respect of all outstanding shares having preferential rights in liqidation.

Determinations under subparagraph (b) may be based upon (i) financial statements prepared on the basis of accounting practices and principles that are reasonable in the circumstances, or (ii) a fair valuation or other method that is reasonable in the circumstances.

In the case of a purchase, redemption or other acquisition of a corporation's shares, the effect of a distribution shall be measured as of the date money or other property is transferred or debt is incurred by the corporation, or as of the date the shareholder ceases to be a shareholder of the corporation with respect to such shares, whichever is earlier. In all other cases, the effect of a distribution shall be measured as of the date of its authorization if payment occurs 120 days or less following the date of authorization, or as of the date of payment if payment occurs more than 120 days following the date of authorization.

Indebtedness of a corporation incurred or issued to a shareholder in a distribution in accordance with this Section shall be on a parity with the indebtedness of the corporation to its general unsecured creditors except to the extent subordinated by agreement.

§ 46. Distributions from Capital Surplus [Repealed]

§ 47. Loans to Employees and Directors

A corporation shall not lend money to or use its credit to assist its directors without authorization in the particular case by its shareholders, but may lend money to and use its credit to assist any employee of the corporation or of a subsidiary, including any such employee who is a director of the corporation, if the board of directors decides that such loan or assistance may benefit the corporation.

§ 48. Liability of Directors in Certain Cases

In addition to any other liabilities, a director who votes for or assents to any distribution contrary to the provisions of this Act or contrary to any restrictions contained in the articles of incorporation, shall, unless he complies with the standard provided in this Act for the performance of the duties of directors, be liable to the corporation, jointly and severally with all other directors so voting or assenting, for the amount of such dividend which is paid or the value of such distribution in excess of the amount of such distribution which could have been made without a violation of the provisions of this Act or the restrictions in the articles of incorporation.

Any director against whom a claim shall be asserted under or pursuant to this section for the making of a distribution and who shall be held liable thereon, shall be entitled to contribution from the shareholders who accepted or received any such distribution, knowing such distribution to have been made in violation of this Act, in proportion to the amounts received by them.

Any director against whom a claim shall be asserted under or pursuant to this section shall be entitled to contribution from any other director who voted for or assented to the action upon which the claim is asserted and who did not comply with the standard provided in this Act for the performance of the duties of directors.

§ 49. Provisions Relating to Actions by Shareholders

No action shall be brought in this State by a shareholder in the right of a domestic or foreign corporation unless the plaintiff was a holder of record of shares or of voting trust certificates therefor at the time of the transaction of which he complains, or his shares or voting trust certificates thereafter devolved upon him by operation of law from a person who was a holder of record at such time.

In any action hereafter instituted in the right of any domestic or foreign corporation by the holder or holders of record of shares of such corporation or of voting trust certificates therefor, the court having jurisdiction, upon final judgment and a finding that the action was brought without reasonable cause, may require the plaintiff or plaintiffs to pay to the parties named as defendant the reasonable expenses, including fees of attorneys, incurred by them in the defense of such action.

In any action now pending or hereafter instituted or maintained in the right of any domestic or foreign corporation by the holder or holders of record of less than five per cent of the outstanding shares of any class of such corporation or of voting trust certificates therefor, unless the shares or voting trust certificates so held have a market value in excess of twenty-five thousand dollars, the corporation in whose right such action is brought shall be entitled at any time before final judgment to require the plaintiff or plaintiffs to give security for the reasonable expenses, including fees of attorneys, that may be incurred by it in connection with such action or may be incurred by other parties named as defendant for which it may become legally liable. Market value shall be determined as of the date that the plaintiff institutes the action or, in the case of an intervenor, as of the date that he becomes a party to the action. The amount of such security may from time to time be increased or decreased, in the discretion of the court, upon showing that the security provided has or may become inadequate or is excessive. The corporation shall have recourse to such security in such amount as the court having jurisdiction shall determine upon the termination of such action, whether or not the court finds the action was brought without reasonable cause.

§ 50. Officers

The officers of a corporation shall consist of a president, one or more vice presidents as may be prescribed by the by-laws, a secretary, and a treasurer, each of whom shall be elected by the board of directors at such time and in such manner as may be prescribed by the by-laws. Such other officers and assistant officers and agents as may be deemed necessary may be elected or appointed by the board of directors or chosen in such other manner as may be prescribed by the by-laws. Any two or more offices may be held by the same person, except the offices of president and secretary.

All officers and agents of the corporation, as between themselves and the corporation, shall have such authority and perform such duties in the management of the corporation as may be provided in the by-laws, or as may be determined by resolution of the board of directors not inconsistent with the by-laws.

§ 51. Removal of Officers

Any officer or agent may be removed by the board of directors whenever in its judgment the best interests of the corporation will be served thereby, but such removal shall be without prejudice to the contract rights, if any, of the person so removed. Election or appointment of an officer or agent shall not of itself create contract rights.

§ 52. Books and Records: Financial Reports to Shareholders; Examination of Records

Each corporation shall keep correct and complete books and records of account and shall keep minutes of the proceedings of its shareholders and board of directors and shall keep at its registered office or principal place of business, or at the office of its transfer agent or registrar, a record of its shareholders, giving the names and addresses of all shareholders and the number and class of the shares held by each. Any books, records and minutes may be in written form or in any form capable of being converted into written form within a reasonable time.

Any person who shall have been a holder of record of shares or of voting trust certificates therefor at least six months immediately preceding his demand or shall be the holder of record of, or the holder of record of voting trust certificates for, at least five percent of all the outstanding shares of the corporation, upon written demand stating the purpose thereof, shall have the right to examine, in person, or by agent or attorney, at any reasonable time or times, for any proper purpose its relevant books and records of accounts, minutes, and record of shareholders and to make extracts therefrom.

Any officer or agent who, or a corporation which, shall refuse to allow any such shareholder or holder of voting trust certificates, or his agent or attorney, so to examine and make extracts from its books and records of account, minutes, and record of shareholders, for any proper purpose, shall be liable to such shareholder or holder of voting trust certificates in a penalty of ten per cent of the value of the shares owned by such shareholder, or in respect of which such voting trust certificates are issued, in addition to any other damages or remedy afforded him by law. It shall be a defense to any action for penalties under this section that the person suing therefor has within two years sold or offered for sale any list of shareholders or of holders of voting trust certificates for shares of such corporation or any other corporation or has aided or abetted any person in procuring any list of shareholders or of holders of voting trust certificates for any such purpose, or has improperly used any information secured through any prior examination of the books and records of account, or minutes, or record of shareholders or of holders of voting trust certificates for shares of such corporation or any other corporation, or was not acting in good faith or for a proper purpose in making his demand.

Nothing herein contained shall impair the power of any court of competent jurisdiction, upon proof by a shareholder or holder of voting trust certificates of proper purpose, irrespective of the period of time during which such shareholder or holder of voting trust certificates shall have been a shareholder of record or a holder of record of voting trust certificates, and irrespective of the number of shares held by him or represented by voting trust certificates held by him, to compel the production for examination by such shareholder or holder of voting trust certificates of the books and records of account, minutes and record of shareholders of a corporation.

Each corporation shall furnish to its shareholders annual financial statements, including at least a balance sheet as of the end of each fiscal year and a statement of income for such fiscal year, which shall be prepared on the basis of generally accepted accounting principles, if the corporation prepares financial statements for such fiscal year on that basis for any purpose, and may be consolidated statements of the corporation and one or more of its subsidiaries. The financial statements shall be mailed by the corporation to each of its shareholders within 120 days after the close of each fiscal year and, after such mailing and upon written request, shall be mailed by the corporation to any shareholder (or holder of a voting trust certificate for its shares) to whom a copy of the most recent annual financial statements has not previously been mailed. In the case of statements audited by a public accountant, each copy shall be accompanied by a report setting forth his opinion thereon; in other cases, each copy shall be accompanied by a statement of the president or the person in charge of the corporation's financial accounting records (1) stating his reasonable belief as to whether or not the financial statements were prepared in accordance with generally accepted accounting principles and, if not, describing the basis of presentation, and (2) describing any respects in which the financial statements were not prepared on a basis consistent with those prepared for the previous year.

§ 53. Incorporators

One or more persons, or a domestic or foreign corporation, may act as incorporator or incorporators of a corporation by signing and delivering in duplicate to the Secretary of State articles of incorporation for such corporation.

§ 54. Articles of Incorporation

The articles of incorporation shall set forth:

(a) The name of the corporation.

(b) The period of duration, which may be perpetual.

(c) The purpose or purposes for which the corporation is organized which may be stated to be, or to include, the transaction of any or all lawful business for which corporations may be incorporated under this Act.

(d) The aggregate number of shares which the corporation shall have authority to issue and, if such shares are to be divided into classes, the number of shares of each class.

(e) If the shares are to be divided into classes, the designation of each class and a statement of the preferences, limitations and relative rights in respect of the shares of each class.

(f) If the corporation is to issue the shares of any preferred or special class in series, then the designation of each series and a statement of the variations in the relative rights and preferences as between series insofar as the same are to be fixed in the articles of incorporation, and a statement of any authority to be vested in the board of directors to establish series and fix and determine the variations in the relative rights and preferences as between series.

(g) If any preemptive right is to be granted to shareholders, the provisions therefor.

(h) The address of its initial registered office, and the name of its initial registered agent at such address.

(i) The number of directors constituting the initial board of directors and the names and addresses of the persons who are to serve as directors until the first annual meeting of shareholders or until their successors be elected and qualify.

(j) The name and address of each incorporator.

In addition to provisions required therein, the articles of incorporation may also contain provisions not inconsistent with law regarding:

(1) the direction of the management of the business and the regulation of the affairs of the corporation;

(2) the definition, limitation and regulation of the powers of the corporation, the directors, and the shareholders, or any class of the shareholders,

including restrictions on the transfer of shares;

(3) the par value of any authorized shares or class of shares;

(4) any provision which under this Act is required or permitted to be set forth in the by-laws.

It shall not be necessary to set forth in the articles of incorporation any of the corporate powers enumerated in this Act.

§ 55. Filing of Articles of Incorporation

Duplicate originals of the articles of incorporation shall be delivered to the Secretary of State. If the Secretary of State finds that the articles of incorporation conform to law, he shall, when all fees have been paid as in this Act prescribed:

(a) Endorse on each of such duplicate originals the word "Filed," and the month, day and year of the filing thereof.

(b) File one of such duplicate originals in his office.

(c) Issue a certificate of incorporation to which he shall affix the other duplicate original.

The certificate of incorporation, together with the duplicate original of the articles of incorporation affixed thereto by the Secretary of State, shall be returned to the incorporators or their representative.

§ 56. Effect of Issuance of Certificate of Incorporation

Upon the issuance of the certificate of incorporation, the corporate existence shall begin, and such certificate of incorporation shall be conclusive evidence that all conditions precedent required to be performed by the incorporators have been complied with and that the corporation has been incorporated under this Act, except as against this State in a proceeding to cancel or revoke the certificate of incorporation or for involuntary dissolution of the corporation.

§ 57. Organization Meeting of Directors

After the issuance of the certificate of incorporation an organization meeting of the board of directors named in the articles of incorporation shall be held, either within or without this State, at the call of a majority of the directors named in the articles of incorporation, for the purpose of adopting by-laws, electing officers and transacting such other business as may come before the meeting. The directors calling the meeting shall give at least three days' notice thereof by mail to each director so named, stating the time and place of the meeting.

§ 58. Right to Amend Articles of Incorporation

A corporation may amend its articles of incorporation, from time to time, in any and as many respects as may be desired, so long as its articles of incorporation as amended contain only such provisions as might be lawfully contained in original articles of incorporation at the time of making such amendment, and, if a change in shares or the rights of shareholders, or an exchange, reclassification or cancellation of shares or rights of shareholders is to be made, such provisions as may be necessary to effect such change, exchange, reclassification or cancellation.

In particular, and without limitation upon such general power of amendment, a corporation may amend its articles of incorporation, from time to time, so as:

(a) To change its corporate name.

(b) To change its period of duration.

(c) To change, enlarge or diminish its corporate purposes.

(d) To increase or decrease the aggregate number of shares, or shares of any class, which the corporation has authority to issue.

(e) To provide, change or eliminate any provision with respect to the par value of any shares or class of shares.

(f) To exchange, classify, reclassify or cancel all or any part of its shares, whether issued or unissued.

(g) To change the designation of all or any part of its shares, whether issued or unissued, and to change the preferences, limitations, and the relative rights in respect of all or any part of its shares, whether issued or unissued.

(h) To change the shares of any class, whether issued or unissued, into a different number of shares of the same class or into the same or a different number of shares of other classes.

(i) To create new classes of shares having rights and preferences either prior and superior or subordinate and inferior to the shares of any class then authorized, whether issued or unissued.

(j) To cancel or otherwise affect the right of the holders of the shares of any class to receive dividends which have accrued but have not been declared.

(k) To divide any preferred or special class of shares, whether issued or unissued, into series and fix and determine the designations of such series and the variations in the relative rights and preferences as between the shares of such series.

(l) To authorize the board of directors to establish,

out of authorized but unissued shares, series of any preferred or special class of shares and fix and determine the relative rights and preferences of the shares of any series so established.

(m) To authorize the board of directors to fix and determine the relative rights and preferences of the authorized but unissued shares of series theretofore established in respect of which either the relative rights and preferences have not been fixed and determined or the relative rights and preferences theretofore fixed and determined are to be changed.

(n) To revoke, diminish, or enlarge the authority of the board of directors to establish series out of authorized but unissued shares of any preferred or special class and fix and determine the relative rights and preferences of the shares of any series so established.

(o) To limit, deny or grant to shareholders of any class the preemptive right to acquire additional shares of the corporation, whether then or thereafter authorized.

§ 59. Procedure to Amend Articles of Incorporation

Amendments to the articles of incorporation shall be made in the following manner:

(a) The board of directors shall adopt a resolution setting forth the proposed amendment and, if shares have been issued, directing that it be submitted to a vote at a meeting of shareholders, which may be either the annual or a special meeting. If no shares have been issued, the amendment shall be adopted by resolution of the board of directors and the provisions for adoption by shareholders shall not apply. If the corporation has only one class of shares outstanding, an amendment solely to change the number of authorized shares to effectuate a split of, or stock dividend in, the corporation's own shares, or solely to do so and to change the number of authorized shares in proportion thereto, may be adopted by the board of directors; and the provisions for adoption by shareholders shall not apply, unless otherwise provided by the articles of incorporation. The resolution may incorporate the proposed amendment in restated articles of incorporation which contain a statement that except for the designated amendment the restated articles of incorporation correctly set forth without change the corresponding provisions of the articles of incorporation as theretofore amended, and that the restated articles of incorporation together with the designated amendment supersede the original articles of incorporation and all amendments thereto.

(b) Written notice setting forth the proposed amendment or a summary of the changes to be effected thereby shall be given to each shareholder of record entitled to vote thereon within the time and in the manner provided in this Act for the giving of notice of meetings of shareholders. If the meeting be an annual meeting, the proposed amendment of such summary may be included in the notice of such annual meeting.

(c) At such meeting a vote of the shareholders entitled to vote thereon shall be taken on the proposed amendment. The proposed amendment shall be adopted upon receiving the affirmative vote of the holders of a majority of the shares entitled to vote thereon, unless any class of shares is entitled to vote thereon as a class, in which event the proposed amendment shall be adopted upon receiving the affirmative vote of the holders of a majority of the shares of each class of shares entitled to vote thereon as a class and of the total shares entitled to vote thereon.

Any number of amendments may be submitted to the shareholders, and voted upon by them, at one meeting.

§ 60. Class Voting on Amendments

The holders of the outstanding shares of a class shall be entitled to vote as a class upon a proposed amendment, whether or not entitled to vote thereon by the provisions of the articles of incorporation, if the amendment would:

(a) Increase or decrease the aggregate number of authorized shares of such class.

(b) Effect an exchange, reclassification or cancellation of all or part of the shares of such class.

(c) Effect an exchange, or create a right of exchange, of all or any part of the shares of another class into the shares of such class.

(d) Change the designations, preferences, limitations or relative rights of the shares of such class.

(e) Change the shares of such class, into the same or a different number of shares of the same class or another class or classes.

(f) Create a new class of shares having rights and preferences prior and superior to the shares of such class, or increase the rights and preferences or the number of authorized shares, of any class having rights and preferences prior or superior to the shares of such class.

(g) In the case of a preferred or special class of shares, divide the shares of such class into series and fix and determine the designation of such series and the variations in the relative rights and preferences between the shares of such series, or authorize the board of directors to do so.

(h) Limit or deny any existing preemptive rights of the shares of such class.

(i) Cancel or otherwise affect dividends on the shares of such class which have accrued but have not been declared.

§ 61. Articles of Amendment

The articles of amendment shall be executed in duplicate by the corporation by its president or a vice president and by its secretary or an assistant secretary, and verified by one of the officers signing such articles, and shall set forth:

(a) The name of the corporation.

(b) The amendments so adopted.

(c) The date of the adoption of the amendment by the shareholders, or by the board of directors where no shares have been issued.

(d) The number of shares outstanding, and the number of shares entitled to vote thereon, and if the shares of any class are entitled to vote thereon as a class, the designation and number of outstanding shares entitled to vote thereon of each such class.

(e) The number of shares voted for and against such amendment, respectively, and, if the shares of any class are entitled to vote thereon as a class, the number of shares of each such class voted for and against such amendment, respectively, or if no shares have been issued, a statement to that effect.

(f) If such amendment provides for an exchange, reclassification or cancellation of issued shares, and if the manner in which the same shall be effected is not set forth in the amendment, then a statement of the manner in which the same shall be effected.

§ 62. Filing of Articles of Amendment

Duplicate originals of the articles of amendment shall be delivered to the Secretary of State. If the Secretary of State finds that the articles of amendment conform to law, he shall, when all fees and franchise taxes have been paid as in this Act prescribed:

(a) Endorse on each of such duplicate originals the word "Filed," and the month, day and year of the filing thereof.

(b) File one of such duplicate originals in his office.

(c) Issue a certificate of amendment to which he shall affix the other duplicate original.

The certificate of amendment, together with the duplicate original of the articles of amendment affixed thereto by the Secretary of State, shall be returned to the corporation or its representative.

§ 63. Effect of Certificate of Amendment

Upon the issuance of the certificate of amendment by the Secretary of State, the amendment shall become effective and the articles of incorporation shall be deemed to be amended accordingly.

No amendment shall affect any existing cause of action in favor of or against such corporation, or any pending suit to which such corporation shall be a party, or the existing rights of persons other than shareholders; and, in the event the corporate name shall be changed by amendment, no suit brought by or against such corporation under its former name shall abate for that reason.

§ 64. Restated Articles of Incorporation

A domestic corporation may at any time restate its articles of incorporation as theretofore amended, by a resolution adopted by the board of directors.

Upon the adoption of such resolution, restated articles of incorporation shall be executed in duplicate by the corporation by its president or a vice president and by its secretary or assistant secretary and verified by one of the officers signing such articles and shall set forth all of the operative provisions of the articles of incorporation as theretofore amended together with a statement that the restated articles of incorporation correctly set forth without change the corresponding provisions of the articles of incorporation as theretofore amended and that the restated articles of incorporation supersede the original articles of incorporation and all amendments thereto.

Duplicate originals of the restated articles of incorporation shall be delivered to the Secretary of State. If the Secretary of State finds that such restated articles of incorporation conform to law, he shall, when all fees and franchise taxes have been paid as in this Act prescribed:

(1) Endorse on each of such duplicate originals the word "Filed," and the month, day and year of the filing thereof.

(2) File one of such duplicate originals in his office.

(3) Issue a restated certificate of incorporation, to which he shall affix the other duplicate original.

The restated certificate of incorporation, together with the duplicate original of the restated articles of incorporation affixed thereto by the Secretary of State, shall be returned to the corporation or its representative.

Upon the issuance of the restated certificate of incorporation by the Secretary of State, the restated articles of incorporation shall become effective and shall supersede the original articles of incorporation and all amendments thereto.

§ 65. Amendment of Articles of Incorporation in Reorganization Proceedings

Whenever a plan of reorganization of a corporation has been confirmed by decree or order of a court of competent jurisdiction in proceedings for the reorganization of such corporation, pursuant to the provisions of any applicable statute of the United States relating to reorganizations of corporations, the articles of incorporation of the corporation may be amended, in the manner provided in this section, in as many respects as may be necessary to carry out the plan and put it into effect, so long as the articles of incorporation as amended contain only such provisions as might be lawfully contained in original articles of incorporation at the time of making such amendment.

In particular and without limitation upon such general power of amendment, the articles of incorporation may be amended for such purpose so as to:

(A) Change the corporate name, period of duration or corporate purposes of the corporation;

(B) Repeal, alter or amend the by-laws of the corporation;

(C) Change the aggregate number of shares or shares of any class, which the corporation has authority to issue;

(D) Change the preferences, limitations and relative rights in respect of all or any part of the shares of the corporation, and classify, reclassify or cancel all or any part thereof, whether issued or unissued;

(E) Authorize the issuance of bonds, debentures or other obligations of the corporation, whether or not convertible into shares of any class or bearing warrants or other evidences of optional rights to purchase or subscribe for shares of any class, and fix the terms and conditions thereof; and

(F) Constitute or reconstitute and classify or reclassify the board of directors of the corporation, and appoint directors and officers in place of or in addition to all or any of the directors or officers then in office.

Amendments to the articles of incorporation pursuant to this section shall be made in the following manner:

(a) Articles of amendment approved by decree or order of such court shall be executed and verified in duplicate by such person or persons as the court shall designate or appoint for the purpose, and shall set forth the name of the corporation, the amendments of the articles of incorporation approved by the court, the date of the decree or order approving the articles of amendment, the title of the proceedings in which the decree or order was entered, and a statement that such decree or order was entered by a court having jurisdiction of the proceedings for the reorganization of the corporation pursuant to the provisions of an applicable statute of the United States.

(b) Duplicate originals of the articles of amendment shall be delivered to the Secretary of State. If the Secretary of State finds that the articles of amendment conform to law, he shall, when all fees and franchise taxes have been paid as in this Act prescribed:

(1) Endorse on each of such duplicate originals the word "Filed," and the month, day and year of the filing thereof.

(2) File one of such duplicate originals in his office.

(3) Issue a certificate of amendment to which he shall affix the other duplicate original.

The certificate of amendment, together with the duplicate original of the articles of amendment affixed thereto by the Secretary of State, shall be returned to the corporation or its representative.

Upon the issuance of the certificate of amendment by the Secretary of State, the amendment shall become effective and the articles of incorporation shall be deemed to be amended accordingly, without any action thereon by the directors or shareholders of the corporation and with the same effect as if the amendments had been adopted by unanimous action of the directors and shareholders of the corporation.

§ 66. Restriction on Redemption or Purchase of Redeemable Shares [Repealed]

§ 67. Cancellation of Redeemable Shares by Redemption or Purchase [Repealed]

§ 68. Cancellation of Other Reacquired Shares [Repealed]

§ 69. Reduction of Stated Capital in Certain Cases [Repealed]

§ 70. Special Provisions Relating to Surplus and Reserves [Repealed]

§ 71. Procedure for Merger

Any two or more domestic corporations may merge into one of such corporations pursuant to a plan of merger approved in the manner provided in this Act.

The board of directors of each corporation shall, by resolution adopted by each such board, approve a plan of merger setting forth:

(a) The names of the corporations proposing to merge, and the name of the corporation into which they propose to merge, which is hereinafter designated as the surviving corporation.

(b) The terms and conditions of the proposed merger.

(c) The manner and basis of converting the shares of each corporation into shares, obligations or other securities of the surviving corporation or of any other corporation or, in whole or in part, into cash or other property.

(d) A statement of any changes in the articles of incorporation of the surviving corporation to be effected by such merger.

(e) Such other provisions with respect to the proposed merger as are deemed necessary or desirable.

§ 72. Procedure for Consolidation

Any two or more domestic corporations may consolidate into a new corporation pursuant to a plan of consolidation approved in the manner provided in this Act.

The board of directors of each corporation shall, by a resolution adopted by each such board, approve a plan of consolidation setting forth:

(a) The names of the corporations proposing to consolidate, and the name of the new corporation into which they propose to consolidate, which is hereinafter designated as the new corporation.

(b) The terms and conditions of the proposed consolidation.

(c) The manner and basis of converting the shares of each corporation into shares, obligations or other securities of the new corporation or of any other corporation or, in whole or in part, into cash or other property.

(d) With respect to the new corporation, all of the statements required to be set forth in articles of incorporation for corporations organized under this Act.

(e) Such other provisions with respect to the proposed consolidation as are deemed necessary or desirable.

§ 72A. Procedure for Share Exchange

All the issued or all the outstanding shares of one or more classes of any domestic corporation may be acquired through the exchange of all such shares of such class or classes by another domestic or foreign corporation pursuant to a plan of exchange approved in the manner provided in this Act.

The board of directors of each corporation shall, by resolution adopted by each such board, approve a plan of exchange setting forth:

(a) The name of the corporation the shares of which are proposed to be acquired by exchange and the name of the corporation to acquire the shares of such corporation in the exchange, which is hereinafter designated as the acquiring corporation.

(b) The terms and conditions of the proposed exchange.

(c) The manner and basis of exchanging the shares to be acquired for shares, obligations or other securities of the acquiring corporation or any other corporation, or, in whole or in part, for cash or other property.

(d) Such other provisions with respect to the proposed exchange as are deemed necessary or desirable.

The procedure authorized by this Section shall not be deemed to limit the power of a corporation to acquire all or part of the shares of any class or classes of a corporation through a voluntary exchange or otherwise by agreement with the shareholders.

§ 73. Approval by Shareholders

(a) The board of directors of each corporation in the case of a merger or consolidation, and the board of directors of the corporation the shares of which are to be acquired in the case of an exchange, upon approving such plan of merger, consolidation or exchange, shall, by resolution, direct that the plan be submitted to a vote at a meeting of its shareholders, which may be either an annual or a special meeting. Written notice shall be given to each shareholder of record, whether or not entitled to vote at such meeting, not less than twenty days before such meeting, in the manner provided in this Act for the giving of notice of meetings of shareholders, and, whether the meeting be an annual or a special meeting, shall state that the purpose or one of the purposes is to condiser the proposed plan of merger, consolidation or exchange. A copy or a summary of the plan of merger, consolidation or exchange, as the case may be, shall be included in or enclosed with such notice.

(b) At each such meeting, a vote of the shareholders shall be taken on the proposed plan. The plan shall be approved upon receiving the affirmative vote of the holders of a majority of the shares entitled to vote thereon of each such corporation, unless any class of shares of any such corporation is entitled to vote thereon as a class, in which event, as to such corporation, the plan shall be approved upon receiving the affirmative vote of the holders of a majority of the shares of each class of shares entitled to vote thereon.

Any class of shares of any such corporation shall be entitled to vote as a class if any such plan contains any provision which, if contained in a proposed amendment to articles of incorporation, would entitle such class of shares to vote as a class and, in the case of an exchange, if the class is included in the exchange.

(c) After such approval by a vote of the shareholders ofeach such corporation, and at any time prior to the filing of the articles of merger, consolidation or exchange, the merger, consolidation or exchange may be abandoned pursuant to provisions therefor, if any, set forth in the plan.

(d) (1) Notwithstanding the provisions of subsections (a) and (b), submission of a plan of merger to a vote at a meeting of shareholders of a surviving corporation shall not be required if—

(i) the articles of incorporation of the surviving corporation do not differ except in name from those of the corporation before the merger,

(ii) each holder of shares of the surviving corporation which were outstanding immediately before the effective date of the merger is to hold the same number of shares with identical rights immediately after,

(iii) the number of voting shares outstanding immediately after the merger, plus the number of voting shares issuable on conversion of other securities issued by virtue of the terms of the merger and on exercise of rights and warrants so issued, will not exceed by more than 20 percent the number of voting shares outstanding immediately before the merger, and

(iv) the number of participating shares outstanding immediately after the merger, plus the number of participating shares issuable on conversion of other securities issued by virtue of the terms of the merger and on exercise of rights and warrants so issued, will not exceed by more than 20 percent the number of participating shares outstanding immediately before the merger.

(2) As used in this subsection—

(i) "voting shares" means shares which entitle their holders to vote unconditionally in elections of directors;

(ii) "participating shares" means shares which entitle their holders to participate without limitation in distribution of earnings or surplus.

§ 74. Articles of Merger, Consolidation or Exchange

(a) Upon receiving the approvals required by Sections 71, 72 and 73, articles of merger or articles of consolidation shall be executed in duplicate by each corporation by its president or a vice president and by its secretary or an assistant secretary, and verified by one of the officers of each corporation signing such articles, and shall set forth:

(1) The plan of merger or the plan of consolidation;

(2) As to each corporation, either (i) the number of shares outstanding, and, if the shares of any class are entitled to vote as a class, the designation and number of outstanding shares of each such class; or (ii) a statement that the vote of shareholders is not required by virtue of subsection 73(d);

(3) As to each corporation the approval of whose shareholders is required, the number of shares voted for and against such plan, respectively, and, if the shares of any class are entitled to vote as a class, the number of shares of each such class voted for and against such plan, respectively.

(b) Duplicate originals of the articles of merger, consolidation or exchange shall be delivered to the Secretary of State. If the Secretary of State finds that such articles conform to law, he shall, when all fees and franchise taxes have been paid as in this Act prescribed:

(1) Endorse on each of such duplicate originals the word "Filed," and the month, day and year of the filing thereof.

(2) File one of such duplicate originals in his office.

(3) Issue a certificate of merger, consolidation or exchange to which he shall affix the other duplicate original.

(c) The certificate of merger, consolidation or exchange together with the duplicate original of the articles affixed thereto by the Secretary of State, shall be returned to the surviving, new or acquiring corporation, as the case may be, or its representative.

§ 75. Merger of Subsidiary Corporation

Any corporation owning at least ninety per cent of the outstanding shares of each class of another corporation may merge such other corporation into itself without approval by a vote of the shareholders of either corporation. Its board of directors shall, by resolution, approve a plan of merger setting forth:

(A) The name of the subsidiary corporation and the name of the corporation owning at least ninety per cent of its shares, which is hereinafter designated as the surviving corporation.

(B) The manner and basis of converting the shares of the subsidiary corporation into shares, obligations or other securities of the surviving corporation or or of any other corporation or, in whole or in part, into cash or other property.

A copy of such plan of merger shall be mailed to each shareholder of record of the subsidiary corporation.

Articles of merger shall be executed in duplicate by the surviving corporation by its president or a vice president and by its secretary or an assistant secretary, and verified by one of its officers signing such articles, and shall set forth:

(a) The plan of merger;

(b) The number of outstanding shares of each class of the subsidiary corporation and the number of such shares of each class owned by the surviving corporation; and

(c) The date of the mailing to shareholders of the subsidiary corporation of a copy of the plan of merger.

On and after the thirtieth day after the mailing of a copy of the plan of merger to shareholders of the subsidiary corporation or upon the waiver thereof by the holders of all outstanding shares duplicate originals of the articles of merger shall be delivered to the Secretary of State. If the Secretary of State finds that such articles conform to law, he shall, when all fees and franchise taxes have been paid as in this Act prescribed:

(1) Endorse on each of such duplicate originals the word "Filed," and the month, day and year of the filing thereof,

(2) File one of such duplicate originals in his office, and

(3) Issue a certificate of merger to which he shall affix the other duplicate original.

The certificate of merger, together with the duplicate original of the articles of merger affixed thereto by the Secretary of State, shall be returned to the surviving corporation or its representative.

§ 76. Effect of Merger, Consolidation or Exchange

Upon the issuance of the certificate of merger or the certificate of consolidation by the Secretary of State, the merger or consolidation shall be effected.

When such merger or consolidation has been effected:

(a) The several corporations parties to the plan of merger or consolidation shall be a single corporation, which, in the case of a merger, shall be that corporation designated in the plan of merger as the surviving corporation, and, in the case of a consolidation, shall be the new corporation provided for in the plan of consolidation.

(b) The separate existence of all corporations parties to the plan of merger or consolidation, except the surviving or new corporation, shall cease.

(c) Such surviving or new corporation shall have all the rights, privileges, immunities and powers and shall be subject to all the duties and liabilities of a corporation organized under this Act.

(d) Such surviving or new corporation shall thereupon and thereafter possess all the rights, privileges, immunities, and franchises, of a public as well as of a private nature, of each of the merging or consolidating corporations; and all property, real, personal and mixed, and all debts due on whatever account, including subscriptions to shares, and all other choses in action, and all and every other interest of or belonging to or due to each of the corporations so merged or consolidated, shall be taken and deemed to be transferred to and vested in such single corporation without further act or deed; and the title to any real estate, or any interest therein, vested in any of such corporations shall not revert or be in any way impaired by reason of such merger or consolidation.

(e) Such surviving or new corporation shall thenceforth be responsible and liable for all the liabilities and obligations of each of the corporations so merged or consolidated; and any claim existing or action or proceeding pending by or against any of such corporations may be prosecuted as if such merger or consolidation had not taken place, or such surviving or new corporation may be substituted in its place. Neither the rights of creditors nor any liens upon the property of any such corporation shall be impaired by such merger or consolidation.

(f) In the case of a merger, the articles of incorporation of the surviving corporation shall be deemed to be amended to the extent, if any, that changes in its articles of incorporation are stated in the plan of merger; and, in the case of a consolidation, the statements set forth in the articles of consolidation and which are required or permitted to be set forth in the articles of incorporation of corporations organized under this Act shall be deemed to be the original articles of incorporation of the new corporation.

§ 77. Merger, Consolidation or Exchange of Shares Between Domestic and Foreign Corporations

One or more foreign corporations and one or more domestic corporations may be merged or consolidated in the following manner, if such merger, consolidation or exchange is permitted by the laws of the state under which each such foreign corporation is organized:

(a) Each domestic corporation shall comply with the provisions of this Act with respect to the merger, consolidation or exchange, as the case may be, of domestic corporations and each foreign corporation shall comply with the applicable provisions of the laws of the state under which it is organized.

(b) If the surviving or new corporation in a merger or consolidation is to be governed by the laws of any state other than this State, it shall comply with the provisions of this Act with respect to foreign corporations if it is to transact business in this State, and in every case it shall file with the Secretary of State of this State:

(1) An agreement that it may be served with process in this State in any proceeding for the enforcement of any obligation of any domestic corporation which is a party to such merger or consolidation and in any proceeding for the enforcement of the rights of a dissenting shareholder of any such domestic corporation against the surviving or new corporation;

(2) An irrevocable appointment of the Secretary of State of this State as its agent to accept service of process in any such proceeding; and

(3) An agreement that it will promptly pay to the dissenting shareholders of any such domestic corporation, the amount, if any, to which they shall be entitled under provisions of this Act with respect to the rights of dissenting shareholders.

The effect of such merger or consolidation shall be the same as in the case of the merger or consolidation of domestic corporations, if the surviving or new corporation is to be governed by the laws of this State. If the surviving or new corporation is to be governed by the laws of any state other than this State, the effect of such merger or consolidation shall be the same as in the case of the merger or consolidation of domestic corporations except insofar as the laws of such other state provide otherwise.

At any time prior to the filing of the articles of merger or consolidation, the merger or consolidation may be abandoned pursuant to provisions therefor, if any, set forth in the plan of merger or consolidation.

§ 78. Sale of Assets in Regular Course of Business and Mortgage or Pledge of Assets

The sale, lease, exchange, or other disposition of all, or substantially all, the property and assets of a corporation in the usual and regular course of its business and the mortgage or pledge of any or all property and assets of a corporation whether or not in the usual and regular course of business may be made upon such terms and conditions and for such consideration, which may consist in whole or in part of cash or other property, including shares, obligations or other securities of any other corporation, domestic or foreign, as shall be authorized by its board of directors; and in any such case no authorization or consent of the shareholders shall be required.

§ 79. Sale of Assets Other Than in Regular Course of Business

A sale, lease, exchange, or other disposition of all, or substantially all, the property and assets, with or without the good will, of a corporation, if not in the usual and regular course of its business, may be made upon such terms and conditions and for such consideration, which may consist in whole or in part of cash or other property, including shares, obligations or other securities of any other corporation, domestic or foreign, as may be authorized in the following manner:

(a) The board of directors shall adopt a resolution recommending such sale, lease, exchange, or other disposition and directing the submission thereof to a vote at a meeting of shareholders, which may be either an annual or a special meeting.

(b) Written notice shall be given to each shareholder of record, whether or not entitled to vote at such meeting, not less than twenty days before such meeting, in the manner provided in this Act for the giving of notice of meetings of shareholders, and, whether the meeting be an annual or a special meeting, shall state that the purpose, or one of the purposes is to consider the proposed sale, lease, exchange, or other disposition.

(c) At such meeting the shareholders may authorize such sale, lease, exchange, or other disposition and may fix, or may authorize the board of directors to fix, any or all of the terms and conditions thereof and the consideration to be received by the corporation therefor. Such authorization shall require the affirmative vote of the holders of a majority of the shares of the corporation entitled to vote thereon, unless any class of shares is entitled to vote thereon as a class, in which event such authorization shall require the affirmative vote of the holders of a majority of the shares of each class of shares entitled to vote as a class thereon and of the total shares entitled to vote thereon.

(d) After such authorization by a vote of shareholders, the board of directors nevertheless, in its discretion, may abandon such sale, lease, exchange, or other disposition of assets, subject to the rights of third parties under any contracts relating thereto, without further action or approval by shareholders.

§ 80. Right of Shareholders to Dissent and Obtain Payment for Shares

(a) Any shareholder of a corporation shall have the right to dissent from, and to obtain payment for his shares in the event of, any of the following corporate actions:

(1) Any plan of merger or consolidation to which the corporation is a party, except as provided in subsection (c);

(2) Any sale or exchange of all or substantially all of the property and assets of the corporation not made in the usual or regular course of its business, including a sale in dissolution, but not including a sale pursuant to an order of a court having jurisdiction in the premises or a sale for cash on terms requiring that all or substantially all of the net proceeds of sale be distributed to the shareholders in accordance with their respective interests within one year after the date of sale;

(3) Any plan of exchange to which the corporation is a party as the corporation the shares of which are to be acquired;

(4) Any amendment of the articles of incorporation which materially and adversely affects the rights appurtenant to the shares of the dissenting shareholder in that it—

(i) alters or abolishes a preferential right of such shares;

(ii) creates, alters or abolishes a right in respect of the redemption of such shares, including a provision respecting a sinking fund for the redemption or repurchase of such shares;

(iii) alters or abolishes a preemptive right of the holder of such shares to acquire shares or other securities;

(iv) excludes or limits the right of the holder of such shares to vote on any matter, or to cumulate his votes, except as such right may be limited by dilution through the issuance of shares or other securities with similar voting rights; or

(5) Any other corporate action taken pursuant to a shareholder vote with respect to which the articles of incorporation, the bylaws, or a resolution of the board of directors directs that dissenting shareholders shall have a right to obtain payment for their shares.

(b) (1) A record holder of shares may assert dissenters' rights as to less than all of the shares registered in his name only if he dissents with respect to all the shares beneficially owned by any one person, and discloses the name and address of the person or persons on whose behalf he dissents. In that event, his rights shall be determined as if the shares as to which he has dissented and his other shares were registered in the names of different shareholders.

(2) A beneficial owner of shares who is not the record holder may assert dissenters' rights with respect to shares held on his behalf, and shall be treated as a dissenting shareholder under the terms of this section and Section 81 if he submits to the corporation at the time of or before the assertion of these rights a written consent of the record holder.

(c) The right to obtain payment under this section shall not apply to the shareholders of the surviving corporation in a merger if a vote of the shareholders of such corporation is not necessary to authorize such merger.

(d) A shareholder of a corporation who has a right under this section to obtain payment for his shares shall have no right at law or in equity to attack the validity of the corporate action that gives rise to his right to obtain payment, nor to have the action set aside or rescinded, except when the corporate action is unlawful or fraudulent with regard to the complaining shareholder or to the corporation.

§ 81. Procedures for Protection of Dissenters' Rights

(a) As used in this section:

(1) "Dissenter" means a shareholder or beneficial owner who is entitled to and does assert dissenters' rights under Section 80, and who has performed every act required up to the time involved for the assertion of such rights.

(2) "Corporation" means the issuer of the shares held by the dissenter before the corporate action, or the successor by merger or consolidation of that issuer.

(3) "Fair value" of shares means their value immediately before the effectuation of the corporate action to which the dissenter objects, excluding any appreciation or depreciation in anticipation of such corporate action unless such exclusion would be inequitable.

(4) "Interest" means interest from the effective date of the corporate action until the date of payment, at the average rate currently paid by the corporation on its principal bank loans, or, if none, at such rate as is fair and equitable under all the circumstances.

(b) If a proposed corporate action which would give

rise to dissenters' rights under Section 80(a) is submitted to a vote at a meeting of shareholders, the notice of meeting shall notify all shareholders that they have or may have a right to dissent and obtain payment for their shares by complying with the terms of this section, and shall be accompanied by a copy of sections 80 and 81 of this Act.

(c) If the proposed corporate action is submitted to a vote at a meeting of shareholders, any shareholder who wishes to dissent and obtain payment for his shares must file with the corporation, prior to the vote, a written notice of intention to demand that he be paid fair compensation for his shares if the proposed action is effectuated, and shall refrain from voting his shares in approval of such action. A shareholder who fails in either respect shall acquire no right to payment for his shares under this section or section 80.

(d) If the proposed corporate action is approved by the required vote at a meeting of shareholders, the corporation shall mail a further notice to all shareholders who gave due notice of intention to demand payment and who refrained from voting in favor of the proposed action. If the proposed corporate action is to be taken without a vote of shareholders, the corporation shall send to all shareholders who are entitled to dissent and demand payment for their shares a notice of the adoption of the plan of corporate action. The notice shall (1) state where and when a demand for payment must be sent and certificates of certificated shares must be deposited in order to obtain payment, (2) inform holders of uncertificated shares to what extent transfer of shares will be restricted from the time that demand for payment is received, (3) supply a form for demanding payment which includes a request for certification of the date on which the shareholder, or the person on whose behalf the shareholder dissents, acquired beneficial ownership of the shares, and (4) be accompanied by a copy of sections 80 and 81 of this Act. The time set for the demand and deposit shall be not less than 30 days from the mailing of the notice.

(e) A shareholder who fails to demand payment, or fails (in the case of certificated shares) to deposit certificates, as required by a notice pursuant to subsection (d) shall have no right under this section or section 80 to receive payment for his shares. If the shares are not represented by certificates, the corporation may restrict their transfer from the time of receipt of demand for payment until effectuation of the proposed corporate action, or the release of restrictions under the terms of subsection (f). The dissenter shall retain all other rights of a shareholder until these rights are modified by effectuation of the proposed corporate action.

(f) (1) Within 60 days after the date set for demanding payment and depositing certificates, if the corporation has not effectuated the proposed corporate action and remitted payment for shares pursuant to paragraph (3), it shall return any certificates that have been deposited, and release uncertificated shares from any transfer restrictions imposed by reason of the demand for payment.

(2) When uncertificated shares have been released from transfer restrictions, and deposited certificates have been returned, the corporation may at any later time send a new notice conforming to the requirements of subsection (d), with like effect.

(3) Immediately upon effectuation of the proposed corporate action, or upon receipt of demand for payment if the corporate action has already been effectuated, the corporation shall remit to dissenters who have made demand and (if their shares are certificated) have deposited their certificates the amount which the corporation estimates to be the fair value of the shares, with interest if any has accrued. The remittance shall be accompanied by:

(i) the corporation's closing balance sheet and statement of income for a fiscal year ending not more than 16 months before the date of remittance, together with the latest available interim financial statements;

(ii) a statement of the corporation's estimate of fair value of the shares; and

(iii) a notice of the dissenter's right to demand supplemental payment, accompanied by a copy of sections 80 and 81 of this Act.

(g) (1) If the corporation fails to remit as required by subsection (f), or if the dissenter believes that the amount remitted is less than the fair value of his shares, or that the interest is not correctly determined, he may send the corporation his own estimate of the value of the shares or of the interest, and demand payment of the deficiency.

(2) If the dissenter does not file such an estimate within 30 days after the corporation's mailing of its remittance, he shall be entitled to no more than the amount remitted.

(h) (1) Within 60 days after receiving a demand for payment pursuant to subsection (g), if any such demands for payment remain unsettled, the corporation shall file in an appropriate court a petition requesting that the fair value of the shares and interest thereon be determined by the court.

(2) An appropriate court shall be a court of competent jurisdiction in the county of this state where the registered office of the corporation is located. If, in the

case of a merger or consolidation or exchange of shares, the corporation is a foreign corporation without a registered office in this state, the petition shall be filed in the county where the registered office of the domestic corporation was last located.

(3) All dissenters, wherever residing, whose demands have not been settled shall be made parties to the proceeding as in an action against their shares. A copy of the petition shall be served on each such dissenter; if a dissenter is a nonresident, the copy may be served on him by registered or certified mail or by publication as provided by law.

(4) The jurisdiction of the court shall be plenary and exclusive. The court may appoint one or more persons as appraisers to receive evidence and recommend a decision on the question of fair value. The appraisers shall have such power and authority as shall be specified in the order of their appointment or in any amendment thereof. The dissenters shall be entitled to discovery in the same manner as parties in other civil suits.

(5) All dissenters who are made parties shall be entitled to judgment for the amount by which the fair value of their shares is found to exceed the amount previously remitted, with interest.

(6) If the corporation fails to file a petition as provided in paragraph (1) of this subsection, each dissenter who made a demand and who has not already settled his claim against the corporation shall be paid by the corporation the amount demanded by him, with interest, and may sue therefor in an appropriate court.

(i) (1) The costs and expenses of any proceeding under subsection (h), including the reasonable compensation and expenses of appraisers appointed by the court, shall be determined by the court and assessed against the corporation, except that any part of the costs and expenses may be apportioned and assessed as the court may deem equitable against all or some of the dissenters who are parties and whose action in demanding supplemental payment the court finds to be arbitrary, vexatious, or not in good faith.

(2) Fees and expenses of counsel and of experts for the respective parties may be assessed as the court may deem equitable against the corporation and in favor of any or all dissenters if the corporation failed to comply substantially with the requirements of this section, and may be assessed against either the corporation or a dissenter, in favor of any other party, if the court finds that the party against whom the fees and expenses are assessed acted arbitrarily, vexatiously, or not in good faith in respect to the rights provided by this section and section 80.

(3) If the court finds that the services of counsel for any dissenter were of substantial benefit to other dissenters similarly situated, and should not be assessed against the corporation, it may award to these counsel reasonable fees to be paid out of the amounts awarded to the dissenters who were benefitted.

(j) (1) Notwithstanding the foregoing provisions of this section, the corporation may elect to withhold the remittance required by subsection (f) from any dissenter with respect to shares of which the dissenter (or the person on whose behalf the dissenter acts) was not the beneficial owner on the date of the first announcement to news media or to shareholders of the terms of the proposed corporate action. With respect to such shares, the corporation shall, upon effectuating the corporate action, state to each dissenter its estimate of the fair value of the shares, state the rate of interest to be used (explaining the basis thereof), and offer to pay the resulting amounts on receiving the dissenter's agreement to accept them in full satisfaction.

(2) If the dissenter believes that the amount offered is less than the fair value of the shares and interest determined according to this section, he may within 30 days after the date of mailing of the corporation's offer, mail the corporation his own estimate of fair value and interest, and demand their payment. If the dissenter fails to do so, he shall be entitled to no more than the corporation's offer.

(3) If the dissenter makes a demand as provided in paragraph (2), the provisions of subsections (h) and (i) shall apply to further proceedings on the dissenter's demand.

§ 82. Voluntary Dissolution by Incorporators

A corporation which has not commenced business and which has not issued any shares, may be voluntarily dissolved by its incorporators at any time in the following manner:

(a) Articles of dissolution shall be executed in duplicate by a majority of the incorporators, and verified by them, and shall set forth:

(1) The name of the corporation.

(2) The date of issuance of its certificate of incorporation.

(3) That none of its shares has been issued.

(4) That the corporation has not commenced business.

(5) That the amount, if any, actually paid in on subscriptions for its shares, less any part thereof disbursed for necessary expenses, has been returned to those entitled thereto.

(6) That no debts of the corporation remain unpaid.

(7) That a majority of the incorporators elect that the corporation be dissolved.

(b) Duplicate originals of the articles of dissolution shall be delivered to the Secretary of State. If the Secretary of State finds that the articles of dissolution conform to law, he shall, when all fees and franchise taxes have been paid as in this Act prescribed:

(1) Endorse on each of such duplicate originals the word "Filed," and the month, day and year of the filing thereof.

(2) File one of such duplicate originals in his office.

(3) Issue a certificate of dissolution to which he shall affix the other duplicate original.

The certificate of dissolution, together with the duplicate original of the articles of dissolution affixed thereto by the Secretary of State, shall be returned to the incorporators or their representative. Upon the issuance of such certificate of dissolution by the Secretary of State, the existence of the corporation shall cease.

§ 83. Voluntary Dissolution by Consent of Shareholders

A corporation may be voluntarily dissolved by the written consent of all of its shareholders.

Upon the execution of such written consent, a statement of intent to dissolve shall be executed in duplicate by the corporation by its president or a vice president and by its secretary or an assistant secretary, and verified by one of the officers signing such statement, which statement shall set forth:

(a) The name of the corporation.

(b) The names and respective addresses of its officers.

(c) The names and respective addresses of its directors.

(d) A copy of the written consent signed by all shareholders of the corporation.

(e) A statement that such written consent has been signed by all shareholders of the corporation or signed in their names by their attorneys thereunto duly authorized.

§ 84. Voluntary Dissolution by Act of Corporation

A corporation may be dissolved by the act of the corporation, when authorized in the following manner:

(a) The board of directors shall adopt a resolution recommending that the corporation be dissolved, and directing that the question of such dissolution be submitted to a vote at a meeting of shareholders, which may be either an annual or a special meeting.

(b) Written notice shall be given to each shareholder of record entitled to vote at such meeting within the time and in the manner provided in this Act for the giving of notice of meetings of shareholders, and, whether the meeting be an annual or special meeting, shall state that the purpose, or one of the purposes, of such meeting is to consider the advisability of dissolving the corporation.

(c) At such meeting a vote of shareholders entitled to vote thereat shall be taken on a resolution to dissolve the corporation. Such resolution shall be adopted upon receiving the affirmative vote of the holders of a majority of the shares of the corporation entitled to vote thereon, unless any class of shares is entitled to vote thereon as a class, in which event the resolution shall be adopted upon receiving the affirmative vote of the holders of a majority of the shares of each class of shares entitled to vote thereon as a class and of the total shares entitled to vote thereon.

(d) Upon the adoption of such resolution, a statement of intent to dissolve shall be executed in duplicate by the corporation by its president or a vice president and by its secretary or an assistant secretary, and verified by one of the officers signing such statement, which statement shall set forth:

(1) The name of the corporation.

(2) The names and respective addresses of its officers.

(3) The names and respective addresses of its directors.

(4) A copy of the resolution adopted by the shareholders authorizing the dissolution of the corporation.

(5) The number of shares outstanding, and, if the shares of any class are entitled to vote as a class, the designation and number of outstanding shares of each such class.

(6) The number of shares voted for and against the resolution, respectively, and, if the shares of any class are entitled to vote as a class, the number of shares of each such class voted for and against the resolution, respectively.

§ 85. Filing of Statement of Intent to Dissolve

Duplicate originals of the statement of intent to dissolve, whether by consent of shareholders or by act of the corporation, shall be delivered to the Secretary of State. If the Secretary of State finds that such statement conforms to law, he shall, when all fees and franchise taxes have been paid as in this Act prescribed:

(a) Endorse on each of such duplicate originals the word "Filed," and the month, day and year of the filing thereof.

(b) File one of such duplicate originals in his office.

(c) Return the other duplicate original to the corporation or its representative.

§ 86. Effect of Statement of Intent to Dissolve

Upon the filing by the Secretary of State of a statement of intent to dissolve, whether by consent of shareholders or by act of the corporation, the corporation shall cease to carry on its business, except insofar as may be necessary for the winding up thereof, but its corporate existence shall continue until a certificate of dissolution has been issued by the Secretary of State or until a decree dissolving the corporation has been entered by a court of competent jurisdiction as in this Act provided.

§ 87. Procedure after Filing of Statement of Intent to Dissolve

After the filing by the Secretary of State of a statement of intent to dissolve:

(a) The corporation shall immediately cause notice thereof to be mailed to each known creditor of the corporation.

(b) The corporation shall proceed to collect its assets, convey and dispose of such of its properties as are not to be distributed in kind to its shareholders, pay, satisfy and discharge its liabilities and obligations and do all other acts required to liquidate its business and affairs, and, after paying or adequately providing for the payment of all its obligations, distribute the remainder of its assets, either in cash or in kind, among its shareholders according to their respective rights and interests.

(c) The corporation, at any time during the liquidation of its business and affairs, may make application to a court of competent jurisdiction within the state and judicial subdivision in which the registered office or principal place of business of the corporation is situated, to have the liquidation continued under the supervision of the court as provided in this Act.

§ 88. Revocation of Voluntary Dissolution Proceedings by Consent of Shareholders

By the written consent of all of its shareholders, a corporation may, at any time prior to the issuance of a certificate of dissolution by the Secretary of State, revoke voluntary dissolution proceedings theretofore taken, in the following manner:

Upon the execution of such written consent, a statement of revocation of voluntary dissolution proceedings shall be executed in duplicate by the corporation by its president or a vice president and by its secretary or an assistant secretary, and verified by one of the officers signing such statement, which statement shall set forth:

(a) The name of the corporation.

(b) The names and respective addresses of its officers.

(c) The names and respective addresses of its directors.

(d) A copy of the written consent signed by all shareholders of the corporation revoking such voluntary dissolution proceedings.

(e) That such written consent has been signed by all shareholders of the corporation or signed in their names by their attorneys thereunto duly authorized.

§ 89. Revocation of Voluntary Dissolution Proceedings by Act of Corporation

By the act of the corporation, a corporation may, at any time prior to the issuance of a certificate of dissolution by the Secretary of State, revoke voluntary dissolution proceedings theretofore taken, in the following manner:

(a) The board of directors shall adopt a resolution recommending that the voluntary dissolution proceedings be revoked, and directing that the question of such revocation be submitted to a vote at a special meeting of shareholders.

(b) Written notice, stating that the purpose or one of the purposes of such meeting is to consider the advisability of revoking the voluntary dissolution proceedings, shall be given to each shareholder of record entitled to vote at such meeting within the time and in the manner provided in this Act for the giving of notice of special meetings of shareholders.

(c) At such meeting a vote of the shareholders entitled to vote thereat shall be taken on a resolution to revoke the voluntary dissolution proceedings, which shall require for its adoption the affirmative vote of the holders of a majority of the shares entitled to vote thereon.

(d) Upon the adoption of such resolution, a statement of revocation of voluntary dissolution proceedings shall be executed in duplicate by the corporation by its president or a vice president and by its secretary or an assistant secretary, and verified by one of the officers signing such statement, which statement shall set forth:

(1) The name of the corporation.

(2) The names and respective addresses of its officers.

(3) The names and respective addresses of its directors.

(4) A copy of the resolution adopted by the shareholders revoking the voluntary dissolution proceedings.

(5) The number of shares outstanding.

(6) The number of shares voted for and against the resolution, respectively.

§ 90. Filing of Statement of Revocation of Voluntary Dissolution Proceedings

Duplicate originals of the statement of revocation of voluntary dissolution proceedings, whether by consent of shareholders or by act of the corporation, shall be delivered to the Secretary of State. If the Secretary of State finds that such statement conforms to law, he shall, when all fees and franchise taxes have been paid as in this Act prescribed:

(a) Endorse on each of such duplicate originals the word "Filed," and the month, day and year of the filing thereof.

(b) File one of such duplicate originals in his office.

(c) Return the other duplicate original to the corporation or its representative.

§ 91. Effect of Statement of Revocation of Voluntary Dissolution Proceedings

Upon the filing by the Secretary of State of a statement of revocation of voluntary dissolution proceedings, whether by consent of shareholders or by act of the corporation, the revocation of the voluntary dissolution proceedings shall become effective and the corporation may again carry on its business.

§ 92. Articles of Dissolution

If voluntary dissolution proceedings have not been revoked, then when all debts, liabilities and obligations of the corporation have been paid and discharged, or adequate provision has been made therefor, and all of the remaining property and assets of the corporation have been distributed to its shareholders, articles of dissolution shall be executed in duplicate by the corporation by its president or a vice president and by its secretary or an assistant secretary, and verified by one of the officers signing such statement, which statement shall set forth:

(a) The name of the corporation.

(b) That the Secretary of State has theretofore filed a statement of intent to dissolve the corporation, and the date on which such statement was filed.

(c) That all debts, obligations and liabilities of the corporation have been paid and discharged or that adequate provision has been made therefor.

(d) That all the remaining property and assets of the corporation have been distributed among its shareholders in accordance with their respective rights and interests.

(e) That there are no suits pending against the corporation in any court, or that adequate provision has been made for the satisfaction of any judgment, order or decree which may be entered against it in any pending suit.

§ 93. Filing of Articles of Dissolution

Duplicate originals of such articles of dissolution shall be delivered to the Secretary of State. If the Secretary of State finds that such articles of dissolution conform to law, he shall, when all fees and franchise taxes have been paid as in this Act prescribed:

(a) Endorse on each of such duplicate originals the word "Filed," and the month, day and year of the filing thereof.

(b) File one of such duplicate originals in his office.

(c) Issue a certificate of dissolution to which he shall affix the other duplicate original.

The certificate of dissolution, together with the duplicate original of the articles of dissolution affixed thereto by the Secretary of State, shall be returned to the representative of the dissolved corporation. Upon the issuance of such certificate of dissolution the existence of the corporation shall cease, except for the purpose of suits, other proceedings and appropriate corporate action by shareholders, directors and officers as provided in this Act.

§ 94. Involuntary Dissolution

A corporation may be dissolved involuntarily by a decree of the . . . . court in an action filed by the Attorney General when it is established that:

(a) The corporation has failed to file its annual report within the time required by this Act, or has failed to pay its franchise tax on or before the first day of August of the year in which such franchise tax becomes due and payable; or

(b) The corporation procured its articles of incorporation through fraud; or

(c) The corporation has continued to exceed or abuse the authority conferred upon it by law; or

(d) The corporation has failed for thirty days to appoint and maintain a registered agent in this State; or

(e) The corporation has failed for thirty days after change of its registered office or registered agent to file in the office of the Secretary of State a statement of such change.

§ 95. Notification to Attorney General

The Secretary of State, on or before the last day of December of each year, shall certify to the Attorney General the names of all corporations which have failed to file their annual reports or to pay franchise taxes in accordance with the provisions of this Act, together with the facts pertinent thereto. He shall also certify, from time to time, the names of all corporations which have given other cause for dissolution as provided in this Act, together with the facts pertinent thereto. Whenever the Secretary of State shall certify the name of a corporation to the Attorney General as having given any cause for dissolution, the Secretary of State shall concurrently mail to the corporation at its registered office a notice that such certification has been made. Upon the receipt of such certification, the Attorney General shall file an action in the name of the State against such corporation for its dissolution. Every such certificate from the Secretary of State to the Attorney General pertaining to the failure of a corporation to file an annual report or pay a franchise tax shall be taken and received in all courts as prima facie evidence of the facts therein stated. If, before action is filed, the corporation shall file its annual report or pay its franchise tax, together with all penalties thereon, or shall appoint or maintain a registered agent as provided in this Act, or shall file with the Secretary of State the required statement of change of registered office or registered agent, such fact shall be forthwith certified by the Secretary of State to the Attorney General and he shall not file an action against such corporation for such cause. If, after action is filed, the corporation shall file its annual report or pay its franchise tax, together with all penalties thereon, or shall appoint or maintain a registered agent as provided in this Act, or shall file with the Secretary of State the required statement of change of registered office or registered agent, and shall pay the costs of such action, the action for such cause shall abate.

§ 96. Venue and Process

Every action for the involuntary dissolution of a corporation shall be commenced by the Attorney General either in the . . . . court of the county in which the registered office of the corporation is situated, or in the . . . . court of . . . . county. Summons shall issue and be served as in other civil actions. If process is returned not found, the Attorney General shall cause publication to be made as in other civil cases in some newspaper published in the county where the registered office of the corporation is situated, containing a notice of the pendency of such action, the title of the court, the title of the action, and the date on or after which default may be entered. The Attorney General may include in one notice the names of any number of corporations against which actions are then pending in the same court. The Attorney General shall cause a copy of such notice to be mailed to the corporation at its registered office within ten days after the first publication thereof. The certificate of the Attorney General of the mailing of such notice shall be prima facie evidence thereof. Such notice shall be published at least once each week for two successive weeks, and the first publication thereof may begin at any time after the summons has been returned. Unless a corporation shall have been served with summons, no default shall be taken against it earlier than thirty days after the first publication of such notice.

§ 97. Jurisdiction of Court to Liquidate Assets and Business of Corporation

The . . . . courts shall have full power to liquidate the assets and business of a corporation:

(a) In an action by a shareholder when it is established:

    (1) That the directors are deadlocked in the management of the corporate affairs and the shareholders are unable to break the deadlock, and that irreparable injury to the corporation is being suffered or is threatened by reason thereof; or

    (2) That the acts of the directors or those in control of the corporation are illegal, oppressive or fraudulent; or

    (3) That the shareholders are deadlocked in voting power, and have failed, for a period which includes at least two consecutive annual meeting dates, to elect successors to directors whose terms have expired or would have expired upon the election of their successors; or

    (4) That the corporate assets are being misapplied or wasted.

(b) In an action by a creditor:

    (1) When the claim of the creditor has been reduced to judgment and an execution thereon returned unsatisfied and it is established that the corporation is insolvent; or

(2) When the corporation has admitted in writing that the claim of the creditor is due and owing and it is established that the corporation is insolvent.

(c) Upon application by a corporation which has filed a statement of intent to dissolve, as provided in this Act, to have its liquidation continued under the supervision of the court.

(d) When an action has been filed by the Attorney General to dissolve a corporation and it is established that liquidation of its business and affairs should precede the entry of a decree of dissolution.

Proceedings under clause (a), (b) or (c) of this section shall be brought in the county in which the registered office or the principal office of the corporation is situated.

It shall not be necessary to make shareholders parties to any such action or proceeding unless relief is sought against them personally.

§ 98. Procedure in Liquidation of Corporation by Court

In proceedings to liquidate the assets and business of a corporation the court shall have power to issue injunctions, to appoint a receiver or receivers pendente lite, with such powers and duties as the court, from time to time, may direct, and to take such other proceedings as may be requisite to preserve the corporate assets wherever situated, and carry on the business of the corporation until a full hearing can be had.

After a hearing had upon such notice as the court may direct to be given to all parties to the proceedings and to any other parties in interest designated by the court, the court may appoint a liquidating receiver or receivers with authority to collect the assets of the corporation, including all amounts owing to the corporation by subscribers on account of any unpaid portion of the consideration for the issuance of shares. Such liquidating receiver or receivers shall have authority, subject to the order of the court, to sell, convey and dispose of all or any part of the assets of the corporation wherever situated, either at public or private sale. The assets of the corporation or the proceeds resulting from a sale, conveyance or other disposition thereof shall be applied to the expenses of such liquidation and to the payment of the liabilities and obligations of the corporation, and any remaining assets or proceeds shall be distributed among its shareholders according to their respective rights and interests. The order appointing such liquidating receiver or receivers shall state their powers and duties. Such powers and duties may be increased or diminished at any time during the proceedings.

The court shall have power to allow from time to time as expenses of the liquidation compensation to the receiver or receivers and to attorneys in the proceeding, and to direct the payment thereof out of the assets of the corporation or the proceeds of any sale or disposition of such assets.

A receiver of a corporation appointed under the provisions of this section shall have authority to sue and defend in all courts in his own name as receiver of such corporation. The court appointing such receiver shall have exclusive jurisdiction of the corporation and its property, wherever situated.

§ 99. Qualifications of Receivers

A receiver shall in all cases be a natural person or a corporation authorized to act as receiver, which corporation may be a domestic corporation or a foreign corporation authorized to transact business in this State, and shall in all cases give such bond as the court may direct with such sureties as the court may require.

§ 100. Filing of Claims in Liquidation Proceedings

In proceedings to liquidate the assets and business of a corporation the court may require all creditors of the corporation to file with the clerk of the court or with the receiver, in such form as the court may prescribe, proofs under oath of their respective claims. If the court requires the filing of claims it shall fix a date, which shall be not less than four months from the date of the order, as the last day for the filing of claims, and shall prescribe the notice that shall be given to creditors and claimants of the date so fixed. Prior to the date so fixed, the court may extend the time for the filing of claims. Creditors and claimants failing to file proofs of claim on or before the date so fixed may be barred, by order of court, from participating in the distribution of the assets of the corporation.

§ 101. Discontinuance of Liquidation Proceedings

The liquidation of the assets and business of a corporation may be discontinued at any time during the liquidation proceedings when it is established that cause for liquidation no longer exists. In such event the court shall dismiss the proceedings and direct the receiver to redeliver to the corporation all its remaining property and assets.

§ 102. Decree of Involuntary Dissolution

In proceedings to liquidate the assets and business of a corporation, when the costs and expenses of such proceedings and all debts, obligations and liabilities of the corporation shall have been paid and discharged and all of its remaining property and assets distributed to its shareholders, or in case its property and assets are not sufficient to satisfy and discharge such costs, expenses, debts and obligations, all the property and assets have been applied so far as they will go to their payment, the court shall enter a decree dissolving the corporation, whereupon the existence of the corporation shall cease.

§ 103. Filing of Decree of Dissolution

In case the court shall enter a decree dissolving a corporation, it shall be the duty of the clerk of such court to cause a certified copy of the decree to be filed with the Secretary of State. No fee shall be charged by the Secretary of State for the filing thereof.

§ 104. Deposit with State Treasurer of Amount Due Certain Shareholders

Upon the voluntary or involuntary dissolution of a corporation, the portion of the assets distributable to a creditor or shareholder who is unknown or cannot be found, or who is under disability and there is no person legally competent to receive such distributive portion, shall be reduced to cash and deposited with the State Treasurer and shall be paid over to such creditor or shareholder or to his legal representative upon proof satisfactory to the State Treasurer of his right thereto.

§ 105. Survival of Remedy after Dissolution

The dissolution of a corporation either (1) by the issuance of a certificate of dissolution by the Secretary of State, or (2) by a decree of court when the court has not liquidated the assets and business of the corporation as provided in this Act, or (3) by expiration of its period of duration, shall not take away or impair any remedy available to or against such corporation, its directors, officers, or shareholders, for any right or claim existing, or any liability incurred, prior to such dissolution if action or other proceeding thereon is commenced within two years after the date of such dissolution. Any such action or proceeding by or against the corporation may be prosecuted or defended by the corporation in its corporate name. The shareholders, directors and officers shall have power to take such corporate or other action as shall be appropriate to protect such remedy, right or claim. If such corporation was dissolved by the expiration of its period of duration, such corporation may amend its articles of incorporation at any time during such period of two years so as to extend its period of duration.

§ 106. Admission of Foreign Corporation

No foreign corporation shall have the right to transact business in this State until it shall have procured a certificate of authority so to do from the Secretary of State. No foreign corporation shall be entitled to procure a certificate of authority under this Act to transact in this State any business which a corporation organized under this Act is not permitted to transact. A foreign corporation shall not be denied a certificate of authority by reason of the fact that the laws of the state or country under which such corporation is organized governing its organization and internal affairs differ from the laws of this State, and nothing in this Act contained shall be construed to authorize this State to regulate the organization or the internal affairs of such corporation.

Without excluding other activities which may not constitute transacting business in this State, a foreign corporation shall not be considered to be transacting business in this State, for the purposes of this Act, by reason of carrying on in this State any one or more of the following activities:

(a) Maintaining or defending any action or suit or any administrative or arbitration proceeding, or effecting the settlement thereof or the settlement of claims or disputes.

(b) Holding meetings of its directors or shareholders or carrying on other activities concerning its internal affairs.

(c) Maintaining bank accounts.

(d) Maintaining offices or agencies for the transfer, exchange and registration of its securities, or appointing and maintaining trustees or depositaries with relation to its securities.

(e) Effecting sales through independent contractors.

(f) Soliciting or procuring orders, whether by mail or through employees or agents or otherwise, where such orders require acceptance without this State before becoming binding contracts.

(g) Creating as borrower or lender, or acquiring, indebtedness or mortgages or other security interests in real or personal property.

(h) Securing or collecting debts or enforcing any rights in property securing the same.

(i) Transacting any business in interstate commerce.

(j) Conducting an isolated transaction completed within a period of thirty days and not in the course of a number of repeated transactions of like nature.

§ 107. Powers of Foreign Corporation

A foreign corporation which shall have received a certificate of authority under this Act shall, until a certificate of revocation or of withdrawal shall have been issued as provided in this Act, enjoy the same, but no greater, rights and privileges as a domestic corporation organized for the purposes set forth in the application pursuant to which such certificate of authority is issued; and, except as in this Act otherwise provided, shall be subject to the same duties, restrictions, penalties and liabilities now or hereafter imposed upon a domestic corporation of like character.

§ 108. Corporate Name of Foreign Corporation

No certificate of authority shall be issued to a foreign corporation unless the corporate name of such corporation:

(a) Shall contain the word "corporation," "company," "incorporated," or "limited," or shall contain an abbreviation of one of such words, or such corporation shall, for use in this State, add at the end of its name one of such words or an abbreviation thereof.

(b) Shall not contain any word or phrase which indicates or implies that it is organized for any purpose other than one or more of the purposes contained in its articles of incorporation or that it is authorized or empowered to conduct the business of banking or insurance.

(c) Shall not be the same as, or deceptively similar to, the name of any domestic corporation existing under the laws of this State or any foreign corporation authorized to transact business in this State, or a name the exclusive right to which is, at the time, reserved in the manner provided in this Act, or the name of a corporation which has in effect a registration of its name as provided in this Act, except that this provision shall not apply if the foreign corporation applying for a certificate of authority files with the Secretary of State any one of the following:

(1) a resolution of its board of directors adopting a fictitious name for use in transacting business in this State which fictitious name is not deceptively similar to the name of any domestic corporation or of any foreign corporation authorized to transact business in this State or to any name reserved or registered as provided in this Act, or

(2) the written consent of such other corporation or holder of a reserved or registered name to use the same or deceptively similar name and one or more words are added to make such name distinguishable from such other name, or

(3) a certified copy of a final decree of a court of competent jurisdiction establishing the prior right of such foreign corporation to the use of such name in this State.

§ 109. Change of Name by Foreign Corporation

Whenever a foreign corporation which is authorized to transact business in this State shall change its name to one under which a certificate of authority would not be granted to it on application therefor, the certificate of authority of such corporation shall be suspended and it shall not thereafter transact any business in this State until it has changed its name to a name which is available to it under the laws of this State or has otherwise complied with the provisions of this Act.

§ 110. Application for Certificate of Authority

A foreign corporation, in order to procure a certificate of authority to transact business in this State, shall make application therefor to the Secretary of State, which application shall set forth:

(a) The name of the corporation and the state or county under the laws of which it is incorporated.

(b) If the name of the corporation does not contain the word "corporation," "company," "incorporated," or "limited," or does not contain an abbreviation of one of such words, then the name of the corporation with the word or abbreviation which it elects to add thereto for use in this State.

(c) The date of incorporation and the period of duration of the corporation.

(d) The address of the principal office of the corporation in the state or country under the laws of which it is incorporated.

(e) The address of the proposed registered office of the corporation in this State, and the name of its proposed registered agent in this State at such address.

(f) The purpose or purposes of the corporation which it proposes to pursue in the transaction of business in this State.

(g) The names and respective addresses of the directors and officers of the corporation.

(h) A statement of the aggregate number of shares which the corporation has authority to issue, itemized by classes and series, if any, within a class.

(i) A statement of the aggregate number of issued shares itemized by class and by series, if any, within each class.

(j) An estimate, expressed in dollars, of the value of all property to be owned by the corporation for the following year, wherever located, and an estimate of the value of the property of the corporation to be located within this State during such year, and an estimate, expressed in dollars, of the gross amount of business which will be transacted by the corporation during such year, and an estimate of the gross amount thereof which will be transacted by the corporation at or from places of business in this State during such year.

(k) Such additional information as may be necessary or appropriate in order to enable the Secretary of State to determine whether such corporation is entitled to a certificate of authority to transact business in this State and to determine and assess the fees and franchise taxes payable as in this Act prescribed.

Such application shall be made on forms prescribed and furnished by the Secretary of State and shall be executed in duplicate by the corporation by its president or a vice president and by its secretary or an assistant secretary, and verified by one of the officers signing such application.

§ 111. Filing of Application for Certificate of Authority

Duplicate originals of the application of the corporation for a certificate of authority shall be delivered to the Secretary of State, together with a copy of its articles of incorporation and all amendments thereto, duly authenticated by the proper officer of the state or country under the laws of which it is incorporated.

If the Secretary of State finds that such application conforms to law, he shall, when all fees and franchise taxes have been paid as in this Act prescribed:

(a) Endorse on each of such documents the word "Filed," and the month, day and year of the filing thereof.

(b) File in his office one of such duplicate originals of the application and the copy of the articles of incorporation and amendments thereto.

(c) Issue a certificate of authority to transact business in this State to which he shall affix the other duplicate original application.

The certificate of authority, together with the duplicate original of the application affixed thereto by the Secretary of State, shall be returned to the corporation or its representative.

§ 112. Effect of Certificate of Authority

Upon the issuance of a certificate of authority by the Secretary of State, the corporation shall be authorized to transact business in this State for those purposes set forth in its application, subject, however, to the right of this State to suspend or to revoke such authority as provided in this Act.

§ 113. Registered Office and Registered Agent of Foreign Corporation

Each foreign corporation authorized to transact business in this State shall have and continuously maintain in this State:

(a) A registered office which may be, but need not be, the same as its place of business in this State.

(b) A registered agent, which agent may be either an individual resident in this State whose business office is identical with such registered office, or a domestic corporation, or a foreign corporation authorized to transact business in this State, having a business office identical with such registered office.

§ 114. Change of Registered Office or Registered Agent of Foreign Corporation

A foreign corporation authorized to transact business in this State may change its registered office or change its registered agent, or both, upon filing in the office of the Secretary of State a statement setting forth:

(a) The name of the corporation.

(b) The address of its then registered office.

(c) If the address of its registered office be changed, the address to which the registered office is to be changed.

(d) The name of its then registered agent.

(e) If its registered agent be changed, the name of its successor registered agent.

(f) That the address of its registered office and the address of the business office of its registered agent, as changed, will be identical.

(g) That such change was authorized by resolution duly adopted by its board of directors.

Such statement shall be executed by the corporation by its president or a vice president, and verified by him, and delivered to the Secretary of State. If the Secretary of State finds that such statement conforms to the provisions of this Act, he shall file such statement in his office, and upon such filing the change of address of the registered office, or the appointment of a new registered agent, or both, as the case may be, shall become effective.

Any registered agent of a foreign corporation may resign as such agent upon filing a written notice thereof, executed in duplicate, with the Secretary of State, who shall forthwith mail a copy thereof to the corporation at its principal office in the state or country under the laws of which it is incorporated. The appointment of such agent shall terminate upon the expiration of thirty days after receipt of such notice by the Secretary of State.

If a registered agent changes his or its business address to another place within the same .... *, he or it may change such address and the address of the registered office of any corporation of which he or it is registered agent by filing a statement as required above except that it need be signed only by the registered agent and need not be responsive to (e) or (g) and must recite that a copy of the statement has been mailed to the corporation.

*Supply designation of jurisdiction, such as county, etc. in accordance with local practice.

§ 115. **Service of Process on Foreign Corporation**

The registered agent so appointed by a foreign corporation authorized to transact business in this State shall be an agent of such corporation upon whom any process, notice or demand required or permitted by law to be served upon the corporation may be served.

Whenever a foreign corporation authorized to transact business in this State shall fail to appoint or maintain a registered agent in this State, or whenever any such registered agent cannot with reasonable diligence be found at the registered office, or whenever the certificate of authority of a foreign corporation shall be suspended or revoked, then the Secretary of State shall be an agent of such corporation upon whom any such process, notice, or demand may be served. Service on the Secretary of State of any such process, notice or demand shall be made by delivering to and leaving with him, or with any clerk having charge of the corporation department of his office, duplicate copies of such process, notice or demand. In the event any such process, notice or demand is served on the Secretary of State, he shall immediately cause one of such copies thereof to be forwarded by registered mail, addressed to the corporation at its principal office in the state or country under the laws of which it is incorporated. Any service so had on the Secretary of State shall be returnable in not less than thirty days.

The Secretary of State shall keep a record of all processes, notices and demands served upon him under this section, and shall record therein the time of such service and his action with reference thereto.

Nothing herein contained shall limit or affect the right to serve any process, notice or demand, required or permitted by law to be served upon a foreign corporation in any other manner now or hereafter permitted by law.

§ 116. **Amendment to Articles of Incorporation of Foreign Corporation**

Whenever the articles of incorporation of a foreign corporation authorized to transact business in this State are amended, such foreign corporation shall, within thirty days after such amendment becomes effective, file in the office of the Secretary of State a copy of such amendment duly authenticated by the proper officer of the state or country under the laws of which it is incorporated; but the filing thereof shall not of itself enlarge or alter the purpose or purposes which such corporation is authorized to pursue in the transaction of business in this State, nor authorize such corporation to transact business in this State under any other name than the name set forth in its certificate of authority.

§ 117. **Merger of Foreign Corporation Authorized to Transact Business in This State**

Whenever a foreign corporation authorized to transact business in this State shall be a party to a statutory merger permitted by the laws of the state or country under the laws of which it is incorporated, and such corporation shall be the surviving corporation, it shall, within thirty days after such merger becomes effective, file with the Secretary of State a copy of the articles of merger duly authenticated by the proper officer of the state or country under the laws of which such statutory merger was effected; and it shall not be necessary for such corporation to procure either a new or amended certificate of authority to transact business in this State unless the name of such corporation be changed thereby or unless the corporation desires to pursue in this State other or additional purposes than those which it is then authorized to transact in this State.

§ 118. **Amended Certificate of Authority**

A foreign corporation authorized to transact business in this State shall procure an amended certificate of authority in the event it changes its corporate name, or desires to pursue in this State other or additional purposes than those set forth in its prior application for a certificate of authority, by making application therefor to the Secretary of State.

The requirements in respect to the form and contents of such application, the manner of its execution, the filing of duplicate originals thereof with the Secretary of State, the issuance of an amended certificate of authority and the effect thereof, shall be the same as in the case of an original application for a certificate of authority.

§ 119. Withdrawal of Foreign Corporation

A foreign corporation authorized to transact business in this State may withdraw from this State upon procuring from the Secretary of State a certificate of withdrawal. In order to procure such certificate of withdrawal, such foreign corporation shall deliver to the Secretary of State an application for withdrawal, which shall set forth:

(a) The name of the corporation and the state or country under the laws of which it is incorporated.

(b) That the corporation is not transacting business in this State.

(c) That the corporation surrenders its authority to transact business in this State.

(d) That the corporation revokes the authority of its registered agent in this State to accept service of process and consents that service of process in any action, suit or proceeding based upon any cause of action arising in this State during the time the corporation was authorized to transact business in this State may thereafter be made on such corporation by service thereof on the Secretary of State.

(e) A post-office address to which the Secretary of State may mail a copy of any process against the corporation that may be served on him.

(f) A statement of the aggregate number of shares which the corporation has authority to issue, itemized by class and series, if any, within each class, as of the date of such application.

(g) A statement of the aggregate number of issued shares, itemized by class and series, if any, within each class, as of the date of such application.

(h) Such additional information as may be necessary or appropriate in order to enable the Secretary of State to determine and assess any unpaid fees or franchise taxes payable by such foreign corporation as in this Act prescribed.

The application for withdrawal shall be made on forms prescribed and furnished by the Secretary of State and shall be executed by the corporation by its president or a vice president and by its secretary or an assistant secretary, and verified by one of the officers signing the application, or, if the corporation is in the hands of a receiver or trustee, shall be executed on behalf of the corporation by such receiver or trustee and verified by him.

§ 120. Filing of Application for Withdrawal

Duplicate originals of such application for withdrawal shall be delivered to the Secretary of State. If the Secretary of State finds that such application conforms to the provisions of this Act, he shall, when all fees and franchise taxes have been paid as in this Act prescribed:

(a) Endorse on each of such duplicate originals the word "Filed," and the month, day and year of the filing thereof.

(b) File one of such duplicate originals in his office.

(c) Issue a certificate of withdrawal to which he shall affix the other duplicate original.

The certificate of withdrawal, together with the duplicate original of the application for withdrawal affixed thereto by the Secretary of State, shall be returned to the corporation or its representative. Upon the issuance of such certificate of withdrawal, the authority of the corporation to transact business in this State shall cease.

§ 121. Revocation of Certificate of Authority

The certificate of authority of a foreign corporation to transact business in this State may be revoked by the Secretary of State upon the conditions prescribed in this section when:

(a) The corporation has failed to file its annual report within the time required by this Act, or has failed to pay any fees, franchise taxes or penalties prescribed by this Act when they have become due and payable; or

(b) The corporation has failed to appoint and maintain a registered agent in this State as required by this Act; or

(c) The corporation has failed, after change of its registered office or registered agent, to file in the office of the Secretary of State a statement of such change as required by this Act; or

(d) The corporation has failed to file in the office of the Secretary of State any amendment to its articles of incorporation or any articles of merger within the time prescribed by this Act; or

(e) A misrepresentation has been made of any material matter in any application, report, affidavit, or other document submitted by such corporation pursuant to this Act.

No certificate of authority of a foreign corporation shall be revoked by the Secretary of State unless (1) he shall have given the corporation not less than sixty days' notice thereof by mail addressed to its registered office in this State, and (2) the corporation shall fail prior to revocation to file such annual report, or pay such fees, franchise taxes or penalties, or file the required statement of change of registered agent or registered office, or file such articles of amendment or articles of merger, or correct such misrepresentation.

§ 122. Issuance of Certificate of Revocation

Upon revoking any such certificate of authority, the Secretary of State shall:

(a) Issue a certificate of revocation in duplicate.

(b) File one of such certificates in his office.

(c) Mail to such corporation at its registered office in this State a notice of such revocation accompanied by one of such certificates.

Upon the issuance of such certificate of revocation, the authority of the corporation to transact business in this State shall cease.

§ 123. Application to Corporations Heretofore Authorized to Transact Business in this State

Foreign corporations which are duly authorized to transact business in this State at the time this Act takes effect, for a purpose or purposes for which a corporation might secure such authority under this Act, shall, subject to the limitations set forth in their respective certificates of authority, be entitled to all the rights and privileges applicable to foreign corporations procuring certificates of authority to transact business in this State under this Act, and from the time this Act takes effect such corporations shall be subject to all the limitations, restrictions, liabilities, and duties prescribed herein for foreign corporations procuring certificates of authority to transact business in this State under this Act.

§ 124. Transacting Business Without Certificate of Authority

No foreign corporation transacting business in this State without a certificate of authority shall be permitted to maintain any action, suit or proceeding in any court of this State, until such corporation shall have obtained a certificate of authority. Nor shall any action, suit or proceeding be maintained in any court of this State by any successor or assignee of such corporation on any right, claim or demand arising out of the transaction of business by such corporation in this State, until a certificate of authority shall have been obtained by such corporation or by a corporation which has acquired all or substantially all of its assets.

The failure of a foreign corporation to obtain a certificate of authority to transact business in this State shall not impair the validity of any contract or act of such corporation, and shall not prevent such corporation from defending any action, suit or proceeding in any court of this State.

A foreign corporation which transacts business in this State without a certificate of authority shall be liable to this State, for the years or parts thereof during which it transacted business in this State without a certificate of authority, in an amount equal to all fees and franchise taxes which would have been imposed by this Act upon such corporation had it duly applied for and received a certificate of authority to transact business in this State as required by this Act and thereafter filed all reports required by this Act, plus all penalties imposed by this Act for failure to pay such fees and franchise taxes. The Attorney General shall bring proceedings to recover all amounts due this State under the provisions of this Section.

§ 125. Annual Report of Domestic and Foreign Corporations

Each domestic corporation, and each foreign corporation authorized to transact business in this State, shall file, within the time prescribed by this Act, an annual report setting forth:

(a) The name of the corporation and the state or country under the laws of which it is incorporated.

(b) The address of the registered office of the corporation in this State, and the name of its registered agent in this State at such address, and, in case of a foreign corporation, the address of its principal office in the state or country under the laws of which it is incorporated.

(c) A brief statement of the character of the business in which the corporation is actually engaged in this State.

(d) The names and respective addresses of the directors and officers of the corporation.

(e) A statement of the aggregate number of shares which the corporation has authority to issue, itemized by class and series, if any, within each class.

(f) A statement of the aggregate number of issued shares, itemized by class and series, if any, within each class.

(g) A statement, expressed in dollars, of the value of all the property owned by the corporation, wherever located, and the value of the property of the corporation located within this State, and a statement, expressed in dollars, of the gross amount of business transacted by the corporation for the twelve months ended on the thirty-first day of December preceding the date herein provided for the filing of such report and the gross amount thereof transacted by the corporation at or from places of business in this State. If, on the thirty-first day of December preceding the time herein provided for the filing of such report, the corporation had not been in existence for a period of twelve months, or in the case of a foreign corporation had not been authorized to transact business in this State for a period of twelve months, the statement with respect to business transacted shall be furnished for the period between the date of incorporation or the date of its authorization to transact business in this State, as the case may be, and such thirty-first day of December. If all the property of the corporation is located in this State and all of its business is transacted at or from places of business in this State, then the information required by this subparagraph need not be set forth in such report.

(h) Such additional information as may be necessary or appropriate in order to enable the Secretary of State to determine and assess the proper amount of franchise taxes payable by such corporation.

Such annual report shall be made on forms prescribed and furnished by the Secretary of State, and the information therein contained shall be given as of the date of the execution of the report, except as to the information required by subparagraphs (g) and (h) which shall be given as of the close of business on the thirty-first day of December next preceding the date herein provided for the filing of such report. It shall be executed by the corporation by its president, a vice president, secretary, an assistant secretary, or treasurer, and verified by the officer executing the report, or, if the corporation is in the hands of a receiver or trustee, it shall be executed on behalf of the corporation and verified by such receiver or trustee.

§ 126. Filing of Annual Report of Domestic and Foreign Corporations

Such annual report of a domestic or foreign corporation shall be delivered to the Secretary of State between the first day of January and the first day of March of each year, except that the first annual report of a domestic or foreign corporation shall be filed between the first day of January and the first day of March of the year next succeeding the calendar year in which its certificate of incorporation or its certificate of authority, as the case may be, was issued by the Secretary of State. Proof to the satisfaction of the Secretary of State that prior to the first day of March such report was deposited in the United States mail in a sealed envelope, properly addressed, with postage prepaid, shall be deemed a compliance with this requirement. If the Secretary of State finds that such report conforms to the requirements of this Act, he shall file the same. If he finds that it does not so conform, he shall promptly return the same to the corporation for any necessary corrections, in which event the penalties hereinafter prescribed for failure to file such report within the time hereinabove provided shall not apply, if such report is corrected to conform to the requirements of this Act and returned to the Secretary of State within thirty days from the date on which it was mailed to the corporation by the Secretary of State.

§ 127. Fees, Franchise Taxes and Charges to be Collected by Secretary of State

The Secretary of State shall charge and collect in accordance with the provisions of this Act:

(a) Fees for filing documents and issuing certificates.

(b) Miscellaneous charges.

(c) License fees.

(d) Franchise taxes.

§ 128. Fees for Filing Documents and Issuing Certificates

The Secretary of State shall charge and collect for:

(a) Filing articles of incorporation and issuing a certificate of incorporation, ... dollars.

(b) Filing articles of amendment and issuing a certificate of amendment, ... dollars.

(c) Filing restated articles of incorporation, ... dollars.

(d) Filing articles of merger or consolidation and issuing a certificate of merger or consolidation, ... dollars.

(e) Filing an application to reserve a corporate name, ... dollars.

(f) Filing a notice of transfer of a reserved corporate name, ... dollars.

(g) Filing a statement of change of address of registered office or change of registered agent, or both, ... dollars.

(h) Filing a statement of the establishment of a series of shares, ... dollars.

(i) Filing a statement of intent to dissolve, ... dollars.

(j) Filing a statement of revocation of voluntary dissolution proceedings, ... dollars.

(k) Filing articles of dissolution, ... dollars.

(l) Filing an application of a foreign corporation for a certificate of authority to transact business in this State and issuing a certificate of authority, ... dollars.

(m) Filing an application of a foreign corporation for an amended certificate of authority to transact business in this State and issuing an amended certificate of authority, ... dollars.

(n) Filing a copy of an amendment to the articles of incorporation of a foreign corporation holding a certificate of authority to transact business in this State, ... dollars.

(o) Filing a copy of articles of merger of a foreign corporation holding a certificate of authority to transact business in this State, ... dollars.

(p) Filing an application for withdrawal of a foreign corporation and issuing a certificate of withdrawal, ... dollars.

(q) Filing any other statement or report, except an annual report, of a domestic or foreign corporation, ... dollars.

§ 129. Miscellaneous Charges

The Secretary of State shall charge and collect:

(a) For furnishing a certified copy of any document, instrument, or paper relating to a corporation, ... cents per page and .... dollars for the certificate and affixing the seal thereto.

(b) At the time of any service of process on him as agent of a corporation, ... dollars, which amount may be recovered as taxable costs by the party to the suit or action causing such service to be made if such party prevails in the suit or action.

§ 130. License Fees Payable by Domestic Corporations

The Secretary of State shall charge and collect from each domestic corporation license fees, based upon the number of shares which it will have authority to issue or the increase in the number of shares which it will have authority to issue, at the time of:

(a) Filing articles of incorporation;

(b) Filing articles of amendment increasing the number of authorized shares; and

(c) Filing articles of merger or consolidation increasing the number of authorized shares which the surviving or new corporation, if a domestic corporation, will have the authority to issue above the aggregate number of shares which the constituent domestic corporations and constituent foreign corporations authorized to transact business in this State had authority to issue.

The license fees shall be at the rate of .... cents per share up to and including the first 10,000 authorized shares, ... cents per share for each authorized share in excess of 10,000 shares up to and including 100,000 shares, and .... cents per share for each authorized share in excess of 100,000 shares, whether the shares are of par value or without par value.

The license fees payable on an increase in the number of authorized shares shall be imposed only on the increased number of shares, and the number of previously authorized shares shall be taken into account in determining the rate applicable to the increased number of authorized shares.

§ 131. License Fees Payable by Foreign Corporations

The Secretary of State shall charge and collect from each foreign corporation license fees, based upon the proportion represented in this State of the number of shares which it has authority to issue or the increase in the number of shares which it has authority to issue, at the time of:

(a) Filing an application for a certificate of authority to transact business in this State;

(b) Filing articles of amendment which increased the number of authorized shares; and

(c) Filing articles of merger or consolidation which increased the number of authorized shares which the surviving or new corporation, if a foreign corporation, has authority to issue above the aggregate number of shares which the constituent domestic corporations and constituent foreign corporations authorized to transact business in this State had authority to issue.

The license fees shall be at the rate of .... cents per share up to and including the first 10,000 authorized shares represented in this State, ... cents per share for each authorized share in excess of 10,000 shares up to and including 100,000 shares represented in this State, and .... cents per share for each authorized share in excess of 100,000 shares represented in this State.

The license fees payable on an increase in the number of authorized shares shall be imposed only on the increased number of such shares represented in this State, and the number of previously authorized shares represented in this State shall be taken into account in determining the rate applicable to the increased number of authorized shares.

The number of authorized shares represented in this State shall be that proportion of its total authorized shares which the sum of the value of its property located in this State and the gross amount of business transacted by it at or from places of business in this State bears to the sum of the value of all of its property, wherever located, and the gross amount of its business, wherever transacted. Such proportion shall be determined from information contained in the application for a certificate of authority to transact business in this State until the filing of an annual report and thereafter from information contained in the latest annual report filed by the corporation.

§ 132. Franchise Taxes Payable by Domestic Corporations

The Secretary of State shall charge and collect from each domestic corporation an initial franchise tax at the time of filing its articles of incorporation at the rate of one-twelfth of one-half of the license fee payable by such corporation under the provisions of this Act at the time of filing its articles of incorporation, for each calendar month, or fraction thereof, between the date of the issuance of the certificate of incorporation by the Secretary of State and the first day of July of the next succeeding calendar year.

The Secretary of State shall charge and collect from each domestic corporation an annual franchise tax, payable in advance for the period from July 1 in each year to July 1 in the succeeding year, beginning July 1 in the calendar year in which such corporation is required to file its first annual report under this Act, (Alternative 1: at the rate of ...... of ...... per cent of the amount represented in this State of the stated capital of the corporation, as determined in accordance with accounting practices and principles that are reasonable in the circumstances, as disclosed by the latest report filed by the corporation with the Secretary of State) (Alternative 2: at the rate of ...... cents per share up to and including the first 10,000 issued and outstanding shares, and ...... cents per share for each issued and outstanding share in excess of 10,000 shares up to and including 100,000 shares, and ...... cents per share for each issued and outstanding share in excess of 100,000 shares).

[If Alternative 2 is enacted, the following paragraph should be deleted.]

The amount represented in this State of the stated capital of the corporation shall be that proportion of its stated capital which the sum of the value of its property located in this State and the gross amount of business transacted by it at or from places of business in this State bears to the sum of the value of all of its property, wherever located, and the gross amount of its business, wherever transacted.

§ 133. Franchise Taxes Payable by Foreign Corporations

The Secretary of State shall charge and collect from each foreign corporation authorized to transact business in this State an initial franchise tax at the time of filing its application for a certificate of authority at the rate of one-twelfth of one-half of the license fee payable by such corporation under the provisions of this Act at the time of filing such application, for each month, or fraction thereof, between the date of the issuance of the certificate of authority by the Secretary of State and the first day of July of the next succeeding calendar year.

The Secretary of State shall charge and collect from each foreign corporation authorized to transact business in this State an annual franchise tax, payable in advance for the period from July 1 in each year to July 1 in the succeeding year, beginning July 1 in the calendar year in which such corporation is required to file its first annual report under this Act, (Alternative 1: at the rate of ...... per cent of the amount represented in this State of the stated capital of the corporation, as determined in accordance with accounting practices and principles that are reasonable in the circumstances, as disclosed by the latest annual report filed by the corporation with the Secretary of State) (Alternative 2: at a rate of ...... cents per share up to and including the first 10,000 issued and outstanding shares represented in this State, and ...... cents per share for each issued and outstanding share in excess of 10,000 shares up to and including 100,000 shares represented in this State, and ...... cents per share for each issued and outstanding share in excess of 100,000 shares represented in this State).

[If Alternative 2 is enacted, the following paragraph should be deleted.]

The amount represented in this State of the stated capital of the corporation shall be that proportion of its stated capital which the sum of the value of its property located in this State and the gross amount of business transacted by it at or from places of business in this State bears to the sum of the value of all of its property, wherever located, and the gross amount of its business, wherever transacted.

§ 134. Assessment and Collection of Annual Franchise Taxes

It shall be the duty of the Secretary of State to collect all annual franchise taxes and penalties imposed by, or assessed in accordance with, this Act.

Between the first day of March and the first day of June of each year, the Secretary of State shall assess against each corporation, domestic and foreign, required to file an annual report in such year, the franchise tax payable by it for the period from July 1 of such year to July 1 of the succeeding year in accordance with the provisions of this Act, and, if it has failed to file its annual report within the time prescribed by this Act, the penalty imposed by this Act upon such corporation for its failure so to do; and shall mail a written notice to each corporation against which such tax is assessed, addressed to such corporation at its registered office in this State, notifying the corporation (1) of the amount of franchise tax assessed against it for the ensuing year and the amount of penalty, if any, assessed against it for failure to file its annual report; (2) that objections, if any, to such assessment will be heard by the officer making the assessment on or before the fifteenth day of June of such year, upon receipt of a request from the corporation; and (3) that such tax and penalty shall be payable to the Secretary of State on the first day of July next succeeding the date of the notice. Failure to receive such notice shall not relieve the corporation of its obligation to pay the tax and any penalty assessed, or invalidate the assessment thereof.

The Secretary of State shall have power to hear and determine objections to any assessment of franchise tax at any time after such assessment and, after hearing, to change or modify any such assessment. In the event of any adjustment of franchise tax with respect to which a penalty has been assessed for failure to file an annual report, the penalty shall be adjusted in accordance with the provisions of this Act imposing such penalty.

All annual franchise taxes and all penalties for failure to file annual reports shall be due and payable on the first day of July of each year. If the annual franchise tax assessed against any corporation subject to the provisions of this Act, together with all penalties assessed thereon, shall not be paid to the Secretary of State on or before the thirty-first day of July of the year in which such tax is due and payable, the Secretary of State shall certify such fact to the Attorney General on or before the fifteenth day of November of such year, whereupon the Attorney General may institute an action against such corporation in the name of this State, in any court of competent jurisdiction, for the recovery of the amount of such franchise tax and penalties, together with the cost of suit, and prosecute the same to final judgment.

For the purpose of enforcing collection, all annual franchise taxes assessed in accordance with this Act, and all penalties assessed thereon and all interest and costs that shall accrue in connection with the collection thereof, shall be a prior and first lien on the real and personal property of the corporation from and including the first day of July of the year when such franchise taxes become due and payable until such taxes, penalties, interest, and costs shall have been paid.

§ 135. Penalties Imposed upon Corporations

Each corporation, domestic or foreign, that fails or refuses to file its annual report for any year within the time prescribed by this Act shall be subject to a penalty of ten per cent of the amount of the franchise tax assessed against it for the period beginning July 1

of the year in which such report should have been filed. Such penalty shall be assessed by the Secretary of State at the time of the assessment of the franchise tax. If the amount of the franchise tax as originally assessed against such corporation be thereafter adjusted in accordance with the provisions of this Act, the amount of the penalty shall be likewise adjusted to ten per cent of the amount of the adjusted franchise tax. The amount of the franchise tax and the amount of the penalty shall be separately stated in any notice to the corporation with respect thereto.

If the franchise tax assessed in accordance with the provisions of this Act shall not be paid on or before the thirty-first day of July, it shall be deemed to be delinquent, and there shall be added a penalty of one per cent for each month or part of month that the same is delinquent, commencing with the month of August.

Each corporation, domestic or foreign, that fails or refuses to answer truthfully and fully within the time prescribed by this Act interrogatories propounded by the Secretary of State in accordance with the provisions of this Act, shall be deemed to be guilty of a misdemeanor and upon conviction thereof may be fined in any amount not exceeding five hundred dollars.

§ 136. Penalties Imposed upon Officers and Directors

Each officer and director of a corporation, domestic or foreign, who fails or refuses within the time prescribed by this Act to answer truthfully and fully interrogatories propounded to him by the Secretary of State in accordance with the provisions of this Act, or who signs any articles, statement, report, application or other document filed with the Secretary of State which is known to such officer or director to be false in any material respect, shall be deemed to be guilty of a misdemeanor, and upon conviction thereof may be fined in any amount not exceeding .... dollars.

§ 137. Interrogatories by Secretary of State

The Secretary of State may propound to any corporation, domestic or foreign, subject to the provisions of this Act, and to any officer or director thereof, such interrogatories as may be reasonably necessary and proper to enable him to ascertain whether such corporation has complied with all the provisions of this Act applicable to such corporation. Such interrogatories shall be answered within thirty days after the mailing thereof, or within such additional time as shall be fixed by the Secretary of State, and the answers thereto shall be full and complete and shall be made in writing and under oath. If such interrogatories be directed to an individual they shall be answered by him, and if directed to a corporation they shall be answered by the president, vice president, secretary or assistant secretary thereof. The Secretary of State need not file any document to which such interrogatories relate until such interrogatories be answered as herein provided, and not then if the answers thereto disclose that such document is not in conformity with the provisions of this Act. The Secretary of State shall certify to the Attorney General, for such action as the Attorney General may deem appropriate, all interrogatories and answers thereto which disclose a violation of any of the provisions of this Act.

§ 138. Information Disclosed by Interrogatories

Interrogatories propounded by the Secretary of State and the answers thereto shall not be open to public inspection nor shall the Secretary of State disclose any facts or information obtained therefrom except insofar as his official duty may require the same to be made public or in the event such interrogatories or the answers thereto are required for evidence in any criminal proceedings or in any other action by this State.

§ 139. Powers of Secretary of State

The Secretary of State shall have the power and authority reasonably necessary to enable him to administer this Act efficiently and to perform the duties therein imposed upon him.

§ 140. Appeal from Secretary of State

If the Secretary of State shall fail to approve any articles of incorporation, amendment, merger, consolidation or dissolution, or any other document required by this Act to be approved by the Secretary of State before the same shall be filed in his office, he shall, within ten days after the delivery thereof to him, give written notice of his disapproval to the person or corporation, domestic or foreign, delivering the same, specifying the reasons therefor. From such disapproval such person or corporation may appeal to the .... court of the county in which the registered office of such corporation is, or is proposed to be, situated by filing with the clerk of such court a petition setting forth a copy of the articles or other document sought to be filed and a copy of the written disapproval thereof by the Secretary of State; whereupon the matter shall be tried de novo by the court, and the court shall either sustain the action of the Secretary of State or direct him to take such action as the court may deem proper.

If the Secretary of State shall revoke the certificate of authority to transact business in this State of any foreign corporation, pursuant to the provisions of this Act, such foreign corporation may likewise appeal to the .... court of the county where the registered office of such corporation in this State is situated, by filing with the clerk of such court a petition setting forth a copy of its certificate of authority to transact business in this State and a copy of the notice of revocation given by the Secretary of State; whereupon the matter shall be tried de novo by the court, and the court shall either sustain the action of the Secretary of State or direct him to take such action as the court may deem proper.

Appeals from all final orders and judgments entered by the .... court under this section in review of any ruling or decision of the Secretary of State may be taken as in other civil actions.

§ 141. Certificates and Certified Copies to be Received in Evidence

All certificates issued by the Secretary of State in accordance with the provisions of this Act, and all copies of documents filed in his office in accordance with the provisions of this Act when certified by him, shall be taken and received in all courts, public offices, and official bodies as prima facie evidence of the facts therein stated. A certificate by the Secretary of State under the great seal of this State, as to the existence or non-existence of the facts relating to corporations shall be taken and received in all courts, public offices, and official bodies as prima facie evidence of the existence or non-existence of the facts therein stated.

§ 142. Forms to be Furnished by Secretary of State

All reports required by this Act to be filed in the office of the Secretary of State shall be made on forms which shall be prescribed and furnished by the Secretary of State. Forms for all other documents to be filed in the office of the Secretary of State shall be furnished by the Secretary of State on request therefor, but the use thereof, unless otherwise specifically prescribed in this Act, shall not be mandatory.

§ 143. Greater Voting Requirements

Whenever, with respect to any action to be taken by the shareholders of a corporation, the articles of incorporation require the vote or concurrence of the holders of a greater proportion of the shares, or of any class or series thereof, than required by this Act with respect to such action, the provisions of the articles of incorporation shall control.

§ 144. Waiver of Notice

Whenever any notice is required to be given to any shareholder or director of a corporation under the provisions of this Act or under the provisions of the articles of incorporation or by-laws of the corporation, a waiver thereof in writing signed by the person or persons entitled to such notice, whether before or after the time stated therein, shall be equivalent to the giving of such notice.

§ 145. Action by Shareholders Without a Meeting

Any action required by this Act to be taken at a meeting of the shareholders of a corporation, or any action which may be taken at a meeting of the shareholders, may be taken without a meeting if a consent in writing, setting forth the action so taken, shall be signed by all of the shareholders entitled to vote with respect to the subject matter thereof.

Such consent shall have the same effect as a unanimous vote of shareholders, and may be stated as such in any articles or document filed with the Secretary of State under this Act.

§ 146. Unauthorized Assumption of Corporate Powers

All persons who assume to act as a corporation without authority so to do shall be jointly and severally liable for all debts and liabilities incurred or arising as a result thereof.

§ 147. Application to Existing Corporations

The provisions of this Act shall apply to all existing corporations organized under any general act of this State providing for the organization of corporations for a purpose or purposes for which a corporation might be organized under this Act, where the power has been reserved to amend, repeal or modify the act under which such corporation was organized and where such act is repealed by this Act.

§ 148. Application to Foreign and Interstate Commerce

The provisions of this Act shall apply to commerce with foreign nations and among the several states only insofar as the same may be permitted under the provisions of the Constitution of the United States.

§ 149. Reservation of Power

The ....* shall at all times have power to prescribe such regulations, provisions and limitations as it may deem advisable, which regulations, provisions and limitations shall be binding upon any and all corporations subject to the provisions of this Act, and the ....* shall have power to amend, repeal or modify this Act at pleasure.

*Insert name of legislative body.

§ 150. Effect of Repeal of Prior Acts

The repeal of a prior act by this Act shall not affect any right accrued or established, or any liability or penalty incurred, under the provisions of such act, prior to the repeal thereof.

§ 151. Effect of Invalidity of Part of this Act

If a court of competent jurisdiction shall adjudge to be invalid or unconstitutional any clause, sentence, paragraph, section or part of this Act, such judgment or decree shall not affect, impair, invalidate or nullify the remainder of this Act, but the effect thereof shall be confined to the clause, sentence, paragraph, section or part of this Act so adjudged to be invalid or unconstitutional.

§ 152. Exclusivity of Certain Provisions [Optional]

In circumstances to which section 45 and related sections of this Act are applicable, such provisions supersede the applicability of any other statutes of this state with respect to the legality of distributions.

§ 153. Repeal of Prior Acts

(insert appropriate provisions)..........

SELECTED PROVISIONS OF REVISED MODEL BUSINESS CORPORATION ACT

* * *

§ 2.04. Liability for Preincorporation Transactions

All persons purporting to act as or on behalf of a corporation, knowing there was no incorporation under this Act, are jointly and severally liable for all liabilities created while so acting.

* * *

§ 2.06. Bylaws

(a) The incorporators or board of directors of a corporation shall adopt initial bylaws for the corporation.

(b) The bylaws of a corporation may contain any provision for managing the business and regulating the affairs of the corporation that is not inconsistent with law or the articles of incorporation.

* * *

§ 6.21. Issuance of Shares

(a) The powers granted in this section to the board of directors may be reserved to the shareholders by the articles of incorporation.

(b) The board of directors may authorize shares to be issued for consideration consisting of any tangible or intangible property or benefit to the corporation, including cash, promissory notes, services performed, contracts for services to be performed, or other securities of the corporation.

(c) Before the corporation issues shares, the board of directors must determine that the consideration received or to be received for shares to be issued is adequate. That determination by the board of directors is conclusive insofar as the adequacy of consideration for the issuance of shares relates to whether the shares are validly issued, fully paid, and nonassessable.

(d) When the corporation receives the consideration for which the board of directors authorized the issuance of shares, the shares issued therefor are fully paid and nonassessable.

(e) The corporation may place in escrow shares issued for a contract for future services or benefits or a promissory note, or make other arrangements to restrict the transfer of the shares, and may credit distributions in respect of the shares against their purchase price, until the services are performed, the note is paid, or the benefits received. If the services are not performed, the note is not paid, or the benefits are not received, the shares escrowed or restricted and the distributions credited may be cancelled in whole or part.

* * *

§ 7.01. Annual Meeting

(a) A corporation shall hold annually at a time stated in or fixed in accordance with the bylaws a meeting of shareholders.

(b) Annual shareholders' meetings may be held in or out of this state at the place stated in or fixed in accordance with the bylaws. If no place is stated in or fixed in accordance with the bylaws, annual meetings shall be held at the corporation's principal office.

(c) The failure to hold an annual meeting at the time stated in or fixed in accordance with a corporation's bylaws does not affect the validity of any corporate action.

* * *

§ 7.03. Court-Ordered Meeting

(a) The [name or describe] court of the county where a corporation's principal office (or, if none in this state, its registered office) is located may summarily order a meeting to be held:

(1) On application of any shareholder of the corporation entitled to participate in an annual meeting if an annual meeting was not held within the earlier of 6 months after the end of the corporation's fiscal year or 15 months after its last annual meeting; or

(2) on application of a shareholder who signed a demand for a special meeting valid under section 7.02 if:

(i) notice of the special meeting was given within 30 days after the date the demand was delivered to the corporation's secretary; or

(ii) the special meeting was not held in accordance with the notice.

(b) The court may fix the time and place of the meeting, determine the shares entitled to participate in the meeting, specify a record date for determining shareholders entitled to notice of and to vote at the meeting, prescribe the form and content of the meeting notice, fix the quorum required for specific matters to be considered at the meeting (or direct that the votes represented at the meeting constitute a quorum for action on those matters), and enter other orders necessary to accomplish the purpose or purposes of the meeting.

* * *

§ 7.27. Greater Quorum or Voting Requirements

(a) The articles of incorporation may provide for a greater quorum or voting requirement for shareholders (or voting groups of shareholders) than is provided by this Act.

(b) An amendment to the articles of incorporation that adds, changes, or deletes a greater quorum or voting requirement must meet the same quorum requirement and be adopted by the same vote and voting groups required to take action under the quorum and voting requirements then in effect or proposed to be adopted, whichever is greater.

* * *

§ 7.40. Procedure in Derivative Proceedings

(a) A person may not commence a proceeding in the right of a domestic or foreign corporation unless he was a shareholder of the corporation when the transaction complained of occurred or unless he became a shareholder through transfer by operation of law from one who was a shareholder at that time.

(b) A complaint in a proceeding brought in the right of a corporation must be verified and allege with particularity the demand made, if any, to obtain action by the board of directors and either that the demand was refused or ignored or why he did not make the demand. Whether or not a demand for action was made, if the corporation commences an investigation of the changes made in the demand or complaint, the court may stay any proceeding until the investigation is completed.

(c) A proceeding commenced under this section may not be discontinued or settled without the court's approval. If the court determines that a proposed discontinuance or settlement will substantially affect the interest of the corporation's shareholders or a class of shareholders, the court shall direct that notice be given the shareholders affected.

(d) On termination of the proceeding the court may require the plaintiff to pay any defendant's reasonable expenses (including counsel fees) incurred in defending the proceeding if it finds that the proceeding was commenced without reasonable cause.

(e) For purposes of this section, "shareholder" includes a beneficial owner whose shares are held in a voting trust or held by a nominee on his behalf.

§ 8.01. Requirement For And Duties Of Board Of Directors

(a) Except as provided in subsection (c), each corporation must have a board of directors.

(b) All corporate powers shall be exercised by or under the authority of, and the business and affairs of the corporation managed under the direction of, its board of directors, subject to any limitation set forth in the articles of incorporation.

(c) A corporation having 50 or fewer shareholders may dispense with or limit the authority of a board of directors by describing in its articles of incorporation who will perform some or all of the duties of a board of directors.

* * *

§ 8.03. Number and Election Of Directors

(a) A board of directors must consist of one or more individuals, with the number specified in or fixed in accordance with the articles of incorporation or bylaws.

(b) If a board of directors has power to fix or change the number of directors, the board may increase or decrease by 30 percent or less the number of directors last approved by the shareholders, but only the shareholders may increase or decrease by more than 30 percent the number of directors last approved by the shareholders.

(c) The articles of incorporation or bylaws may establish a variable range for the size of the board of directors by fixing a minimum and maximum number of directors. If a variable range is established, the number of directors may be fixed or changed from time to time, within the minimum and maximum, by the shareholders or the board of directors. After shares are issued, only the shareholders may change the range for the size of the board or change from a fixed to a variable-range size board or vice versa.

(d) Directors are elected at the first annual shareholders' meeting and at each annual meeting thereafter unless their terms are staggered under section 8.06.

§ 8.04. Election of Directors by Certain Classes of Shareholders

If the articles of incorporation authorize dividing the shares into classes, the articles may also authorize the election of all or a specified number of directors by the holders of one or more authorized classes of shares. Each class (or classes) of shares entitled to elect one or more directors is a separate voting group for purposes of the election of directors.

* * *

§ 8.08. Removal of Directors by Shareholders

(a) The shareholders may remove one or more directors with or without cause unless the articles of incorporation provide that directors may be removed only for cause.

(b) If a director is elected by a voting group of shareholders, only the shareholders of that voting group may participate in the vote to remove him.

(c) If cumulative voting is authorized, a director may not be removed if the number of votes sufficient to elect him under cumulative voting is voted against his removal. If cumulative voting is not authorized, a director may be removed only if the number of votes cast to remove him exceeds the number of votes cast not to remove him.

(d) A director may be removed by the shareholders only at a meeting called for the purpose of removing him and the meeting notice must state that the purpose, or one of the purposes, of the meeting is removal of the director.

* * *

§ 8.24. Quorum and Voting

(a) Unless the articles of incorporation or bylaws require a greater number, a quorum of a board of directors consists of:

(1) a majority of the fixed number of directors if the corporation has a fixed board size; or

(2) a majority of the number of directors prescribed, or if no number is prescribed the number in office immediately before the meeting begins, if the corporation has a variable range size board.

(b) The articles of incorporation or bylaws may authorize a quorum of a board of directors to consist of no fewer than one-third of the fixed or prescribed number of directors determined under subsection (a).

(c) If a quorum is present when a vote is taken, the affirmative vote of a majority of directors present is the act of the board of directors unless the articles of incorporation or bylaws require the vote of a greater number of directors.

(d) A director who is present at a meeting of the board of directors or a committee of the board of directors when corporate action is taken is deemed to have assented to the action taken unless: (1) he objects at the beginning of the meeting (or promptly upon his arrival) to holding it or transacting business at the meeting; (2) his dissent or abstention from the action taken is entered in the minutes of the meeting; or (3) he delivers written notice of his dissent or abstention to the presiding officer of the meeting before its adjournment or to the corporation immediately after adjournment of the meeting. The right of dissent or abstention is not available to a director who votes in favor of the action taken.

§ 8.25. Committees

(a) Unless the articles of incorporation or bylaws provide otherwise, a board of directors may create one or more committees and appoint members of the board of directors to serve on them. Each committee may have two or more members, who serve at the pleasure of the board of directors.

(b) The creation of a committee and appointment of members to it must be approved by the greater of (1) a majority of all the directors in office when the action is taken or (2) the number of directors required by the articles of incorporation or bylaws to take action under section 8.24.

(c) Sections 8.20 through 8.24, which govern meetings, action without meetings, notice and waiver of notice, and quorum and voting requirements of the board of directors, apply to committees and their members as well.

(d) To the extent specified by the board of directors or in the articles of incorporation or bylaws, each committee may exercise the authority of the board of directors under section 8.01.

(e) A committee may not, however:

(1) authorize distributions;

(2) approve or propose to shareholders action that this Act requires to be approved by shareholders;

(3) fill vacancies on the board of directors or on any of its committees;

(4) amend articles of incorporation pursuant to section 10.02;

(5) adopt, amend, or repeal bylaws;

(6) approve a plan of merger not requiring shareholder approval;

(7) authorize or approve reacquisition of shares, except according to a formula or method prescribed by the board of directors; or

(8) authorize or approve the issuance or sale or contract for sale of shares, or determine the designation and relative rights, preferences, and limitations of a class or series of shares, except that the board of directors may authorize a committee (or a senior executive officer of the corporation) to do so within limits specifically prescribed by the board of directors.

(f) The creation of, delegation of authority to, or action by a committee does not alone constitute compliance by a director with the standards of conduct described in section 8.30.

§ 8.30. General Standards for Directors

(a) A director shall discharge his duties as a director, including his duties as a member of a committee:

(1) in good faith;

(2) with the care an ordinarily prudent person in a like position would exercise under similar circumstances; and

(3) in a manner he reasonably believes to be in the best interests of the corporation.

(b) In discharging his duties a director is entitled to rely on information, opinions, reports, or statements, including financial statements and other financial data, if prepared or presented by:

(1) one or more officers or employees of the corporation whom the director reasonably believes to be reliable and competent in the matters presented;

(2) legal counsel, public accountants, or other persons as to matters the director reasonably believes are within the person's professional or expert competence; or

(3) a committee of the board of directors of which he is not a member if the director reasonably believes the committee merits confidence.

(c) A director is not acting in good faith if he has knowledge concerning the matter in question that makes reliance otherwise permitted by subsection (b) unwarranted.

(d) A director is not liable for any action taken as a director, or any failure to take any action, if he performed the duties of his office in compliance with this section.

§ 8.31. Director Conflict of Interest

(a) A conflict of interest transaction is a transaction with the corporation in which a director of the corporation has a direct or indirect interest. A conflict of interest transaction is not voidable by the corporation solely because of the director's interest in the transaction if any one of the following is true:

(1) the material facts of the transaction and the director's interest were disclosed or known to the board of directors or a committee of the board of directors and the board of directors or committee authorized, approved, or ratified the transaction;

(2) the material facts of the transaction and the director's interest were disclosed or known to

the shareholders entitled to vote and they authorized, approved, or ratified the transaction; or

(3) the transaction was fair to the corporation.

(b) For purposes of this section, a director of the corporation has an indirect interest in a transaction if (1) another entity in which he has a material financial interest or in which he is a general partner is a party to the transaction or (2) another entity of which he is a director, officer, or trustee is a party to the transaction and the transaction is or should be considered by the board of directors of the corporation.

(c) For purposes of subsection (a)(1), a conflict of interest transaction is authorized, approved, or ratified if it receives the affirmative vote of a majority of the directors on the board of directors (or on the committee) who have no direct or indirect interest in the transaction, but a transaction may not be authorized, approved, or ratified under this section by a single director. If a majority of the directors who have no direct or indirect interest in the transaction vote to authorize, approve, or ratify the transaction, a quorum is present for the purpose of taking action under this section. The presence of, or vote cast by, a director with a direct or indirect interest in the transaction does not affect the validity of any action taken under subsection (a)(1) if the transaction is otherwise authorized, approved, or ratified as provided in that subsection.

(d) For purposes of subsection (a)(2), a conflict of interest transaction is authorized, approved, or ratified if it receives the vote of a majority of the shares entitled to be counted under this subsection. Shares owned by or voted under the control of a director who has a direct or indirect interest in the transaction, and shares owned by or voted under the control of an entity described in subsection (b)(1), may not be counted in a vote of shareholders to determine whether to authorize, approve, or ratify a conflict of interest transaction under subsection (a)(2). The vote of those shares, however, shall be counted in determining whether the transaction is approved under other sections of this Act. A majority of the shares, whether or not present, that are entitled to be counted in a vote on the transaction under this subsection constitutes a quorum for the purpose of taking action under this section.

§ 8.32. Loans to Directors

(a) Except as provided by subsection (c), a corporation may not lend money to or guarantee the obligation of a director of the corporation unless:

(1) the particular loan or guarantee is approved by a majority of the votes represented by the outstanding voting shares of all classes, voting as a single voting group, except the votes of shares owned by or voted under the control of the benefited director; or

(2) the corporation's board of directors determines that the loan or guarantee benefits the corporation and either approves the specific loan or guarantee or a general plan authorizing loans and guarantees.

(b) The fact that a loan or guarantee is made in violation of this section does not affect the borrower's liability on the loan.

(c) This section does not apply to loans and guarantees authorized by statute regulating any special class of corporations.

* * *

§ 8.40. Required Officers

(a) A corporation has the officers described in its bylaws or appointed by the board of directors in accordance with the bylaws.

(b) A duly appointed officer may appoint one or more officers or assistant officers if authorized by the bylaws or the board of directors.

(c) The bylaws or the board of directors shall delegate to one of the officers responsibility for preparing minutes of the directors' and shareholders' meetings and for authenticating records of the corporation.

(d) The same individual may simultaneously hold more than one office in a corporation.

* * *

§ 8.42. Standards of Conduct for Officers

(a) An officer with discretionary authority shall discharge his duties under that authority:

(1) in good faith;

(2) with the care an ordinarily prudent person in a like position would exercise under similar circumstances; and

(3) in a manner he reasonably believes to be in the best interests of the corporation.

(b) In discharging his duties an officer is entitled to rely on information, opinions, reports, or statements, including financial statements and other financial data, if prepared or presented by:

(1) one or more officers or employees of the corporation whom the officer reasonably believes to be reliable and competent in the matters presented; or

(2) legal counsel, public accountants, or other persons as to matters the officer reasonably believes are within the person's professional or expert competence.

(c) An officer is not acting in good faith if he has knowledge concerning the matter in question that makes reliance otherwise permitted by subsection (b) unwarranted.

(d) An officer is not liable for any action taken as an officer, or any failure to take any action, if he performed the duties of his office in compliance with this section.

* * *

§ 10.02. Amendment by Board of Directors

Unless the articles of incorporation provide otherwise, a corporation's board of directors may adopt one or more amendments to the corporation's articles of incorporation without shareholder action:

(1) to extend the duration of the corporation if it was incorporated at a time when limited duration was required by law;

(2) to delete the names and addresses of the initial directors;

(3) to delete the name and address of the initial registered agent or registered office, if a statement of change is on file with the secretary of state;

(4) to change each issued and unissued authorized share of an outstanding class into a greater number of whole shares if the corporation has only shares of that class outstanding;

(5) to change the corporate name by substituting the word "corporation," "incorporated," "company," "limited," or the abbreviation "corp.," "inc.," "co.," or "ltd.," for a similar word or abbreviation in the name, or by adding, deleting, or changing a geographical attribution for the name; or

(6) to make any other change expressly permitted by this Act to be made without shareholder action.

§ 10.03. Amendment by Board of Directors and Shareholders

(a) A corporation's board of directors may propose one or more amendments to the articles of incorporation for submission to the shareholders.

(b) For the amendment to be adopted:

(1) the board of directors must recommend the amendment to the shareholders unless the board of directors determines that because of conflict of interest or other special circumstances it should make no recommendation and communicates the basis for its determination to the shareholders with the amendment; and

(2) the shareholders entitled to vote on the amendment must approve the amendment as provided in subsection (e).

(c) The board of directors may condition its submission of the proposed amendment on any basis.

(d) The corporation shall notify each shareholder, whether or not entitled to vote, of the proposed shareholders' meeting in accordance with section 7.05. The notice of meeting must also state that the purpose, or one of the purposes, of the meeting is to consider the proposed amendment and contain or be accompanied by a copy or summary of the amendment.

(e) Unless this Act, the articles of incorporation, or the board of directors (acting pursuant to subsection (c)) require a greater vote or a vote by voting groups, the amendment to be adopted must be approved by:

(1) a majority of the votes entitled to be cast on the amendment by any voting group with respect to which the amendment would create dissenters' rights; and

(2) the votes required by sections 7.25 and 7.26 by every other voting group entitled to vote on the amendment.

§ 10.04. Voting on Amendments by Voting Groups

(a) The holders of the outstanding shares of a class are entitled to vote as a separate voting group (if shareholder voting is otherwise required by this Act) on a proposed amendment if the amendment would:

(1) increase or decrease the aggregate number of authorized shares of the class;

(2) effect an exchange or reclassification of all or part of the shares of the class into shares of another class;

(3) effect an exchange or reclassification, or create the right of exchange, of all or part of the shares of another class into shares of the class;

(4) change the designation, rights, preferences, or limitations of all or part of the shares of the class;

(5) change the shares of all or part of the class into a different number of shares of the same class;

(6) create a new class of shares having rights or preferences with respect to distributions or to dissolution that are prior, superior, or substantially equal to the shares of the class;

(7) increase the rights, preferences, or number of authorized shares of any class that, after giving effect to the amendment, have rights or preferences with respect to distributions or to dissolution that are prior, superior, or substantially equal to the shares of the class;

(8) limit or deny an existing preemptive right of all or part of the shares of the class; or

(9) cancel or otherwise affect rights to distributions or dividends that have accumulated but not yet been declared on all or part of the shares of the class.

(b) If a proposed amendment would affect a series of a class of shares in one or more of the ways described in subsection (a), the shares of that series are entitled to vote as a separate voting group on the proposed amendment.

(c) If a proposed amendment that entitles two or more series of shares to vote as separate voting groups under this section would affect those two or more series in the same or a substantially similar way, the shares of all the series so affected must vote together as a single voting group on the proposed amendment.

(d) A class or series of shares is entitled to the voting rights granted by this section although the articles of incorporation provide that the shares are nonvoting shares.

* * *

§ 11.01. **Merger**

(a) One or more corporations may merge into another corporation if the board of directors of each corporation adopts and its shareholders (if required by section 11.03) approve a plan of merger.

(b) The plan of merger must set forth:

(1) the name of each corporation planning to merge and the name of the surviving corporation into which each other corporation plans to merge;

(2) the terms and conditions of the merger; and

(3) the manner and basis of converting the shares of each corporation into shares, obligations, or other securities of the surviving or any other corporation or into cash or other property in whole or part.

(c) The plan of merger may set forth:

(1) amendments to the articles of incorporation of the surviving corporation; and

(2) other provisions relating to the merger.

* * *

§ 14.07. **Unknown Claims Against Dissolved Corporation**

(a) A dissolved corporation may also publish notice of its dissolution and request that persons with claims against the corporation present them in accordance with the notice.

(b) The notice must:

(1) be published one time in a newspaper of general circulation in the county where the dissolved corporation's principal office (or, if none in this state, its registered office) is or was last located;

(2) describe the information that must be included in a claim and provide a mailing address where the claim may be sent; and

(3) state that a claim against the corporation will be barred unless a proceeding to enforce the claim is commenced within five years after the publication of the notice.

(c) If the dissolved corporation publishes a newspaper notice in accordance with subsection (b), the claim of each of the following claimants is barred unless the claimant commences a proceeding to enforce the claim against the dissolved corporation within five years after the publication date of the newspaper notice:

(1) a claimant who did not receive written notice under section 14.06;

(2) a claimant whose claim was timely sent to the dissolved corporation but not acted on;

(3) a claimant whose claim is contingent or based on an event occurring after the effective date of dissolution.

(d) A claim may be enforced under this section:

(1) against the dissolved corporation, to the extent of its undistributed assets; or

(2) if the assets have been distributed in liquidation, against a shareholder of the dissolved corporation to the extent of his pro rata share

of the claim or the corporate assets distributed to him in liquidation, whichever is less, but a shareholder's total liability for all claims under this section may not exeed the total amount of assets distributed to him.

§ 14.20. Grounds for Administrative Dissolution

The secretary of state may commence a proceeding under section 14.21 to administratively dissolve a corporation if:

(1) the corporation does not pay within 60 days after they are due any franchise taxes or penalties imposed by this Act or other law;

(2) the corporation does not deliver its annual report to the secretary of state within 60 days after it is due;

(3) the corporation is without a registered agent or registered office in this state for 60 days or more;

(4) the corporation does not notify the secretary of state within 60 days that its registered agent or registered office has been changed, that its registered agent has resigned, or that its registered office has been discontinued; or

(5) the corporation's period of duration stated in its articles of incorporation expires.

*   *   *

§ 14.30. Grounds For Judicial Dissolution

The [name or describe court or courts] may dissolve a corporation:

(1) in a proceeding by the attorney general if it is established that:

(i) the corporation obtained its articles of incorporation through fraud; or

(ii) the corporation has continued to exceed or abuse the authority conferred upon it by law;

(2) in a proceeding by a shareholder if it is established that:

(i) the directors are deadlocked in the management of the corporate affairs, the shareholders are unable to break the deadlock, and irreparable injury to the corporation is threatened or being suffered, or the business and affairs of the corporation can no longer be conducted to the advantage of the shareholders generally, because of the deadlock;

(ii) the directors or those in control of the corporation have acted, are acting, or will act in a manner that is illegal, oppressive, or fraudulent;

(iii) the shareholders are deadlocked in voting power and have failed, for a period that includes at least two consecutive annual meeting dates, to elect successors to directors whose terms have expired; or

(iv) the corporate assets are being misapplied or wasted;

(3) in a proceeding by a creditor if it is established that:

(i) the creditor's claim has been reduced to judgment, the execution on the judgment returned unsatisfied, and the corporation is insolvent; or

(ii) the corporation has admitted in writing that the creditor's claim is due and owing and the corporation is insolvent; or

(4) in a proceeding by the corporation to have its voluntary dissolution continued under court supervision.

*   *   *

§ 15.01 Authority to Transact Business Required

(a) A foreign corporation may not transact business in this state until it obtains a certificate of authority from the secretary of state.

(b) The following activities, among others, do not constitute transacting business within the meaning of subsection (a):

(1) maintaining, defending, or settling any proceeding;

(2) holding meetings of the board of directors or shareholders or carrying on other activities concerning internal corporate affairs;

(3) maintaining bank accounts;

(4) maintaining offices or agencies for the transfer, exchange, and registration of the corporation's own securities or maintaining trustees or depositaries with respect to those securities;

(5) selling through independent contractors;

(6) soliciting or obtaining orders, whether by mail or through employees or agents or otherwise, if the orders require acceptance outside this state before they become contracts;

(7) creating or acquiring indebtedness, mortgages, and security interests in real or personal property;

(8) securing or collecting debts or enforcing mortgages and security interests in property securing the debts;

(9) owning, without more, real or personal property;

(10) conducting an isolated transaction that is completed within 30 days and that is not one in the course of repeated transactions of a like nature;

(11) transacting business in interstate commerce.

(c) The list of activities in subsection (b) is not exhaustive.

*   *   *

§ 16.02. Inspection of Records by Shareholders

(a) Subject to section 16.03(c), a shareholder of a corporation is entitled to inspect and copy, during regular business hours at the corporation's principal office, any of the records of the corporation described in section 16.01(e) if he gives the corporation written notice of his demand at least five business days before the date on which he wishes to inspect and copy.

(b) A shareholder of a corporation is entitled to inspect and copy, during regular business hours at a reasonable location specified by the corporation, any of the following records of the corporation if the shareholder meets the requirements of subsection (c) and gives the corporation written notice of his demand at least five business days before the date on which he wishes to inspect and copy:

(1) excerpts from minutes of any meeting of the board of directors, records of any action of a committee of the board of directors while acting in place of the board of directors on behalf of the corporation, minutes of any meeting of the shareholders, and records of action taken by the shareholders or board of directors without a meeting, to the extent not subject to inspection under section 16.02(a);

(2) accounting records of the corporation; and

(3) the record of shareholders.

(c) A shareholder may inspect and copy the records identified in subsection (b) only if:

(1) his demand is made in good faith and for a proper purpose;

(2) he describes with reasonable particularity his purpose and the records he desires to inspect; and

(3) the records are directly connected with his purpose.

(d) The right of inspection granted by this section may not be abolished or limited by a corporation's articles of incorporation or bylaws.

(e) This section does not affect:

(1) the right of a shareholder to inspect records under section 7.20 or, if the shareholder is in litigation with the corporation, to the same extent as any other litigant;

(2) the power of a court, independently of this Act, to compel the production of corporate records for examination.

§ 16.03. Scope of Inspection Right

(a) A shareholder's agent or attorney has the same inspection and copying rights as the shareholder he represents.

(b) The right to copy records under section 16.02 includes, if reasonable, the right to receive copies made by photographic, xerographic, or other means.

(c) The corporation may impose a reasonable charge, covering the costs of labor and material, for copies of any documents provided to the shareholder. The charge may not exceed the estimated cost of production or reproduction of the records.

(d) The corporation may comply with a shareholder's demand to inspect the record of shareholders under section 16.02(b)(3) by providing him with a list of its shareholders that was compiled no earlier than the date of the shareholder's demand.

*   *   *

§ 16.21. Other Reports to Shareholders

(a) If a corporation indemnifies or advances expenses to a director under section 8.51, 8.52, 8.53, or 8.54 in connection with a proceeding by or in the right of the corporation, the corporation shall report the indemnification or advance in writing to the shareholders with or before the notice of the next shareholders' meeting.

(b) If a corporation issues or authorizes the issuance of shares for promissory notes or for promises to render services in the future, the corporation shall report in writing to the shareholders the number of shares authorized or issued, and the consideration received by the corporation, with or before the notice of the next shareholders' meeting.

*   *   *

Appendix I

DICTIONARY OF LEGAL TERMS

A

abatement of nuisance See **nuisance**

abstract of title A condensed history of the title to land, consisting of a summary of the material or operative portion of all the conveyances which in any manner affect the land, or any estate or interest therein, together with a statement of all liens, charges, or liabilities to which the same may be subject, and of which it is in any way material for purchasers to be apprised.

acceptance *Commercial paper* Acceptance is the drawee's signed engagement to honor the draft as presented. It becomes operative when completed by delivery or notification. U.C.C. § 3–410.

Contracts Compliance by offeree with terms and conditions of offer.

Sale of goods U.C.C. § 2–606 provides three ways a buyer can accept goods: (1) by signifying to the seller that the goods are conforming or that he will accept them in spite of their nonconformity, (2) by failing to make an effective rejection, and (3) by doing an act inconsistent with the seller's ownership.

accession An addition to one's property by increase of the original property or by production from such property. E.g., A innocently converts the wheat of B into bread. U.C.C. § 9–315 changes the common law where a perfected security interest is involved.

accommodation An arrangement made as a favor to another, usually involving a loan of money or commercial paper. While a party's intent may be to aid a maker of note by lending his credit, if he seeks to accomplish thereby legitimate objects of his own, and not simply to aid the maker, the act is not for accommodation.

accommodation party A person who signs commercial paper in any capacity for the purpose of lending his name to another party to an instrument. U.C.C. § 3–415.

accord and satisfaction A method of discharging a claim whereby the parties agree to accept something in settlement, the "accord" being the agreement and the "satisfaction" its execution or performance. It is a new contract that is substituted for an old contract, which is thereby discharged, or for an obligation or cause of action and that must have all of the elements of a valid contract.

account Any account with a bank, including a checking, time, interest or savings account. U.C.C. § 4–194. Also, any right to payment, for goods or services, that is not evidenced by an instrument or chattel paper. E.g., account receivable.

[218]

adhesion contract Standard "form" contract, usually between a large retailer and a consumer, in which the weaker party has no realistic choice or opportunity to bargain.

adjudication The giving or pronouncing of a judgment in a case; also the judgment given.

administrator A person appointed by the court to manage the assets and liabilities of an intestate (person dying without a will). A person who is named in the will by testator (person dying with a will) is called the executor. Female designations are administratrix and executrix.

adverse possession A method of acquisition of title to real property by possession for a statutory period under certain conditions. There may be different periods of time, depending on whether the adverse possessor has color of title. See also **constructive adverse possession; prescription; tacking.**

affidavit A written statement of facts, made voluntarily, confirmed by oath or affirmation of party making it, and taken before an authorized officer.

affirmative defense A response that attacks the plaintiff's legal right to bring an action as opposed to attacking the truth of the claim. E.g., accord and satisfaction; assumption of risk; contributory negligence; duress; estoppel.

agency Relation in which one person acts for or represents another by the latter's authority.
Actual agency Exists where the agent is really employed by the principal.
Agency by estoppel One created by operation of law and established by proof of such acts of the principal as reasonably lead to the conclusion of its existence.
Implied agency One created by acts of parties and deduced from proof of other facts.

alienation Every mode of passing realty by the act of the party, as distinguished from passing it by the operation of law. See also **restraint on alienation.**

allegation A statement of a party setting out what he expects to prove.

annul To annul a judgment or judicial proceeding is to deprive it of all force and operation.

answer Any pleading setting up matters of facts by way of defense. The answer is the formal written statement made by a defendant setting forth the ground of his defense.

anticipatory breach of contract (or **anticipatory repudiation**). The unjustified assertion by a party that he will not perform an obligation that he is contractually obligated to perform at a future time. See U.C.C. §§ 610 & 611.

apparent authority Such principal power that a reasonable person would assume an agent has in light of the principal's conduct. It includes the power to do whatever is usually done in order to carry into effect the principal power conferred.

appeal Resort to a superior (appellate) court to review the decision of an inferior (trial) court or administrative agency.

appearance A technical coming into court as a party to an action, as plaintiff or as defendant. The party may actually appear in court, or he may, by his attorney, enter his appearance by filing written pleadings in the case, or by filing a formal written entry of appearance.

appellant A party who takes an appeal from one court to another. He may be either the plaintiff or defendant in the original court proceeding.

appellee The party in a cause against whom an appeal is taken; that is, the party who has an interest adverse to setting aside or reversing the judgment. Sometimes also called the "respondent."

appurtenances Things appurtenant pass as incident to the principal thing. Sometimes an easement consisting of a right of way over one piece of land will pass with another piece of land as being appurtenant to it.

arbitration The reference of a dispute to an impartial (third) person chosen by the parties who agree in advance to abide by the arbitrator's award issued after a hearing at which both parties have an opportunity to be heard.

arrest of judgment The act of staying a judgment, or refusing to render judgment in an action at law, after verdict, for some matter intrinsic appearing on the face of the record, which would render the judgment, if given, erroneous or reversible.

articles of incorporation (or **certificate of incorporation**) The instrument under which a corporation is formed. The contents are prescribed in the particular state's general incorporation statute.

articles of partnership A written agreement by which parties enter into a partnership, to be governed by the terms set forth therein.

assignment A transfer of the rights to real or personal property, usually intangible property such as rights in a lease, mortgage, sale agreement or partnership.

attachment The process of seizing property, by virtue of a writ, summons, or other judicial order, and bringing the same into the custody of the court for the purpose of securing satisfaction of the judgment ultimately to be entered in the action. While formerly the main objective was to coerce the defendant debtor to appear in court, today the writ of attachment is used primarily to seize the debtor's property in the event a judgment is rendered.

Distinguished from execution See **execution.**

Also, the process by which a security interest becomes enforceable. Attachment may occur upon the taking of possession or upon the signing of a security agreement by the person who is pledging the property as collateral.

attestation The act of witnessing an instrument in writing, at the request of the party making the same, and subscribing it as a witness. Execution and attestation are clearly distinct formalities; the former being the act of the party, and the latter of the witnesses only.

B

bailee The party to whom personal property is delivered under a contract of bailment.

bailment A delivery of personal property in trust for the execution of a special object in relation to such goods, beneficial either to the bailor or bailee or both, and upon a contract to either redeliver the goods to the bailor or otherwise dispose of the same in conformity with the purpose of the trust.

bailor The party who delivers goods to another in the contract of bailment.

bankrupt The state or condition of one who is unable to pay his debts as they are, or become, due.

bankruptcy act The Act was substantially revised in 1978, effective October 1, 1979. Straight bankruptcy is in the nature of a liquidation proceeding and involves the collection and distribution to creditors of all the bankrupt's non-exempt property by the trustee in the manner provided by the Act. The debtor rehabilitation provisions of the Act (Chapters 11 and 13) differ however from straight bankruptcy in that the debtor looks to rehabilitation and reorganization, rather than liq-

uidation, and the creditor looks to future earnings of the bankrupt, rather than property held by the bankrupt to satisfy their claims.

beneficiary One who benefits from act of another. See also **third party beneficiary.**

Incidental A person who may derive benefit from performance on contract, though he is neither the promisee nor the one to whom performance is to be rendered. Since the incidental beneficiary is not a donee or creditor beneficiary (see **third party beneficiary**), he has no right to enforce the contract.

Trust As it relates to trust beneficiaries, includes a person who has any present or future interest, vested or contingent, and also includes the owner of an interest by assignment or other transfer and, as it relates to a charitable trust, includes any person entitled to enforce the trust.

bequest A gift by will of personal property; a legacy. Disposition of realty in will is termed "devise." See also **devise; legacy.**

Residuary bequest A gift of all the remainder of the testator's personal estate, after payment of debts and legacies, etc.

Specific bequest One whereby the testator gives to the legatee all his property of a certain class or kind; as all his pure personalty.

bill of lading Document evidencing receipt of goods for shipment issued by person engaged in business of transporting or forwarding goods and it includes airbill. U.C.C. § 1–201(6).

bill of sale A written agreement, formerly limited to one under seal, by which one person assigns or transfers his right to or interest in goods and personnal chattels to another.

binder A written memorandum of the important terms of contract of insurance which gives temporary protection to insured pending investigation of risk by insurance company or until a formal policy is issued.

blue sky laws A popular name for state statutes providing for the regulation and supervision of securities offerings and sales, for the protection of citizen-investors from investing in fraudulent companies.

bona fide Latin. In good faith.

bond A certificate or evidence of a debt on which the issuing company or governmental body promises to pay the bondholders a specified amount of interest for a specified length of time, and to repay the loan on the expiration date. In every case a bond represents debt—its holder is a creditor of the corporation and not a part owner as is the shareholder.

by-laws Regulations, ordinances, rules of laws adopted by an association or corporation for its government.

C

capital Accumulated goods, possessions, and assets, used for the production of profits and wealth. Owners' equity in a business. Often used equally correctly to mean the total assets of a business. Sometimes used to mean capital assets.

capitalization To record an expenditure that may benefit in the future as an asset, rather than to treat the expenditure as an expense of the period of its occurrence. Different tax consequences flow from whether an expenditure is "capitalized" or "expensed".

cause of action The ground on which an action may be sustained.

caveat emptor Latin. Let the buyer beware. This maxim is more applicable to judicial sales, auctions, and the like, than to sales of consumer goods where strict liability, warranty, and other laws protect.

certificate of deposit A written acknowledgment by a bank or banker of a deposit with promise to pay to depositor, to his order, or to some other person or to his order. U.C.C. § 3–104(2)(c).

certification of incorporation See **articles of incorporation**.

certiorari Latin. To be informed of. A writ of common law origin issued by a superior to an inferior court requiring the latter to produce a certified record of a particular case tried therein. It is most commonly used to refer to the Supreme Court of the United States, which uses the writ of certiorari as a discretionary device to choose the cases it wishes to hear. The trend in state practice has been to abolish such writ.

chancery Equity; equitable jurisdiction; a court of equity; the system of jurisprudence administered in courts of equity.

charter An instrument emanating from the sovereign power, in the nature of a grant. A charter differs from a constitution in that the former is granted by the sovereign, while the latter is established by the people themselves.

Corporate law An act of a legislature creating a corporation, or creating and defining the franchise of a corporation. Also a corporation's constitution or organic law; that is to say, the articles of incorporation taken in connection with the law under which the corporation was organized.

chattel An article of personal property, as opposed to real property. It may refer to animate as well as inanimate property.

chattel mortgage A pre-Uniform Commercial Code security device whereby a security interest was taken by the mortgagee in personal property of the mortgagor. Such security device has generally been superseded by other types of security agreements under U.C.C. Article 9 (Secured Transactions).

check A draft drawn upon a bank and payable on demand, signed by the maker or drawer, containing an unconditional promise to pay a sum certain in money to the order of the payee. U.C.C. § 3–104(2)(b).

Cashier's check A bank's own check drawn on itself and signed by the cashier or other authorized official. It is a direct obligation of the bank.

civil law Laws concerned with civil or private rights and remedies, as contrasted with criminal laws.

The system of jurisprudence administered in the Roman empire, particularly as set forth in the compilation of Justinian and his successors, as distinguished from the common law of England and the canon law. The civil law (Civil Code) is followed by Louisiana.

close corporation See **corporation**.

code A compilation of all permanent laws in force, consolidated and classified according to subject matter. Many states have published official codes of all laws in force, including the common law and statutes as judicially interpreted, which have been compiled by code commissions and enacted by the legislatures.

codicil A supplement or an addition to a will; it may explain, modify, add to, subtract from, qualify, alter, restrain or revoke provisions in existing will. It must be executed with the same formalities as a will.

cognovit judgment Written authority by debtor for entry of judgment against him in the event he defaults in payment. Such provision in a debt instrument on default confers judgment against the debtor.

collateral security A security given in addition to the direct security, and subordinate to it, intended to guaranty its validity or convertibility or insure its performance.

Banking Some form of security in addition to the personal obligation of the borrower.

collecting bank Any bank handling the item for collection except the payor bank. U.C.C. § 4–105(d).

commercial law A phrase used to designate the whole body of substantive jurisprudence (*e.g.* Uniform Commercial Code; Truth in Lending Act) applicable to the rights, intercourse, and relations of persons engaged in commerce, trade, or mercantile pursuits. See **uniform commercial code.**

commercial paper Bills of exchange (*i.e.* drafts), promissory notes, bank-checks, and other negotiable instruments for the payment of money, which, by their form and on their face, purport to be such instruments. U.C.C. Article 3 is the general law governing commercial paper.

common law As distinguished from statutory law created by the enactment of legislatures, the common law comprises the judgments and decrees of the courts recognizing, affirming, and enforcing usages and customs of immemorial antiquity. As distinguished from ecclesiastical law, it is the system of jurisprudence administered by the purely secular tribunals.

comparative negligence Under comparative negligence statutes or doctrines, negligence is measured in terms of percentage, and any damages allowed shall be diminished in proportion to amount of negligence attributable to the person for whose injury, damage or death recovery is sought.

complainant One who applies to the courts for legal redress by filing complaint (*i.e.* plaintiff).

complaint The pleading which sets forth a claim for relief. Such complaint (whether it be the original claim, counterclaim, cross-claim, or third-party claim) shall contain: (1) a short and plain statement of the grounds upon which the court's jurisdiction depends, unless the court already has jurisdiction and the claim needs no new grounds of jurisdiction to support it, (2) a short and plain statement of the claim showing that the pleader is entitled to relief, and (3) a demand for judgment for the relief to which he deems himself entitled. Fed.R. Civil P. 8(a). The complaint, together with

the summons, is required to be served on the defendant. Rule 4.

confession of judgment See **cognovit judgment.**

conflict of laws That branch of jurisprudence, arising from the diversity of the laws of different nations, states or jurisdictions, that reconciles the inconsistency, or decides which law is to govern in the particular case.

confusion Results when goods belonging to two or more owners become intermixed to the point where the property of any of them no longer can be identified except as part of a mass of like goods.

consanguinity Kinship; blood relationship; the connection or relation of persons descended from the same stock or common ancestor.

conservator Appointed by court to manage affairs of incompetent or to liquidate business.

consideration The cause, motive, price, or impelling influence which induces a contracting party to enter into a contract. Some right, interest, profit or benefit accruing to one party, or some forbearance, detriment, loss, or responsibility, given, suffered, or undertaken by the other.

consignee One to whom a consignment is made. Person named in bill of lading to whom or to whose order the bill promises delivery. U.C.C. § 7–102(b).

consignment Ordinarily implies an agency and denotes that property is committed to the consignee for care or sale.

consignor One who sends or makes a consignment; a shipper of goods. The person named in a bill of lading as the person from whom the goods have been received for shipment. U.C.C. § 7–102(c).

consolidation In *corporate law*, the combination of two or more corporations into a newly created corporation. Thus, A Corporation and B Corporation combine to form C Corporation.

constructive That which is established by the mind of the law in its act of *construing* facts, conduct, circumstances, or instruments. That which has not the character assigned to it in its own essential nature, but acquires such character in consequence of the way in which it is regarded by a rule or policy of law; hence, inferred, implied, or made out by legal interpretation; the word "legal" being sometimes used here in lieu of "constructive."

constructive adverse possession Type of adverse possession that is characterized by performance of certain acts under color of title by an adverse claimant who is not in actual possession of the entire amount of land being claimed. See **adverse possession.**

constructive assent An assent or consent imputed to a party from a construction or interpretation of his conduct; as distinguished from one which he actually expresses.

constructive conditions Conditions in contracts which are neither expressed nor implied but are rather imposed by law to meet the ends of justice.

constructive delivery Term comprehending all those acts which, although not truly conferring a real possession of the vendee, have been held by construction of law to be the equivalent to acts of real delivery.

constructive trust See **trustee.**

contract An agreement between two or more persons which creates an obligation to do or not to do a particular thing. Its essentials are competent parties, subject matter, a legal consideration, mutuality of agreement, and mutuality of obligation.

Output contract A contract in which one party agrees to sell his entire output and the other agrees to buy it; it is not illusory, though it may be indefinite.

Requirements contract A contract in which one party agrees to purchase his total requirements from the other party and hence it is binding and not illusory.

Unconscionable contract One which no sensible man not under delusion, duress, or in distress would make, and such as no honest and fair man would accept. A contract the terms of which are excessively unreasonable, overreaching and one-sided.

Unilateral and bilateral A unilateral contract is one in which one party makes an express engagement or undertakes a performance, without receiving in return any express engagement or promise of performance from the other. Bilateral (or reciprocal) contracts are those by which the parties expressly enter into mutual engagements.

contributory negligence The act or omission amounting to want of ordinary care on part of complaining party, which, concurring with defendant's negligence, is proximate cause of injury.

The defense of contributory negligence is an absolute bar to any recovery in some states; be-

cause of this, it has been replaced by the doctrine of comparative negligence in many other states.

conversion Unauthorized and wrongful exercise of dominion and control over another's personal property, to exclusion of or inconsistent with rights of the owner. See also **trover.**

corporation A legal entity ordinarily consisting of an association of numerous individuals. Such entity is regarded as having a personality and existence distinct from that of its several members and is vested with the capacity of continuous succession, irrespective of changes in its membership, either in perpetuity or for a limited term of years.

Domestic and foreign With reference to the laws and the courts of any given state, a "domestic" corporation is one created by, or organized under, the laws of that state; a "foreign" corporation is one created by or under the laws of another state, government, or country.

Subsidiary and parent Subsidiary corporation is one in which another corporation (called parent corporation) owns at least a majority of the shares, and thus has control.

Close corporation A corporation whose shares, or at least voting shares, are held by a single shareholder or closely-knit group of shareholders.

Corporation de facto One existing under color of law and in pursuance of an effort made in good faith to organize a corporation under the statute. Such a corporation is not subject to collateral attack.

Corporation de jure That which exists by reason of full compliance with requirements of an existing law permitting organization of such corporation.

Subchapter S corporation A small business corporation which, under certain conditions, may elect to have its undistributed taxable income taxed to its shareholders. I.R.C. § 1371 *et seq.* Of major significance is the fact that Subchapter S status usually avoids the corporate income tax, and corporate losses can be claimed by the shareholders.

costs A pecuniary allowance, made to the successful party (and recoverable from the losing party), for his expenses in prosecuting or defending an action or a distinct proceeding within an action. Fed.R.Civil P. 54(d); Fed.R.App.P. 39. Generally, "costs" do not include attorney fees unless such fees are by a statute denominated costs or are by statute allowed to be recovered as costs in the case.

count　In pleading, the plaintiff's statement of his cause of action.　No longer used under Federal Rules of Civil Procedure.

counter offer　A statement by the offeree which has the legal effect of rejecting the offer and of proposing a new offer to the offeror.　However, the provisions of U.C.C. § 2–207(2) modifies this principle by providing that the "additional terms are to be construed as proposals for addition to the contract."

counterclaim　A claim presented by a defendant in opposition to or deduction from the claim of the plaintiff.　Fed.R. Civil P. 13.　If established, such will defeat or diminish the plaintiff's claim.　The two types are compulsory and permissive.

course of dealing　A sequence of previous acts and conduct between the parties to a particular transaction which is fairly to be regarded as establishing a common basis of understanding for interpreting their expressions and other conduct. U.C.C. § 1–205(1).

court above—court below　In appellate practice, the "court above" is the one to which a cause is removed for review, whether by appeal, writ of error, or certiorari; while the "court below" is the one from which the case is being removed.

covenant　Used primarily with respect to promises in conveyances or other instruments dealing with real estate.

Covenant of warranty　An assurance by the grantor of an estate that the grantee shall enjoy the same without interruption by virtue of paramount title.

Covenant running with land　A covenant which goes with the land, as being annexed to the estate, and which cannot be separated from the land, and transferred without it.　A covenant is said to run with the land when not only the original parties or their representatives, but each successive owner of the land, will be entitled to its benefit, or be liable (as the case may be) to its obligation.　Such a covenant is said to be one which "touches and concerns" the land itself, so that its benefit or obligation passes with the ownership.　Essentials are that the grantor and grantee must have intended that the covenant run with the land, the covenant must affect or concern the land with which it runs, and there must be privity of estate between party claiming the benefit and the party who rests under the burden.

Covenants against incumbrances　A stipulation against all rights to or interests in the land which may subsist in third persons to the diminution of the value of the estate granted.

Covenant appurtenant　A covenant which is connected with land of the grantor, and not in gross. A covenant running with the land and binding heirs, executors and assigns of the immediate parties.

Covenant for further assurance　An undertaking, in the form of a covenant, on the part of the vendor of real estate to do such further acts for the purpose of perfecting the purchaser's title as the latter may reasonably require.

Covenant for possession　A covenant by which the grantee or lessee is granted possession.

Covenant for quiet enjoyment　An assurance against the consequences of a defective title, and of any disturbances thereupon.

Covenants for title　Covenants usually inserted in a conveyance of land, on the part of the grantor, and binding him for the completeness, security, and continuance of the title transferred to the grantee.　They comprise covenants for seisin, for right to convey, against incumbrances, or quiet enjoyment, sometimes for further assurance, and almost always of warranty.

Covenant in gross　Such as do not run with the land.

Covenant of right to convey　An assurance by the convenantor that the grantor has sufficient capacity and title to convey the *estate* which he by his deed undertakes to convey.

Covenant of seisin　An assurance to the purchaser that the grantor has the very estate in quantity and quality which he purports to convey.

credit beneficiary　See **third party beneficiary.**

cure　The right of a seller under U.C.C. to correct a non-conforming delivery of goods to buyer within the contract period.　§ 2–508.

cy-pres　As near as (possible).　Rule for the construction of instruments in equity, by which the intention of the party is carried out *as near as may be,* when it would be impossible or illegal to give it literal effect.

D

damage　Loss, injury, or deterioration, caused by the negligence, design, or accident of one person to another, in respect of the latter's person or property.　The word is to be distinguished from its plural, "damages", which means a compensation in money for a loss or damage.

damages Money sought as a remedy for breach of contract or for tortious acts.

Actual damages Real, substantial and just damages, or the amount awarded to a complainant in compensation for his actual and real loss or injury, as opposed on the one hand to "nominal" damages, and on the other to "exemplary" or "punitive" damages. Synonymous with "compensatory damages" and with "general damages."

Compensatory damages Compensatory damages are such as will compensate the injured party for the injury sustained, and nothing more; such as will simply make good or replace the loss caused by the wrong or injury.

Consequential damages Such damage, loss or injury as does not flow directly and immediately from the act of the party, but only from some of the consequences or results of such act. Consequential damages resulting from a seller's breach of contract include any loss resulting from general or particular requirements and needs of which the seller at the time of contracting had reason to know and which could not reasonably be prevented by cover or otherwise, and injury to person or property proximately resulting from any breach of warranty. U.C.C. § 2–715(2).

Exemplary or punitive damages Damages other than compensatory damages which may be awarded against person to punish him for outrageous conduct.

Expectancy damages Calculable by subtracting the injured party's actual dollar position as a result of the breach from that party's projected dollar position had performance occurred.

Incidental damages Under U.C.C. § 2–710, such damages include any commercially reasonable charges, expenses or commissions incurred in stopping delivery, in the transportation, care and custody of goods after the buyer's breach, in connection with the return or resale of the goods or otherwise resulting from the breach. Also, such damages, resulting from a seller's breach of contract, include expenses reasonably incurred in inspection, receipt, transportation and care and custody of goods rightfully rejected, any commercially reasonable charges, expenses or commissions in connection with effecting cover and any other reasonable expense incident to the delay or other breach. U.C.C. § 2–715(1).

Irreparable damages In the law pertaining to injunctions, damages for which no certain pecuniary standard exists for measurement.

Liquidated damages and penalties Damages for breach by either party may be liquidated in the agreement but only at an amount which is reasonable in the light of the anticipated or actual harm caused by the breach, the difficulties of proof of loss, and the inconvenience or nonfeasibility of otherwise obtaining an adequate remedy. A term fixing unreasonably large liquidated damages is void as a penalty. U.C.C. § 2–718(1).

Mitigation of damages A plaintiff may not recover damages for the effects of an injury which reasonably could have been avoided or substantially ameliorated. This limitation on recovery is generally denominated as "mitigation of damages" or "avoidance of consequences."

de facto In fact, in deed, actually. This phrase is used to characterize an officer, a government, a past action, or a state of affairs which must be accepted for all practical purposes, but is illegal or illegitimate. See also **corporation,** *corporation de facto*.

de jure Descriptive of a condition in which there has been total compliance with all requirements of law. In this sense it is the contrary of *de facto*. See also **corporation,** *corporation de jure*.

de novo Anew; afresh; a second time.

debt security Any form of corporate security reflected as debt on the books of the corporation in contrast to equity securities such as stock; *e.g.* bonds, notes and debentures are debt securities.

deceit A fraudulent and cheating misrepresentation, artifice, or device, used to deceive and trick one who is ignorant of the true facts, to the prejudice and damage of the party imposed upon. See also **fraud; misrepresentation.**

declaration In common-law pleading, the first of the pleadings on the part of the plaintiff in an action at law, being a formal and methodical specification of the facts and circumstances constituting his cause or action. The term "complaint" is now used in the federal courts and in all states that have adopted the Rules of Civil Procedure.

deed A conveyance of realty; a writing signed by grantor, whereby title to realty is transferred from one to another.

defendant The party against whom relief or recovery is sought in an action or suit.

delegation of duties Transferring all or part of one's duties arising under a contract to another.

delivery The physical or constructive transfer of an instrument or of goods from the hands of one person to those of another.　See also **constructive delivery.**

demurrer　An allegation of a defendant that, even if the facts as stated in the pleading to which objection is taken be true, yet their legal consequences are not such as to put the demurring party to the necessity of answering them or proceeding further with the cause.

The Federal Rules of Civil Procedure do not provide for the use of a demurrer, but provide an equivalent to a general demurrer in the motion to dismiss for failure to state a claim on which relief may be granted.　Fed.R. Civil P. 12(b).

deposition　The testimony of a witness taken upon interrogatories, not in court, but intended to be used in court.　See also **discovery.**

depository bank　The first bank to which an item is transferred for collection even though it may also be the payor bank.　U.C.C. § 4–105(a).

descent　Succession to the ownership of an estate by inheritance, or by any act of law, as distinguished from "purchase."

Descents are of two sorts, *lineal* and *collateral*. Lineal descent is descent in a direct or right line, as from father or grandfather to son or grandson. Collateral descent is descent in a collateral or oblique line, that is, up to the common ancestor and then down from him, as from brother to brother, or between cousins.

devise　A testamentary disposition of land or realty;　a gift of real property by the last will and testament of the donor.　When used as a noun, means a testamentary disposition of real or personal property and when used as a verb, means to dispose of real or personal property by will.

dictum　Generally used as an abbreviated form of *obiter dictum,* "a remark by the way;" that is, an observation or remark made by a judge which does not embody the resolution or determination of the court and which is made without argument or full consideration of the point.

directed verdict　In a case in which the party with the burden of proof has failed to present a prima facie case for jury consideration, the trial judge may order the entry of a verdict without allowing the jury to consider it, because, as a matter of law, there can be only one such verdict.　Fed.R. Civil P. 50(a).

discount　A discount by a bank means a drawback or deduction made upon its advances or loans of money, upon negotiable paper or other evidences of debt payable at a future day, which are transferred to the bank.

discovery　The pre-trial devices that can be used by one party to obtain facts and information about the case from the other party in order to assist the party's preparation for trial.　Under Federal Rules of Civil Procedure tools of discovery include: depositions upon oral and written questions, written interrogatories, production of documents or things, permission to enter upon land or other property, physical and mental examinations and requests for admission.　Rules 26–37.

dishonor　To refuse to accept or pay a draft or to pay a promissory note when duly presented.　U.C.C. § 3–507(1); § 4–210.　See also **protest.**

dissolution　The dissolution of a partnership is the relation of the partners caused by any partner ceasing to be associated in the carrying on as distinguished from the winding up of the business. See also **winding up.**

dividend　The payment designated by the board of directors of a corporation to be distributed pro rata among the shares outstanding.

domicile　That place where a man has his true, fixed, and permanent home and principal establishment, and to which whenever he is absent he has the intention of returning.

donee beneficiary　See **third party beneficiary.**

dower　A species of life-estate which a woman is, by law, entitled to claim on the death of her husband, in the lands and tenements of which he was seised in fee during the marriage, and which her issue, if any, might by possibility have inherited.

Dower has been abolished in the majority of the states and materially altered in most of the others.

draft　A written order by the first party, called the drawer, instructing a second party, called the drawee (such as a bank) to pay a third party, called the payee.　An order to pay a sum certain in money, signed by a drawer, payable on demand or at a definite time, and to order or bearer.　U.C.C. § 3–104.

drawee　A person to whom a bill of exchange or draft is directed, and who is requested to pay the amount of money therein mentioned.　The drawee of a check is the bank on which it is drawn.

When drawee accepts, he engages that he will pay the instrument according to its tenor at the time of his engagement or as completed.   U.C.C. § 3–413(1).

drawer   The person who draws a bill or draft. The drawer of a check is the person who signs it.

The drawer engages that upon dishonor of the draft and any necessary notice of dishonor or protest, he will pay the amount of the draft to the holder or to any indorser who takes it up.   The drawer may disclaim this liability by drawing without recourse, U.C.C. § 3–413(2).

duress   Unlawful constraint exercised upon a person, whereby he is forced to do some act against his will.

E

earnest   The payment of a part of the price of goods sold, or the delivery of part of such goods, for the purpose of binding the contract.

easement   A right in the owner of one parcel of land, by reason of such ownership, to use the land of another for a special purpose not inconsistent with a general property in the owner.   This right is distinguishable from a "license" which merely confers personal privilege to do some act on the land.

Affirmative easement   One where the servient estate must permit something to be done thereon, as to pass over it, or to discharge water on it.

Appurtenant easement   An incorporeal right which is attached to a superior right and inheres in land to which it is attached and is in the nature of a covenant running with the land.

Easement by estoppel   Easement which is created when landlord voluntarily imposes apparent servitude on his property and another person, acting reasonably, believes that servitude is permanent and in reliance upon that belief does something that he would not have done otherwise or refrains from doing something that he would have done otherwise.

Easement by necessity   Such arises by operation of law when land conveyed is completely shut off from access to any road by land retained by grantor or by land of grantor and that of a stranger.

Easement by prescription   A mode of acquiring title to property by immemorial or long-continued enjoyment, and refers to personal usage restricted to claimant and his ancestors or grantors.

Easement in gross   An easement in gross is not appurtenant to any estate in land or does not belong to any person by virtue of ownership of estate in other land but is mere personal interest in or right to use land of another; it is purely personal and usually ends with death of grantee.

Easement of access   Right of ingress and egress to and from the premises of a lot owner to a street appurtenant to the land of the lot owner.

ejectment   An action of which the purpose is to determine whether the title to certain land is in the plaintiff or is in the defendant.

emancipation   The act by which an infant is set at liberty from the control of parent or guardian and made his own master.

emblements   Crops annually produced by labor of tenant.   The doctrine of emblements denotes the right of a tenant to take and carry away such crops after his tenancy has ended.

eminent domain   Right of the people or government to take private property for public use upon giving of a fair consideration.

entirety   Used to designate that which the law considers as one whole, and not capable of being divided into parts.

equitable   Just, fair, and right.   Existing in equity; available or sustainable only in equity, or only upon the rules and principles of equity.

equitable servitude   A restriction on the use of land that is enforceable in an equity proceeding.

equity   Justice administered according to fairness as contrasted with the strictly formulated rules of common law.   It is based on a system of rules and principles which originated in England as an alternative to the harsh rules of common law and which were based on what was fair in a particular situation.

equity of redemption   The right of the mortgagor of an estate to redeem the same after it has been forfeited, at law, by a breach of the condition of the mortgage, upon paying the amount of debt, interest and costs.

equity securities   Stock or similar security, in contrast to debt securities such as bonds, notes and debentures.

error   A mistake of law, or false or irregular application of it, such as vitiates the proceedings and warrants the reversal of the judgment.

Error is also used as an elliptical expression for "writ of error"; as in saying that *error* lies; that a judgment may be reversed *on error*.

Harmless error   In appellate practice, an error committed in the progress of the trial below which was not prejudicial to the rights of the party assigning it and for which, therefore, the court will not reverse the judgment.

Reversible error In appellate practice, such an error as warrants the appellate court in reversing the judgment before it.

escrow A system of document transfer in which a deed, bond, or funds is delivered to a third person to hold until all conditions in a contract are fulfilled; *e.g.* delivery of deed to escrow agent under installment land sale contract until full payment for land is made.

estate The degree, quantity, nature, and extent of interest which a person has in real and personal property. An estate in lands, tenements, and hereditaments signifies such interest as the tenant has therein.

Also, the total property of whatever kind that is owned by a decedent prior to the distribution of that property in accordance with the terms of a will, or, when there is no will, by the laws of inheritance in the state of domicile of the decedent.

Future estate An estate limited to commence in possession at a future day, either without the intervention of a precedent estate, or on the determination by lapse of time, or otherwise, of a precedent estate created at the same time. Examples include reversions and remainders.

estoppel A bar or impediment raised by the law, which precludes a man from alleging or from denying a certain fact or state of facts, in consequence of his previous allegation or denial or conduct or admission, or in consequence of a final adjudication of the matter in a court of law. See also **waiver.**

eviction Dispossession by process of law; the act of depriving a person of the possession of lands which he has held, in pursuance of the judgment of a court.

evidence Any species of proof, or probative matter, legally presented at the trial of an issue, by the act of the parties and through the medium of witnesses, records, documents, concrete objects, etc., for the purpose of inducing belief in the minds of the court or jury as to their contention.

ex parte A judicial proceeding, order, injunction, etc., is said to be *ex parte* when it is taken or granted at the instance and for the benefit of one party only, and without notice to, or contestation by, any person adversely interested.

exception A formal objection to the action of the court, during the trial of a cause, in refusing a request or overruling an objection; implying that the party excepting does not acquiesce in the decision of the court, but will seek to procure its reversal, and that he means to save the benefit of his request or objection in some future proceeding. Under rules practice in the federal and most state courts, the need for claiming an exception to evidence or to a ruling to preserve appellate rights has been eliminated in favor of an objection. Fed.R. Civil P. 46.

executed Completed; already done or performed. The opposite of executory.

execution *Execution of contract* includes performance of all acts necessary to render it complete as an instrument and imports idea that nothing remains to be done to make complete and effective contract.

Execution upon a money judgment is the legal process of enforcing the judgment, usually by seizing and selling property of the debtor.

executor A person appointed by a testator to carry out the directions and requests in his will, and to dispose of the property according to his testamentary provisions after his decease. The female designation is executrix. A person appointed by the court in intestacy situation is called the administrator(rix).

executory That which is yet to be executed or performed; that which remains to be carried into operation or effect; incomplete; depending upon a future performance or event. The opposite of executed.

executory contract See **contracts.**

executory interests A general term, comprising all future estates and interests in land or personalty, other than reversions and remainders.

exemplary damages See **damages.**

express Manifested by direct and appropriate language, as distinguished from that which is inferred from conduct. The word is usually contrasted with "implied."

ex-ship Seller may choose shipper. Risk of loss passes to buyer upon the goods leaving the ship. Buyer is responsible for any landing charges. See U.C.C. § 2–322. See also **F.A.S.**

F

F.A.S. Free alongside. Term used in sales price quotations, indicating that the price includes all costs of transportation and delivery of the goods alongside the ship.   See U.C.C. § 2–319(2).   See also **ex-ship**

fee simple

Absolute   A fee simple absolute is an estate that is unlimited as to duration, disposition, and descendibility.   It is the largest estate and most extensive interest that can be enjoyed in land.

Conditional   Type of transfer in which grantor conveys fee simple on condition that something be done or not done.

Defeasible   Type of fee grant which may be defeated on the happening of an event.   An estate which may last forever, but which may end upon the happening of a specified event, is a "fee simple defeasible".

Determinable   Created by conveyance which contains words effective to create a fee simple and, in addition, a provision for automatic expiration of estate on occurrence of stated event.

fee tail   An estate of inheritance, descending only to a certain class or classes or heirs;   e.g., an estate is conveyed or devised "to A. and the heirs of his body," or "to A. and the heirs male of his body," or "to A., and the heirs female of his body."   State statutes have dealt variously with estates tail, some converting them into estates in fee simple.

fiduciary   A person or institution who manages money or property for another and who must exercise a standard of care in such management activity imposed by law or contract;   *e.g.* executor of estate;   receiver in bankruptcy;   trustee.

financing statement   Under the Uniform Commercial Code, a financing statement is used under Article 9 to reflect a public record that there is a security interest or claim to the goods in question to secure a debt.   The financing statement is filed by the security holder with the Secretary of State, or similar public body, and as such becomes public record.   See also **secured transaction.**

firm offer   An offer by a merchant to buy or sell goods in a signed writing which by its terms give assurance that it will be held open is not revocable, for lack of consideration, during the time stated or if no time is stated for a reasonable time, but in no event may such period of irrevocability exceed three months.   U.C.C. § 2–205.

fixture   An article in the nature of personal property which has been so annexed to realty that it is regarded as a part of the land.   Examples include a furnace affixed to a house or other building, counters permanently affixed to the floor of a store, a sprinkler system installed in a building.   U.C.C. § 9–313(1)(a).

Trade fixtures   Such chattels as merchants usually possess and annex to the premises occupied by them to enable them to store, handle, and display their goods, which are generally removable without material injury to the premises.

FOB   Free on board some location (for example, FOB shipping point;   FOB destination);   the invoice price includes delivery at seller's expense to that location.   Title to goods usually passes from seller to buyer at the FOB location.   U.C.C. § 2–319(1).

foreclosure   Procedure by which mortgaged property is sold on default of mortgagor in satisfaction of mortgage debt.

franchise   A privilege granted or sold, such as to use a name or to sell products or services.   The right given by a manufacturer or supplier to a retailer to use his products and name on terms and conditions mutually agreed upon.

fraud   Elements include: false representation;   of a present or past fact;   made by defendant;   action in reliance thereon by plaintiff;   damage resulting to plaintiff from such misrepresentation.

freehold   An estate for life or in fee.   It must possess two qualities: (1) immobility, that is, the property must be either land or some interest issuing out of or annexed to land;   and (2) indeterminate duration.

frustration of purpose doctrine   Excuses a promisor in certain situations when the objectives of contract have been utterly defeated by circumstances arising after formation of agreement, and performance is excused under this rule even though there is no impediment to actual performance.

fungibles   With respect to goods or securities, those of which any unit is, by nature or usage of trade, the equivalent of any other like unit.   U.C.C. § 1–201(17);   *e.g.*, a bushel of wheat or other grain.

future estate   See **estate**

G

garnishment   A statutory proceeding whereby a person's property, money, or credits in the possession or control of another are applied to payment of the former's debt to a third person.

gift   A voluntary transfer of property to another made gratuitously and without consideration.   Essential requisites of "gift" are capacity of donor, intention of donor to make gift, completed delivery to or for donee, and acceptance of gift by donee.

gift causa mortis A gift in view of death is one which is made in contemplation, fear, or peril of death, and with intent that it shall take effect only in case of the death of the giver.

goods A term of variable content and meaning. It may include every species of personal property or it may be given a very restricted meaning. Sometimes the meaning of "goods" is extended to include all tangible items, as in the phrase "goods and services."

All things (including specially manufactured goods) which are movable at the time of identification to the contract for sale other than the money in which the price is to be paid, investment securities and things in action. U.C.C. § 2–105(1).

grantor A transferor of property. The creator of a trust is usually designated as the grantor of the trust.

guaranty A promise to answer for the payment of some debt, or the performance of some duty, in case of the failure of another person, who, in the first instance, is liable to such payment or performance.

The terms *guaranty* and *suretyship* are sometimes used interchangeably; but they should not be confounded. The distinction between contract of suretyship and contract of guaranty is whether or not the undertaking is a joint undertaking with the principal or a separate and distinct contract; if it is the former it is one of "suretyship", and if the latter, it is one of "guaranty". See also **surety.**

H

hearsay Hearsay evidence is testimony in court of a statement made out of the court, the statement being offered as an assertion to show the truth of matters asserted therein, and thus resting for its value upon the credibility of the out-of-court asserter.

heir A person who succeeds, by the rules of law, to an estate in lands, tenements, or hereditaments, upon the death of his ancestor, by descent and right of relationship.

holder Person who is in possession of a document of title or an instrument or an investment security drawn, issued or endorsed to him or to his order, or to bearer or in blank. U.C.C. § 1–201(20).

holder in due course A holder who takes an instrument for value, in good faith, and without notice that it is overdue or has been dishonored or of any defense against or claim to it on the part of any person.

holograph A will or deed written entirely by the testator or grantor with his own hand and not witnessed (attested). State laws vary with respect to the validity of the holographic will.

I

in personam Against the person. Action seeking judgment against a person involving his personal rights and based on jurisdiction of his person, as distinguished from a judgment against property (*i.e.* in rem). Type of jurisdiction or power which a court may acquire over the defendant himself in contrast to jurisdiction over his property.

in re In the affair; in the matter of; concerning; regarding. This is the usual method of entitling a judicial proceeding in which there are not adversary parties, but merely some *res* concerning which judicial action is to be taken, such as a bankrupt's estate, an estate in the probate court, a proposed public highway, etc.

in rem A technical term used to designate proceedings or actions instituted *against the thing*, in contradistinction to personal actions, which are said to be *in personam*.

Quasi in rem A term applied to proceedings which are not strictly and purely *in rem*, but are brought against the defendant personally, though the real object is to deal with particular property or subject property to the discharge of claims asserted; for example, foreign attachment, or proceedings to foreclose a mortgage, remove a cloud from title, or effect a partition.

inchoate Imperfect; unfinished; begun, but not completed; as a contract not executed by all the parties.

indemnify To reimburse one for a loss already incurred.

indenture A written agreement under which bonds and debentures are issued, setting forth maturity date, interest rate, and other terms.

indicia Signs; indications. Circumstances which point to the existence of a given fact as probable, but not certain.

indorsee The person to whom a negotiable instrument, promissory note, bill of lading, etc., is assigned by indorsement.

indorsement The act of a payee, drawee, accommodation indorser, or holder of a bill, note, check, or other negotiable instrument, in writing his name upon the back of the same, with or without further or qualifying words, whereby the property in the same is assigned and transferred to another. U.C.C. § 3–202 *et seq.*

injunction An equitable remedy forbidding the party defendant from doing some act which he is threatening or attempting to commit, or restraining him in the continuance thereof, such act being unjust and inequitable, injurious to the plaintiff, and not such as can be adequately redressed by an action at law.

Interlocutory injunction Interlocutory injunctions are those issued at any time during the pendency of the litigation for the short-term purpose of preventing irreparable injury to the petitioner prior to the time that the court will be in a position to either grant or deny permanent relief on the merits. A preliminary injunction includes any interlocutory injunction granted after the respondent has been given notice and the opportunity to participate in a hearing on whether or not that injunction should issue. A temporary restraining order differs from a preliminary injunction in that it is issued ex parte, with no notice or opportunity to be heard granted to the respondent.

insolvency In general, state insolvency laws have been superseded by the Federal Bankruptcy Act.

Under U.C.C., a person is insolvent who either has ceased to pay his debts in the ordinary course of business or cannot pay his debts as they fall due or is insolvent within the meaning of the Federal Bankruptcy Law. U.C.C. § 1–201(23).

insurable interest Exists where insured derives pecuniary benefit or advantage by preservation and continued existence of property or would sustain pecuniary loss from its destruction.

insurance A contract whereby, for a stipulated consideration, one party undertakes to compensate the other for loss on a specified subject by specified perils. The party agreeing to make the compensation is usually called the "insurer" or "underwriter"; the other, the "insured" or "assured"; the written contract, a "policy"; the events insured against, "risks" or "perils"; and the subject, right, or interest to be protected, the "insurable interest." Insurance is a contract whereby one undertakes to indemnify another against loss, damage, or liability arising from an unknown or contingent event.

inter alia Among other things.

inter se or **inter sese** Latin. Among or between themselves; used to distinguish rights or duties between two or more parties from their rights or duties to others.

intermediary bank Any bank to which an item is transferred in the course of collection except the depositary or payor bank. U.C.C. § 4–105(c).

intestate A person is said to die intestate when he dies without making a will. The word is also often used to signify the person himself. *Compare* **testator.**

invitee A person is an "invitee" on land of another if (1) he enters by invitation, express or implied, (2) his entry is connected with the owner's business or with an activity the owner conducts or permits to be conducted on his land and (3) there is mutuality of benefit or benefit to the owner.

J

joint tenancy See **tenancy.**

judgment The official and authentic decision of a court of justice upon the respective rights and claims of the parties to an action or suit therein litigated and submitted to its determination.

judgment in personam A judgment against a particular person, as distinguished from a judgment against a thing or a right or *status*.

judgment in rem An adjudication pronounced upon the status of some particular thing or subject matter, by a tribunal having competent authority.

judgment n. o. v. Judgment non obstante verdicto in its broadest sense is a judgment rendered in favor of one party notwithstanding the finding of a verdict in favor of the other party.

jurisdiction The right and power of a court to adjudicate concerning the subject matter in a given case.

jury (From the Latin jurare, to swear). A body of persons selected and summoned by law and sworn to try the facts of a case and to find according to the law and the evidence. In general, the province of the jury is to find the facts in a case, while the judge passes upon pure questions of law. As a matter of fact, however, the jury must often pass upon mixed questions of law and fact in determining the case, and in all such cases the instructions of the judge as to the law become very important.

L

laches Based upon maxim that equity aids the vigilant and not those who slumber on their rights. It is defined as neglect to assert right or claim which, taken together with lapse of time and other circumstances causing prejudice to adverse party, operates as bar in court of equity.

landlord He who, being the owner of an estate in land, or a rental property, has leased it to another person, called the "tenant." Also called "lessor."

lapse The termination or failure of a right or privilege through neglect to exercise it within some limit of time, or through failure of some contingency.

lease Any agreement which gives rise to relationship of landlord and tenant (real property) or lessor and lessee (real or personal property).

The person who conveys is termed the "lessor," and the person to whom conveyed, the "lessee;" and when the lessor conveys land or tenements to a lessee, he is said to lease, demise, or let them.

Sublease, or underlease One executed by the lessee of an estate to a third person, conveying the same estate for a shorter term than that for which the lessee holds it.

leasehold An estate in realty held under a lease. The four principal types of leasehold estates are the estate for years, periodic tenancy, tenancy at will, and tenancy at sufferance.

legacy "Legacy" is a gift or bequest by will of personal property, whereas a "devise" is a testamentary disposition of real estate.

Demonstrative legacy A bequest of a certain sum of money, with a direction that it shall be paid out of a particular fund. It differs from a specific legacy in this respect: that, if the fund out of which it is payable fails for any cause, it is nevertheless entitled to come on the estate as a general legacy. And it differs from a general legacy in this: that it does not abate in that class, but in the class of specific legacies.

General legacy A pecuniary legacy, payable out of the general assets of a testator.

Residuary legacy A bequest of all the testator's personal estate not otherwise effectually disposed of by his will.

Specific legacy One which operates on property particularly designated. A legacy or gift by will of a particular specified thing, as of a horse, a piece of furniture, a term of years, and the like.

letter of credit An engagement by a bank or other person made at the request of a customer that the issuer will honor drafts or other demands for payment upon compliance with the conditions specified in the credit.

letters of administration Formal document issued by probate court appointing one an administrator of an estate.

letters testamentary The formal instrument of authority and appointment given to an executor by the proper court, empowering him to enter upon the discharge of his office as executor. It corresponds to letters of administration granted to an administrator.

levy To assess; raise; execute; exact; tax; collect; gather; take up; seize. Thus, to levy (assess, exact, raise, or collect) a tax; to levy an execution, *i.e.*, to levy or collect a sum of money on an execution.

license License with respect to real property is a privilege to go on premises for a certain purpose, but does not operate to confer on, or vest in, licensee any title, interest, or estate in such property.

lien A qualified right of property which a creditor has in or over specific property of his debtor, as security for the debt or charge or for performance of some act.

life estate An estate whose duration is limited to the life of the party holding it, or some other person. Upon the death of the life tenant, the property will go to the holder of the remainder interest or to the grantor by reversion.

limited partnership See **partnership.**

liquidated Ascertained; determined; fixed; settled; made clear or manifest. Cleared away; paid; discharged.

liquidated damages See **damages.**

liquidation The settling of financial affairs of a business or individual, usually by liquidating (turning to cash) all assets for distribution to creditors, heirs, etc. It is to be distinguished from dissolution which is the end of the legal existence of a corporation. Liquidation may precede or follow dissolution, depending upon statutes.

lost property Property which the owner has involuntarily parted with and does not know where to find or recover it, not including property which he has intentionally concealed or deposited in a secret place for safe-keeping. Distinguishable from mislaid property which has been deliberately placed somewhere and forgotten.

M

maker One who makes or executes; as the maker of a promissory note. One who signs a check; in this context, synonymous with drawer. See **draft.**

mandamus Latin, we command. A legal writ compelling the defendant to do an official duty.

Pleading Like most of the extraordinary writs, the *writ* of mandamus has been abolished under rules practice in favor of a complaint in the nature of mandamus which accomplishes the same object.

mandate A judicial command or precept proceeding from a court or judicial officer, directing the proper officer to enforce a judgment, sentence, or decree.

master See **principal.**

maturity The date at which an obligation, such as the principal of a bond or a note, becomes due.

mechanic's lien A claim created by state statutes for the purpose of securing priority of payment of the price or value of work performed and materials furnished in erecting or repairing a building or other structure, and as such attaches to the land as well as buildings and improvements erected thereon.

mercantile law An expression substantially equivalent to commercial law. It designates the system of rules, customs, and usages generally recognized and adopted by merchants and traders, and which, either in its simplicity or as modified by common law or statutes, constitutes the law for the regulation of their transactions and the solution of their controversies. The Uniform Commercial Code is the general body of law governing commercial or mercantile transactions.

merchant A person who deals in goods of the kind or otherwise by his occupation holds himself out as having knowledge or skill peculiar to the practices or goods involved in the transaction or to whom such knowledge or skill may be attributed by his employment of an agent or broker or other intermediary who by his occupation holds himself out as having such knowledge or skill. U.C.C. § 2–104(1).

merger The fusion or absorption of one thing or right into another; generally spoken of a case where one of the subjects is of less dignity or importance than the other. Here the less important ceases to have an independent existence.

Corporations The absorption of one company by another, latter retaining its own name and identity and acquiring assets, liabilities, franchises, and powers of former, and absorbed company ceasing to exist as separate business entity. It differs from a consolidation wherein all the corporations terminate their existence and become parties to a new one.

Horizontal merger Merger between business competitors, such as manufacturers of the same type products or distributors selling competing products in the same market area.

Vertical merger Union with corporate customer or supplier.

mislaid property Property which an owner has put deliberately in a certain place but owner is unable to remember where he put it, as distinguished from lost property which the owner leaves unwittingly in a place, forgetting its location. See also **lost property.**

misrepresentation Any manifestation by words or other conduct by one person to another that, under the circumstances, amounts to an assertion not in accordance with the facts. A "misrepresentation" that justifies the rescission of a contract is a false statement of a substantive fact, or any conduct which leads to a belief of a substantive fact material to proper understanding of the matter in hand, made with intent to deceive or mislead. See also **deceit; fraud.**

mitigation of damages See **damages.**

mortgage A mortgage is an interest in land created by a written instrument providing security for the performance of a duty or the payment of a debt.

N

negligence The omission to do something which a reasonable man, guided by those ordinary considerations which ordinarily regulate human affairs, would do, or the doing of something which a reasonable and prudent man would not do.

negotiable Legally capable of being transferred by endorsement or delivery. Usually said of checks and notes and sometimes of stocks and bearer bonds.

non sequitur Latin. It does not follow. An inference which does not follow from the premise.

nonsuit Action in form of a judgment taken against a plaintiff who has failed to appear to prosecute his action or failed to prove his case. Under rules practice, the applicable term is "dismissal", not nonsuit. Fed.R. Civil P. 41.

note See **promissory note.**

novation A novation substitutes a new party and discharges one of the original parties to a contract by agreement of all three parties. A new contract is created with the same terms as the original one but only the parties are changed.

nuisance Nuisance is that activity which arises from unreasonable, unwarranted or unlawful use by a person of his own property, working obstruction or injury to right of another, or to the public, and producing such material annoyance, inconvenience and discomfort that law will presume resulting damage.

Abatement of a nuisance The removal, stoppage, prostration, or destruction of that which causes a nuisance, whether by breaking or pulling it down, or otherwise removing, destroying, or effacing it.

O

obiter dictum See **dictum**

offer A manifestation of willingness to enter into a bargain, so made as to justify another person in understanding that his assent to that bargain is invited and will conclude it. Restatement, Second, Contracts, § 24.

output contract See **contracts.**

P

par In commercial law, equal; equality. An equality subsisting between the nominal or face value of a bill of exchange, share of stock, etc., and its actual selling value. When the values are thus equal, the instrument or share is said to be "at par;" if it can be sold for more than its nominal worth, it is "above par;" if for less, it is "below par."

parol evidence rule Under this rule, when parties put their agreement in writing, all previous oral agreements merge in the writing and a contract as written cannot be modified or changed by parol evidence, in the absence of a plea of mistake or fraud in the preparation of the writing. But rule does not forbid a resort to parol evidence not inconsistent with the matters stated in the writing. Also, as regards sales of goods, such written agreement may be explained or supplemented by course

of dealing or usage of trade or by course of conduct, and by evidence of consistent additional terms unless the court finds the writing to have been intended also as a complete and exclusive statement of the terms of the agreement. U.C.C. § 2–202.

part performance In order to establish part performance taking an oral contract for the sale of realty out of the statute of frauds, the acts relied upon as part performance must be of such a character that they can reasonably be naturally accounted for in no other way than that they were performed in pursuance of the contract, and they must be in conformity with its provisions. See U.C.C. § 2–201(3).

partition The dividing of lands held by joint tenants, coparceners, or tenants in common, into distinct portions, so that they may hold them in severalty. And, in a less technical sense, any division of real or personal property between co-owners, resulting in individual ownership of the interests of each. Division between several persons of property which belongs to them as co-owners; it may be compulsory (judicial) or voluntary. Commonly, the court will order the property sold and the proceeds divided instead of ordering a physical partition of the property.

partnership An association of two or more persons to carry on, as co-owners, a business for profit.

Partnerships are treated as a conduit and are, therefore, not subject to taxation. The various items of partnership income, gains, and losses, etc. flow through to the individual partners and are reported on their personal income tax returns.

Limited partnership Type of partnership comprised of one or more general partners who manage business and who are personally liable for partnership debts, and one or more limited partners who contribute capital and share in profits but who take no part in running business and incur no liability with respect to partnership obligations beyond contribution.

payee The person in whose favor a bill of exchange, promissory note, or check is made or drawn.

payer, or **payor** One who pays, or who is to make a payment; particularly the person who is to make payment of a check, bill or note. Correlative to "payee."

payor bank A bank by which an item is payable as drawn or accepted. U.C.C. § 4–105(b).

per capita This term, derived from the civil law,

is much used in the law of descent and distribution, and denotes that method of dividing an intestate estate by which an equal share is given to each of a number of persons, all of whom stand in equal degree to the decedent, without reference to their stocks or the right of representation. It is the antithesis of *per stirpes*

per stirpes This term, derived from the civil law, is much used in the law of descents and distribution, and denotes that method of dividing an intestate estate where a class or group of distributees take the share which their deceased would have been entitled to, taking thus by their right of representing such ancestor, and not as so many individuals. It is the antithesis of *per capita*

perfection of security interest Acts required of a secured party in the way of giving at least constructive notice so as to make his security interest effective at least against lien creditors of the debtor. See U.C.C. §§ 9–302 through 9–306. In most cases, the secured party may obtain perfection either by filing with Secretary of State or by taking possession of the collateral.

performance See **part performance; specific performance.**

personal property Generally, all property other than real estate.

plaintiff The party who complains or sues in a civil action and is so named on the record.

plea In common law pleading (now obsolete with adoption of Rules of Civil Procedure), any one in the series of pleadings. More particularly, the first pleading on the part of the defendant. In the strictest sense, the answer which the defendant in an action at law made to the plaintiff's declaration, and in which he set up matter of *fact* as defense, thus distinguished from a demurrer, which interposed objections on grounds of *law*.

In equity pleading (now obsolete with adoption of Rules of Civil Procedure), a special answer showing or relying upon one or more things as a cause why the suit should be either dismissed or delayed or barred.

pleadings The formal allegations by the parties of their respective claims and defenses.

Rules or Codes of Civil Procedure Unlike the rigid technical system of common law pleading, pleadings under federal and state rules or codes of civil procedure have a far more limited function, with determination and narrowing of facts and issues being left to discovery devices and pre-trial conferences. In addition, the rules and codes permit liberal amendment and supplementation of pleadings.

Under rules of civil procedure the pleadings consist of a complaint, an answer, a reply to a counterclaim, an answer to a cross-claim, a third party complaint, and a third party answer. Fed.R.Civil P. 7(a).

pledge A bailment of goods to a creditor as security for some debt or engagegment.

Much of the law of pledges has been replaced by the provisions for secured transactions in Article 9 of the U.C.C.

possibility of reverter The interest which remains in a grantor or testator after the conveyance or devise of a fee simple determinable and which permits the grantor to be revested automatically of his estate on breach of the condition.

power of appointment A power of authority conferred by one person by deed or will upon another (called the "donee") to appoint, that is, to select and nominate, the person or persons who are to receive and enjoy an estate or an income therefrom or from a fund, after the testator's death, or the donee's death, or after the termination of an existing right or interest.

power of attorney An instrument authorizing a person to act as the agent or attorney of the person granting it.

power of termination The interest left in the grantor or testator after the conveyance or devise of a fee simple on condition subsequent or conditional fee.

precedent An adjudged case or decision of a court, considered as furnishing an example or authority for an identical or similar case afterwards arising or a similar question of law. See also **stare decisis.**

pre-emptive right The privilege of a stockholder to maintain a proportionate share of ownership by purchasing a proportionate share of any new stock issues.

preference The act of an insolvent debtor who, in distributing his property or in assigning it for the benefit of his creditors, pays or secures to one or more creditors the full amount of their claims or a larger amount than they would be entitled to receive on a *pro rata* distribution. The treatment of such preferential payments in bankruptcy is governed by Bankruptcy Act, § 547.

premium   A bounty or bonus; a consideration given to invite a loan or a bargain, as the consideration paid to the assignor by the assignee of a lease, or to the transferor by the transferee of shares of stock, etc.   So stock is said to be "at a premium" when its market price exceeds its nominal or face value.

Also, the price for insurance protection for a specified period of exposure.

prescription   Prescription is a peremptory and perpetual bar to every species of action, real or personal, when creditor has been silent for a certain time without urging his claim.

Also, acquisition of a personal right to use a way, water, light and air by reason of continuous usage.   See also **easement**.

presentment   The production of a negotiable instrument to the drawee for his acceptance, or to the drawer or acceptor for payment; or of a promissory note to the party liable, for payment of the same. U.C.C. § 3–504(1).

presumption   A presumption is a rule of law, statutory or judicial, by which finding of a basic fact gives rise to existence of presumed fact, until presumption is rebutted.   A presumption imposes on the party against whom it is directed the burden of going forward with evidence to rebut or meet the presumption, but does not shift to such party the burden of proof in the sense of the risk of nonpersuasion, which remains throughout the trial upon the party on whom it was originally cast.

prima facie   Latin.   At first sight; on the first appearance; on the face of it; so far as can be judged from the first disclosure; presumably; a fact presumed to be true unless disproved by some evidence to the contrary.

principal   *Law of agency*   The term "principal" describes one who has permitted or directed another (*i.e.* agent or servant) to act for his benefit and subject to his direction and control.   Principal includes in its meaning the term "master", a species of principal who, in addition to other control, has a right to control the physical conduct of the species of agents known as servants, as to whom special rules are applicable with reference to harm caused by their physical acts.

privity of contract   That connection or relationship which exists between two or more contracting parties.   The absence of privity as a defense in actions for damages in contract and tort actions is generally no longer viable with the enactment of warranty statutes (*e.g.* U.C.C. § 2–318), acceptance by states of doctrine of strict liability and court decisions which have extended the right to sue to third party beneficiaries and even innocent bystanders.

probate   Court procedure by which a will is proved to be valid or invalid; though in current usage this term has been expanded to generally include all matters and proceedings pertaining to administration of estates, guardianships, etc.

process   *Judicial process*   In a wide sense, this term may include all the acts of a court from the beginning to the end of its proceedings in a given cause; but more specifically it means the writ, summons, mandate, or other process which is used to inform the defendant of the institution of proceedings against him and to compel his appearance, in either civil or criminal cases.

Legal process   This term is sometimes used as equivalent to "lawful process."   Thus, it is said that legal process means process not merely fair on its face, but in fact valid.   But properly it means a summons, writ, warrant, mandate, or other process issuing from a court.

profit   *Mesne profits*   Value of use or occupation of land during time it was held by one in wrongful possession and is commonly measured in terms of rents and profits.

Profit à prendre   Right to make some use of the soil of another, such as a right to mine metals, and it carries with it the right of entry and the right to remove.

promissory estoppel   Arises where there is a promise which promisor should reasonably expect to induce action or forbearance on part of promisee and which does induce such action or forbearance, and where injustice can be avoided only by enforcement of the promise.

promissory note   An unconditional written promise to pay a specified sum of money on demand or at a specified date.   Such a note is negotiable if signed by the maker and containing an unconditional promise to pay a sum certain in money either on demand or at a definite time and payable to order or bearer.   U.C.C. § 3–104.

promoters   In the law relating to corporations, those persons are called the "promoters" of a company who first associate themselves together for the purpose of organizing the company, issuing its prospectus, procuring subscriptions to the stock, securing a charter, etc.

protest A formal declaration made by a person interested or concerned in some act about to be done, or already performed, whereby he expresses his dissent or disapproval, or affirms the act against his will. The object of such a declaration is generally to save some right which would be lost to him if his implied assent could be made out, or to exonerate himself from some responsibility which would attach to him unless he expressly negatived his assent.

Notice of protest A notice given by the holder of a bill or note to the drawer or indorser that the bill has been protested for refusal of payment or acceptance. U.C.C. § 3–509.

proximate cause Where the act or omission played a substantial part in bringing about or actually causing the injury or damage and where the injury or damage was either a direct result or a reasonably probable consequence of the act or omission.

proxy (Contracted from procuracy.) Written authorization given by one person to another so that the second person can act for the first, such as that given by a shareholder to someone else to represent him and vote his shares at a shareholders' meeting.

Q

quantum meruit Expression "quantum meruit" means "as much as he deserves" and it is an expression that describes the extent of liability on a contract implied by law. Essential elements of recovery under quantum meruit are: (1) valuable services were rendered or materials furnished, (2) for person sought to be charged, (3) which services and materials were accepted by person sought to be charged, used and enjoyed by him, and (4) under such circumstances as reasonably notified person sought to be charged that plaintiff, in performing such services, was expected to be paid by person sought to be charged.

quasi Latin. As if; almost as it were; analogous to. It negatives idea of identity, but points out that the conceptions are sufficiently similar for one to be classed as the equal of the other.

quasi contract Legal fiction invented by common law courts to permit recovery by contractual remedy in cases where, in fact, there is no contract, but where circumstances are such that justice warrants a recovery as though there had been a promise.

quasi in rem See **in rem**.

quiet To pacify; to render secure or unassailable by the removal of disquieting causes or disputes. This is the meaning of the word in the phrase "action to quiet title," which is a proceeding to establish the plaintiff's title to land by bringing into court an adverse claimant and there compelling him either to establish his claim or be forever after estopped from asserting it.

quitclaim deed A deed of conveyance operating by way of release; that is, intended to pass any title, interest, or claim which the grantor may have in the premises, but not professing that such title is valid, nor containing any warranty or covenants for title.

quorum When a committee, board of directors, meeting of shareholders, legislature or other body of persons cannot act unless a certain number at least of them are present.

R

ratification In a broad sense, the confirmation of a previous act done either by the party himself or by another; as, confirmation of a voidable act.

In the law of principal and agent, the adoption and confirmation by one person with knowledge of all material facts, of an act or contract performed or entered into in his behalf by another who at the time assumed without authority to act as his agent.

real property Land, and generally whatever is erected or growing upon or affixed to land. Also rights issuing out of, annexed to, and exercisable within or about land. See also **fixture**.

receiver A fiduciary of the court, appointed as an incident to other proceedings wherein certain ultimate relief is prayed. He is a trustee or ministerial officer representing court, and all parties in interest in litigation, and property or fund intrusted to him.

recoupment To recover a loss by a subsequent gain. In pleading, to set forth a claim against the plaintiff when an action is brought against one as a defendant.

Under rules practice, recoupment has been replaced by the modern counterclaim.

Set-off distinguished A "set-off" is a demand which the defendant has against the plaintiff, arising out of a transaction extrinsic to the plaintiff's cause of action, whereas a "recoupment" is a reduction or rebate by the defendant of part of the plaintiff's claim because of a right in the defendant arising out of the same transaction.

redemption The realization of a right to have the title of property restored free and clear of the mortgage; performance of the mortgage obligation being essential for that purpose.

Repurchase by corporation of its shares at a price equal to the net asset value of the shares on date a redemption request is received by the corporation.

reformation Equitable remedy used to reframe written contracts to reflect accurately real agreement between contracting parties when, either through mutual mistake or unilateral mistake coupled with actual or equitable fraud by other party, the writing does not embody contract as actually made.

release The relinquishment, concession, or giving up of a right, claim, or privilege, by the person in whom it exists or to whom it accrues, to the person against whom it might have been demanded or enforced.

remainder An estate limited to take effect and be enjoyed after another estate is determined. As, if a man seised in fee-simple grants lands to A for twenty years, and, after the determination of the said term, then to B and his heirs forever, here A is tenant for years, remainder to B in fee.

remand To send back. The sending by the appellate court of the cause back to the same court out of which it came, for purpose of having some further action taken on it there.

remedy The means by which the violation of a right is prevented, redressed, or compensated. Though a remedy may be by the act of the party injured, by operation of law, or by agreement between the injurer and the injured, we are chiefly concerned with one kind of remedy, the judicial remedy, which is by action or suit.

rent Consideration paid for use or occupation of property. In a broader sense, it is the compensation or fee paid, usually periodically, for the use of any property, land, buildings, equipment, etc.

At common law, term referred to compensation or return of value given at stated times for the possession of lands and tenements corporeal.

replevin An action whereby the owner or person entitled to repossession of goods or chattels may recover those goods or chattels from one who has wrongfully distrained or taken or who wrongfully detains such goods or chattels.

repudiation Repudiation of a contract means re-

fusal to perform duty or obligation owed to other party.

requirements contract See **contracts.**

res judicata Rule that a final judgment is conclusive as to the rights of the parties and their privies, and, as to them, constitutes an absolute bar to a subsequent action involving the same claim, demand or cause of action.

rescission An equitable action in which a party seeks to be relieved of his obligations under a contract on the grounds of mutual mistake, fraud, impossibility, etc.

residuary Pertaining to the residue; constituting the residue; giving or bequeathing the residue; receiving or entitled to the residue. See also **legacy,** *residuary legacy.*

respondeat superior Latin. Let the master answer. This maxim means that a master is liable in certain cases for the wrongful acts of his servant, and a principal for those of his agent.

respondent In equity practice, the party who makes an answer to a bill or other proceeding in equity. In appellate practice, the party who contends against an appeal; *i.e.* the appellee. The party who appeals is called the "appellant."

restitution An equitable remedy under which a person who has rendered services to another seeks to be reimbursed for the costs of his acts (but not his profits) even though there was never a contract between the parties.

restraint on alienation A provision in an instrument of conveyance which prohibits the grantee from selling or transferring the property which is the subject of the conveyance. Many such restraints are unenforceable as against public policy and the law's policy of free alienability of land.

reverse An appellate court uses the term "reversed" to indicate that it annuls or avoids the judgment, or vacates the decree, of the trial court.

reversion The term reversion has two meanings, first, as designating the estate left in the grantor during the continuance of a particular estate and also the residue left in grantor or his heirs after termination of particular estate. It differs from a remainder in that it arises by act of the law, whereas a remainder is by act of the parties. A reversion, moreover, is the remnant left in the grantor, while a remainder is the remnant of the whole estate disposed of, after a preceding part of the same has been given away.

revocation The recall of some power, authority, or thing granted, or a destroying or making void of some deed that had existence until the act of revocation made it void. It may be either general, of all acts and things done before; or special, to revoke a particular thing.

right of entry The right of taking or resuming possession of land by entering on it in a peaceable manner.

right of redemption The right (granted by statute only) to free property from the encumbrance of a foreclosure or other judicial sale, or to recover the title passing thereby, by paying what is due, with interest, costs, etc. Not to be confounded with the "equity of redemption," which exists independently of statute but must be exercised before sale. See also **equity of redemption.**

rule against perpetuities Principle that no interest in property is good unless it must vest, if at all, not later than 21 years, plus period of gestation, after some life or lives in being at time of creation of interest.

S

satisfaction The discharge of an obligation by paying a party what is due to him (as on a mortgage, lien, or contract) or what is awarded to him, by the judgment of a court or otherwise. Thus, a judgment is satisfied by the payment of the amount due to the party who has recovered such judgment, or by his levying the amount. See also **accord and satisfaction**.

scienter Latin. Knowingly.

scintilla Latin. A spark; a remaining particle; the least particle.

secured transaction A transaction which is founded on a security agreement. Such agreement creates or provides for a security interest. U.C.C. § 9–105(h).

securities Stocks, bonds, notes, convertible debentures, warrants, or other documents that represent a share in a company or a debt owed by a company.

seisin Possession with an intent on the part of him who holds it to claim a freehold interest.

set-off A counter-claim demand which defendant holds against plaintiff, arising out of a transaction extrinsic of plaintiff's cause of action.

In equity practice it is commenced by a declaration in set-off, though under rules practice (which merged law and equity) it has been displaced by the counterclaim.   Fed.R.Civil P. 13.

For the distinction between set-off and recoupment, see **recoupment.**

severance Act of severing, or state of being severed; partition; separation; *e.g.* a claim against a party may be severed and proceeded with separately.   Fed.R.Civil P. 21.

Also, the destruction of any one of the unities of a joint tenancy.   It is so called because the estate is no longer a joint tenancy, but is severed.

Term may also refer to cutting of the crops, such as corn, wheat, etc., or the separating of anything from the realty.

Shelley's case, rule in Where a person takes an estate of freehold, legally, or equitably, under a deed, will, or other writing, and in the same instrument there is a limitation by way of remainder of any interest of the same legal or equitable quality to his heirs, or heirs of his body, as a class of persons to take in succession from generation to generation, the limitation to the heirs entitles the ancestor to the whole estate.

The rule was adopted as a part of the common law of this country, though it has long since been abolished by most states.

shipment contract Seller is authorized or required only to bear the expense of placing goods with the common carrier and bears the risk of loss only up to such point.

short swing profits Profits made by insider through sale or other disposition of the corporate stock within six months after purchase.

sight draft An instrument payable on presentment.

sole proprietorship A form of business in which one person owns all the assets of the business in contrast to a partnership and corporation.

specific performance The doctrine of specific performance is that, where damages would be an inadequate compensation for the breach of an agreement, the contractor or vendor will be compelled to perform specifically what he has agreed to do; *e.g.* ordered to execute a specific conveyance of land. See Fed.R. Civil P. 70.

With respect to sale of goods, specific performance may be decreed where the goods are unique or in other proper circumstances. The decree for specific performance may include such terms and conditions as to payment of the price, damages, or other relief as the court may deem just. U.C.C. §§ 2–711(2)(b), 2–716.

stare decisis Doctrine that, when court has once laid down a principle of law as applicable to a certain state of facts, it will adhere to that principle, and apply it to all future cases, where facts are substantially the same; regardless of whether the parties and property are the same.

statute of frauds A celebrated English statute, passed in 1677, and which has been adopted, in a more or less modified form, in nearly all of the United States. Its chief characteristic is the provision that no action shall be brought on certain contracts unless there be a note or memorandum thereof in writing, signed by the party to be charged or by his authorized agent.

statute of limitation A statute prescribing limitations to the right of action on certain described causes of action; that is, declaring that no suit shall be maintained on such causes of action unless brought within a specified period after the right accrued.

stock "Stock" is distinguished from "bonds" and, ordinarily, from "debentures," in that it gives right of ownership in part of assets of corporation and right to interest in any surplus after payment of debt. "Stock" in a corporation is an equity, and it represents an ownership interest, and it is to be distinguished from obligations such as notes or bonds which are not equities and represent no ownership interest.

Capital stock See **capital.**

Common stock Securities which represent an ownership interest in a corporation. If the company has also issued preferred stock, both common and preferred have ownership rights. Claims of both common and preferred stockholders are junior to claims of bondholders or other creditors of the company. Common stockholders assume the greater risk, but generally exercise the greater control and may gain the greater reward in the form of dividends and capital appreciation.

Convertible stock Stock which may be changed or converted into common stock.

Cumulative preferred A stock having a provision that if one or more dividends are omitted, the omitted dividends must be paid before dividends may be paid on the company's common stock.

Preferred stock is a separate portion or class of the stock of a corporation, which is accorded, by the charter or by-laws, a preference or priority in respect to dividends, over the remainder of the stock of the corporation, which in that case is called *common stock.*

Stock warrant A certificate entitling the owner to buy a specified amount of stock at a specified time(s) for a specified price. Differs from a stock option only in that options are granted to employees and warrants are sold to the public.

strict liability A concept applied by the courts in product liability cases in which a seller is liable for any and all defective or hazardous products which unduly threaten a consumer's personal safety. This concept applies to all members involved in the manufacturing and selling of any facet of the product.

subpoena A subpoena is a command to appear at a certain time and place to give testimony upon a certain matter. A subpoena duces tecum requires production of books, papers and other things.

subrogation The substitution of one thing for another, or of one person into the place of another with respect to rights, claims, or securities.

Subrogation denotes the putting a third person who has paid a debt in the place of the creditor to whom he has paid it, so that he may exercise against the debtor all the rights which the creditor, if unpaid, might have done.

subscribe Literally to write underneath, as one's name. To sign at the end of a document. Also, to agree in writing to furnish money or its equivalent, or to agree to purchase some initial stock in a corporation.

substantial performance Equitable doctrine protects against forfeiture for technical inadvertence or trivial variations or omissions in performance.

substantive law The basic law of rights and duties (contract law, criminal law, tort law, law of wills, etc.) as opposed to procedural law (law of pleading, law of evidence, law of jurisdiction, etc.).

suit "Suit" is a generic term, of comprehensive signification, and applies to any proceeding in a court of justice in which the plaintiff pursues, in such court, the remedy which the law affords him for the redress of an injury or the recovery of a right.

summary judgment Rule of Civil Procedure 56 permits any party to a civil action to move for a summary judgment on a claim, counterclaim, or cross-claim when he believes that there is no genuine issue of material fact and that he is entitled to prevail as a matter of law.

summons Writ or process directed to the sheriff or other proper officer, requiring him to notify the person named that an action has been commenced against him in the court from where the process issues, and that he is required to appear, on a day named, and answer the complaint in such action.

surety One who undertakes to pay money or to do any other act in event that his principal fails therein.

Guarantor and surety compared A surety and guarantor are both bound for another person. However, a surety is usually bound with his principal by the same instrument, executed at the same time and on the same consideration. On the other hand, the contract of guarantor is his own separate undertaking, in which the principal does not join. A surety is an insurer of the debt or obligation; a guarantor is an insurer of the solvency of the principal debtor or of his ability to pay. Under U.C.C., term "surety" includes a guarantor. § 1–201(40). See also **guaranty.**

T

tacking The term is applied especially to the process of making out title to land by adverse possession, when the present occupant and claimant has not been in possession for the full statutory period, but adds or "tacks" to his own possession that of previous occupants under whom he claims.

tenancy Possession or occupancy of land or premises under lease.

Joint tenancy Joint tenants have one and the same interest, accruing by one and the same conveyance, commencing at one and the same time, and held by one and the same undivided possession. The primary incident of joint tenancy is survivorship, by which the entire tenancy on the decease of any joint tenant remains to the survivors, and at length to the last survivor.

Tenancy at sufferance Only naked possession which continues after tenant's right of possession has terminated.

Tenancy at will Possession of premises by permission of owner or landlord, but without a fixed term.

Tenancy by the entirety A tenancy which is created between a husband and wife and by which together they hold title to the whole with right of survivorship so that, upon death of either, other takes whole to exclusion of deceased heirs. It is essentially a "joint tenancy," modified by the common-law theory that husband and wife are one person.

Tenancy for a period A tenancy for years or for some fixed period.

Tenancy in common A form of ownership whereby each tenant (*i.e.,* owner) holds an undivided interest in property. Unlike a joint tenancy or a tenancy by the entirety, the interest of a tenant in common does not terminate upon his or her prior death (*i.e.,* there is no right of survivorship).

tender An offer of money; the act by which one produces and offers to a person holding a claim or demand against him the amount of money which he considers and admits to be due, in satisfaction of such claim or demand, without any stipulation or condition.

Also, there may be a tender of performance of a duty other than the payment of money.

testator One who makes or has made a testament or will; one who dies leaving a will.

third party beneficiary One for whose benefit a promise is made in a contract but who is not a party to the contract

Creditor beneficiary Where performance of a promise in a contract will benefit a person other than the promisee, that person is a creditor beneficiary if no purpose to make a gift appears from the terms of the promise in view of the accompanying circumstances and performance of the promise will satisfy an actual or supposed or asserted duty of the promisee to the beneficiary.

Donee beneficiary The person who takes the benefit of the contract even though there is no privity between him and the contracting parties. A third party beneficiary who is not a creditor beneficiary. See also **beneficiary.**

title The means whereby the owner of lands or of personalty has the just possession of his property.

tort A private or civil wrong or injury, other than breach of contract, for which the court will provide a remedy in the form of an action for damages.

Three elements of every tort action are: Existence of legal duty from defendant to plaintiff, breach of duty, and damage as proximate result.

tort-feasor One who commits or is guilty of a tort.

trade acceptance A draft drawn by a seller which is presented for signature (acceptance) to the buyer at the time goods are purchased and which then becomes the equivalent of a note receivable of the seller and the note payable of the buyer.

trespass At common law, trespass was a form of action brought to recover damages for any injury to one's person or property or relationship with another.

Trespass to chattels An unlawful and serious interference with the possessory rights of another to personal property.

Trespass to land At common law, every unauthorized and direct breach of the boundaries of another's land was an actionable trespass. The present prevailing position of the courts finds liability for trespass only in the case of intentional intrusion, or negligence, or some "abnormally dangerous activity" on the part of the defendant. Compare **nuisance**.

trover A possessory action wherein plaintiff must show that he has either a general or special property in thing converted and the right to its possession at the time of the alleged conversion. Such remedy lies only for wrongful appropriation of goods, chattels, or personal property which is specific enough to be identified. See also **conversion**.

trust Any arrangement whereby property is transferred with intention that it be administered by trustee for another's benefit.

A trust, as the term is used in the Restatement, when not qualified by the word "charitable," "resulting" or "constructive," is a fiduciary relationship with respect to property, subjecting the person by whom the title to the property is held to equitable duties to deal with the property for the benefit of another person, which arises as a result of a manifestation of an intention to create it. Restatement, Second, Trusts § 2.

Constructive trust Wherever the circumstances of a transaction are such that the person who takes the legal estate in property cannot also enjoy the beneficial interest without necessarily violating some established principle of equity, the court will immediately raise a *constructive trust*, and fasten it upon the conscience of the legal owner, so as to convert him into a trustee for the parties who in equity are entitled to the beneficial enjoyment. Constructive trusts have been said to arise through the application of the doctrine of equitable estoppel, or under the broad doctrine that equity regards and treats as done what in good conscience ought to be done.

Resulting trust One that arises by implication of law, where the legal estate in property is disposed of, conveyed, or transferred, but the intent appears or is inferred from the terms of the disposition, or from the accompanying facts and circumstances, that the beneficial interest is not to go or be enjoyed with the legal title.

Voting trust A trust which holds the voting rights to stock in a corporation. It is a useful device when a majority of the shareholders in a corporation cannot agree on corporate policy.

trustee In a strict sense, a "trustee" is one who holds the legal title to property for the benefit of another, while, in a broad sense, the term is sometimes applied to anyone standing in a fiduciary or confidential relation to another, such as agent, attorney, bailee, etc.

U

ultra vires Acts beyond the scope of the powers of a corporation, as defined by its charter or laws of state of incorporation. By doctrine of ultra vires a contract made by a corporation beyond the scope of its corporate powers is unlawful.

unconscionable contract See **contracts**

underwriter Any person, banker, or syndicate that guarantees to furnish a definite sum of money by a definite date to a business or government in return for an issue of bonds or stock. In insurance, the one assuming a risk in return for the payment of a premium.

undue influence Term refers to conduct by which a person, through his power over mind of testator, makes the latter's desires conform to his own, thereby overmastering the violition of the testator.

uniform commercial code One of the Uniform Laws drafted by the National Conference of Commissioners on Uniform State Laws governing commercial transactions (sales of goods, commercial paper, bank deposits and collections, letters of credit, bulk transfers, warehouse receipts, bills of lading, investment securities, and secured transactions). The U.C.C. has been adopted by all states, except Louisiana.

usage of trade A usage of trade is any practice or method of dealing having such regularity of observance in a place, vocation or trade as to justify an expectation that it will be observed with respect to the transaction in question.

usury Collectively, the laws of a jurisdiction regulating the charging of interest rates. A usurious loan is one whose interest rates are determined to be in excess of those permitted by the usury laws.

V

vendee A purchaser or buyer; one to whom anything is sold. Generally used of the purchaser of real property, one who acquires chattels by sale being called a "buyer." See also **vendor.**

vendor The person who transfers property by sale, particularly real estate; "seller" being more commonly used for one who sells personalty. The latter may, however, with entire propriety, be termed a vendor. A merchant; a retail dealer; a supplier; one who buys to sell. See also **vendee.**

venue "Jurisdiction" of the court means the inherent power to decide a case, whereas "venue" designates the particular county or city in which a court with jurisdiction may hear and determine the case.

verdict The formal and unanimous decision or finding of a jury, impaneled and sworn for the trial of a cause, upon the matters or questions duly submitted to them upon the trial.

vested Fixed; accured; settled; absolute. To be "vested," a right must be more than a mere expectation based on an anticipation of the continuance of an existing law; it must have become a title, legal or equitable, to the present or future enforcement of a demand, or a legal exemption from the demand of another.

vicarious liability Indirect legal responsibility; for example, the liability of an employer for the acts of an employee, or, a principal for torts and contracts of an agent.

void Null; ineffectual; nugatory; having no legal force or binding effect; unable, in law, to support the purpose for which it was intended.

There is this difference between the two words "void" and "voidable": *void* in the strict sense means that an instrument or transaction is nugatory and ineffectual so that nothing can cure it; *voidable* exists when an imperfection or defect can be cured by the act or confirmation of him who could take advantage of it.

Frequently the word "void" is used and construed as having the more liberal meaning of "voidable."

voidable See **void.**

voluntary Resulting from free choice. The word, especially in statutes, often implies knowledge of essential facts.

W

waiver Terms "estoppel" and "waiver" are not synonymous; "waiver" means the voluntary, intentional relinquishment of a known right, and "estoppel" rests upon principle that, where anyone has done an act, or made a statement, which would be a fraud on his part to controvert or impair, because other party has acted upon it in belief that what was done or said was true, conscience and honest dealing require that he not be permitted to repudiate his act or gainsay his statement. See also **estoppel.**

ward An infant or insane person placed by authority of law under the care of a guardian.

warrant, *v.* In contracts, to engage or promise that a certain fact or state of facts, in relation to the subject-matter, is, or shall be, as it is represented to be.

In conveyancing, to assure the title to property sold, by an express covenant to that effect in the deed of conveyance.

warrant, *n.* An order by which the drawer authorizes one person to pay a particular sum of money.

An authority issued to a collector of taxes, empowering him to collect the taxes extended on the assessment roll, and to make distress and sale of goods or land in default of payment.

Stock warrant See **stock.**

warranty A warranty is a statement or representation made by seller of goods, contemporaneously with and as a part of contract of sale, though collateral to express object of sale, having reference to character, quality, or title of goods, and by which seller promises or undertakes to insure that certain facts are or shall be as he then represents them.

The general statutory law governing warranties on sales of goods is provided in U.C.C. § 2–312 *et seq.* The three main types of warranties are: (1) express warranty; (2) implied warranty of fitness; (3) implied warranty of merchantability.

warranty deed Deed in which grantor warrants good clear title. The usual covenants of title are warranties of seisin, quiet enjoyment, right to convey, freedom from encumbrances and defense of title as to all claims.

will   A written instrument executed with the formalities required by statutes, whereby a person makes a disposition of his property to take effect after his death.

winding up   To settle the accounts and liquidate the assets of a partnership or corporation, for the purpose of making distribution and dissolving the concern.

writ of certiorari   See **certiorari.**

writ of error   A writ issued from a court of appellate jurisdiction, directed to the judge or judges of a court of record, requiring them to remit to the appellate court the record of an action before them, in which a final judgment has been entered, in order that examination may be made of certain errors alleged to have been committed, and that the judgment may be reversed, corrected, or affirmed, as the case may require.

INDEX

References are to Pages

RESCISSION
Generally, 10
Consumer right of, 913–14
Mutual,
Discharge of obligation, 314, 320–21

RES IPSA LOQUITUR
Negligence doctrine, 129–30

RESPONDEAT SUPERIOR
Generally, 375–77, 386–87
Corporations, 700–701

RESTATEMENTS OF LAW
Contracts, 153
Source of law, 10–11
Torts, 99
Strict liability, 446–49

RESTITUTION (See Equity)

RESTRAINT OF TRADE (See Antitrust; Contracts, Illegal Bargains)

RESTRICTIVE COVENANTS (See Land Use)

ROBBERY (See Criminal Law)

ROBINSON–PATMAN ACT
Generally, 893–94, 907–8
Cost justification, 893
Meeting competition, 893–94
Chart, 894

SALES
See also Bulk Sales; Documents of Title; Parol Evidence Rule; Products Liability; Statute of Frauds; Warranties
Generally, 396–499
Acceptance,
Manner of, 403–4
Mirror image rule, 402–3
Variant acceptances, 402–3, 411–13
Approval, sale on, 421–22
Bailment, compared, 397
Bona fide purchaser, 418–20
Minors, sales by, 419–20
Buyer in ordinary course of business, 420
C. & F. (cost and freight),
Performance, 465
Risk of loss, 422
Carriers, contracts involving,
Destination contracts, 423, 466
Shipment contracts, 422–23, 432–34, 465–66
C.I.F. (cost, insurance and freight),
Performance, 465
Risk of loss, 422
C.O.D. (collect on delivery),
Performance, 465, 469
Risk of loss, 423
Consignment, 422

Course of dealing, defined, 399
Cover,
Remedies and, 488–89, 495–97
Cure,
Seller, by, 466–68, 475–76
Defined, 396–97, 406–9
Delivery, time and manner of, 465
Destination contracts, 416
Performance, 466
Risk of loss, 423
Discharge of claim after breach, 404
Entrusting of goods to a merchant, 420–21
Chart, 420
Ex-ship (delivery from the ship),
Performance, 466
Risk of loss, 423
F.A.S. (free alongside),
Performance, 465
Risk of loss, 422
F.O.B. (free on board),
Performance, 466
Risk of loss, 422
Formation of sales contract, 401–5
Freedom of contract, 401
Gift, compared, 397
Good faith, 398
Lease, compared, 397
Liquidated damages provision, 360, 335–36, 491–92
Merchants,
Defined, 399
Entrusting of goods to, 420–21, 430–32
Chart, 420
Sales by and between, 399–401
Modifications, contractual, 404
No arrival, no sale term,
Performance, 466
Risk of loss, 423
Offer,
Definiteness, 401–2
Delivery, open, 402
Price, open, 402
Quantity, open, 402
Firm, 167, 402
Output, agreement to purchase seller's entire,
Offer and acceptance, 166, 402
Performance, 464–82
Buyer, by, 468–72
Acceptance, 470–71, 479
Revocation of, 471, 480–81
Inspection, 469
Payment, obligation of, 471–72
Rejection, 469–70, 476–79
Excuses for nonperformance, 472–73
Casualty to identified goods, 472
Non-happening of presupposed condition, 472–73
Substituted performance, 473
Seller, by, 464–68
Requirements, agreement to supply buyer's entire,
Offer and acceptance, 166, 402
Risk of loss, 421–25